Features

113th Edition

Statistical Abstract of the United States 1993

U.S. Department of Commerce
Ronald H. Brown, Secretary
Economics and Statistics Administration
Paul A. London, Acting Under Secretary for Economic Affairs
BUREAU OF THE CENSUS
Harry A. Scarr, Acting Director

Economics and Statistics Administration

Paul A. London, Acting Under Secretary for Economic Affairs

BUREAU OF THE CENSUS

Harry A. Scarr, Acting Director

DATA USER SERVICES DIVISION
Marshall L. Turner, Jr., Chief

Acknowledgments

Glenn W. King, Chief, Statistical Compendia Staff, was responsible for general supervision and compilation of this volume under the direction of **Marie Argana. Lars B. Johanson** was responsible for technical supervision and coordination. Assisting in the research and analytical phases of assigned sections and in the developmental aspects of new tables were **Rosemary E. Clark, Edward C. Jagers** and **Rachael LaPorte**. The latter two were also responsible for content and preparation of graphics. **Geraldine W. Blackburn** provided primary editorial assistance. Other editorial assistance was rendered by **Kelvin Elmore, Patricia S. Lancaster, Catherine Lavender, Joyce Mori**, and **Marjorie M. Sproesser**.

The staff of the Administrative and Publications Services Division, **Walter C. Odom**, Chief, performed publication planning, editorial review, design, composition, and printing planning and procurement. **Patricia Heiston** provided publication coordination and editing. **Janet Sweeney** provided design and graphics services.

The cooperation of many contributors to this volume is gratefully acknowledged. The source note below each table credits the various government and private agencies which have collaborated in furnishing information for the **Statistical Abstract**. In a few instances, contributors have requested that their data be designated as subject to copyright restrictions, as indicated in the source notes to the tables affected. Permission to use copyright material should be obtained directly from the copyright owner.

Library of Congress Card No. 4–18089

SUGGESTED CITATION

U.S. Bureau of the Census, *Statistical Abstract of the United States: 1993* (113th edition.) Washington, DC, 1993

For sale by Superintendent of Documents, U.S. Government Printing Office, Washington, DC 20402, Tel. 202–783–3238
(Paper) ISBN 0–16–042046–6
(Cloth) ISBN 0–16–042047–4

212053

Preface

The *Statistical Abstract of the United States,* published since 1878, is the standard summary of statistics on the social, political, and economic organization of the United States. It is designed to serve as a convenient volume for statistical reference and as a guide to other statistical publications and sources. The latter function is served by the introductory text to each section, the source note appearing below each table, and Appendix I, which comprises the Guide to Sources of Statistics, the Guide to State Statistical Abstracts, and the Guide to Foreign Statistical Abstracts.

This volume includes a selection of data from many statistical publications, both government and private. Publications cited as sources usually contain additional statistical detail and more comprehensive discussions of definitions and concepts than can be presented here. Data not available in publications issued by the contributing agency but obtained from unpublished records are identified in the source notes as "unpublished data." More information on the subjects covered in the tables so noted may generally be obtained from the source.

Except as indicated, figures are for the United States as presently constituted. Although emphasis in the *Statistical Abstract* is primarily given to national data, many tables present data for regions and individual States and a smaller number for metropolitan areas and cities. Appendix II, Metropolitan Area Concepts and Components, presents explanatory text, a complete current listing and population data for metropolitan statistical areas (MSA's), the primary metropolitan statistical areas (PMSA's), and the consolidated metropolitan statistical areas (CMSA's) defined as of December 1992. Table 42 in section 1 presents selected population characteristics for MSA's with population of 250,000 or more. Statistics for the Commonwealth of Puerto Rico and for outlying areas of the United States are included in many State tables and are supplemented by information in section 30. Additional information for States, cities, counties, metropolitan areas, and other small units, as well as more

historical data, are available in various supplements to the *Abstract* (see inside back cover).

Changes in this edition.—New to this addition are up-to-date world maps in Section 31 that include recent changes in Czechoslovakia, Soviet Union, and Yugoslavia. In addition, a comprehensive table presents populations for every country in the world. This table also includes references to allow for easy location of each country on the maps.

Subject matter content changes include an extensive presentation of population projections in section 1 and more detail presented for racial and Hispanic groups in many tables throughout the book. Other selected areas for which we have added new material include health practices, educational attainment, child abuse and neglect cases, book purchasing, the Federal debt, military installations, occupational tenure, usage of automated teller machines, and high tech exports. (See Appendix VI, pp. 949–951 for a complete list of new tables introduced in this edition.) We have also included a new Appendix presenting selected data for each congressional district, including population, educational attainment, income, and housing. See Appendix VII, pp. 952–958. In addition, we have also brought back our section on State Rankings which begins on page xii. As mentioned above, Appendix II presents a listing of the newly defined metro areas.

Work is continuing on the project to provide the Abstract on CD–ROM. Currently, we are developing and testing the search/retrieval and printing capability software. Given these prove satisfactory, we hope to have the CD–ROM version of the 1993 Abstract available by the end of the year.

Statistics in this edition are generally for the most recent year or period available by late 1992. Special effort was made to include final results of the 1992 elections and economic series which became available in early 1993 including series covering the labor force, the consumer price index, construction, and foreign trade. Each year almost 1,500 tables and charts are reviewed and evaluated; new tables and charts of current interest are added, continuing series are updated, and less timely data are condensed or eliminated. Text notes and appendices are revised as appropriate.

USA Statistics in Brief, 1993, a pocket-size pamphlet highlighting many statistical series in the *Abstract,* is available separately. Single copies can be obtained free from U.S. Bureau of the Census, Customer Services, Washington, DC 20233 (telephone 301-763-4100).

Historical statistics.—Specific headnote references in this *Abstract* link many tables to earlier data shown in *Historical Statistics of the United States, Colonial Times to 1970.* (See Appendix IV, pp. 942 and 943).

Statistics for States and metropolitan areas.—Data for States and metro areas may also be found in the *State and Metropolitan Area Data Book, 1991.*

Statistical reliability and responsibility.—The contents of this volume were taken from many sources. All data from either censuses and surveys or from administrative records are subject to error

arising from a number of factors: Sampling variability (for statistics based on samples), reporting errors in the data for individual units, incomplete coverage, nonresponse, imputations, and processing error. (See also Appendix III, pp. 926–941). The Bureau of the Census cannot accept the responsibility for the accuracy or limitations of the data presented here, other than those for which it collects. The responsibility for selection of the material and for proper presentation, however, rests with the Bureau.

For additional information on data presented.—Please consult the source publications available in local libraries or write to the agency indicated in the source notes. Write to the Bureau of the Census only if it is cited as the source.

Suggestions and comments.—Users of the *Statistical Abstract* and its supplements (see inside back cover) are urged to make their data needs known for consideration in planning future editions. Suggestions and comments for improving coverage and presentation of data should be sent to the Director, U.S. Bureau of the Census, Washington, DC 20233.

User survey.—Inserted in this edition is a brief post card sized user survey which we plan to include periodically. Your input on the various topics should enable us to plan our programs and products to meet your needs. Please complete the survey and return to us. If it is no longer in the book and you wish to obtain a copy of it, please write to U.S. Bureau of the Census, Statistical Compendia Branch, DUSD, Washington, DC 20233-8300 or call 301-763-5299.

Contents

[Numbers following subjects are page numbers]

Contents

APPROXIMATE CONVERSION MEASURES

[For assistance on metric usage, call or write the Office of Metric Programs, U.S. Department of Commerce, Washington, DC 20230 (301-975-3690)]

Symbol	When you know conventional	Multiply by	To find metric	Symbol
in	inch	2.54	centimeter	cm
ft	foot	30.48	centimeter	cm
yd	yard	0.91	meter	m
mi	mile	1.61	kilometer	km
in^2	square inch	6.45	square centimeter	cm^2
ft^2	square foot	0.09	square meter	m^2
yd^2	square yard	0.84	square meter	m^2
mi^2	square mile	2.59	square kilometer	km^2
	acre	0.41	hectare	ha
oz	ounce [1]	28.35	gram	g
lb	pound[1]	.45	kilograms	kg
oz (troy)	ounce [2]	31.10	gram	g
	short ton (2,000 lbs)	0.91	metric ton	t
	long ton (2,240 lbs)	1.02	metric ton	t
fl oz	fluid ounce	29.57	milliliter	mL
c	cup	0.24	liter	L
pt	pint	0.47	liter	L
qt	quart	0.95	liter	L
gal	gallon	3.78	liter	L
ft^3	cubic foot	0.03	cubic meter	m^3
yd^3	cubic yard	0.76	cubic meter	m^3
F	degrees Fahrenheit (subtract 32)	0.55	degrees Celsius	C

Symbol	When you know metric	Multiply by	To find conventional	Symbol
cm	centimeter	0.39	inch	in
cm	centimeter	0.33	foot	ft
m	meter	1.09	yard	yd
km	kilometer	0.62	mile	mi
cm^2	square centimeter	0.15	square inch	in^2
m^2	square meter	10.76	square foot	ft^2
m^2	square meter	1.20	square yard	yd^2
km^2	square kilometer	0.39	square mile	mi^2
ha	hectare	2.47	acre	
g	gram	.035	ounce [1]	oz
kg	kilogram	2.21	pounds	lb[1]
g	gram	.032	ounce [2]	oz (troy)
t	metric ton	1.10	short ton (2,000 lbs)	
t	metric ton	0.98	long ton (2,240 lbs)	
mL	milliliter	0.03	fluid ounce	fl oz
L	liter	4.24	cup	c
L	liter	2.13	pint (liquid)	pt
L	liter	1.05	quart (liquid)	qt
L	liter	0.26	gallon	gal
m^3	cubic meter	35.32	cubic foot	ft^3
m^3	cubic meter	1.32	cubic yard	yd^3
C	degrees Celsius	1.80	degrees Fahrenheit (after subtracting 32)	F

[1] For weighing ordinary commodities.   [2] For weighing precious metals, jewels, etc.

Example of table structure:

No. 594. State and Local Government Retirement Systems—Beneficiaries and Finances: 1980 to 1990

[In millions of dollars, except as indicated. For fiscal years closed during the 12 months ending June 30]

YEAR AND LEVEL OF GOVERNMENT	Number of beneficiaries (1,000)	RECEIPTS					BENEFITS AND WITHDRAWALS			Cash and security holdings
		Total	Employee contributions	Government contributions		Earnings on investments	Total	Benefits	Withdrawals	
				State	Local					
1980: All systems.........	(NA)	37,313	6,466	7,581	9,951	13,315	14,008	12,207	1,801	185,226
State-administered....	(NA)	28,603	5,285	7,399	5,611	10,308	10,257	8,809	1,448	144,682
Locally administered ..	8,710	8,710	1,180	181	4,340	3,008	3,752	3,399	353	40,544
1985: All systems.........	3,378	71,411	9,468	12,227	15,170	34,546	24,413	21,999	2,414	374,433
State-administered....	2,661	55,960	7,901	11,976	8,944	27,139	18,230	16,183	2,047	296,951
Locally administered ..	716	15,451	1,567	251	6,226	7,407	6,183	5,816	367	77,481
1989: All systems.........	3,911	100,125	12,862	13,249	18,037	55,978	35,114	32,992	2,122	628,778
State-administered....	3,120	81,090	10,813	13,155	11,202	45,919	26,979	25,277	1,702	503,074
Locally administered ..	791	19,036	2,048	94	6,835	10,059	8,136	7,716	420	125,704
1990: All systems.........	4,026	111,339	13,853	13,994	18,583	64,907	38,396	35,966	2,430	703,772
State-administered....	3,232	89,162	11,648	13,964	11,538	52,012	29,603	27,562	2,041	565,641
Locally administered ..	794	22,177	2,205	32	7,045	12,895	8,793	8,404	389	138,131

NA Not available.

Source: U.S. Bureau of the Census, *Finances of Employee-Retirement Systems of State and Local Governments*, series GF, No. 2, annual.

Headnotes immediately below table titles provide information important for correct interpretation or evaluation of the table as a whole or for a major segment of it.

Footnotes below the bottom rule of tables give information relating to specific items or figures within the table.

Unit indicators show the *specified quantities* in which data items are presented. They are used for two primary reasons. Sometimes data are not available in absolute form and are estimates (as in the case of many surveys). In other cases we round the numbers in order to save space to show more data, as in the case above.

EXAMPLES OF UNIT INDICATOR INTERPRETATION FROM TABLE 594

Year	Item	Unit Indicator	Number shown	Multiplier
1990...................	Beneficiaries	Thousands..........	4,026	1,000,
1990...................	Receipts................	$ Millions...........	111,339	1,000,000

To Determine the Figure it Is Necessary to Multiply the Number Shown by the Unit Indicator:

Beneficiaries = 4,026 * 1,000, or 4,026,000 (over 4 million).
Receipts = 111,339 * 1,000,000 or 111,339,000,000 (over 111 billion).

When a table presents data with more than one unit indicator, they are found in the headnotes and column headings (shown above), spanner (table 53), stub (table 72), or unit column (table 76). When the data in a table are shown in the same unit indicator, it is shown in boldface as the first part of the headnote (table 2). If no unit indicator is shown, data presented are in absolute form (table 1).

Heavy vertical rules are used to separate independent sections of a table, as shown above, or in tables where the stub is continued into one or more additional columns (table 4).

Averages. An average is a single number or value that is often used to represent the "typical value" of a group of numbers. It is regarded as a measure of "location" or "central tendency" of a group of numbers.

The *arithmetic mean* is the type of average used most frequently. It is derived by summing the individual item values of a particular group and dividing the total by the number of items. The arithmetic mean is often referred to as simply the "mean" or "average."

The *median* of a group of numbers is the middle number or value when each item in the group is arranged according to size (lowest to highest or visa versa); it generally has the same number of items above it as well as below it. If there is an even number if items in the group, the median is taken to be the average of the two middle numbers.

Per capita (or per person) quantities. A per capita figure represents an average computed for every person in a specified group (or population). It is derived by taking the total for an item (such as income, taxes, or retail sales) and dividing it by the number of persons in the specified population.

Index numbers. An index number is the measure of difference or change, usually expressed as a percent, relating one quantity (the variable) of a specified kind to another quantity of the same kind. Index numbers are widely used to express changes in prices over periods of time but may also be used to express differences between related subjects for a single point in time.

To compute a price index, a base year or period is selected. The base year price (of the commodity or service) is then designated as the base or reference price to which the prices for other years or periods are related. Many price indexes use the year 1982 as the base year; in tables this is shown as "1982=100". A method of expressing the price relationship is: The price of a set of one or more items for a related year (e.g. 1990) **divided by** the price of the same set of items for the base year (e.g. 1982). The result multiplied by 100 provides the index number. When 100 is subtracted from the index number, the result equals the percent change in price from the base year.

Average annual percent change. Unless otherwise stated in the *Abstract* (as in Section 1, Population), average annual percent change is computed by use of a *compound interest formula*. This formula assumes that the rate of change is constant throughout a specified compounding period (one year for average annual rates of change). The formula is similar to that used to compute the balance of a savings account which receives compound interest. According to this formula, at the end of a compounding period the amount of accrued change (e.g. school enrollment or bank interest) is added to the amount which existed at the beginning the period. As a result, over time (e.g., with each year or quarter), the same rate of change is applied to a larger and larger figure.

The *exponential formula,* which is based on continuous compounding, is often used to measure population change. It is preferred by population experts because they view population and population-related subjects as changing without interruption, ever ongoing. Both exponential and compound interest formulas assume a constant rate of change. The former, however, applies the amount of change continuously to the base rather than at the end of each compounding period. When the average annual rates are small

(e.g., less than 5 percent) both formulas give virtually the same results. For an explanation of these two formulas as they relate to population, see U.S. Bureau of the Census, *The Methods and Materials of Demography,* vol. 2, 3d printing (rev.), 1975, pp. 372-381.

Current and constant dollars. Statistics in some tables in a number of sections are expressed in both current and constant dollars (see, for example, table 704 in section 14). Current dollar figures reflect actual prices or costs prevailing during the specified year(s). Constant dollar figures are estimates representing an effort to remove the effects of price changes from statistical series reported in dollar terms. In general, constant dollar series are derived by dividing current dollar estimates by the appropriate price index for the appropriate period (for example, the Consumer Price Index). The result is a series as it would presumably exist if prices were the same throughout, as in the base year—in other words as if the dollar had constant purchasing power. Any changes in this constant dollar series would reflect only changes in real volume of output, income, expenditures, or other measure.

Explanation of Symbols:

The following symbols, used in the tables throughout this book, are explained in condensed form in footnotes to the tables where they appear:

- Represents zero or rounds to less than half the unit of measurement shown.

B Base figure too small to meet statistical standards for reliability of a derived figure.

D Figure withheld to avoid disclosure pertaining to a specific organization or individual.

NA Data not enumerated, tabulated, or otherwise available separately.

NS Percent change irrelevant or insignificant.

S Figure does not meet publication standards for reasons other than that covered by symbol B, above.

X Figure not applicable because column heading and stub line make entry impossible, absurd, or meaningless.

Z Entry would amount to less than half the unit of measurement shown.

In many tables, details will not add to the totals shown because of rounding.

State Rankings

[When States share the same rank, the next lower rank is omitted. Because of rounded data, States may have identical values shown, but different ranks]

REGION, DIVISION, AND STATE	RESIDENT POPULATION [1]									
	Total, [2] 1992		Percent increase, [2] 1990-92		65 years old and over, [3] 1992		Foreign-born, [4] 1990		Speak a language other than English, [4][5] 1990	
	Number (1,000)	Rank	Percent	Rank	Percent	Rank	Percent	Rank	Percent	Rank
United States . . .	255,082	(X)	2.6	(X)	12.7	(X)	7.9	(X)	13.8	(X)
Northeast	51,118	(X)	0.6	(X)	13.9	(X)	10.3	(X)	16.5	(X)
New England	13,200	(X)	(Z)	(X)	13.7	(X)	7.9	(X)	13.9	(X)
Maine.	1,235	39	0.6	45	13.6	15	3.0	26	9.2	17
New Hampshire . .	1,111	41	0.1	47	11.8	35	3.7	21	8.7	20
Vermont	570	49	1.2	40	12.0	33	3.1	24	5.8	30
Massachusetts . .	5,998	13	-0.3	49	13.9	12	9.5	6	15.2	11
Rhode Island	1,005	43	0.2	46	15.2	4	9.5	7	17.0	9
Connecticut	3,281	27	-0.2	48	13.9	11	8.5	10	15.2	10
Middle Atlantic	37,918	(X)	0.8	(X)	14.0	(X)	11.1	(X)	17.5	(X)
New York	18,119	2	0.7	44	13.1	22	15.9	2	23.3	5
New Jersey	7,789	9	0.8	43	13.6	16	12.5	5	19.5	7
Pennsylvania	12,009	5	1.1	41	15.7	2	3.1	25	7.3	24
Midwest	60,713	(X)	1.8	(X)	13.1	(X)	3.6	(X)	7.1	(X)
East North Central .	42,753	(X)	1.8	(X)	12.8	(X)	4.2	(X)	8.0	(X)
Ohio.	11,016	7	1.6	36	13.2	21	2.4	32	5.4	35
Indiana	5,662	14	2.1	27	12.7	26	1.7	38	4.8	39
Illinois	11,631	6	1.8	32	12.6	27	8.3	11	14.2	12
Michigan	9,437	8	1.5	37	12.2	32	3.8	20	6.6	27
Wisconsin	5,007	18	2.3	25	13.3	20	2.5	31	5.8	31
West North Central .	17,960	(X)	1.7	(X)	13.9	(X)	2.0	(X)	4.9	(X)
Minnesota	4,480	20	2.4	23	12.5	28	2.6	29	5.6	34
Iowa	2,812	30	1.3	39	15.4	3	1.6	41	3.9	42
Missouri	5,193	15	1.5	38	14.1	10	1.6	40	3.8	43
North Dakota	636	47	-0.5	50	14.6	8	1.5	42	7.9	21
South Dakota	711	45	2.2	26	14.7	7	1.1	45	6.5	28
Nebraska	1,606	36	1.7	33	14.1	9	1.8	35	4.8	38
Kansas	2,523	32	1.8	31	13.9	13	2.5	30	5.7	32
South	88,143	(X)	3.2	(X)	12.7	(X)	5.4	(X)	10.9	(X)
South Atlantic	45,061	(X)	3.4	(X)	13.5	(X)	6.3	(X)	9.2	(X)
Delaware	689	46	3.5	15	12.3	31	3.3	23	6.9	26
Maryland.	4,908	19	2.7	22	11.0	41	6.6	14	8.9	19
Dist. of Columbia .	589	(X)	-3.0	(X)	13.1	(X)	9.7	(X)	12.5	(X)
Virginia	6,377	12	3.1	19	10.9	43	5.0	16	7.3	23
West Virginia	1,812	35	1.0	42	15.2	5	0.9	49	2.6	49
North Carolina . . .	6,843	10	3.2	17	12.4	30	1.7	36	3.9	41
South Carolina . . .	3,603	25	3.3	16	11.6	37	1.4	43	3.5	44
Georgia.	6,751	11	4.2	12	10.1	47	2.7	28	4.8	40
Florida	13,488	4	4.2	11	18.4	1	12.9	4	17.3	8
East South Central .	15,529	(X)	2.3	(X)	12.8	(X)	1.0	(X)	2.8	(X)
Kentucky	3,755	24	1.9	30	12.7	25	0.9	48	2.5	50
Tennessee	5,024	17	3.0	20	12.7	24	1.2	44	2.9	45
Alabama	4,136	22	2.4	24	13.0	23	1.1	46	2.9	46
Mississippi	2,614	31	1.6	34	12.5	29	0.8	50	2.8	47
West South Central .	27,554	(X)	3.2	(X)	11.1	(X)	6.4	(X)	18.6	(X)
Arkansas	2,399	33	2.0	29	14.9	6	1.1	47	2.8	48
Louisiana	4,287	21	1.6	35	11.2	39	2.1	34	10.1	16
Oklahoma	3,212	28	2.1	28	13.5	17	2.1	33	5.0	37
Texas	17,656	3	3.9	13	10.2	46	9.0	8	25.4	3
West	55,108	(X)	4.4	(X)	11.0	(X)	14.8	(X)	23.5	(X)
Mountain	14,381	(X)	5.3	(X)	11.3	(X)	5.2	(X)	15.1	(X)
Montana	824	44	3.1	18	13.4	18	1.7	37	5.0	36
Idaho	1,067	42	6.0	3	11.9	34	2.9	27	6.4	29
Wyoming.	466	50	2.8	21	10.7	44	1.7	39	5.7	33
Colorado.	3,470	26	5.3	5	10.0	48	4.3	19	10.5	15
New Mexico.	1,581	37	4.4	10	10.9	42	5.3	15	35.5	1
Arizona	3,832	23	4.6	9	13.4	19	7.6	12	20.8	6
Utah.	1,813	34	5.2	6	8.8	49	3.4	22	7.8	22
Nevada.	1,327	38	10.4	1	11.0	40	8.7	9	13.2	13
Pacific	40,726	(X)	4.1	(X)	10.8	(X)	18.2	(X)	26.4	(X)
Washington	5,136	16	5.5	4	11.7	36	6.6	13	9.0	18
Oregon	2,977	29	4.8	7	13.8	14	4.9	17	7.3	25
California.	30,867	1	3.7	14	10.5	45	21.7	1	31.5	2
Alaska	587	48	6.7	2	4.3	50	4.5	18	12.1	14
Hawaii	1,160	40	4.6	8	11.4	38	14.7	3	24.8	4

X Not applicable.   Z Less than .05 percent.   [1] Source: U.S. Bureau of the Census.   [2] See table 31. As of July 1.   [3] See table 35. As of July 1.   [4] See table 58. As of April 1.   [5] Persons 5 years old and over.

[When States share the same rank, the next lower rank is omitted. Because of rounded data, States may have identical values shown, but different ranks]

REGION, DIVISION, AND STATE	RESIDENT POPULATION IN METRO AREAS,[1][2] 1990		ONE-PARENT FAMILIES,[2][3] 1990		BIRTH RATE PER 1,000 POPULATION,[4] 1990					
					All races		White		Black	
	Percent	Rank	Percent	Rank	Rate	Rank	Rate	Rank	Rate	Rank
United States . . .	79.4	(X)	23.9	(X)	16.7	(X)	15.5	(X)	22.4	(X)
Northeast	89.5	(X)	24.0	(X)	15.6	(X)	14.9	(X)	24.5	(X)
New England	84.2	(X)	22.7	(X)	15.2	(X)	14.6	(X)	30.3	(X)
Maine	36.1	44	21.6	33	14.1	49	14.0	37	31.7	9
New Hampshire . .	59.4	34	18.2	48	15.8	22	15.7	13	25.6	27
Vermont	26.9	49	21.8	31	14.7	44	14.7	26	19.5	49
Massachusetts . . .	96.2	3	23.9	19	15.4	32	14.5	29	34.1	4
Rhode Island	93.5	5	23.8	21	15.1	39	14.3	33	34.5	3
Connecticut	95.7	4	22.5	29	15.2	38	14.6	28	25.6	28
Middle Atlantic	91.3	(X)	24.5	(X)	15.7	(X)	15.0	(X)	23.8	(X)
New York	91.8	8	27.5	3	16.5	16	16.2	10	23.2	38
New Jersey	100.0	1	21.6	35	15.8	22	15.1	19	23.6	35
Pennsylvania	84.9	9	21.7	32	14.5	45	13.4	47	25.6	26
Midwest	73.2	(X)	22.8	(X)	15.9	(X)	14.8	(X)	25.8	(X)
East North Central . .	79.5	(X)	23.9	(X)	16.1	(X)	15.0	(X)	25.6	(X)
Ohio	81.4	18	23.8	20	15.4	32	14.4	30	24.0	31
Indiana	71.5	23	22.1	30	15.6	28	14.9	22	23.8	32
Illinois	83.8	12	24.0	18	17.1	10	16.2	11	26.7	21
Michigan	82.8	16	26.6	4	16.5	16	15.2	17	25.5	30
Wisconsin	68.1	28	21.2	38	14.9	42	13.9	40	30.7	11
West North Central .	58.3	(X)	20.3	(X)	15.3	(X)	14.5	(X)	26.9	(X)
Minnesota	68.8	26	19.6	42	15.5	29	14.8	24	32.7	7
Iowa	43.2	40	18.9	45	14.2	48	13.9	39	26.6	22
Missouri	68.2	27	22.9	26	15.5	29	14.2	34	25.7	25
North Dakota	40.3	43	16.9	49	14.5	45	13.6	45	33.8	5
South Dakota	31.7	45	19.1	44	15.8	22	14.1	35	41.4	1
Nebraska	49.9	37	18.9	46	15.4	32	14.9	21	27.0	19
Kansas	53.8	36	19.9	41	15.7	26	15.3	15	26.8	20
South	73.5	(X)	24.4	(X)	16.5	(X)	15.4	(X)	23.0	(X)
South Atlantic	78.6	(X)	25.0	(X)	16.1	(X)	14.3	(X)	23.2	(X)
Delaware	83.0	14	24.3	13	16.7	15	15.4	14	23.8	33
Maryland	92.8	7	25.4	11	16.8	13	15.0	20	21.9	43
Dist. of Columbia .	100.0	(X)	54.7	(X)	19.5	(X)	9.7	(X)	22.9	(X)
Virginia	77.1	20	21.5	37	16.1	21	14.8	23	21.3	47
West Virginia . . .	41.7	41	20.2	39	12.6	50	12.4	50	17.1	50
North Carolina . . .	65.2	32	24.2	15	15.8	22	13.9	38	21.7	45
South Carolina . . .	69.5	25	25.5	10	16.8	13	14.6	27	21.8	44
Georgia	66.9	30	25.9	8	17.4	9	15.1	18	23.6	36
Florida	92.9	6	26.4	6	15.4	32	13.8	43	27.3	16
East South Central . .	55.6	(X)	24.3	(X)	15.6	(X)	13.9	(X)	22.3	(X)
Kentucky	47.6	38	21.6	34	14.8	43	14.3	32	20.4	48
Tennessee	65.5	31	24.1	16	15.4	32	13.8	41	23.2	39
Alabama	67.1	29	24.3	14	15.7	26	13.7	44	21.6	46
Mississippi	30.1	46	29.0	1	16.9	12	13.6	46	22.8	41
West South Central .	75.6	(X)	23.6	(X)	17.7	(X)	18.2	(X)	22.9	(X)
Arkansas	44.2	39	22.9	25	15.5	29	14.0	36	23.2	37
Louisiana	73.5	22	28.7	2	17.1	10	14.3	31	23.1	40
Oklahoma	59.4	33	22.7	27	15.1	39	13.8	42	23.7	34
Texas	83.4	13	22.6	28	18.6	5	20.6	3	22.7	42
West	86.2	(X)	24.2	(X)	19.1	(X)	20.4	(X)	26.7	(X)
Mountain	70.3	(X)	23.1	(X)	17.8	(X)	18.1	(X)	27.2	(X)
Montana	23.9	50	21.5	36	14.5	45	13.1	48	31.5	10
Idaho	29.4	48	18.6	47	16.3	18	16.6	8	27.3	18
Wyoming	29.6	47	20.0	40	15.4	32	15.2	16	29.7	12
Colorado	81.5	17	23.6	23	16.2	20	16.6	9	25.5	29
New Mexico	55.6	35	26.1	7	18.1	7	19.3	5	25.8	24
Arizona	84.7	10	25.5	9	18.8	4	19.6	4	28.7	13
Utah	77.5	19	16.7	50	21.1	2	21.0	2	33.3	6
Nevada	84.4	11	26.6	5	18.0	8	17.9	7	27.4	15
Pacific	91.7	(X)	24.6	(X)	19.6	(X)	21.4	(X)	26.6	(X)
Washington	82.9	15	23.7	22	16.3	18	15.8	12	27.7	14
Oregon	69.8	24	24.0	17	15.1	39	14.7	25	27.3	17
California	96.8	2	25.1	12	20.6	3	23.7	1	26.4	23
Alaska	41.1	42	23.0	24	21.6	1	18.3	6	31.9	8
Hawaii	75.5	21	19.2	43	18.5	6	12.7	49	35.3	2

X Not applicable. [1] See table 41. [2] Source: U.S. Bureau of the Census. [3] As percent of all families with own children. See table 69. [4] See table 94. Source: U.S. National Center for Health Statistics.

State Rankings

[When States share the same rank, the next lower rank is omitted. Because of rounded data, States may have identical values shown, but different ranks]

REGION, DIVISION, AND STATE	INFANT MORTALITY RATE, [1] 1990		COMMUNITY HOSPITALS, [2] 1991						PHYSICIANS, RATE PER 100,000 POPULATION, [6] 1990	
			Beds per 100,000 population [3]		Occupancy rate [3][4]		Average cost per patient per day [5]			
	Rate	Rank	Rate	Rank	Rate	Rank	Dollars	Rank	Rate	Rank
United States . . .	9.2	(X)	366	(X)	66.1	(X)	752	(X)	216	(X)
Northeast	8.9	(X)	393	(X)	78.3	(X)	(NA)	(X)	280	(X)
New England	7.2	(X)	334	(X)	72.9	(X)	(NA)	(X)	293	(X)
Maine.	6.2	50	369	27	70.0	11	617	36	178	30
New Hampshire . .	7.1	46	310	36	65.0	19	713	25	200	18
Vermont	6.4	49	316	35	68.3	13	621	35	253	6
Massachusetts. . .	7.0	47	361	28	73.0	8	880	9	337	1
Rhode Island	8.1	37	308	38	78.9	4	730	23	254	5
Connecticut	7.9	41	289	40	75.8	5	910	5	305	4
Middle Atlantic	9.5	(X)	413	(X)	79.8	(X)	(NA)	(X)	275	(X)
New York	9.6	16	417	18	84.8	1	694	27	315	3
New Jersey	9.0	24	380	25	79.6	3	680	31	246	7
Pennsylvania	9.6	16	430	16	72.7	9	732	22	235	10
Midwest	9.6	(X)	410	(X)	63.2	(X)	(NA)	(X)	190	(X)
East North Central . .	10.1	(X)	379	(X)	64.2	(X)	(NA)	(X)	192	(X)
Ohio.	9.8	15	391	20	63.0	26	782	16	196	21
Indiana	9.6	16	384	23	60.1	38	745	19	157	42
Illinois	10.7	6	391	20	66.3	15	770	17	212	14
Michigan	10.7	6	351	29	65.4	17	792	15	185	27
Wisconsin	8.2	36	374	26	64.3	20	611	39	189	25
West North Central .	8.4	(X)	482	(X)	61.5	(X)	(NA)	(X)	186	(X)
Minnesota	7.3	45	431	15	67.7	14	582	41	220	11
Iowa	8.1	37	506	5	60.2	37	538	45	151	43
Missouri	9.4	21	468	9	60.9	35	737	21	196	21
North Dakota	8.0	40	699	1	64.1	21	454	48	170	35
South Dakota	10.1	12	605	2	61.9	31	436	50	140	47
Nebraska	8.3	34	529	4	57.3	43	546	44	172	34
Kansas	8.4	32	459	12	55.9	46	585	40	175	31
South	10.0	(X)	381	(X)	62.6	(X)	(NA)	(X)	192	(X)
South Atlantic	10.7	(X)	358	(X)	66.6	(X)	(NA)	(X)	215	(X)
Delaware.	10.1	12	306	39	74.8	7	845	11	199	19
Maryland.	9.5	20	275	41	75.6	6	740	20	334	2
Dist. of Columbia .	20.7	(X)	722	(X)	76.6	(X)	1,038	(X)	615	(X)
Virginia	10.2	11	322	32	65.8	16	701	26	213	12
West Virginia . . .	9.9	14	460	11	63.7	22	612	38	166	37
North Carolina . . .	10.6	8	327	31	72.3	10	651	33	190	24
South Carolina . . .	11.7	3	320	33	68.9	12	684	30	161	38
Georgia.	12.4	1	401	19	65.2	18	652	32	175	31
Florida	9.6	16	381	24	61.6	33	836	13	208	16
East South Central . .	10.4	(X)	463	(X)	61.4	(X)	(NA)	(X)	168	(X)
Kentucky.	8.5	31	428	17	62.6	28	616	37	168	36
Tennessee	10.3	10	474	8	62.1	29	716	24	196	21
Alabama	10.8	5	458	13	62.1	29	637	34	158	40
Mississippi	12.1	2	503	6	57.5	41	479	47	133	49
West South Central .	8.7	(X)	373	(X)	57.3	(X)	(NA)	(X)	171	(X)
Arkansas.	9.2	22	468	9	60.6	36	571	42	150	44
Louisiana	11.1	4	446	14	58.4	39	764	18	188	26
Oklahoma	9.2	22	388	22	55.7	47	684	30	147	45
Texas.	8.1	37	340	30	56.6	45	846	10	175	31
West	8.1	(X)	269	(X)	62.2	(X)	(NA)	(X)	222	(X)
Mountain	8.6	(X)	298	(X)	60.6	(X)	(NA)	(X)	184	(X)
Montana	9.0	24	541	3	63.1	24	437	49	158	40
Idaho	8.7	29	319	34	57.4	42	565	43	125	50
Wyoming.	8.6	30	475	7	51.3	49	489	46	139	48
Colorado.	8.8	27	309	37	63.3	23	801	14	211	15
New Mexico.	9.0	24	259	46	57.3	43	840	12	183	29
Arizona.	8.8	27	259	46	61.8	32	955	3	197	20
Utah.	7.5	44	249	48	58.3	40	915	4	185	27
Nevada.	8.4	32	269	42	61.4	34	907	6	159	39
Pacific	7.9	(X)	259	(X)	62.9	(X)	(NA)	(X)	235	(X)
Washington	7.8	43	239	49	62.9	27	904	7	213	12
Oregon	8.3	34	268	43	55.1	48	896	8	205	17
California.	7.9	41	263	44	63.1	24	1,037	2	244	8
Alaska	10.5	9	209	50	49.3	50	1,130	1	146	46
Hawaii	6.7	48	262	45	82.8	2	686	28	236	9

NA Not available.   X Not applicable.   [1] See table 124. Source: U.S. National Center for Health Statistics. Deaths of infants under 1 year old per 1,000 live births, by place of residence. Excludes fetal deaths.   [2] Source: American Hospital Association, Chicago, IL (copyright).   [3] See table 180.   [4] Ratio of the number of inpatients receiving treatment each day to every 100 beds. Excludes newborn.   [5] See table 183. Average cost to community hospitals; based on total hospital expenses (payroll, employee benefits, professional fees, supplies, etc.)   [6] See table 173. Source: American Medical Association, Chicago, IL (copyright). Covers active non-Federal physicians and includes physicians not classified according to activity status.

[When States share the same rank, the next lower rank is omitted. Because of rounded data, States may have identical values shown, but different ranks]

REGION, DIVISION, AND STATE	PUBLIC ELEMENTARY AND SECONDARY SCHOOLS						EDUCATIONAL ATTAINMENT, [5] 1990			
	Enrollment, percent increase, [1][2] 1990-93		Teachers' average salaries, [3] 1992		High school graduates, percent increase, [2][4] 1990-94		High school graduate or higher		Bachelor's degree or higher	
	Percent	Rank	Dollars	Rank	Percent	Rank	Percent	Rank	Percent	Rank
United States . . .	4.2	(X)	34.1	(X)	-4.8	(X)	75.2	(X)	20.3	(X)
Northeast	4.5	(X)	(NA)	(X)	-10.8	(X)	76.2	(X)	22.8	(X)
New England	6.5	(X)	(NA)	(X)	-13.8	(X)	79.3	(X)	25.6	(X)
Maine	5.0	17	30.1	30	-14.1	48	78.8	18	18.8	27
New Hampshire . .	14.0	1	33.2	22	-12.8	47	82.2	7	24.4	7
Vermont	4.4	19	33.6	20	-15.6	49	80.8	12	24.3	8
Massachusetts . .	6.1	13	37.3	9	-16.9	50	80.0	15	27.2	1
Rhode Island	3.7	22	36.0	11	-7.1	30	72.0	40	21.3	17
Connecticut	6.6	11	47.0	1	-9.3	38	79.2	17	27.2	1
Middle Atlantic . . .	3.8	(X)	(NA)	(X)	-9.7	(X)	75.2	(X)	21.8	(X)
New York	2.9	27	43.3	3	-8.3	35	74.8	34	23.1	10
New Jersey	6.5	12	41.0	5	-12.2	46	76.7	26	24.9	5
Pennsylvania	3.2	25	38.7	8	-9.9	40	74.7	35	17.9	31
Midwest	2.0	(X)	(NA)	(X)	-6.2	(X)	77.1	(X)	18.4	(X)
East North Central . .	1.7	(X)	(NA)	(X)	-7.8	(X)	76.4	(X)	18.1	(X)
Ohio	1.5	34	33.3	21	-8.9	36	75.7	30	17.0	39
Indiana	1.6	33	34.8	13	-7.5	31	75.6	31	15.6	45
Illinois	1.5	34	36.5	10	-5.0	24	76.2	28	21.0	19
Michigan	2.1	29	41.1	4	-11.1	44	76.8	25	17.4	36
Wisconsin	2.1	29	35.2	12	-5.7	28	78.6	21	17.7	34
West North Central .	2.5	(X)	(NA)	(X)	-2.5	(X)	78.9	(X)	19.2	(X)
Minnesota	4.3	20	33.7	19	-0.9	14	82.4	6	21.8	15
Iowa	-2.6	45	29.2	33	-3.9	20	80.1	13	16.9	40
Missouri	4.6	18	28.9	35	-4.9	22	73.9	38	17.8	32
North Dakota	-0.7	41	24.5	48	-2.9	18	76.7	26	18.1	30
South Dakota	3.0	26	23.3	50	3.5	5	77.1	24	17.2	38
Nebraska	-	40	27.2	40	-4.9	22	81.8	8	18.9	26
Kansas	3.4	24	30.7	28	0.5	11	81.3	10	21.1	18
South	3.9	(X)	(NA)	(X)	-5.4	(X)	71.3	(X)	18.7	(X)
South Atlantic	7.6	(X)	(NA)	(X)	-5.9	(X)	73.0	(X)	19.9	(X)
Delaware	8.4	9	34.5	15	-1.8	15	77.5	23	21.4	16
Maryland	11.4	2	39.5	7	-7.6	32	78.4	22	26.5	4
Dist. of Columbia . .	4.1	(X)	41.3	(X)	-24.7	(X)	73.1	(X)	33.3	(X)
Virginia	9.7	7	31.9	24	-8.2	33	75.2	32	24.5	6
West Virginia	-6.9	50	27.4	39	-9.0	37	66.0	48	12.3	50
North Carolina . . .	5.8	15	29.2	32	-10.6	43	70.0	42	17.4	36
South Carolina . . .	3.8	21	28.3	37	-1.9	16	68.3	43	16.6	41
Georgia	7.6	10	29.5	31	2.6	7	70.9	41	19.3	25
Florida	10.1	6	31.1	26	-5.5	27	74.4	37	18.3	29
East South Central . .	0.4	(X)	(NA)	(X)	-8.3	(X)	66.0	(X)	15.1	(X)
Kentucky	-2.9	47	30.9	27	-10.3	41	64.6	49	13.6	48
Tennessee	2.5	28	28.6	36	-9.4	39	67.1	45	16.0	43
Alabama	1.8	32	27.0	42	-5.3	26	66.9	46	15.7	44
Mississippi	-1.1	42	24.4	49	-8.2	33	64.3	50	14.7	47
West South Central .	0.7	(X)	(NA)	(X)	-3.1	(X)	71.3	(X)	18.7	(X)
Arkansas	1.5	34	26.6	44	-3.8	19	66.3	47	13.3	49
Louisiana	-1.9	44	27.0	41	-10.5	42	68.3	43	16.1	42
Oklahoma	-1.6	43	25.3	47	-11.5	45	74.6	36	17.8	32
Texas	1.5	34	29.0	34	0.3	12	72.1	39	20.3	22
West	7.1	(X)	(NA)	(X)	4.0	(X)	78.6	(X)	22.7	(X)
Mountain	4.3	(X)	(NA)	(X)	2.6	(X)	80.8	(X)	21.4	(X)
Montana	-2.6	45	27.6	38	-0.6	13	81.0	11	19.8	24
Idaho	-3.1	48	26.3	46	5.4	4	79.7	16	17.7	34
Wyoming	-6.3	49	30.4	29	-5.7	28	83.0	5	18.8	27
Colorado	3.6	23	33.1	23	-5.0	24	84.4	3	27.0	3
New Mexico	5.3	16	26.7	43	1.9	9	75.1	33	20.4	21
Arizona	10.8	3	31.2	25	-2.8	17	78.7	20	20.3	22
Utah	0.7	39	26.5	45	20.5	1	85.1	2	22.3	14
Nevada	10.3	5	33.9	18	10.8	2	78.8	18	15.3	46
Pacific	8.3	(X)	(NA)	(X)	4.6	(X)	77.8	(X)	23.1	(X)
Washington	5.9	14	34.8	14	2.0	8	83.8	4	22.9	12
Oregon	1.3	38	34.1	17	3.4	6	81.5	9	20.6	20
California	9.4	8	40.2	6	5.7	3	76.2	28	23.4	9
Alaska	1.9	31	44.7	2	1.9	9	86.6	1	23.0	11
Hawaii	10.7	4	34.5	16	-4.5	21	80.1	13	22.9	12

- Represents or rounds to zero.   NA Not available.   X Not applicable.   [1] See tables 241 and 242.   [2] Source: U.S. National Center for Education Statistics.   [3] See table 245. Source: National Education Association, Washington, DC (copyright).   [4] See table 268.   [5] See table 235. Source: U.S. Bureau of the Census. Persons 25 years old and over.

[When States share the same rank, the next lower rank is omitted. Because of rounded data, States may have identical values shown, but different ranks]

REGION, DIVISION, AND STATE	COLLEGE ENROLLMENT,[1] 1991				CRIME, 1991					
	Full-time		Minority		Violent crime rate per 100,000 population[2]		Criminal justice expenditures per person[3]		Federal and State prisoners, percent change,[4] 1980-91	
	Percent	Rank	Percent	Rank	Rate	Rank	Dollars	Rank	Percent	Rank
United States . . .	56.5	(X)	20.6	(X)	758	(X)	299	(X)	149.9	(X)
Northeast	61.4	(X)	17.7	(X)	752	(X)	361	(X)	187.9	(X)
New England	60.6	(X)	10.6	(X)	532	(X)	296	(X)	173.4	(X)
Maine.	57.6	29	2.7	50	132	47	189	41	94.0	43
New Hampshire . .	62.7	21	4.5	48	119	48	233	28	370.2	1
Vermont	68.6	10	3.9	49	117	49	185	42	132.9	28
Massachusetts . . .	63.4	20	12.6	27	736	14	315	12	187.4	9
Rhode Island	62.5	23	8.9	36	462	31	287	17	240.8	5
Connecticut	50.8	41	12.6	27	540	26	346	9	154.8	21
Middle Atlantic	61.7	(X)	20.7	(X)	829	(X)	383	(X)	192.0	(X)
New York	62.7	21	25.2	7	1,164	2	499	2	165.2	17
New Jersey	50.4	43	22.7	12	635	20	349	8	299.1	3
Pennsylvania	66.0	15	11.8	29	450	32	229	30	186.2	10
Midwest	57.2	(X)	13.1	(X)	631	(X)	241	(X)	135.5	(X)
East North Central . .	55.7	(X)	15.2	(X)	704	(X)	258	(X)	138.7	(X)
Ohio.	61.1	25	11.3	31	562	24	249	24	165.0	18
Indiana	65.8	17	9.1	35	505	29	173	45	94.6	40
Illinois	49.6	44	24.3	10	1,039	4	266	21	144.7	24
Michigan	50.8	41	14.1	25	803	11	303	13	140.8	26
Wisconsin	60.2	26	8.0	37	277	42	268	19	97.2	39
West North Central .	60.8	(X)	8.1	(X)	457	(X)	203	(X)	124.6	(X)
Minnesota	58.9	28	5.9	41	316	37	228	31	73.5	44
Iowa.	70.6	5	5.4	44	303	39	190	38	67.1	47
Missouri	56.7	32	11.6	30	763	12	189	40	177.6	13
North Dakota	79.3	1	6.9	40	65	50	143	47	94.5	41
South Dakota. . . .	69.9	6	7.2	39	182	45	161	46	116.4	34
Nebraska	56.8	31	5.9	41	335	36	183	44	72.5	46
Kansas	57.3	30	9.7	32	500	30	239	26	136.7	27
South	59.5	(X)	23.3	(X)	798	(X)	257	(X)	106.3	(X)
South Atlantic	56.6	(X)	22.8	(X)	851	(X)	301	(X)	105.7	(X)
Delaware.	60.1	27	15.6	23	714	16	328	10	152.2	22
Maryland.	46.0	46	24.9	9	956	6	358	6	149.5	23
Dist. of Columbia . .	62.2	(X)	37.6	(X)	2,453	(X)	1,261	(X)	232.4	(X)
Virginia	56.2	34	20.1	17	373	35	260	23	122.3	33
West Virginia	67.7	12	5.1	47	191	44	118	50	19.5	50
North Carolina . . .	61.7	24	21.3	15	658	19	231	29	21.9	49
South Carolina . . .	68.8	9	21.7	14	973	5	224	32	132.4	29
Georgia.	66.3	14	24.3	10	738	13	266	20	94.2	42
Florida	48.3	45	25.1	8	1,184	1	354	7	124.4	32
East South Central . .	67.4	(X)	18.1	(X)	631	(X)	189	(X)	122.9	(X)
Kentucky	63.6	19	7.8	38	438	33	190	39	173.1	15
Tennessee	65.5	18	16.6	20	726	15	221	33	63.4	48
Alabama	67.8	11	22.1	13	844	8	185	43	156.2	20
Mississippi	76.0	2	29.4	5	389	34	134	49	128.2	30
West South Central . .	59.7	(X)	27.0	(X)	806	(X)	224	(X)	99.6	(X)
Arkansas	71.4	4	16.0	22	593	22	142	48	166.8	16
Louisiana	68.9	8	28.5	6	951	7	241	25	125.0	31
Oklahoma	69.9	6	16.5	21	584	23	195	37	178.1	12
Texas	54.5	38	29.9	4	840	9	237	27	72.9	45
West	47.4	(X)	27.1	(X)	841	(X)	374	(X)	245.9	(X)
Mountain	52.6	(X)	16.5	(X)	544	(X)	302	(X)	202.7	(X)
Montana	75.0	3	9.2	34	140	46	196	36	100.0	38
Idaho	67.4	13	5.2	46	290	40	197	35	162.3	19
Wyoming.	55.5	37	5.9	41	310	38	300	14	105.8	37
Colorado	52.8	39	14.8	24	559	25	290	15	219.2	7
New Mexico	51.3	40	38.0	2	835	10	284	18	143.9	25
Arizona	44.6	47	20.4	16	671	18	372	5	252.6	4
Utah.	65.9	16	5.4	44	287	41	220	34	181.7	11
Nevada.	32.7	50	17.4	18	677	17	417	4	199.2	8
Pacific	45.5	(X)	31.0	(X)	945	(X)	399	(X)	262.6	(X)
Washington	56.5	33	14.0	26	523	27	261	22	108.1	36
Oregon.	55.6	36	9.7	32	506	28	288	16	111.9	35
California.	43.0	48	34.3	3	1,090	3	432	3	314.4	2
Alaska	37.5	49	17.2	19	614	21	600	1	229.2	6
Hawaii	56.2	34	63.5	1	242	43	320	11	174.1	14

X Not applicable.   [1] See table 276. Source: U.S. National Center for Education Statistics.   [2] See table 302. Source: U.S. Federal Bureau of Investigation. Based on offenses known to the police.   [3] See table 325. Source: U.S. Bureau of the Census.   [4] See table 346. Source: U.S. Bureau of Justice Statistics.

[When States share the same rank, the next lower rank is omitted. Because of rounded data, States may have identical values shown, but different ranks]

REGION, DIVISION, AND STATE	HAZARDOUS WASTE SITES [1] 1992		STATE GASOLINE TAX RATES [2] 1992 (per gallon)		FEDERAL FUNDS [3] 1992					
					Defense [4]		Grants to State and local governments per person			
							Total [5]		Highway trust fund [6]	
	Number	Rank	Cents	Rank	Mil. dol.	Rank	Dollars	Rank	Dollars	Rank
United States . . .	1,224	(X)	(X)	(X)	226,045	(X)	684	(X)	58	(X)
Northeast	376	(X)	(X)	(X)	31,532	(X)	863	(X)	(NA)	(X)
New England	87	(X)	(X)	(X)	13,918	(X)	855	(X)	(NA)	(X)
Maine	9	38	19.0	23	1,927	30	847	12	64	24
New Hampshire . .	17	22	18.6	28	635	42	842	14	52	37
Vermont	8	41	16.0	39	140	50	882	9	120	7
Massachusetts . . .	26	14	21.0	14	6,664	8	870	11	96	12
Rhode Island	12	28	26.0	2	868	38	981	5	117	8
Connecticut	15	24	28.0	1	3,684	17	790	16	107	9
Middle Atlantic	289	(X)	(X)	(X)	17,614	(X)	865	(X)	(NA)	(X)
New York	83	4	22.9	8	7,180	6	1,065	3	38	49
New Jersey	108	1	10.5	47	4,824	14	670	25	52	39
Pennsylvania	98	2	22.4	9	5,610	9	691	21	52	38
Midwest	332	(X)	(X)	(X)	26,324	(X)	626	(X)	(NA)	(X)
East North Central . .	220	(X)	(X)	(X)	14,775	(X)	617	(X)	(NA)	(X)
Ohio	33	11	21.0	14	5,156	13	641	31	44	46
Indiana	33	11	15.0	43	2,551	25	573	44	70	21
Illinois	37	10	19.0	23	3,171	21	596	39	46	44
Michigan	77	5	15.0	43	2,570	24	636	33	42	48
Wisconsin	40	9	22.2	11	1,327	35	624	34	56	31
West North Central .	112	(X)	(X)	(X)	11,549	(X)	647	(X)	(NA)	(X)
Minnesota	42	8	20.0	18	1,812	31	646	29	60	28
Iowa	21	19	20.0	18	653	40	590	40	85	14
Missouri	23	16	13.0	45	5,272	12	674	24	61	25
North Dakota	2	47	17.0	35	473	43	948	6	177	4
South Dakota. . . .	4	45	18.0	30	334	46	845	13	141	6
Nebraska	10	33	24.6	3	969	37	621	35	68	23
Kansas	10	33	18.0	30	2,036	29	545	47	54	33
South	281	(X)	(X)	(X)	89,805	(X)	633	(X)	(NA)	(X)
South Atlantic	171	(X)	(X)	(X)	55,765	(X)	585	(X)	(NA)	(X)
Delaware.	19	20	19.0	23	367	44	617	36	87	13
Maryland	10	33	23.5	6	7,147	7	599	37	54	34
Dist. of Columbia .	-	(X)	20.0	(X)	2,704	(X)	3,314	(X)	194	(X)
Virginia	22	18	17.5	34	17,270	2	435	50	43	47
West Virginia	5	44	20.4	17	285	48	921	8	79	15
North Carolina . . .	23	16	22.3	10	5,488	10	580	42	45	45
South Carolina . . .	24	15	16.0	39	3,369	20	664	26	53	36
Georgia.	13	26	7.5	50	7,949	5	597	38	49	42
Florida	55	6	11.8	46	11,186	4	459	49	38	50
East South Central. .	47	(X)	(X)	(X)	12,192	(X)	747	(X)	(NA)	(X)
Kentucky.	19	20	15.4	42	2,225	28	786	17	47	43
Tennessee	14	25	20.0	18	2,226	27	728	18	61	26
Alabama	12	28	18.0	30	4,124	16	676	23	53	35
Mississippi.	2	47	18.2	29	3,617	18	839	15	68	22
West South Central .	63	(X)	(X)	(X)	21,848	(X)	647	(X)	(NA)	(X)
Arkansas.	12	28	18.7	27	994	36	705	20	77	17
Louisiana	12	28	20.0	18	2,549	26	1,030	4	71	19
Oklahoma	10	33	17.0	35	2,709	23	643	30	58	30
Texas	29	13	20.0	18	15,596	3	546	46	50	40
West	235	(X)	(X)	(X)	61,102	(X)	655	(X)	(NA)	(X)
Mountain	72	(X)	(X)	(X)	13,205	(X)	645	(X)	(NA)	(X)
Montana	8	41	21.4	13	286	47	929	7	190	3
Idaho	9	38	21.0	14	364	45	650	28	103	10
Wyoming.	3	46	9.0	48	242	49	1,271	2	222	2
Colorado.	17	22	22.0	12	4,622	15	549	45	71	18
New Mexico.	11	32	17.0	35	1,739	32	872	10	101	11
Arizona	10	33	18.0	30	3,502	19	583	41	49	41
Utah.	13	26	19.0	23	1,610	33	575	43	60	29
Nevada.	1	50	24.0	4	840	39	504	48	60	27
Pacific.	163	(X)	(X)	(X)	47,897	(X)	659	(X)	(NA)	(X)
Washington	50	7	23.0	7	5,436	11	657	27	78	16
Oregon	9	38	24.0	4	641	41	688	22	70	20
California.	95	3	17.0	35	37,381	1	639	32	55	32
Alaska	7	43	8.0	49	1,546	34	1,425	1	360	1
Hawaii	2	47	16.0	39	2,893	22	724	19	171	5

- Represents zero.   NA Not available.   X Not applicable.   [1] See table 375. Source: U.S. Environmental Protection Agency.
[2] See table 1015. Source: U.S. Federal Highway Administration. In effect December 31.   [3] Source: U.S. Bureau of the Census.
[4] See table 522.   [5] See table 473.   [6] See table 1014.

[When States share the same rank, the next lower rank is omitted. Because of rounded data, States may have identical values shown, but different ranks]

REGION, DIVISION, AND STATE	CIVILIAN LABOR FORCE, [1] 1992						NONFARM EMPLOYMENT, [2] 1992			
	Employment/ population ratio		Female participation rate		Unemployment rate		Services		Manufacturing	
	Ratio	Rank	Rate	Rank	Percent	Rank	Percent	Rank	Percent	Rank
United States . . .	61.4	(X)	57.8	(X)	7.4	(X)	26.7	(X)	16.8	(X)
Northeast	59.6	(X)	56.2	(X)	8.1	(X)	29.6	(X)	16.1	(X)
New England	63.7	(X)	61.8	(X)	8.0	(X)	29.9	(X)	18.3	(X)
Maine.	63.7	24	61.7	18	7.1	23	25.2	27	18.0	20
New Hampshire . .	66.6	8	64.9	4	7.5	12	26.6	18	20.0	13
Vermont	66.4	10	66.0	1	6.6	28	27.7	12	17.7	21
Massachusetts. .	61.8	32	60.0	25	8.5	6	32.6	2	16.6	24
Rhode Island . . .	62.1	30	60.6	23	8.9	4	30.2	5	21.4	11
Connecticut	66.0	14	63.8	8	7.5	12	27.6	14	20.1	12
Middle Atlantic . .	58.1	(X)	54.3	(X)	8.1	(X)	29.5	(X)	15.3	(X)
New York	56.5	49	52.8	48	8.5	6	30.2	5	13.1	36
New Jersey	60.8	35	57.0	35	8.4	8	28.2	9	15.3	30
Pennsylvania . . .	58.8	42	54.8	42	7.5	12	29.3	8	18.7	16
Midwest	63.7	(X)	59.9	(X)	6.5	(X)	25.2	(X)	20.0	(X)
East North Central. .	62.2	(X)	58.7	(X)	7.3	(X)	25.0	(X)	21.4	(X)
Ohio.	61.1	34	57.1	34	7.2	21	25.5	24	21.7	10
Indiana	62.0	31	57.5	33	6.5	31	21.7	45	24.7	3
Illinois.	63.1	27	59.8	27	7.5	12	26.7	16	17.7	21
Michigan	59.7	38	56.8	36	8.8	5	24.8	30	22.9	8
Wisconsin	67.7	5	64.8	5	5.1	42	24.3	35	23.2	6
West North Central .	67.1	(X)	62.8	(X)	4.8	(X)	25.5	(X)	16.7	(X)
Minnesota	68.9	1	65.7	2	5.1	42	27.1	15	18.1	19
Iowa.	68.2	3	63.5	9	4.6	46	24.5	33	18.4	17
Missouri	64.4	19	60.0	25	5.7	38	25.9	21	17.7	21
North Dakota. . . .	64.4	19	60.1	24	4.9	44	26.7	16	6.5	47
South Dakota. . . .	67.3	6	62.4	15	3.1	49	25.4	25	12.1	38
Nebraska	68.9	1	64.4	7	3.0	50	24.8	30	13.4	34
Kansas	68.0	4	62.8	12	4.2	48	23.2	39	16.3	25
South	60.8	(X)	57.3	(X)	7.2	(X)	25.2	(X)	16.1	(X)
South Atlantic	61.2	(X)	58.4	(X)	7.1	(X)	26.5	(X)	15.3	(X)
Delaware.	65.5	17	62.3	16	5.3	41	25.0	28	19.8	14
Maryland.	66.4	10	64.8	5	6.6	28	30.3	4	8.8	43
Dist. of Columbia .	60.8	(X)	61.7	(X)	8.4	(X)	37.8	(X)	2.1	(X)
Virginia	66.4	10	63.0	10	6.4	33	26.6	18	14.4	31
West Virginia	48.3	50	43.7	50	11.3	1	24.7	32	12.8	37
North Carolina . . .	64.0	22	60.8	21	5.9	36	20.4	48	26.6	1
South Carolina . . .	62.3	29	58.8	31	6.2	35	20.2	49	24.3	5
Georgia.	61.5	33	57.9	32	6.9	24	22.5	41	18.2	18
Florida	56.8	47	54.8	42	8.2	9	31.6	3	9.0	42
East South Central. .	58.0	(X)	53.9	(X)	7.0	(X)	22.1	(X)	22.5	(X)
Kentucky.	57.6	44	52.8	48	6.9	24	23.2	39	19.0	15
Tennessee	59.4	40	55.6	38	6.4	33	24.0	37	23.0	7
Alabama	57.5	45	53.4	45	7.3	20	20.6	46	22.8	9
Mississippi	56.6	48	53.1	46	8.1	10	18.4	50	26.1	2
West South Central .	61.8	(X)	57.4	(X)	7.4	(X)	24.7	(X)	14.0	(X)
Arkansas.	58.9	41	55.4	40	7.2	21	21.8	44	24.6	4
Louisiana	56.9	46	53.1	46	8.1	10	24.3	35	11.4	40
Oklahoma	60.0	37	55.5	39	5.7	38	23.7	38	13.5	33
Texas	63.7	24	59.2	29	7.5	12	25.4	25	13.3	35
West	61.5	(X)	57.6	(X)	8.1	(X)	27.7	(X)	13.8	(X)
Mountain	63.0	(X)	59.1	(X)	6.4	(X)	28.4	(X)	10.3	(X)
Montana	64.0	22	63.0	10	6.7	27	25.9	21	7.3	44
Idaho	64.2	21	59.2	29	6.5	31	21.9	42	15.9	27
Wyoming	66.6	8	62.5	14	5.6	40	20.5	47	4.4	48
Colorado.	65.9	15	62.6	13	5.9	36	27.7	12	11.6	39
New Mexico.	59.5	39	53.6	44	6.8	26	26.6	18	6.7	46
Arizona.	58.3	43	55.1	41	7.4	19	28.0	11	11.3	41
Utah.	67.0	7	61.0	20	4.9	44	25.7	23	13.8	32
Nevada.	65.2	18	61.7	18	6.6	28	44.3	1	4.1	49
Pacific	61.0	(X)	57.1	(X)	8.6	(X)	27.4	(X)	15.1	(X)
Washington	63.4	26	60.7	22	7.5	12	25.0	28	15.6	28
Oregon.	62.5	28	59.3	28	7.5	12	24.4	34	16.3	25
California.	60.2	36	56.0	37	9.1	2	28.2	9	15.6	28
Alaska	66.1	13	65.7	2	9.1	2	21.9	42	7.3	44
Hawaii	65.7	16	61.9	17	4.5	47	29.9	7	3.7	50

X Not applicable. [1] See table 626. Source: U.S. Bureau of Labor Statistics. [2] See table 661. Source: U.S. Bureau of Labor Statistics.

State Rankings xix

[When States share the same rank, the next lower rank is omitted. Because of rounded data, States may have identical values shown, but different ranks]

REGION, DIVISION, AND STATE	MEDIAN HOUSEHOLD INCOME, [1] 1989						PERSONS BELOW POVERTY, [2] 1989			
	All races		White		Black		All races		White	
	Dollars	Rank	Dollars	Rank	Dollars	Rank	Percent	Rank	Percent	Rank
United States . . .	30,056	(X)	31,435	(X)	19,758	(X)	13.1	(X)	9.8	(X)
Northeast	33,825	(X)	35,461	(X)	24,308	(X)	10.6	(X)	7.7	(X)
New England	36,241	(X)	36,990	(X)	26,324	(X)	8.5	(X)	6.9	(X)
Maine	27,854	26	27,901	32	26,250	8	10.8	35	10.7	19
New Hampshire . .	36,329	7	36,379	9	31,657	1	6.4	50	6.3	45
Vermont	29,792	19	29,852	25	28,625	5	9.9	41	9.7	26
Massachusetts . . .	36,952	6	38,083	5	25,402	10	8.9	44	7.0	44
Rhode Island	32,181	13	33,103	13	20,377	22	9.6	42	8.0	40
Connecticut	41,721	1	43,407	2	28,011	6	6.8	49	4.6	50
Middle Atlantic	32,869	(X)	34,814	(X)	24,035	(X)	11.3	(X)	8.0	(X)
New York	32,965	11	35,811	11	24,089	12	13.0	20	8.7	34
New Jersey	40,927	3	42,740	3	29,145	4	7.6	48	5.0	49
Pennsylvania	29,069	22	30,065	22	20,064	24	11.1	32	8.8	32
Midwest	29,334	(X)	30,355	(X)	19,012	(X)	12.0	(X)	9.4	(X)
East North Central . .	30,319	(X)	31,448	(X)	19,176	(X)	12.0	(X)	9.0	(X)
Ohio	28,706	25	30,026	23	17,716	37	12.5	23	10.0	22
Indiana	28,797	24	29,588	27	19,101	27	10.7	36	9.0	31
Illinois	32,252	12	34,358	12	20,990	19	11.9	26	7.8	42
Michigan	31,020	15	32,463	14	18,851	29	13.1	19	9.4	27
Wisconsin	29,442	21	30,216	20	16,189	42	10.7	36	8.3	39
West North Central .	27,128	(X)	27,709	(X)	18,244	(X)	12.0	(X)	10.3	(X)
Minnesota	30,909	17	31,322	18	18,878	28	10.2	38	8.7	34
Iowa	26,229	36	26,427	39	16,010	43	11.5	29	10.8	18
Missouri	26,362	34	27,179	35	18,374	33	13.3	17	11.2	17
North Dakota	23,213	43	23,634	45	21,066	18	14.4	16	12.8	10
South Dakota	22,503	46	23,220	47	20,890	20	15.9	11	12.6	11
Nebraska	26,016	37	26,435	38	17,038	38	11.1	32	9.9	24
Kansas	27,291	29	28,036	31	18,422	32	11.5	29	9.9	24
South	26,832	(X)	29,185	(X)	17,620	(X)	15.7	(X)	11.3	(X)
South Atlantic	29,281	(X)	31,325	(X)	20,333	(X)	12.7	(X)	8.9	(X)
Delaware	34,875	9	36,660	8	24,286	11	8.7	45	5.7	47
Maryland	39,386	4	41,964	4	30,746	3	8.3	46	5.3	48
Dist. of Columbia . .	30,727	(X)	45,991	(X)	24,576	(X)	16.9	(X)	8.2	(X)
Virginia	33,328	10	36,039	10	21,987	15	10.2	38	7.4	43
West Virginia	20,795	49	21,034	50	13,174	47	19.7	4	19.1	1
North Carolina . . .	26,647	33	29,300	28	17,979	35	13.0	20	8.6	36
South Carolina . . .	26,256	35	30,118	21	16,555	40	15.4	14	8.5	37
Georgia	29,021	23	32,445	15	18,689	30	14.7	15	8.8	32
Florida	27,483	28	28,981	30	18,055	34	12.7	22	9.4	27
East South Central . .	23,098	(X)	25,424	(X)	13,917	(X)	18.8	(X)	13.9	(X)
Kentucky	22,534	45	23,202	48	14,871	45	19.0	6	17.8	2
Tennessee	24,807	39	26,244	40	16,432	41	15.7	12	12.5	12
Alabama	23,597	41	26,792	36	13,997	46	18.3	7	11.7	14
Mississippi	20,136	50	24,940	43	11,625	50	25.2	1	13.2	9
West South Central .	25,267	(X)	27,570	(X)	15,279	(X)	18.9	(X)	13.9	(X)
Arkansas	21,147	48	22,550	49	12,128	48	19.1	5	14.5	4
Louisiana	21,949	47	26,436	37	12,029	49	23.6	2	13.4	8
Oklahoma	23,577	42	24,851	44	15,725	44	16.7	9	13.7	7
Texas	27,016	32	29,728	26	17,853	36	18.1	8	13.9	6
West	32,270	(X)	33,359	(X)	25,229	(X)	12.6	(X)	9.9	(X)
Mountain	27,742	(X)	28,921	(X)	21,256	(X)	14.0	(X)	11.3	(X)
Montana	22,988	44	23,524	46	20,364	23	16.1	10	14.0	5
Idaho	25,257	38	25,567	42	21,900	16	13.3	17	12.2	13
Wyoming	27,096	31	27,600	33	16,708	39	11.9	26	10.7	19
Colorado	30,140	18	31,024	19	21,676	17	11.7	28	10.0	22
New Mexico	24,087	40	25,872	41	19,561	26	20.6	3	16.1	3
Arizona	27,540	27	29,245	29	20,564	21	15.7	12	11.3	16
Utah	29,470	20	29,999	24	19,878	25	11.4	31	10.2	21
Nevada	31,011	16	31,813	16	22,528	14	10.2	38	8.4	38
Pacific	34,428	(X)	35,710	(X)	25,884	(X)	12.1	(X)	9.3	(X)
Washington	31,183	14	31,685	17	24,066	13	10.9	34	9.4	27
Oregon	27,250	30	27,574	34	18,432	31	12.4	25	11.4	15
California	35,798	8	37,724	6	26,079	9	12.5	23	9.1	30
Alaska	41,408	2	44,998	1	31,474	2	9.0	43	6.1	46
Hawaii	38,829	5	37,406	7	27,215	7	8.3	46	7.9	41

X Not applicable. [1] See table 719. Source: U.S. Bureau of the Census. [2] See table 741. Source: U.S. Bureau of the Census.

[When States share the same rank, the next lower rank is omitted. Because of rounded data, States may have identical values shown, but different ranks]

REGION, DIVISION, AND STATE	BLACK PERSONS BELOW POVERTY LEVEL, [1] 1989		SOCIAL SECURITY RECIPIENTS, [2] 1991		PUBLIC AID RECIPIENTS, [3] 1991		VOTING-AGE POPULATION CASTING VOTES FOR PRESIDENT, [4] 1992		FARM LAND, PERCENT INCREASE IN AVERAGE VALUE PER ACRE, [5] 1990-92	
	Percent	Rank	Percent	Rank	Percent	Rank	Percent	Rank	Percent	Rank
United States . . .	29.5	(X)	15.7	(X)	7.0	(X)	55.2	(X)	2.5	(X)
Northeast	24.3	(X)	16.8	(X)	7.0	(X)	55.6	(X)	(NA)	(X)
New England	21.6	(X)	16.5	(X)	6.3	(X)	62.6	(X)	(NA)	(X)
Maine	20.0	42	17.7	9	7.3	12	72.0	1	−8.6	41
New Hampshire . .	12.6	48	15.1	37	2.9	49	63.1	15	−8.6	41
Vermont	21.0	41	15.9	29	6.6	18	67.5	5	−8.6	41
Massachusetts . . .	23.0	35	16.5	22	7.0	15	60.2	22	−8.6	41
Rhode Island	25.8	30	18.3	7	7.3	12	58.4	27	−8.6	41
Connecticut	19.8	43	16.2	25	5.5	31	63.8	13	−8.6	41
Middle Atlantic	24.7	(X)	16.9	(X)	7.2	(X)	53.1	(X)	(NA)	(X)
New York	25.0	32	15.9	29	8.3	7	50.9	41	7.9	11
New Jersey	19.3	45	16.0	28	5.8	25	56.3	28	3.0	22
Pennsylvania	29.0	25	18.9	4	6.4	21	54.3	32	0.7	29
Midwest	32.2	(X)	16.5	(X)	6.7	(X)	62.1	(X)	(NA)	(X)
East North Central . .	32.4	(X)	16.2	(X)	7.4	(X)	60.7	(X)	(NA)	(X)
Ohio	32.3	13	16.7	20	7.8	10	60.6	21	3.8	19
Indiana	29.0	25	16.4	24	4.3	42	55.2	29	4.7	16
Illinois	31.1	16	15.4	35	7.5	11	58.9	26	8.0	10
Michigan	33.7	11	16.2	25	8.8	6	61.7	20	10.0	6
Wisconsin	40.8	4	17.2	16	6.7	16	69.0	4	8.3	9
West North Central .	31.0	(X)	17.1	(X)	5.0	(X)	65.5	(X)	(NA)	(X)
Minnesota	36.8	7	15.3	36	5.0	35	71.6	2	8.5	8
Iowa	37.1	6	18.9	4	4.7	38	65.3	10	6.9	12
Missouri	29.9	23	17.9	8	6.2	24	62.0	19	1.5	26
North Dakota	15.5	47	17.6	13	3.8	46	67.3	6	5.4	15
South Dakota	19.6	44	18.5	6	4.4	41	67.0	7	11.0	5
Nebraska	31.1	16	17.1	17	3.9	45	63.2	14	3.4	21
Kansas	30.0	22	16.6	21	4.2	44	63.0	16	4.7	16
South	31.6	(X)	16.1	(X)	6.6	(X)	51.4	(X)	(NA)	(X)
South Atlantic	26.7	(X)	16.5	(X)	6.1	(X)	50.1	(X)	(NA)	(X)
Delaware	22.0	39	15.9	29	4.7	37	55.2	29	−5.9	38
Maryland	16.6	46	12.9	46	5.6	30	53.4	36	−6.8	39
Dist. of Columbia . .	20.2	(X)	13.1	(X)	12.3	(X)	49.6	(X)	(X)	(X)
Virginia	22.4	38	13.6	43	4.3	43	52.8	37	−10.1	47
West Virginia	36.0	8	20.7	1	8.9	5	50.6	42	17.2	3
North Carolina . . .	27.1	29	16.5	22	6.5	19	50.1	44	0.1	30
South Carolina . . .	31.4	15	15.7	32	6.3	23	45.0	49	2.4	24
Georgia	30.3	21	13.7	42	7.9	9	46.9	48	−10.8	48
Florida	31.5	14	20.6	2	5.3	33	50.2	43	−1.1	33
East South Central . .	38.8	(X)	17.5	(X)	8.5	(X)	53.5	(X)	(NA)	(X)
Kentucky	35.2	9	17.7	9	9.1	4	53.7	35	1.2	28
Tennessee	32.4	12	17.1	17	7.9	8	52.4	39	−1.1	33
Alabama	37.7	5	17.7	9	6.6	17	55.2	29	−0.8	32
Mississippi	46.4	1	17.7	9	11.4	1	52.8	37	1.3	27
West South Central .	37.2	(X)	14.5	(X)	6.5	(X)	52.4	(X)	(NA)	(X)
Arkansas	43.0	3	19.9	3	6.4	20	53.8	34	−3.5	36
Louisiana	45.7	2	15.6	33	9.7	3	59.8	24	−1.1	33
Oklahoma	34.6	10	17.0	19	5.8	26	59.7	25	−0.6	31
Texas	31.0	18	13.0	45	5.8	27	49.1	46	−5.8	37
West	21.7	(X)	13.3	(X)	7.9	(X)	53.5	(X)	(NA)	(X)
Mountain	25.4	(X)	14.3	(X)	4.7	(X)	58.8	(X)	(NA)	(X)
Montana	31.0	18	17.6	13	5.7	29	70.1	3	5.9	13
Idaho	22.8	36	15.5	34	2.8	50	65.2	11	3.9	18
Wyoming	25.2	31	13.9	40	4.7	39	62.3	18	−7.1	40
Colorado	23.9	33	12.8	47	4.4	40	62.7	17	2.6	23
New Mexico	27.8	27	14.7	38	7.0	14	51.6	40	21.9	1
Arizona	27.5	28	16.2	25	5.4	32	54.1	33	14.9	4
Utah	30.5	20	11.2	49	3.5	47	65.1	12	9.2	7
Nevada	23.3	34	13.9	40	3.0	48	50.0	45	19.2	2
Pacific	21.1	(X)	12.9	(X)	9.1	(X)	51.7	(X)	(NA)	(X)
Washington	22.8	36	14.5	39	6.4	22	59.9	23	1.7	25
Oregon	29.8	24	17.4	15	4.9	36	65.7	8	5.6	14
California	21.1	40	12.3	48	10.1	2	49.1	46	3.6	20
Alaska	10.4	49	6.1	50	5.8	28	65.4	9	(NA)	(X)
Hawaii	8.8	50	13.3	44	5.3	33	41.9	50	(NA)	(X)

NA Not available.   X Not applicable.   [1] See table 741. Source: U.S. Bureau of the Census.   [2] See table 590. Source: U.S. Social Security Administration.   [3] See table 606. Source: U.S. Bureau of the Census. Recipients of Aid to Families with Dependent Children plus Supplemental Security Income as percent of resident population.   [4] See table 457. Data compiled by U.S. Bureau of the Census.   [5] See table 1102. Source: U.S. Department of Agriculture.

[When States share the same rank, the next lower rank is omitted. Because of rounded data, States may have identical values shown, but different ranks]

| REGION, DIVISION, AND STATE | HOUSING UNITS [1] | | | | MOTOR VEHICLES, 1991 | | | | ENERGY EXPENDITURES PER PERSON, [4] 1990 | |
| | Built between 1980 and 1990 | | With no telephone, 1990 | | Deaths per 100 million vehicle miles [2] | | Miles of travel per mile of road [3] | | | |
	Percent	Rank	Percent	Rank	Rate	Rank	Number (1,000)	Rank	Dollars	Rank
United States . . .	20.7	(X)	5.2	(X)	2.0	(X)	559	(X)	1,900	(X)
Northeast	(NA)	(X)	(NA)	(X)	(NA)	(X)	(X)	(X)	1,764	(X)
New England	(NA)	(X)	(NA)	(X)	(NA)	(X)	(X)	(X)	1,806	(X)
Maine	20.7	27	3.7	34	1.7	38	539	25	2,076	11
New Hampshire . .	27.7	9	3.4	39	1.5	44	662	17	1,777	38
Vermont	22.4	21	4.5	29	1.9	24	419	31	1,876	29
Massachusetts . . .	13.8	43	2.1	50	1.2	49	1,369	5	1,755	41
Rhode Island	15.1	38	3.1	41	1.3	48	1,192	7	1,581	49
Connecticut	15.7	37	2.6	47	1.2	49	1,331	6	1,855	31
Middle Atlantic . . .	(NA)	(X)	(NA)	(X)	(NA)	(X)	(X)	(X)	1,750	(X)
New York	9.4	50	5.0	25	1.9	24	970	10	1,531	50
New Jersey	14.8	39	3.1	43	1.4	46	1,744	2	2,071	13
Pennsylvania	12.4	46	2.6	48	1.9	24	746	13	1,872	30
Midwest	(NA)	(X)	(NA)	(X)	(NA)	(X)	(X)	(X)	1,913	(X)
East North Central . .	(NA)	(X)	(NA)	(X)	(NA)	(X)	(X)	(X)	1,919	(X)
Ohio	12.2	47	4.7	26	1.8	31	816	12	1,945	25
Indiana	14.5	41	5.9	18	1.9	24	590	20	2,204	6
Illinois	11.7	48	4.6	27	1.9	24	628	19	1,963	24
Michigan	13.6	44	4.1	32	1.7	38	694	14	1,806	36
Wisconsin	14.5	42	2.8	45	1.8	31	413	32	1,654	43
West North Central .	(NA)	(X)	(NA)	(X)	(NA)	(X)	(X)	(X)	1,898	(X)
Minnesota	18.5	29	2.4	49	1.4	46	304	37	1,717	42
Iowa	10.0	49	3.4	38	2.1	17	204	43	1,860	32
Missouri	18.3	30	5.2	24	2.0	18	421	30	1,850	33
North Dakota	16.6	36	3.5	36	1.6	41	68	50	2,475	5
South Dakota	14.8	40	6.0	17	2.0	18	81	49	1,938	26
Nebraska	12.9	45	3.6	35	2.0	18	152	47	1,981	20
Kansas	16.9	34	4.4	30	1.8	31	174	44	2,146	8
South	(NA)	(X)	(NA)	(X)	(NA)	(X)	(X)	(X)	2,075	(X)
South Atlantic	(NA)	(X)	(NA)	(X)	(NA)	(X)	(X)	(X)	1,813	(X)
Delaware	24.3	14	3.1	42	1.6	41	1,120	8	2,138	9
Maryland	21.6	24	3.2	40	1.8	31	1,426	4	1,654	43
Dist. of Columbia .	5.5	(X)	4.2	(X)	1.9	(X)	3,430	(X)	1,787	(X)
Virginia	26.3	11	5.4	21	1.6	41	899	11	1,827	34
West Virginia	17.7	32	10.3	4	2.7	6	458	29	1,899	28
North Carolina . . .	28.6	8	7.1	15	2.2	14	683	15	1,977	21
South Carolina . . .	29.0	7	9.1	6	2.6	8	538	26	1,990	18
Georgia	32.1	5	8.3	13	1.9	24	664	16	1,620	46
Florida	35.0	4	5.3	23	2.3	12	1,041	9	1,620	46
East South Central . .	(NA)	(X)	(NA)	(X)	(NA)	(X)	(X)	(X)	2,002	(X)
Kentucky	20.0	28	10.2	5	2.5	9	503	27	1,987	19
Tennessee	24.2	15	7.1	14	2.4	10	556	23	1,993	16
Alabama	23.5	18	8.7	8	2.0	18	472	28	2,076	11
Mississippi	24.1	17	12.6	1	2.9	1	341	35	1,928	27
West South Central .	(NA)	(X)	(NA)	(X)	(NA)	(X)	(X)	(X)	2,545	(X)
Arkansas	24.2	16	10.9	3	2.9	1	285	40	2,014	15
Louisiana	22.1	23	8.3	12	2.2	14	588	21	3,235	3
Oklahoma	22.1	22	8.8	7	2.0	18	306	36	1,992	17
Texas	29.7	6	8.6	9	1.9	24	540	24	2,549	4
West	(NA)	(X)	(NA)	(X)	(NA)	(X)	(X)	(X)	1,734	(X)
Mountain	(NA)	(X)	(NA)	(X)	(NA)	(X)	(X)	(X)	1,829	(X)
Montana	17.5	33	6.9	16	2.4	10	117	48	2,111	10
Idaho	18.0	31	5.8	19	2.7	6	166	45	1,810	35
Wyoming	21.4	25	5.6	20	2.2	14	154	46	3,371	2
Colorado	24.7	12	4.2	31	2.0	18	356	34	1,592	48
New Mexico	27.5	10	12.4	2	2.9	1	300	38	1,966	23
Arizona	37.8	3	8.5	10	2.3	12	635	18	1,786	37
Utah	24.4	13	4.0	33	1.8	31	358	33	1,599	47
Nevada	40.1	1	5.4	22	2.9	1	228	42	2,017	14
Pacific	(NA)	(X)	(NA)	(X)	(NA)	(X)	(X)	(X)	1,700	(X)
Washington	23.1	19	3.5	37	1.5	44	581	22	1,759	40
Oregon	16.6	35	4.5	28	1.8	31	268	41	1,765	39
California	22.9	20	3.0	44	1.8	31	1,554	3	1,634	45
Alaska	38.0	2	8.3	11	2.9	1	287	39	3,869	1
Hawaii	20.8	26	2.6	46	1.7	38	2,036	1	1,973	22

NA Not available.   X Not applicable.   [1] See table 1240. Source: U.S. Bureau of the Census.   [2] See table 1028. Source: National Safety Council, Itasca, IL (copyright).   [3] See table 1018. Source: U.S. Federal Highway Administration.   [4] See table 935. Source: U.S. Energy Information Administration.

State Rankings

[When States share the same rank, the next lower rank is omitted. Because of rounded data, States may have identical values shown, but different ranks]

REGION, DIVISION, AND STATE	BUSINESS FAILURE RATE PER 10,000 CONCERNS, [1] 1992		MANUFACTURING, [2] 1991				RETAIL SALES PER HOUSEHOLD, PERCENT INCREASE, [3] 1990-91		U.S. EXPORTS BY STATE OF ORIGIN, [4] 1992	
			Value added		Value of shipments					
	Rate	Rank	Bil. dol.	Rank	Bil. dol.	Rank	Percent	Rank	Mil. dol.	Rank
United States . . .	110	(X)	1,314	(X)	2,826	(X)	-0.2	(X)	379,263	(X)
Northeast	(NA)	(X)	269	(X)	507	(X)	-1.9	(X)	61,332	(X)
New England	117	(X)	78	(X)	139	(X)	-1.8	(X)	19,420	(X)
Maine	90	26	5	38	12	38	-3.8	46	902	42
New Hampshire . .	146	4	6	37	10	40	-8.6	50	917	41
Vermont	94	23	3	43	6	43	-2.4	40	1,314	38
Massachusetts . . .	135	5	34	13	62	17	2.7	9	10,400	10
Rhode Island	133	6	5	39	10	41	-7.9	49	859	43
Connecticut	86	30	24	20	40	25	-4.5	47	5,028	21
Middle Atlantic	112	(X)	191	(X)	368	(X)	-1.9	(X)	41,912	(X)
New York	117	10	82	2	148	5	-1.8	38	22,628	4
New Jersey	103	20	44	9	86	10	-0.7	30	8,955	14
Pennsylvania	109	14	65	6	134	7	-3.0	43	10,329	12
Midwest	(NA)	(X)	393	(X)	877	(X)	1.7	(X)	80,959	(X)
East North Central . .	79	(X)	292	(X)	647	(X)	1.3	(X)	64,368	(X)
Ohio	82	34	79	3	175	3	3.7	5	16,306	6
Indiana	93	25	44	10	97	9	5.4	1	6,148	17
Illinois	74	39	70	5	152	4	1.1	18	15,328	8
Michigan	77	36	63	7	143	6	-0.7	31	20,414	5
Wisconsin	73	41	36	12	80	12	-3.3	45	6,173	16
West North Central .	84	(X)	101	(X)	230	(X)	2.6	(X)	16,591	(X)
Minnesota	87	27	25	18	53	21	4.3	2	6,137	18
Iowa	47	50	19	25	45	24	3.2	7	2,476	32
Missouri	109	14	32	16	66	15	0.3	26	3,664	25
North Dakota	55	46	1	48	3	48	4.3	3	336	47
South Dakota	63	44	2	44	5	44	4.1	4	232	49
Nebraska	94	23	8	34	21	34	3.1	8	1,233	39
Kansas	99	22	15	27	37	26	2.2	10	2,514	31
South	(NA)	(X)	423	(X)	955	(X)	0.3	(X)	131,348	(X)
South Atlantic	114	(X)	208	(X)	425	(X)	-0.7	(X)	53,939	(X)
Delaware	87	27	4	40	12	37	-1.0	33	1,508	36
Maryland	111	13	15	26	30	30	-2.6	41	3,879	24
Dist. of Columbia .	64	(X)	2	(X)	2	(X)	-4.1	(X)	344	(X)
Virginia	116	11	33	14	62	18	-4.8	48	9,784	13
West Virginia	85	32	6	36	12	36	0.4	25	1,746	35
North Carolina . . .	77	36	60	8	118	8	-0.7	32	10,374	11
South Carolina . . .	52	47	22	22	48	23	0.6	21	4,222	23
Georgia	169	1	37	11	83	11	-1.4	36	7,652	15
Florida	130	7	29	17	59	19	1.9	12	14,431	9
East South Central . .	99	(X)	90	(X)	203	(X)	(Z)	(X)	14,396	(X)
Kentucky	104	18	24	21	54	20	0.4	24	3,648	26
Tennessee	120	9	32	15	70	13	1.7	15	5,156	19
Alabama	86	30	21	24	48	22	-1.7	37	3,629	27
Mississippi	70	42	13	30	31	27	-1.4	35	1,963	34
West South Central .	103	(X)	124	(X)	327	(X)	2.1	(X)	63,014	(X)
Arkansas	65	43	13	31	31	28	0.4	23	1,324	37
Louisiana	74	39	22	23	63	16	0.1	27	16,151	7
Oklahoma	124	8	12	32	28	31	-0.6	29	1,987	33
Texas	108	16	78	4	204	2	3.3	6	43,553	2
West	(NA)	(X)	229	(X)	487	(X)	-1.5	(X)	105,622	(X)
Mountain	110	(X)	43	(X)	91	(X)	0.4	(X)	12,983	(X)
Montana	51	48	1	49	4	46	1.9	13	268	48
Idaho	77	36	4	42	10	39	1.6	16	1,076	40
Wyoming	60	45	1	50	3	50	1.4	17	368	45
Colorado	114	12	14	28	27	32	1.8	14	2,594	30
New Mexico	85	32	4	41	8	42	1.0	20	356	46
Arizona	164	3	12	33	23	33	0.5	22	5,109	20
Utah	82	34	7	35	14	35	-2.8	42	2,706	29
Nevada	106	17	1	45	3	49	-2.2	39	507	44
Pacific	152	(X)	186	(X)	396	(X)	-2.1	(X)	92,639	(X)
Washington	104	18	25	19	68	14	1.1	19	28,041	3
Oregon	100	21	13	29	31	29	2.1	11	4,890	22
California	169	1	145	1	290	1	-3.2	44	56,307	1
Alaska	51	48	1	47	4	47	-1.4	34	3,195	28
Hawaii	87	27	1	46	4	45	-0.1	28	206	50

NA Not available.   X Not applicable.   Z Less than .05 percent.   [1] See table 862. Source: Dun & Bradstreet Corporation, New York, NY (copyright).   [2] See table 1258. Source: U.S. Bureau of the Census.   [3] See table 1317. Source: Market Statistics, New York, NY (copyright).   [4] See table 1345. Source: U.S Bureau of the Census.

Telephone Contacts List

To help *Abstract* users find more data and information about statistical publications, we are issuing this list of contacts for Federal agencies with major statistical programs. The intent is to give a single, first-contact point-of-entry for users of statistics. These agencies will provide general information on their statistical programs and publications, as well as specific information on how to order their publications.

Executive Office of the President

Office of Management and Budget

Administrator
Office of Information and Regulatory Affairs
Office of Management and Budget
Washington, DC 20503
Information: 202-395-3000
Publications: 202-395-7332

Department of Agriculture

Economic Research Service

Information Division
Economic Research Service
U.S. Department of Agriculture
Room 208
1301 New York Ave., N.W.
Washington, DC 20005-4788
Information and Publications: 202-219-0515

National Agricultural Statistics Service

National Agricultural Statistics Service
U.S. Department of Agriculture
14th St. and Independence Ave., S.W.
Washington, DC 20250
Information and Publications: 202-720-4020

Department of Commerce

U.S. Department of Commerce
Room 5058 Main Commerce
14th St. and Constitution Ave., N.W.
Washington, DC 20230
Newsroom: 202-482-4901

Bureau of the Census

Customer Services Branch
Data User Services Division
Bureau of the Census
U.S. Department of Commerce
Washington, DC 20233
Information and Publications: 301-763-4100

Bureau of Economic Analysis

Current Business Analysis Division, BE-53
Bureau of Economic Analysis
U.S. Department of Commerce
Washington, DC 20230
Information and Publications: 202-606-9900

Department of Commerce —Con.

International Trade Administration

Trade Statistics Division
Office of Trade and Investment Analysis
International Trade Administration
Room 2814 B
U.S. Department of Commerce
Washington, DC 20230
Information and Publications: 202-482-4211

National Oceanic and Atmospheric Administration

National Oceanic and Atmospheric Administration Library
U.S. Department of Commerce
1315 East-West Highway
2nd Floor
Silver Spring MD 20910
Library: 301-713-2600

Department of Defense

Department of Defense
Office of the Assistant Secretary of Defense (Public Affairs)
Attention: Directorate for Public Correspondence
The Pentagon, 2E777
Washington, DC 20301-1400
Information: 703-697-5737

Department of Education

Office of Information Services

Statistical Information Office
U.S. Department of Education
555 New Jersey Ave., N.W.
Washington, DC 20208-5641
Information and Publications: 202-219-1651;
1-800-424-1616

Department of Energy

Energy Information Administration

Office of Energy Information Services
Energy Information Administration
U.S. Department of Energy
Washington, DC 20585
Information and Publications: 202-586-8800

Department of Health and Human Services

Health Resources and Services Administration

Administrator for Health Resources and Services
Health Resources and Services Administration
U.S. Department of Health and Human Services
5600 Fishers Lane
42 Parklawn Building 14-05
Rockville, MD 20857
Publications: 301-443-2086

Alcohol, Drug Abuse, and Mental Health Administration

U.S. Department of Health and Human Services
5600 Fishers Lane
Room 12C15
Rockville, MD 20857
Information: 301-443-3783
Publications: 301-468-2600

Centers for Disease Control

Office of Information
Centers for Disease Control
21600 Clifton Road, N.E.
Atlanta, GA 30333
Public Inquiries: 404-639-3534

Health Care Financing Administration

Office of Public Affairs
Health Care Financing Administration
U.S. Department of Health and Human Services
Room 428H, Humphrey Building
200 Independence Ave., S.W.
Washington, DC 20201
Information: 202-690-6145

National Center for Health Statistics

Scientific and Technical Information Branch
National Center for Health Statistics
U.S. Department of Health and Human Services
6525 Belcrest Rd. Rm. 1064
Hyattsville, MD 20782
Information and Publications: 301-436-8500

Social Security Administration

Publications Staff
Office of Research and Statistics
Social Security Administration
U.S. Department of Health and Human Services
Van Ness Centre, Room 209
4301 Connecticut Ave., N.W.
Washington, DC 20008
Information and Publications: 202-282-7138

Department of Housing and Urban Development

Assistant Secretary for Community Planning and Development

Office of the Assistant Secretary for Community Planning and Development
U.S. Department of Housing and Urban Development
451 7th St., S.W.
Washington, DC 20410-0555
Information: 202-708-2690
Publications: 301-251-5154

Department of the Interior

Bureau of Mines

Office of Public Information
Bureau of Mines
U.S. Department of the Interior
810 7th St., N.W.
Washington, DC 20241
Information: 202-501-9649
Publications: 202-501-9757

Geological Survey

Public Inquiries Office
Geological Survey
U.S. Department of the Interior
507 National Center
Reston, VA 22092
Information and Publications: 703-648-6892

Department of Justice

Bureau of Justice Statistics

Statistics Division
Bureau of Justice Statistics
U.S. Department of Justice
633 Indiana Ave., N.W.
Washington, DC 20531
Information and Publications: 202-307-6100

National Criminal Justice Reference Service

Box 6000
Rockville, MD 20850
Information and Publications: 301-251-5500
Publications: 1-800-732-3277

Federal Bureau of Investigation

National Crime Information Center
Federal Bureau of Investigation
U.S. Department of Justice
9th St. and Pennsylvania Ave., N.W.
Washington, DC 20535
Information and Publications: 202-324-3691
Publications: 202-324-5343

Immigration and Naturalization Service

Statistics Branch
Immigration and Naturalization Service
U.S. Department of Justice
425 I St., N.W.
Washington, DC 20536
Attention: Tariff Rm. 235
Information and Publications: 202-376-3066

Department of Labor

Bureau of Labor Statistics

Office of Publications and Information
Services
Bureau of Labor Statistics
U.S. Department of Labor
441 G St., N.W., Room 2831A
Washington, DC 20212
Information and Publications: 202-606-7828

Employment and Training Administration

Office of Public Information
Employment and Training Administration
U.S. Department of Labor
200 Constitution Ave., N.W., Room N4700
Washington, DC 20210
Information and Publications: 202-219-6871

Department of Transportation

Federal Aviation Administration

Public Inquiry Center
APA 200
Federal Aviation Administration
U.S. Department of Transportation
800 Independence Ave., S.W.
Washington, DC 20591
Information and Publications: 202-267-3484

Federal Highway Administration

Office of Public Affairs
Federal Highway Administration
U.S. Department of Transportation
400 7th St., S.W.
Washington, DC 20590
Information and Publications: 202-366-0660

National Highway Traffic Safety Administration

Office of Public Affairs
National Highway Traffic Safety
Administration
U.S. Department of Transportation
400 7th St., S.W.
Washington, DC 20590
Information: 202-366-0123
Publications: 202-366-2588

Department of the Treasury

Internal Revenue Service

Statistics of Income Division
Internal Revenue Service
U.S. Department of the Treasury
P.O. Box 2608
Washington, DC 20013
Information and Publications: 202-874-0410

Department of Veterans Affairs

Department of Veterans Affairs

Office of Public Affairs
Department of Veterans Affairs
810 Vermont Ave., N.W.
Washington, DC 20420
Information: 202-535-8300

Independent Agencies

Environmental Protection Agency

Public Information Center, PM-211B
Environmental Protection Agency
401 M St., S.W.
Washington, DC 20460
Information and Publications: 202-260-2080

Federal Reserve Board

Division of Research and Statistics
Federal Reserve Board
Washington, DC 20551
Information: 202-452-3301
Publications: 202-452-3245

National Science Foundation

Office of Public Information
National Science Foundation
1800 G St., N.W.
Washington, DC 20550
Information: 202-357-1110
Publications: 202-357-7861

Securities and Exchange Commission

Office of Public Affairs
Securities and Exchange Commission
450 5th St., N.W.
Washington, DC 20549
Information: 202-272-3100
Publications: 202-272-7460

Population

This section presents statistics on the growth, distribution, and characteristics of the U.S. population. The principal source of these data is the Bureau of the Census, which conducts a decennial census of population, a monthly population survey, a program of population estimates and projections, and a number of other periodic surveys relating to population characteristics. For a list of relevant publications, see the Guide to Sources of Statistics in Appendix I.

Decennial censuses.—The U.S. Constitution provides for a census of the population every 10 years, primarily to establish a basis for apportionment of members of the House of Representatives among the States. For over a century after the first census in 1790, the census organization was a temporary one, created only for each decennial census. In 1902, the Bureau of the Census was established as a permanent Federal agency, responsible for enumerating the population and also for compiling statistics on other subjects.

The census of population is a complete count. That is, an attempt is made to account for every person, for each person's residence, and for other characteristics (sex, age, family relationships, etc.). Since the 1940 census, in addition to the complete count information, some data have been obtained from representative samples of the population. In the 1990 census, variable sampling rates were employed. For most of the country, one in every six households (about 17 percent) received the long form or sample questionnaire; in governmental units estimated to have fewer than 2,500 inhabitants, every other household (50 percent) received the sample questionnaire to enhance the reliability of sample data for small areas. Exact agreement is not to be expected between sample data and the complete census count. Sample data may be used with confidence where large numbers are involved and assumed to indicate trends and relationships where small numbers are involved.

Three different census counts for the resident population in 1970 are shown

In Brief	
Total population, 1992 255 million	
Northeast	*20 %*
Midwest	*24 %*
South	*35 %*
West	*22 %*
Total households, 1992 96 million	
One-person households	*25 %*

203,211,926; 203,235,298; and 203,302,031. The first is the initial tabulated count, the second is the official count, and the third contains the latest revisions. Breakdowns of the revised count of 203,302,031 are not available for demographic characteristics and may not be available for some levels of geography. The complete count data from the 1980 and 1990 censuses shown in this edition are generally consistent with figures published in the 1980 and 1990 census final reports, series PC80-1-A and series 1990 CP-1, respectively.

Census data presented here have not been adjusted for underenumeration. Results from the evaluation program for the 1990 census indicate that the overall national undercount was between 1 and 2 percent—the estimate from the Post Enumeration Survey (PES) was 1.6 percent and the estimate from Demographic Analysis (DA) was 1.8 percent. Both the PES and DA estimates show disproportionately high undercounts for some demographic groups. For example, the PES estimates of percent net undercount for Blacks (4.4 percent), Hispanics (5.0 percent), and American Indians (4.5 percent) were higher than the estimated undercount of non-Hispanic Whites (0.7 percent). Historical DA estimates demonstrate that the overall undercount rate in the census has declined significantly over the past 50 years (from an estimated 5.4 percent in 1940 to 1.8 percent in 1990), yet the undercount of Blacks has remained disproportionately high.

Current Population Survey (CPS).—This is a monthly nationwide survey of a scientifically selected sample representing the noninstitutional civilian population. The sample is located in 729 areas comprising 1,973 counties, independent cities, and minor civil divisions with coverage in every State and the District of Columbia and is subject to sampling error. At the present time, about 60,000 occupied households are eligible for interview every month; of these between 4 and 5 percent are, for various reasons, unavailable for interview.

While the primary purpose of the CPS is to obtain monthly statistics on the labor force, it also serves as a vehicle for inquiries on other subjects. Using CPS data, the Bureau issues a series of publications under the general title of Current Population Reports, which cover population characteristics (series P20), consumer income (series P60), special studies (series P23), and other topics.

Estimates of population characteristics based on the CPS will not necessarily agree with the counts from the census because the CPS and the census use different procedures for collecting and processing the data for racial groups, the Hispanic population, and other topics. Caution should also be used when comparing estimates for 1980 and later, (for education data, 1981 and later), which reflect 1980 census-based population controls, to those for 1971 through 1979 (for education, to 1980), which reflect 1970 census-based population controls. This change in population controls had relatively little impact on derived measures such as means, medians, and percent distribution, but did have a significant impact on levels.

Population estimates and projections.— National population estimates are derived by using decennial census data as benchmarks and data available from various agencies as follows: Births and deaths (National Center for Health Statistics); immigrants (Immigration and Naturalization Service); Armed Forces (Department of Defense and Department of Transportation); net movement between Puerto Rico and the U.S. mainland (Puerto Rico Planning Board); and Federal employees abroad (Office of Personnel Management and Department of Defense). Estimates for States and smaller areas are based on

data series such as births and deaths, school statistics from State departments of education and parochial school systems, and Federal income tax returns. These estimates contain estimated emigration of 160,000 per year since 1980 and net undocumented immigration of 200,000 per year. For further information, see Current Population Reports, P25-1095.

Data for the population by age for April 1, 1990, (shown in tables 14, 22, and 23) are modified counts. The review of detailed 1990 information indicated that respondents tended to provide their age as of the date of completion of the questionnaire, not their age as of April 1, 1990. In addition, there may have been a tendency for respondents to round up their age if they were close to having a birthday. A detailed explanation of the age modification procedure appears in *1990 Census of Population and Housing Data Paper Listing* (CPH-L-74).

Population estimates and projections are published in the P25 and P26 series of *Current Population Reports.* These estimates and projections are generally consistent with official decennial census figures and do not reflect the amount of estimated census underenumeration. However, these estimates and projections by race have been modified and are not comparable to the census race categories (see section below under "race"). For details on methodology, see the sources cited below the individual tables.

Immigration.— The principal source of immigration data is the *Statistical Yearbook of the Immigration and Naturalization Service,* published annually by the Immigration and Naturalization Service (INS), a unit of the Department of Justice. Immigration statistics are prepared from entry visas and change of immigration status forms. Immigrants are aliens admitted for legal permanent residence in the United States. The procedures for admission depend on whether the alien is residing inside or outside the United States at the time of application for permanent residence. Eligible aliens residing outside the United States are issued immigrant visas by the U.S. Department of State. Eligible aliens residing in the United States are allowed to change their status from temporary to permanent residence at INS district offices.

The category, immigrant, includes persons who may have entered the United States as nonimmigrants or refugees, but who subsequently changed their status to that of a permanent resident. Nonresident aliens admitted to the United States for a temporary period are nonimmigrants (tables 7 and 426). Refugees are considered nonimmigrants when initially admitted into the United States, but are not included in nonimmigrant admission data. A refugee is any person who is outside his or her country of nationality who is unable or unwilling to return to that country because of persecution or a well-founded fear of persecution.

U.S. immigration law gives preferential immigration status to aliens who are related to certain U.S. citizens or legal permanent residents, aliens with needed job skills, or aliens who qualify as refugees. Immigration to the United States can be divided into two general categories: (1) those subject to the annual worldwide limitation, and (2) those exempt from it. A maximum of 270,000 immigrants may be admitted annually under the current worldwide limitation. Visa allocation is determined by a system consisting of six preference categories, each with its own numerical limitation. The first, second, fourth, and fifth preferences are based on the alien's relationship with a U.S. citizen or legal permanent resident, and the third and sixth preferences are based on needed job skills (see table 6). Aliens not eligible for any of the six preferences may qualify for the nonpreference category. Heavy demand for preference visas has resulted in no nonpreference visas being issued since 1978. Additional visas have been issued under the nonpreference category since 1987 to persons from countries adversely affected by the Immigration Amendments of 1965. Those exempt from the worldwide limitation include immediate relatives of U.S. citizens, refugees and asylees adjusting to permanent residence, and other various classes of special immigrants (see table 6).

The Refugee Act of 1980, effective April 1, 1980, provides for a uniform admission procedure for refugees of all countries, based on the United Nations' definition of refugees. Authorized admission ceilings are set annually by the President in consultation with Congress. After one year of residence in the United States, refugees are eligible for immigrant status.

The Immigration Reform and Control Act of 1986 (IRCA) allows two groups of aliens to become temporary and then permanent residents of the United States: aliens who have been in the United States unlawfully since January 1, 1982, (legalization applicants) and aliens who were employed in seasonal agricultural work for a minimum period of time (Special Agricultural Worker (SAW) applicants). The application period for temporary residency for legalization applicants began on May 5, 1987, and ended on May 4, 1988, while the application period for SAW applicants began on June 1, 1987, and ended on November 30, 1988. Legalization applicants became eligible for permanent residence beginning in fiscal year 1989. Beginning 1989, immigrant data include temporary residents who were granted permanent residence under the legalization program of IRCA.

Metropolitan Areas.—The general concept of a metropolitan area is one of a large population nucleus together with adjacent communities which have a high degree of social and economic integration with that nucleus. Metropolitan statistical areas (MSA's), consolidated metropolitan statistical areas (CMSA's), and primary metropolitan statistical areas (PMSA's) are defined by the Office of Management and Budget as a standard for Federal agencies in the preparation and publication of statistics relating to metropolitan areas. The entire territory of the United States is classified as metropolitan (inside MSA's or CMSA's) or nonmetropolitan (outside MSA's or CMSA's). MSA's, CMSA's, and PMSA's are defined in terms of entire counties except in New England, where the definitions are in terms of cities and towns. To summarize data for New England that are available only by counties, New England County Metropolitan Areas (NECMA's) have been defined as a convenience for data users. From time to time, new metropolitan areas are created and the boundaries of others change. As a result, data for metropolitan areas over time may not be comparable and the analysis of historical trends must be made cautiously. For descriptive details and a listing of area titles and components of each metropolitan area, see Appendix II.

Urban and rural.—According to the 1990 census definition, the urban population comprises all persons living in (a) places of 2,500 or more inhabitants incorporated as cities, villages, boroughs (except in Alaska and New York), and towns (except in the New England States, New York, and Wisconsin), but excluding those persons living in the rural portions of extended cities (places with low population density in one or more large parts of their area); (b) census designated places (previously termed unincorporated) of 2,500 or more inhabitants; and (c) other territory, incorporated or unincorporated, included in urbanized areas. An urbanized area comprises one or more places and the adjacent densely settled surrounding territory that together have a minimum population of 50,000 persons.

In censuses prior to 1950, the urban population comprised all persons living in incorporated places of 2,500 or more inhabitants and areas (usually minor civil divisions) classified as urban under special rules relating to population size and density. To improve its measure of the urban population, the Bureau of the Census in 1950 adopted the concept of the urbanized area and delineated boundaries for unincorporated places. The 1950 definition has continued substantially unchanged, except for minor modifications in 1960, the introduction of the extended city concept in 1970, and changes since the 1970 census in the criteria for defining urbanized areas so as to permit such areas to be defined around smaller centers. In all definitions, the population not classified as urban constitutes the rural population.

Residence.—In determining residence, the Bureau of the Census counts each person as an inhabitant of a usual place of residence (i.e., the place where one usually lives and sleeps). While this place is not necessarily a person's legal residence or voting residence, the use of these different bases of classification would produce the same results in the vast majority of cases.

Race.—The Bureau of the Census collects and publishes racial statistics as outlined in Statistical Policy Directive No. 15 issued by the U.S. Office of Management and Budget. This directive provides standards on ethnic and racial categories for statistical reporting to be used by all Federal agencies. According to the directive, the basic racial categories are American Indian or Alaska Native, Asian or Pacific Islander, Black, and White. (The directive identifies Hispanic origin as an ethnicity.) The concept of race the Bureau of the Census uses reflects self-identification by respondents; that is the individual's perception of his/her racial identity. The concept is not intended to reflect any biological or anthropological definition. Although the Bureau of the Census adheres to the overall guidelines of Directive No. 15, it recognizes that there are persons who do not identify with a specific racial group. The 1990 census race question includes an "Other race" category with provisions for a write-in entry. Furthermore, the Bureau of the Census recognizes that the categories of the race item include both racial and national origin or socio-cultural groups.

Differences between the 1990 census and earlier censuses affect the comparability of data for certain racial groups and American Indian tribes. The lack of comparability is due to changes in the way some respondents reported their race as well as changes in 1990 census procedures related to the racial classification. (For a fuller explanation, see *1990 Census of Population, Volume I, General Population Characteristics* (1990 CP-1)).

Data for the population by race for April 1, 1990, (shown in tables 12, 13, 19, 22, and 23) are modified counts and are not comparable to the 1990 census race categories. These numbers were computed using 1990 census data by race which had been modified to be consistent with the race categories used in the reporting of vital statistics by the U.S. National Center for Health Statistics. A detailed explanation of the race modification procedure appears in *1990 Census of Population and Housing Data Paper Listing* (CPH-L-74).

In the CPS and other household sample surveys in which data are obtained through personal interview, respondents are asked to classify their race as: (1) White, (2) Black, (3) American Indian, Aleut, or Eskimo, or (4) Asian or Pacific Islander. The procedures for classifying persons of mixed races who could not provide a single response to the race question are generally similar to those used in the census.

Hispanic population.—In the 1990 census, the Bureau of the Census collected data on the Hispanic origin population in the United States by using a self-identification question. Persons of Spanish/Hispanic origin are those who classified themselves in one of the specific Hispanic origin categories listed on the questionnaire—Mexican, Puerto Rican, Cuban, or Other Spanish/Hispanic origin. The difference between the 1980 and the 1990 questionnaire was that in the 1980 census, a Hispanic origin question was used with prelisted categories for the largest Spanish origin groups and a residual Other Spanish/Hispanic category. For the 1990 census the questionnaire was modified by adding a space for the respondent to write-in the entry for the Other Spanish/Hispanic category. It should be noted that Hispanic persons may be of any race.

In the CPS information on Hispanic persons is gathered by using a self-identification question. Persons classify themselves in one of the Hispanic categories in response to the question: "What is the origin or descent of each person in this household?" Hispanic persons in the CPS are persons who report themselves as Mexican-American, Chicano, Mexican, Puerto Rican, Cuban, Central or South American (Spanish countries), or other Hispanic origin.

Nativity.—The native population consists of all persons born in the United States, Puerto Rico, or an outlying area of the United States. It also includes persons born at sea or in a foreign country who have at least one American parent. All others are classified as "foreign born."

Mobility status.—The U.S. population is classified according to mobility status on the basis of a comparison between the place of residence of each individual at the time of the survey or census and the place of residence at a specified earlier date. Nonmovers are all persons who were living in the same house or apartment at the end of the period as at the beginning of the period. Movers are all persons who were living in a different house at the end of the period from that in which they were living at the beginning of the period. Movers from abroad include all persons, either citizens or aliens, whose place of residence was outside the United States at the beginning of the period; that is, in Puerto Rico, an outlying area under the jurisdiction of the United States, or a foreign country.

Living arrangements.—Living arrangements refer to residency in households or in group quarters. A "household" comprises all persons who occupy a "housing unit," that is, a house, an apartment or other group of rooms, or a single room that constitutes "separate living quarters." A household includes the related family members and all the unrelated persons, if any, such as lodgers, foster children, wards, or employees who share the housing unit. A person living alone or a group of unrelated persons sharing the same housing unit is also counted as a household. See text, section 26, Construction and Housing, for definition of housing unit.

All persons not living in households are classified as living in group quarters. These individuals may be institutionalized, e.g., under care or custody in juvenile facilities, jails, correctional centers, hospitals, or rest homes; or they may be residents in college dormitories, military barracks, rooming houses, etc. (see table 85).

Householder.—The householder is the first adult household member listed on the questionnaire. The instructions call for listing first the person (or one of the persons) in whose name the home is owned or rented. If a home is owned or rented jointly by a married couple, either the husband or the wife may be listed first. Prior to 1980, the husband was always considered the household head (householder) in married-couple households.

Family.—The term "family" refers to a group of two or more persons related by birth, marriage, or adoption and residing together in a household. A family includes among its members the house-holder.

Subfamily.—A subfamily consists of a married couple and their children, if any, or one parent with one or more never-married children under 18 years old living in a household. Subfamilies are divided into "related" and "unrelated" subfamilies. A related subfamily is related to, but does not include, the householder. Members of a related subfamily are also members of the family with whom they live. The number of related subfamilies, therefore, is not included in the count of families. An unrelated subfamily may include persons such as guests, lodgers, or resident employees and their spouses and/or children; none of whom is related to the householder.

Married couple.—A "married couple" is defined as a husband and wife living to-gether in the same household, with or without children and other relatives.

Unrelated individuals.—"Unrelated individuals" are persons (other than inmates of institutions) who are not members of families or subfamilies. An unrelated individual may be a nonfamily householder who lives alone or with nonrelatives only, or a secondary individual such as a guest, lodger, or resident employee. Persons in group quarters, except inmates of institutions, are classified as secondary individuals.

Statistical reliability.—For a discussion of statistical collection and estimation, sampling procedures, and measures of statistical reliability applicable to Census Bureau data, see Appendix III.

Historical statistics.—Tabular head-notes provide cross-references, where applicable, to *Historical Statistics of the United States, Colonial Times to 1970.* See Appendix IV.

Figure 1.1
**Percent Distribution of the Population, by
Race and Hispanic Origin: 1990 to 2050**
(Based on the middle series)

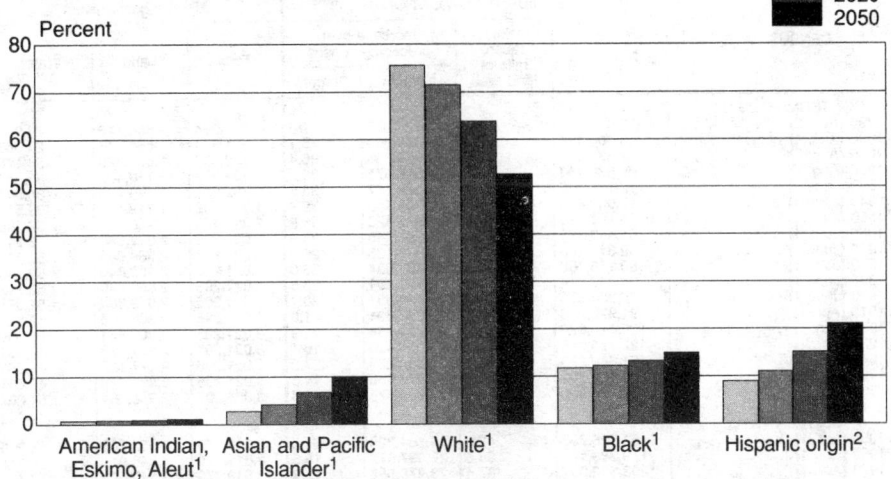

1 Non-Hispanic. 2 Persons of Hispanic origin may be of any race.
Source: Chart prepared by U.S. Bureau of the Census. For data, see tables 19 and 20.

Figure 1.2
**Percent Distribution of Children, by
Presence of Parents: 1980 and 1992**

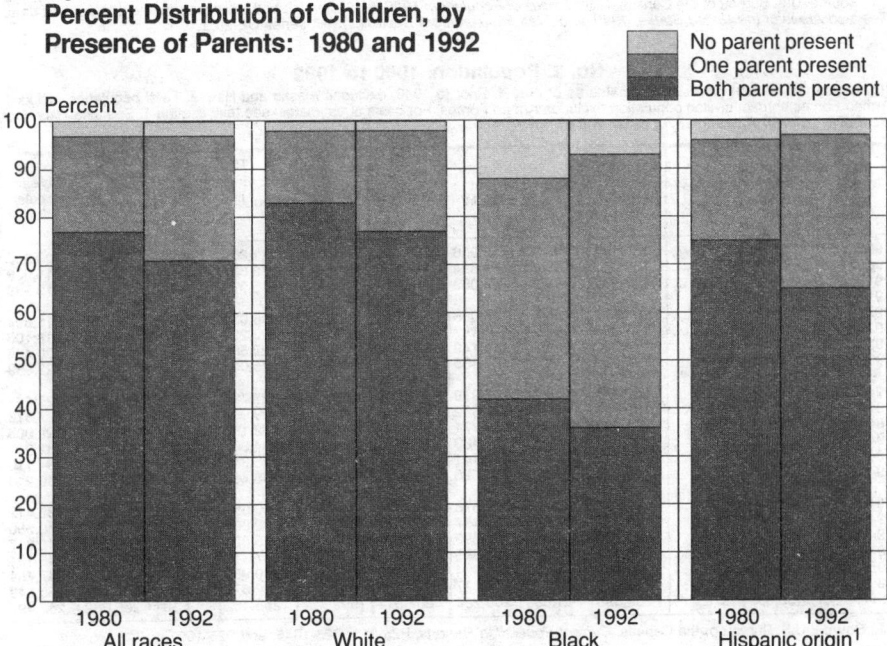

1 Persons of Hispanic origin may be of any race.
Source: Chart prepared by U.S. Bureau of the Census. For data, see table 80.

No. 1. Population and Area: 1790 to 1990

[Area figures represent area on indicated date including in some cases considerable areas not then organized or settled, and not covered by the census. Total area figures for 1790 to 1970 have been recalculated on the basis of the remeasurement of States and counties for the 1980 census, but not on the basis of the 1990 census. The land and water area figures for past censuses have not been adjusted and are not strictly comparable with the total area data for comparable dates because the land areas were derived from different base data, and these values are known to have changed with the construction of reservoirs, draining of lakes, etc. Density figures are based on land area measurements as reported in earlier censuses]

CENSUS DATE	RESIDENT POPULATION				AREA (square miles)		
	Number	Per square mile of land area	Increase over preceding census		Total	Land	Water
			Number	Percent			
CONTERMINOUS U.S. [1]							
1790 (Aug. 2)	3,929,214	4.5	(X)	(X)	891,364	864,746	24,065
1800 (Aug. 4)	5,308,483	6.1	1,379,269	35.1	891,364	864,746	24,065
1810 (Aug. 6)	7,239,881	4.3	1,931,398	36.4	1,722,685	1,681,828	34,175
1820 (Aug. 7)	9,638,453	5.5	2,398,572	33.1	1,792,552	1,749,462	38,544
1830 (June 1)	12,866,020	7.4	3,227,567	33.5	1,792,552	1,749,462	38,544
1840 (June 1)	17,069,453	9.8	4,203,433	32.7	1,792,552	1,749,462	38,544
1850 (June 1)	23,191,876	7.9	6,122,423	35.9	2,991,655	2,940,042	52,705
1860 (June 1)	31,443,321	10.6	8,251,445	35.6	3,021,295	2,969,640	52,747
1870 (June 1)	[2]39,818,449	[2]13.4	8,375,128	26.6	3,021,295	2,969,640	52,747
1880 (June 1)	50,155,783	16.9	10,337,334	26.0	3,021,295	2,969,640	52,747
1890 (June 1)	62,947,714	21.2	12,791,931	25.5	3,021,295	2,969,834	52,553
1900 (June 1)	75,994,575	25.6	13,046,861	20.7	3,021,295	2,969,565	52,822
1910 (Apr. 15)	91,972,266	31.0	15,977,691	21.0	3,021,295	2,969,451	52,936
1920 (Jan. 1)	105,710,620	35.6	13,738,354	14.9	3,021,295	2,977,128	45,259
1930 (Apr. 1)	122,775,046	41.2	17,064,426	16.1	3,021,295	2,977,128	45,259
1940 (Apr. 1)	131,669,275	44.2	8,894,229	7.2	3,021,295	2,974,726	47,661
1950 (Apr. 1)	150,697,361	50.7	19,028,086	14.5	3,021,295	2,968,054	54,207
1960 (Apr. 1)	178,464,236	60.1	27,766,875	18.4	3,021,295		
UNITED STATES							
1950 (Apr. 1)	151,325,798	42.6	19,161,229	14.5	3,618,770	3,552,206	63,005
1960 (Apr. 1)	179,323,175	50.6	27,997,377	18.5	3,618,770	3,540,911	74,212
1970 (Apr. 1)	[3]203,302,031	[3]57.4	23,978,856	13.4	3,618,770	[3]3,540,023	[3]78,444
1980 (Apr. 1)	[4]226,542,203	64.0	23,240,172	11.4	3,618,770	3,539,289	79,481
1990 (Apr. 1)	248,709,873	70.3	22,167,670	9.8	3,787,403	3,536,338	[5]251,065

X Not applicable. [1] Excludes Alaska and Hawaii. [2] Revised to include adjustments for underenumeration in southern States; unrevised number is 38,558,371 (13.0 per square mile). [3] Figures corrected after 1970 final reports were issued. [4] Total population count has been revised since the 1980 census publications. Numbers by age, race, Hispanic origin, and sex have not been corrected. [5] Comprises inland, coastal, Great Lakes, and territorial water. Data for prior years cover inland water only. For further explanation, see table 355.

Source: U.S. Bureau of the Census, *U.S. Census of Population: 1920* to *1990*, vol. I; and other reports and unpublished data. See also *Areas of the United States, 1940*, and *Area Measurement Reports, 1960*, series GE-20, No. 1.

No. 2. Population: 1900 to 1992

[In thousands, except percent. Estimates as of July 1. Prior to 1940, excludes Alaska and Hawaii. Total population includes Armed Forces abroad; civilian population excludes Armed Forces. For basis of estimates, see text, section 1. See also *Historical Statistics, Colonial Times to 1970*, series A 6-8]

YEAR	Resident population	YEAR	TOTAL		Resident population	Civilian population	YEAR	TOTAL		Resident population	Civilian population
			Population	Percent change				Population	Percent change		
1900....	76,094	1953...	160,184	1.67	158,956	156,595	1973...	211,909	0.96	211,357	209,600
1905....	83,822	1954...	163,026	1.77	161,884	159,695	1974...	213,854	0.92	213,342	211,636
1910....	92,407	1955...	165,931	1.78	165,069	162,967	1975...	215,973	0.99	215,465	213,789
1915....	100,546										
1920....	106,461	1956...	168,903	1.79	168,088	166,055	1976...	218,035	0.95	217,563	215,894
1925....	115,829	1957...	171,984	1.82	171,187	169,110	1977...	220,239	1.01	219,760	218,106
1930....	123,077	1958...	174,882	1.68	174,149	172,226	1978...	222,585	1.06	222,095	220,467
1935....	127,250	1959...	177,830	1.69	177,135	175,277	1979...	225,055	1.11	224,567	222,969
1940....	132,457	1960...	180,671	1.60	179,979	178,140	1980...	227,726	1.19	227,225	225,621
1941....	133,669	1961...	183,691	1.67	182,992	181,143	1981...	229,966	0.98	229,466	227,818
1942....	134,617	1962...	186,538	1.55	185,771	183,677	1982...	232,188	0.97	231,664	229,995
1943....	135,107	1963...	189,242	1.45	188,483	186,493	1983...	234,307	0.91	233,792	232,097
1944....	133,915	1964...	191,889	1.40	191,141	189,141	1984...	236,348	0.87	235,825	234,110
1945....	133,434	1965...	194,303	1.26	193,526	191,605	1985...	238,466	0.90	237,924	236,219
1946....	140,686	1966...	196,560	1.16	195,576	193,420	1986...	240,651	0.92	240,133	238,412
1947....	144,083	1967...	198,712	1.09	197,457	195,264	1987...	242,804	0.89	242,289	240,550
1948....	146,730	1968...	200,706	1.00	199,399	197,113	1988...	245,021	0.91	244,499	242,817
1949....	149,304	1969...	202,677	0.98	201,385	199,145	1989...	247,342	0.95	246,819	245,131
1950....	152,271	1970...	205,052	1.17	203,984	201,895	1990...	249,900	1.03	249,391	247,751
1951....	153,982	1971...	207,661	1.27	206,827	204,866	1991...	252,671	1.11	252,160	250,549
1952....	156,393	1972...	209,896	1.08	209,284	207,511	1992...	255,462	1.10	255,082	253,497

Source: U.S. Bureau of the Census, *Current Population Reports*, P25-311, P25-1045, and P25-1097.

No. 3. Resident Population Projections: 1992 to 2050

[In thousands. As of July 1. Each series shown assumes middle levels of fertility, life expectancy, and net immigration unless otherwise specified. Middle level components are shown in footnote 1. Data are consistent with results of the 1990 census, as enumerated]

YEAR	Middle series [1]	Lowest series [2]	Highest series [3]	FERTILITY		LIFE EXPECTANCY		NET IMMIGRATION	
				Low	High	Low	High	Low	High
1992	254,922	254,678	255,147	254,922	254,922	254,890	254,951	254,710	255,118
1993	257,592	256,930	258,211	257,549	257,638	257,508	257,670	257,057	258,087
1994	260,202	258,932	261,399	260,059	260,355	260,046	260,347	259,230	261,101
1995	262,754	260,715	264,685	262,483	263,042	262,507	262,984	261,229	264,165
1996	265,251	262,386	267,976	264,825	265,704	264,897	265,584	263,161	267,187
1997	267,700	263,954	271,278	267,092	268,346	267,220	268,154	265,032	270,172
1998	270,106	265,426	274,597	269,288	270,975	269,485	270,698	266,848	273,126
1999	272,476	266,808	277,938	271,421	273,597	271,698	273,222	268,617	276,055
2000	274,815	268,108	281,306	273,496	276,218	273,864	275,732	270,345	278,965
2005	286,324	273,605	298,773	283,271	289,624	284,206	288,238	278,644	293,467
2010	298,109	278,078	317,895	292,579	304,258	294,382	301,184	287,022	308,443
2015	310,370	282,045	338,580	301,815	320,102	304,674	314,733	295,720	324,049
2020	322,602	285,200	360,123	310,681	336,421	314,582	328,401	304,227	339,786
2025	334,216	286,854	382,281	318,465	352,849	323,542	341,678	311,930	355,089
2030	344,951	286,710	405,130	324,798	369,357	331,339	354,367	318,564	369,700
2040	364,349	282,286	453,687	333,694	403,559	344,512	378,378	329,321	397,285
2050	382,674	275,647	506,740	339,701	440,955	357,028	401,359	338,650	424,161

[1] Ultimate total fertility rate = 2,119; life expectancy in 2050 = 82.1 years; and annual net immigration = 880,000. These are middle level assumptions. For explanation of total fertility rate; see headnote, table 95. [2] Ultimate total fertility rate = 1,846; life expectancy in 2050 = 75.3 years; and annual net immigration = 350,000. These are lowest level assumptions. [3] Ultimate total fertility rate = 2,507; life expectancy in 2050 = 87.6 years; and annual net immigration = 1,370,000. These are highest level assumptions.

Source: U.S. Bureau of the Census, *Current Population Reports*, P25-1092.

No. 4. Components of Population Change, 1980 to 1991, and Projections, 1992 to 2050

[Resident population. Data are consistent with results of 1990 Census, as enumerated]

YEAR	Population at start of period (1,000)	TOTAL (Jan. 1-Dec. 31)					Net migration [3] (1,000)	RATE PER 1,000 MIDYEAR POPULATION				
		Net increase [1]		Natural increase				Net growth rate [1]	Natural increase			Net migration [3]
		Total (1,000)	Percent [2]	Births (1,000)	Deaths (1,000)				Total	Birth rate	Death rate	
1980 [4]	226,546	1,900	0.8	2,743	1,463		724	11.1	7.5	16.0	8.6	4.2
1981	228,446	2,200	1.0	3,629	1,978		690	9.6	7.2	15.8	8.6	3.0
1982	230,645	2,157	0.9	3,681	1,975		595	9.3	7.4	15.9	8.5	2.6
1983	232,803	2,066	0.9	3,639	2,019		592	8.8	6.9	15.6	8.6	2.5
1984	234,868	2,070	0.9	3,669	2,039		589	8.8	6.9	15.6	8.6	2.5
1985	236,938	2,171	0.9	3,761	2,086		649	9.1	7.0	15.8	8.8	2.7
1986	239,109	2,158	0.9	3,757	2,105		661	9.0	6.9	15.6	8.8	2.8
1987	241,267	2,195	0.9	3,809	2,123		666	9.1	7.0	15.7	8.8	2.7
1988	243,462	2,243	0.9	3,910	2,168		662	9.2	7.1	16.0	8.9	2.7
1989	245,705	2,438	1.0	4,041	2,150		712	9.9	7.7	16.4	8.7	2.9
1990	248,143	2,722	1.1	4,179	2,162		746	10.9	8.1	16.8	8.7	3.0
1991	250,865	2,803	1.1	4,094	2,157		866	11.1	7.7	16.2	8.6	3.4
PROJECTIONS [5]												
1992	253,549	2,708	1.1	4,038	2,210		880	10.6	7.2	15.8	8.7	3.5
1993	256,257	2,640	1.0	3,997	2,237		880	10.2	6.8	15.5	8.7	3.4
1994	258,897	2,581	1.0	3,964	2,264		880	9.9	6.5	15.2	8.7	3.4
1995	261,478	2,524	1.0	3,935	2,291		880	9.6	6.3	15.0	8.7	3.3
1996	264,002	2,473	0.9	3,911	2,318		880	9.3	6.0	14.7	8.7	3.3
1997	266,475	2,428	0.9	3,892	2,345		880	9.1	5.8	14.5	8.8	3.3
1998	268,903	2,388	0.9	3,880	2,372		880	8.8	5.6	14.4	8.8	3.3
1999	271,291	2,355	0.9	3,874	2,399		880	8.6	5.4	14.2	8.8	3.2
2000	273,646	2,328	0.9	3,872	2,424		880	8.5	5.3	14.1	8.8	3.2
2005	285,173	2,307	0.8	3,955	2,528		880	8.1	5.0	13.8	8.8	3.1
2010	296,907	2,414	0.8	4,168	2,633		880	8.1	5.1	14.0	8.8	3.0
2015	309,135	2,470	0.8	4,344	2,755		880	8.0	5.1	14.0	8.9	2.8
2020	321,395	2,400	0.7	4,434	2,914		880	7.4	4.7	13.7	9.0	2.7
2025	333,088	2,237	0.7	4,481	3,124		880	6.7	4.1	13.4	9.3	2.6
2030	343,913	2,062	0.6	4,560	3,378		880	6.0	3.4	13.2	9.8	2.6
2040	363,421	1,850	0.5	4,839	3,869		880	5.1	2.7	13.3	10.6	2.4
2050	381,750	1,852	0.5	5,062	4,089		880	4.8	2.5	13.2	10.7	2.3

[1] Prior to April 1, 1990, includes "error of closure" (the amount necessary to make the components of change add to the net change between censuses), for which figures are not shown separately. [2] Percent of population at beginning of period. [3] Covers net international migration and movement of Armed Forces, Federally affiliated civilian citizens, and their dependents. [4] Data are for period April 1 to December 31. [5] Based on middle series of assumptions. See footnote 1, table 3.

Source: U.S. Bureau of the Census, *Current Population Reports*, P25-1092 and P25-1095.

No. 5. Immigration: 1820 to 1991

[In thousands, except rate. For fiscal years ending in year shown, except as noted; see text, section 9. For definition of immigrants, see text, section 1. For 1820-1867, alien passengers arriving, 1868-1891 and 1895-1897, immigrants arriving; 1892-1894 and 1898 to the present, immigrants admitted. Rates based on Bureau of the Census estimates as of July 1 for resident population through 1929, and for total population thereafter (excluding Alaska and Hawaii prior to 1959). See also *Historical Statistics, Colonial Times to 1970*, series C 89]

PERIOD	Number	Rate [1]	PERIOD OR YEAR	Number	Rate [1]	YEAR	Number	Rate [1]
1820 to 1830 [2]	152	1.2	1921 to 1930	4,107	3.5	1982	594	2.6
1831 to 1840 [3]	599	3.9	1931 to 1940	528	0.4	1983	560	2.4
1841 to 1850 [4]	1,713	8.4	1941 to 1950	1,035	0.7	1984	544	2.3
1851 to 1860 [4]	2,598	9.3	1951 to 1960	2,515	1.5	1985	570	2.4
1861 to 1870 [5]	2,315	6.4	1961 to 1970	3,322	1.7	1986	602	2.5
1871 to 1880	2,812	6.2	1971 to 1980	4,493	2.1	1987	602	2.5
1881 to 1890	5,247	9.2	1981 to 1990	7,338	3.1	1988	643	2.6
1891 to 1900	3,688	5.3	1970	373	1.8	1989 [6]	1,091	4.4
1901 to 1910	8,795	10.4	1980	531	2.3	1990 [6]	1,536	6.1
1911 to 1920	5,736	5.7	1981	597	2.6	1991 [6]	1,827	7.2

[1] Annual rate per 1,000 U.S. population. Rate computed by dividing sum of annual immigration totals by sum of annual U.S. population totals for same number of years. [2] Oct. 1, 1819, to Sept. 30, 1830. [3] Oct. 1, 1830, to Dec. 31, 1840. [4] Calendar years. [5] Jan. 1, 1861, to June 30, 1870. [6] Includes persons who were granted permanent residence under the legalization program of the Immigration Reform and Control Act of 1986.

No. 6. Immigrants Admitted, by Class of Admission: 1980 to 1991

[For fiscal year ending September 30. For definition of immigrants, see text, section 1. See also *Historical Statistics, Colonial Times to 1970*, series C 143-157]

CLASS OF ADMISSION	1980	1985	1988	1989	1990	1991
Immigrants, total	530,639	570,009	643,025	1,090,924	1,536,483	1,827,167
Numerically limited	289,479	264,208	264,148	280,275	298,306	293,846
New arrivals	239,590	226,505	234,586	252,401	273,416	271,513
Adjustments	49,889	37,703	29,562	27,874	24,890	22,333
Exempt from numerical limitation	241,160	305,801	378,877	810,649	1,238,177	1,533,321
New arrivals	99,765	129,860	143,299	150,030	162,313	171,594
Adjustments	141,395	175,941	235,578	660,619	1,075,864	1,361,727
Numerically limited, total	289,479	264,208	264,148	280,275	298,306	293,846
Unmarried sons/daughters of U.S. citizens and their children (1st preference)	5,668	9,319	12,107	13,259	15,861	15,385
Spouses, unmarried sons/daughters of alien residents, and their children (2d pref.)	110,269	114,997	102,777	112,771	107,686	110,126
Professional or highly skilled immigrants (3d preference) [1]	18,583	24,905	26,680	26,798	26,546	27,748
Married sons/daughters of U.S. citizens (4th preference) [1]	10,752	18,460	21,940	26,975	26,751	27,115
Brothers or sisters of U.S. citizens (5th preference) [1]	90,167	70,481	63,948	64,087	64,252	63,462
Needed skilled or unskilled workers (6th preference) [1]	25,786	25,990	26,927	25,957	27,183	27,201
Conditional entries by refugees [2]	12,222	(X)	(X)	(X)	(X)	(X)
Nonpreference	-	7	6,029	7,068	20,371	12,268
Recaptured Cuban numbers	15,913	(X)	(X)	(X)	(X)	(X)
Natives of under represented countries, P.L. 100-658	(X)	(X)	(X)	(X)	8,790	9,802
Other	119	49	3,740	3,360	866	739
Exempt from numerical limitations	241,160	305,801	378,877	810,649	1,238,177	1,533,321
Immediate relatives	157,743	204,368	219,340	217,514	231,680	237,103
Spouses of U.S. citizens	96,854	129,790	130,977	125,744	125,426	125,397
Children of U.S. citizens	27,207	35,592	40,863	41,276	46,065	48,130
Orphans	5,139	9,286	9,120	7,948	7,088	9,008
Parents of U.S. citizens	33,682	38,986	47,500	50,494	60,189	63,576
Refugee and asylee adjustments	75,835	95,040	81,719	84,288	97,364	139,079
Cuban Refugee Act, Nov. 1966	6,021	14,288	10,993	5,206	5,730	5,486
Indochinese Refugee Act, Oct. 1977	22,497	166	42	40	33	22
Refugee-Parolee Act, Oct. 1978	46,058	3,766	437	381	153	69
Asylees, Refugee Act of 1980	1,250	5,000	5,445	5,145	4,937	22,664
Refugees, Refugee Act of 1980	(X)	71,820	64,801	73,516	86,511	110,838
Other refugees	9	-	1	-	-	-
Special immigrants	3,142	2,551	5,120	4,986	4,463	4,576
Ministers of religion [1]	1,529	1,853	2,207	2,595	2,786	2,903
Employees of U.S. Government abroad [1]	1,354	479	2,047	1,713	1,234	1,318
Foreign medical graduates, Act of Dec. 1981 [1]	(X)	87	7	11	2	3
Other special immigrants [1]	259	132	859	667	441	352
Other adjustments [3]	263	185	69,103	13,459	8,360	10,626
Children born abroad to resident aliens or subsequent to issuance of visa	4,059	3,508	3,082	2,806	2,630	2,516
Amerasians (P.L. 100-202) [4]	(X)	(X)	319	8,589	13,059	16,010
Immigration Reform and Control Act of 1986 legalization adjustments	(X)	(X)	(X)	478,814	880,372	1,123,162
Others not subject to numerical limitation	118	149	194	193	249	249

- Represents zero.   X Not applicable.   [1] Includes spouses and children.   [2] In 1980, conditional entries were a 7th preference class.   [3] Beginning 1988, includes Cuban/Haitian entrants under the Act of November 1986.   [4] Under Public Law 100-202 Amerasians are aliens born in Vietnam between January 1, 1962, and January 1, 1976, who were fathered by U.S. citizens.

Source of tables 5 and 6: U.S. Immigration and Naturalization Service, *Statistical Yearbook*, annual.

No. 7. Nonimmigrants Admitted, by Class of Admission: 1984 to 1991

[In thousands, except as noted. For fiscal years ending Sept. 30; see text, section 9. Nonimmigrants are nonresident aliens (non-U.S. citizens) admitted to the United States for a temporary period. Included in this group are visitors for business and pleasure, students and their spouses and children, foreign government officials, exchange visitors and their spouses and children, international representatives, treaty traders and investors, representatives of foreign information media, fiances(ees) of U.S. citizens and their children, officials of the North Atlantic Treaty Organization (NATO) and aliens in transit. Most classes include spouses and unmarried minor (or dependent) children accompanying or following to join the alien. Excluded are border crossers, crewmen, and insular travelers. See also *Historical Statistics, Colonial Times to 1970*, series C 149-157]

CLASS OF ADMISSION	1984	1985	1986	1987	1988	1989	1990	1991
Nonimmigrants [1]	9,293	9,540	10,471	12,273	14,592	16,145	17,574	18,963
Temporary visitors, total	8,218	8,405	9,280	11,019	13,197	14,667	16,080	17,386
Percent of total	88	88	89	90	90	91	91	92
For pleasure	6,595	6,609	7,342	8,887	10,821	12,115	13,418	14,734
For business [2]	1,623	1,797	1,938	2,132	2,376	2,553	2,661	2,652
Transit aliens [2]	238	237	244	264	299	293	306	364
Foreign government officials [3]	89	90	94	92	99	102	97	98
Treaty traders and investors [3]	91	97	104	114	126	140	148	155
Students [3]	257	286	288	289	338	361	355	314
Representatives to international organizations [3]	57	57	59	57	59	61	61	64
Temporary workers and industrial trainees	80	88	99	114	133	165	174	205
Workers of distinguished merit and ability	43	47	54	66	78	90	100	118
Performing services unavailable in U.S	23	25	28	29	33	49	41	48
Industrial trainees	3	3	3	3	3	2	3	3
Their spouses and children [3]	11	13	14	16	20	24	29	35
Representatives of foreign information media [3]	19	17	17	18	22	21	20	21
Exchange visitors [3]	121	141	163	183	203	217	215	224
NATO officials [3]	8	8	7	7	9	9	8	9
Fiances(ees) of U.S. citizens [4]	7	8	8	7	7	7	7	8
Intracompany transferees [3]	104	107	108	107	102	101	103	113
Parolees [5]	48	64	67	63	95	107	90	127
Refugees	69	68	51	67	80	101	110	100

[1] Includes nonimmigrants whose class of admission is unknown.   [2] Includes foreign government officials and their spouses and (unmarried minor or dependent) children, in transit.   [3] Includes spouses and children.   [4] Includes children of fiances(ees) of U.S. citizens.   [5] Aliens allowed to enter the United States for a temporary period of time on emergency conditions or when the entry is determined to be in the public interest (e.g., witness in court).

No. 8. Immigrants, by Country of Birth: 1961 to 1991

[In thousands. For fiscal years ending in year shown; see text, section 9. For definition of immigrants, see text, section 1]

COUNTRY OF BIRTH	1961-70, total	1971-80, total	1981-90, total	1991	COUNTRY OF BIRTH	1961-70, total	1971-80, total	1981-90, total	1991
All countries	3,321.7	4,493.3	7,338.1	1,827.2	Vietnam	4.6	179.7	401.4	55.3
Europe [1]	1,238.6	801.3	705.6	135.2	**North America** [1]	1,351.1	1,645.0	3,125.0	1,211.0
France	34.3	17.8	23.1	2.5	Canada	286.7	114.8	119.2	13.5
Germany	200.0	66.0	70.1	6.5	Mexico	443.3	637.2	1,653.3	946.2
Greece	90.2	93.7	29.1	2.1	Caribbean [1]	519.5	759.8	892.7	140.1
Ireland	42.4	14.1	32.8	4.8	Barbados	9.4	20.9	17.4	1.5
Italy	206.7	130.1	32.9	2.6	Cuba	256.8	276.8	159.2	10.3
Netherlands	27.8	10.7	11.9	1.3	Dominican				
Poland	73.3	43.6	97.4	19.2	Republic	94.1	148.0	251.8	41.4
Portugal	79.3	104.5	40.0	4.5	Haiti	37.5	58.7	140.2	47.5
Romania	14.9	17.5	38.9	8.1	Jamaica	71.0	142.0	213.8	23.8
Soviet Union	15.7	43.2	84.0	57.0	Trinidad and				
Spain	30.5	30.0	15.8	1.8	Tobago	24.6	61.8	39.5	8.4
United Kingdom	230.5	123.5	142.1	13.9	Central America [1]	97.7	132.4	458.7	111.1
Yugoslavia	46.2	42.1	19.2	2.7	Belize	(NA)	(NA)	18.1	2.4
Asia [1]	445.3	1,633.8	2,817.4	358.5	Costa Rica	17.4	12.1	15.5	2.3
Afghanistan	0.4	2.0	26.6	2.9	El Salvador	15.0	34.4	214.6	47.4
Bangladesh	(NA)	(NA)	15.2	10.7	Guatemala	15.4	25.6	87.9	25.5
Cambodia	1.2	8.4	116.6	3.3	Honduras	15.5	17.2	49.5	11.5
China: Mainland	[2]96.7	[2]202.5	[2]388.8	33.0	Nicaragua	10.1	13.0	44.1	17.8
Taiwan	(²)	(²)	(²)	13.3	Panama	18.4	22.7	29.0	4.2
Hong Kong	25.6	47.5	63.0	10.4	**South America** [1]	228.3	284.4	455.9	79.9
India	31.2	176.8	261.9	45.1	Argentina	42.1	25.1	25.7	3.9
Indonesia	(NA)	(NA)	14.3	2.2	Brazil	20.5	13.7	23.7	8.1
Iran	10.4	46.2	154.8	19.6	Chile	11.5	17.6	23.4	2.8
Iraq	6.4	23.4	19.6	1.5	Colombia	70.3	77.6	124.4	19.7
Israel	12.9	26.6	36.3	4.2	Ecuador	37.0	50.2	56.0	10.0
Japan	38.5	47.9	43.2	5.0	Guyana	7.1	47.5	95.4	11.7
Jordan	14.0	29.6	32.6	4.3	Peru	18.6	29.1	64.4	16.2
Korea	35.8	272.0	338.8	26.5	Venezuela	8.5	7.1	17.9	2.6
Laos	0.1	22.6	145.6	10.0	**Africa** [1]	39.3	91.5	192.3	36.2
Lebanon	7.5	33.8	41.6	6.0	Egypt	17.2	25.5	31.4	5.6
Pakistan	4.9	31.2	61.3	20.4	Ethiopia	(NA)	(NA)	27.2	5.1
Philippines	101.5	360.2	495.3	63.6	Ghana	(NA)	(NA)	14.9	3.3
Syria	4.6	13.3	20.6	2.8	Nigeria	1.5	8.8	35.3	7.9
Thailand	5.0	44.1	64.4	7.4	South Africa	4.5	11.5	15.7	1.9
Turkey	6.8	18.6	20.9	2.5	Other countries [3]	19.1	37.3	41.9	6.3

NA Not available.   [1] Includes countries not shown separately.   [2] Data for Taiwan included with China: Mainland.   [3] Includes Australia, New Zealand, and unknown countries.

Source of tables 7 and 8: U.S. Immigration and Naturalization Service, *Statistical Yearbook*, annual; and releases.

No. 9. Immigrants Admitted as Permanent Residents Under Refugee Acts, by Country of Birth: 1961 to 1991

[For fiscal years ending in year shown; see text, section 9. Covers immigrants who were allowed to enter the United States under 1953 Refugee Relief Act and later acts; Hungarian parolees under July 1958 Act; refugee-escapee parolees under July 1960 Act; conditional entries by refugees under Oct. 1965 Act; Cuban parolees under Nov. 1966 Act; beginning 1978, Indochina refugees under Act of Oct. 1977; beginning 1980, refugee-parolees under the Act of Oct. 1978, and asylees under the Act of March 1980; and beginning 1981 refugees under the Act of March 1980]

COUNTRY OF BIRTH	1961-70, total	1971-80, total	1981-90, total	1991	COUNTRY OF BIRTH	1961-70, total	1971-80, total	1981-90, total	1991
Total	212,843	539,447	1,013,620	139,079	Korea	1,316	65	120	1
Europe........	55,235	71,858	155,512	62,946	Lebanon	(2)	(2)	1,271	318
Bulgaria	1,799	1,238	1,197	311	Laos	-	21,690	142,964	9,127
Czechoslovakia..	5,709	3,646	8,204	659	Malaysia	9	192	1,277	93
Germany	665	143	851	214	Pakistan......	(2)	(2)	666	166
Greece	586	478	1,408	127	Philippines	100	216	3,403	249
Hungary......	4,044	4,358	4,942	817	Syria	383	1,336	2,145	252
Italy........	1,198	346	394	206	Thailand......	13	1,241	30,259	3,603
Netherlands ...	3,134	8	14	5	Turkey.......	1,489	1,193	1,896	109
Poland.......	3,197	5,882	33,889	4,205	Vietnam	7	150,266	324,453	21,543
Portugal......	1,361	21	21	2	Other Asia	1,307	1,538	1,086	231
Romania	7,158	6,812	29,798	4,276	North America ...	132,068	252,633	121,840	21,317
Soviet Union....	871	31,309	72,306	51,551	Cuba	131,557	251,514	113,367	7,953
Spain........	4,114	5,317	736	96	El Salvador.....	1	45	1,383	1,249
Yugoslavia	18,299	11,297	324	66	Nicaragua.....	3	36	5,590	11,233
Other Europe ...	3,100	1,003	1,428	411	Other N. America.	507	1,038	1,500	882
Asia.........	19,895	210,683	712,092	49,762	South America ...	123	1,244	1,976	320
Afghanistan ...	-	542	22,946	2,100	Chile	4	420	531	38
Cambodia.....	-	7,739	114,064	2,550	Other S. America.	119	824	1,445	282
China [1]......	5,308	13,760	7,928	625	Africa........	5,486	2,991	22,149	4,731
Hong Kong....	2,128	3,468	1,916	75	Egypt........	5,396	1,473	426	52
Indonesia......	7,658	222	1,385	12	Ethiopia	2	1,307	18,542	3,582
Iran.........	58	364	46,773	8,515	Other Africa ...	88	211	3,181	1,097
Iraq.........	119	6,851	7,540	193	Other.........	36	38	51	3

- Represents zero. [1] Covers Mainland and Taiwan. [2] Included in Other Asia.

No. 10. Immigrants Admitted, by Leading Country of Birth and Metropolitan Area of Intended Residence: 1991

[For year ending September 30. Includes Puerto Rico. Includes new arrivals and persons adjusting their status. MSA-metropolitan statistical area; PMSA-primary metropolitan statistical area; and NECMA-New England county metropolitan area as defined by U.S. Office of Management and Budget, June 30, 1986. See text, section 1, and Appendix II]

METROPOLITAN AREA OF INTENDED RESIDENCE	Total [1]	Mexico	Philippines	Soviet Union	Vietnam	Haiti	El Salvador	India	Dominican Republic	China: Mainland
Total [2]...............	1,827,167	946,167	63,596	56,980	55,307	47,527	47,351	45,064	41,405	33,025
Los Angeles-Long Beach, CA PMSA	257,160	153,918	12,147	877	5,156	55	16,111	2,565	45	3,626
New York, NY PMSA	163,006	3,824	3,421	17,708	786	8,141	1,545	7,368	21,309	8,964
Chicago, IL PMSA	60,590	30,960	2,546	2,641	767	203	280	3,409	63	1,023
San Diego, CA MSA	59,329	47,035	3,548	381	1,683	3	185	193	9	309
Anaheim-Santa Ana, CA PMSA...	59,015	40,778	1,526	147	5,366	1	861	783	3	502
Miami-Hialeah, FL PMSA......	58,918	5,192	267	370	73	15,996	1,070	243	1,724	152
Houston, TX PMSA..........	53,690	34,388	673	290	2,518	31	5,294	1,281	79	362
Riverside-San Bernardino, CA PMSA	50,608	42,150	1,324	186	550	6	804	416	15	157
Dallas, TX PMSA	39,352	28,783	275	380	1,177	14	2,145	699	14	210
Washington, DC-MD-VA MSA....	36,370	2,807	1,186	423	2,611	339	5,320	1,653	371	742
Fresno, CA MSA	33,033	28,198	157	207	102	3	731	449	-	53
San Francisco, CA PMSA	29,989	7,254	3,702	2,111	1,096	42	1,726	431	9	4,068
San Jose, CA PMSA.........	28,942	12,233	2,463	471	4,640	3	332	1,774	3	962
Oakland, CA PMSA	24,416	9,093	2,941	368	1,309	5	493	1,391	9	1,667
Boston-Lawrence-Salem-Lowell-Brockton, MA NECMA	21,922	341	306	2,067	1,458	3,240	493	839	1,582	1,083
Phoenix, AZ MSA...........	21,027	17,184	193	80	623	2	191	144	3	160
Visalia-Tulare-Porterville, CA MSA.	17,874	16,874	217	1	4	-	110	71	-	17
Oxnard-Ventura, CA PMSA	17,144	14,961	575	27	148	-	159	123	2	60
Bakersfield, CA MSA	17,008	15,169	516	10	33	-	451	201	1	11
Newark, NJ PMSA	16,909	226	636	689	253	2,035	395	872	529	259
El Paso, TX MSA	16,425	15,977	36	15	8	3	16	26	4	12
Atlanta, GA MSA	15,619	5,954	126	589	1,275	46	384	889	35	175
Philadelphia, PA-NJ PMSA......	15,009	2,604	528	2,001	1,367	174	53	1,169	165	464
Salinas-Seaside-Monterey, CA ..	14,581	13,306	341	53	95	1	185	30	1	33
Fort Lauderdale-Hollywood-Pompano Beach, FL PMSA	14,520	987	130	46	88	4,919	94	209	163	96
McAllen-Edinburg-Mission, TX MSA	14,496	14,217	30	-	-	3	46	10	5	2
Santa Barbara-Santa Maria-Lompoc, CA MSA	14,269	13,086	222	26	39	-	87	29	-	32
West Palm Beach-Boca Raton-Delray Beach, FL MSA	13,903	3,328	84	128	44	6,180	168	125	37	59
Stockton, CA MSA..........	13,548	10,404	625	3	507	-	52	263	-	81
Nassau-Suffolk, NY PMSA......	13,300	422	325	80	95	688	1,650	956	652	370
Sacramento, CA MSA........	13,156	6,526	628	1,525	583	2	89	474	3	390

- Represents zero. [1] Includes other countries, not shown separately. [2] Includes other metropolitan areas, not shown separately.

Source of tables 9 and 10: U.S. Immigration and Naturalization Service, *Statistical Yearbook*, annual.

No. 11. Immigrants Admitted, by Leading Country of Birth and State: 1991

[For year ending September 30. For definition of immigrants, see text, section 1]

REGION, DIVISION, AND STATE	Total [1]	Mexico	Philippines	Soviet Union	Vietnam	Haiti	El Salvador	India	Dominican Republic	China: Mainland
U.S. [2]	**1,827,167**	**946,167**	**63,596**	**56,980**	**55,307**	**47,527**	**47,351**	**45,064**	**41,405**	**33,025**
Northeast	**310,615**	**13,666**	**8,448**	**28,190**	**7,640**	**15,873**	**5,155**	**17,406**	**28,673**	**12,761**
N.E.	**46,314**	**1,245**	**963**	**4,332**	**2,900**	**4,120**	**650**	**1,973**	**2,416**	**1,532**
ME.	1,155	98	45	123	112	4	2	25	7	43
NH.	1,421	155	40	45	92	32	7	86	38	59
VT.	709	17	11	55	147	3	1	25	3	15
MA.	27,020	444	411	3,089	1,961	3,293	530	1,061	1,673	1,150
RI.	3,644	117	86	287	54	101	33	73	491	64
CT.	12,365	414	370	733	534	687	77	703	204	201
M.A.	**264,301**	**12,421**	**7,485**	**23,858**	**4,740**	**11,753**	**4,505**	**15,433**	**26,257**	**11,229**
NY.	188,104	4,963	4,045	19,618	2,235	8,906	3,282	9,133	22,190	9,667
NJ.	56,164	2,981	2,885	1,724	886	2,683	1,149	4,939	3,861	1,020
PA.	20,033	4,477	555	2,516	1,619	164	74	1,361	206	542
Midwest	**133,496**	**56,275**	**5,306**	**6,834**	**5,355**	**277**	**693**	**6,984**	**191**	**2,469**
E.N.C	**108,510**	**47,803**	**4,472**	**5,328**	**2,261**	**243**	**491**	**6,269**	**166**	**2,020**
OH.	8,632	1,046	512	880	343	8	33	843	25	279
IN.	4,512	1,692	232	220	162	5	25	253	10	135
IL.	73,388	39,938	2,924	2,757	967	211	366	3,827	78	1,164
MI.	16,090	3,547	659	1,019	685	16	37	1,064	44	326
WI.	5,888	1,580	145	452	104	3	30	282	9	116
W.N.C	**24,986**	**8,472**	**834**	**1,506**	**3,094**	**34**	**202**	**715**	**25**	**449**
MN.	7,461	780	217	713	732	15	40	226	14	188
IA.	3,331	1,437	89	81	531	2	24	89	-	35
MO.	4,470	757	263	400	709	15	25	218	7	139
ND.	565	155	27	13	160	1	-	17	-	6
SD.	519	48	30	39	70	-	1	9	-	6
NE.	3,020	1,812	81	75	441	-	25	25	-	12
KS.	5,620	3,483	127	185	451	1	87	131	4	63
South	**471,874**	**254,833**	**7,186**	**3,950**	**14,980**	**31,149**	**17,231**	**9,170**	**2,874**	**3,204**
S.A.	**235,854**	**74,023**	**4,579**	**2,809**	**7,181**	**31,039**	**8,525**	**5,409**	**2,698**	**1,994**
DE.	1,937	703	60	67	13	86	11	96	11	54
MD.	17,470	1,331	791	880	697	369	1,514	984	180	499
DC.	5,510	134	109	25	779	79	1,157	69	128	125
VA.	24,942	3,711	1,352	379	1,896	52	2,851	1,194	107	382
WV.	763	201	51	8	51	7	5	71	1	24
NC.	16,772	11,436	239	54	626	10	392	421	26	114
SC.	3,836	1,911	202	30	100	5	22	175	14	63
GA.	23,556	11,668	274	607	1,396	56	509	1,175	41	238
FL.	141,068	42,928	1,501	759	1,623	30,375	2,064	1,224	2,190	495
E.S.C.	**9,541**	**2,605**	**414**	**238**	**1,259**	**26**	**49**	**650**	**23**	**214**
KY.	1,753	278	100	18	347	7	9	113	2	55
TN.	3,828	1,034	141	180	456	15	31	266	12	80
AL.	2,706	810	90	40	310	1	9	183	5	56
MS.	1,254	483	83	-	146	3	-	88	4	23
W.S.C	**226,479**	**178,205**	**2,193**	**903**	**6,540**	**84**	**8,657**	**3,111**	**153**	**996**
AR.	2,559	1,724	84	2	132	3	69	48	-	16
LA.	4,917	946	202	16	708	10	60	251	29	108
OK.	6,403	3,961	132	26	443	6	33	211	2	80
TX.	212,600	171,574	1,775	859	5,257	65	8,495	2,601	122	792
West	**893,950**	**618,838**	**40,884**	**18,005**	**27,296**	**176**	**24,246**	**11,461**	**186**	**14,473**
Mt.	**92,630**	**73,503**	**1,569**	**1,132**	**2,416**	**40**	**784**	**615**	**33**	**721**
MT.	826	264	46	93	3	-	-	10	-	11
ID.	7,088	6,364	52	60	60	-	35	18	1	22
WY.	566	368	19	4	8	-	-	16	-	9
CO.	13,782	9,130	211	582	723	4	81	142	6	182
NM.	13,519	12,222	88	6	240	7	45	76	2	37
AZ.	40,642	35,279	355	111	806	6	282	210	7	210
UT.	5,737	2,876	106	246	369	1	61	58	4	110
NV.	10,470	7,000	692	30	207	22	280	85	13	140
Pac.	**801,320**	**545,335**	**39,315**	**16,873**	**24,880**	**136**	**23,462**	**10,846**	**153**	**13,752**
WA.	33,826	22,102	1,563	729	1,889	1	338	386	13	555
OR.	24,575	18,082	305	1,712	908	2	140	124	-	317
CA.	732,735	504,631	32,698	14,409	21,542	129	22,951	10,291	109	12,265
AK.	1,525	328	382	15	43	3	18	17	29	21
HI.	8,659	192	4,367	8	498	1	15	28	2	594

- Represents zero. [1] Includes other countries, not shown separately. [2] Includes Guam, Puerto Rico, Northern Mariana Islands, Virgin Islands, and other or unknown areas not shown separately.

Source: U.S. Immigration and Naturalization Service, *Statistical Yearbook*, annual.

No. 12. Resident Population—Selected Characteristics, 1790 to 1991, and Projections, 1995 to 2050

[In thousands. See also *Historical Statistics, Colonial Times to 1970*, series A 73-81 and A 143-149]

DATE	SEX		RACE						Hispanic origin [1]	RESIDENCE [2]	
					Total	Other					
	Male	Female	White	Black		American Indians and Alaska Natives	Asian and Pacific Islanders			Urban	Rural
1790 (Aug. 2) [3]	(NA)	(NA)	3,172	757	(NA)	(NA)	(NA)	(NA)	202	3,728
1800 (Aug. 4) [3]	(NA)	(NA)	4,306	1,002	(NA)	(NA)	(NA)	(NA)	322	4,986
1850 (June 1) [3]	11,838	11,354	19,553	3,639	(NA)	(NA)	(NA)	(NA)	3,544	19,648
1860 (June 1) [3]	16,085	15,358	26,923	4,442	79	(NA)	(NA)	(NA)	6,217	25,227
1870 (June 1) [3]	19,494	19,065	33,589	4,880	89	(NA)	(NA)	(NA)	9,902	28,656
1880 (June 1) [3]	25,519	24,637	43,403	6,581	172	(NA)	(NA)	(NA)	14,130	36,026
1890 (June 1) [3]	32,237	30,711	55,101	7,489	358	(NA)	(NA)	(NA)	22,106	40,841
1900 (June 1) [3]	38,816	37,178	66,809	8,834	351	(NA)	(NA)	(NA)	30,160	45,835
1910 (Apr. 15) [3]	47,332	44,640	81,732	9,828	413	(NA)	(NA)	(NA)	41,999	49,973
1920 (Jan. 1) [3]	53,900	51,810	94,821	10,463	427	(NA)	(NA)	(NA)	54,158	51,553
1930 (Apr. 1) [3]	62,137	60,638	110,287	11,891	597	(NA)	(NA)	(NA)	68,955	53,820
1940 (Apr. 1) [3]	66,062	65,608	118,215	12,866	589	(NA)	(NA)	(NA)	74,424	57,246
1950 (Apr. 1) [3]	74,833	75,864	134,942	15,042	713	(NA)	(NA)	(NA)	96,468	54,230
1950 (Apr. 1)......	75,187	76,139	135,150	15,045	1,131	(NA)	(NA)	(NA)	96,847	54,479
1960 (Apr. 1)......	88,331	90,992	158,832	18,872	1,620	(NA)	(NA)	(NA)	125,269	54,054
1970 (Apr. 1) [4]	98,926	104,309	178,098	22,581	2,557	(NA)	(NA)	(NA)	149,647	53,565
1980 (Apr. 1) [5][6]	110,053	116,493	194,713	26,683	5,150	1,420	3,729	14,609	167,051	59,495
1990 (Apr. 1) [5]	121,239	127,471	208,704	30,483	9,523	2,065	7,458	22,354	187,053	61,656
1991 (July 1) [7]	122,979	129,198	210,899	31,164	10,113	2,117	7,996	23,350	(NA)	(NA)
1995 (July 1) [8]	128,292	134,461	217,511	33,147	12,096	2,247	9,849	26,522	(NA)	(NA)
2000 (July 1) [8]	134,338	140,477	224,594	35,525	14,696	2,409	12,287	30,602	(NA)	(NA)
2005 (July 1) [8]	140,097	146,227	230,993	37,907	17,423	2,583	14,840	34,842	(NA)	(NA)
2010 (July 1) [8]	146,012	152,097	237,412	40,429	20,268	2,772	17,496	39,312	(NA)	(NA)
2015 (July 1) [8]	152,178	158,192	244,073	43,074	23,223	2,971	20,252	44,030	(NA)	(NA)
2020 (July 1) [8]	158,308	164,294	250,587	45,743	26,271	3,175	23,096	48,952	(NA)	(NA)
2025 (July 1) [8]	164,054	170,162	256,425	48,388	29,403	3,386	26,017	54,018	(NA)	(NA)
2050 (July 1) [8]	187,271	195,403	274,761	62,181	45,732	4,641	41,091	80,675	(NA)	(NA)

NA Not available. [1] Persons of Hispanic origin may be of any race. [2] Beginning 1950, current definition. For explanation of change, see text, section 1. [3] Excludes Alaska and Hawaii. [4] The revised 1970 resident population count is 203,302,031; which incorporates changes due to errors found after tabulations were completed. The race and sex data shown here reflect the official 1970 census count while the residence data come from the tabulated count; see text, section 1. [5] The race data shown have been modified; see text, section 1 for explanation. [6] See footnote 4, table 1. [7] Estimated. [8] Middle series projection; see table 3.

No. 13. Resident Population Characteristics—Percent Distribution and Median Age, 1850 to 1991, and Projections, 1995 to 2050

[In percent, except as indicated. For definition of median, see Guide to Tabular Presentation]

DATE	SEX		RACE			RESIDENCE [1]		Median age (years)
	Male	Female	White	Black	Other	Urban	Rural	
1850 (June 1) [2]	51.0	49.0	84.3	15.7	(NA)	15.3	84.7	18.9
1860 (June 1) [2]	51.2	48.8	85.6	14.1	0.3	19.8	80.2	19.4
1870 (June 1) [2]	50.6	49.4	87.1	12.7	0.2	25.7	74.3	20.2
1880 (June 1) [2]	50.9	49.1	86.5	13.1	0.3	28.2	71.8	20.9
1890 (June 1) [2]	51.2	48.8	87.5	11.9	0.6	35.1	64.9	22.0
1900 (June 1) [2]	51.1	48.9	87.9	11.6	0.5	39.7	60.3	22.9
1910 (Apr. 15) [2]	51.5	48.5	88.9	10.7	0.4	45.7	54.3	24.1
1920 (Jan. 1) [2]	51.0	49.0	89.7	9.9	0.4	51.2	48.8	25.3
1930 (Apr. 1) [2]	50.6	49.4	89.8	9.7	0.5	56.2	43.8	26.4
1940 (Apr. 1) [2]	50.2	49.8	89.8	9.8	0.4	56.5	43.5	29.0
1950 (Apr. 1) [2]	49.7	50.3	89.5	10.0	0.5	64.0	36.0	30.2
1950 (Apr. 1)	49.7	50.3	89.3	9.9	0.7	64.0	36.0	30.2
1960 (Apr. 1)	49.3	50.7	88.6	10.5	0.9	69.9	30.1	29.5
1970 (Apr. 1)	48.7	51.3	87.6	11.1	1.3	73.6	26.4	28.0
1980 (Apr. 1) [3][4]	48.6	51.4	85.9	11.8	2.3	73.7	26.3	30.0
1990 (Apr. 1) [3]	48.7	51.3	83.9	12.3	3.8	75.2	24.8	32.8
1991 (July 1) [5]	48.8	51.2	83.6	12.4	4.0	(NA)	(NA)	33.1
1995 (July 1) [6]	48.8	51.2	82.8	12.6	4.6	(NA)	(NA)	34.3
2000 (July 1) [6]	48.9	51.1	81.7	12.9	5.3	(NA)	(NA)	35.7
2025 (July 1) [6]	49.1	50.9	76.7	14.5	8.8	(NA)	(NA)	38.5
2050 (July 1) [6]	48.9	51.1	71.8	16.2	12.0	(NA)	(NA)	39.3

NA Not available. [1] Beginning 1950, current definition. For explanation of change, see text, section 1. [2] Excludes Alaska and Hawaii. [3] The race data shown have been modified; see text, section 1 for explanation. [4] See footnote 4, table 1. [5] Estimated. [6] Middle series projection; see table 3.

Source of tables 12 and 13: U.S. Bureau of the Census, *U.S. Census of Population: 1940*, vol. II, part 1, and vol. IV, part 1; *1950*, vol. II, part 1; *1960*, vol. I, part 1; *1970*, vol. I, part B; and *Current Population Reports*, P25-1092 and P25-1095.

No. 14. Resident Population, by Age and Sex: 1970 to 1991

[In thousands, except as indicated. 1970, 1980, and 1990 data are enumerated population as of April 1; data for other years are estimated population as of July 1. Excludes Armed Forces overseas. For definition of median, see Guide to Tabular Presentation. See also Historical Statistics, Colonial Times to 1970, series A119-134]

YEAR AND SEX	Total, all years	Under 5 years	5-9 years	10-14 years	15-19 years	20-24 years	25-29 years	30-34 years	35-39 years	40-44 years	45-49 years	50-54 years	55-59 years	60-64 years	65-74 years	75-84 years	85 years and over	5-13 years	14-17 years	18-24 years	Median age (yr.)
1970, total [1]	**203,235**	17,163	19,969	20,804	19,084	16,383	13,486	11,437	11,113	11,988	12,124	11,111	9,979	8,623	12,443	6,122	1,408	36,675	15,851	23,714	**28.0**
Male	98,926	8,750	10,175	10,598	9,641	7,925	6,626	5,599	5,416	5,823	5,855	5,351	4,769	4,030	5,440	2,437	489	18,687	8,069	11,583	26.8
Female	104,309	8,413	9,794	10,206	9,443	8,458	6,859	5,838	5,697	6,166	6,269	5,759	5,210	4,593	7,002	3,684	919	17,987	7,782	12,131	29.3
1980, total [2]	**226,546**	16,348	16,700	18,242	21,168	21,319	19,521	17,561	13,965	11,669	11,090	11,710	11,615	10,088	15,581	7,729	2,240	31,159	16,247	30,022	**30.0**
Male	110,053	8,362	8,539	9,316	10,755	10,663	9,705	8,677	6,862	5,708	5,388	5,621	5,482	4,670	6,757	2,867	662	15,923	8,298	15,054	28.8
Female	116,493	7,986	8,161	8,926	10,413	10,655	9,816	8,884	7,104	5,961	5,702	6,089	6,133	5,418	8,824	4,862	1,559	15,237	7,950	14,969	31.3
1981, total	229,466	16,893	16,060	18,300	20,541	21,663	20,169	18,731	14,366	12,028	10,985	11,595	11,554	10,359	15,890	7,982	2,349	30,711	15,609	30,245	30.3
1982, total	231,664	17,228	15,958	18,145	19,962	21,682	20,704	18,714	15,566	12,464	11,011	11,414	11,463	10,567	16,147	8,203	2,437	30,528	15,057	30,162	30.5
1983, total	233,792	17,547	16,053	17,869	19,388	21,682	21,141	19,067	16,565	13,150	11,201	11,155	11,447	10,655	16,414	8,429	2,518	30,279	14,740	29,922	30.8
1984, total	235,825	17,695	16,338	17,450	18,931	21,529	21,459	19,503	16,867	13,636	11,429	10,957	11,352	10,803	16,626	8,656	2,595	30,062	14,725	29,461	31.1
1985, total	237,924	17,842	16,665	17,027	18,727	21,265	21,671	20,025	17,604	14,087	11,606	10,854	11,229	10,906	16,858	8,890	2,667	29,893	14,888	28,902	31.4
1986, total	240,133	17,963	17,098	16,474	18,813	20,744	21,893	20,479	18,611	14,398	11,878	10,781	11,135	10,859	17,137	9,129	2,742	30,078	14,824	28,227	31.7
1987, total	242,289	18,052	17,430	16,377	18,698	20,192	21,857	20,984	18,619	15,608	12,294	10,802	10,968	10,783	17,426	9,376	2,823	30,502	14,502	27,694	32.0
1988, total	244,499	18,195	17,759	16,496	18,496	19,655	21,739	21,391	18,993	16,188	12,954	10,995	10,722	10,791	17,626	9,612	2,885	31,028	14,023	27,356	32.3
1989, total	246,819	18,508	17,917	16,797	18,133	19,258	21,560	21,676	19,455	16,960	13,421	11,212	10,534	10,707	17,864	9,850	2,968	31,413	13,536	27,156	32.6
1990, total [3]	**248,710**	18,758	18,035	17,060	17,882	19,132	21,328	21,833	19,846	17,589	13,744	11,313	10,487	10,625	18,045	10,012	3,021	31,826	13,340	26,942	**32.8**
Male	121,239	9,599	9,232	8,739	9,173	9,743	10,702	10,862	9,833	8,676	6,739	5,493	5,008	4,947	7,907	3,745	841	16,295	6,657	13,734	31.6
Female	127,471	9,159	8,803	8,322	8,709	9,389	10,625	10,971	10,013	8,913	7,004	5,820	5,479	5,679	10,139	6,267	2,180	15,532	6,483	13,208	34.0
1991, total [3]	**252,177**	19,222	18,237	17,671	17,205	19,194	20,718	22,159	20,518	18,754	14,094	11,645	10,423	10,582	18,280	10,314	3,160	32,500	13,423	26,385	**33.1**
Male	122,979	9,836	9,337	9,051	8,834	9,775	10,393	11,034	10,174	9,258	6,907	5,656	4,987	4,945	8,022	3,888	881	16,641	6,901	13,456	31.9
Female	129,198	9,386	8,900	8,620	8,371	9,419	10,325	11,125	10,344	9,496	7,188	5,989	5,436	5,637	10,258	6,426	2,279	15,859	6,522	12,929	34.3
Percent:																					
1970 [1]	100.0	8.4	9.8	10.2	9.4	8.1	6.6	5.6	5.5	5.9	6.0	5.5	4.9	4.2	6.1	3.0	0.7	18.0	7.8	11.7	(X)
1980 [2]	100.0	7.2	7.4	8.1	9.3	9.4	8.6	7.8	6.2	5.2	4.9	5.2	5.1	4.5	6.9	3.4	1.0	13.8	7.2	13.3	(X)
1990 [3]	100.0	7.5	7.3	6.9	7.2	7.7	8.6	8.8	8.0	7.1	5.5	4.5	4.3	4.3	7.3	4.0	1.2	12.8	5.4	10.8	(X)
1991	100.0	7.6	7.2	7.0	6.8	7.6	8.2	8.8	8.1	7.4	5.6	4.6	4.1	4.2	7.2	4.1	1.3	12.9	5.3	10.5	(X)
Male	100.0	8.0	7.6	7.4	7.2	7.9	8.0	9.0	8.3	7.5	5.6	4.6	4.0	4.0	6.5	3.2	0.7	13.5	5.6	10.9	(X)
Female	100.0	7.3	6.9	6.7	6.5	7.3	8.0	8.6	8.0	7.3	5.6	4.6	4.2	4.4	7.9	5.0	1.8	12.3	5.0	10.0	(X)

X Not applicable. [1] Official count. The revised 1970 resident population count is 203,302,031; the difference of 66,733 is due to errors found after release of the official series. [2] See footnote 4, table 1. [3] The data shown have been modified from the official 1990 census counts. See text, section 1 for explanation.

Source: U.S. Bureau of the Census, Current Population Reports, P25-917 and P25-1095; and unpublished data.

No. 15. Ratio of Males to Females, by Age Group, 1950 to 1991, and Projections, 2000 and 2025

[Number of males per 100 females. Total resident population]

AGE	1950 (Apr. 1)	1960 (Apr. 1)	1970 (Apr. 1)	1980 (Apr. 1)	1990 (Apr. 1)	1991 (July 1)	PROJECTIONS [1] 2000 (July 1)	2025 (July 1)
All ages	98.6	97.1	94.8	94.5	95.1	95.2	95.6	96.4
Under 14 years	103.7	103.4	103.9	104.6	104.9	104.9	105.1	105.4
14 to 24 years	98.2	98.7	98.7	101.9	104.6	104.7	104.0	104.2
25 to 44 years	96.4	95.7	95.5	97.4	98.9	99.0	99.1	97.9
45 to 64 years	100.1	95.7	91.6	90.7	92.5	92.8	94.1	94.8
65 years and over. . . .	89.6	82.8	72.1	67.6	67.2	67.5	70.3	83.2

[1] Middle series projections; see table 3.

Source: U.S. Bureau of the Census, *U.S. Census of Population: 1950*, vol. II, part 1; *1960*, vol. I, part 1; *1970*, vol. I, part B; and *Current Population Reports*, P25-1092 and P25-1095.

No. 16. Resident Population, by Sex and Age: 1991

[In thousands, except as indicated. As of July 1. For derivation of estimates, see text, section 1]

AGE	Total	Male	Female	AGE	Total	Male	Female
Total	252,177	122,979	129,198	43 yrs. old	3,585	1,761	1,824
				44 yrs. old	3,996	1,986	2,010
Under 5 yrs. old	19,222	9,836	9,386	45 to 49 yrs. old	14,094	6,907	7,188
Under 1 yr. old	4,011	2,052	1,959	45 yrs. old	2,832	1,392	1,440
1 yr. old	3,969	2,030	1,938	46 yrs. old	2,821	1,384	1,437
2 yrs. old	3,806	1,949	1,857	47 yrs. old	2,848	1,392	1,456
3 yrs. old	3,718	1,902	1,816	48 yrs. old	2,856	1,396	1,459
4 yrs. old	3,717	1,902	1,815	49 yrs. old	2,737	1,342	1,395
5 to 9 yrs. old	18,237	9,337	8,900	50 to 54 yrs. old	11,645	5,656	5,989
5 yrs. old	3,702	1,897	1,806	50 yrs. old	2,528	1,234	1,294
6 yrs. old	3,681	1,884	1,797	51 yrs. old	2,340	1,139	1,200
7 yrs. old	3,575	1,829	1,746	52 yrs. old	2,298	1,116	1,182
8 yrs. old	3,512	1,797	1,715	53 yrs. old	2,280	1,105	1,175
9 yrs. old	3,767	1,930	1,836	54 yrs. old	2,200	1,063	1,137
10 to 14 yrs. old	17,671	9,051	8,620	55 to 59 yrs. old	10,423	4,987	5,436
10 yrs. old	3,703	1,899	1,804	55 yrs. old	2,129	1,023	1,106
11 yrs. old	3,662	1,875	1,786	56 yrs. old	2,195	1,054	1,141
12 yrs. old	3,484	1,783	1,701	57 yrs. old	2,068	991	1,077
13 yrs. old	3,414	1,746	1,668	58 yrs. old	1,946	927	1,019
14 yrs. old	3,409	1,747	1,661	59 yrs. old	2,085	992	1,093
15 to 19 yrs. old	17,205	8,834	8,371	60 to 64 yrs. old	10,582	4,945	5,637
15 yrs. old	3,293	1,690	1,603	60 yrs. old	2,124	994	1,129
16 yrs. old	3,362	1,732	1,630	61 yrs. old	2,100	994	1,106
17 yrs. old	3,360	1,733	1,627	62 yrs. old	2,076	971	1,105
18 yrs. old	3,383	1,733	1,650	63 yrs. old	2,145	1,004	1,141
19 yrs. old	3,808	1,948	1,860	64 yrs. old	2,138	982	1,156
20 to 24 yrs. old	19,194	9,775	9,419	65 to 69 yrs. old	10,037	4,491	5,546
20 yrs. old	4,080	2,087	1,992	65 yrs. old	2,072	939	1,132
21 yrs. old	3,969	2,029	1,940	66 yrs. old	2,069	933	1,136
22 yrs. old	3,732	1,902	1,829	67 yrs. old	2,026	910	1,116
23 yrs. old	3,633	1,845	1,788	68 yrs. old	1,911	848	1,063
24 yrs. old	3,781	1,912	1,869	69 yrs. old	1,960	862	1,099
25 to 29 yrs. old	20,718	10,393	10,325	70 to 74 yrs. old	8,242	3,531	4,712
25 yrs. old	3,837	1,935	1,902	70 yrs. old	1,886	828	1,058
26 yrs. old	4,042	2,026	2,016	71 yrs. old	1,731	750	981
27 yrs. old	4,217	2,116	2,101	72 yrs. old	1,649	710	939
28 yrs. old	4,063	2,033	2,030	73 yrs. old	1,518	637	881
29 yrs. old	4,559	2,283	2,276	74 yrs. old	1,458	606	852
30 to 34 yrs. old	22,159	11,034	11,125	75 to 79 yrs. old	6,279	2,482	3,797
30 yrs. old	4,482	2,234	2,247	75 yrs. old	1,405	576	829
31 yrs. old	4,414	2,200	2,214	76 yrs. old	1,334	540	795
32 yrs. old	4,371	2,173	2,197	77 yrs. old	1,244	491	753
33 yrs. old	4,372	2,169	2,203	78 yrs. old	1,204	462	742
34 yrs. old	4,520	2,258	2,263	79 yrs. old	1,091	414	677
35 to 39 yrs. old	20,518	10,174	10,344	80 to 84 yrs. old	4,035	1,406	2,629
35 yrs. old	4,312	2,142	2,170	80 yrs. old	970	352	618
36 yrs. old	4,189	2,079	2,109	81 yrs. old	883	314	568
37 yrs. old	4,120	2,040	2,080	82 yrs. old	799	279	521
38 yrs. old	3,778	1,867	1,912	83 yrs. old	739	249	489
39 yrs. old	4,119	2,047	2,072	84 yrs. old	644	211	433
				85 to 90 yrs. old	2,090	625	1,465
40 to 44 yrs. old	18,754	9,258	9,496	90 to 94 yrs. old	812	201	611
40 yrs. old	3,829	1,891	1,938	95 to 99 yrs. old	214	45	169
41 yrs. old	3,716	1,833	1,883	100 yrs. old and over . .	44	10	34
42 yrs. old	3,629	1,788	1,841	Median age (yr.)	33.1	31.9	34.3

Source: U.S. Bureau of the Census, *Current Population Reports*, P25-1095.

No. 17. Resident Population Projections, by Age and Sex: 1992 to 2050

[In thousands, except as indicated. As of July. See headnote, table 3]

YEAR	Total	Under 5 years	5 to 13 years	14 to 17 years	18 to 24 years	25 to 34 years	35 to 44 years	45 to 54 years	55 to 64 years	65 to 74 years	75 to 84 years	85 years and over
TOTAL												
Lowest series:												
1992	254,678	19,483	32,983	13,639	25,898	42,332	39,841	27,387	20,908	18,436	10,506	3,264
1993	256,930	19,589	33,397	13,877	25,546	41,680	40,692	28,600	20,881	18,609	10,682	3,377
1994	258,932	19,496	33,706	14,339	25,076	41,060	41,511	29,778	20,953	18,666	10,870	3,478
1995	260,715	19,165	34,185	14,643	24,623	40,469	42,296	30,956	21,042	18,689	11,072	3,575
2000	268,108	17,438	35,247	15,454	25,439	36,310	43,995	36,632	23,626	17,892	12,022	4,055
2005	273,605	16,531	33,437	16,587	27,122	34,697	40,978	40,761	28,917	17,833	12,300	4,442
2010	278,078	16,356	31,203	15,834	28,742	36,028	36,782	42,305	34,134	20,090	11,751	4,852
2020	285,200	16,709	30,565	14,096	25,901	39,579	36,486	35,350	39,330	28,981	13,380	4,820
2030	286,710	15,735	30,493	14,368	24,724	35,587	39,946	35,047	32,783	33,186	19,271	5,569
2040	282,286	15,336	28,842	13,899	25,084	34,670	35,986	38,337	32,574	27,669	21,958	7,933
2050	275,647	15,153	28,464	13,300	23,709	34,732	35,055	34,510	35,570	27,629	18,299	9,228
Middle series:												
1992	254,922	19,497	33,010	13,656	25,941	42,382	39,867	27,404	20,924	18,452	10,517	3,272
1993	257,592	19,670	33,446	13,918	25,651	41,808	40,760	28,644	20,920	18,649	10,709	3,399
1994	260,202	19,710	33,826	14,411	25,260	41,297	41,637	29,857	21,023	18,738	10,922	3,518
1995	262,754	19,553	34,372	14,754	24,903	40,844	42,500	31,082	21,153	18,800	11,154	3,638
2000	274,815	18,908	36,051	15,734	26,117	37,416	44,662	37,054	23,988	18,258	12,339	4,289
2005	286,324	18,959	35,782	17,020	28,111	36,495	42,284	41,610	29,647	18,523	12,955	4,937
2010	298,109	19,730	35,425	16,908	30,007	38,367	38,853	43,737	35,378	21,235	12,767	5,702
2020	322,602	21,388	38,068	16,847	29,685	43,024	39,786	38,220	41,959	31,680	15,467	6,480
2030	344,951	21,961	40,368	18,449	31,275	42,629	44,364	39,203	36,866	37,865	23,592	8,381
2040	364,349	23,192	41,739	19,159	33,530	45,329	43,977	43,757	38,079	33,678	28,689	13,221
2050	382,674	24,411	44,223	19,999	34,482	48,020	46,626	43,418	42,620	35,217	26,008	17,652
Highest series:												
1992	255,147	19,510	33,036	13,671	25,981	42,433	39,896	27,419	20,936	18,461	10,527	3,278
1993	258,211	19,749	33,529	13,956	25,752	41,936	40,836	28,682	20,950	18,671	10,735	3,414
1994	261,399	19,928	33,942	14,479	25,438	41,532	41,778	29,928	21,079	18,779	10,968	3,547
1995	264,685	19,949	34,551	14,857	25,175	41,214	42,726	31,196	21,238	18,867	11,226	3,685
2000	281,306	20,448	36,845	15,998	26,773	38,524	45,461	37,465	24,257	18,474	12,576	4,484
2005	298,773	21,621	38,175	17,434	29,065	38,281	43,828	42,492	30,168	18,928	13,406	5,372
2010	317,895	23,640	39,904	17,971	31,230	40,655	41,191	45,253	36,260	21,884	13,433	6,473
2020	360,123	27,101	46,782	19,816	33,571	46,391	43,396	41,221	43,990	33,126	16,702	8,028
2030	405,130	30,104	52,440	23,205	38,690	49,906	49,228	43,501	40,325	40,606	26,043	11,083
2040	453,687	34,355	58,778	25,662	43,627	57,323	52,886	49,367	42,831	37,768	32,716	18,374
2050	506,740	38,645	66,797	29,009	48,381	63,826	60,428	53,012	48,716	40,622	31,144	26,160
MALE												
(middle series)												
1992	124,358	9,981	16,902	7,020	13,219	21,179	19,737	13,388	9,913	8,121	3,984	911
1993	125,699	10,072	17,136	7,153	13,063	20,892	20,194	13,996	9,929	8,240	4,078	946
1994	127,010	10,094	17,323	7,406	12,854	20,637	20,643	14,589	9,993	8,309	4,182	980
1995	128,292	10,014	17,605	7,582	12,662	20,410	21,084	15,190	10,060	8,371	4,300	1,013
2000	134,338	9,684	18,474	8,085	13,249	18,661	22,187	18,132	11,465	8,280	4,907	1,215
2005	140,097	9,713	18,340	8,750	14,263	18,151	20,974	20,407	14,226	8,538	5,294	1,440
2010	146,012	10,111	18,167	8,697	15,237	19,058	19,225	21,478	17,041	9,911	5,369	1,720
2020	158,308	10,969	19,537	8,671	15,073	21,394	19,590	18,710	20,367	15,082	6,844	2,070
2030	169,259	11,258	20,711	9,491	15,870	21,182	21,824	19,097	17,870	18,312	10,775	2,867
2040	178,444	11,882	21,402	9,849	16,995	22,504	21,598	21,299	18,402	16,365	13,405	4,740
2050	187,271	12,505	22,673	10,275	17,455	23,819	22,867	21,121	20,632	17,161	12,302	6,462
FEMALE												
(middle series)												
1992	130,564	9,516	16,107	6,636	12,721	21,203	20,130	14,016	11,010	10,331	6,533	2,362
1993	131,893	9,597	16,328	6,764	12,588	20,916	20,567	14,648	10,992	10,409	6,633	2,453
1994	133,192	9,616	16,504	7,006	12,407	20,660	20,994	15,268	11,032	10,429	6,740	2,539
1995	134,461	9,539	16,766	7,172	12,243	20,433	21,416	15,892	11,091	10,429	6,854	2,625
2000	140,477	9,224	17,577	7,648	12,868	18,755	22,476	18,923	12,523	9,978	7,433	3,074
2005	146,227	9,246	17,440	8,270	13,849	18,345	21,310	21,204	15,422	9,985	7,660	3,497
2010	152,097	9,618	17,260	8,211	14,770	19,310	19,628	22,260	18,336	11,326	7,398	3,982
2020	164,294	10,419	18,531	8,176	14,611	21,630	20,194	19,509	21,592	16,598	8,622	4,410
2030	175,693	10,702	19,657	8,957	15,404	21,445	22,539	20,106	18,995	19,554	12,818	5,514
2040	185,906	11,310	20,338	9,310	16,534	22,825	22,379	22,457	19,676	17,313	15,283	8,481
2050	195,403	11,905	21,549	9,724	17,027	24,201	23,759	22,297	21,989	18,056	13,707	11,189
PERCENT DISTRIBUTION												
(middle series)												
1992	100.0	7.6	12.9	5.4	10.2	16.6	15.6	10.7	8.2	7.2	4.1	1.3
1995	100.0	7.4	13.1	5.6	9.5	15.5	16.2	11.8	8.1	7.2	4.2	1.4
2000	100.0	6.9	13.1	5.7	9.5	13.6	16.3	13.5	8.7	6.6	4.5	1.6
2005	100.0	6.6	12.5	5.9	9.8	12.7	14.8	14.5	10.4	6.5	4.5	1.7
2010	100.0	6.6	11.9	5.7	10.1	12.9	13.0	14.7	11.9	7.1	4.3	1.9
2020	100.0	6.6	11.8	5.2	9.2	13.3	12.3	11.8	13.0	9.8	4.8	2.0
2030	100.0	6.4	11.7	5.3	9.1	12.4	12.9	11.4	10.7	11.0	6.8	2.4
2040	100.0	6.4	11.5	5.3	9.2	12.4	12.1	12.0	10.5	9.2	7.9	3.6
2050	100.0	6.4	11.6	5.2	9.0	12.5	12.2	11.3	11.1	9.2	6.8	4.6

Source: U.S. Bureau of the Census, *Current Population Reports*, P25-1092.

No. 18. Resident Population, by Race and Hispanic Origin: 1980 and 1990

[As of April 1]

RACE AND HISPANIC ORIGIN	NUMBER (1,000)		PERCENT DISTRIBUTION		CHANGE, 1980-90	
	1980 [1]	1990	1980 [1]	1990	Number (1,000)	Percent
All persons	**226,546**	**248,710**	**100.0**	**100.0**	**22,164**	**9.8**
RACE						
White	188,372	199,686	83.1	80.3	11,314	6.0
Black	26,495	29,986	11.7	12.1	3,491	13.2
American Indian, Eskimo, or Aleut	1,420	1,959	0.6	0.8	539	37.9
American Indian	1,364	1,878	0.6	0.8	514	37.7
Eskimo	42	57	(Z)	(Z)	15	35.6
Aleut	14	24	(Z)	(Z)	10	67.5
Asian or Pacific Islander	[2]3,500	7,274	1.5	2.9	3,773	107.8
Chinese	806	1,645	0.4	0.7	839	104.1
Filipino	775	1,407	0.3	0.6	632	81.6
Japanese	701	848	0.3	0.3	147	20.9
Asian Indian	362	815	0.2	0.3	454	125.6
Korean	355	799	0.2	0.3	444	125.3
Vietnamese	262	615	0.1	0.2	353	134.8
Hawaiian	167	211	0.1	0.1	44	26.5
Samoan	42	63	(Z)	(Z)	21	50.1
Guamanian	32	49	(Z)	(Z)	17	53.4
Other Asian or Pacific Islander	(NA)	822	(NA)	0.3	(NA)	(NA)
Other race	6,758	9,805	3.0	3.9	3,047	45.1
HISPANIC ORIGIN						
Hispanic origin [3]	14,609	22,354	6.4	9.0	7,745	53.0
Mexican	8,740	13,496	3.9	5.4	4,755	54.4
Puerto Rican	2,014	2,728	0.9	1.1	714	35.4
Cuban	803	1,044	0.4	0.4	241	30.0
Other Hispanic	3,051	5,086	1.3	2.0	2,035	66.7
Not of Hispanic origin	211,937	226,356	93.6	91.0	14,419	6.8

NA Not available. Z Less than 0.05 percent. [1] See footnote 4, table 1. [2] Not entirely comparable with 1990 counts. The 1980 count shown here which is based on 100-percent tabulations includes only the nine specific Asian or Pacific Islander groups listed separately in the 1980 race item. The 1980 total Asian or Pacific Islander population of 3,726,440 from sample tabulations is comparable to the 1990 count; these figures include groups not listed separately in the race item on the 1980 census form. [3] Persons of Hispanic origin may be of any race.

Source: U.S. Bureau of the Census, press release CB91-216.

No. 19. Resident Population, by Race and Hispanic Origin: 1980 to 1991

[In thousands. As of July, except as indicated. These data are consistent with the 1980 and 1990 decennial enumerations and have been modified from the official census counts; see text, section 1 for explanation]

YEAR	Total	RACE				Hispanic origin [1]	NOT OF HISPANIC ORIGIN, BY RACE			
		White	Black	American Indian, Eskimo, Aleut	Asian, Pacific Islander		White	Black	American Indian, Eskimo, Aleut	Asian, Pacific Islander
1980 (April) [2]	226,546	194,713	26,683	1,420	3,729	14,609	180,906	26,142	1,326	3,563
1980	227,225	195,185	26,771	1,433	3,837	14,869	181,140	26,215	1,336	3,665
1981	229,466	196,635	27,133	1,483	4,214	15,560	181,974	26,532	1,377	4,022
1982	231,664	198,037	27,508	1,537	4,581	16,240	182,782	26,856	1,420	4,367
1983	233,792	199,420	27,867	1,596	4,909	16,935	183,561	27,159	1,466	4,671
1984	235,825	200,708	28,212	1,656	5,249	17,640	184,243	27,444	1,512	4,986
1985	237,924	202,031	28,569	1,718	5,606	18,368	184,945	27,738	1,558	5,315
1986	240,133	203,430	28,942	1,783	5,978	19,154	185,678	28,040	1,606	5,655
1987	242,289	204,770	29,325	1,851	6,343	19,946	186,353	28,351	1,654	5,985
1988	244,499	206,129	29,723	1,923	6,724	20,786	187,012	28,669	1,703	6,329
1989	246,819	207,540	30,143	2,001	7,134	21,648	187,713	29,005	1,755	6,698
1990 (April)	248,710	208,704	30,483	2,065	7,458	22,354	188,300	29,273	1,796	6,988
1990	249,415	209,150	30,620	2,075	7,570	22,554	188,559	29,400	1,806	7,096
1991	252,177	210,899	31,164	2,117	7,996	23,350	189,568	29,910	1,845	7,504

[1] Persons of Hispanic origin may be of any race. [2] See footnote 4, table 1.

Source: U.S. Bureau of the Census, Current Population Reports, P25-1095.

No. 20. Resident Population Projections, by Race and Hispanic Origin: 1992 to 2050

[In thousands, except as indicated. As of July. See headnote, table 3. Minus sign (-) indicates decrease]

YEAR AND SERIES	Total	RACE White	RACE Black	RACE American Indian, Eskimo, Aleut	RACE Asian, Pacific Islander	Hispanic origin [1]	NOT OF HISPANIC ORIGIN, BY RACE White	NOT OF HISPANIC ORIGIN, BY RACE Black	NOT OF HISPANIC ORIGIN, BY RACE American Indian, Eskimo, Aleut	NOT OF HISPANIC ORIGIN, BY RACE Asian, Pacific Islander
Lowest series:										
1992	254,678	212,485	31,649	2,150	8,394	24,062	190,506	30,353	1,873	7,883
1993	256,930	213,886	32,098	2,182	8,765	24,730	191,298	30,764	1,900	8,237
1994	258,932	215,101	32,512	2,212	9,107	25,350	191,948	31,144	1,926	8,565
1995	260,715	216,151	32,900	2,241	9,422	25,926	192,470	31,501	1,952	8,866
2000	268,108	220,092	34,642	2,383	10,991	28,693	193,877	33,094	2,074	10,370
2005	273,605	222,430	36,110	2,522	12,543	31,301	193,830	34,424	2,193	11,857
2010	278,078	223,922	37,419	2,658	14,079	33,828	193,016	35,596	2,309	13,329
2020	285,200	225,437	39,656	2,916	17,190	38,866	189,931	37,560	2,532	16,310
2030	286,710	222,311	41,008	3,142	20,250	43,465	182,604	38,667	2,731	19,244
2040	282,286	214,276	41,596	3,342	23,072	47,391	170,987	39,047	2,912	21,948
2050	275,647	204,724	41,712	3,519	25,691	50,790	158,340	38,981	3,077	24,458
Middle series:										
1992	254,922	212,648	31,673	2,150	8,451	24,136	190,604	30,372	1,873	7,937
1993	257,592	214,328	32,171	2,183	8,911	24,927	191,568	30,822	1,901	8,374
1994	260,202	215,948	32,662	2,215	9,377	25,722	192,469	31,265	1,929	8,818
1995	262,754	217,511	33,147	2,247	9,849	26,522	193,307	31,702	1,956	9,266
2000	274,815	224,594	35,525	2,409	12,287	30,602	196,701	33,834	2,096	11,582
2005	286,324	230,993	37,907	2,583	14,840	34,842	199,274	35,957	2,245	14,005
2010	298,109	237,412	40,429	2,772	17,496	39,312	201,668	38,201	2,407	16,522
2020	322,602	250,587	45,743	3,175	23,096	48,952	206,162	42,911	2,756	21,821
2030	344,951	261,318	51,031	3,610	28,993	59,197	207,674	47,552	3,141	27,388
2040	364,349	268,778	56,445	4,099	35,027	69,827	205,587	52,285	3,581	33,070
2050	382,674	274,761	62,181	4,641	41,091	80,675	201,841	57,316	4,078	38,765
Highest series:										
1992	255,147	212,792	31,699	2,150	8,506	24,208	190,685	30,392	1,873	7,989
1993	258,211	214,735	32,241	2,183	9,052	25,113	191,812	30,878	1,901	8,507
1994	261,399	216,749	32,798	2,216	9,636	26,068	192,965	31,376	1,930	9,061
1995	264,685	218,811	33,368	2,250	10,257	27,073	194,123	31,882	1,958	9,649
2000	281,306	229,063	36,307	2,422	13,514	32,343	199,639	34,485	2,106	12,733
2005	298,773	239,680	39,460	2,615	17,017	38,066	205,123	37,269	2,270	16,045
2010	317,895	251,352	42,947	2,833	20,763	44,328	211,185	40,346	2,455	19,580
2020	360,123	277,183	50,719	3,317	28,904	58,445	224,371	47,187	2,871	27,248
2030	405,130	304,030	59,296	3,879	37,925	74,717	236,654	54,682	3,360	35,716
2040	453,687	332,346	68,889	4,557	47,894	93,466	248,211	63,014	3,956	45,040
2050	506,740	363,006	79,609	5,359	58,766	114,904	259,721	72,277	4,667	55,171
PERCENT DISTRIBUTION										
Lowest series:										
1992	100.0	83.4	12.4	0.8	3.3	9.4	74.8	11.9	0.7	3.1
1995	100.0	82.9	12.6	0.9	3.6	9.9	73.8	12.1	0.7	3.4
2000	100.0	82.1	12.9	0.9	4.1	10.7	72.3	12.3	0.8	3.9
2005	100.0	81.3	13.2	0.9	4.6	11.4	70.8	12.6	0.8	4.3
2010	100.0	80.5	13.5	1.0	5.1	12.2	69.4	12.8	0.8	4.8
2020	100.0	79.0	13.9	1.0	6.0	13.6	66.6	13.2	0.9	5.7
2030	100.0	77.5	14.3	1.1	7.1	15.2	63.7	13.5	1.0	6.7
2040	100.0	75.9	14.7	1.2	8.2	16.8	60.6	13.8	1.0	7.8
2050	100.0	74.3	15.1	1.3	9.3	18.4	57.4	14.1	1.1	8.9
Middle series:										
1992	100.0	83.4	12.4	0.8	3.3	9.5	74.8	11.9	0.7	3.1
1995	100.0	82.8	12.6	0.9	3.7	10.1	73.6	12.1	0.7	3.5
2000	100.0	81.7	12.9	0.9	4.5	11.1	71.6	12.3	0.8	4.2
2005	100.0	80.7	13.2	0.9	5.2	12.2	69.6	12.6	0.8	4.9
2010	100.0	79.6	13.6	0.9	5.9	13.2	67.6	12.8	0.8	5.5
2020	100.0	77.7	14.2	1.0	7.2	15.2	63.9	13.3	0.9	6.8
2030	100.0	75.8	14.8	1.0	8.4	17.2	60.2	13.8	0.9	7.9
2040	100.0	73.8	15.5	1.1	9.6	19.2	56.4	14.4	1.0	9.1
2050	100.0	71.8	16.2	1.2	10.7	21.1	52.7	15.0	1.1	10.1
Highest series:										
1992	100.0	83.4	12.4	0.8	3.3	9.5	74.7	11.9	0.7	3.1
1995	100.0	82.7	12.6	0.9	3.9	10.2	73.3	12.0	0.7	3.6
2000	100.0	81.4	12.9	0.9	4.8	11.5	71.0	12.3	0.7	4.5
2005	100.0	80.2	13.2	0.9	5.7	12.7	68.7	12.5	0.8	5.4
2010	100.0	79.1	13.5	0.9	6.5	13.9	66.4	12.7	0.8	6.2
2020	100.0	77.0	14.1	0.9	8.0	16.2	62.3	13.1	0.8	7.6
2030	100.0	75.0	14.6	1.0	9.4	18.4	58.4	13.5	0.8	8.8
2040	100.0	73.3	15.2	1.0	10.6	20.6	54.7	13.9	0.9	9.9
2050	100.0	71.6	15.7	1.1	11.6	22.7	51.3	14.3	0.9	10.9
PERCENT CHANGE (middle series)										
1992-2000	7.8	5.6	12.2	12.0	45.4	26.8	3.2	11.4	11.9	45.9
2000-2010	8.5	5.7	13.8	15.1	42.4	28.5	2.5	12.9	14.8	42.7
2010-2020	8.2	5.5	13.1	14.5	32.0	24.5	2.2	12.3	14.5	32.1
2020-2030	6.9	4.3	11.6	13.7	25.5	20.9	0.7	10.8	14.0	25.5
2030-2040	5.6	2.9	10.6	13.5	20.8	18.0	-1.0	10.0	14.0	20.7
2040-2050	5.0	2.2	10.2	13.2	17.3	15.5	-1.8	9.6	13.9	17.2

[1] Persons of Hispanic origin may be of any race.
Source: U.S. Bureau of the Census, *Current Population Reports*, P25-1092.

No. 21. Components of Population Change, by Race and Hispanic Origin: 1980 to 1991 and Projections, 1995 and 2000

YEAR	TOTAL (Jan. 1-Dec. 31)						RATE PER 1,000 MIDYEAR POPULATION				
	Population at start of period (1,000)	Net increase [1] Total (1,000)	Per-cent [2]	Natural increase Births (1,000)	Natural increase Deaths (1,000)	Net migration [3] (1,000)	Net growth rate [1]	Natural increase Total	Natural increase Birth rate	Natural increase Death rate	Net migration rate [3]
WHITE											
1980 [4]	194,713	1,270	0.7	2,203	1,277	429	8.6	6.3	15.0	8.7	2.9
1985	201,419	1,378	0.7	2,991	1,819	354	6.8	5.8	14.8	9.0	1.8
1989	206,874	1,502	0.7	3,132	1,854	410	7.2	6.2	15.1	8.9	2.0
1990	208,376	1,699	0.8	3,224	1,876	400	8.1	6.4	15.4	9.0	1.9
1991	210,075	1,773	0.8	3,144	1,869	498	8.4	6.0	14.9	8.9	2.4
Projections:[5]											
1995	216,730	1,535	0.7	3,046	1,975	463	7.1	4.9	14.0	9.1	2.1
2000	223,926	1,323	0.6	2,931	2,071	463	5.9	3.8	13.0	9.2	2.1
BLACK											
1980 [4]	26,683	289	1.1	445	173	62	14.4	13.5	22.1	8.6	3.1
1985	28,406	364	1.3	608	244	61	12.7	12.7	21.3	8.5	2.1
1989	29,939	438	1.5	709	268	58	14.5	14.7	23.5	8.9	1.9
1990	30,377	527	1.7	739	260	63	17.2	15.6	24.1	8.5	2.1
1991	30,904	569	1.8	735	259	93	18.3	15.3	23.6	8.3	3.0
Projections:[5]											
1995	32,904	483	1.5	681	278	80	14.6	12.2	20.6	8.4	2.4
2000	35,290	472	1.3	695	304	80	13.3	11.0	19.6	8.6	2.3
AMERICAN INDIAN, ESKIMO, ALEUT											
1980 [4]	1,420	38	2.7	28	9	1	35.3	21.4	26.2	4.8	0.5
1985	1,687	64	3.8	43	7	-	37.3	20.7	24.8	4.2	0.2
1989	1,962	82	4.2	49	7	-	41.1	20.6	24.6	4.1	0.1
1990	2,044	53	2.6	50	7	-	25.3	20.2	24.2	4.0	-
1991	2,097	44	2.1	51	5	1	20.6	20.2	24.2	4.0	0.4
Projections:[5]											
1995	2,231	32	1.4	41	9	-	14.2	14.2	18.4	4.2	0.1
2000	2,392	33	1.4	44	11	-	13.9	13.8	18.4	4.5	-
ASIAN, PACIFIC ISLANDER											
1980 [4]	3,729	302	8.1	67	8	232	103.4	20.1	22.9	2.9	79.3
1985	5,426	365	6.7	118	16	233	65.1	18.3	21.1	2.9	41.6
1989	6,929	417	6.0	150	21	244	58.4	18.1	21.1	2.9	34.2
1990	7,345	443	6.0	166	18	283	58.5	19.6	21.9	2.3	37.4
1991	7,789	418	5.4	164	20	274	52.2	18.0	20.5	2.5	34.2
Projections:[5]											
1995	9,613	475	4.9	166	28	337	48.2	14.0	16.9	2.9	34.2
2000	12,038	500	4.2	202	39	337	40.7	13.3	16.4	3.1	27.4
HISPANIC ORIGIN [6]											
1980 [4]	14,609	613	4.2	261	45	339	54.5	19.2	23.2	4.0	30.2
1985	17,997	763	4.2	415	73	302	41.6	18.6	22.6	4.0	16.4
1989	21,207	915	4.3	537	82	291	42.3	21.0	24.8	3.8	13.4
1990	22,122	828	3.7	556	75	303	36.7	21.3	24.7	3.3	13.4
1991	22,950	772	3.4	575	110	306	33.0	19.9	24.6	4.7	13.1
Projections:[5]											
1995	26,122	803	3.1	587	108	324	30.3	18.1	22.1	4.1	12.2
2000	30,189	830	2.7	642	135	324	27.1	16.6	21.0	4.4	10.6
WHITE, NON-HISPANIC											
1980 [4]	180,906	716	0.4	1,958	1,234	113	5.3	5.3	14.4	9.1	0.8
1985	184,649	729	0.4	2,607	1,750	82	3.9	4.6	14.1	9.5	0.4
1989	187,410	750	0.4	2,642	1,778	147	4.0	4.6	14.1	9.5	0.8
1990	188,160	956	0.5	2,701	1,807	128	5.1	4.7	14.3	9.6	0.7
1991	189,116	1,054	0.6	2,598	1,768	224	5.6	4.4	13.7	9.3	1.2
Projections:[5]											
1995	192,888	808	0.4	2,510	1,875	174	4.2	3.3	13.0	9.7	0.9
2000	196,406	573	0.3	2,346	1,947	174	2.9	2.0	11.9	9.9	0.9
BLACK, NON-HISPANIC											
1980 [4]	26,142	253	1.0	434	171	47	12.8	13.3	22.0	8.7	2.4
1985	27,607	297	1.1	588	241	42	10.7	12.5	21.2	8.7	1.5
1989	28,844	346	1.2	680	264	40	11.9	14.4	23.4	9.1	1.4
1990	29,191	477	1.6	718	256	43	16.2	15.7	24.4	8.7	1.5
1991	29,667	536	1.8	716	254	74	17.9	15.5	24.0	8.5	2.5
Projections:[5]											
1995	31,484	435	1.4	648	273	60	13.7	11.8	20.4	8.6	1.9
2000	33,624	421	1.3	658	297	60	12.4	10.7	19.5	8.8	1.8

- Represents or rounds to zero.   [1] Prior to April 1, 1990, includes "error of closure" (the amount necessary to make the components of change add to the net change between censuses), for which figures are not shown separately.   [2] Percent of population at beginning of period.   [3] Covers net international migration and movement of Armed Forces, Federally affiliated civilian citizens, and their dependents.   [4] Represents data for period April 1, 1980, to December 31, 1980.   [5] Based on middle series of assumptions. See footnote 1, table 3.   [6] Persons of Hispanic origin may be of any race.

Source: U.S. Bureau of the Census, *Current Population Reports*, P25-1092 and P25-1095.

No. 22. Resident Population, by Age and Race: 1980 to 1991

[In thousands, except percent. As of April, except 1991 as of July. See headnote, table 19 and, for 1980 data, footnote 4, table 1]

YEAR, SEX, AND RACE	Total, all years	Under 5 years	5-9 years	10-14 years	15-19 years	20-24 years	25-29 years	30-34 years	35-39 years	40-44 years	45-49 years	50-54 years	55-59 years	60-64 years	65-74 years	75-84 years	85 years and over	5-13 years	14-17 years	18-24 years
ALL RACES																				
1980	226,546	16,348	16,700	18,242	21,168	21,319	19,521	17,561	13,965	11,669	11,090	11,710	11,615	10,088	15,581	7,729	2,240	31,159	16,247	30,022
1990	248,710	18,758	18,035	17,060	17,882	19,132	21,328	21,833	19,846	17,589	13,744	11,313	10,487	10,625	18,045	10,012	3,021	31,826	13,340	26,942
1991	252,177	19,222	18,237	17,671	17,205	19,194	20,718	22,159	20,518	18,754	14,094	11,645	10,423	10,582	18,280	10,314	3,160	32,500	13,423	26,385
Male	122,979	9,836	9,337	9,051	8,834	9,775	10,393	11,034	10,174	9,258	6,907	5,656	4,987	4,945	8,022	3,888	881	16,641	6,902	13,456
Female	129,198	9,386	8,900	8,620	8,371	9,419	10,325	11,125	10,344	9,496	7,188	5,989	5,436	5,637	10,258	6,426	2,279	15,859	6,521	12,929
WHITE																				
1980	194,713	13,414	13,717	15,095	17,681	18,072	16,658	15,157	12,122	10,110	9,693	10,360	10,394	9,078	14,045	7,057	2,060	25,692	13,491	25,381
1990	208,704	14,960	14,502	13,670	14,351	15,637	17,638	18,190	16,652	15,001	11,826	9,744	9,131	9,381	16,175	9,084	2,761	25,557	10,664	21,939
1991	210,899	15,168	14,634	14,122	13,749	15,630	17,036	18,424	17,170	15,927	12,097	10,013	9,037	9,312	16,338	9,356	2,886	26,036	10,718	21,380
Male	103,268	7,780	7,512	7,254	7,078	8,006	8,620	9,272	8,608	7,948	5,984	4,908	4,367	4,396	7,212	3,529	795	13,368	5,523	10,960
Female	107,631	7,388	7,123	6,868	6,671	7,625	8,416	9,152	8,562	7,980	6,113	5,105	4,669	4,916	9,125	5,827	2,090	12,669	5,196	10,422
BLACK																				
1980	26,683	2,459	2,509	2,691	3,007	2,749	2,342	1,904	1,469	1,260	1,150	1,135	1,041	874	1,344	588	159	4,628	2,380	3,948
1990	30,483	2,939	2,711	2,629	2,714	2,655	2,780	2,718	2,359	1,882	1,413	1,178	1,041	972	1,498	772	223	4,837	2,056	3,816
1991	31,164	3,099	2,747	2,722	2,647	2,671	2,753	2,763	2,463	2,055	1,451	1,211	1,050	979	1,536	786	232	4,938	2,071	3,778
Male	14,753	1,568	1,391	1,376	1,339	1,309	1,311	1,291	1,144	949	661	544	464	422	631	282	69	2,498	1,053	1,865
Female	16,412	1,531	1,356	1,346	1,307	1,361	1,442	1,472	1,318	1,106	790	666	586	557	905	504	163	2,440	1,018	1,912
AMERICAN INDIAN, ESKIMO, ALEUT																				
1980	1,420	149	147	156	170	149	125	107	84	69	58	52	45	34	48	21	6	270	136	216
1990	2,065	220	209	197	191	179	188	181	157	132	99	79	64	53	73	34	9	368	152	256
1991	2,117	234	212	207	186	183	184	183	162	138	103	81	65	54	76	36	11	380	151	256
Male	1,050	119	108	105	95	95	93	90	79	67	50	39	31	26	34	14	4	193	77	133
Female	1,068	115	105	102	91	88	91	93	83	71	53	42	34	29	42	21	7	188	74	124
ASIAN, PACIFIC ISLANDER																				
1980	3,729	326	328	300	310	349	396	393	291	230	188	163	135	101	143	63	15	570	239	478
1990	7,458	638	612	564	626	661	722	745	678	574	405	312	252	220	300	122	29	1,063	469	931
1991	7,996	720	644	621	623	710	744	788	723	633	444	340	271	237	329	135	32	1,146	484	969
Male	3,909	369	327	316	321	365	369	381	343	294	212	165	124	102	145	63	13	582	250	497
Female	4,087	352	317	305	302	345	375	407	380	339	232	175	147	135	184	74	19	564	234	471
PERCENT																				
Total, 1991	100.0	7.6	7.2	7.0	6.8	7.6	8.2	8.8	8.1	7.4	5.6	4.6	4.1	4.2	7.2	4.1	1.3	12.9	5.3	10.5
White	100.0	7.2	6.9	6.7	6.5	7.4	8.1	8.7	8.1	7.6	5.7	4.7	4.3	4.4	7.7	4.4	1.4	12.3	5.1	10.1
Black	100.0	9.9	8.8	8.7	8.5	8.6	8.8	8.9	7.9	6.6	4.7	3.9	3.4	3.1	4.9	2.5	0.7	15.8	6.6	12.1
American Indian, Eskimo, Aleut	100.0	11.1	10.0	9.8	8.8	8.6	8.7	8.6	7.7	6.5	4.9	3.8	3.1	2.6	3.6	1.7	0.5	17.9	7.1	12.1
Asian, Pacific Islander	100.0	9.0	8.1	7.8	7.8	8.9	9.3	9.9	9.0	7.9	5.6	4.3	3.4	3.0	4.1	1.7	0.4	14.3	6.1	12.1

Source: U.S. Bureau of the Census, Current Population Reports, P25-1095.

No. 23. Resident Population, by Age and Hispanic Origin: 1980 to 1991

[In thousands, except percent. As of April, except 1991 as of July. See headnote, table 19 and, for 1980 data, footnote 4, table 1. Hispanic persons may be of any race]

YEAR AND SEX	Total all years	Under 5 years	5-9 years	10-14 years	15-19 years	20-24 years	25-29 years	30-34 years	35-39 years	40-44 years	45-49 years	50-54 years	55-59 years	60-64 years	65-74 years	75-84 years	85 years and over	5-13 years	14-17 years	18-24 years
HISPANIC ORIGIN																				
1980	14,609	1,663	1,537	1,475	1,606	1,586	1,376	1,129	854	712	622	564	454	321	457	203	49	2,715	1,251	2,240
1990	22,354	2,467	2,178	1,989	2,084	2,320	2,337	2,045	1,642	1,276	936	750	633	550	715	339	91	3,782	1,575	3,215
1991	23,350	2,600	2,256	2,088	2,057	2,357	2,400	2,175	1,761	1,394	997	788	656	580	770	364	106	3,947	1,593	3,221
Male	11,890	1,330	1,151	1,068	1,076	1,288	1,285	1,136	899	697	488	380	310	268	337	141	37	2,016	820	1,747
Female	11,460	1,271	1,104	1,021	981	1,070	1,115	1,039	862	698	509	408	346	312	433	224	69	1,930	772	1,473
NON-HISPANIC																				
WHITE																				
1980	180,906	11,842	12,262	13,703	16,166	16,574	15,358	14,091	11,315	9,437	9,104	9,824	9,963	8,775	13,614	6,863	2,014	23,126	12,313	23,267
1990	188,300	12,781	12,516	11,854	12,447	13,522	15,508	16,332	15,162	13,839	10,971	9,057	8,548	8,871	15,511	8,767	2,675	22,106	9,225	19,008
1991	189,568	12,721	12,581	12,218	11,868	13,483	14,851	16,445	15,572	14,659	11,186	9,291	8,433	8,776	15,623	9,017	2,786	22,443	9,265	18,444
Male	92,399	6,559	6,463	6,281	6,094	6,831	7,449	8,236	7,791	7,313	5,538	4,560	4,082	4,148	6,998	3,398	760	11,531	4,773	9,364
Female	97,169	6,221	6,118	5,937	5,775	6,652	7,402	8,209	7,781	7,346	5,649	4,731	4,352	4,628	8,726	5,619	2,025	10,911	4,491	9,080
BLACK																				
1980	26,142	2,399	2,455	2,635	2,944	2,689	2,292	1,865	1,438	1,233	1,127	1,114	1,024	861	1,327	582	157	4,530	2,331	3,862
1990	29,273	2,799	2,597	2,525	2,605	2,528	2,649	2,600	2,265	1,811	1,362	1,137	1,008	945	1,465	757	219	4,639	1,976	3,640
1991	29,910	2,967	2,625	2,612	2,539	2,541	2,618	2,640	2,361	1,977	1,396	1,168	1,017	951	1,501	770	228	4,727	1,987	3,603
Male	14,118	1,501	1,329	1,320	1,284	1,240	1,239	1,227	1,092	910	635	524	449	409	617	276	67	2,391	1,009	1,772
Female	15,792	1,466	1,296	1,292	1,256	1,302	1,379	1,413	1,269	1,067	762	644	568	541	883	493	160	2,337	978	1,832
AMERICAN INDIAN, ESKIMO, ALEUT																				
1980	1,326	136	135	145	158	138	116	100	79	66	55	49	43	32	46	20	6	249	127	199
1990	1,796	185	179	170	165	151	160	156	138	117	90	72	58	48	68	31	9	317	131	217
1991	1,845	203	181	178	161	155	157	158	141	123	93	74	59	49	70	33	10	326	131	218
Male	908	103	92	91	82	79	78	77	68	59	45	35	28	23	31	14	3	165	66	112
Female	936	100	89	88	79	75	78	81	74	63	48	38	31	26	39	21	6	160	64	106
ASIAN, PACIFIC ISLANDER																				
1980	3,563	308	311	285	294	332	378	376	279	221	182	158	131	98	136	60	14	540	226	455
1990	6,988	586	566	522	581	611	673	700	640	545	384	297	240	210	287	116	27	984	436	862
1991	7,504	671	596	575	580	658	692	741	683	602	421	324	258	226	316	130	31	1,062	448	899
Male	3,664	343	302	293	299	337	342	357	324	279	201	157	118	97	140	60	12	538	231	460
Female	3,840	327	293	282	281	320	350	383	359	323	220	167	140	129	177	71	18	521	218	438
1991, PERCENT																				
Hispanic origin	100.0	11.1	9.7	8.9	8.8	10.1	10.3	9.3	7.5	6.0	4.3	3.4	2.8	2.5	3.3	1.6	0.5	16.9	6.8	13.8
Non-Hispanic:																				
White	100.0	6.7	6.6	6.4	6.3	7.1	7.8	8.7	8.2	7.7	5.9	4.9	4.4	4.6	8.2	4.8	1.5	11.8	4.9	9.7
Black	100.0	9.9	8.8	8.7	8.5	8.5	8.8	8.8	7.9	6.6	4.7	3.9	3.4	3.2	5.0	2.6	0.8	15.8	6.6	12.0
American Indian, Eskimo, Aleut	100.0	11.0	9.8	9.6	8.7	8.4	8.5	8.6	7.6	6.7	5.0	4.0	3.2	2.7	3.8	1.8	0.5	17.7	7.1	11.8
Asian, Pacific Islander	100.0	8.9	7.9	7.7	7.7	8.8	9.2	9.9	9.1	8.0	5.6	4.3	3.4	3.0	4.2	1.7	0.4	14.2	6.0	12.0

Source: U.S. Bureau of the Census, Current Population Reports, P25-1095.

No. 24. White, Black, Asian, Pacific Islander, American Indian, and Hispanic Origin Population, by Single Years of Age: 1991

[In thousands, except as indicated. As of July 1. Resident population. For derivation of estimates, see text, section 1]

AGE	White	Black	American Indian, Eskimo, Aleut	Asian, Pacific Islander	Hispanic origin [1]
Total	210,899	31,164	2,117	7,996	23,350
Under 5 yrs. old	15,168	3,099	234	720	2,600
Under 1 yr. old	3,102	677	54	178	553
1 yr. old	3,129	645	48	146	553
2 yrs. old	3,013	613	45	134	515
3 yrs. old	2,957	583	44	134	499
4 yrs. old	2,966	580	43	128	481
5-9 yrs. old	14,634	2,747	212	644	2,256
5 yrs. old	2,967	562	43	130	473
6 yrs. old	2,963	549	42	128	457
7 yrs. old	2,870	536	42	127	443
8 yrs. old	2,820	523	42	127	431
9 yrs. old	3,015	577	43	132	451
10-14 yrs. old	14,122	2,722	207	621	2,088
10 yrs. old	2,966	560	44	134	451
11 yrs. old	2,929	565	42	126	431
12 yrs. old	2,774	546	41	123	406
13 yrs. old	2,733	521	40	120	403
14 yrs. old	2,720	531	39	119	399
15-19 yrs. old	13,749	2,647	186	623	2,057
15 yrs. old	2,624	511	38	120	395
16 yrs. old	2,692	513	37	120	398
17 yrs. old	2,682	516	37	125	401
18 yrs. old	2,700	526	35	121	415
19 yrs. old	3,050	581	38	138	449
20-24 yrs. old	15,630	2,671	183	710	2,357
20 yrs. old	3,295	597	39	148	481
21 yrs. old	3,226	555	38	149	473
22 yrs. old	3,057	499	35	140	464
23 yrs. old	2,957	506	34	135	461
24 yrs. old	3,094	514	36	137	479
25-29 yrs. old	17,036	2,753	184	744	2,400
25 yrs. old	3,127	532	36	142	484
26 yrs. old	3,313	547	36	145	486
27 yrs. old	3,474	555	38	151	487
28 yrs. old	3,363	521	35	145	461
29 yrs. old	3,760	598	40	161	481
30-34 yrs. old	18,424	2,763	183	788	2,175
30 yrs. old	3,722	562	38	160	480
31 yrs. old	3,661	557	37	159	447
32 yrs. old	3,632	545	36	157	424
33 yrs. old	3,650	533	35	153	415
34 yrs. old	3,759	566	37	159	409
35-39 yrs. old	17,170	2,463	162	723	1,761
35 yrs. old	3,586	533	35	157	397
36 yrs. old	3,501	508	33	147	371
37 yrs. old	3,447	496	33	144	348
38 yrs. old	3,180	436	30	133	317
39 yrs. old	3,456	490	32	141	328
40-44 yrs. old	15,927	2,055	138	633	1,394
40 yrs. old	3,208	452	30	139	313
41 yrs. old	3,121	431	29	135	290
42 yrs. old	3,073	404	27	125	271
43 yrs. old	3,048	384	28	125	257
44 yrs. old	3,477	385	25	109	264
45-49 yrs. old	12,097	1,451	103	444	997
45 yrs. old	2,414	297	22	99	223
46 yrs. old	2,416	292	21	92	207
47 yrs. old	2,438	299	21	90	197
48 yrs. old	2,494	265	19	78	187
49 yrs. old	2,336	298	20	83	183
50-54 yrs. old	10,013	1,211	81	340	788
50 yrs. old	2,171	261	18	78	175
51 yrs. old	2,006	247	17	70	162
52 yrs. old	1,980	236	16	66	155
53 yrs. old	1,964	237	15	63	151
54 yrs. old	1,892	230	15	63	145
55-59 yrs. old	9,037	1,050	65	271	656
55 yrs. old	1,825	229	14	60	140
56 yrs. old	1,909	217	14	55	143
57 yrs. old	1,789	212	13	55	130
58 yrs. old	1,697	188	12	49	120
59 yrs. old	1,816	204	12	52	123
60-64 yrs. old	9,312	979	54	237	580
60 yrs. old	1,858	203	12	51	126
61 yrs. old	1,847	194	11	48	120
62 yrs. old	1,822	196	11	47	115
63 yrs. old	1,900	189	10	45	113
64 yrs. old	1,884	198	10	45	107
65-69 yrs. old	8,926	873	44	194	458
65 yrs. old	1,820	198	10	44	102
66 yrs. old	1,838	182	9	40	97
67 yrs. old	1,806	173	9	38	92
68 yrs. old	1,703	161	8	37	85
69 yrs. old	1,758	159	8	35	81
70-74 yrs. old	7,412	663	32	135	312
70 yrs. old	1,688	157	8	34	77
71 yrs. old	1,551	144	7	30	68
72 yrs. old	1,484	130	7	28	61
73 yrs. old	1,372	118	6	23	54
74 yrs. old	1,317	114	5	22	51
75-79 yrs. old	5,679	489	23	88	223
75 yrs. old	1,271	108	5	21	49
76 yrs. old	1,211	99	5	19	47
77 yrs. old	1,125	97	4	18	44
78 yrs. old	1,086	97	4	16	44
79 yrs. old	985	87	4	15	39
80-84 yrs. old	3,677	297	13	47	141
80 yrs. old	881	73	3	12	35
81 yrs. old	802	67	3	10	31
82 yrs. old	732	56	3	9	27
83 yrs. old	676	51	2	8	25
84 yrs. old	585	49	2	8	22
85-89 yrs. old	1,915	147	7	21	72
90-94 yrs. old	741	60	3	8	26
95-99 yrs. old	194	17	1	2	7
100 yrs. old and over	36	7	-	1	2
Median age (yr.)	34.1	28.1	26.0	29.6	25.7

- Represents or rounds to zero.   [1] Persons of Hispanic origin may be of any race.

Source: U.S. Bureau of the Census, *Current Population Reports*, P25-1095.

No. 25. Projections of Resident Population, by Age, Sex, and Race: 1995 to 2025

[As of July 1. Data are for middle series; for assumptions, see table 3]

AGE, SEX, AND RACE	POPULATION (1,000)					PERCENT DISTRIBUTION		
	1995	2000	2005	2010	2025	2000	2010	2025
Total	**262,754**	**274,815**	**286,324**	**298,109**	**334,216**	**100.0**	**100.0**	**100.0**
Under 5 years old	19,553	18,908	18,959	19,730	21,682	6.9	6.6	6.5
5 to 13 years old	34,372	36,051	35,782	35,425	39,547	13.1	11.9	11.8
14 to 17 years old	14,754	15,734	17,020	16,908	17,652	5.7	5.7	5.3
18 to 24 years old	24,903	26,117	28,111	30,007	30,005	9.5	10.1	9.0
25 to 34 years old	40,844	37,416	36,495	38,367	43,129	13.6	12.9	12.9
35 to 44 years old	42,500	44,662	42,284	38,853	42,541	16.3	13.0	12.7
45 to 54 years old	31,082	37,054	41,610	43,737	37,346	13.5	14.7	11.2
55 to 64 years old	21,153	23,988	29,647	35,378	39,892	8.7	11.9	11.9
65 to 74 years old	18,800	18,258	18,523	21,235	35,820	6.6	7.1	10.7
75 to 84 years old	11,154	12,339	12,955	12,767	19,565	4.5	4.3	5.9
85 years old and over	3,638	4,289	4,937	5,702	7,038	1.6	1.9	2.1
Male	128,292	134,338	140,097	146,012	164,054	48.9	49.0	49.1
Female	134,461	140,477	146,227	152,097	170,162	51.1	51.0	50.9
White, total	**217,511**	**224,594**	**230,993**	**237,412**	**256,425**	**100.0**	**100.0**	**100.0**
Under 5 years old	15,321	14,496	14,254	14,617	15,461	6.5	6.2	6.0
5 to 13 years old	27,201	28,043	27,303	26,455	28,361	12.5	11.1	11.1
14 to 17 years old	11,662	12,322	13,068	12,764	12,601	5.5	5.4	4.9
18 to 24 years old	19,862	20,615	21,997	23,107	21,828	9.2	9.7	8.5
25 to 34 years old	33,296	29,825	28,603	29,813	32,125	13.3	12.6	12.5
35 to 44 years old	35,336	36,660	34,110	30,634	32,436	16.3	12.9	12.6
45 to 54 years old	26,548	31,203	34,536	35,860	28,928	13.9	15.1	11.3
55 to 64 years old	18,242	20,554	25,265	29,772	32,180	9.2	12.5	12.5
65 to 74 years old	16,652	15,906	15,899	18,136	29,764	7.1	7.6	11.6
75 to 84 years old	10,093	11,111	11,538	11,191	16,798	4.9	4.7	6.6
85 years old and over	3,299	3,862	4,419	5,064	5,944	1.7	2.1	2.3
Male	106,684	110,359	113,689	117,043	126,877	49.1	49.3	49.5
Female	110,827	114,235	117,304	120,369	129,548	50.9	50.7	50.5
Black, total	**33,147**	**35,525**	**37,907**	**40,429**	**48,388**	**100.0**	**100.0**	**100.0**
Under 5 years old	3,177	3,183	3,299	3,529	4,088	9.0	8.7	8.4
5 to 13 years old	5,337	5,829	5,939	6,081	7,221	16.4	15.0	14.9
14 to 17 years old	2,296	2,418	2,786	2,803	3,189	6.8	6.9	6.6
18 to 24 years old	3,703	3,923	4,197	4,701	5,095	11.0	11.6	10.5
25 to 34 years old	5,372	5,131	5,163	5,426	6,572	14.4	13.4	13.6
35 to 44 years old	5,154	5,586	5,422	5,175	5,934	15.7	12.8	12.3
45 to 54 years old	3,237	4,110	4,910	5,323	4,998	11.6	13.2	10.3
55 to 64 years old	2,130	2,413	3,015	3,838	4,904	6.8	9.5	10.1
65 to 74 years old	1,625	1,690	1,804	2,070	4,041	4.8	5.1	8.4
75 to 84 years old	837	909	990	1,044	1,712	2.6	2.6	3.5
85 years old and over	278	333	382	439	635	0.9	1.1	1.3
Male	15,711	16,846	17,972	19,168	22,951	47.4	47.4	47.4
Female	17,436	18,680	19,936	21,261	25,437	52.6	52.6	52.6
American Indian, Eskimo, Aleut, total	**2,247**	**2,409**	**2,583**	**2,772**	**3,386**	**100.0**	**100.0**	**100.0**
Under 5 years old	220	224	242	264	308	9.3	9.5	9.1
5 to 13 years old	412	425	429	455	561	17.6	16.4	16.6
14 to 17 years old	174	193	208	204	254	8.0	7.4	7.5
18 to 24 years old	255	277	314	337	382	11.5	12.2	11.3
25 to 34 years old	362	356	367	407	481	14.8	14.7	14.2
35 to 44 years old	332	352	345	341	436	14.6	12.3	12.9
45 to 54 years old	219	262	298	318	320	10.9	11.5	9.5
55 to 64 years old	132	153	186	225	271	6.4	8.1	8.0
65 to 74 years old	85	93	104	123	210	3.9	4.4	6.2
75 to 84 years old	42	51	58	64	108	2.1	2.3	3.2
85 years old and over	15	22	28	35	56	0.9	1.3	1.7
Male	1,113	1,193	1,279	1,372	1,677	49.5	49.5	49.5
Female	1,133	1,216	1,304	1,400	1,709	50.5	50.5	50.5
Asian, Pacific Islander, total	**9,849**	**12,287**	**14,840**	**17,496**	**26,017**	**100.0**	**100.0**	**100.0**
Under 5 years old	836	1,006	1,163	1,320	1,824	8.2	7.5	7.0
5 to 13 years old	1,422	1,755	2,110	2,435	3,405	14.3	13.9	13.1
14 to 17 years old	623	801	956	1,136	1,608	6.5	6.5	6.2
18 to 24 years old	1,084	1,303	1,603	1,863	2,700	10.6	10.6	10.4
25 to 34 years old	1,813	2,104	2,361	2,722	3,952	17.1	15.6	15.2
35 to 44 years old	1,678	2,064	2,406	2,704	3,737	16.8	15.5	14.4
45 to 54 years old	1,079	1,479	1,866	2,236	3,101	12.0	12.8	11.9
55 to 64 years old	649	867	1,181	1,542	2,536	7.1	8.8	9.7
65 to 74 years old	439	568	717	907	1,806	4.6	5.2	6.9
75 to 84 years old	184	269	368	468	947	2.2	2.7	3.6
85 years old and over	46	72	108	165	402	0.6	0.9	1.5
Male	4,784	5,940	7,157	8,428	12,549	48.3	48.2	48.2
Female	5,066	6,347	7,684	9,068	13,468	51.7	51.8	51.8

Source: U.S. Bureau of the Census, *Current Population Reports*, P25-1092.

No. 26. Projections of Hispanic and Non-Hispanic Populations, by Age and Sex: 1995 to 2025

[As of July 1. Resident population. Data are for middle series; for assumptions, see table 3]

AGE AND SEX	POPULATION (1,000)					PERCENT DISTRIBUTION		
	1995	2000	2005	2010	2025	2000	2010	2025
Hispanic origin, total [1]	**26,522**	**30,602**	**34,842**	**39,312**	**54,018**	**100.0**	**100.0**	**100.0**
Under 5 years old	2,804	3,055	3,338	3,683	4,746	10.0	9.4	8.8
5 to 13 years old	4,535	5,226	5,720	6,212	8,133	17.1	15.8	15.1
14 to 17 years old	1,816	2,097	2,486	2,698	3,464	6.9	6.9	6.4
18 to 24 years old	3,224	3,544	4,059	4,676	5,919	11.6	11.9	11.0
25 to 34 years old	5,046	5,200	5,344	5,851	7,940	17.0	14.9	14.7
35 to 44 years old	3,887	4,821	5,410	5,560	6,991	15.8	14.1	12.9
45 to 54 years old	2,270	3,029	3,902	4,800	5,680	9.9	12.2	10.5
55 to 64 years old	1,408	1,729	2,266	2,993	5,261	5.6	7.6	9.7
65 to 74 years old	955	1,135	1,327	1,625	3,569	3.7	4.1	6.6
75 to 84 years old	437	578	750	889	1,689	1.9	2.3	3.1
85 years old and over	139	188	240	324	625	0.6	0.8	1.2
Male	13,470	15,492	17,585	19,792	27,059	50.6	50.3	50.1
Female	13,052	15,110	17,257	19,519	26,959	49.4	49.7	49.9
Non-Hispanic White, total	**193,307**	**196,701**	**199,274**	**201,668**	**207,439**	**100.0**	**100.0**	**100.0**
Under 5 years old	12,753	11,706	11,214	11,270	11,155	6.0	5.6	5.4
5 to 13 years old	23,083	23,290	22,097	20,815	21,007	11.8	10.3	10.1
14 to 17 years old	10,008	10,423	10,821	10,318	9,480	5.3	5.1	4.6
18 to 24 years old	16,915	17,385	18,317	18,871	16,475	8.8	9.4	7.9
25 to 34 years old	28,703	25,095	23,745	24,509	24,933	12.8	12.2	12.0
35 to 44 years old	31,800	32,270	29,187	25,580	26,118	16.4	12.7	12.6
45 to 54 years old	24,475	28,442	30,981	31,483	23,758	14.5	15.6	11.5
55 to 64 years old	16,949	18,970	23,195	27,041	27,379	9.6	13.4	13.2
65 to 74 years old	15,767	14,862	14,683	16,652	26,513	7.6	8.3	12.8
75 to 84 years old	9,685	10,574	10,842	10,370	15,252	5.4	5.1	7.4
85 years old and over	3,169	3,685	4,194	4,761	5,365	1.9	2.4	2.6
Male	94,375	96,213	97,645	99,002	102,265	48.9	49.1	49.3
Female	98,931	100,488	101,629	102,667	105,173	51.1	50.9	50.7
Non-Hispanic Black, total	**31,702**	**33,834**	**35,957**	**38,201**	**45,237**	**100.0**	**100.0**	**100.0**
Under 5 years old	3,024	3,014	3,111	3,316	3,807	8.9	8.7	8.4
5 to 13 years old	5,083	5,531	5,615	5,723	6,731	16.3	15.0	14.9
14 to 17 years old	2,198	2,298	2,638	2,647	2,977	6.8	6.9	6.6
18 to 24 years old	3,533	3,729	3,966	4,424	4,743	11.0	11.6	10.5
25 to 34 years old	5,093	4,846	4,870	5,098	6,110	14.3	13.3	13.5
35 to 44 years old	4,933	5,316	5,122	4,870	5,530	15.7	12.7	12.2
45 to 54 years old	3,113	3,940	4,689	5,055	4,687	11.6	13.2	10.4
55 to 64 years old	2,056	2,320	2,889	3,667	4,607	6.9	9.6	10.2
65 to 74 years old	1,579	1,631	1,730	1,977	3,824	4.8	5.2	8.5
75 to 84 years old	817	884	954	998	1,615	2.6	2.6	3.6
85 years old and over	273	326	372	425	605	1.0	1.1	1.3
Male	14,985	16,002	17,004	18,066	21,405	47.3	47.3	47.3
Female	16,717	17,833	18,954	20,135	23,832	52.7	52.7	52.7
Non-Hispanic American Indian, Eskimo, Aleut, total	**1,956**	**2,096**	**2,245**	**2,407**	**2,942**	**100.0**	**100.0**	**100.0**
Under 5 years old	193	196	212	230	273	9.4	9.6	9.3
5 to 13 years old	351	369	375	398	492	17.6	16.5	16.7
14 to 17 years old	150	165	179	178	221	7.9	7.4	7.5
18 to 24 years old	220	238	268	288	332	11.4	12.0	11.3
25 to 34 years old	307	303	316	348	420	14.5	14.5	14.3
35 to 44 years old	289	302	292	289	369	14.4	12.0	12.5
45 to 54 years old	196	231	259	273	274	11.0	11.3	9.3
55 to 64 years old	120	139	167	198	230	6.6	8.2	7.8
65 to 74 years old	78	84	95	111	182	4.0	4.6	6.2
75 to 84 years old	40	47	53	59	97	2.2	2.5	3.3
85 years old and over	14	20	26	33	53	1.0	1.4	1.8
Male	963	1,032	1,106	1,186	1,453	49.2	49.3	49.4
Female	993	1,064	1,139	1,221	1,490	50.8	50.7	50.6
Non-Hispanic Asian, Pacific Islander, total	**9,266**	**11,582**	**14,005**	**16,522**	**24,580**	**100.0**	**100.0**	**100.0**
Under 5 years old	778	938	1,084	1,230	1,701	8.1	7.4	6.9
5 to 13 years old	1,319	1,634	1,974	2,276	3,183	14.1	13.8	12.9
14 to 17 years old	582	750	895	1,066	1,506	6.5	6.5	6.1
18 to 24 years old	1,013	1,220	1,504	1,747	2,536	10.5	10.6	10.3
25 to 34 years old	1,694	1,971	2,219	2,561	3,725	17.0	15.5	15.2
35 to 44 years old	1,591	1,953	2,271	2,554	3,534	16.9	15.5	14.4
45 to 54 years old	1,029	1,412	1,779	2,127	2,947	12.2	12.9	12.0
55 to 64 years old	620	830	1,132	1,478	2,414	7.2	8.9	9.8
65 to 74 years old	421	545	689	872	1,731	4.7	5.3	7.0
75 to 84 years old	176	258	355	451	912	2.2	2.7	3.7
85 years old and over	44	69	105	159	390	0.6	1.0	1.6
Male	4,498	5,600	6,757	7,966	11,871	48.4	48.2	48.3
Female	4,768	5,983	7,248	8,556	12,709	51.7	51.8	51.7

[1] Persons of Hispanic origin may be of any race.

Source: U.S. Bureau of the Census, *Current Population Reports*, P25-1092.

No. 27. Center of Population: 1790 to 1990

["Center of population" is that point at which an imaginary flat, weightless, and rigid map of the United States would balance if weights of identical value were placed on it so that each weight represented the location of one person on the date of the census]

YEAR	North latitude			West longitude			Approximate location
	°	'	"	°	'	"	
1790 (August 2)	39	16	30	76	11	12	23 miles east of Baltimore, MD
1850 (June 1)	38	59	0	81	19	0	23 miles southeast of Parkersburg, WV
1900 (June 1)	39	9	36	85	48	54	6 miles southeast of Columbus, IN
1950 (April 1)	38	50	21	88	9	33	8 miles north–northwest of Olney, Richland County, IL
1960 (April 1)	38	35	58	89	12	35	In Clinton Co. about 6 1/2 miles northwest of Centralia, IL
1970 (April 1)	38	27	47	89	42	22	5.3 miles east–southeast of the Mascoutah City Hall in St. Clair County, IL
1980 (April 1)	38	8	13	90	34	26	1/4 mile west of De Soto in Jefferson County, MO
1990 (April 1)	37	52	20	91	12	55	9.7 miles southeast of Steelville in Crawford County, MO

No. 28. U.S. Resident Population, by Region and Division: 1960 to 1992

[As of **April 1**; except **1985** and **1992**, as of **July 1**. For composition of divisions, see table 31]

REGION AND DIVISION	POPULATION (millions)						PERCENT DISTRIBUTION					
	1960	1970	1980	1985	1990	1992	1960	1970	1980	1985	1990	1992
United States	179.3	203.3	226.5	237.9	248.7	255.1	100.0	100.0	100.0	100.0	100.0	100.0
Northeast	44.7	49.1	49.1	49.9	50.8	51.1	24.9	24.1	21.7	21.0	20.4	20.0
New England	10.5	11.8	12.3	12.7	13.2	13.2	5.9	5.8	5.5	5.4	5.3	5.2
Middle Atlantic	34.2	37.2	36.8	37.1	37.6	37.9	19.1	18.3	16.2	15.6	15.1	14.9
Midwest	51.6	56.6	58.9	58.8	59.7	60.7	28.8	27.8	26.0	24.7	24.0	23.8
East North Central	36.2	40.3	41.7	41.4	42.0	42.8	20.2	19.8	18.4	17.4	16.9	16.8
West North Central	15.4	16.3	17.2	17.4	17.7	18.0	8.6	8.0	7.6	7.3	7.1	7.0
South	55.0	62.8	75.4	81.4	85.4	88.1	30.7	30.9	33.3	34.2	34.4	34.6
South Atlantic	26.0	30.7	37.0	40.2	43.6	45.1	14.5	15.1	16.3	16.9	17.5	17.7
East South Central	12.1	12.8	14.7	15.0	15.2	15.5	6.7	6.3	6.5	6.3	6.1	6.1
West South Central	17.0	19.3	23.7	26.3	26.7	27.6	9.5	9.5	10.5	11.0	10.7	10.8
West	28.1	34.8	43.2	47.8	52.8	55.1	15.6	17.1	19.1	20.1	21.2	21.6
Mountain	6.9	8.3	11.4	12.7	13.7	14.4	3.8	4.1	5.0	5.4	5.5	5.6
Pacific	21.2	26.5	31.8	35.1	39.1	40.7	11.8	13.1	14.0	14.7	15.7	16.0

Source: U.S. Bureau of the Census, *1990 Census of Population and Housing, Population and Housing Unit Counts* (CPH–2) and *Current Population Reports*, P25, forthcoming report.

No. 29. Annual Inmigration, Outmigration, and Net Migration for Regions: 1980 to 1991

[In thousands. As of **March.** For persons 1 year old and over. Excludes members of the Armed Forces except those living off post or with their families on post. Based on Current Population Survey; see text, section 1 and Appendix III. For composition of regions, see table 31. Minus sign (-) indicates net outmigration]

PERIOD	North-east	Mid-west	South	West	PERIOD	North-east	Mid-west	South	West
1980-81: Inmigrants	464	650	1,377	871	**1987-88:** Inmigrants	430	715	1,338	613
Outmigrants	706	1,056	890	710	Outmigrants	671	818	886	721
Net internal migration	-242	-406	487	161	Net internal migration	-241	-103	452	-108
Movers from abroad	207	180	412	514	Movers from abroad	261	146	414	379
Net migration	-35	-226	899	675	Net migration	20	43	866	271
1982-83: Inmigrants	439	661	1,211	880	**1988-89:** Inmigrants	370	777	1,318	791
Outmigrants	625	947	973	645	Outmigrants	714	703	1,071	637
Net internal migration	-186	-286	238	235	Net internal migration	-344	74	247	154
Movers from abroad	192	149	323	315	Movers from abroad	292	170	375	629
Net migration	6	-137	561	550	Net migration	-52	244	622	783
1983-84: Inmigrants	487	820	1,399	834	**1989-90:** Inmigrants	461	908	1,428	964
Outmigrants	578	1,102	973	887	Outmigrants	758	1,024	1,198	781
Net internal migration	-91	-282	426	-53	Net internal migration	-297	-116	230	183
Movers from abroad	213	141	383	341	Movers from abroad	328	169	500	562
Net migration	122	-141	809	288	Net migration	30	53	730	745
1984-85: Inmigrants	482	842	1,329	994	**1990-91:**				
Outmigrants	691	1,053	1,169	734	Total inmigrants	346	782	1,421	835
Net internal migration	-209	-211	160	260	From Northeast	(X)	175	565	191
Movers from abroad	228	168	532	499	From Midwest	76	(X)	448	273
Net migration	19	-43	692	759	From South	195	422	(X)	370
1985-86: Inmigrants	502	1,011	1,355	910	From West	75	185	408	(X)
Outmigrants	752	996	1,320	710	Total outmigrants	932	797	987	668
Net internal migration	-250	15	35	200	To Northeast	(X)	76	195	75
Movers from abroad	198	158	342	502	To Midwest	175	(X)	422	185
Net migration	-52	173	377	702	To South	565	448	(X)	408
1986-87: Inmigrants	398	858	1,374	916	To West	191	273	370	(X)
Outmigrants	732	969	1,095	750	Net internal migration	-585	-15	433	167
Net internal migration	-334	-111	279	166	Movers from abroad	209	208	351	617
Movers from abroad	214	193	277	458	Net migration	-376	193	784	784
Net migration	-120	82	556	624					

X Not applicable.
Source: U.S. Bureau of the Census, *Current Population Reports*, P20-463, and earlier reports.

No. 30. Mobility of the Resident Population, by State: 1990

[As of **April 1.** Based on a sample; see Appendix III]

REGION, DIVISION, AND STATE	Persons 5 years old and over,[1] 1990 (1,000)	Same house as in 1990	PERCENT DISTRIBUTION—RESIDENCE IN 1985 Different house, same county	Different county, same State	Different county, different State	REGION, DIVISION, AND STATE	Persons 5 years old and over,[1] 1990 (1,000)	Same house as in 1990	PERCENT DISTRIBUTION—RESIDENCE IN 1985 Different house, same county	Different county, same State	Different county, different State
U.S.	230,446	53.3	25.5	9.7	9.4	DC	570	53.5	23.1	(X)	19.1
						VA	5,746	49.1	18.4	14.9	15.0
Northeast	47,319	60.7	21.9	8.0	6.8	WV	1,687	64.2	21.9	6.2	7.3
N.E.	12,290	56.9	23.8	7.0	10.1	NC	6,172	54.3	23.6	8.9	12.1
ME	1,142	55.6	24.2	7.7	11.6	SC	3,232	55.6	23.4	7.7	12.3
NH	1,025	50.7	22.7	6.8	18.7	GA	5,984	49.4	22.7	12.9	13.4
VT	522	51.9	26.0	6.9	14.4	FL	12,095	44.9	26.1	8.2	17.6
MA	5,606	58.4	23.0	7.9	7.9	**E.S.C.**	14,118	56.4	25.8	7.9	9.2
RI	936	57.4	23.8	5.1	11.3	KY	3,435	56.7	26.1	8.3	8.1
CT	3,060	57.4	25.1	5.7	9.5	TN	4,545	54.0	26.9	7.5	11.0
M.A.	35,029	62.1	21.2	8.4	5.7	AL	3,760	57.3	25.6	7.6	8.7
NY	16,743	62.0	21.2	8.7	4.3	MS	2,379	59.2	23.7	8.5	8.1
NJ	7,201	60.1	19.8	9.2	7.9	**W.S.C.**	24,601	51.6	27.3	11.6	7.8
PA	11,085	63.4	22.1	7.4	6.3	AR	2,187	54.3	25.0	9.1	11.0
Midwest	55,273	56.2	25.7	9.9	7.2	LA	3,886	59.3	25.5	8.7	5.8
E.N.C.	38,921	56.6	26.7	9.2	6.4	OK	2,922	52.1	25.7	11.6	9.6
OH	10,063	57.6	26.7	8.8	6.2	TX	15,606	49.2	28.3	12.7	7.5
IN	5,146	55.6	26.0	9.3	8.4	**West**	48,605	45.2	29.4	10.5	11.0
IL	10,586	55.7	28.2	8.0	6.3	**Mt**	12,557	46.3	26.9	8.3	16.7
MI	8,595	56.9	26.0	10.7	5.5	MT	740	52.0	24.9	10.9	11.4
WI	4,531	57.3	25.1	10.2	6.8	ID	927	50.5	24.2	9.2	14.8
W.N.C.	16,352	55.1	23.4	11.4	9.2	WY	419	49.5	26.5	8.4	14.9
MN	4,039	55.5	22.8	12.9	7.9	CO	3,043	45.2	24.3	13.4	15.3
IA	2,584	58.2	23.4	10.2	7.5	NM	1,390	51.8	24.9	7.7	13.9
MO	4,749	54.3	23.5	12.0	9.4	AZ	3,375	43.1	30.4	4.9	19.3
ND	591	57.3	22.2	9.9	9.5	UT	1,553	52.7	26.4	7.9	11.4
SD	641	55.5	22.1	10.8	10.8	NV	1,110	34.7	29.9	3.2	29.4
NE	1,459	55.9	23.6	9.9	9.7	**Pac**	36,048	44.8	30.3	11.2	9.0
KS	2,290	51.7	24.7	10.3	11.9	WA	4,502	45.9	28.3	9.6	13.9
South	79,249	51.8	25.0	10.0	11.4	OR	2,640	46.1	26.8	11.8	13.8
S.A.	40,530	50.3	23.4	9.8	14.3	CA	27,384	44.4	31.1	11.8	7.2
DE	618	53.8	27.7	2.1	15.2	AK	495	40.6	27.7	8.2	21.3
MD	4,425	52.4	23.1	10.0	12.0	HI	1,026	50.9	25.8	2.3	16.3

X Not applicable. [1] Includes persons residing abroad in 1985.
Source: U.S. Bureau of the Census, *1990 Census of Population and Housing Data Paper Listing* (CPH-L-121).

No. 31. Resident Population—

[As of **July 1**; except **1970, 1980, and 1990**, as of **April 1**. Insofar as possible, population shown for all years is that of See *Historical Statistics, Colonial Times to 1970*, series A 172, for population by regions,

REGION, DIVISION, AND STATE	POPULATION (1,000)										
	1970	1980 [1]	1984	1985	1986	1987	1988	1989	1990	1991	1992
U.S.	203,302	226,546	235,825	237,924	240,133	242,289	244,499	246,819	248,710	252,160	255,082
Northeast	49,061	49,135	49,718	49,869	50,071	50,302	50,584	50,757	50,809	50,961	51,118
N.E.	11,848	12,348	12,642	12,741	12,833	12,951	13,085	13,182	13,207	13,195	13,200
ME	994	1,125	1,156	1,163	1,170	1,185	1,204	1,220	1,228	1,234	1,235
NH	738	921	977	997	1,025	1,054	1,083	1,105	1,109	1,104	1,111
VT	445	511	527	530	534	540	550	558	563	567	570
MA	5,689	5,737	5,841	5,881	5,903	5,935	5,980	6,015	6,016	5,996	5,998
RI	950	947	962	969	977	990	996	1,001	1,003	1,005	1,005
CT	3,032	3,108	3,180	3,201	3,224	3,247	3,272	3,283	3,287	3,289	3,281
M.A.	37,213	36,787	37,076	37,128	37,238	37,350	37,499	37,575	37,602	37,766	37,918
NY	18,241	17,558	17,746	17,792	17,833	17,869	17,941	17,983	17,990	18,055	18,119
NJ	7,171	7,365	7,515	7,566	7,622	7,671	7,712	7,726	7,730	7,753	7,789
PA	11,801	11,864	11,815	11,771	11,771	11,811	11,846	11,866	11,882	11,958	12,009
Midwest	56,589	58,866	58,775	58,820	58,848	59,018	59,254	59,468	59,669	60,239	60,713
E.N.C	40,262	41,682	41,393	41,418	41,455	41,590	41,721	41,873	42,009	42,427	42,753
OH	10,657	10,798	10,738	10,735	10,730	10,760	10,799	10,829	10,847	10,941	11,016
IN	5,195	5,490	5,458	5,459	5,454	5,473	5,492	5,524	5,544	5,610	5,662
IL	11,110	11,427	11,412	11,400	11,387	11,391	11,390	11,410	11,431	11,541	11,631
MI	8,882	9,262	9,049	9,076	9,128	9,187	9,218	9,253	9,295	9,380	9,437
WI	4,418	4,706	4,736	4,748	4,756	4,778	4,822	4,857	4,892	4,956	5,007
W.N.C.	16,327	17,183	17,382	17,402	17,393	17,428	17,533	17,595	17,660	17,812	17,960
MN	3,806	4,076	4,158	4,184	4,205	4,235	4,296	4,338	4,375	4,432	4,480
IA	2,825	2,914	2,859	2,830	2,792	2,767	2,768	2,771	2,777	2,795	2,812
MO	4,678	4,917	4,975	5,000	5,023	5,057	5,082	5,096	5,117	5,157	5,193
ND	618	653	680	677	669	661	655	646	639	635	636
SD	666	691	697	698	696	696	698	697	696	704	711
NE	1,485	1,570	1,589	1,585	1,574	1,567	1,571	1,575	1,578	1,593	1,606
KS	2,249	2,364	2,424	2,427	2,433	2,445	2,462	2,473	2,478	2,495	2,523
South	62,812	75,372	80,417	81,409	82,428	83,208	83,890	84,700	85,446	86,903	88,143
S.A.	30,678	36,959	39,492	40,159	40,863	41,619	42,318	43,008	43,567	44,403	45,061
DE	548	594	612	618	628	637	648	658	666	680	689
MD	3,924	4,217	4,365	4,413	4,487	4,566	4,658	4,727	4,781	4,859	4,908
DC	757	638	633	635	638	637	630	624	607	595	589
VA	4,651	5,347	5,644	5,715	5,812	5,932	6,037	6,120	6,187	6,280	6,377
WV	1,744	1,950	1,928	1,907	1,882	1,858	1,830	1,807	1,793	1,803	1,812
NC	5,084	5,882	6,164	6,254	6,322	6,404	6,481	6,565	6,629	6,736	6,843
SC	2,591	3,122	3,272	3,303	3,343	3,381	3,412	3,457	3,487	3,560	3,603
GA	4,588	5,463	5,835	5,963	6,085	6,208	6,316	6,411	6,478	6,623	6,751
FL	6,791	9,746	11,040	11,351	11,668	11,997	12,306	12,638	12,938	13,266	13,488
E.S.C	12,808	14,666	14,912	14,971	15,012	15,070	15,107	15,136	15,176	15,350	15,529
KY	3,221	3,661	3,695	3,695	3,688	3,683	3,680	3,677	3,685	3,713	3,755
TN	3,926	4,591	4,687	4,715	4,739	4,783	4,822	4,854	4,877	4,953	5,024
AL	3,444	3,894	3,952	3,973	3,992	4,015	4,024	4,030	4,041	4,091	4,136
MS	2,217	2,521	2,578	2,588	2,594	2,589	2,580	2,574	2,573	2,593	2,614
W.S.C.	19,326	23,747	26,013	26,279	26,553	26,518	26,466	26,556	26,703	27,151	27,554
AR	1,923	2,286	2,320	2,327	2,332	2,342	2,343	2,346	2,351	2,373	2,399
LA	3,645	4,206	4,400	4,408	4,407	4,344	4,289	4,253	4,220	4,254	4,287
OK	2,559	3,025	3,286	3,271	3,253	3,210	3,167	3,150	3,146	3,175	3,212
TX	11,199	14,229	16,007	16,273	16,561	16,622	16,667	16,807	16,987	17,348	17,656
West	34,838	43,172	46,914	47,827	48,786	49,762	50,770	51,894	52,786	54,056	55,108
Mt	8,289	11,373	12,518	12,741	12,952	13,145	13,303	13,498	13,659	14,036	14,381
MT	694	787	821	822	814	805	800	800	799	809	824
ID	713	944	991	994	990	985	986	994	1,007	1,040	1,067
WY	332	470	505	500	496	477	465	458	454	460	466
CO	2,210	2,890	3,170	3,209	3,237	3,260	3,262	3,276	3,294	3,378	3,470
NM	1,017	1,303	1,417	1,438	1,463	1,479	1,490	1,504	1,515	1,549	1,581
AZ	1,775	2,718	3,067	3,184	3,308	3,437	3,535	3,622	3,665	3,748	3,832
UT	1,059	1,461	1,622	1,643	1,663	1,678	1,689	1,706	1,723	1,770	1,813
NV	489	800	925	951	981	1,023	1,075	1,137	1,202	1,283	1,327
Pac	26,549	31,800	34,396	35,086	35,835	36,617	37,467	38,397	39,127	40,020	40,726
WA	3,413	4,132	4,344	4,400	4,453	4,532	4,640	4,746	4,867	5,012	5,136
OR	2,092	2,633	2,667	2,673	2,684	2,701	2,741	2,791	2,842	2,922	2,977
CA	19,971	23,668	25,844	26,441	27,102	27,777	28,464	29,218	29,760	30,380	30,867
AK	303	402	514	532	544	539	542	547	550	570	587
HI	770	965	1,028	1,040	1,052	1,068	1,080	1,095	1,108	1,137	1,160

- Represents or rounds to zero.   X Not applicable.   [1] See footnote 4, table 1.   [2] Persons per square mile were calculated on the basis of land area data from the 1990 census.

States: 1970 to 1992

present area of State; for area figures of States, see table 355. Minus sign (-) indicates decrease.
and A 195-198 for population and density, by States]

RANK				PERCENT CHANGE			POPULATION PER SQ. MILE OF LAND AREA [2]				REGION, DIVISION, AND STATE
1970	1980	1990	1992	1970-80	1980-90	1990-92	1970	1980	1990	1992	
(X)	(X)	(X)	(X)	11.4	9.8	2.6	57.5	64.1	70.3	72.1	**U.S.**
(X)	(X)	(X)	(X)	0.2	3.4	0.6	302.3	302.8	313.1	315.0	**Northeast**
(X)	(X)	(X)	(X)	4.2	7.0	-	188.6	196.6	210.3	210.2	**N.E**
38	38	38	39	13.2	9.2	0.6	32.2	36.5	39.8	40.0	ME
41	42	40	41	24.8	20.5	0.1	82.2	102.6	123.7	123.8	NH
48	48	48	49	15.0	10.0	1.2	48.1	55.3	60.8	61.6	VT
10	11	13	13	0.8	4.9	-0.3	725.8	732.0	767.6	765.3	MA
39	40	43	43	-0.3	5.9	0.2	908.8	906.4	960.3	961.8	RI
24	25	27	27	2.5	5.8	-0.2	625.8	641.4	678.5	677.2	CT
(X)	(X)	(X)	(X)	-1.1	2.2	0.8	374.1	369.9	378.1	381.2	**M.A**
2	2	2	2	-3.7	2.5	0.7	386.3	371.8	381.0	383.7	NY
8	9	9	9	2.7	5.0	0.8	966.6	992.7	1,041.9	1,049.9	NJ
3	4	5	5	0.5	0.1	1.1	263.3	264.7	265.1	267.9	PA
(X)	(X)	(X)	(X)	4.0	1.4	1.8	75.3	78.3	79.4	80.8	**Midwest**
(X)	(X)	(X)	(X)	3.5	0.8	1.8	165.3	171.2	172.5	175.5	**E.N.C**
6	6	7	7	1.3	0.5	1.6	260.2	263.7	264.9	269.0	OH
11	12	14	14	5.7	1.0	2.1	144.8	153.1	154.6	157.8	IN
5	5	6	6	2.8	(Z)	1.8	199.9	205.6	205.6	209.2	IL
7	8	8	8	4.3	0.4	1.5	156.3	163.0	163.6	166.1	MI
16	16	16	18	6.5	4.0	2.3	81.3	86.6	90.1	92.2	WI
(X)	(X)	(X)	(X)	5.2	2.8	1.7	32.1	33.8	34.8	35.4	**W.N.C**
19	21	20	20	7.1	7.3	2.4	47.8	51.2	55.0	56.3	MN
25	27	30	30	3.1	-4.7	1.3	50.6	52.1	49.7	50.3	IA
13	15	15	15	5.1	4.1	1.5	67.9	71.4	74.3	75.4	MO
45	46	47	47	5.7	-2.1	-0.5	9.0	9.5	9.3	9.2	ND
44	45	45	45	3.7	0.8	2.2	8.8	9.1	9.2	9.4	SD
35	35	36	36	5.7	0.5	1.7	19.3	20.4	20.5	20.9	NE
28	32	32	32	5.1	4.8	1.8	27.5	28.9	30.3	30.8	KS
(X)	(X)	(X)	(X)	20.0	13.4	3.2	72.1	86.5	98.1	101.2	**South**
(X)	(X)	(X)	(X)	20.5	17.9	3.4	115.2	138.8	163.6	169.3	**S.A**
46	47	46	46	8.4	12.1	3.5	280.4	304.0	340.8	352.5	DE
18	18	19	19	7.5	13.4	2.7	401.4	431.4	489.2	502.1	MD
(X)	(X)	(X)	(X)	-15.6	-4.9	-3.0	12,404.4	10,466.1	9,949.2	9,649.5	DC
14	14	12	12	14.9	15.7	3.1	117.5	135.0	156.3	161.0	VA
34	34	34	35	11.8	-8.0	1.0	72.4	81.0	74.5	75.2	WV
12	10	10	10	15.7	12.7	3.2	104.4	120.7	136.1	140.5	NC
26	24	25	25	20.5	11.7	3.3	86.0	103.6	115.8	119.7	SC
15	13	11	11	19.1	18.6	4.2	79.2	94.3	111.8	116.6	GA
9	7	4	4	43.5	32.7	4.2	125.8	180.5	239.6	249.8	FL
(X)	(X)	(X)	(X)	14.5	3.5	2.3	71.7	82.1	85.0	86.9	**E.S.C**
23	23	23	24	13.7	0.7	1.9	81.1	92.1	92.8	94.5	KY
17	17	17	17	16.9	6.2	3.0	95.2	111.4	118.3	121.9	TN
21	22	22	22	13.1	3.8	2.4	67.9	76.7	79.6	81.5	AL
29	31	31	31	13.7	2.1	1.6	47.3	53.7	54.8	55.7	MS
(X)	(X)	(X)	(X)	22.9	12.4	3.2	45.3	55.7	62.6	64.6	**W.S.C**
32	33	33	33	18.9	2.8	2.0	36.9	43.9	45.1	46.1	AR
20	19	21	21	15.4	0.3	1.6	83.7	96.5	96.9	98.4	LA
27	26	28	28	18.2	4.0	2.1	37.3	44.1	45.8	46.8	OK
4	3	3	3	27.1	19.4	3.9	42.8	54.3	64.9	67.4	TX
(X)	(X)	(X)	(X)	23.9	22.3	4.4	19.9	24.6	30.1	31.5	**West**
(X)	(X)	(X)	(X)	37.2	20.1	5.3	9.7	13.3	16.0	16.8	**Mt**
43	44	44	44	13.3	1.6	3.1	4.8	5.4	5.5	5.7	MT
42	41	42	42	32.4	6.7	6.0	8.6	11.4	12.2	12.9	ID
49	49	50	50	41.3	-3.4	2.8	3.4	4.8	4.7	4.8	WY
30	28	26	26	30.8	14.0	5.3	21.3	27.9	31.8	33.5	CO
37	37	37	37	28.1	16.3	4.4	8.4	10.7	12.5	13.0	NM
33	29	24	23	53.1	34.8	4.6	15.6	23.9	32.3	33.7	AZ
36	36	35	34	37.9	17.9	5.2	12.9	17.8	21.0	22.1	UT
47	43	39	38	63.8	50.1	10.4	4.5	7.3	10.9	12.1	NV
(X)	(X)	(X)	(X)	19.8	23.0	4.1	29.7	35.5	43.7	45.5	**Pac**
22	20	18	16	21.1	17.8	5.5	51.3	62.1	73.1	77.1	WA
31	30	29	29	25.9	7.9	4.7	21.8	27.4	29.6	31.0	OR
1	1	1	1	18.5	25.7	3.7	128.0	151.7	190.8	197.9	CA
50	50	49	48	32.8	36.9	6.7	0.5	0.7	1.0	1.0	AK
40	39	41	40	25.3	14.9	4.6	119.9	150.2	172.5	180.5	HI

Source: U.S. Bureau of the Census, *1990 Census of Population and Housing, Population and Housing Unit Counts* (CPH-2) and *Current Population Reports*, P25, forthcoming report.

No. 32. Resident Population, by Race

[In thousands.

REGION, DIVISION, AND STATE	Total [1]	White	Black	AMERICAN INDIAN, ESKIMO, ALEUT				ASIAN, PACIFIC ISLANDER			
				Total	American Indian	Eskimo	Aleut	Total [2]	Chinese	Filipino	Japanese
U.S.	248,710	199,686	29,986	1,959	1,878	57	24	7,274	1,645	1,407	848
Northeast	50,809	42,069	5,613	125	122	2	2	1,335	445	143	74
N.E.	13,207	12,033	628	33	32	(Z)	(Z)	232	72	15	15
ME	1,228	1,208	5	6	6	(Z)	(Z)	7	1	1	1
NH	1,109	1,087	7	2	2	(Z)	(Z)	9	2	1	1
VT	563	555	2	2	2	(Z)	(Z)	3	1	(Z)	(Z)
MA	6,016	5,405	300	12	12	(Z)	(Z)	143	54	6	9
RI	1,003	917	39	4	4	(Z)	(Z)	18	3	2	1
CT	3,287	2,859	274	7	6	(Z)	(Z)	51	11	5	4
M.A	37,602	30,036	4,986	92	90	1	2	1,104	373	128	59
NY	17,990	13,385	2,859	63	61	1	1	694	284	62	35
NJ	7,730	6,130	1,037	15	15	(Z)	(Z)	273	59	53	17
PA	11,882	10,520	1,090	15	14	(Z)	(Z)	137	30	12	7
Midwest	59,669	52,018	5,716	338	334	2	2	768	133	113	63
E.N.C	42,009	35,764	4,817	150	147	1	1	573	103	97	50
OH	10,847	9,522	1,155	20	20	(Z)	(Z)	91	19	10	10
IN	5,544	5,021	432	13	12	(Z)	(Z)	38	7	5	5
IL	11,431	8,953	1,694	22	21	(Z)	(Z)	285	50	64	22
MI	9,295	7,756	1,292	56	55	(Z)	(Z)	105	19	14	11
WI	4,892	4,513	245	39	39	(Z)	(Z)	54	7	4	3
W.N.C	17,660	16,254	899	188	187	1	1	195	30	17	13
MN	4,375	4,130	95	50	49	(Z)	(Z)	78	9	4	4
IA	2,777	2,683	48	7	7	(Z)	(Z)	25	4	2	2
MO	5,117	4,486	548	20	20	(Z)	(Z)	41	9	6	3
ND	639	604	4	26	26	(Z)	(Z)	3	1	1	(Z)
SD	696	638	3	51	51	(Z)	(Z)	3	(Z)	1	(Z)
NE	1,578	1,481	57	12	12	(Z)	(Z)	12	2	1	2
KS	2,478	2,232	143	22	22	(Z)	(Z)	32	5	3	2
South	85,446	65,582	15,829	563	557	3	3	1,122	204	159	67
S.A.	43,567	33,391	8,924	172	170	1	1	631	114	108	39
DE	666	535	112	2	2	(Z)	(Z)	9	2	1	1
MD	4,781	3,394	1,190	13	13	(Z)	(Z)	140	31	19	7
DC	607	180	400	1	1	(Z)	(Z)	11	3	2	1
VA	6,187	4,792	1,163	15	15	(Z)	(Z)	159	21	35	8
WV	1,793	1,726	56	2	2	(Z)	(Z)	7	1	2	1
NC	6,629	5,008	1,456	80	80	(Z)	(Z)	52	9	5	5
SC	3,487	2,407	1,040	8	8	(Z)	(Z)	22	3	6	2
GA	6,478	4,600	1,747	13	13	(Z)	(Z)	76	13	6	6
FL	12,938	10,749	1,760	36	35	(Z)	(Z)	154	31	32	9
E.S.C	15,176	12,049	2,977	41	40	(Z)	(Z)	84	15	9	9
KY	3,685	3,392	263	6	6	(Z)	(Z)	18	3	2	3
TN	4,877	4,048	778	10	10	(Z)	(Z)	32	6	3	3
AL	4,041	2,976	1,021	17	16	(Z)	(Z)	22	4	2	2
MS	2,573	1,633	915	9	8	(Z)	(Z)	13	3	2	1
W.S.C	26,703	20,142	3,929	350	347	1	1	407	76	43	20
AR	2,351	1,945	374	13	13	(Z)	(Z)	13	2	2	1
LA	4,220	2,839	1,299	19	18	(Z)	(Z)	41	5	4	2
OK	3,146	2,584	234	252	252	(Z)	(Z)	34	5	3	2
TX	16,987	12,775	2,022	66	64	1	1	319	63	34	15
West	52,786	40,017	2,828	933	866	51	17	4,048	863	991	643
Mt	13,659	11,762	374	481	478	1	1	217	40	32	34
MT	799	741	2	48	48	(Z)	(Z)	4	1	1	1
ID	1,007	950	3	14	14	(Z)	(Z)	9	1	1	3
WY	454	427	4	9	9	(Z)	(Z)	3	1	(Z)	1
CO	3,294	2,905	133	28	27	(Z)	(Z)	60	9	5	11
NM	1,515	1,146	30	134	134	(Z)	(Z)	14	3	2	2
AZ	3,665	2,963	111	204	203	(Z)	(Z)	55	14	8	6
UT	1,723	1,616	12	24	24	(Z)	(Z)	33	5	2	7
NV	1,202	1,013	79	20	19	(Z)	(Z)	38	5	5	4
Pac	39,127	28,255	2,454	453	387	49	16	3,831	823	960	609
WA	4,867	4,309	150	81	78	2	2	211	34	44	34
OR	2,842	2,637	46	38	37	1	1	69	14	7	12
CA	29,760	20,524	2,209	242	236	3	4	2,846	705	732	313
AK	550	415	22	86	31	44	10	20	1	8	2
HI	1,108	370	27	5	5	(Z)	(Z)	685	69	169	247

Z Less than 500.   [1] Includes other races, not shown separately.   [2] Includes other Asian and Pacific Islander races not shown separately.

and Hispanic Origin—States: 1990

As of **April 1**]

ASIAN, PACIFIC ISLANDER-Con.						HISPANIC ORIGIN [3]					REGION, DIVISION, AND STATE
Asian Indian	Korean	Vietnamese	Hawaiian	Samoan	Guamanian	Total	Mexican	Puerto Rican	Cuban	Other Hispanic	
815	799	615	211	63	49	22,354	13,496	2,728	1,044	5,086	**U.S.**
285	182	61	4	2	4	3,754	175	1,872	184	1,524	**Northeast**
36	21	22	1	(Z)	1	568	29	316	16	207	**N.E**
1	1	1	(Z)	(Z)	(Z)	7	2	1	(Z)	3	ME
2	2	1	(Z)	(Z)	(Z)	11	2	3	1	5	NH
1	1	(Z)	(Z)	(Z)	(Z)	4	1	1	(Z)	2	VT
20	12	15	1	(Z)	(Z)	288	13	151	8	116	MA
2	1	1	(Z)	(Z)	(Z)	46	2	13	1	29	RI
12	5	4	(Z)	(Z)	(Z)	213	8	147	6	51	CT
249	161	39	3	1	3	3,186	146	1,556	167	1,317	**M.A**
141	96	16	1	1	2	2,214	93	1,087	74	960	NY
79	39	7	1	(Z)	1	740	29	320	85	306	NJ
28	27	16	1	(Z)	(Z)	232	24	149	7	52	PA
146	109	52	6	2	3	1,727	1,153	258	37	279	**Midwest**
123	80	26	3	1	2	1,438	944	244	30	220	**E.N.C**
21	11	5	1	(Z)	(Z)	140	58	46	4	32	OH
7	5	2	1	(Z)	(Z)	99	67	14	2	16	IN
64	42	10	1	(Z)	1	904	624	146	18	116	IL
24	16	6	1	(Z)	(Z)	202	138	19	5	40	MI
7	6	2	(Z)	(Z)	(Z)	93	58	19	2	15	WI
23	29	26	2	1	1	289	209	14	6	60	**W.N.C**
8	12	9	(Z)	(Z)	(Z)	54	35	3	2	14	MN
3	5	3	(Z)	(Z)	(Z)	33	24	1	(Z)	7	IA
6	6	4	1	(Z)	(Z)	62	38	4	2	17	MO
(Z)	1	(Z)	(Z)	(Z)	(Z)	5	3	(Z)	(Z)	1	ND
(Z)	1	(Z)	(Z)	(Z)	(Z)	5	3	(Z)	(Z)	1	SD
1	2	2	(Z)	(Z)	(Z)	37	30	1	(Z)	6	NE
4	4	7	(Z)	(Z)	(Z)	94	76	4	1	13	KS
196	153	169	12	4	8	6,767	4,344	406	735	1,282	**South**
114	101	62	7	2	5	2,133	315	338	702	778	**S.A**
2	1	(Z)	(Z)	(Z)	(Z)	16	3	8	1	4	DE
28	30	9	1	(Z)	1	125	18	18	6	83	MD
2	1	1	(Z)	(Z)	(Z)	33	3	2	1	26	DC
20	30	21	1	(Z)	1	160	33	24	6	97	VA
2	1	(Z)	(Z)	(Z)	(Z)	8	3	1	(Z)	5	WV
10	7	5	1	(Z)	1	77	33	15	4	26	NC
4	3	2	(Z)	(Z)	(Z)	31	11	6	2	11	SC
14	15	8	1	(Z)	1	109	49	17	8	34	GA
31	12	16	2	1	1	1,574	161	247	674	492	FL
15	12	10	1	(Z)	1	95	39	13	5	39	**E.S.C**
3	3	2	(Z)	(Z)	(Z)	22	9	4	1	9	KY
6	5	2	1	(Z)	(Z)	33	14	4	2	13	TN
4	3	2	(Z)	(Z)	(Z)	25	10	4	1	10	AL
2	1	4	(Z)	(Z)	(Z)	16	7	1	(Z)	7	MS
67	40	97	4	1	3	4,539	3,990	55	28	466	**W.S.C**
1	1	2	(Z)	(Z)	(Z)	20	12	1	(Z)	6	AR
5	3	18	(Z)	(Z)	(Z)	93	23	6	9	55	LA
5	5	7	1	(Z)	(Z)	86	63	5	2	17	OK
56	32	70	3	1	2	4,340	3,891	43	18	388	TX
189	355	334	189	55	34	10,106	7,824	192	88	2,002	**West**
15	28	20	7	3	2	1,992	1,440	26	12	514	**Mt**
(Z)	1	(Z)	(Z)	(Z)	(Z)	12	8	(Z)	(Z)	3	MT
(Z)	1	1	(Z)	(Z)	(Z)	53	43	1	(Z)	9	ID
(Z)	(Z)	(Z)	(Z)	(Z)	(Z)	26	19	(Z)	(Z)	7	WY
4	11	7	1	(Z)	1	424	282	7	2	133	CO
2	1	1	(Z)	(Z)	(Z)	579	329	3	1	247	NM
6	6	5	2	(Z)	1	688	616	8	2	62	AZ
2	3	3	1	2	(Z)	85	57	2	(Z)	25	UT
2	4	2	(Z)	(Z)	(Z)	124	85	4	6	29	NV
173	327	314	182	52	32	8,114	6,384	166	76	1,488	**Pac**
8	30	19	5	4	4	215	156	9	2	47	WA
4	9	9	2	1	1	113	86	3	1	23	OR
160	260	280	34	32	25	7,688	6,119	126	72	1,371	CA
(Z)	4	1	1	1	(Z)	18	9	2	(Z)	6	AK
1	24	5	139	15	2	81	14	26	1	41	HI

[3] Persons of Hispanic origin may be of any race.

Source: U.S. Bureau of the Census, *1990 Census of Population, General Population Characteristics, United States* (CP-1-1).

No. 33. Resident Population, by Region, Race, and Hispanic Origin: 1990

[As of April 1. For composition of regions, see table 31]

RACE AND HISPANIC ORIGIN	POPULATION (1,000)					PERCENT DISTRIBUTION				
	United States	North-east	Midwest	South	West	United States	North-east	Midwest	South	West
Total	248,710	50,809	59,669	85,446	52,786	100.0	20.4	24.0	34.4	21.2
White	199,686	42,069	52,018	65,582	40,017	100.0	21.1	26.0	32.8	20.0
Black	29,986	5,613	5,716	15,829	2,828	100.0	18.7	19.1	52.8	9.4
American Indian, Eskimo, Aleut	1,959	125	338	563	933	100.0	6.4	17.2	28.7	47.6
American Indian	1,878	122	334	557	866	100.0	6.5	17.8	29.7	46.1
Eskimo	57	2	2	3	51	100.0	2.9	3.5	4.9	88.8
Aleut	24	2	2	3	17	100.0	8.1	8.1	11.5	72.3
Asian or Pacific Islander	7,274	1,335	768	1,122	4,048	100.0	18.4	10.6	15.4	55.7
Chinese	1,645	445	133	204	863	100.0	27.0	8.1	12.4	52.4
Filipino	1,407	143	113	159	991	100.0	10.2	8.1	11.3	70.5
Japanese	848	74	63	67	643	100.0	8.8	7.5	7.9	75.9
Asian Indian	815	285	146	196	189	100.0	35.0	17.9	24.0	23.1
Korean	799	182	109	153	355	100.0	22.8	13.7	19.2	44.4
Vietnamese	615	61	52	169	334	100.0	9.8	8.5	27.4	54.3
Laotian	149	16	28	29	76	100.0	10.7	18.6	19.6	51.0
Cambodian	147	30	13	19	85	100.0	20.5	8.8	13.1	57.7
Thai	91	12	13	24	43	100.0	12.9	14.2	26.0	46.8
Hmong	90	2	37	2	50	100.0	1.9	41.3	1.8	55.0
Pakistani	81	28	15	22	17	100.0	34.3	18.9	26.5	20.4
Hawaiian	211	4	6	12	189	100.0	2.0	2.6	5.8	89.6
Samoan	63	2	2	4	55	100.0	2.4	3.6	6.4	87.6
Guamanian	49	4	3	8	34	100.0	7.3	6.4	16.8	69.5
Other Asian or Pacific Islander	263	49	34	54	126	100.0	18.5	12.9	20.6	48.0
Other races	9,805	1,667	829	2,350	4,960	100.0	17.0	8.5	24.0	50.6
Hispanic origin [1]	22,354	3,754	1,727	6,767	10,106	100.0	16.8	7.7	30.3	45.2
Mexican	13,496	175	1,153	4,344	7,824	100.0	1.3	8.5	32.2	58.0
Puerto Rican	2,728	1,872	258	406	192	100.0	68.6	9.4	14.9	7.0
Cuban	1,044	184	37	735	88	100.0	17.6	3.5	70.5	8.5
Other Hispanic	5,086	1,524	279	1,282	2,002	100.0	30.0	5.5	25.2	39.4
Not of Hispanic origin	226,356	47,055	57,942	78,679	42,680	100.0	20.8	25.6	34.8	18.9

[1] Persons of Hispanic origin may be of any race.

Source: U.S. Bureau of the Census, *1990 Census of Population, General Population Characteristics, United States* (CP-1-1).

No. 34. Mobility Status of the Population, by Selected Characteristics: 1991

[See headnote, table 29]

AGE AND REGION	Total (1,000)	PERCENT DISTRIBUTION						
		Non-movers (same house in 1990)	Movers (different house in U.S. in 1990)					Movers from abroad
			Total	Same county	Different county			
					Total	Same State	Different State	
Total	244,884	83	16	10	6	3	3	1
1 to 4 years old	15,297	77	22	15	8	4	4	1
5 to 9 years old	18,466	82	17	11	6	3	3	1
10 to 14 years old	17,601	86	14	9	4	2	2	(Z)
15 to 19 years old	16,839	82	17	11	6	3	3	1
20 to 24 years old	17,986	65	34	21	13	7	6	2
25 to 29 years old	20,767	67	32	19	13	7	5	1
30 to 44 years old	60,803	83	17	11	6	3	3	1
45 to 54 years old	25,686	90	10	6	4	2	2	1
55 to 64 years old	21,346	93	7	4	3	2	2	(Z)
65 to 74 years old	18,237	95	5	3	2	1	1	(Z)
75 years old and over	11,855	95	5	3	2	1	1	(Z)
Northeast	50,059	88	11	7	4	2	2	(Z)
Midwest	59,041	84	15	10	6	3	3	(Z)
South	83,863	81	18	11	7	4	4	(Z)
West	51,920	79	20	13	7	4	3	1

Z Less than 0.5 percent.

Source: U.S. Bureau of the Census, *Current Population Reports*, P20-463.

No. 35. Resident Population, by Age and State: 1992

[In thousands, except percent. As of July 1. Includes Armed Forces stationed in area. See text, section 1 for basis of estimates. See *Historical Statistics, Colonial Times to 1970*, series A 204-209 for decennial census data]

REGION, DIVISION, AND STATE	Total	Under 5 years	5 to 17 years	18 to 24 years	25 to 34 years	35 to 44 years	45 to 54 years	55 to 64 years	65 to 74 years	75 to 84 years	85 years and over	16 years and over	Percent 65 years and over
U.S. . . .	255,082	19,512	46,655	25,919	42,463	39,904	27,418	20,927	18,461	10,565	3,259	195,672	12.7
Northeast .	51,118	3,702	8,547	5,052	8,480	8,012	5,706	4,494	4,047	2,344	734	40,124	13.9
N.E.	13,200	949	2,169	1,344	2,266	2,112	1,455	1,094	1,007	603	201	10,391	13.7
ME . . .	1,235	83	223	122	195	203	136	106	94	56	19	962	13.6
NH . . .	1,111	82	198	110	193	190	122	85	74	43	14	858	11.8
VT . . .	570	40	104	63	90	97	63	44	38	22	8	441	12.0
MA . . .	5,998	434	950	632	1,067	943	646	491	461	279	95	4,750	13.9
RI . . .	1,005	71	162	111	166	154	104	83	86	51	16	795	15.2
CT. . . .	3,281	239	532	306	554	526	383	283	255	152	49	2,586	13.9
M.A	37,918	2,752	6,378	3,708	6,214	5,900	4,250	3,401	3,040	1,741	533	29,733	14.0
NY. . . .	18,119	1,366	3,056	1,810	3,067	2,813	2,037	1,596	1,345	777	252	14,151	13.1
NJ. . . .	7,789	573	1,290	713	1,310	1,244	905	696	615	343	99	6,117	13.6
PA. . . .	12,009	813	2,031	1,185	1,837	1,843	1,308	1,109	1,080	621	181	9,465	15.7
Midwest. . .	60,713	4,493	11,441	6,126	9,736	9,392	6,487	5,077	4,434	2,647	881	46,442	13.1
E.N.C . . .	42,753	3,181	7,968	4,370	6,906	6,650	4,626	3,592	3,105	1,788	566	32,775	12.8
OH . . .	11,016	793	2,027	1,119	1,739	1,714	1,204	964	845	466	146	8,497	13.2
IN . . .	5,662	405	1,056	610	896	875	621	480	408	235	75	4,361	12.7
IL	11,631	899	2,130	1,167	1,953	1,802	1,255	962	822	489	153	8,912	12.6
MI	9,437	724	1,785	978	1,516	1,483	1,024	776	669	369	113	7,190	12.2
WI. . . .	5,007	360	970	497	801	777	522	411	361	230	78	3,815	13.3
W.N.C. . .	17,960	1,312	3,473	1,755	2,829	2,742	1,862	1,485	1,329	859	315	13,667	13.9
MN . . .	4,480	335	871	425	755	717	470	345	297	193	71	3,393	12.5
IA . . .	2,812	194	541	281	411	418	291	244	227	150	57	2,156	15.4
MO . . .	5,193	377	973	506	820	777	559	448	399	249	86	3,983	14.1
ND . . .	636	45	127	67	98	96	60	51	47	34	12	482	14.6
SD. . . .	711	54	150	69	104	104	67	59	55	36	14	528	14.7
NE. . . .	1,606	119	320	157	246	243	160	133	118	78	30	1,212	14.1
KS. . . .	2,523	187	491	251	396	388	255	204	186	119	44	1,913	13.9
South	88,143	6,633	16,226	9,164	14,553	13,602	9,494	7,315	6,451	3,634	1,070	67,678	12.7
S.A.	45,061	3,290	7,739	4,567	7,506	7,016	4,970	3,871	3,561	1,980	561	35,165	13.5
DE. . . .	689	52	120	72	120	106	75	60	52	25	8	534	12.3
MD . . .	4,908	383	843	465	888	819	574	397	324	166	50	3,798	11.0
DC. . . .	589	41	76	70	119	94	63	48	44	25	8	483	13.1
VA. . . .	6,377	468	1,094	688	1,136	1,050	735	509	415	217	64	4,974	10.9
WV . . .	1,812	108	330	191	250	284	204	171	158	91	27	1,429	15.2
NC . . .	6,843	491	1,171	767	1,140	1,070	764	594	501	268	76	5,359	12.4
SC. . . .	3,603	273	672	409	589	557	390	296	255	128	34	2,760	11.6
GA . . .	6,751	530	1,270	732	1,184	1,089	749	514	399	220	62	5,138	10.1
FL . . .	13,488	943	2,163	1,173	2,081	1,946	1,415	1,282	1,414	838	232	10,690	18.4
E.S.C . . .	15,529	1,112	2,922	1,682	2,430	2,360	1,703	1,339	1,126	656	199	11,947	12.8
KY. . . .	3,755	258	706	402	596	580	415	322	270	157	50	2,901	12.7
TN. . . .	5,024	353	893	529	807	787	574	440	367	211	63	3,915	12.7
AL. . . .	4,136	298	778	449	639	621	449	363	307	178	52	3,181	13.0
MS . . .	2,614	203	545	302	388	372	265	214	182	110	34	1,951	12.5
W.S.C . . .	27,554	2,231	5,565	2,916	4,617	4,227	2,822	2,104	1,763	999	310	20,566	11.1
AR. . . .	2,399	171	458	244	349	344	262	213	198	123	37	1,841	14.9
LA. . . .	4,287	340	898	462	691	646	435	335	281	154	45	3,180	11.2
OK . . .	3,212	232	626	330	493	481	344	272	241	145	48	2,447	13.5
TX. . . .	17,656	1,489	3,583	1,881	3,084	2,755	1,781	1,285	1,042	576	179	13,098	10.2
West	55,108	4,684	10,442	5,577	9,693	8,897	5,730	4,041	3,529	1,940	574	41,427	11.0
Mt	14,381	1,172	2,931	1,444	2,356	2,278	1,480	1,091	959	522	147	10,691	11.3
MT . . .	824	58	168	75	117	136	91	69	61	38	11	623	13.4
ID . . .	1,067	83	241	108	151	166	110	80	71	44	13	779	11.9
WY . . .	466	34	104	46	70	80	48	34	29	16	5	343	10.7
CO . . .	3,470	262	647	341	607	622	384	259	204	109	35	2,651	10.0
NM . . .	1,581	133	336	156	251	247	162	124	102	56	16	1,160	10.9
AZ. . . .	3,832	320	727	384	634	568	381	305	303	167	43	2,887	13.4
UT. . . .	1,813	176	478	215	281	244	151	108	93	52	15	1,227	8.8
NV. . . .	1,327	106	232	118	246	213	153	113	96	41	9	1,021	11.0
Pac	40,726	3,513	7,510	4,133	7,337	6,619	4,250	2,950	2,570	1,418	427	30,735	10.8
WA . . .	5,136	390	965	488	860	880	570	383	343	197	60	3,915	11.7
OR . . .	2,977	211	555	274	451	507	335	233	230	138	42	2,291	13.8
CA. . . .	30,867	2,763	5,660	3,195	5,714	4,925	3,158	2,207	1,897	1,036	313	23,217	10.5
AK. . . .	587	57	128	57	111	114	63	32	17	6	1	417	4.3
HI	1,160	91	202	119	202	193	125	95	82	40	11	895	11.4

Source: U.S. Bureau of the Census, *Current Population Reports*, series P-25, forthcoming report.

No. 36. Urban and Rural Population, by Size of Place: 1970 to 1990

[As of **April 1**. See text, section 1 and *Historical Statistics, Colonial Times to 1970*, series A 43-72]

CLASS AND SIZE	PLACES			POPULATION (1,000)			PERCENT OF TOTAL POPULATION		
	1970	1980	1990	1970	1980	1990	1970	1980	1990
United States	(X)	(X)	(X)	[1]203,302	[1]226,542	248,710	100.0	100.0	100.0
Urban.	7,129	8,765	9,421	149,647	167,051	187,053	73.6	73.7	75.2
Places of 1,000,000 or more	6	6	8	18,769	17,530	19,953	9.2	7.7	8.0
Places of 500,000 to 999,999	20	16	15	12,967	10,834	10,107	6.4	4.8	4.1
Places of 250,000 to 499,999	30	34	41	10,442	12,158	14,585	5.1	5.4	5.9
Places of 100,000 to 249,999	100	117	136	14,286	17,015	19,703	7.0	7.5	7.9
Places of 50,000 to 99,999	240	290	355	16,724	19,786	24,027	8.2	8.7	9.7
Places of 25,000 to 49,999	520	675	741	17,861	23,436	25,701	8.8	10.3	10.3
Places of 10,000 to 24,999	1,385	1,765	1,852	21,415	27,645	29,041	10.5	12.2	11.7
Places of 5,000 to 9,999	1,838	2,181	2,336	12,914	15,356	16,599	6.4	6.8	6.7
Places of 2,500 to 4,999	2,295	2,665	3,026	8,038	9,368	10,701	4.0	4.1	4.3
Places under 2,500	695	1,016	911	835	1,260	1,079	0.4	0.6	0.4
Other urban	(X)	(X)	(X)	15,395	12,663	15,557	7.6	5.6	6.3
Rural	13,639	13,764	14,014	53,565	59,495	61,656	26.4	26.3	24.8
Places of 1,000 to 2,500	4,128	4,434	4,424	6,552	7,038	7,051	3.2	3.1	2.8
Places under 1,000	9,511	9,330	9,590	3,849	3,863	3,801	1.9	1.7	1.5
Other rural	(X)	(X)	(X)	43,165	48,594	50,804	21.2	21.4	20.4

X Not applicable.   [1] Total population counts have been revised since the 1970 and 1980 census publications. Urban and rural numbers have not been corrected.

Source: U.S. Bureau of the Census, *1990 Census of Population and Housing, Population and Housing Unit Counts, United States Summary* (1990 CPH-2-1).

No. 37. Urban and Rural Population—States: 1990

[In thousands, except percent. As of **April 1**. Resident population]

REGION, DIVISION, AND STATE	Total	URBAN Number	URBAN Percent	Rural	REGION, DIVISION, AND STATE	Total	URBAN Number	URBAN Percent	Rural
U.S.	248,710	187,053	75.2	61,656	DC.	607	607	100.0	-
					VA.	6,187	4,293	69.4	1,894
Northeast	50,809	40,092	78.9	10,717	WV	1,793	648	36.1	1,145
N.E.	13,207	9,829	74.4	3,378	NC	6,629	3,338	50.4	3,291
ME	1,228	548	44.6	680	SC.	3,487	1,905	54.6	1,581
NH	1,109	566	51.0	544	GA	6,478	4,097	63.2	2,381
VT.	563	181	32.2	382	FL.	12,938	10,967	84.8	1,971
MA	6,016	5,070	84.3	947	**E.S.C**	15,176	8,531	56.2	6,646
RI	1,003	863	86.0	140	KY.	3,685	1,910	51.8	1,775
CT.	3,287	2,602	79.1	686	TN.	4,877	2,970	60.9	1,907
M.A.	37,602	30,263	80.5	7,340	AL.	4,041	2,440	60.4	1,601
NY.	17,990	15,164	84.3	2,826	MS	2,573	1,211	47.1	1,362
NJ.	7,730	6,910	89.4	820	**W.S.C**	26,703	19,894	74.5	6,808
PA.	11,882	8,188	68.9	3,693	AR.	2,351	1,258	53.5	1,093
Midwest.	59,669	42,774	71.7	16,894	LA.	4,220	2,872	68.1	1,348
E.N.C	42,009	31,074	74.0	10,935	OK	3,146	2,130	67.7	1,015
OH	10,847	8,039	74.1	2,808	TX.	16,987	13,635	80.3	3,352
IN	5,544	3,598	64.9	1,946	**West**	52,786	45,531	86.3	7,255
IL	11,431	9,669	84.6	1,762	**Mt**	13,659	10,881	79.7	2,777
MI	9,295	6,556	70.5	2,739	MT	799	420	52.5	379
WI	4,892	3,212	65.7	1,680	ID	1,007	578	57.4	429
W.N.C.	17,660	11,700	66.3	5,959	WY	454	295	65.0	159
MN	4,375	3,056	69.9	1,319	CO	3,294	2,716	82.4	579
IA	2,777	1,683	60.6	1,094	NM	1,515	1,106	73.0	409
MO	5,117	3,516	68.7	1,601	AZ.	3,665	3,207	87.5	458
ND	639	340	53.3	298	UT.	1,723	1,499	87.0	224
SD.	696	348	50.0	348	NV.	1,202	1,061	88.3	140
NE.	1,578	1,044	66.1	534	**Pac**	39,127	34,650	88.6	4,477
KS.	2,478	1,713	69.1	765	WA	4,867	3,718	76.4	1,149
South	85,446	58,656	68.6	26,790	OR	2,842	2,003	70.5	839
S.A.	43,567	30,231	69.4	13,336	CA.	29,760	27,571	92.6	2,189
DE.	666	487	73.0	180	AK.	550	371	67.5	179
MD	4,781	3,888	81.3	893	HI	1,108	986	89.0	122

- Represents zero.

Source: U.S. Bureau of the Census, *1990 Census of Population, General Population Characteristics, United States*, (CP-1-1).

Metropolitan Population—Coastal Population

35

No. 38. Metropolitan and Nonmetropolitan Area Population: 1960 to 1990

[Metropolitan areas are as defined by U.S. Office of Management and Budget as of year shown, except as noted. See headnote, table 39]

ITEM	1960	1970	1980 [1] (SMSA's)	MSA's AND CMSA's [2] 1980	MSA's AND CMSA's [2] 1990
Metropolitan areas: Number of areas	212	243	318	268	268
Population (1,000)	112,885	139,480	169,431	176,663	197,467
Percent change over previous year shown	[3]33.0	23.6	21.5	(X)	11.8
Percent of total U.S. population	63.0	68.6	74.8	78.0	79.4
Land area, percent of U.S. land area	8.7	10.9	16.0	19.0	19.0
Nonmetropolitan areas, population (1,000)	66,438	63,822	57,115	49,879	51,243

X Not applicable.   [1] SMSA=standard metropolitan statistical area. Areas are as defined June 30, 1981.   [2] Areas are as defined December 31, 1992.   [3] Percent change from 1950.

Source: U.S. Bureau of the Census, *U.S. Census of Population: 1960* and *1970; 1980 Census of Population,* vol. 1, chapter A (PC80-1-A) and *Supplementary Report, Metropolitan Statistical Areas* (PC80-S1-18); press release CB93-50; and unpublished data.

No. 39. Number and Population of Metropolitan Areas, by Population Size-Class in 1990: 1970 to 1990

[As of **April 1**. Data exclude Puerto Rico. CMSA=consolidated metropolitan statistical area. MSA=metropolitan statistical area. PMSA=primary metropolitan statistical area. Areas are as defined by U.S. Office of Management and Budget, December 31, 1992. For definitions, see Appendix II. See also *Historical Statistics, Colonial Times to 1970,* series A 264-275]

LEVEL AND POPULATION SIZE-CLASS OF METROPOLITAN AREA IN 1990	CMSA's AND MSA's Number, 1990	CMSA's AND MSA's Population, 1970 (mil.)	CMSA's AND MSA's Population, 1980 (mil.)	CMSA's AND MSA's Population, 1990 Total (mil.)	CMSA's AND MSA's Population, 1990 Percent in each class	MSA's AND PMSA's Number, 1990	MSA's AND PMSA's Population, 1990 Total (mil.)	MSA's AND PMSA's Population, 1990 Percent in each class
Total, all metropolitan areas	268	159.3	176.7	197.5	100	309	197.5	100
Level A (1,000,000 or more)	40	109.3	118.5	132.7	67	47	122.1	62
2,500,000 or more	15	78.8	84.1	93.9	48	12	65.8	33
1,000,000 to 2,499,999	25	30.4	34.4	38.8	20	35	56.3	29
Level B (250,000 to 999,999)	96	35.3	41.1	46.2	23	114	54.1	27
500,000 to 999,999	32	18.1	20.9	23.8	12	38	27.4	14
250,000 to 499,999	64	17.2	20.1	22.4	11	76	26.7	14
Level C (100,000 to 249,999)	111	13.2	15.3	16.7	8	126	19.4	10
Level D (less than 100,000)	21	1.6	1.8	1.8	1	22	1.9	1

Source: U.S. Bureau of the Census, *1980 Census of Population, Supplementary Report, Metropolitan Statistical Areas* (PC80-S1-18); and *1990 Census of Population and Housing Data Paper Listing* (CPH-L-118A).

No. 40. Population in Coastal Counties: 1960 to 1991

[Enumerated population as of **April 1**, except as indicated. Areas as defined by U.S. National Oceanic and Atmospheric Agency, 1992. Covers 672 counties and equivalent areas with at least 15 percent of their land area either in a coastal watershed or in a coastal cataloging unit]

YEAR	U.S., total	COUNTIES IN COASTAL REGIONS Total	COUNTIES IN COASTAL REGIONS Atlantic	COUNTIES IN COASTAL REGIONS Gulf of Mexico	COUNTIES IN COASTAL REGIONS Great Lakes	COUNTIES IN COASTAL REGIONS Pacific	Balance of U.S.
Land area, 1990 (1,000 sq. mi.)	3,536	888	148	114	115	510	2,649
POPULATION							
1960 (mil.)	179.3	94.5	44.5	8.4	23.7	17.9	84.8
1970 (mil.)	203.3	110.0	51.1	10.0	26.0	22.8	93.3
1980 (mil.)	226.5	119.8	53.7	13.1	26.0	27.0	106.7
1990 (mil.)	248.7	133.4	59.0	15.2	25.9	33.2	115.3
1991 (July 1)(mil.)	252.2	135.1	59.5	15.6	26.1	33.9	117.1
1960 (percent)	100	53	25	5	14	10	47
1970 (percent)	100	54	25	5	13	11	46
1980 (percent)	100	53	24	6	11	12	47
1990 (percent)	100	54	24	6	10	13	46
1991 (July 1)(percent)	100	54	24	6	10	13	46

Source: U.S. Bureau of the Census, *U.S. Census of Population: 1960* and *1970; 1980 Census of Population,* vol. 1, chapter A (PC80-1-A-1), *U.S. Summary; 1990 Census of Population and Housing* (CPH1); and press release CB93-85.

No. 41. Metropolitan and Nonmetropolitan Population—States: 1980 and 1990

[As of **April 1**. Metropolitan refers to 250 metropolitan statistical areas and 18 consolidated metropolitan statistical areas as defined by U.S. Office of Management and Budget, December 31, 1992; nonmetropolitan is the area outside metropolitan areas; see Appendix II. Minus sign (-) indicates decrease]

REGION, DIVISION, AND STATE	METROPOLITAN POPULATION						NONMETROPOLITAN POPULATION					
	Total (1,000)		Net change, 1980-90		Percent of State		Total (1,000)		Net change, 1980-90		Percent of State	
	1980	1990	Number (1,000)	Percent	1980	1990	1980	1990	Number (1,000)	Percent	1980	1990
U.S..	176,663	197,467	20,804	11.8	78.0	79.4	49,879	51,243	1,364	2.7	22.0	20.6
Northeast . .	44,045	45,453	1,408	3.2	89.6	89.5	5,092	5,356	264	5.2	10.4	10.5
N.E	10,469	11,125	656	6.3	84.8	84.2	1,880	2,082	202	10.8	15.2	15.8
ME	405	443	38	9.5	36.0	36.1	721	785	65	9.0	64.0	63.9
NH	535	659	124	23.1	58.1	59.4	386	450	65	16.8	41.9	40.6
VT	133	152	18	13.8	26.0	26.9	378	411	33	8.7	74.0	73.1
MA	5,530	5,788	258	4.7	96.4	96.2	207	229	22	10.5	3.6	3.8
RI	886	938	52	5.9	93.5	93.5	61	65	4	6.6	6.5	6.5
CT	2,980	3,146	165	5.6	95.9	95.7	127	141	14	11.1	4.1	4.3
M.A	33,576	34,328	752	2.2	91.3	91.3	3,212	3,274	62	1.9	8.7	8.7
NY	16,144	16,515	371	2.3	91.9	91.8	1,414	1,475	61	4.3	8.1	8.2
NJ	7,365	7,730	365	5.0	100.0	100.0	(X)	(X)	(X)	(X)	(X)	(X)
PA	10,067	10,083	16	0.2	84.8	84.9	1,798	1,799	1	(Z)	15.2	15.1
Midwest . . .	42,557	43,691	1,134	2.7	72.3	73.2	16,310	15,978	-332	-2.0	27.7	26.8
E.N.C	33,031	33,391	360	1.1	79.2	79.5	8,652	8,618	-34	-0.4	20.8	20.5
OH	8,791	8,826	35	0.4	81.4	81.4	2,007	2,021	14	0.7	18.6	18.6
IN	3,885	3,962	78	2.0	70.8	71.5	1,605	1,582	-24	-1.5	29.2	28.5
IL	9,461	9,574	113	1.2	82.8	83.8	1,967	1,857	-110	-5.6	17.2	16.2
MI	7,719	7,698	-21	-0.3	83.3	82.8	1,543	1,598	54	3.5	16.7	17.2
WI	3,176	3,331	155	4.9	67.5	68.1	1,530	1,561	31	2.0	32.5	31.9
W.N.C . . .	9,526	10,300	774	8.1	55.4	58.3	7,658	7,360	-298	-3.9	44.6	41.7
MN	2,674	3,011	337	12.6	65.6	68.8	1,402	1,364	-38	-2.7	34.4	31.2
IA	1,198	1,200	2	0.1	41.1	43.2	1,716	1,577	-139	-8.1	58.9	56.8
MO	3,314	3,491	177	5.3	67.4	68.2	1,603	1,626	23	1.5	32.6	31.8
ND	234	257	23	9.8	35.9	40.3	418	381	-37	-8.8	64.1	59.7
SD	194	221	27	13.9	28.0	31.7	497	475	-22	-4.3	72.0	68.3
NE	728	787	59	8.1	46.4	49.9	842	791	-50	-6.0	53.6	50.1
KS	1,184	1,333	149	12.6	50.1	53.8	1,180	1,145	-36	-3.0	49.9	46.2
South	53,405	62,835	9,430	17.7	70.9	73.5	21,962	22,611	649	3.0	29.1	26.5
S.A	28,171	34,222	6,051	21.5	76.2	78.6	8,786	9,344	558	6.4	23.8	21.4
DE	496	553	57	11.4	83.5	83.0	98	113	15	15.5	16.5	17.0
MD	3,920	4,439	519	13.2	93.0	92.8	297	343	46	15.3	7.0	7.2
DC	638	607	-32	-4.9	100.0	100.0	(X)	(X)	(X)	(X)	(X)	(X)
VA	3,966	4,773	807	20.4	74.2	77.1	1,381	1,414	33	2.4	25.8	22.9
WV	796	748	-47	-6.0	40.8	41.7	1,155	1,045	-109	-9.5	59.2	58.3
NC	3,713	4,325	612	16.5	63.2	65.2	2,167	2,304	137	6.3	36.8	34.8
SC	2,114	2,423	308	14.6	67.8	69.5	1,006	1,064	58	5.7	32.2	30.5
GA	3,489	4,331	843	24.2	63.9	66.9	1,974	2,147	173	8.7	36.1	33.1
FL	9,039	12,023	2,985	33.0	92.7	92.9	708	915	206	29.1	7.3	7.1
E.S.C	7,933	8,436	503	6.3	54.1	55.6	6,733	6,740	7	0.1	45.9	44.4
KY	1,710	1,755	45	2.6	46.7	47.6	1,950	1,930	-20	-1.0	53.3	52.4
TN	2,946	3,195	249	8.4	64.2	65.5	1,645	1,682	38	2.3	35.8	34.5
AL	2,560	2,710	150	5.8	65.7	67.1	1,334	1,331	-3	-0.2	34.3	32.9
MS	776	776	60	8.3	28.4	30.1	1,805	1,798	-7	-0.4	71.6	69.9
W.S.C . . .	17,301	20,177	2,876	16.6	72.9	75.6	6,443	6,526	83	1.3	27.1	24.4
AR	963	1,040	77	8.0	42.1	44.2	1,323	1,311	-13	-0.9	57.9	55.8
LA	3,074	3,101	27	0.9	73.1	73.5	1,132	1,119	-13	-1.1	26.9	26.5
OK	1,724	1,870	146	8.4	57.0	59.4	1,301	1,276	-26	-2.0	43.0	40.6
TX	11,539	14,166	2,626	22.8	81.1	83.4	2,686	2,821	135	5.0	18.9	16.6
West.	36,655	45,487	8,832	24.1	84.9	86.2	6,516	7,299	783	12.0	15.1	13.8
Mt	7,645	9,605	1,960	25.6	67.2	70.3	3,726	4,054	328	8.8	32.8	29.7
MT	189	191	2	1.3	24.0	23.9	598	608	10	1.7	76.0	76.1
ID	257	296	39	15.2	27.2	29.4	687	711	24	3.4	72.8	70.6
WY	141	134	-6	-4.4	29.9	29.6	329	319	-10	-3.0	70.1	70.4
CO	2,326	2,686	360	15.5	80.5	81.5	563	608	45	8.0	19.5	18.5
NM	675	842	167	24.7	51.8	55.6	628	673	45	7.2	48.2	44.4
AZ	2,264	3,106	842	37.2	83.3	84.7	453	559	107	23.5	16.7	15.3
UT	1,128	1,336	207	18.4	77.2	77.5	333	387	54	16.3	22.8	22.5
NV	666	1,014	348	52.3	83.2	84.4	135	188	53	39.5	16.8	15.6
Pac	29,010	35,882	6,872	23.7	91.2	91.7	2,790	3,245	455	16.3	8.8	8.3
WA	3,366	4,036	670	19.9	81.5	82.9	766	830	64	8.4	18.5	17.1
OR	1,799	1,985	186	10.3	68.3	69.8	834	858	23	2.8	31.7	30.2
CA	22,907	28,799	5,891	25.7	96.8	96.8	760	961	201	26.4	3.2	3.2
AK	174	226	52	29.8	43.4	41.1	227	324	96	42.3	56.6	58.9
HI	763	836	74	9.7	79.0	75.5	202	272	70	34.6	21.0	24.5

X Not applicable.   Z Less than 0.05 percent.

Source: U.S. Bureau of the Census, unpublished data.

No. 42. Metropolitan Areas—Population: 1980 to 1991

[As of **April 1**, except **1991** as of **July 1**. Covers 18 consolidated metropolitan statistical areas (CMSA's), their 59 component primary metropolitan statistical areas (PMSA's), and the remaining 117 MSA's with 250,000 and over population in 1991 as defined by the U.S. Office of Management and Budget as of December 31, 1992. Rank based on unrounded figures for CMSA's and MSA's only. For definitions and components of all MSA's and population of NECMA's (New England County Metropolitan Areas), see Appendix II. Minus sign (-) indicates decrease]

METROPOLITAN AREA	1980, total (1,000)	1990 Total (1,000)	1990 Under 18 yrs. old (percent)	1990 65 yrs. old and over (percent)	1991 Total (1,000)	1991 Rank	PERCENT CHANGE 1980-90	PERCENT CHANGE 1990-91
Albany-Schenectady-Troy, NY MSA	825	861	23.3	14.1	869	52	4.4	0.9
Albuquerque, NM MSA	485	589	27.1	10.4	602	65	21.4	2.3
Allentown-Bethlehem-Easton, PA MSA	551	595	22.9	15.5	602	66	8.0	1.2
Appleton-Oshkosh-Neenah, WI MSA	291	315	26.7	11.9	320	113	8.2	1.5
Atlanta, GA MSA	2,233	2,960	25.9	8.0	3,051	13	32.5	3.1
Augusta-Aiken, GA-SC MSA	345	395	27.8	9.9	407	88	14.5	2.9
Austin-San Marcos, TX MSA	585	846	25.6	7.8	874	51	44.6	3.3
Bakersfield, CA MSA	403	543	31.5	9.7	567	70	34.8	4.3
Baton Rouge, LA MSA	444	470	28.2	9.0	478	77	5.8	1.8
Beaumont-Port Arthur, TX MSA	373	361	27.6	13.1	367	101	-3.2	1.6
Biloxi-Gulfport-Pascagoula, MS MSA	300	312	28.3	10.6	316	115	4.1	1.2
Binghamton, NY MSA	263	264	24.0	14.2	265	130	0.4	0.2
Birmingham, AL MSA	815	840	25.4	13.1	849	54	3.0	1.1
Boise City, ID MSA	257	296	29.1	11.4	310	116	15.2	4.7
Boston-Brockton-Nashua, MA-NH-ME-CT CMSA	5,122	5,455	22.6	12.7	5,432	7	6.5	-0.4
Boston, MA-NH-ME-CT PMSA	4,763	5,051	22.4	12.9	5,027	(X)	6.0	-0.5
Brockton, MA PMSA	225	236	25.1	11.1	237	(X)	5.1	0.4
Nashua, NH PMSA	134	168	26.5	8.3	168	(X)	25.4	-0.1
Brownsville-Harlingen-San Benito, TX MSA	210	260	35.3	10.6	269	129	24.0	3.4
Buffalo-Niagara Falls, NY MSA	1,243	1,189	23.6	15.2	1,193	33	-4.3	0.3
Canton-Massillon, OH MSA	404	394	25.3	14.4	397	95	-2.6	0.7
Charleston-North Charleston, SC MSA	430	507	27.6	8.6	524	71	17.8	3.3
Charleston, WV MSA	270	250	23.8	14.9	252	135	-7.1	0.4
Charlotte-Gastonia-Rock Hill, NC-SC MSA	971	1,162	24.7	10.9	1,190	34	19.6	2.4
Chattanooga, TN-GA MSA	393	399	24.7	13.1	403	90	1.5	1.0
Chicago-Gary-Kenosha, IL-IN-WI CMSA	8,115	8,240	26.1	11.4	8,339	3	1.5	1.2
Chicago, IL PMSA	7,246	7,411	25.9	11.3	7,498	(X)	2.3	1.2
Gary, IN PMSA	643	605	27.9	11.8	611	(X)	-5.9	1.2
Kankakee, IL PMSA	103	96	28.1	13.7	98	(X)	-6.5	1.4
Kenosha, WI PMSA	123	128	26.8	12.6	132	(X)	4.1	2.9
Cincinnati-Hamilton, OH-KY-IN CMSA	1,726	1,818	26.8	11.8	1,843	23	5.3	1.4
Cincinnati, OH-KY-IN PMSA	1,468	1,526	26.9	12.1	1,544	(X)	4.0	1.2
Hamilton-Middletown, OH PMSA	259	291	26.2	10.2	299	(X)	12.6	2.5
Cleveland-Akron, OH CMSA	2,938	2,860	24.9	13.9	2,878	14	-2.7	0.6
Akron, OH PMSA	660	658	24.4	12.9	665	(X)	-0.4	1.1
Cleveland-Lorain-Elyria, OH PMSA	2,278	2,202	25.1	14.2	2,213	(X)	-3.3	0.5
Colorado Springs, CO MSA	309	397	27.6	8.0	404	89	28.3	1.9
Columbia, SC MSA	410	453	25.0	9.3	464	78	10.6	2.3
Columbus, GA-AL MSA	255	261	26.9	10.7	264	131	2.4	1.2
Columbus, OH MSA	1,214	1,345	25.1	10.0	1,370	29	10.8	1.8
Corpus Christi, TX MSA	326	350	30.8	10.2	356	103	7.3	1.9
Dallas-Fort Worth, TX CMSA	3,046	4,037	27.2	8.3	4,135	9	32.5	2.4
Dallas, TX PMSA	2,055	2,676	27.1	8.1	2,739	(X)	30.2	2.3
Fort Worth-Arlington, TX PMSA	991	1,361	27.3	8.8	1,396	(X)	37.4	2.5
Davenport-Moline-Rock Island, IA-IL MSA	385	351	26.7	13.7	354	104	-8.8	1.0
Dayton-Springfield, OH MSA	942	951	25.3	12.4	956	44	1.0	0.5
Daytona Beach, FL MSA	270	399	19.7	23.0	414	85	48.1	3.5
Denver-Boulder-Greeley, CO CMSA	1,742	1,980	25.7	9.2	2,034	21	13.7	2.7
Boulder-Longmont, CO PMSA	190	225	23.0	7.6	232	(X)	18.8	3.0
Denver, CO PMSA	1,429	1,623	25.9	9.4	1,668	(X)	13.6	2.8
Greeley, CO PMSA	123	132	28.1	10.2	134	(X)	6.8	1.4
Des Moines, IA MSA	368	393	25.6	11.7	400	92	6.9	1.8
Detroit-Ann Arbor-Flint, MI CMSA	5,293	5,187	26.1	11.5	5,215	8	-2.0	0.5
Ann Arbor, MI PMSA	455	490	24.5	8.5	499	(X)	7.7	1.7
Detroit, MI PMSA	4,388	4,267	26.0	11.9	4,285	(X)	-2.8	0.4
Flint, MI PMSA	450	430	28.0	10.2	431	(X)	-4.4	0.2
El Paso, TX MSA	480	592	32.6	8.2	612	63	23.3	3.4
Erie, PA MSA	280	276	25.9	13.8	278	125	-1.5	0.9
Eugene-Springfield, OR MSA	275	283	24.5	13.1	288	123	2.8	1.8
Evansville-Henderson, IN-KY MSA	276	279	25.4	14.0	281	124	1.0	0.7
Fayetteville, NC MSA	247	275	28.0	6.1	276	126	11.1	0.7
Fort Myers-Cape Coral, FL MSA	205	335	19.6	24.8	347	107	63.3	3.5
Fort Pierce-Port St. Lucie, FL MSA	151	251	20.9	23.6	260	134	66.1	3.5
Fort Wayne, IN MSA	445	456	28.2	12.0	460	79	2.6	0.9
Fresno, CA MSA	578	756	31.3	10.6	781	56	30.8	3.4
Grand Rapids-Muskegon-Holland, MI MSA	841	938	28.6	11.1	953	45	11.5	1.6
Greensboro—Winston-Salem—High Point, NC MSA	951	1,050	22.9	12.4	1,066	39	10.5	1.5
Greenville-Spartanburg-Anderson, SC MSA	744	831	24.5	12.4	843	55	11.6	1.5
Harrisburg-Lebanon-Carlisle, PA MSA	556	588	23.4	13.9	595	68	5.7	1.2
Hartford, CT MSA	1,081	1,158	22.6	13.2	1,159	35	7.1	0.1
Hickory-Morganton, NC MSA	270	292	23.8	12.2	296	119	8.1	1.1

See footnotes at end of table.

Population

No. 42. Metropolitan Areas—Population: 1980 to 1991—Continued

[See headnote, page 37]

METROPOLITAN AREA	1980, total (1,000)	1990 Total (1,000)	Under 18 yrs. old (percent)	65 yrs. old and over (percent)	1991 Total (1,000)	Rank	PERCENT CHANGE 1980-90	1990-91
Honolulu, HI MSA	763	836	24.5	11.0	851	53	9.7	1.7
Houston-Galveston-Brazoria, TX CMSA	3,118	3,731	28.9	7.3	3,859	10	19.6	3.4
Brazoria, TX PMSA	170	192	29.3	7.8	199	(X)	13.0	3.9
Galveston-Texas City, TX PMSA	196	217	27.6	10.5	223	(X)	11.1	2.5
Houston, TX PMSA	2,753	3,322	28.9	7.1	3,437	(X)	20.7	3.5
Huntington-Ashland, WV-KY-OH MSA	311	288	24.3	14.5	289	122	-7.4	0.3
Huntsville, AL MSA	243	293	24.7	9.4	300	117	20.6	2.5
Indianapolis, IN MSA	1,306	1,380	26.2	11.4	1,406	28	5.7	1.8
Jackson, MS MSA	362	395	28.1	10.5	400	93	9.2	1.1
Jacksonville, FL MSA	722	907	26.0	10.9	934	46	25.5	3.0
Johnson City-Kingsport-Bristol, TN-VA MSA	434	436	22.3	14.6	441	80	0.6	1.1
Kalamazoo-Battle Creek, MI MSA	421	429	25.9	11.8	433	82	2.1	0.8
Kansas City, MO-KS MSA	1,449	1,583	26.4	11.6	1,602	25	9.2	1.2
Knoxville, TN MSA	546	586	22.9	13.4	600	67	7.2	2.4
Lafayette, LA MSA	331	345	30.6	10.0	350	106	4.3	1.5
Lakeland-Winter Haven, FL MSA	322	405	24.1	18.6	413	86	26.0	1.9
Lancaster, PA MSA	362	423	26.5	13.1	430	83	16.7	1.8
Lansing-East Lansing, MI MSA	420	433	25.6	9.0	436	81	3.1	0.8
Las Vegas, NV-AZ MSA	528	853	24.3	11.6	925	47	61.5	8.5
Lexington, KY MSA	371	406	23.6	10.3	412	87	9.4	1.5
Little Rock-North Little Rock, AR MSA	474	513	26.5	11.4	519	72	8.1	1.1
Los Angeles-Riverside-Orange County, CA CMSA	11,498	14,532	26.6	9.8	14,818	2	26.4	2.0
Los Angeles-Long Beach, CA PMSA	7,477	8,863	26.9	9.7	8,978	(X)	18.5	1.3
Orange County, CA PMSA	1,933	2,411	24.4	9.2	2,442	(X)	24.7	1.3
Riverside-San Bernardino, CA PMSA	1,558	2,589	29.8	10.8	2,721	(X)	66.1	5.1
Ventura, CA PMSA	529	669	27.4	9.4	677	(X)	26.4	1.2
Louisville, KY-IN MSA	954	949	25.3	12.6	958	43	-0.5	1.0
Macon, GA MSA	273	291	27.4	10.8	295	120	6.6	1.4
Madison, WI MSA	324	367	22.7	9.3	376	97	13.5	2.3
McAllen-Edinburg-Mission, TX MSA	283	384	36.6	10.0	399	94	35.4	4.1
Melbourne-Titusville-Palm Bay, FL MSA	273	399	21.9	16.6	414	84	46.2	3.8
Memphis, TN-AR-MS MSA	939	1,007	27.9	10.4	1,020	40	7.3	1.3
Miami-Fort Lauderdale, FL CMSA	2,644	3,193	22.7	16.6	3,264	11	20.8	2.2
Fort Lauderdale, FL PMSA	1,018	1,255	20.4	20.8	1,287	(X)	23.3	2.5
Miami, FL PMSA	1,626	1,937	24.2	14.0	1,977	(X)	19.2	2.1
Milwaukee-Racine, WI CMSA	1,570	1,607	26.4	12.4	1,622	24	2.4	0.9
Milwaukee-Waukesha, WI PMSA	1,397	1,432	26.3	12.5	1,444	(X)	2.5	0.9
Racine, WI PMSA	173	175	27.8	12.0	178	(X)	1.1	1.7
Minneapolis-St. Paul, MN-WI MSA	2,198	2,539	26.4	9.8	2,583	15	15.5	1.7
Mobile, AL MSA	444	477	28.0	12.5	486	76	7.5	1.9
Modesto, CA MSA	266	371	30.6	10.8	387	96	39.3	4.4
Montgomery, AL MSA	273	293	27.4	11.4	298	118	7.3	1.7
Nashville, TN MSA	851	985	25.1	10.6	1,003	41	15.8	1.8
New London—Norwich, CT-RI MSA	273	291	23.6	12.5	290	121	6.5	-0.1
New Orleans, LA MSA	1,304	1,285	28.1	11.0	1,295	31	-1.5	0.8
New York-Northern New Jersey-Long Island, NY-NJ-CT-PA CMSA	18,713	19,342	23.1	13.1	19,384	1	3.4	0.2
Bridgeport, CT PMSA	439	444	23.2	14.7	443	(X)	1.2	-0.1
Danbury, CT PMSA	188	208	24.0	11.3	209	(X)	10.3	0.5
Dutchess County, NY PMSA	245	259	23.9	11.4	261	(X)	5.9	0.6
New Haven, CT PMSA	500	530	22.6	14.1	530	(X)	5.9	-0.1
New York-Newark, NY-NJ-PA PMSA	16,448	16,938	23.0	13.1	16,972	(X)	3.0	0.2
Orange County, NY PMSA	260	308	27.6	10.4	312	(X)	18.5	1.4
Stamford-Norwalk, CT PMSA	326	330	20.9	13.4	331	(X)	1.3	0.2
Trenton, NJ PMSA	308	326	22.5	13.0	327	(X)	5.8	0.2
Norfolk-Virginia Beach-Newport News, VA-NC MSA	1,201	1,443	26.4	9.2	1,465	27	20.2	1.5
Oklahoma City, OK MSA	861	959	26.6	11.0	971	42	11.4	1.3
Omaha, NE-IA MSA	605	640	27.9	10.7	649	60	5.6	1.5
Orlando, FL MSA	805	1,225	23.8	12.9	1,269	32	52.2	3.6
Pensacola, FL MSA	290	344	25.7	11.3	354	105	18.9	2.7
Peoria-Pekin, IL MSA	366	339	26.4	13.8	342	109	-7.3	0.9

See footnotes at end of table.

No. 42. Metropolitan Areas—Population: 1980 to 1991—Continued

[See headnote, page 37]

METROPOLITAN AREA	1980, total (1,000)	1990 Total (1,000)	1990 Under 18 yrs. old (percent)	1990 65 yrs. old and over (percent)	1991 Total (1,000)	1991 Rank	PERCENT CHANGE 1980-90	PERCENT CHANGE 1990-91
Philadelphia-Wilmington-Atlantic City, PA-NJ-DE-MD CMSA	5,649	5,893	24.4	13.5	5,925	6	4.3	0.5
Atlantic-Cape May, NJ PMSA	276	319	22.7	16.2	323	(X)	15.6	1.0
Philadelphia, PA-NJ PMSA	4,781	4,922	24.4	13.5	4,941	(X)	2.9	0.4
Vineland-Millville-Bridgeton, NJ PMSA	133	138	26.0	13.5	139	(X)	3.9	0.4
Wilmington-Newark, DE-MD PMSA	459	513	24.5	11.2	522	(X)	11.9	1.7
Phoenix-Mesa, AZ MSA	1,600	2,238	26.4	12.6	2,287	19	39.9	2.2
Pittsburgh, PA MSA	2,571	2,395	22.0	17.1	2,404	18	−6.9	0.4
Portland-Salem, OR-WA CMSA	1,584	1,793	25.8	12.4	1,857	22	13.3	3.6
Portland-Vancouver, OR-WA PMSA	1,334	1,515	25.7	12.0	1,570	(X)	13.6	3.6
Salem, OR PMSA	250	278	26.4	14.4	287	(X)	11.3	3.3
Providence-Fall River-Warwick, RI-MA MSA	1,077	1,134	22.8	15.1	1,135	36	5.4	0.1
Provo-Orem, UT MSA	218	264	37.8	7.0	270	128	20.9	2.3
Raleigh-Durham-Chapel Hill, NC MSA	665	856	22.7	9.5	883	49	28.7	3.2
Reading, PA MSA	313	337	23.3	15.6	341	110	7.7	1.3
Reno, NV MSA	194	255	23.1	10.3	263	132	31.5	3.2
Richmond-Petersburg, VA MSA	761	866	24.3	11.3	881	50	13.7	1.8
Rochester, NY MSA	1,031	1,062	25.1	12.5	1,073	38	3.1	1.0
Rockford, IL MSA	326	330	26.5	12.8	336	111	1.2	1.9
Sacramento-Yolo, CA CMSA	1,100	1,481	26.2	10.8	1,532	26	34.7	3.4
Sacramento, CA PMSA	986	1,340	26.4	10.9	1,388	(X)	35.8	3.6
Yolo, CA PMSA	113	141	24.1	9.5	144	(X)	24.4	1.8
Saginaw-Bay City-Midland, MI MSA	422	399	27.5	12.1	401	91	−5.3	0.3
St. Louis, MO-IL MSA	2,414	2,493	26.3	12.8	2,507	17	3.3	0.6
Salinas, CA MSA	290	356	27.5	9.8	363	102	22.5	2.1
Salt Lake City-Ogden, UT MSA	910	1,072	35.6	8.4	1,103	37	17.8	2.9
San Antonio, TX MSA	1,089	1,325	29.0	10.3	1,348	30	21.7	1.8
San Diego, CA MSA	1,862	2,498	24.5	10.9	2,549	16	34.2	2.0
San Francisco-Oakland-San Jose, CA CMSA	5,368	6,253	23.1	11.1	6,332	5	16.5	1.3
Oakland, CA PMSA	1,762	2,083	24.3	10.7	2,112	(X)	18.2	1.4
San Francisco, CA PMSA	1,489	1,604	18.9	13.3	1,622	(X)	7.7	1.2
San Jose, CA PMSA	1,295	1,498	24.0	8.7	1,506	(X)	15.6	0.5
Santa Cruz-Watsonville, CA PMSA	188	230	23.8	11.3	229	(X)	22.1	−0.2
Santa Rosa, CA PMSA	300	388	24.7	13.4	396	(X)	29.5	2.0
Vallejo-Fairfield-Napa, CA PMSA	334	451	27.4	10.2	466	(X)	34.9	3.3
Santa Barbara-Santa Maria-Lompoc, CA MSA	299	370	23.2	12.3	374	99	23.7	1.2
Sarasota-Bradenton, FL MSA	351	489	17.2	30.4	501	73	39.6	2.4
Savannah, GA MSA	231	258	27.2	11.9	263	133	11.8	1.8
Scranton—Wilkes-Barre—Hazleton, PA MSA	659	638	21.9	19.0	641	61	−3.2	0.4
Seattle-Tacoma-Bremerton, WA CMSA	2,409	2,970	25.0	10.8	3,054	12	23.3	2.8
Bremerton, WA PMSA	147	190	27.9	10.7	201	(X)	28.9	6.0
Olympia, WA PMSA	124	161	26.9	11.7	170	(X)	29.8	5.2
Seattle-Bellevue-Everett, WA PMSA	1,652	2,033	23.9	10.8	2,078	(X)	23.1	2.2
Tacoma, WA PMSA	486	586	27.2	10.5	605	(X)	20.7	3.3
Shreveport-Bossier City, LA MSA	377	376	28.6	12.7	374	98	−0.1	−0.5
Spokane, WA MSA	342	361	26.4	13.3	374	100	5.7	3.5
Springfield, MA MSA	570	588	23.4	14.1	586	69	3.2	−0.3
Springfield, MO MSA	228	264	24.1	13.0	270	127	15.9	2.1
Stockton-Lodi, CA MSA	347	481	29.6	11.1	493	75	38.4	2.5
Syracuse, NY MSA	723	742	25.3	12.6	749	57	2.7	0.9
Tampa-St. Petersburg-Clearwater, FL MSA	1,614	2,068	20.4	21.6	2,101	20	28.2	1.6
Toledo, OH MSA	617	614	26.3	12.4	614	62	−0.4	-
Tucson, AZ MSA	531	667	24.9	13.7	677	59	25.5	1.5
Tulsa, OK MSA	657	709	26.8	11.6	723	58	7.9	1.9
Utica-Rome, NY MSA	320	317	24.5	15.7	318	114	−1.1	0.5
Visalia-Tulare-Porterville, CA MSA	246	312	33.1	10.8	323	112	26.9	3.7
Washington-Baltimore, DC-MD-VA-WV CMSA	5,791	6,727	23.9	9.9	6,830	4	16.2	1.5
Baltimore, MD PMSA	2,199	2,382	24.1	11.7	2,414	(X)	8.3	1.3
Hagerstown, MD PMSA	113	121	22.7	13.8	123	(X)	7.3	1.4
Washington, DC-MD-VA-WV PMSA	3,478	4,223	23.7	8.7	4,293	(X)	21.4	1.6
West Palm Beach-Boca Raton, FL MSA	577	864	19.6	24.3	887	48	49.7	2.7
Wichita, KS MSA	442	485	27.8	11.9	493	74	9.7	1.6
York, PA MSA	313	340	24.2	13.1	346	108	8.5	1.8
Youngstown-Warren, OH MSA	645	601	25.1	15.6	603	64	−6.8	0.4

- Represents or rounds to zero.   X Not applicable.

Source: U.S. Bureau of the Census, press release CB93-50; and unpublished data.

No. 43. Metropolitan Areas With Large Numbers of Selected Racial Groups and of Hispanic Origin Population: 1990

[As of April 1. For Black, Hispanic origin, and Asian and Pacific Islander populations, areas selected had 100,000 or more of specified group; for American Indian, Eskimo, and Aleut population, areas selected are ten areas with largest number of that group. CMSA=consolidated metropolitan statistical area. MSA=metropolitan statistical area. Areas as defined by U.S. Office of Management and Budget, December 31, 1992. For definitions, see Appendix II]

METROPOLITAN AREA	Number of specified group (1,000)	Percent of total metro. area	METROPOLITAN AREA	Number of specified group (1,000)	Percent of total metro. area
BLACK			**HISPANIC ORIGIN** [1]		
New York-Northern New Jersey-Long Island, NY-NJ-CT-PA CMSA	3,439	17.8	Los Angeles-Riverside-Orange County, CA CMSA	4,779	32.9
Washington-Baltimore, DC-MD-VA-WV CMSA	1,696	25.2	New York-Northern New Jersey-Long Island, NY-NJ-CT-PA CMSA	2,843	14.7
Chicago-Gary-Kenosha, IL-IN-WI CMSA	1,564	19.0	Miami-Fort Lauderdale, FL CMSA	1,062	33.3
Los Angeles-Riverside-Orange County, CA CMSA	1,230	8.5	San Francisco-Oakland-San Jose, CA CMSA	970	15.5
Philadelphia-Wilmington-Atlantic City, PA-NJ-DE-MD CMSA	1,083	18.4	Chicago-Gary-Kenosha, IL-IN-WI CMSA	898	10.9
Detroit-Ann Arbor-Flint, MI CMSA	1,061	20.5	Houston-Galveston-Brazoria, TX CMSA	773	20.7
			San Antonio, TX MSA	628	47.4
Atlanta, GA MSA	747	25.2	Dallas-Fort Worth, TX CMSA	526	13.0
Houston-Galveston-Brazoria, TX CMSA	668	17.9	San Diego, CA MSA	511	20.4
Miami-Fort Lauderdale, FL CMSA	591	18.5	El Paso, TX MSA	412	69.6
Dallas-Fort Worth, TX CMSA	566	14.0	Phoenix-Mesa, AZ MSA	380	17.0
San Francisco-Oakland-San Jose, CA CMSA	538	8.6	McAllen-Edinburg-Mission, TX MSA	327	85.2
New Orleans, LA MSA	447	34.8	Fresno, CA MSA	267	35.3
Cleveland-Akron, OH CMSA	445	15.6	Washington-Baltimore, DC-MD-VA-WV CMSA	259	3.9
St. Louis, MO-IL MSA	424	17.0	Denver-Boulder-Greeley, CO CMSA	254	12.8
			Boston-Brockton-Nashua, MA-NH-ME-CT CMSA	239	4.4
Memphis, TN-AR-MS MSA	410	40.7			
Norfolk-Virginia Beach-Newport News, VA-NC MSA	409	28.3	Philadelphia-Wilmington-Atlantic City, PA-NJ-DE-MD CMSA	224	3.8
Boston-Brockton-Nashua, MA-NH-ME-CT CMSA	261	4.8	Albuquerque, NM MSA	218	37.1
Richmond-Petersburg, VA MSA	252	29.2	Brownsville-Harlingen-San Benito, TX MSA	213	81.9
Birmingham, AL MSA	241	28.7	Corpus Christi, TX MSA	182	52.0
Charlotte-Gastonia-Rock Hill, NC-SC MSA	232	19.9	Austin-San Marcos, TX MSA	177	20.9
Milwaukee-Racine, WI CMSA	214	13.3	Sacramento-Yolo, CA CMSA	172	11.6
			Tucson, AZ MSA	163	24.5
Raleigh-Durham-Chapel Hill, NC MSA	207	24.2	Bakersfield, CA MSA	152	28.0
Cincinnati-Hamilton, OH-KY-IN CMSA	204	11.2	Tampa-St. Petersburg-Clearwater, FL MSA	139	6.7
Greensboro—Winston-Salem—High Point, NC MSA	203	19.3	Laredo, TX MSA	125	93.9
Kansas City, MO-KS MSA	201	12.7	Visalia-Tulare-Porterville, CA MSA	121	38.8
Tampa-St. Petersburg-Clearwater, FL MSA	186	9.0	Salinas, CA MSA	120	33.6
Indianapolis, IN MSA	182	13.2	Stockton-Lodi, CA MSA	113	23.4
			Detroit-Ann Arbor-Flint, MI CMSA	105	2.0
Jacksonville, FL MSA	181	20.0	Orlando, FL MSA	101	8.2
Pittsburgh, PA MSA	180	7.5	**ASIAN AND PACIFIC ISLANDER**		
Jackson, MS MSA	168	42.5	Los Angeles-Riverside-Orange County, CA CMSA	1,339	9.2
Columbus, OH MSA	163	12.1	San Francisco-Oakland-San Jose, CA CMSA	927	14.8
San Diego, CA MSA	159	6.4	New York-Northern New Jersey-Long Island, NY-NJ-CT-PA CMSA	898	4.6
			Honolulu, HI MSA	526	63.0
Charleston-North Charleston, SC MSA	153	30.2	Chicago-Gary-Kenosha, IL-IN-WI CMSA	258	3.1
Nashville, TN MSA	152	15.5	Washington-Baltimore, DC-MD-VA-WV CMSA	248	3.7
Orlando, FL MSA	147	12.0	San Diego, CA MSA	198	7.9
Greenville-Spartanburg-Anderson, SC MSA	145	17.4	Seattle-Tacoma-Bremerton, WA CMSA	181	6.1
			Boston-Brockton-Nashua, MA-NH-ME-CT CMSA	137	2.5
Baton Rouge, LA MSA	143	30.5	Houston-Galveston-Brazoria, TX CMSA	132	3.5
Columbia, SC MSA	138	30.4	Philadelphia-Wilmington-Atlantic City, PA-NJ-DE-MD CMSA	119	2.0
Seattle-Tacoma-Bremerton, WA CMSA	133	4.5	Sacramento-Yolo, CA CMSA	115	7.7
Mobile, AL MSA	131	27.4	**AMERICAN INDIAN, ESKIMO, ALEUT**		
			Los Angeles-Riverside-Orange County, CA CMSA	87	0.6
Shreveport-Bossier City, LA MSA	130	34.6	Phoenix-Mesa, AZ MSA	49	2.2
Dayton-Springfield, OH MSA	126	13.3	New York-Northern New Jersey-Long Island, NY-NJ-CT-PA CMSA	48	0.2
Augusta-Aiken, GA-SC MSA	125	31.6	Tulsa, OK MSA	48	6.8
Louisville, KY-IN MSA	122	12.9	Oklahoma City, OK MSA	46	4.8
Buffalo-Niagara Falls, NY MSA	122	10.3	San Francisco-Oakland-San Jose, CA CMSA	41	0.7
			Seattle-Tacoma-Bremerton, WA CMSA	38	1.3
West Palm Beach-Boca Raton, FL MSA	108	12.5	Albuquerque, NM MSA	30	5.1
Montgomery, AL MSA	105	36.0	Minneapolis-St. Paul, MN-WI MSA	24	1.0
Sacramento-Yolo, CA CMSA	102		Detroit-Ann Arbor-Flint, MI CMSA	21	0.4
Little Rock-North Little Rock, AR MSA	102	19.9			
Macon, GA MSA	102	35.0			
Oklahoma City, OK MSA	101	10.5			

[1] Persons of Hispanic origin may be of any race.

Source: U.S. Bureau of the Census, unpublished data.

No. 44. 75 Largest Metropolitan Areas—Racial and Hispanic Origin Populations: 1990
[As of April 1. Areas as defined by U.S. Office of Management and Budget, December 31, 1992. For definitions, see Appendix II]

METROPOLITAN AREA [1]	Total population (1,000)	PERCENT OF TOTAL METROPOLITAN POPULATION			
		Black	American Indian, Eskimo, Aleut	Asian and Pacific Islander	Hispanic origin [2]
New York-Northern New Jersey-Long Island, NY-NJ-CT-PA CMSA	19,342	17.8	0.2	4.6	14.7
Los Angeles-Riverside-Orange County, CA CMSA	14,532	8.5	0.6	9.2	32.9
Chicago-Gary-Kenosha, IL-IN-WI CMSA	8,240	19.0	0.2	3.1	10.9
Washington-Baltimore, DC-MD-VA-WV CMSA	6,727	25.2	0.3	3.7	3.9
San Francisco-Oakland-San Jose, CA CMSA	6,253	8.6	0.7	14.8	15.5
Philadelphia-Wilmington-Atlantic City, PA-NJ-DE-MD CMSA	5,893	18.4	0.2	2.0	3.8
Boston-Brockton-Nashua, MA-NH-ME-CT CMSA	5,455	4.8	0.2	2.5	4.4
Detroit-Ann Arbor-Flint, MI CMSA	5,187	20.5	0.4	1.4	2.0
Dallas-Fort Worth, TX CMSA	4,037	14.0	0.5	2.4	13.0
Houston-Galveston-Brazoria, TX CMSA	3,731	17.9	0.3	3.5	20.7
Miami-Fort Lauderdale, FL CMSA	3,193	18.5	0.2	1.4	33.3
Seattle-Tacoma-Bremerton, WA CMSA	2,970	4.5	1.3	6.1	3.0
Atlanta, GA MSA	2,960	25.2	0.2	1.8	2.0
Cleveland-Akron, OH CMSA	2,860	15.6	0.2	1.0	1.9
Minneapolis-St. Paul, MN-WI MSA	2,539	3.5	1.0	2.6	1.5
San Diego, CA MSA	2,498	6.4	0.8	7.9	20.4
St. Louis, MO-IL MSA	2,493	17.0	0.2	1.0	1.1
Pittsburgh, PA MSA	2,395	7.5	0.1	0.7	0.6
Phoenix-Mesa, AZ MSA	2,238	3.5	2.2	1.6	17.0
Tampa-St. Petersburg-Clearwater, FL MSA	2,068	9.0	0.3	1.1	6.7
Denver-Boulder-Greeley, CO CMSA	1,980	5.0	0.7	2.2	12.8
Cincinnati-Hamilton, OH-KY-IN CMSA	1,818	11.2	0.1	0.8	0.5
Portland-Salem, OR-WA CMSA	1,793	2.5	1.0	3.2	4.0
Milwaukee-Racine, WI CMSA	1,607	13.3	0.5	1.2	3.8
Kansas City, MO-KS MSA	1,583	12.7	0.5	1.1	2.9
Sacramento-Yolo, CA CMSA	1,481	6.9	1.1	7.7	11.6
Norfolk-Virginia Beach-Newport News, VA-NC MSA	1,443	28.3	0.3	2.4	2.3
Indianapolis, IN MSA	1,380	13.2	0.2	0.8	0.9
Columbus, OH MSA	1,345	12.1	0.2	1.6	0.8
San Antonio, TX MSA	1,325	6.7	0.4	1.2	47.4
New Orleans, LA MSA	1,285	34.8	0.3	1.7	4.2
Orlando, FL MSA	1,225	12.0	0.3	1.7	8.2
Buffalo-Niagara Falls, NY MSA	1,189	10.3	0.6	0.9	2.0
Charlotte-Gastonia-Rock Hill, NC-SC MSA	1,162	19.9	0.4	1.0	0.9
Hartford, CT MSA	1,158	8.3	0.2	1.5	6.9
Providence-Fall River-Warwick, RI-MA MSA	1,134	3.3	0.3	1.8	4.2
Salt Lake City-Ogden, UT MSA	1,072	1.0	0.8	2.4	5.8
Rochester, NY MSA	1,062	8.9	0.3	1.3	3.0
Greensboro—Winston-Salem—High Point, NC MSA	1,050	19.3	0.3	0.7	0.7
Memphis, TN-AR-MS MSA	1,007	40.7	0.2	0.8	0.8
Nashville, TN MSA	985	15.5	0.2	1.0	0.8
Oklahoma City, OK MSA	959	10.5	4.8	1.9	3.6
Dayton-Springfield, OH MSA	951	13.3	0.2	1.0	0.8
Louisville, KY-IN MSA	949	12.9	0.2	0.6	0.6
Grand Rapids-Muskegon-Holland, MI MSA	938	6.9	0.6	0.9	3.1
Jacksonville, FL MSA	907	20.0	0.3	1.7	2.5
Richmond-Petersburg, VA MSA	866	29.2	0.3	1.4	1.1
West Palm Beach-Boca Raton, FL MSA	864	12.5	0.1	1.0	7.7
Albany-Schenectady-Troy, NY MSA	861	4.6	0.2	1.2	1.7
Raleigh-Durham-Chapel Hill, NC MSA	856	24.2	0.3	1.6	1.3
Las Vegas, NV-AZ MSA	853	8.4	1.1	3.1	10.4
Austin-San Marcos, TX MSA	846	9.4	0.4	2.2	20.9
Birmingham, AL MSA	840	28.7	0.2	0.5	0.4
Honolulu, HI MSA	836	3.1	0.4	63.0	6.8
Greenville-Spartanburg-Anderson, SC MSA	831	17.4	0.1	0.6	0.7
Fresno, CA MSA	756	4.8	1.1	7.7	35.3
Syracuse, NY MSA	742	5.7	0.6	1.1	1.4
Tulsa, OK MSA	709	8.2	6.8	0.9	2.1
Tucson, AZ MSA	667	3.1	3.0	1.8	24.5
Omaha, NE-IA MSA	640	8.0	0.5	1.0	2.6
Scranton—Wilkes-Barre-Hazleton, PA MSA	638	0.9	0.1	0.5	0.6
Toledo, OH MSA	614	11.4	0.2	1.0	3.3
Youngstown-Warren, OH MSA	601	9.4	0.2	0.4	1.3
Allentown-Bethlehem-Easton, PA MSA	595	2.0	0.1	1.1	4.6
El Paso, TX MSA	592	3.7	0.4	1.1	69.6
Albuquerque, NM MSA	589	2.5	5.1	1.4	37.1
Harrisburg-Lebanon-Carlisle, PA MSA	588	6.7	0.1	1.1	1.7
Springfield, MA MSA	588	6.3	0.2	1.4	8.5
Knoxville, TN MSA	586	6.1	0.2	0.8	0.5
Bakersfield, CA MSA	543	5.5	1.3	3.0	28.0
Little Rock-North Little Rock, AR MSA	513	19.9	0.4	0.7	0.8
Charleston-North Charleston, SC MSA	507	30.2	0.3	1.2	1.5
Sarasota-Bradenton, FL MSA	489	5.8	0.2	0.5	3.1
Wichita, KS MSA	485	7.6	1.1	1.9	4.1
Stockton-Lodi, CA MSA	481	5.6	1.1	12.4	23.4

[1] Metropolitan areas are shown in rank order of total population of consolidated metropolitan statistical areas (CMSA) and metropolitan statistical areas (MSA). [2] Persons of Hispanic origin may be of any race.

Source: U.S. Bureau of the Census, unpublished data.

No. 45. Incorporated Places, by Population Size: 1960 to 1990

POPULATION SIZE	NUMBER OF INCORPORATED PLACES				POPULATION (mil.)				PERCENT OF TOTAL			
	1960	1970	1980	1990	1960	1970	1980	1990	1960	1970	1980	1990
Total	18,088	18,666	19,097	19,290	115.9	131.9	140.3	152.9	100.0	100.0	100.0	100.0
1,000,000 or more. . . .	5	6	6	8	17.5	18.8	17.5	20.0	15.1	14.2	12.5	13.0
500,000 to 999,999. . .	16	20	16	15	11.1	13.0	10.9	10.1	9.6	9.8	7.8	6.6
250,000 to 499,999 . . .	30	30	33	41	10.8	10.5	11.8	14.2	9.3	7.9	8.4	9.3
100,000 to 249,999 . . .	79	97	114	131	11.4	13.9	16.6	19.1	9.8	10.5	11.8	12.5
50,000 to 99,999.	180	232	250	309	12.5	16.2	17.6	21.2	10.8	12.2	12.3	13.9
25,000 to 49,999.	366	455	526	567	12.7	15.7	18.4	20.0	11.0	11.9	13.1	13.0
10,000 to 24,999.	978	1,127	1,260	1,290	15.1	17.6	19.8	20.3	13.1	13.3	14.1	13.3
Under 10,000	16,434	16,699	16,892	16,929	24.9	26.4	28.0	28.2	21.5	20.0	20.0	18.4

Source: U.S. Bureau of the Census, *Census of Population: 1970, 1980,* and *1990,* vol. I.

No. 46. Cities With 100,000 or More Inhabitants in 1990—Population, 1970 to 1990, and Land Area, 1990

[Population: As of April 1. Data refer to boundaries in effect on January 1, 1990. Minus sign (-) indicates decrease]

CITY	POPULATION [1]										Land area, 1990 (square miles)
	1970, total (1,000)	1980, total (1,000)	1990								
			Total (1,000)	Rank	Percent change, 1980-90	Percent—				Per square mile	
						Black	American Indian, Eskimo, Aleut	Asian, Pacific Islander	His-panic [2]		
Abilene, TX	90	98	107	180	8.5	7.0	0.4	1.3	15.5	1,035	103.1
Akron, OH.	275	237	223	71	-6.0	24.5	0.3	1.2	0.7	3,586	62.2
Albany, NY	116	102	100	196	-1.7	20.6	0.3	2.3	3.1	4,674	21.4
Albuquerque, NM	245	332	385	38	15.5	3.0	3.0	1.7	34.5	2,909	132.2
Alexandria, VA.	111	103	111	164	7.7	21.9	0.3	4.2	9.7	7,267	15.3
Allentown, PA	110	104	105	183	1.5	5.0	0.2	1.3	11.7	5,949	17.7
Amarillo, TX	127	149	158	110	5.6	6.0	0.8	1.9	14.7	1,793	87.9
Anaheim, CA.	166	219	266	59	21.4	2.5	0.5	9.4	31.4	6,014	44.3
Anchorage, AK	48	174	226	69	29.8	6.4	6.4	4.8	4.1	133	1,697.7
Ann Arbor, MI	100	108	110	170	1.5	9.0	0.4	7.7	2.6	4,231	25.9
Arlington, TX	90	160	262	61	63.5	8.4	0.5	3.9	8.9	2,814	93.0
Atlanta, GA	495	425	394	36	-7.3	67.1	0.1	0.9	1.9	2,990	131.8
Aurora, CO	75	159	222	72	40.1	11.4	0.6	3.8	6.6	1,676	132.5
Austin, TX.	254	346	466	27	34.6	12.4	0.4	3.0	23.0	2,138	217.8
Bakersfield, CA	70	106	175	97	65.5	9.4	1.1	3.6	20.5	1,904	91.8
Baltimore, MD	905	787	736	12	-6.4	59.2	0.3	1.1	1.0	9,108	80.8
Baton Rouge, LA	166	220	220	73	-0.4	43.9	0.1	1.7	1.6	2,969	74.0
Beaumont, TX	118	118	114	155	-3.2	41.3	0.2	1.7	4.3	1,427	80.1
Berkeley, CA	114	103	103	190	-0.6	18.8	0.6	14.8	8.4	9,783	10.5
Birmingham, AL	301	284	266	60	-6.5	63.3	0.1	0.6	(Z)	1,791	148.5
Boise City, ID	75	102	126	145	23.0	0.6	0.6	1.6	2.7	2,726	46.1
Boston, MA.	641	563	574	20	2.0	25.6	0.3	5.3	10.8	11,860	48.4
Bridgeport, CT	157	143	142	123	-0.6	26.6	0.3	2.3	26.5	8,855	16.0
Buffalo, NY	463	358	328	50	-8.3	30.7	0.8	1.0	4.9	8,083	40.6
Cedar Rapids, IA	111	110	109	173	-1.3	2.9	0.2	1.0	1.1	2,033	53.5
Charlotte, NC	241	315	396	35	25.5	31.8	0.4	1.8	1.4	2,272	174.3
Chattanooga, TN	120	170	152	113	-10.0	33.7	0.2	1.0	0.6	1,288	118.4
Chesapeake, VA	90	114	152	114	32.8	27.4	0.3	1.2	1.3	446	340.7
Chicago, IL	3,369	3,005	2,784	3	-7.4	39.1	0.3	3.7	19.6	12,251	227.2
Chula Vista, CA	68	84	135	131	61.0	4.6	0.6	8.9	37.3	4,661	29.0
Cincinnati, OH	454	385	364	45	-5.5	37.9	0.2	1.1	0.7	4,717	77.2
Cleveland, OH.	751	574	506	23	-11.9	46.6	0.3	1.0	4.6	6,565	77.0
Colorado Springs, CO . . .	136	215	281	54	30.7	7.0	0.8	2.4	9.1	1,535	183.2
Columbia, SC	114	101	103	188	2.2	43.7	0.3	1.4	2.0	884	117.1
Columbus, GA [3]	155	169	179	93	5.5	38.1	0.3	1.4	3.0	827	216.1
Columbus, OH.	540	565	633	16	12.0	22.6	0.2	2.4	1.1	3,315	190.9
Concord, CA	85	104	111	163	7.3	2.4	0.7	8.7	11.5	3,773	29.5
Corpus Christi, TX	205	232	257	64	10.9	4.8	0.4	0.9	50.4	1,907	135.0
Dallas, TX.	844	905	1,008	8	11.4	29.5	0.5	2.2	20.9	2,943	342.4
Dayton, OH.	243	194	182	89	-5.9	40.4	0.2	0.6	0.7	3,310	55.0
Denver, CO.	515	493	468	26	-5.1	12.8	1.2	2.4	23.0	3,051	153.3
Des Moines, IA	201	191	193	80	1.1	7.1	0.4	2.4	2.4	2,567	75.3
Detroit, MI.	1,514	1,203	1,028	7	-14.6	75.7	0.4	0.8	2.8	7,410	138.7
Durham, NC	95	101	137	130	35.1	45.7	0.2	2.0	1.2	1,972	69.3
Elizabeth, NJ	113	106	110	168	3.6	19.8	0.3	2.7	39.1	8,929	12.3
El Monte, CA.	70	79	106	181	33.5	1.0	0.6	11.8	72.5	11,175	9.5
El Paso, TX.	322	425	515	22	21.2	3.4	0.4	1.2	69.0	2,100	245.4
Erie, PA	129	119	109	175	-8.7	12.0	0.2	0.5	2.4	4,944	22.0
Escondido, CA.	37	64	109	176	68.8	1.5	0.8	3.7	23.4	3,048	35.6
Eugene, OR	79	106	113	159	6.6	1.3	0.9	3.5	2.7	2,962	38.0
Evansville, IN	139	130	126	144	-3.2	9.5	0.2	0.6	0.6	3,102	40.7
Flint, MI	193	160	141	125	-11.8	47.9	0.7	0.5	2.9	4,161	33.8
Fort Lauderdale, FL	140	153	149	116	-2.6	28.1	0.2	0.9	7.2	4,753	31.4

See footnotes at end of table.

No. 46. Cities With 100,000 or More Inhabitants in 1990—Population, 1970 to 1990, and Land Area, 1990—Continued

[See headnote, p. 42]

CITY	1970, total (1,000)	1980, total (1,000)	POPULATION [1] Total (1,000)	Rank	Percent change, 1980-90	1990 Percent— Black	American Indian, Eskimo, Aleut	Asian, Pacific Islander	His-panic [2]	Per square mile	Land area, 1990 (square miles)
Fort Wayne, IN	178	172	173	99	0.4	16.7	0.3	1.0	2.7	2,762	62.7
Fort Worth, TX	393	385	448	28	16.2	22.0	0.4	2.0	19.5	1,592	281.1
Fremont, CA	101	132	173	98	31.4	3.8	0.7	19.4	13.3	2,250	77.0
Fresno, CA	166	217	354	47	62.9	8.3	1.1	12.5	29.9	3,573	99.1
Fullerton, CA	86	102	114	156	11.6	2.2	0.5	12.2	21.3	5,160	22.1
Garden Grove, CA	121	123	143	120	16.0	1.5	0.6	20.5	23.5	7,974	17.9
Garland, TX	81	139	181	91	30.1	8.9	0.5	4.5	11.6	3,150	57.4
Gary, IN	175	152	117	154	-23.2	80.6	0.2	0.2	5.7	2,322	50.2
Glendale, AZ	36	97	148	117	52.4	3.0	0.9	2.1	15.5	2,837	52.2
Glendale, CA	133	139	180	92	29.5	1.3	0.3	14.1	21.0	5,882	30.6
Grand Rapids, MI	198	182	189	83	4.0	18.5	0.8	1.1	5.0	4,273	44.3
Greensboro, NC	144	156	184	88	18.2	33.9	0.5	1.4	1.0	2,304	79.8
Hampton, VA	121	123	134	133	9.1	38.9	0.3	1.7	2.0	2,583	51.8
Hartford, CT	158	136	140	128	2.5	38.9	0.3	1.4	31.6	8,077	17.3
Hayward, CA	93	94	111	162	19.0	9.8	1.0	15.5	23.9	2,560	43.5
Hialeah, FL	102	145	188	85	29.4	1.9	0.1	0.5	87.6	9,772	19.2
Hollywood, FL	107	121	122	148	0.3	8.5	0.2	1.3	11.9	4,464	27.3
Honolulu, HI [4]	325	365	377	39	3.3	1.3	0.3	70.5	4.6	4,400	85.7
Houston, TX	1,234	1,595	1,631	4	2.2	28.1	0.3	4.1	27.6	3,021	539.9
Huntington Beach, CA	116	171	182	90	6.5	0.9	0.6	8.3	11.2	6,871	26.4
Huntsville, AL	139	143	160	109	12.2	24.4	0.5	2.1	1.2	973	164.4
Independence, MO	112	112	112	160	0.5	1.4	0.6	1.0	2.0	1,436	78.2
Indianapolis, IN [3]	737	701	731	13	4.3	22.6	0.2	0.9	1.1	2,022	361.7
Inglewood, CA	90	94	110	169	16.4	51.9	0.4	2.5	38.5	11,952	9.2
Irvine, CA	([5])	62	110	167	77.6	1.8	0.2	18.1	6.3	2,607	42.3
Irving, TX	97	110	155	112	41.0	7.5	0.6	4.6	16.3	2,293	67.6
Jackson, MS	154	203	197	78	-3.1	55.7	0.1	0.5	0.4	1,804	109.0
Jacksonville, FL [3]	504	541	635	15	17.9	25.2	0.3	1.9	2.6	837	758.7
Jersey City, NJ	260	224	229	67	2.2	29.7	0.3	11.4	24.2	15,337	14.9
Kansas City, KS	168	161	150	115	-7.1	29.3	0.7	1.2	7.1	1,390	107.8
Kansas City, MO	507	448	435	31	-2.9	29.6	0.5	1.2	3.9	1,397	311.5
Knoxville, TN	175	175	165	102	-5.7	15.8	0.2	1.0	0.7	2,135	77.2
Lakewood, CO	93	114	126	143	11.1	1.0	0.7	1.9	9.1	3,100	40.8
Lansing, MI	131	130	127	142	-2.4	18.6	1.0	1.8	7.9	3,755	33.9
Laredo, TX	69	91	123	147	34.4	0.1	0.2	0.4	93.9	3,739	32.9
Las Vegas, NV	126	165	258	63	56.8	11.4	0.9	3.6	12.5	3,100	83.3
Lexington-Fayette, KY.	108	204	225	70	10.4	13.4	0.2	1.6	1.1	792	284.5
Lincoln, NE	150	172	192	81	11.7	2.4	0.6	1.7	2.0	3,033	63.3
Little Rock, AR	132	159	176	96	10.5	34.0	0.3	0.9	0.8	1,709	102.9
Livonia, MI	110	105	101	193	-3.8	0.3	0.2	1.3	1.3	2,823	35.7
Long Beach, CA	359	361	429	32	18.8	13.7	0.6	13.6	23.6	8,586	50.0
Los Angeles, CA	2,812	2,969	3,485	2	17.4	14.0	0.5	9.8	39.9	7,426	469.3
Louisville, KY	362	299	270	58	-9.8	29.7	0.2	0.7	0.7	4,341	62.1
Lowell, MA	94	92	103	189	11.9	2.4	0.2	11.1	10.1	7,506	13.8
Lubbock, TX	149	174	186	87	6.8	8.6	0.3	1.4	22.5	1,789	104.1
Macon, GA	122	117	107	179	-8.2	52.2	0.1	0.4	0.6	2,241	47.9
Madison, WI	172	171	191	82	11.8	4.2	0.4	3.9	2.0	3,300	57.8
Memphis, TN	624	646	610	18	-5.5	54.8	0.2	0.8	0.7	2,384	256.0
Mesa, AZ	63	152	288	53	89.0	1.9	1.0	1.5	10.9	2,653	108.6
Mesquite, TX	55	67	101	191	51.3	5.8	0.5	2.6	8.8	2,369	42.8
Miami, FL	335	347	359	46	3.5	27.4	0.2	0.6	62.5	10,074	35.6
Milwaukee, WI	717	636	628	17	-1.3	30.5	0.9	1.9	6.3	6,537	96.1
Minneapolis, MN	434	371	368	43	-0.7	13.0	3.3	4.3	2.1	6,706	54.9
Mobile, AL	190	200	196	79	-2.1	38.9	0.2	1.0	1.0	1,663	118.0
Modesto, CA	62	107	165	103	54.0	2.7	1.0	7.9	16.3	5,458	30.2
Montgomery, AL	133	178	188	86	5.4	42.3	0.2	0.7	0.8	1,389	135.0
Moreno Valley, CA	([5])	([5])	119	151	(X)	13.8	0.7	6.6	22.9	2,418	49.1
Nashville-Davidson, TN [3]	426	456	488	25	6.9	24.3	0.2	1.4	0.9	1,032	473.3
Newark, NJ	382	329	275	56	-16.4	58.5	0.2	1.2	26.1	11,554	23.8
New Haven, CT	138	126	130	138	3.5	36.1	0.3	2.4	13.2	6,922	18.9
New Orleans, LA	593	558	497	24	-10.9	61.9	0.2	1.9	3.5	2,751	180.7
Newport News, VA	138	145	171	100	18.3	33.6	0.3	2.3	2.8	2,510	68.3
New York, NY	7,896	7,072	7,323	1	3.5	28.7	0.4	7.0	24.4	23,701	309.0
Bronx Borough	1,472	1,169	1,204	(X)	3.0	37.3	0.5	3.0	43.5	28,641	42.0
Brooklyn Borough	2,602	2,231	2,301	(X)	3.1	37.9	0.3	4.8	20.1	32,620	70.5
Manhattan Borough	1,539	1,428	1,488	(X)	4.1	22.0	0.4	7.4	26.0	52,415	28.4
Queens Borough	1,987	1,891	1,952	(X)	3.2	21.7	0.4	12.2	19.5	17,839	109.4
Staten Island Borough	295	352	379	(X)	7.7	8.1	0.2	4.5	8.0	6,466	58.6
Norfolk, VA	308	267	261	62	-2.2	39.1	0.4	2.6	2.9	4,856	53.8
Oakland, CA	362	339	372	40	9.7	43.9	0.6	14.8	13.9	6,640	56.1
Oceanside, CA	40	77	128	140	67.1	7.9	0.7	6.1	22.6	3,164	40.5
Oklahoma City, OK	368	404	445	29	10.1	16.0	4.2	2.4	5.0	731	608.2
Omaha, NE	347	314	336	48	7.0	13.1	0.7	1.0	3.1	3,336	100.7
Ontario, CA	64	89	133	134	49.9	7.3	0.7	3.9	41.7	3,624	36.8
Orange, CA	77	91	111	166	21.0	1.4	0.5	7.9	22.8	4,741	23.3
Orlando, FL	99	128	165	104	28.4	26.9	0.3	1.6	8.7	2,448	67.3
Overland Park, KS	78	82	112	161	36.7	1.8	0.3	1.9	2.0	2,007	55.7

See footnotes at end of table.

No. 46. Cities With 100,000 or More Inhabitants in 1990—Population, 1970 to 1990, and Land Area, 1990—Continued

[See headnote, p. 42]

CITY	1970, total (1,000)	1980, total (1,000)	1990 Total (1,000)	Rank	Percent change, 1980-90	Black	American Indian, Eskimo, Aleut	Asian, Pacific Islander	His-panic [2]	Per square mile	Land area, 1990 (square miles)
Oxnard, CA	71	108	143	121	31.8	5.2	0.8	8.6	54.4	5,843	24.4
Pasadena, CA	113	118	132	137	11.4	19.0	0.4	8.1	27.3	5,724	23.0
Pasadena, TX	90	113	119	150	6.1	1.0	0.5	1.6	28.8	2,726	43.8
Paterson, NJ	145	138	141	124	2.1	36.0	0.3	1.4	41.0	16,693	8.4
Peoria, IL	127	124	114	157	-8.6	20.9	0.2	1.7	1.6	2,776	40.9
Philadelphia, PA	1,949	1,688	1,586	5	-6.1	39.9	0.2	2.7	5.6	11,734	135.1
Phoenix, AZ	584	790	983	9	24.5	5.2	1.9	1.7	20.0	2,342	419.9
Pittsburgh, PA	520	424	370	41	-12.8	25.8	0.2	1.6	0.9	6,649	55.6
Plano, TX	18	72	128	141	76.8	4.1	0.3	4.0	6.2	1,929	66.3
Pomona, CA	87	93	132	136	42.0	14.4	0.6	6.7	51.3	5,770	22.8
Portland, OR	380	368	437	30	18.8	7.7	1.2	5.3	3.2	3,508	124.7
Portsmouth, VA	111	105	104	186	-0.6	47.3	0.3	0.8	1.3	3,139	33.1
Providence, RI	179	157	161	107	2.5	14.8	0.9	5.9	15.5	8,707	18.5
Raleigh, NC	123	150	211	74	40.4	27.6	0.3	2.5	1.4	2,395	88.1
Rancho Cucamonga, CA	(5)	55	101	192	83.5	5.9	0.6	5.4	20.0	2,682	37.8
Reno, NV	73	101	134	132	32.8	2.9	1.4	4.9	11.1	2,328	57.5
Richmond, VA	249	219	203	76	-7.5	55.2	0.2	0.9	0.9	3,374	60.1
Riverside, CA	140	171	227	68	32.8	7.4	0.8	5.2	26.0	2,916	77.7
Rochester, NY	295	242	230	66	-4.7	31.5	0.5	1.8	8.7	6,435	35.8
Rockford, IL	147	140	140	127	0.2	15.0	0.3	1.5	4.2	3,110	45.0
Sacramento, CA	257	276	369	42	34.0	15.3	1.2	15.0	16.2	3,836	96.3
St. Louis, MO	622	453	397	34	-12.4	47.5	0.2	0.9	1.3	6,405	61.9
St. Paul, MN	310	270	272	57	0.7	7.4	1.4	7.1	4.2	5,157	52.8
St. Petersburg, FL	216	239	240	65	0.7	19.6	0.2	1.7	2.6	4,059	59.2
Salem, OR	69	89	108	178	21.0	1.5	1.6	2.4	6.1	2,595	41.5
Salinas, CA	59	80	109	174	35.2	3.0	0.9	8.1	50.6	5,839	18.6
Salt Lake City, UT	176	163	160	108	-1.9	1.7	1.6	4.7	9.7	1,467	109.0
San Antonio, TX	654	786	936	10	19.1	7.0	0.4	1.1	55.6	2,810	333.0
San Bernardino, CA	107	119	164	105	38.2	16.0	1.0	4.0	34.6	2,980	55.1
San Diego, CA	697	876	1,111	6	26.8	9.4	0.6	11.8	20.7	3,428	324.0
San Francisco, CA	716	679	724	14	6.6	10.9	0.5	29.1	13.9	15,502	46.7
San Jose, CA	460	629	782	11	24.3	4.7	0.7	19.5	26.6	4,568	171.3
Santa Ana, CA	156	204	294	52	44.0	2.6	0.5	9.7	65.2	10,842	27.1
Santa Clarita, CA	(5)	(5)	111	165	(X)	1.5	0.6	4.2	13.4	2,733	40.5
Santa Rosa, CA	50	83	113	158	37.1	1.8	1.2	3.4	9.5	3,362	33.7
Savannah, GA	118	142	138	129	-2.6	51.3	0.2	1.1	1.4	2,204	62.6
Scottsdale, AZ	68	89	130	139	46.8	0.8	0.6	1.2	4.8	706	184.4
Seattle, WA	531	494	516	21	4.5	10.1	1.4	11.8	3.6	6,154	83.9
Shreveport, LA	182	206	199	77	-4.1	44.8	0.2	0.5	1.1	2,013	98.6
Simi Valley, CA	60	78	100	195	29.3	1.5	0.6	5.5	12.7	3,034	33.0
Sioux Falls, SD	72	81	101	194	24.0	0.7	1.6	0.7	0.6	2,236	45.1
South Bend, IN	126	110	106	182	-3.8	20.9	0.4	0.9	3.4	2,897	36.4
Spokane, WA	171	171	177	94	3.4	1.9	2.0	2.1	2.1	3,169	55.9
Springfield, IL	92	100	105	184	5.2	13.0	0.2	1.0	0.8	2,474	42.5
Springfield, MA	164	152	157	111	3.1	19.2	0.2	1.0	16.9	4,890	32.1
Springfield, MO	120	133	140	126	5.5	2.5	0.7	0.9	1.0	2,068	68.0
Stamford, CT	109	102	108	177	5.5	17.8	0.1	2.6	9.8	2,865	37.7
Sterling Heights, MI	61	109	118	152	8.1	0.4	0.2	2.9	1.1	3,215	36.6
Stockton, CA	110	150	211	75	42.3	9.6	1.0	22.8	25.0	4,013	52.6
Sunnyvale, CA	96	107	117	153	10.0	3.4	0.5	19.3	13.2	5,353	21.9
Syracuse, NY	197	170	164	106	-3.7	20.3	1.3	2.2	2.9	6,528	25.1
Tacoma, WA	154	159	177	95	11.5	11.4	2.0	6.9	3.8	3,677	48.1
Tallahassee, FL	73	82	125	146	53.0	29.1	0.2	1.8	3.0	1,972	63.3
Tampa, FL	278	272	280	55	3.1	25.0	0.3	1.4	15.0	2,577	108.7
Tempe, AZ	64	107	142	122	32.7	3.2	1.3	4.1	10.9	3,590	39.5
Thousand Oaks, CA	36	77	104	185	35.4	1.2	0.4	4.8	9.6	2,104	49.6
Toledo, OH	383	355	333	49	-6.1	19.7	0.3	1.0	4.0	4,132	80.6
Topeka, KS	125	119	120	149	1.0	10.6	1.3	0.8	5.8	2,173	55.2
Torrance, CA	135	130	133	135	2.5	1.5	0.4	21.9	10.1	6,487	20.5
Tucson, AZ	263	331	405	33	22.6	4.3	1.6	2.2	29.3	2,594	156.3
Tulsa, OK	330	361	367	44	1.8	13.6	4.7	1.4	2.6	2,001	183.5
Vallejo, CA	72	80	109	171	36.0	21.2	0.7	23.0	10.8	3,613	30.2
Virginia Beach, VA	172	262	393	37	49.9	13.9	0.4	4.3	3.1	1,583	248.3
Waco, TX	95	101	104	187	2.3	23.1	0.3	0.9	16.3	1,367	75.8
Warren, MI	179	161	145	118	-10.1	0.7	0.5	1.3	1.1	4,226	34.3
Washington, DC	757	638	607	19	-4.9	65.8	0.2	1.8	5.4	9,883	61.4
Waterbury, CT	108	103	109	172	5.5	13.0	0.3	0.7	13.4	3,815	28.6
Wichita, KS	277	280	304	51	8.6	11.3	1.2	2.6	5.0	2,640	115.1
Winston-Salem, NC	134	132	143	119	8.8	39.3	0.2	0.8	0.9	2,018	71.1
Worcester, MA	177	162	170	101	4.9	4.5	0.3	2.8	9.6	4,520	37.6
Yonkers, NY	204	195	188	84	-3.7	14.1	0.2	3.0	16.7	10,403	18.1

X Not applicable.   Z Less than .05 percent.   [1] Population totals include corrections through October 1992; the data by race and Hispanic origin are not corrected.   [2] Hispanic persons may be of any race.   [3] Represents the portion of a consolidated city that is not within one or more separately incorporated places.   [4] Data represent a census designated place as delineated by State and local officials.   [5] Not incorporated.

Source: U.S. Bureau of the Census, *Census of Population: 1970*, vol. I, chapters A and B; *1980 Census of Population*, vol. 1, chapters A and B; *1990 Census of Population and Housing, Summary Population and Housing Characteristics*, (CPH-1).

No. 47. Population 65 Years Old and Over, by Age Group and Sex, 1980 to 1991, and Projections, 2000

[As of **April**, except **1991** and **2000**, as of **July**. Projection based on middle series, see table 3]

AGE GROUP AND SEX	NUMBER (1,000)				PERCENT DISTRIBUTION			
	1980	1990	1991	2000, proj.	1980	1990	1991	2000, proj.
Persons 65 yrs. and over.....	25,549	31,079	31,754	34,886	100.0	100.0	100.0	100.0
65 to 69 years old	8,782	10,066	10,037	9,469	34.3	32.4	31.6	27.1
70 to 74 years old	6,798	7,980	8,242	8,789	26.6	25.7	26.0	25.2
75 to 79 years old	4,794	6,103	6,279	7,447	18.8	19.6	19.8	21.3
80 to 84 years old	2,935	3,909	4,035	4,892	11.5	12.6	12.7	14.0
85 years old and over	2,240	3,021	3,160	4,289	8.8	9.7	10.0	12.3
Males, 65 yrs. and over..........	10,305	12,493	12,791	14,402	100.0	100.0	100.0	100.0
65 to 69 years old..............	3,903	4,508	4,491	4,369	37.8	36.1	35.1	30.3
70 to 74 years old..............	2,854	3,399	3,531	3,911	27.7	27.2	27.6	27.2
75 to 79 years old..............	1,848	2,389	2,482	3,100	18.0	19.1	19.4	21.5
80 to 84 years old..............	1,019	1,356	1,406	1,807	9.9	10.9	11.0	12.5
85 years old and over	682	841	881	1,215	6.6	6.7	6.9	8.4
Females, 65 yrs. and over	15,245	18,586	18,962	20,484	100.0	100.0	100.0	100.0
65 to 69 years old..............	4,880	5,558	5,546	5,100	31.9	29.9	29.2	24.9
70 to 74 years old..............	3,945	4,580	4,712	4,878	25.9	24.6	24.8	23.8
75 to 79 years old..............	2,946	3,714	3,797	4,347	19.3	20.0	20.0	21.2
80 to 84 years old..............	1,916	2,553	2,629	3,086	12.6	13.7	13.9	15.1
85 years old and over	1,559	2,180	2,279	3,074	10.3	11.7	12.0	15.0

Source: U.S. Bureau of the Census, *Current Population Reports*, P25-1092 and P25-1095.

No. 48. Persons 65 Years Old and Over—Characteristics, by Sex: 1980 to 1992

[As of **March, except as noted.** Covers civilian noninstitutional population. See headnote, table 49]

CHARACTERISTIC	TOTAL				MALE				FEMALE			
	1980	1985	1990	1992	1980	1985	1990	1992	1980	1985	1990	1992
Total [1] (million).............	24.2	26.8	29.6	30.6	9.9	11.0	12.3	12.8	14.2	15.8	17.2	17.8
White (million).................	21.9	24.2	26.5	27.3	9.0	9.9	11.0	11.4	12.9	14.3	15.4	15.9
Black (million).................	2.0	2.2	2.5	2.6	0.8	0.9	1.0	1.1	1.2	1.3	1.5	1.5
Percent below poverty level [2].......	15.2	12.4	11.4	12.4	11.1	8.7	7.8	7.9	17.9	15.0	13.9	15.5
PERCENT DISTRIBUTION												
Marital status:												
Single.....................	5.5	5.2	4.6	4.6	4.9	5.3	4.2	4.2	5.9	5.1	4.9	4.9
Married....................	55.4	55.2	56.1	55.8	78.0	77.2	76.5	75.9	39.5	39.9	41.4	41.2
Spouse present	53.6	53.4	54.1	54.1	76.1	75.0	74.2	73.8	37.9	38.3	39.7	39.8
Spouse absent	1.8	1.8	2.0	1.7	1.9	2.2	2.3	2.1	1.7	1.6	1.7	1.4
Widowed..................	35.7	35.6	34.2	34.4	13.5	13.8	14.2	15.0	51.2	50.7	48.6	48.3
Divorced..................	3.5	4.0	5.0	5.3	3.6	3.7	5.0	4.9	3.4	4.3	5.1	5.5
Family status:												
In families [3]................	67.6	67.3	66.7	66.5	83.0	82.4	81.9	80.8	56.8	56.7	55.8	56.2
Nonfamily householders.........	31.2	31.1	31.9	32.0	15.7	15.4	16.6	17.1	42.0	42.1	42.8	42.7
Secondary individuals..........	1.2	1.6	1.4	1.5	1.3	2.2	1.5	2.1	1.1	1.1	1.4	1.1
Living arrangements:												
Living in household	99.8	99.6	99.7	99.7	99.9	99.5	99.9	99.7	99.7	99.6	99.5	99.8
Living alone.................	30.3	30.2	31.0	31.1	14.9	14.7	15.7	16.3	41.0	41.1	42.0	41.8
Spouse present	53.6	53.4	54.1	54.1	76.1	75.0	74.3	73.8	37.9	38.3	39.7	39.8
Living with someone else.......	15.9	15.9	14.6	14.6	8.9	9.8	9.9	9.6	20.8	20.2	17.8	18.1
Not in household [4]	0.2	0.4	0.3	0.3	0.1	0.5	0.1	0.3	0.3	0.4	0.5	0.2
Years of school completed:												
8 years or less	43.1	35.4	28.5	26.5	45.3	37.2	30.0	28.1	41.6	34.1	27.5	25.2
1 to 3 years of high school	16.2	16.5	16.1	15.7	15.5	15.7	15.7	14.9	16.7	17.0	16.4	16.3
4 years of high school	24.0	29.0	32.9	34.3	21.4	26.4	29.0	29.9	25.8	30.7	35.6	37.4
1 to 3 years of college	8.2	9.8	10.9	11.4	7.5	9.1	10.8	11.2	8.6	10.3	11.0	11.6
4 years or more of college	8.6	9.4	11.6	12.1	10.3	11.5	14.5	15.8	7.4	8.0	9.5	9.5
Labor force participation: [5]												
Employed	12.2	10.4	11.5	11.2	18.4	15.3	15.9	15.6	7.8	7.0	8.4	8.0
Unemployed................	0.4	0.3	0.4	0.4	0.6	0.5	0.5	0.5	0.3	0.2	0.3	0.4
Not in labor force	87.5	89.2	88.1	88.4	81.0	84.2	83.6	83.8	91.9	92.7	91.3	91.7

[1] Includes other races, not shown separately. [2] Poverty status based on income in preceding year. [3] Excludes those living in unrelated subfamilies. [4] In group quarters other than institutions. [5] Annual averages of monthly figures. Source: U.S. Bureau of Labor Statistics, *Employment and Earnings*, January issues.

Source: Except as noted, U.S. Bureau of the Census, *Current Population Reports*, P20-468 and earlier reports; P60-181 and earlier reports; and unpublished data.

No. 49. Social and Economic Characteristics of the White and Black Populations: 1980 to 1992

[As of **March, except labor force status,** annual average. Excludes members of Armed Forces except those living off post or with their families on post. Based on Current Population Survey; see text, section 1, and Appendix III]

CHARACTERISTIC	NUMBER (1,000)									PERCENT DISTRIBU- TION, 1992	
	All races [1]			White			Black				
	1980	1990	1992	1980	1990	1992	1980	1990	1992	White	Black
Total persons	223,160	246,191	251,447	191,905	206,983	210,257	26,033	30,392	31,439	100.0	100.0
Under 5 years old	16,319	18,932	19,566	13,307	15,161	15,487	2,444	2,932	3,172	7.4	10.1
5 to 14 years old	34,979	35,467	36,625	28,828	28,405	29,199	5,190	5,546	5,725	13.9	18.2
15 to 44 years old	103,493	115,690	116,491	88,570	96,656	96,735	12,247	14,660	14,983	46.0	47.7
45 to 64 years old	44,174	46,536	48,175	39,302	40,282	41,538	4,112	4,766	4,953	19.8	15.8
65 years old and over	24,194	29,566	30,590	21,898	26,479	27,297	2,040	2,487	2,606	13.0	8.3
YEARS OF SCHOOL COMPLETED											
Persons 25 years old and over	130,409	156,538	160,838	114,763	134,687	137,657	12,927	16,751	17,445	100.0	100.0
Elementary: 0 to 8 years.	22,817	17,591	15,439	18,739	14,131	12,426	3,559	2,701	2,317	9.0	13.3
High school: 1 to 3 years	18,086	17,461	17,672	15,064	14,080	13,911	2,748	2,969	3,324	10.1	19.1
4 years	47,934	60,119	57,864	43,149	52,449	50,049	3,980	6,239	6,220	36.4	35.7
College: 1 to 3 years	19,379	28,075	35,523	17,350	24,350	30,915	1,618	2,952	3,502	22.5	20.1
4 years or more	22,193	33,291	34,340	20,460	29,677	30,356	1,024	1,890	2,080	22.1	11.9
LABOR FORCE STATUS [2]											
Civilians 16 years old and over	167,745	188,049	191,576	146,122	160,415	162,658	17,824	21,300	21,958	100.0	100.0
Civilian labor force.	106,940	124,787	126,982	93,600	107,177	108,526	10,865	13,493	13,891	66.7	63.3
Employed	99,303	117,914	117,598	87,715	102,087	101,479	9,313	11,966	11,933	62.4	54.3
Unemployed	7,637	6,874	9,384	5,884	5,091	7,047	1,553	1,527	1,958	4.3	8.9
Unemployment rate [3]	7.1	5.5	7.4	6.3	4.7	6.5	14.3	11.3	14.1	(X)	(X)
Not in labor force	60,806	63,262	64,593	52,523	53,237	54,132	6,959	7,808	8,067	33.3	36.7
FAMILY TYPE											
Total families	59,550	66,090	67,173	52,243	56,590	57,224	6,184	7,470	7,716	100.0	100.0
With own children [4]	31,022	32,289	32,738	26,474	26,718	27,038	3,820	4,378	4,444	47.2	57.6
Married couple	49,112	52,317	52,457	44,751	46,981	47,124	3,433	3,750	3,631	82.3	47.1
With own children [4]	24,961	24,537	24,416	22,415	21,579	21,513	1,927	1,972	1,926	37.6	25.0
Female householder, no spouse present.	8,705	10,890	11,693	6,052	7,306	7,726	2,495	3,275	3,582	13.5	46.4
With own children [4]	5,445	6,599	7,042	3,558	4,199	4,488	1,793	2,232	2,334	7.8	30.2
Male householder, no spouse present	1,733	2,884	3,025	1,441	2,303	2,374	256	446	504	4.1	6.5
With own children [4]	616	1,153	1,280	500	939	1,037	99	173	184	1.8	2.4
FAMILY INCOME IN PREVIOUS YEAR IN CONSTANT (1991) DOLLARS											
Total families	59,550	66,090	67,173	52,243	56,590	57,224	6,184	7,470	7,716	100.0	100.0
Less than $5,000	1,489	2,115	2,442	993	1,302	1,453	439	725	877	2.5	11.4
$5,000 to $9,999.	3,335	3,701	4,079	2,299	2,547	2,759	934	1,023	1,156	4.8	15.0
$10,000 to $14,999	4,407	4,758	4,844	3,500	3,678	3,808	853	941	859	6.7	11.1
$15,000 to $24,999	10,004	10,046	10,745	8,463	8,375	9,006	1,330	1,412	1,416	15.7	18.4
$25,000 to $34,999	9,707	9,980	10,502	8,725	8,715	9,073	866	1,023	1,115	15.9	14.5
$35,000 to $49,999	13,518	13,152	13,116	12,329	11,714	11,624	952	1,091	1,143	20.3	14.8
$50,000 or more	17,091	22,338	21,445	15,934	20,259	19,502	810	1,255	1,148	34.1	14.9
Median income (dol.) [5]	36,051	37,579	35,939	37,619	39,514	37,783	21,302	22,197	21,548	(X)	(X)
POVERTY [6]											
Families below poverty level . . .	5,461	6,784	7,712	3,581	4,409	5,022	1,722	2,077	2,343	8.8	30.4
Persons below poverty level . . .	26,072	31,528	35,708	17,214	20,785	23,747	8,050	9,302	10,242	11.3	32.7
HOUSING TENURE											
Total occupied units	80,776	93,347	95,669	70,766	80,163	81,675	8,586	10,486	11,083	100.0	100.0
Owner-occupied	54,891	59,846	61,310	49,913	54,094	55,117	4,173	4,445	4,683	67.5	42.3
Renter-occupied	24,421	31,895	32,705	19,581	24,685	25,167	4,257	5,862	6,183	30.8	55.8
No cash rent	1,464	1,606	1,654	1,272	1,384	1,391	156	178	217	1.7	2.0

X Not applicable. [1] Includes other races not shown separately. [2] Source: U.S. Bureau of Labor Statistics, *Employment and Earnings*, January issues. [3] Total unemployment as percent of civilian labor force. [4] Children under 18 years old. [5] For definition of median, see Guide to Tabular Presentation. [6] For explanation of poverty level, see text, section 14.

Source: Except as noted, U.S. Bureau of the Census, *Current Population Reports*, P20-448 and P20-464; P60-180 and P60-181; and unpublished data.

No. 50. Social and Economic Characteristics of the Asian and Pacific Islander Population: 1990 and 1992

[As of **March**. Excludes members of Armed Forces except those living off post or with their families on post. Based on Current Population Survey; see text, section 1 and Appendix III]

CHARACTERISTIC	NUMBER (1,000)		PERCENT DISTRIBUTION	
	1990	1992	1990	1992
Total persons	**6,679**	**7,193**	**100.0**	**100.0**
Under 5 years old	602	589	9.0	8.2
5 to 14 years old	1,112	1,133	16.6	15.8
15 to 44 years old	3,345	3,609	50.1	50.2
45 to 64 years old	1,155	1,306	17.3	18.2
65 years old and over	465	555	7.0	7.7
YEARS OF SCHOOL COMPLETED				
Persons 25 years old and over	**3,961**	**4,409**	**100.0**	**100.0**
Elementary: 0 to 8 years	543	489	13.7	11.1
High school: 1 to 3 years	234	229	5.9	5.2
4 years	1,038	1,171	26.2	26.6
College: 1 to 3 years	568	784	14.3	17.8
4 years or more	1,578	1,737	39.9	39.4
LABOR FORCE STATUS				
Civilians 16 years old and over	**4,849**	**5,342**	**100.0**	**100.0**
Civilian labor force	3,216	3,473	66.3	65.0
Employed	3,079	3,255	63.5	60.9
Unemployed	136	218	2.8	4.1
Unemployment rate [1]	4.2	6.3	(X)	(X)
Not in labor force	1,634	1,869	33.7	35.0
FAMILY TYPE				
Total families	**1,531**	**1,624**	**100.0**	**100.0**
Married couple	1,256	1,284	82.1	79.1
Female householder, no spouse present	188	237	12.3	14.6
Male householder, no spouse present	86	103	5.6	6.3
FAMILY INCOME IN PREVIOUS YEAR IN CONSTANT (1991) DOLLARS				
Total families	**1,531**	**1,624**	**100.0**	**100.0**
Less than $5,000	(NA)	69	(NA)	4.2
$5,000 to $9,999	(NA)	95	(NA)	5.9
$10,000 to $14,999	(NA)	108	(NA)	6.7
$15,000 to $24,999	(NA)	212	(NA)	13.0
$25,000 to $34,999	(NA)	219	(NA)	13.5
$35,000 to $49,999	(NA)	269	(NA)	16.6
$50,000 or more	(NA)	652	(NA)	40.1
Median income (dol.) [2]	44,320	42,661	(X)	(X)
POVERTY [3]				
Families below poverty level	182	210	11.9	13.0
Persons below poverty level	939	996	14.1	13.8
HOUSING TENURE				
Total occupied units	**1,988**	**2,094**	**100.0**	**100.0**
Owner-occupied	977	1,068	49.1	51.0
Renter-occupied	982	997	49.4	47.6
No cash rent	30	28	1.5	1.3

NA Not available.   X Not applicable.   [1] Total unemployment as percent of civilian labor force.   [2] For definition of median, see Guide to Tabular Presentation.   [3] For explanation of poverty level, see text, section 14.

Source: U.S. Bureau of the Census, *Current Population Reports*, P20-459; and unpublished data.

No. 51. American Indian, Eskimo, and Aleut Population—Population Living Inside and Outside Identified Areas, and Households, by Type: 1990

[In thousands. As of April 1. Households are based on race of householder]

IDENTIFIED AREA AND HOUSEHOLD TYPE	Total [1]	Oklahoma	California	Arizona	New Mexico	Alaska	Washington
Total population..............	1,959	252	242	204	134	86	81
Inside identified areas..............	739	207	14	142	88	48	22
American Indian areas..............	692	207	14	142	88	1	22
Reservations [2]..............	411	6	13	142	68	1	21
Trust lands [3]..............	26	(X)	(Z)	(Z)	19	(X)	1
Tribal Jurisdiction Statistical Areas [4]..	201	201	(X)	(X)	(X)	(X)	(X)
Tribal Designated Statistical Areas [5].	54	(X)	(X)	(X)	(X)	(X)	(X)
Alaska Native Village Statistical Areas [6].	47	(X)	(X)	(X)	(X)	47	(X)
Outside identified areas..............	1,220	45	229	61	47	37	60
Total households	591	78	79	50	33	22	25
Family households..............	442	59	56	41	28	16	18
Married couple family..............	284	43	37	24	16	10	11
With related children..............	179	25	21	18	13	7	6
With no related children..............	104	18	15	6	4	2	4
Male householder, no spouse present...	37	3	5	4	3	2	2
With related children..............	25	2	3	3	2	1	1
With no related children..............	12	1	2	1	1	1	(Z)
Female householder, no spouse present.	121	13	15	13	8	5	6
With related children..............	94	9	11	10	6	4	5
With no related children..............	27	3	4	3	2	1	1
Nonfamily households..............	149	19	23	9	6	6	7
One person households..............	116	16	16	7	5	5	5
Two or more person households.....	33	2	7	2	1	1	2

X Not applicable. Area not located within this State.   Z Fewer than 500.   [1] Includes other States not shown separately. [2] Federal American Indian reservations are areas with boundaries established by treaty, statute, and/or executive or court order, and recognized by the Federal Government as territory in which American Indian tribes have jurisdiction. State reservations are lands held in trust by State governments for the use and benefit of a given tribe. [3] Property associated with a particular American Indian reservation or tribe, held in trust by the Federal Government. These lands are located outside of a reservation boundary. [4] Areas delineated by federally-recognized tribes in Oklahoma without a reservation, for which the Census Bureau tabulates data. [5] Areas delineated outside Oklahoma by federally- and State- recognized tribes without a land base or associated trust lands, to provide statistical areas for which the Census Bureau tabulates data. [6] Alaska Native villages constitute tribes, bands, clans, groups, villages, communities, or associations in Alaska that are recognized pursuant to the Alaska Native Claims Settlement Act of 1972.

Source: U.S. Bureau of the Census, *1990 Census of Population, General Population Characteristics, American Indian and Alaska Native Areas* (CP-1-1A); and unpublished data.

No. 52. Population Living on Selected Reservations and Trust Lands, and American Indian Tribes with 10,000 or More American Indians: 1990

[As of April]

RESERVATION AND TRUST LANDS WITH 5,000 OR MORE AMERICAN INDIANS, ESKIMOS, AND ALEUTS	Total population	AMERICAN INDIANS, ESKIMOS, ALEUTS		AMERICAN INDIAN TRIBE	Number	Percent distribution
		Number	Percent of total			
All reservation and trust lands	808,163	437,431	54.1	American Indian population, total [1]..............	1,878,285	100.0
Navajo and Trust Lands, AZ-NM-UT.............	148,451	143,405	96.6	Cherokee..............	308,132	16.4
Pine Ridge and Trust Lands, NE-SD	12,215	11,182	91.5	Navajo	219,198	11.7
Fort Apache, AZ	10,394	9,825	94.5	Chippewa	103,826	5.5
Gila River, AZ	9,540	9,116	95.6	Sioux [2]	103,255	5.5
Papago, AZ.	8,730	8,480	97.1	Choctaw	82,299	4.4
Rosebud and Trust Lands, SD.................	9,696	8,043	83.0	Pueblo	52,939	2.8
San Carlos, AZ	7,294	7,110	97.5	Apache [3]..............	50,051	2.7
				Iroquois [3]..............	49,038	2.6
Zuni Pueblo, AZ-NM......	7,412	7,073	95.4	Lumbee..............	48,444	2.6
Hopi and Trust Lands, AZ ...	7,360	7,061	95.9	Creek	43,550	2.3
Blackfeet, MT	8,549	7,025	82.2	Blackfoot	32,234	1.7
Turtle Mountain and Trust Lands, ND-SD	7,106	6,772	95.3	Canadian and Latin American.	22,379	1.2
Yakima and Trust Lands, WA.	27,668	6,307	22.8	Chickasaw [3]..............	20,631	1.1
				Potawatomi [3]..............	16,763	0.9
Osage, OK [4]	41,645	6,161	14.8	Tohono o'Odham	16,041	0.9
Fort Peck, MT............	10,595	5,782	54.6	Pima	14,431	0.8
Wind River, WY	21,851	5,676	26.0	Tlingit	13,925	0.7
Eastern Cherokee, NC	6,527	5,388	82.5	Seminole	13,797	0.7
Flathead, MT.............	21,259	5,130	24.1	Alaskan Athabaskans......	13,738	0.7
Cheyenne River, SD	7,743	5,100	65.9	Cheyenne	11,456	0.6
				Comanche	11,322	0.6
				Paiute	11,142	0.6
				Puget Sound Salish	10,246	0.5

[1] Includes other American Indian tribes, not shown separately. [2] Any entry with the spelling "Siouan" was miscoded to Sioux in North Carolina. [3] Reporting and/or processing problems have affected the data for this tribe. [4] The Osage Reservation is coextensive with Osage County. Data shown for the reservation are for the entire reservation.

Source: U.S. Bureau of the Census, *1990 Census of Population, General Population Characteristics, American Indian and Alaska Native Areas* (CP-1-1A), and press release CB92-244.

No. 53. Social and Economic Characteristics of the Hispanic Population: 1991

[As of March, except labor force status, annual average. Excludes members of the Armed Forces except those living off post or with their families on post. Based on Current Population Survey; see text, section 1, and Appendix III]

CHARACTERISTIC	NUMBER (1,000)						PERCENT DISTRIBUTION					
	His-panic, total	Mexi-can	Puer-to Rican	Cuban	Central and South American	Other His-panic	His-panic, total	Mexi-can	Puer-to Rican	Cuban	Central and South American	Other His-panic
Total persons	**21,437**	**13,421**	**2,382**	**1,055**	**2,951**	**1,628**	**100.0**	**100.0**	**100.0**	**100.0**	**100.0**	**100.0**
Under 5 years old	2,370	1,592	262	59	318	139	11.1	11.9	11.0	5.6	10.8	8.5
5 to 14 years old	4,006	2,698	478	91	497	242	18.7	20.1	20.1	8.6	16.8	14.9
15 to 44 years old	10,993	6,936	1,178	463	1,612	806	51.3	51.7	49.5	43.9	54.6	49.5
45 to 64 years old	2,976	1,608	352	287	435	295	13.9	12.0	14.8	27.2	14.7	18.1
65 years old and over	1,091	587	112	156	89	146	5.1	4.4	4.7	14.8	3.0	9.0
YEARS OF SCHOOL COMPLETED												
Persons 25 years old and over	**11,208**	**6,518**	**1,261**	**784**	**1,658**	**986**	**100.0**	**100.0**	**100.0**	**100.0**	**100.0**	**100.0**
Elementary: 0 to 8 years	3,761	2,609	306	223	456	166	33.6	40.0	24.3	28.4	27.5	16.8
High school: 1 to 3 years	1,695	1,067	224	83	201	119	15.1	16.4	17.8	10.6	12.1	12.1
4 years	3,285	1,747	416	220	533	370	29.3	26.8	33.0	28.1	32.1	37.5
College: 1 to 3 years	1,379	690	188	113	217	171	12.3	10.6	14.9	14.4	13.1	17.3
4 years or more	1,089	405	127	145	251	160	9.7	6.2	10.1	18.5	15.1	16.2
LABOR FORCE STATUS [1]												
Civilians 16 years old and over	**14,770**	**8,947**	**1,629**	**849**	**(NA)**	**(NA)**	**100.0**	**100.0**	**100.0**	**100.0**	**(NA)**	**(NA)**
Civilian labor force	9,762	5,984	930	543	(NA)	(NA)	66.1	66.9	57.1	64.0	(NA)	(NA)
Employed	8,799	5,363	822	499	(NA)	(NA)	59.6	59.9	50.5	58.8	(NA)	(NA)
Unemployed	963	621	108	44	(NA)	(NA)	6.5	6.9	6.6	5.2	(NA)	(NA)
Unemployment rate [2]	9.9	10.4	11.6	8.1	(NA)	(NA)	(X)	(X)	(X)	(X)	(NA)	(NA)
Not in labor force	5,008	2,963	699	306	(NA)	(NA)	33.9	33.1	42.9	36.0	(NA)	(NA)
FAMILY TYPE												
Total families	**4,982**	**2,945**	**626**	**335**	**667**	**408**	**100.0**	**100.0**	**100.0**	**100.0**	**100.0**	**100.0**
Married couple	3,454	2,164	328	255	441	266	69.3	73.5	52.4	76.1	66.1	65.1
Female householder, no spouse present	1,186	563	271	65	174	112	23.8	19.1	43.3	19.4	26.1	27.5
Male householder, no spouse present	342	218	27	15	52	30	6.9	7.4	4.3	4.5	7.8	7.3
FAMILY INCOME IN 1990												
Total families	**4,982**	**2,945**	**626**	**335**	**667**	**408**	**100.0**	**100.0**	**100.0**	**100.0**	**100.0**	**100.0**
Less than $5,000	312	167	69	19	35	22	6.3	5.7	11.0	5.7	5.2	5.4
$5,000 to $9,999	614	340	142	27	61	44	12.3	11.5	22.7	8.1	9.1	10.8
$10,000 to $14,999	629	402	63	30	92	41	12.6	13.7	10.1	9.0	13.8	10.0
$15,000 to $24,999	1,082	659	118	59	170	76	21.7	22.4	18.8	17.6	25.4	18.6
$25,000 to $34,999	826	520	71	66	105	64	16.6	17.7	11.3	19.7	15.7	15.7
$35,000 to $49,999	784	498	76	54	92	65	15.7	16.9	12.1	16.1	13.8	15.9
$50,000 or more	734	359	88	80	111	96	14.7	12.2	14.1	23.9	16.6	23.5
Median income (dol.) [3]	23,431	23,240	18,008	31,439	23,445	27,382	(X)	(X)	(X)	(X)	(X)	(X)
Families below poverty level [4]	1,244	736	235	46	148	79	25.0	25.0	37.5	13.8	22.2	19.4
Persons below poverty level [4]	6,006	3,764	966	178	748	350	28.1	28.1	40.6	16.9	25.4	21.5
HOUSING TENURE												
Total occupied units	**6,220**	**3,604**	**805**	**425**	**809**	**576**	**100.0**	**100.0**	**100.0**	**100.0**	**100.0**	**100.0**
Owner-occupied	2,423	1,568	188	201	180	286	39.0	43.5	23.4	47.3	22.2	49.6
Renter-occupied [5]	3,797	2,036	617	224	630	290	61.0	56.5	76.6	52.5	77.8	50.3

NA Not available.   X Not applicable.   [1] Source: U.S. Bureau of Labor Statistics, *Employment and Earnings*, January 1992. [2] Total unemployment as percent of civilian labor force.   [3] For definition of median, see Guide to Tabular Presentation.   [4] For explanation of poverty level, see text, section 14.   [5] Includes no cash rent.

Source: Except as noted, U.S. Bureau of the Census, *Current Population Reports*, P60-174 and P20-455.

No. 54. Native and Foreign-Born Population, by Place of Birth: 1920 to 1990

[In thousands, except percent. Beginning 1950, data are based on a sample from the census; for details, see text, section 1. See source for sampling variability. See also *Historical Statistics, Colonial Times to 1970*, series C 1-10]

YEAR	Total population	NATIVE POPULATION							FOREIGN-BORN	
		Total	Born in State of residence	Born in other States		State of birth not reported	Born in outlying areas	Born abroad or at sea of American parents	Number	Percent of total population
				Number	Percent of native population					
1920	106,022	[2]92,001	71,071	20,274	22.1	314	38	93	14,020	13.2
1930	123,203	[2]108,919	82,678	25,388	23.4	238	136	131	14,283	11.6
1940	132,165	[2]120,508	92,610	26,906	22.4	280	157	122	11,657	8.8
1950	150,845	[2]140,413	102,788	35,284	25.2	1,370	330	96	10,431	6.9
1960	179,326	169,588	119,293	44,691	26.4	4,541	660	402	9,738	5.4
1970	203,210	193,591	131,718	50,639	26.2	8,973	891	1,370	9,619	4.7
1980	226,546	212,466	144,871	65,452	30.8	(³)	1,088	1,055	14,080	6.2
1990	248,710	228,943	153,685	72,011	31.5	(³)	1,382	1,864	19,767	7.9

[1] 1920-50, includes Alaska and Hawaii. Includes Puerto Rico.   [2] Includes some persons born abroad of American parents, not shown separately.   [3] Place of birth was allocated to those who did not report.

No. 55. Foreign-Born Population, by Place of Birth: 1980 and 1990

[As of **April 1**. Based on a sample and subject to sampling variability, see text, section 1]

PLACE OF BIRTH	1980 (1,000)	1990		PLACE OF BIRTH	1980 (1,000)	1990	
		Number (1,000)	Percent distribution			Number (1,000)	Percent distribution
Total [1]	**14,080**	**19,767**	**100.0**	Thailand.	55	107	0.5
				Turkey.	52	55	0.3
Europe [2].	**4,743**	**4,017**	**20.3**	Vietnam	231	543	2.7
Austria.	146	88	0.4	**Canada**	**843**	**745**	**3.8**
Belgium	36	34	0.2	**Mexico**.	**2,199**	**4,298**	**21.7**
Czechoslovakia	113	87	0.4	**Caribbean** [2]	**1,258**	**1,938**	**9.8**
Denmark	43	35	0.2	Antigua-Barbuda	4	12	0.1
Finland	29	22	0.1	Bahamas	14	22	0.1
France.	120	119	0.6	Barbados	27	43	0.2
Germany	849	712	3.6	Cuba	608	737	3.7
Greece	211	177	0.9	Dominican Republic . .	169	348	1.8
Hungary	144	110	0.6	Grenada.	7	18	0.1
Ireland.	198	170	0.9	Haiti	92	225	1.1
Italy.	832	581	2.9	Jamaica	197	334	1.7
Latvia	34	26	0.1	Trinidad and Tobago .	66	116	0.6
Lithuania	48	30	0.2	**Central America** [2]	**354**	**1,134**	**5.7**
Netherlands	103	96	0.5	Belize	14	30	0.2
Norway	63	42	0.2	Costa Rica	30	44	0.2
Poland.	418	388	2.0	El Salvador.	94	465	2.4
Portugal	212	210	1.1	Guatemala	63	226	1.1
Romania	67	91	0.5	Honduras	39	109	0.6
Spain.	74	76	0.4	Nicaragua	44	169	0.9
Sweden	77	54	0.3	Panama	61	86	0.4
Switzerland	43	39	0.2	**South America** [2]	**561**	**1,037**	**5.2**
United Kingdom.	669	640	3.2	Argentina	69	93	0.5
Yugoslavia	153	142	0.7	Bolivia	14	31	0.2
Soviet Union [3]	**406**	**334**	**1.7**	Brazil.	41	82	0.4
Asia [2].	**2,540**	**4,979**	**25.2**	Chile	35	56	0.3
Afghanistan	4	28	0.1	Colombia	144	286	1.4
Burma	11	20	0.1	Ecuador	86	143	0.7
Cambodia.	20	119	0.6	Guyana	49	121	0.6
China.	286	530	2.7	Peru	55	144	0.7
Hong Kong.	80	147	0.7	Uruguay	13	21	0.1
India	206	450	2.3	Venezuela	33	42	0.2
Indonesia	30	48	0.2	**Africa** [2]	**200**	**364**	**1.8**
Iran.	122	211	1.1	Cape Verde	10	14	0.1
Iraq.	32	45	0.2	Egypt.	43	66	0.3
Israel	67	86	0.4	Ethiopia	8	35	0.2
Japan	222	290	1.5	Ghana	8	21	0.1
Jordan	22	32	0.2	Kenya	6	14	0.1
Korea	290	568	2.9	Morocco	10	16	0.1
Laos	55	172	0.9	Nigeria	26	55	0.3
Lebanon	53	86	0.4	South Africa	16	35	0.2
Malaysia	10	34	0.2	**Oceania** [2]	**78**	**104**	**0.5**
Pakistan.	31	92	0.5	Australia.	36	42	0.2
Philippines	501	913	4.6	Fiji	8	16	0.1
Saudi Arabia.	17	13	0.1	New Zealand	11	15	0.1
Syria	22	37	0.2	Tonga	6	11	0.1
Taiwan.	75	244	1.2	Western Samoa. . . .	13	11	0.1

[1] Includes persons whose place of birth was not reported.   [2] Includes other areas not shown separately.   [3] The former Soviet Union is now referred to as the following geopolitical entities: Armenia, Azerbaijan, Byelarus, Georgia, Kazakhstan, Kyrgyzstan, Moldova, Russia, Tajikistan, Turkmenistan, Ukraine, and Uzbekistan.
Source of tables 54 and 55: U.S. Bureau of the Census, *U.S. Census of Population: 1960*, vol. II, part 2A; *1970*, vol. I, parts C and D; *1980 Census of Population*, vol.1, chapter C (PC80-1-C) and chapter D (PC80-1-D); and *1990 Census of Population and Housing Data Paper Listing* (CPH-L-98).

No. 56. Population, by Selected Ancestry Group and Region: 1990

[As of April 1. Covers persons who reported single and multiple ancestry groups. Persons who reported a multiple ancestry group may be included in more than one category. Major classifications of ancestry groups do not represent strict geographic or cultural definitions. Based on a sample and subject to sampling variability; see text, section 1]

ANCESTRY GROUP	Total (1,000)	PERCENT DISTRIBUTION, BY REGION				ANCESTRY GROUP	Total (1,000)	PERCENT DISTRIBUTION, BY REGION			
		North-east	Mid-west	South	West			North-east	Mid-west	South	West
European: [1]						Central and					
Austrian	865	38	21	19	22	South America:					
British.	1,119	17	18	39	26	Cuban.	860	18	3	69	9
Croatian	544	21	43	20	16	Dominican. . . .	506	86	1	10	2
Czech.	1,296	10	52	22	16	Hispanic	1,113	13	6	31	50
Danish	1,635	9	34	12	45	Mexican	11,587	1	9	33	57
Dutch	6,227	16	34	29	21	Puerto Rican . .	1,955	66	11	15	8
English	32,652	18	22	35	25	Salvadoran . . .	499	13	2	23	62
European	467	14	17	31	39	Spanish	2,024	16	8	30	45
Finnish	659	14	47	11	27						
French	10,321	26	26	29	20	West Indian: [1]					
German	57,947	17	39	25	19	Jamaican	435	59	5	31	6
Greek.	1,110	37	23	21	19						
Hungarian	1,582	36	32	17	16	Asia:					
Irish	38,736	24	25	33	17	Asian Indian. . .	570	32	19	26	24
Italian	14,665	51	17	17	15	Chinese	1,505	25	8	12	55
Lithuanian	812	43	28	16	13	Filipino	1,451	10	9	13	68
Norwegian. . . .	3,869	6	52	10	33	Japanese	1,005	9	8	11	72
Polish	9,366	37	37	15	11	Korean	837	22	14	20	44
Portuguese . . .	1,153	49	3	8	41	Vietnamese . . .	536	9	8	28	54
Russian	2,953	44	16	18	22						
Scandinavian . .	679	8	33	15	45	North America:					
Scotch-Irish . . .	5,618	14	19	47	20	Acadian	668	1	2	91	5
Scottish	5,394	20	21	33	26	Afro-American .	23,777	15	21	54	10
Slovak	1,883	40	34	14	11	American Indian	8,708	9	22	47	23
Swedish	4,681	14	40	14	32	American.	12,396	10	18	61	11
Swiss	1,045	16	36	17	30	Canadian.	550	34	18	21	28
Ukrainian.	741	51	22	14	13	French Canadian	2,167	45	20	20	15
Welsh.	2,034	22	24	27	27	United States. .	644	16	18	53	13
Yugoslavian. . .	258	23	28	12	37	White	1,800	7	13	53	28

[1] Non-Hispanic groups.

Source: U.S. Bureau of the Census, *1990 Census of Population, Supplementary Reports, Detailed Ancestry Groups for States* (1990 CP-S-1-2).

No. 57. Persons Speaking a Language Other Than English at Home, by Age and Language: 1990

[As of April. Based on a sample and subject to sampling variability]

AGE GROUP AND LANGUAGE SPOKEN AT HOME	Persons who speak language (1,000)	Percent who speak English less than "very well"	LANGUAGE	Persons, 5 years old and over who speak language (1,000)
Persons 5 years old and over.	230,446	(X)	Speak only English	198,601
Speak only English.	198,601	(X)	Spanish.	17,339
Speak other language.	31,845	43.9	French	1,702
Speak Spanish or Spanish Creole	17,345	47.9	German	1,547
Speak Asian or Pacific Island language. .	4,472	54.1	Italian	1,309
Speak other language	10,028	32.4	Chinese	1,249
			Tagalog.	843
Persons 5 to 17 years old	45,342	(X)	Polish	723
Speak only English.	39,020	(X)	Korean	626
Speak other language.	6,323	37.8	Vietnamese	507
Speak Spanish or Spanish Creole	4,168	39.3	Portuguese	430
Speak Asian or Pacific Island language. .	816	44.2	Japanese.	428
Speak other language	1,340	29.2	Greek	388
			Arabic	355
Persons 18 to 64 years old	153,908	(X)	Hindi (Urdu)	331
Speak only English.	132,200	(X)	Russian	242
Speak other language.	21,708	45.1	Yiddish	213
Speak Spanish or Spanish Creole	12,121	49.6	Thai (Laotian)	206
Speak Asian or Pacific Island language. .	3,301	54.7	Persian	202
Speak other language	6,286	31.4	French Creole	188
			Armenian.	150
Persons 65 years old and over	31,195	(X)	Navaho	149
Speak only English.	27,381	(X)	Hungarian	148
Speak other language.	3,814	47.2	Hebrew	144
Speak Spanish or Spanish Creole	1,057	62.3	Dutch	143
Speak Asian or Pacific Island language. .	355	72.0	Mon-Khmer (Cambodian) . . .	127
Speak other language	2,402	36.9	Gujarathi	102

X Not applicable.

Source: U.S. Bureau of the Census, *1990 Census of Population and Housing Data Paper Listing* (CPH-L-133); and Summary Tape File 3C.

No. 58. Foreign-Born Population, Leading Ancestry Groups, and Persons Speaking A Language Other Than English At Home—States: 1990

[As of **April**. Based on a sample and subject to sampling variability]

REGION, DIVISION, AND STATE	FOREIGN BORN POPULATION Number (1,000)	Percent of total population	Year of entry, 1980-90 (1,000)	ANCESTRY GROUPS Leading ancestry group Group	Number (1,000)	Second leading group Group	Number (1,000)	Third leading group Group	Number (1,000)	PERSON 5 YEARS OLD AND OVER SPEAKING FOREIGN LANGUAGE Number (1,000)	Percent of total population
U.S...	19,767	7.9	8,661	German	57,947	Irish	38,736	English	32,652	31,845	13.8
Northeast.	5,231	10.3	2,059	German	9,929	Irish	9,420	Italian	7,504	7,824	16.5
N.E . .	1,043	7.9	368	Irish	2,949	English	2,330	French	1,591	1,703	13.9
ME . .	36	3.0	7	English	372	French	224	Irish	217	105	9.2
NH . .	41	3.7	10	English	266	Irish	232	French	205	89	8.7
VT . .	18	3.1	3	English	147	French	133	Irish	101	30	5.8
MA . .	574	9.5	223	Irish	1,571	English	921	Italian	844	852	15.2
RI . .	95	9.5	35	Irish	214	Italian	199	English	161	159	17.0
CT . .	279	8.5	90	Italian	628	Irish	614	English	463	466	15.2
M.A .	4,188	11.1	1,691	German	8,622	Irish	6,471	Italian	5,668	6,122	17.5
NY . .	2,852	15.9	1,190	German	2,899	Italian	2,838	Irish	2,800	3,909	23.3
NJ. .	967	12.5	385	Italian	1,457	Irish	1,415	German	1,408	1,406	19.5
PA . .	369	3.1	116	German	4,315	Irish	2,256	Italian	1,373	807	7.3
Midwest. .	2,131	3.6	754	German	22,477	Irish	9,643	English	7,294	3,921	7.1
E.N.C .	1,783	4.2	607	German	14,776	Irish	6,655	English	5,083	3,125	8.0
OH . .	260	2.4	71	German	4,068	Irish	1,896	English	1,449	546	5.4
IN . . .	94	1.7	31	German	2,085	Irish	965	English	767	246	4.8
IL . . .	952	8.3	371	German	3,326	Irish	1,861	Afro American.	1,426	1,499	14.2
MI. . .	355	3.8	94	German	2,666	Irish	1,320	English	1,315	570	6.6
WI. . .	122	2.5	41	German	2,631	Irish	612	Polish	506	264	5.8
W.N.C.	348	2.0	147	German	7,702	Irish	2,988	English	2,211	796	4.9
MN . .	113	2.6	51	German	2,021	Norwegian .	757	Irish	574	227	5.6
IA . .	43	1.6	19	German	1,395	Irish	527	English	389	100	3.9
MO . .	84	1.6	30	German	1,843	Irish	1,038	English	743	178	3.8
ND . .	9	1.5	3	German	325	Norwegian .	189	Irish	54	47	7.9
SD . .	8	1.1	2	German	355	Norwegian .	106	Irish	88	42	6.5
NE . .	28	1.8	10	German	795	Irish	272	English	209	70	4.8
KS . .	63	2.5	31	German	968	Irish	436	English	406	132	5.7
South . .	4,582	5.4	2,027	German	14,630	Irish	12,951	Afro American.	12,936	8,670	10.9
S.A . .	2,723	6.3	1,169	German	7,882	Irish	6,377	English	6,307	3,708	9.1
DE . .	22	3.3	4	Irish	139	German	138	English	123	42	6.9
MD . .	313	6.6	148	German	1,218	Afro American.	966	Irish	769	395	8.9
DC . .	59	9.7	34	Afro American.	315	German	39	Irish	34	71	12.5
VA . .	312	5.0	159	German	1,186	English	1,051	Afro American.	970	419	7.3
WV . .	16	0.9	4	German	469	Irish	348	English	270	44	2.6
NC . .	115	1.7	52	German	1,228	Irish	1,111	English	987	241	3.9
SC . .	50	1.4	18	Afro American.	870	German	500	Irish	486	113	3.5
GA . .	173	2.7	90	Afro American.	1,421	Irish	971	English	890	285	4.8
FL. . .	1,663	12.9	660	German	2,410	Irish	1,899	English	1,846	2,098	17.3
E.S.C . .	157	1.0	65	Irish	2,581	German	2,177	English	1,978	392	2.8
KY . .	34	0.9	14	German	798	Irish	696	American	586	86	2.5
TN . .	59	1.2	26	Irish	875	German	724	English	692	132	2.9
AL . .	44	1.1	18	Irish	839	American	687	Irish	617	108	2.9
MS . .	20	0.8	8	Afro American.	775	American	393	American	317	67	2.8
W.S.C . .	1,702	6.4	793	German	4,572	Irish	3,993	English	3,091	4,569	18.6
AR . .	25	1.1	10	Irish	464	German	400	Afro American.	307	61	2.8
LA. . .	87	2.1	35	Afro American.	1,097	French	550	Irish	518	392	10.1
OK . .	65	2.1	30	German	714	Irish	642	American Indian	469	146	5.0
TX . .	1,524	9.0	718	Mexican	3,403	German	2,950	Irish	2,369	3,970	25.4
West . . .	7,823	14.8	3,821	German	10,911	English	8,110	Irish	6,721	11,430	23.5
Mt . . .	715	5.2	298	German	3,477	English	2,843	Irish	1,921	1,901	15.1
MT . .	14	1.7	3	German	285	Irish	139	German	137	37	5.0
ID . . .	29	2.9	13	English	291	German	279	Irish	142	59	6.4
WY . .	8	1.7	2	German	158	English	101	Irish	73	24	5.7
CO . .	142	4.3	57	German	1,064	English	582	Irish	538	321	10.5
NM . .	81	5.3	31	German	234	Mexican	216	Spanish	191	494	35.5
AZ . .	278	7.6	117	German	878	English	586	Irish	530	700	20.8
UT . .	59	3.4	26	English	750	German	299	Danish	163	120	7.8
NV . .	105	8.7	48	German	280	English	207	Irish	200	146	13.2
Pac . . .	7,108	18.2	3,523	German	7,433	English	5,267	Irish	4,800	9,529	26.4
WA . .	322	6.6	129	German	1,390	English	897	Irish	768	403	9.0
OR . .	139	4.9	61	German	879	English	575	Irish	467	192	7.3
CA . .	6,459	21.7	3,256	Mexican	5,322	German	4,935	English	3,646	8,619	31.5
AK . .	25	8.7	11	German	127	English	77	Irish	74	60	12.1
HI . . .	163	14.7	67	Japanese	262	Filipino	176	Hawaiian	157	255	24.8

Source: U.S. Bureau of the Census, *1990 Census of Population and Housing, Summary Social, Economic, and Housing Characteristics, United States* (1990 CPH-5-1) and *1990 Census of Population, Supplementary Reports, Detailed Ancestry Groups for States* (1990 CP-S-1-2).

No. 59. Marital Status of the Population, by Sex, Race, and Hispanic Origin: 1970 to 1992

[In millions, except percent. As of March, except as noted. Persons 18 years old and over. Excludes members of Armed Forces except those living off post or with their families on post. Except as noted, based on Current Population Survey, see text, section 1 and Appendix III. See *Historical Statistics, Colonial Times to 1970*, series A 160-171, for decennial data]

MARITAL STATUS, RACE, AND HISPANIC ORIGIN	TOTAL				MALE				FEMALE			
	1970	1980	1990	1992	1970	1980	1990	1992	1970	1980	1990	1992
Total [1]	132.5	159.5	181.8	185.3	62.5	75.7	86.9	88.7	70.0	83.8	95.0	96.6
Never married	21.4	32.3	40.4	41.8	11.8	18.0	22.4	23.2	9.6	14.3	17.9	18.6
Married	95.0	104.6	112.6	113.3	47.1	51.8	55.8	56.2	47.9	52.8	56.7	57.1
Widowed	11.8	12.7	13.8	13.9	2.1	2.0	2.3	2.5	9.7	10.8	11.5	11.3
Divorced	4.3	9.9	15.1	16.3	1.6	3.9	6.3	6.8	2.7	6.0	8.8	9.6
Percent of total	100.0	100.0	100.0	100.0	100.0	100.0	100.0	100.0	100.0	100.0	100.0	100.0
Never married	16.2	20.3	22.2	22.6	18.9	23.8	25.8	26.2	13.7	17.1	18.9	19.2
Married	71.7	65.5	61.9	61.1	75.3	68.4	64.3	63.3	68.5	63.0	59.7	59.1
Widowed	8.9	8.0	7.6	7.5	3.3	2.6	2.7	2.9	13.9	12.8	12.1	11.7
Divorced	3.2	6.2	8.3	8.8	2.5	5.2	7.2	7.6	3.9	7.1	9.3	9.9
Percent standardized for age: [2]												
Never married	14.1	16.5	20.6	21.7	16.5	18.7	23.3	24.4	12.1	14.5	18.2	19.2
Married	74.2	69.3	63.7	62.5	77.6	72.9	66.5	64.9	70.8	65.9	61.2	60.2
Widowed	8.3	7.6	6.9	6.7	3.3	2.7	2.7	2.8	13.0	12.1	10.8	10.3
Divorced	3.4	6.6	8.7	9.1	2.6	5.6	7.6	7.9	4.1	7.6	9.8	10.3
White, total	118.2	139.5	155.5	157.6	55.9	66.7	74.8	76.0	62.2	72.8	80.6	81.6
Never married	18.4	26.4	31.6	32.2	10.2	15.0	18.0	18.4	8.2	11.4	13.6	13.8
Married	85.8	93.8	99.5	100.1	42.7	46.7	49.5	50.0	43.1	47.1	49.9	50.3
Widowed	10.3	10.9	11.7	11.7	1.7	1.6	1.9	2.0	8.6	9.3	9.8	9.6
Divorced	3.7	8.3	12.6	13.6	1.3	3.4	5.4	5.8	2.3	5.0	7.3	7.9
Percent of total	100.0	100.0	100.0	100.0	100.0	100.0	100.0	100.0	100.0	100.0	100.0	100.0
Never married	15.6	18.9	20.3	20.5	18.2	22.5	24.1	24.2	13.2	15.7	16.9	16.9
Married	72.6	67.2	64.0	63.5	76.3	70.0	66.2	65.5	69.3	64.7	61.9	61.6
Widowed	8.7	7.8	7.5	7.4	3.1	2.5	2.6	2.7	13.8	12.8	12.2	11.8
Divorced	3.1	6.0	8.1	8.6	2.4	5.0	7.2	7.6	3.8	6.8	9.0	9.6
Black, total	13.0	16.6	20.3	21.0	5.9	7.4	9.1	9.5	7.1	9.2	11.2	11.5
Never married	2.7	5.1	7.1	7.8	1.4	2.5	3.5	3.8	1.2	2.5	3.6	4.0
Married	8.3	8.5	9.3	9.0	3.9	4.1	4.5	4.4	4.4	4.5	4.8	4.7
Widowed	1.4	1.6	1.7	1.8	0.3	0.3	0.3	0.4	1.1	1.3	1.4	1.4
Divorced	0.6	1.4	2.1	2.3	0.2	0.5	0.8	0.9	0.4	0.9	1.3	1.4
Percent of total	100.0	100.0	100.0	100.0	100.0	100.0	100.0	100.0	100.0	100.0	100.0	100.0
Never married	20.6	30.5	35.1	37.4	24.3	34.3	38.4	40.4	17.4	27.4	32.5	35.0
Married	64.1	51.4	45.8	43.0	66.9	54.6	49.2	46.0	61.7	48.7	43.0	40.6
Widowed	11.0	9.8	8.5	8.8	5.2	4.2	3.7	4.5	15.8	14.3	12.4	12.3
Divorced	4.4	8.4	10.6	10.8	3.6	7.0	8.8	9.1	5.0	9.5	12.0	12.2
Hispanic, [3] total	5.1	7.9	13.6	14.4	2.4	3.8	6.7	7.2	2.6	4.1	6.8	7.2
Never married	0.9	1.9	3.7	4.0	0.5	1.0	2.2	2.3	0.4	0.9	1.5	1.7
Married	3.6	5.2	8.4	8.7	1.8	2.5	4.1	4.3	1.8	2.6	4.3	4.4
Widowed	0.3	0.4	0.5	0.6	0.1	0.1	0.1	0.1	0.2	0.3	0.4	0.5
Divorced	0.2	0.5	1.0	1.1	0.1	0.2	0.4	0.4	0.1	0.3	0.6	0.6
Percent of total	100.0	100.0	100.0	100.0	100.0	100.0	100.0	100.0	100.0	100.0	100.0	100.0
Never married	18.6	24.1	27.2	27.9	21.2	27.3	32.1	32.4	16.2	21.1	22.5	23.5
Married	71.8	65.6	61.7	60.3	73.8	67.1	60.9	60.0	70.0	64.3	62.4	60.7
Widowed	5.6	4.4	4.0	4.4	2.3	1.6	1.5	1.7	8.7	7.1	6.5	7.2
Divorced	3.9	5.8	7.0	7.3	2.7	4.0	5.5	5.9	5.1	7.6	8.7	8.7

[1] Includes persons of other races, not shown separately. [2] 1960 age distribution used as standard; standardization improves comparability over time by removing effects of changes in age distribution of population. [3] Hispanic persons may be of any race. 1970 data as of April and based on census.

Source: U.S. Bureau of the Census, *1970 Census of Population*, volume I, part 1, and *Current Population Reports*, P20-468; and earlier reports.

No. 60. Never-Married (Single) Persons as Percent of Total Population, by Sex and Age: 1970 to 1992

[As of March. Persons 18 years old and over. Based on Current Population Survey; see headnote, table 61]

AGE	MALE					FEMALE				
	1970	1980	1985	1990	1992	1970	1980	1985	1990	1992
Total	18.9	23.8	25.2	25.8	26.2	13.7	17.1	18.2	18.9	19.2
18 to 19 years old	92.8	94.3	97.1	96.8	97.7	75.6	82.8	86.7	90.3	90.0
20 to 24 years old	54.7	68.8	75.6	79.3	80.3	35.8	50.2	58.5	62.8	65.7
25 to 29 years old	19.1	33.1	38.7	45.2	48.7	10.5	20.9	26.4	31.1	33.2
30 to 34 years old	9.4	15.9	20.8	27.0	29.4	6.2	9.5	13.5	16.4	18.8
35 to 39 years old	7.2	7.8	10.1	14.7	18.4	5.4	6.2	8.1	10.4	12.6
40 to 44 years old	6.3	7.1	8.6	10.5	9.2	4.9	4.8	5.3	8.0	8.4
45 to 54 years old	7.5	6.1	6.3	6.3	7.3	4.9	4.7	4.6	5.0	5.3
55 to 64 years old	7.8	5.3	6.1	5.8	5.6	6.8	4.5	3.7	3.9	4.0
65 years old and over	7.5	4.9	5.3	4.2	4.2	7.7	5.9	5.1	4.9	4.9
65 to 74 years old	8.0	5.2	5.2	4.7	4.6	7.8	5.6	4.4	4.6	4.4
75 years old and over	6.6	4.2	5.3	3.4	3.5	7.5	6.3	6.2	5.4	5.4

Source: U.S. Bureau of the Census, *Current Population Reports*, P20-468; and earlier reports.

No. 61. Marital Status of the Population, by Sex and Age: 1992

[As of **March. Persons 18 years old and over.** Excludes members of Armed Forces except those living off post or with their families on post. Based on Current Population Survey; see text, section 1 and Appendix III. See *Historical Statistics, Colonial Times to 1970,* series A 160-171, for decennial census data]

SEX AND AGE	NUMBER OF PERSONS (1,000)					PERCENT DISTRIBUTION				
	Total	Single	Married	Widowed	Divorced	Total	Single	Married	Widowed	Divorced
Male	**88,663**	**23,220**	**56,162**	**2,529**	**6,752**	**100.0**	**26.2**	**63.3**	**2.9**	**7.6**
18 to 19 years old	3,283	3,207	76	-	-	100.0	97.7	2.3	-	-
20 to 24 years old	8,800	7,067	1,612	2	119	100.0	80.3	18.3	-	1.4
25 to 29 years old	10,024	4,882	4,644	13	485	100.0	48.7	46.3	0.1	4.8
30 to 34 years old	11,101	3,262	6,991	10	837	100.0	29.4	63.0	0.1	7.5
35 to 39 years old	10,358	1,905	7,331	51	1,071	100.0	18.4	70.8	0.5	10.3
40 to 44 years old	9,148	839	7,117	57	1,134	100.0	9.2	77.8	0.6	12.4
45 to 54 years old	13,114	957	10,424	128	1,606	100.0	7.3	79.5	1.0	12.2
55 to 64 years old	10,036	559	8,249	351	877	100.0	5.6	82.2	3.5	8.7
65 to 74 years old	8,266	383	6,536	841	506	100.0	4.6	79.1	10.2	6.1
75 years old and over	4,533	159	3,180	1,076	118	100.0	3.5	70.2	23.7	2.6
Female	**96,599**	**18,576**	**57,133**	**11,325**	**9,565**	**100.0**	**19.2**	**59.1**	**11.7**	**9.9**
18 to 19 years old	3,303	2,974	308	-	21	100.0	90.0	9.3	-	0.6
20 to 24 years old	9,048	5,940	2,895	11	201	100.0	65.7	32.0	0.1	2.2
25 to 29 years old	10,108	3,356	5,916	26	811	100.0	33.2	58.5	0.3	8.0
30 to 34 years old	11,260	2,122	7,856	83	1,200	100.0	18.8	69.8	0.7	10.7
35 to 39 years old	10,595	1,334	7,808	115	1,337	100.0	12.6	73.7	1.1	12.6
40 to 44 years old	9,470	795	7,032	187	1,456	100.0	8.4	74.3	2.0	15.4
45 to 54 years old	13,910	744	10,238	642	2,285	100.0	5.3	73.6	4.6	16.4
55 to 64 years old	11,114	445	7,739	1,659	1,271	100.0	4.0	69.6	14.9	11.4
65 to 74 years old	10,174	451	5,395	3,648	681	100.0	4.4	53.0	35.9	6.7
75 years old and over	7,616	413	1,947	4,953	301	100.0	5.4	25.6	65.0	4.0

- Represents or rounds to zero.

No. 62. Unmarried Couples, by Selected Characteristics: 1970 to 1992

[In thousands. As of **March.** An "unmarried couple" is two unrelated adults of the opposite sex sharing the same household. See headnote, table 65]

PRESENCE OF CHILDREN AND AGE OF HOUSEHOLDER	1970	1980	1985	1990	1992
Unmarried couples, total	523	1,589	1,983	2,856	3,308
No children under 15 years old	327	1,159	1,380	1,966	2,187
Some children under 15 years old	196	431	603	891	1,121
Under 25 years old	55	411	425	596	661
25 to 44 years old	103	837	1,203	1,775	2,026
45 to 64 years old	186	221	239	358	475
65 years old and over	178	119	116	127	146

No. 63. Married Couples of Same or Mixed Races and Origins: 1970 to 1992

[In thousands. As of **March, except as noted. Persons 15 years old and over.** Persons of Hispanic origin may be of any race. Except as noted, based on Current Population Survey; see headnote, table 65]

RACE AND ORIGIN OF SPOUSES	1970 [1]	1980	1992
Married couples, total	44,598	49,714	53,512
RACE			
Same race couples	43,922	48,264	50,873
White/White	40,578	44,910	47,358
Black/Black	3,344	3,354	3,515
Interracial couples	310	651	1,161
Black/White	65	167	246
Black husband/White wife	41	122	163
White husband/Black wife	24	45	83
White/other race [2]	233	450	883
Black/other race [2]	12	34	32
All other couples [2]	366	799	1,478
HISPANIC ORIGIN			
Hispanic/Hispanic	1,368	1,906	3,297
Hispanic/other origin (not Hispanic)	584	891	1,155
All other couples (not of Hispanic origin)	42,645	46,917	49,060

[1] As of April and based on Census of Population.   [2] Excluding White and Black.

Source of tables 61-63: U.S. Bureau of the Census, *Current Population Reports,* P20-468; and earlier reports.

No. 64. Householder and Marital Status of Population, 15 Years Old and Over: 1992

[In thousands. As of March. See headnote, table 65]

HOUSEHOLDER AND MARITAL STATUS	Total, 15 yrs. and over	MALE Total [1]	20 to 24 years	25 to 44 years	45 to 64 years	65 yr. and over	FEMALE Total [1]	20 to 24 years	25 to 44 years	45 to 64 years	65 yr. and over
Total persons	**195,243**	**93,760**	**8,800**	**40,631**	**23,150**	**12,799**	**101,483**	**9,048**	**41,433**	**25,024**	**17,790**
Householder	95,669	63,698	2,512	29,512	20,174	11,325	31,971	1,922	12,270	7,934	9,596
Never married	14,461	7,130	1,266	4,434	919	383	7,330	1,400	4,265	820	640
Married, spouse present	52,457	48,246	1,150	21,895	16,419	8,736	4,211	252	2,315	1,168	453
Married, spouse absent	4,571	1,694	35	866	581	210	2,877	157	1,653	850	203
Widowed	11,895	2,033	2	89	387	1,554	9,863	6	361	2,053	7,443
Divorced	12,286	4,596	58	2,229	1,867	442	7,690	108	3,675	3,044	858
Not householder	99,574	30,062	6,288	11,118	2,976	1,475	69,512	7,125	29,164	17,090	8,194
Never married	37,230	21,172	5,801	6,454	598	158	16,059	4,541	3,343	369	225
Married, spouse present	54,568	5,266	340	2,720	1,461	712	49,301	2,341	24,222	15,799	6,636
Married, spouse absent	1,783	972	87	604	212	60	811	145	422	160	49
Widowed	1,958	496	-	41	91	364	1,462	5	51	249	1,158
Divorced	4,035	2,156	60	1,299	615	182	1,879	93	1,129	512	124

- Represents or rounds to zero.   [1] Includes 15 to 19 year olds.

Source: U.S. Bureau of the Census, *Current Population Reports*, P20-468.

No. 65. Households, Families, Subfamilies, Married Couples, and Unrelated Individuals: 1960 to 1992

[In thousands, except as indicated. As of March. Based on Current Population Survey; includes members of Armed Forces living off post or with their families on post, but excludes all other members of Armed Forces; see text, section 1 and Appendix III. For definition of terms, see text, section 1. Minus sign (-) indicates decrease. See also *Historical Statistics, Colonial Times to 1970*, series A 288-319]

TYPE OF UNIT	1960	1970	1975	1980	1985	1990	1991	1992	PERCENT CHANGE 1970-80	1980-90	1990-92
Households	**52,799**	**63,401**	**71,120**	**80,776**	**86,789**	**93,347**	**94,312**	**95,669**	**27**	**16**	**3**
Average size	3.33	3.14	2.94	2.76	2.69	2.63	2.63	2.62	(X)	(X)	(X)
Family households	44,905	51,456	55,563	59,550	62,706	66,090	66,322	67,173	16	11	2
Married couple	39,254	44,728	46,951	49,112	50,350	52,317	52,147	52,457	10	7	-
Male householder [1]	1,228	1,228	1,485	1,733	2,228	2,884	2,907	3,025	41	66	5
Female householder [1]	4,422	5,500	7,127	8,705	10,129	10,890	11,268	11,692	58	25	7
Nonfamily households	7,895	11,945	15,557	21,226	24,082	27,257	27,990	28,496	78	28	5
Male householder	2,716	4,063	5,912	8,807	10,114	11,606	12,150	12,428	117	32	7
Female householder	5,179	7,882	9,645	12,419	13,968	15,651	15,840	16,068	58	26	3
One person	6,896	10,851	13,939	18,296	20,602	22,999	23,590	23,974	69	26	4
Families	**45,111**	**51,586**	**55,712**	**59,550**	**62,706**	**66,090**	**66,322**	**67,173**	**15**	**11**	**2**
Average size	3.67	3.58	3.42	3.29	3.23	3.17	3.18	3.17	(X)	(X)	(X)
Married couple	39,329	44,755	46,971	49,112	50,350	52,317	52,147	52,457	10	7	-
Male householder [1]	1,275	1,239	1,499	1,733	2,228	2,884	2,907	3,025	40	66	5
Female householder [1]	4,507	5,591	7,242	8,705	10,129	10,890	11,268	11,692	56	25	7
Unrelated subfamilies	207	130	149	360	526	534	639	669	177	48	25
Married couple	75	27	20	20	46	68	94	92	(B)	(B)	(B)
Male reference persons [1]	47	11	14	36	85	45	41	55	(B)	(B)	(B)
Female reference persons [1]	85	91	115	304	395	421	504	523	234	39	24
Related subfamilies	1,514	1,150	1,349	1,150	2,228	2,403	2,546	2,559	-	109	7
Married couple	871	617	576	582	719	871	986	963	-6	50	11
Father-child [1]	115	48	69	54	116	153	142	134	(B)	(B)	-12
Mother-child [1]	528	484	705	512	1,392	1,378	1,418	1,462	6	169	6
Married couples	**40,200**	**45,373**	**47,547**	**49,714**	**51,114**	**53,256**	**53,227**	**53,512**	**10**	**7**	**1**
With own household	39,254	44,728	46,951	49,112	50,350	52,317	52,147	52,457	10	7	1
Without own household	946	645	596	602	764	939	1,080	1,055	-7	56	12
Percent without	2.4	1.4	1.3	1.2	1.5	1.8	2.0	2.0	(X)	(X)	(X)
Unrelated individuals	**11,092**	**14,988**	**19,100**	**26,426**	**30,518**	**35,384**	**36,298**	**37,094**	**76**	**34**	**5**
Nonfamily householders	7,895	11,945	15,557	21,226	24,082	27,257	27,990	28,496	78	28	5
Secondary individuals	3,198	3,043	3,543	5,200	6,436	8,127	8,308	8,598	71	56	6
Male	1,746	1,631	2,087	3,006	3,743	4,711	4,880	5,076	84	57	8
Female	1,451	1,412	1,456	2,194	2,693	3,416	3,428	3,522	55	56	3

- Represents or rounds to zero.   B Not shown; base less than 75,000.   X Not applicable.   [1] No spouse present.

Source: U.S. Bureau of the Census, *Current Population Reports*, P20-467.

No. 66. Family and Nonfamily Households, by Race, Hispanic Origin, and Type: 1970 to 1992

[As of **March**, except as noted. Based on Current Population Survey, except as noted; see headnote, table 65. See also *Historical Statistics, Colonial Times to 1970*, series A 292-295 and A 320-334]

RACE, HISPANIC ORIGIN, AND TYPE	NUMBER (1,000)					PERCENT DISTRIBUTION				
	1970	1980	1985	1990	1992	1970	1980	1985	1990	1992
FAMILY HOUSEHOLDS										
White, total................	**46,166**	**52,243**	**54,400**	**56,590**	**57,224**	**100**	**100**	**100**	**100**	**100**
Married couple	41,029	44,751	45,643	46,981	47,124	89	86	84	83	82
Male householder [1]	1,038	1,441	1,816	2,303	2,374	2	3	3	4	4
Female householder [1].......	4,099	6,052	6,941	7,306	7,726	9	12	13	13	14
Black, total................	**4,856**	**6,184**	**6,778**	**7,470**	**7,716**	**100**	**100**	**100**	**100**	**100**
Married couple	3,317	3,433	3,469	3,750	3,631	68	56	51	50	47
Male householder [1]	181	256	344	446	504	4	4	5	6	7
Female householder [1].......	1,358	2,495	2,964	3,275	3,582	28	40	44	44	46
Asian or Pacific Islander, total [2].	**(NA)**	**818**	**(NA)**	**1,531**	**1,624**	**(NA)**	**100**	**(NA)**	**100**	**100**
Married couple	(NA)	691	(NA)	1,256	1,284	(NA)	84	(NA)	82	79
Male householder [1]	(NA)	39	(NA)	86	103	(NA)	5	(NA)	6	6
Female householder [1].......	(NA)	88	(NA)	188	237	(NA)	11	(NA)	12	15
Hispanic, total [3].............	**2,004**	**3,029**	**3,939**	**4,840**	**5,177**	**100**	**100**	**100**	**100**	**100**
Married couple	1,615	2,282	2,824	3,395	3,532	81	75	72	70	68
Male householder [1]	82	138	210	329	383	4	5	5	7	7
Female householder [1].......	307	610	905	1,116	1,261	15	20	23	23	24
NONFAMILY HOUSEHOLDS										
White, total................	**10,436**	**18,522**	**20,928**	**23,573**	**24,451**	**100**	**100**	**100**	**100**	**100**
Male householder	3,406	7,499	8,608	9,951	10,476	33	40	41	42	43
Female householder.........	7,030	11,023	12,320	13,622	13,975	67	60	59	58	57
Black, total................	**1,367**	**2,402**	**2,703**	**3,015**	**3,367**	**100**	**100**	**100**	**100**	**100**
Male householder	564	1,146	1,244	1,313	1,594	41	48	46	44	47
Female householder.........	803	1,256	1,459	1,702	1,773	59	52	54	56	53
Hispanic, total [3].............	**299**	**654**	**944**	**1,093**	**1,202**	**100**	**100**	**100**	**100**	**100**
Male householder	150	365	509	587	660	50	56	54	54	55
Female householder.........	148	289	435	506	542	49	44	46	46	45

NA Not available. [1] No spouse present. [2] 1980 data as of April and are from 1980 Census of Population. [3] Hispanic persons may be of any race. 1970 data as of April.

Source: U.S. Bureau of the Census, *Census of Population: 1970, Persons of Spanish Origin*, PC(2)-1C; and *Current Population Reports*, P20-467, and earlier reports.

No. 67. Households, by Characteristic of Householder and Size of Household: 1970 to 1992

[As of **March**. Based on Current Population Survey; see headnote, table 65. See also *Historical Statistics, Colonial Times to 1970*, series A 335-349]

CHARACTERISTIC OF HOUSEHOLDER AND SIZE OF HOUSEHOLD	NUMBER (mil.)						PERCENT DISTRIBUTION					
	1970	1975	1980	1985	1990	1992	1970	1975	1980	1985	1990	1992
Total [1]	**63.4**	**71.1**	**80.8**	**86.8**	**93.3**	**95.7**	**100**	**100**	**100**	**100**	**100**	**100**
Age of householder:												
15 to 24 years old [2]	4.4	5.8	6.6	5.4	5.1	4.9	7	8	8	6	6	5
25 to 29 years old	6.1	7.8	9.3	9.6	9.4	8.8	10	11	12	11	10	9
30 to 34 years old	5.6	7.1	9.3	10.4	11.0	11.2	9	10	12	12	12	12
35 to 44 years old	11.8	11.9	14.0	17.5	20.6	21.8	19	17	17	20	22	23
45 to 54 years old	12.2	12.9	12.7	12.6	14.5	15.5	20	18	16	15	16	16
55 to 64 years old	10.8	11.3	12.5	13.1	12.5	12.6	17	16	16	15	13	13
65 to 74 years old	7.7	8.9	10.1	10.9	11.7	12.0	12	13	13	13	13	13
75 years old and over.....	4.8	5.4	6.4	7.3	8.4	8.9	8	8	8	8	9	9
Male..................	50.0	54.3	58.0	60.0	62.9	63.7	79	76	72	69	67	67
Female................	13.4	16.8	22.8	26.8	30.4	32.0	21	24	28	31	33	33
White	56.6	62.9	70.8	75.3	80.2	81.7	90	89	88	87	86	85
Black	6.2	7.3	8.6	9.5	10.5	11.1	10	10	11	11	11	12
Hispanic [3]	(NA)	(NA)	3.7	4.9	5.9	6.4	(NA)	(NA)	5	6	6	7
One person	10.9	13.9	18.3	20.6	23.0	24.0	17	20	23	24	25	25
Male	3.5	4.9	7.0	7.9	3.0	9.6	6	7	9	9	10	10
Female	7.3	9.0	11.3	12.7	14.0	14.4	12	13	14	15	15	15
Two persons	18.3	21.8	25.3	27.4	30.1	30.7	29	31	31	32	32	32
Three persons	10.9	12.4	14.1	15.5	16.1	16.4	17	17	18	18	17	17
Four persons	10.0	11.1	12.7	13.6	14.5	14.7	16	16	16	16	16	15
Five persons	6.5	6.4	6.1	6.1	6.2	6.4	10	9	8	7	7	7
Six persons	3.5	3.1	2.5	2.3	2.1	2.1	6	4	3	3	2	2
Seven persons or more	3.2	2.5	1.8	1.3	1.3	1.3	5	4	2	2	1	1

NA Not available. [1] Includes other races, not shown separately. [2] 1970 and 1975, persons 14 to 24 years old. [3] Hispanic persons may be of any race.

Source: U.S. Bureau of the Census, *Current Population Reports*, P20-467, and earlier reports; and unpublished data.

No. 68. Household Characteristics, by Race, Hispanic Origin, and Type: 1992

[As of March. Based on Current Population Survey; see headnote, table 65. For composition of regions, see table 31]

CHARACTERISTIC	NUMBER OF HOUSEHOLDS (1,000)							PERCENT DISTRIBUTION							PERSONS PER HOUSEHOLD		
	Total	Black	His-panic[1]	Family households — Total[2]	Married couple	Female house-holder[3]	Non-family house-holds	Total	Black	His-panic[1]	Family households — Total[2]	Married couple	Female house-holder[3]	Non-family house-holds	Total	Black	His-panic[1]
Total	**95,669**	**11,083**	**6,379**	**67,173**	**52,457**	**11,692**	**28,496**	**100**	**100**	**100**	**100**	**100**	**100**	**100**	**2.62**	**2.81**	**3.45**
Age of householder:																	
15 to 24 years old	4,859	702	555	2,642	1,471	909	2,217	5	6	9	4	3	8	8	2.35	2.58	3.08
25 to 29 years old	8,810	1,203	785	5,859	4,205	1,285	2,951	9	11	12	9	8	11	10	2.68	2.98	3.56
30 to 34 years old	11,197	1,458	1,035	8,520	6,486	1,680	2,677	12	13	16	13	12	14	9	3.06	2.90	3.80
35 to 44 years old	21,774	2,636	1,640	17,533	13,519	3,230	4,241	23	24	26	26	26	28	15	3.26	3.34	3.94
45 to 54 years old	15,547	1,718	979	12,188	9,828	1,837	3,360	16	16	15	18	18	16	12	2.89	2.99	3.56
55 to 64 years old	12,559	1,418	728	9,296	7,758	1,203	3,263	13	13	11	14	15	10	11	2.34	2.62	2.98
65 to 74 years old	12,043	1,245	417	7,330	6,269	923	4,713	13	11	7	11	12	7	17	1.86	2.03	2.44
75 years old and over	8,878	703	238	3,805	2,919	724	5,073	9	6	4	6	6	6	18	1.57	1.84	2.05
Region:																	
Northeast	19,314	1,907	1,135	13,428	10,399	2,422	5,886	20	17	18	20	20	21	21	2.63	2.84	3.03
Midwest	23,327	2,238	456	16,170	12,730	2,739	7,157	24	20	7	24	24	23	25	2.59	2.78	3.32
South	33,073	5,972	1,980	23,679	18,346	4,342	9,394	35	54	31	35	35	37	33	2.60	2.85	3.38
West	19,955	966	2,807	13,897	10,981	2,189	6,058	21	9	44	21	21	19	21	2.71	2.50	3.70
Size of household:																	
One person	23,974	2,915	887	(X)	(X)	(X)	23,974	25	26	14	(X)	(X)	(X)	84	1.00	1.00	1.00
Two persons	30,734	2,887	1,364	27,119	20,702	4,967	3,615	32	26	21	40	39	42	13	2.00	2.00	2.00
Three persons	16,398	2,069	1,247	15,822	11,460	3,564	576	17	19	20	24	22	30	2	3.00	3.00	3.00
Four persons	14,710	1,661	1,272	14,459	12,197	1,813	251	15	15	20	22	23	16	1	4.00	4.00	4.00
Five persons	6,389	878	836	6,334	5,346	794	55	7	8	13	9	10	7	(Z)	5.00	5.00	5.00
Six persons	2,126	368	406	2,107	1,742	284	19	2	3	6	3	3	2	(Z)	6.00	6.00	6.00
Seven persons or more	1,338	304	367	1,332	1,011	270	6	1	3	6	2	2	2	(Z)	(NA)	(NA)	(NA)
Marital status of householder:																	
Never married (single)	14,461	2,931	1,118	3,935	(X)	2,900	10,526	15	26	18	6	(X)	25	37	(NA)	(NA)	(NA)
Married, spouse present	52,457	3,631	3,532	52,457	52,457	(X)	(X)	55	33	55	78	100	(X)	(X)	(NA)	(NA)	(NA)
Married, spouse absent	4,571	1,273	575	2,507	(X)	2,049	2,064	5	11	9	4	(X)	18	7	(NA)	(NA)	(NA)
Widowed	11,895	1,527	444	2,938	(X)	2,458	8,957	12	14	7	4	(X)	21	31	(NA)	(NA)	(NA)
Divorced	12,286	1,721	711	5,337	(X)	4,285	6,949	13	16	11	8	(X)	37	24	(NA)	(NA)	(NA)
Tenure:																	
Owner occupied	61,310	4,683	2,547	47,819	41,102	5,040	13,491	64	42	40	71	78	43	47	2.73	3.01	3.58
Renter occupied	34,359	6,400	3,832	19,354	11,355	6,651	15,005	36	58	60	29	22	57	53	2.43	2.66	3.37

NA Not available. X Not applicable. Z Less than 0.5 percent. [1] Hispanic persons may be of any race. [2] Includes male householder, no spouse present. [3] No spouse present.

Source: U.S. Bureau of the Census, Current Population Reports, P20-467 and P60-180.

No. 69. Households—States: 1970 to 1990

[As of **April 1**. For definitions of household and family, see text, section 1]

REGION, DIVISION, AND STATE	HOUSEHOLDS							FAMILIES, 1990 (1,000)				NONFAMILY HOUSEHOLDS, 1990 (1,000)	
	Number (1,000)			Percent change		Persons per household		Total [1]	Married couple		One-parent [3]	Total [4]	One-person
	1970	1980	1990	1970-80	1980-90	1980	1990		Total [2]	With own children			
U.S....	63,450	80,390	91,947	26.7	14.4	2.75	2.63	64,518	50,708	23,495	7,383	27,429	22,580
Northeast .	15,483	17,471	18,873	12.8	8.0	2.74	2.61	13,071	10,089	4,505	1,421	5,802	4,828
N.E.....	3,645	4,362	4,943	19.7	13.3	2.74	2.58	3,404	2,692	1,215	357	1,538	1,225
ME ...	303	395	465	30.5	17.7	2.75	2.56	329	271	126	35	137	108
NH ...	225	323	411	43.5	27.1	2.75	2.62	293	245	119	27	119	90
VT....	132	178	211	35.0	18.1	2.75	2.57	145	119	58	16	66	49
MA ...	1,760	2,033	2,247	15.5	10.5	2.72	2.58	1,515	1,170	524	165	732	581
RI ...	292	339	378	16.0	11.6	2.70	2.55	259	202	89	28	119	99
CT....	933	1,094	1,230	17.2	12.5	2.76	2.59	864	685	299	87	366	297
M.A ...	11,837	13,109	13,930	10.7	6.3	2.74	2.62	9,667	7,397	3,289	1,065	4,263	3,603
NY....	5,914	6,340	6,639	7.2	4.7	2.70	2.63	4,489	3,316	1,496	568	2,150	1,806
NJ....	2,218	2,549	2,795	14.9	9.7	2.84	2.70	2,021	1,579	708	195	773	646
PA....	3,705	4,220	4,496	13.9	6.5	2.74	2.57	3,156	2,502	1,085	302	1,340	1,151
Midwest...	17,537	20,859	22,317	18.9	7.0	2.75	2.60	15,675	12,574	5,875	1,740	6,642	5,588
E.N.C ..	12,383	14,654	15,597	18.3	6.4	2.78	2.63	11,015	8,699	4,053	1,276	4,582	3,852
OH ...	3,289	3,834	4,088	16.5	6.6	2.76	2.59	2,895	2,294	1,054	329	1,192	1,020
IN	1,609	1,927	2,065	19.7	7.2	2.77	2.61	1,480	1,202	563	160	585	497
IL	3,502	4,045	4,202	15.5	3.9	2.76	2.65	2,925	2,272	1,068	337	1,277	1,081
MI....	2,653	3,195	3,419	20.4	7.0	2.84	2.66	2,439	1,883	875	317	980	809
WI....	1,329	1,652	1,822	24.3	10.3	2.77	2.61	1,275	1,048	493	133	547	444
W.N.C...	5,154	6,205	6,720	20.4	8.3	2.68	2.55	4,660	3,875	1,822	463	2,060	1,737
MN ...	1,154	1,445	1,648	25.2	14.0	2.74	2.58	1,131	943	460	112	517	414
IA	896	1,053	1,064	17.5	1.1	2.68	2.52	741	630	287	67	324	275
MO ...	1,521	1,793	1,961	17.9	9.4	2.67	2.54	1,368	1,105	502	149	593	511
ND ...	182	228	241	25.4	5.8	2.75	2.55	166	142	71	14	75	64
SD....	201	243	259	20.8	6.8	2.74	2.59	180	153	74	17	79	68
NE....	474	571	602	20.6	5.4	2.66	2.54	415	351	168	39	187	160
KS....	727	872	945	19.9	8.3	2.62	2.53	659	552	260	65	286	245
South ..	19,258	26,486	31,822	37.5	20.1	2.77	2.61	22,722	17,786	8,181	2,647	9,101	7,641
S.A.....	9,438	13,160	16,503	39.4	25.4	2.73	2.56	11,639	9,091	3,962	1,322	4,864	3,974
DE ...	165	207	247	25.7	19.5	2.79	2.61	176	138	62	20	72	57
MD ...	1,175	1,461	1,749	24.3	19.7	2.82	2.67	1,246	949	437	149	503	395
DC ...	263	253	250	-3.6	-1.4	2.40	2.26	122	63	22	27	128	104
VA ...	1,391	1,863	2,292	34.0	23.0	2.77	2.61	1,629	1,302	611	167	662	524
WV ...	547	686	689	25.4	0.3	2.79	2.55	500	406	187	47	188	169
NC ...	1,510	2,043	2,517	35.4	23.2	2.78	2.54	1,812	1,424	634	202	705	597
SC....	734	1,030	1,258	40.3	22.1	2.93	2.68	928	710	333	114	330	281
GA....	1,369	1,872	2,367	36.7	26.4	2.84	2.66	1,713	1,307	633	222	654	538
FL....	2,285	3,744	5,135	63.9	37.1	2.55	2.46	3,512	2,792	1,043	374	1,623	1,310
E.S.C ...	3,868	5,051	5,652	30.6	11.9	2.83	2.62	4,142	3,233	1,505	484	1,509	1,334
KY....	984	1,263	1,380	28.4	9.2	2.82	2.60	1,016	817	391	108	364	321
TN....	1,213	1,619	1,854	33.4	14.5	2.77	2.56	1,348	1,060	477	151	506	442
AL....	1,034	1,342	1,507	29.8	12.3	2.84	2.62	1,104	858	396	127	403	358
MS ...	637	827	911	29.9	10.2	2.97	2.75	674	498	242	99	237	213
W.S.C...	5,952	8,276	9,668	39.0	16.8	2.80	2.69	6,941	5,462	2,714	840	2,727	2,332
AR....	615	816	891	32.6	9.2	2.74	2.57	652	527	236	70	240	214
LA ...	1,052	1,412	1,499	34.2	6.2	2.91	2.74	1,090	803	403	162	409	356
OK ...	851	1,119	1,206	31.5	7.8	2.62	2.53	855	696	321	95	351	309
TX....	3,434	4,929	6,071	43.5	23.2	2.82	2.73	4,344	3,436	1,754	513	1,727	1,453
West ...	11,172	15,574	18,935	39.4	21.6	2.71	2.72	13,050	10,260	4,934	1,575	5,885	4,523
Mt	2,518	3,986	5,033	58.3	26.3	2.79	2.65	3,499	2,831	1,371	411	1,535	1,227
MT ...	217	284	306	30.6	7.9	2.70	2.53	212	177	84	23	94	80
ID	219	324	361	48.0	11.3	2.85	2.73	263	224	111	25	98	81
WY ...	105	166	169	58.3	1.9	2.78	2.63	120	101	52	13	49	41
CO ...	691	1,061	1,282	53.6	20.8	2.65	2.51	854	690	332	103	428	341
NM ...	289	441	543	52.6	22.9	2.90	2.74	391	304	153	54	151	125
AZ ...	539	957	1,369	77.5	43.0	2.79	2.62	940	748	332	114	429	338
UT....	298	449	537	50.6	19.8	3.20	3.15	411	348	202	41	126	102
NV....	160	304	466	90.1	53.2	2.59	2.53	307	240	106	38	159	120
Pac	8,653	11,587	13,902	33.9	20.0	2.68	2.74	9,551	7,429	3,564	1,165	4,351	3,296
WA ...	1,106	1,541	1,872	39.3	21.5	2.61	2.53	1,265	1,029	475	148	607	476
OR ...	692	992	1,103	43.4	11.3	2.60	2.52	751	613	269	85	352	279
CA ...	6,574	8,630	10,381	31.3	20.3	2.68	2.79	7,139	5,470	2,656	889	3,242	2,430
AK....	79	131	189	66.3	43.7	2.93	2.80	133	106	63	19	56	42
HI	203	294	356	44.8	21.2	3.15	3.01	263	210	101	24	93	69

[1] Includes other family types not shown separately.   [2] Includes other married couple families not shown separately. [3] Comprises male family householders with no wife present and with own children and female family householders with no husband present and with own children.   [4] Includes nonfamily households with two or more persons.

Source: U.S. Bureau of the Census, *Census of Population: 1970*; *1980 Census of Population*, vol. 1, chapter B; and *1990 Census of Population, General Population Characteristics, United States* (1990 CP-1-1).

No. 70. Households, 1980 to 1992, and Persons in Households, 1992, by Type of Household and Presence of Children

[As of March. Based on Current Population Survey; see headnote, table 65. Minus sign (-) indicates decrease]

TYPE OF HOUSEHOLD AND PRESENCE OF CHILDREN	HOUSEHOLDS						PERSONS IN HOUSEHOLDS, 1992		Persons per household, 1992
	Number (1,000)			Percent change, 1980-92	Percent distribution		Number (1,000)	Percent distribution	
	1980	1990	1992		1980	1992			
Total households.	80,776	93,347	95,669	18	100	100	250,984	100	2.62
Family households	59,550	66,090	67,173	13	74	70	216,054	86	3.22
With own children under 18	31,022	32,289	32,746	6	38	34	129,150	52	3.94
Without own children under 18	28,528	33,801	34,427	21	35	36	86,904	35	2.52
Married couple family.	49,112	52,317	52,457	7	61	55	170,416	68	3.25
With own children under 18	24,961	24,537	24,420	-2	31	26	101,883	41	4.17
Without own children under 18	24,151	27,780	28,037	16	30	29	68,533	27	2.44
Male householder, no spouse present. . .	1,733	2,884	3,025	75	2	3	9,329	4	3.08
With own children under 18	616	1,153	1,283	108	1	1	4,268	2	3.33
Without own children under 18	1,117	1,731	1,742	56	1	2	5,061	2	2.91
Female householder, no spouse present .	8,705	10,890	11,692	34	11	12	36,309	15	3.11
With own children under 18	5,445	6,599	7,043	29	7	7	22,999	9	3.27
Without own children under 18	3,261	4,290	4,648	43	4	5	13,310	5	2.86
Nonfamily households.	21,226	27,257	28,496	34	26	30	34,930	14	1.23
Living alone.	18,296	22,999	23,974	31	23	25	23,974	10	1.00
Male householder	8,807	11,606	12,428	41	11	13	16,452	7	1.32
Living alone.	6,966	9,049	9,613	38	9	10	9,613	4	1.00
Female householder	12,419	15,651	16,068	29	15	17	18,478	7	1.15
Living alone.	11,330	13,950	14,361	27	14	15	14,361	6	1.00

Source: U.S. Bureau of the Census, *Current Population Reports*, P20-467, and earlier reports; and unpublished data.

No. 71. Living Arrangements of Persons 15 Years Old and Over, by Selected Characteristics: 1992

[As of March. Based on Current Population Survey which includes members of Armed Forces living off post or with families on post, but excludes other Armed Forces; see text, section 1 and Appendix III]

AGE AND SEX	ALL RACES [1]					WHITE PERSONS PERCENT LIVING—			BLACK PERSONS PERCENT LIVING—		
	Total (1,000)	Percent living—				Alone	With spouse	With other relatives	Alone	With spouse	With other relatives
		Alone	With spouse	With other relatives	With non-relatives						
Total.	195,243	12	55	26	7	12	58	23	13	32	48
15 to 19 years old.	16,567	1	2	93	4	1	3	93	1	1	96
20 to 24 years old.	17,848	6	23	56	15	6	25	52	5	12	74
25 to 34 years old.	42,493	9	56	24	11	9	59	20	10	31	49
35 to 44 years old.	39,571	9	70	16	5	9	73	14	10	46	38
45 to 54 years old.	27,024	11	72	13	4	10	75	11	16	47	30
55 to 64 years old.	21,150	14	72	11	3	14	76	8	20	46	27
65 years old and over	30,589	31	54	12	2	31	56	11	36	37	24
65 to 74 years old	18,440	25	63	10	2	24	65	9	34	43	20
75 years old and over. . .	12,149	41	41	16	2	41	42	15	39	25	33
Male.	93,760	10	57	24	8	10	60	22	13	36	40
15 to 19 years old.	8,380	1	1	95	3	(Z)	1	95	1	(Z)	96
20 to 24 years old.	8,800	6	17	60	17	6	19	57	5	9	75
25 to 34 years old.	21,125	11	52	22	15	11	55	19	12	32	41
35 to 44 years old.	19,506	11	70	12	7	11	72	10	13	52	25
45 to 54 years old.	13,114	11	76	8	5	10	78	7	16	54	19
55 to 64 years old.	10,036	11	79	6	4	10	82	5	19	53	16
65 years old and over	12,799	16	74	7	3	15	76	6	30	54	12
65 to 74 years old	8,266	13	77	6	3	12	79	6	28	58	9
75 years old and over. . .	4,533	22	68	8	2	21	70	7	32	46	17
Female.	101,483	14	53	28	5	15	56	24	13	29	54
15 to 19 years old.	8,187	1	4	91	4	1	5	90	1	1	96
20 to 24 years old.	9,048	6	29	52	14	6	31	48	5	14	74
25 to 34 years old.	21,368	8	59	25	8	8	64	20	8	31	56
35 to 44 years old.	20,065	7	69	21	4	7	73	17	7	41	48
45 to 54 years old.	13,910	11	69	17	3	10	72	14	15	41	39
55 to 64 years old.	11,114	17	66	14	2	17	70	11	21	40	36
65 years old and over	17,790	42	40	16	2	42	41	14	40	25	33
65 to 74 years old	10,174	34	51	13	2	34	54	11	39	32	28
75 years old and over. . .	7,616	52	24	21	2	53	25	19	43	14	41

Z Less than 0.5 percent. [1] Includes other races not shown separately.

Source: U.S. Bureau of the Census, *Current Population Reports*, P20-468.

No. 72. Living Arrangements of Young Adults: 1970 to 1992

[1970 and 1980, as of April. Beginning 1985, as of March and based on Current Population Survey, see headnote, table 71]

LIVING ARRANGEMENTS AND SEX	PERSONS 18 TO 24 YEARS OLD					PERSONS 25 TO 34 YEARS OLD				
	1970	1980	1985	1990	1992	1970	1980	1985	1990	1992
Total (1,000)	22,357	29,122	27,844	25,310	24,434	24,566	36,796	40,857	43,240	42,493
Percent distribution:										
Child of householder [1]	47	48	54	53	54	8	9	11	12	12
Family householder or spouse ...	38	29	24	22	21	83	72	68	65	63
Nonfamily householder........	5	10	8	9	9	5	12	13	13	13
Other...................	10	13	14	16	16	4	7	9	11	12
Male (1,000)	10,398	14,278	13,695	12,450	12,083	11,929	18,107	20,184	21,462	21,125
Percent distribution:										
Child of householder [1]	54	54	60	58	60	10	11	13	15	15
Family householder or spouse ...	30	21	16	15	14	79	66	60	56	54
Nonfamily householder........	5	11	10	10	10	7	15	16	16	16
Other...................	10	13	14	17	16	5	8	11	13	15
Female (1,000)	11,959	14,844	14,149	12,860	12,351	12,637	18,689	20,673	21,779	21,368
Percent distribution:										
Child of householder [1]	41	43	48	48	48	7	7	8	8	9
Family householder or spouse ...	45	36	32	30	28	86	78	76	73	72
Nonfamily householder........	4	8	7	8	8	4	9	10	10	10
Other...................	10	13	13	15	16	4	6	7	9	9

[1] Includes unmarried college students living in dormitories.
Source: U.S. Bureau of the Census, 1970 and 1980 Census of Population, PC(2)-4B and Current Population Reports, P20-468, and earlier reports.

No. 73. Families, by Size and Presence of Children: 1980 to 1992

[In thousands, except as indicated. As of March. Excludes members of Armed Forces except those living off post or with their families on post. Based on Current Population Survey; see text, section 1 and Appendix III. For definition of families, see text, section 1]

CHARACTERISTIC	1980, total	1990, total	1992								
			All races [1]			White		Black		Hispanic [4]	
			Total [2]	Married couple	Female householder [3]	Total [2]	Married couple	Total [2]	Married couple	Total [2]	Married couple
Total.............	59,550	66,090	67,173	52,457	11,692	57,224	47,124	7,716	3,631	5,177	3,532
Size of family:											
Two persons	23,461	27,606	28,202	20,838	5,527	24,828	19,360	2,680	1,026	1,266	696
Three persons	13,603	15,353	15,594	11,503	3,370	13,097	10,250	2,007	889	1,209	725
Four persons	12,372	14,026	14,162	12,219	1,656	11,997	10,840	1,582	886	1,238	927
Five persons	5,930	5,938	6,030	5,257	676	4,953	4,564	836	485	752	614
Six persons	2,461	1,997	1,986	1,709	230	1,534	1,393	341	219	387	314
Seven or more persons..	1,723	1,170	1,200	931	234	815	717	272	126	324	255
Average per family	3.29	3.17	3.17	3.23	2.98	3.11	3.18	3.43	3.62	3.81	4.02
Own children under age 18:											
None	28,528	33,801	34,427	28,037	4,648	30,178	25,607	3,271	1,705	1,843	1,210
One	12,443	13,530	13,615	9,520	3,327	11,204	8,355	1,870	766	1,160	754
Two	11,470	12,263	12,364	9,728	2,244	10,477	8,668	1,429	685	1,139	817
Three	4,674	4,650	4,836	3,757	980	3,926	3,297	740	332	655	481
Four or more	2,435	1,846	1,932	1,416	492	1,439	1,197	406	144	380	269
Own children under age 6:											
None	46,063	50,905	51,769	40,532	8,721	44,612	36,643	5,557	2,706	3,388	2,210
One	9,441	10,304	10,642	8,153	2,097	8,722	7,135	1,471	661	1,174	871
Two or more	4,047	4,882	4,763	3,772	874	3,891	3,346	688	263	615	450
PERCENT DISTRIBUTION											
Total.............	100	100	100	100	100	100	100	100	100	100	100
Size of family:											
Two persons	39	42	42	40	47	43	41	35	28	24	20
Three persons	23	23	23	22	29	23	22	26	24	23	21
Four persons	21	21	21	23	14	21	23	21	24	24	26
Five persons	10	9	9	10	6	9	10	11	13	15	17
Six persons	4	3	3	3	2	3	3	4	6	7	9
Seven or more persons..	3	2	2	2	2	1	2	4	3	6	7
Own children under age 18:											
None	48	51	51	53	40	53	54	42	47	36	34
One	21	20	20	18	28	20	18	24	21	22	21
Two	19	19	18	19	19	18	18	19	19	22	23
Three	8	7	7	7	8	7	7	10	9	13	14
Four or more	4	3	3	3	4	3	3	5	4	7	8
Own children under age 6:											
None	77	77	77	77	75	78	78	72	75	65	63
One	16	16	16	16	18	15	15	19	18	23	25
Two or more	7	7	7	7	7	7	7	9	7	12	13

[1] Includes other races, not shown separately. [2] Includes other types of families, not shown separately. [3] No spouse present. [4] Hispanic persons may be of any race.
Source: U.S. Bureau of the Census, Current Population Reports, P20-467, and earlier reports.

No. 74. Families, by Number of Own Children Under 18 Years Old: 1970 to 1992

[Except as noted, as of **March** and based on Current Population Survey; see headnote, table 73. See also *Historical Statistics, Colonial Times to 1970*, series A 353-358]

RACE, HISPANIC ORIGIN, AND YEAR	NUMBER OF FAMILIES (1,000)					PERCENT DISTRIBUTION					Average size of family
	Total	No chil-dren	One child	Two chil-dren	Three or more chil-dren	Total	No chil-dren	One child	Two chil-dren	Three or more chil-dren	
ALL FAMILIES [1]											
1970	51,586	22,774	9,398	8,969	10,445	100	44	18	17	20	3.58
1980	59,550	28,528	12,443	11,470	7,109	100	48	21	19	12	3.29
1985	62,706	31,594	13,108	11,645	6,359	100	50	21	19	10	3.23
1990	66,090	33,801	13,530	12,263	6,496	100	51	20	19	10	3.17
1992	67,173	34,427	13,615	12,364	6,768	100	51	20	18	10	3.17
Married couple	52,457	28,037	9,520	9,728	5,173	100	53	18	19	10	3.23
Male householder [2]	3,025	1,742	768	391	123	100	58	25	13	4	2.77
Female householder [2]	11,692	4,648	3,327	2,244	1,472	100	40	28	19	13	2.98
WHITE FAMILIES											
1970	46,261	20,719	8,437	8,174	8,931	100	45	18	18	19	3.52
1980	52,243	25,769	10,727	9,977	5,769	100	49	21	19	11	3.23
1985	54,400	28,169	11,174	9,937	5,120	100	52	21	18	9	3.16
1990	56,590	29,872	11,186	10,342	5,191	100	53	20	18	9	3.11
1992	57,224	30,178	11,204	10,477	5,365	100	53	20	18	9	3.11
BLACK FAMILIES											
1970	4,887	1,903	858	726	1,401	100	39	18	15	29	4.13
1980	6,184	2,364	1,449	1,235	1,136	100	38	23	20	18	3.67
1985	6,778	2,887	1,579	1,330	982	100	43	23	20	15	3.60
1990	7,470	3,093	1,894	1,433	1,049	100	41	25	19	14	3.46
1992	7,716	3,271	1,870	1,429	1,146	100	42	24	19	15	3.43
HISPANIC FAMILIES [3]											
1970	2,004	597	390	388	629	100	30	20	19	31	4.28
1980	3,029	946	680	698	706	100	31	22	23	23	3.90
1985	3,939	1,337	904	865	833	100	34	23	22	21	3.88
1990	4,840	1,790	1,095	1,036	919	100	37	23	21	19	3.83
1992	5,177	1,843	1,160	1,139	1,035	100	36	22	22	20	3.81

[1] Includes other races, not shown separately. [2] No spouse present. [3] Hispanic persons may be of any race. 1970 Hispanic data as of April and based on Census of Population.

Source: U.S. Bureau of the Census, *U.S. Census of Population, 1970* (PC-2-4A), and *Current Population Reports*, P20-467, and earlier reports.

No. 75. Family Households With Own Children Under Age 18, by Type of Family, 1970 to 1992, and by Age of Householder, 1992

[As of **March**. Excludes members of Armed Forces except those living off post or with their families on post. Based on Current Population Survey; see text, section 1 and Appendix III]

FAMILY TYPE	1970	1980	1990	1992						
				Total	15 to 24 years old	25 to 34 years old	35 to 44 years old	45 to 54 years old	55 to 64 years old	65 years old and over
NUMBER (1,000)										
Family households with children	28,731	31,022	32,289	32,746	1,707	11,061	13,999	4,994	850	136
Married couple	25,532	24,961	24,537	24,420	822	7,866	10,859	4,064	714	95
Male householder [1]	341	616	1,153	1,283	87	413	506	197	59	21
Female householder [1]	2,858	5,445	6,599	7,043	798	2,781	2,633	732	78	20
PERCENT DISTRIBUTION										
Family households with children	100	100	100	100	100	100	100	100	100	100
Married couple		89	81	76	75	48	71	78	81	84	70
Male householder [1]		1	2	4	4	5	4	4	4	7	15
Female householder [1]		10	18	20	22	47	25	19	15	9	15
HOUSEHOLDS WITH CHILDREN, AS A PERCENT OF ALL FAMILY HOUSEHOLDS, BY TYPE										
Family households with children, total	56	52	49	49	65	77	80	41	9	1
Married couple	57	51	47	47	56	74	80	41	9	1
Male householder [1]	28	36	40	42	33	57	65	38	18	6
Female householder [1]	52	63	61	60	88	94	82	40	7	1

[1] No spouse present.

Source: U.S. Bureau of the Census, *Current Population Reports*, P20-467, and earlier reports.

No. 76. Female Family Householders With No Spouse Present—Characteristics, by Race and Hispanic Origin: 1980 to 1992

[As of March. Covers persons 15 years old and over. Based on Current Population Survey; see headnote, table 73]

CHARACTERISTIC	Unit	WHITE			BLACK			HISPANIC ORIGIN [1]		
		1980	1990	1992	1980	1990	1992	1980	1990	1992
Female family householder .	1,000	6,052	7,306	7,726	2,495	3,275	3,582	610	1,116	1,261
Marital status:										
Never married (single)	Percent . . .	11	15	17	27	39	42	23	27	29
Married, spouse absent	Percent . . .	17	16	17	29	21	19	32	29	26
Widowed	Percent . . .	33	26	23	22	17	16	15	16	16
Divorced	Percent . . .	40	43	43	22	23	23	30	29	30
Presence of children under 18:										
No own children	Percent . . .	41	43	42	28	32	35	25	33	32
With own children	Percent . . .	59	58	58	72	68	65	75	67	68

[1] Persons of Hispanic origin may be of any race.

Source: U.S. Bureau of the Census, *Current Population Reports*, P20-467, and earlier reports.

No. 77. Married Couple Family Households with Children: 1980 to 1990

[As of June. Covers only those married-couple families with at least one "own child" under age 18 living in their household. "Own children" are children of the householder and/or the householder's spouse. Each child who was the biological child of one of the parents but not of the other parent was classified as a stepchild. If one spouse adopted the biological child of the other spouse, the child was still considered to be a stepchild. Children who were the biological children of both parents were classified as biological children, while all "own" children who were not biological children of either of their parents were classified as adoptive children. Based on Current Population Survey; see text, section 1 and Appendix III]

TYPE OF FAMILY	NUMBER (1,000)			PERCENT DISTRIBUTION		
	1980	1985	1990	1980	1985	1990
Total	24,091	23,868	25,314	100.0	100.0	100.0
Biological [1]	19,037	18,470	19,253	79.0	77.4	76.1
Adoptive [2]	429	303	345	1.8	1.3	1.4
Biological mother-stepfather [3]	1,818	2,207	2,619	7.5	9.2	10.3
Biological father-stepmother [4]	171	180	152	0.7	0.8	0.6
Joint biological-step [5]	1,862	2,038	2,475	7.7	8.5	9.8
Joint biological-adoptive [6]	429	223	324	1.8	0.9	1.3
Joint step-adoptive [7] . . .	12	15	8	-	0.1	-
Joint bio-step-adoptive [8]	25	29	-	0.1	0.1	-
Unknown [9]	309	403	137	1.3	1.7	0.5

- Represents or rounds to zero. [1] All the own children were biological children of both parents. [2] All the own children were adoptive children of both parents. [3] All the own children were biological children of the mother and stepchildren of the father. [4] All the own children were biological children of the father and stepchildren of the mother. [5] At least one child was a biological child of both parents, at least one was a biological child of one parent and a stepchild of the other parent, and no other type of child was present; or a stepchild of each parent and no other type of child was present. [6] At least one child was a biological child of both parents, at least one was an adopted child of both parents, and no other type of child was present. [7] At least one child was a biological child of one parent and a stepchild of the other parent, at least one was an adopted child of both parents, and no other type of child was present. [8] At least one child was a biological child of both parents, at least one was the biological child of one parent and the stepchild of the other, and at least one was an adopted child of both parents. [9] At least one child had at least one parent for whom the nature of the relationship could not be designated.

No. 78. Children Living with Biological, Step, and Adoptive Married-Couple Parents, by Race and Hispanic Origin of Mother: 1980 to 1990

[As of June. See headnote, table 77]

TYPE OF PARENT	ALL RACES [1]			WHITE			BLACK			His-panic origin, [2] 1990
	1980	1985	1990	1980	1985	1990	1980	1985	1990	
NUMBER (1,000)										
Own children under 18 years, total	47,248	45,347	45,448	42,329	39,942	39,732	3,775	3,816	3,671	4,568
Biological mother and father	39,523	37,213	37,026	35,852	33,202	32,975	2,698	2,661	2,336	3,703
Biological mother-stepfather	5,355	6,049	6,643	4,362	4,918	5,258	877	952	1,149	699
Stepmother-biological father	727	740	608	664	676	549	46	50	38	38
Adoptive mother and father.	1,350	866	974	1,209	754	815	119	76	97	101
Unknown mother or father	293	479	197	242	391	135	35	77	51	27
PERCENT DISTRIBUTION										
Own children under 18 years, total.	100.0	100.0	100.0	100.0	100.0	100.0	100.0	100.0	100.0	100.0
Biological mother and father	83.7	82.1	81.5	84.7	83.1	83.0	71.5	69.7	63.6	81.1
Biological mother-stepfather	11.3	13.3	14.6	10.3	12.3	13.2	23.2	24.9	31.3	15.3
Stepmother-biological father	1.5	1.6	1.3	1.6	1.7	1.4	1.2	1.3	1.0	0.8
Adoptive mother and father.	2.9	1.9	2.1	2.9	1.9	2.1	3.1	2.0	2.6	2.2
Unknown mother or father	0.6	1.1	0.4	0.6	1.0	0.3	0.9	2.0	1.4	0.6

[1] Includes other races not shown separately. [2] Persons of Hispanic origin may be of any race.

Source of tables 77 and 78: U.S. Bureau of the Census, *Current Population Reports*, P23-180.

No. 79. Living Arrangements of Children Under 18 Years Old, by Selected Characteristic of Parent: 1992

[In thousands. As of March. Covers only those persons under 18 years old who are living with one or both parents. Characteristics are shown for the householder or reference person in married-couple situations. See also headnote, table 80]

CHARACTERISTIC OF PARENT	ALL RACES [1]				WHITE				BLACK				HISPANIC [2]			
	Total	Both parents	Mother only	Father only	Total	Both parents	Mother only	Father only	Total	Both parents	Mother only	Father only	Total	Both parents	Mother only	Father only
Children under 18 years old	**64,216**	**46,638**	**15,396**	**2,182**	**51,606**	**40,635**	**9,250**	**1,721**	**9,648**	**3,714**	**5,607**	**327**	**7,382**	**4,935**	**2,168**	**279**
Age:																
15 to 24 years old	3,709	1,345	2,188	176	2,417	1,144	1,139	133	1,163	149	984	31	594	296	274	25
25 to 29 years old	8,466	5,010	3,132	325	6,337	4,328	1,761	249	1,858	527	1,266	65	1,192	731	422	39
30 to 34 years old	14,771	10,559	3,785	427	12,061	9,385	2,331	344	2,105	701	1,353	51	1,853	1,181	605	68
35 to 39 years old	15,733	12,140	3,152	440	13,045	10,739	1,951	355	2,038	905	1,074	59	1,542	1,067	438	38
40 to 44 years old	12,213	9,905	1,915	393	10,080	8,482	1,270	329	1,387	780	558	48	1,189	909	231	49
45 to 54 years old	7,904	6,516	1,090	299	6,609	5,670	712	228	851	481	332	38	833	617	171	46
55 to 64 years old	1,233	1,043	104	87	922	807	64	52	203	138	33	32	159	124	23	12
65 years old and over	186	121	30	36	134	80	22	32	43	34	6	4	19	11	4	4
Educational attainment:																
Less than 9th grade	4,138	2,765	1,182	191	3,504	2,406	929	169	399	173	214	12	2,414	1,663	653	98
9th to 12th grade, no diploma	7,947	4,061	3,548	337	5,471	3,372	1,836	264	2,188	506	1,618	64	1,556	869	651	36
High school graduate [3]	22,858	16,122	5,905	831	17,996	14,055	3,282	659	4,016	1,447	2,431	138	1,911	1,284	556	71
Some college, no degree or associate degree	15,480	11,360	3,594	527	12,712	10,008	2,301	403	2,128	919	1,141	68	1,007	697	260	50
Bachelor's degree	8,652	7,573	857	222	7,442	6,611	652	179	618	440	150	28	301	257	24	20
Graduate or professional degree	5,141	4,757	310	74	4,480	4,184	250	46	299	229	52	18	193	165	23	4
Employment status: [4]																
In the civilian labor force	53,634	42,385	9,345	1,904	44,882	37,376	5,965	1,542	6,442	3,100	3,083	259	5,568	4,313	1,026	229
Employed	49,539	39,819	8,009	1,711	41,890	35,191	5,300	1,398	5,502	2,844	2,441	217	4,911	3,861	850	200
Both parents employed	25,692	25,692	(X)	(X)	22,435	22,435	(X)	(X)	2,107	2,107	(X)	(X)	2,023	2,023	(X)	(X)
Unemployed	4,095	2,566	1,335	193	2,992	2,185	664	143	941	256	642	43	658	452	176	29
Not in the labor force	9,552	3,251	6,046	254	5,961	2,519	3,280	162	3,003	415	2,524	64	1,731	542	1,142	46
Family income:																
Under $5,000	3,789	717	2,901	171	2,113	587	1,439	88	1,526	94	1,367	65	626	167	434	26
$5,000 to $9,999	5,403	1,338	3,850	215	3,223	1,035	2,022	166	1,874	165	1,671	37	1,071	374	660	37
$10,000 to $14,999	4,774	2,431	2,124	219	3,460	1,993	1,294	173	1,069	271	767	33	1,025	648	350	28
$15,000 to $24,999	9,469	6,045	2,904	519	7,289	4,993	1,831	466	1,684	684	956	44	1,657	1,216	368	72
$25,000 to $29,999	4,886	3,783	893	210	4,043	3,226	657	160	621	360	224	38	639	518	84	37
$30,000 to $39,999	9,333	7,714	1,283	336	7,957	6,813	910	234	1,027	623	333	71	972	811	143	18
$40,000 to $49,999	8,149	7,313	634	202	7,173	6,496	496	181	671	546	112	12	587	504	52	30
$50,000 and over	18,414	17,296	808	310	16,348	15,491	602	255	1,176	972	176	27	804	697	77	31
Tenure: [5]																
Owned	39,702	33,703	4,885	1,114	34,612	30,180	3,497	935	3,432	2,104	1,200	128	2,593	2,112	387	94
Rented	24,514	12,935	10,511	1,068	16,994	10,455	5,753	786	6,215	1,609	4,407	199	4,789	2,822	1,781	185

X Not applicable. [1] Includes other races, not shown separately. [2] Persons of Hispanic origin may be of any race. [3] Includes equivalency. [4] Excludes children whose parent is in the Armed Forces.
[5] Refers to the tenure of the householder (who may or may not be the child's parent).

Source: U.S. Bureau of the Census, Current Population Reports, P20-468.

No. 80. Children Under 18 Years Old, by Presence of Parents: 1970 to 1992

[As of **March**. Excludes persons under 18 years old who maintained households or family groups. Based on Current Population Survey; see headnote, table 73]

RACE, HISPANIC ORIGIN, AND YEAR	Number (1,000)	Both parents	PERCENT LIVING WITH—					Father only	Neither parent
			Mother only						
			Total	Divorced	Married, spouse absent	Never married (single)	Wid-owed		
ALL RACES [1]									
1970	69,162	85	11	3	5	1	2	1	3
1980	63,427	77	18	8	6	3	2	2	4
1985	62,475	74	21	9	5	6	2	3	3
1990	64,137	73	22	8	5	7	2	3	3
1992	65,965	71	23	8	6	8	1	3	3
WHITE									
1970	58,790	90	8	3	3	(Z)	2	1	2
1980	52,242	83	14	7	4	1	2	2	2
1985	50,836	80	16	8	4	2	1	2	2
1990	51,390	79	16	8	4	3	1	3	2
1992	52,493	77	18	8	5	4	1	3	2
BLACK									
1970	9,422	59	30	5	16	4	4	2	10
1980	9,375	42	44	11	16	13	4	2	12
1985	9,479	40	51	11	12	25	3	3	7
1990	10,018	38	51	10	12	27	2	4	8
1992	10,427	36	54	10	12	31	1	3	7
HISPANIC [2]									
1970	[3]4,006	78	(NA)	(NA)	(NA)	(NA)	(NA)	(NA)	(NA)
1980	5,459	75	20	6	8	4	2	2	4
1985	6,057	68	27	7	11	7	2	2	3
1990	7,174	67	27	7	10	8	2	3	3
1992	7,619	65	28	8	9	10	1	4	3

NA Not available.   Z Less than 0.5 percent.   [1] Includes other races not shown separately.   [2] Hispanic persons may be of any race.   [3] All persons under 18 years old.

Source: U.S. Bureau of the Census, *Current Population Reports*, P20-468, and earlier reports.

No. 81. Children Living in the Home of Their Grandparents, by Presence of Parents, Race, and Hispanic Origin: 1970 to 1992

[Excludes children whose parent(s) maintain the home, even though grandparents are living with them. Excludes inmates of institutions. Data for **1970** and **1980** are as of **April** and based on the Census of Population; beginning **1990**, data are as of **March** and based on the Current Population Survey. See text, section 1 and Appendix III]

LIVING ARRANGEMENT	1970, total	1980, total	1990, total	1992			
				Total [1]	White	Black	Hispanic origin [2]
Grandchild of householder under 18 years (1,000)	**2,214**	**2,306**	**3,155**	**3,253**	**1,887**	**1,208**	**458**
Percent of all children under 18 years . .	3.2	3.6	4.9	4.9	3.6	11.6	6.0
With both parents present (1,000)	363	310	467	502	428	25	118
With mother only present (1,000)	817	922	1,563	1,740	957	719	220
With father only present (1,000)	78	86	191	144	96	40	23
With neither parent present (1,000)	957	988	935	867	407	424	97
Total, percent distribution	**100.0**	**100.0**	**100.0**	**100.0**	**100.0**	**100.0**	**100.0**
With both parents present	16	13	15	15	23	2	26
With mother only present	37	40	50	53	51	60	48
With father only present	4	4	6	4	5	3	5
With neither parent present	43	43	30	27	22	35	21

[1] Includes other races not shown separately.   [2] Persons of Hispanic origin may be of any race.

Source: U.S. Bureau of the Census, *Current Population Reports*, P20-468, and earlier reports.

No. 82. Nonfamily Households, by Age of Householder and Presence of Nonrelatives: 1980 to 1992

[As of **March**. See headnote, table 73]

ITEM	NONFAMILY HOUSEHOLDS Total (1,000)	NONFAMILY HOUSEHOLDS Percent	MALE HOUSEHOLDER (1,000) Total	15 to 24 yr. old	25 to 44 yr. old	45 to 64 yr. old	65 yr. old and over	FEMALE HOUSEHOLDER (1,000) Total	15 to 24 yr. old	25 to 44 yr. old	45 to 64 yr. old	65 yr. old and over
1980, total	**21,226**	100	8,807	1,567	3,854	1,822	1,565	12,419	1,189	2,198	3,048	5,983
One person (living alone)	18,296	86	6,966	947	2,920	1,613	1,486	11,330	779	1,809	2,901	5,842
Nonrelatives present	2,930	14	1,841	620	934	209	79	1,089	410	389	147	141
1990, total	**27,257**	100	11,606	1,236	5,780	2,536	2,053	15,651	1,032	3,697	3,545	7,377
One person (living alone)	22,999	84	9,049	674	4,231	2,203	1,943	13,950	536	2,881	3,300	7,233
Nonrelatives present	4,258	16	2,557	560	1,551	334	112	1,701	497	817	245	143
1992, total	**28,496**	100	12,428	1,232	6,111	2,897	2,188	16,068	985	3,757	3,726	7,598
One person (living alone)	23,974	84	9,613	601	4,443	2,483	2,086	14,361	555	2,962	3,408	7,437
Nonrelatives present	4,522	16	2,815	629	1,668	413	102	1,707	431	797	320	161

Source: U.S. Bureau of the Census, *Current Population Reports*, P20-468, and earlier reports; and unpublished data.

No. 83. Nonfamily Householders, by Sex and Marital Status: 1980 to 1992

[In thousands. As of **March**. Based on Current Population Survey; see headnote, table 73]

MARITAL STATUS	MALE HOUSEHOLDER 1980	1990	1992 Total [1]	25 to 44 yr. old	45 to 64 yr. old	65 yr. old and over	FEMALE HOUSEHOLDER 1980	1990	1992 Total [1]	25 to 44 yr. old	45 to 64 yr. old	65 yr. old and over
Total	8,807	11,606	12,428	6,111	2,897	2,188	12,419	15,651	16,068	3,757	3,726	7,598
Never married	4,371	5,844	6,096	3,827	792	325	3,302	4,382	4,430	2,461	527	518
Married [2]	1,051	1,117	1,236	596	418	191	675	794	828	281	354	155
Widowed	1,177	1,417	1,552	25	243	1,281	6,569	7,428	7,405	69	1,142	6,191
Divorced	2,209	3,228	3,544	1,662	1,443	390	1,873	3,046	3,405	946	1,703	734

[1] Includes persons 15 to 24 years old, not shown separately.　　[2] No spouse present.

Source: U.S. Bureau of the Census, *Current Population Reports*, P20-468, and earlier reports; and unpublished data.

No. 84. Persons Living Alone, by Sex and Age: 1970 to 1992

[As of **March**. Based on Current Population Survey; see headnote, table 73]

SEX AND AGE	NUMBER OF PERSONS (1,000) 1970	1980	1985	1990	1992	PERCENT DISTRIBUTION 1970	1980	1985	1990	1992
Both sexes	10,851	18,296	20,602	22,999	23,974	100	100	100	100	100
15 to 24 years old [1]	556	1,726	1,324	1,210	1,156	5	9	6	5	5
25 to 34 years old	[2]1,604	[2]4,729	3,905	3,972	3,924	[2]15	[2]26	19	17	16
35 to 44 years old	(2)	(2)	2,322	3,138	3,480	(2)	(2)	11	14	15
45 to 64 years old	3,622	4,514	4,939	5,502	5,890	33	25	24	24	25
65 to 74 years old	2,815	3,851	4,130	4,350	4,561	26	21	20	19	19
75 years old and over	2,256	3,477	3,982	4,825	4,962	21	19	19	21	21
Male	3,532	6,966	7,922	9,049	9,613	33	38	39	39	40
15 to 24 years old [1]	274	947	750	674	601	3	5	4	3	3
25 to 34 years old	[2]933	[2]2,920	2,307	2,395	2,320	[2]9	[2]16	11	10	10
35 to 44 years old	(2)	(2)	1,406	1,836	2,123	(2)	(2)	7	8	9
45 to 64 years old	1,152	1,613	1,845	2,203	2,483	11	9	9	10	10
65 to 74 years old	611	775	868	1,042	1,100	6	4	4	5	5
75 years old and over	563	711	746	901	986	5	4	4	4	4
Female	7,319	11,330	12,680	13,950	14,361	68	62	62	61	60
15 to 24 years old [1]	282	779	573	536	555	3	4	3	2	2
25 to 34 years old	[2]671	[2]1,809	1,598	1,578	1,604	[2]6	[2]10	8	7	7
35 to 44 years old	(2)	(2)	916	1,303	1,358	(2)	(2)	4	6	6
45 to 64 years old	2,470	2,901	3,095	3,300	3,408	23	16	15	14	14
65 to 74 years old	2,204	3,076	3,262	3,309	3,461	20	17	16	14	14
75 years old and over	1,693	2,766	3,236	3,924	3,976	16	15	16	17	17

[1] 1970, persons 14 to 24 years old.　　[2] Data for persons 35 to 44 years old included with persons 25 to 34 years old.

Source: U.S. Bureau of the Census, *Current Population Reports*, P20-468, and earlier reports; and unpublished data.

No. 85. Population in Institutions and Other Group Quarters, by Type of Group Quarters and State: 1990

[As of **April** 1. See text, section 1 and Appendix III. See *Historical Statistics, Colonial Times to 1970*, series A 359-371, for inmates of institutions]

REGION, DIVISION, AND STATE	Group quarters population, total[1]	INSTITUTIONALIZED PERSONS				College dormitories	Military quarters	Emergency shelters for homeless persons[3]	Persons visible in street locations[3]
		Total[2]	Correctional institutions	Nursing homes	Juvenile institutions				
U.S....	6,697,744	3,334,018	1,115,111	1,772,032	104,200	1,953,558	589,700	190,406	49,734
Northeast	1,510,088	713,335	195,275	399,329	20,091	540,689	47,252	62,247	14,653
N.E.....	445,031	179,333	33,227	119,646	4,998	198,866	20,349	12,454	970
ME ...	37,169	14,136	2,311	9,855	427	14,118	5,153	462	7
NH ...	32,151	11,466	1,991	8,202	284	17,025	923	404	8
VT....	21,642	6,161	807	4,809	172	13,435	-	261	16
MA ...	214,307	84,345	15,471	55,662	2,457	100,487	4,439	6,476	674
RI ...	38,595	14,801	2,645	10,156	498	18,898	2,851	502	44
CT....	101,167	48,424	10,002	30,962	1,160	34,903	6,983	4,349	221
M.A...	1,065,057	534,002	162,048	279,683	15,093	341,823	26,903	49,793	13,683
NY....	545,265	267,122	90,025	126,175	6,981	165,925	12,875	33,228	10,732
NJ....	171,368	92,670	29,093	47,054	2,343	43,711	10,102	7,725	1,639
PA....	348,424	174,210	42,930	106,454	5,769	132,187	3,926	8,840	1,312
Midwest.	1,598,620	852,419	211,192	544,650	26,134	557,270	40,203	30,009	3,324
E.N.C ..	1,055,689	568,050	157,275	346,243	18,374	369,009	19,261	21,423	2,544
OH ...	261,451	152,331	41,618	93,769	6,158	88,785	449	4,773	188
IN ...	161,992	81,686	21,726	50,845	2,823	70,873	883	2,530	268
IL	286,956	149,842	37,334	93,662	3,601	86,777	16,091	8,017	1,755
MI....	211,692	112,903	42,849	57,622	3,835	73,093	1,693	4,290	262
WI....	133,598	71,288	13,748	50,345	1,957	49,481	145	1,813	71
W.N.C. ...	542,931	284,369	53,917	198,407	7,760	188,261	20,942	8,586	780
MN ...	117,621	63,279	9,969	47,051	1,417	39,280	24	2,483	138
IA	99,520	47,841	5,630	36,455	1,142	43,093	57	1,153	148
MO ...	145,397	80,854	19,975	52,060	2,173	44,033	6,424	2,393	215
ND ...	24,234	10,574	831	8,159	443	10,377	2,245	315	30
SD. ...	25,841	13,305	2,543	9,356	565	9,306	1,051	437	71
NE....	47,553	25,620	3,662	19,171	1,191	16,692	1,104	805	20
KS....	82,765	42,896	11,307	26,155	829	25,480	10,037	1,000	158
South	2,294,420	1,145,986	439,250	558,382	31,432	615,791	312,915	46,382	7,975
S.A.....	1,243,962	577,690	231,369	270,930	14,778	322,299	213,816	27,052	5,025
DE. ...	20,071	8,662	3,347	4,596	179	8,806	1,164	349	19
MD ...	113,856	62,760	27,025	26,884	2,252	30,892	10,426	2,706	523
DC. ...	41,717	14,070	4,035	7,008	138	16,126	2,181	4,731	131
VA....	209,300	84,292	33,553	37,762	2,860	61,943	51,869	2,842	319
WV ...	36,911	19,469	4,439	12,591	458	15,083	32	579	33
NC ...	224,470	83,400	24,857	47,014	2,119	71,266	58,378	2,952	259
SC. ...	116,543	44,134	18,351	18,228	2,123	35,488	30,166	1,060	102
GA ...	173,633	87,266	40,803	36,549	1,666	39,723	30,261	4,122	450
FL ...	307,461	173,637	74,959	80,298	2,983	42,972	29,339	7,711	3,189
E.S.C	392,424	194,314	63,082	102,900	6,169	131,846	38,432	5,733	922
KY....	101,176	47,609	13,948	27,874	1,052	30,600	15,228	1,474	118
TN....	129,129	65,389	21,335	35,192	2,194	43,683	11,126	2,094	357
AL....	92,402	51,583	19,226	24,031	1,924	28,859	6,085	1,657	364
MS ...	69,717	29,733	8,573	15,803	999	28,704	5,993	508	83
W.S.C ...	658,034	373,982	144,799	184,552	10,485	161,646	60,667	13,597	2,028
AR ...	58,332	34,223	8,642	21,809	827	16,775	1,814	594	62
LA ...	112,578	67,276	26,792	32,072	1,633	27,990	10,851	1,803	184
OK ...	93,677	51,211	15,108	29,666	1,044	24,924	8,712	2,335	340
TX ...	393,447	221,272	94,257	101,005	6,981	91,957	39,290	8,865	1,442
West	1,294,616	622,278	269,394	269,671	26,543	239,808	189,330	51,768	23,782
Mt	297,687	144,834	60,762	65,842	6,777	77,782	27,269	9,807	3,215
MT ...	23,747	11,125	2,174	7,764	393	6,195	1,000	494	17
ID ...	21,490	10,478	2,871	6,318	457	6,676	740	539	19
WY ...	10,240	5,434	1,556	2,679	297	3,414	832	228	13
CO ...	79,472	35,976	13,446	18,506	1,706	22,749	12,895	2,721	393
NM ...	28,807	14,024	5,385	6,276	637	8,333	3,088	775	164
AZ....	80,683	41,508	22,636	14,472	1,751	18,459	6,071	3,014	1,897
UT....	29,048	12,739	4,252	6,222	901	10,156	1,046	974	276
NV....	24,200	13,550	8,442	3,605	635	1,800	1,597	1,062	436
Pac	996,929	477,444	208,632	203,829	19,766	162,026	162,061	41,961	20,567
WA ...	120,531	55,313	14,569	32,840	1,606	27,908	18,491	4,862	772
OR ...	66,205	33,378	10,912	18,200	1,317	18,970	122	3,505	564
CA....	751,860	376,374	178,199	148,362	16,375	108,880	115,334	32,063	18,081
AK....	20,701	4,574	2,630	1,202	386	1,310	8,807	604	79
HI ...	37,632	7,805	2,322	3,225	82	4,958	19,307	927	1,071

- Represents zero.   [1] Includes persons in other types of group quarters not shown separately.   [2] Includes other institutionalized persons not shown separately.   [3] Results reported from the enumeration of emergency shelters and visible in street locations are not (and were never intended to be) a count of the total population of homeless persons at the national, State, or local level. The data do not represent a complete count of the homeless population. Counts of persons in these two locations represent one of the Bureau's efforts to include homeless persons in the 1990 census.

Source: U.S. Bureau of the Census, *1990 Census of Population, General Population Characteristics* (CP-1).

No. 86. Religious Preference, Church Membership, and Attendance: 1957 to 1991

[In percent. Covers civilian noninstitutional population, 18 years old and over. Data represent averages of the combined results of several surveys during year. Data are subject to sampling variability, see source]

YEAR	RELIGIOUS PREFERENCE					Church/ syna-gogue members	Persons attend-ing church/ syna-gogue [1]	AGE AND REGION	Church/ syna-gogue members, 1991
	Protes-tant	Catho-lic	Jewish	Other	None				
1957	66	26	3	1	3	[2]73	47	18-29 years old. . . .	60
1967	67	25	3	3	2	[3]73	43	30-49 years old. . . .	67
1975	62	27	2	4	6	71	41	50 years and over . .	76
1980	61	28	2	2	7	69	40	East [4]	69
1985	57	28	2	4	9	71	42	Midwest [5]	66
1990	56	25	2	6	11	65	40	South [6]	76
1991	56	25	2	6	11	68	42	West [7]	54

[1] Persons who attended a church or synagogue in the last seven days. [2] 1952 data. [3] 1965 data. [4] ME, NH, RI, NY, CT, VT, MA, NJ, PA, WV, DE, MD, and DC. [5] OH, IN, IL, MI, MN, WI, IA, ND, SD, KS, NE, and MO. [6] KY, TN, VA, NC, SC, GA, FL, AL, MS, TX, AR, OK, and LA. [7] AZ, NM, CO, NV, MT, ID, WY, UT, CA, WA, OR, AK, and HI.

Source: Princeton Religion Research Center, Princeton, NJ, "Emerging Trends," periodical. Based on surveys conducted by The Gallup Organization, Inc.

No. 87. Religious Bodies—Church Membership, 1960 to 1990, and Number of Churches, 1990

[Membership in thousands, except as indicated. See headnote, table 88. See also *Historical Statistics, Colonial Times to 1970,* series H 793-799]

RELIGIOUS BODY	MEMBERSHIP						Number of churches, 1990
	1960	1970	1975	1980	1985	1990	
Total	114,449	131,045	131,013	134,817	142,926	156,336	358,194
Members as percent of population [1]	64	63	61	59	60	63	(X)
Average members per local church	359	399	393	401	413	436	(X)
Buddhist Churches of America	20	100	60	60	100	19	67
Eastern Churches.	2,699	3,850	3,696	3,823	4,026	3,976	1,702
Jews [2]	5,367	5,870	6,115	5,920	5,835	5,981	3,416
Old Catholic, Polish National Catholic, and Armenian Churches.	590	848	846	924	1,024	950	441
The Roman Catholic Church	42,105	48,215	48,882	50,450	52,655	58,568	23,685
Protestants [3]	[4]63,669	71,713	71,043	73,479	79,096	86,684	327,717
Miscellaneous [5]	([4])	449	372	161	191	157	1,166

X Not applicable. [1] Based on Bureau of the Census estimated total population as of July 1. Estimates for 1980's reflect results of 1990 census. [2] Estimates of the Jewish community including those identified with Orthodox, Conservative and Reform synagogues or temples. [3] Includes nonprotestant bodies such as "Latter-day Saints" and "Jehovah's Witnesses." [4] Data for "Miscellaneous" included with Protestants. [5] Includes non-Christian bodies such as "Spiritualists," "Ethical Culture Movement," and "Unitarian-Universalists."

Source: National Council of the Churches of Christ in the United States of America, New York, NY, *Yearbook of American and Canadian Churches,* annual (copyright).

No. 88. Religious Bodies—Selected Data

[Represents latest information available from religious bodies with memberships of 60,000 or more; excludes a few groups giving no data. Not all groups follow same calendar year nor count membership in same way; some groups give only approximate figures. Roman Catholics count all baptized persons, including infants; Jewish statistics are estimates of the number of persons living in Jewish households including as a consequence of intermarriage, approximately 7.4 percent non-Jewish persons. Eastern Orthodox Churches include all persons in their nationality or cultural groups; most Protestant bodies count only persons who have attained full membership, and previous estimates have indicated that all but a minority of these are over 11 years of age; however, many Lutheran bodies and The Episcopal Church report all baptized persons, and not only those confirmed. Data which appear in italics are "noncurrent," i.e., they are reported for 1989 or earlier. All other data are "current" and were reported in 1990 or 1991]

RELIGIOUS BODY	Year reported	Churches reported	Member-ship (1,000)	Pastors serving par-ishes [1]	Sunday school enrollment [2] (1,000)
African Methodist Episcopal Church	*1981*	*6,200*	*2,210*	*6,050*	(NA)
African Methodist Episcopal Zion Church	1991	3,000	1,200	2,500	50
American Baptist Association	*1986*	*1,705*	*250*	*1,740*	(NA)
American Baptist Churches in the U.S.A.	1990	5,808	1,536	5,351	300
Antiochian Orthodox Christian Archdiocese of North America, The . . .	*1989*	*160*	*350*	*250*	(NA)
Apostolic Catholic Assyrian Church of the East, N. American Diocese .	*1989*	*22*	*120*	*92*	(NA)
Armenian Apostolic Church of America	1991	28	150	22	1
Armenian Church of America, Diocese of the	*1979*	*66*	*450*	*45*	(NA)
Assemblies of God.	1990	11,353	2,182	16,336	1,403
Baptist Bible Fellowship, International	*1986*	*3,449*	*1,406*	*3,400*	(NA)
Baptist General Conference	1991	799	135	1,200	79
Baptist Missionary Association of America	1990	1,372	229	1,232	98

See footnotes at end of table.

No. 88. Religious Bodies—Selected Data—Continued

[See headnote, page 67]

RELIGIOUS BODY	Year reported	Churches reported	Member-ship (1,000)	Pastors serving par-ishes [1]	Sunday school enrollment [2] (1,000)
Christian and Missionary Alliance, The	1990	1,856	279	1,596	194
Christian Brethren (a.k.a. Plymouth Brethren)	1984	1,150	98	(NA)	(NA)
Christian Church (Disciples of Christ)	1990	4,069	1,040	3,744	309
Christian Churches and Churches of Christ	1988	5,579	1,071	5,525	(NA)
Christian Congregation, Inc., The	1990	1,453	110	1,451	48
Christian Methodist Episcopal Church	1983	2,340	719	2,340	(NA)
Christian Reformed Church in North America	1990	715	226	634	(NA)
Church of God, The	1978	2,035	76	1,910	(NA)
Church of God (Anderson, IN)	1990	2,339	206	2,126	169
Church of God (Cleveland, TN)	1990	5,841	620	4,665	389
Church of God in Christ, The	1991	15,300	5,500	28,988	(NA)
Church of God in Christ, International, The	1982	300	200	700	(NA)
Church of God of Prophecy, The	1991	2,096	73	7,015	90
Church of Jesus Christ of Latter-day Saints, The	1990	9,213	4,267	27,639	3,380
Church of the Brethren	1990	1,095	148	1,084	(NA)
Church of the Nazarene	1991	5,172	574	4,416	860
Churches of Christ	1990	13,134	1,683	(NA)	8
Community Churches, International Council of	1991	398	250	(NA)	(NA)
Congregational Christian Churches, National Association of	1991	400	90	550	(NA)
Conservative Baptist Association of America	1989	1,126	210	1,126	(NA)
Coptic Orthodox Church	1990	42	165	49	7
Cumberland Presbyterian Church	1990	796	99	571	45
Episcopal Church, The	1990	7,354	2,446	8,040	568
Evangelical Covenant Church, The	1990	590	90	824	77
Evangelical Free Church of America	1991	1,087	192	(NA)	(NA)
Evangelical Lutheran Church in America	1990	11,087	5,241	10,083	1,161
Free Methodist Church of North America	1990	1,096	74	(NA)	98
Free Will Baptists, National Association of	1990	2,506	197	2,800	146
Full Gospel Fellowship of Churches and Ministers, International	1985	450	65	850	(NA)
General Association of Regular Baptist Churches	1990	1,574	168	(NA)	(NA)
General Baptists (General Association of)	1990	876	74	1,384	(NA)
Greek Orthodox Archdiocese of North and South America	1977	535	1,950	610	(NA)
Independent Fundamental Churches of America	1991	700	78	745	75
International Church of the Foursquare Gospel	1990	1,451	199	(NA)	(NA)
Jehovah's Witnesses	1991	9,347	858	-	-
Jews [3]	1990	3,416	5,981	(NA)	(NA)
Liberty Baptist Fellowship	1990	600	180	2,000	(NA)
Lutheran Church - Missouri Synod, The	1990	5,296	2,603	5,347	673
Mennonite Church	1990	1,034	93	1,504	(NA)
National Baptist Convention of America	1956	11,398	2,669	7,598	(NA)
National Baptist Convention, U.S.A., Inc	1991	30,000	7,800	30,000	(NA)
National Primitive Baptist Convention, Inc.	1975	616	250	460	(NA)
North American Old Roman Catholic Church.	1986	133	63	109	(NA)
Old Order Amish Church	1989	785	71	3,140	(NA)
Orthodox Church in America	1978	440	1,000	457	(NA)
Pentecostal Church of God	1990	1,174	91	(NA)	74
Pentecostal Holiness Church, International	1989	1,475	119	1,583	(NA)
Polish National Catholic Church of America	1960	162	282	141	(NA)
Presbyterian Church in America	1990	1,167	224	1,204	112
Presbyterian Church (U.S.A.)	1990	11,501	3,788	10,308	1,144
Primitive Baptists	1960	1,000	72	(NA)	(NA)
Progressive National Baptist Convention, Inc.	1991	1,400	2,500	1,400	(NA)
Reformed Church in America	1990	924	327	860	105
Reorganized Church of Jesus Christ of Latter-day Saints.	1990	1,025	190	16,666	(NA)
Roman Catholic Church, The	1990	23,685	58,568	34,598	7,302
Romanian Orthodox Episcopate of America	1990	37	65	37	2
Salvation Army, The	1990	1,133	446	3,540	112
Serbian Eastern Orthodox Church in the U.S.A. and Canada	1986	68	67	60	(NA)
Seventh-day Adventist Church	1990	4,217	717	2,316	441
Southern Baptist Convention	1990	37,922	15,038	37,800	8,004
Ukrainian Orthodox Church in the U.S.A.	1966	107	88	107	(NA)
Unitarian Universalist Association	1991	1,020	141	650	49
United Church of Christ	1990	6,260	1,599	4,813	426
United Methodist Church, The	1989	37,407	8,905	20,774	(NA)
United Pentecostal Church, International	1991	3,626	500	(NA)	(NA)
Wesleyan Church, The	1990	1,628	111	1,857	121
Wisconsin Evangelical Lutheran Synod	1990	1,211	420	1,167	49

- Represents or rounds to zero. NA Not available. [1] Includes other pastors performing pastoral duties. [2] Includes pupils, officers, and teachers. [3] Estimate of size of Jewish community provided by American Jewish Yearbook. Estimates of the number of Jews holding membership in synagogues or temples of the four branches of Judaism amount to 4,750,000.

Source: National Council of the Churches of Christ in the United States of America, New York, NY, *Yearbook of American and Canadian Churches*, annual (copyright).

No. 89. Christian Church Adherents, 1990, and Jewish Population, 1991—States

[Christian church adherents were defined as "all members, including full members, their children and the estimated number of other regular participants who are not considered as communicant, confirmed or full members." Data on Christian church adherents are based on reports of 133 church groupings and exclude 34 church bodies that reported more than 100,000 members to the *Yearbook of American and Canadian Churches*. Data on Jewish population are based primarily on a compilation of individual estimates made by local Jewish federations. Additionally, most large communities have completed Jewish demographic surveys from which the Jewish population can be determined]

REGION, DIVISION, AND STATE	CHRISTIAN ADHERENTS, 1990 Number (1,000)	CHRISTIAN ADHERENTS, 1990 Percent of population [1]	JEWISH POPULATION, 1991 Number (1,000)	JEWISH POPULATION, 1991 Percent of population [1]
U.S. . . .	137,065	55.1	5,798	2.3
Northeast .	31,721	62.4	2,817	5.6
N.E.	7,882	59.7	417	3.2
ME. . .	447	36.4	8	0.7
NH. . .	438	39.5	7	0.6
VT. . .	237	42.1	5	0.8
MA. . .	3,942	65.5	275	4.6
RI . . .	770	76.7	16	1.6
CT . . .	2,048	62.3	106	3.2
M.A. . .	23,839	63.4	2,400	6.4
NY. . .	11,813	65.7	1,644	9.1
NJ . . .	4,735	61.3	426	5.5
PA. . .	7,291	61.4	330	2.8
Midwest . .	33,551	56.2	669	1.1
E.N.C . .	22,768	54.2	548	1.3
OH. . .	5,438	50.1	131	1.2
IN . . .	2,635	47.5	18	0.3
IL. . . .	6,848	59.9	257	2.2
MI . . .	4,687	50.4	107	1.2
WI . . .	3,160	64.6	35	0.7
W.N.C. .	10,783	61.1	121	0.7
MN. . .	2,837	64.9	30	0.7
IA . . .	1,681	60.5	6	0.2
MO . . .	2,945	57.6	62	1.2
ND. . .	485	75.9	1	0.1
SD. . .	474	68.1	(Z)	0.1
NE. . .	1,007	63.8	7	0.5
KS. . .	1,355	54.7	14	0.6
South. . . .	49,525	58.0	1,180	1.4
S.A. . . .	22,239	51.0	1,008	2.3
DE . . .	306	46.0	9	1.4
MD. . .	2,312	48.3	211	4.4
DC. . .	374	61.7	25	4.2
VA. . .	2,966	47.9	68	1.1
WV . .	742	41.4	2	0.1
NC. . .	3,978	60.0	16	0.2
SC. . .	2,158	61.9	8	0.2
GA. . .	3,731	57.6	74	1.1
FL . . .	5,673	43.8	593	4.6
E.S.C. . .	9,886	65.1	40	0.3
KY. . .	2,228	60.4	12	0.3
TN. . .	2,985	61.2	18	0.4
AL. . .	2,867	71.0	9	0.2
MS. . .	1,806	70.2	2	0.1
W.S.C. .	17,399	65.2	132	0.5
AR. . .	1,425	60.6	2	0.1
LA. . .	2,975	70.5	16	0.4
OK. . .	2,102	66.8	5	0.2
TX . . .	10,896	64.1	109	0.6
West	22,268	42.2	1,133	2.1
Mt.	6,587	48.2	153	1.1
MT . . .	341	42.7	(Z)	0.1
ID . . .	507	50.4	(Z)	0.1
WY . . .	216	47.7	(Z)	0.1
CO. . .	1,294	39.3	51	1.5
NM. . .	889	58.7	6	0.4
AZ. . .	1,577	43.0	72	2.0
UT. . .	1,374	79.8	3	0.2
NV. . .	386	32.1	20	1.7
Pac. . . .	15,681	40.1	980	2.5
WA. . .	1,613	33.1	33	0.7
OR. . .	915	32.2	15	0.5
CA. . .	12,585	42.3	923	3.1
AK. . .	177	32.2	2	0.4
HI . . .	391	35.3	7	0.6

Z Fewer than 500. [1] Based on U.S. Bureau of the Census data for resident population enumerated as of April 1, 1990, and estimated as of July 1, 1991.

Source: Christian church adherents—M. Bradley; N. Green, Jr.; D. Jones; M. Lynn; and L. McNeil; *Churches and Church Membership in the United States 1990*, Glenmary Research Center, Atlanta, GA, 1992 (copyright); Jewish population—American Jewish Committee and the Jewish Publication Society, New York, NY, *American Jewish Year Book, 1992* (copyright).

No. 90. Religious Population of the World, by Region: 1992

[In thousands, except percent. Refers to adherents of all religions as defined and enumerated for each of the world's countries in *World Christian Encyclopedia* (1982), projected to mid-1992, adjusted for recent data]

RELIGION	Total	Percent distribution	Africa	Asia	Latin America	Northern America	Europe	Eurasia [1]	Oceania
Total population . . .	5,480,010	100.0	682,132	3,231,273	465,987	279,985	500,712	292,691	27,230
Christians	1,833,022	33.4	327,204	285,365	435,811	239,004	413,756	109,254	22,628
Roman Catholics.	1,025,585	18.7	122,907	123,597	405,623	97,022	262,638	5,590	8,208
Protestants	373,698	6.8	87,332	81,476	17,263	96,312	73,939	9,858	7,518
Orthodox	170,422	3.1	28,549	3,655	1,764	6,008	36,165	93,705	576
Anglicans.	74,883	1.4	26,863	707	1,300	7,338	32,956	(Z)	5,719
Other Christians	188,434	3.4	61,553	75,930	9,861	32,324	8,058	101	607
Muslims	971,329	17.7	278,251	636,976	1,351	2,847	12,575	39,229	101
Nonreligious [2]	876,032	16.0	1,896	691,144	17,159	25,265	52,411	85,066	3,291
Hindus	732,812	13.4	1,475	728,118	884	1,269	704	2	360
Buddhists	314,939	5.7	21	313,114	541	558	272	407	26
Atheists	240,310	4.4	316	161,414	3,224	1,319	17,604	55,898	535
Chinese folk-religionists [3].	187,107	3.4	13	186,817	73	122	60	1	21
New-religionists [4]	143,415	2.6	21	141,382	530	1,421	50	1	10
Tribal religionists	96,581	1.8	70,588	24,948	936	41	1	-	67
Sikhs	18,801	0.3	26	18,272	8	254	231	1	9
Jews	17,822	0.3	337	5,587	1,092	7,003	1,469	2,236	98
Shamanists	10,493	0.2	1	10,233	1	1	1	254	1
Confucians	6,028	0.1	1	5,994	2	26	2	2	1
Baha'is.	5,517	0.1	1,496	2,680	801	365	91	7	77
Jains	3,794	0.1	53	3,717	4	4	15	-	1
Shintoists	3,223	0.1	(Z)	3,220	1	1	1	(Z)	1
Other religionists	18,586	0.3	433	12,292	3,570	485	1,469	333	4

- Represents zero. Z Fewer than 500. [1] Source's provisional new term for the former Soviet Union. [2] Persons professing no religion, nonbelievers, agnostics, freethinkers and dereligionized secularists indifferent to all religion. [3] Followers of traditional Chinese religion (local deities, ancestor veneration, Confucian ethics, Taoism, etc.). [4] Followers of Asiatic 20th-century New Religions, New Religious movements, radical new crisis religions, and non-Christian syncretistic mass religions.

Source: Encyclopaedia Britannica, Inc., Chicago, IL, *1993 Britannica Book of the Year*. (Reprinted with permission. Copyright 1993.)

Figure 2.1
Distribution of AIDS Deaths, by Age: 1982 Through 1992

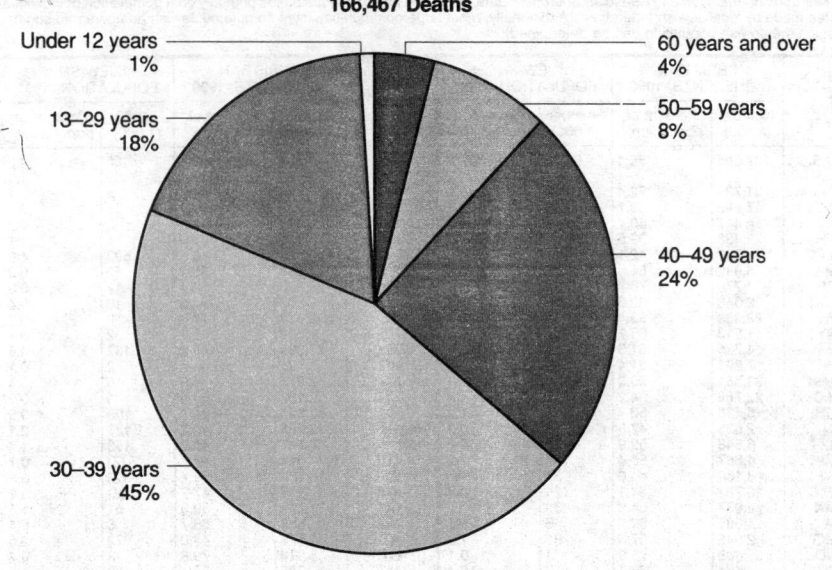

166,467 Deaths

Under 12 years 1%

13–29 years 18%

30–39 years 45%

60 years and over 4%

50–59 years 8%

40–49 years 24%

Source: Chart prepared by U.S. Bureau of the Census. For data, see table 131.

Figure 2.2
Age-Specific Fertility Rates: 1970 to 1990

Per thousand women in each age group

20–24

25–29

30–34

15–19

35–39

Source: Chart prepared by U.S. Bureau of the Census. Data from National Center for Health Statistics.

Vital Statistics

This section presents vital statistics data on births, deaths, abortions, fetal deaths, fertility, life expectancy, marriages, and divorces. Vital statistics are compiled for the country as a whole by the National Center for Health Statistics (NCHS) and published in its annual report, *Vital Statistics of the United States,* in certain reports of the *Vital and Health Statistics* series, and in the *Monthly Vital Statistics Report.* Reports in this field are also issued by the various State bureaus of vital statistics. Data on fertility, on age of persons at first marriage, and on marital status and marital history are compiled by the Bureau of the Census from its Current Population Survey (CPS; see text, section 1) and published in *Current Population Reports,* series P20. Data on abortions are published by the Alan Guttmacher Institute, New York, NY in selected issues of *Family Planning Perspectives.*

Registration of vital events.—The registration of births, deaths, fetal deaths, and other vital events in the United States is primarily a State and local function. The civil laws of every State provide for a continuous and permanent birth- and death-registration system. Many States also provide for marriage- and divorce-registration systems. Vital events occurring to U.S. residents outside the United States are not included in the data.

Births and deaths.—The live-birth, death, and fetal-death statistics prepared by NCHS are based on vital records filed in the registration offices of all States, of New York City, and of the District of Columbia. The annual collection of death statistics on a national basis began in 1900 with a national death-registration area of 10 States and the District of Columbia; a similar annual collection of birth statistics for a national birth-registration area began in 1915, also with 10 reporting States and the District of Columbia. Since 1933, the birth- and death-registration areas have comprised the entire United States, including Alaska (beginning 1959) and Hawaii (beginning 1960). National statistics on fetal deaths were

In Brief	
1991:	
Births	4,111,000
Deaths	2,165,000
Marriages	2,371,000
Divorces	1,187,000
Leading causes of death:	
Heart disease	*718,090*
Cancer	*514,310*
Stroke	*144,070*
Accidents	*91,700*
Chronic lung disease	*89,130*

first compiled for 1918 and annually since 1922.

Prior to 1951, birth statistics came from a complete count of records received in the Public Health Service (now received in NCHS). From 1951 through 1971, they were based on a 50-percent sample of all registered births (except for a complete count in 1955 and a 20- to 50-percent sample in 1967). Beginning in 1972, they have been based on a complete count for States participating in the Vital Statistics Cooperative Program (VSCP) (for details, see the technical appendix in *Vital Statistics of the United States*) and on a 50-percent sample of all other areas. Beginning 1986 all reporting areas participated in the VSCP. Mortality data have been based on a complete count of records for each area (except for a 50-percent sample in 1972). Beginning in 1970, births to, and deaths of nonresident aliens of the United States and U.S. citizens outside the United States have been excluded from the data. Fetal deaths and deaths among Armed Forces abroad are excluded. Data based on samples are subject to sampling error; for details, see annual issues of *Vital Statistics of the United States.*

Mortality statistics by cause of death are compiled in accordance with World Health Organization regulations according to the *International Classification of Diseases* (ICD). The ICD is revised approximately every 10 years. The ninth revision of the ICD was employed beginning in 1979. Deaths for prior years were classified according to the revision of the

ICD in use at the time. Each revision of the ICD introduces a number of discontinuities in mortality statistics; for a discussion of those between the eighth and ninth revisions of the ICD, see *Monthly Vital Statistics Report,* vol. 28, No. 11, supplement.

Some of the tables present age-adjusted death rates in addition to crude death rates. Age-adjusted death rates shown in this section were prepared using the direct method, in which age-specific death rates for a population of interest are applied to a standard population distributed by age. Age adjustment eliminates the differences in observed rates between points in time or among compared population groups that result from age differences in population composition.

Abortions.—The U.S. Centers for Disease Control (CDC) collects data on abortions annually from States which have a central health agency with a statewide reporting system. The Alan Guttmacher Institute, New York, NY also issues data on the number of abortions based on its own surveys of hospitals and physicians. The Guttmacher Institute also publishes data on the characteristics of abortions after adjusting CDC data for changes in the number of States reporting each year.

Fertility and life expectancy.—The total fertility rate, defined as the number of births that 1,000 women would have in their lifetime if, at each year of age, they experienced the birth rates occurring in the specified year, is compiled and published by NCHS. Other data relating to social and medical factors which affect fertility rates, such as contraceptive use and birth expectations, are collected and made available by both NCHS and the Bureau of the Census. NCHS figures are based on information in birth and fetal death certificates and on the periodic National Surveys of Family Growth; Bureau of the Census data are based on decennial censuses and the CPS.

Data on life expectancy, the average remaining lifetime in years for persons who attain a given age, are computed and published by NCHS. For details, see the technical appendix in *Vital Statistics of the United States.*

Marriage and divorce.—The compilation of nationwide statistics on marriages and divorces in the United States began in 1887-88 when the National Office of Vital Statistics prepared estimates for the years 1867-86. Although periodic updates took place after 1888, marriage and divorce statistics were not collected and published annually until 1944 by that Office. In 1957 and 1958, respectively, the same Office established marriage- and divorce-registration areas. Beginning in 1957, the marriage-registration area comprised 30 States, plus Alaska, Hawaii, Puerto Rico, and the Virgin Islands; it currently includes 42 States and the District of Columbia. The divorce-registration area, starting in 1958 with 14 States, Alaska, Hawaii, and the Virgin Islands, currently includes a total of 31 States and the Virgin Islands. Procedures for estimating the number of marriages and divorces in the registration States are discussed in *Vital Statistics of the United States,* vol. III—*Marriage and Divorce.* Total counts of events for registration and nonregistration States are gathered by collecting already summarized data on marriages and divorces reported by State offices of vital statistics and by county offices of registration.

Another important source of data on marriage and divorce trends in the United States is the March supplement to the Current Population Survey conducted by the Bureau of the Census. For information on marital status, see section 1.

Vital statistics rates.—Except as noted, vital statistics rates computed by NCHS are based on decennial census population figures as of April 1 for 1940, 1950, 1960, 1970, 1980, and 1990; and on midyear population figures for other years, as estimated by the Bureau of the Census (see text, section 1).

Race.—Data by race for births, deaths, marriages, and divorces from NCHS are based on information contained in the certificates of registration. The Census Bureau's Current Population Survey obtains information on race by asking respondents to classify their race as: (1) White, (2) Black, (3) American Indian, Eskimo, or Aleut, or (4) Asian or Pacific Islander.

No. 91. Live Births, Deaths, Marriages, and Divorces: 1950 to 1991

[Prior to 1960, excludes Alaska and Hawaii. Beginning 1970, excludes births to and deaths of nonresidents of the United States. See Appendix III. See also *Historical Statistics, Colonial Times to 1970,* series B 1-5, B 142, B 167, and B 216]

YEAR	NUMBER (1,000)					RATE PER 1,000 POPULATION				
	Births [1]	Deaths		Mar- riages [3]	Divorc- es [4]	Births [1]	Deaths		Mar- riages [3]	Divorc- es [4]
		Total	Infant [2]				Total	Infant [2]		
1950	3,632	1,452	104	1,667	385	24.1	9.6	29.2	11.1	2.6
1955	4,097	1,529	107	1,531	377	25.0	9.3	26.4	9.3	2.3
1960	4,258	1,712	111	1,523	393	23.7	9.5	26.0	8.5	2.2
1965	3,760	1,828	93	1,800	479	19.4	9.4	24.7	9.3	2.5
1970	3,731	1,921	75	2,159	708	18.4	9.5	20.0	10.6	3.5
1971	3,556	1,928	68	2,190	773	17.2	9.3	19.1	10.6	3.7
1972	3,258	1,964	60	2,282	845	15.6	9.4	18.5	10.9	4.0
1973	3,137	1,973	56	2,284	915	14.8	9.3	17.7	10.8	4.3
1974	3,160	1,934	53	2,230	977	14.8	9.1	16.7	10.5	4.6
1975	3,144	1,893	51	2,153	1,036	14.6	8.8	16.1	10.0	4.8
1976	3,168	1,909	48	2,155	1,083	14.6	8.8	15.2	9.9	5.0
1977	3,327	1,900	47	2,178	1,091	15.1	8.6	14.1	9.9	5.0
1978	3,333	1,928	46	2,282	1,130	15.0	8.7	13.8	10.3	5.1
1979	3,494	1,914	46	2,331	1,181	15.6	8.5	13.1	10.4	5.3
1980	3,612	1,990	46	2,390	1,189	15.9	8.8	12.6	10.6	5.2
1981	3,629	1,978	43	2,422	1,213	15.8	8.6	11.9	10.6	5.3
1982	3,681	1,975	42	2,456	1,170	15.9	8.5	11.5	10.6	5.1
1983	3,639	2,019	41	2,446	1,158	15.6	8.6	11.2	10.5	5.0
1984	3,669	2,039	40	2,477	1,169	15.6	8.6	10.8	10.5	5.0
1985	3,761	2,086	40	2,413	1,190	15.8	8.8	10.6	10.1	5.0
1986	3,757	2,105	39	2,407	1,178	15.6	8.8	10.4	10.0	4.9
1987	3,809	2,123	38	2,403	1,166	15.7	8.8	10.1	9.9	4.8
1988	3,910	2,168	39	2,396	1,167	16.0	8.9	10.0	9.8	4.8
1989	4,041	2,150	40	[5]2,404	[5]1,163	16.4	8.7	9.8	[5]9.7	[5]4.7
1990 [5]	4,158	2,148	38	[5]2,448	[5]1,175	16.7	8.6	9.2	[5]9.8	[5]4.7
1991 [5]	4,111	2,165	37	2,371	1,187	16.2	8.5	8.9	9.4	4.7

[1] Prior to 1960, data adjusted for underregistration. [2] Infants under 1 year, excluding fetal deaths; rates per 1,000 registered live births. [3] Includes estimates for some States through 1965 and also for 1976 and 1977 and marriage licenses for some States for all years except 1973 and 1975. Beginning 1978, includes nonlicensed marriages in California. [4] Includes reported annulments and some estimated State figures for all years. [5] Preliminary.

Source: U.S. National Center for Health Statistics, *Vital Statistics of the United States,* annual, *Monthly Vital Statistics Report;* and unpublished data.

No. 92. Live Births and Deaths—20 Largest Metropolitan Areas: 1988

[Excludes births to and deaths of nonresidents of the United States. Data are by place of residence. Metropolitan statistical areas (MSA's), consolidated metropolitan statistical areas (CMSA's), and New England County Metropolitan Areas (NECMA's) are defined by the U.S. Office of Management and Budget as of December 31, 1992; see Appendix II for definitions and components]

METROPOLITAN AREA	NUMBER (1,000)			RATE PER 1,000 POPULATION		
	Births	Deaths		Births	Deaths	
		Total	Infant [1]		Total	Infant [1]
New York-Northern New Jersey-Long Island, NY-NJ-CT-PA CMSA/NECMA [2]................	307,126	189,362	3,354	15.8	9.7	10.9
Los Angeles-Riverside-Orange County, CA CMSA	276,991	101,850	2,458	19.9	7.3	8.9
Chicago-Gary-Kenosha, IL-IN-WI CMSA.............	141,570	71,500	1,678	17.3	8.7	11.9
Washington-Baltimore, DC-MD-VA-WV CMSA.........	107,954	50,890	1,243	16.4	7.7	11.5
San Francisco-Oakland-San Jose, CA CMSA	99,474	47,356	774	16.3	7.8	7.8
Philadelphia-Wilmington-Atlantic City, PA-NJ-DE-MD CMSA	94,245	58,748	1,100	16.1	10.0	11.7
Boston-Brockton-Nashua, MA-NH NECMA	85,666	50,656	659	15.2	9.0	7.7
Detroit-Ann Arbor-Flint, MI CMSA	78,425	45,227	967	15.2	8.8	12.3
Dallas-Fort Worth, TX CMSA	74,017	25,596	654	18.9	6.5	8.8
Houston-Galveston-Brazoria, TX CMSA	67,130	22,579	644	18.7	6.3	9.6
Miami-Fort Lauderdale, FL CMSA	48,638	32,785	542	15.8	10.7	11.1
Seattle-Tacoma-Bremerton, WA CMSA	44,475	20,447	395	15.8	7.3	8.9
Atlanta, GA MSA	49,123	19,235	554	17.3	6.8	11.3
Cleveland-Akron, OH CMSA..................	42,012	27,524	463	14.7	9.6	11.0
Minneapolis-St.Paul, MN-WI MSA	41,436	16,896	322	16.8	6.8	7.8
San Diego, CA MSA	44,096	16,658	315	18.7	7.0	7.1
St. Louis, MO-IL MSA	40,097	23,302	390	16.1	9.4	9.7
Pittsburgh, PA MSA	30,134	27,206	260	12.5	11.3	8.6
Phoenix-Mesa, AZ MSA....................	40,216	16,315	398	18.6	7.5	9.9
Tampa-St. Petersburg-Clearwater, FL MSA........	27,201	24,903	290	13.6	12.4	10.7

[1] Infants under 1 year, excluding fetal deaths; rates per 1,000 registered live births. [2] Includes parts of New Haven County, CT, not in the CMSA; excludes parts of Litchfield and Middlesex Counties, CT, in the CMSA.

Source: U.S. National Center for Health Statistics, *Vital Statistics of the United States,* annual; and unpublished data.

No. 93. Births and Birth Rates: 1970 to 1990

[**Births in thousands and by race of child, except as indicated.** Excludes births to nonresidents of the United States. For population bases used to derive these data, see text, section 2, and Appendix III. See also *Historical Statistics, Colonial Times to 1970*, series B 1, B 5-10, and B 12-20]

ITEM	1970	1980	1982	1983	1984	1985	1986	1987	1988	1989	1990
Live births [1]	3,731	3,612	3,681	3,639	3,669	3,761	3,757	3,809	3,910	4,041	4,158
White	3,091	2,899	2,942	2,904	2,924	2,991	2,970	2,992	3,046	3,132	3,225
Black	572	590	593	586	593	608	621	642	672	709	725
Male	1,915	1,853	1,886	1,866	1,879	1,928	1,925	1,951	2,002	2,069	2,129
Female	1,816	1,760	1,795	1,773	1,790	1,833	1,832	1,858	1,907	1,971	2,029
Males per 100 females	106	105	105	105	105	105	105	105	105	105	105
Age of mother:											
Under 20 years old	656	562	524	499	480	478	472	473	489	518	533
20 to 24 years old	1,419	1,226	1,206	1,160	1,142	1,141	1,102	1,076	1,067	1,078	1,094
25 to 29 years old	995	1,108	1,152	1,148	1,166	1,201	1,200	1,216	1,239	1,263	1,277
30 to 34 years old	428	550	605	625	658	696	721	761	804	842	886
35 to 39 years old	180	141	168	180	196	214	230	248	270	294	318
40 years old or more	53	24	26	27	28	29	31	36	41	46	50
Age of father:											
Under 20 years old	189	137	125	116	109	108	105	105	111	120	129
20 to 24 years old	1,015	803	768	722	696	685	651	627	617	613	628
25 to 29 years old	1,085	1,082	1,093	1,070	1,067	1,081	1,059	1,053	1,055	1,056	1,060
30 to 34 years old	599	739	780	782	806	837	845	872	904	922	955
35 to 39 years old	298	275	319	335	356	381	398	413	431	451	474
40 years old or more	214	139	149	153	160	167	174	191	205	221	231
Age not stated	330	437	447	461	475	502	524	549	585	659	681
Birth rate per 1,000 population	18.4	15.9	15.9	15.6	15.6	15.8	15.6	15.7	16.0	16.4	16.7
White	17.4	14.9	14.9	14.6	14.6	14.8	14.6	14.6	14.8	15.1	15.5
Black	25.3	22.1	21.5	21.0	21.0	21.3	21.5	21.9	22.6	23.5	23.8
Male	19.4	16.8	16.7	16.4	16.4	16.7	16.5	16.5	16.8	17.2	17.6
Female	17.4	15.1	15.1	14.8	14.8	15.0	14.9	14.9	15.2	15.6	15.9
Plural birth ratio [2]	[3]18.1	19.3	19.9	20.3	20.3	21.0	21.6	22.0	22.4	23.0	23.3
White	[3]17.3	18.5	19.2	19.6	19.8	20.4	21.2	21.6	22.0	[4]22.5	[4]22.9
Black	[3]22.8	24.1	24.1	24.5	24.2	25.3	24.9	25.4	25.8	[4]26.9	[4]27.0
Birth rate per 1,000 women [5]	87.9	68.4	67.3	65.8	65.4	66.2	65.4	65.7	67.2	69.2	70.9
White [5]	84.1	64.7	63.9	62.4	62.2	63.0	61.9	62.0	63.0	64.7	66.9
Black [5]	115.4	88.1	84.1	81.7	81.4	82.2	82.4	83.8	86.6	90.4	91.9
Age of mother:											
10 to 14 years old	1.2	1.1	1.1	1.1	1.2	1.2	1.3	1.3	1.3	1.4	1.4
15 to 19 years old	68.3	53.0	52.4	51.4	50.6	51.0	50.2	50.6	53.0	57.3	59.9
20 to 24 years old	167.8	115.1	111.6	107.8	106.8	108.3	107.4	107.9	110.2	113.8	116.5
25 to 29 years old	145.1	112.9	112.2	108.5	108.7	111.0	109.8	111.6	114.4	117.6	120.2
30 to 34 years old	73.3	61.9	64.1	64.9	67.0	69.1	70.1	72.1	74.8	77.4	80.8
35 to 39 years old	31.7	19.8	21.2	22.0	22.9	24.0	24.4	26.3	28.1	29.9	31.7
40 to 44 years old	8.1	3.9	3.9	3.9	3.9	4.0	4.1	4.4	4.8	5.2	5.5
45 to 49 years old	0.5	0.2	0.2	0.2	0.2	0.2	0.2	0.2	0.2	0.2	0.2
Birth rate per 1,000 men [6]	71.5	57.0	56.4	55.1	55.0	55.6	54.8	55.0	55.8	57.2	58.4
White [6]	67.1	52.9	52.5	51.4	51.2	51.9	51.0	50.9	51.5	52.6	53.8
Black [6]	107.4	83.8	80.4	78.1	77.6	78.3	78.3	79.5	82.0	85.4	86.3
Age of father: [7]											
15 to 19 years old [8]	25.6	18.8	18.6	18.2	17.8	18.0	17.9	18.3	19.6	21.9	23.5
20 to 24 years old	146.6	92.0	86.5	82.7	80.7	81.2	80.3	80.5	82.4	85.4	88.0
25 to 29 years old	175.0	123.0	117.3	113.0	111.4	112.3	109.6	109.9	111.6	114.3	116.4
30 to 34 years old	112.3	91.0	90.2	89.0	89.9	91.1	90.3	91.2	93.1	94.8	97.8
35 to 39 years old	57.6	42.8	44.5	45.2	46.0	47.3	46.8	48.6	49.9	51.3	53.0
40 to 44 years old	24.9	17.1	17.5	17.4	17.8	18.1	18.3	19.0	19.9	20.4	21.0
45 to 49 years old	9.1	6.1	6.4	6.4	6.3	6.6	6.7	6.9	7.1	7.4	7.5
50 to 54 years old	3.1	2.2	2.3	2.3	2.4	2.5	2.6	2.6	2.7	2.7	2.8
55 years old and over	0.6	0.4	0.4	0.4	0.4	0.4	0.4	0.4	0.4	0.6	0.4

[1] Includes other races not shown separately. [2] Number of multiple births per 1,000 live births. [3] 1971. [4] Race of mother; data not directly comparable with prior years. [5] Per 1,000 women, 15 to 44 years old in specified group. [6] Rate computed by relating total births, regardless of age of father, to 1,000 men, 15 to 54 years old in specified group. [7] Rates by age of father computed using frequencies with age not stated distributed among all age groups. [8] Rate computed by relating births to fathers under 20 years of age to men 15 to 19 years old.

Source: U.S. National Center for Health Statistics, *Vital Statistics of the United States*, annual; *Monthly Vital Statistics Report*; and unpublished data.

No. 94. Live Births—Number and Rate, by State: 1990 and 1991

[Registered births. Excludes births to nonresidents of the United States, except as noted. By race of child, except as indicated. See Appendix III]

DIVISION AND STATE	NUMBER (1,000) 1990					1991 prel.[3]	RATE PER 1,000 POPULATION[4] 1990					1991 prel.[3]
	All races[1]	White	Black	Hispanic[2] Total	Mex- ican		All races[1]	White	Black	Hispanic[2] Total	Mex- ican	
U.S.	4,158.2	3,225.3	724.6	595.1	385.6	4,111.0	16.7	15.5	22.4	26.7	28.7	16.2
New England	201.2	175.3	19.0	15.5	0.6	189.5	15.2	14.6	30.3	27.2	20.1	14.3
Maine	17.4	16.9	0.2	0.1	(Z)	16.6	14.1	14.0	31.7	18.6	13.0	13.2
New Hampshire	17.6	17.1	0.2	(NA)	(NA)	16.1	15.8	15.7	25.6	(NA)	(NA)	13.9
Vermont	8.3	8.2	(Z)	(Z)	(Z)	7.7	14.7	14.7	19.5	8.2	9.7	13.2
Massachusetts	92.7	78.3	10.2	8.4	0.3	86.3	15.4	14.5	34.1	29.3	22.5	14.5
Rhode Island	15.2	13.1	1.3	1.6	0.1	14.6	15.1	14.3	34.5	34.1	35.7	14.5
Connecticut	50.1	41.8	7.0	5.3	0.2	48.3	15.2	14.6	25.6	25.0	20.1	14.8
Middle Atlantic	591.8	450.1	118.7	75.7	5.1	578.8	15.7	15.0	23.8	23.8	34.9	15.2
New York	297.6	216.8	66.3	53.1	3.8	292.4	16.5	16.2	23.2	24.0	41.0	16.2
New Jersey	122.3	92.6	24.5	17.0	0.9	117.8	15.8	15.1	23.6	22.9	30.4	15.1
Pennsylvania	172.0	140.7	27.9	5.6	0.4	168.6	14.5	13.4	25.6	24.3	16.5	13.9
East North Central	675.5	536.7	123.5	34.7	23.8	662.4	16.1	15.0	25.6	24.1	25.2	15.5
Ohio	166.9	137.1	27.7	2.4	1.0	158.6	15.4	14.4	24.0	17.4	17.5	14.4
Indiana	86.2	74.6	10.3	1.9	1.4	84.7	15.6	14.9	23.8	18.8	20.3	14.9
Illinois	195.8	144.8	45.2	24.2	17.7	194.0	17.1	16.2	26.7	26.8	28.3	16.5
Michigan	153.7	117.5	32.9	4.3	2.6	153.4	16.5	15.2	25.5	21.5	18.5	16.4
Wisconsin	72.9	62.7	7.5	1.9	1.2	71.7	14.9	13.9	30.7	20.0	21.3	14.5
West North Central	270.3	235.4	24.1	5.6	4.1	262.4	15.3	14.5	26.9	19.5	19.8	14.5
Minnesota	68.0	61.0	3.1	1.1	0.8	67.0	15.5	14.8	32.7	19.5	22.5	15.1
Iowa	39.4	37.4	1.3	0.6	0.4	36.0	14.2	13.9	26.6	19.1	15.5	12.6
Missouri	79.3	63.8	14.1	1.0	0.7	78.0	15.5	14.2	25.7	15.7	19.0	15.0
North Dakota	9.3	8.2	0.1	0.1	0.1	9.1	14.5	13.6	33.8	26.4	26.1	14.0
South Dakota	11.0	9.0	0.1	0.1	0.1	11.0	15.8	14.1	41.4	21.5	20.9	15.4
Nebraska	24.4	22.1	1.6	0.8	0.5	23.9	15.4	14.9	27.0	21.7	17.4	14.7
Kansas	39.0	34.0	3.8	2.0	1.6	37.3	15.7	15.3	26.8	20.9	21.0	14.6
South Atlantic	700.3	476.1	207.2	39.4	8.9	689.1	16.1	14.3	23.2	18.5	28.3	15.5
Delaware	11.1	8.2	2.7	0.3	0.1	11.2	16.7	15.4	23.8	20.4	27.2	16.0
Maryland	80.2	51.0	26.0	2.5	0.5	84.5	16.8	15.0	21.9	20.2	29.7	17.5
Dist. of Columbia	11.9	1.7	9.2	0.9	(Z)	10.0	19.5	9.7	22.9	27.2	14.8	17.0
Virginia	99.4	71.1	24.7	3.5	0.6	96.6	16.1	14.8	21.3	21.6	19.1	15.4
West Virginia	22.6	21.5	1.0	0.1	(Z)	22.2	12.6	12.4	17.1	8.6	8.5	12.2
North Carolina	104.5	69.8	31.7	1.8	1.0	102.4	15.8	13.9	21.7	22.9	30.2	15.2
South Carolina	58.6	35.2	22.7	0.6	0.3	57.7	16.8	14.6	21.8	18.7	24.1	16.0
Georgia	112.7	69.7	41.3	2.3	1.3	110.0	17.4	15.1	23.6	20.8	26.7	16.6
Florida	199.3	147.9	48.1	27.6	5.0	194.5	15.4	13.8	27.3	17.5	31.0	14.6
East South Central	236.4	167.5	66.3	1.2	0.6	232.1	15.6	13.9	22.3	12.4	15.9	14.9
Kentucky	54.4	48.5	5.4	0.3	0.2	54.9	14.8	14.3	20.4	12.5	20.5	14.7
Tennessee	75.0	56.0	18.0	0.4	0.2	73.1	15.4	13.8	23.2	13.6	16.6	14.5
Alabama	63.5	40.8	22.0	0.3	0.2	60.5	15.7	13.7	21.6	14.0	16.8	14.6
Mississippi	43.6	22.2	20.9	0.1	(Z)	43.5	16.9	13.6	22.8	7.3	7.0	16.6
West South Central	472.7	366.1	90.2	117.2	103.5	482.0	17.7	18.2	22.9	25.8	25.9	17.7
Arkansas	36.5	27.2	8.7	0.4	0.2	34.6	15.5	14.0	23.2	20.8	19.7	14.2
Louisiana	72.2	40.7	30.0	0.9	0.2	74.6	17.1	14.3	23.1	10.1	8.6	17.2
Oklahoma	47.6	35.6	5.5	(NA)	(NA)	47.3	15.1	13.8	23.7	(NA)	(NA)	14.7
Texas	316.4	262.6	45.9	115.8	103.0	325.6	18.6	20.6	22.7	26.7	26.5	18.8
Mountain	242.8	212.4	10.2	48.7	31.8	243.4	17.8	18.1	27.2	24.4	22.1	17.5
Montana	11.6	9.7	0.1	0.3	0.1	11.5	14.5	13.1	31.5	24.0	17.3	14.3
Idaho	16.4	15.8	0.1	1.4	1.2	17.2	16.3	16.6	27.3	27.1	27.7	16.6
Wyoming	7.0	6.5	0.1	0.5	0.3	6.8	15.4	15.2	29.7	19.8	17.2	14.6
Colorado	53.5	48.1	3.4	9.3	4.7	54.0	16.2	16.6	25.5	21.9	16.5	16.1
New Mexico	27.4	22.2	0.8	12.2	2.8	28.2	18.1	19.3	25.8	21.1	8.6	18.0
Arizona	69.0	58.1	3.2	19.7	18.9	67.7	18.8	19.6	28.7	28.6	30.7	18.3
Utah	36.3	33.9	0.4	2.0	1.2	35.1	21.1	21.0	33.3	24.1	21.8	20.1
Nevada	21.6	18.1	2.2	3.3	2.5	23.0	18.0	17.9	27.4	26.2	29.1	18.8
Pacific	767.2	605.7	65.3	257.0	207.2	755.5	19.6	21.4	26.6	31.7	32.5	18.8
Washington	79.3	68.2	4.1	5.7	3.9	75.7	16.3	15.8	27.7	26.6	24.8	15.2
Oregon	42.9	38.9	1.3	3.0	2.6	42.8	15.1	14.7	27.3	26.4	30.9	14.6
California	612.6	486.3	58.2	245.6	200.1	605.7	20.6	23.7	26.4	31.9	32.7	19.8
Alaska	11.9	7.6	0.7	0.3	0.2	11.2	21.6	18.3	31.9	18.4	21.5	21.1
Hawaii	20.5	4.7	1.0	2.4	0.2	20.0	18.5	12.7	35.3	29.9	24.2	17.5

NA Not available. Z Less than 50. [1] Includes other races not shown separately. [2] Persons of Hispanic origin may be of any race. Births by Hispanic origin of mother. [3] Includes births to nonresidents. Provisional. [4] Based on resident population enumerated as of April 1 for 1990 and estimated as of July 1 for 1991.

Source: U.S. National Center for Health Statistics, *Vital Statistics of the United States*, annual, and *Monthly Vital Statistics Report*.

No. 95. Total Fertility Rate and Intrinsic Rate of Natural Increase: 1960 to 1989

[Based on race of child and registered births only. Beginning 1970, excludes births to nonresidents of United States. The *total fertility rate* is the number of births that 1,000 women would have in their lifetime if, at each year of age, they experienced the birth rates occurring in the specified year. A total fertility rate of 2,110 represents "replacement level" fertility for the total population under current mortality conditions (assuming no net immigration). The *intrinsic rate of natural increase* is the rate that would eventually prevail if a population were to experience, at each year of age, the birth rates and death rates occurring in the specified year and if those rates remained unchanged over a long period of time. Minus sign (-) indicates decrease. See also Appendix III and *Historical Statistics, Colonial Times to 1970*, series B 11]

ANNUAL AVERAGE AND YEAR	TOTAL FERTILITY RATE			INTRINSIC RATE OF NATURAL INCREASE			ANNUAL AVERAGE AND YEAR	TOTAL FERTILITY RATE			INTRINSIC RATE OF NATURAL INCREASE		
	Total	White	Black and other	Total	White	Black and other		Total	White	Black and other	Total	White	Black and other
1960-64 ...	3,449	3,326	4,326	18.6	17.1	27.7	1977	1,790	1,703	2,279	-6.2	-8.1	3.2
1965-69 ...	2,622	2,512	3,362	8.2	6.4	18.6	1978	1,760	1,668	2,265	-6.8	-8.8	2.9
1970-74 ...	2,094	1,997	2,680	-0.7	-2.5	9.1	1979	1,808	1,716	2,310	-5.7	-7.7	3.8
1975-79 ...	1,774	1,685	2,270	-6.6	-8.5	3.0	1980	1,840	1,749	2,323	-5.1	-7.0	4.0
1980-84 ...	1,819	1,731	2,262	-5.4	-7.3	3.0	1981	1,815	1,726	2,275	-5.5	-7.4	3.3
1985-88 ...	1,870	1,769	2,339	-4.2	-6.3	4.3	1982	1,829	1,742	2,265	-5.2	-7.0	3.0
1970	2,480	2,385	3,067	6.0	4.5	14.4	1983	1,803	1,718	2,225	-5.7	-7.5	2.5
1971	2,267	2,161	2,920	2.6	0.8	12.6	1984	1,806	1,719	2,224	-5.6	-7.4	2.4
1972	2,010	1,907	2,628	-2.0	-3.9	8.6	1985	1,843	1,754	2,263	-4.8	-6.6	3.1
1973	1,879	1,783	2,443	-4.5	-6.5	5.7	1986	1,836	1,742	2,282	-4.9	-6.8	3.3
1974	1,835	1,749	2,339	-5.4	-7.2	4.0	1987	1,871	1,767	2,349	-4.2	-6.3	4.5
1975	1,774	1,686	2,276	-6.7	-8.6	3.0	1988	1,932	1,814	2,463	-3.0	-5.3	6.3
1976	1,738	1,652	2,223	-7.4	-9.3	2.1	1989	2,014	1,885	2,583	-1.4	-3.8	8.2

Source: U.S. National Center for Health Statistics, *Vital Statistics of the United States*, annual; and unpublished data.

No. 96. Projected Fertility Rates, by Race and Age Group: 1992 and 2010

[For definition of total fertility rate, see headnote, table 95. Birth rates represent live births per 1,000 women in age group indicated. Projections are based on middle fertility assumptions. For explanations of methodology, see text, section 1]

AGE GROUP	ALL RACES [1]		WHITE		BLACK		ASIAN AND PACIFIC ISLANDERS		AMERICAN INDIAN, ESKIMO, ALEUT		HISPANIC [2]	
	1992	2010	1992	2010	1992	2010	1992	2010	1992	2010	1992	2010
Total fertility rate ..	2,054	2,092	1,953	1,981	2,468	2,459	2,335	2,271	2,874	2,855	2,655	2,588
Birth rates:												
10 to 14 years old....	1.4	1.5	0.6	0.7	5.3	5.2	0.6	0.6	1.9	1.9	2.3	2.2
15 to 19 years old....	57.3	58.7	46.7	48.5	113.7	112.7	28.3	27.2	105.9	105.5	86.3	84.1
20 to 24 years old....	118.0	120.0	109.8	112.1	161.6	160.8	95.8	93.1	210.5	209.0	163.2	159.1
25 to 29 years old....	120.0	121.0	119.8	120.0	113.8	113.6	152.2	149.1	142.1	141.1	139.1	135.6
30 to 34 years old....	79.2	80.5	79.7	79.9	66.6	66.6	123.8	120.7	76.2	75.8	88.6	86.4
35 to 39 years old....	29.6	31.0	29.1	29.9	27.2	27.3	53.6	52.2	31.2	31.1	41.3	40.2
40 to 44 years old....	4.9	5.4	4.7	5.0	5.2	5.3	11.3	11.0	6.7	6.8	9.7	9.5
45 to 49 years old....	0.2	0.3	0.2	0.2	0.3	0.3	1.3	1.2	0.4	0.4	0.6	0.6

[1] Includes other races not shown separately. [2] Persons of Hispanic origin may be of any race.

Source: U.S. Bureau of the Census, *Current Population Reports*, series P25-1092; and unpublished data.

No. 97. Birth Rates, by Live-Birth Order and Race: 1970 to 1990

[**Births per 1,000 women 15 to 44 years old in specified racial group.** Live-birth order refers to number of children born alive. Figures for births of order not stated are distributed. See also headnote, table 93, and *Historical Statistics, Colonial Times to 1970*, series B 20-27]

LIVE-BIRTH ORDER	ALL RACES [1]					WHITE					BLACK				
	1970	1980	1985	1989	1990	1970	1980	1985	1989	1990	1970	1980	1985	1989	1990
Total	87.9	68.4	66.3	69.2	70.9	84.1	64.7	63.2	65.1	66.9	115.4	88.1	82.4	90.8	91.9
First birth	34.2	29.5	27.6	28.4	29.0	32.9	28.4	26.6	27.1	27.8	43.3	35.2	32.5	34.9	34.6
Second birth	24.2	21.8	22.0	22.4	22.8	23.7	21.0	21.5	21.5	22.0	27.1	25.7	24.5	26.8	27.1
Third birth..........	13.6	10.3	10.4	11.3	11.7	13.3	9.5	9.7	10.5	10.8	16.1	14.5	14.0	16.0	16.4
Fourth birth.........	7.2	3.9	3.8	4.3	4.5	6.8	3.4	3.3	3.8	3.9	10.0	6.7	6.3	7.4	7.7
Fifth birth	3.8	1.5	1.4	1.6	1.7	3.4	1.3	1.1	1.3	1.4	6.4	3.0	2.7	3.1	3.3
Sixth and seventh	3.2	1.0	0.8	0.9	1.0	2.7	0.8	0.7	0.7	0.7	7.0	2.1	1.8	2.0	2.1
Eighth and over	1.8	0.4	0.3	0.3	0.3	1.2	0.3	0.2	0.2	0.2	5.6	0.9	0.6	0.6	0.6

[1] Includes other races not shown separately.

Source: U.S. National Center for Health Statistics, *Vital Statistics of the United States*, annual; and *Monthly Vital Statistics Reports*.

No. 98. Live Births, by Race and Type of Hispanic Origin—Selected Characteristics: 1985 and 1990

[Represents registered births. Excludes births to nonresidents of the United States. Data are based on Hispanic-origin of mother and beginning 1990, race of mother. Prior to 1990, data are for race of child and are not comparable. Hispanic-origin data are available from only 23 States and the District of Columbia in 1985 and 48 States and DC in 1990. However, in 1985 approximately 90 percent of all births to Hispanic mothers occur to residents of the 23 States, in 1990 this percent is approximately 99.6]

| RACE AND HISPANIC ORIGIN | NUMBER OF BIRTHS (1,000) | | BIRTHS TO TEENAGE MOTHERS, PERCENT OF TOTAL | | BIRTHS TO UNMARRIED MOTHERS, PERCENT OF TOTAL | | PERCENT OF MOTHERS BEGINNING PRENATAL CARE DURING— | | | | PERCENT OF BIRTHS WITH LOW BIRTH WEIGHT [1] | |
| | | | | | | | First trimester | | Third trimester or no care | | | |
	1985	1990	1985	1990	1985	1990	1985	1990	1985	1990	1985	1990
Total	3,761	4,158	12.7	12.8	22.0	26.6	76.2	74.2	5.7	6.0	6.8	7.0
White	2,991	3,290	10.8	10.9	14.5	16.9	79.4	77.7	4.7	4.9	5.6	5.7
Black	608	684	23.0	23.1	60.1	66.7	61.8	60.7	10.0	10.9	12.4	13.3
American Indian, Eskimo, Aleut	43	39	19.1	19.5	40.7	53.6	60.3	57.9	11.5	12.9	5.9	6.1
Asian and Pacific Islander [2]	116	142	5.5	5.7	10.1	(NA)	75.0	(NA)	6.1	(NA)	6.1	(NA)
Filipino	21	26	5.8	6.1	12.1	15.9	77.2	77.1	4.6	4.5	6.9	7.3
Chinese	18	23	1.1	1.2	3.7	5.0	82.4	81.3	4.2	3.4	5.0	4.7
Japanese	10	9	2.9	2.9	7.9	9.6	85.8	87.0	2.6	2.9	5.9	6.2
Hawaiian [3]	7	6	15.9	18.4	(NA)	45.0	(NA)	65.8	(NA)	8.7	6.4	7.2
Hispanic origin [3]	373	595	16.5	16.8	29.5	36.7	61.2	60.2	12.5	12.0	6.2	6.1
Mexican	243	386	17.5	17.7	25.7	33.3	59.9	57.8	12.9	13.2	5.8	5.5
Puerto Rican	35	59	20.9	21.7	51.1	55.9	58.3	63.5	15.5	10.6	8.7	9.0
Cuban	10	11	7.1	7.7	16.1	18.2	82.5	84.8	3.7	2.8	6.0	5.7
Central and South American	41	34	8.2	9.0	34.9	41.2	60.6	61.5	12.5	10.9	5.7	5.8

NA Not available. [1] Births less than 2,500 grams (5 lb.-8 oz.). [2] Includes other races not shown separately. [3] Hispanic persons may be of any race. Includes other types, not shown separately.

No. 99. Live Births, by Place of Delivery, Median and Low Birth Weight, and Prenatal Care: 1970 to 1990

[Represents registered births. Excludes births to nonresidents of the United States. For total number of births, see table 91. See Appendix III]

| YEAR | BIRTHS ATTENDED (1,000) | | | | MEDIAN BIRTH WEIGHT [3] | | | PERCENT OF BIRTHS WITH LOW BIRTH WEIGHT [5] | | | PERCENT OF BIRTHS BY PERIOD IN WHICH PRENATAL CARE BEGAN | |
| | In hospital [1] | Not in hospital | | | Total [4] | White | Black | Total [3] | White | Black | 1st trimester | 3d trimester or no prenatal care |
		Physician	Midwife and other [2]									
1970	3,708	5	18		7 lb.-4 oz.	7 lb.-5 oz.	6 lb.-14 oz.	7.9	6.8	13.9	68.0	7.9
1975	3,105	11	28		7 lb.-5 oz.	7 lb.-7 oz.	6 lb.-15 oz.	7.4	6.3	13.1	72.4	6.0
1980	3,576	12	24		7 lb.-7 oz.	7 lb.-8 oz.	7 lb.-0 oz.	6.8	5.7	12.5	76.3	5.1
1981	3,592	11	27		7 lb.-7 oz.	7 lb.-8 oz.	7 lb.-0 oz.	6.8	5.7	12.5	76.3	5.2
1982	3,642	10	28		7 lb.-7 oz.	7 lb.-8 oz.	7 lb.-0 oz.	6.8	5.6	12.4	76.1	5.5
1983	3,600	10	29		7 lb.-7 oz.	7 lb.-8 oz.	7 lb.-0 oz.	6.8	5.7	12.6	76.2	5.6
1984	3,631	10	28		7 lb.-7 oz.	7 lb.-9 oz.	7 lb.-0 oz.	6.7	5.6	12.4	76.5	5.6
1985	3,722	10	29		7 lb.-7 oz.	7 lb.-9 oz.	7 lb.-0 oz.	6.8	5.6	12.4	76.2	5.7
1986	3,720	9	27		7 lb.-7 oz.	7 lb.-9 oz.	7 lb.-0 oz.	6.8	5.6	12.5	75.9	6.0
1987	3,774	8	27		7 lb.-7 oz.	7 lb.-9 oz.	7 lb.-0 oz.	6.9	5.7	12.7	76.0	6.1
1988	3,872	9	28		7 lb.-7 oz.	7 lb.-9 oz.	7 lb.-0 oz.	6.9	5.6	13.0	75.9	6.1
1989	3,991	13	22		7 lb.-7 oz.	7 lb.-8 oz.	6 lb.-15 oz.	7.0	5.7	13.2	73.9	6.3
1990	4,110	14	21		7 lb.-7 oz.	7 lb.-8 oz.	7 lb.-0 oz.	7.0	5.7	13.3	74.2	6.0

[1] Includes all births in hospitals or institutions and in clinics. [2] Includes births with attendant not specified. [3] Beginning 1989, median birth weight based on race of mother; prior to 1989, based on race of child. [4] Includes other races not shown separately. [5] Through 1975, births of 2,500 grams (5 lb.-8 oz.) or less at birth; thereafter, less than 2,500 grams.
Source of tables 98 and 99: U.S. National Center for Health Statistics, *Vital Statistics of the United States*, annual; *Monthly Vital Statistics Report;* and unpublished data.

No. 100. Cesarean Section Deliveries, by Age of Mother: 1970 to 1991

[Based on data collected from the National Hospital Discharge Survey, a sample survey of hospital records of patients discharged in year shown; subject to sampling variability. Beginning 1988, comparisons with data for earlier years should be made with caution as estimates of change may reflect improvements in the 1988 design rather than true changes in hospital use]

AGE OF MOTHER	1970	1980	1983	1984	1985	1986	1987	1988	1989	1990	1991
Number of cesarean deliveries (1,000)	195	619	808	813	877	906	953	933	938	945	933
Rate: Mothers, all ages [1]	5.5	16.5	20.3	21.1	22.7	24.1	24.4	24.7	23.8	23.5	23.5
Under 20 years	3.9	14.5	15.0	16.5	16.1	18.3	18.5	19.5	18.1	16.6	18.2
20 to 24 years	4.9	15.8	19.0	19.6	21.2	21.9	22.9	20.1	21.1	21.0	21.0
25 to 29 years	5.9	16.7	20.5	20.8	22.9	25.3	23.7	26.7	24.8	23.3	24.3
30 to 34 years	7.5	18.0	24.6	24.6	26.6	26.2	28.3	28.3	28.0	26.6	26.7
35 years and over	8.3	20.6	25.4	28.7	30.7	32.6	31.6	32.1	30.3	31.4	28.4

[1] Cesarean rates are the number of cesarean deliveries per 100 total deliveries for specified category.
Source: U.S. National Center for Health Statistics, unpublished data.

No. 101. Births to Unmarried Women, by Race of Child and Age of Mother: 1970 to 1990

[Excludes births to nonresidents of United States. Data for 1970 include estimates for States in which marital status data were not reported. Beginning in 1980, marital status is inferred from a comparison of the child's and parents' surnames on the birth certificate for those States that do not report on marital status. No estimates included for misstatements on birth records or failures to register births. See also Appendix III and *Historical Statistics, Colonial Times to 1970*, series B 28-35]

RACE OF CHILD AND AGE OF MOTHER	1970	1980	1985	1989	1990	RACE OF CHILD AND AGE OF MOTHER	1970	1980	1985	1989	1990
NUMBER (1,000)						20 to 24 years	32	36	36	35	35
Total live births [1].	398.7	665.7	828.2	1,094.2	1,165.4	25 to 29 years	10	15	18	20	20
White	175.1	320.1	433.0	593.9	647.4	30 to 34 years	5	6	8	10	10
Black	215.1	325.7	365.5	457.5	472.7	35 years and over	3	2	3	4	5
Under 15 years old . . .	9.5	9.0	9.4	10.6	10.7	AS PERCENT OF ALL BIRTHS IN RACIAL GROUPS					
15 to 19 years old	190.4	262.8	270.9	337.3	350.0						
20 to 24 years old . . .	126.7	237.3	300.4	378.1	403.9						
25 to 29 years old	40.6	99.6	152.0	215.5	230.0	Total [1]	11	18	22	27	28
30 to 34 years old	19.1	41.0	67.3	106.3	118.2	White	6	11	15	19	20
35 years old and over .	12.4	16.1	28.2	46.3	52.7	Black	38	55	60	64	65
PERCENT DISTRIBUTION						BIRTH RATE [2]					
						Total [1] [3]	26.4	29.4	32.8	41.6	43.8
Total [1]	100	100	100	100	100	White [3]	13.9	17.6	21.8	29.2	31.8
White	44	48	52	54	56	Black [3]	95.5	82.9	79.0	93.8	93.9
Black	54	49	44	42	41	15 to 19 years	22.4	27.6	31.4	40.1	42.5
Under 15 years.	2	1	1	1	1	20 to 24 years	38.4	40.9	46.5	61.2	65.1
15 to 19 years	48	40	33	31	30	25 to 29 years	37.0	34.0	39.9	52.8	56.0
						30 to 34 years	27.1	21.1	25.2	34.9	37.6

[1] Includes other races not shown separately. [2] Rate per 1,000 unmarried women (never-married, widowed, and divorced) estimated as of July 1. [3] Covers women aged 15 to 44 years.

Source: U.S. National Center for Health Statistics, *Vital Statistics of the United States*, annual; *Monthly Vital Statistics Report*; and unpublished data.

No. 102. Low Birth Weight and Births to Teenage Mothers and to Unmarried Women—States: 1980 and 1990

[Represents registered births. Excludes births to nonresidents of the United States. Based on 100 percent of births in all States and the District of Columbia. See Appendix III]

DIVISION AND STATE	PERCENT OF BIRTHS WITH LOW BIRTH WEIGHT[1] 1980	1990	BIRTHS TO TEENAGE MOTHERS, PERCENT OF TOTAL 1980	1990	BIRTHS TO UNMARRIED WOMEN, PERCENT OF TOTAL 1980	1990	DIVISION AND STATE	PERCENT OF BIRTHS WITH LOW BIRTH WEIGHT[1] 1980	1990	BIRTHS TO TEENAGE MOTHERS, PERCENT OF TOTAL 1980	1990	BIRTHS TO UNMARRIED WOMEN, PERCENT OF TOTAL 1980	1990
U.S.	6.8	7.0	15.6	12.8	18.4	28.0	VA	7.5	7.2	15.5	11.7	19.2	26.0
							WV	6.7	7.1	20.1	17.8	13.1	25.4
N.E.	6.2	5.9	11.6	8.4	15.5	24.2	NC	7.9	8.0	19.2	16.2	19.0	29.4
ME	6.5	5.1	15.3	10.8	13.9	22.6	SC	8.6	8.7	19.8	17.1	23.0	32.7
NH	5.4	4.9	10.7	7.2	11.0	16.9	GA	8.6	8.7	20.7	16.7	23.2	32.8
VT	5.9	5.3	13.0	8.5	13.7	20.1	FL	7.6	7.4	18.2	13.9	23.0	31.7
MA	6.1	5.9	10.7	6.8	15.7	24.7	E.S.C.	7.8	8.2	21.0	18.4	20.9	30.6
RI	6.3	6.2	12.3	10.5	15.7	26.3	KY	6.8	7.1	21.1	17.5	15.1	23.6
CT	6.7	6.6	11.4	8.2	[2]17.9	[2]26.6	TN	8.0	8.2	19.9	17.6	19.9	30.2
M.A.	7.1	7.3	12.6	9.5	21.3	29.9	AL	7.9	8.4	20.6	18.2	22.2	30.1
NY	7.4	7.6	11.8	9.1	[2]23.8	[2]33.0	MS	8.7	9.6	23.2	21.3	28.0	40.5
NJ	7.2	7.0	12.3	8.4	21.1	24.3	W.S.C.	7.3	7.3	19.1	16.3	15.8	22.2
PA	6.5	7.1	13.9	10.9	17.7	28.6	AR	7.6	8.2	21.6	19.7	20.5	29.4
E.N.C.	6.7	7.1	15.2	13.2	18.0	28.3	LA	8.6	9.2	20.1	17.6	23.4	36.8
OH	6.8	7.1	15.7	13.8	[2]17.8	28.9	OK	6.8	6.6	19.6	16.2	14.0	25.2
IN	6.3	6.6	17.3	14.5	15.5	26.2	TX	6.9	6.9	18.3	15.6	[2]13.3	[2]17.5
IL	7.2	7.6	15.7	13.1	22.5	31.7	Mountain	6.6	6.8	14.3	12.8	12.7	25.1
MI	6.9	7.6	14.0	13.5	[2]16.2	[2]26.2	MT	5.6	6.2	12.4	11.5	[2]12.5	23.7
WI	5.4	5.9	12.3	10.2	13.9	24.2	ID	5.3	5.7	13.1	12.3	7.9	16.7
W.N.C.	5.7	5.9	13.5	11.1	13.1	23.2	WY	7.3	7.4	15.5	13.6	8.2	19.8
MN	5.1	5.1	10.4	8.0	11.4	20.9	CO	8.2	8.0	13.3	11.3	13.0	21.2
IA	5.0	5.4	12.5	10.2	10.3	21.0	NM	7.6	7.4	18.2	16.3	16.1	35.4
MO	6.6	7.1	16.9	14.4	17.6	28.6	AZ	6.2	6.4	16.5	14.2	18.7	32.7
ND	4.9	5.5	10.9	8.6	9.2	18.4	UT	5.2	5.7	11.0	10.3	6.2	13.5
SD	5.1	5.1	13.5	10.8	13.4	22.9	NV	6.6	7.2	15.4	12.6	[2]13.5	[2]25.4
NE	5.6	5.3	12.1	9.8	11.6	20.7	Pacific	5.8	5.7	13.6	11.5	19.6	30.2
KS	5.8	6.2	15.0	12.3	12.3	21.5	WA	5.1	5.3	12.5	10.8	13.6	23.7
S.A.	8.0	7.9	18.3	14.4	22.2	30.9	OR	4.9	5.0	13.3	12.0	14.8	25.7
DE	7.7	7.6	16.7	11.9	24.2	29.0	CA	5.9	5.8	13.9	11.6	[2]21.4	[2]31.6
MD	8.2	7.8	14.8	10.5	[2]25.2	29.6	AK	5.4	4.8	11.8	9.7	15.1	26.2
DC	12.8	15.1	20.7	17.8	56.5	64.9	HI	7.1	7.1	11.5	10.5	17.6	24.8

[1] Less than 2,500 grams (5 pounds-8 ounces). [2] Marital status of mother is inferred.

Source: U.S. National Center for Health Statistics, *Vital Statistics of the United States*, annual; and *Monthly Vital Statistics Report*.

No. 103. Women Who Have Had a Child in the Last Year, by Age: 1980 to 1992
[See headnote, table 104]

AGE OF MOTHER	WOMEN WHO HAD A CHILD IN LAST YEAR (1,000)				TOTAL BIRTHS PER 1,000 WOMEN				FIRST BIRTHS PER 1,000 WOMEN			
	1980	1985	1990	1992	1980	1985	1990	1992	1980	1985	1990	1992
Total........	3,247	3,497	3,913	3,688	71.1	68.6	67.0	62.9	28.5	27.1	26.4	24.8
15 to 29 years old....	[1]2,476	[1]2,512	2,568	2,346	[1]103.7	[1]101.4	90.8	85.9	[1]48.6	[1]47.1	43.2	40.9
15 to 19 years old..	(NA)	(NA)	338	311	(NA)	(NA)	39.8	38.0	(NA)	(NA)	30.1	27.9
20 to 24 years old..	[2]1,396	[2]1,339	1,038	940	[2]96.6	[2]95.4	113.4	103.4	(NA)	[2]53.5	51.8	49.4
25 to 29 years old..	1,081	1,173	1,192	1,094	114.8	109.2	112.1	109.0	(NA)	38.7	46.2	43.7
30 to 44 years old....	770	984	1,346	1,342	35.4	37.6	44.7	42.9	6.3	8.0	10.6	10.7
30 to 34 years old..	519	704	892	856	60.0	69.9	80.4	76.1	(NA)	15.8	21.9	21.8
35 to 39 years old..	192	229	377	404	26.9	25.9	37.3	38.0	(NA)	5.2	6.5	6.4
40 to 44 years old..	59	51	77	82	9.9	7.1	8.6	8.7	(NA)	0.8	1.2	2.3

NA Not available.   [1] 18 to 29 years old.   [2] 18 to 24 years old.

Source: U.S. Bureau of the Census, *Current Population Reports,* series P20-454; and unpublished data.

No. 104. Social and Economic Characteristics of Women Who Have Had a Child in the Last Year: 1992

[As of **June.** Covers civilian noninstitutional population. Since the number of women who had a birth during the 12-month period was tabulated and not the actual numbers of births, some small underestimation of fertility for this period may exist due to the omission of: (1) Multiple births, (2) Two or more live births spaced within the 12-month period (the woman is counted only once), (3) Women who had births in the period and who did not survive to the survey date, (4) Women who were in institutions and therefore not in the survey universe. These losses may be somewhat offset by the inclusion in the CPS of births to immigrants who did not have their children born in the United States and births to nonresident women. These births would not have been recorded in the vital registration system. Based on Current Population Survey (CPS); see text, section 1 and Appendix III]

CHARACTERISTIC	TOTAL, 15 TO 44 YEARS OLD			15 TO 29 YEARS OLD			30 TO 44 YEARS OLD		
	Num-ber of women (1,000)	Women who have had a child in the last year		Num-ber of women (1,000)	Women who have had a child in the last year		Num-ber of women (1,000)	Women who have had a child in the last year	
		Total births per 1,000 women	First births per 1,000 women		Total births per 1,000 women	First births per 1,000 women		Total births per 1,000 women	First births per 1,000 women
Total [1]................	58,614	63	25	27,312	86	41	31,302	43	11
White...............	48,157	62	25	22,102	82	41	26,056	44	11
Black..............	8,017	69	22	4,070	106	39	3,947	31	5
Asian or Pacific Islander..........	1,827	64	26	832	69	30	996	59	16
Hispanic [2]...............	5,555	95	35	2,915	125	60	2,640	62	8
Currently married...........	31,878	88	32	9,209	176	80	22,668	52	13
Married, spouse present.......	29,531	90	33	8,338	180	84	21,193	54	14
Married, spouse absent [3]......	2,347	65	19	871	132	45	1,475	26	3
Widowed or divorced..........	5,383	27	10	973	75	31	4,409	16	5
Never married..............	21,354	35	17	17,129	38	20	4,225	22	5
Educational attainment:									
Less than high school........	12,159	67	24	8,422	79	33	3,737	40	4
High school, 4 years.........	19,063	65	25	7,762	113	50	11,301	33	7
College: 1 or more years........	27,392	60	25	11,128	73	40	16,264	51	15
No degree.............	12,422	59	24	6,362	72	36	6,060	45	10
Associate degree........	3,982	56	23	1,420	87	46	2,562	38	11
Bachelor's degree........	8,173	65	27	2,864	70	44	5,310	63	18
Graduate or professional degree	2,814	55	30	482	65	48	2,332	53	27
Labor force status:									
Employed.................	38,139	45	19	15,906	61	32	22,233	34	11
Unemployed..............	3,849	69	31	2,418	88	45	1,432	37	9
Not in labor force...........	16,626	102	35	8,988	129	56	7,637	71	12
Occupation of employed women:									
Managerial-professional.........	9,923	47	22	2,918	68	43	7,005	38	13
Technical, sales, admin. support....	16,818	47	21	7,602	58	32	9,216	37	12
Service workers.............	7,102	46	16	3,763	61	26	3,339	28	4
Farming, forestry, and fishing.....	512	44	10	207	78	25	306	21	-
Precision prod., craft, and repair....	738	44	19	238	54	29	500	39	14
Operators, fabricators, and laborers..	3,047	31	12	1,179	61	25	1,868	12	4
Family income: Under $10,000.......	7,500	95	29	4,426	133	47	3,074	41	3
$10,000 to $19,999.............	9,201	70	29	4,946	103	50	4,255	32	5
$20,000 to $24,999.............	4,964	66	27	2,480	100	47	2,484	33	7
$25,000 to $29,999.............	4,492	57	21	2,086	86	40	2,406	32	5
$30,000 to $34,999.............	4,631	61	22	2,078	89	41	2,553	37	6
$35,000 to $49,999.............	10,677	58	22	4,444	69	37	6,233	50	11
$50,000 to $74,999.............	8,821	53	24	3,407	54	34	5,414	52	18
$75,000 and over.............	5,259	43	21	2,053	29	20	3,205	52	21

- Represents or rounds to zero. [1] Includes women of other races and women with family income not reported, not shown separately. [2] Persons of Hispanic origin may be of any race. [3] Includes separated women.

Source: U.S. Bureau of the Census, *Current Population Reports,* series P20-454; and unpublished data.

No. 105. Women Who Have Had a Child in the Last Year, by Age and Labor Force Status: 1980 to 1992

[See headnote, table 104]

YEAR	TOTAL, 18 TO 44 YEARS OLD				18 TO 29 YEARS OLD				30 TO 44 YEARS OLD			
	All women, percent in labor force	Women who have had a child in the last year			All women, percent in labor force	Women who have had a child in the last year			All women, percent in labor force	Women who have had a child in the last year		
		Number (1,000)	In the labor force			Number (1,000)	In the labor force			Number (1,000)	In the labor force	
			Number (1,000)	Per-cent			Number (1,000)	Per-cent			Number (1,000)	Percent
1980	66	3,247	1,233	38	68	2,476	947	38	64	770	287	37
1981	67	3,381	1,411	42	69	2,499	1,004	40	66	881	407	46
1982	68	3,433	1,508	44	70	2,445	1,040	43	67	988	469	48
1983	69	3,625	1,563	43	71	2,682	1,138	42	68	942	425	45
1984	70	3,311	1,547	47	72	2,375	1,058	45	69	936	489	52
1985	71	3,497	1,691	48	71	2,512	1,204	48	70	984	488	50
1986	72	3,625	1,805	50	73	2,452	1,185	48	72	1,174	620	53
1987	73	3,701	1,881	51	73	2,521	1,258	50	73	1,180	623	53
1988 [1]	73	3,667	1,866	51	74	2,384	1,177	49	73	1,283	688	54
1990 [1]	71	3,913	2,068	53	68	2,568	1,275	50	75	1,346	793	59
1992 [1]	72	3,688	1,985	54	67	2,346	1,182	50	76	1,342	802	60

[1] Lower age limit is 15 years old.
Source: U.S. Bureau of the Census, *Current Population Reports*, series P20-454; and unpublished data.

No. 106. Childless Women and Children Ever Born, by Race, Age, and Marital Status: 1992

[See headnote, table 104]

CHARACTERISTIC	Total number of women (1,000)	WOMEN BY NUMBER OF CHILDREN EVER BORN (percent)				CHILDREN EVER BORN	
		Total	None	One	Two or more	Total number (1,000)	Per 1,000 women
ALL RACES [1]							
Women ever married	37,260	100	18	23	59	65,874	1,768
15 to 19 years old	339	100	44	46	10	228	673
20 to 24 years old	3,064	100	38	34	28	3,046	994
25 to 29 years old	6,780	100	28	30	43	9,237	1,362
30 to 34 years old	9,050	100	17	23	60	15,988	1,767
35 to 39 years old	9,337	100	12	19	69	18,866	2,020
40 to 44 years old	8,690	100	11	18	71	18,509	2,130
Women never married	21,354	100	81	10	9	7,440	348
15 to 19 years old	7,847	100	95	4	1	511	65
20 to 24 years old	6,023	100	80	13	7	1,827	303
25 to 29 years old	3,259	100	70	13	17	1,926	591
30 to 34 years old	2,199	100	64	15	22	1,728	786
35 to 39 years old	1,300	100	65	13	22	1,016	782
40 to 44 years old	726	100	75	11	15	433	596
WHITE							
Women ever married	32,165	100	19	23	58	55,482	1,725
15 to 19 years old	313	100	45	47	8	200	638
20 to 24 years old	2,708	100	40	35	26	2,546	940
25 to 29 years old	5,929	100	28	30	41	7,827	1,320
30 to 34 years old	7,799	100	17	23	60	13,650	1,750
35 to 39 years old	7,993	100	13	19	68	15,753	1,971
40 to 44 years old	7,422	100	12	17	72	15,507	2,089
Women never married	15,993	100	88	7	5	3,006	188
15 to 19 years old	6,191	100	96	3	1	272	44
20 to 24 years old	4,674	100	87	9	4	814	174
25 to 29 years old	2,287	100	80	10	10	832	364
30 to 34 years old	1,476	100	77	13	10	641	434
35 to 39 years old	837	100	82	8	10	307	367
40 to 44 years old	529	100	88	6	6	140	265
BLACK							
Women ever married	3,585	100	11	23	66	7,686	2,144
15 to 19 years old	16	100	(B)	(B)	(B)	16	(B)
20 to 24 years old	238	100	22	28	50	384	1,609
25 to 29 years old	608	100	19	27	54	1,072	1,763
30 to 34 years old	858	100	12	22	66	1,707	1,988
35 to 39 years old	934	100	7	22	71	2,255	2,416
40 to 44 years old	930	100	7	22	72	2,251	2,421
Women never married	4,432	100	53	20	27	4,215	951
15 to 19 years old	1,297	100	88	9	4	226	174
20 to 24 years old	1,097	100	47	29	23	966	881
25 to 29 years old	813	100	41	23	37	1,028	1,264
30 to 34 years old	634	100	31	21	49	1,039	1,639
35 to 39 years old	412	100	30	24	47	677	1,645
40 to 44 years old	179	100	34	26	41	278	1,555

B Base figure too small to meet statistical standards for reliability. [1] Includes other races, not shown separately.
Source: U.S. Bureau of the Census, *Current Population Reports*, series P20, unpublished data.

No. 107. Lifetime Births Expected per 1,000 Wives: 1971 to 1992
[See headnote, table 104]

YEAR	LIFETIME BIRTHS TO ALL WIVES [1] AGED—			LIFETIME BIRTHS TO WHITE WIVES AGED—			LIFETIME BIRTHS TO BLACK WIVES AGED—			LIFETIME BIRTHS TO HISPANIC [2] WIVES AGED—		
	18 to 24 yrs. old	25 to 29 yrs. old	30 to 34 yrs. old	18 to 24 yrs. old	25 to 29 yrs. old	30 to 34 yrs. old	18 to 24 yrs. old	25 to 29 yrs. old	30 to 34 yrs. old	18 to 24 yrs. old	25 to 29 yrs. old	30 to 34 yrs. old
1971....	2,375	2,619	2,989	2,353	2,577	2,936	2,623	3,112	3,714	(NA)	(NA)	(NA)
1975....	2,173	2,260	2,610	2,147	2,233	2,564	2,489	2,587	3,212	2,223	2,607	3,238
1980....	2,134	2,166	2,248	2,130	2,146	2,223	2,155	2,426	2,522	2,428	2,495	2,909
1985....	2,183	2,236	2,167	2,177	2,227	2,139	2,242	2,259	2,521	2,367	2,628	2,712
1990....	2,244	2,285	2,277	2,218	2,272	2,257	2,509	2,443	2,579	2,404	2,482	2,824
1992....	2,279	2,271	2,218	2,274	2,259	2,208	2,353	2,389	2,362	2,511	2,437	2,600

NA Not available. [1] Includes other races not shown separately. [2] Persons of Hispanic origin may be of any race.

No. 108. Lifetime Births Expected by Women, 18 to 34 Years Old, by Selected Characteristics: 1992
[As of June. Covers women in the civilian noninstitutional population. Based on Current Population Survey; see text, section 1 and Appendix III]

CHARACTERISTIC	Women reporting on birth expectations (1,000)	RATE PER 1,000 WOMEN			PERCENTAGE EXPECTING—	
		Births to date	Future births expected	Lifetime births expected	No lifetime births	No future births
Total [1]................	24,223	1,135	963	2,098	9.3	48.3
White.......................	20,141	1,077	1,014	2,091	9.3	46.1
Black.....................	3,217	1,508	628	2,136	9.3	63.4
Hispanic [2]................	2,357	1,493	838	2,331	5.7	51.4
Not a high school graduate	3,599	1,776	616	2,393	7.6	63.8
High school, 4 years.............	8,760	1,325	718	2,043	9.0	57.9
College: 1 or more years	11,864	800	1,249	2,049	10.0	36.5
Some college, no degree	5,871	848	1,216	2,064	10.0	39.2
Associate degree	1,731	1,020	1,018	2,038	8.9	43.4
Bachelor's degree............	3,466	663	1,380	2,043	10.3	31.0
Graduate or professional degree ...	795	563	1,427	1,990	12.0	26.0
In labor force..................	17,834	929	1,069	1,998	10.5	44.1
Employed	16,130	903	1,077	1,980	10.7	43.6
Unemployed................	1,705	1,176	991	2,167	8.4	49.3
Not in labor force..............	6,389	1,710	667	2,377	6.0	60.1
Managerial and professional.......	3,760	725	1,232	1,957	11.3	36.8
Technical, sales, and admin. support..	7,511	835	1,126	1,962	10.2	41.0
Service workers...............	3,127	1,097	974	2,071	9.5	48.2
Farming, forestry, and fishing	198	1,426	972	2,398	14.1	55.5
Precision production, craft, and repair .	299	1,135	714	1,849	12.7	59.5
Operators, fabricators, and laborers...	1,235	1,223	675	1,897	13.5	62.4

[1] Includes other races not shown separately. [2] Persons of Hispanic origin may be of any race.
Source of tables 107 and 108: U.S. Bureau of the Census, *Current Population Reports*, series P20, unpublished data.

No. 109. Pregnancies, Number and Outcome: 1976 to 1988
[**Live births:** source of data is statistics of registered births published annually by National Center for Health Statistics (NCHS). **Induced abortions:** derived from published reports by the Alan Guttmacher Institute. **Fetal losses:** based on the National Survey of Family Growth conducted by NCHS]

YEAR	NUMBER (1,000)				RATE PER 1,000 WOMEN, 15 TO 44 YEARS OLD			
	Total	Live births	Induced abortions	Fetal losses	Total	Live births	Induced abortions	Fetal losses
1976........................	5,002	3,168	1,179	655	102.7	65.0	24.2	13.4
1977........................	5,331	3,327	1,317	687	107.0	66.8	26.4	13.8
1978........................	5,433	3,333	1,410	690	106.7	65.5	27.7	13.5
1979........................	5,714	3,494	1,498	722	109.9	67.2	28.8	13.9
1980........................	5,913	3,612	1,554	747	111.9	68.4	29.4	14.1
1981........................	5,958	3,629	1,577	751	110.7	67.4	29.3	14.0
1982........................	6,024	3,681	1,574	769	110.2	67.3	28.8	14.0
1983........................	5,975	3,639	1,575	761	108.0	65.8	28.5	13.8
1984........................	6,018	3,669	1,577	771	107.3	65.4	28.1	13.8
1985........................	6,144	3,761	1,589	795	108.2	66.2	28.0	14.0
1986........................	6,129	3,757	1,574	798	106.6	65.4	27.4	13.9
1987........................	6,183	3,809	1,559	815	106.7	65.7	26.9	14.1
1988........................	6,341	3,910	1,591	840	109.0	67.2	27.3	14.4

Source: U.S. National Center for Health Statistics, *Monthly Vital Statistics Report*, vol. 41, No. 6, Supplement.

No. 110. Pregnancies, by Outcome, Age of Woman, and Race: 1988

[See headnote, table 109]

ITEM	Total	Under 15 years old	15 to 19 years old	20 to 24 years old	25 to 29 years old	30 to 34 years old	35 to 39 years old	40 years old and over
NUMBER (1,000)								
Total, all pregnancies	6,341	27	988	1,774	1,821	1,195	456	79
Live births	3,910	11	478	1,067	1,239	804	270	41
Induced abortions	1,591	14	393	520	347	197	96	24
Fetal losses	840	3	117	187	234	194	91	14
White, all pregnancies	4,698	11	673	1,270	1,406	927	350	59
Live births	3,046	4	315	805	1,011	661	218	32
Induced abortions	1,026	6	264	332	219	125	63	17
Fetal losses	626	2	94	133	177	141	69	10
Other races, all pregnancies	1,643	16	315	504	415	268	106	20
Live births	863	7	163	263	229	142	52	9
Induced abortions	565	8	129	187	129	72	33	7
Fetal losses	214	1	23	54	58	53	21	4
RATE PER 1,000 WOMEN								
Total, all pregnancies	109.0	3.3	110.8	185.3	166.7	109.7	47.2	9.6
Live births	67.2	1.3	53.6	111.5	113.4	73.7	27.9	5.0
Induced abortions	27.3	1.7	44.0	54.2	31.8	18.1	9.9	3.0
Fetal losses	14.4	0.3	13.2	19.6	21.5	17.8	9.4	1.7
White, all pregnancies	97.2	1.8	93.4	161.7	155.3	102.2	43.2	8.4
Live births	63.0	0.6	43.7	102.5	111.6	72.9	26.9	4.6
Induced abortions	21.2	0.9	36.6	42.3	24.1	13.8	7.8	2.4
Fetal losses	13.0	0.2	13.1	16.9	19.5	15.5	8.5	1.5
Other races, all pregnancies	166.5	9.7	184.3	292.3	221.9	146.5	68.1	16.6
Live births	87.5	4.0	95.3	152.3	122.3	77.8	33.4	7.3
Induced abortions	57.3	4.9	75.5	108.5	68.8	39.6	21.0	6.2
Fetal losses	21.7	0.7	13.6	31.5	30.8	29.1	13.8	3.0
PERCENT DISTRIBUTION								
Total, all pregnancies	100.0	100.0	100.0	100.0	100.0	100.0	100.0	100.0
Live births	61.7	39.2	48.4	60.2	68.1	67.2	59.1	51.6
Induced abortions	25.1	50.5	39.7	29.3	19.1	16.5	21.0	30.9
Fetal losses	13.3	10.3	11.9	10.6	12.9	16.2	19.9	17.4
White, all pregnancies	100.0	100.0	100.0	100.0	100.0	100.0	100.0	100.0
Live births	64.8	35.6	46.9	63.4	71.9	71.3	62.2	54.1
Induced abortions	21.8	50.2	39.2	26.2	15.6	13.5	18.1	28.7
Fetal losses	13.3	14.2	14.0	10.5	12.6	15.2	19.8	17.2
Other races, all pregnancies	100.0	100.0	100.0	100.0	100.0	100.0	100.0	100.0
Live births	52.6	41.8	51.7	52.1	55.1	53.1	49.0	44.2
Induced abortions	34.4	50.7	41.0	37.1	31.0	27.0	30.8	37.6
Fetal losses	13.1	7.5	7.4	10.8	13.9	19.9	20.2	18.2

Source: U.S. National Center for Health Statistics, *Monthly Vital Statistics Report*, vol. 41, No. 6.

No. 111. Contraceptive Use by Women, 15 to 44 Years Old, by Age, Race, Marital Status, and Method of Contraception: 1982 and 1988

[Based on the 1982 and 1988 National Survey of Family Growth; see Appendix III]

CONTRACEPTIVE STATUS AND METHOD	All women, 1982	1988								
		All women[1]	AGE			RACE		MARITAL STATUS		
			15-24 years	25-34 years	35-44 years	White	Black	Never married	Currently married	Formerly married
All women (1,000)	54,099	57,900	18,592	21,726	17,582	47,077	7,679	21,058	29,147	7,695
PERCENT DISTRIBUTION										
Sterile	27.2	29.7	3.1	27.0	61.3	30.5	29.6	5.2	44.0	42.6
Surgically sterile	25.7	28.3	2.4	26.0	58.7	29.2	27.8	4.3	42.4	40.9
Noncontraceptively sterile[2]	6.6	4.7	0.2	2.7	12.0	4.7	5.7	0.9	6.2	9.7
Contraceptively sterile[3]	19.0	23.6	2.2	23.3	46.7	24.5	22.1	3.4	36.2	31.3
Nonsurgically sterile[4]	1.5	1.4	0.7	0.9	2.7	1.3	1.8	1.0	1.6	1.7
Pregnant, postpartum	5.0	4.8	5.0	7.6	1.1	4.8	5.0	2.4	7.1	2.5
Seeking pregnancy	4.2	3.8	2.7	5.8	2.4	3.7	3.9	1.3	6.0	2.0
Other nonusers	26.9	25.0	45.7	16.7	13.5	23.8	26.9	52.5	4.8	26.6
Not sexually active[5]	19.5	19.0	37.9	10.3	8.5	18.1	16.7	43.5	0.3	19.5
Sexually active[5]	7.4	6.5	7.8	6.4	5.0	5.7	10.2	9.0	4.5	7.1
Nonsurgical contraceptors	36.7	36.7	43.5	43.0	21.6	37.2	34.6	38.5	38.1	26.3
Pill	15.6	18.5	29.7	21.6	3.0	18.4	21.6	24.7	15.1	14.5
IUD	4.0	1.2	0.1	1.4	2.1	1.1	1.7	0.6	1.5	2.1
Diaphragm	4.5	3.5	1.3	4.8	4.1	3.8	1.1	2.1	4.6	3.0
Condom	6.7	8.8	9.5	9.1	7.7	9.2	5.8	8.2	10.6	3.4
Foam	1.3	0.6	0.3	0.8	0.8	0.6	0.6	0.2	1.0	0.5
Rhythm[6]	2.2	1.4	0.6	1.7	1.8	1.4	1.2	0.6	2.1	1.1
Other methods[7]	2.5	2.6	2.0	3.6	2.2	2.5	2.6	2.1	3.2	1.7

[1] Includes other races, not shown separately. [2] Persons who had sterilizing operation and who gave as one reason that they had medical problems with their female organs. [3] Includes all other sterilization operations, and sterilization of the husband or current partner. [4] Persons sterile from illness, accident, or congenital conditions. [5] Those having intercourse in the last 3 months before the survey. [6] Periodic abstinence and natural family planning. [7] Withdrawal, douche, suppository, and less frequently used methods.

Source: U.S. National Center for Health Statistics, *Advance Data from Vital and Health Statistics*, No. 182.

No. 112. Abortions—Estimated Number, Rate, and Ratio, by Race: 1972 to 1988

[Refers to women 15 to 44 years old at time of abortion]

YEAR	ALL RACES				WHITE				BLACK AND OTHER			
	Women 15-44 years old (1,000)	Abortions			Women 15-44 years old (1,000)	Abortions			Women 15-44 years old (1,000)	Abortions		
		Num-ber (1,000)	Rate per 1,000 women	Ratio per 1,000 live births [1]		Num-ber (1,000)	Rate per 1,000 women	Ratio per 1,000 live births [1]		Num-ber (1,000)	Rate per 1,000 women	Ratio per 1,000 live births [1]
1972 ..	44,588	586.8	13.2	184	38,532	455.3	11.8	175	6,056	131.5	21.7	223
1975 ..	47,606	1,034.2	21.7	331	40,857	701.2	17.2	276	6,749	333.0	49.3	565
1976 ..	48,721	1,179.3	24.2	361	41,721	784.9	18.8	296	7,000	394.4	56.3	638
1977 ..	49,814	1,316.7	26.4	400	42,567	888.8	20.9	333	7,247	427.9	59.0	679
1978 ..	50,920	1,409.6	27.7	413	43,427	969.4	22.3	356	7,493	440.2	58.7	665
1979 ..	52,016	1,497.7	28.8	420	44,266	1,062.4	24.0	373	7,750	435.3	56.2	625
1980 ..	53,048	1,553.9	29.3	428	44,942	1,093.6	24.3	376	8,106	460.3	56.5	642
1981 ..	53,901	1,577.3	29.3	430	45,494	1,107.8	24.3	377	8,407	469.6	55.9	645
1982 ..	54,679	1,573.9	28.8	428	46,049	1,095.2	23.8	373	8,630	478.7	55.5	646
1983 ..	55,340	1,575.0	28.5	436	46,506	1,084.4	23.3	376	8,834	490.6	55.5	670
1984 ..	56,061	1,577.2	28.1	423	47,023	1,086.6	23.1	366	9,038	490.6	54.3	646
1985 ..	56,754	1,588.6	28.0	422	47,512	1,075.6	22.6	360	9,242	512.9	55.5	659
1986 [2] ..	57,483	1,574.0	27.4	416	48,010	1,044.7	21.8	350	9,473	529.3	55.9	661
1987 ..	57,964	1,559.1	27.1	405	48,288	1,017.3	21.1	338	9,676	541.8	56.0	648
1988 ..	58,192	1,590.8	27.3	401	48,325	1,025.7	21.2	333	9,867	565.1	57.3	638

[1] See headnote, table 114. [2] Total abortions in 1986 have been estimated by interpolation between 1985 and 1987.

Source: 1972, U.S. Centers for Disease Control, Atlanta, GA, *Abortion Surveillance, Annual Summary, 1972*, 1974, and The Alan Guttmacher Institute; 1975-1988, S.K. Henshaw and J. Van Vort, eds., *Abortion Factbook, 1992 Edition: Readings, Trends, and State and Local Data to 1988*, The Alan Guttmacher Institute, New York, NY, 1992 (copyright).

No. 113. Abortions, by Selected Characteristics: 1973 to 1988

[Number of abortions from surveys conducted by source; characteristics from the U.S. Centers for Disease Control's (CDC) annual abortion surveillance summaries, with adjustments for changes in States reporting data to the CDC each year]

CHARACTERISTIC	NUMBER (1,000)				PERCENT DISTRIBUTION				ABORTION RATIO [1]			
	1973	1980	1985	1988	1973	1980	1985	1988	1973	1980	1985	1988
Total abortions	745	1,554	1,589	1,591	100	100	100	100	193	300	297	286
Age of woman:												
Less than 15 years old	12	15	17	14	2	1	1	1	476	607	624	553
15 to 19 years old	232	445	399	393	31	29	25	25	280	451	462	444
20 to 24 years old	241	549	548	520	32	35	35	33	181	310	328	327
25 to 29 years old	130	304	336	347	17	20	21	22	128	213	219	218
30 to 34 years old	73	153	181	197	10	10	11	12	165	213	203	194
35 to 39 years old	41	67	87	96	6	4	5	6	246	317	280	254
40 years old and over	17	21	21	24	2	1	1	2	334	461	409	361
Race of woman:												
White	549	1,094	1,076	1,026	74	70	68	65	178	274	265	250
Black and other	196	460	513	565	26	30	32	36	252	392	397	389
Marital status of woman:												
Married.	216	320	281	277	29	21	18	17	74	98	88	87
Unmarried.	528	1,234	1,307	1,314	71	79	82	83	564	649	605	556
Number of prior live births:												
None	411	900	872	814	55	58	55	51	242	365	358	333
One	115	305	349	379	15	20	22	24	108	208	219	227
Two	104	216	240	262	14	14	15	17	190	283	288	288
Three	61	83	85	93	8	5	5	6	228	288	281	276
Four or more	55	51	43	43	7	3	3	3	196	251	230	213
Number of prior induced abortions:												
None	(NA)	1,043	944	908	(NA)	67	60	57	(NA)	(NA)	(NA)	(NA)
One	(NA)	373	416	429	(NA)	24	26	27	(NA)	(NA)	(NA)	(NA)
Two or more	(NA)	138	228	254	(NA)	9	14	16	(NA)	(NA)	(NA)	(NA)
Weeks of gestation: [2]												
Less than 9 weeks	284	800	811	800	38	52	51	50	(NA)	(NA)	(NA)	(NA)
9 to 10 weeks	222	417	425	424	30	27	27	27	(NA)	(NA)	(NA)	(NA)
11 to 12 weeks	131	202	198	198	18	13	12	12	(NA)	(NA)	(NA)	(NA)
13 weeks or more	108	136	154	168	15	9	10	11	(NA)	(NA)	(NA)	(NA)

NA Not available. [1] Number of abortions per 1,000 abortions and live births. Live births are those which occurred from July 1 of year shown through June 30 of the following year (to match time of conception with abortions). [2] Beginning 1985, data not exactly comparable with prior years because of a change in the method of calculation.

Source: S.K. Henshaw and J. Van Vort, eds., *Abortion Factbook, 1992 Edition: Readings, Trends, and State and Local Data to 1988*, The Alan Guttmacher Institute, New York, NY, 1992 (copyright).

No. 114. Abortions—Number, Rate per 1,000 Women, and Abortion/Live Birth Ratio, by State of Occurrence: 1980 to 1988

[Number of abortions are from surveys of hospitals, clinics, and physicians identified as providers of abortion services, conducted by The Alan Guttmacher Institute. Abortion rates are computed per 1,000 women 15 to 44 years of age on July 1 of specified year; abortion ratios are computed as the number of abortions per 1,000 live births from July 1 of year shown to June 30 of following year, by State of occurrence]

DIVISION, REGION, AND STATE	NUMBER OF ABORTIONS (1,000)			RATE PER 1,000 WOMEN, 15 TO 44 YEARS OLD			RATIO: ABORTIONS PER 1,000 LIVE BIRTHS		
	1980	1985	1988	1980	1985	1988	1980	1985	1988
United States	1,554	1,589	1,591	29.3	28.0	27.3	428	422	401
Northeast	396	407	387	34.9	(NA)	32.4	604	(NA)	495
New England.	84	85	87	28.9	28.6	27.9	530	504	433
Maine.	5	5	5	18.6	18.6	16.2	289	308	281
New Hampshire	5	7	5	21.1	29.0	17.5	347	419	259
Vermont.	4	3	4	30.4	26.2	25.8	466	448	451
Massachusetts.	46	40	44	33.5	29.3	30.2	609	533	448
Rhode Island.	7	8	7	30.7	35.5	30.6	529	572	477
Connecticut.	19	22	24	25.6	29.3	31.2	561	550	506
Middle Atlantic	312	322	300	37.0	37.6	34.0	627	607	516
New York	188	195	184	45.8	47.4	43.3	780	746	629
New Jersey.	56	69	64	32.8	39.6	35.1	591	672	553
Pennsylvania.	69	57	52	26.1	21.3	18.9	423	348	300
Midwest.	318	289	292	23.3	(NA)	20.7	336	(NA)	319
East North Central.	243	221	223	24.9	22.1	22.4	369	356	343
Ohio	67	57	53	26.8	22.4	21.0	397	357	324
Indiana.	20	16	16	15.3	12.2	11.9	227	202	184
Illinois	69	65	73	25.9	23.8	26.4	374	372	392
Michigan.	65	64	63	29.7	28.7	28.5	457	486	442
Wisconsin.	22	18	18	20.1	15.7	16.0	292	246	249
West North Central	75	68	69	19.2	16.7	16.7	260	252	261
Minnesota.	20	17	19	20.7	16.6	18.2	288	257	279
Iowa	9	10	9	14.3	15.0	14.6	195	248	252
Missouri	22	20	19	19.4	17.3	16.4	273	261	262
North Dakota	3	3	2	21.5	18.5	14.9	235	230	197
South Dakota	1	2	1	9.0	10.6	5.7	103	140	81
Nebraska	6	7	6	17.9	18.2	17.7	227	268	261
Kansas.	14	10	11	25.6	18.2	20.1	343	264	305
South	457	453	470	25.9	(NA)	23.4	369	(NA)	342
South Atlantic.	255	257	277	29.4	27.1	27.7	462	429	408
Delaware	4	5	6	25.9	30.9	35.7	395	451	498
Maryland	31	30	33	29.2	26.9	28.6	571	480	462
District of Columbia	29	24	26	168.3	145.9	163.3	1,569	1,186	1,248
Virginia.	32	34	35	24.2	24.0	23.7	417	412	382
West Virginia.	3	5	3	6.9	10.1	7.5	104	185	140
North Carolina.	32	34	40	22.8	22.6	25.4	377	379	389
South Carolina.	14	11	14	18.2	13.7	16.7	274	228	257
Georgia	38	38	37	28.4	26.1	23.5	395	397	331
Florida	74	77	83	35.5	31.8	31.5	547	465	434
East South Central.	65	57	57	19.2	15.8	15.6	271	258	240
Kentucky	13	10	12	15.1	11.0	13.0	215	189	213
Tennessee	26	22	22	23.6	19.1	18.9	352	315	290
Alabama	21	19	18	23.1	20.2	18.7	331	333	282
Mississippi	6	6	5	10.6	9.7	8.4	132	142	122
West South Central	137	139	136	24.5	21.8	21.3	308	290	297
Arkansas	6	5	6	12.3	10.1	11.6	173	159	180
Louisiana	18	19	17	17.6	17.4	16.3	218	240	241
Oklahoma	11	13	12	16.4	17.1	16.2	221	269	255
Texas.	102	101	101	30.0	25.5	24.8	367	320	331
West	383	440	442	36.8	(NA)	36.3	486	(NA)	492
Mountain	68	75	69	25.0	23.6	21.9	302	316	294
Montana.	4	4	3	20.1	19.0	16.5	265	288	263
Idaho	3	3	2	12.7	11.1	8.2	141	155	124
Wyoming	1	1	1	9.5	7.9	5.1	107	125	89
Colorado.	23	24	19	31.4	28.8	22.4	447	438	350
New Mexico	8	6	7	27.0	17.4	19.1	358	219	249
Arizona.	16	22	23	25.0	29.9	28.8	310	373	348
Utah	4	4	5	12.3	11.1	12.8	97	116	138
Nevada	9	10	10	46.6	40.5	40.3	697	641	554
Pacific	315	365	372	41.0	42.8	41.5	561	594	562
Washington.	37	31	31	37.5	28.0	27.6	522	458	471
Oregon.	18	15	16	28.3	22.3	23.9	396	374	390
California	250	304	312	43.7	47.9	45.9	598	640	594
Alaska	2	4	2	17.9	27.7	18.2	196	283	213
Hawaii	8	11	11	34.4	43.7	43.0	441	611	574

NA Not available.

Source: S.K. Henshaw and J. Van Vort, eds., *Abortion Factbook, 1992 Edition: Readings, Trends, and State and Local Data to 1988*, The Alan Guttmacher Institute, New York, NY, 1992 (copyright); and unpublished data.

No. 115. Expectation of Life at Birth, 1970 to 1991, and Projections, 1995 to 2010

[In years. Excludes deaths of nonresidents of the United States. See also *Historical Statistics, Colonial Times to 1970*, series B 107-115]

YEAR	TOTAL			WHITE			BLACK AND OTHER			BLACK		
	Total	Male	Female	Total	Male	Female	Total	Male	Female	Total	Male	Female
1970.............	70.8	67.1	74.7	71.7	68.0	75.6	65.3	61.3	69.4	64.1	60.0	68.3
1975.............	72.6	68.8	76.6	73.4	69.5	77.3	68.0	63.7	72.4	66.8	62.4	71.3
1976.............	72.9	69.1	76.8	73.6	69.9	77.5	68.4	64.2	72.7	67.2	62.9	71.6
1977.............	73.3	69.5	77.2	74.0	70.2	77.9	68.9	64.7	73.2	67.7	63.4	72.0
1978.............	73.5	69.6	77.3	74.1	70.4	78.0	69.3	65.0	73.5	68.1	63.7	72.4
1979.............	73.9	70.0	77.8	74.6	70.8	78.4	69.8	65.4	74.1	68.5	64.0	72.9
1980.............	73.7	70.0	77.4	74.4	70.7	78.1	69.5	65.3	73.6	68.1	63.8	72.5
1981.............	74.1	70.4	77.8	74.8	71.1	78.4	70.3	66.2	74.4	68.9	64.5	73.2
1982.............	74.5	70.8	78.1	75.1	71.5	78.7	70.9	66.8	74.9	69.4	65.1	73.6
1983.............	74.6	71.0	78.1	75.2	71.6	78.7	70.9	67.0	74.7	69.4	65.2	73.5
1984.............	74.7	71.1	78.2	75.3	71.8	78.7	71.1	67.2	74.9	69.5	65.3	73.6
1985.............	74.7	71.1	78.2	75.3	71.8	78.7	71.0	67.0	74.8	69.3	65.0	73.4
1986.............	74.7	71.2	78.2	75.4	71.9	78.8	70.9	66.8	74.9	69.1	64.8	73.4
1987.............	74.9	71.4	78.3	75.6	72.1	78.9	71.0	66.9	75.0	69.1	64.7	73.4
1988.............	74.9	71.4	78.3	75.6	72.2	78.9	70.8	66.7	74.8	68.9	64.4	73.2
1989.............	75.1	71.7	78.5	75.9	72.5	79.2	70.9	66.7	74.9	68.8	64.3	73.3
1990.............	75.4	71.8	78.8	76.1	72.7	79.4	71.2	67.0	75.2	69.1	64.5	73.6
1991, prel........	75.7	72.2	79.1	76.4	73.0	79.7	72.2	68.1	76.2	70.0	65.6	74.3
Projections: [1] 1995 ...	76.1	72.6	79.5	76.7	73.4	80.0	(NA)	(NA)	(NA)	70.9	66.6	75.2
2000 ...	76.6	73.0	80.0	77.2	73.9	80.5	(NA)	(NA)	(NA)	71.1	66.5	75.8
2005 ...	77.1	73.6	80.5	77.7	74.5	81.0	(NA)	(NA)	(NA)	71.6	66.9	76.4
2010 ...	77.6	74.2	81.1	78.3	75.1	81.5	(NA)	(NA)	(NA)	72.2	67.3	77.0

NA Not available.   [1] Based on middle mortality assumptions; for details, see source. Source: U.S. Bureau of the Census, *Current Population Reports*, series P25-1092.

Source: Except as noted, U.S. National Center for Health Statistics, *Vital Statistics of the United States*, annual, and *Monthly Vital Statistics Reports*.

No. 116. Selected Life Table Values: 1969 to 1990

[Beginning 1970, excludes deaths of nonresidents of the United States. See also *Historical Statistics, Colonial Times to 1970*, series B 116-125]

AGE AND SEX	TOTAL [1]				WHITE				BLACK		
	1969-1971	1979-1981	1985	1990	1969-1971	1979-1981	1985	1990	1979-1981	1985	1990
AVERAGE EXPECTATION OF LIFE IN YEARS											
At birth: Male............	67.0	70.1	71.1	71.8	67.9	70.8	71.8	72.7	64.1	65.0	64.5
Female..........	74.6	77.6	78.2	78.8	75.5	78.2	78.7	79.4	72.9	73.4	73.6
Age 20: Male...........	49.5	51.9	52.6	53.3	50.2	52.5	53.2	54.0	46.4	47.1	46.7
Female..........	56.6	59.0	59.3	59.8	57.2	59.4	59.8	60.3	54.9	55.2	55.3
Age 40: Male...........	31.5	33.6	34.2	35.1	31.9	34.0	34.7	35.6	29.5	29.8	30.1
Female..........	37.6	39.8	40.0	40.6	38.1	40.2	40.4	41.0	36.3	36.4	36.8
Age 50: Male...........	23.1	25.0	25.5	26.4	23.3	25.3	25.8	26.7	22.0	22.1	22.5
Female..........	28.8	30.7	30.8	31.3	29.1	31.0	31.1	31.6	27.8	27.8	28.2
Age 65: Male...........	13.0	14.2	14.5	15.1	13.0	14.3	14.5	15.2	13.3	13.0	13.2
Female..........	16.8	18.4	18.5	18.9	16.9	18.6	18.7	19.1	17.1	16.9	17.2
EXPECTED DEATHS PER 1,000 ALIVE AT SPECIFIED AGE [2]											
At birth: Male............	22.5	13.9	12.0	10.3	20.1	12.3	10.6	8.6	23.0	19.9	19.7
Female..........	17.5	11.2	9.4	8.2	15.3	9.7	8.0	6.6	19.3	16.5	16.3
Age 20: Male...........	2.1	1.8	1.5	1.6	1.9	1.8	1.4	1.4	2.2	1.9	2.7
Female..........	0.7	0.6	0.5	0.5	0.6	0.6	0.5	0.5	0.7	0.6	0.7
Age 40: Male...........	4.0	3.0	2.8	3.1	3.4	2.6	2.5	2.7	6.9	6.5	7.1
Female..........	2.3	1.6	1.4	1.4	1.9	1.4	1.3	1.2	3.2	2.9	3.1
Age 50: Male...........	9.7	7.8	6.8	6.2	8.9	7.1	6.2	5.6	14.9	13.3	12.8
Female..........	5.2	4.2	3.8	3.5	4.7	3.8	3.5	3.2	7.7	6.8	6.6
Age 65: Male...........	34.6	28.2	26.1	12.9	33.9	27.4	25.2	23.0	38.5	28.5	36.8
Female..........	16.8	14.3	14.1	13.5	15.6	13.6	13.5	12.8	21.6	21.4	21.4
NUMBER SURVIVING TO SPECIFIED AGE PER 1,000 BORN ALIVE											
Age 20: Male............	961	973	977	979	965	975	979	981	961	966	963
Female..........	973	982	985	986	976	984	986	988	972	976	976
Age 40: Male...........	915	933	941	938	926	940	946	946	885	897	880
Female..........	951	965	970	971	958	969	973	975	941	948	944
Age 50: Male...........	861	890	902	899	877	901	911	912	801	820	801
Female..........	919	941	948	950	929	947	953	957	896	908	904
Age 65: Male...........	643	706	727	741	663	724	744	760	551	571	571
Female..........	797	835	844	851	816	848	855	864	733	746	751

[1] Includes other races not shown separately.   [2] See footnote 1, table 117.
Source: U.S. National Center for Health Statistics, *U.S. Life Tables and Actuarial Tables, 1959-61, 1969-71, and 1979-81; Vital Statistics of the United States*, annual; and unpublished data.

No. 117. Expectation of Life and Expected Deaths, by Race, Sex, and Age: 1990

AGE IN 1990 (years)	EXPECTATION OF LIFE IN YEARS					EXPECTED DEATHS PER 1,000 ALIVE AT SPECIFIED AGE [1]				
	Total	White		Black		Total	White		Black	
		Male	Female	Male	Female		Male	Female	Male	Female
At birth.......	75.4	72.7	79.4	64.5	73.6	9.27	8.55	6.59	19.68	16.30
1............	75.1	72.3	78.9	64.8	73.8	0.66	0.67	0.50	1.20	0.87
2............	74.1	71.4	78.0	63.9	72.9	0.49	0.48	0.38	0.88	0.70
3............	73.1	70.4	77.0	62.9	71.9	0.38	0.36	0.30	0.67	0.57
4............	72.2	69.4	76.0	62.0	71.0	0.31	0.30	0.25	0.55	0.45
5............	71.2	68.5	75.0	61.0	70.0	0.27	0.27	0.21	0.47	0.37
6............	70.2	67.5	74.1	60.1	69.0	0.25	0.26	0.19	0.43	0.30
7............	69.2	66.5	73.1	59.1	68.1	0.22	0.25	0.17	0.39	0.26
8............	68.2	65.5	72.1	58.1	67.1	0.20	0.22	0.15	0.33	0.23
9............	67.3	64.5	71.1	57.1	66.1	0.17	0.18	0.14	0.26	0.22
10............	66.3	63.5	70.1	56.1	65.1	0.15	0.15	0.13	0.20	0.22
11............	65.3	62.6	69.1	55.1	64.1	0.15	0.15	0.14	0.21	0.24
12............	64.3	61.6	68.1	54.2	63.1	0.20	0.21	0.16	0.32	0.27
13............	63.3	60.6	67.1	53.2	62.1	0.31	0.36	0.21	0.58	0.31
14............	62.3	59.6	66.2	52.2	61.2	0.46	0.58	0.28	0.93	0.36
15............	61.3	58.6	65.2	51.3	60.2	0.64	0.82	0.36	1.34	0.42
16............	60.4	57.7	64.2	50.3	59.2	0.80	1.04	0.43	1.73	0.49
17............	59.4	56.7	63.2	49.4	58.2	0.92	1.21	0.48	2.07	0.55
18............	58.5	55.8	62.3	48.5	57.3	0.99	1.31	0.50	2.33	0.60
19............	57.5	54.9	61.3	47.6	56.3	1.02	1.36	0.49	2.54	0.65
20............	56.6	54.0	60.3	46.7	55.3	1.04	1.39	0.47	2.74	0.70
21............	55.7	53.0	59.3	45.9	54.4	1.07	1.43	0.46	2.95	0.75
22............	54.7	52.1	58.4	45.0	53.4	1.10	1.47	0.45	3.13	0.82
23............	53.8	51.2	57.4	44.1	52.5	1.13	1.49	0.46	3.27	0.90
24............	52.8	50.3	56.4	43.3	51.5	1.15	1.52	0.48	3.37	0.99
25............	51.9	49.3	55.4	42.4	50.6	1.18	1.54	0.50	3.46	1.09
26............	51.0	48.4	54.5	41.6	49.6	1.20	1.55	0.52	3.56	1.19
27............	50.0	47.5	53.5	40.7	48.7	1.23	1.58	0.54	3.70	1.30
28............	49.1	46.6	52.5	39.9	47.7	1.28	1.63	0.56	3.90	1.41
29............	48.1	45.6	51.6	39.0	46.8	1.33	1.69	0.59	4.14	1.53
30............	47.2	44.7	50.6	38.2	45.9	1.39	1.76	0.61	4.39	1.65
31............	46.3	43.8	49.6	37.4	45.0	1.46	1.83	0.65	4.64	1.78
32............	45.3	42.9	48.7	36.5	44.0	1.53	1.91	0.68	4.90	1.91
33............	44.4	41.9	47.7	35.7	43.1	1.61	2.00	0.73	5.17	2.04
34............	43.5	41.0	46.7	34.9	42.2	1.69	2.09	0.77	5.45	2.16
35............	42.6	40.1	45.8	34.1	41.3	1.79	2.21	0.83	5.76	2.30
36............	41.6	39.2	44.8	33.3	40.4	1.90	2.32	0.89	6.07	2.45
37............	40.7	38.3	43.8	32.5	39.5	2.00	2.43	0.95	6.37	2.60
38............	39.8	37.4	42.9	31.7	38.6	2.08	2.52	1.02	6.63	2.74
39............	38.9	36.5	41.9	30.9	37.7	2.16	2.60	1.09	6.87	2.89
40............	38.0	35.6	41.0	30.1	36.8	2.24	2.69	1.18	7.11	3.05
41............	37.0	34.7	40.0	29.3	35.9	2.36	2.81	1.28	7.40	3.23
42............	36.1	33.8	39.1	28.5	35.0	2.50	2.97	1.40	7.77	3.46
43............	35.2	32.9	38.1	27.7	34.1	2.68	3.16	1.55	8.23	3.72
44............	34.3	32.0	37.2	27.0	33.3	2.90	3.39	1.72	8.78	4.03
45............	33.4	31.1	36.2	26.2	32.4	3.15	3.66	1.92	9.39	4.38
46............	32.5	30.2	35.3	25.4	31.5	3.42	3.96	2.13	10.03	4.75
47............	31.6	29.3	34.4	24.7	30.7	3.73	4.30	2.37	10.70	5.15
48............	30.7	28.4	33.5	24.0	29.8	4.07	4.69	2.62	11.37	5.59
49............	29.9	27.6	32.5	23.2	29.0	4.44	5.12	2.89	12.07	6.07
50............	29.0	26.7	31.6	22.5	28.2	4.86	5.60	3.20	12.81	6.58
51............	28.1	25.8	30.7	21.8	27.4	5.31	6.14	3.53	13.63	7.14
52............	27.3	25.0	29.8	21.1	26.6	5.82	6.67	3.89	14.60	7.75
53............	26.4	24.2	29.0	20.4	25.8	6.39	7.46	4.28	15.78	8.41
54............	25.6	23.3	28.1	19.7	25.0	7.01	8.25	4.70	17.12	9.12
55............	24.8	22.5	27.2	19.0	24.2	7.68	9.10	5.15	18.57	9.87
56............	24.0	21.7	26.4	18.4	23.4	8.41	10.03	5.65	20.08	10.67
57............	23.2	21.0	25.5	17.8	22.7	9.22	11.07	6.21	21.65	11.57
58............	22.4	20.2	24.7	17.1	22.0	10.12	12.24	6.85	23.27	12.58
59............	21.6	19.4	23.8	16.5	21.2	11.11	13.54	7.56	24.94	13.69
60............	20.8	18.7	23.0	15.9	20.5	12.19	14.96	8.35	26.71	14.87
61............	20.1	18.0	22.2	15.4	19.8	13.33	16.46	9.18	28.59	16.09
62............	19.4	17.3	21.4	14.8	19.1	14.50	18.01	10.04	30.54	17.36
63............	18.6	16.6	20.6	14.3	18.5	15.70	19.59	10.91	32.55	18.66
64............	17.9	15.9	19.8	13.7	17.8	16.93	21.24	11.80	34.63	20.00
65............	17.2	15.2	19.1	13.2	17.2	18.23	22.96	12.76	36.79	21.41
70............	13.9	12.1	15.4	10.7	14.1	27.33	35.15	19.78	51.00	29.49
75............	10.9	9.4	12.0	8.6	11.2	41.08	53.88	31.08	68.81	40.48
80............	8.3	7.1	9.0	6.7	8.6	62.24	82.01	49.92	93.91	58.55
85 and over ...	6.1	5.2	6.4	5.0	6.3	1,000	1,000	1,000	1,000	1,000

[1] Based on the proportion of the cohort who are alive at the beginning of an indicated age interval who will die before reaching the end of that interval. For example, out of every 1,000 people alive and exactly 50 years old at the beginning of the period, between 4 and 5 (4.86) will die before reaching their 51st birthdays.

Source: U.S. National Center for Health Statistics, *Vital Statistics of the United States*, annual; and unpublished data.

No. 118. Deaths and Death Rates, by Sex and Race: 1970 to 1990

[Rates are per 1,000 population for specified groups. Excludes deaths of nonresidents of the United States and fetal deaths. For explanation of age-adjustment, see text, section 2. The standard population for this table is the total population of the United States enumerated in 1940. See Appendix III. See also *Historical Statistics, Colonial Times to 1970*, series B 167-173 and B 181-192]

SEX AND RACE	1970	1980	1981	1982	1983	1984	1985	1986	1987	1988	1989	1990
Deaths [1] (1,000)	**1,921**	**1,990**	**1,978**	**1,975**	**2,019**	**2,039**	**2,086**	**2,105**	**2,123**	**2,168**	**2,150**	**2,148**
Male [1] (1,000)	1,078	1,075	1,064	1,056	1,072	1,077	1,098	1,104	1,108	1,126	1,114	1,113
Female [1] (1,000)	843	915	914	918	947	963	989	1,001	1,015	1,042	1,036	1,035
White (1,000)	1,682	1,739	1,731	1,729	1,766	1,782	1,819	1,831	1,843	1,877	1,854	1,853
Male (1,000)	942	934	925	919	932	935	950	953	953	965	951	951
Female (1,000)	740	805	806	810	834	847	869	879	890	911	903	902
Black (1,000)	226	233	229	227	233	236	244	250	255	264	268	266
Male (1,000)	128	130	127	126	128	129	134	137	140	144	146	145
Female (1,000)	98	103	101	101	105	107	111	113	115	120	121	120
Death rates [1]	**9.5**	**8.8**	**8.6**	**8.5**	**8.6**	**8.6**	**8.8**	**8.8**	**8.8**	**8.8**	**8.7**	**8.6**
Male [1]	10.9	9.8	9.5	9.4	9.4	9.4	9.5	9.4	9.4	9.5	9.3	9.2
Female [1]	8.1	7.9	7.8	7.7	7.9	7.9	8.1	8.1	8.2	8.3	8.2	8.1
White	9.5	8.9	8.8	8.7	8.9	8.9	9.0	9.0	9.0	9.1	8.9	8.9
Male	10.9	9.8	9.7	9.5	9.6	9.5	9.6	9.6	9.5	9.6	9.4	9.3
Female	8.1	8.1	8.0	8.0	8.2	8.2	8.4	8.4	8.5	8.7	8.5	8.5
Black	10.0	8.8	8.4	8.2	8.4	8.4	8.5	8.6	8.7	8.9	8.9	8.8
Male	11.9	10.3	9.9	9.7	9.7	9.7	9.9	10.0	10.1	10.3	10.3	10.1
Female	8.3	7.3	7.1	7.0	7.2	7.2	7.3	7.4	7.5	7.6	7.6	7.5
Age-adjusted death rates [1]	**7.1**	**5.9**	**5.7**	**5.5**	**5.5**	**5.5**	**5.5**	**5.4**	**5.4**	**5.4**	**5.3**	**5.2**
Male [1]	9.3	7.8	7.5	7.3	7.3	7.2	7.2	7.2	7.1	7.1	6.9	6.8
Female [1]	5.3	4.3	4.2	4.1	4.1	4.1	4.1	4.1	4.0	4.1	4.0	3.9
White	6.8	5.6	5.4	5.3	5.3	5.3	5.2	5.2	5.1	5.1	5.0	4.9
Male	8.9	7.5	7.2	7.1	7.0	6.9	6.9	6.8	6.7	6.7	6.5	6.4
Female	5.0	4.1	4.0	3.9	3.9	3.9	3.9	3.9	3.8	3.9	3.8	3.7
Black	10.4	8.4	8.0	7.8	7.9	7.8	7.9	8.0	8.0	8.1	8.1	7.9
Male	13.2	11.1	10.7	10.4	10.4	10.4	10.5	10.6	10.6	10.8	10.8	10.6
Female	8.1	6.3	6.0	5.9	6.0	5.9	5.9	5.9	5.9	6.0	5.9	5.8

[1] Includes other races, not shown separately.

Source: U.S. National Center for Health Statistics, *Vital Statistics of the United States*, annual; and *Monthly Vital Statistics Report*.

No. 119. Death Rates, by Age, Sex, and Race: 1970 to 1991

[Number of deaths per 100,000 population in specified group. See headnote, table 118]

SEX, YEAR, AND RACE	All ages [1]	Under 1 yr. old	1-4 yr. old	5-14 yr. old	15-24 yr. old	25-34 yr. old	35-44 yr. old	45-54 yr. old	55-64 yr. old	65-74 yr. old	75-84 yr. old	85 yr. old and over
MALE [2]												
1970	1,090	2,410	93	51	189	215	403	959	2,283	4,874	10,010	17,822
1980	977	1,429	73	37	172	196	299	767	1,815	4,105	8,817	18,801
1985	949	1,220	59	32	139	180	279	672	1,711	3,856	8,502	18,614
1990	918	1,083	52	29	147	204	310	610	1,553	3,492	7,889	18,057
1991, prel. [3]	909	1,007	49	29	161	201	311	598	1,504	3,307	7,663	17,151
White: 1970	1,087	2,113	84	48	171	177	344	883	2,203	4,810	10,099	18,552
1980	983	1,230	66	35	167	171	257	699	1,729	4,036	8,830	19,097
1985	964	1,057	53	30	134	159	243	612	1,626	3,771	8,486	18,980
1990	931	896	46	26	131	176	268	549	1,467	3,398	7,845	18,268
1991, prel. [3]	924	846	43	26	143	172	269	541	1,431	3,246	7,689	17,620
Black: 1970	1,187	4,299	151	67	321	560	957	1,778	3,257	5,803	9,455	12,222
1980	1,034	2,587	111	47	209	407	690	1,480	2,873	5,131	9,232	16,099
1985	989	2,220	90	42	174	352	630	1,293	2,780	5,172	9,262	15,774
1990	1,008	2,112	86	41	252	431	700	1,261	2,618	4,946	9,130	16,955
1991, prel. [3]	962	1,899	82	44	277	414	707	1,203	2,323	4,286	8,359	14,325
FEMALE [2]												
1970	808	1,864	75	32	68	102	231	517	1,099	2,580	6,678	15,518
1980	785	1,142	55	24	58	76	159	413	934	2,145	5,440	14,747
1985	809	951	45	21	50	69	139	375	926	2,097	5,162	14,554
1990	812	856	41	19	49	74	138	343	879	1,991	4,883	14,274
1991, prel. [3]	802	791	45	19	52	74	136	326	855	1,972	4,862	13,328
White: 1970	813	1,615	66	30	62	84	193	463	1,015	2,471	6,699	15,980
1980	806	963	49	23	56	65	138	373	876	2,067	5,402	14,980
1985	840	799	40	20	48	59	122	342	869	2,027	5,112	14,745
1990	847	690	36	18	46	62	117	309	823	1,924	4,839	14,441
1991, prel. [3]	838	645	37	17	48	63	115	296	807	1,915	4,842	13,553
Black: 1970	829	3,369	129	44	112	231	533	1,044	1,986	3,861	6,692	10,707
1980	733	2,124	84	31	71	150	324	768	1,561	3,057	6,212	12,367
1985	734	1,821	71	29	60	138	277	668	1,533	2,968	6,078	12,703
1990	748	1,736	68	28	69	160	299	639	1,453	2,866	5,688	13,310
1991, prel. [3]	721	1,546	80	28	77	147	298	587	1,328	2,750	5,762	11,856

[1] Includes unknown age.   [2] Includes other races not shown separately.   [3] Includes deaths of nonresidents. Based on a 10-percent sample of deaths.

Source: U.S. National Center for Health Statistics, *Vital Statistics of the United States*, annual; *Monthly Vital Statistics Report*; and unpublished data.

Vital Statistics

No. 120. Deaths and Death Rates, by State: 1980 to 1991

[By State of residence. Excludes deaths of nonresidents of the United States, except as noted. Caution should be used in comparing death rates by State; rates are affected by the population composition of the area. See also Appendix III]

DIVISION AND STATE	NUMBER OF DEATHS (1,000)								RATE PER 1,000 POPULATION [2]							
	1980	1985	1986	1987	1988	1989	1990	1991, [1] prel.	1980	1985	1986	1987	1988	1989	1990	1991, [1] prel.
United States . .	1,990	2,086	2,105	2,123	2,168	2,150	2,148	2,165	8.8	8.8	8.8	8.8	8.9	8.7	8.6	8.6
New England	115	118	118	118	120	116	115	112	9.3	9.3	9.2	9.1	9.2	8.8	8.7	8.5
Maine	11	11	11	11	12	11	11	11	9.6	9.8	9.6	9.5	9.6	9.2	9.0	8.9
New Hampshire . .	8	8	9	8	9	8	8	9	8.3	8.5	8.4	8.0	8.1	7.7	7.7	7.7
Vermont	5	5	5	5	5	5	5	5	9.0	8.8	8.9	8.8	8.5	8.2	8.2	8.0
Massachusetts . . .	55	56	56	56	56	54	53	51	9.6	9.5	9.5	9.4	9.4	9.0	8.8	8.6
Rhode Island	9	10	10	10	10	10	10	9	9.8	10.0	9.9	9.8	9.8	9.6	9.5	9.2
Connecticut	27	28	28	28	29	28	28	28	8.8	8.8	8.7	8.7	8.7	8.6	8.4	8.4
Middle Atlantic. . . .	365	367	370	371	376	367	361	360	9.9	9.9	9.9	9.9	10.0	9.8	9.6	9.5
New York	173	172	174	174	176	172	169	167	9.8	9.7	9.7	9.7	9.8	9.5	9.4	9.2
New Jersey	69	71	72	72	73	71	70	70	9.4	9.4	9.4	9.4	9.5	9.2	9.1	9.0
Pennsylvania	124	124	124	125	126	124	122	124	10.4	10.5	10.6	10.6	10.6	10.4	10.3	10.3
East North Central .	365	370	375	372	379	372	373	379	8.8	8.9	9.0	9.0	9.1	8.9	8.9	8.9
Ohio	98	99	100	99	100	98	99	99	9.1	9.2	9.3	9.2	9.3	9.1	9.1	9.1
Indiana	47	48	49	49	50	49	50	52	8.6	8.8	9.1	8.9	9.1	8.9	8.9	9.2
Illinois	103	102	103	102	105	103	103	104	9.0	9.0	9.1	9.0	9.2	9.1	9.0	9.0
Michigan	75	79	80	80	80	79	79	80	8.1	8.7	8.8	8.7	8.7	8.5	8.5	8.5
Wisconsin	41	41	42	42	43	42	43	44	8.7	8.7	8.9	8.8	8.9	8.7	8.7	8.8
West North Central.	159	162	161	162	164	161	161	164	9.2	9.3	9.3	9.3	9.4	9.2	9.1	9.2
Minnesota	33	35	35	35	35	34	35	35	8.2	8.3	8.3	8.2	8.3	7.9	7.9	8.0
Iowa	27	28	27	27	28	27	27	26	9.3	9.8	9.7	9.8	10.1	9.8	9.7	9.3
Missouri.	50	50	50	51	51	50	50	53	10.1	10.1	10.0	10.0	10.0	9.9	9.8	10.4
North Dakota	6	6	5	5	6	6	6	6	8.6	8.3	7.9	8.3	8.6	8.5	8.9	8.9
South Dakota	7	7	7	7	7	7	6	7	9.5	9.5	9.5	9.6	9.4	9.4	9.1	9.4
Nebraska	14	15	15	15	15	15	15	15	9.2	9.4	9.3	9.5	9.5	9.4	9.4	9.2
Kansas	22	22	22	22	23	22	22	23	9.3	9.1	9.2	9.0	9.3	9.0	9.0	9.0
South Atlantic	330	364	372	379	389	391	392	397	8.9	9.1	9.1	9.1	9.2	9.1	9.0	8.9
Delaware	5	5	6	6	6	6	6	6	8.5	8.9	9.0	8.8	8.9	8.9	8.7	8.6
Maryland	34	37	37	38	39	38	38	38	8.1	8.3	8.3	8.3	8.3	8.1	8.0	7.8
Dist. of Col.	7	7	7	7	8	8	7	7	11.1	11.0	11.4	11.7	12.2	12.3	12.0	11.7
Virginia	43	45	47	47	48	47	48	49	8.0	7.9	8.0	7.9	7.9	7.7	7.8	7.8
West Virginia	19	19	20	20	20	20	19	20	9.9	10.2	10.6	10.6	10.8	10.8	10.8	11.0
North Carolina . . .	48	53	55	55	58	57	57	59	8.2	8.5	8.6	8.6	8.9	8.8	8.6	8.7
South Carolina . . .	25	27	28	28	29	30	30	30	8.1	8.2	8.4	8.4	8.6	8.6	8.5	8.4
Georgia	44	49	49	50	52	52	52	53	8.1	8.2	8.1	8.1	8.2	8.2	8.0	8.0
Florida.	105	121	124	127	131	133	134	135	10.7	10.7	10.6	10.6	10.6	10.5	10.4	10.2
East South Central .	134	140	141	142	145	145	146	144	9.1	9.4	9.4	9.4	9.6	9.6	9.6	9.4
Kentucky	34	35	35	35	36	35	35	35	9.2	9.4	9.4	9.4	9.7	9.6	9.5	9.5
Tennessee.	41	43	44	45	46	45	46	45	8.9	9.2	9.3	9.4	9.5	9.4	9.5	9.2
Alabama	36	38	38	38	39	39	39	38	9.1	9.5	9.4	9.4	9.7	9.7	9.7	9.3
Mississippi	24	25	24	25	25	25	25	26	9.4	9.5	9.4	9.5	9.6	9.9	9.8	9.9
West South Central.	195	209	209	210	215	217	218	222	8.2	8.0	7.9	7.9	8.1	8.2	8.2	8.2
Arkansas	23	24	24	24	25	25	25	24	9.9	10.4	10.3	10.4	10.6	10.5	10.5	10.2
Louisiana	36	37	36	36	38	38	38	38	8.5	8.4	8.3	8.4	8.8	8.9	8.9	9.0
Oklahoma	28	30	30	29	30	30	30	30	9.3	9.1	9.2	9.1	9.5	9.5	9.7	9.6
Texas	108	118	119	120	123	125	125	129	7.6	7.3	7.2	7.2	7.4	7.4	7.4	7.4
Mountain	80	88	90	92	95	95	97	99	7.0	6.9	7.0	7.0	7.1	7.1	7.1	7.1
Montana	7	7	7	7	7	7	7	7	8.5	8.2	8.3	8.2	8.5	8.4	8.6	8.7
Idaho	7	7	7	7	8	7	7	8	7.2	7.2	7.5	7.5	7.8	7.5	7.4	7.5
Wyoming	3	3	3	3	3	3	3	3	6.9	6.6	6.5	6.4	7.0	7.1	7.1	6.9
Colorado	19	20	21	21	21	21	22	22	6.6	6.3	6.4	6.5	6.5	6.5	6.6	6.6
New Mexico	9	10	10	10	10	11	11	11	7.0	6.8	6.9	7.0	7.0	7.0	7.0	7.2
Arizona	21	25	26	27	28	28	29	29	7.9	7.7	7.7	7.8	7.8	7.8	7.9	7.8
Utah	8	9	9	9	9	9	9	9	5.6	5.5	5.4	5.4	5.5	5.4	5.3	5.2
Nevada	6	7	7	8	8	9	9	9	7.4	7.6	7.6	7.7	7.9	7.6	7.8	7.2
Pacific.	247	268	269	277	285	286	286	290	7.8	7.6	7.5	7.6	7.6	7.5	7.3	7.3
Washington	32	35	34	35	36	36	37	38	7.7	7.8	7.7	7.7	7.8	7.6	7.6	7.5
Oregon	22	24	23	24	25	25	25	25	8.3	8.9	8.7	9.0	9.1	8.9	8.8	8.6
California	187	202	203	209	215	217	214	219	7.9	7.6	7.5	7.5	7.6	7.4	7.2	7.2
Alaska.	2	2	2	2	2	2	2	2	4.3	3.9	3.8	3.8	3.8	3.8	4.0	3.8
Hawaii.	5	6	6	6	6	7	7	7	5.2	5.6	5.6	5.8	5.6	5.9	6.1	5.9

[1] Includes deaths of nonresidents. [2] Rates based on enumerated resident population as of April 1 for 1980 and 1990; estimated resident population as of July 1 for all other years.

Source: U.S. National Center for Health Statistics, *Vital Statistics of the United States,* annual; and *Monthly Vital Statistics Report.*

No. 121. Infant, Maternal, and Neonatal Mortality Rates and Fetal Mortality Ratios, by Race: 1970 to 1990

[Deaths per 1,000 live births, except as noted. Excludes deaths of nonresidents of the United States. See also Appendix III and *Historical Statistics, Colonial Times to 1970*, series B 136-147]

ITEM	1970	1975	1980	1981	1982	1983	1984	1985	1986	1987	1988	1989	1990
Infant deaths [1]	20.0	16.1	12.6	11.9	11.5	11.2	10.8	10.6	10.4	10.1	10.0	9.8	9.2
White	17.8	14.2	11.0	10.5	10.1	9.7	9.4	9.3	8.9	8.6	8.5	8.2	7.7
Black and other.	30.9	24.2	19.1	17.8	17.3	16.8	16.1	15.8	15.7	15.4	15.0	15.2	14.4
Black	32.6	26.2	21.4	20.0	19.6	19.2	18.4	18.2	18.0	17.9	17.6	17.7	17.0
Maternal deaths [2]	21.5	12.8	9.2	8.5	7.9	8.0	7.8	7.8	7.2	6.6	8.4	7.9	8.2
White	14.4	9.1	6.7	6.3	5.8	5.9	5.4	5.2	4.9	5.1	5.9	5.6	5.4
Black and other.	55.9	29.0	19.8	17.3	16.4	16.3	16.9	18.1	16.0	12.0	17.4	16.5	19.1
Black	59.8	31.3	21.5	20.4	18.2	18.3	19.7	20.4	18.8	14.2	19.5	18.4	22.4
Fetal deaths [3]	14.2	10.7	9.2	9.0	8.9	8.5	8.2	7.9	7.7	7.7	7.5	7.5	7.5
White	12.4	9.5	8.2	8.0	7.9	7.5	7.4	7.0	6.8	6.7	6.4	6.4	6.4
Black and other.	22.6	16.0	13.4	12.8	12.7	12.4	11.5	11.3	11.2	11.5	11.4	11.4	(NA)
Neonatal deaths [4]	15.1	11.6	8.5	8.0	7.7	7.3	7.0	7.0	6.7	6.5	6.3	6.2	5.8
White	13.8	10.4	7.5	7.1	6.8	6.4	6.2	6.1	5.8	5.5	5.4	5.2	4.9
Black and other.	21.4	16.8	12.5	11.8	11.3	10.8	10.2	10.3	10.1	10.0	9.7	9.6	9.2
Black	22.8	18.3	14.1	13.4	13.1	12.4	11.8	12.1	11.7	11.7	11.5	11.3	10.9

NA Not available. [1] Represents deaths of infants under 1 year old, exclusive of fetal deaths. [2] Per 100,000 live births from deliveries and complications of pregnancy, childbirth, and the puerperium. Beginning 1979, deaths are classified according to the ninth revision of the *International Classification of Diseases;* earlier years classified according to the revision in use at the time; see text, section 2. [3] Includes only those deaths with stated or presumed period of gestation of 20 weeks or more. [4] Represents deaths of infants under 28 days old, exclusive of fetal deaths.

No. 122. Fetal and Infant Deaths—Number and Percent Distribution: 1970 to 1990

[State requirements for reporting of fetal deaths vary. Most States require reporting of fetal deaths of gestations of 20 weeks or more. There is substantial evidence that not all fetal deaths for which reporting is required are reported. For details of methodology, see Appendix III and source]

YEAR	NUMBER						PERCENT DISTRIBUTION					
		Fetal deaths		Infant deaths				Fetal deaths		Infant deaths		
	Total	Early [1]	Late [2]	Neonatal		Post- neo- natal [5]	Total	Early [1]	Late [2]	Neonatal		Post- neo- natal [5]
				Early [3]	Late [4]					Early [3]	Late [4]	
1970	127,628	17,170	35,791	50,821	5,458	18,388	100.0	13.5	28.0	39.8	4.3	14.4
1980	78,879	10754	22,599	25,492	5,126	14,908	100.0	13.6	28.7	32.3	6.5	18.9
1981	75,901	11126	21,470	24,384	4,737	14,184	100.0	14.7	28.3	32.1	6.2	18.7
1982	75,095	11,028	21,666	23,706	4,629	14,066	100.0	14.7	28.9	31.6	6.2	18.7
1983	71,379	10,933	19,819	22,315	4,192	14,120	100.0	15.3	27.8	31.3	5.9	19.8
1984	69,679	10,963	19,136	21,566	4,125	13,889	100.0	15.7	27.5	31.0	5.9	19.9
1985	69,691	10,958	18,703	21,865	4,314	13,851	100.0	15.7	26.8	31.4	6.2	19.9
1986	67,863	11,100	17,872	21,053	4,159	13,679	100.0	16.4	26.3	31.0	6.1	20.2
1987	67,757	11,656	17,693	20,471	4,156	13,781	100.0	17.2	26.1	30.2	6.1	20.3
1988	68,352	11,833	17,609	20,471	4,219	14,220	100.0	17.3	25.8	29.9	6.2	20.8
1989	70,124	12,397	18,072	20,796	4,372	14,487	100.0	17.7	25.8	29.7	6.2	20.7
1990	67,696	12,554	16,791	20,020	4,289	14,042	100.0	18.5	24.8	29.6	6.3	20.7

[1] 20-27 weeks gestation. [2] 28 weeks or more gestation. [3] Less than 7 days. [4] 7-27 days. [5] 28 days-11 months.

No. 123. Infant Deaths and Infant Mortality Rates, by Cause of Death: 1980 to 1990

[Excludes deaths of nonresidents of the United States. Deaths classified according to ninth revision of *International Classification of Diseases*. See also Appendix III]

CAUSE OF DEATH	NUMBER			PERCENT DISTRIBUTION			INFANT MORTALITY RATE [1]		
	1980	1985	1990	1980	1985	1990	1980	1985	1990
Total	45,526	40,030	38,351	100	100	100	12.6	10.6	9.2
Congenital anomalies	9,220	8,561	8,239	20	21	21	2.6	2.3	2.0
Sudden infant death syndrome	5,510	5,315	5,417	12	13	14	1.5	1.4	1.3
Respiratory distress syndrome	4,989	3,691	2,850	11	9	7	1.4	1.0	0.7
Disorders relating to short gestation and unspecified low birth weight	3,648	3,257	4,013	8	8	10	1.0	0.9	1.0
Newborn affected by maternal complications of pregnancy	1,572	1,335	1,655	4	3	4	0.4	0.4	0.4
Intrauterine hypoxia and birth asphyxia.	1,497	1,158	762	3	3	2	0.4	0.3	0.2
Infections specific to the perinatal period.	971	955	875	2	2	2	0.3	0.3	0.2
Accidents and adverse effects	1,166	890	930	3	2	2	0.3	0.2	0.2
Newborn affected by complications of placenta, cord, and membranes	985	891	975	2	2	3	0.3	0.2	0.2
Pneumonia and influenza.	1,012	705	634	2	2	2	0.3	0.2	0.2
All other causes.	14,956	13,272	12,001	33	33	31	4.1	3.5	2.9

[1] Deaths of infants under 1 year old per 1,000 live births.

Sources of tables 121-123: U.S. National Center for Health Statistics, *Vital Statistics of the United States*, annual, and *Monthly Vital Statistics Report;* and unpublished data.

No. 124. Infant Mortality Rates, by Race—States: 1980 to 1990

[Deaths per 1,000 live births, by place of residence. Represents deaths of infants under 1 year old, exclusive of fetal deaths. Excludes deaths of nonresidents of the United States. See Appendix III and *Historical Statistics, Colonial Times to 1970*, series B 143-147, for U.S. totals]

DIVISION AND STATE	TOTAL[1] 1980	TOTAL[1] 1985	TOTAL[1] 1990	WHITE 1980	WHITE 1990	BLACK 1980	BLACK 1990
U.S.	12.6	10.6	9.2	11.0	7.7	21.4	17.0
N.E.	10.5	9.2	7.2	10.1	6.8	17.7	12.3
ME.	9.2	9.1	6.2	9.4	6.2	-	[2]6.1
NH.	9.9	9.3	7.1	9.9	7.2	[2]22.5	[2]5.4
VT.	10.7	8.5	6.4	10.7	6.5	-	-
MA.	10.5	9.1	7.0	10.1	6.7	[2]16.8	10.4
RI.	11.0	8.2	8.1	10.9	8.3	[2]17.4	[2]9.7
CT.	11.2	10.0	7.9	10.2	6.6	19.1	16.0
M.A.	12.8	10.8	9.5	11.1	7.5	21.1	17.7
NY.	12.5	10.8	9.6	10.8	7.7	20.0	17.3
NJ.	12.5	10.6	9.0	10.3	6.8	21.9	17.3
PA.	13.2	11.0	9.6	11.9	7.8	23.1	18.8
E.N.C	13.0	10.9	10.1	10.9	8.0	24.4	20.0
OH.	12.8	10.3	9.8	11.2	8.2	23.0	18.3
IN.	11.9	10.9	9.6	10.5	8.9	23.4	16.0
IL.	14.8	11.7	10.7	11.7	7.7	26.3	21.5
MI.	12.8	11.4	10.7	10.6	7.9	24.2	21.0
WI.	10.3	9.1	8.2	9.7	7.2	18.5	18.1
W.N.C.	11.3	9.5	8.4	10.5	7.5	21.3	17.3
MN.	10.0	8.8	7.3	9.6	6.7	20.0	19.7
IA.	11.8	9.5	8.1	11.5	7.8	27.2	18.0
MO.	12.4	10.2	9.4	11.1	7.8	20.7	17.5
ND.	12.1	8.5	8.0	11.7	7.9	[2]27.5	-
SD.	10.9	9.9	10.1	9.0	8.6	-	[2]7.4
NE.	11.5	9.6	8.3	10.7	7.2	25.2	16.8
KS.	10.4	9.3	8.4	9.5	7.7	20.6	15.4
S.A.	14.5	12.1	10.7	11.6	8.0	21.6	17.4
DE.	13.9	14.8	10.1	9.8	7.3	27.9	19.4
MD.	14.0	11.9	9.5	11.6	6.5	20.4	16.3
DC.	25.0	20.8	20.7	17.8	12.1	26.7	24.4
VA.	13.6	11.5	10.2	11.9	7.5	19.8	18.8
WV.	11.8	10.7	9.9	11.4	9.6	21.5	[2]16.6
NC.	14.5	11.8	10.6	12.1	8.3	20.0	16.0
SC.	15.6	14.2	11.7	10.8	8.3	22.9	17.1
GA.	14.5	12.7	12.4	10.8	9.1	21.0	18.0
FL.	14.6	11.3	9.6	11.8	7.6	22.8	16.2
E.S.C.	14.5	12.1	10.4	11.8	8.1	21.8	16.2
KY.	12.9	11.2	8.5	12.0	8.0	22.0	13.6
TN.	13.5	11.4	10.3	11.9	8.0	19.3	17.5
AL.	15.1	12.6	10.8	11.6	8.3	21.6	15.9
MS.	17.0	13.7	12.1	11.1	8.5	23.7	16.1
W.S.C	12.7	10.4	8.7	11.1	7.4	19.8	14.7
AR.	12.7	11.6	9.2	10.3	8.0	20.0	13.6
LA.	14.3	11.9	11.1	10.5	7.3	20.6	16.5
OK.	12.7	10.9	9.2	12.1	9.4	21.8	13.2
TX.	12.2	9.8	8.1	11.2	7.1	18.8	13.9
Mt.	11.0	9.8	8.6	10.7	8.3	19.5	15.0
MT.	12.4	10.3	9.0	11.8	8.6	-	[2]13.3
ID.	10.7	10.4	8.7	10.7	8.7	-	[2]10.9
WY.	9.8	12.2	8.6	9.3	8.8	[2]25.9	-
CO.	10.1	9.4	8.8	9.8	8.4	19.1	[2]16.5
NM.	11.5	10.6	9.0	11.3	9.3	[2]23.1	[2]12.8
AZ.	12.4	9.7	8.8	11.8	8.2	18.4	16.7
UT.	10.4	9.6	7.5	10.5	7.4	[2]27.3	[2]13.0
NV.	10.7	8.5	8.4	10.0	8.1	20.6	12.5
Pac.	11.2	9.7	7.9	10.9	7.6	17.8	14.1
WA.	11.8	10.7	7.8	11.5	7.6	16.4	14.5
OR.	12.2	9.9	8.3	12.2	8.1	[2]15.9	[2]15.1
CA.	11.1	9.5	7.9	10.6	7.6	18.0	14.2
AK.	12.3	10.8	10.5	9.4	8.5	[2]19.5	[2]11.2
HI.	10.3	8.8	6.7	11.6	5.1	[2]11.8	[2]11.5

- Represents zero. [1] Includes other races, not shown separately. [2] Based on a frequency of less than 20 infant deaths.

No. 125. Age-Adjusted Death Rates, by Selected Causes: 1970 to 1990

[Rates per 100,000 population. For explanation of age-adjustment, see text, section 2. The standard population for this table is the total population of the United States enumerated in 1940. See also headnote, table 126]

CAUSE OF DEATH	1970	1980	1990
All causes	714.3	585.8	520.2
Major cardiovascular diseases	340.1	256.0	189.8
Diseases of heart	253.6	202.0	152.0
Rheumatic fever and rheumatic heart disease	6.3	2.6	1.5
Hypertensive heart disease [1]	4.9	6.8	5.3
Ischemic heart disease	228.1	149.8	102.6
Other diseases of endocardium	2.3	2.0	2.5
All other forms of heart disease	12.0	40.8	40.1
Hypertension [1]	2.9	2.0	1.9
Cerebrovascular diseases	66.3	40.8	27.7
Atherosclerosis	8.4	5.7	2.7
Other	8.8	5.5	5.4
Malignancies [2]	129.9	132.8	135.0
Of respiratory and intrathoracic organs	28.4	36.4	41.4
Of digestive organs and peritoneum	35.2	33.0	30.2
Of genital organs	15.6	13.6	13.6
Of breast	12.6	12.5	12.7
Of urinary organs	5.7	5.2	5.1
Leukemia	5.8	5.4	5.0
Accidents and adverse effects	53.7	42.3	32.5
Motor vehicle	27.4	22.9	18.5
All other	26.3	19.5	14.0
Chronic obstructive pulmonary diseases and allied conditions [3]	11.6	15.9	19.7
Bronchitis, chronic and unspecified	2.1	1.0	0.8
Emphysema	8.4	4.0	3.7
Asthma	1.0	1.0	1.4
Other	(4)	9.9	13.7
Pneumonia and influenza	22.1	12.9	14.0
Pneumonia	20.8	12.4	13.7
Influenza	1.3	0.5	0.3
Diabetes mellitus	14.1	10.1	11.7
Suicide	11.8	11.4	11.5
Chronic liver disease and cirrhosis	14.7	12.2	8.6
Nephritis, nephrotic syndrome, and nephrosis	3.5	4.5	4.3
Homicide and legal intervention	9.1	10.8	10.2
Septicemia	1.4	2.6	4.1
Other infectious and parasitic diseases	2.8	1.8	12.0
Benign neoplasms [5]	2.0	2.0	1.7
Ulcer of stomach and duodenum	3.2	1.7	1.3
Hernia of abdominal cavity and intestinal obstruction [6]	2.6	1.4	1.1
Anemias	1.3	0.9	0.9
Cholelithiasis and other disorders of gallbladder	1.3	0.8	0.6
Nutritional deficiencies	0.8	0.5	0.5
Infections of kidney	2.8	0.7	0.2
Tuberculosis	2.2	0.6	0.5
Meningitis	0.8	0.6	0.3
Viral hepatitis	0.5	0.3	0.5
Acute bronchitis and bronchiolitis	0.5	0.2	0.1
Hyperplasia of prostate	0.6	0.2	0.1
Symptoms, signs, and ill-defined conditions	10.4	9.8	7.3
All other causes	44.0	36.8	38.4

[1] With or without renal disease. [2] Includes other types of malignancies not shown separately. [3] Prior to 1980, data are shown for bronchitis, emphysema, and asthma. [4] Included in "all other causes." Comparable data not available separately. [5] Includes neoplasms of unspecified nature; beginning 1980, also includes carcinoma in situ. [6] Without mention of hernia.

Source of tables 124 and 125: U.S. National Center for Health Statistics, *Vital Statistics of the United States*, annual; *Monthly Vital Statistics Reports*; and unpublished data.

No. 126. Deaths and Death Rates, by Selected Causes: 1970 to 1991

[Excludes deaths of nonresidents of the U.S., except as noted. Beginning 1979, deaths classified according to ninth revision of *International Classification of Diseases*; for earlier years, classified according to revision in use at that time. See also Appendix III and *Historical Statistics, Colonial Times to 1970*, series B 149-166]

CAUSE OF DEATH	DEATHS (1,000)					CRUDE DEATH RATE PER 100,000 POPULATION [2]				
	1970	1980	1985	1990	1991,[1] prel.	1970	1980	1985	1990	1991,[1] prel.
All causes	1,921.0	1,989.8	2,086.4	2,148.5	2,165.0	945.3	878.3	876.9	863.8	854.0
Major cardiovascular diseases	1,008.0	988.5	977.9	916.0	913.4	496.0	436.4	411.0	368.3	360.3
Diseases of heart	735.5	761.1	771.2	720.1	718.1	362.0	336.0	324.1	289.5	283.3
Percent of total	38.3	38.3	37.0	33.5	33.2	38.3	38.3	37.0	33.5	33.2
Rheumatic fever and rheumatic heart disease	14.9	7.8	6.6	6.0	6.0	7.3	3.5	2.8	2.4	2.4
Hypertensive heart disease [3]	15.0	24.8	23.7	23.4	24.1	7.4	10.9	10.0	9.5	9.5
Ischemic heart disease	666.7	565.8	536.8	489.2	478.5	328.1	249.7	225.6	196.7	188.8
Other diseases of endocardium	6.7	7.2	9.5	13.0	14.2	3.3	3.2	4.0	5.2	5.6
All other forms of heart disease	32.3	155.5	194.6	188.4	195.3	15.9	68.7	81.8	75.8	77.1
Hypertension [3]	8.3	7.8	7.8	9.2	9.2	4.1	3.5	3.3	3.7	3.6
Cerebrovascular diseases	207.2	170.2	153.1	144.1	144.1	101.9	75.1	64.3	57.9	56.8
Atherosclerosis	31.7	29.4	23.9	18.0	17.1	15.6	13.0	10.1	7.3	6.7
Other	25.3	20.0	22.0	24.6	24.9	12.5	8.8	9.2	9.9	9.8
Malignancies [4]	330.7	416.5	461.6	505.3	514.3	162.8	183.9	194.0	203.2	202.9
Percent of total	17.2	20.9	22.1	23.5	23.8	17.2	20.9	22.1	23.5	23.8
Of respiratory and intrathoracic organs	69.5	108.5	127.3	146.4	148.8	34.2	47.9	53.5	58.9	58.7
Of digestive organs and peritoneum	94.7	110.6	116.6	120.8	120.4	46.6	48.8	49.0	48.6	47.5
Of genital organs	41.2	46.4	49.7	57.5	59.4	20.3	20.5	20.9	23.1	23.4
Of breast	29.9	35.9	40.4	43.7	44.5	14.7	15.8	17.0	17.6	17.5
Of urinary organs	15.5	17.8	18.9	20.7	21.0	7.6	7.9	7.9	8.3	8.3
Leukemia	14.5	16.5	17.3	18.6	19.6	7.1	7.3	7.3	7.5	7.7
Accidents and adverse effects	114.6	105.7	93.5	92.0	91.7	56.4	46.7	39.3	37.0	36.2
Motor vehicle	54.6	53.2	45.9	46.8	45.2	26.9	23.5	19.3	18.8	17.8
All other	60.0	52.5	47.6	45.2	46.5	29.5	23.3	20.0	18.2	18.3
Chronic obstructive pulmonary diseases and allied conditions [5]	30.9	56.1	74.7	86.7	89.1	15.2	24.7	31.4	34.9	35.2
Bronchitis, chronic and unspecified	5.8	3.7	3.6	3.6	4.0	2.9	1.6	1.5	1.4	1.6
Emphysema	22.7	13.9	14.2	15.7	16.6	11.2	6.1	5.9	6.3	6.5
Asthma	2.3	2.9	3.9	4.8	4.5	1.1	1.3	1.6	1.9	1.8
Other	([6])	35.6	53.0	62.6	64.1	([6])	15.7	22.3	25.2	25.3
Pneumonia and influenza	62.7	54.6	67.6	79.5	75.0	30.9	24.1	28.4	32.0	29.6
Pneumonia	59.0	51.9	65.6	77.4	74.0	29.0	22.9	27.6	31.1	29.2
Influenza	3.7	2.7	2.1	2.1	1.0	1.8	1.2	0.9	0.8	0.4
Diabetes mellitus	38.3	34.9	37.0	47.7	50.0	18.9	15.4	15.5	19.2	19.7
Suicide	23.5	26.9	29.5	30.9	30.2	11.6	11.9	12.4	12.4	11.9
Chronic liver disease and cirrhosis	31.4	30.6	26.8	25.8	24.7	15.5	13.5	11.3	10.4	9.8
Other infectious and parasitic diseases	6.9	5.1	8.1	32.2	36.9	3.4	2.2	3.4	13.0	14.5
Homicide and legal intervention	16.8	24.3	19.9	24.9	27.4	8.3	10.7	8.4	10.0	10.8
Nephritis, nephrotic syndrome, and nephrosis	8.9	16.8	21.3	20.8	22.0	4.4	7.4	9.0	8.3	8.7
Septicemia	3.5	9.4	17.2	19.2	19.5	1.7	4.2	7.2	7.7	7.7
Certain conditions originating in the perinatal period	43.2	22.9	19.2	17.7	16.6	21.3	10.1	8.1	7.1	6.6
Congenital anomalies	16.8	13.9	12.8	13.1	11.8	8.3	6.2	5.4	5.3	4.7
Benign neoplasms [7]	4.8	6.2	6.7	6.8	7.0	2.4	2.7	2.8	2.7	2.7
Ulcer of stomach and duodenum	8.6	6.1	6.6	6.2	6.4	4.2	2.7	2.8	2.5	2.5
Hernia of abdominal cavity and intestinal obstruction [8]	7.2	5.4	5.4	5.8	5.8	3.6	2.4	2.3	2.3	2.3
Anemias	3.4	3.2	3.7	4.1	4.2	1.7	1.4	1.6	1.6	1.6
Cholelithiasis and other disorders of gall bladder	4.0	3.3	3.0	3.0	3.0	2.0	1.5	1.3	1.2	1.2
Nutritional deficiencies	2.5	2.4	2.9	3.0	3.2	1.2	1.0	1.2	1.2	1.2
Tuberculosis	5.2	2.0	1.8	1.8	1.7	2.6	0.9	0.7	0.7	0.7
Infections of kidney	8.2	2.7	2.0	1.3	1.3	4.0	1.2	0.8	0.5	0.5
Viral hepatitis	1.0	0.8	0.9	1.6	1.9	0.5	0.4	0.4	0.6	0.8
Meningitis	1.7	1.4	1.2	1.0	0.7	0.8	0.6	0.5	0.4	0.3
Acute bronchitis and bronchiolitis	1.3	0.6	0.6	0.6	0.6	0.6	0.3	0.3	0.3	0.2
Hyperplasia of prostate	2.2	0.8	0.5	0.5	0.3	1.1	0.3	0.2	0.2	0.1
Symptoms, signs, and ill-defined conditions	25.8	28.8	31.0	24.1	23.6	12.7	12.7	13.0	9.7	9.3
All other causes	108.8	120.0	153.0	172.9	178.3	53.5	53.0	64.3	69.5	70.3

[1] Based on a 10-percent sample of deaths. Includes deaths of nonresidents. [2] 1970, 1980, and 1990 based on resident population enumerated as of April 1. Other years based on resident population estimated as of July 1. [3] With or without renal disease. [4] Includes other types of malignancies not shown separately. [5] Prior to 1980, data are shown for bronchitis, emphysema, and asthma. [6] Included in "all other causes." Comparable data not available separately. [7] Includes neoplasms of unspecified nature; beginning 1980 also includes carcinoma in situ. [8] Without mention of hernia.

Source: U.S. National Center for Health Statistics, *Vital Statistics of the United States*, annual; *Monthly Vital Statistics Report*; and unpublished data.

No. 127. Deaths, by Selected Causes and Selected Characteristics: 1990

[In thousands. Excludes deaths of nonresidents of the United States. Deaths classified according to ninth revision of *International Classification of Diseases*. See also Appendix III]

AGE, SEX, AND RACE	Total[1]	Heart disease	Cancer	Accidents and adverse effects	Cerebro-vascular diseases	Chronic obstructive pulmonary diseases[2]	Pneumonia, flu	Suicide	Chronic liver disease, cirrhosis	Diabetes mellitus	Homicide and legal intervention
ALL RACES[3]											
Both sexes, total[4]	2,148.5	720.1	505.3	92.0	144.1	86.7	79.5	30.9	25.8	47.7	24.9
Under 1 year old	38.4	0.8	0.1	0.9	0.1	0.1	0.6	-	(Z)	(Z)	0.3
1 to 4 years old	6.9	0.3	0.5	2.6	(Z)	0.1	0.2	-	(Z)	(Z)	0.4
5 to 14 years old	8.4	0.3	1.1	3.7	0.1	0.1	0.1	0.3	(Z)	(Z)	0.5
15 to 24 years old	36.7	0.9	1.8	16.2	0.2	0.2	0.2	4.9	(Z)	0.1	7.4
25 to 34 years old	60.1	3.3	5.4	16.0	0.9	0.3	0.8	6.6	0.9	0.7	7.6
35 to 44 years old	83.6	11.8	16.2	11.7	2.4	0.6	1.4	5.7	3.6	1.5	4.4
45 to 54 years old	118.6	30.2	39.8	7.4	4.7	2.3	1.8	3.7	4.5	2.8	1.9
55 to 64 years old	252.7	77.5	94.9	7.2	10.1	10.3	3.9	3.4	6.3	7.0	1.1
65 to 74 years old	477.9	161.4	157.4	8.4	26.1	27.5	10.7	3.2	6.3	13.3	0.7
75 to 84 years old	601.4	229.8	135.0	10.0	50.0	32.1	25.4	2.5	3.4	14.5	0.4
85 years old and over	463.1	203.6	53.0	7.8	49.4	13.1	34.4	0.7	0.7	7.7	0.1
Male, total[4]	1,113.4	360.8	268.3	61.9	56.7	49.4	36.9	24.7	16.6	20.3	19.6
Under 1 year old	21.9	0.4	(Z)	0.5	0.1	(Z)	0.4	-	(Z)	(Z)	0.2
1 to 4 years old	4.0	0.1	0.3	1.6	(Z)	(Z)	0.1	-	(Z)	(Z)	0.2
5 to 14 years old	5.1	0.2	0.6	2.4	(Z)	0.1	0.1	0.2	(Z)	(Z)	0.3
15 to 24 years old	27.9	0.6	1.1	12.5	0.1	0.1	0.1	4.2	(Z)	0.1	6.2
25 to 34 years old	44.1	2.2	2.7	12.5	0.5	0.2	0.5	5.3	0.6	0.4	6.1
35 to 44 years old	57.5	8.9	7.1	9.0	1.3	0.3	1.0	4.4	2.6	0.9	3.5
45 to 54 years old	74.7	22.4	19.9	5.4	2.5	1.2	1.1	2.8	3.3	1.5	1.5
55 to 64 years old	154.6	53.5	53.1	5.0	5.4	5.8	2.4	2.6	4.3	3.4	0.8
65 to 74 years old	276.1	98.8	88.7	5.1	13.2	16.1	6.4	2.5	3.8	6.0	0.5
75 to 84 years old	295.4	111.2	71.7	5.0	20.7	18.7	12.9	2.1	1.8	5.8	0.2
85 years old and over	151.9	62.4	23.0	2.9	12.9	6.9	12.0	0.6	0.3	2.1	0.1
Female, total[4]	1,035.0	359.3	237.0	30.0	87.4	37.3	42.6	6.2	9.2	27.4	5.3
Under 1 year old	16.5	0.4	(Z)	0.4	0.1	(Z)	0.3	-	(Z)	(Z)	0.2
1 to 4 years old	3.0	0.1	0.2	1.0	(Z)	(Z)	0.1	-	(Z)	(Z)	0.2
5 to 14 years old	3.3	0.1	0.5	1.2	(Z)	(Z)	0.1	0.1	(Z)	(Z)	0.2
15 to 24 years old	8.9	0.3	0.7	3.8	0.1	0.1	0.1	0.7	(Z)	0.1	1.1
25 to 34 years old	16.0	1.1	2.7	3.5	0.5	0.1	0.3	1.2	0.3	0.3	1.5
35 to 44 years old	26.1	2.9	9.1	2.7	1.2	0.3	0.5	1.3	1.0	0.6	0.9
45 to 54 years old	44.0	7.8	19.9	2.0	2.2	1.1	0.6	0.9	1.2	1.3	0.4
55 to 64 years old	98.1	24.1	41.9	2.3	4.7	4.5	1.5	0.8	2.0	3.5	0.3
65 to 74 years old	201.9	62.5	68.7	3.3	12.9	11.4	4.3	0.7	2.5	7.2	0.2
75 to 84 years old	306.0	118.7	63.3	5.0	29.3	13.4	12.4	0.4	1.7	8.8	0.2
85 years old and over	311.2	141.2	29.9	4.8	36.5	6.2	22.5	0.1	0.4	5.6	0.1
WHITE											
Both sexes, total[4]	1,853.3	637.4	441.6	76.9	124.5	80.2	70.8	28.1	21.5	38.7	12.2
Under 1 year old	24.9	0.5	0.1	0.6	0.1	(Z)	0.4	-	(Z)	(Z)	0.2
1 to 4 years old	4.9	0.2	0.4	1.9	(Z)	(Z)	0.1	-	(Z)	(Z)	0.2
5 to 14 years old	6.3	0.2	0.9	2.7	0.1	0.1	0.1	0.2	(Z)	(Z)	0.3
15 to 24 years old	26.9	0.6	1.5	13.8	0.2	0.1	0.2	4.2	(Z)	0.1	3.0
25 to 34 years old	42.8	2.2	4.3	13.0	0.6	0.2	0.4	5.7	0.6	0.5	3.5
35 to 44 years old	61.0	8.6	13.0	9.4	1.5	0.4	0.9	5.2	2.6	1.1	2.3
45 to 54 years old	92.2	23.6	32.4	6.0	3.1	1.8	1.2	3.4	3.4	2.0	1.2
55 to 64 years old	209.1	64.2	80.5	6.0	7.5	9.2	3.1	3.2	5.3	5.2	0.7
65 to 74 years old	416.2	140.5	138.8	7.2	21.4	25.6	9.2	3.1	5.7	10.7	0.5
75 to 84 years old	541.7	208.0	121.5	9.0	44.4	30.3	23.0	2.4	3.2	12.4	0.3
85 years old and over	427.0	188.8	48.1	7.2	45.6	12.4	32.2	0.6	0.7	6.8	0.1
BLACK											
Both sexes, total[4]	265.5	75.1	57.1	12.4	17.4	5.7	7.6	2.1	3.8	8.1	12.1
Under 1 year old	12.3	0.3	(Z)	0.3	0.1	(Z)	0.2	-	(Z)	(Z)	0.1
1 to 4 years old	1.8	0.1	0.1	0.6	(Z)	(Z)	(Z)	-	(Z)	(Z)	0.2
5 to 14 years old	1.8	0.1	0.2	0.7	(Z)	0.1	(Z)	(Z)	(Z)	(Z)	0.2
15 to 24 years old	8.6	0.3	0.3	1.8	0.1	0.1	0.1	0.5	(Z)	(Z)	4.2
25 to 34 years old	15.8	1.0	0.9	2.4	0.3	0.1	0.3	0.7	0.2	0.2	4.0
35 to 44 years old	20.5	3.0	2.8	2.0	0.9	0.2	0.5	0.4	0.9	0.3	2.0
45 to 54 years old	23.9	6.1	6.5	1.2	1.4	0.4	0.5	0.2	0.9	0.8	0.7
55 to 64 years old	39.5	12.3	13.0	1.1	2.3	1.0	0.8	0.1	0.9	1.6	0.4
65 to 74 years old	55.7	19.0	16.7	1.0	4.1	1.7	1.4	0.1	0.5	2.4	0.2
75 to 84 years old	53.4	19.7	12.1	0.9	5.0	1.6	2.0	(Z)	0.2	2.0	0.1
85 years old and over	32.0	13.3	4.4	0.5	3.3	0.5	1.8	(Z)	(Z)	0.8	(Z)

- Represents zero.   Z Fewer than 50.   [1] Includes other causes not shown separately.   [2] Includes allied conditions.   [3] Includes other races not shown separately.   [4] Includes those deaths with age not stated.

Source: U.S. National Center for Health Statistics, *Vital Statistics of the United States*, annual.

No. 128. Deaths, by Age and Leading Cause: 1990

[Excludes deaths of nonresidents of the United States. Deaths classified according to ninth revision of *International Classification of Diseases*. See also Appendix III and *Historical Statistics, Colonial Times to 1970*, series B 149-166]

AGE AND LEADING CAUSE OF DEATH	NUMBER OF DEATHS			DEATH RATE PER 100,000 POPULATION		
	Total	Male	Female	Total	Male	Female
ALL AGES [1]						
All races [2]	2,148,463	1,113,417	1,035,046	863.8	918.4	812.0
White	1,853,254	950,812	902,442	888.0	930.9	846.9
Black	265,498	145,359	120,139	871.0	1,008.0	747.9
Leading causes of death:						
Heart disease	720,058	360,788	359,270	289.5	297.6	281.8
Malignant neoplasms (cancer)	505,322	268,283	237,039	203.2	221.3	186.0
Cerebrovascular disease (stroke)	144,088	56,697	87,391	57.9	46.8	68.6
Accidents	91,983	61,938	30,045	37.0	51.1	23.6
Chronic obstructive pulmonary disease	86,679	49,416	37,263	34.9	40.8	29.2
Pneumonia	79,513	36,898	42,615	32.0	30.4	33.4
Diabetes	47,664	20,266	27,398	19.2	16.7	21.5
Suicide	30,906	24,724	6,182	12.4	20.4	4.8
Chronic liver disease, cirrhosis	25,815	16,627	9,188	10.4	13.7	7.2
HIV infection [3]	25,188	22,386	2,802	10.1	18.5	2.2
1 TO 4 YEARS OLD						
All causes	6,931	3,969	2,962	46.8	52.4	41.0
Leading causes of death:						
Accidents	2,566	1,574	992	17.3	20.8	13.7
Malignant neoplasms (cancer)	513	280	233	3.5	3.7	3.2
Congenital anomalies	896	473	423	6.0	6.2	5.8
Homicide and legal intervention	378	208	170	2.6	2.7	2.4
Heart disease	282	141	141	1.9	1.9	1.9
Pneumonia and influenza	171	88	83	1.2	1.2	1.1
5 TO 14 YEARS OLD						
All causes	8,436	5,127	3,309	24.0	28.5	19.3
Leading causes of death:						
Accidents	3,650	2,418	1,232	10.4	13.5	7.2
Malignant neoplasms (cancer)	1,094	621	473	3.1	3.5	2.8
Congenital anomalies	468	245	223	1.3	1.4	1.3
Homicide and legal intervention	512	299	213	1.5	1.7	1.2
Heart disease	308	169	139	0.9	0.9	0.8
Pneumonia and influenza	134	71	63	0.4	0.4	0.4
15 TO 24 YEARS OLD						
All causes	36,733	27,873	8,860	99.2	147.4	49.0
Leading causes of death:						
Accidents	16,241	12,470	3,771	43.9	65.9	20.8
Motor vehicle	12,607	9,361	3,246	34.1	49.5	17.9
Homicide and legal intervention	7,354	6,222	1,132	19.9	32.9	6.3
Suicide	4,869	4,160	709	13.2	22.0	3.9
Malignant neoplasms (cancer)	1,819	1,078	741	4.9	5.7	4.1
Heart disease	917	588	329	2.5	3.1	1.8
HIV infection [3]	541	412	129	1.5	2.2	0.7
25 TO 44 YEARS OLD						
All causes	143,653	101,519	42,134	178.2	253.3	104.0
Leading causes of death:						
Accidents	27,663	21,491	6,172	34.3	53.6	15.2
Motor vehicle	16,488	12,264	4,224	20.5	30.6	10.4
Malignant neoplasms (cancer)	21,650	9,835	11,815	26.9	24.5	29.2
HIV infection [3]	18,748	16,717	2,031	23.3	41.7	5.0
Heart disease	15,045	11,121	3,924	18.7	27.8	9.7
Suicide	12,267	9,763	2,504	15.2	24.4	6.2
Homicide and legal intervention	12,060	9,612	2,448	15.0	24.0	6.0
45 TO 64 YEARS OLD						
All causes	371,304	229,300	142,004	804.2	1,033.5	592.1
Leading causes of death:						
Malignant neoplasms (cancer)	134,742	72,933	61,809	291.8	328.7	257.7
Heart disease	107,750	75,871	31,879	233.4	342.0	132.9
Cerebrovascular (stroke)	14,814	7,916	6,898	32.1	35.7	28.8
Accidents	14,607	10,304	4,303	31.6	24.6	17.9
Chronic obstructive pulmonary disease	12,605	6,985	5,620	27.3	31.5	23.4
Chronic liver disease and cirrhosis	10,806	7,515	3,291	23.4	33.9	13.7
Diabetes	9,803	4,983	4,820	21.2	22.5	20.1
65 YEARS OLD AND OVER						
All causes	1,542,493	723,370	819,123	4,963.2	5,790.3	4,407.2
Leading causes of death:						
Heart disease	594,858	272,397	322,461	1,914.0	2,180.4	1,735.0
Malignant neoplasms (cancer)	345,387	183,473	161,914	1,111.3	1,468.6	871.2
Cerebrovascular (stroke)	125,409	46,785	78,624	403.5	374.5	423.0
Chronic obstructive pulmonary disease	72,755	41,712	31,043	234.1	333.9	167.0
Pneumonia and influenza	70,485	31,256	39,229	226.8	250.2	211.1
Diabetes	35,523	13,926	21,597	114.3	111.5	116.2
Accidents	26,213	13,071	13,142	84.3	104.6	70.7

[1] Includes those deaths with age not stated. [2] Includes other races not shown separately. [3] Human immunodeficiency virus.

Source: U.S. National Center for Health Statistics, *Vital Statistics of the United States*, annual; and unpublished data.

No. 129. Death Rates, by Selected Causes and Age: 1970 to 1990

[Deaths per 100,000 population in specified group. Except as noted, excludes deaths of nonresidents of United States. See headnote, tables 125 and 126]

YEAR, RACE, AND AGE	Total [1]	Heart disease	Malignant neoplasms	Accidents and adverse effects	Cerebrovascular diseases	Chronic obstructive pulmonary diseases [2]	Pneumonia, flu	Suicide	Chronic liver disease, cirrhosis	Diabetes mellitus	Homicide and legal intervention
ALL RACES [3]											
Both sexes:											
1970, age-adjusted . . .	714.3	253.6	129.9	53.7	66.3	([4])	22.1	11.8	14.7	14.1	9.1
1980, age-adjusted . . .	585.8	202.0	132.8	42.3	40.8	15.9	12.9	11.4	12.2	10.1	10.8
1985, age-adjusted . . .	548.9	181.4	134.4	34.8	32.5	18.8	13.5	11.5	9.7	9.7	8.3
1990, age-adjusted [5] . .	520.2	152.0	135.0	32.5	27.7	19.7	14.0	11.5	8.6	11.7	10.2
15 to 24 years old . .	99.2	2.5	4.9	43.9	0.6	0.5	0.6	13.2	0.1	0.3	19.9
25 to 34 years old . .	139.2	7.6	12.6	37.0	2.2	0.7	1.8	15.2	2.1	1.6	17.7
35 to 44 years old . .	223.2	31.4	43.3	31.3	6.5	1.6	3.8	15.3	9.7	4.0	11.8
45 to 54 years old . .	473.4	120.5	158.9	29.4	18.7	9.1	7.0	14.8	18.0	11.3	7.6
55 to 64 years old . .	1,196.9	367.3	449.6	34.3	48.0	48.9	18.6	16.0	29.9	33.0	5.0
65 to 74 years old . .	2,648.6	894.3	872.3	46.6	144.4	152.5	59.1	17.9	34.9	73.6	3.8
75 to 84 years old . .	6,007.2	2,295.7	1,348.5	100.3	499.3	321.1	253.5	24.9	34.1	145.2	4.3
85 years old and over	15,327.4	6,739.9	1,752.9	257.1	1,633.9	433.3	1,140.0	22.2	23.4	255.0	4.6
Male:											
1970, age-adjusted	931.6	348.5	157.4	80.7	73.2	([4])	28.8	17.3	20.2	13.5	14.9
1980, age-adjusted	777.2	280.4	165.5	64.0	44.9	26.1	17.4	18.0	17.1	10.2	17.4
1985, age-adjusted [5] . . .	723.0	250.1	166.1	51.8	35.5	28.1	18.4	18.8	13.7	10.0	12.8
1990, age-adjusted [5] . . .	680.2	206.7	166.3	47.7	30.2	27.2	18.5	19.0	12.2	12.3	16.3
15 to 24 years old. . .	147.4	3.1	5.7	65.9	0.7	0.5	0.6	22.0	0.1	0.3	32.9
25 to 34 years old. . .	204.3	10.3	12.6	57.9	2.1	0.7	2.2	24.8	2.6	1.7	28.3
35 to 44 years old. . .	310.4	48.1	38.5	48.7	6.8	1.7	5.1	23.9	14.3	4.9	19.0
45 to 54 years old. . .	610.3	183.0	162.5	43.7	20.5	9.4	9.1	23.2	26.6	12.6	12.1
55 to 64 years old. . .	1,553.4	537.3	532.9	49.8	54.4	58.6	24.6	25.7	42.8	34.5	8.1
65 to 74 years old. . .	3,491.5	1,250.0	1,122.2	64.6	166.8	204.0	80.4	32.2	48.1	76.4	5.8
75 to 84 years old. . .	7,888.6	2,968.2	1,914.4	134.0	552.7	500.0	345.5	56.1	46.9	153.6	5.7
85 years old and over .	18,056.6	7,418.4	2,739.9	349.8	1,533.2	815.1	1,421.5	65.9	36.3	253.4	6.8
Female:											
1970, age-adjusted	532.5	175.2	108.8	28.2	60.8	([4])	16.7	6.8	9.8	14.4	3.7
1980, age-adjusted	432.6	140.3	109.2	21.8	37.6	8.9	9.8	5.4	7.9	10.0	4.5
1985, age-adjusted	410.3	127.4	111.7	18.7	30.0	12.5	10.1	4.9	6.1	9.4	3.9
1990, age-adjusted [5] . . .	390.6	108.9	112.7	17.9	25.7	14.7	11.0	4.5	5.3	11.1	4.2
15 to 24 years old. . .	49.0	1.8	4.1	20.8	0.6	0.5	0.6	3.9	0.1	0.4	6.3
25 to 34 years old. . .	74.2	5.0	12.6	16.1	2.2	0.7	1.3	5.6	1.5	1.4	7.2
35 to 44 years old. . .	137.9	15.1	48.1	14.3	6.1	1.5	2.5	6.8	5.1	3.1	4.8
45 to 54 years old. . .	342.7	61.0	155.5	15.8	17.0	8.8	5.0	6.9	9.7	10.0	3.2
55 to 64 years old. . .	878.8	215.7	375.2	20.4	42.2	40.3	13.2	7.3	18.3	31.7	2.3
65 to 74 years old. . .	1,991.2	616.8	677.4	32.5	126.9	112.3	42.5	6.7	24.6	71.4	2.2
75 to 84 years old. . .	4,883.1	1,893.8	1,010.3	80.2	467.4	214.2	198.5	6.3	26.5	140.2	3.4
85 years old and over .	14,274.3	6,478.1	1,372.1	221.3	1,672.7	286.0	1,031.3	5.4	18.4	255.7	3.8
WHITE											
Both sexes:											
1970, age-adjusted . . .	679.6	249.1	127.8	51.0	61.8	([4])	19.8	12.4	13.4	12.9	4.7
1980, age-adjusted . . .	559.4	197.6	129.6	41.5	38.0	16.3	12.2	12.1	11.0	9.1	6.9
1985, age-adjusted . . .	524.9	176.6	131.2	34.2	30.1	19.2	12.9	12.3	8.9	8.6	5.4
1990, age-adjusted . . .	492.8	146.9	131.5	31.8	25.5	20.1	13.4	12.2	8.0	10.4	5.9
Male:											
1970, age-adjusted	893.4	347.6	154.3	76.2	68.3	([4])	26.0	18.2	18.8	12.7	7.3
1980, age-adjusted	745.3	277.5	160.5	62.3	41.9	26.7	16.2	18.9	15.7	9.5	10.9
1985, age-adjusted	693.3	246.2	160.4	50.5	33.0	28.7	17.5	19.9	12.7	9.2	8.1
1990, age-adjusted	644.3	202.0	160.3	46.4	27.7	27.4	17.5	20.1	11.5	11.3	8.9
Female:											
1970, age-adjusted	501.7	167.8	107.6	27.2	56.2	([4])	15.0	7.2	8.7	12.8	2.2
1980, age-adjusted	411.1	134.6	107.7	21.4	35.2	9.2	9.4	5.7	7.0	8.7	3.2
1985, age-adjusted	391.0	121.7	110.5	18.4	27.9	12.9	9.9	5.3	5.6	8.1	2.9
1990, age-adjusted	369.9	103.1	111.2	17.6	23.8	15.2	10.6	4.8	4.8	9.5	2.8
BLACK											
Both sexes:											
1970, age-adjusted . . .	1,044.0	307.6	111.2	74.4	114.5	([4])	40.4	6.1	24.8	26.5	46.1
1980, age-adjusted . . .	842.5	255.7	172.1	51.2	68.5	12.5	19.2	6.4	21.6	20.3	40.6
1985, age-adjusted . . .	793.6	240.6	176.6	42.3	55.8	15.3	18.8	6.4	16.3	20.1	29.2
1990, age-adjusted . . .	789.2	213.5	182.0	39.7	48.4	16.9	19.8	7.0	13.7	24.8	39.5
Male:											
1970, age-adjusted	1,318.6	375.9	198.0	119.5	122.5	([4])	53.8	9.9	33.1	21.2	82.1
1980, age-adjusted	1,112.8	327.3	229.9	82.0	77.5	20.9	28.0	11.1	30.6	17.7	71.9
1985, age-adjusted	1,053.4	310.8	239.9	67.6	62.7	24.8	27.5	11.5	23.8	18.2	50.2
1990, age-adjusted	1,061.3	275.9	248.1	62.4	56.1	26.5	28.7	12.4	20.0	23.6	68.7
Female:											
1970, age-adjusted	814.4	251.7	123.5	35.3	107.9	([4])	29.2	2.9	17.8	30.9	15.0
1980, age-adjusted	631.1	201.1	129.7	25.1	61.7	6.3	12.7	2.4	14.4	22.1	13.7
1985, age-adjusted	594.8	188.3	131.8	20.9	50.6	8.8	12.5	2.1	10.2	21.3	10.9
1990, age-adjusted	581.6	168.1	137.2	20.4	42.7	10.7	13.7	2.4	8.7	25.4	13.0

[1] Includes other causes not shown separately.   [2] Includes allied conditions.   [3] Includes other races not shown separately.
[4] Data not available on a comparable basis with later years.   [5] Includes persons under 15 years old not shown separately.
Source: U.S. National Center for Health Statistics, *Vital Statistics of the United States*, annual; and *Monthly Vital Statistics Report*.

No. 130. Death Rates, by Cause—States: 1990

[**Deaths per 100,000 resident population enumerated as of April 1.** By place of residence. Excludes nonresidents of the United States. Causes of death classified according to ninth revision of *International Classification of Diseases*]

DIVISION AND STATE	Total [1]	Heart disease	Cancer	Cerebro-vascular dis-eases	Acci-dents and adverse effects	Chronic obstruc-tive pulmo-nary dis-eases [2]	Pneu-monia, flu	Dia-betes mellitus	Suicide	Chronic liver disease and cirrhosis	Athero-sclerosis
U.S.....	**863.8**	**289.5**	**203.2**	**57.9**	**37.0**	**34.9**	**32.0**	**19.2**	**12.4**	**10.4**	**7.3**
N.E.......	**867.4**	**293.0**	**217.6**	**54.0**	**28.1**	**34.2**	**35.4**	**19.0**	**10.2**	**10.5**	**7.1**
ME	904.5	301.1	227.4	58.6	33.6	45.8	32.9	19.9	12.6	8.9	9.5
NH	765.2	251.7	191.3	50.6	29.4	34.3	24.7	17.9	13.4	9.9	8.0
VT	816.5	253.4	201.9	53.5	34.5	39.3	36.3	19.2	14.9	10.5	5.0
MA	883.9	295.1	223.5	54.9	25.6	33.0	38.5	20.4	8.8	11.2	6.9
RI	954.3	342.5	241.9	55.5	27.9	36.0	28.7	22.1	12.7	10.1	11.2
CT	839.9	291.9	207.4	51.7	29.0	30.5	36.1	15.5	9.1	10.0	5.1
M.A.......	**960.8**	**347.8**	**229.2**	**54.4**	**30.0**	**33.2**	**36.5**	**21.3**	**9.5**	**11.2**	**5.8**
NY......	939.0	353.7	213.5	48.7	28.1	31.6	41.2	15.8	8.6	11.5	5.5
NJ......	910.5	306.1	232.0	51.4	27.1	29.8	31.4	26.8	7.3	11.8	5.8
PA......	1,026.4	366.1	251.2	65.0	34.7	37.9	32.9	26.1	12.2	10.4	6.4
E.N.C......	**887.6**	**307.5**	**211.4**	**59.5**	**34.6**	**35.1**	**31.8**	**22.1**	**11.3**	**10.2**	**8.1**
OH	911.0	319.6	221.0	58.1	33.9	39.0	28.8	25.3	11.0	9.1	8.1
IN	894.1	306.1	210.3	66.7	37.1	38.0	30.0	21.8	13.1	7.5	10.4
IL	901.1	308.8	213.8	58.7	34.9	33.1	34.8	19.8	10.1	11.8	6.8
MI	847.1	297.2	198.5	55.0	34.0	32.4	30.9	21.7	11.5	12.1	8.7
WI	873.6	298.7	210.5	64.7	33.8	32.8	35.4	21.9	12.7	8.1	7.8
W.N.C......	**912.2**	**312.4**	**208.6**	**68.2**	**38.2**	**39.3**	**38.5**	**18.9**	**12.9**	**7.2**	**10.4**
MN	794.9	246.3	185.6	64.8	33.5	32.8	33.4	15.7	12.5	6.7	8.2
IA	968.2	345.2	218.8	73.5	37.7	42.6	44.0	20.7	12.1	6.7	15.2
MO	984.5	348.3	226.8	67.3	42.4	41.5	39.8	21.3	13.8	8.2	8.2
ND	888.0	305.1	209.6	66.7	36.5	34.9	30.7	24.7	11.4	8.1	15.8
SD......	908.9	334.8	196.1	73.0	47.0	38.9	36.5	17.2	13.1	7.2	8.2
NE......	935.7	319.3	209.0	68.0	36.5	47.0	43.3	16.2	13.9	5.9	14.2
KS......	899.2	309.5	203.3	68.9	37.6	38.9	38.1	18.4	12.0	6.9	9.9
S.A.......	**900.0**	**294.4**	**215.4**	**61.6**	**40.2**	**34.9**	**27.7**	**20.2**	**13.7**	**10.7**	**6.6**
DE......	865.2	284.3	225.3	48.6	36.5	33.6	24.9	28.8	12.0	11.0	4.8
MD	803.4	248.9	205.6	46.6	29.7	29.4	24.8	21.1	10.2	8.4	4.4
DC......	1,205.0	310.9	254.9	61.6	32.8	25.9	34.4	32.3	6.1	31.6	9.4
VA......	776.0	248.9	187.9	56.9	35.5	29.2	27.9	14.4	12.9	8.0	5.8
WV	1,080.9	395.8	245.8	65.9	47.1	50.9	39.7	27.2	12.2	10.0	8.6
NC	864.7	280.1	199.6	67.3	44.0	30.9	29.3	19.8	14.0	10.9	5.0
SC......	852.2	267.7	194.8	69.5	47.8	29.9	23.4	20.8	12.4	10.3	4.7
GA	799.8	252.2	170.3	59.0	44.4	29.5	27.7	15.5	13.6	8.7	6.6
FL......	1,038.7	354.3	261.7	65.7	40.0	43.9	27.0	22.9	16.1	13.1	8.7
E.S.C......	**961.4**	**326.1**	**216.8**	**70.7**	**51.6**	**38.3**	**33.9**	**19.9**	**13.2**	**9.7**	**7.0**
KY......	951.8	322.4	228.6	65.9	45.9	42.2	36.7	21.7	14.9	8.6	6.2
TN......	949.6	317.8	215.1	73.6	47.6	38.2	34.8	18.7	13.4	10.5	8.3
AL......	974.6	319.1	214.3	71.7	57.5	37.5	30.3	21.5	12.7	10.7	7.0
MS	976.5	358.3	206.9	70.6	58.0	34.2	33.8	17.1	11.2	8.2	5.5
W.S.C......	**816.7**	**265.3**	**186.1**	**56.6**	**40.5**	**31.7**	**28.2**	**21.6**	**12.9**	**9.1**	**7.3**
AR......	1,048.7	339.9	242.6	88.3	50.4	42.2	38.5	22.0	12.5	8.7	6.9
LA......	890.3	294.4	206.0	56.8	45.7	29.0	24.0	28.8	13.2	8.6	7.6
OK	965.7	345.9	211.6	69.8	42.9	42.6	41.0	16.1	12.5	7.9	12.0
TX......	738.7	232.9	168.6	49.8	37.5	29.0	25.4	20.7	13.0	9.4	6.5
Mt........	**710.3**	**210.3**	**162.1**	**44.3**	**41.8**	**39.0**	**27.8**	**15.4**	**18.5**	**10.3**	**6.9**
MT	858.6	247.7	202.9	61.7	49.8	48.7	29.8	19.4	20.9	10.6	8.4
ID	740.2	219.7	172.6	54.4	47.4	37.7	31.0	17.0	19.1	5.1	6.8
WY	706.1	214.3	161.2	46.5	44.8	44.1	27.8	14.6	17.9	8.6	5.5
CO	655.1	186.5	149.8	40.2	34.2	39.5	28.4	12.3	16.8	9.0	8.3
NM	701.3	198.2	149.5	36.6	52.7	35.2	23.0	21.1	18.7	15.3	7.3
AZ......	785.5	240.3	186.5	47.3	44.4	43.5	32.3	15.1	18.7	11.7	7.0
UT......	533.5	159.0	102.4	39.2	32.7	20.8	23.2	16.7	15.3	6.1	4.5
NV......	775.3	238.3	187.0	42.7	42.7	47.9	21.7	12.7	24.5	14.1	5.3
Pac.......	**729.8**	**227.2**	**169.1**	**53.0**	**35.3**	**33.7**	**31.7**	**12.4**	**12.9**	**12.0**	**7.3**
WA	762.1	230.9	185.0	56.0	36.7	39.9	28.9	15.8	13.9	8.5	9.0
OR	884.3	267.4	212.9	66.2	40.2	45.1	34.6	16.7	15.8	9.4	11.2
CA......	720.3	227.0	164.6	52.0	34.2	32.4	32.6	11.3	12.5	13.1	6.9
AK......	397.8	80.7	85.4	18.7	71.4	16.4	8.7	9.3	12.7	8.4	2.4
HI	612.0	186.6	149.3	47.8	29.0	19.6	26.2	15.2	11.3	6.8	2.1

[1] Includes other causes not shown separately.   [2] Includes allied conditions.

Source: U.S. National Center for Health Statistics, *Monthly Vital Statistics Report;* and unpublished data.

No. 131. Acquired Immunodeficiency Syndrome (AIDS) Deaths, by Selected Characteristics: 1982 to 1992

[Data are shown by year of death and are subject to substantial retrospective changes. For data on AIDS cases reported, see table 203. Based on reporting by State health departments]

CHARACTERISTIC	NUMBER									PERCENT DISTRIBUTION	
	Total, 1982-1992 [1]	1985	1986	1987	1988	1989	1990	1991	1992	Total	1992
Total [2]	166,467	6,682	11,537	15,451	19,657	26,157	28,060	30,593	22,675	100	100
Age:											
Under 5 years old.	1,796	96	127	223	246	277	290	248	192	1	1
5 to 12 years old	373	10	24	50	46	58	68	74	36	(Z)	(Z)
13 to 29 years old	30,518	1,329	2,286	3,012	3,794	4,801	5,021	5,292	3,809	18	17
30 to 39 years old	75,023	3,013	5,244	6,924	8,761	11,880	12,654	13,731	10,265	45	45
40 to 49 years old	39,177	1,396	2,469	3,285	4,326	6,063	6,825	7,743	5,855	24	26
50 to 59 years old	13,493	590	923	1,266	1,642	2,156	2,238	2,442	1,760	8	8
60 years old and over. . .	6,087	248	464	691	842	922	964	1,063	758	4	3
Sex:											
Male	148,863	6,177	10,557	13,921	17,551	23,394	24,936	27,048	20,110	89	89
Female	17,604	505	980	1,530	2,106	2,763	3,124	3,545	2,565	11	11
Race/ethnicity:											
White, non-Hispanic	92,007	3,981	6,871	8,717	10,694	14,219	15,384	16,609	12,323	56	55
Black, non-Hispanic	50,121	1,777	3,044	4,525	6,015	7,969	8,584	9,468	7,092	30	32
Hispanic	22,727	884	1,535	2,087	2,764	3,703	3,823	4,157	2,971	14	13

Z Less than 0.5 percent.   [1] Includes deaths prior to 1982.   [2] Includes other race/ethnicity groups not shown separately.

Source: U.S. Centers for Disease Control, Atlanta, GA, *Surveillance Report,* annual.

No. 132. Death Rates From Heart Disease, by Sex, Age, and Selected Type: 1970 to 1990

[**Deaths per 100,000 population in specified age groups.** Excludes deaths of nonresidents of the United States. Beginning 1980, deaths classified according to the ninth revision of the *International Classification of Diseases.* For earlier years, classified according to the revision in use at the time; see text, section 2. See Appendix III]

AGE AT DEATH AND SELECTED TYPE OF HEART DISEASE	MALE					FEMALE				
	1970	1980	1985	1989	1990	1970	1980	1985	1989	1990
Total U.S. rate [1]	422.5	368.6	342.8	304.3	297.6	304.5	305.1	304.3	287.3	281.8
25 to 34 years old	15.2	11.4	11.5	10.8	10.3	7.7	5.3	5.0	5.0	5.0
35 to 44 years old	103.2	68.7	58.4	49.1	48.1	32.2	21.4	18.3	15.9	15.1
45 to 54 years old	376.4	282.6	236.9	190.3	183.0	109.9	84.5	73.8	61.6	61.0
55 to 64 years old	987.2	746.8	651.9	551.3	537.3	351.6	272.1	250.3	220.5	215.7
65 to 74 years old	2,170.3	1,728.0	1,508.4	1,255.3	1,250.0	1,082.7	828.6	745.3	636.1	616.8
75 to 84 years old	4,534.8	3,834.3	3,498.0	3,043.5	2,968.2	3,120.8	2,497.0	2,245.2	2,009.6	1,893.8
85 years old and over	8,426.2	8,752.7	8,123.7	7,338.2	7,418.4	7,591.8	7,350.5	6,935.7	6,454.7	6,478.1
Persons 45 to 54 years old:										
Ischemic heart	338.0	217.3	170.6	130.0	123.8	84.0	52.2	43.6	34.6	33.6
Rheumatic heart	11.4	3.1	1.9	1.2	1.1	10.6	4.3	2.8	2.0	1.9
Hypertensive heart [2]	4.6	8.3	8.5	8.0	7.6	4.0	5.5	4.7	4.2	4.3
Persons 55 to 64 years old:										
Ischemic heart	904.6	581.1	479.9	392.6	375.4	299.1	189.0	164.5	141.0	135.4
Rheumatic heart	21.5	6.2	4.3	3.3	3.4	20.8	9.2	6.3	4.7	4.7
Hypertensive heart [2]	11.7	21.8	19.8	19.4	18.1	9.1	13.3	12.3	10.7	10.9
Persons 65 to 74 years old:										
Ischemic heart	2,010.0	1,355.5	1,130.9	932.1	898.5	978.0	605.3	514.7	430.1	415.2
Rheumatic heart	31.9	11.8	8.7	6.9	7.1	30.2	18.6	13.3	11.2	10.5
Hypertensive heart [2]	30.6	44.3	38.9	33.9	33.2	24.8	36.2	29.1	25.1	25.9
Persons 75 to 84 years old:										
Ischemic heart	4,222.7	2,953.7	2,544.2	2,188.9	2,129.6	2,866.3	1,842.7	1,530.3	1,337.1	1,287.6
Rheumatic heart	34.8	16.7	14.7	13.8	12.3	34.3	25.4	23.8	22.9	22.5
Hypertensive heart [2]	80.8	90.7	79.4	69.7	67.9	83.9	101.1	79.5	72.4	69.7
Persons 85 years old and over:										
Ischemic heart	7,781.5	6,501.6	5,748.1	5,157.8	5,120.7	6,951.5	5,280.6	4,711.0	4,351.4	4,257.8
Rheumatic heart	34.7	19.5	18.0	20.2	18.7	39.2	25.8	27.6	30.8	33.3
Hypertensive heart [2]	182.0	180.3	153.1	146.2	154.3	223.5	250.8	217.0	210.3	212.1

[1] Includes persons under 25 years old not shown separately.   [2] With or without renal disease.

Source: U.S. National Center for Health Statistics, *Vital Statistics of the United States,* annual; and unpublished data.

No. 133. Death Rates From Cancer, by Sex, Age, and Selected Type: 1970 to 1990

[Deaths per 100,000 population in the specified age groups. See headnote, table 132]

AGE AT DEATH AND SELECTED TYPE OF CANCER	MALE					FEMALE				
	1970	1980	1985	1989	1990	1970	1980	1985	1989	1990
Total U.S. rate [1]	182.1	205.3	213.4	218.9	221.3	144.4	163.6	175.7	184.0	186.0
25 to 34 years.	16.3	13.4	13.2	12.0	12.6	16.7	14.0	13.2	12.6	12.6
35 to 44 years.	53.0	44.0	42.4	38.5	38.5	65.6	53.1	49.2	47.8	48.1
45 to 54 years.	183.5	188.7	175.2	164.0	162.5	181.5	171.8	165.3	154.0	155.5
55 to 64 years.	511.8	520.8	536.9	535.7	532.9	343.2	361.7	381.8	378.4	375.2
65 to 74 years.	1,006.8	1,093.2	1,105.2	1,116.4	1,122.2	557.9	607.1	645.3	674.1	677.4
75 to 84 years.	1,588.3	1,790.5	1,839.7	1,884.0	1,914.4	891.9	903.1	937.8	993.5	1,010.3
85 years old and over.	1,720.8	2,369.5	2,451.8	2,621.9	2,739.9	1,096.7	1,255.7	1,281.4	1,346.7	1,372.1
Persons, 35 to 44 years old:										
Respiratory, intrathoracic	17.0	12.6	10.6	9.1	9.1	6.5	6.8	5.8	5.5	5.4
Digestive organs, peritoneum . .	11.4	9.5	9.1	8.4	8.9	8.6	6.5	5.8	5.5	5.5
Breast.	0.1	-	(B)	(B)	(B)	20.4	17.9	17.5	17.8	17.8
Genital organs	1.4	0.7	0.7	0.7	0.6	13.6	8.3	7.1	6.9	7.3
Lymphatic and hematopoietic tissues, excl. leukemia	5.6	4.3	4.6	4.7	4.5	3.2	2.4	2.3	2.3	2.1
Urinary organs	1.9	1.4	1.6	1.4	1.5	1.0	0.6	0.9	0.7	0.6
Lip, oral cavity, and pharynx . . .	1.7	1.8	1.4	1.2	1.3	0.7	0.5	0.6	0.5	0.3
Leukemia.	3.4	3.2	3.0	2.7	2.5	2.8	2.6	2.1	2.0	2.2
Persons, 45 to 54 years old:										
Respiratory, intrathoracic	72.1	79.8	71.0	64.5	63.0	22.2	34.8	36.2	34.7	35.3
Digestive organs, peritoneum . .	45.9	44.3	41.9	39.2	40.4	32.5	27.8	25.9	22.3	23.3
Breast.	0.4	0.2	0.3	0.2	0.3	52.6	48.1	47.1	45.3	45.4
Genital organs	3.4	3.4	3.2	2.9	2.9	34.4	24.1	20.6	18.7	19.4
Lymphatic and hematopoietic tissues, excl. leukemia	12.8	10.2	10.0	10.5	10.9	8.3	6.6	6.5	6.2	6.0
Urinary organs	8.0	7.4	7.5	7.0	7.2	3.5	3.3	3.1	3.1	2.9
Lip, oral cavity, and pharynx . . .	7.9	8.2	6.8	5.9	5.9	2.8	2.6	2.0	1.8	1.6
Leukemia.	6.6	6.2	5.7	5.3	5.6	4.9	4.4	4.3	3.9	4.1
Persons, 55 to 64 years old:										
Respiratory, intrathoracic	202.3	223.8	233.6	231.5	232.6	38.9	74.5	94.5	105.7	107.6
Digestive organs, peritoneum . .	139.0	129.3	130.8	127.0	124.0	86.0	79.1	75.2	69.1	69.3
Breast.	0.6	0.7	0.6	0.6	0.6	77.6	80.5	84.2	79.7	78.6
Genital organs	22.8	23.5	24.6	27.5	27.9	58.2	46.8	43.1	40.1	40.1
Lymphatic and hematopoietic tissues, excl. leukemia	27.1	24.4	25.3	26.7	27.2	17.7	16.8	17.6	17.7	16.7
Urinary organs	26.4	22.9	22.5	23.2	23.5	9.4	8.9	8.6	9.0	8.8
Lip, oral cavity, and pharynx . . .	20.1	17.9	16.0	15.9	16.2	6.2	6.0	5.4	5.4	4.7
Leukemia.	15.4	14.7	14.7	14.9	14.7	9.0	9.3	9.2	9.2	8.8
Persons, 65 to 74 years old:										
Respiratory, intrathoracic	340.7	422.0	432.5	440.2	447.3	45.6	106.1	145.3	176.7	181.7
Digestive organs, peritoneum . .	293.3	284.1	277.6	270.9	267.4	185.8	173.6	162.9	155.2	153.0
Breast.	1.4	1.1	1.1	1.2	1.1	93.8	101.1	107.8	111.6	111.7
Genital organs	103.7	107.6	110.3	117.6	123.5	85.6	73.6	71.2	70.4	71.0
Lymphatic and hematopoietic tissues, excl. leukemia	50.3	48.1	53.2	55.3	56.8	34.6	34.4	36.6	39.4	39.5
Urinary organs	60.3	56.9	52.0	51.9	50.7	20.1	19.7	19.7	19.4	19.8
Lip, oral cavity, and pharynx . . .	26.8	25.4	24.2	20.9	21.5	6.7	8.8	8.6	8.0	8.3
Leukemia.	35.3	35.3	34.7	36.3	36.0	19.3	18.7	19.2	19.2	18.8
Persons, 75 to 84 years old:										
Respiratory, intrathoracic	354.2	511.5	558.9	583.3	594.4	56.5	98.0	135.7	184.6	194.5
Digestive organs, peritoneum . .	507.5	496.6	476.1	460.5	468.0	353.3	326.3	308.7	296.2	293.3
Breast.	2.7	2.1	2.3	2.2	1.6	127.4	126.4	136.2	145.1	146.3
Genital organs	299.4	315.4	321.3	341.7	358.5	104.9	95.7	92.7	92.1	95.3
Lymphatic and hematopoietic tissues, excl. leukemia	74.0	80.0	92.8	101.4	104.5	49.4	57.8	63.5	71.3	71.2
Urinary organs	112.2	112.4	106.1	107.0	107.5	44.0	37.4	36.4	37.4	38.5
Lip, oral cavity, and pharynx . . .	36.6	31.4	27.6	24.1	26.1	10.8	10.9	9.8	10.4	11.6
Leukemia.	68.3	71.5	70.0	72.2	71.9	39.6	38.5	38.0	36.6	38.8
Persons, 85 years old and over:										
Respiratory, intrathoracic	215.3	386.3	457.3	512.2	538.0	56.5	96.3	104.2	131.4	142.8
Digestive organs, peritoneum . .	583.7	705.8	667.1	685.4	699.5	465.0	504.3	497.6	497.9	497.6
Breast.	2.9	2.6	3.9	4.2	2.4	157.1	169.3	178.5	190.5	196.8
Genital organs	434.2	612.3	614.6	714.0	750.0	107.3	115.9	106.1	112.5	115.6
Lymphatic and hematopoietic tissues, excl. leukemia	58.1	93.2	114.8	231.8	140.5	41.7	63.0	73.7	84.9	90.0
Urinary organs	140.5	177.0	185.5	178.1	186.3	59.9	63.8	63.2	65.0	68.5
Lip, oral cavity, and pharynx . . .	47.0	40.2	32.7	29.4	37.4	19.2	16.0	16.0	16.6	17.5
Leukemia.	83.3	117.1	114.8	102.3	116.0	50.9	61.1	63.9	65.1	65.0

- Represents zero. B Base figure too small to meet statistical standards for reliability of a derived figure.   [1] Includes persons under 25 years of age and malignant neoplasms of other and unspecified sites, not shown separately.

Source: U.S. National Center for Health Statistics, *Vital Statistics of the United States,* annual; and unpublished data.

No. 134. Death Rates From Accidents and Violence: 1970 to 1990

[Rates are per 100,000 population. Excludes deaths of nonresidents of the United States. Beginning 1980, deaths classified according to the ninth revision of the *International Classification of Diseases*. For earlier years, classified according to the revisions in use at the time; see text, section 2. See Appendix III]

CAUSE OF DEATH AND AGE	WHITE						BLACK					
	Male			Female			Male			Female		
	1970	1980	1990	1970	1980	1990	1970	1980	1990	1970	1980	1990
Total [1]	101.9	97.1	81.2	42.4	36.3	32.1	183.2	154.0	142.0	51.7	42.6	38.6
Motor vehicle accidents	39.1	35.9	26.7	14.8	12.8	11.6	44.3	31.1	28.1	13.4	8.3	9.4
All other accidents	38.2	30.4	23.6	18.3	14.4	12.4	63.3	46.0	32.7	22.5	18.6	13.4
Suicide	18.0	19.9	22.0	7.1	5.9	5.3	8.0	10.3	12.0	2.6	2.2	2.3
Homicide	6.8	10.9	9.0	2.1	3.2	2.8	67.6	66.6	69.2	13.3	13.5	13.5
15 to 24 years old	130.7	138.6	107.3	34.9	37.3	30.5	234.3	162.0	208.0	45.5	35.0	34.9
25 to 34 years old	96.6	118.4	97.4	23.8	29.0	26.0	384.4	256.9	218.1	76.0	49.4	48.1
35 to 44 years old	85.7	94.1	82.3	25.8	29.2	24.4	345.2	218.1	176.6	77.2	43.2	38.5
45 to 54 years old	87.5	90.8	73.5	30.4	31.8	25.3	303.3	207.3	138.5	65.5	40.2	30.7
55 to 64 years old	101.5	92.3	79.5	36.3	33.8	29.4	242.4	188.5	129.9	56.0	47.3	36.1
65 years old and over	216.9	163.9	150.7	122.4	87.2	80.1	220.0	215.8	175.5	107.9	102.9	81.6
65 to 74 years old	128.0	116.7	99.7	57.7	46.4	40.5	217.4	182.2	141.8	81.5	68.7	50.4
75 to 84 years old	229.3	209.2	195.7	149.0	101.5	89.4	236.0	261.4	206.1	140.1	137.5	95.8
85 years old and over	466.7	438.5	428.3	391.4	268.1	232.4	271.8	379.2	359.1	214.3	235.7	213.0

[1] Includes persons under 15 years old, not shown separately.

No. 135. Deaths and Death Rates From Accidents, by Type: 1970 to 1990

[See headnote, table 134; and Appendix III. See also *Historical Statistics, Colonial Times to 1970*, series B 163-165]

TYPE OF ACCIDENT	DEATHS (number)					RATE PER 100,000 POPULATION				
	1970	1980	1985	1989	1990	1970	1980	1985	1989	1990
Accidents and adverse effects	114,638	105,718	93,457	95,028	91,983	56.4	46.7	39.3	38.5	37.0
Motor vehicle accidents	54,633	53,172	45,901	47,575	46,814	26.9	23.5	19.3	19.3	18.8
Traffic	53,493	51,930	44,822	46,586	45,827	26.3	22.9	18.8	18.9	18.4
Nontraffic	1,140	1,242	1,079	989	987	0.6	0.5	0.5	0.4	0.4
Water-transport accidents	1,651	1,429	1,111	866	923	0.8	0.6	0.5	0.4	0.4
Air and space transport accidents	1,612	1,494	1,428	1,123	941	0.8	0.7	0.6	0.5	0.4
Railway accidents	852	632	551	608	663	0.4	0.3	0.2	0.2	0.3
Accidental falls	16,926	13,294	12,001	12,151	12,313	8.3	5.9	5.0	4.9	5.0
Fall from one level to another	4,798	3,743	3,365	3,062	3,194	2.4	1.7	1.4	1.2	1.3
Fall on the same level	828	415	411	476	499	0.4	0.2	0.2	0.2	0.2
Fracture, cause unspecified, and other unspecified falls	11,300	9,136	8,225	8,613	8,620	5.6	4.0	3.5	3.5	3.5
Accidental drowning	6,391	6,043	4,407	4,015	3,979	3.1	2.7	1.9	1.6	1.6
Accidents caused by—										
Fires and flames	6,718	5,822	4,938	4,716	4,175	3.3	2.6	2.1	1.9	1.7
Firearms	2,406	1,955	1,649	1,489	1,416	1.2	0.9	0.7	0.6	0.6
Electric current	1,140	1,095	802	702	670	0.6	0.5	0.3	0.3	0.3
Accidental poisoning by—										
Drugs and medicines	2,505	2,492	3,612	5,035	4,506	1.2	1.1	1.5	2.0	1.8
Other solid and liquid substances	1,174	597	479	568	549	0.6	0.3	0.2	0.2	0.2
Gases and vapors	1,620	1,242	1,079	921	748	0.8	0.5	0.5	0.4	0.3
Complications due to medical procedures	3,581	2437	2,674	2,992	2,669	1.8	1.1	1.1	1.2	1.1
Inhalation and ingestion of objects	2,753	3,249	3,551	3,578	3,303	1.4	1.5	1.5	1.4	1.3

No. 136. Suicides, by Sex and Method Used: 1970 to 1990

[Excludes deaths of nonresidents of the United States. Beginning 1979, deaths classified according to the ninth revision of the *International Classification of Diseases*. For earlier years, classified according to the revision in use at the time; see text, section 2. See also *Historical Statistics, Colonial Times to 1970*, series H 979-986]

METHOD	MALE							FEMALE						
	1970	1980	1985	1987	1988	1989	1990	1970	1980	1985	1987	1988	1989	1990
Total	16,629	20,505	23,145	24,272	24,078	24,102	24,724	6,851	6,364	6,308	6,524	6,329	6,130	6,182
Firearms [1]	9,704	12,937	14,809	15,539	15,656	15,680	16,285	2,068	2,459	2,554	2,597	2,513	2,498	2,600
Percent of total	58	63	64	64	65	65	66	30.2	38.6	40.5	39.8	39.7	40.8	42.1
Poisoning [2]	3,299	2,997	3,319	3,790	3,403	3,211	3,221	3,285	2,456	2,385	2,531	2,422	2,232	2,203
Hanging and strangulation [3]	2,422	2,997	3,532	3,478	3,588	3,708	3,688	831	694	732	757	787	776	756
Other [4]	1,204	1,574	1,485	1,465	1,431	1,503	1,530	667	755	637	639	607	624	623

[1] Includes explosives in 1970. [2] Includes solids, liquids, and gases. [3] Includes suffocation. [4] Beginning 1980, includes explosives.

Source of tables 134-136: U.S. National Center for Health Statistics, *Vital Statistics of the United States*, annual; and unpublished data.

No. 137. Suicide Rates, by Sex, Race, and Age Group: 1970 to 1990

[See headnote, tables 129 and 134]

AGE	TOTAL [1]			MALE						FEMALE					
				White			Black			White			Black		
	1970	1980	1990	1970	1980	1990	1970	1980	1990	1970	1980	1990	1970	1980	1990
All ages [2]	11.6	11.9	12.4	18.0	19.9	22.0	8.0	10.3	12.0	7.1	5.9	5.3	2.6	2.2	2.3
10 to 14 years old....	0.6	0.8	1.5	1.1	1.4	2.3	0.3	0.5	1.6	0.3	0.3	0.9	0.4	0.1	(B)
15 to 19 years old....	5.9	8.5	11.1	9.4	15.0	19.3	4.7	5.6	11.5	2.9	3.3	4.0	2.9	1.6	1.9
20 to 24 years old....	12.2	16.1	15.1	19.3	27.8	26.8	18.7	20.0	19.0	5.7	5.9	4.4	4.9	3.1	2.6
25 to 34 years old....	14.1	16.0	15.2	19.9	25.6	25.6	19.2	21.8	21.9	9.0	7.5	6.0	5.7	4.1	3.7
35 to 44 years old....	16.9	15.4	15.3	23.3	23.5	25.3	12.6	15.6	16.9	13.0	9.1	7.4	3.7	4.6	4.0
45 to 54 years old....	20.0	15.9	14.8	29.5	24.2	24.8	13.8	12.0	14.8	13.5	10.2	7.5	3.7	2.8	3.2
55 to 64 years old....	21.4	15.9	16.0	35.0	25.8	27.5	10.6	11.7	10.8	12.3	9.1	8.0	2.0	2.3	2.6
65 to 74 years over...	20.8	16.9	17.9	38.7	32.5	34.2	8.7	11.1	14.7	9.6	7.0	7.2	2.9	1.7	2.6
75 to 84 years over...	21.2	19.1	24.9	45.5	45.5	60.2	8.9	10.5	14.4	7.2	5.7	6.7	1.7	1.4	(B)
85 years and over....	19.0	19.2	22.2	45.8	52.8	70.3	8.7	18.9	(B)	5.8	5.8	5.4	2.8	-	(B)

- Represents zero.   B Base figure too small to meet statistical standards for reliability of a derived figure.   [1] Includes other races not shown separately.   [2] Includes other age groups not shown separately.

Source: U.S. National Center for Health Statistics, *Monthly Vital Statistics Report;* and unpublished data.

No. 138. Firearm Mortality Among Children, Youth, and Young Adults, 1 to 34 Years Old: 1990

[**Death rate per 100,000 population.** Deaths classified according to the ninth revision of the *International Classification of Diseases*]

ITEM	Under 5 years old	5 to 9 years old	10 to 14 years old	15 to 19 years old	20 to 24 years old	25 to 34 years old
MALE						
Total: White	0.6	0.6	4.2	26.5	32.5	27.8
Black	1.2	1.5	10.2	119.9	157.6	108.5
Homicide: White	0.4	0.2	1.3	9.7	12.9	10.8
Black	0.8	1.0	6.9	105.3	140.7	94.4
Suicide: White............	(X)	(X)	1.2	13.5	17.5	15.6
Black	(X)	(X)	1.1	8.8	13.2	12.2
Accidents: White..........	0.3	0.5	2.9	1.5	1.6	1.1
Black................	0.4	0.5	4.9	1.9	2.7	1.4
FEMALE						
Total: White	0.3	0.4	1.0	4.6	4.9	5.5
Black	1.1	1.2	3.7	12.2	14.4	14.6
Homicide: White	0.2	0.3	0.4	2.0	2.3	2.4
Black	0.9	0.9	3.1	10.4	12.4	12.7
Suicide: White............	(X)	(X)	0.5	2.3	2.4	2.9
Black	(X)	(X)	0.4	1.3	1.3	1.4
Accidents: White..........	0.1	0.1	0.1	0.2	0.2	0.2
Black................	0.3	0.3	0.2	0.4	0.6	0.3

X Not applicable.

Source: U.S. National Center for Health Statistics, *Advance Data from Vital and Health Statistics,* No. 231.

No. 139. Deaths—Life Years Lost and Mortality Costs, by Age, Sex, and Cause: 1990

[Life years lost: Number of years person would have lived in absence of death. Mortality cost: value of lifetime earnings lost by persons who die prematurely, discounted at 6 percent]

CHARACTER-ISTIC	Number of deaths (1,000)	LIFE YEARS LOST [1] Total (1,000)	LIFE YEARS LOST [1] Per death	MORTALITY COST [2] Total (mil.)	MORTALITY COST [2] Per death	CHARACTER-ISTIC	Number of deaths (1,000)	LIFE YEARS LOST [1] Total (1,000)	LIFE YEARS LOST [1] Per death	MORTALITY COST [2] Total (mil.)	MORTALITY COST [2] Per death
Total.....	2,148	33,893	16	$232,717	$108,346	Heart disease .	361	4,290	12	44,511	123,372
Under 5 yrs. . .	45	3,348	74	10,720	236,745	Cancer......	268	3,627	14	28,529	106,340
5-14 yrs......	8	551	65	3,181	377,057	Cerebrovas-					
15-24 yrs.....	37	2,001	55	21,168	576,272	cular diseases	57	607	11	3,877	68,386
25-44 yrs.....	144	5,772	40	84,515	588,325	Injuries......	62	2,166	35	26,714	431,300
45-64 yrs.....	371	8,249	22	83,024	223,601	Other.......	365	7,702	21	58,867	161,144
65 yrs. and over	1,542	13,973	9	30,109	19,520						
Heart disease .	720	8,212	11	70,684	98,165	**Female ...**	**1,035**	**15,501**	**15**	**70,219**	**67,852**
Cancer......	505	7,609	15	50,551	100,037	Under 5 yrs. . .	19	1,515	78	4,075	209,417
Cerebrovas-						5-14 yrs......	3	230	70	1,089	329,181
cular diseases	144	1,553	11	7,101	49,285	15-24 yrs.....	9	528	60	4,195	473,487
Injuries......	92	3,114	34	33,255	361,530	25-44 yrs.....	42	1,849	44	18,869	447,826
Other.......	686	13,405	20	71,126	103,614	45-64 yrs.....	142	3,556	25	26,353	185,579
Male ...	**1,113**	**18,392**	**17**	**162,498**	**145,999**	65 yrs. and over	819	7,823	10	15,638	19,092
Under 5 yrs. . .	26	1,833	71	6,646	257,334	Heart disease .	359	3,923	11	26,173	72,852
5-14 yrs......	5	321	63	2,092	407,956	Cancer......	237	3,983	17	22,022	92,903
15-24 yrs.....	28	1,472	53	16,973	608,945	Cerebrovas-					
25-44 yrs.....	102	3,923	39	65,646	646,637	cular diseases	87	946	11	3,224	36,893
45-64 yrs.....	229	4,693	21	56,671	247,149	Injuries......	30	948	32	6,541	217,698
65 yrs. and over	723	6,150	9	14,471	20,005	Other.......	321	5,702	18	12,259	38,173

[1] Based on life expectancy at year of death.   [2] Cost estimates based on the person's age, sex, life expectancy at the time of death, labor force participation rates, annual earnings, value of homemaking services, and a 6-percent discount rate by which to convert to present worth the potential aggregate earnings lost over the years.
    Source: Institute for Health and Aging, University of California, San Francisco, CA, unpublished data.

No. 140. Marriages and Divorces: 1970 to 1988

[See also Historical Statistics, Colonial Times to 1970, series B 214-217]

YEAR	MARRIAGES [1] Number (1,000)	MARRIAGES [1] Rate per 1,000 population Total	MARRIAGES [1] Men, 15 yrs. old and over	MARRIAGES [1] Women, 15 yrs. old and over	MARRIAGES [1] Unmarried women 15 yrs. old and over	MARRIAGES [1] Unmarried women 15 to 44 yrs. old	DIVORCES AND ANNULMENTS Number (1,000)	DIVORCES AND ANNULMENTS Rate per 1,000 population Total	DIVORCES AND ANNULMENTS Married women, 15 yrs. old and over
1970	2,159	10.6	31.1	28.4	76.5	140.2	708	3.5	14.9
1975	2,153	10.0	27.9	25.6	66.9	118.5	1,036	4.8	20.3
1980	2,390	10.6	28.5	26.1	61.4	102.6	1,189	5.2	22.6
1981	2,422	10.6	28.4	26.1	61.7	103.1	1,213	5.3	22.6
1982	2,456	10.6	28.4	26.1	61.4	101.9	1,170	5.0	21.7
1983	2,446	10.5	28.0	25.7	59.9	99.3	1,158	4.9	21.3
1984	2,477	10.5	28.1	25.8	59.5	99.0	1,169	5.0	21.5
1985	2,413	10.1	26.9	24.8	57.0	94.9	1,190	5.0	21.7
1986	2,407	10.0	26.5	24.5	56.2	93.9	1,178	4.9	21.2
1987	2,403	9.9	26.2	24.2	55.7	92.4	1,166	4.8	20.8
1988	2,396	9.7	25.9	23.9	54.6	91.0	1,167	4.7	20.7

[1] Beginning 1980, includes nonlicensed marriages registered in California.

No. 141. Percent Distribution of Marriages, by Marriage Order: 1970 to 1988

[Excludes marriages with marriage order not stated. See headnote, table 143]

MARRIAGE ORDER	1970	1980	1981	1982	1983	1984	1985	1986	1987	1988
Total........................	100.0	100.0	100.0	100.0	100.0	100.0	100.0	100.0	100.0	100.0
First marriage of bride and groom	68.6	56.2	54.7	54.8	54.4	54.4	54.3	53.9	53.9	54.1
First marriage of bride, remarriage of groom . . .	7.6	11.3	11.8	11.6	11.6	11.5	11.5	11.3	11.3	11.1
Remarriage of bride, first marriage of groom . . .	7.3	9.8	10.1	10.3	10.5	10.7	10.9	11.2	11.3	11.4
Remarriage of bride and groom	16.5	22.7	23.4	23.3	23.5	23.4	23.4	23.6	23.5	23.4

    Source of tables 140 and 141: U.S. National Center for Health Statistics, Vital Statistics of the United States, annual; Monthly Vital Statistics Report; and unpublished data.

No. 142. Percent Distribution of Marriages, by Age, Sex, and Previous Marital Status: 1980 to 1988

[Data cover marriage registration area; see text, section 2. Based on a sample and subject to sampling variability; for details, see source]

SEX AND PREVIOUS MARITAL STATUS	Total	Under 20 years old	20-24 years old	25-29 years old	30-34 years old	35-44 years old	45-64 years old	65 years old and over
WOMEN								
All marriages: [1]								
1980	100.0	21.1	37.1	18.7	9.3	7.8	5.0	1.0
1985	100.0	13.9	34.4	22.1	12.0	11.1	5.4	1.0
1988	100.0	11.8	31.5	24.1	13.2	12.6	5.8	1.0
First marriages: [2]								
1980	100.0	30.4	47.3	16.0	4.0	1.6	0.6	0.1
1985	100.0	20.8	46.3	22.4	6.9	2.8	0.6	0.1
1988	100.0	17.7	43.3	26.1	8.5	3.7	0.7	0.1
Remarriages: [2][3]								
1980	100.0	1.7	15.3	24.4	20.6	20.8	14.3	2.9
1985	100.0	0.9	11.1	21.6	21.9	27.1	14.6	2.9
1988	100.0	0.7	9.1	20.5	21.9	29.5	15.4	2.8
Previously divorced: [4] 1980 .	100.0	1.7	16.7	26.7	22.5	21.6	10.0	0.6
1988 .	100.0	0.8	9.8	22.2	23.3	30.7	12.5	0.6
MEN								
All marriages: [1]								
1980	100.0	8.5	35.7	23.8	12.3	10.5	7.4	1.8
1985	100.0	5.3	30.1	26.2	14.4	14.0	8.2	1.9
1988	100.0	4.5	26.9	27.2	15.8	15.1	8.6	1.9
First marriages: [2]								
1980	100.0	12.7	50.0	25.7	7.5	2.9	1.1	0.1
1985	100.0	8.1	43.4	31.5	11.0	4.7	1.1	0.1
1988	100.0	6.9	38.7	33.9	13.6	5.8	1.1	0.1
Remarriages: [2][3]								
1980	100.0	0.2	7.2	20.1	21.9	25.6	20.0	5.1
1985	100.0	0.1	4.9	16.0	20.6	31.6	21.6	5.2
1988	100.0	0.1	4.0	14.4	20.1	33.1	23.1	5.2
Previously divorced: [4] 1980 .	100.0	0.2	7.7	21.7	24.1	27.7	17.3	1.4
1988 .	100.0	0.1	4.3	15.6	21.8	35.3	21.3	1.6

[1] Includes marriage order not stated.   [2] Excludes data for Iowa.   [3] Includes remarriages of previously widowed.
[4] Excludes remarriages in Michigan, Ohio, and South Carolina.

No. 143. Marriage Rates and Median Age of Bride and Groom, by Previous Marital Status: 1970 to 1988

[Data cover marriage registration area; see text, section 2. Beginning 1977, excludes Iowa. Figures for previously divorced and previously widowed exclude data for Michigan and Ohio for all years, for South Carolina beginning 1975, and for the District of Columbia for 1970. Based on a sample and subject to sampling variability; for details, see source. For definition of median, see Guide to Tabular Presentation. See also *Historical Statistics, Colonial Times to 1970*, series A 158-159]

YEAR	MARRIAGE RATES [1]						MEDIAN AGE AT MARRIAGE (years)					
	Women			Men			Women			Men		
	Single	Divorced	Wid-owed	Single	Divorced	Wid-owed	First mar-riage	Remarriage		First mar-riage	Remarriage	
								Divorced	Widowed		Divorced	Widowed
1970	93.4	123.3	10.2	80.4	204.5	40.6	20.6	30.1	51.2	22.5	34.5	58.7
1975	75.9	117.2	8.3	61.5	189.8	40.4	20.8	30.2	52.4	22.7	33.6	59.4
1980	66.0	91.3	6.7	54.7	142.1	32.2	21.8	31.0	53.6	23.6	34.0	61.2
1985	61.5	81.8	5.7	50.1	121.6	27.7	23.0	32.8	54.6	24.8	36.1	62.7
1986	59.7	79.5	5.5	49.1	117.8	26.8	23.3	33.1	54.3	25.1	36.6	62.9
1987	58.9	80.7	5.4	48.8	115.7	26.1	23.6	33.3	53.9	25.3	36.7	62.8
1988	58.4	78.6	5.3	48.3	109.7	25.1	23.7	33.6	53.9	25.5	37.0	63.0

[1] Rate per 1,000 population 15 years old and over in specified group.

No. 144. Divorces and Annulments—Median Duration of Marriage, Median Age at Divorce, and Children Involved: 1970 to 1988

[Data cover divorce-registration area; see text, section 2. Based on a sample and subject to sampling variability; for details, see source. Median age computed on data by single years of age. See also *Historical Statistics, Colonial Times to 1970*, series B 218]

DURATION OF MARRIAGE, AGE AT DIVORCE, AND CHILDREN INVOLVED	1970	1975	1980	1981	1982	1983	1984	1985	1986	1987	1988
Median duration of marriage (years).	6.7	6.5	6.8	7.0	7.0	7.0	6.9	6.8	6.9	7.0	7.1
Median age at divorce:											
Men (years)	32.9	32.2	32.7	33.1	33.6	34.0	34.3	34.4	34.6	34.9	35.1
Women (years)	29.8	29.5	30.3	30.6	31.1	31.5	31.7	31.9	32.1	32.5	32.6
Estimated number of children involved in divorce (1,000)	870	1,123	1,174	1,180	1,108	1,091	1,081	1,091	1,064	1,038	1,044
Avg. number of children per decree	1.22	1.08	0.98	0.97	0.94	0.94	0.92	0.92	0.90	0.89	0.89
Rate per 1,000 children under 18 years of age.	12.5	16.7	17.3	18.7	17.6	17.4	17.2	17.3	16.8	16.3	16.4

Source of tables 142-144: U.S. National Center for Health Statistics of the United States, *Vital Statistics of the United States*, annual, *Monthly Vital Statistics Report;* and unpublished data.

No. 145. First Marriage Dissolution and Years Until Remarriage for Women, by Race and Hispanic Origin: 1988

[For women 15 to 44 years old. Based on 1988 National Survey of Family Growth; see Appendix III. Marriage dissolution includes death of spouse, separation because of marital discord, and divorce]

ITEM	Number (1,000)	YEARS UNTIL REMARRIAGE (cummulative percent)					
		All	1	2	3	4	5
ALL RACES [1]							
Year of dissolution of first marriage:							
All years	11,577	56.8	20.6	32.8	40.7	46.2	49.7
1980-84	3,504	47.5	16.3	28.1	36.4	[2]41.1	[2]45.4
1975-79	3,235	65.3	21.9	36.0	44.7	52.7	55.4
1970-74	1,887	83.2	24.9	38.6	47.9	56.4	61.2
1965-69	1,013	89.9	32.6	48.7	60.2	65.0	72.8
WHITE							
Year of dissolution of first marriage:							
All years	10,103	59.9	21.9	35.2	43.5	49.4	53.0
1980-84	3,030	51.4	18.2	31.1	40.3	[2]45.2	[2]49.8
1975-79	2,839	69.5	23.2	38.5	46.9	55.6	58.4
1970-74	1,622	87.5	24.9	39.8	49.8	59.3	64.3
1965-69	893	91.0	34.7	52.3	64.9	69.3	76.9
BLACK							
Year of dissolution of first marriage:							
All years	1,166	34.0	10.9	16.5	19.6	22.7	25.0
1980-84	380	19.7	[3]4.7	[3]10.6	[3]12.9	[2]14.8	[2]14.8
1975-79	301	32.3	[3]11.4	[3]15.6	18.5	22.2	24.9
1970-74	227	59.0	22.3	29.4	35.3	38.7	42.3
1965-69	98	81.2	[3]20.9	[3]27.3	[3]31.3	40.8	52.1
Hispanic, [4] all years	942	44.7	12.5	16.6	22.7	27.8	29.9

[1] Includes other races.   [2] The percent having remarried is biased downward because the women had not completed the indicated number of years since dissolution of first marriage at the time of the survey.   [3] Figure does not meet standard of reliability or precision.   [4] Hispanic persons may be of any race.

Source: National Center for Health Statistics, *Advance Data from Vital and Health Statistics*, No. 194.

No. 146. Marriage Experience for Women, by Age, Race, and Hispanic Origin: 1980 and 1990

[In percent. As of **June.** Based on Current Population Survey; see text, section 1]

MARITAL STATUS AND AGE	ALL RACES		WHITE		BLACK		HISPANIC [1]	
	1980	1990	1980	1990	1980	1990	1980	1990
EVER MARRIED								
20 to 24 years old	49.5	38.5	52.2	41.3	33.3	23.5	55.4	45.8
25 to 29 years old	78.6	69.0	81.0	73.2	62.3	45.0	80.2	69.6
30 to 34 years old	89.9	82.2	91.6	85.6	77.9	61.1	88.3	83.0
35 to 39 years old	94.3	89.4	95.3	91.4	87.4	74.9	91.2	88.9
40 to 44 years old	95.1	92.0	95.8	93.4	89.7	82.1	94.2	92.8
45 to 49 years old	95.9	94.4	96.4	95.1	92.5	89.7	94.4	91.7
50 to 54 years old	95.3	95.5	95.8	96.1	92.1	91.9	95.0	91.8
DIVORCED AFTER FIRST MARRIAGE								
20 to 24 years old	14.2	12.5	14.7	12.8	10.5	9.6	9.4	6.8
25 to 29 years old	20.7	19.2	21.0	19.8	20.2	17.8	13.9	13.5
30 to 34 years old	26.2	28.1	25.8	28.6	31.4	26.6	21.1	19.9
35 to 39 years old	27.2	34.1	26.7	34.6	32.9	35.8	21.9	29.7
40 to 44 years old	26.1	35.8	25.5	35.2	33.7	45.1	19.7	26.6
45 to 49 years old	23.1	35.2	22.7	35.5	29.0	39.8	23.9	24.6
50 to 54 years old	21.8	29.5	21.0	28.5	29.0	39.2	22.5	22.9
REMARRIED AFTER DIVORCE								
20 to 24 years old	45.5	38.1	47.0	39.3	(B)	(B)	(B)	(B)
25 to 29 years old	53.4	51.8	56.4	52.8	27.9	44.4	(B)	49.5
30 to 34 years old	60.9	59.6	63.3	61.4	42.0	42.0	58.3	45.9
35 to 39 years old	64.9	65.0	66.9	66.5	50.6	54.0	45.2	51.2
40 to 44 years old	67.4	67.1	68.6	69.5	58.4	50.3	(B)	53.9
45 to 49 years old	69.2	65.9	70.4	67.2	62.7	55.0	(B)	51.0
50 to 54 years old	72.0	63.0	72.6	65.4	72.7	50.2	(B)	62.2
REDIVORCED AFTER REMARRIAGE								
20 to 24 years old	8.5	13.1	(NA)	(NA)	(NA)	(NA)	(NA)	(NA)
25 to 29 years old	15.6	17.8	(NA)	(NA)	(NA)	(NA)	(NA)	(NA)
30 to 34 years old	19.1	22.7	(NA)	(NA)	(NA)	(NA)	(NA)	(NA)
35 to 39 years old	24.7	28.5	(NA)	(NA)	(NA)	(NA)	(NA)	(NA)
40 to 44 years old	28.4	30.6	(NA)	(NA)	(NA)	(NA)	(NA)	(NA)
45 to 49 years old	25.1	36.4	(NA)	(NA)	(NA)	(NA)	(NA)	(NA)
50 to 54 years old	29.0	34.5	(NA)	(NA)	(NA)	(NA)	(NA)	(NA)

B Base is less than 75,000.   NA Not available.   [1] Persons of Hispanic origin may be of any race.

Source: U.S. Bureau of the Census, *Current Population Reports*, P23-180.

No. 147. Marriages and Divorces—Number and Rate, by State: 1980 to 1991

[By place of occurrence]

DIVISION AND STATE	MARRIAGES [1]						DIVORCES [3]					
	Number (1,000)			Rate per 1,000 population [2]			Number (1,000)			Rate per 1,000 population [2]		
	1980	1985	1991, prel.	1980	1985	1991, prel.	1980	1985	1991, prel.	1980	1985	1991, prel.
U.S.	2,390.3	2,412.6	[4]2,371.0	10.6	10.1	[4]9.4	1,189.0	[5]1,190.0	[5]1,187.0	5.2	[5]5.0	[5]4.7
New England	106.3	114.3	[6]77.8	8.6	9.0	[6]7.8	49.0	49.9	[6]30.3	4.0	3.9	[6]3.0
Maine	12.0	12.2	11.1	10.7	10.5	8.8	6.2	6.1	5.8	5.5	5.2	4.6
New Hampshire	9.3	11.4	9.8	10.0	11.4	8.5	5.3	4.9	4.9	5.7	4.9	4.3
Vermont	5.2	5.5	6.0	10.2	10.4	10.2	2.6	2.4	2.7	5.1	4.4	4.6
Massachusetts	46.3	49.8	43.4	8.1	8.6	7.3	17.9	21.6	13.5	3.1	3.7	2.3
Rhode Island	7.5	8.0	7.5	7.9	8.3	7.4	3.6	3.7	3.3	3.8	3.8	3.3
Connecticut	26.0	27.3	(NA)	8.4	8.6	(NA)	13.5	11.2	(NA)	4.3	3.5	(NA)
Middle Atlantic	294.0	314.3	[6]136.7	8.0	8.5	[6]6.9	124.7	137.1	[6]95.7	3.4	3.7	[6]3.2
New York	144.5	164.0	(NA)	8.2	9.2	(NA)	62.0	67.6	55.6	3.5	3.8	3.1
New Jersey	55.8	61.2	55.4	7.6	8.1	7.1	27.8	29.3	(NA)	3.8	3.9	(NA)
Pennsylvania	93.7	89.1	81.3	7.9	7.5	6.7	34.9	40.2	40.1	2.9	3.4	3.3
East North Central	395.5	[7]362.2	[6]258.4	9.5	9.2	[6]8.3	212.4	[7]192.6	[6]111.9	5.1	[7]4.6	[6]4.4
Ohio	99.8	[7]94.4	97.4	9.2	[7]8.8	8.8	58.8	[7]53.0	54.3	5.4	[7]4.9	4.9
Indiana	57.9	51.1	50.6	10.5	9.3	8.9	[8]40.0	[8]35.3	(NA)	[8]7.3	[8]6.4	(NA)
Illinois	109.8	97.7	(NA)	9.6	8.5	(NA)	51.0	48.9	(NA)	4.5	4.2	(NA)
Michigan	86.9	79.0	73.6	9.4	8.7	7.9	45.0	38.8	39.8	4.9	4.3	4.3
Wisconsin	41.1	40.0	36.8	8.7	8.4	7.5	17.5	16.6	17.8	3.7	3.5	3.6
West North Central	173.7	158.3	149.9	10.1	9.0	8.3	79.6	74.3	80.1	4.6	4.2	4.4
Minnesota	37.6	35.1	32.8	9.2	8.4	7.4	15.4	14.8	16.0	3.8	3.5	3.6
Iowa	27.5	24.6	23.8	9.4	8.5	8.3	11.9	10.5	12.2	4.1	3.7	4.3
Missouri	54.6	49.5	46.4	11.1	9.8	8.9	27.6	25.0	26.6	5.6	5.0	5.1
North Dakota	6.1	5.4	4.7	9.3	7.9	7.3	2.1	2.3	2.2	3.3	3.4	3.3
South Dakota	8.8	7.8	7.4	12.7	11.0	10.3	2.8	2.6	2.8	4.1	3.6	3.9
Nebraska	14.2	12.7	12.7	9.1	7.9	7.8	6.4	6.4	6.5	4.1	4.0	4.0
Kansas	24.8	23.3	22.1	10.5	9.5	8.7	13.4	12.8	13.9	5.7	5.2	5.5
South Atlantic	413.1	438.8	445.8	11.2	10.9	10.0	206.3	210.5	233.3	5.6	5.2	5.2
Delaware	4.4	5.4	5.3	7.5	8.6	7.6	2.3	3.0	3.0	3.9	4.8	4.3
Maryland	46.3	46.1	44.4	11.0	10.5	9.2	17.5	16.2	16.6	4.1	3.7	3.4
Dist. of Columbia	5.2	5.0	5.0	8.1	8.1	8.6	4.7	2.7	2.3	7.3	4.3	3.9
Virginia	60.2	66.5	68.8	11.3	11.7	11.0	23.6	24.1	28.2	4.4	4.2	4.5
West Virginia	17.4	14.6	12.6	8.9	7.5	6.9	10.3	9.9	10.1	5.3	5.1	5.6
North Carolina	46.7	50.5	49.0	7.9	8.1	7.3	28.1	30.2	33.8	4.8	4.8	5.0
South Carolina	53.9	52.8	53.3	17.3	15.8	14.8	13.6	13.5	14.7	4.4	4.0	4.1
Georgia	70.6	72.3	70.5	12.9	12.1	10.6	34.7	33.4	42.0	6.4	5.6	6.3
Florida	108.3	125.5	136.9	11.1	11.0	10.3	71.6	77.5	82.7	7.3	6.8	6.2
East South Central	[7]168.8	171.8	182.1	[7]11.5	11.4	11.7	[7]87.5	[7]86.2	94.7	[7]6.0	[7]5.7	6.1
Kentucky	[7]32.7	46.0	47.3	[8]8.9	12.3	12.7	[7]16.7	18.3	22.3	[7]4.6	4.9	6.0
Tennessee	59.2	55.0	68.8	12.9	11.5	13.7	30.2	29.9	32.5	6.6	6.3	6.5
Alabama	49.0	46.1	42.7	12.6	11.5	10.3	26.7	25.0	27.1	6.9	6.2	6.5
Mississippi	27.9	24.8	23.4	11.1	9.5	8.9	13.8	[7]13.0	12.9	6.5	[7]5.0	4.9
West South Central	298.2	308.6	291.9	12.6	11.6	10.7	[7]155.0	[7]160.9	[6]148.8	[7]6.5	(NA)	[6]6.5
Arkansas	26.5	31.7	38.1	11.6	13.4	15.7	[7]15.9	[7]16.5	18.9	[7]6.9	[7]7.0	7.8
Louisiana	43.5	39.4	36.8	10.3	8.8	8.5	[7]18.1	[7]17.6	(NA)	[7]4.3	(NA)	(NA)
Oklahoma	46.5	35.9	32.6	15.4	10.9	10.2	24.2	26.4	23.6	8.0	8.0	7.4
Texas	181.8	201.6	184.5	12.8	12.3	10.6	96.8	100.4	106.4	6.8	6.1	6.1
Mountain	241.7	233.7	[6]129.3	21.3	18.3	[6]10.2	86.1	89.9	[6]75.2	7.6	7.0	[6]5.9
Montana	8.3	7.2	7.2	10.6	8.7	8.9	4.9	4.3	4.4	6.3	5.2	5.4
Idaho	13.4	12.3	14.4	14.2	12.2	13.9	6.6	6.2	6.5	7.0	6.2	6.3
Wyoming	6.9	5.4	4.8	14.6	10.6	10.4	4.0	3.8	3.2	8.5	7.5	7.0
Colorado	34.9	33.6	33.6	12.1	10.4	10.0	18.6	19.2	19.1	6.4	5.9	5.7
New Mexico	16.6	[9]15.5	13.1	12.8	[9]10.7	8.3	10.4	[10]13.2	8.7	8.0	[10]9.1	5.6
Arizona	30.2	35.7	37.4	11.1	11.2	10.1	19.9	21.2	24.8	7.3	6.6	6.7
Utah	17.0	17.5	18.8	11.6	10.6	10.8	7.8	8.8	8.4	5.3	5.3	4.8
Nevada	114.3	106.5	(NA)	142.8	113.7	(NA)	13.8	13.3	(NA)	17.3	14.2	(NA)
Pacific	298.8	310.6	[6]97.8	9.4	8.9	[6]10.2	187.9	188.5	[6]53.3	5.9	5.4	[6]5.6
Washington	47.7	43.8	49.9	11.6	9.9	10.0	28.6	26.3	29.5	6.9	6.0	5.9
Oregon	23.0	22.4	24.3	8.7	8.3	8.3	17.8	15.7	15.3	6.7	5.9	5.2
California [11]	210.9	222.8	(NA)	8.9	8.5	(NA)	133.5	[12]137.5	(NA)	5.6	[12]5.2	(NA)
Alaska	5.4	6.2	6.0	13.3	11.8	11.3	3.5	4.0	3.4	8.8	7.7	6.4
Hawaii	11.9	15.4	17.7	12.3	14.7	15.4	4.4	4.9	5.1	4.6	4.6	4.5

NA Not available. [1] Data are counts of marriages performed, except as noted. [2] Based on total population residing in area; population enumerated as of April 1 for 1980; estimated as of July 1 for all other years. [3] Includes annulments. [4] Estimate for U.S. is based on monthly reports adjusted for observed differences from final monthly figures. State figures are not adjusted in this manner. [5] Estimated. [6] Excludes figures for States shown below as not available. [7] Data are incomplete. [8] Includes divorce petitions filed for some counties. [9] Premarital health forms issued. [10] Divorce petitions filed. [11] Marriage data include nonlicensed marriages registered. [12] Data include legal separations.

Source: U.S. National Center for Health Statistics, *Vital Statistics of the United States*, annual; and *Monthly Vital Statistics Reports*.

Figure 3.1
Personal Health Care Expenses: 1970 to 1991

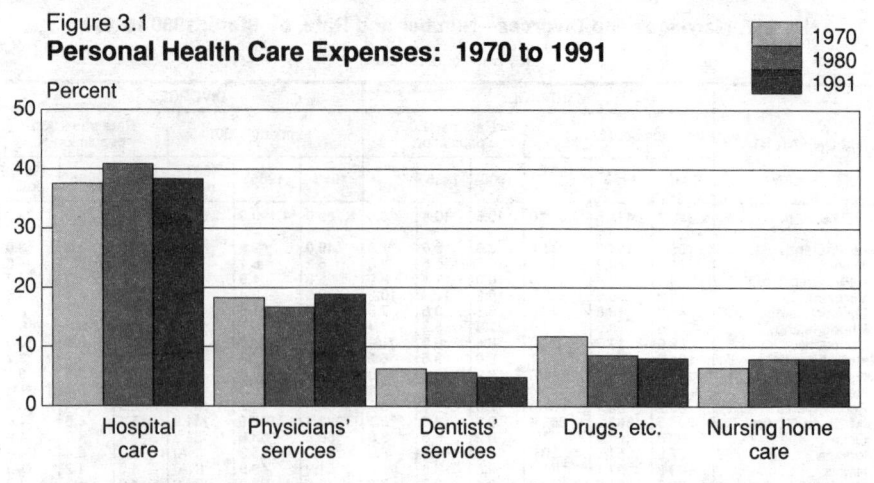

Figure 3.2
**Consumer Price Indexes—
Medical Services: 1970 to 1992**

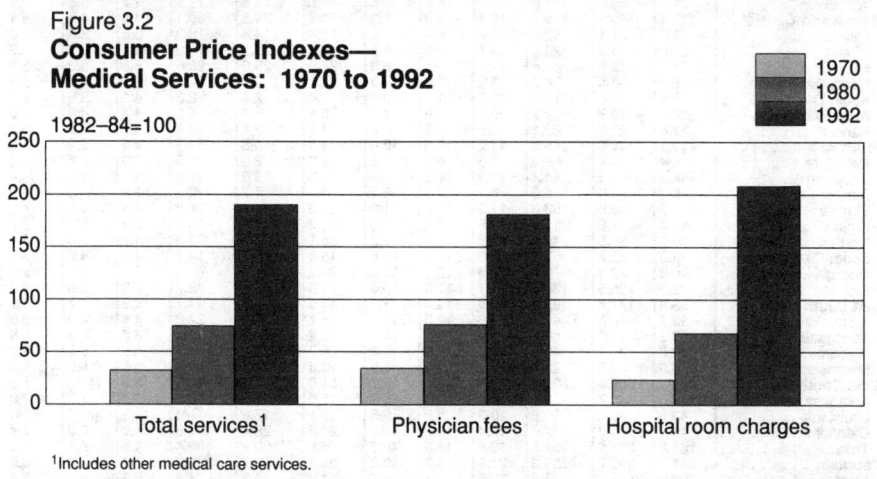

[1]Includes other medical care services.

Figure 3.3
**Per Capita Food Consumption,
by Selected Products: 1970 to 1991**

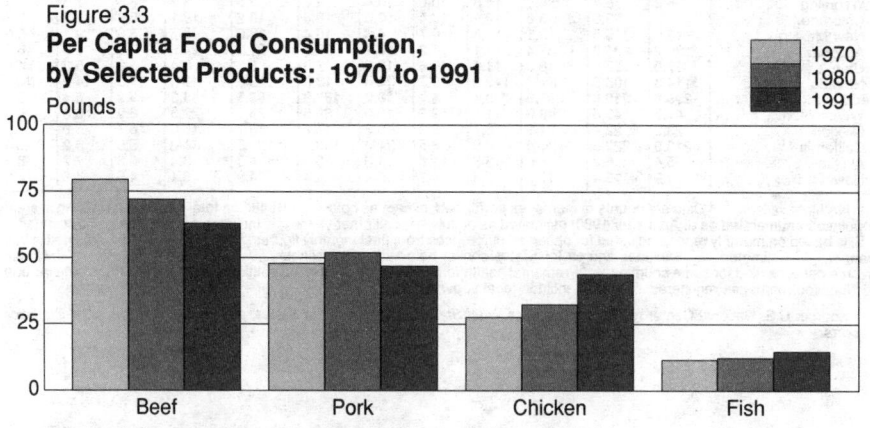

Source: Charts prepared by U.S. Bureau of the Census.
For figure 3.1 data, see table 150; figure 3.2 data, see table 163; figure 3.3 data, see table 218.

Health and Nutrition

This section presents statistics on health expenditures and insurance coverage, including Medicare and Medicaid; medical personnel; hospitals; nursing homes and other care facilities; incidence of acute and prevalence of chronic conditions; nutritional intake of the population; and food consumption. Summary statistics showing recent trends on health care and discussions of selected health issues are published annually by the U.S. National Center for Health Statistics (NCHS) in *Health, United States*. Data on national health expenditures, medical costs, and insurance coverage are compiled by the U.S. Health Care Financing Administration (HCFA) and appear in the quarterly *Health Care Financing Review* and in the *Annual Medicare Program Statistics* series. Statistics on health insurance are also collected by NCHS and are published in series 10 of *Vital and Health Statistics*. The Census Bureau also publishes data on insurance coverage in *Current Population Reports,* series P70. Statistics on health facilities are collected by NCHS and are published in series 14 of *Vital and Health Statistics*. Statistics on hospitals are published annually by the American Hospital Association, Chicago, IL, in *Hospital Statistics*. Primary sources for data on nutrition are the quarterly *National Food Review* and the annual *Food Consumption, Prices, and Expenditures,* both issued by the U.S. Department of Agriculture. NCHS also conducts periodic surveys of nutrient levels in the population, including estimates of food and nutrient intake, overweight and obesity, hypercholesterolemia, hypertension, and clinical signs of malnutrition.

National health expenditures.—HCFA compiles estimates of national health expenditures (NHE) to measure spending for health care in the United States. With the publication of the 1988 estimates, major revisions to the NHE back to 1960 have been incorporated into the accounts. The NHE accounts are structured to show spending by type of expenditure (i.e., hospital care, physician care, dental care, and other professional care; home health; drugs and other medical nondurables; vision products and other medical durables; nursing home care and other person-

In Brief
In 1991:
34 million with no health insurance.
Hospital surgeries—
percent outpatient:

1980	*16*
1991	*52*

Per capita consumption
of red meat:

1980	*126 pounds*
1991	*112 pounds*

al health expenditures; plus nonpersonal health expenditures for such items as public health, research, construction of medical facilities, and administration) and by source of funding (e.g., private health insurance, out-of-pocket payments, and a range of public programs including Medicare, Medicaid, and those operated by the Department of Veterans Affairs (VA)).

In all cases except private insurance (HCFA conducts its own survey of part of the health insurance industry), data used to estimate health expenditures come from existing sources which are tabulated for other purposes. The type of expenditure estimates rely upon statistics produced by such groups as the American Hospital Association, the Internal Revenue Service, the Department of Commerce, and the Department of Health and Human Services (HHS). Source of funding estimates are constructed using administrative and statistical records from the Medicare and Medicaid programs, the Department of Defense and VA medical programs, the Social Security Administration, Census Bureau's *Governmental Finances,* State and local governments, other HHS agencies, and other nongovernment sources. Detailed descriptions of sources and methods, along with the most recent analysis of health care expenditure estimates, are published in the *Health Care Financing Review's* annual article on national health expenditures.

Medicare and Medicaid.—Since July 1966, the Federal Medicare program has provided two coordinated plans for nearly all people age 65 and over: (1) A hospital insurance plan which covers hospital and related services and (2) a voluntary supplementary medical insurance plan, financed partially by monthly premiums paid by participants, which partly covers physicians' and related medical services. Such insurance also applies, since July 1973, to disabled beneficiaries of any age after 24 months of entitlement to cash benefits under the social security or railroad retirement programs and to persons with end stage renal disease.

Under Medicaid, all States offer basic health services to certain very poor people: Individuals who are pregnant, aged, disabled or blind, and families with dependent children. Medicaid eligibility is automatic for almost all cash welfare recipients in these States. Thirty-nine States also extend Medicaid to certain other persons who qualify, except for incomes above regular eligibility levels; those persons include those who have medical expenses which, when subtracted from their income, spend down to a State "medically needy" level or those who meet the higher "medically needy" income restrictions. Within Federal guidelines, each State determines its own Medicaid eligibility criteria and the health services to be provided under Medicaid. The cost of providing Medicaid services is jointly shared by the Federal Government and the States.

Health resources.—Hospital statistics based on data from the American Hospital Association's yearly survey are published annually in *Hospital Statistics,* and cover all hospitals accepted for registration by the Association. To be accepted for registration, a hospital must meet certain requirements relating to number of beds, construction, equipment, medical and nursing staff, patient care, clinical records, surgical and obstetrical facilities, diagnostic and treatment facilities, laboratory services, etc. Data obtained from NCHS cover all U.S. hospitals which meet certain criteria for inclusion. The criteria are published in *Vital and Health Statistics* reports, series 13. NCHS defines a hospital as a non-Federal short-term general or special facility with six or more inpatient beds with an average stay of less than 60 days.

Statistics on the demographic characteristics of persons employed in the health occupations are compiled by the U.S. Bureau of Labor Statistics and reported in *Employment and Earnings* (monthly) (see table 644, section 13). Data based on surveys of health personnel and utilization of health facilities providing long-term care, ambulatory care, and hospital care are presented in NCHS series 13 and series 14, *Data on Health Resources Utilization* and *Data on Health Resources: Manpower and Facilities.* Statistics on patient visits to health care providers, as reported in health interviews, appear in NCHS series 10, *National Health Interview Survey Data.*

The HCFA's *Health Care Financing Review* and *Health Care Financing Program Statistics* present data for hospitals and nursing homes as well as extended care facilities and home health agencies. These data are based on records of the Medicare program and differ from those of other sources because they are limited to facilities meeting Federal eligibility standards for participation in Medicare.

Data on patients in hospitals for the mentally ill and on mental health facilities are collected by the National Institute of Mental Health (NIMH) and appear in *Mental Health, U.S.,* the *Mental Health Statistics* reports, (series CN), and the Mental Health Statistical Note series.

Disability and illness.—General health statistics, including morbidity, disability, injuries, preventive care, and findings from physiological testing are collected by NCHS in its National Health Interview Survey and its National Health and Nutrition Examination Surveys and appear in *Vital and Health Statistics,* series 10 and 11, respectively. The Department of Labor compiles statistics on industrial injuries (see section 13). Annual incidence data on notifiable diseases are compiled by the Public Health Service (PHS) at its Centers for Disease Control in Atlanta, Georgia, and are published as a supplement to its *Morbidity and Mortality Weekly Report.* The list of diseases is revised annually and includes those which, by mutual agreement of the States and PHS, are communicable diseases of national importance.

Nutrition.—Statistics on annual per capita consumption of food and its nutrient value are estimated by the U.S. Department of Agriculture and published quarterly in *National Food Review.* Historical data can be found in *Food Consumption, Prices, and Expenditures,* issued annually.

Statistics on food insufficiency and food and nutrient intake are collected by NCHS to estimate the nation's population diet. NCHS also collects physical examination data to assess the population's nutritional status, including growth, overweight/obesity, nutritional deficiencies, and prevalence of nutrition-related conditions, such as hypertension, hypercholesterolemia, and diabetes.

Statistical reliability.—For discussion of statistical collection, estimation, and sampling procedures and measures of reliability applicable to data from NCHS and HCFA, see Appendix III.

Historical statistics.—Tabular headnotes provide cross-references, where applicable, to *Historical Statistics of the United States, Colonial Times to 1970.* See Appendix IV.

No. 148. National Health Expenditures: 1960 to 1991

[Includes Puerto Rico and outlying areas]

	TOTAL[1]			HEALTH SERVICES AND SUPPLIES						
				Private				Public		
				Out-of-pocket payments					Medical payments	
YEAR	Total (bil.dol.)	Per capita (dol.)	Percent of GDP[2]	Total[3] (bil.dol.)	Total (bil.dol.)	Percent of total private	Insurance premiums[4] (bil.dol.)	Total (bil.dol.)	Medicare (bil. dol.)	Public assistance (bil. dol.)
1960	27.1	143	5.3	19.8	13.3	67.5	5.9	5.7	–	0.5
1965	41.6	204	5.9	29.9	19.0	63.7	10.0	8.3	–	1.7
1970	74.4	346	7.4	44.1	25.6	58.0	16.7	24.9	7.6	6.3
1971	82.3	379	7.5	48.2	27.1	56.2	19.1	28.2	8.5	7.7
1972	92.3	421	7.6	54.0	29.8	55.2	21.9	31.8	9.3	8.9
1973	102.5	464	7.6	59.9	32.9	54.8	24.6	35.9	10.7	10.2
1974	116.1	521	8.0	66.1	35.6	53.8	27.8	42.8	13.5	11.9
1975	132.9	592	8.4	74.5	38.5	51.8	32.9	50.2	16.4	14.5
1976	152.2	672	8.6	86.3	42.5	49.2	39.7	56.9	19.8	16.4
1977	172.0	753	8.7	98.6	46.3	46.9	47.8	64.6	22.8	18.8
1978	193.7	840	8.7	110.4	50.2	45.5	55.0	73.6	26.8	20.9
1979	217.2	933	8.7	123.2	54.1	43.9	63.2	84.1	31.1	24.0
1980	250.1	1,064	9.2	140.7	59.5	42.3	73.4	98.1	37.5	28.0
1981	290.2	1,222	9.6	163.3	67.2	41.1	86.9	114.2	45.2	32.6
1982	326.1	1,359	10.4	185.2	74.2	40.1	100.5	127.0	52.6	34.5
1983	358.6	1,480	10.5	204.1	81.4	39.9	111.4	139.5	59.9	37.9
1984	389.6	1,592	10.3	223.3	87.7	39.3	123.7	150.8	65.9	40.7
1985	422.6	1,711	10.5	242.0	94.4	39.0	134.2	165.2	72.0	44.6
1986	454.9	1,824	10.7	259.2	100.9	38.9	143.8	179.7	76.8	48.3
1987	494.2	1,962	10.9	279.5	108.8	38.9	155.2	197.3	83.0	53.9
1988	546.1	2,146	11.1	311.1	118.5	38.1	175.3	215.1	90.5	58.2
1989	604.3	2,352	11.5	342.8	126.2	36.8	197.1	240.9	102.6	65.8
1990	675.0	2,601	12.2	380.7	136.5	35.9	222.2	271.7	110.7	79.7
1991	751.8	2,868	13.2	412.7	144.3	35.0	244.4	315.9	122.8	104.9

– Represents zero. [1] Includes medical research and medical facilities construction. [2] GDP=Gross domestic product; see table 692. [3] Includes other sources of funds not shown separately. [4] See footnote 2, table 149.
Source: U. S. Health Care Financing Administration, *Health Care Financing Review,* winter 1992.

No. 149. National Health Expenditures, by Type: 1970 to 1991

[In millions of dollars, except percent. Includes Puerto Rico and outlying areas. See also *Historical Statistics, Colonial Times to 1970*, series B 248-261]

TYPE OF EXPENDITURE	1970	1980	1985	1986	1987	1988	1989	1990	1991
Total	**74,377**	**250,126**	**422,600**	**454,879**	**494,159**	**546,080**	**604,315**	**675,037**	**751,771**
Annual percent change [1]	12.3	15.1	8.5	7.6	8.6	10.5	10.7	11.7	11.4
Private expenditures	**46,703**	**144,966**	**247,988**	**265,237**	**286,196**	**318,984**	**350,998**	**389,973**	**421,811**
Health services and supplies	44,148	140,736	242,000	259,194	279,542	311,147	342,787	380,707	412,708
Out-of-pocket payments	25,606	59,500	94,390	100,914	108,825	118,504	126,198	136,491	144,260
Insurance premiums [2]	16,743	73,407	134,197	143,816	155,220	175,325	197,069	222,167	244,367
Other	1,798	7,829	13,413	14,465	15,497	17,318	19,520	22,050	24,081
Medical research	215	274	501	714	725	744	801	843	910
Medical facilities construction	2,341	3,956	5,488	5,328	5,929	7,094	7,410	8,423	8,193
Public expenditures	**27,674**	**105,159**	**174,612**	**189,643**	**207,962**	**227,096**	**253,316**	**285,063**	**329,960**
Percent Federal of public	64.1	68.4	70.7	69.9	69.0	69.0	69.1	68.2	67.5
Health services and supplies	24,908	98,114	165,205	179,725	197,343	215,088	240,857	271,670	315,921
Medicare [3]	7,633	37,533	72,005	76,797	83,000	90,480	102,639	110,736	122,803
Public assistance medical payments [4]	6,310	28,007	44,585	48,276	53,870	58,185	65,848	79,685	104,941
Temporary disability insurance [5] . . .	66	52	51	55	57	62	64	62	64
Workers' compensation (medical) [5] . .	1,409	5,177	8,036	9,069	10,757	12,355	14,447	16,388	17,793
Defense Dept. hospital, medical. . . .	1,784	4,346	7,634	8,427	9,303	9,766	10,376	11,661	12,809
Maternal, child health programs	425	892	1,262	1,434	1,607	1,694	1,794	1,895	1,999
Public health activities	1,385	7,219	12,306	13,486	14,600	16,571	18,938	21,976	24,533
Veterans' hospital, medical care	1,764	5,934	8,613	9,087	9,620	10,011	10,641	11,451	12,185
Medical vocational rehabilitation	158	298	401	425	468	500	523	555	593
State and local hospitals [6]	3,173	5,589	7,030	9,119	10,336	11,443	11,770	12,451	12,697
Other [7]	803	3,067	3,282	3,550	3,725	4,024	3,816	4,812	5,503
Medical research	1,741	5,170	7,294	7,826	8,304	9,596	10,184	11,016	11,674
Medical facilities construction	1,025	1,875	2,112	2,092	2,315	2,411	2,275	2,377	2,365

[1] Change from immediate prior year except for 1970, average annual change from 1965. For explanation of average annual percent change, see Guide to Tabular Presentation.　[2] Covers insurance benefits and amount retained by insurance companies for expenses, additions to reserves, and profits (net cost of insurance).　[3] Represents expenditures for benefits and administrative cost from Federal hospital and medical insurance trust funds under old-age, survivors, disability, and health insurance programs; see text, section 12.　[4] Payments made directly to suppliers of medical care (primarily Medicaid).　[5] Includes medical benefits paid under public law by private insurance carriers and self-insurers.　[6] Expenditures not offset by other revenues.　[7] Covers expenditures for Alcohol, Drug Abuse, and Mental Health Administration; Indian Health Service; school health and other programs.

Source: U.S. Health Care Financing Administration, *Health Care Financing Review*, winter 1992.

No. 150. National Health Expenditures, by Object: 1970 to 1991

[See headnote, table 149. See also *Historical Statistics, Colonial Times to 1970*, series B 221-235]

OBJECT OF EXPENDITURE	EXPENDITURE (bil. dol.)								PERCENT	
	1970	1980	1985	1987	1988	1989	1990	1991	1970	1991
Total	**74.4**	**250.1**	**422.6**	**494.2**	**546.1**	**604.3**	**675.0**	**751.8**	**100.0**	**100.0**
Spent by—										
Consumers	42.3	132.9	228.6	264.0	293.8	323.3	358.7	388.6	56.9	51.7
Government	27.7	105.2	174.6	208.0	227.1	253.3	285.1	330.0	37.2	43.9
Other [1]	4.4	12.1	19.4	22.2	25.2	27.7	31.3	33.2	5.9	4.4
Spent for—										
Health services and supplies	69.1	238.9	407.2	476.9	526.2	583.6	652.4	728.6	92.8	96.9
Personal health care expenses	64.9	219.4	369.7	439.3	482.8	530.9	591.5	660.2	87.3	87.8
Hospital care	27.9	102.4	168.3	194.2	212.0	232.4	258.1	288.6	37.6	38.4
Physicians' services	13.6	41.9	74.0	93.0	105.1	116.1	128.8	142.0	18.3	18.9
Dentists' services	4.7	14.4	23.3	27.1	29.4	31.6	34.1	37.1	6.3	4.9
Other professional services [2]	1.5	8.7	16.6	21.1	23.8	27.1	30.7	35.8	2.0	4.8
Home health care	0.1	1.3	3.8	4.1	4.5	5.6	7.6	9.8	0.2	1.3
Drugs/other medical nondurables . . . [3]	8.8	21.6	36.2	43.2	46.3	50.5	55.6	60.7	11.8	8.1
Vision products/other med. durables [3]	2.0	4.6	7.1	9.1	10.1	10.4	11.7	12.4	2.7	1.6
Nursing home care	4.9	20.0	34.1	39.7	42.8	47.5	53.3	59.9	6.5	8.0
Other health services	1.4	4.6	6.4	7.8	8.7	9.8	11.5	14.0	1.8	1.9
Net cost of insurance and admin. [4]	2.8	12.2	25.2	23.0	26.9	33.8	38.9	43.9	3.7	5.8
Government public health activities	1.4	7.2	12.3	14.6	16.6	18.9	22.0	24.5	1.9	3.3
Medical research	2.0	5.4	7.8	9.0	10.3	11.0	11.9	12.6	2.6	1.7
Medical facilities construction	3.4	5.8	7.6	8.2	9.5	9.7	10.8	10.6	4.5	1.4

[1] Includes nonpatient revenues, privately funded construction, and industrial inplant.　[2] Includes services of registered and practical nurses in private duty, visiting nurses, podiatrists, optometrists, physical therapists, clinical psychologists, chiropractors, naturopaths, and Christian Science practitioners.　[3] Includes expenditures for eyeglasses, hearing aids, orthopedic appliances, artificial limbs, crutches, wheelchairs, etc.　[4] Includes administrative expenses of federally financed health programs.

Source: U.S. Health Care Financing Administration, *Health Care Financing Review*, winter 1992.

No. 151. Health Services and Supplies—Per Capita National and Private Consumer Expenditures, by Object: 1970 to 1991

[In dollars, except percent. Based on Social Security Administration estimates of total U.S. population as of July 1, including Armed Forces and Federal employees abroad and civilian population of outlying areas. Excludes research and construction. See also *Historical Statistics, Colonial Times to 1970*, series B 222-232]

OBJECT OF EXPENDITURE	1970	1975	1980	1985	1986	1987	1988	1989	1990	1991
Total, national	**322**	**555**	**1,016**	**1,648**	**1,760**	**1,893**	**2,068**	**2,271**	**2,513**	**2,779**
Annual percent change [1]	11.4	11.5	14.2	7.8	6.8	7.6	9.3	9.8	10.7	10.6
Hospital care	130	233	435	681	721	771	833	904	994	1,101
Physicians' services	63	104	178	299	329	369	413	452	496	542
Dentists' services	22	37	61	94	99	108	116	123	131	141
Other professional services [2]	7	16	37	67	75	84	93	105	118	137
Home health care	1	2	6	16	16	16	18	22	29	37
Drugs and other medical nondurables	41	58	92	146	159	171	182	196	214	231
Vision products and other medical durables [2]	9	14	19	29	32	36	40	41	45	47
Nursing home care	23	44	85	138	147	157	168	185	205	229
Other health services	6	12	19	26	28	31	34	38	44	53
Net cost of insurance and administration [2]	13	23	52	102	99	91	106	131	150	167
Government public health activities	6	14	31	50	54	58	65	74	85	94
Total, private consumer [3]	**197**	**318**	**565**	**925**	**981**	**1,048**	**1,155**	**1,258**	**1,382**	**1,482**
Hospital care	56	100	182	277	290	310	340	370	403	425
Physicians' services	49	75	124	202	219	244	275	297	327	353
Dentists' services	21	35	58	92	97	105	113	120	128	137
Other professional services [2]	5	10	26	46	51	58	65	72	78	88
Home health care	-	-	1	3	3	3	3	4	6	8
Drugs and other medical nondurables	39	54	85	134	145	155	164	176	191	203
Vision products and other medical durables [2]	9	13	17	23	25	28	31	31	34	34
Nursing home care	11	19	38	69	74	77	83	84	95	101
Net cost of insurance	7	14	35	81	78	68	80	103	119	134

- Represents or rounds to zero.   [1] Beginning 1980, change from immediate prior year. For 1975, average annual change from 1970, and for 1970, average annual change from 1965. For explanation of average annual percent change, see Guide to Tabular Presentation.   [2] See footnotes for corresponding objects in table 150.   [3] Represents out-of-pocket payments and private health insurance.

Source: U.S. Health Care Financing Administration, *Health Care Financing Review*, winter 1992.

No. 152. Personal Health Care—Third Party Payments and Private Consumer Expenditures: 1970 to 1991

[In billions of dollars, except percent. See headnote, table 153]

ITEM	1970	1975	1980	1985	1986	1987	1988	1989	1990	1991
Personal health care expenditures	64.9	116.6	219.4	369.7	400.8	439.3	482.8	530.9	591.5	660.2
Third party payments, total	**39.3**	**78.0**	**159.9**	**275.3**	**299.9**	**330.5**	**364.3**	**404.7**	**455.0**	**516.0**
Percent of personal health care	60.5	66.9	72.9	74.5	74.8	75.2	75.5	76.2	76.9	78.1
Private insurance payments	15.2	29.9	65.3	114.2	124.4	138.1	155.0	170.6	191.2	209.3
Government expenditures	22.4	45.3	87.1	148.2	161.5	177.4	192.5	215.2	242.3	283.3
Other [1]	1.7	2.9	7.6	12.9	14.0	15.0	16.8	19.0	21.5	23.4
Private consumer expenditures [2]	**40.8**	**68.4**	**124.8**	**208.6**	**225.3**	**246.9**	**273.5**	**296.8**	**327.7**	**353.5**
Percent met by private insurance	37.2	43.7	52.3	54.7	55.2	55.9	56.7	57.5	58.4	59.2
Hospital care	12.1	22.4	42.8	68.4	72.3	78.1	86.6	95.1	104.7	111.4
Percent met by private insurance	79.2	80.4	87.5	87.1	88.2	88.9	88.0	88.6	90.1	91.1
Physicians' services	10.6	16.8	29.2	49.8	54.5	61.6	70.0	76.4	84.8	92.5
Percent met by private insurance	45.1	54.5	61.5	67.7	68.7	69.1	70.2	70.5	71.6	72.2

[1] Includes nonpatient revenues and industrial inplant health services.   [2] Includes expenditures not shown separately. Represents out-of-pocket payments and private health insurance benefits. Excludes net cost of insurance.

Source: U.S. Health Care Financing Administration, *Health Care Financing Review*, winter 1992.

No. 153. Personal Health Care Expenditures, by Object and Source of Payment: 1991

[In millions of dollars, except as indicated. Includes Puerto Rico and outlying areas. Covers all expenditures for health services and supplies, except net cost of insurance and administration, government public health activities, and expenditures of philanthropic agencies for fund raising activities]

SOURCE	Total	Hospital care	Physicians' services	Dentists' services	Other professional services [1]	Home health care	Drugs and other medical nondurables	Vision products and other medical durables [1]	Nursing home care	Other personal health care
Total	**660,217**	**288,627**	**141,985**	**37,066**	**35,823**	**9,762**	**60,674**	**12,361**	**59,943**	**13,976**
Out of pocket payments	144,260	9,879	25,728	19,916	9,668	1,238	44,329	7,654	25,848	-
Third party payments	515,957	278,748	116,257	17,150	26,154	8,524	16,345	4,707	34,096	13,976
Private health insurance	209,265	101,497	66,770	16,083	13,344	742	9,000	1,187	641	-
Government	283,252	162,600	49,435	1,067	8,371	7,053	7,345	3,520	32,309	11,552
Other [2]	23,440	14,650	52	-	4,439	729	-	-	1,146	2,424
Private [3]	376,965	126,027	92,550	35,999	27,451	2,709	53,328	8,841	27,635	2,424

- Represents or rounds to zero.   [1] See footnotes for corresponding objects on table 150.   [2] Includes nonpatient revenues and industrial inplant.   [3] Covers out-of-pocket payments, private health insurance, nonpatient revenues, and industrial inplant.

Source: U.S. Health Care Financing Administration, *Health Care Financing Review*, winter 1992.

No. 154. Government Expenditures for Health Services and Supplies: 1980 to 1991

[In millions of dollars, except percent. Includes Puerto Rico and outlying areas. Excludes medical research and construction]

YEAR AND TYPE OF SERVICE	TOTAL [1] Amount	Percent distribution	FEDERAL Total	Percent of total	State and local	Medicare [2] (OASDHI)	Public assistance [3]	OTHER HEALTH SERVICES Veterans	Defense Dept. [4]	Workers' compensation [5]
1980, total [1]	**98,114**	**100.0**	**66,762**	**68.0**	**31,352**	**37,533**	**28,007**	**5,934**	**4,346**	**5,177**
Hospital care	54,599	55.6	41,344	75.7	13,255	26,373	10,933	4,918	3,737	2,007
Physicians' services	12,626	12.9	9,668	76.6	2,959	7,948	2,424	59	261	1,667
Nursing home care	10,525	10.7	6,139	58.3	4,386	411	9,752	361	-	-
Drugs and other medical nondurables	1,661	1.7	819	49.3	842	-	1,536	13	13	78
Administration	3,839	3.9	2,063	53.7	1,776	1,118	1,318	49	37	1,225
Public health activities	7,219	7.4	1,246	17.3	5,973	-	-	-	-	-
1990, total [1]	**271,670**	**100.0**	**184,079**	**67.8**	**87,591**	**110,736**	**79,685**	**11,451**	**11,661**	**16,388**
Hospital care	139,465	51.3	103,989	74.6	35,476	67,414	31,598	9,553	9,234	7,775
Physicians' services	44,038	16.2	34,890	79.2	9,148	29,717	5,765	11,451	1,466	6,479
Nursing home care	27,552	10.1	17,001	61.7	10,551	2,421	24,086	1,045	-	-
Drugs and other medical nondurables	6,083	2.2	2,981	49.0	3,102	-	5,651	10	83	304
Administration	7,407	2.7	4,681	63.2	2,726	2,275	3,698	41	159	1,056
Public health activities	21,976	8.1	2,381	10.8	19,595	-	-	-	-	-
1991, total [1]	**315,921**	**100.0**	**211,990**	**67.1**	**103,931**	**122,803**	**104,941**	**12,185**	**12,809**	**17,793**
Hospital care	162,600	51.5	119,150	73.3	43,451	73,306	46,227	10,137	10,132	8,421
Physicians' services	49,435	15.6	39,035	79.0	10,400	32,781	7,313	12,185	1,628	7,055
Nursing home care	32,309	10.2	19,501	60.4	12,808	2,667	28,493	1,149	-	-
Drugs and other medical nondurables	7,345	2.3	3,624	49.3	3,721	-	6,872	11	93	330
Administration	8,136	2.6	5,166	63.5	2,970	2,560	4,028	45	162	1,151
Public health activities	24,533	7.8	2,687	11.0	21,846	-	-	-	-	-

- Represents zero. [1] Includes other items not shown separately. [2] Covers hospital and medical insurance payments and administrative costs under old-age, survivors, disability and health insurance program. [3] Covers Medicaid and other medical public assistance. Excludes funds paid into Medicare trust fund by States to cover premiums for public assistance recipients and medically indigent persons. [4] Includes care for retirees and military dependents. [5] Medical benefits.

Source: U.S. Health Care Financing Administration, *Health Care Financing Review*, winter 1992.

No. 155. Expenditures for Health Services and Supplies, by Type of Payer: 1970 to 1991

[In billions of dollars]

TYPE OF PAYER	1970	1975	1980	1984	1985	1986	1987	1988	1989	1990	1991
Total expenditures	**69.1**	**124.7**	**238.9**	**374.2**	**407.2**	**438.9**	**476.9**	**526.2**	**583.6**	**652.4**	**728.6**
Private	50.1	86.2	162.0	256.0	279.0	301.8	327.5	362.5	398.3	436.6	474.1
Business	13.7	27.8	64.3	103.7	113.5	125.9	131.8	151.0	167.0	187.9	205.4
Share of private health insurance premiums	9.8	19.9	47.9	77.4	83.9	92.2	95.0	110.9	122.8	140.2	152.7
Households [1]	35.0	55.9	90.8	141.8	153.6	163.1	181.9	196.1	213.8	228.9	247.0
Share of private health insurance premiums	6.0	9.9	16.6	27.6	30.0	30.9	37.5	37.7	42.7	46.6	52.2
Out-of-pocket spending	18.9	38.5	59.5	87.7	94.4	100.9	108.8	118.5	126.2	136.5	144.3
Non-patient revenues [2]	1.5	2.5	7.0	10.6	12.0	12.9	13.8	15.4	17.5	19.8	21.7
Public	18.9	38.5	76.8	118.1	128.2	137.1	149.4	163.7	185.4	215.8	254.5
Federal government	10.4	21.3	42.6	63.5	68.9	71.6	77.0	84.3	96.5	113.7	133.8
State/local government	8.5	17.2	34.2	54.7	59.3	65.5	72.4	79.4	88.8	102.1	120.7

[1] Includes other items not shown separately. [2] Includes philanthropy.

Source: U.S. Health Care Financing Administration, *Health Care Financing Review*, spring 1993.

No. 156. Medicare Program—Enrollment and Payments: 1970 to 1991

[Enrollment as of **July 1;** payments for calendar year. Benefit payments represent trust fund outlays. Includes Puerto Rico, outlying areas, and enrollees in foreign countries. See text, section 3, for explanation of coverage]

TYPE OF INSURANCE	Unit	1970	1975	1980	1985	1986	1987	1988	1989	1990	1991
HOSPITAL AND/OR MEDICAL INSURANCE											
Enrollment, total	1,000 .	20,491	24,959	28,478	31,083	31,750	32,411	32,980	33,579	34,203	34,870
Benefit payments	Mil. dol	7,099	15,588	35,699	70,527	75,997	80,316	86,487	98,305	108,707	118,778
HOSPITAL INSURANCE											
Enrollment, total	1,000 .	20,361	24,640	28,067	30,589	31,216	31,853	32,413	33,040	33,719	34,429
Persons 65 and over . .	1,000 .	20,361	22,472	25,104	27,683	28,257	28,822	29,312	29,869	30,464	31,043
Disabled persons [1] . .	1,000 .	(X)	2,168	2,963	2,907	2,959	3,031	3,101	3,171	3,255	3,385
Benefit payments	Mil. dol	5,124	11,315	25,064	47,580	49,758	49,496	52,517	60,011	66,239	71,549
MEDICAL INSURANCE											
Enrollment, total	1,000 .	19,584	23,904	27,400	29,989	30,590	31,170	31,617	32,099	32,629	33,237
Persons 65 and over . .	1,000 .	19,584	21,945	24,680	27,311	27,863	28,382	28,780	29,216	29,686	30,185
Disabled persons [1] . .	1,000 .	(X)	1,959	2,719	2,678	2,727	2,788	2,837	2,883	2,943	3,052
Benefit payments	Mil. dol	1,975	4,273	10,635	22,947	26,239	30,820	33,970	38,294	42,468	47,229

X Not applicable. [1] Age under 65; includes persons enrolled because of end-stage renal disease (ESRD) only.

Source: U.S. Health Care Financing Administration. Published in U.S. Social Security Administration, *Annual Statistical Supplement* to the *Social Security Bulletin.*

No. 157. Medicare—Persons Served and Reimbursements: 1980 to 1990

[Persons served are enrollees who use covered services, incurred expenses greater than the applicable deductible amounts and for whom Medicare paid benefits. Reimbursements are amounts paid to providers for covered services. Excluded are retroactive adjustments resulting from end of fiscal year cost settlements and certain lump-sum interim payments. Also excluded are beneficiary (or third party payor) liabilities for applicable deductibles, coinsurance amounts, and charges for noncovered services. Includes data for enrollees living in outlying territories and foreign countries]

TYPE OF COVERAGE AND SERVICE	Unit	PERSONS 65 YEARS OLD AND OVER				DISABLED PERSONS [1]			
		1980	1985	1989	1990	1980	1985	1989	1990
Persons served, total [2] **. . . . . .**	1,000 . .	**16,271**	**20,347**	**23,868**	**24,809**	**1,760**	**1,944**	**2,287**	**2,390**
Hospital insurance [2]	1,000 . .	6,024	6,058	6,155	6,367	728	662	659	680
Inpatient hospital	1,000 . .	5,951	5,714	5,725	5,906	721	636	627	644
Skilled-nursing services	1,000 . .	248	304	613	615	9	10	23	23
Home health services [3]	1,000 . .	675	1,448	1,580	1,818	51	101	105	122
Supplementary medical insurance [2] . .	1,000 . .	16,099	20,186	23,746	24,687	1,723	1,916	2,263	2,365
Physicians' and other medical services	1,000 . .	15,627	19,590	23,283	24,193	1,631	1,820	2,159	2,249
Outpatient services	1,000 . .	6,629	9,889	13,291	14,055	909	1,096	1,415	1,496
Home health services [3]	1,000 . .	302	27	36	38	25	-	-	-
Persons served per 1,000 enrollees, total [2] **. . . . .**	Rate . .	**638**	**722**	**785**	**802**	**594**	**669**	**721**	**734**
Hospital insurance [2]	Rate . .	240	219	206	209	246	228	208	209
Inpatient hospital	Rate . .	237	206	192	194	243	219	198	198
Skilled-nursing services	Rate . .	10	11	21	20	3	4	7	7
Home health services [3]	Rate . .	27	52	53	60	17	35	33	38
Supplementary medical insurance [2] . .	Rate . .	652	739	813	832	634	716	785	804
Physicians' and other medical services	Rate . .	633	717	797	815	600	680	749	764
Outpatient services	Rate . .	269	362	455	474	334	409	491	508
Home health services [3]	Rate . .	12	1	1	1	9	-	-	-
Reimbursements, total	Mil. dol.	**29,134**	**56,199**	**82,222**	**88,778**	**4,478**	**7,495**	**10,363**	**11,239**
Hospital insurance	Mil. dol .	20,353	37,360	50,448	54,244	2,765	4,785	6,253	6,694
Inpatient hospital	Mil. dol .	19,583	35,313	45,439	48,952	2,714	4,638	5,936	6,346
Skilled-nursing services	Mil. dol .	331	464	2,806	1,886	13	17	143	85
Home health services [3]	Mil. dol .	440	1,583	2,202	3,406	38	130	173	264
Supplementary medical insurance . .	Mil. dol .	8,781	18,839	31,774	34,533	1,713	2,709	4,111	4,545
Physicians' and other medical services	Mil. dol .	7,361	15,309	25,310	27,379	997	1,712	2,623	2,831
Outpatient services	Mil. dol .	1,261	3,499	6,407	7,077	701	997	1,489	1,714
Home health services [3]	Mil. dol .	159	31	57	78	16	-	-	-
Reimbursements, per person served, total	Dollars.	**1,791**	**2,762**	**3,445**	**3,578**	**2,544**	**3,855**	**4,531**	**4,703**
Hospital insurance	Dollars .	3,379	6,167	8,196	8,520	3,798	7,224	9,482	9,847
Inpatient hospital	Dollars .	3,291	6,181	7,937	8,289	3,765	7,295	9,455	9,849
Skilled-nursing services	Dollars .	1,336	1,525	4,580	3,068	1,571	1,681	6,107	3,702
Home health services [3]	Dollars .	652	1,093	1,394	1,874	733	1,288	1,645	2,156
Supplementary medical insurance . . .	Dollars .	545	933	1,338	1,399	994	1,414	1,817	1,922
Physicians' and other medical services	Dollars .	471	781	1,087	1,132	611	941	1,215	1,259
Outpatient services	Dollars .	190	354	482	503	771	909	1,051	1,146
Home health services [3]	Dollars .	526	1,122	1,614	2,033	619	-	-	-

- Represents or rounds to zero. [1] Age under 65; includes persons enrolled because of end-stage renal disease (ESRD) only. [2] Persons are counted once for each type of covered service used, but are not double counted in totals. [3] Beginning 1982, a change in legislation resulted in virtually all home health services being paid under hospital insurance.

Source: U.S. Health Care Financing Administration, *Medicare Program Statistics,* annual; and unpublished data.

No. 158. Medicare—Hospital Utilization and Hospital and Physician Charges: 1970 to 1991

[Data reflect date expense was incurred based on bills submitted for payment and recorded in Health Care Financing Administration central records through May 1992. Includes Puerto Rico, Virgin Islands, Guam, other outlying areas, and enrollees in foreign countries]

ITEM	Unit	PERSONS 65 YEARS OLD AND OVER					DISABLED PERSONS [1]				
		1970	1980	1985	1990	1991	1975	1980	1985	1990	1991
Hospital inpatient care:											
Admissions [2]	1,000...	6,141	9,258	9,751	9,216	9,653	822	1,271	1,319	1,257	1,316
Per 1,000 enrollees [3]	Rate...	302	369	352	303	311	379	429	454	386	389
Covered days of care.	Millions .	79	98	80	82	83	9	13	11	11	12
Per 1,000 enrollees [3]	Rate...	3,902	3,885	2,882	2,702	2,674	4,198	4,549	3,739	3,464	3,545
Per admission	Days...	12.9	10.5	8.2	8.9	10.0	11.1	10.6	8.2	8.8	9.1
Hospital covered charges	Mil. dol.	5,968	28,615	49,236	90,846	105,596	1,371	4,087	6,582	11,910	14,114
Per covered day	Dollars..	75	293	617	1,104	1,272	151	303	606	1,057	1,176
Percent of covered charges reimbursed [4]	Percent .	78.0	70.0	65.6	47.5	46.0	73.6	68.6	64.4	46.5	44.7
Physician allowed charges	Mil. dol.	2,310	9,011	17,743	30,447	32,138	367	1,112	1,823	2,907	3,065
Percent reimbursed	Percent .	71.9	78.0	78.8	76.9	76.7	76.1	78.7	78.7	75.7	75.9

[1] Disabled persons under age 65 and persons enrolled solely because of end-stage renal disease. [2] Beginning 1990, represents number of discharges and includes pass-through amounts, except for kidney acquisition. [3] Based on Hospital Insurance (HI) enrollment as of July 1. [4] Billing reimbursements exclude: (1) PPS pass-through amounts for capital, direct medical education, kidney acquisitions, and bad debts by Medicare patients; (2) certain lump-sum interim payments; and (3) retroactive adjustments resulting from end-of-fiscal year cost reports.

Source: U.S. Health Care Financing Administration, unpublished data.

No. 159. Medicare and Medicaid—Summary, by State and Other Areas: 1991

[Data are preliminary estimates]

REGION, DIVISION, AND STATE	MEDICARE		MEDICAID [3]		REGION, DIVISION, AND STATE	MEDICARE		MEDICAID [3]	
	Enroll-ment [1] (1,000)	Pay-ments [2] (mil. dol.)	Recipi-ents [4] (1,000)	Pay-ments [5] (mil. dol.)		Enroll-ment [1] (1,000)	Pay-ments [2] (mil. dol.)	Recipi-ents [4] (1,000)	Pay-ments [5] (mil. dol.)
All areas	34,870	118,546	28,280	77,048	WV	312	949	284	542
U.S. [6]	34,153	117,926	27,067	76,898	NC	917	2,607	667	1,788
Northeast	7,541	28,768	5,721	26,030	SC	454	1,212	375	910
N.E.	1,918	6,739	1,368	6,141	GA	750	2,588	746	1,799
ME	186	520	151	536	FL	2,402	8,443	1,249	2,944
NH	141	400	60	292	E.S.C.	2,213	7,482	2,096	4,246
VT	76	200	71	197	KY	543	1,801	525	1,200
MA	879	3,418	651	2,828	TN	706	2,405	697	1,485
RI	161	526	164	657	AL	593	2,124	403	805
CT	476	1,676	272	1,630	MS	371	1,154	470	755
M.A.	5,623	22,029	4,353	19,889	W.S.C.	3,269	11,592	2,959	6,758
NY	2,529	10,345	2,462	13,728	AR	397	1,257	285	688
NJ	1,109	3,834	614	2,725	LA	541	2,283	641	1,723
PA	1,985	7,850	1,277	3,436	OK	458	1,488	305	814
Midwest	8,548	28,759	6,026	16,869	TX	1,873	6,564	1,729	3,532
E.N.C.	5,879	20,867	4,387	12,057	West	6,270	20,146	5,989	11,869
OH	1,571	5,959	1,299	3,653	Mountain	1,697	5,027	1,058	2,095
IN	775	2,488	415	1,662	MT	120	345	64	193
IL	1,553	5,531	1,144	2,731	ID	135	344	70	223
MI	1,257	4,808	1,113	2,540	WY	53	158	37	90
WI	723	2,081	416	1,471	CO	369	1,041	223	673
W.N.C.	2,669	7,892	1,639	4,811	NM	186	509	162	342
MN	597	1,509	422	1,561	AZ	517	1,717	313	84
IA	461	1,294	261	766	UT	166	436	129	311
MO	792	2,698	503	1,118	NV	151	477	59	178
ND	100	293	53	227	Pacific	4,573	15,119	4,931	9,774
SD	111	293	57	196	WA	630	1,827	506	1,131
NE	240	635	134	390	OR	434	1,035	263	667
KS	368	1,169	209	553	CA	3,352	11,871	4,019	7,579
South	11,780	40,235	9,331	22,130	AK	27	93	51	160
S.A.	6,298	21,160	4,277	11,127	HI	131	293	91	238
DE	91	315	51	186	PR	437	581	1,201	146
MD	554	2,326	363	1,292	Outlying areas	9	16	[7]12	[7]4
DC	78	381	100	446	Foreign	272	28	(X)	(X)
VA	741	2,341	442	1,218					

X Not applicable. [1] Hospital and/or medical insurance enrollment as of July 1. [2] Benefit payments are for calendar year. Payments for "All areas" represent actual Trust Fund disbursements as shown in the 1990 Trustees Reports, and other actuarial data. Distribution by State is based on interim payment as reflected on claims for services rendered in 1989 and recorded in central office through December, 1990. Payments have been adjusted to include estimated PPS pass-through amounts, but exclude retroactive cost-based adjustments and administrative expenses. Data reflect State of residence of beneficiary. [3] For fiscal year ending Sept. 30. [4] Persons receiving Medicaid at any time during the year. [5] Payments are for calendar year and represent disbursements from Federal hospital and medical insurance trust funds. Estimates of distribution by State based on preliminary billing data. [6] Includes data for enrollees with residence unknown. [7] Virgin Islands only.

Source: U.S. Health Care Financing Administration, unpublished data.

No. 160. Medicaid—Selected Utilization Measures, by Type of Facility: 1975 to 1991

[In thousands. For fiscal years ending in year shown. Includes Virgin Islands. See text, section 3]

MEASURE	1975	1980	1985	1986	1987	1988	1989	1990	1991
General hospitals:									
Total discharges	3,031	3,203	3,616	3,713	3,558	3,905	3,734	4,823	5,281
Recipients discharged	2,336	2,255	2,390	2,564	2,525	2,640	2,701	3,261	3,638
Total days of care	22,941	24,089	29,562	29,517	23,124	24,022	22,754	27,471	28,998
Nursing facilities: [1]									
Total recipients	1,212	1,395	1,375	1,399	1,371	1,445	1,438	1,461	1,500
Total days of care	199,715	273,497	277,996	334,016	328,758	344,693	367,228	360,044	387,621
Intermediate care facilities: [2]									
Total recipients	69	121	147	145	140	145	147	146	146
Total days of care	9,060	250,124	47,324	48,418	45,611	46,825	50,276	49,730	50,223

[1] Includes skilled nursing facilities and intermediate care facilities for all other than the mentally retarded.   [2] Mentally retarded.

Source: U.S. Health Care Financing Administration, unpublished data.

No. 161. Medicaid—Selected Characteristics of Persons Covered: 1980 to 1991

[In thousands, except percent. Represents number of persons as of March of following year who were enrolled at any time in year shown. Person did not have to receive medical care paid for by Medicaid in order to be counted. See headnote, table 584]

POVERTY STATUS	1980	1985	1990	1991							
				Total [1]	White	Black	His-panic [2]	Under 18 years old	18-44 years old	45-64 years old	65 years and over
Persons covered, total	18,966	19,204	24,160	26,739	16,990	8,282	4,577	13,374	8,055	2,420	2,891
Below poverty level	11,113	12,652	15,175	16,888	9,782	6,241	3,022	9,388	5,011	1,301	1,187
Above poverty level	7,854	6,552	8,985	9,851	7,208	2,041	1,555	3,986	3,044	1,119	1,704
Percent of total population .	8.4	8.1	9.7	10.6	8.1	26.5	20.7	20.3	7.6	5.0	9.5
Below poverty level	39.1	39.7	45.2	47.3	41.2	60.9	47.7	65.5	37.7	30.2	31.4
Above poverty level	4.0	3.2	4.2	4.6	3.9	9.7	9.9	7.7	3.3	2.6	6.4

[1] Includes other races not shown separately.   [2] Persons of Hispanic origin may be of any race.

Source: U.S. Bureau of the Census, Current Population Reports, P60-181, earlier reports and unpublished data.

No. 162. Medical Assistance (Medicaid)—Recipients and Payments, by Basis of Eligibility and Type of Service: 1980 to 1991

[For fiscal year ending in year shown; see text, section 3. Includes Puerto Rico and outlying areas. Medical vendor payments are those made directly to suppliers of medical care]

BASIS OF ELIGIBILITY AND TYPE OF SERVICE	RECIPIENTS (1,000)					PAYMENTS (mil. dol.)				
	1980	1985	1989	1990	1991	1980	1985	1989	1990	1991
Total [1] **. . . . .**	21,605	21,814	23,511	25,255	28,280	23,311	37,508	54,500	64,859	77,048
Age 65 and over	3,440	3,061	3,132	3,202	3,359	8,739	14,096	18,558	21,508	25,453
Blindness	92	80	95	83	85	124	249	409	434	475
Disabled [2]	2,819	2,937	3,496	3,635	3,983	7,497	13,203	20,476	23,969	27,798
AFDC [3] program	14,210	15,275	16,036	17,230	20,194	6,354	9,160	13,788	17,690	22,129
Other and unknown	1,499	1,214	1,175	1,105	658	596	798	1,268	1,257	1,193
Inpatient services in—										
General hospital	3,680	3,434	4,170	4,593	5,072	6,412	9,453	13,378	16,674	19,891
Mental hospital	66	60	90	92	65	775	1,192	1,470	1,714	2,010
Intermediate care facilities:										
Mentally retarded	121	147	148	147	146	1,989	4,731	6,649	7,354	7,680
Nursing facility services [4]	1,398	1,375	1,452	1,461	1,500	7,887	11,587	15,531	17,693	20,709
Physicians.	13,765	14,387	15,686	17,078	19,321	1,875	2,346	3,408	4,018	4,952
Dental	4,652	4,672	4,214	4,552	5,209	462	458	498	593	710
Other practitioner	3,234	3,357	3,555	3,873	4,282	198	251	317	372	437
Outpatient hospital	9,705	10,072	11,344	12,370	14,137	1,101	1,789	2,837	3,324	4,283
Clinic	1,531	2,121	2,391	2,804	3,511	320	714	1,249	1,688	2,211
Laboratory [5]	3,212	6,354	7,759	8,959	10,505	121	337	590	721	897
Home health	392	535	609	719	813	332	1,120	2,572	3,404	4,101
Prescribed drugs	13,707	13,921	15,916	17,294	19,602	1,318	2,315	3,689	4,420	5,424
Family planning	1,129	1,636	1,564	1,752	2,185	81	195	227	265	359

[1] Recipient data do not add due to small number of recipients that are reported in more than one category. Includes recipients of, and payments for other care not shown separately.   [2] Permanently and totally.   [3] Aid to families with dependent children.   [4] Nursing facility services includes skilled nursing facility services and intermediate care facility services for all other than the mentally retarded.   [5] Includes radiological services.

Source: U.S. Health Care Financing Administration, Health Care Financing Review, quarterly.

No. 163. Consumer Price Indexes of Medical Care Prices: 1970 to 1992

[1982-1984=100. Indexes are annual averages of monthly data based on components of consumer price index for all urban consumers; for explanation, see text, section 15. See *Historical Statistics, Colonial Times to 1970*, series B 262-272 for similar data]

YEAR	Medical care	MEDICAL CARE SERVICES					Medical care commodities [2]	ANNUAL PERCENT CHANGE [3]					
		Total [1]	Professional services			Hospital room		Medical care [1]	Medical care services				Medical care commodities [2]
			Total [1]	Physicians	Dental				Total [1]	Physicians	Dental	Hospital room	
1970	34.0	32.3	37.0	34.5	39.2	23.6	46.5	6.6	7.0	7.5	5.7	12.9	2.4
1975	47.5	46.6	50.8	48.1	53.2	38.3	53.3	12.0	12.6	12.1	10.4	17.1	8.3
1978	61.8	61.2	64.5	63.4	65.1	54.0	64.4	8.4	8.5	8.4	7.1	11.1	7.0
1979	67.5	67.2	70.1	69.2	70.5	60.1	69.0	9.2	9.8	9.1	8.3	11.3	7.1
1980	74.9	74.8	77.9	76.5	78.9	68.0	75.4	11.0	11.3	10.5	11.9	13.1	9.3
1981	82.9	82.8	85.9	84.9	86.5	78.1	83.7	10.7	10.7	11.0	9.6	14.9	11.0
1982	92.5	92.6	93.2	92.9	93.1	90.4	92.3	11.6	11.8	9.4	7.6	15.7	10.3
1983	100.6	100.7	99.8	100.1	99.4	100.6	100.2	8.8	8.7	7.8	6.8	11.3	8.6
1984	106.8	106.7	107.0	107.0	107.5	109.0	107.5	6.2	6.0	6.9	8.1	8.3	7.3
1985	113.5	113.2	113.5	113.3	114.2	115.4	115.2	6.3	6.1	5.9	6.2	5.9	7.2
1986	122.0	121.9	120.8	121.5	120.6	122.3	122.8	7.5	7.7	7.2	5.6	6.0	6.6
1987	130.1	130.0	128.8	130.4	128.8	131.1	131.0	6.6	6.6	7.3	6.8	7.2	6.7
1988	138.6	138.3	137.5	139.8	137.5	143.3	139.9	6.5	6.4	7.2	6.8	9.3	6.8
1989	149.3	148.9	146.4	150.1	146.1	158.1	150.8	7.7	7.7	7.4	6.3	10.3	7.8
1990	162.8	162.7	156.1	160.8	155.8	175.4	163.4	9.0	9.3	7.1	6.6	10.9	8.4
1991	177.0	177.1	165.7	170.5	167.4	191.9	176.8	8.7	8.9	6.0	7.4	9.4	8.2
1992	190.1	190.5	175.8	181.2	178.7	208.7	188.1	7.4	7.6	6.3	6.8	8.8	6.4

[1] Includes other services not shown separately.   [2] Prior to 1978, covers drugs and prescriptions only.   [3] Percent change from the immediate prior year.
Source: U.S. Bureau of Labor Statistics, *CPI Detailed Report*, January 1993, and unpublished data.

No. 164. Average Annual Expenditures per Consumer Unit for Health Care, 1984 to 1991, and by Selected Characteristics, 1991

[In dollars, except percent. See text, section 14, and headnote, table 708. For composition of regions, see table 31]

ITEM	HEALTH CARE, TOTAL		Health insurance	Medical services	Drugs and medical supplies[1]	PERCENT DISTRIBUTION			
	Amount	Percent of total expenditures				Health care, total	Health insurance	Medical services	Drugs and medical supplies
1984......................	1,049	4.8	370	454	225	100.0	35.3	43.3	21.4
1985......................	1,108	4.7	375	496	238	100.0	33.8	44.8	21.5
1986......................	1,135	4.8	371	502	261	100.0	32.7	44.2	23.0
1987......................	1,135	4.6	392	467	276	100.0	34.5	41.1	24.3
1988......................	1,298	5.0	474	529	294	100.0	36.5	40.8	22.7
1989......................	1,407	5.1	537	542	327	100.0	38.2	38.5	23.2
1990......................	1,480	5.2	581	562	337	100.0	39.3	38.0	22.8
1991	**1,554**	**5.2**	**656**	**555**	**344**	**100.0**	**42.2**	**35.7**	**22.1**
Age of reference person:									
Under 25 years old..........	360	2.1	144	131	86	100.0	40.0	36.4	23.9
25 to 34 years old	1,030	3.5	417	417	196	100.0	40.5	40.5	19.0
35 to 44 years old	1,487	4.1	583	630	275	100.0	39.2	42.4	18.5
45 to 54 years old	1,727	4.5	633	706	388	100.0	36.7	40.9	22.5
55 to 64 years old	1,846	5.8	749	672	427	100.0	40.6	36.4	23.1
65 to 74 years old	2,300	10.2	1,081	671	549	100.0	47.0	29.2	23.9
75 years old and over........	2,197	13.9	1,152	455	591	100.0	52.4	20.7	26.9
Region of residence:									
Northeast..................	1,504	4.8	669	528	307	100.0	44.5	35.1	20.4
Midwest	1,482	5.4	631	521	330	100.0	42.6	35.2	22.3
South.....................	1,669	5.9	697	581	391	100.0	41.8	34.8	23.4
West	1,506	4.5	607	580	319	100.0	40.3	38.5	21.2
Size of consumer unit:									
One person................	1,014	5.8	453	332	230	100.0	44.7	32.7	22.7
Two or more persons	1,761	5.1	734	640	387	100.0	41.7	36.3	22.0
Two persons	1,862	6.1	801	595	466	100.0	43.0	32.0	25.0
Three persons	1,759	5.1	763	657	339	100.0	43.4	37.4	19.3
Four persons	1,705	4.4	666	712	327	100.0	39.1	41.8	19.2
Five persons or more........	1,546	4.0	583	648	314	100.0	37.7	41.9	20.3
Income before taxes:									
Complete income reporters [2]	1,563	5.1	652	561	349	100.0	41.7	35.9	22.3
Quintiles of income:									
Lowest 20 percent........	1,041	7.7	459	309	273	100.0	44.1	29.7	26.2
Second 20 percent........	1,371	7.2	606	409	356	100.0	44.2	29.8	26.0
Third 20 percent	1,580	6.0	688	547	344	100.0	43.5	34.6	21.8
Fourth 20 percent	1,672	4.6	719	605	348	100.0	43.0	36.2	20.8
Highest 20 percent........	2,149	3.7	788	935	426	100.0	36.7	43.5	19.8
Incomplete reporters of income ..	1,503	6.0	679	515	308	100.0	45.2	34.3	20.5

[1] Includes prescription and nonprescription drugs.   [2] A complete reporter is a consumer unit providing values for at least one of the major sources of income.
Source: Bureau of Labor Statistics, *Consumer Expenditure Survey*, annual.

No. 165. Health Insurance Coverage Status, by Selected Characteristics: 1985 to 1991

[Data represents monthly averages for **first quarter**. Government health insurance includes Medicare, Medicaid, and military plans. Based on Survey of Income and Program Participation; see text, section 14]

CHARACTERISTIC	NUMBER (mil.)						PERCENT				
	Total	Covered by private or Government health insurance				Not covered by health insurance	Total	Covered by private or Government health insurance			Not covered by health insurance
		Total [1]	Private insurance		Covered by Medicaid			Total [1]	Private	Covered by Medicaid	
			Total	Related to employment [2]							
1985 [3]	234.0	199.4	174.6	141.3	16.1	34.6	100.0	85.2	74.6	6.9	14.8
1986	236.7	202.6	177.5	144.1	16.7	34.2	100.0	85.6	75.0	7.1	14.4
1987	238.9	206.0	180.6	146.3	18.0	32.9	100.0	86.2	75.6	7.5	13.8
1988	241.4	210.6	186.6	150.4	17.7	30.8	100.0	87.2	77.3	7.4	12.8
1989	243.6	212.0	187.2	151.8	17.7	31.7	100.0	87.0	76.8	7.3	13.0
1990	246.2	212.6	186.2	150.5	18.5	33.6	100.0	86.4	75.6	7.5	13.6
1991, total [4]	249.0	215.5	186.9	150.5	21.3	33.5	100.0	86.6	75.1	8.6	13.5
Male	121.2	103.1	91.0	75.4	8.2	18.1	100.0	85.1	75.1	6.8	14.9
Female	127.7	112.4	95.9	75.1	13.1	15.4	100.0	88.0	75.1	10.3	12.1
White	208.5	182.5	164.0	131.8	12.7	26.0	100.0	87.5	78.7	6.1	12.5
Black	31.0	25.2	16.8	13.9	7.4	5.7	100.0	81.5	54.2	23.9	18.4
Hispanic origin [5]	21.4	15.2	10.9	9.2	3.8	6.2	100.0	71.0	50.9	17.8	29.0
Under 16 years	58.7	50.5	40.7	33.9	9.7	8.2	100.0	86.0	69.3	16.5	14.0
16 to 24 years	31.6	24.8	22.0	17.0	2.7	6.8	100.0	78.6	69.6	8.5	21.5
25 to 34 years	43.0	35.2	31.5	28.4	3.1	7.9	100.0	81.7	73.3	7.0	18.4
35 to 44 years	38.6	33.4	31.1	28.2	1.6	5.2	100.0	86.6	80.6	4.1	13.5
45 to 54 years	25.8	22.8	21.3	18.7	0.9	3.0	100.0	88.3	82.6	3.5	11.6
55 to 64 years	21.1	18.8	17.0	13.8	1.0	2.3	100.0	89.1	80.6	4.7	10.9
65 years and over	30.2	30.0	23.3	10.5	2.4	0.1	100.0	99.5	77.2	7.9	0.3

[1] Includes other Government insurance not shown separately. [2] Related to current or prior employment of self or other family members. [3] Revised since originally published. [4] Includes other races not shown separately. [5] Persons of Hispanic origin may be of any race.
Source: U.S. Bureau of the Census, *Current Population Reports*, P70-29; and unpublished data.

No.166. Health Insurance Coverage, by Selected Characteristic: 1987-89

[Data represent persons covered by Government or private health insurance coverage during a 28-month period, beginning October 1986. Based on Survey of Income and Program Participation. See text, section 14. For composition of regions, see table 31]

CHARACTERISTIC	All persons (mil.)	COVERED BY INSURANCE (mil.)						PERCENT COVERED BY INSURANCE			
		Government or private			Private			Government or private			Private for entire period
		For entire period	For part of the period	No coverage	For entire period	For part of the period	No coverage	For entire period	For part of the period	No coverage	
Total	231.0	169.8	52.1	9.1	146.8	58.5	25.7	73.5	22.6	3.9	63.6
Under 18 years old	63.3	42.7	17.7	3.0	36.3	17.1	9.9	67.4	28.0	4.7	57.3
Under 6 years old	22.4	14.8	6.6	0.9	12.1	6.4	3.8	66.3	29.5	4.2	54.1
18 to 21 years old	13.6	6.6	6.2	0.8	6.1	6.0	1.5	48.9	45.6	5.6	44.6
22 to 24 years old	11.5	5.9	5.1	0.5	5.4	5.2	0.9	51.3	44.3	4.6	46.6
25 to 34 years old	41.4	28.9	10.8	1.7	26.8	10.9	3.7	69.8	26.1	4.1	64.6
35 to 44 years old	33.0	25.3	6.2	1.4	24.0	6.3	2.7	76.9	18.8	4.3	72.8
45 to 64 years old	43.5	35.8	6.0	1.7	32.7	6.9	3.9	82.4	13.8	3.9	75.2
65 years old and over	24.7	24.5	0.2	0.2	15.7	5.9	3.1	99.3	0.1	0.1	63.6
Male	111.5	80.2	26.6	4.7	71.0	28.5	12.0	71.9	23.9	4.2	63.7
Female	119.5	89.6	25.6	4.3	75.8	30.0	13.7	75.0	21.4	3.6	63.5
White	195.6	148.2	40.2	7.2	132.6	45.8	17.2	75.8	20.6	3.7	67.8
Black	27.8	16.7	9.7	1.4	10.5	10.2	7.1	60.2	34.9	4.9	37.8
Hispanic [1]	17.4	9.3	6.2	1.9	7.0	5.8	4.6	53.6	35.6	10.7	40.2
Residence:											
Northeast	45.2	36.2	8.2	0.8	31.5	9.6	4.0	80.2	18.1	1.8	69.8
Midwest	60.7	47.8	11.5	1.4	42.6	13.0	5.1	78.8	18.9	2.3	70.1
South	77.4	52.7	20.0	4.7	44.8	22.1	10.6	68.1	25.8	6.0	57.9
West	47.7	33.0	12.5	2.2	28.0	13.7	6.0	69.2	26.2	4.6	58.6
Educational attainment: [2]											
Less than 12 years	37.6	27.3	7.9	2.3	18.1	11.3	8.2	72.8	21.0	6.2	48.1
12 to 15 years	96.3	72.1	21.0	3.2	65.9	23.8	6.6	74.9	21.8	3.3	68.4
16 years or more	30.4	26.0	3.9	0.5	25.1	4.6	0.7	85.5	12.8	1.5	82.6
Work-status: [3] Worked entire 28 months—											
Full time	57.2	49.0	7.0	1.2	48.6	7.2	1.4	85.7	12.2	2.1	85.0
Part time	5.6	4.1	1.1	0.4	4.0	1.1	0.5	72.7	19.6	7.0	70.3
Had at least one work interruption	59.7	34.3	22.2	3.2	31.6	22.5	5.6	57.4	37.2	5.4	52.9

[1] Persons of Hispanic origin may be of any race. [2] For persons 19 years old and over. [3] For wage and salary workers.
Source: U.S. Bureau of the Census, *Current Population Reports*, P70-29; and unpublished data.

No. 167. Persons Without Health Insurance Coverage, by Selected Characteristic: 1989

[In percent, except as indicated. Annual average of monthly figures. Based on Current Population Survey; see text, section 1 and Appendix III]

CHARACTERISTIC	Total	UNDER 65 YEARS OLD					65 years and over
		Total	Under 18 years	18 to 24 years	25 to 44 years	45 to 64 years	
All persons (1,000).............	243,532	214,313	64,003	25,401	78,795	46,114	29,219
Persons not covered [1]	13.9	15.7	14.9	27.4	15.5	10.5	1.2
SEX							
Male..........................	15.1	16.7	15.1	31.3	17.6	9.6	1.3
Female........................	12.7	14.6	14.7	23.7	13.6	11.2	1.2
RACE							
White.........................	12.8	14.5	14.0	26.3	14.4	9.4	1.0
Black.........................	20.2	21.9	18.9	34.3	22.5	17.5	2.5
Other.........................	19.7	20.4	18.9	27.8	20.7	17.5	8.4
EDUCATION [2]							
Less than 12 years............	20.8	30.1	(X)	42.1	35.5	19.9	1.5
12 years......................	14.4	16.6	(X)	29.8	16.8	8.5	0.7
More than 12 years	8.4	9.2	(X)	16.0	9.0	5.8	1.3
EMPLOYMENT STATUS [2]							
Currently employed............	13.9	14.3	(X)	26.6	13.6	9.0	1.5
Unemployed...................	38.3	39.2	(X)	44.5	40.8	26.5	(X)
Not in labor force.............	10.8	18.5	(X)	26.0	21.2	12.8	1.2
FAMILY INCOME							
Less than $5,000	27.1	31.3	25.5	27.3	42.4	35.5	1.5
$5,000 to $9,999	27.7	36.9	31.6	43.5	43.5	32.2	1.6
$10,000 to $19,999	24.3	30.1	30.2	37.5	32.0	21.3	1.1
$20,000 to $34,999	10.6	11.6	10.9	22.1	11.8	6.8	1.0
$35,000 to $49,999	5.8	6.0	4.0	18.4	5.8	3.9	0.8
$50,000 or more	3.6	3.7	2.3	12.9	3.7	1.9	1.6

X Not applicable. [1] Excludes 9.7 million persons for whom insurance coverage was unknown. Includes persons whose demographic coverage was unknown. [2] Excludes persons under 18 years old.

Source: U.S. National Center for Health Statistics, *Advance Data from Vital and Health Statistics*, No. 201, June 18, 1991.

No. 168. Health Maintenance Organizations (HMO)—Number Enrollment, by Type and Size of Organization: 1976 to 1992

[As of June 30, except as noted. Under the Health Maintenance Organization Act, an HMO must have four characteristics: (1) an organized system for providing health care in a geographic area, for which the HMO is responsible for providing or otherwise assuring its delivery; (2) an agreed upon set of basic and supplemental health maintenance and treatment services; (3) a voluntarily enrolled group of people; and (4) community rating. A group HMO contracts with one or more medical groups to provide services to members and generally provides all services except hospital care under one roof. Data for group model HMO's include staff model HMO's (a model in which the HMO hires its own physicians) and network HMO's (an HMO that provides comprehensive health services to members in two or more distinct geographic areas. Individual practice association (IPA) HMO contracts with a physician organization that in turn contracts with individual physicians. IPA physicians provide care to HMO members from their private offices and continue to see their fee-for-service patients. An open-ended product line allows enrollees to receive services from health care providers outside the HMO network for additional out-of-pocket fee (typically a deductible and coinsurance are imposed)]

TYPE OF PRACTICE AND SIZE	1976	1980	1985	1986	1987	1988	1989 (Jan.1)	1990 (July 1)	1991 (Jan.1)	1992 (July 1)
NUMBER OF PLANS										
Total	175	236	393	595	662	643	607	[1]556	[1]556	[1]556
Group	134	139	212	250	245	231	220	206	208	217
I.P.A	41	97	181	345	417	412	387	350	348	339
Less than 15,000 members ..	128	144	171	315	325	271	229	179	171	158
15,000-24,999 members	15	36	56	63	86	98	102	94	107	99
25,000-49,999 members	12	28	79	107	100	114	112	125	121	132
50,000-99,999 members	7	15	51	67	89	86	89	72	72	73
100,000 members or more...	10	13	36	47	62	74	74	84	85	94
ENROLLMENT (1,000)										
Total	6,016	9,100	18,894	23,664	28,587	[2]31,366	[2]31,940	[2]33,622	[2]34,072	[2]37,199
Group	5,627	7,406	14,247	15,210	17,261	17,883	18,371	19,743	20,415	22,076
I.P.A	390	1,694	4,646	8,454	11,326	13,483	13,569	13,879	13,657	15,123
Less than 15,000 members ..	620	870	1,020	1,514	1,797	1,794	1,591	1,317	1,242	1,176
15,000-24,999 members	297	732	1,101	1,220	1,681	1,933	2,044	1,793	2,064	1,944
25,000-49,999 members	365	907	2,813	3,791	3,564	4,011	3,927	4,249	4,188	4,332
50,000-99,999 members	525	976	3,315	4,828	6,343	6,041	6,274	5,121	5,132	5,197
100,000 members or more...	4,210	5,615	10,646	12,311	15,202	17,587	18,104	21,142	21,446	24,550
HMO's WITH OPEN-ENDED PRODUCT LINE										
Number of plans	(X)	(X)	(X)	(X)	(X)	48	70	96	116	178
Enrollment (1,000)	(X)	(X)	(X)	(X)	(X)	482	617	1,041	1,191	1,643

X Not applicable. [1] Includes HMO's containing only open-ended members, not distributed by enrollment size. [2] Excludes enrollees participating in open-ended plans.

Source: InterStudy, Excelsior, MN, *The InterStudy Competitive Edge*, 1992, vol. 2, No. 2, and earlier publications (copyright); and Group Health Association of America, Inc., Washington, DC, releases.

No. 169. Children—Health Insurance and Medical Care: 1988

[Based on the National Health Interview Survey; see Appendix III]

CHARACTERISTIC	Total	AGE GROUP					
		Under 1 year	1 to 4 years	5 to 7 years	8 to 11 years	12 to 14 years	15 to 17 years
All children (1,000) [1]	63,569	3,850	14,536	11,037	13,635	9,872	10,639
PERCENT COVERED BY HEALTH INSURANCE							
All children	83.1	80.1	83.7	83.3	83.8	83.0	82.3
Sex: Male	83.5	80.4	83.5	83.7	83.8	84.3	83.1
Female	82.7	79.7	84.0	83.0	83.8	81.4	81.3
Race: White	83.7	80.7	84.4	84.3	83.6	83.7	83.5
Black	80.9	81.2	80.5	79.7	84.1	81.7	77.6
Hispanic origin: Hispanic	70.0	62.2	75.2	76.3	65.0	68.1	68.3
Non-Hispanic	84.9	82.8	85.2	84.3	86.3	85.1	83.8
Family income: Under $10,000	71.8	74.0	75.3	73.9	71.0	69.7	64.4
$10,000 to $24,999	76.1	75.1	76.9	78.2	75.3	73.5	76.6
$25,000 to $39,999	89.8	85.6	90.5	89.4	92.1	90.2	87.4
$40,000 or more	92.4	93.3	93.2	91.7	92.0	93.2	91.6
PERCENT WHO VISITED A DOCTOR FOR HEALTH CARE [2]							
All children	63.9	93.8	81.5	66.0	49.6	54.8	53.9
Sex: Male	64.1	94.4	81.3	65.9	49.4	57.6	52.5
Female	63.7	93.1	81.7	66.0	49.9	51.6	55.3
Race: White	63.7	95.1	81.4	65.7	47.9	56.0	54.0
Black	65.0	87.6	82.6	66.6	55.7	51.7	55.7
Hispanic origin: Hispanic	63.4	93.5	82.3	70.4	49.5	51.9	45.5
Non-Hispanic	63.6	93.5	81.1	65.2	49.5	55.0	54.8
Family income: Under $10,000	62.9	87.4	78.9	65.6	49.5	53.5	45.9
$10,000 to $24,999	61.6	96.1	80.4	62.8	43.7	47.9	52.6
$25,000 to $39,999	64.3	94.9	82.5	67.7	47.1	54.3	56.9
$40,000 or more	68.0	97.2	85.8	70.0	56.3	62.5	58.4
Covered by health insurance	66.8	96.1	83.4	68.6	52.6	58.6	57.7
Not covered by health insurance	56.9	91.8	79.3	58.9	39.0	42.1	44.3

[1] Includes other races and unknown income. [2] For routine health care within the past year.
Source: U.S. National Center for Health Statistics, *Advance Data from Vital and Health Statistics*, No. 188, October 1, 1990.

No. 170. Employment in the Health Insurance and Health Service Industries: 1980 to 1992

[See headnote table 662]

1987 SIC Code [1]	INDUSTRY	1980	1985	1988	1989	1990	1991	1992
(X)	Total, nonfarm	90,406	97,519	105,536	108,329	109,782	108,310	108,437
(X)	Service producing [2]	64,748	72,660	80,363	83,007	84,822	84,480	85,017
(I)	Services [3]	17,890	21,999	25,669	27,120	28,103	28,323	28,903
632,80	Health insurance and health services	5,420	6,470	7,338	7,713	8,073	8,434	8,726
632	Health insurance	142	171	217	229	242	257	262
80	Health services [3]	5,278	6,299	7,121	7,484	7,831	8,177	8,464
801	Offices and clinics of MD's	802	1,030	1,204	1,274	1,343	1,398	1,441
802	Offices and clinics of dentist's	(NA)	440	485	501	514	527	538
804	Offices and clinics of other practitioners	96	166	222	249	278	301	310
805	Nursing and personal care facilities	997	1,199	1,314	1,361	1,419	1,499	1,556
8051	Skilled nursing care facilities	(NA)	792	909	940	992	1,072	1,114
8052	Intermediate care facilities	(NA)	(NA)	204	194	200	211	219
8059	Other, n.e.c. [4]	(NA)	(NA)	201	228	228	215	223
806	Hospitals	2,750	2,997	3,295	3,440	3,550	3,657	3,756
8062	General medical and surgical hospitals	(NA)	2,812	3,048	3,175	3,269	3,361	3,455
8063	Psychiatric hospitals	(NA)	60	92	100	105	105	100
8069	Specialty hospitals, exc. psychiatric	(NA)	126	155	166	176	190	201
807	Medical and dental laboratories	105	119	147	159	167	172	178
808	Home health care services	(NA)	152	217	246	292	342	386

NA Not available. X Not applicable. [1] Based on the 1987 Standard Industrial Classification code; see text, section 13.
[2] Includes transportation and public utilities, wholesale and retail trade, finance and real estate, and government, and other types of insurance not shown separately. [3] Includes other industries not shown separately. [4] N.e.c. means not elsewhere classified.

Source: U.S. Bureau of Labor Statistics, Bulletin 2370, *Supplement to Employment and Earnings*, August 1992; and *Employment and Earnings*, monthly.

No. 171. Physicians, by Selected Activity: 1970 to 1990

[In thousands. Through 1986, as of Dec. 31; thereafter as of Jan. 1., except as noted. Includes Puerto Rico and outlying areas. See also *Historical Statistics, Colonial Times to 1970*, series B 275-280]

ACTIVITY	1970	1975	1980	1985	1986	1988	1989	1990
Doctors of medicine, total	**334.0**	**393.7**	**467.7**	**552.7**	**569.2**	**585.6**	**600.8**	**615.4**
Professionally active	310.8	340.3	414.9	497.1	505.8	521.3	536.8	547.3
Place of medical education:								
U.S. medical graduates	256.4	(NA)	333.3	392.0	398.3	410.3	423.2	432.9
Foreign medical graduates [1]	54.4	(NA)	81.6	105.1	107.4	111.0	113.6	114.4
Sex: Male	289.5	313.1	370.2	425.3	429.0	(NA)	(NA)	454.0
Female	21.4	27.2	44.7	71.9	76.8	(NA)	(NA)	93.3
Active Non-Federal	281.3	312.1	397.1	475.6	483.8	499.6	516.4	526.8
Patient care.	255.0	287.8	361.9	431.5	436.9	453.2	468.9	479.5
Office-based practice	188.9	213.3	271.3	329.0	325.8	337.5	350.1	359.9
General and family practice	50.8	46.3	47.8	53.9	53.6	55.1	56.3	57.6
Cardiovascular diseases	3.9	5.0	6.7	9.1	9.4	9.9	10.2	10.7
Dermatology	2.9	3.4	4.4	5.3	5.4	5.5	5.7	6.0
Gastroenterology	1.1	1.7	2.7	4.1	4.4	4.8	4.9	5.2
Internal medicine	23.0	28.2	40.5	52.7	52.3	55.5	56.9	57.8
Pediatrics	10.3	12.7	17.4	22.4	22.5	23.4	24.7	26.5
Pulmonary diseases	0.8	1.2	2.0	3.0	3.2	3.5	3.6	3.7
General surgery	18.1	19.7	22.4	24.7	23.5	23.7	24.7	24.5
Obstetrics and gynecology	13.8	15.6	19.5	23.5	23.6	24.3	25.2	25.5
Ophthalmology	7.6	8.8	10.6	12.2	12.1	12.5	12.8	13.1
Orthopedic surgery	6.5	8.1	10.7	13.0	13.1	13.5	14.1	14.2
Otolaryngology.	3.9	4.3	5.3	5.8	5.8	6.0	6.2	6.4
Plastic surgery	1.2	1.7	2.4	3.3	3.4	3.5	3.6	3.8
Urological surgery	4.3	5.0	6.2	7.1	7.0	7.2	7.3	7.4
Anesthesiology	7.4	9.0	11.3	15.3	15.3	16.0	16.7	17.8
Diagnostic radiology	0.9	2.0	4.2	7.7	8.1	8.6	9.0	9.8
Emergency medicine.	(NA)	(NA)	(NA)	(NA)	7.3	7.6	8.0	8.4
Neurology	1.2	1.9	3.2	4.7	4.8	5.1	5.4	5.6
Pathology, anatomical/clinical . . .	3.0	4.2	6.0	6.9	6.5	6.7	7.0	7.3
Psychiatry	10.1	12.2	15.9	18.5	18.2	18.7	19.6	20.0
Radiology	5.8	7.0	7.8	7.4	6.1	6.1	6.2	6.1
Other specialty	12.4	15.3	24.1	28.5	20.2	20.3	21.7	22.8
Hospital-based practice	66.1	74.5	90.6	102.5	111.1	115.7	118.8	119.6
Residents and interns	45.8	53.5	59.6	72.2	77.6	79.5	80.0	81.7
Full-time hospital staff	20.3	21.0	31.0	30.3	33.5	36.2	38.8	38.0
Other professional activity [2]	26.3	24.3	35.2	44.0	46.9	46.4	47.5	47.3
Federal	29.5	28.2	17.8	21.6	21.9	21.7	20.4	20.5
Patient care.	23.5	24.1	14.6	17.3	17.0	16.9	15.6	15.6
Office-based practice	3.5	2.1	0.7	1.2	1.2	1.1	1.1	1.1
Hospital-based practice	20.0	22.0	13.9	16.1	15.8	15.8	14.4	14.6
Residents and interns	5.4	4.3	2.4	3.3	2.9	2.7	2.1	1.7
Full-time hospital staff	14.6	17.7	11.4	12.9	12.9	13.0	12.4	12.8
Other professional activity [2]	6.0	4.1	3.2	4.3	5.0	4.8	4.8	4.8
Inactive	19.6	21.4	25.7	38.6	46.8	48.0	48.8	52.7
Not classified	[3]0.4	26.1	20.6	14.0	13.7	13.4	12.4	12.7
Unknown address	3.2	5.9	6.4	3.0	2.9	2.9	2.8	2.8
Doctors of osteopathy [4]	**14.3**	**15.4**	**18.8**	**24.0**	**25.5**	**28.3**	**29.6**	**30.9**
Medical and osteopathic schools [5]	110	123	141	142	142	142	142	141
Students [5]	42.6	59.3	70.1	73.2	72.8	71.9	71.6	72.0
Graduates [5]	8.8	13.9	16.2	17.8	17.7	17.5	17.2	16.9

NA Not available. [1] Foreign medical graduates received their medical education in schools outside the United States and Canada. [2] Includes medical teaching, administration, research, clinical fellows, and other. [3] Not classified established in 1970; however, complete data not available until 1972. [4] As of July. Total DO's. For 1991 the number of total DO's is 32,300; for 1992, 33,500. Source: American Osteopathic Association, Chicago, IL. [5] Number of schools and students as of fall; graduates for academic year ending in year shown. Based on data from annual surveys conducted by the Association of American Medical Colleges and the American Association of Colleges of Osteopathic Medicine. Source: See table 172.

Source: Except as noted, American Medical Association, Chicago, IL, *Physician Characteristics and Distribution in the U.S.*, annual, (copyright).

No. 172. Dentists and Nurses: 1970 to 1990

[As of **end of year**, except as noted. Excludes Puerto Rico and outlying areas. See also *Historical Statistics, Colonial Times to 1970*, series B 281-290]

ITEM	Unit	1970	1975	1980	1984	1985	1986	1987	1988	1989	1990
Dentists, number [1]	**1,000** . . .	**116**	**127**	**141**	**153**	**156**	**158**	**161**	**164**	**168**	**186**
Active (exc. in Federal service) [2] . .	1,000 . . .	96	107	121	133	136	138	140	142	144	158
Rate per 100,000 population [3] . .	Rate . . .	47	50	53	56	57	57	58	58	58	63
Dental schools [4]	Number .	53	59	60	60	60	59	58	58	58	58
Students [4]	1,000 . . .	16.6	20.8	22.8	20.6	19.6	18.7	17.9	17.1	16.2	15.8
Graduates [4]	1,000 . . .	3.7	5.0	5.3	5.3	5.4	5.0	4.7	4.6	4.3	4.2
Nurses, number (active registered) .	**1,000** . . .	**750**	**961**	**1,273**	**1,486**	**1,538**	**1,590**	**1,627**	**1,648**	**1,679**	**1,715**
Rate per 100,000 population [3] . .	Rate . . .	368	446	560	629	644	659	668	670	676	690
Nursing programs [5]	Number .	1,343	1,360	1,385	1,477	1,473	1,469	1,465	1,442	1,457	1,470
Students [5]	1,000 . . .	165	250	231	237	218	194	183	185	201	221
Graduates [5]	1,000 . . .	44	75	76	80	82	77	71	65	62	66

[1] Beginning 1990, data collection methodology revised. [2] Source: American Dental Association, Bureau of Economic and Behavioral Research, Master Membership file and periodic censuses. [3] Based on Bureau of Census estimated resident population as of July 1. Estimates reflect revisions based on the 1990 Census of Population. [4] Number of schools and students as of fall; graduates for academic year ending in year shown. Based on data from the American Dental Association, Council on Dental Education, Annual Report on Dental Education. [5] Number of programs and students are as of October 15 and number of graduates are for academic year ending in year shown; from National League for Nursing, NLN Data Book, annual issues and State-Approved Schools of Nursing, RN, annual issues.

Source: U.S. Dept. of Health and Human Services, Health Resources and Services Administration, unpublished data. Prior to 1980, data were published by U.S. National Center for Health Statistics in *Health Resources Statistics*, annual.

No. 173. Active Non-Federal Physicians 1990, Dentists, 1992, and Nurses, 1991—States

[As of **Dec. 31, except as noted.** Excludes doctors of osteopathy, Federally employed persons, and physicians with addresses unknown. Includes all physicians not classified according to activity status]

REGION, DIVISION, AND STATE	PHYSICIANS, 1990 [1] Total	Rate[2]	DENTISTS, 1992 Total	Rate[2]	NURSES, 1991 Total (1,000)	Rate[2]
U.S. . .	532,638	216	155,058	61	1,758.5	702
North-						
east . . .	**141,690**	**280**	**38,919**	**76**	**443.7**	**872**
N.E . . .	**38,031**	**293**	**9,545**	**73**	**134.9**	**1,026**
ME . .	2,155	178	590	48	10.9	889
NH . .	2,199	200	673	61	10.3	934
VT . .	1,432	253	326	57	5.6	989
MA . .	19,910	337	4,765	80	70.6	1,180
RI . . .	2,515	254	556	56	9.7	971
CT . .	9,820	305	2,635	81	27.8	849
M.A. . . .	**103,659**	**275**	**29,374**	**78**	**308.8**	**819**
NY . .	56,395	315	14,859	82	148.6	825
NJ . .	18,971	246	6,418	83	54.6	706
PA . .	28,293	235	8,097	67	105.6	884
Midwest .	**114,273**	**190**	**36,215**	**60**	**461.6**	**768**
E.N.C. .	**81,124**	**192**	**26,010**	**61**	**314.3**	**742**
OH . .	21,379	196	6,090	55	85.2	780
IN. . .	8,764	157	2,798	49	40.9	730
IL. . .	24,680	212	8,066	70	85.9	746
MI . .	17,129	185	5,955	63	66.4	709
WI . .	9,172	189	3,101	62	35.9	725
W.N.C .	**33,149**	**186**	**10,205**	**57**	**147.3**	**830**
MN . .	9,574	220	2,913	65	35.9	810
IA . .	4,280	151	1,528	54	24.3	869
MO . .	10,100	196	2,756	53	41.6	809
ND . .	1,102	170	299	48	6.2	990
SD . .	992	140	308	44	6.4	919
NE . .	2,741	172	1,079	68	13.0	823
KS . .	4,360	175	1,322	53	19.9	806
South . . .	**162,914**	**192**	**44,681**	**51**	**514.3**	**598**
S.A . . .	**91,258**	**215**	**23,768**	**53**	**290.9**	**664**
DE . .	1,329	199	320	47	6.5	962
MD . .	15,484	334	3,669	75	35.7	741

REGION, DIVISION, AND STATE	PHYSICIANS, 1990 [1] Total	Rate[2]	DENTISTS, 1992 Total	Rate[2]	NURSES, 1991 Total (1,000)	Rate[2]
DC . .	3,674	615	750	129	10.5	1,788
VA . .	12,615	213	3,502	57	36.4	597
WV . .	3,086	166	867	48	11.8	655
NC . .	12,262	190	2,895	43	45.2	682
SC . .	5,541	161	1,521	43	17.2	491
GA . .	11,144	175	3,165	47	38.5	588
FL . .	26,123	208	7,079	53	89.1	677
E.S.C. . .	**25,740**	**168**	**7,675**	**50**	**87.1**	**571**
KY . .	6,202	168	2,113	57	18.6	505
TN . .	9,619	196	2,767	55	30.6	620
AL . .	6,464	158	1,776	43	24.9	612
MS . .	3,455	133	1,019	39	13.0	504
W.S.C. .	**45,916**	**171**	**13,238**	**48**	**136.3**	**506**
AR . .	3,595	150	989	41	13.5	571
LA . .	8,173	188	2,005	47	19.3	457
OK . .	4,697	147	1,556	49	15.7	499
TX . .	29,451	175	8,688	50	87.8	510
West . . .	**113,761**	**222**	**35,243**	**65**	**338.9**	**633**
Mt.	**24,690**	**184**	**8,026**	**56**	**89.8**	**645**
MT . .	1,263	158	468	57	5.4	671
ID . . .	1,259	125	567	53	5.8	560
WY . .	654	139	240	52	3.0	658
CO . .	6,894	211	2,451	71	24.1	722
NM . .	2,768	183	662	42	7.6	494
AZ . .	6,961	197	1,918	50	24.8	666
UT . .	3,145	185	1,167	65	9.1	516
NV . .	1,746	159	553	42	10.0	785
Pac. . . .	**89,071**	**235**	**27,217**	**68**	**249.1**	**629**
WA . .	10,006	213	3,179	63	39.4	795
OR . .	5,778	205	2,050	69	22.0	754
CA . .	70,062	244	20,751	68	179.0	595
AK . .	734	146	317	56	2.4	439
HI. . .	2,491	236	920	83	6.3	582

[1] As of January 1, 1990.   [2] Per 100,000 civilian population. Based on U.S. Bureau of the Census estimates as of July 1, 1989, for physicians, 1992 for dentists, and 1991 for nurses. Estimates for 1989 do not reflect revisions based on the 1990 Census of Population.

Source: Physicians: American Medical Association, Chicago, IL, *Physician Characteristics and Distribution in the U.S.,* annual (copyright); Dentists and nurses: U.S. Dept. of Health and Human Services, Health Resources and Services Administration, unpublished data. Dentists: Based on data supplied by American Dental Association, Bureau of Economic and Behavioral Research.

No. 174. Physician and Dental Contacts, by Patient Characteristics: 1970 to 1990

[See headnote, table 199. Based on National Health Interview Survey; see Appendix III]

TYPE OF VISIT AND YEAR	TOTAL VISITS (mil.) Sex Male	Female	Race [1] White	Black	VISITS PER PERSON PER YEAR Sex Male	Female	Race [1] White	Black	Age (years) Under 6	6 to 16	17 to 24	25 to 44	45 to 64	65 and over
Physicians: 1970. .	396	531	832	87	4.1	5.1	4.8	3.9	5.9	2.9	4.6	4.6	5.2	6.3
1980.	426	610	903	115	4.0	5.4	4.8	4.5	6.7	3.2	4.0	4.6	5.1	6.4
1983.	470	694	1,018	126	4.3	5.8	5.2	4.6	6.5	3.2	4.0	4.7	5.8	7.6
1985.	498	733	1,074	132	4.4	6.1	5.4	4.7	6.3	3.1	4.2	4.9	6.1	8.3
1986.	515	756	1,110	131	4.5	6.2	5.5	4.6	[2]6.3	[3]3.3	[4]4.2	4.7	6.6	9.1
1987.	523	765	1,118	140	4.5	6.2	5.5	4.9	[2]6.7	[3]3.3	[4]4.4	4.8	6.4	8.9
1988.	530	774	1,139	136	4.5	6.2	5.6	4.6	[2]7.0	[3]3.4	[4]3.8	5.1	6.1	8.7
1989.	552	771	1,148	140	4.7	6.1	5.6	4.7	[2]6.7	[3]3.5	[4]3.9	5.1	6.1	8.9
1990.	558	806	1,178	148	4.7	6.4	5.7	4.9	[2]6.9	[3]3.2	[4]4.3	5.1	6.4	9.2
Dentists: 1970 . . .	133	171	283	17	1.4	1.7	1.6	0.8	0.5	1.9	1.8	1.7	1.5	1.1
1980.	158	207	333	26	1.5	1.8	1.8	1.0	0.5	2.3	1.6	1.7	1.8	1.4
1983.	183	239	382	31	1.6	2.0	1.9	1.1	0.5	2.6	1.6	1.9	2.0	1.5
1986.	210	256	416	37	1.9	2.2	2.1	1.4	[2]0.7	[3]2.4	[4]1.7	2.0	2.2	2.1
1989.	221	271	441	34	1.9	2.2	2.2	1.2	[2]0.5	[3]2.4	[4]1.6	2.0	2.4	2.0

[1] See footnote 2, table 199.   [2] Under 5 years.   [3] 5 to 17 years.   [4] 18 to 24 years.

Source: U.S. National Center for Health Statistics, *Vital and Health Statistics,* series 10, No. 181; and unpublished data.

No. 175. Physician Contacts, by Place of Contact and Selected Patient Characteristic: 1990

[Based on the National Health Interview Survey; see Appendix III]

CHARACTERISTIC	NUMBER (1,000)					VISITS PER PERSON				
	All places [1]	Tele-phone	Office	Hos-pital [2]	Other	All places [1]	Tele-phone	Office	Hos-pital [2]	Other
All persons [3]	**1,363**	**164**	**808**	**182**	**199**	**5.5**	**0.7**	**3.3**	**0.7**	**0.8**
AGE										
Under 5 years	131	21	77	18	14	6.9	1.1	4.1	1.0	0.8
5-17 years	148	18	92	19	17	3.2	0.4	2.0	0.4	0.4
18-24 years.	108	11	60	18	19	4.3	0.5	2.4	0.7	0.8
25-44 years.	406	51	243	56	54	5.1	0.6	3.0	0.7	0.7
45-64 years.	297	36	177	41	39	6.4	0.8	3.8	0.9	0.8
65-74 years.	155	15	93	21	25	8.5	0.8	5.1	1.2	1.4
75 years and over	118	12	67	9	30	10.1	1.0	5.7	0.8	2.5
SEX										
Male	558	61	319	88	86	4.7	0.5	2.7	0.7	0.7
Female.	806	104	489	95	112	6.4	0.8	3.9	0.7	0.9
RACE										
White.	1,178	147	717	142	163	5.7	0.7	3.5	0.7	0.8
Black	148	13	72	35	29	4.9	0.4	2.4	1.1	0.9
INCOME										
Under $10,000.	163	16	80	30	37	6.7	0.6	3.3	1.2	1.5
$10,000-$19,999	248	29	136	40	41	6.2	0.7	3.4	1.0	1.0
$20,000-$34,999	282	35	169	39	37	5.3	0.7	3.2	0.7	0.7
$35,000 or more	478	67	304	48	55	5.4	0.8	3.4	0.5	0.6

[1] Includes unknown place of contact. [2] Excludes contacts while an overnight patient in a hospital. [3] Includes other races and unknown income.

Source: U.S. National Center for Health Statistics, *Vital and Health Statistics*, series 10, No. 181.

No. 176. Medical Practice Characteristics, by Selected Specialty: 1983 to 1990

[**Dollar figures in thousands.** Based on a sample telephone survey of 4,000 non-Federal office and hospital based patient care physicians, excluding residents, with a response rate of 69.1 percent in 1990. For details, see source. For definition of mean, see Guide to Tabular Presentation]

SPECIALTY	1983	1984	1985	1986	1987	1988	1989	1990
MEAN PATIENT VISITS PER WEEK								
All physicians [1]	123.4	118.1	117.1	117.7	119.3	121.1	121.6	120.9
General/Family practice	148.4	139.0	138.1	139.2	138.3	145.6	143.0	146.0
Internal medicine.	113.4	107.7	105.2	111.1	114.5	113.0	117.9	112.0
Surgery	111.9	110.0	108.2	105.8	107.8	105.0	107.7	107.6
Pediatrics.	137.4	128.7	130.8	131.9	127.4	135.1	138.1	134.0
Obstetrics/Gynecology.	118.2	115.7	112.0	114.8	112.7	118.9	115.6	120.0
MEAN HOURS IN PATIENT CARE PER WEEK								
All physicians [1]	51.8	51.5	51.3	52.2	52.9	53.1	53.3	53.3
General/Family practice	54.6	53.3	53.6	53.3	53.7	54.4	54.4	55.0
Internal medicine.	53.4	53.0	52.4	54.0	56.0	56.2	56.8	55.7
Surgery	50.7	51.5	51.2	52.6	53.0	53.8	53.3	53.1
Pediatrics.	52.3	51.1	50.6	52.4	53.6	52.5	53.4	52.4
Obstetrics/Gynecology.	55.8	55.7	56.9	59.0	57.0	59.4	59.0	60.4
MEAN NET INCOME								
All physicians [1]	104.1	108.4	112.2	119.5	132.3	144.7	155.8	164.5
General/Family practice	66.9	71.6	77.9	80.3	91.5	94.6	95.9	102.7
Internal medicine.	94.6	104.2	102.0	109.4	121.8	130.9	146.5	152.5
Surgery	144.3	151.0	155.0	162.4	187.9	207.5	220.5	236.4
Pediatrics.	70.8	73.7	76.2	81.8	85.3	94.9	104.7	106.5
Obstetrics/Gynecology.	118.1	118.8	124.3	135.9	163.2	180.7	194.3	207.3
MEAN PROFESSIONAL EXPENSES								
All physicians [1]	85.4	94.0	102.7	118.4	123.7	140.8	148.4	150.0
General/Family practice	79.4	89.2	96.5	119.9	121.2	122.3	128.5	134.5
Internal medicine.	88.5	89.7	90.0	110.5	117.8	136.3	139.1	139.2
Surgery	112.3	128.9	135.7	148.6	164.7	188.2	203.2	201.0
Pediatrics.	64.1	77.8	87.3	93.2	100.2	115.3	132.5	138.0
Obstetrics/Gynecology.	108.5	121.6	131.9	149.5	173.2	189.6	197.4	212.6
MEAN LIABILITY PREMIUM								
All physicians [1]	6.9	8.4	10.5	12.8	15.0	15.9	15.5	14.5
General/Family practice	4.2	4.6	6.8	7.3	8.9	9.4	9.0	7.8
Internal medicine.	4.5	4.9	5.8	7.1	8.4	9.0	8.2	9.2
Surgery	11.0	13.3	16.6	21.3	24.5	26.5	25.8	22.8
Pediatrics.	3.9	3.4	4.7	6.3	7.1	9.3	7.8	7.8
Obstetrics/Gynecology.	14.0	19.0	23.5	29.3	35.3	35.3	37.0	34.3

[1] Includes other specialties not shown separately.

Source: American Medical Association, Chicago IL, *Socioeconomic Characteristics of Medical Practice*, annual (copyright).

No. 177. Hospital Registered Nursing Personnel—Summary: 1991

[In percent, except as indicated. Based on a sample of 6,852 U.S. short term acute care hospitals registered and unregistered by the American Hospital Association, with a response rate of 33.6 percent. For details see source. For an explanation of mean, see Guide to Tabular Presentation]

CHARACTERISTIC	1991	CHARACTERISTIC	1991
Total full-time registered nurses per hospital (mean) [1] .	112.7	Registered nurse, full-time:	
		Lowest mean hourly wage paid.	13.3
LENGTH OF EMPLOYMENT AT HOSPITAL [2]		Highest mean hourly wage paid	18.7
		Mean hourly wage paid	16.1
Full-time: Less than 1 year	16.4		
1 year to less than 2 years	15.1	HOSPITAL STAFFING MECHANISMS [4]	
2 years to less than 5 years.	26.0		
5 years or more.	42.5	Per-diem	31.2
		Float-pool [5]	21.2
Part-time: Less than 1 year.	15.1	On-call	8.7
1 year to less than 2 years	14.3	Temporary nursing service	25.3
2 years to less than 5 years.	25.8	Other	13.6
5 years or more.	44.8		
		HOSPITAL POSITION SCHEDULES [6]	
EDUCATIONAL ATTAINMENT [3]			
		Days only	29.6
Associate degree in nursing	37.3	Evenings only.	17.3
Nursing diploma	27.9	Nights only.	17.1
Baccalaureate degree in nursing	30.8	Shifts: Day/evening	12.9
Master's degree in nursing or higher.	3.6	Day/night	8.4
		Evening/night	4.1
SALARY/WAGES (dol. per hr.) [2]		Rotate all	10.6
Full-time head nurse:		HOSPITAL BARGAINING STATUS	
Lowest mean annual salary paid	16.5		
Highest mean annual salary paid	21.3	Organized for the purpose of collective bargaining . . .	14.8

[1] Source: American Hospital Association, Chicago, IL, 1991 Human Resource Survey.   [2] Full-time: at least 35 hours worked per week. Part-time: less than 35 hours worked per week.   [3] Full time only.   [4] Percent of positions with each mechanism.   [5] In-house nursing staff personnel routinely assigned schedules who work different units in the institution according to the demands of variable patient volume and acuity levels.   [6] Percent of positions.

Source: Except as indicated, American Hospital Association, Chicago, IL, *Report of the Hospital Nursing Personnel Survey, 1991* (copyright).

No. 178. Hospitals and Nursing Homes—Summary Characteristics: 1971 to 1991

[Except as indicated, based on National Master Facility Inventory]

YEAR AND TYPE OF FACILITY	Total	FACILITIES UNDER—			FACILITIES WITH—			Residents [2] (1,000)	Full-time employees (1,000)
		Govt. control	Propri-etary control	Non-profit control	Less than 25 beds [1]	25-74 beds	75 or more beds		
1971: All facilities	29,682	4,178	18,091	7,413	8,902	10,959	9,821	2,262	3,007
Nursing homes [3]	22,004	1,368	17,049	3,587	8,266	8,259	5,479	1,076	568
Hospitals	7,678	2,810	1,042	3,826	636	2,700	4,342	1,186	2,439
1980: All facilities . . . . [3] [4] [5]	30,116	3,498	19,611	7,007	8,852	8,573	12,691	2,427	3,919
Nursing homes [3] [4] [5]	23,065	936	18,669	3,460	8,498	6,362	8,205	1,396	[6]798
Hospitals	7,051	2,562	942	3,547	354	2,211	4,486	1,031	3,121
1986: All facilities	32,600	3,275	21,399	7,926	9,903	8,755	13,942	2,427	(NA)
All hospitals [7]	6,954	2,230	1,176	3,548	290	2,150	4,514	874	3,241
General	5,956	1,871	829	3,256	259	1,849	3,848	690	2,871
Psychiatric	584	267	218	99	12	140	432	139	248
Chronic	44	30	4	10	-	6	38	13	21
Tuberculosis.	4	3	-	1	-	1	3	-	1
Nursing homes [3] [5]	25,646	1,045	20,223	4,378	9,613	6,605	9,428	1,553	(NA)
1990: All hospitals [7]	6,779	2,145	1,203	3,431	326	2,077	4,376	840	3,562
General	5,611	1,788	711	3,112	290	1,690	3,631	673	3,168
Psychiatric	734	272	350	112	17	211	506	128	262
Chronic	34	27	2	5	-	6	28	10	18
Tuberculosis.	4	3	-	1	-	1	3	-	1
1991: All hospitals [7]	6,738	2,119	1,221	3,398	308	2,066	4,364	823	3,663
General	5,535	1,762	688	3,085	272	1,645	3,618	661	3,276
Psychiatric	779	276	389	114	19	242	518	122	253
Chronic	30	24	2	4	-	5	25	10	17
Tuberculosis.	4	3	-	1	-	1	3	-	1

- Represents or rounds to zero.   NA Not available.   [1] For hospitals, minimum of six beds; for nursing homes, minimum of three beds.   [2] Number of residents as of date of interview.   [3] See footnote 1, table 191.   [4] Includes 1978 data for Alaska and South Dakota.   [5] Excludes hospital-based nursing homes; 1986 data based on the 1986 Inventory of Long-Term Care Places.   [6] Estimated.   [7] Includes types not shown separately. Based on data from the American Hospital Association. Data may not be strictly comparable with previous year data.

Source: U.S. National Center for Health Statistics, *Health Resources Statistics, 1971;* and unpublished data.

No. 179. Hospitals—Summary Characteristics, by Type of Service and Control: 1972 to 1991

[Covers hospitals accepted for registration by the American Hospital Association; see text, section 3. Short-term hospitals have an average patient stay of less than 30 days; long-term, an average stay of longer duration. Special hospitals include obstetrics and gynecology; eye, ear, nose, and throat; rehabilitation; orthopedic; and chronic and other special hospitals except psychiatric, tuberculosis, alcoholism, and chemical dependency. See also *Historical Statistics, Colonial Times to 1970*, series B 305-318, B 331-344, and B 413-422]

ITEM	1972	1980	1984	1985	1986	1987	1988	1989	1990	1991
Number:										
All hospitals	7,061	6,965	6,872	6,872	6,841	6,821	6,780	6,720	6,649	6,634
With 100 beds or more....	2,710	3,755	3,808	3,805	3,765	3,713	3,681	3,650	3,620	3,611
Non-Federal [1]	6,660	6,606	6,531	6,529	6,499	6,479	6,438	6,380	6,312	6,300
Community hospitals [2]	5,746	5,830	5,759	5,732	5,678	5,611	5,533	5,455	5,384	5,342
Nongovernmental nonprofit....	3,301	3,322	3,351	3,349	3,323	3,274	3,242	3,220	3,191	3,175
For profit	738	730	786	805	834	828	790	769	749	738
State and local government	1,707	1,778	1,622	1,578	1,521	1,509	1,501	1,466	1,444	1,429
Long-term general and special	216	157	131	128	133	131	129	138	131	126
Psychiatric	529	534	579	610	634	684	726	741	757	800
Tuberculosis	72	11	7	7	4	5	4	4	4	4
Federal	401	359	341	343	342	342	342	340	337	334
Beds (1,000):										
All hospitals [3]	1,550	1,365	1,339	1,309	1,283	1,261	1,241	1,224	1,211	1,197
Rate per 1,000 population [4]	7.4	6.0	5.7	5.5	5.3	5.2	5.1	5.0	4.9	4.7
Beds per hospital	220	196	195	190	188	185	183	182	182	180
Non-Federal [1]	1,407	1,248	1,226	1,197	1,172	1,152	1,138	1,124	1,113	1,101
Community hospitals [2]	879	988	1,017	1,001	978	958	944	933	928	924
Rate per 1,000 population [4]	4.2	4.3	4.3	4.2	4.1	4.0	3.9	3.8	3.7	3.7
Nongovernmental nonprofit....	617	692	716	707	689	673	666	660	657	656
For profit	57	87	100	104	106	106	103	103	102	100
State and local government	205	209	201	189	182	180	175	170	169	168
Long-term general and special	54	39	30	31	30	28	27	27	25	25
Psychiatric	457	215	175	169	165	165	163	160	158	150
Tuberculosis	13	2	1	1	(Z)	1	(Z)	(Z)	(Z)	(Z)
Federal	143	117	112	112	111	109	104	100	98	95
Occupancy rate: [5]										
All hospitals	78.0	77.7	72.5	69.5	68.8	69.2	69.6	69.7	69.7	69.1
Non-Federal [1]	78.0	77.4	71.9	68.9	68.3	68.7	69.1	69.3	69.4	68.8
Community hospitals [2]	75.4	75.6	69.0	64.8	64.3	64.9	65.7	66.2	66.7	66.1
Nongovernmental nonprofit....	77.5	78.2	71.4	67.2	66.8	67.6	68.4	68.8	69.3	68.6
For profit	68.7	65.2	57.0	52.2	50.9	51.0	51.0	51.6	52.6	52.5
State and local government	71.0	71.1	66.2	62.9	62.7	63.1	63.9	64.9	65.3	64.4
Long-term general and special	83.0	85.9	88.7	88.5	88.1	87.2	87.5	86.6	85.9	84.9
Psychiatric	82.8	85.2	86.3	87.0	86.8	86.4	86.3	84.6	82.5	82.4
Tuberculosis	61.2	67.0	63.4	64.1	59.0	64.1	67.2	69.3	66.4	76.6
Federal	80.0	80.1	79.0	76.3	74.2	74.2	74.4	73.7	73.3	72.8
Expenses (bil. dol.): [6]										
All hospitals	32.7	91.9	144.1	153.3	165.2	178.7	196.7	214.9	234.9	258.5
Non-Federal [1]	30.0	84.0	133.0	141.0	152.1	165.0	182.1	199.8	219.6	241.7
Community hospitals [2]	25.5	76.9	123.3	130.5	140.7	152.6	168.7	184.9	203.7	225.0
Nongovernmental nonprofit....	18.4	55.8	90.8	96.1	103.5	112.3	124.7	136.9	150.7	166.8
For profit	1.4	5.8	10.3	11.5	13.0	14.1	15.5	17.2	18.8	20.5
State and local government	5.7	15.2	22.3	22.9	24.1	26.2	28.5	30.8	34.2	37.7
Long-term general and special	0.7	1.2	1.7	1.9	2.0	2.2	2.3	2.5	2.7	2.9
Psychiatric	3.1	5.8	7.7	8.3	9.1	9.9	10.9	12.0	12.9	13.5
Tuberculosis	0.1	0.1	0.1	0.1	(Z)	(Z)	(Z)	(Z)	0.1	(Z)
Federal	3.1	7.9	11.2	12.3	13.1	13.7	14.6	15.1	15.2	16.8
Personnel (1,000): [7]										
All hospitals	2,671	3,492	3,630	3,625	3,647	3,742	3,840	3,937	4,063	4,165
Non-Federal [1]	2,439	3,213	3,339	3,326	3,351	3,445	3,545	3,648	3,760	3,864
Community hospitals [2]	2,051	2,873	3,017	2,997	3,025	3,114	3,205	3,303	3,420	3,535
Nongovernmental nonprofit....	1,473	2,086	2,222	2,216	2,241	2,298	2,373	2,454	2,533	2,624
For profit	105	189	214	221	229	242	249	261	273	281
State and local government	473	598	581	561	555	573	583	589	614	630
Long-term general and special	63	56	54	58	56	55	54	56	55	55
Psychiatric	307	275	260	263	263	269	281	284	280	269
Tuberculosis	12	3	2	2	1	1	1	1	1	1
Federal	232	279	290	299	296	297	295	288	303	301
Personnel per 100 patients: [7]										
All hospitals	221	329	374	398	413	429	445	462	482	504
Non-Federal [1]	223	333	379	403	419	435	451	468	487	510
Community hospitals [2]	309	380	430	462	481	501	517	535	552	579
Nongovernmental nonprofit....	308	385	434	466	487	505	521	540	557	582
For profit	269	334	375	408	423	448	471	493	510	537
State and local government	324	401	437	471	487	507	521	533	555	584
Long-term general and special	140	170	203	212	212	222	225	237	257	259
Psychiatric	81	150	172	180	183	189	200	209	215	217
Tuberculosis	150	290	342	378	365	308	303	289	405	277
Federal	204	297	327	351	360	367	383	390	424	434
Outpatient visits (mil.)	219.2	263.0	276.6	282.1	294.6	310.7	336.2	352.2	368.2	387.7
Emergency	60.1	82.0	78.5	80.1	82.1	83.5	86.6	89.9	92.8	93.5
Closures	(NA)	73	76	59	80	93	106	80	63	67

NA Not available. Z Less than 500 beds, $50 million, or 0.5 percent. [1] Short term (average length of stay less than 30 days) general and special (e.g., obstetrics and gynecology; eye, ear, nose and throat; rehabilitation etc. except psychiatric, tuberculosis, alcoholism and chemical dependency). Includes hospital units of institutions. [2] Excludes hospital units of institutions. [3] Beginning 1988, number of beds at end of reporting period; prior years, average number in 12 month period. [4] Based on Bureau of the Census estimated resident population as of July 1. Estimates reflect revisions based on the 1990 Census of Population. [5] Ratio of average daily census to every 100 beds. [6] Excludes new construction. [7] Includes full-time equivalents of part-time personnel.

Source: American Hospital Association, Chicago, IL, *Hospital Statistics*, annual (copyright).

No. 180. Hospital Facilities—States and Puerto Rico: 1991

[Short term hospitals have an average stay of less than 30 days. See also *Historical Statistics, Colonial Times to 1970*, series B 305-308 and B 359-362]

REGION, DIVISION AND STATE OR OTHER AREA	NUMBER OF HOSPITALS		BEDS (1,000)		PATIENTS ADMITTED (mil.)		AVERAGE DAILY CENSUS [2] (1,000)		OCCUPANCY RATE [3]		OUTPATIENT VISITS (mil.)		Person-nel [4] (1,000)
	Total	Com-muni-ity [1]	Total	Com-muni-ity [1]	Total	Com-muni-ity [1]	Total	Com-muni-ity [1]	Total	Com-muni-ity [1]	Total	Com-muni-ity [1]	
U.S.	6,634	5,342	1,196.8	923.9	33.6	31.1	827.1	611.0	69.1	66.1	387.7	322.0	4,164.9
Northeast . .	1,057	791	269.6	200.1	7.3	6.9	216.9	156.7	80.4	78.3	92.0	82.6	992.0
N.E	338	228	63.5	44.0	1.7	1.6	48.4	32.1	76.2	72.9	23.5	20.8	245.2
ME	45	38	6.0	4.6	0.2	0.1	4.4	3.2	72.9	70.0	2.3	2.1	21.8
NH	39	27	4.8	3.4	0.1	0.1	3.2	2.2	66.0	65.0	1.7	1.6	16.2
VT	18	15	2.3	1.8	0.1	0.1	1.7	1.2	72.5	68.3	0.8	0.7	8.0
MA	154	101	31.9	21.7	0.9	0.8	24.4	15.8	76.3	73.0	12.0	10.6	123.9
RI	19	12	4.3	3.1	0.1	0.1	3.5	2.4	80.7	78.9	1.6	1.3	18.6
CT	63	35	14.1	9.5	0.4	0.4	11.3	7.2	80.1	75.8	5.1	4.5	56.7
M.A	719	563	206.1	156.1	5.5	5.3	168.5	124.6	81.7	79.8	68.5	61.8	746.8
NY	298	231	102.0	75.2	2.5	2.3	88.2	63.8	86.5	84.8	34.2	30.3	370.7
NJ	120	96	37.8	29.4	1.2	1.1	30.5	23.4	80.7	79.6	10.4	9.5	131.7
PA	301	236	66.3	51.4	1.9	1.8	49.7	37.4	75.0	72.7	23.9	22.0	244.4
Midwest . . .	1,795	1,545	303.6	246.9	8.1	7.7	201.2	156.1	66.3	63.2	99.1	88.7	1,047.1
E.N.C	969	819	197.4	160.9	5.6	5.4	132.5	103.3	67.1	64.2	72.2	66.4	719.9
OH	228	193	51.3	42.8	1.5	1.5	33.8	27.0	65.9	63.0	18.9	17.6	193.4
IN	134	113	26.0	21.6	0.7	0.7	16.5	13.0	63.6	60.1	9.3	8.8	92.7
IL	249	209	57.1	45.1	1.6	1.5	39.5	29.9	69.2	66.3	19.2	17.0	204.2
MI	205	175	39.5	32.9	1.1	1.1	26.7	21.6	67.7	65.4	17.6	16.4	155.9
WI	153	129	23.5	18.5	0.6	0.6	15.9	11.9	67.7	64.3	7.3	6.5	73.7
W.N.C	826	726	106.2	85.9	2.5	2.3	68.8	52.8	64.8	61.5	26.9	22.3	327.2
MN	162	148	23.9	19.1	0.6	0.5	16.7	12.9	69.6	67.7	5.2	4.7	66.5
IA	133	123	17.0	14.1	0.4	0.4	10.9	8.5	64.2	60.2	4.9	4.7	51.1
MO	157	133	29.0	24.1	0.8	0.7	18.6	14.7	64.1	60.9	8.1	6.8	105.9
ND	55	47	5.2	4.4	0.1	0.1	3.3	2.8	64.9	64.1	1.0	0.6	13.8
SD	64	52	5.5	4.3	0.1	0.1	3.4	2.6	62.4	61.9	1.3	0.8	14.6
NE	101	90	10.3	8.4	0.2	0.2	6.3	4.8	60.9	57.3	2.3	1.7	29.8
KS	154	133	15.4	11.4	0.3	0.3	9.6	6.4	62.6	55.9	4.1	3.0	45.5
South	2,526	2,020	431.4	331.2	12.1	11.0	283.3	207.5	65.7	62.6	115.8	88.0	1,429.7
S.A	1,057	801	212.6	158.7	6.0	5.5	147.4	105.8	69.3	66.6	59.9	45.4	731.0
DE	13	8	2.8	2.1	0.1	0.1	2.2	1.6	78.1	74.8	1.2	1.0	12.2
MD	81	51	19.9	13.3	0.6	0.6	15.2	10.1	76.3	75.6	6.1	4.4	76.5
DC	17	11	7.5	4.3	0.2	0.2	6.1	3.3	81.0	76.6	2.1	1.1	29.1
VA	136	98	29.1	20.2	0.8	0.7	20.7	13.3	71.1	65.8	8.7	6.6	94.7
WV	67	59	10.4	8.3	0.3	0.3	6.9	5.3	66.2	63.7	3.3	3.0	32.2
NC	155	117	30.0	22.0	0.9	0.8	22.2	15.9	73.9	72.3	8.7	6.6	109.3
SC	89	68	14.6	11.4	0.5	0.4	10.3	7.8	70.6	68.9	4.9	3.6	50.3
GA	203	162	35.4	26.6	1.0	0.9	24.2	17.3	68.3	65.2	9.1	7.0	114.3
FL	296	227	62.9	50.5	1.7	1.6	39.7	31.1	63.2	61.6	15.8	12.3	212.4
E.S.C	530	461	88.9	71.1	2.5	2.3	57.9	43.7	65.1	61.4	22.0	17.6	274.1
KY	124	107	19.1	15.9	0.6	0.5	12.3	10.0	64.7	62.6	6.0	4.7	62.0
TN	156	133	29.2	23.5	0.8	0.8	19.1	14.6	65.3	62.1	6.9	5.9	96.0
AL	137	119	23.4	18.7	0.6	0.6	15.6	11.6	66.7	62.1	6.0	4.8	72.3
MS	113	102	17.2	13.0	0.4	0.4	10.9	7.5	63.3	57.5	3.1	2.2	43.9
W.S.C	939	758	129.9	101.4	3.7	3.3	78.0	58.0	60.0	57.3	33.8	25.0	424.5
AR	101	88	13.3	11.1	0.4	0.3	8.3	6.7	62.3	60.6	2.8	2.3	40.9
LA	170	136	23.8	19.0	0.7	0.6	14.4	11.1	60.7	58.4	6.9	5.8	76.3
OK	140	113	15.0	12.3	0.4	0.4	8.8	6.9	58.7	55.7	4.1	2.4	51.4
TX	528	421	77.9	58.9	2.2	2.0	46.5	33.4	59.7	56.6	20.0	14.5	255.9
West	1,256	986	192.2	145.7	6.0	5.4	125.7	90.7	65.4	62.2	80.8	62.8	696.1
Mt	468	353	55.3	41.9	1.7	1.5	34.8	25.4	63.0	60.6	22.4	15.9	189.9
MT	61	53	4.7	4.4	0.1	0.1	3.0	2.8	63.4	63.1	1.1	0.9	13.0
ID	49	41	4.0	3.3	0.1	0.1	2.5	1.9	60.8	57.4	1.4	1.2	12.1
WY	32	27	3.0	2.2	0.1	-	1.7	1.1	56.1	51.3	0.7	0.6	7.1
CO	88	71	13.7	10.4	0.4	0.4	9.0	6.6	66.1	63.3	6.1	4.1	50.1
NM	62	37	6.5	4.0	0.2	0.2	4.1	2.3	62.7	57.3	3.4	2.0	24.2
AZ	93	61	13.6	9.7	0.5	0.4	8.6	6.0	63.6	61.8	5.1	3.1	48.0
UT	53	42	5.6	4.4	0.2	0.2	3.4	2.6	60.1	58.3	3.1	2.8	21.8
NV	30	21	4.1	3.4	0.1	0.1	2.6	2.1	61.8	61.4	1.6	1.2	13.6
Pac	788	633	136.9	103.8	4.4	4.0	90.9	65.3	66.3	62.9	58.4	46.9	506.1
WA	110	92	15.7	12.0	0.5	0.5	10.3	7.5	65.7	62.9	8.0	5.9	63.2
OR	73	66	10.1	7.8	0.3	0.3	6.2	4.3	61.7	55.1	3.8	3.4	37.8
CA	552	440	105.1	79.8	3.3	3.1	69.9	50.4	66.5	63.1	42.9	35.6	380.6
AK	27	16	1.9	1.2	0.1	-	1.0	0.6	53.1	49.3	1.2	0.4	7.4
HI	26	19	4.1	3.0	0.1	0.1	3.4	2.5	83.6	82.8	2.6	1.5	17.2
P. Rico . .	62	54	10.2	8.5	0.4	0.4	7.1	5.8	69.6	68.7	3.7	3.0	31.9

- Rounds to zero. [1] For definition of community hospital, see footnotes 1 and 2, table 179. [2] Inpatients receiving treatment each day; excludes newborn. [3] Ratio of average daily census to every 100 beds. [4] Includes full-time equivalents of part-time personnel.

Source: American Hospital Association, Chicago, IL, *Hospital Statistics, 1992-1993* (copyright).

No. 181. Hospital Use Rates, by Type of Hospital: 1972 to 1991

[See also *Historical Statistics, Colonial Times to 1970*, series B 384-387]

TYPE OF HOSPITAL	1972	1980	1985	1986	1987	1988	1989	1990	1991
Community hospitals: [1]									
Admissions per 1,000 population [2]	147	159	141	135	130	129	126	125	123
Admissions per bed.	35	37	33	33	33	33	33	34	34
Average length of stay [3] (days)	7.9	7.6	7.1	7.1	7.2	7.2	7.2	7.2	7.2
Outpatient visits per admission	1.8	5.6	6.5	7.2	7.8	8.6	9.2	9.7	10.4
Outpatient visits per 1,000 population [2] . .	777	890	919	966	1,013	1,101	1,158	1,208	1,277
Surgical operations (million)	14.8	18.8	20.1	20.5	20.8	21.4	21.3	21.9	22.4
Number per admission	0.5	0.5	0.6	0.6	0.7	0.7	0.7	0.7	0.7
Non-Federal psychiatric:									
Admissions per 1,000 population [2]	2.8	2.5	2.5	2.5	2.6	2.8	2.9	2.9	2.9
Days in hospital per 1,000 population [2] . .	661	295	224	217	214	209	201	190	179

[1] For definition of community hospitals, see footnotes 1 and 2, table 179.   [2] Based on Bureau of the Census estimated resident population as of July 1. Estimates reflect revisions based on the 1990 Census of Population.   [3] Number of inpatient days divided by number of admissions.

Source: American Hospital Association, Chicago, IL, *Hospital Statistics*, annual (copyright); and unpublished data.

No. 182. Average Cost to Community Hospitals per Patient: 1970 to 1991

[In **dollars, except percent.** Covers non-Federal short-term general or special hospitals (excluding psychiatric or tuberculosis hospitals and, beginning 1975, hospital units of institutions). Total cost per patient based on total hospital expenses (payroll, employee benefits, professional fees, supplies, etc.). Data have been adjusted for outpatient visits]

TYPE OF EXPENSE AND HOSPITAL	1970	1975	1980	1984	1985	1986	1987	1988	1989	1990	1991
Average cost per day, total	**74**	**134**	**245**	**411**	**460**	**501**	**539**	**586**	**637**	**687**	**752**
Annual percent change [1]	12.7	17.5	12.9	11.4	11.9	8.9	7.6	8.7	8.7	7.8	9.5
Nongovernmental nonprofit	75	133	246	415	463	504	544	591	642	692	758
For profit	71	133	257	438	500	552	585	649	708	752	820
State and local government	71	136	239	385	433	466	499	539	582	634	696
Average cost per stay, total	**605**	**1,030**	**1,851**	**2,995**	**3,245**	**3,533**	**3,850**	**4,207**	**4,588**	**4,947**	**5,360**
Nongovernmental nonprofit	615	1,040	1,902	3,073	3,307	3,590	3,914	4,273	4,649	5,001	5,393
For profit	486	876	1,676	2,749	3,033	3,342	3,617	4,023	4,406	4,727	5,134
State and local government	614	1,031	1,750	2,823	3,106	3,405	3,718	4,034	4,430	4,838	5,340

[1] Change from immediate prior year, except 1970, average annual change from 1965. For explanation of average annual change, see Guide to Tabular Presentation.

Source: American Hospital Association, Chicago, IL, *Hospital Statistics*, annual (copyright); and unpublished data.

No. 183. Average Cost to Community Hospitals per Patient, by State: 1985 to 1991

[In **dollars.** See headnote, table 182]

STATE	AVERAGE COST PER DAY			AVERAGE COST PER STAY			STATE	AVERAGE COST PER DAY			AVERAGE COST PER STAY		
	1985	1990	1991	1985	1990	1991		1985	1990	1991	1985	1990	1991
U.S.	**460**	**687**	**752**	**3,245**	**4,947**	**5,360**	MO	457	679	737	3,383	5,022	5,429
AL.	389	588	637	2,653	4,175	4,455	MT.	312	405	437	2,658	3,973	4,395
AK.	693	1,070	1,130	3,742	6,249	6,448	NE	347	490	546	2,892	4,675	5,214
AZ.	591	867	955	3,547	4,877	5,212	NV	677	854	907	3,953	5,511	5,883
AR.	381	534	571	2,292	3,730	3,927	NH	422	671	713	2,644	4,544	4,995
CA.	654	939	1,037	4,050	5,709	6,169	NJ	400	613	680	2,914	4,573	5,136
CO.	486	725	801	3,221	5,209	5,449	NM	501	734	840	2,837	4,172	4,583
CT.	502	825	910	3,610	6,238	6,696	NY	419	641	694	3,930	6,397	6,823
DE.	474	771	845	3,357	5,112	5,748	NC	356	595	651	2,416	4,408	4,759
DC.	612	995	1,038	4,962	7,876	7,743	ND	322	427	454	2,918	4,468	4,898
FL.	494	769	836	3,381	5,312	5,831	OH	493	720	782	3,428	4,801	5,133
GA.	386	630	652	2,501	4,303	4,677	OK	455	632	684	2,814	4,302	4,547
HI	420	638	686	3,522	6,048	6,553	OR	549	800	896	2,879	4,432	4,787
ID	373	547	565	2,402	3,701	4,026	PA	468	662	732	3,412	5,120	5,490
IL	498	717	770	3,607	5,253	5,570	RI	447	663	730	3,432	4,839	5,063
IN	446	667	745	2,942	4,390	4,879	SC	358	590	684	2,508	4,168	4,868
IA	359	495	538	2,735	4,135	4,527	SD	282	391	436	2,442	3,905	4,436
KS.	401	532	585	2,954	4,161	4,548	TN	397	633	716	2,709	4,340	4,859
KY.	367	563	616	2,323	3,762	4,216	TX	461	752	846	2,799	4,663	5,179
LA	475	701	764	2,842	4,575	5,044	UT	556	832	915	2,799	4,409	4,688
ME.	394	574	617	2,870	4,604	4,867	VT	343	598	621	2,705	4,343	4,673
MD.	443	678	740	3,237	4,640	4,835	VA	399	635	701	2,862	4,408	4,875
MA.	500	788	880	4,194	5,709	6,086	WA	546	817	904	3,062	4,519	5,035
MI	507	716	792	3,666	5,358	5,750	WV	399	565	612	2,520	3,918	4,319
MN.	369	536	582	3,302	4,782	5,035	WI	392	554	611	2,974	4,083	4,450
MS.	319	439	479	2,037	3,116	3,454	WY	367	462	489	2,357	3,990	4,081

Source: American Hospital Association, Chicago, IL, *Hospital Statistics*, annual (copyright); and unpublished data.

No. 184. Facilities and Services Provided by Community Hospitals: 1991

[Community hospitals are nonfederal short-stay (average length stay fewer than 30 days) excluding hospital units of institutions. Data are for hospitals responding to that portion of the questionnaire 4,975 of a total of 5,342 community hospitals]

SERVICE	Hospitals with service	Percent of total	SERVICE	Hospitals with service	Percent of total
AIDS inpatient care	3,460	69.5	Outpatient surgery services	4,708	94.6
Angioplasty	1,018	20.5	Patient representative services	2,736	55.0
Alcoholism/chemical dependency			Psychiatric services:		
outpatient services	1,042	20.9	Emergency	1,678	33.7
Birthing rooms	3,294	66.2	Outpatient	1,008	20.3
Blood bank	3,420	68.7			
Cardiac catheterization	1,457	29.3	Radiation therapy:		
Cardiac rehabilitation	2,228	44.8	X-ray	960	19.3
Computed tomographic (CT) scanner	3,633	73.0	Megavoltage (mil. volts)	969	19.5
Emergency department	4,627	93.0	Radio-active implants	1,244	25.0
			Radio isotope facilities:		
Extracorporeal shock wave			Diagnostic	3,131	62.9
lithotripter	370	7.4	Therapeutic	1,272	25.6
Genetic counseling services	494	9.9	Rehabilitation outpatient		
Geriatric services	3,091	62.1	department	2,604	52.3
Hemodialysis	1,315	26.4	Reproductive health services	2,152	43.3
Histopathology laboratory	3,199	64.3	Therapy services:		
Home health services	1,798	36.1	Occupational therapy services	2,595	52.2
Hospice	825	16.6	Physical therapy services	4,206	84.5
Hospital auxiliary	4,118	82.8	Recreational therapy services	1,666	33.5
HIV testing	2,793	56.1	Respiratory therapy services	4,515	90.8
Magnetic resonance imaging (MRI)	1,036	20.8	Trauma center	667	13.4
Open-heart surgery facilities	867	17.4	Ultrasound	4,196	84.3
Organ tissue transplant	555	11.2	Volunteer services department	3,494	70.2
Outpatient department	4,280	86.0	Women's center	1,157	23.3

Source: American Hospital Association, Chicago, IL, *Hospital Statistics, 1992-1993* (copyright).

No. 185. Hospital Utilization Rates, by Sex, 1970 to 1991, and Selected Characteristics, 1991

[Represents estimates of inpatients discharged from noninstitutional, short-stay hospitals, exclusive of Federal hospitals. Excludes newborn infants. Based on sample data collected from the National Hospital Discharge Survey, a sample survey of hospital records of patients discharged in year shown; subject to sampling variability. For composition of regions, see table 31]

SELECTED CHARACTERISTIC	Patients discharged (1,000)	PATIENTS DISCHARGED PER 1,000 PERSONS [1]			DAYS OF CARE PER 1,000 PERSONS [1]			AVERAGE STAY (days)			Beds used per day [2]
		Total	Male	Female	Total	Male	Female	Total	Male	Female	
1970	29,127	144	118	169	1,122	982	1,251	8.0	8.7	7.6	307
1980	37,832	168	139	194	1,217	1,068	1,356	7.3	7.7	7.0	333
1983	38,783	167	139	193	1,155	1,024	1,278	6.9	7.4	6.6	316
1984	37,162	159	132	184	1,044	924	1,155	6.6	7.0	6.3	286
1985	35,056	148	124	171	954	849	1,053	6.5	6.9	6.2	261
1986	34,256	143	121	164	913	817	1,003	6.4	6.8	6.1	250
1987	33,387	138	116	159	889	806	968	6.4	6.9	6.1	244
1988 [3]	31,146	128	107	147	834	757	907	6.5	7.1	6.2	228
1989 [3]	30,947	126	105	145	815	741	884	6.5	7.0	6.1	223
1990 [3]	30,788	124	102	144	792	704	875	6.4	6.9	6.1	217
1991, [3] total	31,098	124	103	144	795	715	869	6.4	7.0	6.0	218
Age:											
Under 1 year old	805	201	227	173	1,227	1,361	1,087	6.1	6.0	6.3	336
1 to 4 years old	735	48	56	40	174	204	143	3.6	3.7	3.5	48
5 to 14 years old	958	27	29	24	124	141	106	4.7	4.9	4.4	34
15 to 24 years old	3,484	98	42	154	404	257	553	4.1	6.1	3.6	111
25 to 34 years old	4,773	113	54	170	496	362	627	4.4	6.7	3.7	136
35 to 44 years old	3,364	86	71	101	478	444	510	5.5	6.3	5.0	131
45 to 64 years old	6,173	132	138	127	859	897	822	6.5	6.5	6.5	235
65 to 74 years old	4,830	264	293	242	2,131	2,325	1,979	8.1	7.9	8.2	584
75 years old and over	5,976	444	494	416	4,007	4,286	3,854	9.0	8.7	9.3	1,098
Region:											
Northeast	7,153	141	125	155	1,032	951	1,107	7.3	7.6	7.1	283
Midwest	7,315	122	103	140	790	712	863	6.5	6.9	6.2	216
South	11,290	131	107	154	817	728	901	6.2	6.8	5.8	224
West	5,340	100	76	123	538	482	593	5.4	6.3	4.8	147

[1] Based on Bureau of the Census estimated civilian population as of July 1. Estimates do not reflect revisions based on the 1990 Census of Population.   [2] Average daily number of beds occupied per 100,000 civilian population.   [3] Comparisons beginning 1988 with data for earlier years should be made with caution as estimates of change may reflect improvements in the design rather than true changes in hospital use.

Source: U.S. National Center for Health Statistics, *Vital and Health Statistics*, series 13, and unpublished data.

No. 186. Hospital Discharges and Days of Care, by Sex, Age, and Diagnosis: 1991

[See headnote, table 185]

AGE AND FIRST-LISTED DIAGNOSIS	DISCHARGES Number (1,000)	DISCHARGES Per 1,000 persons[1]	Days of care per 1,000 persons[1]	Average stay (days)	AGE AND FIRST-LISTED DIAGNOSIS	DISCHARGES Number (1,000)	DISCHARGES Per 1,000 persons[1]	Days of care per 1,000 persons[1]	Average stay (days)
MALE					**FEMALE**				
All ages[2]	**12,478**	**102.7**	**715.2**	**7.0**	**All ages**[2]	**18,620**	**144.3**	**869.3**	**6.0**
					Delivery	3,973	30.8	85.5	2.8
Diseases of heart	1,977	16.3	108.3	6.7	Diseases of heart	1,727	13.4	93.9	7.0
Malignant neoplasms	781	6.4	62.1	9.7	Malignant neoplasms	812	6.3	54.7	8.7
Pneumonia, all forms	545	4.5	35.5	7.9	Fractures, all sites	553	4.3	40.5	9.4
Fractures, all sites	481	4.0	28.9	7.3	Pneumonia, all forms	543	4.2	35.9	8.5
Psychoses	416	3.4	44.6	13.0					
Under 15 years[2]	**1,435**	**50.8**	**247.3**	**4.9**	**Under 15 years**[2]	**1,064**	**39.5**	**187.9**	**4.8**
Acute respiratory infection	138	4.9	14.7	3.0	Pneumonia, all forms	96	3.6	14.3	4.0
Bronchitis, emphysema[3]	128	4.5	13.7	3.0	Acute respiratory infection	82	3.0	9.8	3.2
Pneumonia, all forms	118	4.2	17.7	4.2	Bronchitis, emphysema[3]	69	2.6	7.4	2.9
Congenital anomalies	76	2.7	16.6	6.2	Congenital anomalies	48	1.8	13.9	7.8
Fractures, all sites	70	2.5	14.7	5.9	Noninfectious enteritis of colitis	41	1.5	5.0	3.3
15 to 44 years[2]	**3,248**	**55.9**	**356.5**	**6.4**	**15 to 44 years**[2]	**8,372**	**142.1**	**565.6**	**4.0**
Psychoses	252	4.3	55.1	12.7	Delivery	3,956	67.2	186.5	2.8
Fractures, all sites	230	4.0	24.2	6.1	Psychoses	236	4.0	54.0	13.5
Diseases of heart	145	2.5	13.9	5.5	Pregnancy w/abortive outcome	178	3.0	7.3	2.4
Intervertebral disc disorders	135	2.3	9.5	4.1	Benign neoplasms	173	2.9	11.0	3.8
Alcohol dependence syndrome	114	2.0	19.0	9.7	Cholelithiasis	159	2.7	13.0	4.8
45 to 64 years[2]	**3,088**	**137.5**	**897.4**	**6.5**	**45 to 64 years**[2]	**3,085**	**127.2**	**822.4**	**6.5**
Diseases of heart	716	31.9	198.9	6.2	Diseases of heart	379	15.6	98.3	6.3
Malignant neoplasms	239	10.7	90.7	8.5	Malignant neoplasms	260	10.7	85.4	8.0
Cerebrovascular diseases	86	3.8	29.8	7.8	Cholelithiasis	127	5.2	20.5	3.9
Psychoses	80	3.5	44.4	12.5	Psychoses	109	4.5	62.9	13.9
Fractures, all sites	75	3.3	24.4	7.3	Benign neoplasms	100	4.1	18.9	4.6
65 years old and older[2]	**4,708**	**368.1**	**3,056.5**	**8.3**	**65 years old and older**[2]	**6,098**	**321.6**	**2,839.6**	**8.8**
Diseases of heart	1,107	86.5	611.2	7.1	Diseases of heart	1,254	66.1	480.0	7.3
Malignant neoplasms	455	35.6	369.9	10.4	Malignant neoplasms	428	22.6	221.8	9.8
Pneumonia, all forms	286	22.4	215.4	9.6	Cerebrovascular disease	377	19.9	196.0	9.9
Cerebrovascular diseases	263	20.6	195.5	9.5	Fractures, all sites	346	18.2	208.5	11.4
Hyperplasia of prostate	180	14.1	67.0	4.8	Pneumonia, all forms	303	16.0	171.3	10.7

[1] See footnote 1, table 185.   [2] Includes other first-listed diagnoses not shown separately.   [3] Includes asthma.

Source: U.S. National Center for Health Statistics, *Health, United States*, 1992; and unpublished data.

No. 187. Surgery Performed in Hospitals: 1980 to 1991

[In thousands, except percent]

TYPE OF HOSPITAL	1980	1983	1984	1985	1986	1987	1988	1989	1990	1991
OUTPATIENT SURGERIES										
All hospitals	3,198	4,969	5,803	7,309	8,705	9,758	10,586	10,953	11,678	12,209
Ownership:										
Non-Federal hospitals	3,063	4,735	5,549	6,984	8,272	9,145	10,038	10,362	11,085	11,724
Community hospitals[1]	3,054	4,715	5,530	6,951	8,247	9,126	10,028	10,351	11,070	11,712
Nongovernmental nonprofit	2,416	3,677	4,319	5,392	6,265	6,903	7,577	7,834	8,389	8,989
Federal hospitals	135	235	254	325	434	612	548	591	593	486
Size of hospital: 6 to 99 beds	354	506	591	752	966	1,146	1,229	1,241	1,303	1,366
100 to 199 beds	571	864	1,092	1,502	1,811	2,030	2,252	2,360	2,498	2,636
200 to 299 beds	630	996	1,168	1,521	1,836	2,023	2,297	2,383	2,543	2,695
300 to 499 beds	977	1,438	1,727	2,069	2,368	2,617	2,845	2,920	3,172	3,293
500 beds or more	666	1,167	1,225	1,465	1,725	1,942	1,963	2,049	2,162	2,220
OUTPATIENT SURGERIES AS PERCENT OF TOTAL										
All hospitals	16.4	23.9	27.8	34.5	40.3	44.2	47.0	48.7	50.6	52.1
Ownership:										
Non-Federal hospitals	16.3	23.8	27.8	34.5	40.3	43.9	46.8	48.5	50.5	52.3
Community hospitals[1]	16.3	23.8	27.8	34.6	40.3	43.8	46.8	48.5	50.5	52.3
Nongovernmental nonprofit	17.1	24.6	28.8	35.5	40.8	44.2	47.0	48.6	50.7	52.5
Federal hospitals	18.6	26.7	28.1	33.9	40.7	49.9	49.7	51.5	51.8	47.8
Size of hospital: 6 to 99 beds	17.9	25.6	29.6	36.5	44.7	49.4	52.4	54.1	56.2	58.7
100 to 199 beds	15.4	22.9	28.2	36.3	42.9	47.2	50.3	52.3	55.0	56.3
200 to 299 beds	16.7	25.2	29.1	36.4	42.0	45.7	49.2	50.7	52.9	54.6
300 to 499 beds	17.2	24.1	28.6	34.4	40.0	43.1	46.5	48.0	48.8	50.6
500 beds or more	15.1	24.0	24.9	30.4	35.2	39.2	39.6	41.6	43.9	44.4

[1] For definition of community hospital, see footnotes 1 and 2, table 179.

Source: American Hospital Association, Chicago, IL, *Hospital Statistics*, annual (copyright); and unpublished data from the Annual Survey of Hospitals.

No. 188. Procedures for Inpatients Discharged From Short-Stay Hospitals: 1980 to 1991

[Excludes newborn infants and discharges from Federal hospitals. See headnote, table 185]

SEX AND TYPE OF PROCEDURE	NUMBER OF PROCEDURES (1,000)					RATE PER 1,000 POPULATION [2]				
	1980	1985	1989 [1]	1990 [1]	1991 [1]	1980	1985	1989 [1]	1990 [1]	1991 [1]
BOTH SEXES										
Surgical procedures, total [3]	24,494	24,799	23,370	23,051	23,403	108.6	104.6	94.8	92.4	93.4
Procedures to assist delivery [4]	2,391	2,494	2,446	2,491	2,558	10.6	10.5	9.9	10.0	10.2
Cesarean section	619	877	938	945	933	2.7	3.7	3.8	3.8	3.7
Cardiac catheterization	348	681	958	995	1,000	1.5	2.9	3.9	4.0	4.0
Reduction of fracture [5]	605	681	671	609	665	2.7	2.9	2.7	2.4	2.7
Repair of current obstetric laceration . .	355	548	762	795	795	1.6	2.3	3.1	3.2	3.2
Hysterectomy	649	670	541	591	546	2.9	2.8	2.2	2.4	2.2
Diagnostic and other non-surgical										
procedures [6]	6,918	11,961	16,672	17,455	20,519	30.7	50.5	67.6	70.0	81.9
CAT scan [7]	306	1,378	1,519	1,506	1,459	1.4	5.8	6.2	6.0	5.8
Diagnostic ultrasound	318	1,234	1,558	1,608	1,592	1.4	5.2	6.3	6.4	6.4
Angiocardiography and arteriography [8]	569	1,117	1,620	1,735	1,718	2.5	4.7	6.6	7.0	6.9
Radioisotope scan	525	838	635	603	539	2.3	3.5	2.6	2.4	2.2
Cystoscopy	867	645	487	485	427	3.8	2.7	2.0	1.9	1.7
MALE										
Surgical procedures, total [3]	8,505	8,805	8,886	8,538	8,692	78.1	76.8	74.4	70.6	71.5
Cardiac catheterization	228	439	601	620	603	2.1	3.8	5.0	5.1	5.0
Prostatectomy	335	367	376	364	363	3.1	3.2	3.1	3.0	3.0
Reduction of fracture [5]	325	339	342	300	337	3.0	3.0	2.9	2.5	2.8
Repair of inguinal hernia	483	370	220	181	155	4.4	3.2	1.8	1.5	1.3
Diagnostic and other non-surgical										
procedures [6]	3,386	5,889	7,202	7,378	8,572	31.1	51.4	60.3	61.0	70.5
Angiocardiography and arteriography [8]	355	693	1,000	1,051	989	3.3	6.0	8.4	8.7	8.1
CAT scan [7]	152	671	721	736	702	1.4	5.9	6.0	6.1	5.8
FEMALE										
Surgical procedures, total [3]	15,989	15,994	14,484	14,513	14,711	137.1	130.6	114.0	113.0	114.0
Procedures to assist delivery [4]	2,391	2,494	2,446	2,491	2,558	20.5	20.4	19.2	19.4	19.8
Cesarean section	619	877	938	945	933	5.3	7.2	7.4	7.4	7.2
Repair of current obstetric laceration . .	355	548	762	795	795	3.0	4.5	6.0	6.2	6.2
Hysterectomy	649	670	541	591	546	5.6	5.5	4.3	4.6	4.2
Diagnostic and other non-surgical										
procedures [6]	3,532	6,072	9,471	10,077	11,947	30.3	49.6	74.5	78.5	92.6
Diagnostic ultrasound	204	756	930	941	940	1.7	6.2	7.3	7.3	7.3
CAT scan [7]	154	707	798	770	757	1.3	5.8	6.3	6.0	5.9

[1] Comparisons beginning 1988 with data for earlier years should be made with caution as estimates of change may reflect improvements in the design rather than true changes in hospital use.   [2] Based on Bureau of the Census estimated civilian population as of July 1. Population estimates do not reflect revised estimates based on the 1990 Census of Population.   [3] Includes other types of surgical procedures not shown separately.   [4] Beginning in 1989, the definition of some surgical and diagnostic and other non-surgical procedures was revised, causing a discontinuity in the trends for some totals.   [5] Excluding skull, nose, and jaw.   [6] Includes other non-surgical procedures not shown separately.   [7] Computerized axial tomography.   [8] Using contrast material.

Source: U.S. National Center for Health Statistics, *Vital and Health Statistics,* series 13; and unpublished data.

No. 189. Organ Transplants and Grafts: 1981 to 1991

[As of end of year. Based on reports of procurement programs and transplant centers in the United States]

PROCEDURE	NUMBER OF PROCEDURES							NUMBER OF CENTERS		Number of people waiting, 1991	1-year survival rates, 1990 (percent)
	1981	1985	1987	1988	1989	1990	1991	1981	1991		
Transplant:											
Heart	62	719	1,512	1,647	1,673	1,998	2,125	8	156	2,267	[1]82
Liver	26	602	1,199	1,680	2,160	2,534	2,954	1	93	1,679	[1]74
Kidney	4,883	7,695	8,967	9,123	8,890	9,433	9,949	157	237	19,416	[1]93
Heart-lung	5	30	41	74	67	52	51	(NA)	84	155	[1]53
Lung	-	2	11	31	89	187	401	(NA)	79	678	[1]54
Pancreas/Islet cell	(NA)	130	180	243	413	529	532	(NA)	89	602	[1]89
Cornea grafts	15,500	26,300	35,930	36,900	38,464	40,631	41,393	(NA)	[2]108	5,083	[3]95
Bone grafts	(NA)	(NA)	250,000	300,000	(NA)	350,000	375,000	(NA)	34	(NA)	(NA)
Skin grafts	(NA)	(NA)	5,000	5,200	(NA)	5,500	5,200	(NA)	25	(NA)	(NA)

- Represents zero.   NA Not available.   [1] One year patient survival rates for transplants performed between October 1, 1987, and December 31, 1989.   [2] Eye banks.   [3] Success rate.

Source: U.S. Department of Health and Human Services, Public Health Service, Division of Organ Transplantation; American Association of Tissue Banks, McLean, VA; and Eye Bank Association of America, Washington; and unpublished data.

No. 190. Patients Discharged From Hospitals—Principal Source of Expected Payment, by Selected Characteristic: 1991

[Covers non-Federal short-stay hospitals. Discharges exclude newborn infants. Based on the National Hospital Discharge Survey. See headnote, table 185. For composition of regions, see table 31]

CHARACTERISTIC	Total discharges [1] (1,000)	PRINCIPAL SOURCE OF EXPECTED PAYMENT—PERCENT DISTRIBUTION								
		Private insurance	Government					Self-pay	No charge	Other [2]
			Medicare	Medicaid	Worker's compensation	Other			
AGE										
All ages	31,098	36.6	35.6	12.9	1.2	2.0	5.2	0.3	3.1
Under 15 years old	2,498	47.2	1.2	32.7	(X)	3.0	7.1	0.8	4.6
15 to 44 years old	11,620	52.5	3.7	21.5	2.0	3.2	8.7	0.3	4.2
45 to 64 years old	6,173	59.3	13.9	9.0	1.7	2.7	5.4	0.4	3.8
65 years old and over	10,806	4.2	90.2	1.4	0.3	0.2	0.9	([3])	0.7
SEX										
Male, all ages	12,478	34.4	39.7	9.2	2.2	2.1	5.9	0.4	2.8
Under 15 years old	1,435	47.0	1.0	32.8	(X)	3.0	7.6	0.9	4.5
15 to 44 years old	3,248	48.7	7.4	12.4	5.6	3.9	12.7	0.6	4.4
45 to 64 years old	3,088	58.5	16.1	6.8	2.5	2.8	5.5	0.4	3.6
65 years old and over	4,708	4.9	89.2	1.2	0.4	0.2	0.9	([3])	0.8
Female, all ages	18,620	38.2	32.9	15.5	0.5	2.0	4.7	0.2	3.0
Under 15 years old	1,064	47.5	1.5	32.5	(X)	3.1	6.6	([3])	4.7
15 to 44 years old	8,372	53.9	2.3	25.1	0.7	2.9	7.1	0.2	4.1
45 to 64 years old	3,085	60.2	11.8	11.2	0.9	2.6	5.3	0.5	3.9
65 years old and over	6,098	3.7	91.0	1.5	0.3	([2])	0.8	([3])	0.6
RACE										
White	20,816	38.1	39.8	8.7	1.3	1.6	4.3	0.2	2.7
All other	4,753	29.9	23.4	28.8	0.9	2.9	7.6	0.8	3.5
Not stated	5,528	37.1	30.2	15.2	1.1	3.1	6.8	0.2	3.2
REGION										
Northeast	7,153	36.0	35.2	13.1	1.2	0.8	4.8	0.1	3.8
Midwest	7,315	37.6	37.5	10.4	1.1	2.2	4.9	0.3	2.3
South	11,290	35.2	37.2	13.1	1.4	2.5	6.1	0.4	1.3
West	5,340	39.3	30.1	15.7	1.1	2.5	4.2	([3])	5.8

X Not applicable.   [1] Includes discharges for whom expected source of payment was unknown.   [2] Includes all other nonprofit source of payment such as church, welfare, or United Way.   [3] Figure does not meet standards of reliability or precision.

Source: U.S. National Center for Health Statistics, unpublished data.

No. 191. Nursing and Related Care Facilities: 1971 to 1989

ITEM	Unit	1971	1973	1976	1978	1980	1982	1984	1986	1989
Nursing and related care: [1]										
Facilities	Number	22,004	21,834	20,468	[2]18,722	[3]23,065	[4]25,849	(NA)	[4]25,648	(NA)
Beds	1,000	1,202	1,328	1,415	[2]1,349	[3]1,537	[4]1,642	(NA)	[4]1,709	(NA)
Resident patients	1,000	1,076	1,198	1,293	[2]1,240	[3]1,396	[4]1,493	(NA)	[4]1,553	(NA)
Employees, full-time	1,000	568	636	653	[2]664	[3]798	(NA)	(NA)	(NA)	(NA)
Per 1,000 patients	Rate	528	531	505	[2]535	[3]571	(NA)	(NA)	(NA)	(NA)
Skilled nursing facilities [5]	Number	4,277	3,970	3,922	4,745	5,052	5,408	5,952	6,897	8,198
Beds	1,000	307	287	309	408	436	488	530	(NA)	491
Per 1,000 Medicare enrollees [6]	Rate	15.1	13.5	13.7	17.3	17.7	19.1	19.9	(NA)	16.8

NA Not available.   [1] Covers nursing homes with three beds or more and all other places providing some form of nursing, personal, or domiciliary care; standards vary widely among States. Includes skilled nursing facilities. 1971-1984 based on National Master Facility Inventory. Some changes in data beginning 1976 may be due to dependence on State collection. 1986 data based on the 1986 Inventory of Long Term Care Places. Data may not be strictly comparable with previous years.   [2] Includes 1976 data for California, District of Columbia, New York, and North Carolina.   [3] Excludes hospital-based nursing homes and includes 1978 data for Alaska and South Dakota.   [4] Excludes hospital-based nursing homes.   [5] Source: Through 1976, U.S. Social Security Administration, *Health Insurance Statistics* and unpublished data. Beginning 1978, U.S. Health Care Financing Administration, *Medicare Participating Providers and Suppliers of Health Services, 1980;* and unpublished data. Covers facilities and beds certified for participation under Medicare as of mid-year. Includes facilities which have transfer agreements with one or more participating hospitals, and are engaged primarily in providing skilled nursing care and related services for the rehabilitation of injured, disabled, or sick persons.   [6] Based on number of aged persons residing in United States who were enrolled in the Medicare hospital insurance program as of July 1 of year stated.

Source: Except as noted, U.S. National Center for Health Statistics, *Health Resources Statistics,* annual through 1976 and 1978; 1982 and 1986, *Advance Data from Vital and Health Statistics,* No. 111 and No. 147; and unpublished data.

No. 192. Nursing and Related Care Facilities—Selected Characteristics: 1986

[Excludes hospital-based nursing homes. Based on the 1986 Inventory of Long-Term Care Places. For composition of regions, see table 31]

CHARACTERISTIC	TOTAL FACILITIES				NURSING HOMES [1]				RESIDENTIAL FACILITIES [2]			
	Homes	Beds (1,000)	Average number of beds	Occu-pancy rate	Homes	Beds (1,000)	Average number of beds	Occu-pancy rate	Homes	Beds (1,000)	Average number of beds	Occu-pancy rate
Total	25,646	1709.2	67	91.0	16,388	1,507.4	92	91.7	9,258	201.8	22	85.4
Northeast	4,863	373.8	77	93.7	2,948	317.5	108	94.8	1,915	56.3	29	87.6
Midwest	7,474	539.8	72	90.7	5,393	506.7	94	91.2	2,081	33.1	16	84.4
South	7,311	516.5	71	90.1	5,008	464.0	93	90.5	2,303	52.5	23	86.4
West	5,998	279.1	47	89.4	3,039	219.2	72	91.1	2,959	59.9	20	83.1
Government........	1,045	106.6	102	93.0	789	99.7	126	93.6	256	6.8	27	85.3
Proprietary.........	20,223	1235.4	61	90.5	12,336	1,079.0	87	91.3	7,887	156.5	20	85.1
Nonprofit.........	4,378	367.2	84	91.8	3,263	328.7	101	92.4	1,115	38.5	35	86.5
3 to 9 beds	5,918	32.6	6	82.8	1,340	7.2	5	82.6	4,578	25.5	6	82.9
10 to 24 beds	3,695	58.1	16	86.3	1,069	18.2	17	87.6	2,626	39.9	15	85.7
25 to 49 beds	3,135	115.5	37	89.5	2,061	77.8	38	90.8	1,074	37.6	35	86.8
50 to 74 beds	3,470	208.7	60	92.2	3,037	182.7	60	92.8	433	26.0	60	87.6
75 to 99 beds	2,526	221.6	88	92.1	2,335	205.4	88	92.5	191	16.3	85	86.5
100 to 199 beds.....	5,755	756.2	131	91.1	5,468	717.6	131	91.5	287	38.6	135	84.8
200 to 299 beds.....	858	198.2	231	90.8	804	186.1	231	91.3	54	12.1	225	82.9
300 to 499 beds.....	239	84.9	355	91.2	225	80.1	356	92.1	14	4.8	340	76.9
500 beds or more....	50	33.4	667	95.0	49	32.3	659	94.8	1	1.1	1050	99.7
Certification: Medicare or Medicaid (skilled nursing facility)....	8,045	984.1	122	92.9	8,045	984.1	122	92.9	-	-	-	-
Medicaid (intermediate care facility) [3]........	5,375	411.5	77	90.3	5,375	411.5	77	90.3	-	-	-	-
Not certified nursing home........	2,968	111.8	38	86.3	2,968	111.8	38	86.3	-	-	-	-
Residential facilities .	9,258	201.8	22	85.4	(X)	(X)	(X)	(X)	9,258	201.8	22	85.4

- Represents zero.   X Not applicable.   [1] These facilities have three or more beds and provide to adults who require it either (a) nursing care or (b) personal care (such as help with bathing, eating, using toilet facilities, or dressing) and/or supervision over such activities as money management, walking, and shopping.   [2] These facilities offer no nursing services and provide only personal care or supervisory care.   [3] Facilities certified as both skilled nursing facilities and intermediate care facilities have been classified as skilled nursing facilities.

Source: U.S. National Center for Health Statistics, *Advance Data From Vital and Health Statistics*, No. 147; and unpublished data.

No. 193. Residential Facilities for Persons with Mental Retardation: 1970 to 1990

[For years ending **June 30**. Persons with mental retardation refers to those who have been so designated by State governments in the process of placing them into residential facilities]

ITEM	STATE OPERATED FACILITIES [1]					PRIVATE FACILITIES [3]			
	1970	1980 [2]	1985 [2]	1989 [2]	1990 [2]	1977	1982	1989	1990
Number of facilities [4]	190	394	881	1,305	1,321	10,219	14,605	38,657	41,547
Residents beginning of year.........	189,956	148,734	117,101	99,267	94,675	(NA)	(NA)	(NA)	(NA)
Admissions [5].................	14,985	14,064	7,713	6,518	5,568	22,363	22,431	(NA)	(NA)
Deaths in institutions................	3,496	2,142	1,537	1,205	1,143	891	920	(NA)	(NA)
Live releases [6].................	14,702	16,225	10,310	7,479	7,679	12,384	12,999	(NA)	(NA)
Residents end of year...............	186,743	140,230	112,183	94,268	91,640	89,120	115,032	180,023	188,902
Rate per 100,000 population [7].......	92.5	62.2	47.5	38.5	34.7	40.9	50.0	73.4	76.0
Average daily residents.............	187,897	136,304	111,791	96,171	92,729	(NA)	(NA)	(NA)	(NA)
Maintenance expenditures per day per average daily resident (dollars) [8]...	13	68	122	184	196	[9]19	[9]37	(NA)	(NA)

NA Not available.   [1] Data as submitted by many State agencies; figures reflect some estimates. Resident patients at the end of a year do not equal the number at the beginning of a succeeding year. Includes estimates for underreporting.   [2] Includes data for 142 facilities in 1980, 121 facilities in 1985, 123 in 1989, and 108 in 1990 operated as mental hospitals or other facilities and which have residents with mental retardation. The average daily number of residents with mental retardation in these facilities was 8,240 in 1980, 5,602 in 1985, 1,605 in 1989, and 1,487 in 1990.   [3] A privately-operated living quarter which provides 24-hour, 7-days-a-week responsibility for room, board, and supervision of mentally retarded persons. Excludes single-family homes providing services to a relative; and nursing homes, boarding homes, and foster homes not formally licensed or contracted as mental retardation service providers.   [4] Beginning 1985, reflects the development of a large number of community based State-operated facilities which were developed in the early 1980's.   [5] Includes readmissions and excludes transfers.   [6] 1970, represents excess of residents released alive from facility over those returning to facility. Beginning 1980, total live releases.   [7] Based on Bureau of the Census estimated civilian population as of July 1. Estimates reflect revisions based on 1990 Census of Population.   [8] Reporting facilities only; includes salaries and wages, purchased provisions, fuel, light, water, etc.   [9] Represents average daily reimbursement rate per resident.

Source: State-operated facilities: 1970, U.S. Office of Human Development Services, *Residents in Public Institutions for the Mentally Retarded*, annual, and unpublished data; 1980 through 1988, Center for Residential Services and Community Living (CRSCL), Institute on Community Integration, UAP, University of Minnesota, Minneapolis, MN, White, Lakin, Hill, Wright, and Bruininks, Report No. 30; 1989, MN, White, Lakin, Bruininks, and Li, Report No. 33; 1990, MN, White, Pruity, Lakin & Blake, Report No. 36; Private facilities: 1989, CRSCL, Lakin, White, Prouty, Bruininks and Kimm, Brief Report No. 35; 1990, MN, Lakin, White, Blake, and Prouty, Report No. 38.

No. 194. Mental Retardation Facilities—Summary, by Selected Characteristics: 1986

[Mental retardation (MR) facilities include intermediate care facilities (ICF-MR), foster homes, group residences semi-independent living programs, State institutions and other kinds of MR places. Based on the 1986 Inventory of Long-Term Care Places. For an explanation of mental retardation, see table 193. For details, see source. For composition of regions, see table 31]

CHARACTERISTIC	FACILITIES		BEDS		RESIDENTS						Average number of residents
					Number			Percent distribution			
	Number	Percent distribution	Number	Percent distribution	Total [1]	Black	His-panic [2]	Total [1]	Black	His-panic [2]	
Total	14,639	100.0	269,954	100.0	250,472	29,442	10,181	100.0	100.0	100.0	17
BED SIZE											
1 to 5 beds	5,115	34.9	17,099	6.3	15,234	1,726	623	6.1	5.9	6.1	3
6 to 9 beds	5,491	37.5	37,318	13.8	34,815	3,159	1,587	13.9	10.7	15.6	6
10 to 15 beds	2,097	14.3	24,991	9.3	23,444	1,950	937	9.4	6.6	9.2	11
16 to 99 beds	1,531	10.5	58,050	21.5	54,090	5,485	2,333	21.6	18.6	22.9	35
100 beds or more.	405	2.8	132,496	49.1	122,889	17,122	4,701	49.1	58.2	46.2	303
100 to 199 beds	198	1.4	26,206	9.7	24,539	3,698	995	9.8	12.6	9.8	124
200 to 499 beds	126	0.9	41,331	15.3	38,322	4,904	1,465	15.3	16.7	14.4	304
500 beds or more	81	0.6	64,959	24.1	60,028	8,520	2,241	24.0	28.9	22.0	741
GEOGRAPHIC REGION											
Northeast	3,806	26.0	65,812	24.4	61,707	5,634	1,578	24.6	19.1	15.5	16
Midwest	4,741	32.4	83,067	30.8	77,193	6,438	1,079	30.8	21.9	10.6	16
South	2,380	16.3	71,887	26.6	66,767	14,538	2,668	26.7	49.4	26.2	28
West	3,712	25.4	49,188	18.2	44,805	2,832	4,856	17.9	9.6	47.7	12
TYPE OF OWNERSHIP											
Profit	6,330	43.2	66,536	24.6	60,560	6,503	3,495	24.2	22.1	34.3	10
Nonprofit	6,396	43.7	78,935	29.2	75,193	6,938	2,316	30.0	23.6	22.7	12
Government	1,913	13.1	124,483	46.1	114,719	16,001	4,370	45.8	54.3	42.9	6

[1] Includes races not shown separately. [2] Persons of Hispanic origin may be of any race.

Source: U.S. National Center for Health Statistics, *Advance Data*, No. 143, September 1987.

No. 195. Mental Health Facilities—Summary, by Type of Facility: 1990

[Facilities, beds and inpatients as of yearend 1990; other data are for calendar year or fiscal year ending in a month other than December since facilities are permitted to report on either a calendar or fiscal year basis. Excludes private psychiatric office practice and psychiatric service modes of all types in hospitals or outpatient clinics of Federal agencies other than U.S. Dept. of Veterans Affairs. Excludes data from Puerto Rico, Virgin Islands, Guam, and other territories]

TYPE OF FACILITY	Number of facilities	INPATIENT BEDS		INPATIENTS		Average daily inpatients (1,000)	Inpatient care epi-sodes [2] (1,000)	EXPENDI-TURES		Patient care staff [4] (1,000)
		Total (1,000)	Rate [1]	Total (1,000)	Rate [1]			Total (mil. dol.)	Per capita [3] (dol.)	
Total	5,205	280.7	113.5	231.7	93.8	253.6	2,303.7	28,953	118.0	421.8
Mental hospitals:										
State and county	266	98.6	39.8	90.2	36.5	89.8	365.2	7,678	31.0	112.6
Private [5]	1,038	79.1	32.0	61.8	25.0	83.8	565.3	8,804	36.0	104.4
General hospitals [6] . . . [7]	1,545	52.5	21.2	37.6	15.2	37.9	983.1	4,604	19.0	71.1
Veterans Administration [7] .	130	21.7	8.8	17.2	7.0	17.3	215.5	1,381	6.0	24.3
Free-standing psychiatric outpatient clinics [8]	741	(X)	(X)	(X)	(X)	(X)	(X)	678	3.0	10.3
Other [9]	1,485	28.8	11.7	24.9	10.1	24.8	174.6	5,808	23.0	99.1

X Not applicable. [1] Rate per 100,000 population. Based on Bureau of Census estimated civilian population as of July 1. [2] "Inpatient care episodes" is defined as the number of residents in inpatient facilities at the beginning of the year plus the total additions to inpatient facilities during the year. [3] Based on Bureau of the Census estimated civilian population as of July 1. [4] Full-time equivalent. [5] Includes residential treatment centers for emotionally disturbed children. [6] Non-Federal hospitals with separate psychiatric services. [7] Includes U.S. Department of Veterans Affairs (VA) neuropsychiatric hospitals, VA general hospitals with separate psychiatric settings and VA freestanding psychiatric outpatient clinics. [8] Includes mental health facilities which provide only psychiatric outpatient services. [9] Includes other multiservice mental health facilities with two or more settings, which are not elsewhere classified, as well as freestanding partial care facilities which only provide psychiatric partial care services. Number of facilities, expenditures, and staff data also include freestanding psychiatric partial care facilities.

Source: U.S. Substance Abuse and Mental Health Services Administration, Center for Mental Health Services, unpublished data.

No. 196. Persons Injured, by Sex, 1970 to 1990, and by Age and Type, 1990

[Covers civilian noninstitutional population and comprises incidents leading to restricted activity and/or medical attention. Beginning 1982, data not strictly comparable with other years. See headnote, table 199. Based on National Health Interview Survey; see Appendix III]

YEAR	PERSONS INJURED (millions) Total	Male	Female	RATE PER 100 POPULATION Total	Male	Female	AGE AND TYPE	PERSONS INJURED (millions) Total	Male	Female	RATE PER 100 POPULATION Total	Male	Female
1970 ..	56.0	31.8	24.2	28.0	33.0	23.3	**1990, total** [1].	**60.1**	**33.6**	**26.6**	**24.4**	**28.1**	**21.0**
1975 ..	71.9	39.4	32.5	34.4	39.1	30.0	Under 5 years ...	5.3	3.1	2.2	27.6	31.4	23.5
1978 ..	67.5	38.1	29.4	31.6	36.9	26.6	5 to 17 years ...	13.5	8.4	5.2	29.7	35.9	23.2
1979 ..	69.1	40.2	28.9	32.0	38.6	25.9	18 to 44 years...	27.3	16.3	11.0	26.0	31.6	20.6
1980 ..	68.1	39.0	29.1	31.2	37.1	25.8	45 years and over	14.0	5.8	8.2	18.3	16.7	19.6
1983 ..	61.1	33.0	28.1	26.6	29.8	23.7	Fractures [2]....	6.8	4.2	2.6	2.7	3.5	2.0
1984 ..	61.1	33.7	27.4	26.4	30.1	22.9	Sprains and strains	12.7	6.5	6.2	5.2	5.5	4.9
1985 ..	62.6	34.6	28.0	26.8	30.6	23.1	Open wounds and						
1986 ..	62.4	34.0	28.4	26.4	29.8	23.3	lacerations.....	12.8	8.6	4.2	5.2	7.2	3.3
1987 ..	62.1	33.6	28.4	26.0	29.1	23.1	Contusions [3]....	10.0	5.9	4.1	4.1	4.9	3.3
1988 ..	59.2	32.4	26.8	24.6	27.7	21.6	Other.........	17.9	8.4	9.5	7.3	7.0	7.5
1989 ..	58.0	31.7	26.3	23.8	26.9	20.9							

[1] Includes unknown place of accident not shown separately. [2] Includes dislocations. [3] Includes superficial injuries.
Source: U.S. National Center for Health Statistics, *Vital and Health Statistics*, series 10, No. 181; and unpublished data.

No. 197. Injuries Associated With Consumer Products: 1989 and 1991

[Estimates calculated from a representative sample of hospitals with emergency treatment departments in the United States. Data are estimates of the number of emergency room treated cases nationwide associated with various products. Product involvement does not necessarily mean the product caused the accident. Products were selected from the U.S. Consumer Product Safety Commission's National Electronic Injury Surveillance System]

PRODUCT	1989	1991	PRODUCT	1989	1991
Home maintenance:			**Housewares:**		
Noncaustic cleaning equip. [1]	19,328	21,890	Cookware, pots, pans.........	29,888	34,868
Cleaning agents (except soap)....	35,673	38,397	Cutlery, knives, unpowered	335,083	448,525
Drain, oven cleaners, caustics....	10,006	10,900	Drinking glasses	114,682	134,790
Paints, solvents, lubricants	17,649	21,430	Scissors..................	21,144	30,973
Misc. household chemicals	17,126	20,369	Small kitchen appliances.......	36,945	40,952
Home workshop equipment:			Tableware and accessories	106,400	116,796
Batteries	11,967	12,560	Misc. housewares	48,685	55,635
Hoists, lifts, jacks............	10,899	15,052	**General household appliances:**		
Power home tools, except saws ...	22,002	29,014	Cooking ranges, ovens, etc......	41,727	54,659
Power home workshop saws	71,074	94,076	Irons, clothes steamers........	18,193	18,120
Welding, soldering, cutting tools ...	15,276	19,368	Refrigerators, freezers	31,630	31,741
Wires, cords, not specified	11,361	12,718	Washers, dryers	19,108	19,205
Workshop manual tools	88,813	118,799	Misc. household appliances......	26,356	30,532
Misc. workshop equipment	33,561	40,147	**Heating, cooling equipment:** [5]		
Yard and garden equipment:			Chimneys, fireplaces	14,355	24,120
Chains and saws.............	37,278	44,019	Fans (except stove)	15,866	21,126
Hand garden tools...........	29,988	38,796	Heating stoves, space heaters....	32,458	31,439
Trimmers, small power tools [2]	12,150	11,525	Pipes, heating and plumbing	24,744	21,238
Hatchets, axes	15,013	18,270	Radiators	18,103	14,602
Lawn garden care equipment....	38,636	54,507	**Home entertainment equipment:**		
Lawn mowers	61,864	76,133	Pet supplies, equipment	17,845	23,177
Other power lawn equipment.....	13,556	19,424	Sound recording equip [6]	35,006	42,678
Household packaging and containers:			Television sets	34,949	36,995
Cans, other containers	179,484	209,407	Misc. hobby equipment........	11,955	14,513
Glass bottles, jars	71,058	69,837	**Personal use items:**		
Paper, cardboard, plastic products .	32,670	36,931	Cigarettes, lighters, fuels.......	21,092	20,355
Home furnishing: [3]			Clothing.................	102,397	126,173
Bathtub, shower structures	125,829	152,770	Grooming devices	27,013	32,937
Beds, mattresses, pillows	302,190	362,790	Holders for personal items	12,799	16,550
Carpets, rugs	87,739	97,784	Jewelry	43,868	49,891
Chairs, sofas, sofa beds	305,896	381,024	Paper money, coins	28,745	31,796
Desks, cabinets, shelves, racks ..	164,451	210,188	Pencils, pens, other desk supplies .	42,407	45,833
Electric fixtures, lamps, equipment .	38,787	55,191	Razors, shavers, razor blades	35,401	43,916
Ladders, stools	131,551	179,422	Sewing equipment	27,629	32,044
Mirrors, mirror glass	21,630	23,325	**Sports and recreation equipment:**		
Sinks, toilets..............	43,162	54,847	Barbecue grills, stoves, equipment .	13,324	15,786
Tables.................	265,268	332,775	Bicycles, accessories..........	514,738	600,649
Other misc. accessories	40,287	53,181	Exercise equipment . ... [7]	67,028	86,210
Home construction, construction: [4]			Mopeds, minibikes, ATV's [7].....	106,792	127,371
Cabinets or door hardware	17,993	22,946	Nonpowder guns, BB's, pellets....	24,044	32,562
Ceilings, walls, inside panels	189,317	227,618	Playground equipment	210,236	266,869
Counters, counter tops	27,121	33,748	Skateboards	65,819	56,435
Fences	105,919	122,111	Toboggans, sleds, snow disks, etc .	35,008	38,282
Glass doors, windows, panels	182,725	217,916	Trampolines	15,866	38,823
Handrails, railings, banisters	37,284	40,765	**Miscellaneous products:**		
Nails, carpet tacks, etc.........	214,123	241,859	Dollies, carts..............	35,563	41,363
Nonglass doors, panels	281,310	336,790	Elevators, other lifts..........	14,198	14,697
Porches, open side floors, etc	92,840	118,166	Fireworks, flares	9,800	11,390
Stairs, ramps, landings, floors	1,450,421	1,693,175	Gasoline and diesel fuels	13,534	18,882
Window, door sills, frames.......	44,373	53,523	Nursery equipment...........	(NA)	112,753
Misc. construction materials......	67,711	85,492	Toys	147,898	163,624

NA Not available. [1] Includes detergent. [2] Includes garden tools. [3] Includes accessories. [4] Includes materials. [5] Includes ventilating equipment. [6] Includes reproducing equipment. [7] All-terrain vehicles.
Source: National Safety Council, Itasca, IL, *Accident Facts,* annual (copyright).

No. 198. Costs of Accidents: 1991

[Covers costs for accidents in which deaths or disabling injuries beyond the day of the accident occurred, together with vehicle accidents and fires]

COST	AMOUNT (bil. dol.)					PERCENT DISTRIBUTION				
	Total [1]	Motor vehicle	Work	Home	Other	Total [1]	Motor vehicle	Work	Home	Other
Total	177.2	96.1	63.3	22.0	13.9	100.0	100.0	100.0	100.0	100.0
Wage loss [2]	45.8	24.5	10.0	7.4	6.3	25.8	25.5	15.8	33.6	45.3
Medical expense............	29.6	6.7	8.7	9.3	5.6	16.7	7.0	13.7	42.3	40.3
Insurance administration [3]	35.4	27.7	11.0	1.0	0.8	20.0	28.8	17.4	4.5	5.8
Fire loss	7.7	(NA)	2.2	4.3	1.2	4.3	(NA)	3.5	19.5	8.6
Motor vehicle property damage ...	29.0	29.0	1.7	(NA)	(NA)	16.4	30.2	2.7	(NA)	(NA)
Uninsured work loss [4]	29.7	8.2	29.7	(NA)	(NA)	16.8	8.5	46.9	(NA)	(NA)

NA Not available. [1] Excludes duplication between work and motor vehicle ($18.1 billion). [2] Actual wage losses, the present value of future earnings lost, and the replacement-cost value of household services of employed persons and householders. [3] The difference between premiums paid to companies and the claims paid by them. [4] The value of time lost by noninjured workers (e.g. giving first aid).

Source: National Safety Council, Itasca, IL, *Accident Facts, 1992* (copyright).

No. 199. Days of Disability, by Type and Selected Characteristitcs: 1970 to 1990

[Covers civilian noninstitutional population. Beginning 1985, the levels of estimates may not be comparable to estimates for 1970-1980 because the later data are based on a revised questionnaire and field procedures; for further information, see source. Based on National Health Interview Survey; see appendix III. For composition of regions, see table 31]

ITEM	TOTAL DAYS OF DISABILITY (millions)						DAYS PER PERSON					
	1970	1980	1985	1988	1989	1990	1970	1980	1985	1988	1989	1990
Restricted-activity days [1] ..	2,913	4,165	3,453	3,536	3,693	3,669	14.6	19.1	14.8	14.7	15.2	14.9
Male	1,273	1,802	1,442	1,487	1,558	1,558	13.2	17.1	12.8	12.7	13.2	13.1
Female	1,640	2,363	2,011	2,049	2,135	2,111	15.8	21.0	16.6	16.5	17.0	16.7
White [2]	2,526	3,518	2,899	2,969	3,087	3,057	14.4	18.7	14.5	14.6	15.0	14.8
Black [2]	365	580	489	487	511	536	16.2	22.7	17.4	16.6	17.1	17.7
Hispanic [3]	(NA)	(NA)	228	253	278	(NA)	(NA)	(NA)	13.2	13.0	13.2	(NA)
Under 65 years	2,331	3,228	2,557	2,657	2,774	2,734	12.9	16.6	12.4	12.5	12.9	12.6
65 years and over	582	937	895	879	919	936	30.7	39.2	33.1	30.6	31.5	31.4
Northeast............	709	862	689	667	669	656	14.5	17.9	13.8	13.5	13.7	13.2
Midwest.............	691	989	744	762	812	836	12.4	17.2	12.7	12.8	13.6	14.0
South	996	1,415	1,308	1,328	1,392	1,404	15.9	19.8	16.3	16.1	16.7	16.7
West	518	899	712	779	820	773	15.6	22.0	15.7	15.6	15.8	14.8
Family income:												
Under $10,000.......	(NA)	(NA)	893	754	694	662	(NA)	(NA)	25.8	26.6	26.5	27.3
$10,000 to $19,999 ...	(NA)	(NA)	781	751	768	758	(NA)	(NA)	16.7	17.8	18.7	19.1
$20,000 to $34,999 ...	(NA)	(NA)	791	734	752	715	(NA)	(NA)	12.1	12.3	13.3	13.5
$35,000 or more	(NA)	(NA)	568	726	798	912	(NA)	(NA)	9.9	9.7	9.9	10.3
Bed-disability days [4]	1,222	1,520	1,436	1,519	1,579	1,521	6.1	7.0	6.1	6.3	6.5	6.2
Male	503	616	583	607	652	625	5.2	5.9	5.2	5.2	5.5	5.2
Female	720	904	852	912	927	896	6.9	8.0	7.1	7.3	7.4	7.1
Under 65 years	959	1,190	1,064	1,107	1,164	1,115	5.3	6.1	5.1	5.2	5.4	5.2
65 years and over	263	330	371	412	415	406	13.8	13.8	13.7	14.4	14.2	13.6
Work-loss days [5]	417	485	575	609	659	621	5.4	5.0	5.3	5.3	5.6	5.3
Male	243	271	287	307	322	303	5.0	4.9	4.8	4.8	5.0	4.7
Female	175	215	288	302	337	319	5.9	5.1	6.0	5.8	6.4	5.9
School-loss days [6]	222	204	217	222	260	212	4.9	5.3	4.8	4.9	5.7	4.6
Male	108	95	100	107	129	100	4.7	4.8	4.4	4.6	5.6	4.3
Female	114	109	117	115	131	112	5.1	5.7	5.3	5.2	5.9	5.0

NA Not available. [1] A day when a person cuts down on his activities for more than half a day because of illness or injury. Includes bed-disability, work-loss, and school-loss days. Total includes other races and unknown income, not shown separately. [2] Beginning 1980, race was determined by asking the household respondent to report his race. In earlier years the racial classification of respondents was determined by interviewer observation. [3] Persons of Hispanic origin may be of any race. [4] A day when a person stayed in bed more than half a day because of illness or injury. Includes those work-loss and school-loss days actually spent in bed. [5] A day when a person lost more than half a workday because of illness or injury. Computed for persons 17 years of age and over (beginning 1985, 18 years of age and over) in the currently employed population, defined as those who were working or had a job or business from which they were not on layoff during the 2-week period preceding the week of interview. [6] Child's loss of more than half a school day because of illness or injury. Computed for children 6-16 years of age. Beginning 1985, children 5-17 years old.

Source: U.S. National Center for Health Statistics, *Vital and Health Statistics*, series 10, No. 181; and unpublished data.

No. 200. Children Immunized Against Specified Diseases, by Age Group: 1985 and 1991

[In percent. Covers civilian noninstitutionalized population. Based on estimates from the National Health Interview Survey. See Appendix III]

VACCINE	ALL RESPONDENTS								RESPONDENTS CONSULTING VACCINATIONS RECORDS OR REPORTING NO VACCINATIONS	
	2 years old				1 to 4 years old				2 year olds at the time of the survey	At the second birthday
	1985, total	1991			1985, total	1991				
		Total	White	Black and other		Total	White	Black and other		
Diphtheria-tetanus-pertussis [1] .	63.6	66.6	70.1	53.0	64.9	65.8	68.6	54.6	82.8	81.3
Polio [1]	53.6	52.2	55.9	38.1	55.3	50.6	52.7	42.1	70.5	65.0
Measles containing [2]	61.2	80.4	81.9	74.9	60.8	77.6	77.9	76.4	83.8	80.4
Hib [3]	(NA)	56.4	59.6	44.5	(NA)	56.9	58.5	50.4	63.9	51.3
Up-to-date for age	(NA)	37.2	41.3	21.5	(NA)	42.1	44.6	31.7	55.5	47.0

NA Not available. [1] Three or more doses. [2] Measles, measles/rubella, measles/mumps, and measles/mumps/rubella. [3] Haemophilus B.

Source: U.S. Centers for Disease Control and Prevention, Atlanta, GA, United States Immunization Survey, and the National Health Interview Survey.

No. 201. Specified Reportable Diseases—Cases Reported: 1970 to 1991

[For diseases with 1,000 or more cases reported in 1991. Figures should be interpreted with caution. Although reporting of some of these diseases is incomplete, the figures are of value in indicating trends of disease incidence. Includes cases imported from outside the United States. See *Historical Statistics, Colonial Times to 1970*, series B 291-303, for related data]

DISEASE	1970	1980	1984	1985	1986	1987	1988	1989	1990	1991
AIDS [1]	(NA)	(NA)	4,445	8,249	13,166	21,070	31,001	33,722	41,595	43,672
Amebiasis	2,888	5,271	5,252	4,433	3,532	3,123	2,860	3,217	3,328	2,989
Aseptic meningitis	6,480	8,028	8,326	10,619	11,374	11,487	7,234	10,274	11,852	14,526
Chickenpox (1,000).	[2]	190.9	222.0	178.2	183.2	213.2	192.9	185.4	173.1	147.1
Encephalitis:										
Primary infectious [3]	1,580	1,362	1,257	1,376	1,302	1,418	882	981	1,341	1,021
Post infectious [3]	370	40	108	161	124	121	121	88	105	82
Haemophilius influenza	[2]	[2]	[2]	[2]	[2]	[2]	[2]	[2]	[2]	2,764
Hepatitis: B (serum) (1,000) . .	8.3	19.0	26.1	26.6	26.1	25.9	23.2	23.4	21.1	18.0
A (infectious) (1,000)	56.8	29.1	22.0	23.2	23.4	25.3	28.5	35.8	31.4	24.4
Unspecified (1,000)	[2]	11.9	5.5	5.5	3.9	3.1	2.5	2.3	1.7	1.3
Non-A, non-B (1,000).	[2]	[2]	3.9	4.2	3.6	3.0	2.6	2.5	2.6	3.6
Legionellosis	[2]	[2]	750	830	948	1,038	1,085	1,190	1,370	1,317
Lyme disease	[2]	[2]	[2]	[2]	[2]	[2]	[2]	[2]	[2]	9,465
Malaria	3,051	2,062	1,007	1,049	1,123	944	1,099	1,277	1,292	1,278
Measles (1,000)	47.4	13.5	2.6	2.8	6.3	3.7	3.4	18.2	27.8	9.6
Meningococcal infections. . . .	2,505	2,840	2,746	2,479	2,594	2,930	2,964	2,727	2,451	2,130
Mumps (1,000)	105.0	8.6	3.0	3.0	7.8	12.8	4.9	5.7	5.3	4.3
Pertussis [4] (1,000)	4.2	1.7	2.3	3.6	4.2	2.8	3.5	4.2	4.6	2.7
Rabies, animal.	3,224	6,421	5,567	5,565	5,504	4,658	4,651	4,724	4,826	6,910
Rubella [5] (1,000)	56.6	3.9	1.0	0.6	0.6	0.3	0.2	0.4	1.1	1.4
Salmonellosis [6] (1,000)	22.1	33.7	40.9	65.3	50.0	50.9	48.9	47.8	48.6	48.2
Shigellosis [7] (1,000).	13.8	19.0	17.4	17.1	17.1	23.9	30.6	25.0	27.1	23.5
Tuberculosis [8] (1,000).	37.1	27.7	22.3	22.2	22.8	22.5	22.4	23.5	25.7	26.3
Venereal diseases (civilian cases):										
Gonorrhea (1,000).	600	1,004	879	911	901	781	720	733	690	620
Syphilis (1,000)	91	69	70	68	68	87	103	111	134	129
Other (1,000)	2.2	1.0	1.0	2.3	4.2	5.3	5.2	4.9	4.6	4.0

NA Not available. [1] Acquired immunodeficiency syndrome was not a notifiable disease until 1984. Figures are shown for years in which cases were reported to the CDC. [2] Disease was not notifiable. [3] Beginning 1980, reported data reflect new diagnostic categories. [4] Whooping cough. [5] German measles. [6] Excludes typhoid fever. [7] Bacillary dysentery. [8] Newly reported active cases. New diagnostic standards introduced in 1980.

Source: U.S. Centers for Disease Control, Atlanta, GA, *Summary of Notifiable Diseases, United States, Morbidity and Mortality Weekly Report*, vol. 40, No. 53, October 1992.

No. 202. Selected Measures of Hospital Utilization for Patients Discharged With the Diagnosis of Human Immunodeficiency Virus (HIV): 1985 to 1991

[See headnote, table 185]

MEASURE OF UTILIZATION	Unit	1985	1986	1987	1988	1989	1990	1991
Number of patients discharged [1].	1,000 . . .	23	44	67	95	140	146	165
Rate of patient discharges [2] . . .	Rate . . .	1.0	1.8	2.8	3.9	5.7	5.9	6.6
Number of days of care	1,000 . . .	387	714	936	1,277	1,731	2,188	2,108
Rate of days of care [2]	Rate . . .	16.3	29.8	38.7	52.3	70.2	87.7	84.1
Average length of stay [3]	Days. . . .	17.1	16.4	14.1	13.4	12.4	14.9	12.8

[1] Comparisons beginning 1988 with data for earlier years should be made with caution as estimates of change may reflect improvements in the 1988 design rather than true changes in hospital use. [2] Per 10,000 population. Based on Bureau of the Census estimated civilian population as of July 1. Population estimates do not reflect revised estimates based on the 1990 Census of Population. [3] For similar data on all patients, see table 185.

Source: National Center for Health Statistics, *Vital and Health Statistics*, series 13.

No. 203. AIDS Cases Reported, by Patient Characteristic: 1981 to 1992

[**Provisional.** For cases reported in the year shown. For data on AIDS deaths, see table 131. Data are subject to retrospective changes and may differ from those data in table 201]

CHARACTERISTIC	NUMBER OF CASES										PERCENT DISTRIBUTION	
	Total	1981-1984	1985	1986	1987	1988	1989	1990	1991	1992	1981-1984	1992
Total	244,939	7,354	8,210	13,147	21,088	30,719	33,595	41,653	43,701	45,472	100.0	100.0
Age:												
Under 5 years old...	3,265	91	112	155	266	443	494	580	521	603	1.2	1.3
5 to 12 years old ...	765	5	17	28	56	128	102	143	146	140	0.1	0.3
13 to 29 years old ..	47,307	1609	1,680	2,821	4,359	6,343	6,726	8,114	7,852	7,803	21.9	17.2
30 to 39 years old ..	112,084	3446	3,856	6,100	9,617	14,118	15,524	18,944	19,954	20,525	46.9	45.1
40 to 49 years old ..	56,235	1550	1,709	2,703	4,519	6,524	7,329	9,701	10,643	11,557	21.1	25.4
50 to 59 years old ..	17,835	536	631	964	1,562	2,146	2,413	2,934	3,246	3,403	7.3	7.5
Over 60 years old...	7,448	117	205	376	709	1,017	1,007	1,237	1,339	1,441	1.6	3.2
Sex:												
Male	217,141	6844	7,622	12,099	19,256	27,435	29,942	36,770	38,013	39,160	93.1	86.1
Female	27,798	510	588	1,048	1,832	3,284	3,653	4,883	5,688	6,312	6.9	13.9
Race/ethnic group:												
White [1]	132,573	4331	4,968	7,837	12,962	17,063	18,569	22,325	22,193	22,325	58.9	49.1
Black [1]	75,929	1951	2,081	3,388	5,379	9,118	10,293	13,220	14,609	15,890	26.5	34.9
Hispanic	33,827	1039	1,099	1,803	2,543	4,260	4,358	5,658	6,405	6,662	14.1	14.7
Other/unknown	2,610	33	62	119	204	278	375	450	494	595	0.4	1.3
Leading States: [2]												
New York	50,985	2,893	2,479	3,768	3,948	6,965	5,993	8,389	8,152	8,398	39.3	18.5
California	46,818	1,595	1,977	2,656	4,885	5,703	6,426	7,337	7,700	8,539	21.7	18.8
Florida	24,492	536	549	1,028	1,632	2,665	3,449	4,018	5,514	5,101	7.3	11.2
Texas...........	17,363	359	483	937	1,667	2,215	2,381	3,334	3,067	2,920	4.9	6.4
New Jersey.......	14,702	481	467	766	1,509	2,452	2,225	2,459	2,303	2,040	6.5	4.5
Illinois	8,229	157	188	346	629	987	1,132	1,276	1,602	1,912	2.1	4.2
Georgia	7,044	95	191	304	517	838	1,093	1,228	1,454	1,324	1.3	2.9
Pennsylvania	6,967	145	201	309	653	852	1,071	1,192	1,218	1,326	2.0	2.9
Maryland	5,307	86	150	188	457	544	713	996	969	1,204	1.2	2.6
Massachusetts....	5,177	133	164	282	452	710	752	842	967	875	1.8	1.9
District of Columbia .	4,118	113	178	227	464	494	493	734	709	706	1.5	1.6
Louisiana	3,794	73	104	165	336	401	508	703	794	710	1.0	1.6
Ohio	3,674	46	54	213	336	506	488	679	619	733	0.6	1.6
Virginia..........	3,525	67	109	160	242	348	392	744	679	784	0.9	1.7
Washington.......	3,404	66	109	168	324	342	526	746	572	551	0.9	1.2
Michigan.........	3,343	44	61	150	211	455	506	579	619	718	0.6	1.6
Missouri.........	3,192	35	50	74	238	411	442	580	654	708	0.5	1.6
Connecticut.......	3,079	85	86	175	252	412	431	425	567	646	1.2	1.4
North Carolina	2,854	23	66	81	209	276	444	571	600	584	0.3	1.3
Colorado.........	2,433	64	62	166	226	324	386	362	433	410	0.9	0.9
Arizona..........	1,943	29	49	78	214	275	321	309	282	386	0.4	0.8
Tennessee	1,864	7	18	72	72	329	266	341	351	408	0.1	0.9
South Carolina.....	1,785	18	38	58	84	174	327	360	335	391	0.2	0.9
Indiana..........	1,744	29	26	71	132	78	399	292	315	402	0.4	0.9
Alabama.........	1,702	11	29	33	153	211	214	239	375	437	0.1	1.0
Oregon..........	1,565	20	35	63	160	177	228	336	257	289	0.3	0.6
Percent of total...	94.4	98.0	96.5	95.4	94.9	94.9	94.1	93.8	94.1	93.5	(X)	(X)

X Not applicable.   [1] Non-Hispanic.   [2] States with at least 1,500 total cases reported 1992.
Source: U.S. Centers for Disease Control, Atlanta, GA, unpublished data.

No. 204. Appropriations for AIDS, by Category and Leading States: 1984 to 1992

[**For fiscal years, except as indicated.** Based on survey of State budget analysts, commissioners of health and AIDS coordinators, and other State agencies with AIDS programs, (e.g. Departments of Education)]

ITEM	Unit	1984-1992, total	1986	1987	1988	1989	1990	1991	1992
U.S.P.H.S. expenditures [1] ...... [2] ..	Mil. dol .	8,606.3	233.8	502.5	962.0	1,301.0	1,588.6	1,888.2	1,960.1
State government appropriations [2] ..	Mil. dol .	1,519.9	26.3	65.0	149.2	249.1	278.9	330.7	401.9
Number of States.............	Number	(X)	21	28	37	47	51	51	51
Appropriations for—									
Education/information	Percent.	(NA)	25	19	21	26	28	25	27
Patient care [3]	Percent.	(NA)	4	15	16	25	[4]45	[4]51	[4]50
Support services [3]	Percent.	(NA)	12	11	19	13	([4])	([4])	([4])
Research...............	Percent.	(NA)	41	27	17	8	1	2	4
Testing/counseling .... [5]	Percent.	(NA)	3	11	12	18	14	12	11
Leading areas by appropriations: [5]									
California...............	$1,000 .	377,010	16,020	31,515	58,033	76,877	46,649	47,738	92,684
New York	$1,000 .	375,152	4,500	9,500	39,920	52,884	68,576	90,493	101,229
Florida................	$1,000 .	100,200	576	5,557	12,539	17,765	19,432	20,994	23,280
Massachusetts..........	$1,000 .	84,995	1,604	4,073	7,591	14,754	18,517	18,242	18,714
New Jersey	$1,000 .	86,780	1,969	4,963	7,907	13,012	15,469	14,446	27,564
Percent of total	Percent.	67.0	89.6	83.3	80.6	71.0	60.5	58.0	65.6

NA Not available.   X Not applicable.   [1] Source: United States Public Health Service budget office.   [2] Includes DC. Includes appropriations from State governments direct general revenue funds only; excludes Medicaid expenditures. Includes appropriations for other activities, not shown separately.   [3] Beginning 1989, hospice care included in patient care, rather than support services.   [4] Beginning 1990, patient care and support services were combined.   [5] Areas with over $7 million appropriations for 1989.

Source: Except as indicated, AIDS Policy Center, Intergovernmental Health Policy Project, The George Washington University, Washington, DC, *Intergovernmental AIDS Reports*, vol. 6, No. 4, and earlier issues.

No. 205. Acute Conditions, by Type, 1970 to 1990, and by Selected Characteristics, 1990

[Covers civilian noninstitutional population. Estimates include only acute conditions which were medically attended or caused at least one day of restricted activity. Based on National Health Interview Survey; see Appendix III. See headnote, table 199. For composition of regions, see table 31]

YEAR AND CHARACTERISTIC	NUMBER OF CONDITIONS (mil.)					RATE PER 100 POPULATION				
	Infective and parasitic	Respiratory		Digestive system	Injuries	Infective and parasitic	Respiratory		Digestive system	Injuries
		Common cold	Influenza				Common cold	Influenza		
1970	48.2	(NA)	(NA)	23.0	59.2	24.1	(NA)	(NA)	11.5	29.6
1975	47.6	(NA)	(NA)	21.6	76.2	22.8	(NA)	(NA)	10.3	36.4
1980	53.6	(NA)	(NA)	24.9	72.7	24.6	(NA)	(NA)	11.4	33.4
1985	47.8	(NA)	(NA)	16.3	64.0	20.5	(NA)	(NA)	7.0	27.4
1990, total [1]	51.7	61.5	106.8	13.0	60.1	21.0	25.0	43.4	5.3	24.4
Under 5 years old	10.5	12.6	11.5	0.8	5.3	54.8	65.8	60.3	4.2	27.6
5 to 17 years old	19.7	14.7	28.2	3.3	13.5	43.3	32.2	61.8	7.3	29.7
18 to 24 years old	5.3	6.8	11.6	1.7	7.2	21.2	27.2	46.3	6.6	28.8
25 to 44 years old	10.2	16.3	34.5	3.9	20.1	12.7	20.3	43.0	4.9	25.2
45 to 64 years old	3.8	6.5	15.4	2.0	9.3	8.2	14.0	33.0	4.3	19.9
65 years old and over	2.1	4.6	5.7	1.3	4.7	7.2	15.4	19.3	4.4	15.9
Male	22.1	26.9	46.4	5.4	33.6	18.5	22.5	38.9	4.6	28.1
Female	29.6	34.6	60.4	7.6	26.6	23.3	27.3	47.7	6.0	21.0
White	44.4	51.2	95.8	10.4	52.8	21.4	24.7	46.3	5.0	25.5
Black	6.1	8.1	7.3	2.1	5.9	20.2	26.8	24.1	6.8	19.5
Northeast	10.2	13.9	15.2	2.0	10.3	20.5	27.8	30.5	4.1	20.6
Midwest	10.3	13.3	32.7	3.2	15.5	17.2	22.3	54.7	5.4	26.0
South	23.2	18.3	25.4	4.7	21.6	27.5	21.7	30.2	5.6	25.7
West	8.0	16.0	33.4	3.1	12.7	15.3	30.6	64.1	5.9	24.3
Family income:										
Under $10,000	5.6	7.9	10.8	1.6	6.7	23.0	32.5	44.4	6.8	27.4
$10,000 to $19,999	7.9	10.3	18.0	2.0	9.8	19.8	25.9	45.3	5.1	24.6
$20,000 to $34,999	10.3	12.4	23.5	2.7	13.5	19.4	23.3	44.3	5.2	25.5
$35,000 or more	21.0	23.3	40.3	5.0	21.2	23.7	26.4	45.5	5.6	23.9

NA Not available. [1] Includes other races and unknown income not shown separately.

Source: U.S. National Center for Health Statistics, *Vital and Health Statistics*, series 10, No. 181; and unpublished data.

No. 206. Prevalence of Selected Reported Chronic Conditions, by Age and Sex: 1980 and 1990

[Covers civilian noninstitutional population. Conditions classified according to ninth revision of International Classification of Diseases. Based on National Health Interview Survey; see Appendix III. See headnote, table 199]

CHRONIC CONDITION	1980		1990, RATE [1]								
	Conditions (1,000)	Rate [1]	1990, conditions (1,000)	Male				Female			
				Under 45 yrs.	45-64 yrs.	65-74 yrs.	75 yrs. and over	Under 45 yrs.	45-64 yrs.	65-74 yrs.	75 yrs. and over
Arthritis	27,773	127.4	30,833	25.8	204.9	373.3	376.8	35.8	289.7	472.2	628.6
Dermatitis, including eczema	9,139	41.9	8,681	28.2	21.9	22.7	[2]24.4	42.1	50.9	41.6	38.2
Trouble with—											
Dry (itching) skin	[3]3,698	[3]16.3	5,045	12.9	19.7	30.6	[2]30.4	20.7	25.3	46.4	39.5
Ingrown nails	[3]4,503	[3]19.8	6,040	20.1	33.0	34.3	45.7	14.9	35.0	56.2	61.6
Corns and calluses	[3]4,811	[3]21.2	4,931	10.0	22.7	23.0	[2]28.6	13.7	41.9	65.1	59.9
Visual impairments	7,984	36.6	7,525	30.3	49.5	73.3	109.8	11.7	28.4	33.9	104.5
Cataracts	[3]5,124	[3]22.6	5,927	[2]1.2	17.4	81.2	129.4	2.5	26.3	137.2	271.0
Hearing impairments	17,370	79.7	23,296	49.7	197.8	350.1	480.2	29.6	106.0	194.9	370.3
Tinnitus	[3]5,130	[3]22.6	7,149	12.6	59.6	101.3	92.3	9.8	48.2	88.4	87.2
Deformities or orthopedic impairments	18,504	84.9	28,899	92.4	151.4	152.3	121.1	98.2	170.8	181.0	220.9
Ulcer	[3]3,891	[3]17.1	4,466	11.0	31.6	38.3	38.1	14.3	25.8	29.2	29.9
Hernia of abdominal cavity	[3]4,970	[3]21.9	4,179	6.7	35.1	42.7	79.3	6.4	24.0	56.5	60.4
Frequent indigestion	[3]5,360	[3]23.6	5,770	16.6	36.5	29.2	46.4	18.9	29.1	57.0	30.6
Frequent constipation	[3]4,431	[3]19.5	3,991	4.9	[2]5.6	[2]17.3	55.1	15.5	22.3	47.3	100.2
Diabetes	5,665	26.0	6,232	5.6	48.6	102.0	86.3	7.4	52.1	102.3	75.9
Migraine	5,630	25.8	9,790	20.9	23.9	[2]4.7	[2]0.7	55.8	87.3	37.0	28.9
Heart conditions	16,434	75.4	19,307	27.3	137.4	275.2	404.8	34.2	101.5	242.5	292.3
High blood pressure (Hypertension)	24,919	114.3	27,129	38.1	221.9	285.0	304.2	32.3	215.1	409.8	444.1
Varicose veins of lower extremities	5,930	27.2	6,976	4.8	17.6	27.5	59.7	25.8	73.6	99.5	98.7
Hemorrhoids	8,616	39.5	9,446	22.7	71.1	53.4	[2]32.7	28.9	70.8	73.4	60.8
Chronic bronchitis	7,869	36.1	12,584	40.4	31.6	62.0	50.5	51.7	81.1	87.8	67.8
Asthma	6,803	31.2	10,311	43.4	28.8	28.6	44.3	44.1	47.7	35.6	41.2
Hay fever, allergic rhinitis without asthma	17,433	80.0	22,187	89.1	80.6	65.1	67.6	96.3	108.4	83.5	49.0
Chronic sinusitis	31,956	145.0	32,314	99.9	162.7	132.2	145.5	127.7	199.5	171.7	149.6

[1] Conditions per 1,000 persons. [2] Figure does not meet standards of reliability or precision. [3] 1982 data.
Source: U.S. National Center for Health Statistics, *Vital and Health Statistics*, series 10, No. 181; and unpublished data.

No. 207. Number of Clients in Alcohol and Drug Abuse Treatment Units, by Type of Care and Unit Location: 1991

[As of **September 30.** Based on the National Drug and Alcoholism Treatment Unit Survey (NDATUS), a census of all known drug abuse and alcoholism treatment facilities in the United States. Data collected in cooperation with State agencies which defined what constitutes a facility for reporting purposes]

TYPE OF CARE AND LOCATION	Service locations reporting [1]	All clients	Drug abuse clients only	Alcoholism clients only	Clients with both problems	Clients with a drug problem [2]	Clients with an alcohol problem [3]
Total	8,928	811,819	237,008	365,147	209,664	446,672	574,811
TYPE OF CARE							
Detoxification: [4] Hospital inpatient . .	768	5,215	1,051	2,211	1,953	3,004	4,164
Free-standing residential.	525	6,257	1,425	2,947	1,885	3,310	4,832
Rehab/residential: [5]							
Hospital inpatient	625	9,212	1,543	3,313	4,356	5,899	7,669
Short-term—30 days or less	895	17,929	3,150	7,449	7,330	10,480	14,779
Long-term—over 30 days	2,027	60,537	21,531	13,910	25,096	46,627	39,006
Ambulatory: [6]							
Outpatient	5,787	662,624	190,542	318,018	154,064	344,606	472,082
Intensive outpatient [7]	1,688	42,128	11,058	16,889	14,181	25,239	31,070
Detoxification [8]	253	7,917	6,708	410	799	7,507	1,209
UNIT LOCATION							
Community mental health care	1,287	133,670	32,854	68,293	32,523	65,377	100,816
Free-standing non-residential facility . .	3,634	426,562	134,259	210,318	81,985	216,244	292,303
Hospital [9]	1,292	78,229	20,441	33,090	24,698	45,139	57,788
Correctional facility	219	39,270	12,784	4,826	21,660	34,444	26,486
Halfway house	775	15,830	2,374	6,574	6,882	9,256	13,456
Other residential facility	1,162	51,575	17,452	15,868	18,255	35,707	34,123
Other site	169	11,857	2,726	6,490	2,641	5,367	9,131
Multiple sites	390	54,826	14,118	19,688	21,020	35,138	40,708

[1] Some units provide more than one type of treatment and are counted more than once in the total. [2] The sum of clients with a drug problem and clients with both diagnoses. [3] The sum of clients with an alcohol problem and clients with both diagnoses. [4] 24 hour care for the withdrawal and transition to ongoing treatment. [5] Other than detoxification. Provides treatment services for dependency. [6] Ambulatory care provides care in a nonresidential setting. [7] "Intensive" outpatient involves at least 2 hours of treatment a day for at least 3 days a week. [8] Less than 24 hour care. [9] Includes general hospitals, alcoholism hospitals, mental/psychiatric hospitals, and other specialized hospitals.

Source: U.S. Substance Abuse and Mental Health Services Administration and U.S. Institute on Alcohol Abuse and Alcoholism, *1991 National Drug and Alcoholism Treatment Unit Survey: Final Report.*

No. 208. Drug Use, by Type of Drug and Age Group: 1974 to 1991

[In percent. Current users are those who used drugs at least once within month prior to this study. Based on national samples of respondents residing in households. Subject to sampling variability; see source]

AGE AND TYPE OF DRUG	EVER USED						CURRENT USER					
	1974	1979	1982	1985	1988	1991	1974	1979	1982	1985	1988	1991
12 TO 17 YEARS OLD												
Marijuana	23.0	30.9	26.7	23.6	17.4	13.0	12.0	16.7	11.5	12.0	6.4	4.3
Cocaine	3.6	5.4	6.5	4.9	3.4	2.4	1.0	1.4	1.6	1.5	1.1	0.4
Inhalants	8.5	9.8	(NA)	9.2	8.8	7.0	0.7	2.0	(NA)	3.4	2.0	1.8
Hallucinogens	6.0	7.1	5.2	3.3	3.5	3.3	1.3	2.2	1.4	1.2	0.8	0.8
Heroin	1.0	0.5	(B)	(B)	0.6	0.3	(B)	(B)	(B)	(B)	(B)	0.1
Stimulants [1]	5.0	3.4	6.7	5.6	4.2	3.0	1.0	1.2	2.6	1.6	1.2	0.5
Sedatives [1]	5.0	3.2	5.8	4.1	2.3	2.4	1.0	1.1	1.3	1.0	0.6	0.5
Tranquilizers [1]	3.0	4.1	4.9	4.8	2.0	2.1	1.0	0.6	0.9	0.6	0.2	0.4
Analgesics [1]	(NA)	3.2	4.2	5.8	4.1	4.4	(NA)	0.6	0.7	1.6	0.9	1.1
Alcohol.	54.0	70.3	65.2	55.5	50.2	46.4	34.0	37.2	30.2	31.0	25.2	20.3
Cigarettes	52.0	54.1	49.5	45.2	42.3	37.9	25.0	12.1	14.7	15.3	11.8	10.8
18 TO 25 YEARS OLD												
Marijuana	52.7	68.2	64.1	60.3	56.4	50.5	25.2	35.4	27.4	21.8	15.5	13.0
Cocaine	12.7	27.5	28.3	25.2	19.7	17.9	3.1	9.3	6.8	7.6	4.5	2.0
Inhalants	9.2	16.5	(NA)	12.4	12.5	10.9	(B)	1.2	(NA)	0.8	1.7	1.5
Hallucinogens	16.6	25.1	21.1	11.3	13.8	13.1	2.5	4.4	1.7	1.9	1.9	1.2
Heroin	4.5	3.5	1.2	1.2	0.3	0.8	(B)	(B)	(B)	(B)	(B)	0.1
Stimulants [1]	17.0	18.2	18.0	17.1	11.3	9.4	3.7	3.5	4.7	3.7	2.4	0.8
Sedatives [1]	15.0	17.0	18.7	11.0	5.5	4.3	1.6	2.8	2.6	1.6	0.9	0.7
Tranquilizers [1]	10.0	15.8	15.1	12.0	7.8	7.4	1.2	2.1	1.6	1.6	1.0	0.6
Analgesics [1]	(NA)	11.8	12.1	11.3	9.4	10.2	(NA)	1.0	1.0	1.8	1.5	1.4
Alcohol.	81.6	95.3	94.6	92.6	90.3	90.2	69.3	75.9	70.9	71.4	65.3	63.6
Cigarettes	68.8	82.8	76.9	75.6	75.0	71.2	48.8	42.6	39.5	36.8	35.2	32.2
26 YEARS OLD AND OVER												
Marijuana	9.9	19.6	23.0	27.2	30.7	32.7	2.0	6.0	6.6	6.1	3.9	3.3
Cocaine	0.9	4.3	8.5	9.5	9.9	11.6	(B)	0.9	1.2	2.0	0.9	0.8
Inhalants	1.2	3.9	(NA)	5.0	3.9	4.2	(B)	0.5	(NA)	0.5	0.2	0.3
Hallucinogens	1.3	4.5	6.4	6.2	6.6	7.8	(B)	(B)	(B)	(B)	(B)	0.1
Heroin	0.5	1.0	1.1	1.1	1.1	1.5	(B)	(B)	(B)	(B)	(B)	(B)
Stimulants [1]	3.0	5.8	6.2	7.9	6.6	7.1	(B)	0.5	0.6	0.7	0.5	0.2
Sedatives [1]	2.0	3.5	4.8	5.2	3.3	4.5	(B)	(B)	(B)	0.6	0.3	0.3
Tranquilizers [1]	2.0	3.1	3.6	7.2	4.5	5.7	(B)	(B)	(B)	1.0	0.6	0.5
Analgesics [1]	(NA)	2.7	3.2	5.6	4.5	5.5	(NA)	(B)	(B)	0.9	0.4	0.5
Alcohol.	73.2	91.5	88.2	89.4	88.6	88.6	54.5	61.3	59.8	60.6	54.8	52.5
Cigarettes	65.4	83.0	78.7	80.5	79.6	77.6	39.1	36.9	34.6	32.8	29.8	28.2

B Base too small to meet statistical standards for reliability of a derived figure. NA Not available. [1] Nonmedical use; does not include over-the-counter drugs.

Source: U.S. Substance Abuse and Mental Health Services Administration, *National Household Survey on Drug Abuse: 1991.*

No. 209. Use of Selected Drugs, by Age of User: 1991

[In percent. See headnote, table 208. For composition of regions, see table 31]

SUBSTANCE AND AGE GROUP	Total [1]	SEX		RACE/ETHNICITY			REGION			
		Male	Female	White [2]	Black [2]	Hispanic	Northeast	Midwest	South	West
CURRENT USERS										
Cigarettes: Total	27.0	28.7	25.5	27.3	27.9	24.7	26.9	28.2	27.3	25.4
12 to 17 years old	10.8	11.8	9.8	12.7	4.4	8.7	11.6	12.4	10.2	9.5
18 to 25 years old	32.2	32.0	32.3	35.8	21.8	24.8	35.7	33.6	30.3	30.6
26 to 34 years old	32.9	34.8	31.1	33.3	36.9	28.6	32.6	34.4	35.9	26.9
35 years old and over	26.6	28.8	24.7	25.8	32.6	27.7	25.3	27.6	27.0	26.2
Alcohol: Total	50.9	58.1	44.3	52.7	43.7	47.5	56.3	52.3	44.0	56.3
12 to 17 years old	20.3	22.3	18.2	20.4	20.1	22.5	19.0	21.9	19.8	20.7
18 to 25 years old	63.6	69.7	57.8	67.2	56.0	52.8	71.1	65.2	57.7	65.7
26 to 34 years old	61.7	70.8	52.8	63.8	57.1	57.2	66.3	64.5	55.9	63.5
35 years old and over	49.5	57.4	42.5	50.9	40.3	47.8	55.3	50.5	41.1	57.2
Marijuana: Total	4.8	6.3	3.4	4.5	7.2	4.3	5.2	4.6	4.2	5.8
12 to 17 years old	4.3	5.0	3.7	4.4	4.5	4.6	3.7	4.6	3.9	5.5
18 to 25 years old	13.0	15.7	10.5	13.7	14.6	9.1	14.7	11.5	12.1	14.8
26 to 34 years old	7.0	9.5	4.5	6.6	11.9	4.2	6.2	7.6	5.6	9.2
35 years old and over	2.1	3.0	1.3	1.9	3.5	2.3	2.8	2.0	1.7	2.3
Cocaine: Total	0.9	1.3	0.6	0.7	1.8	1.6	0.9	0.9	0.8	1.3
12 to 17 years old	0.4	0.5	0.3	0.3	0.5	1.3	0.5	(³)	0.6	0.4
18 to 25 years old	2.0	2.8	1.3	1.7	3.1	2.7	1.5	2.1	1.8	3.0
26 to 34 years old	1.8	2.6	1.1	1.6	2.7	2.0	2.1	1.7	1.4	2.4
35 years old and over	0.5	0.6	0.3	0.2	1.3	1.0	0.4	0.6	0.4	0.6
Smokeless tobacco: Total	3.4	6.5	0.5	3.9	2.0	0.8	1.2	3.0	5.4	2.5
12 to 17 years old	3.0	5.4	0.5	3.9	0.8	1.1	0.9	3.8	3.8	2.5
18 to 25 years old	5.8	11.4	0.3	7.4	1.2	1.7	2.7	4.6	7.7	6.5
26 to 34 years old	3.6	7.1	0.2	4.3	1.5	0.8	0.9	2.9	6.0	3.0
35 years old and over	2.8	5.2	0.7	3.0	2.8	0.4	1.0	2.6	4.9	1.3
EVER USED										
Crack: Total	1.9	2.6	1.3	1.5	4.3	2.1	1.8	2.0	1.5	2.6
12 to 17 years old	0.9	0.7	1.0	0.8	1.1	1.3	0.6	0.4	0.9	1.7
18 to 25 years old	3.8	4.7	2.8	3.7	4.7	3.3	4.6	3.1	3.1	5.0
26 to 34 years old	3.7	5.2	2.3	2.8	9.3	3.7	2.9	3.3	3.5	5.2
35 years old and over	1.0	1.6	0.6	0.8	3.0	1.1	1.0	1.6	0.6	1.3
Inhalants: Total	5.4	7.0	4.0	5.6	3.8	4.8	4.5	4.5	4.9	8.3
12 to 17 years old	7.0	7.0	7.0	7.6	5.1	6.6	5.1	6.8	7.6	7.9
18 to 25 years old	10.9	12.3	9.5	12.7	4.5	6.5	9.8	9.7	9.8	15.3
26 to 34 years old	9.2	12.1	6.3	10.3	4.6	6.3	7.7	6.6	9.1	13.5
35 years old and over	2.5	3.8	1.4	2.3	2.9	2.6	2.2	2.2	1.7	4.7
Hallucinogens: Total	8.1	10.1	6.2	8.9	4.1	6.4	7.5	7.9	6.0	12.6
12 to 17 years old	3.3	3.3	3.4	3.8	1.2	3.5	2.9	3.8	3.0	3.8
18 to 25 years old	13.1	15.4	11.0	15.8	5.4	7.5	11.7	12.1	10.5	20.8
26 to 34 years old	15.5	18.8	12.4	18.0	5.9	9.2	15.1	15.0	12.5	21.3
35 years old and over	5.2	7.0	3.5	5.4	3.7	5.5	4.8	5.2	3.3	8.8
Stimulants: [4] Total	7.0	8.2	5.9	7.9	3.3	4.8	4.4	6.2	6.5	11.5
12 to 17 years old	3.0	2.5	3.4	3.5	0.8	2.1	1.5	3.0	3.5	3.3
18 to 25 years old	9.4	9.8	8.9	11.3	3.2	5.1	5.0	10.5	9.1	13.2
26 to 34 years old	12.2	14.1	10.4	14.3	5.0	6.3	7.9	10.3	12.6	17.8
35 years old and over	5.4	6.8	4.2	5.8	3.3	4.7	3.6	4.5	4.5	10.1
Sedatives: [4] Total	4.3	4.8	3.8	4.6	3.0	3.0	3.3	3.6	3.9	6.7
12 to 17 years old	2.4	2.0	2.9	2.7	1.2	2.2	1.8	2.4	2.7	2.5
18 to 25 years old	4.3	4.5	4.1	5.1	2.4	2.3	2.1	5.5	4.4	5.0
26 to 34 years old	7.5	8.7	6.3	8.6	3.8	3.4	6.2	5.9	8.1	9.3
35 years old and over	3.5	4.0	3.1	3.5	3.4	3.3	2.8	2.7	2.7	6.8
Tranquilizers: [4] Total	5.6	5.9	5.2	6.1	3.1	3.9	4.2	4.7	5.6	7.9
12 to 17 years old	2.1	1.8	2.5	2.6	1.1	1.0	1.4	1.9	2.6	2.0
18 to 25 years old	7.4	7.5	7.4	8.8	3.9	3.7	6.2	7.8	7.9	7.6
26 to 34 years old	10.0	10.9	9.1	11.4	5.7	5.4	9.2	8.5	11.0	10.7
35 years old and over	4.2	4.6	3.9	4.4	2.4	4.2	2.5	3.2	3.8	7.9
Analgesics: [4] Total	6.1	6.8	5.4	6.5	4.7	3.9	4.0	6.8	5.3	8.7
12 to 17 years old	4.4	4.3	4.6	4.8	3.9	3.6	2.7	5.0	5.0	4.4
18 to 25 years old	10.2	10.6	9.8	11.4	6.8	6.3	6.0	11.6	9.7	13.8
26 to 34 years old	9.8	11.1	8.5	11.1	6.8	4.1	7.6	8.7	11.0	10.9
35 years old and over	4.1	4.8	3.5	4.2	3.3	3.0	2.6	5.3	2.4	7.4

[1] Includes other races, not shown separately.   [2] Non-Hispanic.   [3] Low precision; no estimate reported.   [4] Nonmedical use; does not include over-the-counter drugs.

Source: U.S. Substance Abuse and Mental Health Services Administration, *National Household Survey on Drug Abuse, 1991*.

No. 210. Current Cigarette Smoking, by Sex, Age, and Race: 1965 to 1991

[In percent. A current smoker is a person who has smoked at least 100 cigarettes and who now smokes; includes occasional smokers. Excludes unknown smoking status. Based on the National Health Interview Survey; for details, see Appendix III]

SEX, AGE, AND RACE	1965	1974	1979	1983	1985	1987	1988	1990	1991
Total smokers, 18 years old and over	**42.4**	**37.1**	**33.5**	**32.1**	**30.1**	**28.8**	**28.1**	**25.5**	**25.6**
Male, total	51.9	43.1	37.5	35.1	32.6	31.2	30.8	28.4	28.1
18 to 24 years	54.1	42.1	35.0	32.9	28.0	28.2	25.5	26.6	23.5
25 to 34 years	60.7	50.5	43.9	38.8	38.2	34.8	36.2	31.6	32.8
35 to 44 years	58.2	51.0	41.8	41.0	37.6	36.6	36.5	34.5	33.1
45 to 64 years	51.9	42.6	39.3	35.9	33.4	33.5	31.3	29.3	29.3
65 years and over	28.5	24.8	20.9	22.0	19.6	17.2	18.0	14.6	15.1
White, total	51.1	41.9	36.8	34.5	31.7	30.5	30.1	28.0	27.4
18 to 24 years	53.0	40.8	34.3	32.5	28.4	29.2	26.7	27.4	25.1
25 to 34 years	60.1	49.5	43.6	38.6	37.3	33.8	35.4	31.6	32.1
35 to 44 years	57.3	50.1	41.3	40.8	36.6	36.2	35.8	33.5	32.1
45 to 64 years	51.3	41.2	38.3	35.0	32.1	32.4	30.0	28.7	28.0
65 years and over	27.7	24.3	20.5	20.6	18.9	16.0	16.9	13.7	13.7
Black, total	60.4	54.3	44.1	40.6	39.9	39.0	36.5	32.5	35.0
18 to 24 years	62.8	54.9	40.2	34.2	27.2	24.9	18.6	21.3	15.0
25 to 34 years	68.4	58.5	47.5	39.9	45.6	44.9	41.6	33.8	39.4
35 to 44 years	67.3	61.5	48.6	45.5	45.0	44.0	42.5	42.0	44.4
45 to 64 years	57.9	57.8	50.0	44.8	46.1	44.3	43.2	36.7	42.0
65 years and over	36.4	29.7	26.2	38.9	27.7	30.3	29.8	21.5	24.3
Female, total	33.9	32.1	29.9	29.5	27.9	26.5	25.7	22.8	23.5
18 to 24 years	38.1	34.1	33.8	35.5	30.4	26.1	26.3	22.5	22.4
25 to 34 years	43.7	38.8	33.7	32.6	32.0	31.8	31.3	28.2	28.4
35 to 44 years	43.7	39.8	37.0	33.8	31.5	29.6	27.8	24.8	27.6
45 to 64 years	32.0	33.4	30.7	31.0	29.9	28.6	27.7	24.8	24.6
65 years and over	9.6	12.0	13.2	13.1	13.5	13.7	12.8	11.5	12.0
White, total	34.0	31.7	30.1	29.4	27.7	26.7	25.7	23.4	23.7
18 to 24 years	38.4	34.0	34.5	36.5	31.8	27.8	27.5	25.4	25.1
25 to 34 years	43.4	38.6	34.1	32.2	32.0	31.9	31.0	28.5	28.4
35 to 44 years	43.9	39.3	37.2	34.8	31.0	29.2	28.3	25.0	27.0
45 to 64 years	32.7	33.0	30.6	30.6	29.7	29.0	27.7	25.4	25.3
65 years and over	9.8	12.3	13.8	13.2	13.3	13.9	12.6	11.5	12.1
Black, total	33.7	36.4	31.1	32.2	31.0	28.0	27.8	21.2	24.4
18 to 24 years	37.1	35.6	31.8	32.0	23.7	20.4	21.8	10.0	11.8
25 to 34 years	47.8	42.2	35.2	38.0	36.2	35.8	37.2	29.1	32.4
35 to 44 years	42.8	46.4	37.7	32.7	40.2	35.3	27.6	25.5	35.3
45 to 64 years	25.7	38.9	34.2	36.3	33.4	28.4	29.5	22.6	23.4
65 years and over	7.1	8.9	8.5	13.1	14.5	11.7	14.8	11.1	9.6

Source: U. S. National Center for Health Statistics, *Health, United States, 1992.*

No. 211. Cancer—Estimated New Cases, 1992, and Survival Rates, 1974-76 to 1983-88

[The 5-year relative survival rate, which is derived by adjusting the observed survival rate for expected mortality, represents the liklihood that a person will not die from causes directly related to their cancer within 5 years. Survival data shown are based on those patients diagnosed while residents of an area listed below during the time periods shown. Data are based on information collected as part of the National Cancer Institute's Surveillance, Epidemiology and End Results (SEER) program, a collection of population-based registries in Connecticut, New Mexico, Utah, Iowa, Hawaii, Atlanta, Detroit, Seattle-Puget Sound, and San Francisco-Oakland]

SITE	ESTIMATED NEW CASES,[1] 1992 (1,000)			5-YEAR RELATIVE SURVIVAL RATES (percent)							
				White				Black			
	Total	Male	Fe-male	1974 -76	1977 -79	1980 -82	1983 -88	1974 -76	1977 -79	1980 -82	1983 -88
All sites [2]	1,130	565	565	50.2	50.7	51.5	53.5	38.7	38.8	39.1	38.3
Lung	168	102	66	11.0	12.0	12.0	11.8	11.3	11.0	12.1	10.5
Breast [3]	181	1	180	74.8	75.1	76.7	79.3	62.9	62.5	65.6	62.1
Colon	111	56	57	50.2	52.7	55.3	59.1	45.5	47.6	48.7	47.9
Prostate	132	132	(X)	67.6	71.7	74.0	77.6	57.7	61.9	63.9	62.9
Bladder	52	39	13	73.6	75.6	78.6	79.1	47.8	54.8	57.5	58.5
Rectum	45	25	20	48.6	50.4	52.7	56.8	41.6	37.7	37.7	46.1
Corpus uteri	32	(X)	32	88.6	86.1	82.5	84.2	60.4	57.8	53.6	54.3
Non-Hodgkin's lymphoma [4]	41	23	18	47.5	48.1	51.4	51.9	47.8	49.6	50.0	42.6
Oral cavity and pharynx	30	21	10	54.8	54.1	54.9	53.7	35.7	36.0	30.4	31.7
Leukemia [4]	28	16	12	34.5	37.2	37.5	37.6	31.1	30.1	31.5	29.4
Melanoma of skin	32	17	15	79.8	81.5	81.9	82.6	68.5	51.7	59.5	68.3
Pancreas	28	14	14	2.7	2.2	2.8	2.8	2.2	3.8	4.8	4.7
Kidney	27	16	10	51.5	50.6	50.7	55.2	48.6	52.4	55.1	53.0
Stomach	24	15	9	14.4	16.1	16.1	16.0	16.4	15.3	19.1	17.1
Ovary	21	(X)	21	36.2	37.5	38.6	39.3	40.7	39.5	37.3	37.1
Cervix uteri [5]	14	(X)	14	69.2	68.8	67.3	68.0	63.2	61.8	60.1	55.3

X Not applicable.　[1] Estimates provided by American Cancer Society are based on rates from the National Cancer Institute's SEER program 1984-88.　[2] Includes other sites not shown separately.　[3] Survival rates for female only.　[4] All types combined.　[5] Invasive cancer only.

Source: U.S. National Institutes of Health, National Cancer Institute, *Cancer Statistics Review,* annual.

No. 212. Women—Selected Health Practices: 1990

[Based on the National Health Interview Survey and subject to sampling error; for details see source and Appendix III]

CHARACTERISTIC	POPULATION 18 YEARS AND OVER					POPULATION 35 YEARS AND OVER		
	Total (1,000)	Percent who—				Total (1,000)	Percent who had a mammogram	
		Had a breast exam [1]	Knew how to do BSE [2]	Did a BSE monthly [2][3]	Had a PAP smear [4]		Ever	In the past 3 years
Total [5]	**95,169**	**53.1**	**88.1**	**43.1**	**50.1**	**59,934**	**57.7**	**50.5**
Race:								
White.	81,255	53.1	88.8	42.3	49.7	52,188	58.9	51.5
Black.	11,212	55.3	86.0	50.9	54.3	6,282	51.3	44.9
Hispanic origin:								
Hispanic.	7,709	50.4	74.7	44.1	49.1	3,704	49.4	42.3
Non-Hispanic	87,151	53.4	89.2	43.1	50.1	56,029	58.2	51.0
Marital status:								
Currently married.	58,398	55.8	90.6	44.5	53.5	38,074	61.5	55.0
Formerly married.	21,650	45.5	84.8	43.8	39.1	18,536	51.7	43.4
Never married.	15,031	53.1	82.8	36.4	51.5	3,312	47.4	38.9
Educational attainment:								
Less than 12 years	20,326	43.0	76.9	43.9	37.9	14,714	44.9	37.4
12 years.	38,634	52.2	89.7	43.6	49.6	24,234	59.0	51.8
More than 12 years	35,964	59.7	92.8	42.2	57.2	20,798	65.5	58.5
Labor force status:								
Employed.	53,833	55.9	91.3	42.9	54.7	30,067	60.5	53.5
Unemployed	2,659	52.9	90.2	40.7	51.1	1,140	52.9	46.2
Not in the labor force . . .	38,677	49.2	83.4	43.8	43.4	28,727	55.1	47.5
Income:								
Less than $10,000	11,930	45.5	80.0	42.2	41.0	7,203	40.9	32.7
$10,000 to $19,999	16,740	47.0	85.3	43.0	44.0	10,408	50.3	42.5
$20,000 to $34,999	20,445	53.0	90.6	42.3	50.1	11,948	58.9	52.0
$35,000 to $49,999	14,149	58.3	93.3	43.1	55.2	8,545	62.9	56.6
$50,000 or more	17,405	61.4	92.5	41.5	58.9	11,710	71.4	64.5

[1] In the past year by a professional. [2] BSE=Breast self-examination. [3] On average over the past year. [4] In the past year. [5] Includes persons whose characteristics are unknown.

Source: U.S. National Center for Health Statistics, *Health Promotion and Disease Prevention, United States 1990, Vital and Health Statistics*, series 10, No. 185.

No. 213. Personal Health Practices, by Selected Characteristic: 1990

[In percent, except total persons. For persons 18 years of age and over. See headnote, table 212]

CHARACTERISTIC	Total persons (1,000)	Eats breakfast [1]	Rarely snacks	Exercised regularly [2]	Had two or more drinks on any day [3]	Current smoker	20 percent or more above weight [4]
All persons [5]	**181,447**	**56.4**	**25.5**	**40.7**	**5.5**	**25.5**	**27.5**
Sex:							
Male.	86,278	54.6	25.6	44.0	9.7	28.4	29.6
Female	95,169	58.0	25.4	37.7	1.7	22.8	25.6
Race:							
White	155,301	57.8	25.8	41.5	5.8	25.6	26.7
Black	20,248	46.9	22.7	34.3	4.3	26.2	38.0
Hispanic Origin:							
Hispanic	14,314	52.5	29.3	34.9	4.6	23.0	27.6
Non-Hispanic	166,599	56.7	25.2	41.2	5.6	25.7	27.5
Marital Status:							
Currently married.	117,413	57.8	25.3	39.4	5.3	24.6	29.2
Formerly married.	30,439	61.5	31.2	34.3	5.3	30.3	29.1
Never married.	33,413	46.9	20.9	51.3	6.6	24.3	19.8
Education level:							
Less than 12 years	38,367	58.6	26.9	25.9	5.1	31.8	32.7
12 years	69,405	52.6	24.0	37.0	5.9	29.6	28.6
More than 12 years	73,244	58.8	26.4	52.1	5.4	18.3	23.8
Income:							
Less than $10,000.	18,469	54.1	27.6	32.9	4.8	31.6	29.3
$10,000 to $19,999	30,452	56.6	25.9	32.3	4.9	29.8	28.5
$20,000 to $34,999	40,216	55.2	25.1	40.5	5.8	26.9	28.2
$35,000 to $49,999	29,795	53.7	23.8	46.1	5.6	23.4	27.8
$50,000 or more	36,199	57.2	25.8	51.7	5.7	19.3	24.9

[1] Almost every day. [2] Or played sports regularly. [3] On average per day in the past two weeks. [4] Above desirable weight. Based on 1983 Metropolitan Life Insurance Company standards. Height and weight data are self-reported. [5] Includes persons whose characteristics are unknown.

Source of tables 212 and 213: U.S. National Center for Health Statistics, *Health Promotion and Disease Prevention: United States, 1990, Vital and Health Statistics*, series 10, No. 185.

No. 214. Medical Device Implants, by Age, Sex, and Race: 1988

[In thousands, except percent. Based in the National Health Interview Survey; for details, see Appendix III]

DEVICE	Total[1]	Age				Sex		Race	
		Under 18 years old	18-44 years old	45-64 years old	65 years old and over	Male	Female	White	Black
Artificial joints[2]	1,625	[3]0.6	13.0	24.6	61.7	39.9	60.1	92.3	6.2
Hip joints	816	[3]0.5	6.5	26.3	66.7	37.5	62.4	93.5	5.5
Knee joints	521	-	10.9	20.5	68.5	41.8	58.2	88.1	10.0
Fixation devices[4]	4,890	[3]3.9	44.3	28.4	[3]23.4	57.2	42.8	91.7	6.6
Head	351	[3]4.3	67.8	22.8	[3]5.4	57.3	42.7	93.2	[3]4.8
Torso	563	[3]5.3	49.6	31.8	13.3	62.7	37.5	92.2	[3]6.9
Upper extremities	646	[3]3.7	55.9	25.4	15.0	70.4	29.7	91.6	[3]5.6
Lower extremities	2,690	[3]3.0	39.6	27.9	29.4	52.8	47.2	91.1	7.7
Other	622	[3]6.4	34.4	34.1	25.1	57.9	42.1	93.6	[3]3.7
Other devices:									
Ear vent tubes	1,494	[5]25.8	[6]27.0	[7]34.6	[8]12.6	39.9	61.1	92.3	6.2
Silicone implants	620	[3]0.5	73.1	23.7	[3]2.9	8.2	91.8	97.6	[3]0.8
Breast implants	544	[3]0.6	73.0	24.1	[3]2.6	[3]2.0	98.0	98.5	-
Shunt or catheter	321	[3]4.3	24.3	22.1	29.3	50.5	49.2	85.7	[3]12.5
Dental implants	275	[3]2.2	57.8	27.3	[3]12.7	56.4	43.6	93.8	[3]4.0
Heart valve	279	(NA)	[9]14.7	35.5	49.8	52.3	47.8	89.2	[10]0.0
Pacemaker	460	(NA)	(NA)	[10]13.5	86.7	50.4	49.6	93.7	[10]5.2
Eye lens	3,765	(NA)	(NA)	[10]18.7	81.3	37.6	62.4	95.6	3.5

- Represents or rounds to zero. NA Not available. [1] Includes other races not shown separately. [2] Includes other devices not shown separately. [3] Figure does not meet standards of reliability or precision. [4] Includes sites unknown. Each device represents a single body part regardless of the number of pins, screws, nails, wires, rods, or plates. [5] Under 3 years old. [6] 3 to 5 years old. [7] 6 to 17 years old. [8] 18 years old and over. [9] Under 45 years old. [10] Under 65 years old.
Source: U.S. National Center for Health Statistics, *National Health Interview Survey*, 1988; unpublished data.

No. 215. Persons Using Assistive Technology Devices and Home Accessibility Features, Type of Device, and Source of Payment, by Age: 1990

[In percent, except as indicated. For the civilian noninstitutionalized population. Based on the Current Population Survey; see text, section 1 and Appendix III]

DEVICE OR FEATURE	Total	Under 25 years old	25 to 44 years old	45 to 64 years old	65 to 74 years old	75 years old and over
Persons using assistive technology devices[1] (1,000)	13,128	1,048	2,228	3,022	2,756	4,073
Anatomical devices	28.4	61.7	61.4	34.8	14.1	6.8
Leg brace	6.6	19.9	12.9	6.9	3.5	1.5
Foot brace	1.4	6.8	2.0	1.0	1.1	[2]0.3
Arm brace	1.6	2.7	3.9	2.0	0.7	[2]0.3
Hand brace	1.6	2.7	4.2	2.1	0.8	[2]0.1
Neck brace	2.3	2.6	5.3	3.6	1.0	[2]0.4
Back brace	8.9	6.5	18.8	15.2	4.6	2.4
Other brace	6.5	[2]3.0	16.6	4.8	1.7	1.2
Artificial leg or foot	1.4	[2]0.8	1.3	2.1	1.7	0.9
Artificial arm or hand	0.3	1.1	[2]0.2	[2]0.3	[2]0.3	[2]-
Mobility devices	48.8	22.9	27.3	45.8	52.1	67.2
Cruch	5.1	8.3	7.8	6.9	5.0	1.6
Cane of walking stick	33.5	3.0	14.3	33.5	37.4	49.3
Walker	12.9	3.2	3.2	9.1	12.7	23.5
Wheelchair	10.8	13.3	7.6	10.0	11.8	11.7
Scooter	0.5	[2]0.6	[2]0.5	[2]0.6	[2]0.7	[2]0.3
Other mobility devices	1.9	[2]1.7	1.3	2.2	2.1	2.1
Hearing devices	30.4	14.5	11.5	27.1	41.4	39.7
Hearing aid	28.8	14.1	10.2	24.6	40.0	38.3
TDD/TTY[3]	1.3	[2]1.1	1.0	1.8	0.9	1.2
Special Alarm	0.6	[2]0.7	[2]0.8	0.8	[2]0.2	0.6
Other hearing devices	4.3	2.3	2.5	4.5	5.1	5.0
Source of payment[4]	100.0	100.0	100.0	100.0	100.0	100.0
Out-of-pocket	48.2	34.0	37.5	45.5	52.5	56.0
Third party	34.0	45.0	49.2	37.1	28.7	24.8
Combination	17.9	21.0	13.3	17.4	18.7	19.2
Persons using home accessibility features (1,000)	7,102	1,395	1,272	1,484	1,284	1,667
Ramps	29.7	41.4	36.0	32.8	25.0	16.0
Extra-wide doors	23.2	28.5	26.2	27.6	19.4	15.8
Elevator or stair lift	5.8	4.7	2.2	3.0	7.6	10.4
Hand rails	47.8	30.5	33.0	46.2	60.6	65.2
Raised toilet	18.6	9.0	10.5	19.2	21.5	30.3
Adaptive door locks	5.8	4.1	2.3	6.1	6.7	8.9
Lowered counters	3.4	3.7	3.7	4.0	1.7	3.7
Slip-resistant floors	3.0	2.9	3.2	5.3	1.9	1.6
Other features	22.5	22.4	24.6	23.3	22.8	19.8
Source of payment[4]	100.0	100.0	100.0	100.0	100.0	100.0
Out-of-pocket	77.5	76.1	77.9	74.6	81.6	78.1
Third party	15.2	17.9	15.4	16.1	11.7	15.0
Combination	7.3	6.0	6.7	9.3	6.8	6.9

- Represents or rounds to zero. [1] Includes other devices, not shown separately. Excludes any implanted devices, such as pacemakers. [2] Figure does not meet standards of reliability or precision. [3] TDD/TTY is a typewriter-like device for the deaf that communicates over telephone lines using text. [4] Excludes persons who indicated no payment or gift.
Source: U.S. National Center for Health Statistics, *Advance Data from Vital and Health Statistics*, No. 217, September 16, 1992.

No. 216. Cumulative Percent Distribution of Population, by Height and Sex: 1976-80

[For persons 18 to 74 years old. Height was measured without shoes. Based on sample and subject to sampling variability; see source]

HEIGHT	MALES						FEMALES					
	18-24 years	25-34 years	35-44 years	45-54 years	55-64 years	65-74 years	18-24 years	25-34 years	35-44 years	45-54 years	55-64 years	65-74 years
Percent under—												
4'8"	-	-	-	-	-	-	0.05	-	0.10	0.28	0.46	1.04
4'9"	-	-	-	-	-	-	0.43	0.23	0.34	0.35	1.07	2.27
4'10"	-	-	-	-	-	-	0.94	0.64	0.95	1.22	3.02	4.23
4'11"	-	-	-	-	-	-	2.22	1.65	1.94	4.20	6.43	9.33
5'	0.18	0.05	0.27	-	0.27	0.24	4.22	3.65	4.56	8.88	11.40	17.20
5'1"	0.18	0.31	0.34	0.19	0.72	1.22	9.13	8.60	7.75	16.16	19.70	29.00
5'2"	0.34	0.42	0.87	0.70	0.92	2.66	17.75	19.11	18.24	27.68	31.71	44.34
5'3"	0.61	0.54	2.07	1.50	2.78	5.97	29.06	32.96	33.11	39.83	45.87	59.15
5'4"	2.37	1.55	3.68	2.55	5.28	10.53	41.81	47.43	49.90	57.21	63.89	76.44
5'5"	3.85	4.36	6.36	5.72	9.29	18.31	58.09	61.36	63.88	70.47	77.44	86.97
5'6"	8.24	9.51	12.39	11.39	17.54	29.42	74.76	74.92	78.07	84.64	88.91	94.63
5'7"	16.18	15.25	17.63	21.24	29.10	41.63	85.37	85.65	87.95	91.21	94.56	97.86
5'8"	26.68	26.69	26.40	33.56	43.53	57.75	92.30	93.28	93.43	96.28	97.70	99.20
5'9"	38.89	39.68	42.52	50.39	58.21	69.96	96.23	97.19	97.18	98.17	99.36	99.81
5'10"	53.66	55.35	57.01	63.38	71.51	81.95	98.34	99.49	99.19	99.58	99.78	99.92
5'11"	68.25	69.67	70.70	76.94	83.09	89.59	99.38	99.68	99.39	99.84	99.81	100.00
6'	80.14	81.58	81.15	85.83	90.99	94.52	100.00	100.00	100.00	100.00	100.00	100.00
6'1"	88.54	89.95	90.04	93.43	96.28	97.82	100.00	100.00	100.00	100.00	100.00	100.00
6'2"	92.74	95.57	95.05	98.01	97.66	99.17	100.00	100.00	100.00	100.00	100.00	100.00
6'3"	96.17	97.98	97.82	99.35	98.90	99.86	100.00	100.00	100.00	100.00	100.00	100.00
6'4"	98.40	99.23	99.19	99.70	99.79	100.00	100.00	100.00	100.00	100.00	100.00	100.00

- Represents or rounds to zero.

Source: U.S. National Center for Health Statistics, *Vital and Health Statistics*, series 11, No. 238.

No. 217. Nutrition—Nutrients in Foods Available for Civilian Consumption per Capita per Day and Percent Change: 1955 to 1988

[Based on estimates of per capita food consumption at the retail level, on imputed consumption data for foods no longer reported, and on estimates of quantities of home grown produce. Food supply estimates do not reflect loss of food or nutrients from further marketing or home processing. Enrichment and fortification levels of iron, thiamin, riboflavin, niacin, vitamin A, vitamin B 6, vitamin B 12, and ascorbic acid are included. Minus sign (-) indicates decrease. See *Historical Statistics, Colonial Times to 1970*, series G 851-856 for related details]

NUTRIENT	Unit	1955-59	1965-69	1975-79	1985-88	PERCENT CHANGE, 1985-88 FROM—		
						1955-59	1965-69	1975-79
Food energy	Calories	3,100	3,200	3,300	3,600	13.9	11.1	8.3
Protein	Grams	94	97	99	104	9.6	6.7	4.8
Total fat [1]	Grams	142	154	157	169	16.0	8.9	7.1
Saturated	Grams	60	62	58	61	1.6	-1.6	4.9
Monounsaturated	Grams	56	62	63	67	16.4	7.5	6.0
Polyunsaturated	Grams	19	23	29	34	44.1	32.4	14.7
Cholesterol	Milligrams	510	490	450	440	-15.9	-11.4	-2.3
Carbohydrate	Grams	380	380	390	420	9.5	9.5	7.1
Vitamin A	Retinol equivalents	1,320	1,350	1,540	1,630	19.0	17.2	5.5
Carotenes	Retinol equivalents	430	430	600	750	42.7	42.7	20.0
Vitamin E	Milligram α-TE [2]	11.3	12.7	14.5	16.3	30.7	22.1	11.0
Ascorbic acid	Milligrams	100	96	111	116	13.8	17.2	4.3
Thiamin	Milligrams	1.9	1.9	2.1	2.2	13.6	13.6	4.5
Riboflavin	Milligrams	2.3	2.2	2.4	2.4	4.2	8.3	0.0
Niacin	Milligrams	20	22	24	26	23.1	15.4	7.7
Vitamin B6	Milligrams	1.9	2.0	2.1	2.1	9.5	4.8	0.0
Folacin	Micrograms	282	267	277	283	0.4	5.7	2.1
Vitamin B12	Micrograms	9.4	10.0	10.0	9.2	-2.2	-8.7	-8.7
Calcium	Milligrams	920	850	850	900	-2.2	5.6	5.6
Phosphorus	Milligrams	1,470	1,460	1,470	1,530	3.9	4.6	3.9
Magnesium	Milligrams	320	310	310	330	3.0	6.1	6.1
Iron	Milligrams	13.8	14.3	15.1	17.0	18.8	15.9	11.2
Zinc	Milligrams	11.8	12.3	12.5	12.6	6.3	2.4	0.8
Copper	Milligrams	1.6	1.5	1.6	1.6	0.0	6.3	0.0
Potassium	Milligrams	3,530	3,380	3,370	3,460	-2.0	2.3	2.6

[1] Includes other types of fat not shown separately. [2] Alpha-Tocopherol equivalents.

Source: U.S. Dept. of Agriculture, Human Nutrition Information Service. Data published by Economic Research Service in *Food Consumption, Prices, and Expenditures*, annual; and *National Food Review*, quarterly.

No. 218. Per Capita Consumption of Major Food Commodities: 1970 to 1991

[In pounds, retail weight except as indicated. Consumption represents the residual after exports, nonfood use and ending stocks are subtracted from the sum of beginning stocks, domestic production, and imports. Based on Bureau of the Census estimated population. Estimates reflect revisions based on the 1990 Census of Population. For similar but unrevised data, see *Historical Statistics, Colonial Times to 1970*, series G 881-915]

COMMODITY	1970	1975	1980	1985	1987	1988	1989	1990	1991
Red meat, total (boneless, trimmed weight) [1][2]	132.0	125.8	126.4	124.9	117.4	119.5	115.9	112.4	112.0
Beef	79.6	83.0	72.1	74.6	69.5	68.6	65.4	63.9	63.1
Veal	2.0	2.8	1.3	1.5	1.3	1.1	1.0	0.9	0.8
Lamb and mutton	2.1	1.3	1.0	1.1	1.0	1.0	1.1	1.1	1.1
Pork (excluding lard)	48.0	38.7	52.1	47.7	45.6	48.8	48.4	46.4	47.0
Fish and shellfish (edible weight) [3]	11.7	12.1	12.4	15.0	16.1	15.1	15.6	15	14.8
Fresh and frozen	6.9	7.5	7.8	9.7	10.6	10.0	10.2	9.6	9.6
Canned	4.4	4.2	4.3	5.0	5.2	4.9	5.1	5.1	4.9
Tuna	2.5	2.8	3.0	3.3	3.5	3.6	3.9	3.7	3.6
Cured	0.4	0.4	0.3	0.3	0.3	0.3	0.3	0.3	0.3
Poultry products: (boneless weight) [2][4]	33.8	32.9	40.6	45.2	50.7	51.7	53.6	55.9	58.1
Chicken	27.7	26.4	32.5	36.1	39.1	39.3	40.5	42.1	43.9
Turkey	6.4	6.5	8.1	9.1	11.6	12.4	13.1	13.8	14.2
Eggs (farm weight) (number)	309	276	271	255	254	246	236	233	231.0
Dairy products:									
Total (milk equivalent) [5]	563.8	539.1	543.3	593.7	601.2	582.8	565.2	570.8	564.7
Fluid milk and cream [6]	275.1	261.4	245.6	240.9	238.5	234.6	236.4	233.4	233.3
Beverage milks	269.1	254.0	237.4	229.7	226.5	222.3	224.3	221.7	221.5
Plain whole milk	213.5	174.9	141.7	119.6	108.5	102.4	94.5	87.6	84.8
Plain lowfat milk	29.8	53.2	70.1	83.3	89.6	89.9	96.3	98.3	99.9
Plain skim milk	11.6	11.5	11.6	12.6	14.0	16.1	20.2	22.9	23.8
Flavored whole milk	5.6	6.3	4.7	3.7	3.4	3.3	3.1	2.8	2.7
Flavored lowfat and skim milks	3.0	3.3	5.3	6.0	6.6	6.6	6.5	6.6	6.8
Buttermilk	5.5	4.7	4.1	4.4	4.3	4.1	3.7	3.5	3.4
Yogurt	0.8	2.1	2.6	4.1	4.4	4.7	4.3	4.1	4.3
Cream [7]	3.8	3.3	3.4	4.4	4.7	4.6	4.8	4.6	4.5
Sour cream and dip	1.1	1.6	1.8	2.3	2.4	2.5	2.5	2.5	2.5
Condensed and evaporated milk:									
Whole milk	7.0	5.1	3.8	3.6	3.7	3.5	3.1	3.1	3.1
Skim milk	5.0	3.5	3.3	3.8	4.2	4.3	4.7	4.8	4.7
Cheese [8]	11.4	14.3	17.5	22.5	24.1	23.7	23.8	24.7	25.2
American	7.0	8.2	9.6	12.2	12.4	11.5	11.0	11.2	11.2
Cheddar	5.9	6.0	6.9	9.8	10.6	9.5	9.2	9.1	9.2
Italian	2.1	3.2	4.4	6.5	7.6	8.1	8.5	9.0	9.4
Mozzarella [9]	1.2	2.1	3.0	4.6	5.6	6.0	6.4	6.9	7.2
Other [9]	2.3	2.9	3.4	3.9	4.1	4.1	4.3	4.6	4.6
Swiss	0.9	1.1	1.3	1.3	1.2	1.3	1.2	1.4	1.2
Cream and Neufchatel	0.6	0.7	1.0	1.2	1.4	1.5	1.6	1.7	1.8
Cottage cheese	5.2	4.7	4.5	4.1	3.9	3.9	3.6	3.4	3.2
Ice cream	17.8	18.6	17.5	18.1	18.3	17.3	16.1	15.8	16.4
Ice milk	7.7	7.6	7.1	6.9	7.4	8.0	8.4	7.7	7.3
Fats and oils:									
Total, fat content only [10]	52.6	52.6	57.2	64.3	62.9	63.0	61.1	62.7	63.6
Butter (product weight)	5.4	4.7	4.5	4.9	4.7	4.5	4.4	4.4	4.2
Margarine (product weight)	10.8	11.0	11.3	10.8	10.5	10.3	10.2	10.9	10.6
Lard (direct use)	4.6	3.2	2.6	1.8	1.8	1.8	1.8	2.2	1.7
Edible tallow (direct use)	(NA)	(NA)	1.1	1.9	0.9	0.8	0.9	0.8	1.4
Shortening	17.3	17.0	18.2	22.9	21.4	21.5	21.5	22.2	22.1
Salad and cooking oils	15.4	17.9	21.2	23.5	25.4	25.8	24.0	24.2	25.2
Other edible fats and oils	2.3	2.0	1.5	1.6	1.3	1.3	1.3	1.2	1.3
Flour and cereal products	135.3	139.1	145.8	157.5	172.5	174.3	174.9	183.0	184.3
Wheat flour [11]	110.9	114.5	116.9	124.7	129.9	130.0	129.2	135.7	135.9
Rye flour	1.2	1.0	0.7	0.7	0.6	0.6	0.6	0.6	0.6
Rice, milled [12]	6.7	7.6	9.4	9.0	14.0	14.3	15.2	16.2	17.0
Corn products	11.1	10.8	12.9	17.1	21.1	21.8	21.5	21.7	21.9
Oat products	4.4	4.4	4.9	5.1	5.9	6.6	7.4	7.7	7.9
Barley products	1.0	0.9	1.1	1.0	1.0	1.0	1.0	1.0	1.0
Caloric sweeteners, total [13]	122.6	117.9	123.9	131.3	133.7	135.1	136.4	139.1	140.2
Sugar, refined cane and beet	101.8	89.2	83.6	62.7	62.4	62.1	62.8	64.5	64.9
Corn sweeteners (dry weight)	19.3	27.4	39.0	67.2	69.9	71.6	72.2	73.1	73.9
Low-calorie sweeteners (sugar sweetness equivalent) [14]	5.8	6.1	7.7	18.1	19.1	20.0	20.3	22.2	24.3
Saccharin	5.8	6.1	7.7	6.0	5.5	6.0	6.1	6.7	7.3
Aspartame	-	-	-	12.1	13.6	14.0	14.2	15.5	17.0
Other:									
Cocoa beans	3.9	3.2	3.4	4.6	4.8	4.8	4.9	5.2	(NA)
Coffee (green beans)	13.6	12.2	10.3	10.5	10.2	9.8	10.3	10.2	10.3
Peanuts (shelled)	5.5	6.0	4.8	6.3	6.4	6.9	7.0	6.0	6.4
Tree nuts (shelled)	1.8	2.0	1.8	2.3	2.2	2.3	2.3	2.5	2.5

- Represents or rounds to zero.　NA Not available.　[1] Excludes edible offals.　[2] Excludes shipments to Puerto Rico and the other U.S. possessions.　[3] Excludes consumption from recreational fishing, approximately 3 to 4 pounds per capita.　[4] Includes backs, necks, skin, and giblets.　[5] Includes other products, not shown separately.　[6] Fluid milk figures are aggregates of commercial sales and milk produced and consumed on farms.　[7] Heavy cream, light cream, and half and half.　[8] Excludes cottage, pot, and baker's cheese.　[9] Includes other cheeses not shown separately.　[10] The fat content of butter and margarine is 80 percent of product weight.　[11] White, whole wheat, semolina, and durum flour.　[12] For crop year beginning in previous year.　[13] Dry weight. Includes edible syrups (maple, molasses, etc.) and honey not shown separately.　[14] Assumes saccharin is 300 times as sweet as sugar and aspartame 200 times as sweet as sugar.

Source: U.S. Department of Agriculture, Economic Research Service, *Food Consumption, Prices, and Expenditures*, annual.

No. 219. Per Capita Utilization of Selected Commercially Produced Fresh Fruits and Vegetables: 1970 to 1991

[In pounds, farm weight. Domestic food use of fresh fruits and vegetables reflects the fresh-market share of commodity production plus imports and minus exports. All data are on a calendar year basis except for citrus fruits, October or November; apples, August; grapes and pears, July. See headnote, table 218]

COMMODITY	1970	1975	1980	1985	1986	1987	1988	1989	1990	1991
Fresh fruits, total.............	79.4	85.0	87.0	86.8	93.1	97.5	97.4	98.8	92.6	90.6
Noncitrus.................	50.6	55.6	60.4	65.3	68.8	73.5	72.0	73.7	70.5	70.7
Bananas.................	17.4	17.6	20.8	23.5	25.8	25.0	24.3	24.7	24.4	25.3
Apples	17.0	19.5	19.2	17.3	17.8	20.8	20.0	21.5	19.8	18.7
Grapes	2.5	3.2	3.5	6.8	7.1	7.0	7.8	8.0	8.0	7.3
Nectarines and peaches......	6.4	5.9	7.1	5.5	5.8	6.0	6.6	5.7	5.5	6.3
Pears	1.9	2.7	2.6	2.8	3.0	3.5	3.3	3.3	3.3	3.3
Strawberries.............	1.7	1.8	2.0	3.0	2.9	3.1	3.3	3.3	3.2	3.6
Pineapples..............	0.7	1.0	1.5	1.5	1.7	1.6	1.8	2.0	2.1	1.9
Plums and prunes..........	1.5	1.3	1.5	1.4	1.3	1.9	1.7	1.8	1.5	1.5
Other [1]	1.5	2.5	2.2	3.5	3.4	4.6	3.2	3.4	2.7	2.8
Citrus..................	28.8	29.4	26.6	21.6	24.3	24.0	25.4	25.1	22.1	19.9
Oranges	16.2	15.9	14.3	11.6	13.4	12.8	13.9	12.6	12.4	8.3
Grapefruit	8.2	8.3	7.3	5.5	6.1	6.3	6.6	7.5	5.0	6.8
Other [2]	4.4	5.2	5.0	4.5	4.8	4.9	4.9	5.0	4.7	4.8
Selected melons.............	21.6	17.7	17.9	24.1	24.6	24.3	23.7	26.3	25.3	23
Watermelons.............	13.5	11.4	10.7	13.5	12.8	13.0	13.5	13.4	14.1	12.5
Cantaloups.............	7.2	5.2	5.8	8.5	9.4	9.1	7.9	10.4	9.1	8.6
Honeydews.............	0.9	1.1	1.4	2.1	2.4	2.2	2.3	2.5	2.1	1.9
Selected fresh vegetables.......	88.8	89.8	92.7	100.7	99.3	105.7	109.7	112.9	110.9	106.0
Asparagus	0.4	0.4	0.3	0.5	0.6	0.6	0.6	0.6	0.6	0.6
Broccoli	0.5	1.0	1.4	2.6	3.0	3.1	3.8	3.8	3.4	3.1
Cabbage...............	11.4	9.1	8.1	9.2	8.2	8.0	7.7	8.4	8.7	7.9
Carrots................	6.0	6.4	6.1	6.5	6.5	8.3	7.2	7.8	8.0	7.4
Cauliflower	0.7	0.9	1.1	1.8	2.2	2.1	2.2	2.3	2.2	2.0
Celery	7.3	6.9	7.5	7.0	6.6	6.7	7.2	7.5	7.2	6.8
Corn	7.8	7.8	6.5	6.4	6.0	6.3	5.7	6.4	6.5	5.6
Cucumbers	2.8	2.8	3.9	4.4	4.6	5.1	4.8	4.8	4.7	4.7
Iceberg lettuce...........	22.4	23.5	25.6	23.7	21.9	25.7	27.0	28.7	27.8	26.1
Onions.................	12.4	13.4	13.3	16.4	16.7	16.3	17.6	17.7	18.6	18.8
Snap beans.............	1.5	1.4	1.3	1.3	1.3	1.2	1.2	1.2	1.1	1.1
Green peppers	2.2	2.5	2.9	3.8	4.0	4.2	4.5	4.7	4.3	4.4
Tomatoes	12.1	12.0	12.8	14.8	15.8	15.8	16.8	16.7	15.5	15.3
Other fresh vegetables [3]	1.3	1.7	1.9	2.3	1.9	2.3	3.4	2.3	2.3	2.2
Potatoes	121.7	122.2	114.3	122.4	125.8	125.8	122.2	127.4	127.8	130.5
Fresh..................	61.8	52.6	51.1	46.3	48.8	47.9	49.6	50.0	45.9	46.9
For freezing.............	28.5	37.1	35.4	45.4	46.3	47.9	43.3	46.8	50.2	51.0
For chips/shoestrings.........	17.4	15.5	16.6	17.6	18.2	17.6	17.2	17.5	17.0	17.1
For dehydrating	12.0	14.7	9.4	11.2	10.7	10.6	10.2	11.1	12.8	13.9
For canning.	2.0	2.0	1.9	1.9	1.8	1.8	1.9	2.0	1.9	1.8
Sweet potatoes [4]	5.4	5.8	4.8	5.8	4.8	4.8	4.5	4.5	5.0	4.4
Mushrooms	1.3	1.9	2.7	3.6	3.8	3.5	3.6	3.5	3.8	3.9
For fresh	0.3	0.7	1.2	1.8	1.9	1.9	2.0	2.0	2.0	2.0
For processing...........	1.0	1.2	1.5	1.8	1.9	1.6	1.6	1.5	1.8	1.9

[1] Includes apricots, avocados, cherries, cranberries, figs, kiwifruit, mangos, olives, papayas, persimmons, and pomegranates.   [2] Includes tangerines, tangelos, lemons, and limes.   [3] Includes artichokes, garlic, and eggplant.   [4] Fresh and processed.

Source: U.S. Dept. of Agriculture, Economic Research Service, *Food Consumption, Prices and Expenditures*, annual; and unpublished data.

No. 220. Per Capita Consumption of Selected Beverages, by Type: 1970 to 1991

[In gallons. See headnote, table 218]

COMMODITY	1970	1975	1980	1985	1986	1987	1988	1989	1990	1991
Nonalcoholic [1]................	95.7	102.9	106.7	109.8	110.1	113.7	114.5	117.5	117.0	118.2
Milk (plain and flavored).........	31.2	29.5	27.6	26.7	26.5	26.3	25.8	26.0	25.7	25.7
Whole	25.4	21.0	17.0	14.3	13.5	13.0	12.3	11.3	10.5	10.2
Lowfat	4.5	7.1	9.2	10.9	11.5	11.7	11.7	12.4	12.6	12.6
Skim	1.3	1.3	1.3	1.5	1.6	1.6	1.9	2.3	2.7	2.8
Tea....................	6.8	7.5	7.3	7.1	7.1	7.0	7.1	7.0	6.7	6.5
Coffee..................	33.4	31.4	26.7	27.4	27.5	26.7	25.7	26.9	26.7	26.8
Bottled water	(NA)	(NA)	2.4	4.5	5.0	5.7	6.5	7.3	8.0	8.0
Club soda and seltzer	(NA)	(NA)	0.4	0.7	0.7	0.8	0.8	0.8	0.8	0.8
Soft drinks...............	24.3	28.2	35.0	35.7	35.8	39.2	41.1	41.8	42.5	43.2
Fruit juices...............	(NA)	6.4	7.4	7.7	7.4	8.0	7.4	7.7	6.5	7.3
Alcoholic (adult population)	35.7	39.7	43.0	40.5	40.6	40.0	39.5	38.9	40.0	37.8
Beer...................	30.6	33.9	36.8	34.4	34.7	34.4	34.1	33.7	35.0	33.2
Wine...................	2.2	2.7	3.2	3.5	3.5	3.3	3.2	3.0	2.9	2.7
Distilled spirits	3.0	3.1	3.0	2.5	2.4	2.3	2.2	2.1	2.2	2.0

NA Not available.   [1] Excludes vegetable juices.

Source: U.S. Dept. of Agriculture, Economic Research Service, *Food Consumption, Prices, and Expenditures*, annual; and unpublished data.

Figure 4.1
School Enrollment: 1970 to 2000

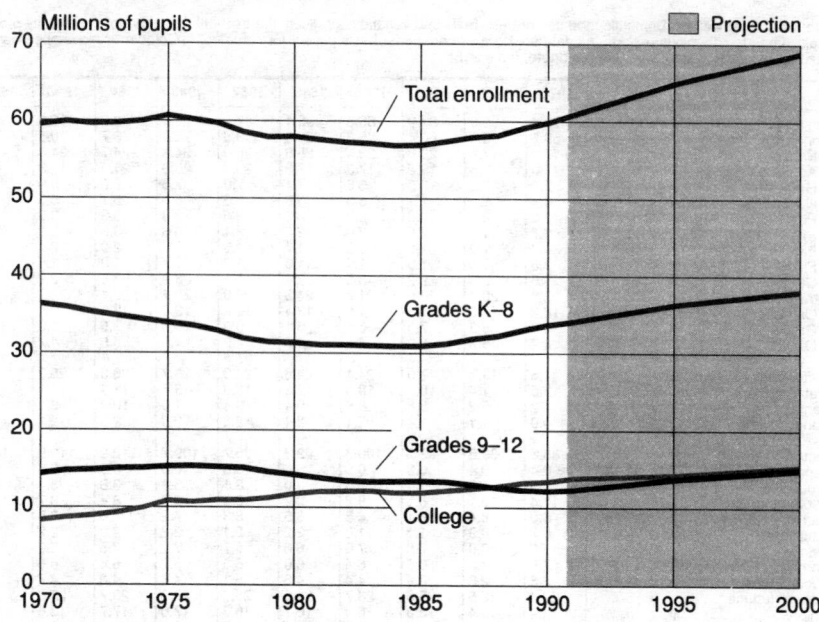

Source: Chart prepared by U.S. Bureau of the Census. For data, see table 226.

Figure 4.2
Percent of Persons 25 Years Old and Over Completing 4 Years of High School or More: 1970 and 1992

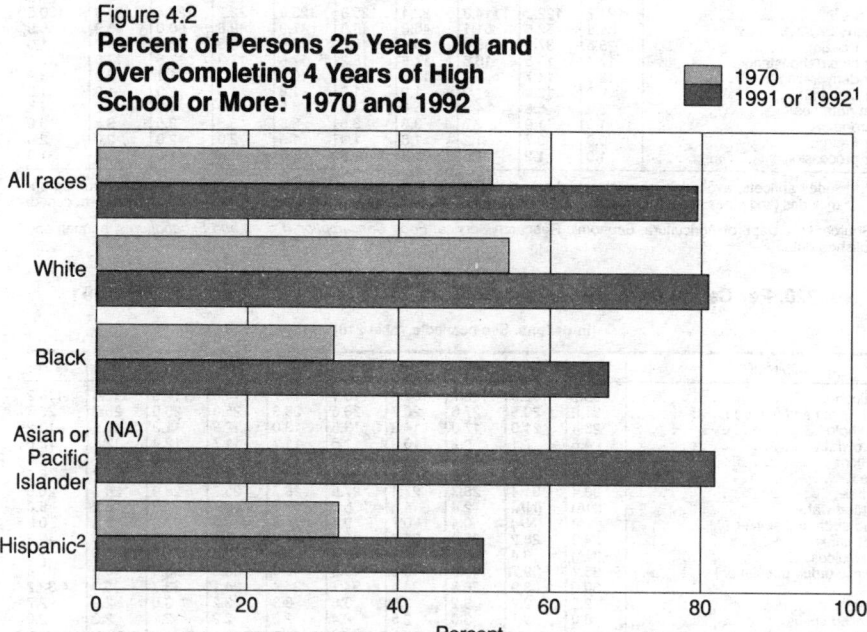

NA Not available. [1] Data for Total, White, and Black are from 1992; data for Asian or Pacific Islander and Hispanic are from 1991. [2] Persons of Hispanic origin may be of any race.
Source: Chart prepared by U.S. Bureau of the Census. For data, see table 233.

Education

This section presents data primarily concerning formal education as a whole, at various levels, and for public and private schools. Data shown relate to the school-age population and school enrollment, educational attainment, education personnel, and financial aspects of education. In addition, data are shown for libraries, computer usage in schools, and adult education. The chief sources are the decennial census of population and the Current Population Survey (CPS), both conducted by the Bureau of the Census (see text, section 1); annual, biennial, and other periodic surveys conducted by the National Center for Education Statistics, a part of the U.S. Department of Education; and surveys conducted by the National Education Association.

The censuses of population have included data on school enrollment since 1840 and on educational attainment since 1940. The CPS has reported on school enrollment annually since 1945 and on educational attainment periodically since 1947.

The National Center for Education Statistics is continuing the pattern of statistical studies and surveys conducted by the U.S. Office of Education since 1870. The annual *Digest of Education Statistics* provides summary data on pupils, staff, finances, including government expenditures, and organization at the elementary, secondary, and higher education levels. It is also a primary source for detailed information on Federal funds for education, projections of enrollment, graduates, and teachers. *The Condition of Education,* issued annually, presents a summary of information on education of particular interest to policymakers.

Other sources of data include special studies by the National Center for Education Statistics and annual or biennial reports of education agencies in individual States. The census of governments, conducted by the Bureau of the Census every 5 years (for the years ending in "2" and "7"), provides data on school district finances and State and local government

In Brief

The enrollment rate of 3 to 5 year olds in preprimary school:

1970	*37 percent*
1991	*56 percent*

Persons 25 years old and over completing college:

1970	*11 percent*
1992	*21 percent*

1990-91 percent change in public schools with:

CD-ROM's	*93*
Satellite dishes	*681*

expenditures for education. Reports published by the Bureau of Labor Statistics contain data relating civilian labor force experience to educational attainment (see also tables 624, 629, 646, and 654 in section 13).

Types and sources of data.—The statistics in this section are of two general types. One type, exemplified by data from the Bureau of the Census, is based on direct interviews with individuals to obtain information about their own and their family members' education. Data of this type relate to school enrollment and level of education attained, classified by age, sex, and other characteristics of the population. The school enrollment statistics reflect attendance or enrollment in any regular school within a given period; educational attainment statistics reflect the highest grade completed by an individual or, beginning in 1992, the highest diploma or degree received.

For enrollment data starting in October 1981, the CPS used 1980 census population controls; for years 1971 through 1980, 1970 census population controls had been used. This change had little impact on summary measures (e.g., medians) and proportional measures (e.g., enrollment rates); however, use of the controls may have significant impact on absolute numbers.

Beginning with data for 1986, a new edit and tabulation package for school enrollment has been introduced. The data produced increased the estimates of high school enrollment for 1986 by 200,000 and college enrollment by 300,000. See table 229 which presents both earlier and revised estimates. In other enrollment tables, revised estimates are shown. In 1988, a new edit and tabulation package was introduced for educational attainment data.

The second type, generally exemplified by data from the National Center for Education Statistics and the National Education Association, is based on reports from administrators of educational institutions and of State and local agencies having jurisdiction over education. Data of this type relate to enrollment, attendance, staff, and finances for the Nation, individual States, and local areas.

Unlike the National Center for Education Statistics, the Census Bureau does not regularly include specialized vocational, trade, business, or correspondence schools in its surveys. The National Center for Education Statistics includes nursery schools and kindergartens that are part of regular grade schools in their enrollment figures. The Census Bureau includes all nursery schools and kindergartens. At the higher education level, the statistics of both agencies are concerned with institutions granting degrees or offering work acceptable for degree-credit, such as junior colleges.

School attendance.—All States require that children attend school. While State laws vary as to the ages and circumstances of compulsory attendance, generally they require that formal schooling begin by age 6 and continue to age 16.

Schools.—The National Center for Education Statistics defines a *school* as "a division of the school system consisting of students composing one or more grade groups or other identifiable groups, organized as one unit with one or more teachers to give instruction of a defined type, and housed in a school plant of one or more buildings. More than one school may be housed in one school plant, as is the case when the elementary and secondary programs are housed in the same school plant."

Regular schools are those which advance a person toward a diploma or degree. They include public and private nursery schools, kindergartens, graded schools, colleges, universities, and professional schools.

Public schools are schools controlled and supported by local, State, or Federal governmental agencies; *private* schools are those controlled and supported mainly by religious organizations or by private persons or organizations.

The Bureau of the Census defines *elementary* schools as including grades 1 through 8; *high* schools as including grades 9 through 12; and *colleges* as including junior or community colleges, regular 4-year colleges, and universities and graduate or professional schools. Statistics reported by the National Center for Education Statistics and the National Education Association by type of organization, such as elementary level and secondary level, may not be strictly comparable with those from the Bureau of the Census because the grades included at the two levels vary, depending on the level assigned to the middle or junior high school by the local school systems.

School year.—Except as otherwise indicated in the tables, data refer to the school year which, for elementary and secondary schools, generally begins in September of the preceding year and ends in June of the year stated. For the most part, statistics concerning school finances are for a 12-month period, usually July 1 to June 30. Enrollment data generally refer to a specific point in time, such as fall, as indicated in the tables.

Statistical reliability.—For a discussion of statistical collection, estimation, and sampling procedures and measures of statistical reliability applicable to Census Bureau and the National Center for Education Statistics data, see Appendix III.

Historical statistics.—Tabular headnotes provide cross-references, where applicable, to *Historical Statistics of the United States, Colonial Times to 1970.* See Appendix IV.

No. 221. School Enrollment, 1955 to 1991, With Projections to 2003, and Number of Schools, 1955 to 1990

[In thousands. As of fall. See also *Historical Statistics, Colonial Times to 1970*, series H 421-429]

ITEM AND YEAR	TOTAL		ELEMENTARY [1]		SECONDARY		COLLEGE	
	Public	Private	Public	Private	Public	Private	Public	Private
Enrollment: [2]								
1955	32,164	5,777	22,159	3,800	8,521	800	[3]1,484	1,177
1965	46,039	8,251	26,604	4,900	15,465	1,400	3,970	1,951
1970	52,322	7,516	27,492	4,052	18,402	1,311	6,428	2,153
1974	53,062	7,235	26,394	3,700	18,679	1,300	7,989	2,235
1975	53,655	7,350	25,656	3,700	19,164	1,300	8,835	2350
1976	52,964	7,526	25,427	3,825	18,884	1,342	8,653	2,359
1977	52,424	7,579	24,954	3,797	18,623	1,343	8,847	2,439
1978	51,338	7,559	25,018	3,732	17,534	1,353	8,786	2,474
1979	50,688	7,533	24,547	3,700	17,104	1,300	9,037	2,533
1980	50,334	7,971	24,196	3,992	16,681	1,339	9,457	2,640
1981	49,691	8,225	24,037	4,100	16,007	1,400	9,647	2,725
1982	49,261	8,330	23,816	4,200	15,749	1,400	9,696	2,730
1983	48,935	8,497	23,635	4,315	15,617	1,400	9,683	2,782
1984	48,685	8,465	23,742	4,300	15,466	1,400	9,477	2,765
1985	48,901	8,325	24,135	4,195	15,287	1,362	9,479	2,768
1986	49,467	8,242	24,497	4,116	15,256	1,336	9,714	2,790
1987	49,981	8,272	25,215	4,232	14,793	1,247	9,973	2,793
1988	50,349	8,136	25,740	4,036	14,448	1,206	10,161	2,894
1989	51,121	8,316	26,408	4,162	14,135	1,193	10,578	2,961
1990	51,965	8,196	27,055	4,090	14,169	1,136	10,741	2,970
1991, est.	53,013	8,176	27,420	4,069	14,419	1,124	11,174	2,983
1992, proj.	53,708	8,440	27,834	4,142	14,752	1,144	11,122	3,154
1995, proj.	56,447	8,795	29,022	4,328	16,049	1,252	11,376	3,215
2000, proj.	59,843	9,335	30,405	4,531	17,252	1,356	12,186	3,448
2002, proj.	60,574	9,477	30,422	4,560	17,695	1,381	12,457	3,536
2003, proj.	60,831	9,523	30,299	4,554	17,977	1,400	12,555	3,569
Schools: [4]								
1955	(X)	(X)	104.4	12.4	26.0	3.9	0.7	1.2
1965	(X)	(X)	73.2	15.3	26.6	4.6	0.8	1.4
1970	(X)	(X)	65.8	14.4	25.4	3.8	(NA)	(NA)
1976 [5]	(X)	(X)	62.6	16.4	25.4	5.9	1.5	1.6
1978	(X)	(X)	62.0	16.1	24.5	5.8	1.5	1.7
1980	(X)	(X)	61.1	16.8	24.4	5.7	1.5	1.7
1984	(X)	(X)	58.8	(NA)	23.9	(NA)	1.5	1.8
1986	(X)	(X)	60.8	(NA)	23.4	(NA)	1.5	1.9
1987	(X)	(X)	61.5	(NA)	22.9	(NA)	1.6	2.0
1988	(X)	(X)	61.5	(NA)	22.8	(NA)	1.6	2.0
1990	(X)	(X)	61.4	(NA)	22.7	(NA)	1.5	2.0

NA Not available. X Not applicable. [1] Enrollment includes kindergarten. [2] For regular schools. [3] Degree-credit enrollment only. [4] Excludes schools not reported by level, such as special education. Schools with both elementary and secondary programs are included under elementary and also secondary. [5] Beginning 1976, branch campuses of college institutions counted separately.

Source: U.S. National Center for Education Statistics, *Digest of Education Statistics*, annual, and *Projections of Education Statistics*, annual.

No. 222. School Expenditures, by Type of Control and Level of Instruction in Constant (1989-90) Dollars: 1960 to 1992

[In millions of dollars. For school years ending in year shown. Total expenditures for public elementary and secondary schools include current expenditures, interest on school debt and capital outlay. Data deflated by the Consumer Price Index, wage earners and clerical workers through 1975; thereafter, all urban consumers, on a school year basis (supplied by the National Center for Education Statistics). See also Appendix III. See *Historical Statistics, Colonial Times to 1970*, series H 494, 499, and 500 for related but not comparable data, and H 513-519 for private schools]

YEAR	Total	ELEMENTARY AND SECONDARY SCHOOLS			COLLEGES AND UNIVERSITIES		
		Total	Public	Private [1]	Total	Public	Private [1]
1960	103,100	72,224	67,471	4,754	30,886	16,869	14,016
1970	230,115	145,155	136,751	8,403	84,960	54,569	30,391
1975	266,404	168,785	158,978	9,807	97,619	66,112	31,507
1980	270,896	168,729	156,953	11,776	102,167	67,768	34,398
1981	268,021	164,646	152,627	12,020	103,375	68,247	35,128
1982	266,882	162,565	150,017	12,548	104,317	68,559	35,758
1983	274,366	166,529	153,204	13,325	107,837	70,296	37,541
1984	285,177	173,403	159,057	14,346	111,773	72,510	39,263
1985	297,316	179,357	164,471	14,886	117,959	76,478	41,481
1986	314,453	188,799	173,396	15,403	125,654	81,761	43,893
1987	333,123	199,995	183,671	16,324	133,128	85,626	47,502
1988	343,081	205,739	188,969	16,770	137,342	88,236	49,106
1989	362,098	219,397	202,212	17,185	142,701	91,466	51,235
1990	377,504	229,731	211,731	18,000	147,773	94,657	53,117
1991 [1]	381,600	234,000	215,900	18,200	147,600	94,700	52,900
1992 [1]	390,700	239,900	221,300	18,500	150,700	97,100	53,600

[1] Estimated.
Source: U.S. National Center for Education Statistics, *Digest Education Statistics*, annual.

No. 223. School Enrollment, Faculty, Graduates, and Finances, 1985 to 1990, and Projections, 1992 to 2002

[As of **fall, except as indicated**]

ITEM	Unit	1985	1989	1990	1992	1993	1994	1995	2000	2002
ELEMENTARY AND SECONDARY SCHOOLS										
School-age population [1]	1,000	44,782	44,948	45,311	46,666	47,382	48,238	49,126	51,784	52,358
School enrollment: Total	1,000	44,979	45,898	46,450	47,872	48,734	49,661	50,651	53,545	54,057
Elementary	1,000	28,330	30,570	31,145	31,976	32,399	32,810	33,350	34,936	34,982
Secondary	1,000	16,649	15,328	15,305	15,896	16,335	16,852	17,301	18,608	19,076
Public, total	1,000	39,422	40,543	41,224	42,586	43,356	44,187	45,071	47,657	48,117
Elementary	1,000	24,135	26,408	27,055	27,834	28,196	28,551	29,022	30,405	30,422
Secondary	1,000	15,287	14,135	14,169	14,752	15,160	15,636	16,049	17,252	17,695
Private, total	1,000	5,557	5,355	5,226	5,286	5,378	5,474	5,580	5,888	5,940
Elementary	1,000	4,195	4,162	4,090	4,142	4,203	4,259	4,328	4,531	4,560
Secondary	1,000	1,362	1,193	1,136	1,144	1,175	1,216	1,252	1,356	1,381
Classroom teachers: Total	1,000	2,549	2,734	2,752	2,791	2,851	2,923	2,993	3,240	3,314
Elementary	1,000	1,483	1,662	1,680	1,679	1,711	1,748	1,788	1,924	1,957
Secondary	1,000	1,066	1,072	1,072	1,112	1,140	1,175	1,205	1,317	1,357
Public, total	1,000	2,206	2,357	2,398	2,437	2,489	2,553	2,614	2,831	2,896
Elementary	1,000	1,237	1,387	1,426	1,429	1,456	1,488	1,522	1,637	1,666
Secondary	1,000	969	970	972	1,008	1,033	1,065	1,093	1,194	1,230
Private, total	1,000	343	377	355	354	361	370	379	410	418
Elementary	1,000	246	275	254	250	255	260	266	287	292
Secondary	1,000	97	102	100	104	106	110	113	123	127
Projected demand for new teachers	1,000	(NA)	237	216	218	242	239	240	261	(NA)
High school graduates, total [2]	1,000	2,643	2,586	2,511	2,480	2,506	2,601	2,631	3,009	3,011
Public	1,000	2,383	2,320	2,263	2,236	2.259	2,345	2,372	2,713	2,715
Public schools: [2]										
Average daily attendance (ADA)	1,000	36,523	37,779	38,209	39,471	40,185	40,955	41,774	44,171	44,392
Constant **(1990-91)** dollars:										
Teachers' average salary	Dol	31,020	33,071	32,977	33,874	34,849	35,745	36,605	39,263	40,092
Current school expenditures	Bil. dol	168.8	197.7	201.4	211.5	221.3	231.5	241.4	281.1	294.0
HIGHER EDUCATION										
Enrollment, total	1,000	12,247	13,539	13,710	14,276	14,431	14,373	14,591	15,634	15,993
Male	1,000	5,818	6,190	6,239	6,395	6,400	6,355	6,471	7,071	7,300
Full-time	1,000	3,608	3,740	3,791	3,851	3,826	3,762	3,851	4,275	4,447
Part-time	1,000	2,211	2,450	2,447	2,544	2,574	2,593	2,620	2,796	2,853
Female	1,000	6,429	7,349	7,472	7,881	8,031	8,018	8,120	8,563	8,693
Full-time	1,000	3,468	3,921	3,989	4,197	4,271	4,199	4,280	4,641	4,771
Part-time	1,000	2,961	3,428	3,483	3,684	3,760	3,819	3,840	3,922	3,922
Public	1,000	9,479	10,578	10,741	11,122	11,242	11,206	11,376	12,186	12,457
Four-year institutions	1,000	5,210	5,694	5,803	6,076	6,130	6,085	6,177	6,649	6,825
Two-year institutions	1,000	4,270	4,884	4,937	5,046	5,112	5,121	5,199	5,537	5,632
Private	1,000	2,768	2,961	2,970	3,154	3,189	3,167	3,215	3,448	3,536
Four-year institutions	1,000	2,506	2,693	2,726	2,887	2,918	2,899	2,940	3,151	3,233
Two-year institutions	1,000	261	267	243	267	271	268	275	297	303
Undergraduate	1,000	10,597	11,742	11,863	12,215	12,307	12,230	12,443	13,447	13,787
Graduate	1,000	1,376	1,522	1,574	1,746	1,796	1,817	1,822	1,857	1,871
First-time professional	1,000	274	274	274	315	328	326	326	330	335
Full-time equivalent	1,000	8,943	9,781	9,921	10,297	10,386	10,277	10,465	11,342	11,664
Public	1,000	6,668	7,372	7,498	7,736	7,799	7,722	7,865	8,528	8,767
Private	1,000	2,276	2,409	2,421	2,562	2,585	2,556	2,600	2,813	2,897
Faculty, total	1,000	715	824	834	868	876	884	891	957	(NA)
Public	1,000	503	577	586	618	611	617	622	667	(NA)
Private	1,000	212	247	248	250	265	267	269	290	(NA)
Degrees conferred, total [2]	1,000	1,830	1,937	2,004	2,088	2,134	2,144	2,139	2,266	2,355
Associate's	1,000	446	455	470	490	492	497	489	540	557
Bachelor's	1,000	988	1,050	1,084	1,131	1,166	1,166	1,170	1,239	1,303
Master's	1,000	289	324	337	345	350	354	354	358	365
Doctorates	1,000	34	38	40	41	41	41	41	42	42
First-professional	1,000	74	71	73	81	85	85	86	87	88

NA Not available.   [1] Population 5-17 years old. As of July.   [2] For school year ending June the following year.

Source: U.S. National Center for Education Statistics, *Digest of Education Statistics,* annual, and *Projections of Educational Statistics,* annual.

No. 224. Federal Funds for Education and Related Programs, by Level of Education or Activity, Agency, and Program: 1980 to 1992

[In millions of dollars, except percent. For fiscal years ending in June. To the extent possible, amounts represent outlays]

LEVEL, AGENCY, AND PROGRAM	1980	1985	1990	1992[1]
Total, all programs	34,317.1	38,809.9	51,393.6	61,384.7
Percent of Federal budget outlays	5.8	4.1	4.1	4.4
Elementary/secondary education programs	16,027.7	16,901.3	21,984.4	28,317.2
Department of Education[2]	6,629.1	7,296.7	9,681.3	12,642.0
Grants for the disadvantaged	3,204.7	4,206.8	4,494.1	6,170.9
School improvement programs	788.9	526.4	1,189.2	1,744.5
Education for the handicapped	93.4	82.3	69.5	74.4
Indian education	821.8	1,018.0	1,616.6	2,553.5
Vocational and adult education	860.7	658.3	1,306.7	1,080.5
Department of Agriculture	4,064.5	4,134.9	5,529.0	6,684.7
Child nutrition programs	3,377.1	3,664.6	4,977.1	6,111.1
Agricultural Marketing Service—commodities[3]	388.0	336.5	350.4	400.0
Special milk program	159.3	16.0	18.7	21.1
Department of Defense[2]	370.8	831.6	1,097.9	1,188.4
Overseas dependents schools	338.8	613.4	865.0	907.0
Section VI schools[4]	—	162.6	193.6	229.7
Department of Energy	77.6	23.0	15.2	13.3
Energy conservation for school buildings	77.2	22.7	15.2	15.2
Department of Health and Human Services	1,077.0	1,531.1	2,396.8	3,530.7
Head Start	735.0	1,075.1	1,447.8	2,201.8
Social security student benefits	342.0	456.0	489.8	496.5
Department of the Interior[2]	318.2	389.8	445.3	533.7
Mineral Leasing Act and other funds	111.6	186.4	226.3	349.2
Indian Education	206.2	202.9	218.4	349.2
Department of Justice	23.9	36.1	66.0	99.7
Inmate programs	18.9	27.8	63.9	96.4
Department of Labor	1,849.8	1,945.3	2,505.5	3,278.2
Job Corps	469.8	604.7	739.4	880.9
Department of Veterans Affairs	545.8	344.8	155.4	203.6
Vocational rehab for disabled veterans	88.0	107.5	136.8	197.8
Other agencies and programs	1,071.0	368.1	91.8	130.3
Higher education programs	10,939.5	10,956.5	13,420.4	14,411.9
Department of Education[2]	5,682.2	8,202.5	11,176.0	11,176.7
Student financial assistance	3,682.8	4,162.7	5,920.3	6,476.4
Guaranteed student loans	1,408.0	3,534.8	4,372.4	3,647.9
Department of Agriculture	10.5	17.7	31.3	34.2
Department of Defense	545.0	1,041.7	646.6	676.8
Tuition assistance for military personnel	106.1	77.1	106.1	90.7
Service academies[5]	(6)	196.4	120.6	142.9
Senior ROTC	(6)	354.0	193.1	183.9
Professional development education	(6)	414.2	226.8	259.3
Department of Energy[2]	53.5	226.8	25.5	31.8
University laboratory cooperative program	57.7	19.5	9.4	18.6
Energy conservation for buildings—higher education	2.8	6.5	7.5	7.4
Department of Health and Human Services[2]	2,235.7	298.2	337.2	839.6
Health professions training programs	460.7	212.2	230.6	675.5
National Health Service Corps scholarships	70.7	2.3	4.8	58.7
Alcohol, drug abuse, and mental health training programs	122.1	43.6	81.4	74.7
Social security postsecondary students' benefits	1,559.0	25.0	—	—
Department of the Interior	80.2	125.2	135.5	139.2
Shared revenues, Mineral Leasing Act and other receipts—estimated education share	35.4	72.0	70.0	68.0
Indian programs	44.8	53.3	65.5	71.3
Department of Transportation	12.5	55.6	46.0	53.0
Department of Veterans Affairs[2]	1,803.8	944.1	599.8	822.3
Vietnam-era veterans	1,580.0	694.2	47.0	—
Post-Vietnam veterans	0.9	82.6	161.5	93.1
All-volunteer-force educational assistance	—	0.2	269.9	614.0
Other agencies and programs[2]	511.9	252.0	422.5	638.2
National Endowment for the Humanities	56.5	49.1	50.9	58.3
National Science Foundation	64.6	60.1	161.9	310.3
United States Information Agency	51.1	124.0	181.2	222.7
Other education programs[2]	1,548.7	2,107.6	3,382.9	4,003.8
Department of Education[2]	747.7	1,173.1	2,251.8	2,593.7
Administration	187.3	284.9	328.3	358.4
Libraries	129.1	85.7	137.3	176.2
Rehabilitation services and handicapped research	426.9	798.3	1,780.4	2,053.0
Department of Agriculture	271.1	336.4	352.5	400.7
Department of Health and Human Services	37.8	47.2	78.0	94.3
Department of Justice	27.6	25.5	26.9	28.6
Department of State	25.0	23.8	47.5	44.1
Department of Transportation	10.2	3.8	3.8	2.8
Department of the Treasury[2]	14.6	16.2	41.5	72.4
Other agencies and programs[2]	414.7	481.7	583.1	767.3
Agency for International Development	99.7	141.8	170.4	164.1
Library of Congress	151.9	169.3	189.8	332.5
National Endowment for the Arts	0.2	1.1	0.9	3.0
National Endowment for the Humanities	85.8	76.3	89.7	97.5
Research programs at universities and related institutions[2]	5,801.2	8,844.6	12,606.0	14,651.9
Department of Agriculture	644.5	293.3	348.1	409.5
Department of Defense	216.4	1,245.9	1,871.9	2,085.6
Department of Energy	1,470.2	2,205.3	2,520.9	2,085.6
Department of Health and Human Services	2,087.1	3,228.0	4,902.7	5,649.5
National Aeronautics and Space Administration	254.6	485.8	1,090.0	1,488.8
National Science Foundation	743.8	1,087.0	42.3	1,760.3

- Represents or rounds to zero.   NA Not available.   [1] Estimated.   [2] Includes other programs and agencies, not shown separately.   [3] Purchased under Section 32 of the Act of August 1935 for use in child nutrition programs.   [4] Includes stateside schools on military installations for free education of dependents.   [5] Instructional costs only including academics, audiovisual, academic computer center, faculty training, military training, physical education, and libraries.   [6] Included in total above.

Source: U.S. National Center for Education Statistics, Digest of Education Statistics, 1992.

No. 225. School Expenditures, by Source of Funds in Constant (1989-90) Dollars: 1970 to 1990

[For school years ending in year shown. Includes nursery, kindergarten, and special programs when provided by school system. All nonpublic school data and all data beginning 1980 are estimated. Data are deflated by the Consumer Price Index. For 1970, for wage earners and clerical workers; beginning 1980, for all urban consumers, on a school year basis (supplied by the U.S. National Center for Education Statistics). Due to revised methodology, data for 1970 are not comparable to later years or to table 222]

SOURCE OF FUNDS AND TYPE OF SCHOOL	TOTAL (bil. dol.)									PERCENT		
	1970	1980	1984	1985	1986	1987	1988	1989	1990	1970	1980	1990
Total	236.6	270.9	285.2	297.3	314.5	333.1	343.1	362.1	377.5	100.0	100.0	100.0
Federal	25.2	30.9	24.6	25.6	27.5	28.8	29.2	30.2	31.1	10.7	11.4	8.2
State	74.6	105.2	108.5	115.4	123.0	129.4	132.7	136.4	140.5	31.5	38.8	37.2
Local	76.0	70.7	75.0	76.0	79.1	83.8	86.8	96.6	102.3	32.1	26.1	27.1
All other	60.8	64.0	77.1	80.3	84.9	91.1	94.4	98.9	103.5	25.7	23.6	27.4
Public	190.9	224.7	231.6	240.9	255.2	269.3	277.2	293.7	306.4	80.7	82.9	81.2
Federal	19.5	24.3	18.4	19.0	20.2	20.7	21.0	21.9	22.7	8.2	9.0	6.0
State	74.3	104.5	107.8	114.6	122.2	128.4	131.5	135.2	139.2	31.4	38.6	36.9
Local	75.6	70.5	74.7	75.7	78.8	83.6	86.5	96.2	101.9	32.0	26.0	27.0
All other	21.5	25.5	30.6	31.6	34.0	36.8	38.1	40.4	42.6	9.1	9.4	11.3
Private	45.7	46.2	53.6	56.4	59.3	63.8	65.9	68.4	71.1	19.3	17.1	18.8
Federal	5.7	6.7	6.2	6.6	7.2	8.1	8.1	8.3	8.5	2.4	2.5	2.3
State and local	0.7	1.0	1.0	1.1	1.2	1.3	1.5	1.8	1.8	0.3	0.4	0.5
All other	39.3	38.5	46.5	48.7	50.9	54.3	56.1	58.6	60.9	16.6	14.2	16.1
Elementary and secondary	153.6	168.7	173.4	179.4	188.8	200.0	205.7	219.4	229.7	100.0	100.0	100.0
Federal	11.4	15.4	10.8	10.9	11.6	11.8	11.9	12.6	12.9	7.4	9.1	5.6
State	53.1	73.1	75.7	80.1	85.4	91.0	93.3	96.3	99.7	34.6	43.3	43.4
Local	72.9	68.0	72.1	72.9	75.9	80.4	83.2	92.8	98.5	47.5	40.3	42.9
All other	16.1	12.2	14.8	15.4	15.9	16.9	17.3	17.8	18.6	10.5	7.2	8.1
Public	137.8	157.0	159.1	164.5	173.4	183.7	189.0	202.2	211.7	89.7	93.1	92.2
Federal	11.4	15.4	10.8	10.9	11.6	11.8	11.9	12.6	12.9	7.4	9.1	5.6
State	53.1	73.1	75.7	80.1	85.4	91.0	93.3	96.3	99.7	34.6	43.3	43.4
Local	72.9	68.0	72.1	72.9	75.9	80.4	83.2	92.8	98.5	47.5	40.3	42.9
All other	0.3	0.5	0.5	0.5	0.6	0.6	0.5	0.6	0.6	0.2	0.3	0.3
Private	15.8	11.8	14.3	14.9	15.4	16.3	16.8	17.2	18.0	10.3	7.0	7.8
Higher education	83.0	102.2	111.8	118.0	125.7	133.1	137.3	142.7	147.8	100.0	100.0	100.0
Federal	13.8	15.6	13.8	14.7	15.9	17.0	17.2	17.6	18.2	16.6	15.3	12.3
State	21.5	32.1	32.8	35.3	37.6	38.5	39.6	40.2	40.8	25.9	31.4	27.6
Local	3.0	2.8	2.9	3.1	3.2	3.4	3.5	3.8	3.9	3.6	2.7	2.6
All other	44.7	51.7	62.3	65.0	69.0	74.2	77.1	81.1	84.9	53.9	50.6	57.4
Public	53.1	67.8	72.5	76.5	81.8	85.6	88.2	91.5	94.7	64.0	66.3	64.1
Federal	8.1	8.9	7.6	8.1	8.6	8.9	9.1	9.4	9.8	9.8	8.7	6.6
State	21.2	31.4	32.1	34.5	36.8	37.4	38.3	38.9	39.4	25.5	30.7	26.7
Local	2.7	2.5	2.6	2.8	2.9	3.1	3.2	3.4	3.5	3.3	2.4	2.4
All other	21.2	25.0	30.2	31.1	33.5	36.2	37.6	39.8	42.0	25.5	24.5	28.4
Private	29.9	34.4	39.3	41.5	43.9	47.5	49.1	51.2	53.1	36.0	33.7	35.9
Federal	5.7	6.7	6.2	6.6	7.2	8.1	8.1	8.3	8.5	6.9	6.6	5.8
State and local	0.7	1.0	1.0	1.1	1.2	1.3	1.5	1.8	1.8	0.8	1.0	1.2
All other	23.5	26.7	32.1	33.8	35.5	38.0	39.3	41.3	42.9	28.3	26.1	29.0

Source: U.S. National Center for Education Statistics, *Digest of Education Statistics*, annual.

No. 226. Enrollment in Public and Private Schools, by Control and Level, 1970 to 1991, and Projections, 1995 to 2003

[In thousands. As of fall. Data are for regular day schools and exclude independent nursery schools and kindergartens, residential schools for exceptional children, subcollegiate departments of colleges, Federal schools for Indians, and federally operated schools on Federal installations. College data include degree-credit and nondegree-credit enrollment]

CONTROL OF SCHOOL AND LEVEL	1970	1980	1985	1986	1987	1988	1989	1990	1991, est.	1995, proj.	2000, proj.	2003, proj.
Total	59,838	58,305	57,226	57,709	58,254	58,485	59,436	60,160	61,189	65,242	69,178	70,354
Public	52,322	50,335	48,901	49,468	49,981	50,350	51,121	51,965	53,013	56,447	59,843	60,831
Private	7,516	7,971	8,325	8,242	8,272	8,136	8,316	8,196	8,176	8,795	9,335	9,523
Kindergarten through 8	36,610	31,639	31,229	31,536	32,163	32,535	33,314	33,978	34,422	36,613	38,334	38,523
Public	32,558	27,647	27,034	27,420	27,933	28,501	29,152	29,888	30,353	32,285	33,803	33,969
Private	4,052	3,992	4,195	4,116	4,232	4,036	4,162	4,090	4,069	4,328	4,531	4,554
Grades 9 through 12	14,647	14,570	13,750	13,669	13,324	12,896	12,583	12,472	12,610	14,038	15,210	15,707
Public	13,336	13,231	12,388	12,333	12,076	11,687	11,390	11,336	11,486	12,786	13,854	14,307
Private	1,311	1,339	1,362	1,336	1,247	1,206	1,193	1,136	1,124	1,252	1,356	1,400
College	8,581	12,097	12,247	12,504	12,767	13,055	13,539	13,711	14,157	14,591	15,634	16,124
Public	6,428	9,457	9,479	9,714	9,973	10,161	10,578	10,741	11,174	11,376	12,186	12,555
Private	2,153	2,640	2,768	2,790	2,793	2,894	2,961	2,970	2,983	3,215	3,448	3,569

Source: U.S. Department of Education, National Center for Education Statistics, *Digest of Education Statistics*, annual; *Projections of Education Statistics*, annual; and unpublished data.

No. 227. School Enrollment, by Age, Race, and Hispanic Origin: 1970 to 1991

[**As of October.** Covers civilian noninstitutional population enrolled in nursery school and above. Based on Current Population Survey, see text, section 1. See *Historical Statistics, Colonial Times to 1970*, series H 442-476 for enrollment 5-34 years old]

AGE, RACE, AND HISPANIC ORIGIN	ENROLLMENT (1,000)						RATE					
	1970	1980	1985	1989	1990	1991	1970	1980	1985	1989	1990	1991
Total 3 to 34 years old [1]............	60,357	57,348	58,013	59,235	60,588	61,276	56.4	49.7	48.3	49.1	50.2	50.7
3 and 4 years old.........	1,461	2,280	2,801	2,898	3,292	3,068	20.5	36.7	38.9	39.1	44.4	40.5
5 and 6 years old.........	7,000	5,853	6,697	6,990	7,207	7,178	89.5	95.7	96.1	95.2	96.5	95.4
7 to 13 years old.........	28,943	23,751	22,849	24,431	25,016	25,445	99.2	99.3	99.2	99.3	99.6	99.7
14 and 15 years old.......	7,869	7,282	7,362	6,493	6,555	6,634	98.1	98.2	98.1	98.8	99.0	98.8
16 and 17 years old.......	6,927	7,129	6,654	6,254	6,098	6,155	90.0	89.0	91.7	92.7	92.5	93.3
18 and 19 years old.......	3,322	3,788	3,716	4,125	4,044	3,969	47.7	46.4	51.6	56.0	57.3	59.6
20 and 21 years old.......	1,949	2,515	2,708	2,630	2,852	3,041	31.9	31.0	35.3	38.5	39.7	42.0
22 to 24 years old.........	1,410	1,931	2,068	2,207	2,231	2,365	14.9	16.3	16.9	19.9	21.0	22.2
25 to 29 years old.........	1,011	1,714	1,942	1,960	2,013	2,045	7.5	9.3	9.2	9.3	9.7	10.2
30 to 34 years old.........	466	1,105	1,218	1,248	1,281	1,377	4.2	6.4	6.1	5.7	5.8	6.2
35 years old and over ...	(NA)	1,290	1,766	2,230	2,439	2,620	(NA)	1.4	1.7	2.0	2.1	2.2
White: Total 3 to 34 years old...........	51,719	47,673	47,452	47,923	48,899	49,156	56.2	48.9	47.8	48.4	49.5	50.0
3 and 4 years old.........	1,181	1,844	2,250	2,370	2,700	2,502	19.9	36.3	38.6	39.4	44.9	41.3
5 and 6 years old.........	5,899	4,781	5,437	5,598	5,750	5,727	90.3	95.8	96.4	95.2	96.5	95.3
7 to 13 years old.........	24,564	19,585	18,464	19,638	20,076	20,325	99.2	99.2	99.3	99.3	99.6	99.6
14 and 15 years old.......	6,761	6,038	6,007	5,197	5,265	5,311	98.2	98.3	98.1	98.8	99.1	98.7
16 and 17 years old.......	6,008	5,937	5,449	4,993	4,858	4,902	90.6	88.6	91.6	92.3	92.5	93.3
18 and 19 years old.......	2,924	3,199	3,105	3,392	3,271	3,197	48.7	46.3	52.4	56.4	57.1	59.7
20 and 21 years old.......	1,750	2,206	2,318	2,208	2,402	2,517	33.1	31.9	36.1	39.5	41.0	43.2
22 to 24 years old.........	1,305	1,669	1,744	1,841	1,781	1,910	15.7	16.4	17.0	20.0	20.2	21.7
25 to 29 years old.........	910	1,473	1,635	1,659	1,706	1,646	7.7	9.2	9.2	9.4	9.9	9.9
30 to 34 years old.........	416	942	1,043	1,028	1,090	1,119	4.2	6.3	6.2	5.6	5.9	6.0
35 years old and over ...	(NA)	1,104	1,533	1,956	2,096	2,219	(NA)	1.3	1.7	2.0	2.1	2.2
Black: Total 3 to 34 years old...........	7,829	8,251	8,444	8,707	8,854	9,031	57.4	53.9	50.9	51.3	51.9	52.5
3 and 4 years old.........	250	371	469	407	452	428	22.7	38.2	42.7	38.9	41.6	37.2
5 and 6 years old.........	999	904	1,030	1,084	1,129	1,108	84.9	95.4	95.7	94.9	96.3	95.8
7 to 13 years old.........	3,998	3,598	3,549	3,761	3,832	3,941	99.3	99.4	99.1	99.2	99.8	99.8
14 and 15 years old.......	1,025	1,088	1,106	1,023	1,023	1,032	97.6	97.9	97.9	99.4	99.2	99.1
16 and 17 years old.......	837	1,047	994	1,033	962	959	85.7	90.6	91.7	93.7	91.7	91.7
18 and 19 years old.......	352	494	472	541	596	578	40.1	45.7	44.1	50.2	55.2	55.6
20 and 21 years old.......	174	242	298	309	305	329	22.8	23.4	27.7	30.7	28.4	30.0
22 to 24 years old.........	84	196	215	253	274	249	8.0	13.6	13.7	17.2	20.0	18.2
25 to 29 years old.........	68	187	192	168	162	229	4.8	8.8	7.4	6.4	6.1	8.7
30 to 34 years old.........	41	124	119	130	119	177	3.4	6.8	5.1	4.9	4.4	6.5
35 years old and over ...	(NA)	186	233	167	238	289	(NA)	1.8	1.9	1.5	2.1	2.5
Hispanic: [2] **Total 3 to 34 years old**............	(NA)	4,263	5,070	5,722	6,073	6,306	(NA)	49.8	47.7	45.8	47.4	47.9
3 and 4 years old.........	(NA)	172	213	202	249	299	(NA)	28.5	27.0	23.8	29.8	30.6
5 and 6 years old.........	(NA)	491	662	785	835	850	(NA)	94.5	94.5	92.8	94.8	92.4
7 to 13 years old.........	(NA)	2,009	2,322	2,637	2,794	2,909	(NA)	99.2	99.0	98.7	99.4	99.7
14 and 15 years old.......	(NA)	568	606	706	739	732	(NA)	94.3	96.1	96.5	99.0	97.2
16 and 17 years old.......	(NA)	454	562	554	592	532	(NA)	81.8	84.5	86.4	85.4	82.6
18 and 19 years old.......	(NA)	226	238	327	329	394	(NA)	37.8	41.8	44.6	44.1	47.9
20 and 21 years old.......	(NA)	111	137	152	213	215	(NA)	19.5	24.0	18.8	27.2	26.4
22 to 24 years old.........	(NA)	93	125	153	121	144	(NA)	11.7	11.6	12.0	9.9	11.6
25 to 29 years old.........	(NA)	84	120	129	130	140	(NA)	6.9	6.6	6.6	6.3	6.9
30 to 34 years old.........	(NA)	54	83	76	72	93	(NA)	5.1	5.7	3.8	3.6	4.5
35 years old and over ...	(NA)	(NA)	(NA)	136	145	148	(NA)	(NA)	(NA)	2.1	2.1	2.0
Mexican: [2] **Total 3 to 34 years old**...........	(NA)	2,698	3,180	3,743	4,017	4,171	(NA)	49.0	47.5	44.7	46.8	47.7
3 and 4 years old.........	(NA)	104	137	148	165	215	(NA)	27.0	26.0	22.7	27.4	32.3
5 and 6 years old.........	(NA)	327	458	553	619	581	(NA)	93.2	95.3	91.8	94.7	92.1
7 to 13 years old.........	(NA)	1,378	1,526	1,768	1,815	1,957	(NA)	99.5	99.2	98.9	99.7	99.7
14 and 15 years old.......	(NA)	361	367	481	499	475	(NA)	92.1	97.7	95.7	99.5	97.6
16 and 17 years old.......	(NA)	257	358	356	403	351	(NA)	76.1	83.8	85.3	83.8	81.0
18 and 19 years old.......	(NA)	113	127	176	213	282	(NA)	32.0	35.2	36.9	40.9	47.0
20 and 21 years old.......	(NA)	55	61	79	121	132	(NA)	15.6	16.4	14.6	23.6	24.8
22 to 24 years old.........	(NA)	40	55	77	70	70	(NA)	7.5	7.8	8.9	8.3	8.2
25 to 29 years old.........	(NA)	41	56	64	64	61	(NA)	5.4	5.0	5.0	4.9	4.8
30 to 34 years old.........	(NA)	22	36	41	47	48	(NA)	3.3	4.5	3.3	3.6	3.7
35 years old and over ...	(NA)	(NA)	(NA)	73	81	89	(NA)	(NA)	(NA)	2.0	2.1	2.2

NA Not available. [1] Includes other races, not shown separately. [2] Persons of Hispanic origin may be of any race.

Source: U.S. Bureau of the Census, *Current Population Reports*, series P20-469, and earlier reports.

No. 228. Enrollment in Public and Private Schools: 1960 to 1991

[In millions, except percent. As of October. For civilian noninstitutional population. For 1960, 5 to 34 years old; for 1970 to 1985, 3 to 34 years old; beginning 1986, for 3 years old and over]

YEAR	PUBLIC						PRIVATE					
	Total	Nur-sery	Kinder-garten	Ele-mentary	High School	College	Total	Nur-sery	Kinder-garten	Ele-mentary	High School	College
1960	39.0	(NA)	(1)	27.5	9.2	2.3	7.2	(NA)	(1)	4.9	1.0	1.3
1970	52.2	0.3	2.6	30.0	13.5	5.7	8.1	0.8	0.5	3.9	1.2	1.7
1980	(NA)	0.6	2.7	24.4	(NA)	(NA)	(NA)	1.4	0.5	3.1	(NA)	(NA)
1984	49.0	0.8	3.0	24.1	12.7	8.5	8.3	1.6	0.5	2.7	1.1	2.4
1985	49.0	0.9	3.2	23.8	12.8	8.4	9.0	1.6	0.6	3.1	1.2	2.5
1989 [2]	52.5	0.9	3.3	25.9	12.1	10.3	8.9	1.9	0.6	2.7	0.8	2.9
1990 [2]	53.8	1.2	3.3	26.6	11.9	10.7	9.2	2.2	0.6	2.7	0.9	2.9
1991 [2]	54.5	1.1	3.5	26.6	12.2	11.1	9.4	1.8	0.6	3.0	1.0	3.0
Percent White:												
1960	85.7	(NA)	(1)	84.3	88.2	92.2	95.7	(NA)	(1)	95.3	96.7	96.3
1970	84.5	59.5	84.4	83.1	85.6	90.7	93.4	91.1	88.2	94.1	96.1	92.8
1980	(NA)	68.2	80.7	80.9	(NA)	(NA)	(NA)	89.0	87.0	90.7	(NA)	(NA)
1985	80.3	72.2	79.0	79.1	80.4	85.1	89.9	89.8	86.7	90.6	92.2	88.7
1990	79.8	71.7	78.3	78.9	79.2	84.1	87.4	89.6	83.2	88.2	89.4	85.0
1991	79.3	74.0	78.3	78.6	78.4	82.8	86.7	89.0	81.8	87.9	88.8	84.3

NA Not available.   [1] Included in elementary school.   [2] See table 272 for college enrollment 35 years old and over. See also footnote 2, table 229.

Source: U.S. Bureau of the Census, *Current Population Reports,* series P20-469; and earlier reports.

No. 229. School Enrollment, by Sex and Level: 1960 to 1991

[In millions. As of Oct. For the civilian noninstitutional population. For 1960, persons 5 to 34 years old; 1970, 3 to 34 years old; beginning 1980, 3 years old and over. Elementary includes kindergarten and grades 1-8; high school, grades 9-12; and college, 2-year and 4-year colleges, universities, and graduate and professional schools. Data for college represent degree-credit enrollment]

YEAR	ALL LEVELS [1]			ELEMENTARY			HIGH SCHOOL			COLLEGE		
	Total	Male	Female	Total	Male	Female	Total	Male	Female	Total	Male	Female
1960	46.3	24.2	22.0	32.4	16.7	15.7	10.2	5.2	5.1	3.6	2.3	1.2
1970	60.4	31.4	28.9	37.1	19.0	18.1	14.7	7.4	7.3	7.4	4.4	3.0
1980	58.6	29.6	29.1	30.6	15.8	14.9	14.6	7.3	7.3	11.4	5.4	6.0
1985	59.8	30.0	29.7	30.7	15.7	15.0	14.1	7.2	6.9	12.5	5.9	6.6
1986	60.1	30.4	29.7	31.1	16.1	15.0	14.0	7.1	6.9	12.4	5.8	6.6
1986 [2]	60.5	30.6	30.0	31.1	16.1	15.0	14.2	7.2	7.0	12.7	6.0	6.7
1987	60.6	30.7	29.9	31.6	16.3	15.3	13.8	7.0	6.8	12.7	6.0	6.7
1988	61.1	30.7	30.5	32.2	16.6	15.6	13.2	6.7	6.4	13.1	5.9	7.2
1989	61.5	30.8	30.7	32.5	16.7	15.8	12.9	6.6	6.3	13.2	6.0	7.2
1990	63.0	31.5	31.5	33.2	17.1	16.0	12.8	6.5	6.4	13.6	6.2	7.4
1991	63.9	32.1	31.8	33.8	17.3	16.4	13.1	6.8	6.4	14.1	6.4	7.6

[1] Beginning 1970, includes nursery schools, not shown separately.   [2] Revised. Data beginning 1986, based on a revised edit and tabulation package.

Source: U.S. Bureau of the Census, *Current Population Reports,* series P20-469; and earlier reports.

No. 230. Years of School Completed, by Age and Race: 1950 to 1992

[In percent, except median. Through 1990, as of April 1; beginning 1990 as of March. Excludes Armed Forces, except members living off post or with their families on post. Beginning 1980, excludes inmates of institutions. 1950 based on 20-percent sample; 1960 on 25-percent sample; 1970 on 20-percent sample; and 1980 on 17-percent sample. Beginning 1990, based on the Current Population Survey; see text, section 1. For definition of median, see Guide to Tabular Presentation]

ITEM	PERSONS 25 YEARS OLD AND OVER						PERSONS 25 TO 29 YEARS OLD					
	1950	1960	1970	1980	1990	1992	1950	1960	1970	1980	1990	1992
All persons: Not high school graduates	65.7	58.9	47.7	33.5	22.4	20.6	47.2	39.3	26.2	15.5	14.3	13.7
With less than 5 years of school	11.1	8.3	5.5	3.6	2.4	2.1	4.7	2.8	1.7	1.1	1.2	0.9
High school graduates of more	34.3	41.1	52.3	66.5	77.6	79.4	52.8	60.7	73.8	84.5	85.7	86.3
College or more	6.2	7.7	10.7	16.2	21.3	21.4	7.7	11.1	16.3	22.1	23.2	23.6
Median school years completed [1] . .	9.3	10.6	12.1	12.5	12.7	(NA)	12.0	12.3	12.6	12.9	12.9	(NA)
Black persons: Not high school graduates	87.1	79.9	68.6	48.8	33.8	32.3	77.8	62.3	44.6	24.8	18.4	19.1
With less than 5 years of school	32.9	23.8	14.6	8.2	5.1	3.9	16.8	7.0	3.2	1.1	1.0	0.9
High school graduates of more	12.9	20.1	31.4	51.2	66.2	67.7	22.2	37.7	55.4	75.2	81.7	80.9
College or more	2.1	3.1	4.4	8.4	11.3	11.9	2.7	4.8	6.0	11.4	13.4	11.3
Median school years completed [1] . .	6.8	8.0	9.8	12.0	12.4	(NA)	8.6	9.9	12.1	12.6	12.7	(NA)

NA Not available.   [1] Due to revised methodology, median school years completed not available beginning 1992.

Source: U.S. Bureau of the Census, *U.S. Census of Population, 1950, 1960, 1970,* and *1980,* vol. I; and *Current Population Reports* , series P20-462; and unpublished data.

No. 231. Educational Attainment, by Race, Ethnicity, and Sex: 1960 to 1992

[In percent. For persons 25 years old and over. 1960, 1970 and 1980 as of April 1 and based on sample data from the Censuses of Population. Other years as of March and based on the Current Population Survey; see text, section 1 and Appendix III. See table 233 for totals for both sexes]

YEAR	ALL RACES		WHITE		BLACK		ASIAN AND PACIFIC ISLANDER		HISPANIC [1]	
	Male	Female	Male	Female	Male	Female	Male	Female	Male	Female
COMPLETED 4 YEARS OF HIGH SCHOOL OR MORE										
1960	39.5	42.5	41.6	44.7	18.2	21.8	(NA)	(NA)	(NA)	(NA)
1965	48.0	49.9	50.2	52.2	25.8	28.4	(NA)	(NA)	(NA)	(NA)
1970	51.9	52.8	54.0	55.0	30.1	32.5	(NA)	(NA)	37.9	34.2
1975	63.1	62.1	65.0	64.1	41.6	43.3	(NA)	(NA)	39.5	36.7
1980	67.3	65.8	69.6	68.1	50.8	51.5	(NA)	(NA)	67.3	65.8
1985	74.4	73.5	76.0	75.1	58.4	60.8	(NA)	(NA)	48.5	47.4
1990	77.7	77.5	79.1	79.0	65.8	66.5	84.0	77.2	50.3	51.3
1991 [2]	78.5	78.3	79.8	79.9	66.7	66.7	83.8	80.0	51.4	51.2
1992 [2]	79.7	79.2	81.1	80.7	67.0	68.2	(NA)	(NA)	53.7	51.5
COMPLETED 4 YEARS OF COLLEGE OR MORE										
1960	9.7	5.8	10.3	6.0	2.8	3.3	(NA)	(NA)	(NA)	(NA)
1965	12.0	7.1	12.7	7.3	4.9	4.5	(NA)	(NA)	(NA)	(NA)
1970	13.5	8.1	14.4	8.4	4.2	4.6	(NA)	(NA)	7.8	4.3
1975	17.6	10.6	18.4	11.0	6.7	6.2	(NA)	(NA)	8.3	4.6
1980	20.1	12.8	21.3	13.3	8.4	8.3	(NA)	(NA)	9.4	6.0
1985	23.1	16.0	24.0	16.3	11.2	11.0	(NA)	(NA)	9.7	7.3
1990	24.4	18.4	25.3	19.0	11.9	10.8	44.9	35.4	9.8	8.7
1991 [2]	24.3	18.8	25.4	19.3	11.4	11.6	43.2	35.5	10.0	9.4
1992 [2]	24.3	18.6	25.2	19.1	11.9	12.0	(NA)	(NA)	10.2	8.5

NA Not available. [1] Persons of Hispanic origin may be of any race. [2] For 1992, persons high school graduates and those with a BA degree or higher.

Source: U.S. Bureau of the Census, *U.S. Census of Population, 1960, 1970, and 1980, vol. 1;* and *Current Population Reports* series P20-459, P20-462; and unpublished data.

No. 232. Years of School Completed, by Selected Characteristic: 1992

[For persons 25 years old and over. As of **March.** Based on Current Population Survey; see text, section 1 and Appendix III. For composition of regions, see table 31]

CHARACTERISTIC	Popula-tion (1,000)	PERCENT OF POPULATION—					
		Not a high school graduate	High school graduate	With some col-lege, but no degree	With an associ-ate's degree [1]	With a bache-lor's degree	With an advanced degree
Total persons	160,827	20.6	36.0	16.2	5.9	14.2	7.2
Age:							
25 to 34 years old	42,493	13.5	37.7	18.6	7.0	17.9	5.3
35 to 44 years old	39,571	11.8	34.2	19.1	8.0	17.4	9.5
45 to 54 years old	27,023	17.3	36.7	16.3	5.6	13.9	10.3
55 to 64 years old	21,150	26.9	38.0	13.3	4.2	10.5	7.2
65 to 74 years old	18,440	35.0	37.2	11.8	3.3	8.3	4.5
75 years old or over	12,149	48.4	28.9	9.9	2.6	6.6	3.6
Sex: Male	76,579	20.3	33.7	16.4	5.4	15.3	9.0
Female	84,248	20.8	38.1	16.0	6.4	13.1	5.6
Race: White	137,646	19.1	36.4	16.4	6.1	14.6	7.5
Black	17,445	32.3	35.7	15.5	4.6	8.3	3.6
Other	5,736	19.7	27.8	13.9	5.3	22.1	11.2
Hispanic origin: Hispanic	11,623	47.4	27.3	11.7	4.2	6.3	3.0
Non-Hispanic	149,204	18.5	36.7	16.5	6.0	14.8	7.5
Region: Northeast	33,361	19.2	38.3	12.4	6.3	14.9	8.9
Midwest	38,376	18.7	40.2	16.1	5.3	13.2	6.4
South	55,054	24.2	35.2	16.1	5.3	12.7	6.5
West	34,036	18.2	30.2	20.1	7.0	16.8	7.6
Marital status:							
Never married	22,606	17.8	33.0	16.2	5.8	18.8	8.3
Married spouse present	102,536	17.5	37.1	16.3	6.3	15.0	7.9
Married spouse absent	5,868	32.9	32.9	16.6	4.5	9.0	4.2
Separated	4,478	31.9	34.6	17.8	4.5	8.1	3.2
Widowed	13,840	45.5	33.2	10.5	2.9	5.6	2.4
Divorced	15,977	18.4	36.6	20.4	6.7	11.6	6.3
Civilian labor force status:							
Employed	99,072	11.9	35.6	17.9	7.2	17.7	9.6
Unemployed	6,954	24.8	41.4	17.3	4.9	8.7	2.9
Not in the labor force	54,090	36.2	35.9	12.6	3.5	8.3	3.3

[1] Includes vocational degrees.

Source: U.S. Bureau of the Census, unpublished data.

No. 233. Educational Attainment, by Race and Ethnicity: 1960 to 1992

[In percent. For persons 25 years old and over. 1960, 1970, and 1980 as of April 1 and based on sample data from the Censuses of Population. Other years as of March and based on the Current Population Survey; see text, section 1, and Appendix III. See table 231 for data by sex]

YEAR	TOTAL [1]	WHITE	BLACK	ASIAN AND PACIFIC ISLANDER	HISPANIC [2] Total [3]	Mexican	Puerto Rican	Cuban
COMPLETED 4 YEARS OF HIGH SCHOOL OR MORE								
1960.	41.1	43.2	20.1	(NA)	(NA)	(NA)	(NA)	(NA)
1965.	49.0	51.3	27.2	(NA)	(NA)	(NA)	(NA)	(NA)
1970.	52.3	54.5	31.4	(NA)	32.1	24.2	23.4	43.9
1975.	62.5	64.5	42.5	(NA)	37.9	31.0	28.7	51.7
1980.	66.5	68.8	51.2	(NA)	44.0	37.6	40.1	55.3
1985.	73.9	75.5	59.8	(NA)	47.9	41.9	46.3	51.1
1990.	77.6	79.1	66.2	80.4	50.8	44.1	55.5	63.5
1991.	78.4	79.9	66.7	81.8	51.3	43.6	58.0	61.0
1992 [4]	79.4	80.9	67.7	(NA)	(NA)	(NA)	(NA)	(NA)
COMPLETED 4 YEARS OF COLLEGE OR MORE								
1960.	7.7	8.1	3.1	(NA)	(NA)	(NA)	(NA)	(NA)
1965.	9.4	9.9	4.7	(NA)	(NA)	(NA)	(NA)	(NA)
1970.	10.7	11.3	4.4	(NA)	4.5	2.5	2.2	11.1
1975.	13.9	14.5	6.4	(NA)	(NA)	(NA)	(NA)	(NA)
1980.	16.2	17.1	8.4	(NA)	7.6	4.9	5.6	16.2
1985.	19.4	20.0	11.1	(NA)	8.5	5.5	7.0	13.7
1990.	21.3	22.0	11.3	39.9	9.2	5.4	9.7	20.2
1991.	21.4	22.2	11.5	39.1	9.7	6.2	10.1	18.5
1992 [4]	21.4	22.1	11.9	(NA)	(NA)	(NA)	(NA)	(NA)

NA Not available. [1] Includes other races, not shown separately. [2] Persons of Hispanic origin may be of any race. [3] Includes persons of other Hispanic origin, not shown separately. [4] For 1992, persons high school graduates and those with a BA degree or higher.

Source: U.S. Bureau of the Census, *U.S. Census of Population, U.S. Summary,* PC80-1-C1 and *Current Population Reports* series P20-455, P20-459, P20-462; and unpublished data.

No. 234. Highest Degree Earned, by Selected Characteristic: 1990

[For persons 18 years old and over. Based on the Survey of Income and Program Participation; see source for details]

CHARACTERISTIC	Total persons	Not a high school graduate	High school graduate only	Some college, no degree	Vocational	Associate	Bachelor's	Master's	Professional	Doctorate
NUMBER (1,000)										
All persons [1]	182,591	38,012	65,291	33,191	4,973	7,570	22,845	7,599	2,054	1,056
Age: 18 to 24 years old	25,145	4,892	8,877	8,357	451	770	1,725	50	22	-
25 to 34 years old	43,245	5,392	16,034	8,277	1,215	2,670	7,522	1,508	509	118
35 to 44 years old	37,708	4,332	12,655	6,910	1,213	2,383	6,415	2,859	648	292
45 to 54 years old	25,489	4,796	9,937	3,718	753	931	3,132	1,599	295	329
55 to 64 years old	21,228	6,063	8,315	2,573	530	497	1,896	888	310	156
65 years old and over	29,776	12,537	9,473	3,356	811	319	2,156	694	270	160
Sex: Male	87,240	17,948	29,713	16,099	1,737	3,600	11,769	3,996	1,547	833
Female	95,350	20,065	35,578	17,092	3,236	3,970	11,076	3,603	506	223
Race: White	156,385	30,270	56,240	28,608	4,541	6,677	20,381	6,813	1,898	956
Male	75,262	14,425	25,556	14,076	1,588	3,242	10,629	3,552	1,449	744
Female	81,123	15,845	30,684	14,532	2,953	3,435	9,752	3,261	449	212
Black	20,401	6,510	7,495	3,534	284	670	1,367	462	46	34
Male	9,158	3,045	3,483	1,441	87	257	581	199	38	28
Female	11,242	3,465	4,012	2,094	197	413	786	262	8	6
Hispanic [2]	13,548	5,934	4,091	1,933	208	316	734	245	55	32
Male	6,708	2,950	1,961	976	89	153	388	121	44	27
Female	6,841	2,984	2,130	958	119	163	346	124	11	5
MEAN MONTHLY INCOME [3] (dol.)										
All persons [1]	1,599	856	1,357	1,545	1,568	1,879	2,489	3,211	5,554	4,545
Age: 18 to 24 years old	724	461	778	698	892	951	1,154	(B)	(B)	(B)
25 to 34 years old	1,546	859	1,340	1,529	1,392	1,639	2,154	2,478	3,310	(B)
35 to 44 years old	2,056	947	1,546	2,028	1,784	2,265	2,634	3,580	5,719	4,917
45 to 54 years old	2,148	1,064	1,790	2,140	1,781	2,357	3,510	3,512	7,597	4,625
55 to 64 years old	1,725	951	1,393	2,046	1,877	2,125	2,920	3,421	8,320	(B)
65 years old and over	1,275	852	1,191	1,656	1,483	1,469	2,439	2,470	4,301	(B)
Sex: Male	2,148	1,166	1,853	2,002	2,085	2,380	3,235	3,748	6,367	4,915
Female	1,096	579	943	1,115	1,290	1,425	1,698	2,614	3,070	3,162
Race: White	1,672	909	1,405	1,595	1,593	1,920	2,552	3,248	5,611	4,679
Black	1,070	652	1,009	1,204	1,170	1,595	2,002	2,786	(B)	(B)
Hispanic [2]	1,078	760	1,092	1,298	1,314	1,549	1,895	2,840	(B)	(B)

B Base figure too small to meet statistical standards for reliability of a derived figure. - Represents or rounds to zero. [1] Includes other races, not shown separately. [2] Persons of Hispanic origin may be of any race. [3] For definition of mean, see Guide to Tabular Presentation.

Source: U.S. Bureau of the Census, *Current Population Reports,* series P70-32.

No. 235. Educational Attainment—States: 1990

[As of April 1. For persons 25 years old and over, except as indicated. Based on the 1990 Census of Population; see text, section 1, and Appendix III]

STATE	Population (1,000)	PERCENT OF POPULATION—						
		Not a high school graduate	High school graduate	With some college, but no degree	With an associate's degree	With a bachelor's degree	With an advanced degree	Drop-outs [1]
United States	158,868	24.8	30.0	18.7	6.2	13.1	7.2	11.2
Alabama	2,546	33.1	29.4	16.8	5.0	10.1	5.5	12.6
Alaska	323	13.4	28.7	27.6	7.2	15.0	8.0	10.9
Arizona	2,301	21.3	26.1	25.4	6.8	13.3	7.0	14.4
Arkansas	1,496	33.7	32.7	16.6	3.7	8.9	4.5	11.4
California	18,695	23.8	22.3	22.6	7.9	15.3	8.1	14.2
Colorado	2,107	15.6	26.5	24.0	6.9	18.0	9.0	9.8
Connecticut	2,199	20.8	29.5	15.9	6.6	16.2	11.0	9.0
Delaware	428	22.5	32.7	16.9	6.5	13.7	7.7	10.4
District of Columbia	409	26.9	21.2	15.6	3.1	16.1	17.2	13.9
Florida	8,887	25.6	30.1	19.4	6.6	12.0	6.3	14.3
Georgia	4,023	29.1	29.6	17.0	5.0	12.9	6.4	14.1
Hawaii	710	19.9	28.7	20.1	8.3	15.8	7.1	7.5
Idaho	601	20.3	30.4	24.2	7.5	12.4	5.3	10.4
Illinois	7,294	23.8	30.0	19.4	5.8	13.6	7.5	10.6
Indiana	3,489	24.4	38.2	16.6	5.3	9.2	6.4	11.4
Iowa	1,777	19.9	38.5	17.0	7.7	11.7	5.2	6.6
Kansas	1,566	18.7	32.8	21.9	5.4	14.1	7.0	8.7
Kentucky	2,334	35.4	31.8	15.2	4.1	8.1	5.5	13.3
Louisiana	2,537	31.7	31.7	17.2	3.3	10.5	5.6	12.5
Maine	796	21.2	37.1	16.1	6.9	12.7	6.1	8.3
Maryland	3,123	21.6	28.1	18.6	5.2	15.6	10.9	10.9
Massachusetts	3,962	20.0	29.7	15.8	7.2	16.6	10.6	8.5
Michigan	5,843	23.2	32.3	20.4	6.7	10.9	6.4	10.0
Minnesota	2,771	17.6	33.0	19.0	8.6	15.6	6.3	6.4
Mississippi	1,539	35.7	27.5	16.9	5.2	9.7	5.1	11.8
Missouri	3,292	26.1	33.1	18.4	4.5	11.7	6.1	11.4
Montana	508	19.0	33.5	22.1	5.6	14.1	5.7	8.1
Nebraska	996	18.2	34.7	21.1	7.1	13.1	5.9	7.0
Nevada	790	21.2	31.5	25.8	6.2	10.1	5.2	15.2
New Hampshire	714	17.8	31.7	18.0	8.1	16.4	7.9	9.4
New Jersey	5,166	23.3	31.1	15.5	5.2	16.0	8.8	9.6
New Mexico	923	24.9	28.7	20.9	5.0	12.1	8.3	11.7
New York	11,819	25.2	29.5	15.7	6.5	13.2	9.9	9.9
North Carolina	4,253	30.0	29.0	16.8	6.8	12.0	5.4	12.5
North Dakota	397	23.3	28.0	20.5	10.0	13.5	4.5	4.6
Ohio	6,925	24.3	36.3	17.0	5.3	11.1	5.9	8.9
Oklahoma	1,995	25.4	30.5	21.3	5.0	11.8	6.0	10.4
Oregon	1,855	18.5	28.9	25.0	6.9	13.6	7.0	11.8
Pennsylvania	7,873	25.3	38.6	12.9	5.2	11.3	6.6	9.1
Rhode Island	659	28.0	29.5	15.0	6.3	13.5	7.8	11.1
South Carolina	2,168	31.7	29.5	15.8	6.3	11.2	5.4	11.7
South Dakota	431	22.9	33.7	18.8	7.4	12.3	4.9	7.7
Tennessee	3,139	32.9	30.0	16.9	4.2	10.5	5.4	13.4
Texas	10,311	27.9	25.6	21.1	5.2	13.9	6.5	12.9
Utah	897	14.9	27.2	27.9	7.8	15.4	6.8	8.7
Vermont	357	19.2	34.6	14.7	7.2	15.4	8.9	8.0
Virginia	3,975	24.8	26.6	18.5	5.5	15.4	9.1	10.0
Washington	3,126	16.2	27.9	25.0	7.9	15.9	7.0	10.6
West Virginia	1,172	34.0	36.6	13.2	3.8	7.5	4.8	10.9
Wisconsin	3,094	21.4	37.1	16.7	7.1	12.1	5.6	7.1
Wyoming	278	17.0	33.2	24.2	6.9	13.1	5.7	6.9

[1] For persons 16 to 19 years old. A dropout is a person who is not in regular school and who has not completed the 12th grade or received a general equivalency degree.

Source: U.S. Bureau of the Census, *1990 Census of Population*, CPH-L-96.

No. 236. Preprimary School Enrollment—Summary: 1970 to 1991

[As of **October**. Civilian noninstitutional population. Includes public and nonpublic nursery school and kindergarten programs. Excludes 5 year olds enrolled in elementary school. Based on Current Population Survey; see text, section 1]

ITEM	1970	1975	1980	1985	1986	1987	1988	1989	1990	1991
NUMBER OF CHILDREN (1,000)										
Population, 3 to 5 years old	10,949	10,183	9,284	10,733	10,866	10,872	10,994	11,038	11,207	11,370
Total enrolled [1]	4,104	4,954	4,878	5,865	5,971	5,932	5,977	6,026	6,659	6,334
Nursery	1,094	1,745	1,981	2,477	2,545	2,555	2,621	2,825	3,378	2,824
Public.	332	570	628	846	829	819	852	930	1,202	996
Private	762	1,174	1,353	1,631	1,715	1,736	1,770	1,894	2,177	1,827
Kindergarten	3,010	3,211	2,897	3,388	3,426	3,377	3,356	3,201	3,281	3,510
Public.	2,498	2,682	2,438	2,847	2,859	2,842	2,875	2,704	2,767	2,968
Private	511	528	459	541	567	535	481	496	513	543
White	3,443	4,105	3,994	4,757	4,851	4,748	4,891	4,911	5,389	5,104
Black	586	731	725	919	892	893	814	872	964	928
Hispanic [2]	(NA)	(NA)	370	496	593	587	544	520	642	675
3 years old.	454	683	857	1,035	1,041	1,022	1,028	1,005	1,205	1,075
4 years old.	1,007	1,418	1,423	1,765	1,772	1,717	1,768	1,882	2,086	1,993
5 years old.	2,643	2,852	2,598	3,065	3,157	3,192	3,183	3,139	3,367	3,266
ENROLLMENT RATE										
Total enrolled [1]	37.5	48.6	52.5	54.6	55.0	54.6	54.4	54.6	59.4	55.7
White	37.8	48.6	52.7	54.7	55.2	54.1	55.4	55.0	59.7	56.2
Black	34.9	48.1	51.8	55.8	54.1	54.2	48.2	54.2	57.8	53.1
Hispanic [2]	(NA)	(NA)	43.3	43.3	47.8	45.5	44.2	41.6	49.0	46.4
3 years old.	12.9	21.5	27.3	28.8	28.9	28.6	27.6	27.1	32.6	28.2
4 years old.	27.8	40.5	46.3	49.1	49.0	47.7	49.1	51.0	56.0	53.0
5 years old.	69.3	81.3	84.7	86.5	86.7	86.1	86.1	86.4	88.8	86.0

NA Not available.   [1] Includes races not shown separately.   [2] Persons of Hispanic origin may be of any race. The method of identifying Hispanic children was changed in 1980 from allocation based on status of mother to status reported for each child. The number of Hispanic children using the new method is larger.
Source: U.S. Bureau of the Census, *Current Population Reports*, series P20-469.

No. 237. Preprimary School Enrollment, by Level of Enrollment and Labor Force Status of Mother: 1978 and 1991

[See headnote, table 236]

RACE AND LABOR FORCE STATUS	ALL CHILDREN (1,000)		PERCENT ENROLLED IN—							PERCENT NOT ENROLLED	
			Nursery school				Kindergarten				
			Total		Full day		Total		Full day,		
	1978	1991	1978	1991	1978	1991	1978	1991	1991	1978	1991
TOTAL [1]											
Children 3 to 5 years old .	9,110	11,370	20.0	24.8	6.9	8.2	30.3	30.9	13.0	49.7	44.3
Living with mother	8,883	10,602	19.8	25.3	6.8	8.3	30.4	30.8	12.8	49.8	43.9
Mother in labor force	4,097	6,146	22.1	28.5	11.4	11.8	31.0	31.6	14.1	47.0	39.9
Employed	3,737	5,568	22.5	29.2	11.7	12.2	31.0	31.8	14.1	46.5	39.0
Full time	2,446	3,860	22.3	27.3	15.2	14.2	31.2	31.7	14.8	46.5	41.0
Part time	1,291	1,709	23.0	33.5	5.2	7.7	30.5	31.9	12.3	46.4	34.6
Unemployed	360	578	17.4	21.6	7.8	8.0	30.6	30.1	14.2	52.0	48.3
Mother not in labor force	4,786	4,456	17.9	20.9	2.9	3.5	29.9	29.8	11.1	52.2	49.3
WHITE											
Children 3 to 5 years old .	7,460	9,083	19.5	26.0	5.2	7.4	30.1	30.0	11.3	50.5	44.0
Living with mother	7,301	8,574	19.4	26.5	5.1	7.5	30.1	30.2	11.3	50.5	43.3
Mother in labor force	3,235	4,939	21.1	27.9	9.2	10.7	30.4	30.8	12.4	48.5	41.3
Employed	3,014	4,578	21.3	29.9	9.4	11.0	30.7	30.8	12.4	48.0	39.3
Full time	1,877	3,037	20.1	27.9	12.6	13.1	31.0	30.7	13.1	48.9	41.4
Part time	1,137	1,541	23.3	33.8	4.1	6.7	30.2	31.0	11.1	46.5	35.2
Unemployed	220	360	17.9	21.9	6.4	6.7	27.1	30.8	12.2	55.0	47.3
Mother not in labor force	4,067	3,635	18.0	22.6	1.9	3.3	29.8	29.4	9.8	52.2	48.0
BLACK											
Children 3 to 5 years old .	1,410	1,747	22.1	19.3	15.3	12.0	31.0	33.8	21.2	46.9	46.9
Living with mother	1,347	1,529	21.7	19.7	15.5	12.4	31.3	33.8	20.9	47.1	46.5
Mother in labor force	731	933	25.9	24.4	20.6	17.0	32.5	35.7	22.6	41.6	39.9
Employed	598	750	28.0	24.7	22.8	18.4	31.7	37.3	23.6	40.3	38.0
Full time	469	641	29.6	24.0	24.8	19.0	32.0	35.7	22.9	38.4	40.3
Part time	128	111	22.3	27.9	15.8	14.4	30.7	45.9	27.0	47.0	26.2
Unemployed	133	182	16.7	24.2	10.6	11.5	35.7	29.1	18.7	47.6	46.7
Mother not in labor force	616	596	16.6	12.2	9.4	5.2	29.8	31.0	18.3	53.5	56.8
HISPANIC [2]											
Children 3 to 5 years old .	720	1,456	11.8	14.2	5.0	5.7	29.1	32.1	12.4	59.1	53.7
Living with mother	713	1,348	11.7	22.8	5.0	8.8	28.9	52.2	20.2	59.4	25.0
Mother in labor force	296	573	16.3	17.8	7.1	10.1	27.5	33.2	13.6	56.2	49.0
Employed	263	494	17.1	19.4	6.7	10.5	26.0	32.6	13.4	56.9	48.0
Full time	196	395	16.9	18.0	7.5	10.1	25.9	32.4	12.2	57.2	49.6
Part time	67	99	(B)	25.3	(B)	12.1	(B)	32.3	18.2	(B)	42.4
Unemployed	33	79	(B)	7.6	(B)	7.6	(B)	38.0	15.2	(B)	54.4
Mother not in labor force	417	776	8.4	11.1	3.5	1.9	29.9	31.1	11.5	61.7	57.8

B Base figure too small to meet statistical standards for reliability of derived figure.   [1] Includes races not shown separately.   [2] Persons of Hispanic origin may be of any race.
Source: U.S. Bureau of the Census, *Current Population Reports*, series P20-469.

No. 238. Public Elementary and Secondary Schools—Summary: 1980 to 1992
[For school year ending in year shown, except as indicated. Data are estimates]

ITEM	Unit	1980	1985	1987	1988	1989	1990	1991	1992
School districts, total.	Number .	16,044	15,812	15,684	15,571	15,530	15,449	15,439	15,360
ENROLLMENT									
Population 5-17 years old [1] . .	1,000. . .	48,041	44,788	44,903	45,004	45,052	44,948	45,311	45,923
Percent of resident population	Percent .	21.4	19.0	18.7	18.6	18.4	18.2	18.2	18.2
Fall enrollment [2]	1,000. . .	41,778	39,354	39,763	40,009	40,207	40,527	41,207	41,953
Percent of population 5-17 years old	Percent .	87.0	87.9	88.6	88.9	89.2	90.2	90.9	91.4
Elementary [3]	1,000. . .	24,397	23,830	24,503	25,215	25,752	26,397	27,080	27,585
Secondary [4]	1,000. . .	17,381	15,524	15,260	14,794	14,455	14,130	14,127	14,368
Average daily:									
Attendance (ADA)	1,000. . .	38,411	36,530	36,905	37,062	37,176	37,536	38,126	38,728
Membership (ADM)	1,000. . .	40,812	38,751	38,988	(NA)	(NA)	(NA)	(NA)	(NA)
High school graduates	1,000. . .	2,762	2,424	2,429	2,497	2,468	2,327	2,254	2,262
INSTRUCTIONAL STAFF									
Total [5]	1,000. . .	2,521	2,473	2,563	2,605	2,652	2,687	2,747	2,767
Classroom teachers.	1,000. . .	2,211	2,175	2,249	2,282	2,323	2,363	2,410	2,430
Average salaries:									
Instructional staff.	Dollar	16,715	24,666	27,706	29,219	30,860	32,634	34,410	35,582
Classroom teachers.	Dollar . .	15,970	23,600	26,569	28,034	29,568	31,391	33,114	34,148
REVENUES									
Revenue receipts	Mil. dol. .	97,635	141,013	163,767	176,266	193,092	208,860	222,043	235,073
Federal	Mil. dol. .	9,020	9,533	10,553	11,308	12,342	13,161	13,901	15,073
State.	Mil. dol. .	47,929	69,107	81,542	86,871	94,020	100,610	107,537	112,512
Local	Mil. dol. .	40,686	62,373	71,672	78,087	86,730	95,089	100,605	107,487
Percent of total:									
Federal	Percent .	9.2	6.8	6.4	6.4	6.4	6.3	6.3	6.4
State.	Percent .	49.1	49.0	49.8	49.3	48.7	48.2	48.4	47.9
Local	Percent .	41.7	44.2	43.8	44.3	44.9	45.5	45.3	45.7
EXPENDITURES									
Total	Mil. dol. .	96,105	139,382	163,091	175,700	190,990	209,465	225,145	241,234
Current expenditures (day schools)	Mil. dol. .	85,661	127,230	147,476	158,501	171,437	186,775	199,803	211,671
Other current expenditures [6]	Mil. dol. .	1,859	2,109	2,597	2,505	2,909	3,076	3,303	3,659
Capital outlay	Mil. dol. .	6,504	7,529	10,161	11,690	13,254	15,855	17,693	20,920
Interest on school debt . . .	Mil. dol. .	2,081	2,514	2,857	3,004	3,391	3,759	4,346	4,984
Percent of total:									
Current expenditures (day schools)	Percent .	89.1	91.3	90.4	90.2	89.8	89.2	88.7	87.8
Other current expenditures [6]	Percent .	1.9	1.5	1.6	1.4	1.5	1.5	1.5	1.5
Capital outlay	Percent .	6.8	5.4	6.2	6.7	6.9	7.6	7.9	8.7
Interest on school debt . . .	Percent .	2.2	1.8	1.8	1.7	1.8	1.8	1.9	2.1
In current dollars:									
Revenue receipts per pupil in—									
ADA.	Dollar . .	2,542	3,860	4,438	4,756	5,194	5,564	5,824	6,070
ADM	Dollar . .	2,392	3,639	4,200	(NA)	(NA)	(NA)	(NA)	(NA)
Current expenditures per pupil in—									
ADA.	Dollar . .	2,230	3,483	3,996	4,277	4,612	4,976	5,241	5,466
ADM	Dollar . .	2,099	3,283	3,783	(NA)	(NA)	(NA)	(NA)	(NA)
In constant (1992) dollars: [7]									
Revenue receipts per pupil in—									
ADA.	Dollar . .	4,527	5,042	5,515	5,676	5,923	6,055	6,011	6,070
ADM	Dollar . .	4,261	4,753	5,220	(NA)	(NA)	(NA)	(NA)	(NA)
Current expenditures per pupil in—									
ADA.	Dollar . .	3,972	4,549	4,966	5,104	5,259	5,415	5,409	5,466
ADM	Dollar . .	3,738	4,289	4,701	(NA)	(NA)	(NA)	(NA)	(NA)

NA Not available. [1] Estimated resident population as of July 1 of the previous year. Estimates reflect revisions based on the 1990 Census of Population. [2] Fall enrollment of the previous year. [3] Kindergarten through grade 6. [4] Grades 7 through 12. [5] Full-time equivalent. [6] Current expenses for summer schools, adult education, post-high school vocational education, personnel retraining, etc., when operated by local school districts and not part of regular public elementary and secondary day-school program. [7] Compiled by U.S. Bureau of the Census. Deflated by the Consumer Price Index, all urban consumers (for school year) supplied by U.S. National Center for Education Statistics.

Source: Except as noted, National Education Association, Washington, DC, *Estimates of School Statistics*, annual (copyright); *Rankings of the States*, annual (copyright); and unpublished data.

No. 239. Public and Private Elementary and Secondary Schools—Enrollment and Teachers, 1960 to 1991, and Projections, 1992 to 2003

[In thousands, except percent. As of fall. Schools are classified by type of organization, rather than by grade group; elementary includes kindergarten and secondary includes junior high. Minus sign (-) indicates decrease]

ITEM	TOTAL				PUBLIC [2]			PRIVATE		
	Total	Percent change [1]	Elementary	Secondary	Total	Elementary	Secondary	Total	Elementary	Secondary
Enrollment: 1960	42,181	3.6	29,150	13,031	36,281	24,350	11,931	5,900	4,800	1,100
1965	48,369	-0.2	31,504	16,865	42,069	26,604	15,465	6,300	4,900	1,400
1970	51,257	0.4	31,544	19,713	45,894	27,492	18,402	5,363	4,052	1,311
1975	49,819	-0.5	29,356	20,464	44,819	25,656	19,164	5,000	3,700	1,300
1980	46,208	-0.9	28,188	18,020	40,877	24,196	16,681	5,331	3,992	1,339
1985	44,979	0.2	28,330	16,649	39,422	24,135	15,287	5,557	4,195	1,362
1987	45,487	0.6	29,447	16,040	40,008	25,215	14,793	5,479	4,232	1,247
1988	45,430	-0.1	29,776	15,654	40,188	25,740	14,448	5,241	4,036	1,206
1989	45,898	1.0	30,570	15,328	40,543	26,408	14,135	5,355	4,162	1,193
1990	46,450	1.2	31,145	15,305	41,224	27,055	14,169	5,226	4,090	1,136
1991, est.	47,032	1.3	31,489	15,543	41,839	27,420	14,419	5,193	4,069	1,124
1992, proj.	47,872	1.8	31,976	15,896	42,586	27,834	14,752	5,286	4,142	1,144
1993, proj.	48,734	1.8	32,399	16,335	43,356	28,196	15,160	5,378	4,203	1,175
1994, proj.	49,661	1.9	32,810	16,852	44,187	28,551	15,636	5,474	4,259	1,216
1995, proj.	50,651	2.0	33,350	17,301	45,071	29,022	16,049	5,580	4,328	1,252
2000, proj.	53,545	0.6	34,936	18,608	47,657	30,405	17,252	5,888	4,531	1,356
2003, proj.	54,230	0.3	34,853	19,377	48,276	30,299	17,977	5,954	4,554	1,400
Teachers: 1960	1,600	4.5	991	609	1,408	858	550	192	133	59
1965	1,933	3.6	1,112	822	1,710	965	746	223	147	76
1970	2,292	2.1	1,283	1,009	2,059	1,130	929	233	153	80
1975	2,453	1.8	1,353	1,100	2,198	1,181	1,017	255	172	83
1980	2,486	1.0	1,402	1,084	2,185	1,190	995	301	212	89
1985	2,549	1.6	1,483	1,066	2,206	1,237	969	343	246	97
1987	2,632	1.5	1,564	1,068	2,279	1,307	973	353	257	95
1988	2,668	1.4	1,604	1,064	2,323	1,353	970	345	251	94
1989	2,734	2.5	1,662	1,072	2,357	1,387	970	377	275	102
1990	2,752	0.7	1,680	1,072	2,398	1,426	972	355	254	100
1991, est.	2,786	1.2	1,705	1,081	2,431	1,451	980	354	254	101
1992, proj.	2,791	0.2	1,679	1,112	2,437	1,429	1,008	354	250	104
1993, proj.	2,851	2.1	1,711	1,140	2,489	1,456	1,033	361	255	106
1994, proj.	2,923	2.5	1,748	1,175	2,553	1,488	1,065	370	260	110
1995, proj.	2,993	2.4	1,788	1,205	2,614	1,522	1,093	379	266	113
2000, proj.	3,240	1.3	1,924	1,317	2,831	1,637	1,194	410	287	123
2003, proj.	3,349	1.1	1,970	1,379	2,927	1,677	1,250	422	294	129

[1] Change from immediate prior year; for 1960, average change from 1955. For explanation of average annual change, see Guide to Tabular Presentation. [2] Data beginning 1970 are estimated.

Source: U.S. National Center for Education Statistics, *Digest of Education Statistics*, annual; and *Projections of Education Statistics*, annual.

No. 240. Public Elementary and Secondary Schools, by Type and Size of School: 1990-91

[Data reported by schools, rather than school districts]

ENROLLMENT SIZE OF SCHOOL	NUMBER OF SCHOOLS					ENROLLMENT (1,000)				
	Total	Elementary [1]	Secondary [2]	Combined [3]	Other [4]	Total	Elementary [1]	Secondary [2]	Combined [3]	Other [4]
Total	84,538	60,812	20,406	2,325	995	41,141	26,504	13,555	926	157
PERCENT DISTRIBUTION [5]										
Total	100.0	100.0	100.0	100.0	100.0	100.0	100.0	100.0	100.0	100.0
Under 100 students	9.1	6.5	12.0	27.1	59.3	0.9	0.7	1.0	3.1	16.6
100 to 199 students	10.6	10.2	11.1	15.3	17.2	3.2	3.5	2.5	5.6	15.4
200 to 299 students	11.9	13.1	9.0	10.0	9.2	6.0	7.4	3.4	6.2	13.9
300 to 399 students	14.2	16.6	8.3	8.5	5.2	10.0	12.9	4.4	7.5	11.3
400 to 499 students	13.6	15.9	7.9	8.7	3.2	12.3	15.9	5.4	9.8	9.0
500 to 599 students	11.8	13.6	7.4	6.9	1.4	12.9	16.6	6.1	9.5	4.9
600 to 699 students	8.5	9.3	6.8	5.6	0.8	11.0	13.3	6.7	9.0	3.3
700 to 799 students	5.8	5.9	5.9	3.7	0.6	8.7	9.8	6.6	7.0	2.9
800 to 999 students	6.5	5.7	9.1	6.2	0.9	11.5	11.1	12.3	13.8	5.1
1,000 to 1,499 students	5.6	3.0	13.3	5.9	1.9	13.4	7.6	24.4	17.6	14.1
1,500 to 1,999 students	1.6	0.3	5.5	1.4	0.2	5.4	1.0	14.1	6.0	2.2
2,000 to 2,999 students	0.8	(Z)	3.1	0.7	0.1	3.9	0.2	11.0	4.1	1.4
3,000 or more students	0.1	(Z)	0.4	0.1	(Z)	0.8	(Z)	2.2	0.9	(Z)
Average enrollment	(X)	(X)	(X)	(X)	(X)	497	449	664	398	158

X Not applicable. Z Represents or rounds to zero. [1] Includes schools beginning with grade 6 or below and with no grade higher than 8. [2] Includes schools with no grade lower than 7. [3] Includes schools with both elementary and secondary grades. [4] Includes special education, alternative, and other schools not classified by grade span. [5] Data for those schools reporting enrollment.

Source: U.S. National Center for Education Statistics, *Digest of Education Statistics*, annual.

No. 241. Public Elementary and Secondary School Enrollment, by State: 1980 and 1990

[As of fall. Includes unclassified students]

STATE	ENROLLMENT (1,000) K through Grade 8		Grades 9 through 12		ENROLL-MENT RATE [1]		STATE	ENROLLMENT (1,000) K through Grade 8		Grades 9 through 12		ENROLL-MENT RATE [1]	
	1980	1990	1980	1990	1980	1990		1980	1990	1980	1990	1980	1990
U.S....	27,647	29,888	13,231	11,336	86.5	91.3	MO......	567	585	277	227	83.8	86.0
AL......	528	527	231	195	87.6	93.3	MT......	106	111	50	42	92.9	93.8
AK......	60	85	26	29	94.0	97.3	NE......	189	198	91	76	86.6	88.7
AZ......	357	479	157	161	88.9	93.3	NV......	101	150	49	51	93.4	98.7
AR......	310	314	138	123	90.3	95.9	NH......	112	126	55	46	85.3	89.1
CA......	2,730	3,615	1,347	1,336	88.0	92.8	NJ......	820	784	426	306	81.5	86.1
CO......	374	420	172	154	92.2	94.6	NM......	186	208	85	94	89.5	94.3
CT......	364	347	168	122	83.3	90.2	NY......	1,838	1,828	1,033	770	80.8	86.6
DE......	62	73	37	27	79.5	87.4	NC......	786	783	343	304	90.0	94.8
DC......	71	61	29	19	91.8	100.0	ND......	77	85	40	33	85.9	92.8
FL......	1,042	1,370	468	492	84.4	92.6	OH......	1,312	1,258	645	514	84.8	88.0
GA......	742	849	327	303	86.9	93.6	OK......	399	425	179	154	92.9	95.1
HI......	110	123	55	49	83.4	87.6	OR......	319	351	145	134	88.5	93.0
ID......	144	160	59	61	95.4	96.9	PA......	1,231	1,172	678	496	80.4	83.6
IL......	1,335	1,310	649	512	82.6	86.9	RI......	98	102	51	37	79.7	87.3
IN......	708	676	347	279	88.0	90.4	SC......	426	452	193	170	88.1	93.8
IA......	351	345	183	139	88.4	92.1	SD......	86	95	42	34	87.4	89.7
KS......	283	320	133	117	88.7	92.6	TN......	602	598	252	226	87.8	93.5
KY......	464	459	206	177	83.7	90.5	TX......	2,049	2,511	851	872	92.4	98.4
LA......	544	586	234	199	80.3	88.2	UT......	250	326	93	122	98.2	98.0
ME......	153	155	70	60	91.5	96.5	VT......	66	71	29	25	87.9	93.9
MD......	493	527	258	188	83.9	89.1	VA......	703	728	307	270	90.7	94.2
MA......	676	604	346	230	88.6	88.8	WA......	515	613	242	227	91.0	94.0
MI......	1,227	1,146	570	436	90.1	90.2	WV......	270	224	113	98	92.6	95.7
MN......	482	546	272	211	87.2	91.3	WI......	528	566	303	232	82.1	86.0
MS......	330	372	147	131	79.6	91.3	WY......	70	71	28	27	97.3	97.3

[1] Percent of persons 5-17 years old. Based on enumerated resident population as of April 1, 1980, and 1990.

Source: U.S. National Center for Education Statistics, *Digest of Education Statistics*, annual.

No. 242. Public Elementary and Secondary School Enrollment Projections: 1991 to 1993

[In thousands. As of fall. Includes unclassified students. Data will not agree with national level projections presented in other tables due to revised projections at the national level]

STATE	K THROUGH GRADE 8			GRADES 9 THROUGH 12			STATE	K THROUGH GRADE 8			GRADES 9 THROUGH 12		
	1991	1992	1993	1991	1992	1993		1991	1992	1993	1991	1992	1993
U.S....	30,186	30,663	31,091	11,389	11,587	11,880	MO......	594	601	606	232	237	244
AL......	531	533	536	195	197	199	MT......	108	108	106	43	42	43
AK......	84	84	86	28	29	30	NE......	197	196	195	77	78	79
AZ......	495	513	530	165	172	179	NV......	151	158	162	54	56	60
AR......	315	316	316	123	125	127	NH......	136	141	147	46	48	50
CA......	3,728	3,850	3,967	1,373	1,410	1,449	NJ......	800	824	852	300	302	309
CO......	421	428	432	155	159	163	NM......	212	216	221	93	95	97
CT......	357	367	378	120	120	122	NY......	1,831	1,854	1,881	768	779	793
DE......	76	76	79	27	29	29	NC......	796	815	836	302	306	314
DC......	61	62	64	20	19	20	ND......	84	83	82	33	34	35
FL......	1,426	1,488	1,545	467	479	504	OH......	1,262	1,268	1,269	514	519	529
GA......	875	898	920	304	310	319	OK......	418	415	408	156	158	162
HI......	129	133	138	47	49	52	OR......	345	347	347	137	141	144
ID......	155	152	149	60	62	65	PA......	1,188	1,201	1,213	493	500	509
IL......	1,294	1,305	1,318	517	521	531	RI......	102	105	106	37	37	38
IN......	682	682	680	280	285	290	SC......	456	462	467	171	174	179
IA......	336	330	323	141	145	148	SD......	96	96	96	35	36	37
KS......	322	323	324	120	125	128	TN......	602	608	612	225	227	233
KY......	445	440	434	177	181	184	TX......	2,493	2,516	2,532	887	892	902
LA......	573	570	567	194	197	203	UT......	319	316	311	126	133	140
ME......	157	160	163	60	60	63	VT......	71	72	74	26	26	26
MD......	549	571	594	190	196	203	VA......	755	782	812	269	274	283
MA......	621	637	655	225	226	230	WA......	620	632	639	232	240	250
MI......	1,153	1,161	1,166	436	440	449	WV......	216	210	204	97	95	96
MN......	552	558	559	215	222	230	WI......	567	569	566	235	241	248
MS......	364	362	361	132	135	136	WY......	67	66	64	27	27	28

Source: U.S. National Center for Education Statistics, *Digest of Education Statistics*, annual, and *Projections of Education Statistics*, annual.

No. 243. Public Elementary and Secondary School Enrollment, by Grade: 1960 to 1990

[1960, for school year; thereafter, as of **fall** of year. Beginning 1975, kindergarten includes nursery schools. For 1960, enrollment figures are prorated and 12th grade includes postgraduates. See also *Historical Statistics, Colonial Times to 1970*, series H 420-424]

GRADE	ENROLLMENT (1,000)										PERCENT DISTRIBUTION		
	1960	1970	1975	1980	1985	1986	1987	1988	1989	1990	1960	1980	1990
Pupils enrolled .	**36,087**	**45,894**	**44,819**	**40,877**	**39,422**	**39,753**	**40,007**	**40,191**	**40,543**	**41,224**	**100.0**	**100.0**	**100.0**
Kindergarten and													
grades 1-8.	27,602	32,558	30,515	27,647	27,034	27,420	27,930	28,501	29,152	29,888	76.5	67.6	72.5
Kindergarten.	1,923	2,564	2,971	2,689	3,192	3,310	3,388	3,433	3,486	3,612	5.3	6.6	8.8
First	3,733	3,817	3,238	2,894	3,239	3,358	3,407	3,460	3,485	3,499	10.3	7.1	8.5
Second	3,436	3,654	3,027	2,800	2,941	3,054	3,173	3,223	3,289	3,328	9.5	6.8	8.1
Third.	3,302	3,663	3,038	2,893	2,895	2,933	3,046	3,167	3,235	3,299	9.2	7.1	8.0
Fourth	3,146	3,675	3,112	3,107	2,771	2,896	2,938	3,051	3,182	3,249	8.7	7.6	7.9
Fifth	3,118	3,635	3,281	3,130	2,776	2,775	2,901	2,945	3,067	3,197	8.6	7.7	7.8
Sixth	3,070	3,598	3,476	3,038	2,789	2,806	2,811	2,937	2,987	3,112	8.5	7.4	7.5
Seventh.	3,173	3,662	3,619	3,085	2,938	2,899	2,910	2,905	3,027	3,067	8.8	7.5	7.4
Eighth	2,701	3,601	3,636	3,086	2,982	2,870	2,839	2,853	2,853	2,981	7.5	7.5	7.2
Unclassified [1]	(X)	690	1,116	924	511	520	519	527	540	544	(X)	2.3	1.3
Grades 9-12	8,485	13,336	14,304	13,231	12,388	12,333	12,077	11,690	11,390	11,336	23.5	32.4	27.5
Ninth.	2,412	3,654	3,879	3,377	3,439	3,256	3,143	3,106	3,141	3,169	6.7	8.3	7.7
Tenth	2,258	3,458	3,723	3,368	3,230	3,215	3,020	2,895	2,868	2,897	6.3	8.2	7.0
Eleventh	2,063	3,128	3,354	3,195	2,866	2,954	2,936	2,749	2,629	2,612	5.7	7.8	6.3
Twelfth . . . , . . .	1,752	2,775	2,986	2,925	2,550	2,601	2,681	2,650	2,473	2,380	4.8	7.2	5.8
Unclassified [1]	(X)	321	362	366	303	308	297	290	279	278	(X)	0.9	0.7

X Not applicable.   [1] Includes ungraded and special education.

Source: U.S. National Center for Education Statistics, *Digest of Education Statistics,* annual.

No. 244. Public Elementary and Secondary School Teachers—Selected Characteristics: 1990-91

[**For school year.** Based on survey and subject to sampling error; for details, see source. See table 258 for similar data on private school teachers]

CHARACTERISTIC	Unit	AGE				SEX		RACE/ETHNICITY			LEVEL OF CONTROL	
		Under 30 years old	30 to 39 years old	40 to 49 years old	Over 50 years old	Male	Female	White [1]	Black [1]	Hispanic	Elementary	Secondary
Total teachers [2]	**1,000. .**	**312**	**732**	**1,003**	**514**	**720**	**1,842**	**2,216**	**212**	**87**	**1,298**	**1,264**
Highest degree held:												
Bachelor's	Percent	84.1	56.4	43.8	41.6	44.7	54.7	51.5	50.8	61.0	56.7	46.9
Master's	Percent	14.4	39.1	48.8	49.9	47.0	40.1	42.7	42.1	32.9	38.7	45.5
Education specialist . .	Percent	1.2	3.4	5.9	5.9	5.3	4.3	4.5	5.0	4.3	4.1	5.2
Doctorate	Percent	-	0.4	1.0	1.4	1.3	0.6	0.7	1.3	0.9	0.4	1.2
Full-time teaching experience:												
Less than 3 years	Percent	40.0	8.4	3.0	1.3	7.1	9.3	8.7	5.9	13.0	9.4	8.0
3 to 9 years	Percent	59.8	37.1	14.5	6.1	18.9	27.1	25.0	19.0	31.8	26.2	23.3
10 to 20 years	Percent	0.2	54.4	49.8	24.8	37.6	41.0	40.0	41.7	41.4	40.3	39.8
20 years or more.	Percent	(X)	0.1	32.7	67.8	36.5	22.5	26.4	33.6	13.8	24.1	28.9
Full-time teachers	1,000. .	283	650	925	481	666	1,273	2,015	199	81	1,170	1,169
Earned income	Dol. . . .	24,892	30,126	36,095	38,642	37,895	31,897	33,631	33,666	32,960	31,972	35,241
Salary	Dol. . . .	22,754	27,934	33,702	36,361	33,383	30,501	31,313	31,707	30,774	30,611	32,034
Supplemental contract during school year:												
Teachers receiving . . .	1,000. .	121	231	313	122	353	434	701	49	25	238	549
Salary	Dol. . . .	1,675	2,045	1,914	2,088	2,663	1,357	1,977	1,664	1,709	1,172	2,276
Supplemental contract during summer:												
Teachers receiving. . .	1,000. .	56	118	169	65	164	244	334	46	19	167	241
Salary	Dol. . . .	1,608	1,952	2,003	2,284	2,309	1,763	1,919	2,272	2,360	1,803	2,104
Teachers with nonschool employment:												
Teaching/tutoring	1,000. .	13	30	47	20	39	70	95	8	5	41	69
Education related	1,000. .	9	18	28	12	31	36	59	5	2	23	44
Not education related. .	1,000. .	32	63	91	42	130	99	203	16	5	52	147

- Represents or rounds to zero.   X Not applicable.   [1] Non-Hispanic.   [2] Includes teachers with no degrees and associates degrees, not shown separately.

Source: U.S. National Center for Education Statistics, *Digest of Education Statistics,* 1993.

No. 245. Public Elementary and Secondary Schools—Number and Average Salary of Classroom Teachers, 1960 to 1992, and by State, 1992

[Estimates for school year ending in **June** of year shown. Schools classified by type of organization rather than by grade-group; elementary includes kindergarten]

YEAR AND STATE	TEACHERS [1] (1,000)			AVG. SALARY ($1,000)			YEAR AND STATE	TEACHERS [1] (1,000)			AVG. SALARY ($1,000)		
	Total	Elementary	Secondary	All teachers	Elementary	Secondary		Total	Elementary	Secondary	All teachers	Elementary	Secondary
1960	1,355	834	521	5.0	4.8	5.3	KY	37.4	26.3	11.1	30.9	30.2	32.5
1970	2,008	1,109	899	8.6	8.4	8.9	LA	44.0	29.6	14.4	27.0	27.0	27.1
1975	2,171	1,169	1,001	11.7	11.3	12.0	ME	14.8	10.0	4.9	30.1	29.4	31.5
1980	2,211	1,206	1,005	16.0	15.6	16.5	MD	43.3	24.3	19.0	39.5	38.2	41.0
1981	2,192	1,196	996	17.6	17.2	18.1	MA	56.0	24.1	31.9	37.3	37.3	37.3
1982	2,158	1,200	959	19.3	18.9	19.8	MI	80.2	54.9	25.3	41.1	40.8	41.3
1983	2,134	1,182	952	20.7	20.2	21.3	MN	44.9	24.2	20.7	33.7	33.0	34.6
1984	2,144	1,189	955	21.9	21.5	22.6	MS	27.9	17.1	10.8	24.4	24.0	24.9
1985	2,175	1,212	963	23.6	23.2	24.2	MO	52.3	27.7	24.6	28.9	28.1	29.8
1986	2,215	1,242	973	25.2	24.7	25.8	MT	9.9	6.9	3.0	27.6	27.1	28.8
1987	2,249	1,274	975	26.6	26.1	27.2	NE	18.9	10.7	8.1	27.2	27.2	27.2
1988	2,282	1,308	974	28.0	27.5	28.8	NV	11.4	6.8	4.6	33.9	33.0	35.1
1989	2,323	1,353	970	29.6	29.0	30.2	NH	11.5	7.8	3.6	33.2	33.2	33.2
1990	2,363	1,391	972	31.4	30.8	32.1	NJ	80.5	50.9	29.6	41.0	40.2	42.5
1991	2,410	1,433	978	33.1	32.5	33.9	NM	17.1	12.0	5.1	26.7	26.1	27.0
							NY	180.3	89.6	90.7	43.3	42.3	44.5
1992, U.S.	**2,430**	**1,455**	**975**	**34.1**	**33.6**	**34.9**	NC	64.8	39.6	25.2	29.2	29.1	29.4
AL	41.1	21.7	19.4	27.0	27.0	27.0	ND	7.8	5.1	2.7	24.5	24.5	24.6
AK	7.2	5.2	2.0	44.7	44.6	45.4	OH	103.2	62.5	40.8	33.3	32.9	33.8
AZ	33.5	25.8	7.7	31.2	31.2	31.8	OK	37.7	20.2	17.5	25.3	24.5	26.4
AR	25.9	12.7	13.2	26.6	25.8	27.3	OR	26.7	16.7	10.0	34.1	33.6	35.1
CA	221.0	162.0	59.0	40.2	39.3	41.7	PA	100.5	49.8	50.7	38.7	38.0	39.4
CO	33.1	16.9	16.2	33.1	32.4	33.8	RI	9.6	5.0	4.6	36.0	36.0	36.1
CT	34.8	23.6	11.1	47.0	46.3	48.4	SC	36.3	24.7	11.7	28.3	27.8	29.5
DE	6.1	3.1	3.0	34.5	33.6	35.5	SD	8.6	6.0	2.6	23.3	22.8	23.7
DC	6.2	3.8	2.4	41.3	41.3	41.3	TN	43.1	30.6	12.5	28.6	28.1	29.8
FL	109.9	59.6	50.3	31.1	31.1	31.1	TX	212.6	114.3	98.2	29.0	28.4	29.7
GA	70.3	47.2	23.1	29.5	29.5	29.5	UT	18.3	10.6	7.8	26.5	26.3	27.2
HI	10.0	5.7	4.8	34.5	34.5	34.5	VT	7.0	3.6	3.4	33.6	33.0	34.4
ID	11.6	6.1	5.5	26.3	26.0	26.8	VA	64.7	38.8	25.9	31.9	31.0	33.6
IL	109.9	75.7	34.1	36.5	34.9	40.0	WA	42.9	25.7	17.2	34.8	34.2	35.7
IN	55.1	29.8	25.3	34.8	33.8	36.0	WV	21.0	11.8	9.2	27.4	27.0	27.8
IA	31.5	15.1	16.3	29.2	28.1	30.2	WI	52.0	32.8	19.2	35.2	34.3	37.0
KS	29.3	17.4	11.9	30.7	30.7	30.7	WY	6.4	3.2	3.2	30.4	30.1	30.8

[1] Full-time equivalent.

Source: National Education Association, Washington, DC, *Estimates of School Statistics, 1991-92,* and earlier issues.

No. 246. Average Starting Salaries of Public School Teachers Compared With Salaries in Private Industry, by Selected Position: 1975 to 1992

[Except as noted, salaries represent what corporations plan to offer graduates graduating in the year shown with bachelors' degrees. Based on a survey of approximately 200 companies]

ITEM AND POSITION	1975	1980	1985	1986	1987	1988	1989	1990	1991	1992
SALARIES (dollars)										
Teachers [1]	8,233	10,764	15,460	16,500	17,500	19,400	(NA)	20,486	21,481	22,171
College graduates:										
Engineering	12,744	20,136	26,880	28,512	28,932	29,856	30,852	32,304	34,236	34,620
Accounting	11,880	15,720	20,628	21,216	22,512	25,140	25,908	27,408	27,924	28,404
Sales—marketing	10,344	15,936	20,616	20,688	20,232	23,484	27,768	27,828	26,580	26,532
Business administration	9,768	14,100	19,896	21,324	21,972	23,880	25,344	26,496	26,256	27,156
Liberal arts [2]	9,312	13,296	18,828	21,060	20,508	23,508	25,608	26,364	25,560	27,324
Chemistry	11,904	17,124	24,216	24,264	27,048	27,108	27,552	29,088	29,700	30,360
Mathematics—statistics	10,980	17,604	22,704	23,976	25,548	25,548	28,416	28,944	29,244	29,472
Economics—finance	10,212	14,472	20,964	22,284	21,984	23,928	25,812	26,712	26,424	27,708
Computer science	(NA)	17,712	24,156	26,172	26,280	26,904	28,608	29,100	30,924	30,888
INDEX (1975=100)										
Teachers [1]	100	131	187	200	213	236	(NA)	249	261	269
College graduates:										
Engineering	100	158	211	224	227	234	242	253	268	271
Accounting	100	132	174	179	189	212	218	230	235	239
Sales—marketing	100	154	199	200	196	227	268	269	257	256
Business administration	100	144	204	218	225	244	259	271	268	278
Liberal arts [2]	100	143	202	226	220	252	275	283	274	293
Chemistry	100	144	203	204	227	228	231	244	249	255
Mathematics—statistics	100	160	207	218	233	233	258	263	266	268
Economics—finance	100	142	205	218	215	234	252	261	258	271
Computer science [3]	(NA)	125	171	185	186	190	202	205	218	217

NA Not available. [1] Estimate. Minimum mean salary. Source: National Education Association, Washington, DC, unpublished data. [2] Excludes Chemistry, Mathematics, Economics, and Computer Science. [3] Computer science index (1978=100).

Source: Except as noted, Northwestern University Placement Center, Evanston, IL, *The Northwestern Lindquist-Endicott Report,* (copyright).

Education

No. 247. Average Salary and Wages Paid in Public School Systems, by Selected Positions: 1975 to 1992

[In dollars. For school year ending in year shown. Data reported by a stratified sample of school systems enrolling 300 or more pupils. Data represent unweighted means of average salaries paid school personnel reported by each school system]

POSITION	1975	1980	1985	1987	1988	1989	1990	1991	1992
ANNUAL SALARY									
Central office administrators:									
Superintendent (contract salary)....	30,338	39,344	56,954	64,580	68,147	71,190	75,425	79,874	83,342
Deputy/assoc. superintendent.....	30,074	37,440	52,877	60,222	63,872	66,214	69,623	72,428	76,796
Assistant superintendent	26,460	33,452	48,003	53,656	56,894	59,655	62,698	66,553	69,315
Administrators for—									
Finance and business........	21,850	27,147	40,344	45,259	47,330	49,933	52,354	55,097	57,036
Instructional services	22,608	29,790	43,452	48,810	50,838	53,716	56,359	59,162	62,102
Public relations/information	21,470	24,021	35,287	38,925	41,305	43,402	44,926	47,938	50,625
Staff personnel services	21,470	29,623	44,182	48,627	51,421	53,972	56,344	59,271	62,269
Subject area supervisors	18,601	23,974	34,422	38,763	41,086	43,555	45,929	48,366	50,580
School building administrators:									
Principals:									
Elementary................	19,061	25,165	36,452	41,536	43,664	45,909	48,431	51,453	53,856
Junior high/middle	21,136	27,625	39,650	44,861	47,078	49,427	52,163	55,083	57,504
Senior high................	22,894	29,207	42,094	47,896	50,512	52,987	55,722	59,106	61,768
Assistant principals:									
Elementary................	15,968	20,708	30,496	34,347	36,364	38,360	40,916	43,548	45,558
Junior high/middle	17,868	23,507	33,793	37,958	40,093	42,292	44,570	46,981	48,956
Senior high................	18,939	24,816	35,491	39,758	41,839	44,002	46,486	49,009	51,318
Classroom teachers............	11,507	15,913	23,587	26,731	28,230	29,608	31,278	32,915	34,565
Auxiliary professional personnel:									
Counselors.................	14,479	18,847	27,593	31,132	32,896	34,244	35,979	38,024	39,563
Librarians.................	12,546	16,764	24,981	28,390	30,046	31,645	33,469	35,417	37,227
School nurses..............	10,673	13,788	19,944	22,219	23,692	24,804	26,090	27,713	28,721
Secretarial/clerical personnel:									
Central office:									
Secretaries/stenographers......	7,318	10,331	15,343	17,182	18,220	19,045	20,238	21,303	22,309
Accounting/payroll clerks	7,588	10,479	15,421	17,273	18,229	19,143	20,088	21,202	22,215
Clerk-typists	6,089	8,359	12,481	13,729	14,651	15,192	16,125	16,859	17,646
School building level:									
Secretaries/stenographers......	6,046	8,348	12,504	13,947	14,749	15,364	16,184	16,953	17,784
Library clerks..............	5,052	6,778	9,911	10,641	11,234	11,751	12,151	12,696	13,347
HOURLY WAGE RATE									
Other support personnel:									
Teacher aides:									
Instructional	2.91	4.06	5.89	6.43	6.72	7.05	7.43	7.77	8.15
Noninstructional............	2.81	3.89	5.60	6.14	6.45	6.69	7.08	7.43	7.70
Custodians.................	3.54	4.88	6.90	7.51	7.82	8.19	8.54	9.05	9.35
Cafeteria workers	2.61	3.78	5.42	5.92	6.23	6.56	6.77	7.19	7.39
Bus drivers.................	3.75	5.21	7.27	8.06	8.31	8.78	9.21	9.52	10.04

Source: Educational Research Service, Arlington, VA, *National Survey of Salaries and Wages in Public Schools*, annual, vols. 2 and 3. (All rights reserved. Copyright.)

No. 248. Public School Employment, by Occupation, Sex, and Race: 1982 and 1990

[In thousands. Covers full-time employment. 1982 excludes Hawaii, District of Columbia, and New Jersey. Based on sample survey of school districts with 250 or more students. 1990 based on sample survey of school districts with 100 or more employees; see source for sampling variability]

OCCUPATION	1982					1990				
	Total	Male	Female	White [1]	Black [1]	Total	Male	Female	White [1]	Black [1]
All occupations........	3,082	1,063	2,019	2,498	432	3,181	914	2,267	2,502	463
Officials, administrators.......	41	31	10	36	3	43	28	15	37	4
Principals and assistant										
principals.................	90	72	19	76	11	90	56	34	70	13
Classroom teachers [2].........	1,680	534	1,146	1,435	186	1,746	468	1,278	1,469	192
Elementary schools	798	129	669	667	98	875	128	747	722	103
Secondary schools.........	706	363	343	619	67	662	304	358	570	66
Other professional staff.......	235	91	144	193	35	227	58	170	187	30
Teachers aides [3]	215	14	200	146	45	324	54	270	208	69
Clerical, secretarial staff........	210	4	206	177	19	226	5	221	181	24
Service workers [4]...........	611	316	295	434	132	524	245	279	348	129

[1] Excludes individuals of Hispanic origin.   [2] Includes other classroom teachers, not shown separately.   [3] Includes technicians.   [4] Includes craftworkers and laborers.

Source: U.S. Equal Employment Opportunity Commission, *Elementary-Secondary Staff Information (EEO-5)*, biennial.

No. 249. Public Elementary and Secondary School Price Indexes: 1975 to 1991

[1983=100. For years ending **June 30**. Reflects prices paid by public elementary-secondary schools. For explanation of average annual percent change, see Guide to Tabular Presentation]

YEAR	Index, total	Average annual percent change [1]	PERSONNEL COMPENSATION Total	Professional salaries	Non-professional salaries	Fringe benefits	CONTRACTED SERVICES, SUPPLIES AND EQUIPMENT Total	Services	Supplies and materials	Equipment replacement	Library materials and textbooks	Utilities	Fixed costs
1975 ..	52.7	(X)	53.3	56.0	55.6	40.2	50.6	55.7	58.0	53.7	53.8	35.9	45.0
1976 ..	57.1	8.3	57.6	60.2	59.7	45.7	55.2	59.5	62.5	58.9	60.6	39.9	50.5
1977 ..	60.8	6.5	61.2	63.4	63.2	50.7	59.2	63.4	65.4	62.3	64.7	44.3	56.6
1978 ..	64.6	6.3	64.9	67.2	67.6	52.8	63.8	67.6	69.2	66.7	72.1	48.4	62.6
1979 ..	70.3	8.8	70.4	71.9	72.6	62.5	69.9	71.5	75.8	72.2	76.7	56.2	69.8
1980 ..	76.5	8.8	75.7	76.7	77.8	69.8	79.6	77.4	85.9	79.6	82.1	73.2	77.6
1981 ..	85.7	12.0	84.4	85.1	85.9	80.2	90.4	85.7	95.7	88.0	86.9	92.8	86.9
1982 ..	93.7	9.4	92.6	92.8	94.4	90.3	97.8	94.6	101.1	95.5	91.6	102.2	94.1
1983 ..	100.0	6.7	100.0	100.0	100.0	100.0	100.0	100.0	100.0	100.0	100.0	100.0	100.0
1984 ..	105.6	5.6	106.2	105.7	104.5	109.4	103.5	106.2	102.2	103.0	107.3	98.2	106.9
1985 ..	112.6	6.6	114.2	113.4	111.3	120.3	106.4	112.3	103.5	105.6	113.0	96.5	111.8
1986 ..	119.6	6.2	122.7	121.4	117.6	132.6	107.6	118.8	102.5	108.7	119.0	88.3	117.8
1987 ..	125.7	5.1	129.9	128.4	121.9	143.5	109.8	122.8	103.9	111.3	126.8	83.2	124.6
1988 ..	132.7	5.5	137.6	135.5	127.5	155.4	113.8	125.3	110.3	111.3	145.2	79.1	131.2
1989 ..	139.6	5.2	144.9	142.2	133.3	166.6	119.3	132.2	118.8	116.3	151.4	77.9	137.0
1990 ..	147.6	5.7	153.4	150.1	139.4	179.5	125.5	136.7	122.5	120.8	175.9	85.8	142.5
1991 ..	156.0	5.7	162.3	158.1	146.5	193.4	132.2	142.5	126.1	124.7	196.1	96.2	147.8

X Not applicable.   [1] Change from immediate prior year shown.

Source: Research Associates of Washington, Washington, DC, *Inflation Measures for Schools and Colleges*, annual, (copyright).

No. 250. Finances of Public Elementary and Secondary School Systems, by Enrollment-Size Group: 1989-90

[**In millions of dollars, except as indicated.** Data are estimates subject to sampling variability. For details, see source. See also Appendix III]

ITEM	All school systems	ENROLLMENT SIZE 50,000 or more	25,000 to 49,999	15,000 to 24,999	7,500 to 14,999	5,000 to 7,499	3,000 to 4,999	Under 3,000
Enrollment, fall 1989 (1,000)	40,573	7,400	3,974	3,648	6,138	3,771	4,949	10,692
General revenue [1]................	209,435	40,478	19,393	16,719	29,575	18,248	24,531	60,492
Intergovernmental	114,734	22,603	11,100	9,831	16,305	9,070	11,949	33,876
From Federal government........	1,343	278	100	83	160	102	135	484
From States..................	110,502	22,109	10,661	9,540	15,784	8,764	11,456	32,188
Federal aid distributed by State governments..........	10,924	2,856	1,123	877	1,411	839	1,110	2,707
From local governments.........	2,889	216	339	208	361	204	358	1,203
From own sources	94,701	17,875	8,292	6,888	13,270	9,177	12,582	26,616
Taxes	63,629	8,634	5,563	4,573	9,091	6,580	9,067	20,120
Property	61,992	8,277	5,380	4,503	8,871	6,403	8,801	19,758
Contribution from parent government	17,790	7,120	1,340	1,040	2,049	1,385	1,821	3,035
Charges and miscellaneous	13,282	2,121	1,389	1,274	2,130	1,212	1,695	3,460
Current charges..............	6,063	1,126	611	552	893	532	726	1,622
School lunch sales	3,425	464	322	307	551	348	462	972
Interest earnings	3,715	581	352	303	564	340	464	1,110
Other.....................	3,504	414	426	419	673	340	504	728
Employee-retirement revenue	730	490	225	15	-	(Z)	-	-
General expenditure [1]	211,457	40,976	19,819	17,020	29,992	18,407	24,735	60,508
Intergovernmental	648	18	29	52	107	67	94	281
Direct.......................	210,809	40,958	19,789	16,968	29,885	18,340	24,641	60,227
Current operation	190,031	37,244	17,415	15,015	26,506	16,623	22,126	55,102
Salaries and wages	122,507	24,779	11,874	10,306	17,863	11,065	14,650	31,972
Capital outlay	17,225	3,168	2,005	1,619	2,818	1,406	2,064	4,195
Construction	9,897	1,924	970	927	1,675	796	1,269	2,337
Interest on debt	3,503	546	369	334	561	311	451	930
Employee-retirement expenditure	305	187	112	5	(Z)	(Z)	-	-
Debt outstanding [2]	54,685	9,186	5,499	4,732	8,663	4,927	7,467	14,211
Long-term....................	52,004	9,133	5,308	4,623	8,270	4,732	6,988	12,950
Short-term..................	2,680	53	191	108	393	195	479	1,261
Long-term debt issued	8,398	1,482	672	592	1,330	778	1,323	2,221
Long-term debt retired	4,215	566	408	360	682	416	592	1,193
Cash and security holdings	47,427	9,875	5,262	2,992	5,553	3,592	5,048	15,104
Employee-retirement holdings.	5,659	3,849	1,717	93	(Z)	(Z)	-	(Z)

- Represents zero.   Z Rounds to zero.   [1] Excludes interschool system transactions.   [2] As of end of fiscal year.

Source: U.S. Bureau of the Census, *Public Education Finances: 1989-90*, GF/90-10.

No. 251. Public Elementary and Secondary Estimated Finances, 1970 to 1992, and by State, 1992

[In millions of dollars, except as noted. For school years ending in June of year shown]

YEAR AND STATE	RECEIPTS						EXPENDITURES					
	Total	Revenue receipts				Non-revenue receipts [1]	Total [2]	Per capita [3] (dol.)	Current expenditures			Capital outlay
		Total	Source						Elementary and secondary day schools	Average per pupil in ADA [4]		
			Federal	State	Local					Amount (dol.)	Rank	
1970.	41,621	38,192	2,767	15,628	19,797	3,429	39,091	194	32,683	773	(X)	4,158
1975.	66,319	63,047	5,089	27,472	30,486	3,273	62,340	292	53,333	1,286	(X)	5,409
1980.	101,724	97,635	9,020	47,929	40,686	4,089	96,105	428	85,661	2,230	(X)	6,504
1982.	117,776	113,999	8,419	54,573	51,007	3,777	113,005	492	102,048	2,753	(X)	6,404
1983.	125,179	120,486	8,691	57,449	54,346	4,693	119,159	514	108,773	2,960	(X)	6,131
1984.	133,373	128,875	9,005	61,611	58,259	4,498	127,014	543	116,295	3,185	(X)	6,373
1985.	146,976	141,013	9,533	69,107	62,373	5,963	139,382	591	127,230	3,483	(X)	7,529
1986.	161,118	153,807	10,351	75,935	67,521	7,311	152,187	640	138,067	3,764	(X)	9,066
1987.	170,651	163,767	10,553	81,542	71,672	6,884	163,091	679	147,476	3,996	(X)	10,161
1988.	184,415	176,266	11,308	86,871	78,087	8,149	175,700	725	158,501	4,277	(X)	11,690
1989.	202,227	193,092	12,342	94,020	86,730	9,135	190,990	781	171,437	4,612	(X)	13,254
1990.	218,217	208,860	13,161	100,610	95,089	9,357	209,465	849	186,775	4,976	(X)	15,855
1991.	234,835	222,043	13,901	107,537	100,605	12,792	225,145	903	199,803	5,241	(X)	17,693
1992, total.	246,435	235,073	15,073	112,512	107,487	11,363	241,234	957	211,671	5,466	(X)	20,920
Alabama	2,590	2,478	337	1,612	530	111	2,798	684	2,508	3,675	48	231
Alaska	1,040	934	118	594	222	106	1,025	1,798	931	9,248	2	35
Arizona	3,594	3,175	312	1,319	1,544	420	3,601	961	2,940	4,750	33	544
Arkansas	1,778	1,735	152	1,090	493	44	1,798	758	1,538	3,770	46	212
California	28,118	27,301	2,156	18,104	7,041	817	28,247	930	23,778	4,686	36	3,084
Colorado	3,436	3,036	138	1,198	1,700	400	3,245	961	2,801	5,259	26	339
Connecticut	4,037	4,036	157	1,631	2,248	1	4,035	1,227	3,800	8,299	4	145
Delaware	636	611	51	413	146	26	612	899	567	6,080	11	25
District of Columbia	636	579	60	-	519	57	630	1,059	560	8,116	5	45
Florida	11,626	11,085	748	5,170	5,167	541	12,385	934	10,019	5,639	15	2,042
Georgia	5,882	5,788	351	3,061	2,376	94	5,854	884	5,187	4,720	34	524
Hawaii	1,046	1,046	78	966	1	-	1,021	898	890	5,453	20	98
Idaho	896	840	62	520	257	57	835	803	759	3,528	49	61
Illinois	10,443	9,941	746	3,515	5,679	502	9,712	842	8,488	5,248	27	487
Indiana	5,586	5,480	266	2,919	2,295	106	5,626	1,003	4,732	5,429	22	499
Iowa	2,445	2,325	125	1,197	1,003	120	2,465	882	2,275	4,949	30	164
Kansas	2,381	2,336	116	968	1,251	46	2,347	941	2,048	5,131	28	207
Kentucky	2,998	2,864	268	1,988	609	134	2,869	773	2,646	4,616	39	152
Louisiana	3,656	3,436	335	1,888	1,212	220	3,428	806	3,104	4,378	42	195
Maine	1,341	1,241	78	599	564	100	1,341	1,087	1,184	5,969	14	120
Maryland	4,747	4,684	242	1,804	2,638	62	4,701	967	4,291	6,273	10	295
Massachusetts	5,423	5,392	310	1,736	3,346	31	5,174	863	4,944	6,323	9	130
Michigan	9,249	8,748	403	3,104	5,241	501	9,261	987	8,197	5,630	16	590
Minnesota	4,975	4,625	192	2,386	2,047	350	4,671	1,054	4,000	5,510	17	478
Mississippi	1,765	1,715	290	900	525	50	1,738	670	1,590	3,344	50	110
Missouri	4,304	4,096	227	1,550	2,319	208	4,021	780	3,361	4,534	41	523
Montana	764	764	65	430	269	-	763	943	712	5,127	29	35
Nebraska	1,342	1,319	82	456	781	23	1,379	866	1,223	4,676	37	132
Nevada	1,110	1,094	45	406	644	16	1,291	1,006	951	4,910	31	271
New Hampshire	1,170	1,101	28	84	989	69	981	888	894	5,500	18	60
New Jersey	10,658	10,555	347	4,367	5,842	102	10,368	1,337	10,114	10,219	1	96
New Mexico	1,334	1,319	147	1,001	171	15	1,504	971	1,222	4,692	35	219
New York	22,468	21,808	1,120	8,496	12,192	660	22,514	1,247	20,346	8,658	3	1,600
North Carolina	5,737	5,556	366	3,617	1,573	181	5,627	835	4,963	4,857	32	623
North Dakota	551	536	50	236	250	15	504	794	468	4,119	44	22
Ohio	10,408	9,508	539	4,058	4,910	900	10,077	921	8,628	5,451	21	992
Oklahoma	2,571	2,411	179	1,530	702	160	2,586	814	2,162	3,939	45	360
Oregon	3,109	2,898	169	896	1,833	210	2,974	1,018	2,751	5,972	12	160
Pennsylvania	14,159	13,023	617	6,109	6,297	1,136	11,413	954	10,679	6,980	7	199
Rhode Island	905	905	36	362	507	-	908	903	878	6,834	8	12
South Carolina	3,176	3,006	261	1,450	1,295	170	3,063	861	2,623	4,537	40	312
South Dakota	585	564	66	146	352	21	588	835	513	4,255	43	67
Tennessee	3,031	2,911	304	1,293	1,313	120	3,026	611	2,868	3,736	47	56
Texas	18,549	16,785	1,329	7,397	8,060	1,764	17,133	988	14,641	4,651	38	1,889
Utah	1,561	1,518	98	867	553	43	1,511	854	1,310	3,092	51	128
Vermont	683	668	37	220	411	15	683	1,205	624	6,992	6	50
Virginia	5,435	5,361	264	1,778	3,318	74	5,966	950	5,117	5,487	19	643
Washington	5,231	4,923	271	3,645	1,008	308	5,816	1,160	4,326	5,331	25	1,289
West Virginia	1,790	1,724	138	1,155	432	66	1,734	962	1,604	5,415	23	61
Wisconsin	4,917	4,738	166	1,990	2,582	179	4,838	976	4,416	5,972	12	277
Wyoming	562	552	32	290	230	10	547	1,189	500	5,333	24	30

- Represents or rounds to zero.　X Not applicable.　[1] Amount received by local education agencies from the sales of bonds and real property and equipment, loans, and proceeds from insurance adjustments.　[2] Includes interest on school debt and other current expenditures not shown separately.　[3] Based on Bureau of the Census estimated resident population, as of July 1, the previous year. Estimates reflect revisions based on the 1990 Census of Population.　[4] Average daily attendance.

Source: National Education Association, Washington, DC, *Estimates of School Statistics*, annual (copyright); and unpublished data.

No. 252. Microcomputers for Student Instruction in Elementary and Secondary Schools: 1981 to 1991

[As of fall for public schools; as of mid-winter of the previous year for private schools. Public school data based on surveys of every school district and all public schools. Private school data based on surveys of all Catholic and private schools. For details, see source]

YEAR	PUBLIC SCHOOLS										PRIVATE SCHOOLS			
	Number of schools (1,000)				Percent with micros				Number of micros [2] (1,000)	Students per micro [3]	Number of schools (1,000)	Percent with micros	Number of micros [2] (1,000)	Students per micro [3]
	Total [1]	Elementary	Junior	Senior	Total	Elementary	Junior	Senior						
1981	84.2	53.3	10.1	15.6	18.2	11.1	25.6	42.7	(NA)	(NA)	(NA)	(NA)	(NA)	(NA)
1982	82.4	51.9	9.9	15.3	30.0	20.2	39.8	57.8	(NA)	(NA)	(NA)	(NA)	(NA)	(NA)
1983	81.5	51.3	9.8	15.2	68.4	62.4	80.5	86.1	324.4	92.3	22.8	23.6	(NA)	(NA)
1984	81.1	51.0	9.8	15.2	85.1	82.2	93.1	94.6	569.8	63.5	24.4	53.0	62.2	56.2
1985	80.8	50.8	9.7	15.1	92.2	91.0	97.3	97.4	842.6	45.5	23.4	70.3	101.2	41.6
1986	80.5	50.7	9.7	15.1	95.6	94.9	98.5	98.7	1,081.9	36.5	22.7	77.1	129.2	33.7
1987	80.6	50.9	9.7	15.0	96.4	96.0	98.6	99.0	1,354.0	30.8	22.7	78.7	151.1	28.8
1988	80.8	51.0	9.8	15.0	97.1	96.8	98.8	99.1	1,522.9	26.9	22.3	82.8	185.5	23.5
1989	81.7	49.5	11.5	13.7	97.0	96.8	98.5	99.1	1,706.4	24.1	23.4	81.8	222.8	20.1
1990	82.0	49.7	11.7	13.8	97.2	97.3	98.4	98.8	2,028.7	20.7	22.3	88.2	241.8	19.5
1991, total . . .	82.5	49.8	11.8	14.0	98.4	98.5	99.5	99.4	2,215.9	19.2	22.7	90.7	289.5	16.5
Number of micros [2] . . .	2,215.9	949.6	401.5	699.3	(X)	(X)	(X)	(X)	(X)	(X)	289.5	(X)	(X)	(X)
Students per micro [3] .	19.2	23.2	18.3	15.2	(X)	(X)	(X)	(X)	(X)	(X)	16.5	(X)	(X)	(X)

NA Not available.   X Not applicable.   [1] Includes other schools, not shown separately.   [2] Includes estimates for schools not reporting number of micros.   [3] For schools reporting number of micros.

Source: Market Data Retrieval, Shelton, CT, *Microcomputers in Schools, 1986-87,* (copyright); and unpublished data.

No. 253. Instructional Use of Computers in Elementary and Secondary Schools, 1985 and 1989, and by Level, 1989

[Includes microcomputers and terminals used by students or teachers. Based on stratified, probability sample of 1,416 public, private, and parochial schools surveyed in spring 1989]

ITEM	Unit	Total, 1985	1989, BY SCHOOL LEVEL [1]			
			Total [2]	Elementary	Middle grades	High school
ALL SCHOOLS						
Computers used for instruction	1,000	1,034	2,355	897	583	895
Schools using computers	Percent . . .	86	96	96	95	98
Schools with 15 or more computers	Percent . . .	24	57	49	60	68
SCHOOLS USING COMPUTERS FOR INSTRUCTION						
Mean number of computers	Number. . .	10	26	19	26	45
Median [3]	Number. . .	8	19	16	20	31
Students per computer, median [3]	Number. . .	42	20	23	18	14
Percent of all instructional computers in—						
Classrooms	Percent . . .	37	36	43	28	32
Computer labs	Percent . . .	49	50	42	58	55
Other locations	Percent . . .	14	14	15	14	13
Percent of all instructional computers used—						
Usually every day.	Percent . . .	(NA)	71	67	68	77
Less than every week for instruction or not used at all	Percent . . .	(NA)	10	10	11	9
Median hours of use per week (in rooms with greatest number of computers) [3]	Number. . .	17	20	20	20	22
Percent of all student computer use: [4]						
Learning math	Percent . . .	(NA)	14	19	12	8
Word processing (how to use)	Percent . . .	(NA)	14	12	14	15
Keyboarding (how to)	Percent . . .	(NA)	13	13	15	12
Learning English	Percent . . .	(NA)	13	18	11	8
Programming.	Percent . . .	(NA)	8	4	9	12
Recreational use	Percent . . .	(NA)	8	10	9	5
Tools, e.g., spreadsheets.	Percent . . .	(NA)	7	4	8	11
Learning science	Percent . . .	(NA)	6	7	7	6
Learning social studies	Percent . . .	(NA)	5	8	5	3
Business education [5]	Percent . . .	(NA)	5	2	4	10
Industrial arts.	Percent . . .	(NA)	3	1	3	5
Fine arts.	Percent . . .	(NA)	2	2	2	2
Learning foreign languages	Percent . . .	(NA)	1	1	2	2
Other	Percent . . .	(NA)	1	1	1	1

NA Not available.   [1] Schools encompassing more than one level are apportioned among the appropriate levels rather than included more than once.   [2] 1989 data do not include schools that have only students below grade 4.   [3] For definition of median, see Guide to Tabular Presentation.   [4] Estimates supplied by each school's most informed computer-using teacher.   [5] Other than keyboarding or word processing instruction.

Source: Center for Social Organization of Schools, Johns Hopkins University, Baltimore, MD, International Computers-in-Education Survey, International Association for the Evaluation of Educational Achievement (I.E.A.), unpublished data.

No. 254. Technology in Public Schools—Summary: 1992 and 1993

[For school year ending in year shown. Based on surveys of school districts conducted in the spring and summer of the school year. For details, see source]

TECHNOLOGY	NUMBER			PERCENT OF TOTAL SCHOOLS	
	Total		Percent change, 1992-93		
	1992	1993		1992	1993
Schools with interactive videodisk players [1]	6,502	11,729	80	8	14
Elementary [2]	2,921	5,986	105	6	12
Junior high [3]	1,258	2,386	90	10	18
Senior high [4]	2,106	3,129	49	14	19
Students represented (1,000)	5,781	9,064	57	14	21
Schools with modems [1]	13,597	18,471	36	16	22
Elementary [2]	5,831	8,492	46	11	17
Junior high [3]	2,608	3,431	32	20	26
Senior high [4]	5,001	6,371	27	30	38
Students represented (1,000)	10,717	13,382	25	25	31
Schools with networks [1]	4,184	11,657	179	5	14
Elementary [2]	1,583	4,683	196	3	9
Junior high [3]	776	2,030	162	6	15
Senior high [4]	1,736	4,895	182	10	29
Students represented (1,000)	3,754	8,043	114	9	19
Schools with CD-ROM's [1]	5,706	11,021	93	7	13
Elementary [2]	1,897	4,457	135	4	9
Junior high [3]	1,231	2,326	89	9	17
Senior high [4]	2,543	4,168	64	15	25
Students represented (1,000)	5,298	8,534	61	12	20
Schools with satellite dishes [1]	1,129	8,812	681	1	11
Elementary [2]	351	2,988	751	1	6
Junior high [3]	166	1,503	805	1	11
Senior high [4]	606	4,292	608	4	26
Students represented (1,000)	1,906	4,668	145	4	11
Schools with cable [1]	(NA)	47,745	(X)	(X)	57
Elementary [2]	(NA)	27,923	(X)	(X)	54
Junior high [3]	(NA)	9,266	(X)	(X)	69
Senior high [4]	(NA)	10,296	(X)	(X)	62
Students represented (1,000)	(NA)	27,324	(X)	(X)	65

NA Not available.   X Not applicable.   [1] Includes schools for special education and adult education, not shown separately.
[2] Includes K-12, preschool, preschool through 3, K-6, and K-8.   [3] Includes schools with grade spans of 4-8, 7-8, and 7-9.
[4] Includes 7-12, 9-12, 10-12, vocational technical, and alternative high schools.

Source: Quality Education Data, Inc., Denver, CO, *Technology in Public Schools, 1991-92* and *1992-93.*

No. 255. Children and Youth with Disabilities in Educational Programs for the Disabled, by Type of Disability: 1980 to 1991

[For school year ending in year shown. For persons under 22 years old, except as noted. Represents children under 20 served under Chapter 1 of the Elementary and Secondary Education Act (ESEA), State Operated Programs (SOP), and children 3 to 21 served under Individuals with Disabilities Education Act, Part B (IDEA). Excludes outlying areas]

ITEM	1980	1983	1984	1985	1986	1987	1988 [1]	1989 [1]	1990 [1]	1991 [1]
All conditions (1,000)	**4,005**	**4,255**	**4,298**	**4,315**	**4,317**	**4,374**	**4,128**	**4,173**	**4,219**	**4,326**
PERCENT DISTRIBUTION										
Learning disabled	31.9	40.9	42.0	42.4	43.1	43.6	47.0	47.8	48.6	49.2
Speech impaired	29.6	26.6	26.2	26.1	26.1	25.8	23.2	23.1	23.1	22.8
Mentally retarded	21.7	17.8	16.9	16.1	15.3	15.0	14.6	13.8	13.0	12.4
Emotionally disturbed	8.2	8.3	8.4	8.6	8.7	8.7	9.1	8.9	9.0	9.0
Hard of hearing and deaf	2.0	1.7	1.7	1.6	1.5	1.5	1.4	1.4	1.3	1.3
Orthopedically handicapped	1.6	1.3	1.3	1.3	1.3	1.3	1.1	1.1	1.1	1.1
Other health impaired	2.6	1.2	1.2	1.6	1.3	1.2	1.1	1.2	1.2	1.3
Visually handicapped	0.8	0.7	0.7	0.7	0.6	0.6	0.6	0.5	0.5	0.5
Multihandicapped	1.5	1.5	1.5	1.6	2.0	2.2	1.9	2.0	2.0	2.2
Deaf-blind	0.1	0.1	0.1	0.1	(Z)	(Z)	(Z)	(Z)	(Z)	(Z)

Z Less than .05 percent.   [1] For children 6 to 21 years old; total number of children served under 22 years old was 4,494,280 in school year 1987-88, 4,568,118 in school year 1988-89, 4,640,969 in 1989-90, and 4,771,398 in 1990-91.

Source: U.S. Dept. of Education, Office of Special Education Programs, *Annual Report to Congress.*

No. 256. Children and Youth With Disabilities 3 to 21 Years Old, by Age and Educational Environment: 1989

[For school year ending in year shown. Covers children 3 to 21 served under Chapter 1 of ESEA (SOP) and IDEA-B; see headnote, table 255. Includes 40,018 children in Puerto Rico, American Samoa, Guam, Northern Marianas, and the Virgin Islands]

ENVIRONMENT	NUMBER (1,000)					PERCENT DISTRIBUTION			
	Total	3-5 years old	6-11 years old	12-17 years old	18-21 years old	3-5 years old	6-11 years old	12-17 years old	18-21 years old
Total	4,497.6	332.5	2,193.4	1,734.1	226.4	100.0	100.0	100.0	100.0
Regular class [1]	1,406.2	140.4	898.7	335.1	32.1	42.2	41.0	19.3	14.2
Resource room [2]	1,675.2	53.7	762.5	779.7	79.3	16.2	34.8	45.0	35.0
Separate class [3]	1,095.5	87.6	449.1	487.5	71.3	26.4	20.5	28.1	31.5
Separate school facility:									
Public	160.8	26.1	45.6	63.1	26.0	7.9	2.1	3.6	11.5
Private	71.9	16.7	22.0	26.1	7.1	5.0	1.0	1.5	3.1
Separate residential facility:									
Public	24.9	1.1	5.6	12.9	5.3	0.3	0.3	0.7	2.3
Private	12.2	0.3	2.6	7.2	2.1	0.1	0.1	0.4	0.9
Correctional facility	11.3	(NA)	(NA)	(NA)	(NA)	(NA)	(NA)	(NA)	(NA)
Home/hospital	39.6	6.6	7.3	22.5	3.2	2.0	0.3	1.3	1.4

NA Not available.   [1] Receives special education and related services less than 21 percent of the school day.   [2] Receives services between 21 and 60 percent of the school day.   [3] Receives services for more than 60 percent of the school day.
Source: U.S. Dept. of Education, Office of Special Education Programs, Data Analysis Systems (DANS), unpublished data.

No. 257. Catholic Elementary and Secondary Schools: 1960 to 1991

[As of October 1. Regular sessions only. See also *Historical Statistics, Colonial Times to 1970*, series H 535-544]

ITEM	Unit	1960	1970	1975	1980	1985	1987	1988	1989	1990	1991
Elementary schools. . .	Number	10,501	9,362	8,340	8,043	7,806	7,601	7,501	7,395	7,291	7,239
Pupils enrolled	1,000. .	4,373	3,359	2,525	2,269	2,057	1,942	1,912	1,893	1,884	1,964
Teachers, total [1] . . .	1,000. .	108	112	99	97	97	93	94	94	91	109
Religious.	1,000. .	79	52	35	25	18	15	14	12	11	13
Lay	1,000. .	29	60	64	72	79	78	80	82	80	96
Secondary schools . . .	Number	2,392	1,981	1,653	1,516	1,430	1,391	1,362	1,324	1,296	1,269
Pupils enrolled	1,000. .	880	1,008	890	837	762	681	639	606	592	587
Teachers, total [1] . . .	1,000. .	44	54	50	49	50	47	44	43	40	44
Religious.	1,000. .	33	28	20	14	11	10	8	8	6	7
Lay	1,000. .	11	26	30	35	39	37	36	35	34	37

[1] Beginning 1991, includes part-time teachers.
Source: National Catholic Educational Association, Washington, DC, *A Statistical Report on Catholic Elementary and Secondary Schools for the Years 1967-68 to 1969-70*, and *U.S. Catholic Schools, 1973-74*, and National Catholic Educational Association/Ganley's, *Catholic Schools in America*, annual (copyright).

No. 258. Private Elementary and Secondary School Teachers—Selected Characteristics: 1990-91

[For school year. Based on survey and subject to sampling error; for details, see source. See table 244 for similar data on public school teachers]

CHARACTERISTIC	Unit	AGE				SEX		RACE/ETHNICITY			LEVEL OF CONTROL	
		Under 30 years old	30 to 39 years old	40 to 49 years old	Over 50 years old	Male	Fe-male	White [1]	Black [1]	His-pan-ic	Ele-men-tary	Sec-ondary
Total teachers [2]	1,000 . . .	68	105	115	67	82	275	329	9	12	172	184
Highest degree held:												
Bachelor's	Percent .	81.4	65.9	55.4	47.0	51.5	65.0	61.8	72.8	60.6	69.5	54.8
Master's	Percent .	9.8	23.5	33.4	38.7	35.3	24.5	27.3	21.7	22.1	19.3	34.1
Education specialist .	Percent .	0.8	2.3	3.7	4.8	4.0	2.6	3.0	1.0	1.7	2.1	3.8
Doctorate	Percent .	0.3	1.1	1.9	4.0	4.2	1.0	1.8	0.9	2.7	0.4	3.0
Full-time teaching experience:												
Less than 3 years. . .	Percent .	51.7	19.7	10.1	7.3	19.8	20.6	20.1	20.1	28.8	20.2	20.6
3 to 9 years	Percent .	48.0	45.4	31.3	10.0	30.7	35.8	34.8	39.1	31.6	36.3	33.1
10 to 20 years	Percent .	0.2	34.8	44.7	27.5	30.4	29.9	30.3	25.4	25.3	30.1	30.0
20 years or more . .	Percent .	-	0.1	13.8	55.2	19.0	13.7	14.9	15.4	14.2	13.4	16.3
Full-time teachers	1,000 . . .	61	86	98	55	70	231	277	9	9	151	150
Earned income	Dol.	18,658	21,334	22,463	24,197	27,196	20,007	21,578	23,094	22,912	18,947	24,442
Salary	Dol.	16,403	19,190	20,892	21,534	23,003	18,815	19,717	20,333	20,740	17,717	21,883

- Represents zero.   [1] Non-Hispanic.   [2] Includes teachers with no degrees and associates degrees, not shown separately.
Source: U.S. National Center for Education Statistics, *Digest of Education Statistics*, 1993.

No. 259. Private Elementary and Secondary Enrollment, Schools, and Tuition Paid, by Orientation and Tuition Levels: 1991

[For school year ending in year shown. Based on survey and subject to sampling error; for details see source]

ORIENTATION AND TUITION LEVEL	ENROLLMENT (1,000)				SCHOOLS				AVERAGE ANNUAL TUITION (dol.)			
	Total	Ele-mentary	Sec-ondary	Com-bined	Total	Ele-mentary	Sec-ondary	Com-bined	Total	Ele-mentary	Sec-ondary	Com-bined
Total	**4,912**	**2,850**	**889**	**1,173**	**24,690**	**15,701**	**2,467**	**6,522**	**2,593**	**1,745**	**3,650**	**3,850**
Catholic schools [1]	2,631	1,884	679	(B)	8,731	7,205	1,322	(B)	1,765	1,263	3,008	(B)
Less than $1,000	713	688	(B)	(B)	3,003	2,864	(B)	(B)	(X)	(X)	(X)	(X)
$1,000 to $2,499	1,478	1,137	325	(B)	4,802	4,134	629	(B)	(X)	(X)	(X)	(X)
$2,500 to $4,999	401	(B)	320	(B)	793	(B)	572	(B)	(X)	(X)	(X)	(X)
$5,000 or more	(B)	(B)	(B)	(B)	(B)	(B)	(B)	(B)	(X)	(X)	(X)	(X)
Other religious schools [1]	1,568	704	123	741	11,476	6,225	568	4,683	2,615	2,258	4,070	2,713
Less than $1,000	136	85	(B)	51	2,989	1,694	(B)	1,213	(X)	(X)	(X)	(X)
$1,000 to $2,499	858	458	(B)	377	6,490	3,731	(B)	2,644	(X)	(X)	(X)	(X)
$2,500 to $4,999	419	124	71	224	1,550	670	323	557	(X)	(X)	(X)	(X)
$5,000 or more	152	37	28	87	514	128	121	265	(X)	(X)	(X)	(X)
Nonsectarian schools [1]	713	262	87	364	4,483	2,271	577	1,634	5,599	3,837	8,061	6,279
Less than $1,000	76	(B)	(B)	40	610	(B)	(B)	288	(X)	(X)	(X)	(X)
$1,000 to $2,499	82	41	(B)	(B)	569	435	(B)	(B)	(X)	(X)	(X)	(X)
$2,500 to $4,999	213	125	(B)	76	1,666	1,225	(B)	392	(X)	(X)	(X)	(X)
$5,000 or more	340	67	66	207	1,600	417	353	830	(X)	(X)	(X)	(X)

B Base figure too small to meet statistical standards of reliability for a derived figure.   X Not applicable.   [1] Includes schools not reporting.
Source: U.S. National Center for Education Statistics, *Digest of Education Statistics*, 1993.

No. 260. Private Elementary and Secondary Schools—Enrollment Size and Minority Enrollment, by Orientation: 1991

[For school year ending in year shown. Based on survey and subject to sampling error; for details see source]

CHARACTERISTIC	ENROLLMENT (1,000)				SCHOOLS			
	Total	Catholic	Other religious	Non-sectarian	Total	Catholic	Other religious	Non-sectarian
Total	**4,911.8**	**2,631.4**	**1,567.6**	**712.8**	**24,690**	**8,731**	**11,476**	**4,483**
School enrollment:								
Less than 150 students	819.2	171.1	448.9	199.1	12,471	1,616	7,899	2,956
150 to 299 students	1,554.7	882.1	469.3	203.3	7,222	3,989	2,254	979
300 to 499 students	1,204.9	753.1	330.1	121.7	3,182	1,998	876	308
500 to 749 students	744.8	461.2	203.9	79.6	1,236	771	333	132
750 or more students	588.3	363.8	115.4	109.1	578	357	114	107
Percent minority students:								
Less than 5 percent	35.9	34.2	44.7	22.5	40.0	38.3	49.0	20.6
5 percent, less than 20 percent	32.0	29.6	31.4	42.1	28.8	28.3	25.8	37.5
20 percent, less than 50 percent	17.7	17.8	14.4	24.8	16.9	15.5	14.9	24.8
50 percent or more	14.4	18.4	9.5	10.6	14.2	17.9	10.3	17.2

Source: U.S. National Center for Education Statistics, *Digest of Education Statistics*, 1993.

No. 261. High School Dropouts, by Race and Hispanic Origin: 1973 to 1991

[In percent. As of October]

ITEM	1973	1975	1980	1983	1984	1985	1986	1987 [1]	1988 [1]	1989 [1]	1990 [1]	1991 [1]
EVENT DROPOUTS [2]												
Total [3]	6.3	5.8	6.0	5.2	5.0	5.2	4.3	4.1	4.8	4.5	4.0	4.0
White	5.7	5.4	5.6	4.8	5.0	4.8	4.2	3.7	4.7	3.9	3.8	3.7
Male	6.1	5.0	6.4	5.4	5.3	4.9	4.2	4.1	5.1	4.1	4.1	3.6
Female	5.3	5.8	4.9	4.2	4.6	4.7	4.1	3.4	4.3	3.8	3.5	3.8
Black	10.1	8.7	8.3	6.9	5.8	7.7	4.7	6.4	6.3	7.7	5.1	6.2
Male	12.0	8.3	8.0	7.0	6.2	8.3	4.8	6.2	6.7	6.9	4.1	5.5
Female	8.4	9.0	8.5	6.8	5.3	7.2	4.6	6.4	6.0	8.6	6.0	7.0
Hispanic [4]	10.0	10.9	11.5	9.8	10.9	9.7	11.9	5.6	10.5	7.7	8.0	7.3
Male	7.9	10.1	16.9	13.7	12.2	9.3	11.7	5.0	12.3	7.6	8.7	10.4
Female	12.0	11.6	6.9	6.2	10.1	9.8	12.4	6.2	8.4	7.7	7.2	4.8
STATUS DROPOUTS [5]												
Total [3]	15.7	15.6	15.6	15.4	14.8	13.9	13.8	14.5	14.6	14.4	13.6	14.2
White	14.2	13.9	14.4	14.3	14.1	13.5	13.5	14.2	14.2	14.1	13.5	14.2
Male	13.8	13.5	15.7	15.8	15.1	14.7	14.6	15.1	15.4	15.4	15.2	15.4
Female	14.5	14.2	13.2	12.9	13.0	12.3	12.4	13.2	13.0	12.8	12.8	13.1
Black	26.5	27.3	23.5	21.5	18.4	17.6	16.6	17.0	17.7	16.4	15.1	15.6
Male	25.9	27.8	26.0	24.1	20.2	18.8	18.1	18.7	18.9	18.6	13.6	15.4
Female	27.1	26.9	21.5	19.3	17.0	16.6	15.8	15.4	16.6	14.5	16.2	15.8
Hispanic [4]	38.9	34.9	40.3	37.5	34.2	31.5	27.9	32.8	39.6	37.7	37.3	39.6
Male	36.5	32.6	42.6	40.9	35.4	35.8	37.4	34.5	40.2	40.3	39.8	44.4
Female	41.3	36.8	38.1	34.3	33.2	27.0	31.1	30.8	38.8	35.0	34.5	34.5

[1] Beginning 1987 reflects new editing procedures for cases with missing data on school enrollment.   [2] Percent of students who drop out in a single year without completing high school. For grades 10 to 12.   [3] Includes other races, not shown separately.   [4] Persons of Hispanic origin may be of any race.   [5] Percent of the population who have not completed high school and are not enrolled, regardless of when they dropped out. For persons 18 to 24 years old.
Source: U.S. Bureau of the Census, *Current Population Reports*, series P20-469.

No. 262. High School Dropouts by Age, Race, and Hispanic Origin: 1970 to 1991

[As of October. For persons 14 to 24 years old. See table 264 for definition of dropouts]

AGE AND RACE	NUMBER OF DROPOUTS (1,000)								PERCENT OF POPULATION			
	1970	1980	1985	1987	1988	1989	1990	1991	1970	1980	1985	1991
Total dropouts [1][2]	4,670	5,212	4,456	4,349	4,300	4,109	3,854	3,964	12.2	12.0	10.6	10.5
16 to 17 years	617	709	505	500	482	395	418	395	8.0	8.8	7.0	6.0
18 to 21 years	2,138	2,578	2,095	1,966	2,081	2,128	1,921	1,960	16.4	15.8	14.1	14.1
22 to 24 years	1,770	1,798	1,724	1,785	1,668	1,516	1,458	1,526	18.7	15.2	14.1	14.3
White [2]	3,577	4,169	3,583	3,522	3,480	3,314	3,127	3,229	10.8	11.3	10.3	10.5
16 to 17 years	485	619	424	401	411	328	334	312	7.3	9.2	7.1	5.9
18 to 21 years	1,618	2,032	1,678	1,577	1,670	1,690	1,516	1,558	14.3	14.7	13.6	13.9
22 to 24 years	1,356	1,416	1,372	1,465	1,342	1,236	1,235	1,287	16.3	14.0	13.3	14.6
Black [2]	1,047	934	748	706	709	648	611	631	22.2	16.0	12.6	11.3
16 to 17 years	125	80	70	77	67	61	73	77	12.8	6.9	6.5	7.4
18 to 21 years	500	486	376	338	368	363	345	354	30.5	23.0	17.5	16.6
22 to 24 years	397	346	279	273	263	220	185	191	37.8	24.0	17.8	14.0
Hispanic [2][3]	(NA)	919	820	941	1,177	1,168	1,122	1,262	(NA)	29.5	23.3	29.5
16 to 17 years	(NA)	92	97	76	123	80	89	102	(NA)	16.6	14.6	15.8
18 to 21 years	(NA)	470	335	410	552	538	502	574	(NA)	40.3	29.3	35.1
22 to 24 years	(NA)	323	365	439	494	524	523	565	(NA)	40.6	33.9	45.7

NA Not available.   [1] Includes other groups not shown separately.   [2] Includes persons 14 to 15 years, not shown separately.
[3] Persons of Hispanic origin may be of any race.
Source: U.S. Bureau of the Census, *Current Population Reports*, series P20-469; and earlier reports.

No. 263. Enrollment Status, by Race, Hispanic Origin, and Sex: 1975 and 1991

[As of October. For persons 18 to 21 years old. For the civilian noninstitutional population. Based on the Current Population Survey; see text, section 1 and Appendix III]

CHARACTERISTIC	TOTAL PERSONS 18 TO 21 YEARS OLD (1,000)		PERCENT DISTRIBUTION									
			Enrolled in high school		High school graduates						Not high school graduates	
					Total		In college		Not in college			
	1975	1991	1975	1991	1975	1991	1975	1991	1975	1991	1975	1991
Total [1]	15,693	13,906	5.7	8.2	78.0	77.7	33.5	42.2	44.5	35.5	16.3	14.1
White	13,448	11,187	4.7	6.9	80.6	79.1	34.6	44.1	46.0	35.0	14.7	13.9
Black	1,997	2,138	12.5	14.2	60.4	69.3	24.9	28.3	35.6	41.0	27.0	16.6
Hispanic [2]	899	1,637	12.0	13.4	57.2	51.6	24.4	23.9	32.8	27.7	30.8	35.1
Male [1]	7,584	6,772	7.4	10.5	76.6	75.0	35.4	40.1	41.3	34.9	15.9	14.6
White	6,545	5,459	6.2	8.9	79.7	76.1	36.9	41.4	42.8	34.7	14.1	15.0
Black	911	1,026	15.9	18.9	55.0	66.3	23.9	26.8	31.1	39.5	29.0	14.7
Hispanic [2]	416	826	17.3	13.9	54.6	45.3	25.2	17.8	29.3	27.5	27.9	41.0
Female [1]	8,109	7,134	4.2	6.0	79.2	80.3	31.8	44.2	47.4	36.1	16.6	13.6
White	6,903	5,728	3.2	5.0	81.4	82.1	32.4	46.8	49.0	35.3	15.3	12.8
Black	1,085	1,112	9.7	9.6	65.0	71.9	25.8	29.7	39.2	42.3	25.4	18.4
Hispanic [2]	484	812	7.6	12.8	59.3	58.1	23.6	30.0	35.7	28.1	33.1	29.1

[1] Includes other races not shown separately.   [2] Persons of Hispanic origin may be of any race.
Source: U.S. Bureau of the Census, *Current Population Reports*, series P20-469.

No. 264. Employment Status of High School Graduates Not Enrolled in College and School Dropouts, by Sex and Race: 1980 to 1991

[In thousands, except percent. As of October. For civilian noninstitutional population 16 to 24 years old. High school graduates: Persons not enrolled in college who have completed 4 years of high school only. Dropouts: Persons not in regular school and who have not completed the 12th grade nor received a general equivalency degree. Based on Current Population Survey; see text, section 1, and Appendix III]

EMPLOYMENT STATUS, SEX, AND RACE	GRADUATES					DROPOUTS				
	1980	1985	1989	1990	1991	1980	1985	1989	1990	1991
Civilian population	11,622	10,381	8,645	8,370	7,804	5,254	4,323	4,042	3,800	3,884
In labor force	9,795	8,825	7,266	7,107	6,444	3,549	2,920	2,703	2,506	2,464
Percent of population	84.3	85.0	84.1	84.9	82.6	67.5	67.5	66.9	66.0	63.4
Employed [1]	8,567	7,707	6,552	6,279	5,641	2,651	2,165	2,147	1,993	1,849
Percent of labor force	87.5	87.3	90.2	88.3	87.5	74.7	74.1	79.4	79.5	75.0
Male	4,462	4,001	3,534	3,435	3,123	1,780	1,475	1,491	1,304	1,288
Female	4,105	3,706	3,018	2,845	2,518	871	690	656	689	561
White	7,638	6,732	5,543	5,334	4,724	2,310	1,888	1,861	1,761	1,631
Black	817	865	853	794	766	305	226	223	178	167
Unemployed [1]	1,228	1,118	714	828	803	898	755	555	513	614
Percent of labor force	12.5	12.7	9.8	11.7	12.5	25.3	25.9	20.6	20.5	24.9
Male	695	569	364	428	441	548	462	343	301	362
Female	532	549	350	400	362	350	293	213	212	253
White	924	729	478	526	506	636	582	397	361	447
Black	289	360	224	279	273	239	160	148	136	153
Not in labor force	1,827	1,556	1,379	1,262	1,360	1,705	1,403	1,339	1,294	1,420
Percent of population	15.7	15.0	16.0	15.1	17.4	32.5	32.5	33.1	34.1	36.6

[1] Includes other races not shown separately.
Source: U.S. Bureau of Labor Statistics, Bulletin 2307; and unpublished data.

No. 265. Scholastic Aptitude Test (SAT) Scores and Characteristics of College-Bound Seniors: 1967 to 1992

[For school year ending in year shown]

TYPE OF TEST AND CHARACTERISTIC	Unit	1967	1970	1975	1980	1985	1987	1988	1989	1990	1991	1992
TEST SCORES [1]												
Verbal, total [2]	Point ...	466	460	434	424	431	430	428	427	424	422	423
Male	Point ...	463	459	437	428	437	435	435	434	429	426	428
Female	Point ...	468	461	431	420	425	425	422	421	419	418	419
Math, total [2]	Point ...	492	488	472	466	475	476	476	476	476	474	476
Male	Point ...	514	509	495	491	499	500	498	500	499	497	499
Female	Point ...	467	465	449	443	452	453	455	454	455	453	456
PARTICIPANTS												
Total	1,000 ...	(NA)	(NA)	996	992	977	1,080	1,134	1,088	1,026	1,033	1,034
Male	Percent .	(NA)	(NA)	49.9	48.2	48.3	48.2	47.0	47.9	47.8	47.7	47.6
White	Percent .	(NA)	(NA)	86.0	82.1	81.0	78.2	77.0	74.7	73.0	72.0	71.5
Black	Percent .	(NA)	(NA)	7.9	9.1	7.5	8.7	9.2	9.6	10.0	10.0	10.4
Obtaining scores [1] of— 600 or above:												
Verbal	Percent .	(NA)	(NA)	7.9	7.2	7.9	8.1	7.3	7.8	7.4	7.2	7.3
Math	Percent .	(NA)	(NA)	15.6	15.1	17.1	18.3	17.6	18.0	18.4	17.8	18.1
Below 400:												
Verbal	Percent .	(NA)	(NA)	37.8	41.8	39.4	39.8	39.4	40.4	41.2	42.4	41.3
Math	Percent .	(NA)	(NA)	28.5	30.2	28.2	28.3	27.8	28.0	28.4	29.1	28.2
Selected intended area of study:												
Business and commerce	Percent .	(NA)	(NA)	11.5	18.6	21.0	23.1	23.0	22.3	21.0	19.0	16.8
Engineering	Percent .	(NA)	(NA)	6.7	11.1	11.7	11.1	10.1	10.1	10.0	10.0	10.5
Social science	Percent .	(NA)	(NA)	7.7	7.8	7.5	10.9	11.7	12.6	13.0	12.0	12.1
Education	Percent .	(NA)	(NA)	9.1	6.1	4.7	6.0	6.6	7.1	7.0	8.0	8.1
SAT average [1] by high school rank:												
Top tenth	Point ...	(NA)	(NA)	(NA)	539	547	552	550	550	549	548	549
Second tenth	Point ...	(NA)	(NA)	(NA)	470	482	484	483	483	481	480	480
Second fifth	Point ...	(NA)	(NA)	(NA)	431	442	440	440	440	438	437	438
Third fifth	Point ...	(NA)	(NA)	(NA)	386	396	395	395	394	392	391	392

NA Not available. [1] Minimum score 200; maximum score, 800. [2] 1967 and 1970 are estimates based on total number of persons taking SAT.
Source: College Entrance Examination Board, New York, NY, *National College-Bound Senior,* annual (copyright).

No. 266. American College Testing (ACT) Program Scores and Characteristics of College-Bound Students: 1967 to 1992

[For academic year ending in year shown. Except as indicated, test scores and characteristics of college-bound students. Through 1985, data based on 10 percent sample; thereafter, based on all ACT tested seniors]

TYPE OF TEST AND CHARACTERISTIC	Unit	1967	1970	1975	1980	1985	1987	1988	1989	1990 [1]	1991 [1]	1992 [1]
TEST SCORES [2]												
Composite	Point ...	19.9	18.6	18.5	18.5	18.6	18.7	18.8	18.6	20.6	20.6	20.6
Male	Point ...	20.3	19.5	19.3	19.3	19.4	19.5	19.6	19.3	21.0	20.9	20.9
Female	Point ...	19.4	17.8	17.9	17.8	17.9	18.1	18.1	18.0	20.3	20.4	20.5
English	Point ...	18.5	17.7	17.9	17.8	18.1	18.4	18.5	18.4	20.5	20.3	20.2
Male	Point ...	17.6	17.1	17.3	17.3	17.6	17.9	18.0	17.8	20.1	19.8	19.8
Female	Point ...	19.4	18.3	18.3	18.2	18.6	18.9	19.0	18.9	20.9	20.7	20.6
Math	Point ...	20.0	17.6	17.4	17.3	17.2	17.2	17.2	17.1	19.9	20.0	20.0
Male	Point ...	21.1	19.3	18.9	18.9	18.6	18.6	18.4	18.3	20.7	20.6	20.7
Female	Point ...	18.8	16.2	16.2	16.0	16.0	16.1	16.1	16.1	19.3	19.4	19.5
Reading [3]	Point ...	19.7	17.4	17.2	17.2	17.4	17.5	17.4	17.2	(NA)	21.2	21.1
Male	Point ...	20.3	18.7	18.2	18.3	18.3	18.4	18.4	18.1	(NA)	21.3	21.1
Female	Point ...	19.0	16.4	16.4	16.4	16.6	16.7	16.6	16.4	(NA)	21.1	21.1
Science reasoning [4]	Point ...	20.8	21.1	21.1	21.0	21.2	21.4	21.4	21.2	(NA)	20.7	20.7
Male	Point ...	21.6	22.4	22.4	22.3	22.6	22.8	22.8	22.6	(NA)	21.3	21.4
Female	Point ...	20.0	20.0	20.0	20.0	20.0	20.0	20.1	20.2	(NA)	20.1	20.1
PARTICIPANTS [5]												
Total	1,000 ...	788	714	822	836	739	777	842	855	817	796	832
Male	Percent .	52	46	45	45	46	46	46	46	46	45	45
White	Percent .	(NA)	77	83	83	82	81	81	80	79	79	80
Black	Percent .	4	7	8	8	8	8	9	9	9	9	9
Obtaining composite scores [6] of— 27 or above	Percent .	14	14	13	13	14	14	14	14	12	11	12
18 or below	Percent .	21	33	33	33	32	31	31	32	35	35	35
Planned educational major:												
Business [7]	Percent .	18	21	20	19	21	23	23	22	20	18	17
Engineering [8]	Percent .	8	6	8	10	9	8	9	9	9	10	11
Social science [8]	Percent .	10	9	6	6	7	9	10	11	10	10	10
Education	Percent .	16	12	9	7	6	8	8	8	8	10	9

NA Not available. [1] Beginning 1990, not comparable with previous years because a new version of the ACT was introduced. Estimated average composite scores for prior years: 1989, 20.6; 1988, 1987, and 1986, 20.8. [2] Minimum score, 1; maximum score, 36. [3] Prior to 1990, social studies; data not comparable with previous years. [4] Prior to 1990, natural sciences; data not comparable with previous years. [5] Beginning 1985, data are for seniors who graduated in year shown and had taken the ACT in their junior or senior years. [6] Prior to 1990, 26 or above and 15 or below. [7] Includes political and persuasive (e.g. sales) fields through 1975; thereafter, business and commerce. [8] Includes religion through 1975.
Source: The American College Testing Program, Iowa City, IA, *High School Profile Report,* annual.

No. 267. Proficiency Test Scores for Selected Subjects, by Characteristic: 1977 to 1990

[Based on The National Assessment of Educational Progress Tests which are administered to a representative sample of students in public and private schools. Test scores can range from 0 to 500, except for writing, 0 to 400. For details, see source]

TEST AND YEAR	Total	SEX		RACE			PARENTAL EDUCATION				
		Male	Female	White [1]	Black [1]	His-panic	Less than high school	High school	More than high school		
									Total	Some college	College grad-uate
READING											
9 year olds:											
1979-80	215	210	220	221	189	190	194	213	226	(NA)	(NA)
1983-84	211	208	214	218	186	187	195	209	223	(NA)	(NA)
1987-88	212	208	216	218	189	194	193	211	220	(NA)	(NA)
1989-90	209	204	215	217	182	189	193	209	218	(NA)	(NA)
13 year olds:											
1979-80	259	254	263	264	232	237	239	254	271	(NA)	(NA)
1983-84	257	253	262	263	236	240	240	253	268	(NA)	(NA)
1987-88	258	252	263	261	243	240	247	253	265	(NA)	(NA)
1989-90	257	251	263	262	242	238	241	251	267	(NA)	(NA)
17 year olds:											
1979-80	286	282	290	293	243	261	262	277	299	(NA)	(NA)
1983-84	289	284	294	296	264	268	269	281	301	(NA)	(NA)
1987-88	290	286	294	295	274	271	267	282	300	(NA)	(NA)
1989-90	290	284	297	297	267	275	270	283	300	(NA)	(NA)
WRITING											
4th graders:											
1983-84	179	176	184	186	154	163	157	171	187	(NA)	193
1987-88	186	176	195	193	154	169	158	183	179	(NA)	195
1989-90	183	174	193	191	155	168	169	183	195	(NA)	191
8th graders:											
1983-84	206	199	214	210	190	191	196	203	210	(NA)	215
1987-88	203	193	213	207	190	188	195	198	213	(NA)	208
1989-90	198	187	208	202	182	189	191	195	207	(NA)	203
11th graders:											
1983-84	212	201	223	218	195	188	200	207	218	(NA)	220
1987-88	214	204	223	219	200	199	202	211	217	(NA)	220
1989-90	212	200	224	217	194	198	190	204	215	(NA)	221
MATHEMATICS											
9 year olds:											
1977-78	219	217	220	224	192	203	200	219	(NA)	230	231
1981-82	219	217	221	224	195	204	199	218	(NA)	225	229
1985-86	222	222	222	227	202	205	201	218	(NA)	229	231
1989-90	230	229	230	235	208	214	210	226	(NA)	236	238
13 year olds:											
1977-78	264	264	265	272	230	238	245	263	(NA)	273	284
1981-82	269	269	268	274	240	252	251	263	(NA)	275	282
1985-86	269	270	268	274	249	254	252	263	(NA)	274	280
1989-90	270	271	270	276	249	255	253	263	(NA)	277	280
17 year olds:											
1977-78	300	304	297	306	268	276	280	294	(NA)	305	317
1981-82	299	302	296	304	272	277	279	293	(NA)	304	312
1985-86	302	305	299	308	279	283	279	293	(NA)	305	314
1989-90	305	306	303	310	289	284	285	294	(NA)	308	316
SCIENCE											
9 year olds:											
1976-77	220	222	218	230	192	175	199	223	(NA)	237	232
1981-82	221	221	221	229	189	187	198	218	(NA)	229	231
1985-86	224	227	221	232	199	196	204	220	(NA)	236	235
1989-90	229	230	227	238	196	206	210	226	(NA)	238	236
13 year olds:											
1976-77	247	251	244	256	208	213	224	245	(NA)	260	267
1981-82	250	256	245	257	217	226	225	243	(NA)	259	264
1985-86	251	256	247	259	222	226	229	245	(NA)	258	264
1989-90	255	259	252	264	226	232	233	247	(NA)	263	268
17 year olds:											
1976-77	290	297	282	298	262	240	265	284	(NA)	296	309
1981-82	283	292	275	293	249	235	259	275	(NA)	290	300
1985-86	289	295	282	298	259	253	258	277	(NA)	295	304
1989-90	290	296	285	301	253	262	261	276	(NA)	297	306

NA Not available.   [1] Non-Hispanic.

Source: U.S. National Center for Education Statistics, *Digest of Education Statistics*, annual.

No. 268. Public High School Graduates, by State, 1980 to 1991, and Projections, 1992 to 1994

[In thousands. For school year ending in year shown. Projections will not agree with data in table 223 due to revised projections on the State level]

STATE	1980	1985	1987	1988	1989	1990	1991, est.	1992, proj.	1993, proj.	1994, proj.
U.S.	2,747.7	2,414.0	2,428.8	2,500.2	2,458.8	2,319.8	2,263.5	2,250.9	2,215.1	2,209.1
AL	45.2	40.0	42.5	43.8	43.4	40.5	40.6	40.6	38.9	38.3
AK	5.2	5.2	5.7	5.9	5.6	5.4	5.5	5.8	5.3	5.5
AZ	28.6	27.9	29.5	29.8	31.9	32.1	30.9	30.9	29.7	31.2
AR	29.1	26.3	27.1	27.8	27.9	26.5	25.9	25.4	25.5	25.5
CA	249.2	225.4	237.4	249.6	244.6	236.3	239.0	243.0	243.6	249.9
CO	36.8	32.3	34.2	36.0	35.5	33.0	31.3	30.9	31.4	31.3
CT	37.7	32.1	31.1	32.4	30.9	27.8	27.4	27.1	25.7	25.3
DE	7.6	5.9	5.9	6.0	6.1	5.6	5.5	5.5	5.4	5.5
DC	5.0	3.9	3.8	3.9	3.6	3.6	3.5	3.4	2.8	2.7
FL	87.3	81.1	82.2	89.2	90.8	88.9	87.5	88.4	78.6	84.0
GA	61.6	58.7	60.0	61.8	61.9	56.6	60.1	60.5	58.6	58.1
HI	11.5	10.1	10.4	10.6	10.4	10.3	9.5	10.1	9.5	9.9
ID	13.2	12.1	12.2	12.4	12.5	12.0	12.3	13.0	12.3	12.6
IL	135.6	117.0	116.1	119.1	116.7	108.1	103.3	102.7	102.3	102.7
IN	73.1	63.3	60.4	64.0	63.6	59.9	58.4	54.7	56.8	55.4
IA	43.4	36.1	34.6	35.2	34.3	31.8	28.8	29.4	30.9	30.6
KS	30.9	26.0	26.9	27.0	26.8	25.4	24.4	23.4	25.2	25.5
KY	41.2	38.0	36.9	39.5	38.9	38.0	36.2	36.5	34.1	34.1
LA	46.3	39.7	39.1	39.1	37.2	36.1	33.5	33.9	33.6	32.3
ME	15.4	13.9	13.7	13.8	13.9	13.8	13.2	13.2	12.3	11.9
MD	54.3	48.3	46.1	47.2	45.8	41.6	40.3	40.3	38.7	38.4
MA	73.8	63.4	61.0	59.5	57.3	55.0	50.6	47.3	46.3	45.7
MI	124.3	105.9	102.7	106.2	101.8	93.7	91.6	90.0	86.0	83.3
MN	64.9	53.4	53.5	54.6	53.1	49.1	46.5	46.5	48.5	48.7
MS	27.6	25.3	26.2	27.9	24.2	25.2	23.4	22.8	23.2	23.1
MO	62.3	51.3	50.8	51.3	52.0	48.5	46.9	45.6	46.9	46.1
MT	12.1	10.0	10.1	10.3	10.5	9.4	9.1	9.1	9.2	9.3
NE	22.4	18.0	18.1	18.3	18.7	17.7	16.4	16.6	17.4	16.8
NV	8.5	8.6	9.5	9.4	9.5	9.5	9.4	9.4	9.9	10.5
NH	11.7	11.1	10.8	11.7	11.3	10.8	10.5	10.4	9.4	9.4
NJ	94.6	81.5	79.4	80.9	76.3	69.8	67.0	63.8	62.1	61.3
NM	18.4	15.6	15.7	15.9	15.5	14.9	15.2	15.0	15.4	15.2
NY	204.1	166.8	163.8	165.4	154.6	143.3	137.3	135.7	131.6	131.4
NC	70.9	67.2	65.4	67.8	70.0	64.8	62.5	60.7	60.7	57.9
ND	9.9	8.1	7.8	8.4	8.1	7.7	7.6	7.5	7.5	7.5
OH	144.2	122.3	121.1	124.5	125.0	114.5	107.5	105.4	107.1	104.3
OK	39.3	34.6	35.5	36.1	36.8	35.6	33.7	34.0	30.3	31.5
OR	29.9	26.9	27.2	28.1	26.9	25.5	24.6	24.8	25.5	26.3
PA	146.5	127.2	121.2	124.4	118.9	110.5	103.2	100.0	101.7	99.5
RI	10.9	9.2	8.8	8.9	8.6	7.8	7.6	7.7	7.3	7.3
SC	38.7	34.5	36.0	36.1	37.0	32.5	33.0	32.2	33.1	31.9
SD	10.7	8.2	8.1	8.4	8.2	7.7	7.1	7.4	7.7	7.9
TN	49.8	43.3	44.7	47.9	48.6	46.1	42.7	41.4	43.7	41.8
TX	171.4	159.2	168.4	171.4	177.0	172.5	184.1	188.5	174.7	172.9
UT	20.0	19.9	20.9	22.2	22.9	22.4	23.5	24.7	24.9	27.0
VT	6.7	5.8	6.0	6.2	6.0	6.1	5.2	4.9	5.2	5.2
VA	66.6	61.0	65.0	65.7	65.0	60.6	58.9	58.0	56.5	55.6
WA	50.4	45.4	49.9	51.8	48.9	45.9	43.5	44.6	46.3	46.9
WV	23.4	22.3	22.4	22.4	22.9	21.9	21.1	20.6	20.3	19.9
WI	69.3	58.9	56.9	58.4	55.0	52.0	51.3	51.8	50.0	49.1
WY	6.1	5.7	5.9	6.1	6.1	5.8	5.7	5.9	5.7	5.5

Source: U.S. National Center for Education Statistics, *Digest of Education Statistics,* annual; and *Projections of Education Statistics,* annual.

No. 269. General Educational Development (GED) Credentials Issued, by Age: 1974 to 1990

[In percent, except number issued]

YEAR	GED'S issued (1,000)	PERCENT DISTRIBUTION BY AGE OF TEST TAKER				
		Under 19 years old	20 to 24 years old	25 to 29 years old	30 to 34 years old	35 years old or over
1974	294	35	27	13	9	17
1975	340	33	26	14	9	18
1979	426	37	28	12	13	11
1980	479	37	27	13	8	15
1981	489	37	27	13	8	14
1982	486	37	28	13	8	15
1983	465	34	29	14	8	15
1984	427	32	28	15	9	16
1985	413	32	26	15	10	16
1986	428	32	26	15	10	17
1987	444	33	24	15	10	18
1988	410	35	22	14	10	18
1989	357	36	22	14	10	17
1990	410	35	25	14	10	17

Source: U.S. National Center for Education Statistics, *Digest of Education Statistics,* 1992.

No. 270. College Enrollment and Percent of High School Graduates Enrolled in or Completed 1 or More Years of College, by Sex, Race, and Hispanic Origin: 1960 to 1991

[As of **October**, except as noted. **Covers civilian noninstitutional population 14 to 24 years old**, except as noted]

ITEM AND YEAR	ALL PERSONS				MALE			FEMALE		
	Total [1]	White	Black	His-panic origin [2]	White	Black	His-panic origin [2]	White	Black	His-panic origin [2]
College enrollment (1,000): 1960 [3]	2,279	2,138	[4]141	(NA)	1,297	[4]68	(NA)	841	[4]73	(NA)
1970	6,065	5,535	437	(NA)	3,213	202	(NA)	2,322	236	(NA)
1975	7,228	6,368	699	308	3,437	308	148	2,931	392	160
1980	7,475	6,546	718	325	3,303	292	156	3,243	426	168
1982	7,932	6,810	789	353	3,403	340	147	3,405	448	206
1983	7,737	6,677	772	366	3,422	343	162	3,256	430	205
1984	7,844	6,735	826	367	3,479	383	156	3,256	443	210
1985	7,799	6,729	755	391	3,374	355	178	3,357	400	211
1986	7,613	6,426	820	455	3,206	350	230	3,221	471	226
1987	7,932	6,677	855	463	3,386	390	250	3,289	464	213
1988	7,973	6,796	785	463	3,310	303	237	3,486	482	228
1989	7,987	6,778	867	470	3,286	332	216	3,493	535	255
1990	8,142	6,767	929	448	3,355	442	226	3,413	486	222
1991	8,304	6,917	846	526	3,311	382	216	3,607	461	310
Percent of high school graduates enrolled: 1960 [3]	23.8	24.3	[4]18.7	(NA)	31.1	[4]21.1	(NA)	18.1	[4]16.9	(NA)
1970	33.3	33.9	26.7	(NA)	42.9	29.5	(NA)	26.3	24.7	(NA)
1975	33.1	33.0	32.5	36.2	36.9	33.4	37.9	29.4	32.0	34.8
1980	32.3	32.5	28.3	30.3	34.3	27.0	31.2	30.9	29.2	29.4
1982	33.5	33.6	28.2	30.1	34.9	28.6	28.0	32.3	27.9	31.8
1983	33.1	33.5	27.7	32.3	35.9	27.9	33.1	31.3	27.5	31.8
1984	33.7	34.2	28.0	30.0	36.8	29.6	28.2	31.8	26.8	31.5
1985	34.3	35.0	26.5	27.5	36.6	28.2	26.4	33.6	25.1	28.4
1986	32.9	33.0	28.7	30.6	35.1	28.5	33.6	31.1	28.8	28.2
1987	36.9	37.1	30.6	28.7	39.2	32.3	31.1	35.2	29.4	26.4
1988	37.6	38.4	28.6	31.3	39.6	25.1	32.2	37.3	31.3	30.5
1989	38.5	39.1	31.5	29.4	39.7	27.5	28.2	38.6	34.7	30.5
1990	39.6	39.8	33.7	29.4	40.7	35.1	29.4	38.9	32.4	29.5
1991	41.4	42.0	31.8	34.6	41.9	32.2	29.7	42.1	31.4	39.2
Percent of high school graduates enrolled in college or completed 1 or more years of college: 1960 [3]	40.4	41.0	[4]32.5	(NA)	47.1	[4]33.5	(NA)	35.6	[4]31.8	(NA)
1970	52.3	53.4	39.4	(NA)	60.9	41.4	(NA)	47.2	39.3	(NA)
1975	52.5	52.7	48.1	50.8	56.6	50.5	55.4	49.1	46.4	46.7
1980	51.1	51.4	45.9	47.3	51.8	44.1	49.5	50.9	47.4	45.4
1982	52.7	53.1	45.5	47.3	53.2	44.5	44.8	52.9	46.3	49.2
1983	52.8	53.4	45.0	48.4	53.5	43.6	47.4	53.4	46.3	49.7
1984	53.0	53.8	45.2	46.0	54.2	45.2	45.7	53.4	45.1	46.6
1985	54.3	55.3	43.8	46.7	55.5	43.6	44.9	55.2	44.0	48.0
1986	55.0	55.5	47.8	45.6	55.1	44.4	44.4	55.8	50.4	46.8
1987 [5]	56.2	56.8	48.1	44.0	56.4	48.0	45.1	57.2	48.1	42.8
1988 [5]	57.4	58.5	46.3	47.0	57.8	42.5	48.3	59.1	49.2	45.8
1989 [5]	57.9	58.9	49.1	43.6	58.5	45.8	42.7	59.2	51.8	44.5
1990 [5]	58.9	60.1	48.0	44.7	58.7	48.9	46.5	61.4	47.3	43.0
1991 [5]	60.7	62.3	46.1	47.6	59.9	46.1	42.2	64.5	47.0	52.4

NA Not available. [1] Includes other races, not shown separately. [2] Persons of Hispanic origin may be of any race. [3] As of April. [4] Black and other races. [5] Population 16 to 24 years old.

Source: U.S. Bureau of the Census, *U.S. Census of Population: 1960*, vol. I, *Characteristics of the Population*, part 1; *Current Population Reports*, series P20-469, and earlier reports; and unpublished data.

No. 271. Enrollment in a Institutions of Higher Education, by Sex, and Attendance Status, 1983 and 1988, and Projections, 1991 to 2003

[As of fall. In thousands]

SEX AND AGE	1983		1988		1991, proj.		1998, proj.		2003, proj.	
	Total	Part-time	Total	Part-time	Total	Part-time	Total	Part-time	Total	Part-time
Total	12,465	5,204	13,055	5,619	14,169	6,137	15,167	6,625	16,124	6,796
Male	6,024	2,264	6,002	2,340	6,412	2,522	6,794	2,725	7,386	2,879
14 to 17 years old	102	16	55	5	79	12	117	14	142	15
18 to 19 years old	1,256	158	1,290	132	1,352	141	1,458	170	1,580	189
20 to 21 years old	1,241	205	1,243	216	1,366	257	1,355	292	1,587	350
22 to 24 years old	1,158	382	1,106	378	1,123	358	1,176	352	1,372	420
25 to 29 years old	1,115	624	875	485	960	552	926	498	895	460
30 to 34 years old	570	384	617	456	592	429	540	391	514	372
35 years old and over	583	494	816	668	940	772	1,220	1,008	1,297	1,073
Female	6,441	2,940	7,053	3,278	7,757	3,615	8,373	3,900	8,738	3,918
14 to 17 years old	142	16	115	17	93	15	108	17	113	18
18 to 19 years old	1,496	179	1,536	195	1,445	178	1,632	216	1,787	243
20 to 21 years old	1,125	204	1,278	218	1,377	258	1,416	265	1,631	298
22 to 24 years old	884	378	932	403	1,103	445	1,110	438	1,259	502
25 to 29 years old	947	658	932	633	1,083	686	1,093	678	1,018	632
30 to 34 years old	721	553	698	499	833	576	810	536	781	519
35 years old and over	1,126	953	1,563	1,313	1,824	1,459	2,203	1,749	2,149	1,707

Source: U. S. Department of Education, National Center for Education Statistics, *Projections of Education Statistics*, annual.

No. 272. College Enrollment, by Sex, Age, Race, and Hispanic Origin: 1972 to 1991

[In thousands. As of **October** for the **civilian noninstitutional population, 14 years old and over.** Based on the Current Population Survey; see text, section 1 and Appendix III]

SEX, AGE, AND RACE	1972	1975	1980	1983	1984	1985	1986[1]	1987	1988	1989	1990	1991
Total[2]	9,095	10,880	11,387	12,367	12,305	12,524	12,651	12,719	13,116	13,180	13,621	14,057
Male[3]	5,218	5,911	5,430	6,038	5,989	5,906	5,957	6,030	5,950	5,950	6,192	6,439
18 to 24 years	3,534	3,693	3,604	3,820	3,929	3,749	3,702	3,867	3,770	3,717	3,922	3,954
25 to 34 years	1,178	1,521	1,325	1,576	1,492	1,464	1,545	1,421	1,395	1,443	1,412	1,605
35 years old and over	365	569	405	535	476	561	628	625	727	716	772	832
Female[3]	3,877	4,969	5,957	6,329	6,316	6,618	6,694	6,689	7,166	7,231	7,427	7,618
18 to 24 years	2,724	3,243	3,625	3,657	3,662	3,788	3,775	3,826	4,021	4,085	4,042	4,218
25 to 34 years	581	947	1,378	1,510	1,522	1,599	1,559	1,564	1,568	1,637	1,749	1,680
35 years old and over	418	614	802	1,009	1,009	969	1,100	1,240	1,176	1,452	1,396	1,636
White	8,147	9,547	9,926	10,607	10,522	10,782	10,707	10,731	11,140	11,243	11,488	11,686
Male	4,723	5,263	4,803	5,187	5,111	5,101	5,074	5,104	5,078	5,136	5,235	5,304
Female	3,427	4,285	5,123	5,420	5,410	5,681	5,632	5,627	6,063	6,107	6,253	6,382
Black	727	1,099	1,163	1,227	1,274	1,208	1,359	1,351	1,321	1,287	1,393	1,477
Male	384	523	476	537	590	518	580	587	494	480	587	629
Female	343	577	686	690	684	689	779	764	827	807	807	848
Hispanic origin[4]	242	411	443	579	563	665	794	739	747	754	748	830
Male	126	218	222	273	248	301	377	390	355	353	364	347
Female	117	193	221	306	315	363	417	349	391	401	384	483

[1] Revised. See footnote 2, table 229.   [2] Includes other races not shown separately.   [3] Includes persons 14 to 17 years old, not shown separately.   [4] Persons of Hispanic origin may be of any race.
Source: U.S. Bureau of the Census, *Current Population Reports*, series P20-469; and earlier reports.

No. 273. College Enrollment, by Selected Characteristics: 1980 to 1990

[**In thousands.** As of **fall.** Totals may differ from other tables because of adjustments to underreported and nonreported racial/ethnic data. Nonresident alien students are not distributed among racial/ethnic groups]

CHARACTERISTIC	1980	1984	1988	1990
Total	12,086.8	12,233.0	13,043.1	13,710.2
Male	5,868.1	5,858.3	5,998.2	6,238.5
Female	6,218.7	6,374.7	7,044.9	7,471.6
Public	9,456.4	9,456.4	10,156.4	10,740.6
Private	2,630.4	2,776.6	2,886.7	2,969.7
2-year	4,521.4	4,526.9	4,868.1	5,181.0
4-year	7,565.4	7,706.1	8,175.0	8,529.1
Undergraduate	10,469.1	10,610.8	11,304.2	11,862.9
Graduate	1,340.9	1,343.7	1,471.9	1,573.6
Professional	276.8	278.5	267.1	273.6
White[1]	9,833.0	9,814.7	10,283.2	10,674.8
Male	4,772.9	4,689.9	4,711.6	4,840.8
Female	5,060.1	5,124.7	5,571.6	5,834.0
Public	7,656.1	7,542.4	7,963.8	8,339.5
Private	2,176.9	2,272.3	2,319.4	2,335.2
2-year	3,558.5	3,514.3	3,701.5	3,917.9
4-year	6,274.5	6,300.4	6,581.6	6,756.8
Undergraduate	8,480.7	8,484.0	8,906.7	9,231.3
Graduate	1,104.7	1,087.3	1,153.2	1,221.1
Professional	247.7	243.4	223.2	222.4
Black[1]	1,106.8	1,075.8	1,129.6	1,223.3
Male	463.7	436.8	442.7	476.3
Female	643.0	639.0	686.9	747.0
Public	876.1	844.0	881.1	952.3
Private	230.7	231.8	248.5	270.9
2-year	472.5	458.7	473.3	508.7
4-year	634.3	617.0	656.3	714.6
Undergraduate	1,018.8	994.9	1,038.8	1,123.8
Graduate	75.1	67.4	76.5	83.6
Professional	12.8	13.4	14.3	15.8
Hispanic	471.7	534.9	680.0	758.1
Male	231.6	253.8	310.3	344.1
Female	240.1	281.2	369.6	413.9
Public	406.2	456.1	586.9	648.3
Private	65.5	78.9	93.1	109.8

CHARACTERISTIC	1980	1984	1988	1990
2-year	255.1	288.8	383.9	413.6
4-year	216.6	246.1	296.0	344.5
Undergraduate	433.1	495.2	631.2	701.8
Graduate	32.1	31.7	39.5	45.8
Professional	6.5	8.0	9.3	10.5
American Indian[1]	83.9	83.6	92.5	102.6
Male	37.8	37.4	39.1	43.0
Female	46.1	46.1	53.4	59.7
Public	74.2	72.1	81.1	90.3
Private	9.7	11.4	11.5	12.4
2-year	47.0	45.5	50.4	54.4
4-year	36.9	38.1	42.1	48.2
Undergraduate	77.9	77.8	85.9	95.1
Graduate	5.2	4.8	5.6	6.4
Professional	0.8	1.0	1.1	1.1
Asian[1]	286.4	389.5	496.7	554.8
Male	151.3	210.0	259.2	286.6
Female	135.2	179.5	237.5	268.2
Public	239.7	322.7	405.7	445.3
Private	46.7	66.8	91.0	109.5
2-year	124.3	167.1	199.3	211.8
4-year	162.1	222.4	297.4	343.0
Undergraduate	248.7	343.0	436.6	484.8
Graduate	31.6	37.1	45.7	51.7
Professional	6.1	9.3	14.4	18.4
Nonresident alien	305.0	334.6	361.2	396.6
Male	210.8	230.4	235.3	247.6
Female	94.2	104.1	125.9	149.0
Public	204.1	219.0	237.8	264.8
Private	100.8	115.5	123.3	131.8
2-year	64.1	52.5	59.6	74.5
4-year	240.9	282.1	301.5	322.1
Undergraduate	209.9	215.8	205.0	226.1
Graduate	92.2	115.3	151.4	165.2
Professional	2.9	3.4	4.7	5.4

[1] Non-Hispanic.
Source: U.S. National Center for Education Statistics, *Digest of Education Statistics*, 1992.

No. 274. Higher Education—Summary: 1970 to 1991

[Institutions, staff, and enrollment as of fall. Finances for fiscal year ending in the following year. Covers universities, colleges, professional schools, junior and teachers colleges, both publicly and privately controlled, regular session. Includes estimates for institutions not reporting. See also Appendix III, and *Historical Statistics, Colonial Times to 1970*, series H 680, H 699-705, and H 710]

ITEM	Unit	1970	1980	1985	1986	1987	1988	1989	1990	1991 [1]
Institutions [2]	Number.	2,556	3,231	3,340	3,406	3,587	3,565	3,535	3,559	3,601
4-year	Number .	1,665	1,957	2,029	2,070	2,135	2,129	2,127	2,141	2,157
2-year	Number .	891	1,274	1,311	1,336	1,452	1,436	1,408	1,418	1,444
Instructional staff [3]	1,000. . .	474	686	715	722	793	804	824	(NA)	(NA)
Percent full-time	Percent .	78	66	64	66	66	(NA)	64	(NA)	(NA)
Total enrollment [4]	1,000. . .	8,581	12,097	12,247	12,504	12,767	13,055	13,539	13,710	14,169
Male	1,000. . .	5,044	5,874	5,818	5,885	5,932	6,002	6,190	6,239	6,412
Female	1,000. . .	3,537	6,223	6,429	6,619	6,835	7,053	7,349	7,472	7,757
4-year institutions.	1,000. . .	6,262	7,571	7,716	7,824	7,990	8,180	8,388	8,529	8,900
2-year institutions.	1,000. . .	2,319	4,526	4,531	4,680	4,776	4,875	5,151	5,181	5,269
Full time.	1,000. . .	5,816	7,098	7,075	7,120	7,231	7,437	7,661	7,780	8,032
Part time	1,000. . .	2,765	4,999	5,172	5,384	5,536	5,619	5,878	5,930	6,137
Public	1,000. . .	6,428	9,457	9,479	9,714	9,973	10,161	10,578	10,741	11,040
Private	1,000. . .	2,153	2,640	2,768	2,790	2,793	2,894	2,961	2,970	3,129
Undergraduate [5]	1,000. . .	7,376	10,475	10,597	10,798	11,046	11,317	11,743	11,863	12,163
Men	1,000. . .	4,254	5,000	4,962	5,018	5,068	5,138	5,311	5,339	5,452
Women	1,000. . .	3,122	5,475	5,635	5,780	5,978	6,179	6,432	6,524	6,711
First-time freshmen.	1,000. . .	2,063	2,588	2,292	2,219	2,246	2,379	2,341	2,263	(NA)
First professional.	1,000. . .	173	278	274	270	268	267	274	274	303
Men	1,000. . .	159	199	180	174	170	167	168	167	179
Women	1,000. . .	15	78	94	97	98	100	105	107	124
Graduate [5]	1,000. . .	1,031	1,343	1,376	1,435	1,452	1,472	1,522	1,574	1,703
Men	1,000. . .	630	675	677	693	693	698	710	733	781
Women	1,000. . .	400	670	700	742	759	774	811	841	922
Current funds revenues [6]	Mil. dol .	23,879	65,585	100,438	108,810	117,340	128,502	139,635	149,766	(NA)
Tuition and fees	Mil. dol. .	5,021	13,773	23,117	25,706	27,837	30,807	33,926	37,434	(NA)
Federal government.	Mil. dol. .	3,198	9,748	12,705	13,904	14,772	15,894	17,255	18,236	(NA)
State government	Mil. dol. .	6,595	20,106	29,912	31,309	33,517	36,031	38,349	39,481	(NA)
Auxiliary enterprises	Mil. dol. .	3,125	7,287	10,674	11,364	11,948	12,856	13,938	14,903	(NA)
Plant funds	Mil. dol. .	(NA)	4,774	7,713	(NA)	(NA)	(NA)	(NA)	(NA)	(NA)
Increase in fund balance [8]	Mil. dol. .	498	2,793	7,239	(NA)	(NA)	(NA)	(NA)	(NA)	(NA)
Current funds expenditures [6]	Mil. dol .	23,375	64,053	97,536	105,764	113,786	123,867	134,656	146,088	(NA)
Educational and general [9]	Mil. dol. .	17,616	50,074	76,128	82,956	89,157	96,803	105,585	114,140	(NA)
Auxiliary enterprises [10]	Mil. dol. .	2,988	7,288	10,528	11,037	11,400	12,280	13,204	14,272	(NA)
Gross addition to plant value .	Mil. dol. .	4,165	6,471	10,149	(NA)	(NA)	(NA)	(NA)	(NA)	(NA)
Value of plant	Mil. dol. .	46,054	88,761	122,261	(NA)	(NA)	(NA)	(NA)	(NA)	(NA)
Endowment (book value)	Mil. dol. .	11,341	20,941	38,698	(NA)	(NA)	(NA)	(NA)	(NA)	(NA)

NA Not available. [1] Projection. [2] Beginning 1980, number of institutions includes count of branch campuses. Due to revised survey procedures, data beginning 1987 are not comparable with previous years. [3] Due to revised survey methods, data beginning 1987 not comparable with previous years. [4] Beginning 1980, branch campuses counted according to actual status, e.g., 2-year branch in 2-year category; previously a 2-year branch included in university category. [5] Includes unclassified students. (Students taking courses for credit, but are not candidates for degrees.) [6] Includes items not shown separately. [7] Annual net increase in plant funds. [8] Includes endowment, and, beginning 1980, annuity and student loans. [9] Data for 1970 are not strictly comparable with later years. [10] Includes activities.

Source: U.S. Department of Education, National Center for Education, Statistics, *Digest of Education Statistics*, annual; *Projections of Education Statistics*, annual; and unpublished data.

No. 275. Junior (2-Year) Colleges—Summary: 1970 to 1991

[Institutions and their enrollment as of fall; financial data fiscal year ending the following year. Prior to 1975, excludes 2-year branches of universities and other 4-year institutions. Beginning 1980, includes schools accredited by the National Association of Trade and Technical Schools. See *Historical Statistics, Colonial Times to 1970*, series H 690-692 and H 705, for related but not comparable data. See also Appendix III]

ITEM	Unit	1970	1975	1980	1985	1986	1987	1988	1989	1990 [1]	1991 [1]
Institutions [2]	Number.	891	1,128	1,274	1,311	1,336	1,452	1,436	1,408	1,418	1,444
Public	Number .	654	897	945	932	960	992	984	968	972	999
Private	Number .	237	231	329	379	376	460	452	440	446	445
Enrollment	1,000. . .	2,223	3,970	4,526	4,531	4,680	4,776	4,875	5,083	5,193	5,261
Public	1,000. . .	2,102	3,836	4,329	4,270	4,414	4,541	4,615	4,821	4,921	4,989
Private	1,000. . .	121	134	198	261	266	235	260	263	272	272
Male	1,000. . .	1,317	2,165	2,047	2,002	2,061	2,073	2,090	2,187	2,227	2,248
Female	1,000. . .	906	1,805	2,479	2,529	2,619	2,704	2,785	2,897	2,966	3,013
Current funds revenue [3]	Mil. dol .	2,504	5,304	8,505	12,293	13,116	14,060	15,387	16,777	(NA)	(NA)
Tuition and fees	Mil. dol. .	413	896	1,618	2,618	2,844	3,057	3,376	3,623	(NA)	(NA)
State government	Mil. dol. .	926	2,248	3,961	5,659	5,982	6,350	6,898	7,558	(NA)	(NA)
Local government	Mil. dol. .	701	1,187	1,623	2,207	2,200	2,352	2,662	2,831	(NA)	(NA)
Current funds expenditures.	Mil. dol .	2,327	5,092	8,212	11,976	12,779	13,644	14,726	16,077	(NA)	(NA)
Education and general [4]	Mil. dol. .	2,073	4,736	7,608	11,118	11,875	12,701	13,676	14,936	(NA)	(NA)
Instruction	Mil. dol. .	1,205	2,401	3,764	5,398	5,729	6,082	6,617	7,236	(NA)	(NA)

NA Not available. [1] Preliminary. [2] See footnote 2, table 274. [3] Includes items not shown separately. [4] Includes mandatory transfers.

Source: U.S. National Center for Education Statistics, *Digest of Education Statistics*, annual; *Financial Statistics of Institutions of Higher Education*, annual; and *Projections of Education Statistics*, annual.

No. 276. Institutions of Higher Education—Number, 1991, and Enrollment 1980 and 1991, and by Selected Characteristics, 1991—States and Other Areas

[Number of institutions beginning in academic year. Opening fall enrollment of resident and extension students attending full-time or part-time. Excludes students taking courses for credit by mail, radio, or TV, and students in branches of U.S. institutions operated in foreign countries. See Appendix III]

STATE OR OTHER AREA	Total enroll-ment, 1980 (1,000)	Num-ber of insti-tu-tions [1]	1991										
			Enrollment, prel. (1,000)										
			Total	Male	Female	Public	Pri-vate	Full-time	White [2]	Minority enrollment			Non-resi-dent alien
										Total [3]	Black [2]	His-panic	
U.S.	12,097	3,601	14,359	6,502	7,857	11,310	3,049	8,115	10,990	2,953	1,335	867	416
Northeast	2,587	857	2,834	1,264	1,570	1,658	1,175	1,739	2,232	503	240	142	99
N.E.	766	255	823	364	458	427	395	498	703	87	34	23	32
ME	43	31	57	24	33	41	16	33	55	2	(Z)	(Z)	1
NH	47	29	64	28	36	35	29	40	60	3	1	1	1
VT	31	22	37	16	21	21	16	26	35	1	(Z)	(Z)	1
MA	418	116	419	187	232	181	239	266	344	53	19	14	22
RI	67	12	79	36	44	43	37	49	69	7	3	2	3
CT	160	45	166	74	92	107	59	84	140	21	10	6	5
M.A.	1,822	602	2,011	899	1,112	1,231	780	1,240	1,529	416	206	119	67
NY	992	321	1,056	465	592	606	451	662	752	267	126	84	38
NJ	322	60	335	149	185	271	64	169	246	76	35	24	13
PA	508	221	620	285	335	354	266	410	531	73	44	12	16
Midwest	3,044	932	3,570	1,625	1,946	2,817	753	2,043	3,011	466	270	91	93
E.N.C	2,169	571	2,490	1,132	1,358	1,982	508	1,387	2,050	379	226	78	62
OH	489	159	569	263	306	436	133	348	490	65	48	6	15
IN	247	79	290	136	154	228	62	191	256	26	16	5	8
IL	644	167	753	340	414	571	182	374	553	183	94	52	17
MI	520	101	568	255	314	486	82	289	473	80	55	9	15
WI	269	65	309	138	171	260	49	186	277	25	12	5	7
W.N.C	875	361	1,080	492	587	834	245	656	961	87	45	14	32
MN	207	81	255	116	139	200	55	150	234	15	5	2	6
IA	140	61	171	80	91	120	51	121	154	9	4	2	8
MO	234	93	297	135	162	203	94	169	254	35	25	4	8
ND	34	20	39	19	19	35	4	31	35	3	(Z)	(Z)	1
SD	33	19	36	16	20	29	7	25	33	3	(Z)	(Z)	1
NE	90	36	114	51	62	95	19	65	105	7	3	2	2
KS	137	51	168	75	92	152	15	96	146	16	7	4	6
South	3,437	1162	4,428	1,979	2,449	3,704	724	2,634	3,287	1,031	643	260	110
S.A.	1,724	592	2,259	1,000	1,260	1,820	439	1,280	1,688	515	357	93	57
DE	33	10	43	19	24	35	8	26	36	7	5	1	1
MD	226	56	268	116	152	229	39	123	193	67	48	5	8
DC	87	17	78	36	42	12	66	48	40	29	23	2	9
VA	281	83	356	158	198	298	58	200	278	72	52	6	7
WV	82	28	89	39	49	78	10	60	82	4	3	(Z)	2
NC	288	122	372	163	209	305	66	229	287	79	67	3	6
SC	132	61	165	71	94	137	28	113	126	36	33	1	3
GA	184	111	277	125	152	219	58	184	203	67	58	3	6
FL	412	104	612	272	340	506	105	296	442	154	67	71	16
E.S.C	614	277	776	343	432	656	120	523	622	140	127	4	14
KY	143	64	188	79	109	156	32	120	171	15	12	1	3
TN	205	81	238	108	130	186	52	156	194	39	35	2	4
AL	164	86	224	102	123	202	22	152	170	50	46	1	5
MS	102	46	125	55	71	111	14	95	86	37	35	(Z)	2
W.S.C	1,099	293	1,393	636	757	1,228	165	832	978	376	158	163	39
AR	78	35	94	40	54	82	12	67	78	15	13	1	2
LA	160	36	197	85	112	169	29	136	136	56	48	4	5
OK	160	47	184	83	100	160	23	128	147	30	13	3	6
TX	701	175	917	427	490	817	101	500	617	274	85	156	26
West	2,978	640	3,474	1,589	1,885	3,078	396	1,646	2,418	943	175	371	113
Mt	658	191	920	429	491	816	104	484	745	152	23	86	23
MT	35	19	38	18	20	33	4	28	33	3	(Z)	(Z)	1
ID	43	11	55	25	30	44	11	37	51	3	(Z)	1	2
WY	21	9	32	14	18	31	1	18	30	2	(Z)	1	1
CO	163	59	235	109	126	207	28	124	195	35	7	19	5
NM	58	30	94	41	52	90	4	48	56	36	3	26	2
AZ	203	39	273	127	146	254	19	122	210	56	8	32	7
UT	94	15	130	66	64	95	36	86	118	7	1	3	5
NV	41	9	63	28	35	62	1	20	51	11	3	4	1
Pac	2,321	449	2,554	1,160	1,394	2,262	292	1,162	1,673	791	152	285	90
WA	304	61	275	122	153	238	36	155	231	38	9	8	6
OR	157	46	167	79	88	144	23	93	145	16	3	4	6
CA	1,791	318	2,024	920	1,104	1,805	220	870	1,257	694	138	272	73
AK	21	7	31	12	18	29	2	12	25	5	1	1	1
HI	47	17	57	26	31	46	12	32	16	36	1	1	5
U.S. military [4]	50	10	53	46	7	53	-	53	42	10	8	1	1
Other:													
American Samoa	1	1	1	1	1	1	-	1	(Z)	1	-	-	(Z)
Guam	3	2	5	2	3	5	-	2	(Z)	4	(Z)	(Z)	(Z)
No. Marianas	-	1	1	(Z)	(Z)	1	-	(Z)	(Z)	1	(Z)	(Z)	(Z)
Puerto Rico	131	58	158	62	96	55	103	125	(Z)	157	(Z)	157	1
Virgin Islands	2	2	3	1	2	3	-	1	(Z)	2	2	(Z)	(Z)

- Represents zero.   Z Less than 500 or 50.   [1] Branch campuses counted as separate institutions.   [2] Non-Hispanic.
[3] Includes other races not shown separately.   [4] Military academies.

Source: U.S. National Center for Education Statistics, *Digest of Education Statistics,* annual.

No. 277. Higher Education Price Indexes: 1965 to 1991

[1983 = 100. For years ending June 30. Reflects prices paid by colleges and universities]

YEAR	Index, total	Average annual percent change [1]	PERSONNEL COMPENSATION				CONTRACTED SERVICES, SUPPLIES, AND EQUIPMENT					
			Total	Professional salaries	Nonprofessional salaries	Fringe benefits	Total	Services	Supplies and materials	Equipment	Library acquisitions	Utilities
1965 ..	29.8	4.1	30.5	34.9	31.0	13.0	27.6	35.8	33.8	36.0	19.3	15.7
1970 ..	39.5	6.7	42.1	47.7	38.8	24.7	31.9	42.8	37.6	41.9	25.7	16.3
1971 ..	42.1	6.4	44.8	50.1	41.8	28.0	34.1	45.1	39.0	43.5	30.8	18.0
1972 ..	44.3	5.3	47.1	52.0	44.9	31.1	36.0	47.8	39.8	45.1	34.9	19.2
1973 ..	46.7	5.3	49.8	54.3	47.6	34.7	37.6	49.9	41.1	46.5	37.7	20.2
1974 ..	49.9	6.9	52.8	57.2	50.6	38.6	41.4	52.2	46.5	49.4	41.6	24.8
1975 ..	54.3	8.8	56.3	60.3	54.6	42.9	48.5	56.8	58.0	58.3	46.7	31.8
1976 ..	57.9	6.7	60.0	63.5	59.0	47.8	51.8	60.0	60.7	61.7	53.7	34.4
1977 ..	61.7	6.6	63.5	66.4	63.1	52.8	56.1	63.5	63.8	64.8	58.6	40.5
1978 ..	65.8	6.6	67.6	69.9	68.1	58.4	60.4	67.0	66.6	69.3	64.3	45.9
1979 ..	70.6	7.3	72.4	74.1	73.4	64.5	65.2	71.0	71.7	74.7	71.4	50.3
1980 ..	77.5	9.8	78.4	79.4	80.2	72.6	75.0	76.5	84.6	81.6	79.5	64.1
1981 ..	85.9	10.8	85.8	86.3	87.7	81.8	86.2	85.3	95.6	89.6	89.3	79.7
1982 ..	94.0	9.4	93.5	93.7	94.6	91.5	95.3	94.8	100.4	96.4	95.5	92.4
1983 ..	100.0	6.4	100.0	100.0	100.0	100.0	100.0	100.0	100.0	100.0	100.0	100.0
1984 ..	104.7	4.7	105.4	104.7	105.2	108.3	102.8	104.7	103.1	102.2	103.8	100.8
1985 ..	110.5	5.5	112.0	111.4	109.1	117.7	106.1	109.2	105.4	104.8	108.5	103.0
1986 ..	115.6	4.6	118.8	118.2	113.0	127.7	106.2	114.3	104.2	106.9	117.2	95.5
1987 ..	120.4	4.1	125.4	125.0	116.4	137.5	105.2	117.8	103.5	108.8	129.9	84.4
1988 ..	125.8	4.5	131.6	130.9	120.4	147.1	108.4	122.1	107.9	110.9	138.7	84.4
1989 ..	133.1	5.8	139.5	138.8	125.2	158.8	114.0	129.0	116.9	115.8	149.9	85.2
1990 ..	140.8	5.8	148.2	147.6	130.2	171.4	118.8	134.2	118.7	120.8	163.6	88.4
1991 ..	149.8	5.3	156.6	155.6	135.5	184.5	123.8	140.2	121.4	123.4	179.0	91.2

[1] Change from immediate prior year.
Source: Research Associates of Washington, Washington, DC, *Inflation Measures for Schools and Colleges*, annual (copyright).

No. 278. Institutions of Higher Education—Finances: 1980 to 1991

[In millions of dollars. For fiscal years ending in year shown. For coverage, see headnote, table 274. See also Appendix III and *Historical Statistics, Colonial Times to 1970* , series H 729-738 and H 747-749]

ITEM	1980	1985	1986	1987	1988	1989	1990	1991 Total	1991 Public	1991 Private
Current funds revenues	58,520	92,473	100,438	108,810	117,340	128,502	139,635	149,766	94,905	54,861
Tuition and fees.	11,930	21,283	23,117	25,706	27,837	30,807	33,926	37,434	15,258	22,176
Federal government	8,902	11,509	12,705	13,904	14,772	15,894	17,255	18,236	9,763	8,473
State government.	18,378	27,583	29,912	31,309	33,517	36,031	38,349	39,481	38,240	1,241
Local government	1,588	2,387	2,545	2,799	3,006	3,364	3,640	3,931	3,532	400
Private gifts, grants, and contracts [1]	2,808	4,896	5,411	5,953	6,359	7,061	7,781	8,361	3,651	4,710
Endowment earnings [2]	1,177	2,096	2,276	2,378	2,586	2,914	3,144	3,269	431	2,837
Educational activities [2]	1,239	2,127	2,373	2,642	2,918	3,316	3,632	4,055	2,700	1,355
Auxiliary enterprises	6,481	10,100	10,674	11,364	11,948	12,856	13,938	14,903	9,059	5,844
Hospitals	(³)	7,475	8,227	9,278	10,627	11,991	13,217	15,150	9,787	5,362
Other funds revenues [4]	6,015	3,015	3,199	3,477	3,770	4,269	4,753	4,946	2,483	2,463
Current funds expenditures [5] . . .	56,914	89,951	97,536	105,764	113,786	123,867	134,656	146,088	92,961	53,127
Educational and general	44,543	70,061	76,128	82,956	89,157	96,803	105,585	114,140	74,395	39,744
Instruction	18,497	28,777	31,032	33,711	35,834	38,813	42,146	45,496	31,371	14,125
Institutional support	5,054	8,587	9,351	10,085	10,774	11,529	12,674	13,726	8,031	5,696
Research	5,099	7,552	8,437	9,352	10,351	11,432	12,506	13,444	9,364	4,080
Plant operation [6]	4,700	7,345	7,605	7,819	8,231	8,740	9,458	10,063	6,656	3,407
Academic support	3,876	6,074	6,667	7,575	8,142	8,904	9,438	10,051	6,934	3,117
Libraries	1,624	2,362	2,551	2,441	2,836	3,010	3,254	3,344	2,167	1,177
Student services	2,567	4,178	4,563	4,976	5,397	5,781	6,388	7,025	4,398	2,627
Scholarships and fellowships	2,200	3,670	4,160	4,776	5,325	5,919	6,656	7,551	2,689	4,863
Unrestricted funds	905	1,962	2,285	2,645	2,941	3,283	3,854	4,445	1,270	3,175
Restricted funds.	1,296	1,709	1,875	2,131	2,384	2,636	2,802	3,106	1,418	1,688
Public service	1,817	2,861	3,120	3,448	3,786	4,227	4,690	5,076	3,990	1,086
Mandatory transfers	732	1,016	1,192	1,212	1,318	1,458	1,630	1,707	962	744
Auxiliary enterprises [5]	6,486	10,012	10,528	11,037	11,400	12,280	13,204	14,272	9,050	5,222
Hospitals [5]	4,757	8,010	8,692	9,173	10,406	11,825	12,679	14,326	9,316	5,010
Independent operations [5]	1,128	1,868	2,187	2,598	2,823	2,959	3,187	3,350	200	3,150

[1] Private grants represent nongovernmental revenue for sponsored research and other sponsored programs; includes private contracts. [2] Sales and service of educational departments only. [3] Included in other. [4] Includes sales and services of federally funded research and development centers, and others sources. [5] Includes mandatory transfers which are primarily current expenditures for plant. [6] Includes maintenance.
Source: U.S. National Center for Education Statistics, *Digest of Education Statistics*, annual.

No. 279. Major Federal Student Financial Assistance Programs—Number of Recipients and Funds Utilized, by Type of Program: 1970 to 1993

[For award years July 1 of year shown to the following June 30, except as indicated. Funds utilized exclude operating costs, etc., and represent funds given to students]

PROGRAM	Unit	1970	1980	1985	1988	1989	1990, est.	1991, est.	1992, est.	1993, est.
Pell Grants:										
Number of recipients...	1,000...	(X)	2,858	2,910	3,341	3,473	3,562	3,669	3,884	3,406
Funds utilized........	Mil. dol. .	(X)	2,387	3,572	4,471	4,768	4,906	5,268	5,583	6,288
Average grant	Dollars..	(X)	835	1,227	1,338	1,373	1,377	1,436	1,437	1,846
Supplemental Educational Opportunity Grants: [1]										
Number of recipients...	1,000...	253.4	716.5	686.0	678.8	727.6	761.2	835.0	907.0	908.0
Funds utilized........	Mil. dol. .	134	368	410	423	466	503	584	648	663
Average grant	Dollars..	527	513	598	621	641	661	700	715	730
Perkins Loans: [2]										
Number of recipients...	1,000...	452.0	813.4	700.9	692.1	695.9	660.2	688.0	699.0	571.0
Loan funds utilized [3] ...	Mil. dol. .	241	694	703	874	903	870	860	873	720
Average loan	Dollars..	532	853	1,003	1,262	1,297	1,318	1,250	1,250	1,261
Loans in default [4]	Mil. dol. .	(NA)	612.0	690.0	749.8	741.1	727.5	(NA)	(NA)	(NA)
Default rate	Percent .	(NA)	11.6	8.3	7.3	6.8	6.2	(NA)	(NA)	(NA)
College Work-Study:										
Number of recipients...	1,000...	425.0	819.1	728.4	672.7	676.7	687.4	697.3	812.0	813.0
Funds utilized	Mil. dol. .	200	660	656	625	664	728	760	808	813
Average annual earnings	Dollars..	470	806	901	930	980	1,059	1,089	995	1,000
Stafford Loans: [5]										
Number of loans...	1,000...	1,017	2,904	3,730	4,584	4,558	4,587	4,403	4,677	5,551
Loan funds utilized [6] ...	Mil. dol. .	1,015	6,200	8,839	11,965	12,166	12,669	12,336	13,427	16,425
Average loan	Dollars..	998	2,135	2,369	2,610	2,669	2,762	2,802	2,871	2,959
Loans in default [7]	Mil. dol. .	(NA)	1,440	4,256	8,417	10,454	13,134	16,373	19,452	(NA)
Default rate [8]	Percent .	(NA)	10.1	8.9	9.2	9.6	10.4	11.6	12.9	(NA)

NA Not available.   X Not applicable.   [1] For 1970, data represents Educational Opportunity Grants Program.   [2] Formerly National Direct Student Loans.   [3] Includes institutional matching funds.   [4] Loans in default represents all loans in institutions' portfolio.   [5] Formerly Guaranteed Student Loans. Beginning with 1985, data include activity under the PLUS (Parent Loans for Undergraduate Students), FISL (Federally Insured Student Loans), and SLS (Supplemental Loans Students) programs. [6] Represents dollar amount of commitments.   [7] As of September 30 of year shown.   [8] Cumulative dollar amount of default claims to lenders, minus cumulative collections as a percent of all loans that have ever gone into repayment.
Source: U.S. Dept. of Education, Office of Postsecondary Education, unpublished data.

No. 280. Finances of Public Institutions of Higher Education, 1988 to 1991, and by State, 1991

[For academic years ending in year shown. Data provided by the State higher education finance officers]

YEAR AND STATE	FTE [1] enroll-ment (1,000)	APPROPRIA-TIONS FOR CURRENT OPERATIONS [2] Total (mil. dol.)	Per FTE [1] student (dol.)	NET TUITION REVENUES [3] Total (mil. dol.)	Per FTE [1] student (dol.)	YEAR AND STATE	FTE [1] enroll-ment (1,000)	APPROPRIA-TIONS FOR CURRENT OPERATIONS [2] Total (mil. dol.)	Per FTE [1] student (dol.)	NET TUITION REVENUES [3] Total (mil. dol.)	Per FTE [1] student (dol.)
Total, 1988 ..	7,358.2	29,356.0	3,990	9,225.0	1,254	MN	179.6	798.4	4,444	284.1	1,581
Total, 1989 ..	7,583.2	31,199.0	4,114	10,157.0	1,339	MS	95.5	288.7	3,023	146.4	1,533
Total, 1990 ..	7,909.3	33,737.0	4,265	11,298.0	1,428	MO	150.8	559.5	3,709	273.7	1,814
Total, 1991	**8,119.2**	**35,083.1**	**4,321**	**12,415.4**	**1,529**	MT	28.1	103.3	3,682	31.4	1,119
						NE.......	65.9	254.8	3,868	84.2	1,278
AL........	170.5	557.1	3,268	289.2	1,697	NV	30.8	142.1	4,613	39.9	1,295
AK........	15.2	154.1	10,141	23.7	1,560	NH	26.2	70.0	2,676	95.2	3,639
AZ........	153.5	615.7	4,011	259.1	1,688	NJ........	175.3	923.4	5,267	339.1	1,934
AR........	64.9	229.6	3,537	109.5	1,687	NM	63.1	319.6	5,068	65.5	1,039
CA........	1,275.3	6,004.0	4,708	715.3	561	NY.......	438.8	2,246.5	5,120	573.2	1,306
CO	131.4	391.3	2,978	297.1	2,261	NC	224.5	1,153.8	5,139	223.2	995
CT........	63.3	397.4	6,275	134.5	2,124	ND	28.4	105.6	3,719	56.6	1,994
DE........	24.3	107.0	4,394	103.8	4,263	OH	344.4	1,248.6	3,625	813.4	2,362
DC........	8.4	73.5	8,793	8.0	957	OK	105.7	451.5	4,272	119.4	1,130
FL........	334.4	1,685.4	5,040	346.2	1,035	OR	102.1	434.3	4,255	154.6	1,515
GA	183.7	807.4	4,395	238.4	1,298	PA........	286.1	1,247.9	4,362	980.0	3,426
HI	30.0	249.1	8,312	22.0	734	RI	27.4	109.4	3,993	76.1	2,778
ID	35.0	175.1	5,005	24.6	703	SC	105.6	455.1	4,311	239.6	2,270
IL	375.3	1,568.1	4,179	365.5	974	SD	20.1	66.1	3,295	40.4	2,014
IN	171.1	723.5	4,230	384.0	2,245	TN	144.5	562.8	3,896	218.5	1,512
IA	100.8	477.2	4,736	211.3	2,097	TX	612.0	2,274.2	3,716	666.8	1,089
KS	104.7	411.4	3,930	144.6	1,381	UT........	65.1	271.4	4,167	90.5	1,390
KY........	114.8	429.2	3,739	148.7	1,295	VT........	15.7	37.7	2,396	101.5	6,451
LA	125.7	381.8	3,037	231.6	1,842	VA........	215.4	812.9	3,774	417.8	1,940
ME	35.7	166.0	4,652	62.6	1,754	WA	155.1	768.6	4,954	189.6	1,222
MD	166.7	684.7	4,108	302.9	1,817	WV	60.6	167.2	2,758	97.2	1,603
MA	121.8	519.8	4,269	248.1	2,038	WI	188.1	868.3	4,617	381.2	2,027
MI	336.4	1,402.7	4,169	928.0	2,758	WY	21.6	130.3	6,034	17.5	810

[1] Full-time equivalent (FTE). Credit and non-credit program enrollment including summer session. Excludes medical enrollments.   [2] State and local appropriations. Includes aid to students attending in-State public institutions. Excludes sums for research, agriculture stations and cooperative extension, and hospitals and medical schools.   [3] Excludes appropriated aid to students attending in-State public institutions.
Source: Research Associates of Washington, Washington, DC, *State Profiles: Financing Public Higher Education,* annual (copyright).

No. 281. Institutions of Higher Education—Charges: 1975 to 1991

[In dollars. Estimated. **For the entire academic year ending in year shown.** Figures are average charges per full-time equivalent student. Room and board are based on full-time students]

ACADEMIC CONTROL AND YEAR	TUITION AND REQUIRED FEES [1]				BOARD RATES [2]				DORMITORY CHARGES			
	All institutions	2-yr. colleges	4-yr. colleges	Other 4-yr. schools	All institutions	2-yr. colleges	4-yr. colleges	Other 4-yr. schools	All institutions	2-yr. colleges	4-yr. colleges	Other 4-yr. schools
Public:												
1975.....	432	277	599	448	625	638	634	613	506	424	527	497
1980.....	583	355	840	662	867	893	898	833	715	574	750	703
1985.....	971	584	1,386	1,117	1,241	1,302	1,276	1,201	1,196	921	1,237	1,200
1989.....	1,285	730	1,846	1,515	1,533	1,488	1,576	1,504	1,457	965	1,483	1,506
1990.....	1,356	756	2,035	1,608	1,635	1,581	1,728	1,561	1,513	962	1,561	1,554
1991.....	1,454	824	2,159	1,707	1,691	1,594	1,767	1,641	1,612	1,050	1,658	1,655
Private:												
1975.....	2,117	1,367	2,614	1,954	700	660	771	666	586	564	691	536
1980.....	3,130	2,062	3,811	3,020	955	923	1,078	912	827	766	1,001	768
1985.....	5,315	3,485	6,843	5,135	1,462	1,294	1,647	1,405	1,426	1,424	1,753	1,309
1989.....	7,461	4,817	9,451	7,172	1,880	1,609	2,269	1,762	1,849	1,540	2,353	1,686
1990.....	8,174	5,196	10,348	7,778	1,948	1,811	2,339	1,823	1,923	1,663	2,411	1,774
1991.....	8,772	5,570	11,379	8,389	2,074	1,989	2,470	1,943	2,063	1,744	2,654	1,889

[1] For in-State students. [2] Beginning 1989, rates reflect 20 meals per week, rather than meals served 7 days a week.
Source: U.S. National Center for Education Statistics, *Digest of Education Statistics*, annual.

No. 282. Voluntary Financial Support of Higher Education: 1970 to 1991

[For school years ending in years shown; enrollment as of fall of preceding year. Voluntary support, as defined in Gift Reporting Standards, excludes income from endowment and other invested funds as well as all support received from Federal, State, and local governments and their agencies]

ITEM	Unit	1970	1980	1985	1986	1987	1988	1989	1990	1991
Estimated support, total [1]	Mil. dol	1,780	3,800	6,320	7,400	8,500	8,200	8,925	9,800	10,200
Individuals	Mil. dol.	822	1,757	2,876	3,606	4,412	3,969	4,369	4,770	4,990
Alumni	Mil. dol.	381	910	1,460	1,825	2,346	2,042	2,292	2,540	2,680
Business corporations	Mil. dol.	269	696	1,574	1,702	1,819	1,853	1,947	2,170	2,230
Foundations..............	Mil. dol.	434	903	1,175	1,363	1,513	1,607	1,742	1,920	2,030
Religious denominations.....	Mil. dol.	102	155	208	211	204	197	237	240	240
Current operations.........	Mil. dol.	960	2,250	3,800	4,022	4,420	4,666	5,045	5,440	5,830
Capital purposes..........	Mil. dol.	820	1,550	2,520	3,378	4,080	3,534	3,880	4,360	4,370
Enrollment, higher education...	1,000..	8,094	11,570	12,242	12,247	12,504	12,767	13,055	13,458	13,673
Support per student	Dollars.	220	328	516	604	680	642	684	728	746
In **1990-91** dollars	Dollars.	781	567	654	744	818	742	755	768	746
Expenditures, higher education .	Bil. dol.	24.7	62.5	98.3	107.7	116.6	125.3	136.2	147.8	155.6
Expenditures per student	Dollars.	3,052	5,402	8,030	8,794	9,325	9,814	10,433	10,982	11,380
In **1990-91** dollars	Dollars.	10,834	9,317	10,165	10,824	11,229	11,342	11,522	11,577	11,380
Institutions reporting support	Number	1,045	1,019	1,114	1,194	1,174	1,142	1,132	1,056	1,046
Total support reported	**Mil. dol**	**1,472**	**3,055**	**5,295**	**6,332**	**7,323**	**7,041**	**7,546**	**8,214**	**8,559**
Private 4-year institutions....	Mil. dol.	1,154	2,178	3,522	4,164	4,844	4,466	4,847	5,072	5,262
Public 4-year institutions.....	Mil. dol.	292	856	1,728	2,104	2,413	2,506	2,625	3,056	3,222
2-year colleges............	Mil. dol.	26	20	45	64	65	69	74	85	75

[1] Includes other contributions not shown separately.
Source: Council for Aid to Education, New York, NY, *Voluntary Support of Education*, annual.

No. 283. Institutions of Higher Education—Average Salaries and Fringe Benefits for Faculty Members, by Type of Control: 1970 to 1992

[In thousands of dollars. For academic year ending in year shown. Figures are for 9 months teaching for full-time faculty members in 4-year colleges and universities]

TYPE OF CONTROL AND ACADEMIC RANK	1970	1975	1980	1985	1986	1987	1988	1989	1990	1991	1992
AVERAGE SALARIES											
Public: All ranks...........	13.1	16.6	22.1	31.2	33.4	35.8	37.2	39.6	41.9	44.0	45.3
Professor	17.3	21.7	28.8	39.6	42.3	45.3	47.2	50.1	53.2	55.8	57.4
Associate professor.......	13.2	16.7	21.9	30.2	32.2	34.2	35.6	37.9	40.3	42.2	43.4
Assistant professor........	10.9	13.7	18.0	25.0	26.7	28.5	29.6	31.7	33.5	35.2	36.3
Instructor..............	9.1	11.2	14.8	19.5	20.9	21.8	22.2	23.9	25.0	26.3	27.2
Private: [1] All ranks...........	13.1	16.6	22.1	33.0	35.4	37.8	39.7	42.4	45.1	47.0	50.0
Professor	17.8	22.4	30.1	44.1	47.0	50.3	52.2	55.9	59.6	61.6	66.1
Associate professor.......	12.6	16.0	21.0	30.9	32.9	34.9	36.6	38.8	41.2	43.2	45.6
Assistant professor........	10.3	13.0	17.0	25.0	26.8	28.3	30.1	31.9	34.0	35.5	37.8
Instructor..............	8.6	10.9	13.3	19.0	19.8	20.4	22.7	24.1	26.0	26.2	28.5
AVERAGE FRINGE BENEFITS											
All ranks combined:											
Public................	1.9	2.5	3.9	7.0	7.3	7.8	8.2	9.0	9.8	10.5	11.0
Private [1]...............	2.2	2.8	4.1	7.2	8.0	8.6	9.2	10.0	10.9	11.6	12.4

[1] Excludes church-related colleges and universities.
Source: Maryse Eymonerie Associates/American Association of University Professors, Washington, DC, *AAUP Annual Report on the Economic Status of the Profession*.

No. 284. Institutions of Higher Education—Tenure Status of Full-Time Faculty, by Type and Control of Institution and Rank and Sex of Faculty: 1991

[In percent. Data are for those institutions of higher education reporting tenure status. Excludes schools with no tenure]

TYPE OF INSTITUTION AND CONTROL	Total faculty	ACADEMIC RANK						SEX	
		Profes-sor	Associate professor	Assistant professor	Instruc-tor	Lecturer	No academic rank	Male	Female
All institutions	61.1	95.6	80.8	18.5	6.5	7.0	35.9	67.7	45.2
4-year	61.7	95.7	80.4	15.8	4.1	6.0	19.1	68.5	43.8
University	65.2	97.2	85.4	9.0	3.5	2.1	1.4	71.6	43.5
Other 4-year . . .	59.4	94.6	77.2	19.6	4.3	9.2	30.3	66.3	44.0
2-year	56.8	93.6	85.2	50.3	15.3	26.8	39.3	60.5	51.7
Public institutions . . .	62.8	96.3	83.7	21.5	8.2	8.5	36.1	69.3	47.3
4-year	64.0	96.5	83.5	17.8	5.3	7.3	11.4	70.7	45.8
University	66.3	97.3	88.3	9.7	4.2	2.4	0.4	72.8	44.5
Other 4-year . . .	62.2	95.9	79.8	23.3	5.7	10.7	23.6	69.0	46.6
2-year	57.0	93.7	85.4	51.0	15.6	26.9	39.2	60.6	52.0
Private institutions . .	56.4	93.8	73.5	11.8	1.5	1.1	32.9	63.4	39.7
4-year	56.5	93.8	73.6	11.7	1.5	1.1	31.2	63.4	39.7
University	61.7	96.8	76.3	7.1	1.4	1.4	6.2	68.1	40.7
Other 4-year . . .	54.0	91.9	72.4	13.5	1.5	0.5	36.3	60.9	39.4
2-year	45.3	90.2	70.9	29.0	4.3	(NA)	48.2	52.8	39.1

NA Not available.
Source: U.S. National Center for Education Statistics, *Digest of Education Statistics*, 1992.

No. 285. College Freshmen—Summary Characteristics: 1970 to 1992

[In percent. As of **fall** for first-time full-time freshmen. Based on sample survey and subject to sampling error; see source]

CHARACTERISTIC	1970	1980	1985	1986	1987	1988	1989	1990	1991	1992
Sex: Male	55	49	48	48	47	46	46	46	47	46
Female	45	51	52	52	53	54	54	54	53	54
Applied to four or more colleges	[1]15	26	29	32	33	37	37	36	34	33
Average grade in high school:										
A- to A+.	16	21	21	23	21	24	23	23	24	26
B- to B+.	58	60	59	56	59	58	59	58	57	57
C to C+	27	19	20	20	19	19	17	19	19	17
D	1	1	1	1	1	1	-	-	-	-
Political orientation:										
Liberal	34	20	21	22	22	22	22	23	24	24
Middle of the road	45	60	57	56	56	54	54	55	54	53
Conservative.	17	17	19	19	18	20	21	20	19	19
Probable field of study:										
Arts and humanities	16	9	8	9	9	10	9	9	8	8
Biological sciences	4	4	4	4	4	4	4	4	4	5
Business	16	24	27	26	27	26	25	21	18	16
Education.	11	7	7	8	9	9	9	10	9	10
Engineering	9	12	11	11	10	10	10	8	10	9
Physical science	2	3	2	2	2	2	2	2	2	2
Social science.	14	7	8	8	9	9	10	10	8	9
Professional	(NA)	15	13	12	11	12	13	15	18	20
Technical	4	6	5	4	3	2	3	4	4	3
Data processing/computer programming	(NA)	2	2	2	1	1	1	1	1	1
Other [2]	(NA)	(NA)	16	15	16	16	15	16	17	17
Communications.	(NA)	2	2	2	3	3	3	2	2	2
Computer science.	(NA)	1	2	2	2	2	2	2	2	1
Recipient of financial aid:										
Pell grant	(NA)	33	19	17	17	20	22	23	23	23
Supplemental educational opportunity grant	(NA)	8	5	5	6	6	6	7	7	6
State scholarship or grant	(NA)	16	14	14	16	14	15	16	13	14
College grant	(NA)	13	19	18	13	20	20	22	22	24
Federal guaranteed student loan	(NA)	21	23	25	22	22	23	23	22	23
Perkins loan [3]	(NA)	9	6	7	5	3	2	8	7	8
College loan	(NA)	4	4	4	5	6	8	6	5	6
College work-study grant.	(NA)	15	10	10	10	10	10	10	11	12
Attitudes—agree or strongly agree:										
Activities of married women are best confined to home and family	48	27	22	20	26	26	26	25	26	26
Capital punishment should be abolished	56	34	27	26	24	23	21	22	21	21
Legalize marijuana.	38	39	22	21	20	19	17	19	21	23
There is too much concern for the rights of criminals.	52	66	(NA)	(NA)	68	69	69	(NA)	65	67
Abortion should be legalized	(NA)	54	55	59	59	57	65	65	63	64

- Represents or rounds to zero.   NA Not available.   [1] 1969 data.   [2] Includes other fields, not shown separately.
[3] National Direct Student Loan prior to 1990.
Source: The Higher Education Research Institute, University of California, Los Angeles, CA, *The American Freshman: National Norms*, annual.

No. 286. Freshman Enrollment in Remedial Courses, by Institutional Characteristic: 1989

[In percent, except number of freshmen. As of fall. Remedial courses are those developed for students lacking skills necessary to perform college-level work as required by the institution. Based on survey and subject to sampling error; for details, see source]

INSTITUTIONAL CHARACTERISTIC	Number of freshmen (1,000)	INSTITUTIONS OFFERING COURSES				FRESHMEN TAKING COURSES			
		Total	Reading	Writing	Math	Total	Reading	Writing	Math
All institutions	2,242	74	58	65	68	30	13	16	21
Control: Public	1,784	91	82	87	89	32	13	17	23
Private	457	58	34	44	47	22	12	11	12
Type: 2-year	1,069	90	82	84	84	36	16	20	26
4-year	1,173	64	41	53	57	24	9	12	15
Size of institution:									
Fewer than 1,000	109	60	76	47	48	26	9	15	18
1,000 to 4,999	650	78	64	69	75	33	16	17	22
5,000 or more	1,483	87	76	81	81	29	11	15	20

Source: U.S. National Center for Education Statistics, "College Level Remedial Education in the Fall of 1989," FRSS-38.

No. 287. Foreign (Nonimmigrant) Student Enrollment in Institutions of Higher Education, by Region of Origin, 1976 to 1992, and by Field of Study, 1980 and 1990

[For fall of the previous year]

REGION OF ORIGIN	ENROLLMENT (1,000)									PERCENT ENROLLED IN—					
										Engineering		Science[1]		Business	
	1976	1980	1985	1987	1988	1989	1990	1991	1992	1980	1990	1980	1990	1980	1990
All regions	179	286	342	350	356	366	387	408	420	25	19	8	9	16	19
Africa	25	36	40	32	28	26	25	24	22	20	15	9	8	19	20
Nigeria	11	16	18	12	8	6	4	4	3	19	12	9	5	22	20
Asia [2]	97	165	200	218	224	232	245	263	277	32	23	8	10	16	18
China: Taiwan	11	18	23	26	27	29	31	34	36	17	26	15	10	17	17
Hong Kong	12	10	10	11	11	11	11	13	13	22	17	9	6	26	33
India	10	9	15	18	21	23	26	29	23	31	35	16	11	21	16
Indonesia	1	2	7	9	9	9	9	10	10	27	20	7	4	21	37
Iran	20	51	17	'12	10	9	7	6	5	45	29	7	14	11	7
Japan	7	12	13	15	18	24	30	37	42	7	5	5	3	19	21
Malaysia	2	4	22	22	19	16	14	14	13	13	30	14	4	22	28
Saudi Arabia	3	10	8	6	5	5	4	4	4	30	26	4	4	14	14
South Korea	3	5	16	20	21	21	22	23	26	17	19	11	12	15	15
Thailand	7	7	7	6	6	7	7	7	8	17	14	6	4	26	35
Europe	14	23	33	36	39	43	46	50	54	15	12	9	8	14	21
Latin America [3]	30	42	49	43	45	45	48	48	43	20	14	8	6	14	19
Mexico	5	6	6	5	6	6	7	7	7	16	13	7	8	11	18
Venezuela	5	10	10	5	4	3	3	3	3	30	17	8	7	11	19
North America	10	16	16	16	16	17	19	19	20	8	8	6	6	13	15
Canada	10	15	15	16	16	16	18	18	19	8	8	6	6	12	14
Oceania	3	4	4	4	4	4	4	4	4	5	5	7	6	16	18

[1] Physical and life sciences.   [2] Includes countries not shown separately.   [3] Includes Central America, Caribbean, and South America.

Source: Institute of International Education, New York, NY, *Open Doors*, annual (copyright).

No. 288. Higher Education Registrations in Foreign Languages: 1960 to 1990

[As of fall]

ITEM	1960	1965	1968	1970	1974	1977	1980	1983	1986	1990
Registrations [1] (1,000)	[2]647.1	1,034.9	1,127.4	1,111.5	946.6	933.5	924.8	966.0	1,003.2	1,184.1
Index (1960=100)	100.0	159.9	174.2	171.8	146.3	144.3	142.9	149.3	155.0	183.0
By selected language (1,000):										
Spanish	178.7	310.3	364.9	389.2	362.2	376.7	379.4	386.2	411.3	533.9
French	228.8	371.6	388.1	359.3	253.1	246.1	248.4	270.1	275.3	272.5
German	146.1	213.9	216.3	202.6	152.1	135.4	126.9	128.2	121.0	133.3
Italian	11.1	22.9	30.4	34.2	33.0	33.3	34.8	38.7	40.9	49.7
Japanese	1.7	3.4	4.3	6.6	9.6	10.7	11.5	16.1	23.5	45.7
Russian	30.6	33.7	40.7	36.1	32.5	27.8	24.0	30.4	34.0	44.6
Latin	[2]25.7	39.6	35.0	27.6	25.2	24.4	25.0	24.2	25.0	28.2
Chinese	1.8	3.4	5.1	6.2	10.6	9.8	11.4	13.2	16.9	19.5
Ancient Greek	[2]12.7	19.5	19.3	16.7	24.4	25.8	22.1	19.4	17.6	16.4
Hebrew	3.8	8.1	10.2	16.6	22.4	19.4	19.4	18.2	15.6	13.0
Portuguese	1.0	3.0	4.0	5.1	5.1	5.0	4.9	4.4	5.1	6.2
Arabic	0.5	0.9	1.1	1.3	2.0	3.1	3.5	3.4	3.4	3.5
12 languages as percent of total.	99.3	99.6	99.3	99.2	98.5	98.3	98.5	98.6	98.6	98.5

[1] Includes other foreign languages, not shown separately.   [2] Estimated.

Source: Association of Departments of Foreign Languages, New York, NY, *ADFL Bulletin*, vol. 23, No. 3, and earlier issues (copyright).

No. 289. Salary Offers to Candidates for Degrees, by Field of Study: 1989 to 1992

[In dollars. Data are average beginning salaries based on offers made by business, industrial, government, and nonprofit and educational employers to graduating students. Data from representative colleges throughout the United States]

FIELD OF STUDY	BACHELOR'S				MASTER'S [1]				DOCTOR'S			
	1989	1990	1991	1992	1989	1990	1991	1992	1989	1990	1991	1992
Accounting	25,290	26,391	26,642	27,179	28,874	29,647	30,996	31,259	(NA)	(NA)	(NA)	(NA)
Business, general [2]	22,274	23,529	24,019	24,305	33,903	36,175	35,241	35,734	(NA)	(NA)	(NA)	(NA)
Marketing [3]	22,523	23,543	23,713	23,914	34,462	35,440	43,182	39,508	(NA)	(NA)	(NA)	(NA)
Engineering:												
Civil	26,735	28,136	29,658	29,376	30,723	32,336	34,551	34,303	37,214	44,481	43,060	46,501
Chemical	32,949	35,122	37,492	39,203	36,131	37,862	40,457	40,611	47,853	50,524	52,992	54,451
Computer	30,413	31,490	32,280	32,848	37,183	35,748	38,348	40,207	53,380	50,526	56,584	55,325
Electrical	30,661	31,778	33,190	33,754	36,435	37,526	38,804	41,024	48,666	53,147	54,612	56,826
Mechanical	30,539	32,064	33,999	34,462	35,260	36,506	38,114	39,298	45,893	49,887	46,866	51,880
Nuclear [4]	31,281	31,750	32,175	34,447	34,024	36,728	38,086	38,607	(NA)	(NA)	(NA)	(NA)
Petroleum	32,987	35,202	38,882	40,679	38,475	38,412	43,608	43,600	(NA)	(NA)	(NA)	(NA)
Engineering tech.	28,310	29,318	30,098	31,051	(NA)	(NA)	(NA)	(NA)	(NA)	(NA)	(NA)	(NA)
Chemistry	26,698	27,494	26,836	27,557	32,157	32,320	33,575	35,104	43,215	45,356	47,911	50,719
Mathematics	26,789	27,032	27,370	28,434	31,498	30,069	30,061	33,636	37,500	42,775	41,146	40,954
Physics	28,296	28,002	29,227	29,019	29,889	31,480	35,207	31,626	42,632	41,486	39,913	40,940
Humanities	23,010	23,213	23,567	22,941	25,799	(NA)	(NA)	(NA)	(NA)	(NA)	(NA)	(NA)
Social sciences [5]	20,205	21,627	21,375	21,623	23,814	(NA)	(NA)	(NA)	(NA)	(NA)	(NA)	(NA)
Computer science	28,557	29,804	30,696	30,523	35,823	36,849	37,894	39,120	50,049	54,788	58,300	61,555

NA Not available.   [1] Candidates with 1 year or less of full-time nonmilitary employment.   [2] For master's degree, offers are after nontechnical undergraduate degree.   [3] Includes distribution.   [4] Includes engineering physics.   [5] Excludes economics.
Source: College Placement Council, Inc., Bethlehem, PA, Salary Survey, *A Study of Beginning Offers*, annual (copyright).

No. 290. Time Spent Earning Bachelor's Degree, by Selected Characteristic: 1990

[As of spring. Based on Survey of Income and Program Participation; for details, see source]

CHARACTERISTIC	Total with bachelor's degrees (1,000)	YEARS TO BA DEGREE FROM END OF HIGH SCHOOL						Mean dura-tion
		Number (1,000)			Percent			
		4 years or less	5 years or less	6 years or less	4 years or less	5 years or less	6 years or less	
All persons	33,553	14,509	21,905	24,822	43.2	65.3	74.0	6.21
Male	18,145	6,893	10,914	12,710	38.0	60.1	70.0	6.23
Female	15,409	7,616	10,991	12,111	49.4	71.3	78.6	6.19
White	30,048	13,267	19,845	22,347	44.2	66.0	74.4	6.18
Male	16,374	6,297	9,920	11,509	38.5	60.6	70.3	6.20
Female	13,675	6,970	9,926	10,838	51.0	72.6	79.3	6.16
Black	1,908	623	1,052	1,266	32.7	55.1	66.4	7.01
Male	846	242	428	536	28.6	50.6	63.4	7.12
Female	1,062	382	624	731	36.0	58.8	68.8	6.92
Hispanic origin [1]	1,065	395	610	733	37.1	57.3	68.8	6.58
Male	579	210	343	410	36.3	59.2	70.8	6.05
Female	487	184	267	323	37.8	54.8	66.3	7.21
Field of Bachelor's degree: [2]								
Agriculture/Forestry	273	79	162	189	28.9	59.3	69.2	6.30
Biology	670	281	449	514	41.9	67.0	76.7	5.75
Business/Management	4,871	1,872	2,959	3,499	38.4	60.7	71.8	6.47
Economics	587	246	371	454	41.9	63.2	77.3	5.47
Education	3,456	1,628	2,335	2,609	47.1	67.6	75.5	6.55
Engineering	2,449	738	1,333	1,553	30.1	54.4	63.4	6.80
English/Journalism	1,121	538	831	923	48.0	74.1	82.3	5.79
Home Economics	322	217	266	282	67.4	82.6	87.6	4.73
Law	73	11	23	28	(B)	(B)	(B)	(B)
Liberal Arts/Humanities	2,321	964	1,416	1,675	41.5	61.0	72.2	6.38
Mathematics/Statistics	485	192	294	364	39.6	60.6	75.1	5.81
Medicine/Dentistry	140	52	103	126	(B)	(B)	(B)	(B)
Nursing/Pharmacy/Technical Health	1,379	403	759	888	29.2	55.0	64.4	7.65
Physical/Earth Sciences	529	203	352	387	38.4	66.5	73.2	5.84
Police Science/Law Enforcement	196	69	76	98	(B)	(B)	(B)	(B)
Psychology	700	247	409	505	35.3	58.4	72.1	6.39
Religion/Theology	153	58	82	90	(B)	(B)	(B)	(B)
Social Sciences	1,441	666	942	1,037	46.2	65.4	72.0	6.54
Vo-tech Studies	141	46	86	102	(B)	(B)	(B)	(B)
Other	1,539	595	984	1,120	38.7	63.9	72.8	6.14
Advanced degree	10,708	5,405	7,673	8,377	50.5	71.7	78.2	5.71

B Base is less than 200,000 persons.   [1] Persons of Hispanic origin may be of any race.   [2] For persons whose highest degree is the BA.
Source: U.S. Bureau of the Census, *Current Population Reports*, series P70-32.

No. 291. Earned Degrees Conferred, by Level of Degree and Sex, 1950 to 1990 and Projections, 1995 to 2003

[In thousands, except percent. Beginning 1960, includes Alaska and Hawaii. See *Historical Statistics, Colonial Times to 1970*, series H-751-763 for similar data. See also Appendix III]

YEAR ENDING	DEGREES Total	DEGREES Percent male	ASSOCIATE'S Male	ASSOCIATE'S Female	BACHELOR'S Male	BACHELOR'S Female	MASTER'S Male	MASTER'S Female	FIRST PROFES- SIONAL Male	FIRST PROFES- SIONAL Female	DOCTOR'S Male	DOCTOR'S Female
1950 [1]	497	75.7	(NA)	(NA)	329	103	41	17	(NA)	(NA)	6	1
1960 [1]	477	65.8	(NA)	(NA)	254	138	51	24	(NA)	(NA)	9	1
1965	664	61.6	(NA)	(NA)	289	213	78	40	27	1	15	2
1970	1,271	59.2	117	89	451	341	126	83	33	2	26	4
1971	1,393	59.0	144	108	476	364	138	92	36	2	28	5
1972	1,509	58.7	166	126	501	387	150	102	41	3	28	5
1973	1,586	58.1	175	141	518	404	154	109	46	4	29	6
1974	1,653	57.5	189	155	527	418	158	119	49	5	27	6
1975	1,666	56.1	191	169	505	418	162	131	49	7	27	7
1976	1,726	55.7	210	181	505	421	167	145	53	10	26	8
1977	1,741	54.7	211	196	496	424	168	149	52	12	25	8
1978	1,744	53.3	205	208	487	434	161	150	52	14	24	8
1979	1,727	52.1	192	211	477	444	153	148	53	16	24	9
1980	1,731	51.1	184	217	474	456	151	147	53	17	23	10
1981	1,752	50.3	189	228	470	465	147	149	53	19	23	10
1982	1,788	49.8	197	238	473	480	146	150	52	20	22	10
1983	1,822	49.6	207	249	479	490	145	145	51	22	22	11
1984	1,819	49.6	203	250	482	492	144	141	51	23	22	11
1985	1,828	49.3	203	252	483	497	143	143	50	25	22	11
1986	1,830	49.0	196	250	486	502	144	145	49	25	22	12
1987	1,825	48.4	192	246	481	510	141	148	47	25	22	12
1988	1,835	48.0	190	245	477	518	145	154	45	25	23	12
1989	1,873	47.3	186	250	483	535	149	161	45	26	23	13
1990	1,937	46.7	191	264	491	558	154	170	44	27	24	14
1995, proj.	2,144	45.4	200	297	535	631	166	188	49	37	24	17
2000, proj.	2,218	45.7	214	314	559	649	167	186	51	36	23	19
2003, proj.	2,355	46.2	228	329	607	696	179	186	52	36	22	20

NA Not available. [1] First-professional degrees are included with bachelor's degrees.
Source: U.S. National Center for Education Statistics, *Digest of Education Statistics*, annual and *Projections of Education Statistics to 2003*, annual.

No. 292. Earned Degrees Below Bachelor's, by Curriculum: 1984 to 1990

[Covers associate degrees and other awards based on post-secondary curriculums of less than 4 years in institutions of higher education]

FIELD OF STUDY	1984	1985	1986	1987	1988	1989	1990	PERCENT FEMALE 1984	PERCENT FEMALE 1990
All degrees.	610,332	614,749	604,634	590,683	601,713	601,280	640,098	54.3	57.0
Agriculture and natural resources. . . .	10,641	10,466	9,263	8,680	8,769	7,541	9,321	28.9	29.7
Architecture and environmental design.	1,927	1,939	2,016	2,260	2,520	2,452	2,528	84.3	86.9
Area and ethnic studies	64	69	115	266	172	208	242	60.9	72.7
Business and management.	166,238	170,170	168,168	161,813	158,844	153,072	153,248	66.5	73.0
Communications [1]	4,162	4,580	4,528	4,561	4,414	5,300	4,570	43.2	41.3
Computer and information sciences	16,111	15,896	13,307	11,972	11,936	10,321	13,373	49.1	54.2
Education	8,503	8,551	8,354	8,095	7,958	8,314	8,827	72.2	72.7
Engineering [1]	100,080	100,146	97,609	97,731	104,036	94,655	93,467	7.9	8.5
Foreign languages	372	427	526	484	584	629	707	57.5	61.8
Health sciences	107,142	107,248	104,051	96,261	96,119	96,884	109,398	87.0	85.1
Home economics	14,344	14,966	14,760	14,333	15,142	15,286	18,511	75.0	76.3
Law	2,551	2,948	3,259	3,728	4,661	6,068	7,935	83.1	83.5
Letters	822	681	812	574	574	626	774	64.8	65.5
Liberal/general studies	109,451	107,814	109,529	109,764	114,882	119,577	129,783	54.9	58.8
Library and archival sciences	260	253	208	203	165	204	215	86.2	89.8
Life sciences	1,297	1,205	1,080	1,136	980	1,050	1,197	52.4	54.5
Mathematics	821	813	705	691	695	664	813	36.4	36.2
Military sciences	87	34	[2]1,000	[2]1,009	141	164	129	4.6	11.6
Multi/interdisciplinary studies	8,398	8,697	9,873	9,842	11,053	11,444	11,916	54.5	55.7
Parks and recreation	819	893	787	660	717	678	593	50.9	36.3
Philosophy, religion, and theology . . .	1,740	1,830	1,810	1,371	1,427	1,502	1,593	44.3	45.9
Physical sciences	2,990	2,296	2,230	2,179	1,998	2,079	2,295	34.7	38.0
Psychology	1,147	1,032	1,005	1,068	1,135	1,143	1,143	67.0	74.3
Protective services	15,554	16,057	15,592	17,786	17,832	17,901	20,174	23.8	24.3
Public affairs	5,812	6,230	6,245	6,478	7,007	8,765	10,471	47.2	32.6
Social sciences	2,755	2,613	2,753	2,782	2,915	2,962	3,131	57.1	55.1
Visual and performing arts	26,244	24,358	24,015	24,327	23,107	21,438	22,790	32.7	33.7
Undistributed	-	2,537	1,034	629	1,960	10,353	10,954	(X)	47.7

- Represents zero. X Not applicable. [1] Includes technologies. [2] Includes a certificate program.
Source: U.S. National Center for Education Statistics, *Digest of Education Statistics*, annual.

No. 293. Earned Degrees Conferred, by Field of Study and Level of Degree: 1971 to 1990

LEVEL AND FIELD OF STUDY	1971	1980	1985	1988	1989	1990	PERCENT FEMALE 1971	PERCENT FEMALE 1990
Bachelor's, total	839,730	929,417	979,477	994,829	1,018,755	1,049,657	43.4	53.2
Agriculture and natural resources	12,672	22,802	18,107	14,222	13,492	13,070	4.2	31.5
Architecture and environmental design	5,570	9,132	9,325	8,603	9,150	9,261	11.9	39.1
Area and ethnic studies	2,582	2,840	2,867	3,453	3,945	4,399	52.4	60.0
Business and management	114,865	185,361	233,351	243,725	247,175	249,081	9.1	46.7
Communications [1]	10,802	28,616	42,083	46,726	48,645	51,283	35.3	60.6
Computer and information sciences	2,388	11,154	38,878	34,523	30,454	27,434	13.6	30.1
Education	176,614	118,169	88,161	91,287	97,082	104,715	74.5	78.1
Engineering [1]	50,046	68,893	96,105	88,706	85,225	82,110	0.8	13.8
Foreign languages	19,945	11,133	9,954	10,045	10,780	11,326	74.6	73.4
Health sciences	25,190	63,607	64,513	60,754	59,138	58,816	77.1	84.3
Home economics	11,167	18,411	15,555	14,855	14,715	14,987	97.3	90.1
Law	545	683	1,157	1,303	1,976	1,582	5.0	67.8
Letters	64,933	33,497	34,091	39,551	43,387	48,075	65.5	67.0
Liberal/general studies	5,461	20,069	19,191	21,790	23,498	24,956	29.0	58.3
Library and archival sciences	1,013	398	202	123	122	84	92.0	81.0
Life sciences	35,743	46,370	38,445	36,755	36,059	37,170	29.1	50.7
Mathematics	24,801	11,378	15,146	15,904	15,218	14,597	38.0	46.5
Military sciences	357	251	299	350	419	417	0.3	7.9
Multi/interdisciplinary studies	8,306	14,404	15,727	17,353	18,215	19,188	28.4	54.4
Parks and recreation	1,621	5,753	4,593	4,078	4,183	4,404	34.7	55.9
Philosophy, religion, and theology	11,890	13,276	12,439	11,526	11,742	12,010	25.5	30.9
Physical sciences	21,412	23,410	23,732	17,806	17,186	16,131	13.8	31.2
Psychology	37,880	41,962	39,811	45,003	48,737	53,586	44.5	71.5
Protective services	2,045	15,015	12,510	13,367	14,698	15,387	9.2	37.8
Public affairs	6,252	18,422	13,838	14,294	15,270	16,241	60.2	67.3
Social sciences [2]	155,236	103,519	91,461	100,288	107,914	116,925	36.8	44.2
Visual and performing arts	30,394	40,892	37,936	36,638	37,925	39,695	59.7	61.4
Unclassified	-	-	-	1,801	2,405	2,727	-	49.1
Master's, total	230,509	298,081	286,251	299,317	310,621	323,844	40.1	52.6
Agriculture and natural resources	2,457	3,976	3,928	3,479	3,245	3,373	5.9	33.4
Architecture and environmental design	1,705	3,139	3,275	3,159	3,383	3,492	13.8	36.4
Area and ethnic studies	1,032	852	879	903	1,004	1,198	38.3	45.2
Business and management	26,481	55,006	67,527	69,655	73,521	77,203	3.9	34.0
Communications [1]	1,856	3,082	3,669	3,925	4,257	4,369	34.6	60.8
Computer and information sciences	1,588	3,647	7,101	9,197	9,414	9,643	10.3	27.7
Education	88,952	103,951	76,137	77,867	82,533	86,057	56.2	75.8
Engineering [1]	16,443	16,243	21,557	23,388	24,572	24,848	1.1	13.8
Foreign languages	4,755	2,236	1,724	1,844	1,898	1,995	65.5	68.6
Health sciences	5,445	15,068	17,383	18,665	19,293	20,354	55.9	77.7
Home economics	1,452	2,690	2,383	2,053	2,166	2,153	93.9	85.6
Law	955	1,817	1,796	1,880	2,013	1,869	4.8	29.9
Letters	11,148	6,807	5,934	6,194	6,676	7,223	60.2	66.0
Liberal/general studies	549	1,373	1,180	1,354	1,450	1,594	44.3	65.2
Library and archival sciences	7,001	5,374	3,893	3,713	3,953	4,349	81.3	77.9
Life sciences	5,728	6,510	5,059	4,784	4,961	4,861	33.6	51.1
Mathematics	5,191	2,860	2,882	3,442	3,447	3,677	29.2	40.0
Military sciences	2	46	119	49	-	-	-	-
Multi/interdisciplinary studies	1,157	3,579	3,184	3,098	3,236	3,505	30.9	42.3
Parks and recreation	218	647	544	461	452	430	29.8	58.4
Philosophy, religion, and theology	4,036	5,126	5,519	5,913	5,924	6,012	27.1	36.2
Physical sciences	6,367	5,219	5,796	5,733	5,723	5,447	13.3	26.4
Psychology	4,431	7,806	8,408	7,872	8,552	9,231	37.2	67.6
Protective services	194	1,805	1,235	1,024	1,047	1,151	10.3	30.8
Public affairs	8,215	18,413	16,045	17,290	17,918	17,993	49.2	65.6
Social sciences [2]	16,476	12,101	10,380	10,294	10,867	11,419	28.5	40.8
Visual and performing arts	6,675	8,708	8,714	7,937	8,265	8,546	47.4	56.1
Unclassified	-	-	-	4,144	851	1,852	-	60.3
Doctorate's, total	32,107	32,615	32,943	34,870	35,720	38,238	14.3	36.3
Agriculture and natural resources	1,086	991	1,213	1,142	1,183	1,272	2.9	19.1
Architecture and environmental design	36	79	89	98	86	97	8.3	28.9
Area and ethnic studies	144	151	137	140	113	128	16.7	46.9
Business and management	807	792	866	1,109	1,149	1,142	2.9	24.4
Communications [1]	145	193	234	234	253	269	13.1	46.5
Computer and information sciences	128	240	248	428	551	623	2.3	14.4
Education	6,403	7,941	7,151	6,553	6,800	6,922	21.2	57.7
Engineering [1]	3,638	2,507	3,230	4,191	4,523	4,965	0.6	8.7
Foreign languages	781	549	437	411	420	512	38.0	59.0
Health sciences	459	771	1,199	1,261	1,436	1,543	16.3	54.8
Home economics	123	192	276	309	265	303	61.0	70.6
Law	20	40	105	89	76	113	0.0	20.4
Letters	1,857	1,500	1,239	1,172	1,234	1,266	28.0	55.3
Life sciences	3,645	3,636	3,432	3,629	3,520	3,844	16.3	37.7
Mathematics	1,199	724	699	750	866	915	7.8	18.5
Multi/interdisciplinary studies	80	295	285	261	257	311	13.8	34.7
Philosophy, religion, and theology	866	1,693	1,608	1,604	1,627	1,730	5.8	15.0
Physical sciences	4,390	3,089	3,403	3,809	3,858	4,168	5.6	19.3
Psychology	1,782	2,768	2,908	2,987	3,222	3,353	24.0	57.8
Public affairs	185	372	431	470	429	495	23.8	53.7
Social sciences [2]	3,659	3,219	2,851	2,781	2,885	3,023	13.9	32.6
Visual and performing arts	621	655	693	725	752	842	22.2	43.9
Other and unclassified	53	218	209	717	215	402	28.3	45.3

- Represents zero. [1] Includes technologies. [2] Includes history.

Source: U.S. Department of Education, National Center for Education Statistics, *Digest of Education Statistics,* annual.

No. 294. Degrees Conferred in Selected Professions: 1960 to 1990

[First professional degrees. See Appendix III]

TYPE OF DEGREE AND SEX OF RECIPIENT	1960	1970	1975	1980	1984	1985	1986	1987	1988	1989	1990 [1]
Medicine (M.D.):											
Institutions conferring degrees..	79	86	104	112	119	120	120	122	122	124	124
Degrees conferred, total......	7,032	8,314	12,447	14,902	15,813	16,041	15,938	15,620	15,358	15,460	15,115
Men................	6,645	7,615	10,818	11,416	11,359	11,167	11,022	10,566	10,278	10,310	9,977
Women	387	699	1,629	3,486	4,454	4,874	4,916	5,054	5,080	5,150	5,138
Percent of total.......	5.5	8.4	13.1	23.4	28.2	30.4	30.8	32.4	33.1	33.3	34.0
Dentistry (D.D.S. or D.M.D.):											
Institutions conferring degrees..	45	48	52	58	60	59	59	58	57	58	57
Degrees conferred, total......	3,247	3,718	4,773	5,258	5,353	5,339	5,046	4,741	4,477	4,265	4,093
Men................	3,221	3,684	4,627	4,558	4,302	4,233	3,907	3,603	3,300	3,124	2,830
Women	26	34	146	700	1,051	1,106	1,139	1,138	1,177	1,141	1,263
Percent of total.......	0.8	0.9	3.1	13.3	19.6	20.7	22.6	24.0	26.3	26.8	30.9
Law (LL.B. or J.D.):											
Institutions conferring degrees..	134	145	154	179	179	181	181	180	180	182	182
Degrees conferred, total......	9,240	14,916	29,296	35,647	37,012	37,491	35,844	36,172	35,397	35,634	36,437
Men................	9,010	14,115	24,881	24,893	23,382	23,070	21,874	21,643	21,067	21,069	21,059
Women	230	801	4,415	10,754	13,630	14,421	13,970	14,529	14,330	14,565	15,378
Percent of total.......	2.5	5.4	15.1	30.2	36.8	38.5	39.0	40.2	40.5	40.9	42.2
Theological (B.D., M.Div., M.H.L.):											
Institutions conferring degrees..	(NA)	(NA)	(NA)	(NA)	(NA)	(NA)	(NA)	(NA)	(NA)	(NA)	(NA)
Degrees conferred, total......	(NA)	5,298	5,095	7,115	6,878	7,221	7,283	7,181	6,466	6,012	5,851
Men................	(NA)	5,175	4,748	6,133	5,673	5,886	5,865	5,794	5,080	4,639	4,406
Women	(NA)	123	347	982	1,205	1,335	1,418	1,387	1,386	1,373	1,445
Percent of total.......	(NA)	2.3	6.8	13.8	17.5	18.5	19.5	19.3	21.4	22.8	24.7

NA Not available. [1] Preliminary.
Source: U.S. National Center for Education Statistics, *Digest of Education Statistics*, annual.

No. 295. Degrees Conferred, by Level and Race/Ethnicity: 1981 to 1990

[For **school year ending in year shown.** Data exclude some institutions not reporting field of study and are slight undercounts of degrees awarded]

LEVEL OF DEGREE AND RACE/ETHNICITY	TOTAL					PERCENT DISTRIBUTION				
	1981	1985	1987	1989	1990	1981	1985	1987	1989	1990
All degrees, total [1]........	1,333,162	1,781,911	1,822,550	1,864,779	1,926,635	100.0	100.0	100.0	100.0	100.0
White, non-Hispanic.....	1,138,994	1,492,230	1,519,632	1,543,364	1,589,127	85.4	83.7	83.4	82.8	82.5
Black, non-Hispanic......	82,002	111,386	110,359	111,096	116,217	6.2	6.3	6.1	6.0	6.0
Hispanic	30,290	54,706	56,180	60,470	65,863	2.3	3.1	3.1	3.2	3.4
Asian or Pacific Islander...	27,409	46,013	56,337	64,853	67,749	2.1	2.6	3.1	3.5	3.5
American Indian/Alaskan Native	4,949	8,822	8,679	8,724	9,330	0.4	0.5	0.5	0.5	0.5
Nonresident alien	49,518	68,754	71,363	76,272	78,349	3.7	3.9	3.9	4.1	4.1
Bachelor's degrees, total ..	934,800	968,311	991,260	1,016,350	1,046,930	100.0	100.0	100.0	100.0	100.0
White, non-Hispanic.....	807,319	826,106	841,820	859,699	882,996	86.4	85.3	84.9	84.6	84.3
Black, non-Hispanic......	60,673	57,473	56,555	58,065	61,074	6.5	5.9	5.7	5.7	5.8
Hispanic	21,832	25,874	26,990	29,910	32,686	2.3	2.7	2.7	2.9	3.1
Asian or Pacific Islander...	18,794	25,395	32,618	37,686	39,059	2.0	2.6	3.3	3.7	3.7
American Indian/Alaskan Native	3,593	4,246	3,971	3,954	4,338	0.4	0.4	0.4	0.4	0.4
Nonresident alien	22,589	29,217	29,306	27,036	26,777	2.4	3.0	3.0	2.7	2.6
Master's degrees, total	294,183	280,421	289,341	309,770	321,992	100.0	100.0	100.0	100.0	100.0
White, non-Hispanic.....	241,216	223,628	228,870	242,756	251,518	82.0	79.7	79.1	78.4	78.1
Black, non-Hispanic......	17,133	13,939	13,867	14,096	15,331	5.8	5.0	4.8	4.6	4.8
Hispanic	6,461	6,864	7,044	7,282	7,905	2.2	2.4	2.4	2.4	2.5
Asian or Pacific Islander...	6,282	7,782	8,558	10,336	10,646	2.1	2.8	3.0	3.3	3.3
American Indian/Alaskan Native	1,034	1,256	1,104	1,086	1,108	0.4	0.4	0.4	0.4	0.4
Nonresident alien	22,057	26,952	29,898	34,214	35,484	7.5	9.6	10.3	11.0	11.0
Doctor's degrees, total	32,839	32,307	34,033	35,659	37,980	100.0	100.0	100.0	100.0	100.0
White, non-Hispanic.....	25,908	23,934	24,435	24,882	25,793	78.9	74.1	71.8	69.8	67.9
Black, non-Hispanic......	1,265	1,154	1,060	1,065	1,145	3.9	3.6	3.1	3.0	3.0
Hispanic	456	677	750	628	783	1.4	2.1	2.2	1.8	2.1
Asian or Pacific Islander...	877	1,106	1,097	1,324	1,282	2.7	3.4	3.2	3.7	3.4
American Indian/Alaskan Native	130	119	104	85	102	0.4	0.4	0.3	0.2	0.3
Nonresident alien	4,203	5,317	6,587	7,675	8,875	12.8	16.5	19.4	21.5	23.4
First-professional degrees, total.................	71,340	71,057	71,617	70,856	70,736	100.0	100.0	100.0	100.0	100.0
White, non-Hispanic.....	64,551	63,219	62,688	61,214	60,291	90.5	89.0	87.5	86.4	85.2
Black, non-Hispanic......	2,931	3,029	3,420	3,148	3,389	4.1	4.3	4.8	4.4	4.8
Hispanic	1,541	1,884	2,051	2,269	2,427	2.2	2.7	2.9	3.2	3.4
Asian or Pacific Islander...	1,456	1,816	2,270	2,976	3,336	2.0	2.6	3.2	4.2	4.7
American Indian/Alaskan Native	192	248	304	264	257	0.3	0.3	0.4	0.4	0.4
Nonresident alien	669	861	884	985	1,036	0.9	1.2	1.2	1.4	1.5

[1] Includes associates degrees, not shown separately.
Source: U.S. National Center for Education Statistics, *Race/Ethnicity Trends in Degrees Conferred by Institutions of Higher Education: 1980-81 through 1989-90*, NCES 92-039.

No. 296. Libraries—Number, by Type: 1980 to 1991

TYPE	1980	1985	1990	1991	TYPE	1980	1985	1990	1991
Total [1]	31,564	32,323	34,613	35,130	Junior college	1,191	1,188	1,233	1,237
					Colleges,				
United States	28,638	29,843	30,761	31,167	universities	3,400	3,846	3,360	3,376
Public	8,717	8,849	9,060	9,075	Departmental	1,489	1,824	1,454	1,472
Public branches	5,936	6,330	5,833	5,873	Law,				
Special [2]	7,649	7,530	9,051	9,348	medicine,				
Medicine	1,674	1,667	1,861	1,861	religious	269	531	501	495
Religious	913	839	946	955	Government	1,260	1,574	1,735	1,773
Law	417	435	647	665	Armed Forces	485	526	489	485
Academic	4,591	5,034	4,593	4,613	Outlying areas	113	114	110	(NA)

NA Not available. [1] Includes Canadian libraries, and libraries in regions administered by the United States, not shown separately. Data are exclusive of elementary and secondary school libraries. Law libraries with fewer than 10,000 volumes are included only if they specialize in a particular field. [2] Includes other types of special libraries, not shown separately. Increase between 1985 and 1990 is due mainly to revised criteria for identifying special libraries and improved methods of counting.

Source: R.R. Bowker Co., New York, NY, *The Bowker Annual: Library and Book Trade Almanac* and *American Library Directory*, annual. (Copyright by Reed Publishing (USA) Inc.)

No. 297. Public Libraries, Selected Characteristics: 1991

[Based on survey of public libraries. Data are for public libraries in the 50 States and the District of Columbia. The response rates for these items are between 95 and 99 percent, except for library visits (76 percent). See source for details]

POPULATION OF SERVICE AREA	NUMBER OF—		OPERATING INCOME			PAID STAFF [3]		SERVICE MEASURES (per capita)		
	Public libraries	Sta-tionary outlets [1]	Total (mil. dol.) [2]	Source (percent)		Total	Librar-ians with ALA-MLS [4]	Books and serial volumes	Library visits	Circu-lation [5]
				State govern-ment	Local govern-ment					
Total	9,050	15,379	4,654	13.0	76.8	108,029	23,351	2.6	3.7	6.1
1,000,000 or more	19	787	621	13.4	72.4	12,305	3,107	2.3	3.3	3.9
500,000 to 999,000	53	1,017	779	18.7	73.9	15,689	4,028	2.4	3.1	6.3
250,000 to 499,999	92	947	578	11.6	81.7	12,280	3,023	2.1	3.0	5.7
100,000 to 249,999	289	1,685	719	11.0	80.4	16,900	3,731	2.1	3.4	5.9
50,000 to 99,999	507	1,544	596	13.3	77.7	14,421	3,151	2.3	3.7	5.9
25,000 to 49,999	880	1,596	570	11.8	77.9	13,978	2,966	2.8	4.4	6.7
10,000 to 24,999	1,655	2,073	487	11.0	76.9	12,524	2,419	3.3	4.8	7.3
5,000 to 9,999	1,509	1,658	180	12.1	73.2	5,255	659	4.0	4.8	7.7
2,500 to 4,999	1,351	1,397	74	7.4	72.9	2,484	186	5.1	4.5	7.7
1,000 to 2,400	1,704	1,697	41	6.0	69.5	1,638	69	7.2	5.0	8.5
Fewer than 1,000	991	978	10	10.2	63.8	556	11	12.3	6.1	10.4

[1] The sum of central and branches libraries. The total number of central libraries was 8,837; the total of branch libraries was 6,542. [2] Includes income from the federal government (1.2%) and other sources (9.0%), not shown separately. [3] Full-time equivalents. [4] Librarians with master's degrees from a graduate library education program accredited by the American Library Association (ALA). Total librarians, including those without ALA-MLS, were 34,486. [5] Transactions that involve lending any item from the library's collection.

Source: U.S. National Center for Education Statistics, *Public Libraries in the United States: 1991.*

No. 298. College and University Libraries—Summary 1975 to 1990

[For school year ending in year shown, except enrollment as of fall of the prior year. Prior to 1982, includes outlying areas]

ITEM	1975	1977	1979	1982	1985	1988	1990
Number of libraries	2,972	3,058	3,122	3,104	3,322	3,438	3,274
Total enrollment (1,000)	10,322	11,121	11,392	12,372	12,242	12,767	13,539
COLLECTIONS (1,000)							
Number of volumes	447,059	481,442	519,895	567,826	631,727	706,504	717,042
Volumes added during year	23,242	22,367	21,608	19,507	20,658	21,907	19,003
Number of serial subscriptions	4,434	4,670	4,775	4,890	6,317	6,416	5,748
STAFF							
Total	56,836	57,087	58,416	58,476	58,476	67,251	69,359
Librarians and professional	23,530	23,308	23,676	23,816	21,822	25,115	26,101
OPERATING EXPENDITURES ($1,000)							
Total [1]	1,091,784	1,259,637	1,502,158	1,943,769	2,404,524	2,770,075	3,257,813
Salaries	592,568	698,090	824,438	1,081,894	1,156,138	1,45 ,551	1,693,813
Collection	327,406	373,699	450,180	561,199	750,282	891,281	1,040,928

[1] Includes other expenditures, not shown separately.

Source: U.S. National Center for Education Statistics, *Digest of Education Statistics,* 1991; and *Academic Libraries: 1990* 1992.

No. 299. Participation in Adult Education: 1990-91

[For the civilian noninstitutional population 17 years old and over not enrolled full-time in elementary or secondary school at the time of the survey. Adult education is considered any part-time enrollment in any educational activity at any time in the prior 12 months. Based on a telephone survey and subject to sampling error; source for details. For composition of regions, see table 31]

CHARACTERISTIC	Adult popu- lation (1,000)	Number taking adult ed. courses (1,000)	Per- cent of total	Reason for taking course (percent) [1]				
				Personal/ social	Advance on the job	Train for a new job	Improve basic skills	Complete degree or diploma
Total	181,800	57,391	32	30	60	9	1	13
Age: 17 to 24 years old	21,688	7,125	33	30	38	18	4	29
25 to 34 years old	47,244	17,530	37	25	63	12	1	14
35 to 44 years old	38,565	17,083	44	27	66	8	1	12
45 to 54 years old	25,375	8,107	32	29	70	6	1	7
55 to 64 years old	19,967	4,516	23	35	61	5	1	5
65 years old and over	28,960	3,031	10	73	22	4	-	3
Sex: Male	82,154	25,923	32	24	67	8	1	11
Female	99,646	31,469	32	35	54	10	1	14
Race/ethnicity:								
White [2]	143,144	47,401	33	30	62	8	1	13
Black [2]	20,141	4,586	23	30	53	14	3	13
Hispanic	13,804	4,032	29	31	48	16	4	12
Other races [2]	4,711	1,371	29	32	51	8	2	17
Region:								
Northeast	37,975	12,042	32	29	62	7	2	13
Midwest	43,889	13,242	30	29	63	9	1	14
South	62,124	18,024	29	29	59	11	1	13
West	37,812	14,083	37	34	56	11	1	12
Marital status:								
Never married	36,652	11,539	31	30	48	14	3	24
Currently married	118,397	39,323	33	30	63	8	1	10
Other	26,752	6,529	24	34	59	11	1	11
Children under 16 in household:								
Yes	68,868	25,349	37	26	65	10	1	12
No	112,932	32,042	28	33	56	9	1	14
Educational attainment:								
Up to 8th grade	10,163	735	7	56	16	5	7	14
9th to 11th grade	17,581	2,520	14	30	43	13	3	16
Twelfth grade	67,129	15,077	22	31	55	13	2	9
Vocational school after high school	6,994	2,219	32	28	68	6	-	10
Some college	36,823	14,488	39	33	53	10	1	19
Associate's degree	5,034	2,461	49	22	71	7	1	15
Bachelor's or higher	38,076	19,891	52	28	70	6	-	11
Labor force status:								
Employed	115,620	47,143	41	24	68	9	1	13
Unemployed	9,820	2,099	21	27	29	27	2	25
Not in the labor force	56,361	8,149	14	64	17	10	2	11
Occupation: [3]								
Professional	19,898	12,693	64	22	79	5	-	15
Executive, administrative, and managerial	10,574	6,255	59	22	78	6	1	13
Technical, sales, and related support	3,082	1,947	63	18	75	12	2	13
Sales workers	12,234	5,154	42	34	56	12	1	11
Administrative support, including clerical	18,971	7,044	37	28	66	10	1	15
Service	15,904	4,426	28	27	61	11	2	15
Agriculture, forestry, and fishing	2,783	303	11	31	62	6	2	10
Precision production, craft and repair	11,393	3,918	34	27	61	13	1	10
Machine operators, assemblers, and inspectors	7,768	2,201	28	20	73	10	1	10
Transportation and materials moving	3,962	1,030	26	23	68	7	4	9
Handlers, equipment cleaners, helpers and laborers	3,297	767	23	17	60	18	2	10
Nonclassifiable, undetermined	5,753	1,403	24	8	19	8	-	6
Income: Under $10,000	27,504	3,843	14	37	34	16	3	14
$10,001 to $15,000	15,465	3,178	21	31	48	16	2	15
$15,001 to $20,000	16,117	3,308	21	32	50	13	2	16
$20,001 to $25,000	16,092	4,063	25	32	56	11	1	14
$25,001 to $30,000	17,973	5,445	30	33	53	14	2	15
$30,001 to $40,000	26,110	9,043	35	30	64	10	1	13
$40,001 to $50,000	21,303	9,313	44	29	64	6	1	12
$50,001 to $75,000	24,540	11,235	46	28	67	6	1	12
More than $75,000	16,695	7,963	48	27	66	6	1	10

- Represents or rounds to zero.   [1] Reason for taking at least one course. Includes duplication.   [2] Non-Hispanic.   [3] For the currently employed.

Source: U.S. National Center for Education Statistics, *Adult Education Profile for 1990-91;* and unpublished data.

Figure 5.1
Selected Crime Rates: 1980 to 1991

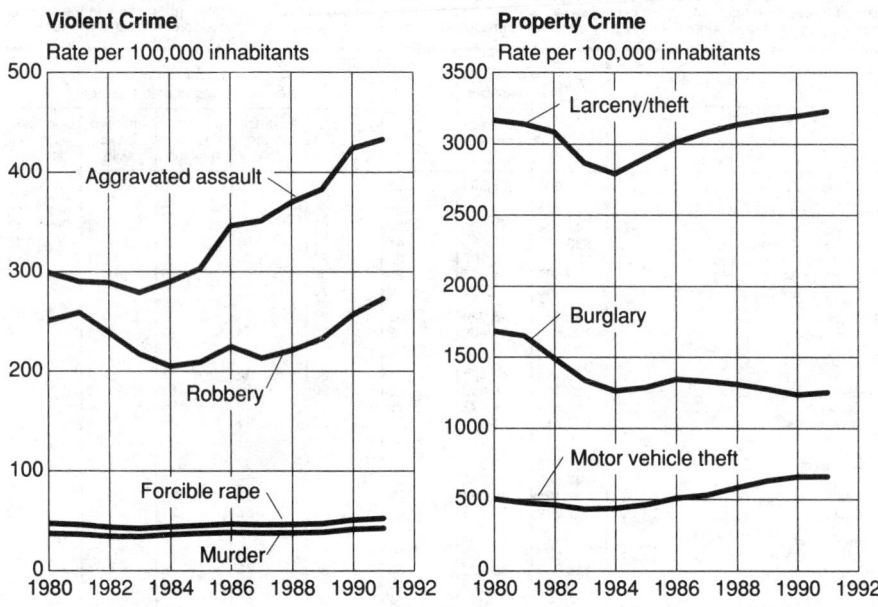

Violent Crime

Rate per 100,000 inhabitants

Property Crime

Rate per 100,000 inhabitants

Aggravated assault

Robbery

Forcible rape

Murder

Larceny/theft

Burglary

Motor vehicle theft

Source: Chart prepared by U.S. Bureau of the Census. For data, see table 300.

Figure 5.2
Criminal Justice System Public Expenditures: 1990

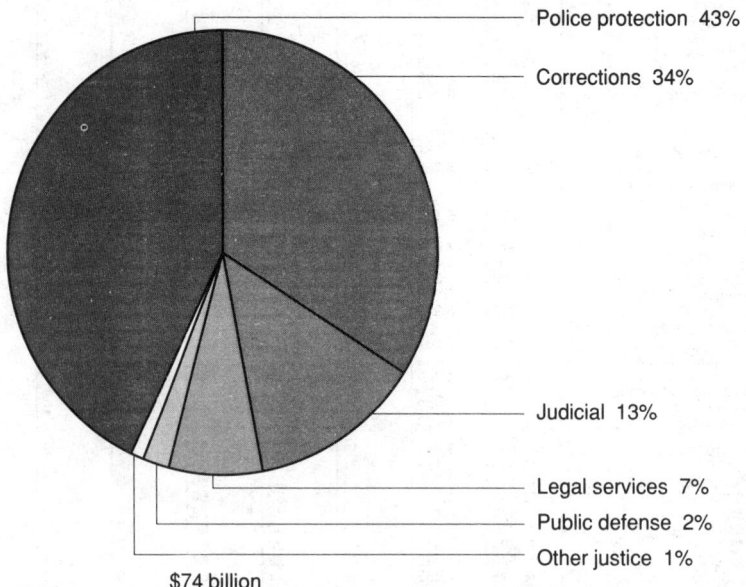

Police protection 43%

Corrections 34%

Judicial 13%

Legal services 7%

Public defense 2%

Other justice 1%

$74 billion

Source: Chart prepared by U.S. Bureau of the Census. For data, see table 322.

Law Enforcement, Courts, and Prisons

This section presents data on crimes committed, victims of crimes, arrests, and data related to criminal violations, and the criminal justice system. The major sources of these data are the Bureau of Justice Statistics (BJS) and the Federal Bureau of Investigation (FBI). BJS issues several reports, including *Sourcebook of Criminal Justice Statistics, Criminal Victimization in the United States, Prisoners in State and Federal Institutions, National Survey of Courts, Census of State Correctional Facilities* and *Survey of Prison Inmates, Census of Jails* and *Survey of Jail Inmates, Parole in the United States, Capital Punishment,* and the annual *Expenditure and Employment Data for the Criminal Justice System.* The Federal Bureau of Investigation's major annual report is *Crime in the United States,* which presents data on reported crimes as gathered from State and local law enforcement agencies.

Other major sources of these data include: *Annual Report of the Director, Federal Court Management Statistics, Federal Offenders,* and *Sentences Imposed Chart* issued by the Administrative Office of the U.S. Courts; *Governmental Finances and Public Employment,* issued annually by the Bureau of the Census; and the *Statistical Report,* issued annually by the Federal Bureau of Prisons. A major new source for this edition is the National Center on Child Abuse and Neglect within the U.S. Department of Health and Human Services.

Legal jurisdiction and law enforcement.—Law enforcement is, for the most part, a function of State and local officers and agencies. The U.S. Constitution reserves general police powers to the States. By act of Congress, Federal offenses include only offenses against the U.S. Government and against and by its employees while engaged in their official duties, and offenses which involve the crossing of State lines or an interference with interstate commerce. Excluding the military, there are 52 separate criminal law jurisdictions in the United

In Brief

All reported crimes up almost 3% while violent crimes up 5% in 1991 from 1990.

$74 billion in public expenditures spent for the criminal justice system in 1990.

Almost 2 million reports of child abuse and neglect in 1991.

States: 1 in each of the 50 States, 1 in the District of Columbia, and the Federal jurisdiction. Each of these has its own criminal law and procedure and its own law enforcement agencies. While the systems of law enforcement are quite similar among the States, there are often substantial differences in the penalties for like offenses.

Law enforcement can be divided into three parts: Investigation of crimes and arrests of persons suspected of committing them; prosecution of those charged with crime; and the punishment or treatment of persons convicted of crime.

Crime.—There are two major approaches taken in determining the extent of crime. One perspective is provided by the FBI through its Uniform Crime Reporting Program (UCR). The FBI receives monthly and annual reports from law enforcement agencies throughout the country, currently representing 98 percent of the national population. Each month, city police, sheriffs, and State police file reports on the number of index offenses that become known to them. The FBI Crime Index offenses are as follows: *Murder and nonnegligent manslaughter,* is based on police investigations, as opposed to the determination of a medical examiner or judicial body, includes willful felonious homicides, and excludes attempts and assaults to kill, suicides, accidental deaths, justifiable homicides, and deaths caused by negligence; *forcible rape* includes forcible rapes and attempts; *robbery* includes stealing or taking anything of value by force or violence or threat of force or violence and includes attempted robbery; *aggravated assault* includes assault with intent to kill; *burglary* includes any unlawful entry to commit a felony or a theft and includes attempted burglary and burglary followed by larceny; *larceny* includes theft of property or articles of value without use of force and violence or fraud and excludes embezzlement, "con games," forgery, etc.; *motor vehicle theft* includes all cases where vehicles are driven away and abandoned, but excludes vehicles taken for temporary use and returned by the taker. Arson was added as the eighth Index offense in April 1979 following a Congressional mandate. *Arson* includes any willful or malicious burning or attempt to burn with or without intent to defraud, a dwelling house, public building, motor vehicle or aircraft, personal property of another, etc. The monthly Uniform Crime Reports also contain data on crimes cleared by arrest and on characteristics of persons arrested for all criminal offenses. In summarizing and publishing crime data, the FBI depends primarily on the adherence to the established standards of reporting for statistical accuracy, presenting the data as information useful to persons concerned with the problem of crime and criminal-law enforcement.

National Crime Survey (NCS).—A second perspective on crime is provided by the National Crime Survey (NCS) of the Bureau of Justice Statistics. Details about the crimes come directly from the victims. No attempt is made to validate the information against police records or any other source. The NCS measures rape, robbery, assault, household and personal larceny, burglary, and motor vehicle theft. The NCS includes offenses reported to the police, as well as those not reported. Police reporting rates (percent of victimizations) varied by type of crime. In 1991, for instance, 59 percent of the rapes were reported; 55 percent of the robberies; 47 percent of assaults; 28 percent of personal larcenies without contact; 50 percent of the household burglaries; and 74 percent of motor vehicle thefts.

Murder and kidnaping are not covered. Commercial burglary and robbery were dropped from the program during 1977. The so-called victimless crimes, such as drunkenness, drug abuse, and prostitution,

also are excluded, as are crimes for which it is difficult to identify knowledgeable respondents or to locate data records.

Crimes of which the victim may not be aware also cannot be measured effectively. Buying stolen property may fall into this category, as may some instances of embezzlement. Attempted crimes of many types probably are under recorded for this reason. Events in which the victim has shown a willingness to participate in illegal activity also are excluded.

In any encounter involving a personal crime, more than one criminal act can be committed against an individual. For example; a rape may be associated with a robbery; or a household offense, such as a burglary, can escalate into something more serious in the event of a personal confrontation. In classifying the survey-measured crimes, each criminal incident has been counted only once—by the most serious act that took place during the incident and ranked in accordance with the seriousness classification system used by the Federal Bureau of Investigation. The order of seriousness for crimes against persons is as follows: Rape, robbery, assault, and larceny. Consequently, if a person were both robbed and assaulted, the event would be classified as robbery; if the victim suffered physical harm, the crime would be categorized as robbery with injury. Personal crimes take precedence over household offenses.

A *victimization,* basic measure of the occurrence of a crime, is a specific criminal act as it affects a single victim. The number of victimizations is determined by the number of victims of such acts. Victimization counts serve as key elements in computing rates of victimization. For crimes against persons, the rates are based on the total number of individuals age 12 and over or on a portion of that population sharing a particular characteristic or set of traits. As general indicators of the danger of having been victimized during the reference period, the rates are not sufficiently refined to represent true measures of risk for specific individuals or households.

An *incident* is a specific criminal act involving one or more victims; therefore, the number of incidents of personal crimes lower than that of victimizations.

Courts.—Statistics on criminal offenses and the outcome of prosecutions are incomplete for the country as a whole, although data are available for many States individually. The only national compilations of such statistics were made by the Bureau of the Census for 1932 to 1945 covering a maximum of 32 States, and by the Bureau of Justice Statistics for 1986 based on a nationally representative sample survey.

The bulk of civil and criminal litigation in the country is commenced and determined in the various State courts. Only when the U.S. Constitution and acts of Congress specifically confer jurisdiction upon the Federal courts may civil litigation be heard and decided by them. Generally, the Federal courts have jurisdiction over the following types of cases: Suits or proceedings by or against the United States; civil actions between private parties arising under the Constitution, laws, or treaties of the United States; civil actions between private litigants who are citizens of different States; civil cases involving admiralty, maritime, or prize jurisdiction; and all matters in bankruptcy.

There are several types of courts with varying degrees of legal jurisdiction. These jurisdictions include original, appellate, general, and limited or special. A *court of original jurisdiction* is one having the authority initially to try a case and pass judgment on the law and the facts; a *court of appellate jurisdiction* is one with the legal authority to review cases and hear appeals; a *court of general jurisdiction* is a trial court of unlimited original jurisdiction in civil and/or criminal cases, also called a "major trial court"; a *court of limited or special jurisdiction* is a trial court with legal authority over only a particular class of cases, such as probate, juvenile, or traffic cases.

The 94 Federal courts of original jurisdiction are known as the U.S. district courts. One or more of these courts is established in every State and one each in the District of Columbia, Puerto Rico, the Virgin Islands, the Northern Mariana Islands, and Guam. Appeals from the district courts are taken to intermediate appellate courts of which there are 13, known as U.S. courts of appeals and the United States Court of Appeals for the Federal Circuit. The Supreme Court of the United States is the final and highest appellate court in the Federal system of courts.

Juvenile offenders.—For statistical purposes, the FBI and most States classify as juvenile offenders persons under the age of 18 years who have committed a crime or crimes.

Delinquency cases are all cases of youths referred to a juvenile court for violation of a law or ordinance or for seriously "antisocial" conduct. Several types of facilities are available for those adjudicated delinquent, ranging from the short-term physically unrestricted environment to the long-term very restrictive atmosphere.

Prisoners.—Data on prisoners in Federal and State prisons and reformatories were collected annually by the Bureau of the Census until 1950, by the Federal Bureau of Prisons until 1971, transferred then to the Law Enforcement Assistance Administration, and, in 1979, to the Bureau of Justice Statistics. Adults convicted of criminal activity may be given a prison or jail sentence. A *prison* is a confinement facility having custodial authority over adults sentenced to confinement of more than one year. A *jail* is a facility, usually operated by a local law enforcement agency, holding persons detained pending adjudication and/or persons committed after adjudication to one year or less. Nearly every State publishes annual data either for its whole prison system or for each separate State institution.

Statistical reliability.—For discussion of statistical collection, estimation, and sampling procedures and measures of statistical reliability pertaining to the National Crime Survey and Uniform Crime Reporting Program, see Appendix III.

Historical statistics.—Tabular headnotes provide cross-references, where applicable, to *Historical Statistics of the United States, Colonial Times to 1970.* See Appendix IV.

No. 300. Crimes and Crime Rates, by Type: 1982 to 1991

[Data refer to offenses known to the police. Rates are based on Bureau of the Census estimated resident population as of **July 1**, except 1990, enumerated as of **April, 1.** Annual totals for years prior to 1984 were adjusted in 1984 and may not be consistent with those in prior editions. See source for details. Minus sign (-) indicates decrease. For definitions of crimes, see text, section 5. See *Historical Statistics, Colonial Times to 1970,* series H 952-961 for related data]

ITEM AND YEAR	Total	VIOLENT CRIME					PROPERTY CRIME			
		Total	Mur-der[1]	Forci-ble rape	Rob-bery	Aggra-vated assault	Total	Bur-glary	Larce-ny—theft	Motor vehi-cle theft
Number of offenses (1,000):										
1982	12,974	1,322	21.0	78.8	553	669	11,652	3,447	7,143	1,062
1983	12,109	1,258	19.3	78.9	507	653	10,851	3,130	6,713	1,008
1984	11,882	1,273	18.7	84.2	485	685	10,609	2,984	6,592	1,032
1985	12,431	1,329	19.0	88.7	498	723	11,103	3,073	6,926	1,103
1986	13,212	1,489	20.6	91.5	543	834	11,723	3,241	7,257	1,224
1987	13,509	1,484	20.1	91.1	518	855	12,025	3,236	7,500	1,289
1988	13,923	1,566	20.7	92.5	543	910	12,357	3,218	7,706	1,433
1989	14,251	1,646	21.5	94.5	578	952	12,605	3,168	7,872	1,565
1990	14,476	1,820	23.4	102.6	639	1,055	12,656	3,074	7,946	1,636
1991	14,873	1,912	24.7	106.6	688	1,093	12,961	3,157	8,142	1,662
Percent change, number of offenses:										
1982 to 1991	14.6	44.6	17.6	35.3	24.3	63.2	11.2	-8.4	14.0	56.4
1987 to 1991	10.1	28.8	22.9	17.0	32.8	27.8	7.8	-2.4	8.6	28.9
1989 to 1990	1.6	10.6	8.8	8.6	10.6	10.8	0.4	-3.0	0.9	4.5
1990 to 1991	2.7	5.0	5.4	3.9	7.6	3.6	2.4	2.7	2.5	1.6
Rate per 100,000 population:										
1982	5,604	571	9.1	34.0	239	289	5,033	1,489	3,085	459
1983	5,175	538	8.3	33.7	217	279	4,637	1,338	2,869	431
1984	5,031	539	7.9	35.7	205	290	4,492	1,264	2,791	437
1985	5,207	557	7.9	37.1	209	303	4,651	1,287	2,901	462
1986	5,480	618	8.6	37.9	225	346	4,863	1,345	3,010	508
1987	5,550	610	8.3	37.4	213	351	4,940	1,330	3,081	529
1988	5,664	637	8.4	37.6	221	370	5,027	1,309	3,135	583
1989	5,741	663	8.7	38.1	233	383	5,078	1,276	3,171	630
1990	5,820	732	9.4	41.2	257	424	5,089	1,236	3,195	658
1991	5,898	758	9.8	42.3	273	433	5,140	1,252	3,229	659
Percent change, rate per 100,000 population:										
1982 to 1991	5.3	32.7	7.6	24.4	14.1	49.8	2.1	-15.9	4.7	43.6
1987 to 1991	6.3	24.3	18.6	13.1	28.2	23.3	4.1	-5.8	4.8	24.5
1989 to 1990	1.4	10.4	8.0	8.1	10.3	10.7	0.2	-3.1	0.8	4.4
1990 to 1991	1.3	3.6	4.3	2.7	6.1	2.2	1.0	1.3	1.1	0.2

[1] Includes nonnegligent manslaughter.

Source: U.S. Federal Bureau of Investigation, *Crime in the United States,* annual.

No. 301. Crimes and Crime Rates, by Type and Area: 1990 and 1991

[In thousands, except rate. Rate per 100,000 population; see headnote, table 300. Estimated totals based on reports from city and rural law enforcement agencies representing 96 percent of the national population. For definitions of crimes, see text, section 5]

TYPE OF CRIME	1990						1991					
	Metropolitan areas[1]		Other cities		Rural areas		Metropolitan areas[1]		Other cities		Rural areas	
	Total	Rate	Total	Rate	Total	Rate	Total	Rate	Total	Rate	Total	Rate
Total	12,605	6,547	1,188	5,303	683	2,022	12,916	6,616	1,238	5,436	719	2,105
Violent crime	1,648	856	102	458	70	207	1,728	885	110	481	74	217
Murder and nonnegligent manslaughter	20	11	1	5	2	6	22	11	1	5	2	6
Forcible rape	88	46	7	33	8	22	91	46	8	34	8	24
Robbery	620	322	14	63	5	16	666	341	16	70	6	17
Aggravated assault	920	478	80	357	55	163	950	487	85	372	58	171
Property crime	10,957	5,691	1,085	4,845	613	1,815	11,188	5,730	1,128	4,955	645	1,888
Burglary	2,611	1,356	236	1,053	227	671	2,671	1,368	245	1,074	242	708
Larceny-theft	6,803	3,533	797	3,559	346	1,024	6,950	3,560	831	3,647	362	1,060
Motor vehicle theft	1,543	801	52	232	41	121	1,568	803	53	233	41	120

[1] For definition, see Appendix II.

Source: U.S. Federal Bureau of Investigation, *Crime in the United States,* annual.

No. 302. Crime Rates, by State, 1985 to 1991, and by Type, 1991

[Offenses known to the police per 100,000 population. Based on Bureau of the Census estimated resident population as of July 1, except 1990, enumerated as of April. For definitions of crimes, see text, section 5]

REGION, DIVISION, AND STATE	1985, total	1990, total	1991 Total	Violent crime Total	Murder[1]	Forcible rape	Robbery	Aggravated assault	Property crime Total	Burglary	Larceny—theft	Motor vehicle theft
United States.....	5,207	5,820	5,898	758	9.8	42	273	433	5,140	1,252	3,229	659
Northeast............	4,627	5,193	5,155	752	8.4	29	352	363	4,403	1,010	2,598	795
New England........	4,487	4,996	4,950	532	4.1	30	159	338	4,419	1,103	2,600	716
Maine.............	3,672	3,698	3,768	132	1.2	22	23	86	3,636	903	2,570	163
New Hampshire	3,252	3,645	3,448	119	3.6	30	33	53	3,329	735	2,373	220
Vermont	3,888	4,341	3,955	117	2.1	31	12	72	3,838	1,020	2,674	144
Massachusetts......	4,758	5,298	5,322	736	4.2	32	195	505	4,586	1,167	2,501	919
Rhode Island.......	4,723	5,353	5,039	462	3.7	31	123	304	4,577	1,127	2,656	794
Connecticut........	4,705	5,387	5,364	540	5.7	29	224	280	4,824	1,191	2,838	796
Middle Atlantic.......	4,675	5,263	5,227	829	9.9	29	419	372	4,398	978	2,598	823
New York	5,589	6,364	6,245	1,164	14.2	28	622	499	5,081	1,132	2,944	1,004
New Jersey	5,094	5,447	5,431	635	5.2	29	293	307	4,797	1,016	2,855	926
Pennsylvania	3,037	3,476	3,559	450	6.3	29	194	221	3,109	720	1,907	482
Midwest.............	4,674	5,102	5,257	631	7.8	45	223	355	4,626	1,037	3,082	507
East North Central	4,939	5,322	5,482	704	8.9	50	263	383	4,777	1,056	3,151	570
Ohio..............	4,187	4,843	5,033	562	7.2	53	215	287	4,471	1,055	2,916	500
Indiana...........	3,914	4,683	4,818	505	7.5	41	116	340	4,312	977	2,871	465
Illinois [2]........	5,384	5,935	6,132	1,039	11.3	40	456	532	5,093	1,120	3,318	655
Michigan..........	6,366	5,995	6,138	803	10.8	79	243	470	5,335	1,186	3,469	680
Wisconsin	4,017	4,395	4,466	277	4.8	25	119	128	4,189	752	3,001	436
West North Central ...	4,046	4,579	4,722	457	5.4	34	129	288	4,265	991	2,918	356
Minnesota.........	4,134	4,539	4,496	316	3.0	40	98	175	4,180	854	2,963	363
Iowa [3]...........	3,943	4,101	4,134	303	2.0	21	45	235	3,831	832	2,828	171
Missouri	4,366	5,121	5,416	763	10.5	34	251	467	4,653	1,253	2,841	558
North Dakota.......	2,679	2,922	2,794	65	1.1	18	8	38	2,729	373	2,229	127
South Dakota.......	2,641	2,909	3,079	182	1.7	40	19	122	2,897	590	2,192	115
Nebraska..........	3,695	4,213	4,354	335	3.3	28	54	249	4,020	727	3,080	213
Kansas...........	4,375	5,193	5,534	500	6.1	45	138	310	5,035	1,307	3,377	351
South..............	5,256	6,334	6,417	798	12.1	45	252	489	5,618	1,498	3,518	603
South Atlantic	5,375	6,546	6,585	851	11.4	44	286	510	5,734	1,508	3,665	561
Delaware..........	4,961	5,360	5,869	714	5.4	86	215	408	5,155	1,128	3,652	375
Maryland..........	5,373	5,830	6,209	956	11.7	46	407	492	5,253	1,158	3,365	731
District of Columbia [4].	8,007	10,774	10,768	2,453	80.6	36	1,216	1,121	8,315	2,074	4,880	1,360
Virginia	3,779	4,441	4,607	373	9.3	30	138	196	4,234	783	3,113	339
West Virginia	2,253	2,503	2,663	191	6.2	23	43	119	2,472	667	1,631	175
North Carolina	4,121	5,486	5,889	658	11.4	35	178	434	5,230	1,692	3,239	299
South Carolina	4,841	6,045	6,179	973	11.3	59	171	731	5,207	1,455	3,365	387
Georgia...........	5,110	6,764	6,493	738	12.8	42	268	415	5,755	1,515	3,629	611
Florida............	7,574	8,811	8,547	1,184	9.4	52	400	723	7,363	2,006	4,573	784
East South Central	3,651	4,389	4,687	631	10.4	41	149	430	4,056	1,196	2,465	395
Kentucky..........	2,947	3,299	3,358	438	6.8	35	83	313	2,920	797	1,909	215
Tennessee.........	4,167	5,051	5,367	726	11.0	46	213	456	4,641	1,365	2,662	614
Alabama..........	3,942	4,915	5,366	844	11.5	36	153	644	4521	1,269	2,889	363
Mississippi	3,266	3,869	4,221	389	12.8	46	116	214	3,832	1,332	2,213	286
West South Central ...	5,991	7,092	7,118	806	14.2	50	254	488	6,312	1,653	3,871	788
Arkansas..........	3,585	4,867	5,175	593	11.1	45	136	402	4,582	1,227	3,014	341
Louisiana	5,564	6,487	6,425	951	16.9	41	279	614	5,473	1,412	3,489	573
Oklahoma	5,425	5,599	5,669	584	7.2	51	129	397	5,085	1,478	3,050	557
Texas............	6,569	7,827	7,819	840	15.3	53	286	485	6,979	1,802	4,232	944
West	6,405	6,405	6,478	841	9.6	46	287	498	5,637	1,324	3,522	791
Mountain...........	6,183	6,268	6,125	544	6.5	44	122	371	5,581	1,247	3,843	491
Montana	4,549	4,502	3,648	140	2.6	20	19	99	3,508	524	2,778	206
Idaho	3,908	4,057	4,196	290	1.8	29	21	239	3,905	826	2,901	178
Wyoming	4,015	4,211	4,389	310	3.3	26	17	264	4,079	692	3,232	155
Colorado..........	6,919	6,054	6,074	559	5.9	47	107	399	5,515	1,158	3,930	426
New Mexico........	6,486	6,684	6,679	835	10.5	52	120	652	5,845	1,723	3,775	346
Arizona...........	7,116	7,889	7,406	671	7.8	42	166	455	6,735	1,607	4,266	861
Utah.............	5,317	5,660	5,608	287	2.9	46	55	183	5,321	840	4,240	241
Nevada...........	6,575	6,064	6,299	677	11.8	66	312	287	5,622	1,404	3,565	652
Pacific.............	6,486	6,452	6,602	945	10.7	47	345	542	5,656	1,351	3,409	896
Washington	6,529	6,223	6,304	523	4.2	70	146	303	5,781	1,235	4,102	444
Oregon...........	6,730	5,646	5,755	506	4.6	53	150	298	5,249	1,176	3,598	474
California..........	6,518	6,604	6,773	1,090	12.7	42	411	624	5,683	1,398	3,246	1,039
Alaska...........	5,877	5,153	5,702	614	7.4	92	113	402	5,088	979	3,575	534
Hawaii	5,201	6,107	5,970	242	4.0	33	87	118	5,729	1,234	4,158	336

[1] Includes nonnegligent manslaughter.   [2] Forcible rape figures for 1990 and 1991 were estimated using the national rate of forcible rapes when grouped by like agencies as figures submitted were not in accordance with national Uniform Crime Reporting program guidelines.   [3] Data for 1991 were not available; therefore, data presented are estimates.   [4] Includes offenses reported by the police at the National Zoo.

Source: U.S. Federal Bureau of Investigation, *Crime in the United States,* annual.

No. 303. Crime Rates, by Type—Selected Large Cities: 1991

[**Offenses known to the police per 100,000 population.** Based on Bureau of the Census estimated resident population as of July 1. For definitions of crimes, see text, section 5]

CITY RANKED BY POPULATION SIZE, 1990 [1]	Crime index, total	VIOLENT CRIME					PROPERTY CRIME			
		Total	Murder	Forcible rape	Robbery	Aggravated assault	Total	Burglary	Larceny—theft	Motor vehicle theft
New York, NY	9,236	2,318	29.3	39.3	1,340	909	6,918	1,524	3,489	1,904
Los Angeles, CA	9,730	2,526	28.9	55.3	1,118	1,324	7,204	1,615	3,660	1,929
Chicago, IL	(1)	(1)	32.9	(1)	1,557	1,502	8,228	1,858	4,684	1,686
Houston, TX	10,824	1,600	36.5	72.8	833	657	9,225	2,385	4,429	2,411
Philadelphia, PA	6,833	1,406	27.6	56.6	872	450	5,427	1,344	2,560	1,523
San Diego, CA	8,537	1,220	14.7	41.6	470	693	7,317	1,507	3,938	1,872
Detroit, MI	12,264	2,727	59.3	137.7	1,309	1,221	9,536	2,515	4,248	2,774
Dallas, TX	15,066	2,568	48.6	117.5	1,094	1,308	12,497	3,064	6,994	2,439
Phoenix, AZ	9,958	1,106	12.9	48.2	346	698	8,853	2,432	4,753	1,667
San Antonio, TX	12,291	792	21.8	73.0	395	302	11,498	2,609	7,381	1,508
San Jose, CA	5,364	659	6.6	55.7	166	430	4,706	927	3,214	565
Baltimore, MD	11,371	2,544	40.6	93.7	1,440	970	8,827	2,170	5,242	1,416
Indianapolis, IN	7,357	1,445	19.4	114.6	409	902	5,912	1,784	3,059	1,069
San Francisco, CA	9,384	1,645	12.9	54.1	950	629	7,738	1,435	4,692	1,611
Jacksonville, FL	10,331	1,629	18.2	109.6	589	913	8,702	2,588	5,033	1,082
Columbus, OH	10,145	1,131	21.6	101.8	587	421	9,014	2,568	5,165	1,280
Milwaukee, WI	9,044	979	25.6	78.9	668	206	8,065	1,482	4,451	2,133
Memphis, TN	10,184	1,422	27.3	105.3	727	563	8,761	2,674	3,929	2,159
Washington, DC	10,755	2,452	80.1	35.8	1,215	1,121	8,303	2,074	4,869	1,360
Boston, MA	10,837	2,066	19.7	84.9	836	1,126	8,771	1,752	4,669	2,350
Seattle, WA	12,255	1,364	8.1	82.1	519	755	10,891	1,998	7,607	1,286
El Paso, TX	9,630	1,067	9.3	50.3	282	725	8,563	1,727	5,787	1,050
Cleveland, OH	8,945	1,832	34.3	179.1	1,007	612	7,113	1,991	3,037	2,085
New Orleans, LA	10,831	2,190	68.9	60.3	1,192	869	8,640	2,476	4,189	1,975
Nashville-Davidson, TN	8,665	1,575	17.3	101.3	522	934	7,090	2,034	4,298	757
Denver, CO	7,625	1,050	18.4	89.1	341	602	6,575	1,915	3,448	1,213
Austin, TX	11,295	624	10.3	58.0	327	229	10,671	2,437	7,237	997
Fort Worth, TX	16,973	1,950	42.7	96.7	749	1,061	15,023	3,692	8,385	2,946
Oklahoma City, OK	11,073	1,128	12.5	105.3	334	677	9,945	2,634	5,997	1,314
Portland, OR	11,182	1,806	11.8	103.2	606	1,086	9,376	2,113	5,838	1,425
Kansas City, MO	13,198	2,833	30.8	108.9	1,131	1,562	10,366	2,969	5,141	2,256
Long Beach, CA	9,131	2,101	21.4	64.8	929	1,086	7,031	1,802	3,719	1,510
Tucson, AZ	10,401	939	5.8	80.0	214	639	9,462	1,807	6,819	836
St. Louis, MO	16,031	3,520	65.0	85.5	1,324	2,046	12,511	3,350	6,848	2,313
Charlotte, NC	12,643	2,176	28.3	101.6	720	1,326	10,467	2,885	6,905	677
Atlanta, GA	18,953	4,041	50.9	158.3	1,607	2,225	14,912	3,439	8,742	2,732
Virginia Beach, VA	5,859	272	6.8	31.8	128	105	5,587	1,042	4,213	332
Albuquerque, NM	10,284	1,422	13.0	66.4	332	1,010	8,862	2,632	5,602	628
Oakland, CA	12,187	2,496	39.2	121.1	1,035	1,301	9,691	2,329	5,446	1,916
Pittsburgh, PA	8,219	1,153	9.7	80.6	726	337	7,066	1,582	3,476	2,008
Sacramento, CA	10,098	1,299	17.5	58.6	605	618	8,800	2,056	4,739	2,004
Minneapolis, MN	11,282	1,578	17.1	199.3	699	662	9,704	2,408	5,935	1,361
Tulsa, OK	8,887	1,328	11.3	111.7	396	809	7,559	2,353	3,692	1,514
Honolulu, HI	5,959	240	3.4	32.1	100	104	5,718	1,157	4,206	356
Cincinnati, OH	9,722	1,578	14.7	130.2	631	803	8,144	2,312	5,253	579
Miami, FL	18,256	4,191	34.0	64.1	2,304	1,789	14,065	3,396	8,322	2,347
Fresno, CA	12,031	1,274	14.4	78.0	604	579	10,757	2,168	5,406	3,184
Omaha, NE	7,081	956	10.3	61.1	187	698	6,125	1,176	4,437	512
Toledo, OH	9,503	1,038	10.7	124.5	538	365	8,465	1,753	5,284	1,428
Buffalo, NY	9,555	1,835	15.2	96.9	821	901	7,721	2,569	3,804	1,348
Wichita, KS	9,830	872	7.8	92.7	458	313	8,958	2,435	5,579	944
Santa Ana, CA	7,654	1,103	19.7	25.3	649	409	6,552	1,418	3,684	1,449
Mesa, AZ	7,596	698	5.1	52.9	132	508	6,897	1,562	4,452	884
Colorado Springs, CO	7,441	481	8.7	80.2	134	258	6,960	1,341	5,205	414
Tampa, FL	16,286	3,491	19.5	116.6	1,048	2,307	12,795	3,841	6,842	2,113
Newark, NJ	14,806	3,400	31.8	88.2	1,881	1,399	11,406	2,235	4,122	5,049
St. Paul, MN	7,892	990	4.4	103.7	308	574	6,902	1,662	4,396	844
Louisville, KY	6,425	828	15.9	57.9	459	295	5,598	1,846	3,114	638
Anaheim, CA	7,152	714	9.2	40.8	362	303	6,438	1,577	3,717	1,144
Birmingham, AL	12,586	2,565	51.6	103.6	691	1,719	10,021	2,931	5,521	1,568
Arlington, TX	9,480	789	9.7	62.1	262	455	8,692	1,788	5,640	1,264
Norfolk, VA	9,243	1,158	32.4	77.2	577	472	8,084	1,722	5,251	1,111
Corpus Christi, TX	10,443	825	12.2	77.6	226	509	9,618	2,217	6,814	588
St. Petersburg, FL	10,427	2,225	12.7	71.9	767	1,373	8,202	2,144	5,061	998
Rochester, NY	11,196	1,036	27.5	71.4	588	349	10,159	2,572	6,729	859
Jersey City, NJ	9,201	2,011	10.0	42.3	1,123	836	7,190	2,009	2,831	2,350
Anchorage, AK	6,687	712	10.7	112.5	231	357	5,976	1,061	4,249	656
Lexington-Fayette, KY	7,018	794	5.7	72.2	200	516	6,225	1,414	4,437	374
Akron, OH	8,066	1,257	17.8	99.2	442	697	6,809	1,771	4,253	785
Aurora, CO	8,631	1,645	4.8	80.8	248	1,312	6,986	1,432	4,996	558
Baton Rouge, LA	13,118	2,316	24.6	60.3	484	1,747	10,802	2,714	6,807	1,282
Stockton, CA	11,327	1,288	25.5	74.8	693	494	10,039	2,288	5,972	1,780
Raleigh, NC	7,790	833	11.8	56.8	309	456	6,957	1,861	4,675	420
Shreveport, LA	10,098	1,258	25.0	60.0	362	811	8,840	2,269	6,039	531

[1] The rates for forcible rape, violent crime, and crime index are not shown because the forcible rape figures were not in accordance with national Uniform Crime Reporting guidelines.

Source: U.S. Federal Bureau of Investigation, *Crime in the United States*, annual.

No. 304. Murder—Circumstances and Weapons Used or Cause of Death: 1980 to 1991

[Based solely on police investigation. For definition of murder, see text, section 5]

CHARACTERISTIC	1980	1985	1990	1991	CHARACTERISTIC	1980	1985	1990	1991
Murders, total	**21,860**	**17,545**	**20,273**	**21,505**	Other motives.	20.6	18.1	19.4	19.8
Percent distribution . . .	100.0	100.0	100.0	100.0	Unknown	15.1	22.8	24.8	26.0
CIRCUMSTANCES					TYPE OF WEAPON OR CAUSE OF DEATH				
Felonies, total.	17.7	17.9	20.8	21.3					
Robbery	10.8	9.2	9.2	10.2	Guns.	62.4	58.7	64.3	66.3
Narcotics	1.7	2.9	6.7	6.2	Handguns	45.8	43.0	49.8	53.1
Sex offenses	1.5	1.5	1.1	0.9	Cutting or stabbing . . .	19.3	21.1	17.4	15.8
Other felonies	3.7	4.3	3.7	3.9	Blunt objects [1]	5.0	5.5	5.4	5.0
Suspected felonies . . .	6.7	2.0	0.7	1.0	Personal weapons [2] . . .	5.9	6.7	5.5	5.5
Argument, total	39.9	39.3	34.4	31.9	Strangulations,				
Property or money . .	2.6	2.7	2.5	2.4	asphyxiations.	2.3	2.4	2.0	2.0
Romantic triangle . . .	2.3	2.3	2.0	1.5	Fire.	1.3	1.4	1.4	0.9
Other arguments . . .	35.0	34.3	29.8	28.1	All other [3]	3.8	4.2	4.0	4.3

[1] Refers to club, hammer, etc.   [2] Hands, fists, feet, etc.   [3] Includes poison, drowning, explosives, narcotics, and unknown.

Source: U.S. Federal Bureau of Investigation, *Crime in the United States*, annual.

No. 305. Homicide Victims, by Race and Sex: 1970 to 1990

[**Rates per 100,000 resident population in specified group.** Excludes deaths to nonresidents of United States Beginning 1980, deaths classified according to the ninth revision of the *International Classification of Diseases;* for earlier years, classified according to revision in use at the time; see text, section 2. See also *Historical Statistics, Colonial Times to 1970*, series H 971-978]

YEAR	HOMICIDE VICTIMS					HOMICIDE RATE [2]				
	Total [1]	White		Black		Total [1]	White		Black	
		Male	Female	Male	Female		Male	Female	Male	Female
1970	16,848	5,865	1,938	7,265	1,569	8.3	6.8	2.1	67.6	13.3
1975	21,310	8,222	2,751	8,092	1,929	9.9	9.0	2.9	69.0	14.9
1980	24,278	10,381	3,177	8,385	1,898	10.7	10.9	3.2	66.6	13.5
1981	23,646	9,941	3,125	8,312	1,825	10.3	10.4	3.1	64.8	12.7
1982	22,358	9,260	3,179	7,730	1,743	9.6	9.6	3.1	59.1	12.0
1983	20,191	8,355	2,880	6,822	1,672	8.6	8.6	2.8	51.4	11.3
1984	19,796	8,171	2,956	6,563	1,677	8.4	8.3	2.9	48.7	11.2
1985	19,893	8,122	3,041	6,616	1,666	8.3	8.2	2.9	48.4	11.0
1986	21,731	8,567	3,123	7,634	1,861	9.0	8.6	3.0	55.0	12.1
1987	21,103	7,979	3,149	7,518	1,969	8.7	7.9	3.0	53.3	12.6
1988	22,032	7,994	3,072	8,314	2,089	9.0	7.9	2.9	58.0	13.2
1989	22,909	8,337	2,971	8,888	2,074	9.2	8.2	2.8	61.1	12.9
1990	24,932	9,147	3,006	9,981	2,163	10.0	9.0	2.8	69.2	13.5

[1] Includes races not shown separately.   [2] Rate based on enumerated population figures as of April 1 for 1970 and 1980; July 1 estimates for other years.

Source: U.S. National Center for Health Statistics, *Vital Statistics of the United States*, annual, and unpublished data.

No. 306. Forcible Rape—Number and Rate, by Selected Characteristic: 1970 to 1991

[For definition of rape, see text, section 5]

ITEM	1970	1975	1980	1983	1984	1985	1986	1987	1988	1989	1990	1991
NUMBER												
Total	37,990	56,090	82,990	78,920	84,230	88,670	91,460	91,110	92,490	94,500	102,560	106,590
By force	26,888	41,501	63,599	61,019	66,367	71,060	73,453	73,456	75,441	78,411	86,541	91,522
Attempt	11,102	14,589	19,391	17,901	17,863	17,610	18,007	17,654	17,049	16,089	16,019	15,068
RATE												
Per 100,000 population . .	18.7	26.3	36.8	33.7	35.7	37.1	37.9	37.4	37.6	38.1	41.2	42.3
Per 100,000 females. . . .	30.4	51.3	71.6	65.6	69.4	72.3	73.9	73.0	73.4	74.3	80.5	82.5
Per 100,000 females 12 years old and over . . .	46.3	62.9	86.3	78.5	83.0	86.6	88.6	87.5	88.1	89.3	96.6	100.9
AVERAGE ANNUAL PERCENT CHANGE IN RATE [1]												
Per 100,000 population . .	(NA)	0.4	6.1	-0.9	5.9	3.9	2.2	-1.3	0.5	1.3	8.1	2.7
Per 100,000 females 12 years old and over . . .	(NA)	-0.3	6.0	-1.0	5.7	4.3	2.3	-1.2	0.7	1.4	8.2	4.5

NA Not available.   [1] Represents annual average from prior year shown except for 1975, from 1974; for 1980, from 1979; and for 1983, from 1982.

Source: U.S. Federal Bureau of Investigation, *Population-at-Risk Rates and Selected Crime Indicators*, annual.

No. 307. Robbery and Property Crimes, by Type and Selected Characteristic: 1980 to 1991

[For definition of crime, see text, section 5]

ITEM	NUMBER OF OFFENSES (1,000)				RATE PER 100,000 INHABITANTS				AVERAGE VALUE LOST (dol.)	
	1980	1985	1990	1991	1980	1985	1990	1991	1990	1991
Robbery, total [1]	566	498	639	688	251.1	208.5	257.0	272.7	783	817
Type of crime:										
Street or highway	293	273	359	387	130.1	114.4	144.2	153.3	633	627
Commercial house.	78	60	73	80	34.6	25.3	29.5	31.9	1,341	1,456
Gas station	23	17	18	18	10.4	7.0	7.1	7.1	442	474
Convenience store	38	29	39	39	17.0	12.0	15.6	15.6	341	387
Residence	60	51	62	68	26.8	21.5	25.1	26.8	1,049	1,126
Bank.	8	7	9	11	3.8	2.8	3.8	4.4	3,244	3,177
Weapon used:										
Firearm	228	176	234	274	101.3	73.6	94.1	108.8	(NA)	(NA)
Knife or cutting instrument	73	66	76	76	32.3	27.7	30.7	30.1	(NA)	(NA)
Other dangerous weapon	51	46	61	64	22.8	19.2	24.5	25.4	(NA)	(NA)
Strongarm	214	210	268	274	94.8	88.0	107.7	108.5	(NA)	(NA)
Burglary, total	3,795	3,073	3,074	3,157	1,684.1	1,287.3	1,235.9	1,252.0	1,133	1,246
Forcible entry	2,789	2,148	2,150	2,200	1,237.5	899.6	864.5	872.4	(NA)	(NA)
Unlawful entry	711	668	678	713	315.6	280.0	272.8	282.8	(NA)	(NA)
Attempted forcible entry	295	257	245	244	131.0	107.8	98.7	96.7	(NA)	(NA)
Residence	2,525	2,046	2,033	2,088	1,120.6	857.0	817.4	828.1	1,143	1,281
Nonresidence	1,270	1,027	1,041	1,069	563.5	430.3	418.5	423.8	1,110	1,180
Occurred during the night	1,508	1,177	1,135	1,165	669.0	493.1	456.4	(NA)	(NA)	(NA)
Occurred during the day	1,263	1,025	1,151	1,156	560.3	429.2	462.8	(NA)	(NA)	(NA)
Larceny-theft, total	7,137	6,926	7,946	8,142	3,167.0	2,901.2	3,194.8	3,228.8	480	478
Pocket picking	85	79	81	83	37.9	32.9	32.4	33.0	355	366
Purse snatching	107	83	82	83	47.5	35.0	32.8	33.0	278	280
Shoplifting.	773	968	1,291	1,343	343.0	405.3	519.1	532.7	115	104
From motor vehicles.	1,231	1,369	1,744	1,828	546.4	573.3	701.3	724.7	541	544
Motor vehicle accessories	1,366	1,158	1,185	1,150	606.2	485.2	476.3	456.2	319	305
Bicycles	715	566	443	475	317.5	237.3	178.2	188.4	215	233
From buildings.	1,187	1,078	1,118	1,155	526.9	451.6	449.4	458.1	791	788
From coin-operated machines	58	60	63	79	25.8	24.9	25.4	31.5	147	139
Other	1,613	1,565	1,940	1,945	715.7	655.7	780.0	771.3	671	681
Motor vehicles, total [2]	1,132	1,103	1,636	1,662	502.2	507.8	657.8	658.9	5,032	4,983
Automobiles	845	832	1,304	1,325	374.8	348.5	524.3	525.2	(NA)	(NA)
Trucks and buses.	149	156	238	244	66.1	65.4	95.5	96.8	(NA)	(NA)

NA Not available.   [1] Includes other crimes not shown separately.   [2] Includes other types of motor vehicles not shown separately.

Source: U.S. Federal Bureau of Investigation, *Population-at-Risk Rates and Selected Crime Indicators*, annual.

No. 308. Number and Rate of Victimizations for Crimes Against Persons and Households, by Type: 1973 to 1991

[Data based on National Crime Survey; see text, section 5, and Appendix III]

YEAR	PERSONAL SECTOR								HOUSEHOLD SECTOR			
	Total	Violent crimes						Larce-ny—theft	Total	Bur-glary	Lar-ceny	Motor vehi-cle theft
		Total	Rape	Rob-bery	Assault							
					Total	Aggra-vated	Simple					
NUMBER (1,000)												
1973	20,322	5,351	156	1,108	4,087	1,655	2,432	14,971	15,340	6,459	7,537	1,344
1975	21,867	5,573	154	1,147	4,272	1,631	2,641	16,294	17,400	6,744	9,223	1,433
1980	21,430	6,130	174	1,209	4,747	1,707	3,041	15,300	18,821	6,973	10,468	1,381
1985	19,296	5,823	138	985	4,699	1,605	3,094	13,474	15,568	5,594	8,703	1,270
1986	18,751	5,515	130	1,009	4,376	1,543	2,833	13,235	15,368	5,557	8,455	1,356
1987	19,371	5,796	148	1,046	4,602	1,587	3,014	13,575	15,966	5,705	8,788	1,473
1988	19,966	5,910	127	1,048	4,734	1,741	2,993	14,056	15,830	5,777	8,419	1,634
1989	19,691	5,861	135	1,092	4,634	1,665	2,969	13,829	16,128	5,352	8,955	1,820
1990	18,984	6,009	130	1,150	4,729	1,601	3,128	12,975	15,419	5,148	8,304	1,968
1991	18,956	6,424	173	1,145	5,105	1,609	3,497	12,533	15,774	5,138	8,524	2,112
RATE [1]												
1973	123.6	32.6	1.0	6.7	24.9	10.1	14.8	91.1	217.8	91.7	107.0	19.1
1975	128.9	32.8	0.9	6.8	25.2	9.6	15.6	96.0	236.5	91.7	125.4	19.5
1980	116.3	33.3	0.9	6.6	25.8	9.3	16.5	83.0	227.4	84.3	126.5	16.7
1985	99.4	30.0	0.7	5.1	24.2	8.3	15.9	69.4	174.4	62.7	97.5	14.2
1986	95.6	28.1	0.7	5.1	22.3	7.9	14.4	67.5	170.0	61.5	93.5	15.0
1987	98.0	29.3	0.8	5.3	23.3	8.0	15.2	68.7	173.9	62.1	95.7	16.0
1988	100.1	29.6	0.6	5.3	23.7	8.7	15.0	70.5	169.6	61.9	90.2	17.5
1989	97.8	29.1	0.7	5.4	23.0	8.3	14.7	68.7	169.9	56.4	94.4	19.2
1990	93.4	29.6	0.6	5.7	23.3	7.9	15.4	63.8	161.0	53.8	86.7	20.5
1991	92.3	31.3	0.8	5.6	24.9	7.8	17.0	61.0	162.9	53.1	88.0	21.8

[1] Rate per 1,000 persons, 12 years old and over; and per 1,000 households.

Source: U.S. Bureau of Justice Statistics, *Criminal Victimization in the United States*, annual.

No. 309. Victimization Rates for Crimes Against Persons: 1973 to 1991

[Rates per 1,000 persons, 12 years old and over. Includes attempted crimes. Data based on National Crime Survey; see text, section 5, and Appendix III. Totals exclude personal larceny]

YEAR	Total [1]	White	Black	His-panic [2]	MALE			FEMALE			VICTIM-OFFENDER RELATIONSHIP	
					White	Black	His-panic [2]	White	Black	His-panic [2]	Stranger	Non-stranger
1973	33	32	42	36	43	53	53	21	32	22	22	11
1980	33	32	41	40	43	53	54	22	31	27	21	12
1985	30	29	38	30	38	47	33	21	31	27	18	12
1986	28	28	33	27	35	39	39	21	29	15	16	12
1987	29	28	42	39	36	52	44	20	34	35	17	13
1988	30	28	40	35	34	47	(NA)	22	35	(NA)	18	12
1989	29	28	36	39	35	50	50	22	25	28	18	12
1990	30	28	40	37	36	53	50	21	28	25	18	12
1991	31	30	44	36	38	61	48	22	31	24	19	13

NA Not available.   [1] Includes races not shown separately.   [2] Hispanic persons may be of any race.

No. 310. Crime Incidents, by Place and Time of Occurrence and Injury: 1991

INCIDENT CHARACTERISTICS	Rape	ROBBERY			ASSAULT			Personal larceny with contact
		Total	Completed	Attempted	Total	Aggravated	Simple assault	
Incidents, total	171,420	1,064,750	699,550	365,200	4,599,980	1,371,610	3,228,370	476,460
PERCENT DISTRIBUTION								
Place of occurrence	100.0	100.0	100.0	100.0	100.0	100.0	100.0	100.0
Inside own home.	26.8	9.5	8.6	11.0	10.7	11.3	10.5	[1]3.7
Near own home, on the street near home	[1]5.3	11.7	12.1	11.1	10.7	13.2	9.7	[1]5.4
Friend's, relative's, or neighbor's home . .	20.4	3.7	[1]2.9	[1]5.3	9.7	11.4	8.9	[1]1.7
Inside commercial property	[1]3.1	6.0	6.7	[1]4.7	13.1	11.7	13.7	25.7
In parking lot or garage	[1]4.2	11.9	12.9	9.9	10.7	12.5	9.9	[1]4.8
Inside school, on school property	[1]3.1	3.8	4.6	[1]2.2	13.0	7.0	15.6	[1]5.5
In park, field, or playground.	[1]1.1	3.6	[1]2.7	[1]5.2	4.0	5.3	3.5	[1]2.3
On street not near own or friend's home .	[1]5.1	39.5	37.4	43.4	19.0	21.6	18.0	28.0
Other	20.8	10.3	12.0	7.2	9.0	6.1	10.2	23.0
Time of occurrence:								
Daytime (6 a.m. to 6 p.m.)	33.4	44.1	46.0	40.5	47.9	36.8	52.6	64.6
Nighttime.	66.6	55.0	52.7	59.5	51.6	62.8	46.8	34.5
Percent of incidents:								
Involving the presence of a weapon	20.0	54.9	56.6	51.6	27.5	92.3	(X)	(X)
Resulting in victim injury	(NA)	33.4	34.2	31.9	31.9	36.9	29.5	(X)

NA Not available.   X Not applicable.   [1] Estimate based on about ten or fewer sample cases.

No. 311. Weapons Used in Crime Incidents by Armed Offenders, by Type of Weapon and Crime: 1991

RELATIONSHIP AND TYPE OF INCIDENT	Number of weapons used [1]	PERCENT DISTRIBUTION									
		Total	Firearm				Knife	Sharp object	Blunt object	Other	Type unknown
			Total	Hand gun	Other gun	Gun type unknown [2]					
Crimes of violence	2,025,800	100.0	36.6	28.7	7.6	[2]0.3	22.7	3.9	18.9	13.5	4.3
Completed	910,130	100.0	36.5	31.5	5.1	[2]-	21.5	3.6	21.9	14.4	[2]2.1
Attempted	1,115,660	100.0	36.6	26.5	9.6	[2]0.6	23.7	4.2	16.6	12.8	6.1
Rape [3]	40,990	100.0	[2]35.9	[2]35.9	[2]-	[2]-	[2]35.0	[2]5.4	11.9	[2]11.7	[2]-
Robbery	626,450	100.0	45.7	39.9	5.8	[2]-	25.9	[2]3.6	15.7	7.9	[2]1.2
Aggravated assault . . .	1,358,360	100.0	32.4	23.3	8.6	[2]0.5	20.9	4.0	20.6	16.1	5.9
Involving strangers:											
Crimes of violence. . . .	1,474,890	100.0	40.8	32.4	7.9	[2]0.4	20.6	3.6	19.4	[2]12.7	3.0
Rape [3]	34,030	100.0	[2]43.2	[2]43.2	[2]-	[2]-	[2]37.1	[2]-	5.6	[2]14.1	[2]-
Robbery	551,690	100.0	46.9	40.7	6.2	[2]-	24.9	[2]3.8	15.4	7.7	[2]1.3
Aggravated assault. .	889,160	100.0	36.9	26.9	9.3	[2]0.7	17.3	3.6	22.4	15.7	4.2
Involving nonstrangers:											
Crimes of violence. . . .	550,910	100.0	25.4	18.8	6.6	[2]-	28.5	4.9	17.8	15.7	7.8
Rape	6,950	100.0	[2]-	-	[2]-	[2]-	[2]25.1	32.0	42.9	[2]-	[2]-
Robbery	74,760	100.0	36.9	[2]34.4	[2]2.5	[2]-	[2]33.4	[2]2.6	18.2	[2]8.9	[2]-
Aggravated assault. .	469,200	100.0	23.9	[2]16.6	7.3	[2]-	27.8	[2]4.8	17.3	17.0	9.1

- Represents zero.   [1] Some respondents may have cited more than one weapon present.   [2] Based on about 10 or fewer sample cases.

Source of tables 309-311: U.S. Bureau of Justice Statistics, *Criminal Victimization in the United States, 1991.*

No. 312. Households Touched by Crime, 1981 and 1991, and by Characteristic, 1991

[A household is considered "touched by crime" if during the year it experienced a burglary, auto theft or household or assaulted, or a victim of personal theft, no matter where the crime occurred. Data based on the National Crime Survey; see text, section 5, and Appendix III]

TYPE OF CRIME	1981		1991					
	Num- ber (1,000)	Percent touched	Num- ber (1,000)	Percent touched				
				Total [1]	White	Black	Urban	Sub- urban	Rural
Total [2]	24,863	30.0	22,885	23.7	23.2	26.7	29.1	22.8	17.4
Violent crime	4,850	5.9	4,711	4.9	4.7	5.7	6.2	4.4	3.8
Rape......................	165	0.2	161	0.2	0.2	0.2	0.2	0.1	0.1
Robbery...................	1,117	1.3	951	1.0	0.8	2.1	1.8	0.7	0.3
Assault	3,890	4.7	3,852	4.0	4.0	3.8	4.6	3.8	3.5
Theft	17,738	21.4	16,069	16.6	16.6	16.7	20.0	16.5	11.9
Burglary	6,101	7.4	4,554	4.7	4.4	6.8	6.3	4.0	3.8
Motor vehicle theft	1,285	1.6	1,755	1.8	1.6	3.3	2.9	1.6	0.5

[1] Includes other races not shown separately.　[2] Types of crime will not add to "total" since each household may report as many crime categories as experienced.

Source: U.S. Bureau of Justice Statistics, 1981, *Households Touched by Crime;* 1991, *Crime and the Nation's Households, 1991.*

No. 313. Persons Arrested, by Charge and Race: 1991

[Represents arrests (not charges) reported by 10,075 agencies with a total 1991 population 186,621,000 as estimated by FBI]

OFFENSE CHARGED	TOTAL ARRESTS (1,000)					PERCENT DISTRIBUTION				
	Total	White	Black	Amer- ican Indian or Alaskan Native	Asian or Pacific Islander	Total	White	Black	Amer- ican Indian or Alaskan Native	Asian or Pacific Islander
Total	10,517	7,252	3,049	115	100	100.0	69.0	29.0	1.1	0.9
Serious crimes [1]	2,237	1,415	774	21	26	100.0	63.2	34.6	1.0	1.2
Murder and nonnegligent										
manslaughter.............	18	8	10	(Z)	(Z)	100.0	43.4	54.8	0.8	0.9
Forcible rape..............	30	16	13	(Z)	(Z)	100.0	54.8	43.5	0.9	0.8
Robbery..................	136	51	83	1	1	100.0	37.6	61.1	0.4	0.9
Aggravated assault.........	364	219	139	3	3	100.0	60.0	38.3	0.9	0.8
Burglary	324	223	95	3	3	100.0	68.8	29.3	0.9	1.0
Larceny/theft	1,190	793	368	13	16	100.0	66.6	30.9	1.1	1.4
Motor vehicle theft.........	160	94	63	1	2	100.0	58.5	39.3	0.8	1.4
Arson...................	15	11	3	(Z)	(Z)	100.0	76.7	21.5	0.9	0.9
All other nonserious crimes:										
Other assaults............	772	498	257	10	7	100.0	64.6	33.3	1.3	0.9
Forgery and counterfeiting.....	75	49	25	(Z)	1	100.0	64.8	33.7	0.6	0.9
Fraud...................	292	198	91	1	1	100.0	67.8	31.3	0.4	0.5
Embezzlement.............	11	7	3	(Z)	(Z)	100.0	68.2	30.2	0.7	0.9
Stolen property—buying, receiving, possessing	130	74	54	1	1	100.0	57.0	41.7	0.5	0.8
Vandalism................	249	189	55	2	2	100.0	76.0	22.1	1.0	0.9
Weapons; carrying, possessing, etc..................	173	99	72	1	2	100.0	56.8	41.6	0.5	1.1
Prostitution and commercialized vice	79	48	30	(Z)	1	100.0	60.3	38.0	0.6	1.1
Sex offenses (except forcible rape and prostitution)	81	63	16	1	1	100.0	78.2	19.8	1.0	1.0
Drug abuse violations........	763	444	313	3	4	100.0	58.1	41.0	0.3	0.5
Gambling	12	6	6	(Z)	1	100.0	44.8	46.9	0.1	8.2
Offenses against family and children	71	47	21	1	2	100.0	66.7	29.5	1.1	2.7
Driving under the influence	1,271	1,130	116	15	10	100.0	88.9	9.1	1.2	0.8
Liquor laws...............	449	392	44	11	3	100.0	87.3	9.7	2.4	0.6
Drunkenness..............	625	508	102	14	2	100.0	81.2	16.4	2.2	0.3
Disorderly conduct	559	366	182	7	3	100.0	65.5	32.7	1.3	0.6
Vagrancy	31	16	14	1	(Z)	100.0	51.2	46.6	2.0	0.2
All other offenses (except traffic	2,428	1,543	832	25	28	100.0	63.5	34.3	1.0	1.2
Suspicion	10	4	6	(Z)	(Z)	100.0	40.8	58.6	0.5	0.2
Curfew and loitering law violations.............	72	55	15	1	1	100.0	76.9	20.6	0.8	1.8
Runaways................	128	103	20	1	3	100.0	80.5	15.9	1.1	2.5

Z Less than 500.　[1] Includes arson.

Source: U.S. Federal Bureau of Investigation, *Crime in the United States,* annual.

No. 314. Persons Arrested, by Charge, Sex, and Age: 1991

[Represents arrests (not charges) reported by 10,148 agencies (reporting 12 months) with a total 1991 population of 190 million as estimated by FBI]

CHARGE	Total (1,000)	PERCENT DISTRIBUTION							
		Male	Under 15 years	Under 18 years	18-24 years	25-44 years	45-54 years	55-64 years	65 yr. and over
Total arrests..................	10,744	81.3	5.7	16.3	29.4	47.0	4.9	1.7	0.7
Serious crimes [1]................	**2,277**	**78.0**	**11.6**	**28.7**	**28.0**	**37.8**	**3.5**	**1.3**	**0.8**
Murder and nonnegligent manslaughter.....	19	89.7	1.6	14.1	40.6	38.7	4.3	1.5	0.9
Forcible rape......................	30	98.7	5.7	15.7	28.7	48.8	4.6	1.6	0.7
Robbery..........................	139	91.4	7.2	25.6	36.3	36.4	1.4	0.3	0.1
Aggravated assault................	368	86.3	4.3	14.3	28.6	49.6	5.1	1.7	0.7
Burglary [2].......................	329	91.1	13.5	33.4	31.5	32.9	1.6	0.4	0.1
Larceny—theft....................	1,215	68.0	13.8	30.4	25.3	37.4	4.0	1.7	1.1
Motor vehicle theft................	162	90.0	12.4	43.7	30.9	23.8	1.2	0.3	0.1
Arson...........................	15	86.9	31.9	46.5	18.5	29.4	3.7	1.3	0.6
All other nonserious crimes.......	**8,466**	**82.1**	**4.1**	**13.0**	**29.8**	**49.4**	**5.3**	**1.8**	**0.7**
Other assaults....................	789	83.5	6.3	15.5	27.0	50.8	4.6	1.4	0.6
Forgery and counterfeiting..........	77	65.0	1.6	8.9	34.3	52.0	3.7	0.8	0.3
Fraud...........................	293	57.1	1.0	3.7	28.3	59.5	6.1	1.7	0.8
Embezzlement....................	11	61.1	1.5	7.4	34.5	49.6	6.3	1.8	0.4
Stolen property [3].................	131	88.0	7.7	27.0	36.0	33.6	2.5	0.7	0.2
Vandalism.......................	252	89.1	21.3	42.7	26.8	27.7	2.0	0.6	0.3
Weapons (carrying, etc.)..........	179	92.8	6.0	21.0	36.0	36.8	4.0	1.5	0.7
Prostitution and commercialized vice.....	82	34.1	0.2	1.3	28.4	65.3	3.4	1.0	0.5
Sex offenses [4].................	82	93.0	9.0	17.5	20.2	48.9	7.8	3.6	2.0
Drug abuse violations.............	781	83.5	1.1	7.7	32.9	55.2	3.3	0.7	0.2
Gambling........................	13	87.3	1.1	7.1	20.4	44.2	14.9	8.9	4.6
Offenses against family and children....	73	81.9	1.4	4.1	23.5	64.3	6.0	1.5	0.6
Driving while intoxicated...........	1,289	86.7	(Z)	1.0	24.5	61.4	8.5	3.3	1.2
Liquor laws.....................	454	80.8	2.1	23.0	55.8	17.5	2.4	1.0	0.4
Drunkenness.....................	657	89.6	0.3	2.5	23.3	59.2	9.5	4.0	1.5
Disorderly conduct................	569	80.0	5.7	17.4	33.5	43.1	4.0	1.4	0.6
Vagrancy........................	31	89.2	1.9	7.2	19.3	59.9	9.6	3.0	1.0
Suspicion.......................	15	83.5	8.5	21.4	26.5	47.5	3.5	0.8	0.3
Curfew, loitering (juveniles)........	73	73.2	29.9	100.0	(X)	(X)	(X)	(X)	(X)
Runaways (juveniles).............	135	43.3	44.5	100.0	(X)	(X)	(X)	(X)	(X)
All other offenses, except traffic........	2,481	82.9	3.0	10.0	31.4	51.5	4.9	1.6	0.6

X Not applicable. Z Less than .05 percent. [1] Includes arson arrests, a newly established index offense in 1979. [2] Breaking or entering. [3] Buying, receiving, possessing. [4] Excludes forcible rape and prostitution, shown separately.

Source: U.S. Federal Bureau of Investigation, *Crime in the United States*, annual.

No. 315. Drug Use Among Persons Arrested—Percent Testing Positive, by Sex and Selected City: 1991 and 1992

[Based on the Drug Use Forecasting System, which measures drug use among persons arrested for primarily serious nondrug crimes. The program obtains voluntary, confidential urinalysis specimens from a new sample of arrestees each quarter]

CITY	MALES					FEMALES				
	July-Sept. 1991	Oct.-Dec. 1991	Jan.-Mar. 1992	Apr.-June 1992	July-Sept. 1992	July-Sept. 1991	Oct.-Dec. 1991	Jan.-Mar. 1992	Apr.-June 1992	July-Sept. 1992
Birmingham, AL....	57	64	67	65	67	54	60	71	52	50
Chicago, IL........	68	77	64	75	65	(NA)	(NA)	(NA)	(NA)	(NA)
Cleveland, OH.....	53	57	63	64	65	75	76	76	76	65
Dallas, TX........	55	60	62	60	60	57	51	61	64	71
Denver, CO.......	(NA)	48	68	56	59	48	55	57	55	69
Detroit, MI........	49	57	67	52	55	66	68	75	68	74
Ft. Lauderdale, FL..	60	56	70	62	63	63	67	72	62	55
Houston, TX......	62	65	61	60	50	58	67	55	58	58
Indianapolis, IN....	43	44	51	46	52	56	50	49	51	47
Kansas City, MO...	(NA)	56	56	62	56	(NA)	55	73	76	70
Los Angeles, CA..	60	62	70	69	62	70	76	69	77	67
New Orleans, LA...	62	56	60	61	65	44	53	56	58	48
New York, NY.....	69	70	75	77	77	84	76	88	82	83
Omaha, NE.......	23	40	78	50	48	(NA)	(NA)	(NA)	(NA)	(NA)
Philadelphia, PA....	70	72	77	75	80	76	75	77	80	79
Phoenix, AZ......	42	28	32	48	54	59	56	68	63	66
Portland, OR......	61	59	57	57	63	71	65	68	68	81
St. Louis, MO.....	57	65	62	65	61	38	56	73	65	70
San Antonio, TX...	44	54	56	57	48	52	36	33	61	50
San Diego, CA....	74	72	78	79	77	74	73	76	66	78
San Jose, CA.....	57	54	46	50	50	45	50	45	54	67
Washington, DC...	59	54	54	59	62	70	77	74	73	71

NA Not available.

Source: U.S. National Institute of Justice, *Drug Use Forecasting*, quarterly.

No. 316. Drug Arrest Rates for Drug Abuse Violations, 1980 to 1991, and by Region, 1991

[Rate per 100,000 inhabitants. Based on Bureau of the Census estimated resident population as of July 1, except 1980 and 1990, enumerated as of April 1. For composition of regions, see table 31]

OFFENSE	1980	1985	1988	1989	1990	1991 Total	North-east	Mid-west	South	West
Drug arrest rate, total	256.0	346.2	423.4	526.8	435.3	400.6	477.8	230.6	361.6	522.5
Sale and/or manufacture	57.9	82.0	118.8	170.8	139.0	133.8	213.6	70.1	111.9	147.6
Heroin or cocaine [1]	10.8	27.8	75.1	101.0	93.7	90.1	177.6	27.7	74.1	90.1
Marijuana..................	28.4	36.4	23.6	33.0	26.4	24.6	24.0	16.3	23.0	33.8
Synthetic or manufactured drugs	2.8	2.6	3.5	3.8	2.7	3.1	5.9	1.4	4.3	1.0
Other dangerous nonnarcotic drugs ..	15.9	15.2	16.7	33.1	16.2	16.0	6.1	24.7	10.6	22.8
Possession	198.1	264.1	304.6	356.0	296.3	266.8	264.2	160.5	249.7	374.9
Heroin or cocaine [1]	22.2	74.4	147.2	183.0	144.4	131.3	158.7	51.6	110.1	199.1
Marijuana..................	146.2	156.1	118.5	121.1	104.9	89.6	88.5	78.9	102.4	83.9
Synthetic or manufactured drugs	6.7	5.6	7.9	7.4	6.6	5.6	5.8	2.7	9.5	3.1
Other dangerous nonnarcotic drugs ..	23.0	28.1	31.0	44.4	40.4	40.3	11.1	27.3	27.8	88.8

[1] Includes other derivatives such as morphine, heroin, and codeine.

Source: U.S. Federal Bureau of Investigation, *Crime in the United States*, annual.

No. 317. Drug Removals, Laboratory Seizures, and Persons Indicted, by DEA: 1985 to 1992

[Represents domestic drug removals. 1 kg=.454 lbs; du=dosage unit]

ITEM	Unit	1985	1986	1987	1988	1989	1990	1991	1992
Domestic drug removals:									
Heroin..................	kg	447	382	382	829	629	637	1,124	613
Cocaine..................	kg	18,129	26,954	37,405	57,113	82,438	73,635	57,080	76,996
Cannabis (Marijuana)	1,000 kg.	745	711	649	602	336	149	108	201
Dangerous drugs...........	mil. du ..	26	32	34	114	109	148	532	46
Clandestine laboratory seizures ..	Number .	338	509	682	810	852	549	408	328
Narcotic Title III intercepts	Number .	136	79	93	129	192	235	256	291
Asset removals:									
Total seizures.............	$1,000 ..	246,344	401,415	504,397	671,290	975,884	1,106,827	956,960	857,338
DEA seizures.............	$1,000 ..	171,888	310,730	402,071	483,355	659,802	886,184	705,003	654,128
Seizures through inter-agency cooperation........	$1,000 ..	74,456	90,684	102,308	187,936	316,082	220,643	251,957	203,210
Arrests..................	Number .	15,727	18,687	21,869	23,994	25,718	23,082	23,025	23,405
Convictions...............	Number .	10,519	12,028	12,427	13,091	15,917	15,662	15,962	17,457

Source: Drug Enforcement Administration, *Annual Report*.

No. 318. Authorized Intercepts of Communication—Summary: 1980 to 1991

[Data for jurisdictions with statutes authorizing or approving interception of wire or oral communication]

ITEM	1980	1981	1982	1983	1984	1985	1986	1987	1988	1989	1990	1991
Jurisdictions: [1]												
With wiretap statutes	28	29	29	31	31	32	32	33	34	37	40	41
Reporting interceptions	22	22	22	20	24	22	24	22	23	25	25	23
Intercept applications authorized.	564	589	578	648	801	784	754	673	738	763	872	856
Intercept installations........	524	562	518	602	773	722	676	634	678	720	812	802
Federal................	79	106	129	205	277	235	247	233	286	305	321	349
State	445	456	389	397	496	487	429	401	392	415	491	453
Intercepted communications, average [2]	1,058	848	1,082	1,107	1,209	1,320	1,328	1,299	1,251	1,656	1,487	1,584
Incriminating..............	315	190	209	229	298	275	253	230	316	337	321	290
Persons arrested [3]	1,871	1,735	1,725	1,716	2,393	2,469	2,410	2,226	2,486	2,804	2,057	2,364
Convictions [3]	259	248	453	521	649	660	761	506	543	706	420	605
Major offense specified:												
Gambling.................	199	156	150	157	186	206	189	135	126	111	116	98
Drugs	282	318	333	360	483	434	348	379	435	471	520	536
Homicide and assault........	13	33	31	31	30	25	34	18	14	20	21	21
Other	70	82	64	100	102	119	183	141	163	161	204	201

[1] Jurisdictions include Federal Government, States, and District of Columbia. [2] Average per authorized installation. [3] Based on information received from intercepts installed in year shown; additional arrests/convictions will occur in subsequent years but are not shown here.

Source: Administrative Office of the U.S. Courts, *Report on Applications for Orders Authorizing or Approving the Interception of Wire, Oral or Electronic Communications*, (Wiretap Report), annual.

No. 319. Aliens Expelled and Immigration Violations: 1980 to 1991

[For fiscal years ending in year shown. See text, section 9. See also *Historical Statistics, Colonial Times to 1970*, series C 144, C 149, and C 158-160]

ITEM	Unit	1980	1983	1984	1985	1986	1987	1988	1989	1990	1991
Aliens expelled.	1,000	737	946	927	1,062	1,608	1,113	934	860	1,045	1,091
Deported	1,000	17	18	18	21	22	22	23	30	26	28
Required to depart	1,000	719	928	910	1,041	1,586	1,091	911	830	1,019	1,063
Prosecutions disposed of	Number . .	14,863	16,493	17,980	17,688	23,405	18,894	18,360	18,580	20,079	18,882
Immigration violations	Number . . .	14,498	15,848	16,989	16,976	22,751	18,200	17,590	17,992	19,351	18,297
Nationality violations	Number . . .	365	645	991	712	654	694	770	588	728	585
Convictions	Number . .	12,935	11,233	10,546	9,833	15,259	11,996	12,208	12,561	12,719	11,509
Immigration violations	Number . . .	12,678	10,947	10,237	9,635	15,104	11,786	11,929	12,379	12,515	11,392
Nationality violations	Number . . .	257	286	309	198	155	210	279	182	204	117

No. 320. Immigration Border Patrol and Investigation Activities: 1980 to 1991

[In thousands, except where indicated. For fiscal years ending in year shown. See text, section 9]

ITEM	1980	1983	1984	1985	1986	1987	1988	1989	1990	1991
BORDER PATROL										
Border patrol agents:										
Authorized (number)	2,484	2,413	2,409	3,228	3,214	4,812	4,812	4,804	4,852	4,968
On duty (number)	2,329	2,291	2,281	3,023	3,238	3,180	4,074	3,857	4,360	4,312
Border patrol obligations										
(mil. dol.)	82.5	110.2	114.1	141.9	150.4	194.6	205.3	246.4	261.1	295.5
Persons apprehended [1]	766.6	1,115.4	1,705.3	1,272.4	1,705.3	1,168.9	980.5	906.5	1,123.2	1,152.7
Deportable aliens located [2] . .	759.4	1,105.7	1,149.9	1,262.4	1,692.5	1,159.0	971.1	893.0	1,103.4	1,132.9
Mexican.	734.2	1,076.3	1,104.4	1,218.7	1,635.7	1,124.6	929.8	832.2	1,054.8	1,095.1
Canadian.	5.3	5.9	5.8	5.9	6.2	4.8	4.3	5.3	5.7	6.7
Other	19.9	23.5	30.2	37.8	50.6	29.6	37.0	55.5	42.8	31.1
Number of seizures	1,920	5,807	6,456	7,827	10,464	7,512	6,643	10,789	17,275	14,693
Value of seizures (mil. dol.) . .	116.1	43.5	44.5	122.0	165.1	590.6	721.2	1,212.7	843.6	950.2
Narcotics (mil. dol.)	110.3	28.7	42.9	119.8	161.7	582.4	700.5	1,191.5	797.8	910.1
INVESTIGATIONS										
Deportable aliens located . . .	150.9	140.8	102.9	83.9	72.8	31.5	37.0	61.1	64.1	63.6
Mexican.	83.3	96.0	66.2	48.3	35.8	15.0	19.9	33.1	35.8	35.5
Canadian.	1.5	1.5	1.1	1.1	1.2	0.4	0.4	0.5	0.4	0.5
Other	66.1	43.3	35.6	34.5	35.8	16.1	16.7	28.5	30.0	29.7

[1] Covers deportable aliens located and U.S. citizens engaged in smuggling or other immigration violations. [2] Beginning 1988, includes apprehension by the antismuggling unit.

Source of tables 319 and 320: U.S. Immigration and Naturalization Service, *Statistical Yearbook*, annual; and unpublished data.

No. 321. Law Enforcement Officers Killed, by Division, or Assaulted, by Type of Weapon Used: 1980 to 1991

[Covers officers killed feloniously and accidentally in line of duty; includes Federal officers. 1988 excludes Florida and Kentucky. For composition of regions, see table 31. See also *Historical Statistics, Colonial Times to 1970*, series H 987-998]

ITEM	1980	1983	1984	1985	1986	1987	1988	1989	1990	1991
OFFICERS KILLED										
Total killed.	165	152	147	148	133	148	155	145	132	71
Northeast	31	20	21	19	15	24	17	23	13	7
Midwest	23	26	22	23	20	31	18	22	20	20
South	72	64	69	64	63	51	77	68	68	29
West	32	34	32	29	29	40	39	23	23	7
Puerto Rico.	6	6	3	10	6	2	-	8	8	7
Outlying areas, foreign										
countries.	1	2	-	3	-	-	4	1	-	1
ASSAULTS										
Population (1,000) [1]	182,288	198,341	195,794	198,935	196,030	190,025	186,418	189,641	199,065	191,397
Number of—										
Agencies represented	9,235	9,908	10,002	9,906	9,755	8,957	8,866	9,213	9,483	9,263
Police officers.	345,554	377,620	372,268	389,808	380,249	378,977	369,743	380,232	412,314	405,069
Total assaulted.	57,847	62,324	60,153	61,724	64,259	63,842	58,752	62,172	71,794	62,852
Firearm	3,295	3,067	2,654	2,793	2,852	2,789	2,759	3,154	3,662	3,532
Knife or cutting instrument . . .	1,653	1,829	1,662	1,715	1,614	1,561	1,367	1,379	1,641	1,493
Other dangerous weapon . . .	5,415	5,527	5,148	5,263	5,721	5,685	5,573	5,778	7,390	7,014
Hands, fists, feet, etc	47,484	51,901	50,689	51,953	54,072	53,807	49,053	51,861	59,101	50,813

- Represents zero. [1] Represents the number of persons covered by agencies shown.

Source: U.S. Federal Bureau of Investigation, *Law Enforcement Officers Killed and Assaulted*, annual.

No. 322. Criminal Justice System—Public Expenditures and Employment, by Activity and Level of Government: 1990

[Based on a sample survey of local governments. Data for State governments were compiled from State financial records and for the Federal Government from the *Budget of the United States Government*]

TYPE OF GOVERNMENT	Total	ACTIVITY					
		Police protec- tion	Judicial	Legal services	Public defense	Correc- tions	Other justice
TOTAL EXPENDITURES [1]							
(mil. dol.)							
All governments [2]	74,249	31,805	9,307	5,500	1,742	24,961	934
Federal government	10,059	4,020	1,553	1,518	406	1,597	964
State and local government [2]	64,918	27,784	7,754	3,982	1,336	23,504	557
State government	28,005	5,197	3,478	1,451	604	16,693	582
Local government	39,667	23,081	4,635	2,686	788	8,244	233
FULL-TIME EQUIVALENT EMPLOYMENT							
(1,000)							
All governments	1,722	800	225	118	16	556	7
Federal government	136	65	22	24	(Z)	22	(Z)
State and local government	1,586	735	203	93	15	534	7
State government	576	121	70	30	7	345	5
Local government	1,007	614	133	63	8	188	2

Z Fewer than 500.   [1] Covers direct and intergovernmental expenditures.   [2] Totals are adjusted to exclude duplication from intergovernmental expenditures.

Source: U.S. Bureau of Justice Statistics, *Justice Expenditure and Employment in the U.S., 1990*.

No. 323. General Purpose Law Enforcement Agencies—Number, Employment, and Expenditures: 1987 and 1990

[Includes both full-time and part-time employees. State police data are based on the 49 main State police agencies; Hawaii does not have a State police agency. Expenditure data cover fiscal years ending in year stated]

TYPE OF AGENCY	1987			1990				
	Number of agen- cies[1]	Number of employ- ees	Expendi- tures (mil. dol.)	Number of agen- cies[1]	Number of employees			Expendi- tures (mil. dol.)
					Total	Sworn	Civilian	
NUMBER								
Total.	15,118	757,508	28,071.1	15,430	812,110	590,626	221,484	33,412.7
Local police	11,989	493,930	18,011.3	12,288	513,596	387,534	126,062	20,586.0
Sheriff	3,080	189,234	6,857.8	3,093	220,380	150,610	69,770	9,137.2
State police.	49	74,344	3,202.0	49	78,134	52,482	25,652	3,689.5
PERCENT								
Total.	100.0	100.0	100.0	100.0	100.0	100.0	100.0	100.0
Local police	79.3	65.2	64.2	79.6	63.2	65.6	56.9	61.6
Sheriff	20.4	25.0	24.4	20.0	27.1	25.5	31.5	27.3
State police.	0.3	9.8	11.4	0.3	9.6	8.9	11.6	11.0

[1] The number of agencies reported here is the result of a weighted sample and not an exact enumeration.

Source: U.S. Bureau of Justice Statistics, *Profile of State and Local Law Enforcement Agencies, 1987*, March 1989, and *State and Local Police Departments, 1990*, February 1992.

No. 324. Special Functions of Local Police Agencies: 1990

[Special functions are those functions that go beyond such traditional law enforcement functions as traffic enforcement, accident investigation, crime investigation, patrol, fingerprinting, and communications]

POPULATION SERVED	PERCENT OF ALL AGENCIES THAT REPORTED HAVING PRIMARY RESPONSIBILITY FOR—								
	Animal control	Emer- gency medical services	Court security	Civil defense	Civil process- serving	Jail oper- ations	Training academy operation	Labora- tory test- ing for drugs	Ballistics work
All sizes.	43	18	18	14	10	5	4	3	1
1,000,000 or more . .	-	21	14	21	14	21	93	64	64
500,000-999,999 . . .	3	-	17	7	14	10	87	45	42
250,000-499,999 . . .	19	8	14	2	-	17	80	48	51
100,000-249,999 . . .	30	10	14	7	3	25	48	19	13
50,000-99,999	53	16	15	15	3	12	19	8	3
25,000-49,999	47	18	18	18	5	10	4	9	1
10,000-24,999	50	23	23	16	7	10	4	5	1
2,500-9,999.	47	17	17	14	8	4	1	2	1
Under 2,500	38	17	15	12	13	2	2	1	1

- Represents zero.

Source: U.S. Bureau of Justice Statistics, *State and Local Police Departments, 1990*, February 1992.

No. 325. State and Local Government Police Protection and Correction—Employment and Expenditures: 1991

[Employment as of **October**. Expenditures for fiscal years. Local government data are estimates subject to sampling variation; see Appendix III and source]

REGION, DIVISION, AND STATE	FULL-TIME EQUIVALENT EMPLOYMENT			Per 10,000 population [1]		EXPENDITURES			
	Total	Police protection	Correction	Police protection	Correction	Total [2] (mil. dol.)	Per capita [1] (dol.)	Police protection (mil. dol.)	Correction (mil. dol.)
United States ...	1,228,464	706,584	521,880	28.0	20.7	75,506	299	32,772	27,356
Northeast	274,921	163,244	111,677	32.0	21.9	18,367	361	7,645	6,995
New England.	55,825	36,578	19,247	27.8	14.6	3,904	296	1,680	1,464
Maine.	4,696	2,945	1,751	23.8	14.2	233	189	100	90
New Hampshire....	4,360	2,939	1,421	26.6	12.9	257	233	126	64
Vermont	1,907	1,231	676	21.7	11.9	105	185	49	30
Massachusetts. ...	25,476	17,220	8,256	28.9	13.8	1,882	315	794	728
Rhode Island.	4,762	2,985	1,777	29.7	17.7	288	287	130	92
Connecticut.	14,624	9,258	5,366	28.1	16.3	1,139	346	481	460
Middle Atlantic	219,096	126,666	92,430	33.5	24.5	14,463	383	5,965	5,531
New York	124,608	66,920	57,688	37.1	31.9	9,013	499	3,561	3,688
New Jersey.	47,759	30,536	17,223	39.4	22.2	2,712	349	1,241	887
Pennsylvania.	46,729	29,210	17,519	24.4	14.6	2,738	229	1,163	956
Midwest.	252,255	157,807	94,448	26.2	15.7	14,539	241	6,876	4,626
East North Central...	184,071	114,776	69,295	27.1	16.3	10,931	258	5,148	3,562
Ohio	43,256	27,398	15,858	25.0	14.5	2,728	249	1,233	851
Indiana.	22,299	13,081	9,218	23.3	16.4	970	173	424	363
Illinois	59,233	39,890	19,343	34.6	16.8	3,068	266	1,605	901
Michigan.	40,153	21,634	18,519	23.1	19.8	2,838	303	1,232	1,039
Wisconsin.	19,130	12,773	6,357	25.8	12.8	1,327	268	654	408
West North Central ..	68,184	43,031	25,153	24.2	14.1	3,608	203	1,728	1,064
Minnesota.	14,216	9,064	5,152	20.5	11.6	1,009	228	485	268
Iowa	8,868	6,034	2,834	21.6	10.1	532	190	251	136
Missouri	23,314	14,578	8,736	28.3	16.9	975	189	515	279
North Dakota.	1,911	1,366	545	21.5	8.6	91	143	41	22
South Dakota	2,342	1,544	798	22.0	11.4	113	161	53	37
Nebraska.	6,364	3,832	2,532	24.1	15.9	292	183	138	96
Kansas.	11,169	6,613	4,556	26.5	18.3	596	239	245	226
South	437,395	237,845	199,550	27.4	23.0	22,378	257	9,838	8,532
South Atlantic......	244,389	129,655	114,734	29.2	25.8	13,382	301	5,777	5,266
Delaware	3,543	1,909	1,634	28.1	24.0	223	328	89	83
Maryland	26,503	14,754	11,749	30.4	24.2	1,741	358	757	679
District of Columbia .	9,963	5,320	4,643	89.0	77.6	754	1,261	267	362
Virginia.	29,324	15,224	14,100	24.2	22.4	1,636	260	714	635
West Virginia.	4,286	2,932	1,354	16.3	7.5	212	118	91	59
North Carolina.....	32,265	17,307	14,958	25.7	22.2	1,559	231	686	633
South Carolina.....	17,570	8,885	8,685	25.0	24.4	797	224	316	371
Georgia	35,852	18,288	17,564	27.6	26.5	1,763	266	695	808
Florida	85,083	45,036	40,047	33.9	30.2	4,697	354	2,162	1,636
East South Central...	63,114	36,250	26,864	23.6	17.5	2,902	189	1,273	1,053
Kentucky	14,648	7,781	6,867	21.0	18.5	704	190	302	250
Tennessee	22,439	12,361	10,078	25.0	20.3	1,094	221	437	465
Alabama.	16,662	10,418	6,244	25.5	15.3	756	185	362	232
Mississippi	9,365	5,690	3,675	22.0	14.2	348	134	172	106
West South Central ..	129,892	71,940	57,952	26.5	21.3	6,094	224	2,788	2,213
Arkansas	8,786	5,096	3,690	21.5	15.6	337	142	156	119
Louisiana	21,495	11,870	9,625	27.9	22.6	1,024	241	515	322
Oklahoma........	14,311	8,767	5,544	27.6	17.5	619	195	277	238
Texas.	85,300	46,207	39,093	26.6	22.5	4,114	237	1,840	1,534
West.	263,893	147,688	116,205	27.3	21.5	20,217	374	8,412	7,203
Mountain	68,041	39,238	28,803	28.0	20.5	4,239	302	1,849	1,497
Montana.	3,095	1,959	1,136	24.2	14.1	158	196	70	54
Idaho...........	4,172	2,681	1,491	25.8	14.4	205	197	101	59
Wyoming	2,377	1,527	850	33.2	18.5	138	300	69	40
Colorado.	15,185	9,235	5,950	27.3	17.6	978	290	435	354
New Mexico	8,130	4,536	3,594	29.3	23.2	440	284	197	157
Arizona.	20,707	11,105	9,602	29.6	25.6	1,394	372	595	492
Utah	6,596	3,967	2,629	22.4	14.9	390	220	162	141
Nevada	7,779	4,228	3,551	32.9	27.7	536	417	220	200
Pacific	195,852	108,450	87,402	27.1	21.8	15,978	399	6,563	5,706
Washington.	19,904	10,872	9,032	21.7	18.0	1,310	261	564	470
Oregon.	11,898	6,492	5,406	22.2	18.5	842	288	334	336
California	155,996	86,259	69,737	28.4	23.0	13,121	432	5,402	4,681
Alaska	2,913	1,572	1,341	27.6	23.5	342	600	115	127
Hawaii	5,141	3,255	1,886	28.7	16.6	363	320	148	92

[1] Based on resident population as of July 1. [2] Includes judicial and legal, not shown separately.

Source: U.S. Bureau of the Census, Public Employment, series GE, No. 1, annual, and Government Finances, series GF, No. 5, annual.

No. 326. Lawyers—Selected Characteristics: 1960 to 1988

[See headnote, table 327. See also *Historical Statistics, Colonial Times to 1970*, series H 1028-1062]

CHARACTERISTIC	1960	1963	1966	1970	1980	1985	1988
All lawyers [1]	**285,933**	**296,069**	**316,656**	**355,242**	**542,205**	**655,191**	**723,189**
Lawyers reporting [2]	252,385	268,782	289,404	324,818	(X)	(X)	(X)
Male	245,897	261,639	281,336	315,715	498,019	569,649	606,768
Female.	6,488	7,143	8,068	9,103	44,185	85,542	116,421
Status in practice: [3]							
Government	25,621	29,314	31,280	35,803	50,490	53,035	57,742
Federal.	13,045	15,113	16,284	18,710	20,132	19,989	23,042
State	4,316	6,486	7,416	9,293	30,358	33,046	34,700
City or county	8,260	7,715	7,580	7,800	(4)	(4)	(4)
Judicial [5]	8,180	8,748	9,712	10,349	19,160	21,677	19,071
Federal.	599	707	800	878	2,611	3,003	2,551
State and county	5,301	5,712	6,823	7,548	16,549	18,674	16,520
City	2,280	2,329	2,089	1,923	(4)	(4)	(4)
Private practice	192,353	200,586	212,662	236,085	370,111	460,206	519,941
Individual	116,911	113,127	113,273	118,963	179,923	216,336	240,141
Partner.	60,709	70,064	78,544	92,442	144,279	177,392	194,976
Associate [6]	14,733	17,395	20,845	24,680	45,908	66,478	84,824
Salaried.	25,198	29,510	33,222	40,486	73,862	83,843	85,671
Private industry	22,533	26,492	29,405	33,593	54,626	63,622	66,627
Educational institutions . .	1,798	2,100	2,717	3,732	6,606	7,254	7,575
Other private employment	867	918	1,100	3,161	12,630	12,967	11,469
Inactive or retired [5]	10,887	12,024	14,881	16,812	28,582	36,430	40,762

X Not applicable.   [1] 1960 to 1970 includes lawyers not reporting and an adjustment (subtraction) for duplications; 1980, 1985, and 1988 weighted to account for nonreporters and duplicate listings.   [2] 1960 to 1970 includes duplications; 1980, 1985, and figures are weighted to adjust for duplication of entries.   [3] 1960 to 1970, in cases where more than one subentry was applicable, the individual was tabulated in each. In 1980 and 1985 lawyers who were in both private practice and government service are coded in private practice.   [4] Data no longer available separately; included with category above.   [5] Beginning 1988, "senior" judges are included in "Retired" rather than "Judicial."   [6] Associates are lawyers designated as such by their employers.

Source: American Bar Foundation, Chicago, IL, 1960 to 1970, *The 1971 Lawyer Statistical Report*, 1971 (copyright); 1980, *The Lawyer Statistical Report: A Statistical Profile of the U.S. Legal Profession in the 1980's*, 1985 (copyright); 1985 and 1988, *Supplement to The Lawyer Statistical Report: The U.S. Legal Profession in 1988*, 1991 and similar report for 1985 (copyright).

No. 327. Lawyers, by State: 1970 to 1988

[Data based on 1971, 1980, and 1988 editions of *Martindale-Hubbell Law Directory*. Represents all persons who are members of the bar, including those in industries, educational institutions, etc., and those inactive or retired]

STATE	1970 [1]	1980 [2]	1988 Total [2]	1988 In private practice [2]	1988 Population per lawyer [3]	STATE	1970 [1]	1980 [2]	1988 Total [2]	1988 In private practice [2]	1988 Population per lawyer [3]
U.S. [4] .	**324,818**	**542,205**	**723,189**	**519,941**	**340**						
						MO	7,230	10,731	13,463	9,495	382
AL	3,291	5,466	7,261	5,276	565	MT	978	1,617	2,161	1,606	373
AK	443	1,355	1,940	1,355	270	NE	2,481	3,722	4,473	3,022	358
AZ	2,618	5,657	8,859	6,222	394	NV	739	1,771	2,489	1,723	423
AR	1,969	3,188	3,939	2,746	608	NH	791	1,678	2,613	1,922	415
CA	31,580	64,840	93,054	70,496	304	NJ	11,126	18,400	27,308	19,647	283
CO	4,197	8,652	12,253	9,006	269	NM	1,201	2,508	3,503	2,620	430
CT	5,398	8,930	13,144	8,629	246	NY	48,312	62,745	81,698	60,651	219
DE	733	1,332	1,813	1,078	364	NC	4,367	7,459	10,238	7,324	634
DC	15,501	25,465	32,114	15,524	19	ND	728	1,101	1,286	904	519
FL	10,917	23,521	33,259	24,634	371	OH	15,349	23,949	28,290	20,269	384
GA	5,517	11,087	15,314	11,528	414	OK	4,637	7,034	8,853	6,443	366
HI	857	2,027	3,130	2,310	351	OR	2,996	5,803	7,743	5,582	357
ID	803	1,706	2,242	1,551	447	PA	13,557	22,872	30,319	23,061	396
IL	20,404	32,421	40,743	29,044	285	RI	1,284	2,070	2,654	2,095	374
IN	5,447	8,443	10,091	7,265	551	SC	2,236	4,195	5,482	4,177	633
IA	3,820	5,550	6,159	4,266	460	SD	812	1,125	1,385	992	515
KS	3,126	4,759	5,978	4,113	417	TN	4,770	7,802	9,515	6,771	514
KY	3,625	6,200	7,517	5,447	496	TX	17,217	30,151	43,455	32,580	388
LA	5,089	8,752	11,515	9,244	383	UT	1,309	2,480	3,640	2,720	464
ME	1,068	2,062	2,922	2,105	412	VT	581	1,095	1,537	1,099	362
MD	6,619	10,648	14,608	9,689	316	VA	6,401	10,895	14,910	9,846	403
MA	11,316	18,537	24,218	18,506	243	WA	4,466	8,468	12,925	9,555	360
MI	10,569	17,443	21,644	15,630	427	WV	1,719	2,566	3,016	2,238	622
MN	5,481	9,433	12,723	8,714	339	WI	6,177	9,117	10,829	7,681	448
MS	2,517	3,850	4,384	3,316	598	WY	449	927	1,168	793	410

[1] Represents lawyers reporting only. Includes an estimated adjustment (subtraction) to account for duplications. Based on reporting from approximately 90 percent of all lawyers.   [2] Weighted to account for nonreporters and duplicate listings.   [3] Based on Bureau of the Census estimated resident population, including Armed Forces station in area as of July 1, 1988.   [4] Total for United States counts each lawyer only once regardless of the number of offices maintained by the lawyer. If, however, a lawyer maintains an office in more than one State, the lawyer is included in the total shown for each State in which the lawyer maintains an office.

Source: American Bar Foundation, Chicago, IL, *The 1971 Lawyer Statistical Report, 1971* (copyright); 1980, *The Lawyer Statistical Report: A Statistical Profile of the U.S. Legal Profession in the 1980's*, 1985 (copyright); and 1988, *Supplement to The Lawyer Statistical Report: The U.S. Legal Profession in 1988*, 1991 (copyright).

No. 328. U.S. Supreme Court—Cases Filed and Disposition: 1980 to 1991

[Statutory term of court begins first Monday in **October**. See *Historical Statistics, Colonial Times to 1970*, series H 1063-1078, for related but not comparable data]

ACTION	1980	1983	1984	1985	1986	1987	1988	1989	1990	1991
Total cases on docket	5,144	5,100	5,006	5,158	5,123	5,268	5,657	5,746	6,316	6,770
Appellate cases on docket............	2,749	2,688	2,575	2,571	2,547	2,577	2,587	2,416	2,351	2,451
From prior term...................	527	520	539	400	476	440	446	384	365	365
Docketed during present term........	2,222	2,168	2,036	2,171	2,071	2,137	2,141	2,032	1,986	2,086
Cases acted upon [1]...............	2,324	2,220	2,253	2,185	2,189	2,224	2,271	2,096	2,042	2,124
Granted review	167	140	167	166	152	157	130	103	114	103
Denied, dismissed, or withdrawn....	1,999	1,902	1,953	1,863	1,876	1,919	1,973	1,881	1,802	1,913
Summarily decided...............	90	71	59	78	71	66	75	44	81	52
Cases not acted upon	425	468	322	386	358	353	316	320	309	327
Pauper cases on docket.............	2,371	2,394	2,416	2,577	2,564	2,675	3,056	3,316	3,951	4,307
Cases acted upon.................	2,027	1,992	2,087	2,189	2,250	2,263	2,638	2,891	3,436	3,768
Granted review	17	9	18	20	15	23	17	19	27	17
Denied, dismissed, or withdrawn....	1,968	1,968	2,050	2,136	2,186	2,210	2,577	2,824	3,369	3,716
Summarily decided...............	32	10	14	24	38	21	32	35	28	22
Cases not acted upon	344	402	329	388	314	412	418	425	515	539
Original cases on docket............	24	18	15	10	12	16	14	14	14	12
Cases disposed of during term	7	7	8	2	1	5	2	2	3	1
Total cases available **for argument.**..............	264	269	271	276	270	280	254	204	201	196
Cases disposed of	162	189	184	175	179	175	173	147	131	130
Cases argued..................	154	184	175	171	175	167	170	146	125	127
Cases dismissed or remanded without argument...............	8	5	9	4	4	8	3	1	6	2
Cases remaining	102	80	87	101	91	105	81	57	70	66
Cases decided by signed opinion	144	174	159	161	164	151	156	143	121	120
Cases decided by per curiam opinion. ...	8	6	11	10	10	9	12	3	4	4
Number of signed opinions	123	151	139	146	145	139	133	129	112	107

[1] Includes cases granted review and carried over to next term, not shown separately.
Source: Office of the Clerk, Supreme Court of the United States, unpublished data.

No. 329. U.S. Courts of Appeals—Cases Commenced and Disposition: 1980 to 1992

[For years ending **June 30**. See also *Historical Statistics, Colonial Times to 1970*, series H 1079-1096]

ITEM	1980	1984	1985	1986	1987	1988	1989	1990	1991	1992
Cases commenced [1]	23,200	31,490	33,360	34,292	35,176	37,524	39,734	40,898	42,033	46,032
Criminal.........	4,405	4,881	4,989	5,134	5,260	6,012	8,020	9,493	9,949	10,956
U.S. civil........	4,654	6,259	6,744	6,415	6,292	6,210	6,349	6,626	6,663	7,113
Private civil.......	10,200	15,466	16,827	17,876	19,246	20,464	20,626	20,490	20,798	22,862
Administrative appeals	2,950	3,045	3,179	3,187	2,723	3,043	2,965	2,578	2,764	3,052
Cases terminated [1] ...	20,887	31,185	31,387	33,774	34,444	35,888	37,312	38,520	41,414	42,933
Criminal.........	3,993	4,876	4,892	5,134	5,039	5,284	6,297	7,509	9,198	9,830
U.S. civil........	4,346	6,074	6,363	6,535	6,227	6,386	6,127	6,379	6,579	6,797
Private civil.......	8,942	15,309	15,743	17,276	18,338	19,798	20,313	20,369	20,698	21,628
Administrative appeals	2,643	3,212	2,760	3,235	3,237	2,625	2,914	2,582	3,148	2,801
Cases disposed of [2] .	10,607	14,327	16,369	18,199	18,502	19,178	19,322	21,006	22,707	23,162
Affirmed or granted .	8,017	10,961	12,286	13,398	13,681	14,953	15,240	16,629	17,988	18,463
Reversed or denied .	1,845	2,382	2,770	3,249	2,924	2,664	2,617	2,565	2,503	2,681
Other.	745	984	1,313	1,552	1,897	1,561	1,465	1,812	2,216	2,018
Median months [3]	8.9	8.3	10.3	10.3	10.3	10.1	10.3	10.1	10.2	10.5

[1] Includes original proceedings and bankruptcy appeals not shown separately. [2] Terminated on the merits after hearing or submission. [3] Prior to 1985, the figure is from filing of complete record to final disposition; beginning 1985, figure is from filing notice of appeal to final disposition.

No. 330. U.S. District Courts—Civil and Criminal Cases: 1980 to 1992

[**In thousands, except percent**. For years ending **June 30**. See also *Historical Statistics, Colonial Times to 1970*, series H 1097-1111]

ITEM	1980	1984	1985	1986	1987	1988	1989	1990	1991	1992
Civil cases: Commenced	168.8	261.5	273.7	254.8	239.0	239.6	233.5	217.9	207.7	226.9
Cases terminated [1]........	155.0	241.8	268.6	265.8	237.5	238.1	234.6	213.4	211.7	239.6
No court action	68.7	113.9	129.4	122.2	97.8	79.6	64.3	51.6	44.6	51.4
Court action, total.........	86.2	127.9	139.2	143.6	139.7	158.6	170.4	161.8	166.5	187.6
Before pretrial..........	53.8	86.1	95.5	101.9	95.3	114.7	129.7	127	136.9	153.4
Pretrial	22.4	29.6	31.1	29.9	32.5	32.2	29.5	25.5	21.1	26.2
Trials	10.1	12.1	12.6	11.7	11.9	11.6	11.2	9.2	8.4	8.0
Percent reaching trial ...	6.5	5.0	4.7	4.4	5.0	4.9	4.8	4.3	4.0	3.4
Criminal cases: Commenced [2]....	28.0	35.9	38.5	40.4	42.2	43.5	44.9	46.5	45.1	47.5
Defendants disposed of [3]....	36.6	44.5	47.4	50.0	54.2	52.8	54.6	56.5	56.7	58.4
Not convicted	8.0	8.4	8.8	9.3	10.2	9.9	10.1	9.8	10.0	10.0
Convicted	28.6	36.1	38.5	40.7	43.9	42.9	44.5	46.7	46.8	48.4
Imprisonment	13.2	17.7	18.7	20.6	23.3	22.5	24.9	28.8	29.2	31.1
Probation..............	11.1	13.9	14.4	15.2	16.0	16.1	15.0	14.2	13.8	13.1
Fine and other	4.4	4.5	5.4	4.9	4.6	4.4	4.7	4.7	3.8	4.3

[1] Excludes land condemnation cases. [2] Excludes transfers. [3] Includes Guam, Virgin Islands, and Northern Mariana Islands; 1980 includes Canal Zone.
Source of tables 329 and 330: Administrative Office of the U.S. Courts, *Annual Report of the Director*.

No. 331. U.S. District Courts—Civil Cases Commenced and Pending: 1980 to 1992

[For years ending June 30]

TYPE OF CASE	CASES COMMENCED				CASES PENDING			
	1980	1990	1991	1992	1980	1990	1991	1992
Cases total	168,789	217,879	207,690	226,895	186,113	244,570	237,040	224,302
Contract actions [1]	49,052	46,039	42,396	51,246	40,521	42,497	41,588	42,170
Recovery of overpayments [2] . . .	15,588	10,878	7,932	17,475	6,696	4,686	4,663	6,368
Real property actions	11,067	9,505	9,795	10,143	15,436	8,743	7,657	7,893
Tort actions	32,539	43,759	37,287	36,469	41,062	77,998	69,734	47,744
Personal injury	27,517	40,593	34,007	33,147	34,994	74,141	65,792	43,819
Personal injury product liability [1]	(NA)	18,679	12,399	10,769	9,118	47,288	39,264	17,038
Asbestos	(NA)	13,687	7,142	4,673	(NA)	38,849	31,218	8,843
Other personal injury.	27,517	21,914	21,608	22,378	25,876	26,853	26,528	26,781
Personal property damage	5,022	3,166	3,280	3,322	6,068	3,857	3,942	3,925
Actions under statutes [1]	75,574	118,465	118,085	128,921	88,534	114,853	117,538	125,934
Civil rights [1]	12,944	18,793	19,337	23,419	18,819	23,791	24,009	27,220
Employment	5,017	8,413	8,144	10,275	8,893	11,490	11,156	12,738
Bankruptcy suits	1,688	5,056	5,013	5,243	1,443	3,941	4,083	4,379
Commerce (ICC rates, etc.). . . .	1,105	2,401	1,556	2,475	6,194	1,441	1,189	1,306
Environmental matters	557	958	1,075	1,252	751	1,538	1,719	1,988
Prisoner petitions	23,287	42,630	42,476	46,452	18,008	35,793	37,259	40,894
Forfeiture and penalty	3,019	6,193	5,581	5,492	2,282	4,886	4,967	4,951
Labor laws.	8,640	13,841	14,684	15,800	9,045	12,112	12,778	13,446
Protected property rights [3]	3,783	5,700	5,231	5,670	4,014	5,448	5,296	5,497
Securities commodities and exchanges	1,694	2,629	2,245	1,998	3,255	4,636	4,555	4,137
Social Security laws.	9,043	7,439	7,695	8,415	13,154	8,068	8,154	8,739
Tax suits	3,262	2,604	2,639	2,305	3,075	2,850	2,713	2,429
Freedom of information	627	407	363	439	617	451	465	548

NA Not available. [1] Includes other types not shown separately. [2] Includes enforcement of judgments in student loan cases, and overpayments of veterans benefits. [3] Includes copyright, patent, and trademark rights.

No. 332. U.S. District Courts—Trials: 1980 to 1992

[For years ending June 30. A trial is defined as a contested proceeding (other than a hearing on a motion) before either court or jury in which evidence is introduced and final judgment sought. See also Historical Statistics, Colonial Times to 1970, series H 1112-1118]

TYPE OF TRIAL	1980	1984	1985	1986	1987	1988	1989	1990	1991	1992
Total	19,825	20,830	20,729	20,242	19,985	19,901	20,102	20,433	19,949	19,992
Civil trials	13,191	14,374	14,254	13,276	13,162	12,536	12,085	11,502	11,024	10,527
Nonjury.	9,254	9,037	8,817	8,054	7,597	7,088	6,878	6,737	6,507	6,289
Jury	3,937	5,337	5,437	5,222	5,565	5,448	5,207	4,765	4,517	4,238
Criminal trials.	6,634	6,456	6,475	6,966	6,823	7,365	8,017	8,931	8,925	9,465
Nonjury.	3,216	2,823	2,778	3,066	2,912	3,215	3,553	3,870	3,678	3,832
Jury	3,418	3,633	3,697	3,900	3,911	4,150	4,464	5,061	5,247	5,633

No. 333. U.S. District Courts—Criminal Cases Commenced and Defendants Disposed of, by Nature of Offense: 1991 and 1992

[For years ending June 30]

NATURE OF OFFENSE	1991		DISPOSITION OF DEFENDANTS, 1992									
	Cases commenced [1]	Defendants disposed of	Cases commenced, [1] 1992	Total defendants disposed of	Not convicted		Convicted [2]			Sentenced		
					Total	Acquitted	Total	Guilty plea [3]	By court or jury	Imprisonment	Probation	Fine and other
Total	45,053	56,747	47,467	58,373	9,981	1,653	48,392	42,339	5,523	31,078	13,055	4,259
General offenses:												
Homicide	169	189	195	207	50	18	157	109	48	139	14	4
Robbery	1,489	1,427	1,804	1,628	132	35	1,496	1,339	156	1,459	32	5
Assault	545	607	641	660	233	39	427	358	69	287	103	37
Burglary	133	118	123	147	25	3	122	114	8	118	4	-
Larceny-theft.	3,252	3,807	3,583	4,063	886	74	3,177	2,994	151	1,082	1,792	303
Embezzlement and fraud	8,835	10,624	9,106	10,338	1,189	247	9,149	8,509	611	4,457	4,443	249
Auto theft.	219	293	205	299	41	7	258	245	13	179	75	4
Forgery [4]	1,228	1,503	1,238	1,438	176	18	1,262	1,193	69	644	589	29
Sex offenses.	435	412	393	414	68	13	346	282	63	274	60	12
DAPCA [5]	11,655	19,227	12,512	20,225	3,025	468	17,200	14,347	2,826	15,032	1,954	214
Misc. general offenses	17,093	18,540	17,667	18,954	4,156	731	14,798	12,849	1,509	7,407	3,989	3,402

- Represents or rounds to zero. [1] Excludes transfers. [2] Convicted and sentenced. [3] Includes nolo contendere. [4] Includes counterfeiting. [5] All marijuana, narcotics, and controlled substances prosecutions under the Drug Abuse, Prevention and Control Act.

Source of tables 331-333: Administrative Office of the U.S. Courts, Annual Report of the Director.

No. 334. U.S. District Courts—Offenders Convicted and Sentenced to Prison and Length of Sentence, 1991

MOST SERIOUS OFFENSE OF CONVICTION	Offenders convicted	Convicted offenders sentenced to prison	Length of sentence, 1991 (mo.)	MOST SERIOUS OFFENSE OF CONVICTION	Offenders convicted	Convicted offenders sentenced to prison	Length of sentence, 1991 (mo.)
Total [1]	48,059	29,702	61.6	Drug offenses [2]	17,158	14,738	84.5
				Possession	1,094	407	19.2
Violent offenses	2,503	2,228	91.2	Trafficking and manufacturing	16,064	14,331	86.1
Property offenses	12,976	5,869	21.6	Public-order offenses	15,415	6,862	35.3
Fraudulent offenses [2]	9,376	4,454	20.6	Regulatory offenses	2,302	853	26.2
Embezzlement	1,738	604	15.7	Other offenses	13,113	6,009	36.6
Fraud [3]	6,365	3,196	22.2	Weapons	2,933	2,422	57.5
Forgery	741	352	15.8	Immigration	2,261	1,673	12.5
Other offenses [2]	3,600	1,415	24.9	Tax law violations [4]	1,040	433	25.2
Larceny	2,836	912	17.9				

[1] Total may include offenders for whom offense category could not be determined.   [2] Includes offenses not shown separately.   [3] Excludes tax fraud.   [4] Includes tax fraud.
Source: U.S. Bureau of Justice Statistics, *Federal Criminal Case Processing, 1980-90*, September 1992.

No. 335. U.S. District Courts—Defendants Charged With Violations of Drug Abuse Prevention and Control Act: 1980 to 1992

[For years ending **June 30**]

ITEM	MARIJUANA				DRUGS				CONTROLLED SUBSTANCES (prescribed drugs)			
	1980	1990	1991	1992	1980	1990	1991	1992	1980	1990	1991	1992
Defendants disposed of	1,690	5,139	5,272	5,438	3,290	12,649	12,288	12,776	1,363	1,483	1,667	2,011
Not convicted	569	1,011	895	946	749	1,850	1,712	1,807	276	222	274	272
Dismissed [1]	483	915	809	850	620	1,506	1,399	1,474	234	189	236	233
Convicted	1,121	4,128	4,377	4,492	2,541	10,799	10,576	10,969	1,087	1,261	1,393	1,739
By guilty plea and nolo contendere	772	3,624	3,948	4,056	1,830	8,423	8,479	8,806	848	1,020	1,127	1,512
Imprisonment, total [2]	754	3,004	3,566	3,585	1,945	9,804	9,669	10,050	780	1,030	1,147	1,397
Regular sentence	555	2,931	3,552	3,538	1,410	9,551	9,592	9,936	582	980	1,142	1,355
Avg. sentence (mo.)	47.2	48.9	68.0	51.4	60.8	86.2	104.0	98.1	46.5	79.3	95.7	87.5
Other sentences to prison [2]	199	73	14	47	535	253	77	114.0	198	50	5	42
Probation, total	341	1,054	779	837	588	874	888	828.0	303	207	229	285
Avg. sentence (mo.)	37.9	25.1	54.5	32.7	39.9	40.0	55.7	42.4	37.2	32.3	53.4	39.1
Fine only	20	39	30	69	4	17	14	88.0	3	8	16	57
Other [3]	6	31	2	1	4	104	5	3.0	1	16	1	-

- Represents zero.   [1] Includes defendants committed under 28 USC 2902, Narcotic Addict Rehabilitation Act of 1966.
[2] Split or mixed sentences of prison and probation in the same case as well as indeterminate and Youth Corrections Act sentences are included under total imprisonment and other sentences to prison.   [3] Includes deportation, suspended sentences, imprisonment for four days or less or for time already served, remitted and suspended fines and life sentences.
Source: Administrative Office of the U.S. Courts, *Annual Report of the Director*.

No. 336. Federal Prosecutions of Public Corruption: 1975 to 1991

[As of **Dec. 31.** Prosecution of persons who have corrupted public office in violation of Federal Criminal Statutes]

PROSECUTION STATUS	1975	1980	1981	1982	1983	1984	1985	1986	1987	1988	1989	1990	1991
Total: [1] Indicted	255	721	878	729	1,073	936	1,182	1,193	1,340	1,274	1,349	1,176	1,452
Convicted	179	552	730	671	972	934	997	1,026	1,081	1,067	1,149	1,084	1194
Awaiting trial	27	213	231	186	222	269	256	246	368	288	375	300	346
Federal officials: Indicted	53	123	198	158	[2]460	408	563	596	651	629	695	615	803
Convicted	43	131	159	147	[2]424	429	470	523	545	529	610	583	665
Awaiting trial	5	16	23	38	58	77	90	83	118	86	126	103	149
State officials: Indicted	36	72	87	49	81	58	79	88	102	66	71	96	115
Convicted	18	51	66	43	65	52	66	71	76	69	54	79	77
Awaiting trial	5	28	36	18	26	21	20	24	26	14	18	28	42
Local officials: Indicted	139	247	244	257	270	203	248	232	246	276	269	257	242
Convicted	94	168	211	232	226	196	221	207	204	229	201	225	180
Awaiting trial	15	82	102	58	61	74	49	55	89	79	122	98	88

[1] Includes individuals who are neither public officials nor employees but who were involved with public officials or employees in violating the law, not shown separately.   [2] Increases in the number indicted and convicted between 1982 and 1983 resulted from a greater focus on federal corruption nationwide and more consistent reporting of cases involving lower-level employees.
Source: U.S. Department of Justice, *Federal Prosecutions of Corrupt Public Officials, 1970-1980* and *Report to Congress on the Activities and Operations of the Public Integrity Section*, annual.

No. 337. Delinquency Cases Disposed by Juvenile Courts: 1975 to 1990

YEAR	CASES DISPOSED Total (1,000)	Per-cent change	Case rate [1]	YEAR	CASES DISPOSED Total (1,000)	Per-cent change	Case rate [1]
1975	1,050	(NA)	33.8	1983	1,030	-4.0	38.3
1976	1,077	2.6	35.1	1984	1,034	0.4	38.7
1977	1,076	-0.1	35.8	1985	1,112	7.5	42.2
1978	1,023	-4.9	34.6	1986	1,151	3.5	43.9
1979	1,048	2.4	36.2	1987	1,157	0.5	44.6
1980	1,093	4.3	38.3	1988	1,167	0.9	45.5
1981	1,100	0.6	39.1	1989	1,212	3.9	47.8
1982	1,073	-2.5	39.1	1990	1,265	4.4	49.6

NA Not available. [1] Number of cases disposed per 1,000 youth (ages 10 to 17) at risk.
Source: National Center for Juvenile Justice, Pittsburgh, PA, *Juvenile Court Statistics*, annual.

No. 338. Delinquency Cases Disposed by Juvenile Courts, by Reason for Referral: 1982 to 1990

[In thousands. A delinquency offense is an act committed by a juvenile for which an adult could be prosecuted in a criminal court. Disposition of a case involves taking a definite action such as transferring the case to criminal court, dismissing the case, placing the youth on probation, placing the youth in a facility for delinquents, or such actions as fines, restitution, and community service]

REASON FOR REFERRAL	1982	1983	1984	1985	1986	1987	1988	1989	1990
All delinquency offense	1,073	1,030	1,034	1,112	1,151	1,157	1,167	1,212	1,265
Violent offenses	57	55	61	67	73	68	71	79	95
Criminal homicide	2	1	1	1	2	2	2	2	3
Forcible rape	3	3	3	4	5	4	4	4	4
Robbery	26	24	22	26	26	23	22	24	29
Aggravated assault	27	27	35	36	40	39	43	49	60
Property offenses	475	451	442	489	496	500	500	526	535
Burglary	158	145	129	139	140	132	130	133	141
Larceny	278	270	276	307	308	314	309	317	318
Motor vehicle theft	34	31	31	36	42	47	55	69	69
Arson	5	5	6	7	6	6	7	7	7
Delinquency offenses	541	524	530	555	583	590	596	608	635
Simple assault	86	81	73	92	95	100	103	108	120
Vandalism	64	64	69	84	84	83	81	82	92
Drug law violations	62	57	65	76	73	73	82	78	68
Obstruction of justice	47	55	63	68	76	79	79	82	83
Other [1]	282	268	260	235	255	256	251	257	272

[1] Includes such offenses as stolen property offenses, trespassing, weapons offenses, other sex offenses, liquor law violations, disorderly conduct, and miscellaneous offenses.
Source: National Center for Juvenile Justice, Pittsburgh, PA, *Juvenile Court Statistics*, annual.

No. 339. Juveniles Held in Public and Private Custody—Residents and Facilities: 1985 to 1989

[Public and private facilities for juveniles includes detention centers, shelters, reception and diagnostic centers, training schools, halfway houses, group homes, ranches, forestry camps, and farms]

CHARACTERISTIC	Unit	PUBLIC CUSTODY 1985	1987	1989	PRIVATE CUSTODY 1985	1987	1989
Number of residents [1][2]	Number	51,402	56,097	58,303	34,112	38,184	37,845
Juvenile [3]	Number	49,322	53,503	56,123	34,080	38,143	37,822
Average age [4]	Years	15.4	15.8	16.0	14.9	14.8	14.9
Male	Number	42,549	46,272	49,443	23,844	26,339	26,602
Female	Number	6,773	7,231	6,680	10,236	11,804	11,220
White	Number	29,969	31,103	30,705	23,999	26,839	25,696
Black	Number	18,269	21,057	24,003	9,204	10,357	11,076
Number of admissions (all residents) [5][6]	Number	527,759	597,624	624,597	101,007	126,102	141,907
Number of departures (all residents) [6]	Number	520,903	592,229	614,430	96,006	120,071	135,319
Average daily residents	Number	49,480	54,036	56,595	33,121	38,172	37,944
Facilities, total [2][7]	Number	1,040	1,107	1,100	1,996	2,195	2,167
Occupancy less than 70 percent	Percent	35	28	24	20	18	16
70 to 100 percent	Percent	55	57	57	79	79	82
More than 100 percent	Percent	10	15	18	1	3	2
Personnel, total [2][8]	Number	(NA)	62,249	58,775	(NA)	49,144	49,334
Operating costs [5]	Mil. dol.	1,247.9	1,458.7	1,674.0	805.5	1,060.0	1,186.8
Per resident operating cost [9]	$1,000	25.2	27.0	29.6	24.3	27.8	31.3

NA Not available. [1] Includes adults. [2] Data for February 1, 1985, February 2, 1987, and February 15, 1989. [3] Includes races not reported and races not shown. [4] Based on juvenile residents only. [5] Data are for calendar years 1984, 1986, and 1988. [6] Juvenile and adult. [7] Occupancy is calculated on the average daily resident population. [8] 1987 personnel includes full, part-time, and volunteer and 1989 includes full and part-time only. [9] Based on average daily residents.
Source: 1985, U.S. Bureau of Justice Statistics, *Census of Public and Private Juvenile Detention, Correctional, and Shelter Facilities, 1975-85*; thereafter, U.S. Office of Juvenile Justice and Delinquency Prevention, *1987* and *1989 Census of Public and Private Juvenile Custody Facilities*, and *1987 Children in Custody* and *Juvenile Taken Into Custody: fiscal Year 1990 Report*.

No. 340. Child Abuse and Neglect Cases Reported and Investigated, by State: 1991

[Based on reports alleging child abuse and neglect that were referred for investigation by the respective child protective services agency in each State. The reporting period may be either calendar or fiscal year. The majority of States were unable to provide unduplicated counts. Only nine jurisdictions (Alaska, Hawaii, Michigan, Montana, Ohio, Oregon, South Carolina, Vermont, and Washington) provided unduplicated counts of children subject of report. Excludes the Armed Forces]

STATE	REPORTS Number of reports [1]	Number of children subject of a report	Investigation disposition, number of children substantiated [2]	STATE	REPORTS Number of reports [1]	Number of children subject of a report	Investigation disposition, number of children substantiated [2]
United States	1,767,673	2,695,010	811,709	Missouri	46,343	76,249	(NA)
Alabama.........	28,462	43,969	21,334	Montana	[4]7,236	[4]11,029	(NA)
Alaska..........	[3]8,983	8,983	6,252	Nebraska	7,993	17,087	5,841
Arizona..........	26,531	44,844	28,091	Nevada..........	12,858	20,573	7,413
Arkansas.........	15,860	39,687	8,135	New Hampshire	6,550	10,480	(NA)
California.........	302,834	416,757	68,970	New Jersey	[3]53,750	53,750	19,489
Colorado.........	31,796	50,874	8,688	New Mexico.......	[3]18,234	18,234	5,117
Connecticut........	14,369	22,080	14,528	New York	131,476	212,420	55,539
Delaware.........	4,367	7,941	2,209	North Carolina	45,315	71,427	24,636
District of Columbia....	5,119	9,444	1,035	North Dakota	3,925	6,435	3,262
Florida	117,886	184,370	72,713	Ohio............	88,255	144,218	51,971
Georgia..........	40,142	68,057	44,750	Oklahoma........	[3]21,328	21,328	8,287
Hawaii	[3]5,017	5,017	2,266	Oregon..........	23,530	37,648	7,961
Idaho...........	9,477	19,507	7,103	Pennsylvania	[3]23,861	23,861	7,986
Illinois...........	67,751	117,912	39,572	Rhode Island	8,844	13,820	5,919
Indiana	41,954	63,192	33,329	South Carolina	18,956	30,978	10,643
Iowa............	19,025	27,553	8,154	South Dakota	[3]11,205	11,205	3,825
Kansas..........	[4]9,133	[4]19,280	(NA)	Tennessee	[3]29,715	29,715	10,367
Kentucky.........	33,505	52,912	24,469	Texas...........	97,676	153,753	58,199
Louisiana	25,579	44,612	14,991	Utah............	14,534	23,254	10,179
Maine...........	4,080	9,503	4,381	Vermont.........	3,175	2,689	1,437
Maryland.........	29,254	46,806	-	Virginia..........	34,067	50,732	13,702
Massachusetts.......	35,614	58,218	28,048	Washington	39,067	59,311	(NA)
Michigan.........	49,074	113,932	26,366	West Virginia	13,888	22,221	(NA)
Minnesota........	17,480	26,663	9,948	Wisconsin	[3]44,963	44,963	17,647
Mississippi........	14,377	20,138	6,957	Wyoming.........	3,260	5,379	(NA)

NA Not available.   [1] Except as noted, reports are on incident/family based basis or based on number of reported incidents regardless of the number of children involved in the incidents.   [2] Type of investigation disposition that determines that there is sufficient evidence under State law to conclude that maltreatment occurred or that the child is at risk of maltreatment.   [3] Child-based report that enumerates each child who is a subject of a report.   [4] 1990 data.

Source: U.S. Department of Health and Human Services, National Center on Child Abuse and Neglect, *National Child Abuse and Neglect Data System, Working Paper 2, 1991 Summary Data Component*, May 1993.

No. 341. Child Abuse and Neglect Cases Substantiated and Indicated—Victim Characteristics: 1990 and 1991

[Based on reports alleging child abuse and neglect that were referred for investigation by the respective child protective services agency in each State. The reporting period may be either calendar or fiscal year. The majority of States were unable to provide unduplicated counts. Also, varying number of States reported the various characteristics presented below. Excludes the Armed Forces. A substantiated case represents a type of investigation disposition that determines that there is sufficient evidence under State law to conclude that maltreatment occurred or that the child is at risk of maltreatment]

ITEM	1990 Number	1990 Percent	1991 Number	1991 Percent	ITEM	1990 Number	1990 Percent	1991 Number	1991 Percent
TYPES OF SUBSTANTIATED MALTREATMENT					2 to 5 years old.....	194,485	24.7	208,183	25.6
Victims, total [1]...	801,143	100.0	838,232	100.0	6 to 9 years old.....	177,396	22.5	189,123	23.3
Neglect	358,846	44.8	384,466	45.9	10 to 13 years old ...	151,971	19.3	162,022	20.0
Physical abuse	205,057	25.6	204,404	24.4	14 to 17 years old ...	117,312	14.9	122,546	15.1
Sexual abuse	127,853	16.0	129,697	15.5	18 and over	7,184	0.9	6,322	0.8
Emotional maltreatment	47,673	6.0	49,124	5.9	Unknown	32,773	4.2	11,552	1.4
Other and unknown ..	61,714	7.7	70,541	8.4	RACE/ETHNIC GROUP OF VICTIM				
SEX OF VICTIM					Victims, total....	775,409	100.0	817,718	100.0
Victims, total....	775,596	100.0	815,112	100.0	White............	424,470	54.7	453,955	55.5
Male	360,531	46.5	376,523	46.2	Black...........	197,400	25.5	218,026	26.7
Female	409,286	52.8	433,684	53.2	Asian and Pacific Islander	6,408	0.8	6,564	0.8
Unknown	5,779	0.7	4,905	0.6	American Indian, Eskimo, and Aleut	10,283	1.3	10,875	1.3
AGE OF VICTIM					Other races	11,749	1.5	13,005	1.6
Victims, total...	788,338	100.0	811,985	100.0	Hispanic origin	73,132	9.4	78,025	9.5
1 year and younger ..	107,217	13.6	112,237	13.8	Unknown	51,967	6.7	37,268	4.6

[1] More than one type of maltreatment may be substantiated per child.   [2] Some States were unable to report on the number of Hispanic victims, thus it is probable that nationwide the percentage of Hispanic victims is higher than 9 percent.

Source: U.S. Department of Health and Human Services, National Center on Child Abuse and Neglect, National Child Abuse and Neglect Data System, Working Paper 2, 1991 Summary Data Component, May 1993.

No. 342. Jail Inmates, by Race and Detention Status: 1978 to 1991

[Excludes Federal and State prisons or other correctional institutions; institutions exclusively for juveniles; State-operated jails in Alaska, Connecticut, Delaware, Hawaii, Rhode Island, and Vermont; and other facilities which retain persons for less than 48 hours. As of June 30. For 1978, 1983, and 1988, data based on National Jail Census; for other years, based on sample survey and subject to sampling variability]

CHARACTERISTIC	1978	1983	1985	1986	1987	1988	1989	1990	1991
Total inmates [1]	158,394	223,552	256,615	274,444	295,873	343,569	395,553	405,320	426,479
Percent of rated capacity	65	85	94	96	98	101	108	104	101
Percent of operational capacity .	64	81	(NA)	(NA)	(NA)	(NA)	(NA)	(NA)	(NA)
Male	148,839	207,783	235,909	251,235	270,172	313,158	356,050	368,002	386,865
Female.	9,555	15,769	19,077	21,501	23,920	30,411	37,253	37,318	39,614
White.	89,418	130,118	151,403	159,178	168,647	166,302	201,732	186,989	190,333
Black	65,104	87,508	102,646	112,522	124,267	141,979	185,910	174,335	187,617
Other races.	3,872	5,926	2,566	2,744	2,959	3,932	7,911	5,321	5,391
Hispanic [2]	16,349	31,297	35,926	38,422	41,422	51,455	55,377	57,449	60,129
Non-Hispanic.	142,045	192,254	220,689	236,022	254,451	292,114	340,176	347,871	366,350
Adult. [3]	156,783	221,815	254,986	272,736	294,092	341,893	393,303	403,019	424,129
Awaiting arraignment or trial	77,453	113,984	127,059	142,112	150,101	175,669	204,291	207,358	217,671
Convicted	75,438	107,660	123,409	127,067	139,394	166,224	189,012	195,661	206,458
Juvenile [4]	1,611	1,736	1,629	1,708	1,781	1,676	2,250	2,301	2,350

NA Not available.   [1] For 1985 to 1987, 1989 and 1991, includes juveniles not shown separately by sex, and for 1988, 1990, and 1991 includes 31,356, 38,671, and 43,138 persons, respectively, of unknown race not shown separately.   [2] Hispanic persons may be of any race.   [3] Includes inmates not classified by conviction status.   [4] Juveniles are persons whose age makes them initially subject to juvenile court authority although they are sometimes tried as adults in criminal court.
Source: U.S. Bureau of Justice Statistics, *Profile of Jail Inmates, 1978 and 1989; Jail Inmates,* annual; and *1988 Census of Local Jails.*

No. 343. Federal and State Prisoners: 1960 to 1991

[Based on Bureau of the Census estimated resident population, as of July 1. Prior to 1970, excludes State institutions in Alaska. B jurisdiction of Federal and State authorities rather than those in the custody of such authorities. Represents inmates sentenced to maximum term of more than a year. See also *Historical Statistics, Colonial Times to 1970,* series H 1135-1140]

YEAR	PRESENT AT END OF YEAR						RECEIVED FROM COURTS					
	All institutions		Federal		State		All institutions		Federal		State	
	Number	Rate [1]	Number	Rate [1]	Number	Rate [1]	Number	Rate [1]	Number	Rate [1]	Number	Rate [1]
1960. . . .	212,953	118.6	23,218	12.9	189,735	105.7	88,575	49.3	13,723	7.6	74,852	41.7
1970. . . .	196,429	96.7	20,038	9.8	176,391	86.8	79,351	39.1	12,047	5.9	67,304	33.1
1975. . . .	240,593	113.3	24,131	11.4	216,462	102.0	129,573	61.0	16,770	7.9	112,803	53.1
1980. . . .	315,974	139.2	20,611	9.1	295,363	130.1	142,122	62.7	10,907	4.8	131,215	57.9
1985. . . .	480,568	216.5	32,695	13.6	447,873	187.6	198,499	82.7	15,368	6.4	183,131	76.3
1986. . . .	522,084	230.4	36,531	15.0	485,553	201.4	219,382	91.0	16,067	7.0	203,315	84.0
1987. . . .	560,812	229.0	39,523	16.0	521,289	214.2	241,887	99.0	16,260	7.0	225,627	92.0
1988. . . .	603,732	244.0	42,738	17.0	560,994	227.0	261,242	106.0	15,932	6.4	245,310	99.3
1989. . . .	680,907	274.3	47,168	19.0	633,739	255.3	316,215	127.4	18,388	7.4	297,827	120.0
1990. . . .	739,980	295.0	50,403	20.1	689,577	274.9	(NA)	(NA)	(NA)	(NA)	323,069	128.8
1991. . . .	789,347	309.6	56,696	22.2	732,651	287.3	(NA)	(NA)	(NA)	(NA)	317,237	124.4

NA Not available.   [1] Rate per 100,000 estimated population.
Source: U.S. Bureau of Justice Statistics, *Prisoners in State and Federal Institutions on December 31,* annual, and *Correctional Populations in the United States,* annual.

No. 344. State Prison Inmates—Selected Characteristics: 1986 and 1991

[Based on a sample survey of about 13,986 inmates in 1991 and 13,711 inmates in 1986; subject to sampling variability]

CHARACTERISTIC	NUMBER		PERCENT OF PRISON INMATES		CHARACTERISTIC	NUMBER		PERCENT OF PRISON INMATES	
	1986	1991	1986	1991		1986	1991	1986	1991
Total [1]	450,416	711,643	100.0	100.0	Never married	241,707	389,302	53.7	55.3
					Married	91,492	127,389	20.3	18.1
Under 18 years old	2,057	4,552	0.5	0.6	Widowed	8,343	13,036	1.9	1.9
18 to 24 years old	120,384	151,328	26.7	21.3	Divorced.	81,263	129,913	18.1	18.5
25 to 34 years old	205,817	325,429	45.7	45.7	Separated.	26,985	44,095	6.0	6.3
35 to 44 years old	87,502	161,651	19.4	22.7	Years of school:				
45 to 54 years old	23,524	46,475	5.2	6.5	Less than 12 years . . .	276,309	[2]290,722	61.6	[2]41.2
55 to 64 years old	8,267	16,997	1.8	2.4	12 years or more.	172,385	415,451	38.4	58.8
65 years old and over . . .	2,808	5,210	0.6	0.7	Pre-arrest employment status:				
Male	430,604	672,847	95.6	94.5	Employed	309,364	476,068	69.0	69.0
Female.	19,812	38,796	4.4	5.5	Not employed	138,773	230,874	31.0	31.0
White.	223,648	349,628	49.7	49.1	Looking for work . . .	80,508	115,590	18.0	18.0
Black	211,021	336,920	46.9	47.3	Not looking for work .	58,265	115,286	13.0	13.0
Other races.	15,412	25,094	3.4	3.5					

[1] For 1986, includes data not reported for all characteristics except sex. For 1991, includes data not reported for marital status, re-arrest, employment status and years of school.   [2] In 1991 the survey question was revised; therefore, the response may not be entirely comparable with 1986 and before.
Source: U.S. Bureau of Justice Statistics, *Profile of State Prison Inmates, 1986,* ; and *Survey of State Prison Inmates, 1991.*

No. 345. State Prison Inmates, by Criminal History and Selected Characteristics of the Inmate: 1991

[Violent/nonviolent refers to the current or past criminal offense for which the inmate is or was incarcerated; see table 300 for types of violent crimes. Data based on a sample survey of 13,986 inmates; subject to sampling variability]

| CHARACTERISTIC | Total | CRIMINAL HISTORY OF PRISON INMATES | | | | | | | |
| | | First-timers | | | Recidivists [1] | | | | |
		Total	Non-violent	Violent	Total	Non-violent	Prior violent	Current violent only	Current and prior violent
Prison inmates, total	**697,853**	**134,131**	**45,559**	**88,572**	**563,722**	**223,117**	**88,689**	**131,289**	**120,626**
Percent of total	100.0	19.2	6.5	12.7	80.8	32.0	12.7	18.8	17.3
Percent distribution	100.0	100.0	100.0	100.0	100.0	100.0	100.0	100.0	100.0
Male	94.5	92.0	89.7	93.2	95.1	92.1	96.5	96.9	97.8
Female	5.5	8.0	10.3	6.8	4.9	7.9	3.5	3.1	2.2
White.....................	49.0	52.6	50.9	53.4	48.2	52.9	40.1	50.4	42.9
Black.....................	47.5	43.6	45.7	42.6	48.4	43.7	56.5	45.6	54.0
Other races	3.5	3.8	3.4	4.0	3.5	3.4	3.4	4.0	3.1
Median age (years)	30	31	30	31	30	29	30	30	32
Median age at first arrest (years)....	18	24	25	23	17	18	16	17	16

[1] An individual who has been previously sentenced to probation or incarceration as a juvenile or adult.

Source: U.S. Bureau of Justice Statistics, *Survey of State Prison Inmates, 1991.*

No. 346. Prisoners Under Jurisdiction of State and Federal Correctional Authorities—Summary, by State: 1980 to 1991

[For years ending **December 31**]

| SEX, REGION, DIVISION, AND STATE | 1980 | 1985 | 1990 | 1991 | | SEX, REGION, DIVISION, AND STATE | 1980 | 1985 | 1990 | 1991 | |
				Total	Percent change, 1990-1991					Total	Percent change, 1990-1991
U.S ..	**329,821**	**503,271**	**773,919**	**824,133**	**6.5**	DE [2 3] .	1,474	2,553	3,471	3,717	7.1
Male.....	316,401	480,147	729,840	776,550	6.4	MD. [2 3].	7,731	13,005	17,848	19,291	8.1
Female .	13,420	23,124	44,079	47,583	7.9	DC [2 3] .	3,145	6,404	9,947	10,455	5.1
Federal [1]..	24,363	40,223	65,526	71,608	9.3	VA...	8,920	12,073	17,593	19,829	12.7
State	305,458	463,048	708,393	752,525	6.2	WV...	1,257	1,725	1,565	1,502	-4.0
						NC [3].	15,513	17,344	18,411	18,903	2.7
Northeast.	**45,796**	**75,706**	**123,464**	**131,866**	**6.8**	SC [3].	7,862	10,510	17,319	18,269	5.5
N.E. ..	**9,926**	**15,432**	**25,151**	**27,133**	**7.9**	GA [3].	12,178	16,014	22,411	23,644	5.5
ME...	814	1,226	1,523	1,579	3.7	FL [3].	20,735	28,600	44,387	46,533	4.8
NH [2]. .	326	683	1,342	1,533	14.2	**E.S.C.**	**21,055**	**30,335**	**43,451**	**46,937**	**8.0**
VT [2] .	480	677	1,049	1,118	6.6	KY...	3,588	5,801	9,023	9,799	8.6
MA [3] .	3,185	5,390	8,345	9,155	9.7	TN...	7,022	[4]7,127	[4]10,388	[4]11,474	10.5
RI [2] .	813	1,307	2,392	2,771	15.8	AL...	6,543	11,015	15,665	16,760	7.0
CT [2] .	4,308	6,149	10,500	10,977	4.5	MS...	3,902	6,392	8,375	8,904	6.3
M.A. ..	**35,870**	**60,274**	**98,313**	**104,733**	**6.5**	**W.S.C.**	**46,488**	**64,363**	**88,248**	**92,786**	**5.1**
NY...	21,815	34,712	54,895	57,862	5.4	AR...	2,911	[4]4,611	7,322	7,766	6.1
NJ...	[4]5,884	[4]11,335	21,128	23,483	11.1	LA...	8,889	13,890	18,599	20,003	7.5
PA...	8,171	14,227	22,290	23,388	4.9	OK [3].	4,796	8,330	12,285	13,340	8.6
Midwest..	**66,211**	**95,704**	**145,894**	**155,917**	**6.9**	TX [3] .	29,892	37,532	50,042	51,677	3.3
E.N.C.	**51,175**	**72,599**	**113,806**	**122,139**	**7.3**	**West ....**	**47,093**	**88,712**	**154,384**	**162,876**	**5.5**
OH...	13,489	20,864	31,822	35,744	12.3	**Mt. ....**	**13,141**	**22,798**	**37,433**	**39,774**	**6.3**
IN [3] .	6,683	9,904	12,736	13,008	2.1	MT...	739	1,129	1,425	1,478	3.7
IL [3] .	11,899	18,634	27,516	29,115	5.8	ID ...	817	1,294	1,961	2,143	9.3
MI [3] .	15,124	17,755	34,267	36,423	6.3	WY...	534	758	1,110	1,099	-1.0
WI ...	3,980	5,442	7,465	7,849	5.1	CO...	2,629	3,369	7,671	8,392	9.4
W.N.C.	**15,036**	**23,105**	**32,088**	**33,778**	**5.3**	NM...	1,279	[4]2,313	3,187	3,119	-2.1
MN...	2,001	2,343	3,176	3,472	9.3	AZ [3] .	4,372	8,531	14,261	15,415	8.1
IA [3] .	2,481	2,832	3,967	4,145	4.5	UT...	932	1,633	2,496	2,625	5.2
MO ...	5,726	9,915	14,943	15,897	6.4	NV...	1,839	3,771	5,322	5,503	3.4
ND...	253	422	483	492	1.9	**Pac....**	**33,952**	**65,914**	**116,951**	**123,102**	**5.3**
SD...	635	1,047	1,341	1,374	2.5	WA...	[4]4,399	6,909	7,995	9,156	14.5
NE...	1,446	1,814	2,403	2,495	3.8	OR...	3,177	4,454	6,492	6,732	3.7
KS...	2,494	4,732	5,775	5,903	2.2	CA [3] .	24,569	50,111	97,309	101,808	4.6
South....	**146,358**	**202,926**	**284,651**	**301,866**	**6.0**	AK [2] .	822	2,329	2,622	2,706	3.2
S.A....	**78,815**	**108,228**	**152,952**	**162,143**	**6.0**	HI [2] .	985	2,111	2,533	2,700	6.6

[1] Includes persons held under other jurisdiction, not shown separately. [2] Includes both jail and prison inmates (State has combined jail and prison system). [3] Numbers are custodial, not jurisdictional counts. [4] Jurisdiction counts exclude prisoners held in jail because of crowding.

Source: U.S. Bureau of Justice Statistics, *Prisoners in 1991,* and earlier reports.

No. 347. Adults Under Correctional Supervision: 1990

[In thousands except rate. As of Dec. 31. Excludes juveniles, persons incarcerated in mental health institutions in lieu of prison, persons held by the armed services, persons held on Indian reservations, parolees under county jurisdiction, parolees whose sentences were for 1 year or less, and court probationers (those not placed under the supervisory authority of a probation agency)]

REGION, DIVISION, AND STATE	Total [1]	Rate [2]	Prison [3]	Parole [4]	Probation [5]	REGION, DIVISION, AND STATE	Total [1]	Rate [2]	Prison [3]	Parole [4]	Probation [5]
U.S....	4,349.8	235.0	745.2	531.4	2,670.2	DC	25.4	517.4	8.6	5.3	9.7
						VA	55.4	118.3	14.6	9.0	21.3
Northeast ..	783.5	201.4	119.2	128.9	466.0	WV	9.4	69.9	1.6	1.0	5.1
N.E	190.7	188.0	24.6	6.2	151.1	NC	114.6	228.3	18.6	9.9	77.8
ME	11.1	121.2	1.5	0.0	7.5	SC	57.0	222.2	15.6	3.5	32.3
NH ...	6.0	72.8	1.4	0.5	3.1	GA	201.0	423.0	22.3	22.6	134.8
VT	7.2	171.5	1.0	0.3	5.9	FL.....	288.6	286.6	44.0	2.1	210.8
MA	91.2	195.7	8.3	4.7	72.5	E.S.C.	167.1	149.2	39.8	24.0	76.1
RI....	18.1	232.2	2.4	0.3	15.4	KY	24.7	90.4	8.3	3.2	7.5
CT	57.0	224.7	10.1	0.3	46.6	TN	63.8	174.2	8.5	11.3	32.7
M.A	592.8	206.2	94.5	122.8	314.9	AL....	55.4	185.7	15.4	6.0	27.7
NY	272.5	198.5	54.9	42.8	145.3	MS	23.3	127.7	7.6	3.5	8.2
NJ....	127.2	214.4	17.7	23.3	72.3	W.S.C. ...	639.8	333.5	81.2	125.8	378.9
PA	193.1	212.5	21.9	56.7	97.3	AR	28.9	166.8	6.6	4.0	16.0
Midwest ..	838.8	190.4	145.5	65.7	567.8	LA....	66.6	222.4	14.1	8.9	30.2
E.N.C.	614.6	197.9	113.3	45.4	410.6	OK	41.1	178.2	10.5	3.2	24.4
OH	132.0	164.0	31.5	7.9	83.4	TX	503.2	414.2	50.0	109.7	308.4
IN	92.3	225.8	12.7	3.8	68.7	West......	891.9	230.4	152.6	99.3	536.2
IL	152.7	180.0	27.5	17.7	95.7	Mt	164.1	167.8	37.0	12.1	92.7
MI....	190.7	278.9	34.3	11.9	133.4	MT	7.3	126.1	1.4	0.8	4.1
WI....	47.0	130.3	7.2	4.1	29.4	ID	8.3	119.2	1.8	0.2	4.4
W.N.C	224.3	172.6	32.3	20.3	157.3	WY	4.8	151.4	1.1	0.3	3.0
MN	68.1	212.4	3.2	1.9	59.3	CO	45.7	187.7	6.8	2.4	31.1
IA	22.2	107.7	4.0	2.1	13.9	NM	13.2	123.7	3.4	1.2	6.3
MO	70.9	186.6	14.9	9.2	42.3	AZ	54.2	201.9	14.3	2.7	30.4
ND	2.8	59.6	0.5	0.1	1.7	UT	11.3	103.3	2.5	1.6	5.8
SD	5.7	113.5	1.4	0.6	3.2	NV	19.2	212.7	5.6	2.9	7.7
NE	19.3	168.2	2.4	0.6	14.7	Pac	727.8	251.5	115.7	87.2	443.4
KS	35.3	194.2	5.8	5.8	22.2	WA	109.2	303.0	7.4	9.6	84.8
South	1,694.9	267.2	267.0	215.8	1,042.0	OR	55.1	260.2	6.2	8.0	37.6
S.A	888.0	268.6	146.0	66.0	587.0	CA	541.3	246.0	97.3	67.6	305.7
DE	16.6	329.3	3.1	1.3	12.2	AK [6]	6.7	176.5	2.4	0.6	3.6
MD	119.9	331.4	17.6	11.2	82.9	HI [6]	15.5	187.0	2.4	1.4	11.7

[1] Includes persons in jail not shown separately. [2] Rate per 10,000 persons 18 years old and over. [3] Includes all inmates of Federal and State institutions. [4] Includes all adults under State parole supervision whether released from prison via parole board decision or mandatory release, who were sentenced to more than one year in prison. [5] Includes all adults who, as part of a State, or local court order, have been placed under the supervisory authority of a probation agency. [6] Jail population for Hawaii included with prison population.

Source: U.S. Bureau of Justice Statistics, Correctional Populations in the United States, annual.

No. 348. Prisoners Under Sentence of Death: 1980 to 1991

[As of December 31. Excludes prisoners under sentence of death who remained within local correctional systems pending exhaustion of appellate process or who had not been committed to prison]

CHARACTERISTIC	1980	1985	1989	1990	1991	CHARACTERISTIC	1980	1985	1989	1990	1991
Total [1]	688	1,575	2,243	2,346	2,482	Unknown	163	235	263	279	313
						Marital status:					
White	418	896	1,308	1,368	1,464	Never married......	268	655	956	998	1,071
Black and other	270	679	935	978	1,018	Married	229	487	610	632	663
						Divorced [2]	217	449	684	726	746
Under 20 years	11	13	6	8	14						
20 to 24 years	173	212	191	168	179	Time elapsed since					
25 to 34 years	334	804	1,080	1,110	1,087	sentencing:					
35 to 54 years	186	531	917	1,006	1,129	Less than 12 months .	185	273	231	231	252
55 years and over.....	10	31	56	64	73	12 to 47 months	389	739	809	753	718
Years of school						48 to 71 months	102	303	408	438	441
completed:						72 months and over..	38	276	802	934	1,071
7 years or less	68	147	183	178	173						
8 years	74	159	178	186	181	Legal status at arrest:					
9 to 11 years	204	483	739	775	810	Not under sentence .	384	861	1,301	1,345	1,415
12 years..........	162	440	695	729	783	Parole or probation [3] .	115	350	585	578	615
More than 12						Prison or escaped ...	45	81	94	128	102
years	43	127	192	209	222	Unknown	170	299	270	305	321

[1] For 1980 to 1990, revisions to the total number of prisoners were not carried to the characteristics except for race. [2] Includes persons married but separated, widows, widowers, and unknown. [3] Includes prisoners on mandatory conditional release, work release, leave, AWOL, or bail. Covers 20 prisoners in 1985, 24 in 1989, 28 in 1990, and 29 in 1991.

Source: U.S. Bureau of Justice Statistics, Capital Punishment, annual.

No. 349. Movement of Prisoners Under Sentence of Death: 1980 to 1991

[Prisoners reported under sentence of death by civil authorities. The term "under sentence of death" begins when the court pronounces the first sentence of death for a capital offense]

STATUS	1980	1982	1983	1984	1985	1986	1987	1988	1989	1990	1991
Under sentence of death, Jan. 1..	595	856	1,063	1,209	1,420	1,575	1,800	1,967	2,117	2,243	2,346
Received death sentence [1][2]	203	287	263	296	281	297	299	296	251	244	266
White	125	166	156	173	165	164	190	196	133	147	163
Black	77	117	105	119	114	123	106	91	114	94	101
Dispositions other than executions [2]	101	76	117	69	108	73	90	128	102	108	116
Executions	-	2	5	21	18	18	25	11	16	23	14
Under sentence of death, Dec. 31 [1]	688	1,063	1,209	1,420	1,575	1,800	1,967	2,117	2,243	2,346	2,482
White	425	615	694	809	896	1,006	1,128	1,238	1,308	1,368	1,464
Black	268	446	508	595	664	750	813	853	898	940	982

- Represents zero. [1] Includes races other than White or Black. [2] Revisions to total number of prisoners under death sentence not carried to this category.

Source: U.S. Bureau of Justice Statistics, *Capital Punishment,* annual.

No. 350. Prisoners Executed Under Civil Authority: 1930 to 1991

[Excludes executions by military authorities. The Army (including the Air Force) carried out 160 (148 between 1942 and 1950, 3 each in 1954, 1955, and 1957, and 1 each in 1958, 1959, and 1961). Of the total, 106 were executed for murder (including 21 involving rape), 53 for rape, and 1 for desertion. The Navy carried out no executions during the period. See also *Historical Statistics, Colonial Times to 1970,* series H 1155-1167]

YEAR OR PERIOD	Total [1]	White	Black	EXECUTED FOR MURDER			EXECUTED FOR RAPE			EXECUTED, OTHER OFFENSES [2]		
				Total [1]	White	Black	Total [1]	White	Black	Total [1]	White	Black
All years	4,016	1,845	2,129	3,491	1,758	1,693	455	48	405	70	39	31
1930 to 1939	1,667	827	816	1,514	803	687	125	10	115	28	14	14
1940 to 1949	1,284	490	781	1,064	458	595	200	19	179	20	13	7
1950 to 1959	717	336	376	601	316	280	102	13	89	14	7	7
1960 to 1967	191	98	93	155	87	68	28	6	22	8	5	3
1968 to 1976	-	-	-	-	-	-	-	-	-	-	-	-
1977 to 1980	3	3	-	3	3	-	-	-	-	-	-	-
1981	1	1	-	1	1	-	-	-	-	-	-	-
1982	2	1	1	2	1	1	-	-	-	-	-	-
1983	5	4	1	5	4	1	-	-	-	-	-	-
1984	21	13	8	21	13	8	-	-	-	-	-	-
1985	18	11	7	18	11	7	-	-	-	-	-	-
1986	18	11	7	18	11	7	-	-	-	-	-	-
1987	25	13	12	25	13	12	-	-	-	-	-	-
1988	11	6	5	11	6	5	-	-	-	-	-	-
1989	16	8	8	16	8	8	-	-	-	-	-	-
1990	23	16	7	23	16	7	-	-	-	-	-	-
1991	14	7	7	14	7	7	-	-	-	-	-	-

- Represents zero. [1] Includes races other than White or Black. [2] Includes 25 armed robbery, 20 kidnapping, 11 burglary, 8 espionage (6 in 1942 and 2 in 1953), and 6 aggravated assault.

Source: Through 1978, U.S. Law Enforcement Assistance Administration; thereafter, U.S. Bureau of Justice Statistics, *Correctional Populations in the United States,* annual.

No. 351. Prisoners Under Sentence of Death and Executed Under Civil Authority, by States: 1950 to 1991

[No executions took place in Delaware, Maine, Massachusetts, Michigan, Minnesota, Montana, New Hampshire, North Dakota, Rhode Island, South Dakota, and Wisconsin from 1950 to 1991. Maine, Minnesota, and Wisconsin never authorized the death penalty during the period. New Hampshire and Rhode Island authorized it for most of the 4 decades but did not apply it. Michigan abolished the penalty in 1963, and North Dakota allowed the punishment statute to lapse in 1975. Alaska and Hawaii could enter these data after receiving statehood in 1959, but neither has authorized the death penalty]

STATE	1950 to 1959	1960 to 1969	1977 to 1989[1]	1990	1991	STATE	1950 to 1959	1960 to 1969	1977 to 1989[1]	1990	1991	STATE	1950 to 1959	1960 to 1969	1977 to 1989[1]	1990	1991
U.S.[2]	717	191	120	23	14	IA	1	2	-	-	-	OH	32	7	-	-	-
AL	20	5	7	1	-	KS	5	5	-	-	-	OK	7	6	-	1	-
AZ	8	4	-	-	-	KY	16	1	-	-	-	OR	4	1	-	-	-
AR	18	9	-	2	-	LA	27	1	18	1	1	PA	31	3	-	-	-
CA	74	30	-	-	-	MD	6	1	-	-	-	SC	26	8	2	1	1
CO	3	6	-	-	-	MS	36	10	4	-	-	TN	8	1	-	-	-
CT	5	1	-	-	-	MO	7	4	1	4	1	TX	74	29	33	4	5
DC	4	-	-	-	-	NE	2	-	-	-	-	UT	6	1	3	-	-
FL	49	12	21	4	2	NV	9	2	4	1	-	VT	2	-	-	-	-
GA	85	14	14	-	1	NJ	17	3	-	-	-	VA	23	6	-	3	2
ID	3	-	-	-	-	NM	3	1	-	-	-	WA	6	2	-	-	-
IL	9	2	-	1	-	NY	52	10	-	-	-	WV	9	-	-	-	-
IN	2	1	2	-	-	NC	19	1	3	-	1	WY	-	1	-	-	-

- Represents zero. [1] No executions occurred during the period 1970 to 1976. [2] Includes 23 Federal executions not shown by State (1940 to 1949, 13; 1950 to 1959, 9; and 1960 to 1969, 1).

Source: Through 1978, U.S. Law Enforcement Assistance Administration; thereafter, U.S. Bureau of Justice Statistics, *Capital Punishment,* annual.

No. 352. Fire Losses—Total and Per Capita: 1960 to 1991

[1960 excludes Alaska and Hawaii. Includes allowance for uninsured and unreported losses but excludes losses to government property and forests. Represents incurred losses]

YEAR	Total (mil. dol.)	Per capita [1]	YEAR	Total (mil. dol.)	Per capita [1]	YEAR	Total (mil. dol.)	Per capita [1]
1960.	1,108	6.19	1974.	3,190	14.95	1983.	6,320	26.98
1965.	1,456	7.51	1975.	3,190	14.81	1984.	7,602	32.15
1967.	1,707	8.66	1976.	3,558	16.35	1985.	7,753	32.47
1968.	1,830	9.20	1977.	3,764	17.13	1986.	8,488	35.21
1969.	1,952	9.71	1978.	4,008	18.05	1987.	8,634	35.44
1970.	2,328	11.41	1979.	4,851	21.60	1988.	9,626	39.11
1971.	2,316	11.20	1980.	5,579	24.55	1989.	9,514	38.33
1972.	2,304	11.01	1981.	5,625	24.50	1990.	9,495	38.18
1973.	2,639	12.49	1982.	5,894	25.41	1991.	10,216	40.51

[1] Based on Bureau of the Census estimated resident population as of July 1.

Source: 1960, National Board of Fire Underwriters, New York, NY, *Report of the Committee on Statistics and Origin of Losses;* thereafter, Insurance Information Institute, New York, NY, *Insurance Facts,* annual.

No. 353. Fires—Number and Loss, by Type and Property Use: 1980 to 1991

[Based on annual sample survey of fire departments. No adjustments were made for unreported fires and losses. Property loss includes direct property loss only]

TYPE AND PROPERTY USE	NUMBER (1,000)					PROPERTY LOSS (mil. dol.)				
	1980	1985	1989	1990	1991	1980	1985	1989	1990	1991
Fires, total	**2,988**	**2,371**	**2,115**	**2,019**	**2,041**	**6,254**	**7,324**	**8,655**	**7,818**	**9,467**
Structure.	1,065	860	688	624	640	5,454	6,437	7,518	6,713	8,320
Outside of structure [1]	87	51	55	52	54	61	63	132	90	55
Brush and rubbish	1,115	832	819	787	806	-	-	-	-	-
Vehicle.	472	456	435	436	428	685	792	963	967	1,049
Other.	249	172	118	120	113	54	32	42	48	43
Structure by property use:										
Public assembly	29	24	18	17	16	326	462	286	317	362
Educational	20	13	9	9	9	101	114	116	136	58
Institutional	28	23	12	11	12	25	17	43	33	28
Stores and offices	62	49	35	31	33	645	654	703	603	[2]931
Residential.	758	622	513	467	478	3,042	3,774	3,998	4,253	[3]5,552
1-2 family units [4]	591	502	402	359	363	2,447	3,217	3,335	3,534	3,354
Apartments	143	104	96	95	102	401	476	541	623	609
Hotels and motels	12	8	7	6	6	154	56	87	66	52
Other residential	12	8	8	7	7	40	25	35	30	37
Storage [5]	65	52	44	40	44	512	683	673	534	594
Industry, utility, defense [5] . .	55	36	25	22	19	672	572	[6]1,406	623	605
Special structures	48	41	32	27	29	131	161	293	214	190

- Represents zero. [1] Includes outside storage, crops, timber, etc. [2] Includes one large store and office fire totaling $325 million. [3] Includes the Oakland, CA fire which resulted in $1.5 billion in residential property damage. [4] Includes mobile homes. [5] Data underreported as some incidents were handled by private fire brigades or fixed suppression systems which do not report. [6] Includes one large industrial fire totaling $750 million.

Source: National Fire Protection Association, Quincy, MA, "NFPA Reports on U.S. Fire Loss — 1991," *NFPA Journal,* September 1992, and prior issues, (copyright 1992).

No. 354. Fires and Property Loss for Incendiary and Suspicious Fires and Civilian Fire Deaths and Injuries, by Selected Property Type: 1980 to 1991

[Based on sample survey of fire departments]

ITEM	1980	1985	1990	1991	ITEM	1980	1985	1990	1991
NUMBER (1,000)					**CIVILIAN FIRE DEATHS**				
Structure fires, total . . .	1,065	860	624	640	Deaths, total [2]	6,505	6,185	5,195	4,465
Structure fires of incendiary					Residential property.	5,446	5,025	4,115	3,575
or suspicious origin	146	117	97	98	One- and two-family				
Fires of incendiary origin .	92	69	58	62	dwellings.	4,175	4,020	3,370	2,905
Fires of suspicious origin .	54	48	39	36	Apartments	1,025	865	680	595
					Vehicles	740	825	695	605
PROPERTY LOSS [1] (mil. dol.)					**CIVILIAN FIRE INJURIES**				
Structure fires, total . . .	5,454	6,437	6,713	8,320	Injuries, total [2]	30,200	28,425	28,600	29,375
Structure fires of incendiary					Residential property.	21,000	19,825	20,650	21,850
or suspicious origin	1,760	1,670	1,394	1,531	One- and two-family				
Fires of incendiary origin .	1,158	1,069	875	1,072	dwellings.	16,100	15,250	15,250	15,600
Fires of suspicious origin .	602	601	519	459	Apartments	3,600	3,925	4,975	5,675
					Vehicles	4,075	3,600	3,350	3,050

[1] Direct property loss only. [2] Includes other not shown separately.

Source: National Fire Protection Association, Quincy, MA, "NFPA Reports on Fire Loss — 1991," *NFPA Journal,* September 1992, and prior issues, (copyright 1992).

Geography and Environment

This section presents a variety of information on the physical environment of the United States, starting with basic area measurement data and ending with climatic data for selected weather stations around the country. The subjects covered between those points are mostly concerned with environmental trends, but include such related subjects as land use and ownership, water consumption, air pollutant emissions, hazardous waste sites, threatened and endangered wildlife, and expenditures for pollution abatement and control.

The information in this section is selected from a wide range of Federal agencies that compile the data for various administrative or regulatory purposes, such as the Environmental Protection Agency, Geological Survey, National Oceanic and Atmospheric Administration, and General Services Administration. Other agencies include the Bureau of the Census, which presents nationwide area measurement information; the Council on Environmental Quality (CEQ), which presents data on environmental conditions and pollutants in its annual report; and the Bureau of Economic Analysis, which compiles data on pollution abatement and control expenditures.

For the 1990 census, area measurements were calculated by computer based on the information contained in a single, consistent geographic data base, the TIGER File (described below), rather than relying on historical, local, and manually calculated information. This especially affects inland water area figures reported in 1990; these had only included those bodies of water of at least 40 acres and those streams with a width of at least one-eighth of a statute mile from 1940 to 1980. Water area figures for 1990 increased because the data reflected all water recorded in the Census Bureau's geographic data base including coastal, Great Lakes, and territorial waters.

Geography.—The Geological Survey conducts investigations, surveys, and research in the fields of geography, geology, topography, geographic information systems, mineralogy, hydrology, and geothermal

In Brief

Emissions of lead in the air were down 93% between 1980 and 1991.

Environmental industry's receipts reached $134 billion in 1992.

Pollution abatement capital expenditures by manufacturers were up 22% in 1991 to $7.4 billion.

energy resources as well as natural hazards. In cooperation with State and local agencies, the Geological Survey prepares and publishes topographic, land use/land cover, geologic, and hydrologic maps and data compilations. The Geological Survey provides United States cartographic data through the Earth Sciences Information Center, water resources data through the National Water Data Exchange (NAWDEX), and a variety of research and Open-File reports which are announced monthly in *New Publications of the Geological Survey*. In a joint project with the Census Bureau, the Geological Survey has provided the basic information on geographic features for input into a national geographic and cartographic data base being prepared by the Census Bureau, called the TIGER (Topologically Integrated Geographic Encoding and Referencing) System.

Maps prepared by the Bureau of the Census show names and boundaries of various types of legal and statistical areas, such as places, county subdivisions, census tracts, and urbanized areas, and are available as of the specific decennial census. An inventory of most of these areas is available for the 1990 census both in printed and tape form in the *Geographic Identification Code Scheme* and for the 1992 economic censuses in the *Geographic Reference Manual* (EC92-R-1). The Census Bureau maintains a current inventory of governmental units and their legal boundaries through its Boundary and Annexation Survey. The TIGER system contains information on the legal and statistical entities used by the Census Bureau, as well as on both manmade and natural features, such as streets, roads, railroads, rivers, and lakes; information is available to the public in form of machine-readable TIGER extract files.

An inventory of the Nation's land resources by type of use/cover was conducted by the Soil Conservation Service in 1982 and 1987. The results, published in the *1987 National Inventory of Land Resources,* cover all non-Federal land in Puerto Rico, the Virgin Islands, and the U.S. except Alaska.

Environment.—The CEQ is responsible for overseeing the environmental assessment process, recommending national environmental policies, analyzing changes and trends in the environment, and for reviewing Federal programs affecting the environment. It reports on environmental conditions, trends, programs, and activities in its annual publication, *Environmental Quality.* The principal Federal agency responsible for pollution abatement and control activities is the Environmental Protection Agency (EPA). It is responsible for establishing and monitoring national air quality standards, water quality activities, solid and hazardous waste disposal, and control of toxic substances.

National Ambient Air Quality Standards (NAAQS) for suspended particulate matter, sulfur dioxide, photochemical oxidants, carbon monoxide, and nitrogen dioxide were originally set by the EPA in April 1971. Every 5 years each of the NAAQS is reviewed and revised if new health or welfare data indicate that a change is necessary. The standard for photochemical oxidants now called ozone was revised in February 1979. Also, a new NAAQS for lead was promulgated in October 1978 and for suspended particulate matter in 1987. Table 367 gives some of the health-related standards for the six air pollutants having NAAQS. Responsibility for demonstrating compliance with or progress toward achieving these standards lies with the State agencies. In 1990 there were 1,279 nonFederal sampling stations for particulates, 741 for sulfur dioxide, 491 for carbon monoxide, 812 for ozone, 330 for nitrogen dioxide, and 406 for lead. Data from these State networks are periodically submitted to EPA's National Aerometric Data Bank for summarization in annual reports on the nationwide status and trends

in air quality; for details, see *National Air Quality and Emissions Trends Report, 1991.*

Pollution abatement and control expenditures.—Data on expenditures for pollution abatement and control are compiled and published by the U.S. Bureau of Economic Analysis (BEA), the U.S. Bureau of the Census, and the CEQ as part of ongoing programs. BEA conducts surveys on national expenditures for pollution abatement and control and presents the data in its *Survey of Current Business.* The U.S. Bureau of the Census collects data on State and local government and industry expenditures on control activities. Data on government expenditures are reported in an annual series of publications, *Government Finances,* which covers expenditures on sewage and sanitation outlays. Industry data are reported annually in *Current Industrial Reports.* CEQ publishes some expenditure data in *Environmental Quality.*

Climate.—NOAA, through the National Weather Service and the National Environmental Satellite, Data and Information Service, is responsible for data on climate. NOAA maintains about 11,600 weather stations, of which over 3,000 produce autographic precipitation records, about 600 take hourly readings of a series of weather elements, and the remainder record data once a day. These data are reported monthly in the *Climatological Data* (published by State), and monthly and annually in the *Local Climatological Data* (published by location for major cities).

The normal climatological temperatures, precipitation, and degree days listed in this publication are derived for comparative purposes and are averages for the 30-year period, 1961-90. For stations that did not have continuous records for the entire 30 years from the same instrument site, the normals have been adjusted to provide representative values for the current location. The information in all other tables is based on data from the beginning of the record at that location through 1990, except as noted.

Historical statistics.—Tabular headnotes provide cross-references, where applicable, to *Historical Statistics of the United States, Colonial Times to 1970.* See Appendix IV.

No. 355. Land and Water Area of States and Other Entities: 1990

[One square mile=2.59 square kilometers. See *Historical Statistics of the United States, Colonial Times to 1970*, series A 210-263, for land area]

REGION, DIVISION, STATE, AND OTHER AREA	Year admitted to state-hood	TOTAL AREA			LAND AREA		WATER AREA	
		Rank	Sq. mi.	Sq. km.	Sq. mi.	Sq. km.	Sq. mi.	Sq. km
United States	(X)	(X)	**3,787,403**	**9,809,374**	**3,536,338**	**9,159,115**	**251,065**	**650,258**
Northeast	(X)	(X)	**181,333**	**469,652**	**162,274**	**420,290**	**19,059**	**49,363**
New England	(X)	(X)	**71,997**	**186,472**	**62,812**	**162,683**	**9,185**	**23,789**
Maine	1820	39	35,387	91,652	30,865	79,940	4,523	11,715
New Hampshire	[1]1788	46	9,351	24,219	8,969	23,230	382	989
Vermont	1791	45	9,615	24,903	9,249	23,955	366	948
Massachusetts	[1]1788	44	10,555	27,337	7,838	20,300	2,717	7,037
Rhode Island	[1]1790	50	1,545	4,002	1,045	2,707	500	1,295
Connecticut	[1]1788	48	5,544	14,359	4,845	12,549	698	1,808
Middle Atlantic	(X)	(X)	**109,336**	**283,180**	**99,462**	**257,607**	**9,874**	**25,574**
New York	[1]1788	27	54,556	141,300	47,224	122,310	7,332	18,990
New Jersey	[1]1787	47	8,722	22,590	7,419	19,215	1,303	3,375
Pennsylvania	[1]1787	33	46,058	119,290	44,820	116,084	1,239	3,209
Midwest	(X)	(X)	**821,762**	**2,128,364**	**751,519**	**1,946,434**	**70,243**	**181,929**
East North Central	(X)	(X)	**301,369**	**780,546**	**243,539**	**630,766**	**57,830**	**149,780**
Ohio	1803	34	44,828	116,105	40,953	106,068	3,875	10,036
Indiana	1816	38	36,420	94,328	35,870	92,903	550	1,425
Illinois	1818	25	57,918	150,008	55,593	143,986	2,325	6,022
Michigan	1837	11	96,705	250,466	56,809	147,135	39,895	103,328
Wisconsin	1848	23	65,499	169,642	54,314	140,673	11,186	28,972
West North Central	(X)	(X)	**520,393**	**1,347,818**	**507,980**	**1,315,668**	**12,412**	**32,147**
Minnesota	1858	12	86,943	225,182	79,617	206,208	7,326	18,974
Iowa	1846	26	56,276	145,755	55,875	144,716	401	1,039
Missouri	1821	21	69,709	180,546	68,898	178,446	811	2,100
North Dakota	1889	19	70,704	183,123	68,994	178,694	1,710	4,429
South Dakota	1889	17	77,121	199,743	75,896	196,571	1,225	3,173
Nebraska	1867	16	77,358	200,357	76,878	199,114	481	1,246
Kansas	1861	15	82,282	213,110	81,823	211,922	459	1,189
South	(X)	(X)	**919,945**	**2,382,658**	**871,070**	**2,256,071**	**48,875**	**126,586**
South Atlantic	(X)	(X)	**293,002**	**758,875**	**266,220**	**689,510**	**26,782**	**69,365**
Delaware	[1]1787	49	2,489	6,447	1,955	5,063	535	1,386
Maryland	[1]1788	42	12,407	32,134	9,775	25,317	2,632	6,817
District of Columbia	(X)	(X)	68	176	61	158	7	18
Virginia	[1]1788	35	42,777	110,792	39,598	102,559	3,179	8,234
West Virginia	1863	41	24,231	62,758	24,087	62,385	145	376
North Carolina	[1]1789	28	53,821	139,396	48,718	126,180	5,103	13,217
South Carolina	[1]1788	40	32,008	82,901	30,111	77,987	1,897	4,913
Georgia	[1]1788	24	59,441	153,952	57,919	150,010	1,522	3,942
Florida	1845	22	65,758	170,313	53,997	139,852	11,761	30,461
East South Central	(X)	(X)	**183,414**	**475,042**	**178,616**	**462,615**	**4,798**	**12,427**
Kentucky	1792	37	40,411	104,664	39,732	102,906	679	1,759
Tennessee	1796	36	42,146	109,158	41,219	106,757	926	2,398
Alabama	1819	30	52,423	135,776	50,750	131,443	1,673	4,333
Mississippi	1817	32	48,434	125,444	46,914	121,507	1,520	3,937
West South Central	(X)	(X)	**443,530**	**1,148,743**	**426,234**	**1,103,946**	**17,295**	**44,794**
Arkansas	1836	29	53,182	137,741	52,075	134,874	1,107	2,867
Louisiana	1812	31	51,843	134,273	43,566	112,836	8,277	21,437
Oklahoma	1907	20	69,903	181,049	68,679	177,879	1,224	3,170
Texas	1845	2	268,601	695,677	261,914	678,357	6,687	17,319
West	(X)	(X)	**1,864,363**	**4,828,700**	**1,751,475**	**4,536,320**	**112,888**	**292,380**
Mountain	(X)	(X)	**863,613**	**2,236,758**	**856,121**	**2,217,353**	**7,492**	**19,404**
Montana	1889	4	147,046	380,849	145,556	376,990	1,490	3,859
Idaho	1890	14	83,574	216,457	82,751	214,325	823	2,132
Wyoming	1890	10	97,818	253,349	97,105	251,502	714	1,849
Colorado	1876	8	104,100	269,619	103,729	268,658	371	961
New Mexico	1912	5	121,598	314,939	121,364	314,333	234	606
Arizona	1912	6	114,006	295,276	113,642	294,333	364	943
Utah	1896	13	84,904	219,901	82,168	212,815	2,736	7,086
Nevada	1864	7	110,567	286,369	109,806	284,398	761	1,971
Pacific	(X)	(X)	**1,000,750**	**2,591,943**	**895,354**	**2,318,967**	**105,396**	**272,976**
Washington	1889	18	71,302	184,672	66,581	172,445	4,721	12,227
Oregon	1859	9	98,386	254,820	96,002	248,645	2,383	6,172
California	1850	3	163,707	424,001	155,973	403,970	7,734	20,031
Alaska	1959	1	656,424	1,700,138	570,374	1,477,269	86,051	222,872
Hawaii	1959	43	10,932	28,314	6,423	16,636	4,508	11,676
Other areas:								
Puerto Rico	(X)	(X)	3,492	9,044	3,427	8,876	65	169
American Samoa	(X)	(X)	84	218	77	200	7	18
Guam	(X)	(X)	217	561	210	543	7	18
No. Mariana Islands	(X)	(X)	181	469	179	464	2	6
Palau	(X)	(X)	217	562	177	458	40	104
Virgin Islands of the U.S	(X)	(X)	151	390	134	346	17	44

X Not applicable.   [1] Year of ratification of Constitution; one of the original 13 States.
Source: U.S. Bureau of the Census, *1990 Census of Population and Housing*, series CPH-1.

No. 356. Territorial Expansion of the United States and Acquisitions of Other Areas

[One square mile=2.59 square kilometers. Boundaries of all acquisitions listed under "United States" were indefinite, at least in part, at time of acquisition. See also *Historical Statistics, Colonial Times to 1970,* series J 1–2]

ACCESSION	Acquisition date	LAND AREA		ACCESSION	Acquisition date	LAND AREA	
		Sq. ml.	Sq. km.			Sq. ml.	Sq. km.
Total	(X)	3,540,558	9,170,043	Alaska	1867	570,374	1,477,267
				Hawaii	1898	6,423	16,636
United States[1]	(X)	3,536,338	9,159,116	Other areas:			
Territory in 1790 [2]	(X)	895,415	2,319,125	Puerto Rico	[3]1898	3,427	8,875
Louisiana Purchase	1803	909,380	2,355,294	Guam	[4]1898	210	543
Purchase of Florida	1819	58,666	151,945	American Samoa	[5]1899	77	200
Texas	1845	388,687	1,006,699	Virgin Islands of the U.S.	1917	134	346
Oregon Territory	1846	286,541	742,141	Palau[6]	1947	179	464
Mexican Cession	1848	529,189	1,370,600	N. Mariana Islands	[7]1947	177	458
Gadsden Purchase	1853	29,670	76,845	All other	(X)	16	41

X Not applicable. [1] Source: U.S. Bureau of the Census, 1990 Census of Population and Housing, series CPH-1. Based on 1990 Census; sum of areas listed will not equal these figures. [2] Includes that part of drainage basin of Red River of the North, south of 49th parallel, sometimes considered part of Louisiana Purchase but excludes the Great Lakes. [3] Ceded by Spain in 1898, ratified in 1899, and became Commonwealth of Puerto Rico by Act of Congress on July 25, 1952. [4] Acquired 1898; ratified 1899. [5] Acquired 1899; ratified 1900. [6] Remaining portion of the Trust Territory of the Pacific Islands (TTPI), under U. N. trusteeship since 1947. The Federated States of Micronesia and the Marshall Islands, also formerly part of the TTPI, became freely associated States in 1986 and are not included in the table. [7] Attained Commonwealth status in 1986, separate from the TTPI, of which it had been a part since 1947.

Source: Except as noted, U.S. Geological Survey, *Boundaries of the United States and the Several States,* Paper 909, 1976.

Figure 6.1
Territorial Expansion of the United States and Acquisitions of Other Principal Areas

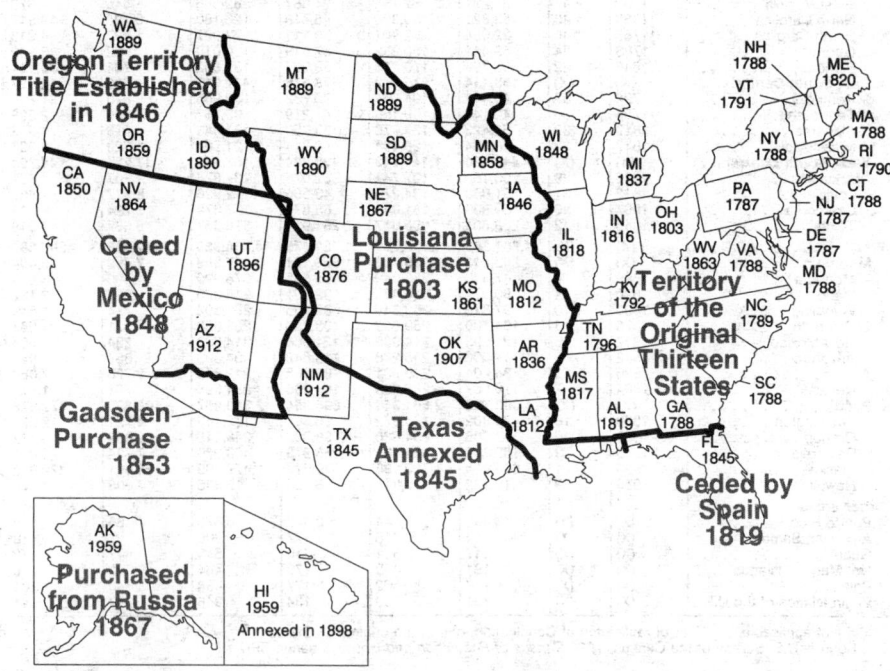

Source: Chart prepared by U.S. Bureau of the Census. For data, see table 356.

No. 357. Area and Acquisition of the Federal Public Domain: 1781 to 1989

[In millions of acres. Areas of acquisitions are as computed in 1912, and do not agree with figures in square miles shown in table 356 which include later adjustments and reflect subsequent remeasurement. Excludes outlying areas of the United States amounting to 645,949 acres in 1978. See also *Historical Statistics, Colonial Times to 1970*, series J 3-6]

YEAR	Land area, total [1]	YEAR	LAND AREA [1]			YEAR AND ACQUISITION	ACREAGE		
			Total	Public domain	Acquired		Total	Land	Inland water
1802....	200.0	1975 ...	760.4	702.9	57.5	**Aggregate**	1,837.8	1,804.7	33.1
1850....	1,200.0	1976 ...	762.2	702.8	59.4				
1880....	900.0	1977 ...	741.5	683.3	58.2	1781-1802 (State Cessions)......	236.8	233.4	3.4
1912....	600.0	1978 ...	775.2	712.0	63.3	1803, Louisiana Purchase [2]	529.9	523.4	6.5
1946....	413.0	1979 ...	744.1	684.3	59.8	1819, Cession from Spain........	46.1	43.3	2.8
1950....	412.0	1980 ...	719.5	648.0	71.5	Red River Basin [3].......	29.6	29.1	0.5
1955....	407.9	1981 ...	730.8	668.7	62.2	1846, Oregon Compromise	183.4	180.6	2.7
1959....	768.6	1982 ...	729.8	670.0	59.8	1848, Mexican Cession [2]........	338.7	334.5	4.2
1960....	771.5	1983 ...	732.0	672.4	59.6	1850, Purchase from Texas......	78.9	78.8	.1
1965....	765.8	1984 ...	726.6	658.9	67.7	1853, Gadsden Purchase	19.0	19.0	(Z)
1970....	761.3	1985 ...	726.7	656.2	70.5	1867, Alaska Purchase.........	375.3	362.5	12.8
1971....	760.2	1986 ...	727.1	662.7	64.4				
1972....	760.7	1987 ...	724.3	661.0	63.3				
1973....	761.0	1988 ...	688.2	623.2	65.0				
1974....	760.5	1989 ...	662.2	597.9	64.3				

Z Less than 50,000. [1] Owned by Federal Government. Comprises original public domain plus acquired lands. Estimated from imperfect data available for indicated years. Prior to 1959, excludes Alaska, and 1960, Hawaii. Source: Beginning 1955, U.S. General Services Administration, *Inventory Report on Real Property Owned by the United States Throughout the World*, annual. [2] Data for Louisiana Purchase exclude areas eliminated by Treaty of 1819 with Spain. Such areas are included in figures for Mexican Cession. [3] Represents drainage basin of Red River of the North, south of 49th parallel. Authorities differ as to method and date of its acquisition. Some hold it as part of the Louisiana Purchase; others, as acquired from Great Britain.

Source: Except as noted, U.S. Dept. of the Interior. Estimated area, Bureau of Land Management; all other data, Office of the Secretary, *Areas of Acquisitions to the Territory of the U.S.*, 1922.

No. 358. Total and Federally Owned Land, 1960 to 1990, and by State, 1990

[As of **end of fiscal year**; see text, section 9. Total land area figures are not comparable with those in table 355]

REGION, DIVISION, AND STATE	Total (1,000 acres)	Not owned by Federal Government (1,000 acres)	OWNED BY FEDERAL GOVERNMENT [1]		REGION, DIVISION, AND STATE	Total (1,000 acres)	Not owned by Federal Government (1,000 acres)	OWNED BY FEDERAL GOVERNMENT [1]	
			Acres (1,000)	Percent				Acres (1,000)	Percent
1960........	2,273,407	1,501,894	771,512	33.9	**South.......**	561,238	540,022	21,217	3.8
1965........	2,271,343	1,505,546	765,797	33.7	**S.A.......**	171,325	161,060	10,265	6.0
1970........	2,271,343	1,510,042	761,301	33.5	DE.....	1,266	1,239	27	2.2
1975........	2,271,343	1,510,929	760,414	33.5	MD.....	6,319	6,141	178	2.8
1980........	2,271,343	1,551,822	719,522	31.7	DC.....	39	29	10	26.2
1985........	2,271,343	1,544,658	726,686	32.0	VA.....	25,496	23,965	1,532	6.0
1988........	2,271,343	1,583,090	688,253	30.3	WV.....	15,411	14,383	1,028	6.7
1989........	2,271,343	1,609,185	662,158	29.2	NC.....	31,403	29,434	1,969	6.3
					SC.....	19,374	18,457	918	4.7
1990, total.	2,271,343	1,621,541	649,802	28.6	GA.....	37,295	35,807	1,489	4.0
Northeast....	104,699	102,453	2,247	2.1	FL.....	34,721	31,607	3,114	9.0
N.E.......	40,401	39,079	1,322	3.3	**E.S.C......**	115,141	110,647	4,494	3.9
ME.....	19,848	19,692	155	0.8	KY.....	25,512	24,430	1,083	4.2
NH.....	5,769	5,035	734	12.7	TN.....	26,728	25,698	1,029	3.9
VT.....	5,937	5,579	358	6.0	AL.....	32,678	31,604	1,074	3.3
MA.....	5,035	4,969	66	1.3	MS.....	30,223	28,915	1,307	4.3
RI.....	677	675	2	0.3	**W.S.C.....**	274,773	268,314	6,458	2.4
CT.....	3,135	3,129	6	0.2	AR.....	33,599	30,837	2,762	8.2
M.A.......	64,299	63,374	925	1.4	LA.....	28,868	28,123	745	2.6
NY.....	30,681	30,476	205	0.7	OK.....	44,088	43,383	704	1.6
NJ.....	4,814	4,699	114	2.4	TX.....	168,218	165,971	2,247	1.3
PA.....	28,804	28,199	606	2.1	**West ....**	1,122,535	519,634	602,901	53.7
Midwest.....	482,870	459,432	23,438	4.9	**Mt. ....**	548,449	283,430	265,019	48.3
E.N.C	156,679	146,854	9,825	6.3	MT.....	93,271	67,128	26,143	28.0
OH.....	26,222	25,876	346	1.3	ID.....	52,933	20,261	32,672	61.7
IN.....	23,158	22,757	401	1.7	WY.....	62,343	31,927	30,416	48.8
IL.....	35,795	34,834	961	2.7	CO.....	66,486	42,417	24,069	36.2
MI.....	36,492	31,904	4,589	12.6	NM.....	77,766	52,038	25,729	33.1
WI.....	35,011	31,482	3,529	10.1	AZ.....	72,688	38,452	34,236	47.1
W.N.C	326,191	312,579	13,613	4.2	UT.....	52,697	19,077	33,620	63.8
MN.....	51,206	45,841	5,365	10.5	NV.....	70,264	12,130	58,135	82.7
IA.....	35,860	35,524	337	0.9	**Pac.......**	574,087	236,204	337,882	58.9
MO.....	44,248	42,155	2,093	4.7	WA.....	42,694	30,319	12,374	29.0
ND.....	44,453	42,573	1,879	4.2	OR.....	61,599	29,309	32,289	52.4
SD.....	48,882	46,075	2,807	5.7	CA.....	100,207	55,666	44,541	44.4
NE.....	49,032	48,321	710	1.4	AK.....	365,482	117,441	248,040	67.9
KS.....	52,511	52,089	422	0.8	HI.....	4,106	3,468	637	15.5

[1] Excludes trust properties.

Source: U.S. General Services Administration, *Inventory Report on Real Property Owned by the United States Throughout the World*, annual.

No. 359. Land Cover/Use, by State: 1987

[In thousands of acres. Excludes Alaska and District of Columbia]

STATE	Total surface area [1]	Federal land	NONFEDERAL LAND							
			Total	Devel-oped [2]	Rural					
					Total	Crop-land	Pasture land	Range-land	Forest land	Minor cover/use
United States . .	1,937,726	404,069	1,484,156	77,305	1,406,851	422,416	129,021	401,685	393,904	59,826
Northeast	108,080	2,392	100,778	9,611	91,166	14,532	7,669	-	64,246	4,720
New England	42,670	1,332	38,609	3,005	35,604	2,311	1,248	-	30,307	1,739
Maine	21,290	161	19,517	508	19,009	943	419	-	16,933	714
New Hampshire . .	5,938	729	4,971	372	4,599	163	115	-	4,052	269
Vermont	6,153	335	5,556	208	5,348	653	388	-	4,184	122
Massachusetts . . .	5,302	89	4,849	1,063	3,786	291	179	-	2,937	379
Rhode Island	776	4	661	161	500	22	37	-	404	37
Connecticut	3,212	14	3,056	693	2,362	239	110	-	1,797	218
Middle Atlantic	65,410	1,060	62,168	6,606	55,562	12,221	6,422	-	33,939	2,981
New York	31,429	234	29,782	2,485	27,297	5,774	3,686	-	16,650	1,187
New Jersey	4,984	148	4,563	1,325	3,239	673	229	-	1,890	447
Pennsylvania	28,997	677	27,823	2,796	25,027	5,774	2,507	-	15,398	1,348
Midwest	490,474	17,883	460,128	23,789	436,339	233,455	40,718	71,859	71,637	18,670
East North Central .	159,066	6,269	148,602	12,368	136,233	72,743	12,982	-	42,482	8,027
Ohio	26,451	347	25,686	2,925	22,762	12,537	2,444	-	6,426	1,354
Indiana	23,159	487	22,302	1,780	20,522	13,930	2,073	-	3,698	821
Illinois	36,061	492	34,792	2,792	32,000	25,121	2,689	-	3,447	744
Michigan	37,457	3,130	33,051	2,921	30,130	9,484	2,735	-	15,483	2,429
Wisconsin	35,938	1,813	32,770	1,951	30,820	11,671	3,041	-	13,428	2,680
West North Central.	331,408	11,615	311,527	11,421	300,105	160,713	27,736	71,859	29,155	10,643
Minnesota	54,017	3,390	47,077	2,136	44,941	22,990	3,425	157	13,952	4,417
Iowa	36,016	172	35,387	1,688	33,699	27,031	3,866	-	1,841	961
Missouri.	44,606	2,060	41,655	2,165	39,491	15,090	12,606	56	10,959	781
North Dakota	45,250	1,882	42,255	1,242	41,013	28,064	1,206	9,933	428	1,382
South Dakota	49,354	2,873	45,467	1,064	44,403	17,819	2,354	22,152	565	1,513
Nebraska.	49,507	652	48,218	1,250	46,967	20,601	1,957	22,900	728	782
Kansas	52,658	587	51,467	1,876	49,592	29,119	2,324	16,660	681	808
South	575,044	26,391	527,041	30,657	496,384	107,532	67,937	113,837	189,507	17,571
South Atlantic	178,469	12,757	156,196	13,346	142,849	26,495	16,165	3,592	88,408	8,190
Delaware.	1,309	33	1,213	165	1,048	521	30	-	357	141
Maryland.	6,695	159	6,048	936	5,111	1,795	514	-	2,415	388
Virginia	26,091	2,368	22,812	1,663	21,150	3,309	3,315	-	13,622	904
West Virginia	15,508	1,116	14,227	532	13,695	1,053	1,892	-	10,466	284
North Carolina . . .	33,708	2,309	28,622	2,487	26,135	6,548	1,992	-	16,528	1,067
South Carolina . . .	19,912	1,340	17,785	1,422	16,363	3,371	1,177	-	11,073	742
Georgia.	37,702	2,062	34,664	2,375	32,289	6,307	3,040	-	21,860	1,083
Florida.	37,545	3,369	30,825	3,766	27,059	3,592	4,205	3,592	12,088	3,583
East South Central .	116,446	5,116	108,068	5,705	102,363	22,870	18,493	96	58,115	2,789
Kentucky.	25,862	1,169	24,023	1,224	22,799	5,818	5,955	-	10,054	972
Tennessee.	26,972	1,369	24,759	1,669	23,090	5,765	5,019	-	11,601	706
Alabama	33,091	904	31,230	1,640	29,591	4,210	3,595	96	21,017	673
Mississippi	30,521	1,674	28,056	1,172	26,884	7,078	3,924	-	15,443	439
West South Central.	280,129	8,518	262,778	11,606	251,172	58,167	33,279	110,149	42,984	6,593
Arkansas	34,040	3,129	29,904	1,232	28,672	8,182	5,678	164	14,268	380
Louisiana.	30,561	1,174	26,472	1,455	25,016	6,484	2,276	234	12,736	3,286
Oklahoma	44,772	1,176	42,431	1,716	40,715	11,557	7,590	14,546	6,505	517
Texas	170,756	3,040	163,971	7,203	156,768	31,944	17,735	95,204	9,476	2,410
West	764,128	357,403	396,209	13,247	382,962	66,896	12,697	215,989	68,514	18,865
Mountain	552,680	266,171	280,033	5,964	274,069	44,235	7,828	182,653	27,532	11,822
Montana	94,109	27,074	65,682	999	64,682	17,881	3,169	36,769	5,253	1,611
Idaho	53,481	33,190	19,628	477	19,152	6,532	1,354	6,596	4,071	600
Wyoming	62,598	29,457	32,576	501	32,075	2,362	928	26,784	984	1,017
Colorado	66,618	23,833	42,320	1,375	40,945	10,967	1,266	23,427	4,079	1,207
New Mexico	77,819	26,423	51,144	698	50,445	2,297	186	40,782	4,685	2,496
Arizona	72,960	30,647	41,994	1,116	40,878	1,306	81	31,867	4,912	2,712
Utah	54,336	35,476	16,440	465	15,975	2,002	563	8,507	3,194	1,711
Nevada	70,759	60,071	10,250	333	9,916	889	282	7,921	356	469
Pacific.	211,448	91,232	116,176	7,283	108,893	22,662	4,869	33,337	40,982	7,043
Washington	43,608	12,471	29,947	1,564	28,383	7,758	1,421	5,574	12,634	997
Oregon	62,127	32,305	28,918	941	27,977	4,348	1,916	9,152	11,857	705
California.	101,572	46,014	53,654	4,621	49,033	10,209	1,501	17,719	15,073	4,531
Hawaii.	4,141	443	3,657	157	3,500	348	31	891	1,419	811

- Represents zero.   [1] Includes water area not shown separately.   [2] Includes urban and built-up areas in units of 10 acres or greater, and rural transportation.

Source: U.S. Dept. of Agriculture, Soil Conservation Service, and Iowa State University, Statistical Laboratory; Statistical Bulletin No. 790, *Summary Report, 1987 National Resources Inventory*, December 1989.

No. 360. Extreme and Mean Elevations States and Other Areas

[One foot = .305 meter]

STATE OR OTHER AREA	HIGHEST POINT			LOWEST POINT			APPROXIMATE MEAN ELEVATION	
	Name	Elevation		Name	Elevation			
		Feet	Meters		Feet	Meters	Feet	Meters
U.S.	**Mt. McKinley (AK)**	**20,320**	**6,198**	**Death Valley (CA)**	**−282**	**−86**	**2,500**	**763**
AL.	Cheaha Mountain	2,405	733	Gulf of Mexico	(¹)	(¹)	500	153
AK.	Mount McKinley.	20,320	6,198	Pacific Ocean.	(¹)	(¹)	1,900	580
AZ.	Humphreys Peak	12,633	3,853	Colorado River	70	21	4,100	1,251
AR.	Magazine Mountain	2,753	840	Ouachita River	55	17	650	198
CA.	Mount Whitney	14,494	4,419	Death Valley.	−282	−86	2,900	885
CO.	Mt. Elbert.	14,433	4,402	Arkansas River	3,350	1,022	6,800	2,074
CT.	Mt. Frissell on South slope	2,380	726	Long Island Sound	(¹)	(¹)	500	153
DE.	Ebright Road, ² New Castle County	442	135	Atlantic Ocean	(¹)	(¹)	60	18
DC.	Tenleytown at Reno Reservoir.	410	125	Potomac River	1	(Z)	150	46
FL.	Sec. 30, T6N, R20W, Walton County.	345	105	Atlantic Ocean	(¹)	(¹)	100	31
GA.	Brasstown Bald	4,784	1,459	Atlantic Ocean	(¹)	(¹)	600	183
HI	Puu Wekiu	13,796	4,208	Pacific Ocean.	(¹)	(¹)	3,030	924
ID	Borah Peak	12,662	3,862	Snake River	710	217	5,000	1,525
IL	Charles Mound	1,235	377	Mississippi River	279	85	600	183
IN	Franklin Twp., Wayne Co .	1,257	383	Ohio River	320	98	700	214
IA	Sec. 29, T100N, R41W, Osceola County ³	1,670	509	Mississippi River	480	146	1,100	336
KS.	Mount Sunflower	4,039	1,232	Verdigris River	679	207	2,000	610
KY.	Black Mountain	4,139	2,162	Mississippi River	257	78	750	229
LA.	Driskill Mountain	535	163	New Orleans	−8	−2	100	31
ME.	Mount Katahdin.	5,267	1,606	Atlantic Ocean	(¹)	(¹)	600	183
MD.	Backbone Mountain	3,360	1,025	Atlantic Ocean	(¹)	(¹)	350	107
MA.	Mount Greylock.	3,487	1,064	Atlantic Ocean	(¹)	(¹)	500	153
MI	Mount Arvon	1,979	604	Lake Erie.	571	174	900	275
MN.	Eagle Mountain, Cook Co .	2,301	702	Lake Superior.	600	183	1,200	366
MS.	Woodall Mountain	806	246	Gulf of Mexico	(¹)	(¹)	300	92
MO.	Taum Sauk Mountain	1,772	540	St. Francis River	230	70	800	244
MT.	Granite Peak.	12,799	3,904	Kootenai River	1,800	549	3,400	1,037
NE.	Johnson Twp., Kimball Co.	5,424	1,654	Missouri River.	840	256	2,600	793
NV.	Boundary Peak	13,140	4,007	Colorado River	479	146	5,500	1,678
NH.	Mount Washington	6,288	1,918	Atlantic Ocean	(¹)	(¹)	1,000	305
NJ	High Point	1,803	550	Atlantic Ocean	(¹)	(¹)	250	76
NM.	Wheeler Peak	13,161	4,014	Red Bluff Reservoir	2,842	867	5,700	1,739
NY.	Mount Marcy.	5,344	1,630	Atlantic Ocean	(¹)	(¹)	1,000	305
NC.	Mount Mitchell	6,684	2,039	Atlantic Ocean	(¹)	(¹)	700	214
ND.	White Butte, Slope Co . . .	3,506	1,069	Red River	750	229	1,900	580
OH.	Campbell Hill	1,549	472	Ohio River	455	139	850	259
OK.	Black Mesa	4,973	1,517	Little River.	289	88	1,300	397
OR.	Mount Hood	11,239	3,428	Pacific Ocean.	(¹)	(¹)	3,300	1,007
PA.	Mount Davis	3,213	980	Delaware River	(¹)	(¹)	1,100	336
RI	Jerimoth Hill	812	248	Atlantic Ocean	(¹)	(¹)	200	61
SC.	Sassafras Mountain	3,560	1,086	Atlantic Ocean	(¹)	(¹)	350	107
SD.	Harney Peak.	7,242	2,209	Big Stone Lake.	966	295	2,200	671
TN.	Clingmans Dome	6,643	2,026	Mississippi River	178	54	900	275
TX.	Guadalupe Peak	8,749	2,668	Gulf of Mexico	(¹)	(¹)	1,700	519
UT.	Kings Peak.	13,528	4,126	Beaverdam Wash	2,000	610	6,100	1,861
VT.	Mount Mansfield	4,393	1,340	Lake Champlain	95	29	1,000	305
VA.	Mount Rogers	5,729	1,747	Atlantic Ocean	(¹)	(¹)	950	290
WA.	Mount Rainier	14,410	4,395	Pacific Ocean.	(¹)	(¹)	1,700	519
WV.	Spruce Knob.	4,861	1,483	Potomac River	240	73	1,500	458
WI	Timms Hill	1,951	595	Lake Michigan	579	177	1,050	320
WY.	Gannett Peak	13,804	4,210	Belle Fourche River	3,099	945	6,700	2,044
Other areas:								
Puerto Rico. . . .	Cerro de Punta	4,390	1,339	Atlantic Ocean	(¹)	(¹)	1,800	549
American Samoa . .	Lata Mountain.	3,160	964	Pacific Ocean.	(¹)	(¹)	1,300	397
Guam	Mount Lamlam	1,332	406	Pacific Ocean.	(¹)	(¹)	330	101
Virgin Is. . . .	Crown Mountain	1,556	475	Atlantic Ocean	(¹)	(¹)	750	229

Z Less than 0.5 meter.   ¹ Sea level.   ² At DE-PA State line.   ³ "Sec." denotes section; "T," township; "R," range; "N," north; "W," west.

Source: U.S. Geological Survey, for highest and lowest points, *Elevations and Distances in the United States, 1990*; for mean elevations, 1983 edition.

No. 361. Flows of Largest U.S. Rivers—Length, Discharge, and Drainage Area

RIVER	Location of mouth	Source stream (name and location)	Length (miles) [1]	Average discharge at mouth (1,000 cubic ft. per second)	Drainage area (1,000 sq. mi.)
Mississippi	Louisiana	Mississippi River, MN	[2]2,340	[3]593	[4][5]1,150
St. Lawrence	Canada	North River, MN	1,900	348	[5]396
Ohio	Illinois-Kentucky	Allegheny River, PA	1,310	281	203
Columbia	Oregon-Washington	Columbia River, Canada	1,240	265	[5]258
Yukon	Alaska	McNeil River, Canada	1,980	225	[5]328
Missouri	Missouri	Red Rock Creek, MT	2,540	76.2	[5]529
Tennessee	Kentucky	Courthouse Creek, NC	886	68	40.9
Mobile	Alabama	Tickanetley Creek, GA	774	67.2	44.6
Kuskokwim	Alaska	South Fork Kuskokwim River, AK	724	67	48
Copper	Alaska	Copper River, AK	286	59	24.4
Atchafalaya [6]	Louisiana	Tierra Blanca Creek, NM	1,420	58	95.1
Snake	Washington	Snake River, WY	1,040	56.9	108
Red	Louisiana	Tierra Blanca Creek, NM	1,290	56	93.2
Stikine	Alaska	Stikine River, Canada	379	56	[5]20
Susitna	Alaska	Susitna River, AK	313	51	20
Tanana	Alaska	Nabesna River, AK	659	41	44.5
Arkansas	Arkansas	East Fork Arkansas River, CO	1,460	41	161
Susquehanna	Maryland	Hayden Creek, NY	447	38.2	27.2
Willamette	Oregon	Middle Fork Williamette River, OR	309	37.4	11.4
Nushagak	Alaska	Nushagak River, AK	285	36	13.4
Alabama	Alabama	Tickanetley Creek, GA	729	34.6	22.8
Wabash	Indiana-Illinois	Wabash River, OH	512	31	32.9
White	Arkansas	White River, AR	722	30.5	27.8
Pend Oreille	Canada	Blacktail Creek, MT	531	30.4	[5]26.3
Alsek	Alaska	Aishihik River, Canada	290	30	[5]10.7

[1] From source to mouth.   [2] The length from the source of the Missouri River to the Mississippi River and thence to the Gulf of Mexico is about 3,710 miles.   [3] Includes about 167,000 cubic ft. per second diverted from the Mississippi into the Atchafalaya River but excludes the flow of the Red River.   [4] Excludes the drainage areas of the Red and Atchafalaya Rivers. [5] Drainage area includes both the U.S. and Canada.   [6] In east-central Louisiana, the Red River flows into the Atchafalaya River, a distributary of the Mississippi River. Data on average discharge, length, and drainage area include the Red River, but exclude all water diverted into the Atchafalaya from the Mississippi River.

Source: U.S. Geological Survey, *Largest Rivers in the United States*, Open File Report 87-242, August 1987.

No. 362. Water Area, Other Than Inland Water—States

[Includes only that portion of body of water under the jurisdiction of the United States, excluding Alaska and Hawaii. Excludes inland waters; see footnote 2, table 1. One square mile=2.59 square kilometers]

BODY OF WATER	AREA Sq. mi.	AREA Sq. km.	BODY OF WATER	AREA Sq. mi.	AREA Sq. km.
Total	74,364	192,603	Gulf of Mexico coastal water	3,837	9,938
			Alabama	560	1,450
Atlantic coastal water	2,298	5,952	Florida	1,698	4,398
Florida	37	96	Louisiana	1,016	2,631
Georgia	48	124	Mississippi	556	1,440
Maine	1,102	2,854	Texas	7	18
Massachusetts	959	2,484			
Rhode Island	14	36	Lake Michigan	22,178	57,441
South Carolina	138	357	Illinois	1,526	3,952
			Indiana	228	591
Chesapeake Bay	3,237	8,384	Michigan	13,037	33,766
Maryland	1,726	4,470	Wisconsin	7,387	19,132
Virginia	1,511	3,913			
			New York Harbor	92	238
Delaware Bay	665	1,722	New Jersey	69	179
Delaware	350	907	New York	23	60
New Jersey	315	816	Lake Ontario: New York	3,033	7,855
Lake Erie	5,002	12,955	Pacific coastal water	343	888
Michigan	216	559	California	69	179
New York	594	1,538	Oregon	48	124
Ohio	3,457	8,954	Washington	226	585
Pennsylvania	735	1,904			
			Puget Sound: Washington	561	1,453
Straits of Georgia and Juan de Fuca: Washington	1,610	4,170	Lake St. Clair: Michigan	116	300
Lake Huron: Michigan	8,975	23,245	Lake Superior	21,118	54,696
Long Island Sound	1,299	3,364	Michigan	16,231	42,038
Connecticut	573	1,484	Minnesota	2,212	5,729
New York	726	1,880	Wisconsin	2,675	6,928

Source: U.S. Bureau of the Census, *Areas of the United States: 1940.*

No. 363. Water Withdrawals and Consumptive Use—States and Other Areas: 1990

[In millions of gallons per day, except as noted. Figures may not add due to rounding. Withdrawal signifies water physically withdrawn from a source. Includes fresh and saline water]

STATE OR OTHER AREA	WATER WITHDRAWN								Con-sumptive use,[4] fresh water
	Total [1]	Per capita (gal. per day) fresh	Source		Selected major uses				
			Ground water	Surface water	Irriga-tion	Public supply [2]	Indus-trial [3]	Thermo-electric	
United States	404,796	1,340	80,440	323,960	136,860	41,481	27,486	192,427	93,799
Alabama	8,090	2,000	403	7,680	94	735	804	6,310	454
Alaska	641	517	112	529	1	99	493	31	26
Arizona	6,570	1,790	2,740	3,830	5,300	739	320	103	4,350
Arkansas	7,840	3,330	4,710	3,130	5,250	360	179	1,640	4,140
California	46,800	1,180	14,900	31,900	27,900	6,148	484	11,600	20,900
Colorado	12,700	3,850	2,800	9,910	11,600	669	202	114	5,250
Connecticut	4,840	325	165	4,680	15	420	150	4,240	103
Delaware	1,370	1,540	89	1,280	32	96	71	1,160	59
District of Columbia	9	15	1	8	-	-	2	8	16
Florida	17,900	582	4,660	13,200	3,730	2,229	774	11,000	3,130
Georgia	5,350	816	996	4,360	441	1,063	702	3,060	822
Hawaii	2,740	1,070	590	2,150	755	248	45	1,650	627
Idaho	19,700	19,600	7,590	12,100	18,700	249	204	6	6,090
Illinois	18,000	1,570	945	17,100	78	1,975	558	15,200	750
Indiana	9,430	1,700	621	8,810	51	722	2,577	5,960	451
Iowa	2,860	1,030	495	2,370	23	367	253	2,070	271
Kansas	6,080	2,460	4,360	1,720	4,190	398	79	1,300	4,410
Kentucky	4,320	1,170	247	4,070	12	483	331	3,440	309
Louisiana	9,350	2,200	1,340	8,010	708	669	2,467	4,950	1,590
Maine	1,140	433	85	1,060	2	155	258	691	51
Maryland	6,420	307	239	6,180	29	868	498	4,970	126
Massachusetts	5,520	338	338	5,180	100	751	92	4,500	195
Michigan	11,600	1,250	707	10,900	240	1,523	1,736	8,060	738
Minnesota	3,270	748	797	2,480	195	683	374	1,880	872
Mississippi	3,640	1,290	2,670	963	1,880	353	272	702	1,800
Missouri	6,930	1,150	728	6,200	371	739	110	5,640	529
Montana	9,320	11,600	218	9,100	9,000	151	76	33	2,090
Nebraska	8,940	5,660	4,800	4,150	6,100	348	177	2,180	4,230
Nevada	3,350	2,780	1,070	2,280	2,820	395	71	34	1,690
New Hampshire	1,310	378	64	1,250	1	122	40	1,150	26
New Jersey	12,800	287	566	12,200	58	1,108	1,460	10,200	211
New Mexico	3,480	2,300	1,760	1,720	3,010	297	86	50	2,060
New York	19,000	583	840	18,100	54	3,030	335	15,500	562
North Carolina	8,940	1,350	435	8,510	114	908	492	7,210	390
North Dakota	2,680	4,190	141	2,540	164	88	13	2,390	228
Ohio	11,700	1,080	904	10,800	15	1,434	597	9,550	901
Oklahoma	1,670	452	905	760	601	556	281	89	659
Oregon	8,430	2,970	767	7,660	6,860	534	286	15	3,160
Pennsylvania	9,830	827	1,020	8,810	14	1,871	2,122	5,750	581
Rhode Island	526	132	25	501	2	107	19	393	18
South Carolina	6,000	1,720	282	5,720	55	455	644	4,820	293
South Dakota	592	851	251	341	392	85	53	3	345
Tennessee	9,190	1,880	503	8,690	38	754	972	7,320	252
Texas	25,200	1,180	7,880	17,300	8,490	3,183	2,970	10,300	9,020
Utah	4,480	2,540	971	3,510	3,590	514	245	87	2,230
Vermont	632	1,120	45	587	1	56	48	519	29
Virginia	6,860	762	443	6,420	36	822	652	5,290	224
Washington	7,940	1,630	1,450	6,490	6,030	979	540	334	2,830
West Virginia	4,580	2,560	728	3,860	-	209	659	3,710	509
Wisconsin	6,510	1,330	681	5,830	151	685	468	5,100	461
Wyoming	7,600	16,700	403	7,200	7,160	96	136	184	2,730
Puerto Rico	3,040	163	157	2,880	140	411	14	2,470	199
Virgin Islands	164	91	3	160	-	8	-	103	2

- Represents zero.   [1] Includes self-supplied withdrawals for commercial use (1.2 mil. gallons) and livestock (4.4 mil. gallons) that are not shown separately under "major uses."   [2] Includes domestic withdrawals for normal household purposes.   [3] Includes water used in mining.   [4] Water that has been evaporated, transpired, or incorporated into products, plant or animal tissue; and therefore, is not available for immediate reuse.

Source: U.S. Geological Survey, *Estimated Use of Water in the United States in 1990*, circular 1081.

No. 364. U.S. Water Withdrawals and Consumptive Use Per Day, by End Use: 1940 to 1990

[Includes Puerto Rico. Withdrawal signifies water physically withdrawn from a source. Includes fresh and saline water; excludes water used for hydroelectric power. See also *Historical Statistics, Colonial Times to 1970*, series J 92-103]

YEAR	Total (bil. gal.)	Per capita [1] (gal.)	Irrigation (bil. gal.)	PUBLIC SUPPLY [2] Total (bil. gal.)	PUBLIC SUPPLY [2] Per capita[3] (gal.)	Rural [4] (bil. gal.)	Industrial and misc. [5] (bil. gal.)	Steam electric utilities (bil. gal.)
WITHDRAWALS								
1940	140	1,027	71	10	75	3.1	29	23
1950	180	1,185	89	14	145	3.6	37	40
1955	240	1,454	110	17	148	3.6	39	72
1960	270	1,500	110	21	151	3.6	38	100
1965	310	1,602	120	24	155	4.0	46	130
1970	370	1,815	130	27	166	4.5	47	170
1975	420	1,972	140	29	168	4.9	45	200
1980	440	1,953	150	34	183	5.6	45	210
1985	399	1,650	137	38	189	7.8	31	187
1990	408	1,620	137	41	195	7.9	30	195
CONSUMPTIVE USE								
1960	61	339	52	3.5	25	2.8	3.0	0.2
1965	77	403	66	5.2	34	3.2	3.4	0.4
1970	87	427	73	5.9	36	3.4	4.1	0.8
1975	96	451	80	6.7	38	3.4	4.2	1.9
1980	100	440	83	7.1	38	3.9	5.0	3.2
1985	92	380	74	(6)	(6)	9.2	6.1	6.2
1990	94	370	76	(6)	(6)	8.9	6.7	4.0

[1] Based on Bureau of the Census resident population as of July 1.   [2] Includes commercial water withdrawals.
[3] Based on population served.   [4] Rural farm and nonfarm household and garden use, and water for farm stock and dairies.
[5] For 1940 to 1960, includes manufacturing and mineral industries, rural commercial industries, air-conditioning, resorts, hotels, motels, military and other State and Federal agencies, and miscellaneous; thereafter, includes manufacturing, mining and mineral processing, ordnance, construction, and miscellaneous.   [6] Public supply consumptive use included in end-use categories.

Source: 1940-1960, U.S. Bureau of Domestic Business Development, based principally on committee prints, *Water Resources Activities in the United States*, for the Senate Committee on National Water Resources, U.S. Senate; thereafter, U.S. Geological Survey, *Estimated Use of Water in the United States in 1990*, circular 1081, and previous quinquennial issues.

No. 365. National Ambient Water Quality in Rivers and Streams—Violation Rate: 1980 to 1992

[In percent. Violation level based on U.S. Environmental Protection Agency water quality criteria. Violation rate represents the proportion of all measurements of a specific water quality pollutant which exceeds the "violation level" for that pollutant. "Violation" does not necessarily imply a legal violation. Data based on U.S. Geological Survey's National Stream Quality Accounting Network (NASQAN) data system; for details, see source. Years refer to water years. A water year begins in Oct. and ends in Sept. μg=micrograms; mg=milligrams. For metric conversion, see page ix]

POLLUTANT	VIOLATION LEVEL	1980	1985	1986	1987	1988	1989	1990	1991	1992
Fecal coliform bacteria . . .	Above 200 cells per 100 ml .	31	28	24	23	22	30	26	15	25
Dissolved oxygen	Below 5 mg per liter	5	3	3	2	2	3	2	2	(Z)
Phosphorus, total, as phosporous	Above 1.0 mg per liter	4	3	3	3	4	2	3	2	2
Lead, dissolved	Above 50 μg per liter	(Z)	(Z)	(Z)	(Z)	(Z)	(Z)	(Z)	(Z)	(Z)
Cadmium, dissolved	Above 10 μg per liter	1	(Z)	(Z)	(Z)	(Z)	(Z)	(Z)	(Z)	(Z)

Z Less than 1.

Source: U.S. Geological Survey, national-level data, unpublished; State-level data, *Water-Data Report*, annual series prepared in cooperation with the State governments.

No. 366. Oil Polluting Incidents Reported in and Around U.S. Waters: 1973 to 1992

YEAR	Incidents	Gallons	YEAR	Incidents	Gallons
1973	11,054	15,289,188	1986	6,330	4,427,544
1974	12,083	15,739,792	1987	6,083	3,759,983
1975	10,998	21,528,444	1988	6,155	6,617,278
1976	11,066	18,517,384	1989	7,923	13,506,643
1977	10,979	8,188,398	1990	9,600	11,375,576
1978	12,174	11,035,890	1991	9,850	1,452,103
1979	11,556	10,051,271			
1980	9,886	12,638,848	1992	8,790	1,503,862
1981	9,589	8,919,789	Tankships	198	117,899
1982	9,416	10,404,646	Tank barges	328	73,559
1983	10,530	8,378,719	Other vessels	4,893	400,296
1984	10,089	19,007,332	Non-vessels	3,371	912,108
1985	7,740	8,465,055			

Source: U.S. Coast Guard. Based on unpublished data from the *Marine Safety Information System*.

No. 367. National Ambient Air Pollutant Concentrations: 1983 to 1991

[Data represent annual composite averages of pollutant based on daily 24-hour averages of monitoring stations, except carbon monoxide is based on the second-highest, non-overlapping, 8-hour average; ozone, average of the second-highest daily maximum one hour value; and lead, quarterly average of ambient lead levels. Based on data from the National Aerometric Data Bank. $\mu g/m^3$ = micrograms of pollutant per cubic meter of air; ppm = parts per million]

POLLUTANT	Unit	Monitoring stations, number	Air quality standard [1]	1983	1984	1985	1986	1987	1988	1989	1990	1991
Carbon monoxide	ppm	313	[2]9	7.85	7.78	7.00	7.15	6.72	6.39	6.31	5.85	5.57
Ozone	ppm	495	[3].12	0.137	0.126	0.124	0.119	0.126	0.137	0.117	0.114	0.116
Sulfur dioxide	ppm	479	.03	0.010	0.010	0.009	0.009	0.009	0.009	0.009	0.008	0.008
Particulates (PM-10) [4]	$\mu g/m^3$	682	50	(X)	(X)	(X)	(X)	(X)	33.6	33.6	30.6	30.3
Nitrogen dioxide	ppm	172	.053	0.023	0.023	0.023	0.024	0.023	0.024	0.023	0.022	0.022
Lead	$\mu g/m^3$	209	[5]1.5	0.421	0.392	0.264	0.149	0.106	0.088	0.072	0.062	0.053

X Not applicable.   [1] Refers to the primary National Ambient Air Quality Standard that protects the public health.   [2] Based on 8-hour standard of 9 ppm.   [3] Based on 1-hour standard of .12 ppm.   [4] The particulates (PM-10) standard replaced the previous standard for total suspended particulates in 1987.   [5] Based on 3-month standard of 1.5 $\mu g/m^3$.
Source: U.S. Environmental Protection Agency, *National Air Quality and Emissions Trends Report*, annual.

No. 368. National Air Pollutant Emissions: 1940 to 1991

[In millions of metric tons, except lead in thousands of metric tons. Metric ton = 1.1023 short tons. PM = Particulate matter, SO_x = Sulfur oxides, NO_x = Nitrogen oxides, VOC = volatile organic compound, CO = Carbon monoxide, Pb = Lead]

YEAR	EMISSIONS						PERCENT CHANGE FROM PRIOR YEAR					
	PM	SO_x	NO_x	VOC	CO	Pb	PM	SO_x	NO_x	VOC	CO	Pb
1940	22.8	18.1	6.8	15.5	80.3	(NA)	(NA)	(NA)	(NA)	(NA)	(NA)	(NA)
1950	24.8	20.3	9.4	18.9	86.4	(NA)	8.8	12.2	38.2	21.9	7.6	(NA)
1960	21.8	20.2	13.2	22.5	103.6	(NA)	-12.1	-0.5	40.4	19.0	19.9	(NA)
1970	19.0	28.4	19.0	27.4	123.6	199.1	-12.8	40.6	43.9	21.8	19.3	(NA)
1980	9.1	23.8	23.6	21.8	100.0	68.0	-17.3	-6.7	16.3	-3.1	-4.6	-52.7
1981	8.6	22.5	21.4	21.2	98.0	53.4	-5.5	-5.5	-9.3	-2.8	-2.0	-21.5
1982	7.7	21.2	20.4	19.5	90.5	52.3	-10.5	-5.8	-4.7	-8.0	-7.7	-2.1
1983	7.8	20.6	19.8	20.3	92.3	44.7	1.3	-2.8	-2.9	4.1	2.0	-14.5
1984	8.1	21.5	20.1	21.0	87.6	38.3	3.8	4.4	1.5	3.4	-5.1	-14.3
1985	7.9	21.7	19.4	19.8	83.1	18.3	-2.5	0.9	-3.5	-1.0	-4.3	-52.2
1986	7.3	21.2	18.8	18.5	76.0	6.6	-7.6	-2.3	-3.1	-6.6	-8.5	-63.9
1987	7.4	21.0	19.0	18.6	75.1	6.2	1.4	-0.9	1.1	0.5	-1.2	-6.1
1988	7.9	21.3	19.7	18.6	75.5	5.9	6.8	1.4	3.7	-	0.5	-4.8
1989	7.6	21.5	19.3	17.4	68.3	5.5	-3.8	0.9	-2.0	-6.5	-9.5	-6.8
1990	7.4	21.1	19.4	17.6	67.7	5.1	-2.6	-1.9	0.5	1.1	-0.9	-7.3
1991	7.4	20.7	18.8	16.9	62.1	5.0	-	-1.9	-3.1	-4.0	-8.3	-2.0

- Represents zero.   NA Not available.

No. 369. Air Pollutant Emissions, by Pollutant and Source: 1970 to 1991

[In millions of metric tons, except lead in thousands of metric tons. Metric ton = 1.1023 short tons]

YEAR AND POLLUTANT	Total emissions	CONTROLLABLE EMISSIONS							PERCENT OF TOTAL		
		Transportation		Fuel combustion [1]		Industrial processes	Solid waste disposal	Misc. uncontrollable	Transportation	Fuel combustion [1]	Industrial
		Total	Road vehicles	Total	Electric utilities						
1970: Carbon monoxide	123.6	96.9	87.8	4.2	0.2	9.0	6.4	7.2	78.4	3.4	7.3
Sulfur oxides	28.4	0.6	0.3	21.3	15.8	6.4	-	0.1	2.1	75.0	22.5
Volatile organic compounds	27.4	12.8	11.5	0.6	-	8.9	1.8	2.3	46.7	2.2	32.5
Particulates	19.0	1.2	0.9	5.1	2.3	10.5	1.1	0.4	6.3	26.8	55.3
Nitrogen oxides	19.0	8.5	6.8	9.1	4.4	0.7	0.4	0.3	44.7	47.9	3.7
Lead	199.1	163.6	156.0	9.6	0.3	23.9	2.0	-	82.2	4.8	12.0
1980: Carbon monoxide	100.0	77.4	70.0	6.6	0.3	6.3	2.1	7.6	77.4	6.6	6.3
Sulfur oxides	22.7	0.9	0.4	18.0	14.7	3.7	-	0.0	4.0	79.3	16.3
Volatile organic compounds	21.8	8.1	6.9	1.0	-	9.1	0.7	1.9	37.2	4.6	41.7
Particulates	9.1	1.3	1.1	3.0	0.8	3.3	0.3	0.1	14.3	33.0	36.3
Nitrogen oxides	23.6	12.5	10.5	10.1	6.4	0.7	0.1	0.2	53.0	42.8	3.0
Lead	68.0	59.4	56.4	3.9	0.1	3.6	1.1	-	87.4	5.7	5.3
1991: Carbon monoxide	62.1	43.5	36.1	4.7	0.3	4.7	2.1	7.2	70.0	7.5	7.6
Sulfur oxides	20.7	1.0	0.6	16.6	14.1	3.2	0.2	0.1	4.8	79.8	15.2
Volatile organic compounds	16.9	5.1	3.8	0.7	0.3	7.9	0.7	2.6	30.1	4.0	46.6
Particulates	7.4	1.6	1.3	1.9	0.4	2.6	0.3	1.0	21.2	25.6	34.4
Nitrogen oxides	18.8	7.3	5.4	10.6	6.7	0.6	0.1	0.2	38.7	56.4	3.2
Lead	5.0	1.6	1.4	0.5	0.5	2.2	0.7	0.0	32.6	9.1	44.5

- Represents zero.   [1] Stationary sources.

Source of tables 368 and 369: U.S. Environmental Protection Agency, *National Air Pollutant Emission Estimates, 1940-1991*.

No. 370. Metropolitan Areas Failing to Meet National Ambient Air Quality Standards for Carbon Monoxide—Number of Days Exceeding Standards: 1990 and 1991

[Areas generally represent the officially defined metropolitan area, but may, in some cases, not have all the counties identified as part of the area; see *Federal Register*, 40 CFR, part 81, *Air Quality Designations: Revised*, June 23, 1992. Nonattainment status was as of June 23, 1992]

METROPOLITAN AREA	1990	1991	METROPOLITAN AREA	1990	1991	METROPOLITAN AREA	1990	1991
Albuquerque, NM	3	2	Hartford, CT CMSA	-	1	Philadelphia, PA-NJ-DE-		
Anchorage, AK	12	3	Klamath County, OR [1]	-	1	MD CMSA	-	-
Baltimore, MD	1	-	Lake Tahoe S. Shore,			Phoenix, AZ	4	3
Boston, MA-NH CMSA	-	-	CA	5	-	Portland, OR-WA CMSA	2	2
Chico, CA	1	-	Las Vegas, NV	17	6	Provo-Orem, UT	11	6
Cleveland, OH CMSA	-	-	Longmont, CO	-	-	Raleigh-Durham, NC	2	-
Colorado Springs, CO	-	-	Los Angeles, CA CMSA	47	41	Reno, NV	7	2
Denver-Boulder, CO CMSA	3	4	Medford, OR	-	3	Sacramento, CA	11	5
Duluth, MN	-	-	Memphis, TN-AR-MS	1	-	San Diego, CA	-	-
El Paso, TX	4	3	Minneapolis-St. Paul,			San Francisco, CA CMSA	2	4
Fairbanks, AK [1]	2	3	MN-WI	1	2	Seattle-Tacoma, WA		
Fort Collins, CO	-	2	Missoula County, MT [1]	1	5	CMSA	2	1
Fresno, CA	1	1	Modesto, CA	2	1	Spokane, WA	6	13
Grant Pass, OR [1]	1	-	New York, NY-NJ-CT			Stockton, CA	2	1
Greensboro-Winston-			CMSA	4	2	Syracuse, NY	1	-
Salem, NC	-	-	Ogden, UT	3	-	Washington, DC-MD-VA	-	-

- Represents zero.   NA Not available.   [1] Not a metropolitan area.

No. 371. Metropolitan Areas Failing to Meet National Ambient Air Quality Standards for Ozone— Number of Days Exceeding Standards: 1989 to 1991

[See headnote, table 370. Nonattainment status was as of June 23, 1992]

METROPOLITAN AREA	1989-1991, avg.	1991 [1]	METROPOLITAN AREA	1989-1991, avg.	1991 [1]
Albany-Schenectady-Troy, NY	-	1.1	Los Angeles South Coast Air, CA [6]	105.2	91.0
Allentown-Bethlehem-Easton, PA-NJ	0.3	-	Manchester, NH	0.5	(NA)
Altoona, PA	-	-	Manitowoc Co, WI	2.4	5.1
Atlanta, GA	3.8	4.0	Memphis, TN-AR-MS	0.3	-
Atlantic City, NJ	2.8	2.1	Miami-Fort Lauderdale, FL CMSA	0.3	-
Baltimore, MD	6.9	8.2	Milwaukee-Racine, WI CMSA	5.7	10.2
Baton Rouge, LA	4.1	2.0	Monterey Bay, CA [7]	0.7	1.1
Beaumont-Port Arthur, TX	5.1	6.0	Muskegon, MI	4.8	4.8
Birmingham, AL	1.4	-	Nashville, TN	3.0	1.1
Boston-Lawrence-Salem, MA-NH CMSA [2]	4.3	7.6	New York, NY-NJ-CT CMSA [8]	8.6	13.3
Buffalo-Niagara Falls, NY CMSA	0.3	-	Norfolk-Virginia Beach-		
Canton, OH	0.3	1.0	Newport News, VA	-	1.0
Charleston, WV	0.3	1.0	Owensboro, KY	1.0	-
Charlotte-Gastonia-Rock Hill, NC-SC [3]	1.1	1.0	Paducah, KY	-	-
Cherokee County, SC [4]	-	-	Parkersburg-Marietta, WV-OH	1.0	1.0
Chicago-Gary-Lake County, IL-IN-WI CMSA	5.5	11.8	Philadelphia, PA-NJ-DE-MD CMSA	8.1	10.3
Cincinnati-Hamilton, OH-KY-IN CMSA	2.3	3.0	Phoenix, AZ	3.0	-
Cleveland-Akron-Lorain, OH CMSA	2.0	2.0	Pittsburgh-Beaver Valley, PA CMSA	1.1	-
Columbus, OH	0.7	1.0	Portland-Vancouver, OR-WA CMSA	1.9	1.4
Dallas-Fort Worth, TX CMSA	3.5	4.2	Portland, ME	5.0	4.8
Dayton-Springfield, OH	0.7	-	Portsmouth-Dover-Rochester, NH-ME	2.1	3.2
Detroit-Ann Arbor, MI CMSA	2.0	3.0	Poughkeepsie, NY	2.1	2.1
Door County, WI [4]	2.3	4.0	Providence, RI [9]	6.0	9.5
Edmonson County, KY [4]	-	-	Raleigh-Durham, NC	1.0	-
El Paso, TX	3.5	3.2	Reading, PA	0.3	1.0
Erie, PA	-	-	Reno, NV	2.1	-
Essex County, NY [4]	1.2	3.7	Richmond-Petersburg, VA	0.3	-
Evansville, IN-KY	0.4	-	Sacramento, CA	3.1	15.7
Grand Rapids, MI	2.0	2.0	St. Louis, MO-IL	1.4	1.0
Greater Connecticut, CT [5]	9.7	17.3	Salt Lake City-Ogden, UT	1.3	-
Greenbrier County, WV [4]	0.4	1.1	San Diego, CA	25.9	7.1
Greensboro-Winston-Salem-High Point, NC	0.3	-	San Joaquin Valley, CA	34.4	33.9
Hancock and Waldo counties, ME [4]	1.2	2.5	San Francisco-Bay area, CA	1.3	1.0
Harrisburg-Lebanon-Carlisle, PA	0.3	-	Santa Barbara-Santa Maria-Lompoc, CA	4.1	4.1
Houston-Galveston-Brazoria, TX CMSA	14.9	16.6	Scranton-Wilkes-Barre, PA	1.1	2.0
Huntington-Ashland, WV-KY-OH	1.9	3.1	Seattle-Tacoma, WA	1.7	0.0
Indianapolis, IN	0.7	-	Sheboygan, WI	7.5	7.5
Jefferson County, NY [4]	-	-	Smyth County, VA [4]	(NA)	(NA)
Jersey Co., IL [4]	0.7	-	South Bend-Mishawaka, IN	-	-
Johnstown, PA	-	-	Southeast Desert Modified AQMD, CA [10]	45.3	32.1
Kent County and Queen Anne's Co., MD [4]	3.2	6.3	Springfield, MA	3.9	5.7
Kewaunee County, WI [4]	0.7	2.1	Sussex County, DE [4]	1.4	3.1
Knox Co. and Lincoln counties, ME [4]	4.2	7.0	Tampa-St. Petersburg-Clearwater, FL	0.5	-
Knoxville, TN	0.3	-	Toledo, OH	0.3	-
Lake Charles, LA	1.7	1.0	Ventura County, CA	29.0	32.6
Lancaster, PA	-	-	Walworth County, WI	0.7	1.0
Lewiston-Auburn, ME	1.0	1.0	Washington, DC-MD-VA	2.4	6.1
Lexington-Fayette, KY	0.3	-	York, PA	0.3	-
Louisville, KY-IN	2.2	3.4	Youngstown-Warren, OH [11]	1.0	1.0

- Represents zero.   NA Not available.   [1] May represent a different monitoring location than one used to calculate average. [2] Includes both the Worcester, MA and New Bedford, MA MSA's. [3] Excludes York Co., SC. [4] Not a metropolitan area. [5] Primarily represents Hartford-New Haven area. [6] Primarily represents Los Angeles and Orange counties. [7] Primarily represents Monterey, Santa Cruz, and San Benito counties. [8] Excludes the Connecticut portion. [9] Covers entire State of Rhode Island. [10] Represents primarily San Joaquin, Turlock, Merced, Madera, Fresno, Kings, Tulare, and Kern counties. [11] Includes Sharon, PA.

Source of tables 370 and 371: U.S. Environmental Protection Agency, press release, June 1992.

No. 372. Municipal Solid Waste Generation, Recovery, and Disposal: 1960 to 1990

[In millions of tons, except as indicated. Covers post-consumer residential and commercial solid wastes which comprise the major portion of typical municipal collections. Excludes mining, agricultural and industrial processing, demolition and construction wastes, sewage sludge, and junked autos and obsolete equipment wastes. Based on material-flows estimating procedure and wet weight as generated. NA Not available]

ITEM AND MATERIAL	1960	1970	1980	1985	1986	1987	1988	1989	1990
Waste generated	87.8	121.9	151.5	164.4	170.7	178.1	184.2	191.4	195.7
Per person per day (lb.)	2.66	3.27	3.65	3.77	3.88	4.01	4.12	4.2	4.3
Materials recovered.	5.9	8.6	14.5	16.4	18.3	20.1	23.5	29.9	33.4
Per person per day (lb.)	0.18	0.23	0.35	0.38	0.42	0.45	0.52	0.7	0.7
Combustion for energy recovery	(NA)	0.4	2.7	7.6	9.6	16.0	24.5	27.1	29.7
Per person per day (lb.)	(NA)	0.02	0.06	0.17	0.22	0.36	0.59	0.6	0.7
Combustion without energy recovery .	27.0	24.7	11.0	4.1	3.0	2.0	1.0	2.0	2.2
Per person per day (lb.)	0.82	0.66	0.27	0.10	0.07	0.05	0.02	0.4	0.5
Landfill, other disposal.	54.9	88.2	123.3	136.4	139.8	140.0	135.1	132.4	130.4
Per person per day (lb.)	1.67	2.37	2.97	3.13	3.18	3.15	3.02	2.9	2.9
Percent distribution of generation:									
Paper and paperboard	34.1	36.3	36.1	37.4	38.4	39.1	38.9	37.6	37.5
Glass.	7.6	10.4	9.9	8.0	7.6	6.9	6.8	6.7	6.7
Metals	12.0	11.6	9.6	8.6	8.5	8.3	8.3	8.2	8.3
Plastics	0.5	2.5	5.2	7.1	7.2	7.5	7.8	8.0	8.3
Rubber and leather	2.3	2.6	2.8	2.3	2.5	2.5	2.5	2.4	2.4
Textiles	1.9	1.6	1.7	1.7	1.6	2.1	2.1	2.9	2.9
Wood	3.4	3.3	4.4	5.0	5.3	5.5	6.1	6.1	6.3
Food wastes.	13.9	10.5	8.7	8.0	7.7	7.4	7.2	6.9	6.7
Yard wastes	22.8	19.0	18.2	18.2	17.7	17.4	17.2	18.1	17.9
Other wastes	1.6	2.2	3.4	3.6	3.4	3.3	3.1	3.1	3.1

No. 373. Generation and Recovery of Selected Materials in Municipal Solid Waste: 1960 to 1990

[In millions of tons, except as indicated. Covers post-consumer residential and commercial solid wastes which comprise the major portion of typical municipal collections. Excludes mining, agricultural and industrial processing, demolition and construction wastes, sewage sludge, and junked autos and obsolete equipment wastes. Based on material-flows estimating procedure and wet weight as generated. - Represents zero]

ITEM AND MATERIAL	1960	1970	1980	1985	1986	1987	1988	1989	1990
Waste generated, total	**87.8**	**121.9**	**151.5**	**164.4**	**170.7**	**178.1**	**184.2**	**191.4**	**195.7**
Paper and paperboard	29.9	44.2	54.7	61.5	65.6	69.6	71.7	71.9	73.3
Ferrous metals	9.9	12.6	11.6	10.9	11.1	11.3	11.6	12.0	12.3
Aluminum	0.4	0.8	1.8	2.3	2.4	2.4	2.5	2.5	2.7
Other nonferrous metals	0.2	0.7	1.1	1.0	1.0	1.1	1.1	1.2	1.2
Glass.	6.7	12.7	15.0	13.2	13.0	12.3	12.5	12.9	13.2
Plastics	0.4	3.1	7.9	11.6	12.2	13.4	14.4	15.4	16.2
Yard waste	20.0	23.2	27.5	30.0	30.2	31.0	31.6	34.7	35.0
Other wastes	20.3	24.6	31.9	33.9	35.2	37.0	38.8	40.8	41.8
Materials recovered, total	**5.9**	**8.6**	**14.5**	**16.4**	**18.3**	**20.1**	**23.5**	**29.9**	**33.4**
Paper and paperboard	5.4	7.4	11.9	13.1	14.8	16.3	18.4	19.1	20.9
Ferrous metals	0.1	0.1	0.4	0.4	0.4	0.4	0.7	1.5	1.9
Aluminum	-	-	0.3	0.6	0.6	0.7	0.8	0.9	1.0
Other nonferrous metals	0.0	0.3	0.5	0.5	0.6	0.6	0.7	0.8	0.8
Glass.	0.1	0.2	0.8	1.0	1.1	1.3	1.5	2.5	2.6
Plastics	-	-	-	0.1	0.1	0.1	0.2	0.3	0.4
Yard waste	-	-	-	-	-	-	0.5	3.5	4.2
Other wastes	0.3	0.6	0.6	0.7	0.7	0.7	0.7	1.3	1.6
Percent of generation recovered, total	**6.7**	**7.1**	**9.6**	**10.0**	**10.7**	**11.2**	**12.8**	**15.6**	**17.1**
Paper and paperboard	18.1	16.7	21.8	21.3	22.6	23.4	25.6	26.6	28.6
Ferrous metals	1.0	0.8	3.4	3.7	3.6	3.5	5.8	12.6	15.4
Aluminum	-	-	16.7	26.1	25.0	29.2	31.7	35.5	38.1
Other nonferrous metals	-	42.9	45.5	50.0	60.0	54.5	65.1	68.3	67.7
Glass.	1.5	1.6	5.3	7.6	8.5	10.6	12.0	19.5	19.9
Plastics	-	-	-	0.9	0.8	0.7	1.1	1.7	2.2
Yard waste	-	-	-	-	-	-	1.6	10.0	12.0
Other wastes	1.5	2.4	1.9	2.1	2.0	1.9	1.8	3.2	3.8

Source of tables 372 and 373: Franklin Associates, Ltd., Prairie Village, KS, *Characterization of Municipal Solid Waste in the United States: 1992 Update*. Prepared for the U.S. Environmental Protection Agency.

No. 374. Synthetic Organic Pesticides—Production and Sales: 1970 to 1990

[Includes a small quantity of soil conditioners. 1 kg. = .454 lbs]

ITEM	Unit	1970	1980	1981	1982	1983	1984	1985	1986	1987	1988	1989	1990
Production, total	Mil. kg.	469	666	649	505	461	539	560	535	472	528	572	557
Herbicides	Mil. kg.	183	366	380	283	259	325	343	329	252	318	316	317
Insecticides	Mil. kg.	222	229	203	172	147	159	168	155	172	160	192	175
Fungicides	Mil. kg.	63	71	65	50	56	56	49	51	48	50	50	44
All other [1]	Mil. kg.	(NA)	(NA)	(NA)	(NA)	(NA)	(NA)	(NA)	(NA)	(NA)	(NA)	14	22
Sales, total	Mil. kg.	400	638	585	520	461	502	463	426	413	424	461	442
Sales value	Mil. dol	870	4,078	4,652	4,432	4,054	4,054	4,730	4,437	4,234	4,171	4,354	5,203	4,774

NA Not available. [1] Beginning 1989, may include some former insecticides along with new products.
Source: U.S. International Trade Commission, *Synthetic Organic Chemicals*, annual.

No. 375. Hazardous Waste Sites on the National Priority List, by State: 1992

[Includes both proposed and final sites listed on the National Priorities List for the Superfund program as authorized by the Comprehensive Environmental Response, Compensationa, and Liability Act of 1980 and the Superfund Amendments and Reauthorization Act of 1986]

STATE	Total sites	Rank	Percent distri- bution	Fed- eral	Non- Fed- eral	STATE	Total sites	Rank	Percent distri- bution	Fed- eral	Non- Fed- eral
Total	1,236	(X)	(X)	126	1,110	Montana.	8	41	0.7	-	8
						Nebraska	10	33	0.8	1	9
United States . .	1,224	(X)	100.0	124	1,100	Nevada	1	50	0.1	-	1
						New Hampshire. . . .	17	22	1.4	1	16
Alabama.	12	28	1.0	2	10	New Jersey.	108	1	8.8	6	102
Alaska	7	43	0.6	5	2	New Mexico	11	32	0.9	2	9
Arizona.	10	33	0.8	3	7	New York	83	4	6.8	4	79
Arkansas	12	28	1.0	-	12	North Carolina. . . .	23	16	1.9	1	22
California	95	3	7.8	22	73	North Dakota.	2	47	0.2	-	2
Colorado.	17	22	1.4	3	14	Ohio	33	11	2.7	3	30
Connecticut.	15	24	1.2	1	14	Oklahoma.	10	33	0.8	1	9
Delaware	19	20	1.6	1	18	Oregon.	9	38	0.7	1	8
District of Columbia .	-	(X)	0.0	-	-	Pennsylvania	98	2	8.0	4	94
Florida	55	6	4.5	4	51	Rhode Island.	12	28	1.0	2	10
Georgia	13	26	1.1	2	11	South Carolina. . . .	24	15	2.0	1	23
Hawaii	2	47	0.2	2	-	South Dakota	4	45	0.3	1	3
Idaho	9	38	0.7	2	7	Tennessee	14	25	1.1	3	11
Illinois	37	10	3.0	4	33	Texas.	29	13	2.4	4	25
Indiana.	33	11	2.7	-	33	Utah	13	26	1.1	4	9
Iowa	21	19	1.7	1	20	Vermont	8	41	0.7	-	8
Kansas.	10	33	0.8	1	9	Virginia	22	18	1.8	3	19
Kentucky	19	20	1.6	-	19	Washington.	50	7	4.1	15	35
Louisiana	12	28	1.0	1	11	West Virginia	5	44	0.4	-	5
Maine.	9	38	0.7	2	7	Wisconsin	40	9	3.3	-	40
Maryland	10	33	0.8	2	8	Wyoming	3	46	0.2	1	2
Massachusetts.	26	14	2.1	3	23						
Michigan.	77	5	6.3	-	77	Guam.	2	(X)	(X)	1	1
Minnesota.	42	8	3.4	2	40	Puerto Rico.	9	(X)	(X)	1	8
Mississippi	2	47	0.2	-	2	Virgin Islands.	1	(X)	(X)	-	1
Missouri	23	16	1.9	3	20						

- Represents zero. X Not applicable.

U.S. Environmental Protection Agency, press release. Also in the *Federal Register*, October 14, 1992.

No. 376. Environmental Industry—Revenues and Employment, by Industry Segment: 1988 to 1992

[Covers approximately 59,000 private and public companies engaged in environmental activities]

INDUSTRY SEGMENT	REVENUE (bil. dol.)					EMPLOYMENT (1,000)				
	1988	1989	1990	1991	1992	1988	1989	1990	1991	1992
Industry total	100.3	114.6	126.0	128.7	133.7	857	967	1,047	1,052	1,073
Analytical services [1]	1.3	1.6	1.7	1.7	1.8	16	19	20	19	20
Solid waste management [2]	20.7	23.5	26.1	27.4	28.2	186	208	226	233	235
Hazardous waste management . . .	9.9	12.1	13.3	13.7	14.6	93	112	120	121	127
Asbestos abatement	3.0	3.8	4.0	3.0	3.1	29	37	38	28	28
Water infrastructure	10.9	11.7	12.1	12.5	13.0	91	95	97	98	100
Water utilities	17.4	18.8	20.2	21.2	21.8	117	125	131	135	136
Engineering/consulting.	8.1	10.2	12.2	13.4	14.2	97	120	141	152	158
Resource recovery	12.0	14.8	17.2	15.8	16.1	86	105	119	107	107
Instrument manufacturing	1.3	1.5	1.6	1.7	1.8	12	13	14	15	15
Air pollution control	5.5	5.3	5.4	5.3	5.4	42	40	40	39	39
Waste management equipment . . .	9.0	9.8	10.4	11.0	11.5	75	80	83	86	88
Environmental energy sources. . . .	1.2	1.5	1.8	2.0	2.2	12	14	17	18	20

[1] Covers environmental laboratory testing and services.   [2] Covers such activities as collection, transportation, transfer stations, disposal, landfill ownership and management for solid waste.

Source: Environmental Business International, Inc., San Diego, CA, *Environmental Business Journal*, monthly, (copyright).

No. 377. Pollution Abatement and Control Expenditures, in Current and Constant (1987) Dollars, 1972 to 1990, and by Media, 1990

[In millions of dollars]

YEAR	Total expenditures	POLLUTION ABATEMENT							Regulation and monitoring	Research and development
		Total	Personal consumption	Business	Government					
					Total	Federal	State and local	Govt. enterprise [1]		
CURRENT DOLLARS										
1972	17,037	15,848	1,349	11,090	3,409	139	1,311	1,959	367	823
1975	28,424	26,668	3,231	16,531	6,906	432	1,752	4,722	653	1,104
1977	35,123	32,812	4,286	21,101	7,426	490	1,965	4,971	833	1,478
1978	39,457	36,860	4,772	23,266	8,822	472	2,212	6,139	949	1,647
1979	45,593	42,750	5,423	27,285	10,042	548	2,461	7,033	1,067	1,777
1980	51,478	48,432	6,568	30,618	11,246	494	2,778	7,973	1,296	1,751
1981	56,472	53,346	8,140	34,453	10,752	506	3,053	7,194	1,378	1,749
1982	56,576	53,395	8,309	34,151	10,935	550	3,274	7,111	1,397	1,783
1983	60,002	56,283	9,758	35,357	11,167	795	3,547	6,825	1,385	2,335
1984	66,445	62,746	10,771	39,467	12,508	944	3,886	7,679	1,362	2,337
1985	70,941	67,250	11,839	41,559	13,852	1,225	4,324	8,304	1,279	2,412
1986	74,178	70,074	12,244	42,636	15,195	1,346	4,793	9,056	1,532	2,573
1987	76,672	72,506	10,875	44,501	17,130	1,237	5,356	10,538	1,519	2,648
1988	81,081	76,605	12,044	46,928	17,633	1,402	6,149	10,082	1,695	2,781
1989	85,407	80,630	10,636	50,817	19,177	1,381	7,076	10,720	1,803	2,974
1990, prel. [2]	89,967	85,087	9,247	54,674	21,166	1,394	8,015	11,757	1,784	3,097
Air	29,499	26,969	9,247	17,369	352	71	13	268	476	2,053
Water	37,260	36,202	-	23,473	12,729	737	503	11,489	649	409
Solid Waste	24,110	23,504	-	15,770	7,735	304	7,431	-	408	197
CONSTANT (1987) DOLLARS										
1972	46,298	43,080	3,449	30,533	9,098	402	3,669	5,028	959.00	2,259
1975	57,333	53,673	6,165	33,113	14,395	937	3,737	9,720	1,346	2,313
1977	62,011	57,792	7,147	37,101	13,545	917	3,726	8,902	1,514	2,705
1978	64,863	60,296	7,412	38,151	14,734	809	3,892	10,032	1,788	2,779
1979	66,796	62,424	7,156	40,224	15,044	840	3,931	10,273	1,624	2,747
1980	67,291	63,005	7,311	40,148	15,546	679	4,051	10,816	1,873	2,414
1981	66,536	62,556	8,494	40,470	13,592	627	3,984	8,981	1,810	2,170
1982	63,219	59,457	8,518	37,790	13,150	649	4,068	8,434	1,709	2,053
1983	65,052	60,870	10,016	38,042	12,813	911	4,203	7,698	1,608	2,574
1984	69,981	65,996	10,967	41,178	13,851	1,048	4,381	8,422	1,507	2,478
1985	72,656	68,802	11,780	42,408	14,615	1,300	4,646	8,668	1,361	2,493
1986	76,384	72,163	12,685	43,797	15,681	1,402	4,990	9,289	1,589	2,633
1987	76,672	72,506	10,875	44,501	17,130	1,237	5,356	10,538	1,519	2,648
1988	79,086	74,785	11,831	45,963	16,991	1,340	5,875	9,777	1,643	2,658
1989	80,106	75,720	10,147	47,755	17,818	1,273	6,502	10,043	1,657	2,730
1990, prel. [2]	81,838	77,472	8,665	49,688	19,118	1,232	6,994	10,893	1,636	2,370
Air	27,313	25,053	8,665	16,077	310	62	11	237	446	1,814
Water	34,391	33,435	-	21,621	11,814	660	498	10,656	597	359
Solid Waste	20,938	20,393	-	13,699	6,695	269	6,425	-	372	173

- Represents or rounds to zero.   [1] Fixed capital.   [2] Includes "other and unallocated" expenditures (such as for noise, radiation, and pesticide pollution and business expenditures not assigned to media) which may be either positive or negative; therefore, data may not add.

No. 378. Air and Water Pollution Abatement Expenditures in Constant (1987) Dollars: 1980 to 1990

[In millions of dollars. Excludes agricultural production of crops and livestock except feedlots]

YEAR	AIR							WATER					
	Total	Mobile sources [1]			Stationary sources			Total [5]	Industrial		Public sewer systems		
		Total	Cars [2]	Trucks [2]	Total [3]	Industrial			Facilities	Operations[4]	Facilities	Operations[4]	
						Facilities	Operations[4]						
1980	25,661	12,367	9,103	2,840	13,294	6,011	6,443	26,482	3,696	3,988	10,148	5,148	
1981	27,012	13,932	11,092	2,700	13,080	5,951	6,295	24,251	3,405	4,025	8,270	5,297	
1982	25,719	13,754	10,914	2,777	11,965	5,501	5,601	23,337	3,284	3,844	7,679	5,616	
1983	26,085	15,456	12,756	3,177	10,629	3,893	5,911	23,751	2,666	4,264	7,063	5,959	
1984	27,659	16,896	14,119	4,090	10,763	3,820	6,151	25,382	2,865	4,482	7,791	6,149	
1985	29,041	18,073	14,896	4,463	10,968	3,539	6,320	26,542	2,879	4,658	8,124	6,550	
1986	30,270	19,513	15,424	4,670	10,757	3,573	6,732	27,765	2,392	4,866	8,807	7,285	
1987	28,548	17,629	13,166	4,433	10,919	3,728	6,575	29,695	2,354	5,383	10,053	7,792	
1988	29,531	19,190	14,727	4,607	10,341	3,342	6,436	29,107	2,381	5,310	9,376	8,269	
1989	27,742	17,181	12,511	3,910	10,561	3,463	6,553	30,618	2,923	5,777	9,661	8,554	
1990, prel.	26,104	15,201	10,768	3,362	10,903	3,900	6,546	33,435	3,799	5,988	10,566	9,534	

[1] Excludes expenditures to reduce emissions from sources other than cars and trucks.   [2] Includes expenditures for devices such as catalytic convertors, and expenditures for devices.   [3] Includes other expenditures not shown separately for fixed capital of government enterprises such as Tennessee Valley Authority.   [4] Operation of facilities.   [5] Includes expenditures for private connectors to sewer systems, by owners of animal feedlots, and by government enterprises.

Source of tables 377 and 378: U.S. Bureau of Economic Analysis, *Survey of Current Business*, June 1992.

No. 379. Pollution Abatement Capital Expenditures and Operating Costs of Manufacturing Establishments, 1980 to 1991, and by Selected Industry Group, 1991

[In millions of dollars. Based on probability sample of about 20,000 manufacturing establishments. Excludes apparel and other textile establishments and establishments with less than 20 employees]

YEAR AND INDUSTRY GROUP	POLLUTION ABATEMENT CAPITAL EXPENDITURES					POLLUTION ABATEMENT GROSS OPERATING COSTS [1]				
				Solid waste					Solid waste	
	Total	Air	Water	Hazardous	Non-hazardous	Total	Air	Water	Hazardous	Non-hazardous
1980...............	3,502.9	2,105.5	1,146.5	(NA)	[2]251.0	8,141.8	3,297.8	3,193.1	(NA)	[2]1,650.6
1985...............	2,809.7	1,292.3	1,017.9	326.2	172.9	11,677.9	4,330.2	4,609.5	943.0	1,795.3
1989...............	4,309.0	1,819.0	1,824.5	304.9	360.6	15,625.6	4,694.2	5,853.4	2,074.1	3,004.0
1990...............	6,030.8	2,562.0	2,651.4	326.8	490.7	17,070.7	5,010.9	6,416.4	2,285.0	3,358.5
All industries, 1991 [3] .	7,390.1	3,706.3	2,814.6	322.9	546.2	17,386.8	5,033.5	6,345.0	2,553.2	3,455.0
Food and kindred products.	481.8	94.6	359.5	2.6	25.1	1,254.2	149.6	798.5	18.4	297.7
Lumber and wood products..........	141.2	102.0	13.8	8.9	16.5	298.4	91.1	34.8	30.3	142.3
Paper and allied products..	1,232.6	480.8	552.7	14.8	184.2	1,635.0	400.8	790.6	44.5	399.1
Chemicals & allied prod. .	2,066.1	816.4	942.3	132.3	175.2	4,046.9	879.6	1,786.9	723.4	657.1
Petroleum & coal prod. ...	1,462.5	996.7	373.3	57.0	35.5	2,849.0	1,464.7	793.9	318.0	272.4
Stone, clay, glass products.	154.4	119.9	22.2	3.1	9.2	464.9	220.5	85.1	31.9	127.2
Primary metal industries...	673.4	499.2	131.9	20.7	21.6	2,002.6	911.7	564.0	257.1	269.8
Fabricated metals prod....	176.9	80.7	66.4	24.0	5.8	842.6	133.8	301.2	256.5	151.1
Machinery, exc. electrical..	128.4	88.7	27.6	5.3	6.8	573.9	70.0	165.1	169.1	169.7
Electrical, electronic equipment..........	233.7	90.7	122.7	9.3	11.0	833.0	100.0	323.5	196.7	212.8
Transportation equipment..	301.4	175.8	94.7	18.5	12.4	1,118.3	254.7	319.6	298.4	245.6
Instruments, related prod..	104.4	27.1	44.3	(D)	(D)	280.0	33.3	77.9	72.2	96.5

NA Not available.   D Withheld to avoid disclosing operations of individual companies.   [1] Includes payments to governmental units.   [2] Hazardous and nonhazardous solid waste were not collected separately prior to 1983.   [3] Includes industries not shown separately; excludes Major Group 23, Apparel and Other Textile Products.

Source: U.S. Bureau of the Census, *Current Industrial Reports*, series MA-200, annual.

No. 380. Threatened and Endangered Wildlife and Plant Species—Number: 1992

[As of October 19. Endangered species: One in danger of becoming extinct throughout all or a significant part of its natural range. Threatened species: One likely to become endangered in the foreseeable future]

ITEM	Mammals	Birds	Reptiles	Amphibians	Fishes	Snails	Clams	Crustaceans	Insects	Arachnids	Plants
Endangered species, total	**305**	**226**	**80**	**14**	**66**	**8**	**42**	**8**	**15**	**3**	**282**
U.S. only..........	37	57	8	6	52	7	40	8	13	3	274
U.S. and foreign.....	19	16	8	-	3	-	-	-	1	-	7
Foreign only [1]......	249	153	64	8	11	1	2	-	1	-	1
Threatened species, total	**32**	**12**	**32**	**5**	**36**	**6**	**2**	**2**	**9**	**-**	**73**
U.S. only..........	6	7	14	4	30	6	2	2	9	-	62
U.S. and foreign.....	3	5	4	1	6	-	-	-	-	-	9
Foreign only [1]......	23	-	14	-	-	-	-	-	-	-	2

- Represents zero.   [1] Species outside United States and outlying areas as determined by Fish and Wildlife Service.

Source: U.S. Fish and Wildlife Service, *Endangered Species Technical Bulletin*, monthly.

No. 381. Tornadoes, Floods, and Tropical Storms: 1981 to 1991

[See also *Historical Statistics, Colonial Times to 1970*, series J 268-278]

ITEM	1981	1982	1983	1984	1985	1986	1987	1988	1989	1990	1991
Tornadoes, number [1]........	783	1,046	931	907	684	764	656	702	856	1,133	1,132
Lives lost, total.......	24	64	34	122	94	15	59	32	50	53	39
Most in a single tornado	5	10	3	16	18	3	30	5	21	29	13
Property loss of $500,000 and over	55	92	95	125	69	75	38	48	60	91	64
Floods: Lives lost...........	90	155	200	126	304	80	82	29	81	147	65
Property loss (mil. dol.).......	1,000	3,500	4,100	4,000	3,000	4,000	1,490	114	415	2,058	1,416
North Atlantic tropical storms and hurricanes: [2]											
Number reaching U.S. coast ...	11	5	4	12	11	6	7	12	11	14	8
Hurricanes only	-	-	1	1	6	2	1	1	3	-	1
Lives lost in U.S...........	-	-	22	4	30	9	-	6	56	113	15

- Represents zero.   [1] A violent, rotating column of air descending from a cumulonimbus cloud in the form of a tubular- or funnel-shaped cloud, usually characterized by movements along a narrow path and wind speeds from 100 to over 300 miles per hour. Also known as a "twister" or "waterspout."   [2] Source: National Hurricane Center, Coral Gables, FL, unpublished data. Tropical storms have maximum winds of 39 to 73 miles per hour; hurricanes have maximum winds of 74 miles per hour or higher.

Source: Except as noted, U.S. National Oceanic and Atmospheric Administration, *Storm Data*, monthly.

No. 382. Normal Daily Mean Temperature—Selected Cities

[In Fahrenheit degrees. Airport data except as noted. Based on standard 30-year period, 1961 through 1990. See *Historical Statistics, Colonial Times to 1970*, series J 110-136 and J 164-267, for related data]

STATE	STATION	Jan.	Feb.	Mar.	Apr.	May	June	July	Aug.	Sept.	Oct.	Nov.	Dec.	Annual avg.
AL	Mobile.........	49.9	53.2	60.5	67.8	74.5	80.4	82.3	81.8	77.9	68.4	59.8	53.0	67.5
AK	Juneau	24.2	28.4	32.7	39.7	47.0	53.0	56.0	55.0	49.4	42.2	32.0	27.1	40.6
AZ	Phoenix........	53.6	57.7	62.2	69.9	78.8	88.2	93.5	91.5	85.6	74.5	61.9	54.1	72.6
AR	Little Rock......	39.1	43.6	53.1	62.1	70.2	78.4	81.9	80.6	74.1	63.0	52.1	42.8	61.8
CA	Los Angeles.....	56.8	57.6	58.0	60.1	62.7	65.7	69.1	70.5	69.9	66.8	61.6	56.9	63.0
	Sacramento......	45.2	50.7	53.6	58.3	65.3	71.6	75.7	75.1	71.5	64.2	53.3	45.3	60.8
	San Diego......	57.4	58.6	59.6	62.0	64.1	66.8	71.0	72.6	71.4	67.7	62.0	57.4	64.2
	San Francisco	48.7	52.2	53.3	55.6	58.1	61.5	62.7	63.7	64.5	61.0	54.8	49.4	57.1
CO	Denver	29.7	33.4	39.0	48.2	57.2	66.9	73.5	71.4	62.3	51.4	39.0	31.0	50.3
CT	Hartford........	24.6	27.5	37.5	48.7	59.6	68.5	73.7	71.6	63.3	52.2	41.9	29.5	49.9
DE	Wilmington......	30.6	33.4	42.7	52.2	62.5	71.5	76.4	75.0	68.0	56.2	46.3	35.8	54.2
DC	Washington.....	34.6	37.5	47.2	56.5	66.4	75.6	80.0	78.5	71.3	59.7	49.8	39.4	58.0
FL	Jacksonville.....	52.4	55.2	61.1	67.0	73.4	79.1	81.6	81.2	78.1	69.8	61.9	55.1	68.0
	Miami	67.2	68.5	71.7	75.2	78.7	81.4	82.6	82.8	81.9	78.3	73.6	69.1	75.9
GA	Atlanta........	41.0	44.8	53.5	61.5	69.2	76.0	78.8	78.1	72.7	62.3	53.1	44.5	61.3
HI	Honolulu	72.9	73.0	74.4	75.8	77.5	79.4	80.5	81.4	81.0	79.6	77.2	74.1	77.2
ID	Boise	29.0	35.9	42.4	49.1	57.5	66.5	74.0	72.5	62.6	51.8	39.9	30.1	50.9
IL	Chicago........	21.0	25.4	37.2	48.6	58.9	68.6	73.2	71.7	64.4	52.8	40.0	26.6	49.0
	Peoria.........	21.6	26.3	39.0	51.4	61.9	71.5	75.5	73.1	66.1	54.0	41.2	27.0	50.7
IN	Indianapolis	25.5	29.6	41.4	52.4	62.8	71.9	75.4	73.2	66.6	54.7	43.0	30.9	52.3
IA	Des Moines	19.4	24.7	37.3	50.9	62.3	71.8	76.6	73.9	65.1	53.5	39.0	24.4	49.9
KS	Wichita	29.5	34.8	45.4	56.4	65.6	75.7	81.4	79.3	70.3	58.6	44.7	33.0	56.2
KY	Louisville	31.7	35.7	46.3	56.3	65.3	73.2	77.2	75.8	69.5	57.6	47.1	36.9	56.1
LA	New Orleans	51.3	54.3	61.6	68.5	74.8	80.0	81.9	81.5	78.1	69.1	61.1	54.5	68.1
ME	Portland.......	20.8	23.3	33.0	43.3	53.3	62.4	68.6	67.3	59.1	48.5	38.7	26.5	45.4
MD	Baltimore......	31.8	34.8	44.1	53.4	63.4	72.5	77.0	75.6	68.5	56.6	46.8	36.7	55.1
MA	Boston	28.6	30.3	38.6	48.1	58.2	67.7	73.5	71.9	64.8	54.8	45.3	33.6	51.3
MI	Detroit........	22.9	25.4	35.7	47.3	58.4	67.6	72.3	70.5	63.2	51.2	40.2	28.3	48.6
	Sault Ste. Marie ...	12.9	14.0	24.0	38.2	50.5	58.0	63.8	62.6	55.1	45.3	33.0	19.0	39.7
MN	Duluth........	7.0	12.3	24.4	38.6	50.8	59.8	66.1	63.7	54.2	43.7	28.4	12.8	38.5
	Minneapolis-St. Paul	11.8	17.9	31.0	46.4	58.5	68.2	73.6	70.5	60.5	48.8	33.2	17.9	44.9
MS	Jackson........	44.1	47.9	56.7	64.6	72.0	78.8	81.5	80.9	75.9	64.7	55.8	47.8	64.2
MO	Kansas City	25.7	31.2	42.7	54.5	64.1	73.2	78.5	76.1	67.5	56.6	43.1	30.4	53.6
	St. Louis	29.3	33.9	45.1	56.7	66.1	75.4	79.8	77.6	70.2	58.4	46.2	33.9	56.1
MT	Great Falls......	21.2	27.4	33.3	43.6	53.1	61.6	68.2	66.9	56.6	47.5	33.9	23.9	44.8
NE	Omaha	21.1	26.9	38.6	51.9	62.4	72.1	76.9	74.1	65.1	53.4	39.0	25.1	50.6
NV	Reno	32.9	38.0	42.8	48.6	56.5	65.1	71.6	69.6	60.4	50.8	40.3	32.7	50.8
NH	Concord	18.6	21.8	32.4	43.9	55.2	64.2	69.5	67.3	58.8	47.8	37.1	24.3	45.1
NJ	Atlantic City	30.9	33.0	41.5	50.0	60.4	69.4	74.7	73.4	66.1	54.9	45.8	35.8	53.0
NM	Albuquerque.....	34.2	40.0	46.9	55.2	64.2	74.2	78.5	75.9	68.6	57.0	44.3	35.3	56.2
NY	Albany........	20.6	23.5	34.3	46.4	57.6	66.9	71.8	69.6	61.3	50.2	39.7	26.5	47.4
	Buffalo	23.6	24.5	33.8	45.2	56.6	65.9	71.1	69.0	61.9	51.1	40.5	29.1	47.7
	New York [1]	31.5	33.6	42.4	52.5	62.7	71.6	76.8	75.5	68.2	57.5	47.6	36.6	54.7
NC	Charlotte......	39.3	42.5	50.9	59.4	67.4	75.7	79.3	78.3	72.4	61.3	52.1	42.6	60.1
	Raleigh	38.9	42.0	50.4	59.0	67.0	74.3	78.1	77.1	71.1	60.1	51.2	42.6	59.3
ND	Bismarck	9.2	15.7	28.2	43.0	55.0	64.4	70.4	68.3	57.0	45.7	28.6	14.0	41.6
OH	Cincinnati......	28.1	31.8	43.0	53.2	62.9	71.0	75.1	73.5	67.3	55.1	44.3	33.5	53.2
	Cleveland	24.8	27.2	37.3	47.6	58.0	67.6	71.9	70.4	63.9	52.8	42.6	30.9	49.6
	Columbus	26.4	29.6	40.9	51.0	61.2	69.2	73.2	71.5	65.5	53.7	42.9	31.9	51.4
OK	Oklahoma City	35.9	40.9	50.3	60.4	68.4	76.7	82.0	81.1	73.0	62.0	49.6	39.3	60.0
OR	Portland.......	39.6	43.6	47.3	51.0	57.1	63.5	68.2	68.6	63.3	54.5	46.1	40.2	53.6
PA	Philadelphia	30.4	33.0	42.4	52.4	62.9	71.8	76.7	75.5	68.2	56.4	46.4	35.8	54.3
	Pittsburgh	26.1	28.7	39.4	49.6	59.5	67.9	72.1	70.5	63.9	52.4	42.3	31.5	50.3
RI	Providence......	27.9	29.7	37.4	47.4	57.3	66.9	72.7	71.3	64.1	53.6	44.0	32.8	50.4
SC	Columbia.......	43.8	46.8	55.2	63.0	70.9	77.4	80.8	79.7	74.2	63.3	54.6	46.9	63.1
SD	Sioux Falls......	13.8	19.7	32.5	46.9	58.4	68.3	74.3	71.4	60.9	48.6	33.0	18.3	45.5
TN	Memphis	39.7	44.2	53.1	62.9	71.2	79.1	82.6	81.0	74.2	63.1	52.5	43.7	62.3
	Nashville	36.2	40.4	50.2	59.2	67.7	75.6	79.3	78.1	71.8	60.4	50.0	40.5	59.1
TX	Dallas-Fort Worth ..	43.4	47.9	56.7	65.5	72.8	81.0	85.3	84.9	77.4	67.2	56.2	46.9	65.4
	El Paso........	42.8	48.1	55.1	63.4	71.8	80.4	82.3	80.1	74.4	64.0	52.4	44.1	63.2
	Houston	50.4	53.9	60.6	68.3	74.5	80.4	82.6	82.3	78.2	69.6	61.0	53.5	67.9
UT	Salt Lake City.....	27.9	34.1	41.8	49.7	58.8	69.1	77.9	75.6	65.2	53.2	40.8	29.7	52.0
VT	Burlington	16.3	18.2	30.7	43.9	56.3	65.2	70.5	67.9	58.9	47.8	36.8	23.0	44.6
VA	Norfolk	39.1	41.0	48.6	57.0	66.1	74.1	78.2	77.2	71.9	61.2	52.5	43.8	59.2
	Richmond	35.7	38.7	48.0	57.3	66.0	73.9	78.0	76.8	70.0	58.6	49.6	40.1	57.7
WA	Seattle-Tacoma ..	40.1	43.5	45.6	49.2	55.1	60.9	65.2	65.5	60.6	52.8	45.3	40.5	52.0
	Spokane	27.1	33.3	38.7	45.9	53.9	62.0	68.8	68.4	58.9	47.3	35.1	27.8	47.3
WV	Charleston	32.1	35.5	45.9	54.8	63.5	71.4	75.1	73.9	67.7	56.2	46.8	37.0	55.0
WI	Milwaukee	18.9	23.0	33.3	44.4	54.6	65.0	70.9	69.3	61.7	50.3	37.7	24.4	46.1
WY	Cheyenne	26.5	29.3	33.6	42.5	52.0	61.3	68.4	66.4	57.4	47.0	35.2	27.8	45.6
PR	San Juan.......	77.0	77.1	78.0	79.4	80.9	82.3	82.6	82.7	82.5	81.9	80.0	78.1	80.2

[1] City office data.

Source: U.S. National Oceanic and Atmospheric Administration, *Climatography of the United States*, No. 81.

No. 383. Normal Daily Maximum Temperature—Selected Cities

[**In Fahrenheit degrees.** Airport data except as noted. Based on standard 30-year period, 1961 through 1990]

STATE	STATION	Jan.	Feb.	Mar.	Apr.	May	June	July	Aug.	Sept.	Oct.	Nov.	Dec.	Annual avg.
AL	Mobile	59.7	63.6	70.9	78.5	84.6	90.0	91.3	90.5	86.9	79.5	70.3	62.9	77.4
AK	Juneau	29.4	34.1	38.7	47.2	55.1	60.9	63.9	62.7	55.9	47.1	36.7	31.6	46.9
AZ	Phoenix	65.9	70.7	75.5	84.5	93.6	103.5	105.9	103.7	98.3	88.1	74.9	66.2	85.9
AR	Little Rock	49.0	53.9	64.0	73.4	81.3	89.3	92.4	91.4	84.6	75.1	62.7	52.5	72.5
CA	Los Angeles	65.7	65.9	65.5	67.4	69.0	71.9	75.3	76.6	76.6	74.4	70.3	65.9	70.4
	Sacramento	52.7	60.0	64.0	71.1	80.3	87.8	93.2	92.1	87.3	77.9	63.1	52.7	73.5
	San Diego	65.9	66.5	66.3	68.4	69.1	71.6	76.2	77.8	77.1	74.6	69.9	66.1	70.8
	San Francisco	55.6	59.4	60.8	63.9	66.5	70.3	71.6	72.3	73.6	70.1	62.4	56.1	65.2
CO	Denver	43.2	46.6	52.2	61.8	70.8	81.4	88.2	85.8	76.9	66.3	52.5	44.5	64.2
CT	Hartford	33.2	36.4	46.8	59.9	71.6	80.0	85.0	82.7	74.8	63.7	51.0	37.5	60.2
DE	Wilmington	38.7	41.9	52.1	62.6	72.9	81.4	85.6	84.1	77.7	66.6	55.5	43.9	63.6
DC	Washington	42.3	45.9	56.5	66.7	76.2	84.7	88.5	86.9	80.1	69.1	58.3	47.0	66.9
FL	Jacksonville	64.2	67.0	73.0	79.1	84.7	89.3	91.4	90.7	87.2	80.2	73.6	66.8	78.9
	Miami	75.2	76.5	79.1	82.4	85.3	87.6	89.0	89.0	87.8	84.5	80.4	76.7	82.8
GA	Atlanta	50.4	55.0	64.3	72.7	79.6	85.8	88.0	87.1	81.8	72.7	63.4	54.0	71.2
HI	Honolulu	80.1	80.5	81.6	82.8	84.7	86.5	87.5	88.7	88.5	86.9	84.1	81.2	84.4
ID	Boise	36.4	44.2	52.9	61.4	71.0	80.9	90.2	88.1	77.0	64.6	48.7	37.7	62.8
IL	Chicago	29.0	33.5	45.8	58.6	70.1	79.6	83.7	81.8	74.8	63.3	48.4	34.0	58.6
	Peoria	29.9	34.9	48.1	62.0	72.8	82.2	85.7	83.1	76.9	64.8	49.8	34.6	60.4
IN	Indianapolis	33.7	38.3	50.9	63.3	73.8	82.7	85.5	83.6	77.6	65.8	51.9	38.5	62.1
IA	Des Moines	28.1	33.7	46.9	61.8	73.0	82.2	86.7	84.2	75.6	64.3	48.0	32.6	59.8
KS	Wichita	39.8	45.9	57.2	68.3	76.9	86.8	92.8	90.7	81.4	70.6	55.3	43.0	67.4
KY	Louisville	40.3	44.8	56.3	67.3	76.0	83.5	87.0	85.7	80.3	69.2	56.8	45.1	66.0
LA	New Orleans	60.8	64.1	71.6	78.5	84.4	89.2	90.6	90.2	86.6	79.4	71.1	64.3	77.6
ME	Portland	30.3	33.1	41.4	52.3	63.2	72.7	78.8	77.4	69.3	58.7	47.0	35.1	54.9
MD	Baltimore	40.2	43.7	54.0	64.3	74.2	83.2	87.2	85.4	78.5	67.3	56.5	45.2	65.0
MA	Boston	35.7	37.5	45.8	55.9	66.6	76.3	81.8	79.8	72.8	62.7	52.2	40.4	59.0
MI	Detroit	30.3	33.3	44.4	57.7	69.6	78.9	83.3	81.3	73.9	61.5	48.1	35.2	58.1
	Sault Ste. Marie	21.1	23.2	32.8	48.0	62.6	70.5	76.3	73.8	65.9	54.3	40.0	26.2	49.6
MN	Duluth	16.2	21.7	32.9	48.2	61.9	71.0	77.1	73.9	63.8	52.3	35.2	20.7	47.9
	Minneapolis-St. Paul	20.7	26.6	39.2	56.5	69.4	78.8	84.0	80.7	70.7	58.8	41.0	25.5	54.3
MS	Jackson	55.6	60.1	69.3	77.4	84.0	90.6	92.4	92.0	88.0	79.1	69.2	59.5	76.4
MO	Kansas City	34.7	40.6	52.8	65.1	74.3	83.3	88.7	86.4	78.1	67.5	52.6	38.8	63.6
	St. Louis	37.7	42.6	54.6	66.9	76.1	85.2	89.3	87.3	79.9	68.5	54.7	41.7	65.4
MT	Great Falls	30.6	37.5	43.7	55.3	65.2	74.6	83.3	81.6	69.6	59.3	43.5	33.1	56.4
NE	Omaha	31.3	37.1	49.4	63.8	74.0	83.7	87.9	85.2	76.5	65.6	49.3	34.6	61.5
NV	Reno	45.1	51.7	56.3	63.7	72.9	83.1	91.9	89.6	79.5	68.6	53.8	45.5	66.8
NH	Concord	29.8	33.0	42.8	56.3	68.9	77.3	82.4	79.8	71.6	60.7	47.1	34.2	57.0
NJ	Atlantic City	40.4	42.5	51.6	60.7	71.2	80.0	84.5	83.3	76.6	66.0	55.7	45.3	63.2
NM	Albuquerque	46.8	53.5	61.4	70.8	79.7	90.0	92.5	89.0	81.9	71.0	57.3	47.5	70.1
NY	Albany	30.2	33.2	44.0	57.5	69.7	79.0	84.0	81.4	73.2	61.8	48.7	34.9	58.1
	Buffalo	30.2	31.6	41.7	54.2	66.1	75.3	80.2	77.9	70.8	59.4	47.1	35.3	55.8
	New York [1]	37.6	40.3	50.0	61.2	71.7	80.1	85.2	83.7	76.2	65.3	54.0	42.5	62.3
NC	Charlotte	49.0	53.0	62.3	71.2	78.3	85.8	88.9	87.7	81.9	72.0	62.6	52.3	70.4
	Raleigh	48.9	52.6	62.1	71.7	78.6	85.0	88.0	86.8	81.1	71.6	62.6	52.7	70.1
ND	Bismarck	20.2	26.4	38.5	54.9	67.8	77.1	84.4	82.7	70.8	58.7	39.3	24.5	53.8
OH	Cincinnati	36.6	40.8	53.0	64.2	74.0	82.0	85.5	84.1	77.9	66.0	53.3	41.5	63.2
	Cleveland	31.9	35.0	46.3	57.9	68.6	78.3	82.4	80.5	73.6	62.1	50.0	37.4	58.7
	Columbus	34.1	38.0	50.5	62.0	72.3	80.4	83.7	82.1	76.2	64.5	51.4	39.2	61.2
OK	Oklahoma City	46.7	52.1	62.0	71.9	79.1	87.3	93.4	92.5	83.8	73.6	60.4	49.9	71.1
OR	Portland	45.4	51.0	56.0	60.6	67.1	74.0	79.9	80.3	74.6	64.0	52.6	45.6	62.6
PA	Philadelphia	37.9	41.0	51.6	62.6	73.1	81.7	86.1	84.6	77.6	66.3	55.1	43.4	63.4
	Pittsburgh	33.7	36.9	49.0	60.3	70.6	78.9	82.6	80.8	74.3	62.5	50.4	38.6	59.9
RI	Providence	36.6	38.3	46.1	57.0	67.3	76.9	82.1	80.7	74.3	64.1	53.0	41.2	59.8
SC	Columbia	55.3	59.3	68.2	76.5	83.5	88.8	91.6	90.1	85.1	76.3	67.8	58.8	75.1
SD	Sioux Falls	24.3	29.6	42.3	59.0	70.7	80.5	86.3	83.3	73.1	61.2	43.4	28.0	56.8
TN	Memphis	48.5	53.5	63.2	73.3	81.0	89.3	92.3	90.8	83.9	74.3	62.3	52.5	72.1
	Nashville	45.9	50.8	61.2	70.8	78.8	86.5	89.5	88.4	82.5	72.5	60.4	50.2	69.8
TX	Dallas-Fort Worth	54.1	58.9	67.8	76.3	82.9	91.9	96.5	96.2	87.8	78.5	66.8	57.5	76.3
	El Paso	56.1	62.2	69.9	78.7	87.1	96.5	96.1	93.5	87.1	78.4	66.4	57.5	77.5
	Houston	61.0	65.3	71.1	78.4	84.6	90.1	92.7	92.5	88.4	81.6	72.4	64.7	78.6
UT	Salt Lake City	36.4	43.6	52.2	61.3	71.9	82.8	92.2	89.4	79.2	66.1	50.0	37.8	63.6
VT	Burlington	25.1	27.5	39.3	53.6	67.2	75.8	81.2	77.9	69.0	57.0	44.0	30.4	54.0
VA	Norfolk	47.3	49.7	57.9	66.9	75.3	82.9	86.4	85.1	79.6	69.5	61.2	52.2	67.8
	Richmond	45.7	49.2	59.5	70.0	77.8	85.1	88.4	87.1	80.9	70.7	61.3	50.2	68.8
WA	Seattle-Tacoma	45.0	49.5	52.7	57.2	63.9	69.9	75.2	75.2	69.3	59.7	50.5	45.1	59.4
	Spokane	33.2	40.6	47.7	57.0	65.8	74.7	83.1	82.5	72.0	58.6	41.4	33.8	57.5
WV	Charleston	41.2	45.3	56.7	66.8	75.5	83.1	85.7	84.4	78.8	68.2	57.3	46.0	65.8
WI	Milwaukee	26.1	30.1	40.4	52.9	64.3	74.9	79.9	77.8	70.6	58.7	44.7	31.2	54.3
WY	Cheyenne	37.7	40.5	44.9	54.7	64.6	74.4	82.2	80.0	71.1	60.0	46.8	38.8	58.0
PR	San Juan	83.2	83.6	84.4	85.8	87.2	88.6	88.5	88.7	88.8	88.3	85.9	83.8	86.4

[1] City office data.

Source: U.S. National Oceanic and Atmospheric Administration, *Climatography of the United States*, No. 81.

No. 384. Normal Daily Minimum Temperature—Selected Cities

[In Fahrenheit degrees. Airport data except as noted. Based on standard 30-year period, 1961 through 1990]

STATE	STATION	Jan.	Feb.	Mar.	Apr.	May	June	July	Aug.	Sept.	Oct.	Nov.	Dec.	Annual avg.
AL	Mobile	40.0	42.7	50.1	57.1	64.4	70.7	73.2	72.9	68.7	57.3	49.1	43.1	57.4
AK	Juneau	19.0	22.7	26.7	32.1	38.9	45.0	48.1	47.3	42.9	37.2	27.2	22.6	34.1
AZ	Phoenix	41.2	44.7	48.8	55.3	63.9	72.9	81.0	79.2	72.8	60.8	48.9	41.8	59.3
AR	Little Rock	29.1	33.2	42.2	50.7	59.0	67.4	71.5	69.8	63.5	50.9	41.5	33.1	51.0
CA	Los Angeles	47.8	49.3	50.5	52.8	56.3	59.5	62.8	64.2	63.2	59.2	52.8	47.9	55.5
	Sacramento	37.7	41.4	43.2	45.5	50.3	55.3	58.1	58.0	55.7	50.4	43.4	37.8	48.1
	San Diego	48.9	50.7	52.8	55.6	59.1	61.9	65.7	67.3	65.6	60.9	53.9	48.8	57.6
	San Francisco	41.8	45.0	45.8	47.2	49.7	52.6	53.9	55.0	55.2	51.8	47.1	42.7	49.0
CO	Denver	16.1	20.2	25.8	34.5	43.6	52.4	58.6	56.9	47.6	36.4	25.4	17.4	36.2
CT	Hartford	15.8	18.6	28.1	37.5	47.6	56.9	62.2	60.4	51.8	40.7	32.8	21.3	39.5
DE	Wilmington	22.4	24.8	33.1	41.8	52.2	61.6	67.1	65.9	58.2	45.7	37.0	27.6	44.8
DC	Washington	26.8	29.1	37.7	46.4	56.6	66.5	71.4	70.0	62.5	50.3	41.1	31.7	49.2
FL	Jacksonville	40.5	43.3	49.2	54.9	62.1	69.1	71.9	71.8	69.0	59.3	50.2	43.4	57.1
	Miami	59.2	60.4	64.2	67.8	72.1	75.1	76.2	76.7	75.9	72.1	66.7	61.5	69.0
GA	Atlanta	31.5	34.5	42.5	50.2	58.7	66.2	69.5	69.0	63.5	51.9	42.8	35.0	51.3
HI	Honolulu	65.6	65.4	67.2	68.7	70.3	72.2	73.5	74.2	73.5	72.3	70.3	67.0	70.0
ID	Boise	21.6	27.5	31.9	36.7	43.9	52.1	57.7	56.8	48.2	39.0	31.1	22.5	39.1
IL	Chicago	12.9	17.2	28.5	38.6	47.7	57.5	62.6	61.6	53.9	42.2	31.6	19.1	39.5
	Peoria	13.2	17.7	29.8	40.8	50.9	60.7	65.4	63.1	55.2	43.1	32.5	19.3	41.0
IN	Indianapolis	17.2	20.9	31.9	41.5	51.7	61.0	65.2	62.8	55.6	43.5	34.1	23.2	42.4
IA	Des Moines	10.7	15.6	27.6	40.0	51.5	61.2	66.5	63.6	54.5	42.7	29.9	16.1	40.0
KS	Wichita	19.2	23.7	33.6	44.5	54.3	64.6	69.9	67.9	59.2	46.6	33.9	23.0	45.0
KY	Louisville	23.2	26.5	36.2	45.4	54.7	62.9	67.3	65.8	58.7	45.8	37.3	28.6	46.0
LA	New Orleans	41.8	44.4	51.6	58.4	65.2	70.8	73.1	72.8	69.5	58.7	51.0	44.8	58.5
ME	Portland	11.4	13.5	24.5	34.1	43.4	52.1	58.3	57.1	48.9	38.3	30.4	17.8	35.8
MD	Baltimore	23.4	25.9	34.1	42.5	52.6	61.8	66.8	65.7	58.4	45.9	37.1	28.2	45.2
MA	Boston	21.6	23.0	31.3	40.2	49.8	59.1	65.1	64.0	56.8	46.9	38.3	26.7	43.6
MI	Detroit	15.6	17.6	27.0	36.8	47.1	56.3	61.3	59.6	52.5	40.9	32.2	21.4	39.0
	Sault Ste. Marie	4.6	4.8	15.3	28.4	38.4	45.5	51.3	51.3	44.3	36.2	25.9	11.8	29.8
MN	Duluth	-2.2	2.8	15.7	28.9	39.6	48.5	55.1	53.3	44.5	35.1	21.5	4.9	29.0
	Minneapolis-St. Paul	2.8	9.2	22.7	36.2	47.6	57.6	63.1	60.3	50.3	38.8	25.2	10.2	35.3
MS	Jackson	32.7	35.7	44.1	51.9	60.0	67.1	70.5	69.7	63.7	50.3	42.3	36.1	52.0
MO	Kansas City	16.7	21.8	32.6	43.8	53.9	63.1	68.2	65.7	56.9	45.7	33.6	21.9	43.7
	St. Louis	20.8	25.1	35.5	46.4	56.0	65.7	70.4	67.9	60.5	48.3	37.7	26.0	46.7
MT	Great Falls	11.6	17.2	22.8	31.9	40.9	48.6	53.2	52.2	43.5	35.8	24.3	14.6	33.1
NE	Omaha	10.9	16.7	27.7	39.9	50.9	60.4	65.9	62.9	53.6	41.2	28.7	15.6	39.5
NV	Reno	20.7	24.2	29.2	33.3	40.1	46.9	51.3	49.6	41.3	32.9	26.7	19.9	34.7
NH	Concord	7.4	10.4	22.1	31.5	41.4	51.2	56.5	54.7	46.0	34.9	27.0	14.4	33.1
NJ	Atlantic City	21.4	23.5	31.3	39.3	49.6	58.7	64.8	63.5	55.5	43.7	35.8	26.3	42.8
NM	Albuquerque	21.7	26.4	32.2	39.6	48.6	58.3	64.4	62.6	55.2	43.0	31.2	23.1	42.2
NY	Albany	11.0	13.8	24.5	35.1	45.4	54.6	59.6	57.8	49.4	38.6	30.7	18.2	36.6
	Buffalo	17.0	17.4	25.9	36.2	47.0	56.5	61.9	60.1	53.0	42.7	33.9	22.9	39.5
	New York [1]	25.3	26.9	34.8	43.8	53.7	63.0	68.4	67.3	60.1	49.7	41.1	30.7	47.1
NC	Charlotte	29.6	31.9	39.4	47.5	56.4	65.6	69.6	68.9	62.9	50.6	41.5	32.8	49.7
	Raleigh	28.8	31.3	38.7	46.2	55.3	63.6	68.1	67.5	61.1	48.4	39.7	32.4	48.4
ND	Bismarck	-1.7	5.1	17.8	31.0	42.2	51.6	56.4	53.9	43.1	32.5	17.8	3.3	29.4
OH	Cincinnati	19.5	22.7	33.1	42.2	51.8	60.0	64.8	62.9	56.6	44.2	35.3	25.3	43.2
	Cleveland	17.6	19.3	28.2	37.3	47.3	56.8	61.4	60.3	54.2	43.5	35.0	24.5	40.5
	Columbus	18.5	21.2	31.2	40.0	50.1	58.0	62.7	60.8	54.8	42.9	34.3	24.6	41.6
OK	Oklahoma City	25.2	29.6	38.5	48.8	57.7	66.1	70.6	69.6	62.2	50.4	38.6	28.6	48.8
OR	Portland	33.7	36.1	38.6	41.3	47.0	52.9	56.5	56.9	52.0	44.9	39.5	34.8	44.5
PA	Philadelphia	22.8	24.8	33.2	42.1	52.7	61.8	67.2	66.3	58.7	46.4	37.6	28.1	45.1
	Pittsburgh	18.5	20.3	29.8	38.8	48.4	56.9	61.6	60.2	53.5	42.3	34.1	24.4	40.7
RI	Providence	19.1	20.9	28.8	37.7	47.3	56.8	63.2	61.9	53.8	43.0	34.9	24.4	41.0
SC	Columbia	32.1	34.2	42.2	49.4	58.2	66.0	70.0	69.2	63.2	50.1	41.5	34.9	50.9
SD	Sioux Falls	3.3	9.7	22.6	34.8	45.9	56.1	62.3	59.4	48.7	36.0	22.6	8.6	34.2
TN	Memphis	30.9	34.8	43.0	52.4	61.2	68.9	72.9	71.1	64.5	51.9	42.7	34.8	52.4
	Nashville	26.5	29.9	39.1	47.5	56.6	64.7	68.9	67.7	61.1	48.3	39.6	30.9	48.4
TX	Dallas-Fort Worth	32.7	36.9	45.6	54.7	62.6	70.0	74.1	73.6	66.9	55.8	45.4	36.3	54.6
	El Paso	29.4	33.9	40.2	48.0	56.5	64.3	68.4	66.6	61.6	49.6	38.4	30.7	49.0
	Houston	39.7	42.6	50.0	58.1	64.4	70.6	72.4	72.0	67.9	57.6	49.6	42.2	57.3
UT	Salt Lake City	19.3	24.6	31.4	37.9	45.6	55.4	63.7	61.8	51.0	40.2	30.9	21.6	40.3
VT	Burlington	7.5	8.9	22.0	34.2	45.4	54.6	59.7	57.9	48.8	38.6	29.6	15.5	35.2
VA	Norfolk	30.9	32.3	39.3	47.1	56.8	65.2	70.0	69.4	64.2	52.9	43.8	35.4	50.6
	Richmond	25.7	28.1	36.3	44.6	54.2	62.7	67.5	66.4	59.0	46.5	37.9	29.9	46.6
WA	Seattle-Tacoma	35.2	37.4	38.5	41.2	46.3	51.9	55.2	55.7	51.9	45.8	40.1	35.8	44.6
	Spokane	20.8	25.9	29.6	34.7	41.9	49.2	54.4	54.3	45.8	36.0	28.8	21.7	36.9
WV	Charleston	23.0	25.7	35.0	42.8	51.5	59.8	64.4	63.4	56.5	44.2	36.3	28.0	44.2
WI	Milwaukee	11.6	15.9	26.2	35.8	44.8	55.0	62.0	60.8	52.8	41.8	30.7	17.5	37.9
WY	Cheyenne	15.2	18.1	22.1	30.1	39.4	48.3	54.6	52.8	43.7	33.9	23.7	16.7	33.2
PR	San Juan	70.8	70.6	71.6	72.9	74.5	76.1	76.8	76.7	76.2	75.5	74.0	72.4	74.0

[1] City office data.

Source: U.S. National Oceanic and Atmospheric Administration, Climatography of the United States, No. 81.

No. 385. Highest Temperature of Record—Selected Cities

[In **Fahrenheit degrees.** Airport data, except as noted. For period of record through 1991]

STATE	STATION	Length of record (yr.)	Jan.	Feb.	Mar.	Apr.	May	June	July	Aug.	Sept.	Oct.	Nov.	Dec.	Annual
AL	Mobile.........	50	84	82	90	94	100	102	104	102	99	93	87	81	104
AK	Juneau........	47	57	56	59	71	82	86	90	83	72	61	56	54	90
AZ	Phoenix.......	54	88	92	100	105	113	122	118	116	118	107	93	88	122
AR	Little Rock......	50	83	85	91	95	98	105	112	108	106	97	86	80	112
CA	Los Angeles......	56	88	92	95	102	97	104	97	98	110	106	101	94	110
	Sacramento.....	41	70	76	88	93	105	115	114	109	108	101	87	72	115
	San Diego......	51	88	88	93	98	96	101	95	98	111	107	97	88	111
	San Francisco	64	72	78	85	92	97	106	105	98	103	99	85	75	106
CO	Denver.........	57	73	76	84	89	96	104	104	101	97	89	79	75	104
CT	Hartford........	37	65	73	87	96	97	100	102	101	99	91	81	74	102
DE	Wilmington......	44	75	78	86	94	95	99	102	101	100	91	85	74	102
DC	Washington	50	79	82	89	95	99	101	104	103	101	94	86	75	104
FL	Jacksonville	50	85	88	91	95	100	103	105	102	100	96	88	84	105
	Miami	49	88	89	92	96	95	98	98	98	97	95	89	87	98
GA	Atlanta	43	79	80	85	93	95	101	105	102	98	95	84	79	105
HI	Honolulu	22	87	88	88	89	93	92	92	93	94	94	93	89	94
ID	Boise	52	63	70	81	92	98	109	111	110	102	91	74	65	111
IL	Chicago........	33	65	71	88	91	93	104	102	101	99	91	78	71	104
	Peoria........	52	70	72	86	92	93	105	103	103	100	90	81	71	105
IN	Indianapolis	52	71	74	85	89	93	102	104	102	100	90	81	74	104
IA	Des Moines	52	65	73	91	93	98	103	105	108	101	95	76	69	108
KS	Wichita	39	75	84	89	96	100	110	113	110	107	95	85	83	113
KY	Louisville	44	77	77	86	91	95	102	105	101	104	92	84	76	105
LA	New Orleans	45	83	85	89	92	96	100	101	102	101	92	87	84	102
ME	Portland........	51	64	64	86	85	94	98	99	103	95	88	74	69	103
MD	Baltimore........	41	75	79	87	94	98	100	104	105	100	92	83	77	105
MA	Boston	40	63	70	81	94	95	100	102	102	100	90	78	73	102
MI	Detroit.........	33	62	65	81	89	93	104	102	100	98	91	77	68	104
	Sault Ste. Marie ...	51	45	47	75	85	89	93	97	98	95	80	67	60	98
MN	Duluth.........	50	52	55	78	88	90	93	97	97	95	86	70	55	97
	Minneapolis-St. Paul	53	58	60	83	95	96	102	105	102	98	89	75	63	105
MS	Jackson........	28	82	85	89	94	99	105	106	102	104	95	88	84	106
MO	Kansas City	19	69	76	86	93	92	105	107	109	102	92	82	70	109
	St. Louis	34	76	85	89	93	93	102	107	107	104	94	85	76	107
MT	Great Falls.......	54	62	68	78	89	93	101	105	106	98	91	76	69	106
NE	Omaha	55	69	78	89	97	99	105	114	110	104	96	80	72	114
NV	Reno	50	70	75	83	89	96	103	104	105	101	91	77	70	105
NH	Concord	50	68	66	85	95	97	98	102	101	98	90	80	68	102
NJ	Atlantic City	48	78	75	87	94	99	106	104	102	99	90	84	75	106
NM	Albuquerque......	52	69	76	85	89	98	105	105	101	100	91	77	72	105
NY	Albany.........	45	62	67	86	92	94	99	100	99	100	89	82	71	100
	Buffalo........	48	72	65	81	94	90	96	97	99	98	87	80	74	99
	New York [1]	123	72	75	86	96	99	101	106	104	102	94	84	72	106
NC	Charlotte	52	78	81	90	93	100	103	103	103	104	98	85	77	104
	Raleigh	47	79	84	92	95	97	104	105	105	104	98	88	79	105
ND	Bismarck........	52	62	68	81	93	98	107	109	109	105	95	75	65	109
OH	Cincinnati.......	30	69	73	84	89	93	102	103	102	98	88	81	75	103
	Cleveland	50	73	69	83	88	92	104	103	102	101	90	82	77	104
	Columbus	52	74	73	85	89	94	102	100	101	100	90	80	76	102
OK	Oklahoma City	38	80	84	93	100	104	105	109	110	102	96	87	86	110
OR	Portland........	51	63	71	80	87	100	100	107	107	105	92	73	64	107
PA	Philadelphia	50	74	74	87	94	97	100	104	101	100	96	81	72	104
	Pittsburgh.......	39	69	69	82	89	91	98	103	100	97	87	82	74	103
RI	Providence.......	38	66	72	80	98	94	97	102	104	100	86	78	70	104
SC	Columbia.......	44	84	84	91	94	101	107	107	107	101	101	90	83	107
SD	Sioux Falls......	46	66	70	87	94	100	110	108	108	104	94	76	61	110
TN	Memphis........	50	78	81	85	94	99	104	108	108	105	103	95	81	108
	Nashville	52	78	84	86	91	97	106	107	104	105	94	84	79	107
TX	Dallas-Fort Worth ..	38	88	88	96	95	103	113	110	108	106	102	89	88	113
	El Paso........	52	80	83	89	98	104	111	112	108	104	96	87	80	112
	Houston........	22	84	91	91	95	97	103	104	107	102	96	89	83	107
UT	Salt Lake City.....	63	62	69	78	85	93	104	107	104	100	89	75	67	107
VT	Burlington.......	48	63	62	84	91	93	97	99	101	94	85	75	65	101
VA	Norfolk	43	78	81	88	97	100	101	103	104	99	95	86	80	104
	Richmond.......	62	80	83	93	96	100	104	105	102	103	99	86	80	105
WA	Seattle-Tacoma ...	47	64	70	75	85	93	96	99	99	98	89	74	63	99
	Spokane	44	59	61	71	90	96	100	103	108	98	86	67	56	108
WV	Charleston.......	44	79	78	89	94	93	98	104	101	102	92	85	80	104
WI	Milwaukee	51	62	65	82	91	93	101	101	103	98	89	77	63	103
WY	Cheyenne	56	66	71	74	82	90	100	100	96	93	83	73	69	100
PR	San Juan........	37	92	96	96	97	96	97	95	97	97	98	96	94	98

[1] City office data.

Source: U.S. National Oceanic and Atmospheric Administration, *Comparative Climatic Data*, annual.

No. 386. Lowest Temperature of Record—Selected Cities

[In Fahrenheit degrees. Airport data, except as noted. For period of record through 1991]

STATE	STATION	Length of record (yr.)	Jan.	Feb.	Mar.	Apr.	May	June	July	Aug.	Sept.	Oct.	Nov.	Dec.	Annual
AL	Mobile.	50	3	11	21	32	43	49	60	59	42	32	22	8	3
AK	Juneau	47	-22	-22	-15	6	25	31	36	27	23	11	-5	-21	-22
AZ	Phoenix.	54	17	22	25	32	40	50	61	60	47	34	25	22	17
AR	Little Rock	50	-4	-5	11	28	40	46	54	52	37	29	17	-1	-5
CA	Los Angeles	56	23	32	34	39	43	48	49	51	47	41	34	32	23
	Sacramento	41	23	23	26	32	36	41	48	49	43	36	26	18	18
	San Diego	51	29	36	39	41	48	51	55	57	51	43	38	34	29
	San Francisco	64	24	25	30	31	36	41	43	42	38	34	25	20	20
CO	Denver	57	-25	-30	-11	-2	22	30	43	41	17	3	-8	-25	-30
CT	Hartford.	37	-26	-21	-6	9	28	37	44	36	30	17	1	-14	-26
DE	Wilmington.	44	-14	-6	2	18	30	41	48	43	36	24	14	-7	-14
DC	Washington	50	-5	4	11	24	34	47	54	49	39	29	16	1	-5
FL	Jacksonville	50	7	19	23	34	45	47	61	63	48	36	21	11	7
	Miami	49	30	32	32	46	53	60	69	68	68	51	39	30	30
GA	Atlanta	43	-8	5	10	26	37	46	53	55	36	28	3	-	-8
HI	Honolulu	22	53	53	55	57	60	65	66	67	66	64	57	54	53
ID	Boise	52	-17	-15	6	19	22	31	35	37	23	11	-3	-25	-25
IL	Chicago.	33	-27	-17	-8	7	24	36	40	41	28	17	1	-25	-27
	Peoria	52	-25	-18	-10	14	25	39	47	41	26	19	-2	-23	-25
IN	Indianapolis	52	-22	-21	-7	16	28	39	44	41	28	17	-2	-23	-23
IA	Des Moines	52	-24	-20	-22	9	30	38	47	40	26	14	-4	-22	-24
KS	Wichita	39	-12	-21	-2	15	31	43	51	48	31	21	1	-16	-21
KY	Louisville	44	-20	-19	-1	22	31	42	50	46	33	23	-1	-15	-20
LA	New Orleans	45	14	19	25	32	41	50	60	60	42	35	24	11	11
ME	Portland.	51	-26	-39	-21	8	23	33	40	33	23	15	3	-21	-39
MD	Baltimore.	41	-7	-3	6	20	32	40	50	45	35	25	13	-	-7
MA	Boston	40	-12	-4	6	16	34	45	50	47	38	28	15	-7	-12
MI	Detroit.	33	-21	-15	-4	10	25	36	41	38	29	17	9	-10	-21
	Sault Ste. Marie . . .	51	-36	-35	-24	-2	18	26	36	29	25	16	-10	-25	-36
MN	Duluth	50	-39	-33	-29	-5	17	27	35	32	22	8	-23	-34	-39
	Minneapolis-St. Paul	53	-34	-28	-32	2	18	34	43	39	26	15	-17	-29	-34
MS	Jackson.	28	2	11	15	27	38	47	51	55	35	29	17	4	2
MO	Kansas City	19	-17	-19	-10	12	30	42	52	43	33	21	1	-23	-23
	St. Louis	34	-18	-10	-5	22	31	43	51	47	36	23	1	-16	-18
MT	Great Falls.	54	-37	-35	-29	-6	15	31	40	35	21	-11	-25	-43	-43
NE	Omaha	55	-23	-21	-16	5	27	38	44	43	25	13	-9	-23	-23
NV	Reno	50	-16	-16	-2	13	18	25	33	24	20	8	1	-16	-16
NH	Concord	50	-33	-37	-16	8	21	30	35	29	21	10	-5	-22	-37
NJ	Atlantic City	48	-10	-11	5	12	25	37	42	40	32	20	10	-7	-11
NM	Albuquerque	52	-17	-5	8	19	28	40	52	52	37	21	-7	-7	-17
NY	Albany.	45	-28	-21	-21	10	26	36	40	34	24	16	5	-22	-28
	Buffalo	48	-16	-20	-7	12	26	35	43	38	32	20	9	-10	-20
	New York [1]	123	-6	-15	3	12	32	44	52	50	39	28	5	-13	-15
NC	Charlotte	52	-5	5	4	24	32	45	53	53	39	24	11	2	-5
	Raleigh	47	-9	5	11	23	31	38	48	46	37	19	11	4	-9
ND	Bismarck	52	-44	-39	-31	-12	15	30	35	33	11	-10	-30	-43	-44
OH	Cincinnati.	30	-25	-11	-11	17	27	39	47	43	33	16	1	-20	-25
	Cleveland	50	-19	-15	-5	10	25	31	41	38	32	19	3	-15	-19
	Columbus	52	-19	-13	-6	14	25	35	43	39	31	20	5	-17	-19
OK	Oklahoma City	38	-4	-3	3	20	37	47	53	51	36	22	11	-8	-8
OR	Portland.	51	-2	-3	19	29	29	39	43	44	34	26	13	6	-3
PA	Philadelphia	50	-7	-4	7	19	28	44	51	44	35	25	15	1	-7
	Pittsburgh	39	-18	-12	-1	14	26	34	42	39	31	16	-1	-12	-18
RI	Providence.	38	-13	-7	1	14	29	41	48	40	33	20	6	-10	-13
SC	Columbia	44	-1	5	4	26	34	44	54	53	40	23	12	4	-1
SD	Sioux Falls.	46	-36	-31	-23	5	17	33	38	34	22	9	-17	-28	-36
TN	Memphis	50	-4	-11	12	29	38	48	52	48	36	25	9	-13	-13
	Nashville	52	-17	-13	2	23	34	42	51	47	36	26	-1	-10	-17
TX	Dallas-Fort Worth . .	38	4	7	15	29	41	51	59	56	43	29	20	-1	-1
	El Paso	52	-8	8	14	23	31	46	57	56	41	25	1	5	-8
	Houston	22	12	20	22	31	44	52	62	62	48	32	19	7	7
UT	Salt Lake City	63	-22	-30	2	14	25	35	40	37	27	16	-14	-21	-30
VT	Burlington	48	-30	-30	-20	2	24	33	39	35	25	15	-2	-26	-30
VA	Norfolk	43	-3	8	18	28	36	45	54	49	45	27	20	7	-3
	Richmond	62	-12	-10	11	23	31	40	51	46	35	21	10	-1	-12
WA	Seattle-Tacoma . . .	47	-	1	11	29	28	38	43	44	35	28	6	6	-
	Spokane	44	-22	-17	-7	17	24	33	37	35	24	10	-21	-25	-25
WV	Charleston	44	-15	-6	-	19	26	33	46	41	34	17	6	-12	-15
WI	Milwaukee	51	-26	-19	-10	12	21	33	40	44	28	18	-5	-20	-26
WY	Cheyenne	56	-29	-34	-21	-8	16	25	38	36	8	-1	-14	-28	-34
PR	San Juan	37	61	62	60	64	66	69	69	70	69	67	66	63	60

- Represents zero.   [1] City office data.

Source: U.S. National Oceanic and Atmospheric Administration, *Comparative Climatic Data*, annual.

No. 387. Normal Monthly and Annual Precipitation—Selected Cities

[In inches. Airport data, except as noted. Based on standard 30-year period, 1961 through 1990. See *Historical Statistics, Colonial Times to 1970*, series J 164-267, for related data]

STATE	STATION	Jan.	Feb.	Mar.	Apr.	May	June	July	Aug.	Sept.	Oct.	Nov.	Dec.	Annual
AL	Mobile.........	4.76	5.46	6.41	4.48	5.74	5.04	6.85	6.96	5.91	2.94	4.10	5.31	63.96
AK	Juneau	4.54	3.75	3.28	2.77	3.42	3.15	4.16	5.32	6.73	7.84	4.91	4.44	54.31
AZ	Phoenix.........	0.67	0.68	0.88	0.22	0.12	0.13	0.83	0.96	0.86	0.65	0.66	1.00	7.66
AR	Little Rock	3.42	3.61	4.91	5.49	5.17	3.57	3.60	3.26	4.05	3.75	5.20	4.83	50.86
CA	Los Angeles.....	2.40	2.51	1.98	0.72	0.14	0.03	0.01	0.15	0.31	0.34	1.76	1.66	12.01
	Sacramento	3.73	2.87	2.57	1.16	0.27	0.12	0.05	0.07	0.37	1.08	2.72	2.51	17.52
	San Diego	1.80	1.53	1.77	0.79	0.19	0.07	0.02	0.10	0.24	0.37	1.45	1.57	9.90
	San Francisco	4.35	3.17	3.06	1.37	0.19	0.11	0.03	0.05	0.20	1.22	2.86	3.09	19.70
CO	Denver	0.50	0.57	1.28	1.71	2.40	1.79	1.91	1.51	1.24	0.98	0.87	0.64	15.40
CT	Hartford.........	3.41	3.23	3.63	3.85	4.12	3.75	3.19	3.65	3.79	3.57	4.04	3.91	44.14
DE	Wilmington.......	3.03	2.91	3.43	3.39	3.84	3.55	4.23	3.40	3.43	2.88	3.27	3.48	40.84
DC	Washington	2.72	2.71	3.17	2.71	3.66	3.38	3.80	3.91	3.31	3.02	3.12	3.12	38.63
FL	Jacksonville	3.31	3.93	3.68	2.77	3.55	5.69	5.60	7.93	7.05	2.90	2.19	2.72	51.32
	Miami	2.01	2.08	2.39	2.85	6.21	9.33	5.70	7.58	7.63	5.64	2.66	1.83	55.91
GA	Atlanta	4.75	4.81	5.77	4.26	4.29	3.56	5.01	3.66	3.42	3.05	3.86	4.33	50.77
HI	Honolulu	3.55	2.21	2.20	1.54	1.13	0.50	0.59	0.44	0.78	2.28	3.00	3.80	22.02
ID	Boise	1.45	1.07	1.29	1.24	1.08	0.81	0.35	0.43	0.80	0.75	1.48	1.36	12.11
IL	Chicago........	1.53	1.36	2.69	3.64	3.32	3.78	3.66	4.22	3.82	2.41	2.92	2.47	35.82
	Peoria	1.51	1.42	2.91	3.77	3.70	3.99	4.20	3.10	3.87	2.65	2.69	2.44	36.25
IN	Indianapolis	2.32	2.46	3.79	3.70	4.00	3.49	4.47	3.64	2.87	2.63	3.23	3.34	39.94
IA	Des Moines	0.96	1.11	2.33	3.36	3.66	4.46	3.78	4.20	3.53	2.62	1.79	1.32	33.12
KS	Wichita	0.79	0.96	2.43	2.38	3.81	4.31	3.13	3.02	3.49	2.22	1.59	1.20	29.33
KY	Louisville	2.86	3.30	4.66	4.23	4.62	3.46	4.51	3.54	3.16	2.71	3.70	3.64	44.39
LA	New Orleans	5.05	6.01	4.90	4.50	4.56	5.84	6.12	6.17	5.51	3.05	4.42	5.75	61.88
ME	Portland.........	3.53	3.33	3.67	4.08	3.62	3.44	3.09	2.87	3.09	3.90	5.17	4.55	44.34
MD	Baltimore.......	3.05	3.12	3.38	3.09	3.72	3.67	3.69	3.92	3.41	2.98	3.32	3.41	40.76
MA	Boston	3.59	3.62	3.69	3.60	3.25	3.09	2.84	3.24	3.06	3.30	4.22	4.01	41.51
MI	Detroit.........	1.76	1.74	2.55	2.95	2.92	3.61	3.18	3.43	2.89	2.10	2.67	2.82	32.62
	Sault Ste. Marie ...	2.42	1.74	2.30	2.35	2.71	3.14	2.71	3.61	3.69	3.23	3.45	2.88	34.23
MN	Duluth	1.22	0.80	1.91	2.25	3.03	3.82	3.61	3.99	3.84	2.49	1.80	1.24	30.00
	Minneapolis-St. Paul	0.95	0.88	1.94	2.42	3.39	4.05	3.53	3.62	2.72	2.19	1.55	1.08	28.32
MS	Jackson.........	5.24	4.70	5.82	5.57	5.05	3.18	4.51	3.77	3.55	3.26	4.81	5.91	55.37
MO	Kansas City	1.09	1.10	2.51	3.12	5.04	4.72	4.36	4.01	4.86	3.29	1.92	1.58	37.62
	St. Louis	1.81	2.12	3.58	3.50	3.97	3.72	3.85	2.85	3.12	2.68	3.28	3.03	37.51
MT	Great Falls.......	0.91	0.57	1.10	1.41	2.52	2.39	1.24	1.54	1.24	0.78	0.66	0.85	15.21
NE	Omaha	0.74	0.77	2.04	2.66	4.52	3.87	3.51	3.24	3.72	2.28	1.49	1.02	29.86
NV	Reno	1.07	0.99	0.71	0.38	0.69	0.46	0.28	0.32	0.39	0.38	0.87	0.99	7.53
NH	Concord	2.51	2.53	2.72	2.91	3.14	3.15	3.23	3.32	2.81	3.23	3.66	3.16	36.37
NJ	Atlantic City	3.46	3.06	3.62	3.56	3.33	2.64	3.83	4.14	2.93	2.82	3.58	3.32	40.29
NM	Albuquerque.....	0.44	0.46	0.54	0.52	0.50	0.59	1.37	1.64	1.00	0.89	0.43	0.50	8.88
NY	Albany	2.36	2.27	2.93	2.99	3.41	3.62	3.18	3.47	2.95	2.83	3.23	2.93	36.17
	Buffalo	2.70	2.31	2.68	2.87	3.14	3.55	3.08	4.17	3.49	3.09	3.83	3.67	38.58
	New York [1]	3.42	3.27	4.08	4.20	4.42	3.67	4.35	4.01	3.89	3.56	4.47	3.91	47.25
NC	Charlotte	3.71	3.84	4.43	2.68	3.82	3.39	3.92	3.73	3.50	3.36	3.23	3.48	43.09
	Raleigh	3.48	3.69	3.77	2.59	3.92	3.68	4.01	4.02	3.19	2.86	2.98	3.24	41.43
ND	Bismarck	0.45	0.43	0.77	1.67	2.18	2.72	2.14	1.72	1.49	0.90	0.49	0.51	15.47
OH	Cincinnati........	2.59	2.69	4.24	3.75	4.28	3.84	4.24	3.35	2.88	2.86	3.46	3.15	41.33
	Cleveland	2.04	2.19	2.91	3.14	3.49	3.70	3.52	3.40	3.44	2.54	3.17	3.09	36.63
	Columbus	2.18	2.24	3.27	3.21	3.93	4.04	4.31	3.72	2.96	2.15	3.22	2.86	38.09
OK	Oklahoma City	1.13	1.56	2.71	2.77	5.22	4.31	2.61	2.60	3.84	3.23	1.98	1.40	33.36
OR	Portland.........	5.35	3.85	3.56	2.39	2.06	1.48	0.63	1.09	1.75	2.67	5.34	6.13	36.30
PA	Philadelphia	3.21	2.79	3.46	3.62	3.75	3.74	4.28	3.80	3.42	2.62	3.34	3.38	41.41
	Pittsburgh	2.54	2.39	3.41	3.15	3.59	3.71	3.75	3.21	2.97	2.36	2.85	2.92	36.85
RI	Providence	3.88	3.61	4.05	4.11	3.76	3.33	3.18	3.63	3.48	3.69	4.43	4.38	45.53
SC	Columbia	4.42	4.12	4.82	3.28	3.68	4.80	5.50	6.09	3.67	3.04	2.90	3.59	49.91
SD	Sioux Falls.....	0.51	0.64	1.64	2.52	3.03	3.40	2.68	2.85	3.02	1.78	1.09	0.70	23.86
TN	Memphis	3.73	4.35	5.41	5.46	4.98	3.57	3.79	3.43	3.53	3.01	5.10	5.74	52.10
	Nashville	3.58	3.81	4.85	4.37	4.88	3.57	3.97	3.46	3.46	2.62	4.12	4.61	47.30
TX	Dallas-Fort Worth ..	1.83	2.18	2.77	3.50	4.88	2.98	2.31	2.21	3.39	3.52	2.29	1.84	33.70
	El Paso	0.40	0.41	0.29	0.20	0.25	0.67	1.54	1.58	1.70	0.76	0.44	0.57	8.81
	Houston	3.29	2.96	2.92	3.21	5.24	4.96	3.60	3.49	4.89	4.27	3.79	3.45	46.07
UT	Salt Lake City.....	1.11	1.23	1.91	2.12	1.80	0.93	0.81	0.86	1.28	1.44	1.29	1.40	16.18
VT	Burlington	1.82	1.63	2.23	2.76	3.12	3.47	3.65	4.06	3.30	2.88	3.13	2.42	34.47
VA	Norfolk	3.78	3.47	3.70	3.06	3.81	3.82	5.06	4.81	3.90	3.15	2.85	3.23	44.64
	Richmond	3.24	3.16	3.61	2.96	3.84	3.62	5.03	4.40	3.34	3.53	3.17	3.26	43.16
WA	Seattle-Tacoma ...	5.38	3.99	3.54	2.33	1.70	1.50	0.76	1.14	1.88	3.23	5.83	5.91	37.19
	Spokane	1.98	1.46	1.49	1.18	1.41	1.26	0.67	0.72	0.73	0.99	2.15	2.42	16.49
WV	Charleston.......	2.91	3.04	3.63	3.31	3.94	3.59	4.99	4.01	3.24	2.89	3.59	3.39	42.53
WI	Milwaukee	1.60	1.45	2.67	3.50	2.84	3.24	3.47	3.53	3.38	2.41	2.51	2.33	32.93
WY	Cheyenne	0.40	0.39	1.03	1.37	2.39	2.08	2.09	1.69	1.27	0.74	0.53	0.42	14.40
PR	San Juan......	2.81	2.15	2.35	3.76	5.93	4.00	4.37	5.32	5.28	5.71	5.94	4.72	52.34

[1] City office data.

Source: U.S. National Oceanic and Atmospheric Administration, *Climatography of the United States*, No. 81.

No. 388. Average Number of Days With Precipitation of .01 Inch or More— Selected Cities

[Airport data, except as noted. For period of record through 1991, except as noted]

STATE	STATION	Length of record (yr.)	Jan.	Feb.	Mar.	Apr.	May	June	July	Aug.	Sept.	Oct.	Nov.	Dec.	Annual
AL	Mobile.	50	11	10	10	7	9	11	16	14	10	6	8	10	122
AK	Juneau [1]	47	18	17	18	17	17	16	17	18	20	24	20	21	221
AZ	Phoenix.	52	4	4	4	2	1	1	4	5	3	3	3	4	36
AR	Little Rock	49	10	9	10	10	10	8	8	7	7	7	8	9	104
CA	Los Angeles	56	6	6	6	3	1	1	1	(Z)	1	2	4	5	35
	Sacramento	52	10	8	9	5	3	1	(Z)	(Z)	1	3	7	9	57
	San Diego	51	7	6	7	5	2	1	(Z)	1	1	2	5	6	42
	San Francisco	63	11	10	10	6	3	1	(Z)	1	1	4	7	10	62
CO	Denver	57	6	6	9	9	11	9	9	9	6	5	6	5	89
CT	Hartford.	37	11	10	11	11	12	11	10	10	9	8	11	12	127
DE	Wilmington.	44	11	10	11	11	11	10	9	9	8	8	9	10	116
DC	Washington	50	10	9	11	10	11	9	10	9	8	7	8	9	112
FL	Jacksonville	50	8	8	8	7	8	12	15	14	13	9	6	8	115
	Miami	49	7	6	6	6	10	15	16	17	17	14	9	7	130
GA	Atlanta	57	11	10	11	9	9	10	12	10	8	6	8	10	115
HI	Honolulu	42	10	9	9	9	7	6	7	6	7	9	9	10	99
ID	Boise	52	12	10	10	8	8	6	2	3	4	6	10	11	90
IL	Chicago.	33	11	10	12	12	11	10	10	9	10	10	11	11	126
	Peoria.	52	9	8	11	12	11	10	9	8	9	8	9	10	113
IN	Indianapolis	52	12	10	13	12	12	10	9	9	8	8	10	12	125
IA	Des Moines	52	7	7	10	11	11	11	9	9	9	8	7	8	107
KS	Wichita	38	5	5	8	8	11	9	7	8	8	6	5	6	86
KY	Louisville	44	11	11	13	12	12	10	11	8	8	8	10	11	124
LA	New Orleans	43	10	9	9	7	8	11	15	13	10	6	7	10	114
ME	Portland.	51	11	10	11	12	13	12	10	10	9	9	12	12	128
MD	Baltimore.	41	10	9	11	11	11	9	9	10	7	7	9	9	113
MA	Boston.	40	11	10	12	11	12	11	9	10	9	9	11	12	126
MI	Detroit.	33	13	11	13	13	11	10	9	9	10	10	12	14	136
	Sault Ste. Marie	50	19	15	13	11	11	12	10	11	13	14	18	19	166
MN	Duluth	50	12	10	11	10	12	13	11	11	12	10	11	12	134
	Minneapolis-St. Paul	53	9	7	10	10	11	12	10	10	10	8	9	9	115
MS	Jackson.	28	11	9	10	9	10	8	10	10	8	6	8	10	110
MO	Kansas City	19	7	7	10	11	12	10	7	9	8	8	8	8	104
	St. Louis.	34	8	8	11	11	11	9	9	8	8	9	9	9	111
MT	Great Falls.	54	9	8	9	9	12	12	7	8	7	6	7	8	101
NE	Omaha	55	6	7	9	10	12	11	9	9	8	7	6	6	98
NV	Reno	49	6	6	6	4	4	3	2	2	3	3	5	6	51
NH	Concord	50	11	10	11	12	12	11	10	10	9	9	11	11	125
NJ	Atlantic City	48	11	10	11	11	10	9	9	9	8	7	9	10	112
NM	Albuquerque.	52	4	4	5	3	4	4	9	10	6	5	3	4	61
NY	Albany.	45	12	11	12	12	13	11	10	10	10	9	12	12	134
	Buffalo	48	20	17	16	14	12	10	10	11	11	12	16	20	169
	New York [2]	122	11	10	11	11	11	10	11	10	8	8	9	10	121
NC	Charlotte.	52	10	10	11	9	10	10	11	10	7	7	8	10	111
	Raleigh.	47	10	10	10	9	10	9	11	10	8	7	8	9	112
ND	Bismarck.	52	8	7	8	8	10	12	9	9	7	6	6	8	96
OH	Cincinnati.	44	12	11	13	12	12	10	10	9	8	8	11	12	129
	Cleveland	50	16	14	15	14	13	11	10	10	10	11	15	16	156
	Columbus	52	13	12	14	13	13	11	11	9	8	9	12	13	137
OK	Oklahoma City	52	5	6	7	8	10	9	6	7	7	6	5	6	83
OR	Portland.	51	18	16	17	14	12	9	4	5	8	12	18	19	152
PA	Philadelphia	51	11	9	11	11	11	10	9	9	8	8	9	10	117
	Pittsburgh	39	16	14	16	14	13	12	11	10	9	11	13	16	153
RI	Providence	38	11	10	12	11	11	11	9	9	8	9	11	12	124
SC	Columbia.	44	10	10	11	8	9	10	12	11	8	6	7	9	109
SD	Sioux Falls.	46	6	6	9	9	11	11	9	9	8	6	6	6	97
TN	Memphis.	41	10	10	11	10	9	8	9	8	7	6	9	10	106
	Nashville.	50	11	11	12	11	11	9	10	9	8	7	9	11	119
TX	Dallas-Fort Worth	38	7	7	7	8	9	6	5	5	7	6	6	7	78
	El Paso.	52	4	3	2	2	2	3	8	8	6	4	3	4	49
	Houston	22	10	8	9	7	8	9	9	9	9	10	7	9	106
UT	Salt Lake City.	63	10	9	10	10	8	5	5	6	6	8	9	9	90
VT	Burlington	48	14	12	13	12	14	12	12	13	12	12	14	15	154
VA	Norfolk	43	11	10	11	10	10	9	11	11	8	8	8	9	115
	Richmond	54	10	9	11	9	11	10	11	10	8	7	8	9	113
WA	Seattle-Tacoma	47	19	16	17	14	11	9	5	6	9	13	18	19	155
	Spokane	44	14	11	12	9	10	8	4	5	6	8	13	15	113
WV	Charleston	44	16	14	15	14	13	11	13	11	10	10	12	14	151
WI	Milwaukee	51	11	10	12	12	12	11	10	9	9	9	10	11	125
WY	Cheyenne	56	6	6	9	10	12	11	11	10	8	6	6	6	100
PR	San Juan.	36	17	13	13	13	17	15	19	18	17	17	18	19	196

Z Less than 1/2 day.   [1] For period of record through 1989.   [2] City office data.

Source: U.S. National Oceanic and Atmospheric Administration, *Comparative Climatic Data*, annual.

No. 389. Snow and Ice Pellets—Selected Cities

[In inches. Airport data, except as noted. For period of record through 1991. T denotes trace]

STATE	STATION	Length of record (yr)	Jan.	Feb.	Mar.	Apr.	May	June	July	Aug.	Sept.	Oct.	Nov.	Dec.	Annual
AL	Mobile	50	0.1	0.2	-	T	T	-	T	-	-	-	T	0.1	0.4
AK	Juneau	47	26.1	18.7	15.4	3.7	-	T	-	-	T	1.1	12.2	22.8	100.0
AZ	Phoenix	54	T	-	-	T	-	-	-	-	-	-	-	-	T
AR	Little Rock	49	2.4	1.5	0.5	T	-	-	-	-	-	-	0.2	0.7	5.3
CA	Los Angeles	56	T	T	T	-	-	-	-	-	-	-	-	T	T
	Sacramento	43	T	-	T	-	-	-	-	-	-	-	-	T	T
	San Diego	51	T	-	T	-	-	-	-	-	-	-	-	-	-
	San Francisco	64	-	T	T	-	-	-	-	-	-	-	-	-	T
CO	Denver	57	8.0	7.4	12.6	9.1	1.7	-	T	T	1.6	3.8	8.6	7.3	60.1
CT	Hartford	37	12.3	11.5	9.4	1.6	-	-	-	-	-	0.1	2.1	10.5	47.5
DE	Wilmington	44	6.8	6.0	3.1	0.2	T	-	T	-	-	0.1	0.9	3.4	20.5
DC	Washington	48	5.5	5.3	2.0	-	T	-	T	-	-	-	0.9	3.1	16.8
FL	Jacksonville	50	T	-	-	-	-	-	T	-	-	-	-	-	T
	Miami	49	-	-	-	-	-	-	-	-	-	-	-	-	-
GA	Atlanta	57	0.9	0.5	0.4	T	-	-	-	-	-	-	-	0.2	2.0
HI	Honolulu	45	-	-	-	-	-	-	-	-	-	-	-	-	-
ID	Boise	52	6.7	3.5	1.7	0.7	0.1	T	T	T	T	0.1	2.2	5.9	20.9
IL	Chicago	33	10.7	8.3	6.6	1.7	0.1	-	-	-	T	0.5	2.0	8.6	38.5
	Peoria	48	6.6	5.4	4.1	0.9	-	-	T	-	-	0.1	2.1	6.0	25.2
IN	Indianapolis	60	6.1	5.7	3.4	0.5	-	-	-	T	-	0.2	1.8	4.9	22.6
IA	Des Moines	52	8.2	7.2	6.4	1.9	-	-	-	-	T	0.2	3.0	6.8	33.7
KS	Wichita	38	4.6	4.3	2.5	0.3	T	T	-	-	-	-	1.2	3.3	16.2
KY	Louisville	44	5.3	4.3	3.3	0.1	T	-	-	-	-	-	1.1	2.1	16.2
LA	New Orleans	45	0.0	0.1	T	T	T	-	-	-	-	-	T	0.1	0.2
ME	Portland	51	19.3	17.2	12.3	2.8	0.2	-	-	-	T	0.2	3.0	14.9	69.9
MD	Baltimore	41	6.1	6.5	3.6	0.1	T	-	T	-	-	-	1.1	3.5	20.9
MA	Boston	56	12.2	11.3	7.3	0.9	-	-	-	-	-	-	-	7.3	40.4
MI	Detroit	33	9.9	9.1	6.6	1.6	T	-	-	-	T	0.2	3.1	11.0	41.1
	Sault Ste. Marie	50	28.5	19.1	15.2	5.5	0.5	T	-	T	0.1	2.3	15.4	29.9	116.5
MN	Duluth	48	16.8	11.3	13.7	6.5	0.8	-	-	T	0.1	1.3	11.8	15.4	77.7
	Minneapolis-St. Paul	53	9.8	8.5	10.8	2.9	0.1	T	-	T	-	0.5	7.8	9.4	49.8
MS	Jackson	28	0.5	0.2	0.2	-	-	-	-	-	-	-	-	-	0.9
MO	Kansas City	57	5.8	4.3	3.7	0.7	T	T	-	-	-	T	1.1	4.5	20.1
	St. Louis	55	5.3	4.4	4.3	0.4	T	T	-	-	-	T	1.4	3.9	19.7
MT	Great Falls	54	9.8	8.4	10.6	7.3	1.8	0.3	T	T	1.6	3.3	7.5	8.8	59.4
NE	Omaha	56	7.5	6.7	6.5	0.8	T	T	-	-	T	0.4	2.6	5.6	30.2
NV	Reno	49	5.7	5.1	4.6	1.3	0.9	-	-	-	-	0.4	2.3	4.3	24.6
NH	Concord	50	18.0	14.6	10.5	2.3	0.1	-	-	-	-	0.1	4.0	13.7	63.3
NJ	Atlantic City	47	5.3	5.5	2.6	0.4	T	-	T	-	-	T	0.4	2.3	16.5
NM	Albuquerque	52	2.5	2.2	1.9	0.6	-	T	T	-	T	0.1	1.1	2.6	11.0
NY	Albany	45	16.3	14.1	10.7	2.7	0.1	T	T	-	T	0.2	4.2	15.1	63.4
	Buffalo	48	23.6	18.4	11.1	3.2	0.3	T	-	T	T	0.2	11.6	22.7	91.1
	New York [1]	123	7.6	8.5	4.9	0.9	T	-	T	-	-	-	0.9	5.4	28.2
NC	Charlotte	52	2.1	1.8	1.3	-	-	-	-	-	-	-	0.1	0.5	5.8
	Raleigh	47	2.3	2.6	1.4	T	-	-	-	-	-	-	0.1	0.8	7.2
ND	Bismarck	52	7.1	6.6	8.3	3.9	0.9	T	T	T	0.3	1.7	5.8	6.8	41.4
OH	Cincinnati	44	6.9	5.3	4.2	0.5	-	-	T	-	-	0.2	2.1	3.9	23.1
	Cleveland	50	12.4	11.9	10.2	2.3	0.1	-	-	-	T	0.6	5.0	11.9	54.4
	Columbus	44	8.2	6.2	4.5	0.9	-	-	T	-	T	-	2.3	5.6	27.7
OK	Oklahoma City	52	3.0	2.5	1.4	-	T	-	-	-	-	T	0.5	1.8	9.2
OR	Portland	51	3.4	0.9	0.4	T	-	T	-	T	T	0.0	0.4	1.4	6.5
PA	Philadelphia	49	6.6	6.4	3.6	0.3	T	-	-	-	-	-	0.7	3.5	21.1
	Pittsburgh	39	11.5	9.2	8.0	1.7	0.1	T	T	-	T	0.2	3.4	8.1	42.2
RI	Providence	38	9.7	9.7	7.3	0.7	0.2	-	-	-	-	0.1	1.0	7.0	35.7
SC	Columbia	44	0.5	0.9	0.2	T	-	-	-	-	-	0.0	T	0.2	1.8
SD	Sioux Falls	46	6.5	7.9	9.5	2.2	-	T	-	-	-	0.7	5.3	7.3	39.4
TN	Memphis	41	2.4	1.4	0.9	T	T	-	-	-	-	T	0.1	0.7	5.5
	Nashville	50	3.9	3.1	1.4	-	-	-	-	-	T	-	0.5	1.5	10.4
TX	Dallas-Fort Worth	38	1.3	1.0	0.2	T	T	-	-	-	-	-	0.1	0.3	2.9
	El Paso	52	1.3	0.9	0.4	0.4	T	-	T	-	-	-	1.0	1.7	5.7
	Houston	57	0.2	0.2	-	-	-	T	-	-	-	-	T	0.0	0.4
UT	Salt Lake City	63	13.0	9.4	9.7	5.1	0.6	T	T	T	0.1	1.3	6.4	11.9	57.5
VT	Burlington	48	18.8	16.3	11.8	3.5	0.2	-	T	T	-	0.2	6.7	18.7	76.2
VA	Norfolk	43	2.8	3.0	1.0	0.0	0.0	T	-	T	-	-	-	0.9	7.7
	Richmond	54	5.0	4.2	2.5	0.1	T	-	-	-	-	T	0.4	2.0	14.2
WA	Seattle-Tacoma	47	5.1	1.7	1.4	0.1	T	-	T	-	-	T	1.2	2.5	12.0
	Spokane	44	16.3	7.7	4.2	0.7	0.1	T	-	-	T	0.4	6.2	14.7	50.3
WV	Charleston	44	10.4	8.8	4.7	0.9	-	-	T	T	T	0.1	2.2	4.9	32.0
WI	Milwaukee	51	13.0	9.7	8.6	1.7	0.1	-	T	T	T	0.2	3.0	10.6	46.9
WY	Cheyenne	56	6.2	5.9	12.2	9.1	3.4	0.2	T	T	0.7	3.7	6.8	6.1	54.3
PR	San Juan	36	-	-	-	-	-	-	-	-	-	-	-	-	-

- Represents zero or rounds to zero.   [1] City office data.

Source: U.S. National Oceanic and Atmospheric Administration, *Comparative Climatic Data*, annual.

No. 390. Sunshine, Average Wind Speed, Mean Number of Days Minimum Temperature Below 32 Degrees Fahrenheit, and Average Relative Humidity—Selected Cities

[Airport data, except as noted. For period of record through 1991, except as noted. M=morning. A=afternoon]

STATE	STATION	AVERAGE PERCENTAGE OF POSSIBLE SUNSHINE		AVERAGE WIND SPEED (m.p.h.)				MINIMUM TEMPERATURE 32 DEGREES OR LESS		AVERAGE RELATIVE HUMIDITY (percent)					
		Length of record (yr.)	Annual	Length of record (yr.)	Annual	Jan.	July	Length of record (yr.)	Mean number (days)	Length of record (yr.)	Annual M	Annual A	Jan. M	Jan. A	July M	July A
AL	Mobile	[1]41	[1]59	43	9.0	10.4	7.0	29	2.2	29	83	57	79	61	87	60
AK	Juneau	33	30	46	8.3	8.2	7.5	47	14.1	25	86	73	81	77	87	70
AZ	Phoenix	96	86	46	6.3	5.2	7.2	31	0.8	31	51	23	66	32	45	20
AR	Little Rock	32	62	49	7.8	8.5	6.7	31	6.0	31	79	57	76	61	83	56
CA	Los Angeles	[2]32	[2]73	43	7.5	6.7	7.8	32	(Z)	32	79	64	70	59	86	68
	Sacramento	43	78	42	7.9	7.2	9.0	41	1.7	31	82	45	90	70	76	28
	San Diego	51	68	51	6.9	5.9	7.4	31	(Z)	31	76	62	70	56	82	66
	San Francisco	(NA)	(NA)	64	10.6	7.2	13.6	32	0.2	32	84	62	86	66	86	59
CO	Denver	42	70	43	8.7	8.6	8.3	31	15.7	31	67	40	63	49	68	34
CT	Hartford	37	56	37	8.5	9.0	7.5	32	13.5	32	76	52	69	56	82	51
DE	Wilmington	(NA)	(NA)	43	9.1	9.8	7.8	44	10.0	44	78	55	73	60	83	54
DC	Washington	43	56	43	9.4	10.0	8.2	31	7.0	31	72	53	67	55	77	53
FL	Jacksonville	40	63	42	8.0	8.2	7.1	50	1.5	55	86	56	85	57	88	58
	Miami	15	72	42	9.3	9.5	7.9	27	(Z)	27	81	61	81	59	82	63
GA	Atlanta	56	61	53	9.1	10.4	7.6	31	5.3	31	77	56	74	59	85	60
HI	Honolulu	39	69	42	11.4	9.6	13.2	22	-	22	76	56	81	61	73	51
ID	Boise	49	64	52	8.7	8.0	8.4	52	12.4	52	69	43	81	70	54	21
IL	Chicago	11	54	33	10.4	11.7	8.2	33	13.3	33	77	60	75	67	79	56
	Peoria	48	57	48	10.0	11.1	7.8	32	12.9	32	79	62	78	68	82	59
IN	Indianapolis	47	55	43	9.6	10.9	7.4	32	11.8	32	80	62	78	70	84	59
IA	Des Moines	41	59	42	10.9	11.7	9.0	30	13.5	30	75	60	74	67	76	57
KS	Wichita	38	65	38	12.3	12.2	11.3	38	11.1	38	73	55	76	63	67	48
KY	Louisville	44	56	44	8.4	9.6	6.8	31	8.9	31	76	58	72	64	81	58
LA	New Orleans	18	59	48	8.2	9.4	6.1	45	1.3	43	85	63	82	66	89	66
ME	Portland	51	57	51	8.8	9.2	7.6	51	15.7	51	82	59	74	60	89	59
MD	Baltimore	40	57	41	9.2	9.7	8.0	41	9.7	38	75	54	69	57	81	53
MA	Boston	56	58	34	12.5	13.9	11.0	27	9.8	27	72	58	65	57	77	56
MI	Detroit	26	53	33	10.4	12.0	8.5	33	13.6	33	79	60	78	69	81	53
	Sault Ste. Marie	50	47	50	9.2	9.7	7.8	50	18.1	50	85	67	81	75	90	61
MN	Duluth	41	52	42	11.1	11.6	9.4	30	18.5	30	77	63	74	70	82	59
	Minneapolis-St. Paul	53	58	53	10.6	10.5	9.4	32	15.6	32	73	60	72	67	74	54
MS	Jackson	27	60	28	7.4	8.5	6.0	28	5.0	28	87	58	84	65	90	59
MO	Kansas City	19	62	19	10.8	11.5	9.4	19	11.0	19	74	59	72	63	75	56
	St. Louis	32	57	42	9.7	10.6	8.0	31	10.0	31	76	59	77	66	77	56
MT	Great Falls	46	61	50	12.8	15.3	10.1	30	15.7	30	67	45	66	60	66	29
NE	Omaha	[2]55	[2]60	55	10.6	10.9	8.9	27	14.1	27	76	59	75	65	78	57
NV	Reno	43	79	49	6.6	5.6	7.1	28	17.4	28	70	31	79	50	63	18
NH	Concord	50	54	49	6.7	7.2	5.7	26	17.3	25	82	54	74	58	90	51
NJ	Atlantic City	31	56	33	10.0	11.0	8.4	27	11.0	27	82	56	76	58	87	57
NM	Albuquerque	52	76	52	9.0	8.1	9.1	31	11.9	31	60	29	70	40	60	27
NY	Albany	53	52	53	8.9	9.8	7.4	26	14.9	26	79	57	76	63	84	55
	Buffalo	48	49	52	12.0	14.3	10.3	31	13.2	31	79	63	77	72	79	55
	New York [3]	105	58	58	9.4	10.7	7.6	78	7.9	49	70	56	65	60	74	55
NC	Charlotte	41	63	42	7.4	7.9	6.6	31	6.6	31	76	54	72	56	83	57
	Raleigh	37	59	42	7.7	8.5	6.6	27	7.8	27	80	54	73	55	88	58
ND	Bismarck	52	59	52	10.2	10.0	9.2	32	18.6	32	74	56	75	68	74	46
OH	Cincinnati	8	52	44	9.1	10.7	7.2	29	10.8	29	77	59	75	67	83	57
	Cleveland	48	49	50	10.6	12.3	8.6	31	12.3	31	77	62	75	69	81	57
	Columbus	40	49	42	8.4	10.0	6.6	32	11.9	32	77	59	74	67	82	56
OK	Oklahoma City	(NA)	(NA)	43	12.4	12.8	10.9	26	7.7	26	72	54	72	59	70	49
OR	Portland	42	48	43	7.9	9.9	7.6	51	4.3	51	86	60	86	75	82	45
PA	Philadelphia	49	56	51	9.5	10.3	8.1	32	9.7	32	76	55	71	59	81	54
	Pittsburgh	39	46	39	9.1	10.6	7.2	32	12.3	31	75	57	73	65	80	54
RI	Providence	38	58	38	10.6	11.2	9.5	28	11.8	28	76	55	69	56	83	56
SC	Columbia	38	64	43	6.9	7.2	6.3	25	6.0	25	83	51	78	54	87	54
SD	Sioux Falls	[4]49	[4]63	43	11.1	11.1	9.8	28	16.8	28	76	60	75	68	75	53
TN	Memphis	35	64	43	8.9	10.1	7.4	50	5.7	52	76	57	75	63	79	57
	Nashville	49	56	50	8.0	9.2	6.5	26	7.6	26	79	57	76	63	85	57
TX	Dallas-Fort Worth	13	63	38	10.8	11.1	9.6	28	4.0	28	72	56	73	60	67	49
	El Paso	49	84	49	8.9	8.3	8.3	31	6.5	31	57	28	66	35	63	30
	Houston	22	56	22	7.9	8.2	6.9	22	2.1	22	86	60	82	64	86	58
UT	Salt Lake City	53	66	62	8.8	7.6	9.6	32	12.5	32	67	43	79	69	52	22
VT	Burlington	48	49	48	9.0	9.7	7.9	27	15.5	26	77	59	70	63	82	53
VA	Norfolk	27	61	43	10.6	11.5	9.0	43	5.4	43	78	57	72	59	84	59
	Richmond	41	62	43	7.7	8.1	6.8	62	8.5	57	82	53	77	57	88	56
WA	Seattle-Tacoma	25	46	43	9.0	9.7	8.3	32	3.1	32	83	62	81	74	82	49
	Spokane	43	54	44	8.9	8.8	8.6	32	13.9	32	78	52	85	78	64	27
WV	Charleston	[5]8	[5]40	44	6.3	7.5	5.0	44	10.0	44	79	56	74	63	90	60
WI	Milwaukee	51	54	51	11.6	12.7	9.7	31	14.1	31	78	64	75	68	80	61
WY	Cheyenne	52	65	44	13.0	15.3	10.4	32	17.2	32	65	44	57	50	70	38
PR	San Juan	36	66	36	8.4	8.5	9.6	36	-	36	83	65	82	64	84	67

- Represents zero.   NA Not available.   Z Less than one-half a day.   [1] Recording site is in Montgomery, AL.   [2] Site is not at the airport.   [3] City office data.   [4] Recording site is in Rapid City, SD.   [5] Recording site is Elkins, WV.

Source: U.S. National Oceanic and Atmospheric Administration, *Comparative Climatic Data*, annual.

No. 391. Normal Monthly and Seasonal Heating Degree Days, 65 Degree Base— Selected Cities

[Airport data, except as noted. Based on standard 30-year period, 1961 through 1990. Degree day normals are used to determine relative estimates of heating requirements for buildings. Each day that the average temperature for a day is below 65 degrees F. produces one heating degree day]

STATE	STATION	Jan.	Feb.	Mar.	Apr.	May	June	July	Aug.	Sept.	Oct.	Nov.	Dec.	Seasonal
AL	Mobile..........	492	344	177	48	-	-	-	-	-	52	196	393	1,702
AK	Juneau..........	1,265	1,025	1,001	759	558	360	279	310	468	707	990	1,175	8,897
AZ	Phoenix..........	362	227	182	75	8	-	-	-	-	17	134	345	1,350
AR	Little Rock......	803	599	384	133	25	-	-	-	8	128	387	688	3,155
CA	Los Angeles.....	258	215	224	158	96	54	9	5	22	32	127	258	1,458
	Sacramento.....	614	400	357	230	80	12	-	-	16	78	351	611	2,749
	San Diego.......	245	189	177	113	73	51	13	-	19	24	109	243	1,256
	San Francisco ...	505	358	363	287	218	121	92	68	79	135	306	484	3,016
CO	Denver..........	1,094	885	806	504	253	71	-	-	144	429	780	1,054	6,020
CT	Hartford.........	1,252	1,050	853	489	194	20	-	6	96	397	693	1,101	6,151
DE	Wilmington.......	1,066	885	691	384	122	-	-	-	35	288	561	905	4,937
DC	Washington	942	770	552	264	60	-	-	-	14	195	456	794	4,047
FL	Jacksonville......	421	296	169	37	-	-	-	-	-	31	149	331	1,434
	Miami	88	51	14	-	-	-	-	-	-	-	6	41	200
GA	Atlanta	744	566	365	138	27	-	-	-	10	138	367	636	2,991
HI	Honolulu........	-	-	-	-	-	-	-	-	-	-	-	-	-
ID	Boise	1,116	815	701	477	242	75	6	20	160	414	753	1,082	5,861
IL	Chicago.........	1,364	1,109	862	492	235	35	5	19	84	391	750	1,190	6,536
	Peoria.........	1,345	1,084	806	408	183	11	-	9	54	356	714	1,178	6,148
IN	Indianapolis.....	1,225	991	732	378	165	5	-	6	58	338	660	1,057	5,615
IA	Des Moines.....	1,414	1,128	859	428	165	10	-	11	71	372	780	1,259	6,497
KS	Wichita	1,101	846	608	278	102	5	-	-	29	221	609	992	4,791
KY	Louisville.......	1,032	820	580	273	105	6	-	-	36	254	537	871	4,514
LA	New Orleans	450	316	162	28	-	-	-	-	-	30	178	349	1,513
ME	Portland.........	1,370	1,168	992	651	363	100	11	39	189	512	789	1,194	7,378
MD	Baltimore........	1,029	846	648	348	108	-	-	-	29	276	546	877	4,707
MA	Boston	1,128	972	818	507	221	32	-	6	72	321	591	973	5,641
MI	Detroit..........	1,305	1,109	908	531	243	38	-	16	102	435	744	1,138	6,569
	Sault Ste. Marie ...	1,615	1,428	1,271	804	457	224	92	128	300	611	960	1,426	9,316
MN	Duluth..........	1,798	1,476	1,259	792	445	170	60	113	329	660	1,098	1,618	9,818
	Minneapolis-St. Paul	1,649	1,319	1,054	558	244	41	11	22	167	502	954	1,460	7,981
MS	Jackson.........	656	485	285	87	7	-	-	-	6	104	295	542	2,467
MO	Kansas City	1,218	946	691	325	135	7	-	6	56	279	657	1,073	5,393
	St. Louis........	1,107	871	617	266	111	-	-	-	21	237	564	964	4,758
MT	Great Falls.......	1,358	1,053	983	642	372	156	37	91	299	543	933	1,274	7,741
NE	Omaha	1,361	1,067	818	398	164	14	-	9	80	372	780	1,237	6,300
NV	Reno	995	756	688	492	274	76	13	20	178	440	741	1,001	5,674
NH	Concord	1,438	1,210	1,011	633	312	70	13	39	196	533	837	1,262	7,554
NJ	Atlantic City	1,057	896	729	450	167	12	-	-	53	324	576	905	5,169
NM	Albuquerque.....	955	700	561	301	89	-	-	-	18	259	621	921	4,425
NY	Albany..........	1,376	1,162	952	558	247	34	-	12	141	459	759	1,194	6,894
	Buffalo.........	1,283	1,134	967	594	279	59	5	17	130	431	735	1,113	6,747
	New York [1]	1,039	879	701	375	125	-	-	-	34	250	522	880	4,805
NC	Charlotte........	797	630	437	183	42	-	-	-	6	161	391	694	3,341
	Raleigh.........	809	644	458	193	47	-	-	-	9	189	414	694	3,457
ND	Bismarck........	1,730	1,380	1,141	660	324	116	15	69	262	598	1,092	1,581	8,968
OH	Cincinnati.......	1,144	930	682	354	151	11	-	-	51	327	621	977	5,248
	Cleveland.......	1,246	1,058	859	522	250	40	-	11	99	387	672	1,057	6,201
	Columbus	1,197	991	747	420	187	23	-	12	81	361	663	1,026	5,708
OK	Oklahoma City ...	902	675	464	176	31	-	-	-	15	137	462	797	3,659
OR	Portland.........	787	599	549	420	249	91	28	35	102	326	567	769	4,522
PA	Philadelphia	1,073	896	701	378	123	5	-	-	32	283	558	905	4,954
	Pittsburgh	1,206	1,016	794	462	214	36	6	14	100	400	681	1,039	5,968
RI	Providence.......	1,150	988	856	528	246	31	-	8	90	359	630	998	5,884
SC	Columbia........	665	514	317	108	18	-	-	-	5	138	323	561	2,649
SD	Sioux Falls......	1,587	1,268	1,008	543	240	50	10	22	165	508	960	1,448	7,809
TN	Memphis........	784	582	383	127	25	-	-	-	10	131	380	660	3,082
	Nashville	893	689	469	193	59	-	-	-	21	195	450	760	3,729
TX	Dallas-Fort Worth ..	670	484	286	75	-	-	-	-	-	51	275	566	2,407
	El Paso.........	688	473	316	110	7	-	-	-	-	88	378	648	2,708
	Houston........	468	322	187	36	-	-	-	-	-	31	181	374	1,599
UT	Salt Lake City....	1,150	865	719	464	215	51	-	-	108	373	726	1,094	5,765
VT	Burlington.......	1,510	1,310	1,063	633	282	58	6	29	199	533	846	1,302	7,771
VA	Norfolk	803	672	508	249	51	-	-	-	11	164	380	657	3,495
	Richmond	908	736	527	241	61	-	-	-	23	233	462	772	3,963
WA	Seattle-Tacoma ...	772	602	601	474	307	144	58	65	156	378	591	760	4,908
	Spokane	1,175	888	815	573	344	139	30	56	223	549	897	1,153	6,842
WV	Charleston.......	1,020	826	592	312	129	10	-	-	44	299	546	868	4,646
WI	Milwaukee.......	1,429	1,176	983	618	338	82	14	27	123	456	819	1,259	7,324
WY	Cheyenne.......	1,194	1,000	973	675	403	150	31	44	251	558	894	1,153	7,326
PR	San Juan........	-	-	-	-	-	-	-	-	-	-	-	-	-

- Represents zero.   [1] City office data.

Source: U.S. National Oceanic and Atmospheric Administration, *Climatography of the United States*, No. 81.

No. 392. Normal Monthly and Seasonal Cooling Degree Days, 65 Degree Base—Selected Cities

[Airport data, except as noted. Based on standard 30-year period, 1961 through 1990. Degree day normals are used to determine relative estimates of heating requirements for buildings. Each day that the average temperature for a day is above 65 degrees F. produces one cooling degree day]

STATE	STATION	Jan.	Feb.	Mar.	Apr.	May	June	July	Aug.	Sept.	Oct.	Nov.	Dec.	Annual avg.
AL	Mobile	24	14	38	132	295	462	536	521	387	157	40	21	2,627
AK	Juneau	-	-	-	-	-	-	-	-	-	-	-	-	-
AZ	Phoenix	8	22	95	222	436	696	884	822	618	311	41	7	4,162
AR	Little Rock	-	-	15	46	187	402	524	484	281	66	-	-	2,005
CA	Los Angeles	-	8	7	11	25	75	136	176	169	88	25	7	727
	Sacramento	-	-	-	29	89	210	332	313	211	53	-	-	1,237
	San Diego	9	10	9	23	45	105	199	240	211	107	19	7	984
	San Francisco	-	-	-	5	-	16	21	28	64	11	-	-	145
CO	Denver	-	-	-	-	11	128	267	203	63	7	-	-	679
CT	Hartford	-	-	-	-	27	125	270	210	45	-	-	-	677
DE	Wilmington	-	-	-	-	44	199	353	310	125	15	-	-	1,046
DC	Washington	-	-	-	9	104	318	465	419	203	31	-	-	1,549
FL	Jacksonville	31	22	48	97	260	423	515	502	393	179	56	25	2,551
	Miami	156	149	221	306	425	492	546	552	507	412	264	168	4,198
GA	Atlanta	-	-	8	33	157	330	428	406	241	54	10	-	1,667
HI	Honolulu	245	224	291	324	388	432	481	508	480	453	366	282	4,474
ID	Boise	-	-	-	-	9	120	285	252	88	-	-	-	754
IL	Chicago	-	-	-	-	46	143	259	226	66	12	-	-	752
	Peoria	-	-	-	-	87	206	326	261	87	15	-	-	982
IN	Indianapolis	-	-	-	-	96	212	322	260	106	18	-	-	1,014
IA	Des Moines	-	-	-	5	81	214	360	287	74	15	-	-	1,036
KS	Wichita	-	-	-	20	121	326	508	443	188	22	-	-	1,628
KY	Louisville	-	-	-	12	115	252	378	335	171	25	-	-	1,288
LA	New Orleans	25	17	56	133	304	450	524	512	393	157	61	23	2,655
ME	Portland	-	-	-	-	-	22	123	111	12	-	-	-	268
MD	Baltimore	-	-	-	-	59	227	372	329	134	16	-	-	1,137
MA	Boston	-	-	-	-	10	113	264	220	66	5	-	-	678
MI	Detroit	-	-	-	-	38	116	231	186	48	7	-	-	626
	Sault Ste. Marie	-	-	-	-	8	14	55	54	-	-	-	-	131
MN	Duluth	-	-	-	-	-	14	94	72	-	-	-	-	180
	Minneapolis-St. Paul	-	-	-	-	43	137	278	192	32	-	-	-	682
MS	Jackson	8	6	28	75	224	414	512	493	333	94	19	9	2,215
MO	Kansas City	-	-	-	10	107	253	419	350	131	18	-	-	1,288
	St. Louis	-	-	-	17	145	312	459	391	177	33	-	-	1,534
MT	Great Falls	-	-	-	-	-	54	137	150	47	-	-	-	388
NE	Omaha	-	-	-	5	84	227	369	292	83	12	-	-	1,072
NV	Reno	-	-	-	-	10	79	217	162	40	-	-	-	508
NH	Concord	-	-	-	-	8	46	153	111	10	-	-	-	328
NJ	Atlantic City	-	-	-	-	25	144	301	260	86	10	-	-	826
NM	Albuquerque	-	-	-	7	64	279	419	338	126	11	-	-	1,244
NY	Albany	-	-	-	-	18	91	213	155	30	-	-	-	507
	Buffalo	-	-	-	-	19	86	194	141	37	-	-	-	477
	New York[1]	-	-	-	-	54	203	366	326	130	17	-	-	1,096
NC	Charlotte	-	-	-	15	116	321	443	412	228	47	-	-	1,582
	Raleigh	-	-	6	13	109	279	406	375	192	37	-	-	1,417
ND	Bismarck	-	-	-	-	14	98	183	171	22	-	-	-	488
OH	Cincinnati	-	-	-	-	86	191	313	266	120	20	-	-	996
	Cleveland	-	-	-	-	33	118	218	178	66	8	-	-	621
	Columbus	-	-	-	-	69	149	258	214	96	11	-	-	797
OK	Oklahoma City	-	-	9	38	136	351	527	499	255	44	-	-	1,859
OR	Portland	-	-	-	-	-	46	127	147	51	-	-	-	371
PA	Philadelphia	-	-	-	-	58	209	363	326	128	17	-	-	1,101
	Pittsburgh	-	-	-	-	44	123	227	184	67	9	-	-	654
RI	Providence	-	-	-	-	7	88	239	203	63	6	-	-	606
SC	Columbia	8	-	13	48	201	372	490	456	281	86	11	-	1,966
SD	Sioux Falls	-	-	-	-	35	149	298	220	42	-	-	-	744
TN	Memphis	-	-	14	64	217	423	546	496	286	72	-	-	2,118
	Nashville	-	-	10	19	143	318	443	406	225	52	-	-	1,616
TX	Dallas-Fort Worth	-	5	29	90	246	480	629	617	372	119	11	5	2,603
	El Paso	-	-	10	62	217	462	536	468	282	57	-	-	2,094
	Houston	16	11	50	135	295	462	546	536	396	174	61	18	2,700
UT	Salt Lake City	-	-	-	-	23	174	400	329	114	7	-	-	1,047
VT	Burlington	-	-	-	-	13	64	176	119	16	-	-	-	388
VA	Norfolk	-	-	-	9	85	277	409	378	218	46	-	-	1,422
	Richmond	-	-	-	10	92	270	403	366	173	34	-	-	1,348
WA	Seattle-Tacoma	-	-	-	-	21	64	81	24	-	-	-	-	190
	Spokane	-	-	-	-	-	49	148	161	40	-	-	-	398
WV	Charleston	-	-	-	6	83	202	313	276	125	26	-	-	1,031
WI	Milwaukee	-	-	-	-	16	82	197	160	24	-	-	-	479
WY	Cheyenne	-	-	-	-	-	39	136	87	23	-	-	-	285
PR	San Juan	372	339	403	432	493	519	546	549	525	524	450	406	5,558

- Represents zero. [1] City office data.

Source: U.S. National Oceanic and Atmospheric Administration, *Climatography of the United States*, No. 81.

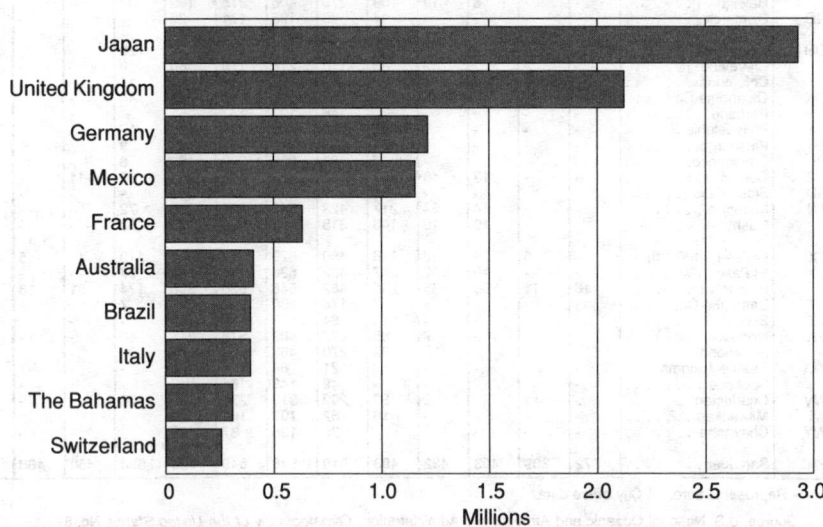

Figure 7.1
Participation in 10 Most Popular Sports Activities, by Sex: 1991

Male
Female

Exercise walking
Swimming
Bicycle riding
Camping
Fishing (fresh water)
Bowling
Exercising with equipment
Basketball
Aerobic exercising
Golf

0   5   10   15   20   25   30   35   40

Percent of the population 7 years old and over

Source: Chart prepared by U.S. Bureau of the Census. For data, see table 412.

Figure 7.2
Foreign Visitors for Pleasure Admitted, by Country of Last Residence—Top 10 Countries: 1991

Japan
United Kingdom
Germany
Mexico
France
Australia
Brazil
Italy
The Bahamas
Switzerland

0   0.5   1.0   1.5   2.0   2.5   3.0

Millions

Source: Chart prepared by U.S. Bureau of the Census. For data, see table 426.

Parks, Recreation, and Travel

This section presents data on national parks and forests, State parks, recreational activities, the arts and humanities, and domestic and foreign travel.

Parks and recreation.—The Department of the Interior has responsibility for administering the national parks. As part of this function, it issues reports relating to the usage of public parks for recreation purposes. The National Park Service publishes information on visits to national park areas in its annual report, *National Park Statistical Abstract. The National Parks: Index (year)* is a biannual report which has appeared under a variety of *Index* titles prior to 1985. Beginning with the 1985 edition, the report has appeared under the current title. The *Index* contains brief descriptions, with acreages, of each area administered by the Service, plus certain "related" areas. A statistical summary of Service-administered areas is also presented. The annual *Federal Recreation Fee Report* summarizes the prior year's recreation fee receipts and recreation visitation statistics for seven Federal land managing agencies.

Statistics for State parks are compiled by the National Association of State Park Directors which issues its annual *Information Exchange.* The Bureau of Land Management, in its *Public Land Statistics,* also issues data on recreational use of its lands. The Department of Agriculture's Forest Service, in its *Report of the Forest Service,* issues data on recreational uses of the national forests.

Visitation.—Data on visitation to reporting areas are collected by several different agencies and groups. The methodology used to collect these results may vary accordingly, from visual counts and estimates to the use of electromagnetic traffic counters. In using and comparing these data, one should also be aware of several different definitions that follow: Recreation visit, which is the entry of any person into an area for recreation purposes; nonrecreation visits, which include visits going to and from inholdings, through traffic, tradespeople and personnel with business in the area; and visitor hour, which constitutes the presence of a person in a recreation

In Brief	
Percent of households in 1991 owning:	
Dogs	37%
Cats	31%
1991 attendance at major league sports:	
Baseball games	57.8 million
Football games	17.8 million
Hockey games	12.3 million

area or site for recreational purposes for periods of time aggregating 60 minutes.

Recreation and leisure activities.—Statistics on the participation in various recreation and leisure time activities are based on several sample surveys. Data on participation in fishing, hunting, and other forms of wildlife-associated recreation are published periodically by the U.S. Department of Interior, Fish and Wildlife Service. The most recent data are from the 1991 survey. Data on participation in various sports recreation activities are published by the National Sporting Goods Association.

Travel.—Information on foreign travel and personal expenditures abroad, as well as expenditures by foreign citizens traveling in the United States, is compiled annually by the U.S. Bureau of Economic Analysis and published in selected issues of the monthly *Survey of Current Business.* Statistics on arrivals to the United States are reported by the U.S. Travel and Tourism Administration (USTTA), in cooperation with the U.S. Immigration and Naturalization Service, and are published in *Summary and Analysis of International Travel to the United States.* Sources of statistics on departures from the United States include USTTA's in-flight survey, the Department of Transportation's *International Air Travel Statistics,* and other sources. Data on domestic travel, business receipts and employment of the travel industry, and travel expenditures are published by the U.S. Travel Data Center, the national nonprofit center for travel and tourism research which is located in Washington, DC. Other data on household transportation characteristics may be found in section 21.

No. 393. Visitation to Federal Recreation Areas, by Administering Federal Agency: 1978 to 1990

[In **millions of visitor hours.** For years ending **September 30,** except as indicated. Covers persons entering and using a recreation area over a specified period of time. For definition of visitor hour, see text, section 7]

ADMINISTERING FEDERAL AGENCY	1978	1980	1982	1983	1984	1985	1986	1987	1988	1989	1990
All areas	**7,094**	**6,367**	**6,640**	**6,668**	**6,252**	**6,403**	**6,858**	**7,332**	**7,419**	**7,475**	**7,620**
Fish and Wildlife Service	84	17	12	63	60	65	67	72	81	45	53
Forest Service	2,622	2,819	2,801	2,733	2,731	2,705	2,718	2,861	2,908	3,030	3,157
U.S. Army Corps of Engineers [1] .	2,071	1,926	1,632	1,638	1,652	1,721	2,068	2,176	2,290	2,296	2,280
National Park Service	1,154	1,042	1,216	1,276	1,240	1,298	1,348	1,394	1,376	1,315	1,322
Bureau of Land Management [2] . .	634	68	341	596	208	246	284	515	461	493	518
Bureau of Reclamation	431	407	558	285	282	289	296	306	294	286	280
Tennessee Valley Authority [3] . .	97	87	80	78	79	79	77	8	9	10	10

[1] Beginning 1986, not comparable with previous years. [2] Data not comparable for all years. [3] Beginning in 1989, the TVA discontinued reporting visitation to nonfee charging areas. Data for 1987 and 1988 have been adjusted to reflect this policy.

Source: 1978 and 1980, U.S. Heritage Conservation and Recreation Service, *Federal Recreation Fee Report,* annual; thereafter, U.S. National Park Service.

No. 394. National Park System—Summary: 1982 to 1990

[For fiscal years ending in year shown, except as noted; see text, section 10. Includes data for five areas in Puerto Rico and Virgin Islands, one area in American Samoa, and one area in Guam. See also *Historical Statistics, Colonial Times to 1970,* series H 806-828]

ITEM	1982	1983	1984	1985	1986	1987	1988	1989	1990
Finances (mil. dol.): [1]									
Expenditures reported	709.7	779.6	843.6	848.1	818.3	909.3	922.9	1,036.8	986.1
Salaries and wages	310.6	343.8	354.6	369.4	372.2	401.5	423.9	441.4	459.1
Improvements, maintenance	98.3	102.4	136.4	127.4	119.6	144.1	154.7	197.5	160.0
Construction	73.0	87.5	93.3	84.7	125.9	102.6	86.3	85.2	108.5
Other	227.8	245.9	259.3	266.6	200.6	261.1	258.0	312.7	258.5
Funds available	1,024.4	1,191.7	1,215.8	1,248.2	1,271.5	1,276.0	1,338.4	1,440.0	1,505.5
Appropriations	715.2	828.9	785.9	821.6	769.3	846.2	874.6	996.7	1,052.5
Other [2]	309.2	362.8	429.9	426.6	502.2	429.8	463.8	443.3	453.0
Revenue from operations	25.5	33.1	36.2	50.6	50.7	70.8	77.2	86.3	78.6
Recreation visits (millions): [3]									
All areas	244.1	243.6	248.6	263.4	281.1	287.2	282.5	269.4	258.7
National parks [4]	49.6	50.0	49.7	50.0	53.5	56.6	56.4	57.4	57.7
National monuments	16.2	16.2	15.8	15.9	21.2	23.5	23.2	23.7	23.9
National historical, commemorative, archaeological [5]	62.3	57.3	63.6	61.9	65.5	68.6	61.2	63.9	57.5
National parkways	36.1	37.7	37.9	40.0	41.6	39.3	42.0	31.2	29.1
National recreation areas [4]	49.7	48.9	45.7	49.4	54.8	56.5	54.5	49.6	47.2
National seashores and lakeshores .	17.2	19.0	21.2	25.3	23.0	21.9	23.2	21.9	23.3
National Capital Parks	5.3	6.3	7.2	8.3	6.9	8.1	9.0	8.9	7.5
Miscellaneous other areas	7.7	8.2	7.5	12.6	14.5	12.7	12.9	12.8	12.5
Recreation overnight stays (millions) [3] .	16.4	15.7	16.0	15.8	16.0	17.1	17.0	17.4	17.6
In commercial lodgings	3.3	3.3	3.5	3.5	3.5	3.7	3.8	3.9	3.9
In Park Service campgrounds	8.8	7.8	7.7	7.3	7.2	8.0	7.9	7.8	7.9
In tents	4.2	3.6	3.7	3.6	3.5	4.0	3.9	3.9	4.1
In recreation vehicles	4.6	4.2	3.9	3.8	3.8	4.0	3.9	3.9	3.8
In backcountry	2.4	2.6	2.0	1.7	1.6	1.6	1.6	1.6	1.7
Other	1.9	2.0	2.8	3.2	3.6	3.8	3.7	4.1	4.2
Land (1,000 acres): [6]									
Total	74,800	74,846	74,913	75,749	75,863	75,970	76,176	76,331	76,362
Parks	45,414	45,427	45,454	45,739	45,791	45,875	45,955	46,081	46,089
Recreation areas	3,313	3,317	3,322	3,335	3,337	3,339	3,339	3,342	3,344
Other	26,073	26,102	26,137	26,675	26,735	26,756	26,882	26,907	26,929
Acquisition, gross	40	50	44	34	177	134	38	73	21
By purchase	37	43	42	29	69	27	37	14	18
By gift	3	1	(Z)	2	20	(Z)	(Z)	58	2
By transfer or exchange	(Z)	6	2	3	88	107	1	1	3
Exclusion	(Z)	2	2	(Z)	4	(Z)	(Z)	1	1
Acquisition, net	40	48	42	34	173	134	38	71	21

Z Less than 500 acres. [1] Financial data are those associated with the National Park System. Certain other functions of the National Park Service (principally the activities absorbed from the former Heritage Conservation and Recreation Service in 1981) are excluded. [2] Includes funds carried over from prior years. [3] For calendar year. [4] Combined data for North Cascades National Park and two adjacent National Recreation Areas are included in National Parks total. [5] Includes military areas. [6] Federal land only, as of Dec. 31. Federal land acreages, in addition to National Park Service administered lands, also include lands within national park system area boundaries but under the administration of other agencies. Year-to-year changes in the federal lands figures include changes in the acreages of these other lands and hence often differ from "net acquisition."

Source: U.S. National Park Service, Visits, *National Park Statistical Abstract,* annual; and unpublished data. Other data are unpublished.

No. 395. National Forest Recreation Use—Summary, 1980 to 1991, and by Activity and States and Other Areas, 1991

[For year ending September 30. Estimated. Represents recreational use of National Forest land and water in States which have a Forest Service recreation program. See also *Historical Statistics, Colonial Times to 1970*, series H 829-835]

YEAR AND ACTIVITY	Recreation visitor-days [1] (1,000)	Per-cent	STATE	Recreation visitor-days [1] 1991 (1,000)	STATE OR OTHER AREA	Recreation visitor-days [1] 1991 (1,000)
1980	233,549	100.0	U.S.	278,849	NV	3,283
1981	235,709	100.0			NH	4,014
1982	233,438	100.0	AL	677	NM	8,065
1983	227,708	100.0	AK	5,718	NY	45
1984	227,554	100.0	AZ	21,549	NC	5,692
1985	225,407	100.0	AR	2,109	ND	199
1986	226,533	100.0	CA	65,221	OH	522
1987	238,458	100.0	CO	25,998	OK	373
1988	242,316	100.0	FL	3,081	OR	21,037
1989	252,495	100.0	GA	2,839	PA	2,977
1990	263,051	100.0	ID	12,909	SC	943
			IL	843	SD	3,095
1991, total	278,849	100.0	IN	594	TN	2,924
			KS	66	TX	2,253
Mechanized travel and viewing scenery	95,940	34.4	KY	2,112	UT	13,337
Camping, picnicking and swimming	76,615	27.5	LA	486	VT	1,571
Hiking, horseback riding and water travel	25,828	9.3	MA	61	VA	4,173
Winter sports	17,852	6.4	MI	8,153	WA	22,458
Hunting	16,284	5.8	MN	4,956	WV	1,340
Resorts, cabins and organization camps	16,249	5.8	MS	1,285	WI	2,215
Fishing	15,322	5.5	MO	1,742	WY	6,914
Nature studies	2,246	0.8	MT	10,595	PR	280
Other [2]	12,514	4.5	NE	147		

[1] One recreation visitor-day is the recreation use of National Forest land or water that aggregates 12 visitor-hours. This may entail 1 person for 12 hours, 12 persons for 1 hour, or any equivalent combination of individual or group use, either continuous or intermittent. [2] Includes team sports, gathering forest products, attending talks and programs, and other uses.

Source: U.S. Forest Service, unpublished data.

No. 396. Recreational Use of Public Lands Administered by Bureau of Land Management, 1982 to 1991, and by State, 1991

[In thousands. For year ending Sept. 30. Beginning 1987, increase due to an estimated longer length of stay per visit, especially in California. See text, section 7]

YEAR AND STATE	Number of visits	Total	TYPE OF RECREATION USE (visitor hours)									Snow- and ice-based recreational activity, winter sports
			Land-based recreation activities						Water-based recreation activities			
			Motorized travel			Site based						
			Off-highway vehicle travel	Other motorized travel	Non-motorized travel	Camping	Hunting	Other	Fishing	Boating	Other	
1982	58,135	316,959	19,471	32,646	11,237	63,928	108,996	44,587	19,287	10,101	1,043	5,663
1983	56,270	334,010	24,397	35,534	12,237	84,066	92,974	39,734	20,290	16,869	4,992	2,917
1984	59,228	271,373	21,348	25,433	9,579	73,032	73,898	37,650	14,263	11,184	2,092	2,894
1985	51,739	244,612	36,995	24,053	10,047	65,397	51,842	23,098	14,254	11,710	2,193	5,023
1986	54,253	284,142	49,688	25,866	14,397	95,196	35,570	19,331	18,227	15,891	3,951	6,025
1987	56,427	514,716	123,325	34,325	19,172	195,315	57,624	38,412	22,932	15,140	5,212	3,259
1988	57,460	492,756	122,014	35,748	19,761	178,703	55,285	38,340	21,617	13,294	4,979	3,015
1989	60,957	493,214	65,808	74,075	36,676	173,597	46,760	45,871	23,392	18,491	5,425	3,119
1990	71,820	523,753	63,016	83,445	41,316	165,366	47,053	57,958	28,664	20,806	8,313	7,816
1991, total	72,541	539,779	50,849	85,835	44,398	196,310	49,593	59,928	20,939	19,676	8,353	3,898
AK	224	5,649	53	375	91	3,976	384	157	335	179	4	95
AZ [1]	10,413	68,374	720	474	2,563	42,669	2,679	10,430	895	5,704	2,239	1
CA	29,105	252,566	35,085	48,688	25,378	93,007	12,677	28,565	3,261	3,074	2,567	264
CO	2,901	24,078	1,271	5,114	922	4,991	7,020	1,492	1,403	1,536	52	277
ID	2,446	18,129	1,041	1,274	598	5,208	2,771	1,539	2,100	1,384	536	1,678
MT [2]	2,300	12,967	1,923	1,641	495	3,168	2,796	375	1,744	456	55	314
NV	1,901	23,436	3,048	5,035	2,603	5,147	2,972	2,501	1,636	225	165	104
NM	2,758	20,088	2,561	1,390	1,285	3,642	5,671	3,808	967	696	65	3
OR [3]	14,421	61,679	1,436	11,900	5,593	17,782	4,894	6,724	7,029	3,467	2,183	671
UT	4,820	42,766	3,363	8,889	4,582	14,812	4,663	2,848	397	2,657	436	119
WY	1,252	10,047	348	1,055	288	1,908	3,066	1,489	1,172	298	51	372

[1] Includes concession visitation data. [2] Includes North Dakota and South Dakota. [3] Includes Washington.

Source: U.S. Bureau of Land Management, *Public Land Statistics*, annual.

No. 397. State Parks and Recreation Areas—States: 1991

[For year ending June 30. Data are shown as reported by State park directors. In some States, park agency has under its control forests, fish and wildlife areas, and/or other areas. In other States, agency is responsible for State parks only]

DIVISION AND STATE	Acreage (1,000)	VISITORS (1,000)		REVENUE		DIVISION AND STATE	Acreage (1,000)	VISITORS (1,000)		REVENUE	
		Total [1]	Day	Total ($1,000)	Percent of operating budget			Total [1]	Day	Total ($1,000)	Percent of operating budget
U.S. . . .	11,148	736,897	680,398	454,248	41.5	WV. . . .	202	8,278	7,577	12,973	58.6
						NC	134	9,463	9,221	1,700	16.0
N.E:						SC	80	7,970	7,001	10,587	61.4
ME. . . .	75	2,448	2,211	1,310	31.4	GA	57	16,262	15,595	14,811	39.7
NH	31	2,815	2,655	4,000	125.0	FL	444	13,087	12,063	16,248	41.3
VT	90	982	586	4,402	95.0	E.S.C:					
MA	273	11,975	11,206	10,408	60.5	KY	42	27,272	26,207	37,668	69.1
RI.	9	5,075	4,759	2,854	47.1	TN	133	26,974	25,814	19,737	53.9
CT	172	6,743	6,392	3,327	32.2	AL	50	6,084	4,985	22,505	80.7
M.A:						MS	23	3,912	3,168	4,796	44.3
NY	260	60,744	58,208	32,914	30.1	W.S.C:					
NJ	303	10,945	10,492	6,514	23.8	AR	47	6,949	6,312	11,227	59.5
PA	277	36,311	34,585	7,150	13.2	LA	39	1,107	788	1,860	30.5
E.N.C:						OK	77	16,031	14,221	15,320	47.4
OH	208	67,222	64,730	12,082	26.9	TX	499	23,957	21,515	12,722	37.0
IN.	57	10,536	8,600	9,011	74.2	Mt:					
IL.	405	34,594	33,819	3,058	9.7	MT	32	1,652	1,099	1,022	43.9
MI	264	25,260	19,868	21,383	79.3	ID.	42	2,500	2,193	1,651	36.6
WI	139	12,252	10,787	5,221	40.8	WY	120	2,018	662	247	7.9
W.N.C:						CO	307	8,653	8,148	10,854	108.0
MN	231	7,981	7,124	7,117	40.2	NM	123	4,251	1,700	2,657	29.3
IA.	82	12,111	11,736	1,571	21.0	AZ	42	2,236	1,891	2,073	35.1
MO. . . .	117	14,998	13,919	3,780	21.0	UT	97	4,940	4,495	2,970	24.3
ND	19	954	809	813	50.7	NV	142	2,563	2,402	756	16.4
SD	92	5,894	5,545	3,810	62.4	Pac:					
NE	142	9,215	7,754	7,550	92.2	WA	241	46,813	44,487	6,292	25.0
KS	30	4,117	2,470	2,426	32.3	OR	90	39,479	37,288	7,682	30.5
S.A:						CA	1,314	70,444	64,467	70,211	43.9
DE	13	3,212	2,961	3,889	48.1	AK	3,169	6,815	6,110	853	16.5
MD	226	7,828	7,293	6,320	27.4	HI.	25	19,112	19,023	1,231	17.7
VA	59	3,862	3,456	2,686	28.5						

[1] Includes overnight visitors.

Source: National Association of State Park Directors, Tallahassee, FL, *1992 Annual Information Exchange.*

No. 398. Personal Consumption Expenditures for Recreation in Constant (1987) Dollars: 1970 to 1991

[In billions of dollars, except percent. Represents market value of purchases of goods and services by individuals and nonprofit institutions]

TYPE OF PRODUCT OR SERVICE	1970	1980	1985	1986	1987	1988	1989	1990	1991
Total recreation expenditures.	91.3	149.1	195.5	208.4	223.7	240.0	250.9	257.3	258.7
Percent of total personal consumption [1]	5.0	6.1	6.8	7.0	7.3	7.6	7.8	7.9	8.0
Books and maps	10.5	10.2	11.4	11.7	13.0	14.1	14.7	15.2	15.4
Magazines, newspapers, and sheet music	13.2	18.4	17.9	18.0	18.8	19.9	20.3	21.2	20.3
Nondurable toys and sport supplies.	9.5	17.4	22.3	23.6	25.5	26.2	27.5	28.1	28.4
Wheel goods, sports and photographic equipment [2] . .	10.3	20.2	24.4	26.3	28.3	28.9	29.0	27.7	26.4
Video and audio products, computer equipment, and musical instruments.	8.8	17.6	29.7	35.4	39.0	45.5	49.2	53.2	56.2
Radio and television repair.	2.7	3.5	3.3	3.2	3.3	3.4	3.4	3.4	3.5
Flowers, seeds, and potted plants.	4.0	5.9	7.0	7.6	8.5	9.2	9.7	10.0	9.3
Admissions to specified spectator amusements	8.2	9.9	10.2	10.1	10.2	10.5	10.6	11.0	10.4
Motion picture theaters.	4.2	3.8	3.6	3.6	3.5	3.4	3.4	3.2	2.9
Legitimate theaters and opera, and entertainments of nonprofit institutions [3].	1.3	2.7	2.9	3.0	3.2	3.4	3.5	4.1	3.7
Spectator sports [4]	2.8	3.4	3.7	3.6	3.5	3.7	3.7	3.7	3.8
Clubs and fraternal organizations except insurance [5] . . .	3.8	4.0	6.3	6.6	7.0	7.2	7.4	7.7	7.6
Commercial participant amusements [6]	6.3	12.5	16.1	16.4	17.3	18.5	19.0	19.3	19.0
Pari-mutuel net receipts.	2.8	3.6	3.2	3.2	3.3	3.2	3.1	3.2	3.4
Other [7].	11.3	25.8	43.5	46.3	49.3	53.4	57.1	57.3	59.0

[1] See table 699.　[2] Includes boats and pleasure aircraft.　[3] Except athletic.　[4] Consists of admissions to professional and amateur athletic events and to racetracks, including horse, dog, and auto.　[5] Consists of dues and fees excluding insurance premiums.　[6] Consists of billiard parlors; bowling alleys; dancing, riding, shooting, skating, and swimming places; amusement devices and parks; golf courses; sightseeing buses and guides; private flying operations; casino gambling and other commercial participant amusements.　[7] Consists of net receipts of lotteries and expenditures for purchases of pets and pet care services, cable TV, film processing, photographic studios, sporting and recreation camps, video cassette rentals, and recreational services, not elsewhere classified.

Source: U.S. Bureau of Economic Analysis, *The National Income and Product Accounts of the United States: Volume 2, 1959-88,* and *Survey of Current Business,* July issues.

No. 399. Average Annual Expenditures per Consumer Unit for Entertainment and Reading, 1984 to 1991, and by Selected Characteristics, 1991

[In dollars, except as indicated. Based on Consumer Expenditure Survey; see text, section 14, for description of survey. See also headnote, table 709. For composition of regions, see table 31]

YEAR AND CHARACTERISTIC	ENTERTAINMENT AND READING		ENTERTAINMENT				Reading
	Total	Percent of total expenditures	Total	Fees and admissions	Television, radios, and sound equipment	Other equipment and services [1]	
1984.	1,187	5.4	1,055	313	322	420	132
1985.	1,311	5.6	1,170	320	371	479	141
1986.	1,289	5.4	1,149	308	371	470	140
1987.	1,335	5.5	1,193	323	379	491	142
1988.	1,479	5.7	1,329	353	416	560	150
1989.	1,581	5.7	1,424	377	429	618	157
1990.	1,575	5.6	1,422	371	454	597	153
1991, total.	**1,635**	**5.5**	**1,472**	**378**	**468**	**627**	**163**
Age of reference person:							
Under 25 years old.	978	5.8	906	233	393	280	72
25 to 34 years old	1,770	6.0	1,630	340	499	791	140
35 to 44 years old	1,965	5.4	1,776	503	577	696	189
45 to 54 years old	2,188	5.7	1,990	516	633	840	198
55 to 64 years old	1,916	6.0	1,718	404	442	871	198
65 to 74 years old	1,006	4.5	841	257	296	288	165
75 years old and over.	560	3.5	444	163	172	110	116
Region of residence: Northeast.	1,658	5.3	1,470	417	458	595	188
Midwest.	1,611	5.8	1,449	348	474	627	162
South.	1,424	5.1	1,286	328	444	513	138
West.	1,988	6.0	1,809	456	510	844	179
Size of consumer unit: One person.	980	5.6	866	227	313	327	114
Two persons.	1,887	5.5	1,705	436	527	741	182
Two or more persons	1,761	5.7	1,576	409	449	718	185
Three persons	1,799	5.2	1,623	376	556	691	176
Four persons	2,141	5.5	1,952	525	616	811	189
Five persons or more.	2,047	5.3	1,874	487	593	795	173
Income before taxes:							
Total complete reporting [2]	1,691	5.5	1,523	384	476	663	168
Quintiles of income:							
Lowest 20 percent.	656	4.9	586	125	225	237	70
Second 20 percent.	838	4.4	732	161	312	258	106
Third 20.	1,366	5.2	1,214	272	431	510	152
Fourth 20.	2,079	5.8	1,876	433	546	898	203
Highest 20.	3,514	6.1	3,205	930	866	1,409	309
Incomplete reporting of income.	1,317	5.3	1,184	338	419	427	133

[1] Other equipment and services includes pets, toys, and playground equipment, and sports, exercise, and photographic equipment.   [2] Income values derived from "complete income reporters" only. Represents the combined income of all consumer unit members 14 years or over during the 12 months preceding the interview. A complete reporter is a consumer unit providing values for at least one of the major sources of income.

Source: U.S. Bureau of Labor Statistics, *Consumer Expenditure Survey*, annual.

No. 400. Quantity of Books Sold and Value of U.S. Domestic Consumer Expenditures, by Type of Publication and Market Area: 1982 to 1991

[Includes all titles released by publishers in the United States and imports which appear under the imprints of American publishers. Multi-volume sets, such as encyclopedias, are counted as one unit]

TYPE OF PUBLICATION AND MARKET AREA	UNITS SOLD (mil.)						CONSUMER EXPENDITURES (mil. dol.)					
	1982	1985	1988	1989	1990	1991	1982	1985	1988	1989	1990	1991
Total [1]	**1,723**	**1,788**	**1,871**	**2,003**	**2,005**	**2,041**	**9,889**	**12,611**	**16,111**	**18,036**	**19,043**	**20,102**
Hardbound, total.	646	694	757	826	824	838	6,190	7,969	10,055	11,243	11,789	12,392
Softbound, total	1,077	1,094	1,114	1,177	1,181	1,203	3,699	4,642	6,056	6,793	7,254	7,709
Trade	459	553	610	685	705	738	2,484	3,660	5,070	6,040	6,498	7,102
Adult	315	360	365	404	403	412	2,028	2,871	3,806	4,520	4,777	5,141
Juvenile	144	193	244	281	301	326	456	789	1,264	1,520	1,721	1,961
Religious	144	134	121	124	130	135	706	926	1,168	1,274	1,362	1,478
Professional	106	110	125	128	131	130	1,630	2,043	2,573	2,769	2,957	3,060
Bookclubs	133	130	112	109	108	109	510	582	671	684	705	729
Elhi text.	233	234	202	213	209	206	1,067	1,415	1,716	1,909	1,948	1,974
College text.	115	110	130	136	137	133	1,388	1,575	1,998	2,144	2,319	2,331
Mail order publications	134	121	138	152	138	132	581	650	720	822	752	755
Mass market paperbacks-rack sized.	382	382	419	441	433	443	1,102	1,244	1,556	1,693	1,775	1,928
General retailers.	756	829	914	994	1,010	1,052	3,743	5,103	6,875	7,914	8,465	9,198
College stores	224	225	243	253	255	253	1,910	2,309	2,904	3,164	3,403	3,501
Libraries and institutions [2]	80	80	82	87	88	90	888	1,090	1,361	1,500	1,592	1,664
Schools [2]	262	260	233	246	244	242	1,313	1,685	2,065	2,290	2,365	2,426
Direct to consumers	319	300	302	316	304	303	1,889	2,214	2,638	2,859	2,901	2,983
Other	82	94	97	108	104	101	146	210	267	309	316	329

[1] Types of publications include university press publications and subscription reference works, not shown separately.   [2] Elhi libraries included in schools.

Source: Book Industry Study Group, Inc., New York, NY, *Book Industry Trends*, annual, (copyright) and *Trend Update*, vol. 1, No. 1, September 1992, (copyright).

No. 401. Adult Book Purchasing: 1991 and 1992

[**In percent.** Excludes books purchased for or by children under 13. Based on a survey of 16,000 households conducted over 12 months ending in March of year shown. For details, see source]

CHARACTERISTIC	TOTAL		MASS MARKET [1]		TRADE [2]		HARDCOVER	
	1991	1992	1991	1992	1991	1992	1991	1992
Total	100.0	100.0	100.0	100.0	100.0	100.0	100.0	100.0
Age of purchaser:								
Under 25 years old	6.0	4.1	4.7	3.6	8.2	4.8	5.7	4.1
25 to 34 years old	18.6	18.8	14.7	13.9	23.5	25.5	19.9	19.2
35 to 44 years old	27.4	23.9	26.3	22.4	29.9	26.3	26.4	23.7
45 to 54 years old	22.4	21.9	25.8	25.7	17.9	17.2	21.3	20.9
55 to 64 years old	12.8	15.9	13.2	15.9	11.1	14.5	14.4	17.4
65 years old and over	12.8	15.4	15.3	18.5	9.4	11.7	12.3	14.7
Education of male household head:								
Not a high school graduate	8.4	8.2	11.6	11.6	5.3	5.0	6.4	6.2
High school graduate	52.9	52.4	59.7	60.3	45.1	44.2	50.6	49.4
College graduate	19.3	19.5	16.0	15.7	22.6	24.3	21.1	20.1
Post college	19.4	19.9	12.7	12.4	27.0	26.5	21.9	24.3
Occupation of male household head:								
Professional	41.9	41.1	34.5	33.9	50.8	48.6	44.1	43.8
Other white collar	6.3	5.8	5.3	4.6	7.0	6.7	7.2	6.7
Blue collar	25.7	19.7	25.5	24.1	17.2	16.3	18.7	16.4
Retired/unemployed	22.2	25.1	26.4	28.2	17.1	21.3	20.9	24.8
Other	3.9	8.3	8.3	9.2	7.9	7.1	9.1	8.3
Household income:								
Under $30,000	35.4	37.1	39.5	42.3	30.8	32.4	38.3	33.8
$30,000 to 49,999	26.8	27.7	26.9	27.6	27.1	27.9	26.3	27.5
$50,000 to 59,999	12.4	10.8	11.7	9.2	13.7	12.8	12.1	11.0
$60,000 to 69,999	7.1	6.9	6.9	7.2	7.6	7.4	6.8	6.0
$70,000 and over	18.3	17.5	15.0	13.7	20.8	19.5	21.5	21.7
Household size:								
Singles	16.6	21.2	15.2	17.7	17.6	24.6	18.1	23.3
Families with no children	38.9	39.5	38.9	42.6	38.1	35.8	39.8	38.3
Families with children............	44.5	39.3	45.9	39.7	44.3	39.6	42.1	38.4
Age of reader:								
Under 25 years old	9.0	7.2	6.4	5.0	13.1	10.1	8.8	7.2
25 to 34 years old	19.3	18.8	14.7	13.9	24.3	24.8	21.2	19.5
35 to 44 years old	25.7	22.9	25.4	22.0	27.6	24.5	24.5	22.6
45 to 54 years old	20.8	20.4	24.9	24.6	16.2	15.6	19.1	18.9
55 to 64 years old	12.1	15.1	13.0	15.8	9.4	13.2	13.4	16.3
65 years old and over	13.1	15.6	15.6	18.7	9.4	11.8	13.0	15.5
Category of book:								
Popular fiction	54.9	54.1	91.3	93.3	15.5	16.0	34.2	32.0
General non-fiction	10.2	10.4	5.0	3.5	15.7	15.4	13.5	16.4
Cooking/crafts	10.5	10.8	0.6	0.4	19.2	20.2	18.4	17.7
Other	24.4	24.7	3.1	2.8	49.6	48.4	33.9	33.9
Sales outlet:								
Independent	28.1	30.5	20.8	25.8	40.2	39.3	26.9	28.3
Chain book store	26.4	26.1	23.0	18.9	33.0	35.5	25.2	27.3
Book clubs	16.1	15.3	15.7	17.3	8.8	8.0	25.4	20.7
Other [3]	29.4	28.1	40.5	38.0	18.0	17.2	22.5	23.7

[1] "Pocket size" books sold primarily through magazine and news outlets, supermarkets, variety stores, etc. [2] All paperbound books, except mass market. [3] Includes mail order, price clubs, discount stores, food/drug stores, used book stores, and other outlets.

Source: Book Industry Study Group, Inc., New York, NY, *1991-1992 Consumer Research Study on Book Purchasing,* (copyright).

No. 402. New Books and Editions Published and Imports, by Subject: 1980 to 1991

[Covers listings in Bowker's Weekly Record in year shown, plus titles issued in that year which were listed in following 6 months. Comprises new books (published for first time) and new editions (with changes in text or format). Excludes government publications; books sold only by subscription; dissertations; periodicals and quarterlies; and pamphlets under 49 pages. See also *Historical Statistics, Colonial Times to 1970*, series R 191-216]

SUBJECT	NEW BOOKS AND NEW EDITIONS						IMPORTS					
	1980	1985	1988	1989	1990	1991	1980	1985	1988	1989	1990	1991
Total	42,377	[1]50,070	55,483	53,446	46,738	48,146	5,390	7,304	8,722	7,315	6,414	5,867
Agriculture	461	536	666	562	514	523	104	118	129	104	86	81
Art	1,691	1,545	1,602	1,569	1,262	1,283	157	166	154	128	94	101
Biography	1,891	1,953	2,250	2,193	1,957	2,120	126	216	190	144	115	124
Business	1,185	1,518	1,647	1,569	1,191	1,421	74	196	194	152	134	140
Education	1,011	1,085	1,113	1,054	1,039	1,129	133	211	239	233	234	176
Fiction.	2,835	5,105	5,564	5,941	5,764	5,424	71	171	287	119	166	250
General works	1,643	2,905	2,475	2,332	1,760	1,886	132	329	372	322	266	252
History	2,220	2,327	3,260	2,563	2,243	2,331	296	395	509	376	329	314
Home economics	879	1,228	1,057	949	758	789	40	41	36	31	19	23
Juvenile.	2,859	3,801	4,954	5,413	5,172	5,111	58	92	104	101	103	69
Language	529	632	628	586	649	566	134	216	206	182	202	171
Law	1,102	1,349	1,343	1,096	896	1,177	112	170	191	156	138	171
Literature.	1,686	1,964	2,272	2,298	2,049	2,087	183	267	330	275	242	196
Medicine	3,292	3,579	3,900	3,447	3,014	3,027	671	598	779	712	588	447
Music	357	364	329	375	289	300	35	70	74	78	52	71
Philosophy, psychology .	1,429	1,559	1,955	2,058	1,683	1,766	218	267	275	348	284	256
Poetry and drama	1,179	1,166	1,270	1,128	874	890	120	220	224	147	119	115
Religion	2,055	2,564	2,746	2,586	2,285	2,389	94	173	162	173	176	129
Science	3,109	3,304	3,743	3,288	2,742	2,710	1,069	1,242	1,396	1,187	1,030	795
Sociology, economics . .	7,152	7,441	8,247	7,971	7,042	7,241	1,050	1,559	1,825	1,575	1,368	1,278
Sports, recreation	971	1,154	1,099	1,077	973	1,063	85	107	97	94	75	93
Technology	2,337	2,526	2,694	2,690	2,092	2,421	373	419	897	638	546	558
Travel	504	465	669	701	495	492	55	61	52	39	48	57

[1] Increase is due largely to a major improvement in the recording of paperbound books.

Source: R. R. Bowker Co., New York, NY, *Publishers Weekly*. (Copyright by Reed Publishing.)

No. 403. Average (Mean) Retail Prices—Books, 1980 to 1991, and Periodicals, 1980 to 1992

[See headnote, table 402. For definition of mean, see Guide to Tabular Presentation]

SUBJECT	BOOKS (per vol.)				SUBJECT	PERIODICALS [3]			
	1980	1985	1990	1991, prel.		1980	1985	1990	1992
Hardcover [1]	24.64	31.46	42.12	43.52	**Total.**	34.54	59.70	93.45	117.11
Agriculture	27.55	36.77	54.24	58.97	Agriculture	15.24	26.05	42.43	49.48
Art.	27.70	35.15	42.18	44.85	Business and economics. . . .	25.42	44.41	63.25	78.09
Biography.	19.77	22.20	29.58	27.54	Chemistry and physics . . .	137.45	238.43	412.66	549.50
Business.	22.45	28.84	45.48	43.14	Children's periodicals	7.85	13.31	17.51	19.48
Education.	17.01	27.28	38.72	41.05	Education.	23.45	37.81	56.33	67.42
Fiction	12.46	15.29	19.83	21.88	Engineering	49.15	84.38	138.84	192.77
General works	29.84	37.91	54.77	50.37	Fine and applied arts	18.67	27.03	36.89	41.15
History	22.78	27.02	36.43	39.76	History	15.77	25.55	35.51	43.27
Home economics	13.31	17.50	23.80	24.30	Home economics	24.63	41.04	64.49	75.13
Juvenile.	8.16	9.95	13.01	16.64	Industrial arts	20.70	35.09	54.69	69.47
Language	22.16	28.68	42.98	52.18	Journalism, communications . .	27.34	46.08	60.85	68.68
Law	33.25	41.70	60.78	59.73	Labor and industrial relations. .	18.84	34.75	52.74	66.69
Literature	18.70	24.53	35.80	35.86	Law.	23.00	35.15	50.32	60.53
Medicine.	34.28	44.36	72.24	70.43					
Music.	21.79	28.79	41.86	40.72	Library and information science.	23.25	40.66	57.34	59.42
Philosophy, psychology. .	21.70	28.11	40.58	42.68	Literature and languages. . .	15.30	24.18	30.63	35.77
Poetry and drama.	17.85	22.14	32.19	32.37	Mathematics, botany, geology,				
Religion	17.61	19.13	31.31	32.97	and general science	67.54	116.93	188.19	235.26
Science	37.45	51.19	74.39	79.73	Medicine	73.37	137.92	217.87	276.01
Sociology, economics . . .	31.76	33.33	42.10	47.86	Philosophy and religion. . . .	14.73	24.30	30.76	35.96
Sports, recreation.	15.92	23.43	30.52	31.44	Physical education and				
Technology.	33.64	50.37	76.80	74.89	recreation	13.83	23.72	32.20	35.81
Travel	16.80	24.66	30.41	32.08	Political science.	19.30	32.72	49.67	56.93
					Psychology.	41.95	76.34	125.31	145.22
Paperbacks:					Sociology and anthropology. . .	27.56	50.87	77.61	91.19
Mass market [2]	(NA)	3.63	4.57	4.85	Zoology	44.58	90.75	153.78	197.89
Trade or other	8.60	13.98	17.45	18.05	General interest periodicals . . .	19.87	26.41	31.24	34.56

NA Not available. [1] Excludes publications of the United States and other governmental units, books sold only by subscription, and dissertations. [2] "Pocket-sized" books sold primarily through magazine and news outlets, supermarkets, variety stores, etc. [3] Average annual subscription prices.

Source: R. R. Bowker Co., New York, NY. Books, *Publishers Weekly*, March 1992; *Bowker Annual: Library and Book Trade Almanac*; Periodicals, *Library Journal*, April 15, 1992, and earlier issues. (Copyright by Reed Publishing.)

No. 404. Phonograph Records and Other Recording Media—Manufacturers' Shipments and Value: 1975 to 1991

[Domestic shipments based on reports of manufacturers representing more than 85 percent of the market. Domestic value data based on list prices of records and other media]

TYPE OF MEDIA	UNIT SHIPMENTS [1] (mil.)					MANUFACTUERS' VALUE (mil. dol.)				
	1975	1980	1985	1990	1991	1975	1980	1985	1990	1991
Total	531.8	683.7	652.9	865.7	801.0	2,378.3	3,862.4	4,387.8	7,541.1	7,834.2
Phonograph records . . .	421.0	487.1	287.7	39.3	26.8	1,696.5	2,559.6	1,561.5	180.9	93.3
Long-playing albums [2]	257.0	322.8	167.0	11.7	4.8	1,485.0	2,290.3	1,280.5	86.5	29.4
Singles	164.0	164.3	120.7	27.6	22.0	211.5	269.3	281.0	94.4	63.9
Pre-recorded	110.8	196.6	342.6	529.6	429.1	681.8	1,302.8	2,436.8	3,730.3	3,250.0
8-track cartridges	94.6	86.4	3.5	-	-	583.0	526.4	25.3	(X)	(X)
Cassettes	16.2	110.2	339.1	442.2	360.1	98.8	776.4	2,411.5	3,472.4	3,019.6
Cassette singles	(X)	(X)	(X)	87.4	69.0	(X)	(X)	(X)	257.9	230.4
Compact disks (CD's) . . .	(X)	(X)	22.6	286.5	333.3	(X)	(X)	389.5	3,451.6	4,337.7
CD singles	(X)	(X)	(X)	1.1	5.7	(X)	(X)	(X)	6.0	35.1
Music video	(X)	(X)	(X)	9.2	6.1	(X)	(X)	(X)	172.3	118.1

- Rounds to zero. X Not applicable. [1] Units net after returns. [2] Includes extended play albums.
Source: Recording Industry Association of America, Inc., Washington, DC, *Inside the Recording Industry: A Statistical Overview: 1991*, and earlier issues.

No. 405. Household Participation in Lawn and Garden Activities—Summary: 1985 to 1991

[Based on national household sample survey conducted by the Gallup Organization. Subject to sampling variability; see source]

ACTIVITY	PERCENT HOUSEHOLDS ENGAGED IN—					RETAIL SALES (mil. dol.)				
	1985	1988	1989	1990	1991	1985	1988	1989	1990	1991
Total	(X)	(X)	(X)	(X)	(X)	12,026	15,518	16,285	20,802	22,134
Lawn care.	64	58	57	66	62	3,898	5,342	5,660	6,412	6,890
Indoor houseplants.	42	41	37	43	42	706	819	822	928	852
Flower gardening	41	42	41	48	41	1,259	1,679	1,857	2,275	2,302
Insect control	27	32	29	39	35	653	880	1,052	1,370	1,260
Shrub care	30	34	29	38	32	699	853	844	1,099	1,030
Vegetable gardening.	37	34	32	37	31	950	982	1,026	1,384	1,652
Tree care	20	23	23	31	27	795	1,140	886	1,445	1,443
Landscaping	23	22	22	31	26	2,125	2,356	2,605	3,837	4,828
Flower bulbs	19	24	23	31	26	275	396	478	579	520
Fruit trees.	17	16	14	19	15	271	416	287	502	371
Container gardening	(NA)	11	11	15	13	(NA)	235	240	359	330
Raising transplants [1]	11	11	11	15	12	208	122	139	181	141
Herb gardening	(NA)	5	7	9	9	(NA)	50	58	84	161
Growing berries	7	8	7	9	7	41	57	73	79	90
Ornamental gardening.	7	6	5	7	7	146	191	266	268	264

NA Not available. X Not applicable. [1] Starting plants in advance of planting in ground.
Source: The National Gardening Association, Burlington, VT, *National Gardening Survey*, annual, (copyright).

No. 406. Household Pet Ownership 1983 to 1991, and by Selected Characteristic: 1991

[Based on a sample survey of 80,000 households in 1991, 40,000 households in 1987, and 20,000 in 1983; for details, see source]

ITEM	Unit	Dog	Cat	Pet bird	Horse
1983: Households owning companion pets [1] . . .	Million	36.1	24.2	4.2	2.4
Percent of all households	Percent . . .	42.5	28.4	5.0	2.8
1987: Households owning companion pets [1] . . .	Million	34.7	27.7	5.2	2.6
Percent of all households	Percent . . .	38.2	30.5	5.7	2.8
1991: Households owning companion pets [1] . . .	Million	34.6	29.2	5.4	1.9
Percent of all households	Percent . . .	36.5	30.9	5.7	2.0
Average number owned.	Number . . .	1.5	2.0	2.2	2.5
Total companion pet population [1]	Million . . .	52.5	57.0	11.7	4.9
Households obtaining veterinary care [2]	Percent . . .	82	62	11	54
Average visits per year.	Number . . .	2.6	1.8	0.2	2.4
Average annual cost	Dollars . . .	131.84	79.75	7.60	163.23
Total expenditures.	Mil. dol. . . .	4,557	2,330	185	314
PERCENT DISTRIBUTION OF HOUSEHOLDS OWNING PETS					
Annual household income: Under $12,500	Percent . . .	14	15	16	9
$12,500 to $24,999	Percent . . .	20	20	21	21
$25,000 to $39,999	Percent . . .	24	23	24	25
$40,000 to $59,999	Percent . . .	22	22	21	22
$60,000 and over	Percent . . .	20	20	18	23
Family size: [1] One person	Percent . . .	14	18	16	10
Two persons	Percent . . .	32	33	27	34
Three persons	Percent . . .	21	20	20	20
Four or more persons	Percent . . .	33	29	37	36

[1] As of December for 1987 and 1991; as of May for 1983. [2] During 1991.
Source: American Veterinary Medical Association, Schaumburg, IL, *U.S. Pet Ownership and Demographics Sourcebook, 1993*, (copyright).

No. 407. Sport Fishing and Hunting Licenses—Number and Cost: 1970 to 1991

[In millions, except as indicated. For fiscal years ending in year shown; see text, section 9. See also *Historical Statistics, Colonial Times to 1970*, series H 875-876]

ITEM	1970	1975	1980	1984	1985	1986	1987	1988	1989	1990	1991
Fishing licenses: Sales	31.1	34.7	35.2	36.1	35.7	35.9	36.5	36.8	36.6	37.0	37.0
Resident	26.8	30.0	30.1	31.0	30.5	30.4	31.0	31.3	31.0	31.0	31.1
Nonresident	4.3	4.7	5.1	5.1	5.2	5.4	5.6	5.5	5.6	6.0	5.9
Paid license holders [1]	24.4	27.5	28.0	29.0	29.7	30.4	30.3	31.4	30.3	30.7	30.7
Cost to anglers (mil. dol.) . . .	91	142	196	260	282	302	315	330	341	363	375
Hunting licenses: Sales	22.2	25.9	27.0	28.5	27.7	27.9	28.8	30.0	29.3	30.0	30.7
Resident	21.0	24.7	25.6	26.8	26.1	26.3	27.1	27.7	27.3	27.4	28.5
Nonresident	1.2	1.3	1.4	1.7	1.6	1.7	1.7	2.0	2.0	2.3	2.2
Paid license holders [1]	15.4	16.6	16.3	16.0	15.9	15.8	15.8	15.9	15.9	15.8	15.7
Cost to hunters (mil. dol.) . . .	102	155	222	292	301	323	345	381	400	422	439
Federal duck stamps sold (1,000)	2,072	2,222	2,090	1,868	1,914	1,780	1,794	1,663	1,395	1,401	1,431

[1] Resident and nonresident. Includes multiple counting of license holders who bought nonresident licenses as well as a home State license. "Licenses" includes licenses, tags, permits and stamps.

Source: U.S. Fish and Wildlife Service, *Federal Aid in Fish and Wildlife Restoration*, annual.

No. 408. Anglers and Hunters: 1991

[For persons 16 years old and over. An angler or hunter is anyone who has fished or hunted in 1991. Based on the 1991 National Survey of Fishing, Hunting, and Wildlife-Associated Recreation conducted for the U.S. Fish and Wildlife Service by the U.S. Bureau of the Census]

TYPE OF FISHING	ANGLERS		Days of fishing [1] (mil.)	Expenditures [2] (mil. dol.)	TYPE OF HUNTING	HUNTERS		Days of fishing [1] (mil.)	Expenditures [2] (mil. dol.)
	Number (1,000)	Percent of population				Number (1,000)	Percent of population		
Total, all fishing .	[3]35,578	19	[3]511	23,990	**Total, all hunting . .**	[3]14,063	7	[3]236	12,336
All freshwater fishing .	[3]31,041	16	[3]440	15,149	Big game	10,745	6	128	5,090
Freshwater, except .					Small game.	7,642	4	77	1,550
Great Lakes.	30,186	16	431	13,812	Migratory birds. . .	3,009	2	22	686
Great Lakes.	2,552	1	25	1,337	Other animals . . .	1,411	1	19	255
Saltwater	8,885	5	75	4,992					

[1] Any part of a day constitutes a day. [2] Totals include expenditures for equipment, trips, magazines, membership dues, contributions, land leasing and ownership, licenses, stamps, tags, and other expenditures. Figures by type of fishing and hunting include only expenditures for trips and equipment. [3] Includes duplication for persons who participate in more than one category.

Source: U.S. Fish and Wildlife Service, *1991 National Survey of Fishing, Hunting, and Wildlife-Associated Recreation*.

No. 409. Wildlife-Associated Recreation Expenditures, by Type of Activity: 1991

[Sportsmen are any persons who fished or hunted in 1991. See headnote, table 408]

TYPE OF EXPENDITURE	EXPENDITURES (mil. dol.)				EXPENDITURE PER PARTICIPANT (dol.)			
	Total	Fishing	Hunting	Primary nonconsumptive [1]	Total	Fishing	Hunting	Primary nonconsumptive [1]
Total [2] **. . . . .**	[3]59,027	23,990	12,336	18,104	[3]543	674	877	238
Food and lodging	11,202	4,953	1,824	4,425	103	139	130	58
Transportation	6,748	2,800	1,339	2,609	62	79	95	34
Other trip costs	4,820	4,094	278	448	44	115	20	6
Licenses, stamps, tags and permits	898	487	533	(NA)	22	14	38	(NA)
Equipment	12,727	3,740	3,283	5,704	123	105	233	75
Auxiliary equipment.	[3]2,157	619	635	350	[3]20	17	45	5
Special equipment	[3]13,001	5,006	1,250	3,506	[3]120	141	89	46

NA Not available. [1] Observing, photographing, and feeding wildlife. [2] Includes expenditures for magazines, membership dues and contributions, and land leasing and ownership, not shown separately. [3] Includes expenditures not specified by type of activity.

Source: U.S. Fish and Wildlife Service, *1991 National Survey of Fishing, Hunting, and Wildlife-Associated Recreation*.

No. 410. Selected Spectator Sports: 1980 to 1991

[See also *Historical Statistics, Colonial Times to 1970,* series H 865-870 and H 872]

SPORT	Unit	1980	1984	1985	1986	1987	1988	1989	1990	1991
Baseball, major leagues: [1]										
Attendance	1,000	43,746	45,262	47,742	48,452	53,182	53,800	55,910	55,512	57,820
Regular season	1,000	43,014	44,742	46,824	47,506	52,011	52,999	55,173	54,824	56,814
National League	1,000	21,124	20,781	22,292	22,333	24,734	24,499	25,324	24,492	24,696
American League	1,000	21,890	23,961	24,532	25,173	27,277	28,500	29,849	30,332	32,118
Playoffs	1,000	407	248	591	624	784	541	514	479	633
World Series	1,000	325	272	327	322	387	260	223	209	373
Players' salaries: [2]										
Average	$1,000	144	329	371	413	412	439	497	598	851
Basketball: [3] [4]										
Men's:										
College:										
Teams	Number	1,258	1,260	1,266	1,265	1,270	1,277	1,264	1,313	1,316
Attendance	1,000	30,692	31,684	32,057	31,645	31,911	32,504	33,020	33,660	33,962
Women's:										
College:										
Teams	Number	(NA)	1,147	1,166	1,188	1,188	1,190	1,190	1,195	1,199
Attendance	1,000	(NA)	2,870	2,944	3,020	3,121	3,301	3,577	3,898	4,011
Pro: [5]										
Teams	Number	22	23	23	23	23	23	25	27	27
Attendance, total [6]	1,000	10,697	11,128	11,534	12,210	13,190	14,070	16,586	18,586	18,009
Regular season	1,000	9,938	10,015	10,506	11,215	12,065	12,654	15,465	17,369	16,876
Average per game	Number	11,017	10,620	11,141	11,893	12,765	13,419	15,088	15,690	15,245
Playoffs	1,000	740	1,096	985	979	1,091	1,397	1,077	1,203	1,109
Players' salaries:										
Average	$1,000	170	275	325	375	440	510	603	817	989
Football:										
College: [4]										
Teams	Number	642	654	661	666	667	673	673	673	681
Attendance	1,000	35,541	36,652	36,312	36,388	36,463	35,581	36,406	36,627	36,566
National Football League: [7]										
Teams	Number	28	28	28	28	28	28	28	28	28
Attendance, total [8]	1,000	14,092	14,053	14,058	17,304	[9]15,180	17,024	17,400	17,666	17,752
Regular season	1,000	13,392	13,398	13,345	13,588	[9]11,406	13,539	13,626	13,960	13,841
Average per game	Number	59,787	59,813	59,567	60,663	[9]54,315	60,446	60,829	62,321	61,792
Postseason games [10]	1,000	700	655	711	734	656	658	686	848	813
Players' salaries: [11]										
Average	$1,000	79	178	194	198	203	239	295	352	415
Median base salary	$1,000	70	110	140	150	175	180	200	236	250
National Hockey league: [12]										
Regular season attendance	1,000	10,534	11,359	11,633	11,621	12,116	12,418	12,423	12,578	12,344
Playoffs attendance	1,000	977	1,107	1,109	1,152	1,336	1,323	1,322	1,356	1,442
Horseracing: [13] [14]										
Racing days	Number	13,133	13,683	13,745	13,853	14,208	14,285	14,240	13,841	(NA)
Attendance	1,000	74,690	74,076	73,346	70,580	70,105	69,949	69,551	63,803	(NA)
Pari-mutuel turnover	Mil. dol	11,218	12,032	12,222	12,441	13,122	13,616	13,867	7,162	(NA)
Revenue to government	Mil. dol	713	650	625	587	608	596	585	611	(NA)
Greyhound: [13]										
Total performances	Number	5,855	8,661	9,590	10,654	11,156	12,904	13,393	14,915	(NA)
Attendance	1,000	20,874	22,076	23,853	25,759	26,215	26,477	33,818	28,660	(NA)
Pari-mutuel turnover	Mil. dol	2,064	2,421	2,702	3,005	3,193	3,291	3,278	3,388	(NA)
Revenue to government	Mil. dol	152	177	201	215	221	230	239	235	(NA)
Jai alai: [13]										
Total performances	Number	1,616	2,721	2,736	2,761	2,906	3,615	3,835	3,620	(NA)
Games played	Number	25,349	42,842	32,260	36,276	38,476	47,716	(NA)	(NA)	(NA)
Attendance	1,000	3,939	4,878	4,722	6,757	6,816	6,414	5,227	5,329	(NA)
Pari-mutuel turnover	Mil. dol	(NA)	665.9	664.0	667.6	707.5	663.6	553.0	545.5	(NA)
Revenue to government	Mil. dol	35	48	50	50	51	44	39	39	(NA)
Professional rodeo: [15]										
Rodeos	Number	631	643	617	616	637	707	741	754	798
Performances	Number	1,921	1,936	1,887	1,868	1,868	2,037	2,128	2,159	2,241
Members	Number	5,114	5,324	5,239	5,603	5,342	5,479	5,560	5,693	5,748
Permit-holders (rookies)	Number	4,038	2,911	2,534	2,700	2,746	3,310	3,584	3,290	3,006

NA Not available. [1] Source: The National League of Professional Baseball Clubs, New York, NY, *National League Green Book;* and The American League of Professional Baseball Clubs, New York, NY, *American League Red Book.* [2] Source: Major League Baseball Players Association, New York, NY. [3] Season ending in year shown. [4] Source: National Collegiate Athletic Assn., Overland Park, KS. For women's attendance total, excludes double-headers with men's teams. [5] Source: National Basketball Assn., New York, NY. [6] Includes All-Star game, not shown separately. [7] Source: National Football League, New York, NY. [8] Beginning 1986, includes preseason attendance, not shown separately. [9] Season was interrupted by a strike. [10] Includes Pro Bowl, a non-championship game and Super Bowl. [11] Source: National Football League Players Association, Washington, DC. [12] Source: National Hockey League, Montreal, Quebec. [13] Source: Association of Racing Commissioners International, Inc., Lexington, KY. [14] Includes thoroughbred, harness, quarter horse, and fairs. [15] Source: Professional Rodeo Cowboys Association, Colorado Springs, CO., *Official Professional Rodeo Media Guide,* annual, (copyright).

Source: Compiled from sources listed in footnotes.

No. 411. Selected Recreational Activities: 1970 to 1991

[See also *Historical Statistics, Colonial Times to 1970,* series H 862-864, H 871, H 874, and H 877]

ACTIVITY	Unit	1970	1975	1980	1985	1987	1988	1989	1990	1991
Softball, amateur: [1]										
Total participants [2]	Million. .	16	26	30	41	41	41	41	41	41
Youth participants	1,000 . .	255	450	650	712	720	722	900	1,100	1,200
Adult teams [3]	1,000 . .	29	66	110	152	178	182	188	188	200
Youth teams [3]	1,000 . .	2	9	18	31	38	40	46	46	51
Golfers (one round or more) [4] [5]	1,000 . .	11,245	13,036	15,112	17,520	21,200	23,000	24,200	27,800	24,800
Golf rounds played [5]	1,000 . .	266,169	308,562	357,701	414,777	431,000	484,000	469,000	502,000	479,000
Golf facilities	Number.	10,188	11,370	12,005	12,346	12,407	12,582	12,658	12,846	13,004
Classification:										
Private	Number.	4,619	4,770	4,839	4,861	4,898	4,897	4,862	4,810	4,686
Daily fee	Number.	4,248	5,014	5,372	5,573	5,583	5,748	5,833	6,024	6,272
Municipal	Number.	1,321	1,586	1,794	1,912	1,926	1,937	1,963	2,012	2,046
Tennis: [6]										
Players	1,000 . .	10,655	[7][8]29,201	(NA)	[9]18,951	[9]16,911	[9]17,314	[9]18,844	[9]18,401	[9]16,702
Courts	1,000 . .	(NA)	130	(NA)	220	220	220	220	220	230
Indoor	1,000 . .	(NA)	8	(NA)	14	14	14	14	14	14
Tenpin bowling:										
Participants, total [10]	Million. .	51.8	62.5	72.0	67.0	68.0	68.0	71.0	71.0	82.0
Male	Million. .	24.8	29.9	34.0	32.0	33.1	33.1	35.4	35.4	40.2
Female	Million. .	27.0	32.6	38.0	35.0	34.9	34.9	35.6	35.6	41.8
Establishments [11]	Number.	9,140	8,577	8,591	8,275	8,031	7,923	7,671	7,544	7,395
Lanes [11]	1,000 . .	141	141	154	155	151	150	147	146	144
Membership, total [11] [12]	1,000 . .	7,733	8,751	9,595	8,064	7,421	7,167	6,570	6,357	5,881
American Bowling Congress	1,000 . .	4,210	4,300	4,688	3,657	3,424	3,313	3,036	2,922	2,712
Women's Bowling Congress	1,000 . .	2,988	3,692	4,118	3,714	3,351	3,189	2,859	2,742	2,523
Young American Bowling Alliance [13]	1,000 . .	535	759	789	693	646	665	675	693	646
Motion picture theaters [14] [15]	1,000 . .	14	15	18	21	24	23	23	24	25
Four-wall	1,000 . .	10	11	14	18	21	22	22	23	24
Drive-in	1,000 . .	4	4	4	3	3	2	1	1	1
Receipts, box office	Mil. dol.	1,225	2,115	2,749	3,749	4,253	4,458	5,033	5,022	4,803
Admission, average price	Dollars .	1.55	2.05	2.69	3.55	3.91	4.11	4.45	4.75	4.89
Attendance	Million. .	921	1,033	1,022	1,056	1,089	1,085	1,133	1,058	982
Bicycles: [16]										
Domestic shipments	Million. .	5.0	5.6	6.9	5.8	5.2	4.5	5.3	6.0	7.2
Imports	Million. .	1.9	1.7	2.0	5.6	7.4	5.4	5.4	4.8	4.4
Boating: [17]										
Recreational boats owned	Million. .	8.8	9.7	11.8	13.8	14.5	15.1	15.6	16.0	16.2
Outboard boats	Million. .	5.2	5.7	6.8	7.4	7.5	7.7	7.9	7.9	8.0
Inboard boats	Million. .	0.6	0.8	1.2	1.4	1.7	1.8	2.0	2.2	2.3
Sailboats	Million. .	0.6	0.8	1.0	1.2	1.2	1.3	1.3	1.3	1.3
Canoes	Million. .	2.4	2.4	1.3	1.8	2.0	2.1	2.2	2.3	2.3
Rowboats and other	Million. .	([18])	([18])	1.5	1.8	2.1	2.2	2.1	2.3	2.3
Expenditures, total [19]	Bil. dol. .	3.4	4.8	7.4	13.3	16.5	17.9	17.1	13.7	10.6
Outboard motors in use	1,000 . .	7,215	7,649	8,241	9,733	10,469	10,860	11,225	11,524	11,769
Motors sold	1,000 . .	430	435	315	392	444	460	430	352	289
Value, retail	Mil. dol.	281	411	554	1,319	1,726	1,828	1,764	1,546	1,311
Outboard boats sold	1,000 . .	276	328	290	305	342	355	291	227	195
Value, retail	Mil. dol.	177	263	408	759	1,001	1,225	1,134	978	871
Inboard/outdrive boats sold	1,000 . .	43	70	56	115	144	148	133	97	73
Value, retail	Mil. dol.	182	420	616	1,663	2,450	2,585	2,354	1,794	1,293
All terrain vehicles: [20]										
Vehicles in use or owned	1,000 . .	(NA)	(NA)	(NA)	2,000	2,475	2,517	2,309	2,240	2,100
Imports	1,000 . .	(NA)	(NA)	(NA)	683	317	209	121	100	80

NA Not available. [1] Source: Amateur Softball Association, Oklahoma City, OK. [2] Amateur Softball Association teams and other amateur softball teams. [3] Amateur Softball Association teams only. [4] Source: National Golf Foundation, Jupiter, FL. [5] For 1970-1985 for persons 5 years of age and over; thereafter for persons 12 years of age and over. [6] Source: U.S. Tennis Association, Princeton, NJ. [7] Survey by A. C. Nielsen Co. [8] 1976 data. [9] Based on National Sporting Goods Association Sports Participation Survey. [10] For season ending in year shown. Persons 5 years old and over. Source: National Bowling Council, Arlington, VA. [11] Source: American Bowling Congress, Greendale, WI. Season ending in year shown. [12] Membership totals are for U.S., Canada and for U.S. military personnel worldwide. [13] Prior to 1985, represents American Jr. Bowling Congress and ABC/WIBC Collegiate Division. [14] Source: Motion Picture Association of America, Inc., New York, NY. [15] Prior to 1975, figures represent theaters; thereafter, screens. [16] Source: Bicycle Manufacturers Association of America, Inc., Washington, DC. [17] Source: National Marine Manufacturers Association, Chicago, IL. [18] Included in canoes. [19] Represents estimated expenditures for new and used boats, motors, accessories, safety equipment, fuel, insurance, docking, maintenance, storage, repairs, and other expenses. [20] Source: Motorcycle Industry Council, Inc., Irvine, CA.

Source: Compiled from sources listed in footnotes.

No. 412. Participation in Sports Activities, by Selected Characteristics: 1991

[In thousands, except rank. For persons 7 years of age or older. Except as indicated, a participant plays a sport more than once in the year. Based on a sampling of 10,000 households]

ACTIVITY	ALL PERSONS Number	ALL PERSONS Rank	SEX Male	SEX Female	AGE 7-11 yrs.	AGE 12-17 yrs.	AGE 18-24 yrs.	AGE 25-34 yrs.	AGE 35-44 yrs.	AGE 45-54 yrs.	AGE 55-64 yrs.	AGE 65 yrs. and over	HOUSEHOLD INCOME (dol.) Under 15,000	15,000-24,999	25,000-34,999	35,000-49,999	50,000-74,999	75,000 and over
Total	228,756	(X)	111,112	117,643	18,613	20,716	25,273	42,912	39,927	27,635	21,157	32,523	46,655	35,896	36,996	42,522	46,308	20,378
Number participated in:																		
Aerobic exercising [1]	25,916	9	4,438	21,478	1,005	1,541	5,241	7,755	5,516	2,907	995	954	3,792	3,172	4,241	5,420	6,092	3,199
Backpacking [2]	10,369	23	6,885	3,484	883	1,603	1,737	3,124	2,112	560	242	107	1,956	1,644	1,722	2,111	1,847	1,089
Baseball	16,548	17	13,640	2,908	5,205	4,835	2,177	2,135	1,636	437	119	5	2,673	2,312	2,663	3,459	4,081	1,361
Basketball [1]	26,150	8	19,151	6,999	4,970	7,990	4,440	4,837	3,000	777	115	21	3,454	3,847	4,584	5,356	6,068	2,840
Bicycle riding [1]	53,972	3	26,896	27,076	11,084	9,327	4,942	10,014	9,169	4,437	2,617	2,381	8,862	7,324	8,844	10,316	12,559	6,066
Bowling	40,369	6	21,022	19,348	4,004	4,735	7,321	10,114	6,734	3,224	2,305	1,933	5,934	6,539	6,711	8,227	9,092	3,866
Calisthenics [3]	12,322	19	5,732	6,590	1,247	1,782	1,831	2,868	2,335	981	721	557	1,809	1,779	2,197	2,332	2,776	1,429
Camping [3]	47,077	4	24,572	22,505	5,740	5,244	4,967	11,515	10,145	4,298	2,727	2,442	7,200	7,131	8,148	11,072	10,163	3,362
Exercise walking [1]	69,559	1	24,708	44,851	2,022	2,850	5,579	14,080	14,230	11,073	8,600	11,125	12,414	10,945	11,303	13,345	15,008	6,544
Exercising with equipment [1]	39,188	7	19,183	20,006	510	2,827	6,985	11,119	8,431	4,135	2,565	2,616	5,009	5,083	6,088	7,156	10,818	5,034
Fishing—fresh water [1]	41,778	5	28,664	13,114	4,356	4,054	4,799	9,727	8,100	4,900	2,831	3,010	7,822	7,177	7,923	8,535	7,721	2,599
Fishing—salt water	11,974	20	8,561	3,414	665	866	1,362	2,772	2,480	1,978	748	1,105	1,916	1,682	2,170	2,304	2,948	955
Football	13,287	18	11,640	1,647	2,806	4,463	2,767	2,258	763	194	31	5	2,669	2,109	2,120	2,372	2,699	1,319
Golf	24,728	10	18,601	6,127	758	1,696	3,100	6,008	4,510	3,567	2,293	2,794	2,340	2,963	3,602	4,487	7,336	4,000
Hiking	22,663	11	11,815	10,848	2,097	2,576	2,516	6,076	4,584	2,196	1,331	1,287	3,932	3,287	3,902	4,474	4,598	2,470
Hunting with firearms	17,111	15	15,336	1,775	356	1,329	2,455	4,862	3,601	2,382	1,326	799	2,810	3,035	3,771	3,328	3,175	993
Racquetball	6,272	25	4,726	1,546	121	451	1,862	2,179	1,174	316	122	48	703	950	1,015	943	1,762	899
Running/jogging [1]	22,473	13	13,186	9,287	2,262	4,063	4,153	5,365	3,779	1,801	819	231	3,569	2,739	3,473	4,038	5,720	2,934
Skiing—alpine/downhill	10,427	22	6,061	4,365	689	1,615	2,333	2,586	1,943	974	201	87	631	663	1,290	1,735	3,849	2,258
Skiing—cross country	4,371	26	2,047	2,324	253	444	718	931	815	766	289	154	362	386	798	713	1,322	790
Soccer	9,992	24	6,657	3,335	3,741	3,581	1,167	843	386	260	14	-	1,001	1,181	1,686	1,964	2,902	1,258
Softball	19,646	14	11,878	7,768	2,358	4,286	3,671	5,326	2,932	859	202	13	2,690	3,034	3,399	4,177	4,693	1,653
Swimming [1]	66,182	2	30,833	35,348	10,244	9,959	9,152	12,747	11,561	5,745	3,153	3,621	10,115	8,194	10,561	13,889	15,650	7,773
Target shooting	11,519	21	8,948	2,571	689	1,461	1,813	3,079	2,775	1,105	356	241	1,890	1,827	2,284	2,501	2,147	870
Tennis	16,702	16	9,207	7,495	1,060	2,993	3,549	4,096	2,645	1,587	439	334	1,771	1,722	2,775	2,882	4,575	2,977
Volleyball	22,586	12	11,495	11,091	1,774	5,089	4,625	6,521	3,258	1,043	201	77	3,471	3,555	3,893	5,370	4,457	1,841

- Represents or rounds to zero.   X Not applicable.   [1] Participant engaged in activity at least six times in the year.   [2] Includes wilderness camping.   [3] Vacation/overnight.

Source: National Sporting Goods Association, Mt. Prospect, IL, *Sports Participation in 1991: Series I*, (copyright).

No. 413. Sporting Goods Sales, by Product Category: 1980 to 1992

[In millions of dollars, except percent. Based on a sample survey of consumer purchases of 80,000 households, except recreational transport, which was provided by industry associations. Excludes Alaska and Hawaii]

SELECTED PRODUCT CATEGORY	1980	1983	1984	1985	1986	1987	1988	1989	1990	1991	1992, proj.
Sales, all products	16,691	23,111	26,401	27,446	30,614	33,942	42,093	45,184	44,111	42,850	45,085
Annual percent change [1]	-1.4	23.7	14.2	4.0	11.5	10.9	24.0	7.3	-2.4	-2.9	5.2
Percent of retail sales	1.7	2.0	2.1	2.0	2.1	2.2	2.5	2.6	2.4	2.3	2.3
Athletic and sport clothing [2]	3,127	3,226	3,432	3,376	3,931	4,645	10,736	11,557	11,382	12,057	12,727
Athletic and sport footwear [3]	1,731	2,189	2,381	2,610	3,199	3,524	3,772	5,763	6,263	6,295	6,360
Walking shoes	(NA)	(NA)	(NA)	263	368	512	752	1,237	1,509	1,375	1,306
Gym shoes, sneakers	465	639	669	656	642	693	783	1,125	1,177	1,181	1,193
Jogging and running shoes	397	557	591	572	476	475	460	515	519	555	572
Tennis shoes	359	340	371	470	448	367	353	508	582	597	615
Aerobic shoes	(NA)	29	54	178	333	401	327	425	389	381	370
Basketball shoes	86	119	159	185	187	169	226	293	428	449	476
Golf shoes	68	115	110	109	120	130	128	129	157	173	182
Athletic and sport equipment [3]	6,487	7,925	8,317	8,922	9,477	9,900	10,705	11,503	11,965	11,982	12,416
Firearms and hunting	1,351	1,666	1,620	1,699	1,675	1,804	1,894	2,139	2,202	2,091	2,049
Exercise equipment	(NA)	960	1,055	1,216	1,206	1,191	1,452	1,748	1,824	2,075	2,199
Golf	386	633	630	730	828	946	1,111	1,167	1,219	1,149	1,184
Camping	646	790	699	724	833	858	945	996	1,072	1,016	1,047
Bicycles (10-12-15-18+ speed)	(NA)	761	765	975	1,089	930	819	906	1,092	(NA)	(NA)
Fishing tackle	539	606	616	681	773	830	766	769	776	711	703
Snow skiing	379	386	502	593	622	661	710	606	606	577	585
Tennis	237	293	315	273	260	238	264	315	287	295	307
Archery	149	179	212	212	214	224	235	261	265	270	337
Baseball and softball	158	173	153	176	180	173	174	206	217	214	218
Water skis	123	133	146	125	132	148	160	96	88	63	66
Bowling accessories	107	106	108	106	114	129	129	143	155	155	157
Recreational transport	5,345	9,771	12,271	12,539	14,007	15,873	16,880	16,360	14,502	12,517	13,582
Pleasure boats	2,718	4,612	6,209	6,753	7,372	8,906	9,637	9,319	7,644	5,862	6,448
Recreational vehicles	1,178	3,368	4,082	3,515	3,940	4,507	4,839	4,481	4,113	3,615	3,941
Bicycles and supplies	1,233	1,638	1,840	2,109	2,518	2,272	2,131	2,259	2,423	2,686	2,820
Snowmobiles	216	153	140	162	177	188	273	301	322	355	373

NA Not available. [1] Represents change from immediate prior year. [2] Category expanded in 1988; not comparable with earlier years. [3] Includes other products not shown separately.

Source: National Sporting Goods Association, Mt. Prospect, IL, *The Sporting Goods Market in 1992,* and prior issues, (copyright).

No. 414. Consumer Purchases of Sporting Goods, by Consumer Characteristics: 1991

[In percent. Based on sample survey of consumer purchases of 80,000 households. Excludes Alaska and Hawaii]

CHARACTERISTIC	Total households	FOOTWEAR					EQUIPMENT					
		Aerobic shoes	Gym shoes/ sneakers	Jogging/ running shoes	Walking shoes	Fishing tackle	Camping equipment	Exercise equipment	Rifles	Shotguns	Golf equipment
Total	100.0	100.0	100.0	100.0	100.0	100.0	100.0	100.0	100.0	100.0	100.0
Age of user:											
Under 14 years old	20.6	6.6	39.3	8.8	3.3	6.0	12.0	1.0	3.1	2.9	2.0
14 to 17 years old	5.3	3.5	10.7	11.7	1.9	3.0	6.0	2.0	4.2	6.0	3.0
18 to 24 years old	10.1	11.7	8.5	8.4	2.7	6.0	7.0	5.0	9.2	10.8	5.0
25 to 34 years old	17.2	30.9	13.2	22.3	12.2	23.0	28.0	23.0	33.3	30.4	24.0
35 to 44 years old	15.5	21.0	11.4	24.1	16.2	26.0	21.0	21.0	25.3	18.2	19.0
45 to 64 years old	18.7	19.5	11.6	19.5	36.6	26.0	13.0	32.0	21.3	27.4	29.0
65 years old and over	12.6	6.8	5.3	5.2	27.1	4.0	3.0	9.0	3.2	2.8	14.0
Multiple ages	-	-	-	-	-	6.0	10.0	7.0	0.4	1.5	3.0
Sex of user:											
Male	48.8	19.6	53.0	62.5	38.1	83.0	62.0	43.0	97.4	94.8	78.0
Female	51.2	80.4	47.0	37.5	61.9	11.0	27.0	46.0	1.8	5.1	16.0
Both sexes	-	-	-	-	-	6.0	11.0	11.0	0.8	-	7.0
Education of household head:											
Less than high school	11.7	7.2	8.9	4.8	11.0	9.0	6.0	7.0	6.8	10.6	6.0
High school	29.5	22.7	28.6	24.1	28.4	29.0	25.0	24.0	33.4	42.6	15.0
Some college	28.5	28.4	28.8	28.9	28.5	36.0	33.0	25.0	31.4	20.4	30.0
College graduate	30.3	41.7	33.7	42.2	32.1	26.0	36.0	43.0	28.4	26.4	49.0
Annual household income:											
Under $15,000	22.2	11.7	12.4	9.8	17.9	11.0	12.0	7.0	3.9	9.0	2.0
$15,000 to $24,999	17.1	12.4	13.6	10.1	16.5	14.0	13.0	10.0	16.8	23.6	4.0
$25,000 to $34,999	15.6	14.6	16.3	14.8	15.7	14.0	16.0	12.0	13.5	17.1	14.0
$35,000 to $49,999	18.4	21.4	22.7	22.4	18.5	23.0	23.0	21.0	22.2	15.8	22.0
$50,000 and over	16.6	19.5	22.7	23.3	19.3	23.0	22.0	27.0	25.1	21.8	31.0
$75,000 and over	10.1	20.4	12.3	19.6	12.1	15.0	14.0	24.0	18.5	12.7	27.0

- Represents or rounds to zero.

Source: National Sporting Goods Association, Mt. Prospect, IL, *The Sporting Goods Market in 1992;* and prior issues, (copyright).

No. 415. Boy Scouts and Girl Scouts—Membership and Units: 1970 to 1991

[In thousands. Boy Scouts as of Dec. 31; Girl Scouts as of Sept. 30. Includes Puerto Rico and outlying areas]

ITEM	1970	1975	1980	1983	1984	1985	1986	1987	1988	1989	1990	1991
BOY SCOUTS OF AMERICA												
Membership	6,287	5,318	4,318	4,689	4,755	4,845	5,171	5,347	5,364	5,356	5,448	5,319
Boys	4,683	3,933	3,207	3,567	3,657	3,755	4,037	4,180	4,228	4,247	4,293	4,150
Adults	1,604	1,385	1,110	1,122	1,098	1,090	1,134	1,168	1,136	1,109	1,155	1,170
Total units (packs, troops, posts)	157	150	129	134	135	134	132	131	131	130	130	129
GIRL SCOUTS OF THE U.S.A.												
Membership	3,922	3,234	2,784	2,888	2,871	2,802	2,917	2,947	3,052	3,166	3,269	3,383
Girls	3,248	2,723	2,250	2,281	2,247	2,172	2,248	2,274	2,345	2,415	2,480	2,561
Adults	674	511	534	607	624	630	669	673	707	751	788	822
Total units (troops, groups)	164	159	154	165	166	166	174	180	189	196	202	210

Source: Boy Scouts of America, National Council, Irving, TX, *Annual Report;* and Girl Scouts of the United States of America, New York, NY, *Annual Report.*

No. 416. Performing Arts—Selected Data: 1970 to 1991

[Receipts and expenditures in millions of dollars. For season ending in year shown, except as indicated]

ITEM	1970	1975	1980	1984	1985	1986	1987	1988	1989	1990	1991
Legitimate theater: [1]											
Broadway shows:											
New productions	62	59	67	36	31	33	40	31	29	35	28
Playing weeks [2][3]	1,047	1,101	1,541	1,119	1,062	1,049	1,031	1,114	1,097	1,062	970
Number of tickets sold (1,000)	(NA)	(NA)	9,380	7,898	7,156	6,527	6,968	8,142	7,968	8,039	7,314
Gross box office receipts	53.3	57.4	143.4	226.5	208.0	190.6	207.2	253.4	262.0	283.3	267.2
Road shows:											
Playing weeks [3]	1,024	799	1,351	1,057	993	983	901	893	869	944	1,152
Gross box office receipts	48.0	50.9	181.2	206.2	225.9	235.6	224.2	222.9	255.5	367.1	450.1
Nonprofit professional theatres: [4]											
Companies reporting	(NA)	39	147	230	217	201	188	189	192	185	184
Gross income	(NA)	34.5	113.6	226.6	234.7	263.8	271.2	276.4	349.0	307.6	333.9
Earned income	(NA)	21.8	67.3	145.7	146.1	160.8	165.2	167.0	224.6	188.4	202.6
Contributed income	(NA)	12.7	46.3	80.9	88.6	103.0	106.0	109.4	124.4	119.2	131.3
Gross expenses	(NA)	34.3	113.6	230.3	239.3	263.3	272.8	277.9	349.2	306.3	336.7
Productions	(NA)	398	1,852	3,434	2,710	2,944	2,427	2,369	2,469	2,265	2,277
Performances	(NA)	11,952	42,109	56,735	52,341	57,727	46,768	46,149	53,263	46,131	48,695
Total attendance (mil.)	(NA)	5.4	14.2	15.5	14.2	14.8	14.6	13.9	18.7	15.2	16.9
Opera companies [5]	648	807	986	1,051	1,123	1,176	1,224	1,250	1,285	(NA)	(NA)
Major [6]	35	54	109	154	168	170	174	187	209	(NA)	(NA)
Expenditures	36.5	(NA)	133.6	236.7	256.5	270.3	321.1	352.3	403.8	(NA)	(NA)
Other companies	266	335	458	491	576	602	658	654	658	(NA)	(NA)
Workshops [7]	347	418	419	406	379	404	392	409	418	(NA)	(NA)
Opera performances	4,779	6,428	9,391	10,421	10,642	11,080	11,794	12,361	15,098	(NA)	(NA)
Operas performed	341	387	497	576	578	660	622	658	731	(NA)	(NA)
Musical performances [8]	(NA)	(NA)	1,397	2,787	4,983	6,993	7,759	8,836	9,825	(NA)	(NA)
Musicals performed [8]	(NA)	(NA)	104	129	242	301	278	296	279	(NA)	(NA)
World premieres	17	16	79	101	121	116	129	141	165	(NA)	(NA)
Attendance (mil.)	4.6	8.0	10.7	13.0	14.1	14.4	16.4	17.7	21.4	(NA)	(NA)
Symphony orchestras [9]	1,441	1,463	1,572	1,572	1,572	1,572	1,572	1,572	1,666	1,666	1,666
College [10]	298	300	385	380	371	371	365	350	422	[11]	[11]
Community [12]	1,019	1,003	926	937	946	927	936	903	924	[11]	[11]
Urban	24	41	85	89	89	93	92	103	103	[11]	[11]
Metropolitan	72	90	115	96	96	107	102	123	121	[11]	[11]
Regional	[13]	[13]	29	40	40	43	45	57	59	[11]	[11]
Major	28	29	32	30	30	31	32	36	37	[11]	[11]
Concerts	6,599	14,171	22,229	19,086	19,969	20,272	20,059	17,774	17,361	16,725	17,437
Attendance (mil.)	12.7	18.3	22.6	23.2	23.7	25.4	25.1	23.6	22.4	22.2	22.3
Gross income	73.3	124.5	246.3	379.0	435.4	480.5	523.6	561.8	619.5	679.9	702.5
Earned income	43.1	70.9	141.2	220.2	250.7	282.4	305.9	332.9	363.3	405.4	412.1
Contributed income	30.2	53.6	105.1	158.8	184.7	198.1	217.7	228.9	256.2	274.5	290.4
Gross expenses	76.4	129.5	252.1	389.8	441.8	491.2	525.4	571.3	600.0	665.4	688.8

NA Not available.   [1] Source: *Variety,* New York, NY, various June issues (copyright).   [2] All shows (new productions and holdovers from previous seasons).   [3] Eight performances constitute one playing week.   [4] Source: Theatre Communications Group, New York, NY. For years ending on or prior to Aug. 30.   [5] Source: Central Opera Service, New York, NY, Central Opera Service Bulletin, periodic.   [6] Companies with budgets of over $100,000 and issue American Guild of Musical Artists (AGMA) contracts to soloists.   [7] Workshops are primarily college and university opera groups.   [8] Covers not-for-profit companies only.   [9] Source: American Symphony Orchestra League, Inc., Washington, DC. For years ending Aug. 31. Orchestras other than college groups are principally defined by their annual budgets: For 1987 and 1988, community, under $135,000; urban, $135,000-$280,000; metropolitan, $280,000-$1,000,000; regional, $1,000,000-$3,600,000; and major, over $3,600,000. Prior to 1987, other budget classifications were in effect.   [10] Includes youth orchestras.   [11] No longer classified by type.   [12] Beginning 1980, includes youth and chamber groups with budgets under $70,000.   [13] Classification began in 1976.

Source: Compiled from sources listed in footnotes.

No. 417. Arts and Humanities—Selected Federal Aid Programs: 1970 to 1991

[In millions of dollars, except as indicated. For fiscal years ending in year shown, see text, section 9]

TYPE OF FUND AND PROGRAM	1970	1975	1980	1985	1986	1987	1988	1989	1990	1991
National Endowment for the Arts:										
Funds available [1]	15.7	86.9	188.1	171.7	167.1	170.9	171.1	166.7	170.8	166.5
Program appropriation	6.3	67.3	97.0	118.7	115.7	120.8	122.2	123.5	124.3	124.6
Matching funds [2]	2.0	7.5	42.9	29.5	30.0	29.3	32.9	23.6	32.4	32.4
Grants awarded (number)	556	3,071	5,505	4,801	4,484	4,542	4,628	4,604	4,475	4,239
Funds obligated	12.9	81.7	166.4	149.4	146.6	151.4	156.3	148.3	157.6	158.0
Music	2.5	14.9	13.6	15.3	14.6	15.1	15.3	15.3	16.5	14.1
State programs	1.9	14.7	22.1	24.4	23.8	24.6	24.9	25.5	26.1	37.7
Museums	(NA)	10.8	11.2	11.9	11.5	11.5	12.6	12.7	12.1	11.3
Theater	2.8	6.4	8.4	10.6	10.2	10.8	10.7	10.7	10.6	9.4
Dance	1.7	6.1	8.0	9.0	9.0	9.1	9.2	9.5	9.6	8.5
Media arts	0.2	5.4	8.4	9.9	12.3	12.9	12.4	12.7	13.9	11.8
Challenge [3]	(X)	(X)	50.8	20.7	20.7	20.8	24.8	15.4	19.7	19.7
Visual arts	1.0	3.2	7.3	6.2	5.7	6.2	6.0	6.1	5.9	5.3
Other	2.8	20.1	36.6	41.3	38.8	40.4	40.4	40.2	43.1	40.2
National Endowment for the Humanities:										
Funds available [1]	13.0	86.0	186.2	125.6	121.1	128.4	125.2	137.1	140.6	149.4
Program appropriation	6.1	67.3	100.3	95.2	[4]91.9	[4]95.8	96.7	108.3	114.2	122.4
Matching funds [2]	2.0	6.5	38.4	30.4	27.3	28.5	28.5	28.7	26.3	27.0
Grants awarded (number)	542	1,330	2,917	2,241	2,297	2,888	2,113	2,285	2,195	2,171
Funds obligated	10.5	73.1	185.5	125.7	121.1	128.4	125.2	137.1	141.0	149.8
Education programs	4.2	17.1	18.3	17.9	14.8	16.4	16.6	16.5	16.3	18.5
State programs	(X)	(X)	26.0	24.4	24.1	25.0	25.3	29.0	29.6	30.8
Research grants	2.0	13.4	32.0	24.4	21.0	21.7	21.9	22.1	22.5	24.0
Fellowship program	1.7	10.9	18.0	15.3	14.4	15.3	15.3	15.3	15.3	16.2
Challenge [3]	(X)	(X)	53.5	19.6	16.2	16.5	16.5	16.7	14.6	15.1
Public programs	1.7	26.3	25.1	24.1	24.7	25.4	24.9	25.1	25.4	25.3
Preservation [5]	(X)	(X)	(X)	(X)	4.1	4.1	4.7	12.3	17.5	19.9
National Capital Arts and Cultural Affairs Program	(X)	(X)	(X)	(X)	1.9	4.0	(X)	(X)	(X)	(X)
Other	1.0	5.5	12.6	(X)	(X)	(X)	(X)	(X)	(X)	(X)

NA Not available. X Not applicable. [1] Includes other funds, shown separately. Excludes administrative funds. Gifts are included through 1980; excluded thereafter. [2] Represents Federal funds appropriated only upon receipt or certification by Endowment of matching non-Federal gifts. [3] Program designed to stimulate new sources and higher levels of giving to institutions for the purpose of guaranteeing long-term stability and financial independence. Program requires a match of at least 3 private dollars to each Federal dollar. Funds for challenge grants are not allocated by program area because they are awarded on a grant-by-grant basis. [4] Excludes National Capital Arts and Cultural Affairs Program. [5] Program designed to support projects which preserve and guarantee access to print and nonprint media in danger of disintegration or deterioration.

Source: U.S. National Endowment for the Arts, *Annual Report*; and U.S. National Endowment for the Humanities, *Annual Report*.

No. 418. State Legislative Appropriations for State Arts Agencies: 1988 to 1992

[In thousands of dollars, except as indicated. For fiscal years ending in year shown. Fiscal years for most States ended June 30; see text, section 9]

STATE OR AREA	1988	1989	1990	1991	1992	STATE OR AREA	1988	1989	1990	1991	1992
Total	242,842	270,652	292,304	272,519	213,392	NE	608	868	1,025	1,048	1,185
						NV	270	269	353	359	478
AL	1,319	1,476	1,949	1,579	2,079	NH	451	474	497	519	490
AK	1,275	1,692	1,217	1,432	1,200	NJ	20,101	22,760	19,722	11,703	10,271
AZ	1,323	1,545	[1]2,570	[1]2,068	[1]2,317	NM	706	710	906	1,119	1,257
AR	1,016	1,021	1,016	973	1,032	NY	53,564	53,529	59,484	[5]0,981	31,266
CA	13,677	15,682	16,795	15,736	14,871	NC	4,505	4,996	4,978	[5]5,428	4,729
CO	1,041	1,108	1,308	1,536	1,618	ND	222	214	263	274	290
CT	2,000	2,119	2,148	2,197	2,897	OH	9,591	9,980	12,075	12,130	10,246
DE	686	785	1,207	1,313	1,279	OK	1,679	2,670	3,377	3,195	3,458
DC	3,544	3,544	2,537	3,200	3,527	OR	1,293	1,431	1,359	1,537	1,390
FL	17,340	24,179	23,635	23,386	16,180	PA	9,780	12,753	12,814	11,704	9,773
GA	3,024	3,248	3,413	3,338	3,059	RI	1,070	1,440	1,383	1,010	900
HI	3,902	6,747	8,777	12,065	10,727	SC	2,801	3,159	3,534	3,633	3,525
ID	198	339	434	665	735	SD	330	338	348	405	408
IL	7,581	7,509	10,705	10,348	8,467	TN	1,523	3,506	3,783	4,299	1,422
IN	1,969	1,970	2,317	2,812	2,667	TX	3,383	2,680	3,437	3,386	3,261
IA	[2]729	[3]825	[4]1,442	[4]1,249	1,423	UT	1,518	1,603	2,869	4,284	2,258
KS	583	1,072	1,238	1,072	1,007	VT	350	457	509	479	416
KY	2,032	2,368	2,387	3,202	3,348	VA	3,017	3,771	5,392	4,016	1,500
LA	931	996	909	936	859	WA	1,704	2,063	2,232	2,396	2,227
ME	515	636	702	755	602	WV	1,811	[6]1,133	[6]1,675	2,384	1,727
MD	5,157	5,971	6,332	7,442	6,396	WI	1,276	[7]1,725	2,254	2,422	2,956
MA	21,148	19,539	17,685	12,624	3,588	WY	203	206	235	351	345
MI	12,611	12,466	12,233	9,152	6,034	Am. Samoa	30	-	-	48	43
MN	3,030	3,184	4,208	4,213	3,943	Guam	339	561	458	620	628
MS	421	496	497	514	489	No. Marianas	60	101	115	114	162
MO	4,660	4,913	5,008	4,480	4,010	PR	8,111	11,013	13,549	13,335	11,300
MT	730	726	781	780	959	VI	104	85	231	276	170

- Represents zero. [1] Includes $1,000,000 to be generated by the Arizona Arts Trust Fund. [2] Includes $250,000 one-time appropriation. [3] Includes $140,000 one-time lottery funds. [4] Includes $220,000 lottery funds. [5] Includes $522,000 one-time appropriation. [6] Excludes administrative expenses. [7] Includes $250,000 one-time Governor's Award.

Source: National Assembly of State Arts Agencies, Washington, DC, unpublished data.

No. 419. Travel by U.S. Residents, by Selected Trip Characteristics: 1985 to 1991

[In millions. See headnote, table 420]

CHARACTERISTIC	TRIPS					PERSON TRIPS [1]				
	1985	1988	1989	1990	1991	1985	1988	1989	1990	1991
Total..............	558.4	656.1	664.3	661.1	664.5	1,077.6	1,232.5	1,260.1	1,274.5	1,306.6
Purpose:										
Visit friends and relatives	206.8	213.8	231.4	246.0	225.9	430.8	425.8	476.5	523.3	496.5
Other pleasure	177.6	241.5	225.9	214.5	239.3	376.0	502.1	469.3	447.5	496.5
Business or convention	133.3	155.6	169.7	155.6	152.8	185.2	211.7	232.0	209.5	209.1
Other	40.7	45.2	37.3	45.0	46.5	85.6	92.9	82.3	94.2	104.5
Mode of transport:										
Auto, truck, recreation vehicle ..	376.1	472.6	479.8	483.9	498.4	797.7	952.2	982.7	1,011.3	1,045.2
Airplane...............	140.5	154.6	154.6	144.9	132.9	217.3	238.6	234.3	214.5	209.1
Other	41.8	28.9	29.9	32.3	33.2	62.6	41.7	43.1	48.7	52.3
Vacation trip [2]............	339.8	396.2	416.7	422.3	418.6	728.7	830.9	878.3	883.9	901.6
Weekend trip [2]............	224.0	271.7	282.4	280.0	392.1	470.1	560.0	582.1	580.2	770.9

[1] A count of times each person (child or adult) goes on a trip.   [2] A trip can be counted as both a weekend and a vacation trip.

Source: U.S. Travel Data Center, Washington, DC, *National Travel Survey*, annual, (copyright).

No. 420. Characteristics of Business Trips and Pleasure Trips: 1980 to 1991

[Represents trips to places 100 miles or more from home by one or more from home by one or more household members traveling together. Based on a monthly telephone survey of 1,500 U.S. adults. For details, see source]

CHARACTERISTIC	Unit	BUSINESS TRIPS				PLEASURE TRIPS			
		1980	1985	1990	1991	1980	1985	1990	1991
Total trips......................	Millions .	97.1	133.3	155.6	152.8	342.8	384.4	460.9	465.2
Average household members on trip	Number .	1.5	1.4	1.4	1.4	2.2	2.1	2.1	2.1
Average nights per trip [1]	Nights .	(NA)	3.6	3.7	3.8	(NA)	5.6	4.4	4.0
Average miles per trip [2]	Miles ...	(NA)	1,180	1,020	862	(NA)	1,010	867	870
Traveled primarily by auto/truck/RV [3] rental car	Percent .	56	51	58	55	80	73	77	81
Traveled primarily by air	Percent .	42	44	37	38	16	21	18	15
Used a rental car while on trip	Percent .	25	20	14	12	7	6	7	9
Stayed in a hotel while on trip	Percent .	66	62	71	75	34	39	37	39
Used a travel agent	Percent .	21	28	21	16	10	13	12	13
Also a vacation trip.............	Percent .	10	13	17	26	75	80	82	79
Male travelers	Percent .	(NA)	67	71	66	(NA)	48	49	53
Female travelers	Percent .	(NA)	33	29	34	(NA)	52	51	47
Household income:									
Less than $40,000..............	Percent .	(NA)	58	42	41	(NA)	73	63	51
$40,000 or more	Percent .	(NA)	42	56	59	(NA)	27	38	49

NA Not available.   [1] Includes no overnight stays.   [2] United States only.   [3] Recreational vehicle.

Source: U.S. Travel Data Center, Washington, DC, *National Travel Survey*, annual, (copyright).

No. 421. Domestic Travel Expenditures, by State: 1990

[Represents U.S. spending on domestic overnight trips and day trips of 100 miles or more away from home. Excludes spending by foreign visitors and by U.S. residents in U.S. territories and abroad]

STATE	Total (mil. dol.)	Share of total (per- cent)	Rank	STATE	Total (mil. dol.)	Share of total (per- cent)	Rank	STATE	Total (mil. dol.)	Share of total (per- cent)	Rank
U.S. total .	290,446	100.0	(X)	KS	2,249	0.8	34	ND	743	0.3	49
				KY	3,092	1.1	30	OH	7,822	2.7	10
AL	3,380	1.2	27	LA	4,344	1.5	23	OK	2,482	0.9	33
AK	1,049	0.4	45	ME	1,402	0.5	40	OR	3,323	1.1	28
AZ	4,799	1.7	19	MD	4,463	1.5	22	PA	9,097	3.1	8
AR	2,181	0.8	37	MA	6,524	2.2	14	RI.	669	0.2	51
CA	40,489	13.9	1	MI	6,764	2.3	12	SC	4,497	1.5	21
CO	5,361	1.8	18	MN	3,849	1.3	25	SD	732	0.3	50
CT	3,208	1.1	29	MS	1,934	0.7	38	TN	5,780	2.0	15
DE	774	0.3	48	MO	5,590	1.9	17	TX	16,835	5.8	4
DC	2,809	1.0	31	MT	1,299	0.4	41	UT	2,229	0.8	35
FL	26,095	9.0	2	NE	1,596	0.5	39	VT	919	0.3	47
GA	7,772	2.7	11	NV	10,981	3.8	6	VA	8,086	2.8	9
HI.	5,726	2.0	16	NH	1,231	0.4	43	WA	4,791	1.6	20
ID.	1,299	0.4	42	NJ	9,759	3.4	7	WV	1,220	0.4	44
IL	11,641	4.0	5	NM	2,200	0.8	36	WI	3,974	1.4	24
IN.	3,827	1.3	26	NY	19,312	6.6	3	WY	1,000	0.3	46
IA	2,555	0.9	32	NC	6,696	2.3	13				

X Not applicable.

Source: U.S. Travel Data Center, Washington, DC, *Impact of Travel on State Economies, 1990*, (copyright).

No. 422. Business Receipts and Employment of Selected Travel Industry Sectors: 1975 to 1990

YEAR	BUSINESS RECEIPTS (mil. dol.)							EMPLOYMENT (1,000)					
	Travel indus-try, total	Transportation [1]			Motel, hotel	Eating and drink-ing places	Amuse-ment and recre-ation serv-ices	Travel indus-try, total	Transportation		Eating and drink-ing places	Hotels, motels, and tourist courts	Amuse-ment and recre-ation serv-ices
		Air [2]	Bus	Rail [3]					Intercity highway passen-gers	Air			
1975 ..	94,549	10,301	1,172	247	13,002	51,067	18,760	5,229	40	363	3,380	850	597
1980 ..	163,015	23,405	1,709	382	26,832	90,058	20,629	6,918	38	453	4,626	1,038	764
1981 ..	180,774	25,598	1,809	429	31,572	98,118	23,248	7,102	38	455	4,750	1,076	784
1982 ..	189,433	25,488	1,854	436	32,749	104,593	24,313	7,206	39	444	4,831	1,093	799
1983 ..	205,228	27,519	1,965	481	35,897	113,281	26,085	7,481	36	455	5,042	1,131	818
1984 ..	221,931	31,437	2,035	524	38,917	121,321	27,697	7,939	37	489	5,388	1,221	804
1985 ..	235,437	33,343	1,989	563	41,837	127,949	29,756	8,396	35	522	5,709	1,290	840
1986 ..	251,213	33,846	1,890	592	43,300	139,415	32,170	8,718	33	567	5,916	1,338	864
1987 ..	276,157	37,555	1,826	639	48,200	153,461	34,476	9,059	30	603	6,106	1,427	893
1988 ..	301,817	41,963	2,036	738	52,400	166,860	37,820	9,377	29	644	6,282	1,503	918
1989 ..	320,348	45,320	2,185	842	58,138	173,894	39,969	9,760	31	684	6,439	1,561	1,045
1990 ..	334,881	45,324	2,000	888	60,490	182,044	44,135	10,027	26	751	6,565	1,595	1,089

[1] Passenger transport service. [2] U.S. certificated carriers in domestic service. [3] Covers fiscal years October 1 through September 30.
Source: U.S. Travel Data Center, Washington, DC, *The 1990-91 Economic Review of Travel in America*, (copyright).

No. 423. International Travelers and Expenditures—Summary: 1970 to 1992

[For coverage, see tables 424 and 425. Beginning 1984, receipts, payments, and fares not comparable with previous years. See source for details. Minus sign (-) indicates deficit. See also *Historical Statistics, Colonial Times to 1970*, series H 921, 928, 941, and 945]

YEAR	TRAVEL AND PASSENGER FARE (mil. dol.)				U.S. net travel and passen-ger payments (mil. dol.)	U.S. travelers to foreign countries (1,000)	Foreign visitors to the U.S. (1,000)
	Payments by U.S. travelers		Receipts from foreign visitors				
	Total [1]	Expenditures abroad	Total [1]	Travel receipts			
1970	5,195	3,980	2,708	2,331	-2,487	(NA)	12,362
1975	8,680	6,417	5,464	4,697	-3,216	(NA)	15,698
1980	14,004	10,397	12,650	10,588	-1,354	[2]22,365	22,326
1982	17,166	12,394	15,085	12,393	-2,081	[2]23,148	21,667
1983	19,152	13,149	14,044	10,947	-5,108	[2]24,853	21,652
1984	28,637	22,913	21,377	17,320	-7,260	33,977	26,934
1985	31,042	24,558	22,302	17,920	-8,740	34,715	25,399
1986	32,467	25,913	26,074	20,529	-6,393	37,158	26,008
1987	36,628	29,310	30,684	23,718	-5,944	39,410	29,424
1988	39,882	32,114	38,590	29,665	-1,292	40,669	34,095
1989	41,676	33,418	47,096	36,571	5,420	41,138	36,564
1990	47,957	37,349	58,558	43,418	10,601	44,622	39,539
1991	47,594	36,958	64,384	48,757	16,790	41,941	42,909
1992	56,300	44,300	72,600	55,300	16,300	44,730	45,405

NA Not available. [1] Includes passenger fares not shown separately. [2] Mexico visitation data are under-reported.
Source: Travelers and visitors: U.S. Travel and Tourism Administration (USTTA), and unpublished data. Fares and Payments: Through 1988, U.S. Bureau of Economic Analysis, *Survey of Current Business*, June 1990, and earlier issues; beginning 1989, USTTA, based on data from the Bureau of Economic Analysis.

No. 424. U.S. Travel to Foreign Countries—Travelers and Expenditures: 1985 to 1992

[Travelers in thousands; expenditures in millions of dollars. Covers residents of the United States, its territories and possessions. See source for details. See also *Historical Statistics, Colonial to 1970*, series H 921-940]

ITEM AND AREA	1985	1986	1987	1988	1989	1990	1991	1992
Total travelers	34,715	37,158	39,410	40,669	41,138	44,622	41,941	44,730
Canada	11,558	13,608	12,720	12,763	12,184	12,252	12,003	11,760
Mexico	10,461	11,512	13,074	13,463	14,163	16,380	15,417	17,130
Total overseas	12,696	12,038	13,616	14,443	14,791	15,990	14,521	15,840
Europe........	6,780	5,887	6,114	7,438	7,233	8,043	6,317	(NA)
Latin America [1]	3,592	3,551	4,303	4,203	4,392	4,749	5,155	(NA)
Other...............	2,324	2,600	3,199	2,802	3,166	3,198	3,049	(NA)
Expenditures abroad	24,558	25,913	29,310	32,114	33,418	37,349	36,958	44,300
Canada	2,506	3,034	2,939	3,232	3,396	3,541	3,705	3,600
Mexico	2,548	2,568	3,058	3,622	4,276	4,879	5,249	5,300
Total overseas	19,504	20,311	23,313	25,260	25,746	28,929	28,104	35,400
Europe............	9,403	9,218	10,251	11,347	11,967	13,996	13,176	17,400
Latin America [1]	3,995	4,337	4,822	5,172	5,123	5,395	5,806	6,900
Other...............	6,106	6,756	8,240	8,741	8,656	9,538	9,122	11,100
Fares to foreign carriers	6,484	6,554	7,318	7,768	8,258	10,608	10,636	12,000

NA Not available. [1] Includes Central and South America and the Caribbean.
Source: Travelers: U.S. Travel and Tourism Administration (USTTA), unpublished data. Expenditures: Through 1988, U.S. Bureau of Economic Analysis, *Survey of Current Business*, June 1990, and earlier issues; beginning 1989, USTTA, based on data from the Bureau of Economic Analysis.

No. 425. Foreign Travel to the United States—Travelers and Receipts: 1985 to 1992

[Travelers in thousands; receipts in millions of dollars. Includes travelers for business and pleasure, foreigners in transit through the United States, and students; excludes travel by foreign government personnel and foreign businessmen employed in the United States. See source for details. See also *Historical Statistics, Colonial Times to 1970*, series H 946-951]

AREA OF ORIGIN	1985	1986	1987	1988	1989	1990	1991	1992
International travelers	**25,399**	**26,008**	**29,424**	**34,095**	**36,564**	**39,539**	**42,909**	**45,405**
Canada	10,721	10,793	12,253	13,700	15,325	17,263	19,113	19,285
Mexico	7,141	6,355	6,637	7,883	7,240	7,217	7,641	8,130
Total overseas	7,537	8,860	10,534	12,512	13,999	15,059	16,155	17,990
Europe	2,905	3,722	4,663	5,772	6,251	6,659	7,360	8,274
Latin America [1]	1,795	2,048	2,176	2,366	2,627	2,877	3,080	3,210
Other	2,837	3,090	3,694	4,374	5,121	5,523	5,715	6,507
Total travel receipts	**17,920**	**20,529**	**23,718**	**29,665**	**36,571**	**43,418**	**48,757**	**55,300**
Canada	2,580	2,701	3,309	4,150	5,385	7,093	8,499	8,700
Mexico	2,259	2,178	2,366	3,202	4,247	5,519	5,740	6,100
Total overseas	13,081	15,650	18,043	22,313	26,939	30,806	34,518	40,500
Europe	4,774	5,844	7,596	9,778	11,004	12,602	14,332	17,300
Latin America [1]	3,122	3,611	3,502	3,726	4,418	5,126	5,927	6,700
Other	5,185	6,195	6,945	8,809	11,517	13,078	14,259	16,500
Fares to U.S. carriers	4,382	5,545	6,966	8,925	10,525	15,140	15,627	17,300

[1] Includes Central and South America and the Caribbean.
Source: Travelers: U.S. Travel and Tourism Administration (USTTA), unpublished data. Receipts: Through 1988, U.S. Bureau of Economic Analysis, *Survey of Current Business*, June 1990, and earlier issues; beginning 1989, USTTA, based on data from the Bureau of Economic Analysis.

No. 426. Foreign Visitors for Pleasure Admitted, by Country of Last Residence: 1985 to 1991

[In thousands. For years ending September 30. See headnote, table 7, section 1]

COUNTRY	1985	1989	1990	1991	COUNTRY	1985	1989	1990	1991
Total [1]	**6,609**	**12,115**	**13,418**	**14,734**	Africa [2]	101	108	105	106
					Egypt	16	16	16	16
Europe [2]	2,048	4,967	5,383	6,119	Nigeria	25	14	11	13
Austria	34	82	87	101	Oceania [2]	282	497	562	572
Belgium	39	80	95	115	Australia	195	324	380	404
Denmark	36	86	75	77	New Zealand	74	144	153	135
Finland	24	67	83	84					
France	226	497	566	632	North America	1,664	2,293	2,463	2,570
Greece	34	43	43	40	Canada	79	101	119	146
Ireland	55	91	81	91	Mexico	773	999	1,061	1,154
Italy	155	276	308	389	Caribbean [2]	584	899	963	931
Netherlands	82	190	214	248	Bahamas, the	211	316	332	306
					Barbados	17	32	34	37
Norway	41	81	80	71	Cayman Islands	18	28	31	33
Poland	40	52	55	44	Dominican Republic	57	114	137	129
Soviet Union	2	38	53	57	Haiti	56	63	57	51
Spain	64	160	183	234	Jamaica	74	134	132	120
Sweden	71	207	230	219	Netherlands Antilles	27	26	31	35
Switzerland	110	221	236	254	Trinidad and Tobago	71	82	81	72
United Kingdom	598	1,790	1,899	2,122	Central America [2]	228	294	320	339
Germany [3]	373	897	969	1,214	Costa Rica	41	50	62	63
					El Salvador	38	46	46	46
Asia [2]	1,866	3,317	3,830	4,017	Guatemala	53	86	91	89
China (Mainland China and Taiwan)	83	136	187	209	Panama	38	41	43	49
Hong Kong	64	97	111	127	South America [2]	606	896	1,016	1,272
India	52	73	75	71	Argentina	66	106	136	231
Israel	80	121	128	141	Brazil	148	272	300	390
Japan	1,277	2,483	2,846	2,932	Chile	28	57	54	65
Korea	26	75	120	184	Colombia	123	122	122	124
Philippines	59	69	76	83	Ecuador	42	52	57	64
Saudi Arabia	31	33	33	33	Peru	44	74	97	96
Singapore	23	30	32	34	Venezuela	122	162	199	238

[1] Includes countries unknown or not reported. [2] Includes countries not shown separately. [3] Data prior to 1991 for former West Germany.

Source: U.S. Immigration and Naturalization Service, *Statistical Yearbook*, annual.

This section relates primarily to Presidential, congressional, and gubernatorial elections. Also presented are summary tables on congressional legislation; State legislatures; Black, Hispanic, and female officeholders; population of voting age; voter participation; and campaign finances.

Official statistics on Federal elections, collected by the Clerk of the House, are published biennially in *Statistics of the Presidential and Congressional Election* and *Statistics of the Congressional Election*. Federal and State elections data appear also in *America Votes*, a biennial volume of the Elections Research Center, Chevy Chase, MD. Federal elections data also appear in the U.S. Congress, *Congressional Directory*, and in official State documents. Data on reported registration and voting for social and economic groups are obtained by the U.S. Bureau of the Census as part of the Current Population Survey (CPS) and are published in *Current Population Reports*, P20 (see text, section 1).

Almost all Federal, State, and local governmental units in the United States conduct elections for political offices and other purposes. The conduct of elections is regulated by State laws or, in some cities and counties, by local charter. An exception is that the U.S. Constitution prescribes the basis of representation in Congress and the manner of electing the President, and grants to Congress the right to regulate the times, places, and manner of electing Federal officers. Amendments to the Constitution have prescribed national criteria for voting eligibility. The 15th Amendment, adopted in 1870, gave all citizens the right to vote regardless of race, color, or previous condition of servitude. The 19th Amendment, adopted in 1919, further extended the right to vote to all citizens regardless of sex. The payment of poll taxes as a prerequisite to voting in Federal elections was banned by the 24th Amendment in 1964. In 1971, as a result of the 26th Amendment, eligibility to vote in national elections was extended to all citizens, 18 years old and over.

In Brief

Percent of voting-age population voting for President:

1980	52.6%
1992	55.2%

Members of Congress:

	1981	1993
Black	17	39
Hispanic	6	17
Female	21	53

Presidential election.—The Constitution specifies how the President and Vice President are selected. Each State elects, by popular vote, a group of electors equal in number to its total of members of Congress. The 23d Amendment, adopted in 1961, grants the District of Columbia three presidential electors, a number equal to that of the least populous State. Subsequent to the election, the electors meet in their respective States to vote for President and Vice President. Usually, each elector votes for the candidate receiving the most popular votes in his or her State. A majority vote of all electors is necessary to elect the President and Vice President. If no candidate receives a majority, the House of Representatives, with each State having one vote, is empowered to elect the President and Vice President, again, with a majority of votes required.

The 22d Amendment to the Constitution, adopted in 1951, limits presidential tenure to two elective terms of 4 years each, or to one elective term for any person who, upon succession to the Presidency, has held the office or acted as President for more than 2 years.

Congressional election.—The Constitution provides that Representatives be apportioned among the States according to their population; that a census of population be taken every 10 years as a basis for apportionment; and that each State have at least one Representative. At the time of each apportionment, Congress decides what the total number of

Representatives will be. Since 1912, the total has been 435, except during 1960 to 1962 when it increased to 437, adding one Representative each for Alaska and Hawaii. The total reverted to 435 after reapportionment following the 1960 census. Members are elected for 2-year terms, all terms covering the same period. The District of Columbia, American Samoa, Guam, and the Virgin Islands each elect one nonvoting Delegate and Puerto Rico elects a nonvoting Resident Commissioner.

The Senate is composed of 100 members, two from each State, who are elected to serve for a term of 6 years. One-third of the Senate is elected every 2 years. Senators were originally chosen by the State legislatures. The 17th Amendment to the Constitution, adopted in 1913, prescribed that Senators be elected by popular vote.

Voter eligibility and participation.—The Census Bureau publishes estimates of the population of voting age and the percent casting votes in each State for Presidential and congressional election years. These voting-age estimates include a number of persons who meet the age requirement but are not eligible to vote, (e.g. aliens and some institutionalized persons). In addition, since 1964, voter participation and voter characteristics data have been collected during November of election years as part of the CPS. These survey data include noncitizens in the voting age population estimates, but exclude members of the Armed Forces and the institutional population.

Statistical reliability.—For a discussion of statistical collection and estimation, sampling procedures, and measures of statistical reliability applicable to Census Bureau data, see Appendix III.

Historical statistics.—Tabular headnotes provide cross-references, where applicable, to *Historical Statistics of the United States, Colonial Times to 1970*. See Appendix IV.

Figure 8.1
Popular Vote Cast for President, by Major Party: 1972 to 1992

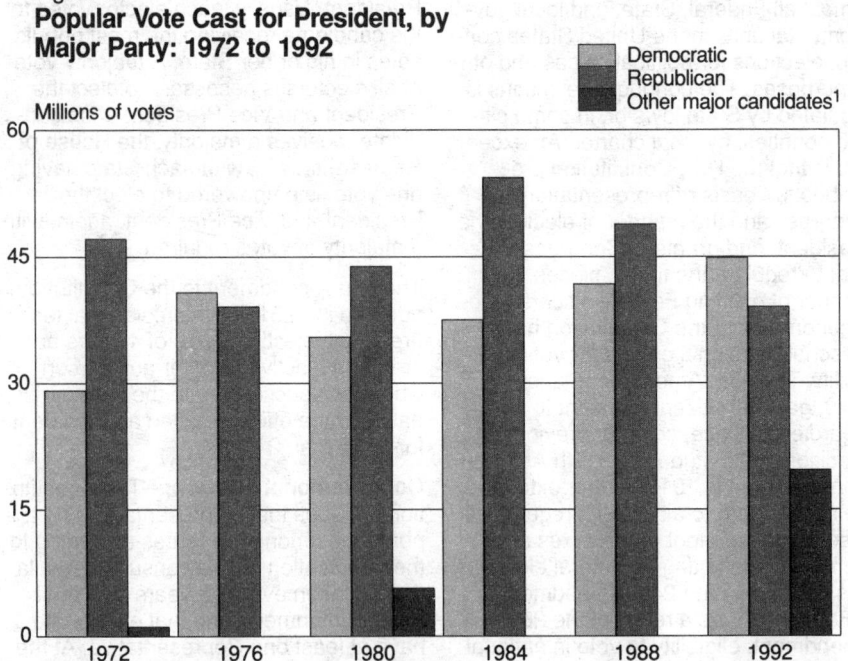

1 1972–American, John Schmitz; 1980–Independent, John Anderson; 1992–Independent, H. Ross Perot.

Source: Chart prepared by U.S. Bureau of the Census. For data, see tables 427 and 428.

No. 427. Vote Cast for President, by Major Political Party: 1936 to 1992

[Prior to 1960, excludes Alaska and Hawaii; prior to 1964, excludes DC. Vote cast for major party candidates include the votes of minor parties cast for those candidates. See also *Historical Statistics, Colonial Times to 1970*, series Y 79-83 and Y 135]

	CANDIDATES FOR PRESIDENT		VOTE CAST FOR PRESIDENT						
				Democratic			Republican		
YEAR	Democratic	Republican	Total popular vote [1] (1,000)	Popular vote		Electoral vote	Popular vote		Electoral vote
				Number (1,000)	Percent		Number (1,000)	Percent	
1936	F. D. Roosevelt. .	Landon	45,655	27,757	60.8	523	16,684	36.5	8
1940	F. D. Roosevelt. .	Willkie	49,900	27,313	54.7	449	22,348	44.8	82
1944	F. D. Roosevelt. .	Dewey.	47,977	25,613	53.4	432	22,018	45.9	99
1948	Truman	Dewey.	48,794	24,179	49.6	303	21,991	45.1	189
1952	Stevenson	Eisenhower.	61,551	27,315	44.4	89	33,936	55.1	442
1956	Stevenson	Eisenhower.	62,027	26,023	42.0	73	35,590	57.4	457
1960	Kennedy	Nixon.	68,838	34,227	49.7	303	34,108	49.5	219
1964	Johnson.	Goldwater	70,645	43,130	61.1	486	27,178	38.5	52
1968	Humphrey	Nixon.	73,212	31,275	42.7	191	31,785	43.4	301
1972	McGovern	Nixon.	77,719	29,170	37.5	17	47,170	60.7	520
1976	Carter	Ford	81,556	40,831	50.1	297	39,148	48.0	240
1980	Carter	Reagan	86,515	35,484	41.0	49	43,904	50.7	489
1984	Mondale.	Reagan	92,653	37,577	40.6	13	54,455	58.8	525
1988	Dukakis	Bush	91,595	41,809	45.6	111	48,886	53.4	426
1992	Clinton.	Bush	104,425	44,909	43.0	370	39,104	37.4	168

[1] Include votes for minor party candidates, independents, unpledged electors, and scattered write-in votes.

No. 428. Vote Cast for Leading Minority Party Candidates for President: 1936 to 1992

[See headnote, table 427]

YEAR	Candidate	Party	Popular vote (1,000)	Candidate	Party	Popular vote (1,000)
1936 . .	William Lemke	Union	892	Norman Thomas . . .	Socialist	188
1940 . .	Norman Thomas . . .	Socialist	116	Roger Babson	Prohibition	59
1944 . .	Norman Thomas . . .	Socialist	79	Claude Watson . . .	Prohibition	75
1948 . .	Strom Thurmond . . .	States' Rights	1,176	Henry Wallace	Progressive	1,157
1952 . .	Vincent Hallinan. . . .	Progressive	140	Stuart Hamblen	Prohibition	73
1956 . .	T. Coleman Andrews.	States' Rights	111	Eric Hass	Socialist Labor	44
1960 . .	Eric Hass	Socialist Labor	48	Rutherford Decker . .	Prohibition	46
1964 . .	Eric Hass	Socialist Labor	45	Clifton DeBerry	Socialist Workers	33
1968 . .	George Wallace	American Independent.	9,906	Henning Blomen . . .	Socialist Labor	53
1972 . .	John Schmitz.	American.	1,099	Benjamin Spock. . . .	People's	79
1976 . .	Eugene McCarthy. . .	Independent	757	Roger McBride	Libertarian.	173
1980 . .	John Anderson	Independent	5,720	Ed Clark	Libertarian.	921
1984 . .	David Bergland	Libertarian.	228	Lyndon H. LaRouche.	Independent	79
1988 . .	Ron Paul	Libertarian.	432	Lenora B. Fulani . . .	New Alliance	217
1992 . .	H. Ross Perot	Independent	19,742	Andre Marrou	Libertarian.	292

Source of tables 427 and 428: Elections Research Center, Chevy Chase, MD, *America at the Polls 2*, 1965, and *America Votes*, biennial (copyright).

No. 429. Democratic and Republican Percentages of Two-Party Presidential Vote, by Selected Characteristics of Voters: 1984 and 1988

[In percent. Covers citizens of voting-age living in private housing units in the contiguous United States. Percentages for Democratic Presidential vote are computed by subtracting the percentage Republican vote from 100 percent; third party votes are not included as valid data. Data are from the National Election Studies and are based on a sample (for 1988, 2,040 respondents) and subject to sampling variability; for details, see source]

CHARACTERISTIC	1984		1988		CHARACTERISTIC	1984		1988	
	Democratic	Republican	Democratic	Republican		Democratic	Republican	Democratic	Republican
Total [1]	42	58	47	53	Race:				
Year of birth:					White.	37	63	41	59
1959 or later	42	58	48	52	Black . . . . : .	91	9	92	8
1943 to 1958.	41	59	47	53					
1927 to 1942.	40	60	49	51	Education:				
1911 to 1926.	44	56	44	56	Grade school.	62	38	61	39
1895 to 1910.	42	58	47	53	High school.	42	58	51	49
					College.	38	62	42	58
Sex:									
Male	38	62	44	56	Union household	57	43	59	41
Female	45	55	50	50	Non-union household. .	37	63	44	56

[1] Includes other characteristics, not shown separately.

Source: Center for Political Studies, University of Michigan, Ann Arbor, MI. Data are published in Warren E. Miller and Santa A. Traugott, *American National Election Studies Data Sourcebook, 1952-1986*, Harvard University Press, Cambridge, MA, 1989 (copyright).

No. 430. Electoral Vote Cast for President, by Major Political Party—States: 1952 to 1992

[D=Democratic, R=Republican. For composition of regions, see table 31. See also *Historical Statistics, Colonial Times to 1970*, series Y 84-134]

REGION, DIVISION, AND STATE	1952	1956 [1]	1960 [2]	1964	1968 [3]	1972 [4]	1976 [5]	1980	1984	1988 [6]	1992
Democratic......	89	73	303	486	191	17	297	49	13	111	370
Republican......	442	457	219	52	301	520	240	489	525	426	168
Northeast: Democratic .	-	-	121	126	102	14	86	4	-	53	106
Republican .	133	133	12	-	24	108	36	118	113	60	-
Midwest: Democratic ..	-	13	71	149	31	-	58	10	10	29	100
Republican ..	153	140	82	-	118	145	87	135	127	108	29
South: Democratic	89	60	101	121	45	3	149	31	3	8	68
Republican	77	105	50	47	77	165	20	138	174	168	116
West: Democratic ..	-	-	10	90	13	-	4	4	-	21	96
Republican....	79	79	75	5	82	102	97	98	111	90	23
New England: ME	R-5	R-5	R-5	D-4	D-4	R-4	R-4	R-4	R-4	R-4	D-4
NH	R-4	R-4	R-4	D-4	R-4	R-4	R-4	R-4	R-4	R-4	D-4
VT	R-3	R-3	R-3	D-3	R-3	R-3	R-3	R-3	R-3	R-3	D-3
MA	R-16	R-16	D-16	D-14	D-14	D-14	D-14	R-14	R-13	D-13	D-12
RI	R-4	R-4	D-4	D-4	D-4	R-4	D-4	D-4	R-4	D-4	D-4
CT	R-8	R-8	D-8	D-8	D-8	R-8	R-8	R-8	R-8	R-8	D-8
Middle Atlantic: NY ...	R-45	R-45	D-45	D-43	D-43	R-41	D-41	R-41	R-36	D-36	D-33
NJ	R-16	R-16	D-16	D-17	R-17	R-17	R-17	R-17	R-16	R-16	D-15
PA	R-32	R-32	D-32	D-29	D-29	R-27	D-27	R-27	R-25	R-25	D-23
East North Central: OH	R-25	R-25	R-25	D-26	R-26	R-25	D-25	R-25	R-23	R-23	D-21
IN	R-13	R-13	R-13	D-13	R-13	R-13	R-13	R-13	R-12	R-12	R-12
IL	R-27	R-27	D-27	D-26	R-26	R-26	R-26	R-26	R-24	R-24	D-22
MI	R-20	R-20	D-20	D-21	D-21	R-21	R-21	R-21	R-20	R-20	D-18
WI	R-12	R-12	R-12	D-12	R-12	R-11	D-11	R-11	R-11	D-11	D-11
West North Central: MN	R-11	R-11	D-11	D-10	D-10	R-10	D-10	D-10	D-10	D-10	D-10
IA	R-10	R-10	R-10	D-9	R-9	R-8	R-8	R-8	R-8	D-8	D-7
MO	R-13	D-13	D-13	D-12	R-12	R-12	D-12	R-12	R-11	R-11	D-11
ND	R-4	R-4	R-4	D-4	R-4	R-3	R-3	R-3	R-3	R-3	R-3
SD	R-4	R-4	R-4	D-4	R-4	R-4	R-4	R-4	R-3	R-3	R-3
NE	R-6	R-6	R-6	D-5	R-5	R-5	R-5	R-5	R-5	R-5	R-5
KS	R-8	R-8	R-8	D-7	R-7	R-7	R-7	R-7	R-7	R-7	R-6
South Atlantic: DE	R-3	R-3	D-3	D-3	R-3	R-3	D-3	R-3	R-3	R-3	D-3
MD	R-9	R-9	D-9	D-10	D-10	R-10	D-10	D-10	R-10	R-10	D-10
DC	(X)	(X)	(X)	D-3	D-3	D-3	D-3	D-3	D-3	D-3	D-3
VA	R-12	R-12	R-12	D-12	R-12	[4]R-11	R-12	R-12	R-12	R-12	R-13
WV	D-8	R-8	D-8	D-7	D-7	R-6	D-6	D-6	R-6	[6]D-5	D-5
NC	D-14	D-14	D-14	D-13	[3]R-12	R-13	D-13	R-13	R-13	R-13	R-14
SC	D-8	D-8	D-8	R-8	R-8	R-8	D-8	R-8	R-8	R-8	R-8
GA	D-12	D-12	D-12	R-12	(3)	R-12	D-12	D-12	D-12	R-12	D-13
FL	R-10	R-10	R-10	D-14	R-14	R-17	D-17	R-17	R-21	R-21	R-25
East South Central: KY	D-10	R-10	R-10	D-9	R-9	R-9	D-9	R-9	R-9	R-9	D-8
TN	D-11	R-11	R-11	D-11	R-11	R-10	D-10	R-10	R-11	R-11	D-11
AL	D-11	[1]D-10	[2]D-5	R-10	(3)	R-9	D-9	R-9	R-9	R-9	R-9
MS	D-8	D-8	(2)	R-7	(3)	R-7	D-7	R-7	R-7	R-7	R-7
West South Central: AR	D-8	D-8	D-8	D-6	(3)	R-6	D-6	R-6	R-6	R-6	D-6
LA	D-10	R-10	D-10	R-10	(3)	R-10	D-10	R-10	R-10	R-10	D-9
OK	R-8	R-8	[2]R-7	D-8	R-8	R-8	R-8	R-8	R-8	R-8	R-8
TX	R-24	R-24	D-24	D-25	D-25	R-26	D-26	R-26	R-29	R-29	R-32
Mountain: MT	R-4	R-4	R-4	D-4	R-4	R-4	R-4	R-4	R-4	R-4	D-3
ID	R-4	R-4	R-4	D-4	R-4	R-4	R-4	R-4	R-4	R-4	R-4
WY	R-3	R-3	R-3	D-3	R-3	R-3	R-3	R-3	R-3	R-3	R-3
CO	R-6	R-6	R-6	D-6	R-6	R-7	R-7	R-7	R-8	R-8	D-8
NM	R-4	R-4	D-4	D-4	R-4	R-4	R-4	R-4	R-5	R-5	D-5
AZ	R-4	R-4	R-4	R-5	R-5	R-6	R-6	R-6	R-7	R-7	R-8
UT	R-4	R-4	R-4	D-4	R-4	R-4	R-4	R-4	R-5	R-5	R-5
NV	R-3	R-3	D-3	D-3	R-3	R-3	R-3	R-3	R-4	R-4	D-4
Pacific: WA	R-9	R-9	R-9	D-9	D-9	R-9	[5]R-8	R-9	R-10	D-10	D-11
OR	R-6	R-6	R-6	D-6	D-6	R-6	R-6	R-6	R-7	D-7	D-7
CA	R-32	R-32	R-32	D-40	R-40	R-45	R-45	R-45	R-47	R-47	D-54
AK	(X)	(X)	R-3	D-3	R-3	R-3	R-3	R-3	R-3	R-3	R-3
HI	(X)	(X)	D-3	D-4	D-4	R-4	D-4	D-4	R-4	D-4	D-4

- Represents zero. X Not applicable. [1] Excludes one electoral vote cast for Walter B. Jones in Alabama. [2] Excludes 15 electoral votes cast for Harry F. Byrd as follows: AL 6, MS 8, and OK 1. [3] Excludes 46 electoral votes cast for American Independent George C. Wallace as follows: AL 10, AR 6, GA 12, LA 10, MS 7, and NC 1. [4] Excludes one electoral vote cast for Libertarian John Hospers in Virginia. [5] Excludes one electoral vote cast for Ronald Reagan in Washington. [6] Excludes one electoral vote cast for Lloyd Bentsen for President in West Virginia.

Source: 1952-72, U.S. Congress, Clerk of the House, *Statistics of the Presidential and Congressional Election*, quadrennial; 1976-92, Elections Research Center, Chevy Chase, MD, *America Votes*, biennial (copyright).

No. 431. Popular Vote Cast for President, by Political Party—States: 1988 and 1992

[In thousands, except percent. See also *Historical Statistics, Colonial Times to 1970*, series Y 135-186]

REGION, DIVISION, AND STATE	1988 Total [1]	1988 Demo-cratic Party	1988 Repub-lican Party	1988 Percent for leading party [2]	1992 Total [1]	1992 Demo-cratic Party	1992 Repub-lican Party	1992 Perot (Inde-pen-dent)	Percent of total vote Demo-cratic Party	Percent of total vote Repub-lican Party	Percent of total vote Perot (Inde-pen-dent)
United States ..	91,595	41,809	48,886	R-53.4	104,425	44,909	39,104	19,742	43.0	37.4	18.9
Northeast	19,852	9,689	9,961	R-50.2	21,581	9,940	7,507	3,994	46.1	34.8	18.5
N.E.	5,730	2,826	2,836	R-49.5	6,351	2,820	2,012	1,479	44.4	31.7	23.3
ME	555	244	307	R-55.3	679	263	207	207	38.8	30.4	30.4
NH	451	164	282	R-62.4	538	209	202	121	38.9	37.6	22.6
VT...........	243	116	124	R-51.1	290	134	88	66	46.1	30.4	22.8
MA	2,633	1,401	1,195	D-53.2	2,774	1,319	805	631	47.5	29.0	22.7
RI	405	225	178	D-55.6	453	213	132	105	47.0	29.0	23.2
CT...........	1,443	677	750	R-52.0	1,616	682	578	349	42.2	35.8	21.6
M.A	14,121	6,863	7,125	R-50.5	15,230	7,120	5,495	2,515	46.7	36.1	16.5
NY...........	6,486	3,348	3,082	D-51.6	6,927	3,444	2,347	1,091	49.7	33.9	15.7
NJ...........	3,100	1,320	1,743	R-56.2	3,344	1,436	1,357	522	43.0	40.6	15.6
PA...........	4,536	2,195	2,300	R-50.7	4,960	2,239	1,792	903	45.1	36.1	18.2
Midwest.........	24,663	11,556	12,915	R-52.4	27,735	11,692	10,234	5,668	42.2	36.9	20.4
E.N.C	16,982	7,819	9,038	R-53.2	19,102	8,199	7,104	3,702	42.9	37.2	19.4
OH	4,394	1,940	2,417	R-55.0	4,940	1,985	1,894	1,036	40.2	38.3	21.0
IN	2,169	861	1,298	R-59.8	2,306	848	989	456	36.8	42.9	19.8
IL	4,559	2,216	2,311	R-50.7	5,050	2,453	1,734	841	48.6	34.3	16.6
MI	3,669	1,676	1,965	R-53.6	4,275	1,871	1,555	825	43.8	36.4	19.3
WI	2,192	1,127	1,047	D-51.4	2,531	1,041	931	544	41.1	36.8	21.5
W.N.C.........	7,681	3,737	3,877	R-50.5	8,633	3,493	3,130	1,966	40.5	36.3	22.8
MN	2,097	1,109	962	D-52.9	2,348	1,021	748	563	43.5	31.9	24.0
IA	1,226	671	545	D-54.7	1,355	586	505	253	43.3	37.3	18.7
MO	2,094	1,002	1,085	R-51.8	2,392	1,054	811	519	44.1	33.9	21.7
ND	297	128	167	R-56.0	308	99	136	71	32.2	44.2	23.1
SD...........	313	146	165	R-52.8	336	125	137	73	37.1	40.7	21.8
NE...........	661	259	398	R-60.2	738	217	344	174	29.4	46.6	23.6
KS...........	993	423	554	R-55.8	1,157	390	450	312	33.7	38.9	27.0
South	28,558	12,004	16,327	R-57.2	33,625	14,118	14,014	5,325	42.0	41.7	15.8
S.A.	14,234	5,927	8,207	R-57.7	17,195	7,352	7,103	2,667	42.8	41.3	15.5
DE.	250	109	140	R-55.9	290	126	102	59	43.5	35.3	20.4
MD...........	1,714	826	876	R-51.1	1,985	989	707	281	49.8	35.6	14.2
DC...........	193	159	28	D-82.6	228	193	21	10	84.6	9.1	4.3
VA...........	2,192	860	1,309	R-59.7	2,559	1,039	1,151	349	40.6	45.0	13.6
WV	653	341	310	D-52.2	684	331	242	109	48.4	35.4	15.9
NC	2,134	890	1,237	R-58.0	2,612	1,114	1,135	358	42.7	43.4	13.7
SC...........	986	371	606	R-61.5	1,203	480	578	139	39.9	48.0	11.5
GA	1,810	715	1,081	R-59.8	2,321	1,009	995	310	43.5	42.9	13.3
FL...........	4,302	1,657	2,619	R-60.9	5,314	2,073	2,173	1,053	39.0	40.9	19.8
E.S.C	5,269	2,174	3,055	R-58.0	6,145	2,689	2,751	673	43.8	44.8	10.9
KY...........	1,323	580	734	R-55.5	1,493	665	617	204	44.6	41.3	13.7
TN...........	1,636	680	947	R-57.9	1,983	934	841	200	47.1	42.4	10.1
AL...........	1,378	550	816	R-59.2	1,688	690	804	183	40.9	47.6	10.8
MS	932	364	558	R-59.9	982	400	488	86	40.8	49.7	8.7
W.S.C	9,054	3,903	5,065	R-55.9	10,285	4,077	4,160	1,985	39.6	40.4	19.3
AR...........	828	349	467	R-56.4	951	506	337	99	53.2	35.5	10.4
LA...........	1,628	717	884	R-54.3	1,790	816	733	211	45.6	41.0	11.8
OK	1,171	483	678	R-57.9	1,390	473	593	320	34.0	42.6	23.0
TX...........	5,427	2,353	3,037	R-56.0	6,154	2,282	2,496	1,355	37.1	40.6	22.0
West	18,522	8,560	9,683	R-52.3	21,484	9,160	7,349	4,755	42.6	34.2	22.1
Mt	5,014	2,043	2,887	R-57.6	5,970	2,167	2,272	1,437	36.3	38.1	24.1
MT	366	169	190	R-52.1	411	155	144	107	37.6	35.1	26.1
ID	409	147	254	R-62.1	482	137	203	130	28.4	42.0	27.0
WY	177	67	107	R-60.5	201	68	79	51	34.0	39.6	25.6
CO	1,372	621	728	R-53.1	1,569	630	563	366	40.1	35.9	23.3
NM	521	244	270	R-51.9	570	262	213	92	45.9	37.3	16.1
AZ...........	1,172	454	703	R-60.0	1,487	543	572	354	36.5	38.5	23.8
UT...........	647	207	428	R-66.2	744	183	323	203	24.7	43.4	27.3
NV...........	350	133	206	R-58.9	506	189	176	133	37.4	34.7	26.2
Pac	13,509	6,517	6,797	R-50.3	15,514	6,993	5,076	3,318	45.1	32.7	21.4
WA	1,865	934	904	D-50.0	2,288	993	731	542	43.4	32.0	23.7
OR	1,202	616	560	D-51.3	1,463	621	476	354	42.5	32.5	24.2
CA...........	9,887	4,702	5,055	R-51.1	11,132	5,121	3,631	2,296	46.0	32.6	20.6
AK...........	200	73	119	R-59.6	259	78	102	73	30.3	39.5	28.4
HI	354	192	159	D-54.3	373	179	137	53	48.1	36.7	14.2

[1] Includes other parties. [2] D=Democratic, R=Republican. Leading party vote refers to the party vote representing either a majority or a plurality for the victorious party in the area shown.

Source: Elections Research Center, Chevy Chase, MD, *America Votes*, biennial (copyright).

No. 432. Votes Cast in Presidential Preference Primaries, by Party and Leading Candidates: 1992

[In thousands. Covers only those States with Democratic or Republican presidential primaries]

STATE	Primary date	DEMOCRATIC (1,000)								REPUBLICAN (1,000)					
		Total	Brown	Clinton	Harkin	Kerry	Tsongas	Uncom-mitted	Other	Total	Buchanan	Bush	Duke	Uncom-mitted	Other
New Hampshire	February 18	168	14	42	17	19	56	-	21	174	65	92	-	-	17
South Dakota	February 25	60	2	11	15	24	6	-	4	45	-	31	-	14	5
Colorado	March 3	240	69	64	6	30	61	5	4	196	59	132	-	-	(Z)
Georgia	March 3	455	37	260	9	22	109	17	3	454	162	292	-	-	-
Maryland	March 3	567	47	190	33	27	230	36	-	240	72	168	11	-	-
South Carolina	March 7	116	7	73	8	1	21	4	-	149	38	100	11	-	3
Florida	March 10	1,124	140	571	14	12	388	-	42	893	285	608	12	-	2
Louisiana	March 10	384	25	267	4	3	43	-	43	135	37	84	6	-	1
Massachusetts	March 10	793	116	87	4	5	526	12	2	270	75	177	16	-	3
Mississippi	March 10	191	18	140	3	2	16	12	26	155	26	112	6	-	(Z)
Oklahoma	March 10	416	70	293	14	13	27	-	2	218	58	152	6	-	2
Rhode Island	March 10	51	10	11	(Z)	(Z)	62	1	(Z)	16	5	10	(Z)	8	0
Tennessee	March 10	318	26	214	20	2	62	13	67	246	55	178	20	5	1
Texas	March 10	1,483	119	972	31	20	285	68	10	797	191	556	11	28	0
Illinois	March 17	1,504	220	777	6	11	388	28	3	831	187	635	2	24	12
Michigan	March 17	586	151	297	2	3	97	5	5	449	112	302	4	9	(Z)
Connecticut	March 24	173	64	62	1	-	34	22	8	99	22	66	(¹)	11	-
Kansas	April 7	160	21	82	4	2	24	11	18	213	31	132	(¹)	35	13
Minnesota	April 7	204	62	64	12	1	44	-	20	133	32	85	(¹)	4	9
New York	April 7	1,008	264	412	5	11	288	15	26	482	79	365	-	-	-
Wisconsin	April 7	773	266	287	21	3	169	-	22	1,009	234	775	-	-	-
Pennsylvania	April 28	1,265	326	715	-	21	162	5	-	5	1	4	-	-	-
District of Columbia	May 5	62	4	46	-	-	6	-	11	468	93	375	-	-	7
Indiana	May 5	477	102	302	6	14	58	107	15	284	55	200	3	28	6
North Carolina	May 5	692	72	443	4	6	58	25	47	192	26	156	7	-	36
Nebraska	May 12	151	32	69	3	-	11	-	29	124	18	100	7	-	28
West Virginia	May 12	307	37	228	-	3	21	-	15	304	58	204	2	-	-
Oregon	May 19	354	110	160	2	1	37	-	3	130	13	87	-	-	-
Washington	May 19	148	34	62	-	-	19	91	-	52	7	46	-	-	(Z)
Arkansas	May 26	503	55	342	-	-	-	16	22	116	15	73	-	27	23
Idaho	May 26	55	9	27	-	-	-	104	108	101	-	75	-	26	8
Kentucky	May 26	371	31	208	7	3	18	91	-	165	13	123	-	30	-
Alabama	June 2	451	31	308	-	-	-	18	24	2,156	569	1,587	-	15	-
California	June 2	2,864	1,150	1,359	-	34	213	28	108	91	11	65	-	-	-
Montana	June 2	117	22	55	-	-	13	-	24	310	46	241	-	-	24
New Jersey	June 2	393	80	244	-	-	45	28	45	87	8	56	-	-	23
New Mexico	June 2	181	31	96	3	-	11	35	47	860	144	717	-	-	-
Ohio	June 2	1,042	197	638	25	23	111	-	28	48	-	40	-	-	8
North Dakota	June 9	33	-	5	-	-	-	-	-						

- Represents zero.   Z Less than 500.   ¹ No primary held.

Source: McGillivray, Alice V., *Presidential Primaries and Caucuses 1992*, Congressional Quarterly, Inc., Washington, DC, 1993 (copyright).

No. 433. Vote Cast for United States Senators, 1990 and 1992, and Incumbent Senators, 1993—States

[D=Democrat; R=Republican]

DIVISION AND STATE	1990 Total (1,000)	1990 Percent for leading party	1992 Total (1,000)	1992 Percent for leading party	INCUMBENT SENATORS AND YEAR TERM EXPIRES Name, party, and year	Name, party, and year
N.E.:						
ME.	520	R-61.3	(X)	(X)	George J. Mitchell (D) 1995	William S. Cohen (R) 1997
NH.	291	R-65.1	518	R-48.1	Judd Gregg (R) 1999	Robert C. Smith (R) 1997
VT.	(X)	(X)	286	D-54.2	Patrick J. Leahy (D) 1999	James M. Jeffords (R) 1995
MA.	2,316	D-57.1	(X)	(X)	Edward M. Kennedy (D) 1995	John F. Kerry (D) 1997
RI	364	D-61.8	(X)	(X)	Claiborne Pell (D) 1997	John H. Chafee (R) 1995
CT.	(X)	(X)	1,501	D-58.8	Christopher J. Dodd (D) 1999	Joseph I. Lieberman (D) 1995
M.A.:						
NY.	(X)	(X)	6,459	R-49.0	Daniel P. Moynihan (D) 1995	Alfonse M. D'Amato (R) 1999
NJ.	1,938	D-50.4	(X)	(X)	Bill Bradley (D) 1997	Frank R. Lautenberg (D) 1995
PA.	[1]3,383	[1]D-55.0	4,802	R-49.1	Harris Wofford (D) 1995	Arlen Specter (R) 1999
E.N.C.:						
OH.	(X)	(X)	4,794	D-51.0	John Glenn (D) 1999	Howard Metzenbaum (D) 1995
IN	[2]1,504	[2]R-53.6	2,211	R-57.3	Dan Coats (R) 1999	Richard G. Lugar (R) 1995
IL.	3,251	D-65.1	4,940	D-53.3	Carol Moseley Braun (D) 1999	Paul Simon (D) 1997
MI	2,560	D-57.5	(X)	(X)	Carl Levin (D) 1997	Donald W. Riegle, Jr. (D) 1995
WI	(X)	(X)	2,455	D-52.6	Herb Kohl (D) 1995	Russell Feingold (D) 1999
W.N.C.:						
MN.	1,808	D-50.4	(X)	(X)	Paul David Wellstone (D) 1997	Dave Durenberger (R) 1995
IA	984	D-54.5	1,292	R-69.6	Tom Harkin (D) 1997	Charles E. Grassley (R) 1999
MO	(X)	(X)	2,355	R-51.9	Christopher S. Bond (R) 1999	John C. Danforth (R) 1995
ND.	(X)	(X)	304	D-59.0	Byron L. Dorgan (D) 1999	[3]Kent Conrad (D) 1995
SD.	259	R-52.4	334	D-64.9	Thomas A. Daschle (D) 1999	Larry Pressler (R) 1997
NE.	594	D-58.9	(X)	(X)	J. James Exon (D) 1997	J. Robert Kerrey (D) 1995
KS.	786	R-73.6	1,126	R-62.7	Bob Dole (R) 1999	Nancy Kassebaum (R) 1997
S.A.:						
DE.	180	D-62.7	(X)	(X)	Joseph R. Biden Jr. (D) 1997	William V. Roth, Jr. (R) 1995
MD.	(X)	(X)	1,842	D-71.0	Barbara A. Mikulski (D) 1999	Paul S. Sarbanes (D) 1995
VA.	1,084	R-80.9	(X)	(X)	Charles S. Robb (D) 1995	John W. Warner (R) 1997
WV	404	D-68.3	(X)	(X)	Robert C. Byrd (D) 1995	John D. Rockefeller IV (D) 1997
NC.	2,070	R-52.5	2,578	R-50.3	Lauch Faircloth (R) 1999	Jesse Helms (R) 1997
SC.	751	R-64.2	1,180	D-50.1	Ernest F. Hollings (D) 1999	Strom Thurmond (R) 1997
GA.	1,034	D-100.0	[4]1,254	[4]R-50.6	Paul Coverdell (R) 1999	Sam Nunn (D) 1997
FL.	(X)	(X)	4,962	D-65.4	Bob Graham (D) 1999	Connie Mack (R) 1995
E.S.C.:						
KY.	916	R-52.2	1,331	D-62.9	Wendell H. Ford (D) 1999	Mitch McConnell (R) 1997
TN.	784	D-67.7	(X)	(X)	[5]Harlan Mathews (D) 1997	Jim Sasser (D) 1995
AL.	1,186	D-60.5	1,578	D-64.8	Howell Heflin (D) 1997	Richard C. Shelby (D) 1999
MS.	274	R-100.0	(X)	(X)	Thad Cochran (R) 1997	Trent Lott (R) 1995
W.S.C.:						
AR.	495	D-99.8	920	D-60.2	Dale Bumpers (D) 1999	David Pryor (D) 1997
LA.	[6]1,396	[6]D-56.5	[6]843	[6]D-73.1	John B. Breaux (D) 1999	J. Bennett Johnston (D) 1997
OK.	884	D-83.2	1,294	R-58.5	David L. Boren (D) 1997	Don Nickles (R) 1999
TX.	3,822	R-60.2	(X)	(X)	[7]Kay Bailey Hutchison (R) 1995	Phil Gramm (R) 1997
Mt.:						
MT.	319	D-68.1	(X)	(X)	Max Baucus (D) 1997	Conrad Burns (R) 1995
ID.	316	R-61.3	479	R-56.5	Larry E. Craig (R) 1997	Dirk Kempthorne (R) 1999
WY	158	R-63.9	(X)	(X)	Alan K. Simpson (R) 1997	Malcolm Wallop (R) 1995
CO.	1,022	R-55.7	1,552	D-51.8	Ben N. Campbell (D) 1999	Hank Brown (R) 1997
NM.	407	R-72.9	(X)	(X)	Jeff Bingaman (D) 1995	Pete V. Domenici (R) 1997
AZ.	(X)	(X)	1,382	R-55.8	Dennis DeConcini (D) 1995	John McCain (R) 1999
UT.	(X)	(X)	758	R-55.4	Robert F. Bennett (R) 1999	Orrin G. Hatch (R) 1995
NV.	(X)	(X)	496	D-51.0	Harry Reid (D) 1999	Richard H. Bryan (D) 1995
Pac.:						
WA.	(X)	(X)	2,219	D-54.0	Patty Murray (D) 1999	Slade Gorton (R) 1995
OR.	1,099	R-53.7	1,376	R-52.1	Mark O. Hatfield (R) 1997	Bob Packwood (R) 1999
CA.	(X)	(X)	10,800	D-47.9	Barbara Boxer (D) 1999	[8]Dianne Feinstein (D) 1995
AK.	190	R-66.2	240	R-53.0	Frank H. Murkowski (R) 1999	Ted Stevens (R) 1997
HI	[9]350	[9]D-54.0	364	D-57.3	Daniel K. Akaka (D) 1999	Daniel K. Inouye (D) 1995

X Not applicable.   [1] Special election in November 1991 to fill vacancy caused by death of Senator John Heinz.   [2] Special election to fill the unexpired term of Vice-President Quayle.   [3] In a special election in 1992 to fill an unexpired term, the Democratic candidate received 63.2 percent of 163,311 total votes cast.   [4] Results of run-off election. In the first election no candidate received more than 50 percent of the vote. First election: Total votes cast, 2,251,587; Democratic candidate, 1,108,416; Republican candidate, 1,073,282.   [5] Appointed to fill the unexpired term of Vice-President Gore.   [6] Louisiana holds an open-primary election with candidates from all parties running on the same ballot. Any candidate who receives a majority is elected. In 1990 and 1992 the indicated Senators received more than 50 percent of the vote in the October open-primary.   [7] Winner of a special election in June 1993 to fill the unexpired term of Senator Bentsen.   [8] In a special election in 1992 to fill an unexpired term, the Democratic candidate received 54.3 percent of 10,782,743 total votes cast.   [9] Special election to fill the unexpired term of Senator Matsunaga.

Source: Elections Research Center, Chevy Chase, MD, *America Votes*, biennial, (copyright).

No. 434. Apportionment of Membership in House of Representatives, by State: 1790 to 1990

[Total membership includes Representatives assigned to newly admitted States after the apportionment acts. Population figures used for apportionment purposes are those determined for States by each decennial census. No reapportionment based on 1920 population census. For method of calculating apportionment and a short history of apportionment, see House Report 91-1314, 91st Congress, 2d session, *The Decennial Population Census and Congressional Apportionment*. See also *Historical Statistics, Colonial Times to 1970*, series Y 220-271]

STATE	1790	1800	1810	1820	1830	1840	1850	1860	1870	1880	1890	1900	1910	1930	1940	1950	1960	1970	1980	1990
U.S....	106	142	186	213	242	232	237	243	293	332	357	391	435	435	435	437	435	435	435	435
Northeast	57	76	97	105	112	94	92	87	95	95	99	108	123	122	120	115	108	104	95	88
N.E.....	29	35	41	39	38	31	29	27	28	26	27	29	32	29	28	28	25	25	24	23
ME...	(X)	(X)	(X)	7	8	7	6	5	5	4	4	4	4	3	3	3	2	2	2	2
NH...	4	5	6	6	5	4	3	3	3	2	2	2	2	2	2	2	2	2	2	2
VT....	2	4	6	6	5	5	4	3	3	3	2	2	2	1	1	1	1	1	1	1
MA...	14	17	20	13	12	10	11	10	11	12	13	14	16	15	14	14	12	12	11	10
RI....	2	2	2	2	2	2	2	2	2	2	2	2	3	2	2	2	2	2	2	2
CT....	7	7	7	6	6	4	4	4	4	4	4	5	5	6	6	6	6	6	6	6
M.A....	28	41	56	66	74	63	63	60	67	69	72	79	91	93	92	87	83	79	71	65
NY....	10	17	27	34	40	34	33	31	33	34	34	37	43	45	45	43	41	39	34	31
NJ....	5	6	6	6	6	5	5	5	7	7	8	10	12	14	14	14	15	15	14	13
PA....	13	18	23	26	28	24	25	24	27	28	30	32	36	34	33	30	27	25	23	21
Midwest.	(X)	1	8	19	32	50	59	75	98	117	128	136	143	137	131	129	125	121	113	105
E.N.C..	(X)	1	8	18	30	43	48	56	69	74	78	82	86	90	87	87	88	86	80	74
OH....	(X)	1	[1]6	14	19	21	21	19	20	21	21	21	22	24	23	23	24	23	21	19
IN....	(X)	(X)	[1]1	3	7	10	11	11	13	13	13	13	13	12	11	11	11	11	10	10
IL....	(X)	(X)	[1]1	1	3	7	9	14	19	20	22	25	27	27	26	25	24	24	22	20
MI....	(X)	(X)	(X)	(X)	[1]1	3	4	6	9	11	12	12	13	17	17	18	19	19	18	16
WI....	(X)	(X)	(X)	(X)	(X)	2	3	6	8	9	10	11	11	10	10	10	10	9	9	9
W.N.C...	(X)	(X)	(X)	1	2	7	11	19	29	43	50	54	57	47	44	42	37	35	33	31
MN...	(X)	(X)	(X)	(X)	(X)	(X)	2	2	3	5	7	9	10	9	9	9	8	8	8	8
IA....	(X)	(X)	(X)	(X)	(X)	[1]2	2	6	9	11	11	11	11	9	8	8	7	6	6	5
MO...	(X)	(X)	(X)	1	2	5	7	9	13	14	15	16	16	13	13	11	10	10	9	9
ND...	(X)	(X)	(X)	(X)	(X)	(X)	(X)	(X)	[1]1	1	2	3	3	2	2	2	2	1	1	1
SD...	(X)	(X)	(X)	(X)	(X)	(X)	(X)	(X)	[1]2	2	2	3	3	2	2	2	2	2	1	1
NE...	(X)	(X)	(X)	(X)	(X)	(X)	(X)	[1]1	1	3	6	6	6	5	4	4	3	3	3	3
KS...	(X)	(X)	(X)	(X)	(X)	(X)	(X)	1	3	7	8	8	8	7	6	6	5	5	5	4
South	49	65	81	89	98	86	83	76	93	107	112	126	136	133	135	134	133	134	142	149
S.A....	46	56	62	61	61	47	43	36	43	49	50	53	56	54	56	60	63	65	69	75
DE...	1	1	2	1	1	1	1	1	1	1	1	1	1	1	1	1	1	1	1	1
MD...	8	9	9	9	8	6	6	5	6	6	6	6	6	6	6	7	8	8	8	8
VA...	19	22	23	22	21	15	13	11	9	10	10	10	10	9	9	10	10	10	10	11
WV...	(X)	(X)	(X)	(X)	(X)	(X)	(X)	3	4	4	4	5	6	6	6	6	5	4	4	3
NC...	10	12	13	13	13	9	8	7	8	9	9	10	10	11	12	12	11	11	11	12
SC...	6	8	9	9	9	7	6	4	5	7	7	7	7	6	6	6	6	6	6	6
GA...	2	4	6	7	9	8	8	7	9	10	11	11	12	10	10	10	10	10	10	11
FL....	(X)	(X)	(X)	(X)	(X)	[1]1	1	1	2	2	2	3	4	5	6	8	12	15	19	23
E.S.C..	3	9	18	25	33	32	32	28	34	36	37	38	39	34	35	32	29	27	28	27
KY...	2	6	10	12	13	10	10	9	10	11	11	11	11	9	9	8	7	7	7	6
TN...	[1]1	3	6	9	13	11	10	8	10	10	10	10	10	9	10	9	9	8	8	9
AL...	(X)	(X)	[1]1	3	5	7	7	6	8	8	9	9	10	9	9	9	8	7	7	7
MS...	(X)	(X)	[1]1	1	2	4	5	5	6	7	7	8	8	7	7	6	5	5	5	5
W.S.C...	(X)	(X)	1	3	4	7	8	12	16	22	25	35	41	45	44	42	41	42	45	47
AR...	(X)	(X)	(X)	(X)	[1]1	1	2	3	4	5	6	7	7	7	6	4	4	4	4	4
LA...	(X)	(X)	[1]1	3	3	4	4	5	6	6	6	7	8	8	8	8	8	8	8	7
OK...	(X)	(X)	(X)	(X)	(X)	(X)	(X)	(X)	(X)	(X)	(X)	[1]5	8	9	8	6	6	6	6	6
TX...	(X)	(X)	(X)	(X)	(X)	[2]2	2	4	6	11	13	16	18	21	21	22	23	24	27	30
West	(X)	(X)	(X)	(X)	(X)	2	3	5	7	13	18	21	33	43	49	59	69	76	85	93
Mt	(X)	(X)	(X)	(X)	(X)	(X)	(X)	1	2	5	7	8	14	14	16	16	17	19	24	24
MT...	(X)	(X)	(X)	(X)	(X)	(X)	(X)	(X)	(X)	[1]1	1	1	2	2	2	2	2	2	2	1
ID....	(X)	(X)	(X)	(X)	(X)	(X)	(X)	(X)	(X)	[1]1	1	1	2	2	2	2	2	2	2	2
WY...	(X)	(X)	(X)	(X)	(X)	(X)	(X)	(X)	(X)	[1]1	1	1	1	1	1	1	1	1	1	1
CO...	(X)	(X)	(X)	(X)	(X)	(X)	(X)	(X)	[1]1	1	2	3	4	4	4	4	4	5	6	6
NM...	(X)	(X)	(X)	(X)	(X)	(X)	(X)	(X)	(X)	(X)	(X)	[2]1	2	1	2	2	2	2	3	3
AZ...	(X)	(X)	(X)	(X)	(X)	(X)	(X)	(X)	(X)	(X)	(X)	[2]1	1	1	2	2	3	4	5	6
UT...	(X)	(X)	(X)	(X)	(X)	(X)	(X)	(X)	(X)	(X)	[1]1	1	2	2	2	2	2	2	3	3
NV...	(X)	(X)	(X)	(X)	(X)	(X)	(X)	[1]1	1	1	1	1	1	1	1	1	1	1	2	2
Pac	(X)	(X)	(X)	(X)	(X)	2	3	4	5	8	11	13	19	29	33	43	52	57	61	69
WA...	(X)	(X)	(X)	(X)	(X)	(X)	(X)	(X)	[1]1	1	2	3	5	6	6	7	7	7	8	9
OR...	(X)	(X)	(X)	(X)	(X)	(X)	[1]1	1	1	1	2	2	3	3	4	4	4	4	5	5
CA...	(X)	(X)	(X)	(X)	(X)	[2]2	2	3	4	6	7	8	11	20	23	30	38	43	45	52
AK...	(X)	(X)	(X)	(X)	(X)	(X)	(X)	(X)	(X)	(X)	(X)	(X)	(X)	(X)	(X)	[1]1	1	1	1	1
HI....	(X)	(X)	(X)	(X)	(X)	(X)	(X)	(X)	(X)	(X)	(X)	(X)	(X)	(X)	[1]1	1	2	2	2	2

X Not applicable. [1] Assigned after apportionment. [2] Included in apportionment in anticipation of statehood.

Source: U.S. Bureau of the Census, press release CB90-232.

No. 435. Representatives Elected, by Percent of Vote Cast for Winner and Major Party, 1980 to 1992, and by State, 1992

YEAR, REGION, DIVISION, AND STATE	TOTAL REPRESENTATIVES ELECTED				DEMOCRATS ELECTED				REPUBLICANS ELECTED				REPRESENTATIVES ELECTED WITH NO MAJOR PARTY OPPOSITION		
		Percentage of vote				Percentage of vote				Percentage of vote					
	Total	Under 55	55-59.9	60 and over	Total	Under 55	55-59.9	60 and over	Total	Under 55	55-59.9	60 and over	Total	Demo-crats	Repub-licans
1980	435	78	63	294	243	35	35	173	192	43	28	121	54	39	15
1982	435	76	73	286	269	40	33	196	166	36	40	90	56	46	10
1984	435	58	56	321	253	33	38	182	182	25	18	139	68	54	14
1986	435	46	41	348	258	22	18	218	177	24	23	130	75	57	18
1988	435	37	34	364	260	21	15	224	175	16	19	140	80	60	20
1990	[1]435	[1]52	71	312	267	29	40	198	167	22	31	114	85	49	36
1992, total . .	[1]435	109	[1]80	246	258	60	47	151	176	49	32	95	40	24	16
Northeast	[1]88	27	[1]10	51	50	15	6	29	37	12	3	22	9	6	3
N.E	[1]23	9	[1]1	13	14	4	-	10	8	5	-	3	1	1	-
ME	2	1	-	1	1	-	-	1	1	1	-	-	-	-	-
NH	2	1	-	1	1	-	-	1	1	1	-	-	-	-	-
VT	[1]1	-	[1]1	-	-	-	-	-	-	-	-	-	-	-	-
MA	10	5	-	5	8	3	-	5	2	2	-	-	1	1	-
RI	2	-	-	2	1	-	-	1	1	-	-	1	-	-	-
CT	6	2	-	4	3	1	-	2	3	1	-	2	-	-	-
M.A	65	18	9	38	36	11	6	19	29	7	3	19	8	5	3
NY	31	9	5	17	18	5	3	10	13	4	2	7	4	4	-
NJ.	13	3	3	7	7	2	2	3	6	1	1	4	-	-	-
PA	21	6	1	14	11	4	1	6	10	2	-	8	4	1	3
Midwest	105	23	23	59	61	16	13	32	44	7	10	27	4	1	3
E.N.C	74	14	15	45	43	11	7	25	31	3	8	20	3	1	2
OH	19	5	2	12	10	4	1	5	9	1	1	7	2	1	1
IN	10	2	3	5	7	1	2	4	3	1	1	1	-	-	-
IL	20	-	7	13	12	-	3	9	8	-	4	4	-	-	-
MI	16	6	1	9	10	6	-	4	6	-	1	5	1	-	1
WI	9	1	2	6	4	-	1	3	5	1	1	3	-	-	-
W.N.C	31	9	8	14	18	5	6	7	13	4	2	7	1	-	1
MN	8	3	2	3	6	2	2	2	2	1	-	1	-	-	-
IA	5	2	-	3	1	-	-	1	4	2	-	2	1	-	1
MO	9	2	2	5	6	1	2	3	3	1	-	2	-	-	-
ND	1	-	1	-	1	-	1	-	-	-	-	-	-	-	-
SD	1	-	-	1	1	-	-	1	-	-	-	-	-	-	-
NE	3	1	1	1	1	1	-	-	2	-	1	1	-	-	-
KS	4	1	2	1	2	1	1	-	2	-	1	1	-	-	-
South	149	28	30	91	92	14	19	59	57	14	11	32	24	14	10
S.A	75	17	19	39	42	10	9	23	33	7	10	16	6	2	4
DE	1	-	1	-	-	-	-	-	1	-	1	-	-	-	-
MD	8	3	-	5	4	1	-	3	4	2	-	2	-	-	-
VA	11	1	3	7	7	1	2	4	4	-	1	3	1	-	1
WV	3	-	-	3	3	-	-	3	-	-	-	-	1	1	-
NC	12	4	2	6	8	3	2	3	4	1	-	3	-	-	-
SC	6	1	-	5	3	-	-	3	3	1	-	2	1	-	1
GA	11	2	6	3	7	1	3	3	4	1	3	-	-	-	-
FL.	23	6	7	10	10	4	2	4	13	2	5	6	3	1	2
E.S.C	27	5	3	19	19	2	3	14	8	3	-	5	7	6	1
KY	6	2	-	4	4	1	-	3	2	1	-	1	6	5	1
TN	9	1	2	6	6	1	2	3	3	-	-	3	1	1	-
AL.	7	2	-	5	4	-	-	4	3	2	-	1	-	-	-
MS	5	-	1	4	5	-	1	4	-	-	-	-	-	-	-
W.S.C	47	6	8	33	31	2	7	22	16	4	1	11	11	6	5
AR	4	2	-	2	2	-	-	2	2	2	-	-	-	-	-
LA.	7	-	-	7	4	-	-	4	3	-	-	3	6	4	2
OK	6	2	1	3	4	-	1	3	2	2	-	-	-	-	-
TX	30	2	7	21	21	2	6	13	9	-	1	8	5	2	3
West.	93	31	17	45	55	15	9	31	38	16	8	14	3	3	-
Mt	24	6	7	11	11	4	3	4	13	2	4	7	-	-	-
MT	1	1	-	-	1	1	-	-	-	-	-	-	-	-	-
ID	2	-	1	1	1	-	1	-	1	-	-	1	-	-	-
WY	1	-	1	-	-	-	-	-	1	-	1	-	-	-	-
CO	6	1	1	4	2	-	-	2	4	1	1	2	-	-	-
NM	3	-	1	2	1	-	1	-	2	-	1	1	-	-	-
AZ	6	2	1	3	3	2	-	1	3	-	1	2	-	-	-
UT	3	1	1	1	2	1	1	-	1	-	-	1	-	-	-
NV	2	1	1	-	1	-	1	-	1	1	-	-	-	-	-
Pac	69	25	10	34	44	11	6	27	25	14	4	7	3	3	-
WA	9	4	2	3	8	4	2	2	1	-	-	1	-	-	-
OR	5	1	-	4	4	1	-	3	1	-	-	1	-	-	-
CA	52	19	8	25	30	6	4	20	22	13	4	5	3	3	-
AK	1	1	-	-	-	-	-	-	1	1	-	-	-	-	-
HI	2	-	2	-	2	-	2	-	-	-	-	-	-	-	-

- Represents zero. [1] Includes one Representative elected as an Independent.

Source: Compiled by U.S. Bureau of the Census from Elections Research Center, Chevy Chase, MD, *America Votes*, biennial (copyright).

No. 436. Vote Cast for United States Representatives, by Major Political Party—States: 1988 to 1992

[In thousands, except percent. In each State, totals represent the sum of votes cast in each Congressional District or votes cast for Representative at Large in States where only one member is elected. In all years there are numerous districts within the State where either the Republican or Democratic party had no candidate. In some States the Republican and Democratic vote includes votes cast for the party candidate by endorsing parties. See also *Historical Statistics, Colonial Times to 1970,* series Y 211-214]

REGION, DIVISION, AND STATE	1988 Total[1]	1988 Democratic	1988 Republican	1988 Percent for leading party	1990 Total[1]	1990 Democratic	1990 Republican	1990 Percent for leading party	1992 Total[1]	1992 Democratic	1992 Republican	1992 Percent for leading party
U.S. [2] . . .	81,786	43,662	37,175	D-53.4	61,513	32,565	27,648	D-52.9	96,239	48,964	43,833	D-50.9
Northeast . . .	17,806	9,490	7,989	D-53.3	12,792	6,483	5,868	D-50.7	19,417	9,567	8,871	D-49.3
N.E.	5,327	3,086	2,066	D-57.4	4,453	2,523	1,742	D-56.7	5,910	3,007	2,334	D-50.9
ME.	555	276	278	R-50.2	517	284	233	D-55.0	670	364	278	D-54.3
NH.	429	176	252	R-58.6	291	141	149	R-51.2	511	266	227	D-52.0
VT	240	45	99	R-41.2	210	6	83	[3]I-56.0	282	22	87	[3]I-57.8
MA.	2,371	1,787	509	D-75.4	2,051	1,420	567	D-69.2	2,614	1,518	857	D-58.1
RI.	391	140	251	R-64.1	347	182	165	D-52.5	399	193	186	D-48.3
CT	1,341	660	677	R-50.5	1,037	489	546	R-52.6	1,435	644	699	R-48.7
M.A.	12,479	6,403	5,923	D-51.3	8,339	3,959	4,126	R-47.1	13,507	6,560	6,537	D-48.6
NY [4] . . .	5,506	2,950	2,441	D-53.6	3,662	1,830	1,662	D-50.0	5,925	3,051	2,687	D-51.5
NJ	2,776	1,336	1,412	R-50.9	1,827	837	911	R-49.9	2,992	1,355	1,503	R-50.2
PA	4,197	2,117	2,070	D-50.4	2,851	1,293	1,552	R-54.5	4,591	2,154	2,347	R-51.1
Midwest . . .	23,539	12,270	11,205	D-52.1	17,484	9,370	7,970	D-53.6	26,232	13,260	12,238	D-50.5
E.N.C. . . .	16,111	8,360	7,715	D-51.9	11,699	6,202	5,363	D-53.0	17,899	9,149	8,315	D-51.1
OH.	4,155	2,087	2,068	D-50.2	3,418	1,807	1,590	D-52.9	4,577	2,198	2,154	D-48.0
IN.	2,120	1,097	1,023	D-51.7	1,514	831	683	D-54.9	2,219	1,206	998	D-54.3
IL.	4,344	2,317	2,023	D-53.3	3,077	1,646	1,349	D-53.5	4,831	2,678	2,097	D-55.4
MI	3,456	1,824	1,605	D-52.8	2,434	1,321	1,089	D-54.3	3,884	1,913	1,855	D-49.3
WI	2,035	1,035	997	D-50.9	1,256	597	652	R-51.9	2,388	1,154	1,211	R-50.7
W.N.C	7,429	3,910	3,490	D-52.6	5,785	3,168	2,607	D-54.8	8,333	4,111	3,923	D-49.3
MN.	1,969	1,149	810	D-58.3	1,781	1,042	736	D-58.5	2,275	1,178	931	D-51.8
IA.	1,189	580	607	R-51.0	792	401	385	D-50.6	1,242	493	729	R-58.7
MO.	2,070	1,148	910	D-55.5	1,353	728	625	D-53.8	2,349	1,269	1,036	D-54.1
ND	300	213	84	D-70.9	234	153	81	D-65.2	298	169	117	D-56.8
SD	312	224	88	D-71.7	257	174	83	D-67.6	333	230	89	D-69.1
NE	656	230	426	R-64.9	587	277	309	R-52.7	711	283	427	R-60.1
KS	932	367	565	R-60.6	781	394	387	D-50.4	1,125	488	592	R-52.6
South [2]	22,979	12,951	9,826	D-56.4	17,180	9,691	7,265	D-56.4	30,107	15,638	13,815	D-51.9
S.A. [2] . . .	12,121	6,660	5,420	D-54.9	9,409	5,222	4,063	D-55.5	15,982	8,088	7,577	D-50.6
DE	235	158	76	D-67.5	177	116	58	D-65.5	276	117	153	R-55.4
MD.	1,561	937	624	D-60.0	1,091	566	517	D-51.9	1,808	956	843	D-52.9
DC	171	122	23	D-71.3	160	98	42	D-61.7	197	167	20	D-84.8
VA	1,891	802	1,077	R-57.0	1,153	663	411	D-57.5	2,368	1,149	1,143	D-48.5
WV	569	437	132	D-76.8	375	251	123	D-67.1	562	439	123	D-78.1
NC	1,985	1,108	876	D-55.8	2,011	1,076	935	D-53.5	2,527	1,282	1,204	D-50.7
SC	991	550	439	D-55.4	670	383	275	D-57.2	1,115	506	581	R-52.1
GA [5][6] . .	1,672	1,115	557	D-66.7	1,394	855	539	D-61.3	2,214	1,215	999	D-54.9
FL [5][6] . .	3,047	1,431	1,616	R-53.0	2,378	1,213	1,163	D-51.0	4,915	2,257	2,511	R-51.1
E.S.C. . . .	4,611	2,707	1,841	D-58.7	2,866	1,712	1,070	D-59.7	5,655	3,170	2,292	D-56.1
KY	1,105	534	564	R-51.1	764	353	397	R-52.0	1,361	722	638	D-53.0
TN	1,409	844	536	D-59.9	717	369	289	D-51.5	1,726	883	738	D-51.2
AL	1,178	722	432	D-61.3	1,017	690	315	D-67.9	1,603	896	643	D-55.9
MS	918	607	308	D-66.1	369	299	69	D-81.2	965	670	273	D-69.4
W.S.C . . .	6,248	3,583	2,565	D-57.3	4,906	2,758	2,132	D-56.2	8,470	4,380	3,946	D-51.7
AR [5] . . .	606	353	253	D-58.3	665	369	296	D-55.5	889	525	357	D-59.1
LA [8] . . .	205	89	116	R-56.8	106	106	-	D-100.0	684	285	399	R-58.3
OK [5][9] . .	767	406	362	D-52.9	857	519	338	D-60.6	1,276	764	504	D-59.9
TX	4,670	2,736	1,834	D-58.6	3,278	1,763	1,498	D-53.8	5,622	2,806	2,686	D-49.9
West	17,461	8,952	8,155	D-51.3	14,057	7,022	6,545	D-50.0	20,483	10,499	8,910	D-51.3
Mt.	4,793	2,062	2,664	R-55.6	3,872	1,783	2,043	R-52.8	5,736	2,627	2,886	R-50.3
MT.	365	193	172	D-52.9	317	157	160	R-50.5	404	204	190	D-50.5
ID.	407	198	203	R-49.9	315	183	131	D-58.2	473	222	231	R-48.8
WY.	178	57	118	R-66.6	158	71	87	R-55.1	197	77	114	R-57.8
CO	1,315	645	667	R-50.7	1,001	504	487	D-50.3	1,479	691	758	R-51.2
NM	449	209	236	R-52.6	359	146	214	R-59.5	556	273	278	R-50.0
AZ	1,125	322	766	R-68.1	966	345	621	R-64.3	1,409	582	740	R-52.5
UT	609	260	341	R-56.0	442	234	191	D-52.9	727	331	362	R-49.8
NV	344	177	160	D-51.4	313	144	151	R-48.2	492	245	214	D-49.9
Pac	12,669	6,891	5,492	D-54.4	10,185	5,239	4,502	D-51.4	14,747	7,872	6,024	D-53.4
WA.	1,731	988	743	D-57.1	1,313	696	596	D-53.0	2,223	1,237	912	D-55.6
OR	1,024	665	358	D-64.9	1,053	667	342	D-63.4	1,391	825	553	D-59.3
CA	9,381	4,945	4,174	D-52.7	7,287	3,568	3,347	D-49.0	10,535	5,447	4,365	D-51.7
AK	193	72	121	R-62.5	192	92	99	R-51.7	239	102	112	R-46.8
HI.	340	221	97	D-65.1	341	216	118	D-63.3	358	261	82	D-72.8

- Represents zero. [1] Includes vote cast for minor parties. [2] Includes vote cast for nonvoting Delegate at Large in District of Columbia. [3] Leading party candidate was Independent. [4] Includes votes cast by other endorsing parties for Democratic and Republican candidates. [5] State law does not require tabulation of votes for unopposed candidates. [6] In 1988 Districts 3, 5, 7, 12, 17, and 18 were unopposed; in 1990 Districts 8, 10, 12, 13, and 16 were unopposed; in 1992 District 21 was unopposed. [7] In 1988 District 1 was unopposed. [8] 1988 data are for a general election runoff in one district. 1988 open primary totals-total, 550,370; Democratic 337,724; Republican, 212,646. 1990 data are for a general election runoff in one district. 1990 open primary totals-total, 1,186,253; Democratic, 706,004; Republican, 450,867. 1992 data are for general election runoffs in three districts. [9] In 1988 Districts 3 and 4 were unopposed.

Source: Elections Research Center, Chevy Chase, MD, *America Votes,* biennial (copyright).

No. 437. Vote Cast for United States Representatives, by Major Political Party—Congressional Districts: 1992

[In some States the Democratic and Republican vote includes votes cast for the party candidate by endorsing parties]

STATE AND DISTRICT	Total vote cast (1,000)	DEMOCRATIC CANDIDATE Name	Percent of total	REPUBLICAN CANDIDATE Name	Percent of total	STATE AND DISTRICT	Total vote cast (1,000)	DEMOCRATIC CANDIDATE Name	Percent of total	REPUBLICAN CANDIDATE Name	Percent of total
AL....	1,603	(X)	56	(X)	40	45th..	227	McCabe...	39	Rohrbacher...	55
1st...	214	Brewer	37	Callahan...	60	46th..	111	Banuelos..	41	Dornan....	50
2d...	228	Wallace...	48	Everett....	49	47th..	254	Anwiler...	30	Cox......	65
3d...	198	Browder...	60	Sledge....	37	48th..	230	Farber....	29	Packard...	61
4th...	231	Bevill.	68	Strickland..	29	49th..	249	Schenk...	51	Jarvis.....	43
5th...	244	Cramer...	66	Smith.....	32	50th..	137	Filner....	57	Valencia...	29
6th...	280	Erdreich...	45	Bachus....	52	51st..	253	Herbert...	34	Cunningham.....	56
7th...	208	Hilliard....	69	Jones.....	17	52d..	214	Gastil....	41	Hunter....	53
AK....	239	Devens...	43	Young.....	47	CO....	1,479	(X)......	47	(X)......	51
AZ....	1,409	(X)......	41	(X)......	53	1st..	228	Schroeder.	69	Aragon....	31
1st...	255	Coopersmith....	51	Rhodes....	45	2d..	271	Skaggs...	61	Day......	33
2d...	137	Pastor....	66	Shooter...	30	3d..	262	Callihan..	44	McInnis....	55
3d...	259	Hartstone.	34	Stump....	61	4th..	242	Redder...	42	Allard.....	58
4th...	264	Mybeck...	27	Kyl......	59	5th..	243	Oriez.....	26	Hefley.....	71
5th...	260	Toevs....	30	Kolbe.....	67	6th..	233	Kolbe.....	39	Schaefer...	61
6th...	234	English...	53	Wead.....	41	CT....	1,435	(X)......	45	(X)......	49
AR....	889	(X)......	59	(X)......	40	1st..	245	Kennelly..	67	Steele.....	31
1st...	214	Lambert...	70	Hayes.....	30	2d..	243	Gejdenson.	51	Munster....	49
2d...	209	Thornton..	74	Scott.....	26	3d..	248	DeLauro...	66	Scott.....	34
3d...	249	Van Winkle.	47	Hutchinson.	50	4th..	220	Schropfer.	27	Shays.....	67
4th...	216	McCuen...	48	Dickey....	52	5th..	240	Lawlor....	31	Franks....	44
CA....	10,535	(X)......	52	(X)......	41	6th..	240	Slason....	25	Johnson...	70
1st...	251	Hamburg...	48	Riggs.....	45	DE....	276	Woo......	43	Castle.....	55
2d...	257	Freedman.	28	Herger....	65	FL....	4,915	(X)......	46	(X)......	51
3d...	239	Fazio....	51	Richardson.	40	1st..	229	Hutto.....	52	Ketchel...	44
4th...	283	Malberg...	46	Doolittle...	50	2d..	152	Peterson..	60	Wagner....	40
5th...	231	Matsui....	69	Dinsmore..	25	3d..	167	Brown....	62	Weidner...	38
6th...	292	Woolsey...	65	Filante....	34	4th..	239	Hair......	43	Fowler....	57
7th...	218	Miller....	70	Scholl....	25	5th..	264	Thurman..	49	Hogan.....	43
8th...	233	Pelosi....	82	Wolin.....	11	6th..	221	Denton....	35	Stearns....	65
9th...	228	Dellums...	72	Hunter....	24	7th..	223	Webster...	43	Mica......	56
10th...	280	Williams..	48	Baker.....	52	8th..	207	Kovaleski..	31	McCollum..	69
11th...	198	Garamendi.	46	Pombo....	48	9th..	268	Knapp....	41	Bilirakis...	59
12th...	228	Lantos....	69	Tomlin....	23	10th..	264	Moffitt....	43	Young.....	57
13th...	206	Stark....	60	Teyler....	32	11th..	191	Gibbons...	53	Sharpe....	41
14th...	259	Eshoo....	57	Huening...	39	12th..	193	Mims.....	48	Canady....	52
15th...	265	Mineta....	64	Wick.....	31	13th..	275	Snell.....	42	Miller.....	58
16th...	156	Edwards...	62	Bundesen..	32	14th..	269	(¹)......	(¹)	Goss.....	82
17th...	210	Panetta...	72	McCampbell......	24	15th..	261	Bacchus...	51	Tolley.....	49
18th...	165	Condit....	85	(¹)......	(¹)	16th..	259	Comerford.	39	Lewis.....	61
19th...	217	Lehman...	47	Cloud....	46	17th..	103	Meek	100	(¹)......	(¹)
20th...	112	Dooley...	65	Hunt.....	35	18th..	157	Davis.....	33	Ros-Lehtinen ..	67
21st...	196	Vollmer...	35	Thomas...	65	19th..	281	Johnston..	63	Metz.....	37
22d...	250	Ochoa....	35	Huffington..	53	20th..	238	Deutsch...	55	Kennedy...	39
23d...	213	Ferguson..	41	Gallegly...	54	21st..	(NA)	(¹)......	(¹)	Diaz-Balart..	(NA)
24th...	255	Beilenson..	56	McClintock.	39	22d..	247	Margolis...	37	Shaw.....	52
25th...	219	Gilmartin..	33	McKeon...	52	23d..	144	Hastings...	59	Fielding...	31
26th...	121	Berman...	61	Frosch....	30	GA....	2,214	(X)......	55	(X)......	45
27th...	212	Kahn.....	39	Moorhead..	50	1st..	180	Christmas.	42	Kingston...	58
28th...	209	Wachtel...	37	Dreier.....	58	2d..	150	Bishop....	64	Dudley....	36
29th...	261	Waxman...	61	Robbins...	26	3d..	208	Ray......	45	Collins....	55
30th...	84	Becerra...	58	Waksberg..	24	4th..	250	Steinberg.	49	Linder.....	51
31st...	109	Martinez..	63	Franco....	37	5th..	204	Lewis.....	72	Stabler....	28
32d...	173	Dixon....	87	(¹)......	(¹)	6th..	275	Center....	42	Gingrich...	58
33d...	51	Roybal-Allard....	63	Guzman...	30	7th..	194	Darden....	57	Beverly....	43
34th...	150	Torres....	61	Hernandez.	34	8th..	195	Rowland...	56	Cunningham.....	44
35th...	125	Waters....	83	Truman....	14	9th..	191	Deal.....	59	Becker....	41
36th...	260	Harman...	48	Flores.....	42	10th..	201	Johnson...	54	Hudgens...	46
37th...	113	Tucker....	86	(¹)......	(¹)	11th..	164	McKinney..	73	Lovett.....	27
38th...	189	Braude...	43	Horn.....	49	HI....	358	(X)......	73	(X)......	23
39th...	214	McClanahan.....	38	Royce.....	57	1st..	177	Abercrombie..	73	Sutton....	23
40th...	205	Rusk.....	31	Lewis.....	63	2d..	181	Mink.....	73	Price.....	22
41st...	171	Baker....	34	Kim......	60	ID....	473	(X)......	47	(X)......	49
42d...	157	Brown....	51	Rutan.....	44	1st..	243	Larocco...	58	Gilbert....	37
43d...	191	Takano...	46	Calvert....	47	2d..	230	Williams...	35	Crapo.....	61
44th...	204	Smith....	40	McCandless.	54						

See footnotes at end of table.

No. 437. Vote Cast for United States Representatives, by Major Political Party—Congressional Districts: 1992—Continued

[See headnote, p. 271]

STATE AND DISTRICT	Total vote cast (1,000)	Democratic Candidate Name	Percent of total	Republican Candidate Name	Percent of total	STATE AND DISTRICT	Total vote cast (1,000)	Democratic Candidate Name	Percent of total	Republican Candidate Name	Percent of total
IL.....	4,831	(X)	55	(X)	43	1st...	234	McMillen	48	Gilchrest	51
1st...	253	Rush	83	Walker	17	2d...	254	Hickey	35	Bentley	65
2d...	234	Reynolds	78	Blackstone	14	3d...	222	Cardin	73	Bricker	26
3d...	255	Lipinski	64	Lepinske	36	4th...	182	Wynn	75	Dyson	25
4th...	117	Gutierrez	78	Rodriguez-Scheiman	22	5th...	223	Hoyer	53	Hogan	44
5th...	232	Rostenkowski	57	Zenkich	39	6th...	232	Hattery	46	Bartlett	54
6th...	252	Watkins	34	Hyde	66	7th...	179	Mfume	85	Kondner	15
7th...	225	Collins	81	Boccio	16	8th...	280	Heffernan	27	Morella	73
8th...	239	Smith	40	Crane	56	MA....	2,614	(X)	58	(X)	33
9th...	240	Yates	68	Sohn	27	1st...	262	Olver	52	Larkin	43
10th..	241	Kennedy	35	Porter	65	2d...	247	Neal	53	Ravosa	31
11th..	243	Sangmeister	56	Herbolsheimer	44	3d...	261	Early	44	Blute	50
12th..	237	Costello	71	Starr	29	4th...	270	Frank	68	McCormick	26
13th..	262	Temple	32	Fawell	68	5th...	257	Meehan	53	Cronin	37
14th..	231	Reich	33	Hastert	67	6th...	290	Mavroules	45	Torkildsen	55
15th..	240	Mattis	41	Ewing	59	7th...	282	Markey	62	Sohn	28
16th..	256	Cox	44	Manzullo	56	8th...	180	Kennedy	83	(1)	(1)
17th..	260	Evans	60	Schloemer	40	9th...	254	Moakley	69	Conboy	21
18th..	271	Hawkins	42	Michel	58	10th..	312	Studds	61	Daly	24
19th..	271	Poshard	69	Lee	31	MI.....	3,884	(X)	49	(X)	48
20th..	274	Durbin	57	Shimkus	43	1st...	269	Stupak	54	Ruppe	44
IN.....	2,219	(X)	54	(X)	45	2d...	247	Miltner	35	Hoekstra	63
1st...	212	Visclosky	69	Vucich	31	3d...	265	Coistra	36	Henry	61
2d...	229	Sharp	57	Frazier	40	4th...	252	Donaldson	35	Camp	63
3d...	211	Roemer	57	Baxmeyer	43	5th...	245	Barcia	60	Muxlow	38
4th...	217	Long	62	Pierson	38	6th...	233	Davis	38	Upton	62
5th...	220	Jontz	49	Buyer	51	7th...	153	(1)	(1)	Smith	88
6th...	258	Bruner	28	Burton	72	8th...	285	Carr	48	Chrysler	46
7th...	217	Wedum	41	Myers	59	9th...	250	Kildee	54	O'Neill	45
8th...	238	McCloskey	53	Mourdock	45	10th..	260	Bonior	53	Carl	44
9th...	231	Hamilton	70	Bailey	30	11th..	293	Briggs	40	Knollenberg	58
10th..	184	Jacobs	64	Horvath	35	12th..	261	Levin	53	Pappageorge	46
IA.....	1,242	(X)	40	(X)	59	13th..	246	Ford	52	Geake	43
1st...	261	Zonneveld	31	Leach	68	14th..	201	Conyers	82	Gordon	16
2d...	268	Nagle	49	Nussle	50	15th..	185	Collins	81	Vincent	17
3d...	257	Baxter	47	Lightfoot	49	16th..	241	Dingell	65	Beaumont	31
4th...	258	Smith	62	Lunde	37	MN....	2,275	(X)	45	(X)	41
5th...	198	(1)	(1)	Grandy	99	1st...	279	Penny[6]	74	Droogsma	26
KS....	1,125	(X)	43	(X)	53	2d...	276	Minge[6]	48	Ludeman	48
1st...	285	West	29	Roberts	68	3d...	315	Mandell	33	Ramstad	64
2d...	269	Slattery	56	Van Slyke	41	4th...	278	Vento	57	Maitland	37
3d...	293	Love	38	Meyers	58	5th...	277	Sabo	63	Moriarty	28
4th...	278	Glickman	52	Yost	42	6th...	301	Sikorski	33	Grams	44
KY....	1,361	(X)	53	(X)	47	7th...	266	Peterson	50	Omann	49
1st...	213	Barlow	60	Hamrick	39	8th...	283	Oberstar	59	Herwig	30
2d...	207	Natcher	61	Bartley	39	MS....	965	(X)	69	(X)	28
3d...	281	Mazzoli	53	Stokes	47	1st...	205	Whitten	59	Whitaker	41
4th...	227	Poore	38	Bunning	62	2d...	175	Espy	76	Benford	24
5th...	211	Hays	45	Rogers	55	3d...	201	Montgomery	81	Williams	19
6th...	223	Baesler	61	Ellinger	39	4th...	195	Parker	67	McMillan	22
LA[2]...	(NA)	(X)	(X)	(X)	(X)	5th...	191	Taylor	63	Harvey	35
1st...	(X)	(X)	(X)	Livingston[3]	(X)	MO....	2,349	(X)	54	(X)	44
2d...	(X)	Jefferson[3]	(X)	(X)	(X)	1st...	233	Clay	68	Montgomery	32
3d...	(X)	Tauzin[3]	(X)	(X)	(X)	2d...	312	Horn	48	Talent	50
4th...	195	Fields[4]	100	(X)	(X)	3d...	272	Gephardt	64	Holekamp	33
5th...	244	Huckaby	37	McCrery	63	4th...	251	Skelton	70	Carley	30
6th...	245	(X)	(X)	Baker[5]	100	5th...	255	Wheat	59	Moody	37
7th...	(X)	Hayes[3]	(X)	(X)	(X)	6th...	269	Danner	55	Coleman	45
ME....	670	(X)	54	(X)	42	7th...	260	Deaton	38	Hancock	62
1st...	358	Andrews	65	Bean	35	8th...	234	Bullock	37	Emerson	63
2d...	311	McGowan	42	Snowe	49	9th...	261	Volkmer	48	Hardy	45
MD....	1,808	(X)	53	(X)	47	MT....	404	Williams	50	Marlenee	47

See footnotes at end of table.

No. 437. Vote Cast for United States Representatives, by Major Political Party—Congressional Districts: 1992—Continued

[See headnote, p. 271]

STATE AND DISTRICT	Total vote cast (1,000)	Democratic Candidate Name	Percent of total	Republican Candidate Name	Percent of total
NE	711	(X)........	40	(X)	60
1st...	239	Finnegan ...	40	Bereuter ..	60
2d ...	233	Hoagland ...	51	Staskiewicz	49
3d ...	238	Fisher	28	Barrett....	72
NV	492	(X)........	50	(X)	43
1st...	221	Bilbray	58	Pettyjohn..	38
2d ...	270	Sferrazza ...	43	Vucanovich	48
NH	511	(X)........	52	(X)	44
1st...	256	Preston	42	Zeliff.....	53
2d ...	255	Swett......	62	Hatch	36
NJ	2,992	(X)........	45	(X)	50
1st...	228	Andrews....	67	Solomon ..	29
2d ...	237	Hughes	56	Lobiondo ..	41
3d ...	256	Ryan	37	Saxton	59
4th ...	241	Hughes	35	Smith	62
5th...	274	Lucas	25	Roukema ..	72
6th...	226	Pallone.....	52	Kyrillos ..	45
7th...	248	Sendelsky...	43	Franks....	53
8th...	206	Klein......	47	Bubba....	41
9th...	239	Torricelli	58	Roma	37
10th...	150	Payne.....	78	Palermo...	20
11th...	268	Spiridellis ...	26	Gallo.....	70
12th...	273	Abate.....	30	Zimmer....	64
13th...	146	Menendez..	64	Theemling.	31
NM	556	(X)........	49	(X)	50
1st...	205	Aragon....	37	Schiff....	63
2d ...	168	Sosa	44	Skeen....	56
3d ...	182	Richardson ..	67	Bemis....	30
NY	5,925	(X)........	51	(X)	45
1st...	228	Hoch-brueckner	52	Romaine..	48
2d ...	206	Downey....	47	Lazio.....	53
3d ...	252	Orlins.....	46	King.....	50
4th...	221	Schiliro.....	45	Levy.....	50
5th...	211	Ackerman ..	52	Binder....	45
6th...	120	Flake......	81	Bhagwandin...	19
7th...	127	Manton.....	57	Shea.....	43
8th...	170	Nadler.....	81	Askren....	15
9th...	132	Schumer....	89	(1).	(1)
10th...	102	Towns.....	96	(1).	(1)
11th...	85	Owens.....	94	(1).	(1)
12th...	73	Velazquez...	77	Diaz.....	20
13th...	192	Albanese ...	38	Molinari...	56
14th...	202	Maloney....	50	Green....	48
15th...	111	Rangel.....	95	(1).	(1)
16th...	93	Serrano....	91	Walters...	9
17th...	122	Engel......	80	Richman...	13
18th...	209	Lowey.....	56	DioGuardi.	44
19th...	232	McCarthy ...	40	Fish.....	60
20th...	227	Levine.....	29	Gilman....	66
21st...	265	McNulty	63	Norman...	34
22d...	251	Roberts....	35	Solomon ..	65
23d ...	220	DiPerna....	28	Boehlert ..	64
24th...	201	Ravenscroft.....	24	McHugh...	61
25th...	242	Jezer......	44	Walsh....	56
26th...	237	Hinchey....	50	Moppert...	47
27th...	247	Call......	36	Paxon....	64
28th...	255	Slaughter ...	55	Polito....	44
29th...	235	LaFalce....	54	Miller....	42
30th...	243	Gorski.....	46	Quinn....	52
31st...	214	Leahey.....	24	Houghton..	71
NC	2,527	(X)........	51	(X)	48
1st...	173	Clayton.....	67	Tyler.....	31
2d ...	212	Valentine ...	54	Davis	44
3d ...	187	Lancaster...	54	Pollard ...	43
4th...	265	Price	65	Goudie ...	34
5th...	224	Neal.......	53	Burr	46
6th...	230	Hood......	29	Coble	71
7th...	163	Rose	57	Anderson..	41
8th...	191	Hefner.....	59	Privette ...	38
9th...	228	Blake.....	33	McMillan..	67
10th...	235	Neill......	34	Ballenger..	63
11th...	238	Stevens	45	Taylor....	55
12th...	181	Watt......	70	Washington	27
ND	298	Pomeroy....	57	Korsmo ...	39
OH	4,577	(X)........	48	(X)	47
1st...	234	Mann.....	51	(1).	(1)
2d ...	254	Chandler....	30	Gradison .	70
3d ...	245	Hall......	60	Davis....	40
4th...	240	Ball......	39	Oxley	61
5th...	188	(1).	(1)	Gillmor ...	100
6th...	242	Strickland ..	51	McEwen ..	49
7th...	230	Heskett	29	Hobson ..	71
8th...	238	Stennet	26	Boehner ..	74
9th...	243	Kaptur	74	Brown....	22
10th...	240	Oakar......	43	Hoke.....	57
11th...	224	Stokes	69	Rothschild .	20
12th...	239	Fitrakis....	29	Kasich....	71
13th...	252	Brown	53	Mueller....	35
14th...	244	Sawyer....	68	Morgan ...	32
15th...	250	Cordray ...	38	Pryce	44
16th...	249	Mendenhall .	36	Regula ...	64
17th...	257	Traficant...	84	Pansino...	16
18th...	243	Applegate ..	68	Ress.....	32
19th...	263	Fingerhut ...	53	Gardner...	47
OK	1,276	(X)........	60	(X)	40
1st...	226	Selph......	47	Inhofe	53
2d ...	214	Synar.....	56	Hill	41
3d ...	208	Brewster...	75	Stokes ...	25
4th ...	199	McCurdy...	71	Bell.....	29
5th...	231	Williams ...	47	Istook	53
6th...	199	English	68	Anthony...	32
OR	1,391	(X)........	59	(X)	40
1st...	294	Furse.....	52	Meeker ...	48
2d ...	274	Ferguson ..	33	Smith	67
3d ...	270	Wyden ...	77	Ritter ...	19
4th...	279	DeFazio ...	71	Schulz...	29
5th...	273	Kopetski ...	64	Seagraves .	36
PA	4,591	(X)........	47	(X)	51
1st...	186	Foglietta....	81	Snyder ...	19
2d ...	214	Blackwell ...	77	Hollin ...	22
3d ...	222	Borski	59	Dougherty .	39
4th...	238	Klink......	78	Johnston ..	20
5th...	189	(1).	(1)	Clinger ...	100
6th...	208	Holden	52	Jones	48
7th...	274	Daly......	33	Weldon ...	66
8th...	250	Kostmayer ..	46	Greenwood...	52
9th...	182	(1).	(1)	Shuster ...	100
10th...	210	(1).	(1)	McDade...	90
11th...	207	Kanjorski ...	67	Fescina ...	33
12th...	167	Murtha ....[7]	100	(1).	(1)
13th...	254	Mezvinsky [7]	50	Fox......	50
14th...	229	Coyne	72	King	27
15th...	213	McHale	52	Ritter ...	47
16th...	213	Peters	35	Walker ...	65
17th...	216	Sturges ...	30	Gekas	70
18th...	254	Pecora	38	Santorum..	61
19th...	218	Kilker.....	34	Goodling ..	45
20th...	226	Murphy....	51	Townsend..	49
21st...	222	Harkins.....	32	Ridge	68
RI	399	(X)........	48	(X)	47
1st...	194	Carlin.....	25	Machtley..	70
2d ...	204	Reed	71	Bell......	24

See footnotes at end of table.

No. 437. Vote Cast for United States Representatives, by Major Political Party—Congressional Districts: 1992—Continued

[See headnote, p. 271]

STATE AND DIS-TRICT	Total vote cast (1,000)	DEMOCRATIC CANDIDATE Name	Percent of total	REPUBLICAN CANDIDATE Name	Percent of total	STATE AND DIS-TRICT	Total vote cast (1,000)	DEMOCRATIC CANDIDATE Name	Percent of total	REPUBLICAN CANDIDATE Name	Percent of total
SC	1,115	(X)	45	(X)	52	30th..	151	Johnson	72	Cain	25
1st...	185	Oberst	32	Ravenel	66	UT	727	(X)	46	(X)	50
2d ...	170	(¹)	(¹)	Spence	88	1st...	245	Holt	28	Hansen	65
3d ...	195	Derrick	61	Bland	39	2d ...	253	Shepherd	50	Greene	47
4th..	198	Patterson	47	Inglis	50	3d ...	229	Orton	59	Harrington	37
5th..	183	Spratt	61	Horne	39	VT [8] ...	282	Young	8	Philbin	31
6th..	185	Clyburn	65	Chase	35	VA	2,368	(X)	49	(X)	48
SD	333	Johnson	69	Timmer	27	1st...	232	Fox	39	Bateman	58
TN	1,726	(X)	51	(X)	43	2d ...	177	Pickett	56	Chapman	44
1st...	170	Christian	28	Quillen	67	3d ...	168	Scott	79	Jenkins	21
2d ...	205	Goodale	26	Duncan	72	4th..	216	Sisisky	68	Zevgolis	32
3d ...	217	Lloyd	49	Wamp	47	5th..	193	Payne	69	Hurlburt	31
4th..	155	Cooper	64	Johnson	33	6th..	212	Mussel-white	40	Goodlatte	60
5th..	188	Clement	67	Stone	26	7th..	255	(¹)	(¹)	Bliley	83
6th..	212	Gordon	57	Blackburn	41	8th..	247	Moran	56	McSlarrow	42
7th..	203	Davis	36	Sundquist	62	9th..	211	Boucher	63	Weddle	37
8th..	163	Tanner	84	(¹)	(¹)	10th..	227	Vickery	33	Wolf	64
9th..	213	Ford	58	Black	28	11th..	228	Byrne	50	Butler	45
TX	5,622	(X)	50	(X)	48	WA	2,223	(X)	56	(X)	41
1st...	152	Chapman	100	(¹)	(¹)	1st...	271	Cantwell	55	Nelson	42
2d ...	211	Wilson	56	Peterson	44	2d ...	256	Swift	52	Metcalf	42
3d ...	234	(¹)	(¹)	Johnson	86	3d ...	247	Unsoeld	56	Fiske	44
4th..	220	Hall	58	Bridges	38	4th..	210	Inslee	51	Hastings	49
5th..	167	Bryant	59	Stokley	37	5th..	246	Foley	55	Sonneland	45
6th..	263	Dietrich	28	Barton	72	6th..	238	Dicks	64	Phillips	28
7th..	169	(¹)	(¹)	Archer	100	7th..	284	McDermott	78	Hampson	19
8th..	233	Robinson	23	Fields	77	8th..	258	Tamblyn	34	Dunn	60
9th..	221	Brooks	54	Stockman	43	9th..	213	Kreidler	52	Von Reich-bauer	43
10th..	262	Pickle	68	Spiro	26	WV	562	(X)	78	(X)	22
11th..	178	Edwards	67	Broyles	33	1st...	173	Mollohan	100	(¹)	(¹)
12th..	200	Geren	63	Hobbs	37	2d ...	203	Wise	71	Cravotta	29
13th..	195	Sarpalius	60	Boulter	40	3d ...	186	Rahall	66	Waldman	34
14th..	200	Laughlin	68	Garza	27	WI	2,388	(X)	48	(X)	51
15th..	143	De La Garza	60	Haughey	40	1st...	256	Aspin	58	Neumann	41
16th..	129	Coleman	52	Taberski	48	2d ...	293	Deer	37	Klug	63
17th..	206	Stenholm	66	Sadowski	34	3d ...	260	Sacia	42	Gunderson	56
18th..	172	Washington	65	Blum	33	4th..	264	Kleczka	66	Cook	32
19th..	209	Moser	23	Combest	77	5th..	234	Barrett	69	Hammer-smith	30
20th..	104	Gonzalez	100	(¹)	(¹)	6th..	272	Lauten-schlager	47	Petri	53
21st..	265	Gaddy	24	Smith	72	7th..	258	Obey	64	Vannes	36
22d ..	218	Konrad	31	Delay	69	8th..	274	Helms	30	Roth	70
23d ..	166	Bustamante	38	Bonilla	59	9th..	277	Buxton	28	Sensen-brenner	70
24th..	174	Frost	60	Masterson	40	WY	197	Herschler	39	Thomas	58
25th..	177	Andrews	56	McKenna	41						
26th..	206	Caton	27	Armey	73						
27th..	157	Ortiz	55	Kimbrough	43						
28th..	141	Tejeda	87	(¹)	(¹)						
29th..	99	Green	65	(X)	35						

NA Not available.　X Not applicable.　[1] No candidate.　[2] Louisiana holds an open-primary election with candidates from all parties running on the same ballot. Any candidate who receives a majority is elected; if no candidate receives 50 percent, there is a run-off election in November between the top two finishers.　[3] Candidate listed won seat in open-primary.　[4] Both candidates in run-off election were Democrats.　[5] Both candidates in run-off election were Republicans.　[6] The winning Democratic candidate received 132,156 votes; the Republican candidate, 131,587.　[7] The winning Democratic candidate received 127,685 votes; the Republican candidate, 126,312.　[8] The winning candidate was Sanders, an Independent, who received 58 percent of the vote.

Source: Elections Research Center, Chevy Chase, MD, *America Votes*, biennial (copyright).

No. 438. Composition of Congress, by Political Party: 1961 to 1993

[D=Democratic, R=Republican. Data for beginning of first session of each Congress (as of January 3). Excludes vacancies at beginning of session. See also *Historical Statistics, Colonial Times to 1970*, series Y 204-210]

YEAR	Party and President	Congress	HOUSE			SENATE		
			Majority party	Minority party	Other	Majority party	Minority party	Other
1961	D (Kennedy)	87th	D-263	R-174	-	D-65	R-35	-
1963	D (Kennedy)	88th	D-258	R-177	-	D-67	R-33	-
1965	D (Johnson)	89th	D-295	R-140	-	D-68	R-32	-
1967	D (Johnson)	90th	D-247	R-187	-	D-64	R-36	-
1969	R (Nixon)	91st	D-243	R-192	-	D-57	R-43	-
1971 [1]	R (Nixon)	92d	D-254	R-180	-	D-54	R-44	2
1973 [1][2]	R (Nixon)	93d	D-239	R-192	1	D-56	R-42	2
1975 [3]	R (Ford)	94th	D-291	R-144	-	D-60	R-37	2
1977 [4]	D (Carter)	95th	D-292	R-143	-	D-61	R-38	1
1979 [4]	D (Carter)	96th	D-276	R-157	-	D-58	R-41	1
1981 [4]	R (Reagan)	97th	D-243	R-192	-	R-53	D-46	1
1983	R (Reagan)	98th	D-269	R-165	-	R-54	D-46	-
1985	R (Reagan)	99th	D-252	R-182	-	R-53	D-47	-
1987	R (Reagan)	100th	D-258	R-177	-	D-55	R-45	-
1989	R (Bush)	101st	D-259	R-174	-	D-55	R-45	-
1991 [5]	R (Bush)	102d	D-267	R-167	1	D-56	R-44	-
1993 [5]	D (Clinton)	103d	D-258	R-176	1	D-57	R-43	-

- Represents zero.   [1] Senate had one Independent and one Conservative-Republican.   [2] House had one Independent-Democrat.   [3] Senate had one Independent, one Conservative-Republican, and one undecided (New Hampshire).   [4] Senate had one Independent.   [5] House had one Independent-Socialist.

Source: U.S. Congress, Joint Committee on Printing, *Congressional Directory,* annual; beginning 1977, biennial.

No. 439. U.S. Congress—Measures Introduced and Enacted and Time in Session: 1975 to 1992

[Excludes simple and concurrent resolutions. See also *Historical Statistics, Colonial Times to 1970*, series Y 189-198]

ITEM	94th Cong., 1975-76	95th Cong., 1977-78	96th Cong., 1979-80	97th Cong., 1981-82	98th Cong., 1983-84	99th Cong., 1985-86	100th Cong., 1987-88	101st Cong., 1989-90	102d Cong., 1991-92
Measures introduced	21,096	19,387	12,583	11,490	11,156	9,885	9,588	6,664	6,775
Bills	19,762	18,045	11,722	10,582	10,134	8,697	8,515	5,977	6,212
Joint resolutions	1,334	1,342	861	908	1,022	1,188	1,073	687	563
Measures enacted	729	803	736	529	677	483	761	666	609
Public	588	633	613	473	623	466	713	650	589
Private	141	170	123	56	54	17	48	16	20
HOUSE OF REPRESENTATIVES									
Number of days	311	323	326	303	266	281	298	281	280
Number of hours	1,788	1,898	1,876	1,420	1,705	1,794	1,659	1,688	1,796
Number of hours per day	5.7	5.9	5.8	4.7	6.4	6.4	5.6	6.0	6.4
SENATE									
Number of days	320	337	333	312	281	313	307	274	287
Number of hours	2,210	2,510	2,324	2,158	1,951	2,531	2,341	2,254	2,292
Number of hours per day	6.9	7.4	7.0	6.9	6.9	8.1	7.6	8.2	8.0

Source: U.S. Congress, *Congressional Record* and *Daily Calendar,* selected issues.

No. 440. Congressional Bills Vetoed: 1961 to 1993

[See also *Historical Statistics, Colonial Times to 1970*, series Y 199-203]

PERIOD	President	Total vetoes	Regular vetoes	Pocket vetoes	Vetoes sustained	Bills passed over veto
1961-63	Kennedy	21	12	9	21	-
1963-69	Johnson	30	16	14	30	-
1969-74	Nixon	42	24	18	36	6
1974-77	Ford	72	53	19	60	12
1977-81	Carter	31	13	18	29	2
1981-89	Reagan	78	39	39	69	9
1989-93	Bush	35	22	13	34	1

- Represents zero.

Source: U.S. Congress, Senate Library, *Presidential Vetoes ... 1789-1968*; U.S. Congress, *Calendars of the U.S. House of Representatives and History of Legislation,* annual.

No. 441. Composition of Congress, by Political Party Affiliation—States: 1987 to 1993

[Figures are for the beginning of the first session (as of January 3). Dem.=Democratic; Rep.=Republican]

REGION, DIVISION, AND STATE	REP. 100th Cong. 1987 Dem.	Rep.	REP. 101st Cong. 1989 Dem.	Rep.	REP. 102d Cong. 1991 Dem.	Rep.	REP. 103rd Cong. 1993 Dem.	Rep.	SEN. 100th Cong. 1987 Dem.	Rep.	SEN. 101st Cong. 1989 Dem.	Rep.	SEN. 102d Cong. 1991 Dem.	Rep.	SEN. 103rd Cong. 1993 Dem.	Rep.
U.S.	258	177	259	174	267	167	258	176	55	45	55	45	56	44	57	43
Northeast	55	40	55	40	56	38	50	37	9	9	10	8	10	8	11	7
N.E.	15	9	14	10	16	7	14	8	6	6	7	5	7	5	7	5
ME	1	1	1	1	1	1	1	1	1	1	1	1	1	1	1	1
NH	-	2	-	2	1	1	1	1	-	2	-	2	-	2	-	2
VT	-	1	-	1	-	-	-	-	1	1	1	1	1	1	1	1
MA	10	1	10	1	10	1	8	2	2	-	2	-	2	-	2	-
RI	1	1	-	2	1	1	1	1	1	1	1	1	1	1	1	1
CT	3	3	3	3	3	3	3	3	1	1	2	-	2	-	2	-
M.A.	40	31	41	30	40	31	36	29	3	3	3	3	3	3	4	2
NY	20	14	21	13	21	13	18	13	1	1	1	1	1	1	1	1
NJ	8	6	8	6	8	6	7	6	2	-	2	-	2	-	2	-
PA	12	11	12	11	11	12	11	10	-	2	-	2	-	2	1	1
Midwest	62	51	64	48	68	45	61	44	13	11	13	11	14	10	15	9
E.N.C	46	34	47	32	49	31	43	31	7	3	7	3	7	3	8	2
OH	11	10	11	10	11	10	10	9	2	-	2	-	2	-	2	-
IN	6	4	6	3	8	2	7	3	-	2	-	2	-	2	-	2
IL	13	9	14	8	15	7	12	8	2	-	2	-	2	-	2	-
MI	11	7	11	7	11	7	10	6	2	-	2	-	2	-	2	-
WI	5	4	5	4	4	5	4	5	1	1	1	1	1	1	2	-
W.N.C	16	17	17	16	19	14	18	13	6	8	6	8	7	7	7	7
MN	5	3	5	3	6	2	6	2	-	2	-	2	1	1	1	1
IA	2	4	2	4	2	4	1	4	1	1	1	1	1	1	1	1
MO	5	4	5	4	6	3	6	3	-	2	-	2	-	2	1	1
ND	1	-	1	-	1	-	1	-	2	-	2	-	2	-	2	-
SD	1	-	1	-	1	-	1	-	1	1	1	1	1	1	1	1
NE	-	3	1	2	1	2	1	2	2	-	2	-	2	-	2	-
KS	2	3	2	3	2	3	2	2	-	2	-	2	-	2	-	2
South	96	46	95	46	95	47	92	57	23	9	22	10	22	10	20	12
S.A.	48	21	47	22	45	24	42	33	11	5	11	5	11	5	9	7
DE	1	-	1	-	1	-	-	1	1	1	1	1	1	1	1	1
MD	6	2	6	2	5	3	4	4	2	-	2	-	2	-	2	-
VA	5	5	5	5	6	4	7	4	2	-	1	1	1	1	2	-
WV	4	-	4	-	4	-	3	-	2	-	2	-	2	-	2	-
NC	8	3	8	3	7	4	8	4	1	1	1	1	1	1	-	2
SC	4	2	4	2	4	2	3	3	1	1	1	1	1	1	1	1
GA	8	1	9	1	9	1	7	4	2	-	2	-	2	-	1	1
FL	12	7	10	9	9	10	10	13	2	-	1	1	1	1	1	1
E.S.C	19	9	18	9	20	8	19	8	6	2	5	3	5	3	5	3
KY	4	3	4	3	4	3	4	2	1	1	1	1	1	1	1	1
TN	6	3	6	3	6	3	6	3	2	-	2	-	2	-	2	-
AL	5	2	4	2	5	2	4	3	2	-	2	-	2	-	2	-
MS	4	1	4	1	5	-	-	5	1	1	-	2	-	2	-	2
W.S.C	29	16	30	15	30	15	31	16	6	2	6	2	6	2	6	2
AR	3	1	3	1	3	1	2	2	2	-	2	-	2	-	2	-
LA	5	3	4	4	4	4	4	3	2	-	2	-	2	-	2	-
OK	4	2	4	2	4	2	4	2	1	1	1	1	1	1	1	1
TX	17	10	19	8	19	8	21	9	1	1	1	1	1	1	1	1
West	45	40	45	40	48	37	55	38	10	16	10	16	10	16	11	15
Mt	9	15	9	15	11	13	11	13	6	10	6	10	6	10	6	10
MT	1	1	1	1	1	1	1	1	2	-	1	1	1	1	1	1
ID	1	1	1	1	2	-	1	1	-	2	-	2	-	2	1	1
WY	-	1	-	1	-	1	-	1	-	2	-	2	-	2	1	1
CO	3	3	3	3	3	3	2	4	1	1	1	1	1	1	1	1
NM	1	2	1	2	1	2	1	2	1	1	1	1	1	1	1	1
AZ	1	4	1	4	1	4	3	3	1	1	1	1	1	1	1	1
UT	1	2	1	2	2	1	2	1	-	2	-	2	-	2	-	2
NV	1	1	1	1	1	1	1	1	1	1	-	2	-	2	-	2
Pac	36	25	36	25	37	24	44	25	4	6	4	6	4	6	5	5
WA	5	3	5	3	5	3	8	1	1	1	1	1	1	1	1	1
OR	3	2	3	2	4	1	4	1	-	2	-	2	-	2	1	1
CA	27	18	27	18	26	19	30	22	1	1	1	1	1	1	2	-
AK	-	1	-	1	-	1	-	1	-	2	-	2	-	2	-	2
HI	1	1	1	1	2	-	2	-	2	-	2	-	2	-	2	-

- Represents zero. [1] Indiana had one vacancy. [2] Alabama had one vacancy. [3] Vermont had one Independent-Socialist Representative.

Source: U.S. Congress, Joint Committee on Printing, *Congressional Directory*, biennial; and unpublished data.

No. 442. Members of Congress—Incumbents Re-elected: 1968 to 1992

ITEM	PRESIDENTIAL-YEAR ELECTIONS							MIDTERM ELECTIONS					
	1968	1972	1976	1980	1984	1988	1992	1970	1974	1978	1982	1986	1990
Representatives:													
Incumbent candidates	409	390	384	398	412	409	367	401	391	382	393	394	407
Re-elected	396	365	368	361	393	402	324	379	343	358	354	385	391
Percent of candidates	96.8	93.6	95.8	90.7	95.4	98.3	88.3	94.5	87.7	93.7	90.1	97.7	96.1
Defeated: In primaries..	4	12	3	6	3	1	[1]19	10	8	5	[1]10	3	1
In general elections ...	9	13	13	31	16	6	[2]24	12	40	19	29	6	15
Senators:													
Incumbent candidates	28	27	25	29	29	27	28	31	27	25	30	28	32
Re-elected	20	20	16	16	26	23	23	24	23	15	28	21	31
Percent of candidates	71.4	74.1	64.0	55.2	89.7	85.2	82.1	77.4	85.2	60.0	93.3	75.0	96.9
Defeated: In primaries..	4	2	-	4	-	-	1	1	2	3	-	-	-
In general elections ...	4	5	9	9	3	4	4	6	2	7	2	7	1

- Represents zero.   [1] Number of incumbents defeated in primaries by other incumbents due to redistricting: six in 1982 and four in 1992.   [2] Five incumbents defeated in general election by other incumbents due to redistricting.

Source: Ornstein, Norman J., Thomas E. Mann, and Michael J. Malbin, *Vital Statistics on Congress, 1991-1992*, Congressional Quarterly, Inc., Washington, DC, 1991 and Congressional Quarterly, Inc., Washington, DC, *Congressional Quarterly Weekly Report*, vol. 50, No. 44, Nov. 7, 1992, and selected prior issues, (copyright.)

No. 443. Members of Congress—Selected Characteristics: 1981 to 1993

[As of beginning of first session of each Congress, (January 3). Figures for Representatives exclude vacancies]

MEMBERS OF CONGRESS AND YEAR	Male	Fe-male	Black [1]	His-panic [2]	AGE (in years)						SENIORITY [3]				
					Under 40	40 to 49	50 to 59	60 to 69	70 to 79	80 and over	Less than 2 years	2 to 9 years	10 to 19 years	20 to 29 years	30 years or more
REPRESENTATIVES															
97th Cong., 1981 ...	416	19	17	6	94	142	132	54	12	1	77	231	96	23	8
98th Cong., 1983 ...	413	21	21	8	86	145	132	57	13	1	83	224	88	28	11
99th Cong., 1985 ...	412	22	20	10	71	154	131	59	17	2	49	237	104	34	10
100th Cong., 1987 ..	412	23	23	11	63	153	137	56	24	2	51	221	114	37	12
101st Cong., 1989 ..	408	25	24	10	41	163	133	74	20	2	39	207	139	35	13
102d Cong., 1991..	407	28	25	11	39	152	134	86	20	4	55	178	147	44	11
103d Cong., 1993..	388	47	38	17	(NA)	(NA)	(NA)	(NA)	(NA)	(NA)	(NA)	(NA)	(NA)	(NA)	(NA)
SENATORS															
97th Cong., 1981 ...	98	2	-	-	9	35	36	14	6	-	19	51	17	11	2
98th Cong., 1983 ...	98	2	-	-	7	28	39	20	3	3	5	61	21	10	3
99th Cong., 1985 ...	98	2	-	-	4	27	38	25	4	2	8	56	27	7	2
100th Cong., 1987 ..	98	2	-	-	5	30	36	22	5	2	14	41	36	7	2
101st Cong., 1989 ..	98	2	-	-	-	30	40	22	6	2	23	22	43	10	2
102d Cong., 1991..	98	2	-	-	-	23	46	24	5	2	5	34	47	10	4
103d Cong., 1993..	94	6	1	-	(NA)	(NA)	(NA)	(NA)	(NA)	(NA)	(NA)	(NA)	(NA)	(NA)	(NA)

- Represents zero.   NA Not available.   [1] Source: Joint Center for Political and Economic Studies, Washington, DC, *Black Elected Officials: A National Roster*, annual (copyright).   [2] Source: National Association of Latino Elected and Appointed Officials, Washington, DC, *National Roster of Hispanic Elected Officials*, annual.   [3] Represents consecutive years of service.

Source: Except as noted, compiled by U.S. Bureau of the Census from data published in *Congressional Directory*, biennial.

No. 444. Congressional Staff, by Location of Employment: 1970 to 1991

[Excludes those persons employed in Congressional support agencies such as the U.S. General Accounting Office, the Library of Congress, and the Congressional Budget Office]

YEAR	PERSONAL STAFF		YEAR	STANDING COMMITTEE STAFF		LOCATION OF EMPLOYMENT	1981	1985	1989	1990	1991
	House	Senate		House	Senate						
1972 ..	5,280	2,426	1970..	702	635	Total.............	17,422	18,136	17,306	17,625	17,821
1978 ..	6,944	3,268	1978..	1,844	1,151						
1979 ..	7,067	3,593	1979..	1,909	1,269	House of Representatives...	11,217	11,636	11,184	11,064	11,041
1980 ..	7,371	3,746	1980..	1,917	1,191	Committee staff [2].......	1,917	2,146	2,267	2,173	2,321
1981 ..	7,487	3,945	1981..	1,843	1,022	Personal staff	7,487	7,528	7,569	7,496	7,278
1982 ..	7,511	4,041	1982..	1,839	1,047	Leadership staff.......	127	144	133	156	149
1983 ..	7,606	4,059	1983..	1,970	1,075	Officers of House, staff ...	1,686	1,818	1,215	1,239	1,293
1984 ..	7,385	3,949	1984..	1,944	1,095						
1985 ..	7,528	4,097	1985..	2,009	1,080	Senate	6,079	6,369	5,984	6,425	6,635
1986 ..	[1]7,920	[1]3,774	1986..	1,954	1,075	Committee staff [2].......	1,150	1,178	1,116	1,207	1,154
1987 ..	7,584	4,075	1987..	2,024	1,074	Personal staff	3,945	4,097	3,837	4,162	4,294
			1988..	1,976	970	Leadership staff.......	106	118	105	94	95
1989 ..	7,569	3,837	1989..	1,986	1,013	Officers of Senate, staff ...	878	976	926	962	1,092
1990 ..	7,496	4,162	1990..	1,993	1,090						
1991 ..	7,278	4,294	1991..	2,201	1,030	Joint committee staff......	126	131	138	136	145

[1] House figure is average for year and Senate figure only covers period following implementation of Gramm-Rudman budget reductions.   [2] Covers standing, select, and special committees.

Source: Ornstein, Norman J., Thomas E. Mann, and Michael J. Malbin, *Vital Statistics on Congress, 1993-94*, Congressional Quarterly, Inc., Washington, DC, 1993 (copyright).

No. 445. Number of Governors, by Political Party Affiliation: 1970 to 1993

[Reflects results of elections in previous year and holdover incumbents]

YEAR	Demo-cratic	Re-pub-lican	Inde-pen-dent	YEAR	Demo-cratic	Re-pub-lican	Inde-pen-dent	YEAR	Demo-cratic	Re-pub-lican	Inde-pen-dent
1970......	18	32	-	1984......	35	15	-	1989......	28	22	-
1975......	36	13	1	1985......	34	16	-	1990......	29	21	-
1980......	31	19	-	1986......	34	16	-	1991[1].....	28	20	2
1982......	27	23	-	1987......	26	24	-	1992......	27	21	2
1983......	34	16	-	1988......	27	23	-	1993......	30	18	2

- Represents zero. [1] Reflects result of runoff election in Arizona in February 1991.
Source: National Governors' Association, Washington, DC, *Directory of Governors of the American States, Commonwealths & Territories*, annual, (copyright).

No. 446. Vote Cast for and Governor Elected, by State: 1986 to 1992

[In thousands, except percent. D=Democratic, R=Republican, I=Independent]

DIVISION AND STATE	1986 Total vote[1]	1986 Percent leading party	1988 Total vote[1]	1988 Percent leading party	1990 Total vote[1]	1990 Percent leading party	1992 Total vote[1]	1992 Percent leading party	Candidate elected at most recent election
N.E.:									
ME........	427	R-39.9	(X)	(X)	522	R-46.7	(X)	(X)	John R. McKernan Jr.
NH........	251	R-53.7	442	R-60.4	295	R-60.3	516	R-56.0	Steve Merrill
VT........	197	D-47.0	243	D-55.4	211	R-51.8	286	D-74.7	Howard B. Dean
MA........	1,684	D-68.7	(X)	(X)	2,343	R-50.2	(X)	(X)	William F. Weld
RI........	323	R-64.7	401	R-50.8	357	D-74.1	425	D-61.5	Bruce G. Sundlun
CT........	994	D-57.9	(X)	(X)	1,141	I-40.4	(X)	(X)	Lowell P. Weicker Jr.
M.A.:									
NY[2]......	4,294	D-64.6	(X)	(X)	4,057	D-53.2	(X)	(X)	Mario M. Cuomo
NJ[2]......	1,973	R-69.6	(X)	(X)	2,254	D-61.2	(X)	(X)	James J. Florio
PA........	3,388	D-50.7	(X)	(X)	3,053	D-67.7	(X)	(X)	Robert P. Casey
E.N.C.:									
OH........	3,067	D-60.6	(X)	(X)	3,478	R-55.7	(X)	(X)	George V. Voinovich
IN........	(X)	(X)	2,141	D-53.2	(X)	(X)	2,229	D-62.0	Evan Bayh
IL........	3,144	R-52.7	(X)	(X)	3,257	R-50.7	(X)	(X)	Jim Edgar
MI........	2,397	D-68.1	(X)	(X)	2,565	R-49.8	(X)	(X)	John Engler
WI........	1,527	R-52.7	(X)	(X)	1,380	R-58.2	(X)	(X)	Tommy G. Thompson
W.N.C.:									
MN........	1,416	D-55.8	(X)	(X)	1,807	R-49.6	(X)	(X)	Arne Carlson
IA........	911	R-51.9	(X)	(X)	976	R-60.6	(X)	(X)	Terry E. Branstad
MO........	(X)	(X)	2,086	R-64.2	(X)	(X)	2,344	D-58.7	Mel Carnahan
ND........	(X)	(X)	299	D-59.9	(X)	(X)	305	R-57.9	Edward T. Schafer
SD........	294	R-51.8	(X)	(X)	257	R-58.9	(X)	(X)	George S. Mickelson
NE........	564	R-52.9	(X)	(X)	587	D-49.9	(X)	(X)	Ben Nelson
KS........	841	R-51.9	(X)	(X)	783	D-48.6	(X)	(X)	Joan Finney
S.A.:									
DE........	(X)	(X)	240	R-70.7	(X)	(X)	277	D-64.7	Thomas R. Carper
MD[2]......	1,101	D-82.4	(X)	(X)	1,111	D-59.8	(X)	(X)	William Donald Schaefer
VA[2]......	1,343	D-55.2	(X)	(X)	1,789	D-50.1	(X)	(X)	L. Douglas Wilder
WV........	(X)	(X)	650	D-58.9	(X)	(X)	657	D-56.0	Gaston Caperton
NC........	(X)	(X)	2,180	R-56.1	(X)	(X)	2,595	D-52.7	James B. Hunt
SC........	754	R-51.0	(X)	(X)	761	R-69.5	(X)	(X)	Carroll A. Campbell Jr.
GA........	1,175	D-70.5	(X)	(X)	1,450	D-52.9	(X)	(X)	Zell Miller
FL........	3,386	R-54.6	(X)	(X)	3,531	D-56.5	(X)	(X)	Lawton Chiles
E.S.C.:									
KY[3]......	781	D-64.6	(X)	(X)	835	D-64.7	(X)	(X)	Brereton C. Jones
TN........	1,210	D-54.2	(X)	(X)	790	D-60.8	(X)	(X)	Ned McWherter
AL........	1,236	R-56.3	(X)	(X)	1,216	R-52.1	(X)	(X)	Guy Hunt
MS[3]......	722	D-53.4	(X)	(X)	711	R-50.8	(X)	(X)	Kirk Fordice
W.S.C.:									
AR........	[5]689	D-63.9	(X)	(X)	696	D-57.5	(X)	(X)	Jim Guy Tucker[4]
LA........	[5]1,559	[5]33.1	(X)	(X)	[6]1,728	[6]D-61.2	(X)	(X)	Edwin W. Edwards
OK........	910	R-47.5	(X)	(X)	911	D-57.4	(X)	(X)	David Walters
TX........	3,441	R-52.7	(X)	(X)	3,893	D-49.5	(X)	(X)	Ann W. Richards
Mt.:									
MT........	(X)	(X)	367	R-51.9	(X)	(X)	408	R-51.3	Marc Racicot
ID........	387	D-49.9	(X)	(X)	321	D-68.2	(X)	(X)	Cecil D. Andrus
WY........	165	D-54.0	(X)	(X)	160	D-65.4	(X)	(X)	Mike Sullivan
CO........	1,059	D-58.2	(X)	(X)	1,011	D-61.9	(X)	(X)	Roy Romer
NM........	395	R-53.0	(X)	(X)	411	D-54.6	(X)	(X)	Bruce King
AZ........	867	R-39.7	(X)	(X)	[7]941	[7]R-52.4	(X)	(X)	Fife Symington
UT........	(X)	(X)	649	R-40.1	(X)	(X)	763	R-42.2	Mike Leavitt
NV........	260	D-71.9	(X)	(X)	321	D-64.8	(X)	(X)	Robert J. Miller
Pac.:									
WA........	(X)	(X)	1,875	D-62.2	(X)	(X)	2,271	D-52.2	Mike Lowry
OR........	1,060	D-51.9	(X)	(X)	1,113	D-45.7	(X)	(X)	Barbara Roberts
CA........	7,444	R-60.5	(X)	(X)	7,699	R-49.2	(X)	(X)	Pete Wilson
AK........	180	D-47.3	(X)	(X)	195	I-38.9	(X)	(X)	Walter J. Hickel
HI........	334	D-52.0	(X)	(X)	340	D-59.8	(X)	(X)	John Waihee III

X Not applicable. [1] Includes minor party and scattered votes. [2] Voting years 1985 and 1989. [3] Voting years 1987 and 1991. [4] Jim Guy Tucker assumed the governorship upon the resignation of Bill Clinton following the 1992 presidential election. [5] Primary election in Oct. 1987, held on a nonparty basis. Winner was Democratic. Runner-up withdrew from runoff. [6] Result of runoff election in 1991. [7] Result of runoff election in February 1991.
Source: Elections Research Center, Chevy Chase, MD, *America Votes*, biennial and unpublished data (copyright).

No. 447. Composition of State Legislatures, by Political Party Affiliation: 1986 to 1992

[Data reflect election results in year shown for most States; and except as noted, results in previous year for other States. Figures reflect immediate results of elections, including holdover members in State houses which do not have all of their members running for re-election. Dem.=Democrat, Rep.=Republican. In general, Lower House refers to body consisting of State Representatives; Upper House, of State Senators]

STATE	LOWER HOUSE								UPPER HOUSE							
	1986 [1][2]		1988 [3][4]		1990 [5][6]		1992 [7][8]		1986 [1][9]		1988 [3][10]		1990 [5][11]		1992 [7][12]	
	Dem.	Rep.	Dem.	Rep.	Dem.	Rep.	Dem.	Rep.	Dem.	Rep.	Dem.	Rep.	Dem.	Rep.	Dem.	Rep.
U.S.	3,294	2,164	3,277	2,176	3,242	2,202	3,202	2,216	1,177	762	1,192	751	1,186	757	1,141	789
AL [13]	89	16	85	17	82	23	82	23	30	5	28	6	28	7	28	7
AK [14]	24	16	23	17	23	17	20	18	8	12	8	12	10	10	9	10
AZ [15]	24	36	26	34	27	33	25	35	11	19	13	17	17	13	12	18
AR [14]	91	9	88	11	90	9	89	10	31	4	31	4	31	4	30	5
CA [14]	44	36	46	33	47	33	48	32	23	15	24	15	25	13	23	14
CO [14]	25	40	26	39	27	38	31	34	10	25	11	24	12	23	16	19
CT [15]	92	59	88	63	87	64	87	64	25	11	23	13	20	16	20	16
DE [14]	19	22	18	23	17	24	18	23	13	8	13	8	15	6	15	6
FL [14]	75	45	73	47	74	46	71	49	25	15	23	17	22	18	20	20
GA [15]	153	27	144	36	145	35	128	52	46	10	45	11	45	11	41	15
HI [14]	40	10	45	6	45	6	47	4	20	5	22	3	22	3	22	3
ID [15]	20	64	20	64	28	56	20	50	16	26	19	23	21	21	12	23
IL [14]	67	51	67	51	72	46	67	51	31	28	31	28	31	28	27	32
IN [14]	48	52	50	50	52	48	55	45	19	30	24	26	24	26	22	28
IA [14]	58	42	61	39	55	45	49	51	30	20	30	20	29	21	26	24
KS [14]	51	74	58	67	63	62	59	66	16	24	18	22	18	22	14	26
KY [14]	71	29	72	28	68	32	72	28	29	9	30	8	27	11	25	13
LA [13]	87	15	86	17	89	16	88	16	34	5	34	5	34	5	34	5
ME [15]	86	65	97	54	97	54	90	61	20	15	20	15	21	14	20	15
MD [13]	124	17	125	16	116	25	116	25	40	7	40	7	38	9	38	9
MA [15]	127	33	128	32	118	37	124	35	32	8	32	8	25	15	31	9
MI [14]	64	46	61	49	61	49	55	55	18	20	18	20	18	20	18	20
MN [14]	83	51	80	53	78	56	87	47	47	20	44	23	46	21	45	22
MS [13]	113	9	112	9	98	23	93	27	45	7	44	8	43	9	39	13
MO [14]	111	52	104	58	99	64	100	63	21	13	22	12	23	11	20	13
MT [14]	49	51	52	48	61	39	47	53	25	25	23	27	29	21	30	20
NE.	(16)	(16)	(16)	(16)	(16)	(16)	(16)	(16)	(16)	(16)	(16)	(16)	(16)	(16)	(16)	(16)
NV [14]	29	13	30	12	22	19	29	13	9	12	8	13	10	10	10	11
NH [15]	132	268	119	281	125	268	136	258	8	16	8	16	11	13	11	13
NJ [14]	39	41	44	36	22	58	22	58	24	16	22	17	13	27	13	27
NM [14]	47	23	45	25	49	21	52	18	21	21	26	16	26	16	27	15
NY [15]	92	56	92	58	95	55	101	49	25	36	27	34	26	35	27	34
NC [14]	84	36	74	46	81	39	78	42	40	10	37	13	36	14	39	11
ND [14]	45	61	45	61	48	58	33	65	27	26	32	21	27	26	25	24
OH [14]	60	39	59	40	61	38	53	46	15	18	14	19	12	21	13	20
OK [14]	70	31	68	32	68	33	69	32	33	15	33	15	37	11	37	11
OR [14]	31	29	32	28	28	32	28	32	17	13	19	11	20	10	16	14
PA [14]	103	100	104	99	107	94	105	98	23	26	23	27	24	26	25	25
RI [15]	80	20	83	17	89	11	85	15	38	12	41	9	45	5	39	11
SC [14]	92	32	87	37	79	43	73	50	36	10	35	11	33	13	30	16
SD [15]	22	48	24	46	25	45	29	41	11	24	15	20	17	18	20	15
TN [14]	61	38	59	40	57	42	63	36	23	10	22	11	20	13	19	14
TX [14]	94	56	93	57	93	57	91	58	25	6	23	8	22	9	18	13
UT [14]	27	48	28	47	31	44	26	49	8	21	7	22	10	19	11	18
VT [15]	74	75	74	76	73	75	87	57	19	11	16	14	15	15	14	16
VA [14]	64	35	59	39	58	41	58	41	30	10	30	10	22	18	22	18
WA [14]	61	37	63	35	58	40	66	32	25	24	24	25	24	25	28	21
WV [14]	78	22	81	19	74	26	79	21	27	7	29	5	33	1	32	2
WI [14]	54	45	56	43	58	41	52	47	20	11	20	13	19	14	18	15
WY [14]	20	44	23	41	22	42	42	19	11	19	11	19	10	20	10	20

[1] Status as of Jan. 1, 1987, except for KY, LA, MS, NJ, and VA which are as of Jan. 1988 and reflect elections held in 1987.
[2] Excludes one Independent each for VT and VA; two Liberals for NY; one vacancy each for HI and KY; and three vacancies for LA. [3] Status as of Jan. 1989, except for NJ and VA which are as of Jan. 1990. [4] Excludes one Independent for AR; two Independents for VA; one Independent Democrat for MS; one vacancy each for CA, MN, MO, and OK; two vacancies for LA; and three vacancies for AL. [5] Status as of May 1992; reflects results of elections held in LA, KY, MS, and NJ in 1991. [6] Excludes one Independent each for MA, MS, NH, SC, and VA; one Independent Democrat for NH; two Independents for VT; one vacancy each for AR, NV, and SC; two vacancies for PA; four vacancies for MA; and five vacancies for NH. [7] Status as of November 30, 1992. [8] Excludes one Independent each for AR, LA, MA, NH, SC, and VA; two Independents each for AK and MS; four Independents for VT; two members of political parties other than Democratic, Republican, or Independent in VT; four members of other parties in NH; and one vacancy each for NH and TX. [9] Excludes one Independent for CA; one vacancy each for CA, IN, OK, and PA; and two vacancies for WI. [10] Excludes one Independent for CA and one vacancy each for AL and NJ. [11] Excludes two Independents for CA; and one vacancy for NV. [12] Excludes one Independent for AK; two Independents for CA; and one vacancy each for CA and MO. [13] Members of both houses serve 4-year terms. [14] Upper House members serve 4-year terms and Lower House members serve 2-year terms. [15] Members of both houses serve 2-year terms. [16] Single chamber (unicameral body) of 49 members, elected without party designation.

Source: 1986-90, The Council of State Governments, Lexington, KY, *State Elective Officials and the Legislatures*, biennial (copyright); 1992, National Conference of State Legislatures, Denver, CO, *State Legislatures*, January 1993 (copyright).

No. 448. Political Party Control of State Legislatures, by Party: 1961 to 1993

[As of beginning of year. Until 1972 there were two nonpartisan legislatures in Minnesota and Nebraska. Since then only Nebraska has had a nonpartisan legislature]

YEAR	LEGISLATURES UNDER—			YEAR	LEGISLATURES UNDER—			YEAR	LEGISLATURES UNDER—		
	Democratic control	Split control or tie	Republican control		Democratic control	Split control or tie	Republican control		Democratic control	Split control or tie	Republican control
1961...	27	6	15	1973...	27	6	16	1985...	27	11	11
1963...	25	7	16	1975...	37	7	5	1987...	28	12	9
1965...	32	10	6	1977...	36	8	5	1989 [2]	28	13	8
1967...	24	8	16	1979...	30	7	12	1990...	29	11	9
1969...	20	8	20	1981...	28	6	15	1992...	29	14	6
1971...	23	9	16	1983 [1]	34	4	11	1993...	25	16	8

[1] Two 1984 midterm recall elections resulted in a change in control of the Michigan State senate. At the time of the 1984 election, therefore, Democrats controlled 33 legislatures. [2] A party change during the year by a Democratic representative broke the tie in the Indiana House of Representatives, giving the Republicans control of both chambers.

Source: National Conference of State Legislatures, Denver, CO, *State Legislatures*, periodic.

No. 449. Black Elected Officials, by Office, 1970 to 1992, and by Region and State, 1992

[As of January 1992, no Black elected officials had been identified in Hawaii, Idaho, Montana, or North Dakota]

REGION, DIVISION, AND STATE	Total	U.S. and State legislatures [1]	City and county offices [2]	Law enforcement [3]	Education [4]	REGION, DIVISION, AND STATE	Total	U.S. and State legislatures [1]	City and county offices [2]	Law enforcement [3]	Education [4]
1970 (Feb.)..	1,479	179	719	213	368	IA	13	1	7	1	4
1975 (Apr.)..	3,522	299	1,885	387	951	MO	177	18	127	14	18
1978 (July)..	4,544	316	2,616	458	1,154	SD	3	-	3	-	-
1979 (July)..	4,636	315	2,675	491	1,155	NE	4	1	1	-	2
1980 (July)..	4,963	326	2,871	534	1,232	KS	19	4	7	2	6
1981 (July)..	5,109	343	2,914	559	1,293	South	5,110	280	3,432	474	924
1982 (July)..	5,241	342	3,017	573	1,309	S.A	2,113	147	1,504	136	326
1983 (July)..	5,719	386	3,283	620	1,430	DE	24	3	14	1	6
1984 (Jan.)..	5,865	396	3,367	657	1,445	MD	135	32	75	22	6
1985 (Jan.)..	6,312	407	3,689	685	1,531	DC	208	5 [4]	196	-	8
1986 (Jan.)..	6,384	410	3,800	676	1,498	VA	156	13	128	15	-
1987 (Jan.)..	6,646	428	3,949	727	1,542	WV	23	2	17	4	-
1988 (Jan.)..	6,793	424	4,089	738	1,542	NC	458	19	331	31	77
1989 (Jan.)..	7,191	441	4,388	760	1,602	SC	413	22	255	12	124
1990 (Jan.)..	7,335	440	4,481	769	1,645	GA	513	38	362	27	86
1991 (Jan.)..	7,445	476	4,493	847	1,629	FL	183	14	126	24	19
1992 (Jan.)..	7,517	499	4,557	847	1,614	E.S.C	1,650	66	1,166	180	238
						KY	65	3	48	4	10
Northeast ..	747	89	288	116	254	TN	167	14	103	25	25
N.E	107	31	62	3	11	AL	702	24	529	65	84
ME	1	-	1	-	-	MS	716	25	486	86	119
NH	2	2	-	-	-	W.S.C.	1,347	67	762	158	360
VT	2	2	-	-	-	AR	342	12	188	39	103
MA	28	6	19	1	2	LA	579	33	319	81	146
RI	11	8	3	-	-	OK	126	6	97	2	21
CT	63	13	39	2	9	TX	300	16	158	36	90
M.A	640	58	226	113	243	West	345	32	98	104	111
NY	287	27	64	61	135	Mt	51	12	11	16	12
NJ	201	13	109	-	79	WY	2	1	-	-	1
PA	152	18	53	52	29	CO	18	4	3	9	2
Midwest ...	1,315	98	739	153	325	NM	4	-	1	2	1
E.N.C	1,086	73	592	129	292	AZ	16	4	3	3	6
OH	215	15	121	30	49	UT	1	-	-	1	-
IN	70	9	49	4	8	NV	10	3	4	1	2
IL	457	25	283	23	126	Pac	294	20	87	88	99
MI	320	18	128	68	106	WA	20	2	9	6	3
WI	24	6	11	4	3	OR	11	4	3	4	-
W.N.C ...	229	25	147	24	33	CA	260	13	73	78	96
MN	13	1	2	7	3	AK	3	1	2	-	-

- Represents zero. [1] Includes elected State administrators. [2] County commissioners and councilmen, mayors, vice mayors, aldermen, regional officials, and other. [3] Judges, magistrates, constables, marshals, sheriffs, justices of the peace, and other. [4] Members of State education agencies, college boards, school boards, and other. [5] Includes two shadow senators and one shadow representative.

Source: Joint Center for Political and Economic Studies, Washington, DC, *Black Elected Officials: A National Roster*, annual (copyright).

No. 450. Hispanic Public Officials, by Office, 1985 to 1992, and by State, 1992

[As of September. For States not shown, no Hispanic public officials had been identified]

REGION, DIVISION, AND STATE	Total	State executives and legislators	County and municipal officials	Judicial and law enforcement	Education and school boards	REGION, DIVISION, AND STATE	Total	State executives and legislators	County and municipal officials	Judicial and law enforcement	Education and school boards
1985	[1]3,147	119	1,316	517	1,185	NE	4	-	3	-	1
1986	[1]3,202	122	1,352	530	1,188	KS	6	4	1	-	1
1987	[1]3,317	127	1,412	568	1,199	South	[1]2,076	37	914	397	723
1988	[1]3,360	124	1,425	574	1,226	S.A	[1]70	11	38	16	4
1989	[1]3,783	133	1,724	575	1,341	DE	1	-	1	-	-
1990	[1]4,004	134	1,819	583	1,458	MD	2	-	1	-	-
1991	[1]4,202	140	1,867	596	1,588	SC	1	-	1	-	-
1992	[1]4,994	139	1,908	628	2,308	FL	[1]66	11	35	16	3
						W.S.C	[1]2,006	26	876	381	719
Northeast	[1]160	15	48	13	83	AR	1	-	-	-	1
N.E	20	5	9	-	6	LA	9	-	1	8	-
MA	4	1	-	-	3	OK	1	-	1	-	-
RI	1	1	-	-	-	TX	[1]1,995	26	874	373	718
CT	15	3	9	-	3	West	[1]1,918	77	892	209	735
M.A	[1]140	10	39	13	77	Mt	[1]1,214	68	652	156	336
NY	[1]91	7	17	11	55	MT	2	-	-	1	1
NJ	40	2	19	-	19	ID	2	-	2	-	-
PA	9	1	3	2	3	WY	5	-	5	-	-
Midwest	840	10	54	9	767	CO	207	10	135	10	52
E.N.C	826	4	49	8	765	NM	[1]688	46	370	100	171
OH	9	-	6	2	1	AZ	[1]303	11	136	44	111
IN	7	1	4	1	1	UT	3	-	3	-	-
IL	796	3	31	3	[2]759	NV	4	1	1	1	1
MI	11	-	6	2	3	Pac	[1]704	9	240	53	399
WI	3	-	2	-	1	WA	13	2	5	1	5
W.N.C	14	6	5	1	2	OR	8	-	5	2	1
MN	3	2	-	1	-	CA	[1]682	7	229	50	393
MO	1	-	1	-	-	AK	1	-	1	-	-

- Represents zero. [1] Includes U.S. Representatives, not shown separately. [2] Includes local school council members in the Chicago area.

Source: National Association of Latino Elected and Appointed Officials, Washington, DC, *National Roster of Hispanic Elected Officials*, annual.

No. 451. Women Holding State and Local Public Offices, by Office and State: 1985 to 1993

[For data on women in U.S. Congress, see table 443]

STATE	Statewide elective executive office,[1][2] 1993	State legislature,[1] 1993	County governing boards, 1988	Mayors and municipal council members, 1985	STATE	Statewide elective executive office,[1][2] 1993	State legislature,[1] 1993	County governing boards, 1988	Mayors and municipal council members, 1985
United States	72	1,517	1,653	14,672	Missouri	2	38	17	-
Alabama	1	8	7	281	Montana	1	29	18	110
Alaska	-	13	17	233	Nebraska	2	10	27	241
Arizona	2	32	8	87	Nevada	3	17	10	15
Arkansas	2	13	71	365	New Hampshire	-	142	8	113
California	2	28	56	465	New Jersey	-	15	15	451
Colorado	3	34	18	315	New Mexico	1	22	17	86
Connecticut	2	47	(X)	240	New York	-	34	131	797
Delaware	3	9	2	57	North Carolina	-	31	45	337
Dist. of Columbia	(X)	(X)	(X)	7	North Dakota	4	24	11	174
Florida	1	28	51	311	Ohio	1	28	25	1,129
Georgia	-	41	28	251	Oklahoma	3	14	5	312
Hawaii	-	18	8	3	Oregon	3	24	20	344
Idaho	1	32	14	141	Pennsylvania	2	25	35	-
Illinois	1	41	152	-	Rhode Island	2	37	(X)	30
Indiana	4	29	10	-	South Carolina	1	22	36	184
Iowa	3	22	35	732	South Dakota	2	21	16	149
Kansas	2	47	24	445	Tennessee	-	16	117	144
Kentucky	-	6	17	-	Texas	2	29	30	786
Louisiana	2	10	32	183	Utah	2	14	2	137
Maine	-	58	3	243	Vermont	1	61	(X)	87
Maryland	-	44	21	133	Virginia	1	17	49	211
Massachusetts	-	46	5	217	Washington	4	58	15	341
Michigan	1	29	123	2,779	West Virginia	-	22	11	202
Minnesota	2	55	37	542	Wisconsin	1	36	241	-
Mississippi	-	19	8	176	Wyoming	2	22	5	86

- Represents zero. X Not applicable. [1] As of January. [2] Excludes women elected to the judiciary, women appointed to State cabinet-level positions, women elected to executive posts by the legislature, and elected members of university Board of Trustees or board of education.

Source: Center for the American Woman and Politics, Eagleton Institute of Politics, Rutgers University, New Brunswick, NJ, information releases.

No. 452. Political Party Identification of the Adult Population, by Degree of Attachment, 1970 to 1990, and by Selected Characteristics, 1990

[In percent. Covers citizens of voting-age living in private housing units in the contiguous United States. Data are from the National Election Studies and are based on a sample and subject to sampling variability; for details, see source]

YEAR AND SELECTED CHARACTERISTIC	Total	Strong Demo- crat	Weak Demo- crat	Inde- pendent Demo- crat	Inde- pendent	Inde- pendent Repub- lican	Weak Repub- lican	Strong Repub- lican	Apolitical
1970.	100	20	24	10	13	8	15	9	1
1972.	100	15	26	11	13	11	13	10	1
1976.	100	15	25	12	15	10	14	9	1
1980.	100	18	23	11	13	10	14	9	2
1984.	100	17	20	11	11	12	15	12	2
1986.	100	18	22	10	12	11	15	11	2
1988.	100	18	18	12	11	13	14	14	2
1990, total [1]	**100**	**20**	**19**	**12**	**11**	**12**	**15**	**10**	**2**
Year of birth:									
1959 or later (Under 32 years old) .	100	11	17	15	15	14	16	9	2
1943 to 1958 (32 to 47 years old). .	100	20	22	14	10	10	15	8	2
1927 to 1942 (48 to 63 years old). .	100	24	17	11	9	14	13	10	1
1911 to 1926 (64 to 79 years old). .	100	30	22	7	6	10	13	13	1
1895 to 1910 (80 to 95 years old). .	100	43	14	9	5	2	19	9	(Z)
Sex:									
Male .	100	18	18	14	9	13	16	11	1
Female .	100	22	20	11	12	11	14	9	2
Race:									
White.	100	17	19	11	11	13	16	11	1
Black.	100	40	23	16	8	7	3	2	2
Education:									
Grade school .	100	37	17	9	13	6	7	4	5
High school .	100	19	21	13	13	11	13	9	2
College .	100	17	17	12	7	15	19	12	(Z)

Z Less than 0.5 percent.   [1] Includes other characteristics, not shown separately.

Source: Center for Political Studies, University of Michigan, Ann Arbor, MI, unpublished data. Data prior to 1988 published in Warren E. Miller and Santa A. Traugott, *American National Election Studies Data Sourcebook, 1952-1986,* Harvard University Press, Cambridge, MA, 1989 (copyright).

No. 453. Persons Reported Registered and Voted, by State: 1992

[See headnote, table 454]

STATE	Voting- age pop- ulation (1,000)	PERCENT OF VOTING-AGE POPULATION Regis- tered	PERCENT OF VOTING-AGE POPULATION Voted	STATE	Voting- age pop- ulation (1,000)	PERCENT OF VOTING-AGE POPULATION Regis- tered	PERCENT OF VOTING-AGE POPULATION Voted	STATE	Voting- age pop- ulation (1,000)	PERCENT OF VOTING-AGE POPULATION Regis- tered	PERCENT OF VOTING-AGE POPULATION Voted
U.S. .	**185,684**	**68.2**	**61.3**	KS. . . .	1,818	77.1	71.9	ND . . .	444	90.8	71.1
				KY. . . .	2,724	64.9	57.6	OH . . .	8,060	69.6	64.3
AL. . . .	3,007	77.1	63.6	LA. . . .	2,972	77.0	68.6	OK . . .	2,295	74.3	67.5
AK. . . .	347	75.1	68.6	ME . . .	938	85.4	74.1	OR . . .	2,206	74.7	69.1
AZ. . . .	2,671	70.5	64.7	MD . . .	3,605	71.7	66.4	PA. . . .	9,170	65.1	59.9
AR. . . .	1,745	66.5	58.0	MA . . .	4,501	72.5	65.8	RI	757	74.0	69.0
CA. . . .	22,340	57.6	52.8	MI	6,811	74.6	65.9	SC. . . .	2,580	67.0	58.0
CO . . .	2,451	74.7	68.8	MN . . .	3,237	86.1	74.2	SD. . . .	500	80.1	70.2
CT. . . .	2,428	76.8	71.7	MS . . .	1,839	79.3	66.7	TN. . . .	3,714	65.0	55.6
DE. . . .	519	70.7	66.1	MO . . .	3,803	74.2	66.2	TX. . . .	12,267	64.9	55.6
DC. . . .	398	73.9	66.1	MT . . .	570	77.3	71.4	UT. . . .	1,097	78.8	72.3
FL. . . .	10,342	62.7	55.8	NE. . . .	1,167	73.1	66.1	VT. . . .	443	76.1	68.6
GA . . .	4,723	62.0	54.1	NV. . . .	955	63.4	58.1	VA. . . .	4,585	65.4	61.2
HI	813	60.6	55.2	NH . . .	853	69.9	64.6	WA . . .	3,699	71.5	66.3
ID	726	71.8	66.9	NJ. . . .	5,838	68.0	61.2	WV . . .	1,367	64.9	57.3
IL	8,676	72.1	65.1	NM . . .	1,079	67.1	62.6	WI	3,611	84.4	75.3
IN	4,183	68.0	63.0	NY. . . .	13,401	62.0	56.8	WY . . .	331	68.1	64.2
IA	2,100	77.9	70.8	NC . . .	4,976	68.7	60.0				

Source: U.S. Bureau of the Census, *Current Population Reports,* P20-466.

No. 454. Voting-Age Population, Percent Reporting Registered, and Voted: 1978 to 1992

[As of **November**. Covers civilian noninstitutional population 18 years old and over. Includes aliens. Figures are based on Current Population Survey (see text, section 1, and Appendix III) and differ from those in table 455 based on population estimates and official vote counts]

CHARACTERISTIC	VOTING-AGE POPULATION (mil.)								PERCENT REPORTING THEY REGISTERED								PERCENT REPORTING THEY VOTED							
									Presidential election years				Congressional election years				Presidential election years				Congressional election years			
	1978	1980	1982	1984	1986	1988	1990	1992	1980	1984	1988	1992	1978	1982	1986	1990	1980	1984	1988	1992	1978	1982	1986	1990
Total [1]	151.6	157.1	165.5	170.0	173.9	178.1	182.1	185.7	66.9	68.3	66.6	68.2	62.6	64.1	64.3	62.2	59.2	59.9	57.4	61.3	45.9	48.5	46.0	45.0
18 to 20 years old	12.2	12.3	12.1	11.2	10.7	10.7	10.8	9.7	44.7	47.0	44.9	48.3	34.7	35.0	35.4	35.4	35.7	36.7	33.2	38.5	20.1	19.8	18.6	18.4
21 to 24 years old	15.5	15.9	16.7	16.7	15.7	14.8	14.0	14.6	52.7	54.3	50.6	55.3	45.1	47.8	46.6	43.3	43.1	43.5	38.3	45.7	26.2	28.4	24.2	22.0
25 to 34 years old	33.4	35.7	38.8	40.3	41.9	42.7	42.7	41.6	62.0	63.3	57.8	60.6	55.5	57.1	55.8	52.0	54.6	54.5	48.0	53.2	38.0	40.4	35.1	33.8
35 to 44 years old	24.2	25.6	28.1	30.7	33.0	35.2	37.9	39.7	70.6	70.9	69.3	69.2	66.7	68.8	68.2	65.5	64.4	63.5	61.3	63.6	50.1	52.2	49.3	48.4
45 to 64 years old	43.4	43.6	44.2	44.3	44.8	45.9	46.9	49.1	75.8	76.6	75.5	75.3	74.3	75.6	74.8	71.4	69.3	69.8	67.9	70.0	58.5	62.2	58.7	55.8
65 years old and over	23.0	24.1	25.6	26.7	27.7	28.8	29.9	30.8	74.6	76.9	78.4	78.0	72.8	75.2	76.9	76.5	65.1	67.7	68.8	70.1	55.9	59.9	60.9	60.3
Male	71.5	74.1	78.0	80.3	82.4	84.5	86.6	88.6	66.6	67.3	65.2	66.9	62.6	63.7	63.4	61.2	59.1	59.0	56.4	60.2	46.6	48.7	45.8	44.6
Female	80.2	83.0	87.4	89.6	91.5	93.6	95.5	97.1	67.1	69.3	67.8	69.3	62.5	64.4	65.0	63.1	59.4	60.8	58.3	62.3	45.3	48.4	46.1	45.4
White	133.4	137.7	143.6	146.8	149.9	152.9	155.6	157.8	68.4	69.6	67.9	70.1	63.8	65.6	65.3	63.8	60.9	61.4	59.1	63.6	47.3	49.9	47.0	46.7
Black	15.6	16.4	17.6	18.4	19.0	19.7	20.4	21.0	60.0	66.3	64.5	63.9	57.1	59.1	64.0	58.8	50.5	55.8	51.5	54.0	37.2	43.0	43.2	39.2
Hispanic [2]	6.8	8.2	8.8	9.5	11.8	12.9	13.8	14.7	36.3	40.1	35.5	35.0	32.9	35.3	35.9	32.3	29.9	32.6	28.8	28.9	23.5	25.3	24.2	21.0
Region: [3]																								
Northeast	35.1	35.5	36.4	36.9	37.3	37.9	38.1	38.3	64.8	66.6	64.8	67.0	62.3	62.5	62.0	61.0	58.5	59.7	57.4	61.2	48.1	49.8	44.4	45.2
Midwest	40.3	41.5	41.9	42.1	42.8	43.3	43.9	44.1	73.8	74.6	72.5	74.6	68.2	71.1	70.7	68.2	65.8	65.7	62.9	67.2	50.5	54.7	49.5	48.6
South	48.8	50.6	55.4	57.6	59.2	60.7	62.4	63.7	64.8	66.9	65.6	67.2	60.1	61.7	63.0	61.3	55.6	56.8	54.5	59.0	39.6	41.8	43.0	42.4
West	27.5	29.5	31.9	33.4	34.6	36.2	37.7	39.3	63.3	64.7	63.0	63.6	59.1	60.6	60.8	57.7	57.2	58.5	55.6	58.5	47.5	50.7	48.4	45.0
School years completed:																								
8 years or less	23.6	22.7	22.4	20.6	19.6	19.1	17.7	15.4	53.0	53.4	47.5	43.9	53.2	52.3	50.5	44.0	42.6	42.9	36.7	35.1	34.6	35.7	32.7	27.7
High school:																								
1 to 3 years	22.3	22.5	22.3	22.1	21.4	21.1	21.0	[4]21.0	54.6	54.9	52.8	[4]50.4	52.9	53.3	52.4	47.9	45.6	44.4	41.3	[4]41.2	35.1	37.7	33.8	30.9
4 years	58.4	61.2	65.2	67.8	68.6	70.0	71.5	[5]65.3	66.4	67.3	64.6	[5]64.9	62.9	62.9	62.9	60.0	58.9	58.7	54.7	[5]57.5	45.3	47.1	44.1	42.2
College:																								
1 to 3 years	25.1	26.7	28.8	30.9	33.0	34.3	36.3	[6]46.7	74.4	75.7	73.5	[6]75.4	68.7	70.0	70.0	71.5	67.2	67.5	64.5	[6]68.7	51.5	53.3	49.9	50.0
4 years or more	22.2	24.0	26.9	28.6	31.3	33.6	35.6	[7]37.4	84.3	83.8	83.1	[7]84.8	76.9	79.4	77.8	77.3	79.9	79.1	77.6	[7]81.0	63.9	66.5	62.5	62.5
Employed	93.2	95.0	97.2	104.2	108.5	113.8	115.5	116.3	68.7	69.4	67.1	69.9	63.0	65.5	64.4	62.6	61.8	61.6	58.4	63.8	46.7	50.0	45.7	45.1
Unemployed	4.9	6.9	10.8	7.4	6.6	5.8	6.7	8.3	50.3	54.3	50.4	53.7	44.1	49.8	50.6	44.6	41.2	44.0	38.6	46.2	27.4	34.1	31.2	27.9
Not in labor force	53.5	55.2	57.5	58.4	58.8	58.5	59.9	61.1	65.8	68.1	67.2	66.8	66.8	64.3	65.4	63.4	57.0	58.9	57.3	58.7	46.2	48.7	48.2	46.7

[1] Includes other races not shown separately. [2] Hispanic persons may be of any race. [3] For composition of regions, see table 31. [4] Represents those who completed ninth to twelfth grade, but have no high school diploma. [5] High school graduate. [6] Some college or associate degree. [7] Bachelor's or advanced degree.

Source: U.S. Bureau of the Census, Current Population Reports, P20-466, and earlier reports.

No. 455. Participation in Elections for President and U.S. Representatives: 1932 to 1992

[As of **November**. Estimated resident population 21 years old and over, 1932-70, except as noted, and 18 years old and over thereafter; includes Armed Forces. Prior to 1960, excludes Alaska and Hawaii. District of Columbia is included in votes cast for President beginning 1964 and in votes cast for Representative beginning 1972]

YEAR	Resident population (incl. aliens) of voting age [1] (1,000)	VOTES CAST				YEAR	Resident population (incl. aliens) of voting age [1] (1,000)	VOTES CAST			
		For President [2] (1,000)	Percent of voting age population	For U.S. Representatives (1,000)	Percent of voting age population			For President [2] (1,000)	Percent of voting age population	For U.S. Representatives (1,000)	Percent of voting age population
1932.	75,768	39,758	52.5	37,657	49.7	1964.	114,090	70,645	61.9	65,895	57.8
1934.	77,997	(X)	(X)	32,256	41.4	1966.	116,638	(X)	(X)	52,908	45.4
1936.	80,174	45,654	56.9	42,886	53.5	1968.	120,285	73,212	60.9	66,288	55.1
1938.	82,354	(X)	(X)	36,236	44.0	1970.	124,498	(X)	(X)	54,173	43.5
1940.	84,728	49,900	58.9	46,951	55.4	1972.	140,777	77,719	55.2	71,430	50.7
1942.	86,465	(X)	(X)	28,074	32.5	1974.	146,338	(X)	(X)	52,495	35.9
1944.	85,654	47,977	56.0	45,103	52.7	1976.	152,308	81,556	53.5	74,422	48.9
1946.	92,659	(X)	(X)	34,398	37.1	1978.	158,369	(X)	(X)	55,332	34.9
1948.	95,573	48,794	51.1	45,933	48.1	1980.	164,595	86,515	52.6	77,995	47.4
1950.	98,134	(X)	(X)	40,342	41.1	1982.	169,936	(X)	(X)	64,514	38.0
1952.	99,929	61,551	61.6	57,571	57.6	1984.	174,468	92,653	53.1	83,231	47.7
1954.	102,075	(X)	(X)	42,580	41.7	1986.	178,566	(X)	(X)	59,619	33.4
1956.	104,515	62,027	59.3	58,426	55.9	1988.	182,779	91,595	50.1	81,786	44.7
1958.	106,447	(X)	(X)	45,818	43.0	1990.	185,812	(X)	(X)	61,513	33.1
1960.	109,672	68,838	62.8	64,133	58.5	1992.	189,044	104,425	55.2	96,239	50.9
1962.	112,952	(X)	(X)	51,267	45.4						

X Not applicable.   [1] Population 18 and over in Georgia, 1944-70, and in Kentucky, 1956-70; 19 and over in Alaska and 20 and over in Hawaii, 1960-70.   [2] Source: 1932-58, U.S. Congress, Clerk of the House, *Statistics of the Presidential and Congressional Election,* biennial.

Source: Except as noted, U.S. Bureau of the Census, *Current Population Reports,* P25-1085; and Elections Research Center, Chevy Chase, MD, *America Votes,* biennial (copyright).

No. 456. Presidential Primaries—Votes Cast and Percent of Voting-Age Population Casting Votes, by Party: 1992

[For States not shown, no presidential primaries were held]

STATE	Voting age population (VAP) (1,000)	VOTES CAST IN DEMOCRATIC PRIMARY		VOTES CAST IN REPUBLICAN PRIMARY		STATE	Voting age population (VAP) (1,000)	VOTES CAST IN DEMOCRATIC PRIMARY		VOTES CAST IN REPUBLICAN PRIMARY	
		Total (1,000)	Percent of VAP	Total (1,000)	Percent of VAP			Total (1,000)	Percent of VAP	Total (1,000)	Percent of VAP
AL	3,056	451	14.8	165	5.4	NE	1,167	163	14.0	206	17.7
AR	1,768	503	28.4	52	2.9	NH	852	170	20.0	178	20.9
CA	22,668	3,065	13.5	2,492	11.0	NJ	5,943	345	5.8	257	4.3
CO	2,501	240	9.6	196	7.8	NM	1,104	181	16.4	87	7.9
CT	2,535	173	6.8	99	3.9	NY	13,609	1,008	7.4	(¹)	(¹)
DC	459	63	13.7	5	1.2	NC	5,217	692	13.3	284	5.4
FL	10,586	1,124	10.6	893	8.4	ND	458	33	7.2	48	10.4
GA	4,950	455	9.2	454	9.2	OH	8,146	1,042	12.8	860	10.6
ID	740	55	7.4	115	15.5	OK	2,328	416	17.9	218	9.4
IL	8,568	1,633	19.1	878	10.3	OR	2,226	354	15.9	304	13.7
IN	4,176	477	11.4	468	11.2	PA	9,129	1,265	13.9	1,009	11.1
KS	1,836	160	8.7	213	11.6	RI	776	51	6.5	16	2.0
KY	2,779	371	13.3	101	3.6	SC	2,672	116	4.4	149	5.6
LA	2,992	384	12.8	135	4.5	SD	502	60	11.9	45	8.9
MD	3,719	586	15.8	247	6.6	TN	3,783	318	8.4	246	6.5
MA	4,607	809	17.6	276	6.0	TX	12,524	1,483	11.8	807	6.4
MI	6,923	586	8.5	449	6.5	UT	1,142	32	2.8	(¹)	(¹)
MN	3,278	204	6.2	133	4.0	WA	3,818	148	3.9	130	3.4
MS	1,861	191	10.3	155	8.3	WV	1,350	307	22.7	124	9.2
MT	586	117	20.0	91	15.5	WI	3,669	759	20.7	469	12.8

[1] No primary held.

Source: Committee for the Study of the American Electorate, Washington, DC, unpublished data.

No. 457. Resident Population of Voting Age and Percent Casting Votes—States: 1986 to 1990, and Projections, 1992

[As of **November. Estimated population, 18 years old and over.** Includes Armed Forces stationed in each State, aliens, and institutional population]

REGION, DIVISION, AND STATE	VOTING-AGE POPULATION						PERCENT CASTING VOTES FOR—					
	1986 (1,000)	1988 (1,000)	1990 (1,000)	1992, proj.			Presidential electors		U.S. Representatives			
				Total (1,000)	Percent Black	Percent female	1988	1992	1986	1988	1990	1992
U.S.	178,566	182,779	185,812	189,044	11.4	52.0	50.1	55.2	33.4	44.7	33.1	50.9
Northeast	38,064	38,590	38,838	38,824	10.9	52.8	51.4	55.6	32.6	46.1	32.9	50.0
N.E.	9,748	9,950	10,137	10,143	4.6	52.5	57.6	62.6	37.4	53.5	43.9	58.3
ME	875	908	924	944	0.3	52.2	61.1	72.0	48.2	61.1	56.0	70.9
NH	775	817	835	852	0.6	51.3	55.2	63.1	31.1	52.5	34.8	60.0
VT	403	420	422	429	0.2	52.0	57.9	67.5	46.9	57.1	49.7	65.6
MA	4,502	4,565	4,646	4,607	4.9	53.0	57.7	60.2	33.4	51.9	44.1	56.7
RI	751	765	776	776	3.7	53.1	52.9	58.4	40.7	51.1	44.7	51.4
CT	2,442	2,476	2,534	2,535	7.8	52.3	58.3	63.8	40.1	54.2	40.9	56.6
M.A.	28,315	28,640	28,701	28,681	13.1	52.9	49.3	53.1	31.0	43.6	29.1	47.1
NY	13,447	13,574	13,083	13,609	16.1	53.0	47.8	50.9	29.0	40.6	26.8	43.5
NJ	5,811	5,894	5,927	5,943	13.1	52.5	52.6	56.3	26.7	47.1	30.8	50.3
PA	9,057	9,171	9,091	9,129	8.7	53.1	49.5	54.3	36.5	45.8	31.4	50.3
Midwest	43,704	44,403	44,160	44,656	9.0	52.3	55.5	62.1	38.9	53.0	39.6	58.7
E.N.C.	30,723	31,204	31,133	31,482	10.8	52.4	54.4	60.7	36.9	51.6	37.6	56.9
OH	7,946	8,059	8,066	8,146	10.0	52.8	54.5	60.6	38.6	51.6	42.4	56.2
IN	4,040	4,111	4,105	4,176	7.3	52.4	52.8	55.2	38.5	51.6	36.9	53.1
IL	8,517	8,636	8,495	8,568	13.9	52.2	52.8	58.9	35.4	50.3	36.2	56.4
MI	6,699	6,805	6,851	6,923	13.2	52.3	53.9	61.7	34.7	50.8	35.5	56.1
WI	3,522	3,593	3,616	3,669	4.3	51.8	61.0	69.0	39.3	56.6	34.7	65.1
W.N.C.	12,981	13,199	13,027	13,174	4.7	52.1	58.2	65.5	43.4	56.3	44.4	63.3
MN	3,115	3,201	3,222	3,278	1.9	51.7	65.5	71.6	44.7	61.5	55.3	69.4
IA	2,105	2,125	2,061	2,075	1.5	52.5	57.7	65.3	42.3	56.0	38.4	59.9
MO	3,772	3,840	3,813	3,858	9.8	52.8	54.5	62.0	37.9	53.9	35.5	60.9
ND	488	484	462	458	0.4	50.7	61.4	67.3	58.6	62.0	50.6	65.0
SD	511	518	498	502	0.2	51.6	60.4	67.0	56.8	60.2	51.7	66.3
NE	1,171	1,183	1,152	1,167	3.3	52.2	55.9	63.2	47.4	55.5	50.9	60.9
KS	1,818	1,848	1,819	1,836	5.4	51.7	53.7	63.0	43.3	50.4	42.9	61.3
South	61,004	62,470	63,821	65,411	17.1	52.3	45.7	51.4	27.0	36.8	26.9	46.0
S.A.	30,896	32,069	33,312	34,320	18.8	52.4	44.4	50.1	26.8	37.8	28.2	46.6
DE	477	498	507	525	16.4	52.4	50.2	55.2	33.8	47.2	35.0	52.6
MD	3,372	3,498	3,640	3,719	24.4	52.4	49.0	53.4	31.5	44.6	30.0	48.6
DC	486	472	481	459	64.3	54.5	40.9	49.6	26.1	36.2	33.2	42.9
VA	4,392	4,568	4,716	4,842	17.8	51.7	48.0	52.8	23.7	41.4	24.4	48.9
WV	1,412	1,398	1,349	1,350	2.9	53.0	46.7	50.6	28.0	40.7	27.8	41.7
NC	4,731	4,880	5,061	5,217	20.2	52.4	43.7	50.1	33.2	40.7	39.7	48.4
SC	2,458	2,531	2,587	2,672	27.1	52.4	39.0	45.0	29.2	39.2	25.9	41.7
GA	4,421	4,593	4,791	4,950	24.9	52.4	39.4	46.9	24.0	36.4	29.1	44.7
FL	9,146	9,632	10,180	10,586	11.8	52.4	44.7	50.2	[1]23.4	[1]31.6	[1]23.4	[1]46.4
E.S.C.	11,065	11,254	11,252	11,479	17.7	52.9	46.8	53.5	30.5	41.0	25.5	49.3
KY	2,720	2,752	2,740	2,779	6.7	52.5	48.1	53.7	23.2	40.2	27.9	49.0
TN	3,569	3,660	3,685	3,783	14.6	52.8	44.7	52.4	31.0	38.5	19.5	45.6
AL	2,947	2,997	2,995	3,056	22.9	53.1	46.0	55.2	37.9	39.3	34.0	52.4
MS	1,827	1,845	1,832	1,861	32.0	53.3	50.5	52.8	28.7	49.8	20.1	51.9
W.S.C.	19,044	19,148	19,257	19,612	13.7	51.8	47.3	52.4	25.2	32.6	25.5	43.2
AR	1,732	1,750	1,737	1,768	13.7	52.8	47.3	53.8	38.5	[2]34.6	38.3	50.3
LA	3,153	3,112	2,988	2,992	28.5	52.8	52.3	59.8	[2]12.4	[2]6.6	[2]3.5	[2]22.8
OK	2,396	2,366	2,310	2,328	6.7	52.1	49.5	59.7	[1]30.3	[1]32.4	37.1	54.8
TX	11,764	11,919	12,222	12,524	11.5	51.3	45.5	49.1	25.6	39.2	26.8	44.9
West	35,795	37,316	38,993	40,153	5.3	50.6	49.6	53.5	38.5	46.8	36.0	51.0
Mt	9,260	9,548	9,856	10,157	2.6	50.9	52.5	58.8	40.5	50.2	39.3	56.5
MT	587	586	579	586	0.2	51.2	62.4	70.1	54.2	62.3	54.8	68.9
ID	693	703	707	740	0.4	50.8	58.2	65.2	54.3	57.9	44.5	63.9
WY	349	339	319	322	0.6	50.0	52.1	62.3	45.8	52.5	49.5	61.2
CO	2,407	2,440	2,447	2,501	3.9	50.9	56.2	62.7	42.3	53.9	40.9	59.1
NM	1,041	1,065	1,075	1,104	1.8	51.6	48.9	51.6	37.1	42.2	33.4	50.3
AZ	2,400	2,543	2,696	2,749	2.8	51.2	46.1	54.1	33.5	44.2	35.8	51.3
UT	1,048	1,067	1,104	1,142	0.7	51.3	60.6	65.1	40.9	57.1	40.1	63.7
NV	734	804	929	1,013	5.9	49.1	43.5	50.0	35.0	42.8	33.7	48.6
Pac	26,536	27,768	29,137	29,996	6.2	50.4	48.6	51.7	37.8	45.6	35.0	49.2
WA	3,329	3,491	3,650	3,818	2.8	50.9	53.4	59.9	38.9	49.6	36.0	58.2
OR	2,022	2,096	2,140	2,226	1.5	51.5	57.3	65.7	51.0	48.9	49.2	62.5
CA	20,043	21,006	22,124	22,668	7.4	50.3	47.1	49.1	35.9	44.7	32.9	46.5
AK	358	359	382	395	3.8	47.6	55.7	65.4	50.3	53.8	50.2	60.5
HI	784	815	841	889	2.1	49.9	43.5	41.9	42.2	41.7	40.5	40.3

[1] State law does not require tabulation of votes for unopposed candidates.   [2] See footnote 8, table 436.

Source: Compiled by U.S. Bureau of the Census. Population data from U.S. Bureau of the Census, *Current Population Reports*, P25-1085; votes cast from Elections Research Center, Chevy Chase, MD, *America Votes*, biennial (copyright).

No. 458. Political Party Financial Activity, by Major Political Party: 1981 to 1990

[In millions of dollars. Covers financial activity during 2-year calendar period indicated. Some political party financial activities, such as building funds and State and local election spending, are not reported to the source. Also excludes contributions earmarked to Federal candidates through the party organizations, since some of those funds never passed through the committees' accounts]

YEAR AND TYPE OF COMMITTEE	DEMOCRATIC				REPUBLICAN			
	Receipts, net [1]	Disbursements, net [1]	Contributions to candidates	Monies spent on behalf of party's nominees [2]	Receipts, net [1]	Disbursements, net [1]	Contributions to candidates	Monies spent on behalf of party's nominees [2]
1981-82................	39.3	40.1	1.7	3.3	215.0	214.0	5.6	14.3
1983-84................	98.5	97.4	2.6	9.0	297.9	300.8	4.9	20.1
1985-86, total	**64.8**	**65.9**	**1.7**	**9.0**	**255.2**	**258.9**	**3.4**	**14.3**
National committee.............	17.2	17.4	(Z)	0.3	83.8	86.7	0.4	(Z)
Senatorial committee...........	13.4	13.5	0.6	6.1	84.4	83.7	0.6	10.0
Congressional committee........	12.3	12.6	0.6	1.5	39.8	40.8	1.7	4.1
Conventions, other national.......	7.9	8.1	(Z)	-	0.2	0.2	-	-
State and local................	14.0	14.3	0.5	1.0	47.0	47.4	0.8	0.3
1987-88, total	**135.2**	**129.1**	**1.8**	**17.9**	**267.1**	**261.0**	**3.4**	**22.7**
National committee.............	52.3	47.0	0.1	8.1	91.0	89.9	0.3	8.3
Senatorial committee...........	16.3	16.3	0.4	6.2	65.9	63.3	0.8	10.2
Congressional committee........	12.5	12.5	0.7	2.4	34.7	33.7	1.6	4.1
Conventions, other national.......	19.2	19.2	-	-	9.6	9.6	-	-
State and local................	35.0	34.1	0.6	1.2	65.9	64.5	0.7	0.1
1989-90, total	**85.8**	**90.9**	**1.5**	**8.7**	**206.3**	**213.5**	**2.9**	**10.7**
National committee.............	14.5	18.5	0.1	0.1	68.7	70.4	0.3	0.1
Senatorial committee...........	17.5	17.6	0.4	4.5	65.1	67.6	0.7	7.7
Congressional committee........	9.1	9.1	0.4	2.9	33.2	34.4	0.9	2.8
Conventions, other national.......	8.8	9.2	-	-	-	-	-	-
State and local................	35.8	36.4	0.5	1.2	39.3	41.1	1.0	0.2

- Represents zero.   Z Less than $50,000.   [1] Excludes monies transferred between affiliated committees.   [2] Monies spent in the general election.

Source: U.S. Federal Election Commission, *FEC Reports on Financial Activity, Final Report, Party and Non-Party Political Committees*, biennial.

No. 459. Independent Expenditures for Presidential and Congressional Campaigns: 1981 to 1990

[In thousands of dollars. Covers campaign finance activity during 2-year calendar period indicated. An "independent expenditure" is money spent to support or defeat a clearly identified candidate. According to Federal election law, such an expenditure must be made without cooperation or consultation with the candidate or his/her campaign. Independent expenditures are not limited, as are contributions]

TYPE OF OFFICE AND YEAR	ALL PARTIES			DEMOCRATS		REPUBLICANS		OTHERS	
	Total	For	Against	For	Against	For	Against	For	Against
TOTAL									
1981-82	7,282	2,135	5,147	1,252	4,597	883	550	-	-
1983-84	23,420	19,951	3,468	1,693	1,016	18,257	2,453	1	-
1985-86	10,205	8,832	1,373	3,450	888	5,376	485	6	-
1987-88	21,341	16,654	4,687	2,865	4,248	13,784	439	6	-
1989-90	5,774	4,177	1,597	1,530	735	2,645	862	2	-
PRESIDENTIAL									
1981-82	185	184	1	92	1	92	-	-	-
1983-84	17,468	16,638	831	806	487	15,830	344	1	-
1985-86	841	795	45	76	28	719	17	-	-
1987-88	14,127	10,628	3,499	568	3,352	10,054	146	6	-
1989-90	497	322	174	5	169	318	5	-	-
SENATE									
1981-82	4,875	724	4,150	426	3,667	298	484	-	-
1983-84	4,627	2,134	2,493	326	410	1,808	2,082	-	-
1985-86	5,312	4,331	980	988	632	3,343	348	-	-
1987-88	4,401	3,641	761	831	617	2,810	143	(Z)	-
1989-90	3,506	2,362	1,144	756	428	1,604	716	2	-
HOUSE OF REPRESENTATIVES									
1981-82	2,221	1,226	995	734	929	492	66	-	-
1983-84	1,325	1,180	145	561	118	619	27	-	-
1985-86	4,053	3,706	347	2,386	227	1,314	120	6	-
1987-88	2,813	2,385	427	1,466	279	920	149	(Z)	-
1989-90	1,772	1,493	279	770	138	723	141	-	-

- Represents zero.   Z Less than $500.

Source: U.S. Federal Election Commission, *FEC Index of Independent Expenditures, 1987-88*, May 1989; press release of May 19, 1989; and unpublished data.

No. 460. Political Action Committees—Number, by Committee Type: 1980 to 1991

[As of **December 31**]

COMMITTEE TYPE	1980	1985	1986	1987	1988	1989	1990	1991
Total	2,551	3,992	4,157	4,165	4,268	4,178	4,172	4,094
Corporate	1,206	1,710	1,744	1,775	1,816	1,796	1,795	1,738
Labor	297	388	384	364	354	349	346	338
Trade/membership/health	576	695	745	865	786	777	774	742
Nonconnected	374	1,003	1,077	957	1,115	1,060	1,062	1,083
Cooperative	42	54	56	59	59	59	59	57
Corporation without stock	56	142	151	145	138	137	136	136

Source: U.S. Federal Election Commission, press release of January 20, 1992.

No. 461. Political Action Committees—Financial Activity Summary, by Committee Type: 1985 to 1990

[In millions of dollars. Covers financial activity during 2-year calendar period indicated. Data have not been adjusted for transfers between affiliated committees]

COMMITTEE TYPE	RECEIPTS			DISBURSEMENTS [1]			CONTRIBUTIONS TO CANDIDATES		
	1985-86	1987-88	1989-90	1985-1986	1987-88	1989-90	1985-1986	1987-88	1989-90
Total	353.4	384.6	372.1	340.0	364.2	357.6	139.8	159.2	159.1
Corporate	82.0	96.9	106.5	79.3	89.8	101.1	49.6	56.2	58.1
Labor	65.3	78.5	88.9	57.9	74.1	84.6	31.0	35.5	34.7
Trade/membership/health	75.4	89.5	92.5	73.3	83.7	88.1	34.6	41.2	44.8
Nonconnected	118.6	106.3	71.6	118.4	104.9	71.4	19.4	20.3	15.1
Cooperative	4.7	4.9	5.0	4.7	4.5	4.8	2.7	2.7	2.9
Corporation without stock	7.4	8.5	7.6	6.4	7.2	7.7	2.6	3.3	3.4

[1] Comprises contributions to candidates, independent expenditures, and other disbursements.

Source: U.S. Federal Election Commission, *FEC Reports on Financial Activity, Final Report, Party and Non-Party Political Committees,* biennial.

No. 462. Presidential Campaign Finances—Federal Funds for General Election: 1980 to 1988

[In millions of dollars. Based on FEC certifications, audit reports, and Dept. of Treasury reports]

1980		1984		1988	
Candidate	Amount	Candidate	Amount	Candidate	Amount
Total	62.7	Total	80.3	Total	92.2
Anderson [1]	4.2	Mondale	40.2	Bush	46.1
Carter	29.4	Reagan	40.1	Dukakis	46.1
Reagan	29.2				

[1] John Anderson, as the candidate of a new party, was permitted to raise funds privately. Total receipts for the Anderson campaign, including Federal funds, were $17.6 million, and total expenditures were $15.6 million.

Source: U.S. Federal Election Commission, press releases of November 15, 1981, June 4, 1986, and April 9, 1989.

No. 463. Presidential Campaign Finances—Primary Campaign Receipts and Disbursements: 1979 to 1988

[In millions of dollars. Covers campaign finance activity during 2-year calendar period indicated. Covers candidates who received Federal matching funds or who had significant financial activity]

ITEM	TOTAL			DEMOCRATIC			REPUBLICAN		
	1979-80	1983-84 [1]	1987-88 [2]	1979-80	1983-84	1987-88	1979-80	1983-84	1987-88
Receipts, total [3]	94.2	105.0	213.8	35.6	77.5	91.9	58.5	27.1	116.0
Individual contributions	61.0	62.8	141.1	23.9	46.2	59.4	37.1	16.4	76.8
Federal matching funds	30.9	34.9	65.7	10.3	24.6	30.1	20.5	10.1	34.7
Disbursements	92.3	103.6	210.7	35.6	77.4	90.2	56.7	25.9	114.6

[1] Includes Citizens Party candidate, not shown separately.   [2] Includes a minor party candidate who sought several party nominations and a Democratic candidate who did not receive Federal matching funds, but who had significant financial activity. [3] Includes other types of receipts, not shown separately.

Source: U.S. Federal Election Commission, *FEC Reports on Financial Activity, Final Report, Presidential Pre-Nomination Campaigns,* quadrennial.

No. 464. Congressional Campaign Finances—Receipts and Disbursements: 1985 to 1990

[Covers all campaign finance activity during 2-year calendar period indicated for primary, general, run-off, and special elections. For 1985-86 relates to 1,611 House of Representatives candidates and 262 Senate candidates; for 1987-88 to 1,582 House of Representatives candidates and 210 Senate candidates; for 1989-90 to 1,580 House of Representatives candidates and 179 Senate candidates. Data have been adjusted to eliminate transfers between all committees within a campaign. For further information on legal limits of contributions, see Federal Election Campaign Act of 1971, as amended]

ITEM	HOUSE OF REPRESENTATIVES						SENATE					
	Amount (mil. dol.)			Percent distribution			Amount (mil. dol.)			Percent distribution		
	1985-86	1987-88	1989-90	1985-86	1987-88	1989-90	1985-86	1987-88	1989-90	1985-86	1987-88	1989-90
Total receipts [1]	257.7	278.3	285.4	100	100	100	214.4	199.3	186.3	100	100	100
Individual contributions	127.6	129.9	129.9	50	47	46	140.1	128.1	119.6	65	64	64
Other committees	87.4	102.2	108.5	34	37	38	45.3	45.7	41.2	21	23	22
Candidate loans	20.9	23.2	20.9	8	8	7	6.2	8.2	10.0	3	4	5
Candidate contributions	4.8	4.9	4.8	2	2	2	1.9	6.8	2.4	1	3	1
Democrats	139.9	160.3	163.4	54	58	57	91.8	107.7	89.5	43	54	48
Republicans	117.7	117.0	120.9	46	42	42	122.5	91.3	96.8	57	46	52
Others	0.1	1.0	1.1	(Z)	(Z)	(Z)	0.1	0.3	(Z)	(Z)	(Z)	(Z)
Incumbents	149.7	175.6	181.9	58	63	64	90.3	98.3	118.7	42	49	64
Challengers	49.2	52.5	47.7	19	19	17	67.2	56.3	54.8	31	28	29
Open seats [2]	58.8	50.2	55.9	23	18	20	56.9	44.7	12.8	27	22	7
Total disbursements	239.3	257.6	265.8	100	100	100	211.6	201.4	180.4	100	100	100
Democrats	128.7	145.6	151.0	54	57	57	89.0	107.9	87.6	42	54	49
Republicans	110.5	111.0	113.7	46	43	43	122.6	93.1	92.9	58	46	52
Others	0.1	1.0	1.1	(Z)	(Z)	(Z)	0.3	0.3	(Z)	(Z)	(Z)	(Z)
Incumbents	132.5	156.6	163.4	55	61	62	89.3	101.2	113.5	42	50	63
Challengers	48.8	51.7	47.0	20	20	18	66.2	56.1	54.9	31	28	30
Open seats [2]	58.0	49.3	55.4	24	19	21	56.1	44.1	12.1	27	22	7

Z Less than $50,000 or 0.5 percent.   [1] Includes other types of receipts, not shown separately.   [2] Elections in which an incumbent did not seek re-election.

Source: U.S. Federal Election Commission, *FEC Reports on Financial Activity, Final Report, U.S. Senate and House Campaigns*, biennial.

No. 465. Contributions to Congressional Campaigns by Political Action Committees (PAC), by Type of Committee: 1979 to 1990

[In millions of dollars. Covers amounts given to candidates in primary, general, run-off, and special elections during the 2-year calendar period indicated. For number of political action committees, see table 460]

TYPE OF COMMITTEE	HOUSE OF REPRESENTATIVES						SENATE					
	Total	Democrats	Republicans	Incumbents	Challengers	Open seats [1]	Total	Democrats	Republicans	Incumbents	Challengers	Open seats [1]
1979-80	37.9	20.5	17.2	24.9	7.9	5.1	17.3	8.4	9.0	8.6	6.6	2.1
1981-82	61.1	34.2	26.8	40.8	10.9	9.4	22.6	11.2	11.4	14.3	5.2	3.0
1983-84, total [2]	75.7	46.3	29.3	57.2	11.3	7.2	29.7	14.0	15.6	17.9	6.3	5.4
Corporate	23.4	10.4	13.1	18.8	2.6	2.0	12.0	3.2	8.8	8.8	1.1	2.2
Trade association [3]	20.4	10.5	9.9	16.5	2.1	1.7	6.3	2.7	3.7	4.5	0.9	1.0
Labor	19.8	18.8	1.0	14.3	3.5	2.0	5.0	4.7	0.3	1.6	2.3	1.2
Nonconnected [4]	9.1	4.7	4.4	4.9	2.9	1.3	5.4	3.0	2.4	2.4	2.0	1.0
1985-86, total [2]	87.4	54.7	32.6	65.9	9.1	12.4	45.3	20.2	25.1	23.7	10.2	11.4
Corporate	26.9	12.9	14.0	22.9	1.0	3.0	19.2	4.8	14.4	11.7	2.7	4.9
Trade association [3]	23.4	12.3	11.2	19.3	1.3	2.8	9.5	3.8	5.7	5.7	1.6	2.1
Labor	22.6	21.1	1.6	14.7	4.3	3.6	7.2	6.6	0.6	2.2	3.2	1.9
Nonconnected [4]	11.1	6.6	4.5	6.1	2.4	2.6	7.7	4.2	3.4	3.1	2.4	2.2
1987-88, total [2]	102.2	67.4	34.7	82.2	10.0	10.0	45.7	24.2	21.5	28.7	8.0	9.0
Corporate	31.6	16.3	15.4	28.6	1.1	1.9	18.8	7.2	11.6	12.7	2.4	3.7
Trade association [3]	28.6	16.5	12.0	24.6	1.5	2.5	10.4	4.8	5.6	7.1	1.3	2.0
Labor	26.8	24.8	2.0	18.3	5.1	3.3	7.1	6.5	0.5	3.6	2.2	1.3
Nonconnected [4]	11.4	7.4	3.9	7.3	2.2	1.9	7.8	4.8	3.0	4.2	2.0	1.6
1989-90, total [2]	108.5	72.2	36.2	87.5	7.3	13.6	41.2	20.2	21.0	29.5	8.2	3.5
Corporate	35.4	18.7	16.7	30.8	1.4	3.2	18.0	6.1	11.9	13.0	3.5	1.5
Trade association [3]	32.5	19.3	13.3	27.5	1.4	3.6	10.0	4.2	5.8	7.2	1.8	0.9
Labor	27.6	25.8	1.8	19.8	3.2	4.5	6.0	5.6	0.4	3.9	1.7	0.4
Nonconnected [4]	8.5	5.5	2.9	5.5	1.1	1.8	5.7	3.5	2.2	4.2	1.1	0.5

[1] Elections in which an incumbent did not seek re-election.   [2] Includes other types of political action committees not shown separately.   [3] Includes membership organizations and health organizations.   [4] Represents "ideological" groups as well as other issue groups not necessarily ideological in nature.

Source: U.S. Federal Election Commission, *FEC Reports on Financial Activity, Final Report, U.S. Senate and House Campaigns*, biennial.

State and Local Government Finances and Employment

This section presents data on revenues, expenditures, debt, and employment of State and local governments. Nationwide statistics relating to State and local governments, their numbers, finances, and employment, are compiled primarily by the Bureau of the Census through a program of censuses and surveys. Every fifth year (for years ending in "2" and "7") the Bureau conducts a Census of Governments involving collection of data for all governmental units in the United States. In addition, the Bureau conducts annual surveys which cover all the State governments and a sample of local governments.

Publications issued annually by the Bureau of the Census include a report on finances which presents figures for the Federal Government, nationwide totals for State and local governments by type, and State-local data by States. Also issued annually is a series of publications on State, city, county, and school finances, and on city, county, and other public employment. Financial data are published in the GF publication series, employment data in the GE series. There is also a series of quarterly reports covering tax revenue and finances of major public employee retirement systems.

Basic information for Census Bureau statistics on governments is obtained by mail canvass from State and local officials; however, financial data for each of the State governments and for many of the large local governments are compiled from their official records and reports by Census Bureau personnel. In over half of the States, all or part of local government financial data are obtained through central collection arrangements with State governments. Financial data on the Federal Government is based on the *Budget* published by the Office of Management and Budget (see text, Section 10).

Governmental units.—The governmental structure of the United States includes, in addition to the Federal Government and the States, thousands of

In Brief	
State government revenue (from own sources) in 1991: $516,438 million	
Taxes	*60%*
Insurance trust funds	*20%*
Charges	*9%*
Interest earnings	*5%*
Utility and liquor stores	*1%*
State government direct expenditures in 1991: $442,295 million	
Public welfare	*23%*
Education	*18%*
Insurance trust funds	*15%*
Health and hospitals	*14%*

local governments—counties, municipalities, townships, school districts, and numerous kinds of "special districts." As shown by table 466, 86,743 local governments were identified by the 1992 Census of Governments. As defined by the census, governmental units include all agencies or bodies having an organized existence, governmental character, and substantial autonomy. While most of these governments can impose taxes, many of the special districts—such as independent public housing authorities, the New York Port Authority, and numerous local irrigation, power, and other types of districts—are financed from rentals, charges for services, benefit assessments, grants from other governments, toll charges, and other nontax sources. The count of governments excludes semi-autonomous agencies through which States, cities, and counties sometimes provide for certain functions—for example, "dependent" school systems, State institutions of higher education, and certain other "authorities" and special agencies which are under the administrative or fiscal control of an established governmental unit.

Finances.—The financial statistics relate to government fiscal years ending June 30, or at some date within the 12 previous months. The following governments are exceptions and are included as though they were part of the June 30 group; ending September 30, the State governments of Alabama and Michigan, The District of Columbia, and Alabama school districts; and ending August 31, the State government of Texas and Texas school districts. New York State ends its fiscal year on March 31. The Federal Government ended the fiscal year June 30 until 1976 when its fiscal year, by an act of Congress, was revised to extend from Oct. 1 to Sept. 30. A 3-month quarter (July 1 to Sept. 30, 1976) bridged the transition.

Nationwide government finance statistics have been classified and presented in terms of uniform concepts and categories, rather than according to the highly diverse terminology, organization, and fund structure utilized by individual governments. Accordingly, financial statistics which appear here for the Federal Government and for individual States or local governments have been standardized and may not agree directly with figures appearing in the original sources.

Statistics on governmental finances distinguish among general government, utilities, liquor stores, and insurance trusts. *General government* comprises all activities except utilities, liquor stores, and insurance trusts. Utilities include government water supply, electric light and power, gas supply, and transit systems. Liquor stores are operated by 17 States and by local governments in 6 States. Insurance trusts relate to employee retirement, unemployment compensation, and other social insurance systems administered by the Federal, State, and local governments.

Data for cities relate only to municipal corporations and their dependent agencies and do not include amounts for other local governments overlying city areas. Therefore, expenditure figures for "education" do not include spending by the separate school districts which administer public schools within most municipal areas. Variations in the assignment of governmental responsibility for public assistance, health, hospitals, public housing, and other functions to a lesser degree also have an important effect upon reported amounts of city expenditure, revenue, and debt. Therefore, any intercity comparisons based upon these figures should be made with caution and with due recognition of variations that exist among urban areas in the relative role of the municipal corporation.

Employment and payrolls.—These data are based mainly on mail canvassing of State and local governments. Payroll includes all salaries, wages, and individual fee payments for the month specified, and employment relates to all persons on governmental payrolls during a pay period of the month covered—including paid officials, temporary help, and (unless otherwise specified) part-time as well as full-time personnel. Beginning 1986, statistics for full-time equivalent employment have been computed with a formula using hours worked by part-time employees. A payroll based formula was used prior to 1985. Full-time equivalent employment statistics were not computed for 1985. Figures shown for individual governments cover major dependent agencies such as institutions of higher education, as well as the basic central departments and agencies of the government.

Statistical reliability.—For a discussion of statistical collection and estimation, sampling procedures, and measures of statistical reliability applicable to Census Bureau data, see Appendix III.

Historical statistics.—Tabular headnotes provide cross-references, where applicable, to *Historical Statistics of the United States, Colonial Times to 1970.* See Appendix IV.

Figure 9.1

State Government Tax Collections, by Type: 1970 and 1991

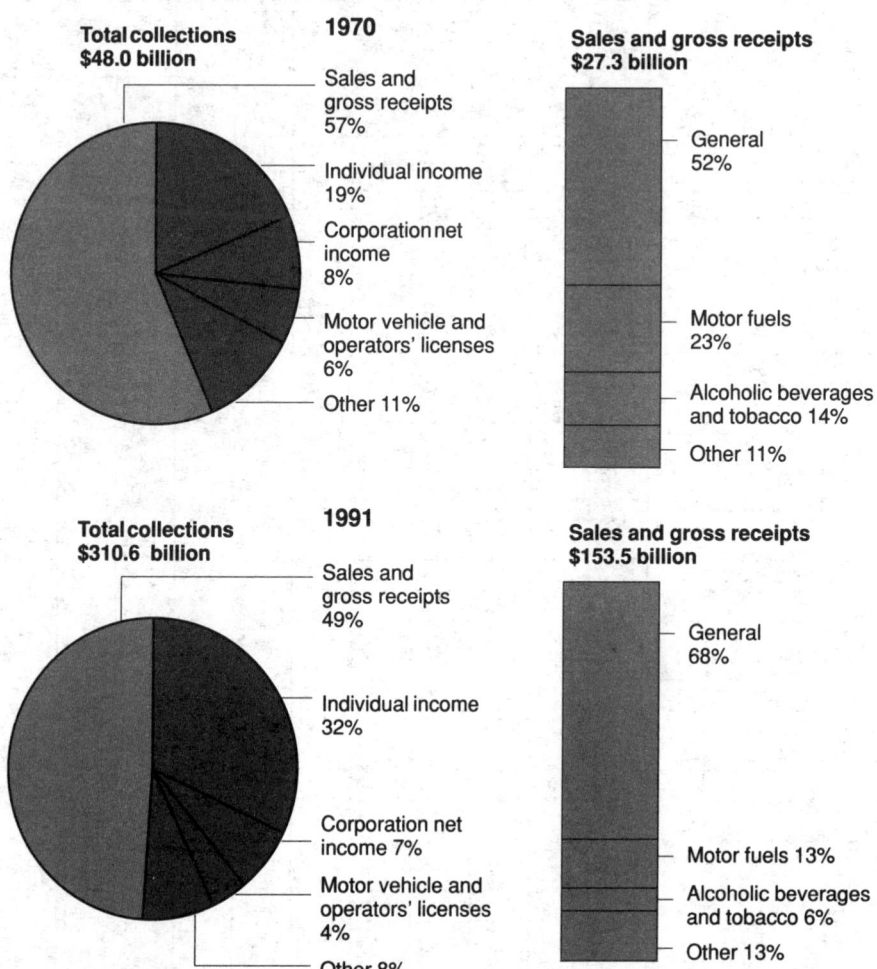

Total collections
$48.0 billion

1970

Sales and
gross receipts
57%

Individual income
19%

Corporation net
income
8%

Motor vehicle and
operators' licenses
6%

Other 11%

Sales and gross receipts
$27.3 billion

General
52%

Motor fuels
23%

Alcoholic beverages
and tobacco 14%

Other 11%

Total collections
$310.6 billion

1991

Sales and
gross receipts
49%

Individual income
32%

Corporation net
income 7%

Motor vehicle and
operators' licenses
4%

Other 8%

Sales and gross receipts
$153.5 billion

General
68%

Motor fuels 13%

Alcoholic beverages
and tobacco 6%

Other 13%

Source: Chart prepared by U.S. Bureau of the Census. For data, see table 483.

No. 466. Number of Governmental Units, by Type of Government: 1942 to 1992

TYPE OF GOVERNMENT	1942	1952[1]	1957[1]	1962	1967	1972	1977	1982	1987	1992
Total	155,116	116,807	102,392	91,237	81,299	78,269	79,913	81,831	83,237	86,743
U.S. Government	1	1	1	1	1	1	1	1	1	1
State government	48	50	50	50	50	50	50	50	50	50
Local governments	155,067	166,756	102,341	91,186	81,248	78,218	79,862	81,780	83,186	86,692
County	3,050	3,052	3,050	3,043	3,049	3,044	3,042	3,041	3,042	3,043
Municipal	16,220	16,807	17,215	18,000	18,048	18,517	18,862	19,076	19,200	19,296
Township and town	118,919	17,202	17,198	17,142	17,105	16,991	16,822	16,734	16,691	16,666
School district	108,579	67,355	50,454	34,678	21,782	15,781	15,174	14,851	14,721	14,556
Special district	8,299	12,340	14,424	18,323	21,264	23,885	25,962	28,078	29,532	33,131

[1] Adjusted to include units in Alaska and Hawaii which adopted statehood in 1959.
Source: U.S. Bureau of the Census, 1992 Census of Governments, *Government Units in 1992*, (GC92-1P).

No. 467. All Governments—Revenue, Expenditure, and Debt: 1980 to 1991

[For fiscal year ending in year shown; see text, section 9. Local government amounts are estimates subject to sampling variation; see Appendix III and source. See also *Historical Statistics, Colonial Times to 1970*, series Y 505-637 and Y 652-848]

ITEM AND YEAR	All govern-ments (bil. dol.)	FEDERAL [1]		STATE AND LOCAL (bil. dol.)			AVERAGE ANNUAL PERCENT CHANGE [2]		PER CAPITA [3] (dollars)		
		Total (bil. dol.)	Per-cent of total	Total	State	Local	Fed-eral	State and local	Total	Fed-eral	State and local
Revenue: [4] 1980	[5]932	565	60.7	[5]452	277	258	12.9	11.5	[5]4,115	2,496	1,993
1985	[5]1,419	807	56.9	[5]720	439	402	7.1	9.3	[5]5,963	3,391	3,025
1990	[5]2,047	1,155	56.4	[5]1,032	632	580	5.7	8.2	[5]8,230	4,642	4,150
1991	[5]2,124	1,201	56.5	[5]1,081	661	612	4.0	4.7	[5]9,049	4,762	4,286
Intergovernmental: 1980	(X)	2	(X)	[5]83	64	102	34.8	10.5	(X)	8	367
1985	(X)	2	(X)	[5]106	90	138	1.5	4.9	(X)	8	446
1990	(X)	3	(X)	[5]137	126	191	0.3	8.7	(X)	12	550
1991	(X)	3	(X)	[5]154	144	202	11.1	12.6	(X)	13	611
General, own sources:											
1980	717	417	58.2	299	169	130	12.1	11.6	3,163	1,842	1,321
1985	1,050	559	53.2	492	276	216	5.8	9.9	4,413	2,347	2,066
1990	1,493	780	52.2	713	391	322	5.4	7.9	6,004	3,138	2,866
1991	1,557	809	52.0	748	408	340	3.7	5.0	6,175	3,209	2,967
Taxes: [4] 1980	574	351	61.1	223	137	86	10.0	8.7	2,535	1,548	986
1985	804	454	56.4	350	215	134	5.2	9.0	3,379	1,908	1,470
1990	1,134	632	55.7	502	300	201	2.7	7.0	4,559	2,542	2,017
1991	1,167	642	55.0	525	311	215	1.5	4.7	4,629	2,546	2,083
Property: 1980	68	(X)	(X)	68	3	66	(X)	5.5	302	(X)	302
1985	104	(X)	(X)	104	4	100	(X)	8.3	437	(X)	436
1990	156	(X)	(X)	156	6	150	(X)	9.3	626	(X)	626
1991	168	(X)	(X)	168	6	162	(X)	7.9	666	(X)	666
Individual income:											
1980	286	244	85.3	42	37	5	12.0	13.9	1,263	1,077	186
1985	401	331	82.5	70	64	6	6.1	10.2	1,685	1,391	295
1990	573	467	81.6	106	96	10	4.8	8.0	2,302	1,877	425
1991	577	468	81.1	109	99	10	0.2	3.5	2,290	1,855	434
Corporate income:											
1980	78	65	82.9	13	13	-	-1.6	9.8	344	285	59
1985	80	61	76.2	19	18	2	-1.0	7.3	336	258	81
1990	117	94	80.3	24	22	2	-9.5	-9.1	471	376	95
1991	120	98	81.7	22	20	2	4.9	-5.6	477	389	88
Sales or gross receipts:											
1980	112	[6]32	28.6	80	68	12	19.9	7.7	494	[6]141	353
1985	175	[6]49	28.0	126	105	21	8.6	9.1	740	[6]207	531
1990	232	[6]54	23.3	178	147	31	2.7	6.9	932	[6]217	715
1991	244	[6]58	23.8	186	154	32	8.4	4.3	966	[6]232	736
Current charges and miscellaneous: 1980	142	67	46.7	76	32	44	24.4	21.1	629	294	335
1985	246	104	42.5	142	60	82	9.0	12.5	1,034	439	596
1990	359	148	41.3	211	91	120	18.9	10.3	1,445	596	849
1991	390	167	42.8	223	98	125	12.8	5.5	1,546	663	884
Expenditures: [4] 1980	[5]959	617	64.4	[5]434	258	261	14.9	13.7	[5]4,232	2,724	1,916
1985	[5]1,581	1,032	65.3	[5]658	391	391	10.3	8.3	[5]6,644	4,338	2,766
1990	[5]2,219	1,393	62.8	[5]976	572	581	9.7	9.5	[5]8,921	5,601	3,924
1991	[5]2,382	1,481	58.2	[5]1,064	629	623	6.3	9.0	[5]10,091	5,872	4,218
Intergovernmental: 1980	(X)	91	(X)	[5]2	85	2	6.6	16.9	(X)	401	8
1985	(X)	107	(X)	[5]2	122	4	3.3	2.3	(X)	451	8
1990	(X)	147	(X)	[5]3	175	6	15.5	10.7	(X)	591	13
1991	(X)	160	(X)	[5]3	186	5	8.9	6.8	(X)	635	14
Direct: [4] 1980	959	526	54.9	432	173	259	16.4	13.7	4,232	2,323	1,908
1985	1,581	925	58.5	656	269	387	11.3	8.3	6,644	3,887	2,758
1990	2,219	1,246	56.2	973	397	575	9.0	9.5	8,921	5,010	3,911
1991	2,381	1,321	55.5	1,060	442	618	6.0	9.0	9,442	5,237	4,204
Current operation: 1980	517	209	40.5	308	108	200	21.1	12.3	2,282	923	1,359
1985	833	360	43.3	473	172	300	10.9	8.6	3,501	1,514	1,986
1990	1,190	490	41.2	700	258	442	13.4	9.3	4,785	1,970	2,815
1991	1,284	522	40.7	762	287	475	6.5	8.9	5,093	2,069	3,023
Capital outlay: 1980	99	36	36.7	63	23	40	-8.7	18.2	439	161	278
1985	157	77	49.1	80	31	49	14.9	4.8	660	324	336
1990	221	98	44.3	123	46	78	-1.9	9.9	888	394	495
1991	227	96	42.1	132	48	84	-2.2	7.0	903	380	522
Debt outstanding: [7] 1980	1,250	914	73.2	336	122	214	9.7	10.4	5,517	4,036	1,481
1985	2,399	1,827	76.3	571	212	357	13.9	10.6	10,069	7,681	2,401
1990	4,127	3,266	79.2	861	318	542	13.4	7.7	16,592	13,132	3,460
1991	4,599	3,683	80.1	916	346	570	12.8	6.4	18,236	14,606	3,632

- Represents or rounds to zero. X Not applicable. [1] Data adjusted to system for reporting State and local data and therefore differ from figures in section 10 tables. [2] Percent change from prior year, except for 1985, change from 1980. For explanation, see Guide to Tabular Presentation. Minus sign (-) indicates decrease. [3] 1980 and 1990 based on enumerated resident population as of April 1; all other years based on estimated resident population as of July 1. Excludes intergovernmental amounts. [4] Includes amounts not shown separately. [5] Excludes duplicative transactions between levels of government; see source. [6] Includes customs. [7] End of fiscal year.

Source: U.S. Bureau of the Census, *Government Finances,* series No. 5, annual.

No. 468. All Governments—Revenue and Expenditure, by Level of Government: 1991

[For fiscal year ending in year shown, see text, section 9. Local government amounts are estimates subject to sampling variation; see Appendix III and source. See also *Historical Statistics, Colonial Times to 1970*, series Y 505-637 and Y 652-848]

SOURCE OF REVENUE AND TYPE OF EXPENDITURE	All governments (mil. dol.)	Federal (mil. dol.)	State (mil. dol.)	Local (mil. dol.)	PERCENT		PER CAPITA[1] (dol.)	
					Federal	State and local	Federal	State and local
Revenue	**2,124,206**	**1,200,682**	**659,972**	**612,220**	**100**	**100**	**4,762**	**4,286**
Intergovernmental revenue	(2)	3,234	143,534	201,901	0.3	14.3	13	611
Revenue from own sources	2,124,206	1,197,448	516,438	410,319	99.7	85.7	4,749	3,675
General revenue from own sources	1,557,183	809,105	408,188	339,890	67.4	69.2	3,209	2,967
Percent of total revenue	73	67	62	56	(X)	(X)	(X)	(X)
Taxes [3]	1,167,272	641,982	310,561	214,728	53.5	48.6	2,546	2,083
Property	167,934	(X)	6,228	161,706	(X)	15.5	(X)	666
Individual income	577,168	467,827	99,279	10,062	39.0	10.1	1,855	434
Corporation income	120,328	98,086	20,357	1,886	8.2	2.1	389	88
Sales and gross receipts	244,065	58,495	153,535	32,036	4.9	17.2	232	736
Customs duties	16,034	16,034	(X)	(X)	1.3	(X)	64	(X)
General	125,449	(X)	103,165	22,283	(X)	11.6	(X)	497
Selective [3]	102,582	42,461	50,369	9,752	3.5	5.6	168	238
Motor fuel	38,233	16,917	20,639	677	1.4	2.0	67	85
Alcoholic beverages	10,910	7,227	3,400	283	0.6	0.3	29	15
Tobacco products	10,952	4,782	5,980	190	0.4	0.6	19	24
Public utilities	19,246	7,253	6,752	5,241	0.6	1.1	29	48
Motor vehicle and operators' licenses	11,780	(X)	10,996	784	(X)	1.1	(X)	47
Death and gift	15,449	11,138	4,284	27	0.9	0.4	44	17
Charges and miscellaneous [3]	389,912	167,123	97,627	125,162	13.9	20.6	663	884
Current charges [3]	211,560	86,292	47,334	77,933	7.2	11.6	342	497
National defense and international relations	9,206	9,206	-	-	0.8	(X)	37	(X)
Postal service	42,592	42,592	-	-	3.5	(X)	169	(X)
Education [3]	35,659	-	25,907	9,752	-	3.3	-	141
School lunch sales	3,663	-	13	3,651	-	0.3	-	15
Higher education	28,851	-	25,473	3,378	-	2.7	-	114
Natural resources	17,346	15,528	1,335	482	1.3	0.2	62	7
Hospitals	33,808	95	10,875	22,837	(Z)	3.1	(Z)	134
Sewerage and sanitation	19,604	(X)	239	19,365	(X)	1.8	(X)	78
Parks and recreation	3,717	102	796	2,819	(Z)	0.3	(Z)	14
Housing and community development	5,674	2,742	191	2,741	0.2	0.3	11	12
Airports	5,738	20	618	5,101	(Z)	0.5	(Z)	23
Water transport and terminals	2,634	1,099	382	1,152	0.1	0.1	4	6
Special assessments	2,320	(X)	103	2,218	(X)	0.2	(X)	9
Sale of property	4,557	3,663	144	750	0.3	0.1	15	4
Interest earnings	69,743	11,159	27,764	30,820	0.9	5.4	44	232
Utility revenue	60,736	(X)	6,474	54,263	(X)	5.6	(X)	241
Insurance trust revenue	506,286	388,343	101,776	16,167	32.3	7.0	1,540	468
Expenditure	**2,380,686**	**1,480,664**	**628,836**	**623,273**	**100**	**100**	**5,872**	**4,218**
Intergovernmental expenditure	(2)	160,145	186,540	5,401	10.8	0.3	635	14
Direct expenditure	2,380,686	1,320,519	442,295	617,872	89.2	99.7	5,237	4,204
General expenditure	1,805,522	900,518	368,360	536,644	60.8	85.1	3,571	3,589
Percent of total expenditure	76	61	59	86	(X)	(X)	(X)	(X)
Education [3]	330,759	21,093	80,468	229,197	1.4	29.1	84	1,228
Elementary and secondary education	218,006	-	1,997	216,009	-	20.5	-	865
Higher education	78,749	-	65,560	13,189	-	7.4	-	312
Public welfare	167,681	40,716	100,114	26,850	2.7	11.9	161	504
Health and hospitals	166,700	31,186	62,888	72,626	2.1	12.7	124	537
Highways	65,602	665	38,911	26,025	(Z)	6.1	3	258
Police protection	38,942	6,170	4,785	27,986	0.4	3.1	24	130
Fire protection	13,796	(X)	(X)	13,796	(X)	1.3	(X)	55
Corrections	29,297	1,941	17,807	9,550	0.1	2.6	8	108
Natural resources	57,149	44,574	9,724	2,851	3.0	1.2	177	50
Sewerage and sanitation	31,014	(X)	1,994	29,020	(X)	2.9	(X)	123
Housing and community development	33,346	16,698	1,759	14,888	1.1	1.6	66	66
Governmental administration	64,181	15,720	18,943	29,518	1.1	4.6	62	192
Parks and recreation	17,718	1,788	2,744	13,187	0.1	1.5	7	63
Interest on general debt	247,374	195,142	23,393	28,840	13.2	4.9	774	207
Utility and liquor store expenditure	81,004	(X)	9,721	71,283	(X)	7.6	(X)	321
Insurance trust expenditure	494,160	420,001	64,214	9,945	28.4	7.0	1,666	294
By character and object:								
Current operation	1,284,024	521,636	287,079	475,309	35.2	71.7	2,069	3,023
Capital outlay	227,408	95,775	47,937	83,695	6.5	12.4	380	522
Construction	107,145	10,491	37,647	59,006	0.7	9.1	42	383
Equip., land and existing structures	120,263	85,284	10,290	24,689	5.8	3.2	338	139
Assistance and subsidies	118,421	87,965	18,876	11,580	5.9	2.9	349	121
Interest on debt (general and utility)	256,674	195,142	24,189	37,343	13.2	5.8	774	244
Insurance benefits and repayments	494,160	420,001	64,214	9,945	28.4	7.0	1,666	294
Expenditure for salaries and wages [4]	*520,705*	*154,289*	*107,679*	*258,737*	*10.4*	*34.4*	*612*	*1,453*

- Represents or rounds to zero. X Not applicable. Z Less than .05 percent or $.50. [1] Based on estimated resident population as of July 1. [2] Aggregates exclude duplicative transactions between levels of government; see source. [3] Includes amounts not shown separately. [4] Included in items shown above.

Source: U.S. Bureau of the Census, *Government Finances*, series GF, No. 5, annual.

No. 469. All Governments—Expenditure for Capital Outlay, by Level of Government and by Function: 1970 to 1991

[In millions of dollars, except percent. For fiscal year ending in year shown; see text, section 9. Except for 1987, local government amounts are estimates subject to sampling variation; see Appendix III and source. See also *Historical Statistics, Colonial Times to 1970*, series Y 523-524, Y 673-674, Y 740-741, and Y 787-788]

LEVEL AND FUNCTION	1970	1975	1980	1985	1986	1987	1988	1989	1990	1991
Total	47,519	66,622	99,386	156,912	176,096	195,713	197,844	211,734	220,960	227,408
Federal Government:										
Total	17,869	21,798	36,492	77,014	85,647	96,871	93,531	99,790	97,891	95,775
Annual percent change [1]	−6	4	11	6	11	13	−3	7	−2	−2
As percent of direct expenditure	10	8	7	8	9	9	8	9	8	7
By function:										
National defense [2]	14,027	14,507	28,161	64,154	71,995	78,222	74,790	78,891	75,624	72,755
Education	9	2	97	39	5	13	7	9	41	97
Highways.............	9	70	132	121	204	173	173	165	181	143
Health and hospitals	166	311	673	916	1,160	1,327	1,228	1,403	1,096	1,387
Natural resources	1,691	3,416	4,046	4,092	3,651	4,058	3,581	3,786	4,698	4,921
Housing [3]	853	1,059	317	1,935	2,515	3,642	5,180	5,032	4,343	4,147
Air transportation ..[4]....	234	363	151	785	391	494	407	658	664	778
Water transportation [4]	285	251	1,003	583	245	315	370	306	385	459
Other	595	1,819	1,912	4,389	5,481	8,627	7,792	9,540	10,859	11,088
State and local governments:										
Total	29,650	44,824	62,894	79,898	90,449	98,842	104,313	111,944	123,069	131,633
Annual percent change [1]	5	9	7	13	13	9	6	7	10	7
As percent of direct expenditure	20	17	15	12	13	13	13	13	13	12
By function:										
Education [5]	7,621	9,861	10,737	13,477	15,490	17,803	18,529	21,854	25,997	27,234
Higher education	2,705	2,834	2,972	4,629	5,217	6,141	6,397	6,851	7,441	7,064
Elementary and secondary..	4,658	6,532	7,362	8,358	10,091	11,355	11,789	14,584	18,057	19,834
Highways..............	10,762	13,646	19,133	23,900	26,807	28,352	31,635	32,754	33,867	36,409
Health and hospitals	790	1,781	2,443	2,709	2,810	3,029	3,436	3,445	3,848	4,139
Natural resources	789	1,113	1,052	1,736	1,803	2,157	1,894	2,019	2,545	2,474
Housing [3]	1,319	1,821	2,248	3,217	3,516	3,394	3,619	3,765	3,997	4,389
Air transportation ..[4].....	691	852	1,391	1,875	2,183	2,632	2,896	2,965	3,434	3,941
Water transportation [4]	258	419	623	717	911	869	911	943	924	984
Sewerage	1,385	3,569	6,272	5,926	6,461	7,483	8,300	8,343	8,356	9,104
Parks and recreation	684	1,261	2,023	2,196	2,554	2,838	3,142	3,350	3,877	4,702
Utilities	2,437	4,846	9,933	13,435	15,340	15,638	14,782	15,371	16,601	17,027
Water.	1,201	2,111	3,335	4,160	5,134	6,135	6,052	6,372	6,873	7,499
Electric.	820	1,485	4,572	5,247	6,127	5,086	4,473	4,291	3,976	3,579
Transit	366	1,203	1,921	3,830	3,830	4,165	3,998	4,430	5,443	5,636
Gas.................	50	48	105	198	250	253	259	279	310	314
Other	2,915	5,656	7,039	10,711	12,573	14,645	15,172	17,135	19,623	21,230

[1] Change from prior year shown. 1970, change from 1969. For definition of average annual percent change, see Guide to Tabular Presentation.   [2] Includes international relations and U.S. service schools.   [3] Includes community development.   [4] Includes terminals.   [5] Includes other education.

Source: U.S. Bureau of the Census, *Historical Statistics on Governmental Finances and Employment*; and *Government Finances*, series GF No. 5, annual.

No. 470. All Governments—Expenditures for Public Works: 1980 to 1991

[In millions of dollars. Public works include expenditures on highways, airports, water transport and terminals, sewerage, solid waste management, water supply, and mass transit systems. Represents direct expenditures excluding intergovernmental grants]

LEVEL AND TYPE OF EXPENDITURE	Total	Highways	Airport transportation	Water transport and terminals	Sewerage	Solid waste management	Water supply	Mass transit
1980: Total	72,177	33,745	5,071	3,278	9,892	3,322	9,228	7,641
Federal.................	5,114	434	2,570	2,110	-	-	-	-
State..................	22,832	20,661	360	360	334	-	91	1,026
Local	44,231	12,650	2,141	808	9,558	3,322	9,137	6,615
Capital expenditures (percent) ...	48	57	30	50	63	11	36	25
1990: Total	146,762	61,913	10,983	4,524	18,309	10,144	22,101	18,788
Federal.................	7,911	856	4,499	2,556	-	-	-	-
State..................	43,787	36,464	635	504	636	891	136	4,521
Local	95,064	24,593	5,848	1,464	17,673	9,253	21,966	14,267
Capital expenditures (percent) ...	42	55	37	29	46	18	31	29
1991: Total	157,810	65,601	12,390	4,866	19,676	11,338	23,560	20,379
Federal.................	8,639	665	5,157	2,817	-	-	-	-
State..................	46,860	38,911	759	487	833	1,161	147	4,562
Local	102,311	26,025	6,474	1,562	18,843	10,177	23,413	15,817
Capital expenditures (percent) ...	42	56	38	30	46	14	32	28

- Represents or rounds to zero.

Source: U.S. Bureau of the Census, *Government Finances*, series GF, No. 5, annual.

No. 471. Federal Grants-in-Aid Summary: 1970 to 1994

[For fiscal year ending in year shown; see text, section 9. Minus sign (-) indicates decrease]

YEAR	CURRENT DOLLARS							CONSTANT (1982) DOLLARS	
	Total grants (bil. dol.)	Average annual percent change [1]	Grants to individuals		Grants as percent of—			Total grants (bil. dol.)	Average annual percent change [1]
			Total (bil. dol.)	Percent of total grants	State-local govt. outlays [2]	Federal outlays	Gross domestic product		
1970	24.0	17.2	8.6	35.8	19.0	12.3	2.4	61.2	11.6
1975	49.8	15.7	16.4	33.0	22.6	15.0	3.1	87.1	7.3
1980	91.5	10.4	31.9	34.9	25.8	15.5	3.3	105.9	-0.7
1985	105.9	8.5	48.1	45.4	20.9	11.2	2.6	94.0	4.2
1988	115.3	6.4	61.0	52.9	18.2	10.8	2.4	92.5	2.0
1989	121.8	5.6	65.9	54.1	17.3	10.7	2.3	93.4	1.1
1990	136.9	12.2	78.6	57.5	17.9	10.9	2.5	100.9	7.7
1991	152.0	12.1	89.9	59.2	20.5	11.5	2.7	112.9	11.9
1992, estimate. . . .	182.2	19.9	114.6	62.9	(NA)	12.3	3.1	(NA)	(NA)
1993, projection. . . .	199.1	9.3	128.8	64.7	(NA)	13.1	3.2	(NA)	(NA)
1994, projection. . . .	220.1	10.5	145.5	66.1	(NA)	14.9	3.3	(NA)	(NA)

NA Not available. [1] Average annual percent change from prior year shown. For explanation, see Guide to Tabular Presentation. 1970, change change from 1965. [2] Outlays as defined in the national income and product accounts.

Source: Advisory Commission on Intergovernmental Relations, Washington, DC, *Significant Features of Fiscal Federalism*, 1992 Edition, vol. II, based on *Budget of the United States Government*, FY 93, table 12.1.

No. 472. Federal Aid to State and Local Governments: 1970 to 1992

[In millions of dollars. For fiscal year ending in year shown; see text, section 9. Includes trust funds. Minus sign (-) indicates previously disbursed funds returned to the Federal Government. See *Historical Statistics, Colonial Times to 1970*, series Y 638-651, for related data]

TYPE OF AID, FUNCTION, AND MAJOR PROGRAM	1970	1980	1985	1988	1989	1990	1991	1992
Grant-in-aid shared revenue [1]	[2]24,065	91,451	105,897	115,382	121,976	135,377	154,570	178,315
National defense	37	93	157	188	253	241	185	318
Natural resources and environment	411	5,363	4,069	3,747	3,606	3,745	4,040	3,947
Environmental Protection Agency	194	4,603	3,197	2,895	2,797	2,874	3,071	3,040
Energy	25	499	529	457	420	461	457	448
Agriculture	604	569	2,420	2,069	1,359	1,285	1,220	1,142
Transportation [1]	4,599	13,087	17,055	18,083	18,225	19,225	19,878	20,616
Airports	83	590	789	825	1,135	1,220	1,541	1,672
Highways	4,395	9,208	12,841	13,926	13,492	14,171	14,417	15,140
Urban mass transit	104	3,129	3,304	3,228	3,500	3,730	3,821	3,585
Community and regional development [1]	1,780	6,486	5,221	4,266	4,074	4,965	4,273	4,437
Appalachian development	184	335	198	141	104	124	157	125
Community development block grants	(X)	3,902	3,817	3,050	2,948	2,818	2,976	3,090
Education, employment, training, social services [1]	6,417	21,862	17,817	19,882	21,987	23,359	26,566	29,060
Compensatory education for the disadvantaged [3]	1,470	3,370	4,194	4,016	4,165	4,437	5,193	6,129
School improvement programs [3] . .	86	523	479	384	846	1,080	1,243	1,361
Bilingual and immigrant education [3]	-	166	111	130	132	152	148	160
Federally affected areas impact aid	622	622	629	694	735	799	747	785
Vocational and adult education	285	854	633	1,261	824	1,287	1,038	1,020
Libraries	105	158	79	94	131	127	132	190
Payments to States for Family Support Activities	81	383	274	90	86	265	546	594
Social services-block grants to States	574	2,763	2,743	2,666	2,671	2,749	2,822	2,708
Human development services	390	1,548	1,807	1,997	2,571	2,267	2,920	3,621
Training and employment assistance	954	6,191	2,775	2,958	3,020	3,042	2,985	3,388
Health [1]	3,849	15,758	24,451	32,586	36,679	43,890	55,783	71,416
Alcohol, drug abuse, and mental health [4] . . .	146	679	501	720	666	1,241	1,744	1,778
Medicaid [4]	2,727	13,957	22,655	30,462	34,604	41,103	52,533	67,827
Income security [1]	5,795	18,495	27,153	31,620	32,523	35,189	38,864	43,504
Family support payments to States [4]	4,142	6,888	8,592	10,764	11,166	12,246	13,520	15,103
Food stamps-administration	559	412	886	1,113	1,167	1,199	1,406	1,611
Child nutrition and special milk programs [4] . .	380	3,388	3,479	4,159	4,455	4,871	5,418	5,993
Housing assistance [4]	436	3,435	6,407	8,618	8,515	9,516	10,444	12,251
Veterans benefits and services	18	90	91	106	127	134	141	164
Administration of justice	42	529	95	427	520	574	940	987
General government [5]	479	8,616	6,838	1,950	2,204	2,309	2,224	2,272

- Represents or rounds to zero.   X Not applicable.   [1] Includes items not shown separately.   [2] Includes $5 million for international affairs subsequently provided to a private institution.   [3] The 1983 Budget proposed dismantlement of the Dept. of Education (DED). Budget data for elementary and secondary education previously performed by DED are included in the Foundation for Education Assistance under compensatory education for the disadvantaged, school improvement (formerly titled "Special programs and populations") programs and bilingual and immigrant education.   [4] Includes grants for payments to individuals.   [5] Includes general purpose fiscal assistance.

Source: U.S. Office of Management and Budget, *Historical Tables, Budget of the United States Government*, annual.

No. 473. Federal Aid to State and Local Governments—Selected Programs, by State: 1992

[In millions of dollars, except per capita. For fiscal year ending Sept. 30]

DIVISION AND STATE	FEDERAL AID [1] Total	Per capita [2] (dol.)	OE [3] compensatory education [4]	EPA [5] waste treatment facilities construction	HHS [6] Administration for Children and Families [7]	Medicaid	HUD [8] Lower income housing assistance [9]	Community development	ETA [10] employment/ training	DOT [11] highway trust fund
Total [12]	174,448	684	5,813	2,367	25,548	67,740	10,775	2,957	6,570	14,843
New England:										
Maine..........	1,047	847	32	22	142	448	77	15	38	79
New Hampshire ...	935	842	15	19	76	561	49	9	22	58
Vermont........	503	882	14	14	84	160	29	7	19	68
Massachusetts....	5,218	870	142	110	690	2,069	545	97	166	575
Rhode Island.....	986	981	23	10	123	403	103	17	37	117
Connecticut......	2,593	790	64	32	340	1,030	226	37	99	351
Middle Atlantic:										
New York	19,305	1,065	670	398	3,024	9,429	1,310	302	516	692
New Jersey	5,217	670	199	71	686	2,100	439	89	213	402
Pennsylvania	8,293	691	304	47	1,070	3,567	491	215	318	623
East North Central:										
Ohio..........	7,064	641	224	103	1,177	2,950	485	146	287	486
Indiana	3,242	573	93	31	322	1,430	167	57	135	396
Illinois..........	6,937	596	290	153	994	2,077	592	171	349	540
Michigan........	6,004	636	240	162	1,169	2,243	286	114	317	394
Wisconsin	3,127	624	87	93	536	1,256	150	56	123	280
West North Central:										
Minnesota.......	2,894	646	67	43	453	1,087	195	56	98	267
Iowa...........	1,660	590	46	25	228	595	70	38	63	238
Missouri........	3,498	674	92	59	392	1,443	186	63	121	319
North Dakota....	603	948	15	6	64	183	30	6	23	112
South Dakota.....	601	845	19	11	57	176	41	9	21	100
Nebraska........	997	621	29	13	129	320	59	18	31	109
Kansas.........	1,376	545	40	13	186	572	60	24	46	136
South Atlantic:										
Delaware........	425	617	17	10	53	123	36	4	18	60
Maryland........	2,940	599	102	64	437	983	251	43	120	263
District of Columbia.	1,951	3,314	47	13	173	300	77	31	36	114
Virginia	2,773	435	118	24	371	834	218	51	111	277
West Virginia	1,668	921	54	26	179	756	92	16	51	143
North Carolina	3,971	580	154	46	495	1,684	218	56	150	309
South Carolina	2,393	664	96	17	222	1,129	119	30	83	192
Georgia.........	4,028	597	179	35	549	1,581	247	62	127	332
Florida.........	6,187	459	269	78	870	2,243	376	126	224	508
East South Central:										
Kentucky........	2,951	786	111	21	360	1,355	170	42	100	176
Tennessee	3,658	728	132	33	316	1,642	186	55	116	308
Alabama	2,795	676	134	15	223	1,127	171	36	117	221
Mississippi......	2,193	839	120	22	217	886	116	40	67	179
West South Central:										
Arkansas........	1,691	705	74	9	146	720	80	20	63	185
Louisiana	4,417	1,030	148	26	380	2,498	164	55	100	304
Oklahoma	2,066	643	59	21	286	786	138	20	67	186
Texas..........	9,645	546	380	75	983	4,041	491	185	319	885
Mountain:										
Montana........	765	929	15	16	85	210	33	7	28	157
Idaho..........	694	650	18	10	76	210	30	8	36	110
Wyoming........	593	1,271	8	4	44	85	13	3	19	103
Colorado........	1,905	549	49	14	244	542	125	29	68	247
New Mexico......	1,379	872	44	10	154	408	74	14	39	159
Arizona.........	2,235	583	62	23	377	786	135	31	91	189
Utah...........	1,042	575	21	2	132	352	35	16	46	108
Nevada.........	669	504	14	10	65	197	51	7	34	80
Pacific:										
Washington......	3,374	657	65	58	593	1,170	151	37	143	401
Oregon.........	2,050	688	48	24	314	567	103	24	96	210
California........	19,738	639	541	193	5,036	6,142	1,191	340	830	1,688
Alaska.........	837	1,425	11	12	105	115	42	3	41	211
Hawaii	839	724	17	19	116	174	53	19	28	198

[1] Includes amounts not shown separately. [2] Based on estimated resident population as of July 1. [3] Office of Education. [4] For the disadvantaged. [5] Environmental Protection Agency. [6] Department of Health and Human Services. [7] Includes family support payments (Aid to Families with Dependent Children), social services block grants, children and family services, foster care and adoption assistance, low-income home energy assistance, community services block grants, refugee assistance, and assistance for legalized aliens. [8] Department of Housing and Urban Development. [9] Includes public housing, housing payments (section 8) to public agencies, and college housing. [10] Employment and Training Administration, Job Training Partnership Act. [11] Department of Transportation. [12] Includes undistributed amounts not shown separately.

Source: U.S. Bureau of the Census, *Federal Expenditures by State for Fiscal Year 1992.*

No. 474. State and Local Governments—Summary of Finances: 1980 to 1991

[For fiscal year ending in year shown; see text, section 9. Local government amounts are estimates subject to sampling variation; see Appendix III and source. See also *Historical Statistics, Colonial Times to 1970*, series Y 652-709]

SOURCE OF REVENUE AND TYPE OF EXPENDITURE	TOTAL (mil. dol.)			PER CAPITA [1] (dol.)			PERCENT DISTRIBUTION		
	1980	1990	1991	1980	1990	1991	1980	1990	1991
Revenue [2]	**451,537**	**1,032,115**	**1,080,865**	**1,993**	**4,150**	**4,286**	**100**	**100**	**100**
From Federal Government	**83,029**	**136,802**	**154,097**	**367**	**550**	**611**	**18**	**13**	**14**
Public welfare	24,921	59,961	72,661	110	241	288	6	6	7
Highways	8,980	14,368	14,561	40	58	58	2	1	1
Education	14,435	23,233	25,195	64	93	100	3	2	2
Health and hospitals	2,513	5,904	6,504	11	24	26	1	1	1
Housing and community development	3,905	9,655	10,233	17	39	41	1	1	1
Other and unallocable	28,275	23,683	24,943	125	95	99	6	2	2
From State and local sources	**368,509**	**895,313**	**926,200**	**1,627**	**3,600**	**3,673**	**82**	**87**	**86**
General, net intergovernmental	299,293	712,700	748,092	1,321	2,866	2,967	66	69	69
Taxes	223,463	501,619	525,281	986	2,017	2,083	50	49	49
Property	68,499	155,613	167,926	302	626	666	15	15	16
Sales and gross receipts	79,927	177,885	185,570	353	715	736	18	17	17
Individual income	42,080	105,640	109,341	186	425	434	9	10	10
Corporation income	13,321	23,566	22,242	59	95	88	3	2	2
Other	19,636	38,915	40,202	87	156	159	4	4	4
Charges and miscellaneous	75,830	211,081	222,810	335	849	884	17	20	21
Utility and liquor stores	25,560	58,642	57,165	113	236	227	6	6	5
Water supply system	6,766	17,674	18,034	30	71	72	2	2	2
Electric power system	11,387	29,268	30,489	50	118	121	3	3	3
Transit system	2,397	5,216	5,629	11	21	22	1	1	1
Gas supply system	1,809	3,043	3,013	8	12	12	(Z)	(Z)	(Z)
Liquor stores	3,201	3,441	3,568	14	14	14	1	(Z)	(Z)
Insurance trust revenue [3]	43,656	123,970	117,943	193	498	468	10	12	11
Employee retirement	25,441	94,268	87,230	112	379	346	6	9	8
Unemployment compensation	13,529	18,441	18,025	60	74	71	3	2	2
Direct expenditure	**432,328**	**972,662**	**1,060,332**	**1,908**	**3,911**	**4,205**	**100**	**100**	**100**
By function:									
Direct general expenditure [3]	367,340	834,786	905,169	1,621	3,343	3,590	85	86	85
Education [3]	133,211	288,148	309,667	588	1,159	1,228	31	30	29
Elementary and secondary education	92,930	202,009	218,007	410	812	865	22	21	21
Higher education	33,919	73,418	78,749	150	295	312	8	8	7
Highways	33,311	61,057	64,937	147	245	258	8	6	6
Public welfare	45,552	110,518	126,965	201	431	504	11	11	12
Health	8,387	24,223	26,706	37	97	106	2	2	3
Hospitals	23,787	50,412	54,407	105	203	216	6	5	5
Police protection	13,494	30,577	32,772	60	123	130	3	3	3
Fire protection	5,718	13,186	13,796	25	53	55	1	1	1
Natural resources	5,509	12,330	12,575	24	50	50	1	1	1
Sanitation and sewerage	13,214	28,453	31,014	58	114	123	3	3	3
Housing and community development	6,062	15,479	16,648	27	62	66	1	2	2
Parks and recreation	6,520	14,326	15,930	29	58	63	2	1	2
Financial administration	6,719	16,217	16,995	30	65	67	2	2	2
Interest on general debt [4]	14,747	49,739	52,393	65	200	208	3	5	5
Utility and liquor stores [4]	36,191	77,801	77,999	160	313	309	8	8	7
Water supply system	9,228	22,101	23,561	41	89	93	2	2	2
Electric power system	15,016	30,997	31,090	66	125	123	4	3	3
Transit system	7,641	18,788	20,379	34	76	81	2	2	2
Gas supply system	1,715	2,989	2,970	8	12	12	(Z)	(Z)	(Z)
Liquor stores	2,591	2,926	3,005	11	12	12	1	(Z)	(Z)
Insurance trust expenditure [3]	28,797	63,321	74,159	127	255	294	7	7	7
Employee retirement	14,008	38,355	42,121	62	154	167	3	4	4
Unemployment compensation	12,070	16,499	22,135	53	66	88	3	2	2
By character and object:									
Current operation	307,811	700,131	762,392	1,359	2,828	3,023	71	72	72
Capital outlay	62,894	123,069	131,632	278	495	522	15	13	12
Construction	51,492	89,114	96,654	227	358	383	12	9	9
Equipment, land, and existing structures	11,402	33,955	34,978	50	137	139	3	3	3
Assistance and subsidies	15,222	27,227	30,456	67	109	121	4	3	3
Interest on debt (general and utility)	17,604	58,914	61,694	78	237	245	4	6	6
Insurance benefits and repayments	28,797	63,321	74,159	127	255	294	7	7	7
Expenditure for salaries and wages	*163,896*	*341,158*	*366,359*	*723*	*1,372*	*1,453*	*38*	*35*	*35*
Debt outstanding, year end	**335,603**	**860,584**	**915,546**	**1,481**	**3,460**	**3,631**	**100**	**100**	**100**
Long-term	322,456	841,278	893,833	1,423	3,383	3,545	96	98	98
Short-term	13,147	19,306	21,713	58	78	86	4	2	2
Long-term debt:									
Issued	42,364	108,468	118,054	187	436	468	(X)	(X)	(X)
Retired	17,404	64,831	65,656	77	261	260	(X)	(X)	(X)

X Not applicable.   Z Less than 0.5 percent.   [1] 1980 and 1990 based on enumerated resident population as of April 1. Other years based on estimated resident population as of July 1.   [2] Aggregates exclude duplicative transactions between State and local governments; see source.   [3] Includes amounts not shown separately.   [4] Interest on utility debt included in "utility expenditure." For total interest on debt, see "Interest on debt (general and utility)."

Source: U.S. Bureau of the Census, *Historical Statistics on Governmental Finances and Employment* and *Government Finances*, series GF, No. 5, annual.

No. 475. State and Local Government Expenditures in the National Income and Product Accounts: 1970 to 1991

[In billions of dollars. For explanation of national income, see text, section 14]

EXPENDITURE	1970	1980	1984	1985	1986	1987	1988	1989	1990	1991
Purchases, total	112.6	298.0	389.9	428.1	465.3	496.6	531.7	573.6	616.8	643.2
Durable goods	3.9	12.8	19.6	22.3	24.6	26.0	28.1	31.9	34.9	36.4
Nondurable goods	6.5	28.8	35.9	38.7	39.1	42.3	45.5	50.7	56.0	58.0
Services	77.1	207.4	281.4	307.5	335.1	357.3	382.2	410.1	440.6	462.1
Compensation of employees	71.1	193.5	261.9	283.2	305.9	327.3	351.9	379.8	411.4	435.6
Other services	6.0	13.9	19.6	24.3	29.2	29.9	30.3	30.4	29.2	26.6
Structures	25.1	49.0	53.0	59.5	66.4	71.0	75.9	80.9	85.3	86.7
Transfers, total	20.1	65.7	93.5	101.2	110.9	119.6	130.0	143.6	164.7	198.0
Benefits from social insurance funds	5.0	17.8	27.9	30.4	33.9	37.4	40.9	44.6	49.2	54.4
State and local employee retirement	4.0	15.1	23.5	25.5	28.4	31.2	34.1	36.9	40.1	43.7
Temporary disability insurance	0.4	0.8	1.1	1.4	1.5	1.6	1.8	1.9	2.2	2.8
Workers' compensation	0.5	2.0	3.3	3.5	3.9	4.6	5.1	5.8	6.9	8.0
Public assistance	13.9	42.8	60.5	65.1	70.7	75.6	82.0	91.3	107.0	134.5
Medical care	5.4	24.6	37.9	41.2	45.4	49.8	55.0	62.9	75.6	100.1
Aid to families with dependent children	4.8	12.4	14.8	15.4	16.4	16.7	17.3	18.0	19.8	22.0
Supplemental security income	3.0	2.0	2.1	2.3	2.6	2.9	3.1	3.4	3.8	3.8
General assistance	0.6	1.4	2.4	2.4	2.5	2.6	2.7	2.8	3.0	2.9
Other	0.1	2.3	3.4	3.7	3.7	3.6	4.0	4.1	4.8	5.6
Other	1.3	4.9	5.0	5.6	6.3	6.5	7.0	7.7	8.5	9.2

Source: U.S. Bureau of Economic Analysis, *National Income and Product Accounts of the United States: volume 1, 1929–59*; and *Survey of Current Business*, July 1992.

Figure 9.2
State and Local Government Expenditures as a Percentage of Gross Domestic Product: 1970 to 1991

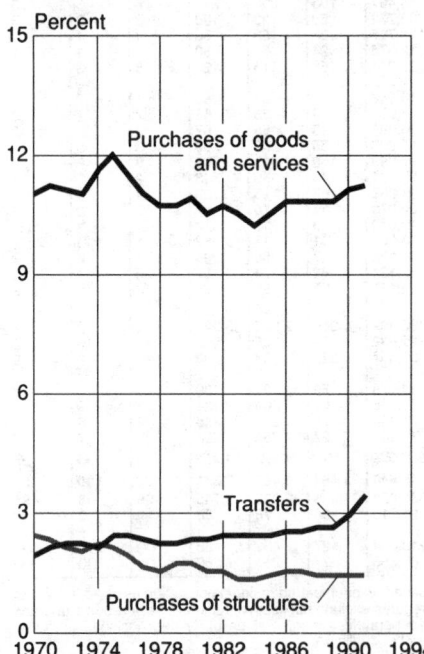

Source: Chart prepared by U.S. Bureau of the Census. For data, see table 475.

Figure 9.3
Budget Surplus or Deficit of State and Local Government as a Percentage of Gross Domestic Product: 1970 to 1991

Source: Chart prepared by U.S. Bureau of the Census. For data, see table 476.

No. 476. State and Local Government Receipts and Expenditures in the National Income and Product Accounts: 1970 to 1991

[In billions of dollars. For explanation of national income, see text, section 14]

ITEM	1970	1980	1984	1985	1986	1987	1988	1989	1990	1991
Receipts	129.0	361.4	492.2	528.7	571.2	594.3	631.3	681.5	729.3	777.9
Personal tax and nontax receipts [1]	16.7	56.2	87.1	94.0	101.6	111.8	117.6	131.4	138.7	145.4
Income taxes	10.9	42.6	67.5	72.1	77.4	86.0	89.9	101.4	106.0	110.3
Nontaxes	1.4	5.0	8.7	9.9	11.4	11.9	12.7	14.1	15.5	16.7
Corporate profits tax accruals	3.7	14.5	18.8	20.2	22.7	23.9	26.0	24.2	22.7	21.5
Indirect business tax and nontax accruals [1]	74.8	172.3	251.7	271.4	292.0	306.5	324.5	352.8	378.2	397.0
Sales taxes	31.6	82.9	121.1	131.1	140.4	149.8	161.4	172.3	183.5	189.0
Property taxes	36.7	68.8	99.7	107.0	114.5	121.1	127.6	143.5	155.4	167.7
Contributions for social insurance	9.2	29.7	40.2	42.8	47.3	49.2	51.9	54.8	57.3	60.6
Federal grants-in-aid	24.4	88.7	94.4	100.3	107.6	102.8	111.3	118.2	132.3	153.3
Expenditures	127.2	336.6	434.1	472.6	517.0	554.2	593.0	636.7	699.2	760.7
Purchases	112.6	298.0	389.9	428.1	465.3	496.6	531.7	573.6	616.8	643.2
Compensation of employees	71.1	193.5	261.9	283.2	305.9	327.3	351.9	379.8	411.4	435.6
Transfer payments to persons	20.1	65.7	93.5	101.2	110.9	119.6	130.0	143.6	164.7	198.0
Net interest paid [2]	−1.8	−19.3	−34.0	−38.7	−40.4	−41.2	−44.2	−52.3	−52.4	−48.4
Less: Dividends received	0.2	1.9	3.9	4.5	5.1	5.9	6.9	8.1	9.0	9.5
Subsidies [3]	−3.6	−5.8	−11.4	−13.5	−13.7	−14.9	−17.5	−20.1	−20.9	−22.6
Surplus	1.8	24.8	58.1	56.1	54.3	40.1	38.4	44.8	30.1	17.1
Social insurance funds	6.9	26.9	42.8	46.9	52.7	54.8	56.8	62.3	63.0	60.3

[1] Includes other items not shown separately.   [2] Interest paid less interest received.   [3] Less current surplus of government.

Source: U.S. Bureau of Economic Analysis, *Survey of Current Business*, July 1992.

No. 477. New Issues of Long-Term State and Local Government Securities: 1980 to 1992

[In billions of dollars. Beginning 1985, includes outlying areas]

ITEM	1980	1985	1986	1987	1988	1989	1990	1991	1992
All issues, new capital and refunding	41.2	201.4	148.1	101.5	115.3	121.9	126.1	171.0	232.5
General obligations	11.4	39.8	45.0	30.2	30.9	37.7	40.1	57.9	80.3
Revenue	29.9	161.7	103.1	71.3	84.4	84.2	86.0	113.1	152.2
Type of issuer:									
City, town	6.7	36.5	29.9	17.2	20.9	23.9	22.8	31.3	44.6
College or university	0.2	2.9	3.2	1.0	1.7	2.0	1.5	3.6	3.7
County/parish	4.1	15.9	12.0	9.6	10.9	10.0	10.0	15.3	20.2
District	2.6	15.4	15.5	10.1	13.1	13.3	14.9	23.3	30.7
Local authority	8.6	51.2	30.6	22.4	22.2	23.5	20.7	28.4	42.4
State	5.1	12.1	14.4	10.1	9.5	11.9	15.5	19.5	25.3
State authority	14.0	67.5	42.4	30.8	37.1	37.3	40.7	49.6	65.5
Issues for new capital, total	37.5	124.4	80.2	55.1	77.6	84.2	98.3	116.3	108.3
Use of proceeds:									
Economic development	0.1	1.9	1.7	2.2	1.4	1.4	1.5	2.2	2.5
Education	2.6	10.3	10.8	8.4	11.1	14.0	16.4	18.0	17.3
General purpose/public improvement	9.7	22.3	29.7	17.5	24.8	28.8	32.2	43.4	34.7
Health care	1.7	15.7	3.3	3.6	5.6	7.9	8.2	11.4	8.5
Single family housing	10.6	14.2	4.7	4.4	10.0	6.4	10.2	7.1	5.6
Transportation	0.9	5.8	6.5	2.5	3.4	5.0	7.0	6.3	9.4
Water, sewer, and gas facilities	1.4	4.8	6.5	5.4	6.7	6.9	7.6	10.9	9.1

Source: Securities Data Company, Inc., Newark, NJ, Municipal New Issues Database.

No. 478. State and Local Governments—Indebtedness: 1980 to 1991

[In billions of dollars, except per capita. For fiscal year ending in year shown; see text, section 9. Local government amounts are estimates subject to sampling variation; see Appendix III and source. See *Historical Statistics, Colonial Times to 1970*, series Y 680, Y 747, and Y 794, for debt outstanding]

ITEM	DEBT OUTSTANDING						LONG-TERM		
	Total	Per capita [1] (dol.)	Long-term			Short-term	Net long-term	Debt issued	Debt retired
			Local schools [2]	Utilities	All other				
1980: Total	335.6	1,482	32.3	55.2	235.0	13.1	262.9	42.4	17.4
State	122.0	540	3.8	4.6	111.5	2.1	79.8	16.4	5.7
Local	213.6	942	28.5	50.6	123.5	11.0	183.1	25.9	11.7
1985: Total	568.6	2,390	43.8	90.8	414.5	19.6	430.5	101.2	43.5
State	211.9	891	6.7	8.6	193.8	2.8	110.4	41.7	16.4
Local	356.7	1,499	37.1	82.2	220.6	16.8	320.1	59.5	27.2
1990: Total	860.6	3,460	60.4	134.8	646.1	19.3	477.0	108.5	64.8
State	318.3	1,280	4.4	12.3	298.8	2.8	125.5	43.5	22.9
Local	542.3	2,181	56.0	122.4	347.4	16.5	351.5	65.0	42.0
1991: Total	915.7	3,632	71.0	141.2	681.8	21.7	522.1	118.1	65.7
State	345.6	1,370	5.9	12.5	323.7	3.4	140.4	50.5	25.4
Local	570.2	2,261	65.1	128.7	358.1	18.3	381.7	67.6	40.3

[1] 1980 and 1990 based on enumerated resident population as of April 1; other years based on estimated resident population as of July 1.   [2] Includes debt for education activities other than higher education.

Source: U.S. Bureau of the Census, *Government Finances*, series GF, No. 5, annual; and unpublished data.

No. 479. State Governments—Revenue,

[In millions of dollars, except as indicated. Data will not match other tables due to later revisions.

YEAR, DIVISION, AND STATE	Total revenue [1]	GENERAL REVENUE								DEBT OUTSTANDING
		Total		Per capita [2]		Intergovernmental revenue		Taxes	Charges and miscellaneous	
		Amount	Rank	Total (dol.)	Rank	From Federal Government	From local governments			Total
1980	276,962	233,592	(X)	1,034	(X)	61,892	2,434	137,075	32,190	121,958
1985	439,416	365,835	(X)	1,538	(X)	84,434	5,453	215,893	60,055	211,917
1986	481,279	393,475	(X)	1,639	(X)	92,666	5,908	228,053	66,848	247,715
1987	517,217	419,487	(X)	1,731	(X)	95,463	6,918	246,933	70,173	265,551
1988	541,426	445,138	(X)	1,821	(X)	100,478	6,763	264,146	73,751	276,786
1989	586,931	482,721	(X)	1,956	(X)	108,235	7,530	284,413	82,543	295,500
1990	625,473	517,443	(X)	2,081	(X)	118,353	7,995	300,489	90,607	318,237
U.S., 1991	**661,393**	**551,722**	**(X)**	**2,188**	**(X)**	**134,926**	**8,607**	**310,561**	**97,627**	**345,554**
New England:										
Maine	3,222	2,902	40	2,351	17	753	4	1,558	586	2,585
New Hampshire	2,088	1,702	48	1,541	50	441	59	625	577	4,127
Vermont	1,703	1,548	49	2,733	9	451	3	685	409	1,486
Massachusetts	18,727	17,460	10	2,912	6	4,036	420	9,684	3,321	21,102
Rhode Island	3,305	2,592	41	2,579	13	740	43	1,257	553	4,393
Connecticut	9,816	8,745	20	2,659	10	2,129	4	4,983	1,629	13,006
Middle Atlantic:										
New York	65,715	54,935	2	3,043	5	14,735	4,470	28,300	7,430	51,804
New Jersey	24,743	20,056	9	2,587	12	4,218	189	11,645	4,004	19,039
Pennsylvania	27,086	22,155	4	1,853	42	5,571	62	13,021	3,500	11,640
East North Central:										
Ohio	31,721	21,379	7	1,954	36	5,549	207	11,556	4,067	11,367
Indiana	12,288	11,222	17	2,000	33	2,583	102	6,182	2,355	4,624
Illinois	25,092	21,801	6	1,889	41	4,810	113	13,292	3,585	18,238
Michigan	24,505	20,891	8	2,227	21	5,204	209	11,103	4,375	10,109
Wisconsin	14,137	11,825	15	2,386	16	2,639	87	7,017	2,083	6,625
West North Central:										
Minnesota	13,701	11,642	16	2,627	11	2,485	117	7,051	1,990	3,941
Iowa	7,137	6,200	30	2,218	22	1,449	70	3,447	1,234	1,620
Missouri	10,002	8,661	22	1,679	47	2,233	10	4,996	1,421	5,775
North Dakota	1,998	1,755	46	2,764	8	491	21	755	488	964
South Dakota	1,597	1,412	50	2,006	32	502	3	528	378	1,754
Nebraska	3,436	3,219	39	2,020	30	749	19	1,767	684	1,596
Kansas	5,249	4,724	33	1,893	40	1,132	18	2,796	778	337
South Atlantic:										
Delaware	2,443	2,227	43	3,275	4	362	14	1,165	685	3,215
Maryland	12,479	10,605	18	2,183	24	2,224	60	6,401	1,919	7,528
Virginia	14,523	12,431	13	1,979	35	2,357	163	6,852	3,059	6,500
West Virginia	4,896	4,152	37	2,303	20	1,075	9	2,328	740	2,770
North Carolina	15,266	12,927	11	1,919	38	3,061	293	7,850	1,723	3,490
South Carolina	9,413	7,408	26	2,081	27	2,049	84	3,933	1,341	4,189
Georgia	13,866	11,864	14	1,791	45	3,383	73	7,155	1,253	3,652
Florida	25,754	22,080	5	1,664	48	4,582	245	13,764	3,489	11,084
East South Central:										
Kentucky	9,951	8,706	21	2,345	18	2,219	14	5,043	1,430	6,024
Tennessee	9,544	8,385	23	1,693	46	2,731	41	4,311	1,302	2,790
Alabama	9,767	8,173	24	1,998	34	2,316	46	3,943	1,869	4,214
Mississippi	5,794	4,949	32	1,908	39	1,825	16	2,461	647	1,413
West South Central:										
Arkansas	4,810	4,307	36	1,815	44	1,193	5	2,366	743	1,764
Louisiana	10,764	9,410	19	2,212	23	2,841	16	4,309	2,244	10,729
Oklahoma	7,819	6,655	27	2,096	26	1,509	46	3,862	1,238	3,730
Texas	33,773	28,819	3	1,661	49	7,605	27	16,017	5,169	7,687
Mountain:										
Montana	2,359	1,886	45	2,331	19	610	15	818	443	1,611
Idaho	2,584	2,148	44	2,066	29	537	17	1,205	389	1,122
Wyoming	1,979	1,741	47	3,789	3	561	30	637	513	922
Colorado	7,863	6,226	29	1,843	43	1,577	34	3,214	1,401	2,659
New Mexico	4,913	4,332	35	2,797	7	921	70	2,086	1,255	1,752
Arizona	9,016	7,544	25	2,013	31	1,489	301	4,711	1,043	2,540
Utah	4,344	3,662	38	2,069	28	976	39	1,861	785	1,911
Nevada	3,553	2,463	42	1,920	37	425	16	1,683	340	1,708
Pacific:										
Washington	16,394	12,750	12	2,544	14	2,769	73	7,990	1,918	6,520
Oregon	8,201	6,353	28	2,175	25	1,823	35	3,030	1,466	6,451
California	90,784	72,676	1	2,392	15	17,569	582	44,874	9,650	31,956
Alaska	6,355	5,673	31	9,945	1	706	9	1,806	3,152	5,291
Hawaii	4,916	4,348	34	3,825	2	731	3	2,639	975	4,202

X Not applicable.   [1] Includes items not shown separately.   [2] 1970, 1980, and 1990 based on enumerated resident population as of April 1. All other years based on estimated resident population as of July 1.

Debt, and Expenditure, 1980 to 1991, and by State, 1991

[For fiscal year ending in year shown; see text, section 9]

Per capita [2] Total (dol.)	Per capita [2] Rank	Total expenditures [1]	Total [1] Amount	Total [1] Per capita [2] Total (dol.)	Total [1] Per capita [2] Rank	Education	Public welfare	Highways	Health and hospitals	Corrections	YEAR, DIVISION, AND STATE
540	(X)	257,812	228,223	1,010	(X)	87,939	44,219	25,044	17,855	5,093	1980
891	(X)	390,742	345,047	1,450	(X)	128,604	67,264	33,154	27,595	9,171	1985
1,030	(X)	424,205	376,429	1,568	(X)	140,189	72,464	36,661	30,131	10,771	1986
1,094	(X)	455,700	403,942	1,667	(X)	149,901	78,454	38,273	32,131	11,704	1987
1,129	(X)	484,667	432,179	1,768	(X)	159,500	84,235	40,681	34,872	13,303	1988
1,194	(X)	525,077	469,269	1,901	(X)	173,184	92,750	42,694	38,602	15,018	1989
1,280	(X)	571,909	507,875	2,042	(X)	184,529	104,971	44,249	42,662	17,266	1990
1,370	**(X)**	**628,634**	**554,553**	**2,199**	**(X)**	**196,461**	**124,464**	**47,038**	**45,877**	**19,240**	**U.S., 1991**
											N.E.:
2,094	14	3,515	3,095	2,508	15	961	878	287	178	68	ME
3,736	5	2,135	1,749	1,583	49	404	398	175	143	43	NH
2,623	9	1,736	1,607	2,836	8	540	346	170	64	30	VT
3,520	7	20,349	18,265	3,046	5	3,300	5,785	699	1,603	708	MA
4,371	3	3,465	2,750	2,736	9	725	651	194	255	92	RI
3,955	4	11,115	9,807	2,982	7	2,335	2,069	1,019	1,030	460	CT
											M.A.:
2,869	8	64,321	53,916	2,986	6	14,581	17,015	2,569	5,353	2,204	NY
2,456	12	23,250	19,399	2,502	16	5,830	4,186	1,372	1,313	633	NJ
973	37	26,710	22,879	1,913	39	6,892	6,115	2,363	1,847	541	PA
											E.N.C.:
1,039	33	27,791	22,324	2,040	29	8,009	5,712	2,047	1,751	643	OH
824	40	11,548	10,967	1,955	36	4,404	2,272	1,044	763	296	IN
1,580	18	24,619	22,168	1,921	38	7,206	4,860	2,376	1,530	662	IL
1,078	31	24,037	20,749	2,212	24	6,948	5,125	1,437	2,377	815	MI
1,337	22	12,448	11,340	2,288	18	3,948	2,480	829	729	308	WI
											W.N.C.:
889	38	12,730	11,688	2,637	11	4,501	2,375	1,012	893	167	MN
580	44	6,820	6,384	2,284	19	2,581	1,171	867	576	151	IA
1,120	28	9,254	8,478	1,644	48	3,454	1,772	903	715	197	MO
1,518	21	1,793	1,653	2,604	13	623	256	196	93	15	ND
2,493	11	1,417	1,356	1,927	37	409	212	209	92	28	SD
1,002	36	3,266	3,192	2,003	30	1,161	594	435	326	66	NE
135	50	5,134	4,707	1,886	41	1,945	825	633	422	209	KS
											S.A.:
4,729	2	2,318	2,152	3,164	4	758	257	257	147	83	DE
1,549	19	12,576	10,776	2,218	22	3,354	2,108	1,187	896	506	MD
1,035	34	13,352	12,390	1,973	34	4,868	1,814	1,697	1,312	567	VA
1,536	20	4,741	3,996	2,216	23	1,721	708	501	188	40	WV
518	48	15,036	13,805	2,050	28	6,258	2,362	1,390	1,085	527	NC
1,177	25	8,970	7,698	2,162	25	3,022	1,538	511	917	314	SC
551	46	13,286	12,280	1,854	42	5,199	2,673	1,020	1,013	628	GA
835	39	25,168	23,628	1,781	46	9,097	4,556	1,779	1,949	924	FL
											E.S.C.:
1,623	17	9,048	8,248	2,221	21	3,310	1,937	826	473	209	KY
563	45	9,238	8,596	1,735	47	3,074	1,978	1,061	703	394	TN
1,030	35	8,855	8,050	1,968	35	3,509	1,357	679	1,049	177	AL
545	47	5,171	4,680	1,805	44	1,902	868	496	375	91	MS
											W.S.C.:
743	42	4,649	4,315	1,818	43	1,841	954	459	294	100	AR
2,522	10	10,537	9,592	2,255	20	3,465	1,832	843	998	259	LA
1,175	26	7,267	6,271	1,975	33	2,597	1,263	779	546	202	OK
443	49	29,542	27,026	1,558	50	12,310	5,393	2,612	2,116	1,064	TX
											Mt.:
1,992	16	2,384	2,058	2,544	14	753	331	272	115	46	MT
1,080	30	2,305	2,055	1,977	32	862	285	279	87	53	ID
2,006	15	1,813	1,638	3,564	3	536	152	325	101	23	WY
787	41	6,992	6,089	1,803	45	2,654	1,132	671	385	257	CO
1,131	27	4,527	4,204	2,714	10	1,778	538	364	372	123	NM
678	43	7,872	7,118	1,899	40	2,807	1,034	1,094	357	347	AZ
1,080	29	4,108	3,692	2,086	27	1,805	534	300	329	92	UT
1,331	23	3,436	2,557	1,993	31	998	262	243	105	126	NV
											Pac.:
1,301	24	15,666	13,170	2,628	12	5,749	2,452	1,105	989	310	WA
2,208	13	7,249	6,292	2,154	26	1,892	1,144	784	574	237	OR
1,052	32	85,640	75,033	2,470	17	27,218	18,991	3,889	5,806	2,983	CA
9,275	1	4,941	4,493	7,876	1	1,098	435	502	174	130	AK
3,697	6	4,510	4,174	3,673	2	1,269	478	277	370	92	HI

Source: U.S. Bureau of the Census, *State Government Finances,* series GF, No. 3, annual.

No. 480. State Governments—Summary of Finances: 1980 to 1991

[For fiscal year ending in year shown; see text section 9. See also *Historical Statistics, Colonial Times to 1970,* series Y 710-782]

ITEM	TOTAL (mil. dol.)			PER CAPITA [1] (dol.)			PERCENT DISTRIBUTION		
	1980	1990	1991	1980	1990	1991	1980	1990	1991
Borrowing and revenue	293,356	672,994	708,047	1,299	2,713	2,808	100	100	100
Borrowing.................	16,394	40,532	46,654	73	163	185	6	6	7
Revenue..................	276,962	632,462	661,393	1,226	2,549	2,623	94	94	93
General revenue............	233,592	517,720	551,722	1,034	2,082	2,188	80	77	78
Taxes	137,075	300,779	310,561	607	1,212	1,232	47	45	44
Sales and gross receipts	67,855	147,404	153,535	300	594	609	23	22	22
General	43,168	99,929	103,165	191	403	409	15	15	15
Motor fuels..........	9,722	19,379	20,639	43	78	82	3	3	3
Alcoholic beverages.....	2,478	3,191	3,400	11	13	13	1	1	(Z)
Tobacco products	3,738	5,541	5,980	17	22	24	1	1	1
Other...............	8,750	19,365	20,349	39	78	81	3	3	3
Licenses..............	8,690	18,849	19,419	38	76	77	3	3	3
Motor vehicles........	4,936	9,850	10,131	22	40	40	2	1	1
Corporations in general....	1,388	3,096	3,114	6	12	12	1	1	(Z)
Other...............	2,366	5,903	6,174	10	24	24	1	1	1
Individual income	37,089	96,076	99,279	164	387	394	13	14	14
Corporation net income	13,321	21,751	20,357	59	88	81	5	3	3
Property	2,892	5,775	6,228	13	23	25	1	1	1
Other	7,227	10,922	11,745	32	44	47	3	2	2
Charges and miscellaneous...	32,190	90,612	97,627	142	365	387	11	14	14
Intergovernmental revenue	64,326	126,329	143,534	285	509	569	22	19	20
From Federal Government ...	61,892	118,353	134,926	274	477	535	21	18	19
Public welfare	24,680	59,397	71,961	109	239	285	8	9	10
Education............	12,765	21,271	23,337	57	86	93	4	3	3
Highways	8,860	13,931	14,098	39	56	56	3	2	2
Other..............	15,587	23,755	25,530	69	96	101	5	4	4
From local governments.....	2,434	7,976	8,607	11	32	34	1	1	1
Utility revenue	1,304	3,305	3,460	6	13	14	(Z)	1	(Z)
Liquor store revenue	2,765	2,907	3,013	12	12	12	1	(Z)	(Z)
Insurance trust revenue [2]	39,301	108,530	103,198	174	436	409	13	15	15
Employee retirement	21,146	78,898	72,558	94	291	288	7	11	10
Unemployment compensation ..	13,468	18,370	17,952	60	74	71	5	3	3
Expenditure and debt redemption	263,494	592,213	650,290	1,166	2,387	2,579	100	100	100
Debt redemption	5,682	19,895	21,656	25	80	86	2	3	3
Expenditure	257,812	572,318	628,634	1,141	2,305	2,493	98	97	97
General expenditure	228,223	508,284	554,553	1,010	2,047	2,199	87	86	85
Education...............	87,939	184,935	196,461	389	744	779	33	31	30
Public welfare	44,219	104,971	124,464	196	423	494	17	18	19
Highways.............	25,044	44,249	47,038	111	178	187	10	8	7
Health and hospitals........	17,855	42,666	45,878	79	172	182	7	7	7
Corrections..............	4,449	17,266	19,240	20	70	76	2	3	3
Natural resources	4,346	9,909	10,256	19	40	41	2	2	2
General control	3,232	8,384	9,355	14	34	37	1	1	1
Financial administration.......	3,031	8,616	9,101	13	35	36	1	2	1
Police protection	2,263	5,166	5,506	10	21	22	1	1	1
Employment security	2,001	3,003	3,238	9	12	13	1	1	(Z)
Housing and community development	601	2,856	2,827	3	12	11	(Z)	1	(Z)
Other and unallocable	33,242	76,264	81,189	147	307	322	13	13	12
Utility expenditure	2,401	7,131	7,217	11	29	29	1	1	1
Liquor store expenditure........	2,206	2,452	2,504	10	10	10	1	(Z)	(Z)
Insurance trust expenditure [2]	24,981	54,452	64,360	111	219	255	10	9	10
Employee retirement	10,256	29,562	32,442	45	119	129	4	5	5
Unemployment compensation ..	12,006	16,423	22,017	53	66	87	5	3	3
By character and object:									
Intergovernmental expenditure ...	84,504	175,028	186,469	374	706	739	32	30	29
Direct expenditure...........	173,307	397,291	442,165	767	1,599	1,754	66	67	68
Current operation	108,131	258,046	286,802	479	1,038	1,137	41	44	44
Capital outlay	23,325	45,524	47,937	103	183	190	9	8	7
Construction	19,736	34,803	37,647	87	140	149	8	6	6
Land and existing structures ..	1,345	3,471	3,402	6	14	13	1	1	1
Equipment............	2,243	7,250	6,888	10	29	27	1	1	1
Assistance and subsidies	9,818	16,902	18,876	43	68	75	4	3	3
Interest on debt.	7,052	22,367	24,189	31	90	96	3	4	4
Insurance benefits [3]	24,981	54,452	64,360	111	219	255	10	9	10
Debt outstanding, year end...	121,958	318,254	345,554	540	1,283	1,370	100	100	100
Long-term...............	119,821	315,490	342,164	530	1,272	1,357	98	99	99
Full-faith and credit	49,364	74,972	84,749	219	302	336	41	24	25
Nonguaranteed..............	70,457	240,518	257,415	312	969	1,021	58	76	74
Short-term...............	2,137	2,764	3,390	9	11	13	2	1	1
Net long-term	79,810	125,524	140,405	353	506	557	65	39	41
Full-faith and credit only........	39,357	63,481	73,220	174	256	290	32	20	21

Z Less than 0.5 percent.   [1] 1980 and 1990 based on enumerated resident population as of April 1. Other years based on estimated resident population as of July 1.   [2] Includes other items not shown separately.   [3] Includes repayments.

Source: U.S. Bureau of the Census, *1982 Census of Governments: Historical Statistics on Governmental Finances and Employment* and *State Government Finances,* series GF, No. 3, annual.

No. 481. State Resources, Expenditures, and Balances: 1991 to 1993

[For fiscal year ending in year shown; see text; section 9. **General funds** exclude special funds earmarked for particular purposes, such as highway trust funds and federal funds; they support most on-going broad-based State services, and are available for appropriation to support any governmental activity. Minus sign (-) indicates deficit]

DIVISION AND STATE	Total, 1991 (mil. dol.)	EXPENDITURES BY FUND SOURCE				STATE GENERAL FUND					
		1992 [1]				Resources [3][4]		Expenditures [4]		Balance [5]	
		Total [2] (mil. dol.)	General fund (percent)	Federal funds (percent)	Other State funds (percent)	1992 (mil. dol.)	1993 [1] (mil. dol.)	1992 (mil. dol.)	1993 [1] (mil. dol.)	1992 (mil. dol.)	1993 [1] (mil. dol.)
United States . . .	541,150	595,926	49	26	24	306,105	314,135	303,785	311,051	1,998	2,975
New England:											
Maine.	2,769	3,152	48	32	18	1,547	1,574	1,534	1,563	13	11
New Hampshire. . . .	1,604	2,013	36	34	27	724	777	703	741	21	35
Vermont	1,341	1,430	44	30	22	591	623	656	640	-65	-17
Massachusetts.	20,317	20,380	46	21	29	13,916	14,743	13,528	14,719	388	24
Rhode Island.	2,290	3,181	54	24	19	1,748	1,467	1,747	1,465	2	1
Connecticut.	8,890	9,117	65	14	14	6,965	7,321	6,915	7,318	50	4
Middle Atlantic:											
New York	48,910	52,329	54	26	17	29,842	30,851	29,842	30,784	-	6
New Jersey.	17,725	21,330	67	17	14	15,313	14,423	14,543	14,346	770	77
Pennsylvania.	23,890	28,109	50	26	22	13,766	14,048	13,757	14,046	9	2
East North Central:											
Ohio	23,266	24,770	41	25	32	10,243	10,452	10,153	10,620	90	[7]168
Indiana.	9,817	10,198	58	30	11	5,894	6,208	5,755	6,208	139	
Illinois.	20,445	22,528	51	18	28	12,082	12,126	11,951	11,926	131	200
Michigan.	18,120	19,914	38	28	34	7,347	8,001	7,347	8,038	-	-37
Wisconsin.	7,930	8,937	50	36	14	6,688	6,974	6,589	6,933	100	41
West North Central:											
Minnesota.	11,244	12,178	54	21	24	6,754	6,725	6,490	6,483	264	242
Iowa	7,364	8,399	38	22	40	3,184	3,473	3,184	3,405	-	69
Missouri	8,198	9,018	48	27	25	4,346	4,513	4,303	4,473	43	40
North Dakota.	1,600	1,513	38	33	29	628	586	586	609	42	8
South Dakota	1,248	1,418	37	39	24	574	596	568	592	6	4
Nebraska	3,133	3,471	45	23	31	1,746	1,749	1,545	1,645	201	104
Kansas.	5,082	5,512	45	21	33	2,632	3,029	2,499	2,728	133	301
South Atlantic:											
Delaware	2,395	2,618	47	13	30	1,383	1,409	1,230	1,288	153	121
Maryland	12,267	12,133	51	19	25	6,277	6,651	6,271	6,602	6	49
Virginia.	13,126	13,063	47	17	35	6,271	6,429	6,203	6,374	68	55
West Virginia.	4,137	4,598	43	32	23	2,016	2,119	1,959	2,116	57	3
North Carolina.	12,873	13,625	57	24	19	7,818	8,255	7,652	8,210	165	45
South Carolina.	7,988	8,946	38	31	29	3,404	3,770	3,396	3,729	8	41
Georgia	12,747	13,711	55	28	14	7,421	8,152	7,403	8,134	18	18
Florida	26,974	28,870	39	19	40	11,169	11,901	11,047	11,901	123	-
East South Central:											
Kentucky	8,735	10,595	43	30	27	4,595	4,658	4,546	4,625	49	34
Tennessee	8,043	9,568	42	33	23	4,017	4,568	3,916	4,528	101	40
Alabama.	8,393	9,285	36	57	7	3,405	3,449	3,400	3,445	5	4
Mississippi	(NA)	(NA)	(NA)	(NA)	(NA)	1,945	2,000	1,925	1,993	20	7
West South Central:											
Arkansas.	5,038	5,579	35	26	38	1,935	2,055	1,935	2,055	-	-
Louisiana	10,172	12,471	36	31	31	4,426	4,318	4,426	4,411	-	93
Oklahoma	6,612	7,371	44	25	31	3,327	3,516	3,160	3,318	167	198
Texas.	27,262	29,749	57	25	15	18,766	18,622	18,934	18,360	-168	262
Mountain:											
Montana.	2,174	2,398	22	28	50	550	556	524	540	26	16
Idaho	1,978	2,171	46	31	22	991	1,000	991	1,007	-	7
Wyoming	1,426	1,322	32	24	45	439	423	387	390	52	33
Colorado.	5,377	6,043	46	26	28	2,879	3,109	2,807	2,973	72	136
New Mexico	3,878	4,169	49	22	26	2,078	2,131	2,053	2,132	6	-
Arizona.	6,890	7,463	49	29	20	3,534	3,664	3,524	3,653	10	11
Utah	3,445	3,767	49	22	27	1,891	1,960	1,853	1,956	38	4
Nevada	(NA)	(NA)	(NA)	(NA)	(NA)	1,047	1,110	1,018	1,059	29	50
Pacific:											
Washington.	13,604	15,627	49	18	28	7,839	7,789	7,619	7,626	220	163
Oregon.	8,767	8,229	33	16	52	2,986	2,836	2,686	2,892	300	189
California	72,929	83,743	51	32	15	40,828	41,230	43,019	40,795	-2,191	435
Alaska	3,770	4,369	58	16	25	3,211	2,772	2,913	2,706	6	6
Hawaii	4,967	5,540	50	12	24	3,130	3,185	2,793	2,953	337	232

- Represents zero.   NA Not available.   [1] Estimated.   [2] Includes bonds not shown separately.   [3] Includes funds budgeted, adjustments, and balances from previous year.   [4] May or may not include budget stabilization fund transfers, depending on state accounting practices.   [5] Resources less expenditures.   [6] Ending balance is held in a budget stabilization fund.   [7] Ending balance reflects the current status estimate as of August 1992. Actions will be taken so that the ending balance is zero or greater, per Ohio's constitution requiring a balanced budget.   [8] Reflects the use of $23 million in rainy day funds to arrive at a zero ending balance.

Source: National Association of State Budget Officers, Washington, DC, *1992 State Expenditure Report*, and National Governors' Association and NASBO, *Fiscal Survey of the States*, semi-annual (copyright).

No. 482. State Tax Collections, 1992, and Projections, 1993

[In millions of dollars]

DIVISION AND STATE	SALES		INDIVIDUAL INCOME		CORPORATE INCOME	
	1992, prel.	1993, proj.	1992, prel.	1993, proj.	1992, prel.	1993, proj.
United States.	101,348	106,410	105,319	110,550	22,011	22,983
New England.	5,135	5,361	8,623	9,072	1,520	1,394
Maine	554	600	574	661	68	49
New Hampshire	(X)	(X)	(X)	(X)	91	80
Vermont	157	171	271	311	28	28
Massachusetts	1,979	2,160	5,337	5,320	644	630
Rhode Island	391	407	474	517	54	65
Connecticut	2,054	2,023	1,967	2,263	635	542
Middle Atlantic.	14,349	14,631	23,805	24,375	4,239	4,277
New York	5,794	6,185	14,913	15,284	1,671	1,723
New Jersey	4,055	3,647	4,085	4,250	955	1,022
Pennsylvania	4,500	4,799	4,807	4,841	1,613	1,532
East North Central	14,659	15,407	17,331	18,378	4,146	4,462
Ohio	3,555	3,775	3,911	4,185	762	830
Indiana	2,246	2,396	2,247	2,335	672	710
Illinois	3,986	4,089	4,477	4,647	577	599
Michigan	2,745	2,905	3,554	3,801	1,697	1,870
Wisconsin	2,127	2,242	3,142	3,410	438	453
West North Central.	6,225	7,004	8,405	8,929	1,237	1,276
Minnesota	2,168	2,337	2,927	3,030	420	427
Iowa	800	1,037	1,588	1,657	237	248
Missouri.	1,276	1,339	2,168	2,313	275	269
North Dakota	224	238	119	129	37	44
South Dakota	264	277	(X)	(X)	(X)	(X)
Nebraska	592	625	659	688	104	105
Kansas	901	1,151	944	1,112	164	183
South Atlantic	17,876	19,416	15,402	16,594	2,584	2,494
Delaware.	(X)	(X)	487	488	43	47
Maryland.	1,580	1,794	2,906	3,295	124	163
Virginia	1,349	1,434	3,321	3,488	376	300
West Virginia	569	636	613	640	108	132
North Carolina	2,161	2,326	3,583	3,797	606	443
South Carolina	1,166	1,251	1,411	1,568	132	146
Georgia	2,676	2,909	3,081	3,318	394	428
Florida.	8,375	9,066	(X)	(X)	801	835
East South Central	5,524	5,634	3,432	3,630	909	930
Kentucky.	1,364	1,413	1,679	1,798	271	289
Tennessee.	2,464	2,493	93	102	295	285
Alabama	858	875	1,170	1,214	160	166
Mississippi	838	853	490	516	183	190
West South Central	11,965	12,811	3,042	3,321	519	558
Arkansas.	1,033	1,079	967	1,039	144	158
Louisiana.	1,472	1,523	870	940	224	235
Oklahoma	910	973	1,205	1,342	151	165
Texas	8,550	9,236	(X)	(X)	(X)	(X)
Mountain	4,802	5,122	4,796	5,224	605	626
Montana	(X)	(X)	294	355	55	61
Idaho	364	369	460	500	58	57
Wyoming	119	119	(X)	(X)	(X)	(X)
Colorado	838	887	1,581	1,768	122	133
New Mexico	886	953	441	457	78	73
Arizona	1,503	1,659	1,237	1,330	211	205
Utah	803	837	783	814	81	97
Nevada	289	298	(X)	(X)	(X)	(X)
Pacific	20,813	21,025	20,485	21,026	6,252	6,966
Washington	3,493	3,600	(X)	(X)	1,216	1,260
Oregon	(X)	(X)	2,179	2,345	155	185
California.	16,025	16,145	17,400	17,745	4,630	5,210
Alaska.	(X)	(X)	(X)	(X)	207	226
Hawaii.	1,295	1,280	906	936	44	85

X Not applicable.

Source: National Governors' Association and National Association of State Budget Officers, *The Fiscal Survey of States*, annual, (copyright).

No. 483. State Government Tax Collections and Excise Taxes, 1970 to 1991, and by State, 1991

[Tax collections for **fiscal year ending in year shown;** see text, section 9. Excise tax rates as of **September** 1. Collections include local shares of State-imposed taxes. 1991 tax collections preliminary]

| YEAR, REGION, DIVISION, AND STATE | STATE TAX COLLECTIONS (mil. dol.) | | | | | | | EXCISE TAX RATES | | |
| | Total [1] | Sales and gross receipts | | | | Individual income | Corporation net income | Motor vehicle and operators' licenses | General sales and gross receipts (percent) [2] | Cigarettes (cents per package) | Gasoline (cents per gallon) |
		Total [1]	General sales and gross receipts	Motor fuels	Alcoholic beverages and tobacco products						
1970 [3]	47,962	27,254	14,177	6,283	3,728	9,183	3,738	2,728	(X)	(X)	(X)
1980 [3]	137,075	67,855	43,168	9,722	6,216	37,089	13,321	5,325	(X)	(X)	(X)
1985 [3]	215,893	105,419	69,633	13,344	7,393	63,908	17,631	7,780	(X)	(X)	(X)
1990 [3]	300,721	147,351	99,929	19,379	8,732	96,076	21,751	10,675	(X)	(X)	(X)
1991 [3]	**310,561**	**153,535**	**103,165**	**20,639**	**9,381**	**99,279**	**20,357**	**10,997**	**(X)**	**(X)**	**(X)**
Northeast	71,758	30,994	19,412	2,772	2,133	28,271	5,580	2,125	(X)	(X)	(X)
New England	18,792	8,400	5,419	1,142	580	7,123	1,507	697	(X)	(X)	(X)
Maine	1,558	745	497	130	79	581	76	55	6F&D	37	19
New Hampshire	625	312	(X)	91	55	37	122	57	(X)	25	18
Vermont	685	313	126	52	26	258	27	38	5F&D	18	15
Massachusetts	9,684	2,946	1,909	464	212	5,343	720	305	5F&D	26	21
Rhode Island	1,257	677	448	75	47	429	46	52	7F&D	37	21
Connecticut	4,983	3,407	2,439	330	161	475	516	190	8F&D	40	25
Middle Atlantic	52,966	22,594	13,993	1,630	1,553	21,148	4,073	1,428	(X)	(X)	(X)
New York	28,300	9,686	5,752	507	840	14,482	2,030	592	4 4F&D	39	8
New Jersey	11,645	6,364	4,043	400	357	3,391	1,031	342	7F&D	40	10.5
Pennsylvania	13,021	6,544	4,198	723	356	3,275	1,012	494	6F&D	31	12
Midwest	70,490	33,593	22,323	5,689	1,985	25,476	5,185	2,996	(X)	(X)	(X)
East North Central	49,150	23,419	15,495	3,922	1,367	17,730	3,915	1,923	(X)	(X)	(X)
Ohio	11,556	5,803	3,575	1,035	277	4,217	630	419	4 5F&D	18	21
Indiana	6,182	3,385	2,538	582	143	2,184	310	166	5F&D	15.5	15
Illinois	13,292	6,633	4,164	1,024	383	4,539	941	639	4 6.25	30	19
Michigan	11,103	4,513	3,191	734	383	3,787	1,593	524	4F&D	25	15
Wisconsin	7,017	3,085	2,027	547	181	3,003	441	175	4 5F&D	30	22.2
West North Central	21,340	10,174	6,828	1,767	618	7,746	1,270	1,073	(X)	(X)	(X)
Minnesota	7,051	3,037	1,963	458	209	2,975	458	383	4 6F&D	43	20
Iowa	3,447	1,506	977	331	99	1,344	202	230	4F&D	36	20
Missouri	4,996	2,503	1,863	365	102	1,829	225	208	4 4.225D	13	11
North Dakota	755	420	235	76	23	114	51	41	5F&D	26	17
South Dakota	528	401	248	79	23	(X)	39	39	4D	23	18
Nebraska	1,767	959	624	223	55	603	82	59	4 5F&D	27	23.9
Kansas	2,796	1,348	918	235	107	881	213	113	4 4.25D	24	17
South [3]	91,760	53,434	35,117	7,861	3,563	21,334	4,063	3,357	(X)	(X)	(X)
South Atlantic [3]	49,448	26,440	17,840	3,772	1,738	15,074	2,503	1,574	(X)	(X)	(X)
Delaware	1,165	170	(X)	66	26	462	122	22	(X)	24	19
Maryland	6,401	2,642	1,541	444	88	2,931	255	153	5F&D	16	18.5
Dist. of Col. [3]	2,414	674	452	30	17	616	134	20	6F&D	30	18
Virginia	6,852	2,791	1,559	618	101	3,236	285	267	3.5D	2.5	17.5
West Virginia	2,328	1,236	817	206	40	576	191	87	6D	17	15.5
North Carolina	7,850	3,126	1,690	825	168	3,534	500	256	4D	5	22.3
South Carolina	3,933	2,093	1,437	340	145	1,387	151	85	5D	7	16
Georgia	7,155	3,497	2,657	451	200	2,948	417	94	4D	12	6 7.5
Florida	13,764	10,885	8,139	822	970	(X)	582	610	4 6F&D	33.9	4
East South Central	15,758	9,074	5,833	1,580	472	3,444	973	544	(X)	(X)	(X)
Kentucky	5,043	2,150	1,300	350	67	1,693	319	146	6F&D	3	15
Tennessee	4,311	3,300	2,363	635	142	97	346	174	4 5.5D	13	20
Alabama	3,943	2,023	1,050	290	178	1,174	168	153	4D	16.5	11
Mississippi	2,461	1,601	1,120	305	85	480	140	71	6D	18	18
West South Central	26,554	17,920	11,444	2,509	1,353	2,816	587	1,239	(X)	(X)	(X)
Arkansas	2,366	1,258	877	225	87	794	122	79	4 4.5D	22	18.5
Louisiana	4,309	2,126	1,308	444	126	804	327	86	4D	20	20
Oklahoma	3,862	1,659	964	331	125	1,218	138	288	4 4.5D	23	17
Texas	16,017	12,877	8,295	1,509	1,015	(X)	(X)	786	4 6.25F&D	41	15
West	76,554	35,510	26,315	4,318	1,704	24,199	5,529	2,518	(X)	(X)	(X)
Mountain	16,215	8,676	5,938	1,379	373	4,525	570	678	(X)	(X)	(X)
Montana	818	183	(X)	110	27	283	71	39	(X)	18	20
Idaho	1,205	588	404	112	28	446	60	59	5D	18	22
Wyoming	637	231	178	36	7	(X)	(X)	37	4 3D	12	9
Colorado	3,214	1,367	845	332	81	1,466	115	108	4 3F&D	20	22
New Mexico	2,086	1,250	939	176	35	369	49	108	4 5	15	16.2
Arizona	4,711	2,677	2,006	362	92	1,246	193	217	5 5F&D	18	18
Utah	1,861	943	740	131	40	715	82	48	4 5D	23	19
Nevada	1,683	1,437	826	120	63	(X)	(X)	62	4 5.75F&D	35	16.25
Pacific	60,339	26,834	20,377	2,939	1,331	19,674	4,959	1,840	(X)	(X)	(X)
Washington	7,990	5,994	4,758	585	257	(X)	(X)	213	6.5F&D	34	23
Oregon	3,030	424	(X)	259	94	1,984	149	256	(X)	28	20
California	44,874	18,721	14,340	2,002	884	16,817	4,440	1,329	4 6F&D	35	15
Alaska	1,806	97	(X)	40	29	(X)	254	21	(X)	29	8
Hawaii	2,639	1,598	1,279	53	67	873	116	21	4D	(8)	9 16

X Not applicable. [1] Includes amounts not shown separately. [2] F=food exempt from sales tax; D=prescription drugs exempt from sales tax. [3] DC excluded from total. [4] Local sales tax rates are additional. [5] Food and prescription drugs are subject to a 1 percent State tax. In addition, these items may be subject to a 1 percent local tax. [6] An additional tax is levied at the rate of 3 percent of the retail sales price, less than the current 7.5 cents per gallon tax. [7] Food products subject to a 2 percent State tax. [8] Tax is 40 percent of wholesale price. [9] Combined State and county rates are: Hawaii 24.8 cents; Honolulu 32.5 cents; Kauai 26 cents; and Maui 25 cents.

Source: U.S. Bureau of the Census, *State Government Tax Collections*, series GF, No. 1, annual.

No. 484. State Government Individual Income Taxes: 1991

[As of October 1991. Only basic rates, brackets and exemptions are shown. Local income tax rates, even those mandated by the State, are not included. Taxable income rates and brackets listed below apply to single individuals and married taxpayers filing "combined separate" returns (in States where this is permitted). Alaska, Florida, Nevada, South Dakota, Texas, Washington, and Wyoming have no State income tax]

STATE	Taxable income rates (range in percent)	TAXABLE INCOME BRACKETS		PERSONAL EXEMPTIONS			SIZE OF STANDARD DEDUCTION[1]			Federal income tax deductible[2]
		Lowest: amount under	Highest: amount over	Single	Married-joint return	Dependents	Percent	Single	Married-joint return	
AL [3][4]	2.0-5.0	$500	$3,000	$1,500	$3,000	$300	20	$2,000	$4,000	Yes
AZ [5]	3.8-7.0	10,000	150,000	2,000	4,000	2,000	(X)	3,500	7,000	No
AR [5]	1.0-7.0	3,000	25,000	[6]20	[6]40	[6]20	10	1,000	1,000	No
CA [5]	1.0-11.0	4,394	200,000	[7]60	[7]120	[7]60	(X)	2,262	4,524	No
CO		5% of Federal taxable income								No
CT [3]	1.5	Flat rate		12,000	24,000	-	(X)	(X)	(X)	(X)
DE [3]	3.2-7.7	[8]2,000	40,000	1,250	2,500	1,250	(X)	1,300	1,600	No
DC	6.0-9.5	10,000	20,000	1,370	2,740	1,370	(X)	2,000	2,000	No
GA	1.0-6.0	750	7,000	1,500	3,000	1,500	(X)	2,300	3,000	No
HI	2.0-10.0	1,500	20,500	1,040	2,080	1,040	(X)	1,500	1,900	No
ID	2.0-8.2	1,000	20,000	Same as Federal[9]						No
IL [5]	3.0	Flat rate		1,000	2,000	1,000	(X)	(X)	(X)	No
IN [3]	3.4	Flat rate		1,000	2,000	1,000	(X)	(X)	(X)	No
IA [5]	.4-9.98	1,060	47,700	[7]20	[7]40	[7]15	(X)	1,280	3,160	Yes
KS [3]	[10]4.5-5.95	[10]27,500	[10]27,500	2,000	4,000	2,000	(X)	3,000	5,000	Yes
KY [3]	2.0-6.0	3,000	8,000	[6]20	[6]40	[6]20	(X)	650	650	No
LA	2.0-6.0	10,000	50,000	[11]4,500	[11]9,000	[11]1,000	Combined with exemptions[11]			Yes
ME [3][13]	[12]2.1-9.89	4,150	37,500	2,100	4,200	2,100	(X)	3,400	5,700	No
MD [3]	2.0-5.0	1,000	[3]3,000	1,200	2,400	1,200	15	2,000	4,000	No
MA [15]	6.25-12.0	Flat rate[14]		2,200	4,400	1,000	(X)	(X)	(X)	No
MI [3][15]	4.6	Flat rate		2,100	4,200	2,100	(X)	(X)	(X)	No
MN [5]	6.0-8.5	13,620	44,750	Same as Federal[9]						No
MS	3.0-5.0	5,000	10,000	6,000	9,500	1,500	(X)	2,300	3,400	No
MO [3][16]	1.5-6.0	1,000	9,000	1,200	2,400	400	(X)	Same as Federal[9]		Yes
MT [5]	2.0-11.0	1,600	57,600	1,320	2,640	1,320	20	2,470	4,940	Yes
NE	2.37-6.92	1,800	27,000	1,290	2,580	1,290	(X)	Same as Federal[9]		No
NH		Limited income tax[17]								No
NJ [3]	2.0-7.0	[18]20,000	75,000	1,000	2,000	1,500	(X)	(X)	(X)	No
NM [3]	1.8-8.5	[19]5,200	41,600	Same as Federal[9]						No
NY [3]	[20]4.0-7.875	5,500	13,000	-	-	1,000	(X)	6,000	9,500	No
NC [3]	[21]6.0-7.75	[21]12,750	60,000	2,150	4,300	2,150	(X)	3,000	5,000	No
ND [3]	[22]2.67-12.0	[22]3,000	[22]50,000	Same as Federal[9]						Yes
OH [3]	.743-6.9	5,000	100,000	650	1,300	650	(X)	(X)	(X)	No
OK [5]	[23].5-7.0	[23]1,000	[23]9,950	1,000	2,000	1,000	15	2,000	2,000	[23]Yes
OR [5]	5.0-9.0	2,000	5,000	104	208	104	(X)	1,800	3,000	[24]Yes
PA [3]	2.1	Flat rate		(X)	(X)	(X)	(X)	(X)	(X)	No
RI		27.5% of Federal income tax liability								No
SC [5]	2.5-7.0	2,070	10,350	2,150	4,300	2,150	Same as Federal[9]			No
TN		Limited income tax[25]								
UT	2.55-7.2	750	3,750	1,613	3,226	1,613	Same as Federal[9]			[26]Yes
VT		28 -34% of federal income tax liability								No
VA	2.0-5.75	3,000	17,000	800	1,600	800	(X)	3,000	5,000	No
WV	3.0-6.5	10,000	60,000	2,000	4,000	2,000	(X)	(X)	(X)	No
WI	4.9-6.93	7,500	15,000	-	-	[6]50	(X)	5,200	8,900	No

- Represents zero. X Not applicable. [1] The lesser of either (a) the percentage indicated, multiplied by adjusted gross income (AGI) or (b) the dollar value listed. [2] A State provision that allows the taxpayer to deduct fully the Federal income tax payment; reduces the effective marginal tax rate for persons in the highest State and Federal tax brackets by approximately 30% of the nominal tax rate—the deduction is of a lesser benefit to other taxpayers. [3] States in which one or more local governments levy a local income tax. [4] Social Security (FICA) taxes are included in itemized deductions. [5] Indexed by an inflation factor. [6] Tax credit per dependent. [7] Taxpayers 65 and older receive an additional tax credit. [8] Lowest personal tax rate (3.2%) applies to income in the $2,000-$5,000 bracket. Taxable income under $2,000 is not subject to tax. [9] Personal exemptions on the 1991 return are $2,150 each; standard deduction for single is $3,400 and for those filing joint returns, $5,700. [10] Income below $27,500 taxed at 4.5% rate, income above $27,500 taxed at 5.95% rate. [11] Personal exemption and standard deduction are combined. [12] A 5% surcharge is imposed on tax liabilities arising from the first $75,000 of taxable income for married taxpayers filing jointly ($37,500 for single filers). Any taxpayer with taxable income in excess of these amounts pays a top marginal rate of 8.6% and a 15% surcharge. [13] All counties have a local income tax surcharge of at least 20% of State tax liability; most counties have a surcharge of 50%. Single taxpayers have a minimum standard deduction of $1,500 and married taxpayers a minimum standard deduction of $3,000. [14] Twelve percent (flat rate) imposed on capital gains, interest, and dividends of residents, and Massachusetts business income of nonresidents. All other net income taxed at 6.25%. No tax is imposed on a single person with gross income of $8,000 or less ($12,000 married). [15] Persons who can be claimed as a dependent on someone else's return get an exemption of $1,000. If their AGI is $1,500 or less, they owe no tax. [16] FICA taxes deductible when itemizing deductions. [17] There is a 5% tax on dividend and interest income in excess of $1,200 ($2,400 married). [18] No taxpayer is subject to tax if gross income is $3,000 or less ($1,500 married, filing separately). [19] Several rebates are available for lower income taxpayers. [20] A supplemental tax is imposed on taxpayers with New York adjusted gross income in excess of $100,000. [21] Taxable income brackets are for single taxpayers. Breaking point for higher marginal tax rate varies according to filing status. [22] Applies to the long-form method. As an alternative, taxpayers may use the short-form method where the tax is 14% of the adjusted federal income tax liability. [23] These tax rates and brackets apply to single persons not deducting Federal income tax. For individuals deducting Federal income tax, rates range from .5% of the first $1,000 to 10% on income over $16,000. [24] Federal tax deduction limited to $3,000 ($1,500 married, filing separately). [25] Interest and dividends taxed at 6%. [26] One-half of federal tax liability is deductible.

Source: Advisory Commission on Intergovernmental Relations, Washington, DC, *Significant Features of Fiscal Federalism*, 1992 edition, volume 1.

No. 485. Gross Revenue of Selected States From Parimutuel and Amusement Taxes and Lotteries: 1991

[In millions of dollars, except percent. For fiscal years; see text, section 9]

STATE	Gross revenue	Parimutuel taxes	Amusement taxes [1]	LOTTERY REVENUE			
				Total [2]	Apportionment of funds (percent)		
					Prizes	Administration	Proceeds available from ticket sales
Total [3]	20,497.8	635.3	695.6	19,167.0	54	6	40
Alabama	4.7	4.6	0.1	(X)	(X)	(X)	(X)
Alaska	1.4	-	1.4	(X)	(X)	(X)	(X)
Arizona	225.4	7.9	0.9	216.6	51	10	40
Arkansas	18.3	18.3	-	(X)	(X)	(X)	(X)
California	2,143.6	131.9	-	2,011.8	53	9	39
Colorado	183.2	8.4	0.5	174.4	55	13	32
Connecticut	582.1	58.5	19.8	503.8	56	5	39
Delaware	62.3	0.1	-	62.2	55	4	41
Florida	2,144.4	98.3	2.7	2,043.4	52	6	42
Idaho	52.5	1.0	-	51.5	50	18	31
Illinois	1,465.9	43.3	8.3	1,414.3	55	4	41
Indiana	412.3	-	-	412.3	56	7	37
Iowa	149.8	7.2	-	142.7	61	13	27
Kansas	67.4	-	0.8	66.5	49	17	33
Kentucky	207.0	6.4	0.3	200.3	63	10	27
Louisiana	21.3	19.3	2.0	(X)	(X)	(X)	(X)
Maine	97.7	1.3	-	96.3	54	11	36
Maryland	776.4	3.0	1.7	771.7	53	4	43
Massachusetts	1,511.0	27.5	9.4	1,474.2	64	4	32
Michigan	1,060.8	19.9	-	1,040.8	54	4	41
Minnesota	305.6	2.4	-	303.2	59	19	22
Missouri	203.6	-	-	203.6	57	11	32
Montana	22.7	0.2	-	22.6	52	29	20
Nebraska	7.4	0.6	6.8	(X)	(X)	(X)	(X)
Nevada	355.4	-	355.4	(X)	(X)	(X)	(X)
New Hampshire	110.1	9.8	1.8	98.6	56	10	34
New Jersey	1,428.6	7.2	247.1	1,174.4	52	4	45
New York	2,028.2	78.0	0.8	1,949.4	49	3	48
North Dakota	6.2	-	6.2	(X)	(X)	(X)	(X)
Ohio	1,582.9	13.9	-	1,569.0	54	6	41
Oklahoma	8.4	8.3	(Z)	(X)	(X)	(X)	(X)
Oregon	143.0	4.1	0.1	138.9	57	17	26
Pennsylvania	1,435.1	11.2	0.6	1,423.3	55	3	42
Rhode Island	69.5	10.8	0.2	58.6	53	5	42
South Carolina	16.7	-	16.7	(X)	(X)	(X)	(X)
South Dakota	44.2	0.5	-	43.7	24	9	67
Texas	11.2	-	11.2	(X)	(X)	(X)	(X)
Vermont	44.3	0.2	-	44.1	57	14	29
Virginia	749.1	-	(Z)	749.1	56	9	35
Washington	269.6	10.8	0.1	258.8	48	14	38
West Virginia	85.4	9.6	(Z)	75.8	54	14	33
Wisconsin	382.0	10.3	0.5	371.2	60	8	33

- Represents or rounds to zero. X Not applicable. Z Less than $50,000. [1] Represents nonlicense taxes. [2] Excludes commissions. [3] Includes States whose gross revenues were less than $1,000,000 not shown separately.
Source: U.S. Bureau of the Census, *State Government Finances*, series GF, No. 3, annual.

No. 486. State Government Revenue From Severance Taxes, by State: 1985 to 1991

[In millions of dollars. For fiscal year ending in year shown; see text, section 9. **Severance taxes** are taxes imposed distinctively on the removal of natural products, such as oil, gas, other minerals, timber, and fish; from land or water and measured by value and/or quantity of products removed or sold. See source for information on particular taxes (including changes in tax rates) and additional analytical detail]

STATE	1985	1989	1990	1991	STATE	1985	1989	1990	1991
Total	7,211	4,145	4,692	5,367	Nebraska	4.6	2.3	2.7	3.2
					Nevada [2]	0.1	0.4	22.9	24.0
Alabama	89.6	61.7	59.2	71.7	New Hampshire	0.1	0.1	0.2	0.1
Alaska	1,389.3	698.9	1,103.8	1,284.7	New Mexico	390.8	256.2	292.7	256.4
Arkansas	26.0	14.5	15.6	16.7	North Carolina	1.5	1.5	1.5	1.6
California	19.1	29.3	30.9	35.6	North Dakota	176.3	79.5	79.6	108.0
Colorado	30.4	13.8	14.4	10.5	Ohio	8.2	8.8	9.5	9.5
Florida [1]	173.2	60.6	65.9	71.9	Oklahoma	708.8	371.6	395.3	415.5
Idaho	0.7	0.4	0.5	0.7	Oregon	31.8	37.5	52.2	63.1
Indiana	1.5	1.0	0.8	0.8	South Dakota	4.5	9.2	8.6	8.1
Kansas	111.9	79.7	86.6	99.6	Tennessee	2.8	1.6	1.5	1.4
Kentucky	228.0	195.1	213.9	212.6	Texas	2,175.3	1,172.2	1,087.9	1,355.1
Louisiana	745.2	411.5	429.1	578.4	Utah	49.4	30.6	38.7	39.9
Michigan	75.7	40.5	45.6	48.9	Virginia	1.6	1.5	1.6	1.5
Minnesota	80.0	6.4	2.1	2.2	Washington	36.2	58.9	69.3	70.1
Mississippi	92.9	45.1	45.6	51.2	West Virginia [3]	(X)	135.7	162.7	173.0
Missouri	(Z)	(Z)	(Z)	(Z)	Wisconsin	1.0	0.9	0.9	1.3
Montana	150.7	85.5	95.7	82.9	Wyoming	404.0	231.7	254.0	266.5

X Not applicable. Z Less than $50,000. [1] Beginning 1986, corporate excise tax was reclassified to corporate net income tax. [2] Taxation of mineral proceeds changed via constitutional amendment effective May 24, 1989. [3] Severance tax replaced the business and occupation tax for specified firms engaged in natural resource activities effective July 1, 1987.
Source: U.S. Bureau of the Census, *State Government Tax Collections*, series GF, No. 1, annual.

No. 487. State Government Intergovernmental Expenditures, 1980 to 1991, and by State, 1991

[For fiscal year ending in year shown; see text, section 9]

YEAR AND STATE	Total (mil. dol.)	Per capita [1] (dol.)	Rank	As percent of general expenditure	YEAR AND STATE	Total (mil. dol.)	Per capita [1] (dol.)	Rank	As percent of general expenditure
1980	84,504	374	(X)	37	MI.	6,587	702	7	32
1985	121,571	511	(X)	35	MN	4,883	1102	11	42
1986	131,966	550	(X)	35	MS	1,627	627	30	35
1987	141,279	583	(X)	35	MO	2,671	518	19	32
1988	151,662	620	(X)	35	MT	589	728	43	29
1989	165,506	671	(X)	35	NE	892	560	39	28
1990	175,096	704	(X)	34	NV	1,037	808	37	41
1991, U.S. . . .	186,469	739	(X)	34	NH	257	233	49	15
AL.	2,042	499	25	25	NJ.	6,145	793	9	32
AK	930	1631	38	21	NM	1,552	1002	32	37
AZ	2,575	687	20	36	NY	20,561	1139	2	38
AR	1,259	531	34	29	NC	5,448	809	10	39
CA	36,388	1198	1	48	ND	388	612	45	23
CO	1,956	579	28	32	OH	7,769	710	5	35
CT	1,994	606	27	20	OK	1,932	608	29	31
DE	385	566	46	18	OR	1,600	548	31	25
FL.	8,293	625	3	35	PA	6,897	577	6	30
GA	3,758	567	15	31	RI	448	446	44	16
HI	104	92	50	2	SC	2,007	564	26	26
ID	666	640	41	32	SD	270	384	48	20
IL	6,508	564	8	29	TN	2,460	497	22	29
IN	3,708	661	16	34	TX	8,289	478	4	31
IA	2,117	757	24	33	UT	1,061	599	36	29
KS	1,407	564	33	30	VT	297	525	47	18
KY	2,221	598	23	27	VA	3,493	556	17	28
LA	2,467	580	21	26	WA	4,263	851	14	32
ME	702	568	40	23	WV	1,179	654	35	30
MD	2,682	552	18	25	WI.	4,599	928	12	41
MA	4,497	750	13	25	WY	608	1324	42	37

X Not applicable.   [1] 1980 and 1990 based on enumerated resident population as of April 1; all other years based on estimated resident population as of July 1.
Source: U.S. Bureau of the Census, *Census of Governments, 1987*, vol. 6, No. 4, *Historical Statistics on Governmental Finances and Employment* and *State Government Finances*, series GF, No. 3, annual.

No. 488. Local Government General Revenue, by Source, 1980 to 1991, and by State, 1991

[In millions of dollars. For fiscal year ending in year shown; see text, section 9. Data are estimates subject to sampling variation; see Appendix III and source]

YEAR, DIVISION, AND STATE	Total [1]	INTERGOVERN-MENTAL FROM—		FROM OWN SOURCES		YEAR, DIVISION, AND STATE	Total [1]	INTERGOVERN-MENTAL FROM—		FROM OWN SOURCES	
		Federal	State	Total	Taxes			Federal	State	Total	Taxes
1980	232,453	21,136	81,289	130,027	86,387	DC.	4,758	1,780	(X)	2,978	2,414
1985	354,119	21,724	116,380	216,014	134,473	VA.	11,576	370	3,513	7,692	5,467
1990	512,322	18,449	172,274	321,599	201,130	WV	2,340	71	1,004	1,265	608
1991, U.S.	541,816	19,171	182,733	339,912	214,746	NC	12,097	457	5,129	6,511	3,417
N.E.	24,809	1,004	7,749	16,053	12,758	SC.	5,213	194	1,854	3,165	1,623
ME	1,958	64	654	1,240	952	GA	13,209	421	3,790	8,999	4,745
NH	2,015	48	231	1,735	1,491	FL	29,857	845	8,643	20,369	10,533
VT.	909	29	263	617	518	E.S.C.	21,903	892	7,765	13,247	6,608
MA	11,782	610	4,273	6,899	5,120	KY.	4,872	161	2,070	2,641	1,379
RI	1,532	87	421	1,023	884	TN.	7,386	331	2,083	2,673	2,673
CT.	6,613	166	1,907	4,539	3,793	AL.	5,660	232	2,022	3,407	1,635
M.A.	108,073	2,930	35,010	70,134	51,418	MS	3,985	168	1,590	2,227	921
NY.	67,408	1,700	22,672	43,036	31,952	W.S.C.	46,758	1,392	13,341	32,026	19,439
NJ.	18,524	347	5,519	12,658	9,916	AR	2,795	99	1,166	1,531	800
PA.	22,141	883	6,819	14,440	9,550	LA	7,389	273	2,359	4,757	2,724
E.N.C.	83,917	2,764	28,097	53,056	36,238	OK	4,687	155	1,727	2,805	1,444
OH	20,620	802	7,039	12,780	8,700	TX.	31,887	865	8,089	22,933	14,471
IN	9,829	225	3,700	5,903	3,573	Mt	28,365	1,089	10,040	17,236	9,828
IL	23,098	1,006	6,497	15,595	11,323	MT	1,372	89	559	724	392
MI	19,515	479	6,294	12,742	8,628	ID	1,599	54	658	887	462
WI.	10,855	252	4,567	6,036	4,014	WY	1,323	31	514	778	399
W.N.C.	34,308	1,223	11,324	21,760	12,816	CO	7,576	199	1,917	5,460	3,405
MN	11,885	455	4,845	6,585	3,355	NM	2,732	128	1,392	1,212	580
IA	5,224	159	1,737	3,327	1,995	AZ	7,980	309	2,865	4,806	2,806
MO	7,492	339	2,100	5,052	3,235	UT.	2,790	114	1,013	1,663	973
ND	1,020	47	375	598	346	NV	2,993	165	1,122	1,706	811
SD.	984	49	234	701	519	Pac	104,668	3,279	42,897	58,492	31,889
NE.	3,003	106	764	2,133	1,347	WA	10,682	355	4,315	6,012	3,233
KS.	4,700	68	1,269	3,364	2,019	OR	6,119	357	1,551	4,211	2,863
S.A.	89,014	4,596	26,510	57,909	33,754	CA	84,489	2,392	36,092	46,005	24,470
DE.	982	51	431	501	249	AK	2,281	98	846	1,337	708
MD	8,982	407	2,146	6,429	4,698	HI	1,097	77	93	927	615

X Not applicable.   [1] Excludes duplicative intergovernmental transactions.
Source: U.S. Bureau of the Census, *Census of Governments: 1982*, vol. 6, No. 4; *Historical Statistics on Governmental Finances and Employment*; and *Government Finances*, series GF, No. 5, annual.

No. 489. Number of Local Governments, by Type—States: 1987 and 1992

[Governments in existence in January. Limited to governments actually in existence. Excludes, therefore, a few counties and numerous townships and "incorporated places" existing as areas for which statistics can be presented as to population and other subjects, but lacking any separate organized county, township, or municipal government]

STATE	1987			1992					Special district governments			
	All govern-mental units [1]	School district govern-ments	Special district govern-ments	All govern-mental units [1]	County govern-ments [2]	Munic-ipal govern-ments [2]	Town-ship govern-ments [2]	School district govern-ments	Total [3]	Natural re-sources	Fire pro-tection	Hous-ing and com-munity devel-opment
U.S.	83,186	14,721	29,532	86,743	3,043	19,296	16,666	14,556	33,131	6,564	5,354	3,663
AL.	1,053	129	421	1,134	67	440	-	129	497	68	4	153
AK.	172	-	14	176	12	149	-	-	14	-	-	13
AZ.	576	227	253	598	15	86	-	228	268	71	130	-
AR.	1,396	333	505	1,473	75	489	-	324	584	230	48	130
CA.	4,331	1,098	2,734	4,495	57	460	-	1,080	2,897	489	395	92
CO	1,593	180	1,085	1,826	62	266	-	180	1,317	170	247	96
CT.	477	16	281	575	-	30	149	17	378	1	59	95
DE.	281	19	202	281	3	57	-	19	201	192	-	4
DC.	2	-	1	2	-	1	-	-	1	-	-	-
FL.	965	95	414	1,041	66	390	-	95	489	136	60	107
GA	1,286	186	410	1,321	157	536	-	185	442	38	6	207
HI	18	-	14	21	3	1	-	-	16	16	-	-
ID	1,065	118	705	1,105	44	199	-	116	745	170	130	13
IL	6,627	1,029	2,783	6,810	102	1,282	1,433	997	2,995	928	813	117
IN	2,806	304	836	2,976	91	566	1,008	310	1,000	132	1	62
IA	1,877	451	372	1,904	99	953	-	445	406	242	72	19
KS.	3,803	324	1,387	3,918	105	627	1,355	324	1,506	261	-	207
KY.	1,303	178	569	1,345	119	438	-	177	610	128	93	24
LA	452	66	24	461	61	301	-	66	32	2	-	1
ME	800	88	203	799	16	22	468	88	204	13	-	27
MD	401	-	223	416	23	155	-	-	237	165	-	21
MA	836	82	391	851	12	39	312	86	401	14	15	255
MI.	2,699	590	250	2,727	83	534	1,242	587	280	82	2	-
MN	3,555	441	374	3,616	87	854	1,804	477	393	111	-	172
MS	853	171	307	898	82	294	-	176	345	256	-	57
MO	3,147	561	1,217	3,368	114	933	324	553	1,443	175	208	159
MT	1,243	547	514	1,305	54	128	-	544	578	129	150	18
NE.	3,152	952	1,119	2,997	93	534	452	842	1,075	96	422	137
NV.	197	17	146	212	16	18	-	17	160	33	14	17
NH	524	160	120	531	10	13	221	168	118	10	16	23
NJ.	1,625	551	486	1,625	21	320	247	550	486	17	171	83
NM	331	88	112	494	33	99	-	94	267	220	-	5
NY.	3,302	720	978	3,319	57	620	929	714	998	2	909	-
NC	916	-	321	954	100	518	-	-	335	150	-	104
ND	2,787	310	703	2,795	53	366	1,351	284	740	79	277	38
OH	3,377	621	410	3,534	88	942	1,317	665	521	98	41	59
OK	1,802	636	498	1,822	77	589	-	614	541	102	18	124
OR	1,502	350	876	1,487	36	240	-	340	870	202	268	22
PA.	4,956	515	1,805	5,397	66	1,022	1,548	516	2,244	10	1	88
RI	125	3	83	128	-	8	31	4	84	3	38	26
SC.	707	92	300	705	46	270	-	91	297	48	85	46
SD.	1,762	193	212	1,803	64	310	971	184	273	109	51	42
TN.	904	14	462	960	93	339	-	14	513	117	-	96
TX.	4,415	1,113	1,892	4,919	254	1,171	-	1,101	2,392	432	96	402
UT.	530	40	236	635	29	228	-	40	337	77	20	18
VT.	673	272	95	690	14	50	237	278	110	14	22	9
VA.	430	-	106	461	95	230	-	-	135	44	-	-
WA	1,779	297	1,177	1,796	39	268	-	296	1,192	160	410	51
WV	630	55	290	708	55	231	-	55	366	15	-	36
WI	2,719	433	366	2,752	72	583	1,267	430	399	179	-	188
WY	424	56	250	576	23	97	-	56	399	128	62	-

- Represents zero. [1] Includes the Federal Government and the 50 State governments not shown separately. [2] Includes "town" governments in the six New England States and in Minnesota, New York, and Wisconsin. [3] Includes other types of governments not shown separately.

Source: U.S. Bureau of the Census, Census of Governments: 1987, vol. 1, No. 1, *Government Organization* and *Government Units in 1992.*

No. 490. County, Municipal, and Township Governments, 1987, and Their Populations, 1986, by Population-Size Group

[Number of governments as of **January 1987**. Population estimated as of **July 1, 1986;** estimates do not reflect revisions based on the 1990 Census of Population. Consolidated city-county governments are classified as municipal rather than county governments. Township governments include "towns" in the six New England States, Minnesota, New York, and Wisconsin]

POPULATION-SIZE GROUP	COUNTY GOVERNMENTS			MUNICIPAL GOVERNMENTS			TOWNSHIP GOVERNMENTS		
	Number, 1987	Population, 1986		Number, 1987	Population, 1986		Number, 1987	Population, 1986	
		Number (1,000)	Per- cent		Number (1,000)	Per- cent		Number (1,000)	Per- cent
Total	3,042	217,397	100.0	19,200	149,864	100.0	16,691	52,065	100.0
250,000 or more	167	113,164	52.1	61	44,059	29.4	4	1,744	3.4
100,000 to 249,999	231	35,559	16.4	122	17,882	11.9	29	4,015	7.7
50,000 to 99,999	387	27,279	12.6	285	19,522	13.0	74	4,989	9.6
25,000 to 49,999	616	21,807	10.0	561	19,386	13.0	233	7,832	15.1
10,000 to 24,999	943	15,580	7.2	1,303	20,425	13.6	706	10,899	20.9
5,000 to 9,999	[1]698	[1]4,007	[1]1.9	1,544	10,950	7.3	1,005	7,021	13.5
2,500 to 4,999	(NA)	(NA)	(NA)	2,151	7,646	5.1	1,775	6,215	11.9
1,000 to 2,499	(NA)	(NA)	(NA)	3,804	6,061	4.1	3,722	5,958	11.4
Less than 1,000	(NA)	(NA)	(NA)	9,369	3,933	2.6	9,143	3,392	6.5

NA Not available. [1] For population-size group less than 9,999.

Source: U.S. Bureau of the Census, Census of Governments: 1987, vol. 1, No. 1, Government Organization.

No. 491. County Governments—Summary of Finances, 1980 to 1991, and per Capita, by Population-Size Group, 1991

[For fiscal year ending in year shown; see text, section 9. Represents all counties and their dependent agencies (including dependent school systems where applicable). Size classifications based on 1986 populations; counties distributed according to their 1990 enumerated population]

ITEM	ALL COUNTIES [1] (mil. dol.)			PER CAPITA (dollars), 1991								
				All counties		Counties with **1990** population (1,000) of—						
	1980	1990	1991	Total (3,043) [2]	Per- cent distri- bution	Less than 100 [3] (2,631)	100 to 149.9 (133)	150 to 199.9 (66)	200 to 299.9 (74)	300 to 499.9 (62)	500 to 999.9 (52)	1,000 or more (24)
General revenue	54,573	135,775	137,223	610	100	539	527	544	551	551	733	704
Intergovernmental revenue[4]	24,746	53,953	49,863	222	36	194	195	184	179	184	228	305
From State govern- ments	18,969	49,225	44,535	198	32	174	175	162	157	167	200	274
From Federal government	4,948	2,780	3,058	14	2	12	14	14	14	9	15	16
Tax revenue [4]	18,813	48,750	52,154	232	38	189	184	234	212	227	333	239
Property	14,300	35,723	38,610	172	28	136	135	163	156	169	232	195
Charges and miscella- neous	11,014	33,072	35,207	157	26	157	148	126	160	140	173	160
General expenditure. . . .	54,291	127,626	139,267	619	100	535	542	568	559	562	764	710
Capital outlay.	6,505	13,467	15,332	68	11	53	60	62	63	61	104	71
Current expenditure. . . .	47,786	114,159	123,934	551	89	482	482	506	496	501	660	638
Education	8,412	18,395	19,821	88	14	111	103	120	86	80	126	22
Public welfare	8,591	18,114	20,171	90	14	50	74	71	70	97	97	151
Hospitals.	5,975	13,018	14,164	63	10	65	47	22	56	32	60	95
Health	2,806	8,791	9,362	42	7	32	40	40	42	39	47	53
Highways	5,227	9,415	10,246	46	7	68	42	45	37	38	39	28
Police protection.	2,661	6,693	7,382	33	5	27	28	36	29	28	35	44
Correction	1,759	6,590	7,447	33	5	17	21	25	31	31	46	53
Natural resources	687	1,314	1,371	6	1	5	4	4	3	5	4	11
Parks and recreation . . .	1,094	2,487	2,830	13	2	5	6	10	10	13	27	15
Financial administration .	1,521	3,363	3,613	16	3	17	14	17	17	15	16	16
General control [5]	3,374	9,149	9,948	42	7	51	23	22	24	28	35	58
General public buildings .	1,072	2,182	2,317	10	2	10	10	11	12	10	14	7
Interest on general debt.	1,542	7,976	8,223	37	6	27	30	29	32	30	52	47
Other and unallocable . .	9,570	20,139	22,372	102	16	49	101	116	109	117	167	111
Debt outstanding, year end	32,993	118,680	121,755	541	100	401	433	468	459	480	732	697
Long-term	31,543	115,392	117,041	520	96	395	426	459	449	458	715	643
Short-term.	1,450	3,216	4,714	21	4	6	8	9	10	22	18	54

[1] Data for counties under 100,000 population are estimates subject to sampling variation; see Appendix III and source.
[2] Figures in parentheses represent number of counties in each size group.   [3] Estimated.   [4] Includes other revenues not shown separately.   [5] Includes judicial and legal as well as other administrative expenditures.

Source: U.S. Bureau of the Census, County Government Finances, series GF, No. 8, annual.

No. 492. City Governments—Summary of Finances: 1980 to 1991

[For fiscal year ending in year shown; see text, section 9. Represents all municipalities and their dependent agencies (including dependent school systems where applicable); excludes other local governments overlying city areas. Includes sample-based estimates for cities of less than 50,000; thus subject to sampling variation. See Appendix III and source]

ITEM	TOTAL (mil. dol.)			PER CAPITA [1] (dol.)			PERCENT DISTRIBUTION		
	1980	1990	1991	1980	1990	1991	1980	1990	1991
Revenue	**94,862**	**202,393**	**210,498**	**672**	**1,323**	**1,368**	**100**	**100**	**100**
General revenue	76,056	158,301	164,319	539	1,035	1,068	80	78	78
Intergovernmental revenue	28,270	45,306	46,260	200	296	301	30	22	22
From State governments only	15,939	34,243	34,901	113	224	227	17	17	17
Taxes	31,256	68,788	72,208	222	450	469	33	34	34
Property	16,859	35,024	37,654	119	229	245	18	17	18
Percent of total taxes	54	51	52	(X)	(X)	(X)	(X)	(X)	(X)
Sales and gross receipts	8,208	19,190	19,604	58	125	127	9	10	9
General	5,096	11,645	11,738	36	76	76	5	6	6
Selective	3,112	7,545	7,866	22	49	51	3	4	4
Income, licenses, and other	6,189	14,574	14,954	44	95	97	7	7	7
Charges and miscellaneous	16,530	44,207	45,846	117	289	298	17	22	22
Current charges only	9,875	25,265	27,221	70	165	177	10	13	13
Utility and liquor store revenue	15,719	33,266	34,486	111	217	224	17	16	16
Water system	4,989	11,578	12,067	35	76	78	5	6	6
Electric power system	8,007	17,312	17,926	57	113	117	8	9	9
Gas supply system	1,444	2,335	2,299	10	15	15	2	1	1
Transit system	1,032	1,766	1,924	7	12	13	1	1	1
Liquor stores	247	275	270	2	2	2	-	-	-
Insurance trust revenue	3,088	10,827	11,693	22	71	76	3	5	6
Expenditure	**93,699**	**198,822**	**211,506**	**664**	**1,299**	**1,375**	**100**	**100**	**100**
General expenditure	72,433	153,717	164,226	513	1,005	1,068	77	77	78
Police protection	8,200	18,183	19,388	58	119	126	9	9	9
Fire protection	4,535	9,487	10,045	32	62	65	5	5	5
Highways	5,977	12,106	12,627	42	79	82	6	6	6
Sewerage and sanitation	7,907	16,476	17,603	56	108	114	8	8	8
Public welfare	3,801	7,890	8,941	27	52	58	4	4	4
Education	9,284	17,368	18,793	66	114	122	10	9	9
Libraries	883	1,939	2,119	6	13	14	1	1	1
Health and hospitals	4,457	9,141	9,818	32	60	64	5	5	5
Parks and recreation	3,433	7,584	8,450	24	50	55	4	4	4
Housing and community develop	3,459	7,661	8,286	25	50	54	4	4	4
Airports	1,100	2,878	2,970	8	19	19	1	2	1
Financial administration	1,843	3,895	3,907	13	25	25	2	2	2
General control [2]	2,015	5,274	6,196	14	34	40	2	3	3
General public buildings	1,090	1,767	1,947	8	12	13	1	1	1
Interest on general debt	3,054	11,317	11,370	22	74	74	3	6	5
Other and unallocable	11,395	20,751	21,767	81	136	142	12	10	10
Utility and liquor store expenditure	18,274	38,436	39,728	130	251	258	20	19	19
Water system	5,933	13,579	14,229	42	89	92	6	7	7
Electric power system	8,596	17,490	17,656	61	114	115	9	9	8
Gas supply system	1,334	2,263	2,218	9	15	14	1	1	1
Transit system	2,189	4,855	5,375	16	32	35	2	3	3
Liquor stores	222	250	250	2	2	2	-	-	-
Insurance trust expenditure	2,993	6,669	7,552	21	44	49	3	3	4
By character and object:									
Direct expenditure	91,692	193,933	206,637	650	1,268	1,343	98	98	98
Current operation	66,687	138,818	147,644	473	907	960	71	70	70
Capital outlay	16,285	31,779	34,106	115	208	222	17	16	16
Construction	13,341	22,842	23,977	95	149	156	14	12	11
Land and existing structures [3]	2,944	8,937	10,129	21	58	66	3	5	5
Assistance payments	1,546	2,212	2,549	11	14	17	2	1	1
Interest on debt	4,182	14,455	14,786	30	94	96	5	7	7
Insurance benefits, repayments	2,992	6,669	7,552	21	44	49	3	3	4
Intergovernmental expenditure	2,007	4,890	4,869	14	32	32	2	3	2
Expenditure for salaries and wages [4]	*34,709*	*66,973*	*72,051*	*246*	*438*	*468*	*37*	*34*	*34*
Debt outstanding, year end	**86,019**	**212,919**	**226,554**	**610**	**1,392**	**1,473**	**100**	**100**	**100**
Long-term	82,346	207,487	220,591	584	1,356	1,434	96	98	97
Full faith and credit	39,570	68,510	75,147	280	448	489	46	32	33
Nonguaranteed	42,776	138,977	145,444	303	908	946	50	65	64
Short-term	3,673	5,432	5,963	26	36	39	4	3	3
Net long-term debt outstanding	72,528	139,109	152,880	514	909	994	84	65	67
Long-term debt issued	12,582	27,991	30,166	89	183	196	(X)	(X)	(X)
Long-term debt retired	5,541	17,980	16,245	39	118	106	(X)	(X)	(X)

- Represents or rounds to zero. X Not applicable. [1] 1980 data based on April 1 enumerated resident population; 1990 data based on July 1, 1988, estimated resident population; 1991 data based on April 1, 1990, enumerated population. [2] Includes judicial and legal as well as other governmental administration. [3] Includes equipment. [4] Included in items shown above.

Source: U.S. Bureau of the Census, *City Government Finances*, series GF No. 4, annual.

No. 493. City Governments—Total and per Capita Revenue, Expenditure, and Debt for Largest Cities: 1991

[For fiscal year ending in year show; see text, section 9. Cities ranked by size of population enumerated as of April 1, 1990, except Honolulu and Baton Rouge ranked by county population. Data reflect inclusion of fiscal activity of dependent school systems where applicable. Intercity comparisons should be made with caution due to variations in responsibilities among urban areas; for details see text, section 9, and source]

CITIES RANKED BY 1990 POPULATION	GENERAL REVENUE		INTERGOV REVENUE		TAXES		GENERAL EXPENDITURE		DEBT OUTSTANDING	
	Total (mil. dol.)	Per capita [1] (dol.)	Total (mil. dol.)	Per capita [1] (dol.)	Total (mil. dol.)	Per capita [1] (dol.)	Total (mil. dol.)	Per capita [1] (dol.)	Total (mil. dol.)	Per capita [1] (dol.)
New York City, NY [2]	34,329	4,688	13,446	1,836	16,038	2,190	33,588	4,587	31,161	4,255
Los Angeles, CA	3,688	1,058	505	145	1,853	532	3,373	968	6,959	1,997
Chicago, IL	3,145	1,130	838	301	1,594	573	3,078	1,106	5,939	2,133
Houston, TX	1,340	822	63	39	718	440	1,343	823	3,508	2,151
Philadelphia, PA [2]	2,731	1,722	669	422	1,611	1,016	2,524	1,592	4,029	2,541
San Diego, CA	1,092	984	196	176	372	335	934	841	1,634	1,471
Detroit, MI	1,514	1,473	677	659	528	513	1,584	1,541	1,536	1,495
Dallas, TX	818	812	37	36	493	490	804	799	1,624	1,613
Phoenix, AZ	1,002	1,019	332	338	329	335	1,024	1,041	2,084	2,120
San Antonio, TX	543	581	122	131	207	221	661	706	4,150	4,434
San Jose, CA	633	809	101	129	323	413	668	854	1,076	1,375
Baltimore, MD [2]	1,745	2,371	873	1,186	664	902	1,592	2,163	1,272	1,729
Indianapolis, IN [2]	881	1,204	254	347	392	536	840	1,149	988	1,351
San Francisco, CA [2]	2,524	3,487	794	1,097	943	1,302	2,090	2,887	2,381	3,288
Jacksonville, FL [2]	707	1,113	151	238	241	380	757	1,192	4,227	6,655
Columbus, OH	529	836	102	161	271	428	570	901	1,140	1,802
Milwaukee, WI	565	899	277	441	160	255	558	889	568	904
Memphis, TN	836	1,370	546	894	153	251	837	1,371	756	1,239
Washington, DC [2]	4,424	7,289	1,491	2,456	2,414	3,978	4,342	7,154	3,856	6,354
Boston, MA [2]	1,708	2,974	815	1,418	610	1,063	1,657	2,885	1,005	1,750
Seattle, WA	673	1,304	88	170	339	657	610	1,182	949	1,838
El Paso, TX	263	511	29	57	121	234	273	530	446	866
Cleveland, OH	572	1,130	172	339	275	545	559	1,105	735	1,454
New Orleans, LA [2]	695	1,398	138	278	300	604	681	1,370	1,065	2,144
Nashville-Davidson, TN [2]	945	1,936	208	425	462	947	831	1,702	2,314	4,737
Denver, CO [2]	981	2,097	181	387	388	829	1,030	2,202	2,219	4,746
Austin, TX	535	1,149	45	96	174	374	543	1,167	3,242	6,962
Fort Worth, TX	403	901	53	117	200	448	419	936	915	2,044
Oklahoma City, OK	349	785	25	56	184	415	348	782	483	1,086
Portland, OR	403	921	66	151	219	501	398	909	781	1,787
Kansas City, MO	540	1,240	53	121	329	755	537	1,234	728	1,673
Long Beach, CA	567	1,320	101	235	160	374	567	1,320	778	1,811
Tucson, AZ	367	906	138	339	134	331	344	848	830	2,047
St. Louis, MO [2]	484	1,219	65	165	274	692	500	1,261	757	1,908
Charlotte, NC	389	982	100	253	142	359	417	1,054	762	1,925
Atlanta, GA	647	1,641	127	323	218	552	573	1,454	1,097	2,785
Virginia Beach, VA [2]	722	1,837	280	712	348	884	707	1,798	522	1,328
Albuquerque, NM	438	1,139	140	363	126	328	460	1,195	1,259	3,271
Oakland, CA	500	1,342	81	219	212	571	494	1,327	1,104	2,966
Pittsburgh, PA	368	996	86	233	239	646	359	970	586	1,585
Sacramento, CA	309	837	31	85	157	426	314	851	314	851
Minneapolis, MN	656	1,780	210	570	192	522	703	1,908	2,311	6,273
Tulsa, OK	422	1,148	24	67	164	446	418	1,137	1,582	4,307
Honolulu, HI [2]	775	927	89	106	436	521	821	982	869	1,040
Cincinnati, OH	500	1,372	91	251	224	615	467	1,282	253	694
Miami, FL	304	848	53	147	166	464	312	871	536	1,496
Fresno, CA	221	624	38	107	108	305	186	525	249	704
Omaha, NE	222	662	38	112	138	411	214	638	189	563
Toledo, OH	234	701	46	139	126	377	244	733	195	586
Buffalo, NY	679	2,070	472	1,439	133	404	719	2,190	456	1,389
Wichita, KS	237	779	65	214	76	249	193	636	547	1,799
Santa Ana, CA	178	606	28	97	99	338	190	648	325	1,106
Mesa, AZ	183	636	59	204	45	158	197	685	516	1,793
Colorado Springs, CO	250	890	22	77	84	300	243	865	425	1,511
Tampa, FL	315	1,124	58	207	124	442	344	1,228	432	1,541
Newark, NJ	347	1,261	199	724	88	319	398	1,445	135	491
St. Paul, MN	414	1,522	142	521	93	343	409	1,504	940	3,452
Louisville, KY	224	833	25	93	144	534	243	901	402	1,494
Anaheim, CA	269	1,010	44	165	109	409	306	1,150	710	2,664
Birmingham, AL	249	937	27	102	145	457	310	1,167	803	3,020
Arlington, TX	142	543	10	38	87	331	142	544	401	1,530
Norfolk, VA [2]	563	2,154	216	828	208	797	585	2,238	634	2,427
Las Vegas, NV	219	849	93	361	59	229	210	814	79	307
Corpus Christi, TX	153	596	17	65	68	263	162	629	428	1,663
St. Petersburg, FL	222	932	28	117	90	376	268	1,124	615	2,577
Rochester, NY	573	2,473	338	1,460	132	568	577	2,493	357	1,541
Jersey City, NJ	204	891	89	391	97	426	239	1,044	215	939
Riverside, CA	221	976	42	184	74	328	184	814	673	2,973
Anchorage, AK [2]	672	2,968	285	1,259	180	793	658	2,907	1,144	5,053
Lexington-Fayette, KY [2]	196	870	38	169	101	450	228	1,013	380	1,688
Akron, OH	189	849	32	145	93	415	205	920	128	574
Aurora, CO	161	723	14	64	88	396	148	664	437	1,969
Baton Rouge, LA [2]	379	998	49	130	190	499	396	1,043	775	2,040
Stockton, CA	130	616	18	85	65	307	135	638	214	1,016
Raleigh, NC	169	813	51	247	75	359	177	850	130	626

[1] Based on 1990 enumerated population as of April 1.   [2] Represents, in effect, city-county consolidated government.

Source: U.S. Bureau of the Census, *City Government Finances,* series GF, No. 4, annual.

No. 494. City Governments—Finances, by Population-Size Groups: 1991

[For fiscal year ending in year shown; see text, section 9. Represents all municipalities and their dependent agencies, including dependent school systems where applicable]

ITEM	All cities [1]	CITIES HAVING A 1990 POPULATION OF—						
		Less than 75,000 [1]	75,000 to 99,999	100,000 to 199,999	200,000 to 299,999	300,000 to 499,999	500,000 to 999,999	1,000,000 or more
Number of cities, 1990.	19,296	19,003	98	119	24	28	16	8
Population, 1990 (1,000)	153,827	81,012	8,455	16,390	5,975	11,088	10,954	19,953
FINANCES, 1991 (mil. dol.)								
General revenue [2]	**164,319**	**53,225**	**7,657**	**16,100**	**6,805**	**13,495**	**18,381**	**48,656**
Taxes [2]	72,213	22,348	3,538	6,847	2,610	5,784	7,879	23,207
Property	37,654	13,236	2,273	4,213	1,371	2,552	4,082	9,927
Sales and gross receipts	19,604	6,007	963	1,962	735	2,212	1,781	5,944
Intergovernmental [2]	46,260	12,370	1,791	4,362	2,068	3,005	6,234	16,430
From State governments	34,901	8,999	1,434	3,296	1,507	1,889	3,556	14,220
From Federal Government	7,615	1,592	257	627	341	708	2,194	1,896
Current charges	27,221	10,807	1,349	2,783	1,254	2,709	2,488	5,831
Utility and liquor store revenue	34,486	16,561	1,627	3,734	1,365	2,112	3,605	5,482
General expenditure [2]	**164,226**	**54,061**	**7,809**	**16,768**	**7,128**	**13,373**	**17,860**	**47,227**
Police and fire protection	29,433	11,780	1,652	3,344	1,364	2,563	2,855	5,875
Education	18,793	3,242	1,097	2,524	995	993	2,210	7,732
Sewerage and sanitation	17,603	7,856	782	1,799	756	1,415	1,772	3,223
Highways	12,627	6,221	677	1,347	576	1,056	951	1,799
Health and hospitals	9,818	2,466	289	456	243	563	1,574	4,227
Public welfare	8,941	326	59	241	143	160	1,170	6,842
Housing and community development	8,286	1,892	434	806	496	622	912	3,124
Interest on general debt	11,370	3,416	554	1,244	604	1,650	1,253	2,649
Utility and liquor store expenditure	39,728	17,381	1,822	3,964	1,532	2,354	4,285	8,390
Debt outstanding	**226,554**	**71,467**	**10,831**	**23,009**	**11,505**	**26,850**	**26,503**	**56,389**
Long term	220,591	69,507	10,612	22,582	11,296	26,401	26,025	54,168
Short term	5,963	1,960	219	427	209	449	478	2,221
PERCENT DISTRIBUTION								
General revenue [2]	**100**	**100**	**100**	**100**	**100**	**100**	**100**	**100**
Taxes [2]	44	42	46	43	38	43	43	48
Property	23	25	30	26	20	19	22	20
Sales and gross receipts	12	11	13	12	11	16	10	12
Intergovernmental	28	23	23	27	30	22	34	34
Current charges	17	20	18	17	18	20	14	12
General expenditure [2]	**100**	**100**	**100**	**100**	**100**	**100**	**100**	**100**
Police and fire protection	18	22	21	20	19	19	16	12
Education	11	6	14	15	14	7	12	16
Sewerage and sanitation	11	15	10	11	11	11	10	7
Highways	8	12	9	8	8	8	5	4
Health and hospitals	6	5	4	3	3	4	9	9
Public welfare	5	1	1	1	2	1	7	14
Housing and community development	5	3	6	5	7	5	5	7
Interest on general debt	7	6	7	8	12	12	7	7
PER CAPITA [3] **(dollars)**								
General revenue [2]	**1,068**	**657**	**906**	**982**	**1,139**	**1,217**	**1,678**	**2,439**
Taxes [2]	469	276	418	418	437	522	719	1,163
Property	245	163	269	257	229	230	373	498
Sales and gross receipts	127	74	114	120	123	200	163	298
Intergovernmental [2]	301	153	212	266	346	271	569	823
From State governments	227	111	170	201	252	170	325	713
From Federal Government	50	20	30	38	57	64	200	95
Current charges	177	133	160	170	210	244	227	292
Utility and liquor store revenue	224	204	192	228	229	190	329	275
General expenditure [2]	**1,068**	**667**	**924**	**1,023**	**1,193**	**1,206**	**1,630**	**2,367**
Police and fire protection	191	145	195	204	228	231	261	294
Education	122	40	130	154	166	90	202	388
Sewerage and sanitation	114	97	93	110	126	128	162	162
Highways	82	77	80	82	96	95	87	90
Health and hospitals	64	30	34	28	41	51	144	212
Public welfare	58	4	7	15	24	14	107	343
Housing and community development	54	23	51	49	83	56	83	157
Interest on general debt	74	42	65	76	101	149	114	133
Utility and liquor store expenditure	259	215	216	242	256	212	391	420
Debt outstanding	**1,473**	**882**	**1,281**	**1,404**	**1,926**	**2,421**	**2,420**	**2,826**
Long-term	1,434	858	1,255	1,378	1,891	2,381	2,376	2,715
Short-term	39	24	26	26	35	40	44	111

[1] Data are estimates subject to sampling variation, see Appendix III and source. [2] Includes items not shown separately.
[3] Based on 1990 enumerated resident population as of April 1.

Source: U.S. Bureau of the Census, *City Government Finances*, series GF, No. 4, annual.

No. 495. City Governments—Finances,

[In millions of dollars. For fiscal year ending

CITIES RANKED BY 1990 POPULATION [1]	REVENUE							Utility and liquor store	Debt out-stand-ing
	Total [2]	General revenue							
		Total [2]	Intergovernmental		Taxes				
			From State and local govts.	From Federal Government	Total [2]	Prop-erty	Sales and gross receipts		
New York City, NY [3]	41,061	34,329	12,366	1,080	16,038	7,313	3,518	1,981	31,161
Los Angeles, CA	6,582	3,688	359	145	1,853	689	784	2,128	6,959
Chicago, IL	4,302	3,145	558	279	1,594	591	859	211	5,939
Houston, TX [3]	1,682	1,340	25	38	718	384	316	235	3,508
Philadelphia, PA [3]	3,427	2,731	536	133	1,611	319	33	546	4,029
San Diego, CA	1,285	1,092	122	73	372	146	193	122	1,634
Detroit, MI	1,965	1,514	552	126	528	199	42	144	1,536
Dallas, TX	1,124	818	15	21	493	286	198	115	1,624
Phoenix, AZ	1,157	1,002	240	92	329	119	193	99	2,084
San Antonio, TX	1,417	543	81	41	207	113	88	842	4,150
San Jose, CA [3]	730	633	90	11	323	123	147	7	1,076
Baltimore, MD [3]	1,926	1,745	809	64	664	455	48	48	1,272
Indianapolis, IN [3]	907	881	216	37	392	299	20	8	988
San Francisco, CA [3]	3,146	2,524	671	124	943	492	236	197	2,381
Jacksonville, FL [3]	1,490	707	97	54	241	185	46	718	4,227
Columbus, OH	607	529	59	43	271	21	6	78	1,140
Milwaukee, WI	786	565	234	44	160	148	5	38	568
Memphis, TN	1,775	836	516	30	153	113	30	837	756
Washington, DC [3]	4,743	4,424	77	1,413	2,414	882	674	63	3,856
Boston, MA [3]	1,942	1,708	766	48	610	567	28	64	1,005
Seattle, WA	1,048	673	71	17	339	111	146	327	949
El Paso, TX	328	263	7	22	121	62	55	33	446
Cleveland, OH	735	572	63	108	275	49	3	163	735
New Orleans, LA [3]	775	695	51	87	300	128	137	56	1,065
Nashville-Davidson, TN [3]	1,573	945	196	12	462	264	165	594	2,314
Denver, CO [3]	1,092	981	160	21	388	113	231	82	2,219
Austin, TX	1,101	535	38	7	174	103	68	513	3,242
Fort Worth, TX	530	403	29	23	200	136	60	72	915
Oklahoma City, OK	392	349	11	14	184	29	152	36	483
Portland, OR	450	403	59	7	219	157	31	46	781
Kansas City, MO	662	540	25	28	329	60	146	45	728
Long Beach, CA	729	567	64	37	160	66	78	162	778
Tucson, AZ	449	367	100	38	134	24	99	67	830
St. Louis, MO [3]	603	484	32	33	274	38	107	29	757
Charlotte, NC	431	389	88	12	142	123	8	32	762
Atlanta, GA [3]	768	647	89	39	218	116	70	66	1,097
Virginia Beach, VA [3]	760	722	184	96	348	214	108	37	522
Albuquerque, NM [3]	481	438	114	26	126	45	77	43	1,259
Baton Rouge, LA [3]	417	379	28	22	190	53	126	3	775
Oakland, CA	524	500	64	17	212	107	65	-	1,104
Pittsburgh, PA	402	368	68	19	239	125	27	-	586
Sacramento, CA	357	309	31	1	157	49	93	21	314
Minneapolis, MN	712	656	181	29	192	144	37	22	2,311
Tulsa, OK	477	422	14	11	164	24	136	47	1,582
Honolulu, HI [3]	858	775	42	47	436	343	57	83	869
Cincinnati, OH	647	500	64	28	224	38	4	60	253
Miami, FL	368	304	37	15	166	124	34	-	536
Fresno, CA	285	221	29	9	108	36	52	21	249
Omaha, NE	240	222	32	5	138	64	65	-	189
Toledo, OH	254	234	32	14	126	10	-	20	195
Buffalo, NY	697	679	412	60	133	113	14	18	456
Wichita, KS	281	237	65	-	76	50	23	22	547
Santa Ana, CA	195	178	17	11	99	48	42	17	325
Mesa, AZ	254	183	52	6	45	5	37	71	516
Colorado Springs, CO	507	250	13	9	84	18	65	257	425
Tampa, FL	401	315	41	17	124	56	59	29	432
Newark, NJ	374	347	186	13	88	52	9	26	135
St. Paul, MN	448	414	102	40	93	72	17	22	940
Louisville, KY	283	224	15	10	144	38	1	59	402
Anaheim, CA	505	269	23	21	109	37	61	236	710
Birmingham, AL	283	249	20	7	145	26	46	-	803
Arlington, TX [3]	174	142	1	9	87	50	34	35	401
Norfolk, VA [3]	632	563	156	61	208	121	66	34	634
Las Vegas, NV	219	219	90	3	59	26	13	-	79
Corpus Christi, TX	206	153	7	9	68	37	30	53	428
St. Petersburg, FL	281	222	25	3	90	57	29	44	615
Rochester, NY	596	573	301	37	132	119	11	23	357
Jersey City, NJ	228	204	89	(Z)	97	95	-	23	215
Riverside, CA [3]	373	221	37	5	74	25	41	152	673
Anchorage, AK [3]	789	672	278	6	180	168	5	93	1,144
Lexington-Fayette, KY [3]	214	196	22	16	101	26	5	1	380
Akron, OH	214	189	22	10	93	16	-	25	128
Aurora, CO	187	161	13	1	88	15	68	26	437
Stockton, CA	136	130	12	6	65	17	39	6	214
Raleigh, NC [3]	186	169	46	5	75	65	2	17	130
Richmond, VA [3]	697	561	157	35	262	181	54	120	982
Shreveport, LA	193	169	8	27	88	30	53	16	367
Jackson, MS	156	138	28	9	47	41	4	18	300

- Represents zero. Z Less than $50,000. [1] Based on enumerated resident population as of April 1. [2] Includes items not shown separately. [3] Represents, in effect, city-county consolidated government.

Largest Cities: 1991

in year show; see text, section 9. See headnote, table 493]

Total[2]	General expenditure								Utility and liquor store	CITIES RANKED BY 1990 POPULATION[1]
	Total[2]	Education	Housing and community development	Public welfare	Health and hospitals	Police protection	Fire protection	Highways		
40,777	33,588	7,667	2,534	6,528	3,695	1,785	705	868	4,525	New York City, NY[3]
6,274	3,373	14	231	-	11	652	255	173	2,313	Los Angeles, CA
3,653	3,078	30	119	97	85	570	220	351	185	Chicago, IL
1,623	1,343	-	27	-	53	251	145	92	215	Houston, TX
3,403	2,524	16	85	216	265	327	120	65	599	Philadelphia, PA[3]
1,138	934	-	78	2	1	152	70	57	159	San Diego, CA
2,075	1,584	5	39	-	98	302	84	119	262	Detroit, MI
1,020	804	-	13	-	18	160	77	75	132	Dallas, TX
1,191	1,024	3	59	2	2	147	82	97	146	Phoenix, AZ
1,604	661	6	25	5	17	98	63	50	930	San Antonio, TX
712	668	-	91	-	-	103	51	55	8	San Jose, CA
1,714	1,592	530	58	2	56	152	81	153	40	Baltimore, MD[3]
898	840	(Z)	26	66	156	82	34	42	24	Indianapolis, IN[3]
2,790	2,090	65	59	265	461	153	97	32	488	San Francisco, CA[3]
1,509	757	-	49	13	30	72	55	40	718	Jacksonville, FL[3]
692	570	-	5	-	22	104	61	46	122	Columbus, OH
657	558	-	46	-	9	118	59	45	36	Milwaukee, WI
1,718	837	394	21	-	15	69	57	26	822	Memphis, TN
4,803	4,342	721	244	692	521	267	100	142	96	Washington, DC[3]
2,038	1,657	489	42	127	231	139	87	57	54	Boston, MA[3]
1,020	610	-	28	-	14	85	56	59	355	Seattle, WA
331	273	-	5	-	13	38	22	19	42	El Paso, TX
773	559	-	84	(Z)	16	121	60	42	214	Cleveland, OH
763	681	-	64	20	13	67	29	52	52	New Orleans, LA[3]
1,494	831	262	5	9	69	55	33	26	625	Nashville-Davidson, TN[3]
1,160	1,030	-	11	103	125	90	50	57	109	Denver, CO[3]
990	543	(Z)	3	2	121	49	33	51	425	Austin, TX
518	419	-	5	-	10	56	38	46	77	Fort Worth, TX
408	348	-	7	-	2	59	50	39	55	Oklahoma City, OK
469	398	-	20	-	-	65	48	52	38	Portland, OR
622	537	24	7	(Z)	41	75	40	72	57	Kansas City, MO
759	567	-	57	-	15	91	54	22	191	Long Beach, CA
496	344	-	27	2	1	52	24	50	143	Tucson, AZ
584	500	4	16	4	37	91	26	19	28	St. Louis, MO[3]
474	417	-	14	(Z)	3	38	32	54	52	Charlotte, NC
725	573	17	12	(Z)	-	75	40	27	91	Atlanta, GA
744	707	332	6	14	17	40	20	79	37	Virginia Beach, VA[3]
531	460	-	16	3	6	54	27	35	71	Albuquerque, NM
423	396	-	12	1	28	36	18	22	6	Baton Rouge, LA[3]
538	494	3	57	1	(Z)	72	38	21	-	Oakland, CA
410	359	-	10	(Z)	7	53	41	30	17	Pittsburgh, PA
356	314	(Z)	-	-	2	62	36	26	24	Sacramento, CA
812	703	1	110	-	10	51	29	45	23	Minneapolis, MN
480	418	-	5	-	16	41	34	31	59	Tulsa, OK
1,011	821	-	70	-	10	102	41	45	190	Honolulu, HI[3]
596	467	-	38	-	31	62	48	43	76	Cincinnati, OH
346	312	(Z)	16	1	(Z)	79	44	8	-	Miami, FL
244	186	-	7	-	-	40	19	17	35	Fresno, CA
226	214	(Z)	12	-	1	35	25	26	-	Omaha, NE
267	244	-	11	-	6	45	32	27	23	Toledo, OH
737	719	351	74	-	2	47	35	21	18	Buffalo, NY
232	193	-	-	-	1	24	16	56	23	Wichita, KS
207	190	-	39	-	1	45	22	19	17	Santa Ana, CA
265	197	-	4	(Z)	-	40	19	22	68	Mesa, AZ
527	243	-	4	-	90	32	18	37	284	Colorado Springs, CO
414	344	(Z)	6	-	4	50	20	30	45	Tampa, FL
429	398	(Z)	35	47	8	60	37	8	24	Newark, NJ
451	409	-	59	-	8	34	25	55	27	St. Paul, MN
298	243	-	20	10	7	32	21	15	55	Louisville, KY
546	306	-	63	-	4	47	22	14	240	Anaheim, CA
326	310	6	9	-	2	33	27	36	-	Birmingham, AL
175	142	-	10	1	1	21	15	21	32	Arlington, TX
638	585	200	72	30	29	33	20	23	38	Norfolk, VA[3]
210	210	-	4	(Z)	2	37	24	39	-	Las Vegas, NV
213	162	-	2	-	7	24	12	15	51	Corpus Christi, TX
348	268	-	3	-	4	37	14	25	66	St. Petersburg, FL
593	577	313	38	-	-	36	25	19	16	Rochester, NY
272	239	-	11	7	10	48	35	17	29	Jersey City, NJ
363	184	-	17	-	1	33	14	20	179	Riverside, CA
773	658	288	-	-	29	38	22	45	109	Anchorage, AK[3]
241	228	(Z)	18	7	11	20	19	11	5	Lexington-Fayette, KY[3]
231	205	-	8	-	8	27	20	37	26	Akron, OH
175	148	-	2	-	(Z)	29	16	24	28	Aurora, CO
142	135	-	3	-	1	32	20	8	7	Stockton, CA
213	177	-	5	1	(Z)	20	14	20	36	Raleigh, NC
737	570	188	63	40	17	42	30	15	150	Richmond, VA[3]
193	162	-	13	-	-	17	17	19	24	Shreveport, LA
156	132	-	3	-	-	15	15	12	24	Jackson, MS

Source: U.S. Bureau of the Census, *City Government Finances*, series GF, No. 4, annual.

No. 496. Estimated State and Local Taxes Paid by a Family of Four in Selected Cities, by Income Level: 1991

[Preliminary. Data based on average family of four (two wage earners and two school age children) owning their own home and living in a city where taxes apply. Comprises State and local sales, income, auto, and real estate taxes. For definition of median, see Guide to Tabular Presentation]

CITY	TOTAL TAXES PAID, BY GROSS FAMILY INCOME LEVEL (dol.)				TOTAL TAXES PAID AS PERCENT OF INCOME, BY INCOME LEVEL			
	$25,000	$50,000	$75,000	$100,000	$25,000	$50,000	$75,000	$100,000
Albuquerque, NM	1,798	3,936	6,692	9,399	7.2	7.9	8.9	9.4
Atlanta, GA	2,730	5,349	8,571	11,398	10.9	10.7	11.4	11.4
Baltimore, MD	2,793	5,763	8,933	11,792	11.2	11.5	11.9	11.8
Bridgeport, CT	3,182	6,196	10,485	13,666	12.7	12.4	14.0	13.7
Burlington, VT	1,993	4,197	7,328	10,289	8.0	8.4	9.8	10.3
Charleston, WV	1,895	3,908	6,775	9,382	7.6	7.8	9.0	9.4
Charlotte, NC	2,250	4,805	7,793	10,394	9.0	9.6	10.4	10.4
Chicago, IL	2,443	4,778	7,448	9,674	9.8	9.6	9.9	9.7
Columbus, OH	2,301	4,950	7,993	11,002	9.2	9.9	10.7	11.0
Columbia, SC	2,421	5,455	8,961	11,983	9.7	10.9	11.9	12.0
Des Moines, IA	2,126	4,632	7,416	9,933	8.5	9.3	9.9	9.9
Detroit, MI	3,000	6,159	9,763	13,684	12.0	12.3	13.0	13.7
Honolulu, HI	1,961	4,512	7,548	10,240	7.8	9.0	10.1	10.2
Indianapolis, IN	2,180	3,918	6,529	8,386	8.7	7.8	8.7	8.4
Jackson, MS	1,747	3,930	6,686	9,027	7.0	7.9	8.9	9.0
Louisville, KY	2,420	5,030	7,874	10,506	9.7	10.1	10.5	10.5
Memphis, TN	1,728	2,811	4,286	5,447	6.9	5.6	5.7	5.4
Milwaukee, WI	3,446	7,468	11,630	15,325	13.8	14.9	15.5	15.3
Newark, NJ	2,991	5,935	9,355	12,860	12.0	11.9	12.5	12.9
New York City, NY	2,576	6,427	10,921	14,895	10.3	12.9	14.6	14.9
Virginia Beach, VA	2,099	4,491	7,421	9,866	8.4	9.0	9.9	9.9
Omaha, NE	2,445	4,968	8,360	11,325	9.8	9.9	11.1	11.3
Philadelphia, PA	3,398	6,436	9,511	12,393	13.6	12.9	12.7	12.4
Portland, ME	2,233	5,312	9,691	13,119	8.9	10.6	12.9	13.1
Portland, OR	2,997	6,458	10,261	13,594	12.0	12.9	13.7	13.6
Providence, RI	2,910	5,803	9,723	13,120	11.6	11.6	13.0	13.1
Kansas City, MO	2,025	4,422	6,938	9,176	8.1	8.8	9.3	9.2
Salt Lake City, UT	2,243	4,926	7,784	10,316	9.0	9.9	10.4	10.3
Sioux Falls, SD	2,451	4,456	7,296	9,112	9.8	8.9	9.7	9.1
Washington, DC	2,358	5,159	8,521	11,670	9.4	10.3	11.4	11.7
Median [1]	2,126	4,512	7,491	9,994	8.5	9.0	10.0	10.0

[1] Median of all 51 cities. For complete list of cities, see table 497.

Source: Government of the District of Columbia, Department of Finance and Revenue, *Tax Rates and Tax Burdens in the District of Columbia: A Nationwide Comparison*, annual.

No. 497. Residential Property Tax Rates in Selected Cities: 1991

CITY	EFFECTIVE TAX RATE PER $100		Assessment level (percent)	Nominal rate per $100	CITY	EFFECTIVE TAX RATE PER $100		Assessment level (percent)	Nominal rate per $100
	Rank	Rate				Rank	Rate		
Detroit, MI	1	4.40	49.4	8.92	Burlington, VT	27	1.44	60.7	2.37
Milwaukee, WI	2	3.75	96.7	3.88	Billings, MT	28	1.43	3.9	37.14
Newark, NJ	3	3.14	15.8	19.96	Columbia, SC	29	1.43	4.0	35.64
Des Moines, IA	4	2.66	65.8	4.04	Minneapolis, MN	30	1.39	12.1	11.50
Philadelphia, PA	5	2.64	32.0	8.26	Charlotte, NC	31	1.20	99.6	1.21
Portland, OR	6	2.64	100.0	2.64	Kansas City, MO	32	1.15	19.0	6.03
Manchester, NH	7	2.59	100.0	2.59	Virginia Beach, VA	33	1.09	100.0	1.09
Providence, RI	8	2.55	100.0	2.55	Salt Lake City, UT	34	1.08	60.0	1.80
Bridgeport, CT	9	2.49	39.4	6.33	Seattle, WA	35	1.05	95.5	1.10
Baltimore, MD	10	2.46	40.0	6.16	Oklahoma City, OK	36	1.04	11.0	9.45
Sioux Falls, IA	11	2.36	84.9	2.78	Albuquerque, NM	37	1.04	33.3	3.11
Omaha, NE	12	2.31	88.1	2.63	Las Vegas, NV	38	1.02	35.0	2.92
Jacksonville, FL	13	2.15	100.0	2.15	Denver, CO	39	0.97	14.3	6.73
Chicago, IL	14	2.05	16.0	9.96	Little Rock, AR	40	0.95	18.7	5.08
Houston, TX	15	2.00	100.0	2.00	Louisville, KY	41	0.95	92.0	1.03
Columbus, OH	16	2.00	35.0	5.70	Wilmington, DE	42	0.94	57.7	1.63
Boise City, ID	17	1.92	96.9	1.98	Washington, DC	43	0.91	94.7	0.96
Fargo, ND	18	1.78	4.5	39.59	Boston, MA	44	0.89	100.0	0.89
Wichita, KS	19	1.76	12.0	14.66	New York City, NY	45	0.87	8.0	10.89
Indianapolis, IN	20	1.75	15.0	11.65	Cheyenne, WY	46	0.72	9.5	7.59
Atlanta, GA	21	1.74	30.0	5.81	Birmingham, AL	47	0.70	10.0	6.95
Anchorage, AK	22	1.74	96.0	1.81	Charleston, WV	48	0.65	37.4	1.73
Portland, ME	23	1.74	46.4	3.75	Los Angeles, CA	49	0.63	61.2	1.03
New Orleans, LA	24	1.61	10.0	16.12	Memphis, TN	50	0.54	25.0	2.15
Phoenix, AZ	25	1.47	10.0	14.74	Honolulu, HI	51	0.37	100.0	0.37
Jackson, MS	26	1.47	10.0	14.73					

Source: Government of the District of Columbia, Department of Finance and Revenue, *Tax Rates and Tax Burdens in the District of Columbia: A Nationwide Comparison*, annual.

No. 498. Gross Assessed Value of Property and Government Revenue From Property Taxes: 1975 to 1991

[In billions of dollars, except percent. Data are estimates subject to sampling variation; see Appendix III and source]

ITEM	1975	1979	1981	1984	1986	1987	1988	1989	1990	1991
Gross assessed value of property [1]	1,096	1,679	2,958	4,053	4,818	(NA)	(NA)	6,013	(NA)	(NA)
State assessed	75	114	159	200	243	(NA)	(NA)	257	(NA)	(NA)
Locally assessed	1,022	1,565	2,799	3,853	4,575	(NA)	(NA)	5,756	(NA)	(NA)
Real property	882	1,359	2,515	3,447	4,105	(NA)	(NA)	5,220	(NA)	(NA)
Percent of locally assessed . . .	86	87	90	89	90	(NA)	(NA)	91	(NA)	(NA)
Net assessed value of locally taxable property [2]	1,063	1,607	2,838	3,869	4,620	(NA)	(NA)	5,791	(NA)	(NA)
Percent of gross assessed	97	96	96	96	96	(NA)	(NA)	96	(NA)	(NA)
REVENUE FROM PROPERTY TAXES										
Total revenue, State and local	52	65	75	97	112	121	132	143	156	168
Percent of general revenue	23	19	18	18	17	18	18	18	18	19
Percent of tax revenue	36	32	31	30	30	30	30	30	31	32
Revenue, State governments	2	3	3	4	4	5	5	5	6	6
Percent of general revenue	1	1	1	1	1	1	1	1	1	1
Percent of tax revenue	2	2	2	2	2	2	2	2	2	2
Revenue, local governments	50	63	72	93	107	117	127	137	150	162
Average annual percent change from prior year	[3]6.6	6	7	8	8	9	9	8	9	9
Percent of general revenue	32	27	25	25	25	25	29	29	29	30
Percent of tax revenue	82	78	76	75	74	74	74	74	75	75

NA Not available. [1] Gross assessed value amounts may include prior year components for those States unable to report data for indicated year at time of publication. See sources for definitions of terms and limitations of data. [2] Value subject to local general property taxation, including State-assessed property, after deduction of partial exemptions. [3] Change from 1971.

Source: U.S. Bureau of the Census, *Census of Governments: 1982* and *1987*, vol. 2; *Property Values Subject to Local General Property Taxation in the United States: 1975* and *1979*, series GSS, Nos. 80, 92, and 98; and *Government Finances*, series GF, No. 5, annual.

No. 499. Governmental Employment and Payrolls: 1970 to 1991

[For **October.** Covers both full-time and part-time employees. Except for 1987, local government data are estimates subject to sampling variation; see Appendix III and source. See also *Historical Statistics, Colonial Times to 1970*, series Y 272-307]

TYPE OF GOVERNMENT	1970	1980	1983	1984	1985	1986	1987	1988	1989	1990	1991
EMPLOYEES (1,000)											
Total	13,028	16,213	16,034	16,436	16,690	16,933	17,212	17,588	17,879	18,369	18,554
Federal (civilian) [1]	2,881	2,898	2,875	2,942	3,021	3,019	3,091	3,112	3,114	3,105	3,103
State and local	10,147	13,315	13,159	13,494	13,669	13,913	14,121	14,476	14,765	15,263	15,452
Percent of total	78	82	82	82	82	82	82	82	83	83	83
State	2,755	3,753	3,816	3,898	3,984	4,068	4,116	4,236	4,365	4,503	4,521
Local	7,392	9,562	9,344	9,595	9,685	9,846	10,005	10,240	10,400	10,760	10,930
Counties.	1,229	1,853	1,811	1,872	1,891	1,926	1,963	2,024	2,085	2,167	2,196
Municipalities	2,244	2,561	2,424	2,434	2,467	2,494	2,493	2,570	2,569	2,642	2,662
School districts	3,316	4,270	4,211	4,387	4,416	4,502	4,627	4,679	4,774	4,950	5,045
Townships	330	394	379	386	392	400	393	415	405	418	415
Special districts	275	484	519	516	519	524	529	552	568	585	612
OCTOBER PAYROLLS (mil. dol.)											
Total	8,334	19,935	24,525	26,904	28,945	30,670	32,669	34,203	36,763	39,228	41,237
Federal (civilian) [1]	2,428	5,205	6,301	7,137	7,580	7,561	7,924	7,976	8,636	8,999	9,687
State and local	5,906	14,730	18,224	19,767	21,365	23,109	24,745	26,227	28,127	30,229	31,551
Percent of total	71	74	74	74	74	75	76	77	77	77	77
State	1,612	4,285	5,346	5,815	6,329	6,810	7,263	7,842	8,443	9,083	9,437
Local	4,294	10,445	12,878	13,952	15,036	16,298	17,482	18,385	19,684	21,146	22,113
Counties.	640	1,936	2,387	2,596	2,819	3,009	3,270	3,532	3,855	4,192	4,404
Municipalities	1,361	2,951	3,640	3,872	4,191	4,407	4,770	4,979	5,274	5,564	5,784
School districts	2,032	4,683	5,729	6,283	6,746	7,517	7,961	8,298	8,852	9,551	9,975
Townships	122	330	398	421	446	474	522	556	599	642	664
Special districts	140	546	724	780	834	892	959	1,020	1,104	1,197	1,287

[1] Includes employees outside the United States.

Source: U.S. Bureau of the Census, *1982* and *1987 Census of Governments*, vol. 6, No. 5, *Historical Statistics on Governmental Finances and Employment*, and *Public Employment*, series GE, No. 1, annual.

No. 500. All Governments—Employment and Payroll, by Function: 1991

[For **October.** Covers both full-time and part-time employees. Local government amounts are estimates subject to sampling variation; see Appendix III and source]

FUNCTION	EMPLOYEES (1,000)					OCTOBER PAYROLLS (mil. dol.)				
	Total	Federal (civilian)[1]	State and local			Total	Federal (civilian)[1]	State and local		
			Total	State	Local			Total	State	Local
Total	18,554	3,103	15,452	4,521	10,930	41,237	9,687	31,551	9,437	22,113
National defense[2]	1,019	1,019	(X)	(X)	(X)	3,294	3,294	(X)	(X)	(X)
Postal Service	803	803	(X)	(X)	(X)	2,359	2,359	(X)	(X)	(X)
Space research and technology.	26	26	(X)	(X)	(X)	109	109	(X)	(X)	(X)
Education	8,086	14	8,072	1,999	6,074	15,724	41	15,683	3,551	12,132
Highways	568	4	564	259	305	1,238	18	1,220	613	607
Health and hospitals	1,817	303	1,514	724	790	4,048	876	3,172	1,584	1,587
Public welfare	502	10	492	217	275	982	34	948	464	485
Police protection	844	83	762	87	674	2,253	304	1,948	250	1,699
Fire protection	341	(X)	341	(X)	341	771	(X)	771	(X)	771
Sanitation and sewerage	241	(X)	241	3	238	518	(X)	518	7	510
Parks and recreation.	342	26	315	44	271	489	66	423	69	353
Natural resources.	433	233	200	162	39	1,150	732	418	349	70
Financial administration	508	147	361	149	212	1,119	400	719	343	376
Other government administration.	395	29	366	53	313	646	95	551	126	424
Judicial and legal	359	47	312	112	200	952	172	780	338	442
Other	2,270	359	1,912	712	1,198	5,585	1,187	4,400	1,743	2,657

X Not applicable.   [1] Includes employees outside the United States.   [2] Includes international relations.

Source: U.S. Bureau of the Census, *Public Employment*, series GE, No. 1.

No. 501. State and Local Government—Full-Time Employment and Salary, by Sex and Race/Ethnic Group: 1973 to 1991

[As of June 30. Excludes school systems and educational institutions. Based on reports from State governments (44 in 1973, 48 in 1975 and 1976, 47 in 1977, 45 in 1978, 48 in 1979, 42 in 1980, 49 in 1981, 47 in 1983, 49 in 1984 through 1991) and a sample of county, municipal, township, and special district jurisdictions employing 15 or more nonelected, nonappointed full-time employees. Data for 1982 and 1988 not available. For definition of median, see Guide to Tabular Presentation]

YEAR AND OCCUPATION	EMPLOYMENT (1,000)							MEDIAN ANNUAL SALARY ($1,000)					
	Total	Male	Female	White[1]	Minority			Male	Female	White[1]	Minority		
					Total[2]	Black[1]	Hispanic[3]				Total[1]	Black[2]	Hispanic[3]
1973	3,809	2,486	1,322	3,115	693	523	125	9.6	7.0	8.8	7.5	7.4	7.4
1975	3,899	2,436	1,464	3,102	797	602	147	11.3	8.2	10.2	8.8	8.6	8.9
1976	4,369	2,724	1,645	3,490	880	664	165	11.8	8.6	10.7	9.2	9.1	9.4
1977	4,415	2,737	1,678	3,480	935	705	175	12.4	9.1	11.3	9.7	9.5	9.9
1978	4,447	2,711	1,736	3,481	966	723	181	13.3	9.7	12.0	10.4	10.1	10.7
1979	4,576	2,761	1,816	3,568	1,008	751	192	14.1	10.4	12.8	10.9	10.6	11.4
1980	3,987	2,350	1,637	3,146	842	619	163	15.2	11.4	13.8	11.8	11.5	12.3
1981	4,665	2,740	1,925	3,591	1,074	780	205	17.7	13.1	16.1	13.5	13.3	14.7
1983	4,492	2,674	1,818	3,423	1,069	768	219	20.1	15.3	18.5	15.9	15.6	17.3
1984	4,580	2,700	1,880	3,458	1,121	799	233	21.4	16.2	19.6	17.4	16.5	18.4
1985	4,742	2,789	1,952	3,563	1,179	835	248	22.3	17.3	20.6	18.4	17.5	19.2
1986	4,779	2,797	1,982	3,549	1,230	865	259	23.4	18.1	21.5	19.6	18.7	20.2
1987	4,849	2,818	2,031	3,600	1,249	872	268	24.2	18.9	22.4	20.9	19.3	21.1
1989	5,257	3,030	2,227	3,863	1,394	961	308	26.1	20.6	24.1	22.1	20.7	22.7
1990	5,374	3,071	2,302	3,918	1,456	994	327	27.3	21.8	25.2	23.3	22.0	23.8
1991, total . .	5,459	3,110	2,349	3,965	1,494	1,011	340	28.4	22.7	26.4	23.8	22.7	24.5
Officials/administrators	304	212	93	262	43	28	10	43.7	37.0	41.9	41.2	41.6	41.8
Professionals. . . .	1,227	609	619	957	270	164	53	35.9	30.8	33.1	30.9	30.4	32.5
Technicians. . . .	501	294	207	381	120	74	30	28.9	23.0	26.6	23.6	23.3	25.8
Protective service	913	792	121	697	216	148	56	29.5	24.9	29.1	28.3	27.1	31.9
Paraprofessionals	403	110	292	245	158	126	23	21.3	19.3	20.0	19.6	19.1	20.0
Admin. support . .	976	121	856	683	293	190	75	21.2	19.6	19.6	19.8	19.9	20.1
Skilled craft. . . .	455	436	19	349	106	67	30	26.0	20.7	25.7	25.6	25.0	26.5
Service/maintenance.	679	537	141	390	288	213	62	21.1	16.6	20.4	20.5	18.9	20.7

[1] Non-Hispanic.   [2] Includes other minority groups not shown separately.   [3] Hispanic persons may be of any race.

Source: U.S. Equal Employment Opportunity Commission, *State and Local Government Information Report*, annual.

No. 502. State and Local Government—Employee Benefits: 1990

[In percent. For January through July. Covers full-time employees in State and local governments. Covers only benefits for which the employer pays part or all of the premium or expenses involved, except unpaid maternity and paternity leave, and long-term care insurance. Based on sample survey of establishments. For data on employee benefits in business firms, see table 679]

EMPLOYEE BENEFIT	All em-ploy-ees	Regu-lar em-ploy-ees [1]	Teach-ers [2]	Police and fire fight-ers	EMPLOYEE BENEFIT	All em-ploy-ees	Regu-lar em-ploy-ees [1]	Teach-ers [2]	Police and fire fight-ers
Paid: Vacations	67	87	10	98	Noncontributory	18	17	23	12
Holidays	74	89	33	94	Retirement and savings plans:				
Jury duty leave	94	94	97	82	Defined benefit pension	90	89	94	92
Funeral leave	63	63	62	75	Noncontributory	23	23	23	21
Rest time	56	69	22	49	Defined contribution	9	8	11	13
Military leave	81	83	74	86	Money purchase pension [4]	8	7	10	12
Sick leave	95	93	97	95	Additional benefits:				
Personal leave	39	33	57	25	Child care	9	10	7	7
Lunch time	11	8	13	39	Educational assistance:				
Unpaid: Maternity leave	51	49	57	45	Job related	63	66	53	69
Paternity leave	33	33	35	29	Not job related	18	20	13	16
Insurance plans:					Eldercare	4	4	4	3
Medical	93	93	91	97	Employee assistance				
Dental	62	62	64	63	program	59	64	45	71
Extended care facility	73	73	73	81	Financial counseling	7	8	7	6
Home health care	76	76	76	83	Flexible benefits plans	5	4	7	(Z)
Hospital/room & board	93	93	91	97	In-house infirmary	18	19	17	11
In HMO's [3]	20	20	18	23	Long-term care insurance	2	2	3	(Z)
Inpatient surgery	93	93	91	97	Nonproduction bonuses,				
Mental health care:					cash	35	38	23	59
Inpatient	92	92	90	96	Parking	81	79	87	82
Outpatient	88	89	84	94	Prepaid legal services	8	8	6	17
Vision	32	31	32	35	Recreation facilities	15	13	19	22
Alcohol abuse treatment	92	92	89	96	Reimbursement accounts [5]	31	31	30	26
Drug abuse treatment	91	91	89	95	Relocation allowance	13	16	6	11
Life	88	88	87	89	Severance pay	27	26	28	32
Noncontributory	77	77	78	80	Subsidized commuting	7	8	1	18
Accident/sickness	21	23	16	17	Subsidized meals	7	8	5	4
Noncontributory	17	19	15	14	Travel accident insurance	14	14	13	13
Long-term disability	27	26	32	20	Wellness programs	29	31	22	32

Z Less than 0.5 percent.   [1] Includes all white-collar employees (professional, administrative, technical, clerical) and blue-collar employees (production, service) except those classified as teachers or police and firefighters.   [2] Includes all personnel in primary and secondary schools, junior colleges, and universities whose primary duty is teaching or closely related activities.   [3] For definition, see table 168.   [4] Fixed contributions are periodically placed in an employee's account and payments are based on how much money has accumulated at retirement.   [5] Account which is used throughout the year to pay for plan premiums or to reimburse the employee for benefit related expenses. Account may be financed by employer, employee, or both.

Source: U.S. Bureau of Labor Statistics, *Employee Benefits in State and Local Governments, 1990.*

No. 503. State and Local Government Major Collective Bargaining Agreements—Average Percent Changes in Wage and Compensation Rates Negotiated: 1985 to 1992

[In percent, except as indicated. Averages presented are means; for definition of mean, see Guide to Tabular Presentation]

ITEM	1985	1986	1987	1988	1989	1990	1991	1992
Compensation rate changes, [1] all settlements:								
First year	4.2	6.2	4.9	5.4	5.1	5.1	1.8	0.6
Over life of contract [2]	5.1	6.0	4.8	5.3	4.9	5.1	2.9	1.9
State government: First year	4.8	6.8	4.3	5.3	4.9	4.4	1.9	0.2
Over life of contract [2]	4.8	6.0	4.3	4.9	4.6	3.9	2.8	2.0
Local government: First year	3.7	5.6	5.4	5.5	5.6	5.4	1.6	1.2
Over life of contract [2]	5.5	6.0	5.1	5.8	5.5	5.8	2.9	1.5
Wage rate changes, [3] all settlements:								
First year	4.6	5.7	4.9	5.1	5.1	4.9	2.3	1.1
Over life of contract [2]	5.4	5.7	5.1	5.3	5.1	5.0	2.8	2.1
State government: First year	4.8	6.3	4.1	5.3	5.0	4.7	2.0	0.5
Over life of contract [2]	4.9	6.0	4.2	5.0	4.7	4.2	3.0	2.0
Local government: First year	4.4	5.3	5.3	5.0	5.2	5.0	2.5	1.7
Over life of contract [2]	5.7	5.6	5.5	5.5	5.4	5.2	2.7	2.1
Number of workers affected (mil.) [4]	1.5	0.9	1.3	1.1	1.1	0.9	0.8	1.2
State government	0.5	0.3	0.5	0.4	0.5	0.2	0.4	0.6
Local government	0.9	0.6	0.8	0.7	0.6	0.7	0.4	0.6
Wage rate changes, all agreements [5]	5.7	5.5	4.9	4.7	5.1	4.6	2.6	1.9
Source: Current settlements	4.1	2.4	2.7	2.3	2.5	2.0	0.6	0.8
Prior settlements	1.6	3.0	2.2	2.4	2.6	2.6	1.8	1.1
Cost-of-living adjustments	(Z)	(Z)	(Z)	(Z)	(Z)	(Z)	0.1	(Z)
State government	4.5	5.6	4.3	4.1	4.0	4.7	2.5	1.6
Local government	6.5	5.4	5.3	5.1	5.9	4.6	2.6	2.1

Z Less than .05 percent.   [1] Data relate to settlements of 5,000 workers or more in each calendar year, whether wages and benefits were changed or not.   [2] Average annual rate of change.   [3] Data relate to settlements covering 1,000 workers or more in each calendar year but exclude possible changes in wages under cost-of-living adjustment (COLA) clauses, except increases guaranteed by the contract. Includes all settlements, whether wages were changed or not.   [4] Number of workers covered by settlements reached in each calendar year.   [5] Data relate to all wage changes implemented in the year stemming from settlements reached in the year, deferred from prior-year agreements, and cost-of-living clauses.

Source: U.S. Bureau of Labor Statistics, *Current Wage Developments,* monthly.

No. 504. State and Local Government Employment (Full-Time Equivalent), by Selected Function, 1980 to 1991, and by State, 1991

[In thousands, for October. Full-time equivalent employment not available for 1985. Except 1987, local government amounts are estimates subject to sampling variation; see Appendix III and source]

YEAR, REGION, DIVISION, AND STATE	EDUCATION				HEALTH AND HOSPITALS		HIGHWAYS		POLICE AND FIRE PROTECTION		PUBLIC WELFARE	
	Total		Higher education									
	State	Local	State	Local	State	Local	State	Local	State [1]	Local	State	Local
1980 [2]	1,062.8	4,278.3	947.7	212.1	649.8	646.4	255.3	277.4	75.5	745.0	171.5	200.4
1986 [2]	1,256.4	4,595.3	1,140.4	212.8	652.5	643.9	249.7	284.4	78.5	813.8	186.6	223.1
1987	1,252.3	4,726.7	1,137.4	215.5	659.9	650.4	248.1	266.0	84.8	796.7	190.1	220.6
1988	1,309.5	4,815.5	1,192.7	230.6	673.8	662.6	251.0	288.9	84.3	838.3	198.1	230.9
1989	1,359.8	4,937.5	1,235.1	238.1	682.6	682.8	255.2	285.2	88.7	840.1	200.9	240.6
1990	1,418.5	5,067.5	1,289.2	250.5	695.6	695.6	256.7	293.3	88.1	864.5	212.9	252.1
1991	1,403.8	5,137.4	1,276.5	253.0	690.5	712.0	254.7	291.6	86.7	877.4	212.9	254.5
Northeast	178.5	1,010.6	157.0	35.6	164.6	111.9	51.0	72.1	19.6	199.6	40.5	95.7
New England	62.4	247.2	55.7	-	44.4	13.0	15.9	14.4	5.2	52.9	17.5	6.3
Maine	6.8	29.8	5.5	-	3.0	1.1	2.8	1.6	0.6	3.6	1.9	0.2
New Hampshire	5.5	21.6	5.2	-	1.8	0.3	2.0	1.5	0.3	3.9	1.1	2.3
Vermont	4.7	13.4	4.3	-	1.1	-	1.1	1.0	0.5	1.0	1.1	-
Massachusetts	22.8	103.7	22.0	-	21.6	9.7	4.9	5.6	2.0	27.7	7.6	1.8
Rhode Island	7.0	16.7	6.0	-	2.7	-	1.0	0.9	0.2	4.8	1.5	0.1
Connecticut	15.6	62.0	12.7	-	14.2	1.9	4.1	3.8	1.6	11.9	4.3	1.9
Middle Atlantic	116.1	763.3	101.3	35.6	120.2	98.9	35.1	57.7	14.4	146.7	23.0	89.4
New York	51.9	380.7	46.5	19.5	73.8	81.3	14.2	36.6	5.6	82.3	7.2	59.6
New Jersey	31.3	170.8	24.6	8.6	22.1	11.5	8.3	10.6	3.7	34.3	5.9	11.1
Pennsylvania	32.9	211.9	30.2	7.5	24.3	6.1	12.6	10.5	5.1	30.1	9.9	18.7
Midwest	397.5	1,251.4	377.1	64.9	138.9	159.7	51.0	77.8	17.7	195.4	53.3	66.2
East North Central	268.9	864.2	256.0	44.6	87.0	107.1	28.5	47.5	11.9	145.4	34.4	49.0
Ohio	67.9	203.2	65.5	4.7	23.1	28.2	8.8	12.8	2.2	36.7	2.2	22.6
Indiana	47.1	111.5	42.8	-	12.8	22.8	4.8	6.1	1.8	16.8	5.2	3.0
Illinois	51.5	224.0	48.5	18.7	23.9	23.2	9.0	10.7	4.0	50.4	12.9	7.8
Michigan	65.4	220.3	63.5	11.9	18.0	22.8	4.1	8.8	3.1	25.1	13.0	3.0
Wisconsin	37.0	105.2	35.7	9.3	9.2	10.1	1.8	9.1	0.8	16.4	1.1	12.6
West North Central	128.6	387.2	121.1	20.3	51.9	52.6	22.5	30.3	5.8	50.0	18.9	17.2
Minnesota	34.0	87.7	32.4	2.6	9.6	17.6	5.0	7.6	0.9	10.4	1.7	10.1
Iowa	27.1	67.1	25.9	5.6	9.1	10.0	2.8	5.5	0.8	6.9	3.4	1.8
Missouri	24.2	101.8	22.1	4.7	15.1	11.7	6.3	6.1	1.9	17.4	6.2	2.3
North Dakota	6.6	13.1	6.2	-	2.8	0.2	1.1	1.1	0.2	1.4	0.1	0.8
South Dakota	4.8	16.1	4.3	-	2.1	0.6	1.3	1.5	0.3	1.6	1.1	0.2
Nebraska	11.3	36.8	10.7	2.2	4.8	4.3	2.3	3.2	0.7	4.3	2.8	1.3
Kansas	20.6	64.6	19.5	5.2	8.4	8.2	3.7	5.3	1.0	8.0	3.6	0.7
South	507.2	1,891.6	462.3	73.1	283.2	285.9	102.5	90.1	29.2	298.6	89.5	38.0
South Atlantic	240.4	911.9	220.2	41.6	138.5	146.4	56.4	38.0	17.2	160.9	35.7	28.2
Delaware	6.5	11.7	6.3	-	3.7	0.2	1.3	0.5	0.7	1.5	1.5	-
Maryland	26.9	91.3	24.9	7.5	13.3	3.1	5.1	5.4	2.4	18.6	6.8	1.9
Dist. of Columbia	(X)	12.8	(X)	1.5	(X)	7.6	(X)	0.9	(X)	7.2	(X)	1.9
Virginia	44.3	134.6	41.2	-	25.0	8.7	11.1	4.0	2.3	19.4	2.4	7.0
West Virginia	12.8	40.4	11.2	-	3.2	4.0	5.7	0.9	0.8	3.1	2.3	-
North Carolina	41.5	147.1	38.5	12.5	17.6	28.1	11.7	3.2	3.0	19.6	1.2	11.3
South Carolina	31.3	72.4	28.3	0.0	17.4	13.6	5.2	2.2	1.8	9.7	5.1	0.1
Georgia	36.5	144.7	31.8	0.3	28.5	42.3	6.1	7.3	2.0	24.3	7.6	0.9
Florida	40.7	257.0	38.0	19.8	29.8	38.8	10.2	13.6	4.2	57.5	8.8	5.1
East South Central	111.4	312.8	99.3	5.0	51.6	63.1	18.5	21.4	5.3	45.7	17.9	5.7
Kentucky	31.1	79.8	26.8	-	7.7	8.0	6.3	3.0	1.8	8.6	5.0	0.6
Tennessee	31.2	86.6	29.3	-	14.2	19.3	4.8	6.9	1.5	16.6	5.1	3.6
Alabama	34.0	80.4	29.9	-	18.9	21.1	4.2	7.2	1.1	13.5	4.5	1.2
Mississippi	15.1	65.9	13.3	5.0	10.8	14.7	3.2	4.3	0.9	7.0	3.3	0.3
West South Central	155.5	666.9	142.8	26.5	93.1	76.4	27.6	30.7	6.7	92.0	35.9	4.1
Arkansas	15.7	52.6	13.1	-	8.2	4.3	3.9	3.2	0.9	6.1	3.3	0.3
Louisiana	30.0	94.5	26.5	0.2	23.9	10.3	5.5	5.1	1.1	14.6	6.2	0.8
Oklahoma	25.8	72.6	23.9	-	11.4	8.7	3.6	5.3	1.7	10.7	8.0	0.2
Texas	84.0	447.2	79.3	26.3	49.6	53.1	14.6	17.1	3.0	60.6	18.4	2.8
West	320.5	983.9	280.7	79.5	104.0	154.5	50.0	51.2	20.0	184.0	29.8	54.4
Mountain	110.8	301.2	103.9	11.9	27.9	34.4	17.4	16.4	5.6	46.1	12.2	7.3
Montana	6.2	24.4	5.5	0.2	1.7	1.3	1.8	1.3	0.4	2.0	1.2	0.9
Idaho	7.5	23.2	6.9	0.8	1.3	4.3	1.7	1.4	0.4	2.9	1.2	0.1
Wyoming	3.4	14.8	3.2	1.7	1.5	3.3	1.9	0.8	0.3	1.7	0.6	-
Colorado	29.0	69.6	27.9	1.2	6.0	10.9	3.0	4.7	1.0	11.5	1.4	4.0
New Mexico	17.1	37.5	16.3	1.4	7.0	2.8	2.6	1.7	0.5	5.3	2.0	0.3
Arizona	21.6	76.8	19.1	6.6	3.6	6.7	3.2	4.0	1.7	12.8	2.6	1.4
Utah	19.8	33.3	19.0	-	5.2	1.5	1.8	1.4	0.8	4.4	2.4	0.3
Nevada	6.3	21.5	6.0	-	1.6	3.6	1.4	1.1	0.5	5.5	0.8	0.3
Pacific	209.6	682.6	176.8	67.6	76.1	120.1	32.6	34.8	14.4	137.9	17.6	47.1
Washington	40.6	85.8	39.0	-	14.5	10.9	6.2	5.9	1.8	14.9	7.5	0.7
Oregon	18.3	62.7	17.3	6.2	8.7	5.0	3.8	3.7	1.1	8.3	4.2	0.9
California	113.3	522.6	108.6	61.4	46.2	103.3	18.9	23.5	11.1	108.1	3.2	45.3
Alaska	7.6	11.5	4.1	-	0.9	0.7	2.9	0.7	0.4	1.7	1.6	0.1
Hawaii	30.0	-	7.8	-	5.8	0.2	0.8	1.0	-	4.9	1.1	0.1

- Represents or rounds to zero.   X Not applicable.   [1] For State government, represents police protection only.   [2] Beginning 1986, data not comparable with previous years due to a change in how full-time equivalent is calculated; see text, section 9.

Source: U.S. Bureau of the Census, *1987 Census of Governments,* vol. 3. No. 2, and *Public Employment,* series GE, No. 1, annual.

No. 505. State and Local Government Employment and Average Earnings, by State: 1986 and 1991

[For October]

REGION, DIVISION, AND STATE	TOTAL FULL-TIME EQUIVALENT EMPLOYMENT (1,000)				FULL-TIME EQUIVALENT EMPLOYMENT PER 10,000 POPULATION [2]				AVERAGE OCTOBER EARNINGS [3] (dol.)			
	State		Local [1]		State		Local [1]		State		Local [1]	
	1986	1991	1986	1991	1986	1991	1986	1991	1986	1991	1986	1991
U.S.	3,437	3,829	8,415	9,356	143	152	349	371	2,052	2,565	1,992	2,445
Northeast	704	722	1,823	1,931	141	142	365	379	2,180	2,888	2,137	2,786
New England	212	216	390	411	166	164	306	311	2,053	2,709	2,005	2,629
Maine	20	21	36	43	168	176	307	347	1,714	2,503	1,590	2,075
New Hampshire	18	16	29	35	172	146	285	315	1,759	2,319	1,701	2,333
Vermont	11	13	15	17	211	225	270	308	1,842	2,393	1,653	2,203
Massachusetts	88	88	192	191	151	147	329	318	2,034	2,609	2,082	2,627
Rhode Island	19	20	24	27	195	196	245	269	2,041	2,611	2,215	2,773
Connecticut	56	58	95	98	175	176	297	297	2,336	3,137	2,089	2,966
Middle Atlantic	492	506	1,433	1,520	132	134	384	402	2,233	2,962	2,173	2,828
New York	272	269	810	854	153	149	456	473	2,355	3,032	2,266	2,942
New Jersey	96	113	283	305	126	145	372	393	2,278	3,139	2,146	2,887
Pennsylvania	124	124	340	361	104	104	286	302	1,915	2,642	1,976	2,507
Midwest	812	882	2,016	2,209	137	146	340	367	2,007	2,589	2,008	2,395
East North Central	529	580	1,414	1,541	127	137	339	363	2,189	2,708	2,057	2,470
Ohio	122	141	365	389	113	129	340	356	1,984	2,569	1,911	2,321
Indiana	75	90	182	199	136	160	330	355	2,056	2,466	1,686	2,143
Illinois	130	141	385	425	113	122	333	368	2,165	2,584	2,166	2,545
Michigan	128	139	315	341	140	148	344	364	2,541	3,016	2,329	2,767
Wisconsin	74	69	168	187	154	140	351	377	2,128	2,988	2,035	2,463
West North Central	283	302	602	668	161	170	342	375	1,863	2,365	1,892	2,221
Minnesota	61	66	137	169	145	150	326	381	2,428	3,001	2,318	2,650
Iowa	57	56	101	108	199	199	355	388	2,049	2,681	1,735	2,109
Missouri	66	74	157	171	130	144	310	333	1,621	2,012	1,826	2,101
North Dakota	15	15	22	21	222	237	318	324	1,805	2,196	2,017	2,192
South Dakota	13	13	23	25	177	192	330	350	1,684	2,033	1,441	1,809
Nebraska	29	29	65	69	184	185	407	432	1,509	2,135	1,785	2,153
Kansas	43	49	96	105	174	198	390	422	1,687	2,152	1,700	2,028
South	1,238	1,427	2,887	3,276	149	164	348	377	1,803	2,224	1,711	2,052
South Atlantic	609	719	1,436	1,651	149	162	351	372	1,834	2,261	1,810	2,211
Delaware	17	20	16	17	272	294	252	251	1,795	2,340	1,991	2,405
Maryland	80	87	143	159	178	179	321	327	2,046	2,648	2,233	2,820
District of Columbia	(X)	(X)	51	55	(X)	(X)	817	926	(X)	(X)	2,594	3,142
Virginia	102	114	195	224	177	182	336	357	1,895	2,298	1,787	2,252
West Virginia	34	34	61	58	180	186	317	321	1,574	1,955	1,625	1,899
North Carolina	93	108	216	253	147	160	341	376	1,935	2,386	1,662	2,092
South Carolina	69	81	109	120	204	227	322	336	1,705	2,017	1,558	1,893
Georgia	91	112	239	271	149	169	391	410	1,811	2,054	1,589	1,915
Florida	124	163	407	494	106	123	348	372	1,748	2,272	1,872	2,230
East South Central	247	281	486	549	162	183	320	358	1,706	2,155	1,512	1,824
Kentucky	63	76	102	119	170	206	275	321	1,651	2,268	1,596	1,927
Tennessee	71	76	157	174	147	154	327	351	1,746	2,149	1,554	1,929
Alabama	70	82	131	151	174	199	324	369	1,884	2,216	1,532	1,802
Mississippi	42	47	95	105	161	179	364	407	1,430	1,887	1,324	1,562
West South Central	381	427	964	1,076	142	157	359	396	1,817	2,208	1,665	1,927
Arkansas	39	43	71	80	163	183	299	336	1,724	2,007	1,388	1,700
Louisiana	86	88	151	156	191	206	337	368	1,673	2,123	1,494	1,761
Oklahoma	64	68	109	117	195	214	329	369	1,733	1,945	1,595	1,819
Texas	193	228	633	723	115	131	379	417	1,927	2,355	1,748	2,006
West	684	798	1,689	1,939	135	148	334	359	2,356	2,862	2,321	2,857
Mountain	219	249	457	526	168	177	351	375	1,976	2,402	1,964	2,297
Montana	16	17	29	35	192	207	349	436	1,864	2,256	1,727	1,982
Idaho	18	18	33	39	175	179	332	371	1,766	2,256	1,535	1,880
Wyoming	11	11	25	25	213	243	494	535	1,924	2,086	1,967	2,186
Colorado	50	53	122	133	155	158	375	393	2,368	2,925	2,017	2,391
New Mexico	34	41	49	60	231	263	332	387	1,792	2,255	1,680	1,835
Arizona	43	51	119	138	128	136	358	369	2,126	2,312	2,185	2,579
Utah	33	39	47	52	197	219	283	293	1,654	2,179	1,900	2,143
Nevada	15	19	33	44	154	147	343	341	1,990	2,635	2,140	2,647
Pacific	465	549	1,231	1,413	124	137	328	353	2,530	3,069	2,456	3,069
Washington	79	96	143	170	177	191	320	339	2,231	2,589	2,134	2,622
Oregon	44	55	91	103	163	187	338	353	1,975	2,457	2,018	2,433
California	279	325	965	1,104	104	107	358	363	2,751	3,366	2,535	3,195
Alaska	21	22	20	22	393	392	377	379	3,228	3,442	3,324	3,522
Hawaii	41	51	12	14	389	447	113	120	1,844	2,474	2,010	2,734

X Not applicable. [1] Estimates subject to sampling variation; see Appendix III and source. [2] Based on estimated resident population as of July 1. [3] For full-time employees.

Source: U.S. Bureau of the Census, *Public Employment*, series GE, No. 1, annual.

No. 506. City Government Employment and Payroll: 1970 to 1991

[For **October**. Includes only those school systems operated as part of the city government. Represents average for period of intervals shown; for 1970, change from 1960. 1972, 1977, 1982, and 1987 based on complete census of all cities; other years based on sample and subject to sampling variation. For explanation of average annual percent change, see Guide to Tabular Presentation. Minus sign (-) indicates decrease]

YEAR	ALL EMPLOYEES, FULL-TIME AND PART-TIME (1,000)		OCTOBER PAYROLLS (mil. dol.)		AVERAGE ANNUAL PERCENT CHANGE		FULL-TIME EQUIVALENT EMPLOYMENT [1] (1,000)			AVERAGE EARNINGS IN OCTOBER, FULL-TIME EMPLOYEES (dollars)	
	Total	Excl. education	Total	Excl. education	All employees	October payroll	Total	Education	Other	Education	Other
1970	2,244	1,815	1,361	1,062	2.9	8.8	1,922	359	1,563	838	681
1975	2,506	2,074	2,129	1,725	0.6	7.3	2,142	376	1,767	1,130	972
1980	2,561	2,130	2,942	2,403	0.3	7.8	2,166	360	1,806	1,501	1,338
1981	2,469	2,056	3,222	2,640	-3.6	9.5	2,111	346	1,765	1,686	1,500
1982	2,396	2,015	3,428	2,861	-2.9	6.4	2,088	317	1,770	1,791	1,625
1983	2,423	2,051	3,640	3,059	1.1	6.2	2,060	300	1,760	1,962	1,739
1984	2,434	2,070	3,872	3,268	0.4	6.4	2,090	300	1,790	2,033	1,831
1985	2,467	2,102	4,191	3,536	1.4	8.2	(NA)	(NA)	(NA)	2,117	1,953
1986	2,494	2,126	4,407	3,724	1.1	5.1	2,181	320	1,860	2,186	2,044
1987	2,493	2,110	4,770	3,977	(Z)	8.2	2,223	337	1,885	2,406	2,163
1988	2,570	2,188	4,979	4,136	3.1	4.4	2,251	342	1,910	2,566	2,220
1989	2,569	2,190	5,274	4,405	(Z)	5.9	2,268	341	1,927	2,669	2,343
1990	2,642	2,237	5,564	4,675	2.8	5.5	2,295	338	1,957	2,683	2,449
1991	2,662	2,324	5,784	4,878	0.7	4.0	2,303	338	1,965	2,739	2,547

NA Not available. Z Less than .05 percent. [1] Beginning 1986, data not comparable to previous years due to a change in how full-time equivalent is calculated; see text, section 9.

Source: U.S. Bureau of the Census, *Census of Governments, 1972, 1977, 1982,* and *1987,* vol. 3, No. 2, *Compendium of Public Employment,* and *City Employment,* series GE, No. 2, annual.

No. 507. City Government Employment and Payroll, by Function: 1980 to 1991

[For **October**]

ITEM	EMPLOYEES (1,000)					OCTOBER PAYROLLS (mil. dol.)				
	All cities [1]				Cities with 75,000 population or more, [2] 1991	All cities [1]				Cities with 75,000 population or more, [2] 1991
	1980	1986	1990	1991		1980	1986	1990	1991	
Total	2,561	2,494	2,642	2,662	1,561	2,942	4,407	5,564	5,784	3,930
Full-time	2,071	2,050	2,149	2,153	1,377	2,826	4,231	5,334	5,543	3,806
Part-time	489	445	493	509	184	116	175	229	241	123
Full-time equivalent [3]	2,166	2,181	2,295	2,303	1,447	(X)	(X)	(X)	(X)	(X)
Education [4]	360	320	338	338	270	539	683	889	906	734
Percent of total	17	15	15	15	19	18	15	16	16	19
Instructional staff	266	233	264	262	211	436	553	754	765	622
Others	94	87	74	76	59	102	130	134	141	112
Libraries	34	43	45	45	28	38	63	80	84	56
Public welfare	41	50	57	58	52	47	91	118	116	106
Hospitals	131	124	124	124	79	143	211	282	297	213
Health	35	38	42	41	33	47	73	93	94	79
Highways	121	127	133	132	57	141	223	274	283	139
Police protection	365	391	412	418	232	550	858	1,093	1,162	717
Fire protection	190	194	199	201	118	300	478	579	603	387
Correction	18	25	35	36	34	27	63	90	94	90
Parks and recreation	103	112	121	123	72	116	170	211	222	135
Housing and community development	44	46	46	46	39	57	92	104	108	92
Sewerage	60	67	74	75	38	74	122	155	164	90
Solid waste management	104	92	86	85	49	118	163	174	177	120
Financial administration	69	71	74	75	36	85	130	164	169	90
Judicial, legal, other governmental administration	112	113	129	129	72	147	230	314	326	196
Local utilities [5]	209	226	226	226	144	306	493	594	619	448
Water supply	93	99	101	103	52	116	182	219	230	131
Electric power	44	50	51	51	28	67	119	142	149	92
Transit	66	70	66	66	61	115	178	217	224	217
Other	171	141	154	152	95	208	267	350	360	237

X Not applicable. [1] Data are estimates subject to sampling variation; see Appendix III and source. [2] Based on enumerated resident population as of April 1, 1990. [3] Beginning 1986, data not directly comparable to previous years due to a change in how full-time equivalent is calculated; see text, section 9. [4] City-operated schools and colleges only. [5] Includes gas supply not shown separately.

Source: U.S. Bureau of the Census, *City Employment,* series GE, No. 2, annual.

No. 508. City Government Employment and Payroll—Largest Cities

[For October. See footnote 3, table 495, for those areas representing city-county consolidated governments]

CITIES RANKED BY 1990 POPULATION	TOTAL EMPLOYMENT (1,000)		FULL-TIME EQUIVALENT EMPLOYMENT [1] Total (1,000)		Per 10,000 population [2]		OCTOBER PAYROLL (mil. dol.)		AVERAGE EARNINGS IN OCTOBER, FULL-TIME EMPLOYEES (dol.)	
	1980	1991	1980	1991	1980	1991	1980	1991	1980	1991
New York, NY [3][4]	364	444	319	390	451	532	504	1,122	1,587	2,907
Los Angeles, CA	42	52	41	51	138	147	73	187	1,806	3,658
Chicago, IL	47	[5]42	45	[5]42	150	[5]149	71	[5]125	1,569	[5]3,002
Houston, TX	18	20	18	20	111	123	26	45	1,499	2,214
Philadelphia, PA	33	31	32	31	189	192	51	86	1,611	2,869
San Diego, CA	8	11	7	10	81	93	12	30	1,773	3,017
Detroit, MI	22	20	22	20	179	190	40	50	1,852	2,587
Dallas, TX	14	[6]15	14	[6]15	153	(NA)	20	[6]28	1,465	[6]1,945
Phoenix, AZ	9	12	9	11	114	112	14	33	1,517	3,059
San Antonio, TX	10	14	10	13	128	138	13	30	1,282	2,345
San Jose, CA [3][6]	[7]4	8	[7]4	6	[7]60	79	[7]7	23	[7]1,714	4,017
Baltimore, MD [3][6]	44	[9]30	40	[9]29	514	[9]390	47	[9]72	1,172	[9]2,538
Indianapolis, IN	13	13	12	13	174	176	13	27	1,098	2,147
San Francisco, CA	21	26	21	26	310	358	37	97	1,761	3,728
Jacksonville, FL	[10]11	11	[10]11	10	[10]202	157	[10]11	26	[10]1,031	2,688
Columbus, OH	8	8	7	8	122	119	10	19	1,498	2,495
Milwaukee, WI	10	9	9	9	145	137	15	21	1,631	2,431
Memphis, TN [3]	25	[9]23	22	[9]22	342	[9]364	29	[9]49	1,335	[9]2,230
Washington, DC [3][4]	45	48	42	47	651	768	73	141	1,761	3,046
Boston, MA [9]	[7]28	21	[7]25	21	[7]444	359	[7]35	52	[7]1,398	2,528
Seattle, WA	10	11	9	10	188	197	17	33	1,830	3,344
El Paso, TX	5	5	4	5	104	95	3	10	942	2,049
Cleveland, OH	10	9	9	8	160	160	13	21	1,460	2,666
New Orleans, LA	[11]13	[12]10	[11]13	[12]10	[11]225	[12]194	[11]11	[12]16	[11]919	[12]1,623
Nashville-Davidson, TN [3]	[13]18	17	[13]17	16	[13]374	327	[13]22	40	[13]1,295	2,523
Denver, CO	13	13	12	12	244	258	18	34	1,540	2,807
Austin, TX	8	11	[10]7	10	199	225	10	26	1,515	2,550
Fort Worth, TX	[10]5	5	[10]5	5	[10]120	117	[10]5	11	[10]1,198	2,260
Oklahoma City, OK	5	5	4	4	104	101	6	11	1,323	2,615
Portland, OR	5	5	4	5	115	104	8	11	1,916	3,363
Kansas City, MO	7	6	7	6	145	146	9	16	1,368	2,485
Long Beach, CA	[7]5	[5]6	[7]4	[5]5	[7]122	[5]125	[7]7	[5]18	[7]1,678	[5]3,413
Tucson, AZ	4	5	4	5	124	117	6	12	1,474	2,541
St. Louis, MO	13	7	13	7	280	185	15	17	1,279	2,299
Charlotte, NC	4	5	4	5	125	123	5	11	1,290	2,369
Atlanta, GA	8	8	8	8	187	205	10	19	1,230	2,391
Virginia Beach, VA [3]	10	15	9	13	346	341	11	29	1,204	2,252
Albuquerque, NM	[10]4	7	[10]4	6	[10]119	154	[10]4	12	[10]1,335	2,110
Baton Rouge, LA	[11]4	6	[11]4	6	[11]106	259	[11]3	11	[11]908	2,030
Oakland, CA	4	5	4	4	109	118	7	18	2,011	4,314
Pittsburgh, PA	[16]6	[14]6	[16]6	[14]6	[11]135	[14]152	[16]6	[14]12	[11]1,116	[14]2,240
Sacramento, CA	3	4	3	4	119	105	6	12	1,762	3,379
Minneapolis, MN	6	[12]6	5	[12]6	136	[12]152	9	[12]15	1,821	[12]2,815
Tulsa, OK	[7]4	[5]4	[7]4	[5]4	[7]115	[5]111	[7]5	[5]10	[7]1,184	[5]2,583
Honolulu, HI	9	10	9	[12]6	117	111	12	26	1,401	2,797
Cincinnati, OH	7	[12]7	7	[12]6	174	[12]173	10	[12]16	1,527	[12]2,634
Miami, FL	4	4	4	4	118	105	6	14	1,408	3,753
Fresno, CA	3	3	3	3	115	81	4	9	1,607	3,031
Omaha, NE	3	3	3	3	92	84	5	8	1,684	2,895
Toledo, OH	4	3	3	3	96	88	6	8	1,758	2,881
Buffalo, NY [3]	14	12	13	12	348	356	18	28	1,475	2,502
Wichita, KS	3	[14]3	3	[14]3	111	[14]87	4	[14]5	1,327	[14]2,083
Santa Ana, CA	2	2	1	2	68	59	2	7	1,819	4,457
Mesa, AZ	1	2	1	2	89	80	2	7	1,592	2,896
Colorado Springs, CO	4	6	3	5	158	183	5	14	1,445	2,722
Tampa, FL [15]	5	4	5	4	165	143	5	11	1,178	2,804
Newark, NJ [15]	12	[16]5	12	[16]5	374	[16](NA)	17	[16]8	1,387	[16]1,698
St. Paul, MN	4	4	3	3	125	120	6	11	1,734	3,462
Louisville, KY	6	4	6	4	186	157	7	8	1,358	1,917
Anaheim, CA	2	4	2	3	91	98	3	11	1,616	4,137
Birmingham, AL	4	4	4	4	128	143	5	9	1,333	2,360
Arlington, TX	[10]1	2	[10]1	2	[10]63	74	[10]1	5	[10]1,180	2,721
Norfolk, VA [3]	11	11	10	10	380	384	12	22	1,222	2,295

NA Not available. [1] 1991 data not comparable with 1980 due to a change in how full-time equivalent is calculated. See text, section 9. [2] 1980 based on enumerated resident population as of April 1, 1980; 1991 based on 1990 enumerated resident population as of April 1, 1990. [3] Includes city-operated elementary and secondary schools. [4] Includes city-operated university or college. [5] 1990 data. [6] 1984 data. [7] 1979 data. [8] Prior to 1990, includes data for city operated colleges. [9] Noneducation data are for 1990. [10] 1978 data. [11] 1977 data. [12] 1989 data. [13] Noneducation data are for 1979. [14] 1988 data. [15] Prior to 1983, city-operated elementary and secondary schools. [16] 1983 data.

Source: U.S. Bureau of the Census, *City Employment*, series GE, No. 2, annual; and unpublished data.

Figure 10.1
The Government of the United States
(As of July 1, 1992)

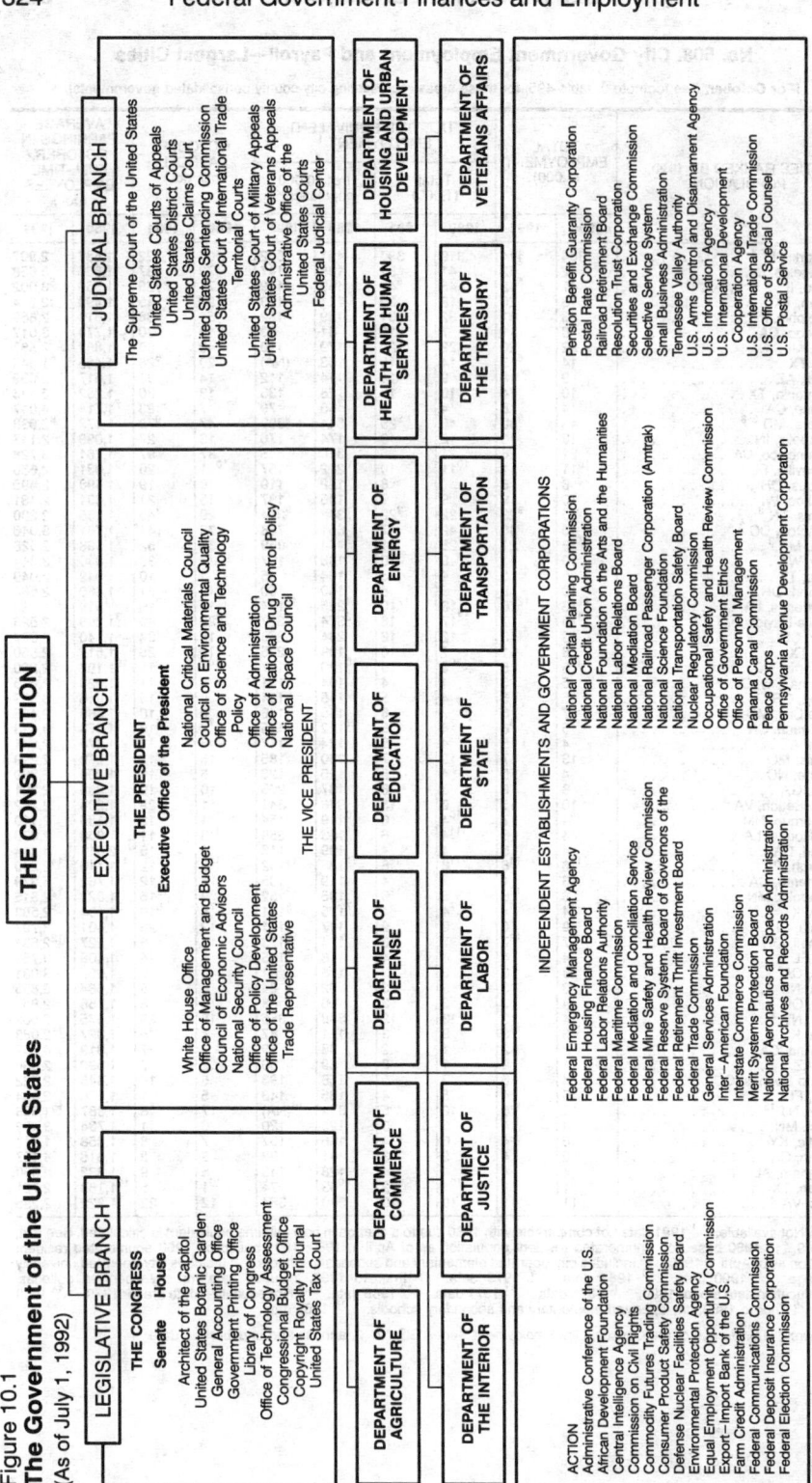

THE CONSTITUTION

LEGISLATIVE BRANCH

THE CONGRESS

Senate   House

Architect of the Capitol
United States Botanic Garden
General Accounting Office
Government Printing Office
Library of Congress
Office of Technology Assessment
Congressional Budget Office
Copyright Royalty Tribunal
United States Tax Court

EXECUTIVE BRANCH

THE PRESIDENT

Executive Office of the President

White House Office
Office of Management and Budget
Council of Economic Advisors
National Security Council
Office of Policy Development
Office of the United States
Trade Representative

National Critical Materials Council
Council on Environmental Quality
Office of Science and Technology
Policy
Office of Administration
Office of National Drug Control Policy
National Space Council

THE VICE PRESIDENT

JUDICIAL BRANCH

The Supreme Court of the United States
United States Courts of Appeals
United States District Courts
United States Claims Court
United States Sentencing Commission
United States Court of International Trade
Territorial Courts
United States Court of Military Appeals
United States Court of Veterans Appeals
Administrative Office of the
United States Courts
Federal Judicial Center

DEPARTMENT OF AGRICULTURE

DEPARTMENT OF COMMERCE

DEPARTMENT OF DEFENSE

DEPARTMENT OF EDUCATION

DEPARTMENT OF ENERGY

DEPARTMENT OF HEALTH AND HUMAN SERVICES

DEPARTMENT OF HOUSING AND URBAN DEVELOPMENT

DEPARTMENT OF THE INTERIOR

DEPARTMENT OF JUSTICE

DEPARTMENT OF LABOR

DEPARTMENT OF STATE

DEPARTMENT OF TRANSPORTATION

DEPARTMENT OF THE TREASURY

DEPARTMENT OF VETERANS AFFAIRS

INDEPENDENT ESTABLISHMENTS AND GOVERNMENT CORPORATIONS

ACTION
Administrative Conference of the U.S.
African Development Foundation
Central Intelligence Agency
Commission on Civil Rights
Commodity Futures Trading Commission
Consumer Product Safety Commission
Defense Nuclear Facilities Safety Board
Environmental Protection Agency
Equal Employment Opportunity Commission
Export–Import Bank of the U.S.
Farm Credit Administration
Federal Communications Commission
Federal Deposit Insurance Corporation
Federal Election Commission

Federal Emergency Management Agency
Federal Housing Finance Board
Federal Labor Relations Authority
Federal Maritime Commission
Federal Mediation and Conciliation Service
Federal Mine Safety and Health Review Commission
Federal Reserve System, Board of Governors of the
Federal Retirement Thrift Investment Board
Federal Trade Commission
General Services Administration
Inter–American Foundation
Interstate Commerce Commission
Merit Systems Protection Board
National Aeronautics and Space Administration
National Archives and Records Administration

National Capital Planning Commission
National Credit Union Administration
National Foundation on the Arts and the Humanities
National Labor Relations Board
National Mediation Board
National Railroad Passenger Corporation (Amtrak)
National Science Foundation
National Transportation Safety Board
Nuclear Regulatory Commission
Occupational Safety and Health Review Commission
Office of Government Ethics
Office of Personnel Management
Panama Canal Commission
Peace Corps
Pennsylvania Avenue Development Corporation

Pension Benefit Guaranty Corporation
Postal Rate Commission
Railroad Retirement Board
Resolution Trust Corporation
Securities and Exchange Commission
Selective Service System
Small Business Administration
Tennessee Valley Authority
U.S. Arms Control and Disarmament Agency
U.S. Information Agency
U.S. International Development
Cooperation Agency
U.S. International Trade Commission
U.S. Office of Special Counsel
U.S. Postal Service

Source: Chart prepared by U.S. Bureau of the Census.

Federal Government Finances and Employment

This section presents statistics relating to the financial structure and the civilian employment of the Federal Government. The fiscal data cover taxes, other receipts, outlays, and debt. The principal sources of fiscal data are *The Budget of the United States Government* and related documents, published annually by the Office of Management and Budget (OMB), and the Department of the Treasury's *United States Government Annual Report* and its *Appendix.* Detailed data on tax returns and collections are published annually by the Internal Revenue Service. Personnel data relating to staffing and payrolls for the various public functions and agencies, to employee characteristics, and to civil service status; are published by the Office of Personnel Management and the Bureau of Labor Statistics. The primary source for data on public lands is *Public Land Statistics,* published annually by the Bureau of Land Management, Department of the Interior. Data on federally owned land and real property are collected by the General Services Administration and presented in its annual *Inventory Report on Real Property Owned by the United States Throughout the World.*

Budget concept.—Under the unified budget concept, all Federal monies are included in one comprehensive budget. These monies comprise both Federal funds and trust funds. Federal funds are derived mainly from taxes and borrowing and are not restricted by law to any specific government purpose. Trust funds, such as the Unemployment Trust Fund, collect certain taxes and other receipts for use in carrying out specific purposes or programs in accordance with the terms of the trust agreement or statute. Fund balances include both cash balances with Treasury and investments in U.S. securities. Part of the balance is obligated, part unobligated. Prior to 1985, the budget totals, under provisions of law, excluded some Federal activities—including the Federal Financing Bank, the Postal Service, the Synthetic Fuels Corporation, and the lending activities of

In Brief	
	1993
Gross Federal debt	$4,410 bil.
Net interest on the public debt	$296 bil.

the Rural Electrification Administration. The Balanced Budget and Emergency Deficit Control Act of 1985 (P.L.99-177) repealed the off-budget status of these entities and placed social security (Federal old-age and survivors insurance and the Federal disability insurance trust funds) off-budget. Though social security is now off-budget and, by law, excluded from coverage of the congressional budget resolutions, it continues to be a Federal program.

Receipts arising from the Government's sovereign powers are reported as governmental receipts; all other receipts, i.e., from business-type or market-oriented activities, are offset against outlays. Outlays are reported on a checks-issued (net) basis (i.e., outlays are recorded at the time the checks to pay bills are issued).

Debt concept.—For most of U.S. history, the total debt consisted of debt borrowed by the Treasury (i.e., public debt). The present debt series includes both public debt and agency debt. The *gross Federal debt* includes money borrowed by the Treasury and by various Federal agencies; it is the broadest generally used measure of the Federal debt. *Total public debt* is covered by a statutory debt limitation and includes only borrowing by the Treasury.

Treasury receipts and outlays.—All receipts of the Government, with a few exceptions, are deposited to the credit of the U.S. Treasury regardless of ultimate disposition. Under the Constitution, no money may be withdrawn from the Treasury unless appropriated by the Congress.

The day-to-day cash operations of the Federal Government clearing through the accounts of the U.S. Treasury are reported in the *Daily Treasury Statement.* Extensive detail on the public debt is published in the *Monthly Statement of the Public Debt of the United States.*

Budget receipts such as taxes, customs duties, and outlays represented by checks issued and cash payments made by disbursing officers as well as government agencies are reported in the *Daily Treasury Statement of Receipts and Outlays of the United States Government* and in the Treasury's *United States Government Annual Report* and its *Appendix.* These deposits in and payments from accounts maintained by Government agencies are on the same basis as the unified budget.

The quarterly *Treasury Bulletin* contains data on fiscal operations and related Treasury activities, including financial statements of Government corporations and other business-type activities.

Income tax returns and tax collections.—Tax data are compiled by the Internal Revenue Service of the Treasury Department. The *Annual Report of the Commissioner and Chief Counsel of the Internal Revenue Service* gives a detailed account of tax collections by kind of tax and by regions, districts, and States. The agency's annual *Statistics of Income* reports present detailed data from individual income tax returns and corporation income tax returns. The quarterly *Statistics of Income Bulletin* has, in general, replaced the supplemental *Statistics of Income* publications which presented data on such diverse subjects as tax-exempt organizations, unincorporated businesses, fiduciary income tax and estate tax returns, sales of capital assets by individuals, international income and taxes reported by corporations and individuals, and estate tax wealth.

Employment and payrolls.—The Office of Personnel Management collects employment and payroll data from all departments and agencies of the Federal Government, except the Central Intelligence Agency, the National Security Agency, and the Defense Intelligence Agency. Employment figures represent the number of persons who occupied civilian positions at the end of the report month shown and who are paid for personal services rendered for the Federal Government, regardless of the nature of appointment or method of payment.

Federal payrolls include all payments for personal services rendered during the report month and payments for accumulated annual leave of employees who separate from the service. Since most Federal employees are paid on a biweekly basis, the calendar month earnings are partially estimated on the basis of the number of work days in each month where payroll periods overlap.

Federal employment and payroll figures are published by the Office of Personnel Management in its *Federal Civilian Workforce Statistics—Employment and Trends.* It also publishes biennial employment data for minority groups, data on occupations of white- and blue-collar workers, and data on employment by geographic area; reports on salary and wage distribution of Federal employees are published annually. General schedule is primarily white-collar; wage system primarily blue-collar. Data on Federal employment are also issued by the Bureau of Labor Statistics in its *Monthly Labor Review* and in *Employment and Earnings* and by the Bureau of the Census in its annual *Public Employment.*

Public lands.—These data refer to transactions which involve the disposal, under public land laws, of Federal public lands to non-Federal owners. In general, original entries and selections are applications to secure title to public lands which have been accepted as properly filed (i.e., allowed). Some types of applications, however, are not reported until issuance of the final certificate, which passes equitable title to the land to the applicant. Applications are approved when full compliance with the requirements of the laws is shown and become final entries (perfected entries) upon issuance of a final certificate. Patents are Government deeds which pass legal title to the land to the applicant. Certifications are issued in lieu of patents in connection with certain State selections.

Historical statistics.—Tabular headnotes provide cross-references, where applicable, to *Historical Statistics of the United States, Colonial Times to 1970.* See Appendix IV.

Figure 10.2
Federal Budget—Receipts, Outlays, and Deficit: 1970 to 1993

Billions of dollars

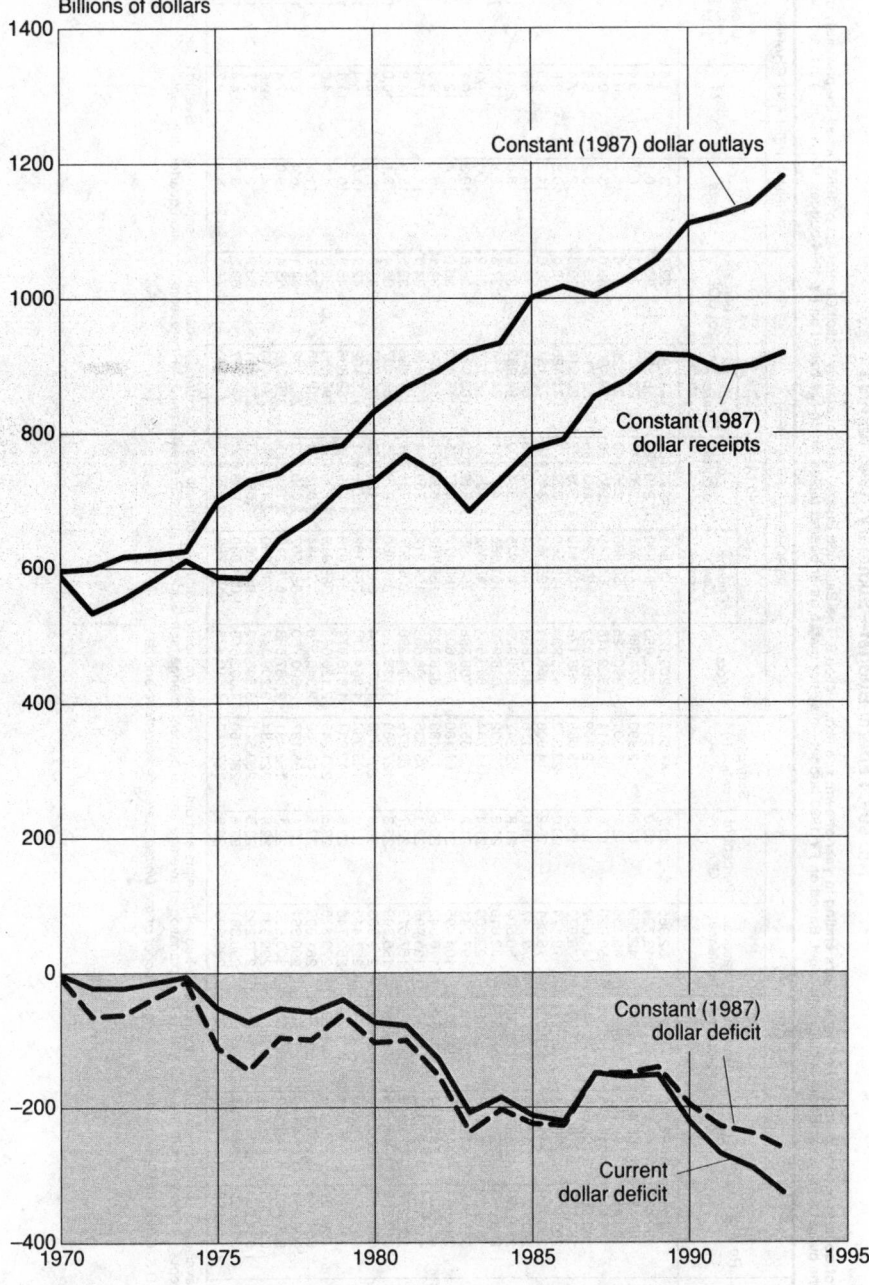

Note: Data for 1993 is projected.
Source: Chart prepared by U.S. Bureau of the Census. For data, see tables 509 and 513.

No. 509. Federal Budget—Summary: 1945 to 1993

[In millions of dollars, except percent. For fiscal years ending in year shown; see text, section 9. The Balanced Budget and Emergency Deficit Control Act of 1985 put all the previously off-budget Federal entities into the budget and moved Social Security off-budget. Based on FY 1993 budget—may not match other budget tables which are based on FY 1994 budget. Minus sign (-) indicates deficit or decrease]

YEAR	Receipts [1]	OUTLAYS [1] Total	Human resources	National defense	Percent of GDP [2]	Surplus or deficit (-)	GROSS FEDERAL DEBT [3] Total	Held by—Federal Gov't Account	The public	Federal Reserve System	As percent of GDP [2]	ANNUAL PERCENT CHANGE [4] Receipts	Outlays	Gross Federal debt [3]	Outlays, off-budget
1945	45,159	92,712	1,859	82,965	43.7	-47,553	260,123	24,941	235,182	21,792	122.7	3.2	1.5	27.5	143
1950	39,443	42,562	14,221	13,724	16.0	-3,119	256,853	37,830	219,023	18,331	96.6	0.1	9.6	1.7	524
1955	65,451	68,444	14,908	42,729	17.8	-2,993	274,366	47,751	226,616	23,607	71.3	-6.0	-3.4	1.3	3,983
1960	92,492	92,191	26,184	48,130	18.2	301	290,525	53,686	236,840	26,523	57.6	16.7	0.1	1.1	10,850
1965	116,817	118,228	36,576	50,620	17.6	-1,411	322,318	61,540	260,778	39,100	48.0	3.7	-0.3	2.0	16,529
1970	192,807	195,649	75,349	81,692	19.8	-2,842	380,921	97,723	283,198	65,518	38.7	3.2	6.5	4.1	27,607
1971	187,139	210,172	91,901	78,872	19.9	-23,033	408,176	105,140	303,037	71,426	38.8	2.9	7.4	7.2	32,826
1972	207,309	230,681	107,211	79,174	20.0	-23,373	435,936	113,559	322,377	75,181	38.0	10.8	9.8	6.8	36,857
1973	230,799	245,707	119,522	76,681	19.2	-14,908	466,291	125,381	340,910	80,648	36.6	11.3	6.5	7.0	45,589
1974	263,224	269,359	135,783	79,347	19.0	-6,135	483,893	140,194	343,699	84,993	35.9	14.0	9.6	3.8	52,089
1975	279,090	332,332	173,245	86,509	21.8	-53,242	541,925	147,225	394,700	94,714	34.5	6.0	23.4	12.0	60,440
1976	298,060	371,779	203,594	89,619	21.9	-73,732	628,970	151,566	477,404	96,702	35.9	6.8	11.9	16.1	69,609
1976 [5]	81,232	95,973	52,065	22,269	21.4	-14,744	643,561	148,052	495,509	105,004	37.3	(X)	(X)	(X)	19,421
1977	355,559	409,203	221,895	97,241	21.2	-53,659	706,398	157,295	549,103	115,480	36.2	19.3	10.1	12.3	80,716
1978	399,561	458,729	242,329	104,495	21.1	-59,186	776,602	169,477	607,125	115,594	36.0	12.4	12.1	9.9	89,657
1979	463,302	503,464	267,574	116,342	20.6	-40,183	828,923	189,162	639,761	120,846	36.8	16.0	9.8	6.7	99,978
1980	517,112	590,920	313,374	133,995	22.1	-73,835	908,503	199,212	709,291	124,466	34.1	11.6	17.4	9.6	114,329
1981	599,272	678,249	362,022	157,513	22.7	-78,976	994,298	209,507	784,791	134,497	33.5	15.9	14.8	9.4	135,196
1982	617,766	745,755	388,681	185,309	23.8	-127,989	1,136,798	217,560	919,238	155,122	36.4	3.1	10.0	14.3	131,404
1983	600,562	808,380	426,003	209,903	24.3	-207,818	1,371,164	240,114	1,131,049	155,122	41.3	-2.8	8.4	20.6	147,108
1984	666,457	851,846	432,042	227,413	23.0	-185,388	1,564,110	264,159	1,299,951	169,806	42.3	11.0	5.4	14.1	165,813
1985	734,057	946,391	471,822	252,748	23.0	-212,334	1,816,974	317,612	1,499,362	190,855	45.8	10.1	11.1	16.1	176,807
1986	769,091	990,336	481,594	273,375	22.5	-221,245	2,120,082	383,919	1,736,163	212,040	50.3	4.8	4.6	16.7	183,498
1987	854,143	1,003,911	502,196	281,999	22.5	-149,769	2,345,578	457,444	1,888,134	229,218	52.7	11.1	1.4	10.6	193,832
1988	908,954	1,064,140	533,404	290,361	22.1	-155,187	2,600,760	550,507	2,050,252	220,088	54.1	6.4	6.0	10.9	202,691
1989	990,691	1,144,172	568,668	303,559	22.1	-152,481	2,867,538	678,210	2,189,327	234,410	55.4	9.0	7.4	10.3	210,911
1990	1,031,308	1,252,691	619,327	299,331	22.9	-221,384	3,206,347	795,990	2,410,357	258,591	58.6	4.1	9.6	11.8	225,065
1991	1,054,264	1,323,785	689,691	273,292	23.5	-269,521	3,598,993	911,060	2,687,933	296,397	63.9	2.2	5.7	12.3	241,687
1992	1,091,601	1,381,791	773,594	298,361	23.5	-290,160	4,002,669	1,004,039	2,998,630	(NA)	68.2	3.5	4.4	11.2	252,316
1993, est.	1,147,588	1,474,935	837,865	289,299	23.9	-327,347	4,410,475	1,100,758	3,309,717	(NA)	71.5	5.1	9.7	10.2	266,815

NA Not available. X Not applicable. [1] Includes off-budget receipts and outlays. [2] Gross domestic product as of fiscal year; for calendar year GDP, see section 14. [3] See text, section 10 for discussion of debt concept. [4] Change from previous year. For explanation of average annual percent change, see Guide to Tabular Presentation. [5] Represents transition quarter, July-Sept.

Source: U.S. Office of Management and Budget, Budget of the United States Government, annual.

No. 510. Federal Receipts, by Source: 1980 to 1993

[In millions of dollars. For fiscal years ending in year shown; see text, section 9. Receipts reflect collections. Covers both Federal funds and trust funds (see text, section 10). Excludes government-sponsored but privately-owned corporations, Federal Reserve System, District of Columbia government, and money held in suspense as deposit funds. See *Historical Statistics, Colonial Times to 1970*, series Y 343-351, and Y 472-487 for related data]

SOURCE	1980	1985	1990	1991	1992	1993, est.	PERCENT DISTRIBUTION 1980	PERCENT DISTRIBUTION 1993, est.
Total receipts [1]	**517,112**	**734,057**	**1,031,308**	**1,054,264**	**1,090,462**	**1,145,685**	**100.0**	**100.0**
Individual income taxes	244,069	334,531	466,884	467,827	475,974	515,315	47.2	45.0
Corporation income taxes	64,600	61,331	93,507	98,086	100,270	106,261	12.5	9.3
Social insurance	157,803	265,163	380,047	396,016	413,689	426,815	30.5	37.3
Employment taxes and contributions	138,748	234,646	353,891	370,526	385,491	396,266	26.8	34.6
Old-age and survivors insurance	96,581	169,822	255,031	265,503	273,137	281,598	18.7	24.6
Disability insurance	16,628	16,348	26,625	28,382	29,289	30,178	3.2	2.6
Hospital insurance	23,217	44,871	68,556	72,842	79,108	80,668	4.5	7.0
Railroad retirement/pension fund	2,323	2,213	2,292	2,371	2,449	2,313	0.4	0.2
Railroad social security equivalent account	-	1,391	1,387	1,428	1,508	1,508	-	0.1
Unemployment insurance	15,336	25,758	21,635	20,922	23,140	25,768	3.0	2.2
Other retirement contributions	3,719	4,759	4,522	4,568	4,788	4,782	0.7	0.4
Excise taxes [1]	24,329	35,992	35,345	42,402	45,569	47,628	4.7	4.2
Federal funds	15,563	19,097	15,591	18,275	21,836	24,138	3.0	2.1
Alcohol	5,601	5,562	5,695	7,364	8,011	7,973	1.1	0.7
Tobacco	2,443	4,779	4,081	4,706	5,049	5,772	0.5	0.5
Ozone depletion	-	-	360	562	637	886	-	0.1
Trust funds [1]	8,766	16,894	19,754	24,127	23,733	23,490	1.7	2.1
Highways	6,620	13,015	13,867	16,979	16,733	17,806	1.3	1.6
Airport and airway	1,874	2,851	3,700	4,910	4,645	3,424	0.4	0.3
Black lung disability	272	581	665	652	626	633	0.1	0.1
Hazardous substance response	-	273	818	810	818	843	-	0.1
Aquatic resources	-	126	218	260	271	285	-	-
Leaking underground storage	-	-	122	123	157	150	-	-
Vaccine injury compensations	-	-	159	81	118	33	-	-
Oil spill liability	-	-	143	254	295	234	-	-
Estate and gift taxes	6,389	6,422	11,500	11,138	11,143	12,594	1.2	1.1
Customs duties	7,174	12,079	16,707	15,949	17,359	19,192	1.4	1.7
Federal Reserve deposits	11,767	17,059	24,319	19,158	22,920	13,833	2.3	1.2

- Represents or rounds to zero. [1] Totals reflect interfund and intragovernmental transactions and/or other functions, not shown separately.

Source: U.S. Office of Management and Budget, *Budget of the United States Government,* annual.

No. 511. Federal Trust Fund Receipts, Outlays, and Balances: 1991 to 1993

[In billions of dollars. For fiscal years ending in year shown; see text section 9. Receipts deposited. Outlays on a checks-issued basis, less refunds collected. Balances: That which have not been spent. See text, section 10 for discussion of the budget concept and trust funds]

DESCRIPTION	INCOME 1991	INCOME 1992	INCOME 1993, est.	OUTLAYS 1991	OUTLAYS 1992	OUTLAYS 1993, est.	BALANCES [1] 1991	BALANCES [1] 1992	BALANCES [1] 1993, est.
Total [2]	**631.1**	**663.4**	**699.6**	**518.8**	**567.4**	**607.3**	**896.8**	**973.3**	**1,064.4**
Airport and airway trust fund	6.2	5.9	4.5	5.3	6.0	6.7	15.3	15.2	13.1
Federal employees retirement funds	57.2	60.5	63.3	33.7	34.1	35.1	269.0	290.6	318.9
Federal old-age, survivors and disability insurance trust funds	325.9	338.3	351.1	272.4	287.6	304.9	268.4	318.5	364.7
Foreign military sales trust fund	12.5	12.2	12.7	11.5	12.4	12.9	6.8	6.5	6.4
Health insurance trust funds	133.2	145.8	154.5	117.7	132.3	147.7	125.6	139.1	145.9
Highway trust funds	18.5	18.4	19.3	15.7	16.8	20.4	20.7	22.0	20.9
Military retirement trust funds	36.0	36.5	35.3	23.1	24.5	25.6	90.5	88.2	97.9
Railroad retirement trust funds	11.3	11.4	11.4	10.1	10.4	10.9	10.4	12.8	13.2
Unemployment trust funds	25.5	29.2	41.2	28.4	41.3	40.2	47.8	35.7	35.8
Veterans life insurance trust funds	1.5	1.5	1.5	1.2	1.3	1.1	12.7	12.9	13.2
Other trust funds [3]	6.8	6.8	8.2	3.1	4.0	5.3	29.6	31.7	34.5

[1] Balances available on a cash basis (rather than an authorization basis) at the end of the year. Balances are primarily invested in Federal debt securities. [2] Includes funds not shown separately. [3] Effective August 9, 1989, the permanent insurance fund of the FDIC was classified under law as a Federal fund.

Source: U.S. Office of Management and Budget, *Budget of the United States Government,* annual.

No. 512. Federal Budget Outlays—Defense, Human and Physical Resources, and Net Interest Payments: 1940 to 1993

[In millions of dollars. For fiscal year ending in year shown. Minus sign (-) indicates offsets]

YEAR	Outlays, total	National defense	HUMAN RESOURCES Total	Social Security	Income security	Medicare	Health	Education[1]	Veterans benefits	PHYSICAL RESOURCES Total[2]	Transportation	Commerce and housing	Net interest	Other	Undistributed offsets
1940	9,468	1,660	4,139	28	1,514	(NA)	55	1,972	570	2,312	392	550	899	775	-317
1945	92,712	82,965	1,859	267	1,137	(NA)	211	134	110	1,747	3,654	-2630	3,112	4,418	-1,389
1950	42,562	13,724	14,221	781	4,097	(NA)	268	241	8,834	3,667	967	1,035	4,812	7,955	-1,817
1955	68,444	42,729	14,908	4,427	5,071	(NA)	291	445	4,675	2,732	1,246	92	4,850	6,718	-3,493
1960	92,191	48,130	26,184	11,602	7,378	(NA)	795	968	5,441	7,991	4,126	1,618	6,947	7,760	-4,820
1964	118,528	54,757	35,294	16,620	9,641	(NA)	1,788	1,563	5,682	9,528	5,242	418	8,199	16,458	-5,708
1965	118,228	50,620	36,576	17,460	9,455	(NA)	1,791	2,146	5,723	11,264	5,763	1,157	8,591	17,086	-5,908
1966	134,532	58,111	43,257	20,694	9,662	64	2,543	4,372	5,923	13,410	5,730	3,245	9,386	16,911	-6,542
1967	157,464	71,417	51,272	21,725	10,248	2,748	3,351	6,458	6,743	14,674	5,936	3,979	10,268	17,126	-7,294
1968	178,134	81,926	59,375	23,854	11,798	4,649	4,390	7,642	7,042	16,002	6,316	4,280	11,090	17,786	-8,045
1969	183,640	82,497	66,410	27,298	13,066	5,695	5,162	7,548	7,642	11,869	6,526	-119	12,699	18,151	-7,986
1970	195,649	81,692	75,349	30,270	15,645	6,213	5,907	8,634	8,679	15,574	7,008	2,112	14,380	17,286	-8,632
1971	210,172	78,872	91,901	35,872	22,936	6,622	6,843	9,849	9,778	18,286	8,052	2,366	14,841	16,379	-10,107
1972	230,681	79,174	107,211	40,157	27,638	7,479	8,674	12,529	10,732	19,574	8,392	2,222	15,478	18,828	-9,583
1973	245,707	76,681	119,522	49090	28,264	8,052	9,356	12,457	12,015	20,614	9,066	931	17,349	24,950	-13,409
1974	269,359	79,347	135,783	55,867	33,699	9,639	10,733	12,745	13,388	25,106	9,172	4,705	21,449	24,423	-16,749
1975	332,332	86,509	173,245	64,658	50,160	12,875	12,930	16,022	16,599	35,449	10,918	7,619	23,244	27,487	-13,602
1976	371,792	89,619	203,594	73,899	60,784	15,834	15,734	18,910	18,433	35,188	13,739	7,931	26,727	27,050	-14,386
1976 [3]	95,975	22,269	52,065	19,763	14,981	4,264	3,924	5,169	3,963	9,512	3,358	931	6,949	9,388	-4,206
1977	409,218	97,241	221,895	85,061	61,044	19,345	17,302	21,104	18,038	40,746	14,829	3,093	29,901	34,315	-14,879
1978	458,746	104,495	242,329	93,861	61,488	22,768	18,524	26,710	18,978	52,591	15,521	6,254	35,458	39,594	-15,720
1979	503,485	116,342	267,574	104,073	66,359	26,495	20,494	30,223	19,931	54,013	17,532	4,686	42,636	40,396	-17,476
1980	590,947	133,995	313,374	118,547	86,540	32,090	23,169	31,843	21,185	65,985	21,329	9,390	52,538	44,996	-19,942
1981	678,249	157,513	362,022	139,584	99,723	39,149	26,866	33,709	22,991	70,886	23,379	8,206	68,774	47,095	-28,041
1982	745,755	185,309	388,681	155,964	107,717	46,567	27,445	27,029	23,958	61,752	20,625	6,256	85,044	51,069	-26,099
1983	808,380	209,903	426,003	170,724	122,598	52,588	28,641	26,606	24,846	57,600	21,334	6,681	89,828	59,023	-33,976
1984	851,846	227,413	432,042	178,223	112,668	57,540	30,417	27,579	25,614	57,938	23,669	6,917	111,123	55,287	-31,957
1985	946,391	252,748	471,822	188,623	128,200	65,822	33,542	29,342	26,292	56,789	25,838	4,229	129,504	68,227	-32,698
1986	990,336	273,375	481,594	198,757	119,796	70,164	35,936	30,585	26,356	54,932	28,117	4,890	136,047	73,713	-33,007
1987	1,003,911	281,999	502,196	207,353	123,250	75,120	39,967	29,724	26,782	58,283	26,222	6,182	138,652	62,588	-36,455
1988	1,064,140	290,361	533,404	219,341	129,332	78,878	44,487	31,938	29,428	81,068	27,272	18,815	151,838	57,222	-36,967
1989	1,143,172	303,559	568,668	232,542	136,031	84,964	48,390	36,674	30,066	125,532	27,608	29,211	169,266	57,822	-37,212
1990	1,252,691	299,331	619,327	248,623	147,019	98,102	57,716	38,755	29,112	134,537	29,485	67,142	184,221	60,896	-36,615
1991	1,323,785	273,292	689,691	269,015	170,301	104,489	71,183	43,354	31,349	74,788	31,099	75,639	194,541	71,081	-39,356
1992	1,381,791	298,361	773,594	287,545	198,073	119,024	89,570	45,248	34,133	94,877	33,337	9,514	199,429	74,901	-39,280
1993, est.	1,474,935	289,299	837,865	304,747	207,433	132,839	104,979	52,292	35,575	74,877	36,380	22,141	202,771	87,336	-37,213

NA Not available.   [1] Also includes training, employment, and social services.   [2] Includes outlays not shown separately.   [3] Transition quarter, July to September.

Source: U. S. Office of Management and Budget, *Budget of the United States Government*, annual.

No. 513. Federal Budget Outlays in Constant (1987) Dollars: 1940 to 1993

[Dollar amounts in billions of dollars. For fiscal years ending in year shown; see text, section 9. Given the inherent imprecision in deflating outlays, the data shown in constant dollars present a reasonable perspective—not precision. The deflators and the categories that are deflated are as comparable over time as feasible. See headnote, table 509. Minus sign (-) indicates decrease]

OUTLAYS	1940	1950	1960	1970	1980	1985	1987	1988	1989	1990	1991	1992	1993, est.
Outlays, total	95.8	250.1	389.5	597.8	832.1	1,001.3	1,003.9	1,027.1	1,057.2	1,110.1	1,122.0	1,138.4	1,180.0
National defense	18.1	94.6	217.9	264.4	187.1	261.2	282.0	283.3	285.9	272.3	240.1	253.6	239.5
Nondefense outlays	77.8	155.5	171.7	333.5	645.0	740.1	721.9	743.8	771.3	837.8	882.0	884.8	940.6
Payments for individuals	14.0	63.0	87.8	183.8	394.9	458.6	471.3	480.0	490.4	509.5	540.4	589.3	618.9
Direct payments	11.5	57.3	78.8	159.0	348.6	405.6	413.5	420.2	428.8	442.2	463.5	498.5	517.4
Grants to State and local gov't's	2.5	5.8	9.0	24.7	46.3	53.0	57.8	59.9	61.6	67.3	77.0	90.8	101.5
Other grants	6.2	6.7	20.1	48.7	81.2	59.8	50.5	50.8	50.3	52.0	53.7	56.0	61.2
Net interest	8.2	24.2	26.6	41.6	74.4	137.3	138.7	146.5	156.3	163.2	165.2	164.6	163.1
All other	53.0	74.2	60.4	87.0	122.9	118.7	97.9	102.4	108.6	145.5	155.7	107.1	127.1
Undistributed offsetting receipts	-3.7	-12.5	-23.1	-29.0	-28.5	-34.3	-36.5	-35.8	-34.4	-32.4	-33.2	-32.2	-29.7
PERCENT OF GDP													
Outlays, total	9.9	16.0	18.2	19.9	22.3	23.9	22.5	22.1	22.1	22.9	23.5	23.5	23.9
National defense	1.7	5.2	9.5	8.1	5.1	6.4	6.3	6.0	5.9	5.5	4.9	5.1	4.7
Nondefense outlays	8.2	10.9	8.7	11.6	17.3	17.5	16.2	16.1	16.2	17.4	18.7	18.5	19.2
Payments for individuals	1.7	4.1	4.1	6.1	10.6	10.9	10.6	10.4	10.4	10.7	11.5	12.4	12.8
Direct payments	1.4	3.7	3.7	5.3	9.3	9.5	9.3	9.1	9.1	9.3	9.9	10.5	10.7
Grants to State and local gov't's	0.3	0.4	0.4	0.9	1.2	1.3	1.3	1.3	1.3	1.4	1.6	1.9	2.1
Other grants	0.6	0.4	0.9	1.6	2.2	1.4	1.1	1.1	1.1	1.1	1.1	1.1	1.2
Net interest	0.9	1.6	1.4	1.5	2.0	2.9	3.1	3.2	3.3	3.4	3.5	3.4	3.3
All other	5.2	4.2	2.6	3.0	3.3	2.9	2.2	2.2	2.3	3.0	3.3	2.2	2.5
Undistributed offsetting receipts	-0.3	-0.7	-1.0	-0.9	-0.8	-0.8	-0.8	-0.8	-0.7	-0.7	-0.7	-0.7	-0.6
PERCENT OF OUTLAYS													
Outlays, total	100.0	100.0	100.0	100.0	100.0	100.0	100.0	100.0	100.0	100.0	100.0	100.0	100.0
National defense	17.5	32.2	52.2	41.8	22.7	26.7	28.1	27.3	26.6	23.9	20.6	21.6	19.6
Nondefense outlays	82.5	67.8	47.8	58.2	77.3	73.3	71.9	72.7	73.4	76.1	79.4	78.4	80.4
Payments for individuals	17.5	25.2	22.5	30.7	47.5	45.8	46.9	46.7	46.4	45.9	48.2	51.8	52.5
Direct payments	14.4	22.9	20.2	26.6	41.6	40.5	41.2	40.9	40.6	39.8	41.3	43.8	43.9
Grants to State and local gov't's	3.1	2.3	2.3	4.1	5.6	5.3	5.8	5.8	5.8	6.1	6.9	8.0	8.6
Other grants	6.1	2.7	4.9	8.1	9.8	6.0	5.0	5.0	4.8	4.7	4.8	4.9	5.0
Net interest	9.5	11.3	6.8	7.4	8.9	13.7	13.8	14.3	14.8	14.7	14.7	14.4	13.8
All other	52.8	26.3	15.5	14.6	14.7	11.9	9.8	10.0	10.2	13.1	13.8	9.3	10.6
Undistributed offsetting receipts	-3.4	-5.2	-5.9	-4.9	-3.4	-3.5	-3.6	-3.5	-3.3	-2.9	-3.0	-2.8	-2.5

Source: U.S. Office of Management and Budget, *Budget of the United States Government*, annual.

No. 514. Federal Outlays, by Detailed Function: 1980 to 1993

[In millions of dollars. For fiscal years ending in year shown; outlays stated in terms of checks issued or cash payments. See headnote, table 510]

FUNCTION	1980	1985	1990	1991	1992	1993, est.	PERCENT DISTRIBUTION 1980	1993, est.
Total outlays	**590,947**	**946,391**	**1,252,691**	**1,323,785**	**1,381,791**	**1,474,935**	**100.00**	**100.00**
Legislative branch	1,224	1,610	2,241	2,296	2,677	2,847	0.21	0.19
The Judiciary	567	966	1,641	1,989	2,299	2,531	0.10	0.17
Funds appropriated to President [1]	8,542	11,858	10,087	11,724	11,109	11,855	1.45	0.80
Departments:								
Agriculture	34,785	55,523	46,012	54,119	56,465	67,169	5.89	4.55
Commerce	3,129	2,140	3,734	2,585	2,567	3,061	0.53	0.21
Defense-Military	130,912	245,154	289,755	261,925	286,632	276,037	22.15	18.72
Defense-Civil	15,161	18,770	24,975	26,543	28,267	29,471	2.57	2.00
Education	14,770	16,682	23,109	25,339	26,047	30,880	2.50	2.09
Energy	6,467	10,587	12,084	12,479	15,523	16,859	1.09	1.14
Health and Human Services	76,374	132,104	193,678	217,969	257,961	292,695	12.92	19.84
Housing and Urban Development	12,735	28,720	20,167	22,751	24,470	25,573	2.16	1.73
Interior	4,477	4,825	5,796	6,097	6,555	7,155	0.76	0.49
Justice	2,641	3,586	6,507	8,244	9,826	10,519	0.45	0.71
Labor [2]	29,731	23,893	25,316	34,040	47,163	43,343	5.03	2.94
State	1,940	2,645	3,979	4,252	5,007	5,238	0.33	0.36
Transportation	19,802	25,020	28,637	30,503	32,477	35,913	3.35	2.43
Treasury	76,568	164,967	255,172	276,339	293,428	303,023	12.96	20.54
Veterans Affairs	21,137	26,333	28,998	31,214	33,894	35,361	3.58	2.40
Independent agencies:								
Environmental Protection Agency	5,603	4,490	5,108	5,769	5,950	6,444	0.95	0.44
General Services Administration	249	-2	-123	487	469	1,327	0.04	0.09
NASA [3]	4,959	7,251	12,429	13,878	13,961	14,092	0.84	0.96
Office of Personnel Management	15,056	23,727	31,949	34,808	35,596	37,229	2.55	2.52
Small Business Administration	2,026	680	692	613	394	975	0.34	0.07
Other independent agencies	16,112	9,974	74,523	81,240	18,556	35,608	2.73	2.41
Undistributed offsetting receipts	-31,988	-58,656	-98,930	-110,005	-117,111	-119,242	-5.41	-8.08
Outlays, by function	**590,947**	**946,391**	**1,252,691**	**1,323,785**	**1,381,791**	**1,474,935**	**100.00**	**100.00**
National defense	133,995	252,748	299,331	273,292	298,361	289,299	22.67	19.61
Dept. of Defense—Military	130,912	245,154	289,755	262,389	286,892	275,923	22.15	18.71
Military personnel	40,897	67,842	75,622	83,439	81,171	75,955	6.92	5.15
Operation and maintenance	44,788	72,371	88,340	101,769	91,984	90,826	7.58	6.16
Procurement	29,021	70,381	80,972	82,028	74,881	68,544	4.91	4.65
R and D, test, and evaluation	13,127	27,103	37,458	34,589	34,632	37,215	2.22	2.52
Military construction	2,450	4,260	5,080	3,497	4,262	5,330	0.41	0.36
Family housing	1,680	2,642	3,501	3,296	3,271	3,504	0.28	0.24
Other	-1,050	553	-1,218	-46,229	-3,308	-5,450	-0.18	-0.37
Atomic energy defense activities	2,878	7,098	8,988	10,004	10,619	11,664	0.49	0.79
Defense related activities	206	495	587	899	850	1,712	0.03	0.12
International affairs	12,714	16,176	13,764	15,851	16,106	18,704	2.15	1.27
International development and humanitarian assistance	3,626	5,409	5,498	5,141	6,131	6,298	0.61	0.43
Conduct of foreign affairs	1,366	2,043	3,050	3,282	3,894	4,094	0.23	0.28
Other	7,722	8,725	5,216	7,428	6,081	8,312	1.31	0.56
Income security	86,540	128,200	147,019	170,301	198,073	207,433	14.64	14.06
General retirement and disability insurance	5,083	5,617	5,148	4,945	5,483	5,372	0.86	0.36
Federal employee retirement and disability	26,594	38,591	51,981	56,106	57,572	59,768	4.50	4.05
Housing assistance	5,632	25,263	15,891	17,200	18,914	21,464	0.95	1.46
Food and nutrition assistance	14,016	18,540	23,964	28,481	32,651	35,865	2.37	2.43
Other income security	17,163	22,715	31,146	36,485	43,987	49,701	2.90	3.37
Unemployment compensation	18,051	17,475	18,889	27,084	39,466	35,263	3.05	2.39
Health	23,169	33,542	57,716	71,183	89,570	104,979	3.92	7.12
Health care services	18,003	26,984	47,642	60,723	77,715	92,541	3.05	6.27
Health research	4,161	5,376	8,611	8,899	10,098	10,630	0.58	0.72
Consumer and occupational health and safety	1,006	1,182	1,462	1,560	1,757	1,809	0.17	0.12
Medicare	32,090	65,822	98,102	104,489	119,024	132,839	5.43	9.01
Social Security	118,547	188,623	248,623	269,015	287,545	304,747	20.06	20.66
Veterans benefits and services	21,185	26,292	29,112	31,349	34,133	35,575	3.59	2.41
Income security for veterans	11,688	14,714	15,241	16,961	17,296	17,595	1.98	1.19
Educ., training, and rehab	2,342	1,059	278	427	783	835	0.40	0.06
Hospital and medical care	6,515	9,547	12,134	12,889	14,091	15,032	1.10	1.02
Housing for veterans	(Z)	214	517	85	898	1,048	-	0.07
Other	665	758	943	987	1,065	1,065	0.11	0.07

See footnotes at end of table.

No. 514. Federal Outlays, by Detailed Function: 1980 to 1993—Continued

[In millions of dollars. See headnote, table 510]

SOURCE OR FUNCTION	1980	1985	1990	1991	1992	1993, est.	PERCENT DISTRIBUTION	
							1980	1993, est.
Education, training, employment, and social services	31,843	29,342	38,755	43,354	45,248	52,292	5.39	3.55
Elementary, secondary, and vocational education.	6,893	7,598	9,918	11,372	12,402	14,265	1.17	0.97
Higher education	6,723	8,156	11,107	11,961	11,268	14,050	1.14	0.95
Research and general educ. aids	1,212	1,229	1,577	1,773	1,996	2,134	0.21	0.14
Training and employment	10,345	4,972	5,619	5,934	6,479	7,156	1.75	0.49
Other labor services.	551	678	810	788	884	920	0.09	0.06
Social services	6,119	6,710	9,723	11,526	12,219	13,767	1.04	0.93
Commerce and housing credit.	9,390	4,229	67,142	75,639	9,514	22,141	1.59	1.50
Mortgage credit.	5,887	3,054	3,845	5,362	3,932	2,073	1.00	0.14
Postal Service.	1,246	1,351	2,116	1,828	1,147	1,788	0.21	0.12
Deposit insurance	-285	-2,198	58,081	66,394	2,511	15,534	-0.05	1.05
Other commerce	2,542	2,022	3,100	2,054	1,924	2,746	0.43	0.19
Transportation	21,329	25,838	29,485	31,099	33,337	36,380	3.61	2.47
Ground transportation.	15,274	17,606	18,954	19,545	20,347	22,302	2.58	1.51
Air transportation.	3,723	4,895	7,234	8,184	9,313	10,050	0.63	0.68
Water transportation.	2,229	3,201	3,151	3,148	3,434	3,733	0.38	0.25
Other transportation	104	137	146	223	244	296	0.02	0.02
Natural resources and environment	13,858	13,357	17,067	18,552	20,017	21,462	2.35	1.46
Water resources	-4,223	4,122	4,401	4,366	4,559	5,021	0.71	0.34
Conservation and land management . .	1,043	1,481	3,553	4,047	4,587	4,700	0.18	0.32
Recreational resources.	1,677	1,621	1,876	2,137	2,378	2,569	0.28	0.17
Pollution control and abatement.	5,510	4,465	5,156	5,853	6,061	6,625	0.93	0.45
Other natural resources	1,405	1,668	2,080	2,148	2,432	2,548	0.24	0.17
Energy	10,156	5,685	3,341	2,436	4,509	4,807	1.72	0.33
Supply.	8,367	2,615	1,976	1,945	3,235	3,780	1.42	0.26
Conservation.	569	491	365	386	468	516	0.10	0.03
Emergency preparedness	342	1,838	442	-235	319	328	0.06	0.02
Information, policy, and regs	878	740	559	340	486	184	0.15	0.01
Community/regional develop	11,252	7,680	8,498	6,811	7,411	10,086	1.90	0.68
Community development.	4,907	4,598	3,530	3,543	3,643	4,022	0.83	0.27
Area and regional development	4,303	3,117	2,868	2,743	2,903	3,236	0.73	0.22
Disaster relief and insurance	2,043	(Z)	2,100	525	866	2,827	0.35	0.19
Agriculture.	8,839	25,565	11,958	15,183	14,997	21,533	1.50	1.46
Farm income stabilization	7,441	23,751	9,761	12,924	12,454	18,899	1.26	1.28
Research and services	1,398	1,813	2,197	2,259	2,543	2,635	0.24	0.18
Net interest	52,538	129,504	184,221	194,541	199,429	202,771	8.89	13.75
On-budget	54,877	133,622	200,212	214,763	223,066	229,793	9.29	15.58
Off-budget	-2,339	-4,118	-15,991	-20,222	-23,637	-27,022	0.39	-1.83
Interest on the public debt.	74,808	178,898	264,724	285,455	292,330	296,475	12.66	20.10
Interest received by on-budget trust funds	-9,707	-21,838	-46,321	-50,426	-54,193	-55,007	-1.64	-3.73
Interest received by off-budget trust funds	-2,339	-4,118	-15,991	-20,222	-23,637	-27,022	-0.40	-1.83
Other interest	-10,224	-23,438	-18,191	-20,266	-15,071	-11,675	-1.73	-0.79
General science, space, and technology	5,832	8,627	14,444	16,111	16,409	17,142	0.99	1.16
Gen. science and basic research	1,381	2,019	2,835	3,154	3,571	4,273	0.23	0.29
General government	13,028	11,588	10,734	11,661	12,939	14,728	2.20	1.00
Legislative functions.	1,038	1,355	1,763	1,916	2,124	2,227	0.18	0.15
Exec. direction and manag't.	97	113	160	190	188	253	0.02	0.02
Central fiscal operations	2,612	3,492	6,004	6,097	6,612	7,358	0.44	0.50
General property and records management	327	96	31	657	692	1,631	0.06	0.11
General purpose fiscal assistance. . . .	8,582	6,353	2,161	2,100	1,865	2,162	1.45	0.15
Other general government.	569	521	800	1,280	1,782	1,615	0.10	0.11
Deductions, offsetting receipts	-351	-506	-361	-718	-530	-680	-0.06	-0.05
Administration of justice.	4,584	6,270	9,995	12,276	14,450	15,229	0.78	1.03
Federal law enforcement.	2,239	3,520	4,648	5,661	6,462	6,653	0.38	0.45
Federal litigative and judicial	1,347	2,064	3,579	4,352	5,078	5,343	0.23	0.36
Federal correctional activities.	342	537	1,291	1,600	2,114	2,268	0.06	0.15
Criminal justice assistance.	656	150	477	663	795	965	0.11	0.07
Undistributed offsetting receipts	-19,942	-32,698	-36,615	-39,356	-39,280	-37,213	-3.37	-2.52

- Represents zero.   Z Less than $500,000.   [1] Represents international affairs funds mainly.   [2] Includes Pension Benefit Guaranty Corporation.   [3] National Aeronautics and Space Administration.

Source: U.S. Office of Management and Budget, *Budget of the United States Government,* annual.

No. 515. Tax Expenditures, by Function: 1990 to 1994

[In millions of dollars. For years ending, Sept. 30, except as noted. Tax expenditures are defined as *revenue losses attributable to provisions of the Federal tax laws which allow a special exclusion, exemption, or deduction from gross income or which provide a special credit, a preferential rate of tax, or a deferral of liability.* Represents tax expenditures of $1 billion or more in 1994]

DESCRIPTION	1990	1991	1992	1993	1994
National defense:					
Exclusion of benefits/allowances to Armed Forces personnel. .	1,965	2,345	2,325	2,370	2,400
International affairs [1]	(X)	(X)	6,045	6,375	6,795
Exclusion of income earned abroad by United States citizens . .	1,205	2,480	1,275	1,405	1,545
Exclusion of income of foreign sales corporations.	(X)	(X)	1,730	1,760	1,900
Inventory property sales source rules exception	2,200	4,230	3,120	3,280	3,440
General science, space, and technology [1]	(X)	(X)	4,455	3,074	2,720
Expensing of research and development expenditures [2].	(X)	(X)	1,895	2,020	2,150
Energy	(X)	(X)	2,175	2,585	2,865
Excess of percentage over cost depletion: Oil and gas	(X)	(X)	1,260	1,450	1,610
Alternative fuel production credit	(X)	(X)	970	1,215	1,355
Natural resources and environment	(X)	(X)	2,730	2,660	2,645
Exclusion of interest on State and local IDB [3]					
for pollution control and sewage and waste disposal facilities .	1,515	2,000	1,740	1,595	1,520
Commerce and housing credit [1]	(X)	(X)	156,505	166,285	176,780
Exclusion of interest on—					
Life insurance savings.	6,920	9,455	9,835	10,460	11,215
Owner-occupied mortgage subsidy bonds.	1,775	2,730	2,340	2,170	1,950
State and local debt for rental housing.	1,150	1,505	1,585	1,465	1,415
Capital gains (other than agriculture, timber, iron ore and coal) [2]	(X)	(X)	2,925	3,160	3,355
Deferral of capital gains on home sales.	(NA)	(NA)	13,265	13,925	14,620
Exclusion of capital gains on home sales for persons					
age 55 and over	3,230	4,255	5,685	6,170	6,360
Deductibility of—					
Mortgage interest on owner-occupied homes	39,785	40,690	42,730	45,145	48,145
Property tax on owner-occupied homes	11,240	10,735	12,245	13,100	14,015
Accelerated depreciation on rental housing [2]	(X)	(X)	1,360	1,310	1,280
Accelerated depreciation of buildings other than rental housing [2]	(X)	(X)	5,625	5,485	5,430
Step-up basis of capital gains at death	(NA)	32,750	31,485	33,690	36,050
Investment credit, other than ESOP [4]	4,520	(NA)	3,055	3,130	3,095
Accelerated depreciation of machinery and equipment [5] . . .	23,525	18,725	17,205	19,505	22,065
Reduced rates on the first $100,000 of corporate incomes [2] . .	3,235	4,310	4,515	5,075	5,495
Exception from passive loss rules for $25,000 rental loss . . .	5,475	7,635	5,655	6,040	6,245
Community and regional development [1]	(X)	(X)	2,135	2,385	2,580
Credit for low income housing investments	(X)	(X)	1,130	1,370	1,530
Education, training, employment, and social services [1]	(X)	(X)	22,055	22,940	24,040
Deductibility of—					
Charitable contributions (education).	1,720	1,805	1,780	1,870	1,960
Charitable contributions other than education	11,730	12,285	11,875	12,470	13,090
Credit for child and dependent care expenses.	3,895	3,265	3,215	3,385	3,585
Exclusion of interest on State and local debt for private					
nonprofit educational facilities.	(X)	(X)	950	990	1,035
Health [1]	(X)	(X)	70,185	76,545	83,990
Exclusion of employer contrib. for medical insurance					
premiums and medical care.	29,820	45,500	52,120	57,270	63,225
Exclusion of employer share of Hospital insurance tax.	(X)	(X)	11,270	12,220	13,325
Deductibility of medical expenses.	2,860	3,025	3,225	3,445	3,735
Exclusion of interest on State and local debt for private					
nonprofit health facilities	2,370	1,650	1,665	1,710	1,770
Deductibility of charitable contributions (health)	1,555	1,635	1,610	1,690	1,775
Social Security [1]	(X)	(X)	22,280	23,390	24,580
Exclusion of Social Security benefits:					
Disability insurance benefits	1,145	1,320	1,485	1,655	1,810
OASI benefits for retired workers	15,680	1,695	17,445	18,190	19,025
Benefits for dependents and survivors	3,110	3,170	3,350	3,545	3,745
Income security [1]	(X)	(X)	95,230	99,145	98,225
Exclusion of workmen's compensation benefits	2,980	3,230	3,505	3,750	4,270
Net exclusion of pension contributions and earnings:					
Employer plans	45,085	60,715	68,310	71,845	70,475
Individual Retirement Accounts.	5,960	8,290	7,530	6,975	6,410
Keoghs	1,470	3,520	3,520	3,650	3,840
Exclusion of other employee benefits:					
Premiums on group term life insurance	2,565	3,685	3,455	3,580	3,715
Special ESOP rules (other than investment credit)	(X)	(X)	3,055	3,130	3,095
Additional deduction for the elderly [6]	1,505	1,680	1,885	1,915	1,945
Earned income credit.	(X)	(X)	3,900	4,105	4,435
Veterans benefits and services [1]	(X)	(X)	1,945	2,000	2,060
Exclusion of veterans disability compensation	1,500	1,655	1,705	1,760	1,815
Deferral of interest on savings bonds.	(X)	(X)	1,335	1,405	1,475
General purpose fiscal assistance [1]	(X)	(X)	42,055	44,435	47,280
Exclusion of interest on public purpose State and local debt. . .	11,290	13,925	14,275	14,505	15,040
Deductibility of nonbusiness State and local taxes other					
than on owner-occupied homes	20,290	20,940	23,535	25,300	27,195
Tax credit for corporations receiving income from doing					
business in United States possessions	2,100	3,180	4,245	4,630	5,045

NA Not available.   X Not applicable.   [1] Total (after interactions).   [2] Normal Tax method.   [3] Industrial development bonds.   [4] Employee stock ownership plans. Includes investment credit for rehabilitation of structures, energy property, and reforestation expenditures.   [5] Pre-1983 budget method.   [6] Data on calendar year basis.

Source: U.S. Office of Management and Budget, *Budget of the United States Government,* annual.

No. 516. Federal Debt Held by the Public: 1970 to 1993

[In billions of dollars, except percents. Based on end of fiscal year]

YEAR	1970	1975	1980	1985	1990	1991	1992	1993, est.
Current dollars	283.2	394.7	709.3	1,499.4	2,410.4	2,687.9	2,998.6	3,303.8
Constant (1987) dollars [1]	818.3	829.6	1,004.9	1,589.7	2,134.8	2,282.4	2,475.5	2,664.2
Percent of GDP	28.7	26.1	26.8	37.8	44.1	47.7	51.1	53.5
Percent of credit market debt [2]	20.8	18.4	18.5	22.8	22.7	24.3	25.8	(NA)
Interest as percent of total outlays [3]	7.9	7.5	10.6	16.2	16.2	16.2	15.5	14.5

NA Not available.   [1] Debt in current dollars deflated by the gross domestic product (GDP) deflator with FY 1987=100.
[2] Unpublished and preliminary estimates from the Federal Reserve Board flow of funds accounts. Total credit market debt owed by domestic nonfinancial sectors, modified to be consistent with budget concepts for the measurement of Federal debt.
[3] Represents *interest on the public debt* less *interest received by trust funds* subfunction 901 less subfunction 902 and 903. Excludes the comparatively small amount of interest on agency debt or the offsets for other interest received by Government accounts.

Source: U.S. Office of Management and Budget, *Budget of the United States Government,* annual.

No. 517. Summary of Federal Debt: 1985 to 1992

[In millions of dollars. Based on end of fiscal year]

ITEM	1985	1988	1989	1990	1991	1992
Debt outstanding, total	**1,827,470**	**2,614,581**	**2,881,112**	**3,266,073**	**3,683,054**	**4,082,871**
Public debt securities	1,823,103	2,602,183	2,857,431	3,233,313	3,665,303	4,064,621
Agency securities	4,366	12,398	23,680	32,758	17,751	18,250
Securities held by—						
Government accounts, total	317,612	550,649	676,842	795,907	919,713	1,016,453
Public debt securities	316,545	550,448	676,605	795,762	919,573	1,016,330
Agency securities	1,067	202	138	145	139	123
The public, total	1,509,857	2,063,932	2,204,270	2,470,166	2,763,341	3,066,418
Public debt securities	1,506,558	2,051,735	2,180,726	2,437,551	2,745,729	3,048,291
Agency securities	3,299	12,196	23,542	32,613	17,612	18,127
Interest-bearing public debt, total	**1,821,010**	**2,599,877**	**2,836,309**	**3,210,943**	**3,662,759**	**4,061,801**
Marketable, total	1,360,179	1,802,905	1,892,763	2,092,759	2,390,660	2,677,476
Treasury bills	384,220	398,451	406,597	482,454	564,589	634,287
Treasury notes	776,449	1,089,578	1,133,193	1,218,081	1,387,717	1,566,349
Treasury bonds	199,510	299,875	337,974	377,224	423,354	461,840
Nonmarketable, total	460,831	796,972	943,546	1,118,184	1,272,099	1,384,325
U.S. savings bonds	77,011	106,176	114,025	122,152	133,512	148,266
Foreign series: Government	6,638	6,320	6,818	36,041	41,639	37,039
Government account series, total	313,928	536,455	663,677	779,412	908,406	1,011,020
Airport and airway trust fund	7,410	11,132	12,913	14,312	15,194	15,090
Bank insurance fund	16,130	15,565	15,016	8,438	6,108	4,664
Employees life insurance fund	6,312	8,522	9,359	9,561	11,140	12,411
Exchange stabilization fund	2,073	1,433	1,179	1,863	2,378	3,314
Federal disability insurance trust fund	5,443	7,084	8,167	11,254	12,854	12,774
Federal employees retirement funds	127,253	181,689	201,524	223,229	246,631	273,732
Federal hospital insurance trust fund	20,721	66,078	82,914	96,249	109,327	120,647
Federal Housing Administration	3,485	6,373	6,144	6,678	6,839	6,077
Fed. old-age & survivors insurance trust fund	30,968	97,137	148,565	203,717	255,557	306,524
Fed. S&L Corp., resolution fund	4,953	1,667	1,866	929	966	1,346
Fed. supplementary medical insur. trust fund	10,736	6,326	10,365	14,286	16,241	18,534
Government life insurance fund	269	201	182	184	148	134
Highway trust fund	9,422	8,284	9,926	9,530	10,146	11,167
National service life insurance fund	9,296	10,440	10,694	10,917	11,150	11,310
Postal Service fund	2,362	3,948	4,419	3,063	3,339	4,679
Railroad retirement account	4,232	7,090	7,709	8,356	9,097	10,081
Treasury deposit funds	681	421	418	304	151	212
Unemployment trust fund	16,454	35,743	44,540	50,186	47,228	34,898
Other	35,728	67,322	87,777	106,376	143,912	163,426
State and local government series	62,778	147,596	158,580	161,248	158,117	157,570
Domestic series	(X)	(X)	(X)	18,886	29,995	29,995
Other	477	427	445	447	439	435
MATURITY DISTRIBUTION						
Amount outstanding, privately held	**1,185,675**	**1,555,208**	**1,654,660**	**1,841,903**	**2,113,799**	**2,363,802**
Maturity class:						
Within 1 year	472,661	524,201	546,751	626,297	713,778	808,705
1-5 years	402,766	552,993	578,333	630,144	761,243	866,329
5-10 years	159,383	232,453	247,428	267,573	280,574	295,921
10-20 years	62,853	74,186	80,616	82,713	84,900	84,706
20 years and over	88,012	171,375	201,532	235,176	273,304	308,141

X Not applicable.

Source: U.S. Department of the Treasury, *Treasury Bulletin,* quarterly.

No. 518. Federal Participation in Domestic Credit Markets: 1980 to 1992

[In billions of dollars, except percent. See headnote, table 519. Federal credit programs are primarily in three forms: direct loans from the Federal Government, Federal guarantees of private lending, and lending by privately-owned government-sponsored enterprises]

TYPE OF PARTICIPATION	1980	1985	1986	1987	1988	1989	1990	1991	1992
Total funds loaned in U.S. credit markets, excluding equities [1]	**327.0**	**767.0**	**878.6**	**780.0**	**795.0**	**711.0**	**656.0**	**496.0**	**(NA)**
Federal and federally assisted lending	79.9	110.3	129.1	149.2	109.4	128.6	133.5	105.3	144.8
Federal participation rate (percent)	24.4	14.4	14.7	19.1	13.8	18.1	20.4	21.2	(NA)
Direct loans	24.2	28.0	11.2	-19.0	-13.4	-14.6	2.8	-7.5	4.6
Guaranteed loans	31.6	21.6	34.6	60.4	40.3	41.7	40.7	22.1	36.8
Government-sponsored enterprise loans	24.1	60.7	83.3	107.8	82.5	101.5	90.0	90.7	103.4
Total funds borrowed in U.S. credit markets [1]	**327.0**	**767.0**	**878.6**	**780.0**	**795.0**	**711.0**	**656.0**	**496.0**	**(NA)**
Federal and federally assisted borrowing	122.5	278.9	374.5	324.0	289.4	305.0	376.2	423.5	540.8
Federal participation rate (percent)	37.5	36.4	42.6	41.5	36.4	42.2	85.2	85.4	(NA)
Federal borrowing from public	69.5	199.4	236.8	152.0	162.1	140.1	220.1	276.8	392.5
Borrowing for guaranteed loans	31.6	21.6	34.6	60.4	40.3	41.7	40.7	22.1	36.8
Government-sponsored enterprise borrowing	21.4	57.9	103.2	111.7	87.1	123.2	115.4	124.6	111.5

NA Not available.   [1] Funds loaned to and borrowed by nonfinancial sectors, excluding equities.

Source: U.S. Office of Management and Budget, *Special Analyses, Budget of the United States Government*, annual.

No. 519. Federal Direct and Guaranteed Loans: 1970 to 1989

[In billions of dollars. As of end of fiscal year; see text, section 9. Government guaranteed loans are not included in Federal budget outlays. They constitute contingent liabilities not resulting in outlays, except in event of default]

ITEM	1970	1975	1980	1982	1983	1984	1985	1986	1987	1988	1989
Direct loans, amount: [1]											
Gross (new) loans dispersed	12.4	28.8	49.3	37.1	43.8	41.4	64.4	42.2	35.2	33.7	26.0
Net loan outlays	3.0	12.8	24.2	23.4	15.3	6.3	28.0	11.2	-19.0	-13.4	-14.6
Direct loans outstanding	51.1	74.1	163.9	207.8	223.0	229.3	257.4	251.6	234.2	222.0	207.0
Guaranteed loans: [2]											
Primary [3]	27.5	31.2	66.2	59.6	78.0	73.3	55.5	89.6	151.7	96.4	96.3
Net loans	8.4	8.7	31.6	20.9	34.1	20.1	21.6	34.6	60.4	40.3	41.7
Outstanding loans	125.1	198.3	298.5	331.2	363.8	386.7	410.4	449.8	507.0	550.0	588.6

[1] Includes loans from "off-budget" government accounts.   [2] Includes capital subscriptions to international financial institutions. To avoid double counting, secondary guaranteed loans and guaranteed loans held as direct loans are excluded.   [3] Gross loan guarantees minus both secondary guaranteed loans, and guaranteed loans held as direct loans by the Government—by either on- or off-budget accounts.

Source: U.S. Office of Management and Budget, *Budget of the United States Government*, annual.

No. 520. U.S. Savings Bonds: 1970 to 1992

[In billions of dollars, except percent. As of end of fiscal year, see text section 9. See *Historical Statistics, Colonial Times to 1970*, series Y 500, for similar but not exactly comparable data]

ITEM	1970	1975	1980	1985	1986	1987	1988	1989	1990	1991	1992
Amounts outstanding, total [1]	51.8	65.5	72.7	77.3	85.8	97.3	106.5	114.3	122.5	133.8	148.6
Funds from sales	4.7	6.8	4.8	5.0	8.3	10.3	7.3	7.7	7.8	9.2	13.6
Accrued discounts	1.0	3.3	4.2	5.2	5.6	6.1	7.9	7.5	8.0	9.9	8.7
Redemptions [2]	6.3	6.5	16.7	5.7	5.1	4.9	5.9	7.3	7.5	7.5	7.4
Percent of total outstanding	12.2	10.0	23.0	7.4	6.0	5.1	5.6	6.3	6.1	5.6	5.0

[1] Interest-bearing debt only for amounts and end of period or end of year.   [2] Matured and unmatured bonds.

Source: U.S. Dept. of the Treasury, *Treasury Bulletin*, quarterly.

No. 521. Government-Sponsored Enterprise Securities and Guarantees Outstanding: 1970 to 1991

[As of December 31. In billions of dollars]

ENTERPRISE	1970	1980	1990	1991	ENTERPRISE	1970	1980	1990	1991
Total	39	177	981	1,082	Mortgage-backed securities	(X)	(X)	300	372
Farm credit system:					Freddie Mac: [2]				
Farm credit banks	11	52	42	40	Debt	(X)	5	28	28
Banks for cooperatives	2	9	13	13	Mortgage-backed securities	(X)	17	316	359
Fannie Mae: [1]					Fed. home loan bank system	11	37	118	108
Debt	15	55	123	134	Sallie Mae [3]	(X)	3	39	43

X Not applicable.   [1] Federal National Mortgage Association.   [2] Federal Home Loan Mortgage Corporation.   [3] Student Loan Mortgage Association.

Source: Congressional Budget Office, *Controlling the Risks of Government-Sponsored Enterprises*, April 1991.

No. 522. Federal Funds—Summary Distribution, by State: 1992

[In millions of dollars. For year ending Sept. 30. Data for grants, salaries and wages and direct payments to individuals are on an expenditures basis; procurement is on obligation basis]

REGION, DIVISION, AND STATE	FEDERAL FUNDS		Defense	Non-defense	Direct payments to individuals	Procure-ment	Grants to State and local govern-ments	Salaries and wages
	Total [1]	Per capita [2] (dol.)						
U.S	1,181,373	4,631	226,045	955,328	607,433	199,595	174,448	160,510
Northeast	240,733	4,709	31,532	209,201	137,038	30,528	44,097	22,418
New England	66,779	5,059	13,918	52,861	34,009	12,842	11,282	6,277
Maine	6,533	5,288	1,927	4,606	3,179	1,399	1,047	807
New Hampshire	4,281	3,854	635	3,646	2,335	499	935	399
Vermont	2,167	3,803	140	2,027	1,262	124	503	224
Massachusetts	32,832	5,473	6,664	26,168	16,224	6,861	5,218	2,922
Rhode Island	5,066	5,040	868	4,198	2,834	524	986	597
Connecticut	15,900	4,846	3,684	12,216	8,175	3,434	2,593	1,329
Middle Atlantic	173,954	4,588	17,614	156,340	103,030	17,686	32,815	16,141
New York	83,923	4,632	7,180	76,743	47,107	8,170	19,305	7,031
New Jersey	34,313	4,405	4,824	29,489	20,711	4,366	5,217	3,576
Pennsylvania	55,718	4,640	5,610	50,108	35,212	5,150	8,293	5,534
Midwest	240,674	3,964	26,324	214,350	142,657	23,995	38,003	24,579
East North Central	161,500	3,778	14,775	146,725	100,878	14,513	26,373	15,264
Ohio	43,514	3,950	5,156	38,358	26,418	4,949	7,064	4,228
Indiana	19,980	3,529	2,551	17,429	12,105	1,832	3,242	1,936
Illinois	44,412	3,818	3,171	41,241	27,888	3,102	6,937	5,157
Michigan	35,752	3,789	2,570	33,182	23,182	3,183	6,004	2,605
Wisconsin	17,842	3,564	1,327	16,515	11,286	1,447	3,127	1,339
West North Central	79,174	4,408	11,549	67,625	41,779	9,483	11,629	9,315
Minnesota	16,806	3,751	1,812	14,994	9,002	1,897	2,894	1,496
Iowa	11,397	4,052	653	10,744	6,772	721	1,660	819
Missouri	26,093	5,025	5,272	20,821	13,105	4,679	3,498	3,179
North Dakota	3,467	5,452	473	2,994	1,506	219	603	540
South Dakota	3,330	4,683	334	2,996	1,633	236	601	520
Nebraska	6,873	4,281	969	5,904	3,691	586	997	996
Kansas	11,208	4,443	2,036	9,172	6,070	1,144	1,376	1,765
South	421,184	4,778	89,805	331,379	209,698	67,788	55,754	74,561
South Atlantic	236,700	5,253	55,765	180,935	112,864	39,671	26,338	50,016
Delaware	2,685	3,896	367	2,318	1,572	219	425	417
Maryland	32,337	6,588	7,147	25,190	12,071	7,876	2,940	6,910
District of Columbia	19,998	33,974	2,704	17,294	2,355	4,199	1,951	10,059
Virginia	40,913	6,416	17,270	23,643	15,127	9,914	2,773	11,722
West Virginia	8,127	4,485	285	7,842	5,364	304	1,668	692
North Carolina	25,739	3,762	5,488	20,251	14,328	2,185	3,971	4,624
South Carolina	15,908	4,415	3,369	12,539	7,679	2,998	2,393	2,621
Georgia	28,295	4,191	7,949	20,346	13,499	4,447	4,028	5,686
Florida	62,698	4,649	11,186	51,512	40,869	7,530	6,187	7,286
East South Central	71,774	4,622	12,192	59,582	37,346	12,075	11,597	9,302
Kentucky	15,541	4,139	2,225	13,316	8,806	983	2,951	2,490
Tennessee	22,533	4,485	2,226	20,307	11,720	4,301	3,658	2,501
Alabama	20,351	4,921	4,124	16,227	10,436	3,716	2,795	2,953
Mississippi	13,349	5,106	3,617	9,732	6,383	3,076	2,193	1,358
West South Central	112,710	4,091	21,848	90,862	59,488	16,042	17,819	15,243
Arkansas	9,957	4,151	994	8,963	6,421	466	1,691	964
Louisiana	18,605	4,340	2,549	16,056	9,348	2,216	4,417	2,089
Oklahoma	14,292	4,449	2,709	11,583	7,871	1,178	2,066	2,544
Texas	69,856	3,957	15,596	54,260	35,848	12,183	9,645	9,646
West	253,455	4,599	61,102	192,353	117,639	52,841	36,119	38,936
Mountain	67,491	4,693	13,205	54,286	30,497	14,458	9,282	10,675
Montana	4,092	4,968	286	3,806	1,960	230	765	571
Idaho	4,721	4,424	364	4,357	2,194	1,092	694	560
Wyoming	2,100	4,505	242	1,858	933	173	593	338
Colorado	17,184	4,952	4,622	12,562	6,899	4,246	1,905	3,317
New Mexico	10,390	6,571	1,739	8,651	3,482	3,809	1,379	1,485
Arizona	16,513	4,309	3,502	13,011	9,135	2,535	2,235	2,202
Utah	7,114	3,924	1,610	5,504	3,015	1,345	1,042	1,476
Nevada	5,377	4,051	840	4,537	2,878	1,029	669	726
Pacific	185,964	4,566	47,897	138,067	87,142	38,383	26,837	28,262
Washington	24,025	4,678	5,436	18,589	11,738	4,016	3,374	3,992
Oregon	11,712	3,934	641	11,071	7,339	589	2,050	1,329
California	139,695	4,526	37,381	102,314	64,816	32,353	19,738	18,988
Alaska	4,035	6,875	1,546	2,489	793	731	837	1,584
Hawaii	6,497	5,603	2,893	3,604	2,456	695	839	2,369
Undistributed	25,335	(NA)	17,282	8,053	400	24,443	475	15

NA Not available.   [1] Includes other programs not shown separately.   [2] Based on Bureau of the Census resident population as of April 1, 1992.

Source: U.S. Bureau of the Census, *Federal Expenditures by State for Fiscal Year*, annual.

No. 523. Tax Returns Filed—Examination Coverage: 1970 to 1991

[In thousands, except as indicated. Identification of returns with either schedule C (nonfarm sole proprietorships) or schedule F (farm proprietorships) for audit examination purposes was based in the largest source of income on the return and certain other characteristics. Therefore, the number with schedule C is not comparable to the number of nonfarm sole proprietorships returns in table 850]

YEAR AND ITEM	Returns filed [1]	RETURNS EXAMINED					AVERAGE TAX AND PENALTY—DOLLARS PER RETURN		
		Total	Percent of returns filed	By—			Revenue agents	Tax auditors	Service centers
				Revenue agents	Tax auditors	Service centers			
INDIVIDUAL RETURNS									
1970	76,431	1,672	2.2	(NA)	(NA)	-	(NA)	(NA)	-
1975	81,272	1,839	2.3	355.2	1,483.4	-	2,609	219	-
1980	90,727	1,834	2.0	292.5	1,346.3	195.1	1,335	602	39
1981	93,052	1,644	1.8	289.5	1,193.1	161.5	6,374	579	223
1982	94,013	1,455	1.6	285.5	1,066.6	103.2	7,505	751	364
1983	95,419	1,428	1.5	277.9	1,001.9	147.9	10,248	990	316
1984	95,541	1,216	1.3	276.2	859.4	80.4	11,584	1,314	692
1985	96,497	1,266	1.3	332.6	810.9	122.1	10,854	1,539	496
1986	99,529	1,091	1.1	298.9	732.5	59.6	14,052	1,945	862
1987	101,751	1,109	1.1	317.5	610.4	181.3	12,235	2,107	4,084
1988	103,251	1,061	1.0	352.8	532.3	175.7	9,750	2,190	4,195
1989	107,029	985	0.9	243.0	542.7	199.0	11,347	1,827	2,393
1990	109,868	883	0.8	202.8	517.2	163.2	16,248	1,965	3,817
1991, total	**112,305**	**1,124**	**1.0**	**200.7**	**499.9**	**422.9**	**19,981**	**2,403**	**3,436**
1040A, income under $25,000	43,694	388	0.9	11.7	130.5	246.0	18,396	1,680	3,269
Non 1040A, income: [2]									
Under $25,000	18,913	115	0.6	16.9	79.2	19.2	8,924	1,515	2,014
$25,000 - $49,999, simple	26,935	171	0.6	25.8	108.8	36.6	9,253	2,054	3,955
$50,000 - $99,999, complex	12,510	139	1.1	26.1	83.1	30.1	10,540	2,192	2,325
$100,000 and over	2,914	153	5.3	45.8	34.4	72.9	35,295	4,600	4,565
Schedule C-TGR: [3]									
Under $25,000	2,187	32	1.4	8.9	21.3	1.6	9,343	2,717	644
$25,000 - $99,999	2,746	51	1.9	20.2	25.8	4.8	12,580	5,303	2,167
$100,000 and over	1,525	55	3.6	34.3	10.6	10.4	30,918	8,857	4,473
Schedule F-TGR: [3]									
Under $100,000	607	8	1.3	3.2	4.2	0.4	7,798	1,186	862
$100,000 and over	274	10	3.8	7.7	1.9	0.8	11,661	2,065	3,864
1991 —OTHER RETURNS									
Fiduciary	2,681	2	0.1	2.4	-	-	20,807	-	-
Partnerships	1,726	11	0.6	10.9	-	-	-	-	-
Corporations, total	2,685	63	2.4	63.4	-	-	344,467	-	-
Estate, total	61	11	18.0	10.9	-	-	75,023	-	-
Gift	148	2	1.1	1.7	-	-	82,746	-	-
Excise	852	40	4.8	39.9	0.6	-	7,497	1,057	-
Employment	28,126	80	0.3	54.8	3.1	-	9,092	1,605	-
Windfall profit	-	3	-	0.4	-	2.3	426,831	-	626
Miscellaneous	-	-	-	-	-	-	-	-	-
Service center corrections	-	203	-	-	-	202.8	-	-	1,583

- Represents zero.   NA Not available.   [1] Returns filed in previous calendar year.   [2] Income from positive sources only.   [3] Total gross receipts.

Source: U.S. Internal Revenue Service, *Annual Report of the Commissioner and Chief Counsel of the Internal Revenue Service.*

No. 524. Internal Revenue Gross Collections, by Source: 1980 to 1991

[For fiscal year ending in year shown; see text section 9. See also *Historical Statistics, Colonial Times to 1970,* series Y 358-373]

SOURCE OF REVENUE	COLLECTIONS (bil. dol.)						PERCENT OF TOTAL				
	1980	1985	1988	1989	1990	1991	1980	1985	1989	1990	1991
All taxes	519.4	742.9	935.1	1,013.3	1,056.3	1,086.9	100.0	100.0	100.0	100.0	100.0
Individual income taxes	287.5	396.7	473.7	515.7	540.2	546.9	54.9	53.4	50.9	51.1	50.3
Withheld by employers	223.8	299.0	341.5	361.4	388.4	404.2	43.1	40.2	35.7	36.8	37.2
Employment taxes [1]	128.3	225.2	318.0	345.6	367.2	384.5	24.7	30.2	34.1	34.8	35.4
Old-age and disability insurance	122.5	215.6	307.6	336.8	357.5	374.7	23.6	29.0	33.2	33.8	34.5
Unemployment insurance	3.3	5.7	6.2	4.7	5.5	5.5	0.6	0.8	0.5	0.5	0.5
Corporation income taxes	72.4	77.4	109.7	117.0	110.0	113.6	13.9	10.4	11.5	10.4	10.5
Estate and gift taxes	6.5	6.6	7.8	9.0	11.8	11.5	1.3	0.9	0.9	1.1	1.1
Excise taxes	24.6	37.0	25.9	26.0	27.1	30.5	4.7	5.0	2.6	2.6	2.8
Alcohol and tobacco	8.1	9.9	10.3	10.1	10.1	12.1	1.6	1.3	1.0	1.0	1.1
Manufactures	6.5	10.6	10.6	11.2	11.0	14.2	1.3	1.3	1.1	1.0	1.3
Windfall profits tax	3.1	5.1	(Z)	(Z)	(Z)	(Z)	0.6	0.7	(Z)	(Z)	(Z)
Other	10.0	17.0	5.0	4.7	6.0	4.2	1.9	2.3	0.5	0.6	0.4

Z Less than $50 million or .05 percent.   [1] Includes railroad retirement, not shown separately.

Source: U.S. Internal Revenue Service, *Annual Report of the Commissioner and Chief Counsel of the Internal Revenue Service.*

No. 525. Federal Individual Income Tax Returns With Adjusted Gross Income (AGI)—Summary: 1980 to 1990

[Includes Puerto Rico and Virgin Islands. Includes returns of resident aliens, based on a sample of unaudited returns as filed. Data are not comparable for all years because of tax changes and other changes, as indicated. See *Statistics of Income, Individual Income Tax Returns* publications for a detailed explanation. See Appendix III. See *Historical Statistics, Colonial Times to 1970*, series Y 393-411, for related data]

ITEM	NUMBER OF RETURNS (1,000)				AMOUNT (mil. dol.)				AVERAGE AMOUNT (dollars)			
	1980	1985	1989	1990	1980	1985	1989	1990	1980	1985	1989	1990
Total returns	93,902	101,660	112,136	113,717	1,613,731	2,305,951	3,256,358	3,405,427	17,185	22,683	29,039	29,947
Form 1040	57,123	67,006	71,563	69,270	1,310,088	1,938,263	2,725,119	2,772,625	22,935	28,927	38,080	40,026
Salaries and wages	83,802	87,198	95,488	96,730	1,349,843	1,928,201	2,449,531	2,599,401	16,108	22,113	25,653	26,873
Interest received	49,020	64,526	69,882	70,370	102,009	182,109	220,116	227,084	2,081	2,822	3,150	3,227
Dividends in AGI	10,739	15,528	23,080	22,904	38,761	55,046	81,309	80,169	3,609	3,545	3,523	3,500
Business or profession profit less loss	8,881	11,900	14,161	11,222	55,129	78,773	132,738	141,430	6,207	6,620	9,373	12,603
Sales of capital assets, net gain less loss, in AGI	9,971	11,126	15,060	14,288	30,029	67,694	145,631	114,231	3,012	6,084	9,670	9,995
Pensions and annuities in AGI	7,374	13,133	16,817	17,041	43,340	95,096	147,358	159,294	5,878	7,241	8,762	9,348
Rents and royalties, net income less loss	8,208	9,964	10,131	10,317	4,105	-10,946	928	-3,156	500	-1,099	92	-306
Partnerships and S Corporations¹, profit less loss	3,910	5,488	5,928	5,977	10,099	-2,527	63,092	67,022	2,583	-460	10,643	11,213
Farm profit less loss	2,608	2,621	2,360	2,321	-1,792	-12,005	-214	-434	-687	-4,580	-91	-187
Statutory adjustments, total	13,149	37,763	9,927	16,648	28,614	95,082	24,573	33,994	2,176	2,518	2,475	2,041
Individual Retirement Arrangements	2,564	16,206	5,825	5,224	3,431	38,212	10,829	9,858	1,338	2,358	1,859	1,887
Self-employed retirement (Keogh) plan	569	676	822	824	2,008	5,182	6,326	6,778	3,529	7,666	7,696	8,226
Married couples who both work	(NA)	24,835	(NA)	(NA)	(NA)	24,615	(NA)	(NA)	(NA)	991	(NA)	(NA)
Exemptions, total²	227,925	244,180	223,756	227,549	227,569	253,720	447,130	485,985	998	1,039	1,998	2,135
Age 65 or older	11,847	16,749	(NA)	(NA)	(NA)	(NA)	(NA)	(NA)	(NA)	(NA)	(NA)	(NA)
Blind	185	327	(NA)	(NA)	(NA)	(NA)	(NA)	(NA)	(NA)	(NA)	(NA)	(NA)
Standard and itemized deductions, total³	88,105	96,849	111,311	112,796	362,776	554,734	740,409	789,942	4,118	5,728	6,652	7,003
Itemized deductions, total³	28,950	39,848	31,972	32,175	218,028	405,024	430,978	458,485	7,531	10,164	13,480	14,250
Medical and dental expenses	19,458	10,777	5,128	5,091	14,972	22,926	20,921	21,457	769	2,127	4,080	4,215
Taxes paid	28,749	39,548	31,393	31,594	69,404	128,085	131,300	140,011	2,414	3,239	4,182	4,432
Interest paid	26,677	36,287	29,438	29,395	91,187	180,095	193,186	208,354	3,418	4,963	6,562	7,088
Contributions	26,601	36,162	29,132	29,230	25,810	47,963	55,459	57,243	970	1,326	1,904	1,958
Taxable income⁴	88,105	96,124	92,314	93,148	1,279,985	1,820,741	2,173,346	2,263,661	14,528	18,942	23,543	24,302
Income tax before credits	76,136	85,994	92,246	93,089	256,294	332,165	438,240	453,128	3,366	3,863	4,751	4,868
Tax credits, total²	19,674	20,995	12,035	12,484	7,216	10,248	6,131	6,831	367	488	509	547
Child care	4,231	8,418	6,028	6,144	956	3,128	2,439	2,549	226	372	405	415
Elderly and disabled	562	463	320	339	135	109	64	61	240	235	200	180
Residential energy	4,670	2,979	(NA)	(NA)	562	812	(NA)	(NA)	120	273	(NA)	(NA)
Foreign tax	393	454	642	772	1,342	783	1,312	1,682	3,415	1,725	2,044	2,179
General business credit⁵	(NA)	4,614	332	263	(NA)	4,791	593	616	(NA)	1,038	1,736	2,342
Income tax, total⁶	73,906	82,846	89,178	89,862	250,341	325,710	432,940	446,296	3,387	3,932	4,855	4,922

NA Not available. ¹ Represents corporations with no more than 35 shareholders (10 in 1980), most of which are individuals electing to be taxed at the shareholder level. ² Includes items not shown separately. ³ For 1985, includes charitable deduction for nonitemizers. Starting 1989, includes additional standard deductions for age 65 or older or for blindness. ⁴ For 1980 and 1985, includes amounts "taxed" at zero percent. ⁵ Includes investment credit. ⁶ Includes minimum tax or alternative tax.

Source: U.S. Internal Revenue Service, *Statistics of Income Bulletin*, and *Statistics of Income, Individual Income Tax Returns*, annual.

No. 526. Individual Income Tax Returns—Number, Income Tax, and Average Tax, by Size of Adjusted Gross Income: 1989 and 1990

[Number in thousands; money amounts in billions of dollars, except as indicated]

SIZE OF ADJUSTED GROSS INCOME	NUMBER OF RETURNS		ADJUSTED GROSS INCOME (AGI)		TAXABLE INCOME		INCOME TAX TOTAL [1]		TAX AS PERCENT OF AGI		AVERAGE TAX ($1,000)	
	1989	1990, prel.	1989	1990, prel.	1989	1990, prel.	1989	1990, prel.	1989	1990, prel.	1989	1990, prel.
Total	112,136	113,717	3,256.4	3,405.4	2,173.3	2,263.6	432.9	447.2	13.6	13.6	4.9	5.0
Less than $1,000 [2]	3,866	3,688	-40.7	-44.0	0.2	0.1	0.1	0.2	(X)	(X)	0.2	0.1
$1,000-$2,999	7,331	7,379	14.4	14.6	1.0	1.1	0.2	0.2	4.6	4.7	0.1	0.1
$3,000-$4,999	6,396	6,317	25.4	25.2	2.3	2.1	0.4	0.4	3.9	4.0	0.2	0.2
$5,000-$6,999	6,080	6,004	36.3	36.1	5.2	4.9	0.8	0.8	3.5	3.6	0.2	0.2
$7,000-$8,999	6,038	6,026	48.2	48.2	11.4	10.2	1.7	1.6	5.2	5.3	0.5	0.4
$9,000-$10,999 ...	5,955	5,891	59.6	58.9	17.5	16.2	2.5	2.3	6.3	6.3	0.6	0.6
$11,000-$12,999...	5,846	5,573	70.2	66.9	26.4	25.3	3.6	3.1	6.8	6.8	0.8	0.8
$13,000-$14,999...	5,391	5,382	75.3	75.3	32.2	31.1	4.3	4.1	7.2	7.2	1.0	1.0
$15,000-$16,999...	4,914	4,686	78.6	74.9	38.5	35.8	5.3	4.9	7.3	7.3	1.2	1.2
$17,000-$18,999...	4,680	4,656	84.2	83.9	45.1	42.9	6.5	6.1	7.7	7.6	1.4	1.4
$19,000-$21,999...	6,118	6,308	125.1	129.2	70.7	71.8	10.5	10.6	8.4	8.4	1.8	1.7
$22,000-$24,999...	5,359	5,465	125.6	128.1	75.1	75.9	11.2	11.3	8.9	8.9	2.1	2.1
$25,000-$29,999...	7,615	7,838	209.2	215.3	131.9	133.5	20.7	20.5	9.7	9.7	2.7	2.7
$30,000-$39,999...	12,100	12,283	420.2	426.4	278.3	280.6	45.6	45.3	10.7	10.7	3.8	3.7
$40,000-$49,999...	8,590	8,837	383.7	394.8	263.1	270.5	44.0	44.9	11.4	11.4	5.1	5.1
$50,000-$74,999...	9,921	10,944	594.4	657.2	424.6	466.6	81.3	87.2	13.3	13.3	8.2	8.0
$75,000-$99,999...	3,059	3,276	261.1	279.6	193.0	205.3	42.7	44.3	15.9	15.9	14.0	13.6
$100,000-$199,999.	2,090	2,330	276.3	305.6	212.2	230.4	54.5	57.9	19.0	19.0	26.1	24.9
$200,000-$499,999.	613	644	179.1	188.1	146.4	152.6	41.6	43.5	23.3	23.1	68.0	67.5
$500,000-$999,999 .	116	130	78.5	87.1	66.9	74.4	18.9	20.9	24.3	24.1	163.5	161.0
$1,000,000 or more.	58	61	151.5	154.7	131.4	134.6	36.6	37.4	24.7	24.2	636.6	616.5

X Not applicable.   [1] Consists of income after credits, and alternative minimum tax, and minimum tax.   [2] In addition to low income taxpayers, this size class (and others) includes taxpayers with "tax preferences," not reflected in adjusted gross income or taxable income which are subject to the "alternative minimum tax" (included in total income tax).

Source: U.S. Internal Revenue Service, *Statistics of Income Bulletin*, quarterly and *Statistics of Income, Individual Income Tax Returns*, annual.

No. 527. Individual Income Tax Returns—Itemized Deductions and Statutory Adjustments, by Size of Adjusted Gross Income: 1990

[Preliminary]

ITEM	Unit	ADJUSTED GROSS INCOME CLASS						
		Total	Under $10,000	$10,000 to $19,999	$20,000 to $29,999	$30,000 to $39,999	$40,000 to $49,999	$50,000 to $99,999	$100,000 and over
Returns with itemized deductions:									
Number.................	1,000 ..	32,157	729	2,449	3,997	5,085	5,231	11,623	3,043
Amount...............	Mil. dol .	452,380	6,182	22,369	35,110	48,083	55,786	164,846	120,004
Medical and dental expenses:									
Returns	1,000 ..	5,039	483	1,157	1,233	862	523	715	66
Amount...............	Mil. dol .	21,163	2,676	5,392	4,392	2,703	1,888	3,114	998
Taxes paid: Returns, total.....	1,000 ..	31,597	583	2,321	3,873	5,033	5,199	11,561	3,027
State, local income taxes ..	1,000 ..	26,680	305	1,725	3,187	4,380	4,439	9,999	2,644
Real estate taxes	1,000 ..	28,250	505	1,882	3,310	4,389	4,645	10,690	2,831
Amount, total...........	Mil. dol .	139,955	844	3,480	7,552	12,468	15,676	52,263	47,672
State, local income taxes ..	Mil. dol .	85,012	168	979	3,186	6,456	8,336	30,320	35,567
Real estate taxes	Mil. dol .	49,680	692	2,357	3,975	5,444	6,507	19,610	11,096
Interest paid: Returns........	1,000 ..	29,356	460	1,916	3,585	4,745	4,948	10,974	2,727
Amount	Mil. dol .	203,499	1,913	9,608	16,166	23,776	28,042	78,650	45,343
Home mortgages interest:									
Returns...............	1,000 ..	26,053	383	1,621	3,029	4,185	4,455	9,959	2,420
Amount...............	Mil. dol .	181,685	2,090	8,957	14,793	22,005	25,705	71,780	36,356
Contributions: Returns	1,000 ..	29,290	518	1,918	3,452	4,565	4,812	11,082	2,942
Amount	Mil. dol .	57,245	444	2,144	4,080	5,538	6,329	19,741	18,969
Employee business expense:									
Returns...............	1,000 ..	8,404	62	422	906	1,388	1,465	3,419	743
Amount...............	Mil. dol .	22,325	120	1,210	2,076	2,857	3,135	9,013	3,913
Returns with statutory adjus'mts: [1]									
Returns...............	1,000 ..	16,611	2,676	2,882	2,965	2,348	1,854	2,791	1,093
Amount of adjustments	Mil. dol .	33,263	1,712	3,413	4,290	3,976	2,970	7,925	8,976
Payments to IRA's: [2] Returns ..	1,000 ..	6,924	327	961	1,552	1,366	1,081	1,149	489
Amount	Mil. dol .	9,929	482	1,461	2,183	1,901	1,210	1,832	859
Payments to Keogh plans:									
Returns...............	1,000 ..	819	8	35	69	64	62	290	292
Amount...............	Mil. dol .	6,637	21	50	172	205	214	1,570	4,405
Alimony paid: Returns.........	1,000 ..	638	34	84	87	79	83	171	100
Amount...............	Mil. dol .	4,694	246	290	371	398	420	1,258	1,711

[1] Includes disability income exclusion, employee business expenses, moving expenses, forfeited interest penalty, alimony paid, deduction for expense of living abroad, and other data not shown separately.   [2] Individual Retirement Account.

Source: U.S. Internal Revenue Service, *Statistics of Income, Individual Income Tax Returns*, annual.

No. 528. Federal Individual Income Tax Returns—Adjusted Gross Income (AGI), by Source of Income and Income Class for Taxable Returns: 1990

[In millions of dollars, except as indicated. Minus sign (-) indicates net loss was greater than net income. See headnote, table 525]

ITEM	Total [1]	Under $10,000	$10,000 to $19,999	$20,000 to $29,999	$30,000 to $39,999	$40,000 to $49,999	$50,000 to $99,999	$100,000 and over
Number of returns(1,000)	89,862	13,789	20,510	17,180	12,216	8,812	14,196	3,159
Adjusted gross income (AGI)								
by source	3,298,920	77,116	310,639	423,991	424,129	393,663	935,212	734,170
Salaries and wages	2,478,055	61,004	231,239	346,500	353,693	327,172	763,718	394,400
Percent of AGI for taxable returns . . .	75.1	77.0	74.4	81.7	83.3	83.1	81.7	53.7
Interest received	210,216	9,220	28,083	24,041	21,821	18,242	46,211	62,598
Dividends in AGI	76,236	1,989	5,471	5,482	5,288	5,054	17,552	35,399
Business; profession, net profit less loss.	135,043	2,300	9,349	13,316	13,146	11,243	35,709	49,979
Pensions and annuities in AGI.	149,636	4,317	29,549	26,548	20,192	19,254	35,647	14,130
Sales of property, net [2]	108,228	1,707	1,449	2,102	2,239	3,801	14,082	82,848
Rents, royalties, net [3]	97,128	-307	1,391	1,801	1,886	-3,656	7,870	85,323
Other sources, net	18,911	345	1,244	1,159	1,133	1,112	3,939	9,978
Percent of all returns:								
Number of returns	79.0	12.1	18.0	15.1	10.7	7.7	12.5	2.8
Adjusted gross income	96.9	2.4	9.1	12.5	12.5	11.6	27.5	21.6
Salaries and wages	95.3	2.3	8.9	13.3	13.6	12.6	29.5	15.2
Interest received	92.6	4.1	12.4	10.6	9.6	8.0	20.3	27.6
Dividends in AGI	95.1	2.5	6.8	6.8	6.6	6.3	21.9	44.2
Business; profession, net profit less loss.	95.5	1.6	6.6	9.4	9.3	7.9	25.2	35.3
Pensions and annuities in AGI.	93.9	2.7	18.5	16.7	12.7	12.1	22.4	8.9
Sales of property [2]	94.7	1.5	1.3	1.8	2.0	3.3	12.3	72.5

[1] Includes a small number of taxable returns with no adjusted gross income. [2] Includes sales of capital assets and other property; net gain less loss. [3] Excludes rental passive losses disallowed in the compilation of AGI; net income less loss.

Source: U.S. Internal Revenue Service, Statistics of Income, Individual Income Tax Returns, 1990.

No. 529. Federal Individual Income Tax Returns, by State: 1990

YEAR, DIVISION, STATE	Number of returns [1] (1,000)	Adjusted gross income (AGI) [2]	INCOME TAX Total [3] (mil. dol.)	INCOME TAX Per capita [4] (dol.)	YEAR, DIVISION, STATE	Number of returns [1] (1,000)	Adjusted gross income (AGI) [2]	INCOME TAX Total [3] (mil. dol.)	INCOME TAX Per capita [4] (dol.)
U.S. . . .	114,788	3,398,139	471,094	1,894	VA	2,885	90,930	12,257	1,981
Northeast . .	24,009	795,204	115,175	2,267	WV	697	17,083	2,131	1,189
N.E	6,400	212,352	30,785	2,331	NC	3,042	79,878	10,006	1,509
ME	566	14,391	1,777	1,447	SC	1,551	38,644	4,650	1,334
NH	540	16,972	2,354	2,123	GA	2,882	81,447	10,693	1,651
VT	267	7,117	917	1,629	FL	6,141	176,297	25,643	1,982
MA	2,900	96,074	13,806	2,295	E.S.C.	6,413	158,701	20,306	1,338
RI	469	13,833	1,851	1,845	KY	1,516	38,050	4,833	1,312
CT	1,658	63,965	10,080	3,067	TN	2,170	55,567	7,464	1,530
M.A.	17,609	582,852	84,390	2,244	AL	1,712	43,146	5,433	1,344
NY	8,212	282,468	41,215	2,291	MS	1,015	21,938	2,576	1,001
NJ	3,865	141,250	21,100	2,730	W.S.C	11,376	301,143	42,439	1,589
PA	5,532	159,134	22,075	1,858	AR	965	22,011	2,680	1,140
Midwest	27,408	784,041	106,781	1,790	LA	1,688	41,388	5,452	1,292
E.N.C.	19,397	565,951	77,688	1,849	OK	1,316	33,010	4,314	1,371
OH	5,087	138,958	18,373	1,694	TX	7,407	204,734	29,993	1,766
IN	2,526	68,951	9,178	1,655	West	24,328	752,394	104,333	3,712
IL	5,358	170,173	24,984	2,186	Mt	6,115	165,992	21,939	1,606
MI	4,168	124,821	16,974	1,826	MT	355	8,043	1,013	1,268
WI	2,258	63,048	8,179	1,672	ID	428	10,634	1,330	1,321
W.N.C . . .	8,011	218,090	29,093	1,647	WY	205	5,592	791	1,742
MN	2,025	60,095	7,981	1,824	CO	1,564	45,372	6,245	1,896
IA	1,269	32,207	4,231	1,524	NM	661	15,454	1,893	1,250
MO	2,288	62,059	8,313	1,625	AZ	1,602	43,209	5,559	1,517
ND	281	6,584	866	1,355	UT	682	18,259	2,209	1,282
SD	312	7,146	971	1,395	NV	618	19,429	2,899	2,411
NE	732	18,906	2,513	1,592	Pac	18,213	586,402	82,394	2,106
KS	1,104	31,093	4,218	1,702	WA	2,303	71,409	10,408	2,138
South	37,967	1,044,633	142,063	1,663	OR	1,306	35,873	4,667	1,642
S.A	20,178	584,789	79,318	1,821	CA	13,735	452,648	63,367	2,129
DE	328	10,417	1,417	2,128	AK	314	9,009	1,488	2,705
MD	2,334	79,891	11,009	2,303	HI	555	17,463	2,464	2,224
DC	318	10,202	1,512	2,491	Other [5]	1,076	21,864	2,742	1,487

[1] Includes returns filled by nonresident aliens and certain self-employment tax returns. [2] Less deficit. [3] Includes additional tax for tax preferences, self-employment tax, tax from investment credit recapture and other income-related taxes. Total is before earned income credit. [4] Based on resident population as of July 1. [5] Includes returns filed from Army Post Office and Fleet Post Office addresses by members of the armed forces stationed overseas; returns by other U.S. citizens abroad; and returns filed by residents of Puerto Rico with income from sources outside of Puerto Rico or with income earned as U.S. Government employees.

Source: U.S. Internal Revenue Service, Statistics of Income Bulletin. Quarterly.

No. 530. Federal Individual Income Tax—Effective (Average) and Marginal Tax Rates, for Selected Income Groups: 1970 to 1992

[Refers to income after exclusions. Effective rate represents tax liability divided by stated income. The marginal tax rate is the percentage of the first additional dollar of income which would be paid in income tax. Computations assume the low income allowance, standard deduction, zero bracket amount, or itemized deductions equal to 10 percent of adjusted gross income, whichever is greatest. Excludes self employment tax. See *Historical Statistics, Colonial Times to 1970*, series 412-439, for similar data on net income]

CURRENT DOLLARS

ADJUSTED GROSS INCOME [1]	TAX LIABILITY (dol.)					EFFECTIVE RATE (percent)					MARGINAL TAX RATE (percent)				
	1970[2]	1985	1990	1991	1992	1970[2]	1985	1990	1991	1992	1970[2]	1985	1990	1991	1992
Single person, no dependents:															
$5,000	683	177	-	-	-	13.7	3.5	-	-	-	19.5	12.0	-	-	-
$10,000	1,778	888	705	668	615	17.8	8.9	7.1	6.7	6.2	28.7	16.0	15.0	15.0	15.0
$20,000	5,030	2,854	2,205	2,168	2,115	25.2	14.3	11.0	10.8	10.6	43.1	26.0	15.0	15.0	15.0
$25,000	7,144	4,125	2,988	2,918	2,865	28.6	16.5	12.0	11.7	11.5	49.2	30.0	28.0	15.0	15.0
$35,000	11,904	6,916	5,718	5,573	5,360	34.0	19.8	16.3	15.9	15.3	54.3	38.0	28.0	28.0	28.0
$50,000	19,695	12,067	9,498	9,353	9,168	39.4	24.1	19.0	18.7	18.3	61.5	45.0	28.0	28.0	28.0
$75,000	34,025	22,195	16,718	16,134	15,867	45.4	29.6	22.3	21.5	21.2	65.6	48.0	33.0	31.0	31.0
Married couple, 2 dependents: [3]															
$5,000	275	[4]-550	[4]-700	[4]-865	[4]-920	5.5	[4]-11.0	[4]-14.0	[4]-17.3	[4]-18.4	15.0	[4]-11.0	[4]-14.0	[4]-17.3	[4]-18.4
$10,000	1,122	[4]-132	[4]-953	[4]-1,235	[4]-1,384	11.2	[4]-1.3	[4]-9.5	[4]-12.4	[4]-13.8	19.5	[4]23.2	[4]25.0	[4]27.4	[4]28.1
$20,000	3,213	1,682	926	701	409	16.1	8.4	4.6	3.5	[4]2.0	25.6	14.0	15.0	15.0	15.0
$25,000	4,490	2,566	1,703	1,605	1,470	18.0	10.3	6.8	6.4	5.9	32.8	16.0	15.0	15.0	15.0
$35,000	7,677	4,916	3,203	3,105	2,970	21.9	14.0	9.2	8.9	8.5	40.0	25.0	15.0	15.0	15.0
$50,000	13,674	9,086	5,960	5,576	5,220	27.3	18.2	11.9	11.2	10.4	49.2	33.0	28.0	28.0	28.0
$75,000	25,594	17,649	12,386	12,072	11,670	34.1	23.5	16.5	16.1	15.6	56.4	42.0	28.0	31.0	31.0

CONSTANT (1990) DOLLARS

ADJUSTED GROSS INCOME [1]	CURRENT INCOME EQUIVALENT TO CONSTANT INCOME (dol.)					EFFECTIVE RATE (percent)					MARGINAL TAX RATE (percent)				
	1970[2]	1985	1990	1991	1992	1970[2]	1985	1990	1991	1992	1970[2]	1985	1990	1991	1992
Single person, no dependents:															
$5,000	1,550	4,050	5,000	5,220	5,370	-	1.7	-	-	-	-	11.0	-	-	-
$10,000	3,100	8,100	10,000	10,430	10,750	10.4	7.4	7.1	7.0	6.8	19.5	15.0	15.0	15.0	15.0
$20,000	6,190	16,190	20,000	20,870	21,500	14.9	12.3	11.0	11.0	10.9	22.6	20.0	15.0	15.0	15.0
$25,000	7,740	20,240	25,000	26,090	26,870	16.1	14.4	12.0	11.9	11.7	25.6	26.0	28.0	28.0	15.0
$35,000	10,830	28,330	35,000	36,520	37,620	18.4	17.6	16.3	16.3	16.1	28.7	30.0	28.0	28.0	28.0
$50,000	15,480	40,480	50,000	52,170	53,740	21.9	21.5	19.0	19.0	18.8	36.9	38.0	28.0	28.0	28.0
$75,000	23,220	60,720	75,000	78,260	80,610	27.4	26.6	22.3	21.8	21.6	49.2	45.0	33.0	31.0	31.0
Married couple, 2 dependents: [3]															
$5,000	1,550	4,050	5,000	5,220	5,370	-	[4]-11.0	[4]-14.0	[4]-17.3	[4]-18.4	-	[4]-11.0	[4]-14.0	[4]-17.3	[4]-18.4
$10,000	3,100	8,100	10,000	10,430	10,750	-	[4]-3.8	[4]-9.5	[4]-11.8	[4]-12.9	-	[4]23.2	[4]25.0	[4]27.4	[4]28.1
$20,000	6,190	16,190	20,000	20,870	21,500	7.6	6.7	4.6	4.5	[4]3.9	17.9	14.0	15.0	15.0	15.0
$25,000	7,740	20,240	25,000	26,090	26,870	9.4	8.5	6.8	6.8	6.5	19.5	16.0	15.0	15.0	15.0
$35,000	10,830	28,330	35,000	36,520	37,620	11.7	11.6	9.2	9.1	8.9	19.5	22.0	15.0	15.0	15.0
$50,000	15,480	40,480	50,000	52,170	53,740	14.1	15.6	11.9	11.9	11.4	22.6	28.0	28.0	28.0	28.0
$75,000	23,220	60,720	75,000	78,260	80,610	17.4	20.7	16.5	16.5	16.2	28.7	38.0	28.0	31.0	31.0

- Represents zero.   [1] See headnote, table 525.   [2] Includes tax surcharge.   [3] Only one spouse is assumed to work.   [4] Refundable earned income credit.

Source: U.S. Dept. of the Treasury, unpublished data.

No. 531. Federal Civilian Employment, by Branch, and Agency: 1970 to 1991

[As of September 30]

AGENCY	1970	1980	1985	1988	1989	1990	1991
Total, all agencies [1]	**2,866,313**	**2,875,866**	**3,020,531**	**3,112,823**	**3,123,731**	**3,128,267**	**3,111,912**
Legislative Branch, total [1]	29,939	39,710	38,764	37,547	37,690	37,495	38,504
Congress [1]	11,428	19,096	19,656	19,200	19,504	19,474	20,178
U.S. Senate	(NA)	7,195	7,294	7,200	7,401	7,369	7,571
House of Representatives	(NA)	11,888	12,351	11,985	12,090	12,089	12,587
Architect of the Capitol	1,636	2,168	2,145	2,158	2,161	2,235	2,316
Judicial Branch	6,879	15,178	18,225	21,502	21,915	23,605	25,805
Supreme Court	(NA)	331	337	341	327	332	343
U.S. Courts	(NA)	14,847	17,888	21,161	21,588	23,221	25,392
Executive Branch, total [1]	2,829,495	2,820,978	2,963,542	3,053,774	3,064,126	3,067,167	3,047,603
Executive Office of the President [1]	997	1,886	1,526	1,554	1,577	1,731	1,758
White House Office	333	406	367	366	371	396	347
Office of Management and Budget	604	616	566	552	527	574	609
Office of Administration	(NA)	166	194	212	202	205	228
Council of Economic Advisors	60	35	30	29	32	34	34
Executive Departments	1,772,363	1,716,970	1,789,270	1,804,057	2,065,038	2,065,542	2,054,094
State	40,042	23,497	25,254	25,634	25,327	25,288	25,699
Treasury	90,683	124,663	130,084	160,516	152,548	158,655	166,433
Defense	1,169,173	960,116	1,084,549	1,049,619	1,075,437	1,034,152	1,012,716
Justice	40,075	56,327	64,433	76,515	79,667	83,932	90,821
Interior	71,671	77,357	77,485	78,216	77,545	77,679	81,683
Agriculture	114,309	129,139	117,750	120,869	122,062	122,594	125,640
Commerce	36,124	48,563	35,150	52,819	45,091	69,920	38,087
Labor	10,928	23,400	18,260	18,178	18,125	17,727	17,938
Health & Human Services	110,186	155,662	140,151	123,270	122,259	123,959	129,483
Housing & Urban Development	15,046	16,964	12,289	13,342	13,544	13,596	14,998
Transportation	66,970	72,361	62,227	63,506	65,615	67,364	69,831
Energy	7,156	21,557	16,749	17,031	17,130	17,731	19,539
Education	-	7,364	4,889	4,542	4,696	4,771	5,081
Veterans Affairs [2]	169,241	228,285	247,156	245,467	245,992	248,174	256,145
Independent agencies [1]	1,056,135	1,102,122	1,172,746	1,248,163	997,511	999,894	991,751
Environmental Protection Agency	-	14,715	13,788	15,309	15,590	17,123	18,218
Equal Employment Opportunity Comm.	797	3,515	3,222	3,229	2,743	2,880	2,889
Federal Deposit Insurance Corporation	2,462	3,520	6,723	8,249	9,031	17,641	22,007
Fed. Emergency Management Agency	-	3,427	3,133	2,610	3,048	3,137	3,130
General Services Administration [3]	37,661	37,654	25,782	20,070	20,063	20,277	21,122
National Aeronautics & Space Admin	30,674	23,714	22,562	23,130	24,165	24,872	25,737
Nuclear Regulatory Commission		3,283	3,605	3,341	3,288	3,353	3,534
Office of Personnel Management	5,513	8,280	6,353	6,673	6,859	6,636	6,757
Small Business Administration	4,397	5,804	4,960	4,588	4,653	5,128	4,867
Smithsonian Institution, Summary	2,547	4,403	4,757	5,034	5,158	5,092	5,360
Tennessee Valley Authority	23,785	51,714	32,035	28,290	26,676	28,392	24,870
U.S. Information Agency	10,156	8,138	8,851	8,821	8,723	8,555	8,213
U.S. International Development Cooperation Agency	14,493	6,152	5,054	4,836	4,816	4,698	4,575
U.S. Postal Service	721,183	660,014	750,021	831,956	826,310	816,886	804,338

- Represents zero.   NA Not available   [1] Includes other branches, or other agencies, not shown separately.   [2] Formerly Veterans Administration.   [3] 1980 figure includes the National Archives and Records Administration which became an independent agency in 1985.

Source: U.S. Office of Personnel Management, *Federal Civilian Workforce Statistics—Employment and Trends,* bimonthly.

No. 532. Federal White Collar Civilian Employment, by Sex and Grade: 1970 to 1991

[1970, as of Oct. 31; thereafter as of Sept. 30. Represents full-time white-collar employment]

GRADE [1]	TOTAL (1,000)					PERCENT FEMALE				
	1970	1980	1985	1989	1991	1970	1980	1985	1989	1991
Total employment [2]	**1,885**	**1,985**	**2,156**	**2,326**	**2,362**	**33.1**	**38.6**	**47.4**	**(NA)**	**(NA)**
General Schedule and equivalent pay system	1,259	1,473	1,561	1,608	1,623	40.3	45.1	47.7	48.7	48.6
Grades 1-6 ($11,015-$24,598)	521	561	563	518	494	72.2	74.1	74.5	74.8	74.6
Grades 7-10 ($21,023-$36,818)	302	357	377	388	390	33.4	46.3	50.3	53.5	55.8
Grades 11-12 ($31,116-$48,481)	264	335	388	434	441	9.5	19.3	27.5	32.9	33.0
Grades 13-15 ($44,348-$89,787)	164	217	231	267	299	3.0	8.2	12.1	17.0	19.6
Grades 16-18 [3]	8	3	1	1	-	1.4	4.4	6.1	9.1	-
Postal pay system [4]	521	483	553	663	651	(NA)	26.8	33.2	38.3	40.0
Other pay system	105	29	42	55	88	45.7	35.5	37.0	41.8	58.2

- Represents or rounds to zero.   NA Not available.   [1] Pay ranges shown for General Schedule grades are as of January 31, 1991.   [2] Includes other systems, not shown separately.   [3] Beginning 1980, change in number reflects shift of senior level employees to Senior Executive Service.   [4] Source: U.S. Postal Service, *National Payroll Hours,* annual.

Source: Except as noted, U.S. Office of Personnel Management, *Occupations of Federal White-Collar and Blue-Collar Workers,* biennial.

No. 533. Federal Civilian Employment and Annual Payroll, by Branch: 1970 to 1991

[Average Annual employment: **For fiscal year ending in year shown;** see text, section 9. Includes employees in U.S. territories and foreign countries. Data represent employees in active-duty status, including intermittent employees. Annual employment figures are averages of monthly figures. Excludes Central Intelligence Agency, National Security Agency, and, as of November 1984, the Defense Intelligence Agency. See also *Historical Statistics, Colonial Times to 1970*, series Y 308-317]

YEAR	EMPLOYMENT						PAYROLL (mil. dol.)				
	Total (1,000)	Percent of U.S. employed [1]	Executive		Legislative (1,000)	Judicial (1,000)	Total	Executive		Legislative	Judicial
			Total (1,000)	Defense (1,000)				Total	Defense		
1970 [2]	2,997	3.7	2,961	1,263	29	7	27,322	26,894	11,264	338	89
1975	2,877	3.4	2,830	1,044	37	10	39,126	38,423	13,418	549	154
1979	2,897	2.9	2,844	974	40	13	53,590	52,513	18,065	817	260
1980 [3]	2,987	3.0	2,933	971	40	14	58,012	56,841	18,795	883	288
1981	2,909	2.9	2,855	986	40	15	63,793	62,510	21,227	922	360
1982	2,871	2.9	2,816	1,019	39	16	65,503	64,125	22,226	980	398
1983	2,878	2.9	2,823	1,033	39	16	69,878	68,420	23,406	1,013	445
1984	2,935	2.8	2,879	1,052	40	17	74,616	73,084	25,253	1,081	451
1985	3,001	2.8	2,944	1,080	39	18	80,599	78,992	28,330	1,098	509
1986	3,047	2.8	2,991	1,089	38	19	82,598	80,941	29,272	1,112	545
1987	3,075	2.7	3,018	1,084	38	19	85,543	83,797	29,786	1,153	593
1988	3,113	2.7	3,054	1,073	38	21	88,841	86,960	29,609	1,226	656
1989	3,133	2.7	3,074	1,067	38	22	92,847	90,870	30,301	1,266	711
1990 [4]	3,233	2.7	3,173	1,060	38	23	99,138	97,022	31,990	1,329	787
1991	3,101	2.7	3,038	1,015	38	25	104,273	101,965	32,956	1,434	874

[1] Civilian only. See table 625.　[2] Includes 33,000 temporary census workers.　[3] Includes 81,116 temporary census workers.　[4] Includes 111,020 temporary census workers.

Source: U.S. Office of Personnel Management, *Federal Civilian Workforce Statistics—Employment and Trends*, bimonthly; and unpublished data.

No. 534. Federal Civilian Employment—Summary: 1970 to 1991

[In thousands. As of Dec. 31. Excludes U.S. Territories and foreign countries, Central Intelligence Agency, National Security Agency, and the Defense Intelligence Agency. Partially estimated]

CHARACTERISTICS	UNITED STATES							WASHINGTON, DC [1]			
	1970	1975	1980	1985	1989	1990	1991	1980	1985	1990	1991
Paid employment	2,645	2,741	2,782	2,902	2,974	2,940	2,977	366	353	358	374
Male	1,931	1,896	1,806	1,769	1,722	1,685	1,688	202	191	183	189
Female	714	845	976	1,133	1,252	1,255	1,289	164	162	175	185
Full-time	2,516	2,496	2,504	2,589	2,673	2,632	2,678	342	335	342	358
Other	129	245	278	313	300	308	299	24	18	16	16
Competitive service [2]	2,393	1,714	1,692	1,710	1,733	1,694	1,732	258	246	248	260
Permanent appointment	2,281	1,647	1,622	1,628	1,662	1,637	1,671	247	234	241	252
Temp. and indef. appointment	112	67	70	82	71	57	61	11	12	7	8
Excepted and Senior Executive Services (SES) [3]	252	1,027	1,091	1,191	1,241	1,246	1,245	107	108	109	114
Permanent appointment	164	860	917	1,015	1,049	1,029	1,037	70	73	76	79
Temp. and indef. appointment	88	167	174	176	192	217	208	37	35	33	35
White-collar [4]	2,113	2,254	2,324	2,478	2,588	2,576	2,621	335	327	336	352
Blue-collar [4]	532	487	458	424	386	364	356	31	26	22	22

[1] Through June 30, 1980, represents SMSA; thereafter, MSA.　[2] In 1971, under Postal Reorganization Act of 1970, U.S. Postal Service employees were changed from competitive service to excepted service.　[3] Excepted from competitive requirements of Civil Service Act. Prior to 1980 SES was not included in total.　[4] Through 1980, based on full-time employment; beginning 1985, based on total workforce.

No. 535. Accessions to and Separations From Paid Civilian Employment in the Federal Government: 1970 to 1992

[In thousands, except rate. For fiscal year ending in year shown; see text, section 9. Includes accessions and separations of full-time, part-time and intermittent employees]

ITEM	UNITED STATES							WASHINGTON, DC [1]				
	1970 [2]	1975	1980 [2]	1985	1990	1991	Oct. 1991-Aug. 1992	1980 [2]	1985	1990	1991	Oct. 1991-Aug. 1992
Accessions, total	727	606	995	630	898	573	517	94	63	59	63	49
Monthly rate [3]	2.2	1.9	2.9	1.9	2.5	1.6	1.5	2.3	1.6	1.5	1.5	1.3
Separations, total	797	589	1,004	530	889	598	519	89	58	52	48	39
Monthly rate [3]	2.4	1.8	3.0	1.6	2.4	1.7	1.5	2.2	1.5	1.3	1.2	1.0
Quit [4]	334	213	228	218	191	153	137	33	25	23	19	15

[1] See footnote 1, table 534.　[2] Includes temporary census enumerators.　[3] Per 100 employees.　[4] Represents voluntary resignations by employees or separations by agency if employee declines new assignment, abandons position, joins military, or fails to return from military furlough.

Source of tables 534 and 535: U.S. Office of Personnel Management, *Federal Civilian Workforce Statistics—Employment and Trends*, bimonthly; and unpublished data.

No. 536. Paid Civilian Employment in the Federal Government: 1990

[As of December 31. Excludes members and employees of Congress, Central Intelligence Agency, Defense Intelligence Agency, employees overseas, temporary census enumerators, seasonal and on-call employees, temporary Christmas help of the U.S. Postal Service, and National Security Agency]

DIVISION AND STATE	Total (1,000)	Percent defense	DIVISION AND STATE	Total (1,000)	Percent defense
U.S.	2,906	31.4	DC	212	8.1
			VA	161	66.2
Northeast	481	26.3	WV	15	11.0
N.E.	124	26.6	NC	46	33.0
ME	17	58.8	SC	32	59.0
NH	8	19.4	GA	88	41.2
VT	5	12.5	FL	112	29.4
MA	60	19.5	E.S.C.	173	32.5
RI	10	41.8	KY	35	35.4
CT	24	20.7	TN	56	13.9
M.A.	357	26.2	AL	57	44.5
NY	152	11.8	MS	24	43.6
NJ	75	34.6	W.S.C	275	35.0
PA	129	38.1	AR	19	25.6
Midwest	492	24.7	LA	34	25.7
E.N.C	320	26.4	OK	45	50.2
OH	91	37.8	TX	177	33.9
IN	41	37.0	West	642	37.4
IL	104	19.4	Mt.	193	31.2
MI	56	20.1	MT	11	11.6
WI	27	11.5	ID	10	13.5
W.N.C	173	21.7	WY	6	17.0
MN	32	9.0	CO	53	26.0
IA	18	8.0	NM	26	36.5
MO	66	28.9	AZ	39	26.0
ND	8	25.8	UT	36	57.9
SD	9	15.3	NV	11	18.9
NE	15	26.7	Pac.	449	40.0
KS	25	27.3	WA	65	43.8
South	1,254	33.9	OR	29	10.2
S.A	806	33.8	CA	315	39.5
DE	5	32.7	AK	15	32.2
MD	133	31.0	HI	25	75.6

Source: U.S. Office of Personnel Management, *Biennial Report of Employment by Geographic Area.*

No. 537. Paid Full-Time Federal Civilian Employment, all Areas: 1980 to 1992

[As of March 31. Excludes employees of Congress and Federal courts, maritime seamen of Dept. of Commerce, and small number for whom rates were not reported. See text, section 10 for explanation of general schedule and wage system. See also *Historical Statistics, Colonial Times to 1970*, series Y 318-331]

COMPENSATION AUTHORITY	EMPLOYEES (1,000)					AVERAGE PAY				
	1980	1985	1990	1991	1992	1980	1985	1990	1991	1992
Total	2,498	2,590	2,697	2,665	2,051	19,447	26,139	31,174	33,340	35,357
General Schedule	1,402	1,450	1,506	1,499	1,537	19,910	26,186	31,239	33,288	35,254
Wage System	456	418	369	328	328	17,970	23,288	26,565	27,543	28,852
Postal pay system [1]	527	586	661	651	(NA)	18,344	26,559	31,992	33,186	(NA)
Other	113	136	161	187	186	24,825	34,413	41,149	43,926	42,689

NA Not available.   [1] Source: U.S. Postal Service, *National Payroll Hours*, annual.

Source: Except as noted, U.S. Office of Personnel Management, *Pay Structure of the Federal Civil Service*, annual.

No. 538. Federal General Schedule Employee Pay Increases: 1965 to 1993

[Percent change from prior year shown, except 1965, change from 1964. Represents legislated pay increases. For some years data based on range; for details see source]

EFFECTIVE DATE	Average increase	EFFECTIVE DATE	Average increase	EFFECTIVE DATE	Average increase
Oct. 1, 1965	3.6	Oct. 1, 1974	5.5	Jan. 1, 1985	3.5
July 1, 1966	2.9	Oct. 1, 1975	5.0	Jan. 1, 1986	-
Oct. 1, 1967	4.5	Oct. 1, 1976	5.2	Jan. 1, 1987	3.0
July 1, 1968	4.9	Oct. 1, 1977	7.0	Jan. 1, 1988	2.0
July 1, 1969	9.1	Oct. 1, 1978	5.5	Jan. 1, 1989	4.1
Dec. 27, 1969	6.0	Oct. 1, 1979	7.0	Jan. 1, 1990	3.6
Jan. 1, 1971	6.0	Oct. 1, 1980	9.1	Jan. 1, 1991	4.1
Jan. 1, 1972	5.5	Oct. 1, 1981	4.8	Jan. 1, 1992	4.2
Oct. 1, 1972	5.1	Oct. 1, 1982	4.0	Jan. 1, 1993	3.7
Oct. 1, 1973	4.8	Jan. 1, 1984	4.0		

- Represents zero.

Source: U.S. Office of Personnel Management, *Pay Structure of the Federal Civil Service*, annual.

No. 539. Federal Government Employment, by Race and National Origin and by Pay System: 1982 and 1991

[As of Sept. 30. Covers total employment for only Executive Branch agencies participating in OPM's Central Personnel Data File (CPDF). Excludes foreign nationals abroad and U.S. Postal Service]

PAY SYSTEM	1982					1991				
	Total employees (1,000)	Race/national origin				Total employees (1,000)	Race/national origin			
		Race and origin [1] (1,000)	Percent of total	Black non-Hispanic (1,000)	Hispanic (1,000)		Race and origin [1] (1,000)	Percent of total	Black non-Hispanic (1,000)	Hispanic (1,000)
All pay systems, total [2]	2,008.6	484.0	24.1	311.1	90.0	2,183.4	602.0	27.6	363.9	118.8
General Schedule and equivalent [3]..	1,507.4	336.1	22.3	222.0	59.0	1,694.9	454.9	26.8	281.6	88.1
Grades 1-4 ($10,581-$18,947) ...	303.6	101.9	33.6	71.0	16.1	223.8	96.4	43.1	64.4	16.3
Grades 5-8 ($16,305-$29,081) ...	464.9	126.5	27.2	90.2	20.2	521.0	176.5	33.9	119.6	30.9
Grades 9-12 ($24,705-$46,571) ..	530.0	87.6	16.5	50.1	18.7	660.8	143.8	21.8	78.1	33.0
Grades 13-15 ($42,601-$76,982)..	208.9	20.1	9.6	10.7	4.0	289.3	38.2	13.2	19.5	7.9
Executive, total	9.7	0.6	6.2	0.4	0.1	14.1	1.1	7.8	0.6	0.3
Wage pay system [4]	414.0	134.6	32.5	83.5	28.0	360.8	122.6	34.0	71.6	26.3
Other pay systems [4]	77.5	12.6	16.3	5.2	2.9	113.7	23.4	20.6	10.1	4.2

[1] Includes American Indians, Alaska Natives, Asians, and Pacific Islanders, not shown separately.   [2] Due to the inclusion of unspecified employee records, the pay systems listed do not add to the total.   [3] Pay rates as of January 1990 for general schedule. Each grade (except Executive) includes several salary steps. Range is from lowest to highest step of grades shown. [4] Includes white-collar employment in other than General Schedule and Equivalent or Executive pay plans.
Source: U.S. Office of Personnel Management, Central Personnel Data File.

No. 540. Federal Land and Buildings Owned and Leased, and Predominant Land Usage: 1970 to 1990

[For fiscal years ending in years shown; see text section 9. Covers Federal real property throughout the world, except as noted. Cost of land figures represent total cost of property owned in year shown. For further details see source. For data on Federal land by State, see table 358]

ITEM AND AGENCY	Unit	1970	1975	1980	1985	1986	1987	1988	1989	1990
Federally owned: Land	Mil. acres.	762	761	720	727	727	724	688	662	650
Buildings, number [1]	1,000 . . .	418	405	403	454	429	412	442	451	446
Cost of land, buildings, etc.[2]	Bil. dol. .	79	91	107	148	158	165	164	164	180
Federally leased: Land	Mil. acres.	1.6	1.2	1.4	1.3	1.3	1.6	1.6	1.5	0.9
Buildings, floor area [1]	Mil. sq/ft .	182	210	214	237	246	246	248	254	234
Rental property, cost	Mil. dol . .	451	664	1,054	1,681	1,774	1,893	2,001	2,127	2,125
Predominant usage (U.S. only)	Mil. acres.	761	760	720	727	727	724	688	662	650
Forest and wildlife	Mil. acres.	503	502	422	431	431	431	400	375	368
Grazing	Mil. acres.	164	164	162	155	155	154	151	151	154
Parks and historic sites	Mil. acres.	25	25	93	94	96	96	99	98	96
Other	Mil. acres.	70	69	43	48	46	43	38	39	33

[1] Excludes data for Dept. of Defense military functions outside United States.   [2] Includes other uses not shown separately.
Source: U.S. General Services Administration, *Inventory Report on Real Property Owned by the United States Throughout the World,* annual.

No. 541. Public Lands—Disposal: 1980 to 1991

[For fiscal year ending in year shown: see text, section 9. Period figures are totals, not annual averages. See also *Historical Statistics, Colonial Times to 1970,* series J 10-15 and J 28-32]

ITEM	Unit	1980	1985	1987	1988	1989	1990	1991
Applications, entries, and selections allowed [1]	1,000 acres .	1,167	1,404	1	1	1	7	1
Applications, entries, and selections approved [1]	1,000 acres .	175	6,491	1,812	1,387	579	238	436
Patents and certificates [1]	1,000 acres .	2,495	4,217	3,000	5,419	780	1052	476
Mineral class, total	Number	106,125	119,419	89,789	82,585	83,762	81,355	83,358
Leases	Number	105,963	119,101	89,546	82,450	83,656	81,248	83,259
Permits [2]	Number	132	316	231	121	96	96	88
Licenses	Number	30	2	12	14	10	11	11
Grazing Leases [3]	Number	7,700	7,387	7,164	7,197	7,263	7,105	7,185
Permits [4]	Number	14,741	12,493	12,368	12,537	12,362	12,153	12,312

[1] Excludes Indian fee and reissue trusts and corrective patents.   [2] Excludes free-use permits for disposition of mineral materials.   [3] Beginning 1985, as of September 30.   [4] Licenses and permits within grazing districts.
Source: U.S. Bureau of Land Management, *Public Land Statistics,* annual.

National Defense and Veterans Affairs

This section presents data on national defense and its human and financial costs; active and reserve military personnel; ships, equipment and aircraft; and federally sponsored programs and benefits for veterans. The principal sources of these data are the annual *Selected Manpower Statistics* and the *Atlas/Data Abstract for the United States and Selected Areas* issued by the Office of the Secretary of Defense; *Annual Report of Secretary of Veterans Affairs, Department of Veterans Affairs,* and *The Budget of the United States Government,* Office of Management and Budget. For more data on expenditures, personnel, and ships, see section 31.

Department of Defense (DOD).—DOD is responsible for providing military forces of the United States. The President serves as Commander in Chief of the Armed Forces; from him, the authority flows to the Secretary of Defense and through the Joint Chiefs of Staff to the commanders of unified and specified commands (e.g., United States European Command).

Reserve components.—Reserve personnel of the Armed Forces consist of the Army National Guard, Army Reserve, Naval Reserve, Marine Corps Reserve, Air National Guard, Air Force Reserve, and Coast Guard Reserve. They provide trained personnel available for active duty in the Armed Forces in time of war or national emergency and at such other times as authorized by law. The National Guard has dual Federal-State responsibilities and uses jointly provided equipment, facilities, and budget support. The President is empowered to mobilize the National Guard and to use such of the Armed Forces as he considers necessary to enforce Federal authority in any State.

The ready reserve includes selected reservists who are intended to assist active forces in a war and the individual ready reserve who, in a major war, would be used to fill out active and reserve units and later would be a source of combat replacements; a portion of the ready reserve serves in an active status. The

> **In Brief**
>
> 1993 National
> defense outlays $291 bil.

standby reserve cannot be called to active duty unless the Congress gives explicit approval. The retired reserve represents a low potential for mobilization.

Department of Veterans Affairs.—The Department of Veterans Affairs administers laws authorizing benefits for eligible former and present members of the Armed Forces and for the beneficiaries of deceased members. Veterans benefits available under various acts of Congress include compensation for service-connected disability or death; pensions for nonservice-connected disability or death; vocational rehabilitation, education, and training; home loan insurance; life insurance; health care; special housing and automobiles or other conveyances for certain disabled veterans; burial and plot allowances; and educational assistance to families of deceased or totally disabled veterans, servicemen missing in action, or prisoners of war. Since these benefits are legislated by Congress, the dates they were enacted and the dates they apply to veterans may be different from the actual dates the conflicts occurred.

VA estimates of veterans cover all persons with active duty service during periods of war or armed conflict and until 1982 include those living outside the United States. Veteran population estimates for September 1982 are for the 50 States, the District of Columbia and Puerto Rico. Veterans whose active duty service was entirely during periods of peacetime are eligible for some veterans benefits and, where appropriate, are included in VA estimates.

Historical statistics.—Tabular headnotes provide cross-references, where applicable, to *Historical Statistics of the United States, Colonial Times to 1970.* See Appendix IV.

Figure 11.1

U.S. Military Sales Deliveries to Foreign Governments, Cumulative: 1984 to 1991

(U.S. total—$71 billion)

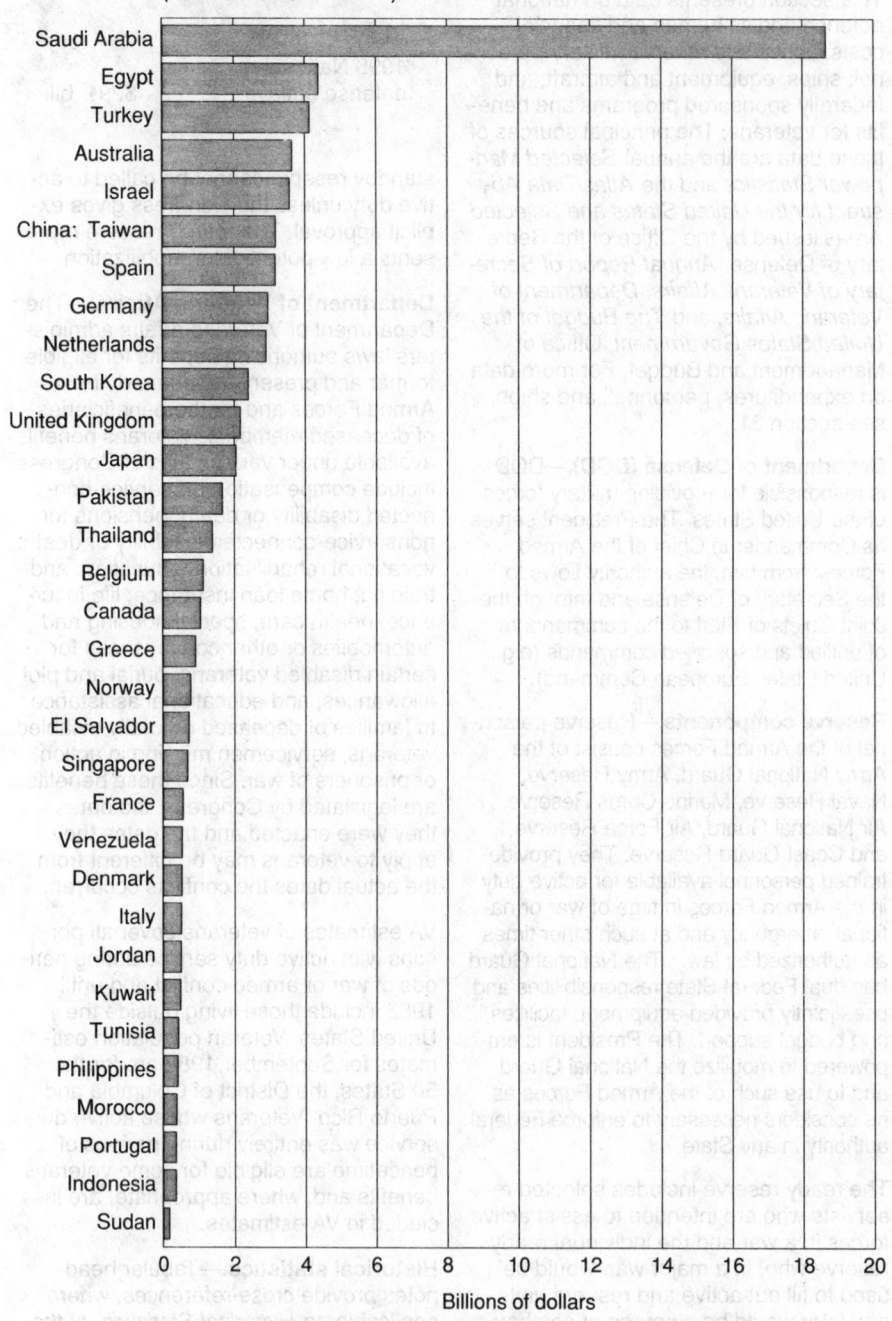

Billions of dollars

Source: Chart prepared by U.S. Bureau of the Census. For data, see table 551.

No. 542. National Defense Outlays and Veterans Benefits: 1960 to 1993

[For fiscal year ending in year shown; see text, section 9. Includes outlays of Department of Defense, Department of Veterans Affairs, and other agencies for activities primarily related to national defense and veterans programs. For explanation of average annual percent change, see Guide to Tabular Presentation. Minus sign (-) indicates decline. *See Historical Statistics, Colonial Times to 1970*, series Y 472, 473 and Y 476, for related data]

YEAR	NATIONAL DEFENSE AND VETERANS OUTLAYS				ANNUAL PERCENT CHANGE [1]				DEFENSE OUTLAYS, PERCENT OF—	
	Total outlays (bil. dol.)	Defense outlays		Veterans outlays (bil. dol.)	Total outlays	Defense outlays		Veterans outlays	Federal outlays	Gross domestic product [2]
		Current dollars (bil. dol.)	Constant (1982) dollars (bil. dol.)			Current dollars	Constant (1982) dollars			
1960	53.5	48.1	192.1	5.4	2.5	2.4	-1.9	3.1	52.2	9.5
1965	56.3	50.6	181.4	5.7	-6.8	-7.6	-8.8	0.7	42.8	7.5
1966	64.0	58.1	197.9	5.9	13.7	14.8	9.1	3.5	43.2	7.9
1967	78.2	71.4	235.1	6.7	22.1	22.9	18.8	13.8	45.4	9.0
1968	89.0	81.9	254.8	7.0	13.8	14.7	8.4	4.4	46.0	9.7
1969	90.1	82.5	243.4	7.6	1.3	0.7	-4.5	8.5	44.9	8.9
1970	90.4	81.7	225.6	8.7	0.3	-1.0	-7.3	13.6	41.8	8.3
1971	88.7	78.9	202.7	9.8	-1.9	-3.5	-10.2	12.7	37.5	7.5
1972	89.9	79.2	190.9	10.7	1.4	0.4	-5.8	9.8	34.3	6.9
1973	88.7	76.7	175.1	12.0	1.3	-3.1	-8.3	12.0	31.2	6.0
1974	92.7	79.3	163.3	13.4	4.6	3.5	-6.7	11.4	29.5	5.7
1975	103.1	86.5	159.8	16.6	11.2	9.0	-2.1	24.0	26.0	5.7
1976	108.1	89.6	153.6	18.4	4.8	3.6	-3.9	11.0	24.1	5.3
1976, TQ [3]	26.2	22.3	37.1	4.0	(X)	(X)	(X)	(X)	23.2	5.0
1977	115.3	97.2	154.3	18.0	6.7	8.5	0.5	-2.1	23.8	5.1
1978	123.5	104.5	155.0	19.0	7.1	7.5	0.5	5.2	22.8	4.8
1979	136.3	116.3	159.1	19.9	10.4	11.3	2.6	5.0	23.1	4.8
1980	155.2	134.0	164.0	21.2	13.9	15.2	3.1	6.3	22.7	5.1
1981	180.5	157.5	171.4	23.0	16.3	17.6	4.5	8.5	23.2	5.3
1982	209.3	185.3	185.3	24.0	15.9	17.6	8.1	4.2	24.9	5.9
1983	234.7	209.9	201.3	24.8	12.1	13.3	8.6	3.3	26.0	6.3
1984	253.0	227.4	211.3	25.6	7.8	8.3	5.0	3.2	26.7	6.2
1985	279.0	252.7	230.0	26.3	10.3	11.1	8.8	2.7	26.7	6.4
1986	299.7	273.4	244.0	26.4	7.4	8.2	6.1	0.4	27.6	6.5
1987	308.8	282.0	251.0	26.8	3.0	3.1	2.9	1.5	28.1	6.3
1988	319.8	290.4	252.8	29.4	3.6	3.0	0.7	9.7	27.3	6.0
1989	333.7	303.6	256.6	30.1	4.3	4.5	1.5	2.4	26.2	5.9
1990	328.4	299.3	271.1	29.1	-1.6	-1.4	5.7	-3.3	23.9	5.5
1991	304.6	273.3	238.5	31.3	-7.2	-8.7	-12.0	7.6	20.7	4.9
1992	332.5	298.4	258.8	34.1	12.0	12.4	8.5	8.0	21.6	5.1
1993	326.1	290.6	(NA)	35.5	-1.9	-2.6	(NA)	3.9	19.6	4.7

NA Not available.   X Not applicable.   [1] Change from prior year shown; for 1960, change from 1955.   [2] Represents fiscal year GDP; for definition, see text, section 14.   [3] Transition quarter, July-Sept.

Source: U.S. Office of Management and Budget, *Budget of the United States Government,* annual.

No. 543. Federal Budget Outlays for National Defense Functions: 1970 to 1992

[In billions of dollars, except percent. For fiscal year ending in year shown; see text, section 9. Minus sign (-) indicates decline. See *Historical Statistics, Colonial Times to 1970*, series Y 473, for total]

DEFENSE FUNCTION	1970	1980	1983	1984	1985	1986	1987	1988	1989	1990	1991	1992, est.
Total	81.7	134.0	209.9	227.4	252.7	273.4	282.0	290.4	303.6	299.3	273.3	307.3
Percent change [1]	10.1	15.2	13.3	8.3	11.1	8.2	3.1	3.0	4.5	-1.4	-8.7	12.4
Defense Dept., military	80.1	130.9	204.4	220.9	245.2	265.5	274.0	281.9	294.9	289.8	262.4	294.6
Military personnel	29.0	40.9	60.9	64.2	67.8	71.5	72.0	76.3	80.7	75.6	83.4	79.3
Percent of military	36.2	31.2	29.8	29.0	27.7	26.9	26.3	27.1	27.0	-1.7	-9.5	12.3
Operation, maintenance	21.6	44.8	64.9	67.4	72.4	75.3	76.2	84.5	87.0	88.3	101.8	97.8
Procurement	21.6	29.0	53.6	61.9	70.4	76.5	80.7	77.2	81.6	81.0	82.0	74.0
Research and development	7.2	13.1	20.6	23.1	27.1	32.3	33.6	34.8	37.0	37.5	34.6	36.1
Military construction	1.2	2.5	3.5	3.7	4.3	5.1	5.9	5.9	5.3	5.1	3.5	4.5
Family housing	0.6	1.7	2.1	2.4	2.6	2.8	2.9	3.1	3.3	3.5	3.3	3.4
Other [2]	-1.1	-1.1	-1.2	-1.7	0.6	2.0	2.6	0.2	0.1	-1.2	-46.2	-0.5
Atomic energy activities [3]	1.4	2.9	5.2	6.1	7.1	7.4	7.5	7.9	8.1	9.0	10.0	11.7
Defense-related activities [4]	0.2	0.2	0.3	0.4	0.5	0.5	0.6	0.5	0.6	0.6	0.9	1.0

[1] Change from immediate prior year; for 1970, change from 1965.   [2] Revolving and management funds, trust funds, special foreign currency program, allowances, and offsetting receipts.   [3] Defense activities only.   [4] Includes civil defense activities.

Source: U.S. Office of Management and Budget, *Budget of the United States Government,* annual.

No. 544. National Defense—Budget Authority and Outlays: 1975 to 1993

[In billions of dollars, except percent. For fiscal year ending in year shown, except as noted; see text, section 9. See *Historical Statistics, Colonial Times to 1970*, series Y 458-460 for outlays]

ITEM	1975	1980	1984	1985	1986	1987	1988	1989	1990	1991	1992	1993, est.
Budget authority [1]	87.6	143.9	265.2	294.7	289.1	287.4	292.0	299.6	303.3	303.6	295.1	272.8
Department of Defense-Military [2]	85.8	140.6	258.2	286.8	281.4	279.5	283.8	290.8	293.0	290.0	282.1	258.9
Atomic energy [3]	1.8	3.2	7.0	7.8	7.7	8.0	8.3	8.7	10.3	12.7	12.0	12.1
Unobligated balances [1] [4]	15.1	23.3	44.0	52.2	62.1	60.4	42.8	41.7	(NA)	(NA)	(NA)	(NA)
Department of Defense-Military	15.1	23.0	43.4	51.6	61.5	60.0	42.3	41.2	(NA)	(NA)	(NA)	(NA)
Atomic energy [3]	(NA)	0.3	0.6	0.6	0.6	0.4	0.5	0.5	(NA)	(NA)	(NA)	(NA)
Outlays (Defense) [1]	86.5	134.0	227.4	252.7	273.4	282.0	290.4	303.6	299.3	273.3	298.4	290.6
Department of Defense-Military	84.9	130.9	220.9	245.2	265.5	274.0	281.9	294.9	289.7	262.4	286.9	277.2
Atomic energy [3]	1.7	3.1	6.5	7.6	7.9	8.0	8.4	8.7	9.0	10.0	10.6	11.7

NA Not available. [1] Includes defense budget authority, balances, and outlays by other departments. [2] Excluding accruals. [3] Includes other defense related activities. [4] Start of year.
Source: U.S. Office of Management and Budget, *Budget of the United States Government*, annual.

No. 545. Defense-Related Agencies: 1970 to 1991

[In thousands, except percent. Annual averages]

EMPLOYMENT	1970	1980	1985	1986	1987	1988	1989	1990	1991
Total U.S. employment [1]	80,796	100,907	108,856	111,303	114,177	116,677	119,030	119,550	118,440
Federal	4,763	4,386	4,608	4,601	4,709	4,690	4,662	4,577	4,541
Resident Armed Forces	2,118	1,604	1,706	1,706	1,737	1,709	1,688	1,637	1,564
Civilian personnel [2]	2,645	2,782	2,902	2,895	2,972	2,981	2,974	2,940	2,977
DOD-Civilian employment [3]	1,211	948	1,073	1,059	1,079	1,041	1,067	1,024	1,083
Percent of Federal civilian personnel.	44.3	33.1	37.3	36.5	36.3	34.9	35.8	34.8	36.4
DOD-Military and civilian employment .	3,329	2,552	2,779	2,765	2,816	2,750	2,755	2,661	2,647
Percent of total Federal	68.7	57.1	60.7	60.0	59.8	58.6	59.1	58.1	58.3
Percent of total U.S.	4.1	2.5	2.6	2.5	2.5	2.4	2.3	2.2	2.2

[1] Includes resident Armed Forces. [2] See table 534. [3] Source: Beginning 1980, U.S. Dept. of Defense, *Civilian Manpower Statistics*, annual (Sept. issues).
Source: Except as noted, U.S. Bureau of Labor Statistics, *Employment and Earnings*, monthly.

No. 546. Military and Civilian Personnel and Expenditures: 1985 to 1992

UNIT	1985	1988	1989	1990	1991	1992
Personnel, total (mil. dol.)	3,808	3,864	3,885	3,693	3,872	3,889
Active duty military	1,354	1,338	1,342	1,185	1,263	1,214
Civilian	976	937	965	931	911	899
Reserve and National Guard.	1,478	1,588	1,578	1,577	1,697	1,777
Expenditures, total (mil. dol.)	216,045	211,195	212,509	209,904	221,089	211,534
Payroll outlays	75,949	85,428	92,593	88,650	96,970	99,250
Active duty military pay	29,818	34,483	38,221	33,705	39,118	39,447
Civilian pay	24,815	27,299	27,960	28,230	29,901	31,205
Retired military pay	17,029	18,573	20,591	21,159	22,584	23,936
Reserve and National Guard pay	4,287	5,073	5,821	5,556	5,366	4,661
Prime contract awards [1] (mil. dol.)	140,096	125,767	119,917	121,254	124,119	112,285
Supply contracts	92,375	72,634	67,540	66,895	66,981	54,880
Service contracts	24,224	25,109	24,347	28,540	31,222	30,503
R and D contracts	18,752	22,364	22,996	21,955	20,469	21,508
Construction contracts	3,245	3,795	3,668	2,088	3,469	2,894
Civil function contracts	1,500	1,866	1,365	1,775	1,979	2,500
Major area of work (mil. dol.):						
Aircraft, fixed wing	11,683	5,324	5,335	6,329	6,543	8,197
RDTE/Aircraft-Engineering Development	(NA)	(NA)	(NA)	(NA)	(NA)	1,266
Gas Turbines and jet engines	2,848	1,521	1,630	1,856	1,236	974
Guided Missiles	(NA)	869	886	928	921	(NA)
Guided missile handling and servicing equip.	(NA)	(NA)	875	446	921	(NA)
Major location of expenditures (mil. dol.):						
San Diego, CA	4,027	4,208	4,534	4,820	4,628	5,289
Pico Rivera, CA	(NA)	(NA)	(NA)	(NA)	2,600	4,284
St. Louis, MO.	7,412	5,109	5,965	5,616	5,869	3,462
Norfolk, VA	2,200	2,689	2,597	2,741	2,928	3,257
Arlington, VA	(NA)	2,449	2,314	2,527	2,836	2,974
Fort Worth, TX	3,912	3,681	4,122	3,594	3,973	2,948
Washington, DC	(NA)	2,687	2,352	2,771	2,706	2,828
Marietta, GA	(NA)	(NA)	(NA)	(NA)	(NA)	2,573
Los Angeles, CA	7,125	(NA)	2,339	2,459	(NA)	2,319
San Antonio, TX.	(NA)	(NA)	(NA)	(NA)	(NA)	2,117

NA Not available. [1] Represents contract awards over $25,000.
Source: U.S. Dept. of Defense, *Atlas/Data Abstract for the United States and Selected Areas*, annual.

No. 547. Military Prime Contract Awards to All Businesses, by Program: 1980 to 1992

[In billions of dollars. Net values for fiscal year ending in year shown; see text, section 9. Includes all new prime contracts; debit or credit changes in contracts are also included. Actions cover official awards, amendments, or other changes in prime contracts to obtain military supplies, services, or construction. Excludes term contracts and contracts which do not obligate a firm total dollar amount or fixed quantity, but includes job orders, task orders, and delivery orders against such contracts]

DOD PROCUREMENT PROGRAM	1980	1985	1986	1987	1988	1989	1990	1991	1992
Total	83.7	163.7	158.8	156.5	151.4	139.3	144.7	150.9	136.3
Intragovernmental [1]	10.2	12.4	9.9	8.8	8.9	9.6	10.0	11.9	9.6
For work outside the U.S.	5.4	8.6	9.1	8.9	8.2	6.4	7.1	9.2	5.9
Educ. and nonprofit institutions	1.5	3.1	3.4	3.5	3.5	3.3	3.5	3.6	3.4
With business firms for work in the U.S. [2]	66.7	139.6	136.5	135.3	130.8	120.0	123.8	125.9	117.2
Major hard goods	41.0	98.1	92.8	93.0	85.9	79.9	79.1	74.1	67.1
Aircraft	12.5	34.6	32.8	27.7	25.0	24.2	24.0	23.6	24.1
Electronics and communication equip.	9.6	22.0	19.7	22.6	17.8	18.1	18.5	15.2	14.2
Missiles and space systems	7.9	18.7	19.4	19.8	19.7	18.7	17.1	16.4	13.1
Ships	6.0	10.4	9.4	11.5	13.7	9.6	10.3	9.3	8.3
Tanks, ammo. and weapons	5.1	12.5	12.0	11.6	9.7	9.2	9.2	9.6	7.4
Services	5.9	9.1	10.4	11.0	12.0	11.7	14.6	16.9	17.3

[1] Covers only purchases from other Federal agencies and reimbursable purchases on behalf of foreign governments.
[2] Includes Department of Defense. Includes other business not shown separately. Contracts awarded for work in U.S. possessions, and other areas subject to complete sovereignty of United States; contracts in a classified location; and any intragovernmental contracts entered into overseas.

Source: U.S. Dept. of Defense, *Prime Contract Awards*, semiannual.

No. 548. Department of Defense Contract Awards, Payroll, and Civilian and Military Personnel—States: 1992

[For years ending Sept. 30. Contracts refer to awards made in year specified; expenditures relating to awards may extend over several years. Civilian employees include United States citizen and foreign national direct hire civilians subject to Office of Management and Budget (OMB) ceiling controls and civilian personnel involved in civil functions in the United States. Excludes indirect hire civilians and those direct hire civilians not subject to OMB ceiling controls. Military personnel include active duty personnel based ashore. Excludes personnel temporarily shore-based in a transient status, or afloat. Payroll outlays include the gross earnings of civilian and active duty military personnel for services rendered to the government and for cash allowances for benefits. Excludes employer's share of employee benefits, accrued military retirement benefits and most permanent change of station costs]

STATE	Contract awards [1] (mil. dol.)	Payroll (mil. dol.)	PERSONNEL (1,000) Civilian	PERSONNEL (1,000) Military	STATE	Contract awards [1] (mil. dol.)	Payroll (mil. dol.)	PERSONNEL (1,000) Civilian	PERSONNEL (1,000) Military
U.S.	112,285	99,250	899.0	1,213.7	DC	1,546	1,282	16.8	14.1
					VA	6,571	11,157	106.3	92.3
Northeast	22,846	9,004	121.6	61.1	WV	83	205	1.7	0.5
N.E.	11,033	2,989	30.5	22.5	NC	1,540	4,041	17.1	95.0
ME	1,305	644	8.3	4.7	SC	756	2,699	17.6	39.1
NH	424	219	1.4	0.4	GA	3,796	4,234	37.3	60.8
VT	63	76	0.6	0.1	FL	4,995	6,277	32.3	74.8
MA	5,686	993	11.1	7.2	E.S.C.	6,215	6,045	58.7	73.1
RI	455	437	4.2	3.7	KY	437	1,843	14.2	34.8
CT	3,099	620	4.8	6.5	TN	1,262	984	7.6	8.4
M.A.	11,813	6,015	91.0	38.5	AL	1,949	2,139	26.0	17.6
NY	5,430	1,810	17.8	23.7	MS	2,567	1,079	11.0	12.3
NJ	3,319	1,601	24.7	9.6	W.S.C.	10,923	11,112	93.5	165.3
PA	3,065	2,605	48.5	5.2	AR	288	703	4.5	6.6
Midwest	15,398	11,021	120.6	117.6	LA	1,204	1,358	9.0	21.6
E.N.C.	8,365	6,397	84.1	53.4	OK	759	2,035	21.9	28.3
OH	3,033	2,182	34.7	10.9	TX	8,672	7,016	58.2	108.8
IN	1,517	1,095	15.7	5.3	West	33,463	28,683	233.2	383.2
IL	1,354	1,775	19.3	29.8	Mt.	6,188	7,213	58.8	101.2
MI	1,568	904	11.1	6.5	MT	56	232	1.2	4.4
WI	893	441	3.4	0.9	ID	66	290	1.5	4.7
W.N.C.	7,032	4,624	36.4	64.2	WY	61	171	1.1	3.5
MN	1,496	358	2.9	0.9	CO	2,471	2,190	14.0	37.7
IA	442	202	1.5	0.4	NM	728	1,019	9.2	15.4
MO	3,714	1,622	18.3	15.3	AZ	1,946	1,658	9.8	22.0
ND	146	328	1.9	9.7	UT	616	1,050	19.9	5.6
SD	83	254	1.3	6.1	NV	243	603	2.1	7.7
NE	297	674	3.8	10.5	Pac.	27,274	21,470	174.4	281.9
KS	855	1,186	6.8	21.3	WA	2,217	3,305	29.0	35.7
South	40,578	50,542	423.7	651.8	OR	206	432	2.9	1.0
S.A.	23,440	33,384	271.4	413.4	CA	23,843	14,202	119.9	178.2
DE	103	267	1.8	4.4	AK	385	1,189	4.7	22.2
MD	4,050	3,222	40.5	32.3	HI	623	2,342	17.9	44.9

[1] Military awards for supplies, services, and construction. Net value of contracts of over $25,000 for work in each State and DC. Figures reflect impact of prime contracting on State distribution of defense work. Often the State in which a prime contractor is located in is not the State where the subcontracted work is done. See also headnote, table 547. Undistributed civilians and military personnel, their payrolls and prime contract awards for performance in classified locations are excluded.
Source: U.S. Dept. of Defense, *Atlas/Data Abstract for the United States and Selected Areas*, annual.

No. 549. Worldwide Military Expenditures: 1980 to 1989

[For military expenditures and Armed Forces by country, see section 31. GNP=Gross national product]

COUNTRY GROUP	1980	1981	1982	1983	1984	1985	1986	1987	1988	1989
Current dollars, total [1]	602	682	764	821	869	925	956	990	1,016	1,035
United States	144	170	196	218	237	266	281	288	293	304
Percent of total	23.9	24.9	25.7	26.5	27.3	28.8	29.4	29.1	28.9	29.4
Developed countries [2]	490	553	616	663	706	709	792	827	853	867
Developing countries [2]	113	129	148	158	163	166	165	164	163	168
NATO countries [3]	239	276	312	342	367	402	421	435	444	462
Constant (1988) dollars, total	887	916	965	999	1,018	1,053	1,061	1,065	1,058	1,035
United States	212	228	248	265	278	303	312	310	305	304
Percent of total	23.9	24.9	25.7	26.5	27.3	28.8	29.4	29.1	28.8	29.4
Developed countries [2]	721	743	778	807	827	864	878	889	888	867
Developing countries [2]	166	173	187	192	191	189	183	176	170	168
NATO countries [3]	352	370	395	416	430	458	467	468	462	462
Percent of GNP	5.3	5.4	5.7	5.7	5.6	5.6	5.5	5.4	5.1	4.9
United States	5.3	5.6	6.2	6.4	6.3	6.6	6.6	6.4	6.0	5.8
Developed countries [2]	5.3	5.3	5.6	5.6	5.6	5.6	5.6	5.5	5.3	5.0
Developing countries [2]	5.5	5.7	6.1	6.2	6.0	5.7	5.3	4.9	4.5	4.3
NATO countries [3]	4.3	4.5	4.8	4.9	4.9	5.0	5.0	4.9	4.6	4.5

[1] Includes countries not shown separately.   [2] Twenty-eight developed countries; see table 550 for selected countries; for complete list, see source.   [3] North Atlantic Treaty Organization.

No. 550. Arms Trade in Constant (1989) Dollars—Selected Countries: 1987 to 1989

[In millions of dollars, except percent. Because some countries exclude arms imports or exports from their trade statistics and their "total" imports and exports are therefore understated and because arms transfers may be estimated independently of trade data, the ratio of arms to total imports or exports may be overstated and may even exceed 100 percent]

COUNTRY	1987	1988	1989 Total	1989 Arms imports as percent of total imports	COUNTRY	1987	1988	1989 Total	1989 Arms imports as percent of total imports
World total [1]	62,690	55,430	45,430	(NA)	RECIPIENTS				
					Developing [1]	50,190	41,180	34,630	4.7
EXPORTERS					Afghanistan	1,506	2,707	3,800	462.3
					Algeria	753	885	575	6.5
					Angola	1,828	1,457	750	30.0
Canada	645	677	410	0.2	Argentina	151	312	40	1.0
China: Mainland	1,936	2,707	2,000	0.2	Cuba	1,936	1,770	1,200	14.8
Czechoslovakia	1,398	963	875	3.5	Egypt	1,828	807	600	8.1
France	3,227	2,394	2,700	0.1	El Salvador	54	62	70	6.4
Poland	1,398	1,249	400	2.6	Ethiopia	1,076	729	925	97.3
Soviet Union	24,310	22,490	19,600	0.8	Greece	333	489	2,000	12.4
United Kingdom	5,055	1,666	3,000	0.3	India	3,764	3,539	3,500	17.1
United States	15,380	15,410	11,200	0.3	Iran	2,151	2,394	1,300	12.4
West Germany	1,613	1,249	1,200	0.3	Iraq	5,808	5,101	1,900	15.8
					Israel	1,936	2,082	725	5.0
IMPORTERS					Jordan	355	468	190	8.9
					Kuwait	172	219	490	7.8
					Libya	672	625	975	15.7
Developed [1]	2,154	2,347	2,390	0.4	Morocco	441	135	40	0.7
Australia	780	1,353	675	1.5	Nicaragua	538	573	430	78.2
Canada	183	219	190	0.2	North Korea	452	1,041	525	(NA)
Czechoslovakia	995	219	460	3.5	Oman	118	31	60	2.7
East Germany	333	1,041	825	(NA)	Pakistan	344	437	460	6.4
Hungary	430	125	30	0.2	Peru	473	31	180	7.5
Italy	215	291	300	0.2	Saudi Arabia	7,529	2,811	4,200	21.2
Japan	1,076	1,249	1,400	0.7	South Korea	672	703	370	0.6
Poland	887	1,041	625	2.6	Spain	1,076	1,041	750	1.0
Romania	129	21	20	(NA)	Syria	2,151	1,353	1,000	47.7
Soviet Union	1,398	1,249	900	0.8	Turkey	1,022	1,015	1,100	7.0
United Kingdom	592	677	650	0.3	Venezuela	108	135	80	1.0
United States	2,366	2,602	1,600	0.3	Vietnam	2,044	1,561	1,300	(NA)
West Germany	672	1,145	875	0.3	Yemen (Sanaa)	430	448	420	(NA)

NA Not available.   [1] Includes countries not shown separately.

Source of tables 549 and 550: U.S. Arms Control and Disarmament Agency, *World Military Expenditures and Arms Transfers,* annual.

No. 551. Arms Transfers—Cumulative Value for Period 1985-89, by Major Supplier and Recipient Country

[In millions of dollars]

RECIPIENT	Total [1]	SUPPLIER					
		Soviet Union	United States	France	United Kingdom	China: Mainland	West Germany
World, total	256,585	102,465	60,480	18,075	14,095	8,360	6,190
Africa [1]	24,390	17,005	990	935	300	315	185
Algeria	3,260	2,700	50	20	40	-	-
Angola	6,000	5,500	-	80	-	-	-
Ethiopia	3,805	3,600	-	-	-	20	-
Libya	5,080	3,200	-	-	-	30	10
Morocco	770	-	240	150	-	20	-
Mozambique	850	825	-	5	5	-	-
Nigeria	705	30	50	110	120	5	130
Sudan	330	-	100	-	-	50	-
East Asia [1]	31,815	13,385	13,720	250	570	215	300
China: Mainland	2,205	500	210	120	260	(X)	40
Taiwan	3,885	-	3,000	-	-	-	-
North Korea	2,770	2,700	-	-	-	40	-
Malaysia	710	-	270	20	10	-	-
South Korea	2,645	-	2,600	10	30	-	-
Thailand	1,430	-	1,000	-	20	170	120
Vietnam	8,230	8,200	-	-	-	-	-
South Asia [1]	28,305	21,565	1,155	1,980	700	720	490
Afghanistan	9,730	9,700	-	-	-	-	-
India	16,080	11,800	210	1,900	650	-	470
Pakistan	2,000	5	925	80	40	410	20
Europe [1]	54,000	16,705	21,250	1,705	1,110	-	2,890
Belgium	1,460	-	1,400	60	-	-	-
Bulgaria	3,600	3,100	-	-	-	-	20
Czechoslovakia	3,440	3,300	-	-	-	-	-
Denmark	570	-	500	20	20	-	-
East Germany	4,425	3,500	-	-	-	-	-
France	980	-	900	(X)	10	-	-
Greece	3,210	90	1,800	1,000	-	-	210
Hungary	800	500	-	-	-	-	-
Italy	1,220	-	1,200	-	-	-	-
Netherlands	2,560	-	2,200	-	10	-	330
Norway	1,275	-	675	10	-	-	60
Poland	4,780	4,500	-	-	-	-	-
Soviet Union	5,910	(X)	-	-	-	-	-
Spain	3,335	-	2,800	70	210	-	10
Sweden	540	-	420	20	30	-	40
Switzerland	2,210	-	450	30	350	-	1,200
Turkey	3,970	-	2,500	20	360	-	1,000
United Kingdom	3,200	-	3,200	-	(X)	-	-
West Germany	3,530	-	2,600	360	60	-	(X)
Yugoslavia	855	675	150	-	-	-	-
Latin America [1]	16,905	9,730	2,065	830	150	-	680
Argentina	730	-	70	30	-	-	370
Chile	485	-	10	60	30	-	10
Colombia	290	-	80	-	20	-	5
Cuba	8,690	7,300	-	-	-	-	-
Ecuador	315	-	60	70	60	-	-
Peru	855	220	40	340	-	-	30
Venezuela	920	-	500	60	-	-	60
Middle East [1]	84,535	24,075	15,350	11,045	8,405	7,100	645
Egypt	5,800	575	2,900	675	170	190	40
Iran	10,250	-	10	75	100	2,800	50
Iraq	22,750	13,000	-	1,700	20	1,600	90
Israel	6,100	-	6,100	-	-	-	-
Jordan	2,070	1,200	460	110	40	-	10
Kuwait	1,345	180	150	450	110	-	-
Saudi Arabia	23,040	-	5,000	7,000	7,700	2,500	40
Syria	7,160	6,100	-	-	20	10	-
Yemen (Sanaa)	1,765	1,600	20	-	-	-	5
North America	10,755	-	735	1,300	2,700	10	900
Canada	825	-	735	-	-	-	-
United States	9,930	-	(X)	1,300	2,700	10	900

- Represents $2.5 million or less.   X Not applicable.   [1] Includes countries not shown separately.

Source: U.S. Arms Control and Disarmament Agency, *World Military Expenditures and Arms Transfers*, annual.

No. 552. Arms Delivered, by Selected Supplier and Major Weapon Type: 1985-89

[The suppliers included are the five largest single exporters of major weapons in terms of magnitude of deliveries as well as other countries of the two major alliances; excluded are Albania, Bulgaria, Greece, Malta, Spain, Turkey, and Yugoslavia]

TYPE OF WEAPON	Total [1]	United States [2]	France	United Kingdom	China: Mainland
Land armaments: Tanks.	7,302	971	38	70	560
Anti-air artillery [3]	2,432	2	25	-	820
Field artillery [4]	8,717	612	85	50	2,535
Armored personnel carriers.	13,718	1,052	505	12	1,300
Naval craft: Major surface combatants [5]	50	-	-	6	2
Other surface combatants [6]	528	23	39	37	16
Submarines.	24	-	-	-	-
Missile attack boats.	8	-	-	-	4
Aircraft: Combat aircraft (supersonic)	1,534	412	118	66	85
Combat aircraft (subsonic)	261	24	12	41	31
Other aircraft [7]	1,301	162	68	11	34
Helicopters.	1,582	193	235	23	-
Missiles (surface-to-air)	22,282	1,176	930	81	705

- Represents $2.5 million or less.   [1] Includes other countries not shown separately.   [2] United States data are by fiscal years, while other suppliers' data are by calendar years.   [3] Includes weapons over 23 millimeters.   [4] Includes mobile rocket launchers mortars, and recoilless rifles over 100 millimeters.   [5] Includes aircraft carriers, cruisers, destroyers, destroyer escorts, and frigates.   [6] Includes motor torpedo boats, subchasers, and minesweepers.   [7] Includes reconnaissance aircraft, trainers, transports, and utility aircraft.

Source: U.S. Arms Control and Disarmament Agency, *World Military Expenditures and Arms Transfers*, annual.

No. 553. Estimates of Total Dollar Costs of American Wars

[In millions of dollars, except percent. Service-connected veterans' benefits estimated at 40 percent of total veterans benefits, except as noted]

ITEM	World War II	Vietnam Conflict	Korean Conflict	World War I	Civil War: Union	Civil War: Confederacy	Spanish American War	American Revolution	War of 1812	Mexican War
Original incremental, direct costs: [1]										
Current dollars	360,000	140,600	50,000	32,700	2,300	1,000	270	100-140	89	82
Constant (1967) dollars	816,300	148,800	69,300	100,000	8,500	3,700	1,100	400-680	170	300
Percent 1 year's GNP	188	14	15	43	74	123	2	104	14	4
Service-connected benefits [2]	96,666	32,288	19,512	19,580	3,290	-	2,111	28	20	26
Interest, pmts. on war loans [3]	([4])	([4])	([4])	([4])	11,000	1,200	60	20	14	10
Current cost to 1990 [5]	466,000	179,000	72,000	63,500	6,790	([4])	2,441	170	120	120

- Represents zero.   [1] Figures are rounded and taken from Claudia D. Goldin, *Encyclopedia of American Economic History*, p. 938.   [2] Total cost to Oct. 1, 1990. For World War I and later wars, benefits are actual service-connected figures from *Annual Report of Veterans Administration*. For earlier wars, service-connected veterans' benefits are estimated at 40 percent of total, the approximate ratio of service-connected to total benefits since World War I.   [3] Total cost to 1990. Interest payments are a very rough approximation based on the percentage of the original costs of each war financed by money creation and debt, the difference between the level of public debt at the beginning of the war and at its end, and the approximate time required to pay off the war debts.   [4] Unknown.   [5] Figures are rounded estimates.

Source: Originally presented in U.S. Congress, Joint Economic Committee, *The Military Budget and National Economic Priorities*, part 1, 91st Congress, 1st session (statement of James L. Clayton); subsequently revised and updated by James L. Clayton, University of Utah, Salt Lake City, Utah.

No. 554. U.S. Military Sales and Assistance to Foreign Governments: 1950 to 1991

[In millions of dollars, except as indicated. For fiscal year ending in year shown; see text section 9. Department of Defense (DOD) sales deliveries cover deliveries against DOD sales orders authorized under Arms Export Control Act, as well as earlier and applicable legislation. For details regarding individual programs, see source]

ITEM	1950-83 [1]	1984	1985	1986	1987	1988	1989	1990	1991
Military sales agreements	121,352	12,784	10,482	6,412	6,375	11,605	10,568	13,817	22,982
Weapons and ammunition	52,962	5,920	3,411	2,148	1,814	5,047	4,366	5,403	6,343
Support equipment [2]	16,082	1,822	1,694	652	773	1,009	926	1,679	5,292
Spare parts and mods	26,084	2,493	2,371	1,524	1,604	3,023	2,428	2,631	5,064
Support services	26,224	2,549	3,006	2,088	2,184	2,526	2,848	4,104	6,283
Military constr. sales agrmts.	14,750	404	958	69	130	194	80	541	806
Military sales deliveries [3]	88,275	9,673	8,443	7,842	11,368	9,255	7,381	7,737	9,259
Military sales financing	33,840	5,716	4,940	4,947	4,053	4,049	4,273	4,813	4,679
Military assistance programs [4] [5]	54,985	700	812	841	972	702	542	137	170
Military assist. program delivery [5]	54,391	128	76	76	84	56	53	27	152
IMET program/deliveries [5]	2,090	52	54	51	54	46	46	46	48
Students trained (1,000)	518	6	7	6	6	6	5	5	5

[1] Includes transition quarter, July-September 1976.   [2] Includes aircraft, ships, support vehicles, communications equipment, and other supplies.   [3] Includes military construction sales deliveries.   [4] Also includes Military Assistance Service Funded (MASF) program data, section 506(a) drawdown authority, and MAP Merger Funds.   [5] Includes Military Assistance Service Funded (MASF) program data and section 506(a) drawdown authority.

Source: U.S. Defense Security Assistance Agency, *Foreign Military Sales, Foreign Military Construction Sales, and Military Assistance Facts*, annual; and unpublished data.

No. 555. U.S. Military Sales Deliveries to Foreign Governments, by Country: 1950 to 1991

[In millions of dollars. For *fiscal years ending in year shown;* see text, section 9. Represents Department of Defense military sales]

COUNTRY	1950-1983 [1]	1984	1985	1986	1987	1988	1989	1990	1991 Total	1991 Percent distribution
Total [2]	88,275	9,673	8,443	7,842	11,368	9,255	7,381	7,737	9,259	100.00
Australia	2,431	395	514	399	601	855	390	269	207	2.24
Belgium	1,462	196	119	28	27	222	153	178	184	1.99
Canada	1,698	139	73	113	127	213	152	105	113	1.22
China: Taiwan	2,352	275	339	244	370	485	348	537	562	6.07
Egypt	2,601	313	599	617	992	503	322	448	586	6.33
Germany	7,464	336	222	206	315	382	634	360	482	5.21
Greece	1,720	126	93	73	79	129	138	114	143	1.54
Israel	8,272	214	478	190	1,295	750	232	159	238	2.57
Italy	829	54	54	66	71	62	64	62	70	0.76
Japan	1,560	333	389	151	237	212	170	222	328	3.54
Jordan	1,220	77	122	63	50	55	60	44	24	0.26
Morocco	568	69	49	37	43	74	33	41	20	0.22
Netherlands	1,979	401	339	256	417	327	391	382	372	4.02
Norway	1,274	186	30	43	77	117	96	128	82	0.89
Saudi Arabia	24,025	3,573	2,265	2,773	3,464	1,332	976	1,154	3,118	33.68
Singapore	302	33	22	135	143	191	38	47	65	0.70
South Korea	2,330	258	258	344	353	335	328	296	219	2.37
Spain	959	66	92	262	822	637	687	427	157	1.70
Thailand	1,018	163	118	116	95	293	212	177	197	2.13
Turkey	1,132	305	390	282	279	730	667	707	766	8.27
United Kingdom	3,578	447	386	363	205	180	131	205	248	2.68
Venezuela	296	129	195	66	50	27	13	20	23	0.25

[1] Includes transactions for the transition quarter, July-September 1976. [2] Includes countries not shown.

Source: U.S. Defense Security Assistance Agency, *Foreign Military Sales, Foreign Military Construction Sales,* and *Military Assistance Facts,* annual.

No. 556. Summary of Active and Reserve Military Personnel and Forces: 1989 to 1991

ITEM	1989	1990, est.	1991, est.	ITEM	1989	1990, est.	1991, est.
Military personnel (1,000):				Naval forces (total):			
Active	2,130	2,076	2,039	Total naval vessels	566	551	546
Guard and Reserve	1,171	1,155	1,152	Aircraft carriers	14	14	14
Strategic forces:				Battleships	4	4	2
Intercontinental ballistic missiles:				Nuclear attack submarines	96	91	86
Peacekeeper	50	50	50	Amphibious assault ships	65	64	66
Minuteman	950	950	950	Sealift fleet	69	68	66
Poseidon-Trident	576	608	656	Air Forces:			
Strategic bomber squadrons	21	19	19	Air Force fighter wings (equiv.):			
General purpose forces:				Active	25	24	24
Land forces:				Navy attack wings: Active	13	13	13
Army divisions (active)	18	18	16	Marine Corps wings: Active	3	3	3
Marine divisions	3	3	3	Air Force B-52 squadrons	3	2	2
				Strategic airlift squadrons	20	20	20

Source: U.S. Office of Management and Budget, *Budget of the United States Government,* annual.

No. 557. Intercontinental Ballistic Missiles (ICBM's): 1980 to 1991

WEAPONS SYSTEM	1980	1985	1986	1987	1988	1989	1990	1991
ICBM's:								
United States [1]	1,052	1,017	999	996	1,000	1,000	1,000	956
Minuteman II	450	450	450	450	450	450	450	406
Minuteman III	550	550	534	514	500	500	500	500
Peacekeeper (MX)	-	-	10	32	50	50	50	50
Soviet Union	1,398	1,398	1,418	1,389	1,360	1,373	1,393	1,399
SS-11	640	448	440	420	400	350	325	325
SS-13	60	60	60	60	60	60	40	30
SS-17	150	150	150	145	125	75	50	70
SS-18	308	308	308	308	308	308	308	308
SS-19	240	360	360	350	330	300	300	270
SS-24	-	-	-	6	12	60	90	96
SS-25	-	72	100	100	125	220	280	300

- Represents zero. [1] Includes weapons not shown separately.

Source: The Congress of the United States, Library of Congress, Congressional Research Service, *U.S./Soviet Military Balance, Statistical Trends, 1980-1990,* July 1990.

No. 558. Military Installations in the United States: 1992

[Represents bases with active-duty populations of 300 or more. Excludes the Coast Guard]

STATE AND BRANCH	Active duty personnel	Family members	Civilians	STATE AND BRANCH	Active duty personnel	Family members	Civilians
United States	1,194,888	1,270,271	582,365	United States	1,194,888	1,270,271	582,365
Alabama	18,609	31,371	32,719	Air Force	2,391	1,960	2,398
Army	15,582	25,836	30,990	Michigan	5,685	13,492	3,338
Navy	812	-	90	Air Force	5,685	13,492	3,338
Air Force	2,215	5,535	1,639	Mississippi	13,021	12,401	8,386
Alaska	22,810	30,400	6,160	Navy	6,050	4,200	2,880
Army	9,900	12,300	3,270	Air Force	6,971	8,201	5,506
Navy	2,442	1,869	239	Missouri	16,411	13,378	4,126
Air Force	10,468	16,231	2,651	Army	13,011	9,478	2,226
Arizona	22,665	37,023	9,665	Air Force	3,400	3,900	1,900
Army	5,682	4,760	5,597	Montana	4,290	6,301	541
Marine Corps	5,207	6,818	605	Air Force	4,290	6,301	541
Air Force	11,776	25,445	3,463	Nebraska	10,400	17,000	1,400
Arkansas	5,200	6,000	700	Air Force	10,400	17,000	1,400
Air Force	5,200	6,000	700	Nevada	8,350	19,800	2,400
California	275,353	171,133	121,090	Navy	950	1,800	900
Army	25,668	30,387	12,922	Air Force	7,400	18,000	1,500
Navy	143,914	56,258	48,245	New Hampshire	600	1,350	6,390
Marine Corps	68,084	29,322	21,859	Navy	600	1,350	6,390
Air Force	37,687	55,166	38,064	New Jersey	10,455	13,605	16,757
Colorado	38,367	48,646	6,887	Army	3,205	3,805	11,257
Army	18,323	36,620	4,887	Navy	2,850	-	3,700
Air Force	20,044	12,026	2,000	Air Force	4,400	9,800	1,800
Connecticut	11,000	22,500	1,800	New Mexico	15,426	27,595	11,051
Navy	11,000	22,500	1,800	Army	1,027	1,748	8,006
Delaware	4,281	6,001	2,362	Air Force	14,399	25,847	3,045
Air Force	4,281	6,001	2,362	New York	31,152	32,044	12,699
District of Columbia	11,561	4,907	11,743	Army	18,102	19,210	7,244
Army	5,294	60	5,308	Navy	4,730	4,000	1,400
Navy	2,913	-	5,390	Air Force	8,320	8,834	4,055
Marine Corps	1,200	700	45	North Carolina	110,873	130,423	20,100
Air Force	2,154	4,147	1,000	Army	43,885	80,108	9,805
Florida	95,172	93,119	35,413	Marine Corps	57,800	41,600	8,435
Navy	65,355	56,266	25,089	Air Force	9,188	8,715	1,860
Air Force	29,817	36,853	10,324	North Dakota	9,806	13,512	1,647
Georgia	82,523	99,704	40,349	Air Force	9,806	13,512	1,647
Army	66,709	78,603	15,374	Ohio	9,904	5,900	21,778
Navy	7,016	8,850	4,213	Air Force	9,904	5,900	21,778
Marine Corps	1,198	2,000	5,902	Oklahoma	31,242	28,925	23,632
Air Force	7,600	10,251	14,860	Army	19,887	21,681	6,820
Hawaii	61,238	56,618	25,217	Air Force	11,355	7,244	16,812
Army	20,490	13,608	3,938	Pennsylvania	6,221	6,845	11,648
Navy	24,031	28,560	14,460	Army	692	1,618	605
Marine Corps	11,542	6,629	2,049	Navy	5,529	5,227	11,043
Air Force	5,175	7,821	4,770	Rhode Island	5,500	4,000	4,500
Idaho	4,900	6,500	600	Navy	5,500	4,000	4,500
Navy	1,500	2,000	-	South Carolina	57,007	102,667	21,773
Air Force	3,400	4,500	600	Army	13,501	11,262	3,850
Illinois	34,021	30,155	17,093	Navy	26,704	62,696	13,729
Army	3,080	5,103	9,234	Marine Corps	5,600	7,000	940
Navy	19,500	13,200	3,675	Air Force	11,202	21,709	3,254
Air Force	11,441	11,852	4,184	South Dakota	6,360	10,000	714
Indiana	5,808	6,514	6,250	Air Force	6,360	10,000	714
Army	3,500	3,000	4,900	Tennessee	10,996	2,644	2,953
Air Force	2,308	3,514	1,350	Navy	10,996	2,644	2,953
Kansas	23,658	26,670	3,313	Texas	114,178	153,400	51,380
Army	20,600	19,500	2,900	Army	64,502	91,938	13,726
Air Force	3,058	7,170	413	Navy	6,611	10,250	5,597
Kentucky	34,600	41,194	11,562	Air Force	43,065	51,212	32,057
Army	34,600	41,194	11,562	Utah	5,001	9,200	12,378
Louisiana	26,415	39,827	8,180	Air Force	5,001	9,200	12,378
Army	15,885	23,095	3,852	Virginia	181,772	185,796	89,630
Navy	4,630	9,132	3,128	Army	21,780	31,476	22,729
Air Force	5,900	7,600	1,200	Navy	149,395	149,742	64,689
Maine	5,513	6,787	1,707	Marine Corps	10,597	4,578	2,212
Navy	3,245	3,345	986	Air Force	8,539	12,521	1,796
Air Force	2,268	3,442	721	Washington	55,342	72,417	29,932
Maryland	38,504	35,760	58,874	Army	18,000	25,000	5,709
Army	17,910	22,872	41,180	Navy	28,742	35,817	21,119
Navy	10,585	2,900	14,494	Air Force	8,600	11,600	3,104
Air Force	10,009	9,988	3,200	Wisconsin	370	744	1,574
Massachusetts	8,991	7,560	4,848	Army	370	744	1,574
Army	6,000	5,600	2,200	Wyoming	3,450	4,704	693
Navy	600	-	250	Air Force	3,450	4,704	693

- Represents zero.

Source: Army Times Publishing Co., Springfield, VA. 22159; Guide to Military Installations in the U. S., November 2, 1992.

No. 559. Department of Defense Manpower: 1950 to 1991

[In thousands. As of end of fiscal year; see text, section 9. Includes National Guard, Reserve, and retired regular personnel on extended or continuous active duty. Excludes Coast Guard. Other officer candidates are included under enlisted personnel. See also *Historical Statistics, Colonial Times to 1970,* series Y 904-916]

YEAR	Total [1][2]	ARMY			NAVY [3]			MARINE CORPS			AIR FORCE		
		Total [2]	Officers	Enlisted	Total [2]	Officers	Enlisted	Total [2]	Officers	Enlisted	Total [2]	Officers	Enlisted
1950	1,459	593	73	519	381	45	333	74	7	67	411	57	354
1955	2,935	1,109	122	986	661	75	583	205	18	187	960	137	823
1960	2,475	873	101	770	617	70	545	171	16	154	815	130	683
1961	2,483	859	100	757	626	70	552	177	16	161	821	129	690
1962	2,806	1,066	116	949	664	75	585	191	17	174	884	135	746
1963	2,699	976	108	866	664	76	584	190	17	173	869	134	733
1964	2,686	973	111	861	666	76	585	190	17	173	857	133	721
1965	2,654	969	112	855	670	78	588	190	17	173	825	132	690
1966	3,092	1,200	118	1,080	743	80	659	262	21	241	887	131	753
1967	3,375	1,442	144	1,297	750	82	664	285	24	262	897	135	759
1968	3,546	1,570	166	1,402	764	85	674	307	25	283	905	140	762
1969	3,458	1,512	173	1,337	774	85	684	310	26	284	862	135	723
1970	3,065	1,323	167	1,153	691	81	606	260	25	235	791	130	657
1971	2,713	1,124	149	972	622	75	542	212	22	191	755	126	625
1972	2,322	811	121	687	587	73	511	198	20	178	726	122	600
1973	2,252	801	116	682	564	71	490	196	19	177	691	115	572
1974	2,162	783	106	674	546	67	475	189	19	170	644	110	529
1975	2,128	784	103	678	535	66	466	196	19	177	613	105	503
1976	2,082	779	99	678	525	64	458	192	19	174	585	100	481
1977	2,075	782	98	680	530	63	462	192	19	173	571	96	470
1978	2,062	772	98	670	530	63	463	191	18	172	570	95	470
1979	2,027	759	97	657	523	62	457	185	18	167	559	96	459
1980	2,051	777	99	674	527	63	460	188	18	170	558	98	456
1981	2,083	781	102	675	540	65	470	191	18	172	570	99	467
1982	2,109	780	103	673	553	67	481	192	19	173	583	102	476
1983	2,123	780	106	669	558	68	485	194	20	174	592	105	483
1984	2,138	780	108	668	565	69	491	196	20	176	597	106	486
1985	2,151	781	110	667	571	71	495	198	20	178	602	108	489
1986	2,169	781	110	667	581	72	504	199	20	179	608	109	495
1987	2,174	781	108	668	587	72	510	200	20	179	607	107	495
1988	2,138	772	107	660	593	72	516	197	20	177	576	105	467
1989	2,130	770	107	658	593	72	516	197	20	177	571	104	463
1990	2,044	732	104	624	579	72	503	197	20	177	535	100	431
1991	1,986	711	104	603	570	71	495	194	20	174	510	97	409

[1] Beginning 1980, excludes Navy Reserve personnel on active duty for Training and Administration of Reserves (TARS). From 1969, includes the full-time Guard and Reserve. [2] Includes Cadets. [3] Prior to 1980, includes Navy Reserve personnel on active duty for Training and Administration of Reserves (TARS).

Source: U.S. Dept. of Defense, *Selected Manpower Statistics,* annual.

No. 560. Military Personnel on Active Duty, by Location: 1970 to 1992

[In thousands. 1970 and 1975, as of Dec. 31; thereafter, as of end of fiscal year; see text, section 9]

ITEM	1970	1975	1980	1985	1986	1987	1988	1989	1990	1991	1992, prel.
Total	3,066	2,128	2,051	2,151	2,169	2,174	2,138	2,130	2,044	1,986	1,807
Shore-based [1]	2,798	1,912	1,840	1,920	1,929	1,928	1,891	1,884	1,794	1,743	1,589
Afloat [2]	268	216	211	231	240	246	248	246	252	243	218
United States [3]	2,033	1,643	1,562	1,636	1,644	1,650	1,598	1,620	1,437	1,539	1,463
Foreign countries	1,033	485	488	516	526	524	541	510	609	448	344

[1] Includes Navy personnel temporarily on shore. [2] Includes Marine Corps. [3] Includes outlying areas.

Source: U.S. Dept. of Defense, *Selected Manpower Statistics,* annual; and unpublished data.

No. 561. Military Personnel on Active Duty in Foreign Countries: 1991

[As of end of fiscal year]

COUNTRY	1991	COUNTRY	1991	COUNTRY	1991
Total	447,572	E. Asia and Pacific [1]	104,781	Saudi Arabia	14,617
Ashore	396,014	Australia	707	United Arab Emirates	39
Afloat	51,558	China	33	Afloat	17,266
Western Europe [1]	284,939	Hong Kong	31	Western Hemisphere [1]	19,456
Austria	32	Indonesia	40	Antigua	74
Denmark	64	Japan	44,566	Bahamas, The	44
France	81	New Zealand	58	Bermuda	1,178
Germany	203,423	Philippines	7,761	Brazil	46
Greece	1,375	Rep. of Korea	40,062	Canada	513
Greenland	163	Singapore	68	Colombia	43
Iceland	3,209	Thailand	111	Costa Rica	12
Italy	13,389	Afloat	11,300	Cuba (Guantanamo)	2,323
Netherlands	2,635	Africa, Near East,		El Salvador	96
Norway	225	and South Asia [1]	35,335	Honduras	1,005
Portugal	2,031	Bahrain	255	Mexico	28
Spain	6,166	Egypt	1,135	Panama	10,568
Switzerland	29	India	29	Peru	31
Turkey	6,343	Israel	438	Venezuela	34
U.S.S.R.	56	Kenya	28	Afloat	3,234
United Kingdom	23,442	Morocco	40	Antarctica	61
Afloat	19,758	Pakistan	31		

[1] Includes areas not shown separately.

Source: U.S. Department of Defense, *Selected Manpower Statistics*, annual.

No. 562. Coast Guard Personnel on Active Duty: 1970 to 1992

[As of end of fiscal year; see text, section 9]

YEAR	Total	Officers	Cadets	Enlisted	YEAR	Total	Officers	Cadets	Enlisted
1970	37,689	5,512	653	31,524	1985	38,595	6,775	733	31,087
1975	36,788	5,630	1,177	29,981	1986	37,284	6,577	754	29,953
1979	38,559	6,340	806	31,413	1987	38,576	6,644	859	31,073
1980	39,381	6,463	877	32,041	1988	37,723	6,530	887	30,306
1981	39,760	6,519	981	32,260	1989	37,474	6,611	869	29,994
1982	38,248	6,431	902	30,915	1990	36,939	6,876	927	29,136
1983	39,708	6,535	811	32,362	1991	38,377	7,192	900	30,285
1984	38,705	6,790	759	31,156	1992	39,388	7,507	919	30,962

Source: U.S. Dept. of Transportation, *Annual Report of the Secretary of Transportation*.

No. 563. Vietnam Conflict—U.S. Military Forces in Vietnam and Combat Area Casualties: 1957 to 1992

[Military forces as of Dec. 31. All U.S. forces withdrawn by Jan. 27, 1973]

ITEM	Unit	1957-1992 total [1]	1957-1964	1965	1966	1967	1968	1969	1970	1971	1972	1973-1989
Military forces [2]	1,000	(X)	[3]23.3	184.3	385.3	485.6	536.1	475.2	234.6	156.8	24.2	-
Battle deaths [4]	Number	47,366	279	1,432	5,047	9,463	14,623	9,426	4,230	1,376	361	1,118
Killed	Number	38,506	197	1,124	4,142	7,525	12,624	8,117	3,486	1,082	205	-
Died of wounds	Number	5,224	10	111	579	1,598	979	1,168	555	160	28	22
Died while missing [5]	Number	3,636	72	197	326	401	959	141	189	134	128	1,068

- Represents zero.   X Not applicable.   [1] Number in this column indicates 11 more deaths than a tally of the number by time period, due to revisions. The Cambodia area includes North and South Vietnam, Cambodia, Thailand, Laos, and China. [2] Source: U.S. Dept. of Defense, *Selected Manpower Statistics*, annual.   [3] For 1964 only.   [4] Casualties from enemy action. Deaths exclude 10,799 servicemen who died in accidents, from disease, or other causes.   [5] Includes servicemen who died while captured.

Source: Except as indicated, National Archives and Records Administration, unpublished data from Combat Area Casualties database, as of November 1992.

No. 564. Armed Forces Personnel—Summary of Major Conflicts

[For Revolutionary War, number of personnel serving not known, but estimates range from 184,000 to 250,000; for War of 1812, 286,730 served; for Mexican War, 78,718 served. Dates of the major conflicts may differ from those specified in various laws providing benefits for veterans. See table 563 for data on Vietnam conflict. See also *Historical Statistics, Colonial Times to 1970*, series Y 856-903]

ITEM	Unit	Civil War [1]	Spanish-American War	World War I	World War II	Korean conflict	Vietnam conflict
Personnel serving [2]	1,000	2,213	307	4,735	[3]16,113	[4]5,720	[5]8,744
Average duration of service	Months	20	8	12	33	19	23
Service abroad: Personnel serving	Percent	(NA)	[6]29	53	73	[7]56	(NA)
Average duration [8]	Months	(NA)	1.5	6	16	13	(NA)
Casualties: [9] Battle deaths [2]	1,000	140	(Z)	53	292	34	[10]47
Wounds not mortal [2]	1,000	282	2	204	671	103	[10]153
Draftees: Classified	1,000	777	(X)	24,234	36,677	9,123	[5]75,717
Examined	1,000	522	(X)	3,764	17,955	3,685	[5]8,611
Rejected	1,000	160	(X)	803	6,420	1,189	[5]3,880
Inducted	1,000	46	(X)	2,820	10,022	1,560	[5]1,759

NA Not available. X Not applicable. Z Fewer than 500. [1] Union forces only. Estimates of the number serving in Confederate forces range from 600,000 to 1.5 million. [2] Source: U.S. Department of Defense, *Selected Manpower Statistics*, FY 1991, annual. [3] Covers Dec. 1, 1941, to Dec. 31, 1946. [4] Covers June 25, 1950, to July 27, 1953. [5] Covers Aug. 4, 1964, to Jan. 27, 1973. [6] Army and Marines only. [7] Excludes Navy. Covers July 1950 through Jan. 1955. Far East area only. [8] During hostilities only. [9] For periods covered, see footnotes 3, 4, and 5. [10] Covers Jan. 1, 1961, to Jan. 27, 1973. Includes known military service personnel who have died from combat related wounds.

Source: Except as noted, the President's Commission on Veterans' Pensions, Veterans' *Benefits in the United States*, vol. I, 1956; and U.S. Dept. of Defense, unpublished data.

No. 565. Enlisted Military Personnel Accessions: 1980 to 1990

[In thousands. For years ending Sept. 30]

BRANCH OF SERVICE	1980	1985	1989	1990	BRANCH OF SERVICE	1980	1985	1989	1990
Total	582	529	530	461	Marine Corps	58	57	49	48
Army	265	201	224	182	First enlistments	42	36	33	33
First enlistments	163	117	112	85	Reenlistments	15	19	16	14
Reenlistments	97	84	111	97					
Navy	127	139	155	135	Air Force	132	133	102	104
First enlistments	75	67	74	62	First enlistments	76	68	44	37
Reenlistments	36	50	62	59	Reenlistments	56	64	58	68

Source: U.S. Dept. of Defense, *Selected Manpower Statistics*, annual.

No. 566. Military Personnel on Active Duty and Monthly Basic Pay: 1985 to 1992

[Personnel as of Sept. 30; basic pay as of January, except as noted]

RANK/GRADE	PERSONNEL (1,000)				MONTHLY BASIC PAY (dollars)			
	1985	1990	1991	1992	1985	1990	1991	1992
Total [1]	2,151.0	2,043.7	1,985.6	1,807.2	(X)	(X)	(X)	(X)
Recruit—E-1	127.6	97.6	74.6	83.2	594	684	710	749
Private—E-2	140.6	140.3	125.8	110.9	689	803	838	902
Pvt. 1st class—E-3	336.3	280.1	275.6	233.5	747	871	900	935
Corporal—E-4	444.4	427.8	426.1	383.5	866	1,014	1,066	1,102
Sergeant—E-5	356.2	361.5	355.5	305.1	1,036	1,245	1,297	1,354
Staff Sgt.—E-6	237.8	239.1	238.9	227.4	1,260	1,480	1,563	1,630
Sgt. 1st class—E-7	131.9	134.1	134.2	130.5	1,525	1,784	1,866	1,940
Master Sgt.—E-8	38.5	38.0	36.1	33.2	1,826	2,117	2,210	2,294
Sgt. Major—E-9	15.1	15.3	14.8	13.5	2,234	2,583	2,682	2,785
Warrant Officer—W-1	2.4	3.2	2.8	2.2	1,403	1,686	1,747	1,820
Chief Warrant—W-4	3.2	3.0	3.0	2.7	2,491	2,943	3,085	3,210
2d Lt.—O-1	39.7	31.9	27.3	25.8	1,275	1,485	1,562	1,620
1st Lt.—O-2	42.7	37.9	37.6	33.5	1,737	2,056	2,135	2,219
Captain—O-3	104.4	106.6	106.1	100.2	2,230	2,618	2,727	2,828
Major—O-4	53.3	53.2	53.1	50.4	2,708	3,196	3,321	3,456
Lt. Colonel—O-5	32.8	32.3	32.2	30.9	3,279	3,894	4,041	4,208
Colonel—O-6	14.7	14.0	13.7	13.2	4,039	4,758	4,942	5,140
Brig. General—O-7	0.5	0.5	0.5	0.5	4,928	5,751	5,987	6,238
Major General—O-8	0.4	0.4	0.3	0.3	5,667	6,516	6,783	7,068
Lt. General—O-9	0.1	0.1	0.1	0.1	[2]5,725	6,516	7,482	7,788
General—O-10	(Z)	(Z)	(Z)	(Z)	[2]5,725	6,516	8,441	8,733

X Not applicable. Z Fewer than 50. [1] Includes cadets and midshipmen and warrant officers, W-2 and W-3. [2] Statutory limitation.

Source: U.S. Dept. of Defense, *Selected Manpower Statistics*, annual, and Office of the Comptroller, unpublished data.

No. 567. Military Reserve Personnel: 1970 to 1992

[In thousands. As of end of fiscal year; see text, section 9. Excludes U.S. Coast Guard Reserve. The ready reserve includes selected reservists who are intended to assist active forces in a war and the individual ready reserve who, in a major war, would be used to fill out active and reserve units and later would be a source of combat replacements; a portion of the ready reserve serves in an active status. The standby reserve cannot be called to active duty unless the Congress gives its explicit approval. The retired reserve represents a low potential for mobilization]

RESERVE STATUS AND BRANCH OF SERVICE	1970	1975	1980	1983	1984	1985	1986	1987	1988	1989	1990	1991	1992
Total reserves	3,639	1,836	1,349	1,464	1,534	1,610	1,653	1,657	1,677	1,661	1,670	1,786	1,883
Ready reserve	2,574	1,471	1,263	1,420	1,491	1,566	1,612	1,620	1,642	1,631	1,641	1,758	1,857
Standby reserve	492	365	86	44	44	44	41	38	344	29	29	28	25
Retired reserve	573	(NA)	338	383	379	760	390	377	1,792	1,823	1,845	1,879	1,772
Army	2,221	1,168	804	940	996	1,045	1,067	1,064	1,070	1,062	1,050	1,124	1,156
Navy	808	273	207	192	201	214	228	238	244	248	252	271	297
Marine Corp	(NA)	124	94	91	92	92	93	88	87	82	83	96	107
Air Force	610	271	243	241	246	259	266	268	275	270	286	295	323

Source: U.S. Dept. of Defense, *Official Guard and Reserve Manpower Strengths and Statistics*, quarterly.

No. 568. Ready Reserve Personnel Profile—Race, Age, and Sex: 1989 and 1992

ITEM	RACE					PERCENT DISTRIBUTION			
	Total	White	Black	Asian	American Indian	White	Black	Asian	American Indian
1989, total . . .	1,676,105	1,282,456	372,765	13,237	7,647	76.5	22.2	0.8	0.5
1990, total . . .	1,558,867	1,269,278	271,470	14,608	3,511	81.4	17.4	0.9	0.2
1991, total . . .	1,154,515	906,748	190,214	12,711	5,652	78.5	16.5	1.1	0.5
Male	1,003,325	806,894	146,853	11,179	4,824	80.4	14.6	1.1	0.5
Officers	146,657	133,644	7,768	1,466	263	91.1	5.3	1.0	0.2
Enlisted	856,668	673,250	139,085	9,713	4,561	78.6	16.2	1.1	0.5
Female	151,190	99,854	43,360	1,532	828	66.0	28.7	1.0	0.5
Officers	25,772	20,541	3,838	243	47	79.7	14.9	0.9	0.2
Enlisted	125,418	79,313	39,522	1,289	781	63.2	31.5	1.0	0.6
1992, total . . .	1,114,905	725,963	172,770	11,479	4,842	65.1	15.5	1.0	0.4
Male	966,503	660,227	141,741	11,501	4,360	68.3	14.7	1.2	0.5
Officers	141,770	12,874	7,684	1,451	261	9.1	5.4	1.0	0.2
Enlisted	824,733	647,352	134,057	10,050	4,099	78.5	16.3	1.2	0.5
Female	148,783	98,389	42,466	1,686	804	66.1	28.5	1.1	0.5
Officers	24,832	19,780	3,753	257	61	79.7	15.1	1.0	0.2
Enlisted	123,951	78,609	38,713	1,429	743	63.4	31.2	1.2	0.6

Source: U.S. Dept. of Defense, *Official Guard and Reserve Manpower Strengths and Statistics*, annual.

No. 569. Military Reserve Costs: 1970 to 1990

[In millions of dollars. As of end of fiscal year; see text, section 9. Army and Air Force data include National Guard]

TYPE OF COST	1970	1980	1982	1983	1984	1985	1986	1987	1988	1989	1990
Total	2,597	7,969	10,464	11,910	11,886	19,414	19,640	18,947	19,234	20,630	22,081
Operations and maintenance . . .	994	3,526	4,716	5,137	5,128	5,734	5,770	6,168	6,670	6,765	6,757
Personnel	1,133	2,456	3,912	4,633	5,065	7,703	8,500	8,382	8,837	9,129	9,106
Procurement	187	1,459	971	1,471	984	5,009	4,383	3,316	2,533	3,520	4,914
Active-duty support	234	408	556	386	408	566	616	601	610	611	638
Construction	49	120	309	283	301	402	371	480	584	605	666

Source: U.S. Dept. of Defense, unpublished data.

No. 570. National Guard—Summary: 1970 to 1991

[As of end of fiscal year; see text, section 9. Includes Puerto Rico]

ITEM	Unit	1970	1975	1980	1985	1986	1987	1988	1989	1990	1991
Army National Guard: Units .	Number . .	3,052	3,245	3,379	4,353	5,712	6,125	5,982	5,715	4,055	6,470
Personnel [1]	1,000	410	403	368	438	446	452	455	457	444	446
Funds obligated [2]	Mil. dol . .	752	1,322	1,802	4,387	4,825	4,955	5,258	5,354	5,187	5,419
Value of equipment	Mil. dol . .	1,600	4,100	7,600	18,800	19,700	22,300	27,390	30,129	29,000	29,000
Air National Guard: Units .	Number . .	958	1,106	1,054	1,184	1,229	1,281	1,272	1,339	1,339	1,450
Personnel [1]	1,000	90	95	96	109	113	115	115	116	118	11,463
Funds obligated [2]	Mil. dol . .	467	890	1,678	2,813	2,809	2,886	3,072	3,183	3,192	11,819
Value of equipment (est.) [3] .	Mil. dol . .	(NA)	3,100	5,200	21,400	26,100	23,668	25,683	27,481	26,356	27,094

NA Not available. [1] Officers and enlisted personnel. [2] Federal funds; includes personnel, operations, maintenance, and military construction. [3] Beginning 1984, increase due to repricing of aircraft to current year dollars to reflect true replacement value.

Source: National Guard Bureau, *Annual Review of the Chief, National Guard Bureau;* and unpublished data.

No. 571. Wartime Veterans—States: 1991

[Estimates in thousands. As of end of fiscal year; see text, section 9. Data were estimated starting with veteran's place of residence as of April 1, 1980, based on 1980 Census of Population data, extended to later years on the basis of estimates of veteran interstate migration, separations from the Armed Forces, and mortality; not directly comparable with earlier estimates previously published by the VA. Excludes 423,000 veterans whose only active-duty military service occurred since September 8, 1980, and who failed to satisfy the minimum service requirement. Also excludes a small indeterminate number of National Guard personnel or reservists who incurred service-connected disabilities while on an initial tour of active duty for training only]

STATE	Total [1]	World War I	World War II [2][3]	KOREAN CONFLICT Total [2][3]	KOREAN CONFLICT No prior wartime service [4]	VIETNAM ERA Total [2][4][5]	VIETNAM ERA No prior wartime service	PERSIAN GULF WAR Total [5][6]	PERSIAN GULF WAR No prior wartime service
U.S.	20,280	65	8,443	4,693	3,859	8,269	7,697	263	216
Northeast	4,225	13	1,933	957	834	1,460	1,407	46	37
N.E.	1,146	3	508	266	224	423	402	11	9
ME	116	-	47	27	22	48	45	2	1
NH	110	-	41	25	21	50	47	1	1
VT	46	-	18	10	9	20	19	1	1
MA	495	2	233	115	97	168	160	4	3
RI	90	-	42	21	17	33	30	1	1
CT	289	1	127	68	58	104	101	2	2
M.A.	3,079	10	1,425	691	610	1,037	1,005	35	28
NY	1,305	5	601	293	264	431	422	16	13
NJ	653	2	308	153	133	215	205	5	4
PA	1,121	3	516	245	213	391	378	14	11
Midwest	4,924	18	1,953	1,089	968	1,990	1,925	70	61
E.N.C.	3,404	11	1,361	742	665	1,360	1,324	49	43
OH	933	3	389	201	179	363	351	14	12
IN	450	1	171	100	89	187	182	7	6
IL	891	3	372	199	178	336	328	11	10
MI	726	2	275	155	141	305	298	11	10
WI	404	2	154	87	78	169	165	6	5
W.N.C.	1,520	7	592	347	303	630	601	21	18
MN	363	2	134	81	72	156	152	5	4
IA	237	1	87	51	47	101	98	4	3
MO	470	2	192	110	93	189	178	6	5
ND	47	-	17	10	10	20	20	1	1
SD	57	-	22	15	13	22	21	1	1
NE	131	1	52	32	28	53	49	2	2
KS	215	1	88	48	40	89	83	2	2
South	6,932	21	2,898	1,639	1,285	2,952	2,652	98	77
S.A.	3,684	11	1,618	890	682	1,510	1,334	49	38
DE	59	-	24	13	11	25	23	1	1
MD	404	1	164	101	79	171	156	5	4
DC	41	-	19	11	8	14	13	1	-
VA	497	1	199	135	99	227	193	7	5
WV	160	1	71	34	29	61	57	2	2
NC	523	1	223	123	103	210	191	7	6
SC	270	1	109	66	52	121	105	4	3
GA	498	1	177	116	92	245	221	7	6
FL	1,232	5	632	291	209	436	375	15	11
E.S.C.	1,136	4	459	271	225	473	434	18	14
KY	265	1	105	61	53	108	102	4	4
TN	395	1	155	88	74	173	161	6	4
AL	304	1	123	79	64	125	112	5	4
MS	172	1	76	43	34	67	59	3	2
W.S.C.	2,112	6	821	478	378	969	884	31	25
AR	185	1	79	42	33	78	70	3	3
LA	311	1	130	69	56	130	120	5	4
OK	290	1	115	67	53	129	118	4	3
TX	1,326	3	497	300	236	632	576	19	15
West	4,199	11	1,658	1,006	771	1,871	1,710	50	40
Mt.	1,179	2	455	273	213	539	491	16	13
MT	74	-	28	15	13	32	31	1	1
ID	81	-	30	18	15	36	34	2	1
WY	40	-	12	8	7	21	20	1	1
CO	299	1	100	71	55	153	139	4	3
NM	130	-	50	30	23	60	54	2	2
AZ	332	1	148	76	57	137	122	4	3
UT	109	-	43	25	20	48	45	1	1
NV	114	-	44	30	23	52	46	1	1
Pac.	3,020	9	1,203	733	558	1,332	1,219	34	27
WA	456	1	165	107	80	225	204	6	5
OR	267	1	103	54	44	121	115	4	3
CA	2,171	7	894	542	411	919	840	22	18
AK	49	-	12	10	8	31	29	1	-
HI	77	-	29	20	15	36	31	1	1

- Represents or rounds to zero. [1] Includes one living Spanish-American War veteran and an indeterminate number of Mexican Border period veterans. Veterans who served in more than one wartime period are counted only once. [2] Includes 269,000 who served in the Vietnam era, Korean conflict, and World War II. [3] Includes 649,000 who served in both World War II and the Korean conflict. [4] Includes 339,000 who served in both the Korean conflict and the Vietnam era. [5] Excludes reservists. [6] Includes 47,000 who served in both the Vietnam-era and the Persian Gulf War.

Source: U.S. Dept. of Veterans Affairs, Management Sciences Service (008B2), *Annual Report of the Secretary of Veterans Affairs*, Fiscal Year 1991.

No. 572. Veterans Living in the United States and Puerto Rico, by Age and by Service: 1992

[In thousands, except as indicated. As of Sept. 30. Estimated. Excludes 487,000 veterans whose only active duty military service occurred since Sept. 30, 1980. See headnote, table 571. See *Historical Statistics, Colonial Times to 1970*, series Y 943-956, for all veterans]

AGE	Total veterans	WARTIME VETERANS						PEACETIME VETERANS	
		Total [1]	Persian Gulf [2]	Vietnam era [2][3]	Korean conflict [2][3]	World War II [3][4]	World War I	Total	Post-Vietnam era [5]
All ages	[6]26,992	20,839	733	8,282	4,785	8,510	34	6,153	3,060
Under 30 years old . . .	1,394	440	440	-	-	-	-	955	955
30 to 34 years old. . . .	1,389	152	95	57	-	-	-	1,237	1,237
35 to 39 years old. . . .	1,691	1,033	60	996	-	-	-	658	658
40 to 44 years old. . . .	2,892	2,749	77	2,733	-	-	-	143	134
45 to 49 years old. . . .	3,205	2,837	40	2,823	-	-	-	367	41
50 to 54 years old. . . .	2,403	975	14	908	69	-	-	1,429	22
55 to 59 years old. . . .	2,732	1,654	5	317	1,482	-	-	1,078	11
60 to 64 years old. . . .	3,198	3,016	1	237	2,391	767	-	182	2
65 years old and over .	8,088	7,983	(Z)	211	843	7,742	34	105	-

- Represents zero. Z Less than 500. [1] Veterans who served in more than one wartime period are counted only once. Includes Vietnam era (no prior wartime service), Korean conflict (no prior wartime service), World War II, and World War I. [2] Includes 339,000 who served in both the Korean conflict and the Vietnam era. [3] Includes 269,000 who served in the Vietnam era, Korean conflict, and World War II. [4] Includes 649,000 who served in both World War II and the Korean conflict. [5] Service only after May 7, 1975. [6] There is also one living Spanish-American War veteran and an estimated 65 living Mexican Border conflict veterans.

Source: U.S. Dept. of Veterans Affairs, Office of Information Management and Statistics, *Veteran Population*, annual.

No. 573. Disabled Veterans Receiving Compensation: 1970 to 1992

[In thousands, except as indicated. As of end of fiscal year; see text, section 9. Represents veterans receiving compensation for service-connected disabilities. Totally disabled refers to veterans with any disability, mental or physical, deemed to be total and permanent which prevents the individual from maintaining a livelihood and are rated for disability at 100 percent]

MILITARY SERVICE	1970	1975	1980	1985	1987	1988	1989	1990	1991	1992
Disabled, all periods [1]	2,092	2,220	2,274	2,240	2,212	2,199	2,192	2,184	2,179	2,181
Peace-time	185	194	262	352	382	398	421	444	468	500
World War I [1]	85	55	30	12	8	6	5	3	3	2
World War II.	1,416	1,309	1,193	1,049	982	947	912	876	841	805
Korea.	239	240	236	223	218	215	212	209	205	202
Vietnam.	167	423	553	604	623	633	643	652	662	671
Totally disabled, all periods [1].	124	123	121	136	132	131	131	131	131	132
Peace-time	16	16	20	26	26	26	26	27	27	28
World War I [1]	11	6	3	1	1	1	(Z)	(Z)	(Z)	(Z)
World War II.	63	58	51	54	49	47	45	43	41	39
Korea.	16	16	16	17	16	16	16	16	16	15
Vietnam.	18	26	31	38	40	41	43	44	46	49
Compensation (mil. dol.) . . .	2,393	3,797	6,104	8,270	8,424	8,722	8,937	9,284	9,612	10,018

Z Less than 500. [1] Includes Spanish-American War and Mexican Border service, not shown separately.

Source: U.S. Dept. of Veterans Affairs, *Annual Report of the Secretary of Veterans Affairs;* and unpublished data.

No. 574. Veterans Benefits—Expenditures, by Program: 1970 to 1989

[In millions of dollars. For fiscal years ending in year shown; see text, section 9. On an accrued expenditure basis]

PROGRAM	1970	1975	1980	1984	1985	1986	1987	1988	1989
Total [1]	10,201	18,003	23,187	28,494	30,119	31,556	32,365	33,791	30,041
Compensation and pensions [2]	5,330	7,551	11,257	13,942	14,234	14,399	14,399	14,880	15,008
Educ'al asst. and readjustm't benefits.	1,047	4,529	2,383	1,043	1,169	907	916	998	1,027
Medical services; administ. expenses .	[3]2,009	3,919	6,647	9,123	9,992	10,269	10,641	11,299	10,745
Hospital; domiciliary construction [4] . . .	75	136	342	486	557	567	589	634	657
Insurance and indemnities	1,181	1,345	1,637	1,750	1,853	2,008	1,689	1,734	2,013
Loan guaranty revolving fund	249	423	445	1,511	1,626	2,667	3,333	3,635	3,771
Direct loans	180	84	49	8	8	9	9	6	2

[1] Excludes expenditures from personal funds of patients. Includes expenditures from VA Revolving Supply Fund and insurance trust funds and miscellaneous expenditures. [2] Includes expenditures for statutory burial awards, special clothing allowance, mortgage life insurance, invalid lifts, headstones and markers, and other expenses. [3] Includes National Cancer Institute expenditures (transfer to Dept. of Veterans Affairs). [4] Includes construction grants for State extended care facilities. Beginning 1975, includes expenditures for health manpower training facilities.

Source: U.S. Dept. of Veterans Affairs, *Annual Report of the Secretary of Veterans Affairs.*

No. 575. Veterans Compensation and Pension Benefits—Number on Rolls and Average Payment, by Period of Service and Status: 1980 to 1992

[As of Sept. 30. Living refers to veterans receiving compensation for disability incurred or aggravated while on active duty and war veterans receiving pension and benefits for nonservice connected disabilities. Deceased refers to deceased veterans whose dependents were receiving pensions and compensation benefits. See also *Historical Statistics, Colonial Times to 1970*, series Y 998-999]

PERIOD OF SERVICE AND VETERAN STATUS	VETERANS ON ROLLS (1,000)					AVERAGE PAYMENT (annual basis) [1] (dol.)				
	1980	1985	1990	1991	1992	1980	1985	1990	1991	1992
Total	4,646	4,006	3,584	3,509	3,428	2,370	3,505	4,335	4,552	4,712
Living veterans	3,195	2,931	2,746	2,709	2,674	2,600	3,666	4,320	4,491	4,611
Service connected	2,273	2,240	2,184	2,179	2,181	2,669	3,692	4,250	4,406	4,593
Nonservice connected	922	690	562	530	493	2,428	3,581	4,591	4,837	4,689
Deceased veterans	1,451	1,075	838	800	754	1,863	3,066	4,382	4,761	5,071
Service connected	358	336	320	318	314	3,801	5,836	7,349	8,244	
Nonservice connected	1,093	739	518	482	440	1,228	1,809	2,548	2,748	2,810
Prior to World War I	14	7	4	4	3	1,432	1,855	2,616	2,921	3,073
Living	(Z)	(Z)	(Z)	(Z)	(Z)	2,634	4,436	10,502	10,441	8,176
World War I	692	381	198	172	146	1,683	2,461	3,435	3,674	3,754
Living	198	68	18	13	9	2,669	4,439	6,922	7,239	6,476
World War II	2,520	2,097	1,723	1,638	1,543	2,307	3,317	4,052	4,238	4,334
Living	1,849	1,575	1,294	1,226	1,153	2,462	3,460	4,123	4,278	4,333
Korean conflict [2]	446	399	390	388	387	2,691	4,114	5,105	5,330	5,462
Living	317	309	305	304	300	2,977	4,260	5,103	5,288	5,390
Peacetime	312	404	495	518	550	3,080	3,973	4,132	4,216	4,292
Living	262	352	444	468	500	2,828	3,589	3,709	3,789	3,866
Vietnam era [3]	662	716	774	789	804	2,795	4,021	4,945	5,242	5,551
Living	569	626	685	698	711	2,709	3,849	4,671	4,936	5,234
Persian Gulf War	(X)	(X)	(X)	(X)	(X)	(Z)	(X)	(X)	(X)	1,673
Living	(X)	(X)	(X)	(X)	(X)	(Z)	(X)	(X)	(X)	1,386

X Not applicable.   Z Fewer than 500.   [1] Averages calculated by multiplying average monthly payment by 12.   [2] Service during period June 27, 1950, to Jan. 31, 1955.   [3] Service from Aug. 5, 1964, to May 7, 1975.

Source: U.S. Dept. of Veterans Affairs, *Annual Report of the Secretary of Veterans Affairs;* and unpublished data.

No. 576. Veterans Administration Health Care Summary: 1980 to 1992

[For years ending Sept. 30]

ITEM	Unit	1980	1990	1992	ITEM	Unit	1980	1990	1992
Facilities operating:	. . . . .				Prescriptions dispensed . .	Millions	36.7	58.6	56.5
Hospitals	Number	172	172	171	Laboratory	Millions	215	188	(NA)
Domiciliaries	Number	16	32	35	Radiology examinations .	Millions	5.7	5.5	6.2
Outpatient clinics	Number	226	339	362	Inpatients treated [3]	1,000. .	1,359	1,113	1,085
Nursing home units . .	Number	92	126	128	Average daily	1,000. .	105	88	84
Employment [1]	1,000. .	194	199	204	Outpatient visits	Millions	18.0	22.6	24.2
Obligations [2]	Mil. dol.	6,215	11,827	14,011					

NA Not available.   [1] Net full-time equivalent.   [2] 1980, cost basis; thereafter, obligation basis.   [3] Based on the number of discharges and deaths during the fiscal year, plus the number on the rolls (bed occupants and patients on authorized leave of absence) at the end of the fiscal year. Excludes interhospital transfers.

Source: U.S. Dept. of Veterans Affairs, *Annual Report of the Secretary of Veterans Affairs; Directory of VA Facilities*, biennial; and unpublished data.

No. 577. Veterans Assistance: Education and Training: 1980 to 1992

[In thousands, except where indicated. For fiscal years ending in year shown; see text, section 9. Represents persons in training during year]

PROGRAM	1980	1985	1987	1988	1989	1990	1991	1992
Post-Korea Education Assistance [1]	1,107	402	239	203	164	102	143	195
Institutions of higher education	842	326	203	176	144	94	132	177
Resident schools other than college	149	54	26	19	13	6	9	14
Correspondence schools	42	7	4	4	3	1	1	3
On-the-job training	74	15	7	4	3	1	1	2
Children's Educational Assistance	82.6	55.3	43.4	40.9	38.7	37.5	37.3	37.2
Institutions of higher education	75.5	50.0	39.7	37.8	36.2	35.3	35.2	35.1
Schools other than college	6.5	5.2	3.6	3.0	2.4	2.1	2.1	2.1
Special restorative training	0.1	(Z)	(Z)	(Z)	(Z)	(Z)	(Z)	(Z)
On-the-job training	0.5	0.2	0.1	0.1	0.1	0.1	(Z)	(Z)
Spouses, Widows/Widowers Educational								
Assistance Program	13.0	6.6	5.3	5.0	4.6	4.5	4.4	4.5
Institutions of higher education	10.8	5.7	4.5	4.3	4.1	4.1	4.0	4.0
Schools other than college	2.2	1.0	0.7	0.6	0.5	0.4	0.4	0.4
Vocational Rehab. Program for Disabled Vets	25.5	26.9	24.6	24.7	27.0	27.8	35.9	36.8
Guaranteed and insured loans, (1,000)	297.4	178.9	479.5	234.7	189.7	196.6	181.2	266.0
Guaranteed and insured loans, (mil. dol.) . .	14,815	11,452	34,900	17,302	14,416	15,779	15,454	22,960
Guaranty and insurance (mil. dol.)	6,370	4,363	12,237	6,172	5,211	5,561	5,299	7,819

Z Fewer than 50.   [1] Includes some Post-Vietnam veterans.

Source: U.S. Dept. of Veterans Affairs, *Annual Report of the Secretary of Veterans Affairs;* and unpublished data.

Figure 12.1
**Percentage of Persons Receiving Monthly Social Security
Benefits, by Type of Beneficiary: 1991**

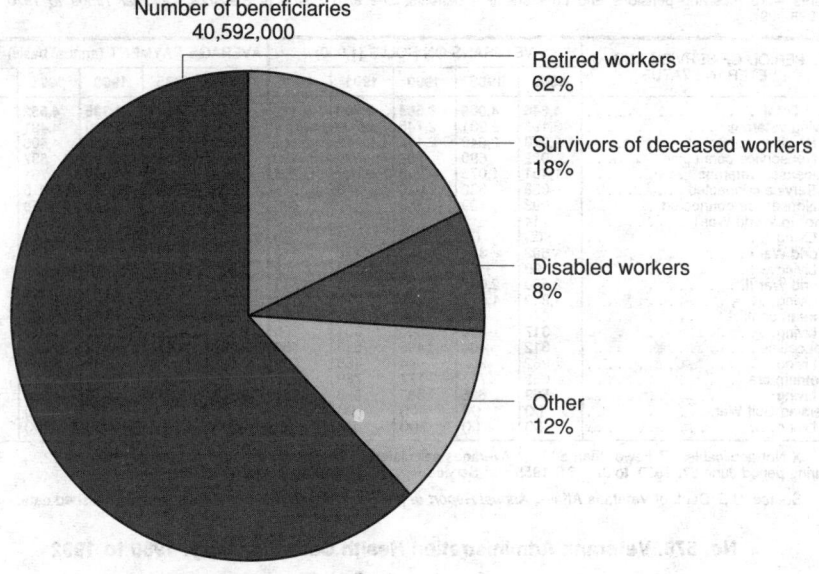

Number of beneficiaries
40,592,000

Retired workers
62%

Survivors of deceased workers
18%

Disabled workers
8%

Other
12%

Source: Chart prepared by U.S. Bureau of the Census. For data, see table 589.

Figure 12.2
Award and Receipt of Child Support Payments: 1989

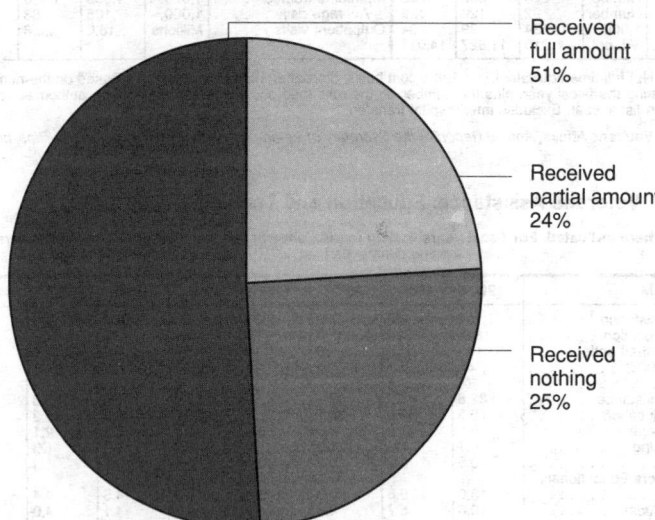

Received
full amount
51%

Received
partial amount
24%

Received
nothing
25%

Payments awarded and due
(5 million out of 10 million women with children from absent
fathers were awarded and due to receive payments)

Source: Chart prepared by U.S. Bureau of the Census. For data, see table 611.

Social Insurance and Human Services

This section presents data related to governmental expenditures for social welfare; governmental programs for old-age, survivors, disability, and health insurance (OASDHI); governmental employee retirement; private pension plans; government unemployment and temporary disability insurance; Federal supplemental security income payments and aid to the needy; child and other welfare services; and Federal food programs. Also included here are selected data on workers' compensation, including black lung benefits; vocational rehabilitation; child support; child care; and philanthropic trusts and foundations.

The principal source for these data is the Department of Health and Human Services' (HHS) quarterly *Social Security Bulletin* which presents current data on many of the programs and summary data in annual statistical supplements. Current data on employment security are published annually in the Department of Labor's *Unemployment Insurance, Financial Data.* Statistics on aid to families with dependent children (AFDC) are presented in the U.S. Family Support Administration's annual publication, *Quarterly Public Assistance Statistics.*

Social insurance under the Social Security Act.—Programs established by the Social Security Act provide protection against wage loss resulting from retirement, prolonged disability, death, or unemployment, and protection against the cost of medical care during old age and disability. The Federal OASDHI program provides cash benefits to retired or disabled insured workers and their dependents and to survivors of insured workers. To be eligible, a worker must have had a specified period of employment in which OASDHI taxes were paid. A worker becomes eligible for full benefits at age 65, although reduced benefits may be obtained up to 3 years earlier; the worker's spouse is under the same limitations. Survivor benefits are payable to dependents of deceased insured workers. Disability benefits are payable

In Brief

In 1991, households below poverty level receiving:

Medicaid	*48%*
Food stamps	*42%*

Social Security beneficiaries, 1992:

Total	*42 million*
Retired workers	*26 million*

to an insured worker under age 65 with a prolonged disability and to the disabled worker's dependents on the same basis as dependents of retired workers. Also, disability benefits are provided at age 50 to the disabled widow or widower of a deceased worker who was fully insured at the time of death. A lump-sum benefit is generally payable on the death of an insured worker to a spouse or minor children. For information on the Medicare program, see section 3.

Retirement, survivors, disability, and hospital insurance benefits are funded by a payroll tax on annual earnings (up to a maximum of earnings set by law) of workers, employers, and the self-employed. The maximum taxable earnings are adjusted annually to reflect increasing wage levels (see table 588). Tax receipts and benefit payments are administered through Federal trust funds. Special benefits for uninsured persons; hospital benefits for persons 65 and over with specified amounts of Social Security coverage less than that required for cash benefit eligibility; and that part of the cost of supplementary medical insurance not financed by contributions from participants are financed from Federal general revenues.

Unemployment insurance is presently administered by the U.S. Employment and Training Administration and each State's employment security agency. By agreement with the U.S. Secretary of Labor, State agencies also administer unemployment compensation for eligible ex-service members and Federal employees, unemployment assistance under the Disaster Relief Act of 1970, and workers assistance and relocation allowances under the Trade Act. Under State unemployment insurance laws, benefits related to the individual's past earnings are paid to unemployed eligible workers. State laws vary concerning the length of time benefits are paid and their amount. In most States, benefits are payable for 26 weeks and, during periods of high unemployment, extended benefits are payable under a Federal-State program to those who have exhausted their regular State benefits. The basic benefit can vary among States by over 100 percent. Some States also supplement the basic benefit with allowances for dependents. Unemployment insurance is funded by a Federal unemployment tax levied on the taxable payrolls of most employers. Taxable payroll under the Federal Act and most State laws is the first $7,000 in wages paid each worker during a year. Employers are allowed a percentage credit of taxable payroll for contributions paid to States under State unemployment insurance laws. The remaining percent of the Federal tax finances administrative costs, the Federal share of extended benefits, and advances to States. About 97 percent of wage and salary workers are covered by unemployment insurance.

Retirement Programs for Government Employees.—The Civil Service Retirement System (CSRS) and the Federal Employees' Retirement System (FERS) are the two major programs providing age and service, disability, and survivor annuities for Federal civilian employees. In general, employees hired after December 31, 1983, are covered under FERS and the social security program (OASDHI), and employees on staff prior to that date are members of CSRS and are covered under Medicare. CSRS employees were offered the option of transferring to FERS during 1987. There are separate retirement systems for the uniformed services (supplementing OASDHI) and for certain special groups of Federal employees. State and local government employees are covered for the most part by State and local retirement systems similar to the Federal civil service retirement system. In many jurisdictions these benefits supplement OASDHI coverage.

Workers' compensation.—All States provide protection against work-connected injuries and deaths, although some States exclude certain workers (e.g., domestic help). Federal laws cover Federal employees, private employees in the District of Columbia, and longshoremen and harbor workers. In addition, the Social Security Administration and the Department of Labor administer a "black lung" benefits program for coal miners disabled by pneumoconiosis and for specified dependents and survivors. Specified occupational diseases are compensable to some extent. In most States, benefits are related to the worker's salary. The benefits may or may not be augmented by dependents' allowances or automatically adjusted to prevailing wage levels.

Public aid.—State-administered public assistance programs (Aid to Families with Dependent Children (AFDC), emergency assistance and general assistance) and the Federal Supplemental Security Income (SSI) program administered by the Social Security Administration provide benefits to persons who qualify. AFDC and emergency assistance are in part federally funded while the costs of general assistance are met entirely with State and local funds. The SSI program replaced Federal grants for aid to the aged, blind, and disabled in the 50 States and the District of Columbia in 1974. Residents of the Northern Mariana Islands became eligible in 1978. Federal grants continue for aid to the aged, blind, and disabled in Guam, Puerto Rico, and the Virgin Islands. The SSI program provides a minimum income for the aged, blind, and disabled and establishes uniform national basic eligibility requirements and payment standards. Most States supplement the basic SSI payment.

Federal Food Stamp program.—Under the Food Stamp program, single persons and those living in households meeting nationwide standards for income and assets may receive coupons redeemable for food at most retail food stores. The monthly amount of coupons a unit receives is determined by household size and income. Households without income receive the determined monthly cost of a nutritionally adequate diet for their household size. This amount is updated to account for food price increases. Households with income receive the difference between the amount of a nutritionally adequate diet and 30 percent of their income, after certain allowable deductions.

To qualify for the program, a household must have less than $2,000 in disposable assets ($3,000 if one member is aged 60 or older), gross income below 130 percent of the official poverty guidelines, and net income below 100 percent of the poverty guidelines. Households with a person aged 60 or older or a disabled person receiving SSI, Social Security, or veterans' disability benefits may have gross income exceeding 130 percent of the poverty guidelines. All households must meet these requirements, even those receiving other Federal assistance payments. Households are certified for varying lengths of time, depending on their income sources and individual circumstances.

Health and welfare services.—Programs providing health and welfare services are aided through Federal grants to States for child welfare services, vocational rehabilitation, activities for the aged, maternal and child health services, maternity and infant care projects, comprehensive health services, and a variety of public health activities. For information about the Medicaid program, see section 3.

Noncash benefits.—The Bureau of the Census annually collects data on the characteristics of recipients of noncash (in-kind) benefits to supplement the collection of annual money income data in the Current Population Survey (see text, section 1 and section 15). Noncash benefits are those benefits received in a form other than money which serve to enhance or improve the economic well-being of the recipient. As for money income, the data for noncash benefits are for the calendar year prior to the date of the interview. The major categories of noncash benefits covered are public transfers (e.g. food stamps, school lunch, public housing, and Medicaid) and employer or union-provided benefits to employees.

Statistical reliability.—For discussion of statistical collection, estimation, and sampling procedures and measures of statistical reliability applicable to HHS and Census Bureau data, see Appendix III.

Historical statistics.—Tabular headnotes provide cross-references, where applicable, to *Historical Statistics of the United States, Colonial Times to 1970.* See Appendix IV.

No. 578. Social Welfare Expenditures Under Public Programs: 1970 to 1990

[In billions of dollars, except percent. For fiscal years ending in year shown; see text, section 9. Represents outlays from trust funds (mostly social insurance funds built up by earmarked contributions from insured persons, their employers, or both) and budgetary outlays from general revenues. Includes administrative expenditures, capital outlay, and some expenditures and payments outside the United States. See table 579 for program detail. See *Historical Statistics, Colonial Times to 1970*, series H 1-47, for related but not comparable data]

YEAR	Total	Social insurance	Public aid	Health and medical programs [1]	Veterans programs	Education	Housing	Other social welfare	All health and medical care [2]
Total:									
1970	146	55	16	10	9	51	1	4	25
1975	289	123	41	17	17	81	3	7	51
1980	493	230	73	27	21	121	7	14	100
1985	732	370	98	39	27	172	13	14	171
1987	834	413	112	48	28	205	13	15	203
1988	887	434	120	53	29	219	17	15	218
1989	957	468	129	57	30	239	18	17	241
1990	1,045	511	147	62	31	258	19	18	272
Federal:									
1970	77	45	10	5	9	6	1	2	16
1975	167	100	27	8	17	9	3	4	33
1980	303	191	49	13	21	13	6	9	69
1985	451	310	63	18	27	14	11	8	122
1987	498	343	71	21	28	16	11	9	141
1988	527	360	76	23	29	17	14	8	149
1989	565	387	82	24	30	19	15	8	166
1990	614	419	93	28	30	18	17	9	188
State and local:									
1970	68	9	7	5	(Z)	45	(Z)	2	9
1975	122	23	14	9	(Z)	72	1	3	18
1980	190	39	23	14	(Z)	108	1	5	31
1985	281	59	35	21	(Z)	158	2	6	49
1987	336	70	41	27	(Z)	188	2	7	62
1988	360	74	44	30	(Z)	202	3	7	68
1989	392	81	47	33	(Z)	220	3	8	75
1990	432	91	53	35	(Z)	240	3	9	84
Percent of total expenditures, by type:									
1970	100	38	11	7	6	35	1	3	17
1980	100	47	15	6	4	25	1	3	20
1985	100	51	13	5	4	24	2	2	24
1988	100	49	13	6	3	25	2	2	25
1989	100	49	13	6	3	25	2	2	25
1990	100	49	14	6	3	25	2	2	26
Percent Federal:									
1970	53	83	59	48	99	12	83	55	65
1980	62	83	68	47	99	11	91	65	69
1985	62	84	64	46	99	8	88	56	71
1988	59	83	63	43	99	8	85	52	68
1989	59	83	63	43	99	8	84	51	69
1990	59	82	64	44	98	7	85	50	69
Per capita (current dollars): [3]									
1970	698	262	79	46	43	244	3	20	120
1980	2,126	990	314	118	92	523	30	59	434
1985	3,008	1,516	405	161	111	708	52	56	705
1988	3,538	1,724	479	213	116	878	66	62	871
1989	3,789	1,849	510	226	117	947	72	66	957
1990	4,116	2,008	575	246	120	1,020	77	71	1,072
Per capita (constant (1990) dollars): [3][4]									
1970	2,219	833	251	146	137	776	10	64	382
1980	3,348	1,559	495	186	145	824	47	93	684
1985	3,676	1,853	495	197	136	865	64	68	862
1988	3,886	1,893	526	234	127	964	72	68	957
1989	3,979	1,942	536	237	123	994	76	69	1,005
1990	4,116	2,008	575	246	120	1,020	77	71	1,072

Z Less than $500 million. [1] Excludes program parts of social insurance, public aid, veterans, and other social welfare. [2] Combines "Health and medical programs" with medical services included in social insurance, public aid, veterans, vocational rehabilitation, and antipoverty programs. [3] Excludes payments within foreign countries for education, veterans, OASDHI, and civil service retirement. [4] Constant dollar figures are based on implicit price deflators for personal consumption expenditures published by U.S. Bureau of Economic Analysis in *Survey of Current Business*, July 1992.

Source: U.S. Social Security Administration, *Social Security Bulletin*, winter 1992; and unpublished data.

No. 579. Social Welfare Expenditures, by Source of Funds and Public Program: 1980 to 1990

[In millions of dollars. See headnote, table 578, and *Historical Statistics, Colonial Times to 1970*, series H 1-47, for related but not comparable data]

PROGRAM	FEDERAL				STATE AND LOCAL			
	1980	1985	1989	1990	1980	1985	1989	1990
Total	303,167	450,788	565,170	613,822	189,547	281,460	392,343	431,552
Social insurance	191,162	310,175	387,280	419,338	38,592	59,421	80,764	91,279
Old-age, survivors, disability, health.	152,110	257,535	324,109	352,362	(X)	(X)	(X)	(X)
Health insurance (Medicare)	34,992	71,384	94,552	106,806	(X)	(X)	(X)	(X)
Public employee retirement [1]	26,983	40,504	50,248	53,514	12,507	22,540	33,546	36,851
Railroad employee retirement	4,769	6,276	6,971	7,230	(X)	(X)	(X)	(X)
Unemployment insurance and employment services [2]	4,408	2,604	2,893	3,094	13,919	15,740	13,488	16,878
Other railroad employee insurance [3]	224	189	99	105	(X)	(X)	(X)	(X)
State temporary disability insurance [4]	(X)	(X)	(X)	(X)	1,377	1,944	2,886	3,224
Workers' compensation [5]	2,668	3,067	2,960	3,033	10,789	19,197	30,844	34,326
Hospital and medical benefits	130	280	410	433	3,596	6,800	12,415	13,897
Public aid	49,394	63,475	81,762	92,650	23,309	34,882	46,921	52,992
Public assistance [6]	23,542	33,523	47,828	54,537	21,522	32,647	43,567	49,387
Medical assistance payments [7]	14,550	22,677	34,858	40,690	13,020	21,182	29,725	34,677
Social services	1,757	2,057	2,003	2,065	586	686	668	688
Supplemental security income	6,440	9,605	12,469	13,625	1,787	2,235	3,354	3,605
Food stamps	9,083	12,513	13,589	16,254	(X)	(X)	(X)	(X)
Other [8]	10,329	7,834	7,876	8,234	(X)	(X)	(X)	(X)
Health and medical programs	12,840	18,029	24,154	27,515	14,423	21,024	33,021	34,913
Hospital and medical care	6,636	9,877	12,894	14,733	5,667	6,688	11,930	12,778
Civilian programs	2,438	2,455	2,736	3,447	5,667	6,688	11,930	12,778
Defense Department [9]	4,198	7,422	10,158	11,286	(X)	(X)	(X)	(X)
Maternal and child health programs	351	422	494	492	519	800	1,295	1,392
Medical research	4,428	5,992	8,548	9,528	496	899	1,360	1,475
Medical facilities construction	210	339	186	499	1,450	1,336	1,462	1,427
Other	1,215	1,399	2,032	2,263	6,291	11,301	16,974	17,841
Veterans programs	21,255	26,705	29,638	30,428	212	338	466	488
Pensions and compensation	11,306	14,333	15,279	15,793	(X)	(X)	(X)	(X)
Health and medical programs	6,204	9,493	11,663	12,004	(X)	(X)	(X)	(X)
Hospital and medical care	5,750	8,809	10,782	11,321	(X)	(X)	(X)	(X)
Hospital construction	323	458	646	445	(X)	(X)	(X)	(X)
Medical and prosthetic research	131	227	235	238	(X)	(X)	(X)	(X)
Education	2,401	1,171	647	523	(X)	(X)	(X)	(X)
Life insurance [10]	665	796	1,002	1,038	(X)	(X)	(X)	(X)
Welfare and other	679	912	1,047	1,070	212	338	466	488
Education [11]	13,452	13,796	18,660	18,374	107,597	158,251	220,111	240,011
Elementary and secondary [12]	7,430	7,278	9,684	9,944	79,720	113,419	173,487	189,333
Construction [13]	41	23	18	23	6,483	8,335	14,566	10,613
Higher	4,468	5,102	7,404	6,747	21,708	36,028	46,624	50,678
Construction	42	32	22	-	1,486	2,314	3,290	3,953
Vocational and adult [13]	1,207	1,087	1,209	1,293	6,169	8,804	([12])	([12])
Housing	6,278	11,059	15,184	16,612	601	1,540	2,943	2,856
Other social welfare	8,786	7,549	8,492	8,905	4,813	6,004	8,117	9,013
Vocational rehabilitation	1,006	1,187	1,560	1,661	245	350	439	466
Medical services and research	237	275	390	415	56	85	110	116
Institutional care [14]	74	121	141	143	408	259	446	486
Child nutrition [15]	4,209	4,349	5,197	5,470	643	960	1,448	1,696
Child welfare [16]	57	200	247	253	743	(NA)	(NA)	(NA)
Special CSA and ACTION programs [17]	2,303	504	163	169	(X)	(X)	(X)	(X)
Welfare, not elsewhere classified [18]	1,137	1,188	1,184	1,209	2,774	4,435	5,784	6,365

- Represents zero. NA Not available. X Not applicable. [1] Excludes refunds to those leaving service. Federal data include military retirement. [2] Includes compensation for Federal employees and ex-servicemen, trade adjustment and cash training allowance, and payments under extended, emergency, disaster, and special unemployment insurance programs. [3] Unemployment and temporary disability insurance. [4] Cash and medical benefits in five areas. Includes private plans where applicable. [5] Benefits paid by private insurance carriers, State funds, and self-insurers. Federal includes black lung benefit programs. [6] Includes payments under State general assistance programs and work incentive activities, not shown separately. [7] Medicaid payments and State and local general assistance medical payments. [8] Refugee assistance, surplus food for the needy, and work-experience training programs under the Comprehensive Employment and Training Act. Beginning 1985, includes low-income energy assistance program. [9] Includes medical care for military dependent families. [10] Excludes servicemen's group life insurance. [11] Federal expenditures include administrative costs (Department of Education) and research, not shown separately. [12] Beginning 1989, all State and local vocational education costs included with elementary-secondary. [13] Construction costs of vocational and adult education programs included under elementary-secondary expenditures. [14] Federal expenditures represent primarily surplus foods for nonprofit institutions. [15] Surplus food for schools and programs under National School Lunch and Child Nutrition Acts. [16] Represents primarily child welfare services under Title V of the Social Security Act. [17] Includes domestic volunteer programs under ACTION and community action and migrant workers programs under Community Services Administration. Beginning 1989, represents ACTION funds only. [18] Federal expenditures include administrative expenses of the Secretary of Health and Human Services; Indian welfare and guidance; and aging and juvenile delinquency activities. State and local include antipoverty and manpower programs, child care and adoption services, legal assistance, and other unspecified welfare services.

Source: U.S. Social Security Administration, *Social Security Bulletin*, winter 1992; and unpublished data.

No. 580. Social Welfare Expenditures Under Public Programs as Percent of GDP and Total Government Outlays: 1970 to 1990

[See headnote, table 578]

YEAR	TOTAL EXPENDITURES				FEDERAL				STATE AND LOCAL GOVERNMENT			
			Percent of—				Percent of—				Percent of—	
	Total (bil. dol.)	Percent change [1]	Total GDP [2]	Total govt. outlays	Total (bil. dol.)	Percent change [1]	Total GDP [2]	Total Federal outlays	Total (bil. dol.)	Percent change [1]	Total GDP [2]	Total State and local outlays
1970....	146	14.6	14.8	46.5	77	13.2	7.8	40.0	68	16.3	6.9	57.9
1975....	289	21.2	19.1	56.6	167	21.9	11.0	53.7	122	19.6	8.1	61.6
1980....	493	14.7	18.6	57.2	303	15.2	11.4	54.4	190	13.8	7.2	62.9
1985....	732	8.0	18.4	52.2	451	7.1	11.3	48.7	281	9.3	7.1	59.9
1988....	887	6.4	18.4	54.9	527	5.8	10.9	49.5	360	7.2	7.5	67.0
1989....	957	7.9	18.5	55.2	565	7.2	10.9	49.5	392	8.8	7.6	68.0
1990....	1,045	9.2	19.1	56.6	614	8.7	11.2	51.1	432	10.0	7.9	68.2

[1] Percent change from immediate prior year. [2] Gross domestic product.
Source: U.S. Social Security Administration, *Social Security Bulletin*, winter 1992; and unpublished data.

No. 581. Private Expenditures for Social Welfare, by Type: 1980 to 1990

[In millions of dollars, except percent]

TYPE	1980	1984	1985	1986	1987	1988	1989	1990
Total expenditures	246,000	398,403	447,120	495,860	525,919	573,768	623,617	680,868
Percent of gross domestic product.	9.1	10.5	11.1	11.6	11.6	11.7	11.9	12.3
Health	145,000	230,000	247,900	264,600	285,700	318,900	350,200	383,600
Income maintenance.........	51,169	93,235	116,207	140,748	140,354	145,790	152,144	163,559
Private pension plan payments [1][2]...	37,560	76,683	98,450	122,209	120,442	124,546	129,662	140,142
Short-term sickness and disability [2]...	6,280	7,497	8,026	8,030	8,896	9,636	9,869	10,372
Long-term disability [2]	1,282	1,874	1,937	2,263	2,293	2,295	2,892	3,054
Life insurance and death [3] ...	5,075	6,899	7,489	7,797	8,166	8,418	9,063	9,221
Supplemental unemployment [2].....	972	282	305	449	557	895	658	770
Education	27,055	40,469	44,099	47,426	52,436	55,860	61,351	66,872
Welfare and other services........	22,776	34,699	38,914	43,086	47,429	53,218	59,922	66,837

[1] Covers benefits paid for solely by employers and all benefits of employment-related pension plans to which employee contributions are made. Excludes individual savings plans such as IRA's and Keogh plans. Pension plan benefits include monthly benefits and lump-sum distributions to retired and disabled employees and their dependents and to survivors of deceased employees. Also includes preretirement lump-sum distributions. [2] Covers wage and salary workers in private industry. [3] Covers all wage and salary workers.
Source: U.S. Social Security Administration, *Annual Statistical Supplement* to the *Social Security Bulletin*, annual.

No. 582. Cash and Noncash Benefits for Persons With Limited Income— Average Monthly Recipients: 1985 to 1990

[In thousands. For years ending September 30, except as noted. See headnote, table 583]

PROGRAM	1985	1989	1990	PROGRAM	1985	1989	1990
MEDICAL CARE				Interest reduction payments [15]...	528	528	531
Medicaid [1]	21,814	23,511	25,255	Rural rental housing loans [15]....	26	16	16
Veterans [2][3]	504	569	585	EDUCATION AID			
Indian Health Services [4]......	931	1,100	1,100	Stafford loans [16][17].........	3,477	3,682	3,624
Community health centers [4]....	5,200	5,350	5,350	Pell grants [16]...............	2,797	3,198	3,434
CASH AID				Head Start................	448	451	541
A.F.D.C. [5]	10,813	10,935	11,439	College Work-Study Program [16]..	737	785	835
Supplemental Security Income...	4,305	4,753	4,913	Supplemental Educational			
Earned income tax credit [6]	17,313	33,444	33,693	Opportunity Grants [16]	720	660	633
Pensions for needy veterans [7][8]..	1,489	1,139	1,080	JOBS AND TRAINING			
General assistance [6]	1,323	1,091	1,205	Training for disadvantaged adults			
FOOD BENEFITS				and youth [18][19]	350	397	416
Food stamps [9]	21,400	20,200	21,500	Job Corps [18]	41	41	40
School lunch program [10][11]	11,500	11,700	11,600	Summer youth employment			
Women, infants and children [12] ..	3,138	4,100	4,500	program [18][20]...............	785	605	625
Nutrition program for elderly [4][13]..	3,630	3,538	3,548	Work incentive program [21]	1,013	1,700	444
HOUSING BENEFITS				Senior community service			
Lower-income housing asst.				employment program [22]	64	66	65
(Sec. 8) [14]	2,010	2,420	2,500	ENERGY AID			
Low-rent public housing [14]	1,355	1,404	1,405	Low-income energy assistance [23]..	6,800	5,900	5,800
Rural housing loans [15]	41	25	25				

[1] Unduplicated annual number. [2] See footnote 4, table 583. [3] For 1985, estimated number of patients discharged from hospital during year. For other years, estimated number of inpatients. [4] Annual numbers. [5] See footnote 6, table 583. [6] Estimated. [7] See footnote 8, table 583. [8] Estimate as of September. [9] See footnote 9, table 583. [10] See footnote 10, table 583. [11] Estimated daily average. [12] See footnote 12, table 583. [13] See footnote 13, table 583. [14] Units eligible for payment at end of year. [15] Represents total families or dwelling units during year. [16] Total numbers for the school year ending in year shown. [17] See footnote 15, table 583. [18] See footnote 18, table 583. [19] Average monthly enrollment for program year. [20] Total participants (June-August). [21] New registrants only. [22] Annual number of jobs authorized. [23] Number of households that received heating and winter crisis aid.
Source: Library of Congress, Congressional Research Service, "Cash and Noncash Benefits for Persons With Limited Income: Eligibility Rules, Recipient and Expenditure Data, FY 1988-90," Report No. 91-741 EPW, September 1991; and earlier reports.

No. 583. Cash and Noncash Benefits for Persons With Limited Income—Expenditures: 1985 to 1990

[In millions of dollars. For years ending September 30, except as noted. Programs covered provide cash, goods, or services to persons who make no payment and render no service in return. In case of job and training programs and some educational benefits, recipients must work or study for wages, training allowances, stipends, grants, or loans. Most of the programs base eligibility on individual, household, or family income, but some use group or area income tests; and a few offer help on the basis of presumed need]

PROGRAM	TOTAL EXPENDITURES [1]				FEDERAL EXPENDITURES			
	1985	1988	1989	1990	1985	1988	1989	1990
Total....................	143,606	172,508	186,449	210,630	105,064	125,047	134,715	152,166
Medical care [2]......................	49,752	66,644	73,554	86,197	27,880	38,608	42,393	50,211
Medicaid [3].......................	41,258	54,304	60,896	72,228	22,844	30,567	34,384	41,195
Veterans [4][5].....................	3,053	5,855	5,678	6,458	3,053	5,855	5,678	6,458
General assistance [5]...............	3,125	3,966	4,300	4,600	-	-	-	-
Indian Health Services..............	862	1,006	1,082	1,250	862	1,006	1,082	1,250
Maternal and child health services.........	783	860	903	907	478	527	554	554
Community health centers..............	383	396	435	478	383	396	435	478
Cash aid [2]......................	37,636	45,707	49,652	55,136	24,486	30,314	33,163	37,044
A.F.D.C. [3][6].......................	16,736	19,016	19,662	21,196	8,909	10,319	10,647	11,505
Supplemental Security Income [3]........	11,857	14,684	15,757	17,232	[7]9,603	[7]11,648	[7]12,417	[7]13,606
Earned income tax credit (refunded portion)...	1,162	2,930	4,257	5,902	1,162	2,930	4,257	5,902
Pensions for needy veterans [6]............	3,842	3,935	4,024	3,954	3,842	3,935	4,024	3,954
General assistance.................	2,499	2,624	2,819	3,184	-	-	-	-
Food benefits [2].....................	20,391	21,355	21,997	25,257	19,362	20,216	20,835	24,011
Food stamps [3][9]...................	13,470	14,369	14,916	17,702	12,599	13,289	13,815	16,517
School lunch program [10][11]...........	2,665	2,937	3,082	3,250	2,665	2,937	3,082	3,250
Women, infants and children [12].........	1,500	1,800	1,924	2,119	1,500	1,800	1,924	2,119
Nutrition program for elderly [13]........	614	561	582	578	456	502	521	517
Housing benefits [2]..................	14,113	14,701	15,925	17,544	14,113	14,701	15,925	17,544
Lower-income housing asst. (Sec. 8)......	6,818	9,133	9,918	10,577	6,818	9,133	9,918	10,577
Low-rent public housing................	3,408	2,526	3,043	3,918	3,408	2,526	3,043	3,918
Rural housing loans [14]..............	1,790	1,271	1,267	1,311	1,790	1,271	1,267	1,311
Interest reduction payments............	619	628	611	630	619	628	611	630
Rural rental housing loans [14].........	903	555	555	572	903	555	555	572
Education aid [2].....................	9,970	11,691	13,029	14,375	9,516	11,147	12,484	13,746
Stafford loans [15].................	3,888	3,775	5,012	5,648	3,888	3,775	5,012	5,648
Pell grants [16]...................	2,800	4,187	4,260	4,484	2,800	4,187	4,260	4,484
Head Start......................	1,309	1,508	1,544	1,940	1,047	1,206	1,235	1,552
College Work-Study Program [16]....	555	593	588	610	555	593	588	610
Supplemental Educational Opportunity Grants [16]......................	375	413	408	438	375	413	408	438
Services [2]........................	5,476	5,659	5,671	5,801	3,551	3,559	3,571	3,661
Social services (Title 20) [17].......	4,650	4,800	4,800	4,902	2,725	2,700	2,700	2,762
Community services block grant..........	372	382	381	389	372	382	381	389
Jobs and training [2].................	3,976	3,820	3,912	4,215	3,895	3,748	3,815	3,966
Training for disadvantaged adults and youth [18][19].................	1,886	1,810	1,788	1,745	1,886	1,810	1,788	1,745
Job Corps [18][19].................	617	716	742	803	617	716	742	803
Summer youth employment program [18][19]....	725	718	709	700	725	718	709	700
Work incentive program................	297	103	186	452	267	93	148	265
Senior community service employment program [19]....................	362	368	382	408	326	331	344	367
Energy assistance [2].................	2,292	2,001	1,809	1,802	2,261	1,824	1,629	1,680
Low-income energy assistance [3][20]........	2,095	1,840	1,648	1,641	2,070	1,663	1,468	1,519
Other [21].........................	(X)	930	900	303	(X)	930	900	303

- Represents zero. X Not applicable. [1] Includes State and local government expenditures not shown separately. [2] Includes other programs not shown separately. [3] Includes administrative expenses. [4] Medical care for veterans with a non-service-connected disability. [5] Estimated. [6] Aid to Families with Dependent Children program. Excludes data for foster care program and child support operations (cost and collections). [7] Excludes Federal sums spent for SSI (State supplements) to Indochinese refugees. [8] Includes dependents and survivors. [9] Includes Puerto Rico's nutritional assistance program. [10] Free and reduced-price segments. [11] Includes estimate of commodity assistance. [12] Special supplemental food program for women, infants and children. [13] No income test required but preference given to those with greatest need. [14] Amount of loans obligated. [15] Formerly Guaranteed Student Loans. [16] Appropriation available for school year ending the fiscal year named. [17] Non-Federal expenditure data are rough estimates. [18] Programs represent specific titles under the Job Training and Partnership Act (JTPA). [19] Federal funds are appropriations. [20] Federal funds include amounts transferred to other programs serving the needy. State spending includes funds received as "oil overcharge" settlements. [21] Represents State Legalization Impact Assistance Grants, offered between 1988 and 1992, to offset State and local costs of welfare, health care, and education provided to legalized aliens.

Source: Library of Congress, Congressional Research Service, "Cash and Noncash Benefits for Persons With Limited Income: Eligibility Rules, Recipient and Expenditure Data, FY 1988-90," Report No. 91-741 EPW, September 30, 1991; and earlier reports.

No. 584. Households Receiving Means-Tested Noncash Benefits: 1980 to 1991

[In thousands, except percent. Households as of **March** of following year. Covers civilian noninstitutional population, including persons in the Armed Forces living off post or with their families on post. A means-tested benefit program requires that the household's income and/or assets fall below specified guidelines in order to qualify for benefits. The means-tested noncash benefits covered are food stamps, free or reduced-price school lunches, public or subsidized housing, and Medicaid. There are general trends toward under-estimation of noncash beneficiaries. Households are classified according to poverty status of family or nonfamily householder; for explanation of poverty level, see text, section 14. Based on Current Population Survey; see text, section 1, and Appendix III]

| | | | | | 1991 | | | |
| TYPE OF BENEFIT RECEIVED | 1980 | 1985 | 1989 | 1990 | Total | Below poverty level | | Above poverty level |
						Number	Percent distribu- tion	
Total households	82,368	88,458	93,347	94,312	95,669	12,949	100	82,720
Receiving at least one noncash benefit. .	14,266	14,466	15,012	16,098	17,387	8,262	64	9,125
Not receiving cash public assistance . .	7,860	7,860	8,342	8,819	9,539	3,362	26	6,177
Receiving cash public assistance [1] . . .	6,407	6,607	6,669	7,279	7,849	4,900	38	2,949
Total households receiving—								
Food stamps.	6,769	6,779	6,508	7,163	7,839	5,489	42	2,350
School lunch.	5,532	5,752	5,943	6,252	6,922	3,677	28	3,245
Public housing.	2,777	3,799	4,085	4,339	4,511	2,765	21	1,746
Medicaid.	8,287	8,178	9,180	10,321	11,458	6,220	48	5,238

[1] Households receiving money from Aid to Families with Dependent Children program, Supplemental Security Income program or other public assistance programs.

Source: U.S. Bureau of the Census, *Current Population Reports*, P60-155, and earlier reports; and unpublished data.

No. 585. Public Income-Maintenance Programs—Cash Benefit Payments: 1970 to 1991

[Includes payments outside the United States and benefits to dependents, where applicable]

| PROGRAM | PAYMENTS (bil. dol.) | | | | | | | | | | PERCENT | | |
	1970	1980	1984	1985	1986	1987	1988	1989	1990	1991	1970	1980	1990
Total [1]	60.5	228.1	309.1	335.2	356.6	372.0	393.8	418.9	450.9	(NA)	100	100	100
Percent of personal income [2]	7.3	10.1	9.9	9.9	10.1	9.8	9.7	9.6	9.6	(NA)	(X)	(X)	(X)
OASDI [3]	31.6	120.3	175.5	186.1	196.1	204.7	216.4	229.6	245.6	263.1	52	53	54
Public employee retirement [4]	9.2	40.6	59.0	63.0	66.9	72.1	78.0	83.8	90.4	(NA)	15	18	20
Railroad retirement.	1.8	4.9	6.1	6.3	6.4	6.5	6.7	6.9	7.2	7.5	3	2	2
Veterans' pensions, compensation.	5.5	11.4	13.8	14.1	14.3	14.3	14.7	15.0	15.5	16.0	9	5	3
Unemployment benefits [5]	4.2	18.9	13.6	14.4	16.0	14.4	13.2	13.5	16.5	24.4	7	8	4
Temporary disability benefits	0.7	1.4	1.8	1.8	2.1	2.5	2.8	2.9	3.2	(NA)	1	1	1
Workers' compensation [6]	2.0	9.7	13.3	22.3	24.7	27.1	30.3	33.8	37.4	(NA)	3	4	8
Public assistance [7]	4.9	12.1	14.6	15.3	16.1	16.5	17.0	17.6	18.8	20.7	8	5	4
Supplemental Security Income [7] . .	(X)	7.9	10.4	11.1	12.9	13.6	14.7	15.8	16.3	17.9	(X)	3	4

NA Not available. X Not applicable. [1] Includes lump sum death benefits, not shown separately. Lump sum death benefits for State and local government employee retirement systems are not available beginning 1987. [2] For base data, see table 700. [3] Old-age, survivors, and disability insurance under Federal Social Security Act; see text, section 12. [4] Excludes refunds of contributions to employees who leave service. [5] Beginning 1984, covers State unemployment insurance, Ex-Servicemen's Compensation Act and railroad unemployment insurance only. [6] Includes black lung benefits. [7] Beginning 1980, Federal grants to States for aid to aged, blind, and disabled replaced by Supplemental Security Income programs; see text, section 12.

Source: U.S. Social Security Administration, *Social Security Bulletin*, quarterly; and unpublished data.

No. 586. Estimated Workers Under Social Insurance Programs: 1970 to 1991

[In millions. As of **December**, except as noted. See also *Historical Statistics, Colonial Times to 1970*, series H 51-56]

EMPLOYMENT AND COVERAGE STATUS	1970	1980	1983	1984	1985	1986	1987	1988	1989	1990	1991
Total labor force [1][2]	86.3	109.1	113.5	115.7	117.5	119.8	122.0	123.8	125.7	126.2	126.7
Paid civilian population	77.8	98.9	102.2	105.5	107.7	110.2	113.3	115.6	117.4	117.0	116.2
Unpaid family workers	0.9	0.6	0.6	0.5	0.4	0.3	0.4	0.4	0.3	0.3	0.3
Unemployed [2]	4.7	7.4	9.0	8.0	7.7	7.5	6.5	6.1	6.3	7.3	8.6
Armed Forces [2]	3.0	2.1	1.7	1.7	1.7	1.8	1.8	1.7	1.7	1.6	1.6
Civilian population covered by—											
Public retirement programs	75.2	96.4	99.5	104.4	106.6	109.3	113.5	116.0	117.9	117.7	117.9
OASDHI [3]	69.1	89.3	92.7	98.0	100.3	102.9	106.3	108.7	110.5	110.2	110.5
Railroad retirement	0.6	0.5	0.4	0.4	0.3	0.3	0.3	0.3	0.3	0.3	0.3
Public employees retirement [4]	5.5	6.6	6.4	6.0	6.0	6.2	6.9	7.0	7.1	7.2	7.1
Unemployment insurance	55.8	87.2	91.3	95.8	98.2	100.2	103.7	106.9	108.8	109.5	106.0
Workers' compensation	59.0	79.1	80.5	83.4	85.1	87.2	90.0	92.8	95.3	96.7	95.1
Temporary disability insurance	14.6	18.4	18.7	19.3	19.8	20.3	21.6	21.8	22.2	(NA)	(NA)

NA Not available. [1] Data from U.S. Bureau of Labor Statistics and based on U.S. Bureau of the Census' Current Population Survey; see text, section 1, and Appendix III. [2] Excludes Armed Forces overseas beginning 1983. [3] OASDHI=Old-age, survivors, disability, and health insurance. Excludes members of Armed Forces and railroad employees. [4] Data represent yearly averages. Excludes State and local government employees covered by both OASDHI and their own retirement program.

Source: U.S. Social Security Administration, *Annual Statistical Supplement* to the *Social Security Bulletin*.

No. 587. Selected Social Insurance Programs—Estimated Payrolls of Covered Employment in Relation to Wages and Salaries: 1980 to 1990

[In billions of dollars, except percent. Data for Federal civilian and military personnel cover all areas. Gross amount before deduction of social insurance contributions. OASDHI: Old-age, survivors, disability, and health insurance programs under Social Security Act; see text, section 12. See also *Historical Statistics, Colonial Times to 1970*, series H 57-69]

PROGRAM	1980	1982	1983	1984	1985	1986	1987	1988	1989	1990
Total earnings [1]	1,553	1,717	1,867	2,073	2,232	2,377	2,573	2,785	2,932	3,112
All wages and salaries [1]	1,372	1,586	1,676	1,839	1,975	2,094	2,250	2,431	2,586	2,739
Civilian	1,342	1,546	1,634	1,794	1,928	2,044	2,198	2,378	2,531	2,682
Payrolls covered by—										
Retirement programs [2]	1,318	1,529	1,614	1,775	1,896	2,011	2,157	2,345	2,495	2,630
OASDHI [3][4]	1,229	1,423	1,502	1,665	1,782	1,896	2,042	2,227	2,372	2,503
Railroad retirement [3]	13	13	12	13	13	12	12	12	12	12
Federal civil service	52	59	62	65	70	72	74	80	83	88
State and local government	123	143	153	162	175	190	203	219	235	252
Unemployment insurance [3]	1,303	1,500	1,583	1,739	1,870	1,983	2,046	2,215	2,348	2,555
Workers' compensation program [5]	1,136	1,301	1,382	1,516	1,618	1,725	1,845	1,997	2,115	2,250
Net earnings in self-employment covered by OASDHI	98	99	109	117	130	139	156	182	221	217
Percent of civilian payrolls covered by—										
OASDHI [6]	92.6	93.1	92.6	92.9	92.4	92.8	92.9	93.7	93.7	93.3
Railroad retirement [3]	1.0	0.8	0.7	0.7	0.7	0.6	0.5	0.5	0.5	0.4
Federal civil service retirement	3.9	3.9	3.8	3.7	3.6	3.5	3.4	3.4	3.3	3.3
State and local government retirement	9.2	9.2	9.4	9.0	9.1	9.3	9.2	9.2	9.3	9.4
Unemployment insurance [3]	97.1	97.0	96.9	97.0	97.0	97.0	93.1	93.1	92.8	95.3
Workers' compensation programs [5]	84.6	84.1	84.6	84.5	83.9	84.4	84.0	84.0	83.6	83.9

[1] Data from U.S. Bureau of Economic Analysis. Earnings include self-employed; wages and salaries represent civilian and military pay in cash and in kind.　[2] Adjusted for duplication in coverage by both OASDHI and State and local government retirement systems.　[3] Taxable plus estimated nontaxable wages and salaries.　[4] Includes Armed Forces in all areas.　[5] Payrolls of employers insured with private carriers, State funds, or self-insured, and pay covered by Federal programs in all areas.　[6] Percent computed after excluding Armed Forces payroll covered by OASDHI.

Source: U.S. Social Security Administration, *Annual Statistical Supplement to the Social Security Bulletin*; and unpublished data.

No. 588. Social Security—Covered Employment, Earnings, and Contribution Rates: 1970 to 1991

[Includes Puerto Rico, Virgin Islands, American Samoa, and Guam. Represents all reported employment. Data are estimated. OASDHI=Old-age, survivors, disability, and health insurance; SMI=Supplementary medical insurance. See also *Historical Statistics, Colonial Times to 1970*, series H 172-185]

ITEM	Unit	1970	1980	1984	1985	1986	1987	1988	1989	1990	1991
Workers with insured status [1]	Million	105.7	137.4	147.0	148.7	150.6	152.7	155.4	158.0	161.1	163.6
Male	Million	61.9	75.4	78.8	79.7	80.7	81.5	82.6	83.7	85.1	86.1
Female	Million	43.8	62.0	68.2	69.0	69.9	71.2	72.8	74.3	76.0	77.4
Under 25 years old	Million	17.7	25.5	23.1	22.3	21.9	21.3	21.3	21.1	21.3	21.2
25 to 34 years old	Million	22.3	34.9	39.7	39.9	40.0	40.6	41.0	41.3	41.6	41.5
35 to 44 years old	Million	19.0	22.4	27.2	28.5	29.8	31.2	32.3	33.5	34.8	36.3
45 to 54 years old	Million	19.0	18.6	18.8	19.0	19.3	19.8	20.5	21.4	22.2	22.8
55 to 59 years old	Million	7.8	9.2	9.1	9.1	9.0	8.9	8.8	8.8	8.7	8.7
60 to 64 years old	Million	6.3	7.9	8.6	8.7	8.8	8.7	8.7	8.7	8.6	8.7
65 to 69 years old	Million	5.1	6.7	7.1	7.3	7.5	7.6	7.7	7.9	8.0	8.1
70 years old and over	Million	8.5	12.1	13.4	13.9	14.3	14.7	15.0	15.4	15.8	16.3
Workers reported with—											
Taxable earnings [2]	Million	93	113	116	120	123	126	130	132	133	132
Maximum earnings [2]	Million	24	10	7	8	8	8	8	8	8	8
Earnings in covered employment [2]	Bil. dol	532	1,329	1,801	1,937	2,082	2,237	2,433	2,589	2,720	2,796
Reported taxable [2]	Bil. dol	416	1,181	1,609	1,723	1,844	1,960	2,089	2,245	2,363	2,428
Percent of total	Percent	78.2	88.9	89.3	88.9	88.6	87.6	85.9	86.7	86.9	86.8
Average per worker:											
Total earnings [2]	Dollars	5,711	11,759	15,484	16,167	16,939	17,811	18,772	19,553	20,442	21,131
Taxable earnings [2]	Dollars	4,464	10,449	13,833	14,379	15,007	15,605	16,120	16,956	17,759	18,350
Annual maximum taxable earnings	Dollars	7,800	25,900	37,800	39,600	42,000	43,800	45,000	48,000	51,300	53,400
Maximum tax	Dollars	374	1,588	[3]2,533	2,792	3,003	3,132	3,380	3,605	3,924	4,085
Contribution rates for OASDHI: [4]											
Each employer and employee	Percent	4.80	6.13	[5]7.00	7.05	7.15	7.15	7.51	7.51	7.65	7.65
Self-employed [6]	Percent	6.90	8.10	14.00	14.10	14.30	14.30	15.02	15.02	15.30	15.30
SMI, monthly premium [7]	Dollars	5.30	9.60	14.60	15.50	15.50	17.90	24.80	31.90	28.60	29.90

[1] Fully insured for retirement and/or survivor benefits at beginning of year.　[2] Includes self-employment.　[3] Employee's maximum tax; see footnote 5.　[4] As of January 1, 1992 and 1993, each employee and employer pays 7.65 percent and the self-employed pay 15.3 percent.　[5] Employee pays 6.7 percent. Employee's additional 0.3 percent is supplied from general revenues.　[6] Self-employed pays 11.3 percent in 1984, 11.8 percent in 1985, 12.3 percent in 1986 and 1987, and 13.02 percent in 1988 and 1989. The additional amount is supplied from general revenues. Beginning 1990, self-employed pays 15.3 percent, and half of the tax is deductible for income tax purposes and for computing self-employment income subject to social security tax.　[7] 1970 and 1980, as of July 1; beginning 1984, as of January 1. As of January 1, 1992, the monthly premium is $31.80 and as of January 1, 1993, the monthly premium is $36.60.

Source: U.S. Social Security Administration, *Annual Statistical Supplement to the Social Security Bulletin;* and unpublished data.

No. 589. Social Security (OASDI)—Benefits, by Type of Beneficiary: 1970 to 1991

[A person eligible to receive more than one type of benefit is generally classified or counted only once as a retired-worker beneficiary. OASDI=Old-age, survivors, and disability insurance. See also headnote, table 588; Appendix III; and *Historical Statistics, Colonial Times to 1970*, series H 197-229]

TYPE OF BENEFICIARY	1970	1980	1984	1985	1986	1987	1988	1989	1990	1991
	BENEFITS IN CURRENT-PAYMENT STATUS[1] (end of year)									
Number of benefits (1,000)...	26,229	35,585	36,479	37,058	37,703	38,190	38,627	39,151	39,832	40,592
Retired workers [2] (1,000)	13,349	19,562	21,906	22,432	22,980	23,440	23,858	24,327	24,838	25,289
Disabled workers [3] (1,000)	1,493	2,859	2,597	2,657	2,728	2,786	2,830	2,895	3,011	3,195
Wives and husbands [2][4] (1,000)	2,952	3,477	3,355	3,375	3,387	3,381	3,367	3,365	3,367	3,370
Children (1,000)	4,122	4,607	3,408	3,319	3,295	3,244	3,204	3,165	3,187	3,268
Under age 18 [5]	3,315	3,423	2,729	2,699	2,665	2,604	2,534	2,488	2,497	2,558
Disabled children [5]	271	450	506	526	545	561	574	586	600	616
Students [6]	537	733	173	94	84	79	96	91	89	95
Of retired workers	546	639	477	457	450	439	432	423	422	426
Of deceased workers	2,688	2,610	2,010	1,917	1,878	1,837	1,809	1,780	1,776	1,791
Of disabled workers	889	1,358	921	945	966	968	963	962	989	1,052
Widowed mothers [7] (1,000)	523	562	382	372	351	329	318	312	304	301
Widows and widowers [2][8] (1,000)	3,227	4,411	4,779	4,863	4,928	4,984	5,029	5,071	5,111	5,158
Parents [2] (1,000)	29	15	10	10	9	8	7	6	6	5
Special benefits [9] (1,000)	534	93	40	32	25	19	14	10	7	5
Average monthly benefit, current dollars										
Retired workers [2]	118	341	461	479	489	513	537	567	603	629
Retired worker and wife [2]	199	567	780	814	831	873	914	966	1,027	1,072
Disabled workers [3]	131	371	471	484	488	508	530	556	587	609
Wives and husbands [2][4]	59	164	227	236	241	253	265	281	298	311
Children of retired workers	45	140	186	198	204	216	228	242	259	273
Children of deceased workers	82	240	314	330	337	352	368	385	406	420
Children of disabled workers	39	110	139	142	141	146	151	157	164	168
Widowed mothers [7]	87	246	322	332	338	353	368	388	409	424
Widows and widowers, nondisabled [2]	102	311	415	433	444	468	493	522	557	584
Parents [2]	103	276	364	378	386	407	428	454	482	506
Special benefits [9]	45	105	134	138	140	145	151	158	167	173
Average monthly benefit, constant (1991) dollars [10]										
Retired workers [2]	409	545	604	604	609	613	615	620	621	629
Retired worker and wife [2]	690	906	1,021	1,027	1,037	1,043	1,046	1,056	1,058	1,072
Disabled workers [3]	454	593	617	611	609	607	607	608	605	609
Wives and husbands [2][4]	204	262	297	298	301	302	303	307	307	311
Children of deceased workers	284	383	411	418	421	421	421	421	418	420
Widowed mothers [7]	301	393	422	419	422	422	422	424	422	424
Widows and widowers, nondisabled [2]	353	497	543	546	544	559	564	571	573	584
	BENEFITS AWARDED DURING YEAR (1,000)									
Number of benefits	3,722	4,215	3,691	3,796	3,853	3,734	3,681	3,646	3,717	3,865
Retired workers [2]	1,338	1,620	1,607	1,690	1,734	1,682	1,654	1,657	1,665	1,695
Disabled workers [3]	350	389	362	377	417	416	409	426	468	536
Wives and husbands [2][4]	436	469	425	440	441	411	391	380	379	380
Children	1,091	1,174	722	714	701	685	706	675	695	727
Widowed mothers [7]	112	108	74	72	69	65	63	60	58	58
Widows and widowers [2][8]	363	452	500	502	491	475	458	449	452	469
Parents [2]	2	1	(Z)	(Z)	(Z)	(Z)	(Z)	(Z)	(Z)	(Z)
Special benefits [9]	30	1	1	1	(Z)	(Z)	(Z)	(Z)	(Z)	(Z)
	BENEFIT PAYMENTS DURING YEAR (bil. dol.)									
Total amount [11]	31.9	120.5	175.8	186.2	196.7	204.2	217.2	230.9	247.8	268.1
Monthly benefits [12]	31.6	120.1	175.6	186.0	196.5	204.0	217.0	230.6	247.6	267.9
Retired workers [2]	18.4	70.4	110.0	116.8	123.6	128.5	137.0	146.0	156.8	169.1
Disabled workers [3]	2.4	12.8	15.6	16.5	17.4	18.1	19.2	20.3	22.1	24.7
Wives and husbands [2][4]	2.2	7.0	10.4	11.1	11.7	12.1	12.8	13.6	14.5	15.5
Children	3.5	10.5	10.7	10.7	10.9	11.0	11.3	11.5	12.0	12.8
Under age 18	2.7	7.4	8.4	8.5	8.7	8.5	8.7	8.7	9.0	9.5
Disabled children [5]	0.3	1.0	1.6	1.8	2.0	2.0	2.2	2.3	2.5	2.8
Students [6]	0.6	2.1	0.6	0.4	0.3	0.4	0.5	0.5	0.5	0.5
Of retired workers	0.3	1.1	1.1	1.1	1.2	1.2	1.2	1.2	1.3	1.4
Of deceased workers	2.8	7.4	7.8	7.8	7.8	7.8	8.1	8.3	8.6	9.0
Of disabled workers	0.5	2.0	1.7	1.8	1.9	1.9	2.0	2.0	2.2	2.4
Widowed mothers [7]	0.6	1.6	1.5	1.5	1.5	1.4	1.4	1.4	1.4	1.5
Widows and widowers [2][8]	4.1	17.6	27.3	29.3	31.3	32.8	35.2	37.7	40.7	44.1
Parents [2]	(Z)	0.1	0.1	0.1	(Z)	(Z)	(Z)	(Z)	(Z)	(Z)
Special benefits [9]	0.3	0.1	0.1	0.1	(Z)	(Z)	(Z)	(Z)	(Z)	(Z)
Lump sum	0.3	0.4	0.2	0.2	0.2	0.2	0.2	0.2	0.2	0.2

Z Fewer than 500 or less than $50 million.   [1] Benefit payment actually being made at a specified time with no deductions or with deductions amounting to less than a month's benefit; i.e., the benefits actually being received.   [2] 62 years and over. [3] Disabled workers under age 65.   [4] Includes wife beneficiaries with entitled children in their care and entitled divorced wives. [5] 18 years old and over. Disability began before age 18 and, beginning 1973, before age 22.   [6] Full-time students aged 18-21 through 1984 and aged 18 and 19 beginning 1985.   [7] Includes surviving divorced mothers with entitled children in their care and, beginning 1980, widowed fathers with entitled children in their care.   [8] Includes widows aged 60-61, surviving divorced wives aged 60 and over, disabled widows and widowers aged 50 and over; and beginning 1980, widowers aged 60-61.   [9] Benefits for persons aged 72 and over not insured under regular or transitional provisions of Social Security Act.   [10] Constant dollar figures are based on the consumer price index for December as published by the U.S. Bureau of Labor Statistics.   [11] Represents total disbursements of benefit checks by the U.S. Dept. of the Treasury during the years specified.   [12] Distribution by type estimated.

Source: U.S. Social Security Administration, *Annual Statistical Supplement* to the *Social Security Bulletin;* and unpublished data.

No. 590. Social Security—Beneficiaries, Annual Payments, and Average Monthly Benefit, 1980 to 1991, and by State and Other Areas, 1991

[Number of beneficiaries in current-payment status and average monthly benefit as of **December**. See also headnote, table 589, and Appendix III]

YEAR, DIVISION, STATE, AND OTHER AREA	NUMBER OF BENEFICIARIES [1] (1,000)				ANNUAL PAYMENTS (mil. dol.)				AVERAGE MONTHLY BENEFIT (dol.)		
	Total	Retired workers and dependents [2]	Survivors	Disabled workers and dependents	Total	Retired workers and dependents [2]	Survivors [3]	Disabled workers and dependents	Retired workers [4]	Disabled workers	Widows and widowers [5]
1980	35,585	23,309	7,598	4,678	120,472	78,025	27,010	15,437	341	371	311
1985	37,058	25,989	7,162	3,907	186,195	128,536	38,824	18,836	479	484	433
1986	37,703	26,541	7,166	3,995	196,692	135,949	40,896	19,847	489	488	444
1987	38,190	26,988	7,157	4,045	204,156	141,329	42,315	20,512	513	508	468
1988	38,627	27,390	7,163	4,074	217,214	150,526	44,996	21,692	537	530	493
1989	39,151	27,853	7,170	4,129	230,850	160,352	47,625	22,873	567	556	522
1990	39,832	28,367	7,197	4,266	247,796	172,042	50,951	24,803	603	587	557
1991, total	**40,568**	**28,812**	**7,246**	**4,515**	**268,098**	**185,545**	**54,891**	**27,662**	**629**	**609**	**584**
United States	**39,621**	**28,241**	**7,028**	**4,352**	**264,049**	**183,287**	**53,806**	**26,956**	**(NA)**	**(NA)**	**(NA)**
New England	**2,182**	**1,633**	**335**	**213**	**14,955**	**10,933**	**2,701**	**1,321**	**(NA)**	**(NA)**	**(NA)**
Maine	218	156	36	26	1,345	932	265	148	578	556	551
New Hampshire	167	126	25	16	1,127	830	199	98	632	605	605
Vermont	90	64	15	10	586	407	117	62	617	594	585
Massachusetts	989	735	154	100	6,719	4,851	1,246	622	632	595	614
Rhode Island	184	139	27	18	1,240	920	210	110	629	580	607
Connecticut	534	413	78	43	3,938	2,993	664	281	691	613	651
Middle Atlantic	**6,375**	**4,687**	**1,088**	**600**	**45,320**	**32,453**	**8,873**	**3,994**	**(NA)**	**(NA)**	**(NA)**
New York	2,868	2,094	476	298	20,451	14,648	3,828	1,975	673	636	627
New Jersey	1,242	933	200	109	9,125	6,706	1,677	742	689	634	642
Pennsylvania	2,265	1,660	412	193	15,744	11,099	3,368	1,277	648	630	615
East North Central	**6,883**	**4,889**	**1,256**	**737**	**48,096**	**33,051**	**10,253**	**4,792**	**(NA)**	**(NA)**	**(NA)**
Ohio	1,827	1,271	356	200	12,501	8,340	2,872	1,289	645	635	613
Indiana	919	652	164	103	6,387	4,397	1,335	655	655	631	618
Illinois	1,772	1,279	319	174	12,591	8,837	2,622	1,132	668	633	630
Michigan	1,515	1,062	278	174	10,793	7,317	2,297	1,179	672	669	628
Wisconsin	850	625	139	86	5,824	4,160	1,127	537	646	615	614
West North Central	**3,054**	**2,228**	**537**	**289**	**20,052**	**14,136**	**4,171**	**1,745**	**(NA)**	**(NA)**	**(NA)**
Minnesota	677	505	116	56	4,424	3,172	908	344	614	596	584
Iowa	527	389	92	46	3,522	2,505	734	283	631	604	595
Missouri	922	651	164	107	6,012	4,117	1,244	651	615	597	577
North Dakota	112	82	21	9	698	485	159	54	593	576	570
South Dakota	130	93	24	13	794	551	175	68	582	550	547
Nebraska	272	201	48	23	1,786	1,274	377	135	621	591	599
Kansas	414	307	72	35	2,816	2,032	574	210	645	591	607
South Atlantic	**7,343**	**5,214**	**1,280**	**852**	**47,205**	**32,707**	**9,300**	**5,198**	**(NA)**	**(NA)**	**(NA)**
Delaware	108	79	18	11	756	538	145	73	656	625	614
Maryland	625	452	116	57	4,204	2,933	894	377	628	626	594
District of Columbia	78	56	16	7	456	312	99	45	537	546	495
Virginia	857	593	159	105	5,387	3,607	1,149	631	595	596	542
West Virginia	373	230	82	61	2,409	1,422	616	371	622	654	554
North Carolina	1,111	758	201	152	6,858	4,599	1,361	898	588	573	512
South Carolina	558	371	104	84	3,415	2,245	678	492	588	583	506
Georgia	905	583	181	141	5,550	3,519	1,215	816	587	582	519
Florida	2,728	2,092	403	234	18,170	13,532	3,143	1,495	628	620	602
East South Central	**2,685**	**1,706**	**555**	**424**	**16,086**	**9,973**	**3,728**	**2,385**	**(NA)**	**(NA)**	**(NA)**
Kentucky	658	407	139	113	3,963	2,365	951	647	579	605	520
Tennessee	846	557	165	123	5,189	3,343	1,143	703	588	577	524
Alabama	722	460	155	107	4,357	2,706	1,046	605	581	582	512
Mississippi	459	282	96	81	2,577	1,559	588	430	546	560	471
West South Central	**3,924**	**2,625**	**824**	**474**	**24,389**	**15,815**	**5,864**	**2,710**	**(NA)**	**(NA)**	**(NA)**
Arkansas	473	311	91	72	2,791	1,784	604	403	565	576	502
Louisiana	663	397	157	108	3,989	2,304	1,085	600	584	617	535
Oklahoma	539	379	104	56	3,410	2,312	761	337	600	592	555
Texas	2,249	1,538	472	238	14,199	9,415	3,414	1,370	610	600	564
Mountain	**2,013**	**1,456**	**329**	**229**	**13,090**	**9,203**	**2,485**	**1,402**	**(NA)**	**(NA)**	**(NA)**
Montana	142	99	24	19	915	617	185	113	611	623	589
Idaho	161	118	27	17	1,035	733	202	100	611	612	586
Wyoming	64	46	11	7	426	299	86	41	628	613	599
Colorado	434	308	75	52	2,803	1,915	571	317	613	603	587
New Mexico	227	154	43	30	1,364	907	292	165	592	595	546
Arizona	609	453	91	65	4,066	2,939	702	425	637	641	607
Utah	198	144	33	21	1,288	924	248	116	635	595	613
Nevada	178	134	25	18	1,193	869	199	125	631	643	609
Pacific	**5,161**	**3,805**	**822**	**534**	**34,856**	**25,016**	**6,431**	**3,409**	**(NA)**	**(NA)**	**(NA)**
Washington	728	543	112	74	5,021	3,638	906	477	653	624	619
Oregon	509	385	76	47	3,437	2,530	610	297	641	618	611
California	3,738	2,735	606	397	25,200	17,948	4,713	2,539	643	611	609
Alaska	35	23	7	5	227	147	52	28	626	607	556
Hawaii	151	119	21	11	971	753	150	68	619	602	559
Puerto Rico	570	316	115	139	2,335	1,203	526	606	402	502	362
Guam	6	3	2	1	24	12	9	3	450	482	424
American Samoa	4	2	2	1	13	5	5	3	393	442	324
Virgin Islands	10	6	3	1	52	33	13	6	531	569	492
Abroad	361	244	96	21	1,625	1,005	534	85	448	535	448

NA Not available. [1] Data for 1991 based on 10-percent sample. [2] Includes special benefits; see footnote 9, table 589. [3] Includes lump-sum payments to survivors of deceased workers. [4] Excludes persons with special benefits. [5] Nondisabled only.

Source: U.S. Social Security Administration, *Social Security Bulletin*, quarterly.

No. 591. Social Security Trust Funds: 1980 to 1991

[In billions of dollars, except percent. See also *Historical Statistics, Colonial Times to 1970*, series H 238-242]

TYPE OF TRUST FUND	1980	1984	1985	1986	1987	1988	1989	1990	1991
Old-age and survivors insurance (OASI):									
Net contribution income [1]	103.5	167.0	180.2	194.2	206.0	233.2	252.6	272.4	278.4
Interest received [2]	1.8	2.6	1.9	3.1	4.7	7.6	12.0	16.4	20.8
Benefit payments [3]	105.1	157.8	167.2	176.8	[4]183.6	[4]195.5	208.0	223.0	240.5
Assets, end of year	22.8	[5]27.1	[5]35.8	39.1	62.1	102.9	155.1	214.2	267.8
Reserve ratio [6] (percent)	21	17	21	22	33	52	74	96	111
Disability insurance (DI):									
Net contribution income [1]	13.3	16.1	17.4	18.6	19.7	22.1	24.1	28.7	29.3
Interest received [2]	0.5	1.2	0.9	0.8	0.6	0.6	0.7	0.9	1.1
Benefit payments [3]	15.5	17.9	18.8	19.9	[4]20.5	[4]21.7	22.9	24.8	27.7
Assets, end of year	3.6	[7]4.0	[6]3	7.8	6.7	6.9	7.9	11.1	12.9
Reserve ratio [6] (percent)	23	21	33	38	31	31	33	45	47
Hospital insurance (HI):									
Net contribution income [1][8]	23.9	42.5	47.7	54.7	58.8	62.6	68.5	71.1	78.4
Interest received [2]	1.1	3.0	3.4	3.6	4.5	5.8	7.3	8.5	9.5
Benefit payments	25.1	43.3	47.5	49.8	49.5	52.5	60.0	66.2	71.5
Assets, end of year	13.7	[9]15.7	[9]20.5	40.0	53.7	69.6	85.6	98.9	115.2
Reserve ratio [6] (percent)	54	36	42	79	107	131	141	148	161
Supplementary medical insurance (SMI):									
Net premium income	3.0	5.2	5.6	5.7	7.4	8.8	10.8	11.3	11.9
Transfers from general revenue	7.5	17.1	18.3	17.8	23.6	26.2	30.9	33.0	37.6
Interest received	0.4	1.0	1.2	1.1	0.9	0.9	1.1	1.6	1.7
Benefit payments	10.6	19.7	22.9	26.2	30.8	34.0	38.4	42.5	47.2
Assets, end of year	4.5	9.7	10.9	8.3	8.4	9.0	12.2	15.5	17.9
Reserve ratio [6] (percent)	40	47	46	30	26	26	31	35	38

[1] Includes deposits by States and deductions for refund of estimated employee-tax overpayment. Beginning in 1984, includes government contributions on deemed wage credits for military service in 1957 and later. Beginning 1984 includes tax credits on wages paid in 1984 and net earnings from self-employment in 1984-89; and taxation of benefits (OASI and DI, only). [2] Beginning in 1984, includes interest on advance tax transfers and interest on reimbursement for unnegotiated checks. Data for 1984 reflect interest on deemed wage credits for military service performed after 1956. Data for 1984-86 reflect interest on interfund borrowing. [3] Includes payments for vocational rehabilitation services furnished to disabled persons receiving benefits because of their disabilities. Beginning in 1984, amounts reflect deductions for unnegotiated benefit checks. [4] Data adjusted to reflect 12 months of benefit payments. [5] Includes $18 billion borrowed from the DI and HI Trust Funds. Repayments on Jan. 31, 1985, reduced such amounts to $13.2 billion. [6] Assets at end of year as a percentage of benefit payments and administrative expenses during the year. [7] Excludes $5 billion lent to the OASI Trust Fund. Repayment on Jan. 31, 1985, reduced the total to $2.5 billion. [8] Includes premiums from aged ineligibles enrolled in HI. [9] Excludes $12 billion lent to the OASI Trust Fund. Repayment on Jan. 31, 1985, reduced the total to $10.6 billion.

Source: U.S. Social Security Administration, *Annual Report of Board of Trustees, OASI, DI, HI, and SMI Trust Funds.* Also published in *Social Security Bulletin*, quarterly.

No. 592. Public Employee Retirement Systems—Beneficiaries and Benefits: 1970 to 1989

[Number of beneficiaries as of end of year]

YEAR	Unit	Total	LEVEL OF GOVERNMENT				TYPE OF BENEFIT			
			Federal			State and local	Age and service	Dis-ability	Survivor	
			Total [1]	Civil service	Armed Forces				Monthly	Lump-sum
Beneficiaries:										
1970	1,000	3,050	1,759	958	773	1,291	2,204	419	427	(X)
1980	1,000	5,659	3,052	1,675	1,330	2,607	4,200	708	751	(X)
1985	1,000	6,890	3,512	1,971	1,487	3,378	5,271	745	874	(X)
1988	1,000	7,422	3,714	2,089	1,567	3,708	5,765	698	959	(X)
1989	1,000	7,693	3,782	2,122	1,602	3,910	5,988	681	1,024	(X)
Benefits:										
1970	Mil. dol.	9,355	6,075	2,820	3,133	3,280	7,210	1,312	645	189
1980	Mil. dol.	41,060	28,042	15,065	12,478	13,018	32,416	5,371	2,896	377
1985	Mil. dol.	63,413	40,912	22,840	17,416	22,501	50,562	7,623	4,684	544
1988	Mil. dol.	77,242	47,518	27,638	18,991	29,724	62,704	8,379	6,072	[2]87
1989	Mil. dol.	83,242	50,250	29,149	20,063	32,992	66,603	9,654	6,910	[2]75
Average annual benefit per annuitant, current dollars:										
1970	Dollars	3,005	3,440	(NA)	(NA)	2,413	3,271	3,136	1,512	(X)
1980	Dollars	7,190	9,181	(NA)	(NA)	4,859	7,719	7,588	3,855	(X)
1985	Dollars	9,137	11,659	(NA)	(NA)	6,512	9,592	10,232	5,556	(X)
1988	Dollars	10,395	12,771	(NA)	(NA)	8,016	10,877	12,001	6,330	(X)
1989	Dollars	10,821	13,285	(NA)	(NA)	8,437	10,472	12,297	6,750	(X)
Average annual benefit per annuitant, constant (1989) dollars: [3]										
1970	Dollars	3,155	3,612	(NA)	(NA)	2,534	3,435	3,292	1,588	(X)
1980	Dollars	7,550	9,640	(NA)	(NA)	5,102	8,105	7,968	4,048	(X)
1985	Dollars	9,594	12,242	(NA)	(NA)	6,838	10,072	10,744	5,834	(X)
1988	Dollars	10,915	13,410	(NA)	(NA)	8,417	11,421	12,602	6,647	(X)
1989	Dollars	10,821	13,285	(NA)	(NA)	8,437	10,472	12,297	6,750	(X)

NA Not available. X Not applicable. [1] Includes other Federal agencies, not shown separately. [2] Lump-sum payments for State and local government are not available. [3] Constant dollar figures are based on implicit price deflators for personal consumption expenditures supplied by U.S. Bureau of Economic Analysis.

Source: U.S. Social Security Administration, *Social Security Bulletin*, summer 1992; and unpublished data.

No. 593. Federal Civil Service Retirement: 1980 to 1991

[As of **Sept. 30** or for **year ending** Sept. 30. See also *Historical Statistics, Colonial Times to 1970*, series H 262-270]

ITEM	Unit	1980	1984	1985	1986	1987	1988	1989	1990	1991
Employees covered [1]	1,000	2,720	2,660	2,750	2,800	2,810	2,800	2,880	2,950	2,986
Annuitants, total	1,000	1,675	1,910	1,955	2,008	2,032	2,089	2,120	2,143	2,185
Age and service	1,000	905	1,082	1,122	1,166	1,186	1,237	1,267	1,288	1,325
Disability	1,000	343	338	332	326	318	311	305	297	290
Survivors	1,000	427	490	501	516	528	541	548	558	570
Receipts, total [2]	Mil. dol	24,389	36,734	40,790	43,216	43,640	46,696	49,249	52,742	56,815
Employee contributions	Mil. dol	3,686	4,608	4,679	4,714	4,641	4,544	4,491	4,501	4,563
Federal government contributions	Mil. dol	15,562	20,848	22,301	22,980	23,144	24,258	25,367	27,368	29,509
Disbursements, total [3]	Mil. dol	14,977	21,951	23,203	24,694	25,772	28,306	29,713	31,416	33,212
Age and service annuitants [4]	Mil. dol	12,639	18,403	19,414	20,702	21,678	23,889	25,095	26,495	28,000
Survivors	Mil. dol	1,912	2,943	3,158	3,304	3,485	3,749	4,033	4,366	4,717
Average monthly benefit:										
Age and service	Dollars	992	1,149	1,189	1,197	1,267	1,263	1,310	1,369	1,439
Disability	Dollars	723	851	881	881	893	930	966	1,003	1,059
Survivors	Dollars	392	501	528	536	552	583	616	653	698
Cash and security holdings	Bil. dol	73.7	124.7	142.3	160.8	178.7	197.1	216.7	238.0	258.6

[1] Excludes employees in Leave Without Pay status. [2] Includes interest on investments. [3] Includes refunds, death claims, and administration. [4] Includes disability annuitants.

Source: U.S. Office of Personnel Management, *Compensation Report*, annual.

No. 594. State and Local Government Retirement Systems—Beneficiaries and Finances: 1980 to 1990

[**In millions of dollars, except as indicated.** For fiscal years closed during the 12 months ending June 30]

YEAR AND LEVEL OF GOVERNMENT	Number of beneficiaries (1,000)	RECEIPTS						BENEFITS AND WITHDRAWALS			Cash and security holdings
		Total	Employee contributions	Government contributions		Earnings on investments		Total	Benefits	Withdrawals	
				State	Local						
1980: All systems	(NA)	37,313	6,466	7,581	9,951	13,315		14,008	12,207	1,801	185,226
State-administered	(NA)	28,603	5,285	7,399	5,611	10,308		10,257	8,809	1,448	144,682
Locally administered	(NA)	8,710	1,180	181	4,340	3,008		3,752	3,399	353	40,544
1985: All systems	3,378	71,411	9,468	12,227	15,170	34,546		24,413	21,999	2,414	374,433
State-administered	2,661	55,960	7,901	11,976	8,944	27,139		18,230	16,183	2,047	296,951
Locally administered	716	15,451	1,567	251	6,226	7,407		6,183	5,816	367	77,481
1989: All systems	3,911	100,125	12,862	13,249	18,037	55,978		35,114	32,992	2,122	628,778
State-administered	3,120	81,090	10,813	13,155	11,202	45,919		26,979	25,277	1,702	503,074
Locally administered	791	19,036	2,048	94	6,835	10,059		8,136	7,716	420	125,704
1990: All systems	4,026	111,339	13,853	13,994	18,583	64,907		38,396	35,966	2,430	703,772
State-administered	3,232	89,162	11,648	13,964	11,538	52,012		29,603	27,562	2,041	565,641
Locally administered	794	22,177	2,205	32	7,045	12,895		8,793	8,404	389	138,131

NA Not available.

Source: U.S. Bureau of the Census, *Finances of Employee-Retirement Systems of State and Local Governments*, series GF, No. 2, annual.

No. 595. Private Pension Plans—Summary, by Type of Plan: 1975 to 1989

["Pension plan" is defined by the Employee Retirement Income Security Act (ERISA) as "any plan, fund, or program which was heretofore or is hereafter established or maintained by an employer or an employee organization, or by both, to the extent that such plan (a) provides retirement income to employees, or (b) results in a deferral of income by employees for periods extending to the termination of covered employment or beyond, regardless of the method of calculating the contributions made to the plan, the method of calculating the benefits under the plan, or the method of distributing benefits from the plan." A defined benefit plan provides a definite benefit formula for calculating benefit amounts - such as a flat amount per year of service or a percentage of salary times years of service. A defined contribution plan is a pension plan in which the contributions are made to an individual account for each employee. The retirement benefit is dependent upon the account balance at retirement. The balance depends upon amounts contributed, investment experience, and, in the case of profit sharing plans, amounts which may be allocated to the account due to forfeitures by terminating employees. Employee Stock Ownership Plans (ESOP) (see table 871) and 401(k) plans are included among defined contribution plans. Data are based on Form 5500 series reports filed with the Internal Revenue Service]

ITEM	Unit	TOTAL				DEFINED CONTRIBUTION PLAN				DEFINED BENEFIT PLAN			
		1975	1980	1985	1989	1975	1980	1985	1989	1975	1980	1985	1989
Number of plans [1]	1,000	311.1	488.9	632.1	732.3	207.7	340.8	462.0	599.4	103.3	148.1	170.2	132.9
Total participants [2][3]	Million	44.5	57.9	74.7	79.9	11.5	19.9	35.0	38.6	33.0	38.0	39.7	41.3
Active participants [2][4]	Million	38.4	49.0	62.3	65.2	11.2	18.9	33.2	36.2	27.2	30.1	29.0	29.0
Contributions	Bil. dol	37.1	66.2	95.1	105.7	12.8	23.5	53.1	80.6	24.2	42.6	42.0	25.2
Benefits [5]	Bil. dol	19.1	35.3	101.9	137.2	6.2	13.1	47.4	70.4	12.9	22.1	54.5	66.8

[1] Excludes all plans covering only one participant. [2] Includes double counting of workers in more than one plan. [3] Total participants include active participants, vested separated workers, and retirees. [4] Any workers currently in employment covered by a plan and who are earning or retaining credited service under a plan. Includes any nonvested former employees who have not yet incurred breaks in service. [5] Benefits paid directly from trust and premium payments made from plan to insurance carriers. Excludes benefits paid directly by insurance carriers.

Source: U.S. Dept. of Labor, Pension and Welfare Benefits Administration, *Trends in Pensions*, 1992; and unpublished data.

No. 596. Pension Plan Coverage of Workers, by Selected Characteristics: 1991

[Covers workers as of **March** of following year who had earnings in year shown. Based on Current Population Survey; see text, section 1 and Appendix III]

SEX AND AGE	NUMBER WITH COVERAGE (1,000)				PERCENT OF TOTAL WORKERS			
	Total [1]	White	Black	Hispanic [2]	Total [1]	White	Black	Hispanic [2]
Total...............	53,913	46,704	5,663	2,732	40	41	40	27
Male..................	30,751	27,075	2,803	1,640	43	43	40	27
Under 65 years old	30,163	26,536	2,762	1,622	44	44	41	27
15 to 24 years old.	1,529	1,299	191	136	13	13	15	11
25 to 44 years old......	17,764	15,530	1,682	1,028	47	48	44	29
45 to 64 years old.	10,870	9,708	888	458	56	57	54	39
65 years old and over.....	589	539	42	18	21	22	20	18
Female.................	23,162	19,629	2,859	1,093	37	37	40	26
Under 65 years old	22,724	19,240	2,823	1,084	38	38	41	26
15 to 24 years old.	1,313	1,117	174	86	12	12	14	10
25 to 44 years old.......	13,763	11,582	1,756	680	42	42	44	29
45 to 64 years old.......	7,649	6,541	894	318	47	47	53	37
65 years old and over.....	438	389	36	9	22	23	20	17

[1] Includes other races, not shown separately.   [2] Hispanic persons may be of any race.

Source: U.S. Bureau of the Census, unpublished data.

No. 597. State Unemployment Insurance—Summary: 1980 to 1991

[See headnote, table 598]

ITEM	Unit	1980	1983	1984	1985	1986	1987	1988	1989	1990	1991
Insured unemployment, avg. weekly..	1,000..	3,350	3,396	2,476	2,611	2,641	2,330	2,081	2,158	2,522	3,342
Percent of covered employment [1]..	Percent	3.9	3.9	2.8	2.9	2.8	2.3	2.0	2.1	2.4	3.1
Percent of civilian unemployed....	Percent	43.9	31.7	29.0	31.4	32.1	31.4	31.0	33.0	36.0	40.0
Unemployment benefits, avg. weekly .	Dollars .	99	124	123	127	135	140	145	152	162	170
Percent of weekly wage	Percent	37.5	37.6	35.8	35.3	35.8	35.3	34.9	35.4	36.2	36.5
Weeks compensated............	Million .	149.0	155.5	111.6	119.3	121.4	105.2	94.2	97.6	116.0	155.1
Beneficiaries, first payments [2]......	1,000..	10,001	8,907	7,765	8,350	8,361	7,205	6,861	7,369	8,629	10,075
Average duration of benefits [2]......	Weeks .	14.9	17.5	14.4	14.3	14.5	14.6	13.7	13.2	13.4	15.4
Claimants exhausting benefits......	1,000..	3,072	4,180	2,600	2,575	2,688	2,409	1,979	1,940	2,323	3,472
Percent of first payment [3].......	Percent	33.2	38.4	34.1	31.3	32.1	30.6	28.5	28.0	29.4	34.8
Contributions collected [4].........	Bil. dol.	11.4	14.6	18.8	19.3	18.1	17.6	17.7	16.5	15.2	14.5
Benefits paid...............	Bil. dol.	13.8	17.8	12.6	14.0	15.4	14.2	13.2	14.3	18.1	25.4
Funds available for benefits [5]	Bil. dol.	11.4	7.3	11.6	16.0	19.6	23.2	31.1	37.5	38.4	31.5
Average employer contribution rate [6] .	Percent	2.5	2.8	3.2	3.1	2.7	2.6	2.5	2.2	2.0	1.9

[1] Insured unemployment as percent of average covered employment in preceding year.   [2] Weeks compensated divided by first payment.   [3] Based on first payments for 12-month period ending June 30.   [4] Contributions from employers; also employees in States which tax workers.   [5] End of year. Sum of balances in State clearing accounts, benefit-payment accounts, and State accounts in Federal unemployment trust funds.   [6] As percent of taxable wages.

No. 598. State Unemployment Insurance, by State and Other Areas: 1991

[Includes unemployment compensation for State and local government employees where covered by State law. For State data on insured unemployment, see table 658. See also *Historical Statistics, Colonial Times to 1970*, series H 305-317]

STATE OR OTHER AREA	Beneficiaries, first payments (1,000)	Benefits paid (mil. dol.)	Avg. weekly unemployment benefits (dol.)	STATE OR OTHER AREA	Beneficiaries, first payments (1,000)	Benefits paid (mil. dol.)	Avg. weekly unemployment benefits (dol.)	STATE OR OTHER AREA	Beneficiaries, first payments (1,000)	Benefits paid (mil. dol.)	Avg. weekly unemployment benefits (dol.)
Total .	10,075	25,446	170	KY	145	273	145	OH....	405	1,034	177
AL....	171	221	119	LA	102	163	111	OK....	60	130	153
AK....	45	110	170	ME....	71	176	164	OR....	153	365	167
AZ....	98	199	143	MD....	166	495	179	PA....	560	1,725	197
AR....	103	176	140	MA....	318	1,313	222	RI....	69	229	204
CA....	1,491	3,451	144	MI	513	1,548	212	SC....	148	235	141
CO....	83	176	173	MN....	148	436	194	SD....	9	11	122
CT....	190	611	206	MS....	85	127	116	TN....	221	333	118
DE....	29	73	183	MO....	205	404	143	TX....	407	1,013	170
DC....	31	135	221	MT....	26	47	143	UT....	39	74	168
FL....	353	823	158	NE....	34	47	126	VT....	31	73	153
GA....	278	469	149	NV....	65	156	168	VA....	169	313	157
HI....	30	81	214	NH....	54	84	130	WA....	229	599	175
ID....	48	81	153	NJ....	373	1,430	218	WV....	66	153	160
IL....	427	1,318	180	NM....	33	71	135	WI....	239	498	176
IN....	168	215	112	NY....	737	2,650	190	WY....	11	25	161
IA....	93	188	167	NC....	332	510	157	PR....	121	163	82
KS....	74	184	170	ND....	17	29	144	VI....	2	4	151

Source of tables 597 and 598: U.S. Employment and Training Administration, *Unemployment Insurance Data Summary*, annual.

No. 599. Workers' Compensation Payments: 1970 to 1990

[In **billions of dollars**, except as indicated. See headnote, table 600. See also *Historical Statistics, Colonial Times to 1970*, series H 332-345]

ITEM	1970	1980	1982	1983	1984	1985	1986	1987	1988	1989	1990
Workers covered [1] (mil.)	59	79	77	78	82	84	86	88	91	94	95
Premium amounts paid. . . .	**4.9**	**22.3**	**22.8**	**23.0**	**25.1**	**29.2**	**34.0**	**38.1**	**43.3**	**48.0**	**53.1**
Private carriers.	3.6	15.7	15.4	15.4	16.6	19.5	22.8	25.4	28.5	31.9	35.1
State funds	0.7	3.0	2.6	2.7	3.0	3.5	4.5	5.3	6.7	7.2	8.0
Federal programs [2]	0.2	1.1	1.5	1.5	1.6	1.7	1.8	1.8	1.9	2.0	2.2
Self-insurers	0.5	2.4	3.2	3.5	3.9	4.5	4.9	5.5	6.2	6.9	7.9
Annual benefits paid	**3.0**	**13.6**	**16.4**	**17.6**	**19.7**	**22.2**	**24.6**	**27.3**	**30.7**	**34.3**	**38.2**
By private carriers [3]	1.8	7.0	8.6	9.3	10.6	12.3	13.8	15.5	17.5	19.9	22.2
From State funds [4]	0.8	4.3	4.8	5.1	5.4	5.7	6.2	6.8	7.5	8.0	8.7
Employers' self-insurance [5]	0.4	2.3	3.0	3.2	3.7	4.1	4.5	5.1	5.7	6.4	7.4
Type of benefit:											
Medical/hospitalization	1.1	3.9	5.1	5.7	6.4	7.5	8.6	9.9	11.5	13.4	15.2
Compensation payments.	2.0	9.7	11.3	11.9	13.3	14.7	16.0	17.4	19.2	20.9	23.1
Disability	1.8	8.4	9.9	10.4	11.7	13.1	14.3	15.8	17.6	19.2	21.2
Survivor	0.2	1.3	1.5	1.5	1.6	1.7	1.6	1.6	1.6	1.7	1.8
Percent of covered payroll:											
Workers' compensation costs [6][7]	1.11	1.96	1.75	1.67	1.66	1.82	1.99	2.07	2.16	2.27	2.36
Benefits [7]	0.66	1.07	1.16	1.17	1.21	1.30	1.37	1.43	1.49	1.58	1.70

[1] Estimated per month.   [2] Includes Federal employer compensation program and that portion of Federal black lung benefits program financed from employer contributions.   [3] Net cash and medical benefits paid under standard workers' compensation policies.   [4] Net cash and medical benefits paid by competitive and exclusive State funds and by Federal workers' compensation programs, including black lung benefit program.   [5] Cash and medical benefits paid by self-insurers, plus value of medical benefits paid by employers carrying workers' compensation policies that exclude standard medical coverage.   [6] Premiums written by private carriers and State funds, and benefits paid by self-insurers increased by 5-10 percent to allow for administrative costs. Also includes benefits paid and administrative costs of Federal system for government employees.   [7] Excludes programs financed from general revenue—black lung benefits and supplemental pensions in some States.

Source: U.S. Social Security Administration, *Annual Statistical Supplement* to the *Social Security Bulletin*.

No. 600. Workers' Compensation Payments, by State: 1980 to 1990

[In **millions of dollars**. Calendar-year data, except fiscal-year data for Federal civilian and other programs and for a few States with State funds. Payments represent cash and medical benefits and include insurance losses paid by private insurance carriers (compiled from the *Spectator (Insurance by States . . . of Casualty Lines)*, from reports of State insurance commissions, and from A. M. Best Co.); net disbursements of State funds (from the *Spectator*, from *Argus Casualty and Surety Chart*, and from State reports), estimated for some states; and self-insurance payments, estimated from available State data. Includes benefit payments under Longshoremen's and Harbor Workers' Compensation Act and Defense Bases Compensation Act for States in which such payments are made]

STATE	1980	1985	1988	1989	1990	STATE	1980	1985	1988	1989	1990
Total	13,618	22,224	30,733	34,316	38,238	Nebraska	42	68	103	112	137
						Nevada	69	123	219	250	339
Alabama	112	203	311	380	444	New Hampshire	48	91	143	154	169
Alaska	60	109	122	113	113	New Jersey	316	501	682	761	844
Arizona	120	198	301	324	371	New Mexico	54	140	196	226	228
Arkansas	83	129	177	196	229	New York	637	985	1,345	1,528	1,752
California	1,628	3,243	4,716	5,242	6,065	North Carolina	131	236	328	386	480
Colorado.	114	284	474	532	595	North Dakota.	17	33	44	50	60
Connecticut.	147	305	496	587	694	Ohio	776	1,387	1,716	1,816	1,960
Delaware	21	41	57	68	75	Oklahoma	127	289	306	313	369
District of Columbia .	69	74	81	84	86	Oregon	275	396	556	576	573
Florida	362	815	1,422	1,732	1,976	Pennsylvania	572	998	1,484	1,820	2,019
Georgia	185	360	581	661	735	Rhode Island	55	97	168	200	219
Hawaii	60	133	151	180	216	South Carolina	79	152	208	240	277
Idaho	37	66	87	93	105	South Dakota	13	26	40	44	56
Illinois	699	912	1,277	1,432	1,607	Tennessee	129	204	341	390	463
Indiana	110	152	245	297	350	Texas	701	1,564	2,462	2,843	2,896
Iowa	99	121	169	190	231	Utah	39	80	116	142	187
Kansas.	84	142	197	220	266	Vermont	15	30	44	55	61
Kentucky	161	225	293	326	383	Virginia	182	276	409	465	507
						Washington	324	619	755	811	883
Louisiana	301	466	565	586	575	West Virginia	176	285	363	375	389
Maine.	81	194	314	342	380	Wisconsin	170	287	422	487	561
Maryland	187	306	397	437	505	Wyoming	22	47	46	47	49
Massachusetts.	296	510	859	1,078	1,235						
Michigan.	626	769	1,035	1,120	1,205	Federal programs:					
Minnesota.	260	453	470	497	582	Civilian employees.	776	1,055	1,253	1,274	1,448
Mississippi	60	98	155	171	198	Black lung					
Missouri	124	237	379	423	496	benefits	1,739	1,603	1,499	1,479	1,435
Montana	41	102	150	153	150	Other [2]	8	7	8	8	11

[1] Includes payments by Social Security Administration and by Department of Labor.   [2] Primarily payments made to dependents of reservists who died while on active duty in the Armed Forces.

Source: U.S. Social Security Administration, *Social Security Bulletin*, spring 1992 and selected prior issues; and unpublished data.

No. 601. Persons With Work Disability, by Selected Characteristics: 1992

[In thousands, except percent. As of **March**. Covers civilian noninstitutional population and members of Armed Forces living off post or with their families on post. Persons are classified as having a work disability if they (1) have a health problem or disability which prevents them from working or which limits the kind or amount of work they can do; (2) have a service-connected disability or ever retired or left a job for health reasons; (3) did not work in survey reference week or previous year because of long-term illness or disability; or (4) are under age 65, and are covered by Medicare or receive Supplemental Security Income. Based on Current Population Survey; see text, section 1, and Appendix III]

AGE AND PARTICIPATION STATUS IN ASSISTANCE PROGRAMS	Total [1]	Male	Female	White	Black	Hispanic [2]
Persons with work disability	14,959	7,573	7,386	11,819	2,670	1,192
16 to 24 years old	1,196	553	643	916	237	123
25 to 34 years old	2,727	1,412	1,315	2,057	562	208
35 to 44 years old	3,226	1,748	1,478	2,568	560	288
45 to 54 years old	3,154	1,547	1,607	2,508	560	254
55 to 64 years old	4,656	2,313	2,343	3,769	751	318
Percent work disabled of total population . . .	9.3	9.6	9.0	8.7	13.8	8.5
16 to 24 years old	3.9	3.6	4.1	3.6	5.2	3.5
25 to 34 years old	6.4	6.7	6.2	5.8	10.4	4.9
35 to 44 years old	8.2	9.0	7.4	7.7	12.6	9.1
45 to 54 years old	11.7	11.8	11.6	10.8	20.1	14.0
55 to 64 years old	22.0	23.1	21.1	20.6	34.7	25.4
Percent of work disabled—						
Receiving Social Security income	28.2	29.3	27.1	28.3	28.2	24.2
Receiving food stamps	22.8	18.4	27.4	19.1	39.1	31.7
Covered by Medicaid.	29.7	23.8	35.8	25.6	47.2	44.1
Residing in public housing	4.8	3.1	6.5	3.2	12.1	7.0
Residing in subsidized housing	3.9	2.6	5.2	3.2	7.1	5.5

[1] Includes other races not shown separately.　[2] Hispanic persons may be of any race.
Source: U.S. Bureau of the Census, unpublished data.

No. 602. Vocational Rehabilitation—Summary: 1980 to 1991

[For fiscal years ending in year shown; see text, section 9. Includes Puerto Rico, Guam, Virgin Islands, American Samoa, Northern Mariana Islands, and Trust Territory of the Pacific Islands. Vocational rehabilitation of the disabled defined as restoration, preservation, or development of the ability to function in productive activity. Rehabilitation services provided by State vocational rehabilitation agencies with matching State and Federal funds include medical restoration, training, counseling, guidance, and placement services. See also *Historical Statistics, Colonial Times to 1970*, series H 392-397]

ITEM	Unit	1980	1984	1985	1986	1987	1988	1989	1990	1991
Federal and State expenditures [1]	Mil. dol. .	[2]1,076	1,366	1,452	1,506	1,649	1,776	1,867	1,910	2,048
Federal expenditures	Mil. dol. .	[2]817	1,038	1,100	1,144	1,275	1,373	1,446	1,525	1,629
Applicants processed for program eligibility.	1,000 . .	717	594	594	594	597	606	623	625	619
Percent accepted into program	Percent .	58	59	60	58	58	58	58	57	57
Total persons rehabilitated [3]	1,000 . .	277	226	228	223	220	218	220	216	203
Rehabilitation rate [4]	Percent .	64	63	64	64	63	63	63	62	60
Severely disabled persons rehabilitated [3][5] .	1,000 . .	143	133	135	135	136	141	147	146	140
Rehabilitation rate [4]	Percent .	61	61	62	62	62	62	62	62	59
Percent of total persons rehabilitated . . .	Percent .	51	59	59	61	62	65	67	68	69
Persons served, total [6]	1,000 . .	1,095	936	932	924	917	919	929	938	942
Persons served, severely disabled [5][6] . . .	1,000 . .	606	565	581	580	584	604	625	640	654
Percent of total persons served	Percent .	55	60	62	63	64	66	67	68	69

[1] Includes expenditures only under the basic support provisions of the Rehabilitation Act.　[2] Estimates based on amounts appropriated.　[3] Persons successfully placed into gainful employment.　[4] Persons rehabilitated as a percent of all active case closures (whether rehabilitated or not).　[5] Severely disabled individuals fall into any of the following three categories: (a) clients with specified major disabling conditions such as blindness and deafness; (b) clients who at any time in the vocational rehabilitation process had been Social Security disability beneficiaries or recipients of Supplemental Security Income; and (c) other individuals with substantial loss in conducting certain specified activities.　[6] Includes active cases accepted for rehabilitation services during year plus active cases on hand at beginning of year.
Source: U.S. Dept. of Education, Rehabilitation Services Administration, *Caseload Statistics of State Vocational Rehabilitation Agencies in Fiscal Years*, and *State Vocational Rehabilitation Agency Program Data in Fiscal Years*, both annual.

No. 603. Protection Against Short-Term Sickness Income Loss: 1980 to 1991

[In **millions of dollars, except percent**. "Short-term sickness" refers to short-term or temporary nonwork-connected disability (lasting not more than 6 months) and the first 6 months of long-term disability. See also *Historical Statistics, Colonial Times to 1970*, series H 115-124]

ITEM	1980	1984	1985	1986	1987	1988	1989	1990	1991
Short-term sickness: Income loss	38,529	54,419	59,145	62,981	68,166	73,841	77,916	82,621	84,456
Total protection provided [1]	14,426	17,904	19,587	20,287	22,458	23,963	25,354	27,327	29,020
Protection as percent of loss.	37.4	32.9	33.1	32.2	32.9	32.6	32.5	33.1	34.4
Benefits provided by protection:									
Individual insurance.	1,280	1,410	1,796	1,774	2,062	2,057	2,451	2,701	2,976
Group benefits to workers in private employment	7,633	9,115	9,897	10,011	11,349	12,237	12,617	13,517	14,185
Private cash insurance [2]	3,271	2,507	2,601	2,268	2,685	2,901	2,727	2,806	2,888
Publicly operated cash sickness funds [3] . . .	770	968	1,179	1,255	1,696	1,779	1,907	2,269	2,699
Sick leave.	3,593	5,640	6,116	6,488	6,969	7,557	7,984	8,442	8,598
Sick leave for government employees.	5,338	7,218	7,700	8,299	8,827	9,462	10,062	10,835	11,548

[1] Provided by individual insurance, group benefits to workers in private employment, and sick leave for government employees. Includes benefits for the sixth month of disability payable under old-age, survivors, disability, and health insurance program, not shown separately.　[2] Group accident and sickness insurance and self-insurance privately written either on a voluntary basis or in compliance with State temporary disability insurance laws in CA, HI, NJ, and NY. Includes a small but undetermined amount of group disability insurance benefits paid to government workers and to self-employed persons through farm, trade, or professional associations.　[3] Includes State-operated plans in RI, CA, and NJ; State Insurance Fund and special fund for disabled unemployed in New York; and provisions of Railroad Unemployment Insurance Act.
Source: U.S. Social Security Administration, *Social Security Bulletin*, May 1986; and unpublished data.

No. 604. Public Aid—Recipients and Average Monthly Cash Payments Under Supplemental Security Income (SSI) and Public Assistance: 1975 to 1991

[As of **December**, except as noted. Public assistance data for all years include Puerto Rico, Guam, and Virgin Islands; SSI data are for federally administered payments only. See text, section 12. Excludes payments made directly to suppliers of medical care. See also Appendix III and *Historical Statistics, Colonial Times to 1970*, series H 355-367]

PROGRAM	RECIPIENTS (1,000)					AVG. MONTHLY PAYMENTS (dol.)				
	1975	1980	1985	1990	1991	1975	1980	1985	1990	1991
SSI, total...................	4,314	4,142	4,138	4,817	5,118	114	168	226	299	321
Aged.....................	2,307	1,808	1,504	1,454	1,465	91	128	164	213	221
Blind....................	74	78	82	84	85	147	213	274	342	351
Disabled.................	1,933	2,256	2,551	3,279	3,569	141	198	261	337	361
Old-age assistance [1]............	18	19	18	17	17	21	39	36	45	55
Aid to the blind [1]............	(Z)	(Z)	(Z)	(Z)	(Z)	15	36	39	42	56
Aid to permanently, totally disabled [1].	17	21	23	26	27	15	35	38	40	58
AFDC: [2] Families..............	3,568	3,843	3,721	4,218	4,708	229	288	341	392	390
Recipients [3]...............	11,404	11,101	10,924	12,159	13,489	72	100	118	136	135
Children.................	8,106	7,599	7,247	8,232	9,126	(NA)	(NA)	(NA)	(NA)	(NA)
General assistance cases	692	796	1,051	1,004	1,106	144	161	(NA)	(NA)	(NA)

NA Not available.   Z Fewer than 500.   [1] Average monthly recipients and payments for the year.   [2] Aid to Families with Dependent Children program.   [3] Includes the children and one or both parents, or one caretaker relative other than a parent, in families where the needs of such adults were considered in determining the amount of assistance.

No. 605. Public Aid Payments: 1975 to 1991

[**In millions of dollars.** See headnote, table 604. Supplemental Security Income data cover federally- and State-administered payments. See also Appendix III and *Historical Statistics, Colonial Times to 1970*, series H 346-354]

PROGRAM	1975	1980	1983	1984	1985	1986	1987	1988	1989	1990	1991
Payments, total [1]	16,313	21,994	23,385	25,035	26,431	28,311	29,556	30,910	32,762	36,047	39,788
Supplemental Security Income [2]..	5,878	7,941	9,404	10,371	11,060	12,081	12,951	13,786	14,980	16,599	18,524
Aged.....................	2,605	2,734	2,814	2,973	3,035	3,096	3,194	3,299	3,476	3,736	3,890
Blind....................	131	190	229	249	264	277	291	302	316	334	347
Disabled.................	3,142	5,014	6,357	7,143	7,755	8,700	9,458	10,177	11,180	12,521	14,268
Public assistance [1]...........	10,434	14,048	13,981	14,664	15,371	16,230	16,605	17,124	17,782	19,448	21,264
Old-age assistance	5	9	8	8	8	8	7	7	7	7	11
Blind...................	(Z)	(Z)	10	(Z)	(Z)	(Z)	(Z)	(Z)	(Z)	(Z)	(Z)
Permanently, totally disabled ..	3	9	10	10	11	11	11	11	12	12	19
Families with dependent children.	9,211	12,475	13,838	14,505	15,196	16,033	16,373	16,827	17,466	19,078	20,931
Emergency assistance	78	113	125	141	157	178	214	279	297	349	303
General assistance	1,138	1,442	(NA)	(NA)	(NA)	(NA)	(NA)	(NA)	(NA)	(NA)	(NA)

NA Not available.   Z Less than $500,000.   [1] Beginning 1983, excludes general assistance payments.   [2] Includes data not available by reason for eligibility.

Source of tables 604 and 605: U.S. Social Security Administration, *Social Security Bulletin,* quarterly and *Annual Statistical Supplement* to the *Social Security Bulletin,* and U.S. Administration for Children and Families, *Quarterly Public Assistance Statistics,* annual.

No. 606. Public Aid Recipients as Percent of Population, by State: 1990 and 1991

[Total recipients as of **June** of Aid to Families with Dependent Children and of Federal Supplemental Security Income as percent of resident population. Based on estimated resident population as of April 1 for 1990 and as of July 1 for 1991]

DIVISION AND STATE	1990	1991	DIVISION AND STATE	1990	1991	DIVISION AND STATE	1990	1991	DIVISION AND STATE	1990	1991
U.S ...	6.5	7.0	IL.......	7.1	7.5	WV.....	8.8	8.9	**Mt**	4.2	4.7
			MI......	8.6	8.8	NC.....	5.7	6.5	MT.....	4.9	5.7
N.E	5.6	6.3	WI......	6.6	6.7	SC.....	5.8	6.3	ID......	2.7	2.8
ME	6.6	7.3	**W.N.C**	4.8	5.0	GA.....	7.1	7.9	WY.....	3.8	4.7
NH	2.2	2.9	MN.....	4.9	5.0	FL.....	4.6	5.3	CO.....	4.3	4.4
VT	5.7	6.6	IA......	4.7	4.7	**E.S.C**	7.9	8.5	NM.....	5.8	7.0
MA	6.4	7.0	MO.....	5.8	6.2	KY.....	7.9	9.1	AZ.....	4.7	5.4
RI	6.4	7.3	ND.....	3.6	3.8	TN.....	7.2	7.9	UT.....	3.3	3.5
CT	4.7	5.5	SD.....	4.2	4.4	AL.....	6.5	6.6	NV.....	2.9	3.0
M.A	6.7	7.2	NE.....	3.7	3.9	MS.....	11.4	11.4	**Pac**	8.4	9.1
NY	7.7	8.3	KS.....	4.1	4.2				WA.....	6.0	6.4
NJ.....	5.3	5.8	**S.A**	5.4	6.1	**W.S.C**	6.2	6.5	OR.....	4.3	4.9
PA.....	6.0	6.4	DE.....	4.4	4.7	AR.....	6.3	6.4	CA.....	9.4	10.1
E.N.C	7.0	7.4	MD....	5.1	5.6	LA.....	9.8	9.7	AK.....	4.6	5.8
OH	7.3	7.8	DC....	10.9	12.3	OK.....	5.6	5.8	HI.....	5.2	5.3
IN	3.9	4.3	VA....	3.9	4.3	TX.....	5.4	5.8			

Source: Compiled by U.S. Bureau of the Census. Data from U.S. Social Security Administration, *Social Security Bulletin,* quarterly, and U.S. Administration for Children and Families, *Quarterly Public Assistance Statistics,* annual.

No. 607. Aid to Families With Dependent Children (AFDC) and Supplemental Security Income (SSI)—Recipients and Payments, by State and Other Areas: 1980 to 1991

[Recipients as of **December**. Data for SSI cover Federal SSI payments and/or federally-administered State supplementation except as noted. For explanation of methodology, see Appendix III]

DIVISION AND STATE OR OTHER AREA	AFDC Recipients [1] (1,000)			AFDC Payments for year (mil. dol.)			AFDC Average monthly payment per family		SSI Recipients (1,000)		SSI Payments for year (mil. dol.)	
	1980	1990	1991	1980	1990	1991	1990	1991	1990	1991	1990	1991
Total	11,101	12,159	13,489	12,475	19,078	20,931	$392	$390	[2]4,817	[2]5,118	16,133	17,996
U.S	10,923	11,958	13,285	12,409	18,995	20,843	396	394	4,817	5,118	16,133	17,996
New England	647	577	653	910	1,250	1,383	535	522	209	222	652	739
ME	58	62	69	60	104	116	422	416	24	24	56	62
NH	24	21	28	27	35	49	431	443	[3]7	[3]7	[3]19	[3]22
VT	24	25	29	32	51	59	527	524	10	11	31	35
MA	348	282	311	510	647	682	556	532	119	127	397	450
RI	54	52	59	72	104	122	499	510	17	18	53	59
CT	140	135	157	209	309	355	571	565	[3]32	[3]34	[3]96	[3]112
Middle Atlantic....	2,216	1,903	2,062	2,954	3,623	3,873	472	466	711	758	2,533	2,866
NY	1,110	1,031	1,108	1,623	2,337	2,496	556	550	415	445	1,557	1,762
NJ	469	323	364	560	459	496	352	342	105	112	340	387
PA	637	549	590	771	827	881	382	380	191	202	635	717
East North Central .	2,419	2,397	2,560	2,838	3,611	3,701	379	367	622	669	2,021	2,320
OH	572	657	746	561	896	955	328	325	156	169	483	564
IN	170	164	195	139	174	202	263	267	[3]60	[3]66	[3]174	[3]204
IL	691	656	698	722	868	929	342	346	[3]177	[3]192	[3]593	[3]688
MI	753	684	680	1,063	1,232	1,163	464	424	143	151	483	538
WI	232	236	241	353	441	452	464	466	86	91	288	326
West North Central.	614	647	705	697	955	1,030	366	372	216	230	584	669
MN	146	177	183	207	355	379	512	524	[3]40	[3]44	[3]110	[3]129
IA	111	96	103	144	154	162	371	380	33	34	86	96
MO	216	218	249	182	237	265	274	280	[3]85	[3]90	[3]237	[3]269
ND	13	16	18	16	24	26	359	360	[3]7	[3]8	[3]18	[3]20
SD	19	19	20	19	22	24	272	286	10	11	26	30
NE	38	44	48	42	60	63	336	332	[3]16	[3]17	[3]42	[3]48
KS	72	77	84	87	103	111	332	341	25	26	65	76
South Atlantic	1,463	1,654	1,985	1,125	1,844	2,170	272	273	847	898	2,370	2,662
DE	34	22	26	32	30	34	292	291	8	8	22	25
MD	220	198	220	214	304	337	370	372	60	63	185	209
DC	82	54	61	92	87	100	380	386	16	17	54	59
VA	176	158	185	160	181	208	265	270	[3]95	[3]101	[3]257	[3]290
WV	80	109	119	60	112	116	249	252	[4]47	[4]50	[4]146	[4]165
NC	202	255	308	154	257	312	237	238	[3]149	[3]157	[3]403	[3]444
SC	156	118	137	72	97	111	203	203	[3]90	[3]93	[3]234	[3]257
GA	234	320	383	138	333	392	265	267	159	166	415	462
FL	279	420	546	203	443	560	263	267	222	241	653	751
East South Central .	704	742	816	366	510	569	168	171	501	524	1,371	1,539
KY	175	204	230	136	185	208	224	217	[3]115	[3]122	[3]337	[3]382
TN	174	230	266	85	176	200	186	187	140	147	384	433
AL	178	132	142	84	63	73	115	125	[3]133	[3]137	[3]351	[3]387
MS	176	176	178	61	86	88	120	122	114	118	300	337
West South Central.	716	1,154	1,238	401	811	895	180	183	564	596	1,478	1,678
AR	85	73	76	51	57	60	190	191	76	79	187	211
LA	219	279	276	124	188	189	167	170	133	140	378	428
OK	92	129	133	92	135	157	279	301	[3]60	[3]62	[3]158	[3]174
TX	320	673	753	134	431	489	165	166	[4]295	[4]315	[4]755	[4]865
Mountain	302	454	544	274	523	643	297	314	162	178	476	559
MT	20	29	32	19	40	43	344	347	10	11	29	33
ID	20	17	19	24	20	23	266	276	[3]10	[3]11	[3]29	[3]35
WY	7	16	19	9	20	26	313	351	[3]3	[3]4	[3]9	[3]11
CO	81	109	127	81	138	154	320	322	[3]38	[3]42	[3]110	[3]131
NM	56	67	86	42	66	92	273	304	[3]32	[3]34	[3]90	[3]102
AZ	60	144	178	40	146	197	268	299	[3]45	[3]50	[3]139	[3]162
UT	44	47	51	48	65	73	347	359	13	14	38	46
NV	14	25	32	11	28	35	278	287	11	13	33	39
Pacific	1,843	2,427	2,723	2,844	5,866	6,577	606	609	984	1,041	4,646	4,962
WA	173	237	269	251	447	533	452	492	62	67	208	242
OR	94	99	117	147	150	187	374	401	[3]32	[3]34	[3]95	[3]110
CA	1,498	2,023	2,258	2,328	5,107	5,664	637	632	873	920	4,278	4,537
AK	16	24	30	27	62	81	651	691	[3]5	[3]5	[3]14	[3]16
HI	61	44	49	91	100	112	581	613	14	14	51	56
PR	170	193	195	60	74	77	103	105	(X)	(X)	(X)	(X)
GU	5	4	5	3	6	7	418	505	(X)	(X)	(X)	(X)
VI	3	3	4	2	3	3	279	285	(X)	(X)	(X)	(X)
N. Mariana	(X)	(X)	(X)	(X)	(X)	(X)	(X)	(X)	[4]1	[4]1	[4]2	[4]2

X Not applicable. [1] See footnote 3, table 604. [2] Includes small number of recipients whose residence was "unknown."
[3] Data for persons with Federal SSI payments only; State has State-administered supplementation. [4] Data for persons with Federal SSI payments only; State supplementary payments not made.

Source: U.S. Social Security Administration, *Social Security Bulletin*, quarterly, and *Annual Statistical Supplement* to the *Social Security Bulletin*; and U.S. Administration for Children and Families, *Quarterly Public Assistance Statistics*, annual.

No. 608. Federal Food Stamp and National School Lunch Programs, by State: 1990 to 1992

[Cost data for years ending Sept. 30. Data on food stamp households and persons are average monthly number participating in year ending Sept. 30. Data on pupils participating in National School Lunch Program are for month in which the highest number of children participated nationwide. For National School Lunch Program, covers public and private elementary and secondary schools and residential child care institutions. Food Stamp costs are for benefits only and exclude administrative expenditures. National School Lunch Program costs include Federal cash reimbursements at rates set by law for each meal served but do not include the value of USDA donated commodities utilized in this program]

REGION, DIVISION, AND STATE	FOOD STAMP PROGRAM								NATIONAL SCHOOL LUNCH PROGRAM					
	Households participating (1,000)		Persons (1,000)			Cost (mil. dol.)			Persons (1,000)			Cost (mil. dol.)		
	1991	1992, prel.	1990	1991	1992, prel.	1990	1991	1992, prel.	1990	1991	1992, prel.	1990	1991	1992, prel.
Total [1]	8,880	10,058	20,067	22,625	25,404	14,187	17,339	20,891	24,589	24,656	25,095	3,214	3,525	3,840
U.S.	8,872	10,048	20,036	22,599	25,370	14,153	17,306	20,842	24,019	24,089	24,528	3,098	3,404	3,721
Northeast	1,777	1,964	3,589	4,066	4,480	2,462	3,023	3,641	4,033	3,955	4,023	489	531	589
N.E	368	413	707	857	963	426	575	706	991	942	954	95	105	119
ME	51	58	94	116	133	63	85	109	108	105	106	11	12	14
NH	20	25	31	47	58	20	34	45	91	85	90	6	7	8
VT	21	23	38	48	54	22	30	37	47	47	48	4	4	5
MA	172	183	347	397	429	207	269	315	454	430	429	44	48	53
RI	34	38	64	78	87	42	57	69	60	56	61	7	8	10
CT	70	86	133	171	202	72	100	131	231	219	220	23	26	29
M.A	1,409	1,551	2,882	3,209	3,517	2,036	2,448	2,935	3,042	3,013	3,069	393	426	470
NY	777	855	1,548	1,716	1,885	1,086	1,290	1,586	1,546	1,548	1,577	232	249	270
NJ	176	201	382	441	495	289	366	433	507	504	513	60	67	77
PA	456	495	952	1,052	1,137	661	792	916	990	961	979	102	110	123
Midwest	2,113	2,271	4,806	5,218	5,616	3,566	4,206	4,738	5,806	5,810	5,911	619	673	724
E.N.C.	1,598	1,705	3,616	3,914	4,183	2,765	3,254	3,626	3,687	3,700	3,743	421	459	495
OH	499	529	1,089	1,171	1,251	861	984	1,102	919	956	953	109	116	126
IN	131	160	311	375	448	226	294	373	635	610	610	54	59	64
IL	460	488	1,013	1,096	1,156	835	961	1,069	932	937	955	131	144	155
MI	408	405	917	978	994	663	808	846	733	723	745	82	91	97
WI	100	123	286	294	334	180	207	236	468	474	480	45	49	53
W.N.C	515	566	1,190	1,304	1,433	801	952	1,112	2,119	2,110	2,168	197	214	229
MN	120	128	263	286	309	165	202	234	489	493	505	42	46	48
IA	72	76	170	180	192	109	123	143	392	376	396	31	34	36
MO	190	214	431	490	549	312	380	447	547	547	557	58	63	68
ND	16	18	39	41	46	25	28	35	94	93	94	8	9	9
SD	18	19	50	52	55	35	39	42	102	104	106	12	12	13
NE	39	43	95	99	107	59	67	78	191	193	197	18	19	21
KS	60	68	142	156	175	96	113	133	302	304	313	29	31	34
South	3,447	4,024	8,040	9,218	10,575	5,928	7,261	8,892	9,890	9,941	10,079	1,334	1,457	1,600
S.A.	1,416	1,737	2,993	3,631	4,402	2,223	2,873	3,776	4,454	4,451	4,515	558	618	683
DE	15	19	33	41	51	25	32	42	59	59	59	6	6	7
MD	130	147	255	304	343	203	259	312	347	337	352	40	43	48
DC	32	38	62	72	82	43	54	70	47	47	47	10	10	11
VA	171	206	346	414	495	247	321	406	586	576	589	60	65	72
WV	105	117	262	281	310	192	220	255	198	217	184	29	31	31
NC	201	236	419	517	597	282	378	461	749	740	750	91	99	107
SC	116	133	299	329	369	240	239	297	451	453	458	60	65	72
GA	244	288	536	648	751	382	505	627	908	910	927	106	117	131
FL	402	[2]553	781	1,025	[2]1,404	609	865	[2]1,306	1,110	1,112	1,149	158	182	204
E.S.C.	795	881	1,938	2,128	2,317	1,386	1,629	1,864	2,085	2,100	2,102	281	301	324
KY	183	197	458	496	529	334	387	430	498	515	523	61	67	73
TN	239	280	527	608	702	372	459	562	590	592	592	68	73	80
AL	186	208	454	504	550	328	394	451	570	568	567	77	81	87
MS	187	196	499	520	536	352	389	421	428	425	420	76	80	84
W.S.C	1,236	1,406	3,109	3,459	3,856	2,319	2,759	3,252	3,351	3,390	3,462	495	538	593
AR	94	[2]102	235	258	277	155	183	[2]207	292	294	310	41	44	46
LA	261	[2]278	727	742	[2]779	549	598	[2]666	694	695	691	104	110	116
OK	117	135	267	298	346	186	224	276	362	363	370	46	50	55
TX	764	891	1,880	2,161	2,454	1,429	1,754	2,103	2,003	2,038	2,091	304	334	376
West	1,535	1,789	3,601	4,097	4,699	2,197	2,816	3,571	4,289	4,383	4,515	657	743	808
Mt	422	488	988	1,147	1,312	726	900	1,079	1,362	1,382	1,415	170	188	210
MT	23	25	57	61	66	41	47	52	84	86	88	10	10	11
ID	23	26	59	65	72	40	47	53	131	134	135	14	15	17
WY	11	12	28	31	33	21	23	26	57	59	59	5	6	6
CO	95	102	221	241	260	156	187	219	282	282	290	31	35	37
NM	64	77	157	188	221	117	147	182	179	179	183	30	33	36
AZ	138	166	317	388	457	239	310	377	331	336	356	47	53	61
UT	40	44	99	110	123	71	83	96	233	229	221	24	27	30
NV	28	36	50	63	80	41	56	74	67	77	83	8	9	12
Pac	1,113	1,301	2,613	2,950	3,387	1,471	1,916	2,492	2,927	3,001	3,100	487	555	598
WA	158	178	340	385	432	229	278	344	361	377	395	43	49	55
OR	103	114	216	240	265	168	197	226	234	237	246	26	30	33
CA	807	958	1,955	2,212	2,558	968	1,307	1,759	2,147	2,201	2,268	396	452	484
AK	10	12	25	30	38	25	34	41	39	40	43	8	9	10
HI	35	[2]39	77	83	[2]94	81	100	[2]122	145	146	148	14	15	16

[1] Includes Puerto Rico (for NSLP), other outlying areas and Dept. of Defense overseas.   [2] Includes hurricane disaster relief.

Source: U.S. Dept. of Agriculture, Food and Nutrition Service. In "Annual Historical Review of FNS Programs" and unpublished data.

No. 609. Federal Food Programs: 1980 to 1992

[For fiscal years ending in year shown; see text, section 9. Program data include Puerto Rico, Virgin Islands, Guam, American Samoa, Northern Marianas and the former Trust Territory when a Federal food program was operated in these areas. Participation data are average monthly figures except as noted. Participants are not reported for the nutrition program for the elderly, and the commodity distribution programs. Cost data are direct Federal benefits to recipients; they exclude Federal administrative payments and applicable State and local contributions. Federal costs for commodities and cash-in-lieu of commodities are shown separately from direct cash benefits for those programs receiving both]

PROGRAM	Unit	1980	1985	1987	1988	1989	1990	1991	1992, prel.
Food Stamp:									
Participants	Million	21.1	19.9	19.1	18.6	18.8	20.1	22.6	25.4
Federal cost	Mil. dol.	8,721	10,744	10,500	11,149	11,676	14,187	17,339	20,891
Monthly average coupon value per recipient	Dollars	34.47	44.99	45.78	49.83	51.85	58.93	63.86	68.53
Nutrition assistance program for Puerto Rico: [1]									
Federal cost	Mil. dol.	(X)	825	853	879	908	937	963	1,002
National school lunch program (NSLP): [2]									
Free lunches served	Million	1,671	1,657	1,656	1,651	1,627	1,662	1,749	1,880
Reduced-price lunches served	Million	308	255	259	262	263	273	293	284
Children participating [3]	Million	26.6	23.6	23.9	24.2	24.3	24.1	24.2	24.5
Federal cost	Mil. dol.	2,279	2,578	2,797	2,908	3,006	3,214	3,525	3,840
School breakfast (SB):									
Children participating [3]	Million	3.6	3.4	3.6	3.7	3.8	4.1	4.4	4.9
Federal cost	Mil. dol.	288	379	447	482	513	596	685	783
Special supplemental food program (WIC): [4]									
Participants	Million	1.9	3.1	3.4	3.6	4.1	4.5	4.9	5.4
Federal cost	Mil. dol.	584	1,193	1,345	1,435	1,489	1,637	1,752	1,959
Commodity supplemental food program: [5]									
Participants	Million	0.1	0.2	0.2	0.2	0.2	0.3	0.3	0.3
Federal cost	Mil. dol.	19	42	47	52	62	71	76	87
Child and adult care (CC): [6]									
Participants [7]	Million	0.7	1.0	1.2	1.3	1.4	1.5	1.6	1.8
Federal cost	Mil. dol.	207	390	476	538	612	720	834	966
Summer feeding (SF): [8]									
Children participating [9]	Million	1.9	1.5	1.6	1.6	1.7	1.7	1.8	1.9
Federal cost	Mil. dol.	104	103	114	113	132	145	160	183
Nutrition program for the elderly:									
Meals served	Million	166	225	232	240	243	246	245	245
Federal cost	Mil. dol.	75	134	139	146	146	142	140	152
Federal cost of commodities donated to— [10]									
Child nutrition (NSLP, CC, SF and SB)	Mil. dol.	930	840	919	853	793	646	701	755
Charitable institutions, summer camps	Mil. dol.	71	170	158	158	136	104	93	111
Emergency feeding [11]	Mil. dol.	(X)	973	846	593	266	286	252	225

X Not applicable.   [1] Puerto Rico was included in the food stamp program until June 30, 1982.   [2] See headnote, table 608. [3] Nine month (September through May) average daily meals (lunches or breakfasts) served divided by the ratio of average daily attendance to enrollment.   [4] WIC serves women, infants, and children.   [5] Program provides commodities to women, infants, children, and the elderly.   [6] Program provides year-round subsidies to feed preschool children in child care centers and family day care homes. Certain care centers serving disabled or elderly adults also receive meal subsidies.   [7] Quarterly average daily attendance at participating institutions.   [8] Program provides free meals to children in poor areas during summer months.   [9] Peak month (July) average daily attendance at participating institutions.   [10] Includes the Federal cost of commodity entitlements, cash-in-lieu of commodities, and bonus foods.   [11] Provides free commodities to needy persons for home consumption through food banks, hunger centers, soup kitchens, and similar nonprofit agencies. Includes the Emergency Food Assistance Program and the commodity purchases for soup kitchens/food banks program.

Source: U.S. Dept. of Agriculture, Food and Nutrition Service. In "Annual Historical Review of FNS Programs" and unpublished data.

No. 610. Primary Child Care Arrangements Used by Employed Mothers for Children Under 5 Years Old: 1977 to 1991

[Data were obtained for the three youngest children in the household, except as noted. Based on the Survey of Income and Program Participation; see text, section 14]

TYPE OF ARRANGEMENT	1977, [1] June	1984-85, winter	1986, fall	1987, fall	1988, fall	1991, fall
Children under 5 years old, total (1,000)	4,370	8,168	8,849	9,124	9,483	9,854
PERCENT DISTRIBUTION						
Care in child's home	33.9	31.0	28.7	29.9	28.2	35.7
By father	14.4	15.7	14.5	15.3	15.1	20.0
By grandparent	(2)	5.7	5.2	5.1	5.7	7.2
By other relative	[2] 12.6	3.7	3.4	3.3	2.2	3.2
By nonrelative	7.0	5.9	5.5	6.2	5.3	5.4
Care in another home	40.7	37.0	40.7	35.6	36.8	31.0
By grandparent	(NA)	10.2	10.2	8.7	8.2	8.6
By other relative	18.3	4.5	6.5	4.6	5.0	4.5
By nonrelative	22.4	22.3	24.0	22.3	23.6	17.9
Organized child care facilities	13.0	23.1	22.4	24.4	25.8	23.0
Day/group care center	(NA)	14.0	14.9	16.1	16.6	15.8
Nursery school/preschool	(NA)	9.1	7.5	8.3	9.2	7.3
School-based activity	(NA)	(NA)	(NA)	(NA)	0.2	0.5
Child cares for self	0.4	-	-	0.3	0.1	-
Mother cares for child at work [3]	11.4	8.1	7.4	8.9	7.6	8.7
Other arrangements [4]	0.6	0.8	0.8	1.0	1.3	1.1

- Represents or rounds to zero.   NA Not available.   [1] Data only for the two youngest children under 5 years of age.   [2] Data for grandparents included in other relative.   [3] Includes mothers working at home or away from home.   [4] Includes children in kindergarten/grade school.

Source: U.S. Bureau of the Census, Current Population Reports, P70-30; and unpublished data.

No. 611. Child Support—Award and Recipiency Status of Women: 1981 to 1989

[Women with own children under 21 years of age present from absent fathers. For 1989, women 15 years old and over as of April 1990; for previous years, women 18 years old and over as of April of following year. Covers civilian noninstitutional population. Based on Current Population Survey; see text, section 1 and Appendix III]

AWARD AND RECIPIENCY STATUS	ALL WOMEN						WOMEN BELOW THE POVERTY LEVEL					
	Number (1,000)			Percent distribution			Number (1,000)			Percent distribution		
	1981	1985	1989	1981	1985	1989	1981	1985	1989	1981	1985	1989
Total	8,387	8,808	9,955	100	100	100	2,566	2,797	3,206	100	100	100
Payments awarded.	4,969	5,396	5,748	59	61	58	1,018	1,130	1,387	40	40	43
Supposed to receive payments .	4,043	4,381	4,953	48	50	50	806	905	1,190	31	32	37
Not supposed to receive payments	926	1,015	795	11	12	8	212	225	197	8	8	6
Payments not awarded	3,417	3,411	4,207	41	39	42	1,547	1,668	1,819	60	60	57
Supposed to receive payments .	4,043	4,381	4,953	100	100	100	806	905	1,190	100	100	100
Actually received payments	2,902	3,243	3,725	72	74	75	495	595	813	61	66	68
Received full amount	1,888	2,112	2,546	47	48	51	(NA)	(NA)	(NA)	(NA)	(NA)	(NA)
Received partial amount.	1,014	1,131	1,179	25	26	24	(NA)	(NA)	(NA)	(NA)	(NA)	(NA)
Did not receive payments	1,140	1,138	1,228	28	26	25	311	310	377	39	34	32

NA Not available.

Source: U.S. Bureau of the Census, *Current Population Reports*, P60-173.

No. 612. Child Support and Alimony—Selected Characteristics of Women: 1989

[See headnote, table 611. Alimony data are for ever-divorced and currently separated women. For definition of mean, see Guide to Tabular Presentation]

RECIPIENCY STATUS OF WOMEN	Unit	Total [1]	AGE			RACE		His-panic [2]	CURRENT MARITAL STATUS			
			18 to 29 years	30 to 39 years	40 years and over	White	Black		Divor-ced	Mar-ried [3]	Never mar-ried	Sepa-rated
CHILD SUPPORT												
All women, total.	1,000 . .	9,955	3,086	4,175	2,566	6,905	2,770	1,112	3,056	2,531	2,950	1,352
Payments awarded.	1,000 . .	5,748	1,408	2,685	1,632	4,661	955	452	2,347	1,999	704	648
Percent of total	Percent.	58	46	64	64	68	35	41	77	79	24	48
Supposed to receive child support in 1989.	1,000 . .	4,953	1,208	2,413	1,309	4,048	791	364	2,123	1,685	583	527
Percent received payment.	Percent.	75	76	74	76	76	70	77	77	72	73	80
Mean child support	Dollars.	2,995	1,981	3,032	3,903	3,132	2,263	2,965	3,322	2,931	1,888	3,060
Percent of total income .	Percent.	19	20	18	19	19	16	20	17	20	20	21
Women with incomes below the poverty level in 1989.	1,000 . .	3,206	1,531	1,189	434	1,763	1,314	536	820	176	1,590	612
Payments awarded.	1,000 . .	1,387	608	568	195	962	384	177	577	127	389	288
Percent of total	Percent.	43	40	48	45	55	29	33	70	72	25	47
Supposed to receive child support in 1989.	1,000 . .	1,190	507	500	168	827	325	148	525	106	334	221
Percent received payment.	Percent.	68	68	67	72	68	64	66	67	67	69	74
Mean child support	Dollars.	1,889	1,515	2,167	2,316	1,972	1,674	1,824	2,112	2,275	1,553	1,717
Percent of total income .	Percent.	37	33	36	56	39	32	37	38	52	34	35
ALIMONY												
All women, total.	1,000 . .	20,610	2,464	6,093	12,051	17,245	2,863	1,499	8,888	7,738	(X)	2,790
Number awarded payments . . .	1,000 . .	3,189	184	610	2,394	2,801	305	171	1,472	1,170	(X)	316
Percent of total	Percent.	16	8	10	20	16	11	11	17	15	(X)	11
Supposed to receive pay-ments	1,000 . .	922	85	267	569	787	98	63	567	170	(X)	164
Women with incomes below the poverty level in 1989.	1,000 . .	3,692	726	1,206	1,758	2,640	931	477	1,860	420	(X)	1,147
Number awarded payments . . .	1,000 . .	429	60	96	273	340	76	31	223	55	(X)	110
Percent of total	Percent.	12	8	8	16	13	8	6	12	13	(X)	10
Supposed to receive pay-ments	1,000 . .	178	43	56	79	149	26	21	112	11	(X)	54

X Not applicable.   [1] Includes other items, not shown separately.   [2] Hispanic women may be of any race.   [3] Remarried women whose previous marriage ended in divorce.

Source: U.S. Bureau of the Census, *Current Population Reports*, P60-173.

No. 613. Child Support Enforcement Program—Caseload and Collections: 1980 to 1991

[For years ending Sept. 30. Includes Puerto Rico, Guam, and the Virgin Islands. The Child Support Enforcement program locates absent parents, establishes paternity of children born out-of-wedlock, and establishes and enforces support orders. By law, these services are available to all families that need them. The program is operated at the State and local government level but 68 per-cent of administrative costs are paid by the Federal government. Child support collected for families not receiving Aid to Families with Dependent Children (AFDC) goes to the family to help it remain self-sufficient. Most of the child support collected on behalf of AFDC families goes to Federal and State governments to offset AFDC payments. Based on data reported by State agencies. Minus sign (-) indicates net outlay]

ITEM	Unit	1980	1985	1986	1987	1988	1989	1990	1991
Total cases	1,000 . . .	5,432	8,401	9,724	10,635	11,078	11,877	12,796	13,423
AFDC and AFDC arrears only caseload	1,000 . . .	(NA)	(NA)	7,220	7,655	7,501	7,610	7,953	8,034
AFDC cases	1,000 . . .	4,583	6,242	5,749	5,776	5,703	5,709	5,872	6,166
AFDC arrears only cases [1]	1,000 . . .	(NA)	(NA)	1,472	1,879	1,798	1,901	2,082	1,868
Non-AFDC cases	1,000 . . .	849	2,159	2,503	2,981	3,577	4,266	4,843	5,389
Cases for which a collection was made:									
AFDC cases.	1,000 . . .	503	684	582	609	621	658	701	755
AFDC arrears only cases [1]	1,000 . . .	(NA)	(NA)	158	196	181	202	224	278
Non-AFDC cases	1,000 . . .	243	654	786	934	1,083	1,247	1,363	1,555
Percentage of cases with collections:									
AFDC cases.	Percent	11.0	11.0	10.1	10.5	10.9	11.5	11.9	12.2
AFDC arrears only cases [1]	Percent	(NA)	(NA)	10.8	10.5	10.1	10.6	10.8	14.9
Non-AFDC cases	Percent	28.7	30.3	31.4	31.3	30.3	29.2	28.1	28.9
Absent parents located, total	1,000 . . .	643	878	1,046	1,145	1,388	1,629	2,062	2,577
Paternities established, total	1,000 . . .	144	232	245	269	307	339	393	479
Support obligations established, total [2].	1,000 . . .	374	669	731	812	870	938	1,022	823
FINANCES									
Collections, total	Mil. dol .	1,478	2,694	3,249	3,917	4,613	5,250	6,020	6,894
AFDC collections	Mil. dol. .	603	1,090	1,225	1,348	1,486	1,593	1,750	1,984
State share.	Mil. dol. .	274	415	424	473	523	563	620	700
Incentive payments to States	Mil. dol. .	72	145	158	185	221	266	264	278
Federal share	Mil. dol. .	246	341	369	413	445	458	533	625
Payments to AFDC families [3]	Mil. dol. .	10	189	275	278	298	307	334	381
Non-AFDC collections	Mil. dol. .	874	1,604	2,023	2,569	3,128	3,656	4,270	4,910
Administrative expenditures, total	Mil. dol. .	466	814	941	1,066	1,171	1,363	1,606	1,804
State share	Mil. dol. .	117	243	308	316	366	426	545	593
Federal share.	Mil. dol. .	349	571	633	750	804	938	1,061	1,212
Program savings, total.	Mil. dol. .	127	86	9	5	18	-77	-189	-201
State share	Mil. dol. .	230	317	274	342	378	403	338	385
Federal share.	Mil. dol. .	-103	-231	-264	-337	-360	-480	-528	-586
Total fees and costs recovered for non-AFDC cases	Mil. dol. .	5	3	6	7	7	7	22	34
Percentage of AFDC payments recovered	Percent	5.2	7.3	8.6	9.1	9.8	10.0	10.3	10.7

NA Not available. [1] Reflects cases that are no longer receiving AFDC but still have outstanding child support due. [2] Through 1990 covers new support orders and modifications. Beginning 1991 covers only new support orders. [3] Beginning 1985, States were required to pass along to the family the first $50 of any current child support collected each month.

Source: U.S. Department of Health and Human Services, Office of Child Support Enforcement, *Annual Report to Congress*.

No. 614. Percent of Adult Population Doing Volunteer Work: 1989

[For year ending in May. Covers civilian noninstitutional population, 16 years old and over. A volunteer is a person who performed unpaid work for an organization such as a church, the Boy or Girl Scouts, a school, Little League, etc. during the year. Persons who did work on their own such as helping out neighbors or relatives are excluded. Based on Current Population Survey; see text, section 1, and Appendix III]

CHARACTERISTIC	VOLUNTEER WORKERS		PERCENT DISTRIBUTION OF VOLUNTEERS, BY TYPE OF ORGANIZATION [1]							
	Number (1,000)	Per-cent of popu-lation	Total	Churches, other religious organi-zations	Schools, other educa-tional insti-tutions	Civic or political organi-zations	Hospi-tals, other health organi-zations	Social or welfare organi-zations	Sport or recrea-tional organi-zations	Other organi-zations
Total [2]	38,042	20.4	100.0	37.4	15.1	13.2	10.4	9.9	7.8	6.3
16 to 19 years old	1,902	13.4	100.0	34.4	26.8	8.9	9.2	7.0	8.2	5.5
20 to 24 years old	2,064	11.4	100.0	30.5	18.5	12.7	11.9	11.6	8.0	6.8
25 to 34 years old	8,680	20.2	100.0	34.9	18.3	13.3	9.1	9.3	8.9	6.1
35 to 44 years old	10,337	28.9	100.0	33.1	20.3	12.6	7.4	8.5	12.1	6.1
45 to 54 years old	5,670	23.0	100.0	40.8	11.8	15.1	10.1	8.8	7.1	6.3
55 to 64 years old	4,455	20.8	100.0	45.7	6.7	16.1	12.4	10.9	2.5	5.7
65 years old and over	4,934	16.9	100.0	43.3	4.3	11.1	17.8	14.5	1.8	7.2
Male	16,681	18.8	100.0	35.9	10.5	17.2	7.0	10.1	11.8	7.5
Female.	21,361	21.9	100.0	38.5	18.8	10.1	13.1	9.7	4.6	5.3
White	34,823	21.9	100.0	36.6	15.1	13.5	10.7	9.8	8.0	6.3
Black	2,505	11.9	100.0	50.4	12.4	9.6	7.0	10.4	4.6	5.6
Hispanic origin [3].	1,289	9.4	100.0	42.2	18.3	9.6	8.5	8.9	6.9	5.6
Educational attainment: [4]										
Less than 4 years of high school	2,939	8.3	100.0	48.4	6.6	10.0	10.0	13.1	4.8	7.0
4 years of high school	11,105	18.8	100.0	41.5	12.5	11.2	11.1	8.8	8.2	6.7
1 to 3 years of college	7,572	28.1	100.0	36.8	14.7	13.3	10.8	10.1	8.0	6.3
4 years of college or more . .	12,459	38.4	100.0	32.9	17.4	16.4	9.7	10.1	7.8	5.7

[1] Organization for which most of the work was done. [2] Includes other races, not shown separately. [3] Persons of Hispanic origin may be of any race. [4] Persons 25 years old and over.

Source: U.S. Bureau of Labor Statistics, *News*, USDL 90-154, March 29, 1990.

No. 615. Charity Contributions—Average Dollar Amount and Percent of Household Income, 1987 to 1991, and by Age of Respondent and Household Income, 1991

[Estimates cover households' contribution activity for the year and are based on respondents' replies as to contribution and volunteer activity of household. Based on a sample survey conducted during the spring of the following year and subject to sampling variability; see source]

AGE	ALL CONTRIBUTING HOUSEHOLDS		CONTRIBUTORS AND VOLUNTEERS		HOUSEHOLD INCOME	ALL CONTRIBUTING HOUSEHOLDS		CONTRIBUTORS AND VOLUNTEERS	
	Average amount (dol.)	Percent of household income	Average amount (dol.)	Percent of household income		Average amount (dol.)	Percent of household income	Average amount (dol.)	Percent of household income
1987	790	1.9	1,021	2.4	**1991—**				
1989	978	2.5	1,192	2.9	Under $10,000 . . .	239	3.6	215	3.4
1991, total	**899**	**2.2**	**1,155**	**2.6**	$10,000-$19,999 . .	507	3.4	601	3.9
18 to 24 years	233	0.8	261	0.9	$20,000-$29,999 . .	617	2.5	778	3.1
25 to 34 years	629	1.5	815	1.9	$30,000-$39,999 . .	640	1.8	762	2.2
35 to 44 years	1,135	2.4	1,381	2.7	$40,000-$49,999 . .	1,038	2.3	1,286	2.9
45 to 54 years	1,243	2.4	1,581	2.8	$50,000-$59,999 . .	1,293	2.4	1,461	2.7
55 to 64 years	1,228	2.9	1,592	3.4	$60,000-$74,999 . .	1,180	1.7	1,397	2.1
65 to 74 years	891	3.2	1,260	3.9	$75,000-$99,999 . .	1,666	1.9	2,131	2.4
75 years and over. .	710	3.2	(B)	(B)	$100,000 and over. .	2,450	2.5	2,722	2.7

B Base too small to meet statistical standards for reliability.

No. 616. Charity Contributions—Percent of Households Contributing, by Dollar Amount, 1987 to 1991, and Type of Charity, 1991

[In percent, except as noted. See headnote, table 615]

ANNUAL AMOUNT OF HOUSEHOLD CONTRIBUTIONS	ALL HOUSEHOLDS			GIVERS			TYPE OF CHARITY	1991	
	1987	1989	1991	1987	1989	1991		Percentage of households	Average contribution [1] (dol.)
None	28.9	24.9	27.8	(X)	(X)	(X)	Arts, culture, humanities .	9.4	194
Givers	71.0	75.1	72.2	100.0	100.0	100.0	Education	21.1	225
$1 to $100 . . .	20.8	16.3	14.9	32.7	27.0	24.9	Environment.	16.3	99
$101 to $200 . .	7.4	8.1	8.1	11.6	13.4	13.5	Health.	32.9	154
$201 to $300 . .	6.6	4.8	7.3	10.5	8.0	12.2	Human services	27.5	260
$301 to $400 . .	3.5	4.6	3.3	5.6	7.6	5.6	International	3.5	198
$401 to $500 . .	3.2	3.1	3.2	5.0	5.1	5.4	Private, community		
$501 to $600 . .	2.3	2.6	2.6	3.7	4.3	4.4	foundations.	6.0	113
$601 to $700 . .	2.0	1.5	2.5	3.2	2.5	4.2	Public, societal benefit . .	11.2	132
$701 to $999 . .	3.7	4.8	3.4	5.8	7.9	5.7	Recreation - adults	6.3	164
$1,000 or more. .	13.9	14.5	14.5	21.9	24.0	24.2	Religion.	51.3	800
Not reported. . .	7.6	14.7	12.4	(X)	(X)	(X)	Youth development	22.1	114

X Not applicable.   [1] Average contribution per contributing household.
Source of tables 615 and 616: Hodgkinson, Virginia, Murray Weitzman, and the Gallup Organization, Inc., *Giving and Volunteering in the United States: 1992 Edition.* (Copyright and published by INDEPENDENT SECTOR, Washington, DC, fall 1992.)

No. 617. Private Philanthropy Funds, by Source and Allocation: 1970 to 1991

[In billions of dollars. Estimates for sources of funds based on U.S. Internal Revenue Service reports of corporate and foundation tax returns and individual charitable deductions; econometric formula utilizing Commerce Department data on personal income, Standard & Poor's 500 Composite Index, Census population data; and surveys conducted by the source and by Council for Aid to Education, The Conference Board, The Foundation Center, and other research organizations. Estimates for allocation of funds based on surveys of recipient organizations conducted by source and other groups. Because of changes in estimation procedures over time, data by type of allocation may not be comparable for all years. See *Historical Statistics, Colonial Times to 1970,* series H 398-411, for similar but not comparable data]

SOURCE AND ALLOCATION	1970	1980	1981	1982	1983	1984	1985	1986	1987	1988	1989	1990	1991
Total funds.	**21.0**	**48.7**	**55.7**	**59.9**	**64.7**	**70.4**	**80.0**	**90.7**	**93.3**	**102.5**	**112.3**	**117.5**	**124.8**
Individuals.	16.2	40.7	46.4	48.5	53.5	58.6	65.9	74.6	75.9	84.7	93.0	96.6	103.1
Foundations.	1.9	2.8	3.1	3.2	3.7	3.9	4.9	5.4	5.9	6.2	6.6	7.2	7.8
Corporations	0.8	2.3	2.6	3.0	3.7	3.9	4.4	4.9	4.9	5.1	5.8	6.0	6.1
Charitable bequests	2.1	2.9	3.6	5.2	3.9	4.0	4.8	5.7	6.6	6.6	7.0	7.6	7.8
Allocation:													
Religion.	9.3	22.2	25.1	28.1	31.8	35.6	38.2	41.7	48.7	55.6	62.5	63.3	67.6
Health.	2.4	5.3	5.8	6.2	6.7	6.8	7.7	8.4	9.2	9.6	9.9	9.9	9.7
Education.	2.6	5.0	5.8	6.0	6.7	7.3	8.2	9.4	9.8	10.2	11.0	12.4	13.3
Human service	2.9	4.9	5.6	6.3	7.2	7.9	8.5	9.1	9.8	10.5	11.4	11.8	10.6
Arts, culture and humanities. . .	0.7	3.2	3.7	5.0	4.2	4.5	5.1	5.8	6.3	6.8	7.5	7.9	8.8
Public/society benefit	0.5	1.5	1.8	1.7	1.9	1.9	2.2	2.5	2.9	3.2	3.8	4.9	4.9
Environment/wildlife.	(¹)	(¹)	(¹)	(¹)	(¹)	(¹)	(¹)	(¹)	(¹)	1.3	1.5	1.8	2.3
International	(¹)	(¹)	(¹)	(¹)	(¹)	(¹)	(¹)	(¹)	(¹)	2.2	2.0	1.7	2.2
Undesignated	2.6	6.7	8.0	6.7	6.3	6.4	10.1	13.7	3.0	3.1	2.8	2.7	4.7

[1] Included in "Undesignated."
Source: AAFRC Trust for Philanthropy, New York, NY, *Giving USA,* annual, (copyright).

No. 618. Foundations—Number and Finances, by Asset Size

[Figures are for latest year reported by foundations, usually 1989 or 1990. Covers nongovernment nonprofit organizations with funds and programs managed by their own trustees or directors, whose goal was to maintain or aid social, educational, religious, or other activities deemed to serve the common good. Excludes organizations which make general appeals to the public for funds, act as trade associations for industrial or other special groups, or do not currently award grants]

ASSET SIZE	Number	Assets (mil. dol.)	Gifts received (mil. dol.)	Expen- ditures (mil. dol.)	Grants (mil. dol.)	PERCENT DISTRIBUTION				
						Number	Assets	Gifts received	Expen- ditures	Grants
Total	32,401	142,494	4,972	10,370	8,672	100.0	100.0	100.0	100.0	100.0
Under $50,000	7,732	141	188	246	227	23.9	0.1	3.8	2.3	2.7
$50,000-$99,999	3,462	254	82	109	100	10.7	0.2	1.6	1.1	1.1
$100,000-$249,999	5,411	888	142	230	203	16.7	0.6	2.9	2.2	2.3
$250,000-$499,999	4,072	1,459	186	251	221	12.6	1.0	3.7	2.4	2.5
$500,000-$999,999	3,618	2,575	246	356	309	11.2	1.8	5.0	3.4	3.6
$1,000,000-$4,999,999	5,326	11,722	1,067	1,317	1,149	16.4	8.2	21.5	12.7	13.2
$5,000,000-$9,999,999	1,187	8,360	650	734	623	3.7	5.9	13.1	7.1	7.2
$10,000,000-$49,999,999	1,217	24,998	1,245	2,066	1,735	3.8	17.5	25.0	19.9	20.0
$50,000,000-$99,999,999	194	13,667	433	993	822	0.6	9.6	8.7	9.6	9.5
$100,000,000-$249,999,999	111	17,276	522	1,177	903	0.3	12.1	10.5	11.3	10.4
$250,000,000 or more	71	61,153	209	2,891	2,381	0.2	42.9	4.2	27.9	27.5

Source: The Foundation Center, New York, NY, *National Data Book of Foundations*, 16th Edition, 1992.

No. 619. Foundations—Grants Reported, by Subject Field and Recipient Organization: 1991

[Covers grants of $10,000 or more in size. Based on reports of 846 foundations. Grant sample totaling $4.85 billion represented about 53 percent of all grant dollars awarded by private, corporate, and community foundations. For definition of foundations, see headnote, table 618]

SUBJECT FIELD	NUMBER OF GRANTS		DOLLAR VALUE OF GRANTS		RECIPIENT ORGANIZATION [1]	NUMBER OF GRANTS		DOLLAR VALUE OF GRANTS	
	Num- ber	Per- cent distri- bution	Amount (mil. dol.)	Per- cent distri- bution		Num- ber	Per- cent distri- bution	Amount (mil. dol.)	Per- cent distri- bution
Total	58,218	100.0	4,849	100.0	Community improvement organizations	2,588	4.4	151	3.1
Arts and culture	8,945	15.4	683	14.1	Educational institutions	17,658	30.3	1,880	38.8
Education	13,350	22.9	1,210	25.0	Colleges & universities	10,686	18.4	1,340	27.6
Environment & animals	3,091	5.3	236	4.9	Educational support agencies	2,485	4.3	211	4.4
Health	7,473	12.8	817	16.9	Schools	2,861	4.9	165	3.4
Human services	12,339	21.2	688	14.2	Federated funds	1,786	3.1	185	3.8
International affairs, development & peace	1,952	3.4	196	4.0	Hospitals/medical care facilities	3,169	5.4	345	7.1
Public/society benefit	6,582	11.3	506	10.4	Human service agencies	10,018	17.2	485	10.0
Science and technology	1,826	3.1	278	5.7	International organizations	1,706	2.9	140	2.9
Social sciences	1,157	2.0	133	2.7	Museums/historical societies	2,672	4.6	319	6.6
Religion	1,382	2.4	98	2.0	Performing arts groups	3,484	6.0	188	3.9
Other	121	0.2	4	0.1	Professional societies & associations	3,052	5.2	224	4.6

[1] Grants may be awarded to multiple types of recipient organizations and would thereby be double-counted.

Source: The Foundation Center, New York, NY, *Foundation Grants Index, 1993*, 21st Edition, 1992.

No. 620. Corporate Philanthropy—Donations, by Type of Beneficiary: 1980 to 1991

[In millions of dollars. Based on a sample of corporations that gave at least $100,000; see source]

BENEFICIARY	1980	1983	1984	1985	1986	1987	1988	1989	1990	1991
Total [1]	994.6	1,278.4	1,443.3	1,694.7	1,673.7	1,658.4	1,645.7	1,820.1	2,051.5	2,245.5
Health and human services [1]	337.9	367.6	399.9	494.1	468.6	450.5	480.2	481.0	580.2	608.9
Federated drives	170.7	(NA)	193.9	(NA)	225.9	203.6	235.0	218.3	262.6	285.0
Education [1]	375.8	498.8	561.7	650.0	718.0	610.1	614.1	699.8	789.2	783.6
Employee matching gifts [2]	45.4	(NA)	72.2	(NA)	98.7	108.3	108.2	115.0	105.0	142.0
Culture and art	108.7	145.2	154.7	187.5	198.7	178.6	183.6	201.2	243.6	265.4
Civic, community activities [1]	116.8	188.8	271.6	279.5	220.5	236.1	212.1	253.5	254.5	253.5
Community improvement	47.0	(NA)	30.5	(NA)	12.6	53.4	57.3	87.0	43.0	(NA)
Environment; ecology	10.8	(NA)	97.1	(NA)	35.9	44.0	17.3	11.7	18.7	22.0

NA Not available.   [1] Includes other beneficiaries not shown separately.   [2] Higher education institutions.

Source: The Conference Board, New York, NY, *Annual Survey of Corporate Contributions* (copyright).

Labor Force, Employment, and Earnings

This section presents statistics on the labor force; its distribution by occupation and industry affiliation; and the supply of, demand for, and conditions of labor. The chief source of these data is the Current Population Survey conducted by the U.S. Bureau of the Census. Comprehensive historical data are published by the Bureau of Labor Statistics (BLS) in *Labor Force Statistics Derived From the Current Population Survey, 1948-87, BLS Bulletin 2307.* These data are supplemented on a current basis by the BLS monthly publications *Employment and Earnings* and the *Monthly Labor Review.* Detailed data on the labor force are also available from the Census Bureau's decennial census of population.

Types of data.—Most statistics in this section are obtained by two methods: household interviews or questionnaires, and reports of establishment payroll records. Each method provides data which the other cannot suitably supply. Population characteristics, for example, are readily obtainable only from the household survey, while detailed industrial classifications can be readily derived only from establishment records.

Household data are obtained from a monthly sample survey of the population. The Current Population Survey (CPS) is used to gather data for the calendar week including the 12th of the month and provides current comprehensive data on the labor force (see text, section 1). The CPS provides information on the work status of the population without duplication since each person is classified as employed, unemployed, or not in the labor force. Employed persons holding more than one job are counted only once, according to the job at which they worked the most hours during the survey week.

Monthly data from the CPS are published by the Bureau of Labor Statistics in *Employment and Earnings* and the related reports mentioned above. Data presented include national totals of the number of persons in the civilian labor force by sex, race, Hispanic origin, and age; the number employed; hours of work; industry and

In Brief	
Labor force participation rate of married women with children under 6 years old:	
1960	18.6
1970	30.3
1980	45.1
1992	59.9
Occupational tenure: 1991	
Barbers	27 years
Farmers	22 years
Locomotive operators	20 years

occupational groups; and the number unemployed, reasons for, and duration of unemployment. Monthly data from the CPS are also presented for regions and 11 large States. Annual data shown in this section are averages of monthly figures for each calendar year, unless otherwise specified.

In addition to monthly data, the CPS also produces annual estimates of employment and unemployment for each State, 50 large metropolitan statistical areas, and selected cities. These estimates are published by BLS in its annual *Geographic Profile of Employment and Unemployment.* More detailed geographic data (e.g., for counties and cities) are provided by the decennial population censuses.

Data based on establishment records are compiled by BLS and cooperating State agencies as part of an ongoing Current Employment Statistics Program. Data, gathered from a sample of employers who voluntarily complete mail questionnaires monthly, are supplemented by data from other government agencies and adjusted at intervals to data from government social insurance program reports. The estimates exclude proprietors of unincorporated firms, self-employed persons, private household workers, unpaid family workers, agricultural workers, and the Armed Forces. In March 1991, reporting establishments employed 9 million manufacturing workers (48 percent of the total manufacturing employment at the time), 18 million workers in nonmanufacturing industries (25 percent of the total in nonmanufacturing), and 14 million Federal, State, and local government employees (75 percent of total government).

The establishment survey counts workers each time they appear on a payroll during the reference week (as with the CPS, the week including the 12th of the month). Thus, unlike the CPS, a person with two jobs is counted twice. The establishment survey is designed to provide detailed industry information for the Nation, States, and metropolitan areas on nonfarm wage and salary employment, average weekly hours, and average hourly and weekly earnings. Establishment survey data are published in *Employment and Earnings* and the *Monthly Labor Review*, cited above. Historical national and geographic data are published in *BLS Bulletin 2370, Employment, Hours, and Earnings, United States, 1909-90* and *Bulletin 2320, Employment, Hours, and Earnings, States and Areas, 1972-87*, updated annually.

Labor force.—According to the CPS definitions, the civilian labor force comprises all civilians in the noninstitutional population 16 years and over classified as "employed" or "unemployed" according to the following criteria: Employed civilians comprise (a) all civilians, who, during the reference week, did any work for pay or profit (minimum of an hour's work) or worked 15 hours or more as unpaid workers in a family enterprise, and (b) all civilians who were not working but who had jobs or businesses from which they were temporarily absent for noneconomic reasons (illness, weather conditions, vacation, labor-management dispute, etc.) whether they were paid for the time off or were seeking other jobs. Unemployed persons comprise all civilians who had no employment during the reference week, who made specific efforts to find a job within the previous 4 weeks (such as applying directly to an employer, or to a public employment service, or checking with friends), and who were available for work during that week, except for temporary illness. Persons on layoff from a job or waiting to report to a new job within 30 days are also classified as unemployed if they were available for work. All other civilian persons, 16 years old and over, are "not in the labor force." The total labor force includes, in addition to the civilian

employed and unemployed, members of the Armed Forces stationed in the United States. They are also included in the employed totals.

Beginning in 1982, changes in the estimation procedures and the introduction of 1980 census data caused substantial increases in the population and estimates of persons in all labor force categories. Rates on labor force characteristics, however, were essentially unchanged. In order to avoid major breaks in series, some 30,000 labor force series were adjusted back to 1970. The effect of the 1982 revisions on various data series and an explanation of the adjustment procedure used are described in "Revisions in the Current Population Survey in January 1982," in the February 1982 issue of *Employment and Earnings.* The revisions did not, however, smooth out the breaks in series occurring between 1972 and 1979, and data users should make allowances for them in making certain data comparisons.

Beginning in January 1985, the CPS estimation procedure was revised due to the implementation of a new sample design. A description of the changes and an indication of their effect on the national estimates of labor force characteristics appear in "Changes in the Estimation Procedure in the Current Population Survey Beginning in January 1985" in the February 1985 issue of *Employment and Earnings.* Overall, the revisions had only a slight effect on most estimates. The greatest impact was on estimates of persons of Hispanic origin, which were revised to the extent possible, back to January 1980.

Beginning in January 1986, the CPS estimation procedure was revised to reflect an explicit estimate of the number of undocumented immigrants (largely Hispanic) since 1980 and an improved estimate of the number of legal foreign-born emigrants for the same time period. The revisions had a comparatively small effect on the total population and labor force estimates, but their effect on the estimates of persons of Hispanic origin was more pronounced. As a result, data for Hispanics, to the extent possible, were again revised back to January 1980. An explanation of the changes and their effect on estimates of labor force characteristics appears in "Changes in the Estimation Procedure in the Current Population Survey Beginning in January 1986" in the February 1986 issue of *Employment and Earnings.*

Hours and earnings.—Average hourly earnings, based on establishment data, are gross earnings (i.e., earnings before payroll deductions) and include overtime premiums; they exclude irregular bonuses and value of payments in kind. Hours are those for which pay was received. Wages and salaries from the CPS consist of total monies received for work performed by an employee during the income year. It includes wages, salaries, commissions, tips, piece-rate payments, and cash bonuses earned before deductions were made for taxes, bonds, union dues, etc. Persons who worked 35 hours or more are classified as working full time (see table 639).

Industrial and occupational groups.— Establishments responding to the establishment survey are classified into industries on the basis of their principal product or activity (determined by annual sales volume) in accordance with the *Standard Industrial Classification (SIC) Manual,* Office of Management and Budget. The SIC is a classification structure for the entire national economy. The structure provides data on a division and industry code basis, according to the level of industrial detail. For example, manufacturing is a major industrial division; food and kindred products (code 20) is one of its major groups. One of the ways this group is further divided is into meat products (code 201) and meat packing plants (code 2011). Periodically, the SIC is revised to reflect changes in the industrial composition of the economy. The *1987 SIC Manual* has been issued; the previous was the *1972 SIC Manual.* Tables shown in this *Abstract* indicate which *SIC Manual* the data shown are based on.

Industry data derived from the CPS for 1983-91 utilize the 1980 census industrial classification developed from the 1972 SIC. CPS data from 1971 to 1982 were based on the 1970 census classification system which was developed from the 1967 SIC. Most of the industry categories were not affected by the change in classification.

The occupational classification system used in the 1980 census and in the CPS for 1983-91 evolved from the 1980 Standard Occupational Classification (SOC) system, first introduced in 1977.

Occupational categories used in the 1980 census classification system are so radically different from the 1970 census system used in the CPS through 1982, that their implementation represented a break in historical data series. In cases where data have not yet been converted to the 1980 classifications and still reflect the 1970 classifications (e.g., table 674), comparisons between the two systems should not be made. To help users bridge the data gap, a limited set of estimates was developed for the 1972-82 period based on the new classifications. The estimates were developed by means of applying conversion factors created by double coding a 20-percent sample of CPS occupational records for 6 months during 1981-82. For further details, contact BLS.

Productivity.—The Bureau of Labor Statistics (BLS) publishes data on productivity as measured by output per hour (labor productivity), output per combined unit of labor and capital input (multifactor productivity), and, for manufacturing industries, output per combined unit of capital, labor, energy, materials, and purchased service inputs. Labor productivity and related indexes are published for the business sector as a whole and its major subsectors: nonfarm business, manufacturing, nonfinancial corporations, 177 specific industries, and various functional areas of the Federal and State and local governments. Multifactor productivity and related measures are published for the private business sector and its major subsectors. Productivity indexes which take into account capital, labor, energy, materials, and service inputs are published for the 20 major two-digit industry groups which comprise the manufacturing sector and for the tire and inner tubes, footwear, steel, farm and garden machinery, motor vehicles, and railroad transportation industries. The major sector data are published in the BLS quarterly news release, *Productivity and Costs* and in the annual *Multifactor Productivity Measures* release. The specific industry productivity measures are published annually in the BLS Bulletin, *Productivity Measures for Selected Industries and Government Services,* and the *Handbook of Labor Statistics.* Detailed information on methods, limitations, and data sources appears in the *BLS Handbook of Methods,* BLS Bulletin 2414 (1992), chapters 10 and 11.

Unions.—As defined here, unions include traditional labor unions and employee associations similar to labor unions. Data on union membership status provided by BLS are for employed wage and salary workers and relate to their principal job. Earnings by union membership status are usual weekly earnings of full-time wage and salary workers. The information is collected through the Current Population Survey. For a full description of the method of collection and comparability with earlier data, see "New Data on Union Members and Their Earnings" in the January 1985 issue of *Employment and Earnings,* and "Changing Employment Patterns of Organized Workers" in the February 1985 issue of the *Monthly Labor Review.* Collective bargaining settlements data are available for bargaining situations involving 1,000 or more workers in private industry and State and local government.

Work stoppages.—Work stoppages include all strikes and lockouts known to BLS which last for at least one full day or shift and involve 1,000 or more workers. All stoppages, whether or not authorized by a union, legal or illegal, are counted. Excluded are work slowdowns and instances where employees report to work late, or leave early, to attend mass meetings or mass rallies.

Seasonal adjustment.—Many economic statistics reflect a regularly recurring seasonal movement which can be estimated on the basis of past experience. By eliminating that part of the change which can be ascribed to usual seasonal variation (e.g., climate or school openings and closings), it is possible to observe the cyclical and other nonseasonal movements in the series. However, in evaluating deviations from the seasonal pattern—that is, changes in a seasonally adjusted series—it is important to note that seasonal adjustment is merely an approximation based on past experience. Seasonally adjusted estimates have a broader margin of possible error than the original data on which they are based, since they are subject not only to sampling and other errors, but also are affected by the uncertainties of the adjustment process itself.

Statistical reliability.—For discussion of statistical collection, estimation, sampling procedures, and measures of statistical reliability applicable to Census Bureau and BLS data, see Appendix III.

Historical statistics.—Tabular headnotes provide cross-references, where applicable, to *Historical Statistics of the United States, Colonial Times to 1970.* See Appendix IV.

Figure 13.1
Longest Occupational Tenure—Top 10: 1991

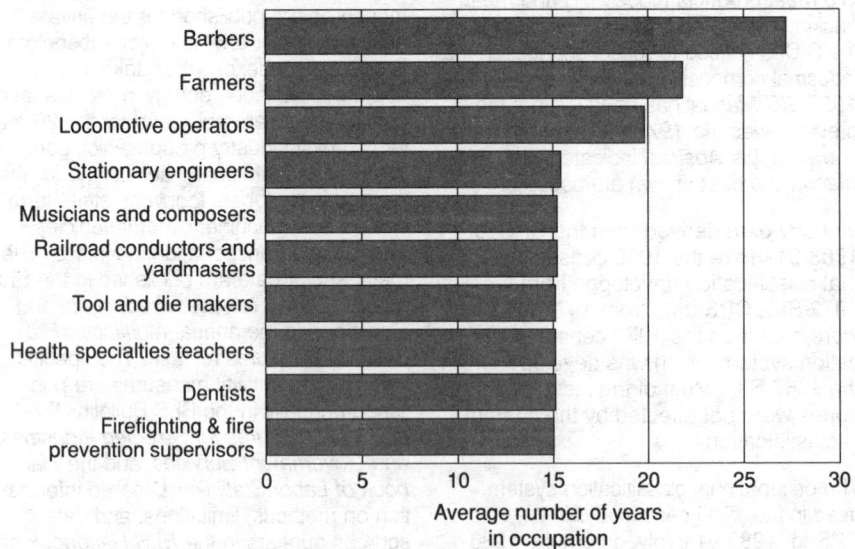

Average number of years
in occupation

Source: Chart prepared by U.S. Bureau of the Census. For data, see table 650.

No. 621. Employment Status of the Noninstitutional Population 16 Years Old and Over: 1950 to 1992

[In thousands, except as indicated. Annual averages of monthly figures. Based on Current Population Survey; see text, section 1, and Appendix III. See also *Historical Statistics, Colonial Times to 1970*, series D 11-19 and D 85-86]

YEAR	Noninsti-tutional popula-tion	LABOR FORCE								Not in labor force
		Number	Employed						Unemployed	
			Total	Resi-dent Armed Forces	Civilian				Number	Percent of labor force [1]
					Total	Agricul-ture	Non-agricul-ture indus-tries			
1950	106,164	63,377	60,087	1,169	58,918	7,160	51,758		3,288	5.2	42,787
1960	119,106	71,489	67,639	1,861	65,778	5,458	60,318		3,852	5.4	47,617
1970	139,203	84,889	80,796	2,118	78,678	3,463	75,215		4,093	4.8	54,315
1975	154,831	95,453	87,524	1,678	85,846	3,408	82,438		7,929	8.3	59,377
1980	169,349	108,544	100,907	1,604	99,303	3,364	95,938		7,637	7.0	60,806
1982	173,939	111,872	101,194	1,668	99,526	3,401	96,125		10,678	9.5	62,067
1983	175,891	113,226	102,510	1,676	100,834	3,383	97,450		10,717	9.5	62,665
1984	178,080	115,241	106,702	1,697	105,005	3,321	101,685		8,539	7.4	62,839
1985	179,912	117,167	108,856	1,706	107,150	3,179	103,971		8,312	7.1	62,744
1986	182,293	119,540	111,303	1,706	109,597	3,163	106,434		8,237	6.9	62,752
1987	184,490	121,602	114,177	1,737	112,440	3,208	109,232		7,425	6.1	62,888
1988	186,322	123,378	116,677	1,709	114,968	3,169	111,800		6,701	5.4	62,944
1989	188,081	125,557	119,030	1,688	117,342	3,199	114,142		6,528	5.2	62,523
1990	189,686	126,424	119,550	1,637	117,914	3,186	114,728		6,874	5.4	63,262
1991	191,329	126,867	118,440	1,564	116,877	3,233	113,644		8,426	6.6	64,462
1992	193,142	128,548	119,164	1,566	117,598	3,207	114,391		9,384	7.3	64,593
PERCENT DISTRIBUTION											
1950	100.0	59.7	56.6	1.1	55.5	6.7	48.8		3.1	(X)	40.3
1960	100.0	60.0	56.8	1.6	55.2	4.6	50.6		3.2	(X)	40.0
1970	100.0	61.0	58.0	1.5	56.5	2.5	54.0		2.9	(X)	39.0
1980	100.0	64.1	59.6	0.9	58.6	2.0	56.7		4.5	(X)	35.9
1990	100.0	66.6	63.0	0.9	62.2	1.7	60.5		3.6	(X)	33.4
1992	100.0	66.6	61.7	0.8	60.9	1.7	59.2		4.9	(X)	33.4

X Not applicable.   [1] Unemployment as a percent of the labor force, including resident Armed Forces.

Source: U.S. Bureau of Labor Statistics, Bulletin 2307; and *Employment and Earnings*, monthly.

No. 622. Civilian Labor Force and Participation Rates by Race, Hispanic Origin, Sex, and Age, 1970 to 1992, and Projections, 2000 and 2005

[For civilian noninstitutional population 16 years old and over. Annual averages of monthly figures. Rates are based on annual average civilian noninstitutional population of each specified group and represent proportion of each specified group in the civilian labor force. Based on Current Population Survey; see text, section 1, and Appendix III. See also *Historical Statistics, Colonial Times to 1970*, series D 42-48]

RACE, SEX, AND AGE	CIVILIAN LABOR FORCE (millions)							PARTICIPATION RATE (percent)						
	1970	1980	1985	1990	1992	2000	2005	1970	1980	1985	1990	1992	2000	2005
Total [1]	82.8	106.9	115.5	124.8	127.0	142.9	150.7	60.4	63.8	64.8	66.4	66.3	68.7	69.0
White	73.6	93.6	99.9	107.2	108.5	120.3	125.8	60.2	64.1	65.0	66.8	66.7	69.3	69.7
Male	46.0	54.5	56.5	59.3	59.8	64.5	66.8	80.0	78.2	77.0	76.9	76.4	76.7	76.2
Female	27.5	39.1	43.5	47.9	48.7	55.8	58.9	42.6	51.2	54.1	57.5	57.8	62.3	63.5
Black [2]	9.2	10.9	12.4	13.5	13.9	16.5	17.8	61.8	61.0	62.9	63.3	63.3	65.7	65.6
Male	5.2	5.6	6.2	6.7	6.9	8.1	8.7	76.5	70.3	70.8	70.1	69.7	71.0	70.2
Female	4.0	5.3	6.1	6.8	7.0	8.4	9.1	49.5	53.1	56.5	57.8	58.0	61.2	61.7
Hispanic [3]	(NA)	6.1	7.7	9.6	10.1	14.2	16.8	(NA)	64.0	64.6	67.0	66.5	69.3	69.9
Male	(NA)	3.8	4.7	5.8	6.1	8.4	9.9	(NA)	81.4	80.3	81.2	80.5	81.8	81.6
Female	(NA)	2.3	3.0	3.8	4.0	5.8	6.9	(NA)	47.4	49.3	53.0	52.6	56.6	58.0
Male	51.2	61.5	64.4	68.2	69.2	75.9	79.3	79.7	77.4	76.3	76.1	75.6	76.0	75.4
16 to 19 years	4.0	5.0	4.1	3.9	3.5	4.4	4.6	56.1	60.5	56.8	55.7	53.3	57.4	57.7
16 and 17 years	1.8	2.1	1.7	1.5	1.4	1.8	1.9	47.0	50.1	45.1	43.7	41.1	47.3	47.9
18 and 19 years	2.2	2.9	2.5	2.4	2.2	2.6	2.6	66.7	71.3	68.9	67.0	66.0	68.0	68.0
20 to 24 years	5.7	8.6	8.3	7.3	7.2	7.7	8.0	83.3	85.9	85.0	84.3	83.3	85.5	86.1
25 to 34 years	11.3	17.0	18.8	19.8	19.4	17.3	17.0	96.4	95.2	94.7	94.2	93.8	93.9	93.6
35 to 44 years	10.5	11.8	14.5	17.3	18.2	20.4	19.2	96.9	95.5	95.0	94.4	93.8	93.7	93.4
45 to 54 years	10.4	9.9	9.9	11.2	12.1	16.5	18.6	94.3	91.2	91.0	90.7	90.8	90.5	90.3
55 to 64 years	7.1	7.2	7.1	6.8	6.7	7.8	9.7	83.0	72.1	67.9	67.7	67.0	68.2	67.9
65 years and over	2.2	1.9	1.8	2.0	2.1	2.2	2.3	26.8	19.0	15.8	16.4	16.1	15.8	16.0
Female	31.5	45.5	51.1	56.6	57.8	67.0	71.4	43.3	51.5	54.5	57.5	57.8	62.0	63.0
16 to 19 years	3.2	4.4	3.8	3.5	3.2	4.1	4.2	44.0	52.9	52.1	51.8	49.2	54.1	54.3
16 and 17 years	1.3	1.8	1.5	1.4	1.3	1.7	1.7	34.9	43.6	42.1	41.9	39.3	45.3	45.4
18 and 19 years	1.9	2.6	2.3	2.2	1.9	2.4	2.5	53.6	61.9	61.7	60.5	59.0	62.9	63.2
20 to 24 years	4.9	7.3	7.4	6.6	6.5	6.6	7.3	57.7	68.9	71.8	71.6	71.2	74.3	75.3
25 to 34 years	5.7	12.3	14.7	16.0	15.7	14.8	14.7	45.0	65.5	70.9	73.6	74.1	78.2	79.7
35 to 44 years	6.0	8.6	11.6	14.6	15.4	18.4	17.8	51.1	65.5	71.8	76.5	76.8	83.3	85.3
45 to 54 years	6.5	7.0	7.5	9.3	10.3	15.0	17.2	54.4	59.9	64.4	71.2	72.7	79.0	81.5
55 to 64 years	4.2	4.7	4.9	5.1	5.2	6.5	8.4	43.0	41.3	42.0	45.3	46.6	51.9	54.3
65 years and over	1.1	1.2	1.2	1.5	1.5	1.6	1.8	9.7	8.1	7.3	8.7	8.3	8.6	8.8

NA Not available.   [1] Beginning 1980, includes other races not shown separately.   [2] For 1970, Black and other.   [3] Persons of Hispanic origin may be of any race.

Source: U.S. Bureau of Labor Statistics, Bulletin 2307; *Employment and Earnings*, monthly, January issues; *Monthly Labor Review*, November 1991; and unpublished data.

No. 623. Civilian Labor Force—Percent Distribution, by Sex and Age: 1960 to 1992

[For civilian noninstitutional population 16 years old and over. Annual averages of monthly figures. Based on Current Population Survey; see text, section 1, and Appendix III. See *Historical Statistics, Colonial Times to 1970*, series D 29-41, for similar but not exactly comparable data]

YEAR AND SEX	Civilian labor force (1,000)	PERCENT DISTRIBUTION						
		16 to 19 years	20 to 24 years	25 to 34 years	35 to 44 years	45 to 54 years	55 to 64 years	65 yrs. and over
Total: 1960	69,628	7.0	9.6	20.7	23.4	21.3	13.5	4.6
1970	82,771	8.8	12.8	20.6	19.9	20.5	13.6	3.9
1975	93,775	9.5	14.7	24.4	18.0	18.2	12.1	3.2
1980	106,940	8.8	14.9	27.3	19.1	15.8	11.2	2.9
1985	115,461	6.8	13.6	29.1	22.6	15.0	10.4	2.5
1988	121,669	6.6	11.9	29.2	24.2	15.7	9.7	2.7
1989	123,869	6.4	11.4	29.0	24.7	16.1	9.6	2.8
1990	124,787	5.9	11.1	28.7	25.5	16.4	9.5	2.8
1991	125,303	5.5	10.9	28.2	26.3	16.9	9.4	2.8
1992	126,982	5.3	10.8	27.6	26.5	17.6	9.3	2.8
Male: 1960	46,388	6.0	8.9	22.1	23.6	20.6	13.8	4.9
1970	51,228	7.8	11.2	22.1	20.4	20.3	13.9	4.2
1975	56,299	8.5	13.4	25.2	18.5	18.5	12.5	3.4
1980	61,453	8.1	14.0	27.6	19.3	16.1	11.8	3.1
1985	64,411	6.4	12.9	29.2	22.5	15.3	11.0	2.7
1988	66,927	6.2	11.3	29.5	24.0	15.8	10.2	2.9
1989	67,840	6.1	11.0	29.3	24.5	16.1	10.0	3.0
1990	68,234	5.7	10.7	29.0	25.3	16.4	9.9	3.0
1991	68,411	5.2	10.6	28.6	26.1	16.8	9.8	2.9
1992	69,184	5.1	10.5	28.0	26.3	17.5	9.7	3.0
Female: 1960	23,240	8.8	11.1	17.8	22.8	22.7	12.8	3.9
1970	31,543	10.3	15.5	18.1	18.9	20.7	13.2	3.3
1975	37,475	10.8	16.5	23.1	17.4	17.8	11.5	2.8
1980	45,487	9.6	16.1	26.9	19.0	15.4	10.4	2.6
1985	51,050	7.4	14.6	28.9	22.7	14.6	9.7	2.3
1988	54,742	7.1	12.6	28.8	24.4	15.6	9.1	2.4
1989	56,030	6.8	12.0	28.5	25.0	16.1	9.1	2.6
1990	56,554	6.3	11.6	28.3	25.8	16.5	9.0	2.7
1991	56,893	5.9	11.3	27.7	26.6	17.0	8.9	2.7
1992	57,798	5.5	11.2	27.2	26.7	17.8	8.9	2.6

Source: U.S. Bureau of Labor Statistics, Bulletin 2307, and *Employment Earnings*, monthly, January issues.

No. 624. Civilian Labor Force and Participation Rates, by Educational Attainment, Sex, and Race: 1970 to 1991

[As of **March**, except as noted. For civilian noninstitutional population 25 to 64 years of age. See headnote, table 622. Beginning 1992, the method of computing educational attainment data was changed. See table 629 for 1992 data]

ITEM	CIVILIAN LABOR FORCE					PARTICIPATION RATE [1]				
	Total (1,000)	Percent distribution				Total	Less than high school	High school grad-uate	College	
		Less than high school	High School grad-uate	College					1-3 years	4 years or more
				1-3 years	4 years or more					
Total: [2] **1970**	61,765	36.1	38.1	11.8	14.1	70.3	65.5	70.2	73.8	82.3
1980	78,010	20.6	39.8	17.6	22.0	73.9	60.7	74.2	79.5	86.1
1985	88,424	15.9	40.2	19.0	24.9	76.2	59.9	75.9	81.6	87.7
1990 [3]	99,981	13.3	39.4	20.8	26.5	78.9	61.4	78.4	83.5	88.6
1991 [3]	101,171	12.8	39.2	21.3	26.7	78.8	61.0	78.2	83.4	88.3
Male: 1970	39,303	37.5	34.5	12.2	15.7	93.5	89.3	96.3	95.8	96.1
1980	45,417	22.2	35.7	17.7	24.3	89.4	78.8	91.9	92.4	95.3
1985	49,647	17.7	36.9	18.3	27.1	88.6	72.2	90.0	91.2	94.6
1990 [3]	55,049	14.9	37.3	19.8	28.0	89.3	76.4	90.1	92.1	94.6
1991 [3]	55,554	14.5	37.1	20.3	28.2	88.9	75.9	89.4	91.9	94.3
Female: 1970	22,462	33.5	44.3	10.9	11.2	49.0	43.0	51.3	50.9	60.9
1980	32,593	18.4	45.4	17.4	18.7	59.5	43.7	61.2	66.4	73.4
1985	38,779	13.7	44.4	19.9	22.0	64.7	44.3	65.0	72.5	78.6
1990 [3]	44,932	11.2	42.1	22.1	24.6	69.1	46.5	68.8	75.7	81.3
1991 [3]	45,617	10.7	41.8	22.5	25.0	69.3	46.0	68.9	75.8	81.3
White: 1970	55,044	33.7	39.3	12.2	14.8	70.1	65.2	69.7	73.3	81.9
1980	68,509	19.1	40.2	17.7	22.9	74.2	61.4	73.7	79.2	86.0
1985	76,739	14.7	40.7	19.1	25.6	76.6	60.7	75.8	81.1	87.7
1990 [3]	85,882	12.5	39.4	20.8	27.3	79.5	63.0	78.6	83.4	88.6
1991 [3]	86,776	12.1	39.1	21.3	27.5	79.5	62.6	78.5	83.4	88.5
Black: 1970	6,721	55.5	28.2	8.0	8.3	72.0	67.1	76.8	81.0	87.4
1980	7,731	34.7	38.1	16.3	11.0	71.5	58.1	79.2	82.0	90.1
1985	9,157	26.2	39.5	19.2	15.0	73.4	57.0	77.2	85.6	89.9
1990 [3]	10,711	19.4	43.0	21.8	15.8	75.4	55.7	78.6	84.6	91.0
1991 [3]	10,863	18.4	43.0	22.5	16.0	75.0	55.1	77.4	84.6	90.4

[1] Percent of the civilian population in each group in the civilian labor force.　[2] Includes other races, not shown separately. For 1970, White and Black races only.　[3] Not strictly comparable with previous years. Annual averages of monthly figures.

Source: U.S. Bureau of Labor Statistics, Bulletin 2307; and unpublished data.

No. 625. Employment Status of the Civilian Noninstitutional Population 16 Years Old and Over, by Sex, Race, and Hispanic Origin: 1960 to 1992

[In thousands, except as indicated. Annual averages of monthly figures. Based on Current Population Survey; see text, section 1, and Appendix III. See also *Historical Statistics, Colonial Times to 1970*, series D 11-19 and D 85-86]

YEAR, SEX, RACE, AND HISPANIC ORIGIN	Civilian noninstitutional population	CIVILIAN LABOR FORCE						NOT IN LABOR FORCE	
		Total	Percent of population	Employed	Employment/population ratio [1]	Unemployed			
						Number	Percent of labor force	Number	Percent of population
Total: [2]									
1960	117,245	69,628	59.4	65,778	56.1	3,852	5.5	47,617	40.6
1970	137,085	82,771	60.4	78,678	57.4	4,093	4.9	54,315	39.6
1980	167,745	106,940	63.8	99,303	59.2	7,637	7.1	60,806	36.2
1985	178,206	115,461	64.8	107,150	60.1	8,312	7.2	62,744	35.2
1988	184,613	121,669	65.9	114,968	62.3	6,701	5.5	62,944	34.1
1989	186,393	123,869	66.5	117,342	63.0	6,528	5.3	62,523	33.5
1990	188,049	124,787	66.4	117,914	62.7	6,874	5.5	63,262	33.6
1991	189,765	125,303	66.0	116,877	61.6	8,426	6.7	64,462	34.0
1992	191,576	126,982	66.3	117,598	61.4	9,384	7.4	64,593	33.7
Male:									
1960	55,662	46,388	83.3	43,904	78.9	2,486	5.4	9,274	16.7
1970	64,304	51,228	79.7	48,990	76.2	2,238	4.4	13,076	20.3
1980	79,398	61,453	77.4	57,186	72.0	4,267	6.9	17,945	22.6
1985	84,469	64,411	76.3	59,891	70.9	4,521	7.0	20,058	23.7
1988	87,857	66,927	76.2	63,273	72.0	3,655	5.5	20,930	23.8
1989	88,762	67,840	76.4	64,315	72.5	3,525	5.2	20,923	23.6
1990	89,650	68,234	76.1	64,435	71.9	3,799	5.6	21,417	23.9
1991	90,552	68,411	75.5	63,593	70.2	4,817	7.0	22,141	24.5
1992	91,541	69,184	75.6	63,805	69.7	5,380	7.8	22,356	24.4
Female:									
1960	61,582	23,240	37.7	21,874	35.5	1,366	5.9	38,343	62.3
1970	72,782	31,543	43.3	29,688	40.8	1,855	5.9	41,239	56.7
1980	88,348	45,487	51.5	42,117	47.7	3,370	7.4	42,861	48.5
1985	93,736	51,050	54.5	47,259	50.4	3,791	7.4	42,686	45.5
1988	96,756	54,742	56.6	51,696	53.4	3,046	5.6	42,014	43.4
1989	97,630	56,030	57.4	53,027	54.3	3,003	5.4	41,601	42.6
1990	98,399	56,554	57.5	53,479	54.3	3,075	5.4	41,845	42.5
1991	99,214	56,893	57.3	53,284	53.7	3,609	6.3	42,321	42.7
1992	100,035	57,798	57.8	53,793	53.8	4,005	6.9	42,237	42.2
White:									
1960	105,282	61,915	58.8	58,850	55.9	3,065	5.0	43,367	41.2
1970	122,174	73,556	60.2	70,217	57.5	3,339	4.5	48,618	39.8
1980	146,122	93,600	64.1	87,715	60.0	5,884	6.3	52,523	35.9
1985	153,679	99,926	65.0	93,736	61.0	6,191	6.2	53,753	35.0
1988	158,194	104,756	66.2	99,812	63.1	4,944	4.7	53,439	33.8
1989	159,338	106,355	66.7	101,584	63.8	4,770	4.5	52,983	33.3
1990	160,415	107,177	66.8	102,087	63.6	5,091	4.7	53,237	33.2
1991	161,511	107,486	66.6	101,039	62.6	6,447	6.0	54,025	33.4
1992	162,658	108,526	66.7	101,479	62.4	7,047	6.5	54,132	33.3
Black:									
1973	14,917	8,976	60.2	8,128	54.5	846	9.4	5,941	39.8
1980	17,824	10,865	61.0	9,313	52.2	1,553	14.3	6,959	39.0
1985	19,664	12,364	62.9	10,501	53.4	1,864	15.1	7,299	37.1
1988	20,692	13,205	63.8	11,658	56.3	1,547	11.7	7,487	36.2
1989	21,021	13,497	64.2	11,953	56.9	1,544	11.4	7,524	35.8
1990	21,300	13,493	63.3	11,966	56.2	1,527	11.3	7,808	36.7
1991	21,615	13,542	62.6	11,863	54.9	1,679	12.4	8,074	37.4
1992	21,958	13,891	63.3	11,933	54.3	1,958	14.1	8,067	36.7
Hispanic: [3]									
1980	9,598	6,146	64.0	5,527	57.6	620	10.1	3,451	36.0
1985	11,915	7,698	64.6	6,888	57.8	811	10.5	4,217	35.4
1986	12,344	8,076	65.4	7,219	58.5	857	10.6	4,268	34.6
1989	13,791	9,323	67.6	8,573	62.2	750	8.0	4,468	32.4
1990	14,297	9,576	67.0	8,808	61.6	769	8.0	4,721	33.0
1991	14,770	9,762	66.1	8,799	59.6	963	9.9	5,008	33.9
1992	15,244	10,131	66.5	8,971	58.9	1,160	11.4	5,113	33.5
Mexican:									
1986	7,377	4,941	67.0	4,387	59.5	555	11.2	2,436	33.0
1990	8,742	5,970	68.3	5,478	62.7	492	8.2	2,773	31.7
1991	8,947	5,984	66.9	5,363	59.9	621	10.4	2,963	33.1
1992	9,368	6,319	67.5	5,581	59.6	739	11.7	3,049	32.5
Puerto Rican:									
1986	1,494	804	53.8	691	46.3	113	14.0	690	46.2
1990	1,546	859	55.6	780	50.5	79	9.1	687	44.4
1991	1,629	930	57.1	822	50.5	108	11.6	699	42.9
1992	1,628	934	57.4	802	49.2	132	14.1	694	42.6
Cuban:									
1986	842	570	67.7	533	63.3	36	6.4	272	32.3
1990	847	552	65.1	512	60.4	40	7.2	295	34.8
1991	849	543	63.9	499	58.8	44	8.1	306	36.0
1992	867	529	61.1	488	56.3	42	7.9	337	38.9

[1] Civilian employed as a percent of the civilian noninstitutional population.   [2] Includes other races, not shown separately.
[3] Persons of Hispanic origin may be of any race. Includes persons of other Hispanic origin, not shown separately.
Source: U.S. Bureau of Labor Statistics, Bulletin 2307; and *Employment and Earnings*, monthly, January issues.

No. 626. Characteristics of the Civilian Labor Force, by State: 1992

[In thousands, except ratio and rate. For civilian noninstitutional population, 16 years old and over. Annual averages of monthly figures. Because of separate processing and weighting procedures, the totals for the United States may differ from results obtained by aggregating totals for regions and States]

REGION, DIVISION, AND STATE	TOTAL		EMPLOYED		Employed/population ratio [1]	UNEMPLOYED					PARTICIPATION RATE [3]	
	Number	Female	Total	Female		Total		Rate [2]			Male	Female
						Number	Female	Total	Male	Female		
United States...	126,982	57,798	117,598	53,793	61.4	9,384	4,005	7.4	7.8	6.9	75.6	57.8
Northeast..........	25,589	11,730	23,518	10,908	59.6	2,071	823	8.1	9.0	7.0	74.4	56.2
New England.....	7,062	3,325	6,500	3,103	63.7	562	222	8.0	9.1	6.7	77.4	61.8
Maine..........	662	305	615	287	63.7	47	18	7.1	8.1	6.0	75.8	61.7
New Hampshire ...	633	295	586	273	66.6	47	22	7.5	7.5	7.5	79.5	64.9
Vermont........	322	152	300	145	66.4	21	8	6.6	7.9	5.2	76.5	66.0
Massachusetts....	3,126	1,478	2,862	1,375	61.8	265	103	8.5	9.8	7.0	76.2	60.0
Rhode Island.....	527	251	481	231	62.1	47	20	8.9	9.7	7.9	76.6	60.6
Connecticut......	1,791	843	1,656	792	66.0	135	51	7.5	8.9	6.0	79.8	63.8
Middle Atlantic.....	18,527	8,406	17,018	7,805	58.1	1,509	601	8.1	9.0	7.2	73.4	54.3
New York	8,522	3,888	7,798	3,602	56.5	724	286	8.5	9.4	7.4	71.9	52.8
New Jersey	4,001	1,795	3,666	1,661	60.8	335	135	8.4	9.1	7.5	76.7	57.0
Pennsylvania	6,004	2,722	5,554	2,542	58.8	450	180	7.5	8.2	6.6	73.4	54.8
Midwest..........	31,269	14,364	29,228	13,487	63.7	2,041	877	6.5	6.9	6.1	71.1	59.9
East North Central..	21,729	9,926	20,146	9,247	62.2	1,583	679	7.3	7.7	6.8	76.4	58.7
Ohio..........	5,489	2,494	5,093	2,328	61.1	396	165	7.2	7.7	6.6	75.5	57.1
Indiana........	2,849	1,329	2,663	1,251	62.0	186	78	6.5	7.1	5.9	76.7	57.5
Illinois.........	6,120	2,796	5,659	2,602	63.1	461	194	7.5	8.0	6.9	77.5	59.8
Michigan.......	4,610	2,081	4,205	1,899	59.7	405	182	8.8	8.8	8.7	75.0	56.8
Wisconsin	2,661	1,226	2,526	1,166	67.7	135	59	5.1	5.3	4.8	78.1	64.8
West North Central .	9,540	4,439	9,082	4,240	67.1	458	198	4.8	5.1	4.5	78.9	62.8
Minnesota......	2,431	1,144	2,306	1,095	68.9	125	49	5.1	5.9	4.3	80.2	65.7
Iowa..........	1,551	711	1,479	682	68.2	72	29	4.6	5.2	4.0	80.1	63.5
Missouri	2,696	1,260	2,543	1,190	64.4	153	69	5.7	5.8	5.5	77.7	60.0
North Dakota.....	314	146	299	140	64.4	15	6	4.9	5.3	4.4	76.2	60.1
South Dakota.....	361	167	350	161	67.3	11	6	3.1	2.7	3.6	76.9	62.4
Nebraska	856	403	831	391	68.9	25	11	3.0	3.1	2.8	78.0	64.4
Kansas.........	1,330	608	1,274	581	68.0	56	27	4.2	4.0	4.5	79.7	62.8
South.............	43,098	19,845	40,011	18,441	60.8	3,088	1,405	7.2	7.2	7.1	74.6	57.3
South Atlantic.....	22,440	10,477	20,847	9,763	61.2	1,592	714	7.1	7.3	6.8	74.1	58.4
Delaware.......	372	175	352	167	65.5	20	8	5.3	5.9	4.6	77.1	62.3
Maryland.......	2,623	1,252	2,450	1,179	66.4	173	73	6.6	7.2	5.9	77.9	64.8
District of Columbia.	276	141	253	131	60.8	23	10	8.4	9.6	7.3	71.8	61.7
Virginia........	3,359	1,540	3,145	1,447	66.4	213	92	6.4	6.7	6.0	79.4	63.0
West Virginia....	766	321	679	294	48.3	86	27	11.3	13.3	8.5	66.3	43.7
North Carolina	3,487	1,645	3,281	1,546	64.0	207	100	5.9	5.8	6.0	76.1	60.8
South Carolina	1,772	825	1,662	771	62.3	111	54	6.2	6.0	6.6	74.9	58.8
Georgia.........	3,232	1,520	3,008	1,421	61.5	224	99	6.9	7.3	6.5	75.5	57.9
Florida........	6,553	3,058	6,017	2,808	56.8	536	250	8.2	8.2	8.2	69.7	54.8
East South Central..	7,304	3,349	6,791	3,101	58.0	513	248	7.0	6.7	7.4	71.9	53.9
Kentucky.......	1,744	780	1,624	734	57.6	120	46	6.9	7.7	5.9	71.8	52.8
Tennessee	2,440	1,142	2,285	1,063	59.4	155	79	6.4	5.9	6.9	72.4	55.6
Alabama.......	1,937	885	1,796	812	57.5	142	74	7.3	6.5	8.3	71.9	53.4
Mississippi......	1,182	542	1,086	492	56.6	96	50	8.1	7.2	9.2	71.3	53.1
West South Central .	13,355	6,018	12,372	5,576	61.8	983	442	7.4	7.4	7.4	76.8	57.4
Arkansas.......	1,149	533	1,066	495	58.9	83	38	7.2	7.2	7.2	72.6	55.4
Louisiana	1,934	881	1,778	811	56.9	156	70	8.1	8.2	7.9	71.9	53.1
Oklahoma	1,527	706	1,440	674	60.0	86	31	5.7	6.7	4.5	72.8	55.5
Texas.........	8,745	3,898	8,088	3,596	63.7	657	303	7.5	7.3	7.8	79.2	59.2
West	27,025	11,858	24,841	10,958	61.5	2,184	900	8.1	8.5	7.6	76.6	57.6
Mountain.........	6,868	3,106	6,427	2,915	63.0	442	191	6.4	6.7	6.1	76.1	59.1
Montana.......	411	193	384	181	64.0	28	12	6.7	7.1	6.2	74.5	63.0
Idaho	518	230	485	216	64.2	33	14	6.5	6.6	6.3	78.5	59.2
Wyoming........	240	107	227	101	66.6	14	6	5.6	5.9	5.3	78.5	62.5
Colorado.......	1,756	818	1,652	768	65.9	104	49	5.9	5.9	6.0	78.3	62.6
New Mexico.....	723	314	674	291	59.5	49	22	6.8	6.6	7.1	74.7	53.6
Arizona.......	1,734	782	1,605	732	58.3	129	50	7.4	8.3	6.4	71.4	55.1
Utah.........	811	365	771	346	67.0	40	18	4.9	4.9	5.0	80.6	61.0
Nevada........	673	297	629	279	65.2	45	18	6.6	7.0	6.1	78.0	61.7
Pacific...........	20,157	8,752	18,415	8,043	61.0	1,742	709	8.6	9.1	8.1	76.7	57.1
Washington	2,598	1,169	2,403	1,097	63.4	195	72	7.5	8.6	6.1	76.7	60.7
Oregon........	1,537	689	1,422	634	62.5	115	55	7.5	7.1	8.0	76.2	59.3
California.......	15,187	6,501	13,805	5,939	60.2	1,382	562	9.1	9.4	8.6	76.7	56.0
Alaska	262	122	238	112	66.1	24	9	9.1	10.3	7.7	80.6	65.7
Hawaii	572	271	547	260	65.7	26	11	4.5	4.8	4.2	76.5	61.9

[1] Civilian employment as a percent of civilian noninstitutional population.   [2] Percent unemployed of the civilian labor force.
[3] Percent of civilian noninstitutional population of each specified group in the civilian labor force.

Source: U.S. Bureau of Labor Statistics, *Geographic Profile of Employment and Unemployment, 1992.*

No. 627. Civilian Labor Force Status, by Selected Metropolitan Area: 1991

[In thousands, except rate. For the civilian noninstitutional population 16 years old and over. Annual averages of monthly figures. Except as noted, data are derived from the Local Area Unemployment Statistics Program. For composition of metropolitan areas, see Appendix II]

METROPOLITAN AREAS RANKED BY LABOR FORCE SIZE, 1991	Em-ployed	UNEMPLOYED		METROPOLITAN AREAS RANKED BY LABOR FORCE SIZE, 1991	Em-ployed	UNEMPLOYED	
		Total	Rate [1]			Total	Rate [1]
U.S. total	116,877	8,426	6.7	San Francisco, CA PMSA	827.7	41.7	4.8
Los Angeles-Long Beach, CA PMSA [2]	4,141.0	362.0	8.0	Kansas City, MO-Kansas City, KS MSA	812.1	48.5	5.6
New York, NY PMSA	3,643.5	319.2	8.1	San Jose, CA PMSA	770.1	44.8	5.5
Chicago, IL MSA	3,025.5	224.8	6.9	Cincinnati, OH-KY-IN PMSA	746.7	39.2	5.0
Philadelphia, PA-NJ PMSA	2,274.7	156.5	6.4	Sacramento, CA MSA	715.9	48.9	6.4
Washington, DC-MD-VA MSA	2,128.7	100.3	4.5	Milwaukee, WI PMSA	719.4	35.2	4.7
Detroit, MI PMSA	1,918.6	195.9	9.3	Columbus, OH MSA	709.3	34.5	4.6
Houston, TX PMSA	1,656.9	99.1	5.6	Fort Worth-Arlington, TX PMSA	689.7	47.8	6.5
Boston, MA PMSA	1,422.5	119.1	7.7	Portland, OR PMSA	666.0	32.9	4.7
Atlanta, GA MSA	1,434.1	71.0	4.7	Bergen-Passaic, NJ PMSA	647.9	42.9	6.2
Dallas, TX PMSA	1,353.6	86.3	6.0	Indianapolis, IN MSA	651.2	31.8	4.7
Minneapolis-St. Paul, MN-WI MSA	1,354.7	65.4	4.6	Fort Lauderdale-Hollywood-Pompano Beach, FL PMSA	623.7	49.8	7.4
Nassau-Suffolk, NY PMSA	1,283.7	82.4	6.0	Norfolk-Virginia Beach-Newport News, VA MSA	609.2	39.2	6.1
Anaheim-Santa Ana, CA PMSA	1,281.5	64.3	4.8	Charlotte-Gastonia-Rock Hill, NC-SC MSA	610.4	33.9	5.3
St. Louis, MO-IL MSA [3]	1,193.0	87.6	6.8	Orlando, FL MSA	600.0	41.5	6.5
Baltimore, MD MSA	1,132.6	79.6	6.6	San Antonio, TX MSA	566.9	39.8	6.6
San Diego, CA MSA	1,104.2	72.1	6.1	Middlesex-Somerset-Hunterdon, NJ PMSA	559.8	30.4	5.2
Seattle, WA PMSA	1,058.9	53.7	4.8	New Orleans, LA MSA	550.6	35.7	6.1
Oakland, CA PMSA	1,039.3	59.2	5.4	Nashville, TN MSA	502.1	27.1	5.1
Riverside-San Bernadino, CA PMSA	988.1	100.3	9.2	Greensboro-Winston-Salem-High Point, NC MSA	494.5	26.4	5.1
Phoenix, AZ MSA	1,003.5	51.4	4.9	Salt Lake City-Ogden, UT MSA	495.2	24.1	4.6
Tampa-St. Petersburg-Clearwater, FL MSA	955.2	65.3	6.4	Louisville, KY-IN MSA	481.7	31.3	6.1
Pittsburgh, PA PMSA	944.5	60.3	6.0	Rochester, NY MSA	487.4	25.5	5.0
Miami-Hialeah, FL PMSA	878.6	83.5	8.7	Mommouth-Ocean, NJ PMSA	460.6	31.7	6.4
Cleveland, OH PMSA	892.1	51.7	5.5				
Newark, NJ PMSA	873.7	64.6	6.9				
Denver, CO PMSA	851.6	41.1	4.6				

[1] Percent unemployed of the civilian labor force. [2] Derived from the Current Population Survey. [3] Excludes part of Sullivan City in Crawford County, Missouri.

Source: U.S. Bureau of Labor Statistics, *Employment and Earnings,* May 1992.

No. 628. Hispanic Persons—Civilian Labor Force Participation: 1991 and 1992

[For civilian noninstitutional population, 16 years old and over. Annual averages of monthly figures. Based on Current Population Survey; see text, section 1, and Appendix III]

ITEM	1991					1992				
	Total	Mex-ican	Puerto Rican	Cuban	Other His-panic origin [1]	Total	Mex-ican	Puerto Rican	Cuban	Other His-panic origin [1]
Total (1,000)	14,770	8,947	1,629	849	3,345	15,244	9,368	1,628	867	3,381
Percent in labor force:										
Male	80.1	81.2	71.8	75.7	82.0	80.5	82.0	69.9	73.2	82.5
Female	52.3	51.5	45.9	52.8	57.4	52.6	52.1	47.1	50.3	57.4
Employed (1,000)	8,799	5,363	822	499	2,115	8,971	5,581	802	488	2,100
Percent	100.0	100.0	100.0	100.0	100.0	100.0	100.0	100.0	100.0	100.0
Managerial and professional	13.0	10.4	17.9	25.1	15.1	13.4	10.8	18.2	25.1	16.0
Tech., sales, and admin. support.	24.5	22.5	32.0	33.1	24.8	24.8	23.2	31.8	32.5	24.8
Services	20.3	18.9	17.5	12.0	27.0	20.3	19.2	19.7	12.1	25.2
Precision production, craft, and repair	12.9	13.9	10.7	12.8	11.3	13.4	14.2	11.0	13.0	12.4
Operators, fabricators and laborers	23.5	25.9	20.7	15.6	20.1	22.2	24.4	18.1	15.4	19.6
Farming, forestry, and fishing	5.7	8.4	1.2	1.4	1.8	5.8	8.3	1.1	1.9	1.9
Percent of labor force unemployed:										
Male	10.1	10.6	12.4	7.7	8.5	11.5	11.7	15.6	7.1	10.5
Female	9.5	10.0	10.7	8.6	7.8	11.3	11.7	12.3	8.9	10.5

[1] Includes Central or South American and other Hispanic origin.

Source: U.S. Bureau of Labor Statistics, *Employment and Earnings,* monthly, January issues.

No. 629. Employment Status of the Civilian Noninstitutional Population, by Educational Attainment, Sex, Race, and Hispanic Origin: 1992

[In thousands, except rate. Annual averages of monthly figures, for civilian noninstitutional population 25 years old and over. Based on Current Population Survey; see text, section 1, and Appendix III]

EMPLOYMENT STATUS, SEX, AND RACE	Population 25 years and over	EDUCATIONAL ATTAINMENT			
		Less than a high school diploma	High school graduates, no college	Less than a bachelor's degree	College graduates
Civilian noninstitutional population, total [1]	160,646	32,397	57,420	36,050	34,780
Civilian labor force	106,530	13,191	37,993	27,089	28,257
Participation rate [2]	66.3	40.7	66.2	75.1	81.2
Employed	100,039	11,688	35,416	25,571	27,364
Unemployed	6,491	1,502	2,577	1,519	893
Unemployment rate	6.1	11.4	6.8	5.6	3.2
Men: Civilian noninstitutional population	76,194	15,070	25,516	16,782	18,827
Civilian labor force	58,393	8,105	19,914	14,038	16,336
Participation rate [2]	76.6	53.8	78.0	83.6	86.8
Employed	54,658	7,182	18,459	13,213	15,803
Unemployed	3,735	922	1,454	825	533
Unemployment rate	6.4	11.4	7.3	5.9	3.3
Women: Civilian noninstitutional population	84,452	17,327	31,904	19,268	15,953
Civilian labor force	48,138	5,086	18,080	13,051	11,920
Participation rate [2]	57.0	29.4	56.7	67.7	74.7
Employed	45,381	4,506	16,957	12,357	11,561
Unemployed	2,756	580	1,123	694	360
Unemployment rate	5.7	11.4	6.2	5.3	3.0
White: Civilian noninstitutional population	137,617	25,858	49,699	31,243	30,817
Civilian labor force	91,242	10,543	32,488	23,273	24,938
Participation rate [2]	66.3	40.8	65.4	74.5	80.9
Employed	86,260	9,417	30,552	22,104	24,187
Unemployed	4,982	1,126	1,936	1,168	751
Unemployment rate	5.5	10.7	6.0	5.0	3.0
Black: Civilian noninstitutional population	17,391	5,317	6,234	3,733	2,106
Civilian labor force	11,422	2,110	4,505	3,004	1,803
Participation rate [2]	65.7	39.7	72.3	80.5	85.6
Employed	10,175	1,792	3,950	2,709	1,724
Unemployed	1,246	318	555	294	79
Unemployment rate	10.9	15.1	12.3	9.8	4.4
Hispanic origin [3]: Civilian noninstitutional population	11,774	5,592	3,136	1,939	1,107
Civilian labor force	7,993	3,124	2,358	1,592	919
Participation rate [2]	67.9	55.9	75.2	82.1	83.0
Employed	7,212	2,724	2,145	1,469	873
Unemployed	781	400	213	122	46
Unemployment rate	9.8	12.8	9.0	7.7	5.0

[1] Includes other races, not shown separately.　[2] For definition, see footnote 3 table 626.　[3] Persons of Hispanic origin may be of any race.
Source: U.S. Bureau of Labor Statistics, unpublished data.

No. 630. School Enrollment and Labor Force Status of Civilians 16 to 24 Years Old, by Selected Characteristics: 1980 and 1991

[In thousands, except percent. As of October. Civilian noninstitutional population. Based on Current Population Survey; see text, section 1, and Appendix III]

CHARACTERISTIC	POPULATION		CIVILIAN LABOR FORCE			EMPLOYED		UNEMPLOYED		
	1980	1991	1980, total	1991		1980	1991	1980, total	1991	
				Total	Per-cent [1]				Total	Rate [2]
Total, 16 to 24 years [3]	37,103	31,188	24,918	20,248	64.9	21,454	17,524	3,464	2,724	13.5
Enrolled in school [3]	15,713	15,519	7,454	7,665	49.4	6,433	6,663	1,021	1,002	13.1
16 to 19 years	11,126	10,116	4,836	4,330	42.8	4,029	3,614	807	716	16.5
20 to 24 years	4,587	5,404	2,618	3,335	61.7	2,404	3,049	214	286	8.6
Male	7,997	7,836	3,825	3,728	47.6	3,259	3,220	566	508	13.6
Female	7,716	7,683	3,629	3,938	51.3	3,174	3,444	455	494	12.6
College level	7,664	8,294	3,996	4,846	58.4	3,632	4,412	364	433	9.0
Full-time	6,396	7,031	2,854	3,696	52.6	2,554	3,327	300	369	10.0
White	13,242	12,523	6,687	6,656	53.2	5,889	5,888	798	768	11.5
Below college	6,566	5,610	3,095	2,449	43.7	2,579	2,019	516	430	17.6
College level	6,678	6,913	3,592	4,207	60.9	3,310	3,869	282	338	8.0
Black	2,028	2,109	595	664	31.5	406	484	189	180	27.2
Below college	1,282	1,267	294	278	22.0	174	171	120	108	38.6
College level	747	841	300	385	45.8	230	313	70	73	18.9
Not enrolled [3]	21,390	15,669	17,464	12,583	80.3	15,021	10,861	2,443	1,722	13.7
White	18,103	12,728	15,121	10,491	82.4	13,318	9,325	1,803	1,166	11.1
Black	2,864	2,439	2,055	1,708	70.0	1,451	1,222	604	486	28.5

[1] Percent of civilian noninstitutional population.　[2] Percent of civilian labor force in each category.　[3] Includes other races, not shown separately.
Source: U.S. Bureau of Labor Statistics, Bulletin 2307; News, USDL 92-395, June 30, 1992; and unpublished data.

No. 631. Labor Force Participation Rates, by Marital Status, Sex, and Age: 1960 to 1992

[Annual averages of monthly figures. See table 626 for definition of participation rate. Based on Current Population Survey; see text, section 1, and Appendix III]

MARITAL STATUS AND YEAR	MALE PARTICIPATION RATE							FEMALE PARTICIPATION RATE						
	Total	16-19 years	20-24 years	25-34 years	35-44 years	45-64 years	65 and over	Total	16-19 years	20-24 years	25-34 years	35-44 years	45-64 years	65 and over
Single:														
1960...	69.8	42.6	80.3	91.5	88.6	80.1	31.2	58.6	30.2	77.2	83.4	82.9	79.8	24.3
1970...	65.5	54.6	73.8	87.9	86.2	75.7	25.2	56.8	44.7	73.0	81.4	78.6	73.0	19.7
1975...	68.7	57.9	77.9	86.7	83.2	69.9	21.0	59.8	49.6	72.5	80.8	78.6	68.3	15.8
1980...	72.6	59.9	81.3	89.2	82.2	66.9	16.8	64.4	53.6	75.2	83.3	76.9	65.6	13.9
1985...	73.8	56.3	81.5	89.4	84.6	65.5	15.6	66.6	52.3	76.3	82.4	80.8	67.9	9.8
1987...	74.2	55.6	82.1	89.7	84.9	63.9	17.1	67.4	53.5	76.9	82.6	81.3	62.8	9.6
1988...	74.7	56.5	82.1	89.6	84.5	62.7	15.8	67.7	53.7	76.5	82.8	81.9	65.7	10.4
1989...	75.5	57.4	82.5	90.0	84.6	64.6	18.2	68.0	54.1	76.4	82.2	81.6	66.3	11.4
1990...	74.9	55.1	81.5	89.9	84.6	67.1	15.7	66.9	51.8	74.7	81.2	81.0	66.1	12.2
1991...	74.2	52.6	80.6	89.6	84.8	66.8	14.0	66.5	50.3	73.5	80.3	81.2	68.4	12.7
1992...	74.6	52.9	80.7	89.8	84.9	67.6	16.3	66.4	49.2	73.7	80.5	80.6	68.2	11.3
Married:[1]														
1960...	89.2	91.5	97.1	98.8	98.6	93.7	36.6	31.9	27.2	31.7	28.8	37.2	36.0	6.7
1970...	86.1	92.3	94.7	98.0	98.1	91.2	29.9	40.5	37.8	47.9	38.8	46.8	44.0	7.3
1975...	83.0	92.9	95.3	97.4	97.1	86.8	23.3	44.3	46.2	57.0	48.4	52.0	43.8	7.0
1980...	80.9	91.3	96.9	97.5	97.2	84.3	20.5	49.8	49.3	61.4	58.8	61.8	46.9	7.3
1985...	78.7	91.0	95.6	97.4	96.8	81.7	16.8	53.8	49.6	65.7	65.8	68.1	49.4	6.6
1987...	78.7	88.5	96.1	97.3	96.6	81.8	17.5	55.9	51.7	67.1	67.7	71.3	51.8	7.2
1988...	78.6	91.1	95.9	97.1	96.7	82.1	17.8	56.7	51.8	66.8	68.1	72.3	53.5	7.6
1989...	78.5	93.7	95.9	97.2	96.8	82.4	17.8	57.8	51.9	65.7	69.0	73.5	55.5	8.1
1990...	78.2	92.3	95.6	96.9	96.8	82.5	17.6	58.4	50.0	66.5	69.8	74.0	56.5	8.5
1991...	77.8	93.2	95.4	96.6	96.6	82.3	16.8	58.5	48.7	65.0	70.1	74.3	57.1	8.3
1992...	77.6	90.2	94.8	96.6	96.2	82.7	17.2	59.2	49.0	66.3	70.9	74.8	58.6	7.9
Other:[2]														
1960...	63.1	(B)	96.9	95.2	94.4	83.2	22.7	41.6	43.5	58.0	63.1	70.0	60.0	11.4
1970...	60.7	(B)	90.4	93.7	91.1	78.5	19.3	40.3	48.6	60.3	64.6	68.8	61.9	10.0
1975...	63.4	(B)	88.8	92.4	89.4	73.4	15.4	40.1	47.6	65.3	68.6	69.2	59.0	8.3
1980...	67.5	(B)	92.6	94.1	91.9	73.3	13.7	43.6	50.0	68.4	76.5	77.1	60.2	8.2
1985...	68.7	(B)	95.1	93.7	91.8	72.8	11.4	45.1	51.9	66.2	76.9	81.6	61.0	7.5
1987...	67.3	(B)	92.2	93.9	90.9	72.5	11.6	45.7	46.9	67.4	77.6	82.7	62.7	7.3
1988...	67.2	(B)	92.5	93.4	90.8	72.5	11.7	46.2	54.2	66.2	77.2	82.1	63.6	7.9
1989...	67.9	(B)	91.1	93.6	90.9	74.2	11.7	47.0	48.2	65.8	78.3	82.2	64.7	8.3
1990...	68.3	(B)	93.1	93.0	90.8	74.6	12.0	47.2	54.4	65.6	77.3	82.3	65.0	8.5
1991...	67.7	(B)	93.9	92.1	90.5	73.5	12.3	46.8	45.8	63.3	74.8	82.1	65.2	8.4
1992...	68.0	(B)	91.8	93.5	90.3	74.7	12.2	47.0	47.8	66.9	75.7	81.6	66.4	8.4

B For 1960, percentage not shown where base is less than 50,000; beginning 1970, 35,000.   [1] Spouse present.
[2] Widowed, divorced, and married (spouse absent).
Source: U.S. Bureau of Labor Statistics, Bulletins 2217 and 2340; and unpublished data.

No. 632. Marital Status of Women in the Civilian Labor Force: 1960 to 1992

[Annual averages of monthly figures. For civilian noninstitutional population 16 years old and over. Based on Current Population Survey; see text, section 1, and Appendix III. See also *Historical Statistics, Colonial Times to 1970*, series D 49-62]

YEAR	FEMALE LABOR FORCE (1,000)				PERCENT DISTRIBUTION, FEMALE LABOR FORCE			FEMALE LABOR FORCE AS PERCENT OF FEMALE POPULATION			
	Total	Single	Married[1]	Other[2]	Single	Married[1]	Other[2]	Total	Single	Married[1]	Other[2]
1960	23,240	5,410	12,893	4,937	23.3	55.5	21.2	37.7	58.6	31.9	41.6
1965	26,200	5,976	14,829	5,396	22.8	56.6	20.6	39.3	54.5	34.9	40.7
1970	31,543	7,265	18,475	5,804	23.0	58.6	18.4	43.3	56.8	40.5	40.3
1975	37,475	9,125	21,484	6,866	24.3	57.3	18.3	46.3	59.8	44.3	40.1
1976	38,983	9,689	22,139	7,156	24.9	56.8	18.4	47.3	61.0	45.3	40.5
1977	40,613	10,311	22,776	7,526	25.4	56.1	18.5	48.4	62.1	46.4	41.5
1978	42,631	11,067	23,539	8,025	26.0	55.2	18.8	50.0	63.7	47.8	42.8
1979	44,235	11,597	24,378	8,260	26.2	55.1	18.7	50.9	64.6	49.0	43.1
1980	45,487	11,865	24,980	8,643	26.1	54.9	19.0	51.5	64.4	49.9	43.6
1981	46,696	12,124	25,428	9,144	26.0	54.5	19.6	52.1	64.5	50.5	44.6
1982	47,755	12,460	25,971	9,324	26.1	54.4	19.5	52.6	65.1	51.1	44.8
1983	48,503	12,659	26,468	9,376	26.1	54.6	19.3	52.9	65.0	51.8	44.4
1984	49,709	12,867	27,199	9,644	25.9	54.7	19.4	53.6	65.6	52.8	44.7
1985	51,050	13,163	27,894	9,993	25.8	54.6	19.6	54.5	66.6	53.8	45.1
1986	52,413	13,512	28,623	10,277	25.8	54.6	19.6	55.3	67.2	54.9	45.6
1987	53,658	13,885	29,381	10,393	25.9	54.8	19.4	56.0	67.4	55.9	45.7
1988	54,742	14,194	29,921	10,627	25.9	54.7	19.4	56.6	67.7	56.7	46.2
1989	56,030	14,377	30,548	11,104	25.7	54.5	19.8	57.4	68.0	57.8	47.0
1990	56,554	14,229	30,970	11,354	25.2	54.8	20.1	57.5	66.9	58.4	47.2
1991	56,893	14,295	31,175	11,423	25.1	54.8	20.1	57.3	66.5	58.5	46.8
1992	57,798	14,477	31,720	11,601	25.0	54.9	20.1	57.8	66.4	59.2	47.0

[1] Husband present.   [2] Widowed, divorced, or separated.
Source: U.S. Bureau of Labor Statistics, Bulletin 2307; and unpublished data.

No. 633. Women in the Civilian Labor Force, by Marital Status and Presence and Age of Children: 1960 to 1992

[As of **March.** For 1960, civilian noninstitutional persons 14 years and over, thereafter 16 years old and over. Based on Current Population Survey; see text, section 1, and Appendix III]

| ITEM | TOTAL | | | WITH ANY CHILDREN | | | | | | | | |
| | | | | Total | | | Children 6 to 17 only | | | Children under 6 | | |
	Single	Mar-ried [1]	Other [2]	Single	Mar-ried [1]	Other [2]	Single	Mar-ried [1]	Other [2]	Single	Mar-ried [1]	Other [2]
IN LABOR FORCE (mil.)												
1960	5.4	12.3	4.9	(NA)	6.6	1.5	(NA)	4.1	1.0	(NA)	2.5	0.4
1970	7.0	18.4	5.9	(NA)	10.2	1.9	(NA)	6.3	1.3	(NA)	3.9	0.6
1980	11.2	24.9	8.8	0.6	13.7	3.6	0.2	8.4	2.6	0.3	5.2	1.0
1985	12.9	27.7	10.3	1.1	14.9	4.0	0.4	8.5	2.9	0.7	6.4	1.1
1987	13.5	29.2	10.4	1.4	16.0	4.1	0.5	9.0	2.9	0.9	7.0	1.1
1988	13.8	29.7	10.6	1.4	16.2	4.0	0.5	9.3	2.9	0.8	7.0	1.1
1989	14.0	30.5	10.7	1.5	16.4	4.0	0.6	9.4	2.8	1.0	7.0	1.1
1990	14.0	31.0	11.2	1.5	16.5	4.2	0.6	9.3	3.0	0.9	7.2	1.2
1991	14.1	31.1	11.1	1.7	16.6	4.1	0.6	9.1	3.0	1.1	7.4	1.2
1992	14.1	31.7	11.5	1.7	16.8	4.2	0.7	9.5	3.0	1.0	7.3	1.2
PARTICIPATION RATE [3]												
1960	44.1	30.5	40.0	(NA)	27.6	56.0	(NA)	39.0	65.9	(NA)	18.6	40.5
1970	53.0	40.8	39.1	(NA)	39.7	60.7	(NA)	49.2	66.9	(NA)	30.3	52.2
1980	61.5	50.1	44.0	52.0	54.1	69.4	67.6	61.7	74.6	44.1	45.1	60.3
1985	65.2	54.2	45.6	51.6	60.8	71.9	64.1	67.8	77.8	46.5	53.4	59.7
1987	65.1	55.8	45.7	54.1	63.8	73.4	64.1	70.6	78.6	49.9	56.8	62.7
1988	65.4	56.6	46.1	51.6	65.0	72.0	66.7	72.5	77.5	44.9	57.1	60.6
1989	66.0	57.6	46.0	54.7	65.6	72.0	69.0	73.4	78.2	48.9	57.4	60.1
1990	66.4	58.2	46.8	55.2	66.3	74.2	69.7	73.6	79.7	48.7	58.9	63.6
1991	65.1	58.5	46.2	53.6	66.8	72.7	64.8	73.6	79.5	48.8	59.9	59.8
1992	64.7	59.3	46.7	52.5	67.8	73.2	67.2	75.4	80.0	45.8	59.9	60.5
EMPLOYMENT (mil.)												
1960	5.1	11.6	4.6	(NA)	6.2	1.3	(NA)	3.9	0.9	(NA)	2.3	0.4
1970	6.5	17.5	5.6	(NA)	9.6	1.8	(NA)	6.0	1.2	(NA)	3.6	0.6
1980	10.1	23.6	8.2	0.4	12.8	3.3	0.2	8.1	2.4	0.2	4.8	0.9
1985	11.6	26.1	9.4	0.9	13.9	3.5	0.3	8.1	2.6	0.5	5.9	0.9
1987	12.1	27.8	9.6	1.0	15.1	3.7	0.4	8.6	2.7	0.6	6.5	1.0
1988	12.6	28.5	9.9	1.1	15.4	3.6	0.4	8.9	2.7	0.6	6.5	1.0
1989	12.8	29.4	10.1	1.2	15.8	3.6	0.5	9.1	2.6	0.7	6.7	1.0
1990	12.9	29.9	10.5	1.2	15.8	3.8	0.5	8.9	2.7	0.7	6.9	1.1
1991	12.9	29.7	10.4	1.4	15.7	3.7	0.5	8.8	2.7	0.8	6.9	1.0
1992	12.8	30.1	10.6	1.4	15.9	3.7	0.6	9.1	2.7	0.8	6.8	1.0
UNEMPLOY-MENT RATE [4]												
1960	6.0	5.4	6.2	(NA)	6.0	8.4	(NA)	4.9	6.8	(NA)	7.8	12.5
1970	7.1	4.8	4.8	(NA)	6.0	7.2	(NA)	4.8	5.9	(NA)	7.9	9.8
1980	10.3	5.3	6.4	23.2	5.9	9.2	15.6	4.4	7.9	29.2	8.3	12.8
1985	10.2	5.7	8.5	23.8	6.6	12.1	15.4	5.5	10.6	28.5	8.0	16.1
1987	10.2	4.5	7.5	25.6	5.4	10.1	17.6	4.9	8.4	29.9	5.9	14.5
1988	8.6	4.0	5.9	22.4	4.8	8.1	17.8	3.8	6.6	25.3	6.1	12.0
1989	8.1	3.4	5.7	21.3	3.8	8.4	14.3	3.7	7.2	25.3	4.1	11.3
1990	8.2	3.5	5.7	18.4	4.2	8.5	14.5	3.8	7.7	20.8	4.8	10.2
1991	8.8	4.6	6.8	17.9	5.3	9.1	10.7	4.2	7.7	22.0	6.7	12.7
1992	9.1	4.9	7.6	17.3	5.7	10.8	14.1	4.6	8.6	19.4	7.0	16.3

NA Not available. [1] Husband present. [2] Widowed, divorced or separated. [3] Percent of women in each specific category in the labor force. [4] Unemployed as a percent of civilian labor force in specified group.
Source: U.S. Bureau of Labor Statistics, Bulletin 2307; and unpublished data.

No. 634. Labor Force Participation Rates for Wives, Husband Present, by Age of Own Youngest Child: 1975 to 1992

[As of **March,** except as indicated. For civilian noninstitutional population, 16 years old and over. For definition of participation rate, see table 633. Based on Current Population Survey; see text, section 1, and Appendix III]

| PRESENCE AND AGE OF CHILD | TOTAL | | | | WHITE | | | | BLACK | | | |
	1975	1985	1990	1992	1975	1985	1990	1992	1975	1985	1990	1992
Wives, total . . .	44.4	54.2	58.2	59.3	43.6	53.3	57.6	58.7	54.1	63.8	64.7	66.8
No children under 18. .	43.8	48.2	51.1	51.9	43.6	47.5	50.8	51.5	47.6	55.2	52.9	56.8
With children under 18.	44.9	60.8	66.3	67.8	43.6	59.9	65.6	67.3	58.4	71.7	75.6	76.0
Under 6, total	36.7	53.4	58.9	59.9	34.7	52.1	57.8	59.1	54.9	69.6	73.1	73.5
Under 3	32.7	50.5	55.5	57.5	30.7	49.4	54.9	56.7	50.1	66.2	67.5	70.8
1 year or under .	30.8	49.4	53.9	56.7	29.2	48.6	53.3	55.9	50.0	63.7	64.4	68.7
2 years	37.1	54.0	60.9	60.9	35.1	52.7	60.3	59.8	56.4	69.9	75.4	75.0
3 to 5 years	42.2	58.4	64.1	63.5	40.1	56.6	62.5	62.7	61.2	73.8	80.4	77.1
3 years	41.2	55.1	63.1	63.5	39.0	52.7	62.3	61.8	62.7	72.3	74.5	77.6
4 years	41.2	59.7	65.1	62.1	38.7	58.4	63.2	61.0	64.9	70.6	80.6	76.9
5 years	44.4	62.1	64.5	65.7	43.8	59.9	62.0	65.2	56.3	79.1	86.2	80.3
6 to 13 years	51.8	68.2	73.0	74.9	50.7	67.7	72.6	74.5	65.7	73.3	77.6	79.7
14 to 17 years	53.5	67.0	75.1	76.6	53.4	66.6	74.9	76.9	52.3	74.4	78.8	74.0

Source: U.S. Bureau of Labor Statistics, Bulletin 2340; and unpublished data.

No. 635. Civilian Labor Force—Employment Status, by Sex, Race, and Age: 1992

[For civilian noninstitutional population 16 years old and over. Annual averages of monthly figures. Based on Current Population Survey; see text, section 1, and Appendix III]

| AGE AND RACE | CIVILIAN LABOR FORCE | | | MALE (1,000) | | | FEMALE (1,000) | | | PERCENT OF LABOR FORCE | | | |
| | Total (1,000) | Percent by age | | Total | Em-ployed | Un-em-ployed | Total | Em-ployed | Un-em-ployed | Employed | | Unemployed | |
		Male	Fe-male							Male	Fe-male	Male	Fe-male
All workers [1]	126,982	100.0	100.0	69,184	63,805	5,380	57,798	53,793	4,005	92.2	93.1	7.8	6.9
16 to 19 years . . .	6,751	5.1	5.5	3,547	2,786	761	3,204	2,613	591	78.5	81.6	21.5	18.5
20 to 24 years . . .	13,703	10.5	11.2	7,242	6,357	884	6,461	5,799	662	87.8	89.8	12.2	10.2
25 to 34 years . . .	35,103	28.0	27.2	19,355	17,847	1,508	15,748	14,594	1,154	92.2	92.7	7.8	7.3
35 to 44 years . . .	33,603	26.3	26.7	18,162	17,067	1,095	15,441	14,595	845	94.0	94.5	6.0	5.5
45 to 54 years . . .	22,391	17.5	17.8	12,101	11,426	675	10,290	9,820	470	94.4	95.4	5.6	4.6
55 to 64 years . . .	11,870	9.7	8.9	6,701	6,314	387	5,169	4,953	216	94.2	95.8	5.8	4.2
65 years and over .	3,562	3.0	2.6	2,077	2,008	69	1,485	1,419	66	96.7	95.6	3.3	4.5
White	108,526	100.0	100.0	59,830	55,709	4,121	48,696	45,770	2,926	93.1	94.0	6.9	6.0
16 to 19 years . . .	5,744	5.0	5.6	3,019	2,464	555	2,726	2,297	429	81.6	84.3	18.4	15.7
20 to 24 years . . .	11,539	10.2	11.2	6,097	5,462	634	5,442	4,993	450	89.6	91.7	10.4	8.3
25 to 34 years . . .	29,539	27.6	26.8	16,510	15,364	1,146	13,029	12,222	807	93.1	93.8	6.9	6.2
35 to 44 years . . .	28,715	26.3	26.6	15,765	14,907	858	12,949	12,324	625	94.6	95.2	5.4	4.8
45 to 54 years . . .	19,411	17.8	18.0	10,652	10,106	546	8,759	8,384	375	94.9	95.7	5.1	4.3
55 to 64 years . . .	10,377	9.9	9.2	5,906	5,584	322	4,471	4,291	180	94.5	96.0	5.5	4.0
65 years and over .	3,201	3.1	2.7	1,881	1,822	59	1,319	1,260	59	96.9	95.5	3.1	4.5
Black	13,891	100.0	100.0	6,892	5,846	1,046	6,999	6,087	912	84.8	87.0	15.2	13.0
16 to 19 years . . .	787	6.1	5.3	419	243	176	368	231	137	58.0	62.8	42.0	37.2
20 to 24 years . . .	1,683	12.7	11.6	872	658	214	811	623	187	75.5	76.8	24.5	23.1
25 to 34 years . . .	4,251	30.8	30.4	2,121	1,820	302	2,130	1,830	300	85.8	85.9	14.2	14.1
35 to 44 years . . .	3,623	25.1	27.1	1,729	1,534	194	1,894	1,709	186	88.7	90.2	11.2	9.8
45 to 54 years . . .	2,143	14.8	16.1	1,018	913	105	1,124	1,052	72	89.7	93.6	10.3	6.4
55 to 64 years . . .	1,124	8.5	7.7	586	539	47	538	515	23	92.0	95.7	8.0	4.2
65 years and over .	280	2.1	1.9	146	139	7	134	128	7	95.2	95.5	4.9	4.9
Hispanic [2] . . .	10,131	100.0	100.0	6,091	5,388	703	4,040	3,584	456	88.5	88.7	11.5	11.3
16 to 19 years . . .	678	6.4	7.1	391	281	110	287	211	76	71.9	73.5	28.2	26.4
20 to 24 years . . .	1,460	14.6	14.1	890	768	122	570	500	71	86.3	87.7	13.7	12.4
25 to 34 years . . .	3,316	34.1	30.7	2,075	1,866	209	1,241	1,103	137	89.9	88.9	10.1	11.1
35 to 44 years . . .	2,548	24.3	26.4	1,481	1,336	145	1,066	962	104	90.2	90.2	9.8	9.7
45 to 54 years . . .	1,358	13.0	14.1	790	720	71	568	519	49	91.1	91.4	8.9	8.5
55 to 64 years . . .	655	6.4	6.5	392	352	40	263	246	16	89.8	93.5	10.3	6.2
65 years and over .	116	1.2	1.1	71	65	6	45	41	4	91.5	91.1	7.8	8.8

[1] Includes other races not shown separately.   [2] Persons of Hispanic origin may be of any race.

Source: U.S. Bureau of Labor Statistics, *Employment and Earnings*, monthly, January 1992.

No. 636. Employed Civilians and Weekly Hours, by Selected Characteristics: 1970 to 1992

[In thousands, except as indicated. For civilian noninstitutional population 16 years old and over. Annual averages of monthly figures. Based on Current Population Survey; see text, section 1, and Appendix III]

AGE, SEX, AND MARITAL STATUS	1970	1980	1986	1987	1988	1989	1990	1991	1992
Total employed	78,678	99,303	109,597	112,440	114,968	117,342	117,914	116,877	117,598
Age:									
16 to 19 years old	6,144	7,710	6,472	6,640	6,805	6,759	6,261	5,628	5,398
20 to 24 years old	9,731	14,087	13,790	13,524	13,244	12,962	12,622	12,233	12,157
25 to 34 years old	16,318	27,204	32,201	33,105	33,574	34,045	33,831	32,914	32,441
35 to 44 years old	15,922	19,523	25,861	27,179	28,269	29,443	30,543	31,286	31,662
45 to 54 years old	16,473	16,234	16,949	17,487	18,447	19,279	19,765	20,164	21,246
55 to 64 years old	10,974	11,586	11,405	11,465	11,433	11,499	11,464	11,268	11,267
65 years old and over	3,118	2,960	2,919	3,041	3,197	3,355	3,428	3,384	3,427
Sex: Male	48,990	57,186	60,892	62,107	63,273	64,315	64,435	63,593	63,805
Female	29,688	42,117	48,706	50,334	51,696	53,027	53,479	53,284	53,793
Marital status:									
Married, spouse present	55,554	62,536	66,802	68,372	69,228	70,164	70,624	70,196	70,440
Single (never married)	15,039	24,082	27,478	28,355	29,500	30,111	29,761	29,278	29,454
Widowed, divorced, separated	8,087	12,684	15,318	15,713	16,242	17,066	17,531	17,403	17,705
Class of worker:									
Nonagriculture	75,215	95,938	106,434	109,232	111,800	114,142	114,728	113,644	114,391
Wage and salary worker	69,491	88,525	98,299	100,771	103,021	105,259	105,715	104,520	105,540
Self-employed	5,221	7,000	7,881	8,201	8,519	8,605	8,760	8,899	8,619
Unpaid family workers	502	413	255	260	260	279	252	225	232
Agriculture	3,463	3,364	3,163	3,208	3,169	3,199	3,186	3,233	3,207
Wage and salary worker	1,154	1,425	1,547	1,632	1,621	1,665	1,679	1,673	1,696
Self-employed	1,810	1,642	1,447	1,423	1,398	1,403	1,400	1,442	1,398
Unpaid family workers	499	297	169	153	150	131	107	118	113
Weekly hours:									
Nonagriculture:									
Wage and salary workers	38.3	38.1	38.8	38.7	39.1	39.3	39.2	39.0	38.8
Self-employed	45.0	41.2	41.2	41.0	41.0	41.1	40.8	40.4	40.1
Unpaid family workers	37.9	34.7	35.5	36.3	36.0	35.1	33.9	35.4	34.5
Agriculture:									
Wage and salary workers	40.0	41.6	40.9	40.6	41.3	41.4	41.3	41.0	40.6
Self-employed	51.0	49.3	48.4	47.8	47.5	47.9	46.9	46.8	47.1
Unpaid family workers	40.0	38.6	39.7	39.9	39.7	39.4	38.5	40.3	40.5

Source: U.S. Bureau of Labor Statistics, *Employment and Earnings*, monthly, January issues; and unpublished data.

No. 637. Self-Employed Workers, by Selected Characteristics: 1970 to 1992

[In thousands. For civilian noninstitutional population 16 years old and over. Annual averages of monthly figures. Data for 1992 are not fully comparable with data for prior years because of the introduction of the occupational and industrial classification used in the 1990 Census. Based on the Current Population Survey; see text, section 1, and Appendix III]

ITEM	1970	1975	1980	1985	1988	1989	1990	1991	1992
Total self-employed	**7,031**	**7,427**	**8,642**	**9,269**	**9,917**	**10,008**	**10,160**	**10,341**	**10,017**
Industry:									
Agriculture	1,810	1,722	1,642	1,458	1,398	1,403	1,400	1,442	1,398
Nonagriculture	5,221	5,705	7,000	7,811	8,519	8,605	8,760	8,899	8,619
Mining	14	16	28	20	28	26	24	23	23
Construction	687	839	1,173	1,301	1,427	1,423	1,463	1,447	1,466
Manufacturing	264	273	358	347	394	406	429	420	392
Transportation and public utilities	196	223	282	315	345	323	302	318	337
Trade	1,667	1,709	1,899	1,792	1,823	1,882	1,859	1,879	1,776
Finance, insurance, and real estate	254	335	458	558	624	621	635	619	630
Services	2,140	2,310	2,804	3,477	3,878	3,924	4,048	4,193	3,995
Occupation:									
Managerial and professional specialty	(NA)	(NA)	(NA)	2,585	2,929	3,059	3,067	3,117	2,919
Technical, sales, and administrative support	(NA)	(NA)	(NA)	2,059	2,155	2,195	2,252	2,245	2,192
Service occupations	(NA)	(NA)	(NA)	980	1,159	1,146	1,213	1,273	1,079
Precision production, craft, and repair	(NA)	(NA)	(NA)	1,611	1,674	1,648	1,680	1,697	1,803
Operators, fabricators, and laborers	(NA)	(NA)	(NA)	568	604	585	568	584	626
Farming, forestry, and fishing	(NA)	(NA)	(NA)	1,465	1,395	1,376	1,380	1,427	1,390

NA Not available.
Source: U.S. Bureau of Labor Statistics, Bulletin 2307; *Employment and Earnings*, monthly, January issues; and unpublished data.

No. 638. Persons With a Job But Not at Work: 1970 to 1992

[In thousands, except percent. For civilian noninstitutional population 16 years old and over. Annual averages of monthly figures. Based on Current Population Survey; see text, section 1, and Appendix III. See *Historical Statistics, Colonial Times to 1970*, series D 116-126, for related but not comparable data]

REASON FOR NOT WORKING	1970	1975	1980	1985	1987	1988	1989	1990	1991	1992 Total	1992 Male	1992 Female
All industries, number	**4,645**	**5,221**	**5,881**	**5,789**	**5,910**	**5,831**	**6,170**	**6,157**	**5,909**	**6,082**	**2,823**	**3,259**
Percent of employed	**5.9**	**6.1**	**5.9**	**5.4**	**5.3**	**5.1**	**5.3**	**5.2**	**5.1**	**5.2**	**4.4**	**6.1**
Reason for not working:												
Vacation	2,341	2,815	3,320	3,338	3,421	3,236	3,437	3,531	3,297	3,414	1,553	1,861
Illness	1,324	1,343	1,426	1,308	1,320	1,364	1,405	1,341	1,302	1,258	610	648
Bad weather	128	139	155	141	92	122	133	89	118	126	116	10
Industrial dispute	156	95	105	42	34	30	63	24	17	19	12	7
All other	696	829	876	960	1,043	1,080	1,132	1,172	1,175	1,265	532	733

Source: U.S. Bureau of Labor Statistics, *Employment and Earnings*, monthly, January issues; and unpublished data.

No. 639. Employed and Unemployed Workers, by Work Schedules, Sex, and Age: 1980 to 1992

[In thousands. See headnote, table 638]

CHARACTERISTIC	EMPLOYED 1980	EMPLOYED 1985	EMPLOYED 1990	EMPLOYED 1992	CHARACTERISTIC	UNEMPLOYED 1980	UNEMPLOYED 1985	UNEMPLOYED 1990	UNEMPLOYED 1992
Total	**99,303**	**107,150**	**117,914**	**117,598**	**Total**	**7,637**	**8,312**	**6,874**	**9,384**
Full-time [1]	82,562	88,534	97,994	97,026	Looking for full-time work	6,269	6,793	5,541	7,746
Male	51,717	53,862	57,982	56,897	Male	3,703	3,925	3,264	4,699
16 to 19 years old	2,017	1,437	1,343	1,019	16 to 19 years old	537	446	328	360
20 to 24 years old	6,533	6,078	5,452	4,955	20 to 24 years old	994	857	582	772
25 to 54 years old	35,644	39,207	44,229	44,160	25 to 54 years old	1,923	2,329	2,098	3,169
55 years and over	7,521	7,139	6,959	6,763	55 years and over	250	292	255	397
Female	30,845	34,672	40,011	40,129	Female	2,564	2,868	2,277	3,047
16 to 19 years old	1,456	1,069	975	720	16 to 19 years old	430	331	233	254
20 to 24 years old	5,098	4,903	4,386	3,978	20 to 24 years old	636	636	439	509
25 to 54 years old	20,395	24,838	30,485	31,307	25 to 54 years old	1,363	1,727	1,491	2,087
55 years and over	3,897	3,862	4,166	4,123	55 years and over	135	173	115	198
Part-time [1]	16,740	18,615	19,920	20,572	Looking for part-time work	1,369	1,519	1,332	1,638
Male	5,471	6,028	6,452	6,907	Male	563	596	535	681
16 to 19 years old	2,068	1,891	1,894	1,767	16 to 19 years old	377	360	301	401
20 to 24 years old	999	1,261	1,174	1,402	20 to 24 years old	81	87	84	112
25 to 54 years old	1,092	1,568	1,842	2,180	25 to 54 years old	54	79	89	109
55 years and over	1,314	1,308	1,543	1,559	55 years and over	52	70	61	59
Female	11,270	12,587	13,468	13,664	Female	806	923	797	957
16 to 19 years old	2,169	2,036	2,049	1,892	16 to 19 years old	326	330	286	338
20 to 24 years old	1,456	1,738	1,611	1,821	20 to 24 years old	124	158	116	153
25 to 54 years old	5,827	6,837	7,584	7,702	25 to 54 years old	299	359	323	382
55 years and over	1,815	1,976	2,224	2,248	55 years and over	57	75	72	84

[1] Full-time workers include employed persons on full-time (35 hours or more per week) schedules and those working part-time (between 1 and 34 hours) for economic reasons who usually work full-time. Part-time workers include employed persons working part-time voluntarily and those working part-time for economic reasons, who usually work part-time. Employed persons with a job but not at work are distributed according to whether they usually work full- or part-time.
Source: U.S. Bureau of Labor Statistics, Bulletin 2307; and *Employment and Earnings*, monthly, January issues.

No. 640. Multiple Jobholders, by Industry and Occupation: 1991

[As of May. Multiple jobholders are employed persons who, either 1) had jobs as wage or salary workers with two employers or more; 2) were self-employed and also held a wage and salary job; or 3) were unpaid family workers on their primary jobs but also held wage and salary job. Based on the Current Population Survey; see text, section 1, and Appendix III]

CHARACTERISTIC	TOTAL			MALE			FEMALE		
	Employed	Multiple jobholders		Employed	Multiple jobholders		Employed	Multiple jobholders	
		Number	Rate [1]		Number	Rate [1]		Number	Rate [1]
Total, 16 years and over	116,626	7,183	6.2	63,499	4,054	6.4	53,127	3,129	5.9
Industry and class of worker of primary job:									
Agriculture	3,466	179	5.2	2,737	139	5.1	728	41	5.6
Nonagricultural industries............	113,160	7,003	6.2	60,762	3,915	6.4	52,399	3,088	5.9
Wage and salary workers	104,193	6,691	6.4	55,063	3,733	6.8	49,129	2,958	6.0
Mining	737	25	3.4	592	17	2.8	145	8	5.8
Construction	5,745	271	4.7	5,231	239	4.6	514	33	6.4
Manufacturing	19,993	1,044	5.2	13,497	798	5.9	6,496	245	3.8
Durable goods	11,669	628	5.4	8,562	506	5.9	3,107	122	3.9
Nondurable goods............	8,324	416	5.0	4,935	292	5.9	3,390	123	3.6
Transportation and public utilities	7,848	487	6.2	5,526	356	6.4	2,321	131	5.6
Wholesale trade.	4,255	261	6.1	3,010	190	6.3	1,245	70	5.7
Retail trade	17,250	914	5.3	8,354	444	5.3	8,896	470	5.3
Finance, insurance, and real estate ...	7,066	414	5.9	2,860	187	6.5	4,206	227	5.4
Services	35,592	2,747	7.7	12,719	1,125	8.8	22,873	1,622	7.1
Public administration............	5,709	528	9.3	3,274	376	11.5	2,434	152	6.2
Self-employed workers............	8,733	306	3.5	5,663	182	3.2	3,070	123	4.0
Unpaid family workers	235	7	2.9	36	-	-	199	7	3.4
Occupation of primary job:									
Managerial and professional specialty...	31,154	2,259	7.3	16,678	1,269	7.6	14,476	990	6.8
Technical, sales, and admin. support ...	36,002	2,154	6.0	12,584	803	6.4	23,418	1,351	5.8
Service occupations	15,534	1,063	6.8	6,252	527	8.4	9,282	536	5.8
Precision production, craft, and repair. .	13,115	652	5.0	12,019	608	5.1	1,096	44	4.0
Operators, fabricators, and laborers	17,065	851	5.0	12,804	682	5.3	4,261	169	4.0
Farming, forestry, and fishing	3,756	203	5.4	3,162	164	5.2	594	39	6.6

- Represents or rounds to zero.   [1] Multiple jobholders as a percent of all employed persons in specified group.
Source: U.S. Bureau of Labor Statistics, *News*, USDL 91-547, October 28, 1991.

No. 641. Workers on Flexible Schedules, 1985 and 1991 and by Selected Characteristics: 1991

[In thousands, except percent. As of May. For employed persons 16 years old and over who usually work full-time and who were at work during the survey reference week. A flexible schedule allows workers to vary the time they begin and end their work day. Based on Current Population Survey; see text, section 1, and Appendix III]

CHARACTERISTIC	ALL WORKERS			WORKERS WITH FLEXIBLE SCHEDULES					
				Number			Percent		
	Total	Male	Female	Total	Male	Female	Total	Male	Female
Total, 1985	73,395	43,779	29,616	9,061	5,760	3,300	12.3	13.2	11.1
Total, 1991...............	80,452	46,308	34,145	12,118	7,168	4,950	15.1	15.5	14.5
Age:									
16 to 19 years.................	1,413	855	558	150	82	67	10.6	9.6	12.0
20 to 24 years.................	8,332	4,694	3,638	999	542	456	12.0	11.5	12.5
25 to 34 years.................	25,523	14,917	10,606	4,008	2,358	1,650	15.7	15.8	15.6
35 to 44 years.................	22,749	13,001	9,749	3,744	2,213	1,531	16.5	17.0	15.7
45 to 54 years.................	14,306	8,003	6,302	2,184	1,299	885	15.3	16.2	14.0
55 to 64 years...............	7,197	4,286	2,910	880	574	306	12.2	13.4	10.5
65 years and over	933	552	382	153	99	54	16.4	17.9	14.1
Race:									
White.......................	68,795	40,267	28,528	10,630	6,416	4,214	15.5	15.9	14.8
Black......................	8,943	4,522	4,421	1,083	525	558	12.1	11.6	12.6
Hispanic [1]..................	6,598	4,172	2,425	702	427	275	10.6	10.2	11.3
Marital Status:									
Single	18,420	10,621	7,799	2,887	1,606	1,281	15.7	15.1	16.4
Married, spouse present	49,101	30,510	18,591	7,195	4,794	2,401	14.7	15.7	12.9
Other.......................	12,932	5,177	7,755	2,035	768	1,267	15.7	14.8	16.3
Occupation:									
Managerial and professional........	22,630	12,037	10,593	4,991	3,053	1,937	22.1	25.4	18.3
Technical, sales, administrative.....	24,116	8,910	15,206	4,258	1,984	2,274	17.7	22.3	15.0
Service occupations	8,389	4,329	4,060	883	432	450	10.5	10.0	11.1
Precision production, craft, and repair .	10,270	9,464	807	833	764	69	8.1	8.1	8.6
Operators, fabricators, and laborers...	13,514	10,211	3,303	980	783	197	7.3	7.7	6.0
Farming, forestry, and fisheries......	1,533	1,355	177	173	151	22	11.3	11.1	12.4
Industry:									
Private sector .....2...........	65,556	38,909	26,647	10,010	6,018	3,992	15.3	15.5	15.0
Goods producing [2]	24,057	17,776	6,281	2,815	2,060	755	11.7	11.6	12.0
Service producing	41,499	21,132	20,367	7,196	3,959	3,237	17.3	18.7	15.9
Public sector	14,896	7,399	7,497	2,108	1,150	958	14.2	15.5	12.8
Federal government.	3,007	1,868	1,140	812	481	331	27.0	25.7	29.0
State government	3,616	1,801	1,814	655	351	304	18.1	19.5	16.8
Local government	8,274	3,730	4,543	640	319	322	7.7	8.6	7.1

[1] Persons of Hispanic origin may be of any race.   [2] Includes agriculture, mining, construction, and manufacturing.
Source: U.S. Bureau of Labor Statistics, *News*, USDL 92-491, August 4, 1992; and unpublished data.

No. 642. Workers on Shift Schedules, by Selected Characteristics: 1985 and 1991

[See headnote, table 641]

CHARACTERISTIC	Total employ-ed [1]	WORK SCHEDULES—PERCENT DISTRIBUTION						
		Regular daytime sched-ules	Shift workers					
			Total	Evening	Night	Rotating	Irregu-lar [2]	Other
Total, 1985 [3]	73,395	84.1	15.9	6.3	2.7	4.3	(NA)	2.6
Total, 1991 [3]	80,452	81.8	17.8	5.1	3.7	3.4	3.7	2.0
Age: 16 to 19 years old	1,413	70.6	28.6	12.0	5.5	3.2	6.4	1.5
20 to 24 years old	8,332	74.8	25.0	8.5	4.7	4.6	5.5	1.7
25 to 34 years old	25,523	81.3	18.3	5.0	3.9	3.8	3.7	1.9
35 to 44 years old	22,749	83.7	16.0	4.1	3.5	3.2	3.2	2.0
45 to 54 years old	14,306	83.6	16.2	4.6	2.9	2.9	3.4	2.3
55 to 64 years old	7,197	84.1	15.3	4.2	3.4	2.4	3.0	2.3
65 years old and over	933	88.1	11.7	2.3	2.7	1.1	2.4	3.3
Race and Hispanic origin:								
White	68,795	82.6	17.1	4.6	3.4	3.3	3.8	2.1
Black	8,943	76.0	23.3	8.4	5.6	4.7	2.9	1.8
Hispanic [4]	6,598	80.3	19.1	6.4	4.6	2.7	3.1	2.4
Marital status: Single	18,420	77.6	22.0	7.0	4.0	4.0	4.7	2.2
Married, spouse present	49,101	83.9	15.8	4.2	3.3	3.2	3.3	1.9
Other	12,932	80.1	19.4	5.8	4.4	3.4	3.5	2.4
Occupation:								
Managerial and professional	22,630	89.6	10.0	1.6	1.4	1.8	2.8	2.3
Technical, sales, administrative	24,116	85.9	13.8	3.5	2.4	2.7	3.6	1.7
Service occupations	8,389	57.1	42.5	14.7	8.7	7.9	6.6	4.6
Precision production, craft, and repair	10,270	85.3	14.4	4.3	3.7	3.4	2.5	0.5
Operators, fabricators, and laborers	13,514	73.4	26.2	8.6	6.8	4.8	4.2	1.7
Farming, forestry, and fisheries	1,533	89.2	10.4	1.1	1.2	0.7	4.4	3.0

NA Not available. [1] Includes a small number of workers who did not report data on shift worked. [2] Employer arranged. [3] Data for 1985 are not strictly comparable to those for 1991 because of the addition of the "irregular" category in the May 1991 survey. Includes other races, not shown separately. [4] Persons of Hispanic origin may be of any race.
Source: U.S. Bureau of Labor Statistics, *News,* USDL 92-491, August 4, 1992; and unpublished data.

No. 643. Workers Doing Job-Related Work at Home, by Selected Characteristics: 1991

[As of **May**. For persons 16 years old and over doing job-related work at home as part of their primary job in nonagriculture industries]

CHARACTERISTIC	Total at work (1,000)	PERSONS DOING JOB RELATED WORK AT HOME						
		Total			Class of worker—percent [4]			
		Number (1,000) [1]	Rate [2]	Mean hours worked (num-ber) [3]	Wage and salary workers			Self-employed
					Total [1]	Paid for the work	Not paid for the work	
Total, 1991	109,126	19,967	18.3	9.1	71.6	9.4	60.9	27.8
Age: 16 to 19 years old	4,989	98	2.0	7.1	71.4	24.5	37.8	28.6
20 to 24 years old	11,279	764	6.8	8.9	84.6	21.6	61.8	14.5
25 to 34 years old	31,248	5,290	16.9	8.3	78.3	12.5	64.4	21.5
35 to 44 years old	29,500	6,755	22.9	8.3	71.8	8.4	61.9	27.6
45 to 54 years old	18,842	4,368	23.2	9.8	69.9	6.3	62.6	29.6
55 to 64 years old	10,291	1,995	19.4	11.8	62.3	6.3	54.8	37.0
65 years old and over	2,977	697	23.4	12.1	43.0	8.9	33.6	54.9
Race and Hispanic origin:								
White	94,387	18,520	19.6	9.0	71.2	9.6	60.3	28.3
Black	11,020	970	8.8	10.4	82.5	7.5	73.5	17.1
Hispanic [5]	7,977	667	8.4	9.8	69.6	8.5	58.8	29.7
Marital status: Single	26,637	2,965	11.1	8.4	81.1	13.0	67.0	18.6
Married, spouse present	66,168	14,359	21.7	9.0	69.4	8.5	59.6	29.9
Other	16,321	2,642	16.2	10.4	73.1	10.4	61.2	26.9
Occupation:								
Managerial and professional	29,971	11,517	38.4	7.8	79.4	6.9	71.3	20.5
Technical, sales, administrative	34,554	5,611	16.2	8.4	69.2	14.4	53.7	29.4
Service occupations	14,955	1,144	7.6	25.1	45.4	10.0	33.2	54.1
Precision production, craft, and repair	12,608	1,070	8.5	9.0	40.3	9.1	30.0	59.3
Operators, fabricators, and laborers	16,271	546	3.4	11.0	54.2	11.9	38.6	45.2
Forestry, and fisheries	766	78	10.2	7.4	38.5	-	38.5	60.3

- Represents or rounds to zero. [1] Includes those that did not report pay status and unpaid family members. [2] Persons working at home as a percent of the total at work. [3] For definition of mean, see Guide to Tabular Presentation. [4] Excludes unpaid family members. [5] Persons of Hispanic origin may be of any race.
Source: U.S. Bureau of Labor Statistics, *Monthly Labor Review,* forthcoming article.

No. 644. Employed Civilians, by Occupation, Sex, Race, and Hispanic Origin: 1983 and 1992

[For civilian noninstitutional population 16 years old and over. Annual average of monthly figures. Based on Current Population Survey; see text, section 1, and Appendix III. Persons of Hispanic origin may be of any race. See headnote, table 637]

OCCUPATION	1983				1992			
	Total employed (1,000)	Percent of total			Total employed (1,000)	Percent of total		
		Female	Black	Hispanic		Female	Black	Hispanic
Total	100,834	43.7	9.3	5.3	117,598	45.7	10.1	7.6
Managerial and professional specialty	23,592	40.9	5.6	2.6	31,153	47.3	6.5	3.9
Executive, administrative, and managerial [1]	10,772	32.4	4.7	2.8	14,767	41.5	5.8	4.2
Officials and administrators, public	417	38.5	8.3	3.8	619	43.8	11.5	3.7
Financial managers	357	38.6	3.5	3.1	517	46.3	3.0	3.9
Personnel and labor relations managers	106	43.9	4.9	2.6	104	58.9	5.9	3.4
Purchasing managers	82	23.6	5.1	1.4	113	33.2	5.8	2.2
Managers, marketing, advertising and public relations	396	21.8	2.7	1.7	516	33.6	2.9	3.4
Administrators, education and related fields	415	41.4	11.3	2.4	605	56.8	9.8	3.7
Managers, medicine and health	91	57.0	5.0	2.0	364	65.8	8.8	2.9
Managers, properties and real estate	305	42.8	5.5	5.2	436	45.5	7.2	5.6
Management-related occupations [1]	2,966	40.3	5.8	3.5	3,961	52.1	6.9	4.6
Accountants and auditors	1,105	38.7	5.5	3.3	1,365	51.2	5.8	4.4
Professional specialty [1]	12,820	48.1	6.4	2.5	16,386	52.6	7.0	3.5
Architects	103	12.7	1.6	1.5	138	15.3	1.3	4.3
Engineers [1]	1,572	5.8	2.7	2.2	1,751	8.5	3.9	2.9
Aerospace engineers	80	6.9	1.5	2.1	89	6.4	3.3	1.3
Chemical engineers	67	6.1	3.0	1.4	70	6.3	0.7	2.8
Civil engineers	211	4.0	1.9	3.2	217	7.9	3.4	3.9
Electrical and electronic	450	6.1	3.4	3.1	527	8.4	5.2	2.4
Industrial engineers	210	11.0	3.3	2.4	204	14.0	4.7	3.5
Mechanical	259	2.8	3.2	1.1	303	5.3	3.7	2.7
Mathematical and computer scientists [1]	463	29.6	5.4	2.6	935	33.5	6.8	3.1
Computer systems analysts, scientists	276	27.8	6.2	2.7	693	29.6	5.9	2.9
Operations and systems researchers and analysts	142	31.3	4.9	2.2	192	45.2	9.3	4.2
Natural scientists [1]	357	20.5	2.6	2.1	459	27.2	3.0	3.0
Chemists, except biochemists	98	23.3	4.3	1.2	120	30.1	2.8	3.4
Geologists and geodesists	65	18.0	1.1	2.6	52	11.8	0.3	1.0
Biological and life scientists	55	40.8	2.4	1.8	95	33.8	2.8	4.6
Health diagnosing occupations [1]	735	13.3	2.7	3.3	914	18.3	2.6	3.5
Physicians	519	15.8	3.2	4.5	614	20.4	3.3	4.3
Dentists	126	6.7	2.4	1.0	162	8.5	1.1	1.6
Health assessment and treating occupations	1,900	85.8	7.1	2.2	2,517	86.8	8.5	3.4
Registered nurses	1,372	95.8	6.7	1.8	1,805	94.3	8.5	2.9
Pharmacists	158	26.7	3.8	2.6	198	37.8	5.6	2.2
Dietitians	71	90.8	21.0	3.7	90	89.8	21.3	8.5
Therapists [1]	247	76.3	7.6	2.7	381	79.6	6.1	4.8
Inhalation therapists	69	69.4	6.5	3.7	77	67.9	8.3	7.3
Physical therapists	55	77.0	9.7	1.5	104	76.5	4.4	7.6
Speech therapists	51	90.5	1.5	-	79	92.1	1.7	0.3
Physicians' assistants	51	36.3	7.7	4.4	(²)	(²)	(²)	(²)
Teachers, college and university	606	36.3	4.4	1.8	737	40.9	4.7	2.7
Teachers, except college and university [1]	3,365	70.9	9.1	2.7	4,216	74.8	9.3	3.4
Prekindergarten and kindergarten	299	98.2	11.8	3.4	481	98.6	12.7	5.9
Elementary school	1,350	83.3	11.1	3.1	1,643	85.4	10.4	3.3
Secondary school	1,209	51.8	7.2	2.3	1,172	55.5	7.6	2.7
Special education	81	82.2	10.2	2.3	269	84.7	10.0	2.1
Counselors, educational and vocational	184	53.1	13.9	3.2	234	65.8	11.4	5.6
Librarians, archivists, and curators	213	84.4	7.8	1.6	207	83.6	5.6	3.0
Librarians	193	87.3	7.9	1.8	182	87.6	5.8	2.7
Social scientists and urban planners [1]	261	46.8	7.1	2.1	387	54.1	6.7	3.1
Economists	98	37.9	6.3	2.7	122	43.3	7.9	3.0
Psychologists	135	57.1	8.6	1.1	223	62.5	6.2	3.3
Social, recreation, and religious workers [1]	831	43.1	12.1	3.8	1,069	50.5	14.8	5.9
Social workers	407	64.3	18.2	6.3	590	68.9	20.2	7.4
Recreation workers	65	71.9	15.7	2.0	93	72.3	15.7	3.5
Clergy	293	5.6	4.9	1.4	317	8.4	6.4	4.0
Lawyers and judges	651	15.8	2.7	1.0	788	21.4	3.1	2.0
Lawyers	612	15.3	2.6	0.9	753	21.4	2.7	1.9
Writers, artists, entertainers, and athletes [1]	1,544	42.7	4.8	2.9	2,019	47.2	4.9	4.5
Authors	62	46.7	2.1	0.9	125	54.5	2.7	0.9
Technical writers	(²)	(²)	(²)	(²)	54	53.9	3.8	4.2
Designers	393	52.7	3.1	2.7	542	54.8	3.0	4.3
Musicians and composers	155	28.0	7.9	4.4	188	29.4	11.2	6.6
Actors and directors	60	30.8	6.6	3.4	96	40.3	6.6	3.8
Painters, sculptors, craft-artists, and artist printmakers	186	47.4	2.1	2.3	222	50.3	2.8	3.9
Photographers	113	20.7	4.0	3.4	129	26.4	6.4	4.6
Editors and reporters	204	48.4	2.9	2.1	264	49.7	4.4	2.8
Public relations specialists	157	50.1	6.2	1.9	161	58.5	5.5	2.4
Announcers	(²)	(²)	(²)	(²)	53	16.9	6.8	7.1
Athletes	58	17.6	9.4	1.7	71	25.8	9.7	5.3

See footnotes at end of table.

No. 644. Employed Civilians, by Occupation, Sex, Race, and Hispanic Origin: 1983 and 1992—Continued

[See headnote, page 405]

OCCUPATION	1983 Total employed (1,000)	1983 Percent of total Female	1983 Percent of total Black	1983 Percent of total Hispanic	1992 Total employed (1,000)	1992 Percent of total Female	1992 Percent of total Black	1992 Percent of total Hispanic
Technical, sales, and administrative support	31,265	64.6	7.6	4.3	36,808	63.9	9.1	6.1
Technicians and related support	3,053	48.2	8.2	3.1	4,253	49.0	9.7	4.5
Health technologists and technicians [1]	1,111	84.3	12.7	3.1	1,517	81.8	12.3	5.2
Clinical laboratory technologists and technicians	255	76.2	10.5	2.9	301	77.6	12.6	6.2
Dental hygienists	66	98.6	1.6	-	74	99.0	0.6	0.9
Health record technologists and technicians	(2)	(2)	(2)	(2)	57	88.9	12.9	8.2
Radiologic technicians	101	71.7	8.6	4.5	146	74.0	6.7	5.1
Licensed practical nurses	443	97.0	17.7	3.1	453	94.8	17.2	3.1
Engineering and related technologists and technicians [1]	822	18.4	6.1	3.5	920	17.5	7.0	4.8
Electrical and electronic technicians	260	12.5	8.2	4.6	330	12.2	9.2	5.3
Drafting occupations	273	17.5	5.5	2.3	255	19.0	4.4	3.9
Surveying and mapping technicians	(2)	(2)	(2)	(2)	72	7.8	0.3	6.6
Science technicians [1]	202	29.1	6.6	2.8	240	36.1	8.3	4.3
Biological technicians	52	37.7	2.9	2.0	79	51.7	5.2	5.9
Chemical technicians	82	26.9	9.5	3.5	77	26.7	10.0	3.6
Technicians, except health, engineering, and science [1]	917	35.3	5.0	2.7	1,576	37.9	8.9	3.8
Airplane pilots and navigators	69	2.1	-	1.6	97	2.3	2.2	2.5
Computer programmers	443	32.5	4.4	2.1	550	33.0	6.8	2.5
Legal assistants	128	74.0	4.3	3.6	241	76.7	10.0	5.2
Sales occupations	11,818	47.5	4.7	3.7	13,919	47.9	6.2	5.6
Supervisors and proprietors	2,958	28.4	3.6	3.4	3,886	34.8	4.0	4.8
Sales representatives, finance and business services [1]	1,853	37.2	2.7	2.2	2,247	40.0	4.7	3.6
Insurance sales	551	25.1	3.8	2.5	573	31.7	6.1	3.9
Real estate sales	570	48.9	1.3	1.5	719	50.4	2.6	3.7
Securities and financial services sales	212	23.6	3.1	1.1	322	29.6	3.7	2.5
Advertising and related sales	124	47.9	4.5	3.3	164	49.3	6.0	3.0
Sales representatives, commodities, except retail	1,442	15.1	2.1	2.2	1,570	21.8	2.4	3.3
Sales workers, retail and personal services	5,511	69.7	6.7	4.8	6,129	65.5	9.1	7.5
Cashiers	2,009	84.4	10.1	5.4	2,519	79.3	12.8	8.5
Sales-related occupations	54	58.7	2.8	1.3	93	65.7	6.0	4.0
Administrative support, including clerical	16,395	79.9	9.6	5.0	18,636	79.3	11.1	6.7
Supervisors	676	53.4	9.3	5.0	759	56.7	11.7	7.2
Computer equipment operators	605	63.9	12.5	6.0	664	63.6	13.0	6.7
Computer operators	597	63.7	12.1	6.0	661	63.6	13.1	6.6
Secretaries, stenographers, and typists [1]	4,861	98.2	7.3	4.5	4,315	98.4	9.3	5.7
Secretaries	3,891	99.0	5.8	4.0	3,700	99.0	8.2	5.4
Typists	906	95.6	13.8	6.4	547	95.1	17.2	7.7
Information clerks	1,174	88.9	8.5	5.5	1,653	88.7	8.3	7.9
Receptionists	602	96.8	7.5	6.6	892	97.3	7.5	8.0
Records processing occupations, except financial [1]	866	82.4	13.9	4.8	916	79.6	15.4	7.4
Order clerks	188	78.1	10.6	4.4	219	76.0	16.8	7.0
Personnel clerks, except payroll and time keeping	64	91.1	14.9	4.6	68	89.5	12.2	6.3
Library clerks	147	81.9	15.4	2.5	152	77.7	10.1	4.6
File clerks	287	83.5	16.7	6.1	292	81.3	17.9	8.6
Records clerks	157	82.8	11.6	5.6	172	79.0	15.9	9.4
Financial records processing [1]	2,457	89.4	4.6	3.7	2,335	90.6	5.3	5.4
Bookkeepers, accounting, and auditing clerks	1,970	91.0	4.3	3.3	1,841	90.7	4.3	5.2
Payroll and time keeping clerks	192	82.2	5.9	5.0	171	90.8	7.1	5.1
Billing clerks	146	88.4	6.2	3.9	180	92.4	10.3	5.4
Cost and rate clerks	96	75.6	5.9	5.3	67	81.1	7.4	9.6
Duplicating, mail and other office machine operators	68	62.6	16.0	6.1	72	53.6	19.5	6.9
Communications equipment operators	256	89.1	17.0	4.4	226	88.3	19.5	6.2
Telephone operators	244	90.4	17.0	4.3	215	89.9	18.9	6.3
Mail and message distributing occupations	799	31.6	18.1	4.5	902	37.3	19.0	7.6
Postal clerks, except mail carriers	248	36.7	26.2	5.2	252	46.1	26.6	8.4
Mail carrier, postal service	259	17.1	12.5	2.7	325	27.8	14.5	5.0
Mail clerks, except postal service	170	50.0	15.8	5.9	180	49.5	21.3	9.6
Messengers	122	26.2	16.7	5.2	144	28.2	13.1	9.8
Material recording, scheduling, and distributing [1][3]	1,562	37.5	10.9	6.6	1,846	43.5	12.7	8.2
Dispatchers	157	45.7	11.4	4.3	213	55.4	10.2	5.6
Production coordinators	182	44.0	6.1	2.2	194	49.2	9.2	3.3
Traffic, shipping, and receiving clerks	421	22.6	9.1	11.1	550	31.6	14.6	10.6
Stock and inventory clerks	532	38.7	13.3	5.5	544	40.3	12.8	8.7
Weighers, measurers, and checkers	79	47.2	16.9	5.8	65	47.2	14.7	14.0
Expediters	112	57.5	8.4	4.3	209	66.7	11.8	5.6
Adjusters and investigators	675	69.9	11.1	5.1	1,300	75.1	11.9	6.1
Insurance adjusters, examiners, and investigators	199	65.0	11.5	3.3	373	76.1	11.6	4.7
Investigators and adjusters, except insurance	301	70.1	11.3	4.8	686	75.6	12.1	6.7
Eligibility clerks, social welfare	69	88.7	12.9	9.4	78	86.9	13.9	8.6
Bill and account collectors	106	66.4	8.5	6.5	163	64.6	11.2	5.8
Miscellaneous administrative support [1]	2,397	85.2	12.5	5.9	3,642	82.9	12.8	7.3
General office clerks	648	80.6	12.7	5.2	717	83.5	12.6	8.1
Bank tellers	480	91.0	7.5	4.3	468	89.8	7.7	6.1
Data entry keyers	311	93.6	18.6	5.6	571	84.9	17.1	7.8
Statistical clerks	96	75.7	7.5	3.4	58	78.6	15.8	6.2
Teachers' aides	348	93.7	17.8	12.6	485	91.9	15.2	11.4

See footnotes at end of table.

No. 644. Employed Civilians, by Occupation, Sex, Race, and Hispanic Origin: 1983 and 1992—Continued

[See headnote, page 405]

OCCUPATION	1983				1992			
	Total employed (1,000)	Percent of total			Total employed (1,000)	Percent of total		
		Female	Black	His-panic		Female	Black	His-panic
Service occupations	**13,857**	**60.1**	**16.6**	**6.8**	**16,096**	**59.7**	**17.5**	**11.3**
Private household [1]	980	96.1	27.8	8.5	876	95.9	18.6	19.6
Child care workers	408	96.9	7.9	3.6	353	97.1	10.2	12.6
Cleaners and servants	512	95.8	42.4	11.8	484	94.8	23.6	24.6
Protective service	1,672	12.8	13.6	4.6	2,096	16.7	18.0	7.2
Supervisors, protective service	127	4.7	7.7	3.1	172	9.5	13.2	7.7
Supervisors, police and detectives	58	4.2	9.3	1.2	81	10.8	8.1	10.0
Firefighting and fire prevention	189	1.0	6.7	4.1	205	3.3	6.5	3.7
Firefighting occupations	170	1.0	7.3	3.8	190	2.4	6.5	3.5
Police and detectives	645	9.4	13.1	4.0	862	15.8	16.6	6.7
Police and detectives, public service	412	5.7	9.5	4.4	459	10.6	10.8	7.3
Sheriffs, bailiffs, and other law enforcement officers	87	13.2	11.5	4.0	108	20.8	16.3	7.4
Correctional institution officers	146	17.8	24.0	2.8	295	21.9	25.7	5.5
Guards	711	20.6	17.0	5.6	860	22.3	23.1	8.5
Guards and police, except public service	602	13.0	18.9	6.2	730	15.4	25.1	9.1
Service except private household and protective	11,205	64.0	16.0	6.9	13,124	64.1	17.3	11.4
Food preparation and service occupations [1]	4,860	63.3	10.5	6.8	5,459	59.0	13.0	12.2
Bartenders	338	48.4	2.7	4.4	291	55.0	2.9	4.9
Waiters and waitresses	1,357	87.8	4.1	3.6	1,369	79.6	4.7	7.6
Cooks	1,452	50.0	15.8	6.5	1,877	46.1	18.5	14.7
Food counter, fountain, and related occupations	326	76.0	9.1	6.7	316	72.6	12.3	8.5
Kitchen workers, food preparation	138	77.0	13.7	8.1	246	76.0	15.9	11.4
Waiters' and waitresses' assistants	364	38.8	12.6	14.2	364	37.5	14.3	19.0
Health service occupations	1,739	89.2	23.5	4.8	2,105	88.8	27.7	7.1
Dental assistants	154	98.1	6.1	5.7	169	98.6	3.9	10.6
Health aides, except nursing	316	86.8	16.5	4.8	363	81.3	22.7	6.1
Nursing aides, orderlies, and attendants	1,269	88.7	27.3	4.7	1,574	89.4	31.4	7.0
Cleaning and building service occupations [1]	2,736	38.8	24.4	9.2	2,988	41.1	22.6	16.4
Maids and housemen	531	81.2	32.3	10.1	638	82.3	27.3	19.5
Janitors and cleaners	2,031	28.6	22.6	8.9	2,118	30.0	21.3	15.9
Personal service occupations [1]	1,870	79.2	11.1	6.0	2,573	81.7	11.9	7.5
Barbers	92	12.9	8.4	12.1	86	20.9	15.3	7.6
Hairdressers and cosmetologists	622	88.7	7.0	5.7	758	90.8	9.6	6.7
Attendants, amusement and recreation facilities	131	40.2	7.1	4.3	153	47.9	9.3	6.5
Public transportation attendants	63	74.3	11.3	5.9	91	82.5	10.8	8.6
Welfare service aides	77	92.5	24.2	10.5	92	87.7	18.3	16.5
Family child care providers	(NA)	(NA)	(NA)	(NA)	320	98.7	7.5	9.7
Early childhood teachers' assistants	(NA)	(NA)	(NA)	(NA)	385	95.9	14.4	6.3
Precision production, craft, and repair	**12,328**	**8.1**	**6.8**	**6.2**	**13,128**	**8.6**	**7.6**	**9.1**
Mechanics and repairers	4,158	3.0	6.8	5.3	4,441	3.3	7.6	7.8
Mechanics and repairers, except supervisors [1]	3,906	2.8	7.0	5.5	4,209	3.1	7.7	8.1
Vehicle and mobile equipment mechanics/repairers [1]	1,683	0.8	6.9	6.0	1,845	1.1	6.8	10.1
Automobile mechanics	800	0.5	7.8	6.0	894	0.8	7.4	10.7
Aircraft engine mechanics	95	2.5	4.0	7.6	143	4.6	8.0	15.3
Electrical and electronic equipment repairers [1]	674	7.4	7.3	4.5	654	7.4	8.7	6.1
Data processing equipment repairers	98	9.3	6.1	4.5	146	10.4	7.8	6.8
Telephone installers and repairers	247	9.9	7.8	3.7	58	3.4	12.9	6.4
Construction trades	4,289	1.8	6.6	6.0	4,790	1.9	6.9	9.1
Construction trades, except supervisors	3,784	1.9	7.1	6.1	4,137	2.0	7.3	9.8
Carpenters	1,160	1.4	5.0	5.0	1,236	1.0	5.4	8.1
Extractive occupations	196	2.3	3.3	4.0	130	0.6	3.4	7.3
Precision production occupations	3,685	21.5	7.3	7.4	3,765	23.7	8.6	10.8
Operators, fabricators, and laborers	**16,091**	**26.6**	**14.0**	**8.3**	**16,957**	**25.0**	**15.1**	**11.8**
Machine operators, assemblers, and inspectors [1]	7,744	42.1	14.0	9.4	7,524	39.7	15.0	13.5
Textile, apparel, and furnishings machine operators [1]	1,414	82.1	18.7	12.5	1,200	76.4	23.7	18.0
Textile sewing machine operators	806	94.0	15.5	14.5	676	87.4	20.2	22.4
Pressing machine operators	141	66.4	27.1	14.2	123	67.1	27.1	23.6
Fabricators, assemblers, and hand working occupations	1,715	33.7	11.3	8.7	1,904	33.2	11.6	12.1
Production inspectors, testers, samplers, and weighers	794	53.8	13.0	7.7	773	53.6	14.6	12.3
Transportation and material moving occupations	4,201	7.8	13.0	5.9	4,878	8.8	14.9	8.4
Motor vehicle operators	2,978	9.2	13.5	6.0	3,706	10.2	15.7	8.6
Trucks, heavy and light	2,195	3.1	12.3	5.7	2,694	4.6	13.6	8.5
Transportation occupations, except motor vehicles	212	2.4	6.7	3.0	162	3.6	10.2	4.7
Material moving equipment operators	1,011	4.8	12.9	6.3	1,009	4.5	12.4	8.6
Industrial truck and tractor operators	369	5.6	19.6	8.2	421	6.6	17.4	12.5
Handlers, equipment cleaners, helpers, and laborers [1]	4,147	16.8	15.1	8.6	4,556	18.0	15.4	12.5
Freight, stock, and material handlers	1,488	15.4	15.3	7.1	1,737	18.6	16.6	9.8
Laborers, except construction	1,024	19.4	16.0	8.6	1,177	18.2	15.8	12.4
Farming, forestry, and fishing	**3,700**	**16.0**	**7.5**	**8.2**	**3,456**	**15.9**	**6.5**	**15.1**
Farm operators and managers	1,450	12.1	1.3	0.7	1,232	15.4	0.9	1.7
Other agricultural and related occupations	2,072	19.9	11.7	14.0	2,054	17.2	9.7	23.9
Farm workers	1,149	24.8	11.6	15.9	866	21.6	8.2	27.8
Forestry and logging occupations	126	1.4	12.8	2.1	109	5.4	13.0	7.4
Fishers, hunters, and trappers	53	4.5	1.8	2.5	60	3.9	0.9	5.5

- Represents or rounds to zero.   NA Not available.   [1] Includes other occupations, not shown separately.   [2] Level of total employment below 50,000.   [3] Includes clerks.

Source: U.S. Bureau of Labor Statistics, *Employment and Earnings*, monthly, January issues.

No. 645. Civilian Employment in Occupations with the Largest Job Growth and in the Fastest Growing and Fastest Declining Occupations: 1990 and 2005

[In thousands, except percent. For occupations employing 100,000 or more in 1990. Includes wage and salary jobs, self-employed and unpaid family members. Estimates based on the Current Employment Statistics estimates and the Occupational Employment Statistics estimates. See source for methodological assumptions. Minus sign (-) indicates decrease]

OCCUPATION	EMPLOYMENT				PERCENT CHANGE 1990-2005		
	1990	2005 [1]			Low	Moderate	High
		Low	Moderate	High			
Total [2]	122,573	136,806	147,191	154,543	12	20	26
LARGEST JOB GROWTH [3]							
Salespersons, retail	3,619	4,180	4,506	4,728	15	24	31
Registered nurses	1,727	2,318	2,494	2,648	34	44	53
Cashiers	2,633	3,094	3,318	3,474	18	26	32
General office clerks	2,737	3,149	3,407	3,597	15	24	31
Truck drivers light and heavy	2,362	2,767	2,979	3,125	17	26	32
General managers and top executives	3,086	3,409	3,684	3,871	10	19	25
Janitors and cleaners [4]	3,007	3,332	3,562	3,728	11	18	24
Nursing aides, orderlies, and attendants	1,274	1,700	1,826	1,934	33	43	52
Food counter, fountain, and related workers	1,607	2,067	2,158	2,229	29	34	39
Waiters and waitresses	1,747	2,110	2,196	2,262	21	26	29
Teachers, secondary school	1,280	1,575	1,717	1,849	23	34	45
Receptionists and information clerks	900	1,228	1,322	1,394	36	47	55
Systems analysts and computer scientists	463	769	829	864	66	79	87
Food preparation workers	1,156	1,442	1,521	1,585	25	32	37
Child care workers	725	1,027	1,078	1,123	42	49	55
Gardeners and groundskeepers, except farm	874	1,158	1,222	1,275	33	40	46
Accountants and auditors	985	1,235	1,325	1,385	25	34	41
Computer programmers	565	811	882	923	44	56	63
Teachers, elementary	1,362	1,538	1,675	1,803	13	23	32
Guards	883	1,094	1,181	1,238	24	34	40
Teacher aides and educational assistants	808	999	1,086	1,165	24	34	44
Licensed practical nurses	644	849	913	968	32	42	50
Clerical supervisors and managers	1,218	1,373	1,481	1,559	13	22	28
Home health aides	287	512	550	582	78	92	103
Cooks, restaurant	615	840	872	898	37	42	46
Maintenance repairers, general utility	1,128	1,283	1,379	1,447	14	22	28
Secretaries, except legal and medical	3,064	3,065	3,312	3,488	-	8	14
Cooks, short order and fast food	743	953	989	1,018	28	33	37
Stock clerks, sales floor	1,242	1,343	1,451	1,524	8	17	23
Lawyers	587	745	793	830	27	35	42
Marketing, advertising, and public relations managers	427	582	630	659	36	47	54
Food service and lodging managers	595	762	793	819	28	33	38
Physicians	580	730	776	818	26	34	41
Financial managers	701	828	894	939	18	28	34
Teachers, preschool and kindergarten	425	555	598	636	31	41	50
Automotive mechanics	757	861	923	969	14	22	28
Medical secretaries	232	363	390	415	57	68	79
Dining room and cafeteria attendants and bar helpers	461	592	619	641	28	34	39
Electricians	548	652	706	748	19	29	36
Carpenters	1,057	1,134	1,209	1,274	7	14	20
FASTEST GROWING							
Home health aides	287	512	550	582	78	92	103
Systems analysts and computer scientists	463	769	829	864	66	79	87
Personal and home care aides	103	170	183	194	64	77	87
Medical assistants	165	268	287	306	62	74	85
Human services workers	145	231	249	264	59	71	82
Radiologic technologists and technicians	149	234	252	268	58	70	80
Medical secretaries	232	363	390	415	57	68	79
Psychologists	125	193	204	214	55	64	72
Travel agents	132	199	214	224	51	62	70
Correction officers	230	342	372	400	49	61	74
Flight attendants	101	146	159	168	45	59	67
Computer programmers	565	811	882	923	44	56	63
Management analysts	151	218	230	240	44	52	58
Child care workers	725	1,027	1,078	1,123	42	49	55
FASTEST DECLINING							
Electrical and electronic equipment assemblers, precision	171	78	90	92	-55	-48	-46
Electrical and electronic assemblers	232	112	128	131	-52	-45	-44
Child care workers, private household	314	176	190	200	-44	-40	-36
Textile draw-out and winding machine operators [5]	199	116	138	142	-41	-31	-29
Telephone and cable TV line installers and repairers	133	85	92	98	-36	-30	-26
Machine tool cutting operators and tenders [6]	145	93	104	107	-36	-29	-26
Cleaners and servants, private household	411	287	310	326	-30	-25	-21
Machine forming operators and tenders [6]	174	119	131	137	-32	-25	-21
Switchboard operators	246	175	189	198	-29	-23	-19
Farmers	1,074	822	850	876	-23	-21	-18
Sewing machine operators, garment	585	368	469	478	-37	-20	-18
Farm workers	837	723	745	766	-14	-11	-8
Typists and word processors	972	805	869	916	-17	-11	-6

- Represents or rounds to zero.   [1] Based on low, moderate, or high trend assumptions.   [2] Includes other occupations, not shown separately.   [3] In descending order, based on absolute employment change 1990 to 2005 (moderate growth). [4] Includes maids and housekeepers.   [5] Includes tenders.   [6] Metal and plastic .

Source: U.S. Bureau of Labor Statistics, *Monthly Labor Review*, November 1991.

No. 646. Occupation of Employed Civilians, by Sex, Race, and Educational Attainment: 1992

[In thousands. Annual averages of monthly figures. For civilian noninstitutional population 25 years and over. Based on Current Population Survey; see text, section 1, and Appendix III]

SEX, RACE, AND YEARS OF SCHOOL	Total employed	Managerial/professional	Tech./sales/administrative	Service[1]	Precision production[2]	Operators/fabricators[3]	Farming, forestry, fishing
Male, total[4]	54,658	15,653	11,156	4,595	10,753	10,161	2,340
Less than a high school diploma	7,182	373	572	932	1,941	2,571	794
High school graduates, no college	18,459	1,923	3,209	1,870	5,260	5,258	940
Less than a bachelor's degree	13,213	3,032	3,790	1,288	2,825	1,881	398
College graduates	15,803	10,324	3,585	505	728	452	209
White	47,779	14,237	9,896	3,520	9,696	8,325	2,104
Less than a high school diploma	5,938	328	482	696	1,709	2,055	668
High school graduates, no college	16,085	1,779	2,884	1,411	4,797	4,356	859
Less than a bachelor's degree	11,588	2,765	3,341	1,015	2,543	1,550	374
College graduates	14,168	9,365	3,189	399	647	365	203
Black	4,945	766	825	828	798	1,551	176
Less than a high school diploma	987	30	64	177	183	435	98
High school graduates, no college	1,926	105	250	362	363	788	60
Less than a bachelor's degree	1,239	192	330	221	205	276	16
College graduates	793	440	182	68	47	52	3
Female, total[4]	45,381	13,748	19,091	7,377	1,021	3,679	464
Less than a high school diploma	4,506	232	944	1,875	218	1,115	122
High school graduates, no college	16,957	2,172	8,511	3,576	512	1,983	204
Less than a bachelor's degree	12,357	3,358	6,714	1,509	214	473	90
College graduates	11,561	7,986	2,922	418	78	108	48
White	38,481	12,141	16,591	5,621	840	2,852	436
Less than a high school diploma	3,479	194	819	1,320	174	866	106
High school graduates, no college	14,466	1,967	7,582	2,753	426	1,543	195
Less than a bachelor's degree	10,516	2,956	5,732	1,202	178	362	87
College graduates	10,019	7,024	2,458	347	62	81	48
Black	5,231	1,125	1,871	1,461	115	644	15
Less than a high school diploma	805	26	87	480	23	179	9
High school graduates, no college	2,023	161	742	693	59	364	5
Less than a bachelor's degree	1,471	305	791	257	24	93	-
College graduates	932	633	251	31	8	9	-

- Represents or rounds to zero.   [1] Includes private household workers.   [2] Includes craft and repair.   [3] Includes laborers.
[4] Includes other races, not shown separately.
Source: U.S. Bureau of Labor Statistics, unpublished data.

No. 647. Employment by Industry, 1970 to 1992, and by Selected Characteristics, 1992

[In thousands, except percent. See headnote, table 628. Data from 1985 to 1991, and also beginning 1992, not strictly comparable with other years due to changes in industrial classification]

INDUSTRY	1970	1980	1985	1990	1991	1992 Total	Percent Female	Percent Black	Percent Hispanic[1]
Total employed	78,678	99,303	107,150	117,914	116,877	117,598	45.7	10.1	7.6
Agriculture	3,463	3,364	3,179	3,186	3,233	3,210	21.0	4.8	14.5
Mining	516	979	939	730	733	664	16.0	3.6	7.0
Construction	4,818	6,215	6,987	7,696	7,087	7,013	8.9	6.3	8.3
Manufacturing	20,746	21,942	20,879	21,184	20,434	19,972	32.9	10.4	8.7
Transportation, communication, and other public utilities	5,320	6,525	7,548	8,136	8,204	8,245	28.3	13.4	6.7
Wholesale and retail trade	15,008	20,191	22,296	24,269	24,055	24,354	46.7	8.1	8.4
Wholesale trade	2,672	3,920	4,341	4,651	4,640	4,765	29.2	6.3	7.4
Retail trade	12,336	16,270	17,955	19,618	19,415	19,589	50.9	8.5	8.6
Finance, insurance, real estate	3,945	5,993	7,005	8,021	7,786	7,764	59.0	8.8	5.9
Banking and other finances	1,697	2,568	3,135	3,434	3,287	3,272	64.4	8.8	6.2
Insurance and real estate	2,248	3,425	3,870	4,587	4,500	4,495	55.0	8.7	5.7
Services[2]	20,385	28,752	33,322	39,084	39,705	40,758	61.7	11.4	6.8
Business and repair services[2]	1,403	3,848	5,969	7,409	7,467	6,553	35.3	10.7	9.4
Advertising	147	191	263	277	255	259	51.1	5.0	5.6
Services to dwellings and buildings	(NA)	370	571	813	833	744	43.5	17.9	18.4
Personnel supply services	(NA)	235	590	704	658	687	64.6	19.0	7.2
Computer and data processing	(NA)	221	549	799	847	882	35.7	6.0	3.7
Detective/protective services	(NA)	213	318	373	399	457	19.4	22.3	8.7
Automobile services	600	952	1,322	1,429	1,435	1,470	12.9	9.0	12.6
Personal services[2]	4,276	3,839	4,352	4,667	4,675	4,400	69.3	14.9	12.6
Private households	1,782	1,257	1,254	1,023	1,000	1,127	86.2	20.4	18.4
Hotels and lodging places	979	1,149	1,451	1,780	1,813	1,433	55.1	16.3	13.4
Entertainment and recreation[2]	717	1,047	1,278	1,503	1,570	1,957	40.3	8.3	7.4
Professional and related services[2]	12,904	19,853	21,563	25,335	25,835	27,677	68.5	11.3	5.2
Hospitals	2,843	4,036	4,269	4,690	4,839	4,915	76.7	15.8	5.8
Health services, except hospitals	1,628	3,345	3,641	4,757	4,978	5,356	78.5	12.6	5.7
Elementary, secondary schools	6,126	5,550	5,431	6,028	6,116	6,178	73.7	11.7	5.2
Colleges and universities	(3)	2,108	2,281	2,609	2,570	2,587	53.0	9.0	4.4
Social services	828	1,590	1,682	2,234	2,350	2,727	81.8	15.0	6.8
Legal services	429	776	995	1,217	1,274	1,247	54.4	5.4	4.6
Public administration[4]	4,476	5,342	4,995	5,608	5,639	5,620	42.7	14.4	5.6

NA Not available.   [1] Persons of Hispanic origin may be of any race.   [2] Includes industries not shown separately.
[3] Included with el/sec schools.   [4] Includes workers involved in uniquely governmental activities, e.g., judicial and legislative.
Source: U.S. Bureau of Labor Statistics, Employment and Earnings, monthly, January issues.

No. 648. Employment by Selected Industry, 1975 to 1990, and Projections, 2005

[In thousands, except percent. Figures may differ from those in other tables since these data exclude establishments not elsewhere classified (SIC 99); in addition, agriculture services (SIC 074, 5, 8) are included in agriculture, not services. See source for details. N.e.c. means not elsewhere classified. Minus sign (-) indicates decrease]

1987 SIC [1] code	INDUSTRY	EMPLOYMENT			ANNUAL AVERAGE RATE OF CHANGE	
		1975	1990	2005 [2]	1975- 1990	1990- 2005 [2]
(X)	Total.	87,666	122,570	147,190	2.3	1.2
(X)	Nonfarm wage and salary.	76,680	109,319	132,647	2.4	1.3
(X)	Goods-producing (excluding agriculture).	22,600	24,958	25,241	0.7	0.1
10-14	Mining.	752	711	668	-0.4	-0.4
15,16,17	Construction.	3,525	5,136	6,059	2.5	1.1
20-39	Manufacturing.	18,323	19,111	18,514	0.3	-0.2
24,25,32-39	Durable manufacturing.	10,662	11,115	10,517	0.3	-0.4
24	Lumber and wood products.	627	741	722	1.1	-0.2
25	Furniture and fixtures.	417	510	618	1.4	1.3
32	Stone, clay and glass products.	598	557	516	-0.5	-0.5
33	Primary metal industries.	1,139	756	643	-2.7	-1.1
331	Blast furnaces/basic steel products.	548	275	222	-4.5	-1.4
34	Fabricated metal products.	1,453	1,423	1,238	-0.1	-0.9
35	Industrial machinery and equipment.	2,076	2,095	1,941	0.1	-0.5
3571,2,5,7	Computer equipment.	210	396	345	4.3	-0.9
36	Electronic and other electric equipment [3].	1,442	1,673	1,567	1.0	-0.4
3661	Telephone and telegraph apparatus.	148	128	110	-1.0	-1.0
3674	Semiconductors and related devices.	122	238	235	4.6	-0.1
37	Transportation equipment.	1,700	1,980	1,889	1.0	-0.3
371	Motor vehicles and equipment.	792	809	744	0.1	-0.6
38	Instruments and related products [3].	804	1,004	1,018	1.5	0.1
382	Measuring/controlling devices, watches.	326	334	271	0.2	-1.4
3841-3	Medical instruments and supplies.	109	206	282	4.3	2.1
39	Miscellaneous manufacturing industries.	407	377	364	-0.5	-0.2
20-23,26-31	Nondurable manufacturing.	7,661	7,995	7,998	0.3	-
20	Food and kindred products.	1,658	1,668	1,560	-	-0.4
21	Tobacco manufactures.	76	49	34	-2.9	-2.5
22	Textile mill products.	868	691	596	-1.5	-1.0
23	Apparel and other textile products.	1,243	1,043	848	-1.2	-1.4
26	Paper and allied products.	633	699	727	0.7	0.3
27	Printing and publishing.	1,083	1,574	1,900	2.5	1.3
28	Chemicals and allied products.	1,015	1,093	1,098	0.5	-
29	Petroleum and coal products.	194	158	122	-1.4	-1.7
30	Rubber/misc. plastics products.	643	889	1,043	2.2	1.1
31	Leather and leather products.	248	132	72	-4.1	-4.0
(X)	Service producing.	54,080	84,363	107,405	3.0	1.6
40-42,44-49	Transportation, communications, utilities.	4,542	5,826	6,689	1.7	0.9
40-42,44-47	Transportation.	2,634	3,554	4,427	2.0	1.5
48	Communications.	1,176	1,311	1,143	0.7	-0.9
49	Electric, gas, and sanitary services.	733	961	1,119	1.8	1.0
50,51	Wholesale trade.	4,430	6,205	7,210	2.3	1.0
52-59	Retail trade.	12,630	19,683	24,804	3.0	1.6
58	Eating and drinking places.	3,380	6,565	8,712	4.5	1.9
60-67	Finance, insurance, and real estate.	4,165	6,739	8,129	3.3	1.3
70-87,89	Services.	13,627	27,588	39,058	4.8	2.3
70	Hotels and other lodging places.	898	1,649	2,174	4.1	1.9
72	Personal services [3].	782	1,113	1,338	2.4	1.2
73	Business services [3].	1,697	5,241	7,623	7.8	2.5
731	Advertising.	122	238	345	4.6	2.5
734	Services to buildings.	391	809	995	5.0	1.4
736	Personnel supply services.	242	1,559	2,068	13.2	1.9
737	Computer and data processing services.	143	784	1,494	12.0	4.4
75	Auto repair, services, and garages.	439	928	1,245	5.1	2.0
76	Miscellaneous repair shops.	218	390	480	4.0	1.4
78	Motion pictures.	206	408	476	4.7	1.0
784	Video tape rental.	(NA)	132	150	(NA)	0.8
79	Amusement and recreation services.	613	1,089	1,428	3.9	1.8
80	Health services.	4,134	7,844	11,519	4.4	2.6
801,2,3,4	Offices of health practitioners.	936	2,180	3,470	5.8	3.1
805	Nursing and personal care facilities.	759	1,420	2,182	4.3	2.9
806	Hospitals, private.	2,274	3,547	4,605	3.0	1.8
807,8,9	Health services, n.e.c.	165	697	1,262	10.1	4.0
81	Legal services.	341	919	1,427	6.8	3.0
82	Educational services.	1,001	1,652	2,326	3.4	2.3
83	Social services.	690	1,811	2,874	6.6	3.1
84,86,8733	Museums, zoos, and membership organizations.	1,573	2,149	2,488	2.1	1.0
87,89	Engineering, management, and services n.e.c. [4].	(NA)	2,396	3,660	(NA)	2.9
(X)	Government.	14,686	18,322	21,515	1.5	1.1
(X)	Federal government.	2,748	3,085	3,184	0.8	0.2
(X)	State and local government.	11,937	15,237	18,331	1.6	1.2
01,02,07,08,09	Agriculture.	3,459	3,276	3,080	-0.4	-0.4
88	Private households.	1,362	1,014	700	-1.9	-2.4
(X)	Nonagriculture self-employed and unpaid family.	6,165	8,961	10,763	2.5	1.2

- Represents or rounds to zero.   NA Not available.   X Not applicable.   [1] 1987 Standard Industrial Classification; see text, section 13.   [2] Based on assumptions of moderate growth; see source.   [3] Includes other industries, not shown separately.   [4] Excludes SIC 8733.

Source: U.S. Bureau of Labor Statistics, *Monthly Labor Review,* November 1991.

No. 649. High Technology Establishments, Employment and Average Pay, by Industry: 1991

[For workers on private industry payrolls and excludes the self-employed. Based on surveys of the Occupational Employment Statistics Program and subject to sampling error; for details see source]

1987 SIC [1] code	INDUSTRY	Establishments (1,000)	Employment		Average annual pay (dol.)
			Total (1,000)	Percent distribution	
(X)	All high technology industries [2]	336.5	9,789	100.0	$38,147
(X)	Level 1 industries [3]	300.2	8,489	86.7	39,157
131	Crude petroleum and natural gas operations...................	9.9	191	2.0	50,563
211	Cigarettes	([4])	36	0.4	47,915
281	Industrial inorganic chemicals	1.5	136	1.4	42,686
282	Plastics materials and synthetics	1.0	177	1.8	41,225
283	Drugs	1.8	268	2.7	43,925
284	Soap, cleaners, and toilet goods	2.6	158	1.6	37,163
285	Paints and allied products...........	1.5	58	0.6	33,596
286	Industrial organic chemicals	1.0	153	1.7	47,199
287	Agricultural chemicals	1.3	57	0.6	38,256
289	Miscellaneous chemical products.......	2.7	99	1.0	36,634
291	Petroleum refining................	0.8	125	1.3	48,236
299	Miscellaneous petroleum and coal products..................	0.5	12	0.1	32,913
335	Nonferrous rolling and drawing	1.2	166	1.7	33,548
355	Special industry machinery	3.9	150	1.5	33,179
357	Computer and office equipment	2.7	414	4.2	45,499
362	Electrical industrial apparatus	2.0	163	1.7	29,038
366	Communications equipment	2.1	253	2.6	36,766
367	Electronic components and accessories ..	6.6	561	5.7	32,820
371	Motor vehicles and equipment.........	5.8	784	8.0	38,901
372	Aircraft and parts	2.7	670	6.8	40,353
376	Guided missiles, space vehicles, parts ...	0.3	167	1.7	44,143
381	Search and navigation equipment	0.8	260	2.7	42,533
382	Measuring and controlling devices	5.2	308	3.1	34,318
384	Medical instruments and supplies.......	4.2	271	2.8	32,075
386	Photographic equipment and supplies....	0.8	98	1.0	44,555
737	Computer and data-processing services ..	56.3	792	8.1	40,564
871	Engineering and architectural services ...	64.4	751	7.1	39,100
873	Research and testing services.........	22.5	546	5.6	36,312
874	Management and public relations.......	86.1	623	6.4	38,889
899	Services, n.e.c. [5].................	8.0	40	0.4	45,677
(X)	Level II industries [6]	36.3	1,300	13.3	30,749
229	Miscellaneous textile goods	0.9	51	0.5	25,345
261	Pulp mills.....................	0.1	15	0.2	41,781
267	Miscellaneous converted paper products..	3.1	237	2.4	30,356
348	Ordnance and accessories, n.e.c. [5]	0.4	71	0.7	32,899
351	Engines and turbines	0.5	88	0.9	38,580
356	General industry machinery...........	4.4	241	2.5	31,428
359	Industrial machines, n.e.c. [5]	22.7	312	3.2	28,238
365	Household audio and video equipment ...	1.2	86	0.9	32,102
369	Miscellaneous electrical equipment and supplies...................	1.9	158	1.6	30,567
379	Miscellaneous transportation equipment ..	1.1	42	0.4	28,377

X Not applicable.   [1] 1987 Standard Industrial Classification; see text, section 13.   [2] Those industries whose proportion of R&D employment is at least equal to the average proportion of all industries surveyed.   [3] Industries whose proportion of R&D employment is at least 50 percent higher than the average of all industries surveyed.   [4] Fewer than 50 establishments.   [5] N.e.c. means not elsewhere classified.   [6] Industries whose proportion of R&D employment is at least equal to the average of all industries surveyed, but less than 50 percent higher than the average.

Source: U.S. Bureau of Labor Statistics, *Employment and Wages, Annual Averages 1991*, BLS Bulletin 2419.

No. 650. Occupational and Employer Tenure, by Occupation: 1991

[As of January. For the 35 occupations with the longest occupational tenure. Covers occupations with 50,000 or more workers. Based on Current Population Survey; see text section 1, and Appendix III]

CURRENT OCCUPATION	Number (1,000)	OCCUPATIONAL TENURE [1]		Employer tenure [2] (years)	Median age
		Total (years)	Rank		
Total employed, 16 years old and over [3]	114,979	6.5	(X)	4.5	37.2
Airplane pilots and navigators	116	12.2	30	4.5	36.2
Automobile body and related repairers	202	12.1	31	3.1	34.1
Barbers	111	27.2	1	11.0	51.7
Brickmasons and stonemasons	160	12.6	21	5.1	38.2
Chemical engineers	72	12.6	21	6.4	38.0
Civil engineers	284	13.2	15	7.4	42.0
Crane and tower operators	77	13.7	13	6.1	41.9
Dental laboratory & medical appliance technicians	59	12.9	17	5.5	39.9
Dentists	136	15.1	7	13.7	40.5
Electrical power installers and repairers	128	12.6	21	12.5	39.2
Electricians	718	12.3	27	4.9	38.3
Farmers, except horticultural	1,037	21.8	2	20.2	48.0
Geologists and geodesists	60	12.3	27	7.3	40.8
Health specialties teachers	50	15.1	7	11.4	45.7
Heavy equipment mechanics	158	13.7	13	6.7	38.1
Locomotive operators	58	19.8	3	19.7	46.5
Machinists	526	12.3	27	6.6	39.3
Managers, farms, except horticultural	145	11.6	34	8.9	36.9
Millwrights	79	12.5	24	6.2	43.1
Musicians and composers	143	15.2	5	5.4	36.8
Operating engineers	247	12.0	32	5.7	37.8
Pharmacists	182	12.7	20	5.8	39.1
Plumbers, pipefitters, and steamfitters	427	13.1	16	5.5	38.4
Public transportation attendants	60	12.5	24	8.2	39.2
Railroad conductors and yardmasters	56	15.2	5	18.8	43.1
Stationary engineers	120	15.4	4	11.8	42.2
Structural metal workers	52	12.4	26	1.1	36.5
Supervisors, firefighting & fire prevention	65	15.0	10	20.3	44.5
Supervisors, police and detectives	69	12.9	17	15.1	41.5
Teachers, elementary school	1,592	12.0	32	8.4	41.3
Teachers, secondary school	1,392	14.1	11	9.5	42.0
Telephone installers and repairers	193	12.9	17	16.5	40.3
Timber cutting and logging	68	11.5	35	3.5	33.3
Tool and die makers	125	15.1	7	12.6	39.5
Veterinarians	66	14.0	12	10.2	39.5

X Not applicable.   [1] Cummulative tenure in current occupation.   [2] Continuous tenure with current employer.   [3] Includes other occupations, not shown separately.
Source: U.S. Bureau of Labor Statistics, *News,* USDL 92-386; and unpublished data.

No. 651. Displaced Workers, by Selected Characteristics: 1992

[As of January. In percent, except total. For persons 20 years old and over with tenure of 3 years or more who lost or left a job between January 1987 and January 1992 because of plant closings or moves, slack work, or the abolishment of their positions. Based on Current Population Survey and subject to sampling error; see source and Appendix III]

SEX, AGE, RACE, AND HISPANIC ORIGIN	Total (1,000)	EMPLOYMENT STATUS			REASON FOR JOB LOSS		
		Employed	Unemployed	Not in the labor force	Plant or company closed down or moved	Slack work	Position or shift abolished
Total [1]	5,584	64.9	22.2	12.9	52.1	31.6	16.3
Males	3,447	66.6	24.5	8.9	49.4	34.7	15.9
20 to 24 years old	127	55.6	32.5	11.8	45.0	49.4	5.6
25 to 54 years old	2,728	71.6	24.5	3.9	49.5	34.0	16.5
55 to 64 years old	488	52.3	24.2	23.5	49.0	34.6	16.4
65 years old and over	103	15.8	15.3	68.9	53.3	35.7	11.0
Females	2,137	62.2	18.6	19.2	56.6	26.4	17.0
20 to 24 years old	76	72.7	7.3	20.1	43.8	46.1	10.0
25 to 54 years old	1,688	65.8	19.9	14.3	54.4	26.7	18.9
55 to 64 years old	262	51.4	17.4	31.2	70.5	19.4	10.1
65 years old and over	111	26.5	8.7	64.8	66.3	25.1	8.6
White	4,828	65.7	21.2	13.0	52.5	30.6	16.9
Male	3,003	67.6	23.3	9.1	49.4	34.1	16.5
Female	1,825	62.7	17.8	19.5	57.6	24.8	17.6
Black	626	58.7	28.6	12.7	51.3	36.3	12.4
Male	356	58.9	33.4	7.7	52.3	36.6	11.1
Female	270	58.5	22.2	19.3	50.0	35.9	14.1
Hispanic origin [2]	511	60.4	27.4	12.3	57.0	34.5	8.5
Male	323	64.6	27.2	8.2	57.6	35.7	6.7
Female	188	53.0	27.7	19.3	56.0	32.5	11.6

[1] Includes other races, not shown separately.   [2] Persons of Hispanic origin may be of any race.
Source: U.S. Bureau of Labor Statistics, *News,* USDL 92-530.

No. 652. Unemployed Workers—Summary: 1980 to 1992

[In thousands, except as indicated. For civilian noninstitutional population 16 years old and over. Annual averages of monthly figures. For data on unemployment insurance, see table 597. See also *Historical Statistics, Colonial Times to 1970*, series D 87-101]

ITEM AND CHARACTERISTIC	1980	1985	1986	1987	1988	1989	1990	1991	1992
UNEMPLOYED									
Total [1]	7,637	8,312	8,237	7,425	6,701	6,528	6,874	8,426	9,384
Labor force time lost [2] (percent)	7.9	8.1	7.9	7.1	6.3	5.9	6.2	7.6	8.3
16 to 19 years old	1,669	1,468	1,454	1,347	1,226	1,194	1,149	1,290	1,352
20 to 24 years old	1,835	1,738	1,651	1,453	1,261	1,218	1,221	1,477	1,546
25 to 44 years old	2,964	3,681	3,761	3,410	3,095	3,010	3,273	4,106	4,603
45 to 64 years old	1,075	1,331	1,279	1,135	1,032	1,016	1,124	1,437	1,748
65 years and over	94	93	91	78	87	91	107	116	135
Male	4,267	4,521	4,530	4,101	3,655	3,525	3,799	4,817	5,380
16 to 19 years old	913	806	779	732	667	658	629	709	761
20 to 24 years old	1,076	944	899	779	676	660	666	849	884
25 to 44 years old	1,619	1,950	2,054	1,858	1,657	1,572	1,774	2,331	2,603
45 to 64 years old	600	766	741	684	606	585	668	862	1,062
65 years and over	58	55	58	49	49	49	61	66	69
Female	3,370	3,791	3,707	3,324	3,046	3,003	3,075	3,609	4,005
16 to 19 years old	755	661	675	616	558	536	519	581	591
20 to 24 years old	760	794	752	674	585	558	555	628	662
25 to 44 years old	1,345	1,732	1,708	1,552	1,439	1,437	1,498	1,775	1,999
45 to 64 years old	473	566	539	453	427	430	456	575	686
65 years and over	36	39	33	30	38	41	46	50	66
White [3]	5,884	6,191	6,140	5,501	4,944	4,770	5,091	6,447	7,047
16 to 19 years old	1,291	1,074	1,070	995	910	863	856	977	983
20 to 24 years old	1,364	1,235	1,149	1,017	874	856	844	1,063	1,084
Black [3]	1,553	1,864	1,840	1,684	1,547	1,544	1,527	1,679	1,958
16 to 19 years old	343	357	347	312	288	300	258	270	313
20 to 24 years old	426	455	453	397	349	322	335	362	401
Hispanic [3][4]	620	811	857	751	732	750	769	963	1,160
16 to 19 years old	145	141	141	136	148	132	131	149	185
20 to 24 years old	138	171	183	152	145	158	135	172	193
Full-time workers	6,269	6,793	6,708	5,979	5,357	5,211	5,541	6,932	7,746
Part-time workers	1,369	1,519	1,529	1,446	1,343	1,317	1,332	1,494	1,638
UNEMPLOYMENT RATE (percent) [5]									
Total [1]	7.1	7.2	7.0	6.2	5.5	5.3	5.5	6.7	7.4
16 to 19 years old	17.8	18.6	18.3	16.9	15.3	15.0	15.5	18.6	20.0
20 to 24 years old	11.5	11.1	10.7	9.7	8.7	8.6	8.8	10.8	11.3
25 to 44 years old	6.0	6.2	6.1	5.4	4.8	4.5	4.8	6.0	6.7
45 to 64 years old	3.7	4.5	4.3	3.8	3.3	3.2	3.5	4.4	5.1
65 years and over	3.1	3.2	3.0	2.5	2.7	2.6	3.0	3.3	3.8
Male	6.9	7.0	6.9	6.2	5.5	5.2	5.6	7.0	7.8
16 to 19 years old	18.3	19.5	19.0	17.8	16.0	15.9	16.3	19.8	21.5
20 to 24 years old	12.5	11.4	11.0	9.9	8.9	8.8	9.1	11.7	12.2
25 to 44 years old	5.6	5.9	6.0	5.3	4.6	4.3	4.8	6.2	6.9
45 to 64 years old	3.5	4.5	4.4	4.0	3.5	3.3	3.7	4.7	5.6
65 years and over	3.1	3.1	3.2	2.6	2.5	2.4	3.0	3.3	3.3
Female	7.4	7.4	7.1	6.2	5.6	5.4	5.4	6.3	6.9
16 to 19 years old	17.2	17.6	17.6	15.9	14.4	14.0	14.7	17.4	18.5
20 to 24 years old	10.4	10.7	10.3	9.4	8.5	8.3	8.5	9.8	10.2
25 to 44 years old	6.4	6.6	6.2	5.5	4.9	4.8	4.9	5.7	6.4
45 to 64 years old	4.0	4.6	4.2	3.5	3.2	3.1	3.2	3.9	4.4
65 years and over	3.1	3.3	2.8	2.4	2.9	2.9	3.1	3.3	4.5
White [3]	6.3	6.2	6.0	5.3	4.7	4.5	4.7	6.0	6.5
16 to 19 years old	15.5	15.7	15.6	14.4	13.1	12.7	13.4	16.4	17.1
20 to 24 years old	9.9	9.2	8.7	8.0	7.1	7.2	7.2	9.2	9.4
Black [3]	14.3	15.1	14.5	13.0	11.7	11.4	11.3	12.4	14.1
16 to 19 years old	38.5	40.2	39.3	34.7	32.4	32.4	31.1	36.3	39.8
20 to 24 years old	23.6	24.5	24.1	21.8	19.6	18.0	19.9	21.6	23.9
Hispanic [3][4]	10.1	10.5	10.6	8.8	8.2	8.0	8.0	9.9	11.4
16 to 19 years old	22.5	24.3	24.7	22.3	22.0	19.4	19.5	22.9	27.5
20 to 24 years old	12.1	12.6	12.9	10.6	9.8	10.7	9.1	11.6	13.2
Experienced workers [6]	6.9	6.8	6.6	5.8	5.2	5.0	5.3	6.5	7.1
Women maintaining families [1]	9.2	10.5	9.9	9.3	8.2	8.1	8.2	9.1	9.9
White	7.3	8.1	7.8	6.8	6.0	6.1	6.3	7.2	7.8
Black	14.0	16.4	15.4	15.4	13.7	13.0	13.1	13.9	14.7
Married men, wife present [1]	4.2	4.3	4.4	3.9	3.3	3.0	3.4	4.4	5.0
White	3.9	4.0	4.0	3.6	3.0	2.8	3.1	4.2	4.7
Black	7.4	8.0	8.0	6.5	5.8	5.8	6.2	6.5	8.3
Percent without work for—									
Less than 5 weeks	43.1	42.1	41.9	43.7	46.0	48.6	46.1	40.1	34.8
5 to 10 weeks	23.4	22.2	22.6	21.6	22.2	22.2	23.5	22.9	20.9
11 to 14 weeks	9.0	8.0	8.4	7.9	7.8	8.1	8.6	9.5	8.5
15 to 26 weeks	13.8	12.3	12.7	12.7	12.0	11.2	11.8	14.5	15.2
27 weeks and over	10.7	15.4	14.4	14.0	12.1	9.9	10.1	13.0	20.6
Unemployment duration, average (weeks)	11.9	15.6	15.0	14.5	13.5	11.9	12.1	13.8	17.9

[1] Includes other races, not shown separately.   [2] Aggregate hours lost by the unemployed and persons on part time for economic reasons as a percent of potentially available labor force hours.   [3] Includes other ages, not shown separately. [4] Persons of Hispanic origin may be of any race.   [5] Unemployed as percent of civilian labor force in specified group.   [6] Wage and salary workers.

Source: U.S. Bureau of Labor Statistics, *Employment and Earnings*, monthly, January issues; and unpublished data.

No. 653. Unemployed Persons, by Sex and Reason, 1980 to 1992, and by Duration, 1992

[In thousands, except as indicated. For civilian noninstitutional population 16 years old and over. Annual averages of monthly figures. Based on Current Population Survey; see text, section 1, and Appendix III]

SEX AND REASON UNEMPLOYED	1980	1984	1985	1986	1987	1988	1989	1990	1991	1992 Total	1992 Duration of unemployment (percent) Less than 5 weeks	1992 Duration of unemployment (percent) 5 to 14 weeks	1992 Duration of unemployment (percent) 15 weeks or more
Male, total	4,267	4,744	4,521	4,530	4,101	3,655	3,525	3,799	4,817	5,380	31.7	29.2	39.0
Job losers	2,649	2,976	2,749	2,725	2,432	2,078	1,975	2,208	3,105	3,518	27.0	28.5	44.5
Job leavers. . .	438	375	409	520	494	503	495	511	492	479	37.4	30.1	32.6
Reentrants. . . .	776	867	876	805	761	697	726	782	865	950	39.9	30.2	29.9
New entrants . .	405	526	487	480	413	376	328	298	356	433	46.2	31.9	21.9
Female, total. . . .	3,370	3,794	3,791	3,707	3,324	3,046	3,003	3,075	3,609	4,005	39.0	29.7	31.3
Job losers	1,297	1,445	1,390	1,308	1,134	1,014	1,008	1,114	1,503	1,773	28.6	28.3	43.2
Job leavers. . . .	453	449	468	494	471	480	529	503	487	496	45.2	29.6	25.2
Reentrants. . . .	1,152	1,317	1,380	1,355	1,213	1,112	1,117	1,101	1,222	1,278	47.5	31.3	21.3
New entrants . .	468	584	552	549	506	440	349	357	398	457	49.2	30.9	19.9

Source: U.S. Bureau of Labor Statistics, *Employment and Earnings,* monthly, January issues; Bulletin 2307; and unpublished data.

No. 654. Unemployment Rates, by Educational Attainment, Sex, and Race: 1970 to 1991

[In percent. As of **March,** except as indicated. Civilian noninstitutional population 25 to 64 years of age. Due to a change in the method of reporting educational attainment, 1992 are not comparable with data for earlier years. See table 629 for data for 1992 data. Based on the Current Population Survey; see text, section 1, and Appendix III]

ITEM	1970	1975	1980	1982	1983	1984	1985	1986	1987	1988	1989	1990 [1]	1991 [1]
Total	3.3	6.9	5.0	7.6	9.0	6.6	6.1	6.1	5.7	4.7	4.4	4.4	5.5
Less than 4 years of high school [2].	4.6	10.7	8.4	12.5	15.8	12.1	11.4	11.6	11.1	9.6	9.1	8.5	11.0
4 years of high school, only	2.9	6.9	5.1	8.5	10.0	7.2	6.9	6.9	6.3	5.4	4.8	4.9	5.9
College: 1-3 years	2.9	5.5	4.3	6.4	7.3	5.3	4.7	4.7	4.5	3.7	3.4	3.7	4.8
4 years or more	1.3	2.5	1.9	3.0	3.5	2.7	2.4	2.3	2.3	1.7	2.2	2.2	2.8
Male: Total.	2.9	6.7	4.9	7.9	9.8	6.9	6.1	6.2	6.0	5.1	4.7	4.4	5.8
Less than 4 years of high school [2].	4.0	10.5	8.2	12.7	16.1	12.3	11.2	11.7	11.2	10.1	9.7	8.2	11.0
4 years of high school, only	2.4	6.7	5.3	9.3	11.9	8.1	7.2	7.4	6.7	6.2	5.4	5.1	6.4
College: 1-3 years	2.7	5.1	4.4	6.8	8.4	5.2	4.5	4.7	5.0	3.9	3.2	3.7	4.9
4 years or more	1.1	2.2	1.7	2.9	3.4	2.7	2.4	2.3	2.5	1.6	2.3	2.1	2.8
Female: Total.	4.0	7.4	5.0	7.2	7.9	6.1	6.0	5.8	5.2	4.2	4.0	4.4	5.2
Less than 4 years of high school [2].	5.7	10.5	8.9	12.2	15.3	11.7	11.7	11.4	10.9	8.9	8.4	9.0	10.9
4 years of high school, only	3.6	7.1	5.0	7.8	8.0	6.3	6.5	6.3	5.8	4.6	4.2	4.6	5.4
College: 1-3 years	3.1	6.3	4.1	5.3	6.0	5.3	4.8	4.8	4.0	3.4	3.7	3.7	4.7
4 years or more	1.9	3.4	2.2	3.3	3.7	2.7	2.5	2.4	2.1	1.9	2.0	2.3	2.8
White: Total	3.1	6.5	4.4	6.8	8.0	5.7	5.3	5.5	5.0	4.0	3.8	3.8	5.0
Less than 4 years of high school [2].	4.5	10.1	7.8	12.2	15.0	10.9	10.6	10.9	10.2	8.3	7.4	7.6	10.3
4 years of high school, only	2.7	6.5	4.6	7.6	8.9	6.4	6.1	6.2	5.5	4.6	4.2	4.2	5.4
College: 1-3 years	2.8	5.1	3.9	5.4	6.5	4.6	3.9	4.2	4.1	3.2	3.0	3.2	4.2
4 years or more	1.3	2.4	1.8	2.8	3.1	2.4	2.1	2.2	2.2	1.5	2.0	2.1	2.7
Black: Total [3]	4.7	10.9	9.6	13.9	16.8	13.3	12.0	10.7	10.6	10.0	9.2	8.6	9.6
Less than 4 years of high school [2].	5.2	13.5	11.7	14.4	19.9	17.4	15.3	15.3	14.8	15.7	15.9	13.3	14.7
4 years of high school, only	5.2	10.7	9.5	16.4	18.9	14.5	13.0	11.7	11.7	11.2	9.2	9.5	9.9
College: 1-3 years	3.5	9.8	9.0	12.5	13.3	9.7	10.6	8.7	7.6	7.4	6.9	6.8	8.8
4 years or more	0.9	3.9	4.0	7.1	8.1	6.2	5.4	3.2	4.2	3.3	4.7	3.0	4.1

[1] Not strictly comparable with data for earlier years. Annual averages of monthly figures. [2] Includes persons reporting no school years completed. [3] For 1970 and 1975, data refer to Black and other workers.
Source: U.S. Bureau of Labor Statistics, Bulletin 2307; and unpublished data.

No. 655. Unemployment Rates, by Industry, 1975 to 1992, and by Sex, 1980 and 1992

[In percent. For civilian noninstitutional population 16 years old and over. Annual averages of monthly figures. Rate represents unemployment as a percent of labor force in each specified group. Data for 1985-91, and also beginning 1992, not strictly comparable with other years due to changes in industrial classification]

INDUSTRY	1975	1980	1985	1989	1990	1991	1992	MALE 1980	MALE 1992	FEMALE 1980	FEMALE 1992
All unemployed [1]	8.5	7.1	7.2	5.3	5.5	6.7	7.4	6.9	7.8	7.4	6.9
Industry: [2]											
Agriculture	10.4	11.0	13.2	9.6	9.7	11.6	12.3	9.7	12.1	15.1	13.1
Mining.	4.1	6.4	9.5	5.8	4.8	7.7	7.9	6.7	8.3	4.5	5.7
Construction.	18.0	14.1	13.1	10.0	11.1	15.4	16.7	14.6	17.2	8.9	11.0
Manufacturing.	10.9	8.5	7.7	5.1	5.8	7.2	7.8	7.4	7.2	10.8	8.8
Transportation and public utilities . . .	5.6	4.9	5.1	3.9	3.8	5.3	5.5	5.1	5.8	4.4	4.7
Wholesale and retail trade	8.7	7.4	7.6	6.0	6.4	7.6	8.4	6.6	7.7	8.3	9.1
Finance, insurance, and real estate .	4.9	3.4	3.5	3.1	3.0	4.0	4.5	3.2	4.4	3.5	4.6
Services	7.1	5.9	6.2	4.8	5.0	5.7	6.5	6.3	7.4	5.8	5.9
Government	4.1	4.1	3.9	2.7	2.6	3.2	3.5	3.9	4.0	4.3	3.1

[1] Includes the self-employed, unpaid family workers, and persons with no previous work experience, not shown separately. [2] Covers unemployed wage and salary workers.
Source: U.S. Bureau of Labor Statistics, *Employment and Earnings,* monthly, January issues.

No. 656. Unemployment and Unemployment Rates by Occupation, 1983 to 1992, and by Sex, 1992

For civilian noninstitutional population 16 years old and over. Beginning 1985, annual averages of monthly data; 1983 data estimated, see text, section 13. Rate represents unemployment as a percent of the labor force for each specified group. Based on Current Population Survey; see text, section 1, and Appendix III. See also headnote, table 637 concerning 1992 data]

OCCUPATION	NUMBER (1,000)			UNEMPLOYMENT RATE				
						1992		
	1983	1985	1992	1983	1985	Total	Male	Female
Total [1]	10,717	8,312	9,384	9.6	7.2	7.4	7.8	6.9
Managerial and professional specialty	795	645	1,007	3.3	2.4	3.1	3.2	3.0
Executive, administrative, and managerial	396	329	576	3.5	2.6	3.8	3.6	4.0
Professional specialty	399	316	431	3.0	2.3	2.6	2.8	2.4
Technical sales, and administrative support	2,116	1,694	2,268	6.3	4.9	5.8	5.2	6.2
Technicians and related support	152	110	174	4.7	3.3	3.9	4.4	3.4
Sales occupations	850	702	964	6.7	5.3	6.5	4.8	8.2
Administrative support, including clerical	1,114	882	1,129	6.4	4.9	5.7	6.3	5.6
Service occupations	1,697	1,386	1,420	10.9	8.8	8.1	8.6	7.8
Private household	79	69	64	7.4	6.4	6.8	7.0	6.8
Protective service	120	85	105	6.7	4.7	4.8	4.5	6.1
Service except private household and protective. .	1,498	1,233	1,251	11.8	9.5	8.7	10.0	7.9
Precision production, craft, and repair	1,466	1,038	1,273	10.6	7.2	8.8	8.9	8.3
Mechanics and repairers	344	225	278	7.6	4.8	5.9	5.9	4.9
Construction trades	709	531	716	14.2	10.1	13.0	13.0	10.9
Other precision production, craft, and repair.	412	281	280	9.6	6.4	6.7	6.1	8.6
Operators, fabricators, and laborers	2,955	2,140	2,093	15.5	11.3	11.0	11.0	11.0
Machine operators, assemblers, inspectors	1,411	980	898	15.4	11.1	10.7	10.2	11.4
Transportation and material moving occupations. .	596	422	421	12.4	8.5	7.9	8.4	6.6
Handlers, equipment cleaners, helpers, laborers . .	948	739	774	18.6	14.3	14.5	15.1	11.7
Construction laborers	207	186	194	25.8	21.3	22.9	22.6	(B)
Farming, forestry, and fishing	407	315	305	9.9	8.3	8.1	7.7	10.1

B Base is less than 35,000.   [1] Includes persons with no previous work experience and those whose last job was in the Armed Forces.

Source: U.S. Bureau of Labor Statistics, *Employment and Earnings,* monthly, January issues.

No. 657. Range of Unemployment Measures Based on Varying Definitions of Unemployment and the Labor Force: 1970 to 1992

[In percent. Annual averages of monthly figures. Based on Current Population Survey, see text, section 1, and Appendix III]

MEASURE	1970	1975	1980	1985	1986	1987	1988	1989	1990	1991	1992
Persons unemployed 15 weeks or longer as a percent of the civilian labor force	0.8	2.7	1.7	2.0	1.9	1.7	1.3	1.1	1.2	1.9	2.6
Job losers as a percent of the civilian labor force . .	2.2	4.7	3.7	3.6	3.4	3.0	2.5	2.4	2.7	3.7	4.2
Unemployed persons 25 years and over as a percent of the 25 and over civilian labor force.	3.3	6.0	5.1	5.6	5.4	4.8	4.3	4.0	4.4	5.4	6.1
Unemployed full-time jobseekers as a percent of the full-time civilian labor force	4.5	8.1	6.9	6.8	6.6	5.8	5.2	4.9	5.2	6.5	7.1
Total unemployed as a percent of the labor force, including the resident Armed Forces [1]	4.8	8.3	7.0	7.1	6.9	6.1	5.4	5.2	5.4	6.6	7.3
Total unemployed as a percent of the civilian labor force [1]	4.9	8.5	7.1	7.2	7.0	6.2	5.5	5.3	5.5	6.7	7.4
Total full-time jobseekers plus 1/2 part-time jobseekers plus 1/2 total on part-time for economic reasons as a percent of the civilian labor force less 1/2 of the part-time labor force	6.3	10.5	9.2	9.6	9.4	8.5	7.6	7.2	7.6	9.2	10.0
Total full-time jobseekers plus 1/2 part-time jobseekers plus 1/2 total on part-time for economic reasons plus discouraged workers as a percent of the civilian labor force plus discouraged workers less 1/2 of the part-time labor force	7.1	11.6	10.1	10.6	10.3	9.3	8.4	7.9	8.2	10.0	10.8

[1] Current unemployment rate definition.

Source: U.S. Bureau of Labor Statistics, Bulletin 2307; and unpublished data.

No. 658. Total Unemployed and Insured Unemployed—States: 1980 to 1991

[For civilian noninstitutional population 16 years old and over. Annual averages of monthly figures. Total unemployment estimates based on the Current Population Survey (CPS); see text, section 1, and Appendix III. U.S. totals derived by independent population controls; therefore State data may not add to U.S. totals. See table 626 for 1992 unemployment data]

| DIVISION AND STATE | TOTAL UNEMPLOYED | | | | | | | | | | INSURED UNEMPLOYED [2] | | | |
| | Number (1,000) | | | | | Percent [1] | | | | | Number (1,000) | | Percent [3] | |
	1980	1985	1989	1990	1991	1980	1985	1989	1990	1991	1990	1991	1990	1991
U.S..........	7,637	8,312	6,528	6,874	8,426	7.1	7.2	5.3	5.5	6.7	[4]2,522	[4]3,342	[4]2.4	[4]3.1
N.E.: ME.......	39	30	25	33	49	7.8	5.4	4.1	5.1	7.5	17.3	25.7	3.4	5.0
NH.........	22	21	21	36	46	4.7	3.9	3.5	5.6	7.2	11.1	14.7	2.2	3.0
VT.........	16	13	11	15	20	6.4	4.8	3.7	5.0	6.4	8.0	10.6	3.2	4.3
MA.........	162	121	127	189	280	5.6	3.9	4.0	6.0	9.0	112.8	127.3	3.8	4.4
RI.........	34	25	21	35	44	7.2	4.9	4.1	6.7	8.5	20.0	23.9	4.5	5.5
CT.........	94	83	64	91	121	5.9	4.9	3.7	5.1	6.7	45.0	61.0	2.8	3.8
M.A.: NY......	597	544	442	451	616	7.5	6.5	5.1	5.2	7.2	219.1	292.6	2.7	3.7
NJ.........	259	218	163	202	266	7.2	5.7	4.1	5.0	6.6	104.6	135.6	3.0	3.9
PA.........	425	442	264	318	409	7.8	8.0	4.5	5.4	6.9	150.1	199.2	3.1	4.1
E.N.C.: OH....	426	455	300	307	346	8.4	8.9	5.5	5.7	6.4	98.7	132.1	2.1	2.8
IN.........	252	215	136	150	166	9.6	7.9	4.7	5.3	5.9	34.3	46.9	1.4	2.0
IL.........	458	513	359	371	431	8.3	9.0	6.0	6.2	7.1	120.0	156.5	2.4	3.1
MI.........	534	433	326	344	418	12.4	9.9	7.1	7.1	9.2	121.6	154.9	3.2	4.0
WI.........	167	171	114	113	140	7.2	7.2	4.4	4.4	5.4	49.4	65.2	2.3	3.0
W.N.C.: MN....	125	133	102	116	124	5.9	6.0	4.3	4.8	5.1	41.0	48.0	2.1	2.4
IA.........	82	113	65	63	70	5.8	8.0	4.3	4.2	4.6	19.9	24.9	1.7	2.1
MO.........	167	159	143	151	177	7.2	6.4	5.5	5.7	6.6	52.0	66.1	2.4	3.0
ND.........	15	20	14	13	13	5.0	5.9	4.3	3.9	4.1	4.0	4.6	1.7	2.0
SD.........	16	18	15	13	12	4.9	5.1	4.2	3.7	3.4	2.1	2.4	0.8	0.9
NE.........	31	44	25	18	23	4.1	5.5	3.1	2.2	2.7	7.3	9.1	1.1	1.3
KS.........	53	62	52	57	57	4.5	5.0	4.0	4.4	4.4	19.0	22.9	1.9	2.2
S.A.: DE.....	22	17	13	19	23	7.7	5.3	3.5	5.1	6.2	4.8	7.8	1.4	2.3
MD.........	140	103	93	118	151	6.5	4.6	3.7	4.6	5.9	37.6	63.5	1.9	3.2
DC.........	24	27	16	20	22	7.3	8.4	5.0	6.6	7.7	8.4	12.0	1.9	2.7
VA.........	128	161	123	137	193	5.0	5.6	3.9	4.3	5.8	27.9	45.3	1.1	1.7
WV.........	74	100	66	64	82	9.4	13.0	8.6	8.3	10.5	16.3	22.9	2.9	3.9
NC.........	187	167	119	139	198	6.6	5.4	3.5	4.1	5.8	56.1	80.3	1.9	2.7
SC.........	96	107	80	81	108	6.9	6.8	4.7	4.7	6.2	26.9	41.0	1.9	2.8
GA.........	163	187	177	175	158	6.4	6.5	5.5	5.4	5.0	46.7	66.3	1.7	2.3
FL.........	251	319	348	378	471	5.9	6.0	5.6	5.9	7.3	76.7	120.8	1.5	2.3
E.S.C.: KY....	133	161	108	103	128	8.0	9.5	6.2	5.8	7.4	30.6	40.6	2.3	3.0
TN.........	152	180	121	125	160	7.3	8.0	5.1	5.2	6.6	51.3	63.0	2.5	3.0
AL.........	147	160	134	128	135	8.8	8.9	7.0	6.8	7.2	35.7	41.7	2.4	2.7
MS.........	79	115	91	88	102	7.5	10.3	7.8	7.5	8.6	23.4	28.2	2.7	3.2
W.S.C.: AR....	76	91	82	78	82	7.6	8.7	7.2	6.9	7.3	26.4	31.7	3.1	3.6
LA.........	121	229	151	117	137	6.7	11.5	7.9	6.2	7.1	30.0	35.2	2.1	2.3
OK.........	66	112	85	86	101	4.8	7.1	5.6	5.6	6.7	17.3	20.8	1.6	1.9
TX.........	352	564	567	521	564	5.2	7.0	6.7	6.2	6.6	111.6	135.8	1.7	2.0
Mt.: MT......	23	31	24	23	28	6.1	7.7	5.9	5.8	6.9	7.5	8.7	2.8	3.2
ID.........	34	37	25	29	31	7.9	7.9	5.1	5.8	6.1	11.3	14.0	3.2	3.8
WY.........	9	18	15	13	12	4.0	7.1	6.3	5.4	5.1	3.1	3.7	1.7	2.0
CO.........	88	101	98	87	87	5.9	5.9	5.8	4.9	5.0	21.8	26.2	1.5	1.8
NM.........	42	57	46	44	49	7.5	8.8	6.7	6.3	6.9	10.4	12.9	2.0	2.4
AZ.........	83	96	89	92	96	6.7	6.5	5.2	5.3	5.7	26.7	34.1	1.9	2.3
UT.........	40	43	37	34	39	6.3	5.9	4.6	4.3	4.9	8.2	10.3	1.3	1.6
NV.........	27	41	30	31	36	6.2	8.0	5.0	4.9	5.5	12.0	20.2	2.1	3.3
Pac.: WA......	157	171	151	122	157	7.9	8.1	6.2	4.9	6.3	61.1	80.3	3.1	3.9
OR.........	108	117	84	82	90	8.3	8.8	5.7	5.5	6.0	37.2	50.5	3.2	4.2
CA.........	790	931	737	823	1,119	6.8	7.2	5.1	5.6	7.5	377.3	528.4	3.0	4.1
AK.........	18	24	17	18	22	9.7	9.7	6.7	6.9	8.5	11.2	13.2	5.4	6.2
HI.........	21	27	13	15	15	4.9	5.6	2.6	2.8	2.8	5.5	7.9	1.2	1.6

[1] Total unemployment as percent of civilian labor force.   [2] Source: U.S. Employment and Training Administration, *Unemployment Insurance, Financial Data,* annual updates.   [3] Insured unemployment as percent of average covered employment in the previous year.   [4] Includes 43,200 in Puerto Rico and the Virgin Islands in 1990 and 50,400 in 1991.
Source: Except as noted, U.S. Bureau of Labor Statistics, *Geographic Profile of Employment and Unemployment,* annual.

No. 659. U.S. Employment Service Job Openings and Placements, and Index of Help-Wanted Advertising: 1970 to 1991

[In thousands, except as indicated. Openings 1970-1984, for years ending Sept. 30; beginning 1985, for years ending June 30]

ITEM	1970	1980	1984	1985	1986	1987	1988	1989	1990	1991
Job openings: [1] Received.......	6,130	8,122	[2]5,144	7,529	6,950	6,968	7,240	6,998	5,651	5,635
Average per month..........	511	677	[2]572	627	579	581	603	583	471	470
Nonagricultural placements [1].....	4,604	5,610	[2]2,297	3,270	4,856	4,516	4,503	4,284	3,714	3,507
Index of help-wanted advertising in newspapers [3] (1967=100)....	93	128	130	138	138	153	157	150	129	94

[1] As reported by State employment agencies. Beginning 1985, all placements. Placements include duplication for individuals placed more than once.   [2] Data for nine months from October 1, 1983 through June 30, 1984.   [3] Source: The Conference Board, New York, NY, The Statistical Bulletin. Further reproduction prohibited without permission. Index based on number of advertisements in classified sections of 51 newspapers, each in a major employment area.
Source: Except as noted, U.S. Employment and Training Administration, unpublished data.

No. 660. Nonfarm Establishments, Employees, Hours, and Earnings, by Industry: 1960 to 1992

[Based on data from establishment reports. Includes all full- and part-time employees who worked during, or received pay for, any part of the pay period reported. Excludes proprietors, the self-employed, farm workers, unpaid family workers, private household workers, and Armed Forces. Establishment data shown here conform to industry definitions in the 1987 Standard Industrial Classification Manual and are adjusted to March 1991 employment benchmarks; consequently, may not be comparable with previously published data. Based on the Current Employment Statistics Program; see Appendix III. See also *Historical Statistics, Colonial Times to 1970*, series D 127-141 and D 803, 878, 881, 884, and 890]

ITEM AND YEAR	Total	GOODS-PRODUCING				SERVICE-PRODUCING						
		Total	Mining	Construc-tion	Manu-factur-ing	Total	Trans-portation and public utilities	Whole-sale trade	Retail trade	Finance, insur-ance, and real estate	Serv-ices	Govern-ment
EMPLOYEES (1,000)												
1960	54,189	20,434	712	2,926	16,796	33,755	4,004	3,153	8,238	2,628	7,378	8,353
1965	60,765	21,926	632	3,232	18,062	38,839	4,036	3,477	9,239	2,977	9,036	10,074
1970	70,880	23,578	623	3,588	19,367	47,302	4,515	4,006	11,034	3,645	11,548	12,554
1975	76,945	22,600	752	3,525	18,323	54,345	4,542	4,430	12,630	4,165	13,892	14,686
1980	90,406	25,658	1,027	4,346	20,285	64,748	5,146	5,292	15,018	5,160	17,890	16,241
1985	97,519	24,859	927	4,673	19,260	72,660	5,238	5,736	17,336	5,955	21,999	16,394
1987	102,200	24,708	717	4,967	19,024	77,492	5,372	5,865	18,462	6,547	24,235	17,010
1988	105,536	25,173	713	5,110	19,350	80,363	5,527	6,055	19,077	6,649	25,669	17,386
1989	108,329	25,322	693	5,187	19,442	83,007	5,644	6,221	19,549	6,695	27,120	17,779
1990	109,782	24,960	710	5,133	19,117	84,822	5,808	6,200	19,677	6,729	28,103	18,304
1991	108,310	23,830	691	4,685	18,455	84,480	5,772	6,069	19,259	6,678	28,323	18,380
1992	108,437	23,420	635	4,595	18,190	85,017	5,742	5,983	19,138	6,672	28,903	18,579
PERCENT DISTRIBUTION												
1960	100.0	37.7	1.3	5.4	31.0	62.3	7.4	5.8	15.2	4.8	13.6	15.4
1965	100.0	36.1	1.0	5.3	29.7	63.9	6.6	5.7	15.2	4.9	14.9	16.6
1970	100.0	33.3	0.9	5.1	27.3	66.7	6.4	5.7	15.6	5.1	16.3	17.7
1975	100.0	29.4	1.0	4.6	23.8	70.6	5.9	5.8	16.4	5.4	18.1	19.1
1980	100.0	28.4	1.1	4.8	22.4	71.6	5.7	5.9	16.6	5.7	19.8	18.0
1985	100.0	25.5	1.0	4.8	19.7	74.5	5.4	5.9	17.8	6.1	22.6	16.8
1987	100.0	24.2	0.7	4.9	18.6	75.8	5.3	5.7	18.1	6.4	23.7	16.6
1988	100.0	23.9	0.7	4.8	18.3	76.1	5.2	5.7	18.1	6.3	24.3	16.5
1989	100.0	23.4	0.6	4.8	17.9	76.6	5.2	5.7	18.0	6.2	25.0	16.4
1990	100.0	22.7	0.6	4.7	17.4	77.3	5.3	5.6	17.9	6.1	25.6	16.7
1991	100.0	22.0	0.6	4.3	17.0	78.0	5.3	5.6	17.8	6.2	26.1	17.0
1992	100.0	21.6	0.6	4.2	16.8	78.4	5.3	5.5	17.6	6.2	26.7	17.1
WEEKLY HOURS [1]												
1960	38.6	(NA)	40.4	36.7	39.7	(NA)	(NA)	40.5	38.0	37.2	(NA)	(NA)
1965	38.8	(NA)	42.3	37.4	41.2	(NA)	41.3	40.8	36.6	37.2	35.9	(NA)
1970	37.1	(NA)	42.7	37.3	39.8	(NA)	40.5	39.9	33.8	36.7	34.4	(NA)
1975	36.1	(NA)	41.9	36.4	39.5	(NA)	39.7	38.6	32.4	36.5	33.5	(NA)
1980	35.3	(NA)	43.3	37.0	39.7	(NA)	39.6	38.4	30.2	36.2	32.6	(NA)
1985	34.9	(NA)	43.4	37.7	40.5	(NA)	39.5	38.4	29.4	36.4	32.5	(NA)
1987	34.8	(NA)	42.4	37.8	41.0	(NA)	39.2	38.1	29.2	36.3	32.5	(NA)
1988	34.7	(NA)	42.3	37.9	41.1	(NA)	38.8	38.1	29.1	35.9	32.6	(NA)
1989	34.6	(NA)	43.0	37.9	41.0	(NA)	38.9	38.0	28.9	35.8	32.6	(NA)
1990	34.5	(NA)	44.1	38.2	40.8	(NA)	38.9	38.1	28.8	35.8	32.5	(NA)
1991	34.3	(NA)	44.4	38.1	40.7	(NA)	38.7	38.1	28.6	35.7	32.4	(NA)
1992	34.4	(NA)	44.0	38.0	41.0	(NA)	38.8	38.2	28.8	35.8	32.5	(NA)
HOURLY EARNINGS [1]												
1960	$2.09	(NA)	$2.60	$3.07	$2.26	(NA)	(NA)	$2.24	$1.52	$2.02	(NA)	(NA)
1965	2.46	(NA)	2.92	3.70	2.61	(NA)	$3.03	2.60	1.82	2.39	$2.05	(NA)
1970	3.23	(NA)	3.85	5.24	3.35	(NA)	3.85	3.43	2.44	3.07	2.81	(NA)
1975	4.53	(NA)	5.95	7.31	4.83	(NA)	5.88	4.72	3.36	4.06	4.02	(NA)
1980	6.66	(NA)	9.17	9.94	7.27	(NA)	8.87	6.95	4.88	5.79	5.85	(NA)
1985	8.57	(NA)	11.98	12.32	9.54	(NA)	11.40	9.15	5.94	7.94	7.90	(NA)
1987	8.98	(NA)	12.54	12.71	9.91	(NA)	12.03	9.59	6.12	8.73	8.49	(NA)
1988	9.28	(NA)	12.80	13.08	10.19	(NA)	12.26	9.98	6.31	9.06	8.88	(NA)
1989	9.66	(NA)	13.26	13.54	10.48	(NA)	12.60	10.39	6.53	9.53	9.38	(NA)
1990	10.01	(NA)	13.68	13.77	10.83	(NA)	12.97	10.79	6.75	9.97	9.83	(NA)
1991	10.33	(NA)	14.18	13.99	11.18	(NA)	13.24	11.15	6.95	10.40	10.22	(NA)
1992	10.59	(NA)	14.51	14.11	11.45	(NA)	13.49	11.40	7.14	10.82	10.54	(NA)
WEEKLY EARNINGS [1]												
1960	$81	(NA)	$105	$113	$90	(NA)	(NA)	$91	$58	$75	(NA)	(NA)
1965	95	(NA)	124	138	108	(NA)	$125	106	67	89	$74	(NA)
1970	120	(NA)	164	195	133	(NA)	156	137	82	113	97	(NA)
1975	164	(NA)	249	266	191	(NA)	233	182	109	148	135	(NA)
1980	235	(NA)	397	368	289	(NA)	351	267	147	210	191	(NA)
1985	299	(NA)	520	464	386	(NA)	450	351	175	289	257	(NA)
1987	313	(NA)	532	480	406	(NA)	472	365	179	317	276	(NA)
1988	322	(NA)	541	496	419	(NA)	476	380	184	325	289	(NA)
1989	334	(NA)	570	513	430	(NA)	490	395	189	341	306	(NA)
1990	345	(NA)	603	526	442	(NA)	505	411	194	357	319	(NA)
1991	354	(NA)	630	533	455	(NA)	512	425	199	371	331	(NA)
1992	364	(NA)	638	536	469	(NA)	523	435	206	387	343	(NA)

NA Not available.   [1] Average hours and earnings. Private production and related workers in mining, manufacturing, and construction; nonsupervisory employees in other industries.

Source: U.S. Bureau of Labor Statistics, *Employment and Earnings*, monthly, March issues.

No. 661. Employees in Nonfarm Establishments—States: 1980 to 1992

[**In thousands.** For coverage, see headnote, table 660. National totals differ from the sum of the State figures because of differing benchmarks among States and differing industrial and geographic stratification. Based on 1987 *Standard Industrial Classification Manual*, see text, section 13]

REGION, DIVISION, AND STATE	1980	1985	1990	1991	1992 Total ¹	Construction	Manufacturing	Transportation and public utilities	Wholesale and retail trade	Finance, insurance, and real estate	Services	Government
U.S....	90,406	97,519	109,782	108,310	108,437	4,595	18,190	5,742	25,121	6,672	28,903	18,579
Northeast .	20,502	21,962	23,386	22,513	22,207	725	3,582	1,143	4,902	1,692	6,578	3,551
N.E.....	5,481	6,067	6,369	6,043	5,967	180	1,091	252	1,374	429	1,782	856
ME ...	418	458	535	513	512	21	92	21	128	24	129	96
NH ...	385	466	508	482	485	16	97	17	124	29	129	72
VT....	200	225	258	249	249	11	44	11	58	12	69	43
MA ...	2,652	2,926	2,985	2,821	2,778	72	462	120	641	196	907	378
RI	398	429	451	422	421	12	90	14	90	25	127	61
CT....	1,427	1,562	1,633	1,556	1,522	47	306	68	333	143	420	205
M.A	15,021	15,896	17,017	16,470	16,240	545	2,491	891	3,528	1,263	4,796	2,695
NY....	7,207	7,751	8,212	7,888	7,728	241	1,015	400	1,566	737	2,336	1,428
NJ....	3,060	3,414	3,635	3,499	3,441	108	527	229	809	226	972	569
PA....	4,753	4,730	5,170	5,084	5,071	197	949	263	1,154	300	1,488	698
Midwest.	23,634	23,995	27,028	26,836	27,054	1,021	5,414	1,365	6,475	1,551	6,813	4,332
E.N.C .	16,728	16,841	18,954	18,750	18,851	711	4,041	906	4,462	1,076	4,718	2,886
OH ...	4,367	4,373	4,882	4,819	4,842	180	1,051	212	1,160	257	1,234	734
IN	2,130	2,169	2,522	2,507	2,538	110	627	130	597	127	552	387
IL	4,850	4,755	5,288	5,232	5,205	201	922	301	1,230	377	1,389	768
MI	3,443	3,562	3,970	3,891	3,917	128	897	154	929	189	972	641
WI	1,938	1,983	2,292	2,302	2,349	91	546	109	546	127	571	356
W.N.C.	6,905	7,154	8,074	8,086	8,203	310	1,373	459	2,013	475	2,095	1,446
MN ...	1,770	1,865	2,130	2,137	2,186	77	396	110	527	130	593	347
IA	1,110	1,074	1,226	1,238	1,251	47	230	55	318	72	306	222
MO ...	1,970	2,095	2,345	2,309	2,320	90	410	151	555	136	601	372
ND ...	245	252	266	271	277	11	18	18	73	13	74	67
SD....	238	249	289	296	307	13	37	15	80	17	78	65
NE....	628	651	730	739	747	28	100	47	189	49	185	148
KS....	945	968	1,089	1,095	1,115	45	182	65	272	58	259	226
South	29,147	32,390	36,816	36,565	37,007	1,714	5,970	2,003	8,693	1,954	9,335	6,962
S.A.....	14,695	16,789	19,773	19,394	19,560	928	2,983	1,009	4,624	1,083	5,191	3,676
DE. ...	259	293	348	342	344	18	68	15	75	33	86	49
MD...	1,712	1,888	2,171	2,100	2,079	118	183	99	504	129	630	414
DC. ...	616	629	686	677	677	9	14	23	55	34	256	287
VA....	2,157	2,455	2,896	2,829	2,840	146	408	146	633	149	756	589
WV ...	646	597	630	629	639	28	82	38	146	25	158	132
NC ...	2,380	2,651	3,118	3,072	3,133	145	833	153	714	135	640	510
SC....	1,189	1,296	1,545	1,513	1,529	81	371	64	345	65	309	292
GA ...	2,159	2,570	2,992	2,938	2,982	120	544	197	743	162	672	535
FL....	3,576	4,410	5,387	5,294	5,339	263	481	273	1,409	352	1,685	869
E.S.C .	5,142	5,384	6,236	6,238	6,378	266	1,432	329	1,441	275	1,407	1,176
KY....	1,210	1,250	1,471	1,475	1,511	69	287	82	355	63	351	274
TN....	1,747	1,868	2,193	2,184	2,232	85	513	120	519	101	535	355
AL....	1,356	1,427	1,636	1,642	1,673	76	381	82	366	74	345	338
MS ...	829	839	937	938	962	36	251	45	200	38	177	209
W.S.C.	9,311	10,217	10,807	10,933	11,069	520	1,555	665	2,628	596	2,737	2,110
AR....	742	797	924	936	963	38	237	56	213	39	210	168
LA....	1,579	1,591	1,590	1,613	1,625	100	185	105	378	77	395	338
OK ...	1,138	1,165	1,193	1,209	1,210	39	163	70	284	60	287	270
TX....	5,851	6,663	7,101	7,175	7,271	344	970	435	1,753	420	1,845	1,334
West	17,578	19,486	22,813	22,606	22,472	960	3,107	1,192	5,330	1,372	6,221	4,117
Mt	4,502	5,110	5,812	5,901	6,057	306	626	341	1,456	329	1,721	1,187
MT ...	280	279	297	304	317	13	23	20	85	14	82	74
ID	330	336	385	398	416	22	66	20	106	22	91	88
WY ...	210	207	199	203	205	11	9	14	47	7	42	57
CO ...	1,251	1,419	1,521	1,545	1,593	74	185	100	386	100	442	291
NM ...	465	520	580	585	598	30	40	29	142	27	159	156
AZ....	1,014	1,279	1,486	1,491	1,520	81	172	81	377	94	425	278
UT....	551	624	724	745	768	35	106	44	184	37	197	157
NV....	400	446	621	629	641	39	26	33	130	29	284	86
Pac	13,076	14,376	17,001	16,705	16,415	654	2,481	851	3,874	1,043	4,500	2,930
WA ...	1,608	1,710	2,152	2,175	2,216	119	346	113	538	119	554	423
OR ...	1,045	1,030	1,252	1,251	1,271	50	207	66	320	86	310	231
CA....	9,849	10,979	12,830	12,497	12,140	475	1,890	607	2,833	790	3,420	2,091
AK....	169	231	238	243	247	10	18	23	48	11	54	73
HI	405	426	528	539	541	(NA)	20	43	135	38	162	111

NA Not available.   ¹ Includes mining, not shown separately.

Source: U.S. Bureau of Labor Statistics, Bulletin 2320; and *Employment and Earnings*, monthly, May issues. Compiled from data supplied by cooperating State agencies.

No. 662. Nonfarm Industries—Number of Employees and Number and Earnings of Production Workers: 1980 to 1992

[Annual averages of monthly figures. Covers all full- and part-time employees who worked during, or received pay for, any part of the pay period including the 12th of the month. For mining and manufacturing, data refer to production and related workers; for construction, to employees engaged in actual construction work; and for other industries, to nonsupervisory employees and working supervisors. See also headnote table 660. See *Historical Statistics, Colonial Times to 1970*, series D 127-151, D 802-810, and D 877-892, for related data]

1987 SIC [1] code	INDUSTRY	ALL EMPLOYEES TOTAL (1,000)			PRODUCTION WORKERS					
					Total (1,000)			Average hourly earnings (dollars)		
		1980	1990	1992	1980	1990	1992	1980	1990	1992
(X)	Total................	90,406	109,782	108,437	(NA)	(NA)	(NA)	(NA)	(NA)	(NA)
(X)	Private sector [2].........	74,166	91,478	89,858	60,331	74,108	72,809	6.66	10.01	10.59
(B)	Mining..................	1,027	710	635	762	509	450	9.17	13.68	14.51
10	Metal mining.................	98	58	54	74	46	43	10.26	14.05	15.22
12	Coal mining..................	246	147	124	204	119	101	10.86	16.71	17.20
13	Oil and gas extraction...........	560	395	354	389	261	230	8.59	12.94	13.97
14	Nonmetallic minerals, except fuels....	123	111	103	96	84	77	7.52	11.58	12.27
(C)	Construction..............	4,346	5,133	4,595	3,421	3,984	3,511	9.94	13.77	14.11
15	General building contractors........	1,173	1,301	1,103	900	940	777	9.22	13.01	13.39
16	Heavy construction, except building...	895	771	718	720	644	594	9.20	13.34	13.89
17	Special trade contractors.........	2,278	3,060	2,774	1,802	2,401	2,140	10.63	14.20	14.44
(D)	Manufacturing.............	20,285	19,117	18,190	14,214	12,979	12,345	7.27	10.83	11.45
(X)	Durable goods............	12,159	11,130	10,339	8,416	7,379	6,859	7.75	11.35	12.02
24	Lumber and wood products [3]....	704	735	687	587	605	563	6.57	9.08	9.43
241	Logging....................	88	85	76	71	70	62	8.64	11.22	11.24
242	Sawmills and planing mills.......	215	198	182	190	173	158	6.70	9.22	9.60
243	Millwork, plywood, and structural members..................	207	262	245	170	211	195	6.44	9.04	9.47
244	Wood containers.............	43	45	43	37	38	36	4.95	6.64	6.89
2451	Mobile homes.............	46	41	43	36	33	35	6.08	8.67	9.21
25	Furniture and fixtures [3].........	466	507	465	376	401	367	5.49	8.52	9.00
251	Household furniture...........	301	290	267	253	242	222	5.12	7.87	8.40
252	Office furniture.............	51	69	59	40	51	44	5.91	9.64	9.75
254	Partitions and fixtures...........	63	79	74	47	57	54	6.68	9.77	10.32
32	Stone, clay, and glass products [3]....	629	557	519	486	433	401	7.50	11.12	11.64
321	Flat glass.................	18	17	16	14	13	13	9.65	15.15	16.49
322	Glass and glassware, pressed and blown..................	124	83	83	105	72	71	7.97	12.40	13.02
323	Products of purchased glass.....	45	60	57	32	46	43	6.50	9.75	10.02
324	Cement, hydraulic...........	31	18	18	25	14	14	10.55	13.90	14.74
325	Structural clay products.......	46	36	33	34	28	25	6.14	9.55	9.99
326	Pottery and related products......	47	39	37	39	31	29	6.25	9.62	10.07
327	Concrete, gypsum, and plaster.....	204	207	187	157	158	141	7.45	10.76	11.17
33	Primary metal industries [3]..........	1,142	757	703	878	575	531	9.77	12.92	13.67
331	Blast furnaces and basic steel products.................	512	276	254	396	212	191	11.39	14.82	15.89
332	Iron and steel foundries........	209	133	121	167	105	97	8.20	11.55	12.22
333	Primary nonferrous metals.......	71	46	43	53	34	32	10.63	14.36	14.93
335	Nonferrous rolling and drawing....	211	173	165	151	124	119	8.81	12.29	12.92
336	Nonferrous foundries (castings)...	90	84	78	72	66	61	7.30	10.21	10.86
34	Fabricated metal products [3]........	1,609	1,423	1,335	1,194	1,048	979	7.45	10.83	11.41
341	Metal cans and shipping containers..	75	50	46	63	43	40	9.84	14.27	14.88
342	Cutlery, handtools, and hardware...	164	131	122	125	96	91	7.02	10.78	11.27
343	Plumbing and heating, exc. electric..	71	60	57	52	43	41	6.59	9.75	10.23
344	Fabricated structural metal products..................	507	427	396	351	303	279	7.27	10.16	10.69
345	Screw machine products........	109	96	88	84	74	67	6.96	10.70	11.39
346	Metal forgings and stampings ...	261	225	214	205	178	169	8.56	12.70	13.47
35	Industrial machinery and equipment [3]..	2,517	2,099	1,946	1,614	1,263	1,164	8.00	11.77	12.43
351	Engines and turbines.........	135	89	93	87	58	58	9.73	14.55	15.67
352	Farm and garden machinery.....	169	106	96	116	78	69	8.78	10.99	11.66
353	Construction and related machinery .	389	229	204	255	141	121	8.60	11.92	12.68
354	Metalworking machinery........	399	331	306	290	236	216	8.13	12.27	12.96
355	Special industry machinery......	195	159	144	125	94	82	7.53	11.90	12.67
356	General industrial machinery......	300	248	233	196	158	148	7.95	11.32	12.07
357	Computer and office equipment....	421	439	395	181	137	131	6.75	11.51	12.33
358	Refrigeration and service machinery................	175	178	172	120	125	120	7.23	10.93	11.29
36	Electronic and other elec. equip. [3]....	1,771	1,676	1,549	(4)	1,056	984	(4)	10.30	11.01
361	Electric distribution equipment.....	117	97	87	82	68	60	6.96	10.15	10.92
362	Electrical industrial apparatus.....	232	169	157	163	119	111	(4)	10.00	10.37
363	Household appliances	162	124	119	128	100	95	6.95	10.26	10.48
364	Electric lighting and wiring equip....	188	189	173	157	136	125	6.43	10.12	10.84
365	Household audio and video equip...	109	85	85	79	59	57	6.42	9.68	10.85
366	Communications equipment.......	(4)	264	238	(4)	133	121	(4)	11.03	11.53
367	Electronic components and accessories................	539	583	534	325	329	308	6.05	10.00	10.93
37	Transportation equipment [3].......	1,881	1,990	1,827	1,220	1,225	1,144	9.35	14.08	15.16
371	Motor vehicles and equipment.....	789	813	812	575	618	621	9.85	14.56	15.33
372	Aircraft and parts...........	636	713	617	344	345	293	9.28	14.79	16.59
373	Ship and boat building and repairing................	221	188	170	176	142	131	8.22	10.94	11.97
374	Railroad equipment	71	33	29	53	25	21	9.93	13.41	14.34
376	Guided missiles, space vehicles, and parts............	111	185	141	35	57	39	9.22	14.39	15.97

See footnotes at end of table.

No. 662. Nonfarm Industries—Number of Employees and Number and Earnings of Production Workers: 1980 to 1992—Continued

[See headnote, p. 419]

1987 SIC[1] code	INDUSTRY	ALL EMPLOYEES TOTAL (1,000)			PRODUCTION WORKERS Total (1,000)			Average hourly earnings (dollars)		
		1980	1990	1992	1980	1990	1992	1980	1990	1992
(X)	**Durable goods—Continued**									
38	Instruments and related products.....	1,022	1,008	943	(⁴)	500	462	(⁴)	11.29	11.93
381	Search and navigation equipment...	(⁴)	285	239	(⁴)	94	75	(⁴)	14.62	15.65
382	Measuring and controlling devices ..	(⁴)	323	292	(⁴)	181	154	(⁴)	10.68	11.54
384	Medical instruments and supplies...	(⁴)	247	267	(⁴)	145	155	(⁴)	9.85	10.50
385	Ophthalmic goods	44	43	41	31	30	27	5.30	8.18	8.46
386	Photographic equipment and supplies	135	100	96	67	43	42	8.83	14.08	14.68
387	Watches, clocks, watchcases, and parts	22	11	9	17	8	7	5.24	7.70	7.94
39	Misc. manufacturing industries [3]	418	377	366	313	274	264	5.46	8.61	9.14
391	Jewelry, silverware, and plated ware	56	52	52	40	37	37	5.76	9.23	9.55
394	Toys and sporting goods.........	117	104	106	88	76	78	5.01	7.94	8.48
395	Pens, pencils, office and art supplies	37	34	33	27	24	22	5.58	8.89	9.91
396	Costume jewelry and notions	(⁴)	34	29	(⁴)	26	21	(⁴)	7.40	7.91
(X)	**Nondurable goods**	8,127	7,988	7,851	5,798	5,600	5,486	6.56	10.12	10.71
20	Food and kindred products [3] ...	1,708	1,666	1,670	1,175	1,198	1,214	6.85	9.62	10.19
201	Meat products................	358	422	435	298	359	370	6.99	7.94	8.31
202	Dairy products................	175	156	155	96	95	97	6.86	10.56	11.31
203	Preserved fruits and vegetables	246	249	249	202	207	210	5.94	8.95	9.73
204	Grain mill products.............	144	128	128	99	89	90	7.67	11.52	12.18
205	Bakery products	230	214	212	139	134	135	7.14	10.85	11.50
206	Sugar and confectionery products...	108	100	101	81	78	79	6.56	11.02	11.02
207	Fats and oils.................	44	31	31	32	22	21	7.03	10.10	10.67
208	Beverages	234	185	178	105	78	77	8.12	13.51	14.33
21	Tobacco products..............	69	49	49	54	37	37	7.74	16.23	16.69
211	Cigarettes..................	46	35	34	35	26	26	9.23	19.57	20.68
22	Textile mill products [3]	848	692	678	737	594	581	5.07	8.02	8.60
221	Broadwoven fabric mills, cotton	150	91	86	135	82	76	5.25	8.31	8.94
222	Broadwoven fabric mills, synthetics..	116	77	74	104	68	64	5.30	8.63	9.26
223	Broadwoven fabric mills, wool	19	17	18	16	14	15	5.21	8.61	9.12
224	Narrow fabric mills.............	23	24	24	20	20	20	4.63	7.39	8.12
225	Knitting mills.................	224	206	201	194	179	175	4.77	7.37	7.88
226	Textile finishing, except wool	74	62	66	62	50	54	5.39	8.45	9.03
227	Carpets and rugs..............	54	61	59	44	50	48	5.20	8.25	8.59
228	Yarn and thread mills	125	103	101	113	92	91	4.76	7.68	8.31
23	Apparel and other textile products [3] ...	1,264	1,039	1,018	1,079	871	852	4.56	6.57	6.95
231	Men's and boys' suits and coats	77	50	45	67	42	37	5.34	7.34	7.54
232	Men's and boys' furnishings	362	274	284	310	236	244	4.23	6.06	6.51
233	Women's and misses outerwear....	417	329	317	360	275	265	4.61	6.26	6.58
234	Women's and children's undergarments.	90	62	56	76	51	46	4.15	6.18	6.67
236	Girls' and children's outerwear.....	64	56	52	55	47	44	4.20	5.95	6.28
26	Paper and allied products [3]	685	698	688	519	524	518	7.84	12.31	13.09
262	Papermills	179	180	180	133	136	137	9.05	15.10	16.07
263	Paperboard mills	65	52	49	51	40	38	9.28	15.56	16.24
265	Paperboard containers and boxes..	205	210	209	157	162	164	6.94	10.39	10.98
267	Misc. converted paper products	220	242	236	163	175	169	6.89	10.79	11.50
27	Printing and publishing [3]	1,252	1,575	1,521	699	874	841	7.53	11.24	11.75
271	Newspapers	420	475	453	164	166	158	7.72	11.17	11.71
272	Periodicals	90	130	124	16	48	43	7.16	11.95	12.67
273	Books	101	121	119	52	66	66	6.76	10.10	10.64
275	Commercial printing	410	554	538	304	403	389	7.85	11.52	11.94
278	Blankbooks and bookbinding.	62	72	68	51	56	52	5.78	8.83	9.18
28	Chemicals and allied products [3]	1,107	1,088	1,071	626	601	565	8.30	13.54	14.45
281	Industrial inorganic chemicals	161	138	125	88	70	57	9.07	14.66	15.67
282	Plastics materials and synthetics ...	205	181	173	137	116	104	8.21	13.97	15.34
283	Drugs	196	237	251	97	105	111	7.69	12.90	14.04
284	Soap, cleaners, and toilet goods ...	141	160	158	86	99	96	7.67	11.71	12.04
285	Paints and allied products	65	61	57	33	31	30	7.39	11.99	12.65
286	Industrial organic chemicals......	174	155	153	88	86	76	9.67	15.97	17.23
287	Agricultural chemicals. ...... [3]	72	56	56	45	34	34	8.12	13.73	14.69
29	Petroleum and coal products [3]	198	158	155	125	103	101	10.10	16.24	17.87
291	Petroleum refining	155	118	116	93	75	75	10.94	17.58	19.55
295	Asphalt paving and roofing materials.	31	27	27	24	21	20	7.69	12.87	13.23
30	Rubber and misc. plastics products [3] ..	765	890	879	588	689	678	6.58	9.76	10.37
301	Tires and inner tubes	115	84	83	81	62	62	9.74	15.42	16.75
302	Rubber and plastics footwear......	22	11	11	20	9	9	4.43	6.66	7.21
31	Leather and leather products [3]	233	133	123	197	110	100	4.58	6.91	7.40
311	Leather tanning and finishing......	19	15	16	16	12	13	6.10	9.04	9.60
314	Footwear, except rubber.........	144	74	66	123	63	55	4.42	6.61	7.01
316	Luggage...................	16	11	10	12	8	7	4.90	6.91	7.49
317	Handbags and personal leather goods	30	15	14	25	12	10	4.33	6.08	6.50

See footnotes at end of table.

No. 662. Nonfarm Industries—Number of Employees and Number and Earnings of Production Workers: 1980 to 1992—Continued

[See headnote, p. 419]

1987 SIC [1] code	INDUSTRY	ALL EMPLOYEES TOTAL (1,000)			PRODUCTION WORKERS					
					Total (1,000)			Average hourly earnings (dollars)		
		1980	1990	1992	1980	1990	1992	1980	1990	1992
(E)	**Transp. and public utilities [3] ....**	**5,146**	**5,808**	**5,742**	**4,293**	**4,821**	**4,791**	**8.87**	**12.97**	**13.49**
40	Railroad transportation.	532	279	259	(4)	(4)	(4)	(4)	(4)	(4)
4011	Class I railroads [5]	482	241	222	(4)	(4)	(4)	[6]9.92	[6]16.08	[6]16.66
41	Local and interurban passenger transit.	265	341	358	244	311	329	6.34	9.23	9.85
42	Trucking and warehousing	1,280	1,629	1,618	1,121	1,419	1,410	9.13	11.71	12.11
44	Water transportation	211	178	186	(4)	(4)	(4)	(4)	(4)	(4)
45	Transportation by air	453	746	732	(4)	(4)	(4)	(4)	(4)	(4)
46	Pipelines, except natural gas	21	19	19	15	14	14	10.50	17.04	18.64
47	Transportation services	198	347	348	(4)	279	274	(4)	10.43	10.77
48	Communication [3]	1,357	1,312	1,262	1,014	980	969	8.50	13.51	14.48
481	Telephone communication.	1,072	914	873	779	658	649	8.72	15.21	15.21
483	Radio and television broadcasting...	192	235	226	154	194	188	7.44	12.71	13.81
484	Cable and other pay television services	(4)	127	130	(4)	106	111	(4)	10.50	11.01
49	Electric, gas, and sanitary services [3]	829	959	959	678	760	755	8.90	15.23	16.09
491	Electric services	391	454	443	316	351	343	9.12	15.80	16.75
492	Gas production and distribution	168	165	162	138	129	126	8.27	14.25	15.43
493	Combination utility services	197	193	194	162	156	150	9.64	17.58	18.66
495	Sanitary services	50	116	128	44	100	110	7.16	11.55	11.99
(F)	**Wholesale trade**	**5,292**	**6,200**	**5,983**	**4,328**	**4,981**	**4,806**	**6.95**	**10.79**	**11.40**
(G)	**Retail trade [3]**	**15,018**	**19,677**	**19,138**	**13,484**	**17,425**	**16,844**	**4.88**	**6.75**	**7.14**
53	General merchandise stores	2,245	2,542	2,309	2,090	2,382	2,158	4.77	6.83	7.18
54	Food stores	2,384	3,221	3,178	2,202	2,958	2,899	6.24	7.31	7.57
55	Automotive dealers and service stations	1,689	2,068	2,011	1,430	1,722	1,670	5.66	8.92	9.34
56	Apparel and accessory stores	957	1,188	1,134	820	995	937	4.30	6.25	6.91
57	Furniture and home furnishings stores.	606	825	800	502	673	649	5.53	8.53	9.19
58	Eating and drinking places	4,626	6,556	6,485	4,256	5,947	5,862	3.69	4.97	5.29
(H)	**Finance, insurance, real estate..**	**5,160**	**6,729**	**6,672**	**3,907**	**4,876**	**4,822**	**5.79**	**9.97**	**10.82**
60	Depository institutions	(4)	2,255	2,168	(4)	1,635	1,569	(4)	8.43	8.97
61	Nondepository institutions	(4)	375	393	(4)	272	293	(4)	10.40	11.56
62	Security and commodity brokers	227	425	438	(4)	(4)	(4)	(4)	(4)	(4)
63	Insurance carriers	1,224	1,463	1,480	854	982	1,000	6.29	11.18	12.37
64	Insurance, agents, brokers, service	464	666	659	(4)	(4)	(4)	(4)	(4)	(4)
65	Real estate	989	1,323	1,301	(4)	(4)	(4)	(4)	(4)	(4)
67	Holding and other investment offices	115	222	233	(4)	(4)	(4)	(4)	(4)	(4)
(I)	**Services [6]**	**17,890**	**28,103**	**28,903**	**15,921**	**24,534**	**25,240**	**5.85**	**9.83**	**10.54**
70	Hotels and other lodging places	1,076	1,644	1,597	(4)	(4)	(4)	(4)	(4)	(4)
701	Hotels and motels	1,038	1,591	1,547	954	1,409	1,366	4.45	6.98	7.42
72	Personal services [3]	818	1,110	1,107	(4)	(4)	(4)	(4)	(4)	(4)
721	Laundry, cleaning, garment services.	356	428	414	318	380	365	4.47	6.82	7.17
723	Beauty shops	284	373	385	264	334	344	4.26	7.10	7.53
73	Business services [3]	2,564	5,173	5,290	(4)	4,552	4,668	(4)	9.48	9.96
731	Advertising	153	236	232	116	170	164	8.07	13.51	14.87
736	Personnel supply services	543	1,546	1,665	(4)	(4)	(4)	(4)	(4)	(4)
7361	Employment agencies	(4)	251	223	(4)	(4)	(4)	(4)	(4)	(4)
7363	Help supply services	(4)	1,295	1,442	(4)	1,251	1395	(4)	8.09	8.33
737	Computer and data processing services	304	775	817	254	605	654	7.16	15.11	15.78
7372	Prepackaged software	(4)	114	134	(4)	(4)	(4)	(4)	(4)	(4)
7374	Data processing and preparation..	(4)	197	198	(4)	(4)	(4)	(4)	(4)	(4)
75	Auto repair, services, and parking	571	916	878	488	759	719	6.10	8.77	9.16
753	Automotive repair shops	350	525	491	297	430	397	6.52	9.67	10.06
78	Motion pictures.	(4)	412	395	(4)	347	323	(4)	10.95	12.08
783	Motion picture theaters	124	113	104	(4)	(4)	(4)	(4)	(4)	(4)
79	Amusement and recreation services...	(4)	1,086	1,116	(4)	953	980	(4)	8.11	8.08
80	Health services [3]	5,278	7,831	8,464	4,712	6,962	7,525	5.68	10.41	11.38
801	Offices and clinics of medical doctors.	802	1,343	1,441	(4)	1,108	1,183	(4)	10.58	11.40
805	Nursing and personal care facilities..	997	1,419	1,556	898	1,283	1,406	4.17	7.24	7.85
806	Hospitals	2,750	3,550	3,756	2,522	3,250	3,447	6.06	11.79	13.03
808	Home health care services	(4)	292	386	(4)	270	357	(4)	8.72	10.03
81	Legal services	498	914	906	427	753	733	7.35	14.16	15.03
82	Educational services	1,138	1,668	1,716	(4)	(4)	(4)	(4)	(4)	(4)
83	Social services	1,134	1,780	1,950	(4)	(4)	(4)	(4)	(4)	(4)
86	Membership organizations	1,539	1,954	2,005	(4)	(4)	(4)	(4)	(4)	(4)
87	Engineering and management services.	(4)	2,489	2,431	(4)	1,894	1,850	(4)	13.56	14.65
(J)	**Government**	**16,241**	**18,304**	**18,579**	**(NA)**	**(NA)**	**(NA)**	**(NA)**	**(NA)**	**(NA)**
(X)	Federal government	2,866	3,085	2,969	(NA)	(NA)	(NA)	(NA)	(NA)	(NA)
(X)	State government	3,610	4,305	4,371	(NA)	(NA)	(NA)	(NA)	(NA)	(NA)
(X)	Local government	9,765	10,914	11,239	(NA)	(NA)	(NA)	(NA)	(NA)	(NA)

NA Not available. X Not applicable. [1] 1987 Standard Industrial Classification, see text, section 13. [2] Excludes government. [3] Includes industries not shown separately. [4] Included in totals; not available separately. [5] For changes in "Class I" classification, see text, section 21. [6] Includes all employees except executives, officials, and staff assistants who received pay during the month.

Source: U.S. Bureau of Labor Statistics, Bulletin 2370, supplement

No. 663. Indexes of Output per Hour for All Employees—Selected Industries: 1975 to 1991

[See text, section 13. Minus sign (-) indicates decrease. See also *Historical Statistics, Colonial Times to 1970,* series W 14, 17, and 19, W 30-54, and 62-65]

1987 SIC [1] code	INDUSTRY	INDEXES (1982=100)							AVERAGE ANNUAL PERCENT CHANGE [2]	
		1975	1980	1985	1988	1989	1990	1991 prel.	1975-91	1985-91
(B)	**Mining:**									
1011	Iron (usable ore)	120.0	125.6	187.2	254.5	244.1	221.1	(NA)	[3]4.2	[3]3.4
1021	Copper (recoverable metal)	66.5	78.8	163.0	191.2	187.9	182.2	175.4	6.2	1.2
12	Coal	88.2	94.2	129.3	168.4	177.5	180.4	186.3	4.8	6.3
1311	Crude petroleum, natural gas [4]	183.3	125.1	106.9	129.0	125.1	124.0	125.6	-2.3	2.7
14	Nonmetallic minerals	101.3	108.0	119.9	130.4	130.1	137.9	132.3	1.7	1.7
(D)	**Manufacturing:**									
2011,2013	Red meat products	75.2	95.3	108.4	111.2	102.6	99.8	(NA)	[3]1.9	[3]-1.6
2015	Poultry dressing and processing	69.9	84.2	106.2	103.1	108.3	114.8	(NA)	[3]3.4	[3]1.6
202	Dairy products	78.1	91.1	109.6	122.3	120.8	122.5	123.3	2.9	2.0
203	Preserved fruits and vegetables	86.8	93.5	105.5	110.0	108.9	108.8	(NA)	[3]1.5	[3]0.6
2051,2052	Bakery products	90.4	90.7	106.4	103.3	103.0	104.6	104.8	0.9	-0.3
2086	Bottled and canned soft drinks	78.5	93.7	119.7	154.2	167.5	177.8	186.8	5.6	7.7
2211,21	Cotton, synthetic broadwoven fabric	77.1	93.4	111.1	115.9	120.5	125.5	129.6	3.3	2.6
2281	Yarn spinning mills	85.7	84.4	114.8	129.3	135.8	140.5	148.8	3.5	4.4
2421	Sawmills, planing mills	84.5	89.0	115.8	128.3	125.7	125.7	128.3	2.6	1.7
2431	Millwork	116.5	108.8	99.6	110.6	109.5	110.1	116.3	0.0	2.6
251	Household furniture	93.2	95.5	107.0	114.2	114.7	114.1	117.7	1.5	1.6
2611,21,31	Pulp, paper, and paperboard mills	77.8	94.4	110.6	126.2	127.0	127.9	128.3	3.2	2.5
2653	Corrugated and solid fiber boxes	86.1	99.2	109.5	109.6	107.6	110.4	111.0	1.6	0.2
281	Industrial inorganic chemicals	100.2	109.2	123.9	138.4	130.3	130.9	(NA)	[3]1.8	[3]1.1
2819	Industrial inorganic chemicals, n.e.c.	103.9	111.7	122.2	129.7	120.0	122.3	(NA)	[3]1.1	[3]0.0
2823,2824	Synthetic fibers	81.5	111.3	130.8	158.7	155.2	150.2	155.5	4.1	2.9
2869	Industrial organic chemicals, n.e.c	97.8	113.5	129.1	162.5	158.9	147.6	141.4	2.3	1.5
2911	Petroleum refining	111.7	118.5	128.8	151.9	157.8	157.5	155.4	2.1	3.2
3011	Tires and inner tubes	71.6	79.9	114.8	140.7	143.4	146.1	147.4	4.6	3.6
308	Miscellaneous plastics, n.e.c.	78.4	87.1	102.7	114.9	113.6	117.2	117.1	2.5	2.2
314	Footwear	95.2	93.1	101.0	102.8	101.4	92.9	90.8	-0.3	-1.8
3271,72	Concrete products	101.0	99.3	110.8	117.3	121.3	120.5	128.0	1.5	2.4
3273	Ready-mixed concrete	107.8	102.7	107.7	115.8	116.7	115.1	118.7	0.6	1.6
331	Steel	102.5	113.2	153.3	184.8	179.5	184.8	177.5	3.5	2.5
3321	Gray ductile iron foundries	103.6	96.9	110.1	123.5	118.6	119.0	110.8	0.4	0.1
3465,6,9	Metal stampings	94.9	101.9	106.5	120.4	119.3	115.5	(NA)	[3]1.3	[3]1.6
3465	Automotive stampings	88.1	95.0	112.6	124.4	124.8	120.0	(NA)	[3]2.1	[3]1.3
3469	Metal stampings, n.e.c.	102.7	110.0	100.1	116.9	114.6	111.5	(NA)	[3]0.5	[3]2.2
3491,92,94	Valves and pipe fittings	91.2	101.5	103.5	111.8	111.3	112.1	(NA)	[3]1.8	[3]1.6
352	Farm, garden machinery	103.0	98.2	106.2	121.2	128.7	133.8	143.2	2.1	5.1
3531	Construction machinery	105.6	100.6	119.1	132.3	136.3	140.3	(NA)	[3]1.9	[3]3.3
3561,63,94	Pumps and compressors	95.2	104.5	113.5	133.7	131.2	134.2	(NA)	[3]2.3	[3]3.4
3621	Motors and generators	90.9	94.4	105.6	114.5	113.9	113.0	114.3	1.4	1.3
3631,32,33,99	Major household appliances	86.4	97.4	114.8	127.1	128.9	126.6	132.2	2.7	2.4
3645,46,47,48	Lighting fixtures and equip.	98.0	102.5	118.2	119.0	117.4	115.4	112.8	0.9	-0.8
371	Motor vehicles and equipment	90.5	93.6	123.4	133.7	133.3	132.6	127.0	2.1	0.5
3825	Instruments to measure electricity	80.4	90.9	109.5	118.8	121.8	120.4	(NA)	[3]2.7	[3]1.9
3861	Photographic equipment and supplies	86.4	102.4	110.7	130.0	139.1	134.1	(NA)	[3]3.0	[3]3.9
(E,G,H,I)	**Transportation, utilities, trade:**									
4011	RR transport (revenue traffic) [5]	77.3	92.6	139.7	195.3	207.4	218.1	236.2	7.2	9.1
411,13,14 (pts.)	Bus carriers [6]	98.2	102.1	88.3	99.2	96.2	(NA)	(NA)	[7]-0.1	[7]2.2
4213	Trucking, except local [6]	82.6	99.7	120.6	135.7	140.9	(NA)	(NA)	[3]9.9	[7]4.0
4512,13,22 (pts)	Air transportation [8]	76.1	92.4	118.8	122.5	118.3	113.7	115.3	2.6	-0.5
4612, 13	Petroleum pipelines	107.1	104.4	118.5	124.3	122.4	121.6	117.6	0.6	-0.1
481	Telephone communications	66.6	91.5	116.1	135.5	141.9	142.4	150.4	5.2	4.4
491,2,3	Gas and electric utilities	105.9	107.7	101.4	109.4	111.0	110.7	112.6	0.4	1.8
5093	Scrap and wasted materials [9]	[10]97.1	105.1	124.3	130.9	120.9	141.8	153.9	[11]3.3	[11]3.6
5251	Hardware stores [9]	89.6	102.3	102.0	115.7	122.8	118.0	109.0	1.2	1.1
5311	Department stores	79.8	92.4	115.6	123.6	120.9	117.9	124.2	2.8	1.2
5331	Variety stores [9]	108.4	95.3	97.6	74.1	87.1	102.0	100.7	-0.5	0.5
54	Food stores [9]	103.5	105.2	100.0	96.2	94.0	93.7	93.9	-0.6	-1.0
5511	New and used car dealers [9]	94.6	99.2	112.2	115.5	116.5	120.4	120.1	1.5	1.1
5531	Auto and home supply stores [9]	83.7	99.6	112.2	123.1	123.0	126.4	127.2	2.7	2.1
5541	Gasoline service stations [9]	76.3	93.9	121.4	130.7	130.8	125.2	124.7	3.1	0.4
56	Apparel and accessory stores [9]	83.0	93.2	116.6	114.4	115.6	114.8	114.5	2.0	-0.3
57	Furniture, furnishings, equip. stores [9]	84.2	98.4	120.7	136.3	138.4	142.5	140.7	3.3	2.6
58	Eating, drinking places [9]	103.8	102.7	92.6	98.3	97.0	97.6	101.0	-0.2	1.5
5912	Drug and proprietary stores [9]	87.4	99.1	98.9	99.4	100.2	101.7	106.5	1.2	1.5
5921	Liquor stores [9]	89.1	94.5	100.7	85.5	87.6	90.9	91.1	0.1	-1.7
602	Commercial banking	96.6	99.6	117.8	129.3	127.8	135.7	(NA)	[3]2.3	[3]2.9
7011	Hotels and motels [9]	98.4	102.0	99.0	94.3	90.9	86.7	87.8	-0.7	-2.0
721	Laundry/clean/garment services [9]	106.5	100.3	98.0	93.6	95.8	96.7	94.5	-0.7	-0.6
7231,41	Beauty and barber shops [9]	90.3	94.0	102.7	106.1	112.0	109.4	109.9	1.2	1.1
753	Automotive repair shops [9]	116.6	109.6	108.4	114.7	117.2	115.8	108.9	-0.4	0.1

NA Not available.   [1] 1987 Standard Industrial Classification; see text, section 13.   [2] Average annual percent change based on compound rate formula.   [3] Change from 1975 to 1990 and 1985 to 1990.   [4] Excludes fuels.   [5] Class 1 line-haul railroads and switching terminal companies.   [6] Class 1 Interstate carriers regulated by the ICC.   [7] Change from 1975 to 1989 and 1985 to 1989.   [8] Refers to output per employee.   [9] Data relate to all persons (paid employees, unpaid family workers, and the self-employed).   [10] 1977 data.   [11] Change from 1977 to 1991.

Source: U.S. Bureau of Labor Statistics, Bulletin 2421, *Productivity Measures for Selected Industries and Government Services,* March 1993; and unpublished data.

No. 664. Productivity and Related Measures: 1960 to 1992

[See text, section 13. Minus sign (-) indicates decrease. See also *Historical Statistics, Colonial Times to 1970*, series D 689-704 and W 22-25]

ITEM	1960	1970	1975	1980	1985	1988	1989	1990	1991	1992
INDEXES (1982=100)										
Output per hour, business sector	65.5	86.9	95.4	98.6	106.1	110.4	109.5	109.7	110.1	113.3
Nonfarm business	69.8	88.5	96.6	99.0	105.4	109.2	108.2	108.2	108.7	111.7
Manufacturing	(NA)	(NA)	(NA)	94.4	108.0	122.0	122.5	125.7	128.1	131.9
Output, [1] business sector.	52.2	75.8	85.0	100.5	116.7	130.1	132.3	132.7	129.8	132.8
Nonfarm business	51.8	75.7	84.9	100.8	116.8	130.6	132.7	132.9	130.0	132.9
Manufacturing	(NA)	(NA)	(NA)	103.8	115.5	133.4	134.6	135.0	131.9	134.6
Hours, [2] business sector	79.7	87.2	89.1	101.9	109.9	117.9	120.9	120.9	117.9	117.2
Nonfarm business	74.2	85.6	88.0	101.8	110.8	119.5	122.7	122.9	119.6	119.0
Manufacturing	(NA)	(NA)	(NA)	109.9	107.0	109.4	109.8	107.4	103.0	102.0
Compensation per hour, [3] business sector .	21.1	36.7	54.5	85.0	113.0	128.0	132.3	139.7	146.6	152.1
Nonfarm business	22.2	37.0	54.8	84.9	112.6	127.2	131.3	138.4	145.4	150.8
Manufacturing	(NA)	(NA)	(NA)	83.1	111.0	122.6	127.3	133.8	140.6	144.1
Real hourly compensation, [3] business sector	68.7	91.2	97.7	99.5	101.3	104.4	103.0	103.2	103.9	104.6
Nonfarm business	72.3	92.0	98.3	99.4	101.0	103.7	102.2	102.2	103.0	103.7
Manufacturing	(NA)	(NA)	(NA)	97.4	99.5	100.0	99.1	98.8	99.6	99.1
Unit labor costs, [4] business sector	32.2	42.2	57.1	86.2	106.5	116.0	120.9	127.3	133.1	134.2
Nonfarm business	31.8	41.8	56.7	85.7	106.8	116.4	121.4	127.9	133.8	135.0
Manufacturing	(NA)	(NA)	(NA)	88.1	102.8	100.5	103.9	106.4	109.8	109.3
ANNUAL PERCENT CHANGE [5]										
Output per hour, business sector	1.6	1.4	2.3	-0.7	1.4	0.9	-0.8	0.3	0.3	2.9
Nonfarm business	1.1	1.0	2.2	-0.9	0.8	0.9	-1.0	0.0	0.5	2.8
Manufacturing	(NA)	(NA)	(NA)	-1.9	2.3	4.0	0.5	2.6	1.9	3.0
Output, [1] business sector.	1.7	-0.5	-1.9	-1.6	3.6	4.3	1.7	0.2	-2.2	2.3
Nonfarm business	1.7	-0.6	-2.0	-1.7	3.4	4.4	1.7	0.1	-2.2	2.2
Manufacturing	(NA)	(NA)	(NA)	-6.5	1.5	7.1	0.9	0.3	-2.3	2.0
Hours, [2] business sector	0.1	-1.9	-4.1	-0.9	2.1	3.3	2.6	0.0	-2.5	-0.6
Nonfarm business	0.6	-1.6	-4.2	-0.8	2.5	3.5	2.7	0.1	-2.6	-0.5
Manufacturing	(NA)	(NA)	(NA)	-4.7	-0.8	2.9	0.4	-2.2	-4.1	-0.9
Compensation per hour, [3] business sector .	4.3	7.6	10.0	10.7	4.5	4.3	3.4	5.6	4.9	3.7
Nonfarm business	4.4	7.2	9.9	10.7	4.2	4.1	3.2	5.4	5.1	3.7
Manufacturing	(NA)	(NA)	(NA)	12.0	5.0	3.9	3.9	5.1	5.1	2.5
Real hourly compensation, [3] business sector	2.6	1.7	0.8	-2.4	0.9	0.1	-1.4	0.2	0.7	0.7
Nonfarm business	2.6	1.4	0.7	-2.4	0.6	0.0	-1.5	0.0	0.8	0.7
Manufacturing	(NA)	(NA)	(NA)	-1.3	1.4	-0.2	-0.9	-0.3	0.8	-0.5
Unit labor costs, [4] business sector	2.7	6.1	7.5	11.5	3.0	3.3	4.2	5.3	4.6	0.8
Nonfarm business	3.3	6.2	7.5	11.7	3.3	3.2	4.3	5.4	4.6	0.9
Manufacturing	(NA)	(NA)	(NA)	14.2	2.7	-0.2	3.4	2.5	3.2	-0.5

NA Not available.   [1] Refers to gross domestic product originating in the sector, in 1987 prices.   [2] Hours at work of all persons engaged in the business and nonfarm business sectors (employees, proprietors, and unpaid family workers); employees' and proprietors' hours in manufacturing.   [3] Wages and salaries of employees plus employers' contributions for social insurance and private benefit plans. Also includes an estimate of same for self-employed. Real compensation deflated by the consumer price index for all urban consumers, see text, section 15.   [4] Hourly compensation divided by output per hour.   [5] All changes are from the immediate prior year.

Source: U.S. Bureau of Labor Statistics, *Employment and Earnings*, monthly; and unpublished data.

No. 665. Persons Receiving Work-Related Training, by Selected Characteristics: 1990

[In thousands, except as indicated. As of spring. For persons 18 to 64 years old. Based on Survey of Income and Program Participation; for details, see source]

CHARACTERISTIC	Total	SEX		RACE		His-panic origin [1]	EDUCATION		
		Male	Female	White	Black		Less than 9 years	9 to 12 years	More than 12 years
All persons	**152,815**	**74,828**	**77,987**	**129,575**	**17,891**	**12,463**	**9,714**	**77,599**	**65,502**
Persons ever receiving work training . .	39,238	19,950	19,288	33,984	4,241	2,218	1,050	20,447	17,742
Uses training on current or most recent job	26,563	14,073	12,489	23,595	2,316	1,486	580	12,671	13,311
Location:									
Apprenticeship	1,749	1,411	338	1,616	76	114	70	999	680
Business/vo-tech school	10,213	4,388	5,825	8,659	1,301	537	192	6,562	3,460
Community college	4,077	1,664	2,413	3,722	275	220	92	1,838	2,147
Four-year college	2,738	1,396	1,341	2,488	198	89	22	355	2,360
High school vo-tech program.	2,158	1,068	1,090	1,875	250	183	36	1,798	324
Training program at work	13,330	7,393	5,936	11,774	1,164	598	270	5,903	7,156
Military	2,229	1,990	238	1,968	180	139	12	1,151	1,065
Previous job	1,821	968	853	1,636	134	134	87	705	1,029
Other	9,720	4,874	4,845	8,304	1,169	497	413	4,524	4,783
Program paid for by—									
Self or family	11,540	4,708	6,832	10,348	914	588	215	6,014	5,311
Employer.	17,834	10,019	7,815	16,059	1,379	880	426	7,885	9,524
Federal, State, or local government .	10,429	5,543	4,886	8,079	2,010	748	387	6,675	3,366
Someone else	1,000	553	447	859	99	84	41	586	373
Length of training program (average number of weeks)	22	25	20	23	21	22	20	25	19

[1] Persons of Hispanic origin may be of any race.
Source: U.S. Bureau of the Census, *Current Population Reports*, series P70-32.

No. 666. Average Annual Total Compensation and Wages and Salaries Full-Time Equivalent Employee, by Industry: 1980 to 1991

[In dollars. Wage and salary payments include executives' compensation, bonuses, tips, and payments-in-kind; total compensation includes in addition to wages and salaries, employer contributions for social insurance, employer contributions to private and welfare funds, director' fees, jury and witness fees, etc. Through 1985, based on 1972 Standard Industrial Classification Code (SIC); beginning 1989, based on the 1987 SIC. See text, section 13]

INDUSTRY	ANNUAL TOTAL COMPENSATION					ANNUAL WAGES AND SALARIES				
	1980	1985	1989	1990	1991	1980	1985	1989	1990	1991
Domestic industries	18,810	25,263	29,747	31,193	32,787	15,747	21,059	24,818	25,996	27,192
Agriculture, forestry, and fisheries	9,509	13,084	15,544	17,480	18,036	8,539	11,773	13,751	15,346	15,701
Mining	28,614	38,883	44,233	46,146	48,414	23,458	32,054	36,338	37,895	39,661
Construction	21,720	26,721	31,481	32,790	33,906	18,574	22,775	26,655	27,717	28,480
Manufacturing	21,973	30,145	34,873	36,352	38,137	17,951	24,600	28,487	29,661	30,926
Transportation	24,927	30,638	33,648	35,290	36,800	20,805	25,240	27,555	28,802	29,869
Communication	28,577	39,635	45,615	47,387	49,271	22,101	31,342	36,614	37,975	39,558
Electric, gas, and sanitary services	27,450	39,179	46,363	47,974	50,334	21,708	31,653	37,770	39,006	40,708
Wholesale trade	21,790	29,195	35,043	36,714	38,402	18,821	25,016	30,035	31,461	32,761
Retail trade	12,558	15,694	17,887	18,482	19,496	10,954	13,603	15,470	15,968	16,765
Finance, insurance, and real estate	18,898	27,873	35,446	36,892	38,752	15,848	23,724	30,356	31,557	33,067
Services	15,356	21,441	26,418	28,072	29,558	13,487	18,698	23,097	24,503	25,700
Government and government enterprises	19,634	27,839	33,625	35,501	37,536	15,888	21,988	26,265	27,701	29,167

Source: U.S. Bureau of Economic Analysis, *The National Income and Product Accounts of the United States, Volume 2, 1958-88;* and *Survey of Current Business,* July issues.

No. 667. Average Hourly and Weekly Earnings in Current and Constant (1982) Dollars, by Private Industry Group: 1970 to 1992

[Average earnings include overtime. Data are for production and related workers in mining, manufacturing, and construction, and nonsupervisory employees in other industries. Excludes agriculture. See headnote, table 660. See also *Historical Statistics, Colonial Times to 1970,* series D 877-892]

PRIVATE INDUSTRY GROUP	CURRENT DOLLARS						CONSTANT (1982) DOLLARS [1]					
	1970	1980	1985	1990	1991	1992	1970	1980	1985	1990	1991	1992
Average hourly earnings	3.23	6.66	8.57	10.01	10.33	10.59	8.03	7.78	7.77	7.52	7.45	7.43
Manufacturing	3.35	7.27	9.54	10.83	11.18	11.45	8.33	8.49	8.65	8.14	8.07	8.03
Mining	3.85	9.17	11.98	13.68	14.18	14.51	9.58	10.71	10.86	10.28	10.23	10.18
Construction	5.24	9.94	12.32	13.77	13.99	14.11	13.03	11.61	11.17	10.35	10.09	9.89
Transportation, public utilities	3.85	8.87	11.40	12.97	13.24	13.49	9.58	10.36	10.34	9.74	9.55	9.46
Wholesale trade	3.43	6.95	9.15	10.79	11.15	11.40	8.53	8.12	8.30	8.11	8.04	7.99
Retail trade	2.44	4.88	5.94	6.75	6.95	7.14	6.07	5.70	5.39	5.07	5.01	5.01
Finance, insurance, real estate	3.07	5.79	7.94	9.97	10.40	10.82	7.64	6.76	7.20	7.49	7.50	7.59
Services	2.81	5.85	7.90	9.83	10.22	10.54	6.99	6.83	7.16	7.39	7.37	7.39
Average weekly earnings	120	235	299	345	354	364	298	275	271	259	256	255
Manufacturing	133	289	386	442	455	469	332	337	350	332	328	329
Mining	164	397	520	603	630	638	409	464	471	453	454	448
Construction	195	368	464	526	533	536	486	430	421	395	385	376
Transportation, public utilities	156	351	450	505	512	523	388	410	408	379	370	367
Wholesale trade	137	267	351	411	425	435	341	312	318	309	307	305
Retail trade	82	147	175	194	199	206	205	172	158	146	143	144
Finance, insurance, real estate	113	210	289	357	371	387	281	245	262	268	268	272
Services	97	191	257	319	331	343	240	223	233	240	239	240

[1] Earnings in current dollars divided by the Consumer Price Index (CPI-W) on a 1982 base; see text, section 15.

Source: U.S. Bureau of Labor Statistics, Bulletin 2370, supplement to *Employment and Earnings,* July 1991; and *Employment and Earnings,* monthly.

No. 668. Annual Percent Changes in Earnings and Compensation: 1980 to 1992

[Annual percent change from immediate prior year. Minus sign (-) indicates decrease]

ITEM	1980	1984	1985	1986	1987	1988	1989	1990	1991	1992
Current dollars:										
Hourly earnings, total [1]	8.1	3.7	3.0	2.2	2.5	3.3	4.1	3.6	3.2	2.5
Hourly earnings, manufacturing [1]	8.5	4.1	3.8	2.0	1.8	2.8	2.8	3.3	3.2	2.4
Compensation per employee-hour [1]	10.6	3.9	4.1	4.9	3.4	4.1	3.2	5.3	5.1	3.7
Constant (1982) dollars:										
Hourly earnings, total [1]	-4.8	0.1	-0.4	0.5	-1.0	-0.5	-0.7	-1.6	-0.9	-0.3
Hourly earnings, manufacturing [1]	-4.5	0.6	0.3	0.3	-1.6	-1.2	-1.9	-1.7	-0.9	-0.5
Compensation per employee-hour [1]	-2.5	-0.4	0.5	2.9	-0.2	0.0	-1.5	-0.1	-0.8	0.7
Consumer Price Index [2]	13.5	4.3	3.6	1.9	3.6	4.1	4.8	5.4	4.2	3.0

[1] Nonfarm business sector.   [2] See text, section 15.

Source: U.S. Bureau of Labor Statistics, *Monthly Labor Review.*

No. 669. Average Annual Pay, by State: 1989 to 1991

[In dollars except percent change. For workers covered by State unemployment insurance laws and for Federal civilian workers covered by unemployment compensation for Federal employees, approximately 90 percent of total civilian employment. Excludes most agricultural workers on small farms, all Armed Forces, elected officials in most States, railroad employees, most domestic workers, employees of certain nonprofit organizations and most self-employed individuals. Pay includes bonuses, cash value of meals and lodging, and tips and other gratuities]

STATE	AVERAGE ANNUAL PAY			PERCENT CHANGE		STATE	AVERAGE ANNUAL PAY			PERCENT CHANGE	
	1989	1990	1991 [1]	1989-90	1990-91 [1]		1989	1990	1991 [1]	1989-90	1990-91 [1]
U.S...	22,563	23,602	24,575	4.6	4.1	MO.....	20,900	21,716	22,567	3.9	3.9
AL......	19,593	20,468	21,287	4.5	4.0	MT.....	17,224	17,895	18,648	3.9	4.2
AK......	29,704	29,946	30,830	0.8	2.9	NE.....	17,690	18,577	19,372	5.0	4.3
AZ......	20,809	21,443	22,207	3.0	3.6	NV.....	21,333	22,358	23,083	4.8	3.2
AR......	17,418	18,204	19,008	4.5	4.4	NH.....	21,553	22,609	23,600	4.9	4.4
CA......	24,917	26,180	27,499	5.1	5.0	NJ.....	26,780	28,449	29,992	6.2	5.4
CO......	21,940	22,908	23,981	4.4	4.7	NM.....	18,667	19,347	20,275	3.6	4.8
CT......	27,500	28,995	30,689	5.4	5.8	NY.....	27,303	28,873	30,011	5.8	3.9
DE......	23,268	24,423	25,647	5.0	5.0	NC.....	19,321	20,220	21,087	4.7	4.3
DC......	32,106	33,717	35,570	5.0	5.5	ND.....	16,932	17,626	18,132	4.1	2.9
FL......	20,072	21,030	21,991	4.8	4.6	OH.....	21,986	22,844	23,603	3.9	3.3
GA......	21,072	22,115	23,164	4.9	4.7	OK.....	19,533	20,288	20,968	3.9	3.3
HI......	21,624	23,167	24,104	7.1	4.0	OR.....	20,303	21,332	22,348	5.1	4.8
ID......	18,146	18,991	19,688	4.7	3.7	PA.....	22,313	23,457	24,393	5.1	4.0
IL......	24,212	25,312	26,310	4.5	3.9	RI.....	21,128	22,388	23,082	6.0	3.1
IN......	20,931	21,699	22,522	3.7	3.8	SC.....	18,797	19,668	20,439	4.6	3.9
IA......	18,420	19,224	19,810	4.4	3.0	SD.....	15,810	16,430	17,131	3.9	4.3
KS......	19,475	20,238	21,002	3.9	3.8	TN.....	19,712	20,611	21,541	4.6	4.5
KY......	19,001	19,947	20,730	5.0	3.9	TX.....	21,740	22,700	23,760	4.4	4.7
LA......	19,750	20,646	21,501	4.5	4.1	UT.....	19,362	20,074	20,874	3.7	4.0
ME......	19,202	20,154	20,870	5.0	3.6	VT.....	19,497	20,532	21,355	5.3	4.0
MD......	23,469	24,730	25,960	5.4	5.0	VA.....	21,882	22,750	23,804	4.0	4.6
MA......	25,233	26,699	28,041	5.8	5.0	WA.....	21,617	22,646	23,942	4.8	5.7
MI......	24,767	25,376	26,125	2.5	3.0	WV.....	19,788	20,715	21,356	4.7	3.1
MN......	22,155	23,121	23,961	4.4	3.6	WI.....	20,204	21,101	21,838	4.4	3.5
MS......	17,047	17,718	18,411	3.9	3.9	WY.....	19,230	20,049	20,591	4.3	2.7

[1] Preliminary.

Source: U.S. Bureau of Labor Statistics, *Employment and Wages Annual Averages 1991*; and USDL News Release 92-631 *Average Annual Pay by State and Industry, 1991*.

No. 670. Average Annual Pay, by Selected Metropolitan Areas: 1988 to 1991

[In dollars. Metropolitan areas ranked by population size 1988. For composition of metropolitan areas, see Appendix II. See also headnote table 669. For civilian labor force data, see table 627]

METROPOLITAN AREA	1989	1990	1991 [1]	METROPOLITAN AREA	1989	1990	1991 [1]
U.S. total	22,563	23,602	24,575	Kansas City, MO-KS MSA	22,219	23,199	24,084
U.S. metropolitan total	23,566	24,675	25,729	Milwaukee-Racine, WI CMSA	22,298	23,244	24,173
New York-Northern New Jersey-				Portland-Vancouver, OR-WA			
Long Island, NY-NJ-CT CMSA ...	29,208	31,047	32,528	CMSA	22,014	23,178	24,316
Los Angeles-Anaheim-Riverside, CA				Sacramento, CA MSA	23,002	24,405	25,648
CMSA	25,682	26,932	28,325	Norfolk-Virginia Beach-Newport			
Chicago-Gary-Lake County (IL),				News, VA MSA	19,446	20,218	21,258
IL-IN-WI CMSA	25,703	26,888	28,016	Columbus, OH MSA	21,835	22,869	23,826
San Francisco-Oakland-San Jose,				San Antonio, TX MSA	19,677	20,212	20,956
CA CMSA................	27,568	29,001	30,710	New Orleans, LA MSA.........	20,695	21,595	22,659
Philadelphia-Wilmington-Trenton,				Indianapolis, IN MSA.........	22,345	23,337	24,531
PA-NJ-DE-MD CMSA	25,070	26,626	27,866	Buffalo-Niagara Falls, NY CMSA ...	21,080	22,161	23,203
Detroit-Ann Arbor, MI CMSA.....	27,164	27,820	28,565	Charlotte-Gastonia-Rock Hill,			
Dallas-Fort Worth, TX CMSA ...	24,298	25,422	26,457	NC-SC MSA	21,618	22,805	23,706
Boston-Lawrence-Salem-Lowell-				Hartford-New Britain-Middletown-			
Brockton, MA NECMA	26,915	28,498	29,968	CT NECMA	27,224	28,767	30,375
Washington, DC-MD-VA MSA.....	28,041	29,384	31,056	Salt Lake City-Ogden, UT MSA	20,014	20,781	21,641
Houston-Galveston-Brazoria,				Rochester, NY MSA	24,550	25,414	26,572
TX CMSA................	25,023	26,253	27,698	Memphis, TN-AR-MS MSA	20,877	21,964	23,042
Miami-Fort Lauderdale, FL CMSA .	21,919	23,022	24,031	Nashville, TN MSA	21,203	22,083	23,018
Cleveland-Akron-Lorain, OH CMSA .	23,382	24,326	25,040	Orlando, FL MSA	20,373	21,261	22,411
Atlanta, GA MSA	24,075	25,303	26,635	Louisville, KY-IN MSA.........	20,579	21,376	22,311
St. Louis, MO-IL MSA	23,409	24,256	25,202	Oklahoma City, OK MSA	20,447	20,988	21,821
Seattle-Tacoma, WA CMSA	23,608	24,991	26,462	Dayton-Springfield, OH MSA....	22,320	23,022	23,889
Minneapolis-St. Paul, MN-WI MSA . .	24,372	25,395	26,423	Greensboro-Winston-Salem-			
San Diego, CA MSA...........	22,956	23,942	24,998	High Point, NC MSA........	20,950	21,348	22,088
Baltimore, MD MSA...........	23,110	24,459	25,705	Birmingham, AL MSA	21,542	22,588	23,424
Pittsburgh-Beaver Valley, PA CMSA. .	22,435	23,684	24,586	Providence-Pawtucket-			
Phoenix, AZ MSA	21,955	22,660	23,469	Woonsocket, RI NECMA.......	21,059	22,380	23,123
Tampa-St. Petersburg-Clearwater,				Jacksonville, FL MSA	20,571	21,519	22,420
FL MSA..................	19,456	20,319	21,533	Albany-Schenectady-Troy, NY			
Denver-Boulder, CO CMSA......	23,898	25,031	26,273	MSA	22,807	23,834	24,817
Cincinnati-Hamilton, OH-KY-IN,				Richmond-Petersburg, VA MSA ...	22,351	23,376	24,265
CMSA...................	22,512	23,590	24,622	Honolulu, HI MSA............	22,399	24,654	25,014

[1] Preliminary.

Source: U.S. Bureau of Labor Statistics, USDL News Release 92-740, *Average Annual Pay Levels in Metropolitan Areas, 1991*, and earlier issues.

No. 671. Full-Time Wage and Salary Workers—Number and Median Weekly Earnings, by Selected Characteristics: 1983 to 1992

[In current dollars of usual weekly earnings. Data represent annual averages of quarterly data. See text, section 13, and headnote table 637, for a discussion of occupational data. Based on Current Population Survey; see text, section 1, and Appendix III. For definition of median, see Guide to Tabular Presentation]

CHARACTERISTIC	NUMBER OF WORKERS (1,000)				MEDIAN WEEKLY EARNINGS (dol.)			
	1983	1985	1990	1992	1983	1985	1990	1992
All workers [1]	70,976	77,002	85,082	84,143	313	343	415	445
Male	42,309	45,589	49,015	47,877	378	406	485	505
16 to 24 years old	6,702	6,956	6,313	5,517	223	240	283	285
25 years old and over	35,607	38,632	42,702	42,360	406	442	514	539
Female	28,667	31,414	36,068	36,266	252	277	348	381
16 to 24 years old	5,345	5,621	5,001	4,339	197	210	254	267
25 years old and over	23,322	25,793	31,066	31,927	267	296	370	400
White	61,739	66,481	72,637	71,629	319	355	427	462
Male	37,378	40,030	42,563	41,439	387	417	497	518
Female	24,361	26,452	30,075	30,190	254	281	355	388
Black	7,373	8,393	9,642	9,537	261	277	329	357
Male	3,883	4,367	4,909	4,766	293	304	360	380
Female	3,490	4,026	4,733	4,771	231	252	308	336
Hispanic origin [2]	(NA)	(NA)	6,993	6,986	(NA)	(NA)	307	324
Male	(NA)	(NA)	4,410	4,390	(NA)	(NA)	322	345
Female	(NA)	(NA)	2,583	2,596	(NA)	(NA)	280	303
Family relationship:								
Husbands	28,720	30,260	31,326	30,664	410	455	532	575
Wives	14,884	16,270	18,666	19,246	257	285	363	395
Women who maintain families	3,948	4,333	5,007	5,143	256	278	339	370
Men who maintain families	1,331	1,313	1,786	1,828	377	396	444	451
Other persons in families:								
Men	5,518	6,173	6,434	5,921	219	238	296	301
Women	4,032	4,309	4,475	4,076	201	213	271	292
All other men [3]	6,740	7,841	9,468	9,465	350	380	442	464
All other women [3]	5,803	6,503	7,920	7,801	274	305	376	406
Occupation, male:								
Managerial and professional	10,312	11,078	12,263	12,082	516	583	731	777
Exec., admin., managerial	5,344	5,835	6,401	6,370	530	593	742	784
Professional specialty	4,967	5,243	5,863	5,712	506	571	720	770
Technical, sales, and administrative support	8,125	8,803	9,596	9,844	385	420	496	519
Tech. and related support	1,428	1,563	1,747	1,956	424	472	570	591
Sales	3,853	4,227	4,666	4,663	389	431	505	523
Admin. support, incl. clerical	2,844	3,013	3,183	3,225	362	391	440	482
Service	3,723	3,947	4,476	4,492	255	272	320	330
Private household	11	13	12	11	(B)	(B)	(B)	(B)
Protective	1,314	1,327	1,523	1,548	355	391	477	501
Other service	2,398	2,607	2,942	2,932	217	230	273	283
Precision production [4]	9,180	10,026	10,169	9,581	387	408	488	503
Mechanics and repairers	3,418	3,752	3,669	3,625	377	400	477	496
Construction trades	2,966	3,308	3,603	3,193	375	394	480	495
Other	2,796	2,966	2,897	2,763	408	433	510	523
Operators, fabricators and laborers	9,833	10,585	11,257	10,618	308	325	378	393
Machine operators, assemblers, and inspectors	4,138	4,403	4,510	4,188	319	341	391	406
Transportation and material moving	3,199	3,459	3,721	3,667	335	369	418	436
Handlers, equipment cleaners, helpers, and laborers	2,496	2,724	3,027	2,763	251	261	308	314
Farming, forestry, and fishing	1,137	1,150	1,253	1,260	200	216	263	269
Occupation, female:								
Managerial and professional	7,139	8,302	10,595	11,165	357	399	511	562
Exec., admin., managerial	2,772	3,492	4,764	4,918	339	383	485	519
Professional specialty	4,367	4,810	5,831	6,247	367	408	534	587
Technical, sales, and administrative support	13,517	14,622	16,202	16,084	247	269	332	365
Tech. and related support	1,146	1,200	1,470	1,608	299	331	417	436
Sales	2,460	2,929	3,531	3,240	204	226	292	313
Admin. support, incl. clerical	9,911	10,494	11,202	11,235	248	270	332	364
Service	3,598	3,963	4,531	4,612	173	185	230	248
Private household	267	330	298	302	116	130	171	177
Protective	139	156	216	256	250	278	405	399
Other service	3,193	3,477	4,017	4,053	176	188	231	248
Precision production [4]	784	906	893	854	256	268	316	336
Mechanics and repairers	120	144	139	124	337	392	459	523
Construction trades	45	53	50	44	(B)	265	394	(B)
Other	619	709	704	686	244	253	300	316
Operators, fabricators, and laborers	3,486	3,482	3,675	3,383	204	216	262	279
Machine operators, assemblers, and inspectors	2,853	2,778	2,840	2,602	202	216	260	275
Transportation and material moving	159	189	227	240	253	252	314	329
Handlers, equipment cleaners, helpers and laborers	474	514	608	540	211	209	250	279
Farming, forestry, and fishing	143	138	171	170	169	185	216	223

B Data not shown where base is less than 50,000.   NA Not available.   [1] Includes other races, not shown separately. [2] Persons of Hispanic origin may be of any race.   [3] The majority of these persons are living alone or with nonrelatives. Also included are persons in families where the husband, wife or other person maintaining the family is in the Armed Forces, and persons in unrelated subfamilies.   [4] Includes craft and repair.

Source: U.S. Bureau of Labor Statistics, Bulletin 2307, and *Employment and Earnings*, monthly, January issues.

No. 672. Median Weekly Earnings of Families, by Type of Family, Number of Earners, Race, and Hispanic Origin: 1980 to 1992

[In current dollars of usual weekly earnings. Annual averages of quarterly figures based on Current Population Survey; see text, section 1, and Appendix III. For families with wage and salary earners]

CHARACTERISTIC	NUMBER OF FAMILIES (1,000)					MEDIAN WEEKLY EARNINGS (dollars)				
	1980	1985	1990	1991	1992	1980	1985	1990	1991	1992
TOTAL										
Total families with earners [1]	41,162	41,616	43,759	43,530	44,137	400	522	653	669	688
Married-couple families	33,825	33,459	34,219	33,930	34,280	433	582	732	754	779
One earner.	14,797	13,347	12,166	12,177	12,200	303	385	455	455	469
Husband	12,127	10,346	8,994	8,784	8,667	336	440	520	532	546
Wife	2,059	2,243	2,407	2,636	2,801	159	217	267	279	294
Other family member.	611	758	764	757	732	163	204	280	278	282
Two or more earners [2]	19,028	20,112	22,053	21,753	22,080	535	715	880	911	942
Husband and wife only	12,990	14,019	15,934	15,923	16,225	507	684	844	884	913
Husband and other family member(s). . .	2,369	2,159	1,751	1,637	1,617	557	689	825	838	848
Wife and other family member(s). . . .	426	514	527	557	597	350	454	557	589	592
Other family members only.	139	176	176	163	158	356	468	554	617	589
Families maintained by women	5,690	6,470	7,323	7,441	7,546	222	297	363	385	385
One earner.	4,022	4,397	4,983	5,090	5,286	184	234	288	306	306
Householder	3,104	3,432	3,937	4,045	4,225	188	243	296	315	316
Other family member.	918	965	1,045	1,045	1,061	168	200	254	270	264
Two or more earners	1,668	2,073	2,340	2,351	2,261	370	487	607	622	634
Families maintained by men	1,647	1,688	2,218	2,159	2,311	360	450	514	514	519
One earner.	1,016	1,031	1,352	1,337	1,462	283	346	396	404	415
Two or more earners	631	656	866	822	850	502	625	778	736	756
WHITE										
Total families with earners [1]	35,786	35,848	37,239	36,978	37,378	411	543	681	695	716
Married-couple families	30,316	29,899	30,361	30,069	30,337	438	589	745	767	791
One earner [2].	13,437	12,097	10,856	10,851	10,852	311	395	473	474	483
Husband	11,152	9,496	8,162	7,953	7,844	343	452	535	549	561
Wife	1,740	1,925	2,044	2,252	2,384	160	218	270	280	296
Two or more earners	16,878	17,802	19,505	19,218	19,485	542	723	892	922	954
Husband and wife only	11,448	12,394	14,148	14,098	14,369	511	691	855	895	923
Families maintained by women	4,140	4,616	5,127	5,209	5,226	233	311	382	399	409
Families maintained by men	1,331	1,333	1,751	1,701	1,814	374	475	539	529	545
BLACK										
Total families with earners [1]	4,503	4,668	5,082	5,098	5,188	299	378	459	484	478
Married-couple families	2,802	2,671	2,724	2,735	2,723	366	487	601	625	646
One earner [2]	1,103	902	893	897	895	210	257	304	313	309
Husband	769	580	527	503	486	244	292	345	366	359
Wife	279	257	290	312	330	151	206	243	272	279
Two or more earners	1,700	1,769	1,831	1,838	1,828	472	622	748	776	806
Husband and wife only	1,238	1,258	1,297	1,362	1,327	461	603	713	756	783
Families maintained by women	1,438	1,703	1,986	2,003	2,079	192	259	314	339	328
Families maintained by men	263	294	372	360	386	307	360	397	401	412
HISPANIC ORIGIN [3]										
Total families with earners [1]	(NA)	(NA)	3,624	3,636	3,755	(NA)	(NA)	496	495	496
Married-couple families	(NA)	(NA)	2,599	2,599	2,698	(NA)	(NA)	555	546	552
One earner [2]	(NA)	(NA)	1,050	1,102	1,116	(NA)	(NA)	322	322	333
Husband	(NA)	(NA)	814	850	876	(NA)	(NA)	356	355	365
Wife	(NA)	(NA)	164	176	170	(NA)	(NA)	236	235	264
Two or more earners	(NA)	(NA)	1,549	1,497	1,582	(NA)	(NA)	716	732	743
Husband and wife only	(NA)	(NA)	924	917	968	(NA)	(NA)	672	713	721
Families maintained by women	(NA)	(NA)	691	701	720	(NA)	(NA)	326	343	341
Families maintained by men	(NA)	(NA)	334	337	337	(NA)	(NA)	468	462	476

NA Not available. [1] Excludes families in which there is no wage or salary earner or in which the husband, wife, or other person maintaining the family is either self-employed or in the Armed Forces. [2] Includes other earners, not shown separately. [3] Persons of Hispanic origin may be of any race.

Source: U.S. Bureau of Labor Statistics, Bulletin 2307; and *Employment and Earnings,* monthly, January issues.

No. 673. Number of Workers With Earnings and Median Earnings, by Occupation of Longest Job Held and Sex: 1991

[Covers persons 15 years old and over as of **March 1992**. Based on Current Population Survey; see text, section 1, and Appendix III. For definition of median, see Guide to Tabular Presentation]

MAJOR OCCUPATION OF LONGEST JOB HELD	ALL WORKERS				YEAR ROUND FULL-TIME					
	Women		Men		Women		Men		Ratio: Women to men	
	Number (1,000)	Median earnings	Number (1,000)	Median earnings	Number (1,000)	Median earnings	Number (1,000)	Median earnings	Number	Median earnings
Total [1]	61,796	$12,884	72,040	$21,857	32,436	$20,553	47,888	$29,421	0.68	0.70
Executive, administrators, and managerial	6,656	23,511	9,145	38,622	4,968	26,928	7,635	41,635	0.65	0.65
Professional specialty	9,138	24,925	8,084	37,467	5,198	30,487	6,068	42,358	0.86	0.72
Technical and related support	2,329	19,763	2,278	28,414	1,508	22,497	1,692	32,029	0.89	0.70
Sales	8,232	7,737	7,943	24,148	3,237	17,254	5,645	30,597	0.57	0.56
Admin. support, incl. clerical	16,827	15,209	4,301	21,335	10,154	19,444	2,905	27,037	3.50	0.72
Precision production, craft and repair	1,237	13,467	13,303	22,412	734	18,554	8,827	27,508	0.08	0.67
Machine operators, assemblers, and inspectors	3,457	11,294	5,143	19,318	1,921	14,965	3,503	23,604	0.55	0.63
Transportation and material moving	449	9,844	4,810	20,853	159	19,448	3,104	25,194	0.05	0.77
Handlers, equipment cleaners, helpers, and laborers	1,064	8,599	4,818	9,994	455	15,528	2,007	17,508	0.23	0.89
Service workers	11,676	6,049	8,004	10,707	3,875	12,148	4,081	19,933	0.95	0.61
Private household	1,038	2,216	60	(B)	144	8,424	24	(B)	6.00	(X)
Service, except private household	10,638	6,526	7,944	10,796	3,732	12,257	4,057	19,996	0.92	0.61
Farming, forestry, and fishing	654	3,530	3,282	8,471	183	10,205	1,621	14,978	0.11	0.68

B Base less than 75,000.   X Not applicable.   [1] Includes persons whose longest job was in the Armed Forces.
Source: U.S. Bureau of the Census, *Current Population Reports,* series P60-180.

No. 674. Employment Cost Index (ECI), by Industry and Occupation: 1982 to 1992

[As of **December.** The ECI is a measure of the rate of change in employee compensation (wages, salaries, and employer costs for employee benefits). Data are not seasonally adjusted: 1982-1985 based on fixed employment counts from 1970 Census of Population; thereafter, based on fixed employment counts from the 1980 Census of Population]

ITEM	INDEXES (June 1989=100)							PERCENT CHANGE FOR 12 MONTHS ENDING—				
	1982	1985	1988	1989	1990	1991	1992	1985	1989	1990	1991	1992
Civilian workers [1]	74.8	86.8	97.7	102.6	107.6	112.2	116.1	4.3	5.0	4.9	4.3	3.5
Workers, by occupational group:												
White-collar workers	72.9	85.8	97.6	102.9	108.3	112.8	116.6	4.9	5.4	5.2	4.2	3.4
Blue-collar workers	78.2	88.4	97.8	102.0	106.5	111.1	115.2	3.3	4.3	4.4	4.3	3.7
Service workers	74.3	87.2	98.2	102.8	108.0	113.1	116.7	3.9	4.7	5.1	4.7	3.2
Workers, by industry division:												
Manufacturing	76.9	87.8	97.6	102.0	107.2	112.2	116.5	3.3	4.5	5.1	4.7	3.8
Nonmanufacturing	73.9	86.4	97.7	102.8	107.8	112.3	116.0	4.7	5.2	4.9	4.2	3.3
Services	70.5	84.1	97.9	103.7	110.2	114.6	119.2	4.7	5.9	6.3	4.0	4.0
Public administration [2]	71.9	85.4	97.8	103.2	108.7	112.6	116.3	4.9	5.5	5.3	3.6	3.3
Private industry workers [3]	75.8	87.3	97.6	102.3	107.0	111.7	115.6	3.9	4.8	4.6	4.4	3.5
Workers, by occupational group:												
White-collar workers	73.7	86.4	97.3	102.4	107.4	112.2	115.9	4.9	5.2	4.9	4.5	3.3
Blue-collar workers	78.4	88.5	97.9	101.9	106.4	111.0	115.0	3.1	4.1	4.4	4.3	3.6
Service workers	76.3	88.4	98.2	102.5	107.3	112.4	115.9	3.0	4.4	4.7	4.8	3.1
Workers, by industry division:												
Manufacturing	76.9	87.8	97.6	102.0	107.2	112.2	116.5	3.3	4.5	5.1	4.7	3.8
Nonmanufacturing	75.1	87.0	97.5	102.3	106.9	111.5	115.1	4.3	4.9	4.5	4.3	3.2
Services	(NA)	84.1	97.5	102.9	109.3	114.0	118.9	(NA)	5.5	6.2	4.3	4.3
Business services	(NA)	(NA)	97.2	101.3	107.4	111.1	115.9	(NA)	4.2	6.0	3.4	4.3
Health services	(NA)	83.7	97.0	103.7	110.8	116.5	121.8	(NA)	6.9	6.8	5.1	4.5
Hospitals	(NA)	(NA)	96.6	103.5	110.7	116.1	121.6	(NA)	7.1	7.0	4.9	4.7
Workers, by bargaining status:												
Union	79.6	90.1	98.2	101.8	106.2	111.1	115.9	2.6	3.7	4.3	4.6	4.3
Nonunion	74.3	86.3	97.4	102.4	107.3	111.9	115.5	4.6	5.1	4.8	4.3	3.2
State and local government workers	70.8	84.6	98.2	104.3	110.4	114.4	118.6	5.6	6.2	5.8	3.6	3.7
Workers, by occupational group:												
White-collar workers	70.4	84.2	98.3	104.6	110.9	114.6	118.9	5.8	6.4	6.0	3.3	3.8
Blue-collar workers	73.9	86.7	97.5	103.7	108.7	112.9	117.8	5.3	6.4	4.8	3.9	4.3
Workers, by industry division:												
Services	70.0	84.0	98.5	104.7	111.3	115.3	119.6	5.9	6.3	6.3	3.6	3.7
Schools	69.0	83.6	98.7	105.3	111.6	115.6	119.9	6.2	6.7	6.0	3.6	3.7
Elementary and secondary	68.6	83.6	99.1	105.5	112.1	116.2	120.7	6.4	6.5	6.3	3.7	3.9
Colleges and universities	(NA)	(NA)	(NA)	104.7	110.2	113.5	117.2	(NA)	(NA)	5.3	3.0	3.3
Services, excluding schools [4]	73.1	85.2	97.8	103.2	110.2	114.4	118.6	4.7	5.5	6.8	3.8	3.7
Public administration [2]	71.9	85.4	97.8	103.2	108.7	112.6	116.3	4.9	5.5	5.3	3.6	3.3

NA Not available.   [1] Includes private industry and State and local government workers and excludes farm, household, and Federal government workers.   [2] Consists of legislative, judicial, administrative, and regulatory activities.   [3] Excludes farm and household workers.   [4] Includes library, social, and health services. Formerly called hospitals and other services.
Source: U.S. Bureau of Labor Statistics, *News, Employment Cost Index,* quarterly.

No. 675. Effective Federal Minimum Hourly Wage Rates, 1950 to 1993, and Coverage in 1991

[Employee estimates as of **September 1991**, except as indicated. The Fair Labor Standards Act of 1938 and subsequent amendments provide for minimum wage coverage applicable to specified nonsupervisory employment categories. Exempt from coverage are executives and administrators or professionals]

IN EFFECT	MINIMUM RATES FOR NONFARM			Minimum rates for farm workers [4]	SEX, RACE, AND INDUSTRY	NONSUPERVISORY EMPLOYEES, 1991		
	Laws prior to 1966 [1]	Percent, avg. earnings [2]	1966 and later [3]			Total (1,000)	Subject to minimum wage rates	
							Total (1,000)	Percent of total
Jan. 25, 1950....	$0.75	54	(X)	(X)	**Total**	91,373	80,540	88.1
Mar. 1, 1956	1.00	52	(X)	(X)				
Sept. 3, 1961....	1.15	50	(X)	(X)	Male.	45,909	40,276	87.7
Sept. 3, 1963....	1.25	51	(X)	(X)	Female	45,464	40,264	88.6
Feb. 1, 1967....	1.40	50	$1.00	$1.00	White	80,222	70,494	87.9
Feb. 1, 1968....	1.60	54	1.15	1.15	Black and other	11,151	10,046	90.1
Feb. 1, 1969....	(5)	51	1.30	1.30	Black only.	10,150	9,148	90.1
Feb. 1, 1970....	(5)	49	1.45	(5)				
Feb. 1, 1971....	(5)	46	1.60	(5)	**Private industry**	80,149	69,316	86.5
					Agriculture [6]	1,702	653	38.4
May 1, 1974	2.00	46	1.90	1.60	Mining.	606	603	99.5
Jan. 1, 1975	2.10	45	2.00	1.80	Construction.	4,452	4,294	96.5
Jan. 1, 1976	2.30	46	2.20	2.00	Manufacturing.	16,400	15,947	97.2
Jan. 1, 1977	(5)	42	2.30	2.20	Transp., public utilities . . .	5,208	5,175	99.4
Jan. 1, 1978	2.65	44	2.65	2.65	Wholesale trade	5,204	4,158	79.9
Jan. 1, 1979	2.90	45	2.90	2.90	Retail trade	17,439	15,800	90.6
Jan. 1, 1980	3.10	44	3.10	3.10	Finance, insurance, and real estate . .	5,736	4,349	75.8
Jan. 1, 1981	3.35	43	3.35	3.35	Service [7]	22,111	17,466	79.0
Apr. 1, 1990....	3.80	35	3.80	3.80	Private households	1,291	871	67.5
Apr. 1, 1991....	4.25	38	4.25	4.25	**Government** [7] [8]	11,224	11,224	100.0
Apr. 1, 1992....	(5)	37	(5)	(5)				
March 1, 1992 ...	(5)	37	(5)	(5)				

X Not applicable. [1] Applies to workers covered prior to 1961 Amendments and, after Sept. 1965, to workers covered by 1961 Amendments. Rates set by 1961 Amendments were: Sept. 1961, $1.00; Sept. 1964, $1.15; and Sept. 1965, $1.25. [2] Percent of gross average hourly earnings of production workers in manufacturing. [3] Applies to workers newly covered by Amendments of 1966, 1974, and 1977, and Title IX of Education Amendments of 1972. [4] Included in coverage as of 1966, 1974, and 1977 Amendments. [5] No change in rate. [6] Estimates based on average employment for the ten-month active season. [7] Estimates for educational services in private industry and government relate to October. [8] Federal, State, and local employees. Source: U.S. Department of Labor, Employment Standards Administration, *Minimum Wage and Maximum Hours Standards Under the Fair Labor Standards Act*, 1981, annual; and unpublished data.

No. 676. Workers Paid Hourly Rates, by Selected Characteristics: 1992

[Annual average of monthly figures; for employed wage and salary workers. Based on Current Population Survey; see text, section 1, and Appendix III]

CHARACTERISTIC	NUMBER OF WORKERS [1] (1,000)				PERCENT DISTRIBUTION			PERCENT OF ALL WORKERS PAID HOURLY RATES				Median hourly earnings of workers paid hourly rates [2]
	Total paid hourly rates	At or below $4.25			Total paid hourly rates	At or below $4.25			At or below $4.25			
		Total	At $4.25	Below $4.25		At $4.25	Below $4.25	Total	At $4.25	Below $4.25		
Total, 16 years and over [3] ...	62,683	4,762	2,866	1,896	100.0	100.0	100.0	7.6	4.6	3.0	7.77	
16 to 24 years	14,172	2,479	1,596	883	22.6	55.7	46.6	17.5	11.3	6.2	5.37	
16 to 19 years.	4,873	1,414	963	451	7.8	33.6	23.8	29.0	19.8	9.3	4.73	
25 years and over	48,511	2,283	1,270	1,013	77.4	44.3	53.4	4.7	2.6	2.1	8.76	
Male, 16 years and over . .	31,510	1,792	1,164	628	50.3	40.6	33.1	5.7	3.7	2.0	8.79	
16 to 24 years	7,399	1,093	760	333	11.8	26.5	17.6	14.8	10.3	4.5	5.65	
16 to 19 years	2,490	649	483	166	4.0	16.9	8.8	26.1	19.4	6.7	4.79	
25 years and over . . .	24,111	699	404	295	38.5	14.1	15.6	2.9	1.7	1.2	10.09	
Women, 16 years and over .	31,173	2,970	1,702	1,268	49.7	59.4	66.9	9.5	5.5	4.1	6.98	
16 to 24 years	6,773	1,386	836	550	10.8	29.2	29.0	20.5	12.3	8.1	5.16	
16 to 19 years	2,382	765	480	285	3.8	16.7	15.0	32.1	20.2	12.0	4.69	
25 years and over . . .	24,400	1,584	866	718	38.9	30.2	37.9	6.5	3.5	2.9	7.67	
White	52,452	3,872	2,269	1,603	83.7	79.2	84.5	7.4	4.3	3.1	7.87	
Black	8,054	719	488	231	12.8	17.0	12.2	8.9	6.1	2.9	7.07	
Hispanic origin [4]	5,984	590	454	136	9.5	15.8	7.2	9.9	7.6	2.3	6.71	
Full-time workers.	46,645	1,742	1,075	667	74.4	37.5	35.2	3.7	2.3	1.4	8.67	
Part-time workers [5]	16,037	3,020	1,791	1,229	25.6	62.5	64.8	18.8	11.2	7.7	5.40	
Private sector.	54,386	4,397	2,613	1,784	86.8	91.2	94.1	8.1	4.8	3.3	7.48	
Goods-producing industries [6] .	17,698	572	409	163	28.2	14.3	8.6	3.2	2.3	0.9	9.02	
Service-producing industries [7]	36,688	3,826	2,205	1,621	58.5	76.9	85.5	10.4	6.0	4.4	6.79	
Public sector	8,296	365	253	112	13.2	8.8	5.9	4.4	3.0	1.4	9.75	

[1] Excludes the incorporated self-employed. [2] For definition of median, see Guide to Tabular Presentation. [3] Includes races not shown separately. [4] Persons of Hispanic origin may be of any race. [5] Working fewer than 35 hours per week. [6] Includes agriculture, mining, construction, and manufacturing. [7] Includes transportation and public utilities; wholesale trade; finance, insurance, and real estate; private households; and other service industries, not shown separately.
Source: U.S. Bureau of Labor Statistics, unpublished data.

No. 677. Employer Costs for Employee Compensation per Hour Worked, 1988 and 1992, and by Industry, 1992

[As of March, for private industry workers. Based on a sample of establishments; see source for details]

COMPENSATION COMPONENT	COST (dol.)						PERCENT DISTRIBUTION					
	1988	1992					1988	1992				
		Total	Goods producing[1]	Service producing[2]	Manufacturing	Nonmanufacturing		Total	Goods producing[1]	Service producing[2]	Manufacturing	Nonmanufacturing
Total compensation....	13.79	16.14	19.38	14.99	19.20	15.34	100.0	100.0	100.0	100.0	100.0	100.0
Wages and salaries....	10.02	11.58	13.17	11.02	12.93	11.23	72.7	71.8	68.0	73.5	67.4	73.2
Total benefits........	3.77	4.55	6.21	3.97	6.26	4.11	27.3	28.2	32.0	26.5	32.6	26.8
Paid leave.........	0.97	1.09	1.33	1.01	1.47	1.00	7.0	6.8	6.9	6.7	7.7	6.5
Vacation.........	0.48	0.54	0.69	0.48	0.75	0.48	3.5	3.3	3.6	3.2	3.9	3.1
Holiday..........	0.33	0.37	0.48	0.33	0.54	0.32	2.4	2.3	2.5	2.2	2.8	2.1
Sick............	0.12	0.14	0.11	0.15	0.12	0.14	0.9	0.9	0.6	1.0	0.6	0.9
Other...........	0.04	0.05	0.05	0.05	0.06	0.05	0.3	0.3	0.3	0.3	0.3	0.3
Supplemental pay....	0.33	0.39	0.64	0.30	0.67	0.31	2.4	2.4	3.3	2.0	3.5	2.0
Premium pay......	0.17	0.18	0.37	0.12	0.37	0.13	1.2	1.1	1.9	0.8	1.9	0.9
Nonproduction bonuses........	0.12	0.15	0.19	0.14	0.20	0.14	0.8	1.0	1.0	0.9	1.1	0.9
Shift pay.........	0.04	0.05	0.08	0.04	0.10	0.04	0.3	0.3	0.4	0.3	0.5	0.3
Insurance.........	0.78	1.12	1.60	0.95	1.70	0.96	5.6	6.9	8.2	6.3	8.9	6.3
Health insurance ...	(NA)	1.02	1.45	0.87	1.55	0.88	(NA)	6.3	7.5	5.8	8.1	5.8
Retirement and savings..........	0.45	0.46	0.70	0.38	0.65	0.41	3.3	2.9	3.6	2.5	3.4	2.7
Pensions........	0.38	0.36	0.55	0.30	0.49	0.33	2.8	2.3	2.8	2.0	2.6	2.2
Savings and thrift...	0.07	0.10	0.16	0.08	0.16	0.08	0.5	0.6	0.8	0.5	0.8	0.5
Legally required[3]	1.22	1.47	1.89	1.33	1.71	1.41	8.8	9.1	9.7	8.9	8.9	9.2
Social Security.....	0.81	0.96	1.13	0.90	1.13	0.92	5.9	6.0	5.8	6.0	5.9	6.0
Federal unemployment....	0.03	0.03	0.03	0.03	0.03	0.03	0.2	0.2	0.2	0.2	0.2	0.2
State unemployment.	0.12	0.10	0.13	0.09	0.12	0.09	0.8	0.6	0.7	0.6	0.6	0.6
Workers compensation	0.24	0.36	0.58	0.28	0.42	0.34	1.7	2.2	3.0	1.9	2.2	2.2
Other benefits[4]	0.02	0.02	0.05	(Z)	0.06	(Z)	0.2	0.1	0.3	(Z)	0.3	(Z)

NA Not available. Z Represents or rounds to zero. [1] Mining, construction, and manufacturing. [2] Transportation, communications, public utilities, wholesale trade, retail trade, finance, insurance, real estate, and services. [3] Includes railroad retirement, railroad unemployment, railroad supplemental unemployment, and other legally required benefits, not shown separately. [4] Includes severance pay, and supplemental unemployment benefits.

Source: U.S. Bureau of Labor Statistics, *News, Employer Costs for Employee Compensation*, USDL 92-391.

No. 678. Employees With Employer- or Union-Provided Pension Plans or Group Health Plans, by Occupation and Selected Characteristic: 1991

[In thousands, except percent. For wage and salary workers 15 years old and over as of March 1992. Based on Current Population Survey; see text, section 1, and Appendix III]

OCCUPATION	Total	WITH PENSION PLANS		WITH GROUP HEALTH PLANS		CHARACTERISTIC	Total	WITH PENSION PLANS		WITH GROUP HEALTH PLANS	
		Number	Percent	Number	Percent			Number	Percent	Number	Percent
Total	134,023	53,913	40.2	69,828	52.1	AGE Total........	134,023	53,913	40.2	69,828	52.1
Executive, admin., managerial.....	15,814	8,382	53.0	10,728	67.8	15 to 24 years	23,028	2,841	12.3	5,430	23.6
Prof. specialty ...	17,232	10,060	58.4	11,448	66.4	25 to 44 years	70,761	31,526	44.6	40,638	57.4
Tech./related support......	4,612	2,459	53.3	3,104	67.3	45 to 64 years	35,484	18,519	52.2	21,930	61.8
Sales workers	16,197	4,327	26.7	6,865	42.4	65 years and over .	4,750	1,027	21.6	1,829	38.5
Admin. support, inc. clerical.....	21,199	9,952	46.9	12,202	57.6	WORK EXPERIENCE Worked......	134,023	53,913	40.2	69,828	52.1
Precision prod., craft/repair....	14,545	6,028	41.4	8,183	56.3	Full-time	104,537	50,574	48.4	65,107	62.3
Mach. operators, assemblers[1] ...	8,602	3,695	43.0	5,384	62.6	50 weeks or more.	80,388	44,133	54.9	55,938	69.6
Transportation/ material moving .	5,259	2,197	41.8	3,085	58.7	27 to 49 weeks .	14,492	4,862	33.5	6,915	47.7
Handlers, equip. cleaners[2]	5,888	1,546	26.3	2,276	38.7	26 weeks or fewer.	9,657	1,580	16.4	2,254	23.3
Service workers ..	19,693	4,198	21.3	5,813	29.5	Part-time	29,486	3,339	11.3	4,720	16.0
Pvt. households.	1,098	11	1.0	19	1.7	50 weeks or more.	12,010	1,965	16.4	2,686	22.4
Other........	18,596	4,187	22.5	5,794	31.2	27 to 49 weeks .	7,078	888	12.5	1,141	16.1
Farming, forestry and fishing	3,977	365	9.2	662	16.6	26 weeks or fewer.	10,398	486	4.7	893	8.6
Armed Forces ...	1,005	704	70.0	77	7.6	EMPLOYER SIZE Under 25........	40,383	4,939	12.2	10,620	26.3
						25 to 99	17,263	5,214	30.2	8,661	50.2
						100 to 499.......	18,635	8,496	45.6	11,508	61.8
						500 to 999.......	7,320	4,053	55.4	4,857	66.4
						Over 1,000.......	50,422	31,211	61.9	34,181	67.8

[1] Includes inspectors. [2] Includes helpers and laborers.

Source: U.S. Bureau of the Census, unpublished data.

No. 679. Employee Benefits in Medium and Large Private Establishments, 1991 and Small Private Establishments, 1990

[Covers full-time employees in private industry. Medium and large establishments exclude establishments with fewer than 100 workers, executive and traveling operating employees, and Alaska and Hawaii. Small establishments include those with fewer than 100 employees. Covers only benefits for which the employer pays part or all of the premium or expenses involved, except unpaid parental leave and long-term care insurance. Based on a sample survey of establishments; for details, see sources. For data on employee benefits in State and local governments, see table 502]

MEDIUM AND LARGE PRIVATE ESTABLISHMENTS, 1991	All employees	Professional, technical and related	Clerical and sales	Production and service
Percent of employees participating in—				
Paid: Vacations	96	97	98	95
Holidays	92	93	94	90
Jury duty leave	86	92	88	82
Funeral leave	80	84	82	77
Rest time	67	58	67	71
Military leave	54	63	56	48
Sick leave	67	87	82	48
Personal leave	21	29	26	13
Lunch time	8	5	4	11
Maternity leave	2	3	2	1
Paternity leave	1	1	1	(Z)
Unpaid: Maternity leave	37	43	38	33
Paternity leave	26	31	26	23
Insurance plans:				
Medical care	83	85	81	84
Noncontributory	41	38	35	46
Hospital/room and board	83	85	81	84
Inpatient surgery	83	85	81	84
Mental health care	81	83	79	82
Dental	60	67	60	57
Extended care facility	66	70	66	66
Home health care	67	71	66	66
Hospice care	46	48	45	45
Vision	23	21	21	25
In HMO's	14	15	15	12
Alcohol abuse treatment	82	83	80	82
Inpatient detoxification	81	82	79	81
Inpatient rehabilitation	64	63	63	66
Outpatient	64	66	63	64
Drug abuse treatment	81	83	79	80
Inpatient detoxification	80	82	79	80
Inpatient rehabilitation	63	62	62	65
Outpatient	62	65	62	61
Life	94	98	95	92
Noncontributory	80	83	82	77
Accident/sickness	45	32	35	57
Noncontributory	33	19	23	46
Long-term disability	40	61	49	24
Noncontributory	31	46	38	20
Retirement and savings plans:				
Defined benefit pension	59	60	56	59
Earnings-based formula [1]	41	52	46	32
Defined contribution	48	57	53	39
Savings and thrift	29	38	35	20
Employee stock ownership	3	4	4	2
Deferred profit sharing	16	13	16	18
Money purchase pension	7	11	7	5
Additional benefits:				
Parking	88	86	85	92
Educational assistance	72	87	73	64
Travel accident insurance	42	55	47	32
Severance pay	41	55	48	30
Relocation allowance	31	50	30	21
Recreation facilities	26	34	25	23
Nonproduction bonuses, cash	35	33	36	35
Child care	8	11	9	5
Flexible benefits plans	10	16	10	6
Reimbursement accounts [2]	36	48	40	26
Eldercare	9	11	12	6
Long-term care insurance	4	6	5	2
Wellness programs	35	47	34	28
Employee assistance programs	56	64	56	51

SMALL PRIVATE ESTABLISHMENTS, 1990	All employees	Professional, technical and related	Clerical and sales	Production and service
Percent of employees participating in—				
Paid: Vacations	88	94	93	83
Holidays	84	95	91	75
Jury duty leave	54	72	62	43
Funeral leave	47	57	54	38
Rest time	48	42	46	51
Military leave	21	29	26	15
Sick leave	47	70	61	29
Personal leave	11	17	13	7
Lunch time	8	7	7	8
Maternity leave	2	3	3	1
Paternity leave	(Z)	(Z)	(Z)	(Z)
Unpaid: Maternity leave	17	26	20	12
Paternity leave	8	13	8	5
Insurance plans:				
Medical care	69	82	75	60
Noncontributory	40	46	40	37
Hospital/room and board	69	82	75	60
Inpatient surgery	69	82	75	60
Mental health care:				
Inpatient	68	80	74	59
Outpatient	66	77	72	58
Dental	30	38	35	24
Extended care facility	57	66	63	49
Home health care	55	66	62	45
Hospice care	35	40	40	30
Vision	9	8	9	9
In HMO's	10	12	8	9
Alcohol abuse treatment	67	80	73	59
Inpatient detoxification	67	80	73	58
Inpatient rehabilitation	54	64	58	47
Outpatient	50	60	54	43
Drug abuse treatment	66	78	70	57
Inpatient detoxification	65	77	71	56
Inpatient rehabilitation	50	60	55	44
Outpatient	47	55	51	41
Life	64	79	70	55
Noncontributory	53	69	60	43
Accident/sickness	26	25	24	27
Noncontributory	17	14	15	19
Long-term disability	19	36	25	9
Noncontributory	16	30	21	8
Retirement and savings plans:				
Defined benefit pension	20	20	23	18
Earnings-based formula [1]	14	17	19	9
Defined contribution	31	40	36	24
Savings and thrift	10	16	15	5
Employee stock ownership	1	1	1	(Z)
Deferred profit sharing	15	17	17	13
Money purchase pension	6	9	6	6
Additional benefits:				
Parking	86	84	85	88
Educational assistance	39	58	46	30
Travel accident insurance	15	24	19	9
Severance pay	19	30	26	12
Relocation allowance	12	22	15	6
Recreation facilities	6	12	6	4
Nonproduction bonuses, cash	45	42	47	44
Child care	1	2	2	1
Flexible benefits plans	1	3	2	1
Reimbursement accounts [2]	8	13	9	4
Eldercare	2	5	1	1
Long-term care insurance	1	(Z)	1	1
Wellness programs	6	10	8	4
Employee assistance programs	15	21	17	11

Z Represents or rounds to zero. [1] Earnings-based formulas pay a percent of employee's annual earnings (usually earnings in the final years of employment) per year of service. [2] Account which is used throughout the year to pay for plan premiums or to reimburse the employee for benefit related expenses. Account may be financed by employer, employee, or both.

Source: U.S. Bureau of Labor Statistics, *Employee Benefits in Medium and Large Private Establishments, 1991*, Bulletin 2422; and *Employee Benefits in Small Private Establishments, 1990*, Bulletin 2388.

No. 680. Major Collective Bargaining Agreements—Average Percent Wage Rate Changes Under All Agreements: 1970 to 1992

[In percent, except as indicated. Data represent all wage rate changes implemented under the terms of private nonfarm industry agreements affecting 1,000 workers or more. Series covers production and related workers in manufacturing and nonsupervisory workers in nonmanufacturing industries. Data measure all wage rate changes effective in the year stemming from settlements reached in the year, deferred from prior year settlements, and cost-of-living adjustment (COLA) clauses]

CHANGES	1970	1975	1980	1985	1986	1987	1988	1989	1990	1991	1992
Average wage rate change (prorated over all workers)	8.8	8.7	9.9	3.3	2.3	3.1	2.6	3.2	3.5	3.6	3.1
Source:											
Current settlements	5.1	2.8	3.6	0.7	0.5	0.7	0.7	1.2	1.3	1.1	0.8
Prior settlements	3.1	3.7	3.5	1.8	1.7	1.8	1.3	1.3	1.5	1.9	1.9
COLA provisions	0.6	2.2	2.8	0.7	0.2	0.5	0.6	0.7	0.7	0.5	0.4
Industry:											
Manufacturing	7.1	8.5	10.2	2.8	1.5	3.4	2.8	3.5	4.4	3.7	3.1
Nonmanufacturing	10.5	8.9	9.7	3.6	2.9	2.9	2.5	3.0	3.0	3.5	3.1
Construction	(NA)	8.1	9.9	3.0	3.0	3.1	2.9	3.1	3.4	3.4	3.4
Transportation and public utilities	(NA)	9.7	10.8	3.6	2.7	2.7	2.1	2.3	2.2	3.3	2.7
Wholesale and retail trade	(NA)	9.2	7.6	3.3	2.9	2.0	2.3	3.2	3.6	3.5	3.5
Services	(NA)	6.4	8.1	5.1	3.7	3.8	3.5	5.3	4.3	4.9	3.7
Nonmanufacturing, excluding construction	(NA)	9.3	9.6	3.7	2.9	2.8	2.4	3.0	2.9	3.6	3.0
Average wage rate increase for workers receiving an increase	9.4	9.0	10.1	4.2	3.4	3.8	3.4	4.0	4.2	4.0	3.7
Source:											
Current settlements	11.9	10.2	9.4	4.1	3.1	3.5	3.3	4.2	4.1	4.2	3.6
Prior settlements	5.8	5.2	5.6	3.7	3.9	3.3	3.1	3.4	3.3	3.7	3.8
COLA provisions	3.7	4.8	7.7	2.2	1.0	2.6	2.7	3.3	2.7	2.0	2.0
Total number of workers receiving a wage rate increase (mil.)	10.2	9.7	8.9	5.5	5.1	5.3	4.7	4.8	4.9	5.1	4.7
Source (mil.):											
Current settlements	4.7	2.7	3.5	1.4	1.7	1.5	1.4	1.7	1.9	1.5	1.3
Prior settlements	5.7	7.3	5.6	3.4	2.8	3.5	2.6	2.3	2.7	3.0	2.8
COLA provisions	1.8	4.7	3.4	2.3	1.4	1.3	1.3	1.3	1.4	1.3	1.0
Number of workers not receiving a wage rate increase (mil.)	0.6	0.4	0.2	1.5	1.4	1.0	1.3	1.2	1.0	0.5	0.9

NA Not available.

Source: U.S. Bureau of Labor Statistics, *Compensation and Working Conditions*, monthly.

No. 681. Major Collective Bargaining Settlements—Average Percent Changes in Wage and Compensation Rates Negotiated: 1970 to 1992

In percent, except as indicated. Data represent private nonfarm industry settlements affecting production and related workers in manufacturing and nonsupervisory workers in nonmanufacturing industries. Wage data cover units with 1,000 workers or more. Compensation data relate to units of 5,000 or more. Data relate to contracts negotiated in each calendar year but exclude possible changes in wage rates under cost-of-living adjustment (COLA) clauses, except increases guaranteed by the contract. Includes all settlements, whether wage and benefit rates were changed or not. Minus sign (-) indicates decrease]

CHANGES	1970	1975	1980	1984	1985	1986	1987	1988	1989	1990	1991	1992
Compensation rates:												
First year	13.1	11.4	10.4	3.6	2.6	1.1	3.0	3.1	4.5	4.6	4.1	3.0
Over life of contract [1]	9.1	8.1	7.1	2.8	2.7	1.6	2.6	2.5	3.4	3.2	3.4	3.1
Wage rates:												
All industries:												
First year	11.9	10.2	9.5	2.4	2.3	1.2	2.2	2.5	4.0	4.0	3.6	2.7
Contracts with COLA	(NA)	12.2	8.0	2.9	1.6	1.9	2.3	2.4	3.9	3.4	3.4	2.7
Contracts without COLA	(NA)	9.1	11.7	2.1	2.7	0.9	2.1	2.7	4.0	4.4	3.7	2.7
Over life of contract [1]	8.9	7.8	7.1	2.4	2.7	1.8	2.1	2.4	3.4	3.2	3.2	3.0
Contracts with COLA	(NA)	7.1	5.0	1.8	2.5	1.7	1.5	1.8	2.8	1.9	3.0	2.5
Contracts without COLA	(NA)	8.3	10.3	2.7	2.8	1.8	2.5	2.8	3.5	4.0	3.3	3.1
Manufacturing:												
First year	8.1	9.8	7.4	2.3	0.8	-1.2	2.1	2.2	3.9	3.7	3.9	2.6
Over life of contract [1]	6.0	8.0	5.4	1.5	1.8	0.2	1.3	2.1	3.2	2.1	3.1	2.6
Nonmanufacturing:												
First year	15.2	10.4	10.9	2.5	3.3	2.0	2.3	2.8	4.0	4.3	3.4	2.7
Over life of contract [1]	11.5	7.8	8.3	2.9	3.3	2.3	2.7	2.5	3.4	4.0	3.3	3.0
Number of workers affected (mil.)	4.7	2.9	3.8	2.3	2.2	2.5	2.0	1.8	1.9	2.0	1.8	1.6
Manufacturing (mil.)	2.2	0.8	1.6	0.9	0.9	0.6	0.9	0.7	0.4	0.9	0.6	0.3
Nonmanufacturing (mil.)	2.5	2.1	2.2	1.4	1.3	1.9	1.1	1.1	1.5	1.1	1.2	1.3

NA Not available.　　[1] Average annual rate of change.

Source: U.S. Bureau of Labor Statistics, *Compensation and Working Conditions*, monthly.

No. 682. Workers Killed or Disabled on the Job, 1960 to 1991, and by Industry Group, 1991

[Data for 1991 are preliminary estimates. Estimates based on data from the U.S. National Center for Health Statistics, State Departments of Health, and State industrial commissions. Numbers of workers based on data from the U.S. Bureau of Labor Statistics]

YEAR	DEATHS						Disabling injuries[2] (1,000)	YEAR AND INDUSTRY GROUP	DEATHS		Disabling injuries[2] (1,000)
	Total		Manufacturing		Nonmanufacturing				Number (1,000)	Rate[1]	
	Number (1,000)	Rate[1]	Number (1,000)	Rate[1]	Number (1,000)	Rate[1]					
1960....	13.8	21	1.7	10	12.1	25	1,950	1991, total.......	9.9	9	1,700
1965....	14.1	20	1.8	10	12.3	24	2,100	Agriculture[3].......	1.4	44	140
1970....	13.8	18	1.7	9	12.1	21	2,200	Mining and quarrying[4]..	0.3	43	30
1975....	13.0	15	1.6	9	11.4	17	2,200	Construction........	1.8	31	180
1980....	13.2	13	1.7	8	11.5	15	2,200	Manufacturing........	0.8	4	310
1984....	11.5	11	1.1	6	10.4	12	1,900	Transportation and utilities	1.3	22	140
1985....	11.5	11	1.2	6	10.3	12	2,000	Trade[5].........	1.0	4	320
1986....	11.1	10	1.0	5	10.1	11	1,800	Services[6]........	1.7	4	330
1987....	11.3	10	1.0	5	10.3	11	1,800	Government.......	1.6	9	250
1988....	11.0	10	1.1	6	9.9	10	1,800				
1989....	10.9	9	1.1	6	9.8	10	1,700				
1990....	10.6	9	1.0	5	9.6	10	1,800				
1991....	9.9	9	0.8	4	9.1	9	1,700				

[1] Per 100,000 workers. [2] Disabling injury defined as one which results in death, some degree of physical impairment, or renders the person unable to perform regular activities for a full day beyond the day of the injury. [3] Includes forestry and fishing. [4] Includes oil and gas extraction. [5] Includes wholesale and retail trade. [6] Includes finance, insurance, and real estate.

Source: National Safety Council, Itasca, IL, *Accident Facts*, annual (copyright).

No. 683. Worker Deaths and Injuries and Production Time Lost: 1985 to 1991

ITEM	DEATHS (1,000)			DISABLING INJURIES[1] (mil.)			PRODUCTION TIME LOST (mil. days)					
							In the current year			In future years[2]		
	1985	1990	1991	1985	1990	1991	1985	1990	1991	1985	1990	1991
All accidents	46.3	46.9	43.2	4.6	4.6	4.2	100.0	95.0	90.0	380.0	380.0	340.0
On the job	11.4	10.6	9.9	1.9	1.8	1.7	40.0	35.0	35.0	110.0	100.0	90.0
Off the job	34.9	36.3	33.3	2.7	2.8	2.5	60.0	60.0	55.0	270.0	280.0	250.0
Motor vehicle	22.2	23.4	21.0	0.9	0.9	0.8	(NA)	(NA)	(NA)	(NA)	(NA)	(NA)
Public nonmotor vehicle ...	6.9	6.5	6.2	0.9	0.9	0.8	(NA)	(NA)	(NA)	(NA)	(NA)	(NA)
Home	5.8	6.4	6.1	0.9	1.0	0.9	(NA)	(NA)	(NA)	(NA)	(NA)	(NA)

NA Not available. [1] See footnote 2, table 682. [2] Based on an average of 5,850 days lost in future years per fatality and 565 days lost in future years per permanent injury.

Source: National Safety Council, Itasca, IL, *Accident Facts*, 1992 (copyright).

No. 684. Industries with the Highest Total Case Incidence Rates for Injuries and Illnesses: 1990 and 1991

[Rates per full-time employees. Industries shown are those with highest rates in 1991. See headnote, table 685]

1987 SIC[1] code	INDUSTRY	1990	1991	1987 SIC[1] code	INDUSTRY	1990	1991
(X)	**Private sector, total........**	8.8	8.4	2451	Mobile homes...............	25.4	22.9
2011	Meat packing plants	42.4	45.5	3412	Metal barrels, drums, and pails	25.4	22.1
3731	Ship building and repairing	46.2	44.1	3751	Motorcycles, bicycles, and parts	18.0	22.0
3431	Metal sanitary ware	31.5	42.0	2083	Malt	21.1	21.7
3321	Gray and ductile iron foundries	30.5	31.3	3211	Flat glass..................	24.0	21.7
3639	Household appliances, n.e.c.[2]......	24.2	30.7	3341	Secondary nonferrous metals	24.1	21.6
3711	Motor vehicles and car bodies......	26.8	28.3	3365	Aluminum foundries............	22.2	21.3
3465	Automotive stampings	29.3	27.5	3743	Railroad equipment............	21.8	21.1
3715	Truck trailers	24.0	25.5	2515	Mattresses and bedsprings.......	18.8	21.0
2429	Special product sawmills, n.e.c.[2]....	25.2	25.1	2092	Fresh or frozen prepared fish	22.5	21.0
3325	Steel foundries, n.e.c.[2].........	23.5	24.1	3441	Fabricated structural metal	23.6	20.9
3334	Primary aluminum	26.4	23.5	3363	Aluminum die-castings	21.4	20.9
2452	Prefabricated wood buildings.......	25.8	23.5	2013	Sausages and other prepared meats .	22.7	20.8
3713	Truck and bus bodies	22.1	23.4	3462	Iron and steel forgings..........	22.4	20.7
2015	Poultry slaughtering and processing ..	26.9	23.1	3792	Travel trailers and campers.......	20.3	20.7
2439	Structural wood members, n.e.c.[2]...	24.5	22.9	3111	Leather tanning and finishing......	19.2	20.4

X Not applicable. [1] 1987 Standard Industrial Classification; see text, section 13. [2] N.e.c. means not elsewhere classified.

Source: U.S. Bureau of Labor Statistics, *Occupational Injuries and Illnesses in the United States by Industry*, annual.

No. 685. Occupational Injury and Illness Incidence Rates, by Selected Industries: 1990 and 1991

[Rates per 100 full-time employees. For nonfarm employment data, see table table 662. Rates refer to any occupational injury or illness resulting in (1) fatalities, (2) lost workday cases, or (3) nonfatal cases without lost workdays. Incidence rates were calculated as: Number of injuries and illnesses divided by total hours worked by all employees during year multiplied by 200,000 as base for 100 full-time equivalent workers (working 40 hours per week, 50 weeks a year)]

1987 SIC [1] code	INDUSTRY	1990	1991	1987 SIC [1] code	INDUSTRY	1990	1991
(X)	**Private sector** [2]	8.8	8.4	E	**Transportation and public utilities**	9.6	9.3
A	**Agriculture, forestry, fishing** [2]	11.6	10.8	40	Railroad transportation	7.5	7.6
B	**Mining**	8.3	7.4	41	Local passenger transit	9.7	9.5
10	Metal mining	6.8	6.5	42	Trucking and warehousing	14.3	14.5
12	Coal mining	10.8	11.1	44	Water transportation	11.9	11.6
13	Oil and gas extraction	8.0	6.4	45	Transportation by air	15.1	14.0
14	Nonmetallic minerals, exc. fuels	7.1	7.0	46	Pipelines, except natural gas	3.4	4.0
C	**Construction**	14.2	13.0	47	Transportation services	3.9	3.8
15	General building contractors	13.4	12.0	48	Communications	3.3	3.2
16	Heavy construction, except building	13.8	12.8	49	Electric, gas, sanitary services	8.2	7.7
17	Special trade contractors	14.7	13.5	F, G	**Wholesale and retail trade**	7.9	7.6
D	**Manufacturing**	13.2	12.7	F	Wholesale trade	7.4	7.2
(X)	Durable goods	14.2	13.6	G	Retail trade	8.1	7.7
24	Lumber and wood products	18.1	16.8	H	**Finance, insurance, real estate**	2.4	2.4
25	Furniture and fixtures	16.9	15.9	60	Depository institutions	2.1	1.8
32	Stone, clay, and glass products	15.4	14.8	61	Nondepository institutions	0.7	1.1
33	Primary metal industries	19.0	17.7	62	Security and commodity brokers	0.9	(NA)
34	Fabricated metal products	18.7	17.4	63	Insurance carriers	2.1	2.4
35	Industrial machinery and equipment	12.0	11.2	64	Insurance agents, brokers, and service	1.3	1.4
36	Electronic and other electric equipment	9.1	8.6	65	Real estate	4.8	5.4
37	Transportation equipment	17.8	18.3	67	Holding and other investment offices	2.5	2.6
38	Instruments and related products	5.9	6.0	I	**Services** [3]	6.0	6.2
39	Miscellaneous manufacturing industries	11.3	11.3	70	Hotels and other lodging places	10.7	10.3
(X)	Nondurable goods	11.7	11.5	72	Personal services	3.6	4.0
20	Food and kindred products	20.0	19.5	73	Business services	5.0	5.2
21	Tobacco products	7.7	6.4	75	Auto repair, services, and parking	7.4	6.5
22	Textile mill products	9.6	10.0	76	Miscellaneous repair services	8.4	7.7
23	Apparel and other textile products	8.8	9.2	78	Motion pictures	3.6	3.6
26	Paper and allied products	12.1	11.2	79	Amusement and recreation services	9.0	8.8
27	Printing and publishing	6.9	6.7	80	Health services	8.4	8.9
28	Chemicals and allied products	6.5	6.4	81	Legal services	0.6	0.7
29	Petroleum and coal products	6.6	6.2	82	Educational services	3.8	3.8
30	Rubber and misc. plastics products	16.2	15.1	83	Social services	6.5	6.6
31	Leather and leather products	12.1	12.5	84	Museums, botanical, zoological gardens	7.4	6.5
				87	Engineering and management services	2.1	2.3

NA Not available.   X Not applicable.   [1] 1987 Standard Industrial Classification; see text, section 13.   [2] Excludes farms with fewer than 11 employees.   [3] Includes categories not shown separately.

Source: U.S. Bureau of Labor Statistics, *Occupational Injuries and Illnesses in the United States by Industry*, annual.

No. 686. Work Stoppages: 1960 to 1992

[Excludes work stoppages involving fewer than 1,000 workers and lasting less than 1 day. Information is based on reports of labor disputes appearing in daily newspapers, trade journals, and other public sources. The parties to the disputes are contacted by telephone, when necessary, to clarify details of the stoppages]

YEAR	Number of work stoppages [1]	Workers involved [2] (1,000)	DAYS IDLE Number [3] (1,000)	Percent estimated working time [4]	YEAR	Number of work stoppages [1]	Workers involved [2] (1,000)	DAYS IDLE Number [3] (1,000)	Percent estimated working time [4]
1960	222	896	13,260	0.09	1980	187	795	20,844	0.09
1965	268	999	15,140	0.10	1981	145	729	16,908	0.07
1969	412	1,576	29,397	0.29	1982	96	656	9,061	0.04
1970	381	2,468	52,761	0.29	1983	81	909	17,461	0.08
1971	298	2,516	35,538	0.19	1984	62	376	8,499	0.04
1972	250	975	16,764	0.09	1985	54	324	7,079	0.03
1973	317	1,400	16,260	0.08	1986	69	533	11,861	0.05
1974	424	1,796	31,809	0.16	1987	46	174	[5]4,469	0.02
1975	235	965	17,563	0.09	1988	40	118	4,364	0.02
1976	231	1,519	23,962	0.12	1989	51	452	16,996	0.07
1977	298	1,212	21,258	0.10	1990	44	185	5,926	0.02
1978	219	1,006	23,774	0.11	1991	40	392	4,584	0.02
1979	235	1,021	20,409	0.09	1992	35	364	3,989	0.01

[1] Beginning in year indicated.   [2] Workers counted more than once if involved in more than one stoppage during the year. [3] Resulting from all stoppages in effect in a year, including those that began in an earlier year.   [4] Agricultural and government employees are included in the total working time; private household and forestry and fishery employees are excluded.   [5] Revised since originally published.

Source: U.S. Bureau of Labor Statistics, *Compensation and Conditions*, monthly.

No. 687. U.S. Membership in AFL-CIO Affiliated Unions, by Selected Union: 1979 to 1991

[In thousands. Figures represent the labor organizations as constituted in 1989 and reflect past merger activity. Membership figures based on average per capita paid membership to the AFL-CIO for the 2-year period ending in June of the year shown and reflect only actively-employed members. Labor unions shown had a membership of 50,000 or more in 1991]

LABOR ORGANIZATION	1979	1985	1989	1991
Total [1]	13,621	13,109	14,100	13,933
Actors and Artistes	75	100	97	99
Allied Industrial Workers	92	63	60	53
Automobile, Aerospace and Agriculture (UAW)	(X)	974	917	840
Bakery, Confectionery and Tobacco	131	115	103	101
Boiler Makers, Iron Ship-builders [2][3]	129	110	75	66
Bricklayers [2]	106	95	84	84
Carpenters [2]	626	616	613	494
Clothing and Textile Workers (ACTWU) [2]	308	228	180	154
Communication Workers (CWA)	485	524	492	492
Electrical Workers (IBEW)	825	791	744	730
Electronic, Electrical and Salaried [2][4]	243	198	171	160
Operating Engineers	313	330	330	330
Fire Fighters	150	142	142	151
Food and Commercial Workers (UFCW) [2]	1,123	989	999	997
Garment Workers (ILGWU)	314	210	153	143
Glass, Molders, Pottery, and Plastics [2]	50	104	86	80
Government, American Federation (AFGE)	236	199	156	151
Graphic Communications [2]	171	141	124	113
Hotel Employees and Restaurant Employees	373	327	278	269
Ironworkers	146	140	111	101
Laborers	475	383	406	406
Letter Carriers (NALC)	151	186	201	210
Longshoreman's Association	63	65	62	60
Machinists and Aerospace (IAM) [2]	688	537	517	534
Marine Engineers Beneficial Assn.	23	22	48	53
Mine Workers	(X)	(X)	(X)	82
Office and Professional Employees	83	90	84	89
Oil, Chemical, Atomic Workers (OCAW)	146	108	71	90
Painters	160	133	128	124
Paperworkers Int'l	262	232	210	202
Plumbing and Pipefitting	228	226	220	220
Postal Workers	245	232	213	228
Retail, Wholesale Department Store	122	106	137	128
Rubber, Cork, Linoleum, Plastic	158	106	92	89
Seafarers	84	80	80	80
Service Employees (SEIU) [2]	537	688	762	881
Sheet Metal Workers	120	108	108	108
Stage Employees, Moving Picture Machine Operators	50	50	50	50
State, County, Municipal (AFSCME) [5]	889	997	1,090	1,191
Steelworkers	964	572	481	459
Teachers (AFT)	423	470	544	573
Teamsters [6]	(X)	(X)	1,161	1,379
Transit Union	94	94	96	98
Transport Workers	85	85	85	85
Transportation/Communications International	127	102	86	73
Transportation Union, United	121	88	(X)	64
Utility Workers	53	52	51	55

X Not applicable.   [1] Includes other AFL-CIO affiliated unions, not shown separately.   [2] Figures reflect mergers with one or more unions since 1979. For details see source.   [3] Includes Blacksmiths, Forgers and Helpers.   [4] Includes Machine and Furniture Workers.   [5] Excludes Hospital and Health Care Employees which merged into both unions on June 1, 1989, (membership of 23,000 in 1985; 60,000 in 1987; and 58,000 in 1989).   [6] Includes Chauffeurs, Warehousemen, and Helpers.
Source: American Federation of Labor and Congress of Industrial Organizations, Washington, DC, *Report of the AFL-CIO Executive Council*, biannual.

No. 688. U.S. Union Membership in Manufacturing, by State: 1984 to 1989

[Data represent annual average dues-paying full-time equivalent membership derived from financial records. Excludes unemployed members. In general, annual per capita revenues received by the parent organization were divided by the per capita rate to yield membership. For unions with multiple dues structures or other structures, other methods were used. See source for details. A right-to-work State has laws which prohibit collective bargaining contracts from including clauses requiring union membership as a condition of employment. Data for DC not available]

STATE	MANUFACTURING—UNION MEMBERSHIP (1,000)			PERCENT OF EMPLOYED [1]			STATE	MANUFACTURING—UNION MEMBERSHIP (1,000)			PERCENT OF EMPLOYED [1]		
	1984	1988	1989	1984	1988	1989		1984	1988	1989	1984	1988	1989
U.S. ..	5,285.9	4,771.1	4,603.1	27.3	24.9	23.8	MT [2]	5.6	5.2	4.9	24.9	25.0	22.8
AL [2]	72.2	57.4	55.1	20.1	15.3	14.3	NE [2]	11.1	9.1	8.6	12.3	9.9	8.7
AK [2]	4.3	3.7	3.6	38.1	25.5	24.6	NV [2]	1.6	1.5	1.4	7.6	6.2	5.4
AZ [2]	9.2	7.2	7.0	5.3	3.8	3.7	NH	9.9	8.2	7.8	8.0	6.7	6.7
AR [2]	28.6	27.3	26.3	13.4	12.0	11.2	NJ	184.9	165.6	160.8	25.4	24.8	24.4
CA	510.5	488.4	481.3	24.7	22.6	22.2	NM	5.6	4.2	3.9	15.3	10.4	9.5
CO	21.2	18.8	18.3	10.9	10.0	9.5	NY	668.2	588.0	561.7	50.4	48.2	47.2
CT	70.2	58.7	56.7	16.9	15.6	15.3	NC [2]	41.4	39.7	38.3	5.0	4.6	4.4
DE [2]	13.8	14.1	13.8	19.6	20.5	19.4	ND [2]	2.1	1.7	1.7	13.6	10.4	10.1
FL [2]	43.3	48.2	48.9	8.6	8.9	9.0	OH	469.0	450.4	438.8	41.6	40.9	39.6
GA [2]	77.3	67.8	66.3	14.1	11.9	11.7	OK	30.6	26.9	26.2	17.5	17.1	15.9
HI	9.0	9.1	9.0	41.3	41.4	41.0	OR	49.9	45.2	44.1	24.8	21.4	20.3
ID [3]	7.3	4.9	4.5	13.3	8.6	7.3	PA	457.1	428.3	413.4	40.7	40.7	39.3
IL	407.7	314.8	291.9	40.9	33.3	29.8	RI	13.0	12.8	12.4	10.7	11.1	11.1
IN	248.7	237.8	234.7	40.1	37.6	37.0	SC [2]	14.6	11.8	11.1	3.9	3.1	2.9
IA [2]	65.3	46.8	43.5	30.8	20.8	18.5	SD [2]	1.1	0.8	0.7	3.8	2.7	2.4
KS [2]	22.6	20.6	20.1	12.8	11.4	10.9	TN [2]	78.4	67.2	65.0	15.8	13.5	12.7
KY	69.6	62.6	60.4	27.0	23.0	21.5	TX [2]	159.8	142.6	134.1	15.9	15.1	13.8
LA [2]	36.8	34.5	33.4	20.2	20.4	19.4	UT [2]	6.8	4.9	4.6	7.2	5.0	4.4
ME	23.8	20.1	19.7	21.5	18.7	18.4	VT	5.5	4.1	3.9	11.2	8.3	8.1
MD	71.2	62.0	60.2	32.5	30.0	29.2	VA [2]	48.5	52.1	50.6	11.5	12.2	11.9
MA	128.8	115.8	111.8	19.2	19.9	19.6	WA	99.7	93.6	90.7	34.6	28.2	25.3
MI	487.8	500.6	486.9	50.7	53.6	51.6	WV	34.9	25.7	24.4	38.1	29.8	28.1
MN [2]	96.2	70.1	65.5	25.7	18.1	16.4	WI	161.4	133.3	127.8	31.1	24.3	23.0
MS [2]	19.0	19.0	18.4	8.7	8.1	7.6	WY [2]	1.6	1.3	1.2	20.0	15.9	13.0
MO	179.2	136.5	127.8	41.3	32.4	29.6							

[1] Employed in manufacturing.   [2] Right-to-work State.   [3] Right-to-work State beginning 1988
Source: Grant/Thornton, Chicago, IL, *Manufacturing Climates Study*, annual.

No. 689. Union Members, by Selected Characteristics: 1983 and 1992

[Annual averages of monthly data. Covers employed wage and salary workers 16 years old and over. Excludes self-employed workers whose businesses are incorporated although they technically qualify as wage and salary workers. See headnote table 637 regarding data by occupation and industry. Based on Current Population Survey, see text, section 1, and Appendix III]

CHARACTERISTIC	EMPLOYED WAGE AND SALARY WORKERS										MEDIAN USUAL WEEKLY EARNINGS [3] (dol.)							
	Total (1,000)		Union members [1] (1,000)		Represented by unions [2] (1,000)		Percent union members		Percent represented by union		Total		Union members [1]		Represented by unions [2]		Not represented by unions	
	1983	1992	1983	1992	1983	1992	1983	1992	1983	1992	1983	1992	1983	1992	1983	1992	1983	1992
Total	88,290	103,688	17,717	16,390	20,532	18,540	20.1	15.8	23.3	17.9	313	445	388	547	383	541	288	413
16 to 24 years old	19,305	17,046	1,749	982	2,145	1,176	9.1	5.8	11.1	6.9	210	277	281	352	275	346	203	272
25 to 34 years old	25,978	29,870	5,097	3,970	5,990	4,549	19.6	13.3	23.1	15.2	321	424	382	506	376	499	304	410
35 to 44 years old	18,722	27,524	4,648	5,282	5,362	5,933	24.8	19.2	28.6	21.6	369	504	411	576	407	572	339	484
45 to 54 years old	13,150	17,834	3,554	4,056	4,014	4,549	27.0	22.7	30.5	25.5	366	523	404	601	402	601	335	496
55 to 64 years old	9,201	9,092	2,474	1,891	2,788	2,090	26.9	20.8	30.3	23.0	346	483	392	552	390	549	316	447
65 years and over	1,934	2,322	196	210	234	244	10.1	9.0	12.1	10.5	260	378	338	495	330	493	238	354
Men	47,856	54,135	11,809	10,113	13,270	11,128	24.7	18.7	27.7	20.6	378	505	416	589	414	586	349	480
Women	40,433	49,554	5,908	6,277	7,262	7,412	14.6	12.7	18.0	15.0	252	381	309	484	307	481	237	361
White	77,046	88,624	14,844	13,416	17,182	15,148	19.3	15.1	22.3	17.1	319	462	396	568	391	562	295	426
Men	42,168	46,732	10,134	8,516	11,364	9,349	24.0	18.2	26.9	20.0	387	518	423	601	421	599	362	495
Women	34,887	41,892	4,710	4,900	5,818	5,799	13.5	11.7	16.7	13.8	254	388	314	496	313	492	240	370
Black	8,979	11,416	2,440	2,433	2,850	2,763	27.2	21.3	31.7	24.2	261	357	331	468	324	464	222	322
Men	4,477	5,480	1,420	1,309	1,615	1,448	31.7	23.9	36.1	26.4	293	380	366	498	360	494	244	338
Women	4,502	5,936	1,020	1,125	1,235	1,315	22.7	19.0	27.4	22.1	231	336	292	423	287	422	209	311
Hispanic [4]	(NA)	8,341	(NA)	1,244	(NA)	1,415	(NA)	14.9	(NA)	17.0	(NA)	324	(NA)	481	(NA)	472	(NA)	303
Men	(NA)	4,954	(NA)	834	(NA)	926	(NA)	16.8	(NA)	18.7	(NA)	345	(NA)	511	(NA)	504	(NA)	313
Women	(NA)	3,386	(NA)	410	(NA)	490	(NA)	12.1	(NA)	14.5	(NA)	303	(NA)	397	(NA)	394	(NA)	289
Full-time workers	70,976	84,143	16,271	14,975	18,745	16,886	22.9	17.8	26.4	20.1	313	445	388	547	383	541	288	413
Part-time workers	17,314	19,545	1,446	1,415	1,787	1,654	8.4	7.2	10.3	8.5	(X)	(X)	(X)	(X)	(X)	(X)	(X)	(X)
Managerial and professional specialty	19,657	26,275	3,354	3,824	4,307	4,687	17.1	14.6	21.9	17.8	437	655	423	661	421	655	446	655
Technical sales, and admin. support	28,024	33,445	3,377	3,462	4,199	4,052	12.1	10.4	15.0	12.1	281	407	350	500	341	494	270	394
Service occupations	12,875	14,898	1,971	2,071	2,306	2,322	15.3	13.9	17.9	15.6	205	283	305	444	299	433	182	256
Precision, production, craft, and repair	10,542	11,038	3,466	2,768	3,760	2,958	32.9	25.1	35.7	26.8	377	491	456	621	450	616	322	438
Operators, fabricators, and laborers	15,416	16,206	5,452	4,174	5,839	4,418	35.4	25.8	37.9	27.3	275	357	366	496	361	491	226	314
Farming, forestry, and fishing	1,775	1,825	98	92	122	104	5.5	5.0	6.9	5.7	196	263	292	397	287	391	189	257
Agricultural wage and salary workers	1,446	1,505	49	37	55	42	3.4	2.4	3.8	2.8	198	271	(B)	(B)	(B)	(B)	195	269
Private nonagri. wage and salary workers	71,225	84,039	11,933	9,703	13,369	10,660	16.8	11.5	18.8	12.7	307	424	389	525	385	520	286	409
Mining	869	620	180	94	201	109	20.7	15.1	23.1	16.1	481	604	470	600	470	588	488	609
Construction	4,109	4,530	1,131	906	1,207	955	27.5	20.0	29.4	21.1	348	478	518	698	510	691	296	417
Manufacturing	19,066	19,076	5,303	3,749	5,812	4,005	27.8	19.7	30.5	21.0	335	458	370	503	368	500	315	440
Transportation and public utilities	5,142	6,233	2,182	1,922	2,376	2,052	42.4	30.8	46.2	32.9	417	554	449	615	445	612	386	510
Wholesale and retail trade, total	18,081	21,347	1,568	1,402	1,775	1,542	8.7	6.6	9.8	7.2	252	342	353	439	348	429	242	333
Finance, insurance, and real estate	5,559	6,658	160	144	228	196	2.9	2.2	4.1	2.9	296	472	284	469	285	475	297	472
Services	18,400	25,575	1,410	1,487	1,770	1,810	7.7	5.8	9.6	7.1	272	406	303	443	303	444	268	403
Government	15,615	18,144	5,735	6,650	7,109	7,838	36.7	36.7	45.5	43.2	351	518	386	579	381	575	316	479

B Data not shown where base is less than 50,000.   NA Not applicable.   X Not applicable.   [1] Members of a labor union or an employee association similar to a labor union.   [2] Members of a labor union or an employee association similar to a union as well as workers who report no union affiliation but whose jobs are covered by a union or an employee association contract.   [3] For full-time employed wage and salary workers; 1983 revised since originally published.   [4] Persons of Hispanic origin may be of any race.

Source: U.S. Bureau of Labor Statistics, *Employment and Earnings*, January issues.

Income, Expenditures, and Wealth

This section presents data on gross domestic product (GDP), gross national product (GNP), national and personal income, saving and investment, money income, poverty, and national and personal wealth. The data on income and expenditures measure two aspects of the U.S. economy. One aspect relates to the national income and product accounts (NIPA's), a summation reflecting the entire complex of the Nation's economic income and output and the interaction of its major components; the other relates to the distribution of money income to families and individuals, or consumer income.

The primary source for data on GDP, GNP, national and personal income, gross saving and investment, and fixed reproducible tangible wealth is the *Survey of Current Business,* published monthly by the Bureau of Economic Analysis (BEA). A comprehensive revision to the NIPA's was completed in December 1991. A discussion of the revision appears in the August through October, 1991 and the December 1991 issues of *Survey of Current Business.* Detailed historical data appear in *The National Income and Product Accounts of the United States, volume 1, 1929-58* and *volume 2, 1959-88* and the July 1992 issue of *Survey of Current Business;* detailed data for the most recent years are normally published each July in the *Survey.*

Sources of income distribution data are the decennial censuses of population and the Current Population Survey (CPS), both products of the Bureau of the Census (see text, section 1). Annual data on income of families, individuals, and households are presented in *Current Population Reports-Consumer Income,* P60 series.

Data on individuals' saving and assets are published by the Board of Governors of the Federal Reserve System in the quarterly *Flow of Funds Accounts;* and detailed information on personal wealth

In Brief

Gross domestic product, constant (1987) dollars
annual percent change:

1989-90	0.8
1990-91	−1.2
1991-92	2.1

Median household income in 1991: $30,126

Poverty status of persons in 1991:
*Number below poverty level: 35.7 million
Percent below poverty level: 14.2*

is published periodically by the Internal Revenue Service (IRS) in *SOI Bulletin.*

National income and product.— *Gross domestic product* is the total output of goods and services produced by labor and property located in the United States, valued at market prices. GDP can be viewed in terms of expenditure categories that comprise purchases of goods and services by consumers and government, gross private domestic investment, and net exports of goods and services. The goods and services included are largely those bought for final use (excluding illegal transactions) in the market economy. A number of inclusions, however, represent imputed values, the most important of which is rental value of owner-occupied housing. GDP, in this broad context, measures the output attributable to the factors of production located in the United States. *Gross State product* (GSP) is the gross market value of the goods and services attributable to labor and property located in a State. It is the State counterpart of the Nation's gross domestic product.

Gross national product measures the output attributable to all labor and property supplied by United States residents. GNP differs from "national income" mainly in that GNP includes allowances for depreciation and for indirect business taxes (sales and property taxes); see table 695.

In December 1991, the Bureau of Economic Analysis began featuring gross domestic product rather than gross national product as the primary measure of U.S. production. GDP is now the standard measure of growth because it is the appropriate measure for much of the short-term monitoring and analysis of the economy. In addition, the use of GDP facilitates comparisons of economic activity in the United States with that in other countries. GDP is the primary measure of production in the United Nation's System of National Accounts, the set of international guidelines for economic accounting that the U.S. economic accounts will be moving toward in the mid-1990's. Virtually all other countries already use GDP as their primary measure of production. The dollar levels of GDP and GNP differ little, but percentage changes often differ. The annual rates of growth of real GNP have been slightly less than the annual rates of growth of real GDP in most years of the 1980's. The quarterly differences are larger and they fluctuate more.

National income is the aggregate of labor and property earnings which arises in the current production of goods and services. It is the sum of employee compensation, proprietors' income, rental income of persons, corporate profits, and net interest. It measures the total factor costs of the goods and services produced by the economy. Income is measured before deduction of taxes.

Capital consumption adjustment for corporations, and for nonfarm sole proprietorships and partnerships is the difference between capital consumption based on income tax returns and capital consumption measured at straight-line depreciation, consistent service lives, and replacement cost. The tax return data are valued at historical costs and reflect changes over time in service lives and depreciation patterns as permitted by tax regulations. *Inventory valuation adjustment* represents the difference between the book value of inventories used up in production and the cost of replacing them.

Personal income is the current income received by persons from all sources minus their personal contributions for social insurance. Classified as "persons" are individuals (including owners of unincorporated firms), nonprofit institutions that primarily serve individuals, private trust funds, and private noninsured welfare funds. Personal income includes transfers (payments not resulting from current production) from government and business such as Social Security benefits, public assistance, etc., but excludes transfers among persons. Also included are certain nonmonetary types of income—chiefly estimated net rental value to owner-occupants of their homes and the value of services furnished without payment by financial intermediaries.

Disposable personal income is personal income less personal tax and nontax payments. It is the income available to persons for spending or saving. Personal tax and nontax payments are tax payments (net of refunds) by persons (except personal contributions for social insurance) that are not chargeable to business expense, and certain personal payments to general government that are treated like taxes. Personal taxes include income, estate and gift, and personal property taxes and motor vehicle licenses. Nontax payments include passport fees, fines and forfeitures, and donations.

Consumer Expenditure Survey.—The Consumer Expenditure Survey program was begun in late 1979. The principal objective of the survey is to collect current consumer expenditure data which provide a continuous flow of data on the buying habits of American consumers. The data are necessary for future revisions of the Consumer Price Index.

The survey conducted by the Bureau of the Census for the Bureau of Labor Statistics, consists of two components: (1) An interview panel survey in which the expenditures of consumer units are obtained in five interviews conducted every 3 months; and (2) a diary or record-keeping survey completed by participating households for two consecutive 1-week periods.

Each component of the survey queries an independent sample of consumer units representative of the U.S. total population. Over 52 weeks of the year, 5,000 consumer units are sampled for the diary survey. Each consumer unit keeps a diary for two 1-week periods yielding approximately 10,000 diaries a year. The interview sample is selected on a rotating panel basis, targeted at 5,000 consumer units per quarter. Data are collected in 88 urban and 16 rural areas of the country that are representative of the U.S. total population. The survey includes students in student housing.

The Diary survey is designed to obtain expenditures on small, frequently purchased items which are normally difficult for respondents to recall. Detailed records of expenses are kept for food • and beverages, both at home and in eating places, tobacco, housekeeping supplies, nonprescription drugs, and personal care products and services.

The Interview survey is designed to obtain data on the types of expenditures which respondents can be expected to recall for a period of 3 months or longer. In general, these include relatively large expenditures, such as those for property, automobiles, and major appliances, or expenditures which occur on a fairly regular basis, such as rent, utilities, or insurance premiums. Including "global estimates" for food, it is estimated that about 95 percent of expenditures are covered in the interview. Excluded are nonprescription drugs, household supplies, and personal care items. The interview survey also provides data on expenditures incurred while on trips. Both surveys exclude all business related expenditures for which the family is reimbursed.

In contrast to previous publications from the survey which have presented data from the diary and quarterly interview surveys separately, the tables in the most recently published Consumer Expenditure Survey combine, or integrate, data from the two surveys. Integration is necessary to permit analysis of total family expenditures because neither the diary nor quarterly interview survey was designed to collect a complete account of consumer spending.

Distribution of money income to families and individuals.—Money income statistics are based on data collected in various field surveys of income conducted since 1936. Since 1947, the Bureau of the Census has collected the

data on an annual basis and published them in Current Population Reports, P60 serie. In each of the surveys, field representatives interview samples of the population with respect to income received during the previous year. Money income as defined by the Bureau of the Census differs from the BEA concept of "personal income."

Data on consumer income collected in the CPS by the Bureau of the Census cover money income received (exclusive of certain money receipts such as capital gains) before payments for personal income taxes, Social Security, union dues, Medicare deductions, etc. Therefore, money income does not reflect the fact that some families receive part of their income in the form of noncash benefits (see section 12) such as food stamps, health benefits, and subsidized housing; that some farm families receive noncash benefits in the form of rent-free housing and goods produced and consumed on the farm; or that noncash benefits are also received by some nonfarm residents which often take the form of the use of business transportation and facilities, full or partial payments by business for retirement programs, medical and educational expenses, etc. These elements should be considered when comparing income levels. For data on noncash benefits, see section 12. None of the aggregate income concepts (GDP, national income, or personal income) is exactly comparable with money income, although personal income is the closest.

Several changes were made in the collection and presentation of data from the March 1980 CPS. The changes include (1) the use of a more detailed income questionnaire for all sample households, (2) the use of an expanded sample, (3) the implementation of the "householder" concept rather than the traditional "head" concept, (4) the exclusion of a small number of "secondary families" from the count of all families, (5) the use of more detailed income intervals in the upper range of the income distribution, (6) the introduction of the new farm definition, and (7) the restriction of the population with income to persons 15 years old and over. For more information on the impact and comparability, see the source.

Beginning in the March 1981 Current Population Survey, 1980 census population controls were used; for income years 1971 through 1979, 1970 census population controls had been used. This change had little impact on income summary measures (means and medians) and proportional measures (percent distributions and poverty rates); however, use of the controls may have significant impact on the absolute numbers.

Income and poverty data for 1986 are the first estimates based entirely on households selected from the 1980 census-based sample design. Estimates by type of residence categories such as metropolitan, nonmetropolitan, farm, and nonfarm reflect metropolitan areas defined as of June 1984. In addition, the March 1987 CPS income supplement was revised to allow for the coding of larger earnings amounts on the questionnaire. A description of this change and its effect on estimates in this report can be found in *Current Population Reports,* series P60-157.

A new computer processing system was introduced to the March 1989 CPS income supplement. The system in use before this year was first introduced in 1976 but was never fully updated to reflect questionnaire changes. In addition, the programs used to process the CPS file were written in a language which was phased out of Census. The March 1988 file was reprocessed based on the new procedures to better evaluate the new processing procedures and allow year to year comparisons to be made using a consistent processing system. A description of this change and its effect on estimates in this report can be found in *Current Population Reports,* series P60-166.

In October 1983, the Census Bureau began to collect data under the new Survey of Income and Program Participation (SIPP). The information supplied by this survey is expected to provide better measures of the status and changes in income distribution and poverty of households and persons in the United States. The data collected in SIPP will be used to study Federal and State aid programs (such as food stamps, welfare, Medicaid, and subsidized housing), to estimate program costs and coverage, and to assess the effects of proposed changes in program eligibility rules or benefit levels. The core questions are repeated at each interview and cover labor force activity, the types and amounts of income received, and participation status in various programs. The core also contains questions covering attendance in postsecondary schools and private health insurance coverage. Various supplements or topical modules covering areas such as educational attainment, assets and liabilities, and pension plan coverage are periodically included.

Poverty.—Families and unrelated individuals are classified as being above or below the poverty level using the poverty index originated at the Social Security Administration in 1964 and revised by Federal Interagency Committees in 1969 and 1980. The poverty index is based solely on money income and does not reflect the fact that many low-income persons receive noncash benefits such as food stamps, Medicaid, and public housing. The index is based on the Department of Agriculture's 1961 Economy Food Plan and reflects the different consumption requirements of families based on their size and composition. The poverty thresholds are updated every year to reflect changes in the Consumer Price Index. The following technical changes to the thresholds were made in 1981: (1) distinctions based on sex of householder have been eliminated; (2) separate thresholds for farm families have been dropped; and (3) the matrix has been expanded to families of nine or more persons from the old cutoff of seven or more persons. These changes have been incorporated in the calculation of poverty data beginning with 1981.

In the recent past, the Bureau of the Census has published a number of technical papers that presented experimental poverty estimates based on income definitions that counted the value of selected government noncash benefits. The Census Bureau has also published annual reports on after-tax income. The *Current Population Reports,* series P60-182RD brings together the benefit and tax data that previously appeared in the separate reports. This report shows the distribution of income among households and the prevalence of poverty under the official definition of money income and under definitions that add or subtract income components. The types of income that are included in one or more of the definitions: (1) money income excluding capital gains or lump-sum payments before taxes, (2) capital gains, (3) government cash transfers, (4) Earned Income Tax Credit, (5) the value of employer contributions to health insurance plans, (6) the value of food stamps, (7) the subsidy value of school lunches, (8) the subsidy value of housing assistance, (9) the fungible values of Medicare and Medicaid coverage (that is, the benefits are counted as income to the extent that they free up resources that could have been spent on medical care), and (10) the imputed net return on equity in own home. The types of taxes accounted for are Federal and State income taxes and payroll taxes.

The poverty statistics presented by the Bureau of the Census and Congressional Budget Office reflect alternative adjustments for inflation. The study used a variation of the Consumer Price Index to adjust poverty thresholds for the effects of changing prices since 1967. The alternative measure of inflation uses estimates of the cost of renting equivalent housing to assess homeownership costs; this methodology has been used in the official Consumer Price Index since 1983. See text, section 15, and source for more details.

Personal wealth.—Personal wealth estimates, issued by the IRS, are based on a sample of Federal estate tax returns which must be filed for deceased persons. Estimates are weighted to adjust for age, sex, and "social class" (as determined by the IRS through insurance holdings). Gross estate is the gross value of all assets, including the full face value of life insurance (reduced by policy loans), before reduction by the amount of debts. The level of gross estate or gross assets required for filing estate tax returns increased from $60,000 in 1972 to $120,000 in 1976. Net worth is one's level of worth after all debts have been removed.

Statistical reliability.—For a discussion of statistical collection and estimation, sampling procedures, and measures of statistical reliability pertaining to Census Bureau data, see Appendix III.

Historical statistics.—Tabular headnotes provide cross-references, where applicable, to *Historical Statistics of the United States, Colonial Times to 1970.* See Appendix IV.

Weighted Average Poverty Thresholds Based on Money Income for Families and Unrelated Individuals: 1980 to 1991

SIZE OF UNIT	1980[1]	1984	1985	1986	1987	1988	1989	1990	1991
1 person (unrelated individual)	$4,190	$5,278	$5,469	$5,572	$5,778	$6,022	$6,310	$6,652	$6,932
Under 65 years	4,290	5,400	5,593	5,701	5,909	6,155	6,451	6,800	7,086
65 years and over	3,949	4,979	5,156	5,255	5,447	5,674	5,947	6,268	6,532
2 persons	5,363	6,762	6,998	7,138	7,397	7,704	8,076	8,509	8,865
Householder under 65 years	5,537	6,983	7,231	7,372	7,641	7,958	8,343	8,794	9,165
Householder 65 years and over ..	4,983	6,282	6,503	6,630	6,872	7,157	7,501	7,905	8,241
3 persons	6,565	8,277	8,573	8,737	9,056	9,435	9,885	10,419	10,860
4 persons	8,414	10,609	10,989	11,203	11,611	12,092	12,674	13,359	13,924
5 persons	9,966	12,566	13,007	13,259	13,737	14,304	14,990	15,792	16,456
6 persons	11,269	14,207	14,696	14,986	15,509	16,146	16,921	17,839	18,587
7 persons	12,761	16,096	16,656	17,049	17,649	18,232	19,162	20,241	21,058
8 persons	14,199	17,961	18,512	18,791	19,515	20,253	21,328	22,582	23,605
9 or more persons	16,896	21,247	22,083	22,497	23,105	24,129	25,480	26,848	27,942

[1]Poverty levels for nonfarm families.
Source: U.S. Bureau of the Census, Current Population Reports, P60-181; and earlier reports.

No. 690. GDP in Current and Constant (1987) Dollars: 1929 to 1992

[**In billions of dollars.** For explanation of gross domestic product, see text, section 14]

ITEM	1929	1940	1950	1960	1970	1980	1981	1982	1983
CURRENT DOLLARS									
Gross domestic product (GDP)	103.1	100.0	287.0	513.4	1,010.7	2,708.0	3,030.6	3,149.6	3,405.0
Personal consumption expenditures	77.5	71.2	192.7	332.4	646.5	1,748.1	1,926.2	2,059.2	2,257.5
Durable goods	9.2	7.8	30.8	43.5	85.3	212.5	228.5	236.5	275.0
Nondurable goods	37.7	37.0	98.2	153.1	270.4	682.9	744.2	772.3	817.8
Services	30.5	26.4	63.7	135.9	290.8	852.7	953.5	1,050.4	1,164.7
Gross private domestic investment	16.7	13.6	54.2	78.7	150.3	467.6	558.0	503.4	546.7
Fixed investment	14.9	11.2	48.3	75.5	148.1	477.1	532.5	519.3	552.2
Nonresidential	11.0	7.7	27.8	49.2	106.7	353.8	410.0	413.7	400.2
Residential	4.0	3.5	20.5	26.3	41.4	123.3	122.5	105.7	152.0
Change in business inventories	1.7	2.4	5.9	3.2	2.3	-9.5	25.4	-15.9	-5.5
Net exports of goods and services	0.4	1.4	0.7	2.4	1.2	-14.7	-14.7	-20.6	-51.4
Exports	5.9	4.8	12.3	25.3	57.0	279.2	303.0	282.6	276.7
Imports	5.6	3.4	11.6	22.8	55.8	293.9	317.7	303.2	328.1
Government purchases	8.6	13.8	39.5	99.8	212.7	507.1	561.1	607.6	652.3
Federal	1.5	6.0	20.2	55.3	100.1	209.1	240.8	266.6	292.0
National defense	-	2.3	14.3	45.3	76.8	142.7	167.5	193.8	214.4
State and local	7.1	7.8	19.3	44.5	112.6	298.0	320.3	341.1	360.3
CONSTANT (1987) DOLLARS									
Gross domestic product (GDP)	821.8	906.0	1,418.5	1,970.8	2,873.9	3,776.3	3,843.1	3,760.3	3,906.6
Personal consumption expenditures	554.5	595.2	874.3	1,210.8	1,813.5	2,447.1	2,476.9	2,503.7	2,619.4
Durable goods	48.1	48.3	95.0	115.4	183.7	262.7	264.6	262.5	297.7
Nondurable goods	238.5	293.0	400.4	526.9	717.2	860.5	867.9	872.2	900.3
Services	267.9	253.9	378.9	568.5	912.5	1,323.9	1,344.4	1,368.9	1,421.4
Gross private domestic investment	152.8	121.8	256.4	290.8	429.7	594.4	631.1	540.5	599.5
Fixed investment	142.1	107.1	233.9	282.7	423.8	602.7	606.5	558.0	595.1
Nonresidential	100.6	69.0	132.5	173.3	292.0	437.8	455.0	433.9	420.8
Residential	41.6	38.1	101.4	109.4	131.8	164.8	151.6	124.1	174.2
Change in business inventories	10.6	14.7	22.5	8.1	5.9	-8.3	24.6	-17.5	4.4
Net exports of goods and services	1.9	8.2	3.2	-7.6	-35.2	30.7	22.0	-7.4	-56.1
Exports	36.0	37.5	53.0	88.4	161.3	320.5	326.1	296.7	285.9
Imports	34.1	29.2	49.7	96.1	196.4	289.9	304.1	304.1	342.1
Government purchases	112.6	180.7	284.5	476.9	665.8	704.2	713.2	723.6	743.8
Federal	21.9	76.2	145.6	259.0	315.0	284.8	295.8	306.0	320.8
National defense	-	-	-	-	-	194.2	206.4	221.4	234.2
State and local	90.7	104.5	138.9	217.9	350.9	419.4	417.4	417.6	423.0

	1984	1985	1986	1987	1988	1989	1990	1991	1992
CURRENT DOLLARS									
Gross domestic product (GDP)	3,777.2	4,038.7	4,268.6	4,539.9	4,900.4	5,250.8	5,522.2	5,677.5	5,950.7
Personal consumption expenditures	2,460.3	2,667.4	2,850.6	3,052.2	3,296.1	3,523.1	3,748.4	3,887.7	4,095.8
Durable goods	317.9	352.9	389.6	403.7	437.1	459.4	464.3	446.1	480.4
Nondurable goods	873.0	919.4	952.2	1,011.1	1,073.8	1,149.5	1,224.5	1,251.5	1,290.7
Services	1,269.4	1,395.1	1,508.8	1,637.4	1,785.2	1,914.2	2,059.7	2,190.1	2,324.7
Gross private domestic investment	718.9	714.5	717.6	749.3	793.6	832.3	799.5	721.1	770.4
Fixed investment	647.8	689.9	709.0	723.0	777.4	789.9	793.2	731.3	766.0
Nonresidential	468.9	504.0	492.4	497.8	545.4	568.1	577.6	541.1	548.2
Residential	178.9	185.9	216.6	225.2	232.0	230.9	215.6	190.3	217.7
Change in business inventories	71.1	24.6	8.6	26.3	16.2	33.3	6.3	-10.2	4.4
Net exports of goods and services	-102.7	-115.6	-132.5	-143.1	-108.0	-79.7	-68.9	-21.8	-30.4
Exports	302.4	302.1	319.2	364.0	444.2	508.0	557.0	598.2	636.3
Imports	405.1	417.6	451.7	507.1	552.2	587.7	625.9	620.0	666.7
Government purchases	700.8	772.3	833.0	881.5	918.7	975.2	1,043.2	1,090.5	1,114.9
Federal	310.9	344.3	367.8	384.9	387.0	401.6	426.4	447.3	449.1
National defense	233.1	258.6	276.7	292.1	295.6	299.9	314.0	323.8	315.8
State and local	389.9	428.1	465.3	496.6	531.7	573.6	616.8	643.2	665.8
CONSTANT (1987) DOLLARS									
Gross domestic product (GDP)	4,148.5	4,279.8	4,404.5	4,540.0	4,718.6	4,838.0	4,877.5	4,821.0	4,922.6
Personal consumption expenditures	2,746.1	2,865.8	2,969.1	3,052.2	3,162.4	3,223.3	3,260.4	3,240.8	3,314.0
Durable goods	338.5	370.1	402.0	403.7	428.7	440.7	439.3	414.7	439.1
Nondurable goods	934.6	958.7	991.0	1,011.1	1,035.1	1,051.6	1,056.5	1,042.4	1,054.1
Services	1,473.0	1,537.0	1,576.1	1,637.4	1,698.5	1,731.0	1,764.6	1,783.7	1,820.7
Gross private domestic investment	757.5	745.9	735.1	749.3	773.4	784.0	739.1	661.1	712.6
Fixed investment	689.6	723.8	726.5	723.0	753.4	754.2	732.9	670.4	707.6
Nonresidential	490.2	521.8	500.3	497.8	530.8	540.0	538.1	500.2	515.0
Residential	199.3	202.0	226.2	225.2	222.7	214.2	194.8	170.2	192.6
Change in business inventories	67.9	22.1	8.5	26.3	19.9	29.8	6.2	-9.3	5.0
Net exports of goods and services	-122.0	-145.3	-155.1	-143.0	-104.0	-73.7	-51.8	-21.8	-41.8
Exports	305.7	309.2	329.6	364.0	421.6	471.8	510.0	539.4	573.2
Imports	427.7	454.6	484.7	507.1	525.7	545.4	561.8	561.2	615.0
Government purchases	766.9	813.4	855.4	881.5	886.8	904.4	929.9	941.0	937.8
Federal	331.0	355.2	373.0	384.9	377.3	376.1	383.6	388.3	375.6
National defense	245.8	265.6	280.6	292.1	287.0	281.4	283.3	282.8	265.0
State and local	436.0	458.2	482.4	496.6	509.6	528.3	546.3	552.7	562.2

- Represents or rounds to zero.

Source: U.S. Bureau of Economic Analysis, *National Income and Product Accounts of the United States: volume 1, 1929-58,* and *volume 2, 1959-88,* and *Survey of Current Business,* March 1993.

No. 691. Gross National Product, by Industry, in Current and Constant (1982) Dollars: 1980 to 1989

[**In billions of dollars.** Based on the *1972 Standard Industrial Classification Manual;* see text, section 13. Data include nonfactor charges (capital consumption allowances, indirect business taxes, etc.) as well as factor charges against gross product; corporate profits and capital consumption allowances have been shifted from a company to an establishment basis. These data are not fully consistent with other gross domestic product tables because they do not yet reflect the results of the comprehensive National Income and Product Accounts revision; see text, section 14]

INDUSTRY	CURRENT DOLLARS				CONSTANT (1982) DOLLARS			
	1980	1985	1988	1989	1980	1985	1988	1989
Gross national product	2,732	4,015	4,874	5,201	3,187	3,619	4,017	4,118
Domestic industries (gross domestic product)	2,684	3,974	4,840	5,163	3,132	3,582	3,989	4,088
Private industries	2,357	3,502	4,296	4,561	2,743	3,200	3,620	3,711
Agriculture, forestry, and fishing	77	92	104	113	76	96	97	100
Mining	107	114	80	80	144	139	130	127
Construction	138	187	237	248	153	166	178	179
Manufacturing [1]	581	790	941	966	674	779	917	929
Durable goods [1]	352	459	527	541	408	472	571	584
Lumber and wood products	19	22	31	32	21	20	26	26
Furniture and fixtures	9	14	15	16	10	12	12	12
Stone, clay, and glass products	19	25	26	26	21	22	23	24
Primary metal industries	44	35	43	44	48	33	38	37
Fabricated metal products	46	58	65	68	54	56	66	66
Machinery, except electrical	77	83	96	97	86	124	164	175
Electric and electronic equipment	55	82	90	97	63	74	88	91
Motor vehicles and equipment	27	54	53	50	35	50	50	47
Instruments and related products	19	26	30	31	22	24	28	27
Nondurable goods	229	331	414	425	265	308	347	345
Food and kindred products	52	70	81	81	60	65	68	70
Tobacco products	7	12	14	16	10	6	4	3
Textile mill products	15	17	20	21	16	16	17	17
Apparel and other textile products	17	21	24	25	21	20	22	22
Paper and allied products	23	33	46	47	26	30	35	33
Printing and publishing	32	53	66	68	37	43	47	45
Chemicals and allied products	45	64	96	99	50	59	78	76
Petroleum and coal products	17	32	35	34	23	39	44	45
Rubber and misc. plastic products	17	26	30	31	19	27	30	31
Leather and leather products	4	3	3	3	4	3	3	3
Transportation and public utilities	241	374	444	461	294	331	395	402
Transportation	106	138	165	172	117	132	154	156
Communications	67	110	129	134	80	90	108	109
Electric, gas, and sanitary services	68	127	150	156	97	109	134	137
Wholesale trade	194	281	317	339	200	267	291	305
Retail trade	245	377	460	486	282	354	399	412
Finance, insurance, and real estate	401	640	827	897	469	528	590	604
Services	374	648	885	971	451	539	623	652
Government and government enterprises	322	477	573	619	383	401	423	431
Statistical discrepancy	*5*	*-5*	*-28*	*-17*	*6*	*-4*	*-24*	*-14*
Rest of the world	48	41	33	38	56	37	28	30

[1] Includes industries not shown separately.

Source: U.S. Bureau of Economic Analysis, *Survey of Current Business,* April 1991.

No. 692. Gross Domestic Product, by Type of Product and Sector: 1970 to 1992

[In billions of dollars]

ITEM	1970	1980	1985	1986	1987	1988	1989	1990	1991	1992
Gross domestic product	1,010.7	2,708.0	4,038.7	4,268.6	4,539.9	4,900.4	5,250.8	5,522.2	5,677.5	5,950.7
BY MAJOR TYPE OF PRODUCT										
Goods	467.8	1,176.2	1,652.6	1,705.3	1,794.5	1,942.0	2,097.0	2,166.4	2,182.5	2,264.7
Services	434.3	1,215.4	1,939.0	2,097.3	2,267.2	2,460.9	2,642.1	2,846.4	3,030.2	3,197.1
Structures	108.6	316.4	447.1	466.0	478.2	497.5	511.7	509.4	464.7	488.8
BY SECTOR										
Business	858.7	2,328.9	3,473.5	3,665.7	3,890.8	4,201.0	4,495.9	4,702.8	4,803.8	5,033.4
Households and institutions	32.4	89.3	141.7	153.3	170.5	187.6	206.1	227.8	246.1	263.4
General government	119.5	289.8	423.6	449.6	478.7	511.7	548.8	591.6	627.6	654.0

Source: U.S. Bureau of Economic Analysis, *National Income and Product Accounts of the United States: volume 2, 1959-88,* and *Survey of Current Business,* March 1993.

No. 693. GDP Components—Average Annual Percent Change in Current and Constant (1987) Dollars: 1959 to 1992

[In percent. Minus sign (-) indicates decrease]

ITEM	1959-1960	1969-1970	1979-1980	1985-1986	1986-1987	1987-1988	1988-1989	1989-1990	1990-1991	1991-1992
CURRENT DOLLARS										
Gross domestic product	3.9	5.3	8.8	5.7	6.4	7.9	7.2	5.2	2.8	4.8
Personal consumption expenditures	4.5	7.1	10.4	6.9	7.1	8.0	6.9	6.4	3.7	5.4
Durable goods.............	1.6	-1.0	-0.8	10.4	3.6	8.3	5.1	1.1	-3.9	7.7
Nondurable goods	3.1	7.2	11.3	3.6	6.2	6.2	7.0	6.5	2.2	3.1
Services.................	7.2	9.6	12.8	8.1	8.5	9.0	7.2	7.6	6.3	6.1
Gross private domestic investment.	-0.1	-3.2	-2.6	0.4	4.4	5.9	4.9	-3.9	-9.8	6.8
Fixed investment	1.2	1.8	2.1	2.8	2.0	7.5	2.8	-0.7	-7.8	4.7
Nonresidential	5.8	3.7	8.4	-2.3	1.1	9.6	4.2	1.7	-6.3	1.3
Residential............	-6.4	-2.8	-12.6	16.5	4.0	3.0	-0.5	-6.6	-11.7	14.4
Exports of goods and services ...	22.8	15.6	22.0	5.7	14.0	22.0	14.4	9.6	7.4	6.4
Imports of goods and services....	2.2	10.5	16.3	8.2	12.3	8.9	6.4	6.5	-0.9	7.5
Government purchases	0.8	5.4	13.1	7.9	5.8	4.2	6.1	7.0	4.5	2.2
Federal	-3.2	-0.4	16.6	6.8	4.6	0.5	3.8	6.2	4.9	0.4
State and local	6.5	11.2	10.7	8.7	6.7	7.1	7.9	7.5	4.3	3.5
CONSTANT (1987) DOLLARS										
Gross domestic product	2.2	-	-0.5	2.9	3.1	3.9	2.5	0.8	-1.2	2.1
Personal consumption expenditures	2.7	2.4	-0.1	3.6	2.8	3.6	1.9	1.2	-0.6	2.3
Durable goods.............	0.9	-3.7	-9.1	8.6	0.4	6.2	2.8	-0.3	-5.6	5.9
Nondurable goods	1.6	2.0	-0.3	3.4	2.0	2.4	1.6	0.5	-1.3	1.1
Services.................	4.1	4.0	2.1	2.5	3.9	3.7	1.9	1.9	1.1	2.1
Gross private domestic investment.	-1.9	-6.9	-11.2	-1.4	1.9	3.2	1.4	-5.7	-10.6	7.8
Fixed investment	-	-2.9	-8.1	0.4	-0.5	4.2	0.1	-2.8	-8.5	5.5
Nonresidential	4.9	-1.5	-2.5	-4.1	-0.5	6.6	1.7	-0.4	-7.0	3.0
Residential............	-7.0	-5.9	-20.5	12.0	-0.4	-1.1	-3.8	-9.1	-12.6	13.2
Exports of goods and services ...	19.8	9.1	9.2	6.6	10.4	15.8	11.9	8.1	5.8	6.3
Imports of goods and services....	0.5	3.8	-4.7	6.6	4.6	3.7	3.7	3.0	-0.1	9.6
Government purchases	0.3	-2.4	2.2	5.2	3.1	0.6	2.0	2.8	1.2	-0.3
Federal	-2.6	-7.4	4.8	5.0	3.2	-2.0	-0.3	2.0	1.2	-3.3
State and local	4.0	2.6	0.4	5.3	2.9	2.6	3.7	3.4	1.2	1.7

- Represents or rounds to zero.

Source: U.S. Bureau of Economic Analysis, *National Income and Product Accounts of the United States: volume 1, 1929-59*, and *Survey of Current Business*, March 1993.

No. 694. Gross State Product: 1980 to 1989

[In billions of dollars. For definition of gross state product, see text, section 14]

STATE	CURRENT DOLLARS			CONSTANT (1982) DOLLARS			STATE	CURRENT DOLLARS			CONSTANT (1982) DOLLARS		
	1980	1985	1989	1980	1985	1989		1980	1985	1989	1980	1985	1989
US	2,670	3,966	5,165	3,115	3,590	4,130	NE......	18	25	31	21	23	25
AL......	35	53	68	41	48	55	NV......	12	18	28	14	16	21
AK......	14	21	20	18	21	21	NH......	9	17	25	11	15	20
AZ......	30	49	65	34	44	51	NJ......	89	145	203	103	129	157
CA......	319	501	697	372	449	552	NM......	17	24	25	20	22	22
CO......	37	56	66	43	51	53	NC......	59	95	130	69	83	99
CT......	40	64	89	46	58	70	ND......	8	11	11	10	10	9
DC......	19	29	39	22	25	28	OK......	38	50	52	45	48	45
FL......	96	162	227	111	143	174	OR......	30	38	52	35	34	41
GA......	56	95	130	64	85	101	PA......	126	173	228	146	156	182
HI	13	18	26	15	15	19	RI	9	14	19	11	12	15
ID	10	13	16	11	11	13	SC......	27	42	60	31	38	48
IL.......	144	197	256	166	179	207	SD......	7	9	11	8	8	9
IN	60	80	105	69	73	86	TN......	45	68	92	52	62	74
IA	35	42	53	40	39	43	TX......	205	308	340	247	290	293
KS......	28	41	49	33	37	40	UT......	15	24	28	17	21	23
LA	64	82	79	79	79	72	VT......	5	8	12	6	7	9
MD......	44	71	99	52	62	76	VA......	58	96	136	68	84	103
MA......	66	106	145	76	96	116	WV......	19	24	28	22	22	24
MI	104	143	182	122	131	148	WI	53	72	94	61	67	77
MS......	22	31	38	25	29	32	WY	11	13	11	13	13	11
MO	53	79	100	62	71	79							

Source: U.S. Bureau of Economic Analysis, *Survey of Current Business*, December 1991; and unpublished data.

No. 695. Relation of GDP, GNP, Net National Product, National Income, Personal Income, Disposable Personal Income, and Personal Saving: 1970 to 1991

[In billions of dollars. For definitions, see text, section 14]

ITEM	1970	1980	1985	1986	1987	1988	1989	1990	1991
Gross domestic product	1,010.7	2,708.0	4,038.7	4,268.6	4,539.9	4,900.4	5,250.8	5,522.2	5,677.5
Plus: Receipts of factor income from the rest of the world [1]	13.0	80.6	97.3	96.0	105.1	128.7	157.5	160.6	143.5
Less: Payments of factor income to the rest of the world [2]	6.6	46.5	82.4	86.9	100.5	120.8	141.5	139.9	126.0
Equals: Gross national product	1,017.1	2,742.1	4,053.6	4,277.7	4,544.5	4,908.2	5,266.8	5,542.9	5,694.9
Less: Consumption of fixed capital . . .	88.8	311.9	454.5	478.6	502.2	534.0	580.4	602.8	626.1
Equals: Net national product [3]	928.3	2,430.2	3,599.1	3,799.2	4,042.4	4,374.2	4,686.4	4,940.1	5,068.8
Less: Indirect business tax and nontax liability	94.3	212.0	329.9	345.5	365.0	385.3	414.7	444.2	475.2
Plus: Subsidies [4] . . . . [3]	2.6	4.8	6.4	9.7	14.1	10.9	5.4	4.2	0.5
Equals: National income [3]	833.5	2,198.2	3,268.4	3,437.9	3,692.3	4,002.6	4,249.5	4,468.3	4,544.2
Less: Corporate profits [5]	77.5	177.7	280.8	271.6	319.8	365.0	362.8	361.7	346.3
Net interest	40.0	191.2	326.2	350.2	360.4	387.7	452.7	460.7	449.5
Contributions for social insurance. . .	62.2	216.6	353.8	379.8	400.7	442.3	473.2	502.3	528.8
Plus: Personal interest income	69.2	274.0	498.1	531.7	548.1	583.2	668.2	694.5	700.6
Personal dividend income	23.5	57.1	87.9	104.7	100.4	108.4	126.5	140.3	137.0
Government transfer payments to persons	81.8	312.6	468.1	497.1	521.3	555.9	603.8	664.6	748.3
Business transfer payments to persons	2.8	8.8	17.8	20.7	20.8	20.8	21.1	21.2	22.8
Equals: Personal income	831.0	2,265.4	3,379.8	3,590.4	3,802.0	4,075.9	4,380.3	4,664.2	4,828.3
Less: Personal tax and nontax payments	109.0	312.4	436.8	459.0	512.5	527.7	593.3	621.3	618.7
Equals: Disposable personal income	722.0	1,952.9	2,943.0	3,131.5	3,289.5	3,548.2	3,787.0	4,042.9	4,209.6
Less: Personal outlays	664.5	1,799.1	2,753.7	2,944.0	3,147.5	3,392.5	3,634.9	3,867.3	4,009.9
Equals: Personal saving	57.5	153.8	189.3	187.5	142.0	155.7	152.1	175.6	199.6

[1] Consists largely of receipts by U.S. residents of interest and dividends and reinvested earnings of foreign affiliates of U.S. corporations.   [2] Consists largely of payments to foreign residents of interest and dividends and reinvested earnings of U.S. affiliates of foreign corporations.   [3] Includes items not shown separately.   [4] Less current surplus of government enterprises.   [5] With inventory valuation and capital consumption adjustments.

Source: U.S. Bureau of Economic Analysis, *National Income and Product Accounts of the United States: volume 1, 1929-59,* and *Survey of Current Business,* March 1993.

No. 696. Selected Per Capita Income and Product Items: 1929 to 1992

[Based on Bureau of the Census estimated population including Armed Forces abroad; based on quarterly averages. Prior to 1960, excludes Alaska and Hawaii]

YEAR	CURRENT DOLLARS					CONSTANT (1987) DOLLARS			
	Gross domestic product	Gross national product	Personal income	Disposable personal income	Personal consumption expenditures	Gross domestic product	Gross national product	Disposable personal income	Personal consumption expenditures
1929	846	852	691	672	636	6,743	6,789	4,807	4,550
1930	734	739	611	594	570	6,079	6,122	4,402	4,221
1935	568	571	467	455	439	5,349	5,371	3,967	3,828
1940	757	760	586	568	539	6,857	6,878	4,747	4,505
1945	1,523	1,526	1,215	1,068	857	11,453	11,470	6,367	5,107
1950	1,892	1,902	1,502	1,369	1,270	9,352	9,398	6,214	5,764
1955	2,446	2,461	1,903	1,693	1,568	10,699	10,764	6,842	6,335
1960	2,840	2,858	2,264	1,994	1,839	10,903	10,969	7,264	6,698
1965	3,616	3,643	2,845	2,527	2,287	12,712	12,807	8,508	7,703
1970	4,928	4,959	4,052	3,521	3,152	14,013	14,099	9,875	8,842
1971	5,283	5,320	4,302	3,779	3,372	14,232	14,329	10,111	9,022
1972	5,750	5,791	4,671	4,042	3,658	14,801	14,904	10,414	9,425
1973	6,368	6,428	5,184	4,521	4,002	15,422	15,564	11,013	9,752
1974	6,819	6,893	5,637	4,893	4,337	15,185	15,346	10,832	9,602
1975	7,343	7,404	6,053	5,329	4,745	14,917	15,036	10,906	9,711
1976	8,109	8,187	6,632	5,796	5,241	15,502	15,646	11,192	10,121
1977	8,961	9,055	7,269	6,316	5,772	16,039	16,201	11,406	10,425
1978	10,029	10,127	8,121	7,042	6,384	16,635	16,795	11,851	10,744
1979	11,055	11,198	9,032	7,787	7,035	16,867	17,082	12,039	10,876
1980	11,892	12,042	9,948	8,576	7,677	16,584	16,790	12,005	10,746
1981	13,177	13,321	11,021	9,455	8,375	16,710	16,890	12,156	10,770
1982	13,564	13,694	11,589	9,989	8,868	16,194	16,348	12,146	10,782
1983	14,531	14,657	12,216	10,642	9,634	16,672	16,813	12,349	11,179
1984	15,978	16,081	13,345	11,673	10,408	17,549	17,659	13,029	11,617
1985	16,933	16,995	14,170	12,339	11,184	17,944	18,007	13,258	12,015
1986	17,735	17,773	14,917	13,010	11,843	18,299	18,337	13,552	12,336
1987	18,694	18,712	15,655	13,545	12,568	18,694	18,712	13,545	12,568
1988	19,994	20,026	16,630	14,477	13,448	19,252	19,284	13,890	12,903
1989	21,224	21,289	17,706	15,307	14,241	19,556	19,615	14,005	13,029
1990	22,092	22,175	18,660	16,174	14,996	19,513	19,587	14,068	13,044
1991	22,466	22,535	19,106	16,658	15,384	19,077	19,138	13,886	12,824
1992	23,296	23,340	19,802	17,346	16,035	19,272	19,311	14,035	12,974

Source: U.S. Bureau of Economic Analysis, *National Income and Product Accounts of the United States: volume 1, 1929-59,* and *volume 2, 1959-88,* and *Survey of Current Business,* March 1993.

No. 697. National Income, by Type of Income: 1970 to 1992

[In billions of dollars]

TYPE OF INCOME	1970	1980	1985	1987	1988	1989	1990	1991	1992
National income	833.5	2,198.2	3,268.4	3,692.3	4,002.6	4,249.5	4,468.3	4,544.2	4,743.4
Compensation of employees	618.3	1,644.4	2,382.8	2,698.7	2,921.3	3,100.2	3,291.2	3,390.8	3,525.2
Wages and salaries	551.5	1,376.6	1,986.3	2,261.2	2,443.0	2,586.4	2,742.9	2,812.2	2,916.6
Government	117.1	261.4	373.7	421.8	449.0	478.5	514.8	578.7	608.6
Other	434.3	1,115.2	1,612.6	1,839.4	1,994.0	2,107.9	2,228.0	2,268.7	2,354.1
Supplements to wages and salaries	66.8	267.8	396.5	437.4	478.3	513.8	548.4	578.7	608.6
Employer contributions for social insurance	34.3	127.9	204.7	227.1	247.8	261.9	277.4	290.4	302.9
Other labor income	32.5	139.8	191.8	210.4	230.5	251.9	271.0	288.3	305.7
Proprietors' income [1]	79.9	171.8	259.9	310.2	324.3	347.3	366.9	368.0	404.5
Farm	14.6	11.5	21.5	31.3	30.9	40.2	41.7	35.8	39.5
Nonfarm	65.3	160.3	238.4	279.0	293.4	307.0	325.2	332.2	364.9
Rental income of persons [2]	17.8	13.2	18.7	3.2	4.3	-13.5	-12.3	-10.4	4.7
Corporate profits [1,3]	77.5	177.7	280.8	319.8	365.0	362.8	361.7	346.3	393.8
Corporate profits [3]	71.8	197.8	225.3	273.4	320.3	325.4	341.2	337.8	364.2
Profits before tax	78.4	240.9	225.0	287.9	347.5	342.9	355.4	334.7	371.6
Profits tax liability	34.4	84.8	96.5	127.1	137.0	141.3	136.7	124.0	140.2
Profits after tax	44.0	156.1	128.5	160.8	210.5	201.6	218.7	210.7	231.4
Dividends	23.7	59.0	92.4	106.2	115.3	134.6	149.3	146.5	149.3
Undistributed profits	20.3	97.1	36.1	54.6	95.2	67.1	69.4	64.2	82.1
Inventory valuation adjustment	-6.6	-43.0	0.2	-14.5	-27.3	-17.5	-14.2	3.1	-7.4
Capital consumption adjustment	5.6	-20.2	55.5	46.4	44.7	37.4	20.5	8.4	29.5
Net interest	40.0	191.2	326.2	360.4	387.7	452.7	460.7	449.5	415.2
Addenda:									
Corporate profits after tax [1]	43.1	92.9	184.2	192.8	228.0	221.5	225.1	222.3	253.6
Net cash flow [1]	70.9	218.9	369.7	394.2	440.3	439.3	444.0	458.8	499.1
Undistributed profits [1]	19.4	33.9	91.9	86.5	112.6	86.9	75.7	75.8	104.3
Consumption of fixed capital	51.5	185.1	277.8	307.7	327.6	352.4	368.3	383.0	394.8
Less: Inventory valuation adjustment	-6.6	-43.0	0.2	-14.5	-27.3	-17.5	-14.2	3.1	-7.4
Equals: Net cash flow	77.5	262.0	369.5	408.7	467.5	456.9	458.1	455.6	506.5

[1] With inventory valuation and capital consumption adjustments. [2] With capital consumption adjustment. [3] With inventory valuation adjustment.

Source: U.S. Bureau of Economic Analysis, *National Income and Product Accounts of the United States, volume 2, 1959-88,* and *Survey of Current Business,* annual.

No. 698. National Income, by Sector: 1970 to 1991

[In billions of dollars]

SECTOR	1970	1980	1985	1986	1987	1988	1989	1990	1991
National income	833.5	2,198.2	3,268.4	3,437.9	3,692.3	4,002.6	4,249.5	4,468.3	4,544.2
Domestic business	675.1	1,785.0	2,688.3	2,825.9	3,038.5	3,295.4	3,478.6	3,628.2	3,653.1
Corporate business	482.2	1,318.8	1,957.9	2,050.7	2,208.7	2,399.1	2,524.6	2,621.2	2,627.0
Compensation of employees	401.0	1,119.4	1,615.3	1,710.5	1,816.1	1,965.2	2,075.8	2,182.8	2,219.5
Corporate profits [1]	70.4	142.7	250.0	238.7	280.3	315.9	303.4	296.0	279.8
Net interest	10.8	56.7	92.6	101.5	112.2	118.0	145.5	142.4	127.7
Sole proprietorships and partnerships	134.7	310.9	470.6	504.5	541.5	584.9	631.0	660.0	664.7
Compensation of employees	49.2	104.9	139.1	142.9	160.7	177.8	185.9	199.5	204.1
Proprietors' income [1]	79.5	170.5	258.2	282.2	308.6	322.5	345.4	365.0	365.9
Net interest	6.0	35.4	73.3	79.4	72.1	84.6	99.7	95.5	94.7
Other private business [2]	45.3	122.1	210.3	218.8	232.9	251.0	259.3	278.9	289.6
Compensation of employees	3.2	7.8	13.8	15.7	17.2	18.7	20.1	21.6	22.0
Proprietors' income [1]	0.4	1.3	1.7	1.6	1.6	1.8	1.9	2.0	2.0
Rental income of persons [3]	17.8	13.2	18.7	8.7	3.2	4.3	-13.5	-12.3	-10.4
Net interest	23.9	99.8	176.0	192.8	210.8	226.2	250.9	267.6	275.9
Government enterprises [4]	12.9	33.2	49.6	52.0	55.6	60.4	63.7	68.2	71.8
Households and institutions [5]	32.4	89.3	141.7	153.3	170.5	187.6	206.1	227.8	246.1
General government [4]	119.5	289.8	423.6	449.6	478.7	511.7	548.8	591.6	627.6
Rest of the world	6.4	34.1	14.8	9.1	4.6	7.9	16.0	20.7	17.4

[1] With inventory valuation and capital consumption adjustments. [2] Consists of all business activities reported on the individual income tax return in Schedule E—Supplemental Income Schedule; tax-exempt cooperatives; and owner-occupied nonfarm housing and buildings and equipment owned and used by nonprofit institutions servicing individuals, which are considered to be business activities selling their current services to their owners. [3] With capital consumption adjustment. [4] Compensation of employees. [5] Compensation of employees in private households; nonprofit social and athletic clubs; labor organizations; nonprofit schools and hospitals; religious, charitable, and welfare organizations; and all other nonprofit organizations serving individuals.

Source: U.S. Bureau of Economic Analysis, *National Income and Product Accounts of the United States, volume 2, 1959-88,* and *Survey of Current Business,* July 1992.

No. 699. Personal Consumption Expenditures, by Type of Expenditure, in Current and Constant (1987) Dollars: 1970 to 1991

[In billions of dollars]

TYPE OF EXPENDITURE	CURRENT DOLLARS				CONSTANT (1987) DOLLARS			
	1970	1980	1990	1991	1970	1980	1990	1991
Personal consumption expenditures [1]	646.5	1,748.1	3,748.4	3,887.7	1,813.5	2,447.1	3,260.4	3,240.8
Food and tobacco [1]	152.9	362.6	644.7	665.4	431.0	487.5	552.7	547.2
Food purchased for off-premise consumption	104.4	241.7	398.4	407.4	283.6	307.5	343.4	339.0
Purchased meals and beverages [2]	34.9	93.4	191.4	198.5	105.8	132.3	167.3	166.7
Tobacco products	10.8	20.9	43.4	47.8	33.5	38.7	31.9	31.5
Clothing, accessories, and jewelry [1]	57.6	131.8	258.6	260.6	107.8	157.1	229.0	222.5
Shoes	7.8	17.4	31.3	31.1	14.4	19.9	28.0	27.5
Clothing	39.8	89.8	175.5	177.7	66.3	106.0	159.1	
Jewelry and watches	4.1	15.0	31.1	30.1	8.4	16.8	25.2	23.6
Personal care	11.8	26.9	59.5	62.2	34.0	38.0	52.5	53.0
Housing [1]	94.0	255.2	547.5	574.0	269.3	399.4	474.7	478.2
Owner-occupied nonfarm dwellings-space rent	61.3	178.4	379.8	399.1	174.4	278.7	326.9	330.7
Tenant-occupied nonfarm dwellings-space rent	26.0	61.8	140.8	147.3	75.1	98.2	125.2	126.5
Household operation [1]	84.8	233.6	434.7	441.7	239.2	315.3	406.1	401.9
Furniture [3]	8.6	20.7	35.3	33.4	17.8	25.8	33.5	31.4
Semidurable house furnishings [4]	4.9	10.6	21.3	21.4	12.2	14.9	20.0	19.7
Cleaning and polishing preparations	8.2	22.9	51.5	52.8	26.4	31.2	45.3	45.0
Household utilities	22.7	81.1	136.4	143.2	92.3	111.7	124.1	126.2
Electricity	9.6	37.2	70.7	75.2	33.3	54.0	66.1	67.8
Gas	5.6	19.1	26.9	28.4	27.0	27.6	26.3	27.4
Water and other sanitary services	3.2	9.4	26.1	28.0	11.7	16.2	21.6	21.4
Fuel oil and coal	4.4	15.4	12.6	11.7	20.2	14.0	10.1	9.7
Telephone and telegraph	10.1	27.6	53.2	54.3	19.9	41.1	54.4	55.1
Medical care [1]	60.0	207.2	595.9	656.0	208.7	346.5	482.4	497.3
Drug preparations and sundries [5]	8.1	21.8	60.3	64.6	23.5	38.8	49.0	48.9
Physicians	14.0	42.8	134.2	148.1	52.7	72.9	108.8	113.4
Dentists	4.9	13.7	32.2	34.5	16.0	22.4	26.6	26.5
Hospitals and nursing homes [6]	23.4	98.7	269.0	296.5	87.1	164.0	217.5	223.9
Health insurance	4.4	12.8	35.6	38.3	13.9	23.0	25.0	24.3
Medical care [7]	2.1	7.6	30.0	31.9	10.0	17.7	19.4	19.4
Personal business [1]	32.0	101.6	297.4	317.7	119.5	175.5	250.1	252.8
Expense of handling life insurance [8]	7.1	23.4	57.1	59.7	22.6	37.8	49.7	50.1
Legal services	4.9	13.6	49.7	51.4	21.7	26.6	42.0	41.0
Funeral and burial expenses	2.3	4.6	8.3	8.9	8.2	8.8	7.2	7.2
Transportation [1]	81.1	235.7	453.7	438.2	219.5	274.8	403.2	377.4
User-operated transportation [1]	74.2	214.9	413.5	398.4	198.8	247.4	368.9	343.4
New autos	21.9	46.4	96.7	79.5	47.4	60.2	91.6	72.6
Net purchases of used autos	4.8	10.8	33.7	35.8	20.9	20.8	33.4	35.0
Tires, tubes, accessories, etc.	6.1	14.9	22.5	23.0	10.8	15.3	21.4	21.6
Repair, greasing, washing, parking, storage, rental, and leasing	12.3	33.7	82.5	83.7	39.3	48.3	72.6	70.8
Gasoline and oil	21.9	86.7	108.5	105.5	62.9	72.0	864.0	85.2
Purchased local transportation	3.0	4.8	8.9	9.1	8.8	7.8	7.8	7.6
Mass transit systems	1.8	2.9	5.7	5.7	5.3	5.3	5.0	4.9
Taxicab	1.2	1.9	3.2	3.4	3.5	2.5	2.8	2.7
Purchased intercity transportation [1]	4.0	16.1	31.2	30.7	11.9	19.7	26.5	26.4
Railway (commutation)	0.2	0.3	0.7	0.7	0.8	0.5	0.6	0.6
Bus	0.5	1.4	1.4	1.5	2.3	2.4	1.3	1.3
Airline	3.1	13.5	26.5	25.8	8.1	15.2	22.4	22.3
Recreation [1] [9]	43.1	117.6	280.7	289.7	91.3	149.1	257.3	258.7
Magazines, newspapers, and sheet music	4.1	12.0	24.1	24.6	13.2	18.4	21.2	20.3
Nondurable toys and sport supplies	5.5	14.6	31.4	32.2	9.5	17.4	28.1	28.4
Radio and television receivers, records, and musical instruments	8.5	19.9	49.6	50.2	8.8	17.6	53.2	56.2
Education and research	12.5	33.6	86.4	92.8	41.6	51.7	73.8	74.9
Religious and welfare activities	12.1	38.6	102.1	107.7	35.4	51.3	90.4	92.1

[1] Includes other expenditures not shown separately.   [2] Consists of purchases (including tips) of meals and beverages from retail, service, and amusement establishments, hotels, dining and buffet cars, schools, school fraternities, institutions, clubs, and industrial lunch rooms. Includes meals and beverages consumed both on and off-premise.   [3] Includes mattresses and bedsprings.   [4] Consists largely of textile house furnishings including piece goods allocated to house furnishing use. Also includes lamp shades, brooms, and brushes.   [5] Excludes drug preparations and related products dispensed by physicians, hospitals, and other medical services.   [6] Consists of (1) current expenditures (including consumption of fixed capital) of nonprofit hospitals and nursing homes, and (2) payments by patients to proprietary and government hospitals and nursing homes.   [7] Consists of (1) premiums, less benefits and dividends, for health, hospitalization and accidental death and dismemberment insurance provided by commercial insurance carriers, and (2) administrative expenses (including consumption of fixed capital) of Blue Cross and Blue Shield plans and of other independent prepaid and self-insured health plans.   [8] Consist of (1) operating expenses of life insurance carriers and private noninsured pension plans, and (2) premiums, less benefits and dividends of fraternal benefit societies. Excludes expenses allocated by commercial carriers to accident and health insurance.   [9] For additional details, see table 398.

Source: U.S. Bureau of Economic Analysis, *National Income and Product Accounts, volume 2, 1959-88*, and *Survey of Current Business*, July 1992.

No. 700. Personal Income and Its Disposition: 1970 to 1991

[In billions of dollars, except percent. For definition of personal income, see text, section 14]

ITEM	1970	1980	1985	1988	1989	1990	1991
Personal income	**831.0**	**2,265.4**	**3,379.8**	**4,075.9**	**4,380.3**	**4,664.2**	**4,828.3**
Wage and salary disbursements	551.5	1,376.6	1,986.5	2,443.0	2,586.4	2,742.8	2,812.2
Commodity-producing industries [1]	203.7	471.9	612.2	699.1	724.2	745.6	737.4
Manufacturing	158.4	355.7	461.3	524.5	542.2	556.1	556.9
Distributive industries [2]	131.2	336.4	475.9	575.3	607.0	634.6	647.4
Service industries [3]	99.4	306.9	524.5	719.6	776.8	847.8	883.9
Government	117.1	261.4	373.9	449.0	478.5	514.8	543.6
Other labor income	32.5	139.8	191.8	230.5	251.9	271.0	288.3
Proprietors' income [4]	79.9	171.8	259.9	324.3	347.3	366.9	368.0
Rental income of persons [5]	17.8	13.2	18.7	4.3	-13.5	-12.3	-10.4
Personal dividend income	23.5	57.1	87.9	108.4	126.5	140.3	137.0
Personal interest income	69.2	274.0	498.1	583.2	668.2	694.5	700.6
Transfer payments to persons	84.6	321.5	485.9	576.7	625.0	685.8	771.1
Old-age, survivors, disability, and health insurance benefits	38.5	154.2	253.4	300.4	325.1	352.0	382.0
Gov't unemployment insurance benefits	4.0	16.1	15.7	13.4	14.4	18.0	27.5
Veterans benefits	7.7	15.0	16.7	16.9	17.3	17.8	18.1
Gov't employees retirement benefits	10.2	43.0	66.6	82.2	87.5	94.0	101.3
Other transfer payments	24.3	93.2	133.5	163.7	180.6	203.9	242.1
Less: Personal contributions for social insurance	*27.9*	*88.6*	*149.1*	*194.5*	*211.4*	*224.8*	*238.4*
Less: Personal tax and nontax payments	*109.0*	*312.4*	*436.8*	*527.7*	*593.3*	*621.3*	*618.7*
Equals: Disposable personal income	**722.0**	**1,952.9**	**2,943.0**	**3,548.2**	**3,787.0**	**4,042.9**	**4,209.6**
Less: Personal outlays	*664.5*	*1,799.1*	*2,753.7*	*3,392.5*	*3,634.9*	*3,867.3*	*4,009.9*
Personal consumption expenditures	646.5	1,748.1	2,667.4	3,296.1	3,523.1	3,748.4	3,887.7
Interest paid by persons	16.8	49.4	83.6	93.7	103.0	109.6	112.5
Personal transfer payments to foreigners (net)	1.2	1.6	2.7	2.7	8.9	9.3	9.7
Equals: Personal saving	**57.5**	**153.8**	**189.3**	**155.7**	**152.1**	**175.6**	**199.6**
Percent of disposable personal income	8.0	7.9	6.4	4.4	4.0	4.3	4.7
Disposable personal income, 1987 dollars	2,025.3	2,733.6	3,162.1	3,404.3	3,464.9	3,516.5	3,509.0
PERCENT DISTRIBUTION							
Personal income	**100**	**100**	**100**	**100**	**100**	**100**	**100**
Wage and salary disbursements	66	61	59	60	59	59	58
Other labor income	4	6	6	6	6	6	6
Proprietors' income [4]	10	8	8	8	8	8	8
Rental income of persons [5]	2	1	1	(Z)	(-Z)	(-Z)	(-Z)
Personal dividend income	3	3	3	3	3	3	3
Personal interest income	8	12	15	14	15	15	15
Transfer payments	10	14	14	14	14	15	16
Less: Personal contributions for social insurance	*-3*	*-4*	*-4*	*-5*	*-5*	*-5*	*-5*

Z Less than 0.5 percent. [1] Comprises agriculture, forestry, fishing, mining, construction, and manufacturing. [2] Comprises transportation, communication, public utilities, and trade. [3] Comprises finance, insurance, real estate, services, and rest of world. [4] With capital consumption and inventory valuation adjustments. [5] With capital consumption adjustment.

Source: U.S. Bureau of Economic Analysis, *National Income and Product Accounts of the United States*, volume 2, 1959-88, and *Survey of Current Business*, July 1992.

No. 701. Gross Saving and Investment: 1970 to 1992

[In billions of dollars]

ITEM	1970	1980	1985	1986	1987	1988	1989	1990	1991	1992
Gross saving	**155.2**	**465.4**	**610.4**	**574.6**	**619.0**	**704.0**	**741.8**	**718.0**	**708.2**	**686.3**
Gross private saving	165.8	499.6	735.7	721.4	730.7	802.3	819.4	854.1	901.5	968.8
Personal saving	57.5	153.8	189.3	187.5	142.0	155.7	152.1	175.6	199.6	212.6
Undistributed corporate profits [1]	19.4	33.9	91.9	55.4	86.5	112.6	86.9	75.7	75.8	104.3
Undistributed profits	20.3	97.1	36.1	1.6	54.6	95.2	67.1	69.4	64.2	82.1
Inventory valuation adjustment	-6.6	-43.0	0.2	9.7	-14.5	-27.3	-17.5	-14.2	3.1	-7.4
Capital consumption adjustment	5.6	-20.2	55.5	44.1	46.4	44.7	37.4	20.5	8.4	29.5
Corporate consumption of fixed capital	51.5	185.1	277.8	294.2	307.7	327.6	352.4	368.3	383.0	394.4
Noncorporate consumption of fixed capital	37.3	126.8	176.7	184.4	194.4	206.4	228.0	234.6	243.1	258.6
Government surplus or deficit (-) [2]	-11.5	-35.3	-125.3	-146.8	-111.7	-98.3	-77.5	-136.1	-193.3	-282.5
Federal	-13.3	-60.1	-181.4	-201.0	-151.8	-136.6	-122.3	-166.2	-210.4	-298.0
State and local	1.8	24.8	56.1	54.3	40.1	38.4	44.8	30.1	17.1	15.5
Capital grants received by the U.S. (net)	0.9	1.2	-	-	-	-	-	-	-	-
Gross investment	**155.2**	**479.1**	**596.5**	**575.9**	**594.2**	**675.6**	**742.9**	**723.4**	**730.1**	**720.4**
Gross private domestic investment	150.3	467.6	714.5	717.6	749.3	793.6	832.3	799.5	721.1	770.4
Net foreign investment	4.9	11.5	-118.1	-141.7	-155.1	-118.0	-89.3	-76.1	9.0	-49.9
Statistical discrepancy	**-**	**13.6**	**-13.9**	**1.2**	**-24.8**	**-28.4**	**1.1**	**5.4**	**21.9**	**34.1**

- Represents or rounds to zero. [1] With inventory valuation and capital consumption adjustments. [2] National income and product accounts basis.

Source: U.S. Bureau of Economic Analysis, *National Income and Product Accounts of the United States: volume 2, 1959-88*, and *Survey of Current Business*, monthly.

No. 702. Disposable Personal Income Per Capita in Current and Constant (1987) Dollars—States: 1980 to 1992

[1992 data preliminary]

REGION, DIVISION, AND STATE	CURRENT DOLLARS				Income rank		CONSTANT (1987) DOLLARS			
	1980	1985	1990	1992	1980	1992	1980	1985	1990	1992
United States	8,569	12,324	16,150	17,387	(X)	(X)	12,001	13,237	14,043	14,067
Northeast	9,140	13,502	18,604	20,058	(X)	(X)	12,801	14,503	16,178	16,228
New England	9,055	13,789	19,078	20,513	(X)	(X)	12,682	14,811	16,590	16,596
Maine	7,283	10,779	15,119	16,298	38	27	10,200	11,578	13,147	13,186
New Hampshire	8,611	13,946	18,952	20,889	15	3	12,060	14,980	16,480	16,900
Vermont	7,485	11,026	15,421	16,640	35	24	10,483	11,843	13,410	13,463
Massachusetts	9,052	13,897	19,282	20,822	13	4	12,678	14,927	16,767	16,846
Rhode Island	8,306	12,437	16,321	17,863	26	14	11,633	13,359	14,192	14,452
Connecticut	10,321	15,500	21,699	22,891	2	2	14,455	16,649	18,869	18,520
Middle Atlantic	9,169	13,404	18,438	19,899	(X)	(X)	12,842	14,397	16,033	16,100
New York	9,249	13,388	18,495	20,021	10	5	12,954	14,380	16,083	16,198
New Jersey	9,974	15,465	21,654	23,074	5	1	13,969	16,611	18,830	18,668
Pennsylvania	8,549	12,103	16,258	17,658	17	16	11,973	13,000	14,137	14,286
Midwest	8,494	12,069	15,700	17,030	(X)	(X)	11,897	12,964	13,652	13,778
East North Central	8,672	12,176	15,899	17,165	(X)	(X)	12,146	13,078	13,825	13,888
Ohio	8,405	11,707	15,123	16,359	24	25	11,772	12,575	13,150	13,235
Indiana	7,988	11,095	14,638	15,882	30	31	11,188	11,917	12,729	12,850
Illinois	9,276	13,173	17,584	18,914	9	8	12,992	14,149	15,290	15,303
Michigan	8,779	12,356	15,903	17,154	14	20	12,296	13,272	13,829	13,879
Wisconsin	8,401	11,743	15,110	16,351	25	26	11,766	12,613	13,139	13,229
West North Central	8,065	11,815	15,224	16,707	(X)	(X)	11,296	12,691	13,238	13,517
Minnesota	8,505	12,352	15,908	17,255	18	18	11,912	13,267	13,833	13,960
Iowa	7,987	11,292	14,693	16,089	31	28	11,186	12,129	12,777	13,017
Missouri	8,030	11,930	15,187	16,742	28	23	11,246	12,814	13,206	13,545
North Dakota	6,600	10,984	13,676	15,297	48	36	9,244	11,798	11,892	12,376
South Dakota	6,890	10,357	14,081	15,082	45	38	9,650	11,125	12,244	12,202
Nebraska	7,769	11,742	15,241	16,992	32	21	10,881	12,612	13,253	13,748
Kansas	8,419	11,959	15,393	16,982	23	22	11,791	12,845	13,385	13,739
South	7,768	11,274	14,794	16,009	(X)	(X)	10,879	12,109	12,865	12,952
South Atlantic	7,956	11,716	15,807	16,877	(X)	(X)	11,143	12,584	13,745	13,655
Delaware	8,502	12,641	17,521	18,300	19	10	11,908	13,578	15,236	14,806
Maryland	9,097	13,753	18,534	19,746	12	6	12,741	14,772	16,117	15,976
District of Columbia	10,542	14,714	19,559	22,101	(X)	(X)	14,765	15,805	17,008	17,881
Virginia	8,443	12,628	17,039	18,010	21	12	11,825	13,564	14,817	14,571
West Virginia	6,944	9,281	12,236	13,526	43	48	9,725	9,969	10,640	10,943
North Carolina	6,939	10,321	14,345	15,600	44	35	9,718	11,086	12,474	12,621
South Carolina	6,627	9,696	13,276	14,318	47	43	9,282	10,415	11,544	11,584
Georgia	7,309	11,092	14,816	15,943	37	30	10,237	11,914	12,883	12,899
Florida	8,595	12,340	16,366	17,246	16	19	12,038	13,255	14,231	13,953
East South Central	6,834	9,706	13,272	14,724	(X)	(X)	9,571	10,425	11,541	11,913
Kentucky	7,066	9,732	13,132	14,664	41	39	9,896	10,453	11,419	11,864
Tennessee	7,117	10,360	14,282	15,820	40	32	9,968	11,128	12,419	12,799
Alabama	6,741	9,656	13,230	14,533	46	41	9,441	10,372	11,504	11,758
Mississippi	6,122	8,552	11,620	13,006	50	50	8,574	9,186	10,104	10,523
West South Central	8,050	11,490	14,002	15,314	(X)	(X)	11,275	12,342	12,176	12,390
Arkansas	6,502	9,499	12,506	13,879	49	46	9,106	10,203	10,875	11,229
Louisiana	7,523	10,421	12,750	14,163	34	44	10,536	11,193	11,087	11,459
Oklahoma	8,017	10,877	13,328	14,344	29	42	11,228	11,683	11,590	11,605
Texas	8,459	12,188	14,642	15,965	20	29	11,847	13,091	12,732	12,917
West	9,422	13,199	16,496	17,508	(X)	(X)	13,196	14,177	14,345	14,165
Mountain	8,247	11,482	14,404	15,490	(X)	(X)	11,550	12,333	12,525	12,532
Montana	7,565	10,068	12,747	14,064	33	45	10,595	10,814	11,084	11,379
Idaho	7,452	10,014	13,674	14,572	36	40	10,437	10,756	11,890	11,790
Wyoming	9,705	11,686	14,667	15,607	6	34	13,592	12,552	12,754	12,627
Colorado	9,130	13,198	16,219	17,517	11	17	12,787	14,176	14,103	14,172
New Mexico	7,246	10,162	12,568	13,709	39	47	10,148	10,915	10,929	11,091
Arizona	8,147	11,629	14,244	15,179	27	37	11,410	12,491	12,386	12,281
Utah	6,987	9,664	12,156	13,355	42	49	9,786	10,380	10,570	10,805
Nevada	10,058	12,991	17,036	17,711	4	15	14,087	13,954	14,814	14,329
Pacific	9,843	13,822	17,225	18,221	(X)	(X)	13,786	14,846	14,978	14,742
Washington	9,317	12,864	16,378	18,038	7	11	13,049	13,817	14,242	14,594
Oregon	8,425	11,268	14,557	15,614	22	33	11,800	12,103	12,658	12,633
California	10,084	14,232	17,596	18,495	3	9	14,123	15,287	15,301	14,964
Alaska	11,639	16,628	18,303	19,093	1	7	16,301	17,860	15,916	15,447
Hawaii	9,286	12,588	17,279	17,972	8	13	13,006	13,521	15,025	14,540

X Not applicable.

Source: U.S. Bureau of Economic Analysis, *Survey of Current Business,* August issues; and unpublished data.

No. 703. Personal Income in Current and Constant (1987) Dollars—States: 1980 to 1992

[In billions of dollars, except percent. 1992 data preliminary. Represents a measure of income received from all sources during the calendar year by residents of each State. Data exclude Federal employees overseas and U.S. residents employed by private U.S. firms on temporary foreign assignment. Totals may differ from those in tables 695, 696, and 700. See text, section 14. Minus sign (-) indicates decrease]

REGION, DIVISION, AND STATE	CURRENT DOLLARS				CONSTANT (1987) DOLLARS				Average annual percent change [1]		Percent distribution	
	1980	1985	1990	1992	1980	1985	1990	1992	1980-1992	1991-1992	1980	1992
United States	2,259.0	3,368.2	4,648.9	5,061.0	3,163.9	3,617.9	4,042.5	4,094.7	2.2	2.1	100.0	100.0
Northeast	526.2	789.0	1,106.2	1,187.7	736.9	847.4	962.0	960.9	2.2	1.7	23.3	23.5
New England	130.9	204.9	293.1	312.0	183.3	220.1	254.9	252.4	2.7	1.4	5.8	6.2
Maine	9.3	14.1	21.1	22.5	13.0	15.2	18.3	18.2	2.9	1.5	0.4	0.4
New Hampshire	9.1	15.7	23.4	25.5	12.7	16.9	20.3	20.6	4.1	2.7	0.4	0.5
Vermont	4.4	6.7	10.0	10.7	6.1	7.2	8.7	8.7	2.9	2.4	0.2	0.2
Massachusetts	61.2	96.3	135.8	144.3	85.7	103.4	118.1	116.8	2.6	1.4	2.7	2.9
Rhode Island	9.1	13.6	18.9	20.4	12.7	14.6	16.4	16.5	2.2	2.6	0.4	0.4
Connecticut	37.9	58.5	84.0	88.5	53.0	62.9	73.0	71.6	2.5	0.6	1.7	1.7
Middle Atlantic	395.3	584.0	813.2	875.7	553.6	627.3	707.1	708.5	2.1	1.8	17.5	17.3
New York	191.6	284.5	397.3	426.4	268.3	305.6	345.4	345.0	2.1	1.6	8.5	8.4
New Jersey	85.9	135.9	193.2	206.1	120.3	145.9	168.0	166.7	2.8	1.7	3.8	4.1
Pennsylvania	117.8	163.6	222.7	243.2	165.0	175.8	193.6	196.8	1.5	2.2	5.2	4.8
Midwest	581.6	812.0	1,080.9	1,177.6	814.6	872.2	939.9	952.7	1.3	2.6	25.7	23.3
East North Central	420.3	577.7	771.2	836.5	588.6	620.5	670.6	676.8	1.2	2.3	18.6	16.5
Ohio	105.2	143.7	189.2	205.2	147.3	154.4	164.5	166.0	1.0	2.5	4.7	4.1
Indiana	50.6	69.1	93.4	102.2	70.9	74.2	81.2	82.6	1.3	2.8	2.2	2.0
Illinois	124.4	172.3	232.6	251.3	174.3	185.1	202.3	203.3	1.3	2.0	5.5	5.0
Michigan	94.0	129.2	170.4	184.1	131.6	138.8	148.2	148.9	1.0	2.2	4.2	3.6
Wisconsin	46.1	63.3	85.6	93.8	64.5	68.0	74.5	75.9	1.4	2.5	2.0	1.9
West North Central	161.4	234.3	309.7	341.1	226.0	251.7	269.3	275.9	1.7	3.2	7.1	6.7
Minnesota	40.8	60.0	82.0	89.8	57.1	64.4	71.3	72.7	2.0	2.8	1.8	1.8
Iowa	27.3	36.1	46.8	51.4	38.2	38.7	40.7	41.6	0.7	3.5	1.2	1.0
Missouri	45.6	67.8	88.9	97.8	63.8	72.8	77.3	79.1	1.8	2.4	2.0	1.9
North Dakota	5.0	8.2	9.6	10.7	7.0	8.8	8.4	8.7	1.8	4.7	0.2	0.2
South Dakota	5.3	7.9	10.8	11.8	7.5	8.4	9.4	9.5	2.1	0.9	0.2	0.2
Nebraska	14.1	20.7	27.3	30.6	19.8	22.3	23.7	24.8	1.9	5.0	0.6	0.6
Kansas	23.3	33.7	44.1	48.9	32.6	36.2	38.3	39.5	1.6	3.9	1.0	1.0
South	678.4	1,047.4	1,445.3	1,589.9	950.2	1,125.1	1,256.8	1,286.3	2.6	2.2	30.0	31.4
South Atlantic	341.9	542.3	795.4	864.5	478.8	582.5	691.7	699.4	3.2	1.8	15.1	17.1
Delaware	6.2	9.3	13.9	14.8	8.6	10.0	12.0	12.0	2.8	0.8	0.3	0.3
Maryland	45.7	71.3	105.2	112.8	64.1	76.6	91.5	91.2	3.0	1.0	2.0	2.2
District of Columbia	8.0	11.2	14.4	15.5	11.2	12.1	12.5	12.6	1.0	1.6	0.4	0.3
Virginia	52.9	83.7	122.3	131.6	74.1	89.9	106.3	106.4	3.1	1.5	2.3	2.6
West Virginia	15.6	19.8	24.6	27.3	21.8	21.3	21.4	22.1	0.1	2.7	0.7	0.5
North Carolina	47.2	74.4	109.0	120.9	66.1	79.9	94.8	97.8	3.3	3.4	2.1	2.4
South Carolina	23.7	36.2	52.6	57.6	33.2	38.9	45.8	46.6	2.9	2.1	1.0	1.1
Georgia	45.8	76.3	110.8	122.4	64.2	82.0	96.4	99.0	3.7	2.8	2.0	2.4
Florida	96.8	160.0	242.7	261.6	135.5	171.9	211.0	211.7	3.8	0.8	4.3	5.2
East South Central	113.6	163.1	225.8	253.1	159.1	175.2	196.4	204.8	2.1	3.4	5.0	5.0
Kentucky	29.5	40.9	55.3	62.1	41.3	43.9	48.1	50.2	1.6	3.9	1.3	1.2
Tennessee	36.9	54.6	77.6	87.1	51.6	58.6	67.4	70.5	2.6	3.6	1.6	1.7
Alabama	29.9	43.3	60.3	67.1	41.8	46.5	52.4	54.3	2.2	2.5	1.3	1.3
Mississippi	17.4	24.3	32.7	36.8	24.3	26.2	28.4	29.8	1.7	3.5	0.8	0.7
West South Central	223.0	342.0	424.0	472.3	312.3	367.4	368.7	382.1	1.7	2.5	9.9	9.3
Arkansas	16.9	24.8	33.0	37.0	23.6	26.7	28.7	30.0	2.0	3.5	0.7	0.7
Louisiana	36.7	51.4	60.2	67.4	51.3	55.2	52.4	54.5	0.5	2.1	1.6	1.3
Oklahoma	28.3	40.5	47.7	52.0	39.7	43.5	41.5	42.1	0.5	2.2	1.3	1.0
Texas	141.1	225.3	283.1	315.9	197.6	242.0	246.2	255.6	2.2	2.5	6.2	6.2
West	472.8	719.8	1,016.4	1,105.9	662.2	773.2	883.8	894.8	2.5	1.7	20.9	21.9
Mountain	108.3	166.1	225.9	252.9	151.6	178.4	196.4	204.6	2.5	3.1	4.8	5.0
Montana	6.9	9.3	11.7	13.2	9.6	10.0	10.2	10.7	0.9	1.3	0.3	0.3
Idaho	8.0	11.1	15.3	17.1	11.2	11.9	13.3	13.9	1.8	4.2	0.4	0.3
Wyoming	5.4	6.7	7.4	8.1	7.5	7.2	6.5	6.6	-1.1	1.1	0.2	0.2
Colorado	30.9	48.4	62.1	69.8	43.3	52.0	54.0	56.5	2.2	3.5	1.4	1.4
New Mexico	10.7	16.4	21.5	24.3	15.0	17.6	18.7	19.6	2.3	3.5	0.5	0.5
Arizona	25.4	42.0	59.5	65.6	35.5	45.1	51.8	53.1	3.4	2.4	1.1	1.3
Utah	11.7	18.0	24.3	27.8	16.4	19.4	21.1	22.5	2.7	4.2	0.5	0.5
Nevada	9.4	14.2	24.1	26.9	13.1	15.2	20.9	21.8	4.3	2.8	0.4	0.5
Pacific	364.5	553.8	790.5	853.0	510.5	594.8	687.4	690.1	2.5	1.4	16.1	16.9
Washington	44.5	62.8	92.0	104.8	62.4	67.5	80.0	84.8	2.6	4.0	2.0	2.1
Oregon	26.1	34.6	48.7	54.2	36.5	37.1	42.4	43.8	1.5	2.9	1.2	1.1
California	278.0	431.4	615.5	656.8	389.3	463.4	535.2	531.4	2.6	0.9	12.3	13.0
Alaska	5.5	10.0	11.5	12.7	7.8	10.7	10.0	10.3	2.4	2.0	0.2	0.3
Hawaii	10.4	15.0	22.8	24.6	14.6	16.1	19.8	19.9	2.6	-0.2	0.5	0.5

[1] For definition of average annual percent change, see Guide to Tabular Presentation.

Source: U.S. Bureau of Economic Analysis, *Survey of Current Business,* August issues; and unpublished data.

No. 704. Personal Income Per Capita in Current and Constant (1987) Dollars—States: 1980 to 1992

[1992 data preliminary. See headnote, table 703]

REGION, DIVISION, AND STATE	CURRENT DOLLARS					CONSTANT (1987) DOLLARS					Income rank	
	1980	1985	1990	1991	1992	1980	1985	1990	1991	1992	1980	1992
United States	9,940	14,155	18,635	19,091	19,841	13,922	15,204	16,204	15,909	16,053	(X)	(X)
Northeast	10,699	15,819	21,754	22,249	23,234	14,984	16,991	18,917	18,541	18,798	(X)	(X)
New England	10,582	16,084	22,166	22,636	23,632	14,821	17,276	19,275	18,863	19,120	(X)	(X)
Maine..........	8,218	12,159	17,125	17,442	18,226	11,510	13,060	14,891	14,535	14,746	29	28
New Hampshire....	9,803	15,749	21,051	21,812	22,934	13,730	16,916	18,305	18,177	18,555	6	6
Vermont	8,546	12,674	17,630	17,960	18,834	11,969	13,613	15,330	14,967	15,238	23	24
Massachusetts.....	10,659	16,371	22,558	23,046	24,059	14,929	17,584	19,616	19,205	19,465	3	3
Rhode Island......	9,576	13,985	18,771	19,201	20,299	13,412	15,021	16,323	16,001	16,423	17	14
Connecticut.......	12,170	18,286	25,528	25,968	26,979	17,045	19,641	22,198	21,640	21,828	1	1
Middle Atlantic	10,738	15,728	21,609	22,114	23,095	15,039	16,894	18,790	18,428	18,685	(X)	(X)
New York	10,906	15,988	22,068	22,572	23,534	15,275	17,173	19,190	18,810	19,040	4	4
New Jersey.......	11,648	17,958	24,977	25,369	26,457	16,314	19,289	21,719	21,141	21,405	2	2
Pennsylvania.....	9,923	13,901	18,725	19,313	20,253	13,898	14,931	16,283	16,094	16,386	16	16
Midwest	9,872	13,804	18,086	18,507	19,396	13,826	14,827	15,727	15,422	15,692	(X)	(X)
East North Central....	10,077	13,947	18,329	18,710	19,566	14,113	14,981	15,938	15,592	15,830	(X)	(X)
Ohio	9,738	13,388	17,422	17,767	18,624	13,639	14,380	15,150	14,806	15,068	26	26
Indiana..........	9,215	12,649	16,814	17,193	18,043	12,906	13,586	14,621	14,328	14,598	32	31
Illinois	10,875	15,115	20,327	20,737	21,608	15,231	16,235	17,676	17,281	17,482	11	7
Michigan.........	10,154	14,239	18,297	18,642	19,508	14,221	15,294	15,910	15,535	15,783	20	19
Wisconsin........	9,772	13,339	17,455	17,919	18,727	13,686	14,328	15,178	14,933	15,151	24	25
West North Central...	9,374	13,463	17,506	18,022	18,990	13,129	14,461	15,223	15,018	15,364	(X)	(X)
Minnesota........	9,982	14,332	18,690	19,130	20,049	13,980	15,394	16,252	15,942	16,221	18	18
Iowa	9,346	12,747	16,848	17,251	18,287	13,090	13,692	14,650	14,376	14,795	30	27
Missouri	9,256	13,552	17,347	17,980	18,835	12,964	14,556	15,084	14,983	15,239	22	23
North Dakota.....	7,641	12,142	15,158	15,646	16,854	10,702	13,042	13,181	13,038	13,636	39	37
South Dakota	7,701	11,251	15,566	16,095	16,558	10,786	12,085	13,536	13,413	13,396	37	38
Nebraska	8,988	13,075	17,276	17,780	19,084	12,588	14,044	15,023	14,817	15,440	25	22
Kansas..........	9,829	13,875	17,768	18,306	19,376	13,766	14,903	15,450	15,255	15,676	21	21
South	8,958	12,865	16,857	17,375	18,038	12,546	13,818	14,658	14,479	14,593	(X)	(X)
South Atlantic......	9,204	13,502	18,171	18,576	19,184	12,891	14,503	15,801	15,480	15,521	(X)	(X)
Delaware	10,356	15,005	20,709	20,935	21,451	14,504	16,117	18,008	17,446	17,355	9	9
Maryland	10,824	16,152	21,915	22,304	22,974	15,160	17,349	19,057	18,587	18,587	5	5
District of Columbia .	12,508	17,702	23,885	24,916	26,360	17,518	19,014	20,770	20,763	21,327	(X)	(X)
Virginia.........	9,857	14,636	19,679	20,046	20,629	13,805	15,721	17,112	16,705	16,690	12	12
West Virginia.....	7,972	10,396	13,722	14,315	15,065	11,165	11,166	11,932	11,929	12,189	49	49
North Carolina....	8,000	11,897	16,383	16,848	17,667	11,204	12,779	14,246	14,040	14,294	34	33
South Carolina....	7,558	10,958	15,043	15,391	15,989	10,585	11,770	13,081	12,826	12,936	43	44
Georgia	8,353	12,799	17,041	17,447	18,130	11,699	13,748	14,818	14,539	14,668	28	30
Florida	9,835	14,098	18,606	18,985	19,397	13,775	15,143	16,179	15,821	15,693	19	20
East South Central...	7,730	10,896	14,859	15,484	16,300	10,826	11,704	12,921	12,903	13,188	(X)	(X)
Kentucky........	8,051	11,067	14,984	15,626	16,534	11,276	11,887	13,030	13,022	13,377	40	39
Tennessee	8,010	11,577	15,869	16,478	17,341	11,218	12,435	13,799	13,732	14,030	36	35
Alabama........	7,656	10,901	14,899	15,526	16,220	10,723	11,709	12,956	12,938	13,123	42	40
Mississippi	6,868	9,407	12,700	13,318	14,088	9,619	10,104	11,043	11,098	11,398	50	50
West South Central ...	9,329	13,014	15,843	16,480	17,142	13,066	13,979	13,777	13,733	13,869	(X)	(X)
Arkansas	7,371	10,672	14,037	14,636	15,439	10,324	11,463	12,206	12,197	12,491	47	46
Louisiana	8,672	11,662	14,300	15,054	15,712	12,146	12,526	12,435	12,545	12,712	45	45
Oklahoma.......	9,308	12,369	15,154	15,570	16,198	13,036	13,286	13,177	12,975	13,105	41	41
Texas..........	9,840	13,844	16,600	17,248	17,892	13,782	14,870	14,435	14,373	14,476	31	32
West	10,889	15,049	19,138	19,522	20,068	15,251	16,165	16,642	16,268	16,236	(X)	(X)
Mountain	9,455	13,032	16,465	16,975	17,586	13,242	13,998	14,317	14,146	14,228	(X)	(X)
Montana.........	8,728	11,316	14,663	15,680	16,062	12,224	12,155	12,750	13,067	12,995	38	43
Idaho..........	8,433	11,118	15,137	15,366	16,067	11,811	11,942	13,163	12,805	12,999	44	42
Wyoming	11,356	13,363	16,467	16,968	17,423	15,905	14,353	14,319	14,140	14,096	33	34
Colorado.	10,616	15,088	18,795	19,395	20,124	14,868	16,206	16,343	16,163	16,282	15	17
New Mexico	8,147	11,421	14,124	14,709	15,353	11,410	12,267	12,282	12,258	12,422	46	47
Arizona.........	9,272	13,178	16,169	16,594	17,119	12,986	14,155	14,060	13,828	13,850	35	36
Utah	7,942	10,975	14,036	14,628	15,325	11,123	11,788	12,205	12,190	12,399	48	48
Nevada	11,559	14,908	19,680	19,812	20,266	16,189	16,013	17,113	16,510	16,396	13	15
Pacific...........	11,403	15,782	20,069	20,415	20,945	15,971	16,952	17,451	17,013	16,946	(X)	(X)
Washington......	10,716	14,277	18,738	19,521	20,398	15,008	15,335	16,294	16,268	16,503	14	13
Oregon.........	9,863	12,934	17,038	17,495	18,202	13,814	13,893	14,816	14,579	14,727	27	29
California	11,681	16,314	20,547	20,805	21,278	16,360	17,523	17,867	17,338	17,215	10	10
Alaska	13,692	18,752	20,867	21,144	21,603	19,176	20,142	18,145	17,620	17,478	7	8
Hawaii	10,774	14,413	20,461	21,062	21,218	15,090	15,481	17,792	17,552	17,167	8	11

X Not applicable.

Source: U.S. Bureau of Economic Analysis, *Survey of Current Business*, August issues; and unpublished data.

No. 705. Personal Income and Personal Income Per Capita for Selected Metropolitan Areas: 1985 to 1991

[As defined **December 28, 1992.** CMSA=Consolidated Metropolitan Statistical Area; NECMA=New England County Metropolitan Area; MSA=Metropolitan Statistical Area. See text, section 14, and Appendix II]

METROPOLITAN AREA RANKED BY 1990 POPULATION	PERSONAL INCOME				PER CAPITA PERSONAL INCOME			
	1985 (mil. dol.)	1990 (mil. dol.)	1991 (mil. dol.)	Annual percent change, 1990-91	1985 (dol.)	1990 (dol.)	1991 (dol.)	Percent of national average, 1991
United States [1]	3,368,244	4,648,867	4,813,897	3.5	14,155	18,635	19,091	(X)
New York-Northern New Jersey-Long Island, NY-NJ-CT-PA CMSA	346,717	490,980	500,515	1.9	18,036	25,212	25,676	134.5
Los Angeles-Riverside-Orange County, CA CMSA	210,652	301,424	306,481	1.7	16,442	20,600	20,683	108.3
Chicago-Gary-Kenosha, IL-IN-WI CMSA . .	130,199	180,082	185,545	3.0	15,973	21,823	22,255	116.6
Washington-Baltimore, DC-MD-VA-WV CMSA.	107,364	158,709	163,407	3.0	17,439	23,496	23,959	125.5
San Francisco-Oakland-San Jose, CA CMSA.	112,765	156,146	161,221	3.2	19,381	24,860	25,463	133.4
Philadelphia-Wilmington-Atlantic City, PA-NJ-DE-MD CMSA	90,043	127,197	131,012	3.0	15,784	21,546	22,125	115.9
Boston-Brockton-Nashua, MA-NH NECMA	92,123	130,704	132,931	1.7	16,719	22,971	23,480	123.0
Detroit-Ann Arbor-Flint, MI CMSA	80,487	104,786	106,651	1.8	15,683	20,174	20,402	106.9
Dallas-Fort Worth, TX CMSA	61,231	79,524	83,342	4.8	16,810	19,570	20,157	105.6
Houston-Galveston-Brazoria, TX CMSA . .	56,712	72,280	77,190	6.8	15,581	19,300	20,007	104.8
Miami-Fort Lauderdale, FL CMSA	44,153	63,230	65,008	2.8	15,167	19,684	19,980	104.7
Seattle-Tacoma-Bremerton, WA CMSA . .	40,816	61,587	65,302	6.0	15,701	20,523	21,425	112.2
Atlanta, GA MSA	39,875	59,719	61,956	3.7	15,542	20,042	20,304	106.4
Cleveland-Akron, OH CMSA.	42,314	55,236	56,416	2.1	14,713	19,312	19,589	102.6
Minneapolis-St. Paul, MN-WI MSA.	38,453	53,949	55,962	3.7	16,513	21,138	21,665	113.5
San Diego, CA MSA	32,775	48,723	50,463	3.6	15,414	19,341	19,799	103.7
St. Louis, MO-IL MSA	37,574	49,848	51,413	3.1	15,378	19,965	20,507	107.4
Pittsburgh, PA MSA	34,465	45,104	47,061	4.3	13,914	18,856	19,579	102.6
Phoenix-Mesa, AZ MSA.	27,975	40,112	41,497	3.5	14,525	17,834	18,156	95.1
Tampa-St. Petersburg-Clearwater, FL MSA.	25,997	37,437	38,761	3.5	13,940	17,977	18,445	96.6
Denver-Boulder-Greeley, CO CMSA.	32,213	40,760	43,078	5.7	16,580	20,542	21,170	110.9
Cincinnati-Hamilton, OH-KY-IN CMSA . . .	24,022	33,610	34,898	3.8	13,743	18,445	18,937	99.2
Portland-Salem, OR-WA CMSA.	22,900	33,033	34,866	5.5	13,935	18,275	18,775	98.3
Milwaukee-Racine, WI CMSA	23,553	31,653	32,730	3.4	15,124	19,639	20,168	105.6
Kansas City, MO-KS MSA	22,859	30,706	31,985	4.2	15,318	19,336	19,963	104.6
Sacramento-Yolo, CA CMSA	18,563	28,405	29,904	5.3	14,689	19,016	19,519	102.2
Norfolk-Virginia Beach-Newport News, VA-NC MSA.	17,408	23,850	24,942	4.6	13,285	16,448	17,030	89.2
Indianapolis, IN MSA	18,788	26,656	27,900	4.7	14,136	19,253	19,844	103.9
Columbus, OH MSA	17,552	24,527	25,526	4.1	13,923	18,161	18,630	97.6
San Antonio, TX MSA	16,014	20,311	21,501	5.9	13,036	15,252	15,950	83.5
New Orleans, LA MSA	17,872	20,917	21,999	5.2	13,250	16,314	16,569	88.8
Orlando, FL MSA	13,686	21,755	22,625	4.0	13,591	17,562	17,832	93.4
Buffalo-Niagara Falls, NY MSA.	16,231	21,273	22,038	3.6	13,511	17,902	18,466	96.7
Charlotte-Gastonia-Rock Hill, NC-SC MSA.	14,209	21,690	22,312	2.9	13,425	18,562	18,757	98.3
Hartford, CT NECMA	18,924	27,502	27,965	1.7	17,490	24,443	24,911	130.5
Salt Lake City-Ogden, UT MSA.	12,257	16,252	17,298	6.4	12,077	15,097	15,687	82.2
Rochester, NY MSA	15,863	21,433	22,293	4.0	15,120	20,161	20,784	108.9
Greensboro-Winston-Salem-High Point, NC MSA	13,677	19,668	20,195	2.7	13,745	18,661	18,943	99.2
Memphis, TN-AR-MS MSA.	12,347	17,813	18,714	5.1	12,759	17,645	18,331	96.0
Nashville, TN MSA	12,418	18,132	19,120	5.4	13,774	18,324	19,059	99.8
Oklahoma City, OK MSA	13,377	15,648	16,318	4.3	13,665	16,302	16,799	88.0
Dayton-Springfield, OH MSA	12,842	16,965	17,499	3.1	13,803	17,808	18,302	95.9
Louisville, KY-IN MSA	12,619	17,369	18,105	4.2	13,308	18,283	18,912	99.1
Grand Rapids-Muskegon-Holland, MI MSA.	11,748	16,600	17,162	3.4	13,415	17,624	18,008	94.3
Providence-Warwick, RI NECMA.	12,254	17,086	17,509	2.5	13,873	18,618	19,088	100.0
Jacksonville, FL MSA	10,949	16,030	16,747	4.5	13,516	17,561	17,937	94.0
West Palm Beach-Boca Raton, FL MSA. .	14,079	24,043	24,909	3.6	19,588	27,550	28,097	147.2
Richmond-Petersburg, VA MSA	12,381	18,527	18,876	1.9	15,487	21,310	21,416	112.2

X Not applicable.   [1] Includes other areas not listed separately.

Source: U.S. Bureau of Economic Analysis, *Survey of Current Business,* August issues; and unpublished data.

No. 706. Percent Distribution of Shares of National Income: 1970 to 1992

TYPE OF INCOME	1970	1980	1985	1986	1987	1988	1989	1990	1991	1992
National income	100.0	100.0	100.0	100.0	100.0	100.0	100.0	100.0	100.0	100.0
Compensation of employees	74.2	74.8	72.9	73.4	73.1	73.0	73.0	73.7	74.6	74.3
Wages and salaries	66.2	62.6	60.8	61.2	61.2	61.0	60.9	61.4	61.9	61.5
Supplements to wages, salaries	8.0	12.2	12.1	12.2	11.8	11.9	12.1	12.3	12.7	12.8
Proprietors' income [1]	9.6	7.8	8.0	8.3	8.4	8.1	8.2	8.2	8.1	8.5
Farm	1.8	0.5	0.7	0.6	0.8	0.8	0.9	0.9	0.8	0.8
Nonfarm	7.8	7.3	7.3	7.6	7.6	7.3	7.2	7.3	7.3	7.7
Rental income of persons [2]	2.1	0.6	0.6	0.3	0.1	0.1	-0.3	-0.3	-0.2	0.1
Corporate profits [1]	9.3	8.1	8.6	7.9	8.7	9.1	8.5	8.1	7.6	8.3
Profits before tax	9.4	11.0	6.9	6.3	7.8	8.7	8.1	8.0	7.4	7.8
Profits after tax	5.3	7.1	3.9	3.2	4.4	5.3	4.7	4.9	4.6	4.9
Inventory valuation adjustment	-0.8	-2.0	-	0.3	-0.4	-0.7	-0.4	-0.3	0.1	-0.2
Capital consumption adjustment	0.7	-0.9	1.7	1.3	1.3	1.1	0.9	0.5	0.2	0.6
Net interest	4.8	8.7	10.0	10.2	9.8	9.7	10.7	10.3	9.9	8.8

- Represents or rounds to zero.   [1] With inventory valuation and capital consumption adjustments.   [2] With capital consumption adjustment.

Source: U.S. Bureau of Economic Analysis, *National Income and Product Accounts of the United States: volume 2, 1959-88,* and *Survey of Current Business,* monthly.

No. 707. Flow of Funds Accounts—Composition of Individuals' Savings: 1970 to 1992

[In billions of dollars. Combined statement for households, farm business, and nonfarm noncorporate business. Minus sign (-) indicates decrease. See *Historical Statistics, Colonial Times to 1970,* series F 566-594, for similar but not exactly comparable data]

COMPOSITION OF SAVINGS	1970	1980	1985	1987	1988	1989	1990	1991	1992
Increase in financial assets	80.5	326.9	581.9	456.8	535.3	593.9	522.1	417.9	483.9
Checkable deposits and currency	7.4	9.2	33.9	6.6	7.4	19.3	22.4	55.3	115.0
Time and savings deposits	43.5	124.9	119.0	114.7	154.8	108.6	21.7	-62.2	-132.6
Money market fund shares	-	24.5	8.7	28.1	23.5	85.9	44.2	28.6	0.7
Securities	1.3	12.5	134.5	127.2	54.5	64.2	175.6	30.4	171.6
U.S. savings bonds	0.3	-7.3	5.3	7.8	8.5	8.2	8.5	11.9	19.1
Other U.S. Treasury securities	-10.4	27.2	9.4	-2.1	38.2	12.1	50.6	-74.9	-29.1
U.S. Government agency securities	4.6	9.3	32.2	56.0	77.1	84.7	43.5	-6.0	3.4
Tax-exempt obligations	-0.1	0.7	79.2	93.1	54.5	62.4	30.3	21.9	20.5
Corporate and foreign bonds	9.6	-10.6	0.9	2.5	-35.6	-5.8	6.5	27.8	-10.3
Open-market paper	-2.2	3.8	60.5	2.0	31.6	-0.1	12.4	-22.2	6.7
Mutual fund shares	2.2	1.7	73.5	71.8	2.3	41.9	50.7	129.2	194.3
Other corporate equities	-2.8	-12.3	-126.5	-103.9	-122.0	-139.1	-27.2	-57.2	-32.9
Private life insurance reserves	5.2	9.7	10.4	25.7	24.9	28.4	25.3	24.4	32.5
Private insured pension reserves	2.9	22.3	63.4	62.7	85.0	77.8	84.4	82.4	71.5
Private noninsured pension reserves	7.2	51.2	71.8	-31.7	24.1	50.6	14.8	103.2	70.0
Government insurance and pension reserves	8.9	35.3	72.3	73.9	84.9	93.3	88.0	82.3	85.4
Miscellaneous financial assets	4.1	37.3	67.9	49.6	76.1	65.7	45.9	73.6	69.9
Gross investment in tangible assets	150.7	406.1	651.8	735.4	778.9	821.9	807.2	743.9	807.2
Owner-occupied homes	31.8	101.6	161.4	198.3	206.6	205.6	190.7	172.2	191.1
Other fixed assets [1]	34.1	98.4	130.8	138.2	145.2	153.8	149.0	126.1	133.5
Consumer durables	85.4	212.5	353.0	403.7	437.1	459.4	464.3	446.1	480.3
Inventories [1]	-0.6	-6.3	6.7	-4.8	-10.0	3.1	3.2	-0.5	2.3
Capital consumption allowances	103.4	314.3	435.5	496.9	532.4	579.7	615.4	649.2	679.7
Owner-occupied homes	14.2	50.3	67.7	75.0	80.0	92.1	93.2	97.5	110.7
Other fixed assets [1]	23.5	77.8	110.6	121.1	127.9	137.5	143.0	147.2	149.5
Consumer durables	65.8	186.2	257.1	300.8	324.5	350.1	379.2	404.5	419.5
Net investment in tangible assets	47.3	91.8	216.3	238.5	246.5	242.2	191.8	94.7	127.5
Owner-occupied homes	17.7	51.3	93.6	123.3	126.5	113.5	97.5	74.6	80.4
Other fixed assets [1]	10.6	20.6	20.2	17.1	17.3	16.4	6.0	-21.1	-16.0
Consumer durables	19.6	26.3	95.8	102.9	112.6	109.3	85.1	41.6	60.8
Inventories [1]	-0.6	-6.3	6.7	-4.8	-10.0	3.1	3.2	-0.5	2.3
Net increase in liabilities	36.7	204.8	437.2	355.9	400.7	379.5	296.3	152.6	205.9
Mortgage debt on nonfarm homes	13.0	96.8	164.2	234.6	241.2	244.7	218.9	128.6	197.9
Other mortgage debt [1]	14.5	50.9	96.5	60.0	56.6	41.3	20.4	-3.3	-26.1
Consumer credit	4.6	2.6	82.3	32.9	50.1	41.7	17.5	-12.5	2.4
Security credit	-1.3	7.3	18.9	-16.3	1.7	-1.0	-3.7	16.3	1.6
Policy loans	2.3	6.7	-0.1	(Z)	-0.1	3.2	4.1	4.8	4.4
Other liabilities [1]	3.7	40.5	75.5	44.9	51.3	49.6	39.2	18.8	25.6
Individuals' saving	91.1	213.9	361.1	339.4	381.0	456.5	417.5	360.0	405.6
Less: Government insurance and pension reserve	8.9	35.3	72.3	73.9	84.9	93.3	88.0	82.3	85.4
Net investment in consumer durables	19.6	26.3	95.8	102.9	112.6	109.3	85.1	41.6	60.8
Net saving by farm corporations	(Z)	0.5	0.9	0.9	1.4	1.8	2.2	1.6	0.8
Equals: Personal saving, flow of funds basis	62.7	151.9	192.1	161.7	182.2	252.1	242.3	234.5	258.6
Personal saving, NIPA basis	57.5	153.9	189.3	142.0	155.7	152.1	175.6	199.6	213.6
Difference [2]	5.2	-2.0	2.9	19.7	26.5	100.0	66.8	34.9	45.0

- Represents or rounds to zero.   Z Less than $50 million.   [1] Includes corporate farms.   [2] Personal saving on national income account basis measures personal saving as income less taxes and consumption; flow-of-funds basis measures the same concept from acquisition of assets less borrowing.

Source: Board of Governors of the Federal Reserve System, *Flow of Funds Accounts,* quarterly.

No. 708. Average Annual Income

[**In dollars**. Based on Consumer Expenditure Survey, integrated data from the Interview and Diary surveys; see text, section for the noninstitutional population. Second, expenditures reported here are

Line no.	CHARACTERISTIC	Income before taxes [1]	Total expenditures	Food, total	FOOD AT HOME					Food away from home	Alcoholic beverages
					Total [2]	Cereal, bakery products	Meats, poultry, fish, eggs	Dairy products	Fruits and vegetables		
1	All consumer units..............	33,901	29,614	4,271	2,651	404	709	294	429	1,620	297
	Age of reference person:										
2	Under 25 years old..............	14,319	16,745	2,528	1,410	225	356	154	177	1,118	252
3	25 to 34 years old...............	34,032	29,280	4,272	2,529	382	662	301	389	1,742	370
4	35 to 44 years old...............	41,871	36,446	5,405	3,324	522	879	369	527	2,080	354
5	45 to 54 years old...............	48,413	38,137	5,184	3,147	462	889	333	496	2,037	360
6	55 to 64 years old...............	38,285	31,945	4,217	2,639	381	729	286	430	1,578	260
7	65 to 74 years old...............	22,723	22,564	3,466	2,364	370	611	251	439	1,102	217
8	75 years old and over	16,247	15,782	2,548	1,864	301	485	213	359	684	81
	Region of residence:										
9	Northeast....................	36,953	31,026	4,506	2,673	435	764	302	446	1,833	355
10	Midwest.....................	31,535	27,675	3,977	2,456	392	601	281	380	1,522	261
11	South	31,706	28,062	4,091	2,589	376	743	274	408	1,502	250
12	West.......................	37,167	33,131	4,695	2,974	436	730	335	509	1,721	358
	Size of consumer unit:										
13	One person..................	18,057	17,569	2,283	1,267	197	311	145	217	1,015	262
14	Two or more persons...........	40,119	34,234	5,032	3,180	484	861	351	510	1,852	310
15	Two persons................	36,955	30,648	4,184	2,541	369	673	273	442	1,643	349
16	Three persons..............	40,124	34,389	4,897	2,999	465	835	323	458	1,898	273
17	Four persons...............	46,196	38,806	5,869	3,754	563	1,038	419	581	2,115	302
18	Five or more persons.........	40,985	38,269	6,583	4,552	739	1,209	530	698	2,031	264
	Single consumers:										
19	No earner	10,327	12,744	1,880	1,383	224	355	169	250	497	80
20	One earner	22,746	20,499	2,517	1,202	182	285	131	198	1,315	367
	Consumer units of two or more persons:										
21	No earner	18,556	19,529	3,546	2,718	412	774	282	477	827	180
22	One earner	31,661	29,407	4,397	2,959	453	805	332	490	1,438	249
23	Two earners................	46,013	37,581	5,235	3,134	477	823	348	500	2,101	353
24	Three or more earners..........	56,122	45,513	6,799	4,130	624	1,164	454	612	2,668	389
	Husband and wife consumer units:										
25	Total	44,460	37,134	5,376	3,353	514	887	372	546	2,023	318
26	Husband and wife only........	40,579	32,937	4,447	2,686	389	698	286	482	1,760	350
	Husband and wife with children:										
27	Oldest child under 6	43,046	36,075	4,610	3,030	456	740	380	478	1,580	295
28	Oldest child 6 to 17	47,983	40,839	6,241	3,877	636	999	449	599	2,364	247
29	Oldest child 18 or over	49,638	41,798	6,631	3,984	608	1,158	409	589	2,647	342
30	One parent, at least one child under 18 ..	20,302	21,653	3,641	2,588	399	761	283	362	1,053	134
31	Single person and other	21,255	20,092	2,762	1,636	246	440	182	269	1,126	292
	Occupation of reference person:										
32	Self employed workers...........	42,939	36,072	5,044	3,011	450	743	333	534	2,033	363
	Wage and salary earners:										
33	Managers and professionals....	53,812	42,802	5,446	2,986	456	730	333	500	2,459	437
34	Technical, sales, and clerical	36,388	31,383	4,440	2,579	410	672	288	405	1,861	327
35	Service workers.............	22,908	23,205	3,822	2,546	360	796	261	385	1,277	246
36	Construction workers/mechanics ..	35,872	29,925	4,401	2,838	424	797	312	420	1,563	290
37	Operators, fabricators, and laborers..	30,249	26,455	4,126	2,653	407	729	308	388	1,474	284
38	Retired	18,614	19,284	3,043	2,194	345	588	240	389	849	163
	Income before taxes:										
39	Complete reporters of income [1]......	33,901	30,487	4,367	2,725	414	725	307	438	1,642	314
	Quintiles of income:										
40	Lowest 20 percent............	5,981	13,464	2,343	1,726	257	502	194	279	617	127
41	Second 20 percent	14,821	18,986	3,306	2,303	344	652	256	374	1,003	190
42	Third 20 percent	26,073	26,144	3,945	2,577	391	690	284	411	1,368	306
43	Fourth 20 percent	40,868	36,151	5,199	3,140	480	801	358	500	2,058	371
44	Highest 20 percent	81,594	57,597	7,033	3,875	597	980	440	624	3,159	575
45	Incomplete reporting of income	([1])	24,903	3,880	2,347	366	642	242	395	1,533	225

[1] Income values derived from "complete income reporters" only. Represents the combined income of all consumer unit members 14 years old and over during the 12 months preceding the interview. A complete reporter is a consumer unit providing values for at least one of the major sources of income.   [2] Includes items not shown separately.   [3] Includes household equipment.

and Expenditures of All Consumer Units: 1991

14 for description. In interpreting the expenditure data, several factors should be considered. First the data are averages
out-of-pocket expenditures]

	HOUSING				Apparel and services	TRANSPORTATION			Health care	Personal insurance and pensions	Other expenditures [5]	Personal taxes	Line no.
Total	Shelter	Fuel, utilities, public services	Household operations, furnishings [3]	Housekeeping supplies		Vehicle purchases	Gasoline, motor oil	All other transportation [4]					
9,252	5,191	1,990	1,648	424	1,735	2,111	995	2,045	1,554	2,787	4,567	3,172	1
4,886	3,059	983	666	178	1,201	1,916	711	1,241	360	967	2,682	799	2
9,888	5,944	1,799	1,773	370	1,722	2,196	1,013	1,967	1,030	2,903	3,919	3,169	3
11,335	6,621	2,208	1,998	507	2,347	2,682	1,197	2,425	1,487	3,811	5,403	4,288	4
11,208	6,239	2,493	1,988	488	2,245	2,553	1,316	2,836	1,727	4,317	6,391	4,585	5
9,457	4,901	2,247	1,810	499	1,622	2,215	1,048	2,262	1,846	3,462	5,555	3,884	6
6,849	3,328	1,920	1,172	430	1,270	1,535	758	1,612	2,300	1,033	3,521	1,384	7
5,871	2,834	1,586	1,136	315	638	528	385	852	2,197	268	2,413	1,634	8
10,341	6,262	2,105	1,576	396	1,877	1,812	884	2,159	1,504	2,883	4,705	3,767	9
8,289	4,307	1,950	1,605	428	1,641	2,162	988	1,920	1,482	2,582	4,371	2,411	10
8,303	4,339	2,031	1,540	392	1,683	2,333	1,035	1,871	1,669	2,621	4,207	2,817	11
10,895	6,592	1,853	1,951	499	1,792	1,990	1,053	2,364	1,506	3,215	5,261	4,044	12
6,143	3,847	1,246	831	219	980	971	499	1,152	1,014	1,233	3,032	1,739	13
10,446	5,707	2,275	1,961	502	2,024	2,549	1,186	2,387	1,761	3,383	5,156	3,734	14
9,253	4,989	2,044	1,744	477	1,596	2,491	1,002	2,208	1,862	3,018	4,682	3,848	15
10,600	5,890	2,279	1,966	465	2,150	2,432	1,208	2,392	1,759	3,385	5,291	3,428	16
12,176	6,701	2,502	2,416	556	2,356	2,572	1,393	2,735	1,705	4,157	5,541	4,451	17
11,343	6,173	2,640	1,972	557	2,624	2,871	1,409	2,423	1,546	3,397	5,809	2,908	18
4,936	2,784	1,279	658	216	561	409	281	632	1,457	107	2,401	380	19
6,881	4,502	1,225	932	221	1,226	1,318	633	1,473	741	1,927	3,415	2,563	20
6,476	3,062	1,872	1,136	406	1,094	1,191	606	1,290	2,096	310	2,741	1,398	21
9,598	5,156	2,196	1,788	459	1,788	2,344	1,008	1,827	1,668	2,398	4,129	2,609	22
11,430	6,434	2,256	2,224	515	2,142	2,866	1,279	2,651	1,670	4,319	5,636	4,637	23
12,385	6,750	2,855	2,164	616	2,903	3,117	1,742	3,568	1,945	4,963	7,700	4,988	24
11,173	6,060	2,377	2,190	546	2,117	2,777	1,288	2,609	1,963	3,858	5,657	4,301	25
9,746	5,120	2,157	1,941	527	1,644	2,641	1,066	2,380	2,131	3,397	5,136	4,480	26
12,937	7,281	2,104	3,093	458	2,222	2,537	1,180	2,252	1,614	3,892	4,537	3,921	27
12,510	7,021	2,482	2,444	564	2,452	2,918	1,396	2,705	1,733	4,472	6,166	4,537	28
11,035	5,837	2,763	1,792	643	2,580	2,930	1,682	3,280	2,252	4,107	6,961	3,974	29
7,788	4,458	1,781	1,216	333	1,763	1,232	646	1,243	779	1,380	3,047	1,418	30
6,733	4,068	1,469	937	258	1,177	1,301	633	1,366	1,095	1,483	3,252	1,868	31
10,933	6,139	2,411	1,863	520	2,007	2,413	1,132	2,380	2,121	4,077	5,601	3,596	32
13,355	7,925	2,303	2,580	548	2,612	3,220	1,187	2,967	1,659	5,101	6,818	6,025	33
9,826	5,727	1,961	1,706	433	1,916	2,292	1,066	2,270	1,321	3,155	4,773	3,463	34
7,543	4,168	1,734	1,303	337	1,589	1,014	874	1,558	1,267	1,794	3,499	1,591	35
8,851	4,997	1,972	1,501	381	1,385	2,538	1,317	2,071	1,285	3,087	4,699	3,197	36
7,597	4,108	1,867	1,265	357	1,452	2,274	1,209	1,955	1,175	2,531	3,850	2,453	37
6,309	3,026	1,753	1,167	363	959	1,152	604	1,310	2,096	522	3,126	1,379	38
9,325	5,208	1,961	1,704	451	1,801	2,154	998	2,084	1,563	3,142	4,740	3,172	39
4,905	2,741	1,291	639	235	813	670	471	754	1,041	296	2,044	333	40
6,178	3,343	1,652	860	324	1,112	1,209	721	1,266	1,371	907	2,729	513	41
7,975	4,405	1,893	1,288	388	1,443	1,960	1,011	1,850	1,580	2,224	3,851	2,099	42
10,644	5,917	2,171	2,026	530	2,103	2,961	1,271	2,607	1,672	3,999	5,326	3,632	43
16,898	9,621	2,795	3,704	779	3,530	3,963	1,514	3,933	2,149	8,265	9,738	9,263	44
8,939	5,087	2,162	1,380	310	1,451	1,851	978	1,831	1,503	642	3,602	(¹)	45

[4] Includes other vehicle expenses and public transportation. [5] Includes entertainment, personal care, reading, education, tobacco smoking supplies, cash contributions, and miscellaneous expenditures. For additional data on entertainment and reading, see table 399.

Source: U.S. Bureau of Labor Statistics, *Consumer Expenditures in 1991* (BLS Report 835, December 1992); and unpublished data.

No. 709. Average Annual Expenditures of All Consumer Units: 1984 to 1991

[In dollars, except as indicated. For explanation of average annual percent change, see Guide to Tabular Presentation. Minus sign (-) indicates decrease. See headnote, table 708]

ITEM	1984	1985	1989	1990	1991	AVERAGE ANNUAL PERCENT CHANGE	
						1984-91	1990-91
All consumer units (1,000)	90,233	91,564	95,818	96,968	97,918	1	1
Total expenditures	21,975	23,490	27,810	28,381	29,614	4	4
Food, total	3,290	3,477	4,152	4,296	4,271	4	-1
Food at home, total	1,970	2,037	2,390	2,485	2,651	4	7
Cereal and bakery products.	262	283	359	368	404	6	10
Meats, poultry, fish, and eggs	586	579	611	668	709	3	6
Dairy products	253	266	304	295	294	2	(-Z)
Fruits and vegetables.	313	322	408	408	429	5	5
Other food at home.	556	585	708	746	815	5	9
Food away from home	1,320	1,441	1,762	1,811	1,620	3	-11
Alcoholic beverages.	275	306	284	293	297	1	1
Tobacco products and smoking supplies . .	228	219	261	274	276	3	1
Housing, total	6,556	6,963	8,434	8,703	9,252	5	6
Shelter	3,370	3,709	4,660	4,836	5,191	6	7
Fuels, utilities, and public services. . . .	1,638	1,648	1,835	1,890	1,990	3	5
Household operations and furnishings . .	1,241	1,282	1,546	1,571	1,648	4	5
Housekeeping supplies	307	325	394	406	424	5	4
Apparel and services	1,319	1,420	1,582	1,618	1,735	4	7
Transportation, total.	4,304	4,587	5,187	5,120	5,151	3	1
Vehicle purchase	1,813	2,043	2,291	2,129	2,111	2	-1
Gasoline and motor oil	1,058	1,035	985	1,047	995	-1	-5
Other transportation	1,433	1,509	1,911	1,944	2,045	5	5
Health care	1,049	1,108	1,407	1,480	1,554	6	5
Life insurance.	300	278	346	345	356	2	3
Pensions and Social Security.	1,598	1,738	2,125	2,248	2,431	6	8
Other expenditures [1]	3,055	3,393	4,030	4,003	4,291	5	7

Z Less than 0.5 percent. [1] Includes entertainment, personal care, reading, education, cash contributions, and miscellaneous expenditures. For data on entertainment and reading, see table 399.

Source: U.S. Bureau of Labor Statistics, *Consumer Expenditures in 1991*, (BLS Report 835, December 1992); and unpublished data.

No. 710. Average Annual Expenditures of All Consumer Units in Selected Metropolitan Statistical Areas: 1991

[In dollars. Metropolitan areas defined June 30, 1983, CMSA=Consolidated Metropolitan Statistical Area; MSA=Metropolitan Statistical Area; PMSA=Primary Metropolitan Statistical Area. See text, section 1, and Appendix II. See headnote, table 708]

METROPOLITAN STATISTICAL AREA	Total expenditures [1]	Food	HOUSING		Apparel and services	TRANSPORTATION			Health care
			Total [1]	Shelter		Total [1]	Vehicle purchases	Gasoline and motor oil	
Anchorage, AK MSA.	43,991	5,577	13,502	8,461	2,273	7,531	3,112	1,165	1,730
Atlanta, GA MSA	34,163	4,187	10,788	6,051	2,306	5,807	2,076	1,112	1,778
Baltimore, MD MSA	33,208	4,512	11,065	6,900	1,938	5,498	2,201	1,051	1,401
Boston-Lawrence-Salem, MA-NH CMSA.	30,835	4,183	11,341	7,582	1,855	4,696	1,739	881	1,498
Buffalo-Niagara Falls, NY CMSA. . . .	25,119	4,556	8,006	4,569	1,351	4,521	1,940	768	1,149
Chicago-Gary-Lake County, IL-IN-WI CMSA.	32,568	5,109	10,536	6,372	2,306	4,955	1,728	1,015	1,439
Cincinnati-Hamilton, OH-KY-IN CMSA .	27,781	4,688	8,180	4,510	1,825	4,857	1,904	1,054	1,583
Cleveland-Akron-Lorain, OH CMSA . . .	26,960	4,233	7,754	3,982	2,222	4,555	1,748	893	1,430
Dallas-Fort Worth, TX CMSA	33,500	4,741	10,097	5,358	1,999	6,413	2,612	1,293	1,543
Detroit-Ann Arbor, MI CMSA	29,732	4,123	9,698	5,687	1,573	5,748	2,398	1,114	1,304
Honolulu, HI MSA.	36,394	5,634	11,196	7,432	1,728	6,052	2,523	852	1,623
Houston-Galveston-Brazoria, TX CMSA.	32,298	4,681	9,094	4,730	2,063	6,692	2,774	1,237	1,458
Kansas City, MO-Kansas City, KS CMSA.	28,189	4,427	8,679	4,776	1,485	4,661	1,588	987	1,964
Los Angeles-Long Beach, CA PMSA . .	35,673	5,044	12,964	7,977	2,456	5,372	1,945	1,103	1,485
Miami-Fort Lauderdale, FL CMSA	32,053	5,193	10,117	5,931	1,822	5,788	2,018	950	1,686
Milwaukee, WI PMSA	27,843	4,091	9,083	5,507	1,652	4,622	1,937	867	1,228
Minneapolis-St. Paul, MN-WI MSA. . . .	34,801	4,883	10,519	6,370	1,942	5,665	2,053	1,146	1,438
New York-Northern New Jersey-Long Island, NY-NJ-CT CMSA	34,583	5,131	12,121	7,770	2,366	4,873	1,560	784	1,533
Philadelphia-Wilmington-Trenton, PA-NJ-DE-MD CMSA	31,795	4,526	10,350	5,710	2,103	4,832	1,747	863	1,648
Pittsburgh-Beaver Valley, PA CMSA . .	28,626	4,458	9,104	4,254	1,886	4,699	1,941	819	1,290
Portland-Vancouver, OR-WA CMSA. . .	29,228	4,081	8,974	5,468	1,447	5,275	2,177	1,033	1,318
San Diego, CA MSA	32,983	4,457	11,365	7,691	1,808	6,076	2,301	1,184	1,178
San Francisco-Oakland-San Jose, CA CMSA.	39,707	5,284	13,883	9,417	2,413	6,116	2,286	1,029	1,536
Seattle-Tacoma, WA CMSA	35,086	4,599	11,523	7,235	1,768	5,701	1,815	1,090	1,646
St. Louis-East St. Louis-Alton, MO-IL CMSA	27,743	3,692	8,557	4,339	1,385	4,822	1,696	1,037	1,416
Washington, DC-MD-VA MSA.	38,560	4,752	12,322	7,891	2,562	6,192	2,471	1,007	1,962

[1] Includes items not shown separately.

Source: U.S. Bureau of Labor Statistics, *Consumer Expenditure Survey, 1990-91*, forthcoming.

No. 711. Money Income of Households—Percent Distribution, by Income Level, in Constant (1991) Dollars, by Race and Hispanic Origin of Householder: 1970 to 1991

[Constant dollars based on CPI-U-X1 deflator. Households as of **March** of **following year.** Based on Current Population Survey. See text, sections 1 and 14, and Appendix III. For definition of median, see Guide to Tabular Presentation]

RACE AND HISPANIC ORIGIN OF HOUSEHOLDER AND YEAR	Number of house-holds (1,000)	PERCENT DISTRIBUTION, BY INCOME LEVEL							Median income (dol.)
		Under $10,000	$10,000-$14,999	$15,000-$24,999	$25,000-$34,999	$35,000-$49,999	$50,000-$74,999	$75,000 and over	
ALL HOUSEHOLDS [1]									
1970	64,778	16.2	8.7	18.0	19.0	19.8	12.8	5.4	28,803
1975	72,867	15.7	10.1	18.5	16.7	19.6	13.7	5.7	28,597
1980	82,368	15.4	9.4	18.3	16.1	18.8	14.7	7.2	29,309
1985 [2]	88,458	15.3	9.2	17.6	15.7	17.7	15.3	9.2	29,896
1988 [3]	92,830	14.7	9.0	16.7	15.1	17.7	16.0	10.8	31,344
1989	93,347	14.0	8.9	16.8	15.0	17.7	16.2	11.4	31,750
1990	94,312	14.2	9.2	17.0	15.6	17.5	15.7	10.8	31,203
1991	95,669	14.9	9.4	17.4	15.2	17.3	15.4	10.4	30,126
WHITE									
1970	57,575	14.9	8.2	17.5	19.4	20.7	13.5	5.8	30,000
1975	64,392	14.1	9.7	18.2	17.0	20.3	14.6	6.2	29,906
1980	71,872	13.6	9.0	18.1	16.3	19.6	15.6	7.9	30,921
1985 [2]	76,576	13.6	8.7	17.3	16.0	18.4	16.1	9.9	31,529
1988 [3]	79,734	12.6	8.5	16.6	15.4	18.5	16.9	11.7	33,136
1989	80,163	12.2	8.5	16.6	15.2	18.4	17.0	12.2	33,398
1990	80,968	12.2	8.9	16.9	15.9	18.0	16.5	11.5	32,545
1991	81,675	12.8	9.1	17.3	15.4	17.9	16.3	11.2	31,569
BLACK									
1970	6,180	28.8	13.5	22.4	15.6	12.0	6.3	1.3	18,260
1975	7,489	30.1	14.0	20.6	14.3	13.3	6.2	1.5	17,953
1980	8,847	30.7	13.4	20.2	14.0	12.1	7.6	2.1	17,814
1985 [2]	9,797	29.7	12.7	20.2	13.1	12.8	8.5	2.9	18,758
1988 [3]	10,561	30.3	12.7	18.0	13.1	12.2	9.7	4.1	18,890
1989	10,486	28.9	11.8	18.8	13.5	13.2	9.5	4.3	19,862
1990	10,671	29.7	11.6	18.3	13.8	13.3	8.8	4.4	19,462
1991	11,083	30.8	11.6	18.2	13.8	13.4	8.4	3.7	18,807
HISPANIC [4]									
1975	2,948	20.4	13.8	24.3	17.2	15.6	6.8	2.0	21,484
1980	3,906	19.9	13.0	22.7	16.4	15.2	9.6	3.2	22,591
1985 [2]	5,213	21.6	13.5	20.2	16.2	14.6	10.0	3.9	22,107
1988 [3]	5,910	21.0	12.0	20.0	16.3	15.2	10.3	5.3	23,440
1989	5,933	19.7	11.5	20.5	15.6	15.6	11.6	5.5	24,078
1990	6,220	20.0	13.1	20.0	16.7	15.5	9.5	5.1	23,270
1991	6,379	20.7	12.1	21.6	15.8	14.8	10.0	5.0	22,691

[1] Includes other races not shown separately. [2] Beginning 1983, data based on revised Hispanic population controls and not directly comparable with prior years. [3] Beginning 1987, data based on revised processing procedures and not directly comparable with prior years. See text, section 14, and source. [4] Persons of Hispanic origin may be of any race. Income data for Hispanic origin households are not available prior to 1972.

No. 712. Money Income of Households—Median Household Income in Current and Constant (1991) Dollars, by Race and Hispanic Origin of Householder: 1970 to 1991

[See headnote, table 711. Minus sign (-) indicates decrease]

YEAR	MEDIAN INCOME IN CURRENT DOLLARS				MEDIAN INCOME IN CONSTANT (1991) DOLLARS				ANNUAL PER-CENT CHANGE FOR ALL HOUSE-HOLDS [3]	
	All house-holds [1]	White	Black	His-panic [2]	All house-holds [1]	White	Black	His-panic [2]	Current dollars	Constant (1991) dollars
1970	8,734	9,097	5,537	(NA)	28,803	30,000	18,260	(NA)	[4]6.9	[4]2.4
1975	11,800	12,340	7,408	8,865	28,597	29,906	17,953	21,484	[5]6.2	[5]-0.1
1978 [6]	15,064	15,660	9,411	11,803	30,396	31,598	18,989	23,816	11.0	3.9
1979 [6]	16,461	17,259	10,133	13,042	30,297	31,766	18,650	24,004	9.3	-0.3
1980	17,710	18,684	10,764	13,651	29,309	30,921	17,814	22,591	7.6	-3.3
1981	19,074	20,153	11,309	15,300	28,833	30,464	17,095	23,128	7.7	-1.6
1982 [7]	20,171	21,117	11,968	15,178	28,737	30,085	17,051	21,624	5.8	-0.3
1983 [7]	21,018	22,035	12,473	15,794	28,741	30,132	17,056	21,598	4.2	(Z)
1984	22,415	23,647	13,471	16,992	29,383	30,998	17,659	22,274	6.6	2.2
1985	23,618	24,908	14,819	17,465	29,896	31,529	18,758	22,107	5.4	1.7
1986	24,897	26,175	15,080	18,352	30,940	32,528	18,740	22,806	5.4	3.5
1987 [8]	26,061	27,458	15,672	19,336	31,246	32,921	18,790	23,183	4.7	1.0
1988	27,225	28,781	16,407	20,359	31,344	33,136	18,890	23,440	4.5	0.3
1989	28,906	30,406	18,083	21,921	31,750	33,398	19,862	24,078	6.2	1.3
1990	29,943	31,231	18,676	22,330	31,203	32,545	19,462	23,270	3.6	-1.7
1991	30,126	31,569	18,807	22,691	30,126	31,569	18,807	22,691	0.6	-3.5

NA Not available. Z Less than .05 percent. [1] Includes other races not shown separately. [2] Hispanic persons may be of any race. [3] Change from preceding year unless noted otherwise. [4] Change from 1967. [5] Change from 1970. [6] Population controls based on 1980 census; see text, sections 1 and 14. [7] Beginning 1983, data based on revised Hispanic population controls and not directly comparable with prior years. [8] Beginning 1987, based on revised processing procedures and not directly comparable with prior years. See text, section 14, and source.

Source of tables 711 and 712: U.S. Bureau of the Census, *Current Population Reports*, P60-180; and unpublished data.

No. 713. Money Income of Households—Percent Distribution, by Income Level, for Selected Characteristics: 1991

[See headnote, table 711. For composition of regions, see table 31]

CHARACTERISTIC	Number of house-holds (1,000)	PERCENT DISTRIBUTION OF HOUSEHOLDS BY INCOME LEVEL								Median income (dollars)
		Under $5,000	$5,000-$9,999	$10,000-$14,999	$15,000-$24,999	$25,000-$34,999	$35,000-$49,999	$50,000-$74,999	$75,000 and over	
Total [1]	95,669	4.8	10.1	9.4	17.4	15.2	17.3	15.4	10.4	30,126
Age of householder:										
15 to 24 years	4,859	11.8	14.6	13.9	27.2	16.8	10.4	4.1	1.2	18,313
25 to 34 years	20,007	4.8	7.4	8.0	18.5	18.3	21.6	14.7	6.6	30,842
35 to 44 years	21,774	3.1	5.2	5.8	13.4	15.7	21.8	21.3	13.6	39,349
45 to 54 years	15,547	3.8	4.8	5.5	11.4	13.3	18.2	23.7	19.2	43,751
55 to 64 years	12,560	4.6	9.0	7.7	16.0	14.8	17.9	16.1	14.0	33,304
65 years and over . .	20,921	5.6	21.4	17.4	23.4	13.0	9.2	5.8	4.1	16,975
White	81,675	3.7	9.1	9.1	17.3	15.4	17.9	16.3	11.2	31,569
Black	11,083	12.6	18.2	11.6	18.2	13.8	13.4	8.4	3.7	18,807
Hispanic [2]	6,379	6.8	13.9	12.1	21.6	15.8	14.8	10.0	5.0	22,691
Northeast	19,314	4.2	10.4	8.4	15.4	13.4	17.8	17.2	13.2	33,467
Midwest	23,327	4.6	10.1	9.3	17.5	15.8	18.7	15.0	9.0	29,927
South	33,073	6.1	10.9	10.4	18.6	15.6	16.2	13.8	8.4	27,178
West	19,955	3.4	8.5	8.9	17.1	15.6	17.2	16.6	12.6	32,253
Size of household:										
One person	23,974	9.3	23.3	16.2	21.7	13.3	9.6	4.4	2.2	15,441
Two persons	30,734	3.3	6.2	8.8	19.9	17.2	18.4	15.6	10.6	31,221
Three persons	16,398	4.0	5.8	6.1	14.0	15.0	21.3	20.4	13.4	38,244
Four persons	14,710	2.8	4.7	5.2	10.8	14.4	21.9	23.5	16.8	43,054
Five persons	6,389	2.6	4.7	5.8	13.9	15.1	20.1	22.6	15.2	40,792
Six persons	2,126	3.0	5.6	6.7	15.8	16.1	19.3	18.4	15.1	36,894
Seven persons or more	1,338	3.8	6.8	10.4	14.4	15.7	17.4	16.4	15.0	34,136
Family households	67,173	3.3	5.8	7.1	15.9	15.7	19.8	19.1	13.3	36,404
Married-couple families	52,457	1.4	3.1	5.7	14.6	15.9	21.2	22.1	16.0	41,075
Male householder, wife absent	3,025	3.2	6.2	8.8	20.1	18.4	20.6	15.0	7.7	31,010
Female householder, husband absent . . .	11,692	12.2	17.7	13.0	20.3	14.3	12.9	6.9	2.6	17,961
Nonfamily households .	28,496	8.2	20.3	14.7	21.0	14.0	11.6	6.5	3.6	17,774
Male householder . . .	12,428	6.7	12.6	12.8	21.2	16.8	14.9	9.4	5.7	23,022
Female householder . .	16,068	9.3	26.3	16.2	20.9	11.9	9.1	4.3	2.0	14,321
Educational attainment of householder: [3]										
Total	90,810	4.4	9.9	9.2	16.9	15.1	17.7	16.0	10.9	31,032
Less than 9th grade . . .	9,357	10.9	26.6	18.2	21.7	10.5	7.4	3.4	1.1	13,221
9th to 12th grade (no diploma)	10,362	9.3	19.7	14.5	22.2	14.0	11.2	6.9	2.2	17,535
High school graduate . .	30,178	4.0	9.5	9.9	19.7	17.8	19.5	14.2	5.4	28,487
Some college, no degree	14,984	2.9	6.1	7.7	16.4	16.7	21.5	19.1	9.7	35,150
Associate degree . . .	5,041	2.1	4.5	6.0	13.2	16.9	23.0	22.2	12.1	39,700
Bachelor's degree or more	20,889	1.3	2.0	3.2	9.1	12.4	19.0	24.9	28.1	52,270
Bachelor's degree . . .	13,137	1.3	2.3	3.9	10.7	13.4	20.0	25.8	22.6	48,705
Master's degree . .	5,211	1.4	1.8	2.1	6.8	12.1	19.8	25.2	30.8	55,173
Professional degree . .	1,586	0.9	0.8	2.0	5.6	7.9	11.0	18.2	53.6	77,949
Doctorate degree . . .	955	0.9	1.3	0.7	4.8	7.9	14.8	22.8	46.9	70,316
Tenure:										
Owner occupied	61,310	2.6	6.6	7.5	15.2	14.7	19.4	19.7	14.3	37,257
Renter occupied	32,705	8.5	16.2	12.6	21.3	16.2	13.9	7.8	3.4	20,696
Occupier paid no cash rent	1,654	12.6	18.7	17.1	20.0	13.9	9.6	5.0	3.3	15,629

[1] Includes other races not shown separately.   [2] Persons of Hispanic origin may be of any race.   [3] 25 years old and over.

Source: U.S. Bureau of the Census, *Current Population Reports*, P60-180; and unpublished data.

No. 714. Money Income of Households—Aggregate and Mean Income, by Race and Hispanic Origin of Householder: 1991

[See headnote, table 711]

CHARACTERISTIC	ALL RACES [1]		WHITE		BLACK		HISPANIC [2]	
	Aggregate money income (bil. dol.)	Mean income (dol.)	Aggregate money income (bil. dol.)	Mean income (dol.)	Aggregate money income (bil. dol.)	Mean income (dol.)	Aggregate money income (bil. dol.)	Mean income (dol.)
Total	3,628	37,922	3,228	39,523	278	25,043	184	28,872
Age of householder:								
15 to 24 years old	103	21,219	90	22,560	9	13,057	11	19,470
25 to 34 years old	705	35,252	615	36,897	26	21,662	50	27,223
35 to 44 years old	985	45,253	868	47,347	82	31,081	52	31,489
45 to 54 years old	788	50,700	702	52,831	56	32,763	35	35,549
55 to 64 years old	535	42,592	481	44,660	37	26,346	24	33,343
65 years old and over	511	24,424	472	25,331	30	15,654	13	19,935
Region:								
Northeast	804	41,647	729	43,058	54	28,252	30	26,851
Midwest	856	36,715	788	38,033	55	24,613	14	30,200
South	1,147	34,685	989	37,202	139	23,328	56	28,265
West	820	41,091	722	41,394	29	30,303	84	29,901
Size of household:								
One person	503	20,984	443	21,606	47	15,964	14	15,834
Two persons	1,221	39,724	1,119	41,282	73	25,178	40	29,420
Three persons	725	44,238	645	46,719	58	28,092	37	29,621
Four persons	723	49,138	641	51,516	52	31,417	40	31,789
Five persons	301	47,057	259	49,279	27	31,295	27	32,269
Six persons	97	45,677	79	48,241	12	31,833	13	32,070
Seven persons or more	58	43,341	42	45,934	9	28,949	13	34,427

[1] Includes other races not shown separately.   [2] Persons of Hispanic origin may be of any race.

Source: U.S. Bureau of the Census, *Current Population Reports*, P60-180.

No. 715. Money Income of Households—Median Income and Income Level, by Household Type: 1991

[See headnote, table 711]

ITEM	All households	FAMILY HOUSEHOLDS				NONFAMILY HOUSEHOLDS		
		Total	Married couple	Male householder, wife absent	Female householder, husband absent	Total [1]	Single-person household	
							Male householder	Female householder
MEDIAN INCOME (dollars)								
All households	30,126	36,404	41,075	31,010	17,961	17,774	23,022	14,321
White	31,569	38,229	41,584	31,634	21,213	18,461	24,531	14,790
Black	18,807	22,203	33,369	26,428	12,196	12,202	15,223	9,520
Hispanic [2]	22,691	24,551	28,833	23,298	13,323	15,733	19,009	11,420
NUMBER (1,000)								
All households	95,669	67,173	52,457	3,025	11,692	28,496	12,428	16,068
Under $5,000	4,576	2,246	716	97	1,432	2,330	828	1,502
$5,000 to $9,999	9,660	3,864	1,603	188	2,073	5,796	1,568	4,228
$10,000 to $14,999	8,992	4,798	3,011	265	1,521	4,194	1,592	2,602
$15,000 to $19,999	8,376	5,127	3,553	286	1,288	3,248	1,344	1,905
$20,000 to $24,999	8,255	5,521	4,109	321	1,090	2,735	1,287	1,447
$25,000 to $34,999	14,553	10,561	8,335	558	1,668	3,993	2,085	1,907
$35,000 to $49,999	16,586	13,278	11,142	623	1,513	3,308	1,846	1,462
$50,000 and over	24,670	21,779	19,987	686	1,105	2,892	1,877	1,015

[1] Includes other nonfamily households not shown separately.   [2] Persons of Hispanic origin may be of any race.

Source: U.S. Bureau of the Census, *Current Population Reports*, P60-180; and unpublished data.

No. 716. Money Income of Households—Percent Distribution, by Income Quintile and Top 5 Percent for Selected Characteristics: 1991

[See headnote, table 711. For composition of regions, see table 31]

CHARACTERISTIC	Number (1,000)	PERCENT DISTRIBUTION						
		Total	Lowest fifth	Second fifth	Third fifth	Fourth fifth	Highest fifth	Top 5 percent
All households	95,669	100.0	20.0	20.0	20.0	20.0	20.0	5.0
White	81,675	100.0	17.7	19.8	20.3	20.8	21.4	5.4
Black	11,083	100.0	37.2	21.8	18.1	14.0	8.9	1.4
Hispanic [1]	6,379	100.0	27.9	24.4	20.7	15.9	11.1	2.3
Northeast	19,314	100.0	19.2	17.7	18.1	20.8	24.3	6.5
Midwest	23,327	100.0	19.7	20.0	20.9	21.2	18.2	4.1
South	33,073	100.0	22.5	21.7	20.3	18.9	16.7	4.1
West	19,955	100.0	17.0	19.5	20.4	19.7	23.4	6.2
Family households	67,173	100.0	12.7	17.7	20.7	23.5	25.4	6.4
Married-couple families	52,457	100.0	7.2	16.0	21.0	25.7	30.2	7.8
Male householder	3,025	100.0	14.4	22.1	23.7	23.7	16.2	3.0
Female householder	11,692	100.0	37.1	24.3	18.8	13.5	6.3	1.2
Nonfamily households	28,496	100.0	37.2	25.4	18.3	11.8	7.3	1.7
Male householder	12,428	100.0	26.6	24.8	22.0	15.4	11.1	2.7
Living alone	9,613	100.0	31.7	26.8	21.7	12.3	7.5	1.9
Female householder	16,068	100.0	45.3	25.8	15.4	9.1	4.4	0.9
Living alone	14,361	100.0	49.4	26.3	14.5	7.2	2.6	0.6
15 to 24 years old	4,859	100.0	34.3	30.9	20.9	10.5	3.3	0.4
25 to 34 years old	20,007	100.0	16.4	20.3	24.5	23.9	14.9	2.6
35 to 44 years old	21,774	100.0	11.4	14.8	20.6	26.0	27.2	6.1
45 to 54 years old	15,547	100.0	11.6	12.8	17.4	23.2	34.9	9.7
55 to 64 years old	12,560	100.0	17.9	17.6	19.6	20.8	24.1	7.4
65 years old and over	20,921	100.0	36.5	29.4	17.0	9.4	7.7	2.2
65 to 74 years old	12,043	100.0	30.0	29.0	19.6	11.4	10.0	2.9
75 years old and over	8,878	100.0	45.2	30.1	13.4	6.7	4.6	1.4
Worked	68,876	100.0	10.2	17.6	21.9	24.5	25.7	6.4
Worked at full-time jobs	60,739	100.0	7.2	16.6	22.4	26.1	27.7	6.8
Worked at part-time jobs	8,138	100.0	32.6	25.1	18.5	12.6	11.2	3.4
Did not work	26,793	100.0	45.2	26.1	15.1	8.3	5.3	1.3

[1] Persons of Hispanic origin may be of any race.

Source: U.S. Bureau of the Census, *Current Population Reports*, P60-180.

No. 717. Households, by Race and Hispanic Origin—Percent Distribution, by Income Level: 1991

TYPE OF HOUSE-HOLD AND RACE	Total number of households (1,000)	PERCENT DISTRIBUTION BY INCOME LEVEL									Median income (dollars)
		Less than $5,000	$5,000 to $9,999	$10,000 to $14,999	$15,000 to $24,999	$25,000 to $34,999	$35,000 to $49,999	$50,000 to $74,999	$75,000 to $99,999	$100,000 or more	
HOUSEHOLDS											
Total [1]	95,669	4.8	10.1	9.4	17.4	15.2	17.3	15.4	6.0	4.4	30,126
White	81,675	3.7	9.1	9.1	17.3	15.4	17.9	16.3	6.4	4.8	31,569
Black	11,083	12.6	18.2	11.6	18.2	13.8	13.4	8.4	2.5	1.2	18,807
Asian, Pacific Islander [2]	2,094	5.1	6.7	7.4	15.1	13.7	16.5	18.2	9.2	8.2	36,449
Hispanic [2]	6,379	6.8	13.9	12.1	21.6	15.9	14.8	10.0	2.9	2.1	22,691
FAMILIES											
Total [1]	67,173	3.3	5.8	7.1	15.9	15.7	19.8	19.1	7.6	5.7	36,404
White	57,224	2.3	4.5	6.6	15.6	16.0	20.5	20.2	8.1	6.2	38,229
Black	7,716	10.7	14.3	11.1	18.5	14.5	15.4	10.7	3.2	1.5	22,203
Asian, Pacific Islander [2]	1,624	3.9	5.9	6.6	12.2	13.2	17.0	20.9	10.8	9.3	41,907
Hispanic [2]	5,177	5.6	11.7	11.9	21.7	16.6	15.4	11.3	3.3	2.4	24,551
NONFAMILIES											
Total [1]	28,496	8.2	20.3	14.7	21.0	14.0	11.6	6.5	2.1	1.5	17,774
White	24,451	6.9	19.7	15.0	21.4	14.2	11.9	7.0	2.3	1.6	18,461
Black	3,367	16.8	27.1	12.9	17.6	12.2	8.7	3.2	1.0	0.6	12,202
Asian, Pacific Islander [2]	470	9.1	9.4	10.4	25.3	14.9	14.9	8.9	3.4	4.3	23,388
Hispanic [2]	1,202	12.0	23.0	13.0	21.3	12.1	12.2	4.7	1.1	0.7	15,733

[1] Includes other races not shown separately. [2] Persons of Hispanic origin may be of any race.

Source: U.S. Bureau of the Census, *Current Population Reports*, P60-180; and unpublished data.

No. 718. Income Summary Measures by Household Type, in Constant (1989) Dollars: 1969 and 1989

[Households as of **March of the following year. Young couple:** married couple with husband under 45 years old; **empty nester:** married couple with husband 45 to 64 years old; **mature couple:** married couple with husband 65 years old and over; **young single:** householder under 45 years old who is living alone; **older single:** householder 45 years old and over who is living alone; **multiple members:** households consisting of multiple unrelated individuals living together, may also include a small number of single parent households with children over 18 years old]

TYPE OF HOUSEHOLD AND RACE	HOUSEHOLDS				Mean income (dollars)		AGGREGATE INCOME			
	Number (1,000)		Percent of total				Total (mil. dol.)		Percent of total	
	1969	1989	1969	1989	1969	1989	1969	1989	1969	1989
All races, total.	63,393	93,347	100.0	100.0	30,009	36,520	1,902,453	3,409,072	100.0	100.0
Households with children:										
Dual earner married-couples .	12,703	17,869	20.0	19.1	38,695	49,617	491,553	886,624	25.8	26.0
Other married-couples.	13,499	7,674	21.3	8.2	35,563	39,996	480,094	306,934	25.2	9.0
Single parents	3,753	8,820	5.9	9.4	17,508	21,396	65,707	188,723	3.5	5.5
Households without children:										
Young couples.	3,787	6,076	6.0	6.5	33,115	48,343	125,404	293,735	6.6	8.6
Empty nesters	9,323	11,999	14.7	12.9	39,538	53,766	368,632	645,126	19.4	18.9
Mature couples	5,414	8,699	8.5	9.3	20,938	32,273	113,369	280,749	6.0	8.2
Young singles	2,159	8,320	3.4	8.9	20,252	25,242	43,734	210,028	2.3	6.2
Older singles	8,692	14,678	13.7	15.7	11,890	17,507	103,367	256,973	5.4	7.5
Other multiple members	4,063	9,212	6.4	9.9	27,214	36,929	110,590	340,178	5.8	10.0
White, total.	56,593	80,143	100.0	100.0	31,157	38,050	1,763,418	3,049,453	100.0	100.0
Households with children:										
Dual earner married-couples .	11,198	15,659	19.8	19.5	39,699	49,938	444,571	781,991	25.2	25.6
Other married-couples.	12,554	6,646	22.2	8.3	36,508	41,879	458,325	278,316	26.0	9.1
Single parents	2,528	5,721	4.5	7.1	19,506	23,905	49,317	136,772	2.8	4.5
Households without children:										
Young couples.	3,443	5,433	6.1	6.8	33,562	49,148	115,556	267,007	6.6	8.8
Empty nesters	8,736	11,138	15.4	13.9	40,423	54,715	353,145	609,402	20.0	20.0
Mature couples	5,096	8,086	9.0	10.1	21,420	32,791	109,151	265,157	6.2	8.7
Young singles	1,779	7,032	3.1	8.8	21,410	26,167	38,091	184,009	2.2	6.0
Older singles	7,770	12,847	13.7	16.0	12,381	18,167	96,223	233,397	5.5	7.7
Other multiple members	3,490	7,582	6.2	9.5	28,382	38,698	99,043	293,401	5.6	9.6
Black, total.	6,223	10,513	100.0	100.0	19,717	24,022	122,725	252,547	100.0	100.0
Households with children:										
Dual earner married-couples .	1,372	1,578	22.1	15.0	29,917	42,662	41,058	67,308	33.5	26.7
Other married-couples.	804	631	12.9	6.0	21,829	23,164	17,543	14,608	14.3	5.8
Single parents	1,199	2,853	19.3	27.1	13,316	16,240	15,963	46,334	13.0	18.3
Households without children:										
Young couples	309	438	5.0	4.2	28,684	39,530	8,866	17,300	7.2	6.9
Empty nesters	547	663	8.8	6.3	25,577	36,815	13,999	24,393	11.4	9.7
Mature couples	285	469	4.6	4.5	12,406	21,301	3,534	9,855	2.9	3.9
Young singles	337	1,002	5.4	9.5	13,624	19,216	4,595	19,257	3.7	7.6
Older singles	847	1,607	13.6	15.3	7,648	12,028	6,480	19,335	5.3	7.7
Other multiple members	523	1,273	8.4	12.1	20,419	26,827	10,688	34,158	8.7	13.5

No. 719. Median Household Income, by Race for States: 1989

[As of April. In dollars. Based on sample data and subject to sampling variability; see Appendix III]

STATE	All households [1]	White	Black	Asian, Pacific Islander	Indian, Eskimo, Aleut [2]	Hispanic [3]	STATE	All households [1]	White	Black	Asian, Pacific Islander	Indian, Eskimo, Aleut [2]	Hispanic [3]
U.S. . .	30,056	31,435	19,758	36,784	20,025	24,156	MO	26,362	27,179	18,374	27,059	20,255	26,838
AL.	23,597	26,792	13,997	27,610	20,908	23,462	MT	22,988	23,524	20,364	20,649	13,909	17,928
AK	41,408	44,998	31,474	35,056	24,152	32,601	NE	26,016	26,435	17,038	23,109	13,523	21,372
AZ	27,540	29,245	20,564	28,204	13,004	21,344	NV	31,011	31,813	22,528	30,396	23,262	26,582
AR	21,147	22,550	12,128	24,609	19,164	20,281	NH	36,329	36,379	31,657	42,963	26,818	34,919
CA	35,798	37,724	26,079	39,769	27,818	28,209	NJ	40,927	42,740	29,145	52,846	31,571	30,140
CO	30,140	31,024	21,676	28,125	19,931	21,073	NM	24,087	25,872	19,561	28,223	14,540	19,252
CT	41,721	43,407	28,011	48,560	29,310	25,116	NY	32,965	35,811	24,089	35,439	21,569	21,938
DE	34,875	36,660	24,286	41,526	30,500	28,062	NC	26,647	29,300	17,979	28,520	20,062	23,284
DC	30,727	45,991	24,576	30,141	24,375	26,295	ND	23,213	23,634	21,066	15,585	11,874	20,548
FL.	27,483	28,981	18,055	30,465	22,713	24,501	OH	28,706	30,026	17,716	34,243	19,886	25,053
GA	29,021	32,445	18,689	33,743	25,319	28,351	OK	23,577	24,851	15,725	22,283	18,051	19,951
HI	38,829	37,406	27,215	40,951	27,426	31,153	OR	27,250	27,574	18,432	25,120	21,954	21,503
ID	25,257	25,567	21,900	26,326	17,470	19,398	PA	29,069	30,065	20,064	31,361	21,902	18,929
IL	32,252	34,358	20,990	38,442	24,298	27,945	RI	32,181	33,103	20,377	25,394	19,325	20,064
IN	28,797	29,588	19,101	31,436	22,779	28,019	SC	26,256	30,118	16,555	30,454	22,297	25,795
IA	26,229	26,427	16,010	20,307	16,993	21,568	SD	22,503	23,220	20,890	19,119	11,017	16,721
KS	27,291	28,036	18,422	23,320	21,334	23,451	TN	24,807	26,244	16,432	29,092	20,527	24,132
KY	22,534	23,202	14,871	30,712	16,972	21,805	TX	27,016	29,728	17,853	30,792	23,340	19,233
LA	21,949	26,436	12,029	22,567	16,910	22,324	UT	29,470	29,999	19,878	25,071	15,971	22,979
ME	27,854	27,901	26,250	27,823	21,519	28,870	VT	29,792	29,852	28,625	27,824	20,972	29,145
MD	39,386	41,964	30,746	45,446	35,249	37,300	VA	33,328	36,039	21,987	41,488	31,556	35,523
MA	36,952	38,083	25,402	34,706	22,762	19,726	WA	31,183	31,685	24,066	31,424	20,945	22,827
MI	31,020	32,463	18,851	38,224	21,738	26,939	WV	20,795	21,034	13,174	37,031	12,891	19,329
MN	30,909	31,322	18,878	22,685	15,434	25,295	WI	29,442	30,216	16,189	18,490	17,238	23,253
MS	20,136	24,940	11,625	16,975	15,672	20,495	WY	27,096	27,600	16,708	20,130	15,753	22,433

[1] Includes other races not shown separately.   [2] American Indian.   [3] Hispanic persons may be of any race.

Sources of tables 718 and 719: U.S. Bureau of the Census, *1990 Census of Population and Housing*, Summary Tape File 3C on CD-ROM; and unpublished data.

No. 720. Money Income of Families—Percent Distribution by Income Level in Constant (1991) Dollars, by Race and Hispanic Origin of Householder: 1970 to 1991

[Constant dollars based on CPI-U-X1 deflator. Families as of **March** of following year. Beginning with 1980, based on householder concept and restricted to primary families. Based on Current Population Survey. See text, sections 1 and 14, and Appendix III. For definition of median, see Guide to Tabular Presentation. See also *Historical Statistics, Colonial Times to 1970*, series G 1-8, G 16-23, G 190-192, and G 197-199]

RACE AND HISPANIC ORIGIN OF HOUSEHOLDER AND YEAR	Number of families (1,000)	PERCENT DISTRIBUTION OF FAMILIES, BY INCOME LEVEL							Median income (dol.)
		Under $10,000	$10,000- $14,999	$15,000- $24,999	$25,000- $34,999	$35,000- $49,999	$50,000- $74,999	$75,000 and over	
ALL FAMILIES									
1970	52,227	9.2	7.6	18.0	21.0	22.9	15.1	6.3	32,540
1975	56,245	8.7	8.6	18.0	18.3	23.0	16.6	7.0	33,248
1980 [1]	60,309	8.9	7.7	17.3	17.1	21.9	18.2	9.1	34,791
1985 [1]	63,558	9.7	7.5	16.5	16.3	20.1	18.5	11.4	35,107
1988 [2]	65,837	9.0	7.3	15.5	15.5	19.9	19.4	13.5	37,062
1989	66,090	8.8	7.2	15.2	15.1	19.9	19.6	14.2	37,579
1990	66,322	8.9	7.2	15.5	15.8	19.9	19.0	13.7	36,841
1991	67,173	9.7	7.2	16.0	15.6	19.5	18.8	13.1	35,939
WHITE									
1970	46,535	7.9	7.0	17.3	21.4	23.9	15.9	6.7	33,756
1975	49,873	7.1	7.9	17.5	18.6	23.8	17.5	7.6	34,578
1980 [1]	52,710	7.1	6.9	16.8	17.3	22.8	19.2	9.8	36,249
1985 [1]	54,991	7.8	6.8	16.0	16.6	20.8	19.5	12.4	36,901
1988 [2]	56,492	7.0	6.5	15.1	15.8	20.7	20.5	14.4	39,047
1989	56,590	6.8	6.5	14.8	15.4	20.7	20.6	15.4	39,514
1990	56,803	6.7	6.7	15.2	16.1	20.6	20.1	14.6	38,468
1991	57,224	7.3	6.7	15.7	15.9	20.3	20.0	14.1	37,783
BLACK									
1970	4,928	21.9	13.5	24.2	17.7	13.8	7.4	1.5	20,707
1975	5,586	21.8	14.6	22.1	16.2	15.8	7.8	1.8	21,276
1980 [1]	6,317	23.0	13.9	20.9	15.1	14.5	9.8	2.7	20,974
1985 [1]	6,921	24.4	12.1	21.2	13.8	14.9	10.1	3.6	21,248
1988 [2]	7,409	24.1	12.9	18.1	13.6	14.0	12.1	5.3	22,254
1989	7,470	23.4	12.6	18.9	13.7	14.6	11.5	5.3	22,197
1990	7,471	24.7	11.2	18.8	14.2	15.1	10.7	5.4	22,325
1991	7,716	26.4	11.1	18.4	14.5	14.8	10.3	4.5	21,548
HISPANIC [3]									
1975	2,499	16.8	13.6	24.6	18.6	17.0	7.4	2.2	23,147
1980 [1]	3,235	15.8	13.1	23.1	17.5	16.5	10.4	3.4	24,354
1985 [1]	4,206	17.9	13.6	20.3	17.1	15.6	11.1	4.4	24,084
1988 [2]	4,823	17.8	11.7	20.5	16.8	15.9	11.8	5.6	25,063
1989	4,840	16.8	11.4	20.6	16.2	16.9	12.3	5.8	25,753
1990	4,981	17.4	13.0	20.6	16.7	16.5	10.3	5.7	24,417
1991	5,177	18.8	11.9	21.5	16.5	15.0	10.7	5.5	23,895

[1] Beginning 1983, data based on revised Hispanic population controls and not directly comparable with prior years.
[2] Beginning 1987, data based on revised processing procedures and not directly comparable with prior years. See text, section 14, and source.   [3] Persons of Hispanic origin may be of any race.

No. 721. Money Income of Families—Median Family Income in Current and Constant (1991) Dollars, by Race and Hispanic Origin of Householder: 1970 to 1991

[See headnote, table 720. Minus sign (-) indicates decrease]

YEAR	MEDIAN INCOME IN CURRENT DOLLARS				MEDIAN INCOME IN CONSTANT (1991) DOLLARS				ANNUAL PERCENT CHANGE FOR ALL FAMILIES	
	All families [1]	White	Black	His- panic [2]	All families [1]	White	Black	His- panic [2]	Current dollars	Constant (1991) dollars
1970	9,867	10,236	6,279	(NA)	32,540	33,756	20,707	(NA)	[3]7.2	[3]3.3
1975	13,719	14,268	8,779	9,551	33,248	34,578	21,276	23,147	6.3	-1.8
1976	14,958	15,537	9,242	10,259	34,298	35,625	21,191	23,523	9.0	3.2
1977	16,009	16,740	9,563	11,421	34,500	36,076	20,609	24,613	7.0	0.6
1978	17,640	18,368	10,879	12,566	35,594	37,063	21,951	25,355	10.2	3.2
1979	19,587	20,439	11,574	14,169	36,051	37,619	21,302	26,079	11.0	1.3
1980	21,023	21,904	12,674	14,716	34,791	36,249	20,974	24,354	7.3	-3.5
1981	22,388	23,517	13,266	16,401	33,843	35,550	20,054	24,793	6.5	-2.7
1982	23,433	24,603	13,598	16,227	33,385	35,052	19,373	23,118	4.7	-1.4
1983 [4]	24,580	25,757	14,506	16,956	33,741	35,331	19,912	23,151	4.9	1.1
1984	26,433	27,686	15,432	18,833	34,650	36,293	20,228	24,686	7.5	2.7
1985	27,735	29,152	16,786	19,027	35,107	36,901	21,248	24,084	4.9	1.3
1986	29,458	30,809	17,604	19,995	36,607	38,286	21,877	24,848	6.2	4.3
1987 [5]	30,970	32,385	18,406	20,300	37,131	38,828	22,068	24,339	5.1	1.4
1988	32,191	33,915	19,329	21,769	37,062	39,047	22,254	25,063	3.9	-0.2
1989	34,213	35,975	20,209	23,446	37,579	39,514	22,197	25,753	6.3	1.4
1990	35,353	36,915	21,423	23,431	36,841	38,468	22,325	24,417	3.3	-2.0
1991	35,939	37,783	21,548	23,895	35,939	37,783	21,548	23,895	1.7	-2.4

NA Not available.   [1] Includes other races not shown separately.   [2] Persons of Hispanic origin may be of any race.
[3] Change from 1965.   [4] Beginning 1983, data based on revised Hispanic population controls and not directly comparable with prior years.   [5] Beginning 1987, data based on revised processing procedures and not directly comparable with prior years.

Source of tables 720 and 721: U.S. Bureau of the Census, *Current Population Reports*, P60-180; and unpublished data.

No. 722. Money Income of Families—Percent Distribution of Aggregate Income Received by Quintile and Income at Selected Positions, in Constant (1991) Dollars: 1980 and 1991

[See headnote, table 720. For composition of regions, see table 31. See also *Historical Statistics, Colonial Times to 1970*, series G 31-138]

ITEM	All families, 1980	1991						
		All families	RACE		REGION			
			White	Black	North-east	Midwest	South	West
Number (1,000)................	60,309	67,173	57,224	7,716	13,428	16,170	23,679	13,897
INCOME AT SELECTED POSITIONS (dollars)								
Upper limit of each fifth:								
Lowest....................	17,023	17,000	18,922	7,780	19,080	18,050	14,974	17,624
Second	28,779	29,111	31,000	16,000	33,100	30,110	26,000	30,150
Third	40,761	43,000	44,874	27,530	47,900	42,796	39,050	44,960
Fourth	57,151	62,991	64,950	43,900	69,777	60,828	58,000	66,760
Lower limit of top 5 percent	89,465	102,824	106,119	72,800	115,550	98,381	96,400	108,850
PERCENT DISTRIBUTION OF AGGREGATE INCOME								
Lowest fifth.................	5.2	4.5	5.0	3.2	4.5	4.9	4.4	4.5
Second fifth.................	11.5	10.7	11.0	8.4	10.8	11.4	10.5	10.5
Third fifth..................	17.5	16.6	16.7	15.7	16.7	17.1	16.4	16.3
Fourth fifth.................	24.3	24.1	23.8	25.4	23.9	23.9	24.3	24.1
Highest fifth................	41.5	44.2	43.4	47.4	44.1	42.8	44.5	44.5
Top 5 percent................	15.3	17.1	16.8	17.3	17.2	16.4	17.0	17.4

Source: U.S. Bureau of the Census, *Current Population Reports*, P60-180; and unpublished data.

No. 723. Money Income of Families—Percent Distribution, by Income Quintile and Top 5 Percent for Selected Characteristics: 1991

[See headnote, table 720]

CHARACTERISTIC	Number (1,000)	PERCENT DISTRIBUTION						
		Total	Lowest fifth	Second fifth	Third fifth	Fourth fifth	Highest fifth	Top 5 percent
All families.................	67,173	100	20.0	20.0	20.0	20.0	20.0	5.0
White	57,224	100	17.0	20.0	20.6	21.0	21.5	5.5
Black	7,716	100	41.7	20.8	16.4	12.8	8.3	1.3
Hispanic [1]	5,177	100	35.8	24.5	17.5	13.0	9.2	2.0
Married-couple families........	52,457	100	12.8	19.1	21.0	22.9	24.1	6.2
Male householder	3,025	100	24.8	26.8	21.7	15.1	11.6	2.1
Female householder	11,692	100	50.9	22.2	14.9	8.4	3.6	0.6
15 to 24 years old..........	2,642	100	50.0	29.4	13.1	5.3	2.2	0.3
25 to 34 years old..........	14,379	100	24.8	20.8	22.9	19.6	11.8	2.0
35 to 44 years old..........	17,533	100	14.6	16.0	21.2	24.5	23.7	5.4
45 to 54 years old..........	12,187	100	11.2	13.4	17.6	24.6	33.2	9.1
55 to 64 years old..........	9,296	100	15.3	19.0	19.7	21.2	24.8	7.4
65 years old and over........	11,135	100	28.6	31.1	19.0	10.8	10.5	2.9
65 to 74 years old........	7,330	100	25.4	29.8	20.3	12.2	12.2	3.3
75 years old and over.......	3,805	100	34.9	33.5	16.3	8.1	7.3	2.3
Size of family:								
Two persons...............	28,202	100	23.7	24.6	19.6	16.3	15.8	4.3
Three persons.............	15,594	100	19.4	17.7	20.3	21.7	20.8	4.6
Four persons..............	14,162	100	14.8	14.8	20.3	24.6	25.5	6.6
Five persons..............	6,030	100	16.0	17.4	20.4	22.7	23.5	5.3
Six persons...............	1,986	100	18.1	19.0	21.3	20.1	21.5	6.1
Seven persons or more.......	1,200	100	25.2	18.7	17.3	16.9	22.0	5.4
Presence of related children under 18 years old:								
No related children.........	32,312	100	16.5	21.8	19.9	19.7	22.1	6.0
One or more related children	34,861	100	23.2	18.3	20.1	20.3	18.0	4.1
One child................	14,547	100	22.5	18.6	19.8	20.0	19.1	4.1
Two children or more........	20,314	100	23.7	18.1	20.3	20.5	17.3	4.1
Education attainment of householder: [2]								
Total	64,531	100	18.8	19.6	20.3	20.6	20.7	5.2
Less than 9th grade..........	6,048	100	47.7	28.8	13.4	6.9	3.2	0.6
9th to 12th grade (no diploma)	7,045	100	37.4	27.8	17.2	12.3	5.3	0.8
High school graduate (includes equivalency)	22,160	100	18.9	23.2	24.6	20.9	12.4	1.8
Some college, no degree	10,726	100	12.7	17.9	23.8	25.4	20.2	3.7
Associate degree	3,715	100	10.2	15.3	22.6	27.5	24.4	3.5
Bachelor's degree or more	14,837	100	4.4	8.9	15.0	24.5	47.2	15.7
Bachelor's degree	9,288	100	5.4	10.8	16.6	26.4	40.9	11.5
Master's degree............	3,579	100	2.9	6.2	14.1	24.0	52.8	16.8
Professional degree	1,247	100	2.4	6.0	9.9	14.3	67.4	36.1
Doctorate degree............	723	100	3.1	3.4	7.5	20.8	65.2	29.8
Worked	51,431	100	12.9	18.0	21.4	23.5	24.2	6.1
Worked at full-time jobs	46,022	100	10.3	17.3	21.9	24.8	25.7	6.3
Worked at part-time jobs	5,410	100	35.2	23.7	16.8	12.4	11.9	3.9
Did not work................	15,742	100	43.0	26.6	15.4	8.7	6.3	1.5

[1] Persons of Hispanic origin may be of any race.   [2] 25 years old and over.
Source: U.S. Bureau of the Census, *Current Population Reports*, P60-180.

No. 724. Money Income of Families—Median Family Income, by Race and Hispanic Origin: 1991

[See headnote, table 720. For composition of regions, see table 31]

CHARACTERISTIC	NUMBER (1,000)				MEDIAN FAMILY INCOME (dollars)			
	All families [1]	White	Black	His-panic [2]	All families [1]	White	Black	His-panic [2]
All families	67,173	57,224	7,716	5,177	35,939	37,783	21,548	23,895
Region:								
Northeast.	13,428	11,777	1,291	856	40,265	41,815	25,533	21,437
Midwest.	16,170	14,347	1,554	355	36,759	38,224	20,860	26,942
South	23,679	19,023	4,253	1,651	31,940	35,226	20,124	23,708
West.	13,897	12,078	618	2,314	37,171	37,610	28,298	24,317
Type of family:								
Married-couple families.	52,457	47,124	3,631	3,532	40,995	41,506	33,307	28,594
Wife in paid labor force	30,923	27,463	2,420	1,845	48,169	48,802	41,353	35,655
Wife not in paid labor force . .	21,534	19,661	1,210	1,687	30,075	30,792	20,288	21,923
Male householder [3]	3,025	2,374	504	383	28,351	28,924	24,508	21,759
Female householder [3]	11,692	7,726	3,582	1,261	16,692	19,547	11,414	12,132
With related children [4]	34,861	28,368	5,143	3,621	34,990	37,699	18,822	22,064
Married couple	25,357	22,213	2,129	2,445	42,514	43,179	35,358	27,296
Male householder [3]	1,513	1,187	244	204	24,171	24,507	20,920	19,182
Female householder [3]	7,991	4,967	2,771	972	13,012	15,513	9,413	10,216
Number of earners:								
No earners	10,158	8,355	1,547	719	15,631	18,183	6,480	8,264
One earner	18,500	15,245	2,640	1,714	25,960	28,095	15,912	17,058
Two earners.	29,681	25,946	2,724	1,946	43,623	44,711	34,060	30,802
Three earners.	6,542	5,658	647	545	55,871	56,583	46,221	38,763
Four or more earners.	2,293	2,019	159	252	70,019	70,354	60,126	51,680

[1] Includes other races not shown separately. [2] Persons of Hispanic origin may be of any race. [3] No spouse present. [4] Children under 18 years old.

No. 725. Money Income of Families—Percent Distribution by Income Level, by Race, Hispanic Origin of Householder, and Selected Characteristics: 1991

[See headnote, table 720. See *Historical Statistics, Colonial Times to 1970*, series G 1-8 for U.S. data on total, White, Black, and other races. For composition of regions, see table 31]

RACE OF HOUSEHOLDER, REGION, AND PRESENCE OF CHILDREN	Number of families (1,000)	PERCENT DISTRIBUTION OF FAMILIES, BY INCOME LEVEL								Median income (dol.)
		Under $5,000	$5,000 to $9,999	$10,000 to $14,999	$15,000 to $24,999	$25,000 to $34,999	$35,000 to $49,999	$50,000 to $74,999	$75,000 and over	
All families [1]	67,173	3.6	6.1	7.2	16.0	15.6	19.5	18.8	13.1	35,939
White, total	57,224	2.5	4.8	6.7	15.7	15.9	20.3	20.0	14.1	37,783
Northeast.	11,777	2.2	4.9	5.5	13.3	13.9	20.5	21.7	18.1	41,815
Midwest.	14,347	2.4	4.0	6.0	15.4	16.7	22.7	20.3	12.5	38,224
South	19,023	2.8	5.0	7.9	17.4	16.5	19.4	18.9	12.0	35,226
West	12,078	2.5	5.4	6.7	15.9	15.8	18.7	19.6	15.4	37,610
Black, total	7,716	11.4	15.0	11.1	18.4	14.5	14.8	10.3	4.6	21,548
Northeast.	1,291	9.2	13.3	8.9	17.7	13.6	17.1	12.6	7.6	25,533
Midwest.	1,554	11.8	18.6	9.8	15.6	12.9	17.7	9.1	4.3	20,860
South	4,253	12.4	14.9	12.3	19.8	15.0	12.8	8.6	4.3	20,124
West	618	8.1	9.5	11.3	16.3	16.6	16.6	16.1	5.5	28,298
Hispanic, [2] total	5,177	6.4	12.4	11.9	21.6	16.5	15.0	10.7	5.5	23,895
Northeast.	856	9.2	18.9	10.9	15.9	13.0	14.1	11.8	6.2	21,437
Midwest.	355	6.8	8.7	12.1	18.9	17.7	16.9	14.4	4.5	26,942
South	1,651	6.1	11.4	12.9	23.1	17.4	14.2	9.5	5.3	23,708
West	2,314	5.5	11.2	11.7	22.9	16.9	15.6	10.7	5.6	24,317
Presence of related children under 18 years old:										
All families	67,173	3.6	6.1	7.2	16.0	15.6	19.5	18.8	13.1	35,939
No children	32,312	1.7	4.2	7.5	17.4	16.2	19.1	19.0	15.0	36,943
One or more children . . .	34,861	5.4	7.8	7.0	14.7	15.1	19.9	18.7	11.3	34,990
Married-couple families. . . .	52,457	1.4	3.1	5.8	14.6	15.9	21.2	22.1	15.9	40,995
No children.	27,100	1.4	3.4	6.7	16.8	15.7	19.1	20.1	16.8	39,083
One or more children . . .	25,357	1.4	2.7	4.7	12.4	16.1	23.5	24.2	14.9	42,514
Female householder, no husband present	11,692	13.5	19.1	13.2	20.7	13.7	12.0	5.9	2.0	16,692
No children	3,701	4.0	9.4	12.6	21.8	18.4	17.9	11.8	4.2	26,111
One or more children . . .	7,991	17.8	23.6	13.5	20.3	11.5	9.3	3.2	0.9	13,012

[1] Includes other races not shown separately. [2] Persons of Hispanic origin may be of any race.

Source of tables 724 and 725: U.S. Bureau of the Census, *Current Population Reports*, P60-180; and unpublished data.

No. 726. Money Income of Families, by Type of Family and Income Level: 1991

[In thousands, except dollars. See headnote, table 720]

TYPE OF FAMILY	Number of families	NUMBER OF FAMILIES BY INCOME LEVEL								Median income (dol.)
		Under $9,999	$10,000-$14,999	$15,000-$19,999	$20,000-$24,999	$25,000-$34,999	$35,000-$49,999	$50,000-$74,999	$75,000 and over	
All families	67,173	6,521	4,844	5,192	5,553	10,502	13,116	12,661	8,785	35,939
Married-couple families. . .	52,457	2,349	3,030	3,557	4,116	8,343	11,139	11,574	8,350	40,995
Wife in paid labor force .	30,923	518	840	1,239	1,723	4,621	7,310	8,587	6,086	48,169
Wife not in paid labor force.	21,534	1,830	2,189	2,318	2,392	3,723	3,828	2,987	2,264	30,075
Male householder [1]	3,025	370	274	312	335	559	575	396	204	28,351
Female householder [1] . .	11,692	3,803	1,540	1,323	1,102	1,599	1,403	691	231	16,692
With own children [2] . . .	34,861	4,613	2,429	2,581	2,536	5,274	6,952	6,535	3,940	34,990
Married-couple.	25,357	1,049	1,202	1,480	1,652	4,093	5,969	6,124	3,787	42,514
Female householder [1] . .	7,991	3,308	1,075	908	711	918	742	255	75	13,012

[1] No spouse present. [2] Children under 18 years old. Includes male householders not shown separately.

No. 727. Median Money Income of Families and Unrelated Individuals, in Current and Constant (1991) Dollars: 1970 to 1991

[Constant dollars based on CPI-U-X1 deflator. Unrelated individuals are persons not living with any relatives. See headnote, table 720. See also *Historical Statistics, Colonial Times to 1970*, series G 179-188]

ITEM	1970	1980	1984[1]	1985	1986	1987[2]	1988	1989	1990	1991
CURRENT DOLLARS										
Families:[3]										
Married-couple families	10,516	23,141	29,612	31,100	32,805	34,879	36,389	38,547	39,895	40,995
Wife in paid labor force	12,276	26,879	34,668	36,431	38,346	40,751	42,709	45,266	46,777	48,169
Wife not in paid labor force. . .	9,304	18,972	23,582	24,556	25,803	26,640	27,220	28,747	30,265	30,075
Male householder, no wife present	9,012	17,519	23,325	22,622	24,962	25,208	26,827	27,847	29,046	28,351
Female householder, no husband present.	5,093	10,408	12,803	13,660	13,647	14,683	15,346	16,442	16,932	16,692
Unrelated individuals:										
Male	4,540	10,939	13,566	14,921	15,281	16,082	16,976	17,860	17,927	18,069
Female	2,483	6,668	9,501	9,865	10,142	11,029	11,881	12,390	12,450	12,731
CONSTANT (1991) DOLLARS										
Families:[3]										
Married-couple families	34,680	38,297	38,818	39,366	40,767	41,818	41,895	42,340	41,574	40,995
Wife in paid labor force	40,484	44,483	45,445	46,114	47,653	48,858	49,171	49,720	48,745	48,169
Wife not in paid labor force. . .	30,683	31,397	30,913	31,083	32,065	31,940	31,339	31,575	31,539	30,075
Male householder, no wife present	29,720	28,993	30,576	28,635	31,020	30,223	30,886	30,587	30,268	28,351
Female householder, no husband present.	16,796	17,224	16,783	17,291	16,959	17,604	17,668	18,060	17,645	16,692
Unrelated individuals:										
Male	14,972	18,103	17,783	18,887	18,990	19,281	19,545	19,617	18,681	18,069
Female	8,188	11,035	12,455	12,487	12,603	13,223	13,679	13,609	12,974	12,731

[1] Beginning 1983, data based on revised Hispanic population controls and not directly comparable with prior years. [2] Beginning 1987, data based on revised processing procedures and not directly comparable with prior years. See text, section 14, and source. [3] Beginning 1980, based on householder concept. Restricted to primary families, see source.

No. 728. Median Money Income of Year-Round Full-Time Workers With Income, by Sex, Age, Race, and Hispanic Origin: 1980 to 1991

[Age as of **March of following year.** Prior to 1989, earnings are for civilian workers only. For definition of median, see Guide to Tabular Presentation]

ITEM	FEMALE					MALE				
	1980	1985[1]	1989[2]	1990	1991	1980	1985[1]	1989[2]	1990	1991
Total with income. .	$11,591	$16,252	$19,638	$20,591	$21,245	$19,173	$24,999	$28,419	$28,979	$30,332
15 to 19 years old	6,779	8,372	[3]13,649	[3]13,944	[3]14,242	7,753	9,050	[3]15,429	[3]15,462	[3]15,307
20 to 24 years old	9,407	11,757	(NA)	(NA)	(NA)	12,109	13,827	(NA)	(NA)	(NA)
25 to 34 years old	12,190	16,740	19,700	20,184	21,022	17,724	22,321	24,794	25,355	26,100
35 to 44 years old	12,239	18,032	21,502	22,505	23,385	21,777	28,966	32,352	32,607	33,588
45 to 54 years old	12,116	17,009	20,905	21,938	22,630	22,323	29,880	35,390	35,732	37,198
55 to 64 years old	11,931	16,761	19,895	20,755	21,325	21,053	28,387	34,505	33,169	35,720
65 years old and over. . . .	12,342	18,336	21,505	22,957	21,780	17,307	26,146	34,105	35,520	34,473
White.	11,703	16,482	19,871	20,839	21,555	19,720	25,693	29,672	30,081	30,953
Black.	10,915	14,590	17,871	18,544	19,134	13,875	17,971	20,704	21,481	22,628
Hispanic [4]	9,887	13,522	16,006	16,181	16,548	13,790	17,344	18,551	19,358	20,027

NA Not available. [1] Beginning 1983, data based on revised Hispanic population controls and not directly comparable with prior years. [2] Beginning 1987, data based on revised processing procedures and not directly comparable with prior years. See text, section 14, and source. [3] 15 to 24 years old. [4] Persons of Hispanic origin may be of any race.

Source of tables 726-728: U.S. Bureau of the Census, *Current Population Reports*, P60-180; and unpublished data.

No. 729. Money Income of Persons—Percent Distribution, by Income Level and Median Income in Constant (1991) Dollars: 1970 to 1991

[Constant dollars based on CPI-U-X1 deflator. As of **March of following year.** For 1970 and 1975, persons 14 years old and over; thereafter, 15 years old and over. For definition of median, see Guide to Tabular Presentation. See also *Historical Statistics, Colonial Times to 1970*, series G 257-268. For composition of regions, see table 31]

		PERSONS WITH INCOME									
ITEM	All per-sons (mil.)	Total (mil.)	Percent distribution by income level—								Median income (dol.)
			$1 to $2,499 or loss [1]	$2,500 to $4,999	$5,000 to $9,999	$10,000 to $14,999	$15,000 to $24,999	$25,000 to $49,999	$50,000 to $74,999	$75,000 and over	
MALE											
1970	70.6	65.0	8.6	6.5	11.4	9.8	21.1	34.3	5.5	2.7	21,996
1975	77.6	71.2	8.0	5.7	12.4	11.3	20.8	32.7	6.4	2.7	21,455
1980	82.9	78.7	7.6	5.8	12.6	11.4	21.3	31.8	6.6	3.1	20,736
1981	84.0	79.7	8.0	6.1	12.7	11.3	21.1	31.0	6.6	3.1	20,367
1982	85.0	79.7	8.4	6.1	13.1	12.1	20.5	29.8	6.8	3.2	19,874
1983 [2]	86.0	80.8	8.6	6.2	13.0	11.6	21.2	29.2	6.9	3.2	20,048
1984	87.3	82.2	8.0	6.0	13.0	11.9	20.3	29.8	7.5	3.5	20,450
1985	88.5	83.6	7.5	5.9	12.6	11.8	20.5	30.1	7.9	3.8	20,646
1986 [3]	89.4	84.5	7.7	5.4	12.5	11.8	20.3	30.1	8.0	4.1	21,268
1987	90.3	85.7	7.3	5.4	12.2	12.3	20.1	30.3	8.3	4.1	21,324
1988	91.0	86.6	6.9	5.3	12.2	11.9	20.4	30.8	8.2	4.4	21,769
1989	92.0	87.5	6.5	5.2	12.4	11.8	20.8	30.4	8.1	4.8	21,850
1990	92.8	88.2	6.6	5.1	12.6	12.4	21.0	29.9	8.1	4.3	21,147
1991	**93.8**	**88.7**	**6.6**	**5.5**	**13.0**	**12.6**	**21.1**	**29.3**	**7.6**	**4.3**	**20,469**
15 to 24 years old	17.2	13.5	27.2	16.4	21.5	15.2	14.5	5.0	0.2	0.1	6,281
25 to 34 years old	21.1	20.5	3.3	4.1	10.6	13.2	27.0	34.9	5.0	1.9	21,595
35 to 44 years old	19.5	19.2	2.6	2.9	7.3	8.3	19.7	41.1	11.8	6.3	29,301
45 to 54 years old	13.1	12.9	3.0	2.7	7.0	7.4	17.2	39.1	14.6	9.0	31,779
55 to 64 years old	10.0	9.8	3.1	3.7	10.7	11.1	20.4	33.3	10.7	7.0	25,460
65 yr. old and over	12.8	12.7	2.2	4.6	24.2	21.5	25.4	15.4	3.9	2.8	14,357
White	80.0	76.6	6.0	4.8	12.3	12.4	21.2	30.4	8.2	4.7	21,395
Black	10.3	8.9	10.6	11.0	18.7	14.8	20.4	21.0	2.5	0.8	12,962
Hispanic [4]	7.7	6.9	6.9	6.6	21.2	18.5	22.4	20.2	2.9	1.2	13,818
Northeast	19.1	18.0	6.4	4.9	11.5	11.6	20.0	31.3	9.1	5.1	22,349
Midwest	22.4	21.5	7.2	5.5	11.7	12.5	22.0	30.7	6.7	3.7	20,571
South	32.0	30.0	6.5	6.4	14.9	13.5	21.8	26.6	6.5	3.8	18,474
West	20.3	19.2	6.1	4.9	12.8	12.1	19.9	30.2	9.0	5.0	21,572
FEMALE											
1970	77.6	51.6	21.8	17.4	20.9	14.7	17.2	7.4	0.4	0.2	7,377
1975	85.0	60.8	17.9	15.8	24.2	15.4	17.9	8.2	0.4	0.1	8,204
1980	91.1	80.8	21.2	14.1	22.4	14.3	17.9	9.2	0.7	0.2	8,142
1981	92.2	82.1	20.6	13.8	22.7	14.0	18.5	9.6	0.6	0.2	8,251
1982	93.1	82.5	20.4	13.4	22.7	14.6	17.5	10.3	0.8	0.3	8,387
1983 [2]	94.3	83.8	19.7	13.1	22.2	14.0	18.6	11.1	1.0	0.4	8,759
1984	95.3	85.6	18.8	12.8	22.3	14.4	18.0	12.1	1.1	0.4	9,003
1985	96.4	86.5	18.2	13.0	21.8	14.0	18.2	13.1	1.3	0.4	9,135
1986 [3]	97.3	87.8	18.1	12.4	22.0	14.0	18.3	13.4	1.3	0.5	9,457
1987	98.2	89.7	17.1	12.4	21.6	14.2	18.7	14.0	1.5	0.5	9,945
1988	99.0	90.6	16.4	12.1	21.3	14.6	18.6	14.8	1.6	0.6	10,228
1989	99.8	91.4	15.7	12.0	21.2	14.2	19.2	15.3	1.8	0.7	10,571
1990	100.7	92.2	15.3	12.1	21.1	14.7	18.8	15.3	1.9	0.7	10,494
1991	**101.5**	**92.6**	**14.8**	**11.7**	**21.7**	**14.9**	**19.3**	**15.0**	**1.8**	**0.7**	**10,476**
15 to 24 years old	17.2	13.2	30.4	18.5	22.8	14.2	11.4	2.5	0.2	-	5,197
25 to 34 years old	21.4	19.8	14.0	8.8	17.1	15.2	25.3	17.7	1.5	0.4	12,964
35 to 44 years old	20.1	18.9	13.6	7.3	14.9	13.8	22.3	23.8	3.0	1.2	15,125
45 to 54 years old	13.9	12.9	14.8	7.0	14.5	14.3	22.1	22.7	3.1	1.4	14,724
55 to 64 years old	11.1	10.2	16.7	12.4	21.2	13.9	17.6	14.9	2.4	0.9	9,902
65 yr. old and over	17.8	17.5	4.4	17.8	39.1	17.3	13.9	6.2	0.8	0.5	8,189
White	85.5	78.7	15.1	11.1	21.2	15.1	19.4	15.4	1.9	0.7	10,721
Black	12.3	10.7	11.9	16.4	26.4	13.5	18.1	12.2	1.0	0.4	8,816
Hispanic [4]	7.8	6.1	18.1	14.8	26.4	15.1	15.7	8.8	0.8	0.3	8,013
Northeast	21.2	19.4	14.0	10.8	21.7	14.2	19.2	16.8	2.5	0.8	11,047
Midwest	24.4	22.9	15.1	12.3	21.9	15.3	19.6	13.9	1.3	0.6	10,199
South	35.1	31.5	15.1	13.0	21.7	15.3	19.0	13.8	1.5	0.6	10,053
West	20.9	18.8	15.0	10.0	21.6	14.4	19.4	16.4	2.3	1.0	10,976

- Represents or rounds to zero. [1] Includes persons with income deficit. [2] Beginning 1983, data based on revised Hispanic population controls and not directly comparable with prior years. [3] Beginning 1987, data based on revised processing procedures and not directly comparable with prior years. [4] Persons of Hispanic origin may be of any race.

Source: U.S. Bureau of the Census, *Current Population Reports*, P60-180; and unpublished data.

No. 730. Median Income of Married-Couple Families, by Work Experience of Husbands and Wives and Race: 1991

[As of **March 1992**. Based on Current Population Survey; see text, sections 1 and 14, and Appendix III]

WORK EXPERIENCE OF HUSBAND	NUMBER (1,000)				MEDIAN INCOME (dollars)			
		Wife worked		Wife did not work		Wife worked		Wife did not work
	Total	Total	Worked year-round, full-time		Total	Total	Worked year-round, full-time	
All families [1]	52,457	33,673	18,095	18,784	40,995	47,484	53,027	28,504
Husband worked	42,015	31,159	16,863	10,857	45,995	49,178	54,391	36,240
Worked year-round, full-time	32,424	24,496	13,625	7,928	50,092	52,707	57,092	40,518
Husband did not work	10,442	2,514	1,232	7,927	23,084	28,556	34,278	21,616
White	47,124	30,005	15,806	17,119	41,506	48,101	53,645	29,370
Husband worked	37,741	27,848	14,776	9,893	46,550	49,764	54,876	37,076
Worked year-round, full-time	29,188	21,932	11,948	7,256	50,595	53,178	57,538	41,278
Husband did not work	9,383	2,157	1,030	7,226	23,663	29,174	35,386	22,296
Black	3,631	2,539	1,629	1,092	33,307	40,470	45,060	19,365
Husband worked	2,851	2,261	1,471	590	38,536	42,451	47,357	23,780
Worked year-round, full-time	2,139	1,747	1,164	392	42,619	45,312	50,918	27,101
Husband did not work	780	278	158	502	17,229	26,136	28,343	14,245
Hispanic [2]	3,532	1,998	1,009	1,533	28,594	35,580	43,769	20,543
Husband worked	3,016	1,854	932	1,162	30,564	36,358	45,028	22,350
Worked year-round, full-time	2,181	1,336	733	845	34,234	41,510	48,333	25,114
Husband did not work	516	145	77	371	17,634	27,531	32,864	14,502

[1] Includes other races not shown separately. [2] Persons of Hispanic origin may be of any race.

No. 731. Average Earnings of Persons, by Educational Attainment, Sex, and Age: 1991

[In dollars. For year-round, full-time workers 25 years old and over. As of March 1992]

AGE AND SEX	Total	Less than 9th grade	HIGH SCHOOL		COLLEGE		
			9th to 12th grade (no diploma)	High school graduate (includes equivalency)	Some college, no degree	Associate degree	Bachelor's degree or more
Male, total	35,850	19,632	23,765	28,230	33,758	35,500	50,747
25 to 34 years old	28,742	15,853	19,596	24,045	28,135	29,923	39,765
35 to 44 years old	37,882	19,972	23,770	28,984	34,377	37,887	52,130
45 to 54 years old	41,676	20,713	25,277	32,468	41,121	41,796	56,918
55 to 64 years old	38,868	22,274	29,491	32,484	35,291	32,695	59,089
65 years old and over	35,303	16,479	18,926	27,165	30,365	(B)	56,164
Female, total	23,778	12,570	15,352	19,336	22,833	25,554	33,144
25 to 34 years old	22,429	12,521	13,849	18,269	20,993	23,120	29,614
35 to 44 years old	25,277	12,255	15,037	19,824	24,100	27,329	35,214
45 to 54 years old	24,521	12,319	16,854	20,342	23,369	26,035	36,264
55 to 64 years old	22,451	13,201	15,116	18,914	24,049	28,168	34,363
65 years old and over	18,590	(B)	15,833	17,757	(B)	(B)	23,332

B Base figure too small to meet statistical standards for reliability of derived figure.

No. 732. Per Capita Money Income in Current and Constant (1991) Dollars, by Race and Hispanic Origin: 1970 to 1991

[Constant dollars based on CPI-U-X1 deflator. **In dollars.** See headnote, table 729]

YEAR	CURRENT DOLLARS				CONSTANT (1991) DOLLARS			
	All races	White	Black	Hispanic [1]	All races	White	Black	Hispanic [1]
1970	3,177	3,354	1,869	(NA)	10,477	11,061	6,164	(NA)
1975	4,818	5,072	2,972	2,847	11,676	12,292	7,203	6,900
1980	7,787	8,233	4,804	4,865	12,887	13,625	7,950	8,051
1981	8,476	8,979	5,129	5,349	12,813	13,573	7,753	8,086
1982	8,980	9,527	5,360	5,448	12,794	13,573	7,636	7,762
1983 [2]	9,548	10,125	5,755	5,852	13,057	13,846	7,870	8,002
1984	10,328	10,939	6,277	6,401	13,539	14,340	8,228	8,391
1985	11,013	11,671	6,840	6,613	13,940	14,773	8,658	8,371
1986	11,670	12,352	7,207	7,000	14,502	15,350	8,956	8,699
1987 [3]	12,391	13,143	7,645	7,653	14,856	15,758	9,166	9,176
1988	13,123	13,896	8,271	7,956	15,109	15,999	9,522	9,160
1989	14,056	14,896	8,747	8,390	15,439	16,362	9,608	9,215
1990	14,387	15,265	9,017	8,424	14,992	15,907	9,396	8,778
1991	14,617	15,510	9,170	8,662	14,617	15,510	9,170	8,662

NA Not available. [1] Hispanic persons may be of any race. [2] Beginning 1983, data based on revised Hispanic population controls and not directly comparable with prior years. [3] Beginning 1987, data based on revised processing procedures and not directly comparable with prior years.

Source of tables 730-732: U.S. Bureau of the Census, *Current Population Reports*, P60-180.

No. 733. Income Per Capita, by Race for States: 1989

[As of April. In dollars. Based on sample data and subject to sampling variability; see Appendix III]

STATE	All races[1]	White	Black	Asian, Pacific Islander	American Indian, Eskimo, Aleut	Hispanic[2]	STATE	All races[1]	White	Black	Asian, Pacific Islander	American Indian, Eskimo, Aleut	Hispanic[2]
U.S. .	14,420	15,687	8,859	13,638	8,328	8,400	MO . . .	12,989	13,563	8,576	12,666	10,072	10,191
AL. . . .	11,486	13,235	6,473	10,814	8,390	9,663	MT . . .	11,213	11,634	7,657	8,443	5,422	6,021
AK. . . .	17,610	19,903	12,816	13,113	9,140	11,885	NE. . .	12,452	12,773	7,857	8,643	5,485	7,280
AZ. . . .	13,461	14,964	9,688	11,713	4,878	7,374	NV. . . .	15,214	16,241	9,366	11,973	9,818	9,348
AR. . . .	10,520	11,472	5,729	9,875	8,643	7,074	NH . . .	15,959	16,028	12,577	13,881	11,887	11,634
CA. . . .	16,409	19,028	11,578	13,733	11,809	8,504	NJ . . .	18,714	20,406	11,542	17,913	14,423	10,761
CO . . .	14,821	15,544	10,704	10,826	9,111	8,233	NM . . .	11,246	12,678	8,579	10,655	5,141	7,542
CT. . . .	20,189	21,466	11,695	18,174	13,657	9,786	NY. . .	16,501	18,584	10,566	14,247	10,202	8,915
DE. . . .	15,854	17,263	9,683	16,379	14,404	10,066	NC . . .	12,885	14,450	7,926	11,127	8,097	9,544
DC. . . .	18,881	34,563	12,226	16,498	14,095	12,525	ND . . .	11,051	11,359	7,875	9,281	4,755	5,811
FL. . . .	14,698	16,052	7,550	12,514	11,090	10,582	OH . . .	13,461	14,049	8,702	16,703	10,053	9,248
GA . . .	13,631	15,832	7,997	12,758	11,745	11,123	OK . . .	11,893	12,859	7,356	10,435	7,227	7,145
HI . . .	15,770	18,598	10,607	14,616	12,415	9,950	OR . . .	13,418	13,778	8,240	10,734	8,890	6,996
ID . . .	11,457	11,723	8,785	9,809	6,843	6,303	PA . . .	14,068	14,688	9,140	13,210	10,546	7,489
IL . . .	15,201	16,817	8,922	14,710	11,495	8,318	RI . . .	14,981	15,573	9,031	9,325	9,015	7,620
IN . . .	13,149	13,553	8,739	9,898		9,221	SC . . .	11,897	14,115	6,800	11,391	10,288	10,723
IA . . .	12,422	12,573	7,844	8,430	6,707	8,025	SD . . .	10,661	11,230	8,124	7,040	4,040	6,908
KS. . . .	13,300	13,817	8,445	8,767		8,007	TN . . .	12,255	13,201	7,414	11,918	10,231	10,246
KY. . . .	11,153	11,439	7,460	13,652	8,212	9,058	TX . . .	12,904	14,629	8,102	12,029	11,086	6,633
LA. . . .	10,635	12,956	5,687	8,899	7,073	10,188	UT . . .	11,029	11,274	8,385	8,284	5,125	7,398
ME . . .	12,957	13,019	10,089	10,414	7,840	9,946	VT . . .	13,527	13,597	8,991	9,667	8,077	5,811
MD . . .	17,730	19,789	12,343	16,264	13,987	13,198	VA . . .	15,713	17,361	9,439	14,022	14,049	12,220
MA . . .	17,224	18,003	10,867	12,665	11,176	7,833	WA . . .	14,923	15,564	10,440	11,584	8,862	8,149
MI . . .	14,154	15,071	9,195	14,950	9,252	9,298	WV . . .	10,520	10,574	7,416	23,658	6,508	9,805
MN . . .	14,389	14,765	8,714	8,057	6,732	8,003	WI . . .	13,276	13,793	7,021	8,128	6,878	7,050
MS . . .	9,648	12,183	5,194	8,167	5,851	8,621	WY . . .	12,311	12,629	8,490	8,057	5,439	7,967

[1] Includes other races not shown separately.   [2] Hispanic persons may be of any race.

Source: U.S. Bureau of the Census, *1990 Census of Population and Housing,* Summary Tape File 3C CD-ROM.

No. 734. Per Capita Money Income, by Race for Selected Cities: 1989

[As of April. In dollars. Based on sample data and subject to sampling variability; see Appendix III]

CITY RANKED BY 1990 POPULATION	All races[1]	White	Black	Asian, Pacific Islander	American Indian, Eskimo, Aleut	Hispanic[2]
New York, NY	16,281	21,972	10,505	12,851	10,861	8,420
Los Angeles, CA	16,188	22,191	11,257	13,875	12,901	7,111
Chicago, IL	12,899	18,258	8,569	11,581	11,251	7,438
Houston, TX	14,261	19,817	8,366	12,250	12,239	7,021
Philadelphia, PA	12,091	15,027	9,061	8,285	10,146	6,053
San Diego, CA	16,401	19,807	10,375	10,628	11,893	8,242
Detroit, MI	9,443	11,947	8,809	8,241	7,045	7,518
Dallas, TX	16,300	22,898	8,444	12,628	10,048	7,093
Phoenix, AZ	14,096	15,497	8,734	12,643	7,076	7,213
San Antonio, TX	10,884	12,322	8,730	11,075	9,651	7,032
San Jose, CA	16,905	19,496	14,239	14,066	13,613	10,007
Baltimore, MD	11,994	16,563	8,991	12,820	7,988	12,075
Indianapolis, IN	14,478	16,083	9,150	15,941	10,586	10,630
San Francisco, CA	19,695	26,222	11,829	12,665	11,485	11,400
Jacksonville, FL	13,661	15,642	8,169	13,844	11,434	10,927
Columbus, OH	13,151	14,527	9,008	10,564	10,278	10,623
Milwaukee, WI	11,106	13,645	6,833	6,357	7,448	6,253
Memphis, TN	11,682	17,569	6,982	11,761	11,110	9,393
Washington, DC	18,881	34,563	12,226	16,498	14,095	12,525
Boston, MA	15,581	18,939	10,420	9,406	9,319	8,364

[1] Includes other races not shown separately.   [2] Hispanic persons may be of any race.

Source: U.S. Bureau of the Census, *1990 Census of Population and Housing,* Summary Tape File 3C on CD-ROM.

No. 735. Persons Below Poverty Level and Below 125 Percent of Poverty Level: 1959 to 1991

[Persons as of **March of the following year.** For explanation of poverty level, see text, section 14]

YEAR	NUMBER BELOW POVERTY LEVEL (mil.)				PERCENT BELOW POVERTY LEVEL				BELOW 125 PERCENT OF POVERTY LEVEL		AVERAGE INCOME CUTOFFS FOR NONFARM FAMILY OF FOUR [3]	
	All races [1]	White	Black	His-panic [2]	All races [1]	White	Black	His-panic [2]	Number (mil.)	Per-cent of total popula-tion	At poverty level	At 125 percent of poverty level
1959	39.5	28.5	9.9	(NA)	22.4	18.1	55.1	(NA)	54.9	31.1	$2,973	$3,716
1960	39.9	28.3	(NA)	(NA)	22.2	17.8	(NA)	(NA)	54.6	30.4	3,022	3,778
1966	28.5	20.8	8.9	(NA)	14.7	12.2	41.8	(NA)	41.3	21.3	3,317	4,146
1969	24.1	16.7	7.1	(NA)	12.1	9.5	32.2	(NA)	34.7	17.4	3,743	4,679
1970	25.4	17.5	7.5	(NA)	12.6	9.9	33.5	(NA)	35.6	17.6	3,968	4,960
1975	25.9	17.8	7.5	3.0	12.3	9.7	31.3	26.9	37.2	17.6	5,500	6,875
1976	25.0	16.7	7.6	2.8	11.8	9.1	31.1	24.7	35.5	16.7	5,815	7,269
1977	24.7	16.4	7.7	2.7	11.6	8.9	31.3	22.4	35.7	16.7	6,191	7,739
1978	24.5	16.3	7.6	2.6	11.4	8.7	30.6	21.6	34.2	15.8	6,662	8,328
1979 [4]	26.1	17.2	8.1	2.9	11.7	9.0	31.0	21.8	36.6	16.4	7,412	9,265
1980	29.3	19.7	8.6	3.5	13.0	10.2	32.5	25.7	40.7	18.1	8,414	10,518
1981	31.8	21.6	9.2	3.7	14.0	11.1	34.2	26.5	43.7	19.3	9,287	11,609
1982 [5]	34.4	23.5	9.7	4.3	15.0	12.0	35.6	29.9	46.5	20.3	9,862	12,328
1983 [5]	35.3	24.0	9.9	4.6	15.2	12.1	35.7	28.0	47.2	20.3	10,178	12,723
1984	33.7	23.0	9.5	4.8	14.4	11.5	33.8	28.4	45.3	19.4	10,609	13,261
1985	33.1	22.9	8.9	5.2	14.0	11.4	31.3	29.0	44.2	18.7	10,989	13,736
1986 [6]	32.4	22.2	9.0	5.1	13.6	11.0	31.1	27.3	43.5	18.2	11,203	14,004
1987 [6]	32.2	21.2	9.5	5.4	13.4	10.4	32.4	28.0	43.0	17.9	11,611	14,514
1988	31.7	20.7	9.4	5.4	13.0	10.1	31.3	26.7	42.6	17.5	12,092	15,115
1989	31.5	20.8	9.3	5.4	12.8	10.0	30.7	26.2	42.7	17.3	12,674	15,843
1990	33.6	22.3	9.8	6.0	13.5	10.7	31.9	28.1	44.8	18.0	13,359	16,699
1991	35.7	23.7	10.2	6.3	14.2	11.3	32.7	28.7	47.5	18.9	13,924	17,405

NA Not available. [1] Includes other races not shown separately. [2] Persons of Hispanic origin may be of any race. [3] Beginning 1981, income cutoffs for nonfarm families are applied to all families, both farm and nonfarm. [4] Population controls based on 1980 census; see text, sections 1 and 14. [5] Beginning 1983, data based on revised Hispanic population controls and not directly comparable with prior years. [6] Beginning 1987, data based on revised processing procedures and not directly comparable with prior years.

Source: U.S. Bureau of the Census, *Current Population Reports*, P60-181.

No. 736. Children Below Poverty Level, by Race and Hispanic Origin: 1970 to 1991

[Persons as of **March of the following year.** Covers only related children in families under 18 years old. For explanation of poverty, see text, section 14]

YEAR	NUMBER BELOW POVERTY LEVEL (1,000)				PERCENT BELOW POVERTY LEVEL			
	All races [1]	White	Black	Hispanic [2]	All races [1]	White	Black	Hispanic [2]
1970	10,235	6,138	3,922	(NA)	14.9	10.5	41.5	(NA)
1971	10,344	6,341	3,836	(NA)	15.1	10.9	40.7	(NA)
1972	10,082	5,784	4,025	(NA)	14.9	10.1	42.7	(NA)
1973	9,453	5,462	3,822	1,364	14.2	9.7	40.6	27.8
1974	9,967	6,079	3,713	1,414	15.1	11.0	39.6	28.6
1975	10,882	6,748	3,884	1,619	16.8	12.5	41.4	33.1
1976	10,081	6,034	3,758	1,424	15.8	11.3	40.4	30.1
1977	10,028	5,943	3,850	1,402	16.0	11.4	41.6	28.0
1978	9,722	5,674	3,781	1,354	15.7	11.0	41.2	27.2
1979	9,993	5,909	3,745	1,505	16.0	11.4	40.8	27.7
1980	11,114	6,817	3,906	1,718	17.9	13.4	42.1	33.0
1981	12,068	7,429	4,170	1,874	19.5	14.7	44.9	35.4
1982	13,139	8,282	4,388	2,117	21.3	16.5	47.3	38.9
1983 [3]	13,427	8,534	4,273	2,251	21.8	17.0	46.2	37.7
1984	12,929	8,086	4,320	2,317	21.0	16.1	46.2	38.7
1985	12,483	7,838	4,057	2,512	20.1	15.6	43.1	39.6
1986	12,257	7,714	4,039	2,413	19.8	15.3	42.7	37.1
1987 [4]	12,275	7,398	4,234	2,606	19.7	14.7	44.4	38.9
1988	11,935	7,095	4,148	2,576	19.0	14.0	42.8	37.3
1989	12,001	7,165	4,257	2,496	19.0	14.1	43.2	35.5
1990	12,715	7,696	4,412	2,750	19.9	15.1	44.2	39.7
1991	13,658	8,316	4,637	2,977	21.1	16.1	45.6	39.8

NA Not available. [1] Includes persons of other races, not shown separately. [2] Persons of Hispanic origin may be of any race. [3] Beginning 1983, data based on revised Hispanic population controls and not directly comparable with prior years. [4] Beginning 1987, data based on revised processing procedures and not directly comparable with prior years.

Source: U.S. Bureau of the Census, *Current Population Reports*, P60-181.

No. 737. Distribution of All Children and of Poor Children, 6 Years Old, by Family Type and Race: 1991

[Excludes unrelated individuals and foster children. Based on published and unpublished tabulations from the 1992 March Supplement to the Current Population Survey. Numbers and percentages may not add due to rounding]

RACE AND FAMILY TYPE	ALL CHILDREN Number (mil.)	ALL CHILDREN Per- cent	CHILDREN BELOW POV- ERTY LEVEL Number (mil.)	CHILDREN BELOW POV- ERTY LEVEL Per- cent	Pov- erty rate	RACE AND FAMILY TYPE	ALL CHILDREN Number (mil.)	ALL CHILDREN Per- cent	CHILDREN BELOW POV- ERTY LEVEL Number (mil.)	CHILDREN BELOW POV- ERTY LEVEL Per- cent	Pov- erty rate
All races:						Black, non-Hispanic:					
All family types . .	22.9	100.0	5.3	100.0	23.0	All family types . .	3.5	100.0	1.8	100.0	49.5
Married-couple .	17.2	74.7	2.1	39.5	12.1	Married-couple .	1.3	35.5	0.3	14.5	20.2
Single-parent .	5.8	25.2	3.2	60.4	55.0	Single-parent . .	2.3	64.5	0.3	85.5	65.7
Mother-only [1]	5.1	22.4	3.0	57.5	59.0	Mother-only .	2.2	60.8	1.4	80.3	67.9
White, non-Hispanic:						Hispanic [2]:					
All family types . .	15.7	100.0	2.2	100.0	14.2	All family types . .	2.8	100.0	1.1	100.0	40.1
Married-couple .	13.1	83.7	1.1	51.1	8.6	Married-couple .	2.0	72.0	0.6	53.6	29.9
Single-parent . .	2.5	16.3	1.1	49.0	42.7	Single-parent . .	0.7	28.0	0.6	46.4	66.4
Mother-only .	2.1	13.7	1.1	45.7	47.3	Mother-only .	0.7	24.6	0.4	36.8	70.4

[1] Includes father-only, relative-only, and nonrelative-only families. [2] Persons of Hispanic origin may be of any race.
Source: National Center for Children in Poverty, Columbia University School of Public Health, New York, NY, unpublished data.

No. 738. Persons Below Poverty Level, by Race, Hispanic Origin, Age, and Region: 1991

[Persons as of **March 1992**. For explanation of poverty level, see text, section 14. For composition of regions, see table 31]

AGE AND REGION	NUMBER BELOW POVERTY LEVEL (1,000) All races [1]	NUMBER BELOW POVERTY LEVEL (1,000) White	NUMBER BELOW POVERTY LEVEL (1,000) Black	NUMBER BELOW POVERTY LEVEL (1,000) Hispanic [2]	PERCENT BELOW POVERTY LEVEL All races [1]	PERCENT BELOW POVERTY LEVEL White	PERCENT BELOW POVERTY LEVEL Black	PERCENT BELOW POVERTY LEVEL Hispanic [2]
Total	35,708	23,747	10,242	6,339	14.2	11.3	32.7	28.7
Under 16 years old.	13,178	8,135	4,375	2,840	22.2	17.2	47.0	41.1
16 to 21 years old	3,605	2,359	1,040	719	17.9	14.5	34.0	31.5
22 to 44 years old	10,838	7,399	2,878	1,987	11.7	9.5	25.3	22.9
45 to 54 years old	2,167	1,541	544	328	8.0	6.6	19.5	18.1
55 to 59 years old	1,019	716	246	113	9.6	7.9	21.3	17.0
60 to 64 years old	1,120	796	278	115	10.6	8.7	27.5	19.6
65 years old and over . . .	3,781	2,802	880	237	12.4	10.3	33.8	20.8
Northeast	6,177	4,389	1,546	1,217	12.2	10.0	28.1	36.3
Midwest	7,989	5,242	2,380	346	13.2	9.9	37.7	23.5
South.	13,783	7,837	5,716	1,765	16.0	11.7	33.6	26.1
West	7,759	6,279	600	3,012	14.3	13.5	24.0	28.8

[1] Includes other races not shown separately. [2] Persons of Hispanic origin may be of any race.
Source: U.S. Bureau of the Census, *Current Population Reports*, P60-181; and unpublished data.

No. 739. Persons 65 Years Old and Over Below Poverty Level, by Selected Characteristics: 1970 to 1991

[Persons as of **March of following year**]

CHARACTERISTIC	NUMBER BELOW POVERTY LEVEL (1,000) 1970	NUMBER BELOW POVERTY LEVEL (1,000) 1979 [1]	NUMBER BELOW POVERTY LEVEL (1,000) 1985 [2]	NUMBER BELOW POVERTY LEVEL (1,000) 1990 [3]	NUMBER BELOW POVERTY LEVEL (1,000) 1991	PERCENT BELOW POVERTY LEVEL 1970	PERCENT BELOW POVERTY LEVEL 1979 [1]	PERCENT BELOW POVERTY LEVEL 1985 [2]	PERCENT BELOW POVERTY LEVEL 1990 [3]	PERCENT BELOW POVERTY LEVEL 1991
Persons, 65 yr. and over [4]	4,793	3,682	3,456	3,658	3,781	24.6	15.2	12.6	12.2	12.4
White.	4,011	2,911	2,698	2,707	2,802	22.6	13.3	11.0	10.1	10.3
Black	735	740	717	860	880	47.7	36.3	31.5	33.8	33.8
Hispanic [5].	(NA)	154	219	245	237	(NA)	26.8	23.9	22.5	20.8
In families.	2,013	1,380	1,173	1,172	1,228	14.8	8.4	6.4	5.8	6.0
Unrelated individuals.	2,779	2,299	2,281	2,479	2,553	47.2	29.4	25.6	24.7	24.9
Persons, 60 yr. and over	5,977	4,753	4,677	4,756	4,901	21.3	13.9	12.3	11.7	11.9

NA Not available. [1] Population controls based on 1980 census; see text, section 14. [2] Beginning 1983, data based on revised Hispanic population controls and not directly comparable with prior years. [3] Beginning 1987, data based on revised processing procedures and not directly comparable with prior years. [4] Beginning 1979, includes members of unrelated subfamilies not shown separately. For earlier years, unrelated subfamily members are included in the "In families" category. [5] Persons of Hispanic origin may be of any race.
Source: U.S. Bureau of the Census, *Current Population Reports*, P60-181.

No. 740. Persons Below Poverty Level, by Race of Householder and Family Status: 1979 to 1991

[Persons as of March of following year. For explanation of poverty level, see text, section 14]

RACE OF HOUSEHOLDER AND FAMILY STATUS	NUMBER BELOW POVERTY LEVEL (mil.)					PERCENT BELOW POVERTY LEVEL				
	1979 [1]	1985	1989 [2]	1990	1991	1979 [1]	1985	1989 [2]	1990	1991
All persons [3]	**26.1**	**33.1**	**31.5**	**33.6**	**35.7**	**11.7**	**14.0**	**12.8**	**13.5**	**14.2**
In families	20.0	25.7	24.1	25.2	27.1	10.2	12.6	11.5	12.0	12.8
Householder	5.5	7.2	6.8	7.1	7.7	9.2	11.4	10.3	10.7	11.5
Related children under 18 years	10.0	12.5	12.0	12.7	13.7	16.0	20.1	19.0	19.9	21.1
Other family members	4.5	6.0	5.3	5.4	5.8	6.1	7.7	6.6	6.7	7.2
Unrelated individuals	5.7	6.7	6.8	7.4	7.8	21.9	21.5	19.2	20.7	21.1
White	**17.2**	**22.9**	**20.8**	**22.3**	**23.7**	**9.0**	**11.4**	**10.0**	**10.7**	**11.3**
In families	12.5	17.1	15.2	15.9	17.3	7.4	9.9	8.6	9.0	9.7
Householder	3.6	5.0	4.4	4.6	5.0	6.9	9.1	7.8	8.1	8.8
Related children under 18 years	5.9	7.8	7.2	7.7	8.3	11.4	15.6	14.1	15.1	16.1
Other family members	3.0	4.3	3.6	3.6	3.9	4.7	6.4	5.3	5.2	5.7
Unrelated individuals	4.5	5.3	5.1	5.7	5.9	19.7	19.6	16.9	18.6	18.8
Black	**8.1**	**8.9**	**9.3**	**9.8**	**10.2**	**31.0**	**31.3**	**30.7**	**31.9**	**32.7**
In families	6.8	7.5	7.7	8.2	8.5	30.0	30.5	29.7	31.0	32.0
Householder	1.7	2.0	2.1	2.2	2.3	27.8	28.7	27.8	29.3	30.4
Related children under 18 years	3.7	4.1	4.3	4.4	4.6	40.8	43.1	43.2	44.2	45.6
Other family members	1.3	1.5	1.4	1.6	1.5	18.2	17.7	15.9	17.6	17.6
Unrelated individuals	1.2	1.3	1.5	1.5	1.6	37.3	34.7	35.2	35.1	35.3
In families with female householder, no husband present [3]	**13.5**	**16.4**	**15.9**	**17.2**	**18.6**	**32.0**	**33.5**	**30.9**	**32.4**	**34.3**
In families	9.4	11.6	11.7	12.6	13.8	34.9	37.6	35.9	37.2	39.7
Householder	2.6	3.5	3.5	3.8	4.2	30.4	34.0	32.2	33.4	35.6
Related children under 18 years	5.6	6.7	6.8	7.4	8.1	48.6	53.6	51.1	53.4	55.5
Other family members	1.1	1.4	1.4	1.4	1.4	16.9	17.3	16.3	17.6	18.7

[1] Population controls based on 1980 census; see text section 14. [2] Beginning 1987, data based on revised processing procedures and not directly comparable with prior years. [3] Includes races, members of unrelated subfamilies, and unrelated individuals (for families with female householder) not shown separately.

Source: U.S. Bureau of the Census, *Current Population Reports*, P60-181; and unpublished data.

No. 741. Poverty Rates, by Race, for States: 1989

[As of April. In percent. Based on sample data and subject to sampling variability; see Appendix III]

STATE	All races [1]	White	Black	Asian, Pacific Islander	American Indian, Eskimo, Aleut	His- panic [2]	STATE	All races [1]	White	Black	Asian, Pacific Islander	American Indian, Eskimo, Aleut	His- panic [2]
U.S..	13.1	9.8	29.5	14.1	30.9	25.3	MO ..	13.3	11.2	29.9	19.3	22.8	17.1
AL ...	18.3	11.7	37.7	20.0	21.6	19.4	MT ...	16.1	14.0	31.0	20.2	46.1	30.0
AK ...	9.0	6.1	10.4	7.3	23.1	11.9	NE ..	11.1	9.9	31.1	20.1	46.2	22.7
AZ ...	15.7	11.3	27.5	16.2	49.2	28.3	NV ..	10.2	8.4	23.3	10.2	24.1	17.8
AR ...	19.1	14.5	43.0	16.8	23.1	26.2	NH ..	6.4	6.3	12.6	11.2	19.9	13.2
CA ...	12.5	9.1	21.1	14.3	18.6	21.6	NJ ..	7.6	5.0	19.3	6.6	18.1	19.1
CO ...	11.7	10.0	23.9	16.0	27.9	25.5	NM ..	20.6	16.1	27.8	17.2	46.0	27.8
CT ...	6.8	4.6	19.8	8.2	15.0	28.7	NY ..	13.0	8.7	25.0	14.5	23.5	30.5
DE ...	8.7	5.7	22.0	9.6	13.6	19.3	NC ..	13.0	8.6	27.1	15.0	24.4	19.2
DC ...	16.9	8.2	20.2	18.2	24.5	20.4	ND ..	14.4	12.8	15.5	24.7	50.0	23.7
FL ...	12.7	9.4	31.5	13.0	19.9	19.5	OH ..	12.5	10.0	32.3	15.9	24.1	24.9
GA ...	14.7	8.8	30.3	11.6	18.9	20.2	OK ..	16.7	13.7	34.6	21.2	28.7	29.2
HI ...	8.3	7.9	8.8	8.2	17.0	13.5	OR ..	12.4	11.4	29.8	19.9	26.5	28.9
ID ...	13.3	12.2	22.8	16.8	34.3	30.2	PA ..	11.1	8.8	29.0	18.7	26.1	36.2
IL ...	11.9	7.8	31.1	11.0	20.4	20.0	RI ..	9.6	8.0	25.8	27.5	26.0	30.4
IN ...	10.7	9.0	29.0	15.0	22.9	17.1	SC ..	15.4	8.5	31.4	11.5	19.8	15.6
IA ...	11.5	10.8	37.1	27.2	36.2	21.7	SD ..	15.9	12.6	19.6	18.4	57.1	24.9
KS ...	11.5	9.9	30.0	22.2	21.6	19.7	TN ..	15.7	12.5	32.4	15.5	24.1	18.8
KY ...	19.0	17.8	35.2	16.4	31.0	21.3	TX ..	18.1	13.9	31.0	15.7	20.8	33.0
LA ...	23.6	13.4	45.7	28.3	37.7	19.5	UT ..	11.4	10.2	30.5	20.9	43.6	22.8
ME ...	10.8	10.7	20.0	11.9	22.9	13.2	VT ..	9.9	9.7	21.0	14.8	27.8	10.8
MD ...	8.3	5.3	16.6	8.1	12.2	11.3	VA ..	10.2	7.4	22.4	8.7	13.7	11.4
MA ...	8.9	7.0	23.0	19.7	24.4	36.7	WA ..	10.9	9.4	22.8	16.2	29.5	27.8
MI ...	13.1	9.4	33.7	15.3	25.8	23.6	WV ..	19.7	19.1	36.0	14.9	36.1	26.1
MN..	10.2	8.7	36.8	31.7	43.7	25.6	WI ...	10.7	8.3	40.8	41.2	34.7	27.2
MS..	25.2	13.2	46.4	33.5	39.8	25.3	WY ..	11.9	10.7	25.2	16.1	42.9	22.6

[1] Includes other races not shown separately. [2] Hispanic persons may be of any race.

Source: U.S. Bureau of the Census, *1990 Census of Population and Housing*, Summary Tape File 3C on CD-ROM.

No. 742. Poverty Rates for Selected Cities: 1989

[As of April. In percent. Based on sample data and subject to sampling variability; see Appendix III]

CITY RANKED BY 1990 POPULATION	Persons			All families	CITY RANKED BY 1990 POPULATION	Persons			All families
	All persons	Children under 6 years old	Persons over 65 years old			All persons	Children under 6 years old	Persons over 65 years old	
New York, NY	19.3	30.9	16.5	16.3	Seattle, WA	12.4	16.5	9.0	7.4
Los Angeles, CA	18.9	27.7	10.5	14.9	El Paso, TX	25.3	36.7	20.6	21.2
Chicago, IL	21.6	35.8	15.9	18.3	Cleveland, OH	28.5	46.2	19.2	25.2
Houston, TX	20.7	31.3	17.8	17.2	New Orleans, LA	31.6	48.7	24.6	27.3
Philadelphia, PA	20.3	31.9	16.3	16.1	Nashville-Davidson, TN	13.4	23.0	15.1	10.4
San Diego, CA	13.4	21.0	7.4	9.7	Denver, CO	17.1	29.3	12.7	13.1
Detroit, MI	32.4	52.4	20.1	29.0	Austin, TX	17.9	23.2	11.7	11.5
Dallas, TX	18.0	27.9	14.6	14.7	Fort Worth, TX	17.4	26.3	14.4	13.6
Phoenix, AZ	14.2	22.8	11.3	10.5	Oklahoma City, OK	15.9	26.7	13.1	12.0
San Antonio, TX	22.6	35.6	19.1	18.7	Portland, OR	14.5	20.9	11.6	9.7
San Jose, CA	9.3	12.9	7.1	6.5	Kansas City, MO	15.3	26.0	14.6	11.7
Baltimore, MD	21.9	34.3	19.3	17.8	Long Beach, CA	16.8	28.1	9.1	13.5
Indianapolis, IN	12.5	20.2	11.7	9.7	Tucson, AZ	20.2	29.6	12.1	14.4
San Francisco, CA	12.7	17.7	9.9	9.7	St. Louis, MO	24.6	41.2	18.7	20.6
Jacksonville, FL	13.0	20.1	16.1	9.9	Charlotte, NC	10.8	18.0	13.8	8.5
Columbus, OH	17.2	25.6	13.0	12.6	Atlanta, GA	27.3	47.3	25.1	24.6
Milwaukee, WI	22.2	41.5	10.0	18.5	Virginia Beach, VA	5.9	8.8	8.0	4.3
Memphis, TN	23.0	37.7	21.8	18.7	Albuquerque, NM	14.0	21.2	9.7	10.3
Washington, DC	16.9	26.8	17.2	13.3	Baton Rouge, LA	26.2	39.0	18.2	20.3
Boston, MA	18.7	27.9	15.3	15.0	Oakland, CA	18.8	32.2	11.0	16.7

Source: U.S. Bureau of the Census, *1990 Census of Population and Housing,* Summary Tape File 3C on CD-ROM.

No. 743. Families Below Poverty Level—Selected Characteristics, by Race and Hispanic Origin: 1991

[Families as of **March 1992.** For explanation of poverty, see text, section 14. For composition of regions, see table 31]

CHARACTERISTIC	NUMBER BELOW POVERTY LEVEL (1,000)				PERCENT BELOW POVERTY LEVEL			
	All races[1]	White	Black	His-panic[2]	All races[1]	White	Black	His-panic[2]
Total	7,712	5,022	2,343	1,372	11.5	8.8	30.4	26.5
Age of householder:								
15 to 24 years old	937	577	328	181	35.5	27.9	66.9	46.3
25 to 34 years old	2,650	1,746	812	511	18.4	14.7	40.9	33.4
35 to 44 years old	1,786	1,147	531	367	10.2	7.8	25.1	25.8
45 to 54 years old	861	593	226	157	7.1	5.6	18.6	18.8
55 to 64 years old	750	490	217	93	8.1	6.1	23.0	16.1
65 years old and over	728	469	229	63	6.5	4.7	23.7	14.9
Northeast	1,328	947	326	295	9.9	8.0	25.3	34.4
Midwest	1,714	1,100	557	76	10.6	7.7	35.8	21.3
South	3,054	1,690	1,315	396	12.9	8.9	30.9	24.0
West	1,616	1,285	145	605	11.6	10.6	23.4	26.2
Size of family:								
Two persons	2,495	1,703	672	276	8.8	6.9	25.1	21.8
Three persons	1,816	1,154	592	284	11.6	8.8	29.5	23.5
Four persons	1,671	1,065	520	326	11.8	8.9	32.9	26.3
Five persons	921	597	305	217	15.3	12.1	36.5	28.9
Six persons	409	274	116	140	20.6	17.9	33.9	36.1
Seven persons or more	400	229	137	129	33.4	28.1	50.6	39.7
Average size	3.52	3.47	3.59	4.05	(X)	(X)	(X)	(X)
Avg. number of children per family with children	2.21	2.17	2.26	2.45	(X)	(X)	(X)	(X)
Education of householder: [3]								
No high school diploma	3,171	2,081	954	840	24.2	20.0	41.4	36.1
High school diploma, no college	2,337	1,489	777	234	10.5	7.8	30.0	18.8
Some college, less than Bachelor's degree	944	652	246	89	6.5	5.2	16.2	11.8
Bachelor's degree or more	323	224	38	28	2.2	1.7	4.6	6.0
Work experience of householder in 1990: [4]								
Total [5]	7,712	5,022	2,343	1,372	11.5	8.8	30.4	26.5
Worked	3,824	2,691	970	762	7.5	6.1	18.7	19.4
50 to 52 weeks	1,599	1,188	350	374	4.0	3.4	9.4	13.2
49 weeks or less	2,225	1,503	620	388	20.0	16.2	42.3	35.9
Did not work	3,856	2,312	1,366	603	24.5	17.9	57.0	49.7

X Not applicable. [1] Includes other races not shown separately. [2] Hispanic persons may be of any race. [3] Householder 25 years old and over. [4] Restricted to families with civilian workers. [5] Includes Armed Forces not shown separately.

Source: U.S. Bureau of the Census, *Current Population Reports,* P60-181; and unpublished data.

No. 744. Families Below Poverty Level and Below 125 Percent of Poverty Level: 1959 to 1991

[Families as of **March of the following year.** For explanation of poverty level, see text, section 14]

YEAR	NUMBER BELOW POVERTY LEVEL (1,000)				PERCENT BELOW POVERTY LEVEL				BELOW 125 PERCENT OF POVERTY LEVEL	
	All races [1]	White	Black	His-panic [2]	All races [1]	White	Black	His-panic [2]	Number (1,000)	Percent
1959	8,320	6,185	1,860	(NA)	18.5	15.2	48.1	(NA)	11,790	26.2
1960	8,243	6,115	(NA)	(NA)	18.1	14.9	(NA)	(NA)	11,525	25.4
1970	5,260	3,708	1,481	(NA)	10.1	8.0	29.5	(NA)	7,516	14.4
1972	5,075	3,441	1,529	(NA)	9.3	7.1	29.0	(NA)	7,347	13.5
1973	4,828	3,219	1,527	468	8.8	6.6	28.1	19.8	7,044	12.8
1974	4,922	3,352	1,479	526	8.8	6.8	26.9	21.2	7,195	12.9
1975	5,450	3,838	1,513	627	9.7	7.7	27.1	25.1	7,974	14.2
1976	5,311	3,560	1,617	598	9.4	7.1	27.9	23.1	7,647	13.5
1977	5,311	3,540	1,637	591	9.3	7.0	28.2	21.4	7,713	13.5
1978	5,280	3,523	1,622	559	9.1	6.9	27.5	20.4	7,417	12.8
1979 [3] ...	5,461	3,581	1,722	614	9.2	6.9	27.8	20.3	7,784	13.1
1980	6,217	4,195	1,826	751	10.3	8.0	28.9	23.2	8,764	14.5
1981	6,851	4,670	1,972	792	11.2	8.8	30.8	24.0	9,568	15.7
1982	7,512	5,118	2,158	916	12.2	9.6	33.0	27.2	10,279	16.7
1983 [4] ...	7,647	5,220	2,161	981	12.3	9.7	32.3	25.9	(NA)	(NA)
1984	7,277	4,925	2,094	991	11.6	9.1	30.9	25.2	9,901	15.8
1985	7,223	4,983	1,983	1,074	11.4	9.1	28.7	25.5	9,753	15.3
1986	7,023	4,811	1,987	1,085	10.9	8.6	28.0	24.7	9,476	14.7
1987 [5] ...	7,005	4,567	2,117	1,168	10.7	8.1	29.4	25.5	9,338	14.3
1988	6,874	4,471	2,089	1,141	10.4	7.9	28.2	23.7	9,284	14.1
1989	6,784	4,409	2,077	1,133	10.3	7.8	27.8	23.4	9,267	14.0
1990	7,098	4,622	2,193	1,244	10.7	8.1	29.3	25.0	9,564	14.4
1991	7,712	5,022	2,343	1,372	11.5	8.8	30.4	26.5	10,244	15.3

NA Not available. [1] Includes other races not shown separately. [2] Persons of Hispanic origin may be of any race. [3] Population controls based on 1980 census; see text, section 14. [4] Beginning 1983, data based on revised Hispanic population controls and not directly comparable with prior years. [5] Beginning 1987, data based on revised processing procedures and not directly comparable with prior years. See text, section 14, and source.

Source: U.S. Bureau of the Census, *Current Population Reports,* P60-181.

No. 745. Families Below Poverty Level—Alternative Inflation Adjustment: 1970 to 1991

[**In thousands, except percent.** Families as of **March of following year.** Families include unrelated individuals and are therefore not directly comparable to Census Bureau definitions; see text, section 1. Adjustment for inflation using the CPI-U-X1 has been made; see text, section 14. Based on the March Current Population Survey, 1971-1992]

ITEM	1970	1980	1984	1985	1986	1987	1988	1989	1990	1991
NUMBER BELOW POVERTY LEVEL										
All families [1]	9,775	10,869	12,091	12,203	12,269	12,468	12,515	12,141	13,158	13,956
Families with children [1]	3,330	4,432	5,230	5,177	5,199	5,231	5,179	5,054	5,441	6,480
Married couples	1,558	1,555	1,877	1,803	1,644	1,638	1,515	1,498	1,610	1,711
Single mothers	1,509	2,498	2,918	2,957	3,121	3,142	3,195	3,072	3,302	3,597
Nonelderly units:										
Childless families	662	587	907	898	826	795	796	767	755	830
Unrelated individuals	2,146	3,307	3,890	3,990	4,016	4,100	4,214	4,077	4,532	4,660
Elderly units:										
Childless families	965	574	408	420	413	466	492	455	474	448
Unrelated individuals	2,672	1,969	1,656	1,718	1,815	1,876	1,834	1,787	1,956	2,102
PERCENT BELOW POVERTY LEVEL										
All families [1]	15	12	13	13	13	13	12	12	13	13
Families with children [1]	11	13	16	15	15	15	15	15	16	18
Married couples	6	6	8	7	7	7	6	6	7	7
Single mothers	45	42	44	44	46	45	45	43	44	46
Nonelderly units:										
Childless families	4	3	4	4	4	4	4	4	4	4
Unrelated individuals	23	17	18	18	18	17	17	16	18	18
Elderly units:										
Childless families	14	6	4	4	4	4	5	4	4	4
Unrelated individuals	46	25	19	19	20	20	19	18	19	21

[1] Includes other types of families not shown separately.

Source: Congressional Budget Office, *Trends in Family Income: 1970-1986,* February 1988; and Congressional Budget Office tabulations.

No. 746. Weighted Average Adjusted Poverty Thresholds Based on the CPI-U-X1, by Family Size: 1980 to 1991

[Adjustment for inflation using the CPI-U-X1 has been made; see text, section 14]

SIZE OF UNIT	1980	1983	1984	1985	1986	1987	1988	1989	1990	1991
One person (unrelated individual)..	3,843	4,604	4,801	4,974	5,068	5,308	5,534	5,807	6,121	6,378
Under 65 years	3,935	4,713	4,912	5,088	5,186	5,428	5,654	5,937	6,257	6,520
65 years and over	3,623	4,345	4,529	4,690	4,780	5,004	5,212	5,472	5,767	6,010
Two persons	4,920	5,899	6,151	6,366	6,493	6,795	7,077	7,431	7,829	8,157
Householder under 65 years ...	5,079	6,093	6,352	6,578	6,706	7,019	7,310	7,676	8,091	8,433
Householder 65 years and over .	4,571	5,480	5,715	5,916	6,031	6,313	6,575	6,902	7,273	7,583
Three persons	6,022	7,222	7,529	7,799	7,948	8,319	8,667	9,095	9,587	9,992
Four persons	7,719	9,260	9,651	9,997	10,191	10,666	11,108	11,662	12,293	12,812
Five persons	9,142	10,963	11,431	11,832	12,061	12,619	13,141	13,792	14,530	15,141
Six persons	10,338	12,401	12,924	13,369	13,633	14,247	14,834	15,569	16,414	17,102
Seven persons	11,706	14,103	14,642	15,152	15,509	16,212	16,763	17,631	18,624	19,376
Eight persons	13,025	15,622	16,339	16,840	17,094	17,926	18,628	19,624	20,778	21,719
Nine or more persons	15,499	18,479	19,328	20,089	20,465	21,224	22,169	23,444	24,703	25,710

Source: Congressional Budget Office, *Trends in Family Income: 1970 to 1986*, February 1988, and Congressional Budget Office tabulations.

No. 747. Persons Below Poverty Level—Alternative Inflation Adjustment: 1974 to 1991

[Based on Current Population Survey. Annual adjustment for cost-of-living changes is based on the CPI-U-X1; see text, section 14]

YEAR	NUMBER BELOW POVERTY LEVEL (1,000)				PERCENT BELOW POVERTY LEVEL			
	All races [1]	White	Black	Hispanic [2]	All races [1]	White	Black	Hispanic [2]
1974	22,076	14,870	6,773	2,448	10.5	8.2	28.6	21.9
1975	24,232	16,547	7,170	2,787	11.5	9.0	29.8	25.1
1976	23,347	15,513	7,202	2,570	11.0	8.4	29.5	22.8
1977	22,933	15,190	7,230	2,480	10.7	8.2	29.3	20.6
1978	22,472	14,829	7,085	2,416	10.4	8.0	28.4	20.0
1979	23,504	15,382	7,388	2,614	10.5	8.0	28.5	19.5
1980	25,869	17,283	7,671	3,134	11.5	9.0	29.0	23.0
1981	27,731	18,456	8,311	3,302	12.2	9.5	31.0	23.6
1982	30,288	20,385	8,824	3,842	13.2	10.4	32.4	26.7
1983	31,649	21,180	9,130	4,215	13.7	10.7	33.0	25.5
1984	29,971	20,043	8,765	4,367	12.8	10.1	31.2	25.8
1985	29,558	20,157	8,284	4,712	12.5	10.0	29.1	26.1
1986	29,101	19,629	8,391	4,570	12.2	9.7	29.1	24.4
1987	28,890	18,777	8,744	4,899	12.0	9.2	29.8	25.3
1988	28,544	18,326	8,707	4,914	11.7	8.9	29.2	24.5
1989	27,967	18,152	8,504	4,827	11.4	8.8	28.0	23.3
1990	30,097	19,677	9,145	5,401	12.1	9.4	29.7	25.2
1991	32,009	21,027	9,421	5,695	12.7	10.0	30.1	25.8

[1] Includes other races not shown separately.　　[2] Persons of Hispanic origin may be of any race.

Source: U.S. Bureau of the Census, *Current Population Reports*, P60-182; and unpublished data.

No. 748. Weighted Average Poverty Thresholds Based on the CPI-U-X1, by Family Size: 1980 to 1991

SIZE OF UNIT	1980	1984	1985	1986	1987	1988	1989	1990	1991
One person (unrelated individual). ...	3,851	4,856	5,032	5,127	5,316	5,543	5,807	6,121	6,379
Under 65 years	3,942	4,969	5,146	5,246	5,437	5,663	5,936	6,257	6,520
65 years and over	3,629	4,581	4,744	4,835	5,012	5,221	5,472	5,767	6,010
Two persons	3,729	6,222	6,439	6,568	6,806	7,089	7,431	7,829	8,157
Householder under 65 years	5,088	6,425	6,653	6,783	7,031	7,322	7,676	8,091	8,433
Householder 65 years and over ...	4,579	5,780	5,983	6,100	6,323	6,586	6,902	7,273	7,583
Three persons	6,033	7,616	7,888	8,039	8,333	8,681	9,095	9,587	9,992
Four persons	7,732	9,761	10,111	10,308	10,683	11,126	11,662	12,293	12,812
Five persons	9,159	11,562	11,968	12,200	12,640	13,162	13,792	14,530	15,141
Six persons	10,356	13,072	13,522	13,789	14,270	14,859	15,569	16,414	17,101
Seven persons	(NA)	14,810	15,325	13,687	16,239	16,790	17,631	18,624	19,376
Eight persons................	(NA)	16,526	17,033	17,290	17,956	18,659	19,624	20,778	21,719
Nine or more persons	(NA)	19,550	20,319	20,700	21,259	22,205	23,444	24,703	25,710

NA Not available.

Source: U.S. Bureau of the Census, *Current Population Reports*, P60-182; and unpublished data.

No. 749. Persons Below Poverty Level, by Definition of Income: 1991

[Persons as of **March 1992.** For explanation of definitions of income, see text, section 14, and source]

Defi-nition num-ber	DEFINITION OF INCOME	NUMBER BELOW POVERTY LEVEL (1,000)				PERCENT BELOW POVERTY LEVEL			
		All races [1]	White	Black	His-panic [2]	All races [1]	White	Black	His-panic [2]
	All persons......................	251,179	210,121	31,312	22,068	(X)	(X)	(X)	(X)
	INCOME BEFORE TAXES								
1	Money income excluding capital gains (current) measure [3]..............	35,708	23,747	10,242	6,339	14.2	11.3	32.7	28.7
2	Definition 1 less government money transfers.	54,803	39,808	12,759	7,809	21.8	18.9	40.7	35.4
3	Definition 2 plus capital gains...........	54,644	39,676	12,730	7,794	21.8	18.9	40.7	35.3
4	Definition 3 plus health insurance supplements to wage or salary income [4] ...	53,087	38,596	12,314	7,482	21.1	18.4	39.3	33.9
	INCOME AFTER TAXES								
5	Definition 4 less Social Security payroll taxes .	55,198	40,223	12,709	7,873	22.0	19.1	40.6	35.7
6	Definition 5 less Federal income taxes (excluding EITC) [5].................	55,939	40,803	12,835	8,037	22.3	19.4	41.0	36.4
7	Definition 6 plus EITC [5]...............	54,361	39,649	12,475	7,662	21.6	18.9	39.8	34.7
8	Definition 7 less State income taxes.......	54,697	39,918	12,517	7,683	21.8	19.0	40.0	34.8
9	Definition 8 plus nonmeans-tested government cash transfers [6]	38,037	25,432	10,744	6,731	15.1	12.1	34.3	30.5
11	Definition 9 plus nonmeans-tested government noncash transfers [7]........	36,751	24,562	10,372	6,553	14.6	11.7	33.1	29.7
12	Definition 11 plus means-tested government cash transfers [8].................	34,188	22,843	9,697	6,080	13.6	10.9	31.0	27.6
14	Definition 12 plus means-tested government noncash transfers [9]	28,545	19,545	7,653	5,048	11.4	9.3	24.4	22.9
15	Definition 14 plus net imputed return on equity in own home [10]...............	25,772	17,382	7,141	4,791	10.3	8.3	22.8	21.7

X Not applicable. [1] Includes other races not shown separately. [2] Persons of Hispanic origin may be of any race. [3] Official definition of income based on money income before taxes and includes government cash transfers. [4] Employer contributions to the health insurance plans of employees. [5] Earned Income Tax Credit. [6] Includes Social Security and Railroad Retirement, veterans payments, unemployment and workers' compensation, Black Lung payments, Pell Grants, and other government educational assistance. [7] Includes Medicare and subsidies from regular price school lunches. [8] Includes AFDC and other public assistance or welfare payments, Supplemental Security Income, and veterans payments. Households must meet certain eligibility requirements in order to qualify for these benefits. (See section 12.) [9] Includes Medicaid, food stamps, subsidies from free or reduced-price school lunches, and rent subsidies. [10] Estimated amount of income a household would receive if it chose to shift amount held as home equity into an interest bearing account.

No. 750. Money Income of Households—Percent Distribution, by Quintile, and Index of Income Concentration, by Definition of Income: 1991

[Based on 95,669,000 households as of **March 1992.** For explanation of income definitions, see text, section 14]

Defi-nition num-ber	DEFINITION OF INCOME	Total income (bil. dol.)	SHARE OF AGGREGATE INCOME BY QUINTILE					Index of income con-centra-tion [1]	Median income (dol.)
			Lowest quintile	Second quintile	Third quintile	Fourth quintile	Highest quintile		
	INCOME BEFORE TAXES								
1	Money income excluding capital gains (current) measure [2].................	3,628	3.8	9.5	16.0	24.1	46.5	0.425	30,126
2	Definition 1 less government money transfers.	3,323	1.1	8.0	15.9	25.3	49.6	0.483	27,302
3	Definition 2 plus capital gains...........	3,405	1.1	7.8	15.6	24.8	50.6	0.491	27,427
4	Definition 3 plus health insurance supplements to wage or salary income [3] ...	3,544	1.1	7.7	15.5	25.2	50.5	0.490	28,792
	INCOME AFTER TAXES								
5	Definition 4 less Social Security payroll taxes .	3,343	1.0	7.7	15.4	25.0	50.8	0.492	27,005
6	Definition 5 less Federal income taxes (excluding the EITC) [4].................	2,930	1.2	8.3	16.2	25.7	48.6	0.471	24,820
7	Definition 6 plus EITC [4]...............	2,937	1.2	8.4	16.2	25.7	48.4	0.470	24,866
8	Definition 7 less State income taxes.......	2,827	1.3	8.7	16.3	25.8	48.0	0.464	24,212
9	Definition 8 plus nonmeans-tested government cash transfers [5]	3,097	3.7	10.5	16.6	24.6	44.7	0.410	26,813
11	Definition 9 plus nonmeans-tested govt. noncash transfers [6]	3,176	3.8	10.9	16.8	24.5	44.0	0.400	27,951
12	Definition 11 plus means-tested government cash transfers [7]	3,211	4.5	11.0	16.7	24.3	43.6	0.391	28,104
14	Definition 12 plus means-tested government noncash transfers [8]	3,254	5.1	11.1	16.7	24.0	43.0	0.380	28,428
15	Definition 14 plus net imputed return on equity in own home [9]	3,500	5.1	11.2	16.7	23.9	43.1	0.379	30,538

[1] A statistical measure of income equality ranging from 0 to 1. A measure of 1 indicates perfect inequality (i.e. one person having all the wealth and the rest having none.) A measure of 0 indicates perfect equality (i.e. all persons having equal shares of wealth.) [2] See footnote 3, table 749. [3] See footnote 4, table 749. [4] Earned Income Tax Credit. [5] See footnote 6, table 749. [6] See footnote 7, table 749 [7] See footnote 8, table 749. [8] See footnote 9, table 749. [9] See footnote 10, table 749.
Source of tables 749 and 750: U.S. Bureau of the Census, *Current Population Reports*, P60-182; and unpublished data.

No. 751. Family Net Worth—Percent of Families Owning Selected Nonfinancial Assets: 1983 and 1989

[Families include one-person units; for definition of family, see text, section 1. Based on Survey of Consumer Finance; see Appendix III. For data on financial assets, see table 788, section 16]

CHARACTERISTIC	Total	Vehicles	Principal residence	Investment real estate	Business	Other assets
1983						
All families	90.3	84.4	64.4	20.9	14.2	7.4
White	94.3	88.7	68.0	23.1	16.1	8.5
Non-White and Hispanic	71.3	64.4	42.2	10.9	5.4	2.5
Under 35 years old	87.2	83.3	38.7	10.4	10.3	9.1
35 to 44 years old	94.0	91.2	68.4	22.9	18.3	10.3
45 to 54 years old	92.7	90.3	78.0	24.9	18.2	6.4
55 to 64 years old	93.1	87.7	76.8	32.6	18.1	5.9
65 to 74 years old	91.8	80.2	78.9	27.2	12.3	5.6
75 years old and over	79.6	57.8	69.5	16.9	6.4	1.4
Under 55 years old:						
Unmarried, no children	79.1	71.9	23.4	10.0	9.1	13.9
Married, no children	97.0	96.4	51.8	14.6	14.3	13.0
Unmarried, children	78.3	73.1	42.7	12.0	6.4	6.2
Married, children	97.8	96.2	73.5	22.5	19.3	7.6
55 years old and over:						
In labor force	95.1	89.5	78.1	36.3	24.1	7.3
Out of labor force, retired	86.2	74.4	74.8	22.1	6.1	3.4
Income (1989 dollars):						
Less than $10,000	67.4	50.5	40.1	6.9	4.5	3.3
$10,000 to $19,999	89.1	83.2	52.6	14.1	6.9	5.5
$20,000 to $29,999	96.1	93.3	60.3	17.9	12.0	7.2
$30,000 to $49,999	98.6	97.0	77.2	25.8	18.7	8.0
$50,000 and over	99.4	96.4	88.9	42.7	31.5	14.3
1989						
All families	90.2	84.0	64.7	20.4	11.5	22.1
White	93.2	87.9	67.9	21.9	12.6	23.3
Non-White and Hispanic	70.0	56.8	42.8	10.5	4.4	13.2
Under 35 years old	84.4	80.7	36.8	8.1	8.4	20.5
35 to 44 years old	92.8	89.5	65.9	20.9	17.0	24.9
45 to 54 years old	93.3	90.9	76.6	28.5	16.2	25.6
55 to 64 years old	92.1	86.9	82.2	31.3	11.3	23.9
65 to 74 years old	93.8	81.9	80.2	25.6	7.9	20.4
75 years old and over	87.3	66.9	72.8	16.9	4.7	13.3
Under 55 years old:						
Unmarried, no children	82.1	75.5	23.7	10.9	10.5	28.6
Married, no children	97.2	95.4	56.9	19.8	13.0	26.9
Unmarried, children	71.6	64.7	35.2	9.2	5.0	22.2
Married, children	97.7	96.6	74.9	22.3	17.5	21.6
55 years old and over:						
In labor force	94.8	91.1	82.0	34.3	17.6	28.7
Out of labor force, retired	93.5	82.6	82.2	25.0	4.7	17.4
Income (1989 dollars):						
Less than $10,000	66.9	51.6	36.2	5.9	2.3	12.1
$10,000 to $19,999	90.5	82.1	57.0	14.4	8.0	18.5
$20,000 to $29,999	96.7	94.4	63.5	15.0	10.1	23.8
$30,000 to $49,999	98.0	95.5	76.2	27.1	12.0	25.4
$50,000 and over	99.4	96.8	90.0	38.7	25.4	30.7

Source: Board of Governors of the Federal Reserve System, *Federal Reserve Bulletin*, January 1992.

No. 752. Family Net Worth—Composition of Assets and Debts of All Families: 1983 and 1989

[In percent. See headnote, table 751]

ASSETS	1983	1989	DEBTS	1983	1989
Total	100.0	100.0	**Total**	100.0	100.0
Financial	25.6	27.7	Home mortgages	58.1	53.1
Nonfinancial	74.4	72.3	Investment real estate mortgages	20.5	25.0
Vehicles	3.6	3.9	Home equity lines of credit	0.5	2.6
Principal residence	33.4	32.2	Other lines of credit	2.8	1.0
Real estate and land investment	16.0	15.1	Credit cards	1.8	2.2
Business investment	20.4	17.8	Car loans	6.1	8.0
Other	1.0	3.3	Other	10.2	8.1

Source: Board of Governors of the Federal Reserve System, *Federal Reserve Bulletin*, January 1992.

No. 753. Family Net Worth—Mean and Median of Net Worth, by Selected Characteristics: 1983 and 1989

[Mean and median value in thousands of constant 1989 dollars. Constant dollar figures are based on consumer price index data published by U.S. Bureau of Labor Statistics; see table 756, section 15. See headnote, table 751]

CHARACTERISTIC	1983			1989		
	Percent of families	Net worth		Percent of families	Net worth	
		Mean	Median		Mean	Median
All families	100	149.1	42.7	100	183.7	47.2
White	82	173.0	54.3	87	203.8	58.5
Nonwhite and Hispanic	18	37.6	6.9	13	45.9	4.0
Under 35 years old	31	40.9	8.5	26	46.9	6.8
35 to 44 years old	19	110.5	49.8	23	148.3	52.8
45 to 54 years old	15	215.9	69.4	14	286.4	86.7
55 to 64 years old	15	242.2	84.4	15	292.5	91.3
65 to 74 years old	12	272.6	76.3	13	278.3	77.6
75 years old and over	7	166.8	49.8	9	194.5	66.1
Under 55 years old:						
Unmarried, no children	11	48.9	6.0	11	47.5	8.4
Married, no children	6	80.1	20.1	5	147.9	27.3
Unmarried, children	13	57.8	10.8	13	54.2	5.7
Married, children	35	140.6	51.3	34	196.9	62.0
55 years and over:						
In labor force	14	363.1	108.0	12	438.3	104.5
Retired	18	153.6	63.9	18	211.6	94.1
Managerial and professional specialities	24	328.5	95.8	25	382.0	104.5
Technical, sales, and administrative support	12	105.1	39.1	12	139.7	32.6
Service occupations	7	33.6	12.1	7	46.1	8.4
Precision production, craft, and repair.	12	70.4	40.0	12	91.5	46.0
Operators, fabricators, and laborers	12	49.3	28.6	9	67.3	18.8
Farming, forestry, and fishing	2	343.9	185.0	2	322.3	107.3
Not working	31	110.7	30.0	33	138.9	44.0
Income (1989 dollars):						
Less than $10,000	19	30.0	3.8	20	30.1	2.3
$10,000 to $19,999	23	53.0	19.3	20	63.1	27.1
$20,000 to $29,999	19	69.5	36.9	17	89.6	37.0
$30,000 to $49,999	23	117.6	67.7	23	150.2	69.2
$50,000 and over	17	550.5	176.1	20	586.7	185.6

Source: Board of Governors of the Federal Reserve System, *Federal Reserve Bulletin*, January 1992.

No. 754. Gross and Net Stock of Fixed Reproducible Tangible Wealth in Current and Constant (1987) Dollars: 1970 to 1991

[In billions of dollars. As of December 31]

ITEM	1970	1980	1982	1983	1984	1985	1986	1987	1988	1989	1990	1991
CURRENT DOLLARS												
Gross stock, total . . .	4,428	14,306	16,527	17,277	18,259	19,330	20,503	21,774	22,966	24,361	25,652	26,699
Private	2,689	9,364	11,005	11,477	12,082	12,747	13,536	14,388	15,078	16,022	16,894	17,489
Nonresidential equipment	679	2,389	2,939	3,067	3,214	3,374	3,599	3,775	4,010	4,257	4,543	4,674
Nonresidential structures.	790	2,683	3,247	3,376	3,573	3,783	3,951	4,156	4,478	4,755	4,964	5,110
Residential	1,219	4,292	4,818	5,034	5,296	5,590	5,986	6,457	6,590	7,010	7,387	7,705
Government	1,060	2,979	3,237	3,368	3,568	3,772	3,916	4,083	4,306	4,516	4,713	4,904
Equipment	274	488	583	621	657	695	732	764	814	873	949	1,018
Structures	785	2,491	2,654	2,748	2,911	3,077	3,184	3,319	3,492	3,643	3,764	3,886
Federal	424	885	1,018	1,067	1,119	1,176	1,227	1,269	1,325	1,394	1,469	1,543
Military	276	493	566	601	638	678	715	738	776	818	873	927
State and local	636	2,094	2,219	2,301	2,449	2,596	2,690	2,814	2,981	3,122	3,244	3,361
Consumer durable goods. .	680	1,963	2,285	2,433	2,608	2,811	3,051	3,303	3,582	3,823	4,045	4,306
Net stock, total.	2,708	8,619	9,792	10,172	10,734	11,367	12,063	12,803	13,458	14,245	14,936	15,412
Private	1,674	5,814	6,737	6,987	7,348	7,752	8,224	8,729	9,108	9,650	10,130	10,412
Government	662	1,790	1,921	1,991	2,105	2,224	2,311	2,414	2,542	2,665	2,775	2,877
Consumer durable goods. .	372	1,014	1,134	1,194	1,281	1,391	1,527	1,660	1,808	1,930	2,031	2,123
CONSTANT (1987) DOLLARS												
Gross stock, total . . .	12,476	17,469	18,370	18,845	19,441	20,091	20,753	21,400	22,062	22,717	23,339	23,849
Private	8,131	11,585	12,217	12,523	12,909	13,322	13,728	14,112	14,504	14,886	15,245	15,522
Nonresidential equipment	1,839	3,009	3,206	3,285	3,396	3,518	3,633	3,737	3,855	3,979	4,093	4,179
Nonresidential structures.	2,411	3,255	3,506	3,606	3,729	3,870	3,983	4,088	4,191	4,293	4,398	4,477
Residential	3,881	5,321	5,505	5,632	5,783	5,934	6,112	6,286	6,458	6,614	6,754	6,866
Government	3,001	3,544	3,648	3,705	3,770	3,849	3,934	4,026	4,115	4,204	4,307	4,403
Equipment	662	625	634	647	670	698	730	768	802	837	879	917
Structures	2,339	2,918	3,014	3,058	3,100	3,152	3,204	3,259	3,313	3,367	3,428	3,487
Federal	1,141	1,122	1,142	1,156	1,177	1,204	1,233	1,266	1,293	1,319	1,351	1,379
Military	723	641	644	652	668	691	716	743	767	786	813	831
State and local	1,860	2,421	2,506	2,549	2,593	2,645	2,701	2,760	2,822	2,885	2,956	3,025
Consumer durable goods. .	1,344	2,340	2,505	2,617	2,762	2,920	3,091	3,262	3,444	3,627	3,787	3,924
Net stock, total.	7,691	10,524	10,902	11,112	11,441	11,823	12,214	12,577	12,942	13,293	13,598	13,785
Private	5,074	7,198	7,499	7,642	7,866	8,112	8,346	8,558	8,774	8,980	9,157	9,258
Government	1,884	2,123	2,166	2,191	2,223	2,269	2,320	2,380	2,430	2,482	2,537	2,587
Consumer durable goods. .	733	1,203	1,236	1,278	1,352	1,442	1,547	1,639	1,738	1,831	1,903	1,940

Source: U.S. Bureau of Economic Analysis, *Survey of Current Business*, January and August 1992.

Figure 15.1
Annual Percent Change in Consumer Price Indexes for Selected Items: 1970 to 1992

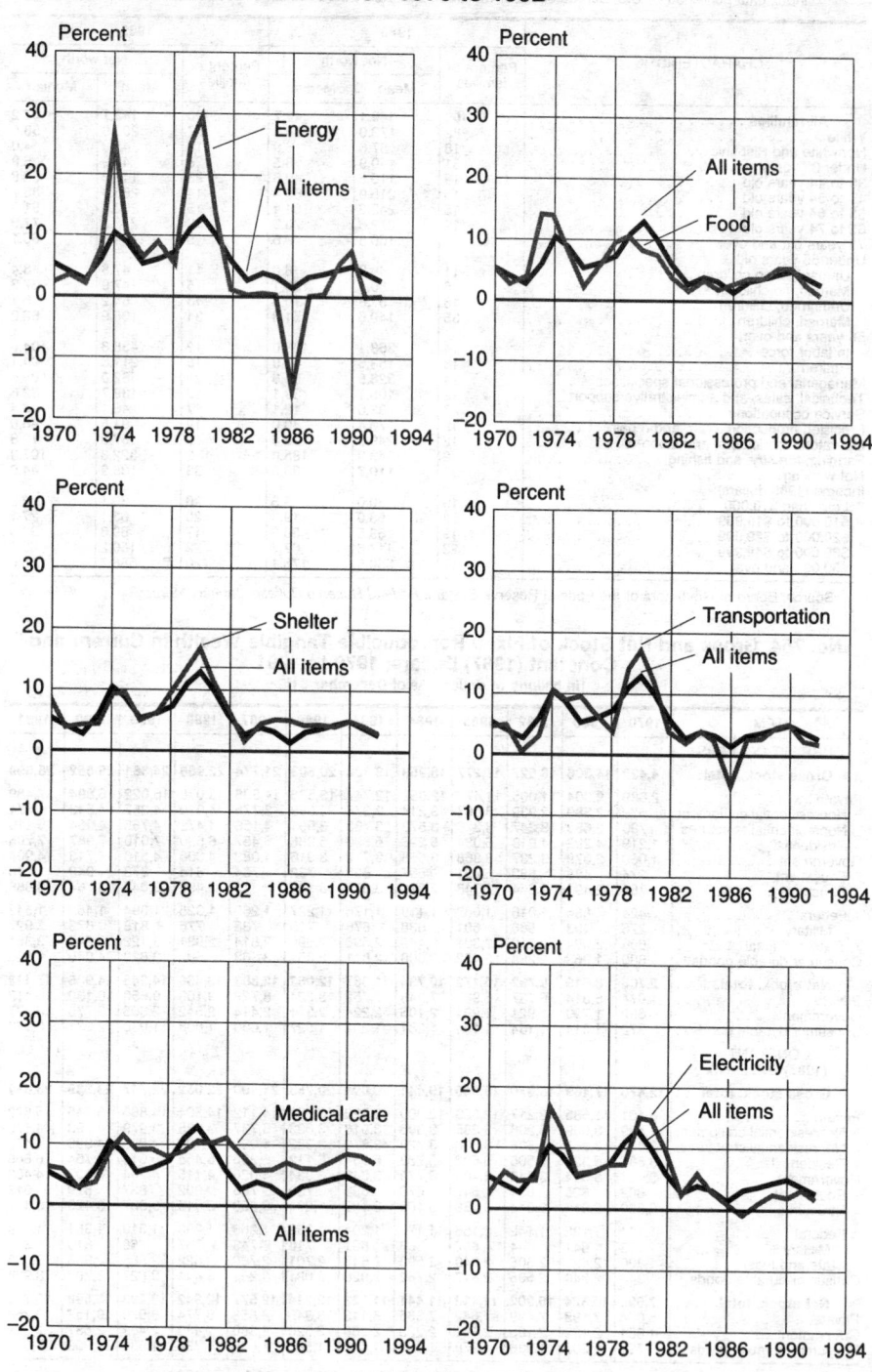

Prices

This section presents indexes of producer and consumer prices, actual prices for selected commodities, and energy prices. The primary sources of these data are monthly publications of the Department of Labor, Bureau of Labor Statistics (BLS), which include *Monthly Labor Review, Consumer Price Index, Detailed Report; Producer Price Indexes;* and *U.S. Import and Export Price Indexes.* The Department of Commerce, Bureau of Economic Analysis is the source for gross domestic product measures.

Producer price index (PPI).—This index, dating from 1890, is the oldest continuous statistical series published by BLS. It is designed to measure average changes in prices received by producers of all commodities, at all stages of processing, produced in the United States.

PPI—Stage of Processing: 1970 to 1992

Percent change

Crude materials

Finished consumer goods

Source: Chart prepared by U.S. Bureau of the Census. For data, see table 765.

The index has undergone several revisions (see *Monthly Labor Review,* February 1962, April 1978, and August 1988). It is now based on approximately 3,200 commodity price series and 80,800 quotations per month. Indexes for the net output of manufacturing and mining industries have been added in recent years. Prices

In Brief

Consumer price changes: 1990-91:

All items index up 3.0 percent
Medical care index up 7.4 percent
Fuel oil index down -4.8 percent

used in constructing the index are collected from sellers, and generally apply to the first significant large volume commercial transaction for each commodity—i.e., the manufacturer's or other producer's selling price or the selling price on an organized exchange or at a central market.

The weights used in the index represent the total net selling value of commodities produced or processed in this country. Values are f.o.b. (free-on-board) production point and are exclusive of excise taxes. Effective with the release of data for January 1988, many important producer price indexes were changed to a new reference base year, 1982=100, from 1967=100. The reference year of the PPI shipment weights has been taken primarily from the 1987 Census of Manufactures. For further detail regarding the PPI, see the *BLS Handbook of Methods, Bulletin 2414,* Chapter 16.

Consumer price indexes (CPI).—The CPI is a measure of the average change in prices over time in a fixed "market basket" of goods and services purchased either by urban wage earners and clerical workers or by all urban consumers.

In 1919, BLS began to publish complete indexes at semiannual intervals, using a weighting structure based on data collected in the expenditure survey of wage-earner and clerical-worker families in 1917-19 (BLS Bulletin 357, 1924). The first major revision of the CPI occurred in 1940, with subsequent revisions in 1953, 1964, 1978, and 1987.

Beginning with the release of data for January 1988 in February 1988, most Consumer Price Indexes shifted to a new reference base year. All indexes previously expressed on a base of 1967=100, or any other base through December 1981, have been rebased to 1982-84=100. Selection of the 1982-84 period was made to coincide with the updated expenditure weights, which are based upon data tabulated from the Consumer Expenditure Surveys for 1982, 1983, and 1984.

BLS publishes CPI's for two population groups: (1) a CPI for All Urban Consumers (CPI-U) which covers approximately 80 percent of the total population; and (2) a CPI for Urban Wage Earners and Clerical Workers (CPI-W) which covers 32 percent of the total population. The CPI-U includes, in addition to wage earners and clerical workers, groups which historically have been excluded from CPI coverage, such as professional, managerial, and technical workers, the self-employed, short-term workers, the unemployed, and retirees and others not in the labor force.

CPI—Selected Items: 1970 to 1992

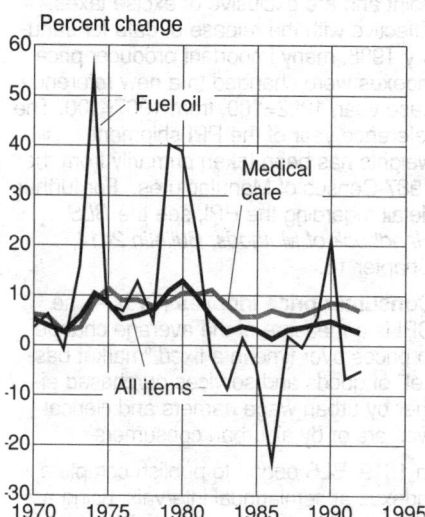

Percent change

Source: Chart prepared by U.S. Bureau of the Census. For data, see table 757.

The current CPI is based on prices of food, clothing, shelter, fuels, transportation fares, charges for doctors' and dentists' services, drugs, etc., purchased for day-to-day living. Prices are collected in 85 areas across the country from over 57,000 housing units and 19,000 establishments. Area selection was based on the 1980 census. All taxes directly associated with the purchase and use of items are included in the index. Prices of food, fuels, and a few other items are obtained every month in all 85 locations.

Prices of most other commodities and services are collected monthly in the five largest geographic areas and every other month in other areas.

In calculating the index, each item is assigned a weight to account for its relative importance in consumers' budgets. Price changes for the various items in each location are then averaged. Local data are then combined to obtain a U.S. city average. Separate indexes are also published for regions, area size-classes, cross-classifications of regions and size-classes, and for 29 local areas, usually consisting of the Metropolitan Statistical Area (MSA); see Appendix II. Area definitions are those established by the Office of Management and Budget in 1983. Definitions do not include revisions made since 1983. Area indexes do not measure differences in the level of prices among cities; they only measure the average change in prices for each area since the base period. For further detail regarding the CPI, see the BLS *Handbook of Methods,* Bulletin 2414, Chapter 19; the Consumer Price Index, and Report 736, the CPI: 1987 Revision. In January 1983, the method of measuring homeownership costs in the CPI-U was changed to a rental equivalence approach. This treatment calculates homeowner costs of shelter based on the implicit rent owners would pay to rent the homes they own. The rental equivalence approach was introduced into the CPI-W in 1985. The CPI-U was used to prepare the consumer prices tables in this section.

Other price indexes.—The *fixed-weighted price index* is a weighted average of the detailed price indexes used in the deflation of goods and services that make up the gross domestic product (GDP). These price indexes are combined using weights that reflect the composition of GDP in 1987. Because the same weights are used for each period, changes in this index measure changes in prices over any period.

Measures of inflation.—Inflation is defined as a time of generally rising prices for goods and factors of production. The Bureau of Labor Statistics samples prices of items in a representative market basket and publishes the results as the CPI. The media invariably announce the inflation rate as the percent change in the CPI from month to month. A much more meaningful indicator of inflation is the percent change from the same month of the prior year.

Selected Fixed-Weighted Price Indexes: 1970 to 1992

Percent change

Source: Chart prepared by U.S. Bureau of the Census. For data, see table 751.

The Producer Price Index (PPI) measures prices at the producer/manufacturing level only. The PPI shows the same general pattern of inflation as does the CPI, but is more volatile. The PPI can be roughly viewed as a leading indicator. It often tends to foreshadow trends that later occur in the CPI.

Other measures of inflation include the index of industrial materials prices; the Dow Jones Commodity Spot Price Index; Futures Price Index, the Employment Cost Index, the Hourly Compensation Index, or the Unit Labor Cost Index as a measure of the change in cost of the labor factor of production, and changes in long-term interest rates that are often used to measure changes in the cost of the capital factor of production.

Statistical reliability.—For a discussion of statistical collection and estimation, sampling procedures, and measures of statistical reliability pertaining to the producer price index and the CPI, see Appendix III.

Historical statistics.—Tabular headnotes provide cross-references, where applicable, to *Historical Statistics of the United States, Colonial Times to 1970.* See Appendix IV.

No. 755. Purchasing Power of the Dollar: 1950 to 1992

[Indexes: PPI, 1982=$1.00; CPI, 1982–84=$1.00. Producer prices prior to 1961, and consumer prices prior to 1964, exclude Alaska and Hawaii. Producer prices based on finished goods index. Obtained by dividing the average price index for the 1982=100, PPI; 1982–84=100, CPI base periods (100.0) by the price index for a given period and expressing the result in dollars and cents. Annual figures are based on average of monthly data]

YEAR	ANNUAL AVERAGE AS MEASURED BY—		YEAR	ANNUAL AVERAGE AS MEASURED BY—		YEAR	ANNUAL AVERAGE AS MEASURED BY—	
	Producer prices	Consumer prices		Producer prices	Consumer prices		Producer prices	Consumer prices
1950	$3.546	$4.151	1965	2.933	3.166	1979	1.289	1.380
1951	3.247	3.846	1966	2.841	3.080	1980	1.136	1.215
1952	3.268	3.765	1967	2.809	2.993	1981	1.041	1.098
1953	3.300	3.735	1968	2.732	2.873	1982	1.000	1.035
1954	3.289	3.717	1969	2.632	2.726	1983	0.984	1.003
1955	3.279	3.732	1970	2.545	2.574	1984	0.964	0.961
1956	3.195	3.678	1971	2.469	2.466	1985	0.955	0.928
1957	3.077	3.549	1972	2.392	2.391	1986	0.969	0.913
1958	3.012	3.457	1973	2.193	2.251	1987	0.949	0.880
1959	3.021	3.427	1974	1.901	2.029	1988	0.926	0.846
1960	2.994	3.373	1975	1.718	1.859	1989	0.880	0.807
1961	2.994	3.340	1976	1.645	1.757	1990	0.839	0.766
1962	2.985	3.304	1977	1.546	1.649	1991	0.822	0.734
1963	2.994	3.265	1978	1.433	1.532	1992	0.812	0.713
1964	2.985	3.220						

Source: U.S. Bureau of Labor Statistics. Monthly data in U.S. Bureau of Economic Analysis, Survey of Current Business.

No. 756. Consumer Price Indexes, by Major Groups: 1960 to 1992

[1982–84 = 100. Represents annual averages of monthly figures. Reflects buying patterns of all urban consumers. See text section 15. See *Historical Statistics, Colonial Times to 1970*, series E 135-173 for similar data]

YEAR	All items	Energy	Food	Shelter	Apparel and upkeep	Trans-portation	Med-ical care	Fuel oil	Elec-tricity	Utility (piped gas)	Tele-phone serv-ices	All com-modities
1960	29.6	22.4	30.0	25.2	45.7	29.8	22.3	13.5	29.9	17.6	58.3	33.6
1961	29.9	22.5	30.4	25.4	46.1	30.1	22.9	14.0	29.9	17.9	58.5	33.8
1962	30.2	22.6	30.6	25.8	46.3	30.8	23.5	14.0	29.9	17.9	58.5	34.1
1963	30.6	22.6	31.1	26.1	46.9	30.9	24.1	14.3	29.9	17.9	58.6	34.4
1964	31.0	22.5	31.5	26.5	47.3	31.4	24.6	14.0	29.8	17.9	58.6	34.8
1965	31.5	22.9	32.2	27.0	47.8	31.9	25.2	14.3	29.7	18.0	57.7	35.2
1966	32.4	23.3	33.8	27.8	49.0	32.3	26.3	14.7	29.7	18.1	56.5	36.1
1967	33.4	23.8	34.1	28.8	51.0	33.3	28.2	15.1	29.9	18.1	57.3	36.8
1968	34.8	24.2	35.3	30.1	53.7	34.3	29.9	15.6	30.2	18.2	57.3	38.1
1969	36.7	24.8	37.1	32.6	56.8	35.7	31.9	15.9	30.8	18.6	58.0	39.9
1970	38.8	25.5	39.2	35.5	59.2	37.5	34.0	16.5	31.8	19.6	58.7	41.7
1971	40.5	26.5	40.4	37.0	61.1	39.5	36.1	17.6	33.9	21.0	61.6	43.2
1972	41.8	27.2	42.1	38.7	62.3	39.9	37.3	17.6	35.6	22.1	65.0	44.5
1973	44.4	29.4	48.2	40.5	64.6	41.2	38.8	20.4	37.4	23.1	66.7	47.8
1974	49.3	38.1	55.1	44.4	69.4	45.8	42.4	32.2	44.1	26.0	69.5	53.5
1975	53.8	42.1	59.8	48.8	72.5	50.1	47.5	34.9	50.0	31.1	71.7	58.2
1976	56.9	45.1	61.6	51.5	75.2	55.1	52.0	37.4	53.1	36.3	74.3	60.7
1977	60.6	49.4	65.5	54.9	78.6	59.0	57.0	42.4	56.6	43.2	75.2	64.2
1978	65.2	52.5	72.0	60.5	81.4	61.7	61.8	44.9	60.9	47.5	76.0	68.8
1979	72.6	65.7	79.9	68.9	84.9	70.5	67.5	63.1	65.6	55.1	75.8	76.6
1980	82.4	86.0	86.8	81.0	90.9	83.1	74.9	87.7	75.8	65.7	77.7	86.0
1981	90.9	97.7	93.6	90.5	95.3	93.2	82.9	107.3	87.2	74.9	84.6	93.2
1982	96.5	99.2	97.4	96.9	97.8	97.0	92.5	105.0	95.8	89.8	93.2	97.0
1983	99.6	99.9	99.4	99.1	100.2	99.3	100.6	96.5	98.9	104.7	99.2	99.8
1984	103.9	100.9	103.2	104.0	102.1	103.7	106.8	98.5	105.3	105.5	107.5	103.2
1985	107.6	101.6	105.6	109.8	105.0	106.4	113.5	94.6	108.9	104.8	111.7	105.4
1986	109.6	88.2	109.0	115.8	105.9	102.3	122.0	74.1	110.4	99.7	117.2	104.4
1987	113.6	88.6	113.5	121.3	110.6	105.4	130.1	75.8	110.0	95.1	116.5	107.7
1988	118.3	89.3	118.2	127.1	115.4	108.7	138.6	75.8	111.5	94.5	116.0	111.5
1989	124.0	94.3	125.1	132.8	118.6	114.1	149.3	80.3	114.7	97.1	117.2	116.7
1990	130.7	102.1	132.4	140.0	124.1	120.5	162.8	98.6	117.4	97.3	117.7	122.8
1991	136.2	102.5	136.3	146.3	128.7	123.8	177.0	92.4	121.8	98.5	119.7	126.6
1992	140.3	103.0	137.9	151.2	131.9	126.5	190.1	88.0	124.2	100.3	120.4	129.1

Source: U.S. Bureau of Labor Statistics, *Monthly Labor Review* and *Handbook of Labor Statistics*, periodic.

No. 757. Consumer Price Indexes—Percent Change in Major Groups: 1960 to 1992

[In percent. Minus sign (-) indicates decrease. See table 756]

YEAR	All items	Energy	Food	Shelter	Apparel and upkeep	Trans-porta-tion	Medical care	Fuel oil	Elec-tricity	Utility (piped gas)	Tele-phone serv-ices	All com-modities
1960	1.7	2.3	1.0	2.0	1.6	-	3.7	-1.5	1.4	6.7	1.6	0.9
1961	1.0	0.4	1.3	0.8	0.9	1.0	2.7	3.7	-	1.7	0.3	0.6
1962	1.0	0.4	0.7	1.6	0.4	2.3	2.6	-	-	-	-	0.9
1963	1.3	-	1.6	1.2	1.3	0.3	2.6	2.1	-	-	0.2	0.9
1964	1.3	-0.4	1.3	1.5	0.9	1.6	2.1	-2.1	-0.3	-	-	1.2
1965	1.6	1.8	2.2	1.9	1.1	1.6	2.4	2.1	-0.3	0.6	-1.5	1.1
1966	2.9	1.7	5.0	3.0	2.5	1.3	4.4	2.8	-	0.6	-2.1	2.6
1967	3.1	2.1	0.9	3.6	4.1	3.1	7.2	2.7	0.7	-	1.4	1.9
1968	4.2	1.7	3.5	4.5	5.3	3.0	6.0	3.3	1.0	0.6	-	3.5
1969	5.5	2.5	5.1	8.3	5.8	4.1	6.7	1.9	2.0	0.6	-	4.7
1970	5.7	2.8	5.7	8.9	4.2	5.0	6.6	3.8	3.2	2.2	1.2	4.5
1971	4.4	3.9	3.1	4.2	3.2	5.3	6.2	6.7	6.6	5.4	1.2	3.6
1972	3.2	2.6	4.2	4.6	2.0	1.0	3.3	-	5.0	7.1	4.9	3.0
1973	6.2	8.1	14.5	4.7	3.7	3.3	4.0	15.9	5.1	5.2	5.5	7.4
1974	11.0	29.6	14.3	9.6	7.4	11.2	9.3	57.8	17.9	4.5	2.6	11.9
1975	9.1	10.5	8.5	9.9	4.5	9.4	12.0	8.4	13.4	12.6	4.2	8.8
1976	5.8	7.1	3.0	5.5	3.7	10.0	9.5	7.2	6.2	19.6	3.2	4.3
1977	6.5	9.5	6.3	6.6	4.5	7.1	9.6	13.4	6.6	16.7	3.6	5.8
1978	7.6	6.3	9.9	10.2	3.6	4.6	8.4	5.9	7.6	19.0	1.2	7.2
1979	11.3	25.1	11.0	13.9	4.3	14.3	9.2	40.5	7.7	16.0	-0.3	11.3
1980	13.5	30.9	8.6	17.6	7.1	17.9	11.0	39.0	15.5	19.2	2.5	12.3
1981	10.3	13.6	7.8	11.7	4.8	12.2	10.7	22.3	15.0	14.0	8.9	8.4
1982	6.2	1.5	4.1	7.1	2.6	4.1	11.6	-2.1	9.9	19.9	10.2	4.1
1983	3.2	0.7	2.1	2.3	2.5	2.4	8.8	-8.1	3.2	16.6	6.4	2.9
1984	4.3	1.0	3.8	4.9	1.9	4.4	6.2	2.1	6.5	0.8	8.4	3.4
1985	3.6	0.7	2.3	5.6	2.8	2.6	6.3	-4.0	3.4	-0.7	3.9	2.1
1986	1.9	-13.2	3.2	5.5	0.9	-3.9	7.5	-21.7	1.4	-4.9	4.9	-0.9
1987	3.6	0.5	4.1	4.7	4.4	3.0	6.6	2.3	-0.4	-4.6	-0.6	3.2
1988	4.1	0.8	4.1	4.8	4.3	3.1	6.5	-	1.4	-0.6	-0.4	3.5
1989	4.8	5.6	5.8	4.5	2.8	5.0	7.7	5.9	2.9	2.8	1.0	4.7
1990	5.4	8.3	5.8	5.4	4.6	5.6	9.0	22.8	2.4	0.2	0.4	5.2
1991	4.2	0.4	2.9	4.5	3.7	2.7	8.7	-6.3	3.7	1.2	1.7	3.1
1992	3.0	0.5	1.2	3.3	2.5	2.2	7.4	-4.8	2.0	1.8	0.6	2.0

- Represents zero.

Source: Bureau of Labor Statistics, *Monthly Labor Review*.

No. 758. Consumer Price Indexes for Selected Items and Groups: 1980 to 1992

[1982-84 = 100. Annual averages of monthly figures. See headnote, table 756]

ITEM	1980	1985	1986	1987	1988	1989	1990	1991	1992
All items.	**82.4**	**107.6**	**109.6**	**113.6**	**118.3**	**124.0**	**130.7**	**136.2**	**140.3**
Food and beverages	86.7	105.6	109.1	113.5	118.2	124.9	132.1	136.8	138.7
Food	86.8	105.6	109.0	113.5	118.2	125.1	132.4	136.3	137.9
Food at home	88.4	104.3	107.3	111.9	116.6	124.2	132.3	135.8	136.8
Cereals and bakery products	83.9	107.9	110.9	114.8	122.1	132.4	140.0	145.8	151.5
Cereals and cereal products	84.2	107.2	110.4	113.9	122.5	133.8	141.1	147.5	153.3
Cereals	76.3	111.3	117.3	124.1	132.9	147.9	158.6	168.1	175.4
Rice, pasta, and cornmeal	83.8	108.2	111.1	115.0	121.8	131.5	139.2	144.7	150.4
Bakery products	90.9	102.1	102.2	101.7	114.4	120.0	122.0	126.5	128.3
White bread	85.9	105.8	107.7	110.7	118.6	129.4	136.4	139.3	146.2
Cookies, cakes, and cupcakes	81.5	110.2	113.4	118.3	125.0	134.5	142.7	151.1	155.6
Meats, poultry, fish and eggs	92.0	100.1	104.5	110.5	114.3	121.3	130.0	132.6	130.9
Meats	92.7	98.9	102.0	109.6	112.2	116.7	128.5	132.5	130.7
Beef and veal	98.4	98.2	98.8	106.3	112.1	119.3	128.8	132.4	132.3
Ground beef excl. canned	104.6	95.9	94.9	100.2	103.4	108.6	118.1	119.9	118.9
Chuck roast	99.8	95.6	95.0	103.8	108.1	116.8	130.3	135.8	137.1
Round steak	98.9	97.0	98.4	105.3	110.6	116.6	125.1	129.5	129.9
Sirloin steak	96.2	99.7	102.3	111.2	120.0	126.0	130.6	133.5	132.4
Pork	81.9	99.1	107.2	116.0	112.5	113.2	129.8	134.1	127.8
Bacon	73.5	101.3	108.5	114.6	100.9	95.8	113.4	119.8	104.6
Chops	82.9	98.7	109.5	120.5	118.8	122.7	140.2	141.7	138.9
Ham	85.5	99.8	107.4	115.8	116.5	117.3	132.4	139.9	135.6
Poultry	93.7	106.2	114.2	112.6	120.7	132.7	132.5	131.5	131.4
Fresh whole chicken	94.4	104.5	115.4	113.3	125.1	137.1	134.9	131.7	131.9
Fresh, frozen chicken parts	91.7	104.6	114.6	114.4	123.3	135.7	135.9	134.7	134.4
Fish and seafood	87.5	107.5	117.4	129.9	137.4	143.6	146.7	148.3	151.7
Canned fish and seafood	93.7	97.8	98.6	103.9	117.0	124.3	119.5	119.0	118.7
Fresh and frozen fish and seafood	84.1	112.9	127.7	143.6	144.2	152.5	161.4	163.8	168.7
Eggs	88.6	91.0	97.2	91.5	93.6	118.5	124.1	121.2	108.3
Dairy products	90.9	103.2	103.3	105.9	108.4	115.6	126.5	125.1	128.5
Fruits and vegetables	82.1	108.4	109.4	119.1	128.1	138.0	149.0	155.8	155.4
Fresh fruits	84.8	116.3	118.7	132.0	143.0	152.4	170.9	193.9	184.2
Apples	92.1	113.1	130.6	131.0	134.2	140.5	147.5	172.8	179.5
Bananas	91.5	99.9	105.0	104.2	119.2	131.3	138.2	145.0	139.9
Oranges, tangerines	72.6	119.7	108.6	135.9	144.6	147.0	160.6	249.4	176.2
Fresh vegetables	79.0	103.5	107.7	121.6	129.3	143.1	151.1	154.4	157.9
Potatoes	81.0	101.6	96.1	116.0	119.1	153.5	162.6	144.6	141.5
Lettuce	77.8	106.1	112.7	136.4	148.6	151.5	150.3	159.8	155.7
Tomatoes	81.9	103.6	111.3	116.8	123.1	136.2	160.8	153.1	171.8
Processed fruits	82.1	109.5	106.3	110.6	122.0	125.9	136.9	131.8	137.7
Processed vegetables	83.1	104.4	104.2	107.1	112.2	124.2	127.5	128.5	138.9
Coffee	111.6	105.5	132.7	116.2	115.0	120.4	117.5	115.3	110.7
Lunch away from home	83.8	107.8	112.0	116.6	121.5	127.6	133.9	138.4	141.3
Dinner away from home	84.2	108.8	112.7	117.0	121.6	126.9	132.3	136.3	138.9
Alcoholic beverages	86.4	106.4	111.1	114.1	118.6	123.5	129.3	142.8	147.3
Alcoholic beverages at home	87.3	105.2	109.3	111.5	114.2	117.9	123.0	137.8	141.6
Beer and ale	84.8	106.7	108.7	110.9	114.4	118.2	123.6	138.4	143.5
Distilled spirits	89.8	105.3	113.3	114.4	116.1	119.9	125.7	139.2	141.5
Wine	89.5	100.2	102.4	105.7	107.8	110.9	114.4	129.9	132.6
Alcoholic beverages away from home	82.9	111.1	118.5	123.4	130.6	137.4	144.4	156.9	162.5
Housing	81.1	107.7	110.9	114.2	118.5	123.0	128.5	133.6	137.5
Shelter	81.0	109.8	115.8	121.3	127.1	132.8	140.0	146.3	151.2
Renters' cost	(NA)	115.4	121.9	128.1	133.6	138.9	146.7	155.6	160.9
Rent, residential	80.9	111.8	118.3	123.1	127.8	132.8	138.4	143.3	146.9
Tenants' insurance	78.9	109.4	115.8	120.4	124.9	128.3	130.6	133.2	136.5
Homeowners' costs	(NA)	113.1	119.4	124.8	131.1	137.3	144.6	150.2	155.3
Owners' equivalent rent	(NA)	113.2	119.4	124.8	131.1	137.4	144.8	150.4	155.5
Household insurance	(NA)	112.4	119.2	124.0	129.0	132.6	135.3	138.4	142.2
Maintenance and repair	82.4	106.5	107.9	111.8	114.7	118.0	122.2	126.3	128.6
Fuels and other utilities	75.4	106.5	104.1	103.0	104.4	107.8	111.6	115.3	117.8
Fuels	74.8	104.5	99.2	97.3	98.0	100.9	104.5	106.7	108.1
Fuel oil and other	86.1	95.9	77.6	77.9	78.1	81.7	99.3	94.6	90.7
Fuel oil	87.7	94.6	74.1	75.8	75.8	80.3	98.6	92.4	88.0
Gas (piped) and electricity	71.4	107.1	105.7	103.8	104.6	107.5	109.3	112.6	114.8
Electricity	75.8	108.9	110.4	110.0	111.5	114.7	117.4	121.8	124.2
Utility (piped) gas	65.7	104.8	99.7	95.1	94.5	97.1	97.3	98.5	100.3
Telephone services	77.7	111.7	117.2	116.5	116.0	117.2	117.7	119.7	120.4
Local charges	72.8	120.4	132.7	139.3	141.3	146.5	149.3	153.9	155.7
Interstate toll charges	83.3	94.9	88.4	75.3	72.3	70.2	68.2	67.6	68.0
Intrastate toll charges	85.2	106.8	106.8	104.7	101.5	97.0	95.1	93.1	91.4
Water and sewerage maintenance	74.0	113.4	119.4	125.8	132.7	140.8	150.2	161.1	172.1
Cable television	(NA)	110.6	115.5	123.1	132.9	144.0	158.4	175.7	186.2
Refuse collection	(NA)	109.9	118.7	130.3	142.5	155.6	171.2	189.2	207.3

See footnotes at end of table.

No. 758. Consumer Price Indexes for Selected Items and Groups: 1980 to 1992—Continued

[1982-84 = 100. Annual averages of monthly figures. See headnote, table 756]

ITEM	1980	1985	1986	1987	1988	1989	1990	1991	1992
Household furnishings and operations	86.3	103.8	105.2	107.1	109.4	111.2	113.3	116.0	118.0
Housefurnishings	88.5	101.7	102.2	103.6	105.1	105.5	106.7	107.5	109.0
Furniture and bedding	88.0	104.9	107.2	109.7	113.2	113.9	115.7	116.6	120.6
Bedroom furniture	83.5	107.4	113.9	114.1	117.7	117.6	118.5	120.1	126.8
Sofas	(NA)	103.0	105.9	110.9	114.3	117.0	118.4	118.3	119.4
Living room chairs and tables	(NA)	103.2	105.3	107.2	111.0	112.5	116.7	118.4	121.9
Appliances and electronic equip.	93.5	95.2	92.8	91.4	90.2	89.1	87.8	86.0	84.6
Video and audio equipment	100.7	91.9	88.0	86.0	83.6	82.2	80.8	79.4	78.4
Television	104.6	88.7	83.2	79.7	77.6	76.1	74.6	72.9	72.4
Video products other than TV	(NA)	(NA)	(NA)	(NA)	(NA)	96.8	91.5	84.6	81.0
Audio products	97.7	94.4	91.8	93.0	92.7	92.8	93.2	94.6	94.4
Housekeeping supplies	83.2	106.2	108.2	111.5	114.7	120.9	125.2	128.9	129.6
Housekeeping services	84.3	106.1	108.5	110.6	114.3	117.3	120.1	127.5	132.1
Postage	76.2	108.8	110.2	110.2	121.4	125.1	125.1	143.6	145.3
Apparel and upkeep	90.9	105.0	105.9	110.6	115.4	118.6	124.1	128.7	131.9
Apparel commodities	92.9	104.0	104.2	108.9	113.7	116.7	122.0	126.4	129.4
Apparel commodities less footwear	93.0	104.3	104.7	109.6	114.4	117.1	122.8	127.4	130.2
Men's and boy's apparel	89.4	105.0	106.2	109.1	113.4	117.0	120.4	124.2	126.5
Women's and girl's apparel	96.0	104.9	104.0	110.4	114.9	116.4	122.6	127.6	130.4
Infants' and toddlers'	85.5	107.2	111.8	112.1	116.4	119.1	125.8	128.9	129.3
Footwear	91.8	102.3	101.9	105.1	109.9	114.4	117.4	120.9	125.0
Transportation	83.1	106.4	102.3	105.4	108.7	114.1	120.5	123.8	126.5
Private transportation	84.2	106.2	101.2	104.2	107.6	112.9	118.8	121.9	124.6
New vehicles	88.5	106.1	110.6	114.4	116.5	119.2	121.4	126.0	129.2
New cars	88.4	106.1	110.6	114.6	116.9	119.2	121.0	125.3	128.4
New trucks	(NA)	105.5	110.2	112.2	113.5	117.0	121.6	127.0	130.9
Used cars	62.3	113.7	108.8	113.1	118.0	120.4	117.6	118.1	123.2
Motor fuel	97.4	98.7	77.1	80.2	80.9	88.5	101.2	99.4	99.0
Automobile maintenance and repair	81.5	106.8	110.3	114.8	119.7	124.9	130.1	136.0	141.3
Automobile insurance	82.0	119.2	135.0	146.2	156.6	166.6	177.9	191.5	205.5
Automobile finance charges	86.4	94.5	86.0	84.9	91.3	100.5	99.6	98.0	86.1
Vehicle rental, registration, other	78.3	111.7	117.2	123.0	128.1	135.0	148.1	154.8	162.3
Public transportation	69.0	110.5	117.0	121.1	123.3	129.5	142.6	148.9	151.4
Airline fares	68.0	112.5	117.1	122.8	124.2	131.6	148.4	155.2	155.2
Other intercity transportation	73.1	114.7	125.5	126.7	132.6	138.5	143.3	149.0	152.5
Intracity transportation	69.7	107.7	115.8	118.8	121.7	125.2	133.5	138.9	146.9
Medical care	74.9	113.5	122.0	130.1	138.6	149.3	162.8	177.0	190.1
Medical care commodities	75.4	115.2	122.8	131.0	139.9	150.8	163.4	176.8	188.1
Prescription drugs	72.5	120.1	130.4	140.8	152.0	165.2	181.7	199.7	214.7
Nonprescription drugs, medical sup..	(NA)	(NA)	(NA)	103.1	108.1	114.6	120.6	126.3	131.2
Medical care services	74.8	113.2	121.9	130.0	138.3	148.9	162.7	177.1	190.5
Professional medical services	77.9	113.5	120.8	128.8	137.5	146.4	156.1	165.7	175.8
Physicians' services	76.5	113.3	121.5	130.4	139.8	150.1	160.8	170.5	181.2
Dental services	78.9	114.2	120.6	128.8	137.5	146.1	155.8	167.4	178.7
Eye care	(NA)	(NA)	(NA)	103.5	108.7	112.4	117.3	121.9	127.0
Hospital and related services	69.2	116.1	123.1	131.6	143.9	160.5	178.0	196.1	214.0
Hospital rooms	68.0	115.4	122.3	131.1	143.3	158.1	175.4	191.9	208.7
Entertainment	83.6	107.9	111.6	115.3	120.3	126.5	132.4	138.4	142.3
Entertainment commodities	84.5	105.8	107.9	110.5	115.0	119.8	124.0	128.6	131.3
Reading materials	77.7	110.7	115.6	119.5	124.3	129.5	136.2	144.7	150.9
Newspapers	79.4	109.3	113.7	118.4	123.7	129.2	134.6	146.5	154.8
Magazines, periodicals, and books	75.9	112.1	117.7	120.7	125.0	130.0	137.9	143.3	147.4
Sporting goods, equipment	88.5	104.6	104.0	104.3	108.1	111.1	114.9	118.5	120.2
Sport vehicles, including bicycles	87.9	106.3	105.6	105.5	108.9	112.3	115.3	117.5	119.7
Toys, hobbies; other entertainment	86.5	103.3	105.3	108.4	113.2	118.5	121.5	123.9	124.7
Pet supplies and expenses	83.3	106.4	108.7	111.0	114.5	120.7	124.6	129.1	128.1
Entertainment services	82.3	110.9	116.8	122.0	127.7	135.4	143.2	150.6	155.9
Club membership	(NA)	(NA)	(NA)	101.0	107.2	112.6	117.0	122.5	125.2
Admissions	83.8	112.8	117.9	124.4	131.1	141.4	151.2	159.3	164.5
Tobacco and smoking products	72.0	116.7	124.7	133.6	145.8	164.4	181.5	202.7	219.8
Personal care	81.9	108.3	111.9	115.1	119.4	125.0	130.4	134.9	138.3
Personal care services	83.7	108.9	112.5	116.2	120.7	126.8	132.8	137.0	140.0
Beauty parlor services for women	83.4	108.8	112.2	116.0	120.3	126.5	133.0	137.2	139.8
Haircuts, etc. for men	84.4	109.0	113.1	116.5	121.7	127.3	131.5	135.9	140.3
Personal and educational expenses	70.9	119.1	126.8	138.5	147.9	158.1	170.2	183.7	197.4
School books and supplies	71.4	118.2	128.1	138.1	148.1	158.0	171.3	180.3	190.3
Personal and educational services	70.8	119.2	128.7	138.7	148.0	158.3	170.4	184.2	198.1
Tuition and other school fees	71.2	119.7	129.6	140.0	151.0	162.7	175.7	191.4	208.5
College tuition	70.8	119.9	129.6	139.4	150.0	161.9	175.0	192.8	213.5
Elementary and high school tuition	72.3	119.0	129.2	141.3	154.6	168.0	182.8	198.0	213.7
Day care and nursery school	(NA)	(NA)	(NA)	(NA)	(NA)	(NA)	(NA)	103.2	108.3
All commodities	86.0	105.4	104.4	107.7	111.5	116.7	122.8	126.6	129.1
All commodities less food	85.7	105.2	101.7	104.3	107.7	112.0	117.4	121.3	124.2
Energy	86.0	101.6	88.2	88.6	89.3	94.3	102.1	102.5	103.0

NA Not available.

Source: U.S. Bureau of Labor Statistics, *Monthly Labor Review* and *CPI Detailed Report*, January issues.

No. 759. Consumer Price Indexes—Selected Areas: 1970 to 1992

[1982-84 = 100, except as indicated. Represents annual averages of monthly figures, except as noted. Local area CPI indexes are byproducts of the national CPI program. Each local index has a smaller sample size than the national index and is therefore, subject to substantially more sampling and other measurement error. As a result, local area indexes show greater volatility than the national index, although their long- term trends are similar. Area definitions are those established by the Office of Management and Budget in 1983. For further detail see the U.S. Bureau of Labor Statistics Handbook of Methods, Bulletin 2285, Chapter 19, the Consumer Price Index, and Report 736, the CPI: 1987 Revision. See also text, section 15]

AREA	1970	1980	1985	1987	1988	1989	1990	1991	1992
U.S. city average	38.8	82.4	107.6	113.6	118.3	124.0	130.7	136.2	140.3
Anchorage, AK MSA	41.1	85.5	105.8	108.2	108.6	111.7	118.6	124.0	128.2
Atlanta, GA MSA	38.6	80.3	108.9	116.5	120.4	126.1	131.7	135.9	138.5
Baltimore, MD MSA	39.1	83.7	108.2	114.2	119.3	124.5	130.8	136.4	140.1
Boston-Lawrence-Salem, MA-NH CMSA	40.2	82.6	109.4	117.1	124.2	131.3	138.9	145.0	148.6
Buffalo-Niagara Falls, NY CMSA	41.2	83.5	108.6	113.0	117.4	121.6	127.7	133.4	137.9
Chicago-Gary-Lake County, IL-IN-WI CMSA	38.9	82.2	107.7	114.5	119.0	125.0	131.7	137.0	141.1
Cincinnati-Hamilton, OH-KY-IN CMSA	37.4	82.1	106.6	111.9	116.1	120.9	126.5	131.4	134.1
Cleveland-Akron-Lorain, OH CMSA	37.2	78.9	107.8	112.7	116.7	122.7	129.0	134.2	136.8
Dallas-Fort Worth, TX CMSA	37.6	81.5	108.2	112.9	116.1	119.5	125.1	130.8	133.9
Denver-Boulder, CO CMSA	34.5	78.4	107.1	110.8	113.7	115.8	120.9	125.6	130.3
Detroit-Ann Arbor, MI CMSA	39.5	85.3	106.8	111.7	116.1	122.3	128.6	133.1	135.9
Honolulu, HI MSA	41.5	83.0	106.8	114.9	121.7	128.7	138.1	148.0	155.1
Houston-Galveston-Brazoria, TX CMSA	36.4	82.7	104.9	106.5	109.5	114.1	120.6	125.1	127.1
Kansas City, MO-KS CMSA	39.0	83.6	107.7	113.1	117.4	121.6	126.0	131.2	134.3
Los Angeles-Anaheim-Riverside, CA CMSA	38.7	83.7	108.4	116.7	122.1	128.3	135.9	141.4	146.5
Miami-Fort Lauderdale, FL CMSA	(NA)	81.1	106.5	111.8	116.8	121.5	128.0	132.3	134.5
Milwaukee, WI PMSA	37.5	81.4	107.0	111.5	115.9	120.8	126.2	132.2	137.1
Minneapolis-St. Paul, MN-WI MSA	37.4	78.9	107.0	111.6	117.2	122.0	127.0	130.4	135.0
New Orleans, LA MSA [1]	(NA)	(NA)	(NA)	100.0	102.7	107.2	111.5	116.0	120.2
New York-Northern New Jersey-Long Island, NY-NJ-CT CMSA	41.2	82.1	108.7	118.0	123.7	130.6	138.5	144.8	150.0
Philadelphia-Wilmington-Trenton, PA-NJ-DE-MD CMSA	40.8	83.6	108.8	116.8	122.4	128.3	135.8	142.2	146.6
Pittsburgh-Beaver Valley, PA CMSA	38.1	81.0	106.9	111.4	114.9	120.1	126.2	131.3	136.0
Portland-Vancouver, OR-WA CMSA	38.7	87.2	106.7	110.9	114.7	120.4	127.4	133.9	139.8
San Diego, CA MSA	34.1	79.4	110.4	117.5	123.4	130.6	138.4	143.4	147.4
San Francisco-Oakland-San Jose, CA CMSA	37.7	80.4	108.4	115.4	120.5	126.4	132.1	137.9	142.5
Seattle-Tacoma, WA CMSA	37.4	82.7	105.6	109.2	112.8	118.1	126.8	134.1	139.0
St. Louis-East St. Louis, MO-IL CMSA	38.8	82.5	107.1	112.2	115.7	121.8	128.1	132.1	134.7
Tampa-St. Petersburg-Clearwater, FL MSA [1]	(NA)	(NA)	(NA)	100.0	103.7	107.2	111.7	116.4	119.2
Washington, DC-MD-VA MSA	39.8	82.9	109.0	116.2	121.0	128.0	135.6	141.2	144.7

NA Not available. [1] 1987=100.

No. 760. CPI—Major Commodity Groups, by Selected Areas: 1992

[1982-84 = 100, except as noted. See table 759]

AREA	All items	Food and beverages	Food	Housing	Apparel and upkeep	Transportation	Medical care	Entertainment	Fuel and other utilities
U.S. city average	140.3	138.7	137.9	137.5	131.9	126.5	190.1	142.3	117.8
Anchorage, AK MSA	128.2	130.3	128.7	116.6	130.2	123.3	183.0	151.0	137.6
Atlanta, GA MSA	138.5	135.7	137.1	132.7	152.6	119.5	202.7	163.3	125.1
Baltimore, MD MSA	140.1	142.4	142.8	133.3	135.2	128.5	184.4	149.3	109.7
Boston-Lawrence-Salem, MA-NH CMSA	148.6	143.3	142.7	143.5	145.1	129.1	224.2	155.0	111.5
Buffalo-Niagara Falls, NY CMSA	137.9	137.1	136.3	146.2	111.3	114.0	166.5	155.7	114.5
Chicago-Gary-Lake County, IL-IN-WI CMSA	141.1	139.2	138.0	139.9	126.2	123.2	190.7	149.4	113.6
Cincinnati-Hamilton, OH-KY-IN CMSA	134.1	129.6	128.9	129.6	131.9	118.8	188.0	140.0	106.6
Cleveland-Akron-Lorain, OH CMSA	136.8	136.1	135.9	135.8	122.2	124.1	178.6	139.6	114.7
Dallas-Fort Worth, TX CMSA	133.9	138.3	137.2	121.8	151.3	123.4	188.3	142.0	118.7
Denver-Boulder, CO CMSA	130.3	128.8	128.7	118.1	94.6	134.2	206.5	136.1	115.3
Detroit-Ann Arbor, MI CMSA	135.9	133.4	132.9	131.8	129.9	129.9	181.6	130.7	116.6
Honolulu, HI MSA	155.1	148.5	148.3	161.7	114.2	147.4	182.6	136.3	106.1
Houston-Galveston-Brazoria, TX CMSA	129.1	130.8	129.8	113.2	135.8	122.9	193.6	146.4	104.3
Kansas City, MO-KS CMSA	134.3	132.9	132.6	127.2	124.8	121.8	183.8	154.0	116.8
Los Angeles-Anaheim-Riverside, CA CMSA	146.5	140.9	138.9	148.6	133.2	133.0	192.4	134.1	136.9
Miami-Fort Lauderdale, FL CMSA	134.5	140.6	141.3	126.2	138.8	127.8	172.3	124.6	111.1
Milwaukee, WI PMSA	137.1	135.4	135.9	137.7	124.2	123.1	174.3	130.0	104.2
Minneapolis-St. Paul, MN-WI MSA	135.0	144.8	142.8	124.9	141.7	121.7	182.4	145.6	107.0
New Orleans, LA [1]	120.2	118.1	118.8	107.5	162.9	118.3	147.3	126.5	121.8
New York- Northern New Jersey-Long Island, NY-NJ-CT CMSA	150.0	146.0	145.4	151.4	128.5	131.5	200.0	146.4	107.3
Philadelphia-Wilmington-Trenton, PA-NJ-DE-MD CMSA	146.6	137.6	135.9	149.6	106.5	136.1	196.6	144.4	118.6
Pittsburgh-Beaver Valley, PA CMSA	136.0	132.9	131.3	135.8	133.0	115.6	185.9	145.4	131.0
Portland-Vancouver, OR-WA CMSA	139.8	131.7	130.8	138.2	124.8	134.0	176.3	139.9	114.3
St. Louis-East St. Louis, MO-IL CMSA	134.7	140.1	139.3	129.7	121.7	121.9	181.0	137.8	116.2
San Diego, CA MSA	147.4	142.5	140.5	148.2	131.2	135.9	201.6	152.1	106.4
San Francisco-Oakland-San Jose, CA CMSA	142.5	143.3	142.3	146.2	117.8	119.8	187.0	156.5	139.5
Seattle-Tacoma, WA CMSA	139.0	141.1	141.2	139.3	118.7	123.9	184.2	140.1	101.9
Washington, DC-MD-VA MSA	144.7	140.9	139.4	143.9	139.6	129.9	186.3	147.6	116.2
Tampa-St. Petersburg-Clearwater, FL [1]	119.2	116.4	115.4	113.4	132.8	114.8	156.6	106.6	108.6

[1] 1987=100.
Source of tables 759-60: U.S. Bureau of Labor Statistics, *Monthly Labor Review*, and *CPI Detailed Report*, January issues.

No. 761. Consumer Price Index, by Region: 1980 to 1992

[1982-84 = 100. For composition of regions, see table 31]

ITEM	1980	1982	1983	1984	1985	1986	1987	1988	1989	1990	1991	1992
U.S. city average, all items . . .	82.4	96.5	99.6	103.9	107.6	109.6	113.6	118.3	124.0	130.7	136.2	140.3
Food	86.8	97.4	99.4	103.2	105.6	109.0	113.5	118.2	125.1	132.4	136.3	137.9
Housing	81.1	96.9	99.5	103.6	107.7	110.9	114.2	118.5	123.0	128.5	133.6	137.5
Gas (piped) and electricity . .	71.4	93.2	101.5	105.4	107.1	105.7	103.8	104.6	107.5	109.3	112.6	114.8
Northeast:												
All items	82.2	95.8	99.8	104.5	108.4	111.1	116.0	121.8	128.6	136.3	142.5	147.3
Food	86.5	97.3	99.4	103.3	106.2	110.1	115.8	121.1	128.7	135.9	139.8	141.9
Housing	80.7	95.7	99.7	104.6	109.0	112.7	117.3	124.0	130.8	138.0	144.4	149.0
Gas (piped) and electricity . .	73.8	94.4	100.9	104.7	105.9	104.6	101.2	100.2	105.4	109.6	113.4	117.2
North Central:												
All items	82.4	96.5	99.9	103.6	106.8	108.0	111.9	116.1	121.5	127.4	132.4	136.1
Food	88.5	98.1	99.3	102.7	104.4	107.5	111.8	116.0	122.2	129.6	133.5	135.0
Housing	80.0	96.3	100.3	103.5	107.0	109.4	112.4	115.9	119.9	124.1	128.5	132.1
Gas (piped) and electricity . .	70.1	90.7	103.3	106.1	108.6	107.1	104.6	104.3	105.5	104.0	105.6	107.6
South:												
All items	81.9	96.5	99.7	103.8	107.1	108.9	112.4	116.4	121.5	127.9	132.9	136.5
Food	86.6	97.1	99.3	103.6	105.7	108.8	113.1	117.6	124.2	131.6	135.0	136.1
Housing	80.8	97.5	99.6	103.0	106.3	109.0	111.0	113.9	117.2	121.8	125.6	128.8
Gas (piped) and electricity . .	70.2	94.1	100.9	105.0	106.0	105.1	104.3	106.1	108.2	104.0	112.9	114.9
West:												
All items	83.3	97.4	99.0	103.6	108.0	110.5	114.3	119.0	124.6	131.5	137.3	142.0
Food	85.2	96.7	99.7	103.6	106.1	109.0	112.9	117.6	124.9	132.0	136.4	138.5
Housing	83.3	98.4	98.2	103.3	108.8	113.0	116.5	120.7	124.8	130.9	136.9	141.2
Gas (piped) and electricity . .	72.1	94.6	99.9	105.6	108.1	105.5	105.5	108.8	112.9	115.8	122.9	123.6

Source: U.S. Bureau of Labor Statistics, *Monthly Labor Review and CPI Detailed Report*, January issues.

No. 762. Annual Percent Changes in Consumer Prices, United States and OECD Countries: 1970 to 1990

[Covers member countries of Organization for Economic Cooperation and Development (OECD). For consumer price indexes for OECD countries, see section 31]

COUNTRY	1970	1975	1979	1980	1981	1982	1983	1984	1985	1986	1987	1988	1989	1990
United States	5.8	9.1	11.3	13.5	10.3	6.1	3.2	4.3	3.5	1.9	3.7	4.1	4.8	5.4
OECD, total	6.0	11.8	10.7	14.2	10.9	8.1	5.7	5.8	5.1	3.2	3.9	4.8	5.8	6.3
OECD, Europe	6.1	14.4	12.7	17.7	13.4	11.5	9.5	9.0	7.9	5.3	5.1	7.1	8.3	8.6
Australia	3.9	15.1	9.1	10.2	9.7	11.1	10.1	3.9	6.8	9.1	8.5	7.2	7.6	7.3
Canada	3.3	10.7	9.1	10.2	12.4	10.8	5.8	4.3	4.0	4.2	4.4	4.0	5.0	4.8
Japan	7.7	11.8	3.7	7.8	4.9	2.7	1.9	2.2	2.0	0.6	-0.1	0.7	2.3	3.1
New Zealand	6.5	14.7	13.7	17.2	15.4	16.2	7.3	6.2	15.4	13.2	15.8	6.4	5.7	6.1
Austria	4.4	8.4	3.7	6.4	6.8	5.4	3.3	5.6	3.2	1.7	1.4	2.0	2.5	3.3
Belgium	3.9	12.8	4.5	6.6	7.1	8.7	7.7	6.3	4.9	1.3	1.6	1.2	3.1	3.4
Denmark	5.8	9.6	9.6	12.3	11.7	10.1	6.9	6.3	4.7	3.6	4.0	4.6	4.8	2.7
Finland	2.8	17.9	7.5	11.6	12.0	9.6	8.3	7.1	5.9	2.9	4.1	5.1	6.6	6.1
France	5.2	11.8	10.8	13.6	13.4	11.8	9.6	7.4	5.8	2.7	3.1	2.7	3.6	3.4
Greece	3.2	13.4	19.0	24.9	24.5	21.0	20.2	18.4	19.3	23.0	16.4	13.5	13.7	20.4
Ireland	8.2	20.9	13.3	18.2	20.4	17.1	10.5	8.6	5.4	3.8	3.1	2.1	4.1	3.3
Italy [1]	5.1	17.2	15.7	21.1	18.7	16.3	15.0	10.6	8.6	6.1	4.6	5.0	6.6	6.1
Luxembourg	4.6	10.7	4.5	6.3	8.1	9.4	8.7	5.6	4.1	0.3	-0.1	1.4	3.4	3.7
Netherlands	3.6	10.2	4.2	6.5	6.7	5.9	2.7	3.3	2.3	0.1	-0.7	0.7	1.1	2.5
Norway	10.6	11.7	4.8	10.9	13.7	11.3	8.4	6.3	5.7	7.2	8.7	6.7	4.6	4.1
Portugal [2]	6.3	20.4	23.9	16.6	20.0	22.4	25.5	28.8	19.6	11.8	9.4	9.7	12.6	13.4
Spain	5.9	16.9	15.6	15.6	14.5	14.4	12.2	11.3	8.8	8.8	5.2	4.8	6.8	6.7
Sweden	7.0	9.8	7.2	13.7	12.1	8.6	8.9	8.0	7.4	4.3	4.2	5.8	6.4	10.5
Switzerland	3.6	6.7	3.6	4.0	6.5	5.6	3.0	2.9	3.4	0.8	1.4	1.9	3.2	5.4
Turkey [2]	28.7	19.5	58.7	110.2	36.6	29.7	31.4	48.4	45.0	34.6	38.9	75.4	63.3	60.3
United Kingdom	6.4	24.2	13.4	18.0	11.9	8.6	4.6	5.0	6.1	3.4	4.1	4.9	7.8	9.5
Germany	3.4	6.0	4.1	5.5	6.3	5.3	3.3	2.4	2.2	-0.1	0.2	1.3	2.8	2.7

[1] Households of wage and salary earners.   [2] Excludes rent.

Source: Organization for Economic Cooperation and Development, Paris, France, *Main Economic Indicators*, monthly.

No. 763. Cost of Living Index—Selected Metropolitan Areas: Third Quarter 1992

[This cost of living index measures relative price levels for consumer goods and services in participating areas for a midmanagement standard of living. The national average equals 100, and each participant's index is read as a percentage of the national average. For example, the Albany-Schenectady-Troy, NY MSA's composite cost of living is 12.4 percent above the national average. The index does not measure inflation, but compares prices at a single point in time. Excludes taxes. Metropolitan areas defined as defined by the Office of Management and Budget. For definitions and components of MSA's, see Appendix II. See source for details. Selection based on 1990 MSA population]

METROPOLITAN AREAS	Composite index	Grocery items	Housing	Utilities	Transportation	Health care
Abilene TX MSA: Abilene.	93.0	90.5	85.9	104.6	102.3	91.6
Albany Schenectady-Troy NY MSA: Albany.	112.4	113.3	112.2	133.7	111.8	103.4
Albuquerque NM MSA: Albuquerque.	99.3	93.3	96.6	97.6	103.7	108.5
Allentown-Bethlehem Easton PA-NJ MSA: Allentown-Bethlehem Easton PA	108.7	108.1	107.1	116.1	97.5	103.0
Amarillo TX MSA: Amarillo.	86.4	95.7	74.0	77.3	94.6	86.3
Anchorage AK MSA: Anchorage.	131.7	134.0	142.9	101.2	117.8	171.1
Anderson IN MSA: Anderson.	95.7	98.8	97.1	94.6	104.2	95.9
Appleton-Oshkosh-Neenah WI MSA: Appleton-Neenah-Menasha WI	95.6	93.8	99.1	86.3	96.3	94.1
Atlanta GA MSA: Atlanta.	98.8	98.5	97.7	113.1	96.7	113.4
Augusta GA-SC MSA: Augusta.	99.6	93.2	94.5	114.2	100.8	90.6
Austin TX MSA: Georgetown	94.6	94.9	83.5	101.4	103.5	90.7
Bakersfield CA MSA: Bakersfield.	115.8	110.8	114.1	117.1	112.0	119.7
Baton Rouge LA MSA: Baton Rogue.	99.0	103.6	85.9	115.5	103.8	99.4
Beaumont-Port Arthur TX MSA: Beaumont.	94.7	100.7	77.7	103.9	108.3	92.7
Bellingham WA MSA: Bellingham	104.3	98.9	113.7	60.2	96.1	136.1
Benton Harbor MI MSA: Benton Harbor-St Joseph MI.	102.8	105.5	110.4	87.3	96.8	99.4
Billings MT MSA: Billings.	104.9	103.9	107.2	84.7	128.2	102.9
Binghampton NY MSA: Binghamton/Broome County NY.	99.1	98.0	93.0	105.9	105.6	94.9
Birmingham AL MSA: Birmingham AL	101.5	94.2	100.1	119.2	98.8	97.5
Bloomington IN MSA: Bloomington IN	100.0	101.3	97.7	97.9	94.0	99.2
Bloomington-Normal IL MSA: Bloomington-Normal IL.	104.1	103.0	100.3	138.1	101.7	91.0
Boise City ID MSA: Boise ID	103.7	97.9	115.4	72.0	99.0	112.5
Burlington NC MSA: Burlington NC	95.4	90.5	99.7	107.1	86.7	85.2
Canton OH MSA: Canton OH.	95.2	93.1	98.5	103.2	94.6	90.2
Cedar Rapids IA MSA: Cedar Rapids.	98.9	96.2	101.5	102.3	90.7	93.1
Champaign-Urbana-Rantoul IL MSA: Champaign-Urbana IL	100.7	100.1	93.7	116.1	100.7	107.0
Charleston SC MSA: Charleston.	99.8	94.4	96.3	96.2	89.0	98.0
Charleston WV MSA: Charleston.	101.7	98.0	106.1	100.8	104.8	99.5
Charlotte-Gastonia-Rock Hill NC-SC MSA: Charlotte NC.	99.6	95.9	96.5	107.8	95.8	103.2
Chattanooga TN-GA MSA: Chattanooga TN.	92.2	92.8	86.5	98.5	86.9	89.9
Colorado Springs CO MSA: Colorado Springs.	94.0	103.3	92.3	73.3	98.8	96.6
Columbia MO MSA: Columbia.	90.9	92.6	86.9	77.6	99.7	101.1
Columbia SC MSA: Columbia.	98.4	96.7	102.9	97.5	85.8	103.3
Columbus GA-AL MSA: Columbus.	93.8	97.6	83.0	102.8	93.3	84.2
Columbus OH MSA: Columbus.	107.6	105.3	112.6	108.6	112.2	105.6
Corpus Christi TX MSA: Corpus Christi.	94.0	97.9	80.1	111.0	90.2	90.7
Cumberland MD-WV MSA: Cumberland.	99.3	103.6	101.4	115.3	87.5	93.3
Decatur AL MSA: Decatur-Hartselle.	90.5	89.4	81.5	89.8	99.0	89.0
Decatur IL MSA: Decatur.	93.3	97.9	80.5	113.8	98.4	86.0
Des Moines IA MSA: Des Moines.	102.3	96.9	103.5	109.4	104.7	104.6
Dothan AL MSA: Dothan.	88.7	97.2	82.0	97.6	99.6	77.1
Eau Claire WI MSA: Eau Claire.	95.6	102.6	90.2	93.2	93.6	100.5
El Paso TX MSA: El Paso.	97.9	91.2	92.1	94.6	111.9	96.4
Erie PA MSA: Erie.	107.4	95.3	123.1	103.7	97.0	106.1
Eugene-Springfield OR MSA: Eugene.	106.7	101.5	128.1	69.0	107.4	108.7
Evansville IN-KY MSA: Evansville.	91.0	99.3	86.1	87.5	94.5	85.2
Fayetteville-Springdale AR MSA: Fayetteville AR.	90.2	91.7	79.0	86.9	95.2	84.2
Florence AL MSA: Florence.	92.3	97.5	79.9	114.4	101.3	95.2
Florence SC MSA: Florence.	91.2	91.6	83.0	106.9	87.2	83.1
Fort Collins-Loveland CO MSA: Fort Collins.	99.6	103.0	101.4	69.9	104.2	105.2
Fort Smith AR-OK MSA: Fort Smith.	89.1	95.0	71.3	104.6	90.5	92.0
Fort Wayne IN MSA: Fort Wayne.	89.7	97.4	87.0	92.9	91.4	86.7
Gadsden AL MSA: Gadsden.	90.3	93.7	64.8	116.3	93.1	95.0
Glens Falls NY MSA: Glen Falls.	108.7	109.4	102.9	127.1	101.5	114.0
Grand Rapids MI MSA: Holland	105.4	100.0	111.9	83.5	100.2	93.0
Green Bay WI MSA: Green Bay.	96.8	96.9	98.9	80.3	98.0	100.9
Greensboro-Winston-Salem-High Point NC MSA.	93.5	92.2	89.5	108.5	91.2	86.0
Greenville-Spartanburg SC MSA: Greenville.	97.5	95.4	98.7	109.8	88.6	74.4
Hagerstown MD MSA: Hagerstown.	97.9	92.2	103.3	89.6	93.6	102.3
Harrisburg-Lebanon-Carlisle PA MSA: Harrisburg PA.	104.3	99.2	98.5	120.9	111.8	103.4
Hickory-Morganton NC MSA: Hickory.	97.6	92.7	99.6	107.2	84.1	91.7
Huntsville AL MSA: Huntsville.	97.0	94.6	90.3	88.9	106.3	89.1
Indianapolis IN MSA: Indianapolis.	95.3	97.4	92.5	92.7	95.8	95.1
Jacksonville FL MSA: Jacksonville	95.3	97.1	84.0	109.5	100.8	102.7
Jamestown-Dunkirk NY MSA: Jamestown.	103.1	109.3	106.9	104.5	111.3	83.3
Johnson City-Kingsport-Bristol TN-VA MSA: Johnson City TN.	97.4	93.0	101.0	80.3	95.5	84.2
Joplin MO MSA: Joplin.	87.0	92.2	83.1	77.6	87.1	91.0
Kansas City MO-KS MSA: Kansas.	95.5	94.2	93.9	92.4	97.1	98.3
Killeen-Temple TX MSA: Killeen-Harker Heights TX.	91.4	96.1	82.5	108.1	90.1	90.9

See source at end of table.

No. 763. Cost of Living Index—Selected Metropolitan Areas: Third Quarter 1992—Continued

[See headnote, page 487]

METROPOLITAN AREAS	Composite index	Grocery items	Housing	Utilities	Transportation	Health care
Knoxville TN MSA: Knoxville	94.9	96.2	86.7	98.5	94.3	85.8
La Crosse WI MSA: La Crosse	98.7	97.6	97.8	89.9	99.3	130.8
Lafayette-West Lafayette IN MSA: Lafayette IN	98.9	101.8	100.6	96.7	90.2	93.2
Lake Charles LA MSA: Lake Charles	94.6	97.4	77.0	99.6	106.4	89.3
Lancaster PA MSA: Lancaster	109.6	101.8	117.0	133.9	114.8	92.0
Lansing-East Lansing MI MSA: Lansing	101.4	103.9	114.7	88.8	94.9	113.1
Las Cruces NM MSA	97.5	92.0	101.3	91.4	105.2	94.5
Las Vegas NV MSA: Las Vegas	109.3	96.4	133.1	78.2	109.7	109.4
Lawton OK MSA: Lawton	95.9	95.7	88.9	102.4	101.4	93.4
Lexington-Fayette KY MSA	99.2	98.9	100.0	83.1	92.8	106.5
Lincoln NE MSA: Lincoln	89.2	95.1	83.6	84.6	100.6	84.4
Longview-Marshall TX MSA: Longview	90.6	92.6	74.6	102.7	98.0	83.6
Louisville KY-IN MSA: Louisville	91.8	93.9	88.8	79.5	94.9	83.8
Lubbock TX MSA: Lubbock	92.2	91.2	85.1	87.3	98.2	85.8
Lynchburg VA MSA: Lynchburg	96.2	95.7	96.1	85.9	84.6	90.0
Macon-Warner Robins GA MSA: Macon	98.4	96.0	90.2	105.5	99.5	90.4
Manchester NH MSA: Manchester	113.7	98.5	124.0	150.9	103.1	117.4
Mansfield OH MSA: Mansfield	96.2	99.9	86.6	119.4	89.7	93.3
Memphis TN-AR-MS MSA: Memphis	94.2	95.9	82.1	90.0	103.6	97.5
Minneapolis-St Paul MN-WI MSA: Minneapolis	100.2	93.6	106.0	91.2	104.5	108.2
Mobile AL MSA: Mobile	96.0	96.3	77.9	117.2	113.2	87.8
Monroe LA MSA: Monroe	99.4	95.2	80.8	133.4	101.0	92.8
Muncie IN MSA: Muncie	99.9	98.0	102.1	92.4	105.5	90.6
Nashville TN MSA: Nashville Franklin	92.2	96.7	87.8	91.2	92.1	82.4
New Haven-Meriden CT MSA: Hamden	130.2	120.0	162.3	135.9	106.9	131.9
New Orleans LA MSA: New Orleans	96.8	97.0	84.8	138.3	104.3	83.8
Norfolk-Virginia Beach-Newport News VA MSA: Virginia Peninsula VA	96.3	94.5	85.4	118.9	105.2	98.1
Ocala FL MSA: Ocala	94.2	98.7	77.7	103.1	101.1	91.1
Oklahoma City OK MSA: Oklahoma	91.1	92.1	78.2	102.9	97.3	96.5
Olympia WA MSA: Olympia	103.3	109.2	112.1	69.8	102.0	135.2
Omaha NE-IA MSA: Omaha	91.1	93.0	83.0	92.6	105.5	97.6
Orlando FL MSA: Orlando	98.9	98.9	95.3	96.8	102.1	113.4
Owensboro KY MSA: Owensboro	92.2	102.4	80.9	82.4	92.7	92.7
Parkersburg-Marietta WV-OH MSA: Marietta OH	91.2	96.8	86.0	82.0	90.6	89.8
Peoria IL MSA: Peoria	104.2	104.3	109.2	98.4	105.0	92.3
Phoenix AZ MSA: Pheonix	98.7	97.0	91.2	92.9	115.4	111.7
Provo-Orem UT MSA: Provo-Orem	99.1	96.3	99.1	89.8	104.0	95.3
Pueblo CO MSA: Pueblo	87.4	98.6	72.9	79.5	92.7	92.5
Raleigh-Durham NC MSA: Chapel Hill	103.5	92.7	109.2	107.9	93.8	111.1
Reno NV MSA: Reno-Sparks	109.6	102.7	124.6	76.6	107.2	124.9
Richland-Kennewick-Pasco WA MSA: Richland-Kennewick-Pasco WA	104.4	102.4	110.6	76.5	104.0	135.3
Richmond-Petersburg VA MSA: Richmond	105.2	98.8	101.3	120.3	101.0	103.5
Roanoke VA MSA: Roanoke	93.4	95.5	87.2	87.0	99.4	89.8
Rochester MN MSA: Rochester	100.4	95.7	101.5	94.9	108.8	107.6
Rochester NY MSA: Rochester	113.0	113.1	119.9	111.8	126.0	114.4
Rockford IL MSA: Rockford	106.2	99.1	108.5	130.4	103.9	104.5
Salt Lake City-Ogden UT MSA: Salt Lake City UT	96.2	98.9	85.0	91.8	109.0	101.8
San Antonio TX MSA: San Antonio	92.7	92.0	85.0	77.3	107.4	99.5
San Diego CA MSA: San Diego	132.3	109.1	195.5	71.2	129.8	134.3
Santa Fe NM MSA: Santa Fe	108.7	93.5	135.8	86.9	103.9	104.6
Scranton-Wilkes Barre PA MSA: Wilkes-Barre PA	104.1	106.3	107.5	147.8	84.7	88.7
Sharon PA MSA: Mercer County	101.1	102.3	109.1	103.1	93.7	94.9
Sioux City IA-NE MSA: Sioux City	100.8	104.8	113.3	89.9	98.4	94.6
Sioux Falls SD MSA: Sioux Falls	93.4	101.0	92.0	86.5	99.0	99.6
South Bend-Mishawaka IN MSA: South Bend	92.7	92.7	89.8	96.7	89.9	91.3
Spokane WA MSA	102.5	103.5	117.4	63.6	94.5	112.6
Springfield IL MSA: Springfield	94.6	101.3	88.3	88.0	98.9	99.5
Springfield MO MSA: Springfield	89.4	91.8	77.4	93.0	92.6	99.8
St. Cloud MN MSA	95.2	103.1	81.1	101.9	107.3	98.2
St. Louis MO-IL MSA	96.6	100.7	95.0	105.5	97.9	102.3
Syracuse NY MSA: Syracuse	101.1	108.2	88.1	134.1	114.8	112.1
Tallahassee FL MSA: Tallahassee	101.9	96.8	97.3	123.9	97.2	97.8
Tampa-St. Petersburg-Clearwater FL MSA: Tampa FL	95.6	97.7	91.8	102.4	99.4	98.5
Toledo OH MSA: Toledo	105.5	103.0	108.8	114.9	103.8	96.1
Tulsa OK MSA: Tulsa	88.3	91.3	75.7	91.7	86.7	91.5
Tuscaloosa AL MSA: Tuscaloosa	99.4	94.2	94.6	117.4	102.9	91.5
Tucson AZ MSA: Tucson	106.5	100.4	101.2	99.0	102.8	120.5
Tyler TX MSA: Tyler	95.4	94.4	82.7	108.2	91.9	89.9
Utica-Rome NY MSA	104.1	103.6	98.7	125.4	107.3	95.8
Waco TX MSA: Waco	94.7	91.9	83.5	112.6	101.5	95.4
Washington DC-MD-VA MSA	134.7	119.2	164.2	115.3	133.1	135.4
Waterloo-Cedar Falls IA MSA: Waterloo-Cedar Falls	97.1	98.4	92.0	86.0	106.4	88.1
Wausau WI MSA: Wausau	101.9	95.9	119.8	91.7	89.0	104.8
Wichita Falls TX MSA: Wichita Falls	92.9	95.1	81.2	105.3	106.2	89.1
Williamsport PA MSA:	108.4	100.2	115.0	137.6	91.1	97.8
Yakima WA MSA: Yakima	100.6	109.3	98.5	87.4	96.5	114.0
York PA MSA: Hanover	101.1	102.9	104.5	88.8	100.5	88.8
Youngstown-Warren OH MSA: Youngstown	94.2	101.1	87.2	112.5	94.3	84.5
Yuma AZ: Yuma	95.4	96.9	81.5	115.4	111.4	103.7

Source: ACCRA, Louisville KY 40206-6749, *ACCRA Cost of Living Index*, Third Quarter 1992 (copyright).

No. 764. Producer Price Indexes, by Stage of Processing: 1950 to 1992

[1982=100. See text, section 15. See *Historical Statistics, Colonial Times to 1970*, series E 73-86 for similar data]

YEAR	Crude materials	Crude foodstuffs and feedstuffs	Intermediate materials	Finished goods	Finished consumer goods	Capital equipment	YEAR	Crude materials	Crude foodstuffs and feedstuffs	Intermediate materials	Finished goods	Finished consumer goods	Capital equipment
1950...	32.7	43.4	25.3	28.2	32.7	23.2	1972...	39.9	51.5	38.2	41.8	46.9	42.8
1951...	37.6	50.2	28.4	30.8	36.7	25.5	1973...	54.5	72.6	42.4	45.6	56.5	44.2
1952...	34.5	47.3	27.5	30.6	36.4	25.9	1974...	61.4	76.4	52.5	52.6	64.4	50.5
1953...	31.9	42.3	27.7	30.3	34.5	26.3	1975...	61.6	77.4	58.0	58.2	69.8	58.2
1954...	31.6	42.3	27.9	30.4	34.2	26.7	1976...	63.4	76.8	60.9	60.8	69.6	62.1
1955...	30.4	38.4	28.4	30.5	33.4	27.4	1977...	65.5	77.5	64.9	64.7	73.3	66.1
1956...	30.6	37.6	29.6	31.3	33.3	29.5	1978...	73.4	87.3	69.5	69.8	79.9	71.3
1957...	31.2	39.2	30.3	32.5	34.4	31.3	1979...	85.9	100.0	78.4	77.6	87.3	77.5
1958...	31.9	41.6	30.4	33.2	36.5	32.1	1980...	95.3	104.6	90.3	88.0	92.4	85.8
1959...	31.1	38.8	30.8	33.1	34.8	32.7	1981...	103.0	103.9	98.6	96.1	97.8	94.6
1960...	30.4	38.4	30.8	33.4	35.5	32.8	1982...	100.0	100.0	100.0	100.0	100.0	100.0
1961...	30.2	37.9	30.6	33.4	35.4	32.9	1983...	101.3	101.8	100.6	101.6	101.0	102.8
1962...	30.5	38.6	30.6	33.5	35.7	33.0	1984...	103.5	104.7	103.1	103.7	105.4	105.2
1963...	29.9	37.5	30.7	33.4	35.3	33.1	1985...	95.8	94.8	102.7	104.7	104.6	107.5
1964...	29.6	36.6	30.8	33.5	35.4	33.4	1986...	87.7	93.2	99.1	103.2	107.3	109.7
1965...	31.1	39.2	31.2	34.1	36.8	33.8	1987...	93.7	96.2	101.5	105.4	109.5	111.7
1966...	33.1	42.7	32.0	35.2	39.2	34.6	1988...	96.0	106.1	107.1	108.0	112.6	114.3
1967...	31.3	40.3	32.2	35.6	38.5	35.8	1989...	103.1	111.2	112.0	113.6	118.7	118.0
1968...	31.8	40.9	33.0	36.6	40.0	37.0	1990...	108.9	113.1	114.5	119.2	124.4	122.9
1969...	33.9	44.1	34.1	38.0	42.4	38.3	1991...	101.2	105.5	114.4	121.7	124.1	126.7
1970...	35.2	45.2	35.4	39.3	43.8	40.1	1992...	100.3	105.1	114.7	123.2	123.2	129.1
1971...	36.0	46.1	36.8	40.5	44.5	41.7							

Source: U.S. Bureau of Labor Statistics, *Producer Price Indexes*, monthly and annual.

No. 765. Stage of Processing Producer Prices—Annual Percent Change: 1960 to 1992

[1982=100. Yearly averages. See table 764. Minus sign indicates decline]

YEAR	FINISHED GOODS Total	Consumer goods	Capital equipment	Finished consumer goods except foods	Intermediate materials, supplies and components	Intermediate materials, less food and feedstuffs	CRUDE MATERIALS Total	Crude foodstuffs and feedstuffs	Crude nonfood materials excluding fuel	Crude fuel
1960	0.9	0.9	0.3	0.6	-	0.7	-2.3	-1.0	-4.3	1.0
1961	-	-	0.3	-0.3	-0.6	-1.3	-0.7	-1.3	1.1	-
1962	0.3	0.3	0.3	-	-	-0.3	1.0	1.8	-0.4	-1.0
1963	-0.3	-0.6	0.3	-	0.3	-0.3	-2.0	-2.8	-1.5	1.0
1964	0.3	0.3	0.9	-0.3	0.3	0.7	-1.0	-2.4	1.9	-
1965	1.8	1.8	1.2	0.9	1.3	1.3	5.1	7.1	1.8	1.0
1966	3.2	3.5	2.4	1.5	2.6	2.0	6.4	8.9	2.2	2.8
1967	1.1	0.6	3.5	1.8	0.6	1.3	-5.4	-5.6	-6.4	3.7
1968	2.8	2.5	3.4	2.3	2.5	2.5	1.6	1.5	2.3	1.8
1969	3.8	3.8	3.5	2.3	3.3	3.4	6.6	7.8	4.8	4.3
1970	3.4	3.2	4.7	3.0	3.8	3.6	3.8	2.5	2.5	15.0
1971	3.1	2.8	4.0	3.5	4.0	4.0	2.3	2.0	1.0	13.8
1972	3.2	3.2	2.6	1.8	3.8	4.1	10.8	11.7	9.9	7.0
1973	9.1	10.8	3.3	4.6	11.0	7.7	36.6	41.0	32.8	10.7
1974	15.4	15.4	14.3	17.0	23.8	24.4	12.7	5.2	27.0	33.3
1975	10.6	9.6	15.2	10.4	10.5	12.1	0.3	1.3	-8.3	23.4
1976	4.5	3.8	6.7	6.2	5.0	6.0	2.9	-0.8	9.8	12.7
1977	6.4	6.5	6.4	7.3	6.6	6.8	3.3	0.9	2.6	21.7
1978	7.9	7.9	7.9	7.1	7.1	7.0	12.1	12.6	9.9	14.8
1979	11.2	11.7	8.7	13.3	12.8	12.8	17.0	14.5	22.0	18.9
1980	13.4	14.3	10.7	18.5	15.2	15.5	10.9	4.6	21.6	21.1
1981	9.2	9.0	10.3	10.3	9.2	9.8	8.1	-0.7	19.6	22.2
1982	4.1	3.5	5.7	4.1	1.4	1.8	-2.9	-3.8	-8.9	17.9
1983	1.6	1.3	2.8	1.2	0.6	0.5	1.3	1.8	-1.2	5.1
1984	2.1	2.0	2.3	1.0	2.5	2.5	2.2	2.8	2.2	-
1985	1.0	0.5	2.2	1.1	-0.4	-	-7.4	-9.5	-6.6	-2.3
1986	-1.4	-2.3	2.0	-4.6	-3.5	-3.6	-8.5	-1.7	-19.4	-10.2
1987	2.1	2.2	1.8	2.2	2.4	2.4	6.8	3.2	16.4	-8.8
1988	2.5	2.5	2.3	2.4	5.5	5.1	2.5	10.3	15.0	-2.4
1989	5.2	5.6	3.9	5.6	4.6	4.7	7.4	4.8	3.7	3.9
1990	4.9	5.4	3.5	5.9	2.2	2.3	5.6	1.7	12.0	-0.6
1991	2.1	1.9	3.1	2.9	-0.1	0.1	-7.1	-6.7	-9.1	-2.2
1992	1.2	1.0	1.9	1.8	0.3	0.3	-0.9	-0.4	-3.4	0.8

- Represents zero.

Source: U.S. Bureau of Labor Statistics, *Monthly Labor Review*.

No. 766. Producer Price Indexes for Selected Commodity Groupings, by Stage of Processing: 1970 to 1992

[1982=100, except as indicated]

COMMODITY	1970	1980	1985	1988	1989	1990	1991	1992
Finished goods	**39.3**	**88.0**	**104.7**	**108.0**	**113.6**	**119.2**	**121.7**	**123.2**
Finished consumer goods	39.1	88.6	103.8	106.2	112.1	118.2	120.5	121.7
Finished consumer foods	43.8	92.4	104.6	112.6	118.7	124.4	124.1	123.2
Fresh fruits	42.3	100.3	108.1	113.5	113.2	118.1	129.9	83.8
Fresh and dried vegetables	47.5	88.9	99.5	105.5	116.7	118.1	103.8	115.0
Eggs	71.0	95.7	95.7	88.6	119.6	117.6	110.7	94.1
Bakery products	40.0	90.0	113.9	126.4	135.4	141.0	146.6	152.5
Milled rice	52.4	131.5	105.0	118.1	104.9	102.5	109.9	108.9
Beef and veal	46.7	106.2	90.3	101.4	108.9	116.0	112.2	109.7
Pork	44.6	78.4	89.1	95.0	97.7	119.8	113.4	98.5
Processed young chickens	61.2	106.8	106.5	113.1	120.3	111.0	105.1	105.1
Processed turkeys	69.1	109.2	121.3	100.4	110.6	107.6	107.3	102.0
Fish	29.7	87.8	114.6	148.7	142.9	147.2	149.5	153.0
Dairy products	44.7	92.7	100.2	102.2	110.6	117.2	114.6	118.0
Processed fruits and vegetables	40.3	83.3	108.0	113.8	119.9	124.7	119.6	120.8
Soft drinks	37.8	81.8	107.7	114.3	117.7	122.3	125.5	125.7
Roasted coffee	37.7	110.4	107.2	113.5	115.9	113.0	107.8	100.5
Shortening and cooking oils	47.7	99.5	124.0	118.8	116.6	123.2	116.5	114.9
Finished consumer goods excl. foods	37.4	87.1	103.3	103.1	108.9	115.3	118.7	120.8
Alcoholic beverages	53.3	88.9	107.7	111.8	115.2	117.2	123.7	126.1
Women's apparel	62.8	86.9	105.4	111.3	113.5	116.1	117.9	119.9
Men's and boys' apparel	51.2	91.3	105.0	113.0	116.8	120.2	122.7	126.0
Girls', children's, and infants' apparel	58.8	87.1	103.1	107.5	110.5	115.3	117.8	118.9
Textile housefurnishings	43.4	86.8	100.6	104.4	106.6	109.5	111.8	113.6
Footwear	46.2	95.2	104.8	115.1	120.8	125.6	128.6	131.9
Natural gas	(NA)	(NA)	(NA)	(NA)	(NA)	(NA)	97.2	98.6
Gasoline	14.4	93.3	83.3	57.3	65.1	78.7	69.9	68.7
Fuel oil No. 2	(NA)	82.8	81.6	49.5	58.0	73.3	65.2	61.7
Pharmaceutical preps, ethical (Prescription)	52.0	80.6	132.0	169.0	184.4	200.8	217.5	231.6
Pharmaceutical preps, propri.; Over-counter	42.3	81.3	121.6	144.4	152.1	156.8	165.4	173.6
Soaps and synthetic detergents	41.5	85.8	107.9	114.7	119.4	117.7	117.5	120.6
Cosmetics and other toilet preparations	47.8	83.8	109.0	116.3	119.3	121.6	124.6	126.6
Tires, tubes, tread, etc	42.7	92.8	93.0	94.0	97.2	96.8	98.2	99.0
Sanitary papers and health products	32.5	91.9	106.6	115.0	126.0	135.3	136.2	136.8
Household furniture	48.6	89.1	108.5	117.6	121.8	125.1	128.0	130.1
Floor coverings	54.9	90.0	105.6	114.7	117.6	119.0	120.4	120.1
Household appliances	52.9	87.5	106.7	106.0	108.7	110.8	111.3	111.2
Home electronic equipment	106.0	103.8	90.8	87.2	86.9	82.7	83.2	82.2
Household glassware	33.1	84.7	121.8	128.1	134.7	132.5	136.0	141.7
Household flatware	32.7	148.0	98.6	113.0	125.7	122.1	119.5	124.5
Lawn and garden equip., excl. tractors	46.8	87.5	110.3	114.6	119.8	123.0	124.7	125.4
Passenger cars	50.0	88.9	106.9	113.0	115.5	118.3	124.1	126.9
Toys, games, and children's vehicles	48.5	89.2	103.8	110.8	115.6	118.1	120.2	121.4
Sporting and athletic goods	52.7	90.6	99.7	105.9	109.8	112.6	115.3	117.7
Tobacco products	35.2	76.0	132.5	171.9	194.8	221.4	249.7	275.3
Mobile homes	(NA)	(NA)	101.7	109.3	114.0	117.5	120.4	122.2
Capital equipment	**40.1**	**85.8**	**107.5**	**114.3**	**118.8**	**122.9**	**126.7**	**129.1**
Agricultural machinery and equipment	36.4	83.3	108.7	112.7	117.7	121.7	125.7	129.3
Construction machinery and equipment	33.7	84.2	105.4	111.8	117.2	121.6	125.2	128.7
Metal cutting machine tools	30.8	85.1	107.3	117.4	123.4	129.8	134.6	138.9
Metal forming machine tools	28.6	85.7	107.0	113.2	118.1	124.7	133.5	135.9
Tools, dies, jigs, fixtures, and ind. molds	(NA)	(NA)	106.3	110.9	113.8	117.2	122.7	124.7
Pumps, compressors, and equipment	33.0	82.8	102.6	108.9	115.0	119.2	124.6	128.8
Industrial material handling equipment	39.8	88.4	102.7	107.5	111.7	115.0	117.4	118.4
Textile machinery	45.4	87.2	107.6	119.4	123.9	128.8	135.0	139.1
Paper industries machinery (June 1982=100)	(NA)	(NA)	109.8	119.4	128.5	134.8	140.1	142.7
Printing trades machinery	42.5	89.7	109.0	120.1	123.0	124.9	126.5	126.7
Transformers and power regulators	44.7	82.4	105.0	108.8	117.3	120.9	123.9	123.4
Oil field and gas field machinery	27.0	76.3	96.8	97.0	99.1	102.4	108.6	107.8
Mining machinery and equipment	30.9	85.2	105.4	110.2	116.3	121.0	125.2	127.4
Office and store machines and equipment	68.3	93.1	101.6	107.0	109.5	109.5	109.8	111.0
Commercial furniture	41.6	85.7	111.9	124.2	129.0	133.4	136.2	138.0
Light motor trucks	42.0	83.3	112.2	125.0	129.5	130.0	135.5	142.4
Heavy motor trucks	36.3	82.3	108.8	112.4	117.2	120.3	123.6	128.5
Truck trailers	(NA)	(NA)	106.2	106.6	110.4	110.8	112.1	115.1
Railroad equipment	33.2	90.4	104.9	107.5	114.0	118.6	122.2	123.6
Photographic and photocopy equipment	72.0	94.9	89.5	91.8	94.1	97.2	99.3	100.9
Intermed. materials, supplies, components	**35.4**	**90.3**	**102.7**	**107.1**	**112.0**	**114.5**	**114.4**	**114.7**
Intermediate foods and feeds	45.6	105.5	97.3	109.5	113.8	113.3	111.1	110.7
Flour	55.3	102.3	99.8	105.7	114.6	103.6	96.8	109.3
Crude vegetable oils	75.8	127.1	137.6	116.6	103.1	115.8	103.0	97.1
Prepared animal feeds	49.1	107.3	90.1	116.0	116.6	107.4	106.8	108.3

See footnotes at end of table.

No. 766. Producer Price Indexes for Selected Commodity Groupings by Stage of Processing: 1970 to 1992—Continued

[1982=100, except as indicated]

COMMODITY	1970	1980	1985	1988	1989	1990	1991	1992
Intermediate materials less foods and feeds....	**34.8**	**89.4**	**103.0**	**106.9**	**111.9**	**114.5**	**114.6**	**114.9**
Leather..........................	34.6	99.8	113.4	167.5	170.4	177.5	168.4	163,6
Liquefied petroleum gas..............	(NA)	102.3	86.3	51.6	52.7	77.4	75.4	66.0
Electric power.....................	26.1	79.1	111.6	111.2	114.8	117.6	124.3	126.5
Jet fuels.........................	(NA)	87.5	81.0	52.1	58.1	76.0	66.4	61.9
No. 2 diesel fuel...................	(NA)	85.8	81.2	49.7	58.9	74.1	65.6	61.9
Residual fuel......................	10.6	81.3	83.2	41.1	47.6	57.7	49.1	45.5
Industrial chemicals................	28.6	91.9	96.0	106.8	114.8	113.2	111.8	109.1
Prepared paint.....................	42.8	89.5	105.3	112.2	119.5	124.8	129.9	131.6
Paint materials....................	33.3	89.9	109.5	115.7	129.1	136.3	135.8	131.1
Medicinal and botanical chemicals.......	44.4	91.0	91.8	93.5	100.3	102.2	109.0	111.3
Fats and oils, inedible...............	49.7	111.6	110.6	110.9	95.5	88.1	86.8	92.9
Mixed fertilizers...................	35.2	90.0	96.1	104.8	105.9	103.3	105.2	102.5
Nitrogenates......................	32.7	90.0	96.3	93.3	94.9	92.3	98.5	95.4
Phosphates	27.5	93.0	91.6	103.3	105.6	96.5	98.1	92.4
Other agricultural chemicals...........	23.2	80.1	98.7	107.4	115.1	119.9	125.6	129.1
Plastic resins and materials...........	32.0	98.5	107.5	132.4	133.4	124.1	120.0	116.3
Synthetic rubber...................	34.0	85.3	96.8	108.9	108.5	111.9	106.1	103.8
Plastic construction products..........	65.5	103.9	108.6	121.1	120.1	117.2	115.1	112.7
Softwood lumber...................	35.2	107.3	107.4	120.0	127.1	123.8	125.7	148.4
Hardwood lumber..................	43.7	96.0	117.1	131.0	128.2	131.0	128.5	140.5
Millwork.........................	41.5	93.2	111.7	121.9	127.3	130.4	135.5	143.2
Plywood..........................	46.7	106.2	99.6	133.4	115.9	114.2	114.3	133.0
Woodpulp.........................	28.9	100.3	91.4	136.7	157.4	151.3	119.2	119.8
Paper............................	38.8	89.7	106.0	123.2	129.6	128.8	126.9	123.1
Paperboard.......................	39.7	92.0	107.7	133.2	140.1	135.7	130.2	134.4
Paper boxes and containers...........	43.3	89.4	108.8	123.5	129.8	129.9	128.6	130.7
Building paper and board	42.2	86.1	107.4	113.3	115.6	112.2	111.8	119.6
Commercial printing (June 1982=100) ...	(NA)	(NA)	111.6	119.5	124.9	128.0	130.0	131.1
Foundry and forge shop products.......	32.4	89.7	105.2	109.6	114.6	117.2	119.0	120.1
Steel mill products.................	32.7	86.6	104.7	110.7	114.5	112.1	109.5	106.4
Primary nonferrous metals............	44.9	132.7	93.6	144.3	149.2	133.4	114.0	108.1
Aluminum mill shapes...............	36.7	89.3	107.8	130.9	135.4	127.9	123.2	121.9
Copper and brass mill shapes.........	63.4	112.6	106.9	162.7	182.0	174.6	160.5	166.6
Nonferrous wire and cable............	62.6	107.5	100.9	129.6	146.1	142.6	139.2	136.7
Metal containers...................	34.3	90.9	109.0	110.2	111.5	114.0	115.5	113.9
Hardware.........................	39.8	85.8	109.1	113.7	120.4	125.9	130.2	132.7
Plumbing fixtures and brass fittings......	39.9	88.5	111.9	128.7	137.7	144.3	149.7	153.1
Heating equipment..................	46.6	87.0	109.5	119.2	125.1	131.6	134.1	137.3
Fabricated structural metal products.....	36.7	88.8	103.2	114.3	120.3	121.8	122.4	122.1
Mechanical power transmission equipment....	36.9	84.5	108.2	116.0	121.1	125.3	129.1	132.1
Ball and roller bearings..............	33.1	80.0	105.9	114.0	124.1	130.6	136.7	139.0
Wiring devices.....................	35.9	81.9	111.7	123.8	129.7	132.2	133.9	134.8
Motors, generators, motor generator sets...	37.7	86.0	113.3	121.8	129.0	132.9	134.9	136.5
Switchgear, switchboard, etc., equipment...	40.5	88.4	106.7	113.2	119.0	124.4	128.5	131.3
Electronic components and accessories.....	57.4	88.8	112.4	117.5	119.4	118.4	118.6	117.5
Internal combustion engines...........	34.5	81.7	104.9	111.4	114.7	120.2	126.0	128.5
Machine shop products...............	31.1	81.0	112.8	116.8	121.3	124.3	125.9	126.8
Flat glass........................	52.2	88.7	101.7	109.7	109.7	107.5	105.9	106.6
Concrete products..................	37.7	92.0	107.5	110.0	111.2	113.5	116.6	117.2
Asphalt felts and coatings............	25.8	99.6	102.6	94.7	95.8	97.1	98.2	96.3
Gypsum products...................	38.9	100.1	132.3	112.9	110.0	105.2	99.3	100.3
Glass containers...................	33.9	82.3	106.8	112.3	115.2	120.4	125.4	125.1
Motor vehicle parts.................	32.9	72.9	102.5	107.2	109.7	111.2	112.5	113.0
Photographic supplies...............	41.0	97.2	107.4	113.1	123.0	127.6	125.8	125.9
Crude materials for further processing........	**35.2**	**95.3**	**95.8**	**96.0**	**103.1**	**108.9**	**101.2**	**100.3**
Crude foodstuffs and feedstuffs........	45.2	104.6	94.8	106.1	111.2	113.1	105.5	105.1
Wheat...........................	39.7	108.3	87.6	93.7	109.5	87.6	79.4	98.5
Corn............................	54.5	119.2	105.9	97.1	102.4	100.9	97.0	96.0
Cattle...........................	46.9	104.9	91.2	109.5	113.8	122.5	115.8	115.4
Hogs............................	45.5	74.5	80.7	81.8	80.5	94.1	82.7	70.7
Live chickens (broilers and fryers)......	48.5	103.4	110.5	125.4	131.7	119.5	111.9	114.6
Live turkeys.......................	59.9	112.2	144.6	108.4	119.1	116.9	109.5	106.6
Fluid milk........................	40.8	96.0	93.7	89.4	98.8	100.8	89.5	96.3
Soybeans.........................	45.3	117.0	94.2	124.8	114.3	100.8	95.1	97.3
Cane sugar, raw...................	39.9	148.3	104.6	111.9	115.5	119.2	113.7	112.1
Crude nonfood materials.................	**23.8**	**84.6**	**96.9**	**85.5**	**93.4**	**101.5**	**94.6**	**93.4**
Raw cotton........................	43.6	135.7	97.7	95.5	105.6	118.2	116.2	89.8
Leaf tobacco.......................	40.3	82.1	101.2	87.2	93.8	95.8	101.1	101.0
Cattle hides.......................	30.4	104.6	126.1	205.8	213.1	217.8	173.4	171.4
Coal............................	28.1	87.4	102.2	95.4	95.5	97.5	97.2	95.0
Natural gas.......................	7.9	63.3	102.9	77.4	82.0	80.4	79.1	80.2
Crude petroleum...................	14.5	75.9	84.5	46.2	56.3	71.0	61.9	58.1
Logs, timber, etc...................	(NA)	(NA)	96.0	117.7	131.9	142.8	144.1	164.9
Wastepaper	103.2	172.2	122.9	183.6	157.1	138.9	121.4	116.1
Iron ore..........................	35.9	87.8	97.5	82.8	82.8	83.3	83.6	83.7
Iron and steel scrap.................	59.6	140.9	112.6	177.1	173.7	166.0	147.6	138.8
Nonferrous metal ores (Dec. 1983=100).....	(NA)	(NA)	73.2	108.1	109.6	98.3	82.6	75.7
Copper base scrap..................	100.9	138.9	95.4	157.9	179.8	181.3	170.0	162.7
Aluminum base scrap................	34.4	183.9	123.4	219.5	204.4	172.6	143.1	138.3
Construction sand, gravel, and crushed stone...	40.9	85.3	110.7	120.6	122.8	125.4	128.6	130.5

NA Not available.

Source: U.S. Bureau of Labor Statistics, *Producer Price Indexes*, monthly and annual.

No. 767. Producer Price Indexes for the Net Output of Selected Industries: 1985 to 1992

[Indexes are based on selling prices reported by establishments of all sizes by probability sampling. Industries selected by value added. N.e.c.= not elsewhere classified. See text, section 27]

SIC code [1]	ITEM	Index base	1985	1988	1989	1990	1991	1992
2011	Meat packing plants	12/80	90.9	101.7	108.2	119.8	115.1	109.0
2013	Sausages and other prepared meats	12/82	95.7	99.2	102.4	112.7	113.0	108.7
2026	Fluid milk	12/82	102.6	106.0	112.8	121.4	119.0	121.5
2033	Canned fruits and vegetables	06/81	112.7	121.0	128.8	129.9	129.4	129.9
2038	Frozen specialties	12/82	110.8	118.4	123.5	127.3	130.4	131.0
2051	Bread, cake, and related products	06/80	127.1	142.8	153.6	159.4	165.0	173.3
2052	Cookies and crackers	06/83	112.0	126.3	134.6	141.9	148.5	151.2
2082	Malt beverages	06/82	110.0	113.2	115.4	115.2	121.3	123.7
2086	Bottled and canned soft drinks	06/81	112.5	119.5	122.5	127.2	130.3	131.1
2095	Coffee	06/81	111.5	117.8	120.4	120.0	116.5	110.0
2099	Food preparations, n.e.c	12/85	(NA)	104.8	110.4	114.3	117.3	117.2
2111	Cigarettes	12/82	110.7	150.8	173.1	197.6	225.0	250.5
2221	Synthetic fiber and silk broadwoven fabric	06/81	101.2	110.1	112.3	115.6	115.2	115.9
2335	Women's, misses', and juniors' dresses	12/80	108.0	116.7	122.0	125.6	129.0	129.8
2411	Logging camps and logging contractors	12/81	94.8	112.8	128.0	135.6	135.0	151.3
2421	Sawmills and planing mills	12/80	97.3	107.1	111.6	109.9	111.5	127.7
2431	Millwork	06/83	103.2	113.5	118.9	120.4	125.8	134.4
2511	Wood household furniture, except upholstered	12/79	133.3	147.2	153.7	158.9	163.3	166.9
2621	Paper mill products except building paper	06/81	109.5	127.4	134.6	134.0	131.0	126.6
2631	Paperboard mills	12/82	112.0	141.6	149.9	146.0	140.7	142.8
2653	Corrugated and solid fiber boxes	03/80	119.7	140.2	143.6	139.6	134.5	137.4
2711	Newspaper publishing	12/79	164.0	193.9	206.9	220.4	235.7	248.6
2721	Periodical publishing	12/79	157.9	183.8	194.0	205.7	217.8	227.9
2731	Book publishing	12/80	134.1	155.1	165.4	175.2	183.4	189.5
2752	Commercial printing, lithographic	06/82	111.0	118.5	124.1	127.9	129.7	130.8
2759	Commercial printing, n.e.c	06/82	112.9	128.2	133.7	136.1	140.8	143.8
2761	Manifold business forms	12/83	106.2	120.3	124.9	124.6	123.9	120.0
2819	Industrial inorganic chemicals, n.e.c	12/82	100.4	104.7	116.2	117.9	119.4	118.9
2821	Plastic materials and resins	12/80	113.6	144.0	147.3	139.5	137.9	131.8
2824	Noncellulosic manmade fibers	06/81	97.6	96.8	101.5	102.7	101.9	101.7
2834	Pharmaceutical preparations	06/81	141.3	175.6	190.2	203.5	217.3	231.2
2841	Soap and other detergents	06/83	104.2	110.5	115.5	115.2	116.0	118.5
2842	Specialty cleaning, polish. and sanitation preps.	06/83	103.9	110.2	115.6	118.6	121.5	123.1
2844	Toilet preparations	03/80	135.4	145.6	149.8	153.2	158.0	162.5
2851	Paints and allied products	06/83	104.9	111.7	119.5	125.0	130.3	132.3
2865	Cyclic (coal tar) crudes & intermediates	12/82	96.9	105.8	112.7	114.1	113.3	113.6
2869	Industrial organic chemicals, n.e.c	12/82	101.3	120.0	128.7	125.6	129.1	127.5
2899	Chemicals and chemical preparations, n.e.c	06/85	(NA)	104.3	111.3	112.5	115.7	117.2
2911	Petroleum refining	06/85	98.3	65.4	73.6	90.1	80.9	78.2
3011	Tires and inner tubes	06/81	96.8	99.5	102.9	103.0	105.0	106.1
3273	Ready-mixed concrete	06/81	108.6	109.7	111.5	114.3	116.9	117.3
3312	Blast furnaces and steel mills	06/82	104.9	109.4	113.0	110.8	108.4	105.9
3321	Gray iron foundries	12/80	115.6	118.3	120.9	123.4	125.6	126.9
3357	Nonferrous wire drawing and insulating	12/82	100.5	132.7	153.5	148.7	145.0	141.8
3411	Metal cans	06/81	110.4	111.2	113.7	116.6	118.1	117.0
3429	Hardware, n.e.c	06/85	(NA)	100.7	106.5	110.6	113.3	114.9
3441	Fabricated structural metal	06/82	103.0	113.0	118.0	118.6	117.3	116.7
3443	Fabricated plate work	03/80	120.8	129.6	137.1	142.3	145.8	147.0
3444	Sheet metal work	12/82	107.2	121.4	128.4	129.4	128.2	126.6
3465	Automotive stampings	12/82	110.4	108.1	110.9	112.6	111.7	111.6
3469	Metal stampings, n.e.c.	06/84	101.4	111.5	118.8	121.1	122.5	123.2
3499	Fabricated metal products, n.e.c	06/85	(NA)	109.6	114.6	117.6	119.0	119.2
3519	Internal combustion engines, n.e.c	12/82	103.4	106.7	110.6	115.7	120.7	123.4
3523	Farm machinery and equipment	12/82	105.3	108.1	113.0	116.8	120.5	124.0
3531	Construction machinery	12/80	119.5	125.8	132.4	137.6	142.0	146.9
3544	Special tools, dies, jigs, fixtures and indus. molds	06/81	113.5	118.2	121.1	124.5	129.3	131.0
3559	Special industry machinery, n.e.c	12/81	116.4	127.2	132.9	137.5	142.4	145.9
3585	Refrigeration and heating equipment	12/82	104.7	110.8	115.5	119.0	119.7	121.1
3599	Machinery, except electrical, n.e.c	06/84	102.0	106.0	110.8	113.9	114.4	114.3
3621	Electric motors and generators	06/83	108.2	116.4	123.3	127.5	129.7	131.5
3661	Telephone & telegraph apparatus	12/85	(NA)	108.3	110.2	112.0	112.8	112.4
3674	Semiconductors and related devices	06/81	106.6	108.3	107.5	105.0	102.8	98.5
3679	Electronic components, n.e.c	06/82	108.6	112.5	113.9	115.1	115.2	117.7
3711	Motor vehicles and passenger car bodies	06/82	107.2	114.1	117.4	119.9	125.3	129.1
3714	Motor vehicle parts and accessories	12/82	100.6	105.3	107.4	108.9	110.3	111.0
3721	Aircraft	12/85	(NA)	101.5	110.2	116.0	120.4	124.3
3724	Aircraft engines and engine parts	12/85	(NA)	103.8	106.6	112.6	117.9	123.5
3728	Aircraft parts and auxiliary equipment, n.e.c	06/85	(NA)	109.6	113.1	116.3	120.3	124.9
3731	Ship building and repairing	12/85	(NA)	105.5	110.2	114.0	116.2	118.3
3861	Photographic equipment and supplies	12/83	101.5	105.3	109.3	112.2	111.9	112.0

NA Not available.　[1] Standard Industrial Classification code.
Source: U.S. Bureau of Labor Statistics, *Producer Price Indexes,* monthly.

No. 768. Fixed-Weighted Price Indexes for Personal Consumption Expenditures: 1960 to 1992
[1987 = 100]

YEAR	Personal consumption expenditures [1]	Motor vehicles and parts	Furniture [2]	Food	Clothing and shoes	Gasoline and oil	Housing	Household operation	Electricity and gas	Transportation	Medical care
1960	30.8	40.6	79.2	27.4	46.1	30.5	28.8	32.0	24.6	25.5	17.8
1961	31.1	40.6	78.2	27.7	46.4	30.2	29.2	32.2	24.7	26.5	18.3
1962	31.3	40.8	76.5	28.0	46.5	30.4	29.5	32.3	24.8	26.8	18.8
1963	31.6	40.8	75.5	28.4	46.9	30.3	29.9	32.5	24.7	26.4	19.2
1964	31.9	41.0	74.9	29.0	47.3	30.1	30.2	32.6	24.7	26.4	19.9
1965	32.2	40.5	73.1	29.5	47.7	31.2	30.5	32.6	24.6	27.1	20.5
1966	32.8	40.1	71.5	30.7	49.0	32.0	30.9	32.5	24.6	27.9	21.5
1967	33.7	40.6	71.8	31.2	51.1	33.0	31.5	33.0	24.8	28.4	22.9
1968	35.0	41.9	73.0	32.3	54.0	33.5	32.3	33.6	25.0	29.2	24.6
1969	36.3	42.6	74.1	33.7	57.1	34.6	33.4	34.5	25.5	30.8	26.1
1970	37.9	43.8	74.9	35.9	59.4	34.9	34.8	35.6	26.4	33.8	27.9
1971	39.5	45.9	75.6	36.9	61.3	35.2	36.4	38.0	28.2	37.3	29.3
1972	40.8	45.9	76.2	38.6	62.7	35.7	37.7	39.9	29.7	38.6	30.7
1973	42.7	46.2	76.9	42.6	64.9	39.1	39.4	41.6	31.3	39.4	32.1
1974	46.7	49.1	80.6	48.7	69.5	52.7	40.9	45.8	36.6	42.1	34.7
1975	50.5	53.9	85.9	52.7	72.2	56.2	43.6	49.8	41.9	44.5	38.3
1976	53.3	57.8	88.3	54.4	74.5	58.6	46.5	53.6	45.6	49.3	41.7
1977	56.7	61.2	89.9	57.9	77.6	62.0	50.4	57.0	50.0	54.7	45.7
1978	60.7	65.3	92.9	63.1	79.5	64.7	54.0	60.2	53.8	57.9	50.0
1979	65.8	70.3	97.2	69.4	81.7	86.8	58.3	63.6	59.1	62.2	54.4
1980	72.6	75.6	98.2	75.9	85.2	120.7	63.8	69.7	69.0	71.9	60.4
1981	78.9	81.3	101.7	82.1	88.2	134.4	70.4	78.1	79.0	79.2	67.6
1982	83.2	85.1	103.6	85.4	90.0	127.5	75.9	86.7	89.1	83.0	74.7
1983	86.7	87.9	102.6	87.6	91.8	123.4	80.5	92.1	95.8	86.9	80.1
1984	89.9	90.5	101.7	91.1	93.1	121.5	84.9	96.3	100.0	89.6	85.0
1985	93.3	93.0	100.8	93.4	95.8	122.5	90.0	98.9	102.2	91.0	90.4
1986	96.1	95.7	99.5	96.5	95.8	96.2	95.4	100.4	101.7	94.0	94.6
1987	100.0	100.0	100.0	100.0	100.0	100.0	100.0	100.0	100.0	100.0	100.0
1988	104.3	101.5	101.0	104.0	104.2	100.9	104.9	101.4	100.8	104.9	107.1
1989	109.5	104.6	101.6	109.8	106.7	110.2	109.6	103.8	103.9	109.6	115.7
1990	115.3	105.4	102.4	115.7	111.4	125.6	115.4	105.9	105.6	114.5	124.2
1991	120.4	108.8	103.0	120.1	115.3	123.8	120.2	109.8	108.8	121.9	132.8
1992	124.3	112.0	104.0	122.1	117.9	123.3	124.1	112.7	111.1	128.1	140.4

[1] Includes items not shown separately.   [2] Includes household equipment.

No. 769. Fixed-Weighted Price Indexes for Personal Consumption Expenditures—Annual Percent Change: 1960 to 1992

YEAR	Personal consumption expenditures [1]	Motor vehicles and parts	Furniture [2]	Food	Clothing and shoes	Gasoline and oil	Housing	Household operation	Electricity and gas	Transportation	Medical care
1960	1.3	-1.7	0.3	1.3	1.2	2.9	1.5	2.2	2.4	3.5	3.6
1962	0.6	0.5	-2.2	1.2	0.2	0.6	1.2	0.4	-	1.3	2.8
1963	0.9	-	-1.3	1.4	1.0	-0.2	1.1	0.7	-0.1	-1.5	2.6
1964	1.1	0.4	-0.8	2.1	0.7	-0.6	1.0	0.3	-0.3	-0.1	3.2
1965	1.0	-1.2	-2.4	1.8	1.0	3.8	1.0	-0.2	-0.3	2.8	3.3
1966	1.8	-1.0	-2.2	3.9	2.6	2.3	1.4	-0.2	0.1	2.8	4.7
1967	2.6	1.3	0.4	1.7	4.2	3.3	1.9	1.5	0.7	2.0	6.6
1968	3.8	3.1	1.7	3.5	5.7	1.5	2.5	1.8	0.9	2.8	7.5
1969	3.8	1.9	1.5	4.6	5.7	3.3	3.4	2.6	2.0	5.3	5.9
1970	4.4	2.8	1.1	6.3	4.1	0.9	4.2	3.3	3.7	9.7	6.9
1971	4.4	4.8	0.9	2.9	3.2	0.8	4.6	6.6	6.8	10.3	5.1
1972	3.3	-	0.8	4.6	2.2	1.3	3.6	5.1	5.0	3.5	5.0
1973	4.6	0.6	0.9	10.4	3.6	9.5	4.4	4.2	5.6	2.1	4.4
1974	9.3	6.2	4.8	14.3	7.1	34.9	3.9	10.1	17.0	6.8	8.4
1975	8.1	9.9	6.6	8.2	3.8	6.7	6.6	8.6	14.5	5.7	10.1
1976	5.6	7.3	2.8	3.3	3.3	4.2	6.7	7.7	8.8	10.9	9.0
1977	6.4	5.7	1.8	6.5	4.1	5.8	8.5	6.3	9.6	10.9	9.6
1978	7.0	6.8	3.3	9.0	2.4	4.4	7.0	5.6	7.5	5.9	9.2
1979	8.5	7.6	4.6	10.0	2.9	34.2	8.0	5.7	9.9	7.3	9.0
1980	10.3	7.6	1.0	9.3	4.3	39.0	9.4	9.5	16.8	15.7	10.9
1981	8.6	7.5	3.6	8.2	3.5	11.3	10.3	12.1	14.4	10.2	11.8
1982	5.4	4.7	1.9	4.0	2.1	-5.1	7.8	11.1	12.8	4.7	10.6
1983	4.3	3.2	-1.0	2.6	2.0	-3.3	6.1	6.2	7.5	4.8	7.2
1984	3.7	3.0	-0.8	3.9	1.4	-1.5	5.4	4.6	4.5	3.1	6.1
1985	3.8	2.8	-1.0	2.6	3.0	0.8	6.1	2.7	2.2	1.5	6.4
1986	3.0	3.0	-1.2	3.3	-	-21.5	6.0	1.5	-0.5	3.3	4.6
1987	4.1	4.5	0.5	3.6	4.3	4.0	4.8	-0.4	-1.7	6.4	5.7
1988	4.3	1.5	1.0	4.0	4.2	0.9	4.9	1.4	0.8	4.9	7.1
1989	4.9	3.1	0.5	5.6	2.4	9.2	4.6	2.4	3.1	4.5	8.0
1990	5.3	0.8	0.8	5.3	4.3	14.0	5.3	2.0	1.6	4.5	7.3
1991	4.4	3.2	0.6	3.8	3.5	-1.4	3.7	3.7	3.0	6.5	6.9
1992	2.9	2.9	1.0	1.7	2.2	-0.4	3.2	2.6	2.1	5.1	5.7

- Represents or rounds to zero.   [1] Includes items not shown separately.   [2] Includes household equipment.
Source of tables 768 and 769: U.S. Bureau of Economic Analysis, *The National Income and Product Accounts of the United States: Volume 2, 1959-88;* and *Survey of Current Business,* July issues.

No. 770. Fixed-Weighted Price Indexes: 1980 to 1992

[1987 = 100]

ITEM	1980	1983	1984	1985	1986	1988	1989	1990	1991	1992
Gross domestic product	(NA)	88.10	91.10	94.30	97.00	103.90	108.40	113.10	118.1	121.6
Personal consumption expenditures.	72.6	86.7	89.9	93.3	96.1	104.3	109.3	115.0	120.5	124.3
Durable goods	84.8	93.7	94.9	96.0	97.1	102.0	104.6	106.8	108.9	111.4
Nondurable goods...............	79.6	91.1	93.7	96.2	96.2	103.8	109.5	116.2	120.5	123.0
Services	65.3	82.4	86.4	90.9	95.8	105.1	110.4	116.3	123.1	128.3
Gross private domestic investment:										
Fixed investment..............	(NA)	95.0	94.8	95.8	97.9	103.2	106.2	108.7	110.8	111.5
Nonresidential	(NA)	98.5	97.0	97.5	98.9	102.7	105.5	107.9	110.4	111.3
Structures	78.5	92.5	94.1	96.9	98.5	104.6	109.0	111.9	114.3	114.9
Producers' durable equipment	(NA)	101.7	98.6	97.8	99.2	101.6	103.6	105.9	108.3	109.5
Residential	75.3	87.3	89.8	92.1	95.8	104.3	107.8	110.4	111.8	113.0
Exports of goods and services	(NA)	99.5	99.8	98.2	97.3	105.7	108.1	109.8	112.4	113.8
Imports of goods and services	(NA)	98.0	97.0	94.6	93.8	105.4	108.6	113.3	113.7	114.5
Government purchases.............	73.3	88.5	92.2	95.4	97.6	103.7	107.9	112.4	116.5	119.9
Federal	75.2	92.2	95.6	97.9	99.0	102.8	107.2	112.1	116.7	121.5
National defense	76.3	93.5	96.9	98.8	99.5	103.1	107.3	112.2	116.5	121.8
Nondefense	72.0	88.4	91.4	94.9	97.5	102.0	106.9	111.5	117.0	120.6
State and local...............	71.9	85.5	89.6	93.5	96.5	104.3	108.5	112.7	116.4	118.6

NA Not available.

Source: U.S. Bureau of Economic Analysis, *The National Income and Product Accounts of the United States: Volume 2 1959-1988* and *Survey of Current Business*, July issues.

No. 771. Fixed-Weighted Price Indexes—Annual Percent Change: 1980 to 1992

[1987 = 100]

ITEM	1980-81	1983-84	1984-85	1985-86	1986-87	1987-88	1988-89	1989-90	1990-91	1991-92
Gross domestic product	(NA)	3.4	3.5	2.9	3.1	3.9	4.3	4.3	4.0	2.9
Personal consumption expend....	8.7	3.7	3.8	3.0	4.1	4.3	4.8	5.2	4.4	3.2
Durable goods	5.5	1.3	1.2	1.1	3.0	2.0	2.5	2.1	2.4	2.3
Nondurable goods..........	8.0	2.9	2.7	-	4.0	3.8	5.5	6.1	3.6	2.1
Services	10.1	4.9	5.2	5.4	4.4	5.1	5.0	5.3	5.3	4.1
Gross private domestic invest.:										
Fixed investment..........	(NA)	−0.2	1.1	2.2	2.1	3.2	2.9	2.4	1.9	0.6
Nonresidential	(NA)	−1.5	0.5	1.4	1.1	2.7	2.7	2.3	1.9	0.8
Structures	11.2	1.7	3.0	1.7	1.5	4.6	4.2	2.7	1.7	0.4
Producers' durable equip...	(NA)	−3.0	−0.8	1.4	0.8	1.6	2.0	2.2	2.0	1.1
Residential	8.0	2.9	2.6	4.0	4.4	4.3	3.4	2.4	1.9	1.1
Exports of goods and services ...	(NA)	0.3	−1.6	−0.9	2.8	5.7	2.3	1.6	2.1	1.1
Imports of goods and services ...	(NA)	−1.0	−2.5	−0.8	6.6	5.4	3.0	4.3	1.0	0.8
Government purchases........	8.6	4.2	3.5	2.3	2.5	3.7	4.1	4.2	3.5	2.9
Federal	9.4	3.7	2.4	1.1	1.0	2.8	4.3	4.6	4.1	4.1
National defense	9.2	3.6	2.0	0.7	0.5	3.1	4.1	4.6	3.9	4.5
Nondefense	9.9	3.4	3.8	2.7	2.6	2.0	4.8	4.3	4.8	3.1
State and local............	7.9	4.8	4.4	3.2	3.6	4.3	4.0	3.9	3.1	1.9

NA Not available.

Source: U.S. Bureau of Economic Analysis, *The National Income and Product Accounts of the United States: Volume 2, 1959-1988;* and *Survey of Current Business*, July issues.

No. 772. Commodity Research Bureau Futures Price Index: 1975 to 1991

[1967 = 100. Index computed daily. Represents unweighted geometric average of commodity futures prices (through 9 months forward) of 21 major commodity futures markets. Represents end of year index]

ITEM	1975	1980	1981	1982	1983	1984	1985	1986	1987	1988	1989	1990	1991
All commodities	191.0	308.5	254.9	234.0	277.6	244.2	229.2	209.1	232.5	251.8	229.9	222.6	208.0
Imported.............	259.4	426.0	357.0	269.0	326.0	291.7	398.2	321.2	356.1	365.2	271.7	276.0	264.4
Industrial.............	154.8	324.6	249.2	249.9	249.0	217.0	211.7	210.4	252.5	248.2	249.6	245.5	217.2
Grains	195.6	312.1	251.3	215.1	249.6	224.9	198.5	164.6	186.1	261.9	205.7	171.2	196.1
Oilseeds	181.6	314.6	271.0	236.9	316.6	273.5	245.4	189.8	223.6	309.6	254.2	223.6	195.4
Livestock and meats.....	180.8	217.4	195.3	219.9	229.7	240.8	206.9	200.2	189.9	199.1	206.5	226.2	174.0
Metals (precious) [1]	141.0	531.4	319.7	366.0	328.5	243.3	256.6	296.6	346.4	318.7	296.9	257.8	226.0

[1] Prior to 1980, index for metals only.

Source: Commodity Research Bureau (CRB), New York City, NY, *CRB Commodity Index Report,* weekly (copyright).

No. 773. Indexes of Spot Primary Market Prices: 1980 to 1991

[1967 = 100. Computed weekly through 1981; daily thereafter. Represents unweighted geometric average of price quotations of 23 commodities; much more sensitive to changes in market conditions than is a monthly producer price index]

ITEMS AND NUMBER OF COMMODITIES	1980 (6-24)	1981 (5-26)	1982 (5-25)	1983 (5-23)	1984 (5-22)	1985 (5-21)	1986 (5-20)	1987 (5-26)	1988 (5-27)	1989 (5-26)	1990 (5-25)	1991 (5-28)
All commodities (22)......	265.1	267.9	247.6	249.8	293.9	251.4	218.0	250.0	270.3	281.3	279.2	235.3
Foodstuffs (9)	260.9	244.2	252.8	246.1	299.9	248.1	205.5	215.2	230.1	222.5	231.5	197.7
Raw industrials (13). . . .	268.0	285.4	243.9	252.3	289.7	253.6	226.9	277.3	302.0	329.0	317.0	265.2
Livestock and products (5). . . .	250.5	265.2	312.1	278.1	364.5	284.5	231.2	303.3	316.1	285.2	306.9	286.6
Metals (5)	257.9	287.3	218.2	225.9	253.4	220.2	191.2	239.5	276.7	347.1	313.9	348.8
Textiles and fibers (4)	234.7	243.0	206.6	208.0	248.1	220.8	216.9	247.1	247.3	253.5	259.4	201.8
Fats and oils (4)........	229.5	238.7	255.7	225.9	363.5	273.1	168.5	201.2	230.4	208.1	193.3	185.0

Source: Commodity Research Bureau, a Knight-Ridder Business Information Service, New York, NY, *CRB Commodity Index Report*, weekly (copyright).

No. 774. Selected Mineral Products—Average Prices: 1980 to 1991

[Represents average price, except as noted. Excludes Alaska and Hawaii, except as noted. See also *Historical Statistics, Colonial Times to 1970*, series M96, 139, 148, 209, 248, and 262]

MINERAL	Unit	1980	1981	1982	1983	1984	1985	1986	1987	1988	1989	1990	1991, prel.
Aluminum [1] . . [2] [3] . .	Cents/lb.	71.6	76.0	76.0	77.8	81.0	81.0	81.0	72.3	110.1	87.8	74.0	59.5
Bituminous coal [2] [3] . . .	Dol./sh. ton .	24.5	26.3	27.1	25.9	25.5	25.1	23.7	23.0	22.0	21.8	21.7	21.8
Cobalt [4] [5]	Dol./lb.	25.0	12.9	8.6	5.8	10.4	11.4	7.5	6.6	7.1	7.6	10.1	16.9
Copper, electrolytic . . .	Cents/lb. . . .	101.3	84.2	72.8	76.5	66.8	67.0	66.1	82.5	120.5	130.9	123.2	109.3
Gold	Dol./fine oz .	612.6	459.6	375.9	424.0	360.7	317.7	368.2	448.0	438.3	382.6	384.9	363.3
Lead (NY) . [2] [6]	Cents/lb. . . .	42.5	36.5	25.5	21.7	25.6	19.1	22.1	35.9	37.1	39.4	46.0	33.5
Natural gas [2] [6]	Dol./1,000 cu. ft .	1.6	2.0	2.5	2.6	2.7	2.5	1.9	1.7	1.7	1.7	1.7	1.6
Nickel	Dol./lb.	3.0	2.7	2.2	2.2	2.2	2.3	1.8	2.2	6.3	6.1	4.0	3.7
Petroleum, crude [2]	Dol./bbl	21.6	31.8	28.5	26.2	25.9	24.1	12.5	15.4	12.6	15.9	20.0	16.5
Platinum [7]	Dol./troy oz .	439.0	475.0	475.0	475.0	475.0	475.0	519.0	600.0	600.0	600.0	600.0	600.0
Silver	Dol./fine oz .	20.6	10.5	8.0	11.4	8.1	6.1	5.5	7.0	6.5	5.5	4.8	4.0
Tungsten concentrate [8] .	Dol./lb	8.4	8.0	6.4	4.7	5.2	4.2	3.2	2.9	(NA)	(NA)	(NA)	(NA)
Zinc [9]	Cents/lb. . . .	37.4	44.6	38.5	41.4	48.6	40.4	38.0	41.9	60.2	82.1	74.6	52.8

NA Not available. [1] 99.5 percent primary aluminum ingot. [2] Average value at point of production; includes Alaska. Source: U.S. Energy Information Administration, *Annual Energy Review* and *Monthly Energy Review*. [3] Includes subbituminous coal and lignite. [4] Weighted average based on the market price quoted by a major U.S. cobalt dealer, otherwise based on range of prices. [5] Cathode prices. [6] Average value of marketed production. [7] Producer prices. [8] Average value of shipments. [9] Delivered price; 1991 price is average delivered price of special high grade zinc.

Source: Except as noted, U.S. Bureau of Mines, *Minerals Yearbook*.

No. 775. Average Prices of Selected Fuels and Electricity: 1980 to 1991

[In dollars per unit, except electricity, in cents per kWh. Represents price to end-users, except as noted]

ITEM	Unit [1]	1980	1981	1982	1983	1984	1985	1986	1987	1988	1989	1990	1991
Crude oil, composite [2]. . .	Barrel	28.07	35.24	31.87	28.99	28.63	26.75	14.55	17.90	14.67	17.97	22.22	19.06
Motor gasoline: [3]													
Unleaded regular. . . .	Gallon	1.25	1.38	1.30	1.24	1.21	1.20	0.93	0.95	0.95	1.02	1.16	1.14
Unleaded premium . . .	Gallon	(NA)	1.47	1.42	1.38	1.37	1.34	1.09	1.09	1.11	1.20	1.35	1.32
No. 2 heating oil	Gallon	0.79	0.91	0.91	0.92	0.92	0.85	0.56	0.58	0.54	0.59	0.73	0.67
No. 2 diesel fuel.	Gallon	0.82	1.00	0.94	0.83	0.82	0.79	0.48	0.55	0.50	0.59	0.73	0.65
Residual fuel oil	Gallon	0.61	0.76	0.68	0.65	0.69	0.61	0.34	0.42	0.33	0.39	0.44	0.34
Natural gas, residential . .	1,000 cu/ft .	3.68	4.29	5.17	6.06	6.12	6.12	5.83	5.54	5.47	5.64	5.80	5.82
Electricity, residential . .	kWh	5.4	6.2	6.9	7.2	7.5	7.8	7.4	7.4	7.5	7.6	7.8	8.1

NA Not available. [1] See headnote. [2] Refiner acquisition cost. [3] Average, all service.

Source: U.S. Energy Information Administration, *Monthly Energy Review*.

No. 776. Weekly Food Cost for Families, by Type of Family: 1980 to 1992

[In dollars. As of **December**, except as indicated. Based on moderate-cost food plan; assumes all meals are eaten at home or taken from home]

FAMILY TYPE	1980	1984	1985	1986	1987	1988	1989	1990	1991	1992 Jan.	1992 May
Couple, 20 to 50 years old [1]........	52.00	56.50	58.30	60.40	63.50	66.70	70.40	74.70	75.70	76.10	76.20
Couple, 51 years and over [1]........	45.90	53.90	55.70	57.80	60.70	64.00	67.50	71.80	72.80	73.30	73.40
Couple [2] with children:											
One child, 1 to 5 years old	62.90	69.20	71.30	73.90	77.50	81.60	86.40	91.70	93.00	93.50	93.70
One child, 15 to 19 years old	74.80	80.50	83.00	85.80	90.10	94.80	100.60	106.50	108.00	108.70	108.80
Two children, 1 to 5 years old	72.60	80.50	82.90	85.80	90.00	94.90	100.60	106.60	108.20	108.80	109.00
Two children, 6 to 11 years old . . .	88.10	97.10	99.80	103.30	108.30	114.10	121.00	128.30	130.10	130.90	131.00
Two children, 12 to 19 years old . . .	93.80	101.60	104.60	108.20	113.50	119.40	126.60	134.90	136.70	137.50	137.60

[1] 1980 costs based on 1974 food plans with age groups 20 to 54 years old and 55 years old and over. [2] Couple 20 to 50 years old.

Source: U.S. Dept. of Agriculture, *Human Nutrition Information Service, Adm. 329*, monthly.

No. 777. Food—Retail Prices of Selected Items: 1986 to 1992

[In dollars per pound, except as indicated. As of December]

FOOD	1986	1987	1988	1989	1990	1991	1992
Bread, whole wheat	0.88	0.90	(NA)	(NA)	(NA)	1.05	1.09
Ground beef	1.26	1.32	1.40	1.50	1.63	1.58	1.50
Chuck, ground	1.65	1.75	1.79	1.88	2.02	1.93	1.91
Rib roast	3.39	3.57	4.03	4.21	4.54	4.59	4.69
Round steak	2.80	2.93	3.01	3.17	3.42	3.38	3.34
Sirloin steak, bone-in	2.93	3.17	3.23	3.46	3.65	3.78	3.75
T-bone steak	3.97	4.27	4.97	5.04	5.45	5.21	5.39
Bacon, sliced	2.16	2.02	1.79	1.96	2.28	1.99	1.86
Chops, center cut	2.75	2.67	2.65	2.85	3.32	3.12	3.15
Ham, rump	1.63	1.60	(NA)	(NA)	(NA)	1.62	1.65
Sausage	2.05	1.99	1.92	2.12	2.42	2.24	2.14
Ham, canned	2.92	2.72	2.60	2.62	(NA)	3.15	(NA)
Chicken, fresh, whole	0.87	0.74	0.89	0.88	0.86	0.86	0.88
Chicken breast	1.99	1.72	2.06	2.01	2.00	2.02	2.08
Turkey, frozen	1.02	0.89	0.97	0.95	0.96	0.91	0.93
Tuna, canned	1.94	2.11	2.18	2.04	2.11	2.05	1.96
Eggs, Grade A, large, (dozen)	0.91	0.73	0.83	1.14	1.00	1.01	0.93
Milk, fresh, whole (1/2 gal.)	1.13	1.16	1.21	1.37	1.39	1.40	1.39
Ice cream (1/2 gal.)	2.41	2.44	2.54	2.67	2.54	2.63	2.49
Cheese, Cheddar	3.07	3.10	3.21	(NA)	(NA)	3.53	3.40
Apples, red delicious	0.66	0.55	0.71	0.57	0.77	0.86	0.76
Bananas	0.33	0.38	0.41	0.42	0.43	0.42	0.40
Pears, anjou	0.72	0.57	0.64	0.76	0.79	0.88	0.80
Potatoes, white	0.26	0.25	0.30	0.31	0.32	0.28	0.31
Lettuce, iceberg	0.56	1.25	0.77	0.52	0.58	0.69	0.69
Tomatoes, field grown	0.94	1.00	0.81	0.90	0.86	0.79	1.23
Onions, yellow	0.34	0.33	0.37	0.32	(NA)	0.37	0.42
Peppers, sweet	0.85	0.82	0.80	0.92	(NA)	0.82	1.15
Margarine, stick	0.76	0.68	0.80	0.83	0.87	0.83	0.81
Shortening	0.82	0.77	0.93	0.90	0.93	0.84	0.79
Peanut butter	1.68	1.82	1.82	1.82	2.07	2.04	1.88
Sugar, white	0.35	0.36	0.38	0.41	0.43	0.42	0.41
Coffee, roasted	3.25	2.55	2.93	2.94	2.94	2.63	2.36

NA Not available.

Source: U.S. Bureau of Labor Statistics, *CPI Detailed Report,* January issues.

No. 778. Average Price of Energy in Selected Metropolitan Areas: 1992

[In dollars per unit shown. As of January. One therm contains approximately 100 cubic feet of natural gas. See Appendix II]

CITY/MSA	Utility (piped) gas (100 therms)	Electricity (500 kWh)	Fuel oil No. 2 (gallon)	GASOLINE		
				All types [1]	Unleaded regular	Unleaded premium
U.S. city average	58.33	44.50	0.99	1.14	1.07	1.27
Baltimore, MD MSA	56.60	47.76	1.02	1.20	1.11	1.31
Boston-Lawrence-Salem, MA-NH CMSA	84.81	51.41	0.97	1.26	1.19	1.40
Chicago-Gary-Lake County, IL-IN-WI CMSA	50.43	55.93	1.01	1.21	1.16	1.33
Cleveland-Akron-Lorain, OH CMSA	46.43	56.74	(NA)	1.11	1.07	1.23
Dallas-Fort Worth, TX CMSA	56.39	43.29	(NA)	1.12	1.07	1.20
Detroit-Ann Arbor, MI CMSA	50.03	51.85	0.98	1.02	0.99	1.17
Houston-Galveston-Brazoria, TX CMSA	46.30	43.13	(NA)	1.16	1.10	1.30
Los Angeles-Anaheim-Riverside, CA CMSA	62.33	60.04	(NA)	1.17	1.10	1.29
Miami-Fort Lauderdale, FL CMSA	77.49	45.52	(NA)	1.12	1.05	1.22
New York-N. NJ-Long Island, NY-NJ-CT CMSA	73.94	61.85	1.07	1.26	1.16	1.38
Philadelphia-Wilmington-Trenton, PA-NJ-DE-MD CMSA	72.44	62.23	0.96	1.21	1.12	1.35
Pittsburgh-Beaver Valley, PA CMSA	57.94	54.96	0.84	1.14	1.06	1.28
St. Louis-East St. Louis, MO-IL CMSA	49.20	41.29	(NA)	1.00	0.94	1.14
San Francisco-Oakland-San Jose, CA CMSA	65.09	62.50	(NA)	1.21	1.17	1.28
Washington, DC-MD-VA MSA	70.08	40.57	1.10	1.21	1.13	1.33

NA Not available. [1] Includes types of gasoline not shown separately.

Source: U.S. Bureau of Labor Statistics, *CPI Detailed Report,* January issues.

No. 779. Import Price Indexes—Selected Commodities: 1985 to 1992

[1985=100, except as noted. As of June quarter. Indexes are weighted by the 1985 Tariff Schedule of the United States Annotated, a scheme for describing and reporting product composition and value of U.S. imports. Import prices are based on U.S. dollar prices paid by importer. F.o.b.=Free on board; c.i.f.=Cost, insurance, and freight; n.e.s.=Not elsewhere specified]

COMMODITY	1985 [1]	1986	1987	1988	1989	1990	1991	1992
All commodities	99.2	98.7	110.0	116.8	119.8	118.9	122.4	124.3
Food	98.9	107.3	108.3	114.0	111.3	111.9	116.1	111.0
Meat	94.0	96.0	108.0	107.0	109.7	136.5	144.1	129.5
Meat, edible meat offals, fresh, chilled or frozen	93.2	91.1	102.0	104.6	108.0	133.4	136.8	119.6
Meat and edible meat offals, prepared or preserved, n.e.s.; fish extracts	95.6	106.5	120.6	111.5	113.3	143.5	159.9	151.3
Dairy products and eggs	98.7	108.7	122.3	125.0	120.2	132.6	131.6	133.6
Fish	98.6	110.5	126.0	129.3	122.7	126.2	140.4	140.7
Shellfish, fresh, chilled, frozen, salted, or dried, c.i.f.	99.4	113.3	123.2	123.1	115.1	114.0	125.5	123.3
Fish in airtight containers, c.i.f.	98.1	103.6	113.7	130.2	124.9	125.8	133.1	136.6
Bakery goods [2]	97.1	112.5	126.2	139.8	140.2	151.7	148.2	152.6
Fruits and vegetables	103.0	100.0	110.1	120.3	123.2	125.9	132.4	130.1
Sugar [3]	102.3	104.6	109.6	110.0	111.8	116.7	113.2	111.6
Coffee, tea, cocoa	96.8	117.2	87.0	93.3	85.3	66.3	62.1	51.5
Beverages and tobacco	99.2	105.2	112.8	116.2	117.2	127.6	142.5	145.9
Beverages	98.9	106.1	114.2	120.0	120.7	129.5	143.8	146.8
Alcoholic	98.9	105.8	113.7	119.3	120.5	129.2	143.8	146.9
Wine of fresh grapes, c.i.f.	98.7	109.7	121.0	127.3	125.3	135.5	151.3	155.8
Beer, c.i.f.	100.1	103.2	111.4	114.2	114.8	117.0	123.6	125.6
Spirits, c.i.f.	98.5	104.1	109.1	115.6	119.2	130.0	147.6	150.0
Crude materials	100.5	106.4	116.2	137.8	144.3	131.7	123.9	123.8
Crude rubber [4]	101.0	99.5	103.7	151.1	103.4	104.0	101.1	103.6
Wood	105.0	104.3	110.2	111.4	112.4	115.1	121.0	131.3
Lumber	105.4	104.6	110.0	111.1	110.8	112.8	118.6	129.3
Pulp and waste paper	101.4	100.3	132.0	160.5	190.0	183.3	141.1	132.7
Crude minerals	100.6	99.0	99.6	101.0	104.7	97.5	98.8	87.1
Metalliferous ores and metal scrap	95.6	121.6	124.5	167.6	212.3	160.7	149.2	145.3
Ores and concentrates of base metals, n.e.s.	94.5	134.0	136.4	192.9	258.1	179.7	166.4	162.1
Crude vegetable and animal materials, n.e.s.	94.8	111.3	109.0	148.2	110.3	117.4	117.1	121.1
Fuels and related products	99.7	51.5	74.1	63.4	73.3	63.7	72.5	75.5
Crude petroleum and petroleum products	99.5	49.0	74.4	63.6	74.4	64.0	73.5	77.0
Crude petroleum	100.5	45.8	68.7	57.5	67.1	54.2	66.0	71.3
Natural gas and LNG	102.3	79.7	67.8	58.7	61.0	60.0	56.5	54.2
Fats and oils	110.0	66.7	87.9	111.2	117.4	95.7	97.3	128.5
Chemicals and related products	100.4	99.7	104.8	116.4	120.4	118.2	120.9	122.1
Intermediate manufactured products	99.1	103.6	112.5	132.2	136.1	135.0	134.7	134.9
Leather and furskins	97.9	106.3	116.6	137.0	133.8	143.8	142.5	140.9
Rubber manufactures	99.5	101.2	104.6	107.0	112.2	115.6	116.5	118.2
Cork and wood manufactures	99.2	111.0	124.3	138.2	139.8	144.4	141.8	155.4
Paper and paperboard products	99.9	100.8	104.9	118.3	120.8	121.2	122.0	113.7
Paper and paperboard	100.0	98.9	102.5	115.5	117.9	118.3	119.5	110.3
Newsprint, c.i.f.	100.1	99.2	105.0	119.1	119.6	120.5	121.3	109.0
Textiles	98.9	105.4	111.8	120.6	122.1	125.8	131.3	135.1
Nonmetallic mineral manufactures	96.2	110.5	126.7	142.5	149.5	159.9	165.5	169.0
Iron and steel	100.2	98.9	106.6	127.2	133.6	125.9	125.4	123.3
Nonferrous metals	100.2	98.9	112.4	159.7	158.6	143.3	129.3	128.7
Silver platinum, other metals of platinum group, c.i.f.	94.6	106.8	141.7	136.4	119.0	124.3	119.8	100.3
Copper	100.6	103.9	107.8	149.0	172.1	172.2	154.8	154.6
Nickel, c.i.f.	105.7	88.1	83.5	262.4	258.0	161.8	165.5	148.3
Zinc	109.4	83.2	101.3	147.1	210.3	219.0	149.2	172.5
Tin, c.i.f.	103.9	49.0	60.4	62.0	83.6	59.9	50.7	54.7
Metal manufactures, n.e.s.	99.2	107.9	112.7	126.9	132.6	134.6	137.7	140.2
Machinery and transport equipment	98.9	110.4	119.9	127.3	129.2	130.1	133.9	136.4
Machinery specialized for particular industries	96.4	116.9	136.1	149.8	145.7	158.8	166.0	172.0
Metalworking machinery	98.3	113.0	128.1	142.4	139.5	149.6	152.5	157.6
General industrial machinery, parts, n.e.s.	98.0	116.2	130.8	143.7	143.0	153.0	159.0	164.2
Office machines [5]	98.5	109.1	114.0	119.5	119.3	115.7	112.7	110.8
Telecommunications [6]	100.2	106.4	110.3	113.8	115.7	111.4	108.7	108.0
Electric machinery and equipment	100.3	106.4	115.8	124.2	129.6	127.8	130.2	132.2
Road vehicles and parts	98.8	110.8	120.5	127.6	129.6	129.5	136.3	139.0
Misc. manufactured articles	99.2	106.8	117.8	125.7	126.6	132.0	134.2	138.4
Plumbing, heating and lighting fixtures	98.6	108.6	117.0	126.9	131.5	140.8	140.2	145.2
Furniture and parts	98.6	109.0	116.5	124.0	125.3	132.1	134.9	137.7
Clothing	99.8	100.7	109.2	114.9	119.9	122.8	120.7	124.3
Footwear, c.i.f.	98.1	108.0	119.8	129.6	127.9	137.6	140.3	142.6
Professional, scientific and controlling instruments, and apparatus	96.1	117.9	135.9	142.5	136.5	145.5	152.5	155.9
Photographic apparatus [7]	98.9	113.8	126.0	129.3	127.9	131.8	134.7	138.4
Misc. manufactured articles, n.e.s.	99.6	108.1	121.1	132.1	131.4	137.3	142.8	148.5

[1] June 1985 may not equal 100 because indexes were reweighted to an "average" trade value in 1985.   [2] Includes pasta products, grain and grain preparations.   [3] Includes sugar preparations and honey.   [4] Includes synthetic and reclaimed rubber.   [5] Includes automatic data processing equipment.   [6] Includes sound recording and reproducing equipment.   [7] Includes photographic supplies, optical goods, watches and clocks.

Source: U.S. Bureau of Labor Statistics, *News*, quarterly.

No. 780. Export Price Indexes—Selected Commodities: 1985 to 1992

[1985=100, except as noted. As of June quarter. Indexes are weighted by 1980 export values according to the Schedule B classification system of the U.S. Bureau of the Census. Prices used in these indexes were collected from a sample of U.S. manufacturers of exports and are factory transaction prices, except as noted. F.a.s.=free alongside ship. N.e.s.=not elsewhere specified. F.o.b.=free on board]

COMMODITY	1985 [1]	1986	1987	1988	1989	1990	1991	1992
All commodities	100.4	99.1	102.2	109.5	113.2	113.3	114.7	115.3
Food	100.5	97.1	89.9	103.4	115.5	108.8	105.1	107.3
Meat	98.8	105.2	121.2	131.0	128.2	123.7	128.0	133.3
Fish	101.2	108.6	125.8	145.0	158.9	126.9	122.1	126.5
Grain and grain preparations	102.5	89.0	71.0	87.2	106.4	101.8	90.8	98.2
Wheat	99.8	80.7	66.8	87.8	116.1	96.9	78.8	93.6
Rice	101.6	67.9	59.1	105.7	95.7	93.1	102.7	97.7
Corn, yellow, f.o.b.	104.0	95.2	72.7	83.7	101.5	104.8	94.3	98.6
Other grain	106.3	96.5	77.7	87.6	104.9	106.0	98.8	105.9
Fruits and vegetables	100.1	108.6	112.4	104.3	113.6	115.2	137.2	113.0
Feedstuff for animals	90.9	114.8	123.8	158.1	144.0	118.4	121.2	123.9
Miscellaneous food products	99.9	97.0	100.6	102.8	108.0	110.2	110.8	110.5
Beverages and tobacco	100.1	97.4	105.0	110.6	117.6	124.5	132.6	137.6
Tobacco and tobacco products	100.1	97.1	105.0	110.7	117.9	124.9	132.8	137.7
Crude materials	101.6	102.2	114.5	139.9	143.0	137.3	130.3	127.6
Raw hides and skins	97.4	117.1	149.6	166.8	149.9	162.0	125.6	124.5
Oilseeds and oleaginous fruit	105.5	98.1	101.6	143.0	129.8	110.4	112.9	111.8
Crude rubber, f.a.s.	99.8	99.9	101.0	106.1	114.6	115.5	120.3	117.7
Wood	98.7	101.2	116.2	149.6	170.7	179.2	171.9	193.4
Pulp and waste paper	100.3	116.4	149.9	179.5	193.5	174.3	150.8	143.7
Textile fibers	103.5	98.0	112.4	110.9	115.5	124.5	129.7	104.3
Cotton	103.4	95.5	114.4	108.8	110.9	122.7	127.6	94.3
Crude minerals and fertilizers	100.4	98.4	94.0	94.2	99.2	99.7	100.7	99.8
Metal ores and scrap	100.9	98.0	107.0	146.0	157.2	142.6	127.2	121.5
Scrap metal (iron or steel) f.a.s.	100.2	96.1	95.8	147.7	154.3	137.1	128.2	112.9
Nonferrous base metal waste and scrap, n.e.s., f.a.s.	98.9	101.3	126.9	185.6	197.0	174.0	147.4	150.6
Fuels and related products	101.8	76.8	82.8	82.1	86.0	88.7	87.5	84.2
Coal and coke	100.5	94.0	88.2	92.0	94.3	97.5	96.1	94.3
Crude petroleum and petroleum products [2]	(NA)	(NA)	(NA)	97.2	105.4	108.7	103.7	100.0
Fats and oils	113.4	67.7	78.8	97.3	87.3	94.6	86.2	87.1
Vegetable oils	116.8	70.6	71.9	93.7	84.4	101.7	89.5	86.2
Chemicals and related products	100.2	98.0	106.7	121.6	121.9	115.5	118.1	115.4
Organic chemicals	100.6	93.1	118.4	146.6	145.0	118.6	118.2	114.4
Hydrocarbons, n.e.s. and derivatives, f.a.s.	101.4	86.4	142.8	169.0	157.6	128.0	104.6	106.8
Alcohols, phenols, phenol-alcohols, and deriv., f.a.s.	99.9	96.9	102.7	143.8	186.8	122.3	129.3	118.2
Carboxylic acids, f.a.s.	100.7	99.0	103.2	127.5	120.9	112.6	126.6	114.0
Fertilizers, manufactured	97.2	93.0	91.6	109.8	108.0	102.8	111.0	94.8
Pesticides, starches, glue, gas and oil additives, chemical materials and products, n.e.s.	99.9	101.8	97.7	101.7	109.4	113.7	119.1	118.6
Intermediate manufactured products	100.2	102.5	107.9	117.7	123.1	123.0	123.3	124.0
Leather and fur skins	99.1	103.8	126.9	125.1	120.7	126.0	118.1	112.7
Rubber manufactures	100.2	100.1	102.5	108.8	112.9	114.4	121.5	122.1
Paper and paperboard products	100.5	104.7	117.0	129.0	133.7	130.3	130.2	128.8
Textiles	100.2	102.9	103.7	107.9	115.4	118.3	123.7	125.5
Nonmetallic mineral manufactures [3]	(NA)	102.4	108.7	114.1	122.4	126.9	128.9	131.8
Iron and steel	99.5	100.2	102.9	110.8	117.2	117.4	119.1	119.2
Nonferrous metals	102.0	103.1	113.0	143.5	145.8	132.6	116.5	116.3
Metal manufactures, n.e.s.	99.7	100.8	101.3	107.6	113.9	117.1	120.5	121.6
Machinery and transport equipment [4]	100.0	100.8	101.8	104.0	107.2	110.1	113.5	115.2
Power generating machinery [5]	100.1	102.4	103.7	108.4	112.8	117.2	123.0	128.7
Internal combustion piston engines, parts	99.8	101.4	102.9	107.1	108.9	112.5	118.2	121.1
Electric motors, generators, other rotating plant, f.o.b., factory	101.0	103.2	107.7	117.9	124.9	131.1	133.9	137.7
Machinery specialized for particular industries	100.0	100.3	100.1	103.6	108.8	113.2	117.8	120.4
Agricultural machinery and parts [6]	99.7	100.4	101.2	102.1	104.9	111.5	113.8	116.9
Civil engineering and contractors, plant and equip. [7]	100.3	98.4	96.0	98.5	105.3	109.3	114.9	112.9
Metalworking machinery	99.7	102.0	106.7	110.8	117.3	121.1	129.4	132.6
General industrial machines, parts, n.e.s.	100.0	101.6	104.5	108.1	113.3	118.2	123.9	125.8
Office machines [8]	99.8	99.0	96.1	95.7	94.8	94.6	92.7	89.2
Telecommunications [9]	99.6	98.9	101.4	104.6	107.5	111.2	118.2	120.4
Electrical machinery, equipment	100.9	99.2	102.1	103.4	106.5	107.5	108.2	111.4
Road vehicles and parts	100.1	101.7	103.5	104.9	107.8	111.0	114.1	115.9
Other transport equipment [4]	99.2	103.1	105.5	109.6	114.7	121.3	136.5	137.3
Miscellaneous manufactured articles	100.3	103.5	105.2	108.1	112.8	116.4	122.4	124.8

NA Not available. [1] June 1985 may not equal 100 because indexes were reweighted to an "average" trade value in 1985. [2] December 1987=100. [3] September 1985=100. [4] Excludes military and commercial aircraft. [5] Includes equipment. [6] Excludes tractors. [7] Includes parts. [8] Includes data processing equipment. [9] Includes sound recording and reproducing equipment.

Source: U.S. Bureau of Labor Statistics, *News,* quarterly.

No. 781. Refiner/Reseller Sales Price of Gasoline, by State: 1990 to 1992

[In cents per gallon. As of March. Represents all refinery and gas plant operators' sales through company-operated retail outlets. Gasoline prices exclude excise taxes]

STATE	Gasoline excise taxes 1992 [1]	AVERAGE, ALL GRADES			LEADED REGULAR			UNLEADED REGULAR			PREMIUM		
		1990	1991	1992	1990	1991	1992	1990	1991	1992	1990	1991	1992
United States .	14.1	76.8	76.5	77.5	74.5	71.6	70.7	72.5	73.6	68.3	88.8	87.3	84.2
Northeast:													
New England:													
Maine.	19	85.8	90.0	80.8	(D)	(NA)	(NA)	81.6	86.9	77.0	99.0	102.2	93.2
New Hampshire . . .	19	84.9	85.2	79.6	(D)	(D)	(NA)	79.1	82.0	75.3	97.0	95.7	92.3
Vermont	16	88.8	91.6	83.6	96.3	(D)	(NA)	84.2	88.2	79.8	100.4	102.8	93.7
Massachusetts. . . .	21	82.9	83.1	76.5	(D)	86.4	(NA)	76.1	78.8	81.1	96.6	94.4	88.3
Rhode Island	26	81.7	82.9	74.4	(NA)	(NA)	(NA)	75.2	78.9	69.4	93.9	91.7	83.6
Connecticut	26	82.9	83.0	78.4	(D)	(D)	(NA)	75.1	78.5	72.8	96.4	93.7	89.9
Middle Atlantic:													
New York	23	78.7	87.0	74.7	77.7	87.1	74.9	72.9	83.2	70.1	92.2	99.5	86.6
New Jersey	15	80.3	83.4	77.8	(D)	(NA)	(NA)	72.3	77.9	70.5	90.4	94.2	89.3
Pennsylvania	22	77.1	82.4	72.9	79.8	(D)	(NA)	70.5	78.5	68.1	89.9	94.2	85.4
North Central:													
East North Central:													
Ohio.	21	75.0	73.4	73.1	79.2	78.4	74.0	70.5	70.7	69.8	90.1	84.6	84.9
Indiana	20	75.1	77.3	68.9	83.8	84.8	80.5	71.3	75.0	66.1	85.5	87.6	78.1
Illinois.	19	73.2	76.1	69.6	77.7	88.2	72.7	69.5	73.4	66.3	83.9	86.2	81.3
Michigan	16	72.7	74.0	67.1	75.5	79.2	76.5	69.6	71.7	64.3	83.5	84.9	78.8
Wisconsin	24	72.8	76.8	69.3	79.2	82.2	74.6	69.7	75.1	67.3	84.2	86.6	78.3
West North Central:													
Minnesota	21	77.9	77.6	73.0	79.2	79.3	73.3	76.1	76.1	71.4	87.2	85.0	80.3
Iowa.	20	75.9	80.0	70.9	77.0	83.7	77.5	74.6	79.1	76.4	84.6	86.4	78.3
Missouri	11	71.8	75.6	68.4	73.1	78.7	70.3	67.8	73.1	65.4	83.6	85.5	79.3
North Dakota	17	85.3	82.8	79.1	86.9	85.5	81.6	84.4	82.2	78.4	93.2	85.6	85.2
South Dakota	19	83.1	80.8	75.9	82.4	80.2	77.1	82.3	79.9	75.0	90.7	90.4	86.3
Nebraska	24	73.0	80.9	73.5	72.9	78.6	75.3	72.3	79.0	72.4	78.9	87.9	80.7
Kansas	17	73.0	76.2	72.2	73.4	77.8	74.0	71.4	74.9	70.5	82.6	85.3	82.5
South:													
South Atlantic:													
Delaware.	19	81.0	83.8	74.0	(NA)	(NA)	(NA)	74.4	78.8	68.6	94.9	98.4	87.7
Maryland	19	84.4	78.8	78.0	(D)	(NA)	(NA)	78.7	73.0	72.2	95.0	93.3	90.9
District of Columbia .	18	0.0	(D)	(D)	(D)	(D)	(NA)	(D)	(D)	(D)	(D)	(D)	(D)
Virginia	18	80.5	77.2	73.3	75.0	72.4	(D)	74.4	72.7	67.6	91.5	89.1	86.6
West Virginia	20	81.0	81.1	77.1	0.0	(D)	(D)	74.5	76.9	72.4	97.2	95.8	89.9
North Carolina	23	76.3	76.2	69.9	70.8	(D)	(D)	70.5	72.3	64.4	88.9	88.3	83.3
South Carolina	17	78.9	75.6	69.2	77.6	(D)	(D)	73.1	71.3	64.3	94.1	91.0	84.5
Georgia.	8	74.6	75.9	70.5	80.1	75.9	64.8	68.9	71.3	64.5	86.2	89.2	84.5
Florida	12	80.9	78.5	72.1	79.2	-	(D)	75.4	73.9	66.0	90.9	89.1	84.4
East South Central:													
Kentucky.	15	76.6	78.6	72.4	76.8	83.8	70.3	72.2	75.5	68.7	89.6	90.2	83.2
Tennessee	21	73.8	74.4	70.2	70.7	(D)	(D)	67.6	70.0	64.8	87.8	87.5	83.0
Alabama	13	83.1	78.4	73.3	79.3	(D)	(D)	77.7	75.1	69.0	95.8	90.1	86.1
Mississippi.	18	78.1	78.9	70.6	77.8	(D)	(D)	73.1	75.2	66.6	92.0	90.4	81.5
West South Central:													
Arkansas	19	75.8	77.5	70.1	75.9	79.5	67.3	72.2	74.8	66.9	88.4	90.6	81.9
Louisiana	20	76.2	77.2	73.6	76.4	(D)	(D)	71.4	73.2	68.5	86.0	88.4	85.2
Oklahoma	17	72.7	75.8	69.6	74.2	77.6	69.4	70.8	74.3	67.4	79.9	81.6	78.5
Texas.	20	76.4	76.1	72.4	76.7	79.0	74.3	72.2	73.1	67.7	86.6	85.5	83.3
West:													
Mountain:													
Montana	20	79.5	81.3	73.8	78.6	80.4	74.8	78.2	90.6	72.5	85.4	86.6	78.7
Idaho	22	71.5	67.0	71.6	71.0	66.0	70.8	70.6	64.4	70.7	81.1	77.8	81.2
Wyoming.	9	78.9	79.4	78.0	77.8	78.9	77.6	77.7	78.2	76.8	86.6	87.0	85.4
Colorado	22	69.7	73.4	74.8	68.3	73.3	75.5	67.4	71.3	72.0	79.6	83.0	84.4
New Mexico.	17	78.6	77.8	73.8	78.1	75.6	72.7	77.3	76.9	72.4	88.6	88.1	85.7
Arizona	19	80.4	78.6	73.7	76.8	75.9	69.9	79.2	77.5	72.1	91.2	89.3	87.2
Utah.	20	71.1	66.2	69.0	69.5	65.3	70.2	69.4	64.4	66.7	79.1	73.8	76.3
Nevada.	21	74.6	79.2	77.8	69.4	74.5	73.4	73.3	77.6	76.1	87.8	90.4	90.1
Pacific:													
Washington	23	73.6	72.4	69.7	69.5	68.1	64.7	71.6	71.1	68.2	86.3	84.3	83.5
Oregon	22	78.7	75.8	78.7	75.7	71.5	73.9	77.6	75.1	77.8	91.8	89.8	92.2
California.	17	77.9	65.3	73.5	72.6	61.4	(NA)	75.3	63.2	69.7	89.9	75.2	85.1
Alaska	8	101.0	108.7	73.7	107.3	(NA)	69.9	98.1	108.6	72.1	106.5	109.2	87.2
Hawaii	16	96.9	99.1	103.8	(NA)	(NA)	(NA)	90.3	93.0	97.5	109.9	110.3	114.4

- Represents zero.   D Withheld to avoid disclosure of individual company data.   NA Not available.   [1] Source: U.S. Advisory Commission on Intergovernmental Relations, *Significant Features of Fiscal Federalism*, annual, vol. I, based on CCH, *State Tax Reporter*.

Source: Except as noted, U.S. Energy Information Administration, *Petroleum Marketing Monthly*.

Figure 16.1
Household Financial Assets and Liabilities: 1992

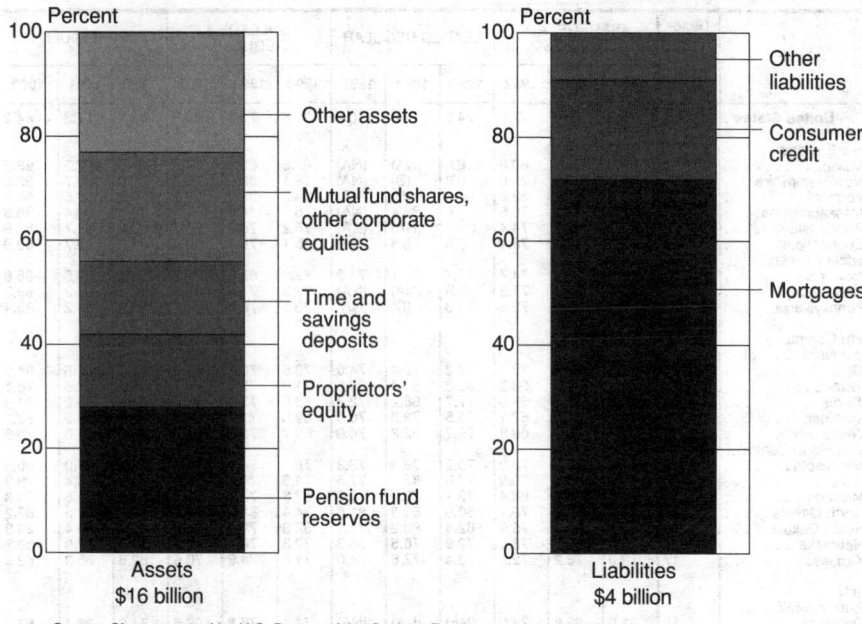

Source: Chart prepared by U.S. Bureau of the Census. For data, see tables 787.

Figure 16.2
Interest Rates: 1970 to 1992

Source: Chart prepared by U.S. Bureau of the Census. For data, see tables 825 and 826.

Banking, Finance, and Insurance

This section presents data on the Nation's finances, various types of financial institutions, money and credit, securities, and insurance. The primary sources of these data are publications of several departments of the Federal Government, especially the Treasury Department, and independent agencies such as the Federal Deposit Insurance Corporation, the Federal Reserve System, and the Securities and Exchange Commission. National data on insurance are available primarily from private organizations, such as the American Council of Life Insurance.

Flow of funds.—The flow of funds accounts of the Federal Reserve System (see tables 784 to 787) bring together statistics on all of the major forms of financial transactions and financial claims to present an economy-wide view of asset and liability relationships. In flow form, the accounts relate borrowing and lending to one another and to the nonfinancial activities that generate income and production. Each claim outstanding is included simultaneously as an asset of the lender and as a liability of the debtor. The accounts also indicate the balance between asset totals and liability totals over the economy as a whole. Several publications of the Board of Governors of the Federal Reserve System contain information on the flow of funds accounts: Summary data on flows and outstandings, in the *Federal Reserve Bulletin, Flow of Funds Accounts* (quarterly), and *Annual Statistical Digest;* and concepts and organization of the accounts, in *Introduction to Flow of Funds* (June 1980).

Banking system.—Banks in this country are organized under the laws of both the States and the Federal Government and are regulated by several bank supervisory agencies. National banks are supervised by the Comptroller of the Currency. *Reports of Condition* have been collected from national banks since 1863. Summaries of these reports are published in the Comptroller's *Annual Report,* which also presents data on the structure of the national banking system.

In Brief	
Conventional new-home mortgage rates::	
1980	13.95%
1990	10.08%
1992	8.43%
Dow-Jones industrial average:	
1980	891.4
1990	2,678.9
1992	3,284.3

The Federal Reserve System was established in 1913 to exercise central banking functions, some of which are shared with the U.S. Treasury. It includes national banks and such State banks that voluntarily join the System. Statements of State bank members are consolidated by the Board of Governors of the Federal Reserve System with data for national banks collected by the Comptroller of the Currency into totals for all member banks of the System. Balance sheet data for member banks and other commercial banks are published quarterly in the *Federal Reserve Bulletin.* The Federal Deposit Insurance Corporation (FDIC), established in 1933, insures each depositor up to $100,000 currently in banks that are members of the Federal Reserve System and in such nonmember banks that join the Bank Insurance Fund. Major item balance sheets for all commercial banks are published monthly in the *Federal Reserve Bulletin.*

The FDIC is the primary federal regulator of State-chartered banks that are not members of the Federal Reserve System and of most savings banks insured by the Bank Insurance Fund. The agency also has certain back–up supervisory authority, for safety and soundness purposes, over State-chartered banks that are members of the Federal Reserve System, national banks, and savings associations.

Savings institutions.—Savings institutions are primarily involved in credit extension in the form of mortgage loans. Statistics on savings institutions are collected by the U.S. Office of Thrift Supervision. The Financial Institutions Reform, Recovery, and Enforcement Act of 1989 (FIRREA) authorized the establishment of the Resolution Trust Corporation (RTC). The RTC is responsible for the disposal of assets from failed savings institutions. FIRREA gave the FDIC the job of managing the federal deposit insurance fund for savings institutions (SAIF=Savings Association Insurance Fund).

Other credit agencies.—Insurance companies, finance companies dealing primarily in installment sales financing, credit unions, and personal loan companies represent important sources of funds for the credit market. Statistics on loans, investments, cash, etc., of life insurance companies are published principally by the American Council of Life Insurance in its *Life Insurance Fact Book.* Consumer credit data are published currently in the *Federal Reserve Bulletin.*

Federally chartered credit unions are under the supervision of the National Credit Union Administration, established in 1970. State-chartered credit unions are supervised by the respective State supervisory authorities. The Administration publishes comprehensive program and statistical information on all Federal and federally insured State credit unions in the *Annual Report of the National Credit Union Administration.* Deposit insurance (up to $100,000 per account) is provided to members of all Federal and those State credit unions that are federally-insured by the National Credit Union Share Insurance Fund which was established in 1970. Deposit insurance for State chartered credit unions is also available in some States under private or State-administered insurance programs.

Government corporations and credit agencies make available credit of specified types or to specified groups of private borrowers, either by lending directly or by insuring or guaranteeing loans made by private lending institutions. Data on operations of Government credit agencies, along with other Government corporations, are available in reports of individual agencies; data on their debt outstanding are published in the *Federal Reserve Bulletin.*

Currency.—Currency, including coin and paper money, represents about 30 percent of all media of exchange in the

United States, with most payments made by check. All currency is now issued by the Federal Reserve Banks.

Securities.—The Securities and Exchange Commission (SEC) was established in 1934 to protect the interests of the public and investors against malpractices in the securities and financial markets and to provide the fullest possible disclosure of information regarding securities to the investing public. Statistical data are published in the *SEC Annual Report.*

Insurance.—Insuring companies, which are regulated by the various States or the District of Columbia, are classified as either life or property. Companies that underwrite accident and health insurance only and those that underwrite accident and health insurance in addition to one or more property lines are included with property insurance. Insuring companies, other than those classified as life, are permitted to underwrite one or more property lines provided they are so licensed and have the necessary capital or surplus.

There are a number of published sources for statistics on the various classes of insurance—life, health, fire, marine, and casualty. Individual States collect data on all insurers operating within their respective jurisdictions, and many of the States publish an annual insurance report giving individual company data and aggregates of certain items for the companies operating within the State. Organizations representing certain classes of insurers publish reports for these classes. Among them are the annual commercial publishers, such as The National Underwriter Company whose *Argus Health Chart* (annual) contains financial and operating data for individual health and accident insurance companies, including Blue Cross and Blue Shield Plans. The American Council of Life Insurance publishes statistics on life insurance purchases, ownership, benefit payments, and assets in its biennial *Life Insurance Fact Book.*

Historical statistics.—Tabular headnotes provide cross-references, where applicable, to *Historical Statistics of the United States, Colonial Times to 1970.* See Appendix IV.

No. 782. Gross National Product in Finance, Insurance, and Real Estate, in Current and Constant (1982) Dollars: 1980 to 1989

[In billions of dollars, except percent. For definition of gross national product, see text, section 14. These data are not fully consistent with other gross domestic product tables because they do not yet reflect the results of the comprehensive National Income and Product Accounts revision; see text, section 14. Based on 1972 Standard Industrial Classification]

INDUSTRY	CURRENT DOLLARS				CONSTANT (1982) DOLLARS			
	1980	1985	1988	1989	1980	1985	1988	1989
Finance, insurance, real estate, total	400.6	639.5	826.8	896.7	468.9	528.3	590.0	604.0
Percent of gross national product	14.7	15.9	17.0	17.2	14.7	14.6	14.7	14.7
Banking	51.1	79.4	100.2	119.4	56.7	61.5	62.4	63.1
Credit agencies other than banks	5.5	11.6	15.7	20.5	5.2	7.0	8.4	8.3
Security and commodity brokers, and services .	9.7	24.1	42.3	43.8	11.2	18.8	36.4	37.9
Insurance carriers.	37.0	40.7	62.0	60.4	38.7	39.5	37.0	36.7
Insurance agents and brokers, and services . . .	14.4	22.4	34.6	37.4	15.9	18.0	21.4	22.1
Real estate.	281.5	449.0	561.6	607.1	335.0	374.5	413.0	424.4
Holding and other investment companies	1.3	12.3	10.2	8.1	6.3	9.0	11.4	11.5

Source: U.S. Bureau of Economic Analysis, *Survey of Current Business*, January and April 1991.

No. 783. Finance, Insurance, and Real Estate—Establishments, Employees, and Payroll: 1988 to 1990

[Covers establishments with payroll. Excludes government employees, railroad employees, self-employed persons, etc. For statement on methodology, see Appendix III]

1987 SIC code [1]	KIND OF BUSINESS	ESTABLISHMENTS (1,000)			EMPLOYEES (1,000)		PAYROLL (bil. dol.)	
		1988	1989	1990	1989	1990	1989	1990
(H)	**Finance, insurance, real estate** . .	**518.2**	**529.3**	**544.7**	**6,801.6**	**6,956.5**	**184.5**	**197.4**
60	Depository institutions [2]	76.3	80.1	81.2	2,029.9	2,032.8	46.2	48.4
601	Central reserve depositories.	0.1	0.1	0.1	26.0	30.5	0.7	0.9
602	Commercial banks	49.6	51.3	52.3	1,463.4	1,472.3	33.6	35.6
603	Savings institutions.	20.2	22.0	21.7	434.7	416.6	9.0	8.8
606	Credit unions.	3.6	3.7	3.6	47.7	50.6	0.9	1.0
609	Functions closely related to banking . . .	2.6	2.3	2.8	40.0	43.9	1.2	1.4
61	Nondepository institutions [2].	43.6	41.8	42.0	484.9	505.8	13.1	14.0
611	Federal and fed.-sponsored credit.	2.8	0.6	0.6	17.8	13.5	0.5	0.4
614	Personal credit institutions	25.6	25.3	25.0	217.8	236.3	5.0	5.5
615	Business credit institutions.	3.6	3.7	3.7	85.1	87.6	2.8	3.1
616	Mortgage bankers and brokers	11.3	10.7	10.9	149.6	152.8	4.5	4.6
62	Security and commodity brokers [2]	21.6	21.5	25.2	406.1	410.8	25.3	26.6
621	Security brokers and dealers	13.3	13.3	15.9	312.6	308.1	20.3	20.8
622	Commodity contracts brokers, dealers . .	1.2	1.1	1.2	15.6	14.7	0.7	0.7
628	Security and commodity services	6.3	6.2	7.1	67.8	75.7	3.8	4.5
63	Insurance carriers [2]	39.9	44.2	43.3	1,390.0	1,406.6	37.8	41.5
631	Life insurance	14.4	14.3	14.1	568.8	571.8	14.8	16.3
632	Medical service and health insurance [2] .	2.1	2.0	2.1	181.9	187.6	4.6	5.1
6321	Accident and health insurance.	1.2	1.1	1.1	45.9	47.9	1.1	1.3
6324	Hospital and medical service plans. . .	0.9	0.9	1.0	135.3	139.3	3.4	3.8
633	Fire, marine, and casualty insurance . . .	16.2	17.3	18.3	524.7	532.5	15.3	17.0
635	Surety insurance	0.5	0.6	0.6	14.0	14.6	0.4	0.5
636	Title insurance.	3.0	3.2	3.2	56.4	56.6	1.5	1.6
637	Pension, health and welfare funds.	2.6	5.7	3.8	26.9	25.1	0.7	0.6
64	Insurance agents, brokers, and service . . .	105.1	107.5	110.8	694.4	712.3	18.8	20.3
65	Real estate [2]	208.0	210.6	217.0	1,326.6	1,374.3	27.4	28.5
651	Real estate operators and lessors.	93.7	93.0	95.7	492.5	509.1	8.2	8.7
653	Real estate agents and managers.	82.9	70.2	72.2	567.1	584.7	13.2	13.3
654	Title abstract offices	3.1	3.0	3.1	23.6	23.9	0.5	0.5
655	Subdividers and developers [2]	18.6	19.2	19.6	132.2	140.3	3.1	3.4
6552	Subdividers and developers, n.e.c. [3] . .	10.6	10.6	10.8	82.3	87.8	2.1	2.3
6553	Cemetery subdividers and developers.	4.6	4.6	4.4	35.6	35.2	0.6	0.6
67	Holding and other investment offices [2] . . .	21.5	21.2	22.6	254.0	263.2	9.2	10.0
671	Holding offices.	5.6	5.8	6.2	124.5	123.5	5.2	5.4
672	Investment offices	1.1	1.0	1.0	13.1	16.1	0.8	1.0
673	Trusts	7.8	7.6	7.8	63.7	65.3	1.4	1.4
6732	Educational, religious, etc. trusts	3.3	3.3	3.6	37.7	41.5	0.8	0.9
679	Miscellaneous investing.	6.7	4.8	5.0	41.4	43.5	1.5	1.5
6794	Patent owners and lessors	0.8	0.8	0.9	14.9	15.4	0.4	0.4
(X)	Administrative and auxiliary.	2.2	2.4	2.6	215.8	250.8	6.5	8.2

X Not applicable.   [1] Standard Industrial Classification; see text, section 13.   [2] Includes industries not shown separately.
[3] N.e.c.=Not elsewhere classified.

Source: U.S. Bureau of the Census, *County Business Patterns*, annual.

No. 784. Flow of Funds Accounts—Financial Assets of Financial and Nonfinancial Institutions, by Holder Sector: 1980 to 1992

[In billions of dollars. As of Dec. 31. See also *Historical Statistics, Colonial Times to 1970*, series X 192, X 229, X 821, and X 835]

SECTOR	1980	1984	1985	1986	1987	1988	1989	1990	1991	1992
All sectors	**13,254**	**19,155**	**21,830**	**24,683**	**26,444**	**28,820**	**31,935**	**32,944**	**36,137**	**38,337**
Households [1]	6,391	8,694	9,819	10,804	11,383	12,356	13,804	13,984	15,434	16,181
Nonfinancial business	1,363	1,815	1,952	2,161	2,323	2,529	2,674	2,809	2,881	3,043
Farm	24	30	33	38	40	43	45	48	51	51
Nonfarm noncorporate	148	279	318	357	372	412	440	450	460	461
Nonfinancial corporations	1,191	1,507	1,601	1,766	1,912	2,074	2,190	2,311	2,371	2,531
State and local government	247	365	516	585	652	697	728	736	735	736
U.S. Government	229	328	372	385	371	360	368	441	498	468
U.S. Government-sponsored credit agencies and mortgage pools	307	585	692	877	1,043	1,165	1,323	1,494	1,660	1,843
Monetary authorities [2]	173	218	243	274	285	304	315	343	365	382
Commercial banking [2]	1,482	2,127	2,375	2,615	2,771	2,950	3,229	3,334	3,440	3,629
Domestic commercial banks	1,266	1,799	1,990	2,166	2,257	2,385	2,545	2,644	2,677	2,774
Foreign banking offices in U.S.	98	122	143	182	232	263	357	363	436	492
Nonbank finance [3]	2,604	4,355	5,061	5,961	6,441	7,090	7,891	8,112	9,333	10,069
Savings and loan associations [3]	623	977	1,058	1,141	1,247	1,360	1,233	1,097	926	832
Mutual savings banks [4]	170	203	217	237	261	285	284	264	249	245
Credit unions	68	111	135	163	178	192	202	217	240	266
Life insurance	464	697	796	906	1,005	1,133	1,251	1,367	1,505	1,625
Other insurance	182	251	299	354	405	454	500	529	592	629
Private pension funds	470	880	1,038	1,198	1,216	1,313	1,536	1,506	2,180	2,347
State and local govt. retirement funds	198	357	405	469	517	606	735	752	891	988
Finance companies	243	371	440	531	584	646	719	772	784	808
Real estate investment trusts	3	6	8	9	11	14	13	13	13	16
Investment companies	62	137	240	414	460	478	566	602	814	1,057
Money market funds	76	234	244	292	316	338	428	498	540	548
Security brokers, dealers	45	118	156	185	138	136	237	262	333	405
SCO [5] issuers	-	14	25	64	103	136	187	232	268	305
Rest of the world	459	668	801	1,021	1,177	1,370	1,603	1,692	1,790	1,985

- Represents zero.   [1] Includes personal trusts and nonprofit organizations.   [2] Includes other sectors not shown separately.   [3] Includes most Federal savings banks insured by Savings Association Insurance Fund. A few of them are included with mutual savings banks.   [4] Includes Federal savings banks insured by Bank Insurance Fund and a few insured by Savings Association Insurance Fund.   [5] Securitized credit obligations.

Source: Board of Governors of the Federal Reserve System, *Annual Statistical Digest.*

No. 785. Flow of Funds Accounts—Credit Market Debt Outstanding: 1980 to 1992

[In billions of dollars; except percent. As of Dec. 31. N.e.c.=Not elsewhere classified]

ITEM	1980	1984	1985	1986	1987	1988	1989	1990	1991	1992
Credit market debt	**4,731**	**7,345**	**8,437**	**9,653**	**10,659**	**11,644**	**12,675**	**13,564**	**14,160**	**14,986**
Government	1,045	1,792	2,151	2,427	2,653	2,857	3,067	3,362	3,679	4,031
Federal	735	1,364	1,590	1,806	1,950	2,105	2,251	2,498	2,776	3,080
State and local	310	427	561	621	704	753	816	864	903	951
Nongovernment	3,686	5,553	6,286	7,226	8,005	8,787	9,608	10,201	10,481	10,955
Financial [1]	604	1,081	1,272	1,604	1,871	2,083	2,333	2,524	2,666	2,890
Sponsored credit agencies [2]	163	242	264	279	308	353	378	399	408	448
Mortgage pools	114	289	369	532	670	745	871	1,020	1,167	1,294
Commercial banks [3]	91	174	185	192	213	215	220	191	176	181
Savings and loan associations [4]	53	82	99	120	139	159	145	115	76	71
Finance companies	177	273	320	402	413	445	504	540	548	562
SCO trusts [5]	-	14	25	64	103	136	187	232	268	305
Foreign	192	229	231	232	238	245	255	279	293	308
Private domestic nonfinancial	2,890	4,243	4,783	5,390	5,896	6,459	7,020	7,399	7,522	7,757
Corporations [1]	875	1,293	1,440	1,650	1,828	2,017	2,195	2,273	2,277	2,331
Bonds	412	574	670	788	865	969	1,042	1,088	1,166	1,231
Mortgages	131	121	110	142	201	207	229	225	220	209
Bank loans, n.e.c.	230	391	424	474	482	519	554	555	531	519
Open-market paper	28	59	72	63	74	86	107	117	99	108
Nonbank finance loans	44	75	88	101	119	140	152	162	159	158
Individuals [1]	2,015	2,950	3,343	3,740	4,068	4,442	4,825	5,125	5,245	5,427
By sector:										
Households [6]	1,406	1,993	2,271	2,584	2,861	3,177	3,508	3,781	3,926	4,141
Farm	162	188	173	157	146	138	139	141	139	140
Nonfarm noncorporate	448	769	899	1,000	1,061	1,127	1,178	1,204	1,181	1,146
By type of instrument:										
Mortgages	1,336	1,939	2,189	2,505	2,783	3,080	3,379	3,642	3,767	3,939
Consumer credit	355	519	602	659	692	742	792	809	797	799
Policy loan	43	56	56	55	55	55	58	63	67	72
Bank loans, n.e.c	136	169	178	189	187	191	207	203	194	189
Other loans	124	184	198	213	233	254	267	283	285	287
Tax-exempt debt	17	51	81	79	78	80	82	86	95	101

- Represents zero.   [1] Includes other types, not shown separately.   [2] U.S. Government.   [3] Includes bank affiliates.   [4] See footnote 3, table 784.   [5] Securitized credit obligations.   [6] Includes personal trusts and nonprofit organizations.

Source: Board of Governors of the Federal Reserve System, *Annual Statistical Digest.*

No. 786. Flow of Funds Accounts—Financial Assets and Liabilities of Financial and Nonfinancial Institutions, by Sector and Type of Instrument: 1992

[In billions of dollars. As of Dec. 31. Preliminary. A=Assets; L=Liabilities, SDR=Special drawing rights, IMF=International Monetary Fund. RPs=Repurchase Agreements. "N.e.c."=Not elsewhere classified]

TYPE OF INSTRUMENT	ALL SECTORS, TOTAL		PRIVATE DOMESTIC NONFINANCIAL INSTITUTIONS								U.S. GOVERNMENT		FINANCIAL INSTITUTIONS								FOREIGN SECTOR	
	A	L	Total A	Total L	Households[1] A	L	Business A	L	State and local govts. A	L	A	L	Total[2] A	L	Commercial banking A	L	Nonbank finance A	L	Federally sponsored credit agencies and mortgage pools A	L	A	L
Total	38,337	30,318	19,960	10,412	16,181	4,281	3,043	5,154	736	976	468	3,475	15,924	15,391	3,629	3,500	10,069	9,677	1,843	1,833	1,985	1,040
Gold stock and SDR's	20	-									9		11									
IMF position	12	12									12											12
Official foreign exchange	40	40									19		22									40
Treasury currency, SDR certificates	30	25										25	30									
Checkable deposits, currency	1,091	1,130	946		672		248		26		32	1	91	1,130	2	708	89				22	
Time and savings accounts	2,688	2,688	2,461		2,217		194		50		1		187	2,688		1,706	187	982			39	
Fed. funds and security RP's	408	435	175				77						209	435		272	126	163			24	
Money market fund shares	548	548	498		462		36						50	548			50	548				
Foreign deposits	52	52	33				33						19				19					52
Life insurance reserves	434	434	434		434							12		423				423				
Pension fund reserves	4,586	4,586	4,586		4,586							304		4,282				4,282				
Interbank claims[3]	122	111											68	111	60	47	5				54	
Mutual fund shares[3]	1,057	1,057	915		898		18						141	1,057	3		138					
Other corporate equities[4]	5,128		2,535		2,535								2,266		5		2,261				327	
Credit market instruments[5]	14,986	14,986	2,584	8,708	1,792	3,067	267	3,617	525	951	234	3,080	11,236	2,890	2,944	181	6,237	968	1,754	1,742	933	308
U.S. Treasury securities[6]	3,062	3,062	803		344		97		362			3,062	1,756		293		1,109		59		503	
Federal agency securities[7]	1,755	1,755	347		306		6		34			19	1,325	1,737	377		895		47	1,737	84	
Tax-exempt securities	1,155	1,155	623		600		12		11	941			532		98		435					
Corporate and foreign bonds	1,883	1,883	131	1,155	131		31	1,118	118				1,496	622	91		1,405	495			256	143
Mortgages	4,193	4,193	451	4,188	302	3,067	68	1,121			86		3,656	5	903	5	1,260		1,494			
Consumer credit	799	799	68	799		799	68						731		362		369					
Bank loans, n.e.c.	780	780	162	708		47		661					780	49	780	49					13	23
Open-market paper	579	579	80	108	80		52	108					404	393	9	339	378		17		13	78
Security credit	224	224		57		57							145	168	88		57					
Proprietors' equity	2,264	992	2,264	901	2,264			901						50				50				
Trade credit	1,131	1,006	1,006				1,006	811			31	48	50	22				22			44	21
Taxes payable	48	77		73							10		5									
Miscellaneous claims	3,470	2,921	1,405	674	242	20	1,163	654	38	25	122	7	1,401	1,632	528	584	853	950	14	91	543	608

- Represents or rounds to zero. [1] Includes personal trusts and nonprofit organizations. [2] Includes monetary authority, not shown separately. [3] Nonbank finance liability is redemption value of shares of open-end investment companies. [4] Shares shown at market value. No specific liability attributed to issuers of stocks other than open-end investment companies for amounts outstanding. [5] Includes "Other loans," not shown separately. [6] Includes savings bonds and other nonmarketable debt held by public. [7] Issues by agencies in the budget and by sponsored credit agencies in financial sectors, issues backed by mortgage pools, and loan participation certificates. [8] Asset is corporate only; noncorporate credit deducted in liability total to conform to quarterly flow tables.

Source: Board of Governors of the Federal Reserve System, Annual Statistical Digest.

No. 787. Flow of Funds Accounts—Assets and Liabilities of Households: 1980 to 1992

[As of **December 31**. Includes personal trusts and nonprofit organizations. See also *Historical Statistics, Colonial Times to 1970*, series X 114-147]

TYPE OF INSTRUMENT	TOTAL (bil. dol.)							PERCENT DISTRIBUTION		
	1980	1985	1988	1989	1990	1991	1992	1980	1990	1992
Total financial assets	**6,391**	**9,819**	**12,356**	**13,804**	**13,984**	**15,434**	**16,181**	**100.0**	**100.0**	**100.0**
Deposit and market instrument [1]	2,140	3,526	4,534	4,959	5,219	5,099	5,143	33.5	37.3	31.8
Checkable deposits and currency. . .	260	380	479	494	516	560	672	4.1	3.7	4.2
Small time and savings deposits . . .	1,141	1,830	2,137	2,225	2,279	2,283	2,215	17.8	16.3	13.7
Money market fund shares	65	211	302	388	433	461	462	1.0	3.1	2.9
Large time deposits.	112	72	129	142	109	61	2	1.8	0.8	(Z)
Credit market instruments.	562	1,033	1,485	1,710	1,882	1,735	1,792	8.8	13.5	11.1
U.S. Government securities	241	427	584	680	771	658	650	3.8	5.5	4.0
Treasury issues.	194	340	381	393	441	355	344	3.0	3.2	2.1
Savings bonds.	73	80	110	118	126	138	157	1.1	0.9	1.0
Other Treasury	122	260	271	275	315	217	186	1.9	2.2	1.2
Agency issues	47	87	203	288	330	303	306	0.7	2.4	1.9
Tax-exempt obligations	102	303	465	527	558	579	600	1.6	4.0	3.7
Corporate and foreign bonds	69	53	81	116	151	150	131	1.1	1.1	0.8
Mortgages	107	127	182	213	215	245	302	1.7	1.5	1.9
Open-market paper	43	122	174	173	188	103	109	0.7	1.3	0.7
Mutual fund shares.	52	207	418	492	515	680	898	0.8	3.7	5.5
Other corporate equities	1,111	1,611	1,719	2,004	1,842	2,349	2,535	17.4	13.2	15.7
Life insurance reserves	216	257	326	354	380	402	434	3.4	2.7	2.7
Pension fund reserves [2]	916	1,992	2,755	3,211	3,303	4,223	4,586	14.3	23.6	28.3
Equity in noncorporate business	1,865	2,059	2,373	2,525	2,449	2,368	2,264	29.2	17.5	14.0
Security credit	16	35	41	53	62	87	80	0.3	0.4	0.5
Miscellaneous assets	74	133	191	206	215	225	242	1.2	1.5	1.5
Total liabilities	**1,466**	**2,373**	**3,284**	**3,619**	**3,892**	**4,060**	**4,281**	**100.0**	**100.0**	**100.0**
Credit market instruments	1,406	2,271	3,177	3,508	3,781	3,926	4,141	95.9	97.1	96.7
Mortgages	950	1,460	2,219	2,483	2,732	2,867	3,067	64.8	70.2	71.6
Installment consumer credit	302	526	673	729	749	742	741	20.6	19.2	17.3
Other consumer credit	53	75	69	63	61	55	58	3.6	1.6	1.4
Tax-exempt debt.	17	81	80	82	86	95	101	1.1	2.2	2.4
Bank loans, not elsewhere classified	30	44	41	53	43	47	47	2.0	1.1	1.1
Other loans	55	84	97	99	110	120	127	3.7	2.8	3.0
Security credit	25	51	44	43	39	55	57	1.7	1.0	1.3
Trade credit	22	36	47	51	56	61	64	1.5	1.4	1.5
Unpaid life insurance premiums [3] . . .	13	15	16	16	17	18	20	0.9	0.4	0.5

Z Less than .05 percent. [1] Excludes corporate equities. [2] See also table 839. [3] Includes deferred premiums.

Source: Board of Governors of the Federal Reserve System, *Annual Statistical Digest*.

No. 788. Percent of Families Owning Financial Assets, by Type of Asset: 1983 and 1989

[Families include one-person units; for definition of family, see text, section 1. Based on Survey of Consumer Finance; see Appendix III]

AGE OF FAMILY HEAD AND FAMILY INCOME	Total [1]	Checking accounts	Savings accounts	Money market accounts	Certificates of deposit	Retirement accounts	Stocks	Bonds	Nontaxable bonds
1983, total	**87.8**	78.6	61.7	15.0	20.1	24.2	20.4	3.0	2.1
1989, total	**87.5**	75.4	43.5	22.2	19.6	33.3	19.0	4.4	4.4
Under 35 years old	82.2	68.4	45.0	14.9	8.5	23.0	11.4	0.8	0.9
35 to 44 years old	88.4	76.1	50.0	20.4	15.5	44.0	21.2	3.4	3.5
45 to 54 years old	90.4	78.9	44.6	27.0	21.1	45.5	23.1	3.5	4.3
55 to 64 years old	87.5	76.7	38.9	23.0	20.9	42.6	22.0	5.9	7.5
65 to 74 years old	91.5	79.9	37.7	28.3	31.6	30.0	20.8	9.1	9.4
75 years old and over	90.6	79.3	36.2	30.5	39.4	6.6	21.3	9.6	4.9
Less than $10,000.	59.1	46.2	21.9	7.8	8.6	3.1	2.0	0.8	(B)
$10,000 to $19,999	85.6	69.7	40.7	14.6	21.2	14.9	10.9	2.4	(B)
$20,000 to $29,999	95.2	80.3	47.6	21.0	20.6	34.4	16.9	3.0	4.2
$30,000 to $49,999	98.2	88.8	52.9	23.2	21.0	44.9	20.8	5.0	4.2
$50,000 and more.	99.7	91.5	53.9	44.7	26.5	69.2	44.6	12.7	12.6

B Base figure too small. [1] Includes other types of financial assets, not shown separately.

Source: Board of Governors of the Federal Reserve System, *Federal Reserve Bulletin*, January 1992.

No. 789. Percent of Families Holding Financial Debt, by Type of Debt: 1983 and 1989

[See headnote, table 788]

AGE OF FAMILY HEAD AND FAMILY INCOME	Total [1]	Home mortgage	Investment real estate	Home equity lines	Other lines of credit	Credit cards	Car loans
1983, total	69.6	36.9	7.6	0.5	11.2	37.0	28.7
1989, total	**72.7**	**38.7**	**7.0**	**3.3**	**3.3**	**39.9**	**35.1**
Under 35 years old	79.5	32.8	2.6	1.0	4.5	44.0	37.4
35 to 44 years old.........	89.6	57.7	10.2	4.3	4.7	52.4	51.5
45 to 54 years old.........	85.9	56.3	12.3	6.3	4.0	50.0	48.7
55 to 64 years old.........	74.0	37.5	10.7	6.1	1.9	34.1	29.3
65 to 74 years old.........	47.9	19.9	3.9	1.0	0.6	25.4	14.0
75 years old and over	23.8	8.6	1.4	(B)	(B)	10.6	5.3
Less than $10,000.........	47.2	8.8	1.0	(B)	1.5	15.0	11.1
$10,000 to $19,999	58.7	21.3	1.5	1.3	2.2	27.3	21.8
$20,000 to $29,999	79.5	36.8	4.7	2.4	1.6	48.9	39.4
$30,000 to $49,999	86.5	53.1	8.8	4.5	4.1	55.0	50.9
$50,000 and more.........	91.8	72.4	18.7	7.7	6.7	53.1	51.7

B Base figure too small.   [1] Includes other types of debt, not shown separately.

Source: Board of Governors of the Federal Reserve System, *Federal Reserve Bulletin*, January 1992.

No. 790. Use of Financial Services by Households, by Type of Financial Institution: 1989

[In percent, except as indicated. Use of a financial institution consists of use of one or more of the types of accounts shown in table 791. Savings institutions consist of savings and loan associations and savings banks. Other nondepository financial institutions include mortgage banks and insurance companies. An institution is local if the office or branch used by the household is located 30 miles or less from the household or workplace of the primary user. Based on the Survey of Consumer Finance, see headnote, table 788. For definition of mean, see Guide to Tabular Presentation]

ITEM	All financial institutions	DEPOSITORY				NONDEPOSITORY			
		Total	Commercial bank	Savings	Credit union	Total	Finance company	Brokerage firm	Other financial
Percentage of households using financial institutions, total [1]	90.3	88.6	77.6	39.4	26.5	42.8	21.3	14.0	18.1
Local	89.5	87.8	75.4	37.4	23.0	28.5	13.3	10.1	7.2
Nonlocal	17.8	11.7	6.8	3.5	4.4	17.5	9.0	4.6	10.9
Mean number of accounts used per household, total	4.73	3.92	2.40	0.91	0.61	0.81	0.29	0.30	0.22
Institutions identified by household as—									
Primary financial institution [2]	100.0	96.4	64.7	22.0	9.7	3.6	2.0	1.3	0.4
Main checking institution [3]	100.0	99.5	69.2	21.2	9.1	0.5	0.2	0.4	(Z)

Z Less than .05 percent.   [1] Sum of local and nonlocal exceeds total because some households use both local and nonlocal institutions.   [2] 84.7 percent of households designated a primary financial institution.   [3] 81.3 percent of households designated a main checking institution.

No. 791. Percent of Households Using Financial Accounts, by Type of Account and Source: 1989

[See headnote, table 790]

TYPE OF ACCOUNT	Any source	FINANCIAL INSTITUTIONS									Non-financial [1]
		Total	Depository				Nondepository				
			Total	Commercial bank	Savings	Credit union	Total	Finance company	Brokerage	Other	
All types of accounts	92.4	90.3	88.6	77.6	39.4	26.5	42.8	21.3	14.0	18.1	27.9
Asset.	86.3	86.2	86.1	65.9	30.6	22.8	17.3	0.3	13.9	4.6	3.8
Checking [2]	75.6	75.6	75.4	55.5	18.3	9.6	0.8	0.1	0.7	-	(Z)
Other liquid asset	61.3	61.2	59.4	34.9	21.4	18.2	6.3	0.1	5.6	0.7	0.9
Savings [3]	43.5	43.4	42.9	21.5	12.0	16.3	0.9	0.1	0.7	0.2	0.4
Money market [4]	21.8	21.6	17.8	10.7	6.0	2.4	5.2	(Z)	4.8	0.5	0.4
Certificate of deposit	19.5	19.5	19.0	11.6	8.5	2.0	0.9	(Z)	0.8	0.1	0.1
IRA or Keogh	24.2	23.0	15.6	9.4	5.2	2.2	9.8	0.1	7.0	3.0	1.9
Brokerage	8.4	8.4	0.9	0.8	0.1	(Z)	7.6	(Z)	7.6		(Z)
Trust	4.3	3.2	1.1	0.7	0.2	0.1	2.2	0.1	0.9	1.4	1.2
Credit	80.0	74.9	68.0	56.6	20.9	13.7	32.8	21.1	1.1	14.8	25.0
Bank credit card.	56.5	55.8	54.0	45.5	5.9	6.3	7.9	0.2	0.8	7.1	1.5
Mortgage.	40.8	37.2	26.3	14.1	12.8	1.1	13.3	5.3	0.1	8.2	5.8
Motor vehicle	34.9	33.8	21.8	13.7	3.1	6.0	13.7	13.5	(Z)	0.1	1.3
Home equity, other credit line . .	10.8	10.6	8.8	5.6	1.5	1.9	2.1	1.8	0.3	-	0.3
Other [5]	28.2	13.8	10.4	6.2	2.2	2.6	4.1	4.0	(Z)	0.1	18.6

- Represents zero.   Z Less than .05 percent.   [1] Includes individuals, retailers, other nonfinancial businesses, government agencies, and nonprofit organizations.   [2] Consists of regular checking, NOW, and share draft accounts. Excludes money market accounts.   [3] Consists of passbook, share, and statement savings accounts.   [4] Consists of money market deposit accounts and mutual fund accounts.   [5] Includes personal loans and home improvement loans.

Source of tables 790 and 791: Board of Governors of the Federal Reserve System, *Federal Reserve Bulletin*, March 1992.

No. 792. Selected Financial Institutions—Number and Assets, by Asset Size: 1991

[As of **December**. FDIC=Federal Deposit Insurance Corporation]

ASSET SIZE	NUMBER OF INSTITUTIONS			ASSETS (bil. dol.)		
	F.D.I.C.-insured		Credit unions [2]	F.D.I.C.-insured		Credit unions [2]
	Commercial banks	Savings institutions [1]		Commercial banks [3]	Savings institutions [1]	
Total	**11,920**	**2,560**	**12,960**	**3,430.1**	**1,119.4**	**227.1**
Less than $5.0 million	(4)	(4)	7,636	(4)	(4)	12.2
$5.0 million to $9.9 million	(4)	(4)	1,825	(4)	(4)	13.0
$10.0 million to $24.9 million	[4]2,844	[4]220	1,702	[4]44.2	[4]3.4	27.2
$25.0 million to $49.9 million	3,164	388	880	113.1	14.4	30.8
$50.0 million to $99.9 million	2,773	573	467	196.5	41.1	32.4
$100.0 million to $499.9 million	2,508	996	412	490.3	216.2	76.9
$500.0 million to $999.9 million	263	171	[5]38	183.5	118.0	[5]34.6
$1.0 billion to $2.9 billion	189	147	(5)	336.3	248.1	(5)
$3.0 billion or more	179	65	(5)	2,066.2	478.1	(5)
	PERCENT DISTRIBUTION					
Total	**100.0**	**100.0**	**100.0**	**100.0**	**100.0**	**100.0**
Less than $5.0 million	(4)	(4)	58.9	(4)	(4)	5.4
$5.0 million to $9.9 million	(4)	(4)	14.1	(4)	(4)	5.7
$10.0 million to $24.9 million	[4]23.9	[4]8.6	13.1	[4]1.3	[4]0.3	12.0
$25.0 million to $49.9 million	26.5	15.2	6.8	3.3	1.3	13.5
$50.0 million to $99.9 million	23.3	22.4	3.6	5.7	3.7	14.3
$100.0 million to $499.9 million	21.0	38.9	3.2	14.3	19.3	33.9
$500.0 million to $999.9 million	2.2	6.7	[5]0.3	5.3	10.5	[5]15.2
$1.0 billion to $2.9 billion	1.6	5.7	(5)	9.8	22.2	(5)
$3.0 billion or more	1.5	2.5	(5)	60.2	42.7	(5)

[1] Excludes institutions in Resolution Trust Corporation conservatorship.　[2] Source: National Credit Union Administration, *National Credit Union Administration Yearend Statistics 1991*. Excludes nonfederally insured State chartered credit unions and federally insured corporate credit unions.　[3] Includes foreign branches of U.S. banks.　[4] Data for institutions with assets less than $10 million included with those with assets of $10.0 million to $24.9 million.　[5] Data for institutions with assets of $1 billion or more included with those with assets of $500.0 million to $999.9 million.

Source: Except as noted, U.S. Federal Deposit Insurance Corporation, *Statistics on Banking, 1991*.

No. 793. Banking Offices, by Type of Bank: 1980 to 1991

[As of **December 31**. Includes Puerto Rico and outlying areas. Covers all FDIC-insured commercial banks and all Bank Insurance Fund-insured savings banks as well as those State-chartered Savings Association Insurance Fund-insured savings banks that are regulated by the FDIC. Data for 1980 includes automatic teller machines which were reported by many banks as branches. See also *Historical Statistics, Colonial Times to 1970*, series X 716-724]

ITEM	1980	1984	1985	1986	1987	1988	1989	1990	1991
All banking offices	**57,232**	**60,067**	**60,890**	**61,897**	**62,914**	**63,960**	**64,570**	**66,945**	**67,783**
Commercial banks, total	53,649	57,010	57,764	58,565	59,423	60,200	60,796	63,160	64,006
Member, Federal Reserve System	29,985	32,809	33,854	34,542	35,196	35,763	36,755	38,201	39,449
National banks	24,217	27,037	27,844	28,218	28,744	29,270	30,019	31,279	31,771
State banks	5,768	5,772	6,010	6,324	6,452	6,493	6,736	6,922	7,678
Nonmember banks	23,664	24,201	23,910	24,023	24,227	24,437	24,041	24,959	24,557
Insured	23,186	23,535	23,910	24,023	24,227	24,437	24,041	24,959	24,557
Noninsured	478	666	(NA)	(NA)	(NA)	(NA)	(NA)	(NA)	(NA)
Savings banks, total	3,583	3,057	3,126	3,332	3,491	3,760	3,774	3,785	3,777
Insured	3,066	2,728	3,126	3,332	3,491	3,760	3,774	3,785	3,777
Noninsured	517	329	(NA)	(NA)	(NA)	(NA)	(NA)	(NA)	(NA)

NA Not available.

Source: U.S. Federal Deposit Insurance Corporation, 1980, *Annual Report* and, beginning 1984, *Statistics on Banking*, annual.

No. 794. Changes in Number of Operating Banking Offices: 1980 to 1991

[As of **December 31**. Includes Puerto Rico and outlying areas. See headnote, table 793. Beginning 1985, excludes noninsured institutions]

TYPE OF CHANGE	1980	1984	1985	1986	1987	1988	1989	1990	1991
Banking offices [1]	**57,232**	**60,067**	**60,890**	**61,897**	**62,914**	**63,960**	**64,570**	**66,945**	**67,783**
Number of banks	15,330	15,489	14,809	14,681	14,207	13,629	13,201	12,819	12,390
Number of branches [1]	41,902	44,578	46,081	47,216	48,707	50,331	51,369	54,126	55,393
Net change during year	**2,306**	**1,017**	**1,759**	**1,007**	**1,017**	**1,046**	**610**	**2,375**	**838**
Offices opened	2,800	2,338	2,874	2,756	3,144	3,537	3,342	4,154	3,728
Banks	271	486	482	396	271	248	202	193	160
Branches	2,529	1,852	2,392	2,360	2,873	3,289	3,961	3,961	3,568
Offices closed	494	1,321	1,115	1,749	2,127	2,491	2,732	1,779	2,890
Banks	142	427	460	524	745	826	630	575	589
Branches	352	894	655	1,225	1,382	1,665	[2]2,102	1,204	2,301

[1] See headnote, table 793.　[2] Includes 366 Federal nonmember contractual branches in Michigan that were previously reported as branches. "Contractual branches" are established among affiliated banks and allow the banks' branches to act as branches for each other.

Source: U.S. Federal Deposit Insurance Corporation, *Statistics on Banking*, annual.

No. 795. BIF-Insured Commercial and Savings Banks Closed or Assisted Due to Financial Difficulties and Problem Banks: 1980 to 1992

[Banks are closed either permanently or temporarily by order of supervisory authorities or by directors of banks. B.I.F.=Bank Insurance Fund. See *Historical Statistics, Colonial Times to 1970*, series X 741, 748, 756, and 761]

ITEM	Unit	1980	1984	1985	1986	1987	1988	1989	1990	1991	1992
Total banks closed or assisted...	Number.	11	80	120	145	203	221	207	169	127	122
Assets, closed and assisted banks	Bil. dol. .	(NA)	(NA)	(NA)	(NA)	(NA)	(NA)	29.4	15.7	63.2	(NA)
Deposits, closed and assisted banks..........	Bil. dol. .	5.2	29.9	8.1	6.6	8.6	37.2	24.1	14.5	53.8	41.2
Problem banks [1]	Number.	217	848	1,140	1,484	1,575	1,406	1,109	1,046	1,090	863
Assets, problem banks	Bil. dol. .	(NA)	(NA)	238	336	359	352	236	409	610	465

NA Not available.   [1] BIF-insured commercial and savings banks considered to be problem banks by the supervisory authorities, end-of-period.

Source: U.S. Federal Deposit Insurance Corporation, *Annual Report, The FDIC Quarterly Banking Profile*, and *Failed Bank Cost Analysis Report*, 1992.

No. 796. 500 Largest Banks in the World—Number and Deposits, by Location of Bank: 1980 to 1991

[**Deposits in billions of dollars, except percent**. Data cover U.S. commercial banks and foreign banks that conduct a commercial banking business; beginning 1983, includes U.S. and foreign savings banks. Beginning 1983, covers top 500 banks in assets available. Number of banks includes banks more than 50 percent owned by other banks. To avoid double-counting of deposits, banks more than 50 percent owned by other banks are excluded from deposit totals if their parent bank consolidates their deposits]

LOCATION OF BANK	1980	1983	1984	1985	1986	1987	1988	1989	1990	1991	PERCENT		
											1980	1990	1991
NUMBER													
U.S. banks	93	102	115	110	102	90	107	108	96	91	19	19	18
Foreign banks	407	398	385	390	398	410	393	392	404	409	81	81	82
Japan	78	95	95	96	108	111	111	108	106	110	16	21	22
United Kingdom ..	34	26	22	22	20	18	18	20	22	20	7	4	4
Germany	38	40	39	39	38	42	38	37	39	41	8	8	8
France	28	21	19	20	23	23	20	20	20	18	6	4	4
Italy	27	29	26	29	31	32	29	28	31	31	5	6	6
DEPOSITS													
Total	4,994	5,683	5,854	7,022	9,220	12,090	12,837	13,565	15,854	16,479	100	100	100
U.S. banks	754	882	961	1,014	1,084	1,108	1,347	1,352	1,329	1,311	15	8	8
Foreign banks	4,240	4,801	4,893	6,008	8,136	10,982	11,489	12,214	14,525	15,168	85	92	92
Japan	1,131	1,587	1,750	2,179	3,350	4,936	5,333	5,236	5,888	6,213	24	37	38
United Kingdom ..	349	375	343	403	458	588	646	673	822	880	7	5	5
Germany	603	550	500	684	912	1,208	1,151	1,309	1,692	1,909	12	11	12
France	483	436	440	502	650	836	822	970	1,175	1,101	10	7	7
Italy	290	309	296	395	527	647	606	708	870	1,008	6	5	6

Source: American Banker-Bond Buyer, New York, NY, *American Banker Ranking The Banks*, annual (copyright).

No. 797. Insured Commercial Banks—Assets and Liabilities: 1980 to 1992

[**In billions of dollars, except as indicated**. As of **Dec. 31**. Includes outlying areas. Except as noted, includes foreign branches of U.S. banks. See *Historical Statistics, Colonial Times to 1970*, series X 588-609, for related data]

ITEM	1980	1985	1986	1987	1988	1989	1990	1991	1992 [1]
Number of banks	14,435	14,417	14,209	13,722	13,137	12,713	12,345	11,926	11,461
Assets, total..............	**1,856**	**2,731**	**2,941**	**3,000**	**3,131**	**3,299**	**3,389**	**3,431**	**3,506**
Net loans and leases............	1,006	1,608	1,728	1,779	1,886	2,004	2,054	1,998	1,978
Real estate loans............	269	438	516	600	675	762	830	851	868
Commercial and industrial loans . . .	391	578	600	589	600	619	615	559	536
Loans to individuals	187	309	336	351	378	401	403	392	385
Farm loans................	32	36	32	29	30	31	33	35	35
Other loans and leases.........	137	270	273	259	249	246	229	216	207
Less: Reserve for losses........	10	23	29	50	47	54	56	55	54
Temporary investments	(2)	452	464	451	466	482	451	499	541
Securities over 1 year in length	(2)	298	358	397	383	402	450	514	569
Other	[2]849	374	392	373	397	411	434	420	418
Domestic office assets...........	1,533	2,326	2,532	2,575	2,726	2,897	2,999	3,033	3,110
Foreign office assets...........	323	406	409	425	405	402	390	398	396
Liabilities and capital, total	1,856	2,731	2,941	3,000	3,131	3,299	3,389	3,431	3,506
Noninterest-bearing deposits [3]	432	471	532	478	479	483	489	480	541
Interest-bearing deposits [4]	1,049	1,646	1,751	1,858	1,952	2,065	2,162	2,207	2,158
Subordinated debt.............	7	15	17	18	17	19	24	25	34
Other liabilities	260	429	458	466	486	526	496	486	510
Equity capital	108	169	182	181	197	205	219	232	264
Domestic office deposits	1,187	1,796	1,970	1,994	2,117	2,237	2,357	2,383	2,412
Foreign office deposits..........	294	322	314	342	315	312	293	305	287

[1] Preliminary.   [2] Temporary investments and securities over one year in length included in other.   [3] Prior to 1985, demand deposits.   [4] Prior to 1985, time and savings deposits.

Source: U.S. Federal Deposit Insurance Corporation, *The FDIC Quarterly Banking Profile, Annual Report*, and *Statistics on Banking*, annual.

No. 798. Insured Commercial Banks—Income and Selected Measures of Financial Condition: 1980 to 1992

[In billions of dollars, except as indicated. Includes outlying areas. Includes foreign branches of U.S. banks. See *Historical Statistics, Colonial Times to 1970*, series X 588-609, for related data]

ITEM	1980	1985	1986	1987	1988	1989	1990	1991	1992 [1]
Interest income	177.4	248.2	237.8	244.8	272.3	317.3	320.4	289.2	255.3
Interest expense	120.1	157.3	142.8	145.0	165.0	205.1	204.9	167.3	121.9
Net interest income	57.3	90.9	94.9	99.9	107.2	112.2	115.5	121.9	133.5
Provisions for loan losses	4.5	17.7	22.1	37.5	17.2	31.0	32.1	34.3	25.9
Noninterest income	13.3	31.0	35.9	41.5	45.0	50.9	54.9	59.7	65.6
Noninterest expense	46.7	82.3	90.2	97.2	101.3	108.1	115.7	124.8	130.9
Income taxes	5.0	5.6	5.3	5.4	10.0	9.5	7.7	8.3	14.5
Securities gain/loss, net	-0.5	1.6	4.0	1.4	0.3	0.8	0.5	3.0	4.0
Extraordinary gains, net	-	0.2	0.3	0.2	0.8	0.3	0.6	0.7	0.4
Net income	14.0	18.1	17.4	2.8	24.8	15.6	16.0	17.9	32.2
RATIOS OF CONDITION									
Return on assets [2] (percent)	0.80	0.70	0.63	0.10	0.82	0.49	0.48	0.54	0.96
Return on equity [3] (percent)	13.66	11.31	9.94	2.00	13.30	7.78	7.55	8.05	13.35
Equity capital to assets (percent)	5.80	6.20	6.20	6.02	6.28	6.21	6.45	6.75	7.52
Nonperforming assets	(NA)	51.0	57.7	73.8	67.1	75.4	98.1	102.6	88.0
Nonperforming assets to assets (percent)	(NA)	1.87	1.94	2.46	2.14	2.30	2.90	2.99	2.51
Net charge-offs [4]	3.6	13.6	16.6	16.4	18.6	22.9	29.7	32.9	25.5
Net charge-offs to loans and leases (percent)	0.36	0.84	0.98	0.92	1.00	1.14	1.44	1.61	1.29
Net interest margin [5] (percent)	3.66	4.09	3.98	3.89	4.06	3.31	3.41	4.18	4.51
Percentage of banks losing money	3.7	17.1	19.8	17.7	14.7	12.5	13.5	11.6	6.5

- Represents or rounds to zero.   NA Not available.   [1] Preliminary.   [2] Net income (including securities transactions and nonrecurring items) as a percentage of average total assets.   [3] Net income as a percentage of average total equity capital. [4] Total loans and leases charged off (removed from balance sheet because of uncollectibility), less amounts recovered on loans and leases previously charged off.   [5] Interest income less interest expense as a percentage of average earning assets (i.e. the profit margin a bank earns on its loans and investments).

No. 799. Insured Commercial Banks, 1991, and Banks Closed or Assisted, 1992, by State and Other Area

[In billions of dollars, except as indicated. Includes foreign branches of U.S. banks]

STATE	COMMERCIAL BANKS, [1] 1991			BANKS CLOSED OR ASSISTED, [2] 1992		STATE	COMMERCIAL BANKS, [1] 1991			BANKS CLOSED OR ASSISTED, [2] 1992	
	Number	Assets	Deposits	Number	Deposits		Number	Assets	Deposits	Number	Deposits
Total	11,926	3,430.1	2,687.6	122	41.2	WV	169	18.6	15.7	-	-
U.S.	11,908	3,412.9	2,672.9	121	41.1	NC	81	79.6	59.7	-	-
Northeast	814	1,125.0	826.5	45	29.0	SC	83	25.6	19.0	-	-
N.E.	219	162.9	126.5	31	7.5	GA	405	71.0	54.9	2	0.1
ME	21	8.8	7.4	-	-	FL	421	138.9	119.9	2	(Z)
NH	32	8.5	6.9	3	0.2	E.S.C.	912	155.0	128.1	1	(Z)
VT	24	6.0	5.3	-	-	KY	320	42.5	34.1	-	-
MA	73	92.0	67.8	15	3.9	TN	250	49.1	41.3	-	-
RI	13	14.4	10.9	3	1.1	AL	219	41.2	33.6	-	-
CT	56	33.2	28.2	10	2.4	MS	123	22.1	19.1	1	(Z)
M.A.	595	962.1	700.0	14	21.5	W.S.C.	2,021	258.2	226.2	36	8.3
NY	189	694.8	480.7	7	14.4	AR	262	23.5	20.9	1	(Z)
NJ	117	95.5	81.2	5	3.8	LA	226	37.5	33.0	2	0.1
PA	289	171.9	138.1	2	3.2	OK	411	28.3	24.8	2	(Z)
Midwest	5,194	758.2	610.4	13	2.3	TX	1,122	168.9	147.5	31	8.2
E.N.C.	2,313	525.2	417.6	3	0.1	West	1,466	570.5	464.0	17	1.3
OH	280	119.0	92.2	-	-	Mt.	814	127.0	103.5	4	0.1
IN	284	59.2	48.5	1	(Z)	MT	145	7.5	6.5	1	(Z)
IL	1,061	199.1	157.0	2	(Z)	ID	22	9.8	7.6	-	-
MI	230	98.8	78.7	-	-	WY	62	4.8	4.3	-	-
WI	458	49.0	41.3	-	-	CO	387	28.1	24.4	-	-
W.N.C.	2,881	233.0	192.7	10	2.2	NM	83	12.1	10.7	-	-
MN	608	54.9	45.0	1	(Z)	AZ	41	35.6	30.4	3	(Z)
IA	553	36.3	30.8	-	-	UT	55	13.8	10.5	-	-
MO	532	65.4	54.4	7	2.2	NV	19	15.2	9.1	-	-
ND	146	7.7	6.8	-	-	Pac.	652	443.5	360.5	13	1.2
SD	125	17.6	11.3	-	-	WA	93	39.6	33.4	-	-
NE	389	21.4	18.6	-	-	OR	51	25.7	20.3	-	-
KS	528	29.8	25.9	2	(Z)	CA	480	352.8	287.1	12	1.2
South	4,434	959.2	771.9	46	8.6	AK	8	4.6	3.5	-	-
S.A.	1,501	546.1	417.7	9	0.2	HI	20	20.8	16.2	1	(Z)
DE	42	74.5	36.0	-	-						
MD	102	54.7	44.0	1	(Z)	AM	1	(Z)	(Z)	-	-
DC	24	14.8	12.7	2	(Z)	PR	14	16.5	14.0	1	(Z)
VA	174	68.5	55.8	2	0.1	GU	2	0.6	0.6	-	-
						Pac. Is	1	(Z)	(Z)	-	-

- Represents zero.   Z Less than $50 million.   [1] As of December 31.   [2] Includes Bank Insurance Fund-insured savings banks.

Source of tables 798 and 799: U.S. Federal Deposit Insurance Corporation, *Annual Report; Statistics on Banking*, annual; and *FDIC Quarterly Banking Profile*.

No. 800. Insured Commercial Banks—Selected Measures of Financial Condition, by Asset Size and Region: 1992

[In percent, except as indicated. Preliminary. See headnote, table 798]

ASSET SIZE AND REGION	Number of banks	Return on assets	Return on equity	Equity capital to assets	Nonperforming assets to total assets	Net charge-offs to loans and leases	Percentage of banks losing money
Total	11,461	0.96	13.35	7.52	2.51	1.29	6.5
Less than $100 million . .	8,290	1.06	11.34	9.40	1.35	0.54	6.5
$100 million to $1 billion .	2,791	1.03	12.73	8.21	1.70	0.74	6.1
$1 billion to $10 billion . .	329	1.05	14.10	7.69	2.15	1.40	10.6
$10 billion or more	51	0.84	13.85	6.62	3.43	1.63	7.8
Northeast [1]	922	0.84	12.89	6.93	3.49	1.80	15.4
Southeast [2]	1,892	1.02	13.46	7.60	1.61	0.84	8.0
Central [3]	2,521	1.07	13.85	7.86	1.35	1.00	3.6
Midwest [4]	2,791	1.32	15.69	8.44	1.18	0.79	2.0
Southwest [5]	2,046	1.15	16.09	7.32	1.49	0.67	5.0
West [6]	1,289	0.85	11.18	8.19	3.44	1.29	15.8

[1] CT, DE, DC, ME, MD, MA, NH, NJ, NY, PA, PR, RI, and VT.   [2] AL, FL, GA, MS, NC, SC, TN, VA, and WV.   [3] IL, IN, KY, MI, OH, and WI.   [4] IA, KS, MN, MO, NE, ND, and SD.   [5] AR, LA, NM, OK, and TX.   [6] AK, AZ, CA, CO, HI, ID, MT, NV, OR, Pacific Islands, UT, WA, and WY.
Source: U.S. Federal Deposit Insurance Corporation, The FDIC Quarterly Banking Profile, Fourth Quarter 1992.

No. 801. U.S. Banking Offices of Foreign Banks—Summary: 1980 to 1991

[In billions of dollars, except as indicated. As of December, except as indicated. Covers agencies, branches, subsidiary commercial banks, and New York State investment companies]

YEAR	Assets	LOANS		Deposits	COUNTRY	NUMBER OF—		Assets	Loans, commercial and industrial	Deposits
		Total	Business			Banks with U.S. offices	U.S. offices			
1980	200.6	121.4	59.6	80.4	1991, total [2] .	299	740	832.0	202.5	440.3
1985	440.8	247.4	108.8	236.7	Japan	52	149	417.0	119.4	206.1
1987	592.6	310.9	147.9	316.1	Canada	6	51	57.3	16.0	25.3
1988	650.6	338.8	167.3	335.1	United Kingdom.	10	39	46.2	11.6	35.9
1989	735.7	369.8	184.3	376.1	Italy	13	26	46.7	8.2	15.7
1990	791.1	397.9	193.3	383.9	France	16	37	50.3	5.9	25.8
1991	860.7	412.3	206.4	444.5	Netherlands . . .	3	25	25.9	5.7	17.6
Share: [1] 1980 . .	11.9	13.4	18.2	6.6	Hong Kong . . .	10	30	21.0	5.0	16.0
1985 . .	16.1	15.4	22.5	12.1	Switzerland . . .	7	18	28.4	3.7	16.2
1990 . .	21.4	18.0	30.8	14.5	Israel	4	25	11.8	3.2	10.0
1991 . .	22.6	18.9	34.5	16.2	Mexico	6	13	5.6	3.0	1.8

[1] Percent of "domestically owned" commercial banks plus U.S. offices of foreign banks.   [2] As of June 30. Includes other countries not shown separately. Source: American Banker-Bond Buyer, New York, NY, American Banker Ranking The Banks, annual (copyright).
Source: Except as noted, Board of Governors of the Federal Reserve System, unpublished data.

No. 802. Foreign Lending by U.S. Banks, by Type of Borrower and Country: 1992

[In millions of dollars. As of December. Covers 150 U.S. banking organizations which do nearly all of the foreign lending in the country. Data represent claims on foreign residents and institutions held at all domestic and foreign offices of covered banks. Data cover only cross-border and nonlocal currency lending. These result from a U.S. bank's office in one country lending to residents of another country or lending in a currency other than that of the borrower's country. Excludes local currency loans and other claims and local currency liabilities held by banks' foreign offices on residents of the country in which the office was located (e.g. Deutsche mark loans to German residents booked at the German branch of the reporting U.S. bank). Criteria for country selection is $2.1 billion or more]

COUNTRY	Total	Bank	Public	Private nonbank	COUNTRY	Total	Bank	Public	Private nonbank
Total [1]	197,057	83,812	49,988	63,257	Hong Kong.	6,387	4,050	48	2,289
					Italy.	5,321	3,030	1,626	665
Argentina	5,777	523	1,487	3,767	Japan	14,789	9,743	451	4,595
Australia.	3,208	1,091	424	1,693	Mexico.	17,277	2,693	11,489	3,095
Bahamas, The.	3,219	2,929	3	287	Netherlands	2,869	978	351	1,540
Belgium-Luxembourg .	5,443	3,397	900	1,146	Philippines	2,906	451	1,794	661
Brazil.	7,352	1,150	3,944	2,258	Singapore.	4,056	2,386	50	1,620
Canada	8,975	3,568	1,094	4,313	South Korea	4,032	2,174	309	1,551
Cayman Islands.	9,472	7,469	2	2,001	Spain.	2,794	1,033	1,297	464
Chile	3,174	576	1,595	1,003	Sweden	3,747	872	2,095	780
China: Taiwan	2,371	1,051	102	1,219	Switzerland.	4,181	1,834	75	2,272
France.	9,834	6,630	1,900	1,304	United Kingdom.	25,046	13,965	265	10,816
Germany	5,184	2,493	1,808	883	Venezuela	6,824	142	5,087	1,595

[1] Includes other countries, not shown separately.
Source: Board of Governors of the Federal Reserve System, Federal Financial Institutions Examination Council, statistical release.

No. 803. Insured Savings Institutions—Financial Summary: 1986 to 1991

[In billions of dollars, except number of institutions. As of December 31. Includes Puerto Rico, Guam, and Virgin Islands. Covers SAIF (Savings Association Insurance Fund)- and BIF (Bank Insurance Fund)-insured savings institutions. Minus sign (-) indicates debt or loss]

ITEM	INSURED SAVINGS INSTITUTIONS [1]						RTC conservatorships, [2] 1991
	1986	1987	1988	1989	1990	1991	
Number of institutions	3,676	3,621	3,438	3,088	2,816	2,560	91
Assets, total.	1,387	1,502	1,629	1,437	1,267	1,119	44
Loans and leases, net	860	912	1,001	920	816	727	24
Liabilities, total.	1,331	1,448	1,563	1,368	1,200	1,051	48
Deposits	1,083	1,138	1,195	1,082	987	907	37
Equity capital.	55	54	66	69	68	69	-4
Interest and fee income.	120	120	127	135	117	98	3
Interest expense.	97	94	101	111	91	70	3
Net interest income.	23	26	26	24	26	28	(Z)
Net income	3	-5	-5	-6	-5	1	-2

Z Less than $500 million.　[1] Excludes institutions in RTC conservatorship.　[2] RTC=Resolution Trust Corporation. These savings institutions are members of the Savings Association Insurance Fund.

No. 804. Insured Savings Institutions—Finances, by Asset Size: 1991

[In billions of dollars, except as indicated. See headnote, table 803. Excludes institutions in Resolution Trust Corporation conservatorship. Minus sign (-) indicates loss]

ITEM	Total	Less than $100 million	$100 million to $1 billion	$1 billion or more	ITEM	Total	Less than $100 million	$100 million to $1 billion	$1 billion or more
Number of institutions	2,560	1,183	1,165	212	Equity capital	69	5	23	41
Assets, total.	1,119	59	334	726					
Investment securities . .	253	11	78	164	Interest and fee income . . .	98	5	29	63
Loans and leases, net [1] .	727	40	217	471	Interest expense	70	4	20	46
Real estate loans	682	38	205	439	Net interest income	28	2	9	17
Commercial and					Provisions for loan losses. .	7	(Z)	2	5
industrial loans	23	1	5	18	Noninterest income	9	(Z)	2	6
Loans to individuals. . .	41	2	12	26	Noninterest expense	27	1	8	17
Less: Reserve for					Net operating income,				
losses	10	(Z)	2	7	pretax	3	(Z)	1	1
Liabilities, total	1,051	54	312	685	Securities gain/loss, net. . .	1	(Z)	(Z)	1
Deposits	907	53	289	565	Income taxes	3	(Z)	1	2
Noninterest-bearing . . .	24	1	7	16	Net income	1	(Z)	1	(Z)
Interest-bearing.	882	52	282	549	Net charge-offs [2].	5	(Z)	1	4

Z Less than $500 million.　[1] Includes other items, not shown separately.　[2] Total loans and leases charged off (removed from balance sheet because of uncollectibility), less amounts recovered on loans and leases previously charged off.

Source: U.S. Federal Deposit Insurance Corporation, *Statistics on Banking, 1991.*

No. 805. Savings Institutions (SAIF-Insured)—Deposit Accounts and Mortgage Activity: 1980 to 1991

[See headnote, table 806]

ITEM	Unit	1980	1984	1985	1986	1987	1988	1989	1990	1991
DEPOSIT ACCOUNTS										
Number of accounts	Millions . .	92.2	111.9	111.5	110.1	110.6	110.1	108.3	93.9	81.3
Average balance	Dollars . .	5,410	7,008	7,572	8,087	8,433	8,825	8,733	8,903	9,004
Net deposit gain [1]	Bil. dol. . .	41.0	113.9	53.0	55.1	46.4	44.0	-15.7	-28.1	-32.3
Net new deposits received [2]	Bil. dol. . .	10.7	57.2	-4.6	-3.3	-1.8	-8.4	-72.8	-80.8	-75.4
MORTGAGE LOANS										
Number of borrowers	Millions . .	15.7	15.8	15.0	14.1	13.6	13.7	12.5	12.8	9.4
Average balance	Dollars . .	31,311	37,510	43,168	46,359	49,967	52,999	56,556	48,205	57,398
Mortgage loans closed [3]	Bil. dol. . .	85.5	181.3	196.8	265.5	253.4	240.3	188.7	153.4	144.1
Refinancing loans	Bil. dol. . .	10.6	31.7	(NA)	(NA)	71.6	42.4	30.9	21.0	27.7
Delinquent mortgage loans: [4]										
Amount	Bil. dol. . .	7.3	12.6	21.7	32.6	37.7	33.3	36.1	36.0	30.6
Percent of mortgage holdings. . . .	Percent . .	1.48	2.12	3.36	4.97	5.56	4.58	4.96	5.63	5.50

NA Not available.　[1] Net new deposits received plus interest credited.　[2] New deposits received less deposits withdrawn.　[3] Reported on a gross basis. Covers permanent loans and combination construction-purchase loans.　[4] Prior to 1987, covers all mortgage loans 60 or more days delinquent. Beginning 1987, covers construction and land loans past due, permanent loans secured by one to four dwelling unit properties 60 or more days delinquent, and all other permanent loans past due.

Source: U.S. Office of Thrift Supervision, 1980-89, *Savings and Home Financing Source Book,* annual; beginning 1990, *Quarterly Thrift Financial Aggregate.*

No. 806. Savings Institutions (SAIF-Insured)—Selected Financial Items and Ratios of Condition: 1980 to 1991

[As of **Dec. 31 for assets, liabilities and net worth; calendar year for other items.** Includes Puerto Rico, Guam, and Virgin Islands. SAIF=Savings Association Insurance Fund. Beginning 1984, includes SAIF-insured savings and loan associations which changed to SAIF-insured savings banks. Minus sign (-) indicates either loss or outflow]

ITEM	Unit	1980	1984	1985	1986	1987	1988	1989	1990	1991
Assets [1]	Bil. dol .	620.6	977.5	1,070.0	1,163.9	1,250.9	1,350.5	1,233.6	1,085.0	920.0
Mortgage assets [2]	Bil. dol .	494.9	593.0	645.5	655.7	679.2	726.6	708.9	615.7	537.7
Mortgage-backed securities	Bil. dol .	27.3	112.7	115.5	158.2	201.8	214.6	170.5	156.2	130.8
Cash and securities	Bil. dol .	57.0	136.7	143.5	164.8	169.7	187.0	166.0	146.7	120.1
Liabilities [1]	Bil. dol .	588.0	940.3	1,023.4	1,111.6	1,204.5	1,295.3	1,225.2	1,054.2	871.4
Deposit accounts	Bil. dol .	503.2	784.5	843.9	890.7	932.6	971.7	945.7	835.7	731.9
FHLB advances	Bil. dol .	47.0	71.7	84.4	100.0	116.4	134.2	124.6	100.4	65.8
Other borrowed money	Bil. dol .	17.2	66.2	73.3	96.9	133.5	165.2	131.4	97.0	56.1
Net worth	Bil. dol .	32.6	37.2	46.7	52.3	46.4	55.2	23.6	31.0	48.6
Net worth to total assets ratio	Ratio ..	5.2	3.8	4.4	4.5	3.7	4.1	1.9	2.8	5.3
Interest expense	Bil. dol .	47.5	85.0	87.7	83.5	80.5	89.3	97.5	86.2	63.8
Net income before taxes	Bil. dol .	1.2	1.8	5.8	3.3	-5.1	-13.4	-13.4	-11.8	4.5
Net income after taxes	Bil. dol .	0.8	1.0	3.7	0.1	-7.8	-13.4	-14.1	-13.2	-2.4
Average cost of funds	Percent.	8.94	10.03	9.19	8.06	7.20	7.49	8.26	8.60	7.36
Average effective dividend rate paid.	Percent.	8.78	9.92	9.02	7.84	6.92	7.20	7.91	7.44	6.53
Average interest return on mortgages	Percent.	9.34	11.65	11.52	10.65	9.70	9.62	10.32	10.22	9.71
Return on assets [3]	Percent.	0.14	0.12	0.39	0.02	-0.64	-1.08	-1.47	-1.12	-0.24

[1] Includes other items, not shown separately.   [2] Beginning 1984, reflects deductions from asset accounts.   [3] Net income after taxes as a percent of average assets.

Source: U.S. Office of Thrift Supervision, 1980-89, *Savings and Home Financing Source Book*, annual; beginning 1990, *Quarterly Thrift Financial Aggregate*.

No. 807. Savings Institutions (SAIF-Insured)—Selected Financial Items, by State and Other Areas: 1991

[See headnote, table 806]

DIVISION AND STATE	Noncurrent real estate loans [1] (percent of total)	Net income after taxes (mil. dol.)	Return on assets [2] (percent)	DIVISION AND STATE	Noncurrent real estate loans [1] (percent of total)	Net income after taxes (mil. dol.)	Return on assets [2] (percent)
Total	3.46	-2,450	-0.24	WV	1.60	4	0.21
				NC....	2.02	41	0.21
U.S....	(NA)	-2,473	(NA)	SC....	2.08	43	0.39
N.E.	(NA)	-369	(NA)	GA....	2.02	21	0.12
ME.....	2.81	-1	-1.35	FL.....	4.27	-234	-0.43
NH....	3.57	-28	-1.54	**E.S.C.**	(NA)	-24	(NA)
VT.....	3.52	-10	-0.22	KY.....	1.04	45	0.59
MA....	4.13	-158	-3.35	TN	3.94	1	0.01
RI	8.00	-136	-5.18	AL.....	4.05	-39	-0.54
CT.....	4.45	-36	-1.70	MS....	3.05	-31	-0.97
M.A.	(NA)	-730	(NA)	**W.S.C**	(NA)	-1,270	(NA)
NY	5.59	-173	-0.38	AR....	2.04	-48	-1.51
NJ	5.74	-387	-0.98	LA	6.45	-311	-3.41
PA.....	3.80	-170	-0.51	OK....	4.39	24	0.34
E.N.C	(NA)	699	(NA)	TX	4.53	-935	-1.49
OH....	1.77	90	0.20	**Mt.**	(NA)	-137	(NA)
IN	1.12	112	0.84	MT....	0.67	10	0.83
IL......	1.60	260	0.52	ID	2.93	4	0.60
MI	1.37	145	0.46	WY	3.83	4	0.46
WI	0.79	92	0.52	CO....	1.96	12	0.13
W.N.C	(NA)	14	(NA)	NM....	3.25	1	0.05
MN....	0.97	27	0.39	AZ....	14.40	-118	-9.94
IA	3.09	12	0.21	UT.....	5.19	20	0.58
MO	6.21	-169	-0.95	NV....	2.47	-70	-1.65
ND....	2.16	62	1.18	**Pac.**	(NA)	-87	(NA)
SD....	3.32	-3	-0.27	WA	2.29	147	0.91
NE	1.06	64	0.75	OR....	2.49	-51	-1.26
KS....	0.96	21	0.14	CA....	3.59	-249	-0.08
S.A.	(NA)	-569	(NA)	AK....	0.53	-2	-2.01
DE....	2.59	18	2.96	HI	0.66	68	0.92
MD....	3.94	-62	-0.29				
DC....	2.36	1	0.19	PR ...	6.11	20	0.36
VA....	7.90	-401	-1.57	GU ...	1.84	3	2.31

NA Not available.   [1] As percent of total loan amount. Covers mortgage and nonmortgage loans that are past due 90 days or more and still accruing interest, and loans reported as nonaccrual.   [2] Net income after taxes as a percent of average assets.

Source: U.S. Office of Thrift Supervision, *Quarterly Thrift Financial Aggregates*.

No. 808. Federal and State-Chartered Credit Unions—Summary: 1980 to 1991

[Except as noted, as of **December 31**. Federal data include District of Columbia, Puerto Rico, Canal Zone, Guam, and Virgin Islands. Excludes State-insured, privately-insured and noninsured State-chartered credit unions and corporate central credit unions which have mainly other credit unions as members. See also *Historical Statistics, Colonial Times to 1970*, series X 864-878]

YEAR	OPERATING CREDIT UNIONS		Number of failed institu-tions [1]	MEMBERS (1,000)		ASSETS (mil. dol.)		LOANS OUTSTANDING (mil. dol.)		SAVINGS (mil. dol.)	
	Federal	State		Federal	State	Federal	State	Federal	State	Federal	State
1980....	12,440	4,910	239	24,519	12,338	40,092	20,870	26,350	14,582	36,263	18,469
1985....	10,125	4,920	94	29,579	15,689	78,188	41,525	48,241	26,168	71,616	37,917
1986....	9,758	4,935	94	31,041	17,363	95,484	52,244	55,305	30,834	87,954	48,097
1987....	9,401	4,934	88	32,067	17,999	105,190	56,972	64,104	35,436	96,346	52,083
1988....	9,118	4,760	85	34,438	18,519	114,565	60,740	73,766	39,977	104,431	55,217
1989....	8,821	4,550	114	35,612	18,858	120,666	63,175	80,272	42,373	109,653	57,658
1990....	8,511	4,349	164	36,241	19,454	130,073	68,133	83,029	44,102	117,892	62,082
1991....	8,229	4,731	130	37,081	21,619	143,940	83,133	84,150	49,268	130,164	75,626

[1] A failed institution is defined as a credit union which has ceased operation because it was involuntarily liquidated or merged with assistance from the National Credit Union Share Insurance Fund. For year ending September 30.

Source: National Credit Union Administration, *Annual Report of the National Credit Union Administration*, and unpublished data.

No. 809. Mortgage Debt Outstanding, by Type of Property and Holder: 1980 to 1991

[In billions of dollars. As of **Dec. 31**. Includes Puerto Rico and Guam. See also *Historical Statistics, Colonial Times to 1970*, series N 273 and N 276]

TYPE OF PROPERTY AND HOLDER	1980	1982	1983	1984	1985	1986	1987	1988	1989	1990	1991
Mortgage debt, total...........	1,460	1,638	1,825	2,051	2,303	2,634	2,990	3,288	3,575	3,798	3,919
Residential nonfarm	1,107	1,226	1,359	1,520	1,716	1,981	2,244	2,505	2,742	2,955	3,087
One- to four-family homes.......	965	1,080	1,198	1,334	1,501	1,724	1,964	2,208	2,435	2,645	2,778
Savings institutions	487	458	482	529	554	559	602	672	669	600	538
Mortgage pools or trusts [1]	125	201	271	322	407	553	702	790	921	1,082	1,235
Commercial banks	160	174	183	196	213	236	276	334	390	456	487
Individuals and others [2]	113	153	161	175	206	235	247	267	300	329	327
Federal and related agencies	61	78	87	98	110	127	124	134	143	165	180
Life insurance companies.......	18	17	15	14	12	13	13	11	12	13	12
Five or more units	142	146	161	185	214	257	280	297	307	310	309
Commercial.....................	255	301	352	419	482	556	659	698	749	759	750
Farm	97	111	114	112	106	96	88	85	84	84	83
TYPE OF HOLDER											
Savings institutions	603	578	627	710	760	778	860	925	910	802	705
Commercial banks	263	301	331	379	429	503	592	674	767	845	876
Life insurance companies.............	131	142	151	157	172	194	212	233	254	268	265
Individuals and others [2]	203	253	271	296	341	393	414	444	487	522	527
Mortgage pools or trusts [1]	146	224	297	351	439	565	718	812	947	1,111	1,263
Government National Mortgage Assoc ...	94	119	160	180	212	263	318	341	368	404	425
Federal Home Loan Mortgage Corp	17	43	58	71	100	171	213	226	273	316	359
Federal National Mortgage Association ...	-	14	25	36	55	97	140	178	228	300	372
Federal and related agencies	115	139	148	159	167	204	193	201	209	251	283

- Represents zero. [1] Outstanding principal balances of mortgage pools backing securities insured or guaranteed by the agency indicated. Includes other pools not shown separately. [2] Includes mortgage companies, real estate investment trusts, State and local retirement funds, noninsured pension funds, State and local credit agencies, credit unions, and finance companies.

Source: Board of Governors of the Federal Reserve System, *Federal Reserve Bulletin*, monthly.

No. 810. Volume of Long-Term Mortgage Loans Originated, by Type of Property, 1980 to 1991, and by Lender, 1991

[In billions of dollars. Covers credit extended in primary mortgage markets for financing real estate acquisitions]

TYPE OF PROPERTY	1980	1984	1985	1986	1987	1988	1989	1990	1991, BY LENDER				
									Total [1]	Commercial banks	Mortgage companies	Savings and loan	Life insurance companies
Loans, total	197.2	319.2	430.0	706.4	729.4	673.6	642.3	711.9	827.2	330.9	300.2	131.9	29.1
1-4 unit family home ..	133.8	203.7	289.8	499.4	507.2	446.3	452.9	458.4	596.0	153.3	297.9	121.9	0.6
New units	49.1	53.7	59.0	72.5	79.0	85.2	90.4	110.7	119.4	50.4	51.6	13.8	0.1
Existing units	84.6	150.0	230.8	426.9	428.2	361.1	362.5	347.8	476.6	103.0	246.3	108.1	0.4
Multifamily residential ..	12.5	27.6	31.9	49.9	45.1	38.2	31.1	32.5	25.5	12.2	2.0	6.3	1.6
New units	8.6	11.1	10.6	15.3	14.1	9.0	8.3	6.4	6.1	3.0	0.1	0.4	0.4
Existing units	3.9	16.4	21.3	34.6	31.0	29.2	22.8	26.0	19.4	9.1	1.9	5.9	1.2
Nonresidential	35.9	77.3	99.4	147.4	168.7	181.6	150.0	209.5	194.6	157.5	0.3	3.7	26.3
Farm properties.....	15.0	10.5	9.0	9.8	8.4	7.6	8.3	11.5	11.1	7.9	-	-	0.7

- Represents zero. [1] Includes other lenders not shown separately.
Source: U.S. Dept. of Housing and Urban Development, monthly and quarterly press releases based on the Survey of Mortgage Lending Activity.

No. 811. Characteristics of Conventional First Mortgage Loans for Purchase of Single-Family Homes: 1980 to 1992

[In percent, except as indicated. Annual averages. Refers to loans originated directly by Savings Association Insurance Fund-insured savings institutions, mortgage bankers, commercial banks, and Federal Deposit Insurance Corporation-insured savings banks. Excludes interim construction loans, refinancing loans, junior liens, and federally underwritten loans]

LOAN CHARACTERISTICS	1980	1982	1983	1984	1985	1986	1987	1988	1989	1990	1991	1992
NEW HOMES												
Contract interest rate, [1] all loans	12.3	14.5	12.1	11.9	11.1	9.7	8.9	8.8	9.8	9.7	9.0	8.0
Fixed-rate loans.	(NA)	14.4	12.3	12.5	11.9	10.0	9.5	10.0	10.2	10.1	9.3	8.3
Adjustable-rate loans [2]	(NA)	14.7	11.8	11.5	10.4	9.0	8.2	8.1	9.0	8.9	8.1	6.6
Initial fees, charges [3]	2.09	2.96	2.39	2.66	2.52	2.48	2.26	2.19	2.08	1.98	1.72	1.59
Effective interest rate, [4] all loans	12.7	15.1	12.6	12.4	11.6	10.2	9.3	9.2	10.1	10.1	9.3	8.2
Fixed-rate loans.	(NA)	14.9	12.7	13.0	12.4	10.5	9.9	10.4	10.6	10.4	9.6	8.5
Adjustable-rate loans [2]	(NA)	15.4	12.3	12.0	10.8	9.4	8.5	8.5	9.3	9.2	8.4	6.9
Term to maturity (years)	28.1	27.5	26.7	27.8	27.0	26.8	27.8	28.0	28.1	27.3	26.8	25.6
Purchase price ($1,000)	83.2	94.1	93.9	96.8	105.0	119.8	137.2	150.5	160.1	154.1	155.2	158.1
Loan to price ratio.	73.2	76.6	77.3	78.6	77.1	75.3	75.2	75.6	74.6	74.9	75.0	76.6
Percent of number of loans with adjustable rates.	(NA)	41	37	59	51	27	41	19	35	31	25	17
EXISTING HOMES												
Contract interest rate, [1] all loans	12.5	14.8	12.3	12.0	11.2	9.8	8.9	9.0	9.8	9.8	9.1	7.8
Fixed-rate loans.	(NA)	14.8	12.6	12.7	11.9	10.1	9.5	10.1	10.2	10.1	9.4	8.2
Adjustable-rate loans [2]	(NA)	14.7	11.9	11.6	10.5	9.1	8.2	8.2	9.2	8.9	8.0	6.3
Initial fees, charges [3]	1.91	2.55	2.40	2.54	2.50	2.13	2.02	1.88	1.79	1.74	1.54	1.58
Effective interest rate, [4] all loans	12.9	15.3	12.8	12.5	11.6	10.2	9.3	9.3	10.1	10.1	9.3	8.1
Fixed-rate loans.	(NA)	15.4	13.0	13.2	12.4	10.5	9.9	10.4	10.5	10.4	9.7	8.5
Adjustable-rate loans [2]	(NA)	15.3	12.3	12.1	10.9	9.4	8.5	8.5	9.4	9.2	8.2	6.5
Term to maturity (years)	26.9	24.9	25.9	26.5	25.5	25.4	26.6	27.7	27.7	27.0	26.5	25.4
Purchase price ($1,000)	68.3	70.7	79.3	82.2	92.7	108.5	117.7	126.6	138.4	140.3	145.8	144.1
Loan to price ratio.	73.5	71.9	74.3	76.8	75.7	73.9	75.4	76.4	75.2	74.9	74.4	76.5
Percent of number of loans with adjustable rates.	(NA)	39	41	64	50	31	44	24	37	27	22	21

NA Not available. [1] Initial interest rate paid by the borrower as specified in the loan contract. [2] Loans with a contractual provision for periodic adjustments in the contract interest rate. [3] Includes all fees, commissions, discounts and "points" paid by the borrower, or seller, in order to obtain the loan. Excludes those charges for mortgage, credit, life or property insurance; for property transfer; and for title search and insurance. [4] Contract interest rate plus fees and charges amortized over a 10-year period.

Source: U.S. Federal Housing Finance Board, annual and monthly press releases.

No. 812. Mortgage Delinquency and Foreclosure Rates and Private Mortgage Insurance: 1980 to 1992

[In percent, except as indicated. Covers one- to four-family residential nonfarm mortgage loans]

ITEM	1980	1985	1986	1987	1988	1989	1990	1991	1992
Number of mortgage loans outstanding (1,000)	30,033	34,316	36,439	37,232	41,603	43,836	47,002	48,260	(NA)
Delinquency rates: [1]									
Total.	5.0	5.8	5.6	5.0	4.8	4.8	4.7	5.0	4.6
Conventional loans.	3.1	4.0	3.8	3.2	2.9	3.1	3.0	3.3	3.0
VA loans.	5.3	6.6	6.6	6.2	6.2	6.4	6.4	6.8	6.5
FHA loans	6.6	7.5	7.2	6.6	6.6	6.7	6.7	7.3	7.1
Foreclosure rates: [2]									
Total.	0.5	1.0	1.2	1.3	1.2	1.0	0.9	1.0	1.0
Conventional loans.	0.2	0.7	0.8	0.8	0.7	0.6	0.7	0.8	0.8
VA loans.	0.6	1.1	1.4	1.6	1.6	1.3	1.2	1.3	1.3
FHA loans	0.7	1.3	1.5	1.8	1.8	1.4	1.3	1.4	1.4
PRIVATE MORTGAGE INSURANCE [3]									
Number of insured loans originated (1,000) .	398	722	612	525	445	384	383	533	(NA)
Insured mortgage originations (bil. dol.)	19.3	49.9	47.4	45.2	40.9	39.1	40.9	57.7	(NA)
Claims paid by private mortgage insurers (mil. dol.)	59	971	1,262	1,574	992	834	597	555	(NA)

NA Not available. [1] Number of loans delinquent 30 days or more as percentage of mortgage loans serviced in survey. Annual average of quarterly figures. [2] Percentage of loans in the foreclosure process at yearend, not seasonally adjusted. [3] Source: Mortgage Insurance Companies of America, Washington, DC, *Factbook and Membership Directory*, annual and unpublished data.

No. 813. Mortgage Delinquency Rates, by Division: 1980 to 1992

[In percent. Annual average of quarterly figures. Covers one- to four-family residential nonfarm mortgage loans. Represents number of loans delinquent 30 days or more as percentage of loans serviced in survey. Excludes loans in foreclosure. For composition of divisions, see table 31]

YEAR	U.S., total	New England	Middle Atlantic	East North Central	West North Central	South Atlantic	East South Central	West South Central	Moun-tain	Pacific
1980	4.97	3.52	6.23	6.29	4.60	4.55	5.32	4.12	4.40	4.29
1985	5.83	4.22	6.31	7.18	4.96	5.11	5.98	6.54	6.10	4.96
1990	4.66	3.53	4.54	5.06	3.82	4.80	6.33	6.45	5.10	3.21
1991	5.02	4.14	5.05	5.20	3.99	5.53	6.70	6.41	5.01	3.45
1992	4.57	4.03	4.86	4.56	3.34	5.05	5.93	5.50	4.12	3.45

Source of tables 812 and 813: Except as noted, Mortgage Bankers Association of America, Washington, DC, *National Delinquency Survey*, quarterly.

No. 814. Home Equity Loans—Insured Domestic Commercial Banks Offering Loans and Home Equity Balances, 1987 to 1991, and by Asset-Size of Bank, 1991

[As of December 31]

ITEM	1987	1988	1989	1990	1991 Total	1991 Less than $100 million	1991 $100 to $249 million	1991 $250 to $999 million	1991 $1 billion or more
Banks offering home equity loans	4,346	4,707	4,863	5,053	5,174	2,849	1,302	698	325
Percent of all commercial banks	32	36	38	41	43	32	68	85	90
Home equity debt outstanding (bil. dol.)	29	40	51	61	70	3	5	10	53
Home equity debt as percent of consumer loans plus home equity debt:									
All commercial banks	8	10	12	14	16	9	14	17	17
Banks offering home equity loans	10	12	15	17	19	19	19	19	19
Home equity debt as percent of consumer loans plus all loans secured by homes:									
All commercial banks	5	6	7	8	9	4	6	9	10
Banks offering home equity loans	6	8	9	9	10	8	8	10	11

Source: Board of Governors of the Federal Reserve System, *Domestic Offices, Commercial Bank Assets and Liabilities, Consolidated Report of Condition*, quarterly.

No. 815. Consumer Installment Credit Outstanding: 1980 to 1992

[In billions of dollars. Estimated amounts of seasonally adjusted credit outstanding as of end of year. See also *Historical Statistics, Colonial Times to 1970*, series X 551-560]

TYPE OF CREDIT	1980	1981	1982	1983	1984	1985	1986	1987	1988	1989	1990	1991	1992
Installment credit outstanding. . .	298.2	311.3	325.8	369.0	442.6	517.7	572.0	608.7	663.0	724.4	738.8	733.5	741.1
Automobile paper	112.0	119.0	125.9	143.6	173.6	210.2	247.8	266.3	285.5	292.5	284.7	260.9	259.6
Revolving [1]	55.1	61.1	66.5	79.1	100.3	121.8	135.8	153.1	174.3	198.5	222.6	243.6	254.3
Other	131.1	131.2	133.4	146.3	168.8	185.7	188.4	189.3	203.2	233.3	231.5	229.0	227.2

[1] Consists mainly of outstanding balances on credit card accounts, but also includes borrowing under check credit and overdraft plans, and unsecured personal lines of credit.

No. 816. Consumer Credit—Installment Credit Finance Rates: 1980 to 1992

[In percent. Annual averages]

TYPE OF CREDIT	1980	1982	1983	1984	1985	1986	1987	1988	1989	1990	1991	1992
Commercial banks:												
New automobiles (48 months) [1]	14.30	16.83	13.92	13.71	12.91	11.33	10.46	10.85	12.07	11.78	11.14	9.29
Mobile homes (120 months) [1]	14.99	18.05	14.96	15.58	14.96	14.00	13.38	13.54	14.11	14.02	13.70	12.67
Other consumer goods (24 months) . .	15.47	18.65	16.68	16.47	15.94	14.83	14.23	14.68	15.44	15.46	15.18	14.04
Credit-card plans	17.31	18.51	18.78	18.77	18.69	18.26	17.93	17.79	18.02	18.17	18.23	17.78
Finance companies:												
New automobiles.	14.82	16.15	12.58	14.62	11.98	9.44	10.73	12.60	12.62	12.54	12.41	9.93
Used automobiles	19.10	20.75	18.74	17.85	17.59	15.95	14.61	15.11	16.18	15.99	15.60	13.79

[1] For 1980 and 1982, maturities were 36 months for new car loans and 84 months for mobile home loans.

Source of tables 815 and 816: Board of Governors of the Federal Reserve System, *Federal Reserve Bulletin*, monthly; and *Annual Statistical Digest*.

No. 817. Credit Cards—Holders, Numbers, Spending, and Debt, 1980 and 1991, and Projections, 2000

TYPE OF CREDIT CARD	CARDHOLDERS (mil.) 1980	CARDHOLDERS (mil.) 1991	CARDHOLDERS (mil.) 2000, proj.	NUMBER OF CARDS (mil.) 1980	NUMBER OF CARDS (mil.) 1991	NUMBER OF CARDS (mil.) 2000, proj.	CREDIT CARD SPENDING (bil. dol.) 1980	CREDIT CARD SPENDING (bil. dol.) 1991	CREDIT CARD SPENDING (bil. dol.) 2000, proj.	CREDIT CARD DEBT (bil. dol.) 1980	CREDIT CARD DEBT (bil. dol.) 1991	CREDIT CARD DEBT (bil. dol.) 2000, proj.
Total [1]	86.1	111.3	124.8	526	1,027	1,319	201.2	481.0	882.0	80.2	257.9	432.9
Bank.	63.3	79.7	90.0	111	221	296	52.9	260.0	493.6	25.0	166.6	278.7
Oil company.	68.5	79.9	91.1	110	122	131	28.9	26.5	53.5	2.2	3.4	6.9
Phone.	(NA)	98.0	111.6	(NA)	145	195	(NA)	12.4	23.1	(NA)	1.0	2.0
Retail store	83.0	95.0	108.9	277	463	610	74.4	76.4	135.2	47.3	51.9	78.7
Travel and entertainment	10.5	23.1	26.4	10	28	36	21.2	89.4	146.6	2.7	20.2	33.5
Other [2]	13.4	7.1	7.3	19	48	52	23.8	21.3	37.9	3.0	14.9	33.2

NA Not available. [1] Cardholders may hold more than one type of card. [2] Includes airline, automobile rental, Discover (except for cardholders), hotel, motel, and other miscellaneous credit cards.

Source: HSN Consultants Inc., Santa Monica, CA, *The Nilson Report*, bimonthly. (Copyright used by permission.)

No. 818. Delinquency Rates on Bank Installment Loans, by Type of Loan: 1980 to 1992

[In percent, except as indicated. As of end of year; seasonally adjusted, except as noted. Number of loans having an installment past due for 30 days or more as a percentage of total installment loans outstanding]

TYPE OF CREDIT	1980	1983	1984	1985	1986	1987	1988	1989	1990	1991	1992
DELINQUENCY RATES											
Closed-end installment loans, total	2.82	1.94	2.09	2.32	2.26	2.47	2.49	2.64	2.57	2.58	2.43
Personal loans [1]	3.53	2.84	3.16	3.63	3.11	3.66	3.34	3.52	3.37	2.95	3.18
Automobile, direct loans [2]	1.81	1.53	1.47	1.64	1.80	1.59	1.92	2.03	2.22	2.14	2.08
Automobile, indirect loans [3]	2.29	1.50	1.77	2.02	2.09	2.20	2.46	2.61	2.59	2.66	2.33
Property improvement [4]	1.93	2.14	2.00	1.91	1.77	1.88	2.06	2.25	2.30	2.38	2.18
Home equity and second mortgage loans [5] . .	(NA)	1.94	1.77	2.06	1.85	2.01	1.86	1.85	1.45	2.06	1.89
Mobile home loans	3.14	2.44	2.56	2.39	3.04	2.57	3.12	2.51	3.03	2.86	4.02
Recreational vehicle loans	1.94	1.58	1.87	1.84	1.92	1.99	2.07	2.24	2.63	2.25	2.27
Marine financing [5]	(NA)	(NA)	(NA)	(NA)	(NA)	(NA)	(NA)	(NA)	(NA)	(NA)	2.52
Bank card loans.	2.72	2.08	2.81	2.95	3.15	2.33	2.19	2.24	2.86	3.29	2.93
Revolving credit loans.	2.70	1.44	1.50	1.96	1.53	2.33	2.87	2.92	3.00	2.75	2.63
Home equity lines of credit loans (open-end) [5] .	(NA)	(NA)	(NA)	(NA)	(NA)	0.74	0.68	0.78	0.85	0.88	0.85
REPOSSESSIONS PER 1,000 LOANS OUTSTANDING											
Mobile home	1.57	1.23	1.29	1.21	2.50	1.58	1.77	1.63	1.19	1.62	1.30
Automobile, direct loans [2]	1.10	0.70	0.72	1.11	1.15	0.86	1.03	1.03	1.75	1.17	0.92
Automobile, indirect loans [3]	2.75	1.56	1.58	2.08	1.95	2.04	1.86	1.70	1.61	2.07	1.47
Marine financing [5]	(NA)	(NA)	(NA)	(NA)	(NA)	(NA)	(NA)	(NA)	(NA)	(NA)	1.21

NA Not available.   [1] Beginning 1983, includes home appliance loans.   [2] Made directly by bank's lending function.   [3] Made by automobile dealerships; loans in bank's portfolio.   [4] Beginning 1983, own plan and FHA Title I loans.   [5] Seasonally not adjusted.

Source: American Bankers Association, Washington, DC, *Consumer Credit Delinquency Bulletin*, quarterly.

No. 819. Electronic Funds Transfer Volume: 1980 to 1992

[Electronic funds transfer cover automated teller machine (ATM) transactions and transactions at point-of-sale (POS) terminals. Point-of-sale terminals are electronic terminals in retail stores that allow a customer to pay for goods through a direct debit to a customer's account at the bank]

ITEM	Unit	1980	1985	1986	1987	1988	1989	1990	1991	1992
Total number of transactions	**Million . .**	(NA)	3,579	3,661	4,108	4,581	5,274	5,942	6,642	7,537
ATM transactions	Million . .	(NA)	3,565	3,625	4,048	4,480	5,116	5,751	6,418	7,206
POS transactions	Million . .	(NA)	14	36	60	92	157	191	223	289
ATM terminals, total	**Number .**	18,500	60,000	64,000	68,000	72,492	75,632	80,156	83,545	87,330
Monthly transactions per terminal . .	Number .	5,405	4,951	4,720	4,962	5,151	5,638	5,980	6,403	6,876
Shared terminals	Number .	(NA)	35,500	48,580	55,000	65,062	70,116	75,296	79,559	84,713
Proprietary terminals	Number .	(NA)	24,500	15,420	13,000	7,430	5,516	4,860	3,986	2,617
POS terminals, total	**Number .**	(NA)	(NA)	(NA)	(NA)	(NA)	(NA)	53,056	78,071	95,163
Grocery stores	Number .	(NA)	(NA)	(NA)	(NA)	(NA)	(NA)	21,538	31,795	45,123
Gasoline service stations	Number .	(NA)	(NA)	(NA)	(NA)	(NA)	(NA)	18,714	21,476	26,283
Specialty stores	Number .	(NA)	(NA)	(NA)	(NA)	(NA)	(NA)	10,079	13,434	16,621
Convenience stores	Number .	(NA)	(NA)	(NA)	(NA)	(NA)	(NA)	2,725	3,091	7,136

NA Not available.

Source: Electronic Funds Transfer Association, Herndon, VA, unpublished data. Based on data supplied by Bank Network News and POS News.

No. 820. Automated Teller Machine (ATM's) Usage: 1990

[In percent, except as indicated. Based on a survey of households and subject to sampling variability; for details, contact source]

ITEM	Total	AGE OF HOUSEHOLDER	Percent distribution of users	HOUSEHOLD INCOME	Percent distribution of users
Households with ATM card (mil.)	58	Total	100	Total	100
Percent of all households.	62	Under 25 years old	7	Less than $15,000.	14
Percent of ATM households using card at least some of the time	79	25 to 34 years old . . . . 35 to 44 years old	31 27	$15,000 to $24,900 . . . . $25,000 to $34,900	16 18
Average number of transactions per month per household	6.3	45 to 54 years old . . . . 55 to 64 years old	15 11	$35,000 to $49,900	22
Average number of cash withdrawals per month.	4.5	65 to 74 years old . . . . 75 years old and over . .	6 2	$50,000 to $74,999 . . . . $75,000 and over	18 11
Average amount per withdrawal	$66				

Source: Electronic Funds Transfer Association, Herndon, VA, unpublished data.

No. 821. Money Stock and Liquid Assets: 1970 to 1992

[In billions of dollars. As of December. Seasonally adjusted averages of daily figures. See *Historical Statistics, Colonial Times to 1970*, series X 410–417 for similar data]

ITEM	1970	1975	1980	1981	1982	1983	1984	1985	1986	1987	1988	1989	1990	1991	1992
M1, total	215	288	409	436	474	521	552	620	725	750	787	795	827	899	1,027
Currency	49	73	115	123	133	146	156	168	181	197	212	223	247	267	292
Travelers checks [2]	1	2	4	4	4	5	5	6	6	7	7	7	8	8	8
Demand deposits [3]	165	212	261	231	234	239	244	267	302	287	287	280	278	291	341
Other checkable deposits [4]	(Z)	1	28	78	104	132	147	180	235	259	281	285	295	334	385
M2, total	628	1,023	1,629	1,793	1,953	2,187	2,376	2,572	2,816	2,917	3,078	3,233	3,346	3,446	3,504
M1	215	288	409	436	474	521	552	620	725	750	787	795	827	899	1,027
Nontransaction components in M2 [5]	414	736	1,221	1,356	1,478	1,665	1,824	1,952	2,092	2,167	2,291	2,439	2,518	2,547	2,477
Overnight repurchase (RP) agreements and Eurodollars [6]	1	6	29	37	40	56	61	73	82	84	83	78	75	76	73
Money market funds, general purpose and broker/dealer	(Z)	3	62	151	185	139	168	177	209	223	243	317	351	364	349
Money market deposit accounts (MMDA) and savings deposits	261	389	400	344	400	685	704	815	941	938	927	891	921	1,042	1,186
Commercial banks	99	161	186	159	190	363	389	457	534	535	543	541	582	666	756
Thrift institutions	162	228	215	185	210	322	315	358	407	403	384	350	339	376	430
Small time deposits [7]	151	338	729	823	851	784	889	886	859	923	1,038	1,153	1,172	1,064	870
Commercial banks	79	142	286	348	380	351	388	386	369	393	452	535	610	601	507
Thrift institutions	72	196	442	475	471	433	501	499	490	530	586	618	562	463	363
M3, total	677	1,172	1,987	2,233	2,441	2,693	2,988	3,204	3,492	3,675	3,916	4,056	4,117	4,168	4,174
M2	628	1,023	1,629	1,793	1,953	2,187	2,376	2,572	2,816	2,917	3,078	3,233	3,346	3,446	3,504
Nontransaction components in M3 [5]	49	149	358	441	488	507	612	631	676	758	837	823	771	722	670
Large time deposits [9]	46	129	261	303	327	328	416	434	431	475	525	549	490	424	357
Commercial banks [9]	45	123	216	249	264	231	269	282	281	313	351	388	369	341	290
Thrift institutions	1	6	45	54	64	97	147	152	150	163	174	161	121	83	67
Term RP's and term Eurodollars [6] [10]	4	18	84	103	115	141	141	139	164	197	227	179	158	130	129
Money market funds, institution only	(Z)	(Z)	15	38	51	42	63	66	86	92	92	109	136	182	202
L, total	816	1,367	2,324	2,596	2,850	3,154	3,530	3,831	4,132	4,334	4,669	4,886	4,965	4,982	5,059
M3	677	1,172	1,987	2,233	2,441	2,693	2,988	3,204	3,492	3,675	3,916	4,056	4,117	4,168	4,174
Savings bonds	52	67	72	68	68	71	74	79	92	101	109	118	126	138	157
Short-term Treasury securities [11]	49	68	133	149	184	212	261	298	280	253	269	325	331	315	341
Bankers acceptances	3	11	32	40	44	45	45	42	37	44	40	40	34	23	19
Commercial paper [12]	34	48	99	105	114	133	161	208	231	261	336	347	357	338	370

Z Less than $500 million.   [1] Currency outside U.S. Treasury, Federal Reserve Banks and the vaults of depository institutions.   [2] Outstanding amount of nonbank issuers.   [3] At commercial banks and foreign-related institutions.   [4] Consists of negotiable order of withdrawal (NOW) and automatic transfer service (ATS) accounts at all depository institutions, credit union share draft balances and demand deposits at thrift institutions.   [5] This sum is seasonally adjusted as a whole.   [6] Not seasonally adjusted.   [7] Issued in amounts of less than $100,000. Includes retail repurchase agreements. Excludes individual retirement accounts (IRA's), and Keogh accounts.   [8] Issued in amounts of $100,000 or more. Excludes those booked at international banking facilities.   [9] Excludes those held by money market mutual funds, depository institutions and foreign banks and official institutions.   [10] Excludes those held by depository institutions and money market mutual funds.   [11] U.S. Treasury bills and coupons with remaining maturities of less than 12 months held by other than depository institutions, Federal Reserve banks, money market mutual funds and foreign entities.   [12] Excludes commercial paper held by money market mutual funds.

Source: Board of Governors of the Federal Reserve System, *Federal Reserve Bulletin*, monthly, and *Money Stock, Liquid Assets, and Debt Measures, Federal Reserve Statistical Release H.6*, weekly.

No. 822. Bank Debits and Deposit Turnover: 1980 to 1991

[Debits in trillions of dollars; turnover as ratio of debits to deposits. Annual averages of monthly data]

ITEM	1980	1981	1982	1983	1984	1985	1986	1987	1988	1989	1990	1991
Debits to—												
Demand deposits, all banks [1]	63.1	81.3	96.5	112.3	131.6	156.3	188.8	214.9	219.9	256.4	277.7	281.2
Major New York City banks	25.3	34.1	39.8	47.6	57.3	70.7	91.6	110.4	115.5	129.5	131.9	140.7
Other banks........	37.9	47.2	56.7	64.7	74.2	85.6	97.1	104.5	104.4	126.9	145.8	140.5
ATS/NOW accounts [2]	0.2	0.7	1.0	1.4	1.6	1.8	2.2	2.2	2.5	2.9	3.3	3.6
Money market deposit accounts	(NA)	(NA)	(NA)	0.6	0.9	1.2	1.6	1.9	2.3	2.7	2.9	2.8
Savings deposits [3]	0.7	0.7	0.7	0.5	0.4	0.4	0.4	0.5	0.5	0.5	0.6	1.4
Deposit turnover:												
All banks [1]	203	286	343	386	441	501	557	608	623	736	800	818
Major New York City banks	816	1,116	1,354	1,522	1,840	2,200	2,500	2,669	2,897	3,428	3,815	4,375
Other banks..........	135	186	225	249	278	306	322	335	333	408	467	451

NA Not available.   [1] Represents accounts of individuals, partnerships, and corporations, and of States and political subdivisions in insured commercial banks.   [2] Accounts authorized for negotiable orders of withdrawal (NOW) and accounts authorized for automatic transfer to demand deposits (ATS).   [3] Excludes ATS and NOW accounts, money market deposit accounts, and special club accounts, such as Christmas and vacation clubs.

Source: Board of Governors of the Federal Reserve System, *Federal Reserve Bulletin*, monthly, and *Annual Statistical Digest*.

No. 823. Selected Time Deposits and Other Accounts at Insured Commercial Banks— Deposits and Interest Rates: 1985 to 1992

[As of **December**. Estimates based on data collected from a sample of about 500 banks]

TYPE OF DEPOSIT	AMOUNT OUTSTANDING (bil. dol.)						ANNUAL EFFECTIVE YIELD (percent)					
	1985	1988	1989	1990	1991	1992	1985	1988	1989	1990	1991	1992
NOW accounts [1]	44.5	190.5	196.8	209.2	244.5	287.1	6.16	5.07	5.02	4.93	3.76	2.33
Savings deposits ....;	(NA)	532.3	532.5	571.5	652.5	738.2	(NA)	5.82	6.10	5.83	4.30	2.88
Interest-bearing time deposits: [2]												
7-91 day	26.3	31.2	45.0	50.2	46.5	38.5	7.31	7.33	7.64	6.94	4.18	2.90
92-182 day	147.8	136.3	152.6	167.6	158.0	127.6	7.50	7.84	7.83	7.19	4.42	3.16
183 day-1 year	66.1	128.0	177.2	220.8	209.7	163.6	7.77	8.19	7.86	7.33	4.59	3.37
1-2½ year..............	81.2	107.2	125.3	150.0	172.3	152.8	8.24	8.30	7.88	7.43	4.95	3.89
2½ year or more	115.4	133.0	128.8	138.1	157.3	169.7	8.73	8.39	7.86	7.52	5.55	4.77
All IRA and Keogh Plan deposits.	59.4	94.0	109.1	131.2	147.9	147.2	(NA)	(NA)	(NA)	(NA)	(NA)	(NA)

NA Not available.   [1] Negotiable order of withdrawal accounts containing an agreement between depositor and depository such that some or all funds deposited are eligible to earn more than 5.25 percent. As of January 1, 1986, interest rate ceilings were removed from all NOW accounts. Beginning with the December 1988 data the NOW accounts category includes all NOW accounts, including those accounts which were subject to a 5.25 percent regulatory interest rate restriction prior to January 1, 1986. Estimates for NOW accounts beginning in December 1988 are based on reports of deposits.   [2] All interest-bearing time deposits and open account time deposits with balances of less than $100,000, including those held in IRA's and Keogh Plan deposits.

Source: Board of Governors of the Federal Reserve System, *Money Stock, Liquid Assets, and Debt Measures, Federal Reserve Statistical Release H.6*, Special Supplementary Table, Monthly Survey of Selected Deposits, monthly.

No. 824. Commercial Paper Outstanding, by Type of Company: 1980 to 1992

[In billions of dollars. As of **December 31**. Seasonally adjusted. Commercial paper is an unsecured promissory note having a fixed maturity of no more than 270 days]

TYPE OF COMPANY	1980	1983	1984	1985	1986	1987	1988	1989	1990	1991	1992
All issuers . . . .,.	124.4	187.7	237.6	298.8	330.0	359.0	458.5	525.8	561.1	530.3	547.5
Financial companies [1]	87.7	141.0	167.0	213.8	252.9	277.1	354.7	394.6	415.0	397.6	400.2
Dealer-placed paper [2]	19.9	44.8	56.5	78.4	101.1	102.7	159.8	183.6	215.1	214.4	227.6
Directly-placed paper [3]	67.8	96.2	110.5	135.3	151.8	174.3	194.9	210.9	199.8	183.2	172.6
Nonfinancial companies [4]	36.7	46.7	70.6	85.0	77.1	81.9	103.8	131.3	146.2	132.7	147.3

[1] Institutions engaged primarily in activities such as, but not limited to, commercial, savings, and mortgage banking; sales, personal, and mortgage financing; factoring, finance leasing, and other business lending; insurance underwriting; and other investment activities.   [2] Includes all financial company paper sold by dealers in the open market.   [3] As reported by financial companies that place their paper directly with investors.   [4] Includes public utilities and firms engaged primarily in such activities as communications, construction, manufacturing, mining, wholesale and retail trade, transportation, and services.

No. 825. Federal Reserve Bank of New York—Discount Rates: 1980 to 1993

[**Percent per year.** Rates for short-term adjustment credit. For rates applicable to other types of discount window credit, see source. See also *Historical Statistics, Colonial Times to 1970*, series X 454-455]

EFFECTIVE DATE	Rate	EFFECTIVE DATE	Rate	EFFECTIVE DATE	Rate	EFFECTIVE DATE	Rate
1980: [1] Feb. 15.....	13	Dec. 4........	12	Nov. 21......	8½	**1989:** Feb. 24......	7
May 30	12	**1982:** July 20	11½	Dec. 24......	8	**1990:** Dec. 19......	6½
June 13......	11	Aug. 2........	11	**1985:** May 20	7½	**1991:** Feb. 1........	6
July 28	10	Aug. 16......	10½	**1986:** March 7......	7	April 30......	5½
Sept. 26	11	Aug. 27......	10	April 21......	6½	Sept. 13	5
Nov. 17......	12	Oct. 12	9½	July 11	6	Nov. 6........	4½
Dec. 5.......	13	Nov. 22......	9	Aug. 21......	5½	Dec. 20......	3½
1981: [1] May 5......	14	Dec. 15......	8½	**1987:** Sept. 4	6	**1992:** July 2	3
Nov. 2.......	13	**1984:** April 9......	9	**1988:** Aug. 9.......	6½	In effect, **Jan. 31, '93**.	3

[1] The discount rates for 1980 and 1981 do not include the surcharge applied to frequent borrowings by large institutions. The surcharge reached 3 percent in 1980 and 4 percent in 1981. Surcharge was eliminated in Nov. 1981.

Source of tables 824 and 825: Board of Governors of the Federal Reserve System, *Federal Reserve Bulletin*, monthly, and *Annual Statistical Digest*.

No. 826. Money Market Interest Rates and Mortgage Rates: 1970 to 1992

[Percent per year. Annual averages of monthly data, except as indicated. See also *Historical Statistics, Colonial Times to 1970*, series X 444-453]

TYPE	1970	1975	1979	1980	1981	1982	1983	1984	1985	1986	1987	1988	1989	1990	1991	1992
Federal funds, effective rate [1][2]	7.17	5.82	11.19	13.35	16.39	12.24	9.09	10.23	8.10	6.80	6.66	7.57	9.21	8.10	5.69	3.52
Commercial paper, 3-month [1][2]	(NA)	6.25	10.97	12.61	15.34	11.90	8.88	10.12	7.95	6.49	6.82	7.66	8.99	8.06	5.87	3.75
Prime rate charged by banks	7.91	7.86	12.67	15.26	18.87	14.85	10.79	12.04	9.93	8.33	8.21	9.32	10.87	10.01	8.46	6.25
Eurodollar deposits, 3-month [2][3]	8.52	7.03	11.96	14.00	16.79	13.12	9.57	10.75	8.27	6.70	7.07	7.85	9.16	8.16	5.86	3.70
Finance paper, 3-month [2][3][4]	7.18	6.15	10.47	11.49	14.08	11.23	8.70	9.73	7.77	6.38	6.54	7.38	8.72	7.87	5.71	3.65
Bankers acceptances, 90-day [2][4]	7.23	6.29	10.99	12.67	15.34	11.89	8.91	10.17	7.91	6.38	6.75	7.56	8.87	7.93	5.70	3.62
Large negotiable CD's, 3-month, secondary market [5]	7.56	6.44	11.22	13.07	15.91	12.27	9.07	10.37	8.05	6.52	6.86	7.73	9.09	8.15	5.83	3.68
Taxable money market funds [5]	(NA)	6.36	11.08	12.68	16.82	12.23	8.58	10.04	7.71	6.26	6.12	7.11	8.87	7.82	5.71	3.37
Certificates of deposit (CD's): [6]																
6-month	(NA)	(NA)	(NA)	(NA)	(NA)	(NA)	(NA)	9.99	7.83	6.51	6.47	7.18	8.34	7.35	5.67	3.46
1-year	(NA)	(NA)	(NA)	(NA)	(NA)	(NA)	(NA)	10.37	8.29	6.75	6.77	7.47	8.41	7.42	5.88	3.72
2½-year	(NA)	(NA)	(NA)	(NA)	(NA)	(NA)	10.06	10.82	9.00	7.13	7.16	7.77	8.33	7.52	6.29	4.47
5-year	(NA)	(NA)	(NA)	(NA)	(NA)	(NA)	(NA)	11.25	9.66	7.60	7.66	8.11	8.30	7.71	6.83	5.62
U.S. Government securities: [7]																
3-month Treasury bill	6.39	5.78	10.07	11.39	14.04	10.60	8.62	9.54	7.47	5.97	5.78	6.67	8.11	7.50	5.38	3.43
6-month Treasury bill	6.51	6.09	10.06	11.32	13.81	11.06	8.74	9.78	7.65	6.02	6.03	6.91	8.03	7.46	5.44	3.54
1-year Treasury bill	6.49	6.28	9.75	10.85	13.16	11.07	8.80	9.94	7.81	6.07	6.33	7.13	7.92	7.35	5.52	3.71
Home mortgages: [8]																
HUD series:																
FHA insured, secondary market [9]	9.02	9.19	10.87	13.44	16.31	15.30	13.11	13.81	12.24	9.91	10.16	10.49	10.24	10.17	9.25	8.46
Conventional, new-home [10][11]	8.52	9.10	11.15	13.95	16.52	15.79	13.43	13.80	12.28	10.07	10.17	10.30	10.21	10.08	9.20	8.43
Conventional, existing-home [10]	8.56	9.14	11.16	13.95	16.55	15.82	13.44	13.81	12.29	10.09	10.31	10.31	10.22	10.08	9.20	8.43
Conventional, 15 yr. fixed [6]	(NA)	(NA)	(NA)	(NA)	(NA)	(NA)	(NA)	(NA)	(NA)	10.05	10.04	10.14	10.05	9.67	8.76	7.80
Conventional, 30 yr. fixed [6]	(NA)	(NA)	(NA)	(NA)	(NA)	(NA)	(NA)	(NA)	(NA)	10.39	10.40	10.38	10.26	10.01	9.09	8.27

NA Not available.　[1] Based on daily offering rates of dealers.　[2] Yields are quoted on a bank-discount basis, rather than an investment yield basis (which would give a higher figure).　[3] Placed directly; averages of daily offering rates quoted by finance companies.　[4] Based on representative closing yields. From Jan. 1, 1981, rates of top-rated banks only.　[5] 12 month return for period ending December 31. Source: IBC/Donoghue, Inc., Ashland, MA, *IBC's Money Market Insight*, monthly (copyright).　[6] Annual averages. Source: Financial Rates, Inc., North Palm Beach, FL, *Bank Rate Monitor*, weekly (copyright).　[7] Averages based on daily closing bid yields in secondary market, bank discount basis.　[8] HUD=Housing and Urban Development.　[9] Averages based on quotations for 1 day each month as compiled by FHA.　[10] Primary market.　[11] Average contract rates on new commitments.

Source: Except as noted, Board of Governors of the Federal Reserve System, *Federal Reserve Bulletin*, monthly, and *Annual Statistical Digest*.

No. 827. Security Prices: 1970 to 1992

[Annual averages of daily figures, except as noted. See also Historical Statistics, Colonial Times to 1970, series X 492-498]

CLASS OR ITEM	1970	1980	1981	1982	1983	1984	1985	1986	1987	1988	1989	1990	1991	1992
Bond prices (dollars per $100 bond):														
Standard & Poor's Municipal [1] [2]	72.3	57.4	43.2	41.8	51.4	47.9	53.0	65.1	62.7	62.0	66.1	66.0	68.8	73.1
Dow Jones and Co., Inc.:[3]														
Yearly high	69.7	76.6	65.8	71.5	77.8	72.9	83.7	93.7	95.5	91.3	94.2	93.0	98.9	103.9
Yearly low	64.4	61.0	55.0	55.7	69.4	64.8	72.3	83.7	81.3	86.9	87.4	88.4	91.3	98.4
Stock prices:														
Standard & Poor's common index (500 stocks) (1941-43=10)[4]														
Composite	83.2	118.7	128.0	119.7	160.4	160.5	186.8	236.3	268.8	265.9	323.1	335.0	376.2	415.8
Industrial	91.3	134.5	144.2	133.6	180.5	181.3	207.8	262.2	330.5	306.5	392.9	391.4	445.8	490.6
N.Y. Stock Exchange common stock index (Dec. 31, 1965=50):														
Composite	45.7	68.1	74.0	68.9	92.6	92.5	108.1	136.0	161.8	150.0	180.1	183.7	206.4	229.0
Yearly high [5]	52.4	81.0	79.1	82.4	96.6	98.1	121.9	145.8	188.0	159.4	199.3	201.1	229.4	242.1
Yearly low [5]	37.7	55.3	65.0	58.8	79.8	85.1	94.6	117.8	125.9	136.7	155.0	162.2	171.0	217.9
Industrial	48.0	78.6	85.4	78.2	107.5	108.0	123.8	155.9	195.3	180.8	228.0	226.1	258.2	284.3
Transportation	32.1	60.5	72.6	60.4	89.4	85.6	104.1	119.9	140.5	134.1	174.9	158.8	174.0	201.0
Utility	37.2	37.3	38.9	39.8	47.0	46.4	56.8	71.4	74.3	72.2	94.3	90.7	92.6	99.5
Finance	54.6	64.3	73.5	72.0	95.3	89.3	114.2	147.2	146.5	127.4	162.0	133.2	150.8	179.3
American Stock Exchange Market Value Index (Aug. 31, 1973=50)	48.3	150.6	171.8	141.3	216.5	208.0	229.1	264.4	316.4	295.1	356.7	338.3	360.3	391.3
NASDAQ OTC composite [6]	(NA)	202.3	195.9	232.4	278.6	247.4	324.9	348.8	330.5	381.4	454.8	373.9	586.3	677.0
Industrial	(NA)	261.4	229.3	273.6	323.7	260.7	330.2	349.3	338.9	379.0	448.0	406.1	669.0	724.9
Insurance	(NA)	166.8	194.3	226.4	257.6	283.1	382.1	404.1	351.1	429.1	546.0	451.8	601.1	803.9
Banks	(NA)	118.4	143.1	156.4	203.8	229.8	349.4	412.5	390.7	435.3	391.0	254.9	350.6	532.9
Dow Jones and Co., Inc.:[7]														
Composite (65 stocks)	243.9	328.2	364.6	345.4	472.2	463.1	541.6	702.5	849.5	772.2	966.9	965.2	1,048.3	1,169.9
Industrial (30 stocks)	753.2	891.4	932.9	884.4	1,190.3	1,178.5	1,328.2	1,792.8	2,276.0	2,060.8	2,508.9	2,678.9	2,929.3	3,284.3
Transportation (20 stocks)	152.4	307.2	398.6	359.8	544.6	513.8	645.1	785.4	929.2	863.8	1,194.3	1,040.2	1,170.2	1,349.6
Utility (15 stocks)	108.8	110.4	108.6	112.0	130.0	131.8	157.6	195.2	202.2	179.7	205.7	211.5	210.3	214.4
Wilshire 5000 equity index (Dec. 31, 1980=1404.596)[8]	9830.3	1,220.7	1,343.7	1,233.7	1,691.5	1,644.6	1,923.8	2,418.8	2,843.7	2,636.9	3,172.6	3,187.3	3,604.6	4,041.1

NA Not available. [1] Source: U.S. Bureau of Economic Analysis, Survey of Current Business, monthly. [2] Derived from average yields on basis of assumed 4 percent, 20-year bond; Wednesday closing prices. [3] Source: Dow Jones and Co., Inc., New York, NY. A 20-bond average consisting of 10 utility bonds and 10 industrial bonds. [4] The index includes 400 industrial stocks, 20 transportation, 40 public utility, and 40 financial stocks. [5] Source: New York Stock Exchange, Inc., New York, NY, Fact Book, annual. [6] Source: National Association of Securities Dealers, Washington, DC, Fact Book, annual. OTC=over-the-counter. December monthly closing values. [7] Based on stocks listed on the New York Stock Exchange and NASDAQ/NMS. [8] Represents return on the market value of all common equity securities for which daily pricing is available. Source: Wilshire Associates, Santa Monica, CA, releases. [9] Represents Dec. 31, 1970.

Source: Except as noted, Board of Governors of the Federal Reserve System, Federal Reserve Bulletin, monthly; Annual Statistical Digest; and unpublished data.

No. 828. Bond and Stock Yields: 1980 to 1992

[**Percent per year.** Annual averages of daily figures, except as indicated. See also *Historical Statistics, Colonial Times to 1970*, series X 474-491]

TYPE	1980	1983	1984	1985	1986	1987	1988	1989	1990	1991	1992
U.S. Treasury, constant maturities: [1][2]											
3-year	11.51	10.45	11.92	9.64	7.06	7.68	8.26	8.55	8.26	6.82	5.30
5-year	11.45	10.79	12.26	10.12	7.30	7.94	8.47	8.50	8.37	7.37	6.19
10-year	11.43	11.10	12.46	10.62	7.67	8.39	8.85	8.49	8.55	7.86	7.01
U.S. Govt., long-term bonds [2][3]	10.81	10.84	11.99	10.75	8.14	8.64	8.98	8.58	8.74	8.16	7.52
State and local govt. bonds, Aaa [4]	7.86	8.80	9.61	8.60	6.95	7.12	7.36	7.00	6.82	6.56	6.09
State and local govt. bonds, Baa [4]	9.02	10.17	10.38	9.58	7.75	8.17	7.84	7.40	7.14	6.99	6.48
High-graded municipal bonds (Standard & Poor's) [5]	8.51	9.48	10.15	9.18	7.38	7.73	7.74	7.24	7.25	6.89	6.41
Municipal (Bond Buyer, 20 bonds)	8.59	9.51	10.10	9.11	7.32	7.63	7.68	7.23	7.27	6.92	6.44
Corporate Aaa seasoned [4]	11.94	12.04	12.71	11.37	9.02	9.38	9.71	9.26	9.32	8.77	8.14
Corporate Baa seasoned [4]	13.67	13.55	14.19	12.72	10.39	10.58	10.83	10.18	10.36	9.80	8.98
Corporate (Moody's) [4][6]	12.75	12.78	[7]13.49	12.05	9.71	9.91	10.18	9.66	9.77	9.23	8.50
Industrials (49 bonds) [8]	12.35	12.25	13.21	11.80	9.96	9.83	9.91	9.66	9.77	9.25	8.52
Public utilities (51 bonds) [9]	13.15	13.31	[7]14.03	12.29	9.46	9.98	10.45	9.66	9.76	9.21	8.57
Stocks (Standard & Poor's): [5]											
Preferred (10 stocks) [10]	10.60	11.02	11.62	10.44	8.76	8.37	9.24	9.04	8.96	8.17	7.46
Common: Composite (500 stocks)	5.26	4.40	4.64	4.25	3.48	3.08	3.64	3.45	3.61	3.24	2.98
Industrials (400 stocks)	4.95	4.04	4.05	3.76	3.09	2.62	3.14	3.01	3.16	2.82	2.63

[1] Yields on the more actively traded issues adjusted to constant maturities by the U.S. Treasury. [2] Yields are based on closing bid prices quoted by at least five dealers. [3] Averages (to maturity or call) for all outstanding bonds neither due nor callable in less than 10 years, including several very low yielding "flower" bonds. [4] Source: Moody's Investors Service, New York, NY. [5] Source: U.S. Bureau of Economic Analysis, *Survey of Current Business*, monthly. Annual averages of weekly figures. [6] For 1980-88 includes railroad bonds which were discontinued as part of composite in 1989. [7] The Aaa public utility average was suspended on Jan. 17, 1984 because of a lack of appropriate issues. The average corporate does not include Aaa utilities from Jan. 17 to Oct. 12. The Aaa utility average was reinstated on Oct. 12. Thirty public utility bonds were used during the period Jan. 17-Oct. 12, 1984. [8] Covers 40 bonds for period 1980-83, 38 bonds for 1984-86, and 37 bonds for 1987 and 1988. [9] Covers 40 bonds for period 1980-88. [10] Yields based on 10 stocks, 4 yields. Issues converted to a price equivalent to $100 par and a 7 percent annual dividend before averaging.

Source: Except as noted, Board of Governors of the Federal Reserve System, *Federal Reserve Bulletin*, monthly.

No. 829. Sales of Stocks and Options on Registered Exchanges: 1980 to 1991

[Excludes over-the-counter trading. See also *Historical Statistics, Colonial Times to 1970*, series X 517-530]

EXCHANGE	Unit	1980	1983	1984	1985	1986	1987	1988	1989	1990	1991
Market value of all sales, all exchanges [1][2]	Bil. dol	522	1,023	1,004	1,260	1,868	2,492	1,702	2,010	1,752	1,908
New York	Bil. dol	398	816	815	1,024	1,453	1,987	1,380	1,581	1,394	1,534
American	Bil. dol	47	48	32	38	63	102	59	80	65	69
Midwest	Bil. dol	21	60	62	79	102	122	87	101	74	77
Chicago	Bil. dol	28	39	35	38	56	124	64	88	81	74
Pacific	Bil. dol	13	31	31	40	55	71	49	64	53	64
Philadelphia	Bil. dol	11	20	19	23	35	48	34	50	41	39
STOCKS [3]											
Shares sold, all exchanges [2]	Million.	15,488	30,146	30,456	37,046	48,338	63,771	52,533	54,239	53,338	58,031
New York	Million.	12,390	24,253	25,150	30,222	39,258	53,038	44,018	44,140	43,829	47,674
American	Million.	1,659	2,209	1,584	2,115	2,999	3,496	2,576	3,248	3,125	3,103
Midwest	Million.	598	1,662	1,843	2,274	2,784	3,329	2,771	2,960	2,511	2,715
Pacific	Million.	435	1,070	1,006	1,352	1,750	2,034	1,576	1,791	1,682	2,068
Market value, all exchanges [2]	Bil. dol	476	957	951	1,200	1,705	2,284	1,587	1,845	1,612	1,776
New York	Bil. dol	398	815	814	1,023	1,450	1,983	1,378	1,577	1,390	1,532
American	Bil. dol	35	31	21	26	43	53	31	43	36	40
Midwest	Bil. dol	21	60	62	79	102	122	87	101	74	77
Pacific	Bil. dol	11	27	28	37	51	57	41	52	45	54
OPTIONS [4]											
Contracts traded, all exchanges [2]	Million.	97	149	197	233	289	305	196	227	210	199
Chicago	Million.	53	82	123	149	180	182	112	127	130	122
American	Million.	29	39	40	49	65	71	45	50	41	39
Market value of contracts traded, all exchanges [2]	Bil. dol	45.8	64.2	53.0	59.1	87.9	118.9	62.6	76.8	79.0	76.1
Chicago	Bil. dol	27.9	39.4	34.9	38.4	55.9	76.9	39.7	47.3	55.4	50.7
American	Bil. dol	12.5	15.8	10.5	11.6	19.0	25.7	12.4	15.1	12.8	14.0
Options exercised:											
Number of contracts	Million.	4.9	13.6	11.9	10.5	14.5	17.0	11.4	15.6	12.1	12.0
Value	Bil. dol	20.4	65.1	55.6	49.2	72.8	85.9	51.5	85.2	55.8	53.9

[1] Includes market value of rights and warrants. Excludes the value of options exercised. [2] Includes other registered exchanges, not shown separately. [3] Includes voting trust certificates, American Depository Receipts, and certificate of deposit for stocks. [4] Includes nonequity options as of October 1982.

Source: U.S. Securities and Exchange Commission, *SEC Monthly Statistical Review* (discontinued Feb. 1989); and unpublished data.

No. 830. Foreign Purchases and Sales of U.S. Securities, by Type of Security, 1980 to 1992, and by Selected Country, 1992

[In billions of dollars. Covers transactions in all types of long-term domestic securities by foreigners as reported by banks, brokers, and other entities in the United States (except nonmarketable U.S. Treasury notes, foreign series; and nonmarketable U.S. Treasury bonds and notes, foreign currency series). Data cover new issues of securities, transactions in outstanding issues, and redemptions of securities. Includes transactions executed in the United States for the account of foreigners, and transactions executed abroad for the account of reporting institutions and their domestic customers. Data by country show the country of domicile of the foreign buyers and sellers of the securities; in the case of outstanding issues, this may differ from the country of the original issuer. The term "foreigner" covers all institutions and individuals domiciled outside the United States, including U.S. citizens domiciled abroad, and the foreign branches, subsidiaries and other affiliates abroad of U.S. banks and businesses; the central governments, central banks, and other official institutions of foreign countries; and international and regional organizations. "Foreigner" also includes persons in the United States to the extent that they are known by reporting institutions to be acting on behalf of foreigners. Minus sign (-) indicates net sales by foreigners or a net outflow of capital from the United States]

YEAR AND COUNTRY	NET PURCHASES					TOTAL TRANSACTIONS [4]				
	Total	Treasury bonds and notes [1]	U.S. Govt. corporations [2] bonds	Corporate bonds [3]	Corporate stocks	Total	Treasury bonds and notes [1]	U.S. Govt. corporations [2] bonds	Corporate bonds [3]	Corporate stocks
1980	15.8	4.9	2.6	2.9	5.4	198	97	17	9	75
1985	78.3	29.2	4.3	39.8	4.9	1,256	968	46	84	159
1986	88.8	19.4	7.0	43.7	18.7	2,623	2,149	67	129	278
1987	69.4	25.6	5.0	22.5	16.3	3,315	2,649	81	104	482
1988	74.8	48.8	6.7	21.2	-2.0	3,581	3,072	56	89	364
1989	96.5	54.2	15.1	17.3	9.9	4,767	4,140	88	121	418
1990	18.7	17.9	6.3	9.7	-15.1	4,204	3,620	104	117	362
1991	58.4	19.9	10.2	17.2	11.1	4,706	4,016	124	155	411
1992, total [5]	73.2	39.0	18.3	21.1	-5.2	5,281	4,443	204	186	448
United Kingdom	33.9	24.2	3.8	9.1	-3.3	1,854	1,611	37	85	122
Japan.	5.6	9.5	1.5	-1.7	-3.6	858	752	51	16	39
Canada	2.2	0.6	0.1	0.1	1.4	356	285	5	13	53
France	-0.3	-0.2	0.4	0.8	-1.3	191	168	2	5	16
Bermuda.	-2.2	-5.8	1.1	1.9	0.7	169	141	6	8	15
Netherlands Antilles	-1.0	-1.8	0.2	0.4	0.3	166	121	7	5	34

[1] Marketable bonds and notes.   [2] Includes federally-sponsored agencies.   [3] Includes transactions in directly placed issues abroad by U.S. corporations and issues of States and municipalities.   [4] Total purchases plus total sales.   [5] Includes other countries, not shown separately.

Source: U.S. Dept. of Treasury, *Treasury Bulletin*, quarterly.

No. 831. New Security Issues of Corporations, by Type of Offering and Industry Group: 1985 to 1991

[In billions of dollars. Represents gross proceeds of issues maturing in more than one year. Figures are the principal amount or the number of units multiplied by the offering price. Excludes secondary offerings, employee stock plans, investment companies other than closed-end, intracorporate transactions, equities sold abroad, and Yankee bonds. Stock data include ownership securities issued by limited partnerships]

TYPE OF OFFERING AND INDUSTRY GROUP	1985	1988	1989	1990	1991	TYPE OF OFFERING AND INDUSTRY GROUP	1985	1988	1989	1990	1991
Total	239.2	409.6	377.8	339.1	465.4	Stocks, total	35.5	57.8	57.9	40.2	75.5
Bonds, total	203.7	351.8	320.0	298.8	390.0	Preferred.	6.5	6.5	6.2	4.0	17.4
Public, domestic . .	119.7	201.1	179.7	188.8	287.1	Common.	29.0	35.9	26.0	19.4	47.9
Private placement, domestic	46.2	127.7	117.4	87.0	74.9	Private placement.	(NA)	15.3	25.6	16.7	10.1
Sold abroad.	37.8	23.1	22.9	23.1	28.0						
Manufacturing . . .	63.6	70.1	74.7	51.8	86.6	Manufacturing . . .	5.7	7.6	9.3	5.6	24.2
Commercial and miscellaneous. . .	17.2	61.9	50.3	40.7	36.7	Commercial and miscellaneous. . .	9.1	8.4	7.4	10.2	19.4
Transportation . . .	6.0	10.9	10.2	12.8	13.6	Transportation . . .	1.5	1.5	1.9	0.4	2.4
Public utility	13.6	21.0	18.6	17.6	23.9	Public utility	2.0	1.9	3.1	0.4	3.5
Communication . .	10.9	6.0	9.3	6.7	9.4	Communication . .	1.0	0.5	1.9	3.8	0.5
Real estate and financial.	92.3	182.0	156.9	169.2	219.7	Real estate and financial.	16.2	37.8	34.0	19.7	25.5

NA Not available.

Source: Board of Governors of the Federal Reserve System, *Federal Reserve Bulletin*, monthly, and *Annual Statistical Digest*.

No. 832. Ownership of Public Debt Securities by Private Investors: 1980 to 1992

[As of **December**. Par values. Estimated]

INVESTOR	AMOUNT (bil. dol.)								PERCENT DISTRIBUTION		
	1980	1985	1987	1988	1989	1990	1991	1992	1980	1990	1992
Total privately held......	616	1,417	1,731	1,859	2,016	2,288	2,563	2,840	100	100	100
Commercial banks [1].........	112	189	194	185	165	172	233	292	18	7	10
Nonbank investors..........	504	1,228	1,537	1,674	1,851	2,117	2,330	2,548	82	93	90
Individuals [2].............	117	155	172	190	216	234	264	289	19	10	10
Insurance companies........	24	81	108	119	125	142	172	183	4	6	6
Money market funds	4	25	15	12	15	46	80	81	1	2	3
Corporations [3]...........	19	59	85	86	93	109	151	193	3	5	7
State and local governments [4]..	88	304	418	472	488	490	520	532	14	21	19
Foreign and international [5]	130	225	300	362	393	422	455	513	21	18	18
Other investors [6]..........	123	380	439	433	521	675	688	758	20	29	27

[1] Consists of domestically chartered banks, U.S. branches and agencies of foreign banks, NY investment companies majority owned by foreign banks, and Edge Act corporations owned by domestically chartered and foreign banks. [2] Includes partnerships and personal trust accounts. [3] Exclusive of banks and insurance companies. [4] Includes State and local pension funds. [5] Consists of the investment of foreign balances and international accounts in the United States. [6] Consists of savings and loan associations, credit unions, mutual savings banks, nonprofit institutions, corporate pension trust funds, and dealers and brokers. Also included are certain government deposit accounts and government-sponsored agencies.

Source: U.S. Dept. of the Treasury, *Treasury Bulletin*, quarterly.

No. 833. Volume of Trading on New York Stock Exchange: 1980 to 1992

[**Round lot**: A unit of trading or a multiple thereof. On the NYSE the unit of trading is generally 100 shares in stocks. For some inactive stocks, the unit of trading is 10 shares. **Odd lot**: An amount of stock less than the established 100-share unit or 10-share unit of trading]

ITEM	Unit	1980	1984	1985	1986	1987	1988	1989	1990	1991	1992
Shares traded........	Million .	11,562	23,309	27,774	36,009	48,143	41,118	42,022	39,947	45,599	51,826
Round lots...........	Million ..	11,352	23,071	27,511	35,680	47,801	40,850	41,699	39,665	45,266	51,376
Average daily shares	Million ..	44.9	91.2	109.2	141.0	189.0	161.5	165.5	156.8	178.9	202.3
High day..............	Million ..	84.3	236.6	181.0	244.3	608.1	343.9	416.4	292.4	317.4	389.0
Low day.............	Million ..	16.1	46.4	62.1	48.9	86.7	72.1	68.9	56.9	69.6	95.1
By size: [1]											
100 to 2,000 shares [2] .	Percent .	24.7	11.3	10.6	10.8	13.6	12.6	13.4	22.3	21.9	21.0
2,100 to 4,900 shares [3] ...	Percent .	32.2	25.1	24.1	25.7	21.1	19.8	20.7	12.9	12.9	12.5
5,000 or more shares [4] ..	Percent .	43.1	63.6	65.3	63.5	65.3	67.6	65.9	64.8	65.2	66.5
Odd lots..............	Million ..	209	238	263	329	342	268	324	282	[5]333	450
Value of shares traded ..	Bil. dol .	382	773	981	1,389	1,889	1,366	1,556	1,336	1,533	1,764
Round lots.............	Bil. dol..	375	765	971	1,374	1,874	1,356	1,543	1,325	1,520	1,745
Odd lots..............	Bil. dol.	8	9	10	15	15	10	13	11	[5]13	19
Bond volume [6]........	Mil. dol .	5,190	6,982	9,046	10,464	9,727	7,702	8,836	10,894	12,698	11,629
Daily average........	Mil. dol	20.5	27.6	35.9	41.4	38.4	30.4	35.1	43.1	50.2	45.8

[1] Share volume of reported trades by size (percent of total) on New York Stock Exchange. [2] 1980-87, at 100-900 shares; 1988-89, at 100-1,000 shares. [3] 1980-87, at 1,000-4,900 shares; 1988-89, at 1,100-4,900 shares. [4] Includes bunched orders at the opening and re-opening of trading. [5] Excludes odd lot statistics for February which were not available. [6] Par value.

No. 834. Securities Listed on New York Stock Exchange: 1980 to 1992

[As of **December 31**, except **cash dividends** are for **calendar year**]

ITEM	Unit	1980	1983	1984	1985	1986	1987	1988	1989	1990	1991	1992
Bonds:												
Number of issuers....	Number .	1,045	1,034	1,024	1,010	951	885	846	794	743	657	589
Number of issues	Number .	3,057	3,600	3,751	3,856	3,611	3,346	3,106	2,961	2,912	1,773	1,462
Face value..........	Bil. dol..	602	965	1,084	1,327	1,380	1,651	1,610	1,435	1,689	2,219	2,009
Market value........	Bil. dol..	508	898	1,022	1,339	1,458	1,621	1,561	1,412	1,610	2,227	2,044
Average price.......	Percent	84.41	93.04	94.29	100.90	105.66	98.20	96.94	98.42	95.31	100.34	101.77
Stocks:												
Companies..........	Number .	1,570	1,550	1,543	1,541	1,575	1,647	1,681	1,720	1,774	1,885	2,089
Number of issues	Number .	2,228	2,307	2,319	2,298	2,257	2,244	2,234	2,246	2,284	2,426	2,658
Shares listed	Billion...	33.7	45.1	49.1	52.4	59.6	72.0	76.1	83.0	90.7	99.6	115.8
Market value........	Bil. dol .	1,243	1,584	1,586	1,950	2,199	2,216	2,457	3,030	2,820	3,713	4,035
Average price.......	Dollars ..	36.87	35.11	32.31	37.20	36.89	30.87	32.30	36.51	31.08	37.27	34.83
Cash dividends on common stock	Bil. dol ..	53.1	67.1	68.2	74.2	76.2	84.4	102.2	101.8	103.2	123.4	109.7

Source of tables 833 and 834: New York Stock Exchange, Inc., New York, NY, *Fact Book*, annual.

No. 835. NASDAQ—Securities Listed and Volume of Trading: 1980 to 1992

ITEM	Unit	1980	1984	1985	1986	1987	1988	1989	1990	1991	1992
Companies listed........	Number...	2,894	4,097	4,136	4,417	4,706	4,451	4,293	4,132	4,094	4,111
Issues.................	Number...	3,050	4,728	4,784	5,189	5,537	5,144	4,963	4,706	4,684	4,758
Shares traded..........	Million....	6,692	15,159	20,699	28,737	37,890	31,070	33,530	33,380	41,311	48,455
Average daily volume ...	Million....	26.5	59.9	82.1	113.6	149.8	122.8	133.1	131.9	163.3	190.8
Value of shares traded ...	Bil. dol. ...	68.7	153.5	233.5	378.2	499.9	347.1	431.4	452.4	693.9	890.8

Source: National Association of Securities Dealers, Washington, DC, *Fact Book*, annual.

No. 836. Commodity Futures Trading on U.S. Exchanges—Volume of Trading: 1980 to 1992

[In millions. For year ending Sept. 30]

COMMODITY	1980	1983	1984	1985	1986	1987	1988	1989	1990	1991	1992
Number of contracts traded.	**82.7**	**136.1**	**148.8**	**152.6**	**183.1**	**213.5**	**241.8**	**267.7**	**272.2**	**261.4**	**289.4**
Grain	18.3	17.8	15.9	10.7	10.3	10.9	15.9	15.9	17.0	16.6	17.6
Oilseeds/products	15.7	19.8	23.5	14.9	13.8	14.2	22.5	21.1	20.4	19.8	18.6
Livestock/products	11.8	11.1	8.4	7.9	8.6	8.8	9.6	8.2	8.0	6.9	6.4
Other agriculturals	7.8	6.3	6.0	5.1	6.7	5.7	9.8	10.7	11.0	9.5	9.4
Energy products	1.1	3.2	4.9	7.0	11.5	20.3	26.3	31.3	35.2	31.8	38.4
Metals	14.1	26.3	22.4	18.4	16.2	19.4	18.9	17.9	17.8	13.9	12.2
Financial instruments	10.2	40.2	51.0	72.1	96.9	114.3	117.6	136.7	135.7	134.1	148.2
Currencies	3.7	11.4	16.7	16.4	19.1	19.9	21.2	25.7	27.2	28.8	38.7

Source: U.S. Commodity Futures Trading Commission, *Annual Report*.

No. 837. Securities Industry—Revenues and Expenses: 1980 to 1992

[**In millions of dollars**. Data provided by U.S. Securities and Exchange Commission cover all securities firms]

TYPE	ALL SECURITIES FIRMS								MEMBERS OF NY STOCK EXCHANGE [1]	
	1980	1985	1986	1987	1988	1989	1990	1991	1991	1992, proj.
Revenues, total	**19,829**	**49,844**	**64,424**	**66,104**	**66,100**	**76,864**	**71,356**	**81,226**	**60,718**	**62,763**
Commissions	6,777	10,955	13,977	16,574	11,932	13,452	12,032	14,209	10,589	11,442
Trading/investment gains	5,091	14,549	18,145	14,423	16,667	16,247	15,746	22,530	17,087	17,186
Underwriting profits	1,571	4,987	6,743	5,719	5,607	4,537	3,728	6,593	6,073	7,714
Margin interest	2,151	2,746	3,022	3,493	3,155	3,860	3,179	2,771	2,632	2,640
Mutual fund sales	278	2,754	4,540	4,069	2,644	3,038	3,242	4,176	2,124	2,813
Other	3,960	13,854	17,998	21,825	26,096	35,731	33,428	30,946	22,213	20,968
Expenses, total	**16,668**	**43,342**	**56,123**	**62,894**	**62,623**	**74,041**	**70,566**	**72,652**	**54,869**	**56,082**
Interest expense	3,876	11,470	14,233	16,473	19,502	29,822	28,093	24,145	18,871	15,913
Compensation	7,619	18,112	23,936	25,583	23,418	23,740	22,931	26,774	20,824	23,887
Commissions/clearance paid	1,055	2,314	2,995	3,563	2,804	3,057	2,959	3,199	1,760	1,860
Other	4,119	11,446	14,959	17,276	16,899	17,422	16,583	18,534	13,414	14,422
Net income, pre-tax	**3,160**	**6,502**	**8,301**	**3,210**	**3,477**	**2,823**	**790**	**8,574**	**5,849**	**6,681**

[1] Covers all members of New York Stock Exchange doing public business. Source: Securities Industry Association, New York, NY, *Securities Industry Association Fact Book*, annual.
Source: Except as noted, U.S. Securities and Exchange Commission, *Annual Report*.

No. 838. Mutual Funds—Summary: 1980 to 1991

[See also *Historical Statistics, Colonial Times to 1970*, series X 536-539]

TYPE OF FUND	Unit	1980	1984	1985	1986	1987	1988	1989	1990	1991
Number of funds, total	Number	**564**	**1,246**	**1,531**	**1,843**	**2,323**	**2,718**	**2,918**	**3,106**	**3,423**
Money market funds	Number	96	329	348	360	389	432	463	508	553
Equity funds	Number	288	466	574	700	847	1,015	1,081	1,127	1,216
Income and bond funds	Number	128	240	323	409	565	681	735	771	864
Municipal bond funds	Number	42	114	174	247	368	415	438	464	523
Short-term municipal bond funds [1]	Number	10	97	112	127	154	175	201	236	267
Shareholder accounts, total	Millions	**12.1**	**28.2**	**35.0**	**46.1**	**54.7**	**54.8**	**58.3**	**62.6**	**68.6**
Equity, bond, and income funds	Millions	7.3	14.4	20.0	29.8	37.0	36.2	37.0	39.6	45.0
Money market funds and short-term municipal bond funds [1]	Millions	4.8	13.8	15.0	16.3	17.7	18.6	21.3	23.0	23.6
Assets, total	Bil. dol	**135**	**371**	**496**	**716**	**770**	**810**	**982**	**1,067**	**1,347**
Money market funds	Bil. dol	74	210	208	228	255	272	359	415	450
Equity funds	Bil. dol	44	83	117	162	181	195	249	246	368
Income and bond funds	Bil. dol	11	33	95	187	196	191	199	202	285
Municipal bond funds	Bil. dol	3	21	39	76	77	87	106	120	154
Short-term municipal bond funds [1]	Bil. dol	2	24	36	64	61	66	69	84	90
Sales, total	Bil. dol	**248**	**680**	**954**	**1,206**	**1,252**	**1,177**	**1,445**	**1,565**	**2,036**
Money market funds	Bil. dol	232	572	730	792	869	903	1,135	1,219	1,570
Equity funds	Bil. dol	6	20	30	58	72	31	55	71	97
Income and bond funds	Bil. dol	3	16	65	118	90	44	45	50	98
Municipal bond funds	Bil. dol	2	10	19	40	29	21	27	28	40
Short-term municipal bond funds [1]	Bil. dol	5	62	109	198	192	178	185	197	231
Redemptions, total	Bil. dol	**217**	**607**	**865**	**1,016**	**1,179**	**1,167**	**1,327**	**1,471**	**1,879**
Money market funds	Bil. dol	204	531	732	776	866	899	1,055	1,183	1,536
Equity funds	Bil. dol	6	11	18	27	40	35	38	45	54
Income and bond funds	Bil. dol	2	5	11	31	59	45	41	39	47
Municipal bond funds	Bil. dol	1	4	4	9	17	13	12	14	15
Short-term municipal bond funds [1]	Bil. dol	4	56	99	172	197	175	181	190	227

[1] The average maturity of the portfolio is generally less than 2 years.
Source: Investment Company Institute, Washington, DC, *Mutual Fund Fact Book*, annual (copyright).

No. 839. Assets of Private and Public Pension Funds, by Type of Fund: 1980 to 1992

[In **billions of dollars**. As of **end of year**. Except for corporate equities, represents book value. Excludes Social Security trust funds, see table 591]

TYPE OF PENSION FUND	1980	1984	1985	1986	1987	1988	1989	1990	1991	1992
Total, all types	**916**	**1,698**	**1,992**	**2,314**	**2,471**	**2,755**	**3,211**	**3,303**	**4,223**	**4,586**
Private funds.	642	1,212	1,438	1,675	1,765	1,941	2,247	2,301	3,057	3,295
Insured	172	332	400	477	549	628	711	795	877	948
Noninsured [1]	470	880	1,038	1,198	1,216	1,313	1,536	1,506	2,180	2,347
Corporate equities [2]	231	375	482	580	603	664	826	752	1,033	1,130
U.S. Government securities	51	150	156	184	179	183	207	218	287	305
Corporate bonds [3]	78	118	116	133	129	131	148	155	214	227
Time deposits	25	78	99	102	101	108	115	115	105	114
Public funds	275	487	554	639	706	814	964	1,002	1,167	1,291
State and local government .	198	357	405	469	517	606	735	752	891	988
Corporate bonds [3]	95	118	129	140	125	146	182	177	183	183
Corporate equities [2]	44	97	120	150	170	220	300	296	401	464
U.S. Government securities	40	111	124	144	169	185	198	220	242	275
Other.	19	31	32	35	54	56	54	59	65	65
U.S. Government	76	130	149	170	188	208	229	251	276	304
Civil service [4]	74	127	145	163	182	200	220	241	266	292
Railroad retirement	3	3	4	6	7	8	9	9	11	12

[1] Covers all pension funds of corporations, nonprofit organizations, unions, and multi-employer groups. Also includes deferred profit-sharing plans and Federal Employees Retirement System (FERS) Thrift Savings Fund. Excludes health, welfare, and bonus plans. Includes other types of assets not shown separately.   [2] Includes mutual fund shares.   [3] Includes foreign bonds.   [4] Includes U.S. Foreign Service Retirement and Disability Trust Fund and the Federal Employees Retirement System.

Source: Board of Governors of the Federal Reserve System, *Annual Statistical Digest*, and unpublished data.

No. 840. Individual Retirement Accounts (IRA) Plans—Value, by Type of Holder: 1981 to 1991

[As of **December 31**. Estimated]

TYPE OF HOLDER	AMOUNT (bil. dol.)									PERCENT DISTRIBUTION		
	1981	1984	1985	1986	1987	1988	1989	1990	1991	1981	1990	1991
Total.	**26**	**132**	**200**	**277**	**334**	**393**	**465**	**543**	**647**	**100**	**100**	**100**
Savings institutions	14	43	56	69	77	90	98	95	86	54	17	13
Commercial banks	6	37	52	67	77	88	99	119	134	22	22	21
Mutual funds	3	17	32	54	72	86	112	127	169	10	23	26
Self directed	(NA)	15	29	45	59	68	82	117	157	(NA)	22	24
Life insurance companies	3	13	17	22	26	36	49	53	66	13	10	10
Credit unions	(Z)	8	14	21	23	25	26	32	35	1	6	6

NA Not available.   Z Less than $500 million.

Source: Investment Company Institute, Washington, DC, *Mutual Fund Fact Book*, annual, (copyright).

No. 841. Health Insurance—Premium Income and Benefit Payments of Insurance Companies: 1970 to 1990

[In **billions of dollars**. Beginning 1980, includes Puerto Rico and other U.S. outlying areas. Represents premium income of and benefits paid by insurance companies only. Excludes Blue Cross-Blue Shield plans, medical-society sponsored plans, and all other independent plans]

ITEM	1970	1980	1981	1982	1983	1984	1985	1986	1987	1988	1989	1990
Premiums [1]	**11.5**	**43.7**	**49.0**	**58.3**	**63.2**	**70.4**	**75.2**	**75.5**	**84.1**	**98.2**	**108.0**	**118.6**
Group policies [2]	8.1	36.8	42.5	50.0	54.9	60.8	64.4	65.9	74.0	87.6	96.1	105.9
Individual and family policies . .	3.4	6.9	6.5	8.3	8.3	9.6	10.8	9.6	10.1	10.6	11.8	12.7
Benefit payments	**9.1**	**37.0**	**41.6**	**48.7**	**51.7**	**56.0**	**60.0**	**64.3**	**72.5**	**83.0**	**89.4**	**97.7**
Group policies [2]	7.5	33.0	37.7	44.2	46.9	50.3	53.7	58.9	66.5	76.4	82.2	89.5
Individual and family policies . .	1.6	4.0	3.9	4.5	4.8	5.7	6.3	5.4	5.9	6.6	7.2	8.2
Type of coverage:												
Loss of income	1.8	5.3	5.2	5.5	4.9	5.2	5.6	5.6	6.4	6.4	7.2	7.6
Medical expense	7.1	28.8	33.0	39.5	42.4	45.5	48.6	51.9	58.7	68.0	73.6	80.1
Dental	0.1	2.8	3.5	4.0	4.4	4.9	5.3	5.3	5.9	6.3	6.5	6.9
Medicare supplement	(NA)	0.1	0.2	0.1	0.1	0.4	0.5	1.5	1.5	2.2	2.1	3.1

NA Not available.   [1] 1970 refers to written premiums; thereafter, refers to earned premiums.   [2] Beginning 1980, insurance company group premiums and benefit payments include administrative service agreements and minimum premium plans. Amounts for 1970 contain only a portion of these data.

Source: Health Insurance Association of America, Washington, DC, *Source Book of Health Insurance Data*, annual.

No. 842. Property and Casualty Insurance—Summary: 1987 to 1992

[In billions of dollars. Minus sign (-) indicates loss]

ITEM	1987	1988	1989	1990	1991	1992, est.
Premiums, net written	193.2	202.0	208.4	217.8	223.0	230.1
Automobile, private [1]	64.3	69.5	73.6	78.4	82.8	(NA)
Automobile, commercial [1]	16.9	16.9	17.3	17.0	16.6	(NA)
Liability other than auto	24.9	23.1	22.7	22.1	20.9	(NA)
Fire and allied lines	7.7	6.9	7.0	7.1	7.2	(NA)
Homeowners' multiple peril	16.7	17.1	17.7	18.6	19.3	(NA)
Commercial multiple peril	17.2	17.7	17.5	17.7	17.0	(NA)
Workers' compensation	23.4	26.1	28.5	31.0	31.3	(NA)
Marine, inland and ocean	5.5	5.5	5.6	5.7	5.5	(NA)
Accident and health	3.8	4.7	4.6	5.0	5.1	(NA)
Other lines	12.8	14.5	14.2	15.2	17.4	(NA)
Underwriting gain/loss	-9.6	-11.2	-19.2	-20.9	-19.4	(NA)
Net investment income	24.0	27.7	31.2	32.9	34.2	(NA)
Operating earnings after taxes	11.0	12.9	9.0	9.0	10.4	(NA)
Assets	426.7	476.9	527.0	556.3	601.4	649.5
Policyholders' surplus	104.0	118.2	134.0	138.4	158.7	(NA)

NA Not available.   [1] Includes premiums for automobile liability and physical damage.

Source: U.S. Department of Commerce, International Trade Administration, *U.S. Industrial Outlook, 1993*.

No. 843. U.S. Life Insurance Companies—Summary: 1980 to 1991

[As of **December 31** or **calendar year**, as applicable. Covers domestic and foreign business of U.S. companies. See also *Historical Statistics, Colonial Times to 1970*, series X 879 and X 890-917]

ITEM	Unit	1980	1983	1984	1985	1986	1987	1988	1989	1990	1991
U.S. companies	Number	1,958	2,117	2,193	2,261	2,254	2,337	2,343	2,270	2,195	2,105
Sales	**Bil. dol.**	**655**	**1,279**	**1,390**	**1,530**	[1]**1,578**	**1,656**	**1,716**	**1,788**	**2,024**	[1]**2,014**
Ordinary	Bil. dol.	462	972	1,074	1,187	1,178	1,267	1,287	1,343	1,368	1,403
Group	Bil. dol.	190	306	315	342	[1]400	388	428	444	655	[1]611
Industrial	Bil. dol.	4	1	1	1	(Z)	(Z)	(Z)	(Z)	(Z)	(Z)
Income	**Bil. dol.**	**130.9**	**176.0**	**206.1**	**234.0**	**282.3**	**314.3**	**338.1**	**367.3**	**402.2**	**411.0**
Life insurance premiums	Bil. dol.	40.8	50.3	51.3	60.1	66.2	76.7	73.5	73.3	76.7	79.3
Percent of total	Percent	31.2	28.6	24.9	25.7	23.5	24.4	21.7	20.0	19.1	19.3
Annuity considerations	Bil. dol.	22.4	30.5	42.8	53.9	83.7	88.7	103.3	115.0	129.1	123.6
Health insurance premiums	Bil. dol.	29.4	38.2	40.7	41.8	44.2	47.6	52.3	56.1	58.2	60.9
Investment and other	Bil. dol.	38.3	57.0	71.3	78.2	88.2	101.3	109.0	122.9	138.2	147.2
Disbursements	**Bil. dol.**	**88.2**	**123.5**	**138.5**	**151.8**	**186.5**	**202.3**	**221.4**	**246.8**	**277.1**	**299.2**
Payments to policyholders [2][3]	Bil. dol.	59.0	80.9	89.8	95.7	131.4	144.4	156.8	178.3	200.9	218.6
Percent of total	Percent	66.9	65.5	64.8	63.0	70.5	71.4	70.8	72.2	72.5	73.1
Death payments	Bil. dol.	12.9	16.8	17.6	18.5	19.6	20.7	22.4	23.5	25.5	26.4
Matured endowments	Bil. dol.	0.8	0.6	0.7	0.8	0.8	0.8	0.8	0.8	0.8	0.7
Annuity payments	Bil. dol.	7.4	12.7	18.0	19.7	17.8	20.3	21.9	26.0	28.6	31.8
Policy dividends	Bil. dol.	8.1	10.8	11.4	12.4	12.4	13.0	13.8	14.9	15.7	15.8
Surrender values [3]	Bil. dol.	6.4	12.5	14.5	15.9	49.6	53.7	58.1	73.4	90.2	101.2
Disability benefits	Bil. dol.	0.5	0.5	0.4	0.5	0.5	0.5	0.4	0.5	0.5	0.5
Commissions, expenses, etc. [3]	Bil. dol.	27.8	40.7	46.0	53.1	51.4	54.7	61.3	63.5	70.2	75.1
Dividends to stockholders	Bil. dol.	1.4	1.9	2.7	3.0	3.7	3.3	3.4	5.0	6.0	5.5
BALANCE SHEET											
Assets	**Bil. dol.**	**479**	**655**	**723**	**826**	**938**	**1,045**	**1,167**	**1,300**	**1,408**	**1,551**
Government securities	Bil. dol.	33	77	100	125	145	151	160	178	211	269
Corporate securities	Bil. dol.	227	297	323	374	433	502	585	664	711	789
Percent of total assets	Percent	47.4	45.3	44.6	45.3	46.2	48.1	50.1	51.1	50.5	50.8
Bonds	Bil. dol.	180	232	259	297	342	406	480	538	583	624
Stocks	Bil. dol.	47	65	63	78	91	97	104	126	128	165
Mortgages	Bil. dol.	131	151	157	172	194	214	233	254	270	265
Real estate	Bil. dol.	15	22	26	29	32	34	37	40	43	47
Policy loans	Bil. dol.	41	54	55	54	54	54	54	57	63	66
Other	Bil. dol.	32	54	64	72	81	90	98	106	110	115
Interest earned on assets [4]	Percent	8.02	8.96	9.45	9.63	9.35	9.10	9.03	9.10	8.89	8.63
Liabilities [2][5]	Bil. dol.	445	609	673	769	873	977	1,092	1,216	1,317	1,445
Policy reserves [2]	**Bil. dol.**	**390**	**532**	**584**	**665**	**762**	**862**	**969**	**1,084**	**1,197**	**1,305**
Annuities	Bil. dol.	182	297	342	411	489	562	642	730	815	895
Group	Bil. dol.	140	222	255	303	356	393	434	474	516	548
Individual [6]	Bil. dol.	41	75	87	108	133	169	208	256	299	347
Life insurance	Bil. dol.	198	221	226	236	252	276	300	324	349	372
Health insurance	Bil. dol.	11	15	17	19	21	24	27	30	33	38
Capital and surplus [2]	Bil. dol.	34	46	50	57	64	67	75	84	91	106

Z Less than $500 million.   [1] Includes Servicemen's Group Life Insurance: $51 billion in 1986 and $167 billion in 1991; as well as Federal Employees' Group Life Insurance: $11 billion in 1986.   [2] Includes operations of accident and health departments of life insurance companies.   [3] Beginning in 1986, data not comparable to prior years due to change in accounting method.   [4] Net rate.   [5] Includes other obligations not shown separately.   [6] Includes reserves for supplementary contracts with and without life contingencies.

Source: American Council of Life Insurance, Washington, DC, *Life Insurance Fact Book*, biennial; and unpublished data.

No. 844. Life Insurance Purchases in the United States— Number and Amount: 1980 to 1991

[Excludes revivals, increases, dividend additions, and reinsurance acquired. Includes long-term credit insurance (life insurance on loans of more than 10 years' duration). See also headnote, table 845]

YEAR	NUMBER OF POLICIES PURCHASED (1,000)						AMOUNT PURCHASED (bil. dol.)					
	Total	Ordinary			Group	Indus-trial	Total	Ordinary			Group	Indus-trial
		Total	Percent—					Total	Percent—			
			Whole life [1]	Term [2]					Whole life [1]	Term [2]		
1980	29,007	14,750	78	22	11,379	2,878	573	386	43	57	183	4
1985	33,880	17,104	78	22	16,243	533	1,231	911	62	38	320	1
1987	33,153	16,225	75	25	16,698	230	1,353	987	57	43	366	(Z)
1988	31,589	15,579	81	19	15,793	217	1,407	996	61	39	411	(Z)
1989	29,960	14,694	80	20	15,110	156	1,442	1,021	59	41	421	(Z)
1990	28,791	14,066	79	21	14,592	133	1,529	1,070	58	42	459	(Z)
1991	29,813	13,471	78	22	16,230	112	[3]1,616	1,042	56	44	[3]574	(Z)

Z Less than $500 million.   [1] Life insurance payable to a beneficiary at the death of the insured whenever that occurs. Premiums may be payable for a specified number of years or for life. Includes a small number of endowment and retirement income policies.   [2] Life insurance payable to a beneficiary only when an insured dies within a specified period.   [3] Includes Servicemen's Group Life Insurance: $167 billion in 1991.

No. 845. Life Insurance in Force in the United States—Summary: 1980 to 1991

[As of **December 31** or **calendar year,** as applicable. Covers life insurance with life insurance companies only. Represents all life insurance in force on lives of U.S. residents whether issued by U.S. or foreign companies. For definition of household, see text, section 1. See also *Historical Statistics, Colonial Times to 1970,* series X 879-889]

YEAR	Number of poli-cies, total (mil.)	LIFE INSURANCE IN FORCE					AVERAGE SIZE POLICY IN FORCE (dollars)				AVERAGE AMOUNT ($1,000)		Dispos-able per-sonal income per house-hold ($1,000)
		Value (bil. dol.)					Ordi-nary	Group	Indus-trial	Cred-it [1]	Per house-hold	Per in-sured house-hold	
		Total	Ordi-nary	Group	Indus-trial	Cred-it [1]							
1980	402	3,541	1,761	1,579	36	165	11,920	13,410	620	2,110	41.9	51.1	24.2
1985	386	6,053	3,247	2,562	28	216	22,780	19,720	640	3,100	66.6	82.2	33.9
1987	395	7,452	4,139	3,043	27	243	28,510	22,380	650	3,330	78.7	97.2	36.5
1988	391	8,020	4,512	3,232	25	251	31,390	23,410	660	3,570	84.5	104.3	38.8
1989	394	8,694	4,940	3,469	24	260	34,410	24,510	670	3,600	89.9	111.0	40.8
1990	389	9,393	5,367	3,754	24	248	37,910	26,630	670	3,500	98.4	121.4	44.1
1991	375	9,986	5,678	4,058	22	228	41,450	28,760	680	3,580	102.7	126.8	44.7

[1] Insures borrower to cover consumer loan in case of death.

No. 846. Life Insurance in Force, by State: 1991

[Applies to policyholders in the United States]

REGION, DIVISION, AND STATE	Policies (1,000)	Value (bil. dol.)	REGION, DIVISION, AND STATE	Policies (1,000)	Value (bil. dol.)	REGION, DIVISION, AND STATE	Policies (1,000)	Value (bil. dol.)
U.S.	**374,849**	**9,986**	IA	4,701	115	**W.S.C**	**38,591**	**968**
Northeast	**75,046**	**2,286**	MO	8,523	209	AR	2,686	67
N.E.	**19,376**	**610**	ND	904	26	LA	8,163	153
ME	1,662	40	SD	922	26	OK	3,697	100
NH	1,533	44	NE	2,380	68	TX	24,045	648
VT	882	22	KS	3,801	104	**West**	**59,079**	**1,950**
MA	8,010	257	**South**	**146,754**	**3,308**	**Mt**	**18,462**	**498**
RI	1,723	40	**S.A.**	**76,934**	**1,784**	MT	1,207	27
CT	5,566	207	DE	1,968	41	ID	1,364	36
M.A.	**55,670**	**1,676**	MD	7,869	215	WY	657	17
NY	23,340	786	DC	2,222	69	CO	5,061	149
NJ	11,227	398	VA	13,432	285	NM	1,833	49
PA	21,103	492	WV	2,658	50	AZ	4,627	119
Midwest	**93,970**	**2,442**	NC	12,055	255	UT	2,413	63
E.N.C	**66,614**	**1,716**	SC	7,460	131	NV	1,300	38
OH	17,517	439	GA	12,129	291	**Pac**	**40,617**	**1,452**
IN	9,161	219	FL	17,141	447	WA	5,707	173
IL	18,886	519	**E.S.C**	**31,229**	**556**	OR	3,218	94
MI	13,494	361	KY	5,917	115	CA	29,189	1,108
WI	7,556	178	TN	9,658	192	AK	520	23
W.N.C.	**27,356**	**726**	AL	11,497	167	HI	1,983	54
MN	6,125	178	MS	4,157	82			

Source of tables 844-846: American Council of Life Insurance, Washington, DC, *Life Insurance Fact Book*, biennial.

Business Enterprise

This section relates to the place and behavior of the business firm and to business initiative in the American economy. It includes data on the number, type, and size of businesses; financial data of domestic and multinational U.S. corporations; business investment, expenditures, and profits; sales and inventories; and business failures. Additional business data may be found in other sections, particularly 27 and 28.

The principal sources of these data are the *Survey of Current Business,* published by the Bureau of Economic Analysis (BEA), the *Federal Reserve Bulletin,* issued by the Board of Governors of the Federal Reserve System, the annual *Statistics of Income* reports of the Internal Revenue Service (IRS), *The Business Failure Record* issued by The Dun & Bradstreet Corporation, New York, and *Fortune* and *The Fortune Directory,* issued by Time, Inc., New York.

Business firms.—A firm is generally defined as a business organization under a single management and may include one or more establishments (i.e., a single physical location at which business is conducted). The terms firm, business, company, and enterprise are used interchangeably throughout this section. Examples of series where the industrial distribution is based on data collected from establishments are those on capital stock (table 879), those on gross national product by industry (table 691), and those on employment and earnings (section 13). Examples of company-based series are those on business expenditures for new plant and equipment (table 878), those from IRS *Statistics of Income* (tables 856 and 857), and those on corporation profits by industry (tables 888 and 889). A firm doing business in more than one industry is classified by industry according to the major activity of the firm as a whole. The industrial classification is based on the *Standard Industrial Classification (SIC) Manual* (see text, section 13). The IRS concept of a business firm relates primarily to the legal entity used for tax reporting purposes. The IRS *Statistics of Income* reports present data, based on a sample of tax returns before audit, separately for

In Brief

Patents issued in 1991: 106,800
Percent issued to foreign country
residents: 46%

Bankruptcies filed in 1992: 972,490
Business: 7%
Nonbusiness: 93%
Change from 1991 10%

sole proprietorships, partnerships, and corporations. Data presented are for active enterprises only. A *sole proprietorship* is an unincorporated business owned by one person including large enterprises with many employees and hired managers and part-time operations in which the owner is the only person involved. A *partnership* is an unincorporated business owned by two or more persons, each of whom has a financial interest in the business. The "persons" could be individuals, estates, trusts, other partnerships, or corporations. A *corporation* is a business that is legally incorporated under State laws. The IRS recognizes many types of businesses as corporations, including joint-stock companies, insurance companies, and unincorporated associations such as business trusts, etc. While many corporations file consolidated tax returns, most corporate tax returns represent individual corporations, some of which are affiliated through common ownership or control with other corporations filing separate returns.

Assets and liabilities.—In its annual report, *Statistics of Income, Corporation Income Tax Returns,* the IRS presents balance sheet and income estimates for all active U.S. corporations. The Bureau of the Census issues the *Quarterly Financial Report for Manufacturing, Mining, and Trade Corporations* (QFR), which presents quarterly income account and balance sheet data for manufacturing, mining, and trade industries. This report was prepared by the Federal Trade Commission until responsibilities for QFR were transferred to Census beginning with the fourth quarter 1982 report.

One of the most comprehensive measures of the investment position of the business sector (and the only measure adjusted to current replacement cost) is the BEA capital stock series. See *Survey of Current Business,* January 1992.

Income, profits, dividends, and taxes.— Several agencies, among them IRS and BEA, compile corporate income account data. These data, however, are not comparable because of differing definitions and methods of compilation. A reconciliation of the two can be found in table 8.22 of *Survey of Current Business,* published by BEA. The IRS publishes financial data for all business enterprises. These data appear in *Statistics of Income, Corporation Income Tax Returns* and the *Statistics of Income Bulletin* (partnerships and sole proprietorships). Data on international income and taxes reported by U.S. corporations are also included in the *Statistics of Income Bulletin* and in the periodic *Compendium of Studies of International Income and Taxes.*

Corporate data issued by BEA are a part of its national income and product accounts (see text, section 14). The primary sources for BEA estimates of profits, taxes, dividends, and undistributed profits are the original corporate tax returns submitted to IRS. Various adjustments of IRS data are required by the national income treatment—particularly with respect to profits which would be disclosed if all tax returns were audited: depletion, capital gain or loss, treatment of bad debts, measurement of income received from abroad, and intercorporate dividends—to make the figures comparable with other entries in the national income accounts. For a discussion of two types of adjustments (inventory valuation and capital consumption), see text, section 14. The BEA's corporate profits data also include net earnings of Federal Reserve banks, credit unions, private noninsured pension funds, and several quasi-government credit agencies not included in IRS data.

Sources and uses of corporate funds.— These data (table 853, Federal Reserve Board) show capital requirements of corporations and the manner in which they are financed. Sources of funds should be equal to their uses. Certain discrepancies, however, interfere with this equality due to omission of (1) money accruing to corporations from an excess of sales over purchases of used plant and equipment,

(2) transactions in securities held as permanent investments except public offerings, and (3) net purchases of land. Also, the balance sheet data upon which many of the financial flow estimates are based are not fully comparable with the tax-return based estimates of internal sources or the establishment series underlying the figures on inventory change.

Fortune 500.—Sales include service and rental revenues but exclude dividends, interest, and other non-operating revenues. All companies must have derived more than 50 percent of their sales from manufacturing and/or mining. Sales of subsidiaries are included when they are consolidated. **Assets** are those shown at the company's year-end. **Net income** is shown after taxes and after extraordinary credits or charges when any are shown on the income statement. **Stockholder's equity** is the sum of capital stock, surplus, and retained earnings at the company's year-end. Redeemable preferred stock is excluded when its redemption is either mandatory or outside the control of the company, except in the case of cooperatives. **Total returns to investors** include both price appreciation and dividend yield. Returns are adjusted for stock splits, stock dividends, recapitalizations, and corporate reorganizations as they occur. For further discussion, see Time, Inc., New York, NY, *The Fortune Directories.*

Economic censuses.—The economic censuses constitute comprehensive and periodic canvasses of the Nation's industrial and business activities. The first economic census of the United States was conducted as part of the 1810 decennial census, when inquiries on manufacturing were included with the census of population. Minerals data were collected in 1840. The first censuses of construction and business were taken for 1929. An integrated economic census program was begun for 1954. In that year, the censuses covered the retail and wholesale trades, selected service industries, manufactures, and mineral industries. The economic censuses are taken at 5-year intervals covering years ending in "2" and "7." Special surveys are conducted every 5 years as part of the economic censuses to determine the extent of business ownership by specific minority groups and women.

No. 847. Number of Returns and Business Receipts, by Size of Receipts and Type of Business: 1970 to 1989

[Covers active enterprises only. Figures are estimates based on sample of unaudited tax returns; see Appendix III. The industrial distribution is based on data collected from companies; see text, section 17. See also *Historical Statistics, Colonial Times to 1970*, series V 1-12]

SIZE-CLASS OF RECEIPTS	RETURNS (1,000)					BUSINESS RECEIPTS [1] (bil. dol.)				
	1970	1980	1985	1988	1989	1970	1980	1985	1988	1989
Corporate returns	1,665	2,711	3,277	3,563	3,628	1,706	6,172	8,050	9,804	10,440
Under $25,000 [2]	452	557	711	818	865	3	4	5	5	5
$25,000 to $49,999	171	208	237	228	241	6	8	9	8	9
$50,000 to $99,999	220	323	330	350	332	16	22	24	26	24
$100,000 to $499,999	517	926	1,110	1,134	1,145	123	224	278	288	288
$500,000 to $999,999	141	280	352	409	415	99	197	249	288	292
$1,000,000 or more	165	418	538	623	630	1,459	5,717	7,484	9,189	9,821
Partnership returns	936	1,380	1,714	1,654	1,635	92	286	349	464	465
Under $25,000 [2]	502	638	1,036	1,045	1,014	4	5	4	2	1
$25,000 to $49,999	125	182	154	120	131	5	7	6	3	3
$50,000 to $99,999	120	184	152	151	142	9	13	11	7	8
$100,000 to $499,999	162	290	281	234	242	33	64	61	44	46
$500,000 to $999,999	17	48	48	50	51	12	33	34	30	31
$1,000,000 or more	10	37	42	54	56	30	164	234	378	376
Nonfarm proprietorship returns [3]	6,494	9,730	11,929	13,679	14,298	199	411	540	672	693
Under $25,000 [2]	4,738	6,916	8,250	9,347	9,856	44	44	54	64	66
$25,000 to $49,999	746	1,079	1,394	1,601	1,660	27	39	50	57	60
$50,000 to $99,999	562	836	1,094	1,226	1,259	40	59	77	88	89
$100,000 to $499,999	420	796	1,060	1,337	1,334	76	159	213	277	276
$500,000 to $999,999	21	74	89	118	140	14	50	61	82	96
$1,000,000 or more	7	29	41	50	50	12	60	85	105	106

[1] Excludes investment income except for partnerships (through 1985) and corporations in finance, insurance, and real estate. [2] Includes firms with no receipts. [3] Number of businesses for 1970 and 1980. Number of nonfarm sole proprietorship returns is not available prior to 1981. However, the number of returns and the number of businesses are very closely related. Since 1970, the ratio of number of returns to the number of businesses has remained approximately 1 to 1.1.

Source: U.S. Internal Revenue Service, *Statistics of Income, Statistics of Income Bulletin;* and unpublished data.

No. 848. Number of Returns, Receipts, and Net Income, by Type of Business, 1970 to 1989, and by Industry, 1989

[See headnote, table 847. Minus sign (-) indicates net loss]

YEAR AND INDUSTRY	NUMBER OF RETURNS (1,000)			BUSINESS RECEIPTS [2] (bil. dol.)			NET INCOME (less loss) [3] (bil. dol.)		
	Nonfarm proprietorships [1]	Partnerships	Corporations	Nonfarm proprietorships [1]	Partnerships	Corporations	Nonfarm proprietorships [1]	Partnerships	Corporations
1970	5,770	936	1,665	199	92	1,706	31	10	66
1980	8,932	1,380	2,711	411	286	6,172	55	8	239
1985	11,929	1,714	3,277	540	349	8,050	79	-9	240
1987	13,091	1,648	3,612	611	411	9,186	106	-5	328
1988	13,679	1,654	3,563	672	464	9,804	126	15	413
1989 [4]	14,298	1,635	3,628	693	465	10,440	133	14	389
Agriculture, forestry, and fishing [5]	342	131	123	15	8	81	2	1	2
Mining	155	46	42	7	20	88	1	2	3
Construction	1,757	62	393	101	30	505	17	3	9
Manufacturing	431	26	301	25	55	3,276	3	1	181
Transportation, public utilities	623	22	156	31	27	844	5	-2	39
Wholesale and retail trade [6]	2,438	173	1,013	234	90	3,095	14	3	36
Wholesale	329	16	321	37	29	1,504	4	1	19
Retail	2,052	156	689	189	61	1,587	8	2	17
Finance, insurance, real estate	1,270	853	593	50	71	1,868	16	-21	109
Services	7,039	299	990	226	162	680	74	27	11

[1] Through 1980, includes both individually owned business and farm returns; thereafter, includes only nonfarm business returns. [2] Excludes investment income except for partnerships (through 1985) and corporations in finance, insurance, and real estate. For 1987, partnerships and S corporations exclude gross income from rental real estate and other rental activities and portfolio income distributed directly to partners or shareholders. S corporations have no more than 35 shareholders (10 prior to 1983) most of which are individuals, electing to be taxed at the shareholder level. [3] Net income (less loss) is defined differently by form of organization, basically as follows: (a) Proprietorships: Total taxable receipts less total deductions, including cost of sales and operations (except charitable contributions and owners' salary), investment and other income are excluded; (b) Partnerships: Total taxable receipts less total deductions, including cost of sales and operations (except foreign taxes and oil depletion), investment and other income (except capital gains); (c) Corporations: Total taxable receipts less total deductions, including cost of sales and operations; investment and other income, such as capital gains and income from foreign corporations considered received for tax purposes only; net income is before income tax. [4] Includes businesses not specifically allocated to industries below. [5] Represents agricultural services only. [6] Includes trade business not identified as wholesale or retail.

Source: U.S. Internal Revenue Service, *Statistics of Income,* various publications.

No. 849. Number of Returns and Business Receipts, by Industry, Type of Business, and Size of Business Receipts: 1989

[Number of returns in thousands; receipts and net income in billions of dollars. Covers active enterprises only. Figures are estimates based on a sample of unaudited tax returns; see Appendix III. The industrial distribution is based on data collected from establishments; see text, section 17. See also *Historical Statistics, Colonial Times to 1970*, series V 42-53, for number of active corporations. Minus sign (-) indicates net loss]

INDUSTRY	Non-farm pro-prietor-ships, total	Partner-ships, total	CORPORATIONS				
			Under $1 mil. [1]	$1 mil.-$4.9 mil.	$5 mil.-$9.9 mil.	$10 mil.-$49.9 mil.	$50 mil. or more
All industrial divisions: [2]							
Number	14,298	1,635	2,998	468	80	68	15
Business receipts [3]	693	465	618	1,003	555	1,340	6,924
Net income (less loss)	133	14	-5	11	11	39	333
Agriculture, forestry, fishing: [4]							
Number	342	131	110	11	1	1	(Z)
Business receipts [5]	15	8	17	22	8	16	18
Mining:							
Number	155	46	37	4	1	1	(Z)
Business receipts [3]	7	20	4	7	4	11	61
Construction:							
Number	1,757	62	312	65	10	5	1
Business receipts [3]	101	30	83	139	68	100	115
Manufacturing:							
Number	431	26	202	65	15	14	5
Business receipts [3]	25	55	55	149	104	299	2,669
Transportation, public utilities:							
Number	623	22	124	25	3	2	1
Business receipts [3]	31	27	25	56	24	48	692
Wholesale and retail trade:							
Number	2,438	173	747	193	35	32	5
Business receipts [3]	234	90	205	416	246	627	1,602
Finance, insurance, real estate:							
Number	1,270	853	545	32	6	7	3
Business receipts [3]	50	71	63	68	45	143	1,549
Services:							
Number	7,039	299	903	73	8	5	1
Business receipts [3]	226	162	165	146	55	95	219

Z Less than 500 returns.   [1] Includes businesses without receipts.   [2] Includes businesses not allocable to individual industries.   [3] Excludes investment income except for corporations (other than S corporations; see table 848, footnote 2) in finance, insurance, and real estate.   [4] Represents agricultural services only.   [5] Total receipts for corporations.

Source: U.S. Internal Revenue Service, *Statistics of Income*, various publications; and unpublished data.

No. 850. Nonfarm Sole Proprietorship Returns—Selected Income and Deduction Items: 1970 to 1990

[In millions of dollars, except as indicated. All figures are estimates based on sample. Tax law changes have affected the comparability of the data over time. See *Statistics of Income* reports for a description of appropriate years tax law changes; see Appendix III. See also *Historical Statistics, Colonial Times to 1970*, series V 4-6]

ITEM	1970	1980	1984	1985	1986	1987	1988	1989	1990
Number of returns, total (1,000) [1]	5,770	8,932	11,262	11,929	12,394	13,091	13,679	14,298	14,783
Businesses with net income (1,000)	(NA)	(NA)	8,003	8,641	9,248	9,884	10,492	11,018	11,223
Inventory, end of year	11,061	21,996	23,233	24,970	24,477	26,333	27,313	30,060	30,422
Business receipts, total [2]	198,582	411,206	516,037	540,045	559,384	610,823	671,970	692,811	730,606
Income from sales and operations	(NA)	407,169	507,234	528,675	548,273	598,315	658,687	678,616	719,008
Business deductions, total [2]	168,045	356,258	445,270	461,273	468,960	505,362	545,735	560,175	589,250
Cost of goods sold/operations	109,149	209,890	229,906	232,294	232,135	255,045	277,880	283,709	291,011
Purchases	88,586	168,302	(NA)	(NA)	(NA)	173,400	197,220	204,681	210,225
Labor costs	7,704	10,922	13,009	14,504	17,318	19,631	21,143	22,540	22,680
Materials and supplies	6,216	12,909	(NA)	(NA)	(NA)	23,842	27,800	29,870	30,195
Commissions	1,274	3,333	(NA)	(NA)	5,461	6,262	6,540	6,843	8,816
Salaries and wages (net)	15,107	26,561	34,686	38,266	38,691	42,330	43,007	45,469	46,998
Car and truck expenses	(NA)	13,378	17,524	17,044	16,381	17,470	19,640	20,789	21,766
Rent paid [3]	4,637	9,636	14,278	15,259	15,654	16,358	19,470	20,952	23,392
Repairs	2,445	5,032	(NA)	(NA)	(NA)	7,438	8,104	8,149	8,941
Taxes paid	3,776	7,672	(NA)	(NA)	(NA)	8,449	9,495	9,948	10,342
Utilities	(NA)	4,790	(NA)	(NA)	(NA)	13,362	14,618	13,601	13,539
Insurance	2,310	6,003	(NA)	(NA)	10,783	11,719	12,528	12,879	13,358
Interest paid	1,784	7,190	11,025	11,914	11,504	11,616	12,071	13,280	13,312
Depreciation	5,452	13,953	23,900	26,291	26,418	25,557	26,078	24,479	23,735
Pension and profit sharing plans	73	141	258	311	638	548	450	539	586
Net income (less loss)	30,537	54,947	70,767	78,773	90,423	105,461	126,323	132,738	141,430
Businesses with net income	33,736	68,010	89,849	98,776	110,497	123,783	145,518	152,416	161,657

NA Not available.   [1] Through 1980, includes both individually owned business and farm returns; thereafter, includes only nonfarm business returns.   [2] Includes other amounts not shown separately.   [3] Beginning 1989, rent paid deduction includes rent on business property, machinery, and equipment. Prior to 1989, deduction included only rent on business property.

Source: U.S. Internal Revenue Service, *Statistics of Income Bulletin*, various publications.

No. 851. Partnerships—Selected Items, by Industry: 1980 to 1990

[In millions of dollars, except number of partners and partnerships in thousands. Covers active partnerships only. Includes partnerships not allocable by nature of business. Figures are estimates based on samples. See Appendix III]

| INDUSTRY AND YEAR | NUMBER OF PARTNERSHIPS | | | Number of part-ners | Total assets | Business re-ceipts [1][2] | Total deduc-tions [2] | Net income less loss [2] | Net income | Net loss |
	Total	With net income	With net loss							
All industries:										
1980	1,380	774	605	8,420	597,504	285,967	283,749	8,249	45,062	36,813
1985	1,714	876	838	13,245	1,269,434	349,169	376,001	-8,884	77,045	85,928
1987	1,648	865	783	16,963	1,381,297	411,457	423,499	-5,419	87,654	93,073
1988	1,654	901	753	17,291	1,580,194	463,956	464,991	14,493	111,384	96,892
1989	1,635	898	737	18,432	1,791,027	464,952	475,434	14,099	113,886	99,787
1990	1,554	854	687	17,095	1,685,223	483,418	549,602	16,610	116,318	99,708
Agriculture, forestry, and fishing:										
1980	126	72	54	381	24,595	21,611	22,859	472	2,539	2,067
1985	136	76	60	585	27,027	6,529	10,495	-1,049	2,797	3,846
1987	149	97	52	592	26,402	6,756	9,146	2,015	4,488	2,472
1988	122	80	42	555	24,106	8,988	11,602	1,079	3,827	2,748
1989	131	83	48	591	25,219	7,708	10,133	1,380	3,679	2,299
1990	125	77	48	503	27,580	9,497	11,805	1,667	3,905	2,238
Mining:										
1980	35	15	20	722	24,742	13,201	18,248	-4,208	3,920	8,128
1985	62	33	30	2,207	66,930	19,922	21,920	1,482	7,884	6,402
1987	60	24	36	2,742	71,492	15,332	19,424	-1,360	5,698	7,058
1988	48	31	17	2,467	65,652	15,977	18,759	934	6,641	5,707
1989	46	26	20	3,771	62,073	19,701	20,751	1,965	7,027	5,062
1990	41	29	11	2,149	58,246	19,967	20,869	2,183	7,009	4,825
Construction:										
1980	67	51	16	160	9,811	18,407	17,202	1,560	2,119	559
1985	57	41	16	134	15,008	21,476	20,080	2,207	2,743	536
1987	62	48	14	153	17,077	26,295	24,293	2,766	3,350	584
1988	74	60	14	179	20,070	30,978	28,712	3,284	3,929	645
1989	62	46	16	165	21,150	30,052	28,397	2,647	3,313	666
1990	59	45	14	162	17,989	30,716	29,672	1,908	3,020	1,112
Transportation and public utilities:										
1980	20	11	10	73	9,291	5,868	5,821	248	1,092	844
1985	25	15	10	186	26,468	11,253	14,814	-3,066	1,360	4,426
1987	30	13	17	429	42,015	19,795	24,228	-3,781	2,028	5,809
1988	20	12	8	433	45,003	21,639	25,389	-2,292	2,951	5,244
1989	22	10	12	435	54,171	26,727	30,319	-1,977	3,695	5,671
1990	25	14	11	503	63,334	37,800	35,989	-117	5,887	6,004
Manufacturing:										
1980	30	20	10	92	11,252	15,327	16,142	-472	1,199	1,671
1985	30	12	18	105	24,838	22,588	24,225	-1,085	1,228	2,314
1987	35	18	17	178	30,965	32,356	32,576	806	2,504	1,698
1988	26	12	14	173	41,714	43,724	43,345	1,540	3,598	2,058
1989	26	14	12	185	56,601	55,336	55,816	1,398	4,154	2,756
1990	28	15	13	246	59,789	65,354	65,833	1,166	4,791	3,626
Wholesale and retail trade:										
1980	200	123	77	487	17,727	65,793	63,988	2,475	3,374	900
1985	201	113	88	493	20,568	69,079	68,119	1,977	3,467	1,490
1987	185	100	85	476	26,105	70,560	69,277	2,697	4,215	1,518
1988	180	104	76	490	26,512	83,640	56,375	3,351	4,742	1,391
1989	173	98	75	496	27,294	90,306	89,418	2,529	4,550	2,021
1990	175	100	76	481	28,423	96,120	97,131	2,610	4,717	2,107
Finance, insurance, and real estate:										
1980	637	313	325	5,566	454,531	87,133	91,382	-4,249	15,169	19,418
1985	844	369	475	7,755	979,787	92,309	118,237	-25,929	30,383	56,311
1987	828	365	463	10,327	1,040,671	123,239	139,480	-26,777	36,061	62,837
1988	869	398	471	10,880	1,200,673	115,415	127,356	-19,258	47,842	67,100
1989	853	419	434	11,327	1,394,319	71,243	91,965	-20,824	47,753	68,576
1990	822	401	422	10,846	1,279,390	64,313	87,011	-19,213	47,577	66,790
Services:										
1980	263	169	94	938	45,510	58,627	48,106	12,424	15,649	3,224
1985	341	207	134	1,713	106,597	104,197	96,202	16,541	26,942	10,400
1987	291	194	97	2,042	125,134	116,379	104,296	18,092	29,118	11,025
1988	296	197	99	2,060	154,548	141,909	126,505	25,639	37,527	11,888
1989	299	189	110	2,370	148,688	162,325	147,280	26,652	39,296	12,643
1990	267	173	95	2,153	150,063	161,702	145,789	26,453	39,383	12,930

[1] Business and investment receipts for partnerships in finance, insurance, and real estate, and business receipts for all other industries through 1985. For 1987, excludes gross income from rental real estate and other rental activities and portfolio income distributed directly to partners.   [2] Beginning 1985, the agriculture, forestry, and fishing industries are based on revised collection procedures. See source for detail.

Source: U.S. Internal Revenue Service, *Statistics of Income Bulletin*, various publications.

No. 852. Partnership Returns—Selected Income Statement and Balance Sheet Items: 1980 to 1990

[In billions of dollars, except as indicated. Covers active partnerships only. All figures are estimates based on samples. See Appendix III and *Historical Statistics, Colonial Times to 1970*, series V 7-9]

ITEM	1980	1983	1984	1985	1986	1987	1988	1989	1990
Partnerships, number (1,000)	1,380	1,542	1,644	1,714	1,703	1,648	1,654	1,635	1,554
Number with net income (1,000). . .	774	784	845	876	851	865	901	898	854
Number with balance sheets (1,000)	1,194	1,191	1,215	1,227	1,203	1,129	1,155	1,149	1,081
Number of partners (1,000)	8,420	10,589	12,427	13,245	15,229	16,963	17,291	18,432	17,095
Assets, total [1] [2].	598	887	1,031	1,269	1,404	1,381	1,580	1,791	1,685
Depreciable assets (net)	239	346	582	696	780	567	621	670	1,033
Inventories, end of year	33	77	62	27	47	45	51	59	57
Land	70	98	122	152	179	178	200	214	215
Liabilities, total [1]	489	745	855	1,269	1,176	1,386	1,580	1,791	1,369
Accounts payable	34	35	33	47	44	41	49	52	62
Short-term debt [3]	48	67	69	103	92	82	87	87	88
Long-term debt [4]	178	268	322	382	429	430	474	512	497
Nonrecourse loans.	119	195	260	328	365	388	437	461	470
Partners' capital accounts	109	142	175	200	228	247	267	356	316
Receipts, total [1] [5] [6]	292	291	375	367	397	474	540	550	519
Business receipts [5] [6]	271	243	318	303	327	411	464	465	483
Interest received [7]	11	15	17	21	22	18	19	21	21
Deductions, total [1] [6]	284	294	379	376	415	423	465	475	550
Cost of goods sold/operations. . . .	114	125	181	146	164	237	253	233	242
Salaries and wages	22	25	29	34	36	41	47	54	56
Taxes paid	10	6	7	8	8	7	8	9	9
Interest paid	28	22	25	29	29	20	23	33	30
Depreciation	22	37	20	23	23	19	20	20	60
Net income (less loss) [6].	8	-3	-4	-9	-17	-5	14	14	17
Businesses with net income.	45	60	70	77	80	88	111	114	116

[1] Includes other amounts not shown separately.　[2] Total assets, total liabilities, and partners' capital accounts are somewhat understated because not all partnership returns filed contained a complete balance sheet.　[3] Represents mortgages, notes, and bonds payable in less than 1 year.　[4] Represents mortgages, notes, and bonds payable in 1 year or more.　[5] For 1987, excludes gross income from rental real estate and other rental activities and portfolio income distributed directly to partners. [6] Beginning 1987, receipts, deductions, and net income from trade or only. Except for total receipts, excludes income and expenses related to certain investment activities. See source for detail.　[7] Beginning 1983, includes both interest and dividends.

Source: U.S. Internal Revenue Service, *Statistics of Income Bulletin,* various publications.

No. 853. Corporate Funds—Sources and Uses: 1970 to 1992

[In billions of dollars, except percent. Covers nonfarm nonfinancial corporate business. See text, section 17]

SOURCE AND USE	1970	1980	1985	1986	1987	1988	1989	1990	1991	1992
Sources, total.	106.5	330.3	465.7	515.9	540.7	588.7	532.2	511.4	447.3	568.9
Internal.	64.0	199.7	351.9	336.7	375.9	404.3	399.9	407.5	416.5	453.3
Domestic undistributed profits . . .	8.6	52.9	10.7	-18.9	26.7	44.4	5.5	2.0	-9.2	12.2
IVA and CCA [1]	-1.1	-61.4	54.4	53.4	30.6	15.7	19.8	12.9	20.9	30.1
Capital consumption allowances. .	49.4	173.2	256.0	269.2	279.2	295.1	315.1	327.0	338.5	347.9
Foreign earnings [2]	7.2	35.0	30.8	32.9	39.5	49.1	59.5	65.7	66.5	63.1
External [3]	42.5	130.6	113.9	179.2	164.8	184.4	132.3	103.9	30.8	115.6
Percent of total	40.0	39.5	24.4	34.7	30.5	31.3	24.9	20.3	6.9	20.3
Credit market funds	36.7	76.5	58.5	129.8	67.6	69.3	49.4	23.4	22.0	80.3
Securities and mortgages.	28.8	35.9	1.9	64.6	32.8	-6.7	-34.2	-11.5	90.7	81.0
Equity issues.	5.7	10.4	-84.5	-85.0	-75.5	-129.5	-124.2	-63.0	18.3	26.8
Bonds and mortgages [4]	23.1	25.5	86.4	149.6	108.3	122.8	89.9	51.5	72.4	54.2
Loans and short-term paper . . .	7.8	40.6	56.6	65.2	34.9	76.0	83.7	34.9	-68.7	-0.7
Other.	5.9	54.1	55.4	49.4	97.1	115.1	82.9	80.5	8.8	35.3
Profit taxes payable.	-2.6	2.9	-3.2	3.8	5.1	1.7	-3.1	-1.0	-10.0	3.8
Trade debt	7.1	38.0	34.0	13.7	39.9	59.1	30.5	40.3	10.7	24.9
Foreign direct investments in U.S	1.4	13.2	24.5	31.9	52.2	54.2	55.4	41.1	8.0	6.6
Uses, total	100.2	352.8	457.8	502.4	473.4	554.2	512.2	482.4	425.5	549.5
Capital expenditures	82.0	255.8	374.9	351.9	365.1	394.4	406.0	395.1	363.9	385.3
Increase in financial assets.	18.3	97.1	83.0	150.4	108.4	159.8	106.2	87.3	61.6	164.2
Discrepancy (sources less uses) . . .	6.3	-22.5	7.9	13.5	67.3	34.4	20.0	29.0	21.8	19.4

[1] Inventory valuation and capital consumption adjustment.　[2] Foreign branch profits, dividends, and subsidiaries' earnings retained abroad.　[3] Net increases in liability.　[4] Includes industrial pollution control revenue bonds, issued by State and local governments.

Source: Board of Governors of the Federal Reserve System. Data derived from *Flow of Funds Accounts,* annual.

No. 854. Nonfinancial Corporate Business-Sector Balance Sheet: 1970 to 1991

[In billions of dollars. Represents yearend outstandings]

ITEM	1970	1980	1982	1983	1984	1985	1986	1987	1988	1989	1990	1991
Total assets	**1,354**	**4,470**	**5,183**	**5,403**	**5,722**	**6,000**	**6,313**	**6,663**	**7,131**	**7,525**	**7,645**	**7,429**
Tangible assets (current cost)	969	3,279	3,860	3,980	4,216	4,399	4,547	4,751	5,057	5,335	5,334	5,050
Reproducible	824	2,771	3,240	3,320	3,514	3,659	3,773	3,939	4,183	4,398	4,581	4,624
Land	145	508	620	659	702	741	775	813	873	937	752	426
Financial assets	385	1,191	1,322	1,423	1,507	1,601	1,766	1,912	2,074	2,190	2,311	2,379
Liquid assets [1]	70	197	267	302	326	355	416	441	465	470	488	532
Checkable deposits and currency	44	57	53	62	75	94	113	120	137	134	132	142
Time deposits	5	38	59	71	74	80	88	92	106	103	99	103
Consumer credit	15	25	26	30	33	37	41	48	54	56	59	59
Mutual fund shares	1	2	3	5	7	11	16	13	11	12	10	15
Trade credit	192	482	491	543	590	630	655	701	793	838	849	837
Miscellaneous assets	109	486	535	544	550	568	638	710	752	814	905	935
Total liabilities	**550**	**1,377**	**1,637**	**1,767**	**2,008**	**2,208**	**2,466**	**2,741**	**3,047**	**3,296**	**3,446**	**3,465**
Credit market instruments	369	875	1,029	1,112	1,293	1,440	1,650	1,828	2,017	2,195	2,273	2,274
Profit taxes payable	10	44	36	39	42	39	43	48	50	47	46	36
Trade debt	160	348	381	418	452	486	500	540	599	629	670	680
Foreign direct investment in U.S	11	110	191	198	221	243	274	326	382	425	458	476
Net worth	**804**	**3,093**	**3,545**	**3,636**	**3,715**	**3,792**	**3,847**	**3,922**	**4,084**	**4,229**	**4,199**	**3,963**

[1] Includes other assets not shown separately.
Source: Board of Governors of the Federal Reserve System, *Balance Sheets for the U.S. Economy.*

No. 855. Corporation Income Tax Returns—Selected Financial Items: 1980 to 1989

[In billions of dollars, except number of returns. Covers active corporations only. All corporations are required to file returns except those specifically exempt. See source for changes in law affecting comparability of historical data. Based on samples; see Appendix III. See also *Historical Statistics, Colonial Times to 1970*, series Y 381-392]

ITEM	1980	1982	1983	1984	1985	1986	1987	1988	1989
Number of returns, total (1,000)	**2,711**	**2,926**	**2,999**	**3,171**	**3,277**	**3,429**	**3,612**	**3,563**	**3,628**
Number with net income (1,000)	1,597	1,608	1,676	1,778	1,820	1,908	1,995	1,909	1,922
S Corporation returns [1] (1,000)	545	564	648	701	725	826	1,128	1,257	1,423
BALANCE SHEET									
Assets, total [2]	**7,617**	**9,358**	**10,201**	**11,107**	**12,773**	**14,163**	**15,311**	**16,568**	**17,647**
Cash	529	541	590	596	683	763	754	785	824
Notes and accounts receivable	1,985	2,420	2,677	2,897	3,318	3,594	3,763	4,099	4,196
Inventories	535	581	599	664	715	733	829	846	879
Investments in Government obligations	472	606	685	726	917	1,059	1,092	1,095	1,262
Mortgage and real estate	894	942	982	1,127	1,259	1,377	1,455	1,605	1,610
Other investments	1,214	1,605	1,798	1,973	2,414	2,848	3,227	3,614	3,971
Depreciable assets	2,107	2,583	2,730	2,913	3,174	3,383	3,603	3,821	4,070
Depletable assets	72	95	108	115	112	116	123	124	134
Land	93	110	119	128	141	150	159	177	191
Liabilities, total [2]	**7,617**	**9,358**	**10,201**	**11,107**	**12,773**	**14,163**	**15,311**	**16,568**	**17,647**
Accounts payable	542	679	671	741	892	909	998	1,023	1,090
Mortgages, notes, and bonds, short-term [3]	505	667	760	867	1,001	1,084	1,247	1,431	1,602
Mortgages, notes, and bonds, long-term [4]	987	1,224	1,323	1,494	1,699	1,958	2,141	2,352	2,490
Capital stock	417	658	787	839	920	1,191	1,292	1,429	1,477
Paid-in or capital surplus	532	782	874	1,066	1,421	1,726	1,988	2,154	2,595
Retained earnings [5]	1,070	1,228	1,274	1,308	1,366	1,394	1,417	1,493	1,522
Net worth	**1,944**	**2,470**	**2,645**	**2,884**	**3,304**	**3,698**	**3,947**	**4,207**	**4,603**
INCOME STATEMENT									
Receipts, total [2][6]	**6,361**	**7,024**	**7,135**	**7,861**	**8,398**	**8,669**	**9,582**	**10,265**	**10,935**
Business receipts [6][7]	5,732	6,157	6,335	6,948	7,370	7,535	8,415	8,950	9,427
Interest [8]	367	530	511	580	635	662	706	805	967
Rents and royalties	54	83	83	90	105	110	113	116	129
Deductions, total [2][6]	**6,125**	**6,869**	**6,945**	**7,629**	**8,158**	**8,395**	**9,244**	**9,853**	**10,545**
Cost of sales and operations [7]	4,205	4,271	4,308	4,693	4,894	4,923	5,596	5,945	6,317
Compensation of officers	109	129	141	157	171	185	200	203	198
Rent paid on business property	72	95	105	119	135	145	154	161	173
Taxes paid	163	166	173	192	201	203	211	222	236
Interest paid	345	515	475	536	569	573	590	672	832
Depreciation	157	213	241	265	304	313	317	328	337
Advertising	52	65	72	82	92	99	107	114	124
Net income (less loss), total [6]	**239**	**154**	**188**	**233**	**240**	**270**	**328**	**413**	**389**
Net income	297	274	297	349	364	409	465	556	556
Deficit	58	120	109	116	124	139	137	143	167
TAX ITEMS									
Income subject to tax	247	205	219	257	266	276	312	383	371
Income tax before credits [9]	104	85	90	106	109	109	115	127	128
Tax credits, total [2]	**42**	**40**	**40**	**44**	**48**	**37**	**31**	**35**	**32**
Foreign tax credit	25	19	20	21	24	21	21	27	24
Income tax after credits [9]	**62**	**45**	**51**	**62**	**61**	**72**	**84**	**92**	**96**

[1] Represents corporations with no more than 35 shareholders (10 prior to 1983), most of which are individuals, electing to be taxed at the shareholder level. [2] Includes items not shown separately. [3] Payable in less than 1 year. [4] Payable in 1 year or more. [5] Appropriated and unappropriated. [6] Beginning 1987, receipts, deductions and net income of S corporations (footnote 1) limited to those from trade or business. Except for total receipts, excludes income and expenses related to certain investment activities. [7] Beginning 1987, includes sales and cost of sales of securities, commodities and real estate by exchanges, brokers or dealers selling on their own account. In 1989, excludes investment income for corporations in finance, insurance, and real estate. Such income is included in total receipts. [8] Includes tax-exempt interest on Government obligations issued by U.S., State, and local governments. [9] Consists of regular (and alternative tax); excludes minimum tax and adjustments for certain prior year credits.
Source: U.S. Internal Revenue Service, *Statistics of Income, Corporation Income Tax Returns,* annual.

No. 856. Corporation Income Tax Returns—Selected Financial Items, by Industry: 1980 to 1989

[In billions of dollars, except as indicated. Covers active corporations only. Industrial distribution based on data collected from companies; see text, section 17. Excludes corporations not allocable by nature of business]

INDUSTRY AND ITEM	1980	1983	1984	1985	1986	1987	1988	1989
Agriculture, forestry, and fishing:								
Returns (1,000)	81	92	98	103	107	117	120	123
Assets	40.7	50.3	50.7	52.7	53.5	55.4	60.5	63.4
Liabilities [1]	29.3	36.7	36.4	37.2	36.4	37.2	40.2	42.3
Receipts [2]	52.1	59.2	66.6	70.5	77.5	77.1	86.3	86.6
Deductions [2]	51.4	59.4	66.4	70.6	76.3	75.4	84.6	85.1
Net income (less loss) [2]	0.7	-0.2	0.2	-0.1	1.1	1.6	1.6	1.6
Mining:								
Returns (1,000)	26	37	41	41	40	42	41	42
Assets	126.9	194.4	209.0	240.8	206.1	220.1	225.6	236.3
Liabilities [1]	72.9	108.8	114.7	136.0	107.5	110.6	113.8	109.9
Receipts [2]	176.7	132.4	123.5	142.0	98.6	96.8	100.4	102.4
Deductions [2]	169.1	134.3	124.6	145.4	102.1	96.7	96.8	99.5
Net income (less loss) [2]	7.8	-1.6	-0.4	-2.5	-3.1	0.3	4.1	3.1
Construction:								
Returns (1,000)	272	284	307	318	342	371	381	393
Assets	132.9	161.4	195.3	215.3	218.9	222.1	241.4	249.7
Liabilities [1]	100.1	119.8	144.9	160.6	166.1	168.1	178.9	183.0
Receipts [2]	267.2	290.8	338.6	387.2	412.5	454.8	499.7	517.5
Deductions [2]	262.1	288.6	335.7	382.8	406.7	446.1	488.4	508.8
Net income (less loss) [2]	5.3	2.3	2.9	4.4	5.8	8.7	11.3	8.7
Manufacturing:								
Returns (1,000)	243	262	272	277	285	294	300	301
Assets	1,709.5	2,233.0	2,417.6	2,644.4	2,931.6	3,111.7	3,390.4	3,721.2
Liabilities [1]	960.3	1,279.9	1,392.6	1,544.7	1,807.2	1,920.0	2,137.2	2,347.7
Receipts [2]	2,404.3	2,552.8	2,768.2	2,831.1	2,810.7	3,141.4	3,349.0	3,531.2
Deductions [2]	2,290.6	2,469.3	2,661.2	2,733.1	2,723.7	3,012.1	3,170.0	3,377.1
Net income (less loss) [2]	125.7	95.3	121.2	113.8	101.8	145.5	205.1	180.5
Transportation and public utilities:								
Returns (1,000)	111	123	128	138	138	148	149	156
Assets	758.4	998.9	1,084.9	1,246.4	1,310.2	1,352.5	1,411.2	1,474.4
Liabilities [1]	467.7	604.6	660.9	755.9	807.7	842.4	891.8	963.1
Receipts [2]	523.8	657.4	725.6	772.4	762.2	786.2	838.8	906.5
Deductions [2]	504.0	638.2	697.2	747.8	740.7	749.0	792.5	867.6
Net income (less loss) [2]	20.0	19.5	28.9	25.1	21.0	37.5	46.9	39.1
Wholesale and retail trade:								
Returns (1,000)	800	852	897	917	939	972	985	1,013
Assets	646.9	804.2	899.0	1,010.0	1,073.5	1,177.7	1,295.8	1,390.6
Liabilities [1]	424.6	539.0	609.7	723.7	773.4	861.2	963.9	1,047.8
Receipts [2]	1,955.5	2,119.4	2,307.6	2,473.9	2,547.4	2,766.7	2,978.0	3,184.9
Deductions [2]	1,919.5	2,084.5	2,265.8	2,440.4	2,512.1	2,728.5	2,935.5	3,148.8
Net income (less loss) [2]	35.8	35.3	42.0	33.1	34.0	38.0	42.8	36.2
Finance, insurance, and real estate:								
Returns (1,000)	493	480	497	518	537	521	572	593
Assets	4,022.2	5,487.2	5,939.0	7,029.5	7,985.6	8,732.3	9,411.5	9,957.5
Liabilities [1]	3,491.7	4,670.4	5,037.3	5,867.5	6,483.4	7,097.4	7,632.1	7,929.3
Receipts [2]	697.5	902.8	1,033.1	1,182.0	1,365.1	1,589.2	1,714.4	1,868.0
Deductions [2]	652.6	856.7	985.7	1,104.6	1,245.5	1,476.7	1,596.0	1,730.5
Net income (less loss) [2]	33.1	31.7	32.7	60.7	99.8	87.4	91.9	108.9
Services:								
Returns (1,000)	671	848	899	939	1,012	1,120	995	990
Assets	178.2	269.8	307.9	331.0	381.6	435.6	530.3	552.1
Liabilities [1]	125.3	198.1	223.1	241.1	284.1	323.1	402.2	419.8
Receipts [2]	279.9	416.5	490.3	534.6	591.9	663.1	695.3	735.5
Deductions [2]	271.8	410.5	485.0	528.7	584.3	654.0	686.3	724.9
Net income (less loss) [2]	8.2	6.0	5.5	5.9	7.0	9.3	9.3	11.0
ANNUAL PERCENT CHANGE RECEIPTS [3]								
Agriculture, forestry, and fishing	-2.4	-9.4	12.6	5.9	9.9	-0.5	11.9	0.3
Mining	33.3	-34.8	-6.7	15.0	-30.6	-1.8	3.7	1.9
Construction	5.7	3.2	16.4	14.4	6.5	10.2	9.8	3.6
Manufacturing	11.7	2.6	8.4	2.3	-0.7	11.7	6.6	5.4
Transportation and public utilities	17.5	4.0	10.3	6.4	-1.3	3.1	6.6	8.1
Wholesale and retail trade	11.6	5.0	8.9	7.2	3.0	8.6	7.6	6.9
Finance, insurance, and real estate	24.3	-5.0	14.4	14.4	15.5	16.4	7.8	9.0
Services	14.2	9.4	17.7	9.0	10.7	12.0	4.8	5.8

[1] Liabilities does not include net worth. [2] Beginning 1987, receipts, deductions and net income of S corporations limited to those from trade or business; those from investments are generally excluded. For definition of S corporation, see table 855, footnote 1. [3] Change from preceding year.

Source: U.S. Internal Revenue Service, *Statistics of Income, Corporation Income Tax Returns,* annual.

No. 857. Corporation Income Tax Returns, by Asset-Size Class and Industry: 1989

[In millions of dollars, except returns and percent distribution. Covers active corporations only. Excludes corporations not allocable by nature of business. The industrial distribution is based on data collected from companies; see text, section 17. Detail may not add to total because of rounding. See also *Historical Statistics, Colonial Times to 1970*, series V 167-183 and V 193-196]

INDUSTRY AND ITEM	Total	ASSET-SIZE CLASS					
		Under 10 mil. dol.[1]	10-24.9 mil. dol.	25-49.9 mil. dol.	50-99.9 mil. dol.	100-249.9 mil. dol.	250 mil. dol. and over
Agriculture, forestry, and fishing:							
Returns	123,195	122,726	272	101	52	35	7
Assets	63,413	43,373	4,024	3,553	3,613	5,711	3,139
Receipts	86,627	61,717	5,716	4,527	4,975	5,605	4,087
Deductions	85,065	60,918	5,741	4,406	4,818	5,478	3,704
Net income (less loss)	1,551	782	−26	123	156	125	391
Mining:							
Returns	41,631	40,729	441	177	123	74	87
Assets	236,339	16,853	6,761	6,488	10,333	12,497	183,408
Receipts	102,379	20,750	5,253	4,042	6,941	9,028	56,365
Deductions	99,497	21,109	5,172	3,974	6,593	8,601	54,047
Net income (less loss)	3,145	−367	77	63	351	426	2,595
Construction:							
Returns	393,103	390,922	1,522	367	163	86	43
Assets	249,711	136,548	22,379	12,382	11,031	15,205	52,168
Receipts	517,477	364,495	44,836	22,039	17,761	23,396	44,951
Deductions	508,789	359,132	43,615	21,521	17,261	22,945	44,315
Net income (less loss)	8,737	5,346	1,212	508	492	439	740
Manufacturing:							
Returns	301,346	290,263	5,785	2,138	1,172	932	1,056
Assets	3,721,220	194,397	90,151	74,583	82,846	146,197	3,133,044
Receipts	3,531,219	487,738	165,191	116,517	116,502	185,132	2,460,139
Deductions	3,377,145	478,695	160,452	112,489	111,801	178,022	2,335,686
Net income (less loss)	180,476	9,673	4,717	4,046	4,787	7,429	149,823
Transportation and public utilities:							
Returns	156,037	153,836	1,065	381	210	186	358
Assets	1,474,413	57,835	16,277	13,723	15,573	30,190	1,340,815
Receipts	906,501	149,072	19,973	15,843	13,823	26,946	680,844
Deductions	867,556	148,284	20,067	15,592	13,925	26,698	642,990
Net income (less loss)	39,074	802	−97	248	−102	267	37,956
Wholesale and retail trade:							
Returns	1,012,980	1,003,995	5,742	1,627	727	483	407
Assets	1,390,556	417,397	86,366	55,754	50,763	76,122	704,153
Receipts	3,184,946	1,467,775	247,425	155,372	127,440	181,338	1,005,596
Deductions	3,148,816	1,458,533	244,195	153,726	125,644	178,800	987,918
Net income (less loss)	36,155	9,287	3,232	1,668	1,792	2,566	17,611
Finance, insurance, and real estate:							
Returns	592,832	568,441	7,886	5,235	4,460	3,521	3,290
Assets	9,957,481	236,270	128,214	187,198	315,048	547,679	8,543,072
Receipts	1,868,003	225,304	33,150	38,035	55,614	92,411	1,423,489
Deductions	1,730,537	223,179	32,140	35,963	50,810	82,133	1,306,314
Net income (less loss)	108,907	2,132	728	1,487	3,595	7,939	93,026
Services:							
Returns	989,850	986,160	2,078	754	370	287	202
Assets	552,132	172,464	32,124	25,958	25,950	50,140	245,497
Receipts	735,497	442,769	36,494	29,075	25,864	43,620	157,675
Deductions	724,923	438,470	36,441	28,478	25,610	43,593	152,331
Net income (less loss)	11,020	4,577	57	575	247	78	5,486
PERCENT DISTRIBUTION RECEIPTS							
Agriculture, forestry, and fishing	100	71	7	5	6	6	5
Mining	100	20	5	4	7	9	55
Construction	100	70	9	4	3	5	9
Manufacturing	100	14	5	3	3	5	70
Transportation and public utilities	100	16	2	2	2	3	75
Wholesale and retail trade	100	46	8	5	4	6	32
Finance, insurance, and real estate	100	12	2	2	3	5	76
Services	100	60	5	4	4	6	21

[1] Includes returns with zero assets.

Source: U.S. Internal Revenue Service, *Statistics of Income, Corporation Income Tax Returns*, annual.

No. 858. Employees and Payroll, by Employment-Size Class: 1980 to 1990

[Excludes government employees, railroad employees, self-employed persons, etc. See "General Explanation" in source for definitions and statement on reliability of data. An **establishment** is a single physical location where business is conducted or where services or industrial operations are performed]

EMPLOYMENT-SIZE CLASS	Unit	1980	1983	1984	1985	1986	1987	1988	1989	1990
Employees, total [1]	1,000 .	74,844	72,974	78,021	81,111	83,379	85,484	87,882	91,631	93,476
Under 20 employees	1,000 .	19,423	20,136	21,171	21,810	22,296	23,069	23,583	23,992	24,373
20 to 99 employees	1,000 .	21,168	20,806	22,449	23,539	24,311	25,221	25,930	26,829	27,414
100 to 499 employees	1,000 .	17,840	16,794	18,348	19,410	20,260	20,615	21,307	22,387	22,926
500 to 999 employees	1,000 .	5,689	5,186	5,614	5,716	5,780	5,922	6,078	6,442	6,551
1,000 or more employees	1,000 .	10,716	10,050	10,413	10,645	10,734	10,657	10,984	11,981	12,212
Annual payroll, total [1]	Bil. dol	1,035	1,269	1,339	1,514	1,608	1,724	1,860	1,990	2,104
Under 20 employees	Bil. dol.	231	298	326	352	375	414	440	461	485
20 to 99 employees	Bil. dol.	261	319	358	388	414	449	485	514	547
100 to 499 employees	Bil. dol.	249	297	334	362	391	417	452	488	518
500 to 999 employees	Bil. dol.	91	107	120	126	132	140	152	163	174
1,000 or more employees	Bil. dol.	208	248	269	286	298	305	331	364	381

[1] Prior to 1987, totals for employees and annual payroll have been revised. Detail may not add to totals because revisions for size class are not available.

Source: U.S. Bureau of the Census, *County Business Patterns,* annual.

No. 859. Establishments, Employees, and Payroll, by Industry: 1980 to 1990

[See headnote, table 858. Beginning 1989, data are based on the 1987 *Standard Industrial Classification (SIC) Manual.* Prior to 1989, data are based on the *1972 SIC Manual*]

INDUSTRY	ESTABLISHMENTS (1,000)				EMPLOYEES (1,000)				PAYROLL (bil. dol.)			
	1980	1985	1989	1990	1980	1985	1989	1990	1980	1985	1989	1990
All industries [1]	4,543	5,701	6,107	6,176	74,844	81,111	91,631	93,476	1,035	1,513	1,990	2,104
Agricultural services [2]	46	64	79	85	290	380	489	531	3	5	8	9
Mining	30	37	30	30	994	943	711	723	22	28	25	27
Contract construction	418	476	547	578	4,473	4,480	5,036	5,239	75	98	127	132
Manufacturing	319	358	363	378	21,165	19,429	19,492	19,173	355	458	533	544
Transportation [3]	168	203	228	235	4,623	4,809	5,418	5,592	88	123	154	166
Wholesale trade	385	438	460	476	5,211	5,624	6,153	6,328	89	130	170	181
Retail trade	1,223	1,407	1,495	1,530	15,047	16,851	19,335	19,815	124	178	229	242
Finance and insurance [4]	421	488	529	545	5,295	6,005	6,802	6,956	77	132	184	197
Services	1,278	1,712	1,977	2,059	17,186	21,549	27,339	28,800	197	346	544	599

[1] Includes nonclassifiable establishments, not shown separately. [2] Includes forestry and fisheries. [3] Includes public utilities. [4] Includes real estate.

Source: U.S. Bureau of the Census, *County Business Patterns,* annual.

No. 860. Establishments, Employees, and Payroll, by Employment-Size Class and Industry: 1990

[See headnote, table 858. Data are based on the *1987 Standard Industrial Classification Manual*]

EMPLOYMENT SIZE-CLASS	Unit	All industries [1]	Agricultural services [2]	Mining	Contract construction	Manufacturing	Transportation [3]	Wholesale trade	Retail trade	Finance and insurance [4]	Services
Establishments, total	1,000 ..	6,176	85	30	578	378	235	476	1,530	545	2,059
Under 20 employees	1,000 ..	5,354	80	24	526	249	189	405	1,295	486	1,843
20 to 99 employees	1,000 ..	684	4	5	47	91	37	64	210	49	175
100 to 499 employees	1,000 ..	122	(Z)	1	5	33	8	7	24	8	36
500 to 999 employees	1,000 ..	10	(Z)	(Z)	(Z)	4	1	(Z)	1	1	3
1,000 or more employees	1,000 ..	6	(Z)	(Z)	(Z)	2	(Z)	(Z)	(Z)	(Z)	2
Employees, total	1,000 ..	93,476	531	723	5,239	19,173	5,592	6,328	19,815	6,956	28,800
Under 20 employees	1,000 ..	24,373	(D)	(D)	2,184	1,505	920	2,184	6,966	2,010	7,927
20 to 99 employees	1,000 ..	27,414	146	205	1,781	4,031	1,527	2,426	8,286	1,930	7,018
100 to 499 employees	1,000 ..	22,926	63	222	920	6,658	1,511	1,279	3,924	1,572	6,777
500 to 999 employees	1,000 ..	6,551	12	83	131	2,490	471	252	409	539	2,164
1,000 or more employees	1,000 ..	12,212	(D)	(D)	224	4,489	1,163	187	230	905	4,913
Annual payroll, total.	Bil. dol .	2,104	8.7	26.7	132.5	544.1	165.8	181.0	241.7	197.4	599.4
Under 20 employees	Bil. dol .	485	(D)	(D)	47.1	33.9	20.7	58.3	81.9	50.2	177.9
20 to 99 employees	Bil. dol .	547	2.4	6.6	47.3	97.4	40.3	67.9	94.2	52.6	137.4
100 to 499 employees	Bil. dol .	518	1.0	8.8	27.5	171.2	45.6	39.6	52.4	46.1	125.3
500 to 999 employees	Bil. dol .	174	0.2	3.5	4.0	72.4	16.0	8.5	7.7	16.6	45.4
1,000 or more employees	Bil. dol .	381	(D)	(D)	6.7	169.1	43.2	6.8	5.6	31.9	113.4

D Withheld to avoid disclosing data for individual companies; data are included in higher-level totals. Z Less than 500 establishments. [1] Includes nonclassifiable establishments not shown separately. [2] Includes forestry and fisheries. [3] Includes public utilities. [4] Includes real estate.

Source: U.S. Bureau of the Census, *County Business Patterns,* annual.

No. 861. New Business Incorporations and Business Failures—Number and Liabilities: 1970 to 1992

[1970 excludes Hawaii; 1970 and 1975 exclude Alaska. Total concerns and failure data prior to 1984 exclude agriculture, forestry, and fishing, finance, insurance, and real estate, and services; therefore, are not directly comparable with data for 1984 and later. See also *Historical Statistics, Colonial Times to 1970*, series V 20-30]

YEAR	Total concerns in business[1] (1,000)	Index of net business formations[2] (1967 =100)	New incorporations (1,000)	FAILURES[3] Number	FAILURES[3] Rate per 10,000 concerns	FAILURES[3] Current liabilities[4] (mil. dol.)	YEAR	Total concerns in business[1] (1,000)	Index of net business formations[2] (1967 =100)	New incorporations (1,000)	FAILURES[3] Number	FAILURES[3] Rate per 10,000 concerns	FAILURES[3] Current liabilities[4] (mil. dol.)
1970....	2,442	108.8	264	10,748	44	1,888	1986....	5,119	120.4	702	61,616	120	44,724
1975....	2,679	109.9	326	11,432	43	4,380	1987....	6,004	121.2	685	61,111	102	34,724
1980....	2,780	129.9	532	11,742	42	4,635	1988....	5,804	124.1	685	57,098	98	39,126
1981....	2,745	124.8	581	16,794	61	6,955	1989....	7,694	124.8	677	50,361	65	44,261
1982....	2,806	116.4	566	24,908	88	15,611	1990....	8,038	120.7	647	60,747	74	56,130
1983....	2,851	117.5	602	31,334	110	16,073	1991....	8,218	115.3	629	88,140	107	96,825
1984....	4,885	121.3	635	52,078	107	29,269	1992....	8,805	(NA)	(NA)	96,857	110	91,289
1985....	4,990	120.9	663	57,078	115	36,937							

NA Not available.   [1] Data through 1983 represent number of names listed in July issue of *Dun & Bradstreet Reference Book*. Data for 1984-92 represent the number of establishments listed in the Dun's Census of American Business. The base has been changed due to expanded business failure coverage.   [2] Source: U.S. Bureau of Economic Analysis, *Survey of Current Business*.   [3] Includes concerns discontinued following assignment, voluntary or involuntary petition in bankruptcy, attachment, execution, foreclosure, etc.; voluntary withdrawals from business with known loss to creditors; also enterprises involved in court action, such as receivership and reorganization or arrangement which may or may not lead to discontinuance; and businesses making voluntary compromise with creditors out of court.   [4] Liabilities exclude long-term publicly held obligations; offsetting assets are not taken into account.

Source: Except as noted, Dun & Bradstreet Corporation, New York, NY, *New Business Incorporations*, monthly; and *Monthly Failure Report.*

No. 862. New Business Incorporations and Number of Failures, by State: 1990 to 1992

[1992 preliminary. See headnote, table 861]

DIVISION AND STATE	NEW BUSINESS INCORPORATIONS 1990	NEW BUSINESS INCORPORATIONS 1991	NUMBER OF FAILURES 1991	NUMBER OF FAILURES 1992	DIVISION AND STATE	NEW BUSINESS INCORPORATIONS 1990	NEW BUSINESS INCORPORATIONS 1991	NUMBER OF FAILURES 1991	NUMBER OF FAILURES 1992
United States ...	647,366	628,580	88,140	96,857	Virginia	17,376	16,883	2,297	2,160
					West Virginia.......	2,542	2,219	399	402
New England	31,363	28,864	5,654	6,199	North Carolina......	12,376	11,944	1,351	1,492
Maine	2,428	2,326	396	464	South Carolina.....	7,158	5,700	603	482
New Hampshire.....	2,679	2,387	861	720	Georgia	18,891	18,098	3,390	2,871
Vermont..........	1,650	1,486	188	259	Florida...........	82,172	81,083	5,229	5,372
Massachusetts	12,468	11,706	2,839	3,021	**East South Central ...**	24,456	24,806	4,779	4,148
Rhode Island	3,000	2,458	459	511	Kentucky	6,669	6,782	1,234	1,089
Connecticut	9,138	8,501	911	1,224	Tennessee........	8,290	8,306	1,995	1,660
Middle Atlantic	113,281	109,142	12,028	14,776	Alabama	6,092	6,116	1,027	902
New York.........	65,569	63,808	5,612	7,867	Mississippi	3,405	3,602	523	497
New Jersey.......	28,281	27,994	2,758	2,821	**West South Central...**	57,760	55,943	10,464	10,309
Pennsylvania	19,431	17,340	3,658	4,088	Arkansas	6,111	5,326	480	512
East North Central ...	87,519	84,261	10,785	10,908	Louisiana	8,974	8,973	1,103	858
Ohio	18,094	17,895	2,776	2,684	Oklahoma	7,152	7,073	1,845	1,417
Indiana	10,608	10,205	1,736	1,479	Texas	35,523	34,571	7,036	7,522
Illinois	29,279	29,068	3,068	3,093	**Mountain ....**	46,017	47,033	6,369	6,100
Michigan	22,204	20,099	2,295	2,428	Montana	1,519	1,572	160	211
Wisconsin........	7,334	6,994	910	1,224	Idaho............	1,909	1,944	397	360
West North Central ...	32,941	32,499	5,467	6,176	Wyoming	1,171	1,386	162	141
Minnesota	9,678	9,564	1,583	1,510	Colorado	12,257	13,583	1,959	1,739
Iowa	4,381	4,531	295	730	New Mexico	2,854	2,713	390	456
Missouri.........	9,761	9,521	1,609	1,830	Arizona	10,129	9,832	2,230	2,299
North Dakota	860	820	140	163	Utah	4,147	4,973	515	437
South Dakota	1,078	1,040	315	232	Nevada	12,031	11,030	556	457
Nebraska........	2,934	3,093	536	632	**Pacific ....**	64,723	61,499	17,636	23,352
Kansas	4,249	3,930	989	1,079	Washington	11,948	11,521	1,424	1,967
South Atlantic.......	189,306	184,533	14,958	14,889	Oregon	8,525	8,375	1,309	1,260
Delaware	29,861	29,887	160	189	California	39,111	36,561	14,685	19,733
Maryland	16,674	16,463	1,331	1,711	Alaska..........	1,345	1,250	144	103
District of Columbia ..	2,256	2,256	198	210	Hawaii...........	3,794	3,792	74	289

Source: Dun & Bradstreet Corporation, New York, NY, *New Business Incorporations*, monthly; and *Business Failure Record*, annual, (copyright).

No. 863. Business Failures—Number and Rate, by Industry: 1985 to 1992

INDUSTRY	NUMBER					RATE PER 10,000 FIRMS				
	1985	1989	1990	1991	1992, prel.	1985	1989	1990	1991	1992, prel.
Total [1]	57,253	50,361	60,747	88,140	96,857	115	65	74	107	110
Agriculture, forestry, fishing	2,699	1,540	1,733	2,256	2,863	197	49	50	65	80
Mining	796	351	388	411	427	193	79	88	95	98
Construction	7,005	7,120	8,162	11,963	12,380	109	86	91	128	128
Manufacturing	4,869	3,933	4,740	6,595	7,077	119	79	92	127	130
Food and kindred products	261	216	232	305	355	127	87	91	122	135
Textile mill products	110	75	102	143	172	129	72	97	135	158
Apparel, other textile products	338	204	318	505	562	128	73	114	177	190
Lumber and wood products	415	368	420	576	548	136	91	97	129	120
Furniture and fixtures	236	253	258	383	390	161	154	151	223	221
Paper and allied products	55	46	68	86	87	100	72	105	129	126
Printing and publishing	659	679	734	1,062	1,233	94	71	74	105	117
Chemicals and allied products	172	102	139	207	216	126	63	86	128	127
Petroleum refining	26	21	21	33	34	145	83	83	137	157
Rubber and misc. products	157	109	158	209	186	117	71	101	134	113
Leather and leather products	47	30	40	40	35	130	84	113	114	95
Stone, clay, and glass products	159	114	161	220	216	98	59	80	111	108
Primary metal products	122	71	115	145	137	169	79	123	157	147
Fabricated metal products	484	374	397	593	656	125	87	90	135	144
Machinery, exc. electric	721	511	656	823	948	110	67	84	105	117
Electric and electronic equipment	329	256	287	380	414	154	104	114	149	166
Transportation equipment	197	190	242	318	266	165	117	147	198	160
Instruments and related equipment	110	108	120	192	177	85	66	68	106	93
Miscellaneous	271	206	272	375	445	101	58	74	98	105
Transportation, public utilities	2,536	2,115	2,630	3,891	3,893	151	82	94	134	125
Wholesale trade	4,836	3,687	4,423	6,170	6,726	102	66	77	109	113
Retail trade	13,494	11,120	12,972	17,242	19,005	109	56	65	90	95
Finance, insurance, real estate	2,676	2,932	3,819	5,962	6,196	62	47	60	90	87
Services	16,649	13,679	16,119	22,852	26,821	115	53	49	87	93

[1] Includes industries not shown separately.

Source: The Dun and Bradstreet Corporation, New York, NY, *Business Failure Record*, annual, (copyright).

No. 864. Bankruptcy Petitions Filed, by State: 1981 to 1992

[In thousands. For years ending June 30. Includes outlying areas, not shown separately. Covers only bankruptcy cases filed under the Bankruptcy Reform Act of 1978. **Bankruptcy:** legal recognition that a company or individual is insolvent and must restructure or liquidate. Petitions "filed" means the commencement of a proceeding through the presentation of a petition to the clerk of the court]

STATE	1981	1985	1989	1990	1991	1992	STATE	1981	1985	1989	1990	1991	1992
U.S.	360.3	364.5	643.0	725.5	880.4	972.5	MO	7.9	7.4	12.0	13.4	17.3	19.2
AL	10.8	10.9	20.9	24.7	27.8	27.8	MT	1.1	1.1	1.9	1.8	2.1	2.1
AK	0.4	0.5	1.4	1.2	1.1	1.1	NE	2.8	2.8	3.3	3.8	4.5	4.4
AZ	4.3	5.2	14.9	17.7	19.3	20.4	NV	2.6	2.9	5.7	6.2	6.9	7.7
AR	2.6	3.9	6.0	6.8	7.7	8.6	NH	0.7	0.5	1.0	1.8	3.4	4.0
CA	50.2	61.8	99.3	103.2	124.2	152.8	NJ	7.0	6.7	9.3	12.6	19.4	24.0
CO	6.7	7.0	18.3	17.1	17.0	16.6	NM	1.5	1.6	3.4	4.0	4.5	4.5
CT	2.5	1.8	3.0	4.4	6.9	8.9	NY	24.2	14.2	21.9	29.0	40.3	49.6
DE	0.6	0.5	0.7	0.9	1.3	1.4	NC	8.3	5.4	8.9	10.7	15.5	16.3
DC	0.7	0.7	1.1	1.0	1.2	1.4	ND	0.6	0.7	1.1	1.1	1.2	1.2
FL	6.8	9.1	25.3	31.9	43.4	52.4	OH	27.3	19.5	31.7	36.8	42.8	44.0
GA	11.7	14.4	29.5	38.7	49.0	48.7	OK	4.7	7.1	14.1	14.3	16.2	15.3
HI	0.8	0.6	0.9	0.9	1.0	1.3	OR	5.5	6.5	10.1	11.3	13.5	14.3
ID	2.2	2.4	3.9	4.1	4.2	4.1	PA	10.0	9.8	13.5	15.8	20.8	24.3
IL	26.6	25.6	32.5	35.8	40.5	43.4	RI	1.0	0.8	1.0	1.7	3.1	3.6
IN	13.5	12.2	20.0	22.2	26.8	28.2	SC	1.6	2.3	4.6	4.8	6.9	7.4
IA	4.5	4.7	4.9	5.5	5.8	6.4	SD	0.6	0.9	1.2	1.4	1.6	1.4
KS	4.5	4.8	7.3	8.1	9.6	9.6	TN	13.8	14.7	29.3	34.2	40.6	41.6
KY	7.8	7.0	12.0	13.6	15.6	15.5	TX	9.6	16.8	41.4	41.7	46.6	49.5
LA	5.2	7.7	12.5	12.9	13.3	14.2	UT	3.8	4.0	7.9	8.0	8.0	8.3
ME	1.0	0.6	1.1	1.5	2.2	2.3	VT	0.3	0.2	0.3	0.5	0.8	1.0
MD	5.3	3.9	8.1	9.2	12.8	16.0	VA	9.9	9.2	16.3	19.3	25.3	29.1
MA	3.4	2.0	4.2	7.6	12.9	15.9	WA	8.4	11.3	18.3	17.0	17.2	18.7
MI	15.1	8.6	16.5	18.8	23.3	26.7	WV	2.2	1.9	3.4	3.5	4.0	4.5
MN	5.4	5.4	11.6	14.0	16.7	17.8	WI	5.8	7.4	9.3	10.2	12.1	12.4
MS	5.1	4.8	9.8	10.6	12.3	12.7	WY	0.6	1.0	1.4	1.5	1.5	1.4

Source: Administrative Office of the U.S. Courts, unpublished data.

No. 865. Bankruptcy Petitions Filed and Pending, by Type and Chapter: 1981 to 1992

[**For years ending June 30.** Covers only bankruptcy cases filed under the Bankruptcy Reform Act of 1978. **Bankruptcy:** legal recognition that a company or individual is insolvent and must restructure or liquidate. Petitions "filed" means the commencement of a proceeding through the presentation of a petition to the clerk of the court; "pending" is a proceeding in which the administration has not been completed]

ITEM	1981	1985	1986	1987	1988	1989	1990	1991	1992
Total, filed	360,329	364,536	477,856	561,278	594,567	642,993	725,484	880,399	972,490
Business [1]	47,415	66,651	76,281	88,278	68,501	62,534	64,688	67,714	72,650
Nonbusiness [2]	312,914	297,885	401,575	473,000	526,066	580,459	660,796	812,685	899,840
Voluntary	358,997	362,939	476,214	559,658	593,158	641,528	723,886	878,626	971,047
Involuntary	1,332	1,597	1,642	1,620	1,409	1,465	1,598	1,773	1,443
Chapter 7 [3]	265,721	244,650	332,679	397,551	423,796	457,240	505,337	612,330	679,662
Chapter 9 [4]	1	3	7	10	3	7	7	20	15
Chapter 11 [5]	7,828	21,425	24,443	22,566	18,891	17,465	19,591	22,495	24,029
Chapter 12 [6]	(X)	(X)	(X)	4,824	3,099	1,717	1,351	1,358	1,634
Chapter 13 [7]	86,778	98,452	120,726	136,300	148,771	166,539	199,186	244,192	267,121
Section 304 [8]	1	6	1	27	7	25	12	4	29
Total, pending . .	361,664	608,945	728,577	808,504	814,195	869,340	961,919	1,123,433	1,237,357

X Not applicable.   [1] Business bankruptcies include those filed under chapters 7, 9, 11, or 12.   [2] Bankruptcies include those filed under chapters 7, 11, or 13.   [3] Chapter 7, liquidation of nonexempt assets of businesses or individuals.   [4] Chapter 9, adjustment of debts of a municipality.   [5] Chapter 11, individual or business reorganization.   [6] Chapter 12, adjustment of debts of a family farmer with regular income, effective November 26, 1986.   [7] Chapter 13, adjustment of debts of an individual with regular income.   [8] Chapter 11 U.S.C., Section 304, cases ancillary to foreign proceedings.

Source: Administrative Office of the U.S. Courts, *Annual Report of the Director.*

No. 866. Small Business Administration Loans to All Small Businesses: 1980 to 1992

[**For fiscal year ending in year shown;** see text, section 9. A small business must be independently owned and operated, must not be dominant in its particular industry, and must meet standards set by the Small Business Administration as to its annual receipts or number of employees. Loans include both direct and guaranteed loans to small business establishments. Does not include Disaster Assistance Loans]

LOANS APPROVED	Unit	1980	1983	1984	1985	1986	1987	1988	1989	1990	1991	1992
Loans, all businesses	1,000. . .	31.7	19.2	21.3	19.3	16.8	17.1	17.1	17.0	18.8	19.4	25.1
Loans, minority-owned businesses . .	1,000. . .	6.0	2.7	3.1	2.8	2.0	2.1	2.2	2.4	2.4	2.9	3.6
Percent of all business loans	Percent . .	19	14	15	15	12	12	13	14	13	15	14
Value of total loans [1]	Mil. dol. .	3,858	3,007	3,450	3,217	3,013	3,232	3,434	3,490	4,354	4,625	6,339
Value of loans to minority-operated businesses [2]	Mil. dol. .	470	295	383	324	265	299	343	385	473	601	808

[1] Includes both SBA and bank portions of loans.   [2] SBA direct loans and guaranteed portion of bank loans only.

Source: U.S. Small Business Administration, unpublished data.

No. 867. Job Creation, by Firm Size and Industry: 1976 to 1990

YEAR	Total (1,000)	SHARE OF JOBS BY SIZE OF FIRM			
		Less than 500 employees			More than 500 employees
		Total	Less than 20	20 to 499	
1976 to 1978.	6,062	4,407	2,316	2,091	1,655
1978 to 1980.	5,777	2,605	1,519	1,086	3,172
1980 to 1982.	1,542	1,473	1,510	-37	69
1982 to 1984.	4,318	3,312	2,107	1,205	1,006
1984 to 1986.	4,611	2,412	1,637	775	2,199
1986 to 1988.	6,169	2,770	1,487	1,283	3,399
1988-90, total	2,664	3,165	4,015	-850	-501
Agriculture, forestry, fishing	201	180	185	-4	21
Mining	-76	-5	3	-8	-70
Construction	3	21	261	-240	-18
Manufacturing	-974	8	220	-212	-982
Transportation, communications, and public utilities	139	99	134	-36	40
Wholesale trade	-93	38	139	-101	-132
Retail trade	760	605	686	-81	155
Finance, insurance, real estate	338	254	278	-25	84
Services	2,366	1,967	2,111	-144	400

Source: U.S. Small Business Administration, Office of Advocacy, Small Business Data Base, linked 1988-90 USEEM files; unpublished data.

No. 868. Federal Contract Actions—Small and Minority-Owned Small Business Share, by State of Principal Place of Performance: 1990 and 1991

[In millions of dollars, except percent. For fiscal year. Excludes Guam, Puerto Rico, and Virgin Islands. Represents contract awards of $25,000 or more awarded to establishments. A contract may consist of more than one action. Minus sign (-) indicates decrease]

REGION, DIVISION, AND STATE	TOTAL CONTRACT ACTIONS			SMALL BUSINESS SHARE				SMALL MINORITY-OWNED SHARE			
	1990	1991	Percent change, 1990-91	1990	1991 Amount	1991 Percent of total	Percent change, 1990-91	1990	1991 Amount	1991 Percent of total	Percent change, 1990-91
U.S.	163,775	186,387	14	25,399	29,205	16	15	5,757	6,684	4	16
Northeast	31,730	34,514	9	3,859	4,755	14	23	655	621	2	-5
New England....	15,399	15,801	3	1,263	1,460	9	16	212	255	2	20
Maine........	921	1,149	25	59	81	7	37	4	13	1	225
New Hampshire.	419	481	15	61	62	13	2	5	6	1	20
Vermont......	96	100	4	19	27	27	42	1	4	4	300
Massachusetts..	9,008	8,207	-9	715	867	11	21	141	190	2	35
Rhode Island...	580	443	-24	137	109	25	-20	31	13	3	-58
Connecticut....	4,375	5,421	24	272	314	6	15	30	29	1	-3
Middle Atlantic ..	16,331	18,713	15	2,596	3,295	18	27	443	366	2	-17
New York.....	8,238	9,666	17	1,098	1,318	14	20	203	80	1	-61
New Jersey....	4,127	4,507	9	784	1,022	23	30	121	167	4	38
Pennsylvania...	3,966	4,540	14	714	955	21	34	119	119	3	-
Midwest.........	24,250	29,449	21	3,526	3,954	13	12	653	681	2	4
East North Central	12,929	16,210	25	2,559	2,661	16	4	438	467	3	7
Ohio	5,879	6,676	14	925	998	15	8	263	250	4	-5
Indiana.......	1,888	2,430	29	222	198	8	-11	31	33	1	6
Illinois.......	2,357	3,791	61	574	839	22	46	112	123	3	10
Michigan.....	1,597	1,919	20	421	381	20	-10	26	52	3	100
Wisconsin.....	1,208	1,394	15	417	245	18	-41	6	9	1	50
West North Central	11,321	13,239	17	967	1,293	10	34	215	214	2	(Z)
Minnesota.....	2,015	2,142	6	140	146	7	4	13	18	1	38
Iowa........	652	670	3	58	109	16	88	4	2	(Z)	-50
Missouri	6,884	8,392	22	349	464	6	33	51	72	1	41
North Dakota..	159	230	45	94	137	60	46	44	61	27	39
South Dakota ..	120	219	83	53	98	45	85	56	10	5	-82
Nebraska	402	434	8	134	143	33	7	10	15	3	50
Kansas.......	1,089	1,152	6	139	196	17	41	37	36	3	-3
South	58,205	67,653	16	12,069	13,817	20	14	3,060	3,740	6	22
South Atlantic...	33,528	38,084	14	6,972	8,856	23	27	2,184	2,624	7	20
Delaware.....	116	155	34	36	50	32	39	10	9	6	-10
Maryland	6,798	7,728	14	1,269	1,767	23	39	559	749	10	34
District of Columbia.....	3,096	4,157	34	874	1,179	28	35	424	562	14	33
Virginia......	10,434	10,222	-2	2,403	3,019	30	26	768	900	9	17
West Virginia...	305	668	119	151	180	27	19	88	28	4	-68
North Carolina..	1,533	2,142	40	361	545	25	51	41	56	3	37
South Carolina..	2,664	3,188	20	377	383	12	2	39	57	2	46
Georgia	2,147	2,540	18	456	545	21	20	80	113	4	41
Florida......	6,435	7,284	13	1,045	1,188	16	14	175	150	2	-14
East South Central	10,156	12,546	24	2,576	2,225	18	-14	355	511	4	44
Kentucky	1,972	2,010	2	1,075	727	36	-32	49	159	8	224
Tennessee ...	3,241	4,880	51	603	493	10	-18	134	85	2	-37
Alabama.....	3,352	3,562	6	713	695	20	-3	133	189	5	42
Mississippi	1,591	2,094	32	185	310	15	68	39	78	4	100
West South Central	14,521	17,023	17	2,521	2,736	16	9	521	605	4	16
Arkansas	361	439	22	152	173	39	14	15	12	3	-20
Louisiana	2,332	2,130	-9	586	479	22	-18	51	56	3	10
Oklahoma....	845	1,029	22	292	406	39	39	159	199	19	25
Texas.......	10,983	13,425	22	1,491	1,678	12	13	296	338	3	14
West...........	49,590	54,771	10	5,945	6,679	12	12	1,389	1,642	3	18
Mountain	15,004	15,522	3	1,687	1,794	12	6	459	543	3	18
Montana	156	173	11	122	135	78	11	29	29	17	(Z)
Idaho........	854	1,042	22	83	107	10	29	15	16	2	7
Wyoming.....	131	125	-5	89	78	62	-12	6	4	3	-33
Colorado.....	4,651	4,598	-1	437	472	10	8	125	131	3	5
New Mexico ...	3,245	3,460	7	303	346	10	14	128	161	5	26
Arizona......	3,625	3,052	-16	290	318	10	10	68	84	3	24
Utah	1,529	1,927	26	264	224	12	-15	56	73	4	30
Nevada......	813	1,145	41	99	114	10	15	32	45	4	41
Pacific	34,586	39,249	13	4,258	4,885	12	15	930	1,099	3	18
Washington....	3,878	3,953	2	419	567	14	35	80	105	3	31
Oregon.......	530	566	7	201	302	53	50	20	28	5	40
California	29,110	33,160	14	3,211	3,398	10	6	687	792	2	15
Alaska	529	822	55	190	340	41	79	48	58	7	21
Hawaii	539	748	39	237	278	37	17	95	116	16	22

- Represents or rounds to zero.　Z Less than 0.5 percent.

Source: U.S. Small Business Administration, *The State of Small Business: A Report of the President*, annual. Data from Federal Procurement Data System, Special Report S92132B, June 18, 1992.

No. 869. Mergers and Acquisitions—Summary: 1980 to 1990

[Covers transactions valued at $1 million or more. Values based on transactions for which price data revealed. **All activity** includes mergers, acquisitions, acquisitions of interest, acquisitions of controlling interest, divestitures, and leveraged transactions that result in a change in ownership. **Divestiture:** sale of a business, division, or subsidiary by corporate owner to another party. **Leveraged buyout:** acquisition of a business in which buyers use mostly borrowed money to finance purchase price and incorporate debt into capital structure of business after change in ownership]

ITEM	Unit	1980	1983	1984	1985	1986	1987	1988	1989	1990
All activity: Number	Number . .	1,558	2,395	3,176	3,489	4,463	4,024	4,233	4,167	4,168
Value.	Mil. dol. . .	32,830	52,708	126,140	145,978	205,958	177,900	240,177	254,020	172,319
Divestitures: Number.	Number . .	104	661	794	1,041	1,419	1,221	1,336	1,333	1,406
Value.	Mil. dol. . .	5,090	12,949	30,572	43,534	72,427	57,797	83,979	66,685	59,605
Leveraged buyouts: Number .	Number . .	11	231	254	255	337	279	383	382	254
Value.	Mil. dol. . .	236	4,519	18,718	19,670	45,160	36,228	47,068	66,915	16,022
Form of payment: All cash. . . .	Percent . .	8	24	36	40	43	54	60	43	46
All stock	Percent . .	19	13	12	10	12	11	5	10	6
Combination cash, stock debt, other.	Percent . .	17	28	26	24	20	18	25	37	33
Undisclosed [1].	Percent . .	56	35	26	26	25	17	10	10	15
Ownership status of acquisition targets:										
Public acquired company:										
Number	Number . .	398	554	835	823	865	1,011	984	1,124	915
Value.	Mil. dol. . .	11,948	31,899	85,692	91,653	109,217	103,029	130,385	168,852	89,974
Private acquired company:										
Number	Number . .	1,059	1,195	1,555	1,621	2,168	1,739	1,848	1,600	1,695
Value.	Mil. dol. . .	15,911	8,344	10,069	10,608	24,454	15,067	24,089	18,236	17,939

[1] Price was given but form of payment was not.

No. 870. Mergers and Acquisitions—Number and Value of Transactions, by Industry: 1990

[See headnote table 869]

INDUSTRY	TOTAL		U.S. COMPANY ACQUIRING U.S. COMPANY		FOREIGN COMPANY ACQUIRING U.S. COMPANY		U.S. COMPANY ACQUIRING FOREIGN COMPANY	
	Number	Value (mil. dol.)	Number	Value (mil. dol.)	Number	Value (mil. dol.)	Number	Value (mil. dol.)
Total activity [1].	4,168	172,319	3,244	107,210	599	47,595	325	17,514
Agriculture, forestry, fishing.	13	57	10	54	2	3	1	(NA)
Mining.	208	11,646	165	6,401	29	5,091	14	154
Construction.	35	281	30	229	5	52	-	(X)
Manufacturing:								
Food and kindred products	92	9,246	65	3,716	16	781	11	4,749
Textile mill products	29	212	21	83	1	43	7	86
Apparel, other textile products	25	544	21	134	1	410	3	(NA)
Lumber and wood products	14	258	10	202	3	56	1	(NA)
Paper and allied products	41	5,682	24	5,314	4	235	13	133
Printing and publishing	130	3,953	95	2,162	29	1,334	6	457
Chemicals and allied products	193	15,612	119	3,787	54	11,545	20	280
Rubber and plastic products.	53	2,298	40	1,399	6	877	7	22
Stone, clay, glass, and concrete	43	4,839	21	1,579	17	3,030	5	230
Primary metals industries.	51	1,572	32	620	17	309	2	643
Fabricated metal products	89	2,715	64	1,536	21	947	4	232
Industrial machinery, computer equipment .	233	5,978	170	4,263	43	1,638	20	77
Electrical and electronic equipment	186	6,381	131	3,885	37	1,811	18	685
Transportation equipment	63	4,837	40	1,552	12	570	11	2,715
Instruments and related products	144	2,778	108	1,094	26	1,661	10	23
Transportation and public utilities	343	19,838	292	14,224	32	1,321	19	4,293
Wholesale trade	266	3,132	190	1,888	38	1,008	38	236
Retail trade	158	7,373	126	4,660	23	2,650	9	63
Finance, insurance, real estate	905	28,142	808	21,337	78	6,015	19	790
Services	744	32,746	585	26,161	86	5,504	73	1,081

- Represents or rounds to zero.   NA Not available.   X Not applicable.   [1] Includes other industries, not shown separately.
Source of tables 869 and 870: MLR Publishing Company, Philadelphia, PA, *Mergers and Acquisitions*, 1991 (copyright). Publication contains extract from database, M&A Database.

No. 871. Employee Stock Ownership Plans—Number of Plans and Participants: 1975 to 1991

[As of **end of year**]

YEAR	Number of plans	Number of employees (1,000)	YEAR	Number of plans	Number of employees (1,000)	YEAR	Number of plans	Number of employees (1,000)
1975.	1,601	248	1982.	6,082	4,745	1988.	8,862	9,076
1977.	3,137	1,658	1983.	6,456	5,397	1989.	9,385	10,631
1978.	4,028	2,800	1984.	6,904	6,576	1990.	9,870	11,271
1979.	4,551	3,039	1985.	7,402	7,353	1991.	9,888	11,329
1980.	5,009	4,048	1986.	8,046	7,860			
1981.	5,680	4,537	1987.	8,514	8,860			

Source: National Center for Employee Ownership, Inc., Oakland, CA, unpublished data.

No. 872. Patents and Trademarks: 1980 to 1991

[In thousands. Calendar year data. Covers patents issued to citizens of the United States and residents of foreign countries. For data on copyrights, see table 919. For data on foreign countries, see table 1409. See also *Historical Statistics, Colonial Times to 1970*, series W 96-108]

ITEM	1980	1983	1984	1985	1986	1987	1988	1989	1990	1991
Patent applications filed	113.0	112.4	120.6	127.1	133.0	139.8	151.9	166.3	176.7	178.4
Inventions	104.3	103.7	111.3	117.0	122.4	127.9	139.8	152.8	164.6	164.3
Designs...................	7.8	8.1	8.7	9.6	9.9	11.2	11.3	12.6	11.3	13.1
Botanical plants	0.2	0.3	0.3	0.2	0.3	0.4	0.4	0.4	0.4	0.4
Reissues	0.6	0.3	0.3	0.3	0.3	0.4	0.4	0.5	0.5	0.6
Patents issued...............	66.2	62.0	72.7	77.3	77.0	89.6	84.4	102.7	99.2	106.8
Inventions	61.8	56.9	67.2	71.7	70.9	83.0	77.9	95.5	90.4	96.5
Individuals...............	13.8	10.5	12.3	12.9	13.3	15.3	14.3	18.0	17.3	18.1
Corporations: United States	27.7	25.7	30.0	31.2	29.5	33.8	31.5	38.7	36.1	39.2
Foreign [1]	19.1	19.6	23.7	26.4	27.0	32.9	31.4	38.0	36.0	38.1
U.S. Government	1.2	1.0	1.2	1.1	1.0	1.0	0.7	0.9	1.0	1.2
Designs..................	3.9	4.6	4.9	5.1	5.5	6.0	5.7	6.1	8.0	9.6
Botanical plants	0.1	0.2	0.2	0.2	0.2	0.2	0.4	0.6	0.3	0.4
Reissues	0.3	0.4	0.3	0.3	0.3	0.2	0.2	0.2	0.4	0.3
U.S. residents [2].	40.8	36.6	42.2	43.3	42.0	47.7	44.6	54.6	52.8	57.7
Foreign country residents [2]	25.4	25.4	30.5	33.9	34.9	41.7	39.7	47.9	46.2	49.0
Percent of total	38.4	41.0	41.9	43.9	45.4	46.6	47.1	46.7	46.7	46.0
Other published documents [3]	(Z)	(Z)	(Z)	(Z)	0.2	0.2	0.2	0.2	0.1	0.1
Trademarks:										
Applications filed..............	46.8	55.5	62.6	65.1	69.1	71.3	78.3	94.4	127.3	123.3
Issued....................	24.7	46.8	54.0	71.7	51.8	51.4	54.3	63.1	60.8	52.4
Trademarks..............	18.9	40.5	48.6	65.8	46.7	47.3	47.4	55.3	53.6	46.6
Trademark renewals	5.9	6.2	5.4	5.9	5.1	4.1	6.9	7.8	7.2	5.8

Z Less than 50. [1] Includes patents to foreign governments. [2] Includes patents for inventions, designs, botanical plants, and reissues. [3] Includes Defensive Publications, a practice which began in November 1968 and ended in July 1986; and Statutory Invention Registrations, the current practice, which began May 1985. These documents are patent applications, which are published to provide the defensive properties of a patent, but do not have the enforceable rights of a patent.

Source: U.S. Patent and Trademark Office. Fiscal-year figures are published in the *Commissioner of Patents and Trademarks Annual Report*.

No. 873. Patents, by State: 1991

[Includes only U.S. patents granted to residents of the United States and territories]

STATE	Total	Inventions	Designs	Botanical plants	Reissues	STATE	Total	Inventions	Designs	Botanical plants	Reissues
U.S. [1] ..	57,656	51,176	6,072	237	171	MO	802	719	81	1	1
						MT	98	82	16	-	-
AL.........	370	319	50	1	-	NE.........	171	145	25	-	1
AK.........	52	45	7	-	-	NV.........	193	165	28	-	-
AZ.........	894	831	61	1	1	NH.........	359	317	41	1	-
AR.........	149	113	36	-	-	NJ.........	3,295	3,031	247	3	14
CA.........	9,002	7,716	1,096	160	30	NM.........	246	228	17	-	1
CO.........	864	762	98	1	3	NY.........	4,965	4,470	481	2	12
CT.........	1,621	1,401	213	2	5	NC.........	980	882	95	2	1
DE.........	537	520	15	-	2	ND.........	71	62	9	-	-
DC.........	67	59	8	-	-	OH.........	2,930	2,554	366	3	7
FL.........	1,950	1,688	247	10	5	OK.........	630	569	59	-	2
GA.........	757	641	109	5	2	OR.........	690	552	131	7	-
HI.........	80	61	18	1	-	PA.........	2,935	2,706	210	9	10
ID.........	224	206	17	1	-	RI.........	234	192	42	-	-
IL.........	3,176	2,786	373	5	12	SC.........	450	409	37	1	3
IN.........	1,140	1,022	115	-	3	SD.........	39	27	11	-	1
IA.........	413	372	41	-	-	TN.........	590	515	68	5	2
KS.........	312	245	66	-	1	TX.........	3,474	3,174	283	8	9
KY.........	371	321	49	-	1	UT.........	407	370	36	-	1
LA.........	503	469	33	-	1	VT.........	119	101	16	1	1
ME.........	106	91	15	-	-	VA.........	938	827	108	-	3
MD.........	972	850	117	1	4	WA.........	1,080	951	123	2	4
MA.........	2,211	2,039	162	4	6	WV.........	170	162	7	-	1
MI.........	3,024	2,810	199	-	15	WI.........	1,265	1,092	173	-	-
MN.........	1,533	1,346	182	-	5	WY.........	51	43	8	-	-
MS.........	124	98	25	-	1	Outlying areas .	22	20	2	-	-

- Represents zero. [1] Includes patents not distributed by State.

Source: U.S. Patent and Trademark Office, *Technology Assessment and Forecast Data Base*.

No. 874. Patents, by Industry: 1970 to 1991

[Includes all patents for inventions granted to residents of the United States, its territories, and foreign citizens. Number of patents by industry may not add to total since a patent may be recorded in more than one industry category. Except for totals, data for all years have been revised to reflect the U.S. Patent Classification System as of 1991]

SIC [1] code	INDUSTRY	1970	1980	1985	1989	1990	1991
(X)	**Total**	**64,429**	**61,819**	**71,661**	**95,538**	**90,354**	**96,514**
(X)	Durable goods:						
32	Stone, clay, and glass products	1,227	1,281	1,377	1,857	1,738	1,997
33, 3462-3	Primary metals	639	674	756	1,007	895	927
34	Fabricated metal products [2]	5,142	5,201	5,709	7,262	7,038	7,162
35	Machinery, except electrical	15,758	14,337	16,735	20,285	18,796	19,645
36, 3825	Electronic and other electric equipment	13,038	10,687	13,890	20,544	19,179	20,986
37, 348	Transportation equipment	3,053	2,913	3,570	4,594	4,400	4,734
38	Instruments and related products [3]	7,293	7,395	8,861	12,792	12,289	13,250
(X)	Nondurable goods:						
20	Food and kindred products	488	482	545	805	726	688
22	Textile mill products	480	420	499	623	501	493
28	Chemicals and allied products	8,806	9,828	10,241	12,720	12,417	13,390
13, 29	Oil and gas extraction, petroleum products	829	729	960	962	831	858
30	Rubber and miscellaneous plastics products	2,478	2,592	3,053	3,952	3,834	4,025
(X)	All other SIC [1] groups	5,100	5,270	5,453	7,918	7,514	7,889

X Not applicable. [1] Standard Industrial Classification. [2] Excludes SIC groups 3462, 3463, and 348. [3] Excludes SIC group 3825.

Source: U.S. Patent and Trademark Office, *Patenting Trends in the United States, State Country Report, 1963-1991.*

No. 875. Consumer Packaged Goods—New Product Introductions: 1980 to 1992

[**Consumer packaged goods:** consumable products packaged by the manufacturer for retail sale primarily through grocery and drug stores. **New product:** a product not previously offered for sale by a particular manufacturer including new varieties, formats, sizes, and packaging for existing products]

ITEM	Food	Beverages	Health and beauty	Household products	Pet products	Miscellaneous products
Domestic and imports:						
1980	1,192	256	834	331	86	197
1981	1,356	262	868	315	74	237
1982	1,762	332	919	390	103	113
1983	3,013	587	1,355	473	138	105
1984	2,678	569	1,094	303	108	227
1985	2,327	585	1,222	463	139	294
1986	2,764	657	1,327	365	107	194
1987	2,895	634	1,526	362	152	292
1988	2,781	597	1,496	310	151	222
1989	2,866	524	1,492	313	204	206
1990	3,453	630	1,531	432	164	154
1991	3,130	589	1,614	422	175	113
1992, total	2,987	587	1,870	417	213	127
Percent:						
New brands [1]	31.4	39.2	26.8	26.4	29.1	48.0
Brand extensions [2]	1.2	1.0	1.0	1.7	0.5	0.8
Line extensions [3]	67.4	59.8	72.2	71.9	70.4	51.2
Types of new product innovation (percent): [4]						
Formulation [5]	50.8	43.8	48.2	39.3	60.0	45.7
New market [6]	-	1.8	2.6	6.8	-	4.3
Packaging [7]	18.0	19.3	17.8	21.3	6.7	19.6
Positioning [8]	30.7	33.3	30.4	29.2	33.3	30.4
Technology [9]	0.5	1.8	1.0	3.4	-	-
CUMULATIVE						
Domestic, except imports, 1980-92	29,624	5,683	16,034	4,685	1,750	2,310
Imports, 1980-92 [10]	3,580	1,126	1,114	211	64	171
International, 1985-92 [11]	11,669	3,325	10,138	2,163	465	761

- Represents or rounds to zero. [1] Product introduced under completely or partly new brand name. [2] Product introduced in a category with an existing brand name which has not been used in the category before. [3] Introduction of a new variety, format, size or package of an existing product/brand name. [4] Product which offers consumers something significantly different from existing products. [5] Added or new ingredient which offers a benefit not previously provided by existing products in its category. [6] Special category for new products which do not compete with any existing category of products. [7] New product packaged in a way that makes it easier to store, handle, prepare, or dispense than others in its category. [8] New product presented for new users or uses compared to existing products in its category. [9] New product with added consumer benefits resulting from use of a new technology. [10] New products introduced in the United States by foreign companies. [11] New products introduced by U.S. and foreign companies outside the United States.

Source: Marketing Intelligence Service Ltd., Naples, NY, *Product Alert Weekly.* Publication contains extract from data base, Productscan.

No. 876. Gross Stock of Fixed Private Capital, Nonresidential and Residential, by Industry: 1970 to 1991

[In billions of dollars. Estimates as of Dec. 31. Based on the *1987 Standard Industrial Classification Manual;* see text, section 13]

INDUSTRY	CURRENT DOLLARS				CONSTANT (1987) DOLLARS			
	1970	1980	1990	1991	1970	1980	1990	1991
Fixed private capital..............	2,689.0	9,364.1	16,893.8	17,489.0	8,131.2	11,584.7	15,244.5	15,521.8
Nonresidential.....................	1,469.6	5,072.1	9,507.0	9,784.1	4,250.1	6,263.6	8,490.2	8,655.7
Agriculture, forestry, and fishing	96.7	333.2	415.5	413.4	300.6	436.1	368.9	360.3
Farms	90.7	308.6	367.7	361.6	282.6	405.0	326.4	315.1
Agr. serv., forestry, and fishing........	6.0	24.6	47.8	51.8	18.0	31.1	42.6	45.2
Mining.........................	83.5	403.3	535.9	535.6	282.4	383.7	448.3	432.2
Metal mining...........	6.9	30.6	41.2	40.3	21.3	39.6	36.6	35.7
Coal mining............	4.7	31.0	49.3	48.4	15.1	39.3	43.7	42.5
Oil and gas extraction............	67.2	323.2	417.3	417.5	231.2	280.8	343.0	328.6
Nonmetallic minerals, exc. fuels	4.7	18.4	28.2	29.4	14.8	24.0	24.9	25.5
Construction.......................	28.1	91.8	113.4	116.2	87.3	120.0	100.8	100.4
Manufacturing......................	338.4	1,144.5	2,105.1	2,179.3	1,001.1	1,480.7	1,874.9	1,911.3
Durable goods.	184.0	622.6	1,134.8	1,166.7	533.7	797.9	1,016.5	1,031.0
Lumber and wood products	7.8	31.0	41.4	41.4	24.2	40.5	36.9	36.1
Furniture and fixtures..............	2.6	9.6	19.1	19.9	7.7	12.6	17.2	17.7
Stone, clay, glass products..........	14.6	47.8	64.2	64.2	44.9	61.4	58.0	57.0
Primary metal industries..........	49.0	143.2	205.5	207.1	144.3	185.6	180.3	178.1
Fabricated metal products	19.8	70.0	125.7	129.3	57.6	90.2	111.7	112.5
Industrial machinery and equip........	28.2	99.8	196.9	203.8	75.7	123.2	179.7	184.4
Electronic and elec. equip........	16.5	65.4	168.6	176.0	46.8	84.8	152.0	157.6
Motor vehicles and equipment	22.4	73.3	119.7	122.2	65.8	93.6	106.3	106.6
Other transportation equip............	12.7	41.2	96.0	100.5	36.6	53.1	86.1	88.9
Instruments, related products	7.1	29.5	78.6	82.6	20.4	37.6	71.5	74.8
Misc. mfg. industries	3.4	11.8	19.1	19.7	9.8	15.3	17.0	17.3
Nondurable goods	154.4	521.9	970.2	1,012.5	467.4	682.8	858.4	880.3
Food and kindred products.......	33.9	103.8	190.4	200.2	103.5	137.2	169.1	173.5
Tobacco products................	1.4	5.3	14.1	14.3	4.0	7.0	12.6	12.5
Textile mill products	11.5	34.7	51.7	52.6	36.9	47.1	45.8	45.3
Apparel, other textile products.......	3.2	11.8	18.2	18.3	9.4	15.4	16.2	16.0
Paper and allied products...........	20.8	69.8	144.2	150.2	63.9	91.9	126.0	128.4
Printing and publishing............	10.7	36.1	81.3	86.0	33.3	47.8	73.9	77.3
Chemicals, allied products	41.0	149.6	270.8	285.5	119.5	192.1	237.8	248.0
Petroleum and coal products	21.7	71.4	127.5	130.0	65.6	92.6	113.0	113.5
Rubber, misc. plastic products	9.3	36.7	67.9	71.4	28.3	48.0	60.4	62.3
Leather and leather products	1.0	2.8	4.0	4.0	3.2	3.7	3.6	3.5
Transportation and public utilities	483.2	1,498.3	2,423.9	2,456.6	1,348.7	1,810.2	2,139.8	2,153.8
Transportation.....................	192.6	492.4	617.4	618.4	555.1	603.1	552.6	540.6
Railroad transportation...........	114.1	232.0	251.3	247.5	332.6	281.1	226.1	221.3
Local, interurban pass. transit	5.1	8.9	12.8	12.6	14.4	11.2	11.5	11.2
Trucking and warehousing	20.7	77.5	106.7	108.4	60.5	101.6	95.9	91.0
Water transportation	14.5	46.6	54.1	55.9	39.3	56.5	48.5	47.5
Transportation by air	19.0	64.0	107.3	107.5	51.5	78.9	95.4	94.4
Pipelines, exc. natural gas	9.8	33.3	41.2	41.7	28.5	40.1	35.8	35.6
Transportation services	9.3	30.0	44.2	44.8	28.2	33.8	39.3	39.7
Communications	101.8	360.2	632.4	625.3	249.7	426.7	563.4	569.0
Telephone and telegraph	95.8	336.4	548.6	537.1	233.3	395.3	487.6	488.4
Radio and television	6.0	23.8	83.8	88.1	16.5	31.4	75.8	80.5
Elec., gas, and sanitary services......	188.7	645.7	1,174.0	1,213.0	544.0	780.4	1,023.7	1,044.2
Electric services	136.5	492.6	907.2	931.2	391.7	596.3	788.3	799.4
Gas services	46.6	135.3	208.6	217.6	136.2	163.6	181.9	186.1
Sanitary services	5.6	17.8	58.3	64.2	16.0	20.4	53.6	58.7
Wholesale trade	40.7	160.5	405.5	419.1	107.6	199.6	374.2	389.2
Retail trade	75.8	259.6	610.8	646.2	216.5	334.8	552.0	581.8
Finance, insurance, real estate..........	216.8	794.3	2,044.2	2,132.9	619.8	1,006.3	1,854.4	1,928.9
Depository institutions.............	22.4	126.1	413.1	441.1	60.9	151.2	379.3	403.5
Nondepository institutions.........	6.2	39.1	106.8	113.2	16.7	44.8	96.7	102.5
Security and commodity brokers.......	1.1	3.8	13.0	12.8	2.6	4.4	12.4	12.4
Insurance carriers	5.6	21.8	124.5	134.3	13.4	25.3	121.3	134.0
Insurance agents, brokers, and service	1.9	4.8	6.0	5.9	3.9	5.0	5.7	5.8
Real estate..................	177.5	589.6	1,352.9	1,398.2	517.8	765.5	1,212.2	1,243.6
Holding, other investment offices	2.1	9.0	27.8	27.4	4.6	10.2	26.9	27.0
Services..........................	106.3	386.7	852.7	884.6	286.1	492.1	776.8	797.7
Hotels, other lodging places	20.1	63.2	128.9	130.6	60.0	82.4	115.9	116.4
Personal services	7.9	20.7	32.0	33.9	19.9	26.0	29.6	30.9
Business services	18.7	88.4	224.1	230.4	48.0	111.2	203.1	204.9
Auto repair, services, parking..........	16.3	68.2	151.5	158.4	43.8	86.5	139.6	143.3
Misc. repair services..............	2.4	9.4	15.0	15.3	7.0	12.0	13.5	13.6
Motion pictures	2.8	9.0	19.8	23.4	6.8	10.8	18.3	21.9
Amusement, recreation services........	10.0	28.5	41.6	42.0	27.3	36.4	37.5	37.7
Other services...................	28.1	99.5	239.8	250.6	73.3	126.8	219.4	229.0
Health services	14.0	50.6	130.1	137.6	38.8	64.9	117.6	123.5
Legal services	2.8	7.9	25.6	26.8	7.0	9.9	24.1	25.4
Educational services	1.4	2.6	5.4	5.7	2.9	3.1	4.9	5.2
Other [1]	9.8	38.4	78.7	80.6	24.6	48.9	72.7	74.9
Residential	1,219.4	4,292.0	7,386.7	7,704.9	3,881.1	5,321.2	6,754.3	6,866.1
Farms..........................	50.9	129.1	159.8	163.0	161.6	160.8	146.4	144.6
Real estate	1,168.5	4,162.9	7,227.0	7,541.9	3,719.5	5,160.4	6,607.9	6,721.5

[1] Consists of social services, membership organizations, and miscellaneous professional service.

Source: U.S. Bureau of Economic Analysis, *Survey of Current Business,* January and August 1992.

No. 877. Fixed Nonresidential Private Capital Valued in Current and Constant (1987) Dollars: 1980 to 1992

[In billions of dollars. Stocks as of Dec. 31; depreciation over entire calendar year. Data refer to privately owned assets and are based on the fixed capital formation components of the gross domestic product. Excludes residential capital and government enterprises; includes nonprofit institutions. Gross stocks allow for retirement; net stocks allow for retirement and depreciation. Net stock and depreciation estimates are based on the straight-line depreciation formula. For manufacturing industry, see table 1263]

ITEM	CURRENT DOLLARS						CONSTANT (1987) DOLLARS					
	1980	1985	1989	1990	1991	1992	1980	1985	1989	1990	1991	1992
Gross stocks...	5,072	7,156	9,012	9,507	9,784	10,042	6,264	7,389	8,272	8,490	8,656	8,807
Equipment...	2,389	3,374	4,257	4,543	4,674	4,777	3,009	3,518	3,979	4,093	4,179	4,269
Structures...	2,683	3,783	4,756	4,964	5,110	5,265	3,255	3,870	4,293	4,398	4,477	4,539
Net stocks....	2,974	4,113	5,084	5,334	5,438	5,539	3,677	4,248	4,673	4,773	4,824	4,870
Equipment...	1,360	1,852	2,299	2,440	2,484	2,519	1,709	1,929	2,155	2,204	2,229	2,263
Structures...	1,615	2,261	2,786	2,894	2,954	3,020	1,968	2,319	2,518	2,568	2,595	2,607
Depreciation...	240	358	451	471	489	505	308	368	425	436	446	460
Equipment...	161	240	306	321	334	346	211	250	294	303	312	323
Structures...	78	118	145	150	155	158	97	118	132	132	134	137

Source: U.S. Bureau of Economic Analysis, *Survey of Current Business*, January and August 1992; and unpublished data.

No. 878. Business Expenditures for New Plant and Equipment: 1980 to 1993

[In billions of dollars. Based on sample and subject to sampling variability; see text, section 17. Represents expenditures for new facilities and for expansion or replacement of existing facilities that are chargeable to fixed asset accounts and for which depreciation or amortization accounts are ordinarily allowed. Excludes expenditures for land and mineral rights; maintenance and repair; used plant and equipment, including that purchased or acquired through mergers or acquisitions; assets located in foreign countries; residential structures; etc. They also differ from the nonresidential fixed investment data in type of detail, data sources, coverage, and timing. For further information, see the February 1985 *Survey of Current Business*]

INDUSTRY	1980	1984	1985	1986	1987	1988	1989	1990	1991	1992	1993, plans
All industries [1]	**286.4**	**373.8**	**410.1**	**399.4**	**410.5**	**455.5**	**507.4**	**532.6**	**528.4**	**546.1**	**582.3**
Constant (1987 dollars) [2]	**354.6**	**390.9**	**424.5**	**405.9**	**410.6**	**443.2**	**482.3**	**496.3**	**488.6**	**512.9**	**554.8**
Manufacturing ...	112.6	139.6	152.9	138.0	141.1	163.5	183.8	192.6	182.8	173.9	183.4
Durable goods [3]	54.8	64.6	70.9	65.7	68.0	77.0	82.6	82.6	77.6	73.4	77.1
Primary metals.............	6.7	6.8	7.5	6.7	8.6	11.0	12.0	12.2	10.7	9.8	9.8
Electrical machinery	10.2	16.2	17.1	15.6	16.8	20.8	20.5	22.0	21.0	20.5	22.3
Machinery, except electrical	10.7	13.6	13.8	11.4	11.9	13.7	14.6	13.7	12.7	10.7	9.5
Transportation equipment.......	16.1	16.6	19.6	18.9	16.7	15.8	18.7	17.9	17.2	16.1	16.8
Nondurable goods [3]	57.8	75.0	82.0	72.3	73.0	86.4	101.2	110.0	105.2	100.5	106.2
Food and beverage...........	8.5	9.7	11.4	11.6	12.1	14.2	15.9	16.4	17.4	19.0	20.3
Paper....................	6.4	6.9	8.1	8.3	8.5	10.9	15.6	16.5	11.5	10.5	11.0
Chemicals................	10.6	13.5	14.4	14.5	13.9	16.6	18.5	20.6	21.5	23.0	23.2
Petroleum	22.8	32.6	34.1	23.1	22.1	26.0	30.1	34.8	35.6	29.5	32.4
Mining	12.7	11.9	12.0	8.2	8.3	9.3	9.2	9.9	10.0	8.9	9.3
Transportation	13.6	13.4	14.6	15.1	15.1	16.6	18.8	21.5	22.7	22.8	23.1
Public utilities...............	41.3	57.5	59.6	56.6	56.3	60.4	66.3	67.2	66.6	72.0	77.4
Wholesale and retail trade	32.0	53.4	60.1	65.4	68.5	76.4	84.5	95.6	105.0	115.9	(NA)
Finance and insurance.	22.6	37.9	45.2	49.6	54.1	59.2	70.3	69.0	64.0	72.9	(NA)
Personal and business services [4]	24.9	28.5	28.8	28.4	30.1	32.9	34.6	33.7	34.7	38.3	(NA)
Communication	26.8	31.6	37.1	38.2	37.2	37.2	39.8	43.1	42.7	41.4	(NA)

NA Not available.   [1] Surveyed quarterly.   [2] For preparation of constant-dollar estimates, see source for detail.   [3] Includes industries not shown separately.   [4] Includes construction.

Source: U.S. Bureau of the Census, *Plant and Equipment Expenditures and Plans*, quarterly.

No. 879. Gross Private Domestic Investment: 1970 to 1991

[In billions of dollars]

YEAR	CURRENT DOLLARS						CONSTANT (1987) DOLLARS					
	Gross private domestic investment				Less: Consumption of fixed capital	Equals: Net private domestic investment	Gross private domestic investment				Less: Consumption of fixed capital	Equals: Net private domestic investment
	Total [1]	Fixed investment	Nonresidential	Residential			Total [1]	Fixed investment	Nonresidential	Residential		
1970	150	148	107	41	89	62	430	424	292	132	258	172
1980	468	477	354	123	312	156	594	603	438	165	401	194
1981	558	533	410	123	362	196	631	607	455	152	418	213
1982	503	519	414	106	399	104	541	558	434	124	430	111
1983	547	552	400	152	418	128	600	595	421	174	447	152
1984	719	648	469	179	433	286	758	690	490	199	456	302
1985	715	690	504	186	455	260	746	724	522	202	472	274
1986	718	709	492	217	479	239	735	727	500	226	487	248
1987	749	723	498	225	502	247	749	723	498	225	502	247
1988	794	777	545	232	534	260	773	753	531	223	519	255
1989	832	799	568	231	580	252	784	754	540	214	545	239
1990	800	793	578	216	603	197	739	733	538	195	555	184
1991	721	731	541	190	626	95	661	670	500	170	569	92

[1] Includes change in business inventories, not shown separately.

Source: U.S. Bureau of Economic Analysis, *National Income and Product Accounts, volume 2, 1959-88*, and *Survey of Current Business*, July 1992.

No. 880. Composite Indexes of Economic Cyclical Indicators: 1980 to 1991

[1991 figures are preliminary. See source for discussion of composite indexes. Minus sign (-) indicates decrease. **Leading indicators** are economic time series that tend to reach their cyclical high and low points earlier than the corresponding peaks and troughs in the overall economy. **Coincident indicators** are economic time series that tend to reach their cyclical high and low points about the same time as the corresponding peaks and troughs in the overall economy. **Lagging indicators** are economic time series that tend to reach their cyclical high and low points later than the corresponding peaks and troughs in the overall economy]

ITEM	Unit	1980	1983	1984	1985	1986	1987	1988	1989	1990	1991
LEADING INDICATORS											
Composite index	1982=100...	99.2	116.2	121.7	124.0	132.4	140.1	142.4	144.4	143.8	143.4
Building permits [1]	1967=100...	96.7	131.1	134.8	138.1	141.2	122.9	115.8	107.7	89.6	75.5
Common stock prices, index [2]	1941-43=100.	118.8	160.4	160.5	186.8	236.4	286.8	265.8	322.8	334.6	376.2
Initial claims, unemployment insurance [3][4].	1,000	480	426	366	383	370	314	305	327	383	444
Change in sensitive materials prices [3][4]	Percent	0.4	1.1	0.2	-0.8	0.4	1.1	0.4	0.1	-0.3	-0.6
Vendor performance, slower deliveries ..	Percent	41	57	57	48	51	57	58	48	48	47
Average workweek, manufacturing [5] ...	Hours	39.7	40.1	40.7	40.5	40.7	41.0	41.1	41.0	40.8	40.7
Plant and equipment contracts and orders (1982 dol.)	Bil. dol.	332	288	350	381	383	433	497	519	509	489
New orders, manufacturing, consumer goods and materials (1982 dol.)	Bil. dol.	909	934	1,016	1,022	1,043	1,097	1,105	1,105	1,091	1,048
Money supply (M2) [6] (1982 dol.)	Bil. dol.	1,836	2,044	2,119	2,228	2,365	2,433	2,458	2,437	2,435	2,410
Consumer expectations index [7]	1966=100...	56.8	84.7	92.7	86.5	85.8	81.3	85.2	85.3	70.2	70.3
Change in manufacturers' unfilled orders, durable goods (1982 dol.) [4]	Bil. dol.	-12	16	30	3	2	18	16	19	10	-16
COINCIDENT INDICATORS											
Composite index	1982=100...	107.2	101.9	112.3	116.3	119.0	123.5	129.1	132.2	131.7	124.5
Industrial production index	1987=100...	84.1	84.9	92.8	94.4	95.3	100.0	105.4	108.1	109.2	107.1
Employees, nonagricultural payrolls	Million	90.4	90.2	94.5	97.5	99.5	102.2	105.5	108.3	109.8	108.3
Personal income less transfer payments (1987 dol.)	Bil. dol.	2,722	2,812	3,015	3,110	3,200	3,260	3,357	3,436	3,460	3,382
Sales, mfg. and trade (1982 dol.)	Bil. dol.	4,341	4,361	4,725	4,869	5,045	5,337	5,586	5,727	5,762	5,627
LAGGING INDICATORS											
Composite index	1982=100...	105.5	91.4	100.7	107.5	111.4	110.8	115.0	120.0	120.0	115.1
Change in labor cost per unit of output, manufacturing [4]	Percent	10.1	-3.3	1.6	1.8	-0.2	-2.6	3.1	1.0	1.9	3.1
Ratio, consumer installment credit to personal income	Percent	13.2	12.0	13.0	14.3	15.3	15.5	15.7	16.0	15.6	15.1
Average prime rate charged by banks...	Percent	15.3	10.8	12.0	9.9	8.3	8.2	9.3	10.9	10.0	8.5
Average duration of unemployment	Weeks.	11.9	20.0	18.2	15.6	15.0	14.5	13.5	11.9	12.1	13.8
Ratio, inventories to sales, mfg. and trade (1982 dol.)	Ratio.	1.6	1.6	1.6	1.6	1.5	1.5	1.5	1.5	1.4	1.5
Commercial and industrial loans outstanding (1982 dol.) [8]	Bil. dol.	225	261	296	329	349	354	364	390	402	385
Change in CPI for services [4][9]	Percent	15.2	3.1	5.6	5.0	4.8	4.2	4.7	5.0	5.9	4.6

[1] New private housing units authorized. [2] Standard and Poor's 500 stocks. [3] Producer prices of selected crude and intermediate materials and spot market prices of selected raw industrial materials. [4] Smoothed by an autoregressive-moving-average filter developed by Statistics Canada. [5] Production workers. [6] See table 821. [7] Copyrighted by the University of Michigan's Survey Research Center. [8] Includes commercial paper issued by nonfinancial companies. [9] Consumer Price Index.

Source: U.S. Bureau of Economic Analysis, *Survey of Current Business*, monthly.

No. 881. Business Cycle Expansions and Contractions—Months of Duration

[A trough is the low point of a business cycle; a peak is the high point. Contraction, or recession, is the period from peak to subsequent trough; expansion is the period from trough to subsequent peak. Business cycle reference dates are determined by the National Bureau of Economic Research, Inc.]

BUSINESS CYCLE REFERENCE DATE		Contraction (trough from previous peak)	Expansion (trough to peak)	LENGTH OF CYCLE	
Trough	Peak			Trough from previous trough	Peak from previous peak
March 1919	January 1920	[1]7	10	[2]51	[1]17
July 1921	May 1923	18	22	28	40
July 1924	October 1926	14	27	36	41
November 1927	August 1929	13	21	40	34
March 1933	May 1937	43	50	64	93
June 1938	February 1945	13	80	63	93
October 1945	November 1948	8	37	88	45
October 1949	July 1953	11	45	48	56
May 1954	August 1957	10	39	55	49
April 1958	April 1960	8	24	47	32
February 1961	December 1969	10	106	34	116
November 1970	November 1973	11	36	117	47
March 1975	January 1980	16	58	52	74
July 1980	July 1981	6	12	64	18
November 1982	July 1990	16	92	28	108
Average, all cycles:					
1919 to 1945 (six cycles)		18	35	53	53
1945 to 1990 (eight cycles)		11	[3]50	56	[3]61

[1] Previous peak: August 1918.   [2] Previous trough: December 1914.   [3] For nine cycles.
Source: U.S. Bureau of Economic Analysis, *Survey of Current Business*, October 1992.

Figure 17.1
Bankruptcy Petitions Filed, by State: 1992
(Thousands)

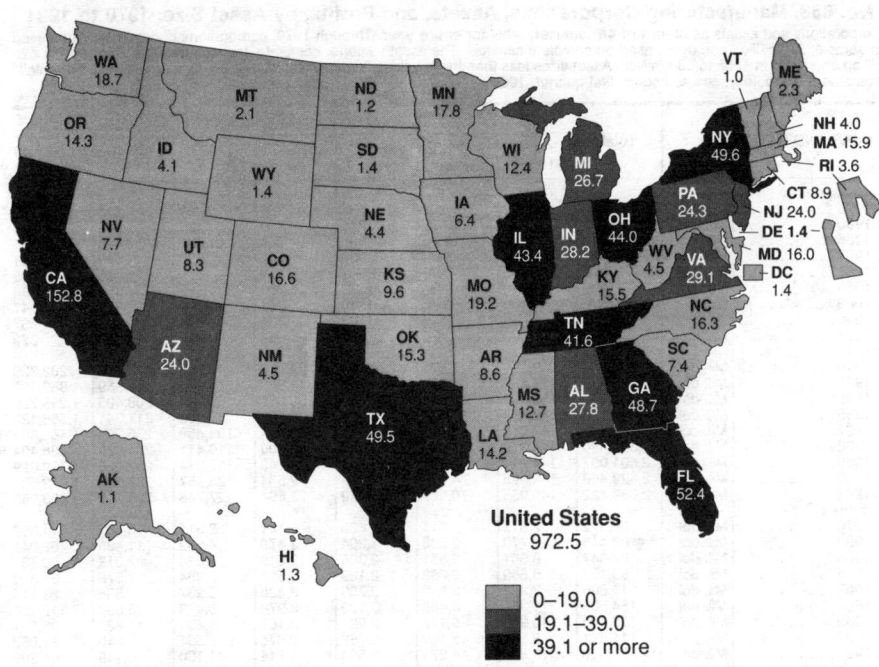

United States
972.5

0–19.0
19.1–39.0
39.1 or more

Source: Chart prepared by U.S. Bureau of the Census. For data, see table 864.

No. 882. Manufacturing and Trade—Sales and Inventories in Current and Constant (1987) Dollars: 1980 to 1992

[In billions of dollars, except ratios]

ITEM	1980	1982	1983	1984	1985	1986	1987	1988	1989	1990	1991	1992
CURRENT DOLLARS												
Sales, average monthly	328	348	371	411	423	432	458	495	524	542	538	559
Manufacturing	154	163	173	191	179	195	206	223	233	239	235	244
Retail trade	80	89	97	107	114	121	128	137	147	154	155	163
Merchant wholesalers	94	96	101	113	115	116	124	135	144	149	148	152
Inventories [1]	509	576	592	651	666	665	712	768	814	837	833	849
Manufacturing	264	312	312	339	335	323	338	367	387	399	386	379
Retail trade	121	135	148	168	182	187	208	220	238	241	246	261
Merchant wholesalers	124	129	132	144	149	155	166	181	189	197	201	209
Inventory-sales ratios [2]	1.55	1.66	1.60	1.58	1.57	1.54	1.55	1.55	1.55	1.54	1.55	1.52
Manufacturing	1.71	1.91	1.80	1.78	1.73	1.66	1.64	1.65	1.66	1.67	1.64	1.55
Retail trade	1.51	1.52	1.53	1.57	1.60	1.55	1.63	1.61	1.62	1.57	1.59	1.60
Merchant wholesalers	1.32	1.34	1.31	1.27	1.30	1.34	1.34	1.34	1.31	1.32	1.36	1.38
CONSTANT (1987) DOLLARS												
Sales, average monthly [3]	381	366	385	418	431	447	464	484	490	488	477	492
Manufacturing	179	169	177	190	194	198	206	216	218	216	211	219
Retail trade	103	103	110	118	123	130	134	139	141	142	139	143
Merchant wholesalers	99	94	98	109	113	120	124	128	130	130	127	129
Inventories.	605	600	612	672	686	694	724	751	784	787	784	787
Manufacturing	320	311	312	339	336	334	340	355	374	378	371	364
Retail trade	147	152	163	181	194	197	214	220	231	227	229	237
Merchant wholesalers	138	137	138	151	156	163	170	176	179	183	184	185
Inventory-sales ratios [4]	1.59	1.64	1.59	1.61	1.59	1.55	1.56	1.55	1.60	1.61	1.64	1.60
Manufacturing	1.79	1.84	1.76	1.78	1.73	1.69	1.65	1.64	1.71	1.75	1.75	1.66
Retail trade	1.42	1.48	1.48	1.54	1.57	1.51	1.60	1.58	1.63	1.60	1.65	1.65
Merchant wholesalers	1.40	1.46	1.41	1.38	1.38	1.36	1.37	1.37	1.37	1.40	1.45	1.43

[1] Seasonally adjusted end-of-year data. See text, section 17.   [2] End-of-year seasonally adjusted inventories to seasonally adjusted sales.   [3] Average monthly sales for fourth quarter.   [4] End of fourth quarter inventories to average monthly sales for fourth quarter.

Source: Current dollars from U.S. Bureau of the Census, Current Business Reports, *"Manufacturing and Trade Inventories and Sales"* July 1992; 1990 and unpublished data; constant dollars from U.S. Bureau of Economic Analysis, *Survey of Current Business.*

No. 883. Manufacturing Corporations, Assets, and Profits, by Asset Size: 1970 to 1991

[Corporations and assets as of **end of 4th quarter**; profit for **entire year.** Through 1979, corporations under $10 million based on sample; $10 million and over based on complete canvass. The asset value for complete canvass was raised in 1980 to $25 million and again in 1988 to $50 million. Asset sizes less than these values continue to be sampled, except as noted. For details regarding methodology, see source for first quarter, 1988]

YEAR AND ITEM	Unit	Total	ASSET-SIZE CLASS						
			Under [1] $10 mil.	$10-$25 mil.	$25-$50 mil.	$50-$100 mil.	$100-$250 mil.	$250 mil. -$1 bil.	$1 bil. and over
Corporations:									
1970 [2]	Number .	197,807	[3]195,000	1,202	533	366	289	218	102
1980	Number .	(NA)	(NA)	1,777	941	590	491	369	244
1985	Number .	(NA)	(NA)	(NA)	896	744	608	428	281
1986	Number .	(NA)	(NA)	(NA)	962	741	628	445	291
1987	Number .	(NA)	(NA)	(NA)	1,007	811	676	481	318
1988	Number .	(NA)	(NA)	(NA)	(NA)	783	729	550	334
1989	Number .	(NA)	(NA)	(NA)	(NA)	781	750	579	347
1990	Number .	(NA)	(NA)	(NA)	(NA)	834	774	597	367
1991	Number .	(NA)	(NA)	(NA)	(NA)	868	799	608	373
Assets:									
1970	Mil. dol .	578,234	69,101	20,471	20,138	25,946	47,783	112,475	282,320
1980	Mil. dol .	1,384,474	126,639	43,569	34,930	41,963	75,284	179,959	882,129
1985	Mil. dol .	1,932,766	153,883	64,324	52,669	58,019	96,748	208,403	1,298,720
1986	Mil. dol .	1,994,120	140,864	67,663	55,974	58,233	97,908	217,341	1,356,137
1987	Mil. dol .	2,135,266	147,919	65,623	50,171	60,874	109,458	235,368	1,465,853
1988	Mil. dol .	2,339,690	149,276	77,068	53,461	62,190	110,411	261,880	1,625,404
1989	Mil. dol .	2,501,097	144,814	73,487	56,548	68,149	117,014	282,056	1,759,029
1990	Mil. dol .	2,629,458	142,498	74,477	55,914	72,554	123,967	287,512	1,872,536
1991	Mil. dol .	2,688,422	140,056	70,567	58,549	72,694	127,748	295,743	1,923,066
Net profit: [4]									
1970	Mil. dol .	28,572	2,812	811	836	1,101	2,315	5,862	14,832
1980	Mil. dol .	92,443	7,770	2,235	1,904	2,479	4,532	11,485	62,041
1985	Mil. dol .	87,647	8,601	2,551	2,305	2,819	3,628	7,312	60,431
1986	Mil. dol .	83,122	6,659	2,988	2,129	2,514	3,884	7,572	57,376
1987	Mil. dol .	115,600	7,273	3,849	2,753	3,338	5,237	9,636	83,514
1988	Mil. dol .	154,583	11,364	4,488	3,199	3,978	5,473	13,994	112,086
1989	Mil. dol. .	136,490	10,381	5,173	2,921	3,105	4,434	11,824	98,651
1990	Mil. dol .	111,561	8,527	5,160	2,769	2,676	3,531	7,245	81,652
1991	Mil. dol .	67,516	6,820	4,271	2,564	1,714	1,730	5,119	45,299

NA Not available.   [1] Beginning 1986, excludes estimates for corporations with less than $250,000 in assets at time of sample selection. Prior periods include estimates for corporations in this size category.   [2] Source: U.S. Securities and Exchange Commission.   [3] Data derived from U.S. Internal Revenue Service, *Statistics of Income,* annual.   [4] After taxes.
Source: Except as noted, through 1980, U.S. Federal Trade Commission; thereafter, U.S. Bureau of the Census, *Quarterly Financial Report for Manufacturing, Mining and Trade Corporations.*

No. 884. 500 Largest Industrial Corporations—Sales, Assets, and Profits by Sales Group Rank: 1987 and 1991

[In billions of dollars, except percent. Excludes large privately owned companies that do not publish sales. Includes service and rental revenues, but companies must derive more than 50 percent of revenues from manufacturing or mining for years ending not later than Dec. 31 of year stated, sales exclude excise taxes collected by manufacturer and include discontinued operations. Minus sign (-) indicates decrease]

RANK BY SALES GROUP	SALES			ASSETS [1]			PROFITS [2]		
	1987	1991	Percent change, 1987-91	1987	1991	Percent change, 1987-91	1987	1991	Percent change 1987-91
500 largest.....	1,880	2,264	20	1,706	2,466	44	91	55	-39
Top 100.....	1,307	1,619	24	1,217	1,844	51	66	38	-41
101-200.....	287	323	13	240	328	37	14	9	-36
201-300.....	142	160	13	123	151	23	5	4	-21
301-400.....	88	96	8	73	77	6	2	3	12
401-500.....	56	65	16	52	57	9	3	1	-72
Percent of total:									
Top 100.....	70	72	(X)	71	75	(X)	73	70	(X)
101-200.....	15	14	(X)	14	13	(X)	16	17	(X)
201-300.....	8	7	(X)	7	6	(X)	6	8	(X)
301-400.....	5	4	(X)	4	3	(X)	3	5	(X)
401-500.....	3	3	(X)	3	2	(X)	3	1	(X)

X Not applicable.   [1] Total assets employed in business at end of fiscal fiscal year, less depreciation and depletion.   [2] After taxes, special charges, and credits.
Source: Time Warner, New York, NY, *The Fortune Directories* (copyright).

No. 885. 500 Largest Industrial Corporations—Selected Financial Items: 1970 to 1991

ITEM	Unit	1970	1980	1984	1985	1986	1987	1988	1989	1990	1991
Sales per employee	$1,000....	29.5	78.1	101.0	106.0	110.7	124.4	137.9	146.0	153.9	159.2
Changes in profits.................	Percent...	(NA)	3.6	24.9	-19.1	-7.9	41.3	26.9	-8.1	-11.6	-41.0
Sales per dollar of stockholder's equity. .	Dollar	2.40	3.00	2.78	2.80	2.79	2.77	2.93	2.96	2.97	2.81
Return on stockholder's equity	Percent...	9.5	14.4	13.5	11.6	11.6	14.4	16.2	15.0	12.7	10.2
Return on sales ....·..........	Percent...	3.9	4.8	4.5	3.9	4.1	5.1	5.5	4.7	4.1	3.1
Total return to investors [1]........	Percent...	6.5	21.1	-0.8	26.3	16.1	6.6	14.1	17.5	-10.2	29.5

NA Not available.   [1] Includes both price appreciation and dividend yield, i.e., to an investor in the company's stock.
Source: Time Warner, New York, NY, *The Fortune Directories* (copyright).

No. 886. 500 Largest Industrial Corporations—Selected Financial Items, by Industry: 1990 and 1991

[Data are medians and are ranked based on sales per employee for latest year shown. See headnote, table 884. Minus sign (-) indicates decrease. For definition of median, see Guide to Tabular Presentation]

INDUSTRY	SALES PER EMPLOYEE ($1,000)		CHANGES IN PROFITS FROM PREVIOUS YEAR (percent)		SALES PER DOLLAR OF STOCKHOLDER'S EQUITY (dol.)		RETURN ON STOCKHOLDER'S EQUITY (percent)		RETURN ON SALES (percent)		TOTAL RETURN TO INVESTORS [1] (percent)	
	1990	1991	1990	1991	1990	1991	1990	1991	1990	1991	1990	1991
500 median	153.9	159.2	-11.6	-41.0	2.97	2.81	12.7	10.2	4.1	3.1	-10.2	29.5
Petroleum refining	613.1	567.0	32.6	-52.1	3.32	3.44	13.8	8.5	4.0	1.5	-3.8	0.7
Mining, crude-oil production......	375.7	414.5	13.4	-61.9	1.97	1.64	15.1	7.7	8.7	4.8	-14.0	-5.5
Tobacco.	252.3	267.7	-11.0	27.2	5.56	2.00	14.8	5.2	1.6	2.1	-8.7	137.3
Soaps, cosmetics	146.9	241.1	15.6	-12.9	3.34	3.11	18.0	14.7	6.0	5.1	5.3	19.4
Food.......................	223.6	239.0	4.1	13.2	5.29	4.82	16.5	19.7	3.1	3.5	3.7	26.7
Chemicals	212.4	227.3	-1.9	-17.8	2.30	2.36	13.8	12.6	5.5	3.9	-3.8	31.9
Beverages	202.0	201.1	9.8	5.9	2.48	2.48	15.5	21.1	7.8	5.5	10.3	32.3
Metals	182.4	176.5	-44.3	-51.8	2.90	2.50	10.2	5.2	4.3	1.5	-18.7	18.2
Forest products.............	175.2	172.4	-39.2	-39.6	2.32	2.02	10.1	4.8	4.4	2.5	-17.0	36.9
Pharmaceuticals	147.6	168.9	17.6	16.0	1.85	1.87	26.4	26.1	13.6	12.8	19.3	61.5
Computers (incl. office equip.)	132.4	163.7	4.6	1.1	2.23	2.38	12.0	10.2	5.7	4.9	-17.1	12.3
Building materials	167.3	157.9	-53.8	-53.8	1.50	1.95	10.8	-0.7	2.4	-3.6	-30.3	39.8
Rubber and plastic products	136.9	152.7	-33.6	13.3	3.01	3.23	9.8	11.6	3.6	3.4	-26.8	90.3
Industrial and farm equipment ...	125.7	137.7	-10.4	-23.6	3.05	3.31	10.5	6.0	2.9	1.7	-22.0	14.8
Aerospace	132.1	135.7	6.9	0.7	4.18	3.91	13.4	12.4	3.5	3.3	-8.7	35.5
Publishing, printing..........	124.8	133.0	-12.0	-10.3	2.17	2.14	9.9	10.7	5.5	5.2	-22.7	19.4
Scientific, photographic equipment .	118.2	130.0	-8.1	16.3	2.32	2.50	11.8	14.3	4.9	5.3	1.8	50.2
Motor vehicles and parts........	130.3	128.7	-26.9	-70.4	3.60	3.44	7.2	0.7	1.9	0.3	-21.8	16.3
Metal products	123.0	125.8	6.1	-1.0	3.32	3.43	12.4	11.7	3.7	3.4	-11.8	40.8
Transportation equipment [2].....	120.9	118.4	-96.3	-11.7	3.11	3.72	8.6	8.9	2.9	2.4	-36.9	54.3
Electronics..................	111.4	111.2	0.2	-9.3	2.89	2.78	13.7	10.7	3.4	2.7	-8.3	37.6
Furniture	103.8	104.0	2.9	-23.8	3.60	3.25	11.4	10.2	2.7	2.1	-12.3	45.2
Textiles	88.0	93.4	-79.0	-7.3	3.19	2.97	2.7	4.6	0.4	1.4	-41.0	47.5
Apparel	65.2	73.9	-0.9	1.1	3.96	3.96	12.9	13.6	3.3	3.4	-37.0	52.6

[1] Includes both price appreciation and dividend yield, i.e., to an investor in the company's stock.   [2] Excludes motor vehicles and aircraft.
Source: Time Warner, New York, NY, *The Fortune Directories* (copyright).

No. 887. Corporate Profits, Taxes, and Dividends: 1980 to 1992

[In billions of dollars. Covers corporations organized for profit and other entities treated as corporations. Represents profits to U.S. residents, without deduction of depletion charges and exclusive of capital gains and losses; intercorporate dividends from profits of domestic corporations are eliminated; net receipts of dividends, reinvested earnings of incorporated foreign affiliates, and earnings of unincorporated foreign affiliates are added]

ITEM	1980	1982	1983	1984	1985	1986	1987	1988	1989	1990	1991	1992
Profits before taxes	240.9	176.3	210.7	240.5	225.0	217.8	287.9	347.5	342.9	355.4	334.7	371.6
Less: Income tax liability [1]	84.8	63.1	77.2	94.0	96.5	106.5	127.1	137.0	141.3	136.7	124.0	140.2
Equals: Profits after taxes	156.1	113.2	133.5	146.4	128.5	111.3	160.8	210.5	201.6	218.7	210.7	231.4
Less: Net dividends [2]	59.0	70.0	81.2	82.7	92.4	109.8	106.2	115.3	134.6	149.3	146.5	149.3
Equals: Undistributed profits [3]	97.1	43.2	52.3	63.8	36.1	1.6	54.6	95.2	67.1	69.4	64.2	82.1
Capital consumption allowances [3]	164.9	228.8	268.1	293.7	333.3	338.3	354.1	372.3	389.8	388.8	391.5	424.4
Profits after tax plus capital consumption allowances [3]	321.0	342.0	401.6	440.1	461.8	449.6	514.9	582.8	591.4	607.5	602.2	655.8

[1] Federal, State, and local.   [2] Disbursements to U.S. residents, measured after eliminations of intercorporate dividends.
[3] Without capital consumption adjustment. Includes depreciation and accidental damages.

No. 888. Corporate Profits, by Industry: 1980 to 1991

[In billions of dollars. Profits are without inventory valuation and capital consumption adjustments. Minus sign (-) indicates loss. See headnote, table 887]

INDUSTRY	BEFORE TAXES				AFTER TAXES			
	1980	1985	1990	1991	1980	1985	1990	1991
Total	240.9	225.0	355.4	334.7	156.1	128.5	218.7	210.7
Domestic industries	205.9	194.2	289.7	268.2	121.1	97.7	153.0	144.2
Agriculture, forestry, fishing	0.6	-0.1	1.9	1.8	0.2	-0.4	1.3	1.2
Mining	6.2	-5.9	2.5	0.3	4.4	-6.1	1.0	-0.3
Construction	6.0	5.0	11.7	10.8	3.8	8.1	9.4	8.8
Manufacturing	93.8	78.9	110.6	86.0	54.6	46.2	65.5	50.0
Transportation	3.6	1.7	1.4	0.4	1.9	-0.1	-1.6	-2.2
Communications	8.0	14.1	19.8	21.7	6.0	10.2	11.5	12.6
Public utilities	10.8	17.6	23.7	22.2	8.2	12.3	14.4	13.7
Wholesale and retail trade	40.3	44.4	44.9	46.3	28.2	27.4	30.1	32.5
Finance, insurance, real estate	26.4	27.3	54.3	59.8	6.6	-2.2	7.2	14.0
Services	10.3	11.2	19.0	19.0	7.2	7.3	14.1	13.8
Rest of world [1]	35.0	30.8	65.7	66.5	35.0	30.8	65.7	66.5

[1] Consists of receipts by all U.S. residents, including both corporations and persons, of earnings of unincorporated foreign affiliates, dividends from their incorporated foreign affiliates, and their share of their incorporated foreign affiliates, net of corresponding outflows.

No. 889. Corporate Profits With Inventory Valuation and Capital Consumption Adjustments—Financial and Nonfinancial Industries: 1980 to 1992

[In billions of dollars. Minus sign (-) indicates loss. See headnote, table 887]

ITEM	1980	1983	1984	1985	1986	1987	1988	1989	1990	1991	1992
Corporate profits with IVA [1] and CCA [2]	177.7	212.7	264.2	280.8	271.6	319.8	365.0	362.8	361.7	346.3	393.8
Domestic industries	142.7	182.3	233.0	250.0	238.7	280.3	315.9	303.4	296.0	279.8	329.8
Financial	22.0	22.4	18.7	28.6	34.9	36.1	41.5	48.2	47.7	49.9	46.8
Nonfinancial	120.7	159.9	214.3	221.4	203.8	244.2	274.4	255.2	248.3	229.9	283.0
Rest of the world	35.0	30.4	31.2	30.8	32.9	39.5	49.1	59.4	65.7	66.5	64.0
Corporate profits with IVA [1]	197.8	202.2	236.4	225.3	227.6	273.4	320.3	325.4	341.2	337.8	364.2
Domestic industries	162.9	171.9	205.2	194.5	194.6	233.9	271.2	266.0	275.5	271.3	300.2
Financial	24.3	24.5	20.3	28.7	35.8	36.4	41.8	50.6	56.7	60.9	56.8
Federal Reserve banks	11.8	14.6	16.4	16.3	15.5	15.7	17.6	20.1	21.4	20.2	17.8
Other	12.6	9.9	3.9	12.4	20.3	20.7	24.2	30.5	35.3	40.7	38.9
Nonfinancial	138.5	147.4	185.0	165.8	158.9	197.5	229.4	215.3	218.8	210.4	243.5
Manufacturing	75.8	71.4	86.7	80.1	59.0	87.0	117.5	108.0	106.9	89.3	113.8
Durable goods [3]	17.9	18.4	37.2	29.0	30.0	42.2	52.2	49.3	40.5	25.8	41.0
Primary metal industries	2.6	-4.9	-0.4	-0.9	0.9	2.6	5.9	6.1	3.1	1.1	0.4
Fabricated metal products	4.3	3.1	4.5	4.7	5.3	5.2	6.4	6.6	6.3	5.4	7.1
Machinery, except electrical	7.5	4.4	6.3	5.3	3.2	7.3	10.5	10.3	11.3	8.9	9.4
Electric and electronic equipment	5.0	3.4	4.8	2.4	2.6	6.2	7.6	9.3	7.5	6.6	9.3
Motor vehicles and equipment	-4.3	5.2	8.9	7.3	4.4	3.7	5.7	2.3	-2.6	-6.9	3.1
Nondurable goods [3]	57.8	53.0	49.5	51.1	29.0	44.8	65.3	58.8	66.5	63.5	72.9
Food and kindred products	6.0	5.8	7.3	8.4	7.5	11.4	11.8	10.7	13.2	16.6	16.6
Chemicals and allied products	5.5	6.8	7.3	6.0	8.0	15.1	19.3	18.5	16.2	16.1	18.1
Petroleum and coal products	33.6	22.1	15.9	17.1	-8.5	-3.6	10.4	5.7	14.6	7.7	9.4
Transportation and public utilities	18.3	28.9	39.9	34.1	36.5	43.4	47.5	42.1	43.9	46.1	44.4
Wholesale and retail trade	22.8	38.7	49.7	43.1	46.3	39.9	37.1	39.7	35.8	44.0	47.7
Other	21.6	8.4	8.7	8.5	17.1	27.2	27.3	25.5	32.1	31.1	37.5

[1] Inventory valuation adjustment.   [2] Capital consumption adjustment.   [3] Includes other industries not shown separately.
Source of tables 887-889: U.S. Bureau of Economic Analysis, National Income and Product Accounts of the Unites States, volume 2, 1959-88; Survey of Current Business, July 1992; and unpublished data.

No. 890. Corporate Profits and Stockholders' Equity Ratios, by Industry: 1980 to 1991

[Averages of quarterly figures at annual rates. Beginning 1990, manufacturing data exclude estimates for corporations with less than $250,000 in assets at time of sample selection. Data are not necessarily comparable from year to year due to changes in accounting procedures, industry classifications, sampling procedures, etc.; for detail, see source. Based on sample; see source for discussion of methodology. Minus sign (-) indicates loss]

INDUSTRY	RATIO OF PROFITS TO STOCKHOLDERS' EQUITY (percent)				PROFITS PER DOLLAR OF SALES (cents)				RATIO OF STOCKHOLDERS' EQUITY TO DEBT			
	1980	1985	1990	1991	1980	1985	1990	1991	1980	1985	1990	1991
All manufacturing corporations [1]	13.9	10.1	10.7	6.4	4.9	3.8	4.0	2.5	2.3	1.9	1.3	1.3
Durable goods industries	11.2	9.2	8.0	1.5	4.0	3.4	3.0	0.6	2.2	2.2	1.6	1.5
Stone, clay, and glass products	10.8	7.9	5.4	-8.9	4.2	3.1	1.8	-3.3	1.9	1.7	0.8	0.7
Primary metal industries	11.7	-7.9	9.5	-1.5	4.1	-2.6	2.6	-0.4	1.7	1.2	1.1	1.0
Iron and steel	9.0	-11.0	6.6	-13.3	2.9	-2.6	1.0	-2.9	1.7	0.8	0.6	0.6
Nonferrous metals	15.6	-5.7	10.4	3.8	5.8	-2.5	4.0	1.5	1.8	1.6	1.6	1.3
Fabricated metal products	13.9	9.2	11.7	8.8	4.2	2.8	3.4	2.6	2.1	1.6	1.3	1.3
Machinery, exc. electrical	15.0	9.3	8.1	-2.1	6.5	4.7	4.4	-1.1	2.2	2.6	2.2	1.9
Electrical and electronic equipment	15.1	8.3	7.5	5.1	5.0	3.4	3.0	2.1	2.6	2.7	1.6	1.6
Transportation equipment	-0.6	15.4	3.8	-4.3	-0.3	4.1	1.3	-1.5	2.7	2.9	1.9	1.6
Motor vehicles and equipment	-9.3	18.2	-1.0	-11.3	-3.4	4.9	-0.5	-4.1	3.4	4.2	2.2	1.7
Aircraft, guided missiles and parts	16.0	11.1	11.5	6.1	4.3	3.1	3.4	1.9	2.8	2.6	1.6	1.6
Instruments and related products	17.5	10.1	12.9	12.1	9.3	5.7	6.6	6.6	4.3	3.5	1.6	1.7
Nondurable goods industries	16.4	11.0	13.3	10.8	5.6	4.1	4.9	4.1	2.3	1.7	1.2	1.2
Food and kindred products [2]	14.7	15.3	16.1	17.5	3.4	4.1	4.1	4.8	1.9	1.4	0.8	0.9
Tobacco products	19.8	(2)	(2)	(2)	11.7	(2)	(2)	(2)	1.8	(2)	(2)	(2)
Textile mill products	8.5	8.6	3.4	6.0	2.2	2.4	0.8	1.5	2.0	1.5	0.7	0.7
Paper and allied products	12.1	9.7	10.6	4.4	5.1	4.0	4.2	1.8	2.0	1.7	1.1	0.9
Printing and publishing	16.4	19.2	8.3	6.1	5.5	6.5	3.6	2.7	2.1	1.7	1.2	1.2
Chemicals and allied products	15.4	9.4	17.3	14.0	7.1	4.7	8.2	6.7	2.2	2.1	1.4	1.4
Industrial	11.9	4.2	13.8	8.0	5.4	2.2	7.0	4.2	1.9	1.8	1.4	1.3
Drugs	19.9	15.2	27.1	26.1	13.2	9.8	15.7	15.2	3.0	3.2	2.2	2.4
Petroleum and coal products	20.0	8.5	12.8	7.7	7.7	4.0	5.7	3.9	3.4	1.6	1.7	1.6
Rubber and misc. plastics products	6.7	9.5	6.9	3.5	2.0	2.6	1.8	0.8	1.6	1.6	1.0	0.9
Mining corporations, total [3]	19.2	-4.0	8.1	2.6	11.3	-3.2	5.7	2.1	1.3	1.0	1.3	1.3
Retail trade corporations, total [3]	13.2	12.5	8.4	7.2	1.7	2.2	1.1	1.0	1.2	1.4	0.6	0.6
Wholesale trade corporations, total [3]	17.3	8.7	5.0	4.3	1.8	1.0	0.6	0.6	1.2	1.0	1.0	0.9

[1] Includes other industries not shown separately. [2] Beginning 1985, tobacco included in food and kindred products. [3] For 1985, represents results of companies with assets over $25 million; thereafter, asset cut-off raised to $50 million.

Source: 1980, U.S. Federal Trade Commission; thereafter, U.S. Bureau of the Census, Quarterly Financial Report for Manufacturing, Mining, and Trade Corporations. In U.S. Council of Economic Advisers, *Economic Report of the President*, annual.

No. 891. Manufacturing Corporations—Sales, Profits, Stockholders' Equity, and Debt: 1970 to 1991

[In billions of dollars. Data are not necessarily comparable from year to year due to changes in accounting procedures, industry classifications, sampling procedures, etc.; for detail, see source. See also *Historical Statistics, Colonial Times to 1970*, series P 93-106]

YEAR	ALL MANUFACTURING CORPS.					DURABLE GOODS INDUSTRIES					NONDURABLE GOODS INDUSTRIES				
	Sales	Profits		Stockholders' equity [1]	Debt [1]	Sales	Profits		Stockholders' equity [1]	Debt [1]	Sales	Profits		Stockholders' equity [1]	Debt [1]
		Before taxes	After taxes				Before taxes	After taxes				Before taxes	After taxes		
1970	709	48	29	307	134	363	23	13	155	71	346	25	16	152	63
1975	1,065	80	49	423	183	521	35	21	208	94	544	45	28	215	89
1976	1,203	105	65	463	188	590	51	31	224	91	614	54	34	238	97
1977	1,328	115	70	497	200	657	58	35	240	95	671	57	36	257	106
1978	1,496	133	81	541	222	761	70	42	263	106	736	63	39	278	117
1979	1,742	154	99	600	252	866	72	45	292	123	876	82	54	308	129
1980	1,897	145	92	665	292	883	57	36	316	143	1,014	88	57	349	149
1981	2,145	159	101	743	335	979	67	42	350	159	1,165	91	60	393	176
1982	2,039	108	71	770	371	913	35	22	356	177	1,126	74	49	415	193
1983	2,114	133	86	813	368	973	49	30	372	168	1,141	84	56	440	200
1984	2,335	166	108	864	405	1,108	76	49	396	166	1,228	90	59	469	239
1985	2,331	137	88	866	454	1,143	61	39	421	187	1,189	76	49	445	267
1986 [2]	2,221	129	83	875	501	1,126	52	33	436	203	1,096	78	51	438	298
1987	2,378	173	116	901	553	1,178	78	53	444	229	1,200	95	63	457	324
1988	2,596	216	155	958	622	1,285	92	67	469	265	1,312	124	88	489	357
1989	2,745	189	136	999	733	1,357	75	56	501	308	1,388	114	81	498	425
1990	2,812	160	112	1,044	782	1,357	58	41	515	328	1,454	102	71	529	453
1991	2,761	100	68	1,064	814	1,304	14	7	507	338	1,457	86	60	557	476

[1] Annual data are average equity or debt for the year (using four endof-quarter figures). [2] Beginning 1986, data exclude estimates for corporations with less than $250,000 in assets at time of sample selection. Prior periods includes estimates for corporations in this size category.

Source: Through 1981, U.S. Federal Trade Commission; thereafter, U.S. Bureau of Census, *Quarterly Financial Report for Manufacturing, Mining, and Trade Corporations*. In U.S. Council of Economic Advisers, *Economic Report of the President*, annual.

No. 892. Corporate Philanthropy as a Percent of Worldwide Pretax Net Income: 1985 to 1991

[Data are based on a sample greater than 1,200 corporations. Medians by industry]

INDUSTRY	1985	1989	1990	1991	INDUSTRY	1985	1989	1990	1991
All firms, median	1.0	0.9	1.0	1.3	Machinery, nonelectrical . . .	1.1	0.7	0.7	0.8
					Paper and like products. . . .	1.2	0.7	1.4	1.9
Manufacturing firms,					Petroleum and gas [1]	0.7	0.8	0.8	2.1
median	1.1	0.9	1.0	1.3	Pharmaceuticals.	1.0	1.0	1.1	1.4
Chemicals.	1.1	0.8	0.9	1.0	Primary metal industries . . .	1.1	0.5	0.8	1.0
Electrical machinery and					Printing and publishing . . .	1.3	1.7	1.2	1.5
equipment.	1.6	0.7	1.0	1.8	Transportation equipment [2] .	1.0	1.2	2.0	1.1
Food, beverage and					**Nonmanufacturing firms,**				
tobacco	1.2	1.4	1.1	1.1	**median**	0.9	1.0	0.9	1.2

[1] Mining firms included with petroleum firms.   [2] Rubber and miscellaneous plastic firms included with transportation firms.

Source: The Conference Board, New York, NY, *Annual Survey of Corporate Contributions* (copyright).

No. 893. U.S. Largest Public Companies—Profitability and Growth: 1992

[In percent, except ranks. For fiscal years ending in the 12 month period ending September 30. Included in the Forbes Universe of 1,221 companies is every firm with revenue of over $400 million in 1992, electric and banking firms $800 million. Represents industry medians; calculated by listing companies in rank order and selecting the midpoint. Where there is an even number of companies, an arithmetic average of the two middle companies is substituted. Minus sign (-) indicates decrease]

INDUSTRY	PROFITABILITY					GROWTH					
	Return on equity [1]			Return on capital, [2] latest 12 months	Debt/ capital	Sales [3]			Earnings per share		
	5-year rank	5-year average	Latest 12 months			5-year rank	5-year average	Latest 12 months	5-year rank	5-year average	Latest 12 months
All-industry medians .	(X)	12.2	10.7	8.8	31.2	(X)	8.1	3.4	(X)	-22.7	7.6
Food, drink, and tobacco . .	1	18.7	15.4	11.4	31.6	9	8.9	5.3	1	12.5	8.0
Consumer nondurables . . .	2	17.2	14.6	11.9	27.8	5	10.7	8.9	12	(NS)	10.5
Health	3	16.2	17.3	13.6	22.5	4	11.8	11.3	2	11.2	15.7
Chemicals	4	14.4	14.3	10.1	30.9	7	9.5	2.8	6	-9.7	11.6
Retailing	5	13.9	12.4	10.0	29.1	2	13.4	9.6	4	-6.5	11.3
Food distribution.	6	12.8	11.0	9.1	39.2	13	7.9	1.7	9	-12.2	-3.0
Business services and supplies.	7	12.8	9.9	8.9	33.3	11	8.1	4.9	7	-10.7	6.3
Forest products and packaging	8	12.3	6.3	5.1	37.1	12	7.9	1.7	12	(NS)	2.7
Entertainment and information.	9	12.3	10.1	8.7	27.8	10	8.1	5.5	12	(NS)	12.1
Electric utilities.	10	12.2	10.7	6.6	41.2	20	3.9	1.7	8	-11.3	-7.7
Computers and communications	11	12.2	11.0	8.3	25.8	1	13.7	6.5	10	-17.1	7.6
Insurance	12	11.4	12.5	11.1	17.5	16	6.3	4.2	3	3.6	9.9
Aerospace and defense. . .	13	11.3	11.1	8.9	31.2	19	4.1	-0.1	12	(NS)	11.0
Financial services	14	10.8	13.7	10.6	28.6	8	9.5	-6.0	11	-22.7	17.5
Capital goods.	15	10.7	10.0	8.8	30.4	6	9.5	0.5	5	-7.2	4.6
Metals	16	10.5	2.8	3.1	30.8	15	6.6	-2.3	12	(NS)	-39.7
Energy	17	9.6	6.9	5.7	38.4	17	6.0	-3.8	12	(NS)	-24.4
Travel.	18	8.0	5.1	5.7	56.1	3	12.5	4.4	12	(NS)	-20.2
Consumer durables	19	7.8	7.3	6.7	31.3	18	5.5	6.7	12	(NS)	41.0
Transport	20	7.5	3.7	4.8	38.4	14	7.0	2.1	12	(NS)	-53.9
Construction	21	6.4	2.4	3.7	39.8	21	3.8	3.4	12	(NS)	-6.8

NS Not significant.   X Not applicable.   [1] Represents primary earnings per share before extraordinary item divided by common shareholders' equity per share. Common shareholders' equity is total shareholders' equity including the stated value of all preferred stock at the beginning of each year minus the involuntary liquidating value of nonconvertible preferred shares.   [2] After-tax profits, the amount remaining if the interest paid on longterm debt was taxed, and minority interest divided by a firm's total capitalization. Total capitalization is long-term debt, common and preferred equity, deferred taxes, investment tax credits, and minority interest in consolidated subsidiaries.   [3] Net sales plus other operating revenue.

Source: Forbes, Inc., New York, NY, *Forbes Annual Report on American Industry* (copyright).

No. 894. Foreign Corporate Activity in the United States: 1989

[Includes U.S. corporations controlled or owned by any foreign person (i.e., an individual, partnership, corporation, estate, or trust), directly or indirectly, based on 50 percent or more of a U.S. corporation's voting stock at the end of the tax year]

AREA AND COUNTRY [1]	Number of returns	Total assets (bil. dol.)	Total receipts [2] (bil. dol.)	Net income (less deficit) (mil. dol.)	TOTAL U.S. INCOME TAX	
					Before credits (mil. dol.)	After credits (mil. dol.)
All corporations in the United States	3,627,863	17,647	10,935	389,011	127,754	96,147
U.S. corporations controlled by a foreign person [3]	**44,840**	**1,429**	**967**	**8,308**	**7,540**	**6,161**
Canada	6,993	146	93	196	703	613
Latin America	7,431	54	32	85	238	172
Other Western Hemisphere	551	13	10	-165	49	47
Europe, total	14,777	766	523	7,839	4,951	3,997
European Economic Community countries [3] .	12,250	681	455	6,881	4,345	3,495
Belgium	136	14	13	595	225	111
France	1,538	69	48	88	281	250
Netherlands	1,764	168	115	-206	620	463
United Kingdom	4,612	308	176	4,852	2,342	1,934
West Germany	2,528	91	87	1,892	781	646
Sweden	329	18	17	323	137	101
Switzerland	1,461	52	41	844	427	371
Africa	785	1	1	-13	2	2
Asia [3]	11,636	397	285	568	1,458	1,259
Hong Kong	1,962	36	7	132	51	37
Japan	6,592	322	254	-76	1,231	1,139
South Korea	160	6	9	-273	9	8
Oceania	497	47	18	-379	50	41
Puerto Rico and U.S. possessions	31	2	1	184	62	6
Country not stated	2,138	3	4	-6	27	24

[1] Geographic location of the foreign owners' country of residence, incorporation, organization, creation, or administration. [2] Total receipts includes business and investment receipts. [3] Includes countries not shown separately.

Source: U.S. Internal Revenue Service, *Statistics of Income Bulletin*, winter 1992-93.

No. 895. U.S. Multinational Companies—Assets, Sales, Employment, Employee Compensation, and U.S. Exports and Imports: 1990

[Preliminary. In billions of dollars, except as indicated. Consists of nonbank U.S. parent companies and their nonbank foreign affiliates. U.S. parent is a U.S. person that owns or controls directly or indirectly, 10 percent or more of the voting securities of an incorporated foreign business enterprise, or an equivalent interest in an unincorporated foreign business enterprise. A U.S. person can be an incorporated business enterprise. A foreign affiliate is a foreign business enterprise owned or controlled by a U.S. parent company]

INDUSTRY [1]	U.S. PARENTS				FOREIGN AFFILIATES				U.S. exports shipped to foreign affiliates	U.S. imports shipped from foreign affiliates
	Total assets	Sales	Employment (1,000)	Employee compensation	Total assets	Sales	Employment (1,000)	Employee compensation		
All industries	**4,969**	**3,278**	**18,550**	**690**	**1,553**	**1,481**	**6,706**	**183**	**108**	**102**
Petroleum	473	395	597	29	216	295	233	10	5	12
Manufacturing	1,917	1,573	9,844	402	578	741	4,308	117	72	81
Food and kindred products	185	204	1,159	30	57	75	453	9	2	1
Chemical and allied products	309	248	1,279	57	120	129	581	17	9	5
Primary and fabricated metals . . .	93	95	638	26	27	28	228	5	2	2
Machinery (except electrical)	215	177	1,184	56	88	122	557	20	12	13
Electric and electronic equipment .	237	153	1,077	43	62	73	699	16	9	11
Transportation equipment	454	356	2,015	99	114	192	883	26	29	40
Other	424	341	2,492	90	109	123	908	23	9	9
Wholesale trade	115	239	458	15	128	241	551	22	30	8
Finance (except banking), insurance, real estate	1,609	399	1,112	49	502	69	169	7	(Z)	(Z)
Services	141	119	1,660	46	54	49	478	13	1	(Z)
Other industries	714	552	4,879	150	75	85	969	14	1	2

Z Less than $500 million. [1] Represents industry of U.S. parent or industry of foreign affiliate.

Source: U.S. Bureau of Economic Analysis, *Survey of Current Business*, May 1993.

Figure 18.1
**Households With Selected Media:
1980 and 1992**

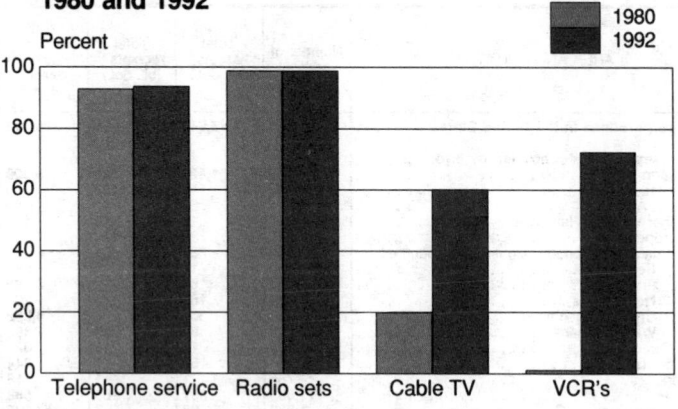

Source: Chart prepared by U.S. Bureau of the Census. For data, see table 900.

Figure 18.2
Telephone Communications

Operating revenue, 1991

Change in revenue, 1990-91

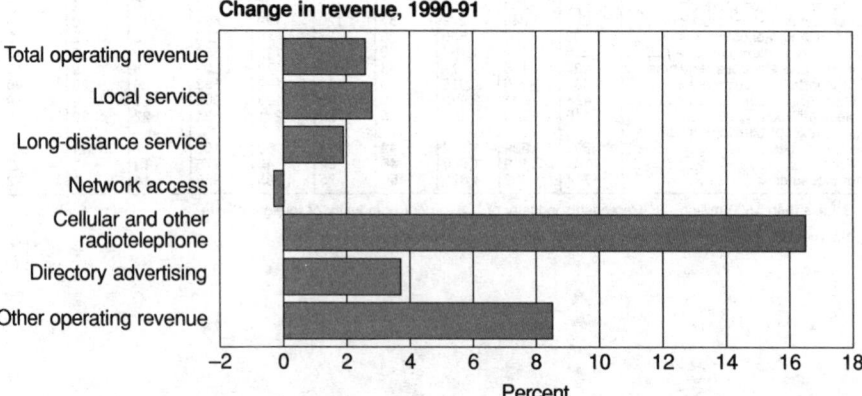

Source: Chart prepared by U.S. Bureau of the Census. For data, see table 903.

Communications

This section presents statistics on the usage, finances, and operations of the Postal Service and of the various communications media: telephone, telegraph, radio, television, newspapers, and periodicals. Expenditure data for advertising in the media are also included.

Postal Service.—The Postal Service provides mail processing and delivery services within the United States. The Postal Reorganization Act of 1970 created the Postal Service, effective July 1971, as an independent establishment of the Federal Executive Branch.

Revenue and cost analysis describes the Postal Service's system of attributing revenues and costs to classes of mail and service. This system draws primarily upon probability sampling techniques to develop estimates of revenues, volumes, and weights, as well as costs by class of mail and special service. The costs attributed to classes of mail and special services are primarily incremental costs which vary in response to changes in volume; they account for roughly 60 percent of the total costs of the Postal Service. The balance represents "institutional costs." Statistics on revenues, volume of mail, and distribution of expenditures are presented in the Postal Service's annual report, *Cost and Revenue Analysis,* and its *Annual Report of the Postmaster General.*

Communication media.—The Bureau of the Census *Annual Survey of Communication Services* (ASCS) covers all employer firms with one or more establishments that are primarily engaged in providing point-to-point communication services, whether by wire or radio, and whether intended to be received aurally or visually. This includes telephone communications, including cellular and other radiotelephone services; telegraph and other message communications, such as electronic mail services, facsimile transmission services, telex services, and so on; radio and television broadcasting stations and networks; cable and other pay television services; and other communication services, such as radar station operations, satellite earth stations, satellite or missile tracking stations, and so

In Brief

Households in 1992 with:

Telephone service	94%
Radio sets	99%
Television	98%
Percent of TV households:	
Cable television	60%
VCR's	73%

on. The report presents statistics that are summarized by kind-of- business classification based on the 1987 edition of the *Standard Industrial Classification Manual.*

The Federal Communications Commission (FCC), established in 1934, regulates wire and radio communications. Only the largest carriers and holding companies file annual or monthly financial reports. The FCC has jurisdiction over interstate and foreign communication services, but not over intrastate or local services. The gross operating revenues of the telephone carriers reporting annually to the FCC, however, are estimated to cover about 90 percent of the revenues of all U.S. telephone companies. Data are not comparable with Bureau of the Census *Annual Survey of Communication Services* because of coverage (*ASCS* includes all domestic long-distance telephone companies, all local exchange carriers, and all cellular telephone companies) and different accounting practices for those telephone companies which report to the FCC.

Reports filed by the broadcasting industry cover substantially all radio and television stations operating in the United States. The private radio services represent the largest and most diverse group of licensees regulated by the FCC. These services provide voice, data communications, point-to-point and point-to-multipoint radio communications for fixed and mobile communicators. Major users of these services are small businesses, the aviation industry, the maritime trades, the land transportation industry, manufacturing industries, State and local public safety and governmental authorities, emergency medical service providers, amateur radio operators, and personal radio operations (CB and the General Mobile Radio Service). The FCC also licenses entities as private and common carriers. Private and common carriers provide fixed and land mobile communications service on a for-profit basis. Principal sources of wire, radio, and television data are the FCC's *Annual Report* and its annual *Statistics of Communications Common Carriers.*

Statistics on the printed media are available from the U.S. Bureau of the Census, as well as from various private agencies. The censuses of manufactures (conducted by the Census Bureau every 5 years, for the years ending in "2" and "7") provide statistics on the number and circulation of newspapers and periodicals and on sales of books and pamphlets. Editor & Publisher Co. New York, NY presents annual data on the number and circulation of daily and Sunday newspapers in its *International Year Book.* Monthly data on new books and new editions appear in *Publishers Weekly,* issued by R. R. Bowker Company, New York. (See table 402 for annual data.)

Advertising.—Data on advertising expenditures are compiled primarily by

McCann-Erickson, Inc., which compiles certain of the data shown (see tables 920-921). Monthly index figures of advertising in certain media are also published periodically by McCann-Erickson in *Advertising Age.*

The Broadcast Advertisers Reports distinguishes between spot and local advertising primarily on the basis of the type of advertiser to whom the time is sold, rather than how and by whom it is sold. In general, time purchased on behalf of retail or service establishments in the market is considered local, even though the establishments may be part of a national or regional chain. That is, spot advertising promotes a product, while local advertising promotes a given establishment. Network advertising, mutually exclusive of spot and local, is broadcast through the network system.

Statistical reliability.—For a discussion of statistical collection and estimation, sampling procedures, and measures of statistical reliability applicable to Census Bureau data, see Appendix III.

Historical statistics.—Tabular headnotes provide cross-references, where applicable, to *Historical Statistics of the United States, Colonial Times to 1970.* See Appendix IV.

No. 896. U.S. Postal Service—Summary: 1980 to 1991

[Employees in thousands; revenue and expenditures in millions of dollars, except as indicated. For fiscal years; see text, section 9. Includes Puerto Rico and all outlying areas except Canal Zone. See text, section 18. See also *Historical Statistics, Colonial Times to 1970*, series R 163-171]

ITEM	1980	1984	1985	1986	1987	1988	1989	1990	1991
Number of post offices	30,326	29,750	29,557	29,344	29,319	29,203	29,083	28,959	28,912
Pieces of mail handled (est.) (bil.)	106.3	131.5	140.1	147.4	153.9	161.0	161.6	166.3	165.9
First-class, number (bil.) [1]	60.3	68.4	72.4	76.2	78.9	84.7	85.9	89.3	90.3
Percent	56.7	52.0	51.7	51.7	51.3	52.6	53.2	53.7	54.4
Second class (bil.)	8.4	9.5	10.4	10.6	10.3	10.4	10.5	10.7	10.4
Employees, total.	**667**	**702**	**744**	**785**	**791**	**824**	**817**	**819**	**808**
Regular	536	561	586	606	751	764	764	757	746
Postmasters	29	28	28	27	28	28	27	27	27
Office supervisors and tech. personnel . .	36	45	46	49	55	55	55	53	54
Office clerks and mail handlers [2]	229	235	249	260	345	347	345	333	324
City carriers and vehicle drivers	160	171	179	187	237	243	243	240	235
Rural carriers	33	35	35	36	37	39	40	42	42
Other	49	47	48	47	49	52	54	62	64
Substitute (part-time).	130	141	159	179	40	60	53	62	62
Compensation and employee benefits (mil. dol.)	16,541	22,157	24,349	25,576	27,229	30,749	32,368	34,214	36,076
Avg. salary per employee (dol.) [3]	24,799	31,562	32,727	32,581	34,424	36,989	39,619	41,775	44,649
Pieces of mail per employee, avg	159	187	188	188	195	195	198	203	205
Total revenue [4]	**19,106**	**26,474**	**28,956**	**31,021**	**32,297**	**35,939**	**38,920**	**40,074**	**44,202**
Operating postal revenue.	17,143	25,314	27,736	30,102	31,528	35,036	37,979	39,201	43,323
Stamps, postal cards, etc	4,287	6,023	6,520	6,969	7,246	7,784	8,381	8,638	9,148
Second-class postage paid in money (pound rates) [5]	881	1,056	1,339	1,271	1,326	1,455	1,594	1,580	1,718
Other postage paid under permit and meter	10,828	16,067	17,747	19,294	20,280	22,676	24,534	25,311	28,019
Box rents.	160	188	230	259	273	296	362	394	413
Miscellaneous.	892	1,847	1,774	2,174	2,255	2,683	2,959	3,124	3,877
Money-order revenues	95	132	126	135	148	142	148	154	148
Government appropriations	1,610	879	970	716	650	517	436	453	562
Percent of total revenue	8.4	3.3	3.3	2.3	2.0	1.4	1.1	1.1	1.3
Investment income, net	353	282	250	203	119	386	504	420	317
Mail and service:									
First-class mail [1]	10,146	15,216	16,740	18,035	18,786	21,402	23,234	24,023	26,649
Priority mail [6]	612	928	960	1,011	1,086	1,329	1,416	1,555	1,765
Second-class publishers' mail [7]	864	1,025	1,093	1,222	1,280	1,400	1,519	1,509	1,668
Third-class mail [8]	2,412	4,241	4,887	5,606	6,148	7,311	7,924	8,082	8,956
Bulk rate.	2,168	4,039	4,697	5,414	5,947	7,096	7,668	7,844	8,699
Single piece rate and fees	244	202	190	193	200	215	256	238	257
Fourth-class mail [9]	805	774	763	814	823	929	908	920	1,001
Zone rate mail (parcels, catalogs, etc.).	500	519	524	550	563	647	612	655	721
Special fourth-class rate	272	210	199	213	203	223	235	215	234
Library rate and fees.	33	45	40	51	57	59	61	50	46
Government mail [10]	745	901	934	992	907	(NA)	(NA)	(NA)	(NA)
International mail [11]	596	859	882	934	957	992	1,081	1,163	1,206
Special services	518	868	918	979	1,030	1,136	1,314	1,310	1,403
Express mail	184	490	544	491	499	524	572	631	668
Mailgrams	15	13	15	17	13	12	10	8	7
Other [12]	2,205	1,159	1,220	919	769	903	938	873	879
Expenditures [13]	**19,412**	**26,357**	**29,207**	**30,716**	**32,520**	**36,119**	**38,370**	**40,490**	**43,291**

NA Not available. [1] Items mailed at 1st-class rates and weighing 12 ounces or less. [2] Includes mobile unit employees. [3] Includes fringe benefits. [4] Net revenues after refunds of postage. Includes operating reimbursements, embossed envelope purchases, indemnity claims, and miscellaneous revenue and expenditure offsets. Shown in year which gave rise to the earnings. [5] Includes controlled circulation publications. [6] Items otherwise qualified as 1st-class or airmail that exceeds 12 ounces and 8 ounces, respectively. [7] Includes mail paid at other than bulk rates. Publishers' mail includes printed publications periodically issued and mailed at a known post office to paid subscribers, such as regular rate newspapers and magazines, and classroom and nonprofit rate publications. See source for further detail. [8] Items less than 16 ounces in weight not mailed at either 1st- or 2d-class rates. [9] Items not mailed at 1st-, 2d-, or 3d-class rates, except government and international mail. May include parcel post, catalogs weighing 16 ounces or more, books, films, and records. [10] Penalty and franked. Beginning in 1988 penalty and franked mail are included in their appropriate classes of mail. [11] Mail from United States to foreign countries paid at international mail rates. [12] Consists of unassignable revenues. [13] Shown in year in which obligation was incurred.

Source: U.S. Postal Service, *Annual Report of the Postmaster General.*

No. 897. U.S. Postal Service—Volume of Mail, by Class: 1980 to 1991

[In millions, except per capita. For fiscal years; see text section 9. Includes Puerto Rico and all outlying areas except Canal Zone. For definition of classes of mail, see footnotes, table 896. See also *Historical Statistics, Colonial Times to 1970,* series R 172-186]

CLASS OF MAIL	PIECES OF MAIL					WEIGHT OF MAIL (lb.)				
	1980	1985	1989	1990	1991	1980	1985	1989	1990	1991
Total	106,311	140,098	161,603	166,301	165,851	12,958	16,783	18,412	18,826	18,340
Domestic	105,348	139,269	160,880	165,503	165,058	12,742	16,564	18,184	18,577	18,104
1st class and express [1]	60,332	72,517	85,926	89,343	90,356	2,213	2,807	3,315	3,452	3,505
Priority mail	248	308	471	518	530	591	672	939	1,007	1,017
2d class	10,221	10,380	10,523	10,680	10,399	3,478	3,966	4,170	4,233	4,015
3d class	30,381	52,170	62,779	63,725	62,430	3,240	6,453	7,479	7,648	7,386
4th class	633	576	626	663	695	2,661	2,156	2,196	2,109	2,074
Penalty	2,992	2,608	(NA)	(NA)	(NA)	503	470	(NA)	(NA)	(NA)
Franked and free for blind	540	710	555	574	648	56	40	84	127	106
International	963	829	724	798	793	216	219	228	249	236
Per capita: [2]										
Total, all domestic mail [3]	463	584	650	662	653	56	69	74	74	72
1st class and express	265	304	347	354	358	10	12	13	14	14
2d class	45	44	43	43	41	15	17	17	17	16
3d class	133	219	254	255	247	14	27	30	31	29
4th class	3	2	3	3	3	12	9	9	9	8

NA Not available.   [1] Includes mailgrams.   [2] 1980 and 1990 based on April 1 population, including Armed Forces abroad; other years based on estimated total population as of Jan. 1, including Armed Forces abroad.   [3] Includes types of mail not shown separately.

Source: U.S. Postal Service, *Annual Report of the Postmaster General; and unpublished data.*

No. 898. U.S. Postal Service Rates for Letters and Post Cards: 1958 to 1991

[Domestic airmail letters discontinued in 1973 at 13 cents per ounce; superceded by express mail. See also *Historical Statistics, Colonial Times to 1970,* series R 188-191]

DATE OF RATE CHANGE	SURFACE MAIL					DATE OF RATE CHANGE	SURFACE MAIL				
	Letters			Postal and post cards	Express mail [1]		Letters			Postal and post cards	Express mail [1]
	Each oz.	First oz.	Each added oz.				Each oz.	First oz.	Each added oz.		
1958 (Aug. 1)	$0.04	(X)	(X)	$0.03	(X)	1978 (May 29)	(X)	$0.15	$0.13	$0.10	(X)
1963 (Jan. 7)	$0.05	(X)	(X)	$0.04	(X)	1981 (Mar. 22)	(X)	$0.18	$0.17	$0.12	(X)
1968 (Jan. 7)	$0.06	(X)	(X)	$0.05	(X)	1981 (Nov. 1)	(X)	$0.20	$0.17	$0.13	$9.35
1971 (May 16)	$0.08	(X)	(X)	$0.06	(X)	1985 (Feb.17)	(X)	$0.22	$0.17	$0.14	$10.75
1974 (Mar. 2)	$0.10	(X)	(X)	$0.08	(X)	1988 (Apr. 3)	(X)	$0.25	$0.20	$0.15	[3]$12.00
1975 (Sept. 14)	(X)	$0.10	$0.09	$0.07	(X)	1991 (Feb. 3)	(X)	$0.29	$0.23	$0.19	[3]$13.95
1975 (Dec. 31)	[2](X)	[2]$0.13	[2]$0.11	[2]$0.09	(X)						

X Not applicable.   [1] Post Office to addressee rates. Rates shown are for weights up to 2 pounds, all zones. Beginning Feb. 17, 1985, for weights between 2 and 5 lbs, $12.85 is charged. Prior to Nov. 1, 1981, rate varied by weight and distances. Over 5 pounds still varies by distance.   [2] As of October 11, 1975, surface mail service upgraded to level of airmail.   [3] Over 8 ounces and up to 2 pounds.

No. 899. International Air Mail Rates From the United States: 1961 to 1991

[Excludes Canada and Mexico. Zones discontinued as of February 1991]

DATE OF RATE CHANGE	ZONE 1 [1]		ZONE 1 [2]		ZONE 1 [3]		Postal and post cards	Aerogrammes
	Each 1/2 oz. up to 2 ozs.	Each added 1/2 oz.	Each 1/2 oz. up to 2 ozs.	Each added 1/2 oz.	Each 1/2 oz. up to 2 ozs.	Each added 1/2 oz.		
1961 (July 1)	$0.13	$0.13	$0.15	$0.15	$0.25	$0.25	$0.11	$0.11
1967 (May 1)	$0.15	$0.15	$0.20	$0.20	$0.25	$0.25	$0.13	$0.13
1971 (July 1)	$0.17	$0.17	$0.21	$0.21	$0.21	$0.21	$0.13	$0.13
1974 (March 2)	$0.21	$0.17	$0.26	$0.21	$0.26	$0.21	$0.18	$0.18
1976 (January 3)	$0.25	$0.21	$0.31	$0.26	$0.31	$0.26	$0.21	$0.22
1981 (January 1)	$0.35	[4]$0.30	$0.40	[5]$0.35	$0.40	[5]$0.35	$0.28	$0.30
1985 (February 17)	$0.39	[6]$0.33	$0.44	[7]$0.39	$0.44	[7]$0.39	$0.33	$0.36
1988 (April 17) [8]	$0.45	$0.42	$0.45	$0.42	$0.45	$0.42	$0.36	$0.39
1991 (February 3) [8]	[9]$0.50	(X)	(X)	(X)	(X)	(X)	$0.40	$0.45

X Not applicable.   [1] Caribbean, Central and South America. The airmail letter rate to South America, 1961 to 1967, was the same as that to Europe. Beginning January 3, 1976, the airmail letter rate to all South American countries except Colombia and Venezuela is the same as Europe; Columbia and Venezuela are included in the first zone.   [2] Europe and Mediterranean Africa.   [3] Rest of world.   [4] Up to 32 oz.; 30 cents for additional ounce over 32.   [5] Up to 32 oz.; 35 cents per additional ounce over 32.   [6] Up to 32 oz.; 33 cents per additional ounce over 32.   [7] Up to 32 oz.; 39 cents per additional ounce over 32.   [8] Air letters collapsed to a single schedule.   [9] First 1/2 ounce= 50 cents; second 1/2 ounce= 40 cents, 39 cents for each additional 1/2 ounce up to the limit of 64 oz.

Sources of tables 898 and 899: U.S. Postal Service, *"United States Domestic Postage Rate: Recent History;"* and unpublished data.

No. 900. Utilization of Selected Media: 1970 to 1992

ITEM	Unit	1970	1980	1984	1985	1986	1987	1988	1989	1990	1991	1992
Households with—												
Telephone service [1]	Percent	87.0	93.0	91.8	91.8	92.2	92.5	92.9	93.0	93.3	93.6	93.9
Radio households [2]	Millions	62.0	78.6	86.7	87.1	88.1	89.9	91.1	92.8	94.4	95.5	96.6
Percent of total households	Percent	98.6	99.0	99.0	99.0	99.0	99.0	99.0	99.0	99.0	99.0	99.0
Average number of sets	Number	5.1	5.5	5.5	5.5	5.4	5.4	5.6	5.6	5.6	5.6	5.6
Television households [3]	Millions	59	76	84	85	86	87	89	90	92	93	92
Percent of total households	Percent	95.3	97.9	98.1	98.1	98.1	98.1	98.1	98.2	98.2	98.2	98.3
Television sets in homes	Millions	81	128	149	155	158	163	168	176	193	193	192
Average number of sets per home	Number	1.4	1.7	1.8	1.8	1.8	1.9	1.9	1.9	2.1	2.1	2.1
Color set households	Millions	21	63	76	78	80	83	85	87	90	91	91
Cable television [4]	Millions	4	15	33	36	39	42	44	48	55	52	56
Percent of TV households	Percent	6.7	19.9	39.3	42.8	45.6	47.7	49.4	52.8	58.9	56.4	60.2
VCR's [4]	Millions	(NA)	1	9	18	31	43	51	58	67	63	67
Percent of TV households	Percent	(NA)	1.1	10.6	20.8	36.0	48.7	58.0	64.6	71.9	68.6	72.5
Commercial radio stations: [2]												
AM	Number	4,323	4,589	4,754	[5]4,718	4,863	4,902	4,932	4,975	4,987	4,985	4,961
FM	Number	2,196	3,282	3,716	[5]3,875	3,944	4,041	4,155	4,269	4,392	4,570	4,785
Television stations: [6] Total	Number	862	1,011	1,138	1,182	1,235	1,290	1,362	1,403	1,442	1,460	1,482
Commercial	Number	677	734	841	883	919	968	1,028	1,061	1,092	1,099	1,118
VHF [3]	Number	501	516	523	520	522	524	539	545	547	547	551
UHF [3]	Number	176	218	318	363	397	444	489	516	545	552	567
Cable television:												
Systems [7]	Number	2,490	4,225	6,200	6,844	7,600	7,900	8,500	9,050	9,575	10,704	11,075
Subscribers served [8]	Millions	4.5	17.7	37.3	39.9	42.2	44.9	48.6	52.6	54.9	55.8	57.2
Daily newspaper circulation: [9]												
Number	Millions	62	62	63	63	63	63	63	(NA)	62	61	(NA)
Per capita	Number	0.305	0.274	0.267	0.265	0.262	0.260	0.258	(NA)	0.250	0.241	(NA)

NA Not available.   [1] For occupied housing units. 1970, 1980, and 1990 as of April 1; all other years as of March. Source: U.S. Bureau of the Census, *Census of Housing: 1970, 1980, and 1990*, vol. 1; and unpublished data.   [2] As of Dec. 31. Source: Radio Advertising Bureau, New York, NY, *Radio Facts*, annual, (copyright). Number of stations on the air compiled from Federal Communications Commission reports.   [3] 1970-1975, as of Sept. of prior year; all other years as of Jan. of year shown. Excludes Alaska and Hawaii. Source: Television Bureau of Advertising, Inc., *Trends in Television*, annual, (copyright).   [4] As of February. Excludes Alaska and Hawaii. Source: See footnote 3.   [5] As of February 1986.   [6] As of Jan. 1 of year shown. Number of television stations on the air. Source: See footnote 3.   [7] As of Jan. 1 of year shown. Source: Warren Publishing, Washington DC, *Television and Cable Factbook.*   [8] Source: AC Nielsen Company, *Nielsen Station Index*, November diary estimates (1992 July diary estimate)   [9] As of Sept. 30. Source: Editor & Publisher, Co., New York, NY, *Editor & Publisher International Year Book*, annual, (copyright). Per capita based on enumerated total resident population as of April 1, 1970, 1980, and 1990. For all other years, based on estimates as of July 1.

Source: Compiled from sources mentioned in footnotes.

No. 901. Multimedia Audiences—Summary: 1992

[In percent, except as indicated. As of spring. For persons 18 years old and over. Represents the number of people viewing/listening during a specified time period. Based on sample and subject to sampling error; see source for details]

ITEM	Total population (1,000)	Television viewing/ coverage	Television prime time viewing/ coverage	Cable viewing/ coverage	Radio listening/ coverage	Newspaper reading/ coverage
Total	185,161	93.4	81.0	57.9	86.0	83.9
18 to 24 years old	25,275	92.8	77.1	59.4	94.6	80.4
25 to 34 years old	44,140	92.8	80.0	56.8	92.9	83.5
35 to 44 years old	38,157	91.9	79.5	61.1	90.9	86.7
45 to 54 years old	25,768	93.2	80.8	63.5	87.4	88.0
55 to 64 years old	21,641	94.4	83.9	56.8	78.6	83.5
65 years old and over	30,181	96.4	85.4	50.3	66.9	80.5
Male	88,306	93.9	80.4	60.0	87.8	84.2
Female	96,856	93.0	81.4	56.0	84.4	83.6
White	158,028	93.1	80.3	59.4	86.0	84.9
Black	20,705	96.0	87.5	49.5	87.4	79.1
Other	6,429	92.8	75.9	48.8	83.0	74.0
Spanish speaking	13,072	95.4	80.4	47.6	86.4	74.3
Not high school graduate	41,173	94.3	83.1	46.7	75.3	66.5
High school graduate	72,357	94.2	82.3	58.8	87.3	85.3
Attended college	35,631	93.4	78.7	62.9	90.6	90.5
College graduate	36,000	90.9	78.1	64.1	91.2	94.5
Employed:						
Full-time	99,414	92.1	79.2	61.2	92.1	87.5
Part-time	16,385	94.3	78.8	60.0	89.9	86.9
Not employed	69,363	95.2	83.9	52.8	76.5	77.9
Household income:						
Less than $10,000	20,273	93.7	82.7	41.8	77.4	64.9
$10,000 to $19,999	29,823	95.2	84.2	45.1	79.1	73.8
$20,000 to $29,999	30,266	94.1	81.5	52.6	82.5	82.2
$30,000 to $34,999	14,976	94.8	83.6	58.9	87.9	85.7
$35,000 to $39,999	13,113	92.2	78.3	63.1	89.3	89.8
$40,000 to $49,999	22,008	94.0	81.2	64.0	91.1	90.5
$50,000 or more	54,703	91.7	78.1	69.9	91.6	92.8

Source: Mediamark Research Inc., New York, NY, *Multimedia Audiences*, fall 1992, (copyright).

No. 902. Telephone and Telegraph Systems: 1970 to 1991

[Covers principal carriers filing annual reports with Federal Communications Commission. Minus sign (-) indicates loss. See *Historical Statistics, Colonial Times to 1970*, series R 46-70 and R 75-88, for data on telegraph systems]

ITEM	Unit	1970	1980	1985	1986	1987	1988	1989	1990	1991
Domestic telephone: [1]										
Carriers [2]	Number .	56	59	39	39	37	54	53	53	54
Access lines	Million . .	(NA)	(NA)	103	106	111	122	126	126	131
Miles of wire	Million . .	628	1,131	1,313	1,338	1,371	1,483	1,502	1,528	1,498
Gross book cost of plant	Bil. dol. .	59.9	147.4	195.1	207.4	222.0	250.2	260.1	264.7	270.4
Depreciation reserves [3]	Bil. dol. .	13.2	26.5	50.0	58.7	69.8	84.7	94.2	97.6	102.1
Ratio to book cost	Percent .	22.1	18.0	25.6	28.3	31.4	33.9	36.2	36.9	37.8
Capital stock and premium	Bil. dol. .	16.4	31.3	48.1	41.5	42.8	45.4	45.7	46.3	47.2
Operating revenues [4]	Bil. dol. .	18.2	55.6	104.8	106.4	106.3	116.7	117.3	117.7	119.8
Operating expenses [5]	Bil. dol. .	11.7	37.3	78.6	79.0	79.8	90.8	91.7	91.6	94.2
Net operating income [5]	Bil. dol. .	3.1	10.0	13.4	13.9	14.5	16.5	16.2	16.4	15.7
Net income	Bil. dol. .	2.3	6.6	9.5	10.4	11.1	12.6	12.4	12.8	11.9
Employees	1,000. .	839	938	(NA)	(NA)	(NA)	688	663	648	616
Compensation of employees	Bil. dol. .	7.0	20.2	(NA)	(NA)	(NA)	24.9	24.4	25.9	25.2
Overseas telephone:										
Number of overseas calls	Million .	23.4	199.6	411.7	477.6	579.6	705.7	1,007.8	1,200.7	1,377.0
Revenue from overseas calls	Mil. dol. .	252	1,535	1,799	1,841	2,127	2,573	3,513.4	4,362.2	4,576.8
Ocean cable systems	Number .	17	24	26	26	26	26	23	24	26
Communications satellites [6]	Number .	4	5	6	11	11	14	15	16	16
Domestic and overseas telegraph: [7]										
Carriers	Number .	7	8	7	7	7	6	6	3	3
Revenue messages transmitted	Million .	102	75	42	29	25	(NA)	(NA)	(NA)	(NA)
Message revenues [8]	Mil. dol. .	358	676	708	678	594	483	521	259	219
Total operating revenues	Mil. dol. .	596	1,232	1,367	1,206	1,076	882	1,019	408	383
Operating revenue deductions	Mil. dol. .	524	1,008	1,292	1,243	1,125	942	995	447	421
Operating income [9]	Mil. dol. .	72	147	102	-37	-48	-56	24	-28	-28
Return on investment: [10]										
Telephone	Percent .	7.1	8.7	9.4	9.4	9.6	10.0	9.8	9.9	9.4
Overseas telegraph	Percent .	10.6	15.9	6.7	-1.5	2.5	-5.5	3.9	0.6	-11.5

NA Not available. [1] Includes Puerto Rico and Virgin Islands. Excludes intercompany duplications. Gross operating revenues of carriers reporting estimated at 90 percent of all carriers. Beginning 1988, based on new accounting rules; prior years not directly comparable. [2] Beginning 1985, number of carriers changed due to change in dollar requirement of reporting carriers from $1,000,000 to $100,000,000. [3] Includes amortization reserves. [4] Excludes taxes. [5] After tax deductions. [6] Excludes contingency and retired satellites. [7] Excludes South American and most Caribbean operations of All America Cables and Radio, Inc. [8] Includes telex service; for domestic telegraph, excludes TWX. [9] After Federal income taxes. [10] Ratio of net operating income (after taxes) to average net book cost of communications plant.
Source: U.S. Federal Communications Commission, *Statistics of Communications Common Carriers*, annual; and unpublished data.

No. 903. Telephone Communications—Operating Revenue and Expenses: 1990 and 1991

[Covers taxable employer firms with one or more establishments that are primarily engaged in providing telephone, voice, and data communication services. Based on the *1987 Standard Industrial Classification Manual*; see text, section 13]

ITEM	1990		1991		Percent change, 1990-91
	Total (mil. dol.)	Percent of total	Total (mil. dol.)	Percent of total	
OPERATING REVENUE					
Total	155,573	100.0	159,639	100.0	2.6
Local service	39,147	25.2	40,230	25.2	2.8
Long-distance service	65,991	42.4	67,266	42.1	1.9
Network access	29,278	18.8	29,180	18.3	-0.3
Cellular and other radiotelephone	5,021	3.2	5,851	3.7	16.5
Directory advertising	8,169	5.3	8,469	5.3	3.7
Other operating revenue	7,967	5.1	8,643	5.4	8.5
OPERATING EXPENSES					
Total	127,948	100.0	133,991	100.0	4.7
Annual payroll	30,685	24.0	31,050	23.2	1.2
Employer contributions to Social Security and other supplemental benefits	7,598	5.9	8,266	6.2	8.8
Access charges	23,680	18.5	24,520	18.3	3.5
Depreciation	23,348	18.2	24,032	17.9	2.9
Lease and rental	3,607	2.8	3,937	2.9	9.1
Purchased repairs	3,004	2.3	2,982	2.2	-0.7
Insurance	194	0.2	220	0.2	13.4
Telephone and other purchased communication services	512	0.4	552	0.4	7.8
Purchased utilities	1,124	0.9	1,169	0.9	4.0
Purchased advertising	2,371	1.9	2,594	1.9	9.4
Taxes	5,181	4.0	5,331	4.0	2.9
Other operating expenses	26,644	20.8	29,338	21.9	10.1

Source: U.S. Bureau of the Census, *1991 Annual Survey of Communication Services*.

No. 904. Telephone Companies—Summary: 1980 to 1991

[As of Dec. 31 or **calendar year,** as applicable. January 1, 1988, marked the beginning of significant rules changes in the way that local exchange carriers account for assets, liabilities, revenue, expenses, and income. Any comparisons with earlier data would not be meaningful. See also *Historical Statistics, Colonial Times to 1970,* series R 1-12 and 31-45]

ITEM	Unit	INDEPENDENT COMPANIES [1]				ALL TELEPHONE COMPANIES				
		1980	1985	1990	1991	1984	1985	1989	1990	1991
All companies	Number .	1,483	1,402	1,310	1,308	1,440	1,426	1,354	1,332	1,328
Access lines	Millions .	20.8	24.3	32.2	32.7	114.5	118.2	135.0	138.1	141.2
Total telephone plant	Bil. dol. .	35.3	49.1	64.7	68.7	193.8	207.3	249.0	256.0	264.1
Operating revenues.	Bil. dol. .	10.5	17.2	22.1	25.1	73.9	78.4	89.1	90.1	93.0
Avg. daily conversations [2] . .	Millions .	192	226	(NA)	(NA)	1,199	1,264	9,569	9,515	9,773
Local calls	Millions .	177	203	(NA)	(NA)	1,111	1,162	(NA)	(NA)	(NA)
Toll calls	Millions .	15	20	(NA)	(NA)	88	102	(NA)	(NA)	(NA)
Reporting companies [3]	Number .	765	653	594	598	655	677	601	616	618
Access lines	Millions .	19.4	23.4	30.3	31.2	113.6	117.4	132.7	136.3	139.7
Telephone plant in service [4] .	Bil. dol. .	32.5	45.5	62.8	64.6	186.2	200.0	243.9	250.9	257.4
Depreciation reserves [5]	Bil. dol. .	7.8	14.3	23.7	24.7	45.7	52.9	89.6	95.0	100.0
Operating revenues.	Bil. dol. .	10.2	16.7	22.1	23.1	73.3	77.9	87.9	89.1	91.0
Operating expenses [6]	Bil. dol. .	7.3	11.9	15.6	16.2	59.8	63.7	63.9	65.2	67.1
Net income	Bil. dol. .	1.3	2.4	3.4	3.5	9.3	10.1	11.5	11.6	11.1
Stockholders' equity	Bil. dol. .	9.6	13.9	22.1	23.4	63.1	66.5	76.8	80.4	82.7
Net income to stockholders equity	Percent .	13.2	17.5	15.4	15.0	14.7	15.1	15.0	14.4	13.4
Employees	1,000 . .	189	170	161	158	724	695	626	606	574
Wages and salaries.	Bil. dol. .	3.4	4.6	(NA)	(NA)	22.1	21.4	(NA)	(NA)	(NA)

NA Not available.   [1] Companies independent of the Bell System, prior to divestiture of January 1984.   [2] Average business day minutes of use beginning in 1989.   [3] Comprises only companies submitting operating information to source cited below.   [4] Total property plant and equipment beginning 1988.   [5] Total accumulated depreciation and amortization beginning 1988.   [6] Excludes Federal income tax.

Source: United States Telephone Association, Washington, DC, *Statistics of the Local Exchange Carriers,* annual, (copyright).

No. 905. Percent of Households with Telephone Service: 1984 and 1992

[For **March.** Based on Current Population Survey, see text, section 1]

CHARACTERISTIC	1984				1992			
	All races	White	Black	Hispanic [1]	All races	White	Black	Hispanic [1]
Total	91.8	93.3	80.1	80.7	93.9	95.3	83.8	86.6
Age of householder:								
16 to 24 years old	77.8	80.3	57.9	59.0	82.0	85.3	63.1	78.0
25 to 54 years old	91.9	93.5	80.4	83.2	93.2	94.7	82.9	85.8
55 to 59 years old	94.9	95.7	87.6	88.7	96.2	97.0	91.2	91.3
60 to 64 years old	94.2	95.9	81.7	87.4	96.6	97.6	90.1	92.2
65 to 69 years old	96.1	97.0	87.8	85.8	95.9	97.1	85.8	90.3
70 years old and over	95.3	96.2	87.2	82.2	97.6	98.3	92.0	95.4
Household size:								
1 person.	88.6	90.7	73.9	72.2	91.9	93.8	80.1	79.6
2 to 3 persons.	93.3	94.5	82.4	80.7	95.3	96.5	86.2	88.5
4 to 5 persons.	92.7	94.1	82.9	85.4	93.5	95.0	83.3	87.2
6 or more persons	86.4	88.6	78.8	78.8	90.6	91.8	85.2	86.6
Labor force status of persons, 16 years and over:								
Total civilian noninstitutional population	93.0	94.2	83.5	83.3	94.7	95.9	86.5	88.5
Employed	94.5	95.3	87.6	87.1	96.0	96.8	89.8	90.2
Unemployed.	82.0	83.8	75.5	73.3	88.5	90.0	82.8	85.9
Not in labor force	92.0	93.8	80.2	79.6	93.4	95.1	82.8	86.0
Income level:								
Under $5,000	71.4	74.7	62.8	53.6	71.7	76.0	63.0	66.9
$5,000 to $7,499	83.6	85.8	74.6	70.0	83.7	85.9	76.7	72.8
$7,500 to $9,999	85.8	87.7	75.9	72.2	88.3	90.4	79.3	78.4
$10,000 to $12,499	90.0	91.3	82.5	81.8	90.0	91.0	83.5	81.2
$12,500 to $14,999	92.7	93.6	84.6	88.5	91.2	92.3	85.4	84.1
$15,000 to $17,499	93.6	94.3	87.6	89.4	93.2	94.3	86.4	87.3
$17,500 to $19,999	95.3	95.4	94.8	87.1	95.6	96.4	89.7	91.6
$20,000 to $24,999	97.1	97.3	94.6	90.0	97.2	97.8	91.5	96.0
$25,000 to $29,999	98.1	98.5	93.5	96.2	98.2	98.4	96.9	96.1
$30,000 to $34,999	98.8	98.8	97.5	99.2	98.6	99.2	95.7	96.7
$35,000 to $39,999	99.4	99.5	96.3	100.0	99.0	99.3	96.4	96.0
$40,000 to $49,999	99.4	99.5	98.0	100.0	99.5	99.5	98.9	99.1
$50,000 to $74,999	99.2	99.3	97.0	100.0	99.4	99.4	98.7	100.0
$75,000 and over	98.9	99.0	94.0	95.1	99.4	99.5	95.3	99.1

[1] Persons of Hispanic origin may be of any race.

Source: Federal Communications Commission, *Telephone Subscribership in the U.S.,* November 1992.

No. 906. Cellular Telephone Industry: 1984 to 1992

[Calendar year data. Based on a survey mailed to 1,506 cellular systems]

ITEM	Unit	1984	1985	1987	1988	1989	1990	1991	1992
Systems	Number .	32	102	312	517	584	751	1,252	1,506
Subscribers	1,000. . .	92	340	1,231	2,069	3,509	5,283	7,557	11,033
Cell sites [1]	Number .	346	913	2,305	3,209	4,169	5,616	7,847	10,307
Employees	Number .	1,404	2,727	7,147	11,400	15,927	21,382	26,327	34,348
Service revenue.	Mil. dol. .	178	482	1,152	1,960	3,341	4,549	5,709	7,853
Roamer revenue [2]	Mil. dol. .	(NA)	(NA)	(NA)	89	295	456	704	973
Capital investment	Mil. dol. .	355	556	798	1,039	1,206	1,801	2,390	2,590
Average monthly bill [3]	Dollars. .	(NA)	(NA)	96.83	98.02	89.30	80.90	72.74	68.68
Average call length [3]	Minutes.	(NA)	(NA)	2.33	2.26	2.48	2.20	2.38	2.58

NA Not available.   [1] The basic geographic unit of a cellular system. A city or county is divided into smaller "cells," each of which is equipped with a lowpowered radio transmitter/receiver. The cells can vary in size depending upon terrain, capacity demands, etc. By controlling the transmission power, the radio frequencies assigned to one cell can be limited to the boundaries of that cell. When a cellular phone moves from one cell toward another, a computer in the Switching Office monitors the movement and at the proper time, transfers or hands off the phone call to the new cell and another radio frequency.   [2] Service revenue generated by subscribers' calls outside of their system areas.   [3] As of December 31.

Source: Cellular Telecommunications Industry Association, Washington, DC, State of the Cellular Industry, annual, (copyright).

No. 907. Private Radio Stations Authorized, by Class: 1985 to 1991

[In thousands. As of Sept. 30. Includes Puerto Rico and Virgin Island. See also Historical Statistics, Colonial Times to 1970, series R 140-148]

CLASS	1985	1989	1990	1991	CLASS	1985	1989	1990	1991
Private radio services [1] .	2,420	2,828	2,880	2,935	Railroad	13.8	16.0	16.2	17.0
Personal [1]	(X)	501.7	528.0	565.5	Taxicab.	6.1	5.9	5.7	5.6
General mobile.	33.6	34.4	32.3	31.0	Interurban property . . .	4.4	5.6	5.8	5.9
Amateur and disaster . .	415.4	467.3	495.7	534.5	Other	13.4	12.9	12.4	12.0
Aviation	245.7	251.2	250.9	241.1	Marine	525.3	620.4	622.9	641.0
Aircraft	207.3	210.2	209.6	200.0	Ship	510.4	604.6	607.2	625.5
Aeronautical and fixed. .	10.9	11.7	12.1	11.9	Alaskan.	2.7	2.5	2.4	2.4
Civil air patrol	23.0	24.2	24.4	24.4	Coastal and other.	12.2	13.3	13.3	13.1
Other	4.5	5.1	4.8	4.8	Public safety	194.5	228.5	234.5	240.2
Industrial	811.3	873.9	864.8	854.4	Police.	42.3	49.1	50.5	51.9
Power.	34.4	44.3	45.7	47.1	Fire	36.6	42.8	44.0	45.0
Business	593.5	638.0	628.1	616.1	Forestry conservation . .	9.6	11.1	11.3	11.5
Petroleum	25.2	27.0	26.8	27.1	Highway maintenance . .	12.7	14.6	15.0	15.5
Forest products	9.8	11.6	11.7	11.7	Special emergency	37.4	40.9	41.1	40.9
Special industrial	115.0	115.4	113.5	112.2	Other	55.9	70.0	72.6	75.4
Other	33.4	37.6	39.0	40.2	Operational fixed				
Land transportation	37.7	40.4	40.1	40.5	services [2]	23.1	29.9	32.9	34.8

X Not applicable.   [1] Includes items not shown separately. Each license, construction permit, or combination construction permit and license is counted one as station; therefore, a station might include a transmitter and many mobile units. 1991 data exclude restricted permits.   [2] Includes microwave operations.

Source: U.S. Federal Communications Commission, Annual Report; and unpublished data.

No. 908. Radio and Television Broadcasting Services—Operating Revenue and Expenses: 1990 and 1991

[In millions of dollars. Based on the 1987 Standard Industrial Classification Manual; see text, section 13. Based on a sample; see Appendix III]

ITEM	TOTAL BROADCASTING		RADIO		TELEVISION	
	1990	1991	1990	1991	1990	1991
Operating revenue, total	**29,024**	**27,812**	**7,238**	**6,946**	**21,786**	**20,866**
Station time sales	19,706	18,677	6,650	6,349	13,056	12,328
Network compensation	571	531	110	103	461	428
National/regional advertising	7,481	6,903	1,583	1,492	5,898	5,411
Local advertising	11,654	11,243	4,957	4,754	6,697	6,489
Network time sales	8,182	7,914	321	329	7,861	7,585
Other operating revenue	1,136	1,221	267	268	869	953
Operating expenses, total	**25,007**	**24,803**	**6,579**	**6,418**	**18,428**	**18,385**
Annual payroll.	6,719	6,673	2,550	2,536	4,169	4,137
Employer contributions to Social Security and other supplemental benefits	1,060	1,065	341	343	719	722
Broadcast rights	7,798	8,086	273	284	7,525	7,802
Music license fees	384	371	165	156	219	215
Depreciation	1,391	1,329	493	478	898	851
Lease and rental	481	475	203	196	278	279
Purchased repairs	240	235	83	82	157	153
Insurance	148	152	66	66	82	86
Telephone and other purchased communication services	247	239	119	117	128	122
Purchased utilities	253	259	102	103	151	156
Purchased advertising	971	865	380	342	591	523
Taxes	180	176	61	59	119	117
Other operating expenses	5,135	4,878	1,743	1,656	3,392	3,222

Source: U.S. Bureau of the Census, 1991 Annual Survey of Communication Services.

No. 909. Public Television Stations: 1978 to 1990

[Fiscal year data. General programming is directed at the general community. Instructional programming is directed at students in the classroom or otherwise in the general context of formal education]

ITEM	1978	1980	1982	1984	1986	1988	1990
Stations broadcasting	272	281	291	303	305	(NA)	(NA)
Number of broadcasters [1]	156	160	164	169	178	169	176
Average annual hours per broadcaster.	4,894	5,128	5,421	5,542	5,650	6,135	6,392
BROADCAST HOURS, PERCENT DISTRIBUTION							
Program content [2]	100.0	100.0	100.0	100.0	100.0	100.0	100.0
General [2]	70.7	71.3	72.0	73.2	74.5	72.9	75.1
News and public affairs [3]	11.0	12.2	12.4	14.1	16.4	16.3	17.6
Information and skills	23.6	22.8	24.5	25.5	29.5	31.7	31.5
Cultural	22.1	21.9	22.8	20.1	20.5	17.9	19.1
General children's and youth's	8.7	8.9	7.5	7.9	6.5	5.8	6.0
Instructional	14.9	14.7	14.3	13.0	14.5	15.5	13.7
The Electric Company, Villa Alegre [4]	1.6	1.5	1.1	1.0	0.4	(NA)	(NA)
Other [5]	13.3	13.2	13.2	12.0	14.1	(NA)	(NA)
Sesame Street and The Electric Company [4]	16.1	15.5	14.8	11.4	11.4	11.7	11.2
Producer [2]	100.0	100.0	100.0	100.0	100.0	100.0	100.0
Local	7.7	7.0	6.7	5.7	5.2	5.2	4.6
Major public television production center, and other	52.2	46.2	45.6	44.4	37.6	27.1	32.0
Consortium	1.8	2.7	2.6	3.3	3.1	9.8	9.7
Children's television workshop.	16.8	17.1	15.8	16.4	29.1	16.1	15.2
Independent producer	5.3	7.9	11.3	9.2	(NA)	19.4	18.7
Commercial producer.	2.7	3.2	3.9	2.8	(NA)	4.4	4.3
Foreign producer, international coproduction	9.1	12.5	10.1	13.2	15.1	14.0	12.3
Distributor [2].	100.0	100.0	100.0	100.0	100.0	100.0	100.0
Local distribution only	7.4	6.8	6.2	5.6	4.9	6.4	5.7
Public broadcasting service.	71.6	69.6	67.1	65.3	63.9	62.0	59.4
Regional public television network	5.4	7.6	10.8	13.0	14.0	17.8	23.8

NA Not available.   [1] In 1988 and 1990, only broadcasters in the 50 U.S. States were surveyed.   [2] Includes other items not shown separately.   [3] In 1986 and 1988, this category includes "Business or Consumer".   [4] "The Electric Company" was double counted if aired during school hours when school is in session.   [5] Excluding "Sesame Street" and "The Electric Company" but including "Mister Rogers." Includes adult educational.

Source: Corporation for Public Broadcasting, Washington, DC, *PTV Programming Survey*, biennial.

No. 910. Public Broadcasting Systems—Income, by Source: 1980 to 1991

[In millions of dollars, except percent. Stations as of Dec. 31; fiscal year data for income. Includes nonbroadcast income]

NUMBER OF STATIONS AND INCOME SOURCE	1980	1985	1987	1988	1989	1990	1991	PERCENT DISTRIBUTION		
								1980	1990	1991
CPB-qualified public radio stations [1] . .	217	288	299	308	313	318	373	(X)	(X)	(X)
Public television stations	290	317	323	324	340	341	349	(X)	(X)	(X)
Total income.	705	1,096	1,295	1,368	1,549	1,581	1,721	100.0	100.0	100.0
Federal government	193	179	243	248	264	267	333	27.3	16.9	19.4
State and local government [2]	272	358	389	416	454	474	503	38.5	30.0	29.3
Subscribers and auction/marathon . . .	102	248	298	321	347	364	384	14.5	23.0	22.3
Business and industry	72	171	196	213	242	262	290	10.3	16.6	16.9
Foundation	24	43	48	51	69	71	70	3.3	4.5	4.0
Other.	43	97	121	120	173	143	139	6.0	9.0	8.1

X Not applicable.   [1] Includes CPB-supported developmental stations.   [2] Includes income received from State colleges and universities.

Source: Corporation for Public Broadcasting (CPB), Washington, DC, *Public Broadcasting Income, Fiscal Year, 1991;* and unpublished data.

No. 911. Cable Television—Systems and Subscribers: 1970 to 1993

[Subscribers in thousands, except percent. Estimated]

YEAR (As of Jan. 1)	Systems	Subscribers	YEAR (As of Jan. 1)	Systems	Subscribers	SUBSCRIBER SIZE-GROUP	NUMBER OF [1]—		PERCENT OF [1]—	
							Systems	Subscribers	Systems	Subscribers
1970	2,490	4,500	1983.	5,600	25,000	1992, total [2]	11,083	53,375	100	100
1973	2,991	7,300	1984.	6,200	30,000	50,000 and over	221	21,538	2	40
1974	3,158	8,700	1985.	6,600	32,000	20,000 to 49,999.	417	12,834	4	24
1975	3,506	9,800	1986.	7,600	37,500	10,000 to 19,999.	507	7,204	5	14
1976	3,681	10,800	1987.	7,900	41,100	5,000 to 9,999	642	4,545	6	9
1977	3,832	11,900	1988.	8,500	44,000	3,500 to 4,999	406	1,703	4	3
1978	3,875	13,000	1989.	9,050	47,500	1,000 to 3,499	1,896	3,616	17	7
1979	4,150	14,100	1990.	9,575	50,000	500 to 999	1,421	1,018	13	2
1980	4,225	16,000	1991.	10,704	51,000	250 to 499	1,500	537	14	1
1981	4,375	18,300	1992.	11,075	53,000	Less than 250	2,957	380	27	1
1982	4,825	21,000	1993.	11,100	55,000					

[1] As of November 1, 1992.   [2] Excludes 1,116 systems not available by subscriber size-group.
Source: Warren Publishing, Inc., Washington, DC, *Television & Cable Factbook*, annual, (copyright).

No. 912. Cable and Pay TV—Summary: 1970 to 1992
[Cable TV for calendar year. Pay TV, as of **Dec. 31** of year shown]

YEAR	CABLE TV Avg. basic sub-scribers (1,000)	Avg. monthly basic rate (dol.)	Revenue [1] (mil. dol.) Total	Basic	PAY TV Units [2] (1,000) Total [3]	Pay cable	Monthly rate (dollars) Total pay	Pay cable	Pay cable units Percent of homes passed	Percent basic
1970	5,100	5.50	345	345	(X)	(X)	(X)	(X)	(X)	(X)
1980	17,500	7.85	2,603	1,668	10,389	9,144	9.78	8.80	27.9	50.6
1985	35,430	10.24	9,305	4,522	31,055	30,596	10.53	10.42	47.1	83.3
1986	38,740	11.09	10,520	5,341	32,428	32,064	10.40	10.31	46.2	80.8
1987	41,200	13.27	12,374	6,778	35,110	34,793	10.21	10.15	47.5	81.6
1988	44,200	14.45	13,979	7,883	39,144	38,819	10.22	10.18	50.3	85.0
1989	47,500	15.97	15,678	9,103	41,234	41,095	10.26	10.21	49.6	83.3
1990	50,500	17.58	17,855	10,653	41,656	41,505	10.44	10.38	48.3	80.2
1991	52,600	18.61	19,473	11,747	42,084	42,415	10.37	10.11	48.0	79.5
1992 [4]	54,300	19.08	20,929	12,433	42,505	43,348	10.31	10.17	47.8	79.8

X Not applicable. [1] Includes installation revenue. [2] Individual program services sold to subscribers. [3] Includes multipoint distribution service (MDS) and satellite TV (STV). [4] Projection.
Source: Paul Kagan Associates Inc., Carmel, CA, *The Cable TV Financial Databook*, annual, (copyright); *The Kagan Census of Cable and Pay TV*, 1991, and *The Cable TV Investor*, February 1993.

No. 913. Cable and Other Pay TV Services—Operating Revenue and Expenses: 1990 and 1991
[Cable and other pay TV services include establishments primarily engaged in the dissemination of visual and textual television programs on a subscription or fee basis. Based on the *1987 Standard Industrial Classification Manual;* see text, section 13]

ITEM	1990 Total (mil. dol.)	Percent of total	1991 Total (mil. dol.)	Percent of total	Percent change, 1990-91
Operating revenue, total [1]	21,717	100.0	23,276	100.0	7.2
Advertising	1,711	7.9	1,909	8.2	11.6
Program revenue	3,458	15.9	3,726	16.0	7.8
Basic service	9,942	45.8	10,898	46.8	9.6
Pay-per-view and other premium service	3,969	18.3	4,074	17.5	2.6
Installation fees	240	1.1	257	1.1	7.1
Other cable and pay television revenue	800	3.7	826	3.5	3.3
Operating expenses, total	18,113	100.0	18,805	100.0	3.8
Annual payroll	2,742	15.1	2,896	15.4	5.6
Employer contributions to Social Security and Security and other supplemental benefits	572	3.2	649	3.5	13.5
Program and production costs	5,288	29.2	5,636	30.0	6.6
Depreciation	3,229	17.8	3,249	17.3	0.6
Lease and rental payments	456	2.5	459	2.4	0.7
Purchased repairs	306	1.7	304	1.6	-0.7
Insurance	97	0.5	102	0.5	5.2
Telephone and other purchased communications ...	119	0.7	124	0.7	4.2
Purchased utilities	167	0.9	179	1.0	7.2
Purchased advertising	417	2.3	421	2.2	0.9
Taxes	279	1.5	299	1.6	7.2
Other operating expenses	4,441	24.5	4,487	23.9	1.0

[1] Includes other amounts not shown separately.
Source: U.S. Bureau of the Census, *1991 Annual Survey of Communication Services.*

No. 914. Publishing Industry—Summary: 1982 to 1991
[In millions of dollars, except as noted. Number in parentheses represents Standard Industrial Classification code; see text, section 13. Based on the censuses of manufactures and the Annual Survey of Manufactures (ASM). For the 1990 ASM, a major change in the survey was introduced. This change resulted from a backlog of previously unclassified single-establishment companies, now classified as manufacturing; for details, see text, section 27, and Appendix III]

ITEM	NEWSPAPERS (2711) 1982	1987	1990	1991	PERIODICALS (2721) 1982	1987	1990	1991	BOOKS (2731) 1982	1987	1990	1991
Establishments	8,846	9,091	(NA)	(NA)	3,328	4,020	(NA)	(NA)	2,130	2,298	(NA)	(NA)
With 20 or more employees.	2,554	2,617	(NA)	(NA)	690	876	(NA)	(NA)	419	424	(NA)	(NA)
Employees [1] (1,000)	402	435	443	428	94	110	115	111	67	70	74	77
Payroll	6,555	9,025	10,407	10,309	1,986	2,983	3,659	3,661	1,327	1,860	2,300	2,514
Value of receipts	21,276	31,849	34,642	33,702	11,478	17,329	20,397	20,345	7,740	12,620	15,318	16,596
Cost of materials	6,006	7,533	8,087	7,606	4,568	5,873	6,580	6,459	2,420	3,663	4,466	5,001
Value added [2]	15,275	24,311	26,560	26,093	6,911	11,452	13,848	13,794	5,292	9,111	10,920	11,683
New capital expends	1,029	1,523	1,886	1,538	190	246	275	223	174	240	329	331
Fixed assets, gross assets ...	8,701	14,028	(NA)	(NA)	1,370	2,528	(NA)	(NA)	1,109	1,680	(NA)	(NA)
Inventories, Dec. 31	755	857	975	915	724	902	1,118	1,012	1,380	2,091	2,769	2,818

NA Not available. [1] Represents the average number of production workers plus the number of other employees in mid-March. [2] By manufacture, derived by subtracting the cost of materials, supplies, containers, fuel, purchased electricity, and contract work from the value of shipments. This result is then adjusted by the addition of value added by merchandising operations, plus the net change in finished goods and work-in-process inventories between the beginning and the end of the year.
Source: U.S. Bureau of the Census, *Census of Manufactures, 1987*, Industry Reports, series MC87-I-27A, and *1991 Annual Survey of Manufactures.*

No. 915. Newspapers and Periodicals—Number, by Type: 1970 to 1993

[Data refer to year of compilation of the Directory cited as the source, i.e., generally to year preceding year shown. See also *Historical Statistics, Colonial Times to 1970,* series R 232-243]

TYPE	1970	1980	1985	1986	1987	1988	1989	1990	1991	1992	1993
Newspapers [1] ..	11,383	9,620	9,134	9,144	9,031	10,088	10,457	11,471	11,689	11,339	11,296
Semiweekly.......	423	537	517	495	510	555	567	579	574	562	584
Weekly..........	8,903	7,159	6,811	6,857	6,750	7,438	7,622	8,420	8,546	8,293	8,218
Daily	1,838	1,744	1,701	1,651	1,646	1,745	1,773	1,788	1,781	1,755	1,735
Periodicals [1] ...	9,573	10,236	11,090	11,328	11,593	11,229	11,556	11,092	11,239	11,143	10,857
Weekly..... , ...	1,856	1,716	1,367	1,383	1,400	880	828	553	511	466	439
Semimonthly [2].....	589	645	801	789	858	619	622	435	412	371	185
Monthly	4,314	3,985	4,088	4,066	4,031	4,192	4,445	4,239	4,340	4,326	4,208
Bimonthly	957	1,114	1,361	1,387	1,402	1,558	1,880	2,087	2,116	2,143	2,119
Quarterly	1,108	1,444	1,759	1,895	1,984	2,245	2,513	2,758	2,861	3,024	2,974

[1] Includes other items not shown separately.   [2] Includes fortnightly (every 2 weeks).

Source: Gale Research Inc., *1993 Gale Directory of Publications and Broadcast Media,* 125th edition; and earlier editions (copyright).

No. 916. Number and Circulation of Daily and Sunday Newspapers: 1970 to 1991

[Number of newspapers as of **Feb. 1** of the following year. Circulation figures as of **Sept. 30.** For English language newspapers only. See also *Historical Statistics, Colonial Times to 1970,* series R 224-231]

TYPE	1970	1980	1981	1982	1983	1984	1985	1986	1987	1988	1989	1990	1991
NUMBER OF NEWSPAPERS													
Daily: Total [1]	1,748	1,745	1,730	1,711	1,701	1,688	1,676	1,657	1,645	1,642	1,626	1,611	1,586
Morning................	334	387	408	434	446	458	482	499	511	529	530	559	571
Evening................	1,429	1,388	1,352	1,310	1,284	1,257	1,220	1,188	1,166	1,141	1,125	1,084	1,042
Sunday.................	586	736	755	768	772	783	798	802	820	840	847	863	875
CIRCULATION (mil.)													
Daily: Total [1]	62.1	62.2	61.4	62.5	62.6	63.1	62.8	62.5	62.8	62.7	62.6	62.3	60.7
Morning................	25.9	29.4	30.6	33.2	33.8	35.4	36.4	37.4	39.1	40.4	40.7	41.3	41.5
Evening................	36.2	32.8	30.9	29.3	28.8	27.7	26.4	25.1	23.7	22.2	21.8	21.0	19.2
Sunday.................	49.2	54.7	55.2	56.3	56.7	57.5	58.8	58.9	60.1	61.5	62.0	62.6	62.1

[1] All-day newspapers are counted in both morning and evening columns but only once in total. Circulation is divided equally between morning and evening.

Source: Editor & Publisher Co., New York, NY, *Editor & Publisher International Year Book,* annual, (copyright).

No. 917. Number and Circulation of Daily Newspapers, by Population-Size Class of City: 1980 to 1991

[Number of newspapers as of **Feb. 1** of the following year. Circulation as of **Sept. 30.** For English language newspapers only. See table 45 for number of cities by population size]

TYPE OF DAILY AND POPULATION-SIZE CLASS	NUMBER [1]					NET PAID CIRCULATION [1] (1,000)				
	1980	1985	1989	1990	1991	1980	1985	1989	1990	1991
Morning dailies, total	**387**	**482**	**530**	**559**	**571**	**29,413**	**36,361**	**40,759**	**41,311**	**41,470**
In cities of—										
1,000,001 or more	20	22	28	18	20	8,795	9,367	11,727	6,508	6,357
500,001 to 1,000,000 ...	27	24	23	22	21	5,705	6,897	5,053	4,804	4,963
100,001 to 500,000	99	121	130	138	143	8,996	12,197	14,890	20,051	19,752
50,001 to 100,000	75	87	94	100	118	2,973	3,653	4,071	4,373	4,914
25,001 to 50,000	64	83	97	102	97	1,701	2,145	2,927	3,209	3,204
Less than 25,000......	102	145	158	179	172	1,243	2,099	2,087	2,365	2,280
Evening dailies, total......	**1,388**	**1,220**	**1,125**	**1,084**	**1,042**	**32,788**	**26,407**	**21,890**	**21,017**	**19,217**
In cities of—										
1,000,001 or more	11	8	8	7	7	2,984	2,169	1,349	1,423	1,263
500,001 to 1,000,000 ...	23	14	14	12	11	4,101	1,626	1,569	1,350	1,201
100,001 to 500,000	123	102	77	71	60	8,178	6,987	5,035	4,687	4,058
50,001 to 100,000	156	127	105	94	96	4,896	3,942	3,336	2,941	2,880
25,001 to 50,000	246	229	209	204	196	5,106	4,606	4,065	4,278	3,807
Less than 25,000......	829	740	712	696	672	7,523	7,075	6,533	6,338	6,009

[1] All-day newspapers are counted in both morning and evening columns; circulation is divided equally between morning and evening.

Source: Editor & Publisher Co., New York, NY, *Editor & Publisher International Year Book,* annual, (copyright).

No. 918. Daily and Sunday Newspapers—Number and Circulation, by State: 1991

[Number of newspapers as of **Feb. 1** of the following year. Circulation figures as of **Sept. 30.** For English language newspapers only. New York, Massachusetts, and Virginia Sunday newspapers include national circulation]

STATE	DAILY Number	DAILY Circulation [1] Net paid (1,000)	DAILY Circulation [1] Per capita [2]	SUNDAY Number	SUNDAY Net paid circulation (1,000)	STATE	DAILY Number	DAILY Circulation [1] Net paid (1,000)	DAILY Circulation [1] Per capita [2]	SUNDAY Number	SUNDAY Net paid circulation (1,000)
Total	1,586	60,687	0.24	875	62,068	MO	44	1,040	0.20	21	1,345
AL......	27	749	0.18	20	756	MT......	11	189	0.23	7	195
AK......	8	145	0.25	4	158	NE......	20	469	0.29	7	435
AZ......	20	734	0.20	12	825	NV......	8	260	0.20	4	303
AR......	31	421	0.18	16	481	NH......	10	232	0.21	4	159
CA......	114	6,535	0.22	71	6,775	NJ......	21	1,628	0.21	17	1,934
CO......	29	1,022	0.30	11	1,191	NM......	18	312	0.20	13	292
CT......	20	839	0.26	11	835	NY......	71	7,019	0.39	41	5,601
DE......	2	144	0.21	2	173	NC......	50	1,416	0.21	36	1,467
DC......	2	887	1.49	2	1,239	ND......	10	186	0.29	7	187
FL......	42	3,153	0.24	35	3,929	OH......	86	2,722	0.25	35	2,894
GA......	36	1,175	0.18	19	1,333	OK......	48	744	0.23	42	888
HI	6	240	0.21	5	261	OR......	19	676	0.23	10	710
ID	12	249	0.24	8	228	PA......	89	3,182	0.27	30	3,219
IL.......	70	2,618	0.23	27	2,744	RI	6	285	0.28	3	307
IN......	73	1,495	0.27	22	1,369	SC......	16	638	0.18	14	739
IA......	37	712	0.25	10	728	SD......	11	169	0.24	4	138
KS......	47	526	0.21	17	482	TN......	27	891	0.18	17	1,090
KY......	23	661	0.18	12	675	TX......	96	3,254	0.19	88	4,229
LA......	26	733	0.17	22	893	UT......	6	290	0.16	6	329
ME......	7	266	0.22	2	188	VT......	8	129	0.23	3	103
MD......	15	708	0.15	7	669	VA......	31	2,540	0.40	15	970
MA......	40	1,964	0.33	14	1,764	WA......	25	1,187	0.24	16	1,230
MI......	52	2,262	0.24	24	2,405	WV......	23	425	0.24	11	406
MN......	25	954	0.22	14	1,212	WI......	36	1,116	0.23	18	1,133
MS......	22	402	0.15	15	381	WY......	10	94	0.20	4	74

[1] Circulation figures based on the principal community served by a newspaper which is not necessarily the same location as the publisher's office.   [2] Per capita based on estimated resident population as of July 1.

Source: Editor & Publisher Co., New York, NY, *Editor & Publisher International Year Book*, annual, (copyright).

No. 919. Copyright Registration, by Subject Matter: 1985 to 1992

[In **thousands.** For years ending Sept. 30. Comprises claims to copyright registered for both U.S. and foreign works. See also *Historical Statistics, Colonial Times to 1970*, series W 82-95]

SUBJECT MATTER OF COPYRIGHT	1985	1990	1992	SUBJECT MATTER OF COPYRIGHT	1985	1990	1992
Total	539.8	643.5	606.2	Sound recordings	22.7	37.5	31.6
Monographs [1]	154.5	179.7	189.3	Renewals	43.8	51.8	49.0
Semiconductor chip products	0.9	1.0	0.9	Musical works [2]	147.9	185.3	165.5
Serials	120.0	111.5	92.9	Works of the visual arts [3]	50.0	76.7	77.0

[1] Includes computer software and machine readable works.   [2] Includes dramatic works, accompanying music, choreography, pantomimes, motion pictures and filmstrips.   [3] Two-dimensional works of fine and graphic art, including prints and art reproductions; sculptural works; technical drawings and models; photographs; commercial prints and labels; works of applied arts, cartographic works and multimedia works.

Source: The Library of Congress, *Annual Report*.

No. 920. Advertising—Estimated Expenditures: 1950 to 1992

[In **millions of dollars.** National advertising is defined as advertising done for companies whose products are distributed nationally and for which national media rates are paid. Local advertising is defined as advertising done for companies which market products locally and which may pay special "local" media rates. See also *Historical Statistics, Colonial Times to 1970*, series T 444-446]

YEAR	Total	National	Local	YEAR	Total	National	Local	YEAR	Total	National	Local
1950.....	5,700	3,260	2,440	1975.....	27,900	15,200	12,700	1984.....	87,820	49,690	38,130
1955.....	9,150	5,380	3,770	1976.....	33,300	18,355	14,945	1985.....	94,750	53,355	41,395
1960.....	11,960	7,305	4,655	1977.....	37,440	20,595	16,845	1986.....	102,140	56,850	45,290
1965.....	15,250	9,340	5,910	1978.....	43,330	23,720	19,610	1987.....	109,650	60,625	49,025
1970.....	19,550	11,350	8,200	1979.....	48,780	26,695	22,085	1988.....	118,050	65,610	52,440
1971.....	20,700	11,755	8,945	1980.....	53,550	29,815	23,735	1989.....	123,930	68,990	54,940
1972.....	23,210	12,980	10,230	1981.....	60,430	33,890	26,540	1990.....	128,640	72,780	55,860
1973.....	24,980	13,700	11,280	1982.....	66,580	37,785	28,795	1991.....	126,400	72,635	53,765
1974.....	26,620	14,700	11,920	1983.....	75,850	42,525	33,325	1992 [1] ...	132,130	76,460	55,670

[1] Projection.

Source: McCann-Erickson, Inc., New York, NY. Compiled for Crain Communications, Inc. in *Advertising Age*, (copyright).

No. 921. Advertising—Indexes of National Advertising Expenditures, by Medium: 1980 to 1991

[1982-84 = 100. Based on the average monthly expenditure for those major media which give national coverage. See also *Historical Statistics, Colonial Times to 1970*, series T 472-484]

MEDIUM	1980	1981	1982	1983	1984	1985	1986	1987	1988	1989	1990	1991
General index	71	79	87	98	114	118	124	128	136	141	146	138
Network television	72	78	86	97	116	113	117	119	128	128	131	125
Spot television	67	77	89	99	112	123	134	140	146	150	159	145
Magazines	73	82	86	99	115	120	124	131	142	156	159	152
Newspapers	71	82	89	99	112	122	123	127	130	135	140	134

Source: McCann-Erickson, Inc., New York, NY. Compiled for Crain Communications, Inc. in *Advertising Age*, (copyright).

No. 922. Advertising—Estimated Expenditures, by Medium: 1980 to 1991

[In millions of dollars, except percent. See text, section 18 for a discussion of types of advertising. See also *Historical Statistics, Colonial Times to 1970*, series R 106-109, R 123-126, and T 444-471]

MEDIUM	EXPENDITURES							PERCENT			
	1980	1985	1987	1988	1989	1990	1991	1980	1985	1990	1991
Total	53,550	94,750	109,650	118,050	123,930	128,640	126,400	100	100	100	100
National	29,815	53,355	60,625	65,610	68,990	72,780	72,635	56	56	57	57
Local	23,735	41,395	49,025	52,440	54,940	55,860	53,765	44	44	43	43
Newspapers	14,794	25,170	29,412	31,197	32,368	32,281	30,409	28	27	25	24
National	1,963	3,352	3,494	3,586	3,720	3,867	3,685	4	4	3	3
Local	12,831	21,818	25,918	27,611	28,648	28,414	26,724	24	23	22	21
Magazines	3,149	5,155	5,607	6,072	6,716	6,803	6,524	6	5	5	5
Weeklies	1,418	2,297	2,445	2,646	2,813	2,864	2,670	3	2	2	2
Women's	782	1,294	1,417	1,504	1,710	1,713	1,671	2	1	1	1
Monthlies	949	1,564	1,745	1,922	2,193	2,226	2,183	2	2	2	2
Farm publications	130	186	196	196	212	215	215	(Z)	(Z)	(Z)	(Z)
Television	11,469	21,022	23,904	25,686	26,891	28,405	27,402	21	22	22	22
Three networks	5,130	8,060	8,500	9,172	9,110	9,383	8,933	10	9	7	7
Cable networks	45	594	760	942	1,197	1,393	1,521	(Z)	1	1	1
Syndication (nat'l)	50	520	762	901	1,288	1,589	1,853	(Z)	1	1	1
Spot (national)	3,269	6,004	6,846	7,147	7,354	7,788	7,110	6	6	6	6
Spot (local)	2,967	5,714	6,833	7,270	7,612	7,856	7,565	6	6	6	6
Cable (non-network)	8	130	203	254	330	396	420	(Z)	(Z)	(Z)	(Z)
Radio	3,702	6,490	7,206	7,798	8,323	8,726	8,476	7	7	7	7
Network	183	365	413	425	476	482	490	(Z)	(Z)	(Z)	(Z)
Spot	779	1,335	1,330	1,418	1,547	1,635	1,575	2	1	1	1
Local	2,740	4,790	5,463	5,955	6,300	6,609	6,411	5	5	5	5
Yellow Pages	2,900	5,800	7,300	7,781	8,330	8,926	9,182	5	6	7	7
National	330	695	830	944	1,011	1,132	1,162	1	1	1	1
Local	2,570	5,105	6,470	6,837	7,319	7,794	8,020	5	5	6	6
Direct mail	7,596	15,500	19,111	21,115	21,945	23,370	24,460	14	16	18	19
Business papers	1,674	2,375	2,458	2,610	2,763	2,875	2,882	3	3	2	2
Outdoor	578	945	1,025	1,064	1,111	1,084	1,077	1	1	1	1
Miscellaneous	7,558	12,107	13,431	14,531	15,271	15,955	15,773	14	13	12	12

Z Less than 0.5 percent.
Source: McCann-Erickson, Inc., New York, NY. Compiled for Crain Communications, Inc. in *Advertising Age*, (copyright).

No. 923. Magazine Advertising—Expenditures, by Product Type: 1980 to 1991

[In millions of dollars, except percent. Space cost based on one-time rate; special rates used where applicable. Year-to-year data not strictly comparable, as a few minor publications are added or deleted]

TYPE OF PRODUCT	1980	1985	1986	1987	1988	1989	1990	1991	PERCENT DISTRIBUTION		
									1980	1990	1991
Total	2,846	4,961	5,120	5,390	5,943	6,611	6,753	6,538	100	100	100
Apparel, footwear, and accessories	112	251	291	323	363	396	428	415	4	6	6
Automotive [1]	230	549	597	678	801	881	900	941	8	13	14
Beer, wine, and liquor	239	240	225	208	213	255	277	280	8	4	4
Computers, office equipment, stationery	79	250	219	247	252	284	283	286	3	4	4
Consumer services [2]	190	463	484	491	466	522	516	460	7	8	7
Drugs and remedies	79	135	148	142	145	135	163	164	3	2	3
Food and food products	199	342	389	377	377	435	444	434	7	7	7
Household equipment and supplies	65	100	93	97	102	104	118	113	2	2	2
Household furnishings	73	87	103	111	116	126	116	118	2	2	2
Jewelry, optical goods, camera	79	101	113	121	142	156	157	150	3	2	2
Mail orders/direct response	(NA)	328	363	407	467	513	531	561	(NA)	8	9
Publishing and media	146	188	176	186	192	191	212	196	5	3	3
Retail	(NA)	121	143	138	176	211	255	201	(NA)	4	3
Smoking materials	290	383	322	334	352	393	305	264	10	5	4
Toiletries and toilet goods	206	385	390	455	554	651	679	629	7	10	10
Travel, hotels, and resorts	123	245	249	273	311	374	380	359	4	6	5
All other	736	793	815	802	914	984	989	967	26	15	15

NA Not available. [1] Includes accessories and equipment. [2] Includes business services.
Source: Publishers Information Bureau, Inc., New York, NY, as compiled by Leading National Advertisers.

No. 924. Television—Expenditures for Network Advertising: 1980 to 1991

[In millions of dollars. See text, section 18 for a definition of network advertising]

TYPE OF PRODUCT	1980	1985	1990	1991	TYPE OF PRODUCT	1980	1985	1990	1991
Total	5,147	8,313	10,132	9,456	Home electronics equipment. . .	50	36	85	107
					Horticulture	15	30	36	29
Apparel, footwear, and					Household equipment,				
accessories	131	161	276	275	supplies, and furnishings	225	275	297	301
Automotive	529	848	1,781	1,532	Insurance	74	99	172	146
Beer and wine	242	428	293	337	Jewelry and cameras [1]	119	129	127	123
Building material, equipment,					Laundry soaps, cleansers, and				
fixtures	59	97	72	63	polishes.	306	397	317	277
Computers, office equipment,					Movies	103	138	242	227
and stationery.	57	249	149	110	Pet products	144	175	104	82
Confectionery, soft drinks.	281	388	407	375	Proprietary medicines	430	700	817	876
Consumer services	178	303	524	450	Publishing and media	34	50	28	34
Dept. and discount stores	94	161	248	232	Restaurants and drive-ins.	132	416	624	541
Financial planning services. . . .	20	60	51	62	Tobacco products and supplies. .	8	6	-	-
Food and food products.	844	1,502	1,704	1,498	Toiletries and toilet goods	765	955	944	867
Freight and industrial					Toys and sporting goods	93	152	138	156
development	7	40	55	65	Travel, hotels, and resorts	72	102	146	168
Gas, lubricants, etc.	71	49	39	48	All other	64	367	456	475

- Represents or rounds to zero. [1] Includes optical goods.

Source: Television Bureau of Advertising, Inc., New York, NY. Data compiled by the Arbitron Co., New York, NY.

No. 925. Television—Estimated Time Charges for Spot Advertising: 1980 to 1991

[In millions of dollars. Data represent activity in the top 75 markets monitored by The Arbitron Co., currently covering approximately 356 stations. Beginning 1989, data exclude National Syndicated activity therefore are not directly comparable to prior years. See text, section 18 for a definition of types of advertising]

TYPE OF PRODUCT	1980	1985	1990	1991	TYPE OF PRODUCT	1980	1985	1990	1991
Total	2,496	4,504	5,697	5,172	Home electronics equipment.	73	67	131	102
Agriculture and farming	15	17	12	14	Horticulture	35	37	41	35
Apparel, footwear, and					Household equipment,				
accessories	105	95	105	102	supplies, and furnishings . .	133	217	175	121
Automotive	228	683	1,449	1,252	Insurance	34	88	120	100
Beer and wine	156	218	201	207	Jewelry, optical goods, and				
Building material, equipment,					cameras	55	68	48	32
and fixtures	47	58	58	54	Laundry soaps, polishes. . . .	111	175	156	163
Computers, office equip-					Pet products	33	60	36	29
ment and stationery.	15	25	21	17	Proprietary medicines	93	148	201	216
Confectionery, soft drinks. . .	212	355	338	272	Publishing and media	78	147	124	99
Consumer services	83	262	414	380	Tobacco products, suppliers.	8	14	4	-
Food and food products. . . .	507	927	1,069	1,018	Toiletries and toilet goods . .	223	267	258	267
Freight and industrial					Toys and sporting goods . . .	104	211	192	182
development	5	36	33	43	Travel, hotels, and resorts . .	76	187	276	259
Gasoline, lubricants, etc. . . .	50	102	169	152	All other	17	40	66	56

- Represents or rounds to zero.

Source: Television Bureau of Advertising, Inc., New York, NY. Data compiled by The Arbitron Co., New York, NY in the top 75 markets.

No. 926. Television—Expenditures for Retail/Local Advertising: 1980 to 1991

[In millions of dollars. See headnote, table 925]

TYPE OF PRODUCT	1980	1985	1990	1991	TYPE OF PRODUCT	1980	1985	1990	1991
Total	1,983	3,899	5,200	4,960	Hotels, resorts, U.S.	18	62	76	57
Amusements, entertainment	68	121	146	147	Jewelry stores	19	25	23	20
Appliance stores, repair	38	122	178	198	Legal services	5	38	95	102
Auto repair, service stations	28	73	94	87	Leisure time stores and services .	42	107	151	138
Auto supply, accessory stores. . .	12	41	34	32	Loan, mortgage companies	12	25	39	35
Auto, truck dealers	99	311	271	244	Mail order, catalog showrooms . .	13	23	10	7
Banks, S&L associations	141	195	179	172	Medical, dental services.	13	87	150	143
Builders, home improvement. . . .	20	32	26	22	Movies	102	103	238	221
Carpet, floor covering stores	24	40	47	53	Optical services, supplies	14	28	84	62
Clothing stores.	46	82	129	129	Newspapers.	15	32	29	25
Department stores	131	186	169	193	Political.	70	22	203	37
Discount department stores	74	115	121	121	Radio, cable TV	69	134	168	174
Drug stores	26	67	101	109	Realtors, real estate developers .	18	31	28	21
Education services	17	70	112	98	Rental services (nonauto).	15	38	30	34
Financial planning services.	7	29	27	31	Restaurants, drive-ins	288	672	828	876
Food stores, supermarkets.	149	259	344	335	Shoe stores.	27	37	36	36
Furniture stores	111	187	273	270	Shopping centers	13	20	28	24
Gas, electric, water companies . .	16	38	46	46	Sport, hobby, toy stores	23	41	50	51
Health clubs, reducing salons . . .	21	39	116	122	All other	137	278	413	381
Home centers and hardware. . . .	42	89	108	107					

Source: Television Bureau of Advertising, Inc., New York, NY. Data compiled by The Arbitron Co., New York, NY in the top 75 markets.

This section presents statistics on fuel resources, energy production and consumption, electric energy, hydroelectric power, nuclear power, solar energy, wood energy and the electric and gas utility industries. The principal sources are the U.S. Department of Energy's Energy Information Administration (EIA), the Edison Electric Institute, Washington, DC, and the American Gas Association, Arlington, VA. For additional data on transportation, see section 21; on fuels, see section 25; and on energy-related housing characteristics, see section 26.

The EIA, in its *Annual Energy Review*, provides statistics and trend data on energy supply, demand, and prices. Information is included on petroleum and natural gas, coal, electricity, hydroelectric power, nuclear power, solar, wood, and geothermal energy. Among its annual reports are *Annual Energy Review, Electric Power Annual, Natural Gas Annual, Petroleum Supply Annual, State Energy Data Report, State Energy Price and Expenditure Report, Financial Statistics of Selected Electric Utilities, Performance Profiles of Major Energy Producers, Annual Energy Outlook,* and *International Energy Annual.* These various publications contain State, national, and international data on production of electricity, net summer capability of generating plants, fuels used in energy production, energy sales and consumption, and hydroelectric power. The EIA also issues the *Monthly Energy Review,* which presents current supply, disposition, and price data, and monthly publications on petroleum, coal, natural gas, and electric power. Data on residential energy consumption, expenditures, and conservation activities are available from EIA's Residential Energy Consumption Survey and are published triennially in *Residential Energy Consumption Survey: Consumption and Expenditures,* and *Residential Energy Consumption Survey: Housing Characteristics,* and several other reports.

The Edison Electric Institute's monthly bulletin and annual *Statistical Year Book of the Electric Utility Industry for the Year*

In Brief

Energy expenditures per person, 1990—$1,900

55% of all electric generation in 1991 was from coal.

Over 50 million residential gas customers in 1991.

contain data on the distribution of electric energy by public utilities; information on the electric power supply, expansion of electric generating facilities, and the manufacture of heavy electric power equipment is presented in the annual *Year End Summary of the Electric Power Situation in the United States.* The American Gas Association, in its monthly and quarterly bulletins and its yearbook, *Gas Facts,* presents data on gas utilities, including sales, revenues, customers, prices, and other financial and operating statistics.

Btu conversion factors.—Various energy sources are converted from original units (e.g., short tons, cubic feet, barrels, kilowatt-hours) to the thermal equivalent using British thermal units (Btu). A Btu is the amount of energy required to raise the temperature of 1 pound of water 1 degree Fahrenheit (F) at or near 39.2 degrees F. Factors are calculated annually from the latest final annual data available; some are revised as a result. The following list provides conversion factors used in 1991 for production and consumption, in that order, for various fuels: Petroleum, 5.800 and 5.387 mil. Btu per barrel; total coal, 21.690 and 21.169 mil. Btu per short ton; and natural gas (dry), 1,031 Btu per cubic foot for both. The factors for the production of nuclear power and geothermal power were 10,680 and 21,096 Btu per kilowatt-hour, respectively. The fossil fuel steam-electric power plant generation factor of 10,335 Btu per kilowatt-hour was used for hydroelectric power generation and for wood and waste, wind, photovoltaic, and solar thermal energy consumed at electric utilities.

No. 927. Total Horsepower of All Prime Movers: 1960 to 1991

[In millions, except percent. As of **January**, except as noted. Prime movers are mechanical engines and turbines, and work animals, which originally convert fuels or force (as wind or falling water) into work and power. Electric motors, which obtain their power from prime movers, are excluded to avoid duplication. See also *Historical Statistics, Colonial Times to 1970*, series S 1-14]

YEAR	Total horse-power	AUTOMOTIVE [1][2]		NONAUTOMOTIVE							
		Total	Percent of total	Total	Facto-ries[3][4]	Mines[3][4]	Rail-roads[5]	Merchant ships and sailing vessels[4]	Farms	Electric central sta-tions[2]	Air-craft[5][6]
1960......	11,008	10,367	94.2	641	42	35	47	24	240	217	37
1965......	15,096	14,306	94.8	790	48	40	44	24	272	307	55
1970......	20,408	19,325	94.7	1,083	54	45	54	22	290	435	183
1975......	25,100	23,752	94.6	1,348	60	47	62	22	318	654	185
1976......	25,732	24,339	94.6	1,393	61	47	64	22	324	692	184
1977......	26,469	25,025	94.5	1,444	62	47	62	23	328	728	194
1978......	27,379	25,892	94.6	1,487	63	48	64	25	[7]335	754	198
1979......	28,162	26,617	94.5	1,545	63	48	62	26	342	803	201
1980......	28,922	27,362	94.6	1,564	64	48	63	28	345	806	210
1981......	29,507	27,909	94.6	1,598	64	48	65	29	345	835	212
1982......	30,495	28,852	94.6	1,643	64	48	64	29	352	854	232
1983......	31,337	29,662	94.7	1,675	64	47	62	29	356	877	240
1984......	31,819	30,117	94.7	1,702	65	47	61	30	359	886	254
1985......	32,529	30,792	94.7	1,737	65	47	58	29	358	912	268
1986......	32,660	30,893	94.6	1,767	65	47	56	29	358	942	270
1987......	33,266	31,488	94.7	1,778	65	47	53	29	357	958	269
1988......	34,200	32,415	94.8	1,785	65	47	53	28	356	969	267
1989......	34,579	32,790	94.8	1,789	65	47	50	28	356	976	267
1990......	34,958	33,158	94.7	1,800	67	48	50	28	356	984	267
1991......	33,905	32,100	94.7	1,805	68	48	50	27	355	991	266

[1] Includes passenger cars, trucks, buses, and motorcycles. [2] As of July 1. [3] Beginning 1965, data are estimates. [4] This is an extension of trends, since government agencies suspended compilation of these power capacity statistics. [5] Beginning 1965, not strictly comparable with earlier years. [6] Includes private planes and commercial airlines. [7] Includes estimates of about 3.0 million hp in work animals and 30,000 in windmills.
Source: John A. Waring, Arlington, VA, unpublished estimates.

No. 928. Energy Production and Consumption, by Major Source: 1960 to 1991

[Btu=British thermal unit. For Btu conversion factors, see text, section 19. See also *Historical Statistics, Colonial Times to 1970*, series M 76-92]

YEAR	Total production (quad. Btu)	PERCENT OF PRODUCTION				Total consumption (quad. Btu)	PERCENT OF CONSUMPTION				Consumption/production ratio
		Coal	Petro-leum[1]	Natural gas[2]	Other[3]		Coal	Petro-leum[1]	Natural gas[2]	Other[3]	
1960	41.5	26.1	36.0	34.0	3.9	43.8	22.5	45.5	28.3	3.8	1.06
1965	49.3	26.5	33.5	35.8	4.3	52.7	22.0	44.1	29.9	4.0	1.07
1970	62.1	23.5	32.9	38.9	4.7	66.4	18.5	44.4	32.8	4.3	1.07
1971	61.3	21.5	32.7	40.5	5.3	67.9	17.1	45.0	33.1	4.8	1.11
1972	62.4	22.6	32.1	39.7	5.6	71.3	16.9	46.2	31.9	5.0	1.14
1973	62.1	22.5	31.4	39.9	6.2	74.3	17.5	46.9	30.3	5.3	1.20
1974	60.8	23.1	30.5	38.9	7.4	72.5	17.5	46.1	30.0	6.5	1.19
1975	59.9	25.0	29.6	36.8	8.6	70.5	17.9	46.4	28.3	7.4	1.18
1976	59.9	26.1	28.8	36.4	8.6	74.4	18.3	47.3	27.4	7.1	1.24
1977	60.2	26.2	29.0	36.4	8.5	76.3	18.2	48.7	26.1	7.0	1.27
1978	61.1	24.4	30.2	35.6	9.9	78.1	17.6	48.6	25.6	8.1	1.28
1979	63.8	27.5	28.4	35.0	9.1	78.9	19.1	47.1	26.2	7.7	1.24
1980	64.8	28.7	28.2	34.2	8.9	76.0	20.3	45.0	26.9	7.8	1.17
1981	64.4	28.5	28.2	34.2	9.1	74.0	21.5	43.2	26.9	8.4	1.15
1982	64.0	29.2	28.7	32.0	10.2	70.8	21.7	42.7	26.1	9.5	1.11
1983	61.3	28.2	30.0	30.6	11.2	70.5	22.5	42.6	24.6	10.3	1.15
1984	65.9	29.9	28.6	30.7	10.7	74.1	23.0	41.9	25.0	10.1	1.13
1985	64.8	29.8	29.3	29.6	11.3	74.0	23.6	41.8	24.1	10.5	1.14
1986	64.3	30.4	28.6	29.0	12.0	74.2	23.3	43.4	22.5	10.8	1.16
1987	64.9	31.1	27.3	29.7	11.9	76.8	23.4	42.8	23.1	10.7	1.19
1988	66.1	31.4	26.2	30.0	12.4	80.2	23.5	42.7	23.1	10.7	1.21
1989	66.1	32.3	24.4	30.2	13.1	81.3	23.3	42.1	23.8	10.8	1.23
1990	[4]67.9	33.1	22.9	30.3	13.7	81.3	23.5	41.3	23.7	11.5	1.20
1991	67.5	31.9	23.1	30.7	14.2	[5]81.5	23.1	40.1	24.7	12.0	1.21

[1] Production includes crude oil and lease condensate. Consumption includes domestically produced crude oil, natural gas liquids, and lease condensate, plus imported crude oil and products. [2] Production includes natural gas liquids; consumption excludes natural gas liquids. [3] Comprised of hydropower, nuclear power, geothermal energy, and other. [4] Represents peak year for U.S. energy production. [5] Represents peak year for U.S. energy consumption.
Source: U.S. Energy Information Administration, *Annual Energy Review*.

No. 929. Energy Supply and Disposition, by Type of Fuel: 1970 to 1991

[In quadrillion British thermal units (Btu). For Btu conversion factors, see text, section 19]

TYPE OF FUEL	1970	1973	1975	1980	1983	1984	1985	1986	1987	1988	1989	1990	1991
Production [2]	62.1	62.1	59.9	64.8	61.2	65.8	64.8	64.3	64.9	66.1	66.1	[1]67.9	67.5
Crude oil [2]	20.4	19.5	17.7	18.2	18.4	18.9	19.0	18.4	17.7	17.3	16.1	15.6	15.6
Natural gas liquids....	2.5	2.6	2.4	2.3	2.2	2.3	2.2	2.2	2.2	2.3	2.2	2.2	2.3
Natural gas [3]	21.7	22.2	19.6	19.9	16.6	18.0	17.0	16.5	17.1	17.6	17.9	18.4	18.4
Coal	14.6	14.0	15.0	18.6	17.3	19.7	19.3	19.5	20.1	20.7	21.4	22.6	21.6
Nuclear electric power.	0.2	0.9	1.9	2.7	3.2	3.6	4.2	4.5	4.9	5.7	5.7	6.2	6.5
Hydroelectric power..	2.6	2.9	3.2	2.9	3.5	3.3	2.9	3.0	2.6	2.3	2.8	2.9	2.9
Geothermal and other.	(Z)	(Z)	0.1	0.1	0.1	0.2	0.2	0.2	0.2	0.2	0.2	0.2	0.2
Net trade [4]	-5.7	-12.7	-11.8	-12.2	-8.3	-9.0	-7.9	-10.4	-11.9	-13.1	-14.2	-14.1	-13.2
Exports	2.7	2.1	2.4	3.7	3.7	3.8	4.2	4.1	3.9	4.4	4.8	4.9	5.2
Coal	1.9	1.4	1.8	2.4	2.0	2.3	2.4	2.2	2.1	2.5	2.6	2.8	2.9
Imports	8.4	14.7	14.1	16.0	12.0	12.8	12.1	14.4	15.8	17.6	19.0	19.0	18.4
Crude oil	2.8	6.9	8.7	11.2	7.1	7.3	6.8	9.0	10.1	11.0	12.6	12.8	12.6
Consumption	66.4	74.3	70.5	76.0	70.5	74.1	74.0	74.2	76.8	80.2	81.4	81.3	[5]81.5
Petroleum products ...	29.5	34.8	32.7	34.2	30.1	31.1	30.9	32.2	32.9	34.2	34.2	33.6	32.7
Natural gas [3]	21.8	22.5	19.9	20.4	17.4	18.5	17.8	16.7	17.7	18.6	19.4	19.3	20.2
Coal	12.3	13.0	12.7	15.4	15.9	17.1	17.5	17.3	18.0	18.8	18.9	19.0	18.0
Nuclear power	0.2	0.9	1.9	2.7	3.2	3.6	4.2	4.5	4.9	5.7	5.7	6.2	6.5
Hydroelectric power [6].	2.7	3.0	3.2	3.1	3.9	3.8	3.4	3.4	3.1	2.6	2.9	3.0	3.1
Geothermal and other.	(Z)	(Z)	0.1	0.1	0.1	0.2	0.2	0.2	0.2	0.3	0.3	0.2	0.2

Z Less than 50 trillion. [1] Represents peak year for U.S. energy production. [2] Includes lease condensate. [3] Dry marketed gas. [4] Exports minus imports. [5] Represents peak year for U.S. energy consumption. [6] Includes industrial generation of hydropower and net electricity imports.

No. 930. Energy Imports and Exports, by Type of Fuel: 1970 to 1991

[In quadrillion of Btu. For definition of Btu, see text, Section 19]

TYPE OF FUEL	1970	1973	1975	1980	1983	1984	1985	1986	1987	1988	1989	1990	1991
Net imports:[1]													
Coal	-1.93	-1.42	-1.74	-2.39	-2.01	-2.12	-2.39	-2.19	-2.05	-2.45	-2.57	-2.70	-2.77
Natural Gas (dry).....	0.77	0.98	0.90	0.96	0.89	0.79	0.90	0.69	0.94	1.22	1.28	1.46	1.59
Petroleum	6.92	12.98	12.51	13.50	9.08	9.89	8.95	11.53	12.53	14.01	15.33	15.29	14.13
Other [2]	-0.04	0.14	0.08	0.18	0.36	0.40	0.41	0.35	0.48	0.36	0.14	0.03	0.21
Imports:													
Coal	(Z)	(Z)	0.02	0.03	0.03	0.03	0.05	0.06	0.04	0.05	0.07	0.07	0.08
Natural Gas (dry).....	0.85	1.06	0.98	1.01	0.94	0.85	0.95	0.75	0.99	1.30	1.39	1.55	1.71
Petroleum	7.47	13.47	12.95	14.66	10.65	11.43	10.61	13.20	14.16	15.75	17.16	16.94	16.25
Other [2]	0.07	0.20	0.16	0.28	0.41	0.45	0.49	0.43	0.56	0.46	0.33	0.25	0.30
Exports:													
Coal	1.94	1.43	1.76	2.42	2.04	2.15	2.44	2.25	2.09	2.50	2.64	2.77	2.85
Natural Gas (dry).....	0.07	0.08	0.07	0.05	0.06	0.06	0.06	0.06	0.05	0.07	0.11	0.09	0.12
Petroleum	0.55	0.49	0.44	1.16	1.57	1.54	1.66	1.67	1.63	1.74	1.84	1.82	2.13
Other [2]	0.11	0.06	0.08	0.09	0.05	0.05	0.08	0.07	0.07	0.10	0.18	0.23	0.09

Z Less than .005 quadrillion Btu. [1] Net imports equals imports minus exports. Minus sign (-) denotes an excess of exports over imports. [2] Coal coke and small amounts of electricity transmitted across U.S. borders with Canada and Mexico.

No. 931. Selected Energy Indicators—Summary: 1970 to 1991

[Btu=British thermal unit. For Btu conversion factors, see text, section 19. Minus sign (-) indicates decrease]

ITEM	1970	1973	1975	1980	1983	1984	1985	1986	1987	1988	1989	1990	1991
AVERAGE ANNUAL PERCENT CHANGE [1]													
Gross domestic product [2] ...	-	5.2	-0.8	-0.5	3.9	6.2	3.2	2.9	3.1	3.9	2.5	0.8	-1.2
Energy production, total [3] ...	5.0	-0.6	-1.6	1.5	-4.2	7.6	-1.6	-0.8	0.9	1.8	0.1	2.6	-0.5
Crude oil [4]	4.1	-2.7	-4.5	0.8	0.4	2.5	0.7	-3.2	-3.9	-2.2	-6.7	-3.4	0.3
Natural gas	5.6	-0.1	-7.4	-0.8	-9.4	8.6	-5.7	-2.6	3.6	2.7	1.4	2.9	0.3
Coal	5.1	-0.7	6.5	6.0	-7.5	14.3	-2.0	0.9	3.2	3.0	2.9	5.2	-4.1
Energy consumption, total [3] ..	3.5	4.2	-2.7	-3.7	-0.5	5.1	-0.2	0.4	3.5	4.4	1.4	-0.1	0.3
Petroleum products	4.0	5.7	-2.2	-7.9	-0.6	3.3	-0.4	4.1	2.1	4.1	(Z)	-1.9	-2.5
Natural gas (dry)	5.1	-0.8	-8.2	-1.4	-6.2	6.6	-3.7	-6.3	6.2	4.6	4.5	-0.4	4.5
Coal	-0.9	7.4	-	2.5	3.7	7.4	2.4	-1.3	4.3	4.7	0.5	1.0	-1.6
PER CAPITA [5] (mil. Btu)													
Energy production	304	294	278	285	262	280	273	268	268	270	268	272	268
Energy consumption	326	351	327	334	302	314	311	309	317	328	330	326	323
Energy consumption per dollar of GDP [2] (1,000 Btu).	23.1	22.7	21.9	20.1	18.1	17.9	17.3	16.9	16.9	17.0	16.8	16.7	16.9

- Represents zero. Z Less than .05 percent. [1] Represents percent change from immediate prior year; for example, 1970, change from 1969. Percent change derived from Btu values. [2] Gross domestic product in constant (1987) dollars. [3] Includes types of fuel or power, not shown separately. [4] Includes lease condensate. [5] Based on resident population estimated as of July 1.

Source of tables 929 to 931: U.S. Energy Information Administration, *Annual Energy Review*, and *Monthly Energy Review*.

No. 932. Energy Consumption—End-Use Sector and Selected Source, by State: 1990

[In trillions of Btu, except as indicated. For Btu conversion factors, see text, section 19]

REGION, DIVISION, AND STATE	Total[1]	Per capita[2] (mil. Btu)	Percent change, 1989-1990	END-USE SECTOR				SOURCE				
				Resi-dential	Com-mercial	Indus-trial	Trans-porta-tion	Petro-leum	Nat-ural gas (dry)	Coal	Hydro-elec-tric power	Nuclear electric power
United States ..	81,151	326.2	-0.2	15,888	12,884	[3]29,847	22,531	33,552	19,288	18,997	2,946	6,161
Northeast	12,416	244.4	-2.9	3,073	2,668	3,214	3,461	6,027	2,435	2,032	423	1,523
New England	3,001	227.2	-4.5	856	668	578	899	1,775	426	178	134	399
Maine	363	295.8	-1.2	80	58	110	115	239	4	7	56	52
New Hampshire . .	243	219.0	-4.6	70	41	59	73	154	14	32	19	44
Vermont	127	224.9	-4.3	38	24	23	42	69	7	-	25	39
Massachusetts . . .	1,341	222.9	-4.1	387	332	218	405	784	268	113	25	54
Rhode Island . . .	195	194.1	-6.7	60	41	36	58	100	32	-	2	-
Connecticut	732	222.7	-6.3	222	172	132	206	429	101	26	7	211
Middle Atlantic	9,415	250.4	-2.4	2,217	2,000	2,636	2,562	4,252	2,009	1,854	289	1,123
New York	3,584	199.2	-1.6	949	1,013	699	923	1,773	889	346	273	252
New Jersey	2,260	292.3	-5.0	471	469	524	796	1,201	439	81	-2	254
Pennsylvania	3,571	300.5	-1.5	797	518	1,413	843	1,278	681	1,427	18	617
Midwest	19,516	327.1	-1.4	4,303	3,146	7,201	4,867	6,789	4,615	6,738	43	1,644
East North Central .	13,774	327.9	-1.5	3,027	2,191	5,301	3,255	4,546	3,341	4,718	-74	1,232
Ohio	3,698	340.9	-3.8	781	575	1,546	796	1,114	777	1,425	2	114
Indiana	2,441	440.3	-1.4	412	267	1,182	580	838	459	1,362	5	-
Illinois	3,535	309.2	0.5	830	648	1,199	858	1,228	960	748	1	768
Michigan	2,734	294.0	-0.5	669	472	913	680	893	834	786	-103	231
Wisconsin	1,366	279.1	-2.3	335	229	461	341	473	311	397	21	120
West North Central .	5,742	325.1	-1.1	1,276	955	1,901	1,612	2,243	1,274	2,020	117	412
Minnesota	1,318	301.1	-0.3	300	193	487	338	495	292	324	9	130
Iowa	899	323.8	-1.5	203	136	327	234	305	220	332	9	32
Missouri.	1,476	288.4	-1.6	372	284	346	475	617	241	541	22	85
North Dakota . . .	307	480.1	-2.8	50	39	153	66	109	34	375	24	-
South Dakota	204	292.6	-1.0	53	31	54	66	106	25	33	41	-
Nebraska.	508	321.8	-2.4	119	109	128	151	204	109	142	12	80
Kansas	1,030	415.7	0.3	179	163	406	282	407	353	273	-	84
South	33,678	394.1	0.5	5,755	4,370	14,736	8,819	13,868	8,697	7,933	518	2,299
South Atlantic	12,538	287.8	-0.2	2,829	2,237	3,661	3,813	5,250	1,525	3,715	195	1,500
Delaware	236	353.5	-1.3	45	34	94	63	132	40	60	-	-
Maryland	1,214	253.9	-5.1	307	163	413	331	501	177	286	24	13
Dist. of Columbia. .	170	279.3	-3.1	33	77	33	27	37	29	2	-	-
Virginia	1,837	296.9	-1.3	405	372	479	581	753	189	333	5	254
West Virginia	806	449.7	0.2	125	86	450	146	292	129	873	12	-
North Carolina . . .	1,948	293.8	-0.9	442	332	637	538	731	166	530	72	277
South Carolina . . .	1,194	342.3	1.9	232	160	493	309	404	134	289	29	458
Georgia	2,074	320.1	1.7	433	322	636	683	827	319	718	51	265
Florida.	3,059	236.4	1.1	807	691	426	1,135	1,573	342	624	2	233
East South Central .	5,715	376.6	0.4	1,077	639	2,462	1,539	2,019	933	2,186	239	358
Kentucky	1,454	394.6	-0.9	255	171	652	377	509	192	804	33	-
Tennessee	1,753	359.4	-0.2	372	198	720	463	587	228	600	99	150
Alabama	1,572	388.9	0.1	283	166	721	403	529	251	678	107	129
Mississippi	936	363.8	4.3	167	104	369	296	394	262	104	-	79
West South Central.	15,425	577.7	1.0	1,849	1,494	8,613	3,467	6,599	6,239	2,032	84	442
Arkansas	782	332.5	-2.4	161	102	289	229	278	234	213	38	121
Louisiana	3,494	827.9	1.7	291	215	2,272	716	1,430	1,637	208	-	152
Oklahoma	1,352	429.8	4.6	257	193	558	344	434	621	277	28	-
Texas	9,797	576.7	0.6	1,140	984	5,494	2,178	4,457	3,747	1,334	18	169
West	15,539	294.4	2.1	2,756	2,700	4,694	5,390	6,869	3,540	2,295	1,963	695
Mountain	4,470	327.3	2.2	828	841	1,436	1,366	1,657	1,006	2,115	325	220
Montana	338	423.1	-1.4	59	50	146	83	147	44	166	111	-
Idaho	373	370.1	0.8	75	69	138	91	120	47	10	90	-
Wyoming	398	877.4	4.6	34	38	243	83	126	101	458	7	-
Colorado	913	277.2	0.6	206	229	207	271	327	240	329	13	-
New Mexico	597	394.0	10.2	75	94	198	230	221	251	276	2	-
Arizona	916	250.0	0.0	199	209	183	326	350	129	344	79	220
Utah	543	315.1	1.8	98	84	212	149	195	127	366	5	-
Nevada.	392	325.7	2.5	82	68	109	133	171	67	166	18	-
Pacific.	11,069	282.9	2.1	1,928	1,859	3,258	4,024	5,212	2,534	180	1,638	475
Washington	1,953	401.3	3.3	375	289	716	573	789	168	86	887	61
Oregon	928	326.4	1.4	203	164	279	282	355	112	16	446	65
California	7,307	245.5	1.9	1,277	1,301	1,889	2,840	3,542	1,924	65	294	349
Alaska.	582	1057.5	2.7	48	60	302	172	232	327	12	10	-
Hawaii.	299	269.9	1.3	25	45	72	157	294	3	1	1	-

- Represents zero.   [1] Sources of energy includes geothermal, wood and waste, and net interstate sales of electricity, including losses, not shown separately.   [2] Based on estimated resident population as of July 1.   [3] Includes 4.8 trillion Btu of net imports of coal coke not allocated by State.

Source: U.S. Energy Information Administration, *State Energy Data Report, 1960-1990.*

No. 933. Primary Energy Consumption, by End-Use Sector: 1960 to 1991

[Btu=British thermal unit. For residential and commercial, industrial, and transportation, represents consumption of fossil fuels only. For Btu conversion factors, see text, section 19]

YEAR	Total consumption (quad. Btu)	Residential and commercial (quad. Btu)	Industrial and miscellaneous (quad. Btu)	Transportation (quad. Btu)	Electricity generation (quad. Btu)	PERCENT OF TOTAL			
						Residential and commercial	Industrial and miscellaneous	Transportation	Electricity generation
1960	43.8	8.8	16.3	10.6	8.2	20.0	37.1	24.1	18.7
1970	66.4	12.1	21.9	16.1	16.3	18.3	33.0	24.2	24.5
1973	74.3	12.3	23.5	18.6	19.9	16.5	31.7	25.0	26.7
1975	70.6	11.6	20.4	18.2	20.4	16.4	28.9	25.8	28.8
1976	74.4	12.3	21.4	19.1	21.6	16.5	28.8	25.6	29.0
1977	76.3	11.9	21.9	19.8	22.7	15.6	28.7	25.9	29.8
1978	78.1	11.9	21.8	20.6	23.7	15.3	28.0	26.4	30.4
1979	78.9	11.5	22.8	20.4	24.1	14.6	28.9	25.9	30.6
1980	76.0	10.7	21.0	19.7	24.5	14.1	27.7	25.9	32.3
1981	74.0	10.0	19.7	19.5	24.8	13.6	26.6	26.3	33.5
1982	70.9	10.1	17.5	19.0	24.3	14.2	24.6	26.9	34.3
1983	70.5	9.7	16.7	19.1	25.0	13.8	23.7	27.1	35.4
1984	74.1	10.1	18.2	19.8	26.0	13.6	24.5	26.8	35.1
1985	74.0	9.8	17.6	20.1	26.5	13.3	23.7	27.1	35.8
1986	74.2	9.6	17.3	20.7	26.6	12.9	23.3	27.9	35.9
1987	76.8	9.7	18.2	21.3	27.6	12.7	23.7	27.7	35.9
1988	80.2	10.4	19.0	22.1	28.6	12.9	23.7	27.6	35.7
1989	81.4	10.5	19.2	22.3	29.3	12.9	23.6	27.5	36.0
1990	81.3	9.6	19.6	22.5	29.6	11.8	24.1	27.7	36.4
1991	81.5	9.9	19.4	22.2	30.0	12.1	23.8	27.2	36.8

Source: U.S. Energy Information Administration, *Annual Energy Review.*

No. 934. Energy Expenditures and Average Fuel Prices, by Source and Sector: 1970 to 1990

[For definition of Btu, see text, section 19. End-use sector and electric utilities exclude expenditures and prices on energy sources such as hydropower, solar, wind, and geothermal. Also excludes expenditures for reported amounts of energy consumed by the energy industry for production, transportation, and processing operations]

SOURCE AND SECTOR	1970	1973	1975	1980	1984	1985	1986	1987	1988	1989	1990
EXPENDITURES (mil. dol.)											
Total[1][2]	82,579	111,616	171,783	373,901	433,584	435,443	381,257	393,843	407,602	436,009	472,657
Natural gas	10,891	13,933	20,061	51,061	77,169	72,938	59,702	58,019	61,089	65,383	64,121
Petroleum products[2]	48,088	65,305	103,859	238,410	225,933	223,195	174,539	186,716	189,265	207,888	237,681
Motor gasoline	31,596	39,667	59,446	124,408	114,438	118,044	91,526	99,809	103,211	112,585	126,472
Distillate fuel oil	6,253	9,524	15,680	40,797	44,864	43,611	34,954	37,240	38,362	43,349	49,266
Jet fuel	1,441	2,001	4,193	13,923	15,064	14,747	10,505	11,448	11,318	13,434	17,784
Residual fuel	2,046	4,667	10,374	21,573	14,392	11,495	7,507	8,071	7,261	8,359	8,715
Coal	4,594	6,229	13,047	22,648	29,049	29,719	27,914	27,589	28,372	28,150	28,380
Electricity sales	23,351	33,780	50,680	98,098	142,438	149,242	151,806	154,692	162,070	169,340	176,742
Residential sector	20,083	27,078	36,844	68,825	96,156	98,307	96,203	97,552	102,773	108,423	109,259
Commercial sector	10,668	15,104	22,835	46,881	69,404	70,263	68,444	68,799	71,601	75,496	79,212
Industrial sector	16,458	23,531	41,170	94,521	108,985	105,723	90,503	90,131	91,309	94,682	102,336
Transportation sector[2]	35,370	45,904	70,935	163,674	159,039	161,150	126,107	137,360	141,919	157,408	181,848
Motor gasoline	30,525	38,598	57,992	121,809	112,044	115,201	89,404	97,527	100,988	110,168	123,775
Electric utilities	4,316	7,817	16,396	37,435	43,378	42,558	35,792	36,681	37,435	38,893	38,444
AVERAGE FUEL PRICES (dol. per mil. Btu)											
All sectors	1.65	2.02	3.33	6.91	8.36	8.42	7.36	7.38	7.30	7.71	8.43
Residential sector	2.12	2.73	3.83	7.55	10.86	11.14	10.99	10.95	10.90	11.26	12.14
Commercial sector	1.97	2.56	4.09	7.88	11.29	11.71	11.35	11.05	10.90	11.38	11.95
Industrial sector	0.83	1.08	2.20	4.71	6.21	6.09	5.40	5.20	5.03	5.15	5.49
Transportation sector	2.31	2.57	4.02	8.61	8.24	8.26	6.22	6.58	6.56	7.20	8.33
Electric utilities	0.32	0.46	0.96	1.75	1.97	1.85	1.55	1.51	1.45	1.48	1.46

[1] Includes electricity sales; excludes electricity generation.   [2] Includes sources or fuel types not shown separately.

Source: U.S. Energy Information Administration, *State Energy Price and Expenditure Report,* annual.

No. 935. Energy Expenditures—End-Use Sector and Selected Source, by State: 1990

[In millions of dollars, except as indicated. End-use sector and electric utilities exclude expenditures on energy sources such as hydropower, solar, wind, and geothermal. Also excludes expenditures for reported amounts of energy consumed by the energy industry for production, transportation, and processing operations]

REGION, DIVISION, AND STATE	Total[1]	Per capita[2] (dol.)	Percent change, 1989-1990	END-USE SECTOR				SOURCE				
				Residential	Commercial	Industrial	Transportation	Petroleum products		Natural gas	Coal	Electricity sales
								Total	Gasoline			
U.S. . . .	472,657	1,900	8.4	109,259	79,212	[3]102,336	181,848	237,681	126,472	64,121	28,380	176,742
Northeast .	89,645	1,764	6.6	25,881	19,545	14,735	29,484	43,640	21,895	12,556	3,296	35,701
N.E.	23,849	1,806	5.6	7,352	4,843	3,320	8,334	13,172	6,535	2,458	332	9,187
ME . . .	2,549	2,076	10.2	666	362	465	1,056	1,685	719	26	18	882
NH . . .	1,970	1,777	5.4	621	306	354	689	1,116	594	92	57	817
VT. . . .	1,056	1,876	5.9	336	178	135	407	637	338	31	1	390
MA . . .	10,557	1,755	6.8	3,244	2,355	1,350	3,608	5,623	2,789	1,480	200	4,021
RI	1,586	1,581	4.6	503	309	212	562	831	459	187	1	588
CT. . . .	6,131	1,865	2.3	1,982	1,333	804	2,012	3,280	1,636	642	55	2,489
M.A	65,796	1,750	7.0	18,529	14,702	11,415	21,150	30,468	15,360	10,098	2,964	26,514
NY. . . .	27,550	1,531	7.9	8,526	7,772	3,209	8,042	12,492	6,419	4,614	575	12,088
NJ. . . .	16,008	2,071	3.3	3,882	3,404	2,703	6,020	8,313	3,694	2,187	144	5,689
PA. . . .	22,238	1,872	8.6	6,121	3,526	5,503	7,088	9,663	5,247	3,297	2,245	8,737
Midwest. . .	114,155	1,913	6.1	27,166	17,912	26,981	42,094	53,266	31,030	18,863	9,779	40,254
E.N.C . . .	80,635	1,919	5.9	19,424	12,915	19,919	28,376	35,847	21,107	14,390	7,304	28,973
OH . . .	21,097	1,945	3.2	5,085	3,434	5,470	7,107	8,958	5,394	3,402	2,194	8,322
IN	12,218	2,204	5.7	2,503	1,408	3,683	4,624	5,834	2,827	1,878	1,984	3,927
IL	22,442	1,963	10.0	5,651	3,991	4,982	7,818	9,694	5,913	4,269	1,283	8,307
MI	16,785	1,806	5.4	4,097	2,883	4,103	5,702	7,334	4,582	3,470	1,283	5,797
WI. . . .	8,093	1,654	3.5	2,088	1,199	1,681	3,125	4,027	2,391	1,371	560	2,620
W.N.C. . .	33,520	1,898	6.4	7,742	4,997	7,062	13,718	17,419	9,923	4,473	2,475	11,281
MN . . .	7,514	1,717	6.1	1,746	978	1,744	3,046	3,916	2,386	1,066	429	2,491
IA	5,164	1,860	5.9	1,281	683	1,107	2,093	2,549	1,552	803	386	1,745
MO . . .	9,468	1,850	7.8	2,363	1,588	1,580	3,937	4,839	2,879	1,108	728	3,485
ND . . .	1,581	2,475	4.8	282	191	509	600	836	420	99	444	401
SD. . . .	1,349	1,938	6.5	323	168	260	598	844	441	111	40	388
NE. . . .	3,126	1,981	7.5	648	542	574	1,361	1,716	914	415	110	996
KS. . . .	5,318	2,146	5.0	1,099	847	1,288	2,083	2,719	1,331	871	338	1,775
South	177,318	2,075	9.9	37,944	24,952	45,218	69,205	92,894	47,397	20,868	12,519	67,073
S.A.	78,970	1,813	8.6	19,835	13,225	14,108	31,805	39,606	23,571	6,252	6,274	33,884
DE. . . .	1,424	2,138	7.3	347	208	305	565	806	429	151	105	534
MD . . .	7,909	1,654	2.8	2,091	989	1,779	3,050	3,998	2,447	884	464	3,122
DC. . . .	1,084	1,787	1.4	208	441	161	275	329	225	184	3	584
VA. . . .	11,302	1,827	6.7	2,796	1,982	1,644	4,881	5,954	3,475	831	533	4,374
WV . . .	3,918	2,185	11.5	715	443	1,424	1,336	2,180	1,022	471	1,286	1,089
NC . . .	12,585	1,899	8.2	3,226	1,938	2,559	4,861	6,090	3,824	657	946	5,715
SC. . . .	6,895	1,977	8.8	1,573	911	1,802	2,610	3,171	1,988	526	499	3,113
GA . . .	12,892	1,990	11.1	2,990	2,118	2,579	5,204	6,084	3,580	1,467	1,282	5,255
FL. . . .	20,961	1,620	10.6	5,889	4,195	1,855	9,023	10,994	6,581	1,081	1,156	10,098
E.S.C . . .	30,390	2,002	6.5	6,157	3,513	8,265	12,453	15,206	8,628	2,859	3,242	11,913
KY. . . .	7,323	1,987	2.8	1,354	812	2,078	3,079	3,800	2,080	656	1,019	2,707
TN. . . .	9,719	1,993	6.3	1,973	1,072	2,675	3,998	4,725	2,846	804	813	4,055
AL. . . .	8,388	2,076	8.0	1,777	982	2,361	3,268	4,066	2,303	842	1,238	3,237
MS . . .	4,960	1,928	10.2	1,053	647	1,151	2,108	2,615	1,399	557	172	1,914
W.S.C. . .	67,958	2,545	13.2	11,952	8,214	22,845	24,947	38,082	15,198	11,757	3,003	21,276
AR. . . .	4,735	2,014	10.0	1,125	612	1,096	1,902	2,323	1,342	665	345	1,790
LA. . . .	13,653	3,235	15.7	1,945	1,348	5,769	4,589	7,894	2,174	2,466	351	3,739
OK . . .	6,265	1,992	12.4	1,478	963	1,110	2,715	3,159	1,851	1,307	388	2,316
TX. . . .	43,305	2,549	12.9	7,404	5,291	14,870	15,741	24,706	9,831	7,319	1,919	13,431
West	91,515	1,734	10.4	18,267	16,803	15,381	41,065	47,878	26,146	11,833	2,785	33,715
Mt	24,987	1,829	8.2	5,170	4,599	4,399	10,820	12,884	7,405	2,751	2,448	9,333
MT . . .	1,686	2,111	6.4	301	220	403	763	1,007	515	163	117	510
ID	1,823	1,810	7.6	355	282	409	777	978	547	142	18	685
WY . . .	1,531	3,371	5.4	180	174	508	668	840	321	163	396	482
CO . . .	5,245	1,592	7.7	1,153	1,129	645	2,319	2,616	1,726	821	353	1,800
NM . . .	2,979	1,966	10.0	537	580	551	1,311	1,717	899	349	363	964
AZ. . . .	6,544	1,786	8.8	1,623	1,441	858	2,622	2,951	1,893	451	499	3,181
UT. . . .	2,755	1,599	6.7	559	414	529	1,253	1,420	794	419	455	831
NV. . . .	2,424	2,017	11.3	462	359	496	1,107	1,355	710	243	247	880
Pac	66,528	1,700	11.3	13,097	12,204	10,982	30,245	34,994	18,741	9,082	337	24,382
WA . . .	8,563	1,759	10.3	1,641	1,110	1,524	4,288	4,959	2,639	554	141	3,034
OR . . .	5,016	1,765	8.1	966	746	942	2,361	2,801	1,566	438	19	1,797
CA . . .	48,635	1,634	11.1	9,892	9,685	8,000	21,058	23,886	13,699	7,830	131	18,418
AK. . . .	2,128	3,869	20.1	342	322	171	1,293	1,560	307	224	45	401
HI	2,186	1,973	18.7	256	341	345	1,245	1,788	530	36	1	732

[1] Includes sources not shown separately. Total expenditures are the sum of purchases for each source (including electricity sales) less electric utility purchases of fuel. [2] Based on estimated resident population as of July 1. [3] Includes net imports of coal coke not shown separately by State.

Source: U.S. Energy Information Administration, *State Energy Price and Expenditure Report*, annual.

No. 936. Residential Energy Consumption, Expenditures, and Average Prices, 1980 to 1990, and by Region, 1990

[For period April to March for 1980-1985; January to December for 1987 and 1990. Excludes Alaska and Hawaii in 1980. Covers occupied units only. Excludes household usage of gasoline for transportation and the use of wood or coal. Based on Residential Energy Consumption Survey; see Appendix III. For composition of regions, see table 31. Btu=British thermal unit; see text, section 19]

TYPE OF FUEL	Unit	1980	1982	1983	1985	1987	1990 Total	North-east	Mid-west	South	West
CONSUMPTION											
Total	Quad. Btu...	9.74	9.51	8.62	9.04	9.13	9.22	2.30	2.81	2.60	1.51
Avg. per household	Mil. Btu...	126	114	103	105	101	98	120	122	81	78
Natural gas	Quad. Btu...	5.31	5.39	4.77	4.98	4.83	4.86	1.03	1.88	1.03	0.92
Electricity	Quad. Btu...	2.42	2.48	2.42	2.48	2.76	3.03	0.47	0.66	1.36	0.54
Fuel oil, kerosene	Quad. Btu...	1.71	1.33	1.14	1.26	1.22	1.04	0.78	0.13	0.11	0.02
Liquid petroleum gas	Quad. Btu...	0.31	0.31	0.29	0.31	0.32	0.28	0.02	0.13	0.10	0.03
EXPENDITURES											
Total	Bil. dol...	63.2	85.0	87.8	97.0	97.7	110.2	28.3	26.9	37.2	17.9
Avg. per household	Dollars...	815	1,022	1,048	1,123	1,080	1,172	1,471	1,166	1,151	920
Natural gas	Bil. dol...	17.8	24.5	27.1	29.8	26.1	27.3	7.3	9.2	5.7	4.8
Electricity	Bil. dol...	32.6	45.9	48.4	54.5	61.6	71.5	14.6	15.4	29.1	12.5
Fuel oil, kerosene	Bil. dol...	10.7	11.8	9.6	9.6	7.2	8.3	6.1	1.0	1.0	0.2
Liquid petroleum gas	Bil. dol...	2.1	2.7	2.7	3.1	2.8	3.1	0.3	1.3	1.2	0.4
AVERAGE PRICE											
Total	Dol./mil. Btu.	6.49	8.93	10.18	10.73	10.71	12.0	12.3	9.6	14.3	11.8
Natural gas	Dol./mil. Btu.	3.36	4.55	5.67	5.97	5.41	5.6	7.1	4.9	5.7	5.2
Electricity	Dol./mil. Btu.	13.46	18.51	19.98	21.94	22.34	23.6	31.2	23.2	21.4	23.2
Fuel oil, kerosene	Dol./mil. Btu.	6.29	8.89	8.42	7.64	5.89	7.9	7.9	7.8	8.4	7.9
Liquid petroleum gas	Dol./mil. Btu.	6.71	8.74	9.42	9.91	8.91	11.2	14.3	9.7	12.2	12.2

Source: U.S. Energy Information Administration, *Household Energy Consumption and Expenditures, 1990* and prior reports. Survey not conducted in 1984, 1986, 1988, and 1989.

No. 937. Residential Energy Consumption and Expenditures, by Type of Fuel and Selected Household Characteristic: 1990

[For period January through December 1990. Quad.=quadrillion. See headnote, table 936]

CHARACTERISTIC	CONSUMPTION (Btu's) Total[1] (quad.)	Avg. per household[1] (mil.)	Nat-ural gas (quad.)	Elec-tricity (quad.)	Fuel oil[2] (quad.)	EXPENDITURES Total[1] (bil. dol.)	Avg. per household[1] (dol.)	Nat-ural gas (bil. dol.)	Elec-tricity (bil. dol.)	Fuel oil[2] (bil. dol.)
Total households	9.22	98	4.86	3.03	1.05	110.2	1,172	27.3	71.5	8.3
Single family detached	6.61	113	3.45	2.20	0.74	78.2	1,340	18.8	51.0	5.9
Single family attached	0.52	87	0.28	0.19	0.06	6.8	1,129	1.7	4.6	0.5
Two to four unit building	0.94	95	0.62	0.20	0.11	10.2	1,015	3.8	5.3	0.9
Five or more unit building	0.73	51	0.36	0.28	0.08	9.8	677	2.2	7.1	0.5
Mobile home	0.41	78	0.15	0.16	0.04	5.3	1,011	0.8	3.5	0.4
Year house built:										
1939 or earlier	2.57	120	1.57	0.51	0.42	26.1	1,216	9.0	13.0	3.3
1940 to 1949	0.74	105	0.45	0.19	0.07	7.9	1,130	2.5	4.5	0.6
1950 to 1959	1.47	110	0.81	0.41	0.22	16.8	1,254	4.6	10.2	1.7
1960 to 1969	1.41	95	0.77	0.48	0.13	17.1	1,155	4.4	11.4	1.0
1970 to 1979	1.82	85	0.78	0.82	0.17	24.5	1,143	4.2	18.3	1.3
1980 to 1984	0.58	72	0.21	0.32	0.01	9.0	1,120	1.2	7.4	0.1
1985 to 1990	0.63	80	0.28	0.30	(B)	8.8	1,117	1.4	6.8	(B)
Heating and cooling degree day zones:[3]										
Less than 2,000 CDD and —										
More than 7,000 HDD	1.12	111	0.53	0.29	0.21	11.5	1,132	2.7	6.3	1.6
5,500 to 7,000 HDD	3.29	123	2.04	0.75	0.43	33.4	1,251	10.8	18.4	3.5
4,000 to 5,499 HDD	2.12	102	1.06	0.67	0.34	25.6	1,222	6.6	15.6	2.7
Less than 4,000 HDD	1.41	73	0.72	0.59	0.04	19.4	1,008	4.2	14.3	0.3
More than 2,000 CDD and less than 4,000 HDD	1.28	75	0.50	0.74	(B)	20.4	1,197	3.0	16.9	(B)
1990 family income:										
Less than $10,000	1.27	80	0.70	0.36	0.15	14.1	888	4.0	8.2	1.2
$10,000 to $19,999	1.66	84	0.88	0.53	0.17	19.4	978	5.0	12.3	1.4
$20,000 to $34,999	2.27	93	1.17	0.77	0.25	27.1	1,115	6.4	17.9	2.1
$35,000 to $49,999	1.75	105	0.90	0.62	0.19	21.7	1,296	5.1	14.6	1.5
$50,000 or more	2.27	132	1.21	0.75	0.27	27.9	1,618	6.8	18.6	2.2

B Base figure too small to meet statistical standards for reliability of derived figure. [1] Includes liquid petroleum gas not shown separately. [2] Includes kerosene. [3] CDD=Cooling degree day; HDD=Heating degree day.
Source: U.S. Energy Information Administration, *Household Energy Consumption and Expenditures, 1990.*

No. 938. Residential Energy Expenditures, by Type of End-Use and Household Characteristic: 1990

[For period January through December 1990. See headnote, table 936]

CHARACTERISTIC	EXPENDITURES (bil. dol.)					EXPENDITURES PER HOUSEHOLD (dollars)				
	All end uses [1]	End-use				All end uses [1]	End-use			
		Space heat-ing [2]	Air-condi-tioning [3]	Water heat-ing [2]	Appli-ances		Space heat-ing [2]	Air-condi-tioning [3]	Water heat-ing [2]	Appli-ances
Total households....	110.2	34.2	11.3	15.3	37.0	1,172	370	186	163	394
Type:										
Single-family detached ..	78.2	24.1	8.1	9.9	27.4	1,340	423	214	171	469
Single-family attached...	6.8	2.2	0.7	0.9	2.2	1,129	371	169	156	369
2 to 4 unit building.....	10.1	3.9	0.7	1.6	2.8	1,015	394	120	163	282
5 or more unit building ..	9.8	2.2	1.3	1.9	3.0	677	154	132	131	209
Mobile home........	5.3	1.8	0.5	0.9	1.6	1,011	340	163	175	315
Year house built:										
1939 or earlier.......	26.1	10.7	1.0	3.5	8.2	1,216	507	98	163	381
1940 to 1949........	7.9	2.8	0.6	1.1	2.5	1,130	412	142	158	360
1950 to 1959........	16.8	5.4	1.4	2.1	5.8	1,254	416	174	157	435
1960 to 1969........	17.1	4.8	2.1	2.3	5.9	1,155	330	200	153	399
1970 to 1979........	24.5	6.4	3.4	3.6	8.4	1,143	302	216	169	392
1980 to 1984........	9.0	1.9	1.4	1.4	3.2	1,120	247	230	175	399
1985 to 1990........	8.7	2.0	1.5	1.3	3.0	1,117	265	234	168	380
1990 family income:										
Less than $10,000	14.1	5.1	1.0	2.1	4.2	888	326	130	130	263
$10,000-$19,999	19.4	6.4	1.7	2.9	6.1	978	332	149	147	305
$20,000-$34,999	27.1	8.3	2.6	4.0	9.1	1,115	349	167	166	376
$35,000-$49,999	21.7	6.3	2.6	3.0	7.5	1,296	382	212	180	446
$50,000 or more	27.9	8.1	3.3	3.3	10.2	1,618	472	251	192	591

[1] Includes expenditures for refrigerator not shown separately. [2] Heating from the primary and secondary heating equipment. [3] Cooling by refrigeration; does not include dehumidifiers, evaporative coolers, or fans not connected to air-conditioning equipment.

Source: U.S. Energy Information Administration, *Household Energy Consumption and Expenditures, 1990.*

No. 939. Manufacturing Energy Consumption Required to Produce Heat, Power, and Electricity, by Type of Fuel and Industry Group: 1988

[Based on the Manufacturing Energy Consumption Survey; therefore, subject to sampling variability]

SIC[1] code	INDUSTRY	TOTAL FUEL CONSUMPTION (tril. Btu)						CONSUMPTION PER—	
		Total	Net elec-tricity [2]	Fuel oil [3]	Natu-ral gas	Coal and coke	Other	Employ-ee (mil. Btu)	Dollar of value added (1,000 Btu)
(X)	Total..................	20,534	2,398	810	5,860	2,783	8,684	868	12.1
20	Food and kindred...........	994	171	83	489	157	95	694	7.6
21	Tobacco products	25	3	1	2	17	1	580	1.4
22	Textile mill products.........	275	101	26	93	39	15	451	10.8
23	Apparel and other textile products ..	54	23	4	22	3	2	42	1.3
24	Lumber and wood products......	407	56	26	35	2	288	551	13.0
25	Furniture and fixtures..........	63	19	4	23	3	13	131	3.1
26	Paper and allied products........	2,366	189	191	431	315	1,241	3,498	36.7
27	Printing and publishing........	116	58	3	49	-	6	73	1.3
28	Chemicals and allied products.....	4,360	416	137	2,049	317	1,441	3,601	22.4
29	Petroleum and coal products......	6,412	106	126	723	8	5,449	28,414	127.0
30	Rubber and misc. plastic products ..	253	107	20	111	9	7	329	5.6
31	Leather and leather products......	16	5	4	5	1	(Z)	108	3.3
32	Stone, clay, and glass products	966	115	5	468	301	31	2,037	29.5
33	Primary metal industries	2,875	509	59	751	1,505	51	3,782	45.9
34	Fabricated metal products........	346	106	12	204	10	14	251	4.4
35	Machinery, except electrical.......	280	114	12	129	18	6	145	2.0
36	Electric and electronic equipment...	224	109	10	85	11	9	144	2.2
37	Transportation equipment	350	127	31	139	42	11	193	2.4
38	Instruments and related products ...	113	49	8	32	22	2	104	1.3
39	Miscellaneous manufacturing.......	41	14	3	20	2	2	110	2.2

X Not applicable. Z Less than 0.5 trillion Btu. [1] Standard Industrial Classification; see text, section 13. [2] Net electricity is obtained by aggregating purchases, transfers in, and generation from noncombustible renewable resources minus quantities sold and transferred out. [3] Includes distillate and residual.

Source: U.S. Energy Information Administration, *Manufacturing Energy Consumption Survey: Consumption of Energy, 1988.*

No. 940. Commercial Buildings—Energy Consumption and Expenditures, by Major Fuel Type Used: 1989

[Covers buildings using one or more major fuel. Excludes industrial buildings, predominantly residential buildings, and buildings of less than 1,000 sq. ft. Based on a sample survey of building representatives and energy suppliers; therefore, subject to sampling variability. For characteristics of commercial buildings, see tables in Section 26. Tril.=trillion]

ITEM	Unit	All major fuels	Elec-tricity	Natural gas	Fuel oil	Pro-pane	District Heat
Number of buildings using the fuel	1,000.	4,528	4,294	2,420	581	348	98
Square footage of floorspace	Million	63,184	61,563	41,143	12,600	4,695	6,578
Square footage per building	1,000.	14.0	14.3	17.0	21.7	13.5	67.0
Energy consumed, total	Tril. Btu	5,788	2,773	2,073	357	-	585
Energy consumed per building	Mil. Btu	1,278	1,346	1,792	2,735	1,300	12,302
Energy consumed per square foot of floorspace	1,000 Btu	92	94	105	126	96	183
Energy consumed per employee	Mil. Btu	82	82	90	94	95	117
Expenditures, total	Mil. dol.	70,826	70,801	48,225	17,356	5,069	12,689
Expenditures per building	$1,000.	15.6	16.5	19.9	29.9	14.6	129.3
Expenditures per square foot of floorspace	Dollars.	1.12	1.15	1.17	1.38	1.08	2.03
Expenditures per million Btu of energy consumed	Dollars.	12.24	12.25	11.12	10.93	11.20	10.51

- Represents zero.

Source: U.S. Energy Information Administration, *Commercial Buildings Energy Consumption and Expenditures, 1989.*

No. 941. Commercial Buildings—Energy Consumption and Expenditures: 1989

[Covers buildings using one or more major fuel. Excludes industrial buildings, predominantly residential buildings, and buildings of less than 1,000 sq. ft. Based on a sample survey of building representatives and energy suppliers; therefore, subject to sampling variability. For characteristics of commercial buildings, see tables in Section 26 For composition of regions, see table 31]

BUILDING CHARACTERISTIC	ALL BUILDINGS USING ANY MAJOR FUEL		CONSUMPTION (tril. Btu)			EXPENDITURES (mil. dol.)		
	Number (1,000)	Square feet (mil.)	Major fuel, total [1]	Elec-tricity	Natural gas	Major fuel, total [1]	Elec-tricity	Natural gas
All buildings	4,528	63,184	5,788	2,773	2,073	70,826	55,943	9,204
Region:								
Northeast	783	13,569	1,354	586	353	17,505	13,188	1,807
Midwest	1,046	15,955	1,659	609	831	16,468	11,697	3,381
South	1,847	22,039	1,648	975	498	21,759	18,409	2,293
West	851	11,620	1,126	604	391	15,093	12,649	1,724
Year constructed:								
1900 or before	172	1,654	128	25	53	1,214	603	270
1901 to 1920	242	4,245	239	75	123	2,448	1,676	527
1921 to 1945	680	8,098	636	211	244	7,033	4,772	1,135
1946 to 1960	868	10,511	988	379	411	10,334	7,333	1,809
1961 to 1970	821	12,167	1,275	589	458	14,894	11,667	1,975
1974 to 1979	884	13,329	1,342	730	441	17,807	14,815	1,939
1980 to 1983	317	4,274	432	295	117	6,194	5,570	502
1984 to 1986	329	5,670	464	303	141	7,184	6,363	665
1987 to 1989	215	3,235	284	167	85	3,718	3,143	382
Principal activity within building:								
Assembly	617	6,909	441	186	174	5,986	4,648	809
Education	282	8,076	704	217	323	6,589	4,391	1,309
Food sales/services	343	1,959	394	218	155	5,445	4,512	812
Health care	80	2,054	449	154	186	4,052	2,670	712
Lodging	140	3,476	425	138	187	4,014	2,593	818
Mercantile/services	1,278	12,365	1,048	550	417	13,527	11,116	1,931
Office	679	11,802	1,230	781	238	18,323	15,757	1,128
Public order and safety	50	616	78	29	25	875	582	120
Warehouse	618	9,253	536	243	206	6,085	4,836	853
Other	62	1,529	344	201	102	4,224	3,558	420
Vacant	333	4,161	98	39	49	1,218	924	237
Square footage:								
1,001 to 5,000	2,529	6,790	692	326	302	9,601	7,592	1,620
5,001 to 10,000	890	6,532	567	246	265	7,870	6,232	1,304
10,001 to 25,000	644	10,393	791	381	278	9,869	7,809	1,348
25,001 to 50,000	247	8,801	756	331	309	8,950	6,919	1,318
50,001 to 100,000	127	9,130	855	433	249	10,124	8,042	1,094
100,001 to 200,000	61	8,277	777	387	238	9,265	7,410	1,016
200,000 to 500,000	23	7,022	698	366	228	7,853	6,326	836
500,000 and over	7	6,239	652	303	203	7,293	5,613	668

[1] Includes fuel oil, propane, and purchased steam not shown separately.

Source: U.S. Energy Information Administration, *Commercial Buildings Energy Consumption and Expenditures, 1989.*

No. 942. Fossil Fuel Prices in Current and Constant (1987) Dollars: 1970 to 1991

[In cents per million British thermal units (Btu), except as indicated. All fuel prices taken as close to the point of production as possible. See text, section 19, for explanation of Btu conversions from mineral fuels]

FUEL	1970	1973	1975	1980	1983	1984	1985	1986	1987	1988	1989	1990	1991
CURRENT DOLLARS													
Composite[1]	31.7	39.8	82.1	204.2	270.1	264.6	251.2	165.3	170.0	153.3	167.1	184.3	165.7
Crude oil	54.8	67.1	132.2	372.2	451.6	446.2	415.3	215.7	265.5	216.9	273.4	345.3	284.5
Natural gas	15.4	20.1	40.2	144.8	232.3	239.9	225.7	174.8	150.2	152.4	152.7	154.6	143.8
Bituminous coal[2]	26.2	36.5	83.9	109.4	117.2	115.9	114.8	108.2	104.9	100.8	100.0	99.5	100.3
Anthracite coal	48.8	61.7	149.5	185.9	230.0	208.7	204.2	191.1	188.9	189.8	183.6	174.5	182.7
CONSTANT (1987) DOLLARS													
Composite[1]	90.3	96.4	166.9	284.8	309.7	290.8	266.1	170.6	170.0	147.5	154.2	163.2	141.6
Crude oil	156.1	162.5	268.7	519.1	517.9	490.3	439.9	222.6	265.5	208.8	252.2	305.8	243.2
Natural gas	43.9	48.7	81.7	202.0	266.4	263.6	239.1	180.4	150.2	146.7	140.9	136.9	122.9
Bituminous coal[2]	74.6	88.4	170.5	152.6	134.4	127.4	121.6	111.7	104.9	97.0	92.3	88.1	85.7
Anthracite coal	139.0	149.4	303.9	259.3	263.8	229.3	216.3	197.2	188.9	182.7	169.4	154.6	156.2
GDP implicit price deflator[3] (1987=100)	35.1	41.3	49.2	71.7	87.2	91.0	94.4	96.9	100.0	103.9	108.4	112.9	117.0

[1] Weighted by relative importance of individual fuels in total fuels production. [2] Includes subbituminous and lignite.
[3] GDP=Gross domestic product; see text, section 15.
Source: U.S. Energy Information Administration, *Annual Energy Review*.

No. 943. World Energy Consumption, by Region and Energy Source: 1960 to 1990

[In tons of coal equivalent. Metric ton=1.1023 short tons. Kilogram=2.205 pounds. See text, section 31 for general comments about the data]

REGION AND ENERGY SOURCE	CONSUMPTION (mil. metric tons)					PER CAPITA (kilograms)				PERCENT DISTRIBUTION			
	1960	1970	1980	1989	1990	1960	1970	1980	1990	1960	1970	1980	1990
World, total	3,924	6,440	8,544	10,382	10,412	1,302	1,748	1,919	1,955	100.0	100.0	100.0	100.0
North America[1]	1,599	2,502	2,796	3,087	3,061	5,951	7,825	7,480	7,165	40.7	38.9	32.7	29.4
United States	1,454	2,217	2,364	2,594	2,572	8,047	10,811	10,386	10,321	37.1	34.4	27.7	24.7
South America	79	143	251	300	307	535	749	1,046	1,034	2.0	2.2	2.9	2.9
Europe	1,039	1,720	2,145	2,200	2,153	2,443	3,745	4,433	4,319	26.5	26.7	25.1	20.7
Asia	514	903	1,579	2,459	2,552	276	386	607	811	13.1	14.0	18.5	24.5
Japan	96	333	435	494	519	1,025	3,246	3,726	4,206	2.4	5.2	5.1	5.0
Soviet Union	595	999	1,473	1,943	1,931	2,777	4,132	5,549	6,692	15.2	15.5	17.2	18.5
Oceania	41	71	105	141	147	2,597	3,675	4,572	5,565	1.0	1.1	1.2	1.4
Energy source:													
Solid fuels	1,940	2,159	2,632	3,392	3,324	644	586	591	624	49.4	33.5	30.8	31.9
Liquid fuels	1,306	2,835	3,778	4,026	4,038	433	770	848	758	33.3	44.0	44.2	38.8
Natural gas	593	1,292	1,834	2,466	2,532	197	351	412	475	15.1	20.1	21.5	24.3
Electricity	84	154	301	498	518	28	42	68	97	2.1	2.4	3.5	5.0

[1] Includes Central America.
Source: Statistical Office of the United Nations, New York, NY, *Energy Statistics Yearbook*, annual, (copyright).

No. 944. World Primary Energy Production, by Region and Type: 1973 to 1990

[In quadrillion Btu. Btu=British thermal units. For Btu conversion factors, see source]

REGION AND TYPE	1973	1975	1980	1982	1983	1984	1985	1986	1987	1988	1989	1990
World, total	244.8	245.0	286.6	280.2	282.2	297.0	304.3	314.1	322.0	333.1	338.4	345.1
North America	73.3	71.1	80.5	81.3	78.9	84.6	84.1	82.8	84.1	86.0	86.2	88.0
United States	62.0	59.8	64.7	63.8	61.1	65.7	64.6	64.0	64.6	65.4	65.8	67.5
Central and South America	12.9	10.6	12.1	12.0	12.2	13.1	13.5	14.2	14.2	15.0	15.3	16.5
Western Europe	19.6	21.4	28.7	30.7	31.9	32.4	35.0	35.9	36.5	36.8	36.7	36.5
Eastern Europe and Soviet Union	51.4	55.9	69.3	72.5	74.2	76.6	78.7	81.5	83.4	85.2	85.2	81.4
Middle East	46.6	43.5	42.2	29.5	27.3	27.7	25.7	30.6	32.1	36.4	39.6	41.0
Africa	14.8	13.3	17.3	15.4	16.1	17.5	18.4	18.1	18.5	19.4	20.2	21.5
Far East and Oceania	26.2	29.3	36.5	38.8	41.5	45.1	49.0	51.1	53.1	54.2	55.1	60.2
Crude oil	117.8	111.6	127.6	113.9	113.4	116.2	114.7	119.5	120.4	125.4	127.5	129.1
Natural gas	43.2	43.9	52.8	53.7	54.1	59.1	61.4	62.6	65.6	67.1	71.1	73.5
Natural gas liquids	4.2	4.4	5.5	5.8	5.8	6.1	6.2	6.5	6.7	7.2	7.0	7.2
Coal	63.8	66.3	75.0	78.4	78.5	82.2	86.1	88.3	90.4	93.0	91.9	93.0
Hydroelectric power	13.5	15.0	18.2	18.9	19.8	20.4	20.6	21.0	21.1	21.3	21.2	22.0
Nuclear electric power	2.2	3.9	7.6	9.5	10.7	13.0	15.4	16.3	17.8	19.1	19.7	20.4

Source: U.S. Energy Information Administration, *International Energy Annual*.

No. 945. U.S. Foreign Trade in Selected Mineral Fuels: 1970 to 1991

[Btu=British thermal units. For Btu conversion factors, see text, section 19. Minus sign (-) indicates an excess of imports over exports. See also *Historical Statistics, Colonial Times to 1970,* series M 100, 101, 127, 128, 140, 141, 178, and 181]

MINERAL FUEL	1970	1973	1975	1980	1984	1985	1986	1987	1988	1989	1990	1991
NATURAL GAS												
Imports:												
Billion cubic feet ...	821	1,033	953	985	843	950	750	993	1,294	1,382	1,532	1,693
Trillion Btu	846	1,060	978	1,006	847	952	748	992	1,296	1,387	1,550	1,713
Exports:												
Billion cubic feet ...	70	77	73	49	55	55	61	54	74	107	86	122
Trillion Btu	72	79	74	49	55	56	62	55	75	109	88	124
Net trade:												
Billion cubic feet ...	-751	-956	-880	-936	-788	-894	-689	-939	-1,220	-1,275	-1,446	-1,571
Trillion Btu	-774	-981	-904	-957	-792	-896	-686	-937	-1,221	-1,278	-1,462	-1,589
CRUDE OIL												
Imports: [1]												
Million barrels	483	1,184	1,498	1,926	1,254	1,168	1,525	1,706	1,869	2,133	2,151	2,110
Trillion Btu	2,814	6,887	8,721	11,195	7,302	6,814	9,002	10,067	11,027	12,597	12,764	12,550
Exports:												
Million barrels	5	1	2	105	66	75	56	55	57	52	40	42
Trillion Btu	29	4	12	609	384	432	326	319	329	301	232	244
Net trade:												
Million barrels	-478	-1,183	-1,496	-1,821	-1,188	-1,094	-1,469	-1,651	-1,812	-2,081	-2,111	-2,068
Trillion Btu	-2,785	-6,883	-8,708	-10,586	-6,918	-6,381	-8,676	-9,748	-10,698	-12,296	-12,532	-12,306
PETROLEUM PRODUCTS												
Imports:												
Million barrels	765	1,099	712	603	736	681	747	731	840	809	775	655
Trillion Btu	4,656	6,578	4,227	3,463	4,131	3,796	4,199	4,095	4,720	4,564	4,351	3,702
Exports:												
Million barrels	89	84	74	94	198	211	230	224	242	262	273	323
Trillion Btu	520	482	427	551	1,161	1,225	1,344	1,311	1,412	1,538	1,594	1,882
Net trade:												
Million barrels	-675	-1,015	-638	-509	-538	-471	-516	-508	-598	-548	-502	-332
Trillion Btu	-4,136	-6,097	-3,800	-2,912	-2,970	-2,570	-2,855	-2,784	-3,308	-3,026	-2,757	-1,820
COAL												
Imports:												
Thousand short tons	36	127	940	1,194	1,286	1,952	2,212	1,747	2,134	2,851	2,699	3,390
Trillion Btu	1	3	24	30	32	49	55	44	53	71	67	85
Exports:												
Thousand short tons	71,733	53,587	66,309	91,742	81,482	92,680	85,518	79,607	95,023	100,815	105,804	108,969
Trillion Btu	1,936	1,425	1,761	2,421	2,151	2,438	2,248	2,093	2,499	2,637	2,772	2,854
Net trade:												
Thousand short tons	71,697	53,460	65,369	90,548	80,196	90,728	83,306	77,860	92,889	97,964	103,105	105,579
Trillion Btu	1,935	1,422	1,738	2,391	2,119	2,389	2,193	2,049	2,446	2,566	2,705	2,769

[1] Beginning 1980, includes strategic petroleum reserve imports.

Source: U.S. Energy Information Administration, *Annual Energy Review.*

No. 946. Daily International Flow of Crude Oil, by Area: 1989

[In thousands of barrels per day]

EXPORTING AREA	Total [1]	IMPORTING AREA							
		North America		Central and South America	Western Europe	Eastern Europe	Middle East and Africa	Japan	Other Far East and Oceania
		U.S.	Canada						
World, total..........	27,290	5,843	490	1,656	9,150	2,123	1,158	354	3,329
United States	142	(X)	8	[2]132	-	-	-	-	2
North America, except U.S.	1,920	1,346	9	74	299	-	34	171	6
Central and South America	1,459	795	47	419	164	-	5	8	21
Western Europe.............	2,470	290	276	9	1,860	11	24	-	-
Eastern Europe and Soviet Union .	2,554	-	-	81	923	1,402	52	(Z)	96
Middle East.................	12,092	1,791	67	672	3,376	557	763	2,483	2,384
Africa.....................	4,645	1,287	83	269	2,518	145	265	12	66
Far East and Oceania.........	2,008	334	-	20	10	8	882	867	754

- Represents zero.   Z Less than 50,000 barrels.   X Not applicable.   [1] Includes stocks at sea, exchanges, transshipments, and other statistical discrepancies not shown separately.   [2] Includes shipments to Puerto Rico and Virgin Islands.

Source: U.S. Energy Information Administration, *International Energy Annual.*

No. 947. Crude Oil Imports Into United States, by Country of Origin: 1970 to 1991

[In millions of barrels. Barrels contain 42 gallons]

COUNTRY OF ORIGIN	1970	1973	1975	1980	1983	1984	1985	1986	1987	1988	1989	1990	1991
Total	483	1,184	1,498	1,921	1,215	1,250	1,168	1,525	1,706	1,864	2,133	2,151	2,110
Canada..........	245	365	219	73	100	124	171	208	222	249	230	235	271
Mexico	-	(Z)	26	185	280	241	261	227	220	246	251	251	277
Norway...........	-	-	4	53	24	41	11	19	26	23	46	35	27
Trinidad-Tobago	(Z)	22	42	42	30	32	36	34	27	26	27	28	26
United Kingdom	-	-	(Z)	63	133	138	101	116	111	93	58	57	39
OPEC [1] . .`	222	765	1,172	1,410	539	552	479	771	876	984	1,232	1,283	1,233
Algeria..........	2	44	96	166	64	71	31	28	42	21	22	23	16
Ecuador.........	-	17	21	6	20	17	20	23	8	12	29	14	19
Gabon...........	-	-	10	9	22	21	19	9	13	5	18	23	31
Indonesia	26	73	138	115	115	111	107	108	96	68	58	36	37
Iran............	12	79	101	3	18	4	10	7	36	(Z)	-	-	12
Iraq............	-	1	1	10	4	4	17	30	30	125	161	188	-
Kuwait	12	15	1	10	3	9	1	10	26	29	57	29	2
Libya...........	17	49	81	200	-	-	-	-	-	-	-	-	-
Nigeria..........	17	164	272	307	110	76	102	160	193	222	292	286	249
Qatar...........	-	3	7	8	-	1	-	4	-	-	1	1	-
Saudi Arabia......	15	169	256	456	117	113	48	226	234	333	407	436	622
United Arab Emirates	23	26	43	63	7	33	13	14	20	8	8	3	1
Venezuela	98	126	144	57	60	92	112	152	178	160	181	243	244
Other	16	32	34	95	109	124	108	150	225	244	279	264	237

- Represents zero.   Z Less than 500,000 barrels.   [1] Organization of Petroleum Exporting Countries.

Source: 1970, U.S. Bureau of Mines, *Minerals Yearbooks, vol. I;* thereafter, U.S. Energy Information Administration, *Petroleum Supply Annual,* vol. I.

No. 948. Crude Oil and Refined Products—Summary: 1973 to 1992

[Barrels of 42 gallons. Data are averages]

YEAR AND QUARTER	CRUDE OIL (1,000 bbl. per day)					REFINED OIL PRODUCTS (1,000 bbl. per day)			Total oil imports[2] (1,000 bbl. per day)	CRUDE OIL STOCKS [3] (mil. bbl.)	
	Input to refineries	Domestic produc- tion	Imports		Exports	Domestic demand	Imports	Exports		Total	Stra- tegic reserve
			Total [1]	Stra- tegic reserve							
1973	12,431	9,208	3,244	(X)	2	17,308	3,012	229	6,256	242	(X)
1974	12,133	8,774	3,477	(X)	3	16,653	2,635	218	6,112	265	(X)
1975	12,442	8,375	4,105	(X)	6	16,322	1,951	204	6,056	271	(X)
1976	13,416	8,132	5,287	(X)	8	17,461	2,026	215	7,313	285	(X)
1977	14,602	8,245	6,615	21	50	18,431	2,193	193	8,807	348	7
1978	14,739	8,707	6,356	162	158	18,847	2,008	204	8,363	376	67
1979	14,648	8,552	6,519	67	235	18,513	1,937	236	8,456	430	91
1980	13,481	8,597	5,263	44	287	17,056	1,646	258	6,909	466	108
1981	12,470	8,572	4,396	256	228	16,058	1,599	367	5,996	594	230
1982	11,774	8,649	3,488	165	236	15,296	1,625	579	5,113	644	294
1983	11,685	8,688	3,329	234	164	15,231	1,722	575	5,051	723	379
1984	12,044	8,879	3,426	197	181	15,726	2,011	541	5,437	796	451
1985	12,002	8,971	3,201	118	204	15,726	1,866	577	5,067	814	493
1986	12,716	8,680	4,178	48	154	16,281	2,045	631	6,224	843	512
1987	12,854	8,349	4,674	73	151	16,665	2,004	613	6,678	890	541
1988	13,246	8,140	5,107	51	155	17,283	2,295	661	7,402	890	560
1989	13,401	7,613	5,843	56	142	17,325	2,217	717	8,061	921	580
1990	13,409	7,355	5,894	27	109	16,988	2,123	748	8,018	908	586
1st qtr	13,128	7,492	6,081	27	123	16,884	2,444	681	8,422	953	582
2d qtr	13,375	7,281	6,287	48	104	16,952	2,251	647	8,484	971	587
3d qtr	14,153	7,228	6,321	32	74	17,223	2,031	723	8,362	932	590
4th qtr	12,827	7,423	4,940	-	134	16,708	1,775	923	6,717	908	586
1991	13,301	7,418	5,782	-	116	16,714	1,844	885	7,627	893	569
1st qtr	12,873	7,561	5,316	-	113	16,481	1,556	1,081	6,871	905	568
2d qtr	13,500	7,413	6,075	-	135	16,402	1,985	801	8,060	915	568
3d qtr	13,732	7,344	6,137	-	101	17,001	1,947	761	8,084	909	569
4th qtr	13,097	7,355	5,592	-	117	16,957	1,881	1,902	7,473	893	569
1992, prel.	13,417	7,149	6,063	10	90	17,009	1,791	835	7,854	895	575
1st qtr	12,829	7,350	5,412	-	82	16,885	1,716	887	7,128	907	569
2d qtr	13,662	7,180	6,052	11	79	16,704	1,808	848	7,861	894	570
3d qtr	13,695	7,014	6,486	11	85	16,949	1,810	771	8,297	893	571
4th qtr	13,470	7,057	6,282	16	113	17,490	1,833	835	8,115	895	575

- Represents zero.   X Not applicable.   [1] Includes Strategic Petroleum Reserve.   [2] Crude oil (including Strategic Petroleum Reserve imports) plus refined products.   [3] End of year or quarter.

Source: U.S. Energy Information Administration, *Monthly Energy Review,* January 1993.

No. 949. Strategic Petroleum Reserve: 1977 to 1992

[**Million barrels, except as noted.** The Strategic Petroleum Reserve is a stock of petroleum maintained by Federal Government for use during periods of major supply interruption]

YEAR	Crude oil imports	Domestic crude oil deliveries	STOCKS AT YEAREND			Days of net petroleum imports [3]
			Quantity [1]	Percent of crude oil stocks [2]	Percent of total petroleum stocks	
1977	7.54	[4]0.37	7.46	2.1	0.6	1
1980	16.07	1.30	107.80	23.1	7.7	17
1981	93.30	28.79	230.34	38.8	15.5	43
1982	60.19	3.79	293.83	45.7	20.5	68
1983	85.29	0.42	379.09	52.4	26.1	88
1984	72.04	0.05	450.51	56.6	28.9	96
1985	43.12	0.17	493.32	60.6	32.5	115
1986	17.56	1.21	511.57	60.7	32.1	94
1987	26.52	2.69	540.65	60.9	33.6	91
1988	18.76	(Z)	559.52	63.0	35.0	85
1989	20.35	-	579.86	63.0	36.8	81
1990	9.77	-	585.69	64.5	36.1	82
1991	-	-	568.51	63.8	35.2	86
1992	3.59	2.60	574.72	64.5	36.1	83

- Represents zero. Z Less than .005 million barrels. [1] Stocks do not include imported quantities in transit to Strategic Petroleum Reserve terminals, pipeline fill, and above ground storage. [2] Including lease condensate stocks. [3] Derived by dividing end-of-year strategic petroleum reserve stocks by annual average daily net imports of all petroleum. Calculated prior to rounding. [4] The quantity of domestic fuel oil which was in storage prior to injection of foreign crude oil.
Source: U.S. Energy Information Administration, *Annual Energy Review.*

No. 950. World Petroleum Consumption, by Major Consuming Country: 1970 to 1991

[**Million barrels per day.** OECD=Organization for Economic Cooperation Development. For a complete list of OECD countries, see Section 31]

COUNTRY	1970	1973	1975	1980	1984	1985	1986	1987	1988	1989	1990	1991
World, total . . .	46.81	57.24	56.20	63.07	59.79	59.87	61.52	62.78	64.50	65.81	65.92	(NA)
OECD countries, total	33.27	39.90	36.98	38.60	34.50	34.27	35.28	35.91	37.09	37.57	37.47	37.98
United States	14.70	17.31	16.32	17.06	15.73	15.73	16.28	16.67	17.28	17.33	16.99	16.71
Australia	0.52	0.57	0.64	0.59	0.61	0.63	0.63	0.64	0.65	0.69	0.72	([1])
Canada	1.52	1.73	1.78	1.87	1.47	1.50	1.51	1.55	1.69	1.73	1.69	1.61
France	1.94	2.60	2.25	2.26	1.75	1.78	1.77	1.79	1.80	1.86	1.81	1.90
West Germany . . .	2.61	3.06	2.65	2.71	2.32	2.34	2.50	2.42	2.42	2.28	2.38	2.83
Italy	1.71	2.07	1.86	1.93	1.65	1.72	1.74	1.86	1.84	1.93	1.87	1.94
Japan	3.82	4.95	4.62	4.96	4.58	4.38	4.44	4.48	4.75	4.98	5.14	5.29
Spain	0.58	0.78	0.87	0.99	0.91	0.85	0.88	0.90	0.98	1.03	1.00	([1])
United Kingdom . .	2.10	2.34	1.91	1.73	1.85	1.63	1.65	1.60	1.70	1.74	1.75	1.76
Other OECD.	3.79	4.50	4.08	4.50	3.63	3.72	3.90	4.00	3.98	4.01	4.12	5.94
Brazil	0.53	0.78	0.92	1.15	1.03	1.08	1.24	1.26	1.30	1.32	1.33	(NA)
China	0.62	1.12	1.36	1.77	1.74	1.78	1.92	2.08	2.15	2.32	2.28	(NA)
Mexico	0.50	0.67	0.75	1.27	1.45	1.47	1.49	1.52	1.55	1.66	1.72	(NA)
U.S.S.R.	5.31	6.60	7.52	9.00	8.91	8.95	8.98	9.00	8.89	8.74	8.40	(NA)

NA Not available. [1] Included in OECD total.
Source: U.S. Energy Information Administration, *Annual Energy Review,* and *Monthly Energy Review,* August 1991 issue.

No. 951. Energy Producing Companies—Selected Financial and Investment Indicators: 1980 to 1991

[Based on data from major publicly owned domestic crude oil producing companies which either had at least one percent of domestic production or reserves of oil, natural gas, coal, or uranium, or at least one percent of refining capacity or petroleum product sales. There were 26 companies during 1980 and 1982; 25 in 1983; 22 during 1984 through 1987; and 23 in 1988 to 1991]

ITEM	1980	1982	1983	1984	1985	1986	1987	1988	1989	1990	1991
INCOME STATEMENT (bil. dol.)											
Operating revenues	518.6	549.7	511.0	517.4	492.5	378.5	417.4	419.8	433.6	510.4	469.3
Operating expenses	455.9	504.2	462.8	467.3	444.2	354.4	383.7	381.6	397.7	470.1	443.3
Operating income.	62.7	45.5	48.2	50.1	48.3	24.0	33.7	38.2	35.9	40.2	26.0
Pretax income	66.9	45.2	47.4	47.6	43.6	20.6	25.0	34.3	32.3	37.5	25.1
Net income	31.0	21.8	21.9	21.3	17.4	9.2	11.3	22.3	19.8	21.6	14.7
Funds from operations[1]	59.0	60.4	60.7	63.6	63.5	53.1	51.6	57.8	48.3	54.9	47.8
BALANCE SHEET (bil. dol.)											
Net property, plant, and equipment	188.9	265.5	278.4	292.4	297.7	291.1	297.6	293.6	293.2	302.5	305.5
Net investment in place [2]	202.6	282.5	296.3	309.1	315.4	310.0	316.4	309.6	309.9	319.7	325.6
Total assets	333.0	411.9	421.8	442.9	438.4	427.0	443.6	437.8	434.5	457.2	447.1
RATIOS (percent)											
Net income to operating revenues.	6.0	4.0	4.3	4.1	3.5	2.4	2.7	5.3	4.6	4.2	3.1
Net income to total assets.	9.3	5.3	5.2	5.0	4.0	2.2	2.5	5.1	4.6	4.7	3.3
Net income to stockholders' equity	21.1	11.9	11.4	12.1	10.5	5.6	6.8	13.5	12.3	12.9	8.8
Long-term debt to stockholders' equity [3] . .	31.5	37.1	34.8	49.5	54.3	56.0	57.6	56.6	56.4	53.0	54.3
Long-term debt to total assets[3]	13.9	16.6	15.9	20.6	20.5	21.6	21.5	21.3	20.9	19.4	20.3

[1] The sum of net income, depreciation, depletion and amortization, deferred taxes, dry hole expenses, etc. [2] Composed of net property, plant, and equipment plus investment and advances to unconsolidated subsidiaries. [3] Long-term debt includes amounts applicable to capitalized leases.
Source: U.S. Energy Information Administration, *Performance Profiles of Major Energy Producers,* annual.

No. 952. Petroleum and Coal Products Corporations—Sales, Net Profit, and Profit Per Dollar of Sales: 1980 to 1991

[Represents SIC group 29. Profit rates are averages of quarterly figures at annual rates. Beginning 1986, excludes estimates for corporations with less than $250,000 in assets]

ITEM	Unit	1980	1981	1982	1983	1984	1985	1986	1987	1988	1989	1990	1991
Sales	Bil. dol. .	333.2	376.1	357.1	312.7	338.4	320.9	226.5	248.3	252.2	265.3	318.5	282.2
Net profit:													
Before income taxes	Bil. dol. .	39.1	35.3	27.8	27.1	24.5	17.7	9.8	14.2	27.3	23.7	23.3	12.2
After income taxes	Bil. dol. .	25.5	23.7	19.7	19.3	17.2	12.7	8.8	10.9	21.2	19.5	18.0	10.9
Depreciation[1]	Bil. dol. .	11.6	13.7	16.3	17.5	20.7	22.1	21.9	20.3	20.0	18.5	18.7	18.0
Profits per dollar of sales:													
Before income taxes	Cents . .	11.7	9.4	7.8	8.7	7.2	5.5	4.1	5.8	10.8	9.0	7.4	4.3
After income taxes	Cents . .	7.7	6.3	5.5	6.2	5.1	4.0	3.8	4.5	8.5	7.4	5.7	3.9
Profits on stockholders' equity:													
Before income taxes	Percent .	30.7	25.6	18.7	17.8	14.3	11.7	6.8	10.1	19.2	17.8	16.6	8.6
After income taxes	Percent .	20.0	17.2	13.2	12.7	10.0	8.5	6.1	7.7	14.9	14.6	12.8	7.7

[1] Includes depletion and accelerated amortization of emergency facilities.
Source: Through 1981, U.S. Federal Trade Commission; thereafter, U.S. Bureau of the Census, *Quarterly Financial Report for Manufacturing, Mining and Trade Corporations.*

No. 953. Major Petroleum Companies—Financial Data Summary: 1973 to 1991

[Data represent a composite of approximately 42 major worldwide petroleum companies aggregated on a consolidated, total company basis]

ITEM	1973	1975	1980	1983	1984	1985	1986	1987	1988	1989	1990	1991
FINANCIAL DATA (bil. dol.)												
Net income	11.8	11.6	32.9	20.6	22.7	19.4	10.8	15.0	24.6	24.7	26.8	18.6
Depreciation, depletion, etc	10.5	11.3	32.5	37.4	45.3	53.0	43.7	45.0	34.3	33.7	38.7	35.9
Cash flow[1]	22.3	22.8	65.4	58.1	68.0	72.4	54.5	60.0	58.9	58.4	65.5	54.5
Dividends paid	4.0	4.7	9.3	10.5	11.6	12.0	12.1	12.4	14.0	16.0	15.9	14.3
Net internal funds available for investment												
or debt repayment[2]	18.3	18.1	56.1	47.6	56.4	60.4	42.4	47.6	44.9	42.4	49.6	38.2
Capital and exploratory expenditures . . .	16.3	26.9	62.1	50.7	57.5	58.3	38.3	50.1	62.4	55.1	59.6	62.2
Long-term capitalization	102.9	121.1	211.4	240.0	285.7	272.1	279.9	282.2	287.8	290.0	300.0	306.8
Long-term debt	22.5	28.9	49.8	61.0	95.8	93.5	95.5	88.4	88.5	91.4	90.4	96.4
Preferred stock	0.4	0.4	2.0	3.5	5.2	3.3	3.7	4.1	4.5	6.4	5.2	4.5
Common stock and retained earnings[3] .	80.0	91.9	159.6	175.5	184.7	175.3	180.7	189.7	194.8	192.2	204.4	205.9
Excess of expenditures over cash												
income[4]	-2.0	8.9	6.0	3.1	1.1	-2.1	3.0	-2.5	17.5	12.7	10.0	24.0
RATIOS[5] (percent)												
Long-term debt to long-term												
capitalization	22.0	23.8	23.6	25.4	33.5	34.4	34.1	31.3	30.8	31.5	30.1	31.4
Net income to total average capital	12.0	10.0	17.0	8.8	8.6	7.0	4.0	4.6	8.6	8.3	9.1	6.1
Net income to average common equity. .	15.6	13.1	22.5	12.0	12.5	10.8	6.2	7.3	12.8	12.4	13.5	9.1

[1] Generally represents internally-generated funds from operations. Sum of net income and noncash charges such as depreciation, depletion, and amortization. [2] Cash flow minus dividends paid. [3] Includes common stock, capital surplus, and earned surplus accounts after adjustments. [4] Capital and exploratory expenditures plus dividends paid minus cash flow. [5] Represents approximate year-to-year comparisons because of changes in the makeup of the group due to mergers and other corporate changes.
Source: Carl H. Pforzheimer & Co., New York, NY, *Comparative Oil Company Statements, 1991-1990*, and earlier reports.

No. 954. Electric Utility Sales and Average Prices, by End-Use Sector: 1970 to 1991

[Prior to 1980, covers Class A and B privately-owned electric utilities; thereafter, Class A utilities whose electric operating revenues were $100 million or more during the previous year]

YEAR	SALES (bil. kWh)				AVERAGE PRICE OF ELECTRICITY SOLD (cents per kWh)							
					Current dollars				Constant (1987) dollars[2]			
	Total[1]	Resi-dential	Com-mer-cial	Indus-trial	Total[1]	Resi-dential	Com-mer-cial	Indus-trial	Total[1]	Resi-dential	Com-mer-cial	Indus-trial
1970	1,392	466	307	571	1.7	2.2	2.1	1.0	4.8	6.3	6.0	2.8
1973	1,713	579	388	686	2.0	2.5	2.4	1.3	4.8	6.1	5.8	3.1
1975	1,747	588	403	688	2.9	3.5	3.5	2.1	5.9	7.1	7.1	4.3
1980	2,094	717	488	815	4.7	5.4	5.5	3.7	6.6	7.5	7.7	5.2
1981	2,147	722	514	826	5.5	6.2	6.3	4.3	7.0	7.9	8.0	5.4
1982	2,086	730	526	745	6.1	6.9	6.9	5.0	7.3	8.2	8.2	6.0
1983	2,151	751	544	776	6.3	7.2	7.0	5.0	7.2	8.3	8.0	5.7
1984	2,286	780	583	838	6.3	7.2	7.1	4.8	6.9	7.9	7.8	5.3
1985	2,324	794	606	837	6.4	7.4	7.3	5.0	6.8	7.8	7.7	5.3
1986	2,369	819	631	831	6.4	7.4	7.2	4.9	6.6	7.6	7.4	5.1
1987	2,457	850	660	858	6.4	7.5	7.1	4.8	6.4	7.4	7.1	4.8
1988	2,578	893	699	896	6.4	7.5	7.0	4.7	6.2	7.2	6.7	4.5
1989	2,647	906	726	926	6.5	7.6	7.2	4.7	6.0	7.0	6.6	4.3
1990	2,713	924	751	946	6.6	7.8	7.3	4.7	5.8	6.9	6.5	4.2
1991	2,759	957	765	941	6.8	8.1	7.5	4.9	5.8	6.9	6.4	4.2

[1] Includes other sectors not shown separately. [2] Based on the GNP implicit price deflator.
Source: U.S. Energy Information Administration, *Annual Energy Review.*

No. 955. Electric Utility Industry—Net Generation, Net Summer Capability, Generating Units, and Consumption of Fuels: 1970 to 1991

[Net Generation for **calendar years**; other data as of **December 31.** See also *Historical Statistics, Colonial Times to 1970,* series S 32-52, S 78-82, and S 86-107]

ITEM	Unit	1970	1975	1980	1985	1986	1987	1988	1989	1990	1991
NET GENERATION											
Total	Bil. kWh	**1,532**	**1,918**	**2,286**	**2,470**	**2,487**	**2,572**	**2,704**	**2,784**	**2,808**	**2,823**
Average annual change [1]	Percent	7.3	4.5	3.5	0.4	0.7	3.4	4.9	2.9	0.9	0.5
Net generation, kWh per kW of net summer capability [2]	Rate	4,554	3,903	3,952	3,771	3,741	3,816	3,990	4,067	4,070	4,068
Investor owned	Bil. kWh	1,183	1,487	1,783	1,918	1,928	2,022	2,146	2,192	2,203	2,213
Percent of total utilities	Percent	77.2	77.5	78.0	77.7	77.5	78.6	79.4	78.7	78.4	78.4
Publicly owned	Bil. kWh	349	431	503	552	559	550	559	592	606	610
Municipal	Bil. kWh	71	82	87	74	79	86	97	100	98	97
Federal	Bil. kWh	186	221	235	233	225	205	201	224	235	241
Cooperatives and other	Bil. kWh	91	128	182	245	255	258	261	269	273	272
Source of energy:											
Coal [3]	Percent	46.0	44.6	51.0	57.2	56.2	57.4	57.4	56.2	55.5	54.9
Nuclear	Percent	1.4	9.0	11.0	15.5	16.6	17.7	19.5	19.0	20.5	21.7
Oil	Percent	12.0	15.1	10.8	4.1	5.5	4.6	5.5	5.7	4.2	3.9
Gas	Percent	24.3	15.6	15.1	11.8	10.0	10.6	9.3	9.6	9.4	9.4
Hydro	Percent	16.2	15.6	12.1	11.4	11.7	9.7	8.2	9.5	10.0	9.8
Type of prime mover: [4]											
Hydro	Bil. kWh	248	300	276	281	291	250	223	265	280	275
Steam conventional [5]	Bil. kWh	1,240	1,414	1,726	1,778	1,756	1,837	1,921	1,950	1,919	1,902
Gas turbine and internal combustion	Bil. kWh	22	28	28	16	15	18	22	29	22	22
Steam nuclear	Bil. kWh	22	173	251	384	414	455	527	529	577	613
Other	Bil. kWh	1	3	6	11	12	12	12	11	11	10
NET SUMMER CAPABILITY											
Total [6]	Mil. kW	**336**	**491**	**579**	**655**	**665**	**674**	**678**	**685**	**690**	**694**
Average annual change [1]	Percent	7.2	7.6	3.3	0.6	1.5	1.4	0.5	1.1	0.7	0.6
Hydro	Mil. kW	64	78	82	89	89	90	90	91	91	92
Steam conventional [7]	Mil. kW	248	333	397	437	441	440	442	444	447	448
Gas turbine	Mil. kW	13	37	43	44	43	44	44	45	46	48
Steam nuclear	Mil. kW	7	37	52	79	85	94	95	98	100	100
Internal combustion	Mil. kW	4	5	5	5	5	5	5	5	5	5
Geothermal and other	Mil. kW	(Z)	1	1	2	2	2	2	2	2	2
NUMBER OF GENERATING UNITS											
Total [8]	Number	**9,717**	**(NA)**	**11,084**	**(NA)**	**10,611**	**10,406**	**10,305**	**10,325**	**10,296**	**10,260**
Hydro	Number	3,108	(NA)	3,275	(NA)	3,489	3,488	3,496	3,479	3,479	3,476
Steam conventional	Number	2,813	(NA)	2,862	(NA)	2,536	2,437	2,383	2,363	2,354	2,284
Gas turbine	Number	658	(NA)	1,447	(NA)	1,439	1,408	1,397	1,438	1,460	1,485
Steam nuclear	Number	16	(NA)	74	(NA)	99	109	108	110	111	111
Internal combustion	Number	3,118	(NA)	3,410	(NA)	2,998	2,917	2,872	2,889	2,847	2,803
CONSUMPTION OF FUELS											
Net generation by fuel [9]	Bil. kWh	**1,284**	**1,618**	**2,010**	**2,189**	**2,197**	**2,322**	**2,481**	**2,519**	**2,525**	**(NA)**
Average annual change [1]	Percent	52.5	3.2	2.1	4.3	0.4	5.4	6.4	1.4	0.2	(NA)
Coal	Bil. kWh	704	853	1,162	1,402	1,386	1,464	1,541	1,554	1,557	(NA)
Percent of total	Percent	54.8	52.7	57.8	64.0	63.1	63.0	62.1	61.7	61.7	(NA)
Petroleum	Bil. kWh	184	289	246	100	137	118	149	158	117	(NA)
Gas	Bil. kWh	373	300	346	292	249	273	253	267	263	(NA)
Nuclear	Bil. kWh	22	173	251	384	414	455	527	529	577	(NA)
Fuel consumed:											
Total energy equivalent	Quad. Btu	13.40	15.19	18.57	18.79	18.59	19.37	20.12	20.56	20.28	(NA)
Coal	Mil. sh. tons	320	406	569	694	685	718	758	767	773	772
Oil	Mil. bbl.	339	506	421	175	232	201	250	267	200	189
Gas	Bil cu. ft.	3,932	3,158	3,682	3,044	2,602	2,844	2,636	2,787	2,787	2,781

NA Not available.   Z Less than 0.5 million kW.   [1] Change from immediate prior year except for 1970, change from 1960. For explanation of average annual percent change, see Guide to Tabular Presentation.   [2] Net summer capability is the steady hourly output that generating equipment is expected to supply to system load, exclusive of auxiliary power as demonstrated by test at the time of summer peak demand.   [3] Includes small percentage (.5 percent) from wood and waste, geothermal, and petroleum coke.   [4] A prime mover is the engine, turbine, water wheel, or similar machine which drives an electric generator.   [5] Fossil fuels only.   [6] Includes wind, solar thermal, and photovoltaic, not shown separately.   [7] Includes fossil steam, wood, and waste.   [8] Each prime mover type in combination plants counted separately. Includes geothermal, wind, and solar, not shown separately.   [9] Includes small amounts of wood, waste, wind, geothermal, solar thermal, and photovoltaic.

Source: 1970, U.S. Federal Power Commission, *Electric Power Statistics,* and press releases; thereafter, U.S. Energy Information Administration, 1975 and 1980, *Power Production, Fuel Consumption, and Installed Capacity Data-Annual,* and unpublished data; thereafter, *Electric Power Annual, Annual Energy Review,* and unpublished data.

No. 956. Electric Utility Industry—Capability, Peak Load, and Capacity Margin: 1970 to 1991

[Excludes Alaska and Hawaii. Capability represents the maximum kilowatt output with all power sources available and with hydraulic equipment under actual water conditions, allowing for maintenance, emergency outages, and system operating requirements. Capacity margin is the difference between capability and peak load]

| YEAR | CAPABILITY AT THE TIME OF— | | | | NON-COINCIDENT PEAK LOAD | | CAPACITY MARGIN | | | |
| | Summer peak load (1,000 kW) | | Winter peak load[1] (1,000 kW) | | | | Summer | | Winter[1] | |
	Amount	Change from prior year[2]	Amount	Change from prior year[2]	Summer	Winter[1]	Amount (1,000 kW)	Percent of capability	Amount (1,000 kW)	Percent of capability
1970	326,900	26,600	339,050	27,600	274,650	248,550	52,250	16.0	90,500	26.7
1975	479,300	34,900	492,450	25,050	356,800	331,100	122,500	25.6	161,350	32.8
1977	516,000	17,250	537,600	26,600	396,350	360,200	119,650	23.2	177,400	33.0
1978	545,700	29,700	561,550	23,950	408,050	383,100	137,650	25.2	178,450	31.8
1979 [3]	544,506	(X)	554,525	(X)	398,424	368,876	146,082	26.8	185,649	33.5
1980	558,237	13,731	572,195	17,670	427,058	384,567	131,179	23.5	187,628	32.8
1981	572,219	13,982	586,569	14,374	429,349	397,800	142,870	25.0	188,769	32.2
1982	586,142	13,923	598,066	11,497	415,618	373,985	170,524	29.1	224,081	37.5
1983	596,449	10,307	612,453	14,387	447,526	410,779	148,923	25.0	201,674	32.9
1984	604,240	7,791	622,125	9,672	451,150	436,374	153,090	25.3	185,751	29.9
1985	621,597	17,357	636,475	14,350	460,503	423,660	161,094	25.9	212,815	33.4
1986	633,291	11,694	646,721	10,246	476,320	422,857	156,971	24.8	223,864	34.6
1987	648,118	14,827	662,977	16,256	496,185	448,277	151,933	23.4	214,700	32.4
1988	661,580	13,462	676,940	13,963	529,460	466,533	132,120	20.0	210,407	31.1
1989	673,316	11,736	685,249	8,309	523,432	496,378	149,884	22.3	188,871	27.6
1990	685,091	11,775	696,757	11,508	545,537	484,014	139,554	20.4	212,743	30.5
1991	690,915	5,824	703,212	6,455	551,320	485,435	139,595	20.2	217,777	31.0

X Not applicable.   [1] 1970 is for the month of December.   [2] For 1970 and 1975, change from 1969 and 1974, respectively.
[3] Beginning 1979, data are not entirely comparable with prior years due to change in data source.

Source: Edison Electric Institute, Washington, DC, *Statistical Yearbook of the Electric Utility Industry,* annual.

No. 957. Electric Energy Sales, by Class of Service, 1970 to 1991, and by State, 1991

[In billions of kilowatthours]

REGION, DIVISION, AND STATE	Total[1]	Residential	Commercial	Industrial	REGION, DIVISION, AND STATE	Total[1]	Residential	Commercial	Industrial
1970	1,392.3	466.3	306.7	570.9	**South**	1,155.6	432.6	289.8	394.8
1973	1,712.9	579.2	388.3	686.1	**South Atlantic**	545.8	218.5	157.3	152.5
1975	1,747.1	588.1	403.0	687.7	Delaware	8.5	2.8	2.4	3.2
1980	2,094.4	717.5	488.2	815.1	Maryland	51.1	20.3	10.7	19.4
1985	2,309.5	791.0	609.0	824.5	Dist. of Columbia	10.2	1.6	5.2	3.1
1987	2,457.3	850.4	660.4	858.2	Virginia	75.1	29.6	21.2	16.0
1988	2,578.1	892.9	699.1	896.5	West Virginia	23.6	8.1	5.2	10.2
1989	2,646.8	905.5	725.9	925.7	North Carolina	92.3	34.4	24.7	31.5
1990	2,712.6	924.0	751.0	945.5	South Carolina	57.1	18.7	12.2	25.4
					Georgia	81.5	30.2	23.2	27.2
1991, total	2,762.0	955.4	765.7	946.6	Florida	146.3	72.8	52.4	16.5
					East South Central	236.8	82.1	40.2	109.6
Northeast	413.7	137.5	142.9	117.2	Kentucky	64.2	18.6	9.9	32.9
New England	103.2	37.1	37.7	26.3	Tennessee	78.4	29.6	12.1	35.7
Maine	11.4	3.8	2.7	4.7	Alabama	61.2	21.3	11.3	28.0
New Hampshire	8.8	3.4	2.0	3.3	Mississippi	33.0	12.5	6.8	13.0
Vermont	4.7	1.8	1.5	1.4	**West South Central**	372.9	132.0	92.3	132.6
Massachusetts	44.8	15.4	18.5	9.8	Arkansas	28.4	11.0	6.3	10.5
Rhode Island	6.4	2.4	2.5	1.4	Louisiana	64.7	21.6	14.0	26.6
Connecticut	27.2	10.4	10.5	5.8	Oklahoma	39.4	15.3	10.6	11.4
Middle Atlantic	310.4	100.3	105.2	90.9	Texas	240.4	84.1	61.4	84.1
New York	129.4	39.2	47.0	31.1	**West**	520.9	166.8	163.5	171.3
New Jersey	64.7	21.5	27.6	15.0	**Mountain**	163.1	50.9	51.0	54.8
Pennsylvania	116.3	39.6	30.6	44.7	Montana	13.4	3.5	2.8	6.6
Midwest	671.9	218.6	169.5	263.2	Idaho	18.0	6.0	4.9	6.9
East North Central	475.1	145.2	116.6	198.0	Wyoming	11.8	1.8	2.3	7.5
Ohio	145.7	40.9	32.3	67.9	Colorado	31.5	10.1	13.7	6.7
Indiana	77.0	24.2	16.4	35.8	New Mexico	14.1	3.7	4.5	4.5
Illinois	116.9	36.0	33.1	39.7	Arizona	41.8	15.6	14.0	10.4
Michigan	84.5	26.8	21.5	35.0	Utah	15.9	4.5	4.7	5.9
Wisconsin	51.0	17.3	13.3	19.7	Nevada	16.6	5.8	4.0	6.2
West North Central	196.7	73.4	52.9	65.2	**Pacific**	357.8	115.9	112.5	116.6
Minnesota	48.8	15.7	8.4	23.9	Washington	92.7	29.9	18.1	40.8
Iowa	30.8	11.2	7.1	11.7	Oregon	43.7	15.9	11.6	15.3
Missouri	56.5	23.4	19.1	13.1	California	208.7	66.0	78.4	56.2
North Dakota	7.3	3.1	1.9	1.8	Alaska	4.3	1.6	2.0	0.5
South Dakota	6.7	3.0	1.5	1.7	Hawaii	8.5	2.4	2.3	3.8
Nebraska	18.6	7.1	5.3	4.7					
Kansas	28.2	9.9	9.6	8.3					

[1] Includes other service not shown separately.

Source: U.S. Energy Information Association, *Electric Power Annual* and *Electric Power Monthly,* December 1991 issue.

No. 958. Electric Energy—Net Generation and Net Summer Capability, by State: 1980 to 1991

[Capacity as of Dec. 31. Covers utilities for public use]

DIVISION AND STATE	NET GENERATION (bil. kWh) 1980	1990	1991 Total	1991 Percent from coal	NET SUMMER CAPABILITY (mil. kW) 1990	1991	DIVISION AND STATE	NET GENERATION (bil. kWh) 1980	1990	1991 Total	1991 Percent from coal	NET SUMMER CAPABILITY (mil. kW) 1990	1991
U.S.	2,286.4	2,808.2	2,821.6	54.9	690.5	693.0	VA	34.3	47.2	48.9	44.8	13.7	13.7
							WV	70.8	77.4	71.3	99.2	14.4	14.4
N.E	78.2	94.1	87.1	19.7	23.4	23.2	NC	72.1	79.8	83.5	56.0	20.2	20.1
ME	7.9	9.1	9.5	-	2.4	2.4	SC	41.9	69.3	69.8	33.2	14.9	16.2
NH	6.0	10.8	12.7	25.0	2.6	2.6	GA	63.3	97.6	90.8	66.1	20.7	20.8
VT	3.8	5.0	5.3	-	1.1	1.1	FL	95.9	123.6	130.6	46.8	32.7	32.7
MA	34.8	36.5	35.9	33.0	9.9	9.8	E.S.C	214.1	246.9	257.8	71.7	59.5	58.5
RI	1.0	0.6	0.2	-	0.3	0.3	KY	57.1	73.8	75.5	95.0	15.5	15.3
CT	24.7	32.2	23.6	9.0	7.1	7.1	TN	60.2	73.9	73.9	63.1	17.0	16.3
M.A	260.5	330.8	325.5	40.1	78.4	78.4	AL	78.3	76.2	85.1	68.1	20.0	19.9
NY	108.6	128.7	126.1	19.8	31.2	31.3	MS	18.5	22.9	23.3	37.1	7.0	7.0
NJ	29.4	36.5	37.0	14.1	13.7	13.7	W.S.C	313.1	374.3	378.1	48.2	101.2	101.5
PA	122.5	165.7	162.4	61.8	33.4	33.3	AR	19.7	37.1	38.4	51.0	9.6	9.6
E.N.C	397.0	485.8	499.9	73.1	113.1	113.7	LA	45.7	58.2	57.0	33.2	16.8	16.8
OH	110.2	126.5	132.1	88.0	27.0	27.5	OK	44.6	45.1	44.9	58.0	12.8	12.8
IN	70.6	97.7	98.2	98.3	20.6	20.8	TX	203.0	234.0	237.9	49.5	62.0	62.2
IL	103.4	127.0	127.9	42.2	32.6	32.6	Mt	158.8	247.4	248.6	73.3	49.3	49.4
MI	74.8	89.1	94.6	69.1	22.3	22.3	MT	15.5	25.7	28.2	57.3	4.9	4.8
WI	37.8	45.6	47.1	71.0	10.6	10.5	ID	9.5	8.6	8.3	-	2.3	2.3
W.N.C . . .	168.2	218.4	219.7	74.6	54.2	54.6	WY	22.4	39.4	38.7	97.9	5.8	5.8
MN	31.5	41.6	38.9	63.4	8.8	8.9	CO	23.6	31.3	31.0	93.3	6.6	6.6
IA	21.8	29.0	31.2	82.8	8.0	8.1	NM	24.7	28.5	25.1	88.3	5.0	5.0
MO	48.9	59.0	60.1	79.7	15.2	15.3	AZ	36.9	62.3	66.8	48.4	14.9	14.9
ND	15.8	26.8	27.5	93.5	4.5	4.5	UT	12.1	32.3	30.2	95.8	4.8	4.8
SD	8.6	6.4	6.6	41.5	2.7	2.7	NV	14.1	19.3	20.4	77.7	4.9	5.1
NE	16.3	21.6	23.0	59.0	5.5	5.5	Pac	278.8	276.7	264.0	4.2	82.1	82.1
KS	25.1	33.9	32.3	72.4	9.6	9.6	WA	92.3	100.5	101.3	7.8	24.2	24.2
S.A	417.8	533.8	540.9	57.5	129.2	131.5	OR	36.6	49.2	46.3	6.1	11.2	11.2
DE	6.7	7.1	7.6	60.9	2.0	2.2	CA	140.3	114.5	104.8	-	43.7	43.6
MD	32.2	31.5	38.2	59.2	9.8	10.7	AK	3.1	4.5	4.3	7.6	1.5	1.5
DC	0.7	0.4	0.2	-	0.8	0.8	HI	6.5	8.0	7.3	-	1.5	1.5

- Represents zero.

Source: U.S. Energy Information Administration, 1980, *Power Production, Fuel Consumption, and Installed Capacity Data*, annual;

No. 959. Nuclear Power Plants—Number of Units, Net Generation, and Net Summer Capability, by State: 1991

REGION, DIVISION, AND STATE	Number of units	NET GENERATION Total (mil. kWh)	Percent of total[1]	NET SUMMER CAPABILITY Total (mil. kW)	Percent of total[1]	REGION, DIVISION, AND STATE	Number of units	NET GENERATION Total (mil. kWh)	Percent of total[1]	NET SUMMER CAPABILITY Total (mil. kW)	Percent of total[1]
U.S.. . . .	111	612,596	21.7	99.6	14.4	KS	1	5,859	18.1	1.1	11.8
Northeast . .	28	144,551	35.0	24.0	23.6	South	42	240,909	20.5	39.2	13.4
N.E	9	33,820	38.8	6.6	28.3	S.A	27	152,866	28.3	23.6	17.9
ME	1	6,264	65.8	0.9	36.0	MD	2	9,036	23.6	1.7	15.4
NH	1	6,788	53.5	1.2	44.1	VA	4	23,886	48.8	3.4	24.8
VT	1	4,108	78.1	0.5	45.5	NC	5	30,312	36.3	4.6	23.0
MA	2	4,417	12.3	0.8	8.5	SC	7	43,108	61.7	6.4	39.4
CT	4	12,243	52.0	3.2	45.5	GA	4	26,016	28.6	3.7	17.9
M.A	19	110,731	34.0	17.5	22.3	FL	5	20,508	15.7	3.8	11.7
NY	6	28,448	22.6	4.9	15.5	E.S.C	8	41,625	16.1	8.2	14.0
NJ	4	24,807	67.0	3.9	28.1	TN	5	16,587	22.4	2.2	13.8
PA	9	57,476	35.4	8.7	26.2	AL	5	15,875	18.7	4.8	24.3
Midwest . .	31	164,804	22.9	25.7	15.2	MS	1	9,164	39.3	1.1	16.3
E.N.C	23	124,712	24.9	20.1	17.7	W.S.C. . . .	7	46,418	12.3	7.4	7.2
OH	2	14,833	11.2	2.0	7.4	AR	2	12,662	33.0	1.7	17.6
IL	13	71,866	56.2	12.6	38.6	LA	2	13,956	24.5	2.0	12.0
MI	5	27,021	28.6	3.9	17.7	TX	3	19,800	8.3	3.7	5.9
WI	3	10,991	23.3	1.5	14.4	West	10	62,333	12.2	10.8	8.2
W.N.C . . .	8	40,092	18.2	5.6	10.2	Mt	3	25,096	10.1	3.8	7.7
MN	3	12,059	31.0	1.5	17.4	AZ	3	25,096	37.6	3.8	25.6
IA	1	4,147	13.3	0.5	6.4	Pac	7	37,237	14.8	7.0	8.5
MO	1	9,979	16.6	1.1	7.3	WA	1	4,230	4.2	1.1	4.5
NE	2	8,048	35.0	1.3	23.0	OR	1	1,465	3.2	1.1	9.8
						CA	5	31,542	30.1	4.7	10.9

[1] For total capability and generation, see table 958.

Source: U.S. Energy Information Administration, *Electric Power Annual* and *Electric Power Monthly*, December 1991 issue.

No. 960. Nuclear Power Plants—Number, Capacity, and Generation: 1965 to 1992

ITEM	1965	1970	1975	1980	1985	1986	1987	1988	1989	1990	1991	1992
Operable generating units[1]	6	18	54	70	95	100	107	108	110	111	111	109
Net summer capability[1][2] (mil. kW). .	0.8	7.0	37.3	51.8	79.4	85.2	93.6	94.7	98.2	99.6	99.6	99.0
Electricity generated (bil. kWh)	0.4	21.8	172.5	251.1	383.7	414.0	455.3	527.0	529.4	576.9	612.6	618.8
Percent of total electric utility generation	0.3	1.4	9.0	11.0	15.5	16.6	17.7	19.5	19.0	20.5	21.7	22.1
Capacity factor[3]	(NA)	(NA)	55.9	56.3	58.0	56.9	57.4	63.5	62.2	66.0	70.2	70.9

NA Not available.   [1] As of yearend.   [2] Net summer capability is the peak steady hourly output that generating equipment is expected to supply to system load, exclusive of auxiliary and other powerplant, as demonstrated by test at the time of summer peak demand.   [3] Weighted average of monthly capacity factors. Monthly factors are derived by dividing actual monthly generation by the maximum possible generation for the month (hours in month times net maximum dependable capacity).

Source: U.S. Energy Information Administration, *Annual Energy Review.*

No. 961. Commercial Nuclear Power Generation, by Country: 1970 to 1992

[Generation for **calendar years**; other data as of **December**]

COUNTRY	REACTORS				GROSS ELECTRICITY GENERATED (bil. kWh)				GROSS CAPACITY (1,000 kW)			
	1970	1980	1990	1992	1970	1980	1990	1992	1970	1980	1990	1992
Total	64	208	368	364	73.9	617.8	1,743.9	1,868.3	15,186	128,847	301,745	304,326
United States . .	15	74	112	112	23.2	265.2	606.4	650.1	5,211	56,529	105,998	106,054
Argentina	-	1	2	2	-	2.3	7.0	6.8	-	357	1,005	1,005
Belgium	1	3	7	7	0.3	12.5	42.7	43.5	11	1,744	5,740	5,740
Brazil.	-	-	1	1	-	-	2.0	1.7	-	-	657	657
Canada	1	9	19	20	0.9	40.4	74.0	81.3	220	5,588	13,855	14,841
China: Taiwan . .	-	2	6	6	-	8.2	32.9	33.8	-	1,272	5,146	5,146
Finland.	-	4	4	4	-	7.0	18.9	19.0	-	2,296	2,400	2,400
France	4	22	58	57	5.7	61.2	314.1	337.6	1,606	15,412	58,862	60,281
Germany	4	11	22	22	5.3	43.7	147.2	158.8	907	8,996	23,973	24,083
Great Britain . . .	27	33	42	37	26.5	37.2	68.8	78.5	4,783	9,012	15,274	14,656
Hungary	-	-	4	4	-	-	13.6	13.9	-	-	1,760	1,840
India	2	4	6	8	2.2	2.9	6.0	6.3	400	860	1,330	1,800
Italy	3	4	2	-	3.3	2.2	-	-	631	1,490	1,132	-
Japan.	3	22	40	42	3.3	81.0	191.9	215.8	828	15,117	31,645	33,399
Mexico	-	-	1	1	-	-	2.1	3.9	-	-	675	675
Netherlands . . .	1	2	2	2	0.4	4.2	3.4	3.8	55	529	540	540
Pakistan	-	1	1	1	-	0.1	0.4	0.5	-	137	137	137
Slovenia [1]	-	-	1	1	-	-	4.6	4	-	-	664	664
South Africa . . .	-	-	2	2	-	-	8.9	9.9	-	-	1,930	1,930
South Korea . . .	-	1	9	9	-	3.5	52.8	56.4	-	587	7,616	7,616
Spain.	1	3	10	9	0.9	5.2	54.3	55.8	160	1,117	7,984	7,405
Sweden	1	8	12	12	(Z)	26.7	68.2	63.5	12	5,770	10,344	10,359
Switzerland . . .	1	4	5	5	1.9	14.3	23.6	23.4	364	2,034	3,079	3,099

- Represents zero.   Z Less than 50 million kWh.   [1] Formerly Yugoslavia.
Source: McGraw-Hill, Inc., New York, NY, *Nucleonics Week,* March issues (copyright).

No. 962. Uranium Supply, Enrichment, and Discharged Commercial Reactor Fuel: 1970 to 1991

[Years ending **Dec. 31**, except as noted. For additional data on uranium, see section 25 on mining. For explanation of kilogram, see weights and measures]

ITEM	Unit	1970	1975	1980	1985	1986	1987	1988	1989	1990	1991
URANIUM CONCENTRATE											
Production	Mil. lb	25.81	23.20	43.70	11.31	13.51	12.99	13.13	13.84	8.89	7.95
Exports.	Mil. lb	4.20	1.00	5.80	5.30	1.60	1.00	3.30	2.10	2.00	2.00
Imports.	Mil. lb		1.40	3.60	11.70	13.50	15.10	15.80	13.10	23.70	14.00
Delivered price.	Dol./lb	(NA)	10.50	26.00	31.43	30.01	27.37	25.65	19.56	15.70	13.66
ENRICHMENT [1]											
Enriched product [2]	Mil. Swu[3] . .	5.10	9.92	10.69	10.2	8.6	8.1	9.9	11.9	10.2	10.3
For domestic customers . . .	Mil. Swu[3] . .	3.74	4.36	6.89	6.0	4.9	3.4	6.3	7.6	6.8	6.7
For foreign customers	Mil. Swu[3] . .	1.36	5.56	3.80	4.2	3.7	4.7	3.6	4.3	3.4	3.6
Sales	Mil. dol . . .	(NA)	376	1,379	1,403	1,085	921	1,094	1,320	1,148	1,156
DISCHARGED COMMERCIAL REACTOR FUEL [4]											
Annual discharge	Metric tons.	82	499	1,193	1,330	1,431	1,615	(NA)	(NA)	(NA)	(NA)
Inventory, yearend [5]	Metric tons.	118	1,538	6,434	12,481	13,881	(NA)	(NA)	(NA)	(NA)	(NA)

- Represents zero.   NA Not available.   [1] Beginning 1984, represents fiscal years.   [2] Based on sales.   [3] Separative work units. The standard measure of enrichment services is based on operating tails assay in effect at the time the enriched product was placed in inventory.   [4] Uranium content. Source: Nuclear Assurance Corporation, Atlanta, GA.   [5] Reprocessed fuel not included as inventory.

Source: Except as noted, U.S. Energy Information Administration, *Annual Energy Review, Uranium Industry Annual* and unpublished data.

No. 963. Electric Utilities—Generation, Sales, Revenue, and Customers: 1970 to 1991

[Sales and revenue are to and from ultimate customers]

CLASS	Unit....	1970	1975	1980	1985	1986	1987	1988	1989	1990	1991, prel.
Generation [1]	Bil. kWh.	1,532	1,918	2,286	2,470	2,487	2,572	2,704	2,784	2,808	2,822
Sales [2]	Bil. kWh	1,391	1,733	2,126	2,306	2,355	2,435	2,554	2,621	2,684	2,732
Residential or domestic....	Bil. kWh.	448	586	734	793	820	846	886	899	916	949
Percent of total........	Percent .	32.2	33.8	34.5	34.4	34.8	34.8	34.7	34.3	34.1	34.7
Commercial [3]...........	Bil. kWh.	313	418	524	606	629	658	698	716	739	755
Industrial [4]...........	Bil. kWh.	573	662	794	820	819	844	882	913	932	929
Revenue [2]..........	Bil. dol .	22.1	46.9	95.5	149.2	152.5	155.7	162.4	169.6	176.5	183.0
Residential or domestic....	Bil. dol .	9.4	18.8	37.6	58.6	60.9	63.0	66.4	68.8	71.7	75.7
Percent of total........	Percent .	42.7	40.1	39.4	39.3	39.9	40.5	40.9	40.5	40.6	41.3
Commercial [3]..........	Bil. dol .	6.3	13.5	27.4	44.1	45.4	46.7	49.1	51.6	54.2	56.3
Industrial [4]..........	Bil. dol .	5.4	12.7	27.3	41.4	40.9	40.6	41.6	43.7	44.9	45.0
Ultimate customers, Dec. 31 [2]	Million..	72.5	81.8	92.7	101.6	103.0	104.6	106.4	108.5	110.1	111.1
Residential or domestic....	Million..	64.0	72.6	82.2	89.8	91.0	92.4	93.9	95.6	97.0	97.9
Commercial [3]...........	Million..	7.9	8.6	9.7	10.9	11.1	11.4	11.6	12.0	12.1	12.3
Industrial [4]...........	Million..	0.4	0.4	0.5	0.5	0.5	0.5	0.5	0.5	0.5	0.5
Avg. kWh used per customer.	1,000...	19.4	21.4	23.2	22.9	23.1	23.5	24.2	24.4	24.6	24.7
Residential...........	1,000...	7.1	8.2	9.0	8.9	9.1	9.2	9.5	9.5	9.5	9.7
Commercial [3]..........	1,000...	40.0	49.0	54.5	56.1	57.2	58.4	60.4	60.6	61.3	61.9
Avg. annual bill per customer	Dollar ..	307	579	1,040	1,482	1,494	1,501	1,536	1,576	1,614	1,655
Residential...........	Dollar ..	149	262	462	658	675	688	712	725	744	777
Commercial [3]..........	Dollar ..	804	1,580	2,848	4,080	4,127	4,147	4,256	4,363	4,494	4,611
Avg. revenue per kWh sold .	Cents ..	1.59	2.70	4.49	6.47	6.47	6.39	6.36	6.47	6.57	6.70
Residential [3]...........	Cents ..	2.10	3.21	5.12	7.39	7.43	7.45	7.49	7.65	7.83	7.98
Commercial [3]..........	Cents ..	2.01	3.23	5.22	7.27	7.22	7.10	7.04	7.20	7.33	7.45
Industrial [4]..........	Cents ..	0.95	1.92	3.44	5.04	4.99	4.82	4.71	4.79	4.81	4.85

[1] Source: 1970 and 1975, U.S. Federal Power Commission; thereafter, U.S. Energy Information Administration, *Monthly Energy Review*, monthly.   [2] Includes other types not shown separately.   [3] Small light and power.   [4] Large light and power.
Source: Except as noted, Edison Electric Institute, Washington, DC, *Statistical Yearbook*.

No. 964. Major Investor-Owned Electric Utilities—Balance Sheet and Income Account of Privately Owned Companies: 1981 to 1990

[In billions of dollars. As of Dec. 31. Covers approximately 180 investor-owned electric utilities that during each of the last 3 years met any one or more of the following conditions — 1 mil. megawatthours of total sales; 100 megawatthours of sales for resale, 500 megawatthours of gross interc 500 megawatthours of wheeling for other. See also *Historical Statistics, Colonial Times to 1970*, series S 133-146 and V 197-212]

ITEM	1981	1982	1983	1984	1985	1986	1987	1988	1989	1990
COMPOSITE BALANCE SHEET										
Assets and other debits....	**285.1**	**315.0**	**342.4**	**375.6**	**404.7**	**426.1**	**446.3**	**454.3**	**465.7**	**477.9**
Electric utility plant [1]	291.6	321.2	347.9	364.7	396.9	419.5	434.6	449.4	462.4	480.6
Depreciation and amortization....	*61.1*	*67.6*	*74.3*	*77.1*	*85.1*	*93.9*	*103.2*	*113.5*	*125.0*	*135.7*
Net electric utility plant........	230.5	253.6	273.6	287.5	311.8	325.6	331.4	335.9	337.5	344.9
Other utility plant...........	15.7	16.7	17.5	17.6	19.9	21.2	23.1	24.6	26.3	28.5
Depreciation and amortization....	*4.9*	*5.3*	*5.8*	*6.1*	*6.5*	*7.2*	*7.8*	*8.5*	*9.2*	*9.9*
Net other utility plant..........	10.8	11.4	11.8	12.1	13.4	14.0	15.2	16.1	17.1	18.6
Total utility plant.............	307.3	337.9	365.5	395.3	431.1	455.9	475.7	493.0	507.9	528.7
Depreciation and amortization....	*66.0*	*72.9*	*80.1*	*88.0*	*97.4*	*107.7*	*118.7*	*131.3*	*144.6*	*157.4*
Net total utility plant...........	241.3	265.0	285.4	307.3	333.8	348.2	357.0	361.6	363.2	371.3
Other property and investments...	7.9	9.1	10.3	10.8	12.1	13.5	15.6	15.2	16.2	17.7
Current and accrued assets	28.6	31.7	33.3	37.9	39.4	38.4	40.9	39.1	41.5	41.5
Deferred debits..............	7.3	9.3	13.4	19.3	19.4	26.1	32.9	38.3	44.8	47.3
Liabilities and other credits [2].	**285.1**	**315.0**	**342.4**	**375.3**	**404.7**	**426.1**	**446.3**	**454.3**	**465.7**	**477.9**
Capital stock	63.7	70.3	75.9	79.0	82.8	81.6	79.9	80.7	82.9	83.2
Other paid-in capital	23.9	27.7	31.0	34.0	36.3	38.4	40.3	40.4	39.1	40.5
Retained earnings [3].........	24.8	27.9	31.9	37.1	41.1	46.0	48.0	47.1	47.7	48.1
Subsidiary earnings [3]........	1.3	1.6	1.7	1.9	2.2	2.3	2.6	2.5	2.8	2.9
Long-term debt..............	115.2	124.0	131.6	140.6	152.7	157.2	158.4	160.7	162.9	167.9
Current and accrued liabilities ...	26.1	28.6	29.5	32.0	32.0	34.0	39.3	38.4	42.0	44.3
Deferred credits and operating reserves	11.0	15.1	16.6	19.0	20.9	22.4	25.6	28.1	28.5	28.9
Deferred income taxes [4]........	16.6	19.4	23.6	28.1	32.7	39.6	45.9	50.2	53.3	56.6
COMPOSITE INCOME ACCOUNTS										
Electric operating revenues.....	101.7	109.3	116.7	128.3	135.3	136.3	138.5	143.9	150.9	157.3
Electric operating expenses	*85.5*	*91.1*	*96.2*	*105.5*	*111.1*	*110.2*	*111.6*	*115.3*	*121.6*	*127.9*
Net electric operating revenues ...	16.2	18.1	20.5	22.8	24.1	26.1	27.0	28.6	29.4	29.4
Other utility operating income....	0.7	0.9	0.9	1.1	1.2	1.1	1.1	1.2	1.2	1.2
Total utility operating income.....	17.0	19.1	21.4	24.0	25.3	27.2	28.1	29.8	30.6	30.5
Other income................	4.4	5.3	6.5	6.8	7.4	7.2	6.6	5.0	5.2	4.1
Total income	21.3	24.4	28.0	30.8	32.7	34.4	34.6	34.8	35.8	34.6
Income deductions	*8.7*	*9.4*	*10.1*	*11.1*	*14.0*	*14.0*	*15.6*	*18.8*	*18.5*	*17.7*
Net income [5]...............	12.7	15.0	17.9	19.7	18.7	20.4	19.0	16.0	17.3	16.9

[1] Includes construction work in progress.   [2] Includes contributions in aid of construction through 1970.   [3] Unappropriated undistributed.   [4] Cumulative.   [5] Includes net extraordinary income.

Source: U.S. Energy Information Administration, 1981-84, *Financial Statistics of Selected Electric Utilities*, annual; thereafter, *Financial Statistics of Selected Investor-Owned Electric Utilities*, annual.

No. 965. Water Power—Developed and Undeveloped Capacity, by Division: 1950 to 1991

[In millions of kilowatts. As of **Dec. 31.** Excludes Alaska and Hawaii for 1950 and all capacity of reversible equipment at pumped storage projects. Also excludes capacity precluded from development due to wild and scenic river legislation. For composition of division, see table 31. See also *Historical Statistics, Colonial Times to 1970*, series S 160-175]

DIVISION	DEVELOPED INSTALLED CAPACITY							ESTIMATED UNDEVELOPED CAPACITY						
	1950	1960	1970	1980	1985	1990	1991	1950	1960	1970	1980	1985	1990	1991
United States	18.7	33.2	52.0	64.4	68.8	73.0	73.6	87.6	114.2	128.0	129.9	76.4	73.9	73.3
New England.	1.2	1.5	1.5	1.5	1.7	1.9	1.9	3.3	2.9	3.3	4.7	4.4	4.4	4.4
Middle Atlantic.	1.7	2.5	4.3	4.3	4.5	4.9	4.9	6.6	7.6	4.5	5.1	5.4	5.1	4.9
East North Central	0.9	0.9	0.9	0.9	1.1	1.1	1.2	2.3	3.0	1.6	2.0	1.8	1.7	1.7
West North Central	0.6	1.6	2.7	2.8	2.9	3.1	3.1	5.8	6.4	4.4	3.4	3.1	3.1	3.1
South Atlantic	2.8	3.8	5.3	5.9	6.5	6.7	6.7	8.2	8.4	9.6	9.6	7.4	7.0	7.1
East South Central	2.7	3.8	5.2	5.6	5.9	5.9	5.9	4.7	4.6	3.8	3.3	2.7	2.4	2.4
West South Central.	0.5	0.9	1.9	2.3	2.3	2.7	2.7	3.6	3.9	3.3	4.7	5.4	4.6	4.6
Mountain.	2.3	4.6	6.2	7.4	8.1	9.2	9.4	23.4	23.6	26.7	34.2	19.4	19.4	19.1
Pacific	6.0	13.6	23.9	33.7	35.8	37.5	37.8	29.8	53.8	70.9	62.9	26.8	26.2	26.0

Source: U.S. Federal Energy Regulatory Commission (formerly U.S. Federal Power Commission), *Hydroelectric Power Resources of the United States, Developed and Undeveloped*, January 1, 1988; and unpublished data.

No. 966. Solar Collector Shipments, by Type, End-Use, and Market Sector: 1975 to 1990

[In thousands of square feet, except number of manufacturers. Solar collector is a device for intercepting sunlight, converting the light to heat, and carrying the heat to where it will be either used or stored. 1985 data are not available]

YEAR	Number of manu-facturers	Total ship-ments [1]	COLLECTOR TYPE		END USE			MARKET SECTOR		
			Low tempera-ture	Medium tempera-ture, spe-cial, other	Pool heating	Hot water	Space heating	Resi-dential	Com-mercial	Indus-trial
1975	131	3,743	3,026	717	(NA)	(NA)	(NA)	(NA)	(NA)	(NA)
1978	340	10,860	5,872	4,988	5,970	2,513	1,736	8,095	1,848	263
1979	349	14,251	8,395	5,857	8,551	2,958	1,722	11,387	2,015	314
1980	233	19,398	12,233	7,165	12,029	4,790	1,688	16,077	2,417	488
1981	203	20,133	8,677	11,456	9,781	7,204	2,017	15,773	2,561	1,518
1982	265	18,621	7,476	11,145	7,035	7,444	2,367	13,729	3,789	560
1983	203	16,828	4,853	11,975	4,839	9,323	2,082	11,780	3,039	1,665
1984	225	17,191	4,479	11,939	4,427	8,930	2,370	13,980	2,091	289
1986 [2]	98	9,360	3,751	1,111	3,494	1,181	127	4,131	703	13
1987 [2]	59	7,269	3,157	957	3,111	964	23	3,775	305	11
1988 [2]	51	8,174	3,326	732	3,304	726	7	3,796	255	7
1989 [2]	44	11,482	4,283	1,989	4,688	1,374	205	5,804	424	42
1990	48	11,378	3,621	2,519	5,016	1,091	2	5,835	294	22

NA Not available.   [1] Includes other end uses and market sectors not shown separately.   [2] Declines between 1984 and 1989 are primarily due to the expiration of the Federal energy tax credit and industry consolidation.
Source: U.S. Energy Information Administration, *Solar Collector Manufacturing Activity*, annual.

No. 967. Wood Energy Consumption, by Region and Sector: 1980 to 1990

[In trillions of Btu, except percent. For composition of regions, see table 31]

YEAR	Total	Percent of total energy con-sump-tion	REGION				SECTOR			
			North-east	Midwest	South	West	Residen-tial	Indus-trial	Com-mercial	Electric utilities
1980	2,483	3.3	386	329	1,380	388	859	1,600	21	4
1981	2,412	3.3	389	331	1,291	402	869	1,519	21	3
1982	2,395	3.4	351	339	1,334	372	937	1,434	22	2
1983	2,556	3.6	369	318	1,471	396	925	1,606	22	3
1984	2,633	3.6	349	341	1,482	461	923	1,679	22	9
1987	2,437	3.2	350	474	1,147	467	852	1,576	(1)	9
1989	2,604	3.2	432	552	1,161	459	918	1,673	(1)	13
1990	2,267	2.8	256	330	1,176	505	581	1,674	(1)	12

[1] Commercial wood energy is not included because there are no accurate data sources to provide reliable estimates.

No. 968. Households That Burn Wood: 1980 to 1990

[Based on Residential Energy Consumption Survey; see Appendix III]

ITEM	Unit	HOUSEHOLDS THAT BURN WOOD					HOUSEHOLDS THAT BURN WOOD AS MAIN HEATING FUEL				
		1980	1982	1984	1987	1990	1980	1982	1984	1987	1990
Number of households	Millions	21.6	21.4	22.9	22.5	22.9	4.7	5.6	6.4	5.0	3.9
Percent of all households	Percent	26.4	25.6	26.6	24.8	24.4	5.8	6.7	7.5	5.6	4.1
Number of cords burned	Millions	42.7	48.6	49.0	42.6	29.1	22.4	28.7	29.4	23.5	15.0
Average number per household	Number	2.0	2.3	2.1	1.9	1.3	4.7	5.1	4.6	4.7	3.9
Median number per household	Number	0.7	1.0	1.0	0.7	0.5	3.3	4.0	4.0	4.0	3.3
Wood energy consumption.	Tril. Btu	854	971	981	853	582	448	574	589	470	300

Source of tables 967 and 968: U.S. Energy Information Administration, *Annual Energy Review*.

No. 969. Renewable Energy Consumption Estimates by Type: 1988 to 1990

SOURCES	QUANTITY (Quadrillion Btu)			PERCENT CHANGE	
	1988	1989	1990	1988-89	1989-90
Adjusted total energy consumption estimates [1] ...	83.63	84.45	84.40	1.0	-0.1
Total renewable energy consumption estimates ...	6.31	6.20	6.26	-1.7	1.0
Percent of adjusted total.	7.50	7.30	7.40	-2.7	1.4
Reported renewable energy consumption	2.88	3.10	3.15	7.6	1.6
Hydroelectric power	2.64	2.88	2.94	9.1	2.1
electric utilities	2.28	2.74	2.89	20.2	5.5
Industrial	0.03	0.03	0.03	-	-
Imported electricity	0.40	0.27	0.21	-32.5	-22.2
Exported electricity	0.07	0.16	0.21	128.6	31.2
Geothermal energy at electric utilities	0.22	0.20	0.18	-9.1	-10.0
Wood and waste energy at electric utilities	0.02	0.02	0.02	-	-
Wind energy at electric utilities	(Z)	(Z)	(Z)	(X)	(X)
Additional renewable energy consumption estimates.	3.43	3.10	3.11	-9.6	0.3
Biofuels	3.15	2.90	2.88	-7.9	-0.7
Residential, commercial, and industrial use	3.09	2.83	2.78	-8.4	-1.8
Transportation use	0.06	0.07	0.10	16.7	42.9
Geothermal energy (nonelectric utilities).	0.13	0.11	0.14	-15.4	27.3
Solar energy (nonelectric utilities)	0.09	0.04	0.04	-55.6	-
Wind energy (nonelectric utilities)	0.03	0.02	0.02	-33.3	-
Hydroelectric power (additional industrial use)	0.03	0.03	0.03	-	-

- Represents or rounds to zero.   X Not applicable.   Z Less than 50 billion.   [1] Adjusted total energy consumption estimates will differ from other energy consumption estimates shown in tables 928 to 933.

Source: U.S. Energy Information Administration, *Annual Energy Review*.

No. 970. Privately Owned Gas Utility Industry—Balance Sheet and Income Account: 1980 to 1991

[In millions of dollars. The gas utility industry consists of pipeline and distribution companies. Excludes operations of companies distributing gas in bottles or tanks. See also *Historical Statistics, Colonial Times to 1970*, series S 205-218]

ITEM	1980	1984	1985	1986	1987	1988	1989	1990	1991
COMPOSITE BALANCE SHEET									
Assets, total [1]	75,851	98,933	104,478	104,008	109,390	121,667	123,820	121,686	124,120
Total utility plant.	67,071	83,118	88,121	91,606	93,540	99,933	106,017	112,863	119,772
Depreciation and amortization . . .	26,162	35,542	36,377	36,776	41,162	44,423	47,054	49,483	52,400
Utility plant (net).	40,909	47,576	51,744	54,830	52,378	55,510	58,963	63,380	67,372
Investment and fund accounts [1] . . .	15,530	21,872	23,871	21,850	25,660	31,552	28,111	23,872	22,873
Current and accrued assets	17,243	25,367	24,771	21,477	21,025	23,402	24,836	23,268	23,023
Deferred debits [2]	2,169	4,118	4,092	5,851	8,633	9,658	10,364	9,576	9,277
Liabilities, total [1]	75,851	98,933	104,478	104,008	109,390	121,667	123,820	121,686	124,120
Capitalization, total [1]	51,382	64,458	65,799	66,660	66,312	69,875	74,753	74,958	75,463
Capital stock [1]	29,315	38,959	39,517	39,902	38,212	39,898	43,889	43,810	43,435
Long-term debts	22,067	25,499	26,282	26,758	28,100	29,977	30,864	31,148	32,030
Current and accrued liabilities. . . .	18,119	23,043	26,125	23,855	26,664	33,735	31,005	29,550	28,128
Deferred income taxes [3]	4,149	7,000	7,769	8,363	9,901	10,685	11,292	11,360	10,527
Other liabilities and credits	2,201	4,432	4,785	5,130	6,513	7,372	6,770	5,818	10,002
COMPOSITE INCOME ACCOUNT									
Operating revenues, total . .	85,918	115,491	103,945	80,978	69,566	69,754	70,363	66,027	63,922
Operating expenses [4]	81,789	109,165	98,320	75,470	64,409	64,696	64,262	60,137	59,165
Operation and maintenance . . .	74,508	98,953	88,572	66,032	56,054	57,032	55,990	51,627	50,867
Federal, State, and local taxes .	4,847	7,146	6,590	6,133	5,179	4,241	4,843	4,957	4,446
Operating income.	4,129	6,326	5,625	5,508	5,157	5,058	6,101	5,890	4,756
Utility operating income.	4,471	6,647	6,030	5,943	5,452	5,202	6,274	6,077	4,962
Income before interest charges [1] . .	6,929	9,068	7,636	7,085	6,845	7,472	8,764	8,081	5,530
Net income [1]	4,194	5,619	3,785	3,390	2,971	3,352	4,641	4,410	1,894
Dividends	2,564	4,471	4,060	3,882	3,453	3,151	3,113	3,191	4,341

[1] Beginning 1980, not comparable with earlier years due to Federal Power Commission ruling requiring adoption of the equity method in reporting earnings of subsidiaries.   [2] Includes capital stock discount and expense and reacquired securities.   [3] Includes reserves for deferred income taxes.   [4] Includes expenses not shown separately.

Source: American Gas Association, Arlington, VA, *Gas Facts*, annual (copyright).

No. 971. Gas Utility Industry—Summary: 1970 to 1991

[Covers natural, manufactured, mixed, and liquid petroleum gas. Based on questionnaire mailed to all privately and municipally owned gas utilities in U.S., except those with annual revenues less than $25,000. See also *Historical Statistics, Colonial Times to 1970,* series S 190-204]

ITEM	Unit	1970	1975	1980	1985	1986	1987	1988	1989	1990	1991
Customers [1]	1,000 . . .	41,482	44,555	47,223	49,971	50,704	51,576	52,422	53,356	54,261	55,174
Residential	1,000 . . .	38,097	40,950	43,489	45,929	46,583	47,362	48,133	48,980	49,802	50,634
Commercial	1,000 . . .	3,131	3,367	3,498	3,816	3,892	3,980	4,069	4,161	4,246	4,322
Industrial and other	1,000 . . .	254	237	236	226	229	234	220	215	214	218
Sales [2]	Tril. Btu . .	16,044	14,863	15,413	12,616	11,125	10,543	10,705	10,551	9,842	9,605
Residential	Tril. Btu . .	4,923	4,991	4,826	4,513	4,381	4,385	4,695	4,798	4,468	4,550
Percent of total	Percent . .	30.7	33.6	31.3	35.8	39.4	41.6	43.9	45.5	45.4	47.4
Commercial	Tril. Btu . .	2,007	2,387	2,453	2,338	2,239	2,156	2,306	2,322	2,192	2,198
Industrial	Tril. Btu . .	8,439	6,837	7,957	5,635	4,338	3,848	3,544	3,243	3,010	2,631
Other	Tril. Btu . .	674	648	177	130	167	155	160	188	171	226
Revenues [2]	Mil. dol . . .	10,283	19,101	48,303	63,293	51,201	45,492	46,162	47,493	45,153	44,647
Residential	Mil. dol . . .	5,207	8,445	17,432	26,864	24,759	23,622	24,828	26,172	25,000	25,729
Percent of total	Percent . .	50.6	44.2	36.1	42.4	48.4	51.9	53.8	55.1	55.4	57.6
Commercial	Mil. dol . . .	1,620	3,302	8,183	12,722	11,274	10,271	10,681	11,074	10,604	10,669
Industrial	Mil. dol . . .	3,181	6,745	22,215	23,086	14,495	11,069	10,113	9,666	8,996	7,576
Other	Mil. dol . . .	274	608	473	621	673	530	538	581	553	674
Prices per mil. Btu [3]	Dollars . . .	0.64	1.29	3.13	5.02	4.60	4.32	4.31	4.50	4.59	4.65
Residential	Dollars . . .	1.06	1.69	3.61	5.95	5.65	5.39	5.29	5.45	5.60	5.66
Commercial	Dollars . . .	0.81	1.38	3.34	5.44	5.04	4.77	4.63	4.77	4.84	4.85
Industrial	Dollars . . .	0.38	0.99	2.79	4.10	3.34	2.88	2.85	2.98	2.99	2.88
Gas mains mileage	1,000 . . .	913	980	1,052	1,119	1,134	1,151	1,169	1,185	1,207	1,225
Field and gathering	1,000 . . .	66	68	84	94	94	94	92	91	90	86
Transmission	1,000 . . .	252	263	266	271	271	274	276	276	280	282
Distribution	1,000 . . .	595	649	702	754	769	784	801	818	837	857
Construction expenditures [4]	Mil. dol . . .	2,506	2,466	5,350	5,671	5,342	5,328	6,166	7,341	7,899	9,036
Transmission	Mil. dol . . .	1,019	590	1,583	1,562	1,448	1,295	1,568	2,081	2,886	3,656
Distribution	Mil. dol . . .	913	910	1,869	2,577	2,920	3,055	3,389	3,980	3,714	3,842
Production and storage	Mil. dol . . .	370	831	1,546	965	383	251	268	276	309	430

[1] Annual average.   [2] Excludes sales for resale.   [3] For definition, see text, section 19.   [4] Includes general.

Source: American Gas Association, Arlington, VA, *Gas Facts,* annual (copyright).

No. 972. Gas Utility Industry—Customers, Sales, and Revenues, by State: 1991

[See headnote, table 971. For definition of Btu, see text, section 19]

REGION, DIVISION, AND STATE	CUSTOMERS[1] (1,000) Total[2]	Resi-dential	SALES[3] (tril. Btu) Total[2]	Resi-dential	REVENUES[3] (mil. dol.) Total[2]	Resi-dential	REGION, DIVISION, AND STATE	CUSTOMERS[1] (1,000) Total[2]	Resi-dential	SALES[3] (tril. Btu) Total[2]	Resi-dential	REVENUES[3] (mil. dol.) Total[2]	Resi-dential
U.S. . . .	55,174	50,634	9,605	4,550	44,647	25,729	DC . . .	148	133	30	11	183	81
							VA . . .	707	634	114	49	636	341
Northeast .	11,014	10,090	1,677	929	10,234	6,499	WV . . .	383	350	53	34	300	211
N.E.	2,052	1,855	368	166	2,312	1,284	NC . . .	616	543	136	39	583	232
ME. . . .	17	12	5	1	25	5	SC . . .	390	347	101	20	425	139
NH. . .	78	67	14	6	86	40	GA . . .	1,442	1,332	197	95	1,068	639
VT. . .	26	23	7	2	35	15	FL . . .	513	466	121	15	484	115
MA. . .	1,238	1,127	222	102	1,348	771	E.S.C. . . .	2,574	2,314	460	185	1,998	992
RI . . .	216	197	32	18	213	133	KY . . .	696	629	117	62	499	293
CT . . .	478	429	88	38	605	319	TN . . .	716	626	159	52	659	254
M.A. . . .	8,962	8,235	1,309	763	7,922	5,215	AL . . .	745	685	107	46	550	315
NY . . .	4,216	3,904	538	337	3,504	2,442	MS . . .	416	375	77	25	289	130
NJ . . .	2,222	2,000	372	178	2,021	1,166	W.S.C. . . .	5,972	5,473	1,698	375	5,380	2,005
PA . . .	2,523	2,332	399	248	2,397	1,607	AR . . .	557	494	83	40	353	193
Midwest . .	16,943	15,461	2,973	1,843	13,555	9,039	LA . . .	991	928	222	55	719	313
E.N.C . . .	12,173	11,176	2,107	1,380	9,921	6,862	OK . . .	904	816	215	71	646	329
OH. . .	3,030	2,790	503	334	2,453	1,699	TX . . .	3,519	3,234	1,178	209	3,662	1,170
IN . . .	1,475	1,344	262	147	1,257	791	West	13,528	12,622	1,899	886	9,052	5,001
IL . . .	3,584	3,283	611	431	2,782	2,046	Mt.	3,421	3,104	520	278	2,277	1,376
MI . . .	2,818	2,609	486	342	2,258	1,630	MT. . .	202	178	40	21	155	83
WI . . .	1,266	1,150	245	124	1,171	696	ID . . .	145	125	20	10	90	52
W.N.C. . . .	4,770	4,285	866	463	3,634	2,177	WY . . .	124	109	24	12	100	56
MN. . .	1,090	987	244	118	965	534	CO. . .	1,117	1,002	173	101	729	447
IA . . .	799	713	154	78	627	372	NM. . .	413	374	54	32	250	164
MO . . .	1,331	1,211	192	122	922	621	AZ . . .	627	580	93	29	395	198
ND. . .	100	88	20	11	86	50	UT . . .	492	456	81	53	380	269
SD. . .	121	107	23	11	96	54	NV . . .	302	280	37	20	178	107
NE . . .	489	426	96	45	390	208	Pac. . . .	10,107	9,518	1,379	608	6,775	3,625
KS . . .	841	753	138	77	548	337	WA . . .	550	486	143	48	483	215
South	13,690	12,462	3,056	894	11,806	5,191	OR . . .	385	336	61	27	303	163
S.A. . . .	5,144	4,675	898	334	4,428	2,194	CA . . .	9,053	8,592	1,137	519	5,815	3,181
DE . . .	100	92	20	7	90	42	AK . . .	84	72	35	13	129	56
MD. . .	846	779	126	64	659	393	HI . . .	35	31	3	1	46	10

[1] Averages for the year.   [2] Includes other service, not shown separately.   [3] Excludes sales for resale.

Source: American Gas Association, Arlington, VA, *Gas Facts,* annual (copyright).

Science and Technology

This section presents statistics on scientific, engineering, and technological resources, with emphasis on patterns of research and development (R&D) funding and on scientific, engineering, and technical personnel, education, and employment. Also included are statistics on space program outlays and accomplishments. Principal sources of these data are the National Science Foundation (NSF) and the National Aeronautics and Space Administration (NASA).

NSF gathers data chiefly through recurring surveys. Current NSF publications containing data on funds for research and development and on scientific and engineering personnel include the *Science Resources Studies Highlights* summaries series; Detailed Statistical Tables; and annual, biennial, triennial, and special reports. Titles or the areas of coverage of these reports include the following: *Science and Engineering Indicators; National Patterns of R&D Resources; Science and Engineering Personnel-A National Overview; Women and Minorities in Science and Engineering;* science and technology data presented in chart and tabular form in a pocket-size publication; *International Science and Technology Data Update;* profiles on human resources and funding in individual fields of science and engineering; *Federal Funds for Research and Development; Federal R&D Funding by Budget Function; Federal Support to Universities, Colleges, and Selected Nonprofit Institutions; Scientific and Engineering Facilities at Universities and Colleges; Geographic Distribution of Industrial R&D Expenditures; Research and Development in Industry;* R&D funds and graduate enrollment and support in academic science and engineering; characteristics of doctoral scientists and engineers and of recent graduates in the United States; *U.S. Scientists and Engineers;* and scientists, engineers, and technicians in manufacturing, nonmanufacturing, and trade and regulated industries. Statistical surveys in these areas pose problems of concept and definition and the data should, therefore, be regarded as broad estimates

In Brief
R&D expenditures in constant (1987) dollars:

1970	74.7 bil.
1980	87.7 bil.
1992	130.4 bil.

Nondefense R&D spending as percent of GNP: 1990

Japan	3.0
Former West Germany	2.7
United States	1.9
France	1.8
Italy	1.3

rather than precise quantitative statements. See sources for details.

The National Science Board's biennial *Science and Engineering Indicators* contains data and analyses of international and domestic science and technology, including measures of inputs and outputs. *The Budget of the United States Government,* published by the U.S. Office of Management and Budget, contains summary financial data on Federal R&D programs.

Research and development outlays.—NSF defines research as a "systematic and intensive study directed toward a fuller knowledge of the subject studied" and development as "the systematic use of scientific knowledge directed toward the production of useful materials, devices, systems, methods, or processes." National coverage of R&D expenditures is developed primarily from periodic surveys in four principal economic sectors: (1) *Government,* made up primarily of Federal executive agencies; (2) *industry,* consisting of manufacturing and nonmanufacturing firms and the federally funded research and development centers (FFRDC's) they administer; (3) *universities and colleges,* composed of universities, colleges, and their affiliated institutions, agricultural experiment stations, and associated schools of agriculture, and FFRDC's administered by educational institutions; and (4) *other nonprofit institutions,* consisting of such organizations as private philanthropic foundations, nonprofit research institutes, voluntary health agencies, and FFRDC's administered by nonprofit organizations. The R&D funds reported consist of current operating costs, including planning and administration costs, except as otherwise noted. They exclude funds for routine testing, mapping and surveying, collection of general-purpose data, dissemination of scientific information, and training of scientific personnel.

Scientists, engineers, and technicians.—Scientists and engineers are defined as persons engaged in scientific and engineering work at a level requiring a knowledge of sciences equivalent at least to that acquired through completion of a 4-year college course. Technicians are defined as persons engaged in technical work at a level requiring knowledge acquired through a technical institute, junior college, or other type of training less extensive than 4-year college training. Craftsmen and skilled workers are excluded.

Historical statistics.—Tabular headnotes provide cross-references, where applicable, to *Historical Statistics of the United States, Colonial Times to 1970.* See Appendix IV.

Figure 20.1
Top 15 Universities—Federal Research and Development Obligations: 1990

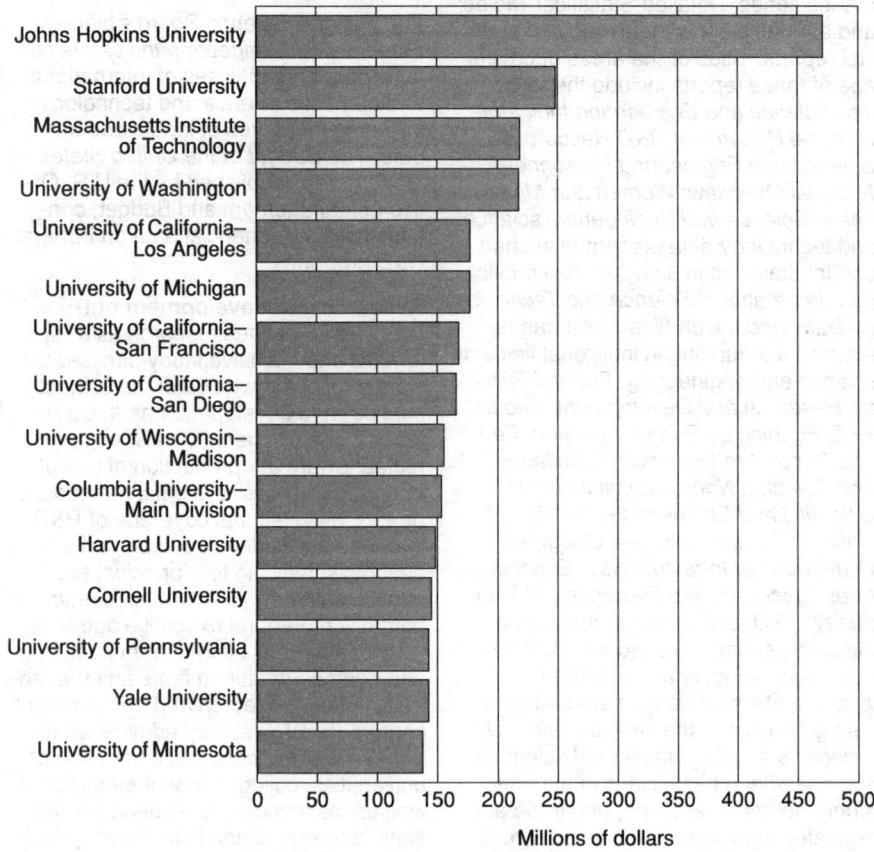

Source: Chart prepared by U.S. Bureau of the Census. For data, see table 982.

No. 973. Research and Development (R&D)—Expenditures: 1960 to 1992

[Includes basic research, applied research, and development. Defense-related outlays comprise all research and development spending by Dept. of Defense, including space activities, and a portion of Department of Energy funds. Space-related outlays are those of the National Aeronautics and Space Administration; they exclude space activities of other Federal agencies, estimated at less than 5 percent of all space research and development spending. Minus sign (-) indicates decrease]

YEAR	CURRENT DOLLARS (bil. dol.)			CONSTANT (1987) DOLLARS [1]		ANNUAL PERCENT CHANGE [3]		PERCENT OF TOTAL R&D OUTLAYS					
								Federally funded defense/space-related			Other outlays		
	Total	Defense space related	Other	Total (bil. dol.)	Percent of GDP [2]	Current dollars	Constant dollars	Total	Defense	Space	Total	Non-Federal	Federal
1960	13.5	7.5	6.0	51.9	2.6	9.4	7.5	55	52	3	45	35	9
1965	20.0	10.8	9.3	70.6	2.9	6.3	3.6	54	33	21	46	35	11
1966	21.8	11.3	10.5	74.6	2.8	9.0	5.6	52	32	19	48	36	12
1967	23.1	11.5	11.7	76.6	2.8	6.0	2.7	49	35	14	51	38	13
1968	24.6	11.9	12.7	77.8	2.8	6.3	1.6	48	35	14	52	39	12
1969	25.6	11.7	13.9	77.2	2.7	4.2	-0.9	46	34	11	54	42	12
1970	26.1	11.4	14.7	74.7	2.6	2.0	-3.2	44	33	10	56	43	13
1971	26.7	11.2	15.5	72.5	2.4	2.1	-3.0	42	33	10	58	44	14
1972	28.5	11.6	16.9	73.7	2.4	6.7	1.6	41	33	8	59	44	15
1973	30.7	11.9	18.9	75.0	2.3	7.9	1.8	39	32	7	61	47	15
1974	32.9	11.8	21.1	74.0	2.3	7.0	-1.4	36	29	7	64	49	15
1975	35.2	12.3	23.0	72.3	2.2	7.2	-2.3	35	27	7	65	49	17
1976	39.0	13.4	25.6	75.1	2.2	10.8	3.9	34	27	8	66	49	17
1977	42.8	14.3	28.5	76.8	2.2	9.6	2.3	33	27	7	67	50	17
1978	48.1	15.3	32.8	80.1	2.2	12.5	4.3	32	26	6	68	50	18
1979	55.0	16.6	38.4	84.1	2.2	14.2	5.0	30	25	6	70	51	19
1980	62.6	18.4	44.2	87.7	2.3	13.9	4.2	29	24	5	71	53	18
1981	71.9	21.2	50.6	91.5	2.4	14.8	4.3	30	24	5	70	54	17
1982	80.0	24.6	55.4	95.6	2.5	11.3	4.5	31	26	5	69	54	15
1983	89.1	28.3	60.9	102.3	2.6	11.4	7.0	32	27	4	68	54	14
1984	101.1	31.8	69.3	111.1	2.7	13.5	8.6	31	28	3	69	55	14
1985	113.8	37.5	76.3	120.6	2.8	12.5	8.5	33	30	3	67	54	13
1986	119.5	40.6	78.9	123.3	2.8	5.0	2.2	34	31	3	66	55	11
1987	125.4	43.2	82.2	125.4	2.8	4.9	1.7	34	31	3	66	54	12
1988	133.7	45.1	88.6	128.8	2.7	6.7	2.8	34	30	3	66	54	12
1989	140.8	45.6	95.2	129.9	2.7	5.3	0.8	32	28	4	68	56	12
1990	146.2	46.5	99.7	129.5	2.7	3.8	-0.3	32	27	4	68	56	12
1991	150.8	45.0	105.8	128.8	2.7	3.2	-0.6	30	25	5	70	57	13
1992	157.4	47.8	109.6	130.4	2.6	4.4	1.2	30	25	5	70	57	13

[1] Based on GDP implicit price deflator.   [2] GDP = Gross Domestic Product.   [3] Change from immediate prior year.
Source: U.S. National Science Foundation, *National Patterns of R&D Resources: 1992;* and unpublished data.

No. 974. Research and Development (R&D)—Source of Funds and Performance Sector: 1970 to 1991

[In millions of dollars. See headnote, table 975]

YEAR	Total	SOURCE OF FUNDS				PERFORMANCE SECTOR				
		Federal Govt.	Industry	Univ., colleges	Other [1]	Federal Govt.	Industry	Univ., colleges	Associated FFRDC's [2]	Other [1]
Current dollars:										
1970	26,134	14,891	10,444	462	337	4,079	18,067	2,335	737	916
1975	35,213	18,109	15,820	749	535	5,354	24,187	3,409	987	1,276
1980	62,610	29,461	30,912	1,334	903	7,632	44,505	6,077	2,246	2,150
1983	89,139	40,832	45,251	1,929	1,127	10,582	65,268	7,877	2,737	2,675
1984	101,139	45,642	52,204	2,103	1,190	11,572	74,800	8,617	3,150	3,000
1985	113,819	52,121	57,977	2,376	1,345	12,945	84,239	9,687	3,523	3,425
1986	119,529	54,274	61,056	2,789	1,410	13,535	87,823	10,926	3,895	3,350
1987	125,353	57,904	62,642	3,201	1,606	13,413	92,155	12,154	4,206	3,425
1988	133,740	61,310	67,143	3,471	1,816	14,281	97,889	13,464	4,531	3,575
1989	140,763	62,626	72,110	3,946	2,081	15,121	101,854	15,009	4,729	4,050
1990	146,152	63,924	75,499	4,356	2,373	16,002	104,344	16,325	4,831	4,650
1991	150,800	65,200	78,250	4,750	2,600	16,500	106,750	17,450	5,000	5,100
Constant (1987) dollars: [3]										
1970	74,722	42,686	29,732	1,336	967	11,799	51,429	6,754	2,132	2,607
1975	72,256	37,408	32,169	1,574	1,105	11,253	49,171	7,165	2,074	2,594
1980	87,666	41,396	43,112	1,890	1,268	10,813	62,062	8,610	3,182	2,998
1983	102,310	46,881	51,918	2,217	1,294	12,160	74,883	9,052	3,145	3,069
1984	111,137	50,177	57,337	2,315	1,308	12,737	82,153	9,485	3,467	3,295
1985	120,624	55,243	61,436	2,519	1,426	13,725	89,265	10,270	3,735	3,629
1986	123,267	55,947	62,995	2,872	1,453	13,936	90,614	11,250	4,011	3,456
1987	125,353	57,904	62,642	3,201	1,606	13,413	92,155	12,154	4,206	3,425
1988	128,848	59,092	64,656	3,349	1,751	13,781	94,260	12,992	4,372	3,442
1989	129,888	57,809	66,511	3,646	1,921	13,971	93,944	13,868	4,369	3,735
1990	129,545	56,683	66,892	3,866	2,104	14,203	92,446	14,489	4,288	4,120
1991	128,782	55,681	66,823	4,057	2,220	14,092	91,161	14,903	4,270	4,355

[1] Nonprofit institutions.   [2] University associated federally-funded R&D centers.   [3] Based on gross domestic product implicit price deflator.

Source: U.S. National Science Foundation, *National Patterns of R&D Resources: 1992.*

No. 975. Research and Development (R&D) Funds, by Performance Sector: 1970 to 1991

[In millions of dollars, except percent. Data primarily on calendar year basis—calendar year data for industry and other nonprofit institutions combined with Federal and university fiscal year data. Data refer, in general, to natural sciences including engineering, and to social sciences in all but industry sector. Excludes capital expenditures data. Expenditures at associated federally funded research and development centers administered by industry and other nonprofit institutions included in totals of respective sectors. See also Historical Statistics, Colonial Times to 1970, series W 109-125]

PERFORMANCE SECTOR	1970	1980	1984	1985	1986	1987	1988	1989	1990	1991
Total R&D [1]	26,134	62,610	101,139	113,819	119,529	125,353	133,740	140,763	146,152	150,800
In 1987 dollars [2]	74,722	87,666	111,137	120,624	123,267	125,353	128,848	129,888	129,545	128,782
Percent Federal as source	57.0	47.1	45.1	45.8	45.4	46.2	45.8	44.5	43.7	43.2
Percent of gross domestic product	2.6	2.3	2.7	2.8	2.8	2.8	2.7	2.7	2.7	2.7
Federal Government	4,079	7,632	11,572	12,945	13,535	13,413	14,281	15,121	16,002	16,500
Industry	18,067	44,505	74,800	84,239	87,823	92,155	97,889	101,854	104,344	106,750
Federal funds	7,779	14,029	23,396	27,196	27,891	30,752	32,117	31,292	30,580	30,400
Industry funds	10,288	30,476	51,404	57,043	59,932	61,403	65,772	70,562	73,764	76,350
Universities and colleges	2,335	6,077	8,617	9,687	10,926	12,154	13,464	15,009	16,325	17,450
Federal funds	1,647	4,104	5,424	6,057	6,703	7,333	8,181	8,984	9,611	10,100
Industry funds	61	236	475	559	699	789	871	998	1,135	1,250
University and college funds [3]	462	1,334	2,103	2,376	2,789	3,201	3,471	3,946	4,356	4,750
Other nonprofit institutions funds [3]	165	403	615	695	735	831	941	1,081	1,223	1,350
Universities and colleges, associated federally funded R&D centers	737	2,246	3,150	3,523	3,895	4,206	4,531	4,729	4,831	5,000
Other nonprofit institutions	916	2,150	3,000	3,425	3,350	3,425	3,575	4,050	4,650	5,100
Federal funds	649	1,450	2,100	2,400	2,250	2,200	2,200	2,500	2,900	3,200
Industry funds	95	200	325	375	425	450	500	550	600	650
Other [4]	172	500	575	650	675	775	875	1,000	1,150	1,250
Total research, basic and applied	9,269	22,052	35,287	39,528	43,660	45,679	47,839	53,164	55,247	58,330
In 1987 dollars [2]	26,598	30,993	38,792	41,895	45,010	45,679	46,107	49,072	48,985	49,814
Percent Federal as source	60.1	54.8	50.9	50.8	46.5	47.1	46.5	47.0	46.9	46.5
Federal Government	1,904	3,666	4,764	5,056	5,160	5,438	5,338	5,982	5,953	6,550
Industry	4,029	9,775	18,373	21,117	23,807	24,136	24,875	27,585	28,064	29,050
Federal funds	1,207	2,190	4,700	5,836	5,229	5,400	5,246	6,203	6,335	6,100
Industry funds	2,822	7,585	13,673	15,281	18,578	18,736	19,629	21,382	21,729	22,950
Universities and colleges	2,223	5,578	7,984	8,975	10,119	11,305	12,400	13,863	14,998	16,110
Federal funds	1,563	3,743	5,014	5,599	6,191	6,821	7,487	8,260	8,754	9,300
Industry funds	56	219	442	520	650	734	810	928	1,056	1,160
University and college funds [3]	449	1,241	1,956	2,210	2,594	2,977	3,228	3,670	4,051	4,400
Other nonprofit institutions funds [3]	155	375	572	646	684	773	875	1,005	1,137	1,250
Universities and colleges, associated federally funded R&D centers	485	1,548	2,216	2,340	2,424	2,550	2,756	2,934	3,032	3,100
Other nonprofit institutions	628	1,485	1,950	2,040	2,150	2,250	2,470	2,800	3,200	3,520
Federal funds	409	930	1,250	1,250	1,300	1,300	1,400	1,600	1,850	2,050
Industry funds	77	160	260	300	340	360	400	440	480	520
Other [4]	142	395	440	490	510	590	670	760	870	950
Total basic research	3,531	8,433	12,909	14,198	16,590	17,999	18,709	21,190	21,303	23,350
In 1987 dollars [2]	10,172	11,902	14,200	15,051	17,093	17,999	18,042	19,568	18,898	19,941
Percent of total R&D	13.5	13.5	12.8	12.5	13.9	14.4	14.0	15.1	14.6	15.5
Percent Federal as source	70.0	70.1	65.8	64.6	60.2	60.4	61.8	61.1	63.3	61.7
Federal Government	559	1,182	1,861	1,923	2,019	2,046	2,050	2,371	2,366	2,600
Industry	602	1,325	2,608	2,862	4,047	4,323	4,280	5,280	4,364	5,050
Federal funds	158	290	476	489	551	740	908	1,253	1,182	1,200
Industry funds	444	1,035	2,132	2,373	3,496	3,583	3,372	4,027	3,182	3,850
Universities and colleges	1,796	4,042	5,735	6,559	7,495	8,398	8,827	9,710	10,431	11,300
Federal funds	1,296	2,863	3,827	4,338	4,862	5,369	5,630	6,142	6,535	7,000
Industry funds	40	142	284	342	436	496	527	592	658	720
University and college funds [3]	350	796	1,257	1,454	1,739	2,011	2,101	2,335	2,529	2,800
Other nonprofit institutions funds [3]	110	241	367	425	458	522	569	641	709	780
Universities and colleges, associated federally funded R&D centers	269	1,124	1,675	1,749	1,859	2,012	2,222	2,329	2,402	2,500
Other nonprofit institutions	305	760	1,030	1,105	1,170	1,220	1,330	1,500	1,740	1,900
Federal funds	189	450	650	675	700	700	750	850	1,000	1,100
Industry funds	44	95	150	170	200	210	230	250	280	300
Other [4]	72	215	230	260	270	310	350	400	460	500
Total development	16,865	40,558	65,852	74,291	75,869	79,674	85,901	87,599	90,905	92,470
In 1987 dollars [2]	48,124	56,674	72,345	78,729	78,257	79,674	82,741	80,816	80,560	78,968
Percent of total R&D	64.5	64.8	65.1	65.3	63.5	63.6	64.2	62.2	62.2	61.3
Percent Federal as source	55.3	42.9	42.1	43.1	44.8	45.7	45.5	43.0	41.8	41.2

[1] Basic research, applied research, and development. [2] Based on gross domestic product implicit price deflator. [3] Includes State and local government funds received by these institutions and used for research and development. [4] Includes estimates for independent nonprofit hospitals and voluntary health agencies.

Source: U.S. National Science Foundation, National Patterns of R&D Resources: 1992; and unpublished data.

No. 976. Funds for Research and Development—Performance Sector, by State: 1989

[In millions of dollars. See headnote, table 975]

REGION, DIVISION, AND STATE	Total	Federal government	Industry	Universities and colleges [1]	Other nonprofit [2]	REGION, DIVISION, AND STATE	Total	Federal government	Industry	Universities and colleges [1]	Other nonprofit [2]
U.S. . . .	**140,763**	**15,121**	**101,854**	**19,738**	**4,050**	VA	2,545	1,018	1,126	281	120
Northeast . .	**34,628**	**1,458**	**27,873**	**4,486**	**811**	WV	(NA)	63	([7])	58	2
N.E	**11,710**	**665**	**8,789**	**1,721**	**535**	NC	1,821	60	1,305	420	36
ME	72	4	33	20	15	SC	576	60	386	120	10
NH	(NA)	22	([3])	62	-	GA	1,302	158	719	417	8
VT	(NA)	4	([4])	43	3	FL	3,375	642	2,341	386	6
MA	2,745	38	2,410	284	13	**E.S.C.** . . .	**3,135**	**864**	**1,640**	**592**	**39**
RI.	7,949	401	5,825	1,232	491	KY	343	31	226	84	2
CT	428	196	139	80	13	TN	1,302	135	930	223	14
M.A.	**22,918**	**793**	**19,084**	**2,765**	**276**	AL	1,226	568	428	210	20
NY	9,898	89	8,071	1,587	151	MS	264	130	56	75	3
NJ	7,229	430	6,381	396	22	**W.S.C** . . .	**7,595**	**571**	**5,580**	**1,351**	**93**
PA	5,791	274	4,632	782	103	AR	121	25	51	44	1
Midwest . . .	**29,887**	**1,454**	**24,615**	**3,596**	**221**	LA	385	36	168	180	1
E.N.C. . . .	**23,356**	**1,288**	**19,308**	**2,609**	**151**	OK	507	46	332	113	16
OH	5,475	1,056	3,946	427	46	TX	6,581	464	5,028	1,014	75
IN.	2,120	75	1,815	227	3	**West**	**42,035**	**3,739**	**30,859**	**6,664**	**773**
IL.	5,305	59	4,050	1,131	65	**Mt.**	**7,110**	**1,021**	**4,095**	**1,868**	**126**
MI	9,058	71	8,468	487	32	MT	(NA)	21	([5])	32	1
WI	1,399	27	1,030	337	5	ID.	(NA)	19	([9])	33	1
W.N.C . . .	**6,530**	**166**	**5,307**	**987**	**70**	WY	(NA)	9	([10])	23	21
MN	2,399	31	2,066	259	43	CO	1,649	117	1,162	290	80
IA.	616	20	363	231	2	NM	2,680	594	1,034	1,039	13
MO. . . .	2,710	58	2,380	255	17	AZ	1,293	118	917	251	7
ND	79	20	27	28	4	UT	620	66	387	165	2
SD	23	6	4	12	-	NV	141	77	29	34	1
NE	182	22	64	94	2	**Pac**	**34,925**	**2,718**	**26,764**	**4,796**	**647**
KS	523	9	404	108	2	WA	3,225	111	2,716	277	121
South	**28,509**	**7,973**	**15,320**	**4,695**	**521**	OR	579	42	355	161	21
S.A	**17,779**	**6,538**	**8,100**	**2,752**	**389**	CA	30,881	2,478	23,675	4,231	497
DE	(NA)	3	([5])	37	2	AK	118	51	9	57	1
MD	5,091	3,012	1,088	922	69	HI.	123	36	9	71	7
DC	(NA)	1,522	([6])	111	136	Other [11]	5,704	497	3,187	296	1,724

- Represents or rounds to zero.   NA Not available.   [1] Distribution by States includes R&D performed in only Doctoral degree granting institutions; U.S. total includes R&D performed in all institutions.   [2] For other sector, funds distributed by State include only Federal obligations to organizations in the nonprofit sector. Nonprofit R&D performance using non-Federal funds are undistributed.   [3] Between $95 and $140 million.   [4] Between $242 and $287 million.   [5] Between $845 and $1,032 million.   [6] Between $23 and $210 million.   [7] Between $80 and $267 million.   [8] Between $5 and $405 million.   [9] Between $161 and $561 million.   [10] Below $400 million.   [11] Includes unknown.
Source: U.S. National Science Foundation, *National Patterns of R&D Resources: 1992.*

No. 977. Federal Obligations for Research and Development, by Agency in Current and Constant (1987) Dollars: 1975 to 1992

[In millions of dollars. For fiscal years ending in year shown; see text, section 9. Includes those agencies with obligations of $1 billion or more in 1992. See *Historical Statistics, Colonial Times to 1970*, series W 142, for total R&D expenditures]

AGENCY	1975	1980	1985	1986	1987	1988	1989	1990	1991	1992
CURRENT DOLLARS										
Obligations, total [1]	**19,039**	**29,830**	**48,360**	**51,412**	**55,253**	**56,768**	**61,406**	**63,667**	**63,218**	**70,427**
Dept. of Defense.	9,013	13,981	29,792	32,938	35,232	35,249	37,577	37,268	33,966	38,770
Dept. of Health and Human Services.	2,281	3,780	5,451	5,658	6,606	7,158	7,903	8,406	9,246	9,780
National Aeronautics and Space Administration	3,064	3,234	3,327	3,420	3,787	4,330	5,394	6,533	7,435	8,543
Dept. of Energy	2,047	4,754	4,966	4,688	4,757	5,036	5,193	5,631	6,159	6,499
National Science Foundation.	595	882	1,346	1,353	1,471	1,533	1,670	1,690	1,847	2,102
Dept. of Agriculture	420	688	943	929	948	1,017	1,038	1,108	1,219	1,256
CONSTANT (1987) DOLLARS [2]										
Obligations, total [1]	**40,015**	**42,265**	**51,272**	**52,937**	**55,253**	**54,780**	**56,737**	**56,507**	**53,991**	**58,339**
Dept. of Defense.	18,943	19,809	31,586	33,915	35,232	34,014	34,720	33,077	29,008	32,116
Dept. of Health and Human Services.	4,794	5,356	5,779	5,825	6,606	6,907	7,302	7,461	7,896	8,101
National Aeronautics and Space Administration	6,440	4,582	3,528	3,521	3,787	4,179	4,984	5,798	6,350	7,077
Dept. of Energy	4,302	6,735	5,265	4,827	4,757	4,860	4,798	4,998	5,260	5,384
National Science Foundation.	1,251	1,249	1,427	1,393	1,471	1,479	1,543	1,500	1,577	1,741
Dept. of Agriculture	883	974	1,000	956	948	981	959	983	1,041	1,040

[1] Includes other agencies, not shown separately.   [2] See footnote 1, table 973.
Source: U.S. National Science Foundation, *Federal Funds for Research and Development*, annual.

No. 978. Federal Funding for Research and Development, by Selected Budget Function, in Current and Constant (1987) Dollars: 1970 to 1993

[In millions of dollars. For fiscal years ending in year shown; see text, section 9. Excludes R&D plant. Represents budget authority. Functions shown are those for which $1 billion or more was authorized for 1992. See *Historical Statistics, Colonial Times to 1970*, series W 126, for total obligations]

FUNCTION	1970	1980	1985	1986	1987	1988	1989	1990	1991	1992, est.	1993, est.
CURRENT DOLLARS											
Total [1]	15,339	29,739	49,887	53,249	57,069	59,106	62,115	63,781	65,898	69,824	72,866
8 functions, percent of total.	96.6	96.5	98.3	98.3	98.2	98.3	98.2	98.0	97.9	97.9	97.8
National defense	7,981	14,946	33,698	36,926	39,152	40,099	40,665	39,925	39,328	41,470	42,410
Health	1,084	3,694	5,418	5,565	6,556	7,076	7,773	8,308	9,226	10,030	10,479
Space research and technology	3,606	2,738	2,725	2,894	3,398	3,683	4,555	5,765	6,511	6,734	7,530
Energy	574	3,603	2,389	2,286	2,053	2,126	2,419	2,715	2,943	3,137	3,215
General science	452	1,233	1,862	1,873	2,042	2,160	2,373	2,410	2,635	2,745	3,154
Natural resources and environment	340	999	1,059	1,062	1,133	1,160	1,255	1,386	1,582	1,688	1,699
Transportation	535	887	1,030	917	908	896	1,064	1,045	1,231	1,419	1,640
Agriculture	238	585	836	815	822	882	907	950	1,052	1,140	1,154
CONSTANT (1987) DOLLARS [2]											
Total [1]	44,371	42,135	52,891	54,828	57,069	57,036	57,392	56,609	56,280	57,840	58,414
National defense	23,086	21,176	35,727	38,021	39,152	38,694	37,573	35,435	33,588	34,352	33,999
Health	3,136	5,234	5,744	5,730	6,556	6,828	7,182	7,374	7,879	8,309	8,401
Space research and technology	10,431	3,879	2,889	2,980	3,398	3,554	4,209	5,117	5,560	5,578	6,037
Energy	1,660	5,105	2,533	2,354	2,053	2,052	2,235	2,410	2,513	2,599	2,577
General science	1,307	1,747	1,974	1,929	2,042	2,084	2,193	2,139	2,250	2,274	2,528
Natural resources and environment	984	1,415	1,123	1,093	1,133	1,119	1,160	1,230	1,351	1,398	1,362
Transportation	1,548	1,257	1,092	944	908	865	983	927	1,051	1,175	1,315
Agriculture	688	829	886	839	822	851	838	843	898	944	925

[1] Includes other functions, not shown separately.　　[2] See footnote 1, table 973.
Source: U.S. National Science Foundation, *Federal R&D Funding by Budget Function*, annual.

No. 979. National Research and Development (R&D) Expenditures as a Percent of Gross Domestic Product, by Country: 1975 to 1991

YEAR	TOTAL R&D						NON DEFENSE R&D [1]					
	United States	Japan	Ger-many [2]	France	United King-dom	Italy	United States	Japan	Ger-many [2]	France	United King-dom	Italy
1975	2.2	2.1	2.2	1.8	2.2	0.8	1.6	2.1	2.1	1.4	1.4	0.8
1980	2.3	2.2	2.4	1.8	(NA)	0.7	1.8	2.2	2.3	1.4	(NA)	0.7
1985	2.8	2.8	2.7	2.3	2.3	1.1	2.0	2.8	2.6	1.8	1.7	1.1
1988	2.7	2.9	2.9	2.3	2.2	1.2	1.9	2.8	2.7	1.8	1.8	1.1
1989	2.7	3.0	2.9	2.3	2.3	1.2	1.9	3.0	2.7	1.8	1.9	1.2
1990	2.7	3.1	2.8	2.4	(NA)	1.4	1.9	3.0	2.7	1.8	(NA)	1.3
1991	2.7	(NA)	(NA)	(NA)	(NA)	(NA)	2.0	(NA)	(NA)	(NA)	(NA)	(NA)

NA Not available.　　[1] Estimated.　　[2] Former West Germany.

Source: National Science Foundation, *National Patterns of R&D Resources: 1992*; and Organisation for Economic Co-operation and Development.

No. 980. Research and Development (R&D) Expenditures in Science and Engineering at Universities and Colleges in Current and Constant (1987) Dollars: 1981 to 1991

[In millions of dollars]

CHARACTERISTIC	1981	1989	1990	1991	CHARACTERISTIC	1981	1989	1990	1991
CURRENT DOLLARS					CONSTANT (1987) DOLLARS [1]				
Total	6,847	15,016	16,344	17,620	Total	8,805	13,874	14,506	15,048
Basic research	4,593	9,801	10,681	11,538	Basic research	5,907	9,056	9,480	9,854
Applied R&D	2,254	5,215	5,663	6,082	Applied R&D	2,899	4,818	5,026	5,194
Source of funds:					Source of funds:				
All governments	5,117	10,225	10,976	11,704	All governments	6,581	9,447	9,742	9,996
Institutions' own funds	1,004	2,712	3,017	3,369	Institutions' own funds	1,291	2,506	2,678	2,877
Industry	292	998	1,134	1,216	Industry	376	922	1,006	1,039
Other	435	1,080	1,218	1,333	Other	559	998	1,081	1,138
Fields:					Fields:				
Physical sciences	765	1,638	1,796	1,937	Physical sciences	984	1,513	1,594	1,654
Environmental sciences	549	1,009	1,073	1,120	Environmental sciences	706	932	952	957
Mathematical sciences	87	214	220	229	Mathematical sciences	112	198	195	196
Computer sciences	132	472	509	544	Computer sciences	170	436	452	465
Life sciences	3,698	8,079	8,762	9,493	Life sciences	4,756	7,465	7,777	8,107
Psychology	127	237	258	293	Psychology	163	219	229	250
Social sciences	366	637	702	745	Social sciences	471	589	623	636
Other sciences	145	331	360	364	Other sciences	186	306	320	311
Engineering	977	2,399	2,663	2,893	Engineering	1,256	2,217	2,364	2,471

[1] See footnote 1, table 973.
Source: U.S. National Science Foundation, *Survey of Scientific and Engineering Expenditures at Universities and Colleges*, annual.

No. 981. Federal Obligations to Universities and Colleges: 1970 to 1990

[In millions of dollars, except percent. For fiscal years ending in year shown; see text, section 9. Total and nonscience/engineering activities for 1983 are estimates based on revised student aid data from the Dept. of Education. Minus sign (-) indicates decrease]

ITEM	1970	1980	1983	1984	1985	1986	1987	1988	1989	1990
CURRENT DOLLARS										
Federal obligations, total	3,237	8,299	9,345	10,039	10,972	11,619	13,434	14,067	15,502	15,205
Annual percent change [1]	-6.5	9.1	6.5	7.4	9.3	5.9	15.6	4.7	10.2	-1.9
Academic science/engineering obligations	2,188	4,791	5,681	6,308	7,258	7,431	8,565	9,133	10,072	10,462
Percent of total	67.6	57.7	60.8	62.8	66.2	64.0	63.8	64.9	65.0	68.8
Research and development	1,447	4,161	5,024	5,449	6,246	6,457	7,241	7,719	8,523	9,031
Research and development plant	45	38	38	50	114	106	230	203	237	125
Other science/engineering activities	696	593	619	809	898	868	1,095	1,211	1,312	1,306
Nonscience/engineering activities	1,049	3,508	3,664	3,731	3,714	4,188	4,868	4,933	5,431	4,743
CONSTANT (1987) DOLLARS [2]										
Federal obligations, total	9,362	11,758	10,738	11,051	11,632	11,964	13,434	13,574	14,323	13,495
Annual percent change [1]	-11.3	0.1	2.2	2.9	5.3	2.8	12.3	1.0	5.5	-5.8
Academic science/engineering obligations	6,328	6,788	6,528	6,943	7,695	7,651	8,565	8,814	9,306	9,285
Percent of total	67.6	57.7	60.8	62.8	66.2	64.0	63.8	64.9	65.0	68.8
Research and development	4,185	5,895	5,774	5,998	6,622	6,648	7,241	7,449	7,874	8,015
Research and development plant	130	54	43	55	121	109	230	196	219	111
Other science/engineering activities	2,014	840	711	891	952	894	1,095	1,169	1,212	1,159
Nonscience/engineering activities	3,035	4,970	4,211	4,107	3,937	4,313	4,868	4,760	5,018	4,210

[1] Percent change from immediate prior year.   [2] See footnote 1, table 973.
Source: U.S. National Science Foundation, *Survey of Federal Support to Universities, Colleges, and Selected Nonprofit Institutions,* annual.

No. 982 Federal R&D Obligations to Selected Universities and Colleges: 1981 to 1990

[For fiscal years ending in year shown; see text, section 9. Data are for the top 45 institutions receiving Federal R&D funds in 1990. Awards to the administrative offices of university systems are excluded from totals for individual institutions because that allocation of funds is unknown, but those awards are included in "total all institutions"]

MAJOR INSTITUTION RANKED BY TOTAL 1990 FEDERAL R&D OBLIGATIONS	OBLIGATIONS ($1,000)				RANK			
	1981	1985	1989	1990	1981	1985	1989	1990
Total, all institutions [1]	4,410,931	6,246,181	8,522,555	9,031,047	(X)	(X)	(X)	(X)
45 institutions, percent of total	62.9	61.4	60.6	60.7	(X)	(X)	(X)	(X)
Johns Hopkins University	363,429	297,374	411,879	470,935	1	1	1	1
Stanford University	106,073	174,961	239,847	247,992	3	3	2	2
Massachusetts Institute of Technology	146,035	189,558	207,157	218,318	2	2	3	3
University of Washington	99,965	146,179	203,691	217,291	4	4	4	4
University of California—Los Angeles	94,945	128,211	170,839	176,735	5	5	5	5
University of Michigan	73,999	108,035	167,865	176,620	11	11	6	6
University of California—San Francisco	64,814	98,536	159,027	167,027	15	16	8	7
University of California—San Diego	91,403	103,633	166,601	165,224	6	13	7	8
University of Wisconsin—Madison	86,918	124,604	150,474	155,175	8	7	9	9
Columbia University—Main Division	83,659	127,331	150,263	153,171	9	6	10	10
Harvard University	87,830	109,414	141,760	148,055	7	9	12	11
Cornell University	72,671	119,966	139,954	144,749	13	8	13	12
University of Pennsylvania	76,136	103,119	132,805	142,509	10	15	14	13
Yale University	73,526	109,227	146,245	142,483	12	10	11	14
University of Minnesota	72,001	103,272	128,727	137,495	14	14	16	15
Pennsylvania State University	47,099	76,726	119,435	136,754	21	19	17	16
University of California—Berkeley	64,065	106,710	131,070	123,983	16	12	15	17
University of Southern California	49,221	89,706	114,766	122,734	20	17	18	18
Washington University	54,170	71,978	102,974	117,907	17	22	20	19
University of Colorado	46,146	71,424	101,345	116,449	22	23	21	20
Duke University	44,287	69,169	108,611	116,109	23	26	19	21
University of Pittsburgh	38,512	58,620	91,094	114,262	29	28	25	22
University of Chicago	53,992	71,194	90,611	104,074	18	24	26	23
University of Rochester	42,983	70,379	98,550	102,453	25	25	23	24
University of NC at Chapel Hill	38,447	63,105	95,025	100,183	30	27	24	25
University of Illinois—Urbana	53,583	83,122	100,062	99,742	19	18	22	26
University of Texas at Austin	43,756	72,379	84,619	93,401	24	21	27	27
University of Arizona	36,308	49,740	82,913	92,824	33	37	28	28
Ohio State University	42,899	56,065	72,702	80,401	26	30	31	29
University of Iowa	35,300	55,117	76,059	76,762	34	31	30	30
New York University	40,636	74,577	77,761	75,749	28	20	29	31
University of Alabama—Birmingham	29,970	44,093	70,702	74,529	35	45	34	32
Baylor College of Medicine	35,062	45,837	69,499	72,260	44	46	32	33
Case Western Reserve University	33,744	47,994	69,589	71,263	38	40	33	34
Vanderbilt University	27,426	39,909	63,978	70,585	47	48	39	35
California Institute of Technology	32,959	55,083	69,335	69,228	40	32	35	36
University of California—Davis	31,757	43,156	60,100	68,952	42	47	45	37
Yeshiva University	42,590	56,988	68,553	67,045	27	29	36	38
University of Massachusetts	22,418	46,046	67,183	66,811	55	44	38	39
University of Utah	38,163	50,938	61,361	65,250	31	36	41	40
University of Maryland—College Park	27,313	51,073	60,252	64,723	50	35	43	41
University of Miami	28,956	33,709	60,135	63,707	46	59	44	42
Purdue University	36,549	51,544	62,751	63,167	32	34	40	43
Indiana University	29,276	39,118	55,449	61,435	45	49	50	44
Northwestern University	32,446	48,260	57,494	61,100	41	39	49	45

X Not applicable.   [1] Includes other institutions, not shown separately.
Source: U.S. National Science Foundation, *Federal Support to Universities and Colleges and Selected Nonprofit Institutions,* annual.

No. 983. Funds for Performance of Industrial Research and Development (R&D), by Source of Funds and Selected Industries, in Current and Constant (1987) Dollars: 1970 to 1990

[In millions of dollars. Covers basic research, applied research, and development. See also *Historical Statistics, Colonial Times to 1970*, series W 144-160]

1972 SIC[1] code	INDUSTRY	1970	1975	1980	1985	1987	1988	1989	1990
	CURRENT DOLLARS								
(X)	**Total funds**................	**18,067**	**24,187**	**44,505**	**84,239**	**92,155**	**97,889**	**101,854**	**104,344**
28	Chemicals and allied products	1,773	2,727	4,636	8,540	9,635	10,772	11,466	12,565
13,29	Petroleum refining and extraction	515	693	1,552	(D)	1,897	1,944	2,066	2,099
35	Machinery......................	1,729	3,196	5,901	12,216	(D)	(D)	(D)	(D)
36	Electrical equipment	4,220	5,105	9,175	14,432	15,848	16,242	16,929	17,397
371	Motor vehicles and motor vehicles equipment......................	1,591	2,340	4,955	6,984	(D)	(D)	(D)	(D)
372,376	Aircraft and missiles..............	5,219	5,713	9,198	22,231	24,458	25,900	25,638	25,357
38	Professional and scientific instruments..	744	1,173	5,013	5,013	5,222	5,426	5,743	6,163
(X)	All other[2].....................	2,276	3,240	6,059	(D)	(D)	(D)	(D)	(D)
(X)	**Company funds**..............	**10,288**	**15,582**	**30,476**	**57,043**	**61,403**	**65,772**	**70,562**	**73,764**
28	Chemicals and allied products	1,593	2,490	4,264	8,310	9,445	10,573	11,383	12,498
13,29	Petroleum refining and extraction	493	(D)	1,401	2,194	1,883	1,923	2,050	2,083
35	Machinery......................	1,469	2687	5,254	10,701	10,577	11,992	13,478	13,804
36	Electrical equipment	2,008	2,798	5,431	9,271	10,449	11,061	11,641	11,768
371	Motor vehicles and motor vehicles equipment......................	1,278	2,022	4,300	6,164	7,167	7,769	8,725	8,550
372,376	Aircraft and missiles..............	1,213	1,285	2,570	5,649	5,939	6,023	6,005	6,140
38	Professional and scientific instruments..	550	1,001	2,456	4,622	4,950	5,306	5,630	6,064
(X)	All other[2].....................	1,684	(D)	4,800	10,132	10,993	11,125	11,650	12,857
	CONSTANT (1987) DOLLARS[3]								
(X)	**Total funds**................	**51,429**	**49,171**	**62,062**	**89,265**	**92,155**	**94,260**	**93,944**	**92,446**
28	Chemicals and allied products	5,047	5,544	6,465	9,050	9,635	10,373	10,576	11,132
13,29	Petroleum refining and extraction	1,466	1,409	2,164	(D)	1,897	1,872	1,906	1,860
35	Machinery......................	4,922	6,497	8,229	12,945	(D)	(D)	(D)	(D)
36	Electrical equipment	12,013	10,378	12,795	15,293	15,848	15,640	15,614	15,413
371	Motor vehicles and motor vehicles equipment......................	4,529	4,757	6,910	7,401	(D)	(D)	(D)	(D)
372,376	Aircraft and missiles..............	14,856	11,614	12,827	23,557	24,458	24,940	23,647	22,466
38	Professional and scientific instruments..	2,118	2,385	4,224	5,312	5,222	5,225	5,297	5,460
(X)	All other[2].....................	6,479	6,587	8,449	(D)	(D)	(D)	(D)	(D)
(X)	**Company funds**..............	**29,286**	**31,677**	**42,499**	**60,446**	**61,403**	**63,334**	**65,082**	**65,353**
28	Chemicals and allied products	4,535	5,062	5,946	8,806	9,445	10,181	10,499	11,073
13,29	Petroleum refining and extraction	1,403	(D)	1,954	2,325	1,883	1,852	1,891	1,846
35	Machinery......................	4,182	5,463	7,327	11,339	10,577	11,547	12,431	12,230
36	Electrical equipment	5,716	5,688	7,574	9,824	10,449	10,651	10,737	10,426
371	Motor vehicles and motor vehicles equipment......................	3,638	4,111	5,996	6,532	7,167	7,481	8,047	7,575
372,376	Aircraft and missiles..............	3,453	2,612	3,584	5,986	5,939	5,800	5,539	5,440
38	Professional and scientific instruments..	1,566	2,035	3,425	4,898	4,950	5,109	5,193	5,373
(X)	All other[2].....................	4,794	(D)	6,694	10,737	10,993	10,713	10,745	11,391

D Figure withheld to avoid disclosure of information pertaining to a specific organization or individual.   X Not applicable.   [1] 1972 Standard Industrial Classification. See text, section 13.   [2] All other manufacturing and nonmanfacturing.   [3] See footnote 1, table 973.

Source: U.S. National Science Foundation, *Research and Development in Industry*, annual.

No. 984. R&D Funds as a Percent of Net Sales in R&D-Performing Manufacturing Companies, by Industry: 1970 to 1990

1972 SIC[1] code	INDUSTRY	TOTAL R&D FUNDS AS A PERCENT OF NET SALES					COMPANY R&D FUNDS AS A PERCENT OF NET SALES				
		1970	1980	1985	1989	1990	1970	1980	1985	1989	1990
(X)	**Total**[2] ....,........	**3.7**	**3.0**	**4.4**	**4.6**	**4.6**	**2.2**	**2.1**	**3.0**	**3.2**	**3.2**
20	Food and kindred products[3]	0.5	0.4	(D)	(D)	(D)	0.5	(D)	0.6	0.5	0.5
26	Paper and allied products	0.9	1.0	(D)	0.7	0.8	(D)	1.0	0.8	0.7	0.8
28	Chemicals and allied products	3.9	3.6	5.0	5.4	5.7	3.5	3.3	4.9	5.3	5.7
13,29	Petroleum refining and extraction	1.0	0.6	(D)	1.0	0.9	0.9	0.5	0.9	1.0	0.8
30	Rubber products	2.3	2.2	(D)	(D)	(D)	1.7	(D)	1.8	1.7	1.8
32	Stone, clay, and glass products	1.8	1.4	(D)	(D)	(D)	1.7	1.3	2.3	2.3	2.3
33	Primary metals................	0.8	0.7	(D)	0.9	(D)	0.8	0.5	0.9	0.9	1.0
34	Fabricated metal products	1.2	1.4	1.5	1.2	1.2	1.1	1.2	1.4	1.0	1.0
35	Machinery....................	4.0	5.0	7.6	8.7	8.9	3.4	4.5	6.7	8.0	8.4
36	Electrical equipment	7.3	6.6	7.6	7.1	7.3	3.4	3.9	4.8	4.9	4.9
371	Motor vehicles and motor vehicle equipment...............	3.5	4.9	3.8	(D)	(D)	2.8	4.2	3.4	3.8	3.9
372,376	Aircraft and missiles	16.2	13.7	14.9	15.3	14.3	3.8	3.8	3.9	3.6	3.5
38	Professional and scientific instruments..............	5.7	7.5	8.9	7.5	7.7	4.2	6.1	8.3	7.3	7.6

D Figure withheld to avoid disclosure of information pertaining to a specific organization or individual.   X Not applicable.   [1] 1972 Standard Industrial Classification. See text, section 13.   [2] Includes all manufacturing industries.   [3] Includes tobacco products (SIC 21) beginning 1985.

Source: U.S. National Science Foundation, *Research and Development in Industry*, annual.

No. 985. Federal Obligations for Research, by Field of Science in Current and Constant (1987) Dollars: 1980 to 1992

[In millions of dollars. For fiscal years ending in year shown; see text, section 9. See headnote, table 978]

FIELD	1980	1984	1985	1986	1987	1988	1989	1990	1991	1992, est.
CURRENT DOLLARS										
Research, total	11,597	14,979	16,133	16,502	17,940	18,650	20,765	21,739	24,072	25,683
Basic	4,674	7,067	7,819	8,153	8,942	9,474	10,602	11,286	12,446	13,208
Applied	6,923	7,911	8,315	8,349	8,998	9,176	10,163	10,453	11,626	12,475
Life sciences	4,192	5,636	6,363	6,464	7,341	7,724	8,495	8,838	9,670	10,230
Psychology	199	267	327	334	370	390	422	449	487	522
Physical sciences	2,001	2,969	3,046	3,069	3,253	3,317	3,705	3,809	4,123	4,523
Environmental sciences	1,261	1,276	1,404	1,482	1,512	1,607	1,773	2,174	2,450	2,627
Mathematics and computer sciences	241	440	575	615	641	643	735	841	946	1,007
Engineering	2,830	3,624	3,618	3,739	3,906	3,956	4,442	4,335	4,924	5,359
Social sciences	524	436	460	416	480	486	551	630	772	706
Other sciences, n.e.c.[1]	350	331	342	383	438	527	642	664	701	708
CONSTANT (1987) DOLLARS[2]										
Research, total	16,432	16,487	17,105	16,992	17,940	17,997	19,186	19,294	20,559	21,275
Basic	6,623	7,779	8,290	8,395	8,942	9,142	9,796	10,017	10,629	10,941
Applied	9,809	8,708	8,815	8,597	8,998	8,855	9,390	9,278	9,929	10,334
Life sciences	5,940	6,204	6,746	6,656	7,341	7,453	7,849	7,844	8,259	8,474
Psychology	282	294	347	344	370	376	390	399	416	432
Physical sciences	2,835	3,268	3,229	3,160	3,253	3,201	3,423	3,381	3,521	3,747
Environmental sciences	1,787	1,404	1,488	1,526	1,512	1,551	1,638	1,930	2,092	2,176
Mathematics and computer sciences	341	485	610	634	641	620	679	746	808	834
Engineering	4,010	3,989	3,835	3,850	3,906	3,818	4,104	3,848	4,205	4,439
Social sciences	742	480	488	428	480	469	509	559	659	585
Other sciences, n.e.c.[1]	495	364	362	395	438	508	593	589	599	586

[1] N.e.c. = Not elsewhere classified.   [2] See footnote 1, table 973.

Source: U.S. National Science Foundation, *Federal Funds for Research and Development*, annual.

No. 986. Research and Development Scientists and Engineers—Average Full-Time-Equivalent Employment and Cost, by Industry: 1975 to 1990

[Data are estimates; on average full-time-equivalent (FTE) basis. See *Historical Statistics, Colonial Times to 1970*, series W 167, for total cost per scientist or engineer]

1972 SIC[1] code	INDUSTRY	1975	1980	1983	1984	1985	1986	1987	1988	1989	1990
	EMPLOYED SCIENTISTS										
(X)	**Average FTE of scientists and engineers (1,000)**[2][3]	363.9	469.2	562.5	603.3	646.8	684.2	702.2	714.4	725.6	720.3
28	Chemicals[4]	44.8	53.1	68.6	70.5	73.5	74.4	75.5	76.7	78.3	79.4
35	Machinery	54.3	65.7	83.3	84.4	85.7	93.1	97.1	99.1	106.1	109.7
36	Electrical equipment[5]	81.5	100.7	110.9	113.2	115.6	123.1	131.5	136.6	139.3	139.5
371	Motor vehicles	25.7	36.7	28.8	28.7	31.3	42.1	46.9	46.6	47.8	47.6
372,376	Aircraft and missiles	67.2	90.6	107.3	120.9	137.5	137.5	136.4	139.4	135.4	123.4
(X)	**CONSTANT (1987) DOLLARS**[6]										
(X)	**Cost per scientist or engineer ($1,000)**[3][7]	135.2	132.3	133.1	136.2	138.0	132.6	131.2	131.9	129.7	128.4
28	Chemicals[4]	123.8	121.9	120.2	123.6	123.2	120.8	127.6	135.2	135.2	140.2
35	Machinery	119.7	125.4	124.4	136.7	151.0	(D)	(D)	(D)	127.7	118.7
36	Electrical equipment[5]	127.5	127.0	131.1	133.7	132.4	124.5	120.6	114.5	112.2	110.5
371	Motor vehicles	185.2	188.5	211.9	232.2	236.4	(D)	(D)	(D)	(D)	(D)
372,376	Aircraft and missiles	173.0	141.7	164.8	171.3	171.3	154.6	179.4	179.0	174.7	182.0

D Withheld to avoid disclosure.   X Not applicable.   [1] 1972 Standard Industrial Classification; see text, section 13.   [2] The mean number of FTE R&D scientists and engineers employed in January of the year shown and the following January.   [3] Includes industries not shown separately.   [4] Includes allied products.   [5] Includes communication.   [6] See footnote 1, table 973.   [7] Represents the arithmetic mean of the numbers of R&D scientists and engineers reported in each industry for January in two consecutive years divided into total R&D expenditures in each industry.

Source: U.S. National Science Foundation, *Research and Development in Industry*, annual.

No. 987. Scientists and Engineers Employed in Research and Development: 1970 to 1989

[In thousands of full-time equivalent employees. Data are estimates. Yearly averages for industry sector only. Excludes those employed by State and local government agencies]

SECTOR	1970	1980	1982	1983	1984	1985	1986	1987	1988	1989
Total	543.8	651.1	711.8	751.6	797.6	841.6	882.3	910.2	927.3	949.3
Industry (excl. social scientists) . . .	375.6	469.2	525.4	562.5	603.3	646.8	683.4	702.2	714.4	726.0
Federal Government	67.5	58.6	60.0	61.3	62.1	55.0	54.4	57.4	57.6	60.0
Other [1]	100.7	123.3	126.4	127.8	132.2	139.8	144.5	150.6	155.3	163.3

[1] Includes professional R&D personnel employed at universities and colleges, other nonprofit institutions, and federally funded R&D centers administered by organizations in these sectors, and graduate students engaged in R&D at universities and colleges.

Source: U.S. National Science Foundation, *National Patterns of R&D Resources: 1992.*

No. 988. Science and Engineering Degree Recipients in 1988 and 1989—Selected Characteristics: 1990

[Based on survey and subject to sampling error; see source for details]

DEGREE AND FIELD	Graduates 1988 and 1989 (1,000)	1990—PERCENT DISTRIBUTION				Median salary ($1,000)
		In school [1]	Employed		Not employed	
			In S&E [2]	In other		
Bachelor's recipients.	643.2	20	44	32	5	26.0
All science fields	494.5	22	35	38	5	23.8
Physical sciences	29.4	39	38	18	5	25.1
Math/statistics	35.2	18	50	26	6	23.6
Computer science.	69.3	6	77	13	4	30.1
Environmental science.	7.3	30	49	15	5	23.7
Life sciences	111.2	32	34	28	6	21.0
Psychology	85.7	21	20	54	5	18.6
Social Sciences	156.4	20	19	55	5	21.9
All engineering fields [3]	148.7	11	73	12	3	33.0
Civil	15.2	10	78	9	3	30.1
Electrical/electronics.	55.5	11	76	10	3	34.0
Industrial	12.3	5	72	18	5	31.1
Mechanical	30.0	11	76	10	4	34.0
Master's recipients	136.6	23	61	13	4	37.0
All science fields	93.7	25	55	16	4	33.8
Physical sciences	9.2	41	49	8	2	34.9
Math/statistics	10.6	18	67	13	2	32.8
Computer science.	22.2	9	78	10	3	42.1
Environmental science.	5.2	21	71	6	2	33.8
Life sciences	19.3	35	47	15	4	26.9
Psychology	7.3	34	36	26	4	32.0
Social Sciences	19.9	26	37	30	7	31.0
All engineering fields [3]	42.9	17	73	6	3	41.4
Civil	4.7	11	85	4	-	35.2
Electrical/electronics.	13.8	19	72	4	5	46.5
Industrial	2.6	8	62	23	8	40.3
Mechanical	8.0	15	79	5	1	42.1

[1] Full-time graduate students.   [2] In science and engineering.   [3] Includes other fields, not shown separately.

Source: National Science Foundation/SRS, *Characteristics of Recent Science and Engineering Graduates: 1990.* (Data are biennial.)

No. 989. Professional Scientific, Engineering, and Technical Personnel in the Federal Government, by Occupational Group: 1970 to 1989

[In thousands, except percent. As of October. Excludes health professional personnel]

OCCUPATIONAL GROUP	1970	1980	1985 [1]	1987 [1]	1988 [1][2]	1989 [1][2]	PERCENT FEMALE					
							1970	1980	1985 [1]	1987 [1]	1988 [1][2]	1989 [1][2]
Total	180.3	206.9	238.0	240.0	217.6	223.3	6.7	9.5	13.8	15.4	13.8	14.7
Scientific personnel .	77.2	88.0	91.4	89.1	86.7	87.7	8.0	12.7	15.6	22.7	17.6	18.6
Physical sciences.	29.8	27.6	27.6	27.1	26.5	26.6	6.4	9.5	12.5	13.9	14.4	14.8
Mathematics [3] . . .	8.6	11.1	11.0	10.4	9.8	9.7	17.4	19.8	22.8	23.7	23.4	24.0
Life sciences . . .	26.9	30.5	33.5	33.1	33.2	33.8	4.1	8.7	12.1	14.2	15.0	16.3
Social sciences [4] .	6.6	10.5	10.1	10.1	10.4	10.2	16.2	23.3	25.1	26.3	26.4	28.8
Economics . . .	4.3	5.9	5.9	5.6	5.5	5.5	11.1	17.4	20.6	21.3	21.5	22.1
Other . . . [5] . .	2.3	4.6	4.2	4.5	4.9	4.7	25.1	30.8	31.5	32.6	31.9	36.6
Geography [5] . . .	3.3	4.9	5.7	4.9	3.6	4.1	8.5	14.8	17.0	18.0	19.2	19.2
Psychology	2.2	3.3	3.4	3.5	3.3	3.4	13.7	16.8	21.4	23.6	23.0	24.7
Engineering personnel	83.0	89.6	105.1	109.7	108.2	111.4	0.5	1.9	5.3	6.7	7.2	7.8
Computer specialists	20.1	29.3	41.5	41.2	22.7	24.3	21.1	23.3	31.4	34.8	31.2	32.0

[1] Excludes U.S. Post Office.   [2] Not comparable with previous years. Excludes employees with less than a bachelor's degree.   [3] Includes statistics.   [4] Includes community planning.   [5] Includes cartography and land surveying.

Source: U.S. National Science Foundation. Compiled from data supplied by the U.S. Office of Personnel Management.

No. 990. Civilian Employment of Scientists, Engineers, and Technicians, by Occupation and Major Industrial Sector: 1990

[In thousands. Based on sample and subject to sampling error. For details, see source]

OCCUPATION	Total [1]	WAGE AND SALARY WORKERS								Self em-ployed
		Min-ing [2]	Con-struc-tion	Manu-facturing	Trans-por-tation [3]	Trade	FIRE [4]	Serv-ices	Govern-ment	
Scientists and engineers. .	2,600.7	48.0	24.9	927.2	117.7	61.8	87.1	711.1	451.4	161.0
Scientists	1,081.7	22.6	1.3	182.9	33.6	27.5	72.5	356.9	250.2	125.0
Physical scientists.	199.5	19.0	0.1	59.3	2.6	2.0	0.2	61.8	43.1	11.0
Life scientists.	173.5	0.2	-	23.6	1.0	1.6	0.6	64.4	66.6	7.0
Mathematical scientists	21.6	-	-	2.5	1.7	-	2.0	9.1	6.3	-
Social scientists	223.9	0.4	-	0.0	1.8	-	10.0	87.6	58.8	65.0
Systems analysts, EDP	463.2	3.1	1.2	97.4	26.6	23.8	59.7	133.9	75.4	42.0
Engineers [5].	1,519.0	25.4	23.6	744.3	84.1	34.4	14.6	354.2	201.2	36.0
Civil engineers	198.0	1.0	8.9	9.4	7.4	0.4	1.1	79.0	83.6	7.0
Electrical/electronics.	426.2	1.1	4.5	196.7	40.5	18.8	0.9	117.3	40.4	6.0
Mechanical engineers	233.3	1.7	4.7	141.6	5.8	5.4	0.9	54.0	14.3	5.0
Engineering and science technicians	1,326.4	18.0	24.6	481.9	77.0	99.6	7.1	412.3	173.8	24.0
Electrical/electronics technicians	363.0	0.8	5.0	145.6	32.0	78.8	1.6	64.7	29.6	5.0
Engineering technicians	391.8	5.5	5.4	137.5	24.0	9.1	1.6	105.2	97.6	5.0
Drafters	325.2	4.1	14.1	106.4	17.4	7.6	1.7	148.0	13.8	10.0
Science technicians	246.4	7.6	0.0	92.3	3.8	4.1	2.3	94.3	32.8	4.0
Surveyors.	108.0	2.7	2.8	-	2.9	-	0.5	68.2	24.3	6.0
Computer programmers . . .	564.7	3.2	2.1	99.7	26.6	56.3	77.4	233.6	50.4	15.0

- Represents or rounds to zero.   [1] Includes agriculture, forestry, and fishing not shown separately.   [2] Includes oil and gas extraction.   [3] Includes communications and public utilities.   [4] Finance, insurance, and real estate.   [5] Includes kinds of engineers and technicians not shown separately.

Source: U.S. Bureau of Labor Statistics, *Monthly Labor Review*, November 1991. (Data collected biennially.)

No. 991. Doctoral Scientists and Engineers—Selected Characteristics: 1975 to 1989

[In thousands]

CHARACTERISTIC	1975	1985	1989		CHARACTERISTIC	1975	1985	1989	
			Num-ber	Em-ployed				Num-ber	Em-ployed
Total.	**270.4**	**424.6**	**485.2**	**448.7**	Women.	25.6	64.0	84.5	77.2
Field:					Race:				
Life scientists.	68.3	109.9	127.0	115.8	White	245.4	377.9	432.0	397.2
Physical scientists	58.5	73.1	78.3	70.2	Black	2.6	5.9	7.6	7.2
Psychologists.	31.3	54.9	64.8	60.6	Asian/Pacific Islander	13.9	35.5	42.6	41.1
Social scientists	38.6	68.5	76.8	70.0	Other and not reported . . .	8.4	5.2	2.9	3.2
Economists	12.6	19.1	20.5	18.6	Employment status:				
Other social scientists . .	26.0	49.4	56.3	51.4	Full-time employed	240.6	371.9	411.0	411.0
Engineers	43.5	67.9	78.4	74.8	Part-time employed	7.3	16.7	22.9	22.9
Mathematical scientists . . .	14.2	17.5	18.8	17.6	Postdoctorates.	8.2	11.8	14.8	14.8
Computer specialists.	3.5	15.0	19.9	19.8	Unemployed/seeking	2.5	3.4	3.8	(X)
Environmental scientists . .	12.5	18.0	21.1	19.8	Unemployed/not seeking . .	2.4	3.9	4.2	(X)
Sex:					Retired/not employed	8.7	16.2	27.4	(X)
Men	244.9	360.6	400.6	371.5	Other and not reported . . .	0.9	0.8	1.1	(X)

X Not applicable.

Source: U.S. National Science Foundation, *Characteristics of Doctoral Scientists and Engineers in the United States,* biennial series.

No. 992. Graduate Science/Engineering Students in Doctorate-Granting Institutions of Higher Education, by Sex, Citizenship, and Enrollment Status: 1975 to 1991

[As of **fall.** Includes outlying areas]

FIELD OF SCIENCE OR ENGINEERING	TOTAL (1,000)				PERCENT—								
					Female			Foreign		Part-time			
	1975	1980	1990	1991	1980	1990	1991	1990	1991	1975	1980	1990	1991
Total, all surveyed fields .	**291.6**	**321.2**	**384.9**	**411.3**	**32.5**	**36.6**	**37.9**	**26.1**	**24.4**	**29.2**	**30.9**	**30.1**	**30.3**
Science/engineering	268.8	285.2	343.6	360.7	27.7	32.1	32.6	28.1	26.7	29.3	29.9	28.4	28.1
Engineering, total	65.2	69.3	98.4	105.1	8.6	13.6	13.8	36.7	34.4	43.0	40.0	35.6	34.4
Sciences, total	203.6	215.9	245.3	255.6	33.9	39.6	40.3	24.6	23.6	24.9	26.6	25.5	25.5
Physical sciences	24.9	25.4	31.9	32.9	16.6	23.3	24.3	37.7	36.4	13.9	12.3	11.0	10.9
Environmental.	11.1	12.8	12.8	13.2	22.7	29.0	30.1	20.5	19.9	18.2	19.3	23.4	25.3
Mathematical sciences . .	14.7	13.6	17.1	17.5	25.4	30.5	30.9	35.6	34.8	30.8	31.2	23.1	22.8
Computer sciences	7.4	11.4	27.5	27.7	21.8	22.8	22.9	33.2	33.1	43.5	48.0	46.7	47.3
Agricultural sciences	10.2	11.7	10.5	10.7	23.4	29.6	31.1	27.1	26.5	15.4	17.1	18.0	18.2
Biological sciences	41.7	42.6	45.6	48.1	38.1	45.5	45.9	25.0	23.7	15.7	16.1	14.8	14.2
Psychology	27.8	29.8	34.2	36.4	52.1	65.4	66.0	4.7	4.4	27.2	26.0	28.0	28.3
Social sciences.	66.0	68.7	65.5	69.1	37.2	43.0	43.2	22.3	21.1	33.1	37.3	32.2	31.8
Health fields, total	22.8	36.0	41.3	50.6	70.8	73.6	76.2	9.9	8.1	28.2	38.9	44.7	46.1

Source: U.S. National Science Foundation, *Survey of Graduate Science Science and Engineering Students and Postdoctu-rates,* annual.

No. 993. Doctorates Conferred, by Recipients' Characteristics, 1980 to 1991, and by Selected Science and Engineering Fields, 1991

[In percent, except as indicated]

CHARACTERISTIC	ALL FIELDS 1980	1985	1991 All fields[1]	Engineering	Physical sciences[2]	Earth sciences	Mathematics	Computer sciences	Biological sciences[3]	Agricultural	Social sciences[4]	Psychology
Total conferred (number)	31,020	31,297	37,451	5,212	3,602	837	1,040	797	4,642	1,072	3,306	3,240
Male	69.7	65.7	63.2	91.3	81.7	77.9	81.3	85.4	62.1	80.5	63.7	38.8
Female	30.3	34.3	36.8	8.7	18.3	22.1	18.7	14.6	37.9	19.5	36.3	61.2
Median age[5]	32.2	33.3	33.9	31.4	29.7	32.6	30.9	31.7	31.3	33.8	343.0	33.9
CITIZENSHIP[6]												
Total conferred (number)	30,156	29,921	35,389	4,831	3,431	798	974	779	4,482	1,031	3,124	2,977
U.S. citizen	83.6	78.1	69.9	40.9	59.7	73.2	45.1	48.7	72.5	53.4	60.9	93.9
Foreign citizen	16.4	21.9	30.1	59.1	40.3	26.8	54.9	51.3	27.5	46.6	39.1	6.1
RACE/ETHNICITY[7]												
Total conferred (number)	26,512	24,693	26,535	2,358	2,220	620	491	441	3,455	607	2,128	2,856
White[8]	84.7	86.2	85.2	75.8	86.2	89.8	83.5	78.9	86.5	88.0	82.1	88.9
Black[8]	4.2	4.2	4.1	2.3	1.4	2.1	1.6	1.8	1.6	2.8	5.7	4.1
Asian/Pacific[8]	4.2	4.3	5.6	17.0	7.3	2.7	11.6	14.7	7.4	3.8	5.2	2.0
Indian/Alaskan[8]	0.3	0.4	0.5	0.3	0.5	0.5	0.0	0.2	0.3	0.7	0.4	0.5
Hispanic	1.8	2.6	3.2	2.5	2.8	2.6	1.8	2.5	2.7	2.5	4.3	4.1
Other/unknown	4.9	2.2	1.5	2.1	1.8	2.3	1.4	1.8	1.5	2.3	2.3	0.6

[1] Includes other fields, not shown separately. [2] Astronomy, physics, and chemistry. [3] Biochemistry, botany, microbiology, physiology, zoology, and related fields. [4] Anthropology, sociology, political science, economics, and international relations. [5] For definition of median, see Guide to Tabular Presentation. [6] For those with known citizenship. Includes those with temporary visas. [7] Excludes those with temporary visas. [8] Non-Hispanic.
Source: U.S. National Science Foundation, Division of Science Resources Studies, Survey of Earned Doctorates, *Selected Data on Science and Engineering Doctorate Awards: 1991*, annual.

No. 994. Nobel Prize Laureates in Chemistry, Physics, and Physiology/Medicine—Selected Countries: 1901 to 1991

[Presented by location of award-winning research and by date of award]

COUNTRY	1901-1991 Total	Physics	Chemistry	Physiology/Medicine	1901-1915	1916-1930	1931-1945	1946-1960	1961-1975	1976-1991
Total	410	141	116	153	52	41	49	74	92	102
United States	162	57	36	69	3	3	14	38	41	63
United Kingdom	69	21	24	24	7	8	11	14	20	9
West Germany[1]	59	17	28	14	15	12	11	4	8	9
France	23	9	7	7	10	3	2	-	8	3
Soviet Union	10	7	1	2	2	-	2	4	5	3
Japan	4	3	1	-	-	-	-	1	2	1
Other countries	83	27	19	37	15	15	11	13	13	16

- Represents zero. [1] Includes East Germany before 1946.
Source: U.S. National Science Foundation, unpublished data.

No. 995. Federal Space Program—Budget Authority, by Agency: 1960 to 1991

[In millions of dollars, except percent. For fiscal years ending in year shown; see text, section 9. NASA=National Aeronautics and Space Administration]

YEAR	Total	NASA Total	NASA Percent of total	DEFENSE Total	DEFENSE Percent of total	Other	YEAR	Total	NASA Total	NASA Percent of total	DEFENSE Total	DEFENSE Percent of total	Other
1960	1,066	462	43.3	561	52.6	43	1979	7,244	4,030	55.6	3,036	41.9	178
1965	6,956	5,138	73.9	1,574	22.6	244	1980	8,689	4,680	53.9	3,848	44.3	160
1966	6,970	5,065	72.7	1,689	24.2	217	1981	9,978	4,992	50.0	4,828	48.4	158
1969	5,976	3,822	64.0	2,013	33.7	141	1982	12,441	5,528	44.4	6,679	53.7	234
1970	5,341	3,547	66.4	1,678	31.4	115	1983	15,589	6,328	40.6	9,019	57.9	242
1971	4,741	3,101	65.4	1,512	31.9	127	1984	17,136	6,648	38.8	10,195	59.5	293
1972	4,575	3,071	67.1	1,407	30.8	97	1985	20,167	6,925	34.3	12,768	63.3	474
1973	4,825	3,093	64.1	1,623	33.6	109	1986	21,659	7,165	33.1	14,126	65.2	368
1974	4,640	2,759	59.4	1,766	38.1	116	1987	26,448	[3]9,809	37.1	16,287	61.6	352
1975[2]	4,914	2,915	59.3	1,892	38.5	107	1988	26,607	8,302	31.2	17,679	66.4	626
1976[2]	6,660	4,075	61.2	2,444	36.7	142	1989	28,443	10,098	35.5	17,906	63.0	440
1977	5,983	3,440	57.5	2,412	40.3	131	1990	28,089	12,142	43.2	15,616	55.6	330
1978	6,518	3,623	55.6	2,738	42.0	157	1991	27,592	13,036	47.2	14,181	51.4	375

[1] Includes budget authority for the space transportation system of $3.1 billion in 1982; $4.1 billion in 1983; and $4.0 billion in 1984. [2] Includes transition quarter, July 1 to Sept. 30, 1976. [3] Includes $2.1 billion for replacement of shuttle orbiter Challenger.
Source: U.S. National Aeronautics and Space Administration, *Aeronautics and Space Report of the President*, annual. Data from U.S. Office of Management and Budget.

No. 996. Space Vehicle Systems—Net Sales and Backlog Orders: 1965 to 1991

[In millions of dollars. Backlog orders as of Dec. 31. Based on data from major companies engaged in manufacture of aerospace products. Includes parts but excludes engines and propulsion units]

YEAR	NET SALES			BACKLOG ORDERS			YEAR	NET SALES			BACKLOG ORDERS		
	Total	Military	Non-military	Total	Military	Non-military		Total	Military	Non-military	Total	Military	Non-military
1965..	2,449	602	1,847	2,203	503	1,700	1985..	6,300	4,241	2,059	6,707	4,941	1,766
1970..	1,956	1,025	931	1,184	786	398	1986..	6,304	4,579	[1]1,725	8,063	6,028	[1]2,035
1975..	2,119	1,096	1,023	1,304	1,019	285	1987..	8,051	5,248	[1]2,803	12,393	9,460	[1]2,933
1980..	3,483	1,461	2,022	1,814	951	863	1988..	8,622	6,190	[1]2,432	10,838	7,880	[1]2,958
1981..	3,856	1,736	2,120	3,174	2,164	1,010	1989..	9,758	6,457	[1]3,301	13,356	9,192	[1]4,164
1982..	4,749	2,606	2,143	4,337	2,403	1,934	1990..	9,691	6,556	[1]3,135	12,462	8,130	[1]4,332
1983..	4,940	2,420	2,520	4,865	2,733	2,132	1991..	10,953	6,898	[1]4,055	12,450	6,539	[1]5,911
1984..	5,225	3,019	2,206	4,624	3,099	1,525							

[1] Includes data for nonmilitary missile systems and parts.
Source: U.S. Bureau of the Census, *Current Industrial Reports*, MA-37D, *Aerospace Industry (Orders, Sales, and Backlog)*.

No. 997. National Aeronautics and Space Administration—Budget Summary: 1993 and 1994

[In millions of dollars. 1993 data are appropriations; 1994 data are budget requests]

ITEM	1993	1994
Total	14,330.4	15,265.0
Research and development.....................	**7,089.3**	**7,712.3**
Space station and new technology investments	2,122.5	2,300.0
Space transportation capability development	649.2	649.2
Space science	1,577.5	1,631.9
Physics and astronomy............................	1,103.8	1,074.7
Planetary exploration	473.7	557.2
Life and microgravity sciences and applications	140.5	351.0
Mission to Planet Earth	1,148.0	1,074.9
Space research and technology.....................	272.7	298.2
Commercial programs	164.4	172.0
Aeronautical research and technology..................	865.6	1,020.7
Transatmospheric research and technology..............	-	80.0
Safety, reliability and quality assurance	32.7	35.3
Academic programs...............................	92.9	74.5
Tracking and data advanced systems	23.3	24.6
Space flight, control and data communications............	**5,086.0**	**5,316.9**
Shuttle production and operational capability	1,053.0	1,189.6
Shuttle operations	3,016.0	3,006.5
Launch services	180.8	300.3
Space and ground networks, communications and data system.	836.2	820.5
Construction of facilities	525.0	545.3
Research and program management......................	1,615.0	1,675.0
Inspector General.................................	15.1	15.5

- Represents or rounds to zero.

Source: U.S. National Aeronautics and Space Administration, *1994 Budget Summary*.

No. 998. NASA Financial Summary: 1970 to 1993

[In millions of dollars. For fiscal year ending in year ending in year shown; see text, section 9]

YEAR	TOTAL		R&D		COMMUNI-CATIONS [1]		FACILITIES CONSTRUCTION		RESEARCH AND PROGRAM DEVELOPMENT	
	Appropri-ations	Outlays	Appropri-ations	Outlays	Appropri-ations	Outlays	Appropri-ations	Outlays	Appropri-ations	Outlays
1970	3,749	3,753	3,006	2,992	-	-	53	54	690	707
1975	3,231	3,267	2,331	2,420	-	-	140	85	760	761
1980	5,243	4,852	4,091	3,701	-	-	156	140	996	1,010
1984	7,243	7,048	2,045	2,792	3,786	2,915	156	109	1,256	1,232
1985	7,552	7,318	2,468	2,118	3,602	3,707	150	170	1,332	1,323
1986	7,764	7,404	2,638	2,615	3,689	3,267	133	189	1,303	1,332
1987	10,621	7,592	3,166	2,436	5,561	3,597	469	149	1,425	1,409
1988	9,002	9,092	3,414	2,916	3,908	4,362	178	166	1,501	1,648
1989	10,898	11,051	4,267	3,922	4,464	5,030	305	190	1,862	1,908
1990 [2] ...	12,296	12,428	5,221	5,094	4,555	5,117	588	218	1,923	1,991
1991 [2] ...	15,078	13,877	6,024	5,766	6,334	5,590	498	326	2,212	2,185
1992 [2] ..	14,302	13,818	6,396	6,261	5,124	5,311	525	448	2,242	1,784
1993, est. [2]	14,330	14,081	7,089	6,912	5,086	5,031	525	517	1,615	1,606

- Represents zero. [1] Space flight, control, and data communications. [2] Include appropriations and outlays for the Inspector General, not shown separately.

Source: National Aeronautics and Space Administration, *NASA News*.

No. 999. Space Shuttle System Expenditures, by NASA in Constant (1982) Dollars: 1973 to 1992

[In millions of dollars. For year ending Sept. 30. These data cannot be used alone to estimate the total shuttle cost. Only operating expenditures correspond to an annual cost in the economic sense, and even those estimates require adjustment for the 3-year period over which the cost of a shuttle flight is incurred and reimbursements are received. For details, see source]

YEAR	Total	D.D.T. and E. [1]	Con- struction	Produc- tion	Opera- tions	YEAR	Total	D.D.T. and E. [1]	Con- struction	Produc- tion	Opera- tions
1973. . . .	58	-	58	-	-	1983. . . .	3,014	-	26	1,635	1,354
1974. . . .	325	216	109	-	-	1984. . . .	3,127	-	73	690	2,364
1975. . . .	1,543	1,407	136	-	-	1985. . . .	2,636	-	42	1,376	1,218
1976. . . .	2,619	2,541	79	-	-	1986. . . .	2,606	-	-	1,184	1,422
1977. . . .	2,258	2,089	60	109	-	1987. . . .	4,165	-	-	2,611	1,553
1978. . . .	2,062	1,898	103	61	-	1988. . . .	2,538	-	-	948	1,590
1979. . . .	2,251	1,713	42	496	-	1989. . . .	3,084	-	-	943	2,141
1980. . . .	2,751	1,339	42	907	463	1990. . . .	2,996	-	-	968	2,028
1981. . . .	2,724	1,041	13	1,093	578	1991. . . .	3,058	-	-	989	2,069
1982. . . .	2,932	894	20	1,283	735	1992. . . .	3,140	-	-	976	2,164

- Represents or rounds to zero. [1] Design, development, testing, and evaluation.

Source: U.S. Congress, Congressional Budget Office, unpublished data.

No. 1000. Space Shuttle Flights—Summary: 1981 to 1992

FLIGHT NUMBER	Date	Mission/ Orbiter name	Crew size	Days duration	FLIGHT NUMBER	Date	Mission/ Orbiter name	Crew size	Days duration
1	4/12/81	Columbia	2	2	27	12/2/88	Atlantis	4	4
4	6/27/81	Columbia	2	7	29	3/13/89	Discovery	5	5
2	11/12/81	Columbia	2	2	30	5/4/89	Atlantis	5	5
3	3/22/82	Columbia	2	8	28	8/8/89	Columbia	5	5
5	11/11/82	Columbia	4	5	34	10/18/89	Atlantis	5	5
6	4/4/83	Challenger	4	5	33	11/22/89	Discovery	5	5
7	6/18/83	Challenger	5	6	32	1/9/90	Columbia	5	10
8	8/30/83	Challenger	5	6	36	2/28/90	Atlantis	5	5
9	11/28/83	Columbia	6	10	31	4/24/90	Discovery	5	6
10	2/3/84	Challenger	5	8	38	10/6/90	Discovery	5	5
11	4/6/84	Challenger	5	7	35	11/15/90	Atlantis	5	4
12	8/30/84	Discovery	6	6	35	12/2/90	Columbia	7	9
13	10/5/84	Challenger	7	8	39	4/28/91	Discovery	7	8
14	11/8/84	Discovery	5	8	37	4/5/91	Atlantis	5	6
15	1/24/85	Discovery	5	3	40	6/5/91	Columbia	7	9
16	4/12/85	Discovery	7	7	43	8/2/91	Atlantis	5	9
17	4/29/85	Challenger	7	7	44	11/24/91	Atlantis	6	7
18	6/17/85	Discovery	7	7	42	1/22/92	Discovery	7	8
19	7/29/85	Challenger	7	8	45	3/24/92	Atlantis	7	8
20	8/27/85	Discovery	5	7	49	5/7/92	Endeavour	7	8
21	10/3/85	Atlantis	5	4	50	6/25/92	Columbia	7	13
22	10/30/85	Challenger	8	7	46	7/31/92	Atlantis	7	7
23	11/26/85	Atlantis	7	7	47	9/12/92	Endeavour	7	7
24	1/12/86	Columbia	7	6	52	10/22/92	Columbia	6	9
25	1/28/86	Challenger	7	-	53	12/2/92	Discovery	5	7
26	9/29/88	Discovery	5	4					

- Represents zero.

Source: U.S. National Aeronautics and Space Administration, *Payload Flight Assignments NASA Mixed Fleets*, January 1992, and "Upcoming Shuttle Flights," January 1992.

No. 1001. World-Wide Successful Space Launches: 1957 to 1991

[Criterion of success is attainment of Earth orbit or Earth escape]

COUNTRY	Total	1957- 1964	1965- 1969	1970- 1974	1975- 1979	1980- 1984	1985- 1989	1985	1986	1987	1988	1989	1990	1991
Total	3,396	289	586	555	607	605	550	120	103	110	116	101	116	88
Soviet Union/CIS [1]	2,314	82	302	405	461	483	447	97	91	95	90	74	75	59
United States	950	207	279	139	126	93	61	17	6	8	12	18	27	18
Japan.	43	-	-	5	10	12	11	2	2	3	2	2	3	2
ESA [2]	43	-	-	-	1	8	21	3	2	2	7	7	5	8
China: Mainland.	29	-	-	2	6	6	9	1	2	2	4	-	5	1
France	10	-	4	3	3	-	-	-	-	-	-	-	-	-
India	3	-	-	-	-	3	-	-	-	-	-	-	-	-
Israel	2	-	-	-	-	-	1	-	-	-	1	-	1	-
Australia	1	-	1	-	-	-	-	-	-	-	-	-	-	-
United Kingdom	1	-	-	1	-	-	-	-	-	-	-	-	-	-

- Represents zero. [1] Commonwealth of Independent States. [2] European Space Agency.

Source: Library of Congress, Congressional Research Service, Science Policy Research Division, *Space Activities of the United States and Other Launching Countries/Organizations 1957-1991*, May 11, 1992.

Transportation—Land

This section presents statistics on revenues, passenger and freight traffic volume, and employment in various revenue-producing modes of the transportation industry, including motor vehicles, trains, and pipelines. Data are also presented on commuting travel, highway mileage and finances, motor vehicle travel, accidents, sales, and registrations, automobile operating costs, and characteristics of public transit, railroads, and pipelines.

The principal compiler of data on public roads and on operation of motor vehicles is the U.S. Department of Transportation's (DOT) Federal Highway Administration (FHWA). These data appear in FHWA's annual *Highway Statistics* and other publications. The U.S. Interstate Commerce Commission (ICC) presents data on interstate land transport in its publications, the *Annual Report to Congress* and the *Transport Statistics in the United States,* which contain data on railroads and motor carriers subject to ICC regulations.

The U.S. National Highway Traffic Safety Administration issues data on traffic accident deaths and death rates in two annual reports: the *Fact Book* and the *Fatal Accident Reporting System Annual Report.* DOT's Federal Railroad Administration presents data on accidents involving railroads in its annual *Accident/Incident Bulletin,* and the *Rail-Highway Crossing Accident/Incident and Inventory Bulletin.*

Various censuses and surveys conducted by the U.S. Bureau of the Census also provide data. Results of the censuses of transportation are presented in the *Truck Inventory and Use Survey.* The *Annual Survey of Manufactures* and reports of the censuses of manufactures, wholesale and retail trade, and service industries contain statistics on the motor vehicle and equipment industry and on retail, wholesale, and services aspects of this industry. Data on persons commuting to work were collected as part of the 1980 census and are in various census reports.

In Brief

Transportation outlays reached $959 billion in 1991

State gasoline tax rates for 1991—
Lowest rate, 7.5 percent in Georgia
Highest rate, 28 percent in Connecticut

Data are also presented in many non-government publications. Among them are the weekly and annual *Cars of Revenue Freight Loaded* and the annual *Yearbook of Railroad Facts,* both published by the Association of American Railroads, Washington, DC; and the *Transit Fact Book,* containing electric railway and motorbus statistics, published annually by the American Public Transit Association, Washington, DC. Useful annual handbooks in the field of transportation are *Motor Vehicle Facts and Figures* and *World Motor Vehicle Data,* issued by the American Automobile Manufacturers Association (AAMA), Detroit, MI; *Accident Facts,* issued by the National Safety Council, Chicago, IL; and *Transportation in America,* issued by the ENO Foundation for Transportation, Westport, Connecticut.

Urban and rural highway mileage.— Beginning 1980, mileage is classified in urban and rural categories, rather than municipal and rural. Urban denotes the Federal-aid legislation definition of an area. Such areas include, as a minimum, a census place with a population of 5,000 to 49,999 or a designated urbanized area with a population of 50,000 or more. These Federal-aid urban areas may extend beyond corporate and census boundaries, and thus are not necessarily coextensive with municipal boundaries. Rural in 1980 refers to non-Federal-aid urban area mileage. Prior to 1980, municipal referred to roads within incorporated places, densely populated New England towns, and certain of the more populous unincorporated areas and rural to non-municipal roads.

Federal-aid highway systems.— Federal law provides that Federal funds be matched in varying proportions with State funds for the costs of planning, engineering, right-of-way acquisition, and construction of highways. Other costs, such as maintenance and policing, are borne entirely by the States and local agencies.

Effective July 1, 1976, a uniform road classification system was implemented which shortened the mileage of the highway system and redefined the three main systems of Federal-aid routes. The Federal-aid primary system is comprised of a network of main roads important to interstate, Statewide, and regional travel. The system consists of main rural roads and their extensions into or through urban areas. The Federal-aid secondary system consists of rural roads of a more local nature, such as those which connect county seats and the larger population centers not served by the primary system. The Federal-aid urban system is located in urban places of 5,000 or more persons and consists of major urban roads and streets, except those on the primary system.

Regulatory bodies.—The ICC, created by the U.S. Congress to regulate transportation in interstate commerce, has jurisdiction over railroads, trucking companies, bus lines, freight forwarders, water carriers, coal slurry pipelines, and transportation brokers. The Federal Energy Regulatory Commission is responsible for setting rates and charges for transportation and sale of natural gas and for establishing rates or charges for transportation.

Motor carriers.—For 1960-73, class I for-hire motor carriers of freight were classified by the ICC as those with $1 million or more of gross annual operating revenue; 1974-79, the class I minimum was $3 million. Effective January 1, 1980, class I carriers are those with $5 million or more in revenue. For 1960-68, class I motor carriers of passengers were classified by the ICC as those with $200,000 or more of gross annual operating revenue; for 1969-76, as those with revenues of $1

million or more; and since 1977, as those with $3 million or more. Effective January 1, 1988, class I motor carriers of passengers are those with $5 million or more in operating revenues; class II less than $5 million in operating revenues.

Railroads.—Railroad companies reporting to the ICC are divided into specific groups as follows: (1) Regular line-haul (interstate) railroads (and their non-operating subsidiaries); (2) switching and terminal railroads; (3) private railroads prior to 1964 (identified by ICC as "circular" because they reported on brief circulars); and (4) unofficial railroads, so designated when their reports are received too late for tabulation. For the most part, the last three groups are not included in the statistics shown here.

For years prior to 1978, class I railroads were those with annual revenues of $1 million or more for 1950-55; $3 million or more for 1956-64; $5 million or more for 1965-75; and $10 million or more for 1976-77. In 1978, the classification became class I, those having more than $50 million gross annual operating revenue; class II, from $10 million to $50 million; and class III, less than $10 million. Effective January 1, 1982, the ICC adopted a procedure to adjust the threshold for inflation by restating current revenues in constant 1978 dollars. In 1990, the criteria for class I and class II railroads were $94.4 million and $18.9 million, respectively. Also effective January 1, 1982, the ICC adopted a *Carrier Classification Index Survey Form* for carriers not filing annual report form R-1 with the commission. Class II and class III railroads are currently exempted from filing any financial report with the Commission. The form is used for reclassifying carriers.

Statistical reliability.—For a discussion of statistical collection and estimation, sampling procedures, and measures of statistical reliability, see Appendix III.

Historical statistics.—Tabular headnotes provide cross-references, where applicable, to *Historical Statistics of the United States, Colonial Times to 1970.* See Appendix IV.

No. 1002. Passenger and Freight Transportation Outlays, by Type of Transport: 1970 to 1991

[In billions of dollars except percents. Freight data include outlays for mail and express. ICC=Interstate Commerce Commission]

TYPE OF TRANSPORT	1975	1978	1979	1980	1981	1982	1983	1984	1985	1986	1987	1988	1989	1990	1991
Total outlays [1]	297.8	453.2	492.4	542.9	592.5	591.4	643.2	715.6	753.1	760.9	807.5	868.9	915.6	965.2	958.7
Passenger, total	187.4	287.5	307.6	338.1	374.0	379.2	410.8	459.5	492.2	492.5	528.1	571.8	603.7	630.3	615.1
Private transportation	161.3	249.9	263.9	284.8	316.7	320.7	347.6	387.3	418.2	415.3	444.5	480.9	507.6	527.7	510.9
Automobiles [2]	156.6	244.1	256.8	276.7	307.3	312.6	340.1	379.0	410.3	407.1	436.0	471.5	498.1	517.3	500.4
New and used cars	46.0	80.4	77.1	73.3	82.6	85.7	105.1	126.1	139.3	156.6	150.6	163.8	163.5	165.9	151.8
Tires, tubes, accessories	12.4	17.2	19.8	22.2	24.6	24.9	25.8	27.4	29.6	29.4	20.9	23.0	23.8	25.0	25.6
Gasoline and oil	53.9	68.3	78.3	99.7	111.3	104.8	106.1	105.9	106.6	81.7	94.1	96.6	106.9	120.6	117.2
Insurance less claims	4.5	10.2	10.3	11.5	10.8	11.2	12.1	11.8	11.6	14.0	17.2	18.7	18.7	20.1	24.2
Interest on debt	7.3	13.0	15.4	17.5	10.8	21.8	19.6	25.1	26.7	26.5	29.0	34.0	36.7	35.5	32.4
Registration and operator's permit fees	2.3	3.0	3.1	3.2	3.5	3.8	4.1	4.5	5.3	5.6	5.9	6.2	6.6	6.7	6.8
Repair, greasing, washing, parking, tolls [3]	22.1	33.0	36.7	39.1	42.3	44.8	46.6	51.9	59.8	59.7	75.2	83.7	90.2	93.9	95.2
Air	4.7	5.8	7.1	8.1	9.4	8.2	7.4	8.2	7.9	8.2	8.5	9.5	9.5	10.4	10.5
For-hire transportation	26.2	37.6	43.3	53.4	57.3	58.5	63.2	72.2	73.9	77.3	83.6	90.9	96.2	102.6	104.2
Local [4]	10.5	14.2	15.4	19.8	21.8	22.8	23.9	27.0	27.3	30.2	30.8	32.1	33.2	34.4	35.8
Bus and transit [5]	4.7	6.7	7.5	9.3	10.3	10.6	11.6	13.2	13.5	14.5	15.1	15.7	15.9	16.7	17.5
School bus	2.2	2.7	3.2	3.8	4.7	5.0	5.2	5.8	5.6	6.4	6.8	7.1	7.5	7.5	7.7
Taxi	3.4	4.4	4.5	5.2	5.2	5.6	5.3	5.5	5.6	6.0	6.4	6.9	7.1	7.5	7.9
Intercity	12.9	19.6	23.3	28.3	30.2	30.3	33.2	38.5	39.5	39.8	43.7	47.5	50.8	53.3	52.8
Air [6]	11.2	17.1	20.4	25.1	26.8	26.8	29.7	33.6	35.9	36.4	40.3	43.8	46.9	49.5	48.9
Rail [6]	0.6	1.3	1.4	1.5	1.6	1.6	1.6	1.6	1.6	1.5	1.6	1.6	1.7	1.7	1.8
Bus	1.0	1.2	1.4	1.7	1.8	1.9	2.0	2.0	2.0	1.9	1.8	2.0	2.2	2.0	2.1
International	2.7	3.8	4.6	5.3	5.3	5.4	6.1	6.7	7.1	7.2	9.1	11.3	12.2	14.9	15.6
Freight, total [4]	115.5	172.9	192.9	213.7	228.4	222.1	243.3	268.0	273.6	281.0	294.2	313.0	329.1	351.8	351.4
Highway	84.8	127.2	142.7	155.3	165.2	162.7	182.0	199.6	205.6	213.2	224.6	239.1	253.9	270.8	278.0
Truck, intercity	47.4	77.9	90.2	94.6	97.1	99.9	111.1	120.7	123.2	128.2	134.8	142.7	151.3	162.3	167.4
Truck, local	37.3	49.1	52.3	60.5	67.8	62.5	70.7	78.7	82.2	84.8	89.6	96.2	102.5	108.4	110.5
Rail	16.5	21.9	24.8	27.9	30.5	27.1	27.3	30.5	29.2	27.9	28.5	29.9	29.9	30.4	29.9
Water	7.9	12.9	13.4	15.5	16.7	15.6	16.0	18.0	18.4	18.8	18.7	20.1	19.8	20.8	20.6
Oil pipeline	2.2	5.5	6.2	7.5	8.0	8.5	8.9	9.3	8.9	8.7	8.5	8.2	7.8	8.4	8.1
Air carrier	1.8	2.7	2.8	4.0	4.3	4.4	5.0	6.0	6.8	7.6	8.9	10.4	11.9	13.7	14.9
Percent change, total [4]	5.4	13.1	8.6	10.3	9.1	-0.2	8.8	11.3	5.2	1.0	6.1	7.6	5.4	5.4	-0.7
Passenger, total	9.4	12.1	7.0	9.9	10.6	1.4	8.3	11.9	7.1	0.1	7.2	8.3	5.6	4.4	-2.4
Private transportation [2]	9.2	11.2	5.6	7.9	11.2	1.3	8.4	11.4	8.0	-0.7	7.0	8.2	5.6	4.0	-3.2
Automobiles	9.3	12.2	5.2	7.7	11.1	1.7	8.8	11.4	8.3	-0.8	7.1	8.1	5.6	3.9	-3.3
Air	6.8	7.4	22.4	14.1	7.3	-12.8	-9.8	10.8	-3.7	3.8	3.7	11.8	0.0	9.5	1.0
For-hire transportation	11.0	12.6	15.2	23.3	16.0	2.1	8.0	14.2	2.4	4.6	8.2	8.7	5.8	6.7	1.6
Freight	-0.4	14.7	11.6	10.8	6.9	-2.8	9.5	10.2	2.1	2.7	4.7	6.4	5.1	6.9	-0.1

[1] Total outlays less than sum of passenger and freight totals, as estimated freight costs included in costs[5] of new cars, gasoline, oil, tires, and tubes have been excluded to prevent duplication.
[2] Includes business-owned vehicles. [3] Includes storage and rental. [4] Includes items not shown separately. [5] Includes Federal, State, and local government operating subsidies and capital grants.
[6] Includes Federal operating subsidies and capital grants for Amtrak.

Source: Eno Foundation for Transportation, Westport, CT, *Transportation in America*, May 1990, with periodic supplements (copyright).

No. 1003. Employment and Earnings in Transportation, by Industry: 1980 to 1992

[Annual averages of monthly figures. Based on Current Employment Statistics program; see Appendix III. See also *Historical Statistics, Colonial Times to 1970*, series Q36-42]

SIC [1] code	INDUSTRY	1980	1985	1986	1987	1988	1989	1990	1991	1992
(X)	NUMBER (1,000)									
(X)	**Total transportation**	**2,960**	**3,001**	**3,056**	**3,163**	**3,312**	**3,428**	**3,537**	**3,512**	**3,520**
40	Railroads	532	359	332	309	298	293	279	263	259
4011	Class I railroads	482	323	294	271	259	252	241	231	222
41	Local and interurban passengers	265	278	287	296	312	329	341	354	358
42	Trucking and warehousing	1,280	1,363	1,396	1,468	1,552	1,600	1,629	1,610	1,618
44	Water transportation	211	185	175	173	172	173	178	188	186
45	Air transportation	453	522	567	603	646	684	746	733	732
46	Pipelines, exc. natural gas	21	19	18	19	19	19	19	19	19
47	Transportation services	198	276	282	296	313	331	347	345	348
(X)	AVERAGE WEEKLY EARNINGS (dol.)									
4011	Class I railroads	427	595	608	627	674	693	727	707	736
41	Local and interurban passengers	217	261	274	281	293	305	310	323	335
42	Trucking and warehousing	358	405	408	414	419	437	451	455	469
46	Pipelines, exc. natural gas	441	629	637	644	662	671	711	733	772

X Not applicable. [1] 1987 Standard Industrial Classification, see text, section 13.

Source: U.S. Bureau of Labor Statistics, Bulletin 2370 and, Supplement to Employment and Earnings, July 1991, *Employment and Earnings*, monthly.

No. 1004. Volume of Domestic Intercity Freight and Passenger Traffic, by Type of Transport: 1970 to 1991

[**Freight traffic in bil. ton-miles; passenger traffic in bil. passenger-miles.** A ton-mile is the movement of 1 ton (2,000 pounds) of freight for the distance of 1 mile. A passenger-mile is the movement of 1 passenger for the distance of 1 mile. Comprises public and private traffic, both revenue and nonrevenue. See also *Historical Statistics, Colonial Times to 1970*, series Q1-22]

TYPE OF TRANSPORT	TRAFFIC VOLUME						PERCENT DISTRIBUTION					
	1970	1975	1980	1985	1990	1991	1970	1975	1980	1985	1990	1991
Freight traffic, total	**1,936**	**2,066**	**2,487**	**2,458**	**2,864**	**2,886**	**100.0**	**100.0**	**100.0**	**100.0**	**100.0**	**100.0**
Railroads	771	759	932	895	1,071	1,078	39.8	36.7	37.5	36.4	37.4	37.4
Truck:												
ICC truck	167	200	242	250	311	320	8.6	9.7	9.7	10.2	10.9	11.1
Non-ICC truck	245	254	313	360	424	438	12.7	12.3	12.6	14.6	14.8	15.2
Water:												
Rivers/canals	205	243	311	306	377	380	10.6	11.8	12.5	12.4	13.2	13.2
Great Lakes	114	99	96	76	87	82	5.9	4.8	3.9	3.1	3.0	2.8
Oil pipelines	431	507	588	564	584	578	22.3	24.5	23.6	23.0	20.4	20.0
Domestic airways [1] . . .	3	4	5	7	10	10	0.2	0.2	0.2	0.3	0.3	0.3
Passenger traffic, total . . .	**1,181**	**1,354**	**1,467**	**1,635**	**1,993**	**2,012**	**100.0**	**100.0**	**100.0**	**100.0**	**100.0**	**100.0**
Private automobiles . . .	1,026	1,171	1,210	1,310	1,598	1,623	86.9	86.5	82.5	80.1	80.2	80.7
Domestic airways [2] . . .	119	148	219	290	359	351	10.1	10.9	14.9	17.7	18.0	17.4
Bus [3]	25	25	27	24	23	24	2.1	1.9	1.8	1.5	1.1	1.2
Railroads [4]	11	10	11	11	13	14	0.9	0.7	0.8	0.7	0.7	0.7

[1] Revenue service only for scheduled and non-scheduled carriers, with small section 418 all-cargo carriers included from 1980. Includes express, mail, and excess baggage. [2] Includes general aviation (mostly private business) flying. [3] Excludes school and urban transit buses. [4] Includes intercity (Amtrak) and rail commuter service.

Source: Eno Foundation for Transportation, Westport, CT, *Transportation in America*, May 1990, with periodic supplements (copyright).

No. 1005. Passenger Transportation Arrangement: 1989 to 1991

[In millions of dollars. Represents SIC 4722]

SOURCE OF RECEIPTS	1989	1990	1991	OPERATING EXPENSES	1989	1990	1991
Receipts, total [1] . . .	**8,688**	**9,036**	**8,547**	Expenses, total [1]	7,808	8,262	8,039
Air carriers	4,958	5,106	4,909	Payroll, annual	3,352	3,696	3,580
Water carriers	326	362	384	Employer contributions [2] .	445	487	489
Hotels and motels	608	627	577	Lease and rental payments	675	676	666
Motor coaches	266	279	288	Advertising and promotion	471	516	467
Railroads	80	79	83	Taxes and licenses	127	125	107
Rental cars	142	151	152	Utilities	251	268	267
Package tours	1,752	1,872	1,623	Depreciation	294	293	282
Other	556	560	531	Office Supplies	266	254	236
				Repair Services	91	99	93

[1] Receipts for firms primarily engaged in arranging passenger transportation. These estimates exclude receipts of transportation companies (airlines, railroads, etc.). [2] Includes contributions to Social Security and other supplemental benefits.

Source: U.S. Bureau of the Census, *Service Annual Survey*.

No. 1006. Transportation Accidents, Deaths, and Injuries: 1970 to 1991

[For related data, see also table 1027, and 1050]

YEAR AND CASUALTY	Total (1,000)	Motor vehi-cle [1] (1,000)	Rail-road [2]	TYPE OF TRANSPORT Air carriers				Gen-eral avia-tion [6]	Recre-ational boat-ing [7]	Gas pipe-lines [8]	Liquid pipe-lines [9]	Water-borne [10]	Haz-ardous mate-rials [11]
				Total	Air-lines [3]	Com-muter air car-riers [4]	On demand air car-riers [5]						
Accidents:													
1970....	16,013	16,000	8,095	(NA)	55	(NA)	(NA)	4,712	3,803	1,019	351	2,582	(NA)
1975....	16,524	16,500	8,041	237	37	48	152	3,995	6,308	1,373	254	3,310	10,951
1980....	17,925	17,900	8,451	228	19	38	171	3,590	5,513	1,996	219	4,624	15,737
1985....	19,348	19,300	3,275	195	22	21	152	2,737	6,237	331	183	3,439	6,014
1990....	11,524	11,500	2,879	149	27	15	107	2,187	6,411	199	177	3,235	8,830
1991....	11,321	11,300	2,659	133	27	22	84	2,143	6,573	233	210	(NA)	9,022
Deaths:													
1970....	54.8	52.6	785	(NA)	146	(NA)	(NA)	1,310	1,418	22	4	178	(NA)
1975....	48.2	44.5	575	221	124	28	69	1,252	1,466	14	7	243	27
1980....	54.5	51.1	584	143	1	37	105	1,239	1,360	11	3	206	19
1985....	47.3	43.8	454	639	526	37	76	951	1,116	26	5	131	8
1990....	46.9	44.5	599	93	39	4	50	745	865	5	3	54	8
1991....	43.9	41.2	583	196	50	77	69	746	924	14	-	(NA)	10
Injuries:													
1970....	2,024	2,000	21,327	(NA)	(NA)	(NA)	(NA)	(NA)	780	347	21	105	(NA)
1975....	1,858	1,800	54,306	109	71	6	32	728	2,136	819	17	97	648
1980....	2,066	2,000	62,246	74	17	14	43	675	2,650	310	12	176	626
1985....	1,705	1,700	31,592	89	30	16	43	517	2,757	106	18	187	253
1990....	1,728	1,700	22,736	83	40	11	32	424	3,822	67	7	25	418
1991....	1,626	1,600	21,370	(NA)	(NA)	(NA)	(NA)	(NA)	3,967	89	8	(NA)	436

- Represents or rounds to zero. NA Not available. [1] Data on deaths are from U.S. National Highway Traffic Safety Administration and are based on 30 day definition; see table 1027. Other data are from National Safety Council. [2] Accidents which result in damages to railroad property. Grade crossing accidents are also included when classified as a train accident. Deaths exclude fatalities in railroad-highway grade crossing accidents. [3] Includes scheduled and nonscheduled (charter) air carriers. Represents serious injuries. [4] All scheduled service. Represents serious injuries. [5] All nonscheduled service. Represents serious injuries. [6] 1975 excludes commuter and on-demand air taxis. [7] Accidents resulting in death; injury or requiring medical treatment beyond first aid; damages exceeding $200; or a person's disappearance. [8] Pipeline accidents/incidents are credited to year of occurrence. Beginning 1985; prior data are credited to the year filed. Fatalities and injuries as reported in annual report. [9] Pipelines carrying hazardous materials, petroleum, and liquid petroleum products. [10] Covers accidents involving commercial vessels which must be reported to U.S. Coast Guard if there is property damage exceeding $1,500; material damage affecting the seaworthiness or efficiency of a vessel; stranding or grounding; loss of life; or injury causing a person's incapacity for more than 3 days. [11] Accidents, deaths, and injuries involving hazardous materials cover all types of transport.

Source: U.S. Dept. of Transportation, Transportation Systems Center, Cambridge, MA, *Transportation Safety Information Report*, annual.

No. 1007. Federal Outlays for Transportation, by Function: 1970 to 1993

[In millions of dollars. For fiscal years ending in year shown; see text, section 9]

FUNCTION	1970	1975	1980	1985	1986	1987	1988	1989	1990	1991	1992	1993, est.
Total outlays	7,008	10,918	21,329	25,838	28,117	26,222	27,272	27,608	29,485	31,099	33,337	36,380
Ground transportation .	4,678	7,027	15,274	17,606	18,725	17,150	18,148	17,946	18,954	19,545	20,347	22,302
Air transportation.....	1,408	2,387	3,723	4,895	5,287	5,520	5,897	6,622	7,234	8,184	9,313	10,050
Water transportation . .	895	1,430	2,229	3,201	3,964	3,461	3,111	2,916	3,151	3,148	3,434	3,733
Other transportation. . .	26	74	104	137	140	91	116	124	146	223	244	296

Source: U.S. Office of Management and Budget, *Budget of the United States Government*, annual.

No. 1008. Expedited Domestic Package Express Volume and Growth: 1977 and 1988

[Year ended December 31. Represents the activity of domestic package express companies. Companies such as Federal Express Inc. and United Parcel Service Inc. Also includes package express services offered by trucking companies, the postal service, passenger airlines, freight forwarders, couriers, Amtrak, and bus companies. The Department of Transportation defines package express as the transportation of parcels of 150 pounds or less, with overnight or second-day delivery]

EXPEDITED PACKAGE EXPRESS	Unit	1977	1988	Percent change, 1977-88	Average annual percent change, 1977-88
Expedited package express, total:					
Shipments.......................	Millions	628	3,176	406.6	40.6
Weight	Mil. lbs	9,409	37,258	296.0	29.6
Revenue	Mil. dol	2,487	20,771	741.9	74.2
Air: Shipments..................	Millions	81	544	571.8	57.2
Weight	Mil. lbs	4,485	8,914	98.7	9.9
Revenue	Mil. dol	1,384	11,403	724.1	72.4
Surface express: Shipments..........	Millions	547	2,632	381.0	38.1
Weight	Mil. lbs	4,924	28,344	475.6	47.6
Revenue	Mil. dol	1,083	9,368	764.8	76.5

Source: U.S. Department of Commerce, *Journal of Commerce*.

No. 1009. Highway Mileage—Urban and Rural, by Type and Control, and Federal-Aid Highway System: 1970 to 1991

[In thousands, except percent. As of Dec. 31. Beginning 1980, data for urban and rural mileage are not comparable to prior years because of classification changes; see text, section 21. See also *Historical Statistics, Colonial Times to 1970*, series Q 50, 51, and 55]

TYPE AND CONTROL	1970	1975	1980	1984	1985	1986	1987	1988	1989	1990	1991
Total mileage [1]	3,730	3,838	[2]3,955	3,892	3,862	3,880	3,874	3,871	3,877	3,380	3,889
Urban mileage [3]	561	639	624	674	691	701	710	739	754	757	750
Under State control	74	84	79	103	111	94	95	96	97	96	96
Under local control	487	555	543	571	578	606	614	642	656	661	653
Rural mileage	3,169	3,199	[2]3,331	3,218	3,171	3,178	3,164	3,132	3,123	3,123	3,139
Percent surfaced [4]	76.1	77.6	77.5	87.5	88.1	88.4	88.4	88.1	88.4	88.6	89.7
Under State control	707	711	702	818	773	704	704	704	706	703	703
Under local control	2,275	2,261	2,270	2,134	2,173	2,243	2,249	2,244	2,238	2,242	2,255
Under Federal control	188	227	262	266	225	231	212	183	178	178	182
Fed.-aid highway system: [5]											
Primary (urban and rural) . .	272	266	300	300	301	303	302	304	304	305	305
Interstate	32	37	41	43	44	44	44	45	45	45	45
Urban	(X)	65	124	140	144	146	148	147	148	148	148
Secondary	647	643	398	398	398	398	398	400	400	400	400

X Not applicable. [1] Prior to 1980, includes public and nonpublic road mileage; beginning 1984, includes only public road mileage as defined 23 USC 402. [2] Includes 98,000 miles of nonpublic road mileage previously contained in other rural categories. [3] Prior to 1980, represents municipal mileage; see text, section 21. [4] Covers soil-surfaced roads and roads with slag, gravel, stone, bituminous, or concrete surfaces. [5] For definition, see text, section 21. Beginning 1980, data represent actual mileage open to traffic rather than total highway miles carrying interstate traffic.

Source: U.S. Federal Highway Administration, *Highway Statistics*, annual.

No. 1010. Highway Mileage—Urban, Rural, and Federal-Aid Highway System: 1991

[As of Dec. 31. For definition of urban, rural, and Federal-aid highway system roads, see text, section 21]

STATE	Urban	Rural	FEDERAL-AID HIGHWAY SYSTEM [1]				STATE	Urban	Rural	FEDERAL-AID HIGHWAY SYSTEM [1]			
			Total		Urban	Sec-ondary				Total		Urban	Sec-ondary
			Primary	Inter-state [2]						Primary	Inter-state [2]		
U.S. . .	749,864	3,139,435	305,226	45,280	148,291	400,309	MO . .	15,033	106,022	8,187	1,177	2,476	18,069
AL. . .	16,865	73,838	7,650	899	2,801	11,648	MT . .	2,275	68,492	6,645	1,191	343	4,737
AK . .	1,561	11,963	2,101	1,089	237	1,802	NE . .	4,961	87,707	7,679	481	1,062	11,456
AZ . .	14,170	41,153	4,682	1,169	2,465	3,238	NV . .	3,156	42,422	2,406	545	557	2,314
AR . .	7,683	69,488	5,777	542	1,157	7,389	NH . .	2,433	12,435	1,352	224	723	1,235
CA . .	74,847	91,034	13,478	2,399	17,866	11,192	NJ . .	22,501	11,767	1,869	406	5,379	1,703
CO . .	11,341	66,539	5,400	943	2,230	3,427	NM . .	5,669	50,407	4,889	999	610	3,645
CT . .	10,964	9,160	1,635	341	2,956	879	NY . .	38,061	73,381	9,977	1,498	8,730	6,296
DE . .	1,643	3,869	483	41	319	604	NC . .	19,572	75,572	5,324	954	3,129	10,329
DC . .	1,102	-	190	12	233	-	ND . .	1,811	84,814	6,145	570	501	10,596
FL. . .	47,747	61,627	9,486	1,444	4,765	4,359	OH . .	31,387	82,178	8,139	1,573	7,851	11,790
GA . .	22,057	88,425	11,432	1,245	3,990	14,012	OK . .	12,417	99,844	6,238	930	2,997	11,775
HI . .	1,507	2,595	554	43	322	435	OR . .	9,358	86,944	5,770	727	2,054	7,781
ID . . .	2,738	59,471	3,362	607	749	4,182	PA . .	28,398	88,290	11,537	1,588	7,048	7,992
IL . . .	32,131	104,040	11,860	1,962	6,670	12,942	RI . . .	4,597	1,523	504	70	933	201
IN . . .	17,922	74,107	6,145	1,137	4,729	9,759	SC . .	9,358	54,724	6,492	798	1,169	8,536
IA . . .	8,805	103,749	9,547	782	2,451	13,576	SD . .	1,751	81,486	6,472	678	393	11,091
KS . .	9,107	124,360	8,915	872	1,656	22,643	TN . .	15,476	69,376	7,258	1,062	3,178	5,450
KY . .	7,697	62,029	4,602	763	2,020	7,226	TX . .	76,215	217,294	20,032	3,229	8,287	32,705
LA . .	12,272	46,264	3,984	844	2,161	7,329	UT . .	5,632	37,523	3,554	938	930	2,724
ME . .	2,501	19,943	2,377	366	706	2,742	VT . .	1,196	12,940	1,444	320	349	1,913
MD . .	12,409	16,575	2,603	481	2,163	1,922	VA . .	15,409	52,634	6,489	1,076	3,450	10,200
MA . .	21,017	13,306	2,777	567	5,905	2,007	WA . .	16,569	63,313	5,786	762	4,235	7,376
MI . .	26,765	90,780	8,470	1,238	4,915	17,080	WV . .	3,089	31,684	2,965	550	809	6,353
MN . .	14,797	114,641	10,206	911	2,395	16,650	WI . .	14,552	95,820	9,999	640	2,955	13,036
MS . .	7,360	65,170	6,456	684	1,720	11,699	WY . .	1,980	36,717	3,902	913	562	2,264

- Represents zero. [1] Highway mileage open to traffic. [2] Although the interstate system is part of the Federal-aid primary system, its mileage is shown separately.

Source: U.S. Federal Highway Administration, *Highway Statistics*, annual.

No. 1011. Highway Pavement Condition, by Type of Road System: 1980 to 1991

[Highway pavement condition is classified by the Present Serviceability Rating (PSR) system (5.0 - 0.1). The reported ranges are defined as: PSR 5.0-3.5, pavements give a first class ride and exhibit few, if any, visible signs of surface wear. Of the quality of new or nearly new pavements. PSR 3.4-2.0, pavements have a riding quality somewhat inferior to that of new pavements or may even be barely tolerable at high speeds. Surfaces may show signs of cracking, substantial patching, and rutting. PSR 1.9-0.1, pavements show extensive wear to the point of needing resurfacing or may even need complete reconstruction]

PAVEMENT CONDITION	INTERSTATE ROAD				ARTERIAL ROAD				COLLECTOR ROAD			
	1980	1985	1990	1991	1980	1985	1990	1991	1980	1985	1990	1991
URBAN AREAS												
Percent of road mileage rated—												
PSR 0.1-1.9 (0.1-2.4) [1]	6	7	6	5	7	5	4	4	9	7	13	9
PSR 2.0-3.4 (2.5-3.4) [1]	26	38	35	35	42	53	52	53	50	58	55	54
PSR 3.5-5.0	68	55	59	60	51	42	44	43	41	35	32	37
RURAL AREAS												
Percent of road mileage rated—												
PSR 0.1-1.9 (0.1-2.4) [1]	5	7	6	6	6	4	2	2	16	10	8	7
PSR 2.0-3.4 (2.5-3.4) [1]	26	33	35	34	46	51	48	48	55	59	54	55
PSR 3.5-5.0	69	60	59	60	48	45	50	50	29	31	38	38

[1] PSR range shown in parentheses applies to Interstate roads only.

No. 1012. Receipts and Disbursements for Highways, by Type: 1970 to 1992

[In millions of dollars. Data compiled from reports of State and local authorities. For Federal highway trust fund receipts, disbursements, and balances, see table 511. State data include District of Columbia]

TYPE	1970	1980	1985	1989	1990	1991, prel.	1992, proj.		
							Total [1]	Federal	State
Total receipts	21,747	39,715	61,506	72,721	73,846	78,203	79,996	17,813	41,395
Current income	19,861	37,604	54,957	67,569	68,474	72,660	74,265	17,813	37,919
Imposts on highway users [2]	15,311	22,559	35,599	44,009	44,099	47,910	49,042	15,789	31,863
Other taxes and fees	3,732	11,808	15,127	17,987	18,438	18,503	18,641	1,174	2,954
Investment income, other receipts	818	3,237	4,231	5,573	5,937	6,247	6,582	850	3,102
Bond issue proceeds [3]	1,886	2,111	6,549	5,152	5,372	5,543	5,731		3,476
Intergovernmental payments	(X)	(X)	(X)	(X)	(X)	(X)	(X)	-15,501	7,017
Funds from (+) or to (-) reserves [4]	-912	2,080	-4058	-1858	966	-1,163	-826	-1,545	118
Total funds available	20,835	41,795	57,448	70,863	74,812	77,040	79,170	767	48,530
Total disbursements	20,835	41,795	57,448	70,863	74,812	77,040	79,170	767	48,530
Current disbursements	19,583	40,084	54,725	67,251	71,500	73,625	75,684	767	46,839
Capital outlay	11,575	20,337	27,138	33,144	35,408	36,242	37,327	297	27,477
Maintenance and traffic services	4,720	11,445	16,032	18,952	19,742	20,469	20,799	116	9,056
Administration and research	1,275	3,022	4,033	5,683	6,355	6,716	7,118	354	4,459
Law enforcement and safety	1,303	3,824	5,334	6,647	6,922	7,114	7,256	-	3,865
Interest on debt	710	1,456	2,188	2,825	3,073	3,084	3,184	-	1,982
Debt retirement [3]	1,252	1,711	2,723	3,612	3,312	3,415	3,486	-	1,691

- Represents zero.   X Not applicable.   [1] Includes other levels of government not shown separately.   [2] Excludes amounts later allocated for nonhighway purposes.   [3] Par value. Excludes issue and redemption of short-term notes or refunding bonds. Premiums and discounts on sale of bonds and accrued interest are included with investment income and other receipts. Redemption premiums and discounts are included with interest on debt.   [4] Plus sign (+) indicates net receipt of funds from other levels of government; minus sign (-) indicates net disbursement of funds to other levels.

Source of tables 1011 and 1012: U.S. Federal Highway Administration, *Highway Statistics*, annual; and releases.

No. 1013. Disbursements of State Highway Funds, by State: 1980 to 1991

[In millions of dollars. Comprises disbursements from current revenues or loans for construction, maintenance, interest and principal payments on highway bonds, transfers to local units, and miscellaneous. Includes transactions by State toll authorities. Excludes amounts allocated for collection and nonhighway purposes, and bonds redeemed by refunding. See also *Historical Statistics, Colonial Times to 1970*, series Q 90-94]

STATE	1980	1990	1991	STATE	1980	1990	1991	STATE	1980	1990	1991
U.S.	30,049	53,580	58,038	KY	913	1,008	1,052	OH	1,032	2,271	2,686
AL	517	866	781	LA	682	923	1,007	OK	461	827	852
AK	274	336	396	ME	164	332	348	OR	482	765	828
AZ	365	1,525	1,309	MD	663	1,464	1,241	PA	1,557	2,885	2,823
AR	425	456	499	MA	704	1,055	1,182	RI	72	214	236
CA	1,930	4,294	4,793	MI	997	1,526	1,561	SC	309	585	579
CO	411	714	755	MN	611	1,228	1,144	SD	151	232	201
CT	393	1,204	1,251	MS	468	529	617	TN	609	1,174	1,109
DE	152	315	364	MO	555	937	989	TX	1,882	3,001	3,039
DC	57	273	296	MT	224	302	293	UT	241	355	342
FL	1,261	1,677	2,125	NE	274	449	470	VT	87	165	182
GA	762	1,278	1,262	NV	169	309	245	VA	894	1,874	1,737
HI	134	297	369	NH	152	299	384	WA	787	1,251	1,524
ID	153	300	280	NJ	662	1,831	4,346	WV	672	650	714
IL	1,652	2,645	2,780	NM	197	409	399	WI	468	979	1,060
IN	688	1,218	1,269	NY	1,650	2,874	2,595	WY	192	297	328
IA	504	869	1,002	NC	807	1,428	1,471				
KS	440	697	693	ND	143	189	232				

Source: U.S. Federal Highway Administration, *Highway Statistics*, annual.

No. 1014. Federal Grants to State and Local Governments for Highway Trust Fund and Federal Transit Administration (FTA), by State: 1991

[Year ending Sept. 30]

STATE	HIGHWAY TRUST FUND Total (mil. dol.)	Per cap- ita [1]	FTA [2] Total (mil. dol.)	Per cap- ita [1]	STATE	HIGHWAY TRUST FUND Total (mil. dol.)	Per cap- ita [1]	FTA [2] Total (mil. dol.)	Per cap- ita [1]	STATE	HIGHWAY TRUST FUND Total (mil. dol.)	Per cap- ita [1]	FTA [2] Total (mil. dol.)	Per cap- ita [1]
U.S.	14,843	58.2	3,508	13.8	KS...	136	54.0	7	2.8	ND...	112	176.7	2	2.8
					KY...	176	46.8	16	4.3	OH...	486	44.1	86	7.8
AL...	221	53.3	15	3.7	LA...	304	70.8	37	8.7	OK...	186	58.0	13	4.0
AK...	211	360.2	2	3.2	ME...	79	64.2	4	3.4	OR...	210	70.4	30	10.1
AZ...	189	49.4	7	2.0	MD...	263	53.5	83	17.0	PA...	623	51.8	250	20.8
AR...	185	77.0	9	3.6	MA...	575	95.9	136	22.8	RI...	117	116.8	16	16.4
CA...	1,688	54.7	417	13.5	MI...	394	41.7	58	6.1	SC...	192	53.2	8	2.2
CO...	247	71.2	40	11.4	MN...	267	59.7	18	4.1	SD...	100	140.8	2	2.8
CT...	351	107.0	80	24.5	MS...	179	68.3	6	2.3	TN...	308	61.2	43	8.5
DE...	60	86.7	2	3.5	MO...	319	61.4	179	34.5	TX...	885	50.2	106	6.0
DC...	114	194.2	237	402.5	MT...	157	190.1	6	7.8	UT...	108	59.6	21	11.5
FL...	508	37.7	143	10.6	NE...	109	68.2	6	3.8	VT...	68	119.7	2	3.2
GA...	332	49.1	77	11.3	NV...	80	60.1	4	2.7	VA...	277	43.4	20	3.2
HI...	198	171.0	20	17.4	NH...	58	52.1	3	2.6	WA...	401	78.1	31	6.1
ID...	110	103.0	2	2.3	NJ...	402	51.6	184	23.6	WV...	143	79.1	7	3.7
IL...	540	46.4	374	32.1	NM...	159	100.5	4	2.7	WI...	280	55.9	35	6.9
IN...	396	70.0	30	5.3	NY...	692	38.2	579	31.9	WY...	103	221.8	1	3.1
IA...	238	84.6	9	3.3	NC...	309	45.2	30	4.4					

[1] Based on Bureau of the Census resident population as of July 1, 1992.　　[2] Federal Transit Administration.

Source: U.S. Bureau of the Census, *Federal Expenditures by State for Fiscal Year*, annual.

No. 1015. State Gasoline Tax Rates, 1990 and 1992, and Motor Fuel Tax Receipts, 1991

[See also *Historical Statistics, Colonial Times to 1970*, series Q 233-234]

STATE	RATE [1] (cents/gal.) 1990	1992	Re- ceipts, [2] 1991 (mil. dol.)	STATE	RATE [1] (cents/gal.) 1990	1992	Re- ceipts, [2] 1991 (mil. dol.)	STATE	RATE [1] (cents/gal.) 1990	1992	Re- ceipts, [2] 1991 (mil. dol.)
Federal.	14.1	14.1	(NA)	KS...	16.0	18.0	251	ND...	17.0	17.0	68
State.	(NA)	(NA)	(NA)	KY [3]..	15.4	15.4	349	OH...	20.0	21.0	1,102
AL...	13.0	18.0	343	LA...	20.0	20.0	437	OK [4]..	17.0	17.0	317
AK...	8.0	8.0	19	ME...	17.0	19.0	131	OR...	18.0	24.0	277
AZ...	18.0	18.0	365	MD...	18.5	23.5	436	PA...	17.8	22.4	1,064
AR...	13.7	18.7	220	MA...	17.0	21.0	521	RI...	20.0	26.0	98
CA...	9.0	17.0	1,915	MI...	15.0	15.0	675	SC...	16.0	16.0	346
CO...	20.0	22.0	354	MN...	20.0	20.0	443	SD [5]..	18.0	18.0	80
CT...	22.0	28.0	329	MS...	18.2	18.2	278	TN [5]..	20.0	20.0	586
DE...	16.0	19.0	71	MO...	11.0	13.0	351	TX...	15.0	20.0	1,515
DC...	18.0	20.0	30	MT...	20.0	21.4	105	UT...	19.0	19.0	166
FL...	10.9	11.8	984	NE...	21.7	24.6	218	VT [3]..	16.0	16.0	63
GA...	7.5	7.5	326	NV...	18.0	24.0	155	VA [3]..	17.7	17.5	630
HI...	11.0	16.0	52	NH...	16.6	18.6	94	WA...	22.0	23.0	595
ID...	18.0	21.0	117	NJ...	10.5	10.5	423	WV...	20.4	20.4	212
IL...	19.0	19.0	1,012	NM...	17.0	17.0	160	WI...	21.5	22.2	548
IN...	15.0	15.0	580	NY...	14.4	22.9	504	WY...	9.0	9.0	43
IA...	20.0	20.0	319	NC...	21.5	22.3	838				

NA Not available.　[1] In effect Dec. 31.　[2] Represents net gallonage receipts.　[3] Trucks or combinations with more than 2 axles pay tax of 2 cents per gallon more in Kentucky, and 3.5 cents per gallon more in Virginia.　[4] .08 cents per gallon is for inspection fee.　[5] Includes 1 cent per gallon inspection fee.

No. 1016. Public Highway Debt—State and Local Governments: 1970 to 1992

[In millions of dollars. Long-term obligations. State data are for calendar years; local data for varying fiscal years. Excludes duplicated and interunit obligations. Municipal debt includes other political subdivisions urban in character. See also *Historical Statistics, Colonial Times to 1970*, series Q 136-147]

ITEM	1970	1980	1984	1985	1986	1987	1988	1989	1990	1991	1992 [1]
Total debt issued [2]...	1,886	2,094	3,151	6,074	6,296	3,802	4,261	5,268	5,493	6,367	5,731
State.............	1,305	1,128	1,715	3,404	3,946	1,927	2,384	3,096	3,233	3,871	3,476
County and township ...	174	276	524	1,387	1,200	451	567	650	669	755	620
Municipal..........	407	690	912	1,283	1,150	1,424	1,310	1,522	1,591	1,741	1,635
Total debt redeemed [3].	1,252	1,706	2,411	2,737	3,132	2,685	2,735	3,606	2,922	3,523	3,486
State.............	782	1,022	1,507	1,580	1,875	1,625	1,396	2,063	1,602	2,039	1,691
County and township ...	152	209	216	378	432	349	353	618	372	498	785
Municipal..........	318	475	688	779	825	711	986	925	948	986	1,010
Total debt outstanding.	19,107	25,851	27,964	31,301	34,465	36,565	38,091	39,716	29,176	45,131	47,376

[1] Projection.　[2] Excludes refunding issues.　[3] Excludes redemptions by refunding.

Source of tables 1015 and 1016: U.S. Federal Highway Administration, *Highway Statistics*, annual.

No. 1017. Transportation to Work: 1990

[In thousands, except as indicated]

REGION, DIVISION, AND STATE	MEANS OF TRANSPORTATION TO WORK			Worked at home	Average travel time to work (minutes)	VEHICLES AVAILABLE		
	Car, truck, van		Percent using public transport-ation			None	One vehicle	Two or more vehicles
	Drove alone	Car-pooled						
United States	**84,215**	**15,378**	**5.4**	**3,406**	**22.4**	**10,602**	**31,039**	**50,306**
Northeast	15,902	2,771	13.1	630	24.5	3,603	6,408	8,862
New England	4,892	749	5.3	191	21.5	568	1,699	2,676
Maine	424	80	0.9	24	19.0	40	159	266
New Hampshire	443	70	0.7	20	21.9	26	132	254
Vermont	200	36	0.8	17	18.0	17	72	122
Massachusetts	2,148	318	8.5	75	22.7	321	819	1,107
Rhode Island	376	58	2.6	10	19.2	40	132	206
Connecticut	1,301	187	4.0	45	21.1	124	386	721
Middle Atlantic	11,010	2,023	16.1	438	25.7	3,035	4,709	6,186
New York	4,461	861	25.5	213	28.6	1,994	2,153	2,492
New Jersey	2,731	472	9.0	80	25.3	360	966	1,468
Pennsylvania	3,818	690	6.6	145	21.6	681	1,589	2,226
Midwest	21,091	3,207	3.7	987	20.7	2,238	7,365	12,714
East North Central	14,749	2,206	4.4	551	21.7	1,693	5,230	8,674
Ohio	3,889	521	2.6	119	20.7	416	1,351	2,320
Indiana	2,040	332	1.4	73	20.4	175	670	1,221
Illinois	3,742	653	10.3	144	25.1	588	1,476	2,138
Michigan	3,328	429	1.7	100	21.2	344	1,133	1,943
Wisconsin	1,751	270	2.6	114	18.3	170	600	1,052
West North Central	6,342	1,002	2.0	436	18.4	545	2,135	4,040
Minnesota	1,593	247	3.8	116	19.1	142	517	988
Iowa	971	157	1.3	89	16.2	75	332	657
Missouri	1,816	312	2.1	84	21.6	191	652	1,118
North Dakota	210	31	0.6	24	13.0	16	73	152
South Dakota	233	33	0.3	31	13.8	17	76	166
Nebraska	590	87	1.2	44	15.8	43	182	377
Kansas	929	136	0.7	49	17.2	60	302	583
South	29,495	5,886	2.7	936	22.0	3,208	10,987	17,627
South Atlantic	15,481	3,156	3.5	501	22.5	1,725	5,725	9,053
Delaware	258	43	2.5	8	20.0	20	80	147
Maryland	1,733	376	8.4	65	27.0	216	554	979
District of Columbia	107	37	37.7	9	27.1	93	103	53
Virginia	2,281	500	4.1	103	24.0	205	717	1,370
West Virginia	493	107	1.1	16	21.0	94	247	347
North Carolina	2,528	530	1.0	71	19.8	242	786	1,489
South Carolina	1,235	277	1.1	31	20.5	137	402	720
Georgia	2,379	468	2.9	65	22.7	244	730	1,393
Florida	4,468	819	2.1	132	21.8	474	2,106	2,555
East South Central	5,110	1,005	1.2	149	21.1	607	1,814	3,231
Kentucky	1,195	229	1.7	47	20.7	159	447	773
Tennessee	1,763	324	1.4	52	21.5	181	593	1,079
Alabama	1,374	267	0.8	31	21.2	156	466	885
Mississippi	777	184	0.8	19	20.6	111	307	494
West South Central	8,904	1,725	2.0	286	21.6	876	3,448	5,343
Arkansas	765	153	0.5	28	19.0	88	303	501
Louisiana	1,239	247	3.1	31	22.3	209	542	749
Oklahoma	1,079	191	0.6	41	19.3	91	414	701
Texas	5,821	1,134	2.3	185	22.2	489	2,190	3,392
West	17,727	3,513	4.3	854	22.7	1,553	6,279	11,103
Mountain	4,586	873	2.2	229	19.7	343	1,697	2,993
Montana	250	41	0.6	22	14.8	20	91	194
Idaho	330	53	2.0	21	17.3	17	101	243
Wyoming	154	28	1.5	9	15.4	8	48	113
Colorado	1,217	210	3.0	67	20.7	89	412	781
New Mexico	472	96	1.0	24	19.1	38	185	320
Arizona	1,178	239	2.1	48	21.6	107	532	730
Utah	541	111	2.4	26	18.9	29	153	355
Nevada	444	94	2.7	12	19.8	36	174	256
Pacific	13,141	2,640	5.0	625	23.8	1,210	4,582	8,111
Washington	1,701	282	4.7	86	22.0	141	582	1,149
Oregon	949	165	3.5	56	19.6	88	355	660
California	9,982	2,036	5.1	453	24.6	923	3,452	6,006
Alaska	165	40	2.6	11	16.7	23	64	102
Hawaii	344	116	7.6	19	23.8	35	129	193

Source: U.S. Bureau of the Census, *Census of Population and Housing, 1990.*

No. 1018. Motor Vehicle Registrations, 1980 to 1991, Vehicle Miles of Travel, 1991, and Drivers Licenses, 1991, by State

[In thousands, except as indicated. Motor vehicle registrations cover publicly, privately, and commercially owned vehicles. For uniformity, figures have been adjusted to a calendar-year basis as registration years in States differ; figures represent net numbers where possible, excluding re-registrations and nonresident registrations]

STATE	AUTOMOBILES, TRUCKS, AND BUSES [1]					1991				
	1980	1985	1990	1991		Motor-cycle [1] regis-tration (incl. official)	Public road and street mileage (1,000 mi.)	Vehicle miles of travel		Drivers licenses
				Total	Automo-biles (incl. taxis)			Total (bil. mi.)	Per mile of road (1,000)	
U.S.....	155,796	171,654	188,798	188,372	142,956	4,177	3,889	2,172	559	168,995
AL.......	2,938	3,338	3,744	3,699	2,712	41	91	42.9	472	2,938
AK.......	262	353	477	471	297	11	14	4.0	287	318
AZ.......	1,917	2,235	2,825	2,849	2,023	81	55	34.9	635	2,400
AR.......	1,574	1,384	1,448	1,480	958	14	77	21.9	285	1,720
CA.......	16,873	18,899	21,926	22,253	17,232	651	166	258.0	1,554	19,931
CO	2,342	2,759	3,155	3,045	2,220	89	78	27.7	356	2,084
CT.......	2,147	2,465	2,623	2,589	2,444	51	20	26.6	1,331	2,213
DE.......	397	465	526	534	411	9	6	6.7	1,120	495
DC.......	268	326	262	246	229	2	1	3.4	3,430	406
FL.......	7,614	9,865	10,950	9,980	7,910	196	109	113.5	1,041	9,693
GA	3,818	4,580	5,489	5,714	3,991	78	110	73.0	664	4,610
HI	570	651	771	785	680	21	4	8.1	2,036	700
ID	834	854	1,054	1,055	641	33	62	10.3	166	712
IL	7,477	7,727	7,873	8,193	6,628	184	136	85.4	628	7,360
IN	3,826	4,024	4,366	4,414	3,233	97	92	54.3	590	3,453
IA	2,329	2,696	2,632	2,668	1,907	165	113	23.0	204	1,857
KS.......	2,007	2,148	2,012	1,879	1,243	59	133	23.2	174	1,781
KY.......	2,593	2,615	2,909	2,963	1,942	34	70	35.2	503	2,414
LA.......	2,779	3,012	2,995	3,046	2,002	32	59	34.7	588	2,595
ME	724	840	977	979	755	37	22	11.8	539	889
MD	2,803	3,276	3,607	3,630	3,009	55	29	41.3	1,426	3,214
MA	3,749	3,738	3,726	3,664	3,160	54	34	46.5	1,369	4,206
MI.......	6,488	6,727	7,209	7,245	5,644	166	118	81.9	694	6,434
MN	3,091	3,385	3,508	3,273	2,564	112	129	39.3	304	2,546
MS	1,577	1,746	1,875	1,887	1,443	26	73	24.9	341	1,925
MO	3,271	3,558	3,905	3,950	2,788	61	121	51.0	421	3,732
MT	680	652	783	766	450	21	71	8.3	117	580
NE.......	1,254	1,257	1,384	1,404	929	21	93	14.1	152	1,069
NV.......	655	709	853	881	602	20	46	10.5	228	909
NH	704	974	946	906	709	37	15	9.9	662	848
NJ.......	4,761	4,909	5,652	5,519	5,058	86	34	59.3	1,744	5,660
NM	1,068	1,176	1,301	1,320	824	32	56	16.8	300	1,081
NY.......	8,002	9,042	10,196	9771	8,494	198	111	107.7	970	10,267
NC	4,532	4,450	5,162	5,216	3,713	58	95	64.9	683	4,547
ND	627	655	630	629	374	19	87	6.0	68	426
OH	7,771	8,102	8,410	8,685	7,057	236	114	93.0	816	7,470
OK	2,583	2,864	2,649	2,669	1,708	59	112	34.2	306	2,283
OR	2,081	2,204	2,445	2,507	1,884	62	96	25.8	268	2,374
PA.......	6,926	7,209	7,971	8,038	6,430	167	117	87.3	746	7,951
RI.......	623	610	672	628	520	23	6	7.2	1,192	676
SC.......	1,996	2,222	2,521	2,471	1,869	30	64	34.5	538	2,402
SD.......	601	650	704	702	420	24	83	6.7	81	501
TN.......	3,271	3,754	4,444	4,542	3,642	74	85	47.3	556	3,393
TX.......	10,475	12,444	12,800	12,697	8,666	185	294	158.8	540	11,293
UT.......	992	1,099	1,206	1,230	799	25	43	15.4	358	1,067
VT.......	347	398	462	447	328	19	14	5.9	419	412
VA.......	3,626	4,253	4,938	5,022	3,825	61	68	61.1	899	4,651
WA	3,225	3,526	4,257	4,404	3,091	116	80	46.4	581	3,491
WV.......	1,320	1,143	1,225	1,273	779	18	35	16.0	458	1,286
WI.......	2,941	3,187	3,815	3,685	2,475	210	110	45.5	413	3,394
WY	467	500	528	469	244	17	39	6.0	154	341

[1] Excludes vehicles owned by military services.

Source: U.S. Federal Highway Administration, *Highway Statistics*, annual; and *Selected Highway Statistics and Charts*, annual.

No. 1019. Motor Vehicle Production and Trade: 1980 to 1991

ITEM	Unit	1980	1985	1986	1987	1988	1989	1990	1991
Production:									
Passenger car production	1,000...	6,376	8,185	7,829	7,100	7,137	6,825	6,078	5,440
Truck and bus production	1,000...	1,634	3,468	3,506	3,826	4,101	4,051	3,706	3,372
Imports:									
Passenger cars (new) [1] [2]	1,000...	3,116	4,398	4,691	4,589	4,450	4,043	3,945	3,736
Canada	1,000...	595	1,145	1,162	927	1,191	1,151	1,220	1,196
Germany, Federal Republic of	1,000...	339	473	452	378	264	217	245	172
Japan	1,000...	1,992	2,527	2,619	2,418	2,123	2,052	1,868	1,789
Trucks (new) [2]	1,000...	747	1,253	1,351	1,177	938	953	766	716
Japan	1,000...	483	800	976	772	542	420	302	283
All-terrain vehicles [3]	1,000...	(NA)	683	498	320	210	121	100	(NA)
Motorcycles, total [3]	1,000...	1,120	733	550	318	287	253	169	(NA)
Import value:									
Passenger cars (new) [1]	Mil. dol..	16,675	36,474	45,302	47,858	47,005	44,417	45,716	45,564
Trucks and buses, (new) [1]	Mil. dol..	1,985	7,734	8,504	8,729	8,089	8,591	8,155	8,221
Motorcycles [3] [4]	Mil. dol..	1,142	783	763	463	512	542	361	(NA)
Exports:									
Passenger cars (new) [1]	1,000...	617	704	673	633	781	778	794	755
Trucks (new) exports	1,000...	186	183	205	222	230	189	151	200
Export value [1]	Mil. dol..	16,015	22,820	21,955	24,812	29,519	31,574	38,086	(NA)
Passenger cars (new) [5]	Mil. dol..	3,932	6,027	6,258	6,695	8,318	8,895	9,708	9,886
Trucks and buses (new) [5]	Mil. dol..	2,977	2,789	2,953	3,375	3,683	3,471	2,845	3,388
Parts and accessories [6]	Mil. dol..	9,106	14,004	12,744	14,742	17,518	19,208	24,996	(NA)
Factory sales:									
Passenger cars	1,000...	6,400	8,002	7,516	7,085	7,105	6,807	6,050	5,407
Trucks and buses	1,000...	1,667	3,357	3,393	3,821	4,121	4,062	3,719	3,375
Retail sales:									
Passenger cars (new) [1]	1,000...	8,979	11,042	11,460	10,277	10,530	9,772	9,300	8,175
Domestics [7]	1,000...	6,581	8,205	8,215	7,081	7,526	7,073	6,897	6,137
Imports [8]	1,000...	2,398	2,838	3,245	3,196	3,004	2,699	2,403	2,038
Trucks and buses [9]	1,000...	2,232	3,984	4,031	4,174	4,608	4,483	4,261	3,842
Light duty (up to 14,000 GVW) [10]	1,000...	1,964	3,700	3,766	3,885	4,273	4,171	3,984	3,621
Med. duty (14,001-26,000 GVW) [10]	1,000...	92	53	51	55	83	73	71	50
Heavy duty (over 26,000 GVW) [10]	1,000...	176	231	214	234	251	239	207	171
Under 6,000 pounds	1,000...	985	2,408	2,541	2,696	2,926	2,854	2,866	2,724
Utility	1,000...	51	429	387	403	445	447	490	549
Van	1,000...	79	115	112	89	47	43	31	17
Mini van (cargo)	1,000...	(X)	103	110	101	105	97	83	66
Station wagon (truck chassis)	1,000...	(X)	86	98	108	138	138	112	110
Mini passenger carrier	1,000...	(X)	301	460	546	692	688	750	706
6,000 to 10,000 pounds [11]	1,000...	975	1,280	1,214	1,175	1,333	1,297	1,097	876
Utility	1,000...	108	108	101	91	90	93	68	37
Van	1,000...	172	261	261	254	302	289	254	203
Pickup, conventional	1,000...	546	628	582	569	666	663	568	476
Station wagon (truck chassis)	1,000...	39	95	98	91	104	100	85	55
10,001 pounds and over	1,000...	271	295	276	302	349	331	298	242

NA Not available. X Not applicable. [1] Based on data from U.S. Dept. of Commerce. [2] Includes other countries, not shown separately.
[3] Source: Motorcycle Industry Council, Inc., Irvine, CA. Data from U.S. Dept. of Commerce. Excludes mopeds/motorized bicycles and all-terrain vehicles. Excludes moped imports (motorcycle imports less than 51 cc's) from all countries (except Japan). [4] Dutiable value for customs purposes prior to 1980, thereafter, c.i.f. value. [5] Covers assembled and unassembled vehicles. [6] Includes rubber tires and tubes and used vehicles. [7] Includes domestic models produced in Canada and Mexico. [8] Excludes domestic models produced in Canada. [9] Excludes motorcoaches and light-duty imports from foreign manufactures. Includes imports sold by franchised dealers of U.S. manufacturers. Starting in 1986, includes sales of trucks over 10,000 lbs. GVW by foreign manufacturers. [10] Gross vehicle weight (fully loaded vehicle). [11] Includes vehicles, not shown separately.

Source: Except as noted, American Automobile Manufacturers Association of the United States, Inc., Detroit, MI, *Motor Vehicle Facts and Figures*, annual; and *World Motor Vehicle Data*, annual.

No. 1020. Motor Vehicles in Use: 1980 to 1991

ITEM	Unit	1980	1985	1986	1987	1988	1989	1990	1991
Cars in use, total	**Million**	**104.6**	**114.7**	**117.3**	**119.8**	**121.5**	**122.8**	**123.3**	**123.3**
Under 5 years	Million	52.3	48.7	50.6	52.8	55.5	57.6	56.5	54.6
6-8 years	Million	25.2	27.8	26.5	24.4	21.6	20.7	22.6	25.5
9-11 years	Million	14.6	17.2	18.7	21.4	22.4	21.1	19.1	16.7
12 years and over	Million	12.5	21.0	21.5	21.2	22.0	23.4	25.1	26.6
Average age	Years	6.6	7.6	7.6	7.6	7.6	7.6	7.8	7.9
Cars retired from use [1]	1,000...	8,405	7,729	8,442	8,103	8,754	8,981	8,897	8,565
Trucks in use, total	**Million**	**35.2**	**42.4**	**44.8**	**47.3**	**50.2**	**53.2**	**56.0**	**58.2**
Under 3 years	Million	8.8	9.0	11.1	11.9	12.5	12.5	12.8	12.0
3-5 years	Million	8.1	6.3	6.6	8.3	10.3	12.6	13.2	14.0
6-8 years	Million	7.4	10.2	8.9	7.4	5.9	6.3	8.0	9.9
9-11 years	Million	4.4	6.2	6.7	8.0	8.9	7.9	6.6	5.3
12 years and over	Million	6.5	10.7	11.5	11.8	12.6	14.0	15.5	17.0
Average age	Years	7.1	8.1	8.0	8.0	7.9	7.9	8.0	8.1
Trucks retired from use [1]	1,000...	1,732	2,100	2,309	2,364	2,251	2,189	2,177	2,284

[1] For years ending June 30. Represents vehicles failing to re-register.

Source: American Automobile Manufacturers Association of the United States, Inc., Detroit, MI, *Motor Vehicle Facts and Figures*, annual; and *World Motor Vehicle Data*, annual.

No. 1021. Motor Vehicle Registrations: 1980 to 1991
[In thousands]

ITEM	1980	1985	1986	1987	1988	1989	1990	1991
Total [1]	155,796	171,654	176,191	179,044	184,397	187,261	188,655	188,372
Automobiles	121,601	131,864	135,431	137,324	141,252	143,081	143,550	142,956
Buses	529	593	594	602	616	625	627	631
Private and commercial:								
Commercial	107	109	110	111	112	113	114	114
School and other	147	157	159	160	160	162	161	161
Publicly owned:								
Federal	4	4	4	5	5	4	5	5
School	271	323	320	327	339	346	347	352
Private and commercial trailers, total	14,372	15,008	15,256	15,322	15,707	16,115	16,098	16,275
Motorcycles	876	722	631	550	410	294	269	247
Truck tractors	1,402	1,150	1,121	1,135	1,183	1,237	1,240	1,236
Light trucks [2]	(NA)	32,146	33,330	34,286	35,320	36,530	37,380	37,603

NA Not available.   [1] Components may not add to total because of double counting.   [2] Excludes farm trucks.

Source: U.S. Federal Highway Administration, *Highway Statistics*, annual.

No. 1022. Motor Vehicle Tires and Batteries: 1980 to 1991
[In millions]

ITEM	1980	1985	1986	1987	1988	1989	1990	1991
Tires, passenger car, total [1]	145.9	200.9	202.7	210.8	218.8	214.8	213.6	214.5
Radials	83.5	164.7	174.0	187.3	200.2	200.4	202.1	205.7
Replacement	106.9	141.5	144.3	151.9	155.3	151.2	152.3	155.4
Tires, truck and bus, total [1]	31.1	41.1	40.6	44.4	46.0	46.9	46.9	42.4
Radials	3.8	19.7	21.1	26.0	29.4	30.6	32.5	32.4
Replacement	24.4	32.1	32.4	34.5	33.9	35.2	36.6	32.9
Batteries, total [2]	61.7	74.4	75.7	75.7	80.1	80.3	79.7	79.8
Replacement automobile batteries	50.1	58.7	60.3	59.9	63.5	64.4	65.2	66.6

[1] Includes original equipment. Also includes exports, not shown separately.   [2] Source: Battery Council International, Chicago, IL, and U.S. Bureau of the Census.

Source: Except as noted, The Rubber Manufacturers Association, Inc., Washington, DC, *RMA Monthly Tire Report*.

No. 1023. Automobile Output and Trade in National Income Accounts: 1970 to 1992
[In billions of current and constant (1982) dollars, except percent. Vehicle output equals final dollar sales value of new vehicles, plus net dollar value of used vehicle sales adjusted for changes in inventories and net balance of vehicle exports and imports]

ITEM	1970	1975	1980	1985	1987	1988	1989	1990	1991	1992
Current dollar auto output	28.5	40.3	59.2	115.8	118.9	129.1	135.1	129.7	119.7	132.8
Final sales	29.7	41.9	60.1	111.3	112.1	128.1	132.0	132.9	119.7	130.8
Personal consumption expenditures	26.8	36.8	57.2	111.7	121.6	131.6	132.4	130.4	115.3	123.8
New autos	21.9	29.3	46.4	87.4	93.5	101.0	99.9	96.7	79.5	85.4
Net purchases of used autos	4.8	7.4	10.8	24.3	28.2	30.5	32.5	33.7	35.8	38.5
Producers' durable equipment	5.3	8.6	14.3	27.7	28.9	32.3	31.1	35.5	36.6	36.9
New autos	7.6	12.6	20.8	44.0	45.1	51.2	49.7	55.1	59.8	61.7
Net purchases of used autos	-2.3	-3.9	-6.5	-16.3	-16.2	-18.9	-18.6	-19.6	-23.3	-24.8
Net exports	-2.9	-4.2	-12.8	-30.0	-40.6	-38.0	-33.7	-35.4	-33.9	-31.5
Exports	0.8	2.9	4.0	6.1	7.4	9.0	10.8	10.5	11.7	14.6
Imports	3.7	7.1	16.8	36.1	47.9	47.1	44.5	45.9	45.6	46.1
Government purchases	0.5	0.7	1.4	2.0	2.1	2.2	2.2	2.4	1.7	1.5
Change in business inventories (new and used)	-1.2	-1.5	-0.9	4.5	6.8	1.0	3.1	-3.2	-	2.0
New	-1.0	-1.9	-0.1	4.0	6.3	0.2	2.2	-2.3	-0.3	1.4
Used	-0.1	0.4	-0.8	0.5	0.5	0.9	0.9	-0.8	0.4	0.7
Constant dollar auto output	65.4	74.8	79.1	125.0	118.9	127.3	128.0	121.7	109.3	117.1
Final sales	68.3	78.5	80.5	120.7	112.1	126.7	125.6	125.8	109.2	115.5
Personal consumption expenditures	68.3	73.5	80.9	122.4	121.6	129.6	126.5	125.0	107.6	111.7
New autos	47.4	53.3	60.2	94.5	93.5	99.1	96.0	91.6	72.6	76.1
Net purchases of used autos	20.9	20.3	20.8	27.9	28.2	30.5	30.4	33.4	35.0	35.5
Producers' durable equipment	10.0	14.8	16.8	32.2	28.9	31.9	30.2	33.3	32.4	32.2
New autos	16.4	22.8	26.9	47.6	45.1	50.2	47.7	52.1	54.7	55.0
Net purchases of used autos	-6.3	-8.0	-10.1	-15.4	-16.2	-18.3	-17.5	-18.9	-22.3	-22.8
Net exports	-11.5	-11.4	-19.2	-36.1	-40.6	-37.0	-33.1	-34.6	-32.2	-29.7
Exports	1.8	5.2	5.3	6.5	7.4	8.9	10.4	9.9	10.6	13.0
Imports	13.3	16.6	24.5	42.6	47.9	45.8	43.5	44.5	42.8	42.7
Government purchases	1.5	1.5	2.0	2.2	2.1	2.2	2.0	2.2	1.5	1.3
Change in business inventories of new and used	-3.0	-3.7	-1.5	4.3	6.8	0.6	2.4	-4.1	0.1	1.6
New	-2.6	-4.5	-0.1	3.9	6.3	-0.3	1.5	-3.3	-0.5	1.0
Used	-0.3	0.8	-1.3	0.4	0.5	0.9	0.9	-0.8	0.6	0.6

- Represents or rounds to zero.

Source: U.S. Bureau of Economic Analysis, *The National Income and Product Accounts of the United States: Volume 2, ᵒ59-88*, and and *Survey of Current Business*, July issues.

No. 1024. Roadway Congestion: 1989

[Various Federal, State, and local information sources were used to develop the data base with the primary source being the Federal Highway Administration's Highway Performance Monitoring System]

URBANIZED AREAS	DAILY VEHICLE MILES OF TRAVEL		VEHICLE HOURS OF DELAY		CONGESTION COST		Delay and fuel cost (mil. dol.)
	Total miles (1,000)	Per lane-mile of freeway	Total hours	Per 1,000 persons	Per reg. vehicle (dol.)	Per capita (dol.)	
Total, average	15,340	12,400	196,750	80	440	310	780
Northeastern cities	25,060	12,550	419,930	90	660	360	1,670
Baltimore, MD.	15,180	12,340	117,720	60	460	250	470
Boston, MA	22,080	22,080	349,860	120	840	470	1,390
New York, NY.	80,920	14,570	1,512,740	90	1,020	370	6,040
Philadelphia, PA	18,280	13,800	272,000	60	380	250	1,060
Pittsburgh, PA.	7,750	7,910	114,920	60	360	240	440
Washington, DC	25,020	16,460	537,770	170	1,280	690	2,130
Midwestern cities	13,790	11,570	111,990	40	270	170	440
Chicago, IL.	34,440	14,970	496,160	70	480	270	1,970
Cincinnati, OH	10,890	12,240	39,520	30	170	140	160
Cleveland, OH	13,210	12,460	46,290	30	130	110	190
Detroit, MI	22,550	13,340	360,930	90	490	360	1,410
Indianapolis, IN.	7,890	10,960	15,400	20	110	70	60
Kansas City, MO.	12,370	9,130	26,280	20	150	90	100
Louisville, KY	6,140	10,500	19,980	20	170	100	80
Milwaukee, WI	7,520	12,740	43,990	40	330	140	180
Minn-St. Paul, MN	16,860	11,630	96,200	50	240	200	390
St. Louis, MO.	18,720	11,110	138,450	70	570	280	540
Southern cities.	6,940	11,790	84,310	80	360	310	330
Atlanta, GA	24,600	14,640	229,090	120	590	490	910
Memphis, TN	4,260	11,200	19,300	20	120	90	80
Miami, FL.	8,350	14,400	222,270	120	610	470	870
Nashville, TN	5,410	11,270	42,400	80	330	310	170
Tampa, FL	3,430	11,630	43,490	60	270	250	170
Southwestern cities	9,640	11,430	105,160	70	340	270	420
Albuquerque, NM	2,310	11,000	20,010	40	190	160	80
Austin, TX	5,300	12,470	44,800	90	370	360	180
Corpus Christi, TX	1,520	8,220	2,680	10	50	40	10
Dallas, TX	22,650	13,400	241,530	120	660	500	980
Denver, CO	10,730	12,480	120,500	80	350	310	480
El Paso, TX	3,300	9,430	7,730	10	90	60	30
Fort Worth, TX	11,280	11,110	91,430	80	380	320	370
Houston, TX.	27,640	14,860	374,950	130	690	520	1,500
Phoenix, AZ	7,050	11,650	179,560	100	590	370	700
Salt Lake City, UT	5,080	9,960	14,830	20	90	80	60
San Antonio, TX	9,180	11,120	58,770	50	270	200	240
Western cities	27,070	15,310	385,570	130	690	520	1,550
Los Angeles, CA.	106,680	20,840	1,752,200	150	900	620	7,000
Portland, OR	7,470	13,580	75,310	70	460	300	310
Sacramento, CA	8,850	12,120	79,230	80	250	300	320
San Diego, CA	26,760	15,560	152,860	70	440	280	620
San Francisco-Oakland, CA ...	41,970	17,860	647,900	180	850	720	2,620
Seattle-Everett, WA	18,200	15,690	255,630	150	810	610	1,020

Source: Texas Transportation Institute, College Station, Texas; *Roadway Congestion in Major Urban Areas*, annual.

No. 1025. Recreational Vehicles—Number and Retail Value of Shipments: 1970 to 1991

ITEM	1970	1975	1980	1983	1984	1985	1986	1987	1988	1989	1990	1991
NUMBER (1,000)												
Total	380.3	339.6	181.4	358.0	398.2	359.2	379.5	400.2	427.3	395.7	354.5	300.5
Motorized homes	30.3	96.6	99.9	223.7	257.3	233.5	249.6	255.7	277.1	261.6	226.5	172.6
Travel trailers	138.0	150.6	52.0	90.0	92.4	82.9	86.0	92.8	96.9	90.3	87.6	84.4
Folding camping trailers	116.1	48.1	24.5	37.5	40.9	35.9	36.5	41.6	42.3	33.9	30.7	33.9
Truck campers	95.9	44.3	5.0	6.8	7.6	6.9	7.4	10.1	11.0	9.9	9.7	9.6
RETAIL VALUE (mil. dol.)												
Total	1,122	2,320	1,952	6,324	7,610	7,029	7,564	8,400	9,188	9,027	8,223	6,739
Motorized homes	318	1,251	1,381	5,099	6,262	5,724	6,155	6,826	7,543	7,420	6,660	5,284
Travel trailers	445	856	485	1,067	1,157	1,122	1,213	1,331	1,381	1,378	1,342	1,250
Folding camping trailers	175	101	69	122	145	137	144	167	175	147	134	146
Truck campers	183	112	17	36	46	46	53	76	88	81	86	87

Source: Recreation Vehicle Industry Association, Reston, VA, *RV's ... A Year-End Report/1989*. Data also in American Automobile Manufacturers Association of the United States, Inc., Detroit, MI, *Motor Vehicle Facts and Figures*, annual.

No. 1026. Motorcycles—Travel, Registration, and Fuel Consumption: 1970 to 1989

ITEM	Unit	1970	1975	1980	1982	1983	1984	1985	1986	1987	1988	1989
Vehicle-miles of travel	Million .	2,979	5,629	10,214	8,784	9,086	9,397	9,506	10,024	10,371	9,557	9,178
Number of registered vehicles ...	1,000 .	2,824	4,964	5,694	5,480	5,444	5,199	4,917	4,584	4,434	4,259	4,177
Average travel per vehicle	Miles. .	1,055	1,134	1,794	1,603	1,669	1,807	1,933	2,187	2,339	2,244	2,197
Fuel consumption, total	Mil. gal	59.6	112.6	204.3	175.7	181.7	187.9	190.1	200.5	207.4	191.1	183.6
Average per vehicle	Gallon .	21	23	36	32	33	36	39	44	47	45	44

Source: U.S. Federal Highway Administration, *Highway Statistics Summary to 1985* and *Highway Statistics*, annual.

No. 1027. Motor Vehicle Accidents—Number and Deaths: 1972 to 1991

[See also *Historical Statistics, Colonial Times to 1970*, series Q 208 and Q 224-232]

ITEM	Unit	1972 [1]	1980	1985	1986	1987	1988	1989	1990	1991
Motor vehicle accidents [2]	Million	17.0	17.9	19.3	17.7	20.8	20.6	12.8	11.5	11.3
Cars	Million	24.5	22.8	25.6	27.7	25.9	28.2	15.3	14.3	13.7
Trucks	Million	3.5	5.5	6.1	6.1	6.0	6.8	6.5	4.4	4.7
Motorcycles	1,000	343	560	480	440	380	370	211	180	239
Motor vehicle deaths within 1 yr. [3]	1,000	56.3	53.2	45.9	47.9	48.3	49.1	47.6	46.8	43.5
Noncollision accidents	1,000	15.8	14.7	12.6	13.1	5.2	5.3	4.9	4.8	4.5
Collision accidents:										
With other motor vehicles	1,000	23.9	23.0	19.9	20.8	20.7	20.9	20.3	19.8	18.5
With pedestrians	1,000	10.3	9.7	8.5	8.9	7.5	7.7	7.8	7.6	7.0
With fixed objects	1,000	3.9	3.7	3.2	3.3	13.2	13.4	12.9	13.2	12.1
Deaths within 30 days [4]	1,000	54.6	51.1	43.8	46.1	46.4	47.1	45.6	(NA)	(NA)
Vehicle occupants	1,000	41.4	36.8	31.5	33.7	34.5	35.5	34.9	(NA)	(NA)
Pedestrians	1,000	9.2	8.1	6.8	6.8	6.7	6.9	6.6	(NA)	(NA)
Motorcyclists [5]	1,000	3.0	5.1	4.6	4.6	4.0	3.7	3.1	(NA)	(NA)
Bicyclists	1,000	1.0	1.0	0.9	0.9	0.9	0.9	0.8	(NA)	(NA)
Traffic death rates: [4] [6]										
Per 100,000 resident population	Rate	26.2	22.6	18.4	19.1	19.1	19.2	18.4	(NA)	(NA)
Per 100,000 registered vehicles	Rate	44.5	31.6	24.8	25.4	25.2	24.9	23.6	(NA)	(NA)
Per 100 million vehicle miles	Rate	4.3	3.3	2.5	2.5	2.4	2.3	2.2	(NA)	(NA)
Per 100,000 licensed drivers	Rate	46.1	35.2	27.9	28.9	28.7	28.9	27.6	(NA)	(NA)
Motor vehicle accidents [7]	Million	24.9	24.1	32.5	33.3	33.9	34.2	34.4	33.4	31.3
Injuries [7]	1,000	5,190	5,230	5,044	5,300	5,400	5,500	5,560	5,560	5,285
Economic loss [7] [8]	Bil. dol.	28.7	57.1	76.0	80.0	85.0	89.0	93.9	95.9	93.8

NA Not available. [1] Represents peak year for deaths from motor vehicle accidents. [2] Covers only accidents occurring on the road. [3] Deaths that occur within one year of accident. Includes collision categories not shown separately. [4] Within 30 days of accident. Source: U.S. National Highway Traffic Safety Administration, unpublished data from Fatal Accident Reporting System. [5] Includes motor scooters and motorized bicycles (mopeds). [6] Based on 30-day definition of traffic deaths. [7] Source: Insurance Information Institute, New York, NY, *Insurance Facts*. Estimates based on official reports from a representative cross-section of States. Includes all motor vehicle accidents on and off the road and all injuries regardless of length of disability. 1986 data for economic loss based on information from the National Center for Health Statistics, National Health Survey. [8] Wage loss; legal, medical, hospital, and funeral expenses; insurance administrative costs; and property damage.

Source: Except as noted, National Safety Council, Itasca, IL, *Accident Facts*, annual, (copyright).

No. 1028. Motor Vehicle Deaths, by State: 1985 to 1991

[Includes both traffic and nontraffic motor vehicle deaths. See source for definitions]

REGION DIVISION STATE	1985	1989	1990	1991	MILEAGE RATE [1] 1985	1991	REGION DIVISION STATE	1985	1989	1990	1991	MILEAGE RATE [1] 1985	1991
U.S.	45,901	47,100	46,300	43,500	2.6	2.0	DC	96	75	55	63	3.0	1.9
							VA	1,021	999	1,073	937	2.1	1.6
Northeast	6,797	6,708	6,243	5,819	(NA)	(NA)	WV	461	468	481	414	3.6	2.7
N.E.	1,873	1,702	1,528	1,400	(NA)	(NA)	NC	1,553	1,464	1,383	1,365	3.1	2.2
ME	224	190	212	202	2.4	1.7	SC	943	996	983	890	3.5	2.6
NH	198	190	158	144	2.6	1.5	GA	1,462	1,632	1,563	1,393	2.7	1.9
VT	117	116	89	106	2.5	1.9	FL	2,968	3,016	2,951	2,519	3.4	2.3
MA	761	700	607	550	1.9	1.2	E.S.C.	3,664	3,616	3,868	3,749	(NA)	(NA)
RI	124	100	84	88	2.1	1.3	KY	749	782	850	828	2.6	2.5
CT	449	406	378	310	2.0	1.2	TN	1,219	1,081	1,172	1,112	3.4	2.4
M.A.	4,924	5,006	4,715	4,419	(NA)	(NA)	AL	1,005	1,025	1,095	1,108	2.9	2.0
NY	2,121	2,239	2,183	1,973	2.3	1.9	MS	691	728	751	701	3.6	2.9
NJ	986	890	886	785	1.9	1.4	W.S.C.	6,197	5,521	5,405	5,154	(NA)	(NA)
PA	1,817	1,877	1,646	1,661	2.4	1.9	AR	580	648	604	608	3.4	2.9
Midwest	9,760	9,993	9,601	9,169	(NA)	(NA)	LA	1,011	857	912	824	3.0	2.2
E.N.C.	6,602	6,871	6,509	6,218	(NA)	(NA)	OK	781	655	646	643	2.5	2.0
OH	1,581	1,700	1,550	1,544	2.1	1.8	TX	3,825	3,361	3,243	3,079	2.7	1.9
IN	1,045	973	1,044	1,020	2.6	1.9	West	10,352	9,847	9,944	9,031	(NA)	(NA)
IL	1,594	1,748	1,589	1,451	2.3	1.9	Mt.	3,409	3,100	3,098	2,982	(NA)	(NA)
MI	1,605	1,633	1,563	1,409	2.4	1.7	MT	233	181	212	200	3.1	2.4
WI	777	817	763	794	2.1	1.8	ID	268	238	243	263	3.5	2.7
W.N.C.	3,158	3,122	3,092	2,951	(NA)	(NA)	WY	145	127	125	122	2.7	2.2
MN	657	605	568	534	2.0	1.4	CO	628	522	543	542	2.4	2.0
IA	478	511	459	491	2.4	2.1	NM	561	538	499	469	4.2	2.9
MO	1,005	1,052	1,096	1,010	2.6	2.0	AZ	942	884	863	816	4.4	2.3
ND	117	81	112	94	2.2	1.6	UT	335	303	270	273	2.8	1.8
SD	142	151	153	143	2.3	2.0	NV	297	307	343	297	3.9	2.9
NE	259	296	262	275	2.1	2.0	Pac.	6,943	6,747	6,846	6,049	(NA)	(NA)
KS	500	426	442	404	2.6	1.8	WA	786	781	825	682	2.3	1.5
South	19,250	18,655	18,631	17,295	(NA)	(NA)	OR	605	630	578	483	2.8	1.8
S.A.	9,389	9,518	9,358	8,392	(NA)	(NA)	CA	5,294	5,105	5,173	4,649	2.6	1.8
DE	119	118	143	103	2.2	1.6	AK	124	84	95	100	3.2	2.9
MD	766	750	726	708	2.3	1.8	HI	134	147	175	135	2.0	1.7

NA Not available. [1] Deaths per 100 million vehicle miles.

Source: 1985: National Center for Health Statistics; thereafter, National Safety Council, Itasca, IL, *Accident Facts, 1991*, (copyright).

No. 1029. Fatal Motor Vehicle Accidents—National Summary: 1980 to 1991

[Based on data from the Fatal Accident Reporting System (FARS). FARS gathers data on accidents that result in loss of human life. FARS is operated and maintained by National Highway Traffic Safety Administration's (NHTSA) National Center for Statistics and Analysis (NCSA). FARS data are gathered on motor vehicle accidents that occurred on a roadway customarily open to the public, resulting in the death of a person within 30 days of the accident; collection of these data depend on the use of police, hospital, medical examiner/coroner, and Emergency Medical Services reports, State vehicle registration, driver licensing, and highway department files, and vital statistics documents and death certificates. See source for further detail]

ITEM	1980	1984	1985	1986	1987	1988	1989	1990	1991
Fatal crashes, total	45,284	39,631	39,196	41,090	41,438	42,130	40,741	39,836	36,895
One vehicle involved	28,306	23,697	22,875	24,275	24,154	24,716	23,742	23,445	21,889
Two or more vehicles involved	16,978	15,934	16,321	16,815	17,284	17,414	16,999	16,391	15,006
Persons killed in fatal crashes	51,091	44,257	43,825	46,087	46,390	47,087	45,582	44,599	41,462
Occupants	41,927	36,284	36,043	38,234	38,565	39,170	38,087	37,134	34,700
Drivers	28,816	25,589	25,337	26,630	26,833	27,253	26,389	25,750	23,904
Passengers	12,972	10,586	10,619	11,498	11,623	11,805	11,624	11,276	10,674
Other	139	109	87	106	109	112	74	108	122
Nonmotorists	9,164	7,973	7,782	7,853	7,825	7,917	7,495	7,465	6,762
Pedestrians	8,070	7,025	6,808	6,779	6,745	6,870	6,556	6,482	5,797
Pedalcyclists	965	849	890	941	948	911	832	859	841
Other	129	99	84	133	132	136	107	124	124
Occupant fatalities by type of vehicle, total	41,927	36,284	36,043	38,234	38,565	39,170	38,087	37,134	34,700
Passenger cars	27,449	23,620	23,212	24,944	25,132	25,808	25,063	24,092	22,347
Mini-compact	3,141	3,555	3,571	3,728	3,815	3,813	3,812	3,556	3,028
Subcompact	4,158	4,346	4,422	4,842	5,007	4,975	4,928	4,753	4,595
Compact	927	2,081	2,635	3,350	3,943	4,764	5,099	5,310	5,284
Intermediate	3,878	4,287	4,391	4,803	4,917	5,016	5,055	4,849	4,644
Full size	4,831	3,269	2,974	3,217	2,937	2,840	2,641	2,386	2,050
Largest size	6,746	4,160	3,612	3,686	3,160	2,904	2,610	2,249	1,929
Unknown	3,768	1,922	1,607	1,318	1,353	1,496	929	989	817
Motorcycles	4,961	4,431	4,417	4,309	3,834	3,492	3,036	3,129	2,703
Other motorized cycles	183	177	147	257	202	170	105	115	105
Multipurpose vehicles	895	723	855	927	1,050	1,040	1,135	1,214	1,475
Light trucks	6,591	5,773	5,834	6,390	7,008	7,266	7,416	7,387	6,905
Pickup	5,483	4,686	4,640	5,090	5,502	5,880	5,870	5,979	5,662
Van	1,000	764	791	879	1,025	1,001	1,214	1,154	1,140
Medium trucks	285	153	157	145	125	125	128	134	115
Heavy trucks	977	921	820	781	727	786	730	571	544
Buses	46	46	57	39	51	54	50	32	31
Other vehicles	257	575	333	244	293	310	277	296	328
Unknown	283	135	211	198	143	119	147	164	147
Persons involved in fatal crashes	113,289	103,348	104,045	109,073	111,457	112,958	109,866	107,777	99,255
Occupants	103,049	94,317	95,482	100,273	102,644	104,086	101,401	99,297	91,599
Drivers	62,957	57,512	57,883	60,335	61,442	62,253	6,435	58,893	54,323
Passengers	39,892	36,634	37,477	39,776	41,013	41,656	40,816	40,229	37,068
Other	200	171	122	162	189	177	150	175	208
Nonoccupants	10,240	9,031	8,563	8,800	8,813	8,872	8,465	8,480	7,656
Vehicle miles traveled (VMT) (100 mill)	15,273	17,203	17,742	18,349	19,212	20,256	21,070	21,444	21,722
Licensed drivers (1,000)	145,295	155,424	156,868	159,487	161,818	162,853	165,555	167,015	169,183
Registered vehicles (1,000)	161,490	171,729	177,098	181,357	183,872	188,981	191,694	192,915	194,897
Fatalities by road type	(NA)	(NA)	(NA)	(NA)	46,390	47,093	(NA)	(NA)	(NA)
Interstate	4,427	4,301	4,148	4,279	4,634	5,142	4,971	4,993	4,574
Federal-aid primary	(NA)	14,848	14,526	15,229	15,561	15,185	14,732	14,203	13,149
Federal-aid secondary	(NA)	6,547	6,429	6,539	8,432	8,534	8,398	8,432	7,480
Federal-aid urban	(NA)	7,933	8,116	8,635	6,597	6,919	6,769	6,892	6,235
NonFederal-aid	(NA)	10,436	10,408	11,242	11,004	10,844	10,579	10,039	9,932
Unknown	(NA)	192	198	163	162	463	133	40	92
Fatality rate by age group:									
Under 5 years old	6.9	5.0	5.2	5.3	5.4	5.4	5.4	4.9	4.6
5 years to 15 years old	8.7	7.3	7.4	7.7	7.8	7.4	7.0	6.4	6.1
16 years to 24 years old	46.0	37.9	37.1	40.2	38.8	40.0	36.7	35.2	33.0
25 years to 44 years old	24.6	20.3	19.6	20.5	20.6	20.3	20.0	19.7	17.6
45 years to 64 years old	17.2	14.6	14.5	14.2	14.9	15.0	15.0	14.9	13.5
65 years to 79 years old	19.6	18.6	18.0	18.7	18.8	19.5	19.1	18.8	18.0
80 years old and over	25.3	23.9	25.1	25.8	27.1	29.1	28.8	26.8	26.8
Fatal crashes by the highest blood alcohol concentration (BAC) in crash:									
0.00 percent	(NA)	46.7	48.5	48.3	49.3	50.1	51.1	50.6	52.1
0.01 to 0.09 percent	(NA)	10.6	10.3	10.9	10.7	10.2	9.8	9.7	9.4
0.10 percent and over	(NA)	42.7	41.2	40.8	40	39.7	39.1	39.7	38.5
National rates:									
Fatalities per 100 million VMT	3.3	2.6	2.5	2.5	2.4	2.3	2.2	2.1	1.9
Fatalities per 100,000 licensed drivers	35.2	28.5	27.9	28.9	28.7	28.9	27.5	26.7	24.5
VMT per registered vehicle	9,458	10,017	10,018	10,117	10,445	10,718	10,936	11,107	11,281
Fatal crashes per 100 million VMT	2.9	2.3	2.2	2.2	2.2	2.1	1.9	1.9	1.7
Involved vehicles per fatal crash	1.4	1.5	1.5	1.5	1.5	1.5	1.5	1.5	1.5

NA Not available.

Source: National Highway Traffic Safety Administration, *Fatal Accident Reporting System*, annual.

No. 1030. Highway Mileage, Vehicle Miles of Travel, Accidents, and Fatalities, 1975 to 1991, and by Type of Highway System, 1991

YEAR AND TYPE OF SYSTEM	Highway mileage (1,000)	Vehicle miles of travel (bil.)	Daily vehicle miles per mile	FATAL ACCIDENTS		NONFATAL INJURY ACCIDENTS		FATALITIES [2]	
				Number	Rate [1]	Number (1,000)	Rate [1]	Number	Rate [1]
1975	3,838	1,328	948	39,993	3.01	1,861	140	44,525	3.43
1980	3,857	1,527	1,082	45,284	2.96	2,008	131	51,091	3.35
1985	3,862	1,774	1,259	39,168	2.21	2,219	125	43,825	2.47
1986	3,880	1,835	1,298	41,062	2.23	2,254	123	46,087	2.51
1987	3,874	1,921	1,361	41,434	2.15	2,294	119	46,390	2.41
1988	3,871	2,026	1,430	42,119	2.08	2,302	114	47,087	2.32
1989	3,877	2,096	1,469	40,718	1.93	2,384	113	45,582	2.16
1990	3,880	2,148	1,516	39,779	1.85	2,501	116	44,529	2.07
1991, total	**3,889**	**2,172**	**1,530**	**36,895**	**1.70**	**2,210**	**102**	**41,462**	**1.91**
Urban	750	1,289	4,708	15,748	1.22	1,569	122	17,049	1.32
Rural	3,139	884	771	21,147	2.39	642	73	24,413	2.76
Interstate	45	490	29,688	3,868	0.79	161	33	4,472	0.91
Urban	12	285	67,372	1,729	0.61	117	41	1,908	0.87
Rural	34	205	16,678	2,139	1.04	49	21	2,564	1.25
Noninterstate	3,844	1,682	1,199	33,027	1.96	2,049	121	36,990	2.20
Urban	738	1,003	3,723	14,019	1.40	1,452	145	15,141	1.51
Rural	3,106	679	599	19,008	2.80	598	88	21,849	3.22
Federal-aid highway system	851	1,769	5,699	27,532	1.58	1,543	87	31,266	1.77
Urban	194	1,048	14,820	12,274	1.17	1,143	109	13,334	1.27
Rural	657	721	3,009	15,258	2.12	399	55	17,932	2.49
Interstate	45	490	29,688	3,868	0.79	161	33	4,472	0.91
Other primary arterial	257	608	6,481	11,286	1.86	490	81	13,117	2.16
Urban	34	278	22,216	3,530	1.27	298	107	3,869	1.39
Rural	223	330	4,062	7,756	2.35	192	58	9,248	2.80
Urban (arterial and collector)	148	485	8,983	7,015	1.45	728	150	7,557	1.58
Secondary (collector)	400	186	1,273	5,363	2.88	163	88	6,120	3.29
NonFederal-aid highway system	3,039	403	363	9,363	2.32	668	166	10,196	2.53
Arterial	13	32	6,772	335	1.06	23	72	373	1.18
Urban	8	27	9,278	237	0.88	21	78	251	0.93
Rural	5	5	2,605	98	2.15	2	39	122	2.68
Collector	353	85	659	1,906	2.25	89	105	2,115	2.49
Urban	22	25	3,137	185	0.73	26	102	201	0.80
Rural	331	60	494	1,721	2.89	63	106	1,914	3.21
Local	2,673	287	294	7,122	2.49	556	194	7,708	2.69
Urban	526	188	981	3,052	1.62	379	201	3,263	1.73
Rural	2,147	98	125	4,070	4.15	177	180	4,445	4.53

[1] Rate per 100 million vehicle miles of travel. [2] Represents fatalities occurring within 30 days of accident. Excludes nontraffic accidents which, for example, occur outside the rights-of-way or other boundaries of roads that are open for public use.

Source: U.S. Federal Highway Administration, *Fatal and Injury Accident Rates on Public Roads in the United States*, annual.

No. 1031. Motor Vehicle Safety Defect Recalls, by Domestic and Foreign Manufacturers: 1980 to 1990

[Covers manufacturers reporting to U.S. National Highway Traffic Administration under section 151 of National Traffic and Motor Vehicle Safety Act of 1966, as amended]

MANUFACTURER	Unit	1980	1982	1983	1984	1985	1986	1987	1988	1989	1990
Motor vehicles:											
Total recall campaigns [1]	Number	167	135	140	164	173	174	199	197	237	208
Domestic	Number	129	107	110	127	137	139	150	152	182	159
Foreign	Number	38	28	30	37	36	35	49	45	55	49
Total vehicles recalled	1,000	4,863	1,914	6,114	7,220	5,629	2,880	9,091	4,486	7,136	4,070
Domestic	1,000	3,939	1,401	3,090	6,283	4,995	1,731	7,297	3,171	6,172	1,915
Vehicles recalled by four leading auto manufacturers	1,000	3,730	1,324	3,021	6,148	4,811	1,382	6,945	[2]2,900	5,842	(NA)
Foreign	1,000	924	513	3,024	937	634	1,149	1,793	1,315	963	(NA)
Motor vehicle tires:											
Recall campaigns [1]	Number	24	17	21	16	19	14	16	12	11	13
Tires recalled	1,000	7,070	131	95	81	28	164	43	215	116	172

NA Not available. [1] A recall campaign is the notification to the Secretary of the U.S. Dept. of Transportation and to owners, purchasers, and dealers of a motor vehicle safety defect. [2] Three leading automobile manufacturers.

Source: U.S. National Highway Traffic Safety Administration, *Motor Vehicles Defect Recall Campaigns*, annual.

No. 1032. State Legislation—Alcohol and Road Safety Laws: Various Years

REGION, DIVISION, AND STATE	ALCOHOL LEGISLATION			MANDATORY BELT USE LAW			Child safety seat law date[5]	Motor-cycle helmet law[6]	65 SPEED LIMIT	
	21 year drinking age since[1]	Open con-tainer law[2]	BAC limit[3]	Effec-tive date	Enforce-ment[4]	Seating posi-tions			Effec-tive date[7]	Applic-able vehicles
Northeast:										
N.E:										
ME	1985	no	0.08	none	(X)	(X)	9/83	[8][9]15	6/87	all
NH	1985	yes	0.10	none	(X)	(X)	7/89	18	4/87	all
VT	1986	no	0.08	none	(X)	(X)	7/84	yes	4/87	all
MA	1985	yes	[10]0.10	repealed	(X)	(X)	1/82	yes	12/91	all
RI	1984	no	[10]0.10	7/91	2	all	7/87	([11])	none	(X)
CT	1985	no	0.10	1/86	1	front	1982	18	none	(X)
M.A:										
NY	1990	no	0.10	12/84	1	front	4/82	yes	none	(X)
NJ	1982	no	0.10	3/85	2	front	4/83	yes	none	(X)
PA	1935	no	0.10	11/87	2	front	11/83	yes	none	(X)
Midwest:										
E.N.C:										
OH	1987	yes	[10]0.10	5/86	2	front	6/83	[9]18	7/87	some
IN	1935	no	0.10	7/87	2	front	1/84	18	6/87	some
IL	1980	yes	0.10	7/85	2	front	7/83	no	4/87	some
MI	1978	yes	0.10	7/85	2	front	3/82	yes	12/87	some
WI	1986	yes	[10]0.10	12/87	1	front	4/84	[8]18	6/87	all
W.N.C:										
MN	1986	yes	0.10	8/86	2	front	8/83	[8]18	6/87	all
IA	1986	yes	0.10	7/86	1	front	1/84	no	5/87	all
MO	1945	no	0.10	9/85	2	front	1/84	yes	4/87	some
ND	1936	yes	0.10	none	(X)	(X)	1/84	18	4/87	all
SD	1987	yes	0.10	none	(X)	(X)	7/84	18	4/87	all
NE	1985	no	0.10	repealed	(X)	(X)	8/83	yes	4/87	all
KS	1985	yes	0.10	7/86	2	front	7/81	18	5/87	some
South:										
S.A:										
DE	1983	yes	0.10	1/92	2	front	6/82	[8][12]19	none	(X)
MD	1982	no	0.10	7/86	2	[13]front	1/84	18	none	(X)
DC	1986	no	0.10	12/85	2	[13]front	7/83	yes	none	(X)
VA	1986	no	0.10	1/88	2	front	1/83	yes	7/88	some
WV	1986	no	0.10	none	(X)	(X)	7/81	yes	5/87	all
NC	1986	yes	0.10	10/85	1	front	7/85	yes	4/87	all
SC	1986	yes	0.10	7/89	2	front	1/89	21	7/87	all
GA	1986	yes	0.10	9/88	2	front	7/84	yes	2/88	all
FL	1985	yes	0.10	7/86	2	front	7/83	yes	4/87	all
E.S.C:										
KY	1938	no	0.10	none	(X)	(X)	7/82	yes	6/87	all
TN	1984	no	0.10	4/86	2	front	1/78	yes	5/87	all
AL	1985	no	0.10	7/92	2	front	1982	yes	1987	all
MS	1986	no	0.10	3/90	1	front	7/83	yes	4/87	all
W.S.C:										
AR	1957	no	0.10	7/91	2	front	8/83	yes	4/87	all
LA	1987	no	0.10	7/86	2	front	1/85	yes	4/87	all
OK	1983	yes	0.10	2/87	2	front	11/83	18	4/87	all
TX	1985	no	0.10	9/85	1	front	1/85	yes	5/87	some
West:										
Mt:										
MT	1987	no	0.10	10/87	2	all	10/83	18	4/87	all
ID	1987	[14]Yes	0.10	7/86	2	front	1/85	18	5/87	all
WY	1988	no	0.10	6/89	2	front	4/85	18	5/87	all
CO	1987	no	0.10	7/87	2	front	1/84	no	4/87	all
NM	1934	yes	0.10	1/86	1	front	5/83	18	4/87	all
AZ	1984	no	0.10	1/91	2	front	1984	18	5/87	all
UT	1935	yes	0.08	4/86	2	front	4/83	18	4/87	all
NV	1933	yes	0.10	7/87	2	all	7/83	yes	4/87	all
Pac:										
WA	1934	yes	0.10	6/86	2	all	1/84	yes	4/87	some
OR	1935	yes	[10]0.08	12/90	1	all	1/84	yes	10/87	some
CA	1933	yes	0.08	1/86	2	all	1/83	yes	5/87	some
AK	1983	yes	0.10	9/90	2	all	6/85	18	none	(X)
HI	1986	Yes	0.10	12/85	1	all	1983	yes	none	(X)

X Not applicable. [1] Year in which original law became effective, not when grandfather clauses expired. [2] Law prohibiting open liquor containers in motor vehicles. [3] Percent blood alcohol concentration (BAC) which constitutes the threshold of legal intoxication. [4] "1" indicates primary enforcement (law can be enforced on its own), "2" indicates secondary enforcement. (Law enforced only if vehicle stopped for a separate offense.) [5] Effective data of original law, not of subsequent revisions. [6] Presence of law or age below which riders are required to wear helmet. [7] Includes administrative action as well as legislation. [8] Plus instruction permit holders. [9] Plus novice license holders. [10] Different legal limit for minors. [11] Passengers only. [12] Possession of helmet required by all. [13] Excluding front center seat. [14] Does not include beer.

Source: National Safety Council, Itasca, IL, *Accident Facts*, annual.

No. 1033. Estimated Arrests for Driving Under the Influence, by Age: 1980 and 1989

[Total drivers and arrests in thousands. Represents licensed drivers and arrests for those 16 years old and over]

AGE	1980			1989			Percent change in rate, 1980-89
	Drivers	Arrests	Arrests per 100,000 drivers	Drivers	Arrests	Arrests per 100,000 drivers	
Total.........	145,207	1,425	981	165,518	1,735	1,048	6.9
Percent distribution.....	100.0	100.0	(X)	100.0	100.0	(X)	(X)
16 to 17 years old....	3.2	2.2	668	2.3	1.1	503	−24.7
18 to 24 years old....	7.2	12.9	1,757	5.4	8.3	1,607	−8.5
25 to 29 years old....	13.0	17.9	1,347	12.4	22.2	1,869	38.8
30 to 34 years old....	12.0	13.1	1,076	12.4	17.6	1,486	38.1
35 to 39 years old....	9.4	9.6	996	11.2	12.0	1,123	12.8
40 to 44 years old....	7.7	7.4	944	9.7	8.1	872	−7.6
45 to 49 years old....	6.9	5.9	837	7.6	5.3	725	−13.4
50 to 54 years old....	6.9	4.9	686	6.2	3.3	558	−18.7
55 to 59 years old....	6.7	3.5	509	5.7	2.2	400	−21.4
60 to 64 years old....	5.7	1.9	335	5.6	1.4	262	−21.8
65 years old and over .	10.7	1.5	140	13.0	1.2	100	−28.6

X Not applicable.
Source: U.S. Bureau of Justice Statistics, *Drunk Driving, Special Report.*

No. 1034. Licensed Drivers, Fatal Motor Vehicle Accidents, and Alcohol Involvement, by Age of Driver: 1990

ITEM	Unit	Total	AGE OF DRIVER							
			16-17 years	18-21 years	22-24 years	25-34 years	35-44 years	45-54 years	55-64 years	65 years and over
Licensed drivers (estimated) [1] ...	1,000...	168,995	3,463	11,809	10,191	40,322	36,987	24,514	18,705	22,939
Percent distribution	Percent .	100.0	2.0	7.0	6.0	23.9	21.9	14.5	11.1	13.6
Licensed drivers involved in fatal accidents	Number .	58,893	2,651	8,112	5,253	15,764	10,177	5,867	4,068	5,501
Percent distribution	Percent .	100.0	4.5	13.8	8.9	26.8	17.3	10.0	6.9	9.3
Drinking drivers involved in fatal accidents	Number .	14,060	355	2,483	1,774	4,805	2,509	1,084	492	452
Percent distribution	Percent .	100.0	2.5	17.7	12.6	34.2	17.8	7.7	3.5	3.2

[1] Source: U.S. Federal Highway Administration, *Selected Highway Statistics and Charts*, annual.

No. 1035. Police-Reported Traffic Crashes, by Age Group: 1991

[Based on probability sample of police-reported crashes. See source for details]

ITEM	Total	15 yrs. and under	16 to 20 yrs.	21 to 24 yrs.	25 to 34 yrs.	35 to 44 yrs.	45 to 54 yrs.	55 to 64 yrs.	65 yrs. and older
Crash-involved........	10,659,000	47,000	1,763,000	1,287,000	2,934,000	2,018,000	1,138,000	725,000	749,000
Percent male	62	64	62	63	64	60	62	64	63
Percent female	49	36	38	37	36	40	38	36	37
Percent alcohol-involved.	5	6	4	6	6	4	5	4	1
Passengers injured or killed	1,018,000	296,000	194,000	104,000	153,000	95,000	58,000	47,000	70,000
Percent male	41	45	46	50	43	36	31	19	18
Percent female	59	55	54	50	57	64	69	81	83
Pedestrians injured or killed	92,000	32,000	8,000	6,000	15,000	10,000	7,000	6,000	9,000
Percent during day	64	78	50	50	47	50	65	50	80
Percent at night	36	22	50	50	53	50	35	50	20
Pedalcyclists injured or killed	67,000	29,000	9,000	7,000	12,000	4,000	3,000	1,000	1,000

Source of tables 1034 and 1035: Except as noted, U.S. National Highway Traffic Safety Administration, *General Estimates System*, annual, and unpublished data.

No. 1036. Cost of Owning and Operating an Automobile: 1980 to 1991

ITEM	Unit	1980	1985	1986	1987	1988	1989	1990	1991
Cost per mile [1]........	Cents	27.95	27.20	29.59	32.64	33.40	38.20	40.96	43.60
Cost per 10,000 miles [1]...	Dollars....	2,795	2,720	2,959	3,264	3,341	3,820	4,096	4,364
Variable cost	Cents/mile .	7.62	8.04	6.52	7.20	7.60	7.90	8.40	9.80
Gas and oil............	Cents/mile .	5.86	6.16	4.48	4.80	5.20	5.20	5.40	6.70
Maintenance...........	Cents/mile .	1.12	1.23	1.37	1.60	1.60	1.90	2.10	2.20
Tires...............	Cents/mile .	0.64	0.65	0.67	0.80	0.80	0.80	0.90	0.90
Fixed cost	Dollars....	2,033	2,441	2,596	2,782	3,061	3,534	3,877	4,217
Insurance............	Dollars....	490	503	509	535	573	663	675	726
License and registration	Dollars....	82	115	130	140	139	151	165	169
Depreciation	Dollars....	1,038	1,253	1,320	1,506	1,784	2,094	2,357	2,543
Finance charge	Dollars....	423	570	637	601	565	626	680	779

[1] Beginning 1985, not comparable to previous data.

Source: American Automobile Manufacturers Association of the United States, Inc., Detroit, MI, *Motor Vehicle Facts and Figures*, annual.

No. 1037. Domestic Motor Fuel Consumption, by Type of Vehicle: 1970 to 1991

[Comprises all fuel types used for propulsion of vehicles under State motor fuels laws. Excludes Federal purchases for military use. Minus sign (-) indicates decrease. See also *Historical Statistics, Colonial Times to 1970*, series Q 156-162]

YEAR	FUEL CONSUMPTION					AVG. FUEL CONSUMPTION PER VEHICLE (gal.)			AVG. MILES PER GALLON		
	All vehicles (bil. gal.)	Avg. annual percent change [1]	Cars [2] (bil. gal.)	Buses [3] (bil. gal.)	Trucks [4] (bil. gal.)	Cars [2]	Buses [3]	Trucks [4]	Cars [2]	Buses [3]	Trucks [4]
1970 ..	92.3	5.4	67.8	0.8	23.6	760	2,172	1,257	13.52	5.54	7.85
1975 ..	109.0	2.5	76.4	1.1	31.4	716	2,279	1,217	13.52	5.75	8.99
1980 ..	115.0	-5.9	71.9	1.0	41.9	591	1,926	1,243	15.46	5.95	9.54
1981 ..	114.5	-0.4	71.0	1.1	42.2	576	1,938	1,219	15.94	5.92	9.59
1982 ..	113.4	-0.9	70.1	1.0	42.1	566	1,756	1,191	16.65	5.93	9.80
1983 ..	116.1	2.4	69.9	0.9	45.1	553	1,507	1,229	17.14	5.92	9.77
1984 ..	118.7	2.3	68.7	0.8	49.0	536	1,359	1,308	17.83	5.85	9.83
1985 ..	121.3	2.2	69.3	0.8	51.0	525	1,407	1,302	18.20	5.84	9.79
1986 ..	125.2	3.2	71.4	0.9	52.9	526	1,463	1,320	18.27	5.84	9.81
1987 ..	127.5	1.8	70.6	0.9	55.8	514	1,500	1,357	19.20	5.89	9.87
1988 ..	130.1	2.0	71.9	0.9	57.2	509	1,496	1,345	19.95	5.93	10.16
1989 ..	131.8	1.3	72.7	0.9	57.9	509	1,518	1,328	20.40	5.96	10.41
1990 ..	130.8	-0.8	72.0	0.9	57.7	502	1,428	1,290	21.02	6.39	10.84
1991 ..	128.6	-1.7	70.7	0.9	56.8	495	1,369	1,269	21.68	6.64	10.70

[1] From prior year, except 1970, change from 1965.   [2] Includes taxicabs.   [3] Includes school buses.   [4] Includes combinations.

Source: U.S. Federal Highway Administration, *Highway Statistics Summary to 1985*, and *Highway Statistics*, annual.

No. 1038. Household Motor Vehicle Transportation, by Vehicle Model Year: 1988

[Preliminary. Household vehicles include all motorized vehicles used for personal transportation, excluding motorcycles, mopeds, large trucks, and buses. The reporting unit for 1988 is all households which owned a vehicle at any time during 1988. Based on the Residential Transportation Energy Consumption Survey; subject to sampling variability. For composition of regions, see table 31]

REGION	Households with motor vehicles (mil.)	VEHICLES (millions)					MILES PER GALLON				
		Total	Model year				Average	Model year			
			1974 and earlier	1975 to 1980	1981 to 1985	1986 to 1989		1976 and earlier	1981 or 1982	1986	1988 or 1989
Total	81.3	147.5	13	29	35	23	18.3	12.3	20.7	21.9	22.1
Northeast	15.2	26.6	8	24	40	28	19.6	12.2	21.8	22.3	21.5
Midwest	20.4	37.8	11	32	35	22	18.2	12.2	20.7	21.5	23.0
South..........	28.3	50.6	12	29	34	24	18.0	12.0	19.7	21.8	21.9
West	17.3	32.5	21	29	30	20	18.0	12.7	21.5	22.3	22.3

Source: U.S. Energy Information Administration, *Household Vehicles Energy Consumption, 1988*.

No. 1039. Household Vehicles—Annual Mileage, Fuel Consumption, and Fuel Expenditures: 1988

[See headnote, table 1038]

HOUSEHOLD AND VEHICLE CHARACTERISTICS	NUMBER OF—			MILES DRIVEN		GALLONS CONSUMED		FUEL EXPENDITURES	
	Households [1] (millions)	Vehicles (millions)	Vehicles per household	Total (billion)	Percent	Total (billion)	Percent	Total (bil. dol.)	Percent
Total	81.3	147.5	1.8	1,511	100.0	82.4	100.0	81.1	100.0
Metropolitan status:									
Metropolitan...........	63.0	113.9	1.8	1,171	77.5	62.6	76.0	61.9	76.3
Nonmetropolitan	18.3	33.6	1.8	341	22.5	19.8	24.0	19.2	23.7
Origin of householder: White .	71.5	132.2	1.8	1,346	89.0	73.5	89.2	72.3	89.1
Black	7.2	10.6	1.5	115	7.6	6.2	7.5	6.2	7.6
Other	2.6	4.7	1.8	51	3.4	2.8	3.3	2.7	3.3
Family income 1988:									
Less than $10,000.......	10.2	13.3	1.3	111	7.4	6.6	8.0	6.4	7.9
$10,000-$14,999........	11.8	17.0	1.4	153	10.2	9.0	10.9	8.8	10.8
$15,000-$19,999........	8.3	13.3	1.6	132	8.7	7.3	8.9	7.2	8.9
$20,000-$24,999........	8.6	15.1	1.7	154	10.2	8.5	10.3	8.3	10.3
$25,000-$34,999........	16.0	29.2	1.8	297	19.7	16.4	19.9	16.1	19.9
$35,000-$49,999........	12.9	28.3	2.2	313	20.7	16.5	20.0	16.3	20.1
$50,000-$74,999........	8.8	20.5	2.3	226	15.0	11.8	14.3	11.6	14.3
$75,000 or more	4.5	10.8	2.4	124	8.2	6.3	7.7	6.3	7.8

[1] Includes only households with vehicles.

Source: U.S. Energy Information Administration, *Household Vehicles Energy Consumption 1988*.

No. 1040. Motor Vehicle Travel, by Type of Vehicle, and by Speed: 1970 to 1991

[Travel in billions of vehicle-miles, except as indicated. Travel estimates based on automatic traffic recorder data. Speed trend data for 1970-1975 were collected by several State highway agencies, normally during summer months; beginning Oct. 1975 all States have monitored speeds at locations on several highway systems as part of 55 mile per hour Speed Limit Monitoring Program. See also *Historical Statistics, Colonial Times to 1970*, series Q 199-207]

| YEAR | VEHICLE-MILES OF TRAVEL (bil.) | | | | AVG. MILES PER VEHICLE (1,000) | | | MOTOR VEHICLE SPEED [2] | | | | |
| | Total | Cars [1] | Buses | Trucks | Passenger vehicles | | Trucks [3] | Vehicles recorded (1,000) [3] | Avg. speed (miles per hour) | Percent of vehicles exceeding— | | |
					Cars [1]	Buses				55 mph	60 mph	65 mph
1970	1,110	920	4.5	186	10.0	12.0	9.9	200	63.8	87	69	44
1980	1,527	1,122	6.1	399	8.8	11.5	11.9	667	57.5	66	25	7
1983	1,653	1,207	5.2	441	9.1	8.9	12.0	7,856	59.1	74	41	15
1984	1,720	1,234	4.6	482	9.2	8.0	12.8	8,067	59.3	75	43	16
1985	1,774	1,270	4.9	500	9.2	8.2	12.7	8,449	59.5	75	44	17
1986	1,834	1,311	5.1	519	9.3	8.5	13.0	8,549	59.7	76	46	18
1987	1,921	1,365	5.3	551	9.6	8.8	13.4	7,992	59.7	74	46	19
1988	2,025	1,439	5.5	581	9.9	8.9	13.6	7,566	59.5	74	46	19
1989	2,096	1,488	5.7	603	10.1	9.0	13.8	7,488	60.1	77	49	22
1990	2,144	1,513	5.7	616	10.5	9.1	13.8	7,511	60.3	78	50	23
1991	2,172	1,534	5.7	624	10.7	9.1	13.9	7,594	59.6	75	48	22

[1] Includes motorcycles. [2] Represents speed on rural interstate highways. Beginning 1980, for year ending Sept. 30. [3] Citations issued for 55 mph violations.

Source: U.S. Federal Highway Administration, *Highway Statistics Summary*, annual.

No. 1041. Passenger Transit Industry—Summary: 1980 to 1991

[Includes Puerto Rico. Includes aggregate information for all transit systems in the United States. Except as noted, prior-to-1985 data exclude commuter railroad, automated guideway, urban ferry boat, and demand response, as well as most transit systems outside of urbanized areas. Nontransit services such as taxicab, school bus, unregulated jitney, sightseeing bus, intercity bus, and special application mass transportation systems (e.g., amusement parks, airports, island, and urban park ferries) are excluded. Beginning in 1985, only active vehicles are counted]

ITEM	Unit	1980	1985	1986	1987	1988	1989	1990	1991, prel.
Operating systems	Number	1,044	4,972	5,018	5,047	5,036	5,046	5,078	5,085
Motor bus systems [1]	Number	1,040	2,631	2,655	2,671	2,671	2,665	2,688	2,690
Publicly owned systems [1]	Number	576	1,435	(NA)	(NA)	(NA)	(NA)	1,580	(NA)
Passenger vehicles owned [2][3]	Number	75,388	94,368	98,709	96,127	97,209	92,293	92,961	93,232
Motor bus [2]	Number	59,411	64,258	66,218	63,017	62,572	58,919	58,714	57,865
Trolley bus	Number	823	676	680	671	710	725	832	919
Heavy rail [2]	Number	9,641	9,326	10,386	10,168	10,539	10,506	10,419	10,170
Light rail [2]	Number	1,013	717	697	766	831	755	913	1,058
Commuter rail	Number	4,500	4,035	4,440	4,686	4,649	4,472	4,415	4,550
Demand response	Number	(NA)	14,490	15,346	15,944	16,812	15,856	16,471	17,222
Total revenue	Mil. dol	6,510	12,195	13,342	14,091	14,537	14,985	16,053	16,810
Passenger revenue [4]	Mil. dol	2,557	4,575	5,113	5,114	5,225	5,420	5,891	6,064
Other operating revenue [4]	Mil. dol	248	702	737	777	841	837	895	954
Operating assistance	Mil. dol	3,705	6,918	7,491	8,200	8,471	8,728	9,267	9,792
Federal	Mil. dol	1,094	940	941	955	901	937	970	945
Local [5]	Mil. dol	2,611	5,979	4,245	4,681	4,893	4,995	5,327	5,605
State [5]	Mil. dol	(NA)	(NA)	2,306	2,565	2,677	2,796	2,970	3,242
Total expense	Mil. dol	6,711	14,077	14,726	15,405	16,442	17,169	17,979	19,617
Operating expense	Mil. dol	6,247	12,381	12,952	13,472	14,287	14,972	15,742	16,785
Transportation	Mil. dol	3,248	5,655	5,690	5,790	6,052	6,275	6,654	6,834
Maintenance	Mil. dol	1,774	3,672	4,029	4,094	4,313	4,493	4,631	4,654
Administration	Mil. dol	1,224	2,505	2,748	2,869	3,078	3,251	3,450	3,622
Reconciling expense	Mil. dol	464	1,696	1,774	1,933	2,155	2,196	2,237	2,832
Capital expenditure, Federal	Mil. dol	2,787	2,510	3,138	2,475	2,521	2,590	2,380	2,371
Vehicle-miles operated [3]	Million	2,287	2,791	2,986	3,055	3,157	3,203	3,242	3,348
Motor bus	Million	1,677	1,863	2,002	2,079	2,097	2,109	2,130	2,182
Trolley bus	Million	13	16	15	15	15	15	14	14
Heavy rail	Million	385	451	476	490	517	532	537	525
Light rail	Million	18	17	17	18	21	21	24	28
Commuter rail	Million	179	183	189	189	202	210	213	217
Demand response	Million	(NA)	247	275	250	289	300	306	359
Passengers carried [3]	Million	8,567	8,636	8,777	8,735	8,666	8,931	8,799	8,643
Motor bus	Million	5,837	5,675	5,753	5,614	5,590	5,620	5,677	5,686
Trolley bus	Million	142	142	139	141	136	130	126	125
Heavy rail	Million	2,108	2,290	2,333	2,402	2,308	2,542	2,346	2,167
Light rail	Million	133	132	130	133	154	162	175	186
Commuter rail	Million	280	275	306	311	325	330	328	324
Demand response	Million	(NA)	59	63	64	73	70	68	72
Avg. revenue per passenger	Cents	29.8	53.0	58.3	58.5	60.3	60.7	66.9	70.2
Employees, number (avg.)	1,000	187	270	278	277	276	272	273	282
Payroll, employee	Mil. dol	3,281	5,843	6,119	6,324	6,675	6,898	7,226	7,490
Fringe benefits, employee	Mil. dol	1,353	2,868	3,126	3,267	3,529	3,737	3,986	4,056

NA Not available. [1] Includes systems with combined services including motor buses, heavy rail cars, light rail cars, trolley coaches, cable cars, and inclined plane cars. Beginning 1985, combined services also include commuter rail cars, urban ferry boats, vanpools, aerial tramways, automated guideways, and demand response vehicles. [2] Beginning 1985, includes active vehicles only. Includes other vehicles not shown separately. [3] Includes other not shown separately. [4] Includes other operating revenue, nonoperating revenue, and auxiliary income. [5] Prior to 1986, State and local combined.

Source: American Public Transit Association, Washington, DC, *Transit Fact Book*, annual.

No. 1042. Class I Intercity Motor Carriers of Passengers: 1975 to 1990

[Carriers subject to ICC regulations. See text, section 21. Minus sign (-) indicates deficit. See also *Historical Statistics, Colonial Times to 1970*, series Q 69-75]

ITEM	Unit	1975	1980	1982	1983	1984	1985	1986	1987	1988	1989	1990
Carriers reporting [1]	Number.	77	48	50	45	43	43	29	32	21	20	21
Number of employees, average. . . .	1,000 . .	31	31	30	25	25	24	20	(NA)	(NA)	(NA)	(NA)
Compensation of employees.	Mil. dol .	383	599	646	570	551	518	443	(NA)	(NA)	(NA)	(NA)
Operating revenue . . , ...	Mil. dol .	942	1,397	1,447	1,276	1,255	1,233	1,117	1,079	1,122	1,205	943
Passenger revenue [2]	Mil. dol .	651	947	969	876	861	836	765	751	825	890	738
Special bus revenue and other. . .	Mil. dol .	291	215	229	180	180	184	155	165	155	165	90
Operating expenses	*Mil. dol .*	*880*	*1,318*	*1,416*	*1,283*	*1,254*	*1,168*	*1,082*	*1,081*	*1,059*	*1,133*	*1,015*
Net operating revenue.	Mil. dol .	61	79	30	-7	1	65	35	-2	63	72	-72
Ordinary income:												
Before income taxes	Mil. dol .	83	107	35	16	53	65	50	-11	(NA)	(NA)	(NA)
After income taxes.	Mil. dol .	56	90	37	26	43	53	36	-21	12	(NA)	-180
Passenger vehicles in service [2]	1,000 . .	9.7	8.6	8.1	7.3	7.0	8.4	8.3	(NA)	(NA)	(NA)	(NA)
Vehicle-miles, passenger	Million. .	835	781	717	591	585	567	495	(NA)	(NA)	(NA)	(NA)
Revenue passengers carried.	Million. .	147	134	112	94	89	88	74	82	55	54	43
Expense per vehicle-mile	Dollar . .	1.05	1.69	1.98	2.17	2.14	2.06	2.18	(NA)	(NA)	(NA)	(NA)

NA Not available. [1] Excludes carriers preponderantly in local or suburban service and carriers engaged in transportation of both property and passengers. [2] Regular route, intercity, and local.

Source: U.S. Interstate Commerce Commission, *Transport Statistics in the United States*, part 2, annual.

No. 1043. Intercity Bus Lines—Summary of Operations: 1970 to 1991

ITEM	Unit	1970	1975	1980	1984	1985	1986	1987	1988	1989	1990	1991
Operating companies	Number.	1,000	950	1,330	(NA)	(NA)	(NA)	3,550	(NA)	3,628	(NA)	(NA)
Buses.	1,000 . .	22.0	20.5	21.4	20.1	20.1	19.1	18.4	(NA)	(NA)	23.5	20.6
Miles of highway served (Dec. 31) [1].	1,000 . .	267	274	279	266	263	257	249	(NA)	(NA)	(NA)	(NA)
Employees (Dec. 31) [2]	1,000 . .	50	47	49	44	43	41	39	42	45	41	41
Operating revenue, all services . . .	Mil. dol .	901	1,172	1,943	1,914	1,898	1,838	1,717	(NA)	(NA)	(NA)	929
Operating expenses . . , ...	Mil. dol .	812	1,103	1,811	1,896	1,839	1,781	1,669	(NA)	(NA)	(NA)	885
Net operating revenue [3]	Mil. dol .	89	69	132	18	59	57	48	(NA)	(NA)	(NA)	44

NA Not available. [1] Includes duplication between carriers. [2] Operating companies only. [3] Before income taxes.

Source: American Bus Association, Washington, DC, *Bus Facts*, annual; and *Annual Report.*

No. 1044. Warehousing Services—Revenues, Expenses, and Payroll: 1990 and 1991

[In millions of dollars]

SIC [1] code	KIND OF BUSINESS	OPERATING REVENUES		OPERATING EXPENSES		ANNUAL PAYROLL	
		1990	1991	1990	1991	1990	1991
42	Motor frgt. transport. and warehousing services . . .	123,781	123,584	114,450	114,817	38,230	38,943
421	Trucking and courier services, except by air [2]	117,511	117,048	109,074	109,220	36,490	37,179
422	Public warehousing and storage.	6,120	6,376	5,231	5,442	1,709	1,731
4212	Local trucking without storage.	27,745	27,297	24,138	24,000	7,380	7,328
4213	Trucking, except local	68,962	68,516	65,738	65,642	20,709	20,724
4214	Local trucking with storage.	4,083	3,992	3,856	3,805	1,370	1,349
4215	Courier services, except by air.	16,721	17,243	15,342	15,773	7,031	7,778
4221	Farm product warehousing and storage.	573	500	486	440	148	131
4222	Refrigerated warehousing.	1,424	1,490	1,225	1,264	434	441
4225	General warehousing and storage.	2,964	3,248	2,524	2,750	779	816
4226	Special warehousing and storage [3]	1,159	1,138	996	988	348	343

[1] Standard Industrial Classification. [2] Excludes private motor carriers that operate as auxiliary establishments to nontransportation companies and independent owner-operators with no paid employees. [3] Includes SIC 4224.

Source: U.S. Bureau of the Census, *Current Business Reports, 1991 Motor Freight Transportation and Warehousing Survey.*

No. 1045. Trucking Costs and Rates for Fresh Fruit and Vegetables: 1980 to 1991

[Dollars per box, except as indicated]

SELECTED ITEMS	1980	1984	1985	1986	1987	1988	1989	1990	1991
Truck costs for fleet operators [1] (dollars per mile) . .	0.97	1.15	1.17	1.14	1.17	1.18	1.23	1.31	1.27
Truck rates by commodity and origin/destination: [2]									
Lettuce [3], California to New York City.	3.36	3.65	3.62	3.75	3.83	3.69	3.76	3.74	3.77
Citrus and vegetables, Southern California to									
New York City	2.77	3.18	3.06	3.16	3.23	3.14	3.20	3.23	3.22
Apples, Washington to New York City	3.09	3.19	3.20	3.21	3.28	3.30	3.31	3.36	3.36

[1] Truck costs developed by Office of Transportation, USDA. [2] Average rates reported by Agricultural Marketing Service, Market News Service, USDA, for the first week of the month. [3] January to April: Imperial Valley, California to New York City; May to December: Salinas, California, to New York City.

Source: U.S. Dept. of Agriculture, Economic Research Service, *Food Cost Review*, annual.

No. 1046. Trucking Services—Operating Revenues, Operating Expenses, and Equipment, by Type of Carrier: 1985 to 1991

[In millions of dollars, except as indicated. Data cover SIC group 421. Estimates include both regulated and nonregulated carriers; excluded are nonemployers (i.e., firms with no paid employees) and private fleets operated as auxiliary establishments to nontransportation companies. Some unpublished estimates may be derived from this table by subtraction, but such figures are subject to high sampling variability and should be used with caution]

ITEM	ALL CARRIERS			SPECIALTY FREIGHT CARRIERS			GENERAL FREIGHT CARRIERS		
	1985	1990	1991	1985	1990	1991	1985	1990	1991
Operating revenues:									
Total [1]	86,858	117,511	117,048	30,435	32,835	31,918	56,423	84,676	85,130
Motor carrier	81,347	107,997	108,604	26,974	28,302	27,905	54,373	79,695	80,699
Local trucking	17,548	25,246	24,582	9,084	13,183	13,077	8,464	12,063	11,505
Intercity trucking	63,799	82,751	84,022	17,890	15,119	14,828	45,909	67,632	69,194
Operating expenses:									
Total	83,266	109,074	109,220	28,933	28,977	28,507	54,333	80,097	80,713
Annual payroll	26,722	36,490	37,179	7,600	8,242	8,123	19,122	28,248	29,056
Employer contributions to Social Security and other benefits	6,113	9,365	9,721	1428	1,937	1,881	4,685	7,428	7,840
Purchased fuels	6,825	8,647	8,719	2,191	1,653	1,667	4,634	6,994	7,052
Cost of purchased transportation	(NA)	19,630	19,321	(NA)	5,701	5,384	(NA)	13,929	13,937
Lease and rental payments	1,314	2,168	2,161	504	631	631	810	1,537	1,530
Cost of insurance	(NA)	3,898	3,998	(NA)	1,108	1,161	(NA)	2,790	2,837
Maintenance and repair costs	(NA)	6,133	6,133	(NA)	1,867	1,843	(NA)	4,266	4,290
Depreciation	4,193	5,603	5,632	1,596	1,623	1,596	2,597	3,980	4,036
Taxes and licenses	1,950	2,325	2,439	619	518	510	1,331	1,807	1,929
Other	(NA)	14,788	13,882	(NA)	5,690	5,701	(NA)	9,098	8,181
Equipment (1,000 units): [2]									
Trucks	201	226	231	94	100	100	(S)	126	131
Truck-tractors	461	525	524	167	111	108	302	414	416
Trailers, full and semi	1,055	1,179	1,191	246	214	205	765	965	986

NA Not available. S Data do not meet publication standards. [1] Includes other revenues not shown separately. [2] Represents revenue generating freight equipment as of December 31. Includes owned and leased equipment.

Source: U.S. Bureau of the Census, *Current Business Reports, Motor Freight Transportation and Warehousing Survey,* annual.

No. 1047. Class I Intercity Motor Carriers of Property, by Carrier: 1980 to 1990

[See headnote, table 1042. Common carriers are carriers offering regular scheduled service. Contract carriers provide service at request of user. Minus sign (-) indicates loss]

ITEM	Unit	1980	1985	1989	1990	1980	1985	1989	1990
		COMMON CARRIER, GENERAL FREIGHT				COMMON CARRIER OTHER THAN GENERAL FREIGHT			
Carriers reporting	Number	298	237	192	191	441	397	337	322
Number of employees, average	1,000	413	376	461	465	101	76	84	87
Compensation of employees	Mil. dol.	9,803	10,217	12,854	13,556	1,931	1,783	2,105	2,236
Operating revenues	Mil. dol.	19,725	22,314	27,405	29,682	8,792	7,962	8,321	9,042
Intercity freight	Mil. dol.	19,480	22,080	27,289	29,517	8,339	7,664	8,024	8,762
Operating expenses	Mil. dol.	18,870	21,037	26,242	28,340	8,426	7,752	8,081	8,702
Ordinary income before taxes	Mil. dol.	701	1,198	988	1,146	230	123	117	198
Net income	Mil. dol.	-72	658	659	746	14	94	88	153
Total power units, intercity service	1,000	102	108	(NA)	(NA)	95	77	(NA)	(NA)
Trucks, tractors owned in operation, avg	1,000	73	82	(NA)	(NA)	33	29	(NA)	(NA)
Intercity vehicle-miles	Million	6,547	5,760	6,557	6,804	6,889	5,714	6,320	6,566
Tons of intercity revenue freight carried	Million	178	136	145	157	324	303	278	302
		CONTRACT CARRIER OTHER THAN GENERAL FREIGHT				CARRIERS OF HOUSEHOLD GOODS			
Carriers reporting	Number	69	64	77	87	28	40	36	36
Number of employees, average	1,000	14	22	29	34	10	11	12	13
Compensation of employees	Mil. dol.	336	630	893	1,082	157	240	276	296
Operating revenues	Mil. dol.	1,272	1,942	2,946	3,486	1,824	2,684	3,114	3,152
Intercity freight	Mil. dol.	1,172	1,792	2,693	3,209	1,676	2,388	2,703	2,702
Operating expenses	Mil. dol.	1,207	1,807	2,888	3,422	1,781	2,635	3,059	3,129
Ordinary income before taxes	Mil. dol.	48	103	15	3	74	79	41	12
Net income	Mil. dol.	28	69	3	-13	42	54	28	8
Total power units, intercity service	1,000	13	16	(NA)	(NA)	25	35	(NA)	(NA)
Trucks, tractors owned in operation, avg	1,000	7	11	(NA)	(NA)	1	1	(NA)	(NA)
Intercity vehicle-miles	Million	934	1,227	1,826	2,044	969	1,171	1,229	1,366
Tons of intercity revenue freight carried	Million	37	41	80	80	5	7	7	8

NA Not available.

Source: U.S. Interstate Commerce Commission, *Transport Statistics in the United States,* part 2, annual.

No. 1048. Trucks—Percent Distribution, Operational Characteristics: 1977 to 1987

[See headnote, table 1049]

CHARACTERISTIC	1977	1982	1987	CHARACTERISTIC	1977	1982	1987
Total	100.0	100.0	100.0	Purchased used	50.0	51.5	50.1
				Leased [5]	2.4	2.8	2.6
Major use:				Fleet size: [6] 1	71.6	77.8	65.1
Agriculture [1]	17.0	12.2	8.5	2 to 5	16.3	10.9	24.9
Construction	6.7	11.2	10.0	6 to 19.	6.6	5.3	5.4
Manufacturing	1.4	1.6	1.3	20 or more	5.5	6.0	4.6
Wholesale and retail trade. ...	7.6	6.8	5.6	Truck-type:			
Personal transportation.	54.4	56.7	65.7	Single-unit	96.8	95.7	96.3
All other.	13.0	11.4	8.8	Combination	3.2	4.3	3.7
Body type:				Annual miles:			
Pickup and panel [2].	83.3	85.8	89.0	Less than 5,000.	23.9	26.0	25.3
Platform and cattlerack.	6.8	5.1	3.7	5,000 to 9,999.	24.0	25.5	23.4
Van	4.5	3.8	3.2	10,000 to 19,999	37.0	35.0	34.5
All other.	5.5	5.2	4.0	20,000 to 29,999	9.2	8.4	10.7
Vehicle size: [4] Light.	85.4	89.3	91.9	30,000 miles or more.	5.9	5.0	6.1
Medium.	6.0	3.5	2.3	Range of operation: [7]			
Light-heavy.	3.1	2.4	1.7	Local.	84.8	76.6	75.6
Heavy-heavy.	5.5	4.8	4.1	Short-range	8.4	10.3	14.8
Year model:				Long-range.	2.1	3.1	4.5
1 to 2 years old.	17.1	8.9	17.2	Off-the-road [8]	4.7	10.0	5.1
3 to 4 years old.	17.5	16.5	16.5	Fuel type:			
4 years or more.	65.4	74.6	66.3	Gasoline	96.0	94.3	93.7
Vehicle acquisition:				Diesel and LPG.	3.9	5.5	6.2
Purchased new	47.6	45.7	47.3	Not reported.	-	0.2	0.1

- Represents zero. [1] Includes forestry and lumbering. [2] Also includes walk-in, minivan, station wagon, and utility trucks.
[3] Includes multi-stop or walk-in. [4] See footnote 6, table 1049. [5] Includes not reported. [6] See footnote 8, table 1048. [7] See footnote 9, table 1049.

No. 1049. Trucks and Truck-Miles, by Vehicle and Operational Characteristics: 1987

[Data are based on a stratified probability sample of trucks drawn from current registrations on file with motor vehicle departments in the 50 States and DC]

ITEM	TRUCKS (1,000)		TRUCK-MILES (bil.)	ITEM	TRUCKS (1,000)		TRUCK-MILES (bil.)
	Total	Excl. pickups, panels [1]			Total	Excl. pickups, panels [1]	
Total	44,572	4,886	529.3	Range of operation: [9]			
Major use:				Local	33,685	3,027	350.9
Agriculture [2]...........	3,819	1,114	39.0	Short-range	6,612	920	108.3
Construction	4,479	997	63.7	Long-range	1,997	490	56.0
Manufacturing	581	241	12.5	Off-the-road [7].	2,278	449	14.1
Wholesale and retail trade ..	2,507	830	43.3	Products carried:			
Personal transportation	29,292	250	287.0	Farm products	1,558	769	16.2
All other	3,894	1,455	83.8	Building materials	1,141	640	18.6
Body type:				Mixed cargoes	686	325	21.1
Pickup and panel [3]	39,686	(X)	427	Craftsman's equipment	2,476	319	34.5
Platform [4]	1,668	1,668	25.0	Personal transportation	29,290	251	286.9
Van [5]	1,424	1,424	48.8	All other	9,422	2,583	152.0
All other	1,794	1,794	28.5	Hazardous materials			
Vehicle size: [6] Light	40,947	1,356	439.3	carried:			
Medium.	1,030	939	10.8	Less than 10 percent of time.	114	107	7.2
Light-heavy	766	764	7.6	10-25 percent of time	28	19	1.2
Heavy-heavy	1,829	1,828	71.6	26-49 percent of time	18	15	0.7
Year model:				50-74 percent of time	25	24	1.0
1 to 2 years old	7,678	473	123.6	75-100 percent of time	94	89	2.8
3 to 4 years old	7,338	549	120.5	Not reported	61	25	1.7
4 years or more	29,543	3,864	285.1				
Vehicle acquisition:				Types of hazardous			
Purchased new	21,087	2,138	292.3	material: [10]			
Purchased used	22,325	2,511	215.2	Flammable liquids	198	175	9.3
Leased [7]	1,160	237	21.8	Combustible liquids.......	95	95	5.8
Fleet size: [7 8] 1	29,026	1,170	308.7	Corrosive liquids	70	66	4.6
2 to 5	11,094	1,547	122.9	Flammable solids	29	28	2.3
6 to 19	2,397	1,007	40.1	Oxidizers	28	28	2.3
20 or more	2,054	1,163	57.6	Flammable gas.	26	26	2.2
Truck type:				Nonflammable gas	26	26	2.2
Single-unit.	42,917	3,587	462.0	Corrosive solids	21	21	1.9
Combination	1,656	1,300	67.3	Not reported	139	101	5.1

X Not applicable. [1] Also excludes minivans, utilities, and station wagons. [2] Includes forestry and lumbering. [3] Also includes multi-stop, minivans, station wagon, and utilities, and station wagon. [4] Includes livestock truck. [5] Includes multi-stop or walk-in. [6] Average vehicle weight (empty-weight of the vehicle plus the average weight of load carried). Light=10,000 lbs. or less; medium=10,001-19,500 lbs.; light-heavy=19,501-26,000 lbs.; and heavy-heavy=26,001 lbs. or more. [7] Includes not reported. [8] A fleet size of one truck was assumed when no response was obtained. [9] Area in which usually operated. Local=less than 50 miles; short-range=50 to 200 miles; long-range=more than 200 miles. [10] Detail does not add to totals because items were not applicable or multiple responses were possible.

Source of tables 1048 and 1049: U.S. Bureau of the Census, *1987 Census of Transportation, TC87-T-52.*

No. 1050. Railroads, Class I—Summary: 1970 to 1991

[As of **Dec. 31**, or **calendar year** data, except as noted. Compiled from annual reports of class I railroads only, except where noted. Beginning 1983, financial data are not comparable with earlier years due to change in method of accounting for track and related structures. Minus sign (-) indicates deficit. See also *Historical Statistics, Colonial Times to 1970*, series Q 284-312, Q 319, Q 330, Q 356-378, and Q 400-401]

ITEM	Unit	1970	1980	1985	1986	1987	1988	1989	1990	1991
Class I line-hauling companies [1] . . .	Number.	71	40	23	22	18	17	15	14	14
Employees [2]	1,000 . .	566	459	302	276	249	236	228	216	206
Compensation	Mil. dol .	5,711	11,318	10,563	9,900	9,373	9,301	9,043	8,654	8,695
Average per hour	Dollars .	4.14	10.2	14.3	14.8	15.1	15.6	15.8	15.8	16.8
Average per year	Dollars .	10,086	24,659	34,991	35,894	37,716	39,431	39,742	39,987	42,131
Mileage:										
Railroad line owned [3]	1,000 . .	206	179	155	154	152	150	149	144	140
Railroad track owned [4]	1,000 . .	336	290	257	256	254	251	249	239	234
Equipment:										
Locomotives in service	Number.	27,077	28,094	22,932	20,790	19,358	19,364	19,015	18,835	18,344
Average horsepower	1,000 lb	1,926	2,302	2,469	2,531	2,554	2,579	2,624	2,665	2,714
Cars in service:										
Passenger train	Number.	11,177	4,347	2,502	2,307	2,350	2,332	(NA)	(NA)	(NA)
Freight train [5]	1,000 . .	1,784	1,711	1,422	1,339	1,288	1,239	1,224	1,212	1,190
Freight cars [6]	1,000 . .	1,424	1,168	867	799	749	725	682	659	633
Average capacity [6]	Tons. .	67.1	78.5	83.2	84.1	85.0	86.4	87.8	87.5	87.9
Aggregate capacity [6]	Mil. tons	95.6	92.7	72.1	67.2	63.6	62.4	59.2	57.7	55.7
Box [6]	1,000 . .	590	347	216	180	163	150	133	123	116
Gondola and hopper [6] . . .	1,000 . .	724	636	505	473	445	437	423	411	401
Other [6]	1,000 . .	140	185	145	146	141	138	124	124	116
Income and expenses:										
Operating revenues	Mil. dol .	11,992	28,258	27,586	26,204	26,622	27,934	27,956	28,370	27,845
Operating expenses	Mil. dol .	11,478	26,355	25,225	24,896	23,878	24,811	25,038	24,652	28,061
Net revenue from operations . .	*Mil. dol .*	*514*	*1,902*	*2,361*	*1,308*	*2,744*	*3,123*	*2,918*	*3,718*	*-216*
Income before fixed charges . . .	Mil. dol .	994	2,897	3,393	2,480	3,932	4,460	4,162	4,627	928
Provision for taxes [7]	Mil. dol .	88	592	660	163	1,051	1,162	1,040	1,088	-157
Ordinary income	Mil. dol .	227	1,129	1,788	747	1,965	2,286	2,009	1,961	-91
Net income	Mil. dol .	227	1,129	1,882	544	2,055	2,382	2,203	1,977	-281
Net railway operating income . .	Mil. dol .	486	1,339	1,746	507	1,756	1,980	1,894	2,648	-37
Total taxes [8]	Mil. dol .	1,069	2,585	3,169	2,728	3,553	3,871	3,742	3,780	2,649
Indus. return on net investment .	Percent.	1.7	4.2	4.6	1.3	4.8	6.7	6.3	8.1	1.3
Gross capital expenditures	Mil. dol .	1,351	3,238	4,485	3,645	3,076	3,546	3,865	3,591	3,439
Equipment	Mil. dol .	993	2,280	965	693	657	1,027	1,171	996	1,068
Roadway and structures	Mil. dol .	358	953	3,458	2,908	2,314	2,654	2,538	2,644	2,369
Other	Mil. dol .	-	5	62	44	105	-135	156	-49	2
Balance sheet:										
Total property investment	Mil. dol .	38,213	43,923	64,241	64,781	66,760	68,550	67,661	70,348	71,622
Accrued depreciation and										
amortization	Mil. dol .	10,027	10,706	19,756	20,940	21,070	21,497	21,481	22,222	23,057
Net investment	Mil. dol .	28,186	33,419	46,237	45,344	45,690	47,053	47,370	48,126	48,565
Shareholder's equity	Mil. dol .	17,323	19,860	27,605	25,442	25,616	26,467	25,753	23,663	22,603
Net working capital	Mil. dol .	-59	897	1,084	743	1,241	-190	-2119	-3505	-3,988
Cash dividends	Mil. dol .	421	610	1,444	1,376	1,252	1,814	1,910	2,074	915
AMTRAK passenger traffic:										
Passenger revenue	Mil. dol .	(NA)	(NA)	604.9	633.6	681.1	784.2	893.0	941.9	962.3
Revenue passengers carried	1,000 . .	(NA)	21,303	20,945	20,165	20,727	21,490	21,394	22,383	21,693
Revenue passenger miles	Million. .	(NA)	4,645	4,977	5,015	5,368	5,686	5,912	6,125	6,249
Averages:										
Revenue per passenger	Dollars .	(NA)	(NA)	28.9	31.4	32.9	36.5	41.8	42.1	44.4
Revenue per passenger mile . .	Cents .	(NA)	(NA)	12.2	12.6	12.7	13.8	15.1	15.4	15.4
Trip per passenger	Miles .	(NA)	218.1	237.6	248.7	259.0	264.6	276.3	273.7	228.0
Freight service:										
Freight revenue	Mil. dol .	10,922	26,200	26,688	25,344	25,797	27,092	27,059	24,471	26,949
Per ton-mile	Cents .	1.4	2.8	3.0	2.9	2.7	2.7	2.7	2.7	2.6
Per ton originated	Dollar .	7.7	17.7	20.2	19.4	18.8	19.0	19.3	19.3	19.5
Revenue-tons originated	Million. .	1,485	1,492	1,320	1,087	1,372	1,430	1,402	1,425	1,383
Revenue-tons carried	Million. .	2,616	2,434	1,985	1,938	1,984	2,045	1,988	2,024	1,987
Tons carried one mile	Billion. .	765	919	877	868	944	996	1,014	1,034	1,039
Average miles of road operated .	1,000 . .	209	179	161	155	147	141	138	133	130
Revenue ton-miles per mile of										
road	1,000 . .	3,652	5,133	5,446	5,587	6,395	7,052	7,373	7,763	8,001
Revenue per ton-mile	Cents .	1.428	3	3	3	3	3	3	3	3
Train miles	Million. .	427	428	347	347	361	379	382	380	375
Net ton-miles per train-mile [9] . . .	Number.	1,820	2,175	2,574	2,552	2,644	2,662	2,683	2,755	2,796
Net ton-miles per loaded										
car-mile [9]	Number.	44.9	63.5	62.7	63.2	64.0	65.5	67.0	69.1	71.6
Train-miles per train-hour	Miles . .	20.1	18.2	21.9	22.5	22.2	21.5	23.0	23.7	23.7
Haul per ton, U.S. as a system . .	Miles . .	490	616	664	664	688	697	723	726	751
Accident: [10]										
Persons killed	Number.	2,255	1,417	1,036	1,091	1,165	1,199	1,324	1,297	1,194
Persons injured	Number.	21,327	62,246	34,304	26,923	26,033	27,054	25,143	25,143	23,468

- Represents zero.   NA Not available.   [1] See text, section 21 for definition of Class I.   [2] Average mid-month count. [3] Represents the aggregate length of roadway of all line-haul railroads. Excludes yard tracks, sidings, and parallel lines. (Includes estimate for class II and III railroads.)   [4] Includes multiple main tracks, yard tracks, and sidings owned by both line-haul and switching and terminal. (Includes estimate for class II and III railroads.)   [5] Includes cars owned by all railroads, private car companies, and shippers.   [6] Class I railroads only.   [7] Includes State income taxes beginning 1980.   [8] Includes payroll, income, and other taxes.   [9] Revenue and non-revenue freight.   [10] Includes highway grade crossing casualties. 1970 not comparable with later years due to change in requirements for reporting injuries.

Source: Association of American Railroads, Washington, DC, *Railroad Facts, Statistics of Railroads of Class I*, annual, and *Analysis of Class I Railroads*, annual. Accident data: U.S. Federal Railroad Administration, *Accident Bulletin*, annual.

No. 1051. Railroads, Class I-Cars of Revenue Freight Loaded, 1970 to 1991, and by Commodity Group, 1990 and 1991

[In thousands. Figures are 52-week totals. N.e.c.= Not elsewhere classified]

YEAR	CARLOADS		COMMODITY GROUP	CARLOADS		COMMODITY GROUP	CARLOADS	
	Total	Piggy-back		1990	1991		1990	1991
1970 . .	27,160	1,450	Coal	6,296	6,137	Metals and products	454	442
1975 . .	23,217	1,308	Metallic ores.	506	491	Stone, clay, and glass products . .	489	446
1980 . .	22,598	1,661	Chemicals, allied products. . . .	1,415	1,402	Crushed stone, gravel, sand	711	614
1985 . .	19,574	2,863	Grain.	1,429	1,374	Nonmetalic minerals, n.e.c	459	431
1987 . .	21,133	3,294	Motor vehicles and equipment .	882	797	Waste and scrap materials	414	392
1988 . .	16,422	(NA)	Pulp, paper, allied products . . .	485	471	Lumber, wood products, n.e.c. [1] .	301	268
1989 . .	16,030	(NA)	Primary forest products.	410	373	Coke.	281	244
1990 . .	16,177	(NA)	Food and kindred prod., n.e.c. .	448	456	Petroleum product.	255	249
1991 . .	15,526	(NA)	Grain mill products.	520	513	All other carloads	423	426

NA Not available.   [1] Excludes furniture.

Source: Association of American Railroads, Washington, DC, *Weekly Railroad Traffic*, annual.

No. 1052. Railroads, Class I Line-Haul-Revenue Freight Originated, by Commodity Group: 1970 to 1991

[See *Historical Statistics, Colonial Times to 1970*, series Q 332, for total carloads originated]

COMMODITY GROUP	1970	1975	1980	1984	1985	1986	1987	1988	1989	1990	1991
Carloads (1,000) [1]	27,015	22,930	22,223	20,946	19,501	19,587	20,602	21,600	21,226	21,401	20,868
Coal.	5,296	4,844	5,789	6,061	5,684	5,433	5,430	5,621	5,672	5,912	5,683
Farm products	2,374	1,873	1,866	1,757	1,494	1,602	1,907	1,977	1,781	1,689	1,605
Chemicals, allied products	1,576	1,313	1,322	1,312	1,296	1,287	1,410	1,497	1,486	1,531	1,556
Food and kindred products	2,706	2,154	1,767	1,234	1,224	1,276	1,326	1,318	1,284	1,307	1,316
Nonmetallic minerals [2]	2,204	1,895	1,474	1,204	1,196	1,113	1,188	1,290	1,254	1,202	1,075
Transportation equipment	1,059	1,135	1,004	1,141	1,202	1,148	1,085	1,160	1,141	1,091	1,068
Lumber and wood products [3] . . .	2,048	1,615	1,384	1,051	948	965	986	910	843	780	716
Pulp, paper, allied products	1,197	1,015	954	741	703	672	561	646	615	611	616
Petroleum and coal products	699	787	596	529	491	477	520	568	561	573	533
Stone, clay, and glass products . .	1,231	906	776	576	551	530	559	577	565	539	479
Metallic ores.	1,602	1,338	1,258	1,001	511	508	494	582	523	508	499
Primary metal products	1,486	796	756	487	449	389	428	479	452	477	469
Waste and scrap materials.	805	744	632	480	429	402	440	471	444	439	433
Machinery, exc. electrical.	200	156	77	40	35	31	33	40	38	39	39
Fabricated metal products [4]	398	244	72	37	31	26	24	26	27	31	34
Tons (mil.) [1]	1,485	1,395	1,492	1,429	1,320	1,306	1,372	1,429	1,403	1,425	1,383
Coal.	405	408	522	567	538	518	523	543	551	579	560
Farm products	134	134	156	151	127	136	163	170	154	147	144
Chemicals, allied products	92	91	108	107	106	106	116	123	123	126	127
Nonmetallic minerals [2]	163	151	125	108	108	101	109	115	111	109	99
Food and kindred products	110	100	92	72	74	78	81	81	79	81	83
Lumber and wood products [3] . . .	102	89	86	70	63	65	67	62	57	53	48
Metallic ores.	127	106	105	86	47	46	45	52	47	47	45
Stone, clay, and glass products . .	71	57	54	45	44	42	44	46	47	44	39
Petroleum and coal products	36	46	38	35	33	33	35	39	39	40	37
Primary metal products	82	51	53	36	34	30	33	38	36	38	37
Pulp, paper, allied products	43	41	42	38	36	36	36	35	34	33	33
Waste and scrap materials.	40	38	34	29	26	25	28	30	28	28	27
Transportation equipment	24	27	24	26	27	26	24	25	24	23	22
Machinery, exc. electrical.	5	4	2	1	1	1	1	1	1	1	1
Fabricated metal products [4]	11	8	2	1	1	1	1	1	1	1	1
Gross revenue (mil. dol.) [1] .	11,388	15,899	26,938	29,866	28,225	27,186	27,657	29,529	29,328	29,775	29,319
Coal.	1,381	2,146	4,956	6,965	6,556	6,089	6,097	6,430	6,581	6,954	6,903
Chemicals, allied products	1,137	1,681	2,946	3,360	3,342	3,342	3,477	3,795	3,788	3,933	4,043
Transportation equipment	734	1,283	1,917	2,859	3,110	2,997	2,866	3,218	3,269	3,100	2,633
Farm products	1,068	1,472	2,801	2,483	1,977	2,007	2,246	2,534	2,444	2,422	2,332
Food and kindred products	1,363	1,822	2,837	2,309	2,256	2,192	2,171	2,198	2,128	2,188	2,254
Pulp, paper, allied products	730	977	1,652	1,762	1,641	1,572	1,542	1,540	1,514	1,486	1,502
Lumber and wood products [3] . . .	832	1,066	1,543	1,611	1,525	1,563	1,660	1,626	1,500	1,390	1,282
Primary metal products	813	848	1,332	955	872	787	863	1,013	972	979	977
Stone, clay, and glass products . .	512	651	1,025	1,024	960	907	914	965	960	931	878
Petroleum and coal products	305	573	865	913	861	800	809	903	917	918	888
Nonmetallic minerals [2]	409	596	948	997	949	839	854	890	868	885	824
Waste and scrap materials.	232	359	513	496	446	425	474	526	492	504	515
Metallic ores.	333	468	597	567	403	375	348	415	397	408	400
Machinery, exc. electrical.	148	200	176	81	72	58	57	63	66	67	62
Fabricated metal products [4]	210	221	110	57	48	40	37	38	38	42	48

[1] Includes commodity groups and small packaged freight shipments, not shown separately.   [2] Except fuels.   [3] Except furniture.   [4] Except ordnance, machinery, and transport.

Source: 1970-1975, U.S. Interstate Commerce Commission, *Freight Commodity Statistics—Class I Railroads in the United States*, annual; thereafter, Association of American Railroads, Washington, DC, *Freight Commodity Statistics*, annual.

No. 1053. Railroad Freight—Producer Price Indexes: 1970 to 1992

[Dec. 1984 = 100. Reflects prices for shipping a fixed set of commodities under specified and unchanging conditions]

COMMODITY	1970	1975	1980	1984	1985	1986	1987	1988	1989	1990	1991	1992
Total railroad freight	29.1	45.3	75.9	99.3	99.9	100.7	100.1	104.8	106.4	107.5	109.3	109.9
Coal	26.9	44.0	75.8	99.9	100.0	100.7	100.1	104.3	105.3	104.2	105.2	105.9
Farm products	29.7	45.2	75.6	98.7	99.0	99.6	99.3	105.5	108.5	110.4	111.4	111.1
Food products	28.9	44.8	75.2	99.1	100.0	99.9	98.6	103.1	103.9	105.4	108.1	108.7
Metallic ores	26.4	43.2	74.5	99.4	100.2	100.5	99.0	103.9	105.8	106.5	106.7	106.6
Chemicals or allied products	30.0	46.5	75.6	98.7	100.1	101.2	100.8	106.9	110.0	111.7	113.5	115.6
Nonmetallic minerals	25.4	40.5	72.2	98.9	100.1	101.6	101.1	106.1	108.3	111.7	115.9	117.7
Wood or lumber products	28.3	42.8	72.7	99.7	100.0	100.9	100.4	105.3	105.9	107.5	108.6	108.8
Transportation equipment	31.7	50.3	81.7	99.8	100.0	100.8	99.3	103.4	106.4	107.5	109.7	110.8
Pulp, paper, or allied products	31.5	47.1	76.7	99.9	100.0	101.0	100.6	104.0	105.1	108.0	111.5	111.8
Primary metal products	29.9	47.8	77.8	99.7	99.7	100.2	99.7	108.8	112.3	113.1	116.1	117.5
Clay, concrete, glass, or stone products .	26.9	43.0	74.2	98.8	100.0	102.2	102.2	107.5	110.5	114.1	117.1	116.5

Source: U.S. Bureau of Labor Statistics, *Producer Price Indexes,* monthly and annual.

No. 1054. Petroleum Pipeline Companies—Characteristics: 1975 to 1991

[1975, covers pipeline companies operating in interstate commerce and subject to jurisdiction of Interstate Commerce Commission; thereafter, Federal Energy Regulatory Commission]

ITEM	Unit	1975	1980	1985	1986	1987	1988	1989	1990	1991
Miles of pipeline, total	1,000	171	173	171	170	168	171	169	168	172
Gathering lines	1,000	40	36	35	34	35	34	33	32	31
Trunk lines	1,000	130	136	136	136	133	136	135	136	141
Total deliveries	Mil. bbl.	9,391	10,600	10,745	11,002	11,194	11,484	11,281	11,378	11,496
Crude oil	Mil. bbl.	5,729	6,405	6,239	6,286	6,278	6,509	6,435	6,563	6,685
Products	Mil. bbl.	3,662	4,195	4,506	4,716	4,917	4,974	4,847	4,816	4,811
Total trunk line traffic	Bil. bbl-miles .	2,892	3,405	3,342	3,467	3,524	3,619	3,505	3,500	3,470
Crude oil	Bil. bbl-miles .	1,551	1,948	1,842	1,893	1,932	1,970	1,918	1,891	1,899
Products	Bil. bbl-miles .	1,341	1,458	1,500	1,573	1,592	1,649	1,587	1,609	1,571
Carrier property value	Mil. dol.	10,740	19,752	21,605	22,384	21,353	24,332	24,638	25,828	26,943
Operating revenues	Mil. dol.	1,869	6,356	7,461	7,287	7,057	6,861	6,512	7,149	6,798
Net income	Mil. dol.	456	1,912	2,431	2,051	2,475	2,505	2,227	2,340	1,788

Source: PennWell Publishing Co., Tulsa, OK, *Oil & Gas Journal,* November 25, 1991, and earlier issues (copyright).

No. 1055. Major Interstate Natural Gas Pipeline Companies—Summary: 1983 to 1990

[In 1984, the reporting criteria were changed from that of prior years. The classification of A and B interstate natural gas pipeline companies was changed to major companies and nonmajor companies. Major natural gas pipleine companies are those whose combined sales for resale and natural gas transported or stored for a fee exceed 50 billion cubic feet. They account for more than 85 percent of all interstate natural gas]

ITEM	Unit	1983	1984	1985	1986	1987	1988	1989	1990
Sales	Tril. cu. ft. .	12.9	13.2	11.3	7.8	6.5	6.4	5.6	4.5
Residential	Tril. cu. ft. .	0.3	0.3	0.3	0.2	0.2	0.3	0.1	0.2
Commercial, industrial	Tril. cu. ft. .	1.0	1.2	1.1	0.5	0.4	0.5	0.5	0.4
For resale	Tril. cu. ft. .	11.6	11.6	9.9	7.1	5.8	5.6	4.9	3.9
Operating revenues	Mil. dol . . .	56,792	56,326	49,106	33,859	27,565	27,501	25,695	22,574
From sales [1]	Mil. dol . . .	53,710	52,529	44,996	29,508	22,942	22,512	19,786	15,981
Residential	Mil. dol . . .	1,725	1,927	1,879	1,122	1,094	1,553	819	912
Commercial, industrial	Mil. dol . . .	4,233	5,180	4,466	1,909	1,464	1,544	1,452	1,272
For resale	Mil. dol . . .	47,661	45,268	38,545	26,413	20,351	19,420	17,505	13,791
From transportation of gas of others	Mil. dol . . .	1,787	1,923	2,272	3,027	3,622	4,059	4,959	5,505
Other	Mil. dol . . .	1,296	1,874	1,838	1,325	1,002	929	950	1,088
Operation, maintenance expenses	Mil. dol . . .	49,391	48,411	42,528	27,460	21,794	22,742	20,829	17,446
Production	Mil. dol . . .	43,516	42,407	36,739	22,208	16,955	17,625	15,257	12,124
Storage	Mil. dol . . .	441	415	418	420	409	436	458	416
Transmission	Mil. dol . . .	3,729	3,760	3,409	2,984	2,598	2,589	2,589	2,720
Distribution	Mil. dol . . .	131	131	132	80	80	127	94	112
Administrative, general, and other	Mil. dol . . .	1,576	1,697	1,830	1,768	1,752	1,966	2,430	2,074
Pipeline mileage:									
Transmission lines	1,000	176.7	183.4	189.7	184.6	181.2	191.6	194.1	195.5
Field lines	1,000	63.7	65.2	69.6	64.5	62.9	55.5	55.1	54.0
Storage	1,000	6.5	4.6	4.8	4.6	4.3	4.8	4.8	5.0

[1] Includes other ultimate customers not shown separately.

Source: U.S. Energy Information Administration, *Statistics of Interstate Natural Gas Pipeline Companies,* annual.

Transportation— Air and Water

This section presents data on civil air transportation, both passenger and cargo, and on water transportation, including inland waterways, oceanborne commerce, the merchant marine, cargo and vessel tonnages, and shipbuilding. Comparative data on various types of transportation carriers are presented in section 21.

Principal sources of these data are the annual *FAA Statistical Handbook of Aviation* issued by the Federal Aviation Administration (FAA); the annual *Waterborne Commerce of the United States* issued by the Corps of Engineers of the Department of the Army; the monthly and annual issues of *U.S. Waterborne Exports and General Imports,* and the annual *Vessel Entrances and Clearances,* and the monthly *Highlights of U.S. Export and Import Trade,* issued by the Bureau of the Census. In addition, the Bureau of the Census in its commodity transportation survey (part of the census of transportation, taken every 5 years, for years ending in "2" and "7") provides data on the type, weight, and value of commodities shipped by manufacturing establishments in the United States, by means of transportation, origin, and destination.

Air transportation data are also presented annually by the Air Transport Association of America, Washington, DC in *Air Transport Facts and Figures.* Additional sources of data on water transportation include *Merchant Fleets of the World* issued periodically by the U.S. Maritime Administration; *The Bulletin,* issued monthly by the American Bureau of Shipping, New York, NY; and the *Annual Summary of Merchant Ships Completed in the World* and the *Register Book,* published by Lloyd's Register of Shipping, London, England.

Civil aviation.—Federal promotion and regulation of civil aviation have been carried out by the FAA and the Civil Aeronautics Board (CAB). The CAB promoted and regulated the civil air transportation

In Brief
SCHEDULED AIR CARRIERS
  Revenue passengers enplaned:
    1983   319 million
    1991   452 million
  Net profit:
    1983   -$188 million
    1991   -$1,870 million

industry within the United States and between the United States and foreign countries. The Board granted licenses to provide air transportation service, approved or disapproved proposed rates and fares, and approved or disapproved proposed agreements and corporate relationships involving air carriers. In December 1984, the CAB ceased to exist as an agency. Some of its functions were transferred to the Department of Transportation (DOT), as outlined below. The responsibility for investigation of aviation accidents resides with the National Transportation Safety Board.

The Office of the Secretary, DOT aviation activities include the following: negotiation of international air transportation rights, selection of U.S. air carriers to serve capacity controlled international markets, oversight of international rates and fares, maintenance of essential air service to small communities, and consumer affairs. DOT's Research and Special Programs Administration (RSPA) handles aviation information functions formerly assigned to CAB.

The principal activities of the FAA include the promotion of air safety, controlling the use of navigable airspace, prescribing regulations dealing with the competency of airmen, airworthiness of aircraft, and air traffic control, operation of air route traffic control centers, airport traffic control towers, and flight service stations, the design, construction, maintenance, and inspection of navigation, traffic control, and communications equipment, and the development of general aviation.

The CAB published monthly and quarterly financial and traffic statistical data for the certificated route air carriers. RSPA continues these publications, including both certificated and noncertificated (commuter) air carriers. The FAA publishes data annually on the use of airway facilities; data related to the location of airmen, aircraft, and airports; the volume of activity in the field of nonair carrier (general aviation) flying; and aircraft production and registration.

General aviation comprises all civil flying (including such commercial operations as small demand air taxis, agriculture application, powerline patrol, etc.) but excludes certificated route air carriers, supplemental operators, large-aircraft commercial operators and commuter airlines.

Air carriers and service.—The CAB previously issued "certificates of public convenience and necessity" under Section 401 of the Federal Aviation Act of 1958 for scheduled and nonscheduled (charter) passenger services and cargo services. It also issued certificates under Section 418 of the Act to cargo air carriers for domestic all-cargo service only. The DOT Office of the Secretary now issues the certificates under a "fit, willing, and able" test of air carrier operations. Carriers operating only 60 seat or less aircraft are given exemption authority to carry passengers, cargo, and mail in scheduled and nonscheduled service under Part 298 of the DOT (formerly CAB) regulations. Exemption authority carriers who offer scheduled passenger service to an essential air service point must meet the "fit, willing, and able" test.

Vessel shipments, entrances, and clearances.—Shipments by dry cargo vessels comprise shipments on all types of watercraft, except tanker vessels;

shipments by tanker vessels comprise all types of cargo, liquid and dry, carried by tanker vessels.

A vessel is reported as entered only at the first port which it enters in the United States, whether or not cargo is unloaded at that port. A vessel is reported as cleared only at the last port at which clearance is made to a foreign port, whether or not it takes on cargo. Army and Navy vessels entering or clearing without commercial cargo are not included in the figures.

Units of measurement.—Cargo (or freight) tonnage and shipping weight both represent the gross weight of the cargo including the weight of containers, wrappings, crates, etc. However, shipping weight excludes lift and cargo vans and similar substantial outer containers. Other tonnage figures generally refer to stowing capacity of vessels, 100 cubic feet being called 1 ton. Gross tonnage comprises the space within the frames and the ceiling of the hull, together with those closed-in spaces above deck available for cargo, stores, passengers, or crew, with certain minor exceptions. Net or registered tonnage is the gross tonnage less the spaces occupied by the propelling machinery, fuel, crew quarters, master's cabin, and navigation spaces. Substantially, it represents space available for cargo and passengers. The net tonnage capacity of a ship may bear little relation to weight of cargo. Deadweight tonnage is the weight in long tons required to depress a vessel from light water line (that is, with only the machinery and equipment on board) to load line. It is, therefore, the weight of the cargo, fuel, etc., which a vessel is designed to carry with safety.

Historical statistics.—Tabular headnotes provide cross-references, where applicable, to *Historical Statistics of the United States, Colonial Times to 1970*. See Appendix IV.

No. 1056. U. S. Scheduled Airline Industry—Summary: 1983 to 1991

[For calendar years or Dec. 31. For domestic and international operations. Covers carriers certificated under Section 401 of the Federal Aviation Act. Minus sign (-) indicates loss]

ITEM	Unit	1983	1984	1985	1986	1987	1988	1989	1990	1991
SCHEDULED SERVICE										
Revenue passengers enplaned	Mil.	318.6	344.7	382.0	418.9	447.7	454.6	453.7	465.6	452.2
Revenue passenger miles	Bil.	281.8	305.1	336.4	366.5	404.5	423.3	432.7	457.9	447.8
Available seat miles	Bil.	464.5	515.3	547.8	607.4	648.7	676.8	684.4	733.4	715.0
Revenue passenger load factor	Percent	60.7	59.2	61.4	60.3	62.3	62.5	63.2	62.4	62.6
Mean passenger trip length [1]	Miles	884	885	881	875	903	931	954	984	990
Freight and express ton miles	Mil.	6,092.9	6,566.6	6,030.5	7,344.1	8,260.3	9,632.2	10,275.0	10,546.3	10,204.9
Aircraft departures	1,000	5,033.9	5,448.2	5,835.5	6,427.0	6,581.3	6,699.6	6,622.1	6,923.6	6,781.6
FINANCES										
Total operating revenue [2]	Mil. dol.	38,954	43,825	46,664	50,525	56,986	63,749	69,316	76,142	75,114
Passenger revenue	Mil. dol.	32,745	36,939	39,236	40,056	44,940	50,296	53,802	58,453	56,982
Freight and express revenue	Mil. dol.	2,593	2,859	2,681	5,628	6,398	7,478	6,893	5,432	5,516
Mail revenue	Mil. dol.	653	712	890	838	923	972	955	970	956
Charter revenue	Mil. dol.	1,075	1,112	1,280	1,269	1,612	1,698	2,052	2,877	3,783
Total operating expense	Mil. dol.	38,643	41,674	45,238	49,202	54,517	60,312	67,505	78,054	76,837
Operating profit	Mil. dol.	310	2,152	1,426	1,323	2,469	3,437	1,811	-1,912	-1,723
Interest expense	Mil. dol.	1,482	1,540	1,588	1,693	1,695	1,846	1,944	1,978	1,774
Net profit	Mil. dol.	-188	825	863	-235	593	1,686	128	-3,921	-1,870
Revenue per passenger mile	Cents	11.6	12.1	11.7	10.9	11.1	11.9	12.4	12.8	12.7
Rate of return on investment	Percent	6.0	9.9	9.6	4.9	7.2	10.8	6.3	-6.0	-0.5
Operating profit margin	Percent	0.8	4.9	3.1	2.6	4.3	5.4	2.6	-2.5	-2.3
Net profit margin	Percent	-0.5	1.9	1.8	-0.5	1.0	2.6	0.2	-5.1	-2.5
EMPLOYEES										
Total	1,000	329	345	355	422	457	481	507	546	534
Pilots, copilots, and other flight personnel	1,000	35	37	40	46	51	52	52	56	57
Flight attendants	1,000	56	60	63	68	73	76	78	83	82
Mechanics	1,000	40	43	43	48	51	55	57	61	59
Aircraft and traffic servicing personnel	1,000	95	101	101	180	199	212	225	252	237
Other	1,000	103	104	108	80	84	86	95	94	98

[1] For definition of mean, see Guide to Tabular Presentation.   [2] Includes other types of revenues, not shown separately.

Source: Air Transport Association of America, Washington, DC, *Air Transport*, annual, and *Air Transport, Facts and Figures*, annual.

No. 1057. Airline Cost Indexes: 1980 to 1991

[Covers U.S. major and national service carriers. Major carriers have operating revenues of $1 billion or more; nationals have operating revenues from $75 million to $1 billion. Minus sign (-) indicates decrease]

ITEM	INDEX (1982=100)									PERCENT DISTRIBUTION OF CASH OPERATING EXPENSES [1]			
	1980	1984	1985	1986	1987	1988	1989	1990	1991	1980	1985	1990	1991
INDEX													
Composite	86.3	102.8	103.1	96.6	98.4	102.4	109.0	117.0	119.6	100.0	100.0	100.0	100.0
Labor	84.8	108.0	111.1	108.8	110.2	115.0	118.4	121.1	127.6	35.1	34.9	32.6	33.7
Interest [2]	88.7	109.0	105.5	100.8	97.5	99.6	111.5	107.3	88.3	2.9	3.5	2.5	2.3
Fuel	91.6	86.3	81.4	56.4	56.8	54.2	61.2	78.7	68.9	29.7	22.3	17.6	14.8
Passenger food	94.3	106.5	102.0	102.4	105.6	111.9	122.8	132.6	141.4	2.9	3.2	3.6	3.9
Advertising and promotion	69.5	100.0	99.8	103.4	90.9	96.9	105.0	107.6	97.9	1.7	2.3	2.1	1.9
Landing fees	90.0	101.4	101.2	112.6	121.5	129.1	137.1	148.1	161.9	1.7	1.7	1.9	2.0
Passenger traffic commissions	77.3	116.7	117.6	119.5	128.9	148.3	163.4	176.8	193.5	4.8	7.4	9.8	10.8
All other	85.6	108.7	112.7	115.7	119.3	123.9	129.4	134.7	139.7	21.3	24.6	29.9	30.6
PERCENT CHANGE [3]													
Composite	23.3	1.0	0.3	-6.3	1.9	4.1	6.4	7.3	2.2	(X)	(X)	(X)	(X)
Labor	10.0	0.2	2.9	-2.1	1.3	4.4	3.0	2.3	5.4	(X)	(X)	(X)	(X)
Interest [2]	16.9	5.1	-3.2	-4.5	-3.3	2.2	11.9	-3.8	-17.7	(X)	(X)	(X)	(X)
Fuel	55.8	-4.6	-5.7	-30.7	0.7	-4.6	12.9	28.6	-12.5	(X)	(X)	(X)	(X)
Passenger food	11.9	2.8	-4.2	0.4	3.1	6.0	9.7	8.0	6.6	(X)	(X)	(X)	(X)
Advertising and promotion	24.3	-1.9	-0.2	3.6	-12.1	6.6	8.4	2.5	-9.0	(X)	(X)	(X)	(X)
Landing fees	9.6	1.1	-0.2	11.3	7.9	6.3	6.2	8.0	9.3	(X)	(X)	(X)	(X)
Passenger traffic commissions	40.0	9.4	0.8	1.6	7.9	15.1	10.2	8.2	9.4	(X)	(X)	(X)	(X)
All other	9.3	4.5	3.7	2.7	3.1	3.9	4.4	4.1	3.7	(X)	(X)	(X)	(X)

X Not applicable.   [1] Total operating expenses plus interest on long term debt, less depreciation and amortization.   [2] Interest on debt.   [3] Change from immediate prior year.

Source: Air Transport Association of America, Washington, DC, *Air Transport*, annual; and unpublished data.

No. 1058. Aircraft in Operation and Aircraft Age, by Type of Aircraft: 1983 to 1989

[As of January 1. For U.S. domestic and major services. Major carriers have operating revenue of $1 billion or more; national carriers have operating revenues of $75 million to $1 billion]

TYPE OF AIRCRAFT	AIRCRAFT IN OPERATION				MEAN AGE (years) [1]			
	1983	1985	1987	1989	1983	1985	1987	1989
Industry total	2,360	2,790	2,816	3,190	10.5	10.8	11.8	12.0
Majors.	1,953	2,185	2,386	2,850	10.9	11.6	12.0	12.2
Nationals.	407	605	430	340	8.4	8.0	10.6	10.6
Type of aircraft:								
Boeing 727 [2]	1,001	996	993	956	10.5	12.0	13.9	15.5
Boeing 737	270	365	547	698	8.9	9.1	8.8	8.2
Boeing 747	130	136	124	136	10.9	11.8	15.0	15.8
Boeing 757	2	23	73	107	1.0	2.0	2.4	3.6
Boeing 767	14	54	61	111	1.0	2.6	3.9	4.3
Airbus A300/A310.	30	134	59	76	3.4	1.9	5.7	5.3
Lockheed L-1011 [2]	119	184	107	111	7.3	7.5	11.0	13.0
McDonnell Douglas DC-8 [2].	98	72	52	40	15.8	17.2	18.8	20.9
McDonnell Douglas DC-9 [2]	541	658	433	455	11.9	9.9	16.7	18.5
McDonnell Douglas DC-10 [2]	155	168	161	159	9.1	9.8	12.5	14.6
McDonnell Douglas MD-80	(X)	(X)	206	341	(X)	(X)	3.1	3.9

X Not applicable.   [1] For definition of mean, see Guide to Tabular Presentation.   [2] No longer in production.
Source: AVMARK, Arlington, VA. Compiled from data by the U.S. Dept. of Transportation and Aviation Information Services Limited, London, England, *The World's Jet and Turboprop Airliner Fleet.*

No. 1059. Net New Firm Orders Booked for U.S. Civil Jet Transport Aircraft: 1985 to 1992

[Value in millions of dollars. Minus sign (-) indicates net cancellations]

TYPE OF AIRCRAFT AND CUSTOMER	1985	1986	1987	1988	1989	1990	1991	1992
Total number [1]	468	332	519	956	1,015	670	280	231
U.S. customers	242	134	217	404	507	259	36	82
Foreign customers	226	198	302	552	508	411	244	149
Boeing 737, total	253	106	234	311	397	189	75	91
U.S. customers	146	45	105	173	216	38	-8	43
Foreign customers	107	61	129	138	181	151	83	48
Boeing 747, total	37	68	61	57	57	153	48	41
U.S. customers	13	6	15	22	4	24	-5	-
Foreign customers	24	62	46	35	53	129	53	41
Boeing 757, total	51	21	44	186	190	66	80	7
U.S. customers	39	11	18	101	137	33	42	29
Foreign customers	12	10	26	85	53	33	38	-22
Boeing 767, total	10	22	42	87	138	60	58	20
U.S. customers	4	3	11	32	40	23	28	10
Foreign customers	6	19	31	55	98	37	30	10
Boeing 777, total	-	-	-	-	-	34	52	36
U.S. customers	-	-	-	-	-	34	-	-
Foreign customers	-	-	-	-	-	-	52	36
McDonnell Douglas MD-11, total . . .	-	-	29	59	38	52	-31	1
U.S. customers	-	-	2	11	17	16	-26	4
Foreign customers	-	-	27	48	21	36	-5	-3
McDonnell Douglas MD-80/90, total.	114	112	105	254	195	116	-2	35
U.S. customers	37	68	65	65	93	91	5	-4
Foreign customers	77	44	40	189	102	25	-7	39
Total value	14,811	13,948	18,737	39,806	47,470	45,485	23,351	16,640
U.S. customers	7,869	3,394	6,999	16,308	20,304	14,828	2,144	3,200
Foreign customers	6,942	10,554	11,738	23,498	27,166	30,657	21,207	13,440

- Represents zero.   [1] Includes types of aircraft not shown separately.
Source: Aerospace Industries Association of America, Washington, DC, Research Center, Statistical Series 23.

No. 1060. Top 10 Airports—Traffic Summary: 1991

[In thousands, except percent change. For calendar year. Airports ranked by revenue passengers enplaned, 1991. For scheduled carriers only; excludes charter-only carriers]

AIRPORT	Rank	AIRCRAFT DEPARTURES		REVENUE PASSENGERS ENPLANED		ENPLANED REVENUE TONS		
		Total [1]	Completed scheduled	Total	Percent change, 1980-1991	Total	Freight and express	U.S. mail
All airports [2]	(X)	6,545	6,489	428,319	53.5	6,418	4,855	1,563
Atlanta, Hartsfield International. . .	4	206	204	17,691	-11.5	226	138	88
Chicago, O'Hare	1	329	328	25,872	34.6	420	289	131
Dallas/Ft. Worth International. . . .	2	269	268	22,656	117.2	225	139	86
Denver, Stapleton International. . .	6	151	151	12,314	28.1	111	74	37
Detroit, Metro Wayne	9	132	131	9,618	91.4	85	51	34
Los Angeles International	3	199	197	18,303	29.3	405	343	62
Newark International.	8	128	127	9,737	131.5	196	161	35
Phoenix, Sky Harbor International .	7	145	144	10,972	224.6	66	43	23
San Francisco International	5	168	167	14,026	49.2	240	188	52
St. Louis International	10	160	159	9,352	75.8	79	47	32

X Not applicable.   [1] Includes completed scheduled and unscheduled.   [2] Includes other airports, not shown separately.
Source: U.S. Federal Aviation Administration and Research and Special Programs Administration, *Airport Activity Statistics,* annual.

No. 1061. Domestic Airline Markets: 1991

[For calendar year. Data are for the 30 top markets and include all commercial airports in each metro area. Data do not include connecting passengers]

MARKET	Passengers	MARKET	Passengers
New York to—from Los Angeles	2,966,690	Chicago to—from Detroit	1,344,280
Los Angeles to—from San Francisco	2,857,840	New York to—from West Palm Beach . . .	1,256,930
New York to—from Boston.	2,472,140	Honolulu to—from Kona, Hawaii	1,211,850
New York to—from Washington	2,453,900	New York to—from Atlanta.	1,193,110
New York to—from Miami	2,340,480	Chicago to—from Los Angeles	1,186,150
New York to—from Chicago	2,326,740	San Francisco to—from San Diego	1,124,260
Dallas/Ft. Worth to—from Houston	2,140,380	Honolulu to—from Hilo, Hawaii	1,036,590
Honolulu to—from Kahului, Maui	2,121,090	New York to—from Dallas/Ft. Worth	997,020
New York to—from San Francisco	2,024,090	Boston to—from Washington	978,370
New York to—from Orlando	1,702,570	Chicago to—from St. Louis.	975,900
New York to—from San Juan	1,635,320	San Francisco to—from Honolulu	899,660
Honolulu to—from Lihue, Kauai	1,632,370	Phoenix to—from San Diego.	891,650
Los Angeles to—from Phoenix	1,541,950	New York to—from Tampa.	879,950
New York to—from Ft. Lauderdale.	1,540,760	Phoenix to—from Las Vegas.	878,750
Los Angeles to—from Honolulu.	1,378,430	Dallas/Ft. Worth to—from San Antonio. . .	870,030

Source: Air Transport Association of America, Washington, DC, *Air Transport 1992.*

No. 1062. Worldwide Airline Fatalities: 1970 to 1991

[For scheduled air transport operations]

YEAR	Fatal accidents	Passenger deaths	Death rate [1]	YEAR	Fatal accidents	Passenger deaths	Death rate [1]
1970.	29	700	0.29	1981.	21	362	0.06
1971.	32	884	0.35	1982.	26	764	0.13
1972.	41	1,209	0.42	1983.	20	809	0.13
1973.	29	862	0.27	1984.	16	223	0.03
1974.	21	1,299	0.38	1985. . [2]	22	1,066	0.15
1975.	20	467	0.13	1986 [2]	22	546	0.06
1976.	24	734	0.19	1987 [2]	26	901	0.09
1977.	25	516	0.12	1988 [2]	28	729	0.07
1978.	31	754	0.15	1989 [2]	27	817	0.05
1979.	31	877	0.16	1990 [2]	25	495	0.03
1980.	22	814	0.14	1991 [2][3] . . .	30	653	0.04

[1] Rate per 100 million passenger miles flown.   [2] Includes former USSR which began reporting in 1986.   [3] Preliminary.
Source: International Civil Aviation Organization, Montreal, Canada, *Civil Aviation Statistics of the World,* annual.

No. 1063. Aircraft Accidents and Hijackings: 1975 to 1991

[For years ending December 31]

ITEM	Unit	1975	1980	1985	1987	1988	1989	1990	1991
Aircraft accidents: [1] General aviation [2]	Number. . .	3,995	3,590	2,737	2,464	2,369	2,216	2,187	2,143
Fatal	Number. . .	633	618	497	487	431	424	435	414
Rate per 100,000 aircraft hours flown	Rate	2.20	1.69	1.62	1.47	1.53	1.4	1.41	1.35
Fatalities	Number. . .	1,252	1,239	951	807	789	759	745	746
Air carrier, all services [3]	Number. . .	(NA)	19	22	36	29	29	27	27
Fatal	Number. . .	(NA)	1	7	5	3	11	6	4
Rate per 1,000,000 aircraft miles flown	Rate	(X)	-	0.002	0.001	-	0.002	0.001	0.001
Fatalities	Number. . .	(NA)	1	526	232	285	278	39	62
Air carrier, scheduled services	Number. . .	29	15	17	32	28	24	25	26
Fatal	Number. . .	2	-	4	4	3	8	6	4
Rate per 1,000,000 aircraft miles flown	Rate	0.001	0.000	0.001	0.001	0.001	0.002	0.001	0.001
Fatalities	Number. . .	122	-	197	231	285	131	39	62
Commuter air carriers [4]	Number. . .	48	38	21	32	19	16	15	22
Fatal	Number. . .	12	8	7	10	2	5	2	8
Rate per 1,000,000 aircraft miles flown	Rate	0.07	0.04	0.02	0.03	0.01	0.01	0.01	0.02
Fatalities	Number. . .	28	37	37	59	21	31	4	99
Air taxis [5].	Number. . .	152	171	152	97	96	107	107	84
Fatal	Number. . .	24	46	35	30	27	25	29	26
Rate per 100,000 aircraft hours flown	Rate	0.95	1.27	1.26	1.04	0.95	0.76	0.91	0.8
Fatalities	Number. . .	69	105	76	65	58	83	50	69
Hijacking incidents, worldwide	Number. . .	25	39	35	15	17	24	46	36
U.S. registered aircraft	Number. . .	12	21	4	4	3	6	4	4
Successful [6]	Number. . .	4	13	2	-	-	-	(NA)	(NA)
Foreign-registered aircraft.	Number. . .	13	18	31	11	14	18	42	32
Successful [6]	Number. . .	3	9	18	5	-	-	(NA)	(NA)
Bomb threats:									
U.S. airports.	Number. . .	449	268	256	376	178	487	448	488
Explosions	Number. . .	4	1	-	-	-	-	-	-
U.S. worldwide and foreign aircraft in U.S	Number. . .	1,853	1,179	372	898	372	479	338	388
Explosions	Number. . .	2	1	1	1	1	1	2	-

- Represents or rounds to zero.   NA Not available.   X Not applicable.   [1] Data from National Transportation Safety Board.   [2] See text, section 22.   [3] U.S. Air Carriers operating under 14 CFR 121.   [4] All scheduled service of U.S. Air Carriers operating under 14 CFR 135.   [5] All nonscheduled service of U.S. Air Carriers operating under 14 CFR 135.   [6] Hijacker controls flight and reaches destination or objective.
Source: U.S. Federal Aviation Administration, *FAA Statistical Handbook of Aviation,* annual; and unpublished data. Includes data from U.S. Department of Transportation, Research and Special Programs Administration.

No. 1064. On-Time Flight Arrivals and Departures at Major U.S. Airports: 1991 and 1992

[In percent. Quarterly, based on gate arrival and departure times for domestic scheduled operations in the 48 contiguous states of major U.S. airlines, per DOT reporting rule effective September 1987. All U.S. airlines with one percent or more of total U.S. domestic scheduled airline passenger revenues are required to report on-time data. A flight is considered on time if it operated less than 15 minutes after the scheduled time shown in the carrier's computerized reservation system. Cancelled and diverted flights are considered late. Excludes flight operations delayed/cancelled due to aircraft mechanical problems reported on FAA maintenance records (4-5 percent of the reporting airlines' scheduled operations). See source for data on individual airlines]

AIRPORT	ON-TIME ARRIVALS						ON-TIME DEPARTURES					
	1991		1992				1991		1992			
	3d qtr.	4th qtr.	1st qtr.	2d qtr.	3d qtr.	4th qtr.	3d qtr.	4th qtr.	1st qtr.	2d qtr.	3d qtr.	4th qtr.
Total, all airports..........	85.2	82.0	81.9	84.7	81.7	80.8	90.2	87.5	87.4	90.4	87.6	86.2
Total 29 major airports	83.8	80.9	80.4	83.5	80.8	80.0	88.7	86.1	85.6	89.0	85.8	85.0
Atlanta, Hartsfield International	80.7	81.1	79.0	79.9	74.2	75.3	88.4	88.1	85.2	87.4	81.2	83.0
Baltimore/Washington International .	85.8	84.1	83.8	83.4	80.2	81.6	90.6	89.4	89.7	88.7	85.6	84.3
Boston, Logan International	79.6	75.4	73.6	76.3	72.6	77.4	85.6	83.3	83.8	86.7	81.1	83.0
Charlotte, Douglas	83.7	86.4	86.7	84.5	83.0	80.4	87.9	87.6	86.7	85.4	81.7	80.4
Chicago, O'Hare..............	85.6	77.0	78.1	85.1	80.9	80.1	89.0	80.8	82.6	88.7	84.6	84.4
Dallas/Ft. Worth International	83.7	77.1	80.1	83.6	84.2	79.4	90.7	84.3	85.6	87.9	87.5	83.2
Denver, Stapleton International	82.4	77.0	78.2	81.7	79.9	73.2	87.5	83.1	83.8	89.4	87.9	81.2
Detroit, Metro Wayne	90.8	87.9	84.0	89.2	83.8	85.2	91.9	89.8	86.6	91.1	87.9	88.8
Dulles International	85.4	85.8	84.7	83.6	81.9	84.7	90.1	88.8	90.0	91.1	85.7	88.6
Houston Intercontinental	85.3	81.3	80.6	82.7	85.6	78.6	89.4	87.1	86.7	88.6	89.7	84.9
Las Vegas, McCarran International .	87.0	86.0	87.2	90.0	88.3	83.6	88.9	89.0	89.4	92.8	91.7	87.5
Los Angeles International........	78.5	76.0	75.0	80.0	81.9	77.9	85.9	83.9	82.4	87.8	89.5	86.3
Miami International	78.2	77.8	82.4	81.2	73.7	83.3	89.2	88.6	88.2	90.3	83.5	90.3
Minneapolis/St. Paul International ..	88.6	81.1	82.8	88.7	86.1	85.0	91.0	83.8	86.6	91.8	90.1	88.4
Newark International	79.4	80.1	71.2	73.1	74.4	75.0	85.3	87.0	82.3	84.4	81.6	82.6
New York, Kennedy International...	78.5	78.1	74.1	71.8	71.4	80.9	80.2	81.2	79.7	81.8	76.7	84.9
New York, LaGuardia	82.5	83.1	80.2	80.6	77.0	81.7	88.8	88.9	87.0	88.3	83.2	84.2
Orlando International...........	83.8	84.1	82.7	83.0	78.8	83.0	90.6	91.3	88.8	89.8	84.4	88.9
Philadelphia International	82.3	81.5	77.6	79.4	75.7	80.5	88.4	86.1	85.0	86.3	80.0	83.3
Phoenix, Sky Harbor International ..	88.8	85.0	87.2	91.0	90.3	85.1	88.6	85.7	87.0	91.4	91.3	86.4
Pittsburgh, Greater International ...	85.1	80.9	77.9	80.6	74.6	76.7	86.9	81.0	83.4	86.9	76.5	77.8
Raleigh/Durham...............	88.9	90.3	88.3	87.3	83.0	85.2	92.5	92.6	88.8	88.1	82.0	87.1
St. Louis, Lambert............	86.7	81.2	82.7	88.0	84.2	85.2	91.2	85.7	85.3	90.8	87.7	88.7
Salt Lake City International......	87.2	80.7	79.3	88.2	84.1	81.1	90.9	87.1	84.5	92.6	89.3	84.2
San Diego International, Lindbergh .	85.2	82.5	82.7	87.6	84.4	79.6	88.3	86.5	86.5	91.8	92.0	88.0
San Francisco International	75.1	79.6	78.4	85.1	81.8	75.5	83.3	85.7	84.7	91.5	90.3	85.3
Seattle-Tacoma International	84.9	75.6	83.4	85.2	78.7	76.2	88.1	86.6	87.3	93.0	88.4	86.9
Tampa International	83.2	83.6	82.7	85.1	78.7	80.1	92.9	92.8	92.3	92.9	89.1	89.7
Washington National	86.3	84.9	82.3	83.6	80.1	82.5	91.3	89.9	89.8	90.0	85.9	87.5

Source: U.S. Department of Transportation, Office of Consumer Affairs, *Air Travel Consumer Report*, monthly.

No. 1065. Consumer Complaints Against U.S. Airlines: 1986 to 1992

[Calendar year data. See source for data on individual airlines]

COMPLAINT CATEGORY	COMPLAINTS							PERCENT		RANK	
	1986	1987	1988	1989	1990	1991	1992	1986	1992	1986	1992
Total.........	10,802	40,985	21,493	10,553	7,703	6,106	5,639	100.0	100.0	(X)	(X)
Flight problems [1]	3,390	18,019	8,831	4,111	3,034	1,877	1,624	31.4	28.8	1	1
Baggage.............	2,149	7,438	3,938	1,702	1,329	883	752	19.9	13.3	2	2
Refunds	1,627	3,313	1,667	1,023	701	783	721	15.1	12.8	3	3
Customer service [2]	702	3,888	2,120	1,002	758	714	695	6.5	12.3	5	4
Ticketing/boarding [3]	687	2,458	1,445	821	624	659	680	6.4	12.1	6	5
Fares [4]	468	937	455	341	312	388	573	4.3	10.2	7	6
Oversales [5]	849	2,122	1,353	607	399	301	265	7.9	4.7	4	7
Advertising	122	344	141	89	96	96	54	1.1	1.0	9	8
Smoking.............	311	888	546	232	74	30	25	2.9	0.4	8	9
Tours...............	33	90	37	22	29	23	12	0.3	0.2	11	10
Credit..............	40	101	35	19	5	10	10	0.4	0.2	10	11
Other..............	424	1,387	925	584	342	342	228	3.9	4.0	(X)	(X)

X Not applicable.   [1] Cancellations, delays, etc. from schedule.   [2] Unhelpful employees, inadequate meals or cabin service, treatment of delayed passengers.   [3] Errors in reservations and ticketing; problems in making reservations and obtaining tickets.   [4] Incorrect or incomplete information about fares, discount fare conditions and availability, etc.   [5] All bumping problems, whether or not airline complied with DOT regulations.

Source: U.S. Dept. of Transportation, Office of Consumer Affairs, *Air Travel Consumer Report*, monthly.

No. 1066. Commuter/Regional Airline Operations—Summary: 1980 to 1991

[Calendar year data. Commuter/regional airlines operate primarily aircraft of predominately 75 passengers or less and 18,000 pounds of payload capacity serving short haul and small community markets. Represents operations within all North America by U.S. Regional Carriers. Averages are means. For definition of mean, see Guide to Tabular Presentation]

ITEM	Unit	1980	1984	1985	1986	1987	1988	1989	1990	1991
Passenger carriers operating	Number .	214	203	179	179	169	163	151	150	144
Passengers enplaned	Millions .	14.8	26.1	[1]26.0	28.4	31.8	35.2	37.4	42.1	42.0
Average passengers enplaned per carrier	1,000 . .	69.2	128.1	152.4	158.4	187.7	213.9	247.4	277.5	291.4
Revenue passenger miles (RPM).	Billions .	1.92	4.17	[1]4.41	4.47	5.0	6.04	6.77	7.61	7.80
Average RPMs per carrier	Millions .	8.97	20.46	[1]24.64	24.98	29.60	37.05	44.84	50.75	54.18
Airports served.	Number .	732	853	854	824	834	861	817	811	811
Average trip length	Miles. . .	129	160	173	158	158	173	181	183	186
Passenger aircraft operated	Number .	1,339	1,747	1,745	1,806	1,841	1,801	1,907	1,917	1,992
Average seating capacity (seats).	Number .	13.9	18.4	19.2	18.4	19.7	20.5	21.8	22.1	22.8
Fleet flying hours	1,000 . .	1,740	2,764	2,854	2,929	2,942	3,078	3,266	3,447	3,671
Average annual utilization aircraft	Hours . .	1,299	1,582	1,635	1,622	1,598	1,709	1,712	1,798	1,843

[1] Adjusted to exclude a merger in 1986.
Source: Regional Airline Association, Washington, DC, *1992 Annual Report of the Regional Airline Industry* (copyright).

No. 1067. Civil Flying—Summary: 1970 to 1991

[As of Dec. 31 or for years ending Dec. 31, except as noted. See also *Historical Statistics, Colonial Times to 1970*, series Q 604-623]

ITEM	Unit	1970	1980	1985	1987	1988	1989	1990	1991
Airports in operation [1]	Number .	11,261	15,161	16,318	17,015	17,327	17,446	17,490	17,581
Heliports.	Number .	790	2,336	3,120	3,653	3,913	4,016	4,085	4,199
Public	Number .	4,260	4,814	5,861	4,984	5,043	5,084	5,078	5,090
Private.	Number .	7,001	10,347	10,457	12,031	12,284	12,362	12,412	12,491
Airports with runway lights	Number .	3,554	4,738	4,941	4,922	4,890	4,443	4,822	4,811
Airports with paved runways	Number .	3,805	5,833	6,721	7,232	7,429	7,612	7,694	7,822
Miles (nautical) of Federal airways. . . .	1,000 . .	324.7	411.1	368.5	332.9	334.8	366.6	(NA)	(NA)
Airport Improvement Program [2]	Mil. dol. .	50.5	639.0	842.1	919.4	1,278.3	1,271.2	1,244.7	1,621.6
Total civil aircraft	1,000 . .	154.5	259.4	274.9	275.1	272.7	274.8	275.9	275.5
Active aircraft [3]	1,000 . .	134.5	214.8	215.4	222.4	215.9	225.4	218.9	204.6
Air carriers, total [4].	1,000 . .	2.8	3.8	4.7	5.2	5.6	5.7	6.7	6.1
General aviation aircraft [5].	1,000 . .	131.7	211.0	210.7	217.2	210.3	219.7	212.2	198.5
Fixed-wing aircraft:									
Multi-engine:	1,000 . .	18.4	31.7	33.6	33.0	32.2	34.1	32.7	30.5
Single-engine:									
4-place and over.	1,000 . .	64.6	107.9	105.6	107.5	105.2	107.8	104.6	98.5
3-place and less.	1,000 . .	44.9	60.5	58.8	63.5	59.6	62.6	60.5	55.7
Rotorcraft [6]	1,000 . .	2.2	6.0	6.4	6.3	6.4	7.5	7.4	6.3
Balloons, blimps, gliders, etc	1,000 . .	1.6	5.0	6.3	6.8	6.9	7.7	7.0	7.6
Airman certificates held	1,000 . .	1,002	1,195	1,105	1,128	1,143	1,168	1,195	1,210
Pilot [7]	1,000 . .	733	827	710	700	694	700	703	692
Held by women	Percent .	4.0	6.4	6.1	6.1	6.1	6.1	5.8	5.9
Airline transport	1,000 . .	34	70	83	91	97	102	108	112
Commercial	1,000 . .	187	183	152	144	143	145	149	148
Private.	1,000 . .	304	357	311	301	300	293	299	293
Student.	1,000 . .	196	200	147	146	137	143	128	120
Nonpilot [8].	1,000 . .	269	368	395	428	449	468	492	517
Ground technicians [9].	1,000 . .	241	321	341	367	385	401	421	444
FAA employees: Total	Number .	53,125	55,340	47,245	47,907	49,210	50,977	51,269	54,119
Air traffic control specialists [10]	Number .	(NA)	27,190	23,580	24,132	24,803	24,368	24,339	25,741
Full performance [11].	Number .	(NA)	16,317	11,672	11,617	12,180	12,640	12,985	13,480
Developmental [11]	Number .	(NA)	4,387	4,304	5,462	5,495	5,574	5,042	5,080
Assistants [11]	Number .	(X)	(X)	1,465	1,481	1,283	1,316	1,153	928
Traffic management coordinators [12].	Number .	(X)	(X)	(X)	278	347	350	370	448
Electronic technicians.	Number .	(NA)	8,871	6,856	6,788	6,627	6,508	6,458	6,641
Aviation safety inspectors	Number .	(NA)	2,038	1,897	2,350	2,499	2,766	2,984	3,101
Engineers.	Number .	(NA)	2,436	2,457	2,579	2,640	2,657	2,745	3,073
Other.	Number .	(NA)	14,805	12,455	12,058	12,641	14,678	14,743	15,563
General aviation: [5]									
Hours flown . . . [13]	Million . .	26.0	41.0	34.1	33.4	33.6	35.0	34.8	30.1
Fuel consumed: [13]									
Gasoline	Mil. gal. .	362	520	420	402	398	343	353	354
Jet fuel [14]	Mil. gal. .	415	766	691	672	746	688	663	577

NA Not available.   X Not applicable.   [1] Existing airports, heliports, seaplane bases, etc. recorded with FAA. Includes military airports with joint civil and military use. Includes U.S. outlying areas. Airport-type definitions: Public—publicly owned and under control of a public agency; private—owned by a private individual or corporation. May or may not be open for public use. [2] Fiscal year data. Does not include System Planning Grants. Includes U.S. outlying areas. 1970-1980 data are obligated Federal funds for the Airport Development Aid Program. 1985-1991 data are appropriated Federal funds under the Airport and Airway Improvement Act of 1982.   [3] Registered aircraft that flew one or more hours during the year.   [4] Includes helicopters.   [5] See text, section 22.   [6] Includes autogyros; excludes air carrier helicopters.   [7] Includes all active pilots. An active pilot is one with a pilot certificate and a valid medical certificate. Also includes pilots who hold only a helicopter, glider, or lighter than air certificate, not shown separately.   [8] Includes dispatchers, flight navigators and engineers, and ground technicians—mechanics, parachute riggers, and ground instructors.   [9] No medical examinations are required, therefore, data represent all certificates on record and include retired or otherwise inactive technicians.   [10] Includes all air traffic control specialists (staff positions, managers, supervisors, and for 1970-1987 traffic management coordinators, not shown separately) and air traffic assistants.   [11] Serving in-flight service stations, towers, and centers.   [12] Prior to 1987, included in total air traffic control specialists.   [13] Source: 1970, U.S. Bureau of Mines; thereafter, FAA General Aviation Activity and Avionics Survey.   [14] Includes kerosene-type and naphtha-type jet fuels.

Source: Except as noted, U.S. Federal Aviation Administration, *FAA Statistical Handbook of Aviation*, annual; and unpublished data. Includes data from U.S. Department of Transportation, Research and Special Programs Administration.

No. 1068. U.S. Aircraft Shipments, 1970 to 1992, and Projections, 1993

[Value in millions of dollars]

YEAR	TOTAL		CIVIL						MILITARY	
			Large transports [1]		General Aviation [2]		Helicopters			
	Units	Value	Units	Value	Units	Value	Units	Value	Units	Value
1970	11,632	7,511	311	3,158	7,292	337	495	49	3,534	3,967
1975	17,030	9,136	315	3,779	14,072	1,033	864	274	1,779	4,050
1980	14,681	18,950	387	9,895	11,881	2,507	1,366	656	1,047	5,892
1981	11,978	20,093	387	9,706	9,457	2,920	1,072	597	1,062	6,870
1982	6,244	19,257	232	6,246	4,266	1,999	587	365	1,159	10,647
1983	4,409	22,519	262	8,000	2,691	1,470	403	303	1,053	12,746
1984	3,935	21,933	185	5,689	2,438	1,698	376	330	936	14,216
1985	3,610	28,386	278	8,448	2,029	1,431	384	506	919	18,001
1986	3,258	34,809	330	10,308	1,495	1,262	326	287	1,107	22,952
1987	3,010	35,925	357	10,507	1,085	1,364	358	277	1,210	23,777
1988	3,254	34,875	423	13,603	1,143	1,918	383	334	1,305	19,020
1989	3,675	34,229	398	15,074	1,535	1,804	515	251	1,227	17,100
1990	3,486	39,206	521	22,215	1,144	2,007	603	254	1,218	14,730
1991 [3]	2,934	40,776	589	26,856	1,021	1,968	571	211	753	11,741
1992 [3]	2,444	42,102	567	27,000	780	1,580	460	220	637	13,302
1993 [4]	2,430	39,923	480	25,500	850	1,650	500	229	600	12,544

[1] Capacity over 70 seats. [2] Includes aircraft kits for exports. [3] Estimated. [4] Forecast.

Source: U.S. Department of Commerce, International Trade Administration, *U.S. Industrial Outlook, 1993.*

No. 1069. Employment and Earnings in Aircraft Industries: 1975 to 1992

[Annual averages of monthly figures. See headnote, table 662]

1987 SIC [1] code	ITEM	Unit	1975	1980	1985	1988	1989	1990	1991	1992
(X)	Employment: Total	1,000 ..	592	744	794	893	906	898	838	758
3721	Aircraft............................	1,000 ..	293	349	326	369	382	381	357	337
3724	Aircraft engines and engine parts	1,000 ..	126	163	148	156	154	152	143	127
3728	Aircraft equipment, n.e.c. [2]	1,000 ..	80	121	143	160	176	180	171	153
376	Guided missiles, space vehicles, and parts ..	1,000 ..	93	111	177	208	194	185	167	141
(X)	Average weekly earnings: [3]									
3721	Aircraft............................	Dollars .	256	404	(NA)	(NA)	(NA)	(NA)	(NA)	(NA)
3724	Aircraft engines and parts	Dollars .	247	394	542	582	616	637	654	689
376	Guided missiles, space vehicles, and parts ..	Dollars .	245	378	515	567	589	612	632	652
(X)	Average hourly earnings: [3]									
3721	Aircraft [4]	Dollars .	6.21	9.66	13.18	14.18	14.89	15.66	16.72	17.70
3724	Aircraft engines and parts	Dollars .	6.04	9.42	12.85	13.80	14.42	14.84	15.38	16.28
376	Guided missiles, space vehicles, and parts ..	Dollars .	6.02	9.22	12.14	13.13	13.70	14.39	14.90	15.97

NA Not available. X Not applicable. [1] 1987 Standard Industrial Classification; see text, section 13. [2] N.e.c.=Not elsewhere classified. [3] For production workers. [4] Excludes lump-sum payments. Earnings which include proration of lump-sum payments were: $13.40 in 1985; $14.65 in 1988; $15.41 in 1989; $16.32 in 1990; $17.16 in 1991; and $18.18 in 1992.

Source: U.S. Bureau of Labor Statistics, Bulletin 2370; and *Employment and Earnings,* monthly.

No. 1070. Aerospace Industry—Summary, 1980 to 1992, and Projections, 1993

[For calendar year, except employment and earnings annual averages of monthly figures. Includes Standard Industrial Classification Codes 372 and 376. Industry shipments refer to the total value of all products shipped by establishments classified in that industry. Product shipments refer to the total value of specific products shipped irrespective of how the establishments which made them are classified]

ITEM	Unit	1980	1985	1986	1987	1988	1989	1990	1991 [1]	1992 [1]	1993 [2]
INDUSTRY DATA											
Value of shipments	Mil. dol.	58,483	90,795	100,999	103,589	107,746	113,477	125,194	128,610	125,749	120,516
In **1987** dollars	Mil. dol.	(NA)	(NA)	(NA)	103,589	106,355	109,070	116,019	115,390	109,021	103,199
Employment, total.......	1,000 ..	721	746	798	810	820	823	816	752	695	652
Production workers	1,000 ..	387	372	400	407	399	400	396	361	330	308
Average hourly earnings ..	Dol ...	9.90	13.88	14.37	14.92	15.35	15.84	16.36	(NA)	(NA)	(NA)
Capital expenditures	Mil. dol.	1,923	3,784	4,144	3,612	3,388	3,921	3,490	(NA)	(NA)	(NA)
PRODUCT DATA											
Value of shipments	Mil. dol.	53,296	80,625	90,907	97,185	102,242	106,320	118,141	115,345	112,643	107,964
In **1987** dollars	Mil. dol.	(NA)	(NA)	(NA)	97,185	100,643	101,659	108,635	101,852	96,995	91,748

NA Not available. [1] Estimated. [2] Forecast.

Source: U.S. Department of Commerce, International Trade Administration, *U.S. Industrial Outlook, 1993.*

No. 1071. Aerospace—Sales, New Orders, and Backlog: 1970 to 1991

[In billions of dollars, except as indicated. Reported by establishments in which the principal business is the development and/or production of aerospace products]

ITEM	1970	1975	1980	1984	1985	1986	1987	1988	1989 [1]	1990 [1]	1991 [1]
Net sales	24.8	29.5	58.4	88.9	100.5	105.6	110.3	113.5	122.1	136.6	134.6
Percent of U.S. Government	66.3	58.7	45.6	62.7	63.2	61.9	62.2	60.0	58.0	54.0	50.0
Complete aircraft and parts [2]	10.4	11.3	22.6	28.3	34.2	38.0	37.0	35.7	38.4	49.9	53.0
Aircraft engines and parts	3.1	3.4	6.9	9.1	9.7	9.8	12.0	15.0	15.4	16.4	15.6
Missiles and space vehicles, parts	5.4	6.3	8.4	13.6	16.7	17.5	20.7	21.5	22.6	22.0	23.8
Other products, services	5.9	8.5	20.5	38.0	39.8	40.3	40.5	41.3	45.7	48.3	42.2
Net, new orders	21.2	29.0	70.4	104.9	111.0	110.8	121.2	147.1	173.6	146.0	132.6
Backlog, Dec. 31	24.7	35.0	90.5	132.5	143.0	148.2	158.7	191.5	252.4	250.1	247.6

[1] Data beginning 1989 are not comparable with earlier years. Data are being reported which were previously not available. The extent of this noncomparability is not known.   [2] Except engines sold separately.

Source: U.S. Bureau of the Census, *Current Industrial Reports*, series MA-37D.

No. 1072. Aerospace Industry Sales, by Product Group and Customer: 1980 to 1993

[In billions of dollars. Due to reporting practices and tabulating methods, figures may differ from those in table 1071]

ITEM	CURRENT DOLLARS						CONSTANT (1987) DOLLARS [3]					
	1980	1985	1990	1991	1992 [1]	1993 [2]	1980	1985	1990	1991	1992 [1]	1993 [2]
Total sales	54.7	96.6	134.4	138.9	134.0	126.5	77.5	97.8	121.6	121.2	114.2	105.9
PRODUCT GROUP												
Aircraft, total	31.5	50.5	71.4	76.1	72.8	66.0	40.4	51.1	64.6	66.4	62.1	55.3
Civil [4]	16.3	13.7	31.4	37.7	37.9	34.4	12.5	13.9	28.4	32.9	32.3	28.8
Military	15.2	36.8	40.1	38.5	34.9	31.6	27.9	37.2	36.3	33.6	29.7	26.5
Missiles	6.5	11.4	14.2	10.9	10.8	10.1	11.8	11.6	12.8	9.5	9.2	8.5
Space	7.9	18.6	26.4	28.7	29.0	29.2	12.0	18.8	23.9	25.0	24.7	24.5
Related products and services [5]	8.8	16.1	22.4	23.1	21.4	21.1	13.0	16.3	20.3	20.2	18.2	17.7
CUSTOMER GROUP												
Aerospace, total	45.9	80.5	112.0	115.7	112.6	105.4	65.0	81.5	101.3	101.0	96.0	88.3
DOD [6]	22.8	53.2	60.5	55.9	51.8	46.4	32.3	53.9	54.8	48.8	44.1	38.8
NASA [7] and other agencies	4.1	6.3	11.1	11.7	12.0	12.4	5.8	6.3	10.0	10.2	10.2	10.3
Other customers [8]	19.0	21.0	40.4	48.2	48.8	46.7	26.9	21.3	36.5	42.1	41.6	39.1
Related products and services [5]	8.8	16.1	22.4	23.1	21.4	21.1	12.5	16.3	20.3	20.2	18.2	17.7

[1] Preliminary.   [2] Estimate.   [3] Based on AIA's aerospace composite price deflator.   [4] All civil sales of aircraft (domestic and export sales of jet transports, commuters, business and personal aircraft and helicopters).   [5] Electronics, software, and ground support equipment, plus sales of non-aerospace products which are produced by aerospace-manufacturing use technology, processes, and materials derived from aerospace products.   [6] Department of Defense.   [7] National Aeronautics and Space Administration.   [8] Includes civil aircraft sales (see footnote 4), commercial space sales, all exports of military aircraft and missiles and related propulsion and parts.

Source: Aerospace Industries Association of America, Inc., Washington, DC, *Aerospace Facts and Figures, 1992/93*.

No. 1073. Aerospace Industry—Net Profits After Taxes: 1976 to 1992

[For calendar year. Minus sign (-) indicates loss]

YEAR	AEROSPACE INDUSTRY PROFITS				MANUFACTURING CORPORATIONS PROFITS			
	Total (mil. dol.)	As percent of—			Total (mil. dol.)	As percent of—		
		Sales	Assets	Equity		Sales	Assests	Equity
1976	1,091	3.4	4.7	12.8	64,550	5.4	7.5	14.0
1977	1,427	4.2	5.7	14.9	69,306	5.3	7.6	14.2
1978	1,816	4.4	5.5	15.7	81,079	5.4	7.8	15.0
1979	2,614	5.0	6.3	18.4	98,719	5.7	8.4	16.5
1980	2,588	4.3	5.2	16.0	93,149	4.8	6.9	13.9
1981	2,966	4.4	5.2	16.0	101,330	4.7	6.7	13.6
1982	2,193	3.3	3.7	12.0	70,966	3.5	4.5	9.2
1983	2,829	3.5	4.1	12.1	85,737	4.1	5.1	10.5
1984	3,639	4.1	4.7	14.1	107,657	4.6	6.0	12.5
1985	3,274	3.1	3.6	11.1	87,809	3.8	4.6	10.1
1986	3,093	2.8	3.1	9.4	82,762	3.7	4.2	9.5
1987	4,582	4.1	4.4	14.6	115,472	4.9	5.6	12.8
1988	4,883	4.3	4.4	14.9	154,647	6.0	6.9	16.2
1989	3,866	3.3	3.3	10.7	136,412	5.0	5.6	13.7
1990	4,487	3.4	3.4	11.5	110,737	4.0	4.3	10.7
1991	[1]2,484	1.8	1.9	6.1	66,379	2.5	2.6	6.4
1992, prel.	[1]-1,836	-1.4	-1.2	-5.2	27,985	1.0	1.0	2.6

[1] Reflects unusually large nonoperating expenses totalling $3.4 billion in 1991 and $8.7 billion in 1992 due to the initial implementation of a change in accounting for future retirement benefit costs and defense-downsizing restructuring charges. Many large aerospace corporations chose to write off against first quarter earnings amounts required to comply with FSAB 106.

Source: Aerospace Industries Association of America, Washington, DC, *Aerospace Facts and Figures*, annual.

No. 1074. U.S. Exports of Aerospace Vehicles and Equipment, 1989 to 1992, and Projections, 1993

ITEM	NUMBER OF UNITS					VALUE (mil. dol.)				
	1989	1990	1991	1992 [1]	1993 [2]	1989	1990	1991	1992 [1]	1993 [2]
Aerospace vehicles and equipment .	(NA)	(NA)	(NA)	(NA)	(NA)	32,884	39,030	43,783	43,423	43,089
Civilian aircraft	3,940	3,446	2,954	2,402	2,374	14,257	18,110	22,387	22,126	21,140
Under 4,536 kg. unladen weight, new .	1,638	799	536	402	426	265	318	304	288	240
4,536-15,000 kg. unladen weight, new .	48	79	69	64	70	164	245	279	259	282
Over 15,000 kg. unladen weight, new .	260	306	385	374	319	13,122	16,691	20,881	20,589	19,555
Rotocraft, new	294	349	318	264	285	155	161	168	156	168
Other new aircraft, n.e.c. [3]	(NA)	(NA)	(NA)	(NA)	(NA)	18	15	21	19	20
Used, rebuilt, and converted	1,700	1,913	1,646	1,298	1,274	533	680	734	815	875
Military aircraft, new and used.	846	445	490	340	395	892	1,481	1,784	1,987	2,330
Aircraft engines and parts	(NA)	(NA)	(NA)	(NA)	(NA)	6,629	6,870	7,039	6,719	6,872
Piston engines and parts.	(NA)	(NA)	(NA)	(NA)	(NA)	438	421	417	302	348
Turbine engines and parts.	(NA)	(NA)	(NA)	(NA)	(NA)	6,191	6,449	6,622	6,417	6,524
Propellers and parts	(NA)	(NA)	(NA)	(NA)	(NA)	271	343	317	287	301
Landing gear and parts	(NA)	(NA)	(NA)	(NA)	(NA)	273	276	333	414	422
Aircraft parts, n.e.c. [3]	(NA)	(NA)	(NA)	(NA)	(NA)	8,198	8,982	9,386	8,823	8,990
Guided missiles and parts	(NA)	(NA)	(NA)	(NA)	(NA)	1,042	1,306	1,204	1,660	1,585
Flight simulators	(NA)	(NA)	(NA)	(NA)	(NA)	206	255	245	180	200
Space launch equipment	(NA)	(NA)	(NA)	(NA)	(NA)	384	660	308	408	414
Avionics	(NA)	(NA)	(NA)	(NA)	(NA)	732	747	780	819	835

NA Not available.   [1] Estimated.   [2] Forecast.   [3] N.e.c. = Not elsewhere classified.
Source: U.S. Dept. of Commerce, International Trade Administration, *U.S. Industrial Outlook*, 1993.

No. 1075. U.S. Receipts and Payments for International Transportation: 1980 to 1992

[In millions of dollars. Data are international transportation transactions recorded for balance of payment purposes (see table 1328). Receipts include freight on exports carried by U.S.-operated carriers and foreign carrier expenditures in U.S. ports. Payments include freight on imports carried by foreign carriers and U.S. carrier port expenditures abroad. Freight on exports carried by foreign carriers is excluded since such payments are directly or indirectly for foreign account. Similarly, freight on U.S. imports carried by U.S. carriers is a domestic rather than an international transaction. Minus sign (-) indicates excess of payments over receipts. See *Historical Statistics, Colonial Times to 1970*, series U 3 and U 10, for totals]

ITEM	1980	1984	1985	1986	1987	1988	1989	1990	1991	1992
Total receipts	**14,208**	**17,876**	**19,085**	**21,366**	**24,337**	**28,430**	**31,147**	**37,252**	**38,180**	**40,126**
Ocean transportation.	7,757	8,894	8,906	9,259	10,162	11,346	11,836	12,295	12,416	12,604
Export freight earnings	2,641	2,702	2,866	2,610	2,806	3,043	3,127	3,233	2,970	2,874
Passenger fares	(NA)	45	60	90	102	128	132	154	156	173
Freight earnings on shipments between foreign countries	588	563	574	576	595	707	769	871	1,030	1,030
Port expenditures.	4,435	5,457	5,274	5,843	6,514	7,315	7,609	7,815	8,020	8,268
Charter hire	93	127	132	140	145	153	199	222	240	259
Air transportation	5,946	8,467	9,698	10,912	12,844	15,639	17,792	23,318	24,254	25,798
Export freight earnings	742	645	706	783	982	1,385	1,719	2,432	2,722	2,589
Passenger fares [1]	2,591	4,022	4,351	5,492	6,901	8,847	10,482	15,144	15,698	17,180
Port expenditures.	2,613	3,800	4,641	4,637	4,961	5,407	5,591	5,742	5,834	6,029
Other transportation	505	515	481	1,195	1,331	1,445	1,519	1,639	1,510	1,724
Total payments	**15,397**	**20,578**	**22,087**	**23,220**	**25,072**	**27,263**	**28,907**	**33,931**	**33,309**	**34,397**
Ocean transportation.	8,447	10,406	10,852	11,507	11,265	12,344	12,420	13,326	12,582	12,221
Import freight payments	5,809	7,755	8,114	8,636	8,365	9,372	9,391	10,290	9,593	9,269
Passenger fares	268	151	154	208	235	164	193	248	279	301
Port expenditures.	1,905	1,972	2,048	2,125	2,115	2,244	2,228	2,174	2,093	2,028
Charter hire	465	528	536	538	550	564	608	614	617	623
Air transportation	6,705	9,929	11,009	11,424	13,480	14,546	16,135	20,163	20,246	21,669
Import freight payments	562	1,633	1,666	2,051	2,242	2,226	2,197	2,207	2,257	2,370
Passenger fares [1]	3,339	5,584	6,290	6,297	7,048	7,565	8,055	10,282	9,733	10,642
Port expenditures.	2,804	2,712	3,053	3,076	4,190	4,755	5,883	7,674	8,256	8,657
Other transportation	245	243	226	289	327	373	352	442	481	507
Balance.	**−1,189**	**−2,702**	**−3,002**	**−1,854**	**−735**	**1,167**	**2,240**	**3,321**	**4,871**	**5,729**

NA Not available.   [1] Beginning 1990, includes interairline settlements.

Source: U.S. Bureau of Economic Analysis, *Survey of Current Business*, June issues; and unpublished data.

No. 1076. Exports and Imports, by Method of Transport: 1970 to 1990

[Exports are free alongside ship (f.a.s.) value (see text, section 29) for all years; imports are f.a.s. value for 1980 and customs value for other years. Export data include both domestic and foreign; import data for general imports only. For details, see source]

ITEM	Unit	EXPORTS						IMPORTS					
		1970	1980	1985	1988	1989	1990	1970	1980	1985	1988	1989	1990
All methods [1]	Bil. dol.	43.2	220.7	213.1	320.4	363.8	393.0	40.0	240.8	345.3	441.3	473.4	495.3
Vessel	Bil. dol.	24.6	120.9	91.7	126.0	146.3	150.8	24.8	165.1	208.4	255.8	269.9	283.4
Air.	Bil. dol.	6.1	46.1	52.3	91.6	101.9	110.5	3.4	28.0	51.3	77.5	84.4	90.9
Shipping weight: Vessel . . .	Bil. kg .	218.0	363.7	317.7	361.8	390.6	372.4	271.4	443.1	361.5	466.8	494.7	496.3
Air.	Bil. kg .	0.4	1.0	0.8	1.4	1.6	1.5	0.3	0.6	1.3	1.5	4.3	1.7

[1] Includes types other than vessel and air and revisions that are not distributed by method of transport.
Source: U.S. Bureau of the Census, Highlights of U.S. Export and Import Trade, through 1988, FT 990, monthly; thereafter, U.S. Merchandise Trade: Selected Highlights, FT-920, monthly.

No. 1077. Federal Expenditures for Civil Functions of the Corps of Engineers, United States Army: 1965 to 1991

[In millions of dollars. For fiscal years ending in year shown, see text, section 9. These expenditures represent the work of the Corps of Engineers to plan, design, construct, operate, and maintain civil works projects and activities, particularly in the management and improvement of rivers, harbors, and waterways for navigation, flood control, and multiple purposes. The amounts listed below do not include the expenditure of funds contributed, advanced, or reimbursed by other government agencies or local interests. Includes Puerto Rico and outlying areas]

FISCAL YEAR	Total program [1]	Navigation	Flood control	Multiple purpose	FISCAL YEAR	Total program [1]	Navigation	Flood control	Multiple purpose
1965....	1,169	426	447	283	1983....	2,959	1,290	1,088	482
1970....	1,128	398	379	331	1984....	3,085	1,383	1,154	445
1975....	2,070	694	904	439	1985....	2,956	1,234	1,187	419
1977....	2,340	792	918	594	1986....	3,163	1,345	1,300	402
1978....	2,645	951	1,069	583	1987....	2,937	1,135	1,272	411
1979....	2,934	1,083	1,218	577	1988....	3,086	1,271	1,271	423
1980....	3,061	1,225	1,228	551	1989....	3,252	1,395	1,253	462
1981....	3,198	1,339	1,273	527	1990....	3,297	1,391	1,397	375
1982....	2,940	1,331	1,083	453	1991....	3,511	1,473	1,447	443

[1] Includes expenditures which are not associated with a specific purpose (e.g., headquarters staff supervision, management, and administration activities, and some research and development activities).
Source: U.S. Army Corps of Engineers, *Report of Civil Works Expenditures by State and Fiscal Year,* annual.

No. 1078. Freight Carried on Inland Waterways, by System: 1960 to 1989

[In billions of ton-miles. Excludes Alaska and Hawaii, except as noted. Includes waterways, canals, and connecting channels]

ITEM	1960	1970	1980	1981	1982	1983	1984	1985	1986	1987	1988	1989
Total	220.3	318.6	406.9	410.2	351.2	359.0	399.0	381.7	392.6	410.7	438.2	448.7
Atlantic coast waterways....	28.6	28.6	30.4	28.3	25.4	22.5	24.7	24.8	25.7	25.9	28.1	28.2
Gulf coast waterways	16.9	28.6	36.6	35.1	31.8	32.4	36.7	36.5	39.0	37.9	44.6	42.5
Pacific coast waterways [1]	6.0	8.4	14.9	14.4	12.8	13.2	20.5	19.9	20.8	22.8	24.5	24.0
Mississippi River system [2]	69.3	138.5	228.9	234.4	218.0	223.0	234.6	224.7	239.3	251.6	257.8	268.1
Great Lakes System [3]	99.5	114.5	96.0	98.0	63.2	67.9	82.5	75.8	67.9	72.5	83.1	85.8

[1] Includes Alaskan waterways. [2] Comprises main channels and all tributaries of the Mississippi, Illinois, Missouri, and Ohio Rivers. [3] Does not include traffic between foreign ports.
Source: U.S. Army Corps of Engineers, *Waterborne Commerce of the United States,* annual.

No. 1079. Domestic and Foreign Waterborne Commerce, by Type of Commodity: 1970 to 1989

[In millions of short tons. Domestic trade includes all commercial movements between United States ports and on inland rivers, Great Lakes, canals, and connecting channels of the United States, Puerto Rico, and Virgin Islands. Figures may differ from those shown in table 1080 due to minor differences in basic concepts]

COMMODITY	1970 Total	1970 Domestic	1980 Total	1980 Domestic	1985 Total	1985 Domestic	1989 Total	1989 Domestic	1989 Foreign Imports	1989 Foreign Exports
Net total	1,531.7	950.7	1,998.9	1,077.5	1,788.4	1,014.1	2,140.4	1,102.5	589.5	448.4
Petroleum products [1] ...	394.7	287.3	423.2	339.2	368.8	259.0	441.9	289.2	108.8	43.9
Gasoline	89.3	88.7	87.3	81.0	94.0	78.0	107.9	86.2	19.8	1.9
Distillate fuel oil	78.8	76.9	74.6	72.1	70.0	55.0	75.2	58.1	12.9	4.2
Residual fuel oil	170.5	78.8	188.0	141.3	130.0	83.7	147.5	91.4	42.8	13.3
Crude petroleum	210.5	116.3	480.2	174.2	357.7	194.7	480.8	181.9	298.8	0.1
Coal and lignite	225.4	154.1	256.4	164.1	273.9	179.9	304.8	203.8	2.4	98.6
Nonmetallic minerals [1][2] .	166.6	132.6	157.1	111.6	150.7	108.5	158.7	111.6	25.7	21.4
Sand and gravel [3]	78.4	73.9	65.1	60.8	66.4	62.0	58.8	54.9	2.1	1.8
Limestone	42.0	34.1	34.2	23.9	24.5	21.9	41.3	35.5	2.3	3.5
Phosphate rock......	16.6	5.8	23.7	9.5	19.4	8.4	15.8	6.1	0.8	8.9
Iron and concentrates...	129.3	75.2	98.4	64.9	72.7	50.0	86.5	59.6	21.4	5.5
Farm products [1]	90.4	28.5	216.8	63.4	172.8	60.0	216.3	70.5	8.7	137.1
Corn	27.2	11.7	98.6	30.8	76.3	29.0	96.4	35.8	0.1	60.5
Wheat...........	25.0	5.8	53.4	14.3	38.0	10.6	55.8	16.5	0.2	39.1
Soybeans	21.2	8.3	39.6	16.1	32.9	14.9	28.8	12.8	(Z)	16.0
Chemicals and allied products	62.0	39.7	91.9	49.4	108.5	53.3	123.3	61.9	15.9	45.5
Food and kindred products	35.0	11.0	54.8	20.4	52.5	17.6	54.3	20.6	11.5	22.2
Lumber and wood products [4]	49.9	27.3	52.0	22.7	47.2	18.8	56.9	21.0	4.7	31.2
Primary metal products ..	42.4	10.8	28.9	9.0	33.4	8.5	31.5	8.7	17.9	4.9
Waste and scrap	25.9	16.0	31.1	18.8	37.4	23.9	54.6	37.3	0.9	16.4
Other.............	99.7	51.9	108.1	39.8	112.8	40.0	130.8	36.4	72.8	21.6

Z Less than 50,000. [1] Includes categories not shown separately. [2] Excludes fuels. [3] Includes crushed rock. [4] Excludes furniture.
Source: U.S. Army Corps of Engineers, *Waterborne Commerce of the United States,* annual.

No. 1080. Waterborne Imports and Exports—Cargo Tonnage and Value, by Coastal District: 1980 to 1991

[Exports are free alongside ship (f.a.s.) value for all years; imports are f.a.s. value for 1980 and customs value for other years, see text, section 29. Includes commodities classified for security reasons as "Special Category" (exports only) and exports by Dept. of Defense (grant-aid shipments), and merchandise shipped in transit through the United States. See Appendix III]

DISTRICT	CARGO TONNAGE (mil. sh. tons)							VALUE (bil. dol.)						
	1980	1985	1987	1988	1989	1990	1991	1980	1985	1987	1988	1989	1990	1991
Imports:														
Atlantic	183	190	224	234	211	207	176	71.5	94.4	105.8	107.4	109.3	110.8	101.1
Gulf............	243	141	184	212	217	225	217	56.4	32.8	30.5	31.2	36.1	41.0	36.4
Pacific..........	56	51	56	55	55	55	49	45.0	90.4	118.4	126.5	140.9	143.3	143.7
Great Lakes	16	17	14	16	16	16	13	1.9	2.8	2.0	2.5	3.7	7.6	8.4
Exports:														
Atlantic	117	93	78	92	94	101	107	51.0	35.2	38.7	48.2	56.3	62.4	70.1
Gulf............	163	144	155	162	152	148	167	41.5	31.8	31.6	37.9	40.9	41.2	44.2
Pacific..........	78	81	95	110	103	100	102	25.2	25.8	31.9	43.3	50.1	53.7	56.6
Great Lakes	45	34	32	37	34	26	18	4.6	2.4	2.1	3.2	3.6	1.7	1.2

Source: U.S. Bureau of the Census, *U.S. Waterborne Exports and General Imports*, through 1988, FT 985, annual; thereafter TM 985, monthly.

No. 1081. Vessels Entered and Cleared in Foreign Trade—Net Registered Tonnage, by Flag of Carrier Vessel: 1966 to 1991

[In millions of net tons, except as indicated. Includes Puerto Rico and Virgin Islands. Seaports comprise all ports except Great Lakes ports. See also *Historical Statistics, Colonial Times to 1970*, series Q 507-517]

YEARLY AVERAGE OR YEAR	Number of vessels	ALL PORTS					SEAPORTS					
		Tonnage, all vessels					Tonnage, all vessels			Tonnage, with cargo		
		Total	U.S.	Percent U.S.	Foreign		Total	U.S.	Foreign	Total	U.S.	Foreign
Entered:												
1966-70.......	53,459	232	29	12.5	203		206	27	180	157	18	139
1971-75.......	53,760	319	30	9.5	290		292	28	264	220	24	196
1976-80.......	53,700	458	40	8.7	418		425	38	387	316	30	286
1981-85.......	50,124	452	57	12.4	395		424	55	369	277	36	241
1986-90.......	61,978	548	46	8.4	502		521	45	476	346	30	315
1970..........	53,293	254	26	10.3	226		227	24	202	171	19	152
1975..........	51,443	355	32	9.9	323		326	30	297	240	26	215
1980..........	53,645	492	52	10.6	440		460	50	410	310	34	276
1985..........	53,531	451	53	11.7	398		426	52	374	283	34	249
1987..........	59,563	518	48	9.3	470		492	47	445	333	29	304
1988..........	62,097	556	47	8.5	509		527	46	481	352	30	322
1989..........	64,946	587	44	7.4	543		558	42	516	367	31	335
1990..........	66,424	589	41	7.0	548		564	40	524	367	30	337
1991..........	57,254	516	39	7.6	476		494	38	455	311	28	283
Cleared:												
1966-70.......	52,415	232	30	12.8	202		206	27	179	122	23	99
1971-75.......	53,039	324	31	9.9	293		296	29	267	149	21	127
1976-80.......	52,931	453	41	9.1	412		420	38	382	203	26	177
1981-85.......	50,291	460	57	12.4	403		432	55	377	251	34	217
1986-90.......	60,249	551	47	8.6	504		524	46	478	284	31	253
1970..........	52,195	253	27	10.6	226		226	25	201	132	20	112
1975..........	51,017	363	34	10.3	329		334	31	303	168	23	144
1980..........	52,928	487	54	11.1	433		456	51	405	246	33	213
1985..........	53,095	461	55	11.9	406		435	53	382	253	36	217
1987..........	58,307	521	49	9.4	472		495	48	447	269	31	238
1988..........	60,540	561	49	8.7	512		531	47	484	295	31	264
1989..........	63,042	590	45	7.6	545		561	44	517	304	30	274
1990..........	63,648	592	43	7.3	550		566	41	525	304	29	275
1991..........	55,100	521	40	7.7	480		498	39	459	282	28	253

Source: U.S. Bureau of the Census, *Vessel Entrances and Clearances*, through 1987, FT 975, annual; thereafter TA 987, annual.

No. 1082. Domestic Merchant Vessels Completed by U.S. Shipyards: 1970 to 1988

[Vessels of 1,000 gross tons and over. See also *Historical Statistics, Colonial Times to 1970*, series Q 438-48]

TYPE	Unit	1970	1975	1979	1980	1981	1982	1983	1984	1985	1986	1987	1988
Merchant vessels......	Number......	13	15	15	10	12	11	13	5	8	5	4	4
Gross tons.........	1,000	342	452	1,149	375	275	337	376	118	172	215	153	153
Cargo.............	Number......	6	3	4	6	2	6	6	-	4	2	3	3
Gross tons.........	1,000	120	65	53	105	53	221	228	-	113	66	58	58
Deadweight tons.....	1,000	134	71	47	114	73	219	219	-	97	53	63	63
Tankers	Number......	7	12	11	4	10	5	7	5	4	3	1	1
Gross tons.........	1,000	222	387	1,096	270	222	116	148	118	59	149	95	95
Deadweight tons.....	1,000	427	742	1,901	354	358	226	277	210	92	271	209	209

- Represents zero.

Source: U.S. Maritime Administration, *New Ship Construction*, annual.

No. 1083. United States Flag Merchant Vessels—Number and Vessel Deadweight Tonnage: 1992

[As of **end of fiscal year;** see text, section 9. Covers ocean-going vessels of 1,000 gross tons and over engaged in foreign and domestic trade, and inactive vessels. Excludes vessels operating exclusively on Great Lakes, inland waterways, and those owned by the United States Army and Navy, and special types such as cable ships, tugs, etc. See also *Historical Statistics, Colonial Times to 1970,* series Q 487-502]

VESSEL TYPE	NUMBER						DEADWEIGHT TONNAGE (1,000)					
	Total	Passenger[1]	Cargo[2]	Intermodal	Bulk carrier[3]	Tanker[4]	Total	Passenger[1]	Cargo[2]	Intermodal	Bulk carrier[3]	Tanker[4]
Total	619	10	191	168	24	226	23,254	92	2,444	4,711	1,014	14,993
Active vessels	411	8	47	154	20	182	18,286	70	728	4,379	844	12,265
Privately owned	362	2	31	128	20	181	17,480	14	527	3,847	844	12,248
U.S. foreign trade	112	-	11	66	12	23	4,944	-	175	2,356	610	1,803
Foreign-to-foreign	22	-	-	8	-	14	2,136	-	-	207	-	1,929
Domestic trade	161	2	4	26	8	121	8,741	14	76	570	234	7,847
Coastal	96	-	4	4	6	82	3,559	-	76	129	179	3,175
Noncontiguous	65	2	-	22	2	39	5,182	14	-	441	55	4,672
Military Sea Lift Command . .	67	-	16	28	-	23	1,659	-	276	714	-	669
Government owned	49	6	16	26	-	1	806	56	201	532	-	17
Ready reserve force	40	2	14	24	-	-	716	23	180	513	-	-
Inactive vessels	208	2	144	14	4	44	4,968	22	1,716	332	170	2,728
Privately owned	32	1	6	2	3	20	2,236	16	69	44	145	1,962
Temporarily inactive	6	-	3	-	2	1	201	-	38	-	128	35
Laid-up	24	1	3	2	1	17	1,968	16	31	44	17	1,860
Laid-up (MARAD Custody)[5]	2	-	-	-	-	2	67	-	-	-	-	67
Government owned (MARAD Custody)[5]	176	1	138	12	1	24	2,732	6	1,647	288	25	766
National defense reserve fleet	165	-	131	12	-	22	2,546	-	1,558	288	-	700
Ready reserve fleet	56	-	34	9	-	13	1,132	-	486	251	-	395
Other reserve	109	-	97	3	-	9	1,414	-	1,072	37	-	305
Nonretention[6]	9	1	6	-	-	2	145	6	73	-	-	66
Other Government owned . .	2	-	1	-	1	-	41	-	16	-	25	-

- Represents zero.   [1] Includes combination passenger and cargo vessels.   [2] General cargo.   [3] Includes tug barges.
[4] Includes tanker barges and liquified natural gas vessels.   [5] In the custody of the Maritime Administration.   [6] Vessels not actively maintained.

Source: U.S. Maritime Administration, *Employment Report of the United States Flag Merchant Fleet Ocean-going Vessels 1,000 Gross Tons and Over,* annual.

No. 1084. Private Shipyards—Summary: 1970 to 1991

[For calendar year, unless noted. See also *Historical Statistics, Colonial Times to 1970,* series Q 449-458 and series Q 467-472]

ITEM	Unit	1970	1980	1984	1985	1986	1987	1988	1989	1990	1991
Employment	1,000. . .	133.4	177.3	142.0	130.3	120.6	120.4	121.0	123.4	121.8	[1]131.0
Production workers	1,000. . .	108.5	141.8	111.0	99.0	90.3	90.8	90.9	88.6	86.4	[1]98.3
Value of work done	Mil. dol. .	2,682	9,269	8,944	9,358	8,840	8,531	(NA)	(NA)	(NA)	(NA)
On ships only	Mil. dol. .	2,594	8,889	8,308	9,483	8,913	8,377	(NA)	(NA)	(NA)	(NA)
Value added	Mil. dol. .	1,616	5,338	5,206	5,740	5,426	5,227	(NA)	(NA)	(NA)	(NA)
Building activity:											
Merchant vessels: [2]											
Under construction [3]	Number .	49	69	10	10	7	6	-	-	-	3
Ordered	Number .	13	7	5	-	-	-	-	-	3	-
Delivered	Number .	13	23	5	3	1	4	-	-	-	-
Cancelled	Number .	-	4	-	-	-	2	-	-	-	-
Under contract [4]	Number .	49	49	10	7	6	-	-	-	3	3
Naval vessels: [2]											
Under construction [3]	Number .	108	99	111	100	85	79	83	105	98	91
Ordered	Number .	6	11	11	11	16	20	32	16	8	12
Delivered	Number .	32	19	22	26	20	16	10	23	15	14
Under contract [4]	Number .	82	91	100	85	[5]79	83	105	98	91	89
Repairs/conversions:											
Commercial ships	Mil. dol. .	431	1,335	1,631	852	847	806	(NA)	(NA)	(NA)	(NA)
Naval ships	Mil. dol. .	359	1,134	1,641	2,311	2,008	1,930	(NA)	(NA)	(NA)	(NA)
Unfinished work: [3]											
Commercial ships	Mil. dol. .	765	2,070	100	450	315	53	-	-	-	(NA)
Naval ships	Mil. dol. .	1,719	7,107	14,003	12,091	9,595	8,265	10,500	16,010	(NA)	(NA)

- Represents zero.   NA Not available.   [1] Annual average of monthly data.   [2] Vessels of 1,000 tons or larger.   [3] As of Jan. 1.   [4] As of Dec. 31.   [5] Two ships were cancelled during 1986.

Source: Shipbuilders Council of America, Arlington, VA., *Annual Report,* through 1980; thereafter, unpublished data.

No. 1085. Employees in Government and Private Shipyards: 1960 to 1992

[In thousands. Annual average employment in establishments primarily engaged in building and repairing all types of ships, barges, canal boats, and lighters of 5 gross tons and over, whether propelled by sail or motor power, or towed by other craft. Includes all full- and part-time employees]

YEAR	Total	Private yards	Navy yards	YEAR	Total	Private yards	Navy yards	YEAR	Total	Private yards	Navy yards
1960	208	112	96	1981	265	187	78	1987	200	124	75
1970	216	134	83	1982	253	172	82	1988	197	124	73
1975	217	154	65	1983	226	143	84	1989	196	126	71
1978	244	172	72	1984	229	146	83	1990	198	130	68
1979	246	173	73	1985	219	138	80	1991	193	131	62
1980	250	178	72	1986	206	131	75	1992	182	124	59

Source: U.S. Bureau of Labor Statistics, Bulletin 2370; *Employment and Earnings,* monthly; and unpublished data.

No. 1086. Employment on U.S. Flag Merchant Vessels, 1970 to 1992, and Basic Monthly (January) Wage Scale for Able-Bodied Seamen, 1970 to 1993

[Employment in thousands. See also *Historical Statistics, Colonial Times to 1970,* series Q 414-416]

YEAR	Employment [1]	YEAR	Employment [1]	YEAR	East coast wage rate [2]	West coast wage rate [2]	YEAR	East coast wage rate [2]	West coast wage rate [2]
1970	37.6	1986	11.5	1970	$470	$652	1987	$1,419	$2,132
1975	20.5	1987	10.4	1975	612	900	1988	1,419	2,175
1980	19.6	1988	10.7	1980	967	1,414	1989	1,448	2,218
1982	16.7	1989	9.9	1983	1,320	1,862	1990	1,505	2,218
1983	15.3	1990	11.1	1984	1,419	2,029	1991	1,581	2,329
1984	13.7	1991	11.7	1985	1,419	2,069	1992	1,655	2,438
1985	13.1	1992	9.2	1986	1,419	2,132	1993	1,721	2,438

[1] As of June 30, except beginning 1980, as of Sept. 30. Estimates of personnel employed on merchant ships, 1,000 gross tons and over. Excludes vessels on inland waterways, Great Lakes, and those owned by, or operated for, U.S. Army and Navy, and special types such as cable ships, tugs, etc. [2] Basic monthly wage, over and above subsistence (board and room); excludes overtime and fringe pay benefits. West coast incorporates extra pay for Saturdays and Sundays at sea into base wages but east coast does not.

Source: U.S. Maritime Administration, *U.S. Merchant Marine Data Sheet,* monthly; and unpublished data.

No. 1087. Worldwide Tanker Casualties: 1975 to 1992

[Data for 1975 and 1980 covers tankers, ore/oil carriers and bulk/oil vessels of 6,000 deadweight tons and over; beginning 1984, 10,000 deadweight tons and over; excludes liquid gas carriers. Incident is counted in the year it is reported. Based on data from "Lloyd's List" published by Lloyd's of London. "Casualties" include weather damage, strandings, collisions and other contact, fires and explosions, machinery damage, and other mishaps]

ITEM	Unit	1975	1980	1984	1985	1986	1987	1988	1989	1990	1991	1992
Casualties	Number	906	(NA)	(NA)	340	451	408	456	528	541	507	396
Total losses [1]	Number	22	15	14	12	8	5	3	8	10	10	10
Deaths	Number	90	132	68	53	23	12	63	74	119	205	83
Oil spills	Number	45	32	15	9	8	12	13	31	31	26	17
Amount	1,000 tons	188	136	22	80	5	9	178	188	61	439	152

NA Not available. [1] Excludes losses due to hostilities.

Source: Tanker Advisory Center, Inc., New York, NY, "Worldwide Tanker Casualty Returns," quarterly.

No. 1088. Merchant Vessels—World and United States: 1960 to 1991

[Vessels of 100 gross tonnage and above. Excludes sailing ships, nonpropelled craft, and all ships built of wood. See also *Historical Statistics, Colonial Times to 1970,* series Q 473-480]

YEAR	WORLD: COMPLETED		WORLD: OWNED		U.S.: COMPLETED		U.S.: REGISTERED	
	Number	Gross tonnage (1,000)	Number	Gross tonnage (1,000)	Number	Gross tonnage (1,000)	Number	Gross tonnage (1,000)
1960	2,005	8,382	36,311	129,770	49	379	4,059	24,837
1970	2,814	20,980	52,444	227,490	156	375	2,983	18,463
1980	2,412	13,101	73,832	419,911	205	555	5,579	18,464
1985	1,964	18,157	76,395	416,269	66	180	6,447	19,518
1986	1,634	16,845	75,266	404,910	36	223	6,496	19,901
1987	1,528	12,259	75,240	403,498	29	164	6,427	20,178
1988	1,575	10,909	75,680	403,406	60	11	6,442	20,832
1989	1,593	13,236	76,100	410,481	10	4	6,375	20,588
1990	1,672	15,885	78,336	423,627	16	15	6,348	21,328
1991	1,574	16,095	80,030	436,027	17	19	6,222	20,291

Source: Lloyd's Register of Shipping, London, England, *Statistical Tables,* annual; and *Annual Summary of Merchant Ships Completed in the World.*

No. 1089. Merchant Vessels—Ships and Tonnage Lost Worldwide, by Type of Ship: 1980 to 1991

[For merchant vessels of 100 gross tonnage and above. Excludes ships which have been declared constructive losses but have undergone repair during the year. Loss counted in the year the casualty occurred, providing that information was available at time of relevant publication]

TYPE OF SHIP	SHIPS LOST					GROSS TONNAGE LOST (1,000)				
	1980	1985	1989	1990	1991	1980	1985	1989	1990	1991
Total [1]	387	307	211	188	258	1,804	1,651	667	1,126	1,548
Tankers	24	19	13	8	13	707	776	135	138	571
Ore/bulk carriers [2]	21	22	12	15	20	458	405	182	687	574
General cargo	211	155	92	87	116	478	363	250	202	300
Container ships	2	5	2	-	1	6	41	3	-	2
Passenger [3]	9	-	1	-	2	112	-	12	-	14
Fishing	96	66	67	50	69	30	26	29	20	33

- Represents zero.   [1] Includes types not shown separately.   [2] Includes ore/bulk/oil carriers.   [3] Includes passenger cargo ships.
Source: Lloyd's Register of Shipping, London, England, *Casualty Return*, annual.

No. 1090. Merchant Fleets of the World: 1980 to 1991

[Vessels of 1,000 gross tons and over. As of Jan. 1 of the following year. Specified countries have 100 or more ships]

YEAR AND COUNTRY OF REGISTRY, 1991	TOTAL		PASSENGER/ CARGO COMB.		FREIGHTERS		BULK CARRIERS [1]		TANKERS	
	Number	Average age (yr.)	Number	Average age (yr.)	Number	Average age (yr.)	Number	Average age (yr.)	Number	Average age (yr.)
1980, world total. . .	24,867	13	468	24	14,242	14	4,798	10	5,359	12
United States	864	23	65	34	471	23	20	22	308	20
Foreign.	24,003	13	403	22	13,771	13	4,778	10	5,051	11
1985, world total. . .	25,555	14	375	25	13,937	15	5,787	11	5,456	13
United States	737	23	37	38	417	25	25	9	258	19
Foreign.	24,818	14	338	23	13,520	15	5,762	11	5,198	13
1989, world total [2].	22,983	14	320	23	12,195	15	5,335	12	5,133	14
United States	655	22	19	41	371	24	26	12	239	19
Foreign.	22,328	14	301	22	11,824	15	5,309	12	4,894	13
1991, world total. . .	23,943	16	347	24	12,581	17	5,473	14	5,542	15
United States	619	24	10	40	359	25	24	15	226	21
Privately-owned	394	18	3	41	167	17	23	15	201	20
Government-owned. . .	225	34	7	40	192	34	1	15	25	33
Foreign.	23,324	16	337	23	12,222	17	5,449	14	5,316	15
Antigua and Barbuda. .	105	13	-	-	88	13	3	21	14	14
Argentina.	108	22	-	-	56	23	12	16	40	21
Bahamas.	756	13	46	21	302	13	175	12	233	13
Brazil	259	18	2	30	83	26	89	12	85	16
British Colonies.	712	18	6	23	393	20	192	14	121	18
Bulgaria.	117	17	2	23	59	19	37	15	19	12
China: Mainland	1,359	20	18	23	880	21	278	16	183	18
Taiwan.	211	13	-	-	127	14	65	9	19	13
Cyprus	1,210	16	6	38	599	15	469	16	136	16
Denmark (DIS) [3]	269	8	-	-	171	8	15	7	83	9
Egypt	134	19	4	32	105	20	14	8	11	22
France	102	15	5	17	48	14	7	10	42	16
Germany	492	9	9	8	396	9	30	12	57	10
Greece	914	18	26	35	216	21	449	15	223	18
Honduras.	200	27	3	37	152	27	8	24	37	26
India	293	14	3	22	99	16	121	13	70	11
Indonesia.	389	19	8	20	267	20	18	12	96	18
Iran.	126	16	-	-	40	19	49	12	37	18
Italy	493	17	17	17	189	16	61	14	226	18
Japan.	944	9	15	11	382	8	266	11	281	9
Liberia.	1,550	13	20	21	380	12	553	13	597	13
Malaysia.	169	16	-	-	103	19	19	12	47	10
Malta	640	19	5	43	303	19	196	18	136	20
Netherlands	362	10	5	17	281	10	15	9	61	10
Norway (NIS) [3]	770	13	13	11	198	14	236	13	323	13
Panama.	3,040	14	30	31	1,662	15	711	13	637	12
Philippines	536	14	10	30	236	17	250	9	40	24
Poland	230	15	3	12	134	15	88	14	5	18
Romania	282	13	-	-	202	13	63	14	17	9
Singapore	478	13	1	17	238	15	78	9	161	12
South Korea.	445	15	-	-	233	15	150	14	62	16
Spain	267	15	2	17	154	15	43	14	68	16
Sweden.	172	14	4	10	85	14	19	16	64	13
Thailand	154	23	1	30	106	23	4	22	43	21
Turkey.	347	17	3	34	200	15	94	17	50	19
United Kingdom	166	16	15	18	68	16	20	12	63	17
Vanuatu.	109	13	1	39	53	12	46	13	9	12
All others.	4,414	18	54	25	2,934	19	506	14	920	16

- Represents zero.   [1] Includes bulk/oil, ore/oil, and ore/bulk/oil carriers.   [2] Average age for the previous year.
[3] International Shipping Registry which is an open registry under which the ship flies the flag of the specified nation but is exempt from certain taxation and other regulations.
Source: U.S. Maritime Administration, *Merchant Fleets of the World*, summary report, annual; and unpublished data.

Figure 23.1
Cash Receipts From Farm Marketings: 1980 and 1991

1980
1991

Percent

ALL CROPS Corn Vegetables ALL LIVESTOCK Cattle and calves Dairy products Hogs

Source: Chart prepared by U.S. Bureau of the Census. For data, see table 1111.

Figure 23.2
Corn, Soybeans, and Wheat—
U.S. Production and Exports: 1992

Production
Exports

Amount (million metric tons)

Corn Soybeans Wheat

Percent of world

Corn Soybeans Wheat

Source: Chart prepared by U.S. Bureau of the Census. For data, see table 1122.

Agriculture

This section presents statistics on farms and farm population; land use and irrigation; farm cooperatives; farm income, expenditures, and debt; farm output, productivity, and marketings; foreign trade in agricultural products; specific crops; and livestock, poultry, and their products.

The principal sources are the reports issued by the U.S. Bureau of the Census and by the National Agricultural Statistics Service (NASS) and the Economic Research Service (ERS) of the U.S. Department of Agriculture. The Bureau of the Census has taken a census of agriculture every 10 years from 1840 to 1920 and every 5 years from 1925 through 1974. Two 4-year censuses, taken for 1978 and 1982, adjusted the data reference year to coincide with the economic censuses. The 1987 Census of Agriculture is the most recent census for which reports are presently available. The Department of Agriculture publishes annually *Agricultural Statistics,* a general reference book on agricultural production, supplies, consumption, facilities, costs, and returns. The Economic Research Service publishes a series of annual reports, *Economic Indicators of the Farm Sector.* This series comprises five reports: *National Financial Summary, State Financial Summary, Production and Efficiency Statistics, Costs of Production—Livestock and Dairy,* and *Costs of Production—Major Field Crops.* Sources of current data on agricultural exports and imports include *Foreign Agricultural Trade of the United States,* published by the ERS, and the reports of the Bureau of the Census, particularly *U.S. Imports for Consumption and General Imports—HTSUSA Commodity by Country of Origin* (FT 247), *U.S. Exports, Harmonized Schedule B, Commodity by Country* (FT447), and *U.S. Merchandise Trade: Exports, General Imports, and Imports for Consumption* (FT925).

The 45 field offices of the NASS collect data on crops, livestock and products, agricultural prices, farm employment, and other related subjects mainly through sample surveys. Information is obtained on some 75 crops and 50

In Brief

Number of farms, 1992: 2.1 million
Leading States—

Texas	183,000
Missouri	107,000
Iowa	102,000

Farm marketings cash receipts, 1991: $167 billion
Leading commodities—

Cattle, calves	$40 billion
Dairy products	$18 billion
Corn	$14 billion

livestock items as well as scores of items pertaining to agricultural production and marketing. State estimates and supporting information are sent to the Agricultural Statistics Board of NASS which reviews the estimates and issues reports containing State and national data. Among these reports are annual summaries such as *Crop Production, Crop Values, Agricultural Prices,* and *Livestock Production, Disposition and Income.* For more information about concepts and methods underlying USDA's statistical series, see *Major Statistical Series of the U.S. Department of Agriculture* (Agricultural Handbook No. 671), a 12-volume set of publications.

Farms and farmland.—The Bureau of the Census has used varying definitions of a farm. Data from the census of agriculture reflect the definition of farm used for the census year. For the 1974, 1978, 1982, and 1987 Censuses of Agriculture, a farm was defined as any place from which $1,000 or more of agricultural products were produced and sold or normally would have been sold during the census year. Control may have been exercised through ownership or management, or through a lease, rental, or cropping arrangement. In the case of landowners who had one or more tenants or renters, the land operated by each was counted as a separate farm. The effect of the change in definition must be considered when comparing farms in the 1974, 1978, 1982, and

1987 censuses with those in previous censuses.

Unless otherwise stated in the specific tables of this section, the definition of a farm applicable to data originated by the Department of Agriculture is the one used by the Bureau of the Census for the agriculture census immediately preceding the year or years for which the data are shown. Farmland refers to all land under the control of a farm operator, including land not actually under cultivation or not used for pasture or grazing. Land used for pasture or grazing on a per head basis that was neither owned nor leased by a farm operator is not included except for grazing lands controlled by grazing associations leased on a per acre basis. Coverage estimates for 1978, 1982, and 1987 indicate about 3.4, 9.1, and 7.2 percent of all farms, respectively, were not included in census totals. Farms undercounted in these censuses were usually small and accounted for approximately 1 percent of the total value of agricultural products sold and approximately 2 percent of the land in farms. For more explanation about mail list compilation and census coverage, see Appendixes A and C, *1987 Census of Agriculture,* volume 1 reports, and *Coverage Evaluation, Volume 2, Part 2.*

Farm population.—Farm population consists of all persons living on farms in rural areas. Farm population data shown are based on the farm definition adopted for the 1974 Census of Agriculture.

Farm income.—Gross farm income comprises cash receipts from farm marketings of crops and livestock, Federal government payments made directly to farmers for farm-related activities, rental value of farm homes, value of farm products consumed in farm homes, and other farm-related income such as machine hire and custom work. Farm marketings represent quantities of agricultural products sold by farmers multiplied by prices received per unit of production at the local market. Information on prices received for farm products is generally obtained by the NASS Agricultural Statistics Board from surveys of firms (such as grain elevators, packers, and processors) purchasing agricultural commodities directly from producers. In some cases, the price information is obtained directly from the producers.

Crops.—Estimates of crop acreage and production by the NASS are based on current sample survey data obtained from individual producers and objective yield counts, reports of carlot shipments, market records, personal field observations by field statisticians, and reports from other sources. Prices received by farmers are marketing year averages. These averages are based on U.S. monthly prices weighted by monthly marketings during specific periods. U.S. monthly prices are State average prices weighted by marketings during the month. Marketing year average prices do not include allowances for outstanding loans, government purchases, deficiency payments or disaster payments.

All State prices are based on individual State marketing years, while U.S. marketing year averages are based on standard marketing years for each crop. For a listing of the crop marketing years and the participating States in the monthly program, see *Crop Values,* January 1992. Value of production is computed by multiplying State prices by each State's production. The U.S. value of production is the sum of State values for all States. Value of production figures shown in tables 1130-1132, 1134, and 1135 should not be confused with cash receipts from farm marketings which relate to sales during a calendar year, irrespective of the year of production.

Price supports.—Agricultural income is supplemented through two basic Government-support mechanisms available to producers of eligible commodities: (1) *a market price support* (loan rate) through which producers may place any portion of their production in approved storage and receive a loan at a specified rate. The farmer may repay the loan with interest and retain the commodity or, at the end of the loan period, forfeit the commodity as full payment of the loan; (2) *a farm income support* (target price) whose payments vary inversely with the market price of the specified commodity. "Deficiency payments" are made when market prices for a specified period are below the target prices. The payment rate is the difference between the target price and market price, or between the target price and loan rate, whichever is smaller.

Livestock.—Annual inventory numbers of livestock and estimates of livestock, dairy, and poultry production prepared by the Department of Agriculture are based on information from farmers and ranchers obtained by probability survey sampling methods.

Statistical reliability.—For a discussion of statistical collection and estimation, sampling procedures, and measures of statistical reliability pertaining to Census Bureau and Department of Agriculture data, see Appendix III.

Historical statistics.—Tabular headnotes provide cross-references, where applicable, to *Historical Statistics of the United States, Colonial Times to 1970.* See Appendix IV.

Figure 23.3
Consumer Expenditures for Farm Foods: 1970, 1980, and 1991
(In billions of dollars)

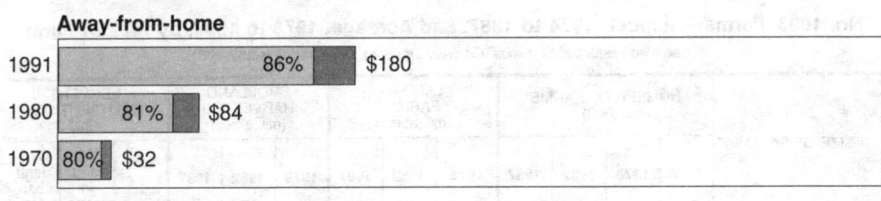

[1]Food purchased from retail food stores for use at home.
Source: Chart prepared by U.S. Bureau of the Census. For data, see table 1116.

No. 1091. Food and Fiber Sector of Domestic Economy—Employment and Value Added: 1980 to 1991

[Employment in millions; value added in billions of dollars, except as indicated]

SECTOR	1980	1983	1984	1985	1986	1987	1988	1989	1990	1991
EMPLOYMENT										
Food and fiber sector, total . .	23.2	22.8	22.1	22.0	22.1	22.1	22.4	23.1	23.1	22.8
Percent of domestic economy [1]	21.7	20.4	19.5	19.0	18.7	18.4	18.4	18.6	18.5	18.2
Farm sector.	2.7	2.8	2.2	2.1	2.0	1.9	2.0	2.0	2.1	2.1
Nonfarm sector	20.5	20.0	19.9	19.9	20.0	20.2	20.4	21.1	21.0	20.8
Food processing	1.7	1.6	1.6	1.6	1.6	1.5	1.5	1.5	1.5	1.5
Manufacturing.	3.8	3.4	3.3	3.3	3.2	3.0	3.0	3.2	3.0	3.0
Transportation, trade, and retailing .	7.1	7.1	7.2	7.3	7.4	7.4	7.5	7.8	7.8	7.7
Eating establishments.	4.5	4.6	4.6	4.6	4.7	5.0	5.1	5.2	5.3	5.3
Other.	3.4	3.2	3.1	3.2	3.2	3.2	3.2	3.4	3.4	3.4
VALUE ADDED [2]										
Food and fiber sector, total . . .	532.9	630.6	658.3	687.4	716.0	747.8	787.1	847.2	887.5	910.0
Percent of domestic economy .	19.7	18.5	17.4	17.0	16.8	16.5	16.1	16.1	16.1	16.0
Farm sector.	48.4	46.6	48.3	52.4	48.8	51.6	52.6	59.9	64.7	61.7
Nonfarm sector	484.5	584.0	610.0	635.0	667.3	696.2	734.5	787.4	822.7	848.2
Food processing	61.4	76.6	81.1	84.5	91.5	91.8	97.1	101.9	107.2	110.2
Manufacturing.	93.7	105.6	105.4	105.1	109.6	109.7	115.4	125.5	129.0	133.5
Transportation, trade, and retailing .	161.3	194.2	203.4	211.2	218.1	228.0	240.0	256.9	268.7	275.3
Eating establishments.	48.0	60.6	64.3	66.8	70.6	77.3	83.1	87.1	91.8	95.7
Other.	120.0	147.0	155.8	167.4	177.4	189.3	198.8	215.9	226.1	233.6

[1] Based on civilian labor force. [2] Value added equals profits, rent, interest, wages, indirect business taxes, and depreciation.

Source: U.S. Dept. of Agriculture, Economic Research Service, unpublished data.

No. 1092. Farm Population and Employment: 1980 to 1992

[In thousands, except percent. For definition of farm population, see text, section 23. See also *Historical Statistics, Colonial Times to 1970*, series C 76 and K 1-2 and K 174-176]

ITEM	1980	1982	1983	1984	1985	1986	1987	1988	1989	1990	1991	1992
Farm population (1974 definition) [1] . . .	6,051	5,628	5,787	5,754	5,355	5,226	4,986	4,951	4,801	4,591	4,632	(NA)
Percent of resident population	2.8	2.5	2.5	2.5	2.3	2.2	2.1	2.1	2.0	1.9	1.9	(NA)
Farm employment, total [2]	3,705	4,043	3,749	3,405	3,115	2,912	2,897	2,954	2,863	2,891	2,877	2,810
Self-employed and unpaid workers [3].	2,402	2,494	2,271	2,175	2,017	1,873	1,846	1,917	1,935	1,999	1,967	1,944
Hired workers [4].	1,303	1,549	1,478	1,230	1,098	1,039	1,051	1,037	928	892	910	866

NA Not available. [1] April-centered five-quarter averages for 1980 to 1983; annual average beginning 1984. [2] 1980 and 1989-92, average from Jan., April, July and Oct. surveys; 1982-83 based on July survey; 1984, average from July and Oct. surveys; 1985-88 average from April, July and Oct. surveys. [3] Includes farm operators doing 1 or more hours of farm work and unpaid workers doing 15 or more hours of farm work during survey week. [4] Includes all persons doing 1 or more hours of farm work for pay during survey week. Members of operators' families doing any farm work for cash wages are counted as hired workers.
Source: Population—U.S. Dept. of Agriculture, Economic Research Service and U.S. Bureau of the Census. Published in U.S. Bureau of the Census, *Current Population Reports*, P20-457, and earlier P20 and P27 reports. Farm employment—U.S. Dept. of Agriculture, National Agricultural Statistics Service, *Farm Labor*, periodic.

No. 1093. Farms—Number, 1974 to 1987, and Acreage, 1978 to 1987, by Size of Farm

[See also *Historical Statistics, Colonial Times to 1970*, series K 162-173]

SIZE OF FARM	NUMBER OF FARMS (1,000)				LAND IN FARMS (mil. acres)			CROPLAND HARVESTED (mil. acres)			PERCENT DISTRIBUTION, 1987		
	1974	1978	1982	1987	1978	1982	1987	1978	1982	1987	Number of farms	All land in farms	Cropland harvested
Total	2,314	2,258	2,241	2,088	1,014.8	986.8	964.5	317.1	326.3	282.2	100.0	100.0	100.0
Under 10 acres.	128	151	188	183	0.6	0.7	0.7	0.2	0.3	0.2	8.8	0.1	0.1
10 to 49 acres	380	392	449	412	10.9	12.1	11.1	4.5	4.5	3.9	19.8	1.2	1.4
50 to 99 acres	385	356	344	311	25.9	24.8	22.5	10.2	9.5	7.9	14.9	2.3	2.8
100 to 179 acres.	443	403	368	334	55.0	49.9	45.3	23.3	21.2	17.1	16.0	4.7	6.1
180 to 259 acres.	253	234	211	192	50.6	45.7	41.5	23.7	21.7	17.2	9.2	4.3	6.1
260 to 499 acres.	363	348	315	286	124.6	113.0	103.0	64.5	60.5	47.3	13.7	10.7	16.8
500 to 999 acres.	207	213	204	200	146.7	140.5	138.5	75.2	77.6	67.4	9.6	14.4	23.9
1,000 to 1,999 acres . .	93	98	97	102	133.0	132.4	138.8	58.2	64.5	61.1	4.9	14.4	21.7
2,000 acres and over. .	62	63	65	67	467.4	467.5	463.2	57.3	66.6	60.2	3.2	48.0	21.3

Source: U.S. Bureau of the Census, *Census of Agriculture: 1974*, vol. 1; and *1987*, vol. 1.

No. 1094. Farms—Number and Acreage, by Tenure of Operator: 1974 to 1987

[*Full owners* own all the land they operate. *Part owners* own a part, and rent from others the rest of the land they operate. See also *Historical Statistics, Colonial Times to 1970*, series K 109-113 and 142-146]

ITEM AND YEAR	Unit	Total	Full owner	Part owner	Tenant	PERCENT DISTRIBUTION Total	PERCENT DISTRIBUTION Full owner	PERCENT DISTRIBUTION Part owner	PERCENT DISTRIBUTION Tenant
Number of farms:									
1974........................	1,000....	2,314	1,424	628	262	100.0	61.5	27.2	11.3
1978........................	1,000....	2,258	1,298	681	279	100.0	57.5	30.1	12.4
1982........................	1,000....	2,241	1,326	656	259	100.0	59.2	29.3	11.5
1987........................	1,000....	2,088	1,239	609	240	100.0	59.3	29.2	11.5
Under 50 acres	1,000....	596	483	59	53	100.0	81.1	9.9	9.0
50 to 179 acres	1,000....	645	449	130	66	100.0	69.6	20.1	10.3
180 to 499 acres	1,000....	478	217	195	67	100.0	45.3	40.8	13.9
500 to 999 acres	1,000....	200	53	117	31	100.0	26.3	58.3	15.4
1,000 acres or more	1,000....	169	37	108	23	100.0	22.1	64.2	13.7
Land in farms:									
1974........................	Mil. acres.	1,017	359	535	122	100.0	35.4	52.6	12.0
1978........................	Mil. acres.	1,015	332	561	122	100.0	32.7	55.3	12.0
1982........................	Mil. acres.	987	342	531	114	100.0	34.7	53.8	11.6
1987........................	Mil. acres.	964	318	520	127	100.0	32.9	53.9	13.2

No. 1095. Farm Operators—Tenure and Characteristics: 1982 and 1987

[In thousands, except as indicated. See also *Historical Statistics, Colonial Times to 1970*, series K 82-113]

CHARACTERISTIC	ALL FARMS 1982	ALL FARMS 1987	FARMS WITH SALES OF $10,000 AND OVER 1982	FARMS WITH SALES OF $10,000 AND OVER 1987	CHARACTERISTIC	ALL FARMS 1982	ALL FARMS 1987	FARMS WITH SALES OF $10,000 AND OVER 1982	FARMS WITH SALES OF $10,000 AND OVER 1987
Total operators	**2,241**	**2,088**	**1,143**	**1,060**	Tenant...............	259	240	170	161
White	2,187	2,043	1,127	1,046					
Black.................	33	23	7	4	**Principal occupation:**				
American Indian, Eskimos, and					Farming	1,235	1,138	901	811
Aleuts	7	7	2	2	Other	1,006	950	242	248
Asian or Pacific Islander	8	8	5	5					
Other	6	7	2	2	**Place of residence:** [2]				
					On farm operated......	1,581	1,488	833	776
Operators of Hispanic origin [1].	16	17	6	6	Not on farm operated	429	443	202	215
Female	122	132	37	42	**Years on present farm:** [2]				
					2 years or less........	127	114	53	49
Under 25 years old	62	36	39	21	3 to 4 years..........	193	135	83	56
25 to 34 years old	294	243	173	147	5 to 9 years...........	360	304	167	138
35 to 44 years old	443	411	223	212	10 years or more......	1,098	1,163	638	653
45 to 54 years old	505	455	264	228					
55 to 64 years old	536	496	288	263	**Days worked off farm:** [2]				
65 years old and over	400	447	156	188	None	862	844	591	561
Average age (years)......	50.5	52.0	49.1	50.6	Less than 100 days	224	200	141	124
					100 to 199 days........	189	178	77	80
Full owner	1,326	1,239	482	445	200 days or more......	775	737	213	219
Part owner	656	609	491	454					

[1] Operators of Hispanic origin may be of any race.   [2] Excludes not reported.

No. 1096. Farms—Number, Acreage, and Value, by Type of Organization: 1982 and 1987

[Data for 1982 exclude abnormal farms (institutional farms, experimental and research farms, Indian reservations, etc.)]

ITEM	Unit	Total [1]	Individual or family	Partnership	Corporation	PERCENT DISTRIBUTION Total [1]	PERCENT DISTRIBUTION Individual or family	PERCENT DISTRIBUTION Partnership	PERCENT DISTRIBUTION Corporation
ALL FARMS									
Number of farms: 1982..........	1,000 ...	2,239	1,946	223	60	100.0	86.9	10.0	2.7
1987..........	1,000 ...	2,088	1,809	200	67	100.0	86.7	9.6	3.2
Land in farms: 1982..........	Mil. acres.	932	642	152	127	100.0	68.9	16.3	13.6
1987..........	Mil. acres.	964	628	153	119	100.0	65.1	15.9	12.4
Value of land and buildings: [2] 1982..	Bil. dol. ..	763	547	119	90	100.0	71.7	15.6	11.8
1987..	Bil. dol. ..	604	424	95	69	100.0	70.1	15.7	11.4
Value of farm products sold: 1982 ..	Bil. dol. ..	132	78	22	31	100.0	59.2	16.4	23.9
1987 ..	Bil. dol. ..	136	77	23	35	100.0	56.3	17.1	25.6
FARMS WITH SALES OF $10,000 AND OVER									
Number of farms: 1982..........	1,000 ...	1,143	934	152	52	100.0	81.7	13.3	4.6
1987..........	1,000 ...	1,060	861	136	56	100.0	81.3	12.8	5.3
Land in farms: 1982..........	Mil. acres.	811	536	141	124	100.0	66.1	17.4	15.3
1987..........	Mil. acres.	829	525	143	116	100.0	63.3	17.3	14.0

[1] Includes other types, not shown separately.   [2] Based on a sample of farms.

Source of tables 1094-1096: U.S. Bureau of the Census, *Census of Agriculture: 1974*, vol. II; *1982*, vol. 1; and *1987*, vol. 1.

No. 1097. Farms—Number, Acreage, and Value, by State: 1987

[See also *Historical Statistics, Colonial Times to 1970*, series K 17-18]

REGION, DIVISION, AND STATE	ALL FARMS			FARMS WITH SALES OF $10,000 OR MORE			REGION, DIVISION, AND STATE	ALL FARMS			FARMS WITH SALES OF $10,000 OR MORE		
	Number of farms (1,000)	Land in farms (mil. acres)	Average size of farm (acres)	Number of farms (1,000)	Land in farms (mil. acres)	Average size of farm (acres)		Number of farms (1,000)	Land in farms (mil. acres)	Average size of farm (acres)	Number of farms (1,000)	Land in farms (mil. acres)	Average size of farm (acres)
U.S.	2,088	964.5	462	1,060	829.0	782	VA	45	8.7	194	16	5.9	377
Northeast ..	123	21.4	174	61	16.0	261	WV	17	3.4	196	3	1.4	431
N.E	25	4.2	169	11	2.8	260	NC	59	9.4	159	26	7.1	276
ME	6	1.3	214	3	0.9	332	SC	20	4.8	232	7	3.3	491
NH	2	0.4	169	1	0.2	283	GA	44	10.7	247	18	7.9	439
VT	6	1.4	240	3	1.1	325	FL	37	11.2	306	15	9.4	638
MA	6	0.6	99	2	0.4	153	E.S.C	250	45.6	183	82	30.4	372
RI	1	0.1	84	(Z)	(Z)	116	KY	92	14.0	152	34	9.4	276
CT	4	0.4	111	1	0.3	179	TN	80	11.7	147	22	7.2	329
M.A	98	17.2	175	50	13.1	262	AL	43	9.1	211	14	5.9	424
NY	38	8.4	223	21	6.7	327	MS	34	10.7	315	12	7.9	662
NJ	9	0.9	99	3	0.7	191	W.S.C ...	335	184.4	551	129	153.3	1,184
PA	51	7.9	153	26	5.7	221	AR	48	14.4	298	21	11.2	522
Midwest ...	862	350.5	407	556	314.5	565	LA	27	8.0	293	11	6.4	607
E.N.C	365	86.6	237	219	76.3	348	OK	70	31.5	449	29	25.1	878
OH	79	15.0	189	40	12.1	305	TX	189	130.5	691	69	110.5	1,606
IN	70	16.2	229	40	14.4	355	West ...	278	311.3	1,118	139	277.5	1,999
IL	89	28.5	321	63	27.0	431	Mt	124	244.1	1,965	67	218.3	3,271
MI	51	10.3	202	24	8.2	340	MT	25	60.2	2,451	16	54.4	3,427
WI	75	16.6	221	52	14.5	280	ID	24	13.9	577	14	12.0	881
W.N.C	497	263.8	531	337	238.3	707	WY	9	33.6	3,650	5	28.4	5,183
MN	85	26.6	312	58	23.8	407	CO	27	34.0	1,248	15	30.6	2,030
IA	105	31.6	301	83	30.2	365	NM	14	46.0	3,230	6	41.3	7,319
MO	106	29.2	275	50	22.7	457	AZ	8	36.3	4,732	4	33.7	9,411
ND	35	40.3	1,143	28	37.9	1,339	UT	14	10.0	710	6	8.6	1,452
SD	36	44.2	1,214	28	37.9	1,339	NV	3	10.0	3,300	1	9.3	6,288
NE	60	45.3	749	47	43.0	918	Pac	154	67.3	466	72	59.2	821
KS	69	46.6	680	43	42.8	1,002	WA	34	16.1	480	15	13.8	901
South	824	281.2	341	304	221.0	727	OR	32	17.8	556	12	15.4	1,319
S.A	240	51.2	214	93	37.4	403	CA	83	30.6	368	43	27.7	647
DE	3	0.6	205	2	0.5	291	AK	1	1.0	1,789	(Z)	0.6	3,411
MD	15	2.4	162	7	1.9	278	HI	5	1.7	353	2	1.6	798

Z Less than 500 farms or 50,000 acres.

Source: U.S. Bureau of the Census, *Census of Agriculture: 1987*, vol. 1.

No. 1098. Irrigated Farms and Acreage, by State: 1982 and 1987

[See also *Historical Statistics, Colonial Times to 1970*, series J 85-91]

STATE	IRRIGATED FARMS				LAND IN IRRIGATED FARMS				IRRIGATED LAND			
	Number (1,000)		Percent of all farms		Acreage (1,000)		Percent of all land in farms		Acreage (1,000)		Percent of all land in farms	
	1982	1987	1982	1987	1982	1987	1982	1987	1982	1987	1982	1987
U.S. [1]	278.3	291.6	12.4	13.9	246,603	241,069	24.9	24.9	49,002	46,386	5.0	4.8
Arizona.	4.4	4.2	60.4	55.3	18,871	17,167	49.9	47.3	1,098	914	2.9	2.5
California	58.4	58.9	70.8	70.7	18,402	17,567	57.2	57.4	8,461	7,596	26.3	24.8
Colorado.	15.2	14.9	56.1	54.6	17,351	16,729	51.7	49.1	3,201	3,014	9.5	8.9
Florida	10.6	12.0	29.0	32.7	5,529	4,670	43.1	41.7	1,623	1,623	12.4	14.5
Idaho	17.4	16.6	70.2	68.8	9,168	9,053	65.8	64.9	3,450	3,219	24.8	23.1
Kansas.	7.3	7.4	9.8	10.7	10,345	10,654	21.9	22.8	2,675	2,463	5.7	5.3
Louisiana	3.7	3.9	11.6	14.3	2,273	2,337	25.4	29.1	694	647	7.8	8.1
Montana	9.2	9.5	39.1	38.7	24,171	23,259	39.9	38.6	2,023	1,997	3.3	3.3
Nebraska	22.2	22.6	36.8	37.3	22,679	22,499	50.4	49.6	6,039	5,682	13.4	12.5
Nevada	2.2	2.2	79.2	73.3	7,881	7,806	78.9	78.1	830	779	8.3	7.8
New Mexico . . .	6.2	7.0	45.9	49.2	14,755	12,385	31.3	26.9	807	718	1.7	1.6
North Dakota. . .	0.8	0.8	2.2	2.2	1,416	1,497	3.5	3.7	163	168	0.4	0.4
Oklahoma	3.1	3.0	4.2	4.3	2,926	2,906	9.0	9.2	492	478	1.5	1.5
Oregon.	15.3	14.4	44.9	45.0	11,382	11,340	64.1	63.6	1,808	1,648	10.2	9.3
South Dakota . .	1.8	1.9	4.8	5.1	4,198	3,791	9.5	8.5	376	362	0.9	0.8
Texas.	19.8	19.8	10.6	10.4	22,161	20,270	16.8	15.5	5,575	4,271	4.2	3.3
Utah	11.2	11.1	79.9	79.2	7,598	7,594	77.7	76.0	1,082	1,161	11.1	11.6
Washington. . . .	16.3	15.4	45.0	45.9	6,003	5,468	36.4	33.9	1,638	1,519	9.9	9.4
Wyoming	5.3	5.2	59.6	56.7	18,132	18,207	54.1	54.1	1,565	1,518	4.7	4.5

[1] Includes other States not shown separately.

Source: U.S. Bureau of the Census, *1987 Census of Agriculture*, vol. 1.

No. 1099. Farms—Number and Acreage: 1975 to 1992

[Based on 1974 census definition; for definition of farms and farmland, see text, section 23. Data for census years (indicated by italics) have been adjusted for underenumeration and are used as reference points along with data from acreage and livestock surveys in estimating data for other years. Minus sign (-) indicates decrease. See also *Historical Statistics, Colonial Times to 1970*, series K 4-7]

YEAR	FARMS Number (1,000)	FARMS Annual change [1] (1,000)	LAND IN FARMS Total (mil. acres)	LAND IN FARMS Average per farm (acres)	YEAR	FARMS Number (1,000)	FARMS Annual change [1] (1,000)	LAND IN FARMS Total (mil. acres)	LAND IN FARMS Average per farm (acres)
1975.....	2,521	(X)	1,059	420	1984......	2,334	-45	1,018	436
1976.....	2,497	-24	1,054	422	1985......	2,293	-41	1,012	441
1977.....	2,456	-41	1,048	427	1986......	2,250	-43	1,005	447
1978.....	2,436	-20	1,045	429	1987......	2,213	-37	999	451
1979.....	2,437	1	1,042	428	1988......	2,197	-16	995	453
1980.....	2,440	3	1,039	426	1989......	2,171	-26	991	457
1981.....	2,440	-	1,034	424	1990......	2,140	-31	987	461
1982.....	2,407	-33	1,028	427	1991......	2,105	-35	983	467
1983.....	2,379	-28	1,023	430	1992, prel...	2,096	-9	980	468

- Represents zero.   X Not applicable.   [1] Annual change from preceding year shown.

Source: U.S. Dept. of Agriculture, National Agricultural Statistics Service, *Farm Numbers, 1975-80; Farms and Land in Farms, Final Estimates by States, 1979-1987*; and *Farm Numbers and Land In Farms*, July release.

No. 1100. Farms—Number and Acreage, by State: 1990 and 1992

[Based on 1974 census definition of farms and farmland; see text, section 23. See also *Historical Statistics, Colonial Times to 1970*, series K 4-7]

STATE	FARMS (1,000) 1990	FARMS (1,000) 1992, prel.	ACREAGE (mil.) 1990	ACREAGE (mil.) 1992, prel.	ACREAGE PER FARM 1990	ACREAGE PER FARM 1992, prel.	STATE	FARMS (1,000) 1990	FARMS (1,000) 1992, prel.	ACREAGE (mil.) 1990	ACREAGE (mil.) 1992, prel.	ACREAGE PER FARM 1990	ACREAGE PER FARM 1992, prel.
U.S........	2,140	2,096	987	980	461	468	Missouri	108	107	30	30	281	283
							Montana	25	25	61	60	2,449	2,439
Alabama....	47	46	10	10	215	213	Nebraska	57	56	47	47	826	841
Alaska	1	1	1	1	1,724	1,778	Nevada......	3	3	9	9	3,560	3,560
Arizona......	8	8	36	36	4,615	4,500	New Hampshire	3	3	(Z)	(Z)	169	162
Arkansas.....	47	46	16	16	330	337	New Jersey...	8	9	1	1	107	104
California....	85	81	31	30	362	368	New Mexico...	14	14	45	44	3,296	3,274
Colorado.....	27	26	33	33	1,249	1,286	New York	39	38	8	8	218	216
Connecticut..	4	4	(Z)	(Z)	108	105	North Carolina .	62	60	10	10	156	158
Delaware.....	3	3	1	1	197	207	North Dakota..	34	33	41	40	1,191	1,224
Florida......	41	39	11	11	266	269	Ohio........	84	78	16	15	187	197
Georgia......	48	46	13	12	260	263	Oklahoma	70	71	33	34	471	479
Hawaii......	5	5	2	2	372	380	Oregon......	37	38	18	18	488	467
Idaho	22	21	14	14	628	643	Pennsylvania ..	53	52	8	8	153	154
Illinois......	83	81	29	29	343	352	Rhode Island..	1	1	(Z)	(Z)	95	90
Indiana......	68	65	16	16	240	246	South Carolina .	25	25	5	5	208	212
Iowa........	104	102	34	33	322	327	South Dakota..	35	35	44	44	1,266	1,263
Kansas.....	69	67	48	48	694	713	Tennessee ...	89	88	12	13	139	143
Kentucky....	93	91	14	14	152	155	Texas.......	186	183	132	130	710	710
Louisiana	32	30	9	9	278	290	Utah........	13	13	11	11	856	856
Maine......	7	7	1	1	201	200	Vermont	7	7	2	2	216	219
Maryland....	15	16	2	2	148	141	Virginia	46	44	9	9	193	198
Massachusetts.	7	7	1	1	99	99	Washington ...	37	38	16	16	432	421
Michigan.....	54	54	11	11	200	200	West Virginia ..	21	20	4	4	180	185
Minnesota....	89	88	30	30	337	339	Wisconsin ...	80	79	18	17	220	219
Mississippi....	40	38	13	13	325	337	Wyoming.....	9	9	35	35	3,910	3,783

Z Less than 500,000 acres.

Source: U.S. Dept. of Agriculture, National Agricultural Statistics Service, *Farm Numbers and Land in Farms* (July release).

No. 1101. Farm Real Estate—Summary: 1980 to 1992

[1980 and 1986-89,, value data as of **Feb. 1**; 1983-85, as of **April 1**; 1990-92, as of **January 1**. Excludes Alaska and Hawaii. Total value of land and buildings is estimated by multiplying the number of acres of farmland by the average value per acre of land and buildings. Per acre values are based on data from the census of agriculture. For intercensal years, estimates are based on surveys conducted by the U.S. Dept. of Agriculture]

ITEM	Unit	1980	1983	1984	1985	1986	1987	1988	1989	1990	1991	1992
Total value	Bil. dol	763.3	803.9	812.9	719.4	641.1	597.1	626.9	653.5	658.2	667.5	670.8
Average value per acre..	Dollars......	737	788	801	713	640	599	632	661	668	681	685
Average value, operating unit...	$1,000 ..	313.5	338.7	349.1	314.5	285.6	270.5	286.0	301.8	308.2	318.0	319.5

Source: U.S. Dept. of Agriculture, Economic Research Service, 1980-84, *Farm Real Estate Market Developments*, annual; thereafter, *Agricultural Resources, Agricultural Land Values and Markets, Situation and Outlook Report*, annual.

No. 1102. Farm Real Estate—Value of Land and Buildings, by State: 1985 to 1992

[See headnote, table 1101. See also *Historical Statistics, Colonial Times to 1970*, series K 16]

STATE	VALUE OF LAND AND BUILDINGS (mil. dol.)			AVERAGE VALUE OF LAND AND BUILDINGS, PER ACRE			STATE	VALUE OF LAND AND BUILDINGS (mil. dol.)			AVERAGE VALUE OF LAND AND BUILDINGS, PER ACRE		
	1985	1990	1992	1985	1990	1992		1985	1990	1992	1985	1990	1992
U.S.. .	719,398	658,187	670,798	$713	$668	$685	MT	14,800	14,399	15,202	243	238	252
							NE	22,911	25,905	26,790	485	550	569
AL	8,929	8,474	8,153	797	839	832	NV	2,171	1,727	2,057	244	194	231
AZ	11,062	9,468	10,879	295	263	302	NH	777	1,096	982	1,439	2,237	2,045
AR	14,425	11,625	11,219	907	750	724	NJ	2,833	4,032	4,201	2,951	4,634	4,774
CA	59,829	52,483	53,469	1,841	1,704	1,765	NM	8,324	8,722	10,582	185	196	239
CO	15,042	11,850	12,043	437	358	367	NY	7,464	8,182	8,723	820	974	1,051
CT	1,442	1,855	1,695	3,005	4,417	4,036	NC	14,373	12,251	12,136	1,331	1,263	1,264
DE	1,037	1,288	1,212	1,596	2,259	2,126	ND	15,253	13,770	14,477	373	340	358
FL	19,346	22,727	21,648	1,599	2,085	2,062	OH	19,203	18,903	19,616	1,215	1,204	1,249
GA	11,968	12,650	10,917	886	1,012	902	OK	19,691	16,401	16,296	597	497	494
ID.	10,711	9,056	9,272	739	661	687	OR	11,077	10,164	10,737	615	571	603
IL.	39,647	39,587	42,760	1,381	1,389	1,500	PA	12,416	14,637	14,744	1,427	1,807	1,820
IN.	22,049	20,277	20,843	1,344	1,244	1,303	RI.	218	352	303	2,990	5,028	4,595
IA.	36,653	36,917	39,473	1,091	1,102	1,178	SC	4,939	4,727	4,747	898	909	931
KS	23,443	22,130	23,179	448	462	484	SD	12,856	14,543	16,113	289	328	365
KY	13,849	13,832	13,998	955	981	993	TN	12,650	12,350	12,219	944	996	985
LA	13,791	8,144	7,961	1,407	915	905	TX	94,025	65,340	61,066	694	495	466
ME	1,153	1,478	1,322	774	1,019	931	UT	5,947	4,396	4,801	513	389	425
MD	5,711	5,445	5,073	2,197	2,420	2,255	VT	1,515	1,797	1,642	947	1,190	1,087
MA	1,616	2,559	2,338	2,377	3,763	3,439	VA	10,566	13,492	11,998	1,112	1,516	1,363
MI	12,517	10,854	11,937	1,108	1,005	1,105	WA	15,187	12,464	12,672	943	779	792
MN	27,311	24,150	26,203	898	805	873	WV	2,186	2,268	2,659	607	613	719
MS	12,054	9,464	9,441	855	728	738	WI	16,905	14,133	15,221	944	803	870
MO	21,234	20,642	20,958	689	679	689	WY	6,287	5,185	4,819	181	149	138

Source: U.S. Dept. of Agriculture, Economic Research Service, *Agricultural Resources, Agricultural Land Values and Markets, Situation and Outlook Report*, annual.

No. 1103. Foreign Ownership of U.S. Agricultural Land: 1991

[**In thousands of acres, except percent.** Covers "foreign persons" reporting under the Agricultural Foreign Investment Disclosure Act of 1978. As defined in the Act, a "foreign person" is any person who is not a U.S. citizen and who is not a permanent resident alien of the U.S. Foreign governments and entities are also "foreign persons." Also, each successive link in a chain of U.S. entities containing foreign interests is considered a "foreign person." An entity is deemed a "foreign person" if it is 10 percent or more foreign owned by a single foreign person or foreign persons acting in concert, or 50 percent foreign owned by a group of foreign persons not acting in concert, none of whom individually holds a 10 percent or greater interest in the entity. Therefore, acreage figures reported do not necessarily mean that they are wholly owned by foreign investors. Covers reports received and accepted as of December 31, 1991]

CHARACTERISTIC	ACREAGE OWNED [1]		ACREAGE ACQUIRED [2]		CHARACTERISTIC	ACREAGE OWNED [1]		ACREAGE ACQUIRED [2]	
	Total	Per- cent	Total	Per- cent		Total	Per- cent	Total	Per- cent
Total [3]	**14,809**	**100.0**	**227**	**100.0**	Country of foreign owner:				
Type of owner:					Canada	1,971	13.3	6	2.5
Corporation	10,762	72.7	166	73.0	Germany	757	5.1	19	8.2
Partnership	2,859	19.3	41	17.8	Netherlands Antilles . . .	367	2.5	(Z)	(Z)
Individual	942	6.4	10	4.6	Switzerland	300	2.0	1	0.5
Other	245	1.7	11	4.6	United Kingdom	1,803	12.2	14	6.0
Size:					Through U.S. interest: [4]				
Less than 100 acres. . .	106	0.7	3	1.1	Canada	1,691	11.4	6	2.5
100-299 acres	296	2.0	8	3.5	France	1,020	6.9	29	12.6
300-999 acres	892	6.0	20	8.7	Germany	445	3.0	1	0.3
1,000 acres or more . . .	13,515	91.3	197	86.7	Japan	268	1.8	65	28.4
Land use:					Luxembourg	234	1.6	(Z)	(Z)
Cropland	2,495	16.9	35	15.3	Mexico	323	2.2	1	0.5
Pasture	3,904	26.4	31	13.8	Netherlands	316	2.1	2	0.8
Forest	7,316	49.4	146	64.3	Switzerland	333	2.3	46	20.0
Other agriculture	673	4.5	6	2.7	United Kingdom	1,327	9.0	6	2.8
Other nonagriculture . . .	420	2.8	9	4.0					

Z Less than 500 acres or .05 percent. [1] Landholdings by foreign interests as of Dec. 31. [2] Acquisitions by foreign interests from Jan. 1-Dec. 31. [3] Includes other countries not shown separately. [4] Reports filed by U.S. corporations with foreign shareholders.

Source: U.S. Dept. of Agriculture, Economic Research Service, *Foreign Ownership of U.S. Agricultural Land Through December 31, 1991*, (Economic Research Service Staff Report AGES 9211), 1992.

No. 1104. Balance Sheet of the Farming Sector in Current and Constant (1987) Dollars: 1980 to 1991

[In billions of dollars, except as indicated. As of December 31. Includes farm operator households. See *Historical Statistics, Colonial Times to 1970*, series K 204-219, for data before revisions]

ITEM	1980	1982	1983	1984	1985	1986	1987	1988	1989	1990	1991
CURRENT DOLLARS											
Assets	1,089.0	1,056.2	1,063.6	975.7	892.8	847.7	911.3	951.5	985.8	1,003.6	1,004.1
Physical assets:											
Real estate	850.1	819.1	829.3	735.0	657.0	613.0	658.6	682.2	703.9	711.4	705.6
Nonreal estate . . . . .₁ . . .	199.6	194.4	189.6	193.0	186.5	181.0	196.1	212.1	223.6	231.5	232.9
Livestock and poultry [1] . . .	60.6	53.0	49.5	49.5	46.3	47.8	58.0	62.2	66.2	70.9	68.4
Machinery, motor vehicles. .	86.9	92.6	92.1	91.1	88.3	86.1	84.5	86.1	89.2	88.6	88.0
Crops stored	32.7	25.8	23.6	26.1	22.9	16.3	17.5	23.3	23.4	22.8	23.6
Household furnishings, equipment.	19.4	23.0	24.4	24.3	27.8	28.7	32.9	37.0	42.2	46.4	50.4
Purchased inputs	(NA)	(NA)	(NA)	2.0	1.2	2.1	3.2	3.5	2.6	2.8	2.5
Financial assets.	39.3	42.8	44.6	47.7	49.3	53.8	56.7	57.2	58.3	60.8	65.6
Investment in cooperatives. . .	19.3	21.9	22.8	24.3	24.3	24.4	25.3	25.1	26.3	27.5	28.4
Other financial assets	20.0	20.9	21.8	23.4	25.0	29.4	31.4	32.1	32.0	33.3	37.2
Claims	1,089.0	1,056.2	1,063.6	975.7	892.8	847.7	911.3	951.5	985.8	1,003.6	1,004.1
Debt	178.7	203.1	206.5	204.3	187.9	166.6	153.7	148.5	146.0	145.1	147.0
Real estate debt.	97.5	111.3	113.7	112.3	105.7	95.9	87.7	83.0	80.5	78.4	79.1
Nonreal estate debt	81.2	91.8	92.7	92.0	82.2	70.8	66.0	65.6	65.5	66.7	67.8
Equity	910.3	853.1	857.1	771.4	704.9	681.0	757.6	802.9	839.8	858.5	857.1
Farm debt/asset ratio (percent)	16.4	19.2	19.4	20.9	21.0	19.7	16.9	15.6	14.8	14.5	14.6
CONSTANT (1987) DOLLARS [2]											
Assets	1,518.8	1,260.4	1,219.7	1,072.2	945.8	874.8	911.3	915.8	908.6	886.6	852.3
Debt	249.3	242.4	236.8	224.5	199.0	171.9	153.7	142.9	134.6	128.2	124.8
Equity	1,269.6	1,018.0	982.9	847.7	746.7	702.8	757.6	772.8	774.0	758.4	727.6

NA Not available. [1] Excludes horses and mules. [2] Constant dollar figures are based on gross domestic product implicit price deflators for year.

Source: U.S. Dept. of Agriculture, Economic Research Service, *Economic Indicators of the Farm Sector: National Financial Summary, 1991.*

No. 1105. Percent Distribution of Farms and Farm Debt, by Debt/Asset Ratio: 1987 to 1991

[Value of sales for calendar year shown; balance sheet data as of January 1 of the following year. A farm is a crop or livestock farm if 50 percent or more of its commodity receipts derive from the sale of crop or animal products, respectively. A crop or livestock farm is further categorized as a particular type if 50 percent of its crop or, if applicable, livestock receipts come from a specific commodity area. Based on Farm Costs and Returns Survey conducted in February-March of following year]

VALUE OF SALES AND TYPE OF FARM	FARMS Total	FARMS Less than 11 percent	FARMS 11 to 40 percent	FARMS 41 to 70 percent	FARMS Over 70 percent	FARM DEBT Total	FARM DEBT Less than 11 percent	FARM DEBT 11 to 40 percent	FARM DEBT 41 to 70 percent	FARM DEBT Over 70 percent
1987	100	58	24	11	7	100	6	34	30	29
1988	100	62	24	9	5	100	7	40	31	21
1989	100	62	24	9	4	100	8	44	31	17
1990	100	61	26	10	4	100	7	47	33	14
1991, total.	100	66	24	7	2	100	7	50	32	11
Less than $10,000	100	77	17	4	2	100	9	56	26	9
$10,000 to $19,999	100	75	18	5	1	100	8	56	28	8
$20,000 to $39,999	100	70	23	5	2	100	12	52	18	18
$40,000 to $99,999	100	52	34	10	4	100	8	52	26	14
$100,000 to $249,999. . .	100	39	41	16	4	100	5	49	33	13
$250,000 to $499,999. . .	100	38	37	20	4	100	7	47	38	9
$500,000 and over.	100	40	41	15	4	100	4	49	38	9
Cash grain	100	54	32	11	4	100	5	52	32	11
Tobacco.	100	71	23	5	-	100	13	50	32	5
Cotton	100	43	34	16	7	100	5	44	32	19
Other field crops	100	72	19	6	3	100	7	48	29	17
Vegetable, fruit, and nut .	100	74	20	5	2	100	7	46	40	7
Nursery, greenhouse. . . .	100	72	18	8	2	100	4	53	33	10
Beef, hog, and sheep . . .	100	74	19	6	2	100	8	48	32	12
Poultry	100	53	32	10	5	100	6	54	27	13
Dairy	100	42	41	15	2	100	6	51	33	11
Other livestock	100	68	26	5	2	100	8	66	17	9

- Represents or rounds to zero.

Source: U.S. Dept. of Agriculture, Economic Research Service, *Financial Characteristics of U.S. Farms*, annual.

No. 1106. Farms, Farm Income, Assets, and Debt, by Value of Sales: 1991

FARMS WITH VALUE OF SALES OF—	Number of farms [1] (1,000)	Gross cash income [2] (bil. dol.)	Cash receipts (bil. dol.)	Govt. pay-ments (bil. dol.)	Net cash income [2] (bil. dol.)	Assets [3] (bil. dol.)	Debt [3] (bil. dol.)	Debt/ asset ratio [3] (per-cent)	PERCENT DISTRIBUTION		
									Number of farms [1]	Gross cash income [2]	As-sets [3]
Total	2,105	183.2	167.3	8.2	58.0	1,004.1	147.0	14.6	100	100	100
Less than $20,000	1,229	9.3	6.9	0.8	-0.1	287.8	25.6	8.9	58	5	29
$20,000 to $39,999	240	8.3	6.9	0.6	2.2	101.0	11.0	10.9	11	5	10
$40,000 to $99,999	309	23.9	20.2	2.1	7.6	184.8	26.1	14.1	15	13	18
$100,000 to $249,999	215	37.3	33.3	2.3	13.0	195.7	34.3	17.5	10	20	20
$250,000 to $499,999	69	25.9	24.0	1.2	9.1	100.9	19.1	19.0	3	14	10
$500,000 to $999,999	26	19.4	18.1	0.8	6.5	64.8	14.3	22.0	1	11	7
$1 million and over	16	59.1	57.7	0.4	19.6	69.1	16.6	24.1	1	32	7

[1] Based on 1974 census definition. See text, section 23. [2] For components of income, see table 1109. Minus sign (-) indicates loss. [3] Data as of December 31. Includes farm households.

No. 1107. Net Cash Income and Net Cash Flow From Farming: 1980 to 1991

[In billions of dollars. Net cash income measures the cash income from a farm operator's farm business and net cash flow measures the cash flow within the agricultural sector. Minus sign (-) indicates net loan redemption or decrease]

ITEM	1980	1981	1982	1983	1984	1985	1986	1987	1988	1989	1990	1991
Net cash income	34.2	32.8	38.1	38.4	37.4	47.1	47.8	55.8	58.1	58.9	61.3	58.0
Gross cash income	143.3	146.0	151.3	151.1	156.1	157.9	152.8	165.2	172.7	180.2	186.4	183.2
Cash expenses	109.1	113.2	113.2	112.8	118.7	110.7	105.0	109.4	114.6	121.2	125.2	125.2
Change in loans outstanding	15.3	15.6	6.4	2.3	2.7	-16.2	-20.6	-12.6	-5.0	-2.2	-0.4	2.0
Real estate loans	10.0	9.1	3.0	1.4	3.5	-6.6	-9.7	-8.0	-4.8	-2.3	-1.7	0.7
Nonreal estate loans [1]	5.3	6.5	3.4	0.9	-0.8	-9.6	-11.0	-4.6	-0.3	0.1	1.3	1.2
Net change in other financial assets	0.1	0.2	0.2	0.3	0.2	0.7	1.1	-0.2	0.5	0.1	0.4	1.0
Net rent received by nonoperator landlords	6.1	6.2	5.5	5.2	8.2	7.7	6.1	7.1	7.3	8.2	8.3	7.5
Capital expenditures	18.0	16.8	13.3	12.7	12.5	9.2	8.5	11.2	11.3	12.6	13.4	12.2
Net cash flow [2]	37.6	37.9	37.0	33.4	36.0	30.1	25.9	39.0	49.5	52.4	56.2	56.1

[1] Excludes Commodity Credit Corporation loans. [2] Net cash income plus change in loans outstanding plus net change in other financial assets plus net rent received by nonoperator landlords minus capital expenditures.

Source of tables 1106 and 1107: U.S. Dept. of Agriculture, Economic Research Service, *Economic Indicators of the Farm Sector: National Financial Summary,* annual.

No. 1108. Gross Farm Product—Summary: 1980 to 1991

[In billions of dollars. For definition of gross product, see text, section 14. Minus sign (-) indicates decrease]

ITEM	1980	1982	1983	1984	1985	1986	1987	1988	1989	1990	1991
CURRENT DOLLARS											
Farm output, total [1]	142.9	152.0	135.1	160.0	152.7	144.0	152.1	158.2	178.7	185.3	179.8
Cash receipts from farm marketings	140.3	135.3	140.2	144.6	136.3	135.2	147.7	159.3	166.5	172.3	169.4
Farm housing	5.1	5.0	5.1	5.1	5.0	4.9	4.9	4.9	5.0	5.2	5.3
Other farm income	2.4	4.8	4.1	3.5	4.6	4.4	5.1	4.6	5.0	4.1	4.3
Change in farm inventories	-6.1	5.8	-15.4	5.7	5.8	-1.5	-6.4	-11.3	1.5	3.1	-
Less: Intermediate goods and services purchased [2]	86.8	86.9	85.9	91.4	85.6	81.1	86.1	90.6	97.6	100.3	100.6
Equals: **Gross farm product**	56.1	65.1	49.2	68.5	67.1	62.9	66.0	67.6	81.1	85.0	79.1
Less: Consumption of fixed capital	19.4	22.8	23.2	22.2	22.9	22.5	22.0	21.6	21.9	21.6	21.3
Indirect business tax [3]	3.0	3.0	3.2	3.1	3.3	3.3	3.6	3.6	3.8	4.2	4.4
Plus: Subsidies to operators	1.0	2.2	7.5	7.0	6.3	9.5	13.9	11.8	9.3	7.8	7.0
Equals: **Farm national income**	34.7	41.6	30.3	49.2	47.2	46.6	54.3	54.2	64.7	67.0	60.4
CONSTANT (1987) DOLLARS											
Farm output, total [1]	137.1	142.2	133.2	139.0	146.0	146.4	152.1	146.5	151.1	156.8	155.5
Cash receipts from farm marketings	130.7	127.9	131.2	127.8	133.1	137.9	147.7	143.9	141.9	145.5	146.4
Farm housing	6.3	5.5	5.4	5.4	5.3	5.1	4.9	4.7	4.6	4.5	4.5
Other farm income	2.3	4.5	3.8	3.1	4.3	4.6	5.1	4.1	4.2	3.7	3.8
Change in farm inventories	-3.4	3.1	-8.3	1.7	2.4	-2.1	-6.4	-7.0	-0.1	2.5	0.3
Less: Intermediate goods and services purchased [2]	86.1	82.0	79.5	83.9	81.8	82.2	86.1	83.3	84.9	86.2	86.1
Equals: **Gross farm product**	51.0	60.2	53.7	55.1	64.2	64.3	66.0	63.2	66.2	70.5	69.4
Less: Consumption of fixed capital	26.7	26.5	25.8	25.1	24.3	23.1	22.0	21.1	20.5	19.5	18.7
Indirect business tax [3]	2.8	3.3	2.9	3.0	3.5	3.5	3.6	3.5	3.6	3.9	3.8
Plus: Subsidies to operators	11.9	11.1	11.6	10.7	11.4	12.3	13.9	12.9	12.7	13.3	13.1
Equals: **Farm national income**	33.4	41.5	36.5	37.7	47.8	49.9	54.3	51.6	54.8	60.4	60.0

- Represents zero. [1] Includes farm products consumed in farm households where raised, not shown separately. [2] Includes rent paid to nonoperator landlords. [3] Includes nontax liability.

Source: U.S. Bureau of Economic Analysis, *Survey of Current Business,* July 1992; and *National Income and Product Accounts of the United States: Volume 2, 1959-88.*

No. 1109. Farm Income and Expenses: 1980 to 1991

[In billions of dollars. See also *Historical Statistics, Colonial Times to 1970*, series K 192, K 259-260, K 264-285, and K 326]

ITEM	1980	1981	1982	1983	1984	1985	1986	1987	1988	1989	1990	1991
Gross farm income	149.3	166.3	164.1	153.9	168.0	161.2	156.1	168.5	175.4	191.1	196.0	189.5
Cash income	143.3	146.0	151.3	151.1	156.1	157.9	152.9	165.2	172.7	180.2	186.4	182.2
Farm marketings	139.7	141.6	142.6	136.8	142.8	144.1	135.4	141.8	151.1	161.0	169.9	167.3
Crops	71.7	72.5	72.3	67.2	69.9	74.3	63.8	65.9	71.7	76.9	80.0	80.5
Livestock and products	68.0	69.2	70.3	69.6	72.9	69.8	71.6	76.0	79.4	84.1	89.9	86.7
Government payments	1.3	1.9	3.5	9.3	8.4	7.7	11.8	16.7	14.5	10.9	9.3	8.2
Other farm income [1]	2.3	2.5	5.2	5.1	4.9	6.0	5.7	6.6	6.1	8.2	7.2	7.6
Value of home consumption	1.2	1.2	1.1	1.0	1.0	0.9	0.9	0.7	0.7	0.7	0.7	0.6
Rental value of dwellings [2]	11.0	12.6	13.1	12.6	4.9	4.7	4.6	4.9	5.4	5.5	5.4	5.3
Value of inventory adjustment [3]	-6.3	6.5	-1.4	-10.9	6.0	-2.3	-2.2	-2.3	-3.4	4.8	3.5	0.4
Expenses of farm production	133.1	139.4	140.3	139.6	141.9	132.4	125.1	128.8	134.3	141.2	145.1	144.9
Intermediate products	76.1	76.6	75.4	75.8	78.0	72.3	70.6	74.8	79.7	84.3	86.6	87.6
Farm origin	34.9	33.3	31.4	32.1	32.3	29.3	30.4	32.6	36.5	37.7	39.1	38.1
Feed purchased	21.0	20.9	18.6	20.6	19.4	16.9	17.5	17.5	20.4	21.0	20.7	19.8
Livestock, poultry purchased	10.7	9.0	9.7	8.8	9.5	9.2	9.8	11.8	12.8	13.1	14.8	14.4
Seed purchased [4]	3.2	3.4	3.2	2.7	3.4	3.1	3.2	3.3	3.4	3.6	3.6	4.0
Manufactured inputs	22.4	23.9	22.1	20.1	22.4	20.2	18.2	18.1	18.7	20.0	21.1	21.7
Fertilizer and lime	9.5	9.4	8.0	7.1	8.4	7.5	6.8	6.5	6.9	7.2	7.1	7.4
Pesticides	3.5	4.2	4.3	3.9	4.7	4.3	4.3	4.5	4.6	5.4	5.7	6.3
Fuel and oil	7.9	8.6	7.7	7.2	7.3	6.4	5.3	5.0	4.9	4.8	5.7	5.5
Electricity	1.5	1.7	2.0	2.0	2.1	1.9	1.8	2.2	2.3	2.5	2.5	2.5
Repairs and maintenance [5]	7.1	7.0	6.4	6.5	6.4	6.4	6.4	6.8	6.9	7.3	7.3	7.2
Other [6]	11.8	12.4	15.5	17.1	16.9	16.5	15.5	17.4	17.6	19.2	19.0	20.5
Interest	16.3	19.9	21.8	21.4	21.1	18.6	16.5	15.0	14.7	14.7	14.5	13.9
Real estate	7.5	9.1	10.5	10.8	10.7	9.9	9.1	8.2	7.9	7.8	7.6	7.3
Nonreal estate	8.7	10.7	11.3	10.6	10.4	8.7	7.4	6.8	6.8	6.9	6.9	6.6
Contract, hired labor expenses [7] [8]	9.3	8.9	9.4	8.9	9.4	10.0	9.5	10.0	10.4	11.1	12.5	12.6
Net rent to nonoperator landlords [8]	6.1	6.2	5.5	5.2	8.1	7.7	6.1	7.1	7.3	8.2	8.3	7.5
Capital consumption [9]	21.5	23.6	24.2	23.8	20.8	19.3	17.8	17.1	17.3	17.8	17.5	17.4
Property taxes	3.9	4.2	4.0	4.5	4.3	4.5	4.6	4.9	4.8	5.1	5.6	6.0
Net farm income	16.1	26.9	23.8	14.2	26.1	28.8	31.1	39.7	41.1	49.9	51.0	44.6

[1] Includes forest product sales. [2] Data for 1980 to 1983 are not comparable with later data. [3] Minus sign (-) indicates decrease in inventories. [4] Includes bulbs, plants, and trees. [5] Expenditures for repairs and maintenance of farm buildings, motor vehicles, and machinery. [6] Includes machine hire and customwork expenses; marketing, storage, and transportation expenses and miscellaneous expenses. [7] Includes Social Security payments and perquisites. [8] Data for years 1980-83, and 1984 and later are based on different sources, creating potential inconsistencies in estimates among these periods. [9] Depreciation and accidental damage.

Source: U.S. Dept. of Agriculture, Economic Research Service, *Economic Indicators of the Farm Sector: National Financial Summary*, annual.

No. 1110. Commodity Credit Corporation—Net Outlays, by Commodity and Function: 1980 to 1992

[In millions of dollars. For fiscal year ending in year shown; see text, section 9. Excludes value of commodity certificates which may also be issued to farmers in lieu of cash under certain programs. Minus sign (-) indicates a net receipt (excess of repayments or other receipts over gross outlays of funds)]

COMMODITY	1980	1990	1991	1992	FUNCTION	1980	1990	1991	1992
Total	2,752	6,471	10,110	9,738	Total	2,752	6,471	10,110	9,738
Feed grains	1,286	2,721	2,722	2,510	Price support loans [4]	-66	-399	418	584
Wheat	879	806	2,958	1,710	Direct payments [5]	418	4,370	6,341	5,847
Cotton, upland	64	-79	382	1,443	Deficiency payments	79	4,178	6,224	5,491
Dairy	1,011	505	839	232	Diversion payments	56	-	-	-
Rice	-76	667	867	715					
Wool	35	104	172	191	1988/89 crop disaster	(X)	[3]5	6	960
Honey	9	47	19	17	Emergency livestock/forage				
Peanuts	28	1	48	41	assistance	23	156	115	94
Sugar	-405	15	-20	-19	Purchases [6]	1,681	-48	646	321
Tobacco	-88	-307	-143	29	Producer storage payments	254	185	1	14
Soybeans	116	5	40	-29	Processing, storage and				
Operating expense [1]	157	618	625	6	transportation	259	317	394	185
Interest expenditure	518	632	745	532	Operating expense [1]	157	618	625	6
Export programs [2]	-669	-34	733	1,455	Interest expenditure	518	632	745	532
1988/89 disaster/livestock					Export programs [2]	-669	-34	733	1,455
assistance	(X)	[3]161	121	1,054	Other	177	669	86	-260
Other	-113	609	2	-149					

- Represents zero. X Not applicable. [1] Excludes CCC transfers to the general sales manager. [2] Covers the direct export credit sales program, the export guarantee program, and transfers to the general sales manager. [3] Approximately $1.5 billion in benefits to farmers under the Disaster Assistance Act of 1989 were paid in generic certificates and were not recorded directly as disaster assistance outlays. [4] Price support loans made less loans repaid. [5] Includes disaster payments; and, beginning 1990, dairy termination program. Cash payments only. For 1990-92 excludes generic certificates. [6] Purchases less sales proceeds.

Source: U.S. Agricultural Stabilization and Conservation Service, *Commodity Credit Corporation Report of Financial Condition and Operations*, annual, and *Agricultural Outlook*, monthly.

No. 1111. Farm Income—Cash Receipts From Farm Marketings: 1980 to 1991

[Represents gross receipts from commercial market sales as well as net Commodity Credit Corporation loans. See also *Historical Statistics, Colonial Times to 1970*, series K 286-302]

COMMODITY	FARM MARKETINGS (mil. dol.)								PERCENT		
	1980	1985	1986	1987	1988	1989	1990	1991	1980	1990	1991
Total	139,737	144,114	135,361	141,844	151,102	161,027	169,920	167,292	100.0	100.0	100.0
All crops [1]	71,746	74,293	63,807	65,851	71,663	76,879	79,999	80,547	51.3	47.1	48.1
Barley	736	1,039	835	754	862	765	802	822	0.5	0.5	0.5
Corn	13,959	16,880	12,397	9,983	8,928	11,388	13,358	13,854	10.0	7.9	8.3
Cotton lint, seed	4,447	3,687	3,371	4,189	4,546	5,033	5,489	5,589	3.2	3.2	3.3
Hay	1,917	2,390	2,246	2,533	3,132	3,388	3,286	3,044	1.4	1.9	1.8
Oats	(NA)	298	178	260	305	268	222	154	(NA)	0.1	0.1
Peanuts	607	1,005	1,074	1,027	1,116	1,117	1,258	1,393	0.4	0.7	0.8
Rice	1,519	1,042	720	720	1,096	942	1,076	1,092	1.1	0.6	0.7
Sorghum	1,392	1,981	1,332	1,100	1,068	1,240	1,016	1,132	1.0	0.6	0.7
Soybean	14,241	11,161	9,235	10,017	12,138	10,524	10,790	10,778	10.2	6.4	6.4
Sunflower/safflower	(NA)	242	254	211	224	212	219	304	(NA)	0.1	0.2
Tobacco	2,672	2,699	1,894	1,816	2,083	2,415	2,741	2,886	1.9	1.6	1.7
Wheat	8,854	7,909	4,975	5,044	6,356	7,286	6,421	5,716	6.3	3.8	3.4
Vegetables [2]	7,307	8,572	8,859	9,898	9,787	11,534	11,455	11,293	5.2	6.7	6.8
Dry beans	(NA)	439	437	444	421	688	690	512	(NA)	0.4	0.3
Snap beans	(NA)	167	150	171	166	228	205	207	(NA)	0.1	0.1
Broccoli	(NA)	239	240	240	292	276	268	242	(NA)	0.2	0.1
Carrots	(NA)	206	335	248	268	297	273	309	(NA)	0.2	0.2
Celery	(NA)	190	211	199	231	268	215	206	(NA)	0.1	0.1
Sweet corn	(NA)	368	360	372	360	468	468	494	(NA)	0.3	0.3
Cucumbers	(NA)	181	170	188	196	203	231	229	(NA)	0.1	0.1
Lettuce	(NA)	675	758	1,003	1,040	950	844	818	(NA)	0.5	0.5
Onions	(NA)	372	415	536	498	538	542	604	(NA)	0.3	0.4
Potatoes	(NA)	1,601	1,377	1,707	1,626	2,336	2,534	2,048	(NA)	1.5	1.2
Tomatoes	(NA)	1,198	1,265	1,466	1,415	1,841	1,626	1,799	(NA)	1.0	1.1
Fruits, tree nuts [2]	6,557	6,946	7,252	8,065	9,202	9,296	9,534	9,882	4.7	5.6	5.9
Apples	(NA)	892	927	1,060	1,109	1,114	1,162	1,659	(NA)	0.7	1.0
Avocados	(NA)	139	163	120	212	224	245	201	(NA)	0.1	0.1
Grapefruit	(NA)	319	358	408	471	436	362	390	(NA)	0.2	0.2
Grapes	(NA)	961	1,177	1,362	1,600	1,866	1,677	1,619	(NA)	1.0	1.0
Lemons	(NA)	237	157	226	188	223	307	259	(NA)	0.2	0.2
Oranges	(NA)	1,404	1,184	1,363	1,825	1,786	1,761	1,565	(NA)	1.0	0.9
Peaches	(NA)	295	315	311	382	364	372	393	(NA)	0.2	0.2
Pears	(NA)	193	198	196	218	259	261	272	(NA)	0.2	0.2
Plums and prunes	(NA)	196	200	207	255	252	295	258	(NA)	0.2	0.2
Strawberries	(NA)	451	504	554	536	538	580	634	(NA)	0.3	0.4
Almonds	(NA)	361	462	648	600	481	598	540	(NA)	0.4	0.3
Pecans	(NA)	163	197	140	167	179	248	307	(NA)	0.1	0.2
Walnuts	(NA)	175	194	243	194	245	236	280	(NA)	0.1	0.2
Sugar beets	(NA)	774	902	1,028	1,022	1,057	1,178	1,217	(NA)	0.7	0.7
Sugarcane	(NA)	717	742	803	854	870	820	902	(NA)	0.5	0.5
Mushrooms	(NA)	491	491	519	573	630	667	668	(NA)	0.4	0.4
Greenhouse, nursery	(NA)	5,407	5,983	6,767	7,081	7,617	8,227	8,405	(NA)	4.8	5.0
All livestock and products [1]	67,991	69,822	71,553	75,993	79,438	84,148	89,921	86,745	48.7	52.9	51.9
Cattle and calves	31,819	29,002	28,865	33,583	36,810	36,894	39,945	39,632	22.8	23.5	23.7
Dairy products	16,365	18,055	17,724	17,727	17,641	19,396	20,210	18,114	11.7	11.9	10.8
Hogs	8,942	9,033	9,734	10,336	9,207	9,475	11,552	11,061	6.4	6.8	6.6
Broilers	4,303	5,668	6,784	6,177	7,435	8,778	8,365	8,385	3.1	4.9	5.0
Eggs	3,247	3,262	3,543	3,208	3,067	3,862	4,010	3,861	2.3	2.4	2.3
Turkeys	1,273	1,820	1,949	1,703	1,951	2,234	2,379	2,344	0.9	1.4	1.4
Sheep and lambs	(NA)	514	481	558	476	487	414	399	(NA)	0.2	0.2
Horses and mules	(NA)	560	500	540	540	524	490	466	(NA)	0.3	0.3
Aquaculture	(NA)	205	230	290	324	407	541	494	(NA)	0.3	0.3

NA Not available.   [1] Includes other commodities not shown separately.   [2] Melons included with vegetables.

Source: U.S. Dept. of Agriculture, Economic Research Service, *Economic Indicators of the Farm Sector: National Financial Summary*, annual.

No. 1112. Government Payments to Farms, by Program: 1980 to 1991

[In millions of dollars. See also *Historical Statistics, Colonial Times to 1970*, series K 326-329]

PROGRAM	1980	1985	1986	1987	1988	1989	1990	1991
Total	1,285	7,705	11,814	16,747	14,480	10,887	9,298	8,214
Feed grain	382	2,861	5,158	8,490	7,219	3,141	2,701	2,649
Wheat	211	1,950	3,500	2,931	1,842	603	2,311	2,166
Cotton	172	1,106	1,042	1,204	924	1,184	441	407
Rice	2	577	423	475	465	671	465	550
Wool	28	98	112	144	117	81	96	154
Conservation	214	189	254	1,531	1,607	1,771	1,898	1,858
Miscellaneous [1]	276	924	1,325	1,972	2,306	3,436	1,386	431

[1] Includes value of commodities transferred to farmers under the payment-in-kind program (PIK).

Source: U.S. Dept. of Agriculture, Economic Research Service, *Economic Indicators of the Farm Sector: National Financial Summary, 1991*.

No. 1113. Farm Assets, Debt, and Income, by State: 1990 and 1991

[Assets and debt, as of December 31. Includes farm operator households. Farm income data are after inventory adjustment]

DIVISION AND STATE	ASSETS (mil. dol.)		DEBT (mil. dol.)		DEBT/ASSET RATIO (percent)		GROSS FARM INCOME (mil. dol.)		NET FARM INCOME (mil. dol.)	
	1990	1991	1990	1991	1990	1991	1990	1991	1990	1991
United States	1,003,562	1,004,109	145,067	146,983	14.5	14.6	196,033	189,496	50,957	44,609
New England:										
Maine	2,588	2,442	332	298	12.8	12.2	557	486	175	109
New Hampshire	1,839	1,727	76	72	4.1	4.2	178	174	43	43
Vermont	2,870	2,770	371	366	12.9	13.2	495	472	100	91
Massachusetts	4,484	4,324	317	314	7.1	7.3	505	528	171	191
Rhode Island	557	508	37	38	6.6	7.4	79	78	37	37
Connecticut	3,620	3,488	231	214	6.4	6.1	521	501	208	194
Middle Atlantic:										
New York	14,748	14,749	2,313	2,145	15.7	14.5	3,220	3,075	770	650
New Jersey	9,263	9,194	435	460	4.7	5.0	761	755	251	231
Pennsylvania	21,948	22,526	2,406	2,528	11.0	11.2	4,071	3,755	1,029	733
East North Central:										
Ohio	30,004	30,425	3,367	3,383	11.3	11.1	4,761	4,231	1,061	663
Indiana	30,476	30,330	4,632	4,842	15.2	16.0	5,466	4,763	997	465
Illinois	54,577	56,605	7,358	7,255	13.5	12.8	8,831	8,089	1,706	1,150
Michigan	19,126	19,504	2,695	2,676	14.1	13.7	3,722	3,638	922	764
Wisconsin	28,934	29,044	5,083	5,077	17.6	17.5	6,489	5,992	1,653	1,187
West North Central:										
Minnesota	41,706	41,853	6,770	6,845	16.2	16.4	8,469	7,868	2,478	1,880
Iowa	57,569	57,962	9,966	10,286	17.3	17.7	11,939	11,195	2,820	2,291
Missouri	33,487	33,654	4,731	4,714	14.1	14.0	4,748	4,660	919	810
North Dakota	22,309	22,314	3,541	3,540	15.9	15.9	3,477	3,390	769	660
South Dakota	23,052	23,909	3,399	3,592	14.7	15.0	4,047	3,948	1,321	1,223
Nebraska	38,332	38,874	6,594	6,883	17.2	17.7	10,279	9,777	2,215	1,955
Kansas	33,212	34,445	5,738	5,764	17.3	16.7	8,554	7,960	1,408	917
South Atlantic:										
Delaware	1,747	1,674	333	317	19.0	18.9	698	697	190	175
Maryland	7,169	7,303	988	1,004	13.8	13.7	1,548	1,501	457	388
Virginia	17,235	17,615	2,049	2,060	11.9	11.7	2,473	2,419	560	491
West Virginia	3,759	4,149	434	432	11.5	10.4	462	447	96	78
North Carolina	18,052	18,079	2,659	3,101	14.7	17.2	5,784	5,914	2,074	2,141
South Carolina	7,441	7,377	974	1,067	13.1	14.5	1,314	1,417	289	386
Georgia	18,314	16,704	2,901	3,103	15.8	18.6	4,353	4,617	1,168	1,471
Florida	28,517	26,935	3,764	3,960	13.2	14.7	5,940	6,389	2,285	2,721
East South Central:										
Kentucky	21,569	21,865	2,773	2,946	12.9	13.5	3,551	3,631	1,098	1,072
Tennessee	19,566	19,408	2,211	2,156	11.3	11.1	2,480	2,398	463	372
Alabama	12,216	12,460	1,489	1,502	12.2	12.1	3,311	3,500	918	1,153
Mississippi	14,522	13,965	2,730	2,661	18.8	19.1	2,913	2,992	665	735
West South Central:										
Arkansas	17,157	16,316	3,079	3,122	17.9	19.1	4,978	5,151	1,303	1,425
Louisiana	10,528	10,019	1,912	1,829	18.2	18.3	2,253	2,150	613	561
Oklahoma	24,832	25,555	3,989	3,935	16.1	15.4	4,429	4,399	1,148	940
Texas	89,227	87,630	10,139	10,213	11.4	11.7	14,206	14,209	3,294	3,061
Mountain:										
Montana	20,425	21,108	2,618	2,598	12.8	12.3	2,085	2,226	365	515
Idaho	13,618	13,663	2,511	2,602	18.4	19.0	3,333	2,922	1,082	741
Wyoming	7,542	7,033	826	901	11.0	12.8	847	1,024	134	200
Colorado	19,618	17,871	3,048	2,970	15.5	16.6	4,696	4,375	889	712
New Mexico	12,625	13,037	1,067	1,096	8.5	8.4	1,605	1,678	331	353
Arizona	11,617	12,207	1,444	1,339	12.4	11.0	2,076	1,983	625	519
Utah	6,455	6,629	698	698	10.8	10.5	898	830	244	191
Nevada	3,156	3,291	267	253	8.5	7.7	323	306	84	70
Pacific:										
Washington	18,127	18,347	3,039	3,024	16.8	16.5	4,550	4,559	1,453	1,378
Oregon	15,622	16,246	2,558	2,675	16.4	16.5	2,935	2,901	886	831
California	83,494	82,303	13,807	13,804	16.5	16.8	20,163	18,883	7,091	5,605
Alaska.	713	658	25	25	3.5	3.8	33	30	7	4
Hawaii	4,004	4,011	337	303	8.4	7.5	628	616	92	76

Source: U.S. Dept. of Agriculture, Economic Research Service, *Economic Indicators of the Farm Sector: State Financial Summary, 1991*; and unpublished data.

No. 1114. Farm Income—Farm Marketings, 1990 and 1991, Government Payments, 1991, and Principal Commodities, 1991, by State

[In millions of dollars. Cattle include calves; sheep include lambs; and greenhouse includes nursery]

DIVISION AND STATE	1990 Farm marketings Total	Crops	Livestock and products	1991 Farm marketings Total	Crops	Livestock and products	Government payments	State rank for total farm marketings and four principal commodities in order of marketing receipts
U.S....	169,920	79,999	89,921	167,292	80,547	86,745	8,214	Cattle, dairy products, corn, hogs
N.E.....	2,083	1,003	1,080	2,031	1,005	1,026	14	(X)
ME ...	493	234	258	445	192	252	6	44-Potatoes, eggs, dairy products, aquaculture
NH ...	143	80	63	143	80	63	1	48-Dairy products, greenhouse, apples, cattle
VT....	456	60	397	433	66	368	3	45-Dairy products, cattle, greenhouse, hay
MA ...	446	321	125	476	355	121	1	42-Greenhouse, cranberries, dairy products, eggs
RI....	71	58	14	71	58	13	(Z)	49-Greenhouse, dairy products, eggs, potatoes
CT....	474	250	223	463	255	209	1	43-Greenhouse, eggs, dairy products, tobacco
M.A	7,365	2,485	4,880	7,032	2,584	4,448	80	(X)
NY....	2,958	986	1,971	2,868	1,087	1,782	41	24-Dairy products, greenhouse, cattle, apples
NJ....	650	455	196	660	464	197	4	39-Greenhouse, dairy products, eggs, peaches
PA....	3,757	1,043	2,714	3,503	1,033	2,470	34	19-Dairy products, cattle, greenhouse, mushrooms
E.N.C ...	25,707	13,389	12,318	24,406	12,985	11,421	1,082	(X)
OH ...	4,146	2,299	1,847	3,893	2,212	1,681	157	15-Soybeans, corn, dairy products, hogs
IN	4,911	2,871	2,040	4,475	2,582	1,893	210	11-Corn, soybeans, hogs, cattle
IL	7,789	5,338	2,452	7,509	5,165	2,344	441	5-Corn, soybeans, hogs, cattle
MI	3,126	1,720	1,407	3,081	1,793	1,288	124	22-Dairy products, corn, cattle, soybeans
WI	5,734	1,161	4,573	5,449	1,234	4,215	150	9-Dairy products, cattle, corn, hogs
W.N.C...	42,675	16,567	26,108	42,553	17,441	25,112	3,358	(X)
MN ...	6,885	3,135	3,749	6,936	3,359	3,577	436	6-Corn, dairy products, soybeans, cattle
IA	10,282	4,420	5,862	10,179	4,458	5,721	645	3-Hogs, corn, cattle, soybeans
MO ...	3,989	1,660	2,329	3,861	1,658	2,203	269	16-Cattle, soybeans, hogs, corn
ND ...	2,532	1,730	801	2,556	1,857	699	534	26-Wheat, cattle, barley, sunflower
SD....	3,259	965	2,294	3,264	1,088	2,176	286	20-Cattle, hogs, corn, soybeans
NE....	8,708	2,632	6,076	8,821	2,888	5,934	491	4-Cattle, corn, hogs, soybeans
KS....	7,020	2,024	4,996	6,935	2,133	4,802	698	7-Cattle, wheat, corn, hogs
S.A....	20,166	10,462	9,704	20,646	11,331	9,315	291	(X)
DE....	636	176	460	620	181	438	3	40-Broilers, soybeans, corn, greenhouse
MD ...	1,364	542	823	1,332	554	779	15	35-Broilers, greenhouse, dairy products, soybeans
VA....	2,122	739	1,383	2,095	732	1,363	27	29-Cattle, broilers, dairy products, tobacco
WV ...	339	70	269	330	77	253	5	46-Cattle, broilers, dairy products, turkeys
NC ...	4,926	2,268	2,658	4,924	2,316	2,608	53	10-Tobacco, broilers, hogs, turkeys
SC....	1,169	588	581	1,225	677	549	49	36-Tobacco, cattle, broilers, greenhouse
GA ...	3,866	1,596	2,270	3,978	1,825	2,153	98	13-Broilers, peanuts, eggs, cattle
FL....	5,744	4,483	1,261	6,141	4,969	1,172	41	8-Oranges, greenhouse, tomatoes, sugar
E.S.C ...	10,422	4,098	6,324	10,556	4,313	6,243	386	(X)
KY....	3,103	1,404	1,699	3,179	1,475	1,704	73	21-Tobacco, cattle, horses, dairy products
TN....	2,061	950	1,111	1,978	933	1,045	70	30-Cattle, dairy products, tobacco, cotton
AL....	2,826	632	2,193	2,978	759	2,219	66	23-Broilers, cattle, greenhouse, peanuts
MS ...	2,433	1,111	1,322	2,422	1,147	1,275	176	28-Cotton, broilers, cattle, soybeans
W.S.C...	21,558	8,132	13,427	22,037	8,055	13,982	1,596	(X)
AR....	4,256	1,555	2,701	4,311	1,631	2,680	353	12-Broilers, cattle, soybeans, rice
LA....	1,929	1,296	633	1,793	1,172	621	175	32-Cotton, cattle, sugar, soybeans
OK ...	3,542	1,200	2,342	3,808	1,040	2,767	291	17-Cattle, wheat, greenhouse, broilers
TX....	11,831	4,081	7,751	12,126	4,212	7,914	778	2-Cattle, cotton, dairy products, greenhouse
Mt	13,988	5,685	8,304	13,119	5,404	7,715	850	(X)
MT ...	1,654	766	888	1,531	741	790	320	33-Cattle, wheat, barley, hay
ID	2,885	1,748	1,137	2,616	1,543	1,073	141	25-Cattle, potatoes, dairy products, wheat
WY ...	754	159	595	813	170	643	33	37-Cattle, sugar beets, hay, barley
CO ...	4,216	1,144	3,073	3,761	1,097	2,664	217	18-Cattle, corn, wheat, dairy products
NM ...	1,483	482	1,001	1,501	482	1,019	58	34-Cattle, dairy products, hay, chili peppers
AZ....	1,910	1,097	813	1,890	1,104	786	40	31-Cattle, cotton, dairy products, lettuce
UT....	762	175	587	731	178	553	33	38-Cattle, dairy products, hay, turkeys
NV....	324	115	209	276	89	187	6	47-Cattle, hay, dairy products, potatoes
Pac	25,957	18,180	7,777	24,911	17,428	7,483	558	(X)
WA ...	3,798	2,402	1,396	3,947	2,657	1,290	206	14-Apples, dairy products, cattle, wheat
OR ...	2,374	1,620	753	2,454	1,631	824	89	27-Cattle, greenhouse, dairy products, wheat
CA ...	19,158	13,624	5,533	17,887	12,615	5,272	261	1-Dairy products, greenhouse, cattle, grapes
AK....	27	19	8	27	20	6	1	50-Greenhouse, dairy products, hay, potatoes
HI	600	514	86	597	506	91	1	41-Sugar, pineapples, greenhouse, nuts

X Not applicable.   Z Less than $500 thousand.

Source: U.S. Dept. of Agriculture, Economic Research Service, *Economic Indicators of the Farm Sector: State Financial Summary, 1991.*

No. 1115. Indexes of Prices Received and Paid by Farmers: 1980 to 1992

[1977=100, except as noted. See also *Historical Statistics, Colonial Times to 1970*, series K 344-353]

ITEM	1980	1990	1991	1992, prel.	ITEM	1980	1990	1991	1992, prel.
Prices received, all products.	**134**	**149**	**145**	**139**	**Prices paid, total** [3]	**138**	**184**	**189**	**191**
Crops [1]	125	127	129	121	Production [1]	138	171	174	174
Food grains	165	127	129	121	Feed	123	128	123	123
Feed grains and hay	132	123	118	115	Feeder livestock	177	213	214	202
Cotton	114	107	108	87	Seed	118	165	163	162
Tobacco	125	152	161	155	Fertilizer.	134	131	134	131
Oil-bearing crops	102	94	91	85	Agricultural chemicals....	102	139	151	159
Fruits.	124	186	262	183	Fuels and energy.......	188	204	203	199
Commercial vegetables [2] .	113	142	135	151	Farm and motor supplies ..	134	154	154	160
Livestock and products	144	170	161	157	Interest payable per acre ...	174	177	172	167
Meat animals	156	193	186	176	Taxes payable per acre ...	115	158	160	171
Dairy products........	135	141	126	135	Wage rates [4]	127	193	201	210
Poultry and eggs	112	131	124	117	**Parity ratio (1910-14=100)** [5] .	**65**	**54**	**51**	**48**

[1] Includes other items not shown separately.   [2] Excludes potatoes and dry beans.   [3] Includes production items, interest, taxes, wage rates, and a family living component. The family living component is the Consumer Price Index for all urban consumers from the Bureau of Labor Statistics. See text, section 15, and table 756.   [4] Straight average of seasonally adjusted indexes.   [5] Ratio of prices received by farmers to prices paid.

Source: U.S. Dept. of Agriculture, National Agricultural Statistics Service, *Agricultural Prices: Annual Summary*.

No. 1116. Civilian Consumer Expenditures for Farm Foods—Farm Value and Marketing Bill: 1980 to 1991

[In billions of dollars, except percent. Excludes imported and nonfarm foods, such as coffee and seafood, as well as food consumed by the military, or exported. See *Historical Statistics, Colonial Times to 1970*, series K 358-360 for data before revisions]

ITEM	1980	1982	1983	1984	1985	1986	1987	1988	1989	1990	1991
Consumer expenditures, total	**264.4**	**298.9**	**315.0**	**332.0**	**345.4**	**359.6**	**375.5**	**398.8**	**419.4**	**449.8**	**461.8**
Farm value, total	81.7	81.4	85.3	89.8	86.4	88.8	90.4	96.8	103.8	106.2	101.2
Marketing bill, total [1]	182.7	217.5	229.7	242.2	259.0	270.8	285.1	301.9	315.6	343.6	360.6
Percent of total consumer expenditures	69.1	72.8	72.9	73.0	75.0	75.3	75.9	75.7	75.3	76.4	78.1
At-home expenditures [2]	180.1	196.7	204.6	213.1	220.8	226.0	230.2	242.1	255.5	276.2	281.4
Farm value...........	65.9	64.1	66.5	69.5	66.6	67.6	67.5	72.5	77.9	80.2	76.3
Marketing bill [1]	114.2	132.6	138.1	143.6	154.2	158.4	162.7	169.6	177.6	196.0	205.1
Percent of at-home expenditures......	63.4	67.4	67.5	67.4	69.8	70.1	70.7	70.1	69.5	71.0	72.9
Away-from-home expenditures	84.3	102.2	110.4	118.9	124.6	133.6	145.3	156.7	163.9	173.6	180.4
Farm value	15.8	17.3	18.8	20.3	19.8	21.2	22.9	24.3	25.9	26.0	24.9
Marketing bill [1]	68.5	84.9	91.6	98.6	104.8	112.4	122.4	132.4	138.0	147.6	155.5
Percent of away-from-home expenditures.	81.3	83.1	83.0	82.9	84.1	84.1	84.2	84.5	84.2	85.0	86.2
Marketing bill cost components:											
Labor cost [3]	81.5	96.6	102.4	109.3	115.6	122.9	130.0	137.9	145.1	154.0	163.0
Packaging materials	21.0	23.7	24.7	26.2	26.9	27.7	29.9	32.6	35.2	36.5	38.1
Rail and truck transport [4]	13.0	14.7	15.4	15.9	16.5	16.8	17.2	17.8	18.6	19.8	20.4
Corporate profits before taxes	9.9	9.3	9.6	9.6	10.4	10.3	11.1	11.6	12.2	14.2	15.1
Fuels and electricity	9.0	11.0	11.7	12.5	13.1	13.2	13.6	14.1	14.8	15.2	16.3
Other [5]	48.3	62.2	65.9	68.7	76.5	79.9	83.3	87.9	89.7	103.9	107.7
Processing	66.3	75.6	77.8	80.8	88.4	91.0	93.9	99.7	103.8	113.4	118.6
Wholesaling	20.4	25.9	27.1	28.6	29.8	30.5	31.8	33.8	35.2	39.0	39.9
Transportation.	13.0	14.9	15.4	16.0	16.6	16.8	17.6	17.7	18.6	19.6	19.8
Retailing and food service	83.0	101.1	109.4	116.8	124.2	132.5	141.8	150.8	158.0	171.6	182.3
SELECTED FOOD COMMODITY GROUPS											
Meat products:											
Total expenditures	83.3	91.9	97.9	101.7	103.2	106.3	110.0	117.6	121.5	128.4	130.0
Farm value	30.8	31.5	31.4	32.4	30.5	30.9	32.7	33.5	34.0	36.9	35.1
Percent of total	37.0	34.3	32.1	31.9	29.6	29.1	29.7	28.5	28.0	28.7	27.0
Marketing bill [1]	52.5	60.4	66.5	69.3	72.7	75.4	77.3	84.1	87.5	91.5	94.9
Poultry and eggs:											
Total expenditures	18.3	20.3	21.7	24.2	26.0	27.6	29.4	31.3	33.9	36.6	37.7
Farm value	8.4	8.5	9.3	11.0	10.2	11.5	10.3	12.1	14.2	13.9	13.2
Percent of total	45.9	41.9	42.9	45.5	39.2	41.7	35.0	38.7	41.9	38.0	35.0
Marketing bill [1]	9.9	11.8	12.4	13.2	15.8	16.1	19.1	19.2	19.7	22.7	24.5
Dairy products:											
Total expenditures	37.8	42.0	45.0	47.4	49.4	51.4	54.0	55.8	58.1	62.5	64.2
Farm value	16.0	16.7	18.0	18.1	17.7	17.8	18.2	17.9	19.6	20.5	19.6
Percent of total	42.3	39.8	40.0	38.2	35.8	34.6	33.7	32.1	33.7	32.8	30.5
Marketing bill [1]	21.8	25.3	27.0	29.3	31.7	33.6	35.8	37.9	38.5	42.0	44.6
Fruits and vegetables:											
Total expenditures	55.5	66.7	70.0	74.7	78.5	81.6	84.7	89.3	96.0	103.7	108.5
Farm value	11.7	11.5	12.9	13.5	13.3	14.6	14.3	16.2	17.8	16.5	15.8
Percent of total	21.1	17.2	18.4	18.1	16.9	17.9	16.9	18.1	18.5	15.9	14.6
Marketing bill [1]	43.8	55.2	57.1	61.2	65.2	67.0	70.4	73.1	78.2	87.2	92.7
Bakery, grain mill products:											
Total expenditures	35.2	39.6	40.6	43.3	45.5	48.3	49.9	54.7	57.7	63.3	64.8
Farm value	5.1	4.8	4.9	5.1	4.7	4.0	3.8	4.9	5.9	5.1	4.8
Percent of total	14.5	12.1	12.1	11.8	10.3	8.3	7.6	9.0	10.2	8.1	7.4
Marketing bill [1]	30.1	34.8	35.7	38.2	40.8	44.3	46.1	49.8	51.8	58.2	60.0

[1] The difference between expenditures for domestic farm-originated food products and the farm value or payment farmers received for the equivalent farm products.   [2] Food primarily purchased from retail food stores for use at home.   [3] Covers employee wages and salaries, and their health and welfare benefits. Also includes imputed earnings of proprietors, partners, and family workers not receiving stated remuneration.   [4] Excludes local hauling.   [5] Represents advertising, rent, depreciation, interest on borrowed capital, taxes other than income, and other costs.

Source: U.S. Dept. of Agriculture, Economic Research Service, *Food Cost Review, 1991*, AER No. 662, August 1992; *National Food Review*, periodic; and *Agricultural Statistics*, annual.

No. 1117. Farmer Marketing and Farm Supply Cooperatives—Summary: 1980 to 1991

[Comprises independent local associations, federations, large-scale centralized associations, and sales agencies. Memberships and businesses are estimated. See also *Historical Statistics, Colonial Times to 1970*, series K 195-203]

ITEM	1980	1982	1983	1984	1985	1986	1987	1988	1989	1990	1991
Cooperatives listed	6,293	6,125	5,989	5,782	5,625	5,369	5,109	4,937	4,799	4,663	4,494
Marketing [1]	3,924	3,826	3,781	3,646	3,589	3,398	3,168	3,101	2,996	2,946	2,805
Farm supply	2,369	2,299	2,208	2,136	2,036	1,971	1,941	1,836	1,803	1,717	1,689
Memberships [2] (1,000).	5,379	5,136	4,955	4,842	4,781	4,600	4,440	4,195	4,134	4,119	4,058
Marketing [1] (1,000)	2,574	2,469	2,402	2,445	2,383	2,290	2,158	2,053	2,099	2,114	2,033
Farm supply (1,000)	2,804	2,666	2,553	2,397	2,398	2,310	2,282	2,142	2,035	2,006	2,025
Business [3] (mil. dol.)	66,254	69,150	66,755	73,047	65,601	58,395	60,318	66,430	72,129	77,266	76,636
Marketing [1] (mil. dol.)	50,120	52,788	50,812	56,078	48,961	43,300	46,047	51,006	55,222	60,178	58,720
Farm supply (mil. dol.)	16,134	16,362	15,943	16,969	16,641	15,095	14,271	15,424	16,907	17,088	17,916

[1] Includes cooperatives whose major activity is providing services related to marketing and purchasing activities.   [2] Excludes nonvoting patrons.   [3] Value of commodities sold or purchased for patrons. Business dollar volume for marketing includes service receipts for charges related to marketing and purchasing. Represents net volume after eliminating intercooperative business.

Source: U.S. Dept. of Agriculture, Agricultural Cooperative Service, *Farmer Cooperative Statistics*, annual.

No. 1118. Selected Indexes of Farm Inputs: 1970 to 1990

[1977 = 100. Inputs based on physical quantities of resources used in production. See *Historical Statistics, Colonial Times to 1970*, series K 486-495 for data before revisions]

INPUT	1970	1980	1982	1983	1984	1985	1986	1987	1988	1989	1990
Total	96	103	98	96	95	91	89	89	87	87	88
Farm labor	112	96	93	97	92	85	80	78	75	76	80
Farm real estate [1]	105	103	102	101	99	97	96	95	94	93	93
Mechanical power and machinery	85	101	89	86	85	80	77	74	74	73	71
Agricultural chemicals [2]	75	123	118	102	120	115	109	111	112	119	122
Feed, seed, and livestock purchases [3]	96	114	107	103	103	102	106	116	111	113	113
Taxes and interest	102	100	94	98	90	92	93	93	89	86	89
Miscellaneous	89	96	116	101	110	116	110	135	126	122	133

[1] Includes service buildings, improvements.   [2] Includes fertilizer, lime, and pesticides.   [3] Includes nonfarm portion.

Source: U.S. Dept. of Agriculture, Economic Research Service, *Economic Indicators of the Farm Sector: Production and Efficiency Statistics*, annual. Also in U.S. Council of Economic Advisers, *Economic Report of the President*, annual.

No. 1119. Farm Machinery and Equipment: 1980 to 1991

[See also *Historical Statistics, Colonial Times to 1970*, series K 184-191]

ITEM	Unit	1980	1981	1982	1983	1984	1985	1986	1987	1988	1989	1990	1991
Value of farm implements and machinery [1]	Bil. dol. . .	86.9	92.5	92.6	92.1	91.1	88.3	86.1	84.5	86.1	89.2	88.6	88.0
Farmers' expenditures:													
Motor vehicles [2]	Mil. dol. . .	5,813	5,652	4,436	4,724	4,583	3,699	3,227	4,275	4,812	5,266	5,409	4,614
Tractors	Mil. dol. . .	3,683	3,740	2,597	2,606	2,539	1,937	1,513	2,104	2,477	2,763	2,898	2,356
Machinery, equipment	Mil. dol. . .	6,956	6,481	5,068	4,735	4,682	3,232	3,094	4,297	4,150	4,916	5,311	5,059
Repair and maintenance. . .	Mil. dol. . .	5,205	5,278	4,635	4,793	4,908	4,834	4,825	5,017	5,209	5,758	5,401	5,403
Tractors, machinery and equipment.	Mil. dol. . .	3,746	3,771	3,557	3,616	3,592	3,442	3,428	3,540	3,591	3,961	3,761	3,783
Autos and trucks	Mil. dol. . .	1,459	1,507	1,079	1,178	1,316	1,392	1,397	1,477	1,618	1,797	1,640	1,620
Retail sales: [3]													
Tractors, total [4].	1,000. . .	119.3	103.8	77.2	71.3	66.7	58.5	47.1	48.3	52.0	59.7	66.3	58.1
Two-wheel drive.	1,000. . .	108.4	94.1	70.4	66.2	62.7	55.5	45.1	46.6	49.3	55.5	61.2	54.0
Four-wheel drive	1,000. . .	10.9	9.7	6.8	5.1	4.0	3.0	2.0	1.7	2.7	4.2	5.1	4.1
Combines	1,000. . .	25.7	26.8	16.2	12.8	11.4	8.4	7.7	7.2	6.0	9.1	10.4	9.7
Field forage harvesters. . .	1,000. . .	9.5	7.6	5.1	4.4	3.5	2.5	2.2	2.3	2.4	2.8	3.3	(NA)

NA Not available.   [1] Farm inventory valuations as of December 31. Includes family automobiles.   [2] For farm business use.   [3] Source: Equipment Manufacturers Institute, Chicago, IL, unpublished data.   [4] Covers tractors over 40 hp. only.

Source: Except as noted, U.S. Dept. of Agriculture, Economic Research Service, *Economic Indicators of the Farm Sector: National Financial Summary*, annual. Also in *Agricultural Statistics*, annual.

No. 1120. Hired Farmworkers—Workers and Weekly Earnings: 1990 and 1991

[Represents average number of persons 15 years old and over in the civilian noninstitutional population who were employed at hired farmwork at any time during the year. Based on Current Population Survey; see text, section 1 and Appendix III. For definition of median, see Guide to Tabular Presentation]

CHARACTERISTIC	WORKERS (1,000)		MEDIAN WEEKLY EARNINGS [1]		CHARACTERISTIC	WORKERS (1,000)		MEDIAN WEEKLY EARNINGS [1]	
	1990	1991	1990	1991		1990	1991	1990	1991
All workers	886	884	$200	$210	White [2]	540	533	201	222
					Black and other races [2]	85	101	175	170
15 to 19 years old	144	128	100	100	Hispanic	260	250	213	220
20 to 24 years old	135	114	206	200					
25 to 34 years old	251	256	240	250	Years of school completed:				
35 to 44 years old	170	180	250	242	Less than 5 years	98	101	204	216
45 to 54 years old	90	95	200	216	5 to 8 years	191	187	200	200
55 years old and over	95	111	200	200	9 to 11 years	202	200	168	162
					12 years	278	274	240	240
Male	735	728	216	220	13 or more years	116	122	260	263
Female	151	156	175	181					

[1] The weekly earnings the farmworker usually earns at his farmwork job before deductions and includes any overtime pay or commissions.   [2] Excludes persons of Hispanic origin.

Source: U.S. Dept. of Agriculture, Economic Research Service, unpublished data.

No. 1121. Farm Output Indexes: 1970 to 1991

[1977=100. See also *Historical Statistics, Colonial Times to 1970*, series K 414-429]

ITEM	1970	1980	1982	1983	1984	1985	1986	1987	1988	1989	1990	1991, prel.
Farm output [1]	84	104	116	96	112	118	111	110	102	114	119	120
Per unit of total input	87	101	119	100	118	129	124	124	116	130	135	(NA)
Gross production:												
Livestock and products [2]	99	108	107	109	107	110	110	113	116	116	118	119
Meat animals	102	107	101	104	101	102	100	102	105	105	104	104
Dairy products	95	105	110	114	110	117	116	116	118	117	120	121
Poultry and eggs	93	115	119	120	123	128	133	144	148	153	162	168
Crops [3]	77	101	117	88	111	118	109	108	92	107	114	111
Feed grains	71	97	122	67	116	134	123	106	73	108	112	106
Hay and forage	92	98	109	100	107	106	106	102	89	101	102	103
Food grains	69	121	138	117	129	121	107	107	98	107	136	104
Vegetables	96	104	116	107	117	122	117	126	115	130	135	(NA)
Fruits and nuts	81	119	113	110	114	119	111	137	137	129	134	(NA)
Sugar crops	95	97	96	93	95	97	106	111	105	105	107	112
Cotton	72	79	85	55	91	94	69	103	107	86	109	122
Tobacco	100	93	104	75	90	81	63	62	72	71	84	87
Oil crops	66	99	121	91	106	117	110	108	89	106	107	114

NA Not available.   [1] Annual production available for eventual human use.   [2] Includes livestock products not shown separately and excludes horses and mules.   [3] Includes crops not shown separately.

Source: U.S. Dept. of Agriculture, Economic Research Service, *Economic Indicators of the Farm Sector: Production and Efficiency Statistics*, annual. Also in *Agricultural Outlook*, monthly.

No. 1122. Selected Farm Products—United States and World Production and Exports: 1990 to 1992

[In metric tons, except as indicated. Metric ton=1.102 short tons or .984 long tons]

ITEM	Unit	AMOUNT						UNITED STATES AS PERCENT OF WORLD		
		United States			World			1990	1991	1992
		1990	1991	1992	1990	1991	1992			
PRODUCTION [1]										
Wheat	Million	74	54	67	588	542	555	12.6	10.0	12.1
Corn for grain	Million	202	190	237	477	485	520	42.3	39.2	45.6
Soybeans	Million	52	54	59	104	106	112	50.0	51.0	52.7
Rice, milled	Million	5.1	4.9	5.3	351	348	351	1.5	1.4	1.5
Tobacco, unmanufactured [2]	1,000	738	755	763	7,107	7,576	8,077	10.4	10.0	9.4
Cotton [3]	Million bales [4]	12.2	15.5	17.6	79.8	87.0	96.0	15.3	17.8	18.3
EXPORTS [5]										
Wheat [6]	Million	28.3	35.1	36.5	94.4	108.2	101.4	30.0	32.4	36.0
Corn	Million	44.5	40.6	42.5	58.8	61.5	61.0	75.7	66.0	69.7
Soybeans	Million	15.2	18.6	20.3	25.1	28.1	30.1	60.6	66.2	66.3
Rice, milled basis	Million	2.4	2.2	2.1	12.2	12.8	15.1	19.7	17.2	13.9
Tobacco, unmanufactured [7]	1,000	223	226	261	1,689	1,824	1,816	13.2	12.4	14.4
Cotton [3]	Million	1.7	1.7	1.5	5.2	5.0	4.9	32.7	34.0	30.6

[1] Production years vary by commodity. In most cases, includes harvests from July 1 of the year shown through June 30 of the following year.   [2] Farm sales weight basis.   [3] For production and trade years ending in year shown.   [4] Bales of 480 lb. net weight.   [5] Trade years may vary by commodity.   [6] Includes wheat flour on a grain equivalent.   [7] Dried weight basis.

Source: U.S. Department of Agriculture, Foreign Agricultural Service, *Foreign Agricultural Commodity Circular Series*, periodic.

No. 1123. Agricultural Exports and Imports—Volume, by Principal Commodities: 1980 to 1991

[In thousands of metric tons]

EXPORTS	1980	1985	1990	1991	IMPORTS	1980	1985	1990	1991
Animal products [1]	2,575	2,517	2,737	3,007	Fruits, nuts, vegetables . . .	2,325	3,326	4,573	4,731
Wheat and products [2]	37,130	26,123	28,286	31,949	Bananas	2,352	2,969	3,094	3,229
Feed grains and products	72,970	51,735	61,397	52,369	Green coffee	1,089	1,122	1,174	1,131
Rice.	3,075	1,961	2,509	2,319	Cocoa and products	325	565	765	761
Feeds and fodders	6,888	6,710	11,248	11,210	Meat and products [5]	931	1,139	1,165	1,147
Protein meal	7,427	4,849	4,868	5,907					
Oilseeds and products [3]	23,631	17,682	15,778	18,182	Vegetable oils	704	961	1,183	1,207
Vegetable oils	1,837	1,142	1,204	1,154	Rubber, crude natural	931	818	840	798
Fruits, nuts, vegetables [4]	4,147	3,255	5,552	5,442	Sugar	3,744	2,178	1,856	1,613
Cotton and linters.	1,880	1,135	1,733	1,543	Spices	86	89	109	123
Tobacco, unmanufactured	272	249	223	226	Tobacco, unmanufactured .	392	196	187	227

[1] Includes meat and products, poultry meats, dairy products, and fats, oils and greases. Excludes live animals, hides, skins, and eggs. [2] Includes flour and bulgur. [3] Includes soybeans, sunflowerseeds, peanuts, cottonseed, safflowerseed, flaxseed, and nondefatted soybean flour. [4] Excludes fruit juices. [5] Excludes poultry.

Source: U.S. Dept. of Agriculture, Economic Research Service, *Foreign Agricultural Trade of the United States*, Jan./Feb. 1992 and calendar year supplements.

No. 1124. Agricultural Exports and Imports—Value: 1970 to 1991

[In billions of dollars, except percent. Includes Puerto Rico. Excludes forest products and distilled liquors; includes crude rubber and similar gums (now mainly plantation products). Includes shipments under foreign aid programs. See also *Historical Statistics, Colonial Times to 1970*, series K 251-255]

YEAR	Trade balance	Exports, domestic products	Percent of all exports	Imports for consumption	Percent of all imports	YEAR	Trade balance	Exports, domestic products	Percent of all exports	Imports for consumption	Percent of all imports
1970.	1.5	7.3	17	5.8	15	1983.	19.5	36.1	18	16.6	7
1975.	12.6	21.9	21	9.3	10	1984.	18.5	37.8	17	19.3	6
1976.	12.0	23.0	20	11.0	9	1985.	9.1	29.0	13	20.0	6
1977.	10.2	23.6	20	13.4	9	1986.	4.8	26.2	13	21.5	6
1978.	14.6	29.4	21	14.8	9	1987.	8.3	28.7	12	20.4	5
1979.	18.0	34.7	19	16.7	8	1988.	16.1	37.1	12	21.0	5
1980.	23.9	41.2	18	17.4	7	1989.	18.2	39.9	11	21.7	5
1981.	26.6	43.3	18	16.8	6	1990.	16.6	39.4	10	22.8	5
1982.	21.2	36.6	17	15.4	6	1991.	16.5	39.2	10	22.7	5

Source: U.S. Dept. of Agriculture, Economic Research Service, *Foreign Agricultural Trade of the United States*, Jan.-Feb. issues and calendar year supplements. Also in *Agricultural Statistics*, annual.

No. 1125. Agricultural Imports— Value, by Selected Commodity, 1980 to 1991, and by Leading Countries of Origin, 1991

[In millions of dollars]

COMMODITY	1980	1985	1987	1988	1989	1990	1991	Leading countries of origin, 1991
Total	17,366	19,968	20,402	20,951	21,749	22,770	22,719	Canada, Mexico, Brazil
Competitive products.	10,374	13,067	13,781	14,688	15,610	17,202	17,139	Canada, Mexico, Australia
Cattle, live	237	307	421	598	662	978	952	Canada, Mexico, Japan
Beef and veal	1,780	1,276	1,562	1,679	1,662	1,872	1,964	Australia, New Zealand, Argentina
Pork	486	861	1,096	933	754	938	795	Canada, Denmark, Hungary
Dairy products.	488	765	831	875	828	867	772	New Zealand, Ireland, Italy
Fruits and preparations . .	564	1,738	1,718	1,866	1,820	2,219	2,131	Mexico, Chile, Brazil
Vegetables and preparations	864	1,385	1,535	1,615	2,047	2,266	2,211	Mexico, Canada, Spain
Wine	692	998	966	939	930	917	915	France, Italy, Spain
Malt beverages	367	633	882	918	855	923	825	Netherlands, Canada, Mexico
Grains and feeds	371	623	748	909	1,219	1,189	1,321	Canada, Thailand, Italy
Sugar and related products	2,205	1,190	630	690	956	1,172	1,065	Canada, Guatemala, Philippines
Oilseeds and products . .	599	756	643	919	916	949	974	Canada, Italy, Philippines
Noncompetitive products . .	6,992	6,902	6,621	6,263	6,139	5,568	5,580	Brazil, Indonesia, Colombia
Coffee and products. . . .	4,186	3,322	2,908	2,470	2,432	1,915	1,859	Brazil, Colombia, Mexico
Rubber, crude natural. . .	817	654	760	1,023	958	707	663	Indonesia, Malaysia, Thailand
Cocoa and products	920	1,351	1,194	1,003	991	1,094	1,092	Brazil, Ivory Coast, Canada
Bananas and plantains . .	430	763	819	832	872	939	1,006	Ecuador, Costa Rica, Colombia

Source: U.S. Dept. of Agriculture, Economic Research Service, *Foreign Agricultural Trade of the United States*, calendar year supplement.

No. 1126. Spices—Imports, by Type of Spice: 1975 to 1991

[In millions of pounds. Data shown are annual averages. The United States produces only three major spices - capsicum (red pepper), paprika, and mustard - in any profitable degree. Unground or unprocessed spices enter duty-free. Most spices imported into the United States are unground or unprocessed, generally ensuring better quality]

SPICE	1975-79	1980-84	1985-89	1990	1991	SPICE	1975-79	1980-84	1985-89	1990	1991
Total [1]	298.4	351.3	398.9	461.7	466.3	Mace	0.5	0.6	0.6	0.7	0.4
						Mustard seed	76.1	79.5	94.5	122.6	121.9
Anise seed	1.0	1.4	2.2	2.2	2.5	Nutmeg	4.4	4.8	4.2	3.8	4.1
Capsicum	10.2	13.9	23.8	44.0	38.8	Paprika	12.3	10.5	13.1	9.1	8.6
Caraway seed	6.5	7.5	7.7	6.8	8.1	Pepper, black and white	59.0	72.5	79.4	86.9	98.5
Cassia and cinnamon	18.6	23.4	29.4	25.6	31.6	Pimento	1.5	1.7	1.9	2.2	2.3
Celery seed	4.2	4.7	5.4	4.9	5.9	Poppy seed	6.1	7.2	8.8	7.4	11.0
Cloves	2.5	2.1	2.5	4.1	2.5	Sage	2.9	3.7	4.4	3.7	5.0
Coriander seed	6.8	10.4	7.7	4.8	5.4	Sesame seed	62.5	80.4	81.1	94.5	80.4
Cumin seed	8.1	8.8	9.2	10.3	8.8	Turmeric	3.2	3.7	4.4	3.7	4.1
Fennel seed	1.9	3.4	4.8	6.4	5.5	Vanilla beans	2.3	1.6	2.4	2.2	2.9
Ginger root	7.8	9.5	11.4	15.8	18.0						

[1] The United States also imports limited amounts of other spices which are not included in the total.

Source: U.S. Dept. of Agriculture, Economic Research Service, *Foreign Agricultural Trade of the United States*, calendar year supplement, and, U.S. Bureau of the Census, *U.S. Imports for Consumption*, series FT247, annual.

No. 1127. Agricultural Exports—Value, by Principal Commodities and Selected Countries of Destination: 1980 to 1991

[See headnote, table 1124. Data by country of destination for 1980 are not adjusted for transshipments]

COMMODITY AND COUNTRY	VALUE (mil. dol.)								PERCENT		
	1980	1985	1986	1987	1988	1989	1990	1991	1980	1990	1991
Total agricultural exports [1]	41,234	29,041	26,222	28,709	37,080	39,909	39,363	39,191	100.0	100.0	100.0
Grains and feeds [2]	19,126	11,882	8,656	9,423	13,994	17,187	14,403	12,769	46.4	36.6	32.6
Feed grains and products	9,852	6,112	3,176	3,917	5,973	7,870	7,151	5,861	23.9	18.2	15.0
Corn	8,492	5,206	2,605	3,209	5,043	6,580	6,027	4,915	20.6	15.4	12.5
Wheat and products	6,660	3,898	3,290	3,280	5,126	6,136	4,033	3,512	16.2	10.2	9.0
Rice	1,289	665	625	576	809	971	800	752	3.2	2.1	1.9
Oilseeds and products [2]	9,394	5,794	6,467	6,446	7,695	6,313	5,684	6,358	22.8	14.5	16.2
Soybeans	5,880	3,732	4,326	4,378	4,863	3,942	3,551	3,957	14.3	9.1	10.1
Soybean oilcake and meal	1,666	870	1,229	1,211	1,580	1,181	992	1,137	4.1	2.6	2.9
Vegetable oils and waxes	1,216	870	672	626	983	872	808	768	3.0	2.1	2.0
Animals and animal products [2]	3,768	4,150	4,547	5,156	6,422	6,378	6,712	7,009	9.2	17.1	17.9
Hides and skins, incl. furskins	1,046	1,295	1,522	1,731	1,829	1,717	1,747	1,375	2.6	4.4	3.5
Cattle hides	637	1,007	1,219	1,328	1,513	1,383	1,428	1,140	1.6	3.7	2.9
Meats and meat products	890	905	1,130	1,366	1,974	2,348	2,558	2,854	2.2	6.5	7.3
Beef and veal	249	467	634	771	1,109	1,420	1,579	1,758	0.6	4.1	4.5
Fats, oils, and greases	769	619	413	431	577	512	424	442	1.9	1.1	1.2
Poultry and poultry products	603	384	504	602	689	713	954	1,094	1.5	2.5	2.8
Cotton, excluding linters	2,864	1,633	812	1,631	1,975	2,250	2,783	2,480	7.0	7.1	6.4
Tobacco, unmanufactured	1,334	1,521	1,223	1,090	1,253	1,301	1,441	1,428	3.3	3.7	3.7
Fruits and preparations	1,335	1,186	1,306	1,484	1,762	1,836	2,359	2,498	3.3	6.0	6.4
Fresh fruits	739	743	851	939	1,093	1,133	1,486	1,561	1.8	3.8	4.0
Vegetables and preparations	1,188	930	1,085	1,158	1,361	1,601	2,302	2,615	2.9	5.9	6.7
Nuts and preparations	757	683	753	804	884	846	976	1,020	1.9	2.5	2.6
Other	1,468	1,262	1,373	1,517	1,724	2,197	2,703	3,014	3.6	6.9	7.7
Asia [1]	15,046	11,191	10,617	12,535	16,858	18,828	17,640	16,451	36.5	44.9	42.0
Japan	6,133	5,409	5,141	5,723	7,640	8,162	8,104	7,729	14.9	20.6	19.8
South Korea	1,797	1,413	1,306	1,833	2,274	2,593	2,644	2,104	4.4	6.8	5.4
China: Taiwan	1,095	1,231	1,171	1,285	1,661	1,754	1,661	1,899	2.7	4.3	4.9
Mainland	2,277	157	58	362	759	1,435	814	722	5.6	2.1	1.9
Hong Kong	437	389	400	466	489	611	701	772	1.1	1.8	2.0
Western Europe [1][3]	12,917	7,002	7,117	7,344	7,911	6,995	7,353	7,468	31.4	18.7	19.1
European Economic Community [4]	12,177	6,542	6,688	6,914	7,370	6,503	6,850	6,916	29.6	17.4	17.7
Netherlands	3,476	1,869	2,073	1,985	2,059	1,722	1,581	1,698	8.5	4.1	4.4
Germany	2,373	1,009	1,109	1,320	1,248	1,075	1,158	1,076	5.8	3.0	2.8
Spain [5]	1,488	837	703	666	883	820	937	928	3.6	2.4	2.4
United Kingdom	996	604	681	661	835	703	829	831	2.5	2.1	2.2
Italy	1,203	669	727	697	699	637	710	674	3.0	1.8	1.8
France	765	403	439	524	534	458	528	581	1.9	1.4	1.5
Latin America [1]	6,154	4,224	3,681	3,678	4,935	5,337	5,092	5,684	15.0	13.0	14.5
Mexico	2,469	1,439	1,080	1,202	2,234	2,724	2,553	2,998	6.0	6.5	7.7
Canada	1,908	1,622	1,542	1,808	2,019	2,221	4,197	4,554	4.7	10.7	11.7
Soviet Union (former)	1,138	1,923	658	938	2,252	3,597	2,271	2,495	2.8	5.8	6.4
Eastern Europe	1,644	414	373	401	464	401	537	234	4.0	1.4	0.6
Africa [1]	2,237	2,488	2,008	1,766	2,387	2,260	1,935	1,911	5.5	5.0	4.9
Algeria	195	227	287	310	596	504	513	486	0.5	1.3	1.3
Egypt	774	891	811	679	841	989	693	687	1.9	1.8	1.8

[1] Includes areas not shown separately. [2] Includes commodities not shown separately. [3] Includes Canary Islands and Madeira Islands for all years. [4] Includes Belgium, Luxembourg, Denmark, Greece, Ireland, and Portugal, not shown separately. As of Jan. 1, 1981, Greece became a member of EEC. As of Jan. 1, 1986, Spain and Portugal became members of EEC. For consistency, data for all years are shown on same basis. [5] As of Jan. 1, 1984, includes Canary Islands and Spanish Africa, not elsewhere classified.

Source: U.S. Dept. of Agriculture, Economic Research Service, *Foreign Agricultural Trade of the United States*, Jan./Feb. 1992 and calendar year supplements. Also in *Agricultural Statistics*, annual.

No. 1128. Cropland Used for Crops and Acreages of Crops Harvested: 1980 to 1992

[See also *Historical Statistics, Colonial Times to 1970*, series K 496-501]

YEAR	CROPLAND USED FOR CROPS					ACREAGES OF CROPS HARVESTED [2]				
	Number (mil. acres)				Index of crop production per acre (1977=100)	Total (mil. acres)	Used to produce goods for—			
							Domestic use		Exports	
	Total	Cropland harvested [1]	Crop failure	Cultivated summer fallow	Index (1977=100)			Amount (mil. acres)	Per capita (acres) [3]	Amount (mil. acres)	Percent of total
1980 . . .	382	342	10	30	101	100	352	215	0.94	137	38.9
1985 . . .	372	334	7	31	98	120	342	263	1.10	81	23.7
1988 . . .	327	287	10	30	87	106	298	180	0.73	118	39.7
1989 . . .	341	306	8	27	90	119	318	215	0.86	103	32.4
1990 . . .	341	310	6	25	90	127	322	239	0.95	83	25.8
1991 [4] . .	337	306	7	24	89	(NA)	(NA)	(NA)	(NA)	(NA)	(NA)
1992 [4] . .	343	312	8	23	91	(NA)	(NA)	(NA)	(NA)	(NA)	(NA)

NA Not available.   [1] Land supporting one or more harvested crops.   [2] Area in principal crops harvested as reported by Crop Reporting Board plus acreages in fruits, tree nuts, and farm gardens.   [3] Based on Bureau of the Census estimated total population, including Armed Forces overseas, as of July 1.   [4] Preliminary.

Source: U.S. Dept. of Agriculture, Economic Research Service, *Economic Indicators of the Farm Sector: Production and Efficiency Statistics*, annual. Also in *Agricultural Statistics*, annual. Data for 1991 and 1992 from *Agricultural Resources: Cropland, Water, and Conservation Situation and Outlook Report*.

No. 1129. Crops—Acreage and Value, by State: 1989 to 1992

STATE	ACREAGE HARVESTED (1,000)				FARM VALUE (mil. dol.)				
	1989	1990	1991	1992, prel.	1989	1990	1991	1992, prel.	
								Value	Rank
U.S. [1]	305,072	308,318	[2]303,864	[2]307,314	80,635	80,855	79,593	86,480	(X)
AL.	2,334	2,338	2,229	2,130	575	464	584	613	33
AZ.	830	802	770	736	1,003	894	891	829	32
AR.	7,603	8,080	7,863	8,110	1,615	1,648	1,762	1,962	16
CA.	4,892	4,789	4,396	4,433	10,397	10,642	9,934	11,194	1
CO	5,677	5,862	5,591	5,394	1,341	1,194	1,127	1,100	26
CT.	128	129	125	128	95	111	92	88	47
DE.	537	496	556	515	127	139	142	133	44
FL.	1,128	1,076	1,048	1,093	3,603	2,768	3,348	3,905	5
GA	4,200	3,788	3,777	3,690	1,400	1,273	1,593	1,613	21
HI	81	79	74	71	407	411	367	361	37
ID	4,226	4,175	4,079	4,006	1,964	1,735	1,665	1,758	19
IL	22,977	22,759	22,906	23,237	6,053	5,812	5,357	6,264	2
IN	11,631	11,485	11,527	11,709	3,152	3,023	2,564	3,190	8
IA	24,097	23,276	23,356	23,816	5,764	5,818	5,634	6,219	3
KS.	18,794	20,978	20,712	20,255	2,268	2,610	2,485	2,934	9
KY.	5,487	5,505	5,495	5,415	1,677	1,721	1,771	2,013	15
LA.	4,075	4,346	3,665	4,029	1,094	1,184	1,126	1,165	24
ME	364	361	351	374	220	180	152	199	41
MD	1,601	1,551	1,562	1,620	360	386	374	426	35
MA	136	135	136	135	167	147	169	169	42
MI	6,360	6,510	6,733	6,797	1,839	1,839	1,942	1,929	17
MN	18,652	18,765	18,692	19,301	4,168	4,177	4,007	3,923	4
MS	4,611	4,719	4,478	4,855	1,042	1,149	1,194	1,269	23
MO	13,249	12,685	12,900	12,904	2,274	2,083	2,122	2,543	13
MT	9,475	8,926	8,687	8,369	1,071	881	1,052	1,028	29
NE.	17,450	18,044	18,366	18,330	3,420	3,621	3,667	3,666	7
NV.	554	520	495	403	170	154	102	101	46
NH	93	91	92	103	27	29	23	37	48
NJ	378	361	380	391	164	170	186	265	39
NM	968	880	1,042	1,053	404	395	395	390	36
NY.	3,560	3,538	3,443	3,185	904	916	964	953	30
NC	4,492	4,336	4,397	4,519	1,852	1,981	2,144	2,033	14
ND	20,520	21,014	20,655	21,011	1,853	2,082	2,188	2,630	12
OH	10,259	10,132	9,972	10,137	2,540	2,597	2,278	2,693	10
OK	9,396	9,688	8,518	9,397	1,167	1,142	913	1,098	27
OR	2,337	2,290	2,260	2,145	1,073	1,035	1,034	1,097	28
PA	4,198	4,094	4,067	4,065	1,270	1,358	1,174	1,414	22
RI	10	10	10	11	5	5	4	6	49
SC	2,280	2,046	1,824	1,887	627	517	639	554	34
SD	15,196	15,528	15,606	15,858	1,455	1,638	1,611	1,822	18
TN	4,569	4,477	4,379	4,324	905	954	956	1,122	25
TX	16,690	18,544	17,714	18,772	3,455	4,023	3,707	3,803	6
UT	983	992	973	990	252	257	220	233	40
VT	442	441	434	463	78	77	78	105	45
VA	2,767	2,725	2,656	2,705	808	846	800	907	31
WA	3,876	3,999	3,861	3,950	2,227	2,529	2,625	2,632	11
WV	664	668	615	639	107	114	114	138	43
WI	8,615	8,550	8,449	8,096	1,911	1,830	2,019	1,672	20
WY	1,628	1,735	1,695	1,706	285	294	300	282	38

X Not applicable.   [1] Excludes Alaska.   [2] Includes sunflower and sugarbeet acreage unallocated by State.

Source: U.S. Dept. of Agriculture, National Agricultural Statistics Service, *Crop Production*, annual; and *Crop Values*, annual.

No. 1130. Principal Crops—Production, Supply, and Disappearance: 1988 to 1992

[Marketing year beginning May 1 for hay, June 1 for wheat, August 1 for cotton and rice, September 1 for soybeans, corn, and sorghum. Acreage, production, and yield of all crops periodically revised on basis of census data. See also *Historical Statistics, Colonial Times to 1970*, series K 506-563]

CROP AND YEAR	ACREAGE (mil.)— Set aside [1]	Planted	Harvested	Yield per acre	Production	Farm price [2]	Farm value (mil. dol.)	Total supply [3]	DISAPPEARANCE Total [4]	Exports	Ending stocks
Corn for grain:				Bu.	Mil. bu.	$/bu.			Mil. bu.		
1988	20.5	67.7	58.3	84.6	4,929	2.54	12,661	9,191	7,260	2,026	1,930
1989	10.8	72.2	64.7	116.3	7,525	2.36	17,897	9,458	8,113	2,368	1,344
1990	10.7	74.2	67.0	118.5	7,934	2.28	18,192	9,282	7,761	1,725	1,521
1991	7.4	76.0	68.8	108.6	7,475	2.37	17,864	9,015	7,915	1,584	1,100
1992, prel	5.3	79.3	72.1	131.4	9,479	2.05	19,378	10,439	8,285	1,600	2,154
Soybeans:				Bu.	Mil. bu.	$/bu.			Mil. bu.		
1988	-	58.8	57.4	27.0	1,549	7.42	11,488	1,855	1,673	527	182
1989	-	60.8	59.5	32.3	1,924	5.69	10,732	2,108	1,869	623	239
1990	-	57.8	56.5	34.1	1,926	5.74	11,042	2,168	1,839	557	329
1991	-	59.2	58.0	34.2	1,987	5.58	11,092	2,319	2,041	685	278
1992, prel	-	59.3	58.4	37.6	2,197	5.40	11,843	2,447	2,097	730	350
Hay:				Sh. tons	Mil. sh. tons	$/ton			Mil. sh. tons		
1988	-	(NA)	65.1	1.94	126	[5][6]85.20	10,457	153	136	(NA)	18
1989	-	(NA)	63.3	2.30	146	[5][6]87.40	11,514	163	136	(NA)	27
1990	-	(NA)	61.4	2.39	147	[5][6]80.60	10,462	174	147	(NA)	27
1991	-	(NA)	62.5	2.45	153	[5][6]71.20	10,006	181	152	(NA)	29
1992, prel	-	(NA)	59.6	2.50	149	[5][6]72.10	10,506	(NA)	(NA)	(NA)	(NA)
Wheat:				Bu.	Mil. bu.	$/bu.			Mil. bu.		
1988	22.4	65.5	53.2	34.1	1,812	3.72	6,684	3,096	2,394	1,415	702
1989	9.6	76.6	62.2	32.7	2,037	3.72	7,542	2,762	2,225	1,232	536
1990	7.5	77.2	69.3	39.5	2,736	2.61	7,184	3,309	2,443	1,068	866
1991	15.9	69.9	57.7	34.3	1,981	3.00	5,957	2,888	2,416	1,281	472
1992, prel	7.0	72.3	64.4	39.4	2,459	3.25	7,979	2,981	2,458	1,275	523
Cotton:				Lb.	Mil. bales [7]	cents/lb.			Mil. bales [7]		
1988	2.2	12.5	11.9	619	[8]15.4	56.6	4,190	21.2	13.9	6.1	[9]7.1
1989	3.5	10.6	9.5	614	[8]12.2	66.2	3,877	19.3	16.5	7.7	[9]3.0
1990	2.0	12.3	11.7	634	[8]15.5	67.1	5,076	18.5	16.5	7.8	[9]2.3
1991	1.2	14.1	13.0	652	[8]17.6	58.1	4,913	20.0	16.2	6.8	[9]3.9
1992, prel	1.6	13.3	11.2	700	[8]16.2	[10]54.6	[10]4,248	19.9	15.7	6.0	[9]4.3
Tobacco: [11]				Lb.	Mil. lb.	$/lb.			Mil. lb.		
1988	(NA)	(NA)	0.6	2,160	1,370	[6]1.65	2,261	4,279	1,565	555	[12]2,714
1989	(NA)	(NA)	0.7	2,016	1,367	[6]1.71	2,338	4,081	1,677	582	[12]2,401
1990	(NA)	(NA)	0.7	2,218	1,626	[6]1.74	2,827	4,026	1,794	631	[12]2,232
1991	(NA)	(NA)	0.8	2,179	1,664	[6]1.77	2,951	3,895	1,615	639	[12]2,280
1992, prel	(NA)	(NA)	0.8	2,171	1,697	[6]1.78	2,996	3,968	(NA)	(NA)	(NA)
Potatoes:				Cwt.	cwt.	$/cwt.			Mil. cwt.		
1988	(NA)	1.3	1.3	283	356	6.02	2,144	558	[13]300	[14]16	(NA)
1989	(NA)	1.3	1.3	289	370	7.36	2,717	555	[13]315	[14]16	(NA)
1990	(NA)	1.4	1.4	293	402	6.08	2,431	582	[13]319	[14]17	(NA)
1991	(NA)	1.4	1.4	304	418	4.96	2,043	618	[13]330	[14]19	(NA)
1992, prel	(NA)	1.4	1.3	316	412	5.28	2,160	629	[13]347	[14]22	(NA)
Sorghum for grain:				Bu.	Mil. bu.	$/bu.			Mil. bu.		
1988	3.9	10.3	9.0	63.8	577	2.27	1,337	1,239	800	311	440
1989	3.3	12.6	11.1	55.4	615	2.10	1,288	1,055	835	303	220
1990	3.3	10.5	9.1	63.1	573	2.12	1,221	793	650	232	143
1991	2.5	11.1	9.9	59.3	585	2.25	1,331	722	669	291	53
1992, prel	1.9	13.3	12.2	72.8	884	1.90	1,693	931	810	300	121
Rice, rough:				Lb.	cwt.	$/cwt.			Mil. cwt.		
1988	1.1	2.9	2.9	5,514	160	6.83	1,092	195	168	86	27
1989	1.2	2.7	2.7	5,749	155	7.35	1,134	186	159	77	26
1990	1.0	2.9	2.8	5,529	156	6.70	1,047	187	163	71	25
1991	0.9	2.9	2.8	5,674	157	7.58	1,201	184	157	66	27
1992, prel	0.4	3.2	3.1	5,722	179	6.20	1,099	201	168	74	32

- Represents zero. NA Not available. [1] Acreage set aside under diversion, PIK (payment-in-kind) and acreage reduction programs. [2] Except as noted, marketing year average price. U.S. prices are computed by weighting U.S. monthly prices by estimated monthly marketings and do not include an allowance for outstanding loans and government purchases and payments. [3] Comprises production, imports, and beginning stocks. [4] Includes feed, residual, and other domestic uses not shown separately. [5] Prices are for hay sold baled. [6] Season average prices received by farmers. U.S. prices are computed by weighting State prices by estimated sales and include an allowance for outstanding loans and government purchases, if any, for crops under government programs. [7] Bales of 480 pounds, net weight. [8] State production figures, which conform with U.S. Bureau of the Census annual ginning enumeration with allowance for cross-State ginnings, rounded to thousands and added for U.S. totals. [9] Stock estimates based on Census Bureau data which results in an unaccounted difference between supply and use estimates and changes in ending stocks. [10] Average to April 1, 1993. [11] Flue-cured and cigar wrapper, crop year July-June; all other types October-September. Farm-sales-weight basis. [12] Includes tobacco carried over on farms. [13] Covers potatoes used for table use, frozen and canned products, chips, and dehydration. [14] Covers fresh potatoes, chips, frozen and dehydrated products.

Source: Production—U.S. Dept. of Agriculture, National Agricultural Statistics Service. In *Crop Production*, annual; and *Crop Values*, annual. Supply and disappearance—U.S. Dept. of Agriculture, Economic Research Service, *Feed Situation*, quarterly; *Fats and Oils Situation*, quarterly; *Wheat Situation*, quarterly; *Tobacco Situation*, quarterly; *Cotton and Wool Outlook Statistics*, periodic; and *Agricultural Supply and Demand Estimates*, periodic. All data are also in *Agricultural Statistics*, annual; and *Agricultural Outlook*, monthly.

No. 1131. Selected Crops—Acreage, Production, and Value, by Leading States: 1990 to 1992

[One bushel of corn=56 pounds; one bushel of soybeans or wheat=60 pounds. See also *Historical Statistics, Colonial Times to 1970*, series K 502-508, 521, 553-558, and 561-563]

STATE	ACREAGE HARVESTED (1,000 acres)			YIELD PER ACRE			PRODUCTION			PRICE			FARM VALUE (mil. dol.)		
	1990	1991	1992	1990	1991	1992	1990	1991	1992	1990	1991	1992	1990	1991	1992
CORN				(bu.)			(mil. bu.)			($/bu.)					
U.S. [1] . . .	66,952	68,847	72,144	119	109	131	7,934	7,475	9,479	2.28	2.37	2.05	18,192	17,864	19,378
IA	12,400	12,200	12,950	126	117	147	1,562	1,427	1,904	2.21	2.30	1.95	3,453	3,283	3,712
IL	10,400	11,000	11,050	127	107	149	1,321	1,177	1,646	2.36	2.46	2.05	3,117	2,895	3,375
NE.	7,300	7,800	7,900	128	127	135	934	991	1,067	2.28	2.34	2.05	2,130	2,318	2,186
IN	5,450	5,550	5,970	129	92	147	703	511	878	2.31	2.45	2.00	1,624	1,251	1,755
MN	6,150	6,000	6,500	124	120	114	763	720	741	2.17	2.22	1.90	1,655	1,598	1,408
OH	3,450	3,400	3,550	121	96	143	417	326	508	2.32	2.48	2.00	968	809	1,015
MO	1,960	2,200	2,400	105	97	135	206	213	324	2.38	2.45	2.15	490	523	697
WI	3,000	3,200	2,950	118	119	104	354	381	307	2.18	2.30	2.10	772	876	644
SD.	3,000	3,250	3,300	78	74	84	234	241	277	2.08	2.16	1.85	487	519	513
KS.	1,450	1,650	1,730	130	125	150	189	206	260	2.25	2.42	2.15	424	499	558
MI	2,070	2,300	2,300	115	110	105	238	253	242	2.21	2.34	2.00	526	592	483
TX.	1,450	1,500	1,620	90	110	125	131	165	203	2.51	2.68	2.45	328	442	496
KY.	1,200	1,250	1,300	100	89	132	120	111	172	2.48	2.58	2.20	298	287	378
CO	830	840	835	155	153	148	129	129	124	2.36	2.43	2.20	304	312	272
PA.	970	860	990	113	75	120	110	65	119	2.62	2.87	2.20	287	185	261
NC	1,070	950	1,040	68	90	95	73	86	99	2.53	2.63	2.20	184	225	217
SOYBEANS				(bu.)			(mil. bu.)			($/bu.)					
U.S. [1] . . .	56,512	58,011	58,383	34	34	38	1,926	1,987	2,197	5.74	5.58	5.40	11,042	11,092	11,843
IL	9,100	9,100	9,430	39	38	43	355	341	405	5.85	5.70	5.45	2,076	1,945	2,210
IA	7,900	8,630	8,270	42	41	44	328	350	364	5.63	5.51	5.35	1,846	1,926	1,947
IN	4,180	4,400	4,520	41	39	43	171	172	194	5.81	5.68	5.40	996	975	1,050
MN	4,600	5,350	5,400	39	37	32	179	195	173	5.55	5.41	5.35	996	1,056	924
MO	4,150	4,430	4,250	30	31	38	125	135	162	5.73	5.59	5.30	713	755	856
OH	3,480	3,770	3,680	39	36	40	136	136	147	5.81	5.69	5.45	789	772	802
AR.	3,350	3,200	3,160	27	28	33	90	90	104	5.91	5.71	5.60	535	512	584
NE.	2,360	2,460	2,460	35	34	42	81	82	103	5.59	5.47	5.25	455	451	542
KS.	1,950	1,900	1,850	24	23	37	47	44	68	5.67	5.55	5.30	265	243	363
SD.	1,920	2,160	2,250	28	27	28	54	58	63	5.54	5.33	5.10	298	311	321
MS	1,900	1,800	1,750	21	26	34	40	47	60	5.88	5.74	5.60	235	269	333
MI	1,140	1,390	1,440	38	38	33	43	53	48	5.63	5.52	5.45	244	292	259
KY.	1,220	1,130	1,160	32	33	38	39	37	44	5.86	5.78	5.50	229	212	242
NC	1,350	1,310	1,350	24	30	27	32	39	36	5.68	5.56	5.45	184	215	199
WHEAT				(bu.)			(mil. bu.)			($/bu.)					
U.S. [1] . . .	69,283	57,703	62,407	40	34	39	2,736	1,981	2,459	2.61	3.00	3.25	7,184	5,957	7,979
ND	10,910	9,790	11,420	35	31	41	385	304	470	2.46	3.04	3.15	945	926	1,485
KS.	11,800	11,000	10,700	40	33	34	472	363	364	2.51	2.81	3.10	1,185	1,020	1,128
OK	6,300	5,000	5,900	32	28	29	202	140	171	2.57	2.85	3.15	518	399	539
MN	2,865	2,155	2,805	48	31	50	139	67	140	2.53	3.21	3.15	349	215	440
MT	5,185	4,379	4,707	28	36	30	146	160	140	2.65	3.17	3.45	384	506	481
TX.	4,200	2,800	3,800	31	30	34	130	84	129	2.74	2.69	3.20	357	226	413
WA	2,480	2,150	2,420	61	46	49	150	99	120	2.73	3.73	3.85	409	367	461
SD.	3,789	3,117	3,733	34	31	32	128	96	120	2.52	3.06	3.20	321	295	384
ID	1,370	1,160	1,440	73	70	69	100	82	100	2.53	3.56	3.60	252	290	358
CO	2,590	2,336	2,347	34	32	31	87	74	73	2.46	3.07	3.15	214	227	228
MO	2,000	1,500	1,350	38	32	48	76	48	65	2.69	2.37	3.10	204	114	201
IL	1,850	1,400	1,150	48	32	54	89	45	62	2.75	2.56	3.25	244	115	202
OH	1,350	1,080	1,115	59	49	53	80	53	59	2.70	2.93	3.05	215	155	180
COTTON				(lb.)			(1,000 bales) [2]			(cents/lb.)					
U.S. [1] . . .	11,732	12,960	11,153	634	652	700	15,505	17,614	16,218	68.2	58.1	54.6	5,076	4,913	4,248
TX.	5,057	5,457	3,585	479	419	449	5,046	4,758	3,322	63.9	54.0	49.5	1,547	1,233	790
CA.	1,116	1,041	1,105	1,201	1,242	1,338	2,791	2,694	3,111	77.5	68.2	62.4	1,039	882	931
MS	1,221	1,231	1,345	728	888	767	1,852	2,276	2,131	65.4	55.2	50.9	581	603	521
AR.	750	980	980	692	772	833	1,081	1,576	1,681	65.7	57.1	55.3	341	432	446
LA.	790	820	870	715	828	712	1,177	1,414	1,299	66.1	53.1	51.5	373	360	321
AZ.	472	462	425	1,022	1,125	968	1,005	1,083	863	75.9	66.7	58.4	366	347	242
TN.	515	610	618	461	522	649	495	701	834	66.3	53.9	52.6	158	181	211
TOBACCO				(lb.)			(mil. lb.)			($/lb.)					
U.S. [1] . . .	733	764	782	2,218	2,179	2,171	1,626	1,664	1,697	1.74	1.77	1.78	2,827	2,951	2,996
NC	284	275	270	2,251	2,308	2,204	640	635	596	1.68	1.73	1.74	1,076	1,099	1,034
KY.	194	223	231	2,278	2,151	2,203	442	480	509	1.76	1.80	1.83	779	863	933
TN.	54	62	67	2,094	1,969	2,016	112	122	135	1.78	1.83	1.85	200	223	250
SC.	51	51	52	2,155	2,180	2,160	110	111	112	1.59	1.72	1.70	174	191	191
VA.	53	54	51	2,074	2,184	2,166	110	117	111	1.71	1.72	1.77	188	201	196
GA	43	40	44	2,415	2,015	2,300	104	81	101	1.68	1.69	1.69	175	137	171

[1] Includes other States, not shown separately.   [2] Bales of 480 lb. net weight.

Source: U.S. Dept. of Agriculture, National Agricultural Statistics Service, *Crop Production*, annual; and *Crop Values*, annual.

No. 1132. Sugar Beets, Sugarcane, and Sugar—Summary: 1990 to 1992

[Data are for crop year. See also *Historical Statistics, Colonial Times to 1970*, series K 542-546]

ITEM	Unit	SUGAR BEETS			SUGARCANE FOR SUGAR AND SEED			YEAR	SUGAR PRODUCTION (1,000 tons)	
		1990	1991	1992	1990	1991	1992		Raw value [1]	Refined basis [2]
Acreage harvested ..	1,000 acres .	1,377	1,387	1,411	794	897	935	**Beet:** 1990.	3,842	3,591
Yield per acre	Sh. tons....	20.0	20.3	20.4	35.4	33.7	33.0	1991.	3,729	3,485
Production	Mil. tons ...	27.5	28.2	28.8	28.1	30.3	30.9	1992.	4,147	3,876
Price per ton [3]	Dollars	43.00	38.50	(NA)	[4]30.80	[4]29.00	(NA)	**Cane:** 1990	3,152	2,945
Farm value	Mil. dol	1,182	1,086	(NA)	[5]863	[5]876	(NA)	1991.	3,430	3,206
								1992.	3,416	3,193

NA Not available. [1] Raw value equals 96 degree sugar as defined in Sugar Act of 1948. [2] Calculated on the basis of 100 lbs. of raw sugar required to produce 93.46 lbs. of refined sugar. [3] Season average prices received by farmers. Prices exclude Government payments under Sugar Act. [4] Price per ton for sugar. [5] Price per ton of cane for sugar used in evaluating value of production for seed.

Source: U.S. Dept. of Agriculture, National Agricultural Statistics Service, *Field Crops* (Statistical Bulletin 793); *Crop Production*, June issue and annual; and *Crop Values*, annual.

No. 1133. Fruits and Planted Nuts—Bearing Areas, by Type: 1980 to 1992

[In thousands of acres]

TYPE	1980	1984	1985	1986	1987	1988	1989	1990	1991	1992, prel.
Total	**3,556**	**3,545**	**3,494**	**3,432**	**3,458**	**3,485**	**3,497**	**3,501**	**3,459**	**3,455**
Citrus fruit [1]	1,143	1,008	899	819	826	833	848	852	850	884
Major deciduous fruits [2]	1,608	1,704	1,725	1,728	1,739	1,748	1,751	1,754	1,748	1,746
Miscellaneous noncitrus [3]	242	210	212	216	217	217	213	206	200	[4]167
Planted nuts [5]	563	624	657	670	675	686	687	689	660	659

[1] Grapefruit, lemons, limes, oranges, tangelos, tangerines, and temples. Acreage is for the year harvest was completed. [2] Commercial apples, apricots, cherries, grapes, nectarines, peaches, pears, plums, and prunes. [3] Avocados, bananas, berries (beginning 1992), cranberries (beginning 1984), dates, figs, guavas (beginning 1988), kiwifruit, olives, papayas, pineapples, and pomegranates (until 1989). [4] Excludes avocados and guavas. [5] Almonds, hazelnuts, macadamia nuts, walnuts, and pistachios.

Source: U.S. Dept. of Agriculture, National Agricultural Statistics Service, *Noncitrus Fruits and Nuts*, annual.

No. 1134. Fruits and Nuts—Utilized Production and Value, 1989 to 1991, and Leading Producing States, 1991

FRUIT OR NUT	UTILIZED PRODUCTION [1]			FARM VALUE (mil. dol.)			Leading States in order of production, 1991
	Unit	1989	1990	1991	1989	1990	1991
Apples (35 States) [2]	Mil. lb	9,917	9,658	9,837	1,034	1,457	1,778	WA, NY, MI
Apricots	1,000 tons ..	119	120	92	40	41	37	CA, WA, UT
Avocados	1,000 tons ..	139	156	179	251	206	179	CA, FL, HI
Bananas	Mil. lb	12	11	11	4	4	5	HI
Cherries, sweet	1,000 tons ..	191	132	143	136	118	138	WA, OR, CA
Cherries, tart	Mil. lb .... [3]	243	203	190	35	37	85	MI, UT, NY
Cranberries	1,000 bbl. [3]	3,747	3,391	4,178	165	156	207	MA, WI, NJ
Dates	1,000 tons ..	22	24	22	23	20	21	CA
Figs (fresh)	1,000 tons ..	48	49	37	18	17	13	CA
Grapefruit (4 States)	Mil. boxes [4] .	70	49	56	416	372	393	FL, CA, AZ
Grapes (13 States)	1,000 tons ..	5,930	5,660	5,555	1,863	1,670	1,732	CA, WA, NY
Kiwifruit.................	1,000 tons .	37	34	29	15	14	24	CA
Lemons (2 States)	Mil. boxes [5] .	20	19	19	235	280	289	CA, AZ
Limes (FL).................	Mil. boxes [6] .	2	2	1	21	23	28	FL
Nectarines.................	1,000 tons ..	220	232	215	88	110	86	CA
Olives	1,000 tons ..	123	132	65	57	56	36	CA
Oranges and tangerines (4 States)..	Mil. boxes [7] .	215	188	183	1,932	1,537	1,657	FL, CA, AZ
Papayas	Mil. lb	74	69	55	14	15	16	HI
Peaches (32 States)	Mil. lb	2,230	2,140	2,492	365	372	393	CA, SC, GA
Pears...................	1,000 tons ..	916	964	904	254	270	274	WA, CA, OR
Pineapples	1,000 tons ..	580	575	555	98	106	108	HI
Plums and prunes (fresh)	1,000 tons [6] .	1,017	734	832	281	271	283	CA, WA, MI
Tangelos (FL)	Mil. boxes [6] .	3	3	3	31	21	21	FL
Temples (FL).............	Mil. boxes [8] .	4	1	3	28	11	21	FL
Almonds (shelled basis).........	Mil. lb	490	660	490	481	598	540	CA
Hazelnuts (in the shell)	1,000 tons ..	13	22	26	11	17	19	OR, WA
Macadamia nuts............	Mil. lb	51	50	50	45	41	35	HI
Pecans (in the shell) (11 States) ...	Mil. lb	251	205	299	179	248	310	GA, TX, NM
Pistachios	Mil. lb	39	120	77	64	122	96	CA
Walnuts, English (in the shell)	1,000 tons ..	229	227	259	245	236	280	CA

[1] Excludes quantities not harvested or not marketed. [2] Production in commercial orchards with 100 or more bearing age trees. [3] Barrels of 100 pounds. [4] Approximate average, net weight, is 65 lb. in AZ and CA, 85 in FL, and 80 in TX. [5] About 76 lb. net. [6] Approximate net weight is 80 lb. [7] Net contents of box varies. In CA and AZ approximate average for oranges and tangerines is 75 lb.; FL oranges, 90 lb.; TX oranges, 85 lb.; and FL tangerines, 95 lb. [8] Approximate net weight is 90 lb.

Source: U.S. Dept. of Agriculture, National Agricultural Statistics Service, *Noncitrus Fruits and Nuts*, annual; and *Citrus Fruits*, annual.

No. 1135. Commercial Vegetable and Other Specified Crops—Area, Production, and Value, 1989 to 1991, and Leading Producing States, 1991

[Relates to commercial production for fresh market and processing combined. Includes market garden areas but excludes minor producing acreage in minor producing States. Excludes production for home use in farm and nonfarm gardens. Value is for season or crop year and should not be confused with calendar-year income]

CROP	AREA [1] (1,000 acres)			PRODUCTION [2] (1,000 short tons)			VALUE [3] (mil. dol.)			Leading States in order of production, 1991
	1989	1990	1991	1989	1990	1991	1989	1990	1991	
Asparagus	99	96	92	125	122	113	150	148	150	WA, CA, MI
Beans, snap [4]	249	246	235	870	796	779	151	146	137	WI, OR, MI
Beans, dry edible	1,651	2,084	1,863	1,186	1,619	1,648	677	599	524	ND, MI, NE
Broccoli	117	111	101	676	617	560	276	268	242	CA, AZ, OR
Carrots	102	94	97	1,449	1,462	1,391	297	273	309	CA, WA, MI
Cauliflower	68	66	56	392	393	352	205	190	188	CA, AZ, OR
Celery	35	38	33	1,014	991	955	268	215	206	CA, FL, MI
Corn, sweet	643	676	719	3,756	3,958	4,131	470	468	493	WI, MN, WA
Cucumbers [4]	124	115	104	643	653	623	131	136	131	MI, NC, WI
Honeydew melons	30	26	26	257	225	187	62	81	69	CA, TX, AZ
Lettuce	243	231	222	3,762	3,660	3,539	950	844	810	CA, AZ, FL
Peppermint	101	102	111	3.3	3.5	3.2	87	97	87	OR, WA, ID
Spearmint	26	34	41	0.9	1.3	1.5	26	38	42	WA, WI, ID
Mushrooms [5]	133	138	140	334	357	375	596	645	648	PA, CA, FL
Onions	133	138	134	2,395	2,639	2,535	497	489	581	OR, CA, CO
Peas, green [4]	317	341	333	505	528	491	120	131	128	WI, WA, MN
Potatoes	1,282	1,371	1,375	18,522	20,106	20,911	2,717	2,431	2,095	ID, WA, ND
Strawberries	46	46	47	571	627	684	538	580	634	CA, FL, OR
Sweet potatoes	86	90	78	568	630	575	186	122	142	NC, LA, CA
Tomatoes	462	489	488	11,280	12,041	12,560	1,848	1,626	1,797	CA, FL, OH

[1] Area of crops for harvest for fresh market, including any partially harvested or not harvested because of low prices or other factors, plus area harvested for processing.   [2] Excludes some quantities not marketed.   [3] Fresh market vegetables valued at f.o.b. shipping point. Processing vegetables are equivalent returns at packinghouse door.   [4] Processing only.   [5] Area is shown in million square feet. All data are for marketing year ending June 30.

Source: U.S. Dept. of Agriculture, National Agricultural Statistics Service, *Vegetables*, annual summary. Also in *Agricultural Statistics*, annual.

No. 1136. Fresh Fruits and Vegetables—Consumption and Imports: 1990

[Data for vegetables may include some vegetables for processing]

FRUIT	Total U.S. consumption (mil. lb.)	PERCENT OF CONSUMPTION		VEGETABLE	Total U.S. consumption (mil. lb.)	PERCENT OF CONSUMPTION	
		Imported	Imported from Mexico			Imported	Imported from Mexico
All fruits, total	23,124	35.3	3.3	**All vegetables, total**	49,337	8.4	5.4
Excluding bananas	17,035	12.3	2.5				
Citrus fruits	5,641	3.3	2.1	Asparagus	148	29.6	22.0
Oranges	3,345	0.8	0.2	Beans, snap	267	11.2	10.9
Grapefruit	1,119	0.9	-	Beans, dry edible	1,507	3.7	-
Tangerines	238	15.7	11.5	Broccoli	842	2.5	2.1
Lemons	655	3.5	-	Cantaloupe	2,278	23.3	14.2
Limes	185	47.1	44.8	Carrots	2,004	6.1	1.6
Tangelos	100	-	-	Cabbage	2,178	4.1	1.8
Noncitrus fruits	17,587	44.4	3.0	Celery	1,800	2.3	1.7
Apples	4,979	4.8	-	Cauliflower	556	4.0	3.3
Grapes	1,962	36.7	2.9	Corn, sweet	1,615	0.9	0.9
Pears	815	11.9	-	Cucumbers	1,169	33.7	31.4
Apricots	41	5.3	-	Eggplant	100	35.9	35.8
Avocados	271	10.9	-	Garlic	360	15.2	6.5
Bananas	6,089	99.8	5.5	Honeydew melons	516	22.3	12.6
Cherries, sweet	95	3.3	-	Lettuce	6,940	0.2	0.2
Cherries, tart	4	15.8	-	Mushrooms	497	0.7	-
Cranberries	28	-	-				
Figs	3	5.9	-	Onions	4,643	8.2	6.9
Kiwifruit	124	59.2	-	Peas, green	487	4.1	2.2
Mangoes [1]	104	95.3	82.0	Peppers	1,069	20.6	18.8
Nectarines	376	-	-	Potatoes	11,372	6.0	-
Peaches	933	12.2	-	Squash	340	50.9	48.4
Pineapple	520	48.3	1.7	Sweet potatoes	1,241	4.8	-
Plums and prunes	384	13.5	-	Tomatoes	3,874	20.5	20.1
Strawberries	814	4.0	3.4	Watermelon	3,534	6.5	6.2
Papayas	45	25.5	14.4				

- Represents zero.   [1] Data for 1989.

Source: U.S. Dept. of Agriculture, Economic Research Service, *Agricultural Outlook*, December 1992.

No. 1137. Greenhouse and Nursery Crops—Summary, by Type of Product: 1988 to 1992

[In millions of dollars, except per capita. Based on a survey of 28 commercial floriculture States and estimates by source]

ITEM	Total	Cut flowers	Potted flowering plants	Foliage plants	Bedding plants	Cut cultivated greens	Other [1]
Domestic production: [2]							
1988	7,069	514	643	567	839	102	4,404
1989	7,617	542	681	575	996	111	4,711
1990	8,227	572	872	608	1,003	130	5,040
1991	8,405	552	929	575	1,076	135	5,138
1992, prel	8,800	529	990	569	1,150	140	5,422
Imports: [2]							
1988	429	284	16	22	(NA)	22	86
1989	498	316	20	22	(NA)	13	128
1990	529	326	18	25	(NA)	14	147
1991	533	322	22	27	(NA)	13	150
1992, prel	555	335	23	28	(NA)	14	155
RETAIL CONSUMER EXPENDITURES [3]							
Total:							
1988	32,848	4,778	2,568	2,319	3,357	619	19,208
1989	35,732	5,232	2,880	2,406	3,985	579	20,651
1990	38,195	5,379	3,629	2,418	4,013	670	22,085
1991	38,904	5,229	3,888	2,308	4,304	710	22,464
1992, prel	40,683	5,259	4,139	2,283	4,600	721	23,681
Per capita (dol.): [4]							
1988	134	20	11	9	14	3	79
1989	145	21	12	10	16	2	84
1990	153	22	15	10	16	3	89
1991	154	21	15	9	17	3	89
1992, prel	160	21	16	9	18	3	93

NA Not available. [1] Includes turfgrass (sod), bulbs, nursery stock, groundcovers, and other greenhouse and nursery products except the following: seeds, cut Christmas trees, and food crops grown under cover. [2] Equivalent wholesale values. [3] Excludes services such as landscaping, installation, and maintenance. [4] Based on U.S. Bureau of the Census estimated resident population as of July 1.

Source: U.S. Dept. of Agriculture, Economic Research Service, unpublished data.

No. 1138. Red Meats—Slaughtering, Supply, and Use: 1980 to 1992

[Quantities in millions of pounds (carcass weight equivalent), except as noted. Carcass weight equivalent is the weight of the animal minus entrails, head, and hide; includes internal organs, fat, and bone. Covers inspected, noninspected, retail, and farm slaughter. See also *Historical Statistics, Colonial Times to 1970*, series K 583-594]

YEAR AND TYPE OF MEAT	Animals slaughtered (mil. head)	Production	Imports	Supply, [1] total	Consumption [2]	Exports	Ending stocks
All red meats:							
1980	139.7	38,978	2,668	42,480	41,170	429	881
1985	131.3	39,408	3,255	43,503	42,310	462	732
1989	130.9	39,602	3,137	43,609	41,662	1,287	660
1990	126.4	38,787	3,313	42,760	40,806	1,247	707
1991	128.6	39,585	3,241	43,533	41,234	1,474	825
1992	135.4	41,081	3,126	45,032	42,475	1,758	799
Beef:							
1980	34.1	21,643	2,064	24,166	23,561	173	432
1985	36.6	23,728	2,071	26,271	25,523	328	420
1989	34.1	23,087	2,178	25,687	24,329	1,023	335
1990	33.4	22,743	2,356	25,434	24,031	1,006	397
1991	32.9	22,917	2,406	25,720	24,113	1,188	419
1992	33.1	23,150	2,410	25,979	24,234	1,345	400
Pork:							
1980	97.2	16,617	550	17,521	16,838	252	431
1985	84.9	14,807	1,128	16,282	15,866	128	288
1989	89.0	15,813	896	17,146	16,571	262	313
1990	85.4	15,354	898	16,565	16,031	238	296
1991	88.4	15,999	775	17,010	16,394	283	393
1992	95.3	17,265	650	18,308	17,513	410	385
Veal:							
1980	2.7	400	21	431	420	2	9
1985	3.5	515	20	549	534	5	11
1989	2.2	355	(NA)	360	356	(NA)	4
1990	1.8	327	(NA)	331	325	(NA)	6
1991	1.5	306	(NA)	312	305	(NA)	7
1992	1.4	313	(NA)	320	314	(NA)	6
Lamb and mutton:							
1980	5.7	318	33	362	351	2	9
1985	6.3	358	36	401	387	1	13
1989	5.6	347	63	416	406	2	8
1990	5.8	363	59	430	419	3	8
1991	5.8	363	60	431	422	3	6
1992	5.6	353	66	425	414	3	8

NA Not available. [1] Total supply equals production plus imports plus ending stocks of previous year. [2] Includes shipments to territories.

Source: U.S. Dept. of Agriculture, Economic Research Service, *Livestock and Meat Statistics*, quarterly. Also published in *Agricultural Outlook*, monthly.

No. 1139. Livestock Inventory and Production: 1980 to 1992

[**Production in live weight**; includes animals for slaughter market, younger animals shipped to other States for feeding or breeding purposes, farm slaughter and custom slaughter consumed on farms where produced, minus livestock shipped into States for feeding or breeding with an adjustment for changes in inventory. See also *Historical Statistics, Colonial Times to 1970*, series K 564-569 and 575-582]

TYPE OF LIVESTOCK	Unit	1980	1983	1984	1985	1986	1987	1988	1989	1990	1991	1992
ALL CATTLE [1]												
Inventory: [2] Number on farms	Mil	111.2	115.0	113.4	109.6	105.4	102.1	99.6	98.1	98.2	98.9	100.1
Total value	Bil. dol. .	55.8	46.7	44.8	44.0	41.2	41.6	52.1	56.9	60.3	64.7	63.0
Value per head.	Dol . . .	502	406	396	402	391	407	523	580	614	654	629
Production: Quantity	Bil. lb . .	40.3	40.4	40.1	40.1	40.6	40.5	40.6	40.2	40.4	41.4	(NA)
Beef, price per 100 lb . .	Dol . . .	62.40	55.50	57.30	53.70	52.60	61.10	66.60	69.50	74.60	72.70	(NA)
Calves, price per 100 lb .	Dol . . .	76.80	61.70	59.90	62.10	61.10	78.50	89.20	90.80	95.60	98.00	(NA)
Value of production. . . .	Bil. dol. .	25.5	22.0	22.1	21.2	21.0	24.8	27.2	28.0	30.2	30.6	(NA)
HOGS AND PIGS												
Inventory: [3] Number on farms	Mil	67.3	54.5	56.7	54.1	52.3	51.0	54.4	55.5	53.8	54.5	57.0
Total value	Bil. dol. .	3.8	4.9	3.3	4.1	3.6	4.7	4.1	3.7	4.3	4.7	3.9
Value per head.	Dol . . .	56.00	89.90	58.80	75.00	69.60	91.90	76.00	66.30	79.10	85.40	69.10
Production: Quantity	Bil. lb . .	23.4	21.2	20.2	20.2	19.5	20.4	21.7	21.9	21.3	22.8	(NA)
Price per 100 lb	Dol . . .	38.00	46.80	47.10	44.00	49.30	51.20	42.30	42.50	53.70	49.10	(NA)
Value of production. . . .	Bil. dol. .	8.9	9.9	9.5	8.9	9.6	10.4	9.1	9.3	11.4	11.1	(NA)
SHEEP AND LAMBS												
Inventory: [2] Number on farms	Mil	12.7	12.1	11.6	10.7	10.1	10.6	10.9	10.9	11.4	11.2	10.9
Total value	Mil. dol .	993	629	603	654	684	799	985	895	902	735	666
Value per head.	Dol . . .	78.20	51.80	52.10	61.10	67.40	75.70	90.00	82.40	79.30	65.60	61.40
Production: Quantity	Mil. lb . .	746	769	700	704	726	733	707	776	758	768	(NA)
Sheep, price per 100 lb .	Dol . . .	21.30	15.70	16.40	23.90	25.60	29.50	25.60	24.40	23.20	19.70	(NA)
Lambs, price per 100 lb .	Dol . . .	63.60	53.90	60.10	67.70	69.00	77.60	69.10	66.10	55.50	52.20	(NA)
Value of production. . . .	Mil. dol .	403	356	378	434	445	503	420	446	362	342	(NA)

NA Not available.   [1] Includes milk cows.   [2] As of Jan. 1.   [3] As of Dec. 1 of preceding year.
Source: U.S. Dept. of Agriculture, National Agricultural Statistics Service, *Meat Animals—Production, Disposition, and Income*, annual; and annual livestock summaries. Also in *Agricultural Statistics*, annual.

No. 1140. Cattle and Calves; and Hogs and Pigs—Number, Production, and Value, by State: 1989 to 1992

[See headnote, table 1139]

STATE	NUMBER ON FARMS [1] (1,000)			QUANTITY PRODUCED (mil. lb.)			VALUE OF PRODUCTION (mil. dol.)			COMMERCIAL SLAUGHTER [2] (mil. lb.)		
	1990	1991	1992	1989	1990	1991	1989	1990	1991	1989	1990	1991
CATTLE AND CALVES [3]												
U.S. [4]	98,162	98,896	100,110	40,241	40,386	41,412	28,031	30,229	30,551	38,467	37,758	38,029
AL	1,750	1,800	1,800	647	767	786	440	548	611	297	288	(5)
AR	1,700	1,690	1,710	648	575	683	440	414	466	39	32	30
CA	4,800	4,600	4,500	2,025	1,943	1,979	1,274	1,273	1,272	1,362	1,408	1,338
CO	2,900	2,750	2,950	1,791	1,905	1,899	1,320	1,498	1,434	2,542	2,363	2,634
ID	1,660	1,740	1,760	810	848	836	527	585	552	825	763	(5)
IL	1,950	2,000	1,980	760	786	773	578	617	577	1,389	(5)	(5)
IA	4,500	4,700	4,450	2,078	1,899	1,931	1,467	1,446	1,384	2,162	2,134	1,952
KS	5,700	5,700	5,650	3,083	3,122	3,144	2,262	2,428	2,370	7,001	7,091	6,937
KY	2,420	2,500	2,580	697	744	793	499	568	611	105	100	94
MN	2,600	2,760	2,800	1,233	1,115	1,161	812	798	792	1,209	1,264	1,344
MO	4,400	4,400	4,550	1,242	1,158	1,119	959	969	953	390	351	299
MT	2,300	2,330	2,550	955	974	1,029	671	719	749	16	30	21
NE	5,800	6,000	5,800	3,714	3,784	3,741	2,728	2,895	2,782	6,698	6,804	7,424
ND	1,700	1,700	1,850	660	637	663	513	532	542	238	215	(5)
OK	5,250	5,550	5,500	2,033	1,928	1,959	1,371	1,437	1,533	82	62	44
SD	3,380	3,400	3,550	1,792	1,756	1,762	1,272	1,385	1,387	751	702	625
TN	2,300	2,250	2,290	652	665	654	426	455	456	105	(5)	(5)
TX	13,200	13,300	13,600	5,639	5,900	6,691	3,982	4,544	5,032	6,282	6,100	6,158
WI	4,170	4,170	4,000	1,244	1,210	1,228	800	879	834	1,436	1,368	1,347
HOGS AND PIGS												
U.S. [4]	53,821	54,477	56,974	21,942	21,347	22,791	9,294	11,376	11,095	22,027	21,230	22,200
IL	5,700	5,700	5,800	2,324	2,225	2,435	986	1,192	1,174	2,178	2,250	2,221
IN	4,350	4,400	4,550	1,666	1,666	1,742	696	870	824	919	876	924
IA	13,500	13,800	14,800	5,544	5,394	5,863	2,379	2,913	2,942	6,421	6,571	7,121
MN	4,450	4,500	4,900	1,787	1,714	1,811	780	948	915	1,228	1,382	1,827
MO	2,700	2,800	2,650	1,078	1,040	1,082	460	572	529	899	685	(5)
NE	4,200	4,300	4,400	1,657	1,624	1,763	707	882	863	1,243	1,299	1,355
NC	2,570	2,800	3,550	1,178	1,190	1,473	493	607	688	698	654	(5)
SD	1,720	1,770	1,950	771	753	817	328	410	406	998	1,154	1,247

[1] Cattle and calves, as of January 1; hogs and pigs as of December 1 of preceding year.   [2] Data for cattle and calves cover cattle only. Includes slaughter in federally inspected and other slaughter plants; excludes animals slaughtered on farms. [3] Includes milk cows.   [4] Includes other States not shown separately.   [5] Included in U.S. total. Not printed to avoid disclosing individual operation.
Source: U.S. Dept. of Agriculture, National Agricultural Statistics Service, *Meat Animals-Production, Disposition and Income*, annual.

No. 1141. Milk Production and Commercial Use: 1980 to 1992

[In billions of pounds milkfat basis]

YEAR	Production	Farm use	COMMERCIAL Farm marketings	COMMERCIAL Beginning stock	Imports	Commercial supply, total	CCC net removals [1]	COMMERCIAL Ending stock	COMMERCIAL Disappearance	Milk price per 100 lb. [2] (dol.)
1980	128.4	2.3	126.1	5.3	2.1	133.5	9.0	5.6	118.8	13.1
1985	143.0	2.5	140.6	4.8	2.8	148.2	13.4	4.5	130.3	12.8
1988	145.2	2.2	142.9	4.6	2.4	149.9	9.1	4.3	136.5	12.3
1989	144.2	2.1	142.2	4.3	2.5	148.9	9.4	4.1	135.4	13.6
1990	148.3	2.0	146.3	4.1	2.7	153.1	9.0	5.1	138.9	13.7
1991	148.5	2.0	146.5	5.1	2.6	154.3	10.4	4.5	139.4	12.2
1992	151.8	2.0	149.8	4.5	2.5	156.8	10.2	4.5	142.1	13.2

[1] Removals from commercial supply by Commodity Credit Corporation.   [2] Wholesale price received by farmers for all milk delivered to plants and dealers.

Source: U.S. Dept. of Agriculture, *Agricultural Outlook*, monthly.

No. 1142. Milk Production and Manufactured Dairy Products: 1980 to 1991

[See also *Historical Statistics, Colonial Times to 1970*, series K 595-601]

ITEM	Unit	1980	1984	1985	1986	1987	1988	1989	1990	1991
Number of farms with milk cows	1,000	334	282	269	249	228	217	204	194	182
Cows and heifers that have calved, kept for milk	Mil. head	10.8	10.8	11.0	10.8	10.3	10.3	10.1	10.1	10.0
Milk produced on farms	Bil. lb	128	135	143	143	143	145	144	148	149
Production per cow	1,000 lb.	11.9	12.5	13.0	13.3	13.8	14.1	14.2	14.6	14.9
Whole milk sold from farms [1]	Bil. lb	126	132	141	141	140	143	142	146	146
Sales to plants and dealers	Bil. lb	125	131	139	140	139	142	141	145	145
Value of milk produced	Bil. dol.	16.9	18.3	18.4	18.0	18.0	17.9	19.7	20.5	18.3
Gross farm income, dairy products	Bil. dol.	16.7	18.0	18.1	17.8	17.8	17.7	19.5	20.3	18.1
Cash receipts from marketing of milk and cream [1]	Bil. dol.	16.6	17.9	18.1	17.7	17.7	17.6	19.4	20.2	18.1
Sales to plants and dealers	Bil. dol.	16.3	17.7	17.8	17.5	17.5	17.4	19.1	20.0	17.8
Number of dairy manufacturing plants	Number	2,257	2,059	2,061	1,998	1,933	1,846	1,754	1,723	1,676
Manufactured dairy products:										
Butter (incl. whey butter)	Mil. lb	1,145	1,103	1,248	1,202	1,104	1,208	1,295	1,302	1,336
Cheese, total [2]	Mil. lb	3,984	4,674	5,081	5,209	5,344	5,572	5,615	6,059	6,091
American (excl. full-skim American)	Mil. lb	2,376	2,648	2,855	2,798	2,717	2,757	2,674	2,894	2,805
Cream and Neufchatel	Mil. lb	229	276	294	322	342	376	401	431	447
All Italian varieties	Mil. lb	983	1,319	1,491	1,633	1,800	1,937	2,043	2,207	2,329
Cottage cheese: Creamed [3]	Mil. lb	825	736	716	705	675	647	572	531	498
Curd, pot, and bakers	Mil. lb	667	606	599	600	574	557	527	493	491
Condensed bulk milk	Mil. lb	952	1,159	1,232	1,362	1,383	1,364	1,417	1,426	1,433
Evaporated and condensed canned milk	Mil. lb	740	666	656	602	597	612	545	615	543
Nonfat dry milk [4]	Mil. lb	1,168	1,168	1,398	1,294	1,077	998	893	902	885
Dry whey [5]	Mil. lb	690	898	987	1,031	1,097	1,137	1,069	1,143	1,167
Ice cream of all kinds	Mil. gal	830	894	901	924	928	882	831	824	863
Ice milk	Mil. gal	293	300	301	315	328	355	377	352	335

[1] Comprises sales to plants and dealers, and retail sales by farmers direct to consumers.   [2] Includes varieties not shown separately.   [3] Includes partially creamed (low fat).   [4] Includes dry skim milk for animal feed.   [5] Includes animal but excludes modified whey production.

Source: U.S. Dept. of Agriculture, National Agricultural Statistics Service, *Dairy Products*, annual; and *Milk: Production, Disposition, and Income*, annual.

No. 1143. Milk Cows—Number, Production, and Value, by State: 1989 to 1991

STATE	NUMBER ON FARMS [1] (1,000)			MILK PRODUCED ON FARMS (mil. lb.)			VALUE OF PRODUCTION [2] (mil. dol.)		
	1989	1990	1991	1989	1990	1991	1989	1990	1991
United States [3]	10,126	10,127	9,990	144,239	148,313	148,526	19,688	20,495	18,326
California	1,104	1,135	1,155	19,420	20,947	21,509	2,446	2,561	2,460
Idaho	171	179	178	2,669	2,949	2,919	328	360	324
Iowa	309	305	303	4,202	4,233	4,151	555	563	494
Michigan	345	344	341	5,152	5,233	5,256	702	739	654
Minnesota	734	710	683	10,108	10,030	9,772	1,322	1,326	1,164
Missouri	228	230	226	2,975	3,040	2,865	396	413	341
New York	776	768	756	11,071	11,067	11,094	1,576	1,621	1,414
Ohio	349	342	337	4,535	4,668	4,695	610	649	563
Pennsylvania	698	683	669	9,998	9,933	10,106	1,469	1,513	1,362
Texas	386	386	380	5,170	5,539	5,418	741	814	688
Washington	225	237	237	4,097	4,392	4,459	559	603	560
Wisconsin	1,739	1,753	1,714	24,000	24,400	24,065	3,228	3,287	2,891

[1] Average number during year. Represents cows and heifers that have calved, kept for milk; excluding heifers not yet fresh.   [2] Valued at average returns per 100 pounds of milk in combined marketings of milk and cream. Includes value of milk fed to calves.   [3] Includes other States not shown separately.

Source: U.S. Dept. of Agriculture, National Agricultural Statistics Service, *Dairy Products*, annual; and *Milk: Production, Disposition, and Income*, annual.

No. 1144. Poultry—Number on Farms, Value, Production, and Prices: 1980 to 1991

[For year ending November 30, except as noted. See also *Historical Statistics, Colonial Times to 1970*, series K 609-623]

ITEM	Unit	1980	1982	1983	1984	1985	1986	1987	1988	1989	1990	1991
Chickens:[1] Number [2]	Million	392	379	365	374	370	373	380	356	356	352	359
Value per head [2]	Dollars	1.88	1.85	1.96	2.02	1.90	1.87	1.87	2.04	2.16	2.29	2.30
Value, total [2]	Mil. dol.	737	701	717	757	704	698	711	726	771	805	826
Number sold [3]	Million	238	242	237	225	220	218	218	224	199	208	198
Price per lb. [3]	Cents	11.0	10.3	12.7	15.9	14.8	12.5	11.0	9.2	14.9	9.3	7.2
Value of sales [3]	Mil. dol.	129	121	145	170	152	128	112	95	138	90	68
PRODUCTION												
Broilers:[4] Number	Million	3,963	4,149	4,184	4,283	4,470	4,649	5,004	5,238	5,517	5,864	6,138
Weight	Bil. lb.	15.5	16.8	17.0	17.9	18.9	19.7	21.5	22.5	24.0	25.6	27.2
Price per lb	Cents	27.7	26.9	28.6	33.7	30.1	34.5	28.7	33.1	36.6	32.6	30.8
Production value	Mil. dol.	4,303	4,502	4,873	6,020	5,668	6,784	6,177	7,435	8,778	8,365	8,385
Turkeys: Number	Million	165	165	171	171	185	207	240	242	261	282	285
Weight	Bil. lb.	3.1	3.2	3.3	3.4	3.7	4.1	4.9	5.1	5.5	6.0	6.1
Price per lb	Cents	41.3	39.5	38.0	48.9	49.1	47.1	34.8	38.6	40.9	39.4	38.4
Gross income	Mil. dol.	1,272	1,255	1,269	1,655	1,819	1,948	1,703	1,951	2,234	2,379	2,344

[1] Excludes commercial broilers. [2] As of December 1. [3] 1980-84, represents number produced and production value. [4] Young chickens of the heavy breeds and other meat-type birds, to be marketed at 2-5 lbs. live weight and from which no pullets are kept for egg production. Not included in sales of chickens.

Source: U.S. Dept. of Agriculture, National Agricultural Statistics Service, *Hatchery Production—Annual; Poultry—Production and Value*, annual; *Turkeys*, annual; and *Layers and Egg Production*, annual.

No. 1145. Poultry—Production, by State: 1989 to 1991

[In millions of pounds, liveweight production. See *Historical Statistics, Colonial Times to 1970*, series K 614 and 621 for U.S. totals]

STATE	BROILERS 1989	BROILERS 1990	BROILERS 1991	TURKEYS 1989	TURKEYS 1990	TURKEYS 1991	STATE	BROILERS 1989	BROILERS 1990	BROILERS 1991	TURKEYS 1989	TURKEYS 1990	TURKEYS 1991
U.S.[1]	23,979	25,631	27,209	5,465	6,030	6,109	MO	308	362	479	353	360	452
AL	3,150	3,642	3,764	(NA)	(NA)	(NA)	NC	2,444	2,593	2,679	992	1,160	1,166
AR	3,866	3,995	4,214	412	453	490	OH	72	96	129	110	135	126
CA	1,049	1,109	1,152	664	712	653	OK	527	540	592	(NA)	(NA)	(NA)
DE	1,132	1,159	1,206	(NA)	(NA)	(NA)	OR	92	107	107	38	44	42
FL	519	490	506	(NA)	(NA)	(NA)	PA	549	520	544	168	169	168
GA	3,573	3,760	3,816	54	61	56	SC	308	343	395	153	168	178
IL	(NA)	(NA)	(NA)	86	99	64	SD	(NA)	(NA)	(NA)	63	80	81
IN	(NA)	(NA)	(NA)	280	288	320	TN	427	436	476	(NA)	(NA)	(NA)
IA	33	63	92	186	228	226	TX	1,254	1,454	1,496	(NA)	(NA)	(NA)
KY	10	6	89	(NA)	(NA)	(NA)	UT	(NA)	(NA)	(NA)	85	90	90
MD	1,108	1,141	1,183	2	2	3	VA	802	882	984	319	316	324
MI	3	3	3	102	125	141	WA	140	157	166	(NA)	(NA)	(NA)
MN	181	198	237	784	852	805	WV	131	156	177	55	72	77
MS	1,627	1,694	1,963	(NA)	(NA)	(NA)	WI	54	62	66	(NA)	(NA)	(NA)

NA Not available. [1] Includes other States not shown separately.

Source: U.S. Dept. of Agriculture, National Agricultural Statistics Service, *Poultry—Production and Value*, annual; and *Turkeys*, annual.

No. 1146. Egg Production, Supply, and Use: 1980 to 1992

YEAR	PRODUCTION [1] Number produced (bil.)	PRODUCTION [1] Price per dozen (cents)	PRODUCTION [1] Production value (mil. dol.)	SUPPLY (mil. dozen) Total [2]	SUPPLY (mil. dozen) Production	SUPPLY (mil. dozen) Imports	USE (mil. dozen) Total	USE (mil. dozen) Consumption [3]	USE (mil. dozen) Hatching use	USE (mil. dozen) Exports
1980	69.7	56.3	3,268	5,830	5,806	5	5,811	5,169	499	143
1985	68.4	57.2	3,262	5,734	5,710	13	5,723	5,104	548	71
1988	69.7	52.8	3,067	5,804	5,784	5	5,789	5,041	606	142
1989	67.2	68.9	3,861	5,639	5,598	25	5,623	4,892	644	92
1990	67.9	70.9	4,011	5,685	5,665	9	5,674	4,894	679	101
1991	69.0	67.6	3,887	5,772	5,758	2	5,760	4,896	708	154
1992	(NA)	(NA)	(NA)	5,888	5,871	3	5,875	4,995	728	151

NA Not available. [1] For year ending November 30. [2] Includes beginning stocks, not shown separately. [3] Includes shipments to territories.

Source: U.S. Dept. of Agriculture, National Agricultural Statistics Service, *Layers and Egg Production—Annual*; and Economic Research Service, *Agricultural Outlook*, monthly.

Forests and Fisheries

This section presents data on the area, ownership, and timber resource of commercial timberland; forestry statistics covering the National Forests and Forest Service cooperative programs; product data for lumber, pulpwood, woodpulp, paper, and paperboard; and similar data. In addition, data are presented on commercial fishing and the fish processing industry.

The principal sources of data relating to forests and forest products are *An Analysis of the Timber Situation in the United States, 1989-2040,1990; Forest Statistics of the United States, 1987, 1989; U.S. Timber Production, Trade, Consumption, and Price Statistics, 1960-88; Land Areas of the National Forest System,* issued annually by the Forest Service of the Department of Agriculture; *Agricultural Statistics* issued by the Department of Agriculture; and reports of the census of manufactures (taken every 5 years) and the annual *Current Industrial Reports,* issued by the Bureau of the Census. Additional information is published in the monthly *Survey of Current Business* of the Bureau of Economic Analysis; and the annual *Wood Pulp and Fiber Statistics* and *The Statistics of Paper, Paperboard, and Wood Pulp* of the American Forest and Paper Association, New York, NY.

The Bureau of the Census also collects data on foreign trade of forest products. The Bureau of Labor Statistics publishes monthly and annual statistics of producer prices for lumber.

The completeness and reliability of statistics on forests and forest products vary considerably. The data for forest land area and stand volumes are much more reliable for areas recently surveyed than for those for which only estimates are available. In general, more data are available for lumber and other manufactured products such as particleboard and softwood panels, etc., than for the primary forest products such as poles and piling and fuelwood.

The principal sources of data relating to fisheries are *Fishery Statistics of the United States,* and *Fisheries of the United States,* both issued annually by

In Brief
1992

Production:
Paper and board   83.7 mil. sh. tns
Consumption:
Recovered paper   26.2 mil. sh. tns

the National Marine Fisheries Service (NMFS), National Oceanic and Atmospheric Administration (NOAA).

The NMFS collects and disseminates data on commercial landings of fish and shellfish. Quarterly data are published on U.S. output of fish sticks, fish portions, and breaded shrimp. Annual reports include quantity and value of commercial landings of fish and shellfish, etc. Reports for the fish-processing industry include annual output of canned, packaged, and industrial products and, for the wholesaling and fish processing establishments, annual and seasonal employment, and number of firms, by product and State.

The Magnuson Fishery Conservation and Management Act of 1976 (Magnuson Act), Public Law 94-265 as amended, provides for the conservation and management of all fishery resources within the U.S. Exclusive Economic Zone (EEZ), except highly migratory species of tuna, and gives the Federal Government exclusive authority over domestic and foreign fisheries within 200 nautical miles of U.S. shores and over certain living marine resources beyond the EEZ. Within the EEZ, the total allowable level of foreign fishing, if any, is that portion of the "optimum yield" not harvested by U.S. vessels. Adjustments in the "optimum yield" level may occur periodically. For details, see *Fisheries of the United States, 1988.* The NMFS collects and disseminates data on catches by foreign fishing vessels in the EEZ.

Historical statistics.—Tabular headnotes provide cross-references, where applicable, to *Historical Statistics of the United States, Colonial Times to 1970.* See Appendix IV.

No. 1147. National Forest System Land and Purchases: 1970 to 1990

[Area as of **June 30** except, beginning **1980**, as of **Sept. 30**; purchases for years ending **June 30**, except as noted. Includes Puerto Rico. Prior to Oct. 1976, lands to be purchased under the Weeks Law and related acts were approved by the National Forest Reservation Commission which also set prices on such lands. With the passage of the National Forest Management Act, all functions of the Commission were transferred to the Secretary of Agriculture. Actual purchases are made by U.S. Department of Agriculture. See also *Historical Statistics, Colonial Times to 1970,* series L 10-14]

ITEM	Unit	1970	1975	1980	1984	1985	1986	1987	1988	1989	1990
Gross area [1]	Mil. acres. .	226	226	226	230	230	230	230	230	231	231
National forest system [2]	Mil. acres. .	187	188	187	191	191	191	191	191	191	191
Approved for purchase	1,000 acres	92	12	42	8	16	23	87	42	99	51
Average price per acre.	Dollars . . .	125	275	664	544	431	308	437	561	346	464
Total price.	Mil. dol . . .	11.5	3.3	27.9	4.2	6.9	7.0	38.0	23.5	34.0	24.0
Purchases completed	1,000 acres	113	34	27	35	7	33	53	18	46	38
Average price per acre.	Dollars . . .	96	267	617	407	653	295	360	153	428	556
Total price.	Mil. dol . . .	10.9	9.1	17.1	14.0	4.2	9.8	19.0	7.2	20.0	21.0
Gross area of purchase units . .	Mil. acres. .	56	56	56	58	58	58	58	58	58	58
Purchase completed, net area [3]	Mil. acres. .	20	20	20	20	20	20	20	20	20	20
Average price per acre.	Dollars . . .	6	9	12	15	15	16	17	17	17	19
Total price.	Mil. dol . . .	125	179	250	298	305	314	333	340	360	381

[1] Comprises all publicly and privately owned land within authorized boundaries of National forests, Purchase units, National grasslands, land utilization projects, research and experimental areas, and other areas.   [2] Federally owned land within the "Gross area."   [3] Cumulative total. Under the March 1, 1911, Act of Congress (Weeks Law), as amended, and related acts.

Source: U.S. National Forest Reservation Commission, *Final Report to October 1976;* and U.S. Forest Service, *Land Areas of the National Forest System,* annual; and unpublished data.

No. 1148. National Forest System—Summary: 1970 to 1991

[For fiscal years ending in year shown; see text, section 9. Includes Alaska and Puerto Rico, except as noted. See *Historical Statistics, Colonial Times to 1970,* series J 33-34, for similar but not comparable grazing data, and L 15-31]

ITEM	Unit	1970	1980	1985	1986	1987	1988	1989	1990	1991
Timber cut, total value	Mil. dol.	309	737	725	790	1,019	1,243	1,313	1,191	1,012
Commercial and cost sales: [1]										
Volume	Mil. bd..	11,527	9,178	10,941	11,786	12,712	12,649	11,951	10,500	8,475
Value	Mil. dol.	308	730	721	787	1,016	1,240	1,310	1,188	1,009
Free use:										
Volume	Mil. bd..	179	2,070	399	308	209	223	214	151	121
Value [2]	Mil. dol.	0.3	5.7	2.2	1.4	1.1	1.2	1.2	1.0	1.0
Misc. forest products:										
Value	Mil. dol.	0.7	1.1	1.7	1.6	1.9	2.0	2.2	2.6	2.7
Livestock grazing: [3]										
Cattle and horses [4]	1,000 .	1,607	1,521	1,545	1,491	1,410	1,313	1,526	1,206	1,265
Sheep and goats	1,000 .	2,105	1,328	1,183	1,168	1,134	1,067	972	974	1,029
Roads and trails:										
Road construction [5]	Miles. .	942	925	1,903	1,252	2,394	1,352	866	857	910
Trail construction [5][6]	Miles. .	278	2,419	987	1,092	1,046	1,834	1,944	1,637	1,921
Receipts, total	Mil. dol.	300	703	636	832	898	980	1,051	971	772
Timber use	Mil. dol.	284	625	515	745	808	888	910	850	667
Grazing use	Mil. dol.	4	16	9	9	8	9	11	10	11
Special land use, etc	Mil. dol.	11	62	112	78	82	83	130	112	93
Payments to local govt. [7]	Mil. dol.	73	240	229	271	295	325	368	368	335
25-percent fund [8]	Mil. dol.	72	234	212	262	285	317	354	358	327
Other [9]	Mil. dol.	1	7	17	9	10	8	15	10	8
Allotments to Forest										
Service, total [10]	Mil. dol.	30	73	60	82	88	104	111	106	88
Roads and trails	Mil. dol.	29	65	55	78	84	92	96	91	73
Other.	Mil. dol.	1	8	5	4	4	12	15	14	16

[1] Includes land exchanges.   [2] Includes some free use timber not reducible to board feet.   [3] For 1970, data for livestock permitted to graze; 1980-91 for number actually grazed. Calendar-year data, prior to 1980. Excludes Puerto Rico.   [4] Excludes animals under 6 months of age. 1970 includes swine. Includes burros beginning in 1980.   [5] Includes reconstruction. [6] Beginning 1980, includes work accomplished by Human Resource Programs and volunteers.   [7] Payments made in following year.   [8] Includes Tongass Alaska suspense account.   [9] Includes Arizona and New Mexico School Fund (through 1982), State of Minnesota, and receipts paid to counties under Bankhead-Jones Farm Tenant Act.   [10] For use in following year.

Source: U.S. Forest Service. In *Agricultural Statistics,* annual, and unpublished data.

No. 1149. National Forest System Land—States and Other Areas: 1991

[In thousands of acres. As of Sept. 30. See also *Historical Statistics, Colonial Times to 1970*, series L 10-11]

STATE	Gross area within unit boundaries [1]	National forest system land [2]	Other lands within unit boundaries	STATE	Gross area within unit boundaries [1]	National forest system land [2]	Other lands within unit boundaries
United States	231,443	191,324	40,119	Missouri	3,082	1,475	1,606
Alabama	1,280	658	622	Montana	19,101	16,806	2,295
Alaska	24,345	22,220	2,126	Nebraska	442	352	90
Arizona	11,880	11,239	642	Nevada	6,275	5,797	478
Arkansas	3,490	2,509	981	New Hampshire	825	720	105
California	24,401	20,619	3,782	New Jersey	-	-	-
Colorado	16,039	14,462	1,577	New Mexico	10,367	9,321	1,046
Connecticut	-	-	-	New York	13	13	-
Delaware	-	-	-	North Carolina	3,165	1,232	1,934
District of Columbia . .	-	-	-	North Dakota	1,106	1,106	-
Florida	1,246	1,128	118	Ohio	833	203	630
Georgia	1,846	859	987	Oklahoma	461	297	165
Hawaii	-	-	-	Oregon	17,502	15,651	1,851
Idaho	21,674	20,438	1,236	Pennsylvania	744	513	231
Illinois	840	266	573	Rhode Island	-	-	-
Indiana	644	188	456	South Carolina	1,376	607	768
Iowa	-	-	-	South Dakota	2,344	1,996	349
Kansas	116	108	8	Tennessee	1,212	628	585
Kentucky	2,102	670	1,431	Texas	1,994	753	1,241
Louisiana	1,022	601	422	Utah	9,186	8,099	1,087
Maine	93	53	40	Vermont	815	340	475
Maryland	-	-	-	Virginia	3,223	1,645	1,578
Massachusetts	-	-	-	Washington	10,050	9,151	899
Michigan	4,885	2,816	2,069	West Virginia	1,863	1,025	838
Minnesota	5,467	2,810	2,657	Wisconsin	2,023	1,517	506
Mississippi	2,310	1,150	1,160	Wyoming	9,704	9,255	449

- Represents zero. [1] Comprises all publicly and privately owned land within authorized boundaries of national forests, purchase units, national grasslands, Land utilization projects, research and experimental areas, and other areas. [2] Federally owned land within the "gross area within unit boundaries."

Source: U.S. Forest Service, *Land Areas of the National Forest System*, annual.

No. 1150. Forest Land—Total and Timberland Area, Volume of Sawtimber, and Growing Stock: 1952 to 1987

[As of **Jan. 1**. See table 31 for composition of regions]

YEAR AND REGION	Total forest land (mil. acres)	TIMBERLAND, OWNERSHIP [1]					SAWTIMBER, NET VOLUME [3]		GROWING STOCK, NET VOLUME [4]	
		All ownerships (mil. acres)	Federally owned or managed [2] (mil. acres)	State, county, and municipal (mil. acres)	Private		Total (bil. bd. ft.)	Softwood (bil. bd. ft.)	Total (bil. cu. ft.)	Softwood (bil. cu. ft.)
					Total (mil. acres)	Percent of total				
United States, 1952	664	509	125	27	356	70.0	2,520	2,089	610	430
North	209	158	13	18	127	80.0	231	62	106	28
South	197	205	15	3	187	91.4	411	198	143	59
West	258	146	97	6	42	29.1	1,878	1,829	361	343
United States, 1962	759	515	125	27	363	70.4	2,558	2,062	659	448
North	178	160	13	18	130	80.9	268	74	131	35
South	220	209	15	3	191	91.4	494	250	168	73
West	360	146	97	6	42	28.9	1,795	1,738	361	340
United States, 1970	754	504	122	29	354	70.2	2,587	2,035	694	458
North	186	158	13	18	127	80.5	305	87	148	40
South	212	203	15	3	185	90.9	569	302	191	87
West	355	143	94	7	42	29.2	1,713	1,646	355	331
United States, 1977	737	491	113	31	347	70.6	2,635	2,021	725	465
North	178	157	12	19	126	80.4	350	102	166	46
South	207	198	15	3	180	90.6	648	345	215	99
West	352	136	85	9	41	30.1	1,637	1,574	344	320
United States, 1987	731	483	103	34	347	71.8	2,829	2,032	756	451
North	170	158	13	19	126	79.6	471	133	190	49
South	203	195	16	4	176	89.9	757	380	238	104
West	358	130	74	11	45	34.9	1,601	519	327	298

[1] Timberland is forest land that is producing or is capable of producing crops of industrial wood and not withdrawn from timber utilization by statute or administrative regulation. Areas qualifying as timberland have the capability of producing in excess of 20 cubic feet per acre per year of industrial wood in natural stands. Currently inaccessible and inoperable areas are included. [2] Includes Indian lands. [3] Sawtimber is timber suitable for sawing into lumber. Live trees of commercial species containing at least one 12-foot sawlog or two noncontiguous 8-foot logs, and meeting regional specifications for freedom from defect. Softwood trees must be at least 9.0-inches diameter, and hardwood trees must be at least 11.0-inches diameter at 4 1/2 feet above ground. International 1/4-inch rule. [4] Live trees of commercial species meeting specified standards of quality or vigor. Cull trees are excluded. Includes only trees 5.0-inches diameter or larger at 4 1/2 feet above ground.

Source: U.S. Forest Service, *Forest Statistics of the United States, 1987*.

356-198 0 - 93 - 23 : QL 3

No. 1151. Timber-Based Industries—Summary of Manufactures: 1989 to 1991

[Data based on *1987 Standard Industrial Classification Manual*, published by the Office of Management and Budget, see text, section 27. Based on Census of Manufactures, except where noted. N.e.c. = Not elsewhere classified]

SIC [1] code	INDUSTRY	1989			1990			1991 [2]		
		All employees		Value of ship-ments (bil. dol.)	All employees		Value of ship-ments (bil. dol.)	All employees		Value of ship-ments (bil. dol.)
		Num-ber (1,000)	Payroll (mil. dol.)		Num-ber (1,000)	Payroll (mil. dol.)		Num-ber (1,000)	Payroll (mil. dol.)	
241/242	Logging and sawmills	256.8	5,040	32.5	254.2	5,076	32.2	207.6	4,307	28.9
2411	Logging	81.7	1,596	12.0	83.4	1,647	12.2	78.1	1,561	11.4
2421	Sawmills and planing mills, general	143.7	2,937	18.5	138.9	2,913	17.9	129.5	2,747	17.5
2426	Hardwood dimension and flooring mills	29.2	472	1.8	29.3	475	1.8	26.1	462	1.7
2429	Special product sawmills, n.e.c.	2.3	36	0.2	2.5	41	0.2	2.0	36	0.2
243	Millwork and veneer [3]	233.0	4,866	23.7	229.4	4,823	23.2	209.9	4,487	21.4
2431	Millwork	90.9	1,977	9.7	90.5	1,961	9.5	84.9	1,836	9.0
2434	Wood kitchen cabinets	61.6	1,197	4.4	62.8	1,217	4.6	57.1	1,139	4.2
2435	Hardwood veneer and plywood	20.1	356	2.2	18.7	335	2.1	17.3	320	1.9
2436	Softwood veneer and plywood	36.5	888	5.3	35.6	881	5.0	31.7	810	4.6
2439	Structural wood members, n.e.c.	23.9	449	2.1	21.8	429	2.2	18.9	382	1.8
244	Wood containers	42.2	600	2.6	41.5	636	2.9	39.8	634	2.9
2441	Nailed and lock corner wood boxes	6.2	95	0.4	6.0	98	0.4	6.2	100	0.4
2448	Wood pallets and skids	29.1	395	1.8	28.3	417	1.9	27.1	413	2.0
2449	Wood containers, n.e.c	6.9	111	0.4	7.2	122	0.5	6.5	120	0.4
245	Wood buildings, mobile homes	62.8	1,211	6.4	61.4	1,217	6.5	54.1	1,106	6.0
2451	Mobile homes	39.9	769	4.1	38.8	769	4.2	35.1	714	3.9
2452	Prefabricated wood buildings and components	22.9	442	2.3	22.6	448	2.3	19.0	392	2.0
249	Miscellaneous wood products	91.0	1,643	9.2	96.4	1,745	9.6	90.9	1,706	9.5
2491	Wood preserving	12.1	223	2.4	13.0	246	2.6	11.7	233	2.6
2493	Reconstituted wood products	22.2	547	3.2	22.3	554	3.0	21.0	537	3.0
2499	Wood products, n.e.c	56.6	873	3.6	61.1	945	3.9	58.1	936	3.8
261	Pulp mills	15.2	603	6.4	16.1	668	6.2	16.8	697	5.3
262	Paper mills	130.1	4,927	35.4	130.1	5,062	35.3	130.3	5,224	33.3
263	Paperboard mills	52.1	1,958	16.3	53.1	2,049	15.9	50.6	2,027	15.0
265	Paperboard containers and boxes	202.3	5,144	30.5	200.3	5,245	30.5	198.6	5,392	30.6
2652	Setup paperboard boxes	8.7	141	0.5	8.8	146	0.6	8.7	150	0.6
2653	Corrugated and solid fiber boxes	111.1	2,928	18.9	110.1	2,984	18.6	108.7	3,047	18.0
2655	Fiber cans, tubes, drums, and similar products	13.3	329	1.8	13.3	341	1.9	12.9	341	1.9
2656	Sanitary food containers, except folding	17.2	383	2.5	17.5	392	2.5	17.6	411	2.7
2657	Folding paperboard boxes, including sanitary	51.8	1,364	6.7	50.7	1,382	7.0	50.7	1,443	7.4
267	Converted paper and paperboard products [4]	229.9	5,765	42.8	228.5	5,923	43.5	224.3	6,043	44.6
2671	Packaging paper and plastics film, coated and laminated	16.3	458	2.9	16.4	489	3.0	15.4	492	3.1
2672	Coated and laminated paper, n.e.c.	35.9	973	7.1	35.0	985	7.1	34.2	992	7.4
2673	Plastics, foil, and coated paper bags	39.0	882	5.6	37.4	870	5.5	35.4	875	5.1
2674	Uncoated paper and multiwall bags	17.0	358	2.8	16.9	374	2.8	17.9	398	2.7
2675	Die-cut paper and paperboard and cardboard	16.1	384	2.0	16.8	395	2.1	17.0	408	2.3
2676	Sanitary paper products	37.8	1,235	14.3	39.0	1,299	14.7	38.8	1,343	15.6
2677	Envelopes	27.3	645	2.8	26.1	648	2.8	24.5	616	2.7
2678	Stationery, tablets, and related products	10.5	203	1.3	10.1	203	1.3	10.1	209	1.4
2679	Converted paper and paperboard products, n.e.c	30.1	627	3.8	30.7	659	4.1	30.9	711	4.3

[1] Standard Industrial Classification code; see text, section 13. [2] Source: U.S. Bureau of the Census, *Annual Survey of Manufactures*. [3] Includes plywood and structural members. [4] Except containers and boxes.

Source: Except as noted, U.S. Bureau of the Census, *Census of Manufactures, 1987 Final Industry Series*, MC87-I-24A-D and MC87-I-26A-C.

No. 1152. Timber-Based Industries—Employment and Average Hourly Earnings: 1980 to 1992

[Data for production workers]

SIC [1] code	ITEM	EMPLOYEES (1,000)						EARNINGS (dollars)					
		1980	1985	1989	1990	1991	1992	1980	1985	1989	1990	1991	1992
24	Lumber and wood products [2]..	587	593	628	605	556	563	6.57	8.25	8.84	9.08	9.24	9.43
241	Logging.................	71	67	72	70	64	76	8.64	10.92	11.13	11.22	11.08	11.24
242	Sawmills and planing mills ..	190	172	177	173	160	182	6.70	8.52	9.03	9.22	9.37	9.60
243	Millwork, plywood, and structur- al members	170	195	220	211	189	245	6.44	8.09	8.73	9.04	9.27	9.47
26	Paper and allied products	519	509	522	524	518	688	7.84	10.83	11.96	12.31	12.73	13.09
25	Furniture and fixtures	376	394	419	401	371	465	5.49	7.17	8.25	8.52	8.76	9.00

[1] 1987 Standard Industrial Classification; see text, section 27.   [2] Includes other industries, not shown separately.

Source: U.S. Bureau of Labor Statistics, Bulletin 2370 Supplement to Employment and Earnings, July 1991, and

No. 1153. Timber Products—Production, Foreign Trade, and Consumption, by Type of Product: 1970 to 1988

[In millions of cubic feet, roundwood equivalent. See also Historical Statistics, Colonial Times to 1970, series L 72-86]

ITEM	1970	1975	1980	1982	1983	1984	1985	1986	1987	1988, prel.
Industrial roundwood:										
Domestic production [1].......	11,105	10,575	12,120	10,910	12,065	12,725	12,515	13,845	14,670	14,985
Softwoods	8,635	8,380	9,290	8,450	9,285	9,790	9,690	10,595	11,390	11,430
Hardwoods	2,470	2,195	2,825	2,465	2,780	2,935	2,825	3,250	3,280	3,555
Imports	2,430	2,215	3,250	3,015	3,710	4,165	4,340	4,375	4,575	4,445
Exports ...._.........	1,540	1,685	2,350	1,995	2,110	2,060	2,070	2,300	2,650	3,200
Consumption [2]...........	11,995	11,105	13,020	11,930	13,665	14,830	14,785	15,920	16,595	16,230
Softwoods	9,425	8,875	10,345	9,575	10,975	11,965	11,960	12,735	13,430	12,970
Hardwoods	2,565	2,230	2,675	2,355	2,690	2,865	2,825	3,180	3,165	3,260
Lumber:										
Domestic production	5,215	4,890	5,300	4,635	5,370	5,770	5,665	6,545	6,990	6,920
Imports	955	930	1,540	1,460	1,915	2,130	2,345	2,285	2,380	2,225
Exports	195	255	395	320	360	340	305	385	510	720
Consumption	5,970	5,565	6,450	5,780	6,925	7,560	7,700	8,445	8,860	8,425
Plywood and veneer:										
Domestic production	1,020	1,165	1,175	1,135	1,365	1,400	1,420	1,505	1,650	1,630
Imports	170	170	120	115	160	145	165	185	190	165
Exports	15	70	45	50	65	45	40	65	80	100
Consumption	1,170	1,265	1,250	1,200	1,460	1,500	1,550	1,625	1,760	1,695
Pulp products:										
Domestic production	3,835	3,485	4,390	3,980	4,165	4,355	4,165	4,545	4,670	4,885
Imports	1,280	1,105	1,565	1,415	1,605	1,860	1,810	1,895	1,985	2,045
Exports	720	715	1,070	900	965	930	920	1,080	1,195	1,345
Consumption	4,400	3,875	4,885	4,495	4,805	5,290	5,055	5,360	5,465	5,585
Logs:										
Imports	25	15	25	20	30	30	20	15	15	15
Exports	465	455	560	550	565	600	655	620	705	825
Pulpwood chips, exports.......	145	195	275	175	155	145	145	150	160	215
Other industrial prod. [3] consump- tion...................	425	385	415	435	445	455	465	475	495	510
Fuelwood consumption	540	570	3,105	3,355	3,235	3,620	3,450	3,115	3,150	3,360

[1] Includes log exports.   [2] Includes log imports.   [3] Includes cooperage logs, poles and piling, fence posts, hewn ties, round mine timbers, box bolts, etc.

No. 1154. Timber Products—Per Capita Consumption: 1970 to 1988

[Based on total population estimated as of July 1. See also Historical Statistics, Colonial Times to 1970, series L 87-97]

PRODUCT	Unit	1970	1975	1980	1982	1983	1984	1985	1986	1987	1988, prel.
All products	Cu. ft	61.1	54.0	70.8	65.7	72.0	77.9	76.2	78.8	81.0	79.5
Industrial roundwood.....	Cu. ft...........	58.5	51.4	57.2	51.3	58.2	62.6	61.8	65.9	68.0	65.9
Lumber...........	Cu. ft...........	29.1	25.8	28.3	24.9	29.5	31.9	32.2	35.0	36.3	34.2
Plywood and veneer....	Cu. ft...........	5.7	5.9	5.5	5.2	6.2	6.3	6.5	6.7	7.2	6.9
Pulp products	Cu. ft...........	21.4	17.9	21.4	19.3	20.5	22.3	21.1	22.2	22.4	22.7
Other products	Cu. ft...........	2.1	1.8	1.8	1.9	1.9	1.9	1.9	2.0	2.0	2.1
Fuelwood	Cu. ft...........	2.6	2.6	13.6	14.4	13.8	15.3	14.4	12.9	12.9	13.6
Lumber.............	Bd. ft...........	193	171	188	161	190	205	207	224	233	221
Plywood and veneer	Bd. ft...........	34	32	30	28	34	34	35	37	39	37
Pulp products........	Cords (128 cu. ft.)...	0.3	0.2	0.3	0.2	0.3	0.3	0.3	0.3	0.3	0.3

Source of tables 1153 and 1154: U.S. Forest Service, U.S. Timber Production, Trade, Consumption, and Price Statistics, 1960-88, annual.

No. 1155. Lumber Consumption, by Species Group and End Use: 1962 to 1986

[In million board feet, except per capita in board feet. Per capita consumption based on estimated resident population as of July 1]

ITEM	1962	1970	1976	1986	END-USE	1962	1970	1976	1986
Total	39,078	39,869	44,653	57,203	New housing	14,160	13,350	17,000	19,320
					Residential upkeep and				
Per capita.	210	194	205	237	improvements	4,330	4,980	6,260	9.930
					New nonresidential				
Species group:					construction [1]	4,200	4,700	4,470	5,310
Softwoods	30,773	31,959	36,627	47,094	Manufacturing.	4,540	4,670	4,865	4,805
Hardwoods	8,305	7,910	8,026	10,109	Shipping	4,550	5,725	5,915	6,785
					Other [2]	7,298	6,444	6,143	11,053

[1] In addition to new construction, includes railroad ties laid as replacements in existing track and lumber used by railroads for railcar repair.   [2] Includes upkeep and improvement of nonresidential buildings and structures; made-at-home projects, such as furniture, boats, and picnic tables; made-on-the-job items such as advertising and display structures; and miscellaneous products and uses.

Source: U.S. Forest Service, *Analysis of the Timber Situation in the United States: 1989-2040*, forthcoming.

No. 1156. Selected Timber Products—Producer Price Indexes: 1980 to 1992

[See also *Historical Statistics, Colonial Times to 1970*, series L 206-210]

PRODUCT	Unit	1980	1985	1989	1990	1991	1992
Lumber and wood products, except furniture. . .	Dec. 1984=100 .	(NA)	100.3	115.3	117.0	119.4	129.6
Logging camps and logging contractors	Dec. 1981=100 .	(NA)	94.8	128.0	135.6	135.0	151.3
Sawmills and planing mills	Dec. 1984=100 .	(NA)	99.7	114.6	113.7	115.3	131.1
Millwork, veneer, and plywood [1]	Dec. 1984=100 .	(NA)	99.9	114.1	115.4	118.3	128.3
Softwood plywood	Dec. 1980=100 .	91.4	90.0	104.8	102.5	103.5	124.2
Wood containers	June 1985=100 .	(NA)	(NA)	109.7	113.9	115.8	123.4
Wood buildings and mobile homes	Dec. 1984=100 .	(NA)	100.6	112.1	115.5	118.9	121.4
Particleboard	Dec. 1982=100 .	92.1	110.0	127.8	117.1	117.0	121.0
Paper and allied products	Dec. 1984=100 .	(NA)	98.8	120.8	121.9	121.1	121.2
Pulp mills.	Dec. 1982=100 .	105.5	100.9	161.3	153.8	121.8	119.3
Paper mill products; except building paper. . .	June 1981=100 .	93.5	109.5	134.6	134.0	131.0	126.6
Paperboard mills.	Dec. 1982=100 .	97.3	112.0	149.9	146.0	140.7	142.8
Converted paper and paperboard products [2] .	June 1985=100 .	(NA)	(NA)	110.5	111.3	112.9	114.1
Paperboard containers and boxes	Dec. 1984=100 .	(NA)	98.4	117.2	117.7	116.6	118.6
Building paper and building board mills	Dec. 1985=100 .	(NA)	(NA)	114.4	(NA)	(NA)	(NA)

NA Not available.   [1] Includes structural wood members.   [2] Excludes containers and boxes.

Source: U.S. Bureau of Labor Statistics, *Producer Price Indexes*, monthly.

No. 1157. Selected Species—Stumpage Prices In Current and Constant (1982) Dollars: 1980 to 1991

[In dollars per 1,000 board feet. Stumpage prices are based on sales of sawtimber from National Forests. See also *Historical Statistics, Colonial Times to 1970*, series L 199-205]

SPECIES	1980	1981	1982	1983	1984	1985	1986	1987	1988	1989	1990	1991
CURRENT DOLLARS												
Softwoods:												
Douglas fir [1]	432	350	118	162	133	126	161	190	256	390	466	395
Southern pine [2]	155	172	127	141	139	91	104	136	142	131	127	166
Sugar pine [3]	667	225	72	138	84	110	170	288	260	289	285	(NA)
Ponderosa pine [3][4] . . .	206	195	67	104	123	101	157	209	182	292	252	238
Western hemlock [5] . . .	213	163	45	62	62	51	75	105	163	223	203	164
Hardwoods:												
All eastern hardwoods [6].	52	51	56	60	90	65	70	88	151	136	146	160
Oak, white, red, and												
black [6]	66	63	71	88	145	95	108	147	146	179	188	164
Maple, sugar [7]	70	68	71	55	81	70	66	81	108	129	135	121
CONSTANT (1982) DOLLARS [8]												
Softwoods:												
Douglas fir [1]	481	357	118	160	128	122	160	185	240	347	401	339
Southern pine [2]	173	176	127	139	134	88	103	132	133	117	109	143
Sugar pine [3]	742	230	72	136	81	106	169	280	244	258	245	(NA)
Ponderosa pine [3][4] . . .	230	199	67	103	118	98	156	204	170	260	217	204
Western hemlock [5] . . .	237	167	45	61	60	49	75	103	152	199	175	141
Hardwoods:												
All eastern hardwoods [6].	58	52	56	59	87	63	70	86	142	121	126	137
Oak, white, red, and												
black [6]	73	65	71	87	140	92	108	143	137	159	162	140
Maple, sugar [7]	78	69	71	54	78	68	66	78	101	115	116	104

NA Not available.   [1] Western Washington and western Oregon.   [2] Southern region.   [3] Pacific Southwest region (formerly California region).   [4] Includes Jeffrey pine.   [5] Pacific Northwest region.   [6] Eastern and Southern regions.   [7] Eastern region.   [8] Deflated by the producer price index, all commodities.

Source: U.S. Forest Service, *U.S. Timber Production, Trade, Consumption, and Price Statistics, 1960-89*, annual, forthcoming.

No. 1158. Lumber Production and Consumption, by Kind of Wood: 1980 to 1991

[In millions of board feet, except as indicated. Based on sample survey; see source for sampling variability. See also *Historical Statistics, Colonial Times to 1970*, series L 98-112 and L 122-137]

ITEM	1980	1983	1984	1985	1986	1987	1988	1989	1990 [1]	1991 [1]
Total production	**35,354**	**34,572**	**37,065**	**36,445**	**41,999**	**44,886**	**44,576**	**43,576**	**43,466**	**40,031**
Softwoods [2]	28,239	28,927	30,801	30,479	34,815	37,410	36,845	36,040	36,224	33,250
Cedar	722	744	752	759	860	924	863	828	959	863
Douglas fir	6,853	6,434	7,809	7,751	9,600	10,422	9,986	10,045	8,831	7,816
Hemlock	1,855	1,316	(NA)	(NA)	(NA)	(NA)	(NA)	(NA)	(NA)	(NA)
Ponderosa pine	3,269	2,869	3,679	3,773	3,967	4,125	3,940	3,914	3,645	3,304
Redwood	770	852	999	1,155	984	1,157	1,157	1,048	1,077	887
Southern yellow pine	8,217	10,181	10,648	10,230	11,443	12,043	12,474	12,031	12,989	12,436
White fir [3]	1,643	1,316	2,017	2,272	2,659	2,899	2,919	3,296	3,272	2,900
Hardwoods [2]	7,115	5,644	6,264	5,966	7,184	7,476	7,731	7,536	7,242	6,781
Ash	(S)	224	219	218	257	265	293	278	210	184
Beech	183	112	111	89	125	116	120	105	82	72
Cottonwood and aspen	303	197	133	216	247	235	234	217	167	154
Elm	149	(NA)	(NA)	(NA)	(NA)	(NA)	(NA)	(NA)	(NA)	(NA)
Maple [4]	225	524	538	532	587	636	619	589	543	517
Oak [5]	3,356	2,163	2,786	2,793	3,410	3,804	3,790	3,546	2,615	2,434
Sweet gum [5]	371	278	300	293	375	330	356	306	219	167
Yellow poplar	661	475	569	544	724	805	828	802	666	629
Domestic consumption	**44,536**	**48,674**	**52,661**	**53,468**	**57,448**	**61,754**	**58,834**	**58,847**	**54,482**	**(NA)**
Percent net imports [6]	16.8	20.6	21.9	24.4	21.3	19.4	16.5	16.7	15.7	(NA)
Softwoods	33,812	39,611	42,832	44,240	47,492	50,558	48,513	47,975	45,003	(NA)
Mill stocks, yearend	4,228	4,606	4,594	4,765	4,905	4,840	4,999	4,888	4,854	(NA)
Exports	1,956	1,745	1,599	1,515	1,877	2,423	3,264	3,319	2,970	(NA)
Imports	9,540	11,977	13,270	14,608	14,238	14,680	13,806	13,638	12,148	(NA)
Hardwoods	10,724	9,063	9,829	9,228	9,956	11,196	10,321	10,872	9,480	(NA)
Mill stocks, yearend	1,572	1,334	1,561	1,719	1,636	(NA)	(NA)	(NA)	(NA)	(NA)
Exports	379	478	467	397	498	775	1,232	856	878	(NA)
Imports	293	261	328	364	347	511	390	375	255	(NA)

NA Not available. S Figure does not meet publication standards. [1] New sample, based on the new MA-24T sample.
[2] Includes types not shown separately. [3] Beginning 1988, also includes hemfir, and other western truefirs.
[4] Includes both hard and soft maple, except data for 1980 excludes hard maple. [5] Includes black, tupelo, and sweet gum.
[6] Imports minus exports.

Source: U.S. Bureau of the Census, *Current Industrial Reports*, series MA-24T, annual.

No. 1159. Lumber Production, by Geographic Area: 1970 to 1991

[In billion board feet. Data based in part on a sample of sawmills and are subject to sampling variability; see source. See *Historical Statistics, Colonial Times to 1970*, series L 113-121, for data by regions]

SECTION AND DIVISION	1970	1975	1980	1983	1984	1985	1986	1987	1988	1989	1990	1991
United States	**34.7**	**32.6**	**[1]35.4**	**34.6**	**37.1**	**36.4**	**42.0**	**44.9**	**44.7**	**43.6**	**43.5**	**40.0**
North [2][3]	4.4	4.1	(NA)	4.3	4.5	4.2	4.9	5.3	5.2	5.0	5.4	5.3
Hardwood	3.4	3.0	(NA)	3.0	3.3	3.0	3.6	3.8	3.9	3.8	3.7	3.5
Softwood	1.0	1.1	(NA)	1.3	1.2	1.2	1.4	1.5	1.4	1.3	1.7	1.7
South [2]	10.8	9.7	(NA)	12.7	13.4	13.0	15.1	15.7	16.3	15.8	16.5	15.6
Hardwood	3.6	2.7	(NA)	2.4	2.8	2.7	3.4	3.4	3.6	3.4	3.2	2.9
Softwood	7.2	7.0	(NA)	10.3	10.7	10.2	11.7	12.3	12.7	12.4	13.3	12.8
West [2]	19.4	18.8	17.2	17.6	19.1	19.3	22.0	23.9	23.2	22.7	21.6	19.1
Hardwood	0.1	0.1	0.3	0.2	0.2	0.2	0.2	0.3	0.3	0.3	0.4	0.4
Softwood	19.3	18.6	16.9	17.4	19.0	19.1	21.7	23.6	22.9	22.4	21.2	18.7
New England	0.7	0.8	1.1	1.1	1.1	1.1	1.2	1.2	1.2	1.1	1.3	1.3
Middle Atlantic	0.8	0.7	0.9	0.8	0.8	0.7	0.9	0.9	0.9	0.9	1.0	1.0
East North Central	1.2	1.1	1.3	1.2	1.3	1.3	1.5	1.6	1.5	1.4	1.5	1.4
West North Central	0.6	0.5	0.6	0.4	0.4	0.6	0.7	0.6	0.8	0.8	0.6	0.6
South Atlantic	5.2	4.7	5.2	6.5	6.7	6.4	7.4	7.7	8.2	8.0	8.1	7.6
East South Central	3.4	3.0	3.2	3.8	4.2	4.1	5.0	5.3	5.4	5.2	5.3	5.3
West South Central	3.2	3.0	2.9	3.1	3.3	3.1	3.4	3.7	3.8	3.6	4.2	3.9
Mountain	4.2	3.9	3.8	3.8	4.4	4.3	4.8	([4])	([4])	([4])	([4])	([4])
Pacific	15.3	14.8	13.4	13.6	14.8	14.8	17.0	[5]23.9	[5]23.2	22.5	21.4	19.0

NA Not available. [1] Includes amounts not specified by division. [2] Source: U.S. Forest Service, *U.S. Timber Production, Trade, Consumption, and Price Statistics, 1960-89*, annual. Sections are as defined by the Forest Service. [3] Includes Kentucky. [4] Included with Pacific. [5] Includes Mountain.

Source: Except as noted, U.S. Bureau of the Census, *Current Industrial Reports*, series MA-24T, annual.

No. 1160. Wood Products—Production: 1970 to 1990

ITEM	Unit	1970	1975	1980	1983	1984	1985	1986	1987	1988	1989	1990, prel.
Hardwood flooring . .	Mil. bd. ft	307	99	78	98	110	122	145	174	193	206	205
Softwood plywood . .	Bil. sq. ft., 3/8"..	14.1	15.1	15.5	18.3	18.9	19.3	20.4	21.1	22.9	21.4	20.7
Insulation boards [1] . .	1,000 short tons .	1,219	1,249	1,051	713	785	735	732	605	529	460	474
Hardboard [1]	Mil. sq. ft., 1/8"..	4,340	5,681	6,140	7,303	6,837	6,300	5,822	5,458	5,118	5,196	5,025
Particleboard.	Mil. sq. ft., 3/4"..	1,731	2,503	2,950	3,009	3,196	3,331	3,603	3,706	3,829	3,858	3,806

[1] Beginning 1983, data are for shipments.
Source: U.S. Dept. of Commerce, International Trade Administration, *Forest Products Review*, monthly (discontinued April 1983); and unpublished data. Based on reports of U.S. Bureau of the Census, National Oak Flooring Manufacturers Association and National Particleboard Association.

No. 1161. Paper and Paperboard—Production and Consumption: 1970 to 1992

[In millions of short tons. See also *Historical Statistics, Colonial Times to 1970*, series L 172, L 174, and L 178-191]

ITEM	PRODUCTION						CONSUMPTION [1]					
	1970	1980	1985	1990	1991	1992	1970	1980	1985	1990	1991	1992
Total paper and paperboard. .	51.7	63.6	68.7	80.3	81.1	83.7	56.0	67.2	76.1	86.7	84.9	87.3
Paper: Newsprint	3.5	4.7	5.4	6.6	6.8	7.1	9.8	11.4	12.8	13.3	12.5	12.6
Coated printing, converting	3.2	4.6	5.9	7.5	7.4	7.6	3.2	4.6	6.3	8.3	7.8	8.1
Uncoated free sheet	5.1	8.0	9.7	11.5	11.5	11.9	5.1	8.0	10.0	12.0	11.9	12.2
Other printing, writing, etc	2.6	2.9	2.9	3.3	3.2	3.1	2.8	3.5	4.4	5.2	5.0	4.8
Packaging and industrial converting	5.3	5.5	5.2	4.6	4.5	4.7	5.1	5.2	5.2	4.7	4.6	4.8
Tissue and other machine creped	3.7	4.4	4.9	5.8	5.7	5.8	3.7	4.4	5.0	5.9	5.7	5.8
Paperboard: Unbleached kraft . . .	11.5	15.3	16.4	20.4	21.0	21.7	9.9	13.0	14.6	17.8	17.8	18.5
Bleached kraft	3.3	3.8	3.9	4.4	4.6	4.5	3.2	3.3	3.4	3.7	3.8	5.9
Semichemical	3.5	4.7	5.1	5.7	5.7	5.9	3.4	4.4	5.0	5.7	5.6	3.7
Recycled finish	7.0	7.1	7.6	8.9	9.2	9.9	7.0	7.0	7.6	9.3	9.5	10.4
Construction paper and board [2]	3.0	2.6	1.7	1.6	1.6	1.6	3.0	3.0	2.0	1.7	1.6	1.7

[1] Total consumption of paper and paperboard includes net imports of paper and paperboard converted products; not available by grade. [2] Beginning 1985, estimated. Source: 1970-80, U.S. Bureau of the Census, *Current Industrial Reports*. Includes wet machine board, approximately 100,000-160,000 tons per year.
Source: Except as noted, American Paper Institute, Inc., New York, NY, *Statistics of Paper, Paperboard, and Woodpulp*, annual.

No. 1162. Newsprint—Production, Stocks, Consumption, Imports, and Price Index: 1970 to 1991

[In thousands of metric tons, except price index and imports (imports in short tons). See also *Historical Statistics, Colonial Times to 1970*, series L 192-198]

COUNTRY AND ITEM	1970	1975	1980	1985	1986	1987	1988	1989	1990	1991
Canada: Production	7,808	6,966	8,625	8,988	9,289	9,669	9,840	9,640	9,068	8,977
Shipments from mills	7,795	7,010	8,622	8,996	9,302	9,757	9,740	9,607	9,074	8,756
Stocks at mills, end of year. . . .	236	96	165	290	277	189	288	321	315	536
United States:										
Estimated consumption [1]	8,805	8,395	10,088	11,507	11,873	12,303	12,244	12,241	12,127	(NA)
Production	3,142	3,348	4,239	4,924	5,107	5,300	5,427	5,523	5,997	6,206
Shipments from mills	3,136	3,347	4,234	4,927	5,115	5,310	5,415	5,515	6,007	6,154
Stocks, end of year: At mills . . .	33	21	21	57	49	36	48	56	46	98
At and in transit to publishers .	749	734	732	910	849	900	933	749	802	816
Imports [2]	6,635	5,847	7,280	8,472	8,589	8,976	8,592	8,765	7,672	6,986
Producer price index (1982=100)	34.1	58.3	[3]88.5	105.3	103.3	112.3	127.6	122.5	119.5	120.9

NA Not available. [1] By all users. Based on American Paper Institute data. [2] Source: Reports of U.S. Bureau of the Census. Includes Puerto Rico and beginning 1985, Virgin Islands. [3] Average for 11 months.
Source: Except as noted, U.S. Bureau of Economic Analysis, *Survey of Current Business*, monthly. Data from American Paper Institute, Inc., New York, NY, and Canadian Pulp & Paper Association.

No. 1163. Recovered Paper Utilization and Recovery Rates: 1970 to 1992

[In millions of short tons, except percent. Recovery rate is ratio of total recovered paper to new supply. Recovered paper utilization is the ratio of recovered paper consumption at paper and board mills to paper and board production. See *Historical Statistics, Colonial Times to 1970*, series L 175, for U.S. wastepaper consumption]

ITEM	1970	1980	1985	1986	1987	1988	1989	1990	1991	1992
Paper and board, production [1]	51.7	63.6	68.7	72.5	75.9	78.1	78.4	80.3	81.1	83.7
Recovered paper consumption	11.8	14.9	16.4	17.9	18.7	19.7	20.2	21.7	23.7	26.2
Recovered paper utilization rate (percent). .	22.8	23.5	23.8	24.7	24.6	25.2	25.8	27.1	29.2	31.3
Other recovered paper uses [2]	0.42	0.47	0.53	0.59	0.66	0.70	0.72	1.00	1.08	1.10
Recovered paper exports	0.41	2.64	3.56	4.09	4.81	5.95	6.31	6.51	6.60	6.40
Total paper recovered.	12.6	17.9	20.4	22.5	24.0	26.2	27.1	29.1	31.2	33.6
Paper and board, new supply [3]	56.0	67.2	76.1	79.8	83.5	85.5	85.2	86.7	84.9	87.3
Recovery rate (percent).	22.4	26.7	26.8	28.2	28.8	30.6	31.8	33.6	36.8	38.5

[1] Excludes hard pressed board; includes construction paper and board, and wet machine board. [2] Estimated. [3] Excludes production of hard pressed board.
Source: American Paper Institute, Inc., New York, NY, *Statistics of Paper, Paperboard, and Woodpulp*, annual; and unpublished data.

No. 1164. Selected Wood Products—Production and Consumption: 1970 to 1989

[See also *Historical Statistics, Colonial Times to 1970*, series L 151-170]

ITEM	Unit	1970	1975	1980	1984	1985	1986	1987	1988	1989
PULPWOOD										
Receipts, total	Mil. cords [1]	68.9	65.4	81.0	88.0	85.4	90.6	93.9	95.1	97.0
Softwood	Mil. cords [1]	52.4	49.3	60.2	62.9	60.2	63.3	65.3	65.8	67.1
Hardwood	Mil. cords [1]	16.5	16.2	20.8	25.2	25.1	27.3	28.6	29.3	29.9
Consumption, total	Mil. cords [1]	67.6	65.4	79.7	87.0	84.8	91.1	92.4	95.3	96.1
Softwood	Mil. cords [1]	51.3	48.9	58.8	62.0	59.7	63.1	64.2	65.9	66.3
Hardwood	Mil. cords [1]	16.3	16.5	20.9	24.9	25.1	28.1	28.2	29.4	29.7
Inventories [2]	Mil. cords [1]	6.6	6.6	6.7	5.2	5.1	4.7	5.6	5.3	5.8
WOODPULP										
Production	Mil. short tons	43.9	43.1	53.0	57.8	57.7	60.6	62.4	64.1	64.6
Consumption, [3] total	Mil. short tons	43.2	42.4	52.4	57.5	56.6	60.0	61.2	62.8	62.7
Own pulp	Mil. short tons	38.9	38.5	46.6	50.3	49.7	52.6	53.8	54.9	54.9
Purchased pulp	Mil. short tons	4.3	3.9	5.9	7.2	7.0	7.5	7.4	7.9	7.8
PLYWOOD										
Softwood:										
Production	Mil. sq. ft. [4]	14,149	15,706	15,483	18,865	19,341	20,363	22,312	22,233	20,919
Consumption, total	Mil. sq. ft. [4]	(NA)	(NA)	15,145	18,526	19,122	19,880	21,503	22,277	20,904
Value	Mil. dol.	949	(NA)	2,582	2,995	3,080	3,237	3,483	3,513	3,734
Hardwood:										
Production	Mil. sq. ft. [5]	1,904	1,280	1,311	1,185	1,016	1,088	1,256	1,217	1,213
Consumption, total	Mil. sq. ft. [5]	5,772	4,970	3,416	3,831	4,311	4,884	4,918	4,193	(NA)
Value	Mil. dol.	516	586	977	1,199	1,192	1,320	1,471	1,405	1,392

NA Not available. [1] Standard cords. 128 cubic feet roughwood bases. [2] As of Dec. 31. [3] In the manufacture of paper and board. [4] 3/8-inch basis. [5] Surface measure.
Source: U.S. Bureau of the Census, *Current Industrial Reports*, series MA26-A, MA24-H, and MA24-F.

No. 1165. Selected Timber Products—Imports and Exports: 1970 to 1991

ITEM	Unit	1970	1980	1984	1985	1986	1987	1988	1989	1990	1991, prel.
IMPORTS [1]											
Lumber, total [2]	Mil. bd. ft.	6,114	9,866	13,632	14,996	14,619	15,234	14,226	15,277	12,159	11,756
From Canada	Percent	96.0	97.5	97.9	97.6	97.5	96.9	97.5	91.3	98.5	98.3
Softwoods	Mil. bd. ft.	5,778	9,573	13,304	14,632	14,272	14,723	13,841	14,928	11,927	11,545
Value	Mil. dol	434	1,826	2,681	2,898	2,969	3,060	2,939	2,875	2,534	2,507
Hardwoods	Mil. bd. ft.	337	293	328	364	347	511	386	349	232	210
Value	Mil. dol	62	152	173	180	168	273	238	152	141	142
Logs, total	Mil. bd. ft. [3]	144	128	147	99	78	83	68	42	28	15
From Canada	Percent	79.6	97.4	97.4	81.8	77.9	91.6	91.9	61.5	67.5	74.5
Softwoods	Mil. bd. ft. [3]	107	114	117	71	52	69	56	24	18	9
Value	Mil. dol	9	17	15	17	7	19	15	12	7	6
Hardwoods	Mil. bd. ft. [3]	38	13	30	28	26	14	12	18	10	6
Value	Mil. dol	5	3	5	4	4	3	3	17	10	6
Paper and board [4]	1,000 tons	7,115	8,780	11,075	11,522	11,936	12,837	13,110	13,100	13,148	12,167
Value	Mil. dol	1,039	3,418	5,324	5,698	6,036	6,928	8,002	8,330	8,427	7,929
Woodpulp	1,000 tons	3,518	4,051	4,490	4,466	4,594	4,848	4,938	5,105	4,893	4,997
Value	Mil. dol	483	1,684	1,845	1,521	1,606	2,069	2,608	3,037	2,831	2,132
Plywood	Mil. sq. ft. [5]	2,049	1,235	1,538	1,817	2,002	2,083	1,698	1,955	1,687	1,457
Value	Mil. dol	208	409	438	463	519	638	577	516	537	457
EXPORTS											
Lumber, total [2]	Mil. bd. ft.	1,243	2,494	2,150	1,945	2,427	3,217	4,527	4,243	3,802	3,997
To: Canada	Percent	21.7	25.3	25.8	23.7	22.0	20.9	17.6	15.6	18.1	15.1
Japan	Percent	30.8	26.0	28.0	32.1	36.4	36.8	34.5	38.1	33.5	30.5
Europe	Percent	24.1	23.8	16.0	15.1	16.6	16.9	20.5	16.6	19.1	19.6
Softwoods	Mil. bd. ft.	1,115	2,007	1,624	1,518	1,878	2,424	3,266	3,379	2,941	3,055
Value	Mil. dol	163	789	541	497	644	856	1,143	1,404	1,336	1,358
Hardwoods	Mil. bd. ft.	128	487	527	427	548	793	1,261	863	861	942
Value	Mil. dol	31	272	300	263	350	493	683	659	818	879
Logs, total	Mil. bd. ft. [3]	2,741	3,261	3,495	3,843	3,627	4,110	4,798	4,745	4,262	3,816
To: Canada	Percent	10.6	9.7	12.1	11.6	12.2	10.3	7.9	5.8	9.3	11.2
Japan	Percent	86.3	78.0	50.4	49.4	57.3	58.3	50.3	63.5	62.5	56.7
China: Mainland	Percent	(NA)	2.7	24.8	27.8	17.0	14.1	23.4	9.6	8.5	9.7
Softwoods	Mil. bd. ft. [3]	2,672	3,109	3,369	3,732	3,488	3,960	4,594	4,532	4,044	3,532
Value	Mil. dol	320	1,452	1,079	1,169	1,129	1,526	2,090	2,176	2,170	1,870
Hardwoods	Mil. bd. ft. [3]	69	152	126	111	139	149	204	214	218	283
Value	Mil. dol	36	129	101	91	97	118	160	223	251	234
Paper and board [4]	1,000 tons	2,817	5,214	4,387	4,071	4,687	5,304	5,691	6,300	6,796	8,331
Value	Mil. dol	602	2,773	2,552	2,266	2,540	3,104	3,753	4,261	5,035	6,006
Woodpulp	1,000 tons	3,095	3,806	3,594	3,796	4,459	4,869	5,528	6,231	5,906	6,337
Value	Mil. dol	464	1,652	1,502	1,354	1,663	2,251	2,915	3,513	3,156	2,800
Plywood	Mil. sq. ft. [5]	172	413	402	358	647	846	1,093	1,562	1,767	1,552
Value	Mil. dol	16	108	94	86	145	194	247	292	338	295

NA Not available. [1] Customs value of imports; see text, section 29. [2] Includes railroad ties. [3] Log scale. [4] Includes paper and board products. Excludes hardboard. [5] 3/8-inch basis.
Source: U.S. Forest Service, *U.S. Timber Production,*

No. 1166. Fishery Products—Domestic Catch and Imports, Summary: 1970 to 1991

[Live weight, in millions of pounds, except percent. 1979-1991 preliminary. For data on commercial catch for selected countries, see table 1478, section 31. See *Historical Statistics, Colonial Times to 1970*, series L 224-226, for domestic cat

ITEM	1970	1980	1982	1983	1984	1985	1986	1987	1988	1989	1990	1991
Total	11,474	11,357	12,011	12,352	12,552	15,150	14,368	15,744	14,628	15,485	16,349	16,364
For human food......	6,213	8,006	7,968	8,413	8,498	9,337	9,620	10,561	10,505	12,268	12,662	13,020
Finfish..............	(NA)	6,139	6,090	6,358	6,303	6,991	7,087	7,919	7,786	9,735	10,120	10,186
Shellfish [1]	(NA)	1,867	1,878	2,055	2,195	2,346	2,533	2,642	2,719	2,533	2,542	2,834
For industrial use	5,261	3,351	4,043	3,939	4,054	5,813	4,748	5,183	4,123	3,217	3,687	3,344
Domestic catch	4,917	6,482	6,367	6,439	6,438	6,258	6,031	6,896	7,192	8,463	9,404	9,404
Percent of total	42.8	57.1	53.0	52.1	51.3	41.3	42.0	43.8	49.2	54.7	57.5	58.0
For human food	2,537	3,654	3,285	3,238	3,320	3,294	3,393	3,946	4,588	6,204	7,041	7,031
Finfish	(NA)	2,516	2,324	2,351	2,348	2,273	2,240	2,769	3,306	4,897	5,747	5,564
Shellfish [1]	(NA)	1,138	961	887	972	1,021	1,153	1,177	1,282	1,307	1,294	1,467
For industrial use	2,380	2,828	3,082	3,201	3,118	2,964	2,638	2,950	2,604	2,259	2,363	2,453
Imports [2]..........	6,557	4,875	5,644	5,913	6,114	8,892	8,337	8,848	7,436	7,022	6,945	6,879
Percent of total	57.2	42.9	47.0	47.9	48.7	58.7	58.0	56.2	50.8	45.3	42.5	42.0
For human food	3,676	4,352	4,683	5,175	5,178	6,043	6,227	6,615	5,917	6,064	5,621	5,989
Finfish	(NA)	3,623	3,766	4,007	3,955	4,718	4,847	5,150	4,480	4,838	4,373	4,622
Shellfish [1]	(NA)	729	917	1,168	1,223	1,325	1,380	1,465	1,437	1,226	1,248	1,367
For industrial use [3] ...	2,881	523	961	738	936	2,849	2,110	2,233	1,519	958	1,324	890

NA Not available.   [1] For univalve and bivalve mollusks (conchs, clams, oysters, scallops, etc.), the weight of meats, excluding the shell, is reported.   [2] Excludes imports of edible fishery products consumed in Puerto Rico; includes landings of tuna caught by foreign vessels in American Samoa.   [3] Fish meal and sea herring.

Source: U.S. National Oceanic and Atmospheric Administration, National Marine Fisheries Service, *Fishery Statistics of the United States*, annual; and *Fisheries of the United States*, annual.

No. 1167. Fisheries—Employment, Fishing Craft, and Establishments: 1970 to 1990

[In thousands. As of Dec. 31. 1979-89 preliminary. Data for employment and establishments exclude Alaska. See also *Historical Statistics, Colonial Times to 1970*, series L 254-261]

ITEM	1970	1980	1981	1982	1983	1984	1985	1986	1987	1988	1989 [1]	1990 [1]
Persons employed in U.S....	227	296	303	314	333	340	351	347	359	364	(NA)	(NA)
Fishermen	140	193	198	216	223	230	239	247	256	274	(NA)	(NA)
Shore workers [2]	87	103	105	98	110	110	112	100	103	90	73	72
Craft used	88	113	115	123	127	127	127	130	128	[3]93	[3]110	95
Vessels, 5 net tons and over .	14	19	20	20	21	24	24	38	[3]23	[3]32	36	32
Motorboats..............	72	93	93	102	105	102	104	88	[3]68	[3]78	75	63
Other boats.............	2	1	2	1	1	1	2	2	[3]2	(NA)	(NA)	(NA)
Fishery shore establishments.	3.7	3.6	3.6	3.6	3.9	4.0	4.0	4.0	4.0	4.2	4.6	4.5	(NA)

NA Not available.   [1] Estimated and excludes Mississippi River. Maryland and Virginia represent only Federal collected data.   [2] Seasonal average for processors and wholesaling plants.   [3] Excludes Maryland and Virginia.

Source: U.S. National Oceanic and Atmospheric Administration, National Marine Fisheries Service, *Fishery Statistics of the United States*, annual; and *Fisheries of the United States*, annual.

No. 1168. Fisheries—Quantity and Value of Domestic Catch: 1960 to 1991

[1979-1991 preliminary. See also *Historical Statistics, Colonial Times to 1970*, series L 224-226, L 229, and L 310]

YEAR	QUANTITY (mil. lb. [1])			Value (mil. dol.)	Average price per lb. (cents)	YEAR	QUANTITY (mil. lb. [1])			Value (mil. dol.)	Average price per lb. (cents)
	Total	For human food	For industrial products [2]				Total	For human food	For industrial products [2]		
1960.....	4,942	2,498	2,444	354	7.2	1981.....	5,977	3,547	2,430	2,388	40.0
1965.....	4,777	2,587	2,190	446	9.3	1982.....	6,367	3,285	3,082	2,390	37.5
1970.....	4,917	2,537	2,380	613	12.5	1983.....	6,439	3,238	3,201	2,355	36.6
1972.....	4,806	2,435	2,371	748	15.6	1984.....	6,438	3,320	3,118	2,350	36.5
1973.....	4,858	2,398	2,460	937	19.3	1985.....	6,258	3,294	2,964	2,326	37.2
1974.....	4,967	2,496	2,471	932	18.7	1986.....	6,031	3,393	2,638	2,763	45.8
1975.....	4,877	2,465	2,412	977	20.0	1987.....	6,896	3,946	2,950	3,115	45.2
1976.....	5,388	2,775	2,613	1,349	25.0	1988.....	7,192	4,588	2,604	3,520	48.9
1977.....	5,271	2,952	2,319	1,554	29.5	1989.....	8,463	6,204	2,259	3,238	38.3
1978.....	6,028	3,177	2,851	1,854	30.7	1990.....	9,404	7,041	2,363	3,522	37.5
1979.....	6,267	3,318	2,949	2,234	35.6	1991.....	9,484	7,031	2,453	3,308	34.9
1980.....	6,482	3,654	2,828	2,237	34.5						

[1] Live weight.   [2] Meal, oil, fish solubles, homogenized condensed fish, shell products, bait, and animal food.

Source: U.S. National Oceanic and Atmospheric Administration, National Marine Fisheries Service, *Fishery Statistics of the United States*, annual; and *Fisheries of the United States*, annual.

No. 1169. Fisheries—Quantity and Value of Catch, by State, and Catch of Principal Species, by Area: 1980 to 1991

[Catch in millions of pounds, live weight, except as indicated; value in millions of dollars. Preliminary. See also *Historical Statistics, Colonial Times to 1970*, series L 262-293]

AREA, STATE, CATCH, AND VALUE	1980	1985	1990	1991
Total:				
Catch	6,482	6,258	9,403	9,484
Value	2,237	2,326	3,522	3,308
New England:				
Catch	788	590	649	646
Value	327	419	543	594
Maine:				
Catch	245	175	169	192
Value	93	101	130	155
New Hampshire:				
Catch	19	8	11	11
Value	5	5	10	13
Massachusetts:				
Catch	438	296	328	289
Value	178	232	303	296
Rhode Island:				
Catch	81	104	132	139
Value	46	70	73	85
Connecticut:				
Catch	5	7	9	15
Value	5	12	27	45
Catch for certain species:				
Clams	15	22	15	12
Cod	118	83	95	92
Crabs	7	8	9	9
Flounder	118	98	60	50
Haddock	55	14	5	4
Herring, sea	184	52	113	106
Lobster, American	36	44	55	56
Ocean perch, Atlantic	24	10	1	1
Pollock	40	43	21	17
Scallops, sea	17	10	25	24
Squid	6	15	36	42
Whiting	18	31	28	26
Middle Atlantic:				
Catch	244	151	207	234
Value	97	101	150	154
New York:				
Catch	39	39	49	51
Value	45	38	56	53
New Jersey:				
Catch	201	108	149	175
Value	50	61	89	97
Delaware:				
Catch	4	5	9	8
Value	2	2	4	4
Catch for certain species:				
Clams (meats)	40	73	93	97
Scup or porgy	8	2	4	7
Squid	3	8	6	26
Chesapeake Bay:				
Catch	717	815	867	770
Value	130	124	160	142
Maryland:				
Catch	80	92	81	89
Value	45	47	54	47
Virginia:				
Catch	637	723	787	681
Value	85	76	107	95
Catch for certain species:				
Crabs	65	91	91	98
Clams	36	47	27	21
Scallops, sea	6	3	9	9
Flounder	10	6	2	4
Oysters	21	8	4	3
South Atlantic:				
Catch	473	311	262	293
Value	148	156	170	169
North Carolina:				
Catch	356	215	176	213
Value	69	65	72	67
South Carolina:				
Catch	21	13	14	19
Value	20	14	24	28
Georgia:				
Catch	19	17	13	16
Value	20	21	20	24

AREA, STATE, CATCH, AND VALUE	1980	1985	1990	1991
Florida (east coast):				
Catch	77	66	58	45
Value	39	57	54	50
Catch for certain species:				
Menhaden	218	105	74	113
Shrimp	33	28	28	37
Crabs	55	48	54	57
Scallops	1	13	2	1
Gulf States:				
Catch	1,979	2,412	1,625	1,679
Value	463	597	640	641
Florida (west coast):				
Catch	115	117	122	117
Value	86	114	116	112
Alabama:				
Catch	25	30	23	22
Value	25	41	36	37
Mississippi:				
Catch	334	471	320	239
Value	25	40	42	34
Louisiana:				
Catch	1,412	1,693	1,061	1,193
Value	174	225	263	244
Texas:				
Catch	94	103	99	108
Value	153	177	182	214
Catch for certain species:				
Crabs	45	53	51	65
Mullet	31	17	24	25
Oysters (meats)	17	25	11	13
Shrimp	208	263	247	229
Great Lakes: [1]				
Catch	44	54	45	39
Value	14	15	20	21
Mississippi River and tributaries:				
Catch	85	92	(NA)	(NA)
Value	21	29	(NA)	(NA)
Pacific Coast:				
Catch	2,140	1,816	5,722	5,795
Value	1,025	863	1,775	1,529
Washington:				
Catch	156	167	137	152
Value	86	93	118	110
Oregon:				
Catch	126	101	139	150
Value	56	46	70	63
California:				
Catch	804	363	347	348
Value	323	133	127	140
Alaska:				
Catch	1,054	1,185	5,099	5,145
Value	560	591	1,459	1,216
Catch for certain species:				
Anchovies	107	15	13	19
Bonito	14	5	8	1
Cod	20	120	526	554
Crabs	347	129	281	(NA)
Flounder	60	68	182	330
Hake	12	16	21	56
Halibut	19	61	70	66
Herring, sea	107	142	108	123
Jack mackerel	44	21	9	4
Mackerel	65	75	84	63
Oysters	7	8	11	(NA)
Pollock	3	93	3,108	2,855
Rockfish	106	82	132	97
Sablefish	22	63	90	84
Salmon	614	727	733	733
Shrimp	98	35	59	47
Tuna	387	64	34	13
Hawaii:				
Catch	11	17	26	28
Tuna catch	7	11	14	9
Value	12	22	65	58

NA Not available. [1] Collected largely by State fishery agencies and compiled by State fishery agencies and National Marine Fisheries Service. Includes, in addition to the Great Lakes, small amounts for Lake St. Clair, Lake of the Woods, Namakan Lake, and Rainy Lake.

Source: U.S. National Oceanic and Atmospheric Administration, National Marine Fisheries Service, *Fishery Statistics of the United States*, annual; and *Fisheries of the United States*, annual.

No. 1170. Domestic Fisheries—Catch by Selected Ports: 1985 to 1991

[See *Historical Statistics, Colonial Times to 1970*, series L 236-253, for data on quantity and value of catch]

PORT	CATCH (mil. lb.)					VALUE (mil. dol.)				
	1985	1988	1989	1990	1991	1985	1988	1989	1990	1991
New Bedford, MA.............	90.6	90.3	90.4	114.8	106.4	103.2	140.9	141.0	160.4	157.7
Dutch Harbor-Unalaska, AK........	106.3	377.3	504.3	509.9	731.7	21.3	100.9	107.0	126.2	130.6
Kodiak, AK..................	96.1	304.6	213.2	272.5	287.3	65.8	[1]166.3	100.2	101.7	96.9
Dulac-Chauvin, LA.............	398.6	244.1	210.9	164.4	166.3	59.9	56.5	50.0	52.7	48.8
Empire-Venice, LA.............	224.5	297.2	272.7	244.2	308.6	34.3	67.7	49.2	46.3	43.5
Gloucester, MA...............	116.5	107.4	98.5	126.2	107.2	37.1	30.8	30.0	40.5	40.0
Petersburg, AK...............	(NA)	50.4	113.5	67.5	90.3	(NA)	58.5	61.4	39.4	34.6
Cordova, AK.................	(NA)	42.5	55.3	70.8	47.5	(NA)	46.4	35.3	36.8	19.5
Cape May-Wildwood, NJ.........	30.3	47.9	54.0	69.2	93.1	18.1	28.4	30.8	34.4	40.1
Point Judith, RI...............	56.8	49.6	48.3	58.7	64.7	28.0	25.4	23.6	32.2	37.5
Portland, ME.................	36.1	43.9	49.0	48.9	63.4	17.2	30.4	34.4	31.7	44.1
Ketchiken, AK................	(NA)	28.3	91.6	52.6	68.5	(NA)	43.5	45.6	28.3	21.9
Beaufort-Morehead City, NC.......	133.2	110.0	95.0	102.0	137.0	22.7	27.0	25.0	23.0	23.0
Cameron, LA.................	673.6	438.9	352.7	232.6	288.4	29.9	33.2	20.5	20.6	20.3
Morgan City-Berwick, LA.........	7.7	43.3	68.1	146.5	112.3	(NA)	16.7	17.8	19.7	20.3
Pascagoula-Moss Point, MS.......	423.2	292.0	282.1	303.9	227.3	18.4	28.2	16.9	18.8	15.1
Los Angeles, CA..............	150.3	232.0	177.6	133.8	115.7	32.5	34.0	20.3	17.6	15.0
Astoria, OR..................	25.5	44.2	51.0	41.2	53.0	9.5	24.3	20.0	16.2	17.0
Port Hueneme-Oxnard-Ventura, CA...	19.9	55.0	65.3	39.4	44.0	5.4	10.0	12.0	12.5	13.2
Intercoastal City, LA............	(NA)	209.7	207.2	173.0	211.4	(NA)	14.7	9.5	(NA)	(NA)

NA Not available.　[1] Record.

Source: U.S. National Oceanic and Atmospheric Administration, National Marine Fisheries Service, *Fisheries of the United States*, annual.

No. 1171. Domestic Fish and Shellfish Catch and Value, by Species: 1985 to 1991

SPECIES	QUANTITY (1,000 lb.)				VALUE ($1,000)		
	1986-90 5-year average	1985	1990	1991	1985	1990	1991
Total	(X)	6,257,642	9,403,571	9,484,194	2,326,237	3,521,995	3,308,272
Fish, total [1] **..........**	(X)	5,214,363	8,091,068	7,993,274	1,193,427	1,900,097	1,679,911
Anchovies..............	13,059	14,566	13,189	19,245	2,704	2,723	6,813
Bluefish	14,056	13,743	13,802	13,232	2,363	3,239	2,731
Butterfish	7,844	10,338	6,532	6,181	3,537	3,334	3,171
Cod: Atlantic...........	74,122	82,823	95,881	92,636	35,140	61,329	74,093
Pacific...........	288,158	120,275	526,396	553,716	18,556	91,384	122,934
Croaker	9,807	11,088	6,720	4,761	3,658	3,390	2,146
Flounder...............	210,878	195,718	254,519	404,955	129,121	112,921	144,789
Haddock...............	6,664	14,416	5,440	4,053	13,545	5,967	4,581
Halibut	76,206	61,032	70,454	66,339	38,376	96,700	99,532
Herring, sea; Atlantic......	91,413	57,133	113,095	107,067	2,968	5,746	6,339
Herring, sea; Pacific......	122,452	142,074	108,120	123,141	47,025	32,178	30,832
Jack mackerel...........	22,054	20,852	8,959	3,618	1,770	535	24,433
Mackerel, Pacific.........	90,386	75,453	83,721	63,336	6,324	5,081	4,872
Menhaden	2,228,120	2,739,401	1,962,160	1,977,060	100,680	93,896	77,694
Mullet................	28,912	21,205	28,554	12,717	5,720	12,738	10,569
Ocean perch, Atlantic	3,168	9,666	1,322	1,176	3,179	703	543
Ocean perch, Pacific.......	26,158	9,034	60,972	29,994	1,757	8,494	6,445
Pollock, Atlantic.........	35,491	43,477	21,042	17,344	6,978	10,516	9,901
Pollock, Alaska..........	1,481,948	92,833	3,108,031	2,855,316	5,409	268,344	241,551
Rockfish..............	119,821	82,109	131,545	97,466	23,107	38,504	109,934
Sablefish	96,494	63,380	89,802	83,610	28,692	58,865	78,166
Salmon...............	669,140	726,946	733,146	783,285	439,795	612,367	359,720
Scup or porgy	13,174	15,996	11,452	16,145	9,338	8,677	9,127
Sea trout, gray..........	16,626	16,400	9,880	8,668	7,330	5,777	4,854
Shark, Dogfish..........	16,790	11,563	35,793	34,376	842	3,801	3,444
Snapper, red...........	3,887	5,181	3,101	2,358	10,661	8,411	5,681
Swordfish	11,563	12,258	13,797	17,963	33,191	40,851	50,155
Tuna	90,205	83,054	62,393	35,695	52,515	105,040	75,053
Whiting...............	38,804	44,545	44,500	36,533	8,274	11,281	11,219
Shellfish, total [1] **.......**	(X)	1,043,279	1,312,503	1,490,920	1,132,810	1,621,898	1,628,361
Clams	137,771	150,551	139,198	134,243	128,349	130,194	125,266
Crabs................	431,090	337,632	499,416	649,993	203,044	483,837	414,835
Lobsters: American.......	50,839	46,152	61,017	63,337	114,895	154,677	165,026
Oysters	34,272	44,173	29,193	31,859	70,053	93,718	97,996
Scallops: Calico.........	5,871	12,513	1,135	286	12,524	1,281	858
Sea	31,252	15,829	39,917	39,302	74,562	153,696	158,932
Shrimp...............	358,442	333,691	346,494	320,087	472,850	491,433	512,848
Squid: Atlantic..........	49,081	7,157	59,800	70,929	7,256	21,178	30,346
Pacific..........	52,489	22,276	36,082	68,640	4,047	2,636	5,288

X Not applicable.　[1] Includes other types of fish and shellfish, not shown separately.

Source: U.S. National Oceanic and Atmospheric Administration, National Marine Fisheries Service, *Fisheries of the United States*, annual.

No. 1172. Disposition of U.S. Domestic Catch: 1970 to 1991

[Live weight catch in millions of pounds. 1980-90 preliminary. In addition to whole fish, a large portion of waste (400-500 million lb.) derived from canning, filleting, and dressing fish and shellfish utilized in production of fish meal and oil in each year shown. See *Historical Statistics, Colonial Times to 1970*, series L 305-310, for similar but not entirely comparable data]

DISPOSITION	1970	1975	1980	1983	1984	1985	1986	1987	1988	1989	1990	1991
Total	4,917	4,877	6,482	6,439	6,438	6,258	6,031	6,896	7,192	8,463	9,404	9,484
Fresh and frozen	1,595	1,744	2,621	2,304	2,336	2,242	2,487	3,157	3,813	5,585	6,501	6,541
Canned	1,150	907	1,161	1,087	1,128	1,232	1,134	1,009	1,017	798	751	674
Cured	71	55	96	80	82	70	60	89	86	128	126	119
Reduced to meal, oil, etc.	2,101	2,171	2,604	2,968	2,892	2,714	2,350	2,641	2,276	1,952	2,026	2,150

Source: U.S. National Oceanic and Atmospheric Administration, National Marine Fisheries Service, *Fishery Statistics of the United States*, annual; and *Fisheries of the United States*, annual.

No. 1173. Joint Venture Catches in the U.S. Exclusive Economic Zone (EEZ), by Species: 1985 to 1990

[Joint venture—An operation authorized under the Magnuson Fishery Conservation and Management Act (MFCMA) in which a permitted foreign vessel receives fish in the U.S. Exclusive Economic Zone (EEZ) from a U.S. vessel. The fish received from the U.S. vessel are part of the U.S. harvest]

SPECIES	QUANTITY (1,000 lb.)				VALUE ($1,000)			
	1985	1988	1989	1990	1985	1988	1989	1990
Total	2,008,889	3,201,487	1,700,293	800,565	104,320	221,090	112,165	51,341
Atka mackerel	88,047	43,253	-	-	6,109	3,571	-	-
Cod	80,189	245,871	97,937	17,809	7,799	30,429	12,495	1,763
Flounder	396,084	727,778	426,436	219,547	24,833	53,763	34,179	23,527
Hake, Pacific	(D)	299,343	448,808	376,927	(D)	14,660	21,628	18,429
Ocean perch	619	-	-	-	56	-	-	-
Mackerel, Atlantic	8,350	12,533	(Z)	(D)	584	760	(Z)	(D)
Pollock, Alaska	1,354,368	1,822,242	634,385	49,376	59,730	116,102	40,378	2,139
Rockfish	154	4,636	-	-	14	705	-	-
Sablefish	207	112	-	-	30	14	-	-
Squid	7,987	(D)	-	-	1,194	(D)	-	-
Other	72,884	45,719	92,727	136,906	3,971	1,086	3,485	5,483

- Represents zero.   D Figure withheld to avoid disclosure.   Z Less than $500.

Source: U.S. National Oceanic and Atmospheric Administration, National Marine Fisheries Service, *Fisheries of the United States*, annual.

No. 1174. U.S. Catch and Value of Fish and Shellfish, by Distance Caught Off U.S. Shores—Selected Species: 1991

[Preliminary. **Catch** is shown in **live weight**, except as indicated. Includes landings by U.S. flag vessels at Puerto Rico and other ports outside the 50 States and joint venture catches, therefore will not agree with other tables; see table 1173]

SPECIES	Total U.S. catch (mil. lb.)	BY DISTANCE FROM U.S. SHORES						Value of U.S. catch [1] (mil. dol.)
		Catch (mil. lb.)			Percent of U.S. catch			
		3 miles or less [1]	3 to 200 miles	International waters [2]	3 miles or less [1]	3 to 200 miles	International waters [2]	
Total	10,141	3,857	5,781	503	38	57	5	3,522
Fish [3]	8,645	3,151	4,991	503	36	58	6	1,883
Cod	646	40	606	(Z)	6	94	(Z)	196
Flounder	405	22	383	(Z)	5	95	(Z)	145
Halibut	66	18	48	-	27	73	-	100
Herring, sea	257	187	70	-	73	27	-	40
Mackerel	112	63	49	-	56	44	-	19
Menhaden	2,091	1,739	352	-	83	17	-	80
Pollock	2,873	40	2,833	-	1	99	-	251
Salmon, Pacific	783	775	8	-	99	1	-	360
Tuna	520	1	22	497	(Z)	4	96	274
Shellfish [3]	1,496	706	790	-	47	53	-	1,639
Clams (meats)	134	39	95	-	29	71	-	125
Crabs	650	255	395	-	39	61	-	415
Lobsters	70	56	14	-	80	20	-	197
Scallops (meats)	40	2	38	-	5	95	-	162
Shrimp	320	149	171	-	47	53	-	513
Squid	140	75	65	(Z)	54	46	(Z)	36

- Represents or rounds to zero.   Z Less than 500,000 pounds or .05 percent.   [1] Includes all landings in Great Lakes and other inland waters.   [2] Greater than 200 nautical miles seaward from the U.S. shores except for two States. The boundaries for the Gulf Coast of Florida and Texas are 9 nautical miles.   [3] Includes other species, not shown separately.

Source: U.S. National Oceanic and Atmospheric Administration, National Marine Fisheries Service, *Fishery Statistics of the United States*, annual; and *Fisheries of the United States*, annual.

No. 1175. U.S. Private Aquaculture—Production and Value: 1980 to 1987

[Production is shown in live weight, except as indicated. Aquaculture is the commercial growing of fish or other aquatic life in a controlled environment]

SPECIES	PRODUCTION (1,000 lbs.)					VALUE ($1,000)				
	1980	1984	1985	1986	1987	1980	1984	1985	1986	1987
Total	203,178	455,733	535,764	619,959	721,089	191,977	398,168	422,736	496,329	613,653
Baitfish [1]	22,046	23,598	24,807	25,247	26,000	44,000	47,045	51,280	51,522	71,500
Catfish [2]	76,842	239,800	271,357	326,979	372,000	53,572	191,840	189,194	228,886	277,000
Clams [2]	561	1,698	1,588	2,506	2,215	2,295	4,178	4,717	8,307	9,243
Crawfish	23,917	59,400	64,999	97,500	95,000	12,951	29,700	32,500	48,750	35,525
Freshwater prawns	300	317	267	178	200	1,200	1,698	1,540	893	1,250
Mussels [2]	(NA)	917	928	1,206	1,077	(NA)	1,584	1,248	1,725	1,746
Oysters [2]	23,755	24,549	22,473	24,090	24,315	37,085	38,970	39,977	42,797	43,756
Pacific salmon	7,616	45,086	84,305	74,398	124,308	3,400	17,252	25,439	32,751	55,906
Shrimp	-	528	440	1,354	2,655	-	1,566	1,687	3,408	7,206
Trout	48,141	49,940	50,600	51,000	56,247	37,474	54,435	55,154	55,590	57,336
Other species	(NA)	9,900	14,000	15,500	[3]17,072	(NA)	9,900	20,000	21,700	[3]53,285

- Represents or rounds to zero.   NA Not available.   [1] Not used for food consumption.   [2] Production is shown in meat weight.   [3] Includes tropical fish or ornamentals; production of 22,000 pounds and value of $21 million.

Source: U.S. Dept. of Agriculture, Office of Aquaculture, *Agricultural Outlook*, June 1989.

No. 1176. Supply of Selected Fishery Items: 1980 to 1991

[In millions of pounds. Totals available for U.S. consumption are supply minus exports plus imports. Round weight is the complete or full weight as caught. Data are preliminary]

ITEM	Unit	1980	1983	1984	1985	1986	1987	1988	1989	1990	1991
Tuna, canned	Canned weight . .	666	713	777	759	873	866	843	1,034	865	945
Shrimp	Heads-off weight .	425	541	584	633	706	773	767	743	734	744
Clams	Meat weight	102	126	144	164	162	151	145	150	152	144
Salmon, canned	Canned weight . .	126	127	150	113	87	76	59	159	148	131
American lobster	Round weight	69	93	100	108	113	115	121	94	111	128
Spiny lobster	Round weight	127	137	153	154	152	151	139	106	95	88
Scallops	Meat weight	51	67	87	72	70	81	75	81	81	70
Sardines, canned	Canned weight . . .	69	46	58	76	68	77	63	61	61	52
Oysters	Meat weight	71	81	84	90	91	92	78	67	57	48
Crab meat, canned	Canned weight . . .	9	8	7	8	9	8	8	8	9	11
Snow crab	Round weight	54	30	23	45	49	29	31	(NA)	(NA)	205
King crab	Round weight	133	23	13	11	19	14	10	(NA)	(NA)	13

NA Not available.

Source: U.S. National Oceanic and Atmospheric Administration, National Marine Fisheries Service, *Fisheries of the United States*, annual.

No. 1177. Canned, Fresh, and Frozen Fishery Products: 1980 to 1991

[Fresh fishery products exclude Alaska and Hawaii. Canned fishery products data are for natural pack only. See also *Historical Statistics, Colonial Times to 1970*, series L 338-357 (production data in cases) and L 358]

PRODUCT	PRODUCTION (mil. lb.)						VALUE (mil. dol.)					
	1980	1985	1988	1989	1990	1991 [1]	1980	1985	1988	1989	1990	1991 [1]
Canned, [2]	1,516	1,161	1,131	1,455	1,178	1,386	1,928	1,360	1,481	1,992	1,562	1,644
Tuna	602	545	598	686	581	593	1,144	821	960	1,058	902	877
Salmon	200	159	88	197	196	196	376	228	219	514	366	413
Clam products	77	117	127	135	110	129	66	109	98	91	76	84
Mackerel [3]	38	15	18	18	23	9	12	7	9	7	11	3
Sardines, Maine	20	20	19	13	13	14	32	38	24	17	17	19
Shrimp	16	4	4	3	1	1	80	19	25	9	3	4
Crabs	5	1	(Z)	1	1	(Z)	19	2	2	3	4	(Z)
Oysters [4]	(Z)	2	3	4	1	1	(Z)	2	2	1	1	2
Fish fillets and steaks [5] .	202	246	378	371	441	402	261	440	767	724	843	823
Cod	31	57	62	73	65	72	43	89	137	136	132	179
Flounder	49	69	53	44	54	42	87	157	163	142	154	130
Haddock	17	8	8	7	7	7	29	19	30	26	24	26
Ocean perch, Atlantic	7	2	2	2	1	1	9	3	5	3	1	1
Rockfish	14	18	36	25	33	16	13	25	57	40	53	25
Pollock, Atlantic	9	15	14	11	12	7	9	17	21	18	21	18
Pollock, Alaska	(NA)	11	110	106	164	161	(NA)	24	110	98	174	209
Other	74	66	93	103	105	96	71	106	244	279	284	235

NA Not available.   Z Less than 500,000 pounds or $500,000.   [1] Preliminary.   [2] Includes other products, not shown separately.   [3] Includes Jack and a small amount of Pacific mackerel.   [4] Includes oyster specialties.   [5] Fresh and frozen.

Source: U.S. National Oceanic and Atmospheric Administration, National Marine Fisheries Service, *Fisheries of the United States*, annual.

No. 1178. Processed Fishery Products—Production and Value: 1980 to 1991

[Includes Puerto Rico and American Samoa. See *Historical Statistics, Colonial Times to 1970*, series L 362-365, for meal, scrap, and oil]

PRODUCT	PRODUCTION (mil. lb.)						VALUE (mil. dol.)					
	1980	1985	1988	1989	1990 [1]	1991 [1]	1980	1985	1988	1989	1990 [1]	1991 [1]
Total [2]	(X)	(X)	(X)	(X)	(X)	(X)	4,456	4,936	5,369	(X)	(X)	(X)
Fresh and frozen [3] . .	(X)	(X)	(X)	(X)	(X)	(X)	2,110	3,242	3,562	(X)	(X)	(X)
Fillets	197	232	362	345	414	388	247	408	707	656	764	773
Steaks.	5	13	22	26	26	14	14	32	70	86	80	77
Fish sticks	88	96	80	89	65	63	89	111	114	116	75	49
Fish portions	344	330	301	280	294	184	388	368	439	400	414	78
Breaded shrimp. .	83	95	99	121	114	116	254	293	404	371	277	
Canned products [4] . .	1,516	1,161	1,130	1,455	1,178	1,386	1,928	1,360	1,481	1,992	1,562	335
Fish and shellfish . .	1,009	913	907	1,110	957	981	1,782	1,269	1,388	1,754	1,415	1,644
Animal food . .	507	248	223	345	221	405	146	91	93	238	147	1,439
Industrial products . .	(X)	(X)	(X)	(X)	(X)	(X)	270	182	236	206	207	205
Meal and scrap. . .	724	722	644	618	577	613	134	84	131	115	121	208
Oil (body & liver) . .	312	285	225	225	282	267	58	42	44	24	29	128
Solubles	267	323	223	233	186	170	14	19	15	18	14	30
Other	(X)	(X)	(X)	(X)	(X)	(X)	64	37	47	50	43	38

X Not applicable. [1] Preliminary. [2] Includes cured fish. [3] Includes items not shown (dressed fish, shellfish not breaded, specialties). [4] Includes salmon eggs for bait.

Source: U.S. National Oceanic and Atmospheric Administration, National Marine Fisheries Service, *Fisheries of the United States,* annual.

No. 1179. Imports and Exports: 1970 to 1991

[Imports include landings of tuna by foreign vessels at American Samoa. See also *Historical Statistics, Colonial Times to 1970*, series L 227-235]

	IMPORTS					EXPORTS				
		Fishery products					Fishery products			
			Edible products		Noned-			Edible products		Noned-
YEAR	Total U.S. value (mil. dol.)	Total value (mil. dol.)	Quantity (mil. lb.)	Value (mil. dol.)	ible, value (mil. dol.)	Total U.S. value (mil. dol.)	Total value (mil. dol.)	Quantity (mil. lb.)	Value (mil. dol.)	ible, value (mil. dol.)
1970.	39,756	1,037	1,873	813	225	43,224	118	140	94	24
1980.	244,007	3,648	2,145	2,687	962	220,783	1,006	574	904	102
1985.	343,553	6,679	2,754	4,064	2,614	213,146	1,084	648	1,010	73
1986.	368,657	7,626	2,979	4,813	2,813	217,304	1,356	735	1,290	66
1987.	402,066	8,818	3,201	[1]5,711	3,106	252,866	1,660	783	1,577	83
1988.	437,140	8,872	2,968	5,442	3,430	320,385	2,275	1,060	2,156	119
1989.	472,977	9,604	3,243	5,498	4,107	(NA)	4,707	1,374	2,283	2,424
1990.	490,554	9,048	2,885	5,233	3,815	(NA)	5,639	1,910	2,777	2,862
1991.	483,028	9,435	3,015	5,672	3,763	(NA)	[1]6,162	[1]2,020	[1]3,037	3,125

NA Not available. [1] Record.

No. 1180. Selected Fishery Products—Imports and Exports: 1985 to 1991

[See *Historical Statistics, Colonial Times to 1970*, series L 312-318, for selected imports]

PRODUCT	QUANTITY (mil. lb.)					VALUE (mil. dol.)				
	1985	1988	1989	1990, prel.	1991, prel.	1985	1988	1989	1990, prel.	1991, prel.
Imports, edible [1]	2,754	2,968	3,243	2,885	3,015	4,064	5,442	5,498	5,233	5,672
Fresh or frozen [1]	2,229	2,473	2,612	2,336	2,419	3,462	4,780	4,695	4,521	4,859
Salmon [2]	27	50	99	104	107	76	155	229	253	243
Tuna [3]	479	550	650	454	496	266	372	402	339	341
Groundfish fillets, blocks [4] . .	640	501	484	442	420	655	759	702	693	770
Other fillets and steaks . . .	231	320	253	257	310	334	533	490	458	533
Scallops (meats)	42	32	41	40	30	147	116	139	131	111
Lobster, American, spiny . .	77	78	72	74	66	465	547	453	440	420
Shrimp and prawn.	343	490	492	492	530	1,121	1,726	1,685	1,639	1,836
Canned [1]	414	424	533	458	513	466	551	642	543	642
Sardines and herring [5]	40	37	41	42	35	30	33	34	31	28
Tuna	214	245	348	285	352	209	299	376	294	359
Oysters	29	27	20	14	12	30	40	37	27	32
Pickled or salted	57	56	51	45	45	53	67	55	49	56
Cod, haddock, hake, pollock, cusk	35	31	17	11	11	41	53	25	18	22
Nonedible scrap and meal . . .	511	265	171	239	159	62	49	32	39	32
Exports: Canned salmon.	48	33	40	49	66	83	92	90	104	134
Fish oil, nonedible	279	149	195	222	254	37	22	20	24	35

[1] Includes products not shown separately. [2] Excludes fillets. [3] Includes landings of tuna by foreign vessels at American Samoa. [4] Includes cod, cusk, haddock, hake, pollock, Atlantic ocean perch, and whiting. [5] Not in oil.

Source of tables 1179 and 1180: U.S. National Oceanic and Atmospheric Administration, National Marine Fisheries Service, *Fisheries of the United States,* annual. Compiled from U.S. Bureau of the Census data.

Figure 25.1
Wells Drilled and Drilling Costs for Crude Petroleum and Natural Gas: 1980 to 1991

Source: Chart prepared by U.S. Bureau of the Census. For data, see tables 1199 and 1204.

Figure 25.2
U.S. Mineral Production as a Percentage of World: 1991

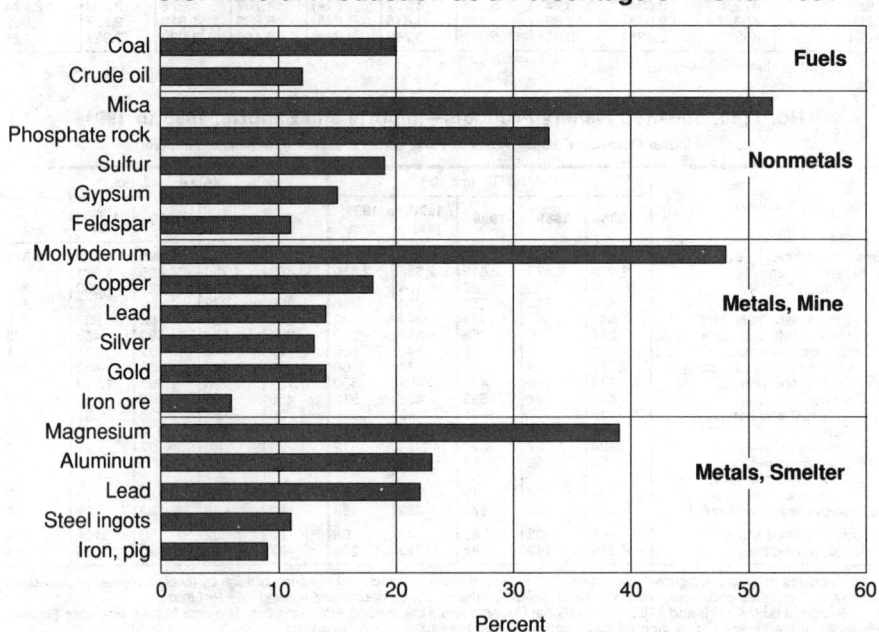

Source: Chart prepared by U.S. Bureau of the Census. For data, see table 1191.

Mining and Mineral Products

This section presents data relating to mineral industries and their products, general summary measures of production, and employment and more detailed data on production, prices, imports and exports, consumption, and distribution for specific industries and products. Data on mining and mineral products may also be found in sections 27 and 31 of this *Abstract;* data on mining employment may be found in section 13.

Mining comprises the extraction of minerals occurring naturally (coal, ores, crude petroleum, natural gas) and quarrying, well operation, milling, refining and processing, and other preparation customarily done at the mine or well site or as a part of extraction activity. (Mineral preparation plants are usually operated together with mines or quarries.) Exploration for minerals is included as is the development of mineral properties.

The principal governmental sources of these data are the *Annual Reports,* published by the Bureau of Mines, Department of the Interior, and various monthly and annual publications of the Energy Information Administration, Department of Energy. See text, section 19, for list of Department of Energy publications. In addition, the Bureau of the Census conducts a census of mineral industries every 5 years. Nongovernment sources include the *Annual Statistical Report* of the American Iron and Steel Institute, Washington, DC; *Metals Week* and the monthly *Engineering and Mining Journal,* issued by the McGraw-Hill Publishing Co., New York, NY; *The Iron Age,* issued weekly by the Chilton Co., Philadelphia, PA; and the *Joint Association Survey of the U.S. Oil and Gas Industry,* conducted jointly by the American Petroleum Institute, Independent Petroleum Association of America, and Mid-Continent Oil and Gas Association.

Mineral statistics, with principal emphasis on commodity detail, have been collected by the Geological Survey or by the Bureau of Mines since 1880. Current data in Bureau of Mines publications include quantity and value of nonfuel minerals produced, sold or used by producers, or shipped;

In Brief

Petroleum balance, 1991:

Production	6.1 billion barrels
Net imports	2.1 billion barrels
Stocks	1.6 billion barrels

---

quantity of minerals stocked; crude materials treated and prepared minerals recovered; and consumption of mineral raw materials. The U.S. Mine Safety and Health Administration also collects and publishes data on workhours, employment, accidents, and injuries in the mineral industries, except petroleum and natural gas. In October 1977, mineral fuel data collection activities of the Bureau of Mines were transferred to the Energy Information Administration.

Censuses of mineral industries have been conducted by the Bureau of the Census at various intervals since 1840. Beginning with the 1967 census, legislation provides for a census to be conducted every 5th year for years ending in "2" and "7." The censuses provide, for the various types of mineral establishments, information on operating costs, capital expenditures, labor, equipment, and energy requirements in relation to their value of shipments and other receipts. Commodity statistics on many manufactured mineral products are also collected by the Bureau at monthly, quarterly, or annual intervals and issued in its *Current Industrial Reports* series.

In general, figures shown in the individual commodity tables include data for outlying areas and may therefore not agree with detailed table 1185. The export and import figures exclude foreign trade passing through the customs districts of Puerto Rico, except where noted as including it.

Historical statistics. Tabular headnotes provide cross-references, where applicable, to *Historical Statistics of the United States, Colonial Times to 1970.* See Appendix IV.

No. 1181. Summary of Mineral Operations: 1958 to 1987

[Represents mineral operations only. Beginning 1967, excludes single unit establishments without paid employees. See also *Historical Statistics, Colonial Times to 1970*, series M 1-11]

ITEM	Unit	1958	1963	1967	1972	1977	1982	1987
Establishments	Number	36,392	38,651	28,579	25,269	31,359	42,241	33,617
With 20 or more employees	Number	6,045	5,499	5,682	5,312	6,632	(NA)	6,299
Including all operations in manufactures	Number	37,966	40,532	29,688	26,178	31,967	42,585	34,041
Excluding oil and gas extraction	Number	19,444	19,290	13,330	11,680	13,520	12,267	10,707
Employees, total	1,000	734	616	567	595	799	1,114	698
Production workers [1]	1,000	565	482	433	443	593	762	451
All other	1,000	169	134	134	152	206	352	247
Worker-hours, production workers [1]	Million	1,081	973	892	909	1,183	1,578	942
Worker-hours per production workers	1,000	1.9	2.0	2.1	2.1	2.0	2.1	2.1
Payroll, total	Mil. dol.	3,749	3,743	4,187	6,226	13,167	28,637	21,739
Wages, production workers [1]	Mil. dol.	2,623	2,680	2,888	4,250	9,082	18,030	12,443
Salaries, all other employees	Mil. dol.	1,126	1,063	1,299	1,976	4,085	10,607	9,296
Cost of supplies, etc. [2]	Mil. dol.	7,521	8,974	10,576	14,884	46,079	109,697	62,423
Value added in mining	Mil. dol.	13,385	15,910	19,330	26,471	68,013	188,056	110,959
Metal mining	Mil. dol.	1,180	1,418	1,557	2,382	3,504	3,215	4,610
Coal mining	Mil. dol.	1,780	1,727	2,091	3,754	11,266	18,631	17,068
Oil and gas extraction	Mil. dol.	9,033	11,020	13,394	17,612	48,587	159,937	80,049
Nonmetallic minerals mining	Mil. dol.	1,392	1,745	2,288	2,723	4,656	6,273	9,233
Value of shipments and receipts [3]	Mil. dol.	16,373	18,804	22,784	36,319	96,375	250,000	157,964
Capital expenditures	Mil. dol.	2,804	3,264	4,058	5,036	17,718	47,753	15,418

NA Not available. [1] See footnote 4, table 1184. [2] Includes purchased machinery installed. [3] See footnote 6, table 1184.

Source: U.S. Bureau of the Census, *Census of Mineral Industries, 1972, 1977, 1982*, and *1987*.

No. 1182. Gross National Product (GNP) in Mining: 1980 to 1989

[In millions of dollars, except percent. For definition of gross national product, see text, section 14. Based on 1972 Standard Industrial Classification]

MINING INDUSTRY	1980	1982	1983	1984	1985	1986	1987	1988	1989
Current dollars, total	107,257	132,122	118,351	119,362	114,174	74,289	76,836	80,017	80,254
Percent of total GNP	3.9	4.2	3.5	3.2	2.8	1.8	1.7	1.6	1.5
Metal mining	3,836	2,321	2,527	2,216	1,750	1,768	2,449	2,928	3,570
Coal mining	12,909	15,108	14,301	14,597	13,881	13,168	13,189	13,171	13,647
Oil and gas extraction	84,947	110,228	96,412	96,385	92,444	52,449	54,010	55,799	55,660
Nonmetallic minerals, exc. fuels	5,565	4,465	5,111	6,164	6,099	6,904	7,188	8,119	7,377
Constant (1982) dollars, total	143,544	132,122	129,926	137,874	138,950	128,250	127,514	129,536	127,187
Percent of total GNP	4.5	4.2	4.0	3.9	3.8	3.4	3.3	3.2	3.1
Metal mining	2,054	2,321	2,246	2,463	2,423	2,597	2,687	2,625	3,294
Coal mining	13,944	15,108	15,484	16,514	16,391	16,972	18,050	19,567	21,599
Oil and gas extraction	121,505	110,228	107,048	112,647	114,053	102,075	100,172	99,919	95,662
Nonmetallic minerals, exc. fuels	6,041	4,465	5,148	6,250	6,083	6,606	6,605	7,425	6,632

Source: U.S. Bureau of Economic Analysis, *The National Income and Product Accounts of the United States, Volume 2, 1959-88*; and *Survey of Current Business*, July issues.

No. 1183. Mining and Primary Metal Production Indexes: 1970 to 1992

[1987 = 100. See also *Historical Statistics, Colonial Times to 1970*, series M 68-71]

INDUSTRY GROUP	1970	1975	1980	1984	1985	1986	1988	1989	1990	1991	1992
Mining	100.4	98.0	110.0	111.9	109.0	101.0	101.8	100.5	102.6	101.1	98.7
Coal	67.2	71.5	90.2	97.5	96.3	97.1	105.0	105.7	113.2	109.2	105.5
Anthracite	274.1	175.0	169.6	116.9	132.8	120.8	115.6	96.3	103.2	72.7	66.1
Bituminous	66.0	71.0	89.7	97.4	96.1	96.9	105.0	105.8	113.3	109.4	105.8
Oil and gas extraction	104.8	101.8	112.1	115.5	111.9	102.0	99.4	99.5	95.5	95.8	93.2
Crude oil and natural gas	122.3	107.5	108.4	106.4	105.0	101.7	99.2	95.6	93.7	95.5	94.0
Oil and gas drilling	65.2	109.7	181.2	226.6	198.9	109.8	100.0	93.7	109.0	93.3	78.3
Metal mining	129.5	106.4	108.8	91.7	91.3	95.2	122.7	141.4	153.1	150.2	158.1
Iron ore	194.4	172.1	149.4	111.0	104.9	84.4	119.8	123.3	118.1	118.2	116.5
Nonferrous ores	111.5	88.7	95.0	84.8	86.4	99.1	123.3	145.1	160.5	156.9	(NA)
Copper ore	123.2	101.5	93.1	85.9	86.9	91.2	113.8	118.4	125.3	129.1	139.7
Lead and zinc ores	192.2	189.9	166.7	109.7	120.1	103.3	119.8	130.4	174.3	185.1	175.9
Primary metals, manufacturing	115.2	107.2	110.8	102.4	101.8	93.8	110.3	109.2	108.4	99.5	102.9
Nonferrous metals	77.1	75.3	92.5	98.2	98.5	97.3	105.4	109.0	106.2	101.5	101.5
Copper	135.2	103.0	94.7	97.0	99.8	99.1	113.5	115.5	120.2	116.7	124.6
Aluminum	107.8	105.2	138.7	122.2	104.7	90.9	117.6	120.8	121.1	123.2	120.5
Iron and steel	148.2	133.5	126.0	105.9	104.5	90.8	113.8	109.3	109.9	98.0	103.9

NA Not available.

Source: Board of Governors of the Federal Reserve System, *Federal Reserve Bulletin*, monthly.

No. 1184. Mineral Industries—Summary: 1977 to 1987

["N.e.c." means not elsewhere classified. See also *Historical Statistics, Colonial Times to 1970*, series M1-12]

MINERAL INDUSTRY	1977			1982					1987									
	Estab-lish-ments	All employ-ees, pay-roll[1] (mil. dol.)	Value added in min-ing[2] (mil. dol.)	Establishments Total	With 20 or more employ-ees	All employees Num-ber[3] (1,000)	Pay-roll[1] (mil. dol.)	Value added in min-ing[2] (mil. dol.)	Establishments Total	With 20 or more employ-ees	All employees Num-ber[3] (1,000)	Pay-roll[1] (mil. dol.)	Production workers[4] Num-ber[3] (1,000)	Hours[5] (mil. lions)	Wages (mil. dol.)	Value added in min-ing[2] (mil. dol.)	Value of ship-ments and re-ceipts[6] (mil. dol.)	Capital expen-ditures (mil. dol.)
All industries	31,359	13,167	68,013	⁷42,241	(NA)	1,114	28,637	188,056	33,617	6,299	698	21,739	451	942	12,443	110,959	157,964	15,418
Metal mining	1,206	1,485	3,504	1,434	(NA)	68	1,860	3,215	1,027	260	44	1,354	34	68	952	4,610	6,852	899
Iron ores	97	78	1,046	78	40	12	340	770	51	16	7	224	6	11	166	768	1,362	24
Copper ores	133	544	1,067	81	51	22	604	672	61	33	14	405	11	21	283	1,301	2,150	205
Lead and zinc ores	88	105	329	71	28	4	112	201	39	19	2	58	3	3	40	176	268	12
Gold and silver ores	175	71	161	371	80	10	263	650	372	101	13	423	10	21	305	1,814	2,261	555
Ferroalloy ores, except vanadium	56	107	256	69	16	5	150	146	58	10	1	46	1	2	24	110	110	8
Metal mining services	270	52	112	313	(NA)	5	61	90	268	42	3	81	2	5	60	161	251	26
Miscellaneous metal ores	387	234	533	451	91	12	332	686	178	42	4	116	3	5	75	313	449	70
Coal mining	5,451	4,171	11,266	5,087	(NA)	251	6,805	18,631	3,905	1,418	163	5,567	129	259	4,251	17,068	25,955	1,665
Bituminous coal and lignite mining	4,944	4,005	10,837	4,513	1,787	241	6,570	18,041	3,507	1,335	158	5,410	124	249	4,125	16,679	25,347	1,614
Anthracite mining	156	48	116	152	40	3	67	172	107	26	2	41	2	3	32	109	206	12
Coal mining services	351	119	313	422	(NA)	7	168	418	291	57	4	116	3	7	94	280	402	39
Oil and gas extraction	18,447	5,902	48,587	29,974	(NA)	685	17,693	159,937	22,910	3,167	378	11,961	206	437	5,283	80,049	112,363	11,717
Crude petroleum and natural gas	8,573	2,738	38,327	⁷12,087	(NA)	264	8,084	126,035	10,203	1,171	199	7,510	69	142	2,154	67,955	76,518	10,549
Natural gas liquids	692	227	3,286	793	236	14	402	8,865	714	210	13	433	10	20	320	4,025	24,750	383
Oil and gas field services	9,182	2,936	6,974	⁷17,094	(NA)	406	9,207	25,037	11,993	1,786	167	4,018	127	275	2,809	8,069	11,095	786
Drilling oil and gas wells	2,625	1,317	3,307	4,385	(NA)	166	4,007	11,316	2,591	620	55	1,318	46	93	1,012	2,549	3,626	321
Oil, gas exploration services	1,252	220	545	2,934	(NA)	42	810	2,307	1,917	143	17	452	13	27	311	771	1,096	69
Oil, gas field services, n.e.c.	5,305	1,399	3,122	9,775	(NA)	199	4,391	11,415	7,485	1,023	95	2,248	69	154	1,486	4,748	6,373	395
Nonmetallic mining[8]	6,255	1,609	4,656	5,746	(NA)	110	2,278	6,273	5,775	1,454	113	2,858	83	178	1,956	9,233	12,795	1,136
Dimension stone[8] [9]	209	19	39	154	22	2	71	50	149	19		25	2		18	65	86	4
Crushed and broken stone[9]	2,055	543	1,501	1,932	567	37	701	1,787	2,002	711	44	1,082	33	72	754	3,465	4,768	521
Sand and gravel[9]	2,807	418	1,017	2,758	343	28	520	1,336	2,750	436	33	772	24	51	551	2,320	3,139	238
Clay and related minerals[9]	255	136	358	224	97	11	212	336	197	100	10	272	7	15	165	827	1,249	111
Chemical and fertilizer minerals	205	372	1,433	196	114	26	681	2,237	148	79	16	501	12	24	336	1,999	2,772	192
Nonmetallic minerals, services	176	36	70	167	(NA)	6	35	70	177	23	2	45	3	3	32	119	165	25
Miscellaneous[9]	548	87	238	315	72	6	109	283	352	86	7	162	5	10	101	438	616	46

NA Not available. [1] Gross earnings paid to all employees on payroll. [2] Computed by subtracting cost of supplies, minerals received for preparation, purchased fuel and electric energy, contract work, and purchased machinery from the value of shipments and capital expenditures. [3] Excludes proprietors and firm members of unincorporated concerns. [4] Represents employees up through the working foreman level engaged in manual work. Includes development and exploration workers. [5] Excludes paid vacations, holidays, and sick leave; includes actual overtime hours (not straight-time equivalent). [6] Represents value of shipments of primary and secondary products of the industry and amount received for services performed for other establishments on a contract, fee, or other basis. [7] Redefined to conform to 1987 and pre-1982 definition of establishment; for detail, see source. [8] Excludes data for dimension stone quarries operated in conjunction with dressing plants. [9] Excludes data for mining included in establishments classified in manufacturing industries.

Source: U.S. Bureau of the Census, *Census of Mineral Industries: 1977, 1982, and 1987,* final industry series reports.

No. 1185. Mineral Production and Value, 1980 to 1991,

[Data represent production as measured by mine shipments, mine sales, or marketable production

	MINERAL	Unit	PRODUCTION QUANTITY				
			1980	1985	1989	1990	1991
1	Total mineral production	(X)	(X)	(X)	(X)	(X)	(X)
2	**Mineral fuels . . . .**	**(X)**	**(X)**	**(X)**	**(X)**	**(X)**	**(X)**
3	Coal: Bituminous and lignite	Mil. sh. tons	824	879	977	1,026	993
4	Pennsylvania anthracite	Mil. sh. tons	6	5	3	4	3
5	Natural gas (wet)	Tril. cu. ft.	20.18	17.27	1,810	1,859	1,871
6	Petroleum (crude).	Mil. bbl. [1]	3,146	3,274	2,779	2,685	2,707
7	Uranium [2]	Mil. lb.	43.7	11.3	13.8	8.9	8.0
8	**Industrial minerals . . . .**	**(X)**	**(X)**	**(X)**	**(X)**	**(X)**	**(X)**
9	Abrasive stone [3]	Metric tons.	572	1,050	898	3,709	2,205
10	Asbestos (sales) . . . . [4]	1,000 metric tons .	80	57	17	(D)	(D)
11	Asphalt and related bitumens (native) [4]	1,000 sh. tons . . .	1,252	(D)	-	-	-
12	Barite, primary, sold/used by producers .	1,000 metric tons . .	2,037	670	290	430	448
13	Boron minerals, (producers)	1,000 metric tons . .	1,401	1,151	1,114	1,094	1,240
14	Bromine (sold or used by producers) . . .	Mil. kilograms	172	145	175	177	170
15	Calcium chloride	1,000 sh. tons . . .	581	(D)	(D)	(D)	(D)
16	Carbon dioxide, natural (estimate)	Mil. cu. ft.	1,628	-	-	-	-
17	Cement: Portland	Mil. sh. tons	71.6	74.3	74.2	75.6	68.7
18	Masonry	Mil. sh. tons	3.0	3.2	3.3	3.3	2.6
19	Clays	1,000 metric tons . .	44,262	40,800	42,254	42,904	44,092
20	Diatomite	1,000 metric tons . .	625	576	617	631	610
21	Feldspar.	1,000 metric tons . .	644	635	655	630	580
22	Fluorspar, finished shipments	1,000 metric tons . .	84	60	66	64	58
23	Garnet (abrasive)	1,000 metric tons . .	24.4	33.3	42.6	47.0	50.9
24	Gem stones (estimate)	(X)	(NA)	(NA)	(NA)	(NA)	(NA)
25	Gypsum, crude	Mil. sh. tons	12.4	14.4	17.6	16.4	15.5
26	Helium [6]	Mil. cu. meters	41	53	82	87	88
27	Lime, (sold or used by producers)	Mil. sh. tons	19.0	15.7	17.2	17.5	17.3
28	Magnesium compounds [7]	1,000 sh. tons . . .	(D)	(D)	(D)	(D)	(D)
29	Mica, scrap & flake, (producers)	1,000 metric tons . .	105	125	119	109	103
30	Peat (sales by producers)	1,000 sh. tons . . .	788	882	775	795	777
31	Perlite, processed (sold or used).	1,000 sh. tons . . .	638	518	601	635	567
32	Phosphate rock (marketable)	Mil. metric tons . . .	54.4	50.8	49.8	46.3	48.1
33	Potassium salts sales, K_2O equivalent .	1,000 metric tons . .	2,217	1,266	1,536	1,716	1,709
34	Pumice & pumicite, producer sales	1,000 metric tons . .	492	461	424	443	401
35	Pyrites	1,000 metric tons . .	847	(D)	(D)	(D)	(D)
36	Salt, common, sold/used by producers .	Mil. metric tons. . . .	40.4	40.1	38.9	40.7	39.6
37	Sand & gravel, sold/used by producer . .	Mil. metric tons . .	719	753	841	852	731
38	Sodium carbonate (natural) (soda ash). .	1,000 metric tons . .	(D)	(D)	8,995	9,156	9,005
39	Sodium sulfate (natural).	1,000 metric tons . .	529	353	340	349	354
40	Stone [8]	Mil. metric tons . .	893	909	1,102	1,110	1,002
41	Sulfur: Frasch mines (shipments)	1,000 metric tons . .	7,400	4,678	3,780	3,676	3,120
42	Talc, and pyrophyllite, crude [9]	1,000 metric tons . .	1,125	1,151	1,253	1,267	1,037
43	Tripoli.	1,000 metric tons . .	110	109	105	94	89
44	Vermiculite concentrate.	1,000 sh. tons	337	314	293	230	185
45	Industrial minerals, undistributed [10] . .	(X)	(X)	(X)	(X)	(X)	(X)
46	**Metals. . . . .**	**(X)**	**(X)**	**(X)**	**(X)**	**(X)**	**(X)**
47	Antimony ore and concentrate	Metric tons [11] . . .	311	(D)	(D)	(D)	(D)
48	Bauxite (dried) . . . . [13]	1,000 metric tons . .	1,559	674	(D)	(D)	(D)
49	Copper [2]	1,000 metric tons . .	1,181	1,105	1,498	1,588	1631
50	Gold [2] . . . . [14]	1,000 kilograms . . .	30	75	266	294	290
51	Iron ore, ... [15]	Mil. metric tons . .	70.7	50.2	58.3	57.0	56.7
52	Lead [2]	1,000 metric tons . .	550	414	411	483	466
53	Magnesium metal [16]	1,000 metric tons . .	(NA)	(NA)	152	139	131
54	Manganiferous ore [17]	1,000 sh. ton [15] . .	174	20	(D)	(D)	(D)
55	Mercury [18]	Metric tons.	1,057	570	414	114	58
56	Molybdenum [19]	1,000 metric tons . .	68	51	62	62	54
57	Nickel [20]	1,000 sh. tons . . .	14.7	6.1	-	0.3	5.5
58	Paladium metal	Kilograms	(D)	(D)	4,850	5,930	6,050
59	Platinum metal.	Kilograms	(D)	(D)	1,430	1,810	1,730
60	Silver [2]	Metric tons.	1,006	1,227	2,007	2,125	1,848
61	Titanium concentrate: Ilmenite	1,000 metric tons [15]	539	(D)	(D)	(D)	(D)
62	Tungsten ore and concentrate	Metric tons [21] . . .	2,738	983	(D)	(D)	(D)
63	Vanadium [2]	Sh. tons.	4,806	(D)	(D)	(D)	(D)
64	Zinc mine production [2]	1,000 metric tons . .	317	227	276	515	518
65	Metals, undistributed [10]	(X)	(X)	(X)	(X)	(X)	(X)

- Represents zero.   D Withheld to avoid disclosing individual company data.   NA Not available.   X Not applicable.
[1] 42 gal. bbl.   [2] Recoverable content of ores, etc.   [3] Includes grindstones, oilstones, whetstones, and deburring media. Excludes grinding pebbles, and tubemill liners.   [4] Contains bituminous limestone and sandstone, and gilsonite.   [5] Value included in "Industrial minerals, undistributed."   [6] 1980, crude and refined; thereafter, refined only.   [7] From sea water and brines, except for metals (MgO equiv.).   [8] Excludes abrasive stone, bituminous limestone and sandstone, and ground soapstone, all included elsewhere in table; 1991 value is for crushed and broken stone only. Includes calcareous marl and slate.

and Principal Producing States, 1991

(including consumption by producers). See *Historical Statistics, Colonial Times to 1970,* series M 13-37 for selected values]

PRODUCTION VALUE (mil. dol.)					Principal producing States ranked by quantity, 1991	
1980	1985	1989	1990	1991		
146,750	168,154	128,603	141,741	(NA)	(X)	1
121,612	**144,847**	**96,378**	**108,422**	**(NA)**	**(X)**	**2**
20,197	22,063	21,268	22,274	21,598	WY, KY, WV, PA.	3
259	215	142	133	(NA)	PA.	4
32,090	43,343	30,627	31,658	30,300	TX, LA, OK, NM.	5
67,930	78,871	44,071	53,772	(NA)	AK, TX, CA, LA.	6
1,136	356	270	140	(NA)	TX, WY, NM.	7
16,218	**17,679**	**20,360**	**20,971**	**19,617**	**(X)**	**8**
2	1	-	-	-	AR, WI, OH.	9
31	21	(5)	(5)	(5)	CA and VT.	10
25	(5)	-	-	-	(X)	11
66	22	13	16	21	NV, GA, MO, MI.	12
367	405	430	436	443	CA.	13
96	80	189	173	167	AR.	14
48	(5)	(5)	(5)	(5)	MI and CA.	15
3	-	-	-	-	(X)	16
3,613	3,817	3,592	3,683	3,343	CA, TX, MI, PA.	17
189	213	229	225	188	IN, SC, PA, MI.	18
899	1,011	1,515	1,620	1,505	GA, AL, WY, TX.	19
101	127	137	138	140	CA, NV, OR, WA.	20
23	23	28	29	26	NC, OK, CT, CA.	21
13	(5)	(5)	(5)	(5)	IL.	22
2	3	4	7	8	ID and NY.	23
7	7	43	53	84	(X)	24
103	112	128	100	94	OK, IA, MI, TX.	25
30	70	107	113	175	KS, WY, TX, CO.	26
843	809	852	902	891	MO, OH, PA, KY.	27
(5)	(5)	(5)	(5)	(5)	MI, CA, FL, UT.	28
6	6	6	6	6	NC, GA, NM, SC.	29
16	22	18	19	18	MI, FL, NJ, ME.	30
17	18	16	17	15	NM, AZ, CA, ID.	31
1,257	1,236	1,083	1,075	1,109	FL, ID, NC, UT.	32
354	178	272	303	305	NM, UT, CA, MI.	33
4	5	(5)	11	9	OR, CA, NM, ID.	34
14	(5)	(5)	(5)	(5)	AZ.	35
656	740	777	827	802	LA, TX, NY, KS.	36
2,289	2,812	3,659	3,686	3,196	CA, MI, OH, WA.	37
(5)	(5)	764	836	836	WY and CA.	38
36	36	31	34	31	CA, TX, UT.	39
3,405	4,225	5,537	5,801	5,382	PA, IL, TX, FL.	40
721	574	379	335	272	TX and LA.	41
19	29	28	31	32	MT, VT, TX, NY.	42
1	1	3	3	3	IL, OK, AR, PA.	43
24	32	33	19	13	SC, VA, MT.	44
941	1,045	480	473	506	(X)	45
8,922	**5,627**	**11,863**	**12,442**	**10,950**	**(X)**	**46**
(12)	(12)	(12)	(12)	(12)	ID.	47
22	13	(12)	(12)	(12)	AL and GA	48
2,667	1,631	4,324	4,311	3,931	AZ, NM, UT, MT.	49
594	771	3,269	3,650	3,386	NV, CA, UT, MT.	50
2,544	2,077	1,840	1,741	1,674	MN, MI, UT, MO.	51
515	174	356	491	344	MO, AK, ID, CO.	52
(NA)	(NA)	509	433	337	TX, WA, UT.	53
2	(12)	(12)	(12)	(12)	SC.	54
12	(12)	(12)	(12)	(12)	NV, CA.	55
1,344	348	427	348	250	AZ, CO, MT, UT.	56
(12)	(12)	-	(NA)	(NA)	(NA)	57
(12)	(12)	23	22	17	MT	58
(12)	(12)	23	27	21	MT	59
667	242	355	329	240	NV, ID, AK, MT.	60
32	(12)	(12)	(12)	(12)	FL, CA, NJ.	61
51	9	(12)	(12)	(12)	CA	62
64	(12)	(12)	(12)	(12)	ID	63
262	202	499	847	602	AK, TN, NY, MO.	64
145	161	238	242	148	(X)	65

[9] For 1991 production quantity, talc only.   [10] Comprises value of items that cannot be disclosed.   [11] Antimony content. [12] Included with "Metals, undistributed."   [13] Dried equivalent.   [14] Represents shipments; includes byproduct ores.   [15] Gross weight.   [16] For 1980-85, magnesium chloride for magnesium metal included in "Metals undistributed," canvass for magnesium chloride for magnesium metal discontinued in 1986.   [17] 5 to 35 percent manganiferous ore.   [18] 1989, mercury produced as the primary product only; thereafter, mercury produced as a byproduct of gold ores only.   [19] Content of concentrate.   [20] Content of ore and concentrate.   [21] Tungsten content.

Source: U.S. Bureau of Mines, *Minerals Yearbook.* Mineral fuels: U. S. Energy Information Administration, *Annual Energy Review, Uranium Industry Annual; Petroleum Supply Annual,* vol. 1; *Natural Gas Annual;* and *Quarterly Coal Report. Natural Gas Annual;* and *Quarterly Coal Report.*

No. 1186. Nonfuel Mineral Commodities—Summary: 1993

[Preliminary estimates]

MINERAL	Unit	Production	Exports	Net import reliance[1] (percent)	Consumption, apparent	Average price per unit (dollars)	Employment (number)
Aluminum	1,000 metric tons	4,000	1,500	[2]	5,500	[3]59.00	19,800
Antimony (contained)	Metric tons	[4]37,000	5,000	58	43,000	[3]80.00	120
Arsenic	Metric tons	-	60	100	22,000	[5]86.00	(NA)
Asbestos	1,000 metric tons	(D)	24	95	32	(D)	70
Barite	1,000 metric tons	410	1	53	874	41.90	350
Bauxite and alumina	1,000 metric tons	(D)	1,114	100	4,900	15-18	35
Beryllium (contained)	Metric tons	240	60	[2]	190	[6]308.00	25
Bismuth (contained)	Metric tons	(D)	80	(D)	[7]1,500	2.65	30
Boron (B$_2$O$_3$ content)	1,000 metric tons	521	600	[2]	(NA)	272.00	900
Bromine (contained)	1,000 metric tons	166	20	[2]	157	[3]123.00	300
Cadmium (contained)	Metric tons	1,700	350	49	3,400	[8]1.00	195
Cement	1,000 sh. tons	76,484	750	7	81,934	[9]49.70	18,100
Cesium (contained)	Kilograms	(NA)	(NA)	(NA)	(NA)	[10](NA)	(NA)
Chromium	1,000 metric tons	[11]113	9	74	435	[12]110.00	(NA)
Clays	1,000 sh. tons	42,151	4,000	[2]	38,044	(NA)	11,000
Columbium (contained)	1,000 lb	-	200	100	3,470	[13]2.83	(NA)
Copper (Mine, contained)	1,000 metric tons	1,720	600	3	2,300	[14]107.00	14,000
Diamond (industrial)	Mil. carats	98.4	76.4	10	109.4	[15]0.75	(NA)
Diatomite	1,000 metric tons	647	170	[2]	477	[16]197.00	1,000
Feldspar	1,000 metric tons	696	13	-	696	[16]43.82	400
Fluorspar	1,000 metric tons	50	60	87	399	(NA)	180
Gallium (contained)	Kilograms	-	(NA)	(NA)	(NA)	425.00	20
Garnet (industrial)	Metric tons	54,304	10,000	[2]	40,416	100-2,000	150
Gem stones	Mil. dol.	69.4	1,619	98	3,136	[17]	800
Germanium (contained)	Kilograms	13,000	(NA)	(NA)	[7]29,000	[18]1060.00	100
Gold (gold contained)	Metric tons	320	360	(NA)	100	[19]350.00	14,400
Graphite (crude)	1,000 metric tons	-	16	100	25	[20]580.00	-
Gypsum	1,000 sh. tons	16,300	26,000	35	26,000	[21]6.10	6,700
Indium	Metric tons	(NA)	(NA)	(NA)	[7]30	[22]200.00	(NA)
Iodine	Metric tons	2,042	1,500	52	30	[23]9.12	50
Iron ore (usable)	Mil. metric tons.	56.2	4.5	12	66.1	[24]72.5-74.0	7,500
Iron and steel scrap (metal)	Mil. sh. tons.	71.2	8.3	[2]	64.3	[25]83.60	104,100
Iron and steel slag (metal)	1,000 sh. tons	18,000	4	(NA)	(NA)	[21]5.55	3,000
Lead (contained)	1,000 metric tons	1,540	70	8	1,220	[3]36.00	1,700
Lime	1,000 sh. tons	18,000	62	14	18,130	[9]51.70	5,500
Magnesium metal	1,000 metric tons	[26]135	60	[2]	126	[27]1.43	1,450
Magnesium compounds	1,000 metric tons	460	50	23	600	(NA)	650
Manganese	1,000 sh. tons	-	14	100	610	[28]3.25	(NA)
Mercury	Metric tons	60	400	(D)	(D)	[29]180.00	7
Mica, scrap and flake	1,000 metric tons	93	4	14	96	56.00	(NA)
Molybdenum	1,000 metric tons	45,400	30,000	[2]	17,200	[10]5.08	800
Nickel	1,000 metric tons	5,500	8,000	64	121,000	[30]3.21	314
Nitrogen (fixed)-ammonia	1,000 metric tons	14,500	420	15	17,052	[31]110.00	2,500
Peat	1,000 sh. tons	730	-	50	1,459	[9]23.00	650
Perlite	1,000 sh. tons	571	30	3	591	[9]26.83	115
Phosphate rock	1,000 metric tons	47,000	4,400	[2]	42,000	[9]23.00	5,800
Platinum-group, refined	Kilograms	1,730	36,518	94	113,343	[32]356.00	500
Potash (K$_2$O equivalent)	1,000 metric tons	1,760	650	67	5,390	134.00	2,179
Pumice and pumicite	1,000 sh. tons	439	12	32	642	[16]26.42	50
Rare-earth metals (REO content)	Metric tons	16,000	(NA)	[2]	15,700	[33]2.87	390
Salt	1,000 sh. tons	39,800	1,000	12	45,800	[34]103.00	4,150
Sand and gravel:							
Construction	Million sh. tons.	805,700	1,100	[2]	806,000	[9]3.64	41,600
Industrial	1,000 sh. tons	26,100	1,500	[2]	24,690	[9]15.29	1,500
Silicon	1,000 metric tons	350	40	36	550	[35]37.00	2,300
Silver	Metric tons	1,800	2,000	[7]	(NA)	[19]4.00	1,700
Sodium carbonate (soda ash)	1,000 metric tons	9,500	2,800	[2]	6,694	[36]98.00	2,800
Sodium sulfate	1,000 metric tons	350	140	1	710	[37]114.00	240
Stone (crushed)	Mil. sh. tons.	1,155	3	-	1,158	[9]4.83	75,000
Sulfur (all forms)	1,000 metric tons	10,600	1,000	18	12,900	[38]60.00	3,200

- Represents or rounds to zero. D Withheld to avoid disclosure. NA Not available. [1] Net import reliance as a percent of consumption. [2] Net exporter. [3] Average cents per pound, except bromine (dollars per kilogram). [4] Refinery production. [5] Metal, 99% As$_2$O$_3$. [6] Metal, vacuum-cast ingot. [7] Reported consumption. [8] Average dollars per pound, 1 to 5 short ton lots. [9] Dollars per short ton. [10] Metal, dollars per pound. [11] Secondary production. [12] Turkish, dollars per metric ton. [13] Columbite, dollars per pound. [14] Domestic producer cathode, cents per pound. [15] Dollars, per carat. [16] Dollars per metric ton. [17] Variable, depending on size, type and quality. [18] Zone refined, first reduction quality. [19] Dollars, per ounce. [20] Price of flake imports, average dollars per metric ton of foreign imports. [21] F.O.B. mine, average dollar per short ton. [22] Average annual dollars per kilogram (99.97% indium). [23] Average c.i.f. value, dollars per kilogram crude. [24] Lake Superior pellets. Cents per long ton unit of iron, delivered rail of vessel at lower lake ports. [25] Average dollars per long ton delivered, No. 1 heavy melting composite price, Iron Age average, Pittsburg, Philadelphia, Chicago. [26] Primary. [27] Yearend price, dollars per pound. [28] Average value, 46%-48% Mn metalurgical ore, dollars per metric ton unit contained Mn, c.i.f. U.S. ports. [29] Price per flask. [30] Average price, London Metal Exchange cash, dollars per pound. [31] Dollars per short ton, yearend quoted, f.o.b. gulf coast. [32] Dealer price of platinum metal, average dollars per ounce; Palladium price was $89 per ounce; rhodium price was $4,412 per ounce. [33] Yearend dollars per kilogram, bastnasite concentrate, REO basis. [34] Vacuum and open pan. [35] Average cents per pound silicon content, ferrosilicon, 50% Si. [36] Quoted yearend price, dense, bulk, f.o.b. Green River, WY, dollars per short ton. [37] Quoted price, bulk, f.o.b. works, East, dollars per short ton. [38] Reported average dollars per metric ton of elemental sulfur, f.o.b. mine and/or plant.

Source: U.S. Bureau of Mines, *Mineral Commodity Summaries*, annual.

No. 1187. Value of Domestic Nonfuel Mineral Production: 1980 to 1991

[In millions of dollars]

STATE	1980	1985	1989	1990	1991	Principal minerals in order of value
U.S. [1]	25,140	23,303	32,220	33,337	30,489	(X)
Northeast	1,581	1,964	2,450	2,475	2,095	(X)
N.E.	268	325	455	443	347	(X)
ME	37	41	65	63	41	Sand and gravel, cement, and stone.
NH	25	33	33	35	30	Sand and gravel, stone, and gem stones.
VT	43	50	89	82	60	Stone, sand and gravel, and talc.
MA	91	117	144	127	112	Stone, sand and gravel, and lime.
RI	6	12	11	18	13	Sand and gravel, stone, and gem stones.
CT	66	72	113	118	91	Stone, sand and gravel, and feldspar.
M.A	1,313	1,639	1,995	2,032	1,748	(X)
NY.	496	657	745	773	699	Stone, salt, and cement.
NJ.	149	178	249	229	205	Stone, sand and gravel, and zircon.
PA.	668	804	1,001	1,030	844	Stone, cement, and sand and gravel.
Midwest	6,610	6,034	6,980	7,139	6,482	(X)
E.N.C	2,930	2,869	3,551	3,476	3,477	(X)
OH	562	594	699	729	684	Stone, sand and gravel, and salt.
IN	288	303	434	432	403	Stone, cement, and sand and gravel.
IL	443	460	633	665	673	Stone, cement, and sand and gravel.
MI	1,485	1,387	1,599	1,438	1,503	Iron ore, cement, and sand and gravel.
WI	152	125	185	212	214	Stone, sand and gravel, and lime.
W.N.C.	3,680	3,165	3,429	3,663	3,005	(X)
MN	1,782	1,548	1,376	1,470	1,019	Iron ore, sand and gravel, and stone.
IA	252	228	283	316	344	Cement, stone, and sand and gravel.
MO	1,054	735	1,050	1,103	880	Lead, stone, and cement.
ND	22	24	14	27	[2]17	Sand and gravel, lime, and stone.
SD.	228	208	284	311	290	Gold, cement, and sand and gravel.
NE.	80	100	104	90	89	Cement, sand and gravel, and stone.
KS.	262	322	318	346	366	Salt, stone, and cement.
South	7,320	8,029	8,966	9,204	8,270	(X)
S.A.	3,454	3,998	4,985	5,120	4,484	(X)
DE [2]	2	4	6	7	5	Sand and gravel and gem stones.
MD	186	258	342	369	348	Stone, sand and gravel, and cement.
VA.	305	381	509	507	428	Stone, sand and gravel, and cement.
WV	106	105	125	136	117	Stone, cement, and sand and gravel.
NC	380	466	582	590	553	Stone, phosphate rock, and lithium minerals.
SC.	195	276	425	450	338	Stone, cement, and gold.
GA	771	946	1,387	1,495	1,299	Clays, stone, and cement.
FL.	1,509	1,562	1,608	1,567	1,396	Phosphate rock, stone, and cement.
E.S.C	1,030	1,251	1,537	1,696	1,533	(X)
KY.	204	268	331	359	343	Stone, lime, and cement.
TN.	394	473	638	664	548	Stone, zinc, and cement.
AL.	328	407	461	561	540	Stone, cement, and lime.
MS	104	103	108	112	102	Sand and gravel, clays, and cement.
W.S.C.	2,836	2,780	2,443	2,388	2,253	(X)
AR.	293	270	382	303	361	Bromine, stone, and sand and gravel.
LA.	584	521	380	368	352	Sulfur, salt, and sand and gravel.
OK	224	252	219	260	276	Stone, cement, and iodine.
TX.	1,735	1,737	1,462	1,457	1,265	Cement, stone, and magnesium metal.
West	9,629	7,276	13,809	14,511	13,364	(X)
Mt	7,223	4,669	9,985	10,371	9,516	(X)
MT	280	200	566	573	590	Gold, copper, and molybdenum.
ID	522	359	365	378	297	Phosphate rock, silver, and molybdenum.
WY	761	551	827	911	929	Soda ash, clays, and helium.
CO	1,265	408	458	386	338	Molybdenum, sand and gravel, and cement.
NM	766	657	1,122	1,103	986	Copper, potash, and sand and gravel.
AZ.	2,471	1,550	3,046	3,064	2,829	Bromine, stone, and sand and gravel.
UT.	764	313	1,290	1,334	1,154	Copper, gold, and magnesium metal.
NV.	394	631	2,310	2,621	2,393	Gold, silver, and sand and gravel.
Pac.	2,406	2,607	3,824	4,140	3,848	(X)
WA	207	222	481	473	483	Sand and gravel, gold, and magnesium metal.
OR	152	130	183	205	198	Stone, sand and gravel, and cement.
CA.	1,872	2,112	2,854	2,780	2,532	Sand and gravel, cement, and boron.
AK.	115	90	213	577	494	Zinc, lead, and silver.
HI	60	53	92	106	141	Stone, cement, and sand and gravel.

X Not applicable.   [1] Includes undistributed not shown separately.   [2] Partial data only.

Source: U.S. Bureau of Mines, *Annual Reports*.

No. 1188. Mineral Industries—Gross Assets and Capital Expenditures: 1972 to 1987

[In millions of dollars]

INDUSTRY AND YEAR	END OF YEAR GROSS VALUE OF DEPRECIABLE ASSETS					CAPITAL EXPENDITURES					
	Total [1]	Buildings and other structures	Machinery and equipment	Mineral exploration and development [1]	Mineral land and rights [1]	Total [1]	New buildings and other structures	New machinery and equipment	Used buildings and other structures	Used machinery and equipment	Mineral exploration and development [1]
Mineral industries: [2]											
1972.........	21,690	4,244	15,038	([3])	[3]2,409	2,802	317	1,407	([3])	[3]128	230
1977.........	44,664	6,099	33,068	2,625	2,871	6,802	785	5,068	30	399	520
1982.........	94,613	10,228	73,419	5,036	5,930	13,472	1,229	10,551	78	937	677
1987.........	84,286	9,314	64,143	5,034	5,795	4,869	349	3,234	88	797	401
Crude oil, nat. gas:											
1972.........	47,500	(NA)	(NA)	(NA)	(NA)	2,954	403	842	([3])	[3]44	1,666
1977.........	94,414	(NA)	(NA)	(NA)	(NA)	10,916	571	2,269	14	93	7,969
1982.........	233,052	(NA)	(NA)	(NA)	(NA)	34,281	1,967	5,550	20	215	26,529
1987.........	(NA)	(NA)	(NA)	(NA)	(NA)	10,549	590	3,176	18	218	6,548

NA Not available. [1] Excludes data for mineral exploration and development, and mineral land and rights portions for mining service industries and natural gas liquids industry. [2] Excludes crude petroleum and natural gas. [3] Not collected separately. Data for mineral exploration and development are combined with mineral land and rights. Data for used buildings and other structures are combined with used machinery and equipment.

Source: U.S. Bureau of the Census, *Census of Mineral Industries, 1987*.

No. 1189. Mineral Industries—Employment, Hours, and Earnings: 1990 to 1992

ITEM	Unit	1990	1991	1992	ITEM	Unit	1990	1991	1992
All mining:					Avg. weekly hours.....	No ...	43.9	44.5	43.9
All employees.........	1,000 .	710	691	635	Avg. weekly earnings...	Dol ...	568	602	613
Production workers	1,000 .	509	491	450	Metal mining:				
Avg. weekly hours.....	No ...	44.1	44.4	44.0	All employees.........	1,000 .	58	56	54
Avg. weekly earnings...	Dol ...	603	630	638	Production workers	1,000 .	46	44	43
Coal mining:					Avg. weekly hours.....	No ...	42.8	43.0	42.9
All employees.........	1,000 .	147	135	124	Avg. weekly earnings...	Dol ...	601	639	653
Production workers	1,000 .	119	109	101	Nonmetallic minerals,				
Avg. weekly hours.....	No ...	44.0	44.6	43.9	except fuels:				
Avg. weekly earnings...	Dol ...	735	762	755	All employees.........	1,000 .	111	105	103
Oil and gas extraction:					Production workers	1,000 .	84	78	77
All employees.........	1,000 .	395	394	354	Avg. weekly hours.....	No ...	45.3	44.6	44.9
Production workers	1,000 .	261	259	230	Avg. weekly earnings...	Dol ...	525	532	551

Source: U.S. Bureau of Labor Statistics, *Bulletin 2370* and *Employment and Earnings*, monthly.

No. 1190. Selected Mineral Products—Average Prices: 1970 to 1992

[Excludes Alaska and Hawaii, except as noted. See *Historical Statistics, Colonial Times to 1970*, series M 96, M 139, M 209, M 248, and M 262, for bituminous coal, crude petroleum, iron ore, lead, and aluminum, respectively]

YEAR	Tantalum (dol. per lb.) [1]	Copper, electrolytic [2] (cents per lb.)	Platinum [3] (dol./ troy oz.)	Gold (dol./ fine oz.)	Silver (dol./ fine oz.)	Lead [4] (cents per lb.)	Tin (New York) [5] (cents per lb.)	Zinc [6] (cents per lb.)	Sulfur, crude [7] (dol./ metric ton)	Bituminous coal [8] (dol./ short ton)	Crude petroleum [8] (dol./ bbl.)	Natural gas [8] (dol./ 1,000 cu. ft.)
1970	9.15	58	133	36	1.77	15.7	174.1	15.3	[9]22.77	6.26	3.18	0.17
1975	18.32	64	164	161	4.42	21.5	339.8	39.0	[9]44.91	19.23	7.67	0.45
1976	20.31	70	162	125	4.35	23.1	379.8	37.0	[9]45.72	19.43	8.19	0.58
1977	25.64	67	157	148	4.62	30.7	534.6	34.4	[9]44.38	19.82	8.57	0.79
1978	34.19	66	261	194	5.40	33.7	629.6	31.0	45.17	21.78	9.00	0.91
1979	80.00	92	445	308	11.09	52.6	753.9	37.3	55.75	23.65	12.64	1.18
1980	126.37	101	677	613	20.63	42.5	846.0	37.4	89.06	24.52	21.59	1.59
1981	99.51	84	446	460	10.52	36.5	733.1	44.6	111.48	26.29	31.77	1.98
1982	49.95	73	327	376	7.95	25.5	653.9	38.5	108.27	27.14	28.52	2.46
1983	30.60	77	424	424	11.44	21.7	654.8	41.4	87.24	25.85	26.19	2.59
1984	37.44	67	357	361	8.14	25.6	623.8	48.6	94.31	25.51	25.88	2.66
1985	33.68	67	291	318	6.14	19.1	596.0	40.4	106.46	25.10	24.09	2.51
1986	23.74	66	461	368	5.47	22.1	383.2	38.0	105.22	23.70	12.51	1.94
1987	27.08	83	553	448	7.01	35.9	418.8	41.9	89.78	23.00	15.40	1.67
1988	47.37	120	523	438	6.54	37.1	441.4	60.2	85.95	22.00	12.58	1.69
1989	44.93	131	507	383	5.50	39.4	520.2	82.0	86.62	21.76	15.86	1.69
1990	38.06	123	467	385	4.82	46.0	386.3	74.6	80.14	21.71	20.03	1.71
1991	36.70	109	371	363	4.04	33.5	362.9	52.8	71.45	21.75	16.50	1.59
1992, prel.	34.42	107	356	350	4.00	36.0	414.0	59.0	60.00	(NA)	(NA)	(NA)

NA Not available. [1] Dollars per pound of tantalum content. [2] Average producer prices, delivered. [3] Average annual producer prices. [4] 1970, New York prices; beginning 1975, nationwide delivered basis. [5] Straits tin through 1975; thereafter, composite price. [6] Prime western. Beginning 1975, delivered price. [7] F.O.B. works. [8] Average value at the point of production. Source: U.S. Energy Information Administration, *Annual Energy Review*. [9] Per long ton.

Source: Except as noted, U.S. Bureau of Mines, *Mineral Facts and Problems*, 1980 edition; and *Mineral Commodity Summaries*, annual.

No. 1191. Principal Fuels, Nonmetals, and Metals—U.S. Production, as Percent of World Production: 1980 to 1991

MINERAL	Unit	WORLD PRODUCTION				PERCENT U.S. OF WORLD			
		1980	1985	1990	1991, est.	1980	1985	1990	1991, est.
Fuels: [1]									
Coal	Bil. sh. ton	4.2	4.8	5.2	5.2	20	18	20	20
Petroleum (crude)	Bil. bbl	21.7	19.6	22.0	21.8	14	17	12	12
Natural gas (dry, marketable)	Tril. cu. ft	53.1	62.0	74.3	(NA)	37	26	24	(NA)
Natural gas plant liquids	Bil. bbl	1.4	1.5	1.8	(NA)	43	38	32	(NA)
Nonmetals:									
Asbestos	Mil. metric ton .	4.7	4.2	3.8	3.5	2	1	(D)	(D)
Barite	Mil. short ton...	7.5	6.1	5.6	5.3	27	11	8	8
Feldspar	Mil. short ton...	3.2	4.0	5.3	5.2	20	16	12	11
Fluorspar	Mil. short ton...	5.0	5.0	5.0	4.4	2	1	1	1
Gypsum	Mil. short ton...	78.4	87.0	94.9	93.9	13	15	16	15
Mica (incl. scrap)	1,000 short ton .	228	255	211	198	46	49	52	52
Nitrogen, agricultural [2]	Mil. short ton...	73.6	91.0	97.6	93.7	20	14	13	14
Phosphate rock	Mil. metric ton .	144	149	154	147	38	34	30	33
Potash	Mil. metric ton .	27.9	29.2	27.7	25.5	8	4	6	7
Sulfur, elemental	Mil. metric ton ..	55.0	53.8	58.2	55.6	22	22	20	19
Metals, mine basis:									
Bauxite	Mil. metric ton ..	90.8	84.2	109.6	109.2	2	1	(D)	(D)
Columbian concentrates (columbian content)	Mil. lb........	15.1	14.8	13.3	13.8	(NA)	-	(NA)	(NA)
Copper [3]	Mil. metric ton ..	7.4	8.0	8.7	8.8	16	14	18	18
Gold	Metric ton	1,219	1,532	2,127	2,112	2	5	14	14
Iron ore	Mil. metric ton ..	891	861	929	901	8	6	6	6
Lead [3]	1,000 metric ton .	3,424	3,431	3,390	3,318	17	12	15	14
Mercury	1,000 flasks [4] ..	6.8	6.1	5.1	4.5	16	9	(NA)	(NA)
Molybdenum [3]	Mil. lb........	111	98	122	112	62	50	50	48
Nickel [3]	1,000 short ton .	779	813	1,029	1,029	2	1	(Z)	1
Silver	Mil. troy oz	10.7	13.1	15.1	14.7	9	9	14	13
Tantalum concentrates (tantalum content)	Mil. lb........	0.5	0.3	0.4	0.4	(NA)	-	(NA)	(NA)
Titanium concentrates:									
Ilmenite	Mil. short ton...	3.7	3.5	4.0	3.5	14	(D)	(D)	(D)
Tungsten	1,000 metric ton .	51.9	46.6	51.9	43.0	5	2	(D)	(D)
Vanadium [3]	1,000 short ton .	36.8	30.2	30.6	26.4	12	(D)	(D)	(D)
Zinc [3]	Mil. metric ton ..	6.3	6.8	7.0	7.0	6	4	7	8
Metals, smelter basis:									
Aluminum	1,000 metric ton.	15,383	15,398	17,977	18,194	30	23	23	23
Cadmium	1,000 metric ton .	18.2	18.9	20.5	20.7	9	8	8	8
Copper	Mil. metric ton ..	7.7	8.6	9.1	9.1	14	14	16	16
Iron, pig (incl. ferroalloys) ...	Mil. short ton...	514	499	533	509	12	9	9	9
Lead	1,000 metric ton .	5,397	5,641	5,942	5,942	23	20	23	22
Magnesium	1,000 metric ton .	316	325	354	339	49	42	39	39
Steel ingots and castings ...	Mil. short ton...	717	718	771	734	14	11	12	11
Tin	1,000 metric ton .	251	193	223	205	1	2	-	
Zinc	1,000 metric ton.	6,049	6,786	7,041	7,041	6	5	5	5

- Represents or rounds to zero.   D Withheld to avoid disclosing company data.   NA Not available.   Z Less than half the unit of measure.   [1] Source: Energy Information Administration, *International Energy Annual*.   [2] For fiscal years ending in year shown; see text, section 9. U.S. production includes Puerto Rico.   [3] Content of ore and concentrate.   [4] 76-lb. flasks.

Source: Except as noted, U.S. Bureau of Mines, *Annual Reports*.

No. 1192. Federal Strategic and Critical Materials Inventory: 1980 to 1991

[As of **Dec. 31.** Covers strategic and critical materials essential to military and industrial requirements in time of national emergency. Market values are estimated current trade values of similar materials and not necessarily amounts that would be realized at time of sale]

MINERAL	Unit	QUANTITY [1]				VALUE (mil. dol.)			
		1980	1985	1990	1991	1980	1985	1990	1991
Tin	1,000 metric ton.	200	185	169	163	3,158	2,324	962	914
Silver	1,000 troy oz...	139,500	136,006	92,151	83,951	2,288	801	374	330
Cobalt	Mil. lb........	41	53	53	53	1,020	590	443	1,609
Bauxite [2]	1,000 lg. ton...	14,333	17,957	18,033	18,033	583	871	888	827
Manganese [3]	1,000 sh. ton...	5,130	4,470	4,017	3,918	599	520	962	1,000
Tungsten [4]	Mil. lb........	97	87	82	82	817	369	253	343
Zinc	1,000 sh. ton...	380	378	379	379	441	268	483	441
Titanium	1,000 sh. ton...	43	48	37	37	432	405	402	402
Platinum	1,000 troy oz...	466	466	453	453	215	154	186	162
Chromium [5]	1,000 sh. ton...	804	854	1,074	1,121	773	836	917	924
Diamonds: Stones ..	Carat........	19,224	12,549	7,777	7,777	349	336	267	267
Industrial, bort. ..	Carat........	23,693	22,001	17,353	14,021	73	39	16	13

[1] Consists of stockpile and nonstockpile grades and reflects uncommitted balances.   [2] Consists of abrasive grade, metallic grade Jamaica, metallic grade Suriname, and refractory.   [3] Consists of chemical grade, dioxide battery natural, dioxide battery synthetic, electrolytic, ferro-high carbon, ferro-med. carbon, ferro-silicon, and metal.   [4] Consists of carbide powder, ferro, metal powder, and ores and concentrates.   [5] Consists of ferro-high carbon, ferro-low carbon, ferro-silicon, and metal.

Source: U.S. Defense Logistics Agency, *Statistical Supplement, Stockpile Report to the Congress* (AP-3).

No. 1193. Federal Strategic and Critical Materials—Summary: 1989 to 1991

ITEM	Unit	Tin	Silver	Cobalt	Bauxite	Manganese	Tungsten	Zinc	Titanium	Platinum	Chromium	Stones	DIAMONDS Industrial bort
Production:													
1989	1,000 metric tons.	[1]11.0	2.0	1.2	(³)	-	(D)	260	25.2	[2]1,430	99	-	(D)
1990	1,000 metric tons.	[1]13.2	2.1	1.2	(³)	-	(D)	263	24.7	[2]1,810	94	-	[3]90.0
1991	1,000 metric tons.	13.0	1.8	1.6		-	(D)	253	13.7	[2]1,730	90	-	[3]90.0
Imports:													
1989	1,000 metric tons.	[1]34.0	3.3	6.2	11,603	579	7.9	790	0.9	[2]13,278	379	[3]8.8	[3]61.6
1990	1,000 metric tons.	[1]33.8	3.3	6.4	12,987	307	6.4	723	1.1	[2]125,354	346	[3]11.0	[3]85.4
1991	1,000 metric tons.	[1]29.1	4.2	6.9	12,305	234	7.8	637	0.6	[2]125,661	309	[3]7.6	[3]70.0
Export:													
1989	1,000 metric tons.	0.9	1.3	0.9	57	52	0.2	136	13.3	[2]38,301	25	[3]2.8	[3]78.2
1990	1,000 metric tons.	0.7	1.8	1.3	64	70	0.1	128	15.8	[2]55,044	14	[3]1.7	[3]71.0
1991	1,000 metric tons.	1.0	1.7	1.5	58	66	-	112	12.1	[2]39,624	31	[3]2.9	[3]78.8
Consumption:													
1989	1,000 metric tons.	47.6	45.1	7.2	4,517	559	10.5	1,060	24.9	[2]101,209	452	[3]6.6	[3]75.8
1990	1,000 metric tons.	45.5	44.0	7.6	4,570	497	8.4	992	23.2	[2]117,043	447	[3]9.8	[3]112.7
1991	1,000 metric tons.	48.7	43.8	7.8	4,609	472	11.8	933	13.6	[2]113,038	366	[3]5.0	[3]89.1
Net Import reliance:													
1989	Percent	77.0	(⁵)	83.0	96.0	100.0	84.0	61.0	4.0	90.0	78.0	91.0	(⁵)
1990	Percent	71.0	(⁵)	84.0	98.0	100.0	81.0	41.0	(²)	88.0	79.0	95.0	13.0
1991	Percent	74.0	(⁵)	80.0	100.0	100.0	91.0	24.0	4.0	89.0	75.0	94.0	(⁵)
Stocks, end of year:													
1989	1,000 metric tons.	14.7	8.3	4.6	2,500	470	1.3	91	2.1	[2]32,543	65	(NA)	(NA)
1990	1,000 metric tons.	17.3	9.2	3.2	2,300	379	1.1	87	3.3	[2]30,324	55	(NA)	(NA)
1991	1,000 metric tons.	13.8	9.4	2.4	2,600	275	1.8	79	2.9	[2]24,313	50	(NA)	(NA)
World production:													
1991	1,000 metric tons.	197.0	14.7	26.6	109,000	22,000	43.0	7,282	56.0	[3]292,000	13,236	(NA)	[2]55.9

- Represents or rounds to zero.   D Withheld to avoid disclosure of individual companies.   NA Not available.   ¹ Production from scrap.   ² Kilograms.   ³ Million carats.   ⁴ Apparent demand.   ⁵ Net importer.

Source: U.S. Bureau of Mines, *Mineral Commodity Summaries*, annual.

No. 1194. Selected Mineral and Metal Products—Quantity and Value of Imports and Exports: 1985 to 1991

[Imports represent imports for consumption. Exports include shipments under foreign aid programs. Includes trade of Puerto Rico with foreign countries. Beginning 1989, import and export data are not necessarily comparable to prior data due to change in tariff schedule to Harmonized System]

PRODUCT	Unit	QUANTITY				VALUE (mil. dol.)			
		1985	1989	1990	1991	1985	1989	1990	1991
IMPORTS									
Petroleum (crude) [1]	Mil. bbl	1,625	2,128	2,222	2,124	22,608	35,041	43,833	37,123
Gem stones: Diamonds	Mil. carat	8.2	10.1	7.5	8.5	3,007	4,358	3,955	3,992
Ores and concentrates:									
Chromium (Cr_2O_3 content)	1,000 metric ton	160	237	134	94	20	44	22	15
Copper	1,000 metric ton	2.9	46.5	91.5	60.8	2	51	131	69
Iron	Mil. metric ton.	16.0	19.6	18.1	13.3	452	522	560	437
Tungsten	1,000 metric ton	4.7	7.9	6.4	7.8	37	45	31	43
Metals:									
Aluminum	1,000 metric ton	869	923	960	1,025	1,017	1,898	1,597	1,428
Cobalt [2]	1,000 metric ton	7.5	5.4	6.0	6.4	181	92	107	158
Copper refined ingots, etc.	1,000 metric ton	378	300	262	289	503	854	675	685
Gold (refined bullion)	Metric ton	198	97	65	147	2,109	1,199	795	1,722
Iron and steel products									
(major)	Mil. metric ton.	23.3	18.1	17.8	16.2	11,019	10,649	11,612	11,962
Platinum group [3]	Metric ton	124	113	125	126	1,026	1,382	1,906	1,743
Silver (bullion)	Metric ton	4,244	3,062	2,698	2,525	849	579	437	339
Zinc: Blocks, pigs, slabs	1,000 metric ton	611	712	632	549	508	1,184	992	620
EXPORTS									
Fuels: [1]									
Bituminous coal	Mil. sh. ton.	84.0	90.8	95.3	98.4	3,862	4,243	4,464	4,588
Petroleum (crude)	Mil. bbl	6.0	3.8	8.0	2.7	117	62.1	198.6	54.1
Nonmetallic minerals:									
Gem stones: Diamonds	Mil. carat	2.4	1.1	1.2	1.8	571	1,244	1,433	1,383
Nitrogen compounds (maj.)	Mil. metric ton.	9.8	12.5	11.9	13.9	1,553	(NA)	(NA)	(NA)
Phosphatic fertilizers [4]	Mil. metric ton.	7.6	9.6	9.2	11.5	1,225	1,760	1,515	1,974
Metals:									
Aluminum: Ingots, slabs,									
crude	1,000 metric ton	347	593	684	793	442	1,260	1,169	1,274
Plates, sheets, bars, etc	1,000 metric ton	168	416	419	489	411	1,196	1,278	1,384
Gold (refined bullion)	Metric ton	90	124	141	174	919	1,490	1,719	2,039
Iron and steel products									
(major)	Mil. metric ton.	1.1	4.7	4.7	6.6	1,476	2,582	4,665	5,753
Magnesium [5]	1,000 metric ton	36.6	56.6	51.8	55.2	114	170	164	150
Molybdenum [6]	Metric ton	260	253	180	88	2	3	2	1
Silver (refined bullion)	Metric ton	392	430	736	787	82	78	120	115
Scrap exports:									
Aluminum	1,000 metric ton	374	575	537	461	351	769	719	542
Iron and steel	Mil. metric ton.	9.2	11.3	11.7	9.5	940	1,785	1,653	1,253

NA Not available.   [1] Source: U.S. Bureau of the Census, *U.S. Imports for Consumption and General Imports, TSUSA Commodity and Country,* FT 246, annual; and *U.S. Exports, Schedule B Commodity and Country,* FT 446, annual; 1989 and 1990, *U.S. Exports of Merchandise* and *U.S. Imports of Merchandise* compact discs, December issues.   [2] Includes unwrought metal, waste and scrap.   [3] Unwrought and semimanufactured, including unwrought sweepings waste and scrap.   [4] Superphosphates and ammonium phosphates.   [5] Metal and alloys, scrap, semimanufactured forms.   [6] Metals and alloys, crude and scrap.

Source: Except as noted, U.S. Bureau of Mines, *Minerals Yearbook.*

No. 1195. Mineral Industries—Lost Workday Injuries and Fatalities: 1985 to 1991

[Excludes office workers. Lost workday injuries are nonfatal occurrences that result in days away from work, days of restricted work activity or a permanent disability. Data for all years includes injuries to independent contractors at mine sites. Rates for the noncoal industries are based only on employment and hours worked by mine employees. See also *Historical Statistics, Colonial Times to 1970,* series M 271-286]

ITEM	COAL MINING			QUARRYING; RELATED INDUSTRY [1]			METAL; NONMETAL MINING [2]		
	1985	1990	1991	1985	1990	1991	1985	1990	1991
Injuries, total	9,141	12,292	11,353	2,571	3,812	3,519	2,234	3,804	3,598
Fatal	68	66	61	26	18	18	22	26	22
Rate per million work-hours:									
Fatal	0.20	0.022	0.024	0.19	0.13	0.14	0.17	0.17	0.15
Nonfatal	26.8	41.5	41.5	18.7	28.2	28.0	16.9	24.7	24.1
Fatalities per 1,000 employed [3]	0.36	0.41	0.41	0.37	0.27	0.24	0.31	0.34	0.30

[1] Includes cement.   [2] Nonmetal mines exclude extraction of Frasch process sulfur.   [3] Average number of persons at work each day mines were active.

Source: U.S. Mine Safety and Health Administration, Denver, CO, unpublished data.

No. 1196. Net U.S. Imports of Selected Minerals and Metals as Percent of Apparent Consumption, 1980 to 1991, and by Major Foreign Sources, 1982 to 1992

[In percent. Figures based on net imports which equal the difference between imports and exports plus or minus government stockpile and industry stock changes]

MINERAL	1980	1985	1988	1989	1990	1991	1992, est.	Rank of major foreign sources, 1983-91
Columbium	100	100	100	100	100	100	100	Brazil, Canada, Thailand.
Manganese	98	100	100	100	100	100	100	South Africa, France, Gabon.
Mica (sheet)	100	100	100	100	100	100	100	India, Belgium, France.
Strontium	100	100	100	100	100	100	100	Mexico, Spain.
Bauxite [1]	94	96	97	96	98	100	100	Australia, Guinea, Jamaica.
Asbestos	78	65	75	90	90	95	95	Canada, South Africa.
Platinum group	87	92	91	90	88	89	94	So. Africa, United Kingdom, U.S.S.R.
Tantalum	90	89	86	86	86	86	87	Thailand, Germany, Brazil.
Cobalt	93	94	87	83	84	80	76	Zaire, Zambia, Canada.
Chromium	91	75	78	78	79	75	74	South Africa, Turkey, Zimbabwe.
Tungsten	53	68	86	84	81	91	85	China, Bolivia, Canada.
Nickel	76	71	74	71	74	71	64	Canada, Norway, Australia.
Tin	79	72	78	77	71	74	73	Brazil, Thailand, Malaysia.
Barium (Barite)	44	74	76	78	71	66	53	China, Morocco, India.
Potassium (Potash)	65	76	71	65	68	67	67	Canada, Israel, U.S.S.R.
Antimony	47	63	65	56	51	53	58	China, South Africa.
Cadmium	55	57	64	48	62	48	49	Canada, Australia, Mexico.
Selenium	59	(D)	52	55	46	50	48	Canada, United Kingdom, Japan.
Petroleum [2][3]	37	27	38	42	42	40	(NA)	Saudi Arabia, Venezuela, Canada.
Zinc	60	70	69	61	[4]41	[4]24	[4]34	Canada, Mexico, Peru.
Gypsum	35	38	36	35	36	31	35	Canada, Mexico, Spain.
Iron ore	25	21	18	22	21	9	12	Canada, Brazil, Venezuela.
Iron and steel	13	22	19	13	13	12	12	E.E.C. [5], Japan, Canada.
Sulfur	14	3	16	9	11	16	18	Canada, Mexico.
Natural gas [3]	5	5	7	7	8	8	(NA)	Canada, Algeria.
Copper	16	28	13	7	3	(6)	3	Chile, Canada, Peru.
Aluminum	(6)	16	7	7	7	(6)	(6)	Canada, Japan, Venezuela.
Silver	7	(NA)	(NA)	(NA)	(NA)	(NA)	(NA)	Canada, Mexico, Peru.
Mercury	27	(NA)	(NA)	(D)	(D)	(D)	(D)	Spain, China, Japan.
Titanium (Ilmenite)	32	(D)	(D)	(D)	(D)	(D)	(D)	Australia, Canada, South Africa.
Vanadium	35	(D)	(D)	(D)	(D)	(D)	(D)	South Africa, E.E.C. [5]

D Withheld to avoid disclosure.　NA Not available.　[1] Includes alumina.　[2] Includes crude and products.　[3] Source: Energy Information Administration, *Annual Energy Review*, and *Monthly Energy Review*.　[4] Effect of sharp rise in exports of concentrates. If calculated on a refined zinc-only basis, reliance would be about the same as pre-1990 level; 1990, 64%; 1991, 61%; and 1992, 64%.　[5] European Economic Community.　[6] Net exports.

Source: Except as noted, U.S. Bureau of Mines, *Mineral Commodity Summaries;* import and export data from U.S. Bureau of the Census.

No. 1197. Federal Offshore Leasing, Exploration, Production, and Revenue: 1980 to 1991

[See source for explanation of terms and for reliability statement]

ITEM	Unit	1980	1984	1985	1986	1987	1988	1989	1990	1991
Tracts offered	Number	483	27,984	15,754	10,724	10,926	33,376	11,013	10,459	16,800
Tracts leased	Number	218	1,400	667	142	640	1,856	1,049	825	676
Acres offered	1,000	2,563	154,384	87,029	58,670	59,762	85,366	60,096	56,788	80,288
Acres leased	1,000	1,134	7,495	3,512	734	45,075	10,040	5,580	4,263	3,416
Bonus paid for leased tracts	Bil. dol.	4.2	4.0	1.5	0.2	0.5	1.2	0.6	0.6	0.4
New wells being drilled:										
Active	Number	191	253	195	95	142	116	123	120	64
Suspended	Number	739	313	348	279	265	289	361	266	249
Wells completed	Number	9,638	13,012	12,285	12,536	12,736	12,827	12,938	13,167	13,184
Wells plugged and abandoned	Number	8,057	9,903	10,487	11,909	12,373	13,164	13,846	14,677	15,430
Revenue, total [1]	Bil. dol.	6.4	8.0	5.2	2.8	2.9	3.4	2.8	3.3	2.8
Bonuses	Bil. dol.	4.2	4.0	1.5	0.2	0.5	1.2	0.6	0.6	0.4
Oil and gas royalties [1]	Bil. dol.	2.1	4.0	3.6	2.6	2.3	2.1	2.1	2.6	2.3
Rentals	Bil. dol.	(Z)	(Z)	0.1	0.1	0.1	0.1	0.1	0.1	0.1
Production, value [2]	Bil. dol.	13.1	24.0	22.2	15.7	14.6	12.9	13.0	16.5	14.2
Crude oil	Bil. dol.	4.8	9.6	9.6	5.8	5.6	4.2	4.4	5.9	5.2
Condensate	Bil. dol.	0.4	1.2	1.0	0.7	0.7	0.7	0.8	1.1	1.1
Natural gas	Bil. dol.	7.9	13.2	11.5	9.3	8.1	7.9	7.8	9.5	7.9
Production: [2]										
Crude oil	Mil. bbls.	259	330	352	350	325	279	260	274	263
Condensate	Mil. bbls.	19	40	37	39	41	41	45	51	52
Natural gas	Bil. cu. ft	4,641	4,537	4,000	3,949	4,425	4,310	4,200	5,093	4,516

Z Less than $50 million.　[1] Includes condensate royalties.　[2] Production value is value at time of production, not current value.

Source: U.S. Dept. of the Interior, Minerals Management Service, *Federal Offshore Statistics,* annual.

No. 1198. Petroleum Industry—Summary: 1980 to 1991

ITEM	Unit	1980	1984	1985	1986	1987	1988	1989	1990	1991, est.
Crude oil producing wells (Dec. 31).	1,000...	548	621	647	623	620	612	603	602	614
Daily output per well.........	Bbl.....	15.9	14.3	13.9	13.9	13.5	13.5	12.6	12.2	12.0
Completed wells drilled, total.....	1,000...	70	85	70	40	36	32	28	30	27
Crude oil.................	1,000...	32	43	35	19	16	13	10	12	12
Gas	1,000...	17	17	14	8	8	8	9	10	9
Dry......................	1,000...	20	26	21	13	12	10	8	8	7
Crude oil production, total.......	Mil. bbl..	3,146	3,250	3,275	3,168	3,047	2,979	2,785	2,685	2,691
Value at wells	Bil. dol..	67.9	84.1	78.9	39.6	46.9	37.5	44.1	53.7	44.4
Average price per barrel	Dollars..	21.59	25.88	24.09	12.51	15.40	12.58	15.86	20.03	16.50
Refinery input of crude oil.......	Mil. bbl.	4,934	4,408	4,381	4,641	4,692	4,848	4,891	4,895	4,855
Imports: Crude oil	Mil. bbl.	1,926	1,254	1,168	1,525	1,706	1,869	2,133	2,151	2,110
Refined petroleum products	Mil. bbl.	603	736	681	747	731	840	809	775	655
Import value................	Mil. dol.	74,440	54,310	50,368	34,790	41,495	39,981	49,028	60,747	50,390
Export value................	Mil. dol.	2,871	4,801	5,121	3,883	3,922	2,802	2,859	4,419	4,710
Operable refineries...........	Number.	319	247	223	216	219	213	204	205	202
Capacity (Jan. 1)	Mil. bbl.	6,584	5,906	5,716	5,643	5,681	5,825	5,714	5,683	5,723
Output	Mil. bbl.	5,352	5,007	5,019	5,301	5,339	5,498	5,539	5,570	5,559
Utilization rate	Percent .	75.4	76.2	77.6	82.9	83.1	84.7	86.6	87.1	85.9
Proved reserves	Bil. bbl.	29.8	28.4	28.4	26.9	27.3	26.8	26.5	26.3	24.7

Source: U.S. Energy Information Administration, *Annual Energy Review,* and *Petroleum Supply Annual.*

No. 1199. Crude Petroleum and Natural Gas Wells Drilled—Summary: 1980 to 1991

[Includes all costs incurred for drilling and equipping wells to point of completion as productive wells or abandonment after drilling becomes unproductive. Based on sample of operators of different size drilling establishments]

ITEM	Unit	1980	1983	1984	1985	1986	1987	1988	1989	1990	1991
Wells drilled	Number..	62,011	67,536	77,210	67,821	37,173	33,041	29,741	26,693	28,513	27,194
Offshore	Number...	1,272	1,270	1,421	1,247	898	709	866	746	704	718
Footage drilled........	Mil. ft....	296.0	301.2	350.6	314.5	176.3	157.4	150.2	131.5	143.8	138.7
Drilling cost...........	Mil. dol...	22,800	25,105	25,206	23,697	13,552	9,239	10,550	9,669	10,937	11,461
Average depth per well ..	Feet	4,773	4,460	4,541	4,637	4,742	4,762	5,051	4,925	5,043	5,100
Average cost per well...	$1,000....	368	372	326	349	365	280	355	362	384	421
Offshore	$1,000....	3,024	3,906	3,536	4,073	4,004	2,896	3,112	3,197	3,112	3,550
Average cost per foot...	Dollars ...	77.02	83.34	71.90	75.35	76.88	58.71	70.23	73.55	76.07	82.64

Source: American Petroleum Institute, *Joint Association Survey of Drilling Costs,* annual.

No. 1200. Domestic Motor Gasoline Supply: 1980 to 1991

[In 1,000 barrels per day, except as noted]

ITEM	1980	1982	1983	1984	1985	1986	1987	1988	1989	1990	1991
Supply [1]........	6,579	6,539	6,622	6,693	6,831	7,034	7,206	7,336	7,328	7,235	7,188
Unleaded.......	3,067	3,409	3,647	3,987	4,406	4,854	5,470	5,995	6,507	6,850	6,935
Production	6,506	6,338	6,340	6,453	6,419	6,752	6,841	6,956	6,963	6,959	6,975
Net imports......	139	177	237	293	371	293	349	383	330	287	215
Stocks (mil. bbl.) [2] ..	261	235	222	243	223	233	226	228	213	220	219

[1] Production plus net imports less net increase in primary stocks. [2] End of year, includes motor gasoline blending components.

Source: U.S. Energy Information Administration, *Monthly Energy Review.*

No. 1201. Natural Gas Plant Liquids—Production and Value: 1970 to 1991

[Barrels of 42 gallons. See also *Historical Statistics, Colonial Times to 1970,* series M 143-146]

ITEM	Unit	1970	1975	1980	1985	1986	1987	1988	1989	1990	1991
Field production [1]........	Mil. bbl ...	606	596	576	587	566	582	595	564	566	606
Pentanes plus..........	Mil. bbl ...	197	149	126	103	98	106	111	113	112	118
Liquefied petroleum gases .	Mil. bbl ...	400	444	441	479	466	474	483	451	454	488
Natural gas processed	Tril. cu. ft..	19	18	15	13	[2]13	13	13	13	15	16

[1] Includes other finished petroleum products, not shown separately. [2] Estimated.

Source: Through 1975, U.S. Bureau of Mines, *Minerals Yearbook;* thereafter, U.S. Energy Information Administration, *Energy Data Reports, Petroleum Statement Annual, Petroleum Supply Annual,* and *Natural Gas Annual.*

No. 1202. World Crude Oil Production: 1980 to 1991

[In thousands of barrels]

COUNTRY	1980	1985	1986	1987	1988	1989	1990	1991
Total	59,599	53,981	56,227	56,601	58,662	59,773	60,471	60,221
Algeria	1,106	1,037	945	1,048	1,040	1,095	1,175	1,230
Iraq	2,514	1,433	1,690	2,079	2,685	2,897	2,040	298
Kuwait	1,656	1,023	1,419	1,585	1,492	1,783	1,175	187
Libya	1,787	1,059	1,034	972	1,175	1,150	1,375	1,483
Qatar	472	301	308	293	346	380	406	390
Saudi Arabia	9,900	3,388	4,870	4,265	5,086	5,064	6,410	8,181
United Arab Emirates	1,709	1,193	1,330	1,541	1,565	1,860	2,117	2,447
Indonesia	1,577	1,325	1,390	1,343	1,342	1,409	1,462	1,613
Iran	1,662	2,250	2,035	2,298	2,240	2,810	3,088	3,334
Nigeria	2,055	1,495	1,467	1,341	1,450	1,716	1,810	1,892
Venezuela	2,168	1,677	1,787	1,752	1,903	1,907	2,137	2,375
Canada	1,435	1,471	1,474	1,535	1,616	1,560	1,553	1,548
Mexico	1,936	2,745	2,435	2,548	2,512	2,520	2,553	2,676
United Kingdom	1,622	2,530	2,539	2,406	2,232	1,802	1,820	1,797
United States	8,597	8,971	8,680	8,349	8,140	7,613	7,355	7,417
China	2,114	2,505	2,620	2,690	2,730	2,757	2,774	2,805
U.S.S.R (former)	11,706	11,585	11,895	11,985	11,978	11,625	10,880	9,887
Other	5,204	7,540	7,850	8,242	8,669	9,338	9,785	10,076
Arab OPEC	19,144	9,434	11,596	11,783	13,389	14,229	14,698	14,216
Total OPEC	26,985	16,634	18,734	18,846	20,785	22,558	23,750	24,016

Source: U. S. Energy Information Administration, *Monthly Energy Review.*

No. 1203. World Natural Gas Production: 1980 to 1989

[In quadrillion Btu's]

REGION AND COUNTRY	1980	1982	1983	1984	1985	1986	1987	1988	1989
World total	52.79	53.74	54.06	59.12	61.37	62.56	65.58	69.04	71.11
North America	23.53	21.77	20.11	21.54	20.80	20.13	20.88	21.87	22.30
Canada	2.64	2.44	2.52	2.61	2.98	2.77	3.00	3.47	3.59
Mexico	0.97	1.07	1.06	1.00	0.92	0.89	0.83	0.89	0.92
United States	19.91	18.26	16.53	17.93	16.91	16.47	17.05	17.52	17.80
Central and South America	1.39	1.51	1.55	1.78	1.84	1.86	1.82	2.02	2.09
Argentina	0.26	0.37	0.41	0.46	0.47	0.51	0.49	0.62	0.65
Bolivia	0.07	0.08	0.08	0.09	0.08	0.09	0.09	0.09	0.09
Brazil	0.04	0.05	0.06	0.08	0.10	0.09	0.11	0.10	0.10
Columbia	0.11	0.12	0.12	0.16	0.16	0.16	0.16	0.17	0.17
Trinidad and Tobago	0.08	0.11	0.13	0.20	0.23	0.16	0.15	0.16	0.17
Venezuela	0.56	0.68	0.66	0.69	0.70	0.77	0.75	0.79	0.82
Western Europe	7.02	6.50	6.39	6.65	6.83	6.77	7.12	6.93	7.17
France	0.24	0.20	0.21	0.20	0.17	0.13	0.13	0.10	0.10
Germany, West	0.63	0.56	0.58	0.62	0.57	0.51	0.53	0.56	0.57
Italy	0.43	0.52	0.47	0.50	0.52	0.58	0.59	0.60	0.62
Netherlands	3.21	2.54	2.45	2.52	2.59	2.44	2.53	2.33	2.41
Norway	1.01	1.02	0.98	1.06	1.07	1.09	1.22	1.20	1.24
United Kingdom	1.31	1.45	1.49	1.51	1.61	1.70	1.79	1.72	1.78
Yugoslavia	0.07	0.07	0.06	0.08	0.09	0.10	0.09	0.12	0.12
Eastern Europe	16.24	18.57	19.80	21.47	23.28	24.70	25.74	27.45	28.42
Germany, East	0.12	0.11	0.15	0.17	0.18	0.16	0.12	0.16	0.17
Hungary	0.23	0.26	0.26	0.27	0.29	0.28	0.25	0.25	0.26
Poland	0.23	0.20	0.20	0.22	0.23	0.21	0.20	0.21	0.21
Romania	1.35	1.52	1.57	1.50	1.43	1.50	1.48	1.44	1.49
U.S.S.R.	14.28	16.44	17.58	19.27	21.12	22.50	23.63	25.34	26.23
Middle East	1.40	1.29	1.33	2.10	2.50	2.76	3.18	3.49	3.62
Bahrain	0.10	0.14	0.15	0.14	0.17	0.19	0.23	0.17	0.18
Iran	0.26	0.26	0.33	0.50	0.63	0.57	0.60	0.75	0.77
Kuwait	0.15	0.14	0.13	0.15	0.15	0.18	0.20	0.24	0.25
Qatar	0.19	0.19	0.18	0.22	0.20	0.20	0.21	0.24	0.25
Saudi Arabia	0.39	0.21	0.20	0.65	0.75	0.93	0.99	1.08	1.11
United Arab Emirates	0.21	0.21	0.28	0.36	0.51	0.56	0.71	0.69	0.71
Africa	0.73	1.31	1.79	1.91	1.97	1.99	2.23	2.32	2.40
Algeria	0.44	1.00	1.39	1.44	1.44	1.41	1.62	1.68	1.74
Egypt	0.03	0.10	0.12	0.15	0.18	0.21	0.23	0.26	0.26
Libya	0.19	0.13	0.15	0.17	0.19	0.21	0.20	0.20	0.21
Nigeria	0.04	0.05	0.09	0.10	0.11	0.12	0.14	0.14	0.15
Far East and Oceania	2.49	2.79	3.10	3.66	4.16	4.35	4.63	4.95	5.12
Australia	0.33	0.40	0.40	0.42	0.47	0.50	0.51	0.52	0.54
Bangladesh	0.05	0.06	0.07	0.09	0.10	0.11	0.13	0.16	0.16
Brunei	0.35	0.36	0.37	0.34	0.33	0.33	0.34	0.34	0.35
China	0.53	0.40	0.45	0.46	0.48	0.51	0.52	0.53	0.55
India	0.05	0.09	0.11	0.12	0.14	0.19	0.23	0.32	0.33
Indonesia	0.66	0.70	0.81	1.11	1.29	1.24	1.35	1.41	1.45
Japan	0.04	0.07	0.08	0.09	0.10	0.08	0.08	0.08	0.08
Malaysia	0.04	0.06	0.15	0.34	0.45	0.55	0.57	0.60	0.62
New Zealand	0.05	0.10	0.11	0.11	0.13	0.16	0.15	0.19	0.20
Pakistan	0.28	0.34	0.33	0.34	0.36	0.38	0.41	0.43	0.45
Thailand	-	0.05	0.06	0.06	0.13	0.12	0.14	0.20	0.21

- Represents or rounds to zero.
Source: U. S. Energy Information Administration, *1989 International Energy Annual*, February 1991.

No. 1204. U.S. Petroleum Balance: 1980 to 1991
[In millions of barrels]

ITEM	1980	1985	1986	1987	1988	1989	1990	1991
Petroleum products supplied	**6,242**	**5,740**	**5,942**	**6,083**	**6,308**	**6,324**	**6,201**	**6,101**
New supply of products	6,249	5,676	5,995	6,053	6,290	6,270	6,259	6,110
Production of products	5,765	5,363	5,604	5,680	5,849	5,874	5,934	5,933
Crude input to refineries	4,934	4,381	4,641	4,692	4,835	4,891	4,894	4,855
Oil, field production.	3,146	3,275	3,168	3,047	2,979	2,779	2,685	2,707
Alaska.	592	666	681	716	738	684	647	656
Lower 48 States	2,555	2,608	2,487	2,331	2,241	2,095	2,037	2,050
Net imports.	1,821	1,094	1,468	1,651	1,807	2,081	2,112	2,068
Imports (gross excluding SPR) [1] . . .	1,910	1,125	1,507	1,679	1,845	2,112	2,142	2,111
SPR [1] imports.	16	43	18	27	19	20	10	-
Exports	-105	75	56	55	57	52	40	42
Other sources	33	12	4	7	57	32	98	80
Natural gas plant liquids (NGPL), supply .	577	604	575	585	593	563	574	613
Other liquids.	253	378	388	403	418	420	465	466
Net imports of refined products.	484	313	391	373	441	396	326	177
Imports	578	523	621	596	681	656	598	500
Exports	94	210	229	223	240	260	272	323
Stock withdrawal, refined products	-7	64	-53	30	17	53	-59	-10
Ending stocks, all oils	1,392	1,519	1,593	1,607	1,597	1,581	1,621	1,617
Crude oil and lease condensate. . . , . . .	358	321	331	349	330	341	323	325
Strategic Petroleum Reserve (SPR) [1]	108	493	512	541	560	580	586	569
Unfinished oils	124	107	94	93	100	(NA)	(NA)	(NA)
Gasoline blending components	17	33	39	38	39	(NA)	(NA)	(NA)
Pentanes plus.	(NA)	8	7	7	7	(NA)	(NA)	(NA)
Finished refined products	785	557	609	580	562	580	712	724
PRODUCT TYPE SUPPLIED								
Total products	**6,242**	**5,740**	**5,942**	**6,083**	**6,326**	**6,324**	**6,201**	**6,101**
Finished motor gasoline	2,407	2,493	2,567	2,630	2,678	2,675	2,641	2,623
Distillate fuel oil	1,049	1,047	1,064	1,086	1,140	1,152	1,103	1,066
Residual fuel oil	918	439	518	462	5,030	500	449	423
Liquified petroleum gases [2]	414	584	552	588	604	609	568	616
Pentanes plus, other liquids, etc	1,454	1,155	1,223	1,304	1,369	1,378	1,431	1,365
Crude oil	(NA)	22	18	12	15	10	9	7

-Represents zero. NA Not available.   [1] SPR=Strategic petroleum reserve. (See table 949.)   [2] Includes ethane.

Source: U.S. Energy Information Administration, *Petroleum Supply Annual.*

No. 1205. Crude Petroleum and Natural Gas—Production, by State: 1985 to 1991

[See also *Historical Statistics, Colonial Times to 1970,* series M 138, M 142, and M 147-161]

STATE	CRUDE PETROLEUM						NATURAL GAS MARKETED PRODUCTION [1]					
	Quantity (mil. bbl.)			Value (mil. dol.)			Quantity (bil. cu. ft.)			Value (mil. dol.)		
	1985	1990	1991	1985	1990	1991	1985	1990	1991	1985	1990	1991
Total [2] . . .	3,274	2,685	2,707	78,884	53,772	44,666	17,270	18,594	18,523	43,343	31,658	30,327
AL.	22	18	19	579	387	355	107	135	171	398	373	398
AK.	666	658	656	10,655	10,086	7,659	321	403	438	236	554	647
AR.	19	10	10	443	222	186	155	175	165	393	360	317
CA.	424	322	320	8,386	5,732	4,358	491	363	378	1,653	857	929
CO	30	31	31	758	722	626	178	243	286	517	377	404
FL	11	6	5	(NA)	(NA)	(NA)	11	6	5	26	15	12
IL	30	20	19	795	467	385	1	1	(Z)	4	1	1
IN	5	3	3	134	73	61	(Z)	(Z)	(Z)	1	1	(Z)
KS.	75	59	60	1,939	1,359	1,130	528	574	565	671	893	776
KY.	8	5	6	201	124	109	73	75	79	174	169	160
LA.	508	148	147	5,387	3,409	2,962	5,014	5,242	5,034	13,355	9,587	8,718
MI	27	20	18	726	458	348	132	140	196	475	420	546
MS	31	30	27	796	630	478	144	95	108	456	167	179
MT	30	20	20	734	429	356	52	50	52	125	90	87
NE	7	5	6	163	119	110	2	1	1	6	2	2
NM	79	66	70	2,028	1,472	1,363	905	965	1,038	2,370	1,629	1,422
NY.	1	(Z)	(Z)	25	9	8	32	25	23	106	55	49
ND	51	39	36	1,307	849	674	73	52	54	138	93	89
OH	15	8	9	361	196	179	182	155	148	560	393	352
OK	163	117	108	4,256	2,690	2,118	1,936	2,258	2,154	4,930	3,548	3,161
PA.	5	2	3	114	54	49	150	178	153	474	417	336
TX.	889	674	683	23	15,060	12,997	6,053	6,343	6,334	14,097	9,939	10,069
UT.	41	23	25	773	524	489	83	146	145	293	249	223
WV	4	2	2	86	43	(NA)	145	178	199	558	568	590
WY	129	103	100	3,061	2,169	1,732	417	736	777	1,252	856	823

NA Not available.   Z Less than 500 million cubic feet or less than $500,000.   [1] Excludes nonhydrocarbon gases.
[2] Includes other States not shown separately. State production does not include State offshore production.

Source: U.S. Energy Information Administration, *Energy Data Reports, Petroleum Supply Annual, Natural Gas Annual,* and *Natural Gas Monthly.*

No. 1206. Natural Gas—Supply, Consumption, Reserves, and Marketed Production: 1970 to 1991

[See also *Historical Statistics, Colonial Times to 1970*, series M 147-161]

ITEM	Unit	1970	1975	1980	1984	1985	1986	1987	1988	1989	1990	1991
Producing wells (yearend)	1,000	117	130	182	234	243	242	249	257	262	270	277
Production value at wells	Bil. dol	3.7	8.9	32.1	48.5	43.2	32.6	29.0	30.3	30.6	31.8	30.3
Avg. per 1,000 cu. ft ..	Dollars	0.17	0.44	1.59	2.66	2.51	1.94	1.67	1.69	1.69	1.71	1.64
Proved reserves [1]	Tril. cu. ft ..	291	228	199	198	193	192	187	168	167	169	167
Marketed production [2] ..	Tril. cu. ft ..	21.9	20.1	20.2	18.3	17.3	16.9	17.4	17.9	18.1	18.6	18.5
Drawn from storage	Tril. cu. ft ..	1.5	1.8	2.0	2.1	2.4	1.8	1.9	2.3	2.9	2.0	2.8
Imports [3]	Tril. cu. ft ..	0.8	1.0	1.0	0.8	1.0	0.8	1.0	1.3	1.4	1.5	1.8
Consumption, total	Tril. cu. ft ..	21.1	19.5	19.9	18.0	17.3	16.2	17.2	18.0	18.8	18.7	19.1
Residential	Tril. cu. ft ..	4.8	4.9	4.8	4.6	4.4	4.3	4.3	4.6	4.8	4.4	4.6
Commercial [4]	Tril. cu. ft ..	2.4	2.5	2.6	2.5	2.4	2.3	2.4	2.7	2.7	2.6	2.7
Industrial	Tril. cu. ft ..	9.3	8.4	8.2	7.2	6.9	6.5	7.1	7.5	7.9	8.5	8.4
Lease and plant fuel ..	Tril. cu. ft ..	1.4	1.4	1.0	1.1	1.0	0.9	1.2	1.1	1.1	1.2	1.2
Other industrial	Tril. cu. ft ..	7.9	7.0	7.2	6.2	5.9	5.6	6.0	6.4	6.8	7.0	7.2
Electric utilities	Tril. cu. ft ..	3.9	3.2	3.7	3.1	3.0	2.6	2.8	2.6	2.8	2.8	2.8
Transportation [5]	Tril. cu. ft ..	0.7	0.6	0.6	0.5	0.5	0.5	0.5	0.6	0.6	0.7	0.6
Extraction losses [6]	Tril. cu. ft ..	0.9	0.9	0.8	0.8	0.8	0.8	0.8	0.8	0.8	0.8	0.8
Exports [7]	Tril. cu. ft ..	0.1	0.1	0.1	0.1	0.1	0.1	0.1	0.1	0.1	0.1	0.1
Additions to storage	Tril. cu. ft ..	1.9	2.1	2.0	2.3	2.2	2.0	1.9	2.2	2.5	2.5	2.7
World production (dry) ..	Tril. cu. ft ..	(NA)	44.1	53.1	59.7	62.0	63.3	66.2	69.8	71.9	74.3	(NA)
U.S. production (dry) ..	Tril. cu. ft ..	21.0	19.2	19.4	17.4	16.4	16.0	16.5	17.0	17.3	17.8	17.7
Percent U.S. of world	Percent ...	56.0	43.6	36.5	29.2	26.4	25.3	25.0	24.4	24.0	(NA)	(NA)

NA Not available. [1] Estimated, end of year. Source: 1970-1975; American Gas Association, Arlington, VA (copyright); thereafter, U.S. Energy Information Administration, *U.S. Crude Oil, Natural Gas, and Natural Gas Liquids Reserves,* annual. [2] Marketed production includes gross withdrawals from reservoirs less quantities used for reservoir repressuring and quantities vented or flared. For 1980 and thereafter, it excludes the nonhydrocarbon gases subsequently removed. [3] Includes imports of liquefied natural gas. [4] Includes deliveries to municipalities and public authorities for institutional heating and other purposes. [5] Pipeline fuel. [6] Volumetric reduction in natural gas resulting from the extraction of natural gas constituents at natural gas processing plants. [7] Beginning 1980, includes liquefied natural gas (LNG) storage in above ground tanks.

Source: Except as noted, U.S. Energy Information Administration, *Annual Energy Review, International Energy Annual, Natural Gas Annual,* Volume I and II and *Monthly Energy Review,* August 1991.

No. 1207. Liquefied Petroleum Gases—Summary: 1980 to 1991

[In millions of 42-gallon barrels. Includes ethane]

ITEM	1980	1985	1990	1991	ITEM	1980	1985	1990	1991
Production	561	622	638	683	**Consumption**	538	584	568	616
At natural gas plants	441	479	456	488	Ethane [1]	164	210	186	208
At refineries	121	143	182	196	Propane [1][2]	298	322	335	358
Imports	79	68	68	54	Butane (incl. isobutane) [2] ..	76	52	47	50
Refinery input	85	111	107	111	Stocks, Dec. 31	116	74	98	92
Exports	9	23	14	15					

[1] Reported consumption of ethane-propane mixtures have been allocated 70 percent ethane and 30 percent propane. [2] Reported consumption of butane-propane mixtures have been allocated 60 percent butane and 40 percent propane.

Source: U.S. Energy Information Administration, *Petroleum Supply Annual.*

No. 1208. World Coal Trade: 1980 to 1990

[In millions of short tons]

COUNTRIES	1980	1981	1982	1983	1984	1985	1986	1987	1988	1989	1990
Exporting countries, total [1]	277.2	288.4	292.0	284.5	332.9	370.2	376.3	383.0	415.0	423.5	440.2
United States	88.7	106.5	106.5	78.2	82.0	93.2	85.5	79.6	94.9	100.8	105.8
Australia	46.6	54.3	48.8	62.3	82.2	96.6	101.3	111.9	109.8	108.5	116.9
South Africa	30.7	33.3	30.5	32.7	40.9	49.8	50.1	46.9	47.4	51.6	54.5
Soviet Union	26.2	22.5	23.0	22.8	22.8	26.5	36.9	39.1	46.0	43.9	42.7
Germany [2]	13.8	13.1	11.2	11.5	12.4	10.5	7.9	6.9	5.5	5.9	6.0
Canada	16.1	17.9	16.6	18.6	26.8	30.3	28.6	29.5	35.0	36.1	34.2
Poland	34.6	16.6	30.6	38.7	47.2	39.7	37.9	34.2	35.5	31.8	61.8
China: Mainland	4.2	4.1	5.1	6.8	7.7	8.6	10.9	14.4	16.2	16.9	19.1
Importing countries, total [1]	277.2	288.4	292.0	284.5	332.9	370.2	376.3	383.0	415.0	423.5	440.2
Western Europe/Mediterranean ..	126.9	129.4	126.5	112.9	132.4	152.3	149.0	145.6	146.2	154.7	172.1
Japan	75.6	86.0	86.5	82.8	96.2	103.0	99.6	100.2	111.6	111.7	113.9
Eastern Europe	34.8	30.1	37.0	39.7	39.9	39.1	45.4	44.9	45.1	39.6	30.6
Canada	17.4	16.3	17.3	16.7	20.3	16.1	14.7	15.8	19.3	15.1	15.7

[1] Includes areas not shown separately. [2] Represents United Germany beginning, 1990.

Source: U.S. Energy Information Administration, 1975-84, *Outlook for U.S. Coal Imports;* thereafter, *Annual Prospects for World Coal Trade.*

No. 1209. Coal and Coke—Summary: 1970 to 1991

[Includes coal consumed at mines. Demonstrated coal reserve base for United States on Jan. 1, 1989, was an estimated 473 billion tons. Recoverability varies between 40 and 90 percent for individual deposits; 50 percent or more of overall U.S. coal reserve base is believed to be recoverable. See also *Historical Statistics, Colonial Times to 1970*, series M 93-126]

ITEM	Unit	1970	1980	1985	1987	1988	1989	1990	1991 [1]
Coal production, total [2] .	**Mil. sh. tons** . .	**613**	**830**	**884**	**919**	**950**	**981**	**1,029**	**996**
Value	Mil. dol.	3,882	20,453	22,277	21,101	20,890	21,330	(NA)	(NA)
Anthracite production	Mil. sh. tons . . .	9.7	6.1	4.7	3.6	3.6	3.3	3.5	3.4
Bituminous coal and lignite: [3]									
Number of mines	Number.	5,601	5,598	4,547	3,894	3,462	3,429	3,243	2,846
Production	Mil. sh. tons . . .	603	824	879	915	947	977	1,026	993
Value, total	Mil. dol.	3,774	20,196	22,061	21,050	20,828	21,260	22,274	21,598
Average per ton	Dollars	6.26	24.52	25.10	23.00	22.00	21.76	21.71	21.75
Exports	Mil. sh. tons . . .	71	90	93	80	95	101	106	109
Value	Mil. dol.	961	4,627	4,465	3,405	4,013	4,287	4,510	4,619
Imports	1,000 sh. tons .	36	1,194	1,952	1,747	2,134	2,851	2,699	3,390
Method of mining:									
Underground	Mil. sh. tons . . .	339	337	350	372	382	394	425	407
Surface	Mil. sh. tons . . .	264	487	529	543	568	587	605	589
Percent of total prod . .	Percent	43.8	59.1	60.2	59.4	59.8	59.8	58.7	59.1
Value	Mil. dol.	(Z)	30	70	(NA)	(NA)	(NA)	(NA)	(NA)
Consumption [4]	Mil. sh. tons . . .	523	703	818	837	884	890	895	888
Electric power utilities . .	Mil. sh. tons . . .	320	569	694	718	758	767	774	772
Industrial.	Mil. sh. tons . . .	184	126	116	112	118	118	116	109
Productivity average: [5]									
Daily employment	1,000	140	225	169	143	135	131	131	121
Days worked	Number	228	210	204	207	211	214	216	224
Tons per worker:									
Per day	Sh. tons.	18.84	16.32	23.13	28.19	30.30	31.75	32.90	35.18
Per year	Sh. tons.	4,296	3,427	4,719	5,835	6,393	6,795	7,106	7,880
Production, by State:									
Alabama	Mil. sh. tons . . .	20.6	26.4	27.8	25.5	26.5	28.0	29.0	27.3
Illinois	Mil. sh. tons . . .	65.1	62.5	59.2	59.2	58.6	59.3	60.4	60.3
Indiana	Mil. sh. tons . . .	22.3	30.9	33.3	34.2	31.3	33.6	35.9	31.5
Kentucky	Mil. sh. tons . . .	125.3	150.1	152.3	163.7	157.9	167.4	173.3	159.0
Montana	Mil. sh. tons . . .	3.4	29.9	33.3	34.4	38.9	37.7	37.6	38.2
Ohio	Mil. sh. tons . . .	55.4	39.4	35.6	35.6	34.0	33.7	35.3	30.6
Pennsylvania	Mil. sh. tons . . .	90.2	93.1	71.4	66.4	67.1	70.6	70.5	65.4
Virginia	Mil. sh. tons . . .	35.0	41.0	40.9	44.2	45.9	43.0	46.9	42.0
West Virginia	Mil. sh. tons . . .	144.1	121.6	127.8	135.9	145.0	153.6	169.2	167.4
Wyoming	Mil. sh. tons . . .	7.2	94.9	140.7	146.8	164.0	171.6	184.2	193.9
Other States.	Mil. sh. tons . . .	44.1	139.7	161.3	165.8	177.6	182.3	186.7	180.7
World production	Mil. sh. tons . .	3,295	4,103	4,783	4,994	5,109	5,253	5,211	(NA)
Coke production [6] . . .	**Mil. sh. tons** . .	**66.5**	**46.1**	**28.7**	**28.0**	**32.4**	**33.0**	**27.6**	**24.0**
Oven coke [7]	Mil. sh. tons . . .	65.7	46.1	28.7	28.0	32.4	33.0	27.6	24.0
Value of product at plant . . .	Mil. dol.	2,193	6,029	(NA)	(NA)	(NA)	(NA)	(NA)	(NA)
Coke and breeze	Mil. dol.	1,899	4,784	(NA)	(NA)	(NA)	(NA)	(NA)	(NA)
Avg. market value per ton . .	Dollars	28	103	103	(NA)	(NA)	(NA)	(NA)	(NA)
Coal carbonized	Mil. sh. tons . . .	96.5	66.7	41.1	37.0	41.9	41.4	38.9	33.9
Average value per ton . . .	Dollars	12.47	56.26	54.30	46.55	47.70	47.50	47.73	48.88
Yield of coke from coal	Percent	69.1	69.2	69.8	75.9	77.3	79.8	71.0	71.0

NA Not available. Z Less than $500,000. [1] Preliminary. [2] Includes bituminous coal, lignite, and anthracite. [3] All domestic product data for 1970 is for mines producing 1,000 short tons or more per year; thereafter, data are for all mines. [4] Includes some categories not shown separately. [5] Data for 1970 are for mines producing 1,000 short tons or more per year; thereafter, for mines producing 10,000 short tons or more. Beginning 1985, includes anthracite. [6] Includes beehive coke. [7] Prior to 1980, excludes screenings or breeze; thereafter, includes beehive and other nonrecoverables.

Source: 1970, U.S. Bureau of Mines, *Minerals Yearbook;* thereafter, U.S. Energy Information Administration, *Coal Production,* annual; *Annual Energy Review,* and *Quarterly Coal Report.*

No. 1210. Uranium Concentrate (U₃O₈) Industry—Summary: 1980 to 1991

[Middle demand case. See table 962. See also *Historical Statistics, Colonial Times to 1970*, series M 266-267]

ITEM	Unit	1980	1983	1984	1985	1986	1987	1988	1989	1990	1991
Production	1,000 sh. tons .	21.9	10.6	7.4	5.6	6.8	6.5	6.5	6.9	4.4	4.0
Net imports (U₃O₈)	1,000 sh. tons .	-1.1	2.4	5.2	3.2	6.4	7.5	6.4	5.6	12.1	9.8
Utility and Suppliers inventories											
(U₃O₈ equivalent)	1,000 sh. tons .	54.4	80.0	[1]74.7	[1]68.3	[1]66.2	[1]64.5	[1]59.1	[1]54.9	45.6	36.7
Price (1988 dol./lb. U₃O₈):											
Long-term contract price	Dollars	41.4	31.7	26.4	24.7	19.3	18.5	(NA)	(NA)	(NA)	(NA)
Spot market price	Dollars	45.0	26.8	19.4	17.0	18.1	17.3	14.5	14.2	(NA)	(NA)
Delivered price.	Dollars	39.9	44.6	[2]36.5	[2]33.6	[2]31.9	[2]19.6	[2]25.7	[2]27.8	(NA)	(NA)
Capital expenditures											
(1988 dollars).	Mil. dol.	1,107	78	43	37	29	63	36	35	(NA)	(NA)
Employment	1,000	19.9	5.6	3.6	2.4	2.1	2.0	2.1	1.6	1.3	1.0

NA Not available. [1] Includes natural U₃O₈ (uranium oxide), natural UF₆ (uranium hexafluoride), natural UF₆ under usage agreement, UF₆ at enrichment suppliers, enriched UF₆ and fabricated fuel. [2] Average U.S. contract prices and market price settlements.

Source: U.S. Department of Energy, *Domestic Uranium Mining and Milling Industry,* annual, and *Uranium Industry,* annual.

Figure 26.1
Single-Family Houses Sold and Sales Price: 1970 to 1992

Source: Chart prepared by U.S. Bureau of the Census. For data, see tables 1224, 1225, and 1227.

Figure 26.2
**Selected Characteristics and Features of
Housing in the United States: 1990**

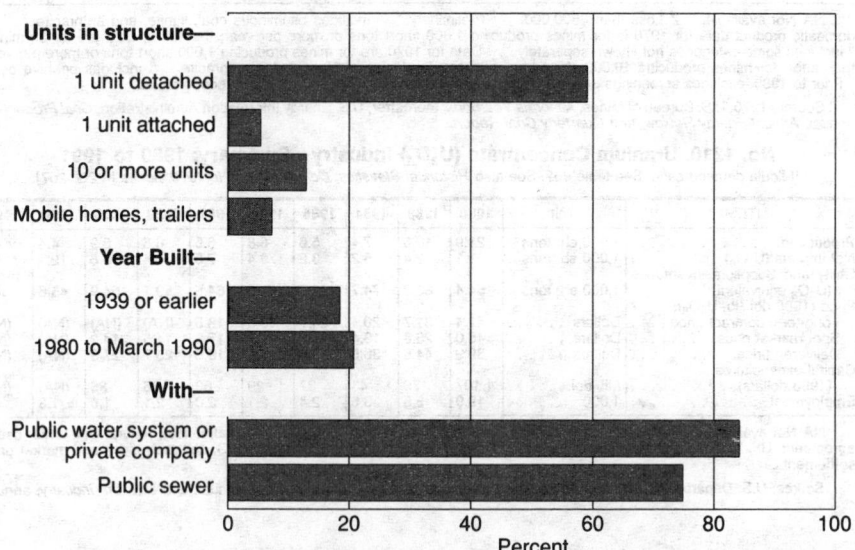

Source: Chart prepared by U.S. Bureau of the Census. For data, see tables 1233 and 1240.

Construction and Housing

This section presents data on the construction industry and on various indicators of its activity and costs; on housing units and their characteristics and occupants; and on the characteristics and vacancy rates for commercial buildings. Considerable data from the 1990 census are featured in tables 1223 to 1241.

The principal source of these data is the U.S. Bureau of the Census, which issues a variety of current publications. Construction statistics compiled by the Bureau appear in its monthly *Current Construction Reports* series with various quarterly or annual supplements; *Housing Starts* and *Housing Completions* present data by type of structure and by 4 major census regions; *New One-Family Houses Sold and For Sale* also provides statistics annually on physical and financial characteristics for all new housing by the 4 major census regions; *Price Index of New One-Family Houses Sold* presents quarterly figures and annual regional data; and *Housing Units Authorized by Building Permits* covers approximately 17,000 permit-issuing jurisdictions in the United States. Statistics on expenditures by owners of residential properties are issued quarterly and annually in *Expenditures for Residential Upkeep and Improvements*. *Value of New Construction Put in Place* presents data on all types of construction and includes monthly composite cost indexes. Reports of the censuses of construction industries (see below) are also issued on various topics.

Other Census Bureau publications include the *Current Housing Reports* series, which comprises the quarterly *Housing Vacancies*, the quarterly *Market Absorption of Apartments*, the American Housing Survey (formerly Annual Housing Survey) and reports of the censuses of housing and of construction industries. *Construction Review*, published quarterly by the International Trade Administration, U.S. Department of Commerce, contains many of the census series and other construction statistics series from the Federal Government and private agencies.

Other sources include the monthly *Dodge Construction Potentials* of F. W. Dodge Division, McGraw-Hill Information

In Brief

Construction contract value up almost 9% to $251 billion in 1992 from 1991.

New homes sold in 1992 increased to 610,000 from 509,000 in 1991.

Sales of existing single-family homes up over 9% in 1992 to 3.5 million.

Systems Company, New York, NY, which presents national and State data on construction contracts; the National Association of Home Builders with State-level data on housing starts; the NATIONAL ASSOCIATION OF REALTORS, which presents data on existing home sales; the Society of Industrial and Office Realtors and Oncor International on commercial office space; the Bureau of Economic Analysis, which presents data on residential capital and gross housing product; and the U.S. Energy Information Administration, which provides data on commercial buildings through its periodic sample surveys.

Censuses and surveys.—Censuses of the construction industry were first conducted by the Bureau of the Census for 1929, 1935, and 1939; beginning in 1967, a census has been taken every five years (for years ending in "2" and "7"). The latest reports are for 1987.

The 1987 Census of Construction Industries, in accordance with the 1987 *Standard Industrial Classification Manual* (see text, section 13), covers all employer establishments primarily engaged in (1) building construction by general contractors or operative builders; (2) heavy (non-building) construction by general contractors; and (3) construction by special trade contractors.

From 1850 through 1930, the Bureau of the Census collected some housing data as part of its censuses of population and agriculture. Beginning in 1940, separate censuses of housing have been taken at

10-year intervals. For the 1970 and 1980 censuses, data on year-round housing units were collected and issued on occupancy and structural characteristics, plumbing facilities, value, and rent; for 1990 such characteristics were presented for all housing units.

Evaluation studies of the 1950, 1960, 1970, and 1980 censuses estimated the underenumeration of occupied housing units at 2.9 percent, 2.4 percent, 1.7 percent, and 1.5 percent respectively. The missed rate in 1980 for all housing units was 2.6 percent or approximately 2.3 million units, 1 million of which were vacant housing units. Estimates for underenumeration from the 1990 census are not available at this time.

The American Housing Survey (*Current Housing Reports* series H-150 and H-170), which began in 1973, provided an annual and ongoing series of data on selected housing and demographic characteristics until 1983. In 1984 the name of the survey was changed from the Annual Housing Survey. It is currently based on a biennial national sample and on 11 annual MSA samples. All samples represent a cross section of the housing stock in their respective areas. Estimates are subject to both sampling and non-sampling errors; caution should therefore, be used in making comparisons with 1970 and 1980 census data.

Data on residential mortgages were collected continuously from 1890 to 1970, except 1930, as part of the decennial census by the Bureau of the Census. Since 1973, mortgage status data, which are limited to single family homes on less than ten acres with no business on the property, have been presented in the American Housing Survey.

Housing units.—In general, a housing unit is a group of rooms or a single room occupied or intended for occupancy as separate living quarters; that is, the occupants do not live and eat with any other persons in the structure and there is direct access from the outside or through a common hall. Transient accommodations, barracks for workers, and institutional-type quarters are not counted as housing units.

Statistical reliability.—For a discussion of statistical collection and estimation, sampling procedures, and measures of statistical reliability applicable to Census Bureau data, see Appendix III.

Historical statistics.—Tabular headnotes provide cross-references, where applicable, to *Historical Statistics of the United States, Colonial Times to 1970.* See Appendix IV.

No. 1211. Construction Industries—Summary, by Industry: 1987

[Based on a probability sample of about 160,000 construction establishments with payroll in 1987; see Appendix III. N.e.c. = Not elsewhere classified]

SIC [1] code	INDUSTRY	Estab-lish-ments with payroll (1,000)	EMPLOYEES (1,000)		PAYROLL (mil. dol.)		VALUE OF CONSTRUC-TION WORK (mil. dol.)		Value added [3] (mil. dol.)
			Total	Con-struction workers	Total	Con-struction workers	Total	Net[2]	
(X)	**All industries, total**	**544.2**	**5,054**	**3,989**	**111,067**	**79,742**	**499,982**	**367,746**	**230,174**
	Contract construction.	536.3	5,015	3,979	110,200	79,589	495,346	365,241	227,934
15	General building contractors.	157.6	1,278	926	27,870	17,204	212,629	111,019	65,514
1521	Single-family houses	90.4	396	307	6,272	4,343	39,098	27,319	14,970
1522	Other residential buildings.	8.1	82	61	1,752	1,130	13,316	6,257	3,659
1531	Operative builders	20.8	169	80	4,385	1,478	48,960	26,837	15,173
1541	Industrial buildings and warehouses . .	7.0	143	111	3,619	2,497	21,462	11,095	6,882
1542	Nonresidential buildings, n.e.c	31.3	488	367	11,843	7,756	89,793	39,510	24,831
16	Heavy construction contractors.	36.6	827	683	20,408	15,461	82,285	68,435	44,940
1611	Highway and street construction	11.0	284	239	7,041	5,397	34,161	27,984	17,120
1622	Bridge, tunnel, and elevated highway .	1.2	47	40	1,192	910	5,481	4,187	2,430
1623	Water, sewer, and utility lines	10.0	198	166	4,513	3,428	17,010	15,055	10,090
1629	Heavy construction, n.e.c	14.5	298	238	7,662	5,726	25,633	21,209	15,301
17	Special trade contractors.	342.0	2,909	2,370	61,921	46,923	200,434	185,786	117,480
1711	Plumbing, heating, air-conditioning . . .	69.6	617	471	14,330	10,311	49,503	44,518	25,912
1721	Painting and paperhanging	29.9	170	145	2,979	2,386	7,953	7,446	5,716
1731	Electrical work	49.4	509	406	12,664	9,622	35,838	34,658	21,817
1741	Masonry and other stonework	23.3	169	150	2,947	2,462	8,714	8,269	5,476
1742	Plastering, drywall, insulation.	17.8	254	217	5,485	4,348	16,427	15,137	9,748
1743	Terrazzo, tile, marble, and mosaic work	5.1	34	28	734	554	2,272	2,182	1,318
1751	Carpentry.	36.0	190	164	3,272	2,610	11,244	10,039	6,078
1752	Floorlaying and other floor work.	8.2	45	35	906	645	3,651	3,371	1,880
1761	Roofing, siding, and sheet metal work.	25.7	231	187	4,314	3,111	15,028	14,183	8,524
1771	Concrete work	23.4	218	187	4,175	3,278	15,056	13,854	8,443
1781	Water well drilling	3.4	18	14	335	249	1,330	1,299	780
1791	Structural steel erection	4.0	65	55	1,594	1,232	4,863	4,510	3,253
1793	Glass and glazing work	4.6	41	29	919	607	3,222	3,142	1,701
1794	Excavation work	13.4	95	79	2,060	1,598	8,244	7,491	5,708
1795	Wrecking and demolition work.	1.2	14	12	261	195	912	845	782
1796	Installing building equipment, n.e.c . . .	3.8	62	50	1,858	1,447	5,360	5,010	3,723
1799	Special trade contractors, n.e.c.	23.2	176	142	3,089	2,269	10,814	9,833	6,622
6552	Land subdividers and developers, n.e.c.	8.0	40	9	867	153	4,636	2,505	2,240

X Not applicable.   [1] Standard Industrial Classification; see, text, section 13.   [2] Value of construction work less payments for construction work subcontracted to others, not shown separately.   [3] Dollar value of business done less (a) payments for materials, components, and supplies, (b) payments for construction work subcontracted to others, not shown separately.
Source: U.S. Bureau of the Census, *Census of Construction Industries, 1987*, series CC87-I-28.

No. 1212. Construction Materials—Producer Price Indexes: 1980 to 1992

[1982 = 100, except as noted. For discussion of producer price index, see text, section 15. This index, more formally known as the special commodity grouping index for construction materials, covers materials incorporated as integral part of a building or normally installed during construction and not readily removable. Excludes consumer durables such as kitchen ranges, refrigerators, etc. This index is not the same as the stage-of-processing index of intermediate materials and components for construction. See *Historical Statistics, Colonial Times to 1970*, series N 140-155 for similar data]

COMMODITY	1980	1983	1984	1985	1986	1987	1988	1989	1990	1991	1992
Construction materials	**92.5**	**103.4**	**106.4**	**107.6**	**107.3**	**109.5**	**115.7**	**119.5**	**119.6**	**120.4**	**122.5**
Interior solvent based paint	91.3	100.0	103.9	107.3	109.9	111.6	120.3	128.8	133.0	140.2	141.7
Plastic construction products	103.9	110.1	115.5	108.6	106.4	108.4	121.1	120.1	117.2	115.1	112.7
Douglas fir, dressed	132.6	135.8	123.2	126.5	124.5	125.1	135.7	151.6	138.4	139.6	169.2
Southern pine, dressed	104.0	111.9	111.9	105.2	104.9	114.1	112.4	108.0	111.2	111.0	130.5
Millwork	93.2	108.2	110.2	111.7	113.7	117.7	121.9	127.3	130.4	135.5	143.2
Softwood plywood	109.5	110.0	107.6	107.4	109.4	109.8	109.1	124.2	119.6	120.8	147.0
Hardwood plywood and related products	97.5	99.3	99.6	89.9	91.0	92.9	94.2	99.8	102.7	102.8	106.9
Softwood plywood veneer, ex. reinforced/backed	126.0	103.1	103.3	100.1	105.9	108.4	117.3	142.1	142.3	138.5	166.2
Building paper and building board mill products .	86.1	104.4	108.2	107.4	108.8	111.2	113.3	115.6	112.2	111.8	119.6
Tube, drawn, 6000 alloy series	85.6	100.9	109.7	109.7	109.8	111.2	128.9	131.0	127.1	124.1	123.4
Builders hardware	84.9	104.8	109.3	113.5	115.8	117.4	122.5	127.8	133.0	138.1	141.3
Plumbing fixtures and brass fittings	88.5	103.8	108.6	111.9	115.5	119.7	128.7	137.7	144.3	149.7	153.1
Heating equipment	87.0	102.7	106.6	109.5	113.0	115.5	119.2	125.1	131.6	134.1	137.3
Metal doors, sash, and trim	87.8	102.8	106.6	107.3	108.9	112.0	122.4	130.0	131.4	134.6	134.9
Incandescent outdoor lighting fixtures	82.7	104.7	109.2	109.2	112.0	117.2	122.4	128.0	137.3	136.5	139.0
Bright nails	90.9	98.0	99.4	100.2	99.8	101.2	104.7	110.4	(NA)	(NA)	(NA)
Welded steel wire fabric for concrete reinforcing.	98.9	98.5	101.9	101.3	98.8	98.3	109.2	108.6	109.7	100.0	100.9
Elevators, escalators, and other lifts	87.3	97.3	97.1	99.7	99.2	100.4	103.6	107.1	110.1	108.7	109.4
Stamped metal outlet box	82.7	105.2	114.9	119.7	152.0	160.1	168.7	171.7	179.4	179.7	187.4
Concrete ingredients and related products	88.4	101.1	105.1	108.5	109.4	110.4	112.0	113.2	115.3	118.4	119.4
Concrete products	92.0	101.4	103.9	107.5	109.2	109.4	110.0	111.2	113.5	116.6	117.2
Clay construction products exc. refractories . . .	88.8	106.5	110.0	113.5	118.0	121.4	124.9	127.0	129.9	130.2	132.0
Prep. asphalt and tar roofing and siding products.	105.5	94.1	97.7	100.5	96.8	91.9	94.4	95.6	97.1	96.2	94.3
Gypsum products	100.1	111.7	135.4	132.3	137.0	125.2	112.9	110.0	105.2	99.3	100.3
Insulation materials.	80.7	103.7	104.0	105.2	105.7	105.0	105.8	106.7	108.4	110.8	102.3
Paving mixtures and blocks	83.7	100.9	106.1	111.6	104.9	100.8	102.7	101.0	101.2	103.2	100.0

NA Not available.

Source: U.S. Bureau of Labor Statistics, *Producer Price Indexes*, monthly and annual.

No. 1213. Price and Cost Indexes for Construction: 1980 to 1992

[1987=100. Excludes Alaska and Hawaii. Indexes of certain sources are published on bases different from those shown here. See *Historical Statistics, Colonial Times to 1970*, series N 118-137, for construction cost indexes on a 1947-49 base]

NAME OF INDEX	1980	1983	1984	1985	1986	1988	1989	1990	1991	1992
Bureau of the Census:										
Composite fixed-weighted [1]	77.6	86.6	90.2	93.1	96.5	103.8	107.4	110.3	111.2	111.8
Implicit price deflator [2]	79.1	88.7	91.2	93.9	96.8	104.1	108.3	111.2	111.8	112.2
Bureau of the Census houses under construction: [3]										
Fixed-weighted	75.6	85.0	88.8	91.0	95.6	103.6	107.0	110.2	110.6	112.0
Price deflator	77.9	87.7	90.1	92.0	95.8	104.1	108.4	111.5	111.7	112.7
Federal Highway Administration, composite [4]	97.2	87.6	92.6	102.0	101.1	106.6	107.7	108.5	107.5	105.1
Bureau of Reclamation composite [5]	81	95	96	98	99	103	107	111	114	116
Turner Construction Co.: Building construction [6]	69	86	91	94	97	104	107	111	113	113
E. H. Boeckh, building cost index: [7]										
Residences	(NA)	88.5	93.5	96.2	98.0	102.5	106.3	109.9	113.0	116.7
Apartments, hotels, and office buildings	(NA)	90.7	94.8	96.3	98.0	102.7	106.2	109.0	112.0	114.9
Commercial and factory buildings	(NA)	91.5	95.0	96.7	98.3	103.0	107.2	110.8	114.2	117.4
Engineering News-Record: [8]										
Buildings	76.5	93.8	95.1	95.5	97.7	102.2	103.6	106.3	108.3	111.5
Construction	73.5	92.3	94.1	95.2	97.5	102.6	104.7	107.4	109.7	113.1
Handy-Whitman public utility: [9]										
Buildings	83	89	94	96	98	104	107	108	105	107
Electric [10]	80	95	97	98	99	107	111	115	116	118
Gas [11]	79	97	100	100	97	106	111	114	116	118
Water [11]	81	91	94	97	98	103	106	108	108	110
C. A. Turner Telephone Plant [12]	102	103	99	101	100	101	110	113	114	114

NA Not available. [1] Weighted average of the various indexes used to deflate the Construction Put in Place series. In calculating the index, the weights (i.e., the composition of current dollar estimates in 1987 by category) are held constant. [2] Derived ratio of total current to constant dollar Construction Put in Place (multiplied by 100). [3] Excludes value of site. [4] Based on average contract unit bid prices for composite mile (involving specific average amounts of excavation, paving, reinforcing steel, structural steel, and structural concrete). [5] Derived from the four quarterly indexes which are weighted averages of costs of labor, materials, and equipment for the construction of dams and reclamation projects. [6] Based on firm's cost experience with respect to labor rates, materials prices, competitive conditions, efficiency of plant and management, and productivity. [7] Average of 20 cities for types shown. Weights based on surveys of building costs. [8] Building index computed on the basis of a hypothetical unit of construction requiring 6 bbl. of portland cement, 1,088 M bd. ft. of 2" x 4" lumber, 2,500 lb. of structural steel, and 68.38 hours of skilled labor. Construction index based on same materials components combined with 200 hours of common labor. [9] Based on data covering public utility construction costs in six geographic regions. Covers skilled and common labor. [10] As derived by U.S. Bureau of the Census. Covers steam generation plants only. [11] As derived by U.S. Bureau of the Census. Reflects costs for structures and improvements at water pumping and treatment plants. [12] Computed by the Census Bureau by averaging the weighted component indexes published for six geographic regions.

No. 1214. Value of New Construction Put in Place: 1964 to 1992

[In millions of dollars. Represents value of construction put in place during year; differs from building permit and construction contract data in timing and coverage. Includes installed cost of normal building service equipment and selected types of industrial production equipment (largely site fabricated). Excludes cost of shipbuilding, land, and most types of machinery and equipment. For methodology, see Appendix III. See also *Historical Statistics, Colonial Times to 1970*, series N 1-29 and N 66-69]

YEAR	CURRENT DOLLARS					CONSTANT (1987) DOLLARS				
	Total	Private			Public	Total	Private			Public
		Total	Residential buildings	Nonresidential buildings			Total	Residential buildings	Nonresidential buildings	
1964	72,124	51,921	30,526	14,412	20,203	294,569	211,627	124,768	60,892	82,942
1970	100,727	72,819	35,863	23,008	27,908	309,244	225,168	114,138	71,796	84,077
1971	117,311	87,612	48,514	24,204	29,699	337,451	254,502	145,554	69,621	82,949
1972	133,318	103,288	60,693	26,568	30,030	360,780	281,593	170,190	71,490	79,187
1973	146,826	114,477	65,085	30,683	32,348	364,938	285,937	166,249	76,259	79,001
1974	147,476	109,344	55,967	32,195	38,132	319,362	242,274	130,126	70,029	77,089
1975	145,623	102,330	51,581	28,397	43,293	290,137	208,991	109,920	58,990	81,147
1976	165,441	121,462	68,273	27,936	43,979	315,865	235,338	136,685	55,617	80,527
1977	193,126	150,044	92,004	30,871	43,083	340,833	266,393	165,926	57,134	74,440
1978	230,178	180,032	109,838	39,135	50,146	362,862	285,880	174,695	65,343	76,982
1979	259,839	203,194	116,444	51,732	56,646	364,554	288,789	165,116	77,359	75,766
1980	259,746	196,100	100,381	58,290	63,646	328,435	252,645	128,926	78,972	75,790
1981	271,950	207,259	99,241	68,450	64,691	320,950	247,427	118,343	85,091	73,523
1982	260,594	197,531	84,676	73,953	63,064	297,759	226,510	97,595	87,505	71,249
1983	294,945	231,494	125,571	70,438	63,450	332,625	261,398	143,108	80,888	71,227
1984	348,817	278,600	153,849	87,493	70,217	382,435	306,152	170,732	96,664	76,284
1985	377,366	299,543	158,474	103,455	77,823	401,967	321,706	172,338	111,262	80,260
1986	407,693	323,100	187,148	98,674	84,593	421,367	335,709	195,377	102,596	85,658
1987	419,366	328,738	194,656	100,933	90,628	419,352	328,637	194,622	100,877	90,715
1988	432,304	337,516	194,101	106,994	94,789	415,084	324,404	190,292	103,037	90,680
1989	443,401	345,328	196,551	113,988	98,073	409,494	318,583	181,321	105,711	90,912
1990	442,065	334,153	182,856	117,971	107,912	397,547	299,638	163,980	106,067	97,909
1991	400,955	290,706	157,835	97,841	110,249	358,549	259,583	141,300	87,608	98,967
1992	425,807	307,067	183,045	85,360	118,740	379,479	271,744	162,230	75,746	107,735

Source: U.S. Bureau of the Census, *Current Construction Reports*, series C30, and press release, CB-92-14.

No. 1215. Value of New Construction Put in Place in Current and Constant (1987) Dollars: 1985 to 1992

[In millions of dollars. Represents value of construction put in place during year; differs from building permit and construction contract data in timing and coverage. Includes installed cost of normal building service equipment and selected types of industrial production equipment (largely site fabricated). Excludes cost of shipbuilding, land, and most types of machinery and equipment. For details on derivation of constant values and description of revised series, see source. For description of nature of revisions and deflators used, see *Construction Reports*, series C30-9005. For methodology, see Appendix III. See also *Historical Statistics, Colonial Times to 1970*, series N 1-29 and N 66-69]

TYPE OF CONSTRUCTION	CURRENT DOLLARS					CONSTANT (1987) DOLLARS				
	1985	1989	1990	1991	1992, prel.	1985	1989	1990	1991	1992, prel.
Total new construction .	377,366	443,401	442,065	400,955	425,807	401,967	409,494	397,547	358,549	379,479
Private construction	299,543	345,328	334,153	290,706	[1]307,067	321,706	318,583	299,638	259,583	[1]271,744
Residential buildings	158,474	196,551	182,856	157,835	183,045	172,338	181,321	163,980	141,300	162,230
New housing units	114,662	139,202	127,987	110,592	130,016	124,699	128,435	114,784	99,002	115,234
One unit	86,123	116,898	108,737	95,444	117,030	93,659	107,849	97,518	85,435	103,706
Two or more units. . . .	28,539	22,304	19,250	15,148	12,986	31,040	20,586	17,266	13,567	11,528
Improvements	43,812	57,349	54,869	47,243	(NA)	47,639	52,886	49,196	42,297	(NA)
Nonresidential buildings . . .	103,455	113,988	117,971	97,841	85,360	111,262	105,711	106,067	87,608	75,746
Industrial.	17,116	20,410	23,848	22,280	20,155	18,408	18,919	21,441	19,951	17,892
Office.	34,276	31,538	28,722	23,010	16,901	36,867	29,263	25,829	20,604	15,010
Hotels, motels	7,925	8,401	9,673	6,286	3,409	8,524	7,791	8,699	5,630	3,025
Other commercial.	30,443	33,958	34,140	25,470	23,328	32,734	31,482	30,693	22,805	20,689
Religious	2,615	3,278	3,390	3,415	3,471	2,811	3,040	3,046	3,058	3,077
Educational.	2,058	3,648	4,219	3,929	4,111	2,213	3,382	3,792	3,518	3,649
Hospital and institutional .	6,060	8,312	9,450	9,189	10,085	6,521	7,711	8,494	8,228	8,946
Miscellaneous [2]	2,962	4,443	4,528	4,260	3,900	3,186	4,122	4,072	3,814	3,459
Farm nonresidential.	2,197	2,449	2,670	2,592	(NA)	2,366	2,271	2,400	2,321	(NA)
Public utilities	32,692	29,881	27,699	29,225	(NA)	32,989	27,003	24,504	25,488	(NA)
Telecommunications. . . .	8,397	9,465	9,565	8,816	(NA)	8,264	8,525	8,498	7,759	(NA)
Other public utilities	24,295	20,416	18,134	20,409	(NA)	24,725	18,478	16,006	17,728	(NA)
Railroads.	4,046	2,650	2,382	2,650	(NA)	4,079	2,452	2,164	2,363	(NA)
Electric light and power .	16,460	13,038	10,521	10,699	(NA)	16,871	11,778	9,234	9,284	(NA)
Gas	3,517	4,386	4,820	6,436	(NA)	3,504	3,941	4,246	5,543	(NA)
Petroleum pipelines. . . .	272	342	411	624	(NA)	271	307	362	537	(NA)
All other private [3]	2,726	2,460	2,957	3,213	4,179	2,751	2,276	2,688	2,867	3,797
Public construction.	77,823	98,073	107,912	110,249	118,740	80,260	90,912	97,909	98,967	107,735
Buildings	27,861	39,808	46,208	50,475	53,085	30,000	36,891	41,523	45,189	47,106
Housing and development	2,893	3,471	3,498	3,496	3,282	3,146	3,203	3,136	3,131	2,915
Industrial.	1,968	1,300	1,433	1,823	1,885	2,118	1,205	1,289	1,633	1,672
Educational.	9,329	17,258	20,976	23,769	24,401	10,033	15,996	18,847	21,278	21,645
Hospital	2,497	2,538	2,646	2,672	3,189	2,686	2,353	2,380	2,393	2,829
Other [4]	11,174	15,241	17,654	18,713	20,328	12,016	14,133	15,871	16,755	18,045
Highways and streets.	23,741	28,837	31,155	29,918	32,884	23,455	26,754	28,729	27,210	31,528
Military facilities.	3,235	3,520	2,665	1,837	2,490	3,341	3,261	2,427	1,660	2,295
Conservation and development	5,144	5,008	4,607	4,959	6,094	5,279	4,627	4,135	4,338	5,260
Sewer systems	6,960	8,868	9,914	10,013	9,799	7,139	8,193	8,886	8,761	8,461
Water supply facilities	2,580	3,779	4,747	4,970	4,940	2,671	3,549	4,379	4,605	4,499
Miscellaneous public [5] . . .	8,302	8,254	8,616	8,077	9,449	8,374	7,637	7,830	7,205	8,586

NA Not available.   [1] Includes estimates for types of construction indicated as (NA).   [2] Includes amusement and recreational buildings, bus and airline terminals, animal hospitals and shelters, etc.   [3] Includes privately owned streets and bridges, parking areas, sewer and water facilities, parks and playgrounds, golf courses, airfields, etc.   [4] Includes federal administrative buildings, prisons, police and fire stations, courthouses, civic centers, passenger terminals, space facilities, postal facilities, etc.   [5] Includes open amusement and recreational facilities, power generating facilities, transit systems, airfields, open parking facilities, etc.

Source: U.S. Bureau of the Census, *Current Construction Reports,* series C30, monthly.

No. 1216. Value of Privately Owned Nonresidential Building Projects, by Construction Status, 1980 to 1992, and by Type of Project, 1992

[In billions of dollars]

CONSTRUCTION STATUS	1980	1985	1986	1987	1988	1989	1990	1991	1992				
									Total	Industrial	Office building	Other commercial	Other[1]
Value of projects—													
Started	53.8	98.5	97.1	95.7	107.7	110.9	89.5	72.9	76.2	14.4	13.6	24.2	24.0
Completed	53.0	89.9	107.5	91.4	101.6	107.7	114.0	109.5	99.3	24.4	23.4	25.2	24.0

[1] Privately owned hotels and motels, religious, educational, hospital and institutional, and miscellaneous nonresidential building projects.

Source: U.S. Bureau of the Census, *Current Construction Reports,* series C30.

No. 1217. Construction Contracts—Value of Construction and Floor Space of Buildings, by Class of Construction: 1980 to 1992

[Includes new structures and additions, and major alterations to existing structures which affect only valuation, since no additional floor area is created by "alteration." See also *Historical Statistics, Colonial Times to 1970*, series N 7888-100]

YEAR	Total	Resi-dential build-ings	NONRESIDENTIAL BUILDINGS									Non-build-ing con-struc-tion
			Total	Com-mer-cial [1]	Manu-fac-turing	Educa-tional [2]	Hos-pital	Public build-ings	Reli-gious	Social and recrea-tional	Mis-cella-neous	
VALUE (bil. dol.)												
1980	151.8	60.4	56.9	27.7	9.2	7.4	5.4	1.6	1.2	2.7	1.7	34.5
1981	157.3	56.3	65.5	35.2	9.3	6.6	6.4	1.4	1.2	3.4	2.0	35.4
1982	157.1	55.0	64.6	32.3	9.6	6.8	8.0	1.9	1.2	2.8	2.0	37.5
1983	194.1	88.4	67.9	38.3	5.4	7.1	8.5	2.1	1.5	2.9	2.1	37.8
1984	214.3	95.3	82.1	48.2	7.9	8.5	7.4	2.7	1.7	3.3	2.4	36.9
1985	235.8	102.1	92.3	54.6	8.1	10.0	7.8	3.1	2.0	4.0	2.5	41.4
1986	249.3	115.6	91.6	52.4	7.3	11.7	7.9	3.2	2.1	4.2	2.8	42.1
1987	259.0	114.1	98.8	53.7	8.6	13.2	9.0	4.7	2.1	4.3	3.2	46.1
1988	262.2	116.2	97.9	51.6	9.5	14.1	8.2	4.4	2.2	4.7	3.2	48.1
1989	271.3	116.2	106.1	53.6	12.7	15.9	8.8	5.2	2.0	5.0	2.9	49.0
1990	246.2	100.9	95.5	45.0	8.4	16.6	9.2	5.7	2.2	5.3	3.1	49.7
1991	230.9	94.5	86.2	32.7	8.3	19.0	9.6	6.2	2.4	5.0	3.0	50.2
1992	250.8	110.6	86.7	32.7	8.7	17.6	10.8	5.8	2.5	5.6	3.1	53.5
FLOOR SPACE (mil. sq. ft.)												
1980	3,102	1,839	1,263	738	220	103	55	18	28	49	52	(X)
1981	2,805	1,562	1,243	787	188	83	60	14	25	46	41	(X)
1982	2,455	1,440	1,015	631	119	82	71	19	25	38	30	(X)
1983	3,387	2,276	1,111	716	112	84	84	20	29	36	31	(X)
1984	3,661	2,311	1,350	901	157	100	70	23	29	37	34	(X)
1985	3,853	2,324	1,529	1,039	165	111	73	28	32	44	38	(X)
1986	3,935	2,481	1,454	960	148	129	73	30	32	44	39	(X)
1987	3,757	2,288	1,469	933	160	139	78	42	32	46	38	(X)
1988	3,594	2,181	1,414	883	162	142	71	38	32	49	37	(X)
1989	3,516	2,115	1,400	867	158	152	72	41	27	48	35	(X)
1990	3,024	1,817	1,204	696	128	152	69	47	29	51	32	(X)
1991	2,626	1,655	981	477	100	177	71	50	29	44	33	(X)
1992	2,801	1,864	937	461	95	156	77	42	30	43	33	(X)

X Not applicable.   [1] Includes nonindustrial warehouses.   [2] Includes science.

No. 1218. Construction Contracts—Value, by State: 1985 to 1992

[**In millions of dollars.** See headnote, table 1217. Represents value of construction in States in which work was actually done]

STATE	1985	1990	1991	1992 Total (incl. non-bldg.)	1992 Resi-den-tial	1992 Non-resi-den-tial	STATE	1985	1990	1991	1992 Total (incl. non-bldg.)	1992 Resi-den-tial	1992 Non-resi-den-tial
U.S	235,819	246,234	230,922	250,829	110,630	86,744	MO	3,935	3,833	3,994	4,391	2,051	1,415
							MT	698	332	522	604	248	153
AL	2,949	2,939	2,777	3,228	1,644	1,002	NE	1,040	1,318	1,298	1,538	604	448
AK	1,507	1,919	768	905	206	455	NV	1,789	3,334	2,642	3,990	1,385	1,808
AZ	6,617	4,553	4,690	5,345	3,127	1,468	NH	1,355	1,021	863	1,009	492	356
AR	1,649	1,438	1,772	2,022	1,007	544	NJ	8,222	6,191	6,121	5,497	1,683	2,031
CA	33,039	37,381	30,280	27,215	11,575	10,071	NM	1,778	1,123	1,405	1,352	539	427
CO	4,678	3,235	4,599	5,788	2,391	1,643	NY	12,000	14,166	12,568	14,162	3,911	5,713
CT	3,583	3,058	2,860	2,897	974	1,391	NC	6,664	6,626	6,955	8,013	4,110	2,493
DE	739	787	791	783	298	249	ND	557	506	467	587	217	176
DC	985	795	624	745	48	571	OH	6,999	9,902	9,442	10,757	4,609	4,097
FL	18,155	17,004	15,401	16,741	8,960	4,672	OK	2,660	2,164	2,046	2,487	1,020	879
GA	7,618	7,128	7,243	8,110	4,497	2,459	OR	1,634	3,103	2,590	2,864	1,578	824
HI	873	2,831	2,790	2,866	993	1,111	PA	7,040	10,106	9,461	9,992	3,872	4,136
ID	758	986	1,051	1,276	794	314	RI	829	594	763	651	271	262
IL	7,958	10,800	9,039	10,638	4,362	3,765	SC	3,463	3,664	3,761	3,435	1,881	1,117
IN	4,051	6,350	5,391	6,435	3,051	2,407	SD	485	468	356	586	226	151
IA	1,507	2,034	2,229	2,174	901	693	TN	4,456	4,388	4,358	5,273	2,717	1,620
KS	2,370	2,193	2,307	2,543	1,181	755	TX	21,418	13,198	14,740	16,472	7,199	5,865
KY	2,848	3,176	3,858	3,856	1,754	1,332	UT	1,647	1,884	1,662	2,038	1,040	648
LA	3,867	3,192	2,930	3,056	998	1,071	VT	484	515	581	584	330	156
ME	784	897	862	1,161	551	315	VA	7,591	7,183	6,455	7,346	3,497	2,079
MD	5,699	6,057	5,068	5,252	2,896	1,568	WA	4,376	6,185	6,426	7,521	3,600	2,598
MA	6,237	5,138	5,135	5,736	2,004	2,049	WV	858	1,253	856	1,091	184	445
MI	5,855	7,649	7,140	7,453	3,380	2,882	WI	3,038	4,655	4,198	4,942	2,331	1,824
MN	4,236	4,951	4,409	5,242	2,683	1,565	WY	698	462	473	468	109	124
MS	1,543	1,569	1,906	1,716	648	548							

Source of tables 1217 and 1218: F. W. Dodge, National Information Services Division, McGraw-Hill Information Systems Company, New York, NY. Figures reported currently in *Dodge Construction Potentials*.

No. 1219. New Privately-Owned Housing Units Authorized, by State: 1991 and 1992

[Based on about 17,000 places in United States having building permit systems]

STATE	HOUSING UNITS (1,000) 1991	1992 Total	1992 1 unit	VALUATION (mil. dol.) 1991	1992 Total	1992 1 unit	STATE	HOUSING UNITS (1,000) 1991	1992 Total	1992 1 unit	VALUATION (mil. dol.) 1991	1992 Total	1992 1 unit
U.S.	948.8	1,105.9	918.5	78,772	96,187	87,669	MO...	16.1	21.3	17.4	1,122	1,601	1,455
							MT...	1.5	2.0	1.7	111	165	145
AL....	11.3	13.0	10.4	692	865	791	NE...	6.2	6.7	5.1	387	459	415
AK...	1.0	1.2	1.0	137	143	135	NV...	21.0	17.1	13.4	1,280	1,233	1,075
AZ...	23.5	31.3	28.9	2,262	3,087	2,956	NH...	3.5	3.6	3.3	304	322	307
AR...	6.9	7.8	6.1	386	504	454	NJ....	14.9	18.5	15.5	1,245	1,534	1,404
CA...	106.0	97.3	75.8	11,990	11,274	9,828	NM...	6.1	7.1	6.8	471	602	593
CO...	14.1	23.2	20.6	1,512	2,584	2,451	NY...	28.6	29.0	22.8	2,421	2,668	2,361
CT...	7.5	8.4	7.5	667	839	800	NC...	39.0	49.4	42.7	2,803	3,849	3,643
DE...	4.3	4.6	4.3	238	285	267	ND...	2.1	2.4	1.3	112	148	118
DC...	0.3	0.1	0.1	17	7	6	OH...	35.8	45.3	33.7	3,147	4,072	3,663
FL....	95.3	103.5	84.6	7,087	8,563	7,540	OK...	5.9	7.1	7.1	488	616	613
GA...	37.6	45.6	43.2	2,701	3,559	3,477	OR...	16.4	17.3	13.5	1,382	1,676	1,508
HI....	9.2	7.8	4.6	1,138	850	559	PA...	34.6	39.2	35.7	2,798	3,408	3,241
ID....	6.6	9.6	7.6	519	753	676	RI...	2.4	2.6	* 2.3	181	208	202
IL....	32.8	40.0	31.8	3,189	3,900	3,439	SC...	18.7	18.9	16.5	1,353	1,469	1,380
IN....	23.9	30.6	25.8	1,995	2,674	2,509	SD...	2.5	2.9	2.0	147	187	156
IA...	8.0	11.0	7.5	603	817	689	TN...	19.3	26.4	24.2	1,359	2,020	1,956
KS...	7.8	9.3	8.1	644	850	804	TX...	51.9	62.9	53.4	4,301	5,497	5,215
KY...	12.0	14.7	11.5	784	1,017	922	UT...	8.9	14.4	12.3	778	1,208	1,127
LA...	7.2	9.8	9.0	509	701	677	VT...	2.0	2.2	1.9	167	184	164
ME...	3.7	3.9	3.7	280	311	298	VA...	33.7	40.7	35.5	2,490	3,130	2,924
MD...	25.2	34.0	29.9	1,915	2,620	2,459	WA...	33.0	39.9	29.8	2,644	3,499	2,936
MA...	12.7	16.3	15.1	1,265	1,712	1,644	WV...	2.0	2.2	1.9	126	147	139
MI...	33.8	39.4	32.7	2,597	3,088	2,852	WI...	25.1	31.7	20.7	1,798	2,369	1,960
MN...	21.1	25.9	22.4	1,882	2,468	2,307	WY...	0.6	1.0	0.9	62	99	97
MS...	5.2	5.8	5.1	285	348	330							

Source: U.S. Bureau of the Census, *Construction Reports*, series C40, annual.

No. 1220. Valuation of Construction Authorized by Permit, by Type of Construction and State: 1992

[In millions of dollars]

STATE	Total [1]	Residential	NONRESIDENTIAL Total [2]	Industrial	Office	Stores	STATE	Total [1]	Residential	NONRESIDENTIAL Total [2]	Industrial	Office	Stores
U.S..	176,697	96,187	31,614	4,436	5,743	10,284	MO..	3,218	1,601	640	73	83	210
							MT...	333	165	69	1	15	44
AL...	1,965	865	522	117	120	157	NE...	846	459	153	24	29	42
AK...	339	143	95	3	10	59	NV...	2,024	1,233	408	40	56	99
AZ...	4,323	3,087	535	36	124	218	NH...	614	322	98	6	3	50
AR...	1,051	504	303	64	36	128	NJ...	3,871	1,534	584	82	102	93
CA...	22,798	11,274	4,040	624	713	1,433	NM...	929	602	101	9	22	38
CO...	3,787	2,584	384	48	97	91	NY...	6,026	2,668	1,283	112	172	579
CT...	2,063	839	306	51	63	66	NC...	6,317	3,849	1,091	180	182	274
DE...	595	285	103	2	23	37	ND...	313	148	68	19	8	20
DC...	103	7	15	-	7	4	OH...	7,362	4,072	1,316	197	200	475
FL...	13,615	8,563	2,124	144	287	790	OK...	1,156	616	280	48	27	116
GA...	5,854	3,559	1,117	227	121	439	OR...	2,710	1,676	408	114	49	103
HI...	1,666	850	356	10	63	124	PA...	7,432	3,408	1,785	197	489	318
ID...	1,172	753	187	14	44	61	RI...	395	208	44	5	9	13
IL....	7,463	3,900	1,334	201	272	449	SC...	2,724	1,469	569	51	101	199
IN...	4,909	2,674	1,081	173	228	367	SD...	406	187	72	5	13	24
IA...	1,646	817	361	82	68	102	TN...	3,916	2,020	835	106	150	205
KS...	1,471	850	232	41	41	71	TX...	10,161	5,497	1,923	186	458	711
KY...	1,858	1,017	361	78	55	116	UT...	1,816	1,208	292	41	81	80
LA...	1,366	701	304	31	39	103	VT...	379	184	97	33	5	15
ME...	666	311	152	7	27	71	VA...	5,453	3,130	855	76	258	280
MD...	4,262	2,620	451	22	102	146	WA..	5,724	3,499	1,021	256	193	306
MA...	3,668	1,712	538	66	54	121	WV..	371	147	93	6	9	42
MI...	5,957	3,088	1,063	181	176	362	WI...	4,477	2,369	795	172	181	175
MN...	4,236	2,468	573	151	53	161	WY..	201	99	41	3	10	19
MS...	692	348	160	19	16	79							

- Represents zero.   [1] Includes residential and nonresidential additions and alterations, residential nonhousekeeping buildings, and residential garages and carports, not shown separately.   [2] Includes other types of construction not shown separately.

Source: U.S. Bureau of the Census, unpublished data.

No. 1221. New Privately-Owned Housing Units Started—Selected Characteristics: 1970 to 1992

[In thousands. For composition of regions, see table 31. See also *Historical Statistics, Colonial Times to 1970*, series N 156-163 and 170]

YEAR	Total units	STRUCTURES WITH—			REGION				CONDOMINIUM UNITS [1]		
		One unit	2 to 4 units	5 or more units	North-east	Mid-west	South	West	Total	Single-family	Multi-family
1970	1,434	813	85	536	218	294	612	311	(NA)	(NA)	(NA)
1971	2,052	1,151	120	781	264	434	869	486	(NA)	(NA)	(NA)
1972	2,357	1,309	141	906	330	443	1,057	527	(NA)	(NA)	(NA)
1973	2,045	1,132	118	795	277	440	899	429	241	69	172
1974	1,338	888	68	382	183	317	553	285	175	46	130
1975	1,160	892	64	204	149	294	442	275	65	20	45
1976	1,538	1,162	86	289	169	400	569	400	95	30	64
1977	1,987	1,451	122	414	202	465	783	538	118	41	77
1978	2,020	1,433	125	462	200	451	824	545	156	42	114
1979	1,745	1,194	122	429	178	349	748	470	198	43	156
1980	1,292	852	110	331	125	218	643	306	186	35	150
1981	1,084	705	91	288	117	165	562	240	181	36	145
1982	1,062	663	80	320	117	149	591	205	170	40	130
1983	1,703	1,068	113	522	168	218	935	382	276	77	199
1984	1,750	1,084	121	544	204	243	866	436	291	96	194
1985	1,742	1,072	93	576	252	240	782	468	225	79	146
1986	1,805	1,179	84	542	294	296	733	483	214	80	134
1987	1,620	1,146	65	409	269	298	634	420	196	73	123
1988	1,488	1,081	59	348	235	274	575	404	148	53	95
1989	1,376	1,003	55	318	179	266	536	396	118	37	82
1990	1,193	895	37	260	131	253	479	329	75	22	53
1991	1,014	840	36	138	113	233	414	254	60	21	39
1992	1,200	1,030	31	139	127	288	497	288	74	35	40

NA Not available.   [1] Type of ownership under which the owners of the individual housing units are also joint owners of the common areas of the building or community. Includes a small number of cooperatively-owned units.

Source: U.S. Bureau of the Census, *Construction Reports*, series C20, monthly.

No. 1222. New Privately-Owned Housing Units Started, by State: 1985 to 1992

[In thousands of units]

REGION, DIVISION, AND STATE	1985	1990	1991	1992 Total units	1992 Single-family units
U.S.	1,741.0	1,193.0	1,014.0	1,200.0	1,033.0
Northeast	251.0	131.0	113.0	132.0	119.0
N.E.	90.8	39.1	33.5	40.3	37.4
ME.	7.8	5.4	3.8	4.4	4.3
NH.	15.5	4.8	3.5	4.2	4.0
VT.	3.7	2.8	2.2	2.5	2.3
MA.	34.6	14.7	12.9	16.4	15.4
RI	4.8	3.2	2.8	3.2	3.0
CT	24.3	8.3	8.2	9.5	8.5
M.A.	160.2	91.6	79.2	91.8	81.7
NY.	60.4	35.5	27.6	30.1	26.1
NJ.	56.3	18.5	16.3	19.4	16.7
PA.	43.5	37.6	35.5	42.3	38.9
Midwest	241.0	254.0	234.0	306.0	260.0
E.N.C.	149.2	184.3	161.6	210.0	173.4
OH.	30.2	45.4	39.8	52.5	43.4
IN.	21.3	29.5	27.1	37.7	34.0
IL.	42.4	39.7	35.7	46.3	38.3
MI.	38.3	41.4	33.3	39.6	31.0
WI.	17.1	28.3	25.7	33.9	26.7
W.N.C.	91.8	70.6	72.3	96.5	86.8
MN.	25.7	22.0	23.3	29.2	26.0
IA.	4.6	9.4	9.6	14.8	12.6
MO.	33.4	17.7	17.9	23.1	21.4
ND.	1.9	1.9	2.5	2.8	2.2
SD.	2.7	3.2	2.8	3.6	3.2
NE.	5.4	7.4	7.3	9.6	8.6
KS.	18.1	9.1	8.9	13.4	12.9
South	782.0	479.0	414.0	490.0	429.0
S.A.	496.5	329.3	268.8	313.4	273.9
DE.	4.9	6.1	5.5	6.7	6.0
MD.	39.3	32.2	21.9	26.3	22.8
DC.	0.7	0.3	0.4	0.3	0.1
VA.	74.6	43.9	32.5	37.2	33.0
WV.	2.0	2.5	2.4	2.8	2.5
NC.	82.6	51.6	43.1	53.3	46.7
SC.	30.8	22.4	21.6	25.4	22.0
GA.	67.9	43.5	39.3	45.2	43.2
FL.	193.8	126.8	102.1	116.2	97.2
E.S.C.	93.6	67.0	61.0	76.8	67.4
KY.	19.9	15.2	13.9	19.3	15.8
TN.	45.5	26.4	24.1	28.7	26.2
AL.	19.3	18.3	16.5	21.0	18.5
MS.	8.9	7.1	6.5	7.7	6.9
W.S.C.	191.9	83.6	84.8	100.1	87.5
AR.	9.9	10.5	9.5	11.5	9.0
LA.	17.2	6.7	6.9	8.0	7.7
OK.	14.0	7.3	7.4	9.3	9.0
TX.	150.8	59.0	61.0	71.3	61.8
West	467.0	329.0	254.0	271.0	225.0
Mt.	157.5	83.7	83.5	102.3	88.7
MT.	2.8	1.5	3.9	4.2	3.5
ID.	4.2	7.3	8.5	10.5	9.3
WY.	3.8	0.8	2.2	2.5	2.2
CO.	33.6	12.5	13.1	18.8	17.6
NM.	9.8	5.4	4.5	5.1	4.9
AZ.	72.1	24.0	25.1	35.0	30.7
UT.	17.3	7.6	9.4	12.0	10.5
NV.	14.0	24.7	16.7	14.3	10.1
Pac.	309.5	245.4	170.7	168.8	136.2
WA.	34.4	46.8	33.5	33.9	28.6
OR.	11.5	22.8	13.5	15.8	12.0
CA.	253.4	167.2	113.3	109.2	88.4
AK.	4.3	1.2	1.4	1.5	1.4
HI.	5.9	7.4	9.0	8.5	6.0

Source: National Association of Home Builders, Economics Division, Washington, DC. Data provided by the Econometric Forecasting Service.

No. 1223. Characteristics of New Privately Owned One-Family Houses Completed: 1970 to 1992

[Percent distribution, except as indicated. Data beginning 1980 show percent distribution of characteristics for all houses completed (includes new houses completed, houses built for sale completed, contractor-built and owner-built houses completed, and houses completed for rent). Data for 1970 cover contractor-built, owner-built, and houses for rent for year construction started and houses sold for year of sale. Percents exclude houses for which characteristics specified were not reported]

CHARACTERISTIC	1970	1980	1990	1991	1992	CHARACTERISTIC	1970	1980	1990	1991	1992
Total houses (1,000) ...	793	957	966	838	964	Bedrooms..........	100	100	100	100	100
						2 or less..........	13	17	15	14	12
Financing	100	100	100	100	100	3.................	63	63	57	59	59
Mortgage	84	81	82	81	86	4 or more..........	24	20	29	28	29
FHA-insured......	30	16	14	13	10	Bathrooms	100	100	100	100	100
VA-guaranteed....	7	8	4	5	5	1 1/2 or less........	20	10	5	14	13
Conventional	47	55	62	61	69	2.................	32	48	42	43	40
Farmers Home						2 1/2 or more	16	25	45	44	47
Administration	(1)	3	2	2	1	Heating fuel	100	100	100	100	100
Cash or equivalent....	16	18	18	19	14	Electricity	28	50	33	32	29
						Gas...............	62	41	59	60	65
Floor area..........	100	100	100	100	100	Oil................	8	3	5	4	4
Under 1,200 sq. ft	36	21	11	12	10	Other..............	1	5	3	4	2
1,200 to 1,599 sq. ft..	28	29	22	22	22	Heating system.......	100	100	100	100	100
1,600 to 1,999 sq. ft...	16	22	22	21	23	Warm air furnace	71	57	65	65	66
2,000 to 2,399 sq. ft ..	21	13	17	17	17	Electric heat pump	(NA)	24	23	23	24
2,400 sq. ft. and over ..	(2)	15	29	28	29	Other..............	29	19	12	13	11
Average (sq. ft.)......	1,500	1,740	2,080	2,075	2,095	Central air-conditioning .	100	100	100	100	100
Median (sq. ft.)......	1,385	1,595	1,905	1,890	1,920	With...............	34	63	76	75	77
						Without	66	37	24	25	23
Number of stories	100	100	100	100	100	Fireplaces...........	100	100	100	100	100
1.................	74	60	46	48	48	No fireplace	65	43	34	37	36
2 or more	17	31	49	47	47	1 or more	35	56	66	63	64
Split level	10	8	4	5	5	Parking facilities	100	100	100	100	100
Foundation	100	100	100	100	100	Garage.............	58	69	82	81	83
Full or partial basement.	37	36	38	40	42	Carport............	17	7	2	3	2
Slab..............	36	45	40	38	38	No garage or carport ..	25	24	16	17	15
Crawl space	27	19	21	22	20						

NA Not available. ¹ Included with "Conventional" financing. ² Included with floor area of 2,000 to 2,399 square feet.

Source: U.S. Bureau of the Census and U.S. Dept. of Housing and Urban Development, *Current Construction Reports*, series C25, *Characteristics of New Housing*, annual.

No. 1224. New Privately Owned One-Family Houses Sold, by Region and Type of Financing, 1970 to 1992, and by Sales-Price Group, 1992

[In thousands. Based on a national probability sample of monthly interviews with builders or owners of one-family houses for which building permits have been issued or, for nonpermit areas, on which construction has started. For details, see source. For composition of regions, see table 31]

YEAR AND SALES-PRICE GROUP	Total sales	REGION				FINANCING TYPE			
		North-east	Midwest	South	West	Conven-tional	FHA and VA	Farmers Home Admin.	Cash
1970	485	61	100	203	121	¹213	244	(¹)	27
1971	656	82	127	270	176	¹314	314	(¹)	28
1972	718	96	130	305	187	¹447	242	(¹)	30
1973	634	95	120	257	161	¹465	134	(¹)	34
1974	519	69	103	207	139	¹378	112	(¹)	28
1975	549	71	106	222	150	363	122	43	22
1976	646	72	128	247	199	458	134	23	31
1977	819	86	162	317	255	592	166	24	38
1978	817	78	145	331	262	575	174	26	43
1979	709	67	112	304	225	469	186	18	36
1980	545	50	81	267	145	302	196	14	32
1981	436	46	60	219	112	244	142	14	36
1982	412	47	48	219	99	193	173	11	34
1983	623	76	71	323	152	350	217	8	49
1984	639	94	76	309	160	423	149	9	58
1985	688	112	82	323	170	403	208	11	64
1986	750	136	96	322	196	411	268	12	59
1987	671	117	97	271	186	408	190	8	64
1988	676	101	97	276	202	437	171	6	62
1989	650	86	102	260	202	416	162	14	58
1990	534	71	89	225	149	337	138	10	50
1991	509	57	93	215	144	329	128	9	43
1992................	610	65	116	259	170	428	134	7	41
Under $80,000.......	100	2	22	63	13	40	45	7	8
$80,000 to $119,999......	196	10	39	91	56	117	66	(B)	14
$120,000 to $149,999.....	111	13	21	41	36	87	15	(B)	8
$150,000 to $199,999.....	97	19	17	33	28	85	7	(B)	5
$200,000 and over.......	106	21	18	32	36	99	(B)	(B)	6

B Withheld because estimate did not meet publication standards on the basis of sample size. ¹ Houses financed by Farmers Home Administration included under conventional financing.

Source: U.S. Bureau of the Census and U.S. Dept. of Housing and Urban Development, *Current Construction Reports*, series C25, *Characteristics of New Housing*, annual; and *New One-Family Houses Sold*, monthly.

No. 1225. Median Sales Price of New Privately Owned One-Family Houses Sold, by Region: 1970 to 1992

[In dollars. For definition of median, see Guide to Tabular Presentation. For composition of regions, see table 31]

YEAR	U.S.	North-east	Midwest	South	West	YEAR	U.S.	North-east	Midwest	South	West
1970....	23,400	30,300	24,400	20,300	24,000	1982....	69,300	78,200	68,900	66,100	75,000
1971....	25,200	30,600	27,200	22,500	25,500	1983....	75,300	82,200	79,500	70,900	80,100
1972....	27,600	31,400	29,300	25,800	27,500	1984....	79,900	88,600	85,400	72,000	87,300
1973....	32,500	37,100	32,900	30,900	32,400	1985....	84,300	103,300	80,300	75,000	92,600
1974....	35,900	40,100	36,100	34,500	35,800	1986....	92,000	125,000	88,300	80,200	95,700
1975....	39,300	44,000	39,600	37,300	40,600	1987....	104,500	140,000	95,000	88,000	111,000
1976....	44,200	47,300	44,800	40,500	47,200	1988....	112,500	149,000	101,600	92,000	126,500
1977....	48,800	51,600	51,500	44,100	53,500	1989....	120,000	159,600	108,800	96,400	139,000
1978....	55,700	58,100	59,200	50,300	61,300	1990....	122,900	159,000	107,900	99,000	147,500
1979....	62,900	65,500	63,900	57,300	69,600	1991....	120,000	155,900	110,000	100,000	141,100
1980....	64,600	69,500	63,400	59,600	72,300	1992....	121,500	169,000	115,600	105,500	130,400
1981....	68,900	76,000	65,900	64,400	77,800						

Source: U.S. Bureau of the Census and U.S. Dept. of Housing and Urban Development, Current Construction Reports, series C25, Characteristics of New Housing, annual; and New One-Family Houses Sold, monthly.

No. 1226. New Mobile Homes Placed for Residential Use and Average Sales Price, by Region: 1980 to 1992

[A mobile home is a moveable dwelling, 10 feet or more wide and 35 feet or more long, designed to be towed on its own chassis and without need of a permanent foundation. Excluded are travel trailers, motor homes, and modular housing. Data are based on a probability sample and subject to sampling variability; see source. For composition of regions, see table 31]

YEAR	UNITS PLACED (1,000)					AVERAGE SALES PRICE (dol.)				
	Total	North-east	Mid-west	South	West	U.S.	North-east	Mid-west	South	West
1980	233.7	12.3	32.3	140.3	48.7	19,800	18,500	18,600	18,200	25,400
1981	229.2	12.0	30.1	143.5	43.6	19,900	19,000	18,900	18,400	25,600
1982	234.1	12.4	25.6	161.1	35.0	19,700	19,800	20,000	18,500	24,700
1983	278.1	16.3	34.3	186.0	41.4	21,000	21,400	20,400	19,700	27,000
1984	287.9	19.8	35.2	193.4	39.4	21,500	22,200	21,100	20,200	27,400
1985	283.4	20.2	38.6	187.6	36.9	21,800	22,700	21,500	20,400	28,700
1986	256.1	21.2	37.2	162.3	35.4	22,400	24,400	21,800	20,700	29,900
1987	239.2	23.6	40.0	145.5	30.1	23,700	25,600	23,700	21,900	31,000
1988	224.3	22.7	39.1	130.7	31.8	25,100	27,000	24,600	22,700	33,900
1989	202.8	20.2	39.1	112.8	30.6	27,200	30,200	26,700	24,100	37,800
1990	195.4	18.8	37.7	108.4	30.6	27,800	30,000	27,000	24,500	39,300
1991	174.3	14.3	35.4	97.6	27.0	27,700	30,400	27,600	24,500	38,600
1992	212.0	15.0	42.2	124.4	30.4	28,400	30,900	28,800	25,400	39,000

No. 1227. Existing One-Family Houses Sold and Price, by Region: 1970 to 1992

[Based on data (adjusted and aggregated to regional and national totals) reported by participating real estate multiple listing services. For definition of median, see Guide to Tabular Presentation. For composition of regions, see table 31]

YEAR	HOUSES SOLD (1,000)					MEDIAN SALES PRICE (dol.)				
	Total	North-east	Mid-west	South	West	Total	North-east	Mid-west	South	West
1970	1,612	251	501	568	292	23,000	25,200	20,100	22,200	24,300
1971	2,018	311	583	735	389	24,800	27,100	22,100	24,300	26,500
1972	2,252	361	630	788	473	26,700	29,800	23,900	26,400	28,400
1973	2,334	367	674	847	446	28,900	32,800	25,300	29,000	31,000
1974	2,272	354	645	839	434	32,000	35,800	27,700	32,300	34,800
1975	2,476	370	701	862	543	35,300	39,300	30,100	34,800	39,600
1976	3,064	439	881	1,033	712	38,100	41,800	32,900	36,500	46,100
1977	3,650	515	1,101	1,231	803	42,900	44,400	36,700	39,800	57,300
1978	3,986	516	1,144	1,416	911	48,700	47,900	42,200	45,100	66,700
1979	3,827	526	1,061	1,353	887	55,700	53,600	47,800	51,300	77,400
1980	2,973	403	806	1,092	672	62,200	60,800	51,900	58,300	89,300
1981	2,419	353	632	917	516	66,400	63,700	54,300	64,400	96,200
1982	1,990	354	490	780	366	67,800	63,500	55,100	67,100	98,900
1983	2,719	493	709	1,035	481	70,300	72,200	56,600	69,200	94,900
1984	2,868	511	755	1,073	529	72,400	78,700	57,100	71,300	95,800
1985	3,214	622	866	1,172	554	75,500	88,900	58,900	75,200	95,400
1986	3,565	703	991	1,261	610	80,300	104,800	63,500	78,200	100,900
1987	3,526	685	959	1,282	600	85,600	133,300	66,000	80,400	113,200
1988	3,594	673	929	1,350	642	89,300	143,000	68,400	82,200	124,900
1989	3,346	531	855	1,185	775	93,100	145,200	71,300	84,500	139,900
1990	3,211	469	831	1,202	709	95,500	141,200	74,000	85,900	139,600
1991	3,220	479	840	1,199	702	100,300	141,900	77,800	88,900	147,200
1992	3,520	534	939	1,292	755	103,700	140,000	81,700	92,100	143,800

Source: National Association of REALTORS, Washington, DC, Home Sales, monthly, and Home Sales Yearbook: 1990 (copyright).

No. 1228. Median Sales Price of Existing One-Family Homes, by Selected Metropolitan Area: 1985 to 1992

[In thousands of dollars. Areas are metropolitan statistical areas (MSA's) except as indicated; for definitions and components, see Appendix II]

METROPOLITAN AREA	1985	1990	1991	1992	METROPOLITAN AREA	1985	1990	1991	1992
U.S., all areas	75.5	95.5	100.3	103.7	Memphis, TN-AR-MS	64.6	78.1	82.5	85.3
					Miami-Hialeah, FL PMSA	80.5	89.3	93.7	97.1
Albany-Schenectady-Troy, NY	60.3	106.9	110.3	111.4	Milwaukee, WI PMSA	67.5	84.4	90.0	97.0
Anaheim-Santa Ana, CA PMSA	134.7	242.4	239.7	234.9	Minneapolis-St. Paul, MN-WI	75.2	88.7	91.1	94.2
Baltimore, MD	72.6	105.9	110.1	113.4	Nashville, TN	66.1	81.8	86.9	88.8
Birmingham, AL	64.5	80.8	86.0	90.9	New Orleans, LA	(NA)	67.8	71.8	76.3
Boston, MA PMSA	134.2	174.1	170.1	171.1	New York-Northern New Jersey-Long Island, NY-NJ-CT CMSA	134.0	174.9	173.5	172.7
Buffalo-Niagara Falls, NY CMSA	46.7	77.2	79.7	81.7	Oklahoma City, OK	64.7	53.2	57.0	61.6
Charlotte, NC	69.4	93.1	101.4	102.2	Orlando, FL	70.3	82.8	86.3	87.6
Chicago, IL PMSA	81.1	116.8	131.1	136.8	Philadelphia, PA-NJ PMSA	74.0	108.7	118.4	117.0
Cincinnati, OH-KY-IN PMSA	60.2	79.8	84.9	88.6	Phoenix, AZ	74.8	84.0	85.5	86.8
Cleveland, OH PMSA	64.4	80.6	86.2	90.7	Pittsburgh, PA PMSA	(NA)	70.1	74.2	78.6
Columbus, OH	62.2	81.6	85.2	91.0	Portland, OR PMSA	61.5	79.5	88.5	97.7
Dallas, TX PMSA	94.0	89.5	88.3	91.3	Richmond, VA	(NA)	87.5	92.5	93.9
Denver, CO PMSA	84.3	86.4	89.1	96.2	Riverside/San Bernardino, CA PMSA	85.0	132.1	137.6	136.2
Detroit, MI PMSA	51.7	76.7	80.6	81.3	Rochester, NY	64.2	79.8	81.5	84.7
Ft. Lauderdale-Hollywood-Pompano Beach, FL PMSA	74.6	92.6	96.2	99.1	St. Louis, MO-IL	65.7	76.7	79.4	83.2
Ft. Worth, TX PMSA	(NA)	76.7	77.6	80.2	Sacramento, CA	77.9	137.5	137.7	132.0
Hartford, CT PMSA	99.6	157.3	148.2	141.1	Salt Lake City-Ogden, UT	66.7	69.4	72.8	76.5
Honolulu, HI	162.1	352.0	340.0	349.0	San Antonio, TX	67.7	63.6	64.9	70.4
Houston, TX PMSA	78.6	70.7	74.0	80.2	San Diego, CA	107.4	183.2	187.5	183.8
Indianapolis, IN	55.0	74.8	79.1	83.7	San Francisco-Oakland-San Jose, CA CMSA	145.1	259.3	258.5	254.8
Jacksonville, FL	58.4	72.4	73.7	76.8	Seattle-Tacoma, WA CMSA	(NA)	142.0	143.1	145.7
Kansas City, MO-KS	61.4	74.1	76.6	79.5	Tampa-St. Petersburg-Clearwater, FL	58.4	71.4	71.3	72.6
Las Vegas, NV	75.1	93.0	101.4	104.3	Washington, DC-MD-VA	97.1	150.5	156.7	157.8
Los Angeles-Long Beach, CA PMSA	125.2	212.1	218.9	213.2	West Palm Beach-Boca Raton-Delray Beach, FL	88.3	108.0	116.3	114.1
Louisville, KY-IN	50.6	60.8	65.4	69.5					

NA Not available.
Source: National Association of REALTORS, Washington, DC, *Home Sales*, monthly, and *Home Sales Yearbook: 1990* (copyright).

No. 1229. Existing Home Sales, by State: 1985 to 1992

[In thousands]

REGION, DIVISION, AND STATE	1985	1989	1990	1991	1992	REGION, DIVISION, AND STATE	1985	1989	1990	1991	1992
U.S.[1]	3,380.0	3,710.0	3,560.0	3,560.0	3,886.0	DC	9.2	15.5	13.1	12.5	12.4
						VA	116.0	116.0	96.9	90.3	101.3
Northeast	630.0	610.0	530.0	550.0	612.0	WV	31.1	36.8	42.0	43.3	46.8
N.E.	156.9	142.8	(NA)	(NA)	139.4	NC	107.9	127.5	135.9	139.9	160.2
ME	21.8	9.0	(NA)	(NA)	10.3	SC	48.4	52.2	57.8	53.9	58.9
NH	14.5	9.7	7.9	9.3	12.0	GA	58.7	73.6	73.2	70.7	(NA)
VT	7.5	6.2	6.1	8.1	9.5	FL	142.7	177.6	183.3	176.0	179.2
MA	60.2	67.4	44.0	49.6	57.6	E.S.C.	230.6	253.3	254.9	259.0	292.6
RI	10.3	9.5	7.8	7.8	10.0	KY	51.8	62.2	66.4	67.8	78.7
CT	42.6	41.0	34.3	37.6	40.0	TN	89.3	95.2	92.7	92.0	102.2
M.A.	467.7	460.6	423.0	425.2	472.8	AL	54.8	59.4	61.1	64.0	72.5
NY	150.0	140.2	125.5	127.2	136.3	MS	34.7	36.5	34.7	35.2	39.2
NJ	160.2	126.6	114.8	118.8	132.1	W.S.C.	312.1	350.5	379.8	385.0	395.1
PA	157.5	193.8	182.7	179.2	204.4	AR	49.9	47.5	44.8	43.4	47.8
Midwest	850.0	920.0	890.0	900.0	1,006.0	LA	36.4	40.8	41.6	47.1	47.0
E.N.C.	581.5	633.4	609.3	618.9	687.2	OK	42.3	49.1	53.4	52.5	57.6
OH	147.6	163.4	151.6	149.8	167.4	TX	183.5	213.1	240.0	242.0	242.7
IN	88.4	81.6	80.1	76.0	84.8	West	770.0	890.0	830.0	810.0	861.0
IL	130.2	162.7	160.9	168.1	186.2	Mt.	243.0	230.5	250.6	256.7	295.6
MI	153.4	151.6	145.0	145.0	157.3	MT	11.7	13.0	12.7	13.9	16.6
WI	61.9	74.1	71.7	80.0	91.5	ID	14.2	15.0	18.1	19.0	21.6
W.N.C.	270.2	285.4	280.9	281.7	320.8	WY	8.0	7.3	7.4	8.2	9.9
MN	67.4	62.7	64.8	66.3	75.7	CO	64.4	53.9	54.2	59.6	71.4
IA	36.4	54.6	51.9	54.1	53.1	NM	22.2	21.9	23.6	24.4	29.2
MO	78.9	81.0	84.1	82.7	98.8	AZ	83.6	77.7	86.3	79.7	89.8
ND	8.8	10.3	10.4	10.3	11.9	UT	22.1	20.3	22.1	26.3	31.5
SD	10.5	10.8	11.6	11.3	12.7	NV	16.8	21.4	26.2	25.6	25.6
NE	22.6	20.9	19.3	19.9	22.4	Pac.	524.6	711.1	(NA)	(NA)	(NA)
KS	45.6	45.1	38.8	37.1	46.2	WA	61.8	90.8	87.7	86.9	91.3
South	1,140.0	1,290.0	1,310.0	1,310.0	1,407.0	OR	36.1	53.2	56.6	48.1	52.5
S.A.	596.6	687.8	679.0	663.8	(NA)	CA[2]	404.9	539.3	452.1	424.1	427.8
DE	11.3	11.8	9.7	10.4	10.0	AK	9.5	6.6	(NA)	(NA)	(NA)
MD	71.3	76.8	67.1	66.8	69.0	HI	12.3	21.2	19.2	12.2	11.6

NA Not available. [1] U.S. totals are derived independently and therefore are not equal to the sum of the States. [2] Provided by the California Association of Realtors.
Source: NATIONAL ASSOCIATION OF REALTORS, Washington, DC, *Existing Home Sales*, monthly. (copyright).

No. 1230. New Apartments Completed and Rented in 3 Months, by Region: 1980 to 1991

[Structures with five or more units, privately financed, nonsubsidized, unfurnished apartments. Based on sample and subject to sampling variability. For composition of regions, see table 31]

YEAR AND RENT	NUMBER (1,000)					PERCENT RENTED IN 3 MONTHS				
	U.S.	North-east	Mid-west	South	West	U.S.	North-east	Mid-west	South	West
1980	196.1	14.2	43.8	91.5	46.6	75	77	77	74	75
1981	135.3	4.9	36.9	68.4	25.1	80	85	86	78	75
1982	117.0	4.6	21.9	66.8	23.7	72	74	79	70	72
1983	191.5	3.5	41.1	115.1	31.8	69	73	86	63	69
1984	313.2	3.8	41.2	194.4	73.9	67	64	79	63	70
1985	365.2	8.1	54.0	166.1	137.0	65	69	72	59	68
1986	407.6	16.9	64.5	171.7	154.5	66	70	70	62	67
1987	345.6	11.3	66.0	124.5	143.9	63	73	65	59	64
1988	284.5	8.7	60.4	91.7	123.8	66	52	73	58	69
1989	247.8	13.4	45.8	86.3	102.3	70	74	74	68	69
1990	214.3	12.7	44.3	77.2	80.0	67	66	75	64	65
1991	165.3	6.8	37.8	63.3	57.5	70	83	78	65	68
Less than $350	13.2	1.5	4.8	6.3	0.5	83	98	95	70	85
$350-$449	13.8	1.5	4.1	7.0	1.3	78	78	87	73	79
$450-$549	32.8	0.7	7.2	14.4	10.5	72	72	83	67	72
$550-$649	36.3	1.0	9.0	11.7	14.7	70	77	75	65	71
$650-$749	22.9	0.7	4.6	8.2	9.4	69	90	79	62	68
$750 or more	46.4	1.4	8.2	15.6	21.1	63	75	64	60	63
Median asking rent	612	508	581	583	668	(X)	(X)	(X)	(X)	(X)

X Not applicable.

Source: U.S. Bureau of the Census, *Current Housing Reports*, series H-130 and H-131, and unpublished data.

No. 1231. Gross Housing Product—Summary: 1970 to 1991

[In billions of dollars. For definition of current and constant dollars, see Guide to Tabular Presentation]

ITEM	CURRENT DOLLARS						CONSTANT (1987) DOLLARS					
	1970	1980	1985	1989	1990	1991	1970	1980	1985	1989	1990	1991
Housing output [1]	90.5	245.3	377.0	493.4	525.7	551.7	257.6	383.1	418.7	450.3	456.6	461.7
Nonfarm housing	87.3	240.2	372.0	488.4	520.6	546.4	249.6	376.9	413.5	445.7	452.1	457.2
Owner-occupied	61.3	178.4	271.0	355.8	379.8	399.1	174.4	278.7	301.3	322.8	326.9	330.7
Tenant-occupied	26.0	61.8	101.0	132.6	140.8	147.3	75.1	98.2	112.2	122.9	125.2	126.5
Farm housing	3.3	5.1	5.0	5.0	5.2	5.3	8.0	6.3	5.3	4.6	4.5	4.5
Less: Intermediate goods and services consumed	13.0	35.8	49.9	65.1	71.6	74.2	37.0	55.9	55.4	61.2	62.3	63.0
Equals: **Gross housing product**	77.5	209.5	327.1	428.3	454.1	477.5	220.6	327.2	363.3	389.1	394.3	398.7

[1] Equals personal consumption expenditures (see text, section 14) for housing, less expenditures for transient hotels, motels, clubs, schools, and other group housing.

Source: U.S. Bureau of Economic Analysis, *Survey of Current Business*, July 1992 issue, and *National Income and Product Accounts of the United States: Volume 2, 1959-88*.

No. 1232. Residential Capital—Yearend Stocks and Average Age: 1970 to 1991

[As of Dec. 31. Data based on fixed residential capital formation components of the gross national product. For definition of current and constant dollars, see Guide to Tabular Presentation]

ITEM	CURRENT DOLLARS (bil. dol.)					CONSTANT (1987) DOLLARS (bil. dol.)					AVERAGE AGE [1] (years)				
	1970	1980	1985	1990	1991	1970	1980	1985	1990	1991	1970	1980	1985	1990	1991
Gross stocks [2]	1,244	4,391	5,726	7,563	7,889	3,961	5,443	6,078	6,917	7,032	24.8	23.2	23.6	23.6	23.8
Private nonfarm:															
1 to 4 units	1,001	3,502	4,566	6,074	6,344	3,208	4,356	4,852	5,556	5,657	25.3	23.9	24.3	24.2	24.4
5 or more units	131	522	701	933	973	421	647	746	853	864	17.7	17.8	18.7	19.8	20.3
Farm (1 to 4 units)	55	136	150	163	166	176	170	159	150	147	43.9	42.8	43.4	43.2	43.2
Private nonhouse-keeping	10	24	27	32	32	32	29	29	29	29	14.6	19.3	22.0	23.7	23.9
Mobile homes	15	79	104	124	129	31	88	106	112	110	5.1	7.7	9.2	10.7	11.0
Public: Federal, State and local	25	99	135	176	184	80	122	144	162	166	14.9	17.2	18.1	19.5	19.8
Net stocks [2] [3]	813	2,910	3,733	4,913	5,095	2,590	3,607	3,964	4,491	4,542	16.2	15.8	16.6	16.8	17.1
Private nonfarm:															
1 to 4 units	656	2,334	2,998	3,991	4,147	2,102	2,902	3,186	3,649	3,698	16.8	16.3	17.1	17.2	17.4
5 or more units	93	371	487	629	648	301	459	518	575	576	11.0	12.8	14.0	15.2	15.7
Farm (1 to 4 units)	24	58	62	68	69	76	73	66	62	61	28.7	26.4	27.2	26.6	26.6
Private nonhouse-keeping	6	12	12	14	14	21	15	13	12	12	9.0	16.0	18.5	18.4	18.3
Mobile homes	11	48	57	62	63	23	54	58	55	53	3.8	6.0	6.7	7.5	7.7
Public: Federal, State and local	18	70	93	117	121	60	87	100	107	109	12.7	13.5	13.7	14.6	14.7

[1] Constant-dollar stocks.   [2] Includes equipment, not shown separately.   [3] Based on straight-line depreciation.

Source: U.S. Bureau of Economic Analysis, *Fixed Reproducible Tangible Wealth in the United States, 1925-89*, and *Survey of Current Business*, January and August 1992 issues.

No. 1233. Housing Units—Selected Characteristics, by State: 1990

[As of April 1]

REGION, DIVISION, AND STATE	ALL HOUSING UNITS Total (1,000)	Percent change, 1980-90	Units in structure: 1 unit detached	1 unit attached	2-4 units	5-9 units	10 or more units	Mobile homes, trailers	OCCUPIED UNITS Total (1,000)	With 1.01 or more persons per room	VACANT UNITS Total (1,000)	Vacancy rate (percent)
U.S.	102,264	15.7	60,383	5,378	9,876	4,936	13,169	7,400	91,947	4,549	10,316	10.1
Northeast	20,811	9.0	10,253	1,657	3,488	1,019	3,464	637	18,873	735	1,938	9.3
N.E.	5,570	14.8	3,050	211	1,133	327	620	153	4,943	112	628	11.3
ME	587	17.2	378	12	74	29	26	55	465	8	122	20.7
NH	504	30.4	298	23	68	27	46	35	411	7	93	18.6
VT	271	21.5	168	9	41	14	10	23	211	4	61	22.3
MA	2,473	12.0	1,238	89	597	159	339	24	2,247	57	226	9.1
RI	415	11.2	219	11	109	23	43	5	378	9	37	8.8
CT	1,321	14.0	749	67	244	75	155	12	1,230	28	90	6.8
M.A.	15,240	7.1	7,203	1,446	2,355	692	2,844	483	13,930	623	1,310	8.6
NY	7,227	5.2	2,929	302	1,320	375	1,998	195	6,639	432	588	8.1
NJ	3,075	10.9	1,637	235	527	146	453	34	2,795	109	281	9.1
PA	4,938	7.4	2,637	910	507	171	393	255	4,496	83	442	9.0
Midwest	24,493	7.3	16,218	754	2,394	1,080	2,470	1,339	22,317	558	2,176	8.9
E.N.C	17,028	6.6	11,044	544	1,825	827	1,759	861	15,597	413	1,431	8.4
OH	4,372	6.4	2,897	148	461	204	416	206	4,088	72	284	6.5
IN	2,246	7.4	1,574	57	171	100	168	157	2,065	45	181	8.0
IL	4,506	4.3	2,557	158	648	291	663	151	4,202	167	304	6.7
MI	3,848	7.2	2,673	131	268	151	337	246	3,419	91	429	11.1
WI	2,056	10.3	1,342	50	277	81	175	101	1,822	38	234	11.4
W.N.C	7,465	9.0	5,175	211	569	253	711	478	6,720	145	744	10.0
MN	1,848	14.6	1,231	69	115	45	276	91	1,648	34	201	10.9
IA	1,144	1.1	853	18	87	41	77	57	1,064	16	79	6.9
MO	2,199	10.6	1,490	57	212	85	172	164	1,961	48	238	10.8
ND	276	6.8	173	10	21	12	30	27	241	5	35	12.8
SD	292	5.6	202	5	19	10	22	31	259	8	33	11.4
NE	661	5.7	479	16	40	25	59	37	602	11	58	8.8
KS	1,044	9.3	747	35	74	35	75	71	945	24	99	9.5
South	36,065	22.6	22,007	1,725	2,349	1,724	4,068	3,835	31,822	1,524	4,243	11.8
S.A.	18,719	27.4	10,607	1,250	1,269	978	2,352	2,095	16,503	675	2,216	11.8
DE	290	21.5	156	40	14	10	33	35	247	6	42	14.6
MD	1,892	20.4	939	393	104	106	294	43	1,749	53	143	7.6
DC	278	0.5	35	71	31	21	118	-	250	21	29	10.4
VA	2,496	23.5	1,532	216	144	136	287	159	2,292	65	205	8.2
WV	781	4.5	546	11	46	20	29	119	689	13	93	11.9
NC	2,818	23.9	1,830	74	178	131	151	430	2,517	73	301	10.7
SC	1,424	23.4	898	34	92	67	80	241	1,258	51	166	11.7
GA	2,638	30.1	1,639	73	198	168	233	305	2,367	96	272	10.3
FL	6,100	39.3	3,033	336	462	321	1,128	763	5,135	298	965	15.8
E.S.C	6,214	13.1	4,213	130	408	260	406	735	5,652	192	562	9.0
KY	1,507	10.1	1,011	25	109	65	96	185	1,380	36	127	8.4
TN	2,026	15.9	1,358	55	146	93	166	189	1,854	51	172	8.5
AL	1,670	13.8	1,134	32	96	66	102	224	1,507	53	164	9.8
MS	1,010	10.8	710	17	57	36	41	137	911	53	99	9.8
W.S.C	11,132	20.6	7,187	345	673	485	1,310	1,006	9,668	657	1,465	13.2
AR	1,001	11.4	709	18	61	27	44	132	891	33	109	10.9
LA	1,716	10.8	1,084	79	152	59	125	196	1,499	89	217	12.6
OK	1,406	13.7	1,005	33	69	56	100	130	1,206	40	200	14.2
TX	7,009	26.3	4,389	215	391	343	1,041	548	6,071	495	938	13.6
West	20,895	22.3	11,905	1,242	1,645	1,113	3,166	1,589	18,935	1,732	1,960	9.4
Mt	5,864	29.3	3,422	300	399	231	751	691	5,033	271	831	14.2
MT	361	10.0	238	8	29	10	17	54	306	9	55	15.2
ID	413	10.2	286	9	29	12	17	57	361	15	53	12.7
WY	203	8.1	129	6	16	6	10	33	169	5	35	17.0
CO	1,477	23.7	884	87	90	64	249	89	1,282	38	195	13.2
NM	632	24.5	388	28	39	16	48	103	543	43	89	14.1
AZ	1,659	49.4	868	110	88	61	257	251	1,369	102	291	17.5
UT	598	22.1	393	24	58	21	62	35	537	30	61	10.2
NV	519	52.6	236	27	50	41	90	70	466	30	53	10.1
Pac	15,031	19.8	8,483	942	1,246	882	2,415	898	13,902	1,461	1,129	7.5
WA	2,032	20.3	1,273	48	139	91	275	188	1,872	73	160	7.9
OR	1,194	10.2	764	32	86	47	119	134	1,103	40	90	7.6
CA	11,183	20.5	6,119	812	966	706	1,900	555	10,381	1,275	802	7.2
AK	233	42.9	124	16	30	16	21	20	189	16	44	18.8
HI	390	16.6	203	34	24	22	100	(Z)	356	57	34	8.6

Z Less than 500 units.

Source: U.S. Bureau of the Census, *1990 Census of Housing, General Housing Characteristics*, series CH-1, and *Census of Population and Housing, 1990: Summary Tape File 1C on CD-ROM.*

No. 1234. Housing Units—Historical Trends for Selected Characteristics: 1940 to 1990

[As of **April 1**. Based on the Census of Population and Housing; see Appendix III]

CHARACTERISTIC	NUMBER OF UNITS						PERCENT DISTRIBUTION					
	1940	1950	1960	1970	1980	1990	1940	1950	1960	1970	1980	1990
UNITS IN STRUCTURE												
All housing units [1]	37,325	45,983	58,315	67,699	86,759	102,264	100.0	100.0	100.0	100.0	100.0	100.0
One detached	23,731	29,116	40,103	44,801	53,596	60,383	63.6	63.3	68.8	66.2	61.8	59.0
One attached	[2]2,835	[3]2,799	3,655	1,990	3,587	5,378	[2]7.6	[3]6.1	6.3	2.9	4.1	5.3
Two	3,464	5,302	4,464	5,444	5,309	4,948	9.3	11.5	7.7	8.0	6.1	4.8
Three or four	2,259	3,374	3,088	3,563	4,373	4,928	6.1	7.3	5.3	5.3	5.0	4.8
Five or more	3,928	5,078	6,238	9,829	15,478	18,105	10.5	11.0	10.7	14.5	17.8	17.7
Mobile home or trailer	(NA)	315	767	2,073	4,416	7,400	(NA)	0.7	1.3	3.1	5.1	7.2
Other	[4]1,108	(NA)	(NA)	(NA)	(NA)	1,121	[4]3.0	(NA)	(NA)	(NA)	(NA)	1.1
PLUMBING FACILITIES												
All housing units [1]	35,026	44,502	58,315	67,657	86,693	102,264	100.0	100.0	100.0	100.0	100.0	100.0
Complete plumbing facilities	19,174	28,729	48,537	62,984	84,359	101,162	54.7	64.6	83.2	93.1	97.3	98.9
Lacking complete plumbing facilities	15,852	15,773	9,778	4,672	2,334	1,102	45.3	35.4	16.8	6.9	2.7	1.1
Not reported	2,299	1,481	(NA)	(NA)	(NA)	(NA)	(X)	(X)	(NA)	(NA)	(NA)	(NA)
TELEPHONE IN HOUSING UNIT [5]												
Occupied housing units	33,884	41,829	53,024	63,450	80,390	91,947	(NA)	(NA)	100.0	100.0	100.0	100.0
With telephone	(NA)	(NA)	41,618	55,177	74,720	87,130	(NA)	(NA)	78.5	87.0	92.9	94.8
No telephone	(NA)	(NA)	11,406	8,273	5,670	4,817	(NA)	(NA)	21.5	13.0	7.1	5.2

NA Not available.   X Not applicable.   [1] Data for 1970 and 1980 are "Year-round housing units," which exclude seasonal and migratory vacant units.   [2] Includes 1,656,858 units classified as "two-family side-by-side."   [3] Includes 1,588,902 units classified as "one and two dwelling unit."   [4] Covers 166,975 units classified as "Other dwelling place" and 940,726 units classified as "one- to four-family with business."   [5] Beginning 1980, data are not completely comparable with earlier years due to change in question asked.

Source: U.S. Bureau of the Census, *1990 Census of Housing*, series CH-1, and earlier census reports.

No. 1235. Occupied Housing Units—Tenure, by Race of Householder: 1920 to 1990

[In thousands, except as indicated. As of **April 1**. Prior to 1960, excludes Alaska and Hawaii. Statistics on the number of occupied units are essentially comparable although identified by various terms. See also *Historical Statistics, Colonial Times to 1970*, series N 238-245]

RACE AND TENURE	1920	1930	1940	1950	1960	1970	1980	1990
ALL RACES								
Occupied units, total	24,352	29,905	34,855	42,826	53,024	63,445	80,390	91,947
Owner occupied	11,114	14,280	15,196	23,560	32,797	39,886	51,795	59,025
Percent of occupied	45.6	47.8	43.6	55.0	61.9	62.9	64.4	64.2
Renter occupied	13,238	15,624	19,659	19,266	20,227	23,560	28,595	32,923
WHITE								
Occupied units, total	21,826	26,983	31,561	39,044	47,880	56,606	68,810	76,880
Owner occupied	10,511	13,544	14,418	22,241	30,823	37,005	46,671	52,433
Percent of occupied	48.2	50.2	45.7	57.0	64.4	65.4	67.8	68.2
Renter occupied	11,315	13,439	17,143	16,803	17,057	19,601	22,139	24,447
BLACK AND OTHER								
Occupied units, total	2,526	2,922	3,293	3,783	5,144	6,839	11,580	15,067
Owner occupied	603	737	778	1,319	1,974	2,881	5,124	6,592
Percent of occupied	23.9	25.2	23.6	34.9	38.4	42.1	44.2	43.8
Renter occupied	1,923	2,185	2,516	2,464	3,170	3,959	6,456	8,475

Source: U.S. Bureau of the Census, *Census of Housing: 1960*, vol. 1; *1970*, vol. 1; *1980 Census of Housing*, vol. 1, chapter A (HC80-1-A); and *1990 Census of Housing, General Housing Characteristics*, series CH-90-1.

No. 1236. Occupied Housing Units—Tenure, by Race and Hispanic Origin of Householder: 1980 and 1990

[As of **April 1**. Based on the Census of Population and Housing; see Appendix III]

RACE AND HISPANIC ORIGIN OF HOUSEHOLDER	ALL HOUSEHOLDS			OWNER OCCUPIED		PERCENT OWNER OCCUPIED		RENTER OCCUPIED	
	1980	1990	Percent change, 1980-1990	1980	1990	1980	1990	1980	1990
Total units	80,389,673	91,947,410	14.4	51,794,545	59,024,811	64.4	64.2	28,595,128	32,922,599
White	68,810,123	76,880,105	11.7	46,670,775	52,432,648	67.8	68.2	22,139,348	24,447,457
Black	8,381,668	9,976,161	19.0	3,724,251	4,327,265	44.4	43.4	4,657,417	5,648,896
American Indian, Eskimo, or Aleut	397,252	591,372	48.9	212,209	318,001	53.4	53.8	185,043	273,371
Asian or Pacific Islander	993,458	2,013,735	102.7	521,230	1,050,182	52.5	52.2	472,228	963,553
Other race	1,807,172	2,486,037	37.6	666,080	896,715	36.9	36.1	1,141,092	1,589,322
Hispanic origin [1]	4,007,896	6,001,718	49.7	1,738,920	2,545,584	43.4	42.4	2,268,976	3,456,134

[1] Persons of Hispanic origin may be of any race.

U.S. Bureau of the Census, *1980 Census of Housing*, vol. 1, chapter A (HC80-1-A); and *1990 Census of Housing, General Housing Characteristics*, series CH-1.

No. 1237. Occupied Housing Units—Tenure, by Age of Householder: 1980 and 1990

[As of April 1]

AGE OF HOUSEHOLDER	OWNER OCCUPIED				RENTER OCCUPIED			
	Number (1,000)		Percent		Number (1,000)		Percent	
	1980	1990	1980	1990	1980	1990	1980	1990
Total units	51,797	59,024	64.4	64.2	28,594	32,922	35.6	35.8
15 to 24 years old................	1,459	862	22.1	17.1	5,137	4,187	77.9	82.9
25 to 34 years old................	9,439	9,000	51.6	45.3	8,844	10,849	48.4	54.7
35 to 44 years old................	9,895	13,503	71.2	66.2	3,997	6,890	28.8	33.8
45 to 54 years old................	[1]19,563	10,774	[1]77.3	75.3	[1]5,744	3,529	[1]22.7	24.7
55 to 64 years old................	[1]	9,864	[1]	79.7	[1]	2,515	[1]	20.3
65 to 74 years old................	[2]11,441	9,072	[2]70.1	78.8	[2]4,872	2,445	[2]29.9	21.2
75 years old and over	[2]	5,949	[2]	70.4	[2]	2,507	[2]	29.6

[1] Householders age 55 to 64 years old are included with householders 45 to 54 years. [2] Householders age 75 years old and over are included with householders 65 to 74 years old.

Source: U.S. Bureau of the Census, *1980 Census of Housing*, vol. 1, chapter A (HC80-1-A); and *1990 Census of Housing, General Housing Characteristics*, series CH-1.

No. 1238. Occupied Housing Units—Housing Value and Gross Rent, by Region: 1990

[Specified owner-occupied units are limited to one-unit structures on less than 10 acres and no business on property. Specified renter-occupied units exclude one-unit on 10 acres or more. Based on the Census of Population and Housing; see Appendix III. For composition of regions, see table 31]

CATEGORY	NUMBER (1,000)					PERCENT DISTRIBUTION				
	Total units	North-east	Midwest	South	West	Total units	North-east	Mid-west	South	West
VALUE										
Specified owner occupied units.....	44,918.0	8,762.9	11,794.7	15,595.6	8,764.8	100.0	100.0	100.0	100.0	100.0
Less than $15,000.......	1,177.0	114.8	412.0	583.6	66.6	2.6	1.3	3.5	3.7	0.8
$15,000 to $19,999	761.0	85.8	293.1	343.5	38.6	1.7	1.0	2.5	2.2	0.4
$20,000 to $24,999	1,018.8	118.2	392.2	451.2	57.2	2.3	1.3	3.3	2.9	0.7
$25,000 to $29,999	1,232.9	137.5	475.9	544.8	74.7	2.7	1.6	4.0	3.5	0.9
$30,000 to $34,999	1,572.0	168.5	597.5	698.1	107.9	3.5	1.9	5.1	4.5	1.2
$35,000 to $39,999	1,737.5	172.9	642.2	787.2	135.1	3.9	2.0	5.4	5.0	1.5
$40,000 to $44,999	1,985.6	202.0	717.8	887.9	178.0	4.4	2.3	6.1	5.7	2.0
$45,000 to $49,999	1,917.7	187.4	683.0	844.2	203.2	4.3	2.1	5.8	5.4	2.3
$50,000 to $59,999	3,940.0	410.5	1,361.4	1,673.5	494.6	8.8	4.7	11.5	10.7	5.6
$60,000 to $74,999	5,959.6	703.8	1,923.1	2,440.9	891.9	13.3	8.0	16.3	15.7	10.2
$75,000 to $99,999	7,057.8	1,162.6	1,961.0	2,639.2	1,295.0	15.7	13.3	16.6	16.9	14.8
$100,000 to $124,999	3,808.2	941.1	873.3	1,188.4	805.3	8.5	10.7	7.4	7.6	9.2
$125,000 to $149,999	2,965.1	944.5	534.9	789.4	696.3	6.6	10.8	4.5	5.1	7.9
$150,000 to $174,999	2,316.2	886.8	312.4	507.5	609.5	5.2	10.1	2.6	3.3	7.0
$175,000 to $199,999	1,701.0	688.3	181.4	315.2	516.1	3.8	7.9	1.5	2.0	5.9
$200,000 to $249,999	2,084.3	776.4	187.8	354.6	765.4	4.6	8.9	1.6	2.3	8.7
$250,000 to $299,999	1,292.6	416.7	96.1	203.5	576.3	2.9	4.8	0.8	1.3	6.6
$300,000 to $399,999	1,206.8	344.1	78.7	176.8	607.2	2.7	3.9	0.7	1.1	6.9
$400,000 to $499,999	501.3	131.1	31.1	70.1	269.2	1.1	1.5	0.3	0.4	3.1
$500,000 and over	682.5	169.8	39.8	96.2	376.7	1.5	1.9	0.3	0.6	4.3
Median value (dol.)	$79,100	$124,400	$62,500	$66,000	$126,200	(X)	(X)	(X)	(X)	(X)
GROSS RENT										
Specified renter occupied units.....	32,170.0	7,215.4	6,854.9	10,461.4	7,638.3	100.0	100.0	100.0	100.0	100.0
Less than $100.........	541.7	75.1	143.2	271.3	52.1	1.7	1.0	2.1	2.6	1.7
$100 to $149	1,125.0	295.0	288.4	425.0	116.6	3.5	4.1	4.2	4.1	3.5
$150 to $199	1,148.4	250.2	297.4	405.5	195.3	3.6	3.5	4.3	3.9	3.6
$200 to $249	1,553.0	280.2	430.6	607.1	235.1	4.8	3.9	6.3	5.8	4.8
$250 to $299	2,183.2	355.5	609.1	875.0	343.6	6.8	4.9	8.9	8.4	6.8
$300 to $349	2,793.5	465.2	761.9	1,088.9	477.5	8.7	6.4	11.1	10.4	8.7
$350 to $399	3,085.7	552.3	830.6	1,130.5	572.3	9.6	7.7	12.1	10.8	9.6
$400 to $449	3,118.8	621.9	793.2	1,072.7	631.0	9.7	8.6	11.6	10.3	9.7
$450 to $499	2,816.3	611.6	664.0	912.3	628.4	8.8	8.5	9.7	8.7	8.8
$500 to $549	2,438.9	582.9	511.5	736.8	607.7	7.6	8.1	7.5	7.0	7.6
$550 to $599	1,968.1	498.1	362.9	563.2	543.9	6.1	6.9	5.3	5.4	6.1
$600 to $649	1,637.9	449.0	258.0	431.2	499.6	5.1	6.2	3.8	4.1	5.1
$650 to $699	1,336.3	387.6	175.8	328.2	444.7	4.2	5.4	2.6	3.1	4.2
$700 to $749	1,090.2	324.5	125.7	248.5	391.6	3.4	4.5	1.8	2.4	3.4
$750 to $999	2,637.8	809.3	243.2	494.3	1,090.9	8.2	11.2	3.5	4.7	8.2
$1,000 or more.........	1,276.0	428.3	86.9	228.9	532.0	4.0	5.9	1.3	2.2	4.0
No cash rent	1,419.3	228.8	272.3	642.1	276.1	4.4	3.2	4.0	6.1	4.4
Median gross rent (dol.) ...	$447	$499	$396	$405	$535	(X)	(X)	(X)	(X)	(X)

X Not applicable.

Source: U.S. Bureau of the Census, *1990 Census of Housing, General Housing Characteristics*, series CH-1.

No. 1239. Occupied Housing Units—

[In thousands of units, except as indicated. As of **April**.

STATE	Total housing units	SPECIFIED OWNER-OCCUPIED UNITS						Lower quartile value[1] (dol.)	Median (dol.)	Upper quartile value[1] (dol.)
		Value categories								
		Less than $50,000	$50,000 to $99,999	$100,000 to $149,000	$150,000 to $199,000	$200,000 to $299,000	$300,000 or more			
United States ..	44,918.0	11,402.5	16,957.5	6,773.3	4,017.2	3,376.9	2,390.7	49,500	79,100	137,800
Alabama	753.8	343.9	310.7	62.5	20.1	11.3	5.4	35,500	53,700	78,800
Alaska..........	77.5	11.0	31.9	23.0	7.5	3.2	0.9	66,400	94,400	128,500
Arizona	668.7	98.7	372.7	118.8	40.6	23.9	14.0	59,800	80,100	109,900
Arkansas	427.7	235.6	156.9	23.3	6.8	3.5	1.6	31,100	46,300	68,700
California	4,690.3	119.0	636.6	812.1	851.5	1,151.0	1,120.0	127,100	195,500	294,800
Colorado	637.6	84.1	363.1	122.8	37.4	19.9	10.3	62,500	82,700	109,700
Connecticut	643.5	4.6	36.7	165.3	188.0	150.3	98.5	139,000	177,800	246,000
Delaware	137.5	11.8	56.8	38.5	15.6	10.5	4.3	74,800	100,100	143,900
District of Columbia .	71.5	1.7	25.2	15.0	6.9	8.4	14.4	86,700	123,900	258,700
Florida..........	2,378.2	433.1	1,239.1	381.9	151.5	100.6	72.0	56,100	77,100	112,200
Georgia	1,138.8	314.5	531.2	163.2	66.9	39.9	23.1	47,300	71,300	102,100
Hawaii..........	144.4	3.3	13.1	16.7	21.1	39.7	50.5	156,800	245,300	358,800
Idaho	177.3	66.8	89.4	14.2	3.7	2.0	1.2	42,100	58,200	79,700
Illinois	2,084.7	525.1	786.6	403.2	183.7	114.5	71.6	49,800	80,900	128,300
Indiana	1,137.8	514.3	484.0	92.8	27.0	13.7	6.0	36,500	53,900	78,200
Iowa	566.6	317.8	209.7	27.7	7.0	3.3	1.1	30,200	45,900	65,900
Kansas	500.6	238.0	199.6	41.1	12.3	6.4	3.1	32,400	52,200	78,000
Kentucky	662.2	326.9	260.5	47.5	15.9	8.0	3.4	33,400	50,500	73,400
Louisiana	733.9	289.1	344.5	63.0	19.8	11.5	6.1	38,200	58,500	83,000
Maine	214.7	37.5	95.2	49.3	18.0	10.0	4.7	60,100	87,400	123,300
Maryland	970.9	87.3	300.9	274.2	139.6	103.3	65.6	79,000	116,500	169,300
Massachusetts	1,004.6	9.5	93.5	310.8	298.3	196.4	96.1	126,800	162,800	216,000
Michigan	1,916.1	737.2	814.5	219.2	79.3	46.0	20.0	38,500	60,600	90,600
Minnesota	894.3	204.9	482.3	138.2	38.6	21.1	9.2	52,200	74,000	98,200
Mississippi	441.8	249.3	156.1	24.2	7.0	3.6	1.6	31,400	45,600	67,800
Missouri.........	1,005.4	385.1	452.6	102.0	33.6	20.3	11.9	38,800	59,800	87,100
Montana	132.4	52.3	68.3	8.4	2.1	1.0	0.3	40,000	56,600	74,200
Nebraska........	314.4	155.3	132.4	18.5	4.7	2.4	1.0	32,800	50,400	70,400
Nevada	183.8	8.4	93.3	51.3	16.0	9.1	5.6	75,400	95,700	129,400
New Hampshire ...	199.4	6.3	45.6	79.9	39.9	21.1	6.6	98,400	129,400	167,600
New Jersey	1,466.3	45.5	241.4	348.8	367.3	301.5	161.9	112,300	162,300	225,000
New Mexico	262.3	73.5	128.2	37.3	12.8	7.2	3.3	46,700	70,100	97,800
New York........	2,387.6	243.8	674.4	431.6	439.0	381.0	217.8	76,200	131,600	200,400
North Carolina	1,218.0	382.8	575.7	155.2	56.3	33.1	15.0	44,700	65,800	94,900
North Dakota	103.7	50.6	46.3	5.1	1.1	0.5	0.1	30,800	50,800	70,000
Ohio	2,241.3	734.0	1,102.8	260.5	80.8	42.9	20.3	43,900	63,500	90,200
Oklahoma	616.3	323.7	235.6	36.8	10.9	6.1	3.3	30,800	48,100	71,000
Oregon	511.8	133.3	281.2	62.7	19.5	10.5	4.7	49,200	67,100	92,600
Pennsylvania	2,581.3	829.2	1,017.8	395.9	180.6	109.1	48.7	42,500	69,700	109,500
Rhode Island	176.5	3.0	31.0	78.4	35.6	19.4	9.0	106,000	133,500	171,800
South Carolina	615.4	225.7	280.1	63.5	23.7	14.8	7.6	41,100	61,100	89,100
South Dakota	113.1	64.2	42.4	4.6	1.0	0.5	0.2	27,300	45,200	64,500
Tennessee.......	938.4	371.8	416.4	91.5	32.2	17.8	8.7	39,600	58,400	85,300
Texas	2,949.1	1,151.2	1,261.1	314.8	111.3	66.5	44.2	38,300	59,600	89,200
Utah	303.7	61.1	188.6	35.2	10.6	5.7	2.5	53,100	68,900	92,000
Vermont.........	89.2	7.9	41.3	25.5	8.4	4.4	1.7	73,100	95,500	130,000
Virginia	1,192.1	206.7	466.2	203.9	132.8	116.5	66.0	60,100	91,000	155,800
Washington	896.4	124.0	371.3	192.7	101.0	67.8	39.6	63,700	93,400	145,400
West Virginia	350.1	185.3	136.8	18.9	5.4	2.8	0.9	31,200	47,900	69,400
Wisconsin	916.7	287.2	492.2	95.3	24.7	12.3	5.1	45,600	62,500	86,100
Wyoming	78.4	25.9	43.8	6.2	1.5	0.7	0.4	43,900	61,600	82,100

[1] This measure divides the distribution of value and rent categories into four equal parts. The lower quartile value is the value that defines the upper limit of the lowest one-quarter of the cases. The upper quartile value defines the lower limit of the upper one-quarter of the cases in the distribution.

Housing Value and Gross Rent, by State: 1990

Based on the Census of Population and Housing; see appendix III]

Total housing units	SPECIFIED RENTER-OCCUPIED UNITS							Median (dol.)	STATE
	Rent categories								
	Less than $200	$200 to $299	$300 to $399	$400 to $499	$500 to $599	$600 to $749	$750 or more		
32,170.0	2,815.1	3,736.2	5,879.2	5,935.0	4,407.0	4,064.4	3,913.8	447	United States
428.0	81.6	87.3	102.1	67.2	29.1	15.7	6.8	325	Alabama
81.9	1.4	4.4	9.8	12.9	11.3	13.1	17.9	559	Alaska
485.8	25.5	46.1	111.5	113.1	71.2	53.0	39.8	438	Arizona
258.1	38.6	57.8	64.8	39.3	17.2	8.5	4.3	328	Arkansas
4,553.4	136.2	198.5	379.5	621.9	736.4	1,004.1	1,361.9	620	California
472.6	36.5	63.3	110.0	96.4	62.2	51.9	36.0	418	Colorado
418.5	31.2	21.4	31.1	51.2	68.2	94.1	106.3	598	Connecticut
72.2	6.0	4.4	8.7	16.0	16.0	10.9	6.7	495	Delaware
152.1	14.7	11.0	25.5	29.5	21.7	20.3	26.6	479	District of Columbia
1,669.6	103.2	130.9	271.1	368.9	308.6	253.3	168.5	481	Florida
808.4	97.8	99.6	134.3	155.9	128.1	98.0	53.2	433	Georgia
162.8	9.1	7.5	12.6	15.6	17.5	26.2	52.3	650	Hawaii
102.4	14.0	24.5	26.3	16.3	6.5	4.0	2.2	330	Idaho
1,470.4	128.7	159.0	281.6	306.8	229.8	185.8	134.3	445	Illinois
589.9	61.5	104.8	156.4	128.6	65.9	29.3	14.1	374	Indiana
285.7	40.5	66.1	76.7	50.7	22.1	10.8	4.6	336	Iowa
289.8	32.3	54.8	69.0	57.7	30.4	19.3	10.3	372	Kansas
392.3	69.2	87.8	100.6	56.9	24.1	11.9	5.4	319	Kentucky
501.3	70.7	93.1	123.5	88.5	43.6	24.3	14.4	352	Louisiana
133.3	15.5	14.2	26.6	26.6	19.2	14.1	7.5	419	Maine
598.3	41.2	36.0	65.4	94.0	106.0	128.8	108.2	548	Maryland
910.0	98.4	58.2	74.9	106.8	130.2	184.5	231.1	580	Massachusetts
966.2	82.1	123.4	209.0	223.3	149.7	92.0	54.6	423	Michigan
445.9	54.6	54.7	85.1	94.3	66.0	50.2	28.4	422	Minnesota
247.5	49.8	54.0	54.0	32.7	15.7	7.9	3.4	309	Mississippi
585.0	74.0	108.7	138.7	115.2	62.5	37.6	18.1	368	Missouri
93.9	16.1	24.4	24.8	12.9	5.5	2.1	0.9	311	Montana
186.6	24.6	39.8	48.6	34.8	16.2	7.7	4.6	348	Nebraska
209.2	8.4	11.5	29.0	48.5	44.4	38.9	22.9	509	Nevada
127.8	7.7	7.1	12.3	21.6	24.9	27.3	21.5	549	New Hampshire
973.7	60.8	45.3	81.1	133.1	166.0	228.3	232.7	592	New Jersey
173.1	18.3	28.6	44.9	31.0	16.4	11.9	7.4	372	New Mexico
3,150.6	242.8	281.8	490.1	605.9	463.7	454.7	532.9	486	New York
777.9	83.5	121.5	187.4	162.2	90.6	49.8	22.3	382	North Carolina
78.5	13.8	18.7	19.8	11.4	4.0	1.8	0.7	313	North Dakota
1,293.4	149.2	206.4	341.2	280.5	146.7	79.0	40.8	379	Ohio
370.7	44.2	85.0	98.7	60.5	30.1	17.8	9.0	340	Oklahoma
394.9	30.2	52.5	99.2	96.1	52.1	33.7	18.1	408	Oregon
1,287.7	141.0	189.7	272.2	245.0	169.6	125.3	85.4	404	Pennsylvania
152.0	17.9	12.1	18.0	29.1	29.2	25.3	15.7	489	Rhode Island
368.9	45.3	59.5	83.9	77.1	38.5	21.2	10.4	376	South Carolina
81.2	16.2	19.4	18.7	11.6	4.5	2.3	0.9	306	South Dakota
568.9	86.8	101.6	134.5	110.3	55.1	27.6	13.9	357	Tennessee
2,332.9	179.0	345.2	614.2	480.6	263.7	193.8	139.7	395	Texas
169.8	12.4	31.3	53.8	33.9	15.7	9.6	6.3	369	Utah
61.8	5.1	5.8	11.3	14.2	9.9	7.5	4.5	446	Vermont
746.2	59.6	65.7	109.8	124.0	103.8	114.3	128.9	495	Virginia
687.0	49.0	73.5	135.2	152.7	109.0	85.1	56.2	445	Washington
168.3	30.7	41.7	40.8	21.4	8.1	3.8	1.4	303	West Virginia
582.4	51.6	83.9	147.8	142.2	76.6	43.7	18.8	399	Wisconsin
51.5	6.7	12.5	13.2	8.1	3.5	2.1	0.9	333	Wyoming

Source: U.S. Bureau of the Census, *1990 Census of Housing, General Housing Characteristics*, series CH-1, and *Detailed Housing Characteristics*, series CH-2, forthcoming; and *Census of Population and Housing, 1990: Summary Tape File 1C and 3C on CD-ROM*.

No. 1240. Housing Units—

[In thousands of units, except as indicated. As of April.

STATE	Total housing units (1,000)	YEAR STRUCTURE BUILT				LACKING COMPLETE PLUMBING		PERCENT OF UNITS WITH—	
		Percent			Median year built	Total units (1,000)	Percent of total housing units	Public water system or private company	Public sewer
		1939 or earlier	1970 to 1979	1980 to March 1990					
United States ..	102,263.7	18.4	21.8	20.7	1965	1,101.7	1.1	84.2	74.8
Alabama	1,670.4	9.3	25.5	23.5	1970	27.5	1.6	87.1	54.5
Alaska.	232.6	3.0	32.7	38.0	1976	29.0	12.5	65.6	62.3
Arizona	1,659.4	3.2	30.7	37.8	1976	31.5	1.9	94.5	81.3
Arkansas	1,000.7	9.4	27.8	24.2	1971	18.4	1.8	81.5	60.1
California	11,182.9	10.7	21.7	22.9	1967	69.4	0.6	95.4	89.6
Colorado	1,477.3	13.0	28.9	24.7	1971	11.8	0.8	91.0	86.9
Connecticut	1,320.9	25.5	15.7	15.7	1959	5.7	0.4	77.7	70.8
Delaware	289.9	14.3	20.2	24.3	1967	1.7	0.6	76.2	73.4
District of Columbia .	278.5	37.7	8.4	5.5	1947	2.3	0.8	99.9	99.3
Florida.	6,100.3	3.7	29.3	35.0	1975	28.0	0.5	86.9	73.8
Georgia	2,638.4	8.1	24.5	32.1	1973	28.5	1.1	81.3	62.1
Hawaii.	389.8	6.7	30.5	20.8	1970	4.3	1.1	97.6	80.2
Idaho	413.3	15.9	32.4	18.0	1970	6.0	1.5	70.0	64.0
Illinois	4,506.3	27.1	18.4	11.7	1958	29.3	0.7	89.8	86.2
Indiana	2,246.0	24.2	20.2	14.5	1961	16.2	0.7	74.1	67.9
Iowa	1,143.7	35.0	20.2	10.0	1956	9.8	0.9	81.1	76.0
Kansas	1,044.1	24.5	20.3	16.9	1961	7.9	0.8	89.5	81.2
Kentucky	1,506.8	15.9	25.0	20.0	1967	44.2	2.9	80.6	56.4
Louisiana	1,716.2	10.6	25.3	22.1	1969	21.9	1.3	89.0	72.6
Maine	587.0	34.9	19.8	20.7	1960	20.8	3.5	53.2	45.4
Maryland	1,891.9	15.5	19.6	21.6	1965	12.7	0.7	82.8	81.1
Massachusetts	2,472.7	38.9	14.1	13.8	1953	12.4	0.5	91.6	72.9
Michigan	3,847.9	20.8	20.4	13.6	1960	32.5	0.8	70.5	70.8
Minnesota	1,848.4	24.5	22.1	18.5	1963	24.4	1.3	73.0	73.4
Mississippi	1,010.4	8.6	27.5	24.1	1971	21.9	2.2	87.3	57.9
Missouri.	2,199.1	20.4	21.5	18.3	1964	26.8	1.2	83.6	73.6
Montana	361.2	21.8	26.6	17.5	1966	7.0	1.9	65.5	60.5
Nebraska	660.6	30.7	22.1	12.9	1960	5.2	0.8	83.0	80.9
Nevada	518.9	2.9	30.5	40.1	1977	2.7	0.5	92.5	87.9
New Hampshire . . .	503.9	27.1	20.5	27.7	1968	5.9	1.2	60.3	49.6
New Jersey	3,075.3	24.6	14.9	14.8	1959	15.6	0.5	89.6	87.9
New Mexico	632.1	8.1	26.5	27.5	1972	20.0	3.2	83.1	71.7
New York.	7,226.9	35.7	11.9	9.4	1952	67.3	0.9	87.6	79.1
North Carolina	2,818.2	9.9	24.3	28.6	1971	43.0	1.5	65.4	49.8
North Dakota	276.3	24.7	26.6	16.6	1965	5.6	2.0	79.0	73.9
Ohio	4,371.9	25.8	18.6	12.2	1959	32.9	0.8	82.4	77.6
Oklahoma	1,406.5	12.4	25.4	22.1	1969	13.8	1.0	87.0	73.1
Oregon	1,193.6	16.8	28.7	16.6	1967	10.4	0.9	80.7	70.0
Pennsylvania	4,938.1	35.1	15.8	12.4	1954	47.1	1.0	78.1	74.3
Rhode Island	414.6	34.0	14.7	15.1	1955	2.3	0.5	88.8	70.9
South Carolina	1,424.2	8.5	26.3	29.0	1972	20.2	1.4	77.2	58.0
South Dakota	292.4	30.4	24.6	14.8	1961	5.9	2.0	81.4	71.1
Tennessee	2,026.1	10.2	24.8	24.2	1970	32.4	1.6	85.7	59.9
Texas	7,009.0	7.1	25.9	29.7	1972	85.1	1.2	91.6	81.2
Utah	598.4	13.5	28.1	24.4	1971	5.9	1.0	95.8	88.4
Vermont.	271.2	36.5	19.6	22.4	1963	6.1	2.3	50.9	42.5
Virginia	2,496.3	11.0	23.6	26.3	1970	46.1	1.8	76.1	69.7
Washington	2,032.4	15.7	24.6	23.1	1969	18.6	0.9	85.7	68.3
West Virginia	781.3	23.7	22.8	17.7	1962	25.1	3.2	72.1	54.8
Wisconsin	2,055.8	28.5	21.1	14.5	1960	29.8	1.4	66.5	70.0
Wyoming	203.4	15.6	31.1	21.4	1971	3.2	1.6	77.6	74.2

Selected Characteristics: 1990

Based on the Census of Population and Housing; see Appendix III]

Occupied housing units (1,000)	Percent owner occupied	Percent condominium	PERCENT WITH—								STATE
			Vehicles available		No telephone in unit	House heating fuel					
			None	Two or more		Utility gas	Bottled, tank, or LP gas	Electricity	Fuel oil, kerosene [1]	Wood	
91,947.4	64.2	4.4	11.5	54.7	5.2	51.0	5.7	25.8	12.2	3.9	**United States**
1,506.8	70.5	1.1	10.3	58.7	8.7	42.8	15.6	34.6	1.2	5.3	Alabama
188.9	56.1	5.3	11.9	54.0	8.3	42.8	1.9	11.8	32.3	7.7	Alaska
1,368.8	64.2	6.0	7.8	53.3	8.5	39.5	4.4	51.4	0.2	3.6	Arizona
891.2	69.6	0.7	9.8	56.2	10.9	52.8	11.6	22.7	0.2	12.5	Arkansas
10,381.2	55.6	7.4	8.9	57.9	3.0	73.2	3.1	19.2	0.3	3.1	California
1,282.5	62.3	7.3	6.9	60.9	4.2	77.0	4.8	12.9	0.3	3.3	Colorado
1,230.5	65.6	8.7	10.0	58.6	2.6	26.3	1.9	15.1	54.4	1.6	Connecticut
247.5	70.3	2.6	8.2	59.3	3.1	30.5	6.8	21.8	38.5	1.7	Delaware
249.6	38.9	10.4	37.4	21.2	4.2	63.5	2.0	20.5	12.5	0.0	District of Columbia
5,134.9	67.2	12.9	9.2	49.8	5.3	7.5	7.2	78.8	4.1	0.8	Florida
2,366.6	64.9	2.6	10.3	58.8	8.3	53.3	13.8	27.2	1.5	3.8	Georgia
356.3	53.9	18.4	9.9	54.1	2.6	3.3	2.0	37.9	0.2	0.5	Hawaii
360.7	70.1	1.2	4.6	67.3	5.8	28.2	3.1	39.8	9.0	18.0	Idaho
4,202.2	64.2	5.4	14.0	50.9	4.6	80.3	4.3	11.2	1.8	1.0	Illinois
2,065.4	70.2	1.4	8.5	59.1	5.9	63.1	6.4	19.3	6.2	4.2	Indiana
1,064.3	70.0	1.1	7.1	61.7	3.4	65.6	14.8	10.5	5.5	2.9	Iowa
944.7	67.9	1.7	6.4	61.7	4.4	75.9	8.8	11.8	0.3	2.9	Kansas
1,379.8	69.6	1.3	11.5	56.0	10.2	45.6	7.7	30.0	4.8	8.2	Kentucky
1,499.3	65.9	1.6	13.9	49.9	8.3	55.1	5.8	36.2	0.3	2.3	Louisiana
465.3	70.5	1.6	8.7	57.1	3.7	1.8	1.9	11.7	69.5	14.1	Maine
1,749.0	65.0	5.5	12.3	56.0	3.2	43.2	2.3	29.6	22.1	1.9	Maryland
2,247.1	59.3	6.1	14.3	49.3	2.1	38.0	2.1	13.5	44.0	1.5	Massachusetts
3,419.3	71.0	2.7	10.1	56.8	4.1	76.9	6.1	5.4	6.9	3.9	Michigan
1,647.9	71.8	3.1	8.6	60.0	2.4	62.9	8.2	10.5	11.9	4.9	Minnesota
911.4	71.5	0.6	12.1	54.2	12.6	40.8	20.1	30.6	0.5	7.8	Mississippi
1,961.2	68.8	2.0	9.8	57.0	5.2	60.4	12.0	18.1	1.5	7.6	Missouri
306.2	67.3	1.2	6.7	63.5	6.9	54.2	7.5	17.9	4.1	14.7	Montana
602.4	66.5	1.2	7.2	62.5	3.6	70.2	10.9	13.6	2.5	2.1	Nebraska
466.3	54.8	6.7	7.8	54.8	5.4	47.7	6.0	39.3	3.7	2.6	Nevada
411.2	68.2	5.8	6.3	61.7	3.4	15.2	6.1	12.4	55.8	9.0	New Hampshire
2,794.7	64.9	6.7	12.9	52.5	3.1	57.5	1.9	10.0	29.2	0.5	New Jersey
542.7	67.4	1.5	6.9	59.0	12.4	70.1	11.9	9.1	0.3	7.6	New Mexico
6,639.3	52.2	4.6	30.0	37.5	5.0	45.7	2.4	8.5	39.6	2.0	New York
2,517.0	68.0	2.5	9.6	59.2	7.1	18.6	8.5	42.0	22.5	7.8	North Carolina
240.9	65.6	2.3	6.5	63.2	3.5	39.7	14.0	26.2	15.7	1.2	North Dakota
4,087.5	67.5	2.5	10.2	56.8	4.7	68.2	3.8	16.8	7.5	2.5	Ohio
1,206.1	68.1	1.5	7.5	58.1	8.8	64.4	10.0	20.5	0.1	4.7	Oklahoma
1,103.3	63.1	1.7	8.0	59.9	4.5	24.7	1.5	44.6	11.4	16.9	Oregon
4496.0	70.7	2.0	15.2	49.5	2.6	49.5	1.7	14.8	27.9	2.6	Pennsylvania
378.0	59.5	2.8	10.6	54.5	3.1	40.7	2.4	7.9	47.0	1.4	Rhode Island
1,258.0	69.9	2.3	10.9	57.2	9.1	24.6	9.2	46.9	13.2	5.7	South Carolina
259.0	66.1	0.8	6.5	64.1	6.0	43.0	19.9	17.8	13.6	4.2	South Dakota
1,853.7	68.0	2.0	9.8	58.2	7.1	30.0	5.5	50.5	3.8	9.0	Tennessee
6,070.9	60.9	2.7	8.1	55.9	8.6	50.4	7.8	40.2	0.1	1.2	Texas
537.3	68.1	4.6	5.4	66.1	4.0	81.9	2.3	9.5	1.3	3.2	Utah
210.7	69.0	3.1	8.0	58.0	4.5	8.0	10.5	9.1	54.3	17.0	Vermont
2,291.8	66.3	4.8	9.0	59.8	5.4	28.9	2.3	40.1	20.2	6.7	Virginia
1,872.4	62.6	3.0	7.5	61.4	3.5	22.4	1.1	55.1	9.9	10.6	Washington
688.6	74.1	0.6	13.7	50.4	10.3	50.7	2.8	25.3	7.8	9.0	West Virginia
1,822.1	66.7	1.6	9.3	57.8	2.8	61.0	8.4	9.3	14.6	5.9	Wisconsin
168.8	67.8	1.2	4.7	66.9	5.6	62.9	9.0	16.5	0.7	7.9	Wyoming

Source: U.S. Bureau of the Census, *1990 Census of Housing, Detailed Housing Characteristics*, series CH-2, forthcoming, and *Census of Population and Housing, 1990: Summary Tape File 3C on CD-ROM.*

No. 1241. Occupied Housing Units—Monthly Owner and Renter Costs as Related to Household Income: 1980 and 1990

[In thousands of units, except as indicated. As of **April 1**. Based on the Census of Population and Housing, see Appendix III]

STATE	1980						1990					
	Median gross rent		Median selected monthly owner costs				Median gross rent		Median selected monthly owner costs			
	Amount (dollars)	As a percent of household income in 1979	With a mortgage (dollars)	Not mortgaged (dollars)	As a percentage of household income in 1979		Amount (dollars)	As a percent of household income in 1989	With a mortgage (dollars)	Not mortgaged (dollars)	As a percentage of household income in 1989	
					With a mortgage	Not mortgaged					With a mortgage	Not mortgaged
United States...	243	25.0	366	128	19.2	11.5	447	26.4	737	209	21.0	12.9
Alabama	188	24.2	295	104	18.6	11.7	325	24.8	555	159	18.4	12.8
Alaska	368	24.0	640	160	20.4	[1]10.0	559	23.8	1,059	232	21.5	12.2
Arizona	264	27.5	365	109	20.2	[1]10.0	438	27.5	769	188	22.8	12.4
Arkansas	185	24.7	280	96	19.3	12.1	328	26.5	514	173	20.0	13.4
California	283	27.1	411	98	19.8	[1]10.0	620	29.1	1,077	191	24.9	11.8
Colorado	252	26.4	422	125	21.0	11.5	418	26.1	800	203	22.5	12.7
Connecticut	260	24.5	434	205	19.9	13.9	598	26.6	1,096	338	22.9	13.7
Delaware	247	25.0	351	146	18.4	11.8	495	24.7	763	200	19.5	12.0
District of Columbia	224	22.4	399	158	17.9	[1]10.0	479	25.4	950	250	20.5	12.8
Florida	255	28.3	337	101	20.2	10.2	481	28.0	718	186	22.3	12.2
Georgia	211	24.5	340	107	19.2	11.2	433	25.8	737	182	20.9	12.8
Hawaii	311	26.1	463	110	19.0	[1]10.0	650	27.4	1,008	170	21.4	10.8
Idaho	218	25.4	332	102	20.1	10.6	330	23.8	561	157	19.3	11.8
Illinois	246	23.8	406	152	19.0	11.3	445	25.9	767	241	20.2	12.7
Indiana	218	23.1	304	118	17.0	10.9	374	24.3	561	188	16.7	12.3
Iowa	226	24.6	348	133	19.2	12.5	336	24.1	553	196	17.3	12.8
Kansas	218	23.8	330	106	18.2	10.5	372	24.5	628	187	19.1	12.6
Kentucky	198	23.9	298	103	18.3	10.7	319	24.9	536	150	18.0	12.3
Louisiana	214	24.6	313	96	18.1	[1]10.0	352	27.9	595	168	20.6	13.3
Maine	216	26.5	317	144	20.9	14.3	419	26.8	664	222	21.4	13.4
Maryland	266	23.3	413	149	18.5	10.9	548	25.4	919	235	21.1	12.4
Massachusetts	255	25.0	424	225	20.9	16.0	580	26.8	985	298	22.3	13.8
Michigan	250	24.8	363	159	18.3	12.7	423	27.2	651	246	18.0	13.5
Minnesota	236	25.0	375	132	18.9	12.1	422	26.7	724	186	20.4	12.4
Mississippi	180	24.9	284	98	19.6	12.7	309	27.1	511	158	20.8	13.5
Missouri	211	24.2	317	118	18.1	11.5	368	25.2	600	177	18.4	12.3
Montana	200	23.9	347	109	19.6	10.7	311	25.0	575	175	20.2	12.5
Nebraska	213	23.2	359	120	19.7	12.0	348	23.7	610	191	19.4	12.6
Nevada	310	28.6	454	135	22.5	[1]10.0	509	26.8	833	204	22.4	11.9
New Hampshire	251	25.5	408	189	22.2	15.7	549	26.4	1,000	321	24.4	14.7
New Jersey	270	24.8	456	218	20.5	14.6	592	26.3	1,105	382	23.4	15.1
New Mexico	215	25.4	324	98	19.4	10.2	372	26.5	651	163	21.6	12.5
New York	249	25.1	430	196	20.2	14.5	486	26.3	894	323	21.5	14.4
North Carolina	205	23.9	320	111	19.2	11.1	382	24.4	655	184	20.5	12.9
North Dakota	206	23.2	392	133	21.3	13.1	313	23.9	608	192	20.3	13.0
Ohio	225	24.0	347	133	18.5	10.8	379	25.3	625	205	18.2	12.5
Oklahoma	215	24.9	305	90	18.8	10.7	340	25.4	573	164	20.0	12.8
Oregon	257	26.8	371	125	19.6	12.2	408	25.5	650	226	20.4	13.4
Pennsylvania	224	24.4	336	141	18.5	11.8	404	26.1	682	226	20.2	13.3
Rhode Island	222	24.9	391	192	21.1	14.6	489	27.5	891	290	22.7	13.9
South Carolina	206	24.4	312	112	19.0	11.5	376	24.4	617	179	19.8	13.0
South Dakota	188	24.4	352	135	21.3	14.7	306	24.6	569	195	19.8	13.3
Tennessee	203	24.3	299	103	18.8	10.5	357	25.0	594	170	20.1	12.6
Texas	246	24.3	348	101	18.4	[1]10.0	395	24.6	712	193	20.9	13.1
Utah	235	24.8	381	116	21.3	[1]10.0	369	23.8	667	185	20.9	12.1
Vermont	224	26.9	336	164	20.6	14.6	446	27.1	719	262	21.9	14.7
Virginia	259	24.7	395	129	20.2	11.6	495	25.8	831	192	21.9	12.5
Washington	254	25.7	362	106	18.5	[1]10.0	445	25.7	738	194	20.4	11.8
West Virginia	195	23.5	290	93	17.6	[1]10.0	303	26.8	498	143	17.5	12.0
Wisconsin	234	23.7	381	158	19.6	13.0	399	24.9	678	251	20.1	13.4
Wyoming	252	22.6	397	97	19.0	[1]10.0	333	23.7	612	162	18.8	11.9

[1] Data represents a value of 10 percent or less.

Source: U.S. Bureau of the Census, *1980 Census of Housing, Metropolitan Housing Characteristics*, series HC80-2, *1990 Census of Housing, Detailed Housing Characteristics*, series CH-2, forthcoming.

No. 1242. Housing Units—Summary of Characteristics and Equipment, by Tenure and Region: 1991

[In thousands of units, except as indicated. Based on the American Housing Survey; see Appendix III. For composition of regions, see table 31]

ITEM	Total housing units	Sea-sonal	YEAR-ROUND UNITS							Vacant
			Occupied							
			Total	Owner	Renter	North-east	Mid-west	South	West	
Total units	**104,592**	**2,728**	**93,147**	**59,796**	**33,351**	**18,962**	**22,593**	**32,190**	**19,402**	**8,717**
Percent distribution	100.0	2.6	89.1	57.2	31.9	18.1	21.6	30.8	18.6	8.3
Units in structure:										
Single family detached	62,646	1,637	57,485	49,084	8,401	9,761	15,092	20,954	11,678	3,524
Single family attached	6,156	74	5,442	2,722	2,720	1,544	923	1,814	1,161	640
2 to 4 units	10,890	90	9,490	1,909	7,581	3,211	2,409	2,119	1,751	1,309
5 to 9 units	5,368	56	4,639	398	4,240	975	969	1,520	1,175	674
10 to 19 units	4,764	69	3,993	317	3,676	714	765	1,479	1,036	701
20 to 49 units	3,713	58	3,118	328	2,790	882	615	741	880	536
50 or more units	4,073	98	3,350	505	2,845	1,373	726	682	569	625
Mobile home or trailer	6,983	645	5,630	4,532	1,098	502	1,095	2,882	1,151	708
Stories in structure: [1]										
One story	3,015	25	2,606	290	2,316	145	418	1,216	827	384
2 stories	10,398	118	8,920	929	7,992	947	1,347	3,434	3,193	1,360
3 stories	8,110	116	6,938	1,254	5,684	2,475	2,414	1,205	844	1,056
4 to 6 stories	4,724	58	4,024	628	3,396	2,265	954	386	419	642
7 or more stories	2,585	56	2,123	373	1,750	1,329	351	305	139	406
Foundation: [2]										
Full or partial basement	30,995	309	29,401	25,785	3,616	9,713	12,239	4,720	2,729	1,286
Crawlspace	18,152	603	16,067	12,520	3,547	621	2,165	8,520	4,761	1,481
Concrete slab	17,710	390	16,134	12,581	3,554	853	1,373	8,804	5,105	1,185
Other	1,945	410	1,324	921	403	119	238	723	245	211
Year structure built: [3]										
1939 and earlier	22,759	494	20,065	11,484	8,581	7,388	6,528	3,754	2,395	2,199
1940 to 1949	8,607	226	7,668	4,742	2,926	1,700	1,818	2,550	1,599	713
1950 to 1959	13,836	420	12,512	8,982	3,530	2,621	3,236	3,964	2,691	904
1960 to 1969	16,161	468	14,523	9,570	4,953	2,445	3,389	5,353	3,337	1,170
1970 to 1979	23,598	689	21,005	13,377	7,629	2,717	4,662	8,524	5,101	1,902
1980 or later	19,632	429	17,374	11,643	5,730	2,090	2,959	8,045	4,279	1,828
Median year	1964	1965	1964	1965	1963	1952	1959	1971	1969	1965
Main heating equipment:										
Warm-air furnace	54,015	774	49,423	34,860	14,563	6,418	16,446	16,256	10,303	3,818
Electric heat pump	8,755	237	7,638	5,497	2,141	405	587	5,579	1,068	880
Steam or hot water system	15,145	86	13,929	7,520	6,409	9,651	2,737	831	710	1,130
Floor, wall, or pipeless furnace	4,819	75	4,291	1,948	2,343	138	339	1,373	2,441	453
Built-in electric units	7,934	283	6,755	2,992	3,763	1,366	1,257	2,050	2,082	897
Room heaters with flue	3,182	238	2,549	1,349	1,200	256	389	1,325	578	396
Room heaters without flue	2,484	48	2,111	1,197	915	38	63	1,837	174	325
Stoves	3,552	390	2,887	2,219	668	453	459	1,238	738	275
Fireplaces	1,280	123	1,098	899	199	54	136	483	426	58
None	1,500	352	861	378	484	50	39	278	494	287
Portable elec. heaters	860	68	695	362	333	11	22	442	220	97
Other	1,067	56	910	577	333	122	120	498	170	101
Air conditioning:										
Central	43,274	664	39,330	28,217	11,113	3,159	9,639	20,465	6,067	3,280
Percent of total units	41.4	24.3	42.2	47.2	33.3	16.7	42.7	63.6	31.3	37.6
One or more room units	28,569	347	26,786	16,438	10,347	8,204	7,134	8,545	2,901	1,436
Source of water:										
Public system or private company . .	88,666	1,412	79,814	48,785	31,029	16,077	18,820	27,264	17,652	7,440
Percent of total units	84.8	51.8	85.7	81.6	93.0	84.8	83.3	84.7	91.0	85.4
Well serving 1 to 5 units	13,739	828	11,809	10,042	1,767	2,642	3,598	4,396	1,173	1,102
Other	2,187	488	1,525	969	556	242	176	530	577	174
Means of sewage disposal:										
Public sewer	78,943	1,003	71,302	41,427	29,876	14,632	17,775	22,446	16,450	6,638
Percent of total units	75.5	36.8	76.6	69.3	89.6	77.2	78.7	69.7	84.8	76.2
Septic tank, cesspool, chemical toilet	25,058	1,407	21,672	18,284	3,388	4,308	4,801	9,622	2,940	1,979
Other	591	318	173	86	87	21	17	123	12	100

[1] Limited to multiunit structures. [2] Limited to single-family units. [3] For mobile home, oldest category is 1939 or earlier.

Source: U.S. Bureau of the Census, *Current Housing Reports*, series H-150-91, American Housing Survey.

No. 1243. Heating Equipment and Fuels for Occupied Units: 1950 to 1990

[Based on the Census of Population and Housing; see Appendix III]

ITEM	NUMBER (1,000)					PERCENT DISTRIBUTION				
	1950	1960	1970	1980	1990	1950	1960	1970	1980	1990
Occupied units, total	**42,826**	**53,024**	**63,445**	**80,390**	**91,947**	**100.0**	**100.0**	**100.0**	**100.0**	**100.0**
Heating equipment:										
Warm air furnace	[1]11,508	17,378	27,515	39,279	(NA)	[1]26.9	32.8	43.4	48.9	(NA)
Heat pumps	(NA)	(NA)	(NA)	2,835	(NA)	(NA)	(NA)	(NA)	3.5	(NA)
Steam or hot water	10,071	11,990	13,211	13,859	(NA)	23.5	22.6	20.8	17.2	(NA)
Floor, wall, or pipeless furnace	[1]	6,088	5,552	4,693	(NA)	[1]	11.5	8.8	5.8	(NA)
Built-in electric units	-	664	3,236	6,370	(NA)	-	1.3	5.1	7.9	(NA)
Room heaters with flue	[2]15,399	[2]11,183	7,209	6,098	(NA)	[2]36.0	[2]21.1	11.4	7.6	(NA)
Room heaters without flue.....	5,268	5,218	3,558	2,736	(NA)	12.3	9.8	5.6	3.4	(NA)
Fireplaces, stoves, portable heaters or other	[2]	[2]	2,766	3,977	(NA)	[2]	[2]	4.4	4.9	(NA)
None	581	503	398	541	(NA)	1.4	0.9	0.6	0.7	(NA)
House heating fuel:										
Utility gas	11,387	22,851	35,014	42,658	46,851	26.6	43.1	55.2	53.1	51.0
Fuel oil, kerosene, etc.	9,686	17,158	16,473	14,655	11,244	22.6	32.4	26.0	18.2	12.2
Electricity	283	933	4,876	14,768	23,697	0.7	1.8	7.7	18.3	25.8
Bottled, tank, or LP gas.......	787	2,686	3,807	4,535	5,243	1.8	5.1	6.0	5.6	5.7
Wood and other fuel.........	4,855	2,460	1,060	2,729	4,009	11.3	4.6	1.7	3.4	4.4
Coal or coke	14,828	6,456	1,821	504	359	34.6	12.2	2.9	0.6	0.4
None	999	478	395	541	544	2.3	0.9	0.6	0.7	0.6
Cooking fuel:										
Electricity	6,403	16,351	25,768	41,906	(NA)	15.0	30.8	40.6	52.1	(NA)
Gas [3]..................	25,501	33,787	36,558	37,944	(NA)	59.6	63.7	57.6	47.2	(NA)
Other fuel	10,796	2,603	908	398	(NA)	25.2	4.9	1.4	0.5	(NA)
None	124	280	213	142	(NA)	0.3	0.5	0.3	0.2	(NA)

- Represents zero. NA Not available. [1] "Floor, wall, or pipeless furnace" included in "Warm air furnace." [2] "Fireplaces, stoves, or portable heaters" included in "Room heaters with flue." [3] Includes utility, bottled, tank, and LP gas.

No. 1244. Appliances Used by Households, by Region and Family Income: 1990

[In millions, except percent. As of November. Represents appliances possessed and generally used by the household. Based on Residential Energy Consumption Survey; see Appendix III. For composition of regions, see table 31]

TYPE OF APPLIANCE	HOUSEHOLDS USING APPLIANCE		REGION				FAMILY INCOME IN 1990			
	Number	Percent of total	North-east	Midwest	South	West	Under $15,000	$15,000 -$24,999	$25,000 -$34,999	$35,000 and over
Total households ..	**94.0**	**100.0**	**19.2**	**23.1**	**32.3**	**19.4**	**27.3**	**17.4**	**15.3**	**34.0**
Air conditioners: Room ...	29.1	31.0	8.1	8.0	10.3	2.8	9.7	5.5	4.9	9.0
Central system [1].....	36.6	38.9	3.2	9.2	19.0	5.2	6.0	6.0	6.0	18.7
Clothes washer	71.7	76.3	14.4	17.7	25.6	14.0	16.3	12.3	12.3	30.7
Clothes dryer.........	64.7	68.8	12.4	16.9	22.7	12.8	12.7	10.6	11.4	29.9
Dehumidifier	11.3	12.0	3.5	5.3	2.0	0.5	1.5	1.7	1.7	6.4
Dishwasher...........	42.7	45.4	8.0	9.3	15.3	10.0	5.2	5.9	7.5	23.9
Evaporative cooler [2]....	3.8	4.0	(B)	(B)	(B)	2.9	1.3	0.8	0.9	0.8
Freezer	32.4	34.5	5.0	9.1	12.3	5.9	7.9	5.7	5.4	13.4
Microwave oven [3]	74.1	78.8	13.6	19.4	25.7	15.3	16.9	13.4	12.8	31.0
Motor vehicles: [4] One...	33.1	35.3	35.3	35.3	35.6	34.7	13.4	8.3	5.0	6.4
Two or more	50.8	54.0	46.7	55.8	55.2	57.2	6.2	7.7	9.8	27.1
Outdoor gas grill	24.9	26.4	6.8	7.1	7.0	4.0	2.4	3.2	4.1	15.1
Outdoor gas light	1.0	1.1	0.3	0.3	0.3	(B)	0.2	0.2	0.1	0.5
Oven: Electric	55.3	58.9	9.3	12.7	22.1	11.2	13.7	9.7	9.8	22.2
Gas	39.6	40.8	9.8	10.5	10.1	8.0	13.3	7.7	5.5	11.9
Personal computer	14.8	15.7	15.6	14.0	15.0	19.1	5.1	7.5	13.1	29.7
Portable electric heater ..	13.5	14.4	2.2	2.8	5.4	3.1	3.9	2.8	2.0	4.8
Portable kerosene heater.	4.6	4.9	0.9	1.3	2.2	0.2	1.3	0.9	1.1	1.3
Range: Electric	54.3	57.8	9.1	12.6	21.8	10.8	16.4	9.7	9.8	21.3
Gas	39.6	42.1	10.0	10.6	10.5	8.6	13.6	7.8	5.5	12.6
Refrigerator: Frost-free ..	75.0	79.8	15.0	18.2	27.0	14.8	18.3	13.2	12.5	31.0
Non frost-free [5]......	24.8	26.4	5.5	7.1	6.6	5.6	9.8	5.3	3.7	5.9
Television set: Color....	90.3	96.1	18.6	22.3	30.8	18.6	25.0	16.9	14.8	33.5
Black and white	28.7	30.6	5.9	8.2	10.4	4.2	8.4	5.3	4.6	10.3
Water heater: [6] Gas	44.6	47.4	7.2	13.3	12.6	11.4	11.5	7.7	6.9	18.5
Electric	33.5	35.6	4.2	6.9	17.2	5.3	9.9	6.9	5.8	10.9
Other fuel	2.0	2.1	1.9	(B)	0.1	(B)	0.4	0.2	0.3	1.1
Whole house cooling fan .	9.4	10.1	2.1	2.1	4.0	1.2	1.5	1.4	1.5	5.1
Window or ceiling fan ...	47.9	51.0	9.0	12.0	20.3	6.6	11.0	8.7	8.1	20.2

B Base figure too small to meet statistical standards for reliability. [1] Includes the 0.9 million households with both central air conditioning and window or wall air conditioning units. [2] An air-cooling unit used in dry climates that turns air into moist, cool air by saturating the air with water vapor. [3] Microwave is first or second most used oven. [4] All motorized vehicles used by U.S. households for personal transportation excluding motorcycles, mopeds, large trucks, and buses. [5] Includes refrigerators without freezer compartments. [6] Excludes water heaters that serve more than one household.

Source: U.S. Energy Information Administration, *Housing Characteristics: 1990.*

No. 1245. Expenditures by Residential Property Owners for Improvements and Maintenance and Repairs, by Type of Property and Activity: 1970 to 1991

[In millions of dollars]

YEAR AND TYPE OF EXPENDITURE	Total	1-unit properties with owner occupant	Other properties	ADDITIONS AND ALTERATIONS				To property outside of structures	Major replacements	Maintenance and repairs
				Total	To structures					
					Additions	Alterations				
1970.	14,770	9,469	5,301	6,246	1,411	3,539	1,296	2,629	5,895
1975.	25,239	15,684	9,556	10,997	1,971	6,844	2,182	4,484	9,758
1976.	29,034	18,854	10,180	12,314	3,493	6,367	2,454	5,341	11,379
1977.	31,280	21,761	9,519	14,237	2,655	8,505	3,077	5,699	11,344
1978.	37,461	24,189	13,272	16,458	3,713	8,443	4,302	8,094	12,909
1979.	42,231	28,280	13,951	18,285	3,280	9,642	5,363	8,996	14,950
1980.	46,338	31,481	14,857	21,336	4,183	11,193	5,960	9,816	15,187
1981.	46,351	30,201	16,150	20,414	3,164	11,947	5,303	9,915	16,022
1982.	45,291	29,779	15,512	18,774	2,641	10,711	5,423	9,707	16,810
1983.	49,295	32,524	16,771	20,271	4,739	11,673	3,859	10,895	18,128
1984.	69,784	43,781	26,003	27,822	6,007	14,486	7,329	13,067	28,894
1985.	80,267	47,742	32,525	28,775	3,966	17,599	7,211	16,134	35,358
1986.	91,274	54,298	36,976	38,608	7,377	21,192	10,040	16,695	35,971
1987.	94,082	54,791	39,291	39,978	9,557	21,641	8,779	15,875	38,229
1988.	101,117	60,822	40,295	43,339	11,333	22,703	9,303	16,893	40,885
1989, total [1].	100,891	59,858	41,033	39,786	6,828	23,129	9,828	18,415	42,689
Heating and air conditioning [2]	5,841	3,589	2,252	1,484	(NA)	1,484	(NA)	2,167	2,191
Plumbing.	9,875	5,258	4,617	1,607	(NA)	1,607	(NA)	3,314	4,954
Roofing.	10,075	6,266	3,809	(NA)	(NA)	(NA)	(NA)	6,299	3,777
Painting.	11,319	5,192	6,127	(NA)	(NA)	(NA)	(NA)	(NA)	11,319
1990, total [1].	106,773	59,683	47,090	37,253	8,561	21,920	6,771	18,215	51,305
Heating and air conditioning [2]	7,646	4,920	2,726	1,634	(NA)	1,634	(NA)	3,394	2,618
Plumbing.	10,838	5,842	4,996	1,867	(NA)	1,867	(NA)	3,382	5,589
Roofing.	7,914	4,159	3,755	(NA)	(NA)	(NA)	(NA)	4,508	3,406
Painting.	13,768	5,260	8,508	(NA)	(NA)	(NA)	(NA)	(NA)	13,768
1991, total [1].	97,528	58,083	39,445	30,944	7,914	16,076	6,954	16,744	49,840
Heating and air conditioning [2]	7,336	4,353	2,983	985	(NA)	985	(NA)	3,688	2,618
Plumbing.	9,714	4,896	4,818	1,366	(NA)	1,366	(NA)	3,383	4,966
Roofing.	8,867	5,275	3,592	(NA)	(NA)	(NA)	(NA)	5,237	3,630
Painting.	12,918	6,522	6,396	(NA)	(NA)	(NA)	(NA)	(NA)	12,918

NA Not available.   [1] Includes types of expenditures not separately specified.   [2] Central air-conditioning.

No. 1246. Vacancy Rates for Housing Units—Characteristics: 1985 to 1992

[In percent. Annual averages. Based on Current Population Survey and Quarterly Household Survey. Rate is relationship between vacant housing for rent or for sale and the total rental and homeowner supply, which comprises occupied units, units rented or sold and awaiting occupancy, and vacant units available for rent or sale. For composition of regions, see table 31. See also Historical Statistics, Colonial Times to 1970, series N 249-258]

CHARACTERISTIC	RENTAL UNITS					HOMEOWNER UNITS				
	1985	1989	1990	1991	1992	1985	1989	1990	1991	1992
Total units	6.5	7.4	7.2	7.4	7.4	1.7	1.8	1.7	1.7	1.5
Inside MSA's.	6.3	7.4	7.1	7.5	7.4	1.7	1.7	1.7	1.7	1.6
Outside MSA's.	7.1	7.7	7.6	7.3	7.0	1.9	1.9	1.8	1.8	1.5
Northeast	3.5	4.7	6.1	6.9	6.9	1.0	1.5	1.6	1.5	1.3
Midwest	5.9	6.8	6.4	6.7	6.7	1.6	1.4	1.3	1.3	1.2
South.	9.1	9.7	8.8	8.9	8.2	2.1	2.2	2.1	2.2	1.7
West	6.2	7.1	6.6	6.5	7.1	2.1	1.6	1.8	1.7	1.9
Units in structure:										
1 unit	3.8	4.2	4.0	3.9	3.9	1.4	1.4	1.4	1.4	1.3
2 units or more . . .	7.9	9.2	9.0	9.4	9.3	6.6	7.1	7.1	6.8	5.9
5 units or more . . .	8.8	10.1	9.6	10.4	10.1	10.1	9.6	8.4	7.9	7.4
Units with—										
3 rooms or less. . .	8.8	10.3	10.3	10.8	11.0	5.8	10.8	10.2	10.5	8.4
4 rooms	6.9	8.2	8.0	8.1	7.9	2.3	3.1	3.2	3.0	2.5
5 rooms.	5.0	5.6	5.7	5.9	5.5	2.0	2.0	2.0	1.9	1.8
6 rooms or more. .	3.2	3.4	3.0	3.1	3.1	1.4	1.2	1.1	1.2	1.1

Source: U.S. Bureau of the Census, Current Housing Reports, series H-111.

No. 1247. Recent Home Buyers—General Characteristics: 1976 to 1992

[As of **October.** Based on a sample survey; subject to sampling variability]

ITEM	Unit	1976	1980	1985	1987	1988	1989	1990	1991	1992
Median purchase price . .	Dollars . . .	43,340	68,714	90,400	99,260	121,910	129,800	131,200	134,300	141,000
First-time buyers	Dollars . . .	37,670	61,450	75,100	84,730	97,100	105,200	106,000	118,700	122,400
Repeat buyers [1]	Dollars . . .	50,090	75,750	106,200	115,430	141,400	144,700	149,400	152,500	158,000
Average monthly mortgage payment	Dollars . . .	329	599	896	939	1,008	1,054	1,127	1,144	1,064
Percent of income. . . .	Percent . . .	24.0	32.4	30.0	29.3	32.8	31.8	33.8	34.0	33.2
Percent buying—										
New houses.	Percent . . .	15.1	22.4	23.8	23.8	26.2	21.8	21.2	19.7	20.5
Existing houses.	Percent . . .	84.9	77.6	76.2	76.2	73.8	78.2	78.8	80.3	79.5
Single-family houses . .	Percent . . .	88.8	82.4	87.0	87.3	83.3	84.8	83.8	85.3	85.0
Condominiums [2]	Percent . . .	11.2	17.6	10.6	12.5	12.4	13.5	13.1	11.5	13.1
For the first time	Percent . . .	44.8	32.9	36.6	36.8	37.8	40.2	41.9	45.1	47.7
Average age:										
First-time buyers	Years . . .	28.1	28.3	28.4	29.6	30.3	29.6	30.5	30.7	31.0
Repeat buyers [1]	Years . . .	35.9	36.4	38.4	39.1	38.9	39.4	39.1	39.8	40.8
Downpayment/sales price	Percent . . .	25.2	28.0	24.8	27.2	24.0	24.4	23.3	22.6	21.4
First-time buyers	Percent . . .	18.0	20.5	11.4	20.4	14.6	15.8	15.7	14.7	14.3
Repeat buyers [1]	Percent . . .	30.8	32.7	32.7	31.3	29.7	30.3	28.9	29.1	28.0

[1] Buyers who previously owned a home.   [2] Includes multiple-family houses.
Source: Chicago Title Insurance Company, Chicago, IL, *The Guarantor*, bimonthly (copyright).

No. 1248. Low-Income Public Housing Units, by Progress Stage: 1970 to 1991

[**In thousands.** As of **Dec. 31.** Housing for the elderly intended for persons 62 years old or over, disabled, or handicapped. Includes Puerto Rico and Virgin Islands. Covers units subsidized by HUD under annual contributions contracts. See also *Historical Statistics, Colonial Times to 1970,* series N 186-191]

YEAR	Total[1]	Occupied units [2]	Under construction	YEAR	Total[1]	Occupied units [2]	Under construction
1970.	1,155.3	893.5	126.8	1989.	1,205.0	1,137.5	7.8
Elderly.	249.4	143.4	65.7	Elderly.	(NA)	482.2	(NA)
1980.	1,321.1	1,195.6	20.9	1990.	1,305.3	1,028.1	7.6
Elderly.	358.3	317.7	11.5	Elderly.	(NA)	342.2	(NA)
1985.	1,378.0	1,344.6	9.6	1991.	1,304.9	1,200.9	7.5
Elderly.	373.5	361.1	2.1	Elderly.	(NA)	376.8	(NA)

NA Not available.   [1] Includes units to be constructed or to go directly "under management" because no rehabilitation needed not shown separately.   [2] Under management or available for occupancy.
Source: U.S. Dept. of Housing and Urban Development, unpublished data

No. 1249. Office Buildings—Vacancy Rates for Major Cities, 1980 to 1992, and Status of Supply, 1992

[**As of December;** except **1991, as of June.** Excludes government owned and occupied, owner-occupied, and medical office buildings]

CITY	VACANCY RATE FOR EXISTING SPACE (percent)									SUPPLY STATUS, June 1992 (mil. sq. ft.)			
										Existing space		Space under construction	
	1980	1985	1986	1987	1988	1989	1990	1991	1992, June	Total	Available for lease	Total	Available for lease
Total [1]	4.6	16.9	18.6	19.0	18.6	19.5	20.0	20.2	20.4	2,081.7	425.3	14.7	6.1
Atlanta, GA.	10.0	21.0	20.1	19.6	18.3	19.9	19.1	19.5	19.1	86.0	16.4	1.5	0.9
Baltimore, MD	7.2	11.5	15.9	15.8	13.4	16.4	20.0	21.0	24.1	33.8	8.1	-	-
Boston, MA.	3.8	13.1	13.0	12.6	14.1	15.3	19.6	19.1	18.9	133.6	25.3	0.9	0.9
Charlotte, NC	(NA)	16.7	15.5	15.1	16.5	14.3	16.5	19.4	(NA)	(NA)	(NA)	(NA)	(NA)
Chicago, IL	7.0	16.5	19.6	17.0	15.9	17.0	18.6	20.0	22.1	195.2	43.1	1.1	0.8
Dallas, TX.	8.6	23.0	30.9	29.1	29.7	26.9	25.8	26.0	(NA)	(NA)	(NA)	(NA)	(NA)
Denver, CO	6.6	24.7	25.1	27.9	27.6	26.1	24.8	23.0	22.9	68.4	15.6	-	-
Houston, TX	4.0	27.6	30.6	31.8	29.2	27.5	24.9	27.3	26.3	138.5	36.5	-	-
Indianapolis, IN . . .	(NA)	(NA)	(NA)	(NA)	21.3	20.0	21.2	21.4	21.5	20.7	4.4	0.1	0.1
Kansas City, MO . .	4.2	16.2	18.2	18.2	19.9	15.8	14.1	16.9	15.8	32.6	5.2	-	-
Los Angeles, CA . .	0.9	15.3	13.2	19.0	15.8	19.7	16.8	20.2	19.8	206.0	40.8	1.2	0.9
Miami, FL	2.4	20.9	25.2	26.1	24.0	22.0	23.4	22.6	21.4	27.2	5.8	0.3	-
Milwaukee, WI	(NA)	(NA)	(NA)	16.8	19.3	20.4	22.9	19.5	18.1	24.1	4.4	-	-
New Orleans, LA . .	(NA)	21.8	25.5	24.3	25.6	25.7	29.0	25.0	(NA)	(NA)	(NA)	(NA)	(NA)
New York, NY [2]	3.1	7.9	8.9	9.7	11.5	15.1	16.0	18.8	18.8	280.4	52.7	1.2	-
Philadelphia, PA . . .	6.3	14.5	15.5	16.5	15.8	16.3	18.2	17.3	19.0	70.7	13.5	1.6	0.3
Pittsburgh, PA	1.2	(NA)	12.0	12.3	17.6	16.3	16.3	14.2	(NA)	(NA)	(NA)	(NA)	(NA)
San Diego, CA. . . .	(NA)	24.7	25.4	22.8	20.1	17.6	19.5	23.7	25.1	38.5	9.7	0.3	0.1
San Francisco, CA .	0.4	13.7	16.6	15.0	15.5	15.7	14.7	13.3	13.4	56.1	7.5	-	-
Seattle, WA.	(NA)	(NA)	(NA)	(NA)	13.2	12.4	12.3	12.8	13.1	30.0	3.9	-	-
St. Louis, MO	(NA)	(NA)	(NA)	15.6	18.4	22.6	21.0	20.5	21.6	33.2	7.2	-	-
Washington, DC . . .	2.5	9.0	13.6	13.4	13.2	14.4	14.7	19.0	17.6	183.7	33.1	3.2	0.5

- Represents zero.   NA Not available.   [1] Includes other cities not shown separately. In 1991, 51 cities were covered.
[2] Refers to Manhattan.
Source: ONCOR International, Houston, TX, 1980-1985, *National Office Market Report*, semi-annual; 1986-1990, *International Office Market Report*, semi-annual; thereafter, *Office Market Data Book* (copyright).

No. 1250. Commercial Office Space—Inventory and Vacancy Rates for the 50 Largest Metropolitan Areas: 1992

[As of December 31. Central business district is the area located near the historical urban core, commonly associated with the traditional government and financial districts in most cities; outside the central business districts is comprised of the suburban area and "urban clusters" with areas of high office space concentrations. Class A space is in "excellent" locations, with high quality finish, well maintained, and professionally managed; Class B space is in "good" locations, professionally managed, with fairly high quality construction and tenancy. Data based on responses from individuals knowledgeable in the local markets]

METROPOLITAN AREAS RANKED BY POPULATION-SIZE, 1990 [1]	INVENTORY (1,000 square feet)				VACANCY RATE [2] (percent)			
	Inside central business district		Outside central business district		Inside central business district		Outside central business district	
	Class A	Class B	Class A	Class B	Class A	Class B	Class A	Class B
Los Angeles-Long Beach, CA PMSA .	24,975.2	6,224.9	70,370.8	43,699.0	27.5	23.4	19.0	24.0
New York, NY PMSA [3]	175,387.7	81,236.4	86,380.9	41,038.7	16.5	20.4	18.5	23.7
Chicago, IL PMSA.	51,914.5	44,377.5	24,676.9	31,766.7	24.6	22.8	18.4	22.0
Philadelphia, PA-NJ PMSA	32,118.5	6,678.0	49,834.7	23,732.2	14.9	24.7	20.3	24.0
Detroit, MI PMSA [4]	-	-	42,651.0	13,000.0	-	-	15.0	19.2
Washington, DC-MD-VA MSA	[5]98,402.2	[5]	[5]162,364.9	[5]	14.9	[5]	16.5	[5]
Boston, MA NECMA	36,892.0	7,918.0	40,000.0	(NA)	13.5	21.8	19.8	(NA)
Houston, TX PMSA.	25,200.0	8,890.0	34,337.0	66,744.0	14.0	32.6	12.3	27.8
Atlanta, GA MSA	[5]32,411.2	[5]	[5]64,732.8	[5]	[5]16.7	[5]	[5]14.0	[5]
Nassau-Suffolk, NY PMSA	-	-	22,365.0	13,419.0	-	-	21.3	22.3
Riverside-San Bernardino, CA PMSA .	460.4	2,049.6	1,540.2	4,875.4	31.6	13.0	25.2	26.0
Dallas, TX PMSA	13,309.0	16,573.0	46,477.0	40,802.0	18.6	37.5	21.8	28.9
San Diego, CA MSA	6,460.8	3,701.1	22,079.7	10,834.6	16.2	21.6	18.0	13.9
Minneapolis-St. Paul, MN-WI MSA . . .	12,700.0	4,595.0	8,550.0	20,113.0	22.6	25.8	16.9	18.9
St. Louis, MO-IL MSA	7,023.3	6,050.0	12,730.0	8,400.0	14.6	73.4	15.7	27.6
Anaheim-Santa Ana, CA PMSA.	54,496.7	(NA)	(NA)	(NA)	21.1	(NA)	(NA)	(NA)
Baltimore, MD MSA.	7,302.7	5,409.4	10,843.0	12,727.5	17.1	22.1	23.3	16.9
Phoenix, AZ MSA	5,280.4	9,991.3	1,363.3	6,271.7	23.4	20.2	23.4	21.8
Oakland, CA PMSA [6].	5,511.5	3,523.9	1,070.5	9,285.1	13.1	12.4	34.0	17.7
Tampa-St.Petersburg-Clearwater, FL MSA [7].	4,980.0	1,251.8	6,448.5	7,530.0	26.3	44.1	12.2	15.8
Pittsburgh, PA PMSA.	14,468.0	3,200.0	4,074.3	6,548.0	9.1	22.3	16.9	11.8
Seattle, WA PMSA	22,582.1	4,526.2	10,609.4	5,556.9	13.9	12.5	13.0	15.2
Miami-Hialeah, FL PMSA	7,200.0	4,700.0	6,160.0	12,200.0	29.9	34.0	20.3	19.7
Cleveland, OH PMSA	11,110.4	10,917.3	10,359.3	3,490.7	23.7	25.3	16.5	41.8
Newark, NJ and Bergen-Passaic, NJ PMSA [8]	-	-	51,073.0	45,409.0	-	-	17.2	24.7
Denver, CO PMSA	12,298.9	9,386.8	7,684.6	26,109.4	14.5	25.1	17.3	17.8
San Francisco, CA PMSA.	30,772.0	17,581.0	14,326.0	17,993.3	14.9	16.5	11.5	16.9
Kansas City, MO-KS MSA	7,996.3	5,948.8	17,614.4	4,963.0	18.1	12.0	11.9	14.2
San Jose, CA PMSA	2,500.0	4,000.0	4,000.0	24,000.0	(NA)	(NA)	(NA)	(NA)
Sacramento, CA MSA	5,437.0	3,879.0	10,700.0	13,000.0	11.0	7.0	10.3	24.6
Cincinnati, OH-KY-IN PMSA	7,167.1	5,469.2	5,411.0	3,840.1	11.3	23.3	16.3	20.5
Milwaukee, WI PMSA	5,324.7	7,603.9	3,095.2	8,121.4	12.3	15.2	13.0	18.3
Norfolk-Virginia Beach-Newport News, VA MSA	2,317.6	1,762.1	3,844.5	7,590.7	11.9	15.4	14.6	11.9
Columbus, OH MSA	8,100.0	3,850.0	8,900.0	4,160.0	5.4	10.3	7.3	17.3
Ft. Worth-Arlington, TX PMSA [9]. . . .	4,860.7	1,651.8	6,842.7	4,549.6	13.5	23.9	16.4	21.2
San Antonio, TX MSA [10]	1,990.8	766.0	4,754.5	10,129.9	25.5	33.9	15.6	25.2
Fort Lauderdale-Hollywood-Pompano Beach, FL PMSA.	2,657.8	588.0	5,505.1	7,182.0	27.1	11.6	22.2	23.8
Indianapolis, IN MSA.	6,407.0	2,195.7	[5]11,568.6	[5]	16.7	37.8	[5]21.9	[5]
Portland, OR PMSA	7,658.9	1,873.4	3,373.3	3,144.5	11.9	22.2	11.7	14.6
New Orleans, LA MSA.	9,452.9	6,095.0	2,220.7	2,604.6	21.6	36.5	11.7	10.7
Charlotte-Gastonia-Rock Hill, NC-SC MSA	5,573.7	3,469.4	5,665.2	4,061.7	20.0	19.0	12.0	23.0
Orlando, FL MSA	3,949.4	1,912.8	4,407.7	12,666.1	14.1	34.8	16.6	14.7
Salt Lake City-Ogden, UT MSA	2,407.2	2,390.6	2,784.8	3,446.8	19.9	17.2	23.0	13.3
Middlesex-Somerset-Hunterdon, NJ PMSA [11]	-	-	38,047.0	30,915.0	-	-	9.4	19.1
Nashville, TN MSA	2,759.9	2,322.9	5,749.2	5,374.4	15.9	23.7	15.9	19.0
Memphis, TN-AR-MS MSA	1,947.9	3,673.0	9,348.5	3,358.2	15.0	34.8	11.5	22.8
Buffalo, NY PMSA	2,973.3	1,841.5	919.6	1,190.2	24.5	13.6	5.5	10.7
Oklahoma City, OK MSA	3,800.0	2,460.0	5,000.0	3,700.0	30.3	44.7	13.0	21.6
Louisville, KY MSA	3,265.0	3,300.0	3,100.0	2,600.0	10.7	42.4	3.2	10.4
Dayton-Springfield, OH MSA.	1,961.9	1,252.8	1,921.0	1,581.7	19.5	22.8	13.1	16.0

- Represents zero.   NA Not available.   [1] List excludes Monmouth-Ocean, NJ PMSA and and Louisville, KY-IN MSA. [2] Represents the total vacant space divided by the total inventory of space in that area.   [3] Excludes Brooklyn and Queens. [4] Represents suburban Detroit only.   [5] Class A includes Class B; data not available separately.   [6] Excludes Contra Costa county.   [7] Represents only Tampa and Hillsborough County.   [8] Data are for area identified by source as New Jersey-Northern with a market area of Bergen, Essex, Hudson, Morris, and Passaic counties.   [9] Represents only Tarrant County.   [10] Represents only Bexar County.   [11] Data are for area identified by source as New Jersey-Central with a market area of Hunterdon, Mercer, Middlesex, Monmouth, Somerset, and Union Counties.

Source: Society of Industrial and Office REALTORS [PR], Washington, DC, 1993 Guide to Industrial and Office Real Estate Markets (copyright).

No. 1251. Commercial Buildings—Selected Characteristics, by Square Footage of Floorspace: 1989

[Excludes buildings 1,000 square feet or smaller. Building type based on predominant activity in which the occupants were engaged. Based on a sample survey of building representatives conducted between January and April 1986; therefore, subject to sampling variability. For composition of regions, see table 31]

CHARACTERISTIC	Number of buildings (1,000)	FLOORSPACE (mil. sq. ft.)							Mean sq. ft. per building (1,000)	Median sq. ft. per building (1,000)
		Total	Within all buildings having square footage of—							
			5,000 or less	5,001 to 10,000	10,001 to 25,000	25,001 to 50,000	50,001 to 100,000	100,001 and over		
All buildings	4,528	63,184	6,790	6,532	10,393	8,801	9,130	21,538	14.0	4.5
Region:										
Northeast	783	13,569	1,047	1,271	1,980	1,722	1,507	6,041	17.3	5.2
Midwest	1,046	15,955	1,612	1,468	2,250	2,049	2,362	6,215	15.3	4.5
South	1,847	22,040	2,853	2,530	4,109	3,322	3,632	5,595	11.9	4.0
West	851	11,620	1,279	1,263	2,054	1,708	1,630	3,686	13.7	4.8
Year constructed:										
1900 or before	172	1,654	270	299	353	451	212	(S)	9.6	4.5
1901 to 1920	242	4,245	338	399	375	680	729	249	17.5	4.8
1921 to 1945	680	8,098	1,178	928	1,089	994	1,395	2,514	11.9	4.0
1946 to 1960	868	10,511	1,363	1,233	2,046	1,369	1,191	2,365	12.1	4.1
1961 to 1970	821	12,167	1,197	1,027	2,064	1,648	1,889	4,343	14.8	4.3
1970 to 1979	884	13,329	1,266	1,340	2,180	1,884	1,628	5,031	15.1	5.0
1980 to 1983	317	4,274	465	440	943	480	563	1,385	13.5	4.8
1984 to 1986	329	5,670	419	541	858	853	924	1,329	17.2	5.4
1987 to 1989	215	3,235	294	325	485	443	600	1,088	15.1	4.5
Principal activity within building:										
Assembly	615	6,909	1,006	1,183	1,390	1,230	635	1,070	11.1	5.0
Education	282	8,076	279	400	892	1,425	1,818	2,603	28.7	9.0
Food sales	102	792	223	33	177	(S)	(S)	(S)	7.7	4.8
Food service	241	1,167	417	263	260	(S)	(S)	(S)	4.8	3.0
Health care	80	2,054	136	(S)	166	(S)	123	1,510	25.7	3.5
Lodging	140	3,476	123	278	617	469	709	992	24.8	8.5
Mercantile/services	1,278	12,365	2,120	1,753	2,639	1,395	1,378	3,081	9.7	3.9
Office	679	11,802	961	821	1,721	1,459	1,575	5,267	17.4	4.2
Parking garage	45	983	55	90	79	(S)	(S)	656	22.0	4.8
Public order and safety	50	616	73	91	(S)	(S)	(S)	(S)	12.3	4.0
Warehouse	618	9,253	800	1,031	1,667	1,921	1,369	2,465	15.0	5.8
Other	62	1,529	63	87	160	128	701	120	24.7	6.7
Vacant	333	4,161	533	440	566	334	530	433	12.5	3.7
Government owned	577	14,342	645	908	1,752	1,892	2,475	6,670	24.8	7.1
Non-government owned	3,950	48,842	6,145	5,624	8,641	6,609	6,655	14,868	12.4	4.2
Fuels used alone or in combination:										
Electricity	4,297	61,563	6,411	6,302	9,989	8,682	8,918	21,286	14.3	4.6
Natural gas	2,420	41,143	3,441	3,985	5,793	5,487	6,397	16,489	17.1	5.0
Fuel oil	581	12,600	832	698	1,499	1,352	1,685	6,618	21.6	5.0
Propane	348	4,695	587	454	738	461	748	(S)	13.5	4.5
District heat	98	6,578	43	115	566	512	848	4,772	65.4	19.5
District chilled water	24	1,927	(S)	32	86	148	282	1,548	84.6	34.5
Any other	130	1,542	206	184	342	138	(S)	(S)	11.9	4.0
Workers:										
Fewer than 5	2,280	13,292	4,271	2,717	2,841	1,432	727	232	5.8	3.0
5 to 9	906	7,939	1,471	1,606	2,132	1,105	749	797	8.8	4.6
10 to 19	507	6,445	544	1,228	1,921	1,317	828	587	12.7	7.5
20 to 49	381	9,665	167	693	2,330	2,415	2,201	1,385	25.4	16.0
50 to 99	132	7,389	(S)	(S)	684	1,584	1,919	2,720	56.1	36.5
100 to 249	79	6,771	(S)	(S)	124	629	2,062	3,924	85.9	69.9
250 or more	32	9,829	(S)	(S)	(S)	95	394	9,340	308.0	200.1
Weekly operating hours:										
39 or less	876	6,073	1,574	1,159	1,157	885	634	375	6.9	3.5
40 to 48	1,117	13,905	1,628	1,830	2,628	2,163	2,386	3,269	12.4	5.0
49 to 60	987	13,473	1,450	1,409	2,614	2,081	1,925	3,995	13.6	5.0
61 to 84	625	10,777	891	824	1,601	1,235	1,530	4,697	17.2	4.8
85 to 167	515	9,387	776	680	1,159	1,296	1,272	3,377	18.2	4.5
168 (open continuously)	408	9,569	472	631	1,235	1,141	1,384	4,707	23.5	5.8

S Figure does not meet publication standards.

Source: U.S. Energy Information Administration, *Commercial Buildings Characteristics, 1989.*

No. 1252. Commercial Buildings—Number and Square Footage of Floorspace, by Type of Building and Characteristic: 1989

[For composition of regions, see table 31]

BUILDING CHARACTERISTICS	All build- ings [1]	As- sembly	Educa- tion	Food sales	Food service	Health care	Lodg- ing	Mer- cantile/ serv- ices	Offices	Public order and safety	Ware- house
NUMBER (1,000)											
All buildings......	**4,528**	**615**	**284**	**102**	**241**	**80**	**118**	**1,278**	**679**	**50**	**618**
Region:											
Northeast..........	783	96	38	(S)	54	12	21	259	108	(S)	95
Midwest...........	1,046	134	54	(S)	59	21	24	303	139	(S)	177
South	1,847	275	108	45	87	30	50	523	275	(S)	243
West.............	851	109	84	(S)	41	17	44	193	157	(S)	104
Year constructed:											
1900 or before	172	53	(S)	(S)	(S)	(S)	(S)	43	21	(S)	(S)
1901 to 1920	242	41	14	(S)	(S)	(S)	(S)	61	36	(S)	27
1921 to 1945	680	125	32	(S)	34	(S)	17	194	85	(S)	67
1946 to 1960	868	138	87	(S)	38	15	18	254	109	(S)	113
1961 to 1970	821	82	65	(S)	35	24	36	227	129	(S)	107
1970 to 1979	884	97	52	(S)	57	10	32	277	128	(S)	137
1980 to 1983	317	32	10	(S)	(S)	(S)	9	78	62	(S)	50
1984 to 1986	329	31	14	(S)	(S)	(S)	10	78	71	(S)	74
1987 to 1989	215	17	9	(S)	(S)	(S)	(S)	67	39	(S)	35
Government owned	577	87	192	(S)	13	9	14	33	70	39	65
Nongovernment owned..	3,951	528	92	99	228	71	126	1,246	609	(S)	553
FLOORSPACE (mil. sq. ft.)											
All buildings......	**63,184**	**6,838**	**8,148**	**792**	**1,167**	**2,054**	**3,476**	**12,365**	**11,802**	**616**	**9,253**
Region:											
Northeast..........	13,569	1,507	1,888	(S)	284	378	549	2,647	2,703	(S)	1,811
Midwest...........	15,955	1,408	2,221	(S)	339	912	982	3,059	2,281	(S)	2,639
South	22,040	2,750	2,404	278	370	472	1,215	4,778	3,817	(S)	3,422
West.............	11,620	1,174	1,634	(S)	173	292	730	1,882	3,001	(S)	1,381
Year constructed:											
1900 or before	1,654	386	(S)	(S)	(S)	(S)	(S)	428	289	(S)	(S)
1901 to 1920	4,245	492	435	(S)	(S)	(S)	(S)	514	552	(S)	348
1921 to 1945	8,098	926	1,244	(S)	147	(S)	442	1,322	1,166	(S)	1,448
1946 to 1960	10,511	1,470	2,267	(S)	152	371	358	1,694	1,849	(S)	1,279
1961 to 1970	12,167	1,249	2,201	(S)	282	355	1,042	2,458	1,736	(S)	1,702
1970 to 1979	13,329	1,410	1,391	(S)	268	586	578	3,464	2,425	(S)	2,178
1980 to 1983	4,274	373	155	(S)	(S)	(S)	(S)	216	873	(S)	650
1984 to 1986	5,670	293	158	(S)	(S)	(S)	(S)	510	896	(S)	1,003
1987 to 1989	3,235	238	280	(S)	(S)	(S)	(S)	717	750	(S)	561
Government owned	14,342	1,394	6,312	(S)	109	495	622	399	2,353	575	597
Nongovernment owned..	48,842	5,443	1,835	787	1,058	1,559	2,854	11,966	9,449	(S)	8,656

S Figure does not meet publication standards. [1] Includes parking garages, vacant, and other commercial buildings, not shown separately.

Source: U.S. Energy Information Administration, *Commercial Building Characteristics, 1989.*

No. 1253. Commercial Buildings and Workers—Selected Building Characteristics, by Floorspace: 1989

[See headnote, table 1251]

BUILDING CHARACTERISTICS	NUMBER OF BUILDINGS (1,000)							WORKERS		
		Square footage of—							Average sq. ft. per worker	Median sq. ft. per worker
	Total	5,000 or less	5,001 to 10,000	10,001 to 25,000	25,001 to 50,000	50,001 to 100,000	100,001 and over	Number (1,000)		
All buildings	**4,528**	**2,529**	**890**	**644**	**247**	**127**	**91**	**70,665**	**894**	**1,001**
Region:										
Northeast	783	390	175	127	48	21	23	15,889	854	1,051
Midwest	1,046	592	196	140	59	33	26	15,557	1,026	1,126
South	1,847	1,086	345	249	91	51	24	23,311	945	1,001
West	851	461	174	129	48	23	17	15,908	730	920
Principal activity within building:										
Assembly	615	322	159	85	34	9	(S)	4,012	1,704	2,002
Education	284	95	55	54	38	27	16	7,204	1,131	987
Food sales/service	343	260	38	19	(S)	(S)	(S)	2,787	1,539	1,611
Health care	80	53	(S)	10	(S)	(S)	5	4,225	486	600
Lodging...............	140	38	40	33	13	11	2	3,092	1,124	1,701
Mercantile/services.......	1,278	803	237	164	42	18	14	12,414	996	1,081
Office	679	378	106	113	42	22	19	27,780	425	483
Public order and safety	50	(S)	(S)	(S)	(S)	(S)	(S)	861	716	800
Warehouse	618	285	147	102	52	18	12	4,377	2,114	3,091
Other	62	29	(S)	(S)	10	8	(S)	2,111	724	930
Vacant	333	215	61	35	10	8	3	1,472	2,827	546
Nongovernment owned......	3,951	2,300	765	536	195	92	63	54,583	895	1,001
Owner occupied........	2,814	1,612	571	383	141	64	44	42,256	893	1,101
Nonowner occupied	1,136	688	194	154	54	28	20	14,327	900	854
Government owned	577	229	125	107	52	35	28	16,082	892	1,015

S Figure does not meet publication standards.
Source: U.S. Energy Information Administration, *Commercial Building Characteristics, 1989.*

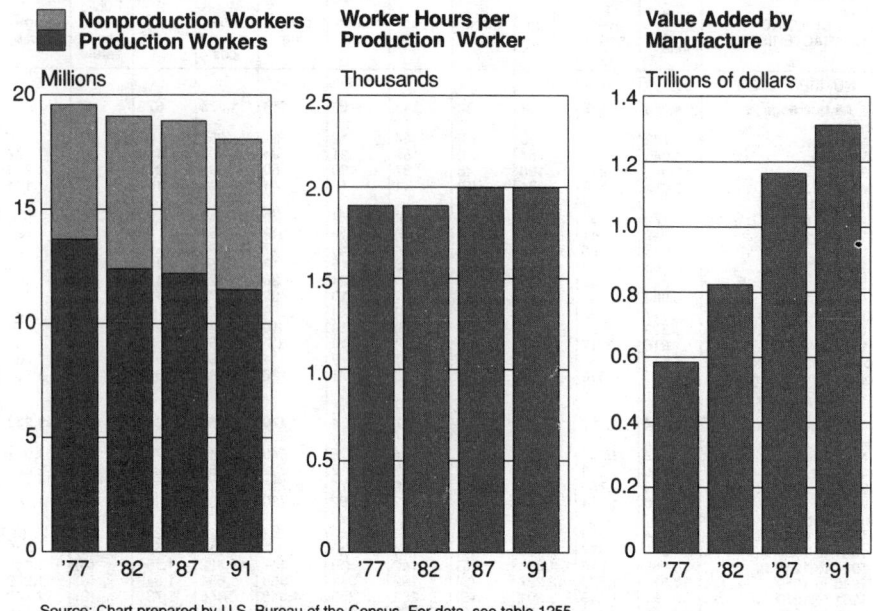

Figure 27.1
Summary of Manufactures: 1977 to 1991

Source: Chart prepared by U.S. Bureau of the Census. For data, see table 1255.

Figure 27.2
**Capital in Manufacturing Establishments:
1980 to 1991**

Source: Chart prepared by U.S. Bureau of the Census. For data, see table 1263.

Manufactures

This section presents summary data for manufacturing as a whole and more detailed information for major industry groups and selected specific products. The types of measures shown at the different levels include data for establishments; employment and wages; raw materials, fuels, and electricity consumed; plant and equipment expenditures; value and quantity of production and shipments; value added by manufacture; inventories; and various indicators of financial status.

In Brief

Personal computer shipments topped 9.8 million units in 1991.

1-megabit DRAM chips:

	1965	1991
Revenue (mil. dol.)	5	3,776
Price (dollars)	162.50	4.52

The principal sources of these data are Bureau of the Census reports of the censuses of manufactures conducted every 5 years; the *Annual Survey of Manufactures;* and the *Current Industrial Reports* series, which presents monthly, quarterly, or annual data on production, shipments, and stocks for particular commodities. Indexes of industrial production are presented monthly in the Federal Reserve Board's *Federal Reserve Bulletin.* Reports on current activities of industries, or current movements of individual commodities, are compiled by such government agencies as the Bureau of Labor Statistics; the Economic Research Service of the Department of Agriculture; the International Trade Administration; and by private research or trade associations such as The Conference Board, Inc., New York, NY and the American Iron and Steel Institute, Washington, DC.

Data on financial aspects of manufacturing industries are collected by the Bureau of Economic Analysis (BEA) and the Bureau of the Census. Industry aggregates in the form of balance sheets, profit and loss statements, analyses of sales and expenses, lists of subsidiaries, and types and amounts of security issues are published for leading manufacturing corporations registered with the Securities and Exchange Commission. The BEA issues data on capital in manufacturing industries and capacity utilization rates in manufacturing. See also section 17, Business Enterprise, in this edition.

Censuses and annual surveys.—The first census of manufactures covered the year 1809. Between 1809 and 1963, a census was conducted at periodic intervals. Since 1967 it has been taken every 5 years (for years ending in "2" and "7"). Census data, either direct reports or estimates from administrative records, are obtained for every manufacturing plant with one paid employee or more.

The *Annual Survey of Manufactures (ASM),* conducted for the first time in 1949, collects data for the years between censuses for the more general measures of manufacturing activity covered in detail by the censuses. The annual survey data are estimates derived from a scientifically selected sample of establishments. The 1991 annual survey is based on a sample of about 55,000 establishments of an approximate total of 200,000. These establishments represent all manufacturing establishments of multiunit companies and all single-establishment manufacturing companies mailed schedules in the 1987 Census of Manufactures. The 1989 through 1993 ASM sample is similar to the previous sample. For the current panel, all establishments of companies with 1987 shipments in manufacturing in excess of $500 million were included in the survey with certainty. For the remaining portion of the mail survey, the establishment was defined as the sampling unit. For this portion, all establishments with 250 employees or more and establishments with a very large value of shipments also were included. Therefore, of the 55,000 establishments included in the ASM panel, approximately 28,000 are selected with certainty. These establishments account for approximately 80 percent of total value of shipments in the 1987 census. Smaller establishments in the remaining portion of the mail survey were selected by sample.

The basic statistical measures of manufacturing activity, such as employment, payrolls, value added, etc., are defined in essentially the same way for both the annual surveys and the census of manufactures. However, the bases for computing average employment vary for different years. For example, beginning with 1949, average employment was calculated from the figures reported for the pay periods ending nearest the 15th of March, May, August, and November; whereas, for 1947 such averages were based on 12 monthly employment figures. In 1967, the average employment calculation was revised to the pay periods which include the 12th of March, May, August, and November to provide data more comparable with other statistical series.

Establishments and classification.— The censuses of manufactures for 1947 through 1987 cover operating manufacturing establishments as defined in the *Standard Industrial Classification Manual (SIC)*, issued by the U.S. Office of Management and Budget (see text, section 13). The *Manual* is also used for classifying establishments in the annual surveys. The comparability of manufactures data over time is affected by changes in the official definitions of industries as presented in the *Manual*. It is important to note, therefore, that the 1987 edition of the *Manual* was used for the 1987 census; and the 1972 edition of the *Manual* and the *1977 Supplement* was used for the 1972 through 1982 censuses. For the censuses from 1947 to 1963, reports were required from all establishments employing one or more persons at any time during the census year. Beginning with the 1967 census, an effort was made to relieve the very small establishments from the necessity of filing a census report. Approximately 150,000 small single-unit manufacturing firms identified as having less than 20 employees (cutoff varied by industry) benefited from this procedure. Data for these single-unit companies were estimated on the basis of government administrative records and industry averages. Each of the establishments tabulated was classified in one of the approximately 459

manufacturing industries as defined by the *SIC Manual* in 1987. The *Manual* defines an industry as a number of establishments producing a single product or a closely related group of products. In the main, an establishment is classified in a particular industry if its production of a product or product group exceeds in value added its production of any other product group. While some establishments produce only the products of the industry in which they are classified, few within an industry specialize to that extent. The statistics on employment, payrolls, value added, inventories, and expenditures, therefore, reflect both the primary and secondary activities of the establishments in that industry. For this reason, care should be exercised in relating such statistics to the total shipments figures of products primary to the industry.

The censuses for 1947 through 1987 were conducted on an establishment basis. The term "establishment" signifies a single physical plant site or factory. It is not necessarily identical to the business unit or company, which may consist of one or more establishments. A company operating establishments at more than one location is required to submit a separate report for each location. An establishment engaged in distinctly different lines of activity and maintaining separate payroll and inventory records is also required to submit separate reports.

Durable goods.—Items with a normal life expectancy of 3 years or more. Automobiles, furniture, household appliances, and mobile homes are common examples.

Nondurable goods.—Items which generally last for only a short time (3 years or less). Food, beverages, clothing, shoes, and gasoline are common examples.

Statistical reliability.—For a discussion of statistical collection and estimation, sampling procedures and measures of statistical reliability applicable to Census Bureau data, see Appendix III.

Historical statistics.—Tabular headnotes provide cross-references, where applicable, to *Historical Statistics of the United States, Colonial Times to 1970*. See Appendix IV.

No. 1254. Gross National Product in Manufacturing: 1977 to 1989

[In millions of dollars. For definition of gross national product, see text, section 14. Based on 1972 Standard Industrial Classification]

ITEM	1977	1978	1979	1980	1981	1982	1983	1984	1985	1986	1987	1988	1989
CURRENT DOLLARS													
Manufacturing [1]	465,346	518,752	561,765	581,018	643,098	634,648	683,205	771,884	789,537	832,420	875,539	940,656	965,997
Durable goods [1]	277,673	317,351	345,242	351,820	385,824	362,512	385,633	451,120	458,774	478,079	499,874	527,137	540,995
Lumber and wood products	15,890	19,010	20,823	18,658	17,125	16,041	20,543	22,843	22,245	24,690	29,441	31,118	32,163
Stone, clay, and glass	15,251	17,975	19,573	19,012	19,039	18,160	20,179	22,934	24,777	26,915	25,737	25,695	26,299
Primary metal industries	33,471	40,623	45,225	44,286	49,804	35,281	30,344	36,286	34,803	39,248	36,053	43,241	44,376
Fabricated metal products	35,438	39,965	44,765	46,017	49,632	46,281	47,626	55,053	57,845	57,917	60,412	65,325	68,029
Machinery, exc. electrical	55,421	62,384	70,631	76,861	86,166	80,005	75,346	85,445	82,687	82,699	89,626	96,156	97,300
Electric and electronic equip	39,490	45,640	49,326	54,961	60,695	61,814	67,694	79,888	82,193	82,656	88,112	90,461	96,894
Motor vehicles and equip.	35,846	38,428	35,811	26,698	31,539	29,453	39,037	49,647	53,718	53,219	52,505	53,311	50,072
Instruments and related products	13,174	15,120	16,485	18,962	22,260	22,631	23,845	26,949	25,809	27,138	26,840	30,256	30,541
Nondurable goods	187,673	201,401	216,523	229,198	257,274	272,136	297,572	320,764	330,763	354,341	375,665	413,519	425,002
Food and kindred products	42,665	44,839	47,859	52,198	57,879	61,427	64,662	66,648	69,830	70,926	75,096	80,863	81,458
Tobacco	5,721	6,485	6,826	7,286	7,925	8,916	11,942	12,762	12,156	14,386	14,105	14,445	16,096
Textile mill	14,047	(NA)	14,785	14,962	15,891	14,827	16,935	17,409	17,135	19,118	20,055	20,217	20,803
Apparel and other textile	14,468	15,442	16,040	17,093	18,671	18,931	20,270	20,716	20,640	21,907	20,478	23,556	24,603
Paper and allied products	18,030	19,839	22,219	23,126	25,052	26,718	27,769	31,907	33,123	35,501	40,152	45,682	46,827
Printing and publishing	23,326	26,202	28,810	31,553	35,228	38,364	42,374	47,578	52,512	56,865	61,112	65,505	68,236
Chemicals and allied	37,506	39,842	44,124	45,475	53,304	55,257	59,581	61,972	63,823	70,789	80,938	95,819	98,763
Petroleum and coal	14,542	15,200	15,078	16,757	19,784	24,352	28,260	33,747	32,219	35,174	29,599	34,515	33,682
CONSTANT (1982) DOLLARS													
Manufacturing [1]	664,755	694,744	712,184	673,936	678,555	634,648	674,223	752,407	779,230	803,179	852,178	917,448	929,042
Durable goods [1]	403,295	423,307	433,149	408,468	408,606	362,512	383,817	448,614	471,548	482,717	515,552	570,796	583,684
Lumber and wood products	19,504	19,348	23,665	21,328	16,515	16,041	18,831	20,921	19,824	21,307	24,993	26,439	25,646
Stone, clay, and glass	22,674	23,327	23,546	21,254	20,187	18,160	19,671	21,300	22,158	22,874	22,018	22,847	23,552
Primary metal industries	47,867	52,825	52,669	48,231	50,583	35,281	28,856	33,360	32,682	32,156	34,752	37,750	36,863
Fabricated metal products	51,534	53,382	56,040	53,692	52,957	46,281	48,761	54,781	56,234	54,774	58,908	66,218	65,816
Machinery, exc. electrical	78,381	80,915	85,588	86,051	89,564	80,005	84,816	105,663	124,180	129,447	138,112	163,910	174,853
Electric and electronic equip	50,087	56,175	60,159	63,346	64,897	61,814	64,559	73,340	74,315	74,141	82,991	88,060	90,839
Motor vehicles and equip.	56,988	58,103	51,587	35,160	34,783	29,453	37,313	47,322	50,332	46,516	44,788	49,503	47,283
Instruments and related products	19,735	20,315	22,397	21,922	23,763	22,631	23,070	25,157	24,244	25,687	25,748	27,946	26,639
Nondurable goods	261,460	271,437	279,035	265,468	269,949	272,136	290,406	303,793	307,682	320,462	336,627	346,651	345,358
Food and kindred products	51,702	56,566	59,526	59,762	58,900	61,427	62,655	62,063	64,818	65,592	66,665	67,836	70,284
Tobacco	9,525	9,924	9,852	9,561	9,991	8,916	8,004	7,784	6,248	7,039	7,039	5,164	3,080
Textile mill	17,628	16,595	17,029	16,368	15,792	14,827	16,230	16,025	15,598	17,043	17,374	16,747	16,720
Apparel and other textile	20,760	21,538	21,334	21,068	20,284	18,931	20,060	20,421	20,096	20,993	21,952	22,406	22,396
Paper and allied products	27,531	28,901	28,667	25,800	25,502	26,718	28,978	29,498	30,214	31,579	33,658	34,560	32,992
Printing and publishing	35,190	36,228	37,097	37,048	38,588	38,364	39,642	40,772	42,532	43,130	44,723	46,515	45,116
Chemicals and allied	52,999	55,057	56,700	50,021	53,986	55,257	59,723	59,398	59,057	64,563	71,944	77,501	76,128
Petroleum and coal	23,453	22,673	24,931	22,937	21,811	24,352	29,780	39,520	39,363	41,139	42,599	44,463	44,906

NA Not available.   [1] Includes industries not shown separately.

Source: U.S. Bureau of Economic Analysis, *The National Income and Product Accounts of the United States: Volume 2, 1959-88;* and *Survey of Current Business,* July issues.

No. 1255. Manufactures—Summary: 1963 to 1991

[For establishment coverage, see text, section 27. Data based on Census of Manufactures, except as noted. For composition of regions, see table 31. See also, *Historical Statistics, Colonial Times to 1970*, series P 1-12]

ITEM	Unit	1963	1967	1972	1977	1982	1987	1990 [1]	1991 [1]
ALL ESTABLISHMENTS									
Number of establishments [2]	1,000	312	311	321	360	358	369	(NA)	(NA)
With 20 or more employees	1,000	102	110	114	119	123	126	(NA)	(NA)
Employee size-class:									
Establishments [3]	1,000	305	306	313	351	348	359	(NA)	(NA)
Under 20	1,000	207	199	203	237	230	238	(NA)	(NA)
20 to 99	1,000	70	74	76	78	84	86	(NA)	(NA)
100 to 249	1,000	18	20	21	22	21	22	(NA)	(NA)
250 to 999	1,000	10	11	11	12	11	11	(NA)	(NA)
1,000 and over	1,000	3	3	3	2	2	2	(NA)	(NA)
Form of organization:									
Corporate	1,000	176.2	153.9	233.2	284.2	283.2	287.4	(NA)	(NA)
Noncorporate, total [4]	1,000	130.4	33.2	87.5	75.7	74.0	81.5	(NA)	(NA)
Individual proprietorship	1,000	99.2	24.9	42.5	52.3	45.6	35.4	(NA)	(NA)
Partnership	1,000	27.7	6.7	17.7	18.3	15.0	13.2	(NA)	(NA)
Value added by region:									
Northeast	Percent ...	29.8	29.1	26.3	23.7	23.7	23.7	20.6	20.5
North Central	Percent ...	35.4	35.0	34.9	34.4	29.8	29.8	29.9	29.9
South	Percent ...	21.5	22.7	25.5	27.4	29.5	29.5	32.0	32.2
West	Percent ...	13.3	13.0	13.4	14.5	17.0	17.0	17.5	17.4
All employees, [5] annual average [6]	Million ...	17.0	19.3	19.0	19.6	19.1	18.9	18.8	18.1
Payroll, all employees	Bil. dol.	100	132	174	264	380	476	532	529
Payroll per employee	$1,000. ...	5.9	6.8	9.2	13.5	19.9	25.2	28.3	29.3
Production workers, annual average	Million	12.2	14.0	13.5	13.7	12.4	12.2	12.1	11.5
Percent of all employees	Percent ...	71.8	72.5	71.1	69.9	64.9	64.6	64.4	63.7
Hours, production workers	Billion	24.5	27.8	26.7	26.7	23.5	24.3	24.3	23.2
Hours per worker	1,000	2.0	2.0	2.0	1.9	1.9	2.0	2.0	2.0
Wages, production workers	Bil. dol. ...	62	81	106	157	205	251	272	266
Percent of payroll for all									
employees	Percent ...	62.0	61.4	60.9	59.5	53.9	52.8	51.1	50
Wages per worker	$1,000. ...	5.1	5.8	7.9	11.5	16.5	20.6	22.5	23.1
Wages per worker hour	Dollar	2.53	2.91	3.97	5.89	8.72	10.35	11.19	11.49
Value added by manufacture [7]	Bil. dol....	192	262	354	585	824	1,166	1,326	1,314
Per production worker	$1,000. ...	15.7	18.7	26.2	42.7	66.5	95.5	109.6	114.1
Per production worker hour	Dollar ...	7.84	9.42	13.26	21.91	35.06	47.97	54.57	56.70
Per dollar of workers' wages	Dollar ...	3.10	3.23	3.34	3.73	4.02	4.64	4.88	4.93
Cost of materials	Bil. dol....	230	299	407	782	1,130	1,320	1,554	1504
Value of shipments [8]	Bil. dol....	421	557	757	1,359	1,960	2,476	2,874	2,826
Per production worker	$1,000. ...	34.5	39.8	56.1	99.2	158.1	203.0	237.5	245.5
End-of-year inventories	Bil. dol. ...	60	84	108	188	307	333	393	380
Capital expenditures, new [9]	Bil. dol. ...	11.4	21.5	24.1	47.5	75.0	78.6	102.0	99.0
Ratios:									
Value added to shipments	Ratio.....	45.6	47.0	46.7	42.9	42.0	47.1	(NA)	(NA)
Inventories to shipments	Ratio.....	14.2	15.0	14.2	13.8	15.7	13.4	(NA)	(NA)
Payroll to value added	Ratio.....	52.0	50.3	49.1	45.2	46.1	40.8	(NA)	(NA)
Gross book value of depreciable									
assets	Bil. dol. ...	158	218	301	439	692	868	(NA)	(NA)
Machinery and equipment	Bil. dol. ...	(NA)	157	218	328	527	671	(NA)	(NA)
Assets per employee	$1,000. ...	9.3	11.3	16.4	22.4	36.2	48.6	(NA)	(NA)
MULTIUNIT COMPANIES									
Establishments	1,000	45.9	51.7	70.2	81.2	81.7	80.9	(NA)	(NA)
Employees	Million....	11.0	13.3	14.3	15.0	14.3	13.8	(NA)	(NA)
Production workers	Million....	8.1	9.8	9.8	10.1	8.8	8.5	(NA)	(NA)
Payroll, all employees	Bil. dol. ...	68.2	93.8	138.8	214.2	307.5	377.3	(NA)	(NA)
Wages, production workers	Bil. dol. ...	44.7	60.9	81.9	124.9	159.1	191.8	(NA)	(NA)
Value added by manufacture	Bil. dol. ...	146.6	206.4	286.1	485.0	678.4	953.6	(NA)	(NA)
Capital expenditures, new	Bil. dol. ...	8.9	18.6	20.0	41.0	65.2	66.5	(NA)	(NA)
SINGLE UNIT COMPANIES [10]									
Establishments	1,000	260.8	254.0	250.5	278.7	276.3	288.0	(NA)	(NA)
Employees	Million....	5.2	5.2	4.6	4.6	4.8	5.1	(NA)	(NA)
Payroll, all employees	Bil. dol. ...	25.1	28.5	35.4	49.8	72.1	98.3	(NA)	(NA)
Value added by manufacture	Bil. dol. ...	45.5	55.5	67.9	100.1	145.7	212.1	(NA)	(NA)

NA Not available. [1] Estimated data based on *Annual Survey of Manufactures;* see text, section 27. [2] Includes administrative and auxiliary units, except as noted. [3] Excludes administrative offices and auxiliary units. [4] Includes forms of organization not shown separately. [5] Includes data for employees of manufacturing establishments engaged in distribution and construction work. [6] Data are based on pay periods ending nearest 15th of March, May, August, and November. [7] Adjusted value added; takes into account (a) value added by merchandising operations (that is, difference between the sales value and cost of merchandise sold without further manufacture, processing, or assembly), plus (b) net change in finished goods and work-in-process inventories between beginning and end of year. [8] Includes extensive and unmeasurable duplication from shipments between establishments in the same industry classification. [9] Includes plants under construction and not yet in operation. [10] Beginning 1967, includes data obtained from Federal administrative records.

Source: U.S. Bureau of the Census, *Census of Manufactures, 1963, 1967, 1972, 1977, 1982,* and *1987;* and *Annual Survey of Manufactures.*

No. 1256. Manufactures—Summary, by Industry Group: 1982, 1987, and 1991

[Data based on various editions of the *Standard Industrial Classification Manual*, published by the Office of Management and Budget: see text, section 27. N.e.c.=Not elsewhere classified. See also *Historical Statistics, Colonial Times to 1970*, series P-58-67]

SIC[1] code	INDUSTRY GROUP	1982 Establishments (number)	1982 All employees Number[2] (1,000)	1982 All employees Payroll (mil. dol.)	1982 Value of shipments (mil. dol.)	1987 Establishments, total	1987 All employees Number (1,000)	1987 All employees Payroll (mil. dol.)	1987 Value of shipments (mil. dol.)	1991 All employees Number (1,000)	1991 All employees Payroll (mil. dol.)	1991 Production workers	1991 Value added by manufacture (mil. dol.)	1991 Value of shipments (mil. dol.)
(X)	**All manufacturing establishments**	358,061	19,094	379,627	1,960,206	368,897	18,950	475,651	2,475,901	18,062	529,019	11,513	1,313,829	2,826,207
20	**Food and kindred products**	22,130	1,488	26,088	280,529	20,624	1,449	30,268	329,725	1,475	34,578	1,070	145,336	387,601
201	Meat products	3,623	318	4,993	67,602	3,267	341	5,701	77,002	390	7,025	330	17,476	89,391
202	Dairy products	2,724	140	2,553	38,771	2,366	142	3,217	44,755	136	3,595	84	13,855	49,853
203	Preserved fruits and vegetables	(NA)	(NA)	(NA)	(NA)	1,912	209	3,784	36,343	216	4,572	181	22,043	46,806
204	Grain mill products	2,745	108	2,197	31,386	2,610	102	2,704	36,737	103	3,126	71	19,835	47,111
205	Bakery products	(NA)	(NA)	(NA)	(NA)	2,850	217	4,761	23,677	209	5,279	127	16,452	26,539
206	Sugar and confectionery products	1,033	96	1,661	15,576	1,094	90	1,991	18,887	92	2,328	73	10,107	21,959
207	Fats and oils	724	39	774	16,752	595	30	702	15,881	28	744	19	3,815	18,735
208	Beverages	2,584	194	4,244	38,801	2,214	161	4,521	47,327	145	4,591	73	26,839	54,610
209	Miscellaneous foods and kindred products	3,941	158	2,300	23,959	3,716	158	2,887	29,116	156	3,318	114	14,915	32,598
21	**Tobacco products**	163	58	1,324	16,061	138	45	1,486	20,757	40	1,520	29	24,484	32,032
211	Cigarettes	14	42	1,094	12,127	11	32	1,486	17,372	27	1,224	20	22,210	27,111
212	Cigars	60	5	59	254	70	3	36	192	3	51	2	201	312
213	Chewing and smoking tobacco	29	3	52	665	29	3	77	1,114	3	88	2	201	1,602
214	Tobacco stemming and redrying	60	8	120	3,015	78	7	139	2,079	7	157	5	871	3,008
22	**Textile mill products**	6,630	717	9,046	47,515	6,412	672	11,410	62,786	598	11,375	515	26,925	65,706
221	Broadwoven fabric mills, cotton	269	77	965	3,972	301	72	1,260	5,508	66	1,246	59	2,480	5,695
222	Broadwoven fabric mills, manmade	523	141	1,815	8,191	441	88	1,596	8,049	78	1,600	69	3,551	8,315
223	Broadwoven fabric mills, wool	131	13	176	763	119	14	236	1,051	15	296	13	705	1,804
224	Narrow fabric mills	281	18	216	852	277	19	296	1,136	16	291	14	698	1,248
225	Knitting mills	(NA)	(NA)	(NA)	(NA)	2,130	203	2,988	13,531	181	3,022	159	7,244	15,449
226	Textile finishing, except wool	753	58	834	4,972	971	56	1,036	7,042	49	1,046	41	2,641	6,360
227	Carpets and rugs	505	42	603	5,808	477	53	1,039	9,795	49	1,028	38	2,846	8,988
228	Yarn and thread mills	714	109	98	7,036	610	114	1,850	10,277	94	1,670	86	3,684	10,687
229	Miscellaneous textile goods	(NA)	(NA)	(NA)	(NA)	1,086	53	1,109	6,398	50	1,176	38	3,077	7,160
23	**Apparel and other textile products**	24,391	1,189	12,129	53,388	22,872	1,081	13,904	64,243	960	14,135	815	33,432	65,345
231	Men's and boys' suits and coats	529	75	878	3,062	347	55	779	2,863	44	743	37	1,400	2,467
232	Men's and boys' furnishings	2,544	299	2,837	12,727	2,195	280	3,246	15,441	252	3,371	222	8,681	15,988
233	Women's and misses' outerwear	10,838	419	4,110	18,225	10,290	349	4,297	18,225	307	4,244	262	9,953	19,433
234	Women's and children's undergarments	755	82	783	3,323	557	68	8,439	3,738	58	810	49	2,172	3,683

See footnotes at end of table.

No. 1256. Manufactures—Summary, by Industry Group: 1982, 1987, and 1991—Continued

[See headnote, p. 743]

SIC code	INDUSTRY GROUP	1982 Establishments (number)	1982 All employees Number² (1,000)	1982 Payroll (mil. dol.)	1982 Value of shipments (mil. dol.)	1987 Establishments, total	1987 All employees Number (1,000)	1987 Payroll (mil. dol.)	1987 Value of shipments (mil. dol.)	1991 All employees Number (1,000)	1991 Payroll (mil. dol.)	1991 Production workers	1991 Value added by manufacture (mil. dol.)	1991 Value of shipments (mil. dol.)
23	**Apparel, other textile products—Con.**													
235	Hats, caps, and millinery	419	16	157	522	461	17	204	663	16	228	14	455	801
236	Girls' and children's outerwear	968	71	671	2,711	834	72	826	3,753	59	791	50	1,907	3,579
237	Fur goods	504	3	60	419	380	2	48	423	2	29	1	70	257
238	Miscellaneous apparel and accessories	1,223	50	513	2,118	986	41	518	2,229	37	546	30	1,167	2,244
239	Miscellaneous fabricated textile products	6,611	174	2,120	10,281	6,822	198	3,143	15,744	186	3,373	152	7,627	16,894
24	**Lumber and wood products**	32,984	576	8,445	42,935	33,982	698	12,707	69,747	631	12,738	526	26,995	70,569
241	Logging	11,658	81	1,208	11,952	11,952	86	1,584	10,938	78	1,561	65	4,097	11,434
242	Sawmills and planing mills	7,403	158	2,306	11,132	6,696	180	3,297	19,220	158	3,244	141	6,803	19,409
243	Millwork, plywood, and structural members	6,545	165	2,596	11,683	7,930	240	4,658	22,614	210	4,487	171	8,885	21,448
244	Wood containers	2,250	36	391	1,635	2,216	37	483	2,069	40	634	33	1,203	2,864
245	Wood buildings and mobile homes	1,163	60	880	4,955	1,077	65	1,215	6,575	54	1,106	42	2,173	5,952
249	Miscellaneous Wood Products	3,965	77	1,064	5,255	4,104	90.1	1,536.4	8,330	91	1,706	74	3,832	9,462
25	**Furniture and fixtures³**	10,003	436	6,084	24,129	11,613	511	9,082	37,462	466	9,489	369	20,669	40,027
251	Household furniture	5,475	263	3,162	12,776	5,606	284	4,492	18,559	259	4,576	217	9,723	19,499
252	Office Furniture	700	59	1,051	4,150	986	81	1,790	7,538	66	1,761	48	4,128	7,263
253	Public building and related furniture	413	19	295	1,103	484	22	397	2,088	26	559	20	1,259	3,136
254	Partitions and fixtures	2,148	60	1,025	3,710	2,455	74	1,552	5,537	67	1,622	49	3,210	5,929
259	Miscellaneous furniture and fixtures	1,267	36	551	2,390	2,084	50	892	3,740	48	972	35	2,348	4,200
26	**Paper and allied products**	(NA)	(NA)	(NA)	(NA)	6,342	611	16,860	108,989	621	19,383	477	58,281	128,824
261	Pulp mills	43	17	468	3,110	39	14	535	4,314	17	697	13	2,446	5,329
262	Paper mills	299	129	3,431	20,995	281	129	4,597	28,918	130	5,224	99	15,510	33,344
263	Paperboard mills	222	56	1,502	9,531	199	52	1,859	13,730	51	2,027	39	7,257	15,013
265	Paperboard containers and boxes	2,781	188	3,517	19,192	2,796	194	4,618	25,863	199	5,392	153	11,531	30,577
267	Miscellaneous converted paper products	3,006	213	3,961	26,701	3,027	222	5,251	36,165	224	6,043	173	21,537	44,560
27	**Printing and publishing**	53,406	1,292	22,707	85,797	61,774	1,494	33,440	136,196	1,488	38,742	787	103,771	156,685
271	Newspapers	8,846	402	6,555	21,276	9,079	434	9,022	31,850	428	10,309	145	26,093	33,702
272	Periodicals	3,328	94	1,986	11,478	4,017	110	2,983	17,329	111	3,661	21	13,794	20,345
273	Books	2,811	112	2,090	10,132	2,856	114	2,821	15,876	126	3,700	55	14,071	20,736
274	Miscellaneous publishing	2,057	45	706	2,871	2,376	70	1,513	7,810	65	1,780	23	7,354	9,762
275	Commercial printing	(NA)	(NA)	(NA)	(NA)	36,103	553	12,301	44,786	556	14,135	401	28,892	51,948
276	Manifold business forms	810	50	934	5,059	853	53	1,281	7,397	46	1,269	32	3,840	7,234
277	Greeting cards	154	21	344	1,894	162	22	471	2,911	24	609	13	2,925	3,810
278	Blankbooks and bookbinding	1,487	61	903	2,803	1,545	69	1,265	4,080	70	1,395	54	3,217	4,571
279	Printing trade services	(NA)	(NA)	(NA)	(NA)	4,783	69	1,784	4,157	62	1,884	45	3,584	4,577

SIC[1] code	INDUSTRY GROUP	1982 Establishments (number)	1982 All employees Number[2] (1,000)	1982 Payroll (mil. dol.)	1982 Value of shipments (mil. dol.)	1987 Establishments (number)	1987 All employees Number (1,000)	1987 Payroll (mil. dol.)	1987 Value of shipments (mil. dol.)	1991 All employees Number (1,000)	1991 Payroll (mil. dol.)	1991 Production workers	1991 Value added by manufacture (mil. dol.)	1991 Value of shipments (mil. dol.)
28	**Chemicals and allied products**	**11,901**	**873**	**20,836**	**170,737**	**12,109**	**814**	**25,016**	**229,546**	**846**	**31,002**	**477**	**154,793**	**292,326**
281	Industrial inorganic chemicals	1,365	108	2,795	17,280	1,405	94	3,099	19,774	104	4,085	56	15,724	26,511
282	Plastics materials and synthetics	606	141	3,451	28,428	680	123	4,013	40,851	129	4,889	87	19,673	46,235
283	Drugs	1,281	166	3,966	24,695	1,356	172	5,304	39,263	184	7,198	83	43,245	60,836
284	Soap, cleaners, and toilet goods	2,379	127	2,581	26,031	2,399	119	3,099	34,748	123	3,750	76	25,374	41,854
285	Paints and allied products	1,441	54	1,158	9,162	1,431	55	1,492	12,702	51	1,568	25	6,784	14,255
286	Industrial organic chemicals	969	144	4,005	38,157	961	126	4,541	51,158	127	5,429	75	26,441	64,432
287	Agricultural chemicals	1,127	51	1,156	14,653	973	40	1,171	14,267	41	1,406	25	8,121	18,522
289	Miscellaneous chemical products	2,733	82	1,725	12,330	2,904	85	2,298	16,782	87	2,678	51	9,431	19,682
29	**Petroleum and coal products**	**2,322**	**152**	**4,339**	**208,919**	**2,254**	**116**	**3,996**	**130,414**	**113**	**4,729**	**73**	**24,024**	**158,076**
291	Petroleum refining	(NA)	(NA)	(NA)	(NA)	331	75	2,845	118,186	74	3,448	48	19,796	145,392
295	Asphalt paving and roofing materials	1,307	30	629	5,948	1,367	28	786	7,749	26	843	19	2,543	7,233
299	Miscellaneous petroleum and coal products	582	14	312	3,614	556	13	365	4,479	13	438	7	1,685	5,452
30	**Rubber and misc. plastics products**	**13,449**	**682**	**11,597**	**55,416**	**14,515**	**831**	**17,581**	**86,634**	**840**	**20,298**	**647**	**50,295**	**100,668**
301	Tires and inner tubes	164	70	1,734	9,340	164	65	2,070	10,427	66	2,286	52	6,654	11,883
302	Rubber and plastics footwear	65	18	197	706	66	11	153	557	12	182	10	384	757
305	Hose and belting and plastics and packing	635	55	999	3,612	693	52	1,159	4,648	53	1,332	39	2,843	5,241
306	Fabricated rubber products, n.e.c.	(NA)	(NA)	(NA)	(NA)	1,573	104	2,245	9,227	98	2,323	75	5,293	10,370
308	Miscellaneous plastics products, n.e.c.	(NA)	(NA)	(NA)	(NA)	12,019	599	11,955	61,775	611	14,176	471	35,121	72,417
31	**Leather and leather products**	**2,735**	**200**	**2,219**	**9,719**	**2,193**	**129**	**1,831**	**9,082**	**106**	**1,753**	**89**	**4,293**	**9,142**
311	Leather tanning and finishing	384	20	311	1,753	344	15	292	2,219	12	278	10	710	2,183
313	Footwear cut stock	161	7	81	368	128	5	70	324	5	83	5	182	383
314	Footwear, except rubber	751	121	1,250	5,269	479	71	913	4,073	53	770	46	1,942	3,775
315	Leather gloves and mittens	96	4	37	178	77	3	34	185	3	33	2	58	141
316	Luggage	292	16	194	789	241	11	196	929	13	230	10	598	1,148
317	Handbags and personal leather goods	636	25	271	1,035	529	17	232	942	12	210	10	495	906
319	Leather goods, n.e.c.	415	7	76	327	395	7	95	411	9	149	7	308	607

See footnotes at end of table.

No. 1256. Manufactures—Summary, by Industry Group: 1982, 1987, and 1991—Continued

[See headnote, page 743]

SIC code	INDUSTRY GROUP	1982 Establishments (number)	1982 All employees Number (1,000)	1982 Payroll (mil. dol.)	1982 Value of shipments (mil. dol.)	1987 Establishments (number)	1987 All employees Number (1,000)	1987 Payroll (mil. dol.)	1987 Value of shipments (mil. dol.)	1991 All employees Number (1,000)	1991 Payroll (mil. dol.)	1991 Production workers	1991 Value added by manufacture (mil. dol.)	1991 Value of shipments (mil. dol.)
32	**Stone, clay, and glass products**	16,545	532	10,097	45,181	16,166	524	12,349	61,477	476	12,612	363	31,839	59,611
321	Flat glass	69	15	414	1,666	81	15	507	2,549	13	486	11	1,254	2,104
322	Glass and glassware, pressed or blown	459	97	2,032	7,941	522	77	1,959	8,339	67	2,015	57	5,129	8,755
323	Products of purchased glass	1,337	41	696	2,977	1,432	51	1,060	5,439	52	1,243	41	3,312	6,155
324	Cement, hydraulic	237	25	636	3,542	215	19	599	4,335	16	560	12	1,937	3,778
325	Structural clay products	628	30	491	1,868	598	35	689	2,915	32	705	25	1,604	2,782
326	Pottery and related products	910	37	598	1,762	1,006	38	762	2,416	37	820	29	1,758	2,559
327	Concrete, gypsum, and plaster products	9,933	167	2,995	14,947	9,814	203	4,632	24,427	180	4,571	129	10,632	22,466
328	Cut stone and stone products	711	11	156	555	745	13	243	841	12	267	10	582	956
329	Miscellaneous nonmetallic mineral products	(NA)	(NA)	(NA)	(NA)	1,753	73	1,898	10,226	67	1,945	49	5,630	10,057
33	**Primary metal industries** [3]	7,061	854	20,603	104,667	6,771	701	19,777	120,248	677	21,640	516	46,605	132,837
331	Blast furnace and basic steel products	1,068	366	8,267	46,720	1,241	253	8,166	51,815	246	8,976	187	19,685	56,327
332	Iron and steel foundries	1,438	157	3,113	9,642	1,231	130	3,426	10,628	125	3,580	100	6,194	11,172
333	Primary nonferrous metals	161	44	1,307	11,321	169	32	996	10,869	35	1,310	27	3,593	13,838
334	Secondary nonferrous metals	458	19	402	4,852	397	13	312	4,431	13	388	10	815	5,041
335	Nonferrous rolling and drawing	1,022	167	3,636	25,463	1,066	163	4,298	33,282	150	4,602	111	10,956	36,318
336	Nonferrous foundries (castings)	(NA)	(NA)	(NA)	(NA)	1,687	80	1,805	6,315	75	1,873	60	3,454	6,693
34	**Fabricated metal products**	35,560	1,460	28,283	119,444	36,105	1,458	35,000	147,366	1,359	36,827	995	76,670	157,077
341	Metal cans and shipping containers	566	59	1,533	12,172	538	48	1,527	12,114	41	1,490	34	3,984	13,642
342	Cutlery, handtools, and hardware	2,238	141	2,585	10,082	2,327	145	3,389	13,481	132	3,420	99	8,156	14,353
343	Plumbing and heating, except electric	1,177	48	821	4,003	828	46	1,005	5,283	42	1,106	29	2,965	5,733
344	Fabricated structural metal products	12,681	422	7,897	34,904	12,569	407	9,042	40,416	379	9,643	269	19,313	42,549
345	Screw machine products, bolts, etc.	2,690	94	1,727	5,834	2,569	95	2,270	7,890	91	2,437	69	4,997	8,484
346	Metal forgings and stampings	4,019	236	5,110	20,057	4,062	255	7,235	28,410	232	7,251	182	12,729	27,927
347	Metal services, n.e.c.	5,070	97	1,518	5,125	5,251	113	2,167	7,790	110	2,464	86	4,787	8,758
348	Ordnance and accessories, n.e.c.	349	79	1,780	4,993	374	88	2,458	7,644	69	2,205	39	4,378	6,673
349	Miscellaneous fabricated metal products	6,770	284	5,312	22,224	7,577	262	5,906	24,340	264	6,814	188	15,361	28,959
35	**Industrial machinery and equipment**	52,912	2,189	46,911	187,896	52,135	1,844	50,553	217,670	1,774	54,983	1,101	124,235	243,479
351	Engines and turbines	341	112	2,850	13,040	356	87	2,906	14,570	78	2,871	52	7,560	16,608
352	Farm and garden machinery	2,078	114	2,386	13,018	1,804	82	1,917	11,474	90	2,305	64	7,133	15,166
353	Construction and related machinery	3,952	326	7,332	32,038	3,467	188	5,272	24,622	190	5,819	118	12,531	27,727
354	Metalworking machinery	(NA)	(NA)	(NA)	(NA)	11,470	268	7,301	22,004	266	8,192	186	12,515	25,456
355	Special industry machinery	(NA)	(NA)	(NA)	(NA)	4,550	169	4,588	17,096	164	5,377	92	10,876	20,687
356	General industrial machinery	(NA)	(NA)	(NA)	(NA)	3,929	240	6,203	24,121	255	7,527	161	16,832	30,809
357	Computer and office equipment	(NA)	(NA)	(NA)	(NA)	2,134	328	10,668	60,627	265	10,082	90	27,419	58,755
358	Refrigeration and service machinery	(NA)	(NA)	(NA)	(NA)	2,129	190	4,752	23,235	174	4,832	121	11,750	25,064
359	Industrial machinery, n.e.c.	1,937	172	3,344	16,450	22,296	292	6,946	19,921	292	7,977	217	14,621	23,207

SIC[1] code	INDUSTRY GROUP	1982				1987				1991				
		Establishments (number)	All employees Number[2] (1,000)	All employees Payroll (mil. dol.)	Value of shipments (mil. dol.)	Establishments (number)	All employees Number (1,000)	All employees Payroll (mil. dol.)	Value of shipments (mil. dol.)	All employees Number (1,000)	All employees Payroll (mil. dol.)	Production workers	Value added by manufacture (mil. dol.)	Value of shipments (mil. dol.)
36	Electronics; other electric equip.	(NA)	(NA)	(NA)	(NA)	15,962	1,565	38,738	171,286	1,427	41,611	896	106,669	197,880
361	Electric distribution equipment	(NA)	(NA)	(NA)	(NA)	766	166	1,791	8,197	70	1,873	49	4,939	9,276
362	Electrical industrial apparatus	(NA)	(NA)	(NA)	(NA)	2,213	166	3,882	15,266	153	4,166	102	9,824	17,754
363	Household appliances	(NA)	(NA)	(NA)	(NA)	480	117	2,642	16,498	104	2,497	84	7,413	17,692
364	Electric lighting and wiring equipment	1,993	159	2,718	12,048	1,986	167	3,732	18,004	144	3,677	105	10,161	18,131
365	Household audio and video equipment	(NA)	(NA)	(NA)	(NA)	854	44	850	7,833	45	1,027	32	3,370	9,823
366	Communications equipment	(NA)	(NA)	(NA)	(NA)	1,437	260	7,537	34,001	238	8,394	109	21,286	37,946
367	Electronic components and accessories	(NA)	(NA)	(NA)	(NA)	5,911	546	13,623	50,258	519	15,477	314	38,650	65,233
369	Misc. electrical equipment and supplies	(NA)	(NA)	(NA)	(NA)	2,315	188	4,682	21,230	154	4,500	101	11,026	22,025
37	Transportation equipment	9,443	1,596	40,812	201,346	10,500	1,817	58,790	332,936	1,634	60,079	1,056	151,979	364,032
371	Motor vehicles and equipment	3,867	616	15,393	112,270	4,422	751	23,910	205,923	653	23,883	519	73,333	206,101
372	Aircraft and parts	1,471	539	14,718	52,027	1,618	596	20,590	77,304	568	21,886	300	49,046	102,381
373	Ship and boat building and repairing	2,566	205	4,326	13,326	2,766	177	4,266	13,857	162	4,504	122	7,959	14,524
374	Railroad equipment	200	35	790	3,457	173	22	631	2,471	26	820	19	1,690	4,450
375	Motorcycles, bicycles, and parts	273	13	225	1,341	246	7	158	1,063	11	277	9	741	1,914
376	Guided missiles, space vehicles, parts	105	146	4,481	14,398	156	214	8,114	26,285	178	7,750	62	17,103	28,965
379	Miscellaneous transportation equipment	961	43	879	4,528	1,119	49	1,122	6,033	36	959	25	2107	5,698
38	Instruments and related products	(NA)	(NA)	(NA)	(NA)	10,326	982	28,778	107,325	901	31,797	452	82,536	127,160
381	Search and navigation equipment	(NA)	(NA)	(NA)	(NA)	1,137	369	12,368	36,267	280	11,631	112	23,672	36,213
382	Measuring and controlling devices	(NA)	(NA)	(NA)	(NA)	4,240	285	7,807	26,042	268	9,070	133	20,096	32,263
384	Medical instruments and supplies	2,973	189	3,559	15,133	3,443	204	5,027	22,865	241	7,218	143	21,873	33,596
385	Ophthalmic goods	410	26	409	1,273	494	24	475	1,689	26	627	17	1,645	2,313
386	Photographic equipment and supplies	795	119	3,193	17,038	791	88	2,878	19,241	78	3,044	40	14,603	21,398
387	Watches, clocks, watchcases and parts	237	17	248	1,188	221	12	223	1,221	8	207	6	646	1,377
39	Misc. manufacturing industries	15,871	363	5,647	26,891	16,544	374	6,884	32,012	363	7,750	260	19,999	37,131
391	Jewelry, silverware, and plated ware	2,882	50	770	4,379	2,978	50	941	5,554	46	982	32	2,458	5,275
393	Musical instruments	452	18	258	916	425	12	218	814	12	238	9	536	881
394	Toys and sporting goods	2,570	99	1,389	8,256	2,711	89	1,512	8,798	93	1,923	69	6,088	11,343
395	Pens, pencils, office, and art supplies	1,026	32	485	2,372	1,013	29	540	2,536	30	625	21	1,788	3,306
396	Costume jewelry and notions	(NA)	(NA)	(NA)	(NA)	1,020	32	498	2,062	26	527	19	1,286	2,203
399	Miscellaneous manufactures[4]	(NA)	(NA)	(NA)	(NA)	8,397	163	3,174	12,248	157	3,454	111	7,843	14,124
(X)	Administrative and auxiliary	9,676	1,276	38,220	-	9,480	1,234	47,202	-	1,269	61,979	-	-	-

- Represents zero. NA Not available. X Not applicable. [1] Standard Industrial Classification Code; see text, section 27. [2] All employees represents the average of production workers plus all other employees for the payroll period ending nearest the 15th of March. [3] Includes other industries, not shown separately. [4] Manufacturing concerns often reported separately for central offices or auxiliaries which serve the manufacturing establishment of a company, rather than the general public. Separate reports were obtained from such units if at a different location or if they serviced more than one establishment.

Source: U.S. Bureau of the Census, Census of Manufactures, 1987, and Annual Survey of Manufactures.

No. 1257. Manufactures—Summary, by Industry Group; Selected Based on Value Added: 1982, 1987, and 1991

[Data based on various editions of the Standard Industrial Classification Manual, published by the Office of Management and Budget; see text, section 27. N.e.c.=Not elsewhere classified. Historical Statistics, Colonial Times to 1970, series P-58-67]

SIC code[1]	INDUSTRY GROUP	1982 Establishments (number)	1982 All employees, Number (1,000)[2]	1982 All employees, Payroll (mil. dol.)	1982 Value of shipments (mil. dol.)	1987 Establishments (number)	1987 All employees, Number (1,000)	1987 All employees, Payroll (mil. dol.)	1987 Value of shipments (mil. dol.)	1991 All employees, Number (1,000)	1991 All employees, Payroll (mil. dol.)	1991 Production workers	1991 Value added by manufacture (mil. dol.)	1991 Value of shipments (mil. dol.)
2011	Meat packing plants	1,780	134.4	2,549	44,854	1,434	113.2	2,141	44,991	120.8	2,375	103.3	5,958	49,326
2013	Sausages and other prepared meats	1,311	65.5	1,206	12,278	1,344	79.1	1,619	16,623	79.6	1,833	59.0	5,046	18,361
2015	Poultry slaughtering and processing	532	117.7	1,237	10,471	463	147.7	1,919	14,912	189.6	2,817	168.0	6,473	21,703
2026	Fluid milk	1,190	78.2	1,469	18,736	946	72.4	1,681	20,591	65.5	1,840	32.3	5,656	21,137
2033	Canned fruits and vegetables	715	70.5	1,040	9,283	647	65.6	1,163	11,890	67.3	1,484	57.2	6,859	15,579
2038	Frozen specialties, n.e.c.	(NA)	(NA)	(NA)	(NA)	288	37.5	669.1	5624.8	44.9	876	36.7	4,230	8,428
2043	Cereal breakfast foods	52	15.6	435	4,132	53	16.0	599	6,566	15.7	707	12.7	6,581	8,954
2051	Bread, cake, and related products	2,305	170.7	3,254	13,143	2,357	161.6	3,556	16,202	150.2	3,834	83.0	10,801	17,279
2052	Cookies and crackers	358	45.6	797	4,665	380	45.4	1,010	6,300	49.3	1,247	36.2	4,991	8,022
2064	Candy and other confectionery products	(NA)	(NA)	(NA)	(NA)	685	45.8	900	6,980	49.1	1,121	39.3	4,999	8,746
2082	Malt beverages	109	43.0	1,308	11,183	134	31.9	1,355	13,619	32.4	1,446	23.5	9,037	15,925
2086	Bottled and canned soft drinks	1,626	113.8	2,146	16,808	1,190	95.6	2,277	22,006	81.7	2,210	31.9	9,555	25,191
2087	Flavoring extracts and syrups, n.e.c.	(NA)	(NA)	237	4,237	280	9.1	258	4,665	8.1	275	4.6	4,123	5,642
2099	Food preparations, n.e.c.	1,658	(NA)	1,094	(NA)	1,658	57.9	1,110	9,787	54.7	1,193	37.5	5,666	11,322
2111	Cigarettes	14	41.5	1,208	12,127	12	32.0	1,234	17,372	26.9	1,561	19.5	22,210	27,111
2411	Logging	11,658	80.8	2,020	8,274	11,936	85.7	1,516	10,880	78.1	1,224	65.4	4,097	11,434
2421	Sawmills and planing mills, general	6,316	131.9	1,403	10,065	5,742	148.2	2,017	17,357	129.5	2,747	116.1	5,866	11,485
2511	Wood household furniture	2,607	125.6	3,431	5,057	2,948	135.8	2,017	7,980	121.4	2,005	103.8	4,169	7,980
2621	Paper mills	299	129.0	1,502	20,995	282	129.1	4,597	28,916	130.3	5,224	99.4	15,510	33,344
2631	Paperboard mills	222	55.6	1,863	9,531	205	52.3	1,859	13,730	50.6	2,027	39.0	7,257	15,013
2653	Corrugated and solid fiber boxes	1,492	94.4	1,862	10,558	1,601	105.8	2,610	16,107	108.7	3,047	79.4	6,064	18,026
2676	Sanitary paper products	138	36.7	863	9,086	133	38.4	1,155	11,698	38.8	1,343	31.1	8,747	15,594
2711	Newspapers	8,846	401.5	6,555	21,276	9,091	434.6	9,025	31,849	428.4	10,309	145.1	26,093	33,702
2721	Periodicals	3,328	94.0	1,986	11,478	4,020	110.0	2,983	17,239	110.6	3,661	20.7	13,794	20,345
2731	Book publishing	2,130	67.1	1,327	7,740	2,298	70.1	1,860	12,620	77.3	2,514	17.1	11,683	16,596
2741	Miscellaneous publishing	2,057	45.3	706	2,871	2,298	69.4	1,513	7,810	65.0	1,780	22.6	7,354	9,762
2752	Commercial printing, lithographic	17,842	311.9	5,746	19,442	24,980	403.0	9,132	32,698	400.1	10,387	290.8	20,952	37,719
2759	Commercial printing, n.e.c.	(NA)	(NA)	(NA)	(NA)	10,796	126.2	2,490	8,973	133.8	3,055	92.1	6,270	10,723
2761	Manifold business forms	810	49.5	934	5,059	853	53.2	1,276	7,359	46.3	1,269	32.2	3,840	7,234
2819	Industrial inorganic chemicals, n.e.c.	645	81.7	2,134	12,060	662	72.2	2,425	13,212	78.9	3,157	41.0	10,612	17,649
2821	Plastics materials and resins	440	60.2	1,434	15,769	480	56.3	2,006	26,244	60.5	2,480	36.7	11,012	29,566
2824	Organic fibers, noncellulosic	70	(NA)	(NA)	8,263	72	45.7	1,347	10,112	46.9	1,569	35.0	6,119	11,084
2834	Pharmaceutical preparations	683	124.4	3,053	18,998	732	131.6	4,168	32,094	129.1	5,012	59.2	34,978	47,376
2841	Soap and other detergents	723	35.4	827	9,167	764	31.7	956	11,559	36.6	1,221	23.1	8,165	15,233
2842	Polishes and sanitation goods	(NA)	23.0	444	4614	726	20.6	500	5,594	19.6	573	12.2	3,895	6,172
2844	Toilet preparations	639	60.4	1,102	10,183	694	58.5	1,353	14,593	57.4	1,616	35.6	12,047	17,085
2851	Paints and allied products	1,441	54.1	1,158	9,162	1,426	55.1	1,491	12,701	51.1	1,568	35.2	6,784	14,255
2869	Industrial organic chemicals, n.e.c.	(NA)	(NA)	(NA)	(NA)	699	100.3	3,696	42,189	101.0	4,403	58.4	22,248	53,069
2879	Agricultural chemicals, n.e.c.	330	16.5	404	5,436	277	16.1	518	6,300	16.4	620	9.1	4,951	8,346
2899	Chemical preparations, n.e.c.	1,443	39.7	837	6,344	1,529	37.9	1,021	8,024	39.4	1,202	22.5	4,765	9,176

SIC[1] code	INDUSTRY GROUP	1982 Establishments (number)	1982 All employees Number[2] (1,000)	1982 All employees Payroll (mil. dol.)	1982 Value of shipments (mil. dol.)	1987 Establishments (number)	1987 All employees Number (1,000)	1987 All employees Payroll (mil. dol.)	1987 Value of shipments (mil. dol.)	1991 All employees Number (1,000)	1991 All employees Payroll (mil. dol.)	1991 Production workers	1991 Value added by manufacture (mil. dol.)	1991 Value of shipments (mil. dol.)
2911	Petroleum refining	(NA)	(NA)	(NA)	(NA)	309	74.6	2,846	118,216	73.9	3,448	47.6	19,796	145,392
3011	Tires and inner tubes	164	70.3	1,734	9,340	163	65.4	2,070	10,427	65.5	2,286	52.4	6,654	11,883
3081	Unsupported plastics film and sheet	594	(NA)	(NA)	(NA)	594	48.4	1,256	8,140	50.5	1,489	36.0	4,246	9,169
3089	Plastics products, n.e.c.	(NA)	(NA)	(NA)	(NA)	8,571	384.7	7,286	33,774	388.9	8,540	301.9	20,121	39,188
3273	Ready-mixed concrete	5,379	81.4	1,475	8,163	5,321	96.9	2,289	12,975	86.1	2,243	62.8	5,170	11,681
3312	Blast furnaces and steel mills	301	295.8	8,678	36,824	342	188.9	6,451	38,663	177.3	6,940	135.3	14,568	40,775
3357	Nonferrous wiredrawing and insulating	440	67.6	1,521	8,217	487	64.9	1,504	10,827	57.1	1,575	41.9	4,313	11,686
3429	Hardware, n.e.c.	1,185	80.1	1,990	5,741	1,240	85.6	2,056	8,175	73.8	1,938	56.2	4,278	8,223
3441	Fabricated structural metal	2,740	103.6	2,180	8,853	2,454	80.9	1,881	8,667	77.0	2,064	54.2	3,900	9,079
3443	Fabricated plate work (boiler shops)	1,929	102.9	2,293	8,225	1,740	74.6	1,842	6,795	73.5	2,127	51.2	4,396	8,684
3444	Sheet metal work	3,795	81.1	1,783	6,854	4,297	100.3	2,237	9,700	94.9	2,411	70.7	4,753	9,961
3465	Automotive stampings	668	90.5	1,979	8,777	660	119.8	3,977	15,252	99.3	3,681	82.1	5,663	13,404
3469	Metal stampings, n.e.c.	2,843	100.4	2,067	6,438	2,815	95.5	2,132	8,331	95.0	2,400	71.9	4,811	9,338
3519	Internal combustion engines, n.e.c.	253	79.6	2,653	9,363	278	64.0	2,043	11,123	56.3	1,909	38.9	5,268	11,516
3523	Farm machinery and equipment	1,903	96.1	2,293	10,743	1,634	57.0	1,416	6,880	65.1	1,787	45.4	5,509	10,347
3531	Construction machinery	939	115.5	2,393	11,658	955	81.2	3,164	12,773	81.0	2,563	52.8	6,281	13,351
3544	Special dies, tools, jigs, and fixtures	7,255	1.0	1,546	5,375	7,317	114.4	2,429	7,550	114.0	3,659	87.5	5,657	8,890
3559	Special industry machinery, n.e.c.	(NA)	(NA)	(NA)	(NA)	2,531	83.3	2,286	8,275	83.0	2,778	45.7	5,800	10,543
3571	Electronic computers	(NA)	(NA)	(NA)	(NA)	974	151.9	4,953	33,627	126.0	3,377	38.1	16,878	35,573
3585	Refrigeration and heating equipment	865	120.5	2,500	12,390	892	133.3	3,500	17,027	119.0	3,200	87.1	8,186	18,224
3599	Industrial machinery, n.e.c.	(NA)	(NA)	(NA)	(NA)	21,545	228.4	5,119	13,692	233.0	6,227	178.7	11,205	16,925
3621	Motors and generators	472	84.2	1,700	6,060	462	74.6	1,664	6,753	69.7	1,742	51.9	4,037	7,674
3625	Relays and industrial controls	(NA)	(NA)	(NA)	(NA)	1,168	66.6	1,631	6,101	61.2	1,799	35.3	4,289	7,379
3661	Telephone and telegraph apparatus	(NA)	(NA)	(NA)	(NA)	469	112.3	3,178	17,583	94.1	3,468	46.9	9,503	17,425
3663	Radio and television communications equip.	(NA)	(NA)	(NA)	(NA)	655	126.0	3,776	14,229	123.4	4,395	53.7	10,339	18,165
3674	Semiconductors and related devices	766	166.5	3,785	12,430	853	184.6	5,495	19,795	175.0	6,491	86.2	20,152	29,668
3679	Electronic components, n.e.c.	(NA)	(NA)	(NA)	(NA)	2,900	162.6	2,891	15,439	165.4	4,531	101.6	9,513	19,450
3711	Motor vehicles and car bodies	355	240.1	6,822	70,740	413	284.4	10,376	133,346	218.1	9,803	178.5	45,147	133,861
3714	Motor vehicle parts and accessories	2,420	321.4	7,614	36,293	2,900	389.1	11,947	62,007	369.9	12,587	290.5	25,213	63,604
3721	Aircraft	165	275.1	7,744	28,024	155	268.2	9,680	39,093	258.3	10,324	125.3	23,091	58,090
3724	Aircraft engines and engine parts	340	130.7	3,544	13,809	453	139.6	4,814	20,262	122.3	4,822	67.3	12,278	22,746
3728	Aircraft parts and equipment, n.e.c.	966	132.8	3,429	10,193	1,013	187.7	6,088	17,923	187.3	6,740	107.5	13,678	21,544
3731	Ship building and repairing	689	166.7	3,738	10,967	590	120.2	3,218	8,504	120.8	3,680	90.1	6,354	10,849
3761	Guided missiles and space vehicles	29	99.6	3,400	10,219	40	166.7	6,415	21,566	135.8	6,026	45.0	13,551	23,399
3812	Search and navigation equipment	(NA)	(NA)	(NA)	(NA)	1,084	369.4	12,373	36,267	279.8	11,631	112.3	23,672	36,213
3825	Instruments to measure electricity	749	89.7	1,888	6,094	930	85.2	2,477	7,703	69.3	2,497	34.0	5,456	8,240
3841	Surgical and medical instruments	859	56.9	1,000	4,085	1,136	73.1	1,786	7,780	87.7	2,591	53.1	7,432	10,710
3842	Surgical appliances and supplies	1,367	68.8	1,211	5,667	1,500	78.5	1,786	8,533	93.3	2,510	60.6	8,044	12,555
3861	Photographic equipment and supplies	795	119.3	3,193	17,038	787	88.0	2,878	19,241	78.0	3,044	40.0	14,603	21,398

NA Not available. [1]Standard Industrial Classification Code, see text, section 27. [2]All employees represents the average of production workers plus all other employees for the payroll period ended nearest the 15th of the month.

Source: U.S. Bureau of the Census, Census of Manufactures, 1987, and Annual Survey of Manufactures.

No. 1258. Manufactures Summary,

[Sum of State totals may not add to U.S. total

DIVISION AND STATE	1982				1987				
	Establishments, total [1]	All employees [2] Number (1,000)	All employees [2] Payroll (mil. dol.)	Value of shipments [3] (mil. dol.)	Establishments, total [1]	All employees [2] Number	All employees [2] Payroll (mil. dol.)	Value added by manufacture [4] (mil. dol.)	Value of shipments [3] (mil. dol.)
1 U.S.	358,061	19,094	379,627	1,960,206	368,897	18,950	475,651	1,165,917	2,475,902
2 Northeast ..	91,102	4,798	95,919	400,767	88,287	4,357	112,222	259,074	483,748
3 N.E.	25,659	1,445	27,603	105,938	26,393	1,350	34,455	78,908	136,989
4 ME	2,009	110	1,775	8,649	2,172	102	2,192	5,271	10,662
5 NH	1,981	107	1,792	7,636	2,328	108	2,509	8,189	12,214
6 VT	1,104	47	863	3,730	1,262	49	1,140	2,543	4,753
7 MA	11,017	643	12,353	48,204	11,006	591	15,211	35,770	62,794
8 RI	2,855	114	1,760	7,652	2,878	112	2,292	4,788	9,166
9 CT	6,693	424	9,060	30,067	6,747	389	11,111	22,349	37,400
10 M.A.	65,443	3,353	68,316	294,829	61,894	3,007	77,767	180,165	346,759
11 NY	32,651	1,419	29,156	121,469	29,608	1,279	33,916	80,033	145,657
12 NJ	15,126	754	15,845	70,420	14,442	691	18,550	42,527	82,451
13 PA	17,666	1,180	23,315	102,940	17,844	1,038	25,302	57,605	118,651
14 Midwest. ...	91,318	5,609	117,830	596,245	94,269	5,508	148,994	351,139	787,123
15 E.N.C.	67,378	4,337	92,400	440,702	69,756	4,186	116,148	266,248	590,487
16 OH	16,960	1,102	24,740	112,278	17,544	1,100	30,765	71,707	158,560
17 IN	7,960	585	12,559	63,332	8,641	602	15,757	39,279	83,788
18 IL	18,618	1,069	22,681	112,929	18,404	990	26,235	63,350	132,204
19 MI	15,158	884	22,223	99,715	16,010	980	30,628	60,259	146,339
20 WI	8,682	497	10,197	52,448	9,157	514	12,763	31,653	69,596
21 W.N.C.	23,940	1,272	25,430	155,543	24,513	1,322	32,846	84,891	196,637
22 MN	6,775	350	7,423	35,321	7,112	374	10,142	23,152	47,604
23 IA	3,598	213	4,403	31,397	3,569	206	4,971	14,469	35,409
24 MO	7,069	406	8,013	41,459	7,290	419	10,390	25,917	59,889
25 ND	587	15	246	2,465	627	15	310	979	2,574
26 SD	748	25	398	3,005	764	28	498	1,476	3,859
27 NE	1,928	92	1,624	15,143	1,876	91	1,938	5,819	16,076
28 KS	3,235	171	3,323	26,753	3,275	189	4,597	12,909	31,056
29 South	99,304	5,819	101,293	647,918	104,500	5,839	128,278	354,380	800,875
30 S.A.	48,855	2,930	48,588	256,625	53,478	3,104	66,893	179,075	373,181
31 DE	632	68	1,743	8,383	673	67	2,091	3,866	10,730
32 MD	3,883	234	4,859	21,282	4,244	230	5,956	14,020	28,000
33 DC	514	17	394	1,537	486	17	494	1,525	2,128
34 VA	5,568	391	6,649	36,803	6,137	429	9,740	26,857	51,902
35 WV	1,662	96	2,007	9,869	1,619	84	2,108	5,404	11,561
36 NC	10,133	799	11,717	64,176	10,995	842	16,293	47,007	95,317
37 SC	4,206	368	5,540	27,836	4,534	366	7,324	19,112	41,212
38 GA	8,534	503	7,906	48,056	9,187	570	11,933	33,708	75,709
39 FL	13,723	454	7,773	38,683	15,603	499	10,954	27,574	56,613
40 E.S.C.	18,573	1,241	20,132	119,698	19,718	1,303	26,524	74,296	164,862
41 KY	3,502	247	4,639	29,639	3,693	252	5,865	18,092	41,827
42 TN	6,417	462	7,378	40,777	6,864	485	9,869	27,050	57,753
43 AL	5,528	330	5,234	29,794	5,843	347	6,963	18,652	40,901
44 MS	3,126	202	2,881	19,488	3,318	219	3,827	10,503	24,381
45 W.S.C.	31,876	1,648	32,573	271,595	31,304	1,432	34,861	101,009	262,832
46 AR	3,313	190	2,824	19,747	3,390	206	3,815	10,827	25,308
47 LA	4,107	202	4,304	57,058	3,816	161	4,176	16,426	50,700
48 OK	4,168	197	4,010	23,116	3,728	151	3,629	9,857	24,074
49 TX	20,288	1,059	21,435	171,674	20,370	914	23,241	63,899	162,751
50 West	76,337	3,074	64,587	315,277	81,841	3,246	86,158	201,325	404,325
51 Mt.	14,854	556	10,863	56,997	16,479	596	14,689	35,822	73,554
52 MT	1,090	20	379	3,668	1,239	20	426	1,112	3,498
53 ID	1,404	48	865	5,370	1,491	53	1,149	3,057	7,005
54 WY	511	10	183	2,558	500	8	180	493	2,074
55 CO	4,406	192	3,983	17,963	4,718	184	4,958	12,046	23,236
56 NM	1,223	33	521	3,815	1,322	35	713	1,653	4,226
57 AZ	3,407	150	3,037	12,907	4,151	184	4,669	11,299	20,758
58 UT	1,962	83	1,539	8,960	2,083	89	2,073	4,883	10,287
59 NV	851	20	356	1,756	975	24	521	1,279	2,470
60 Pac	61,483	2,518	53,724	258,280	65,362	2,650	71,469	165,503	330,771
61 WA	6,788	291	6,681	34,665	7,630	310	8,842	19,016	46,532
62 OR	5,659	185	3,783	17,897	6,353	203	4,767	11,610	25,352
63 CA	47,625	2,005	42,630	199,695	49,930	2,104	57,148	132,638	252,729
64 AK	445	13	270	2,580	427	11	272	834	2,711
65 HI	966	24	360	3,443	1,022	22	440	1,405	3,448

[1] Includes central administrative offices and auxiliary units. [2] Includes employment and payroll at administrative offices and auxiliary units. **All employees** represents the average of production workers plus all other employees for the payroll period ended nearest the 12th of March. Production workers represents the average of the employment for the payroll periods ended nearest the 12th of March, May, August, and November.

by State: 1982 to 1991

because U.S. and State figures were independently derived]

	1990			1991			
All employees [2]		Value of ship-ments [3] (mil. dol.)	All employees [2]		Value added by manu-facture [4] (mil. dol.)	Value of ship-ments [3] (mil. dol.)	
Number (1,000)	Payroll (mil. dol.)		Number (1,000)	Payroll (mil. dol.)			
18,840	532,317	2,873,502	18,062	529,019	1,313,829	2,826,207	1
4,002	119,838	519,990	3,719	118,054	268,581	506,762	2
1,215	36,515	141,252	1,112	36,149	77,682	138,645	3
103	2,499	12,477	98	2,451	5,428	11,642	4
92	2,554	9,727	86	2,542	5,647	9,771	5
44	1,236	5,592	43	1,231	3,163	5,786	6
529	16,321	63,796	490	15,843	34,472	61,859	7
101	2,364	9,761	95	2,305	5,140	9,577	8
345	11,541	39,898	339	11,777	23,832	40,010	9
2,787	83,323	378,738	2,607	81,905	190,899	368,117	10
1,150	35,145	154,714	1,054	33,831	81,625	148,403	11
627	20,353	87,498	591	20,371	44,332	85,692	12
1,010	27,826	136,526	962	27,703	64,942	134,022	13
5,553	166,888	902,270	5,352	164,581	393,332	877,220	14
4,169	129,372	669,480	4,006	127,183	292,462	647,237	15
1,085	33,318	177,787	1,045	33,091	78,876	174,928	16
616	18,920	98,619	594	17,755	43,805	97,282	17
1,008	30,515	156,675	976	30,659	70,104	151,925	18
913	31,699	153,386	858	30,757	63,351	143,103	19
548	14,920	83,013	533	14,921	36,328	79,999	20
1,384	37,516	232,790	1,346	37,398	100,860	229,983	21
395	11,790	55,244	386	11,744	25,042	53,303	22
230	6,012	45,927	224	5,967	19,062	44,996	23
423	11,557	67,355	401	11,238	31,803	66,415	24
16	351	3,013	17	385	1,152	3,056	25
30	564	4,533	30	597	1,691	4,508	26
99	2,296	20,370	101	2,337	7,537	21,010	27
191	4,946	36,349	187	5,130	14,573	36,695	28
5,942	146,361	962,574	5,788	148,255	422,967	955,032	29
3,058	74,584	427,439	2,935	74,642	208,337	425,451	30
66	2,486	12,901	62	2,434	4,231	11,934	31
212	6,357	30,679	201	6,271	15,242	29,583	32
14	541	2,152	13	555	1,573	2,057	33
423	10,683	61,042	408	10,680	33,245	61,642	34
82	2,262	12,938	78	2,221	6,009	12,474	35
832	18,315	116,245	802	18,813	59,915	118,206	36
368	8,348	46,734	353	8,349	22,491	47,515	37
564	13,210	83,997	545	13,118	36,576	82,765	38
498	12,382	60,750	473	12,201	29,055	59,275	39
1,384	31,141	200,241	1,366	31,774	90,149	202,695	40
279	7,013	53,777	273	7,001	23,714	53,500	41
504	11,407	67,404	493	11,711	32,499	69,549	42
368	8,194	48,748	363	8,287	21,056	48,449	43
233	4,527	30,313	237	4,775	12,880	31,197	44
1,500	40,636	334,894	1,487	41,839	124,481	326,886	45
219	4,359	30,493	220	4,471	12,826	31,084	46
171	4,812	65,807	175	5,005	22,126	63,382	47
168	4,482	28,010	169	4,637	11,959	28,418	48
943	26,983	210,584	923	27,726	77,570	204,002	49
3,343	99,230	488,669	3,167	98,133	229,029	487,195	50
619	17,039	88,989	610	17,311	43,251	91,468	51
20	450	4,040	20	479	1,093	3,767	52
61	1,508	9,184	61	1,607	3,895	9,810	53
10	248	2,756	10	251	925	2,733	54
180	5,528	27,701	176	5,647	13,704	26,825	55
40	862	5,548	41	927	3,931	8,037	56
181	5,321	22,886	174	5,171	11,551	22,983	57
102	2,494	13,950	102	2,592	6,689	14,492	58
26	628	2,925	26	637	1,463	2,821	59
2,724	82,192	399,680	2,557	80,822	185,778	395,727	60
367	11,344	67,538	354	11,801	24,852	67,978	61
216	5,657	31,073	208	5,644	13,344	30,692	62
2,106	64,352	293,190	1,962	62,521	144,908	289,613	63
14	362	3,676	14	390	1,291	3,639	64
21	477	4,203	19	466	1,383	3,805	65

[3] For definition, see footnote 6, table 1255.   [4] See footnote 7, table 1255.

Source: U.S. Bureau of the Census, *Census of Manufactures, 1982* and *1987* and *Annual Survey of Manufactures.*

No. 1259. Average Hourly Earnings of Production Workers in Manufacturing Industries, by State: 1980 to 1992

[In dollars]

REGION, DIVISION, AND STATE	1980	1985	1986	1987	1988	1989	1990	1991	1992
U.S.	7.27	9.54	9.73	9.91	10.19	10.48	10.83	11.18	11.45
Northeast:									
New England:									
ME	6.00	8.40	8.65	8.77	9.31	9.92	10.59	11.08	11.40
NH	5.87	8.39	8.77	9.29	9.97	10.37	10.83	10.84	11.22
VT	6.14	8.41	8.83	9.12	9.47	9.99	10.52	11.00	11.52
MA	6.51	9.00	9.24	9.77	10.40	10.87	11.39	11.81	12.15
RI	5.59	7.59	7.90	8.20	8.64	9.06	9.45	9.73	9.92
CT	7.08	9.57	10.07	10.46	10.78	11.21	11.53	11.99	12.47
Middle Atlantic:									
NY	7.18	9.67	9.92	10.09	10.43	10.67	11.11	11.43	11.72
NJ	7.31	9.86	10.12	10.40	10.86	11.17	11.76	12.17	12.59
PA	7.59	9.57	9.74	9.98	10.33	10.66	11.04	11.46	11.86
Midwest:									
East North Central:									
OH	8.57	11.38	11.56	11.73	12.00	12.26	12.64	13.12	13.53
IN	8.49	(NA)	10.81	(NA)	(NA)	11.70	12.03	12.43	12.82
IL	8.02	10.37	10.67	10.85	10.98	11.21	11.44	11.68	11.85
MI	9.52	12.64	12.80	12.97	13.31	13.51	13.86	14.52	14.81
WI	8.03	10.26	10.35	10.55	10.61	10.77	11.11	11.47	11.86
West North Central:									
MN	7.61	10.05	10.20	10.37	10.59	10.95	11.23	11.52	11.92
IA	8.67	10.32	10.35	10.62	10.56	10.82	11.27	11.62	11.93
MO	7.26	9.57	9.83	10.00	10.24	10.49	10.74	10.86	11.23
ND	6.56	8.05	8.19	8.43	8.36	8.80	9.27	9.25	9.61
SD	6.50	7.43	7.75	7.92	8.09	8.30	8.48	8.79	8.84
NE	7.38	9.02	9.26	9.33	9.38	9.53	9.66	9.84	10.22
KS	7.37	9.45	9.76	9.97	10.24	10.68	10.94	11.24	11.61
South:									
South Atlantic:									
DE	7.58	9.86	10.05	10.67	11.49	12.36	12.39	12.20	12.34
MD	7.61	9.73	9.91	10.11	10.71	11.19	11.57	11.92	12.50
DC	8.46	10.48	10.40	10.73	11.10	11.79	12.51	13.05	13.94
VA	6.22	8.51	8.83	9.14	9.37	9.69	10.07	10.43	10.71
WV	8.08	10.24	10.38	10.55	10.81	11.17	11.53	11.77	12.12
NC	5.37	7.29	7.54	7.84	8.12	8.42	8.79	9.19	9.50
SC	5.59	7.61	7.92	8.10	8.30	8.54	8.84	9.17	9.48
GA	5.77	8.10	8.35	8.49	8.65	8.87	9.17	9.56	9.86
FL	5.98	7.86	8.02	8.16	8.39	8.67	8.98	9.30	9.61
East South Central:									
KY	7.34	9.53	9.86	10.02	10.16	10.37	10.70	11.00	11.28
TN	6.08	8.29	8.58	8.78	8.96	9.22	9.55	9.92	10.12
AL	6.49	8.48	8.64	8.76	8.95	9.10	9.39	9.72	10.00
MS	5.44	7.22	7.46	7.59	7.83	8.03	8.37	8.67	8.90
West South Central:									
AR	5.71	7.57	7.76	7.88	8.07	8.26	8.51	8.81	9.05
LA	7.74	10.43	10.60	10.90	10.94	11.13	11.61	11.86	12.21
OK	7.36	9.86	9.80	10.14	10.35	10.48	10.73	11.09	11.39
TX	7.15	9.41	9.65	9.85	9.97	10.25	10.47	10.84	10.92
West:									
Mountain:									
MT	8.78	10.95	10.94	10.61	10.68	11.15	11.51	11.57	12.21
ID	7.55	9.41	9.66	9.75	10.00	10.21	10.60	11.11	11.42
WY	7.01	9.64	9.68	9.75	10.27	10.58	10.83	10.98	11.08
CO	7.63	9.52	9.82	10.05	10.38	10.44	10.94	11.33	11.31
NM	5.79	8.41	8.75	8.74	8.87	8.74	9.04	9.40	9.70
AZ	7.29	9.48	9.88	9.97	9.85	9.92	10.21	10.70	10.98
UT	7.02	9.64	9.98	9.96	10.11	10.14	10.32	10.77	11.09
NV	7.72	9.15	9.36	9.76	10.08	10.33	11.05	11.04	11.55
Pacific:									
WA	(NA)	11.63	11.65	11.73	11.90	12.12	12.61	13.13	13.58
OR	8.65	10.50	10.57	10.56	10.60	10.81	11.15	11.53	11.98
CA	7.70	10.12	10.36	10.75	10.80	11.16	11.48	11.87	12.19
AK	10.22	12.19	11.62	11.79	11.98	12.01	12.46	11.40	10.75
HI	6.83	8.65	8.86	9.30	9.84	10.37	10.99	11.39	11.61

NA Not available.

Source: U.S. Bureau of Labor Statistics, *Employment and Earnings,* monthly.

No. 1260. Industrial Production Indexes, by Industry: 1970 to 1992

[1987 = 100. Based on 1977 *Standard Industrial Classification Manual*; see text, section 6. See also *Historical Statistics, Colonial Times to 1970*, series P 13 and P 18-39]

SIC[1] code	MAJOR INDUSTRY GROUP	1970	1975	1980	1984	1985	1986	1988	1989	1990	1991	1992
(X)	**Industrial production**	**61.4**	**66.3**	**84.1**	**92.8**	**94.4**	**95.3**	**105.4**	**108.1**	**109.2**	**107.1**	**108.7**
(X)	**Manufacturing**	**56.4**	**61.1**	**78.8**	**89.3**	**91.6**	**94.3**	**105.8**	**108.9**	**109.9**	**107.4**	**109.7**
(X)	**Durable goods**	**53.3**	**56.7**	**75.7**	**88.4**	**91.8**	**93.9**	**107.6**	**110.9**	**111.6**	**107.1**	**108.4**
24	Lumber and products	66.7	66.5	76.9	86.0	88.0	95.1	104.6	103.0	101.6	94.2	98.7
25	Furniture and fixtures	55.6	59.4	78.5	87.9	88.1	92.5	103.6	105.3	105.9	99.1	100.3
32	Clay, glass, and stone products	71.1	77.8	92.0	94.2	93.6	97.1	106.4	108.0	105.7	94.9	96.2
33	Primary metals	115.2	107.2	110.8	102.4	101.8	93.8	110.3	109.2	108.4	99.5	102.9
34	Fabricated metal products	75.9	76.7	92.5	93.3	94.5	93.8	106.2	107.2	105.9	100.4	101.7
35	Nonelectrical machinery	32.8	38.1	60.6	80.8	86.8	90.4	113.8	121.8	126.5	123.5	127.2
36	Electrical machinery	40.5	45.1	73.3	94.1	93.1	94.3	106.5	109.5	111.4	110.1	111.8
37	Transportation equipment	55.5	59.7	72.3	83.1	91.8	96.9	105.0	107.2	105.5	98.6	97.3
38	Instruments	38.8	52.4	78.8	92.1	95.7	95.1	110.1	116.4	116.8	118.2	118.3
(X)	**Nondurable goods**	**61.1**	**67.7**	**83.1**	**90.8**	**91.5**	**94.9**	**103.6**	**106.4**	**107.8**	**107.9**	**111.2**
20	Food	64.0	71.4	84.6	92.1	94.9	97.4	102.8	105.5	107.6	108.6	110.1
21	Tobacco products	90.6	97.8	103.6	97.2	97.3	95.8	101.4	99.7	98.6	99.7	105.5
22	Textile mill products	74.4	77.7	92.1	93.7	89.7	93.9	99.8	101.9	100.8	100.5	106.0
26	Paper and products	62.9	65.9	83.1	93.5	92.2	97.1	102.9	103.2	105.3	105.1	107.1
27	Printing and publishing	52.7	53.7	70.3	84.5	87.6	90.7	103.6	108.5	111.9	112.3	113.3
28	Chemicals and products	55.9	69.1	87.8	91.4	91.4	94.6	105.4	108.5	110.3	110.9	117.2
29	Petroleum products	83.9	91.5	99.0	92.8	92.6	98.9	103.4	106.1	108.2	107.5	108.6
30	Rubber and plastics products	37.6	47.4	61.7	83.8	85.8	90.8	105.9	108.9	110.2	110.0	117.3
31	Leather and products	208.0	182.5	161.7	126.5	112.5	102.6	99.6	103.7	100.0	88.1	88.5
(X)	**Mining**	**100.4**	**98.0**	**110.0**	**111.9**	**109.0**	**101.0**	**101.8**	**100.5**	**102.6**	**101.1**	**98.7**
(X)	**Utilities**	**72.9**	**84.3**	**95.9**	**97.0**	**99.5**	**96.3**	**104.4**	**107.1**	**108.0**	**109.2**	**108.3**

X Not applicable. [1] Standard Industrial Classifications.
Source: Board of Governors of the Federal Reserve System, *Federal Reserve Bulletin*, monthly.

No. 1261. Index of Manufacturing Capacity: 1950 to 1992

[1987 output = 100. Annual figures are averages of quarterly data. Capacity represents estimated quantity of output, relative to output in 1967, which the *current* stock of plant and equipment in manufacturing industries was capable of producing. Primary processing industries comprise textiles, lumber, paper and pulp, petroleum, rubber, stone, clay, glass, primary metals, fabricated metals, and a portion of chemicals. Advanced processing industries comprise chemical products, food, beverages, tobacco, apparel, furniture, printing and publishing, leather, machinery, transportation equipment, instruments, ordnance, and miscellaneous industry groups]

YEAR	Index of capacity	RELATION OF OUTPUT TO CAPACITY (percent)			YEAR	Index of capacity	RELATION OF OUTPUT TO CAPACITY (percent)		
		All manu-facturing	Primary pro-cessing	Advanced pro-cessing			All manu-facturing	Primary pro-cessing	Advanced pro-cessing
1950	29	83	88	80	1984	111	80	80	80
1955	36	87	92	84	1985	115	80	80	79
1960	44	80	80	80	1986	119	79	81	78
1965	54	90	91	89	1987	123	81	85	80
1970	71	80	80	79	1988	126	84	88	82
1975	84	73	73	74	1989	130	84	87	83
1980	98	80	78	81	1990	134	82	85	81
1981	102	79	78	79	1991	137	78	80	77
1982	105	73	69	75	1992: 1st qtr	140	77	80	76
1983	108	75	75	75	2d qtr	141	78	81	77

Source: Board of Governors of the Federal Reserve System, *Industrial Production and Capacity Utilization, G.17(419)*.
(Based on data from Federal Reserve Board, U.S. Dept. of Commerce, U.S. Bureau of Labor Statistics, and McGraw-Hill Information Systems Company, New York, NY; and other sources.)

No. 1262. Finances of Manufacturing Corporations: 1970 to 1991

[In billions of dollars. Beginning 1986, data exclude estimates for corporations with less than $250,000 in assets at time of sample selection. Prior period includes estimates for corporations in this size category. See table 890 for individual industry data]

ITEM	1970	1975	1980	1982	1983	1984	1985	1986	1987	1988	1989	1990	1991
Net sales	709	1,065	1,897	2,039	2,114	2,335	2,331	2,221	2,378	2,596	2,745	2,811	2,761
Net operating profit	50	77	129	105	125	159	138	125	159	190	182	173	133
Net profit:													
Before taxes	48	80	145	108	133	166	137	129	173	216	189	160	100
After taxes	29	49	92	71	86	108	88	83	116	155	136	112	68
Cash dividends	15	20	36	41	44	45	46	46	50	57	65	62	60
Net income retained in business	14	29	58	30	44	63	42	37	66	98	71	49	7

Source: Through 1980, U.S. Federal Trade Commission; thereafter, U.S. Bureau of the Census. *Quarterly Financial Report for Manufacturing, Mining, and Trade Corporations*.

No. 1263. Capital in Manufacturing Establishments: 1980 to 1991

[In billions of dollars, except percent. Minus sign (-) indicates decline. Data refer to privately owned manufacturing establishments and are based on the capital expenditures data from the Census of Manufactures, the Annual Survey of Manufactures, and the inventory investment component of GNP. For details, see source]

ITEM	CURRENT DOLLARS						CONSTANT (1987) DOLLARS					
	1980	1985	1988	1989	1990	1991	1980	1985	1988	1989	1990	1991
Purchases of equipment and structures	80	98	98	121	128	120	103	102	96	114	118	110
Percent equipment	70.5	65.3	68.7	68.1	66.1	67.3	68.6	64.6	69.0	68.6	66.9	68.2
Depreciation (straight line) [1].	54	78	91	96	101	106	72	83	88	90	93	96
Percent equipment	76.4	74.3	73.4	73.2	73.0	73.0	75.5	74.1	73.8	73.7	73.6	73.5
Net investment [2]	26	20	8	25	26	15	31	19	7	24	25	14
Net stock, end of year [1] . . .	976	1,238	1,406	1,498	1,571	1,590	1,222	1,285	1,329	1,373	1,403	1,412
Equipment and structures.	666	898	1,023	1,088	1,149	1,183	860	950	973	999	1,025	1,041
Percent equipment. . . .	62.0	57.7	56.6	56.5	56.7	56.7	61.3	57.8	56.9	56.8	56.5	56.2
Inventories	310	340	383	410	422	407	361	336	355	374	378	371

[1] Depreciation and net stock estimates for equipment and structures are derived using the perpetual inventory method and the straight-line depreciation formula. [2] Represents the difference between purchases and depreciation.

Source: U.S. Bureau of Economic Analysis, *National Income Product Accounts of the United States: Volume 2, 1959-88; Fixed Reproducible Tangible Wealth in the United States, 1925-89 (forthcoming);* and *Survey of Current Business,* January 1992, July 1992, and August 1992.

No. 1264. U.S. Share of World Exports of Manufactures: 1980 to 1991

[World exports = exports from 15 major trading countries: United States, Austria, Belgium-Luxembourg, Canada, Denmark, France, West Germany, Italy, Japan, Netherlands, Norway, Sweden, Switzerland, and United Kingdom. Percents are calculated from the values of exports of the 5 commodity groups from each of the 15 countries. Percentage shares are based on dollar values calculated at current exchange rates. Details are reported according to the United Nations Standard International Trade Classification (SITC), Revision 2 (1980-87), Revision 3 (1988 forward).

PRODUCT CATEGORY	TOTAL (bil. dol.)						PERCENT OF WORLD EXPORTS					
	1980	1985	1988	1989	1990	1991	1980	1985	1988	1989	1990	1991
Total [1]	**147.2**	**150.7**	**225.5**	**275.0**	**300.3**	**328.0**	**16.8**	**16.7**	**15.1**	**17.1**	**16.3**	**17.2**
Machinery	57.1	62.7	94.6	112.2	119.7	129.8	21.4	21.4	18.9	20.6	20.2	20.0
Transport equipment . .	28.9	35.2	47.8	55.2	62.9	70.3	18.3	18.7	16.6	17.9	17.6	18.6
Chemicals	20.8	21.5	32.7	38.0	39.5	43.4	17.9	17.9	16.0	18.0	16.6	17.4
Basic manufactures [2] . .	23.3	15.0	23.8	31.6	33.9	37.8	10.1	7.9	7.8	9.6	9.3	10.4
Misc. articles [3]	17.0	16.3	26.7	38.1	43.1	46.7	16.0	14.6	13.6	17.8	16.8	17.6

[1] Represents manufactures exports. Excludes mineral fuel products, processed food, fats, oils, firearms of war, and ammunition. [2] Includes semimanufactures of various materials, such as metals, fibers, wood, glass, leather, rubber, and certain finished products of metal. [3] Includes mainly nondurable consumer goods and professional and scientific instruments.

Source: U.S. Dept. of Commerce, International Trade Administration, Office of Finance, Industry, and Trade Information; *Business America,* biweekly; and unpublished data.

No. 1265. Foreign Direct Investment Position in the United States for Manufacturing: 1990 and 1991

[In millions of dollars. Minus sign (-) indicates a negative position. See table 1335]

AREA OR COUNTRY	TOTAL [1]		FOOD PRODUCTS		CHEMICALS AND ALLIED PRODUCTS		PRIMARY AND FABRICATED METALS		MACHINERY	
	1990	1991	1990	1991	1990	1991	1990	1991	1990	1991
All countries [2]	157,431	162,853	22,943	23,370	45,847	49,133	15,523	15,780	27,521	27,637
Canada	9,652	9,662	986	948	551	655	1,871	1,814	1,807	1,927
Europe [2]	121,292	126,809	20,334	21,065	39,607	43,820	10,310	10,468	19,623	19,417
France	13,669	14,821	1,496	1,855	4,068	4,195	(D)	2,498	(D)	1,538
Netherlands	24,717	24,137	7,439	8,175	8,133	7,071	1,437	2,081	3,950	4,092
United Kingdom	47,304	50,120	8,679	8,691	13,420	15,844	3,335	3,110	4,816	4,104
Sweden	5,238	5,343	-	-	603	909	275	298	2,872	2,714
Switzerland	10,393	9,781	(D)	1,990	3,273	3,225	(D)	549	2,838	2,668
Germany	15,695	16,546	126	-45	8,306	9,102	1,180	789	3,325	3,995
Africa	2,087	2,047	(D)	-18	(D)	-3	(D)	722	483	469
Latin America	5,423	3,664	239	241	1,822	318	104	95	-11	-72
Middle East.	(D)	(D)	-	-	(D)	(D)	(D)	-	-1	40
Asia and Pacific [2]	(D)	(D)	(D)	1,128	(D)	(D)	(D)	2,681	5,619	5,857
Japan	17,153	18,657	793	769	3,101	3,446	2,326	2,504	5,203	5,396

- Represents or rounds to zero. D Withheld to avoid disclosure of data of individual companies. [1] Includes other manufacturing not shown separately. [2] Includes other countries not shown separately.

Source: U.S. Bureau of Economic Analysis, *Survey of Current Business,* August 1992.

No. 1266. Employment Related to Manufactured Exports, by Industry: 1980 to 1989

[Total employment related to manufactured exports is the sum of employment directly calculated for the plants shipping the exported product, the supplying industries and service organizations and the central administrative offices and auxiliaries. For manufacturing industries, employment is limited to paid employees in manufacturing plants, while for nonmanufacturing it includes an estimate for working proprietors and partners]

| INDUSTRY | EMPLOYMENT RELATED TO MANUFACTURED EXPORTS | | | | | | CIVILIAN EMPLOYMENT (1,000) | | |
| | Employees (1,000) | | | Percent of civilian employment | | | | | |
	1980	1985	1989	1980	1985	1989	1980	1985	1989
U.S	4,808	4,413	6,022	4.8	4.0	5.1	100,260	110,136	118,744
Manufacturing	2,639	2,295	2,949	12.8	12.2	15.5	20,647	18,788	19,042
Nonmanufacturing	2,170	2,118	3,073	2.7	2.3	3.1	79,613	91,348	99,702
Trade	845	949	1,385	4.3	4.3	5.9	19,737	21,999	23,553
Business services	575	227	425	3.3	1.1	1.7	17,245	21,139	24,843
Transportation [1]	305	282	443	4.8	4.6	6.9	6,369	6,155	6,435
Agriculture	144	127	131	4.5	3.7	3.9	3,225	3,423	3,387
Mining	69	50	83	7.3	4.9	11.3	947	1,016	733
Other	233	483	606	0.7	1.3	1.5	32,090	37,616	40,751

[1] Includes communications and utilities.

No. 1267. Manufacturing Establishments—Export-Related Shipments and Employment, 1977 to 1989, and by Industry, 1989

[The export-related employment data shown do not include the jobs involved in the export of nonmanufactured goods and various services sold to foreign buyers. Thus, jobs in the manufacturing sector that relate to the export of nonmanufactured goods are excluded from the estimates. In addition, all of the indirect exports being reported are domestically produced, that is, they exclude imports. See source for further details on methodology]

| SIC [1] code | INDUSTRY GROUP | MANUFACTURER'S SHIPMENT VALUE | | | | MANUFACTURING EMPLOYMENT | | | |
| | | | Export related | | Export related as percent of shipments | | Export related | | Export related as percent of total employment |
		Total [2] (bil. dol.)	Total (bil. dol.)	Direct exports [3] (bil. dol.)		Total (1,000)	Total (1,000)	Direct exports [4] (1,000)	
(X)	1977..............	1,358.4	142.4	85.8	10.4	19,590	1,990	1,106	10.2
(X)	1980..............	1,852.7	249.8	151.2	13.5	20,647	2,639	1,486	12.8
(X)	1981..............	2,017.5	271.7	164.3	13.4	20,264	2,604	1,486	12.9
(X)	1983..............	2,055.3	246.4	141.6	12.0	18,737	2,173	1,118	11.6
(X)	1984..............	2,253.8	268.3	151.0	11.9	19,141	2,179	1,083	11.4
(X)	1985..............	2,278.9	286.7	156.9	12.6	18,788	2,295	1,083	12.2
(X)	1986..............	2,260.3	294.3	159.4	13.0	18,371	2,318	1,061	12.6
(X)	1987..............	2,475.9	378.8	193.6	15.3	18,900	2,771	1,185	14.7
(X)	1988..............	2,684.7	395.3	242.9	14.7	19,147	2,638	1,412	13.8
(X)	**1989, total**	2,793.0	460.5	287.4	16.5	19,042	2,948	1,610	15.5
20	Food and kindred products	364.4	23.5	18.1	6.5	1,459	79	62	5.4
21	Tobacco products	25.8	5.6	4.9	21.8	43	12	10	27.8
22	Textile mill products..........	67.3	7.4	3.2	10.9	653	66	26	10.1
23	Apparel, other textile products...	63.4	3.8	2.6	5.9	1,018	44	28	4.4
24	Lumber and wood products.....	74.3	12.2	6.0	16.4	686	88	37	12.8
25	Furniture and fixtures.........	41.2	1.5	1.0	3.8	508	15	9	3.0
26	Paper and allied products......	131.4	17.5	7.6	13.3	630	74	26	11.8
27	Printing and publishing	149.9	11.0	2.7	7.4	1,504	111	22	7.4
28	Chemical and allied products....	278.1	58.0	39.3	20.8	848	169	116	19.9
29	Petroleum and coal products....	143.7	14.7	4.8	10.2	112	10	4	9.2
30	Rubber, misc. plastics products ..	98.4	15.0	5.1	15.2	877	133	43	15.2
31	Leather, leather products	9.9	1.5	1.3	15.4	120	10	9	8.5
32	Stone, clay, glass products	63.6	5.2	2.6	8.2	520	41	20	7.9
33	Primary metal industries	153.0	38.6	9.8	25.2	727	178	38	24.4
34	Fabricated metal products	162.2	22.8	8.3	14.4	1,469	210	72	14.3
35	Machinery, except electric	253.6	69.0	52.0	27.2	1,913	475	336	24.8
36	Electric, electronic equipment ...	192.6	52.1	33.2	27.1	1,551	435	269	28.0
37	Transportation equipment	366.0	74.8	62.7	20.4	1,805	364	295	20.2
38	Instruments and related products .	118.5	21.6	18.2	18.3	968	182	154	18.8
39	Misc. manufacturing..........	35.8	4.8	4.1	13.3	386	42	34	11.0
(X)	Administrative and auxiliary	-	-	-	(Z)	1,246	211	-	16.9

- Represents zero. X Not applicable. Z Equal to or rounds to zero. [1] Standard Industrial Classification; see text, section 13. [2] Includes total domestic and export shipments for all manufacturing establishments. [3] Includes only the value of manufactured products exported by the producing plants. [4] Employment is limited to paid employees in manufacturing plants producing the export product. The number of employees related to export shipments was calculated for each establishment, aggregated by industry and by States, and inflated to a level comparable to the plant value of exports reported in the official foreign trade statistics at port value.

Source of tables 1266 and 1267: U.S. Bureau of the Census, *Census of Manufactures, 1977* and *1987;* and *Annual Survey of Manufactures.*

No. 1268. Export-Related Shipments and Employment of Manufacturing Establishments, by State: 1989

[Advance data. See headnote, table 1267. Includes employees of central administrative and auxiliary offices]

REGION, DIVISION, AND STATE	MANUFACTURES SHIPMENT VALUE					MANUFACTURING EMPLOYMENT				
	Total (bil. dol.)	Export related			Export related as percent of shipments	Total (1,000)	Export related			Export related as percent of total employment
		Total (bil. dol.)	Direct exports (bil. dol.)	Supporting exports (bil. dol.)			Total (1,000)	Direct exports (1,000)	Supporting exports (1,000)	
U.S.	2,793.2	460.8	287.9	173.3	16.5	19,041.2	2,948.7	1,610.7	1,338.0	15.5
Northeast	517.4	83.6	51.7	32.0	16.2	4,168.9	667.2	357.9	309.3	16.0
N.E.	141.5	28.5	19.2	9.3	20.1	1,265.1	242.9	146.2	96.7	19.2
ME	12.5	2.1	1.1	1.0	17.1	106.4	15.2	8.0	7.2	14.3
NH	10.2	1.9	1.2	0.7	18.6	97.8	16.7	8.6	8.1	17.1
VT	5.4	1.4	0.9	0.5	24.9	46.6	9.9	6.2	3.7	21.2
MA	65.2	13.0	9.0	4.0	19.9	561.5	110.0	66.9	43.1	19.6
RI	9.7	1.7	1.0	0.7	17.0	104.0	18.9	11.7	7.2	18.2
CT	38.5	8.4	6.0	2.4	21.8	348.8	72.2	44.8	27.4	20.7
M.A.	375.9	55.1	32.5	22.7	14.7	2,903.8	424.3	211.7	212.6	14.6
NY	155.3	25.2	16.6	8.7	16.2	1,207.5	181.6	102.1	79.5	15.0
NJ	88.0	10.9	6.1	4.8	12.4	657.9	92.3	39.6	52.7	14.0
PA	132.6	19.0	9.8	9.2	14.4	1,038.4	150.4	70.0	80.4	14.5
Midwest	889.2	135.7	83.2	52.6	15.3	5,600.7	857.5	434.1	423.4	15.3
E.N.C.	664.4	104.8	62.7	42.0	15.8	4,231.5	671.6	333.6	338.0	15.9
OH	176.5	30.8	18.8	12.0	17.4	1,100.2	184.7	93.9	90.8	16.8
IN	98.0	16.0	8.8	7.2	16.3	626.6	96.8	48.7	48.1	15.4
IL	152.0	23.7	13.8	9.8	15.6	1,033.4	158.8	76.5	82.3	15.4
MI	156.9	23.7	15.1	8.6	15.1	929.7	154.8	77.2	77.6	16.7
WI	81.0	10.6	6.2	4.4	13.1	541.6	76.5	37.3	39.2	14.1
W.N.C.	224.8	30.9	20.5	10.6	13.7	1,369.2	185.9	100.5	85.4	13.6
MN	53.6	8.6	5.7	2.9	16.0	391.4	62.9	33.7	29.2	16.1
IA	42.9	5.7	3.8	1.9	13.3	225.3	28.7	16.9	11.8	12.7
MO	68.3	9.5	6.2	3.3	13.9	426.0	53.6	26.5	27.1	12.6
ND	2.9	0.5	0.4	0.1	15.9	15.2	1.6	1.0	0.6	10.5
SD	4.4	0.4	0.3	0.2	10.1	28.8	3.3	1.8	1.5	11.5
NE	18.7	1.9	1.2	0.7	10.3	93.8	10.5	5.5	5.0	11.2
KS	34.0	4.3	2.9	1.5	12.8	188.7	25.3	15.1	10.2	13.4
South	925.6	144.7	85.4	59.1	15.6	5,924.1	788.1	417.2	370.9	13.3
S.A.	419.4	63.4	38.8	24.6	15.1	3,088.3	397.8	206.7	191.1	12.9
DE	12.4	1.2	0.6	0.6	9.6	67.9	9.7	2.6	7.1	14.3
MD	31.3	4.8	3.0	1.8	15.3	226.2	31.9	17.5	14.4	14.1
DC	2.2	0.2	0.1	0.1	10.0	14.4	1.3	0.4	0.9	9.0
	59.4	8.8	5.6	3.2	14.8	424.9	49.1	24.5	24.6	11.6
WV	13.1	2.8	1.5	1.3	21.0	83.2	13.3	5.7	7.6	16.0
NC	113.6	16.7	9.7	7.0	14.7	836.3	102.4	51.7	50.7	12.2
SC	46.5	8.5	5.1	3.4	18.3	370.7	55.5	30.4	25.1	15.0
GA	82.8	10.6	6.3	4.3	12.8	568.1	62.0	30.4	31.6	10.9
FL	58.1	9.8	6.9	2.9	16.9	496.6	72.6	43.5	29.1	14.6
E.S.C.	192.8	27.8	15.5	12.3	14.4	1,360.8	163.7	82.9	80.8	12.0
KY	49.4	6.9	3.9	3.0	13.9	270.4	34.5	16.4	18.1	12.8
TN	67.0	9.1	5.2	3.9	13.5	499.6	58.6	30.6	28.0	11.7
AL	47.2	7.5	3.8	3.7	15.9	364.4	46.9	23.4	23.5	12.9
MS	29.2	4.3	2.6	1.7	14.7	226.4	23.7	12.5	11.2	10.5
W.S.C.	313.4	53.5	31.1	22.2	17.1	1,475.0	226.6	127.6	99.0	15.4
AR	29.7	3.9	2.1	1.8	13.2	214.4	26.0	13.5	12.5	12.1
LA	59.8	9.4	5.0	4.3	15.6	166.5	19.8	9.5	10.3	11.9
OK	27.7	3.2	1.6	1.6	11.4	162.1	19.3	9.3	10.0	11.9
TX	196.2	37.0	22.4	14.5	18.8	932.0	161.5	95.3	66.2	17.3
West	461.0	96.8	67.6	29.6	21.0	3,347.5	635.9	401.5	234.4	19.0
Mt.	84.7	14.4	8.5	6.1	17.0	610.0	99.3	56.1	43.2	16.3
MT	3.9	0.6	0.2	0.4	15.6	20.7	2.5	0.6	1.9	12.1
ID	9.0	1.6	1.0	0.6	17.8	58.1	9.4	5.2	4.2	16.2
WY	2.5	0.2	0.1	0.2	9.4	8.9	0.9	0.3	0.6	10.1
CO	26.6	4.0	2.6	1.4	15.1	183.9	29.8	18.5	11.3	16.2
NM	5.2	0.8	0.4	0.5	15.6	38.8	6.0	3.8	2.2	15.5
AZ	22.3	4.8	2.9	1.9	21.5	180.2	34.4	19.2	15.2	19.1
UT	12.6	2.0	1.1	0.9	15.7	96.0	13.6	7.2	6.4	14.2
NV	2.6	0.4	0.2	0.2	13.2	23.4	2.7	1.3	1.4	11.5
Pac.	376.3	82.4	59.1	23.5	21.9	2,737.5	536.6	345.4	191.2	19.6
WA	59.4	23.2	20.1	3.1	39.1	361.6	107.7	84.5	23.2	29.8
OR	30.8	6.0	3.6	2.5	19.5	217.7	39.4	22.6	16.8	18.1
CA	279.2	51.2	33.6	17.6	18.3	2,126.3	380.8	230.7	150.1	17.9
AK	3.1	1.5	1.4	0.1	21.5	11.4	6.0	5.6	0.4	52.6
HI	3.8	0.5	0.4	0.2	14.0	20.5	2.7	2.0	0.7	13.2

Source: U.S. Bureau of the Census, *Exports from Manufacturing Establishments* AR89-1.

No. 1269. Manufacturing Technology—Percent of Establishments Using and Planning to Use: 1988

ESTABLISHMENT CHARACTERISTIC	ESTABLISHMENTS USING SELECTED TECHNOLOGIES									PLANNING TO USE WITHIN 2 YEARS				
	Computer aided design (CAD) or computer aided engineering	Numerically controlled machines	Automated material handling	Automated sensor based inspection or testing	Programmable controllers	Computer control on factory floor	LAN[1] For technical data	LAN[1] For factory use	Inter-company computer network	Design and engineering	Fabrication/ machining, assembly	Automated material handling	Automated sensor based inspection or testing	Communication and control
Major SIC [2] group:														
34. Fabricated metal products	26.8	32.2	1.8	15.0	26.8	21.1	13.4	11.6	14.9	20.4	14.7	1.3	6.5	38.8
35. Industrial mach. and equip.	43.2	56.7	5.3	18.4	33.9	28.1	18.5	16.3	12.4	30.8	14.9	2.6	8.2	40.3
36. Electronic and other	48.5	34.9	6.7	38.4	38.0	34.5	24.9	21.1	16.2	26.6	21.9	3.3	12.0	49.5
37. Transportation equip.	39.9	37.3	8.0	27.1	32.0	27.4	22.0	18.7	21.7	25.8	20.2	3.5	7.1	36.3
38. Instruments, related prod.	48.9	33.6	5.5	27.6	32.7	32.3	25.8	21.3	13.8	29.7	19.4	2.5	12.0	45.4
Employment size:														
20 to 99	29.8	35.9	1.7	13.8	22.5	18.9	13.1	11.0	9.7	23.3	11.4	1.2	6.2	36.2
100 to 499	54.4	50.0	5.4	31.6	48.1	41.0	25.9	22.9	22.7	32.6	26.9	3.8	13.4	53.0
500 and over	82.6	69.8	37.5	85.8	77.8	68.0	58.6	50.7	41.8	32.6	40.7	10.3	16.0	55.9
Age of plant (years):														
Less than 5	44.4	37.3	3.7	24.7	29.5	27.3	21.3	18.0	11.9	32.0	19.5	1.7	13.4	50.3
5 to 15	42.6	42.3	4.4	24.8	34.5	29.8	21.3	17.1	16.2	28.8	19.9	3.3	9.9	48.1
16 to 30	41.3	48.0	4.7	23.7	34.9	29.0	19.4	17.1	16.6	27.5	17.6	2.2	7.9	45.1
Over 30	43.1	50.0	7.3	24.9	39.0	32.1	20.7	18.7	18.0	27.0	17.0	2.6	7.9	38.5
Manufacturing process:														
Fabrication/machining	31.1	53.5	2.4	20.6	31.2	24.7	13.7	12.2	14.6	24.1	15.6	1.6	9.9	45.1
Assembly	49.9	15.1	7.4	30.5	30.5	32.6	26.2	22.5	18.3	22.9	19.5	3.9	11.0	45.7
Both	47.2	55.0	5.7	35.2	38.7	32.1	21.8	18.8	16.6	33.3	20.1	2.7	9.0	46.0
Neither	18.5	9.6	2.7	14.8	24.6	17.4	15.9	12.1	11.9	13.7	10.9	1.3	6.0	36.3
Market for most products:														
Consumer	27.6	23.9	4.6	21.2	34.5	27.1	16.1	17.2	17.5	21.7	21.3	3.0	10.6	42.3
Commercial	49.1	41.7	6.5	25.9	34.3	33.0	24.4	22.0	16.4	32.1	18.7	2.8	9.8	43.5
Industrial	42.8	49.5	3.9	21.3	34.5	27.6	19.1	15.9	13.6	29.9	16.4	2.2	8.5	45.8
Transportation	45.7	47.9	8.3	35.4	44.3	34.5	24.8	20.4	32.6	34.1	29.9	3.6	11.9	57.0
Government	57.0	62.0	7.9	42.2	39.4	41.0	28.8	22.8	13.9	29.0	20.1	3.7	13.5	51.9
Other	36.6	36.9	4.5	14.6	24.5	24.0	16.7	13.3	12.2	16.6	12.4	1.5	5.4	31.6
Market price for most products:														
Less than $5	28.6	29.0	2.2	27.0	39.3	26.4	16.7	15.1	21.5	25.4	22.1	1.7	13.4	47.6
$5 to $100	33.3	45.1	3.5	25.6	35.7	29.9	16.4	17.7	19.0	28.2	18.5	3.7	11.9	47.1
$101 to $1,000	41.0	51.5	4.5	24.9	31.6	29.6	20.0	16.1	13.7	27.6	18.5	1.9	8.0	47.0
$1,001 to $2,000	50.2	49.2	6.0	25.8	32.1	30.5	22.1	18.5	14.1	29.9	16.9	3.6	10.5	43.3
$2,001 to $10,000	50.9	45.0	4.9	21.2	38.0	30.7	22.0	17.4	11.8	30.7	13.5	2.0	6.7	41.1
Over $10,000	61.8	48.8	9.8	22.2	39.8	31.9	29.9	21.8	14.4	33.5	16.0	3.0	6.0	46.5

[1] Local area network.   [2] Standard Industrial Classification; see text, section 13.

Source: U.S. Bureau of the Census. *Current Industrial Reports, Manufacturing Technology, 1988.*

No. 1270. Alcoholic Beverages—Summary: 1970 to 1991

[For fiscal years ending in year shown; see text, section 9. Includes Puerto Rico. Excludes imports. See *Historical Statistics, Colonial Times to 1970*, series P 235 for beer production, and P 236a for distilled spirits]

ITEM	Unit	1970	1980	1985	1987	1988	1989	1990	1991
Beer: Breweries operated ...	Number......	154	86	103	120	183	245	286	333
Production............	Mil. bbl. [1]....	135	193	194	196	197	198	202	204
Value of shipments (SIC 2082) [2]	Mil. dol........	3,822	9,362	12,216	13,619	13,871	14,321	15,186	15,925
Tax-paid withdrawals.....	Mil. bbl. [1]....	123	172	175	178	178	179	182	183
Stocks on hand, June 30 ..	Mil. bbl. [1]....	15	15	14	14	14	14	14	14
Per capita consumption [3] ..	Gallons......	(NA)	24.5	23.7	23.7	(NA)	(NA)	(NA)	(NA)
Distilled spirits: Production facilities operated	Number......	140	143	117	102	105	140	143	145
Warehouses operated	Number......	274	200	214	211	186	260	243	224
Production, total [4].......	Mil. tax gal. [5] ..	355	236	117	90	99	135	122	129
Whisky............	Mil. tax gal. [5] ..	160	87	65	42	38	75	77	75
Tax-paid withdrawals, total [6]	Mil. tax gal. [5] ..	256	330	306	271	255	251	251	242
Whisky............	Mil. tax gal. [5] ..	112	42	(NA)	(NA)	(NA)	(NA)	(NA)	(NA)
Stocks on hand, June 30, total [4]	Mil. tax gal. [5] ..	1,091	696	588	508	456	456	451	459
Whisky............	Mil. tax gal. [5] ..	960	566	467	409	370	361	365	368
Bottled for consumption, total	Mil. wine gal. [7] .	312	392	371	337	317	312	306	299
Whisky............	Mil. wine gal. [7] .	192	165	138	119	111	109	106	100
Per capita [3]	Wine gal. [7] .	(NA)	2.0	1.7	1.6	(NA)	(NA)	(NA)	(NA)
Still wines: Production [8]....	Mil. wine gal. [7] .	713	982	622	677	538	611	577	478
Distilling materials.. ...	Mil. wine gal. [7] .	(NA)	184	148	155	119	122	103	108
Tax-paid withdrawals [9]....	Mil. wine gal. [7] .	204	340	414	451	451	464	468	439
Stocks on hand, June 30 [10]	Mil. wine gal. [7] .	207	486	602	618	570	558	562	539
Per capita [3]	Wine gal. [7]....	(NA)	2.1	2.4	2.2	(NA)	(NA)	(NA)	(NA)
Effervescent wines: [11] Production	Mil. wine gal. [7] .	20.0	26.8	32.0	29.2	29.8	30.9	26.9	22.8
Tax-paid withdrawals	Mil. wine gal. [7] .	17.1	24.1	30.9	31.2	29.2	27.0	26.2	24.6
Stocks on hand, June 30 ..	Mil. wine gal. [7] .	8.1	11.9	21.3	18.7	18.2	19.4	22.1	20.4
Per capita [3]	Wine gal. [7]....	0.15	0.17	(NA)	(NA)	(NA)	(NA)	(NA)	(NA)
Of domestic output.....	Wine gal. [7]....	0.13	0.12	(NA)	(NA)	(NA)	(NA)	(NA)	(NA)

NA Not available. [1] Barrels of 31 wine gallons (see footnote 8). [2] Source: U.S. Bureau of the Census, *Census of Manufactures, 1977, 1982* and *1987*, and *Annual Survey of Manufactures.* [3] Source: U.S. Dept. of Commerce, International Trade Administration. Based on resident population as of July 1, including Armed Forces abroad. [4] Excludes alcohol produced for industrial use. [5] A tax gallon for spirits of 100 proof or over is equivalent to the proof gallon; for spirits of less than 100 proof to the wine gallon. (See footnote 8.) A proof gallon is the alcoholic equivalent of a U.S. gallon at 60° F, containing 50 percent of ethyl alcohol by volume. [6] Includes ethyl alcohol. [7] A wine gallon is the U.S. gallon equivalent to the volume of 231 cubic inches. [8] Production represents total amount removed from fermenters, including distilling material, and includes increase after fermentation (by amelioration, sweetening, and addition of wine spirits). [9] Includes special natural wines. [10] Excludes distilling materials. [11] Includes champagne, other effervescent wines, and artificially carbonated wines.

Source: Except as noted, U.S. Bureau of Alcohol, Tobacco, and Firearms, *Alcohol and Tobacco Summary Statistics*, annual.

No. 1271. Tobacco Products—Production, Consumption, and Expenditures: 1970 to 1991

[Production data are for calendar years. Excludes cigars produced in customs bonded manufacturing warehouses. See also *Historical Statistics, Colonial Times to 1970*, series P 239-241]

ITEM	Unit	1970	1975	1980	1983	1984	1985	1986	1987	1988	1989	1990	1991
Production: Cigarettes	Billions .	583	651	714	667	669	665	658	689	695	677	710	695
Nonfilter tip.........	Billions .	116	80	54	43	39	36	33	30	28	24	23	19
Regular	Billions .	54	36	23	19	18	16	15	14	12	11	11	9
King	Billions .	62	44	30	24	21	20	18	16	16	13	12	10
Filter tip	Billions .	467	571	661	625	630	629	625	660	667	654	687	675
Long and king.......	Billions .	362	404	439	384	380	378	373	397	400	392	417	423
Extra long	Billions .	105	167	222	241	251	252	252	262	267	261	270	253
Cigars	Billions .	8.4	5.7	4.0	3.6	3.5	3.1	2.9	2.1	2.0	2.0	1.9	1.7
Tobacco [1]	Mil. lb. .	165	152	163	162	163	158	147	143	142	141	142	142
Per capita consumption: [2] All products	Lb. [3] ...	9.7	9.1	7.9	7.2	6.9	6.8	6.6	6.3	6.1	5.7	5.5	5.4
Cigarettes	1,000 ..	4.0	4.1	3.8	3.5	3.4	3.4	3.3	3.2	3.1	2.9	2.8	2.7
Cigars [4]	Number.	60	39	24	21	20	18	17	15	14	14	13	12
Expenditures (consumer)....	Mil. dol .	11.5	15.5	21.0	28.7	30.7	32.2	33.7	35.4	37.8	40.9	43.8	47.4
Cigarettes	Mil. dol .	10.4	14.3	19.4	26.8	28.8	30.3	31.8	33.6	35.9	38.3	41.6	45.2
Cigars	Mil. dol .	0.7	0.7	0.7	0.7	0.7	0.7	0.7	0.6	0.6	0.7	0.7	0.7
Other	Mil. dol .	0.4	0.6	0.9	1.2	1.2	1.2	1.2	1.3	1.4	1.4	1.5	1.6

[1] Smoking and chewing tobaccos and snuff output. [2] Based on U.S. Bureau of the Census estimated population 18 years old and over, as of July 1, including Armed Forces abroad. [3] Unstemmed processing weight equivalent. [4] Weighing over 3 pounds per 1,000.

Source: U.S. Dept. of Agriculture, Economic Research Service, *Tobacco Situation and Outlook*, quarterly.

No. 1272. Cotton, Wool, and Manmade Fibers—Consumption and Distribution in Selected Consumer Products: 1987 to 1991

[Represents products manufactured by U.S. mills. Excludes glass fiber]

END-USE AND YEAR	Total (mil. lb.)	COTTON		WOOL		MAN-MADE FIBERS					
		Total (mil. lb.)	Percent end-use	Total (mil. lb.)	Percent end-use	Total (mil. lb.)	Percent end-use	Cellulosic [1]		Non-cellulosic [2]	
								Total (mil. lb.)	Percent end-use	Total (lb.)	Percent end-use
Total:											
1987	13,913	4,520	32.5	226	1.6	9,167	65.9	587	4.2	8,580	61.7
1988	13,532	4,033	29.8	210	1.6	9,289	68.6	613	4.5	8,676	64.1
1989	14,125	4,633	32.8	196	1.4	9,296	65.8	600	4.2	8,696	61.6
1990	14,010	4,699	33.5	185	1.3	9,126	65.2	598	4.3	8,528	60.9
1991	14,416	5,032	34.9	213	1.4	9,171	63.7	556	3.9	8,615	59.8
Apparel:											
1987	5,564	2,769	49.8	157	2.8	2,638	47.4	236	4.2	2,402	43.2
1988	5,164	2,513	48.7	139	2.7	2,512	48.6	276	5.3	2,236	43.3
1989	5,514	2,821	51.2	124	2.2	2,569	46.6	274	5.0	2,295	41.6
1990	5,269	2,956	56.1	118	2.2	2,195	41.7	294	5.6	1,901	36.1
1991	5,604	3,241	57.8	142	2.6	2,221	39.6	283	5.0	1,938	34.6
Home furnishings:											
1987	2,162	1,232	57.0	18	0.8	912	42.2	139	6.4	773	35.8
1988	2,052	1,079	52.6	19	0.9	954	46.5	130	6.3	824	40.2
1989	2,285	1,339	58.6	19	0.8	927	40.6	123	5.4	804	35.2
1990	2,155	1,245	57.8	14	0.6	896	41.6	104	4.8	792	36.8
1991	2,179	1,283	58.9	11	0.5	885	40.6	94	4.3	791	36.3
Floor coverings:											
1987	2,975	18	0.6	23	0.8	2,934	98.6	1	-	2,933	98.6
1988	3,053	12	0.4	21	0.7	3,020	98.9	1	-	3,019	98.9
1989	2,997	14	0.5	24	0.8	2,959	98.7	1	-	2,958	98.7
1990	3,076	19	0.6	21	0.7	3,036	98.7	-	-	3,036	98.7
1991	2,986	20	0.7	25	0.8	2,941	98.5	-	-	2,941	98.5
Exports of domestic products:											
1987	406	127	31.3	15	3.7	264	65.0	22	5.4	242	59.6
1988	456	124	27.2	19	4.2	313	68.6	25	5.5	288	63.1
1989	492	135	27.4	20	4.1	337	68.5	27	5.5	310	63.0
1990	532	146	27.4	22	4.1	364	68.5	29	5.5	335	63.0
1991	572	155	27.1	23	4.0	394	68.9	32	5.6	362	63.3
Industrial: [3]											
1987	2,806	374	13.3	13	0.5	2,419	86.2	189	6.7	2,230	79.5
1988	2,807	305	10.9	12	0.5	2,490	88.6	181	6.4	2,309	82.2
1989	2,837	324	11.4	9	0.3	2,504	88.3	175	6.2	2,329	82.1
1990	2,978	333	11.2	10	0.4	2,635	88.4	171	5.7	2,464	82.7
1991	3,075	333	10.8	12	0.4	2,730	88.8	147	4.8	2,583	84.0

- Represents zero.   [1] Rayon and acetate.   [2] Nylon, polyester, acrylic, olefin, except as noted.   [3] Includes consumer-type products.

Source: Fiber Economics Bureau, Inc., Roseland, NJ, *Textile Organon*, monthly, (copyright).

No. 1273. U.S. Exports and Imports of Textiles and Apparel Products: 1989 to 1991

[**In millions of dollars.** Excludes glass fibers, linoleum, rubber and leather apparel and clothing donated for charity. Minus sign (-) indicates deficit]

PRODUCT	EXPORTS			GENERAL IMPORTS			BALANCE		
	1989	1990	1991	1989	1990	1991	1989	1990	1991
Total	**5,984**	**7,401**	**8,669**	**30,653**	**31,931**	**33,197**	**24,669**	**24,530**	**24,528**
Textile yarn fabrics	3,897	4,922	5,457	6,094	6,398	6,991	2,197	1,476	1,534
Textile yarn	1,032	1,242	1,254	742	697	831	-290	-545	-423
Cotton fabric, woven	369	503	542	1,063	1,120	1,281	694	617	739
Woven fabric of manmade textiles	577	673	703	969	974	1,106	392	301	403
Woven fabric of textile material	132	129	141	641	647	677	509	518	536
Special yarns	830	1,053	1,166	633	695	724	-197	-358	-442
Other	957	1,322	1,651	2,046	2,265	2,372	1,089	943	721
Apparel	2,087	2,479	3,212	24,559	25,533	26,206	22,472	23,054	22,994

Source: U.S. Bureau of the Census, *U.S. Merchandise Trade: Exports, General Imports, and Imports for Consumption*, Report FT925, monthly.

No. 1274. Iron and Steel Industry—Summary: 1980 to 1991

[The universe for financial data for 1991 represents companies who produced 68 percent of the reported raw steel production. The financial data represents the operations of the steel segment of companies. Minus sign (-) indicates net loss]

ITEM	Unit	1980	1983	1984	1985	1986	1987	1988	1989	1990	1991
Steel mill products, apparent supply . . .	Mil. tons [1] . .	95.2	83.5	98.9	96.4	90.0	95.9	102.7	96.8	97.8	88.3
Net shipments	Mil. tons [1] . .	83.9	67.6	73.7	73.0	70.3	76.7	83.8	84.1	85.0	78.8
Exports.	Mil. tons [1] . .	4.1	1.2	1.0	1.0	1.0	1.1	2.1	4.6	4.3	6.3
Imports.	Mil. tons [1] . .	15.5	17.1	26.2	24.3	20.7	20.4	20.9	17.3	17.2	15.8
Scrap consumed	Mil. tons [1] . .	66.6	49.0	51.8	53.2	49.7	51.7	56.3	51.7	50.1	(NA)
Scrap inventory.	Mil. tons [1] . .	6.9	5.0	4.4	4.0	3.4	3.8	3.5	3.5	3.6	(NA)
Iron and steel products: Exports	Mil. tons [1] . .	5.1	1.8	1.7	1.6	1.5	1.7	2.8	5.4	5.3	7.4
Imports.	Mil. tons [1] . .	17.9	19.3	29.5	27.6	24.2	23.8	25.7	22.1	21.9	20.2
Capacity by steelmaking process	Mil. net tons	153.7	150.6	135.3	133.6	127.9	112.2	112.0	115.9	116.7	117.6
Revenue	Bil. dol. . . .	37.7	25.0	30.3	28.4	25.0	27.1	32.7	31.8	30.9	27.4
Net income	Bil. dol. . . .	0.7	-2.2	(-Z)	-1.8	-4.1	1.0	-0.6	1.6	0.1	-2.1
Stockholders' equity	Bil. dol. . . .	14.5	8.2	9.4	6.9	2.4	3.0	2.2	2.1	4.3	2.7
Total assets	Bil. dol. . . .	30.8	25.5	26.2	24.0	21.0	21.9	24.2	24.6	28.3	27.8
Capital expenditures	Bil. dol. . . .	2.7	1.9	1.2	1.6	0.9	1.2	1.8	2.3	2.6	2.3
Working capital ratio [2]	Ratio	1.6	1.3	1.4	1.3	1.6	1.5	1.7	1.6	1.6	1.4
Inventories.	Bil. dol. . . .	4.7	3.3	4.2	3.5	3.0	3.4	3.8	4.0	4.7	4.4
Average employment	1,000 . .	399	243	236	208	175	163	169	169	164	146
Hours worked	Million	758	475	474	419	356	354	363	360	350	304
Producer price indexes: [3]											
Iron and steel, total	1982=100 .	90.0	101.3	105.3	104.8	101.1	104.6	115.7	119.1	117.2	114.1
Steel mill products	1982=100 .	86.6	100.9	104.7	104.7	99.8	102.3	110.7	114.5	112.1	109.5
Blast and electric furnace products . .	1982=100 .	97.1	97.7	97.3	95.6	94.2	97.1	119.6	129.4	120.1	116.9
Iron ore	1982=100 .	87.8	101.2	101.2	97.5	91.5	84.2	82.8	82.8	83.3	83.6
Scrap, iron and steel.	1982=100 .	140.9	107.4	123.7	112.6	109.6	128.4	177.1	173.7	166.0	147.6
Foundry and forge shop products . . .	1982=100 .	89.7	101.6	104.4	105.2	105.2	105.7	109.6	114.6	117.2	119.0

NA Not available.   Z Less than $50 million.   [1] In millions of short tons.   [2] Current assets to current liabilities.   [3] Source: U.S. Bureau of Labor Statistics, *Producer Price Indexes*, monthly and annual.

Source: Except as noted, American Iron and Steel Institute, Washington, DC, *Annual Statistical Report* (copyright).

No. 1275. Raw Steel, Pig Iron, and Ferroalloys Production: 1970 to 1991

[In millions, except percent. See also *Historical Statistics, Colonial Times to 1970*, series P 265-269]

ITEM	1970	1975	1980	1984	1985	1986	1987	1988	1989	1990	1991
Raw steel (net tons):											
World production.	654.2	712.0	790.4	782.6	792.9	788.9	811.1	859.2	865.3	848.8	809.4
U.S. production	131.5	116.6	111.8	92.5	88.3	81.6	89.2	99.9	97.9	98.9	87.9
Percent of world	20.1	16.4	14.2	11.8	11.1	10.3	11.0	11.6	11.3	11.6	10.9
Basic oxygen process . . .	63.3	71.8	67.6	52.8	51.9	47.9	52.5	58.0	58.3	58.5	52.7
Electric.	20.2	22.7	31.2	31.4	29.9	30.4	34.0	36.8	35.2	36.9	33.8
Open hearth	48.0	22.2	13.0	8.3	6.4	3.3	2.7	5.1	4.4	3.5	1.4
Carbon.	117.4	100.4	94.7	79.9	76.7	71.4	78.0	86.8	86.2	86.6	77.9
Alloy and stainless	14.1	16.3	17.1	12.6	11.6	10.2	11.2	13.1	11.7	12.3	10.0
Pig iron and ferroalloys, production (sh. tons) [1] . . .	93.5	79.9	68.7	51.9	50.4	44.0	48.4	55.7	55.9	54.8	48.6

[1] Beginning 1975, includes blast furnace ferroalloys.

No. 1276. Steel Products—Net Shipments, by Market Classes: 1970 to 1991

[In thousands of short tons. Comprises carbon, alloy, and stainless steel]

MARKET CLASS	1970	1975	1980	1985	1987	1988	1989	1990	1991
Total [1]	90,798	79,957	83,853	73,043	76,654	83,840	84,100	84,981	78,846
Automotive.	14,475	15,214	12,124	12,950	11,343	12,555	11,763	11,100	10,015
Steel service centers, distributors.	16,025	12,700	16,172	18,439	19,840	21,037	20,769	21,111	19,464
Construction, incl. maintenance	8,913	8,119	8,742	7,900	7,681	8,607	8,318	9,245	9,161
Containers, packaging, shipping.	7,775	6,053	5,551	4,089	4,372	4,421	4,459	4,474	4,278
Machinery, industrial equipment, tools. . .	5,169	5,173	4,543	2,271	2,277	2,798	2,409	2,388	1,982
Steel for converting and processing . . .	3,443	3,255	4,117	5,484	7,195	8,492	8,235	9,441	8,265
Rail transportation.	3,098	3,152	3,155	1,061	758	1,146	1,229	1,080	999
Contractors' products.	4,440	3,927	3,148	3,330	3,337	3,495	3,182	2,870	2,306
Oil and gas industries	3,550	4,171	5,371	2,044	1,489	1,477	1,203	1,892	1,425
Electrical equipment	2,694	2,173	2,441	1,869	2,373	2,459	2,449	2,453	2,102
Appliances, utensils, and cutlery	2,160	1,653	1,725	1,466	1,633	1,638	1,721	1,540	1,388

[1] Includes other classes not shown and nonclassified shipments.

Source of tables 1275 and 1276: American Iron and Steel Institute, Washington, DC, *Annual Statistical Report* (copyright).

No. 1277. Computer Shipments and Revenues: 1989 to 1991

[Revenue is in if-sold, end-user dollars]

ITEM	FACTORY REVENUE (mil. dol.)			Shipments (units)		
	1989	1990	1991	1989	1990	1991
United States:						
Supercomputer	794.5	788.8	877.6	568	531	553
Mainframe	12,532.8	12,538.1	9,855.6	3,969	3,952	3,434
Midrange	9,962.7	9,815.8	6,340.3	239,652	208,102	178,276
Workstation	2,716.1	3,147.2	3,474.1	130,162	161,488	210,649
Personal computer	18,296.3	18,660.9	18,428.0	9,329,970	9,848,593	10,182,500
Canada						
Supercomputer	30.0	29.9	29.7	16	19	19
Mainframe	918.0	892.4	771.7	257	257	266
Midrange	775.1	744.3	579.0	21,124	17,832	14,277
Workstation	137.8	225.6	191.1	6,609	12,077	7,996
Personal computer	1,227.3	1,447.7	1,474.0	813,702	857,706	884,378
Western Europe						
Supercomputer	429.7	505.6	554.4	256	291	295
Mainframe	10,313.7	10,861.9	8,924.2	4,058	4,307	4,390
Midrange	10,378.5	10,061.5	9,892.1	283,954	243,340	250,778
Workstation	1,870.7	2,395.5	2,544.4	88,291	121,577	155,249
Personal computer	12,210.3	14,810.1	14,519.4	6,855,323	7,954,834	8,572,164
Japan						
Supercomputer	373.4	469.9	495.6	102	116	141
Mainframe	5,394.5	5,697.6	6,242.4	6,094	6,222	5,639
Midrange	4,604.8	5,392.1	5,668.3	217,730	231,571	287,640
Workstation	1,306.8	1,511.6	1,875.5	76,714	96,267	123,904
Personal computer	4,569.5	4,746.0	4,600.8	1,891,800	2,243,500	2,363,000

Source: Dataquest Inc., San Jose, CA, Consolidated Data Base, May 1992.

No. 1278. Domestic Personal Computer Sales and Use: 1981 to 1988

[In millions of units, except as indicated]

ITEM	1981	1982	1983	1984	1985	1986	1987	1988
Personal computers (PC's) sold	1.11	3.53	6.90	7.61	6.75	7.04	8.34	9.50
Value (mil. dol.)	3,143	5,925	9,779	14,269	17,077	18,888	23,458	27,700
Personal computers in use, total [1]	2.12	5.53	12.17	19.18	25.27	31.15	37.84	45.08
Workplace	1.24	2.26	4.00	6.44	9.26	12.22	15.91	20.33
Education	0.13	0.27	0.54	0.78	1.15	1.55	1.96	2.36
Homes	0.75	3.00	7.64	11.95	14.86	17.38	19.97	22.38
Personal computer-related equipment in use:								
Impact printers	0.72	1.90	4.25	8.70	12.80	17.21	22.49	27.30
Nonimpact printers	0.02	0.10	0.31	0.68	1.19	1.83	2.76	3.42
Plotters	0.02	0.05	0.12	0.22	0.39	0.61	0.88	1.07
Monochrome monitors	0.97	2.24	4.68	7.00	9.74	12.56	15.59	18.65
Color monitors	0.13	0.48	1.29	2.98	5.01	7.73	11.68	13.97
Modems	0.18	0.53	1.41	3.00	4.66	6.55	8.91	10.91
Add-in-boards [2]	2.41	5.68	11.43	19.36	29.62	41.22	55.17	65.26
PC hardware maintenance (mil. dol.) [3]	76	166	279	568	951	1,061	1,750	2,298

[1] Excluding multiuser personal computers.   [2] Excluding add-in modem boards.   [3] Excluding education and home.
Source: Future Computing/Datapro, Inc. Delran, NJ, unpublished data.

No. 1279. Microcontrollers and Chip Shipments: 1985 to 1991

ITEM	Unit	1985	1986	1987	1988	1989	1990	1991
Microcontrollers, worldwide: Units	Mil. units	340.8	493.9	729.2	948.3	1,152.8	1,357.5	1,592.0
8-bit	Mil. units	163.6	218.0	333.5	477.8	461.3	562.9	721.5
4-bit	Mil. units	177.0	271.9	392.3	465.0	682.1	777.2	838.4
16-bit	Mil. units	0.2	0.4	3.4	5.5	9.4	17.4	32.1
Revenue	Mil. dol.	1,114	1,392	2,072	2,706	3,262	3,667	4,519
8-bit	Mil. dol.	728	831	1,251	1,725	2,002	2,079	2,618
4-bit	Mil. dol.	382	555	792	935	1,173	1,394	1,598
16-bit	Mil. dol.	4	7	29	47	86	194	303
32-bit processor—Units:								
RISC [1]	Mil. units	-	-	0.1	0.2	0.7	0.8	1.5
CISC [2]	Mil. units	0.1	0.5	1.7	4.9	8.1	7.3	13.5
Revenue	Mil. dol.	19	88	301	579	817	1,402	2,456
RISC [1]	Mil. dol.	3	4	12	39	(NA)	175	270
CISC [2]	Mil. dol.	16	84	288	540	(NA)	1,227	2,186
256K DRAM [3] chips	Mil. units	201.6	620.0	766.3	955.9	780.1	620.5	299.1
Revenue	Mil. dol.	764	1,432	1,809	2,916	2,442	1,322	622
Price	Dollars	3.79	2.31	2.36	3.05	3.13	2.13	2.08
1-Megabit DRAM chips	Mil. units	0.2	4.3	42.6	212.7	407.5	665.0	835.4
Revenue	Mil. dol.	17	134	637	3,590	5,599	4,229	3,776
Price	Dollars	100.66	31.16	14.95	16.88	13.74	6.36	4.52

- Represents or rounds to zero.   NA Not available.   [1] RISC=Reduced Instruction Set Computer.   [2] CISC=Complex
Instruction Set Computer.   [3] DRAM=Dynamic Random Access Memory.
Source: Dataquest, Inc., San Jose, CA, unpublished data.

No. 1280. Computers and Industrial Electronic Equipment—Shipments, by Type: 1982 to 1991

[In millions of dollars]

TYPE OF EQUIPMENT	1982	1983	1984	1985	1986	1987	1988	1989	1990	1991
Total	55,639	60,084	73,610	74,247	73,086	79,456	82,022	85,075	84,962	83,959
Computer and peripheral equipment:										
Computers	16,036	17,865	24,401	25,616	26,020	28,975	28,693	28,464	27,559	27,091
Peripheral equipment	18,728	20,844	23,954	23,828	22,195	23,865	25,443	25,729	25,709	25,291
Industrial Electronics:										
Controlling, processing equipment	7,363	7,428	8,683	8,719	8,924	9,193	9,861	11,992	12,471	12,105
Testing, measuring equipment . .	4,695	5,200	6,279	6,008	5,736	6,009	5,807	5,953	5,955	5,768
Nuclear electronic equipment . .	546	490	480	519	560	601	616	606	651	631
Other electronic equipment. . . .	3,869	3,412	4,665	4,530	4,720	5,238	5,588	5,992	5,609	5,539
Electromedical electronic equipment	4,402	4,845	5,148	5,028	4,931	5,576	6,015	6,339	7,010	7,535

Source: Electronic Industries Association, Washington, DC, *Electronic Market Data Book*, annual.

No. 1281. Factory Sales of Electronic Components and Consumer Electronic Products: 1980 to 1991

[In millions of dollars]

PRODUCT	1980	1983	1984	1985	1986	1987	1988	1989	1990	1991
Electronic components	25,571	33,856	43,306	39,459	38,829	45,335	50,988	54,937	55,094	55,974
Solid state products	9,089	12,570	17,032	14,650	14,408	16,819	19,790	22,376	21,507	21,979
Parts	7,080	8,318	10,155	9,329	9,169	10,664	10,871	10,560	9,976	9,985
Electron tubes . . . , ...	1,744	2,049	2,137	2,055	2,125	2,176	2,289	2,596	2,627	2,564
Other components [1]	7,658	10,919	13,982	13,423	13,121	15,676	18,038	19,405	20,984	21,446
Consumer electronic products .	10,891	14,560	17,594	23,652	21,480	21,835	22,139	22,340	22,602	21,977
Color TV receivers	4,210	5,002	5,538	5,565	6,040	6,303	6,277	6,530	6,247	6,035
Car audio	1,368	1,900	2,500	2,761	3,135	3,523	3,937	4,125	4,292	4,107
Video cassette recorders	621	2,162	3,585	4,739	5,258	3,442	2,848	2,625	2,439	2,454
Camcorders	621	(NA)	(NA)	565	1,280	1,651	1,972	2,007	2,260	2,013
Separate audio components	1,424	1,268	913	1,132	1,358	1,715	1,854	1,871	1,935	1,805
Portable audio tape equipment	1,403	1,102	1,191	1,140	1,389	1,469	1,547	1,595	1,645	1,780
Audio systems [2]	809	630	976	1,372	1,370	1,048	1,225	1,217	1,270	1,264
Blank video cassettes	(NA)	580	770	1,055	1,235	1,006	936	923	948	980
Projection TV	(NA)	268	385	488	529	527	529	478	626	683
Home radios	468	565	661	379	408	409	377	379	360	310
Blank audio cassettes	(NA)	234	256	270	300	375	354	367	376	373
Monochrome TV receivers	588	465	419	328	373	341	236	156	132	92
Video disc players.	(NA)	81	45	23	26	26	34	50	72	81
Color cameras	(NA)	303	355	228	59	(NA)	(NA)	(NA)	(NA)	(NA)

NA Not available. [1] Includes sockets, delay lines, loudspeakers, magnetic components, transducers, printed circuit boards, microwave components, assemblies, and parts. [2] Includes compact and rack systems.

Source: Electronic Industries Association, Washington, DC, *Electronic Market Data Book*, annual (copyright).

No. 1282. Semiconductors and Related Devices: 1980 to 1991

[In millions of dollars, except percent. Semiconductors and related devices represent SIC 3674]

ITEM	1980	1985	1986	1987	1988	1989	1990	1991
Consumption, North American market,[1]	6,053	9,420	10,844	12,858	15,844	17,070	16,540	16,990
Capital expenditures (North America) [2]	1,438	2,629	2,082	2,594	3,434	3,875	4,088	3,851
Percent of sales	22.6	27.9	19.2	20.2	21.7	22.7	24.7	22.7
Japanese capital expenditures as a percent of revenues . .	17.2	40.0	16.0	16.0	21.4	23.3	23.4	(NA)
R&D (North America)	423	1,159	1,250	1,448	1,661	(NA)	(NA)	(NA)
Imports, total [3]	2,223	4,870	5,044	6,656	9,502	10,758	(NA)	(NA)
Integrated circuits	1,909	4,365	4,459	6,000	8,683	9,957	(NA)	(NA)
Transistors	193	242	279	318	402	401	(NA)	(NA)
Diodes and rectifiers	121	263	306	338	417	400	(NA)	(NA)
Shipments [4]	9,455	15,253	14,930	17,929	20,332	23,488	23,978	27,437
Integrated microcircuits. . . . . . ,.	6,768	10,872	10,925	13,300	14,857	16,682	16,372	19,894
Semiconductor devices, n.e.c. [5]	1,398	2,569	2,303	2,586	3,337	4,875	5,584	5,653
Assets, beginning of year	4,014	12,200	(NA)	16,515	(NA)	(NA)	(NA)	(NA)
New capital expenditures	1,596	2,832	2,220	1,921	2,681	3,132	3,439	2,945
Used capital expenditures	40	390	66	94	56	46	37	108
Retirements	230	896	(NA)	1,442	(NA)	(NA)	(NA)	(NA)
Assets, end of year.	5,420	14,526	(NA)	17,088	(NA)	(NA)	(NA)	(NA)
Depreciation charges.	601	1,512	(NA)	1,719	(NA)	(NA)	(NA)	(NA)
Rental payments	74	184	(NA)	203	(NA)	(NA)	(NA)	(NA)

NA Not available. [1] Source: Dataquest Inc., San Jose, CA, unpublished data. Revenue from shipments by all companies into Canada and the United States. [2] Capital expenditures by all companies in Canada and the United States. [3] Imports for consumption. Includes imports not shown separately. [4] Includes items not shown separately. [5] N.e.c. = Not elsewhere classified.

Source: Except as noted, U.S. Bureau of the Census, *Current Industrial Reports*, series MA-36Q; *U.S. Imports, FT 210, 1980-1988: Import CD-ROM Disc 1989;* and *Annual Survey of Manufactures.*

No. 1283. Machine Tool Orders and Shipments: 1970 to 1992

[In millions of dollars. These data represent total industry volume based on reports from over 200 manufacturers]

YEAR	METAL CUTTING TYPE TOOLS					METAL FORMING TYPE TOOLS				
	New orders (net)		Shipments		Order backlog, end of period	New orders (net)		Shipments		Order backlog, end of period
	Total	Domestic	Total	Domestic		Total	Domestic	Total	Domestic	
1970.	651	507	993	827	471	261	227	450	412	235
1971.	609	524	672	554	408	252	223	326	286	162
1972.	1,009	877	714	627	702	403	368	304	267	260
1973.	1,825	1,550	1,074	935	1,454	787	717	427	388	621
1974.	2,017	1,716	1,445	1,241	2,025	566	470	585	522	600
1975.	916	781	1,879	1,548	1,062	361	284	573	485	388
1976.	1,662	1,477	1,482	1,270	1,243	541	485	578	474	351
1977.	2,202	1,981	1,651	1,470	1,794	793	729	630	560	515
1978.	3,373	3,043	2,189	1,960	2,981	973	901	825	729	663
1979.	4.495	3,866	2,930	2,606	4,546	1,126	991	947	860	843
1980.	3,885	3,496	3,681	3,206	4,750	870	744	1,011	879	701
1981.	2,228	1,946	4,105	3,552	2,873	717	617	991	824	427
1982.	1,064	890	2,895	2,599	1,043	433	372	710	600	151
1983.	1,152	1,069	1,372	1,200	823	545	489	474	430	222
1984.	1,916	1,700	1,607	1,484	1,132	1,000	932	679	609	542
1985.	1,853	1,652	1,742	1,549	1,243	675	610	803	743	414
1986.	1,544	1,377	1,890	1,685	897	581	507	688	621	307
1987.	1,451	1,294	1,677	1,499	672	667	536	647	538	327
1988.	2,708	2,316	1,575	1,400	1,806	883	749	825	702	386
1989.	1,977	1,723	2,359	2,059	1,423	832	719	837	704	380
1990.	2,070	1,772	2,330	2,004	1,164	894	761	970	851	304
1991.	1,894	1,549	1,872	1,595	1,186	748	546	802	625	251
1992.	1,756	1,532	1,918	1,606	1,025	726	609	678	547	299

Source: NMTBA-The Association For Manufacturing Technology, McLean, VA; data published in U.S. Bureau of Economic Analysis, *Business Statistics, 1979*, for 1970-78; thereafter, *Survey of Current Business*, monthly.

No. 1284. Manufacturers' Shipments, Inventories, and Orders: 1950 to 1992

[In billions of dollars, except ratio. See also *Historical Statistics, Colonial Times to 1970*, series P 74-92]

YEAR	Ship-ments, total	Invento-ries, total (Dec. 31)[1]	Ratio of invento-ries to ship-ments[2]	New orders, total	Unfilled orders, total (Dec. 31)	YEAR	Ship-ments, total	Invento-ries, total (Dec. 31)[1]	Ratio of invento-ries to ship-ments[2]	New orders, total	Unfilled orders, total (Dec. 31)
1950.	224	32	1.41	242	41	1972.	756	108	1.58	770	120
1951.	261	39	1.78	287	67	1973.	875	124	1.63	913	158
1952.	270	42	1.71	279	76	1974.	1,018	158	1.86	1,047	187
1953.	298	44	1.90	283	60						
1954.	280	42	1.71	268	48	1975.	1,039	160	1.77	1,023	171
						1976.	1,186	175	1.66	1,194	180
1955.	318	45	1.63	330	60	1977.	1,358	188	1.58	1,381	202
1956.	333	51	1.74	340	68	1978.	1,523	209	1.55	1,580	259
1957.	345	52	1.90	331	53	1979.	1,727	239	1.61	1,771	303
1958.	327	50	1.75	324	47						
1959.	363	53	1.68	369	52	1980.	1,853	262	1.61	1,876	326
						1981.	2,018	280	1.74	2,015	323
1960.	371	54	1.79	363	45	1982.	1,960	307	1.91	1,947	309
1961.	371	55	1.67	373	47	1983.	2,071	308	1.80	2,105	343
1962.	400	58	1.76	401	48	1984.	2,288	334	1.78	2,315	370
1963.	421	60	1.66	426	53						
1964.	448	63	1.62	460	65	1985.	2,334	330	1.72	2,348	384
						1986.	2,336	318	1.66	2,342	390
1965.	492	68	1.58	505	79	1987.	2,475	333	1.64	2,513	427
1966.	538	78	1.70	557	97	1988.	2,682	361	1.64	2,724	469
1967.	558	84	1.71	565	104	1989.	2,793	380	1.66	2,831	507
1968.	603	90	1.76	608	110	1990.	2,874	392	1.66	2,885	519
1969.	642	98	1.81	647	115	1991.	2,822	380	1.64	2,805	502
1970.	634	101	1.91	625	106	1992.	2,929	373	1.55	2,897	470
1971.	671	102	1.76	672	107						

[1] Beginning in 1982, inventories are stated at current cost and are not comparable to the book value estimates for prior years. [2] Ratio based on December seasonally adjusted data.

Source: U.S. Bureau of the Census, *Current Industrial Reports, Manufacturers' Shipments, Inventories, and Orders: 1982-1991*, series M3; and monthly press releases.

No. 1285. Value of Manufactures Shipments and Inventories—Selected Industries: 1980 to 1992

[In billions of dollars. See also *Historical Statistics, Colonial Times to 1970*, series P 74-79]

SIC [1] code	INDUSTRY	1980	1985	1988	1989	1990	1991	1992
(X)	**Shipments, total**	**1,852.7**	**2,334.5**	**2,682.5**	**2,792.7**	**2,873.5**	**2,821.7**	**2,929.3**
(X)	Durable goods industries [2]	929.0	1215.4	1415.9	1460.4	1468.6	1422.6	1498.3
32	Stone, clay, and glass products	44.5	55.8	63.1	63.6	63.5	57.1	63.2
33	Primary metals	134.1	112.3	149.1	153.0	146.1	130.0	132.3
34	Fabricated metal products	116.1	143.3	158.8	162.2	163.1	156.9	160.3
35	Industrial machinery and equipment	180.6	218.4	243.3	253.6	256.3	242.8	252.9
351	Engines and turbines	13.7	15.1	16.2	16.9	16.6	18.5	18.8
353	Construction, mining [3]	33.6	27.6	27.7	29.5	30.7	30.0	27.8
357	Computer and office equipment	30.4	60.4	67.6	65.4	64.1	62.6	71.1
36	Electronic and other	112.9	164.0	186.9	192.3	194.8	199.5	212.1
361-2	Elec. transmission and distrib.	20.1	23.8	25.9	27.4	27.9	27.3	28.1
363	Household appliances	12.9	16.1	17.3	18.3	18.0	18.3	18.9
365	Household audio and	8.5	11.5	8.4	9.1	9.3	10.8	12.3
366	Communications equipment	21.3	35.4	36.1	35.1	38.5	41.2	46.9
367	Electronic components	26.7	42.2	57.0	59.9	60.8	62.0	65.5
37	Transportation equipment [2]	186.5	307.4	354.0	366.0	367.9	363.2	390.4
371	Motor vehicles and parts	104.6	193.4	221.6	225.6	215.0	206.4	236.3
372, 6	Aircraft, missiles, and parts.	58.5	91.3	107.7	113.5	125.2	129.7	126.1
38	Instruments and related products [2]	59.8	96.2	114.5	118.5	123.8	123.9	123.3
382	Measuring and controlling devices	15.7	25.9	28.8	29.6	31.5	30.8	31.8
(X)	Nondurable goods industries [2]	923.7	1119.1	1266.6	1332.3	1404.9	1399.1	1431.0
20	Food and kindred products [2]	256.2	308.6	351.5	364.4	384.0	387.0	394.3
208	Beverages	33.0	43.7	49.7	50.1	52.2	53.6	56.0
21	Tobacco products	12.2	18.6	23.8	25.8	29.9	32.3	33.3
22	Textile mill products	47.3	54.6	64.8	67.3	66.0	67.8	72.5
26	Paper and allied products [2]	72.6	94.7	122.6	131.4	131.4	124.4	125.6
261-3,6	Paper, pulp, paperboard mill products	31.5	39.1	54.9	58.1	57.5	53.5	53.3
265	Paperboard containers and boxes	17.2	23.2	28.2	30.5	30.5	28.7	30.1
28	Chemicals and allied products [2]	168.2	204.8	259.7	278.1	288.2	289.0	296.8
281,2,6,8,9	Industrial chemicals	101.7	114.7	145.5	156.2	157.3	152.4	154.3
283-4	Drugs, soaps, toiletries	41.9	61.3	81.8	88.0	95.2	101.9	109.0
29	Petroleum and coal products	193.0	176.6	131.4	143.7	172.6	160.4	158.0
30	Rubber and plastics products	49.2	75.6	94.2	98.4	101.4	103.6	106.7
(X)	**Inventories, total (Dec. 31)**	**261.7**	**329.6**	**361.5**	**380.5**	**392.5**	**379.9**	**373.0**
(X)	Durable goods industries [2]	171.9	214.0	236.5	250.7	254.5	241.9	230.5
32	Stone, clay, and glass products	5.5	6.9	7.4	7.7	8.1	7.9	7.7
33	Primary metals	23.1	19.8	22.3	22.5	22.3	20.3	19.4
34	Fabricated metal products	19.2	22.5	24.4	24.7	24.1	22.3	22.4
35	Industrial machinery and equipment	40.3	45.6	46.5	48.7	48.0	45.3	43.1
351	Engines and turbines	2.6	2.7	3.1	3.0	3.2	3.3	3.3
353	Construction, mining [3]	9.2	7.8	6.6	6.6	6.7	6.3	5.8
357	Computer and office equipment	8.0	11.5	11.2	11.6	10.4	9.4	8.9
36	Electronic and other	21.3	29.8	30.7	32.2	31.7	30.1	29.8
361-2	Elec. transmission and distrib.	3.9	4.7	4.7	4.7	4.7	4.2	4.0
363	Household appliances	1.8	2.5	2.7	3.0	2.8	2.5	2.3
365	Household audio and	1.3	1.3	1.0	1.1	1.1	1.1	1.1
366	Communications equipment	5.0	8.0	6.6	7.0	7.1	7.2	7.5
367	Electronic components	5.2	7.5	9.0	9.6	9.5	8.8	8.7
37	Transportation equipment [2]	35.3	51.5	61.4	70.5	75.0	72.6	65.7
371	Motor vehicles and parts	9.6	11.8	12.1	11.8	13.0	12.8	11.5
372, 6	Aircraft, missiles, and parts.	21.7	36.2	45.4	54.5	57.6	55.6	50.0
38	Instruments and related products [2]	12.9	21.0	24.3	24.7	24.8	23.8	22.6
382	Measuring and controlling devices	4.2	6.4	6.6	6.9	7.0	6.6	6.5
(X)	Nondurable goods industries [2]	89.8	115.6	125.0	129.7	138.0	138.0	142.5
20	Food and kindred products [2]	22.4	24.4	27.4	27.7	29.4	30.6	30.8
208	Beverages	3.8	4.7	4.9	4.9	5.1	5.5	5.6
21	Tobacco products	3.9	6.3	5.5	5.7	6.1	6.6	7.0
22	Textile mill products	6.5	7.2	8.1	8.3	8.4	8.2	8.7
26	Paper and allied products [2]	7.7	10.1	12.4	13.2	13.4	13.5	13.3
261-3,6	Paper, pulp, paperboard mill products	2.9	3.8	4.4	4.9	5.2	5.5	5.5
265	Paperboard containers and boxes	1.9	2.5	3.3	3.5	3.3	3.3	3.3
28	Chemicals and allied products [2]	19.9	26.0	29.4	30.8	33.2	33.9	35.4
281,2,6,8,9	Industrial chemicals	10.7	14.0	15.3	16.1	17.6	17.4	17.6
283-4	Drugs, soaps, toiletries	5.9	7.8	9.9	10.3	11.0	11.7	13.0
29	Petroleum and coal products	9.6	13.7	9.0	10.4	13.1	11.2	11.1
30	Rubber and plastics products	6.3	9.1	11.1	11.4	11.8	11.1	11.6

X Not applicable.　[1] Standard Industrial Classification.　[2] Includes industries not shown separately.　[3] Also includes material handling industries.

Source: U.S. Bureau of the Census, *Current Industrial Reports, Manufactures' Shipments, Inventories, and Orders: 1982-1991*, series M3-1.86 M3-1(88), and monthly press releases.

No. 1286. Fiber, Rugs, Carpeting, and Sheets—Quantity and Value: 1985 to 1991

ITEM	Unit	1985	1986	1987	1988	1989	1990	1991
All fibers [1]	Mil. lbs. .	(NA)	677	720	730	743	812	837
Raw wool [2][3]	Mil. lbs. .	(NA)	137	143	133	135	133	152
Noils, and fiber [4]	Mil. lbs. .	(NA)	35	30	24	24	20	21
Other fibers	Mil. lbs. .	(NA)	505	548	573	584	659	664
Knit fabric production	Mil. lbs. .	1,496	1,757	1,737	1,662	1,935	1,901	1,948
Rugs, carpet and carpeting	Mil. dol. .	6,605.7	7,311.6	7,929.1	8,417.3	8,431.1	8,527.1	7,937.1
Sheets	1,000 doz	15,491	15,053	15,361	15,505	15,663	15,408	14,001
Pillow cases	1,000 doz	13,174	12,372	12,627	12,564	13,089	12,665	11,301
Terry towels	1,000 doz	44,974	50,182	52,425	47,179	62,741	42,376	43,158

NA Not available.   [1] Includes man-made fiber top converted from tow without combing. A number of companies were added for 1990 based on information in the 1987 Census of Manufactures. Data were received from these companies for 1990; therefore, the information shown for years prior to 1990 may not be directly comparable. These changes represent approximately 20 percent of the total fibers consumed on the woolen system and worsted combing.   [2] Data are shown on a scoured basis for greasy wool.   [3] Shorn and pulled wool of sheep excludes raw wool consumed in cotton system spinning to avoid disclosing figures for individual companies.   [4] Includes reprocessed and reused wool, mohair, alpaca, vicuna, and other specialty fibers as well as tops and noils consumed in woolen spinning and mohair consumed in worsted combing. Does not include wool tops consumed in cotton system spinning.

Source: U.S. Bureau of the Census, *Current Industrial Reports*, MA22K, MA22Q, and MQ23X, annual.

No. 1287. Glass Containers, Clay Construction Products, and Refractories—Value of Shipments: 1985 to 1991

[In millions of dollars]

ITEM	1985	1986	1987	1988	1989	1990	1991
Glass container shipments	(NA)	(NA)	(NA)	1,484.9	1,543.2	1,471.4	1,372.2
Brick shipments [1]	(NA)	(NA)	(NA)	(NA)	1,087.7	1,014.0	803.0
Clay tile shipments [2]	(NA)	(NA)	(NA)	(NA)	697.8	686.5	581.8
Clay pipe and fittings shipments [3]	(NA)	(NA)	(NA)	(NA)	63.0	60.2	45.4
Refractory shipments	1,581.7	1,521.3	1,682.3	1,950.0	2,010.9	2,002.8	1,891.0
Clay	694.4	670.0	739.8	813.7	823.3	771.3	754.8
Nonclay	887.3	851.3	942.6	1,136.3	1,187.7	1,231.5	1,136.2

NA Not available.   [1] Building or common and face bricks.   [2] Floor and wall tile including quarry tile.   [3] Vitrified sewer pipe and fittings.

Source: U.S. Bureau of the Census, *Current Industrial Reports*, M32G, MQ32D, and MA32C, annual.

No. 1288. Mining and Mineral Processing Equipment Shipments—Quantity and Value: 1990 and 1991

Product code	PRODUCT	Number of companies	QUANTITY (units)		VALUE ($1,000)	
			1990	1991	1990	1991
3531K	Portable crushing, screening, washing, and combination plants	15	789	470	85,078	63,694
35325	Underground mining machinery [1]	27	2,060	1,879	381,819	318,757
35326	Mineral processing and beneficiation equip. [1][2]	36	5,986	5,413	90,151	86,628
35327	Crushing, pulverizing, and screening machinery [1][2]	42	2,868	2,542	160,289	132,073
35328	Drills, mining machinery, n.e.c. [1][3]	22	15,789	15,346	182,707	176,932
3533A	Portable drilling rigs and parts	23	(X)	(X)	295,253	252,791

X Not applicable.   [1] Excludes parts.   [2] Excludes portables.   [3] n.e.c. = Not Elsewhere Classified.

Source: U.S. Bureau of the Census, *Current Industrial Reports*, MA35F, annual.

No. 1289. Inorganic Materials and Pharmaceutical Preparations: 1988 to 1991

Product code	ITEM	Unit	1988	1989	1990	1991
	INORGANIC FERTILIZERS					
28731 31	Ammonia, synthetic anhydrous:					
	Total production	1,000 sh. tons	16,821	16,467	17,003	17,167
	Shipments	1,000 sh. tons	9,630	9,599	10,382	10,085
	Shipments value	Mil. dol	1,011	1,010	1,072	1,036
28731 50	Ammonium nitrate, original solution:					
	Total production	1,000 sh. tons	7,504	7,871	7,714	7,776
28731 57	Ammonium sulfate:					
	Total production	1,000 sh. tons	2,333	2,384	2,519	2,243
	Shipments	1,000 sh. tons	2,307	2,282	2,529	2,251
	Shipments value	Mil. dol	141	142	130	130
28732	Urea (100%):					
	Total production	1,000 sh. tons	7,914	8,004	8,217	8,133
	Shipments	1,000 sh. tons	5,080	5,231	5,362	5,432
	Shipments value	Mil. dol	620	625	640	723
28731 11	Nitric acid (100%):					
	Total production	1,000 sh. tons	7,991	8,349	7,931	7,925
	Shipments	1,000 sh. tons	696	743	647	622
	Shipments value	Mil. dol	76	85	81	80
28741 81 28741 85	Phosphoric acid (100% P2O5):					
	Total production	1,000 sh. tons	11,659	11,736	12,035	12,056
	Shipments	1,000 sh. tons	4,212	4,307	4,170	4,352
	Shipments value	Mil. dol	1,291	1,300	1,226	1,220
28193	Sulfuric acid, gross (100%):					
	Total production	1,000 sh. tons	42,580	43,301	44,337	43,350
	Shipments	1,000 sh. tons	11,574	11,842	11,879	11,603
	Shipments value	Mil. dol	619	638	589	583
28742	Superphosphates and other fertilizer materials (100% P2O5):					
	Total production	1,000 sh. tons	7,968	8,362	8,982	8,906
	Shipments	1,000 sh. tons	7,813	8,247	9,016	8,899
	Shipments value	Mil. dol	2,553	2,449	2,711	2,811
T128A	**INORGANIC CHEMICAL SHIPMENTS**					
2812	Alkalies and chlorine	Mil. dol	2,590.4	2,989.2	3,187.0	2,930.3
28121	Chlorine (100% Cl)	Mil. dol	755.1	652.8	477.9	240.6
28123	Sodium hydroxide (caustic soda)	Mil. dol	1,529.0	1,989.5	2,340.8	2,309.3
28125	Other alkalies	Mil. dol	300.3	340.1	361.0	373.5
28120 00	Alkalies and chlorine n.s.k.	Mil. dol	5.9	6.9	7.3	6.8
2816	Inorganic color pigments	Mil. dol	1,783.0	2,195.4	2,260.9	2,064.6
28161 00	Titanium dioxide (composite and pure) (commodity weight)	Mil. dol	1,669.9	2,059.2	2,131.2	1,948.7
2819	Inorganic chemicals n.e.c.	Mil. dol	11,806.3	12,408.1	13,612.0	12,694.3
28193	Sulfuric acid, gross (new and fortified)	Mil. dol	618.6	638.1	589.4	583.2
28194	Inorganic acids, except nitric, phosphoric and sulfuric	Mil. dol	563.3	587.7	603.2	568.1
28195	Aluminum oxide, except natural alumina	Mil. dol	838.5	1,214.8	1,498.5	1,080.7
28196	Aluminum compounds	Mil. dol	487.9	577.3	665.2	643.7
28197	Potassium and sodium compounds (except bleaches, alkalies, and alums)	Mil. dol	1,868.2	1,940.8	1,956.3	1,849.4
28198	Chemical catalytic preparations	Mil. dol	1,093.6	1,225.2	1,221.0	1,225.8
28199	Other inorganic chemicals n.e.c.	Mil. dol	6,140.4	6,018.4	6,846.4	6,513.7
28190 00	Industrial inorganic chemicals n.s.k.	Mil. dol	195.8	205.7	232.0	229.6
28422 00	Household bleaching compounds	Mil. dol	713.2	723.0	724.0	823.6
	PHARMACEUTICAL PREP. SHIPMENTS					
	Pharmaceutical preparations:					
28341	Affecting neoplasms, endocrine systems, and metabolic disease	Mil. dol	2,071.2	2,507.4	2,743.2	3,340.8
28342	Acting on the central nervous system and sense organs	Mil. dol	6,172.7	6,441.3	7,218.5	7,820.3
28343	Acting on the cardiovascular system	Mil. dol	4,449.9	4,874.9	4,814.6	5,009.3
28344	Acting on the respiratory system	Mil. dol	3,224.0	3,286.2	3,724.1	3,757.8
28345	Acting on the digestive system	Mil. dol	3,860.8	4,363.0	4,840.2	5,605.8
28346	Acting on the skin	Mil. dol	1,388.5	1,451.7	1,558.0	1,621.4
28347	Vitamin, nutrient, and hematinic preps.	Mil. dol	2,538.5	2,672.4	2,587.9	2,596.8
28348	Affecting parasitic and infective disease	Mil. dol	4,593.6	4,936.2	5,411.0	5,731.0
28349	Pharmaceutical preps. for veterinary use	Mil. dol	1,051.5	1,071.1	1,056.8	1,163.1

Source: U.S. Bureau of the Census, *Current Industrial Reports*, MA28B, MQ28A, and MA28G, annual.

No. 1290. Engines, Refrigeration and Heating Equipment, and Pumps and Compressors—Quantity and Value of Shipments: 1989 to 1991

Product codes	ITEM	Unit	1989	1990	1991
(X)	Internal combustion engines produced..............	1,000	16,343.2	16,968.6	15,109.7
35191	Gasoline (except outboard, aircraft, and auto)	1,000	15,646.8	16,325.5	14,537.9
35193	Nonautomotive diesel (except aircraft)	1,000	219.1	206.1	184.2
35194	Automotive diesel	1,000	472.9	432.9	383.2
35196	Natural gas and LPG	1,000	4.3	4.0	4.3
(X)	Air-conditioning; heating equip. shipments:				
35851	Heat transfer equipment..........................	Mil. dol. ...	4,578.2	4,308.3	4,119.4
35852	Unitary air-conditioners...........................	Mil. dol. ...	3,854.8	3,559.8	3,441.4
35854	Compressors and compressor units	Mil. dol. ...	2,482.4	2,376.6	2,321.6
3561,3 pt.	Pumps and compressors [1]........................	Mil. dol. ...	4,472.8	4,797.3	5,169.0
35611	Industrial pumps	Mil. dol. ...	2,023.9	2,131.2	2,284.5
35613	Domestic water systems...........................	Mil. dol. ...	273.8	263.6	275.1
35615 pt.	Oil well, oilfield, and other pumps (including laboratory pumps)	Mil. dol. ...	488.2	563.4	590.8
35631	Compressors and vacuum pumps	Mil. dol. ...	1,686.8	1,839.1	2,018.6

X Not applicable.   [1] Excludes hand pumps, automotive circulating pumps, compressors for icemaking and refrigeration equipment, air conditioning units, and replacements and repair parts for pumps and compressor.

No. 1291. Computers and Office and Accounting Machines—Quantity and Value of Shipments: 1990 and 1991

Product code	PRODUCT DESCRIPTION	Number of com-panies	QUANTITY (number)		VALUE (mil. dol.)	
			1990	1991	1990	1991
3571	Electronic computers, general purpose [1] ..	(X)	(X)	(X)	27,877	26,492
(X)	Digital processing units (retail price):					
35711 01	Less than $500	21	3,575,515	2,757,268	1,008	615
35711 02	$500 to $1,000	25	1,581,970	1,500,493	1,863	1,402
35711 03	$1,000 to $2,500	48	1,070,966	1,713,967	2,143	2,929
35711 04	$2,500 to $5,000	46	1,238,092	1,290,116	3,677	4,302
35711 05	$5,000 to $15,000	56	690,065	505,539	4,929	3,399
35711 06	$15,000 to $50,000	51	91,707	139,082	2,059	2,632
35711 07	$50,000 to $250,000..............	46	30,409	24,995	3,021	2,265
35711 08	$250,000 to $1 million...........	23	3,369	4,177	820	747
35711 09	Over $1 million	9	1,355	2,002	2,951	2,814
3572	Computer storage devices	(X)	(X)	(X)	8,443	6,551
3575	Computer terminals	(X)	(X)	(X)	2,430	2,232
3578	Calculating & accounting mach. (incl. pts.)....	(X)	(X)	(X)	1,176	1,037
3695	Magnetic; optical recording media (incl. pts.) ..	58	(X	(X)	3,965	4,028

X Not applicable.   [1] Automatic data processors including parts.

No. 1292. Metalworking Machinery—Value of Shipments, by Class of Product: 1985 to 1991

[In millions of dollars]

Product code	PRODUCT DESCRIPTION	1985	1986	1987	1988	1989	1990	1991
(X)	Metalworking machinery.......	2,682.2	2,709.8	2,668.7	2,858.2	3,514.2	3,436.1	3,239.3
(X)	Metal cutting type	1,877.3	1,911.6	1,780.7	1,734.8	2,428.5	2,371.3	2,282.0
3541A	Machining centers [2]............	214.7	213.4	217.8	334.5	442.2	437.0	379.7
3541B	Station type machines ....[1]	406.1	517.7	299.6	225.4	562.9	502.1	450.4
3541C	Other metal cutting machine tools [3] ..	161.5	148.4	173.9	165.4	173.7	141.9	151.0
(X)	Metal forming type.	804.9	798.2	887.9	1,123.4	1,085.7	1,064.8	957.3

X Not applicable.   [1] Beginning with the 1982 Census of Manufactures, product class 35417 became 3541A, 3541B, and 3541C.   [2] Multi-function numerically controlled machines.   [3] Excludes those designed primarily for home workshops, labs, etc.

Source of tables 1290-1292: U.S. Bureau of the Census, *Current Industrial Reports*, M35L, MA35M, MA35P, MA35R, and MQ35W annual.

No. 1293. Switchgear, Switchboard Apparatus, Relays, and Industrial Controls—Value of Shipments: 1985 to 1991

[In millions of dollars]

Product code	PRODUCT DESCRIPTION	Number of companies	1985	1987	1988	1989	1990	1991
36132	Power circuit breakers	22	378	373	386	393	388	367
36133	Low volt panelboards & dist. boards [1]	122	1,607	1,569	1,664	1,747	1,722	1,562
36134	Fuses and fuse equipment [2]	22	369	368	390	419	419	409
36135	Molded case circuit breakers; 1,000 volts and under	31	935	879	948	952	959	917
36136	Duct [3]	22	148	132	152	188	194	172
36139	Switchgear, except ducts	95	988	1,049	1,100	1,319	1,324	1,333
36251	General purpose and other relays	115	634	889	873	835	805	783
36252	Specific purpose industrial controls.	199	1,747	1,732	1,808	1,928	2,020	1,878
36253	General purpose industrial controls	249	2,191	2,403	2,655	2,971	2,912	2,930
36254	Motor controller accessories [4]	126	381	429	459	503	452	431

[1] Includes other switching and interruption devices, 1,000 volts and below.　[2] Under 2,300 volts, except power distribution cutouts.　[3] Includes plug-in units and accessories, 1,000 volts and under, consisting of enclosed sectionalized prefabricated bus bars rated 20 amperes or more, associated structures and fittings.　[4] Includes parts for industrial controls.

Source: U.S. Bureau of the Census, *Current Industrial Reports*, MA36A, annual

No. 1294. Selected Industrial Air Pollution Control Equipment—Quantity and Value: 1991

[Quantity in number of units, value in millions of dollars]

Product code	PRODUCT DESCRIPTION	Number of companies	NEW ORDERS Quantity	Value	SHIPMENTS Quantity	Value	BACKLOG (Dec. 31) Quantity	Value
35646	Selected industrial air pollution control equip. . .	108	(X)	990.8	(X)	936.7	(X)	675.0
(X)	Particulate emissions collectors	(X)	(X)	541.5	(X)	519.4	(X)	286.9
35646 51	Electrostatic precipitators.	17	177	193.7	172	148.7	88	163.4
35646 54	Fabric filters	54	35,157	226.1	40,279	250.6	4,134	69.1
35646 55	Mechanical collectors	36	4,137	62.3	5,899	66.5	623	21.9
35646 58	Wet scrubbers	36	1,175	59.3	1,222	53.7	545	32.5
(X)	Gaseous emissions control devices	(X)	(X)	255.3	(X)	226.9	(X)	327.2
35646 70	Catalytic oxidation systems	7	143	18.4	111	14.8	45	7.5
35646 72	Thermal and direct oxidation systems	11	256	22.1	313	29.2	57	10.2
35646 73	Scrubbers (gas absorber)	12	556	14.1	589	18.4	90	8.4
35646 75	Dry flue gas desulfurization systems	5	33	179.0	26	139.0	34	274.0
35646 76	Gas absorbers.	9	54	21.7	61	25.6	17	27.1
35646 79	Other types of industrial air pollution control equip. .	21	(X)	194.0	(X)	190.4	(X)	60.9

X Not applicable.

Source: U.S. Bureau of the Census, *Current Industrial Reports*, MA35J, annual.

No. 1295. Fluid Power Products—Value of Shipments: 1985 to 1991

[In millions of dollars. Includes aerospace]

Product code	PRODUCT DESCRIPTION	1985	1987	1988	1989	1990	1991
(X)	Fluid power products, incl. aerospace	4,916.2	6,165.7	6,784.5	6,914.8	7,207.2	6,538.3
34921	Hydraulic valves, nonaerospace type	498.8	553.6	615.4	628.8	663.1	607.9
34922	Pneumatic valves, nonaerospace type	405.6	391.6	444.8	462.9	458.3	448.1
34923	Aerospace type hydraulic & pneumatic valves	255.5	387.3	400.1	450.8	498.3	469.3
34924	Fittings for metal and plastic tubing [1]	384.2	398.3	459.7	504.7	499.9	474.9
34925	Hydraulic and pneumatic fittings and couplings for hose (nonaerospace).	439.8	605.4	649.3	625.0	620.2	568.0
34926	Hydraulic and pneumatic hose or tube end fitting and assemblies (aerospace)	154.8	249.7	326.8	335.5	393.7	385.9
34927	Parts for hydraulic & pneumatic valves	123.7	183.3	218.9	205.8	208.5	163.7
35692	Filters for hydraulic and pneumatic fluid power systems.	281.5	284.4	310.3	352.2	385.4	411.3
	Hydraulic and pneumatic cylinders etc.:						
35931	Nonaerospace.	625.4	793.6	906.6	908.6	940.7	859.0
35932	Aerospace	480.0	637.3	635.8	646.4	636.3	503.3
(X)	Parts for hydraulic and pneumatic cylinders [2]	154.9	288.6	290.9	280.5	264.2	181.2
35941	Hydraulic fluid power pumps and motors	905.5	1,052.0	1,177.5	1,180.4	1,240.1	1,094.5
35942	Parts for pumps and motors.	206.5	340.4	348.4	333.1	398.6	371.3

X Not applicable.　[1] Used in fluid and power transfer systems (nonaerospace).　[2] Includes parts for actuators, accumulators, cushions, and nonvehicular shock absorbers.

Source: U.S. Bureau of the Census, *Current Industrial Reports*, MA35N, annual.

No. 1296. Selected Instruments and Related Products—Value of Shipments: 1985 to 1991

[In millions of dollars]

Products code	PRODUCT DESCRIPTION	1985	1986	1987	1988	1989	1990	1991
34918	Automatic regulating and control valves	1,324	1,302	1,221	1,262	1,331	1,418	1,527
34919	Solenoid-operated valves (except nuclear and fluid power transfer)	280	285	327	338	374	346	341
38121	Aeronautical, nautical, and navigational instruments.	1,592	1,789	2,270	2,365	2,521	2,518	2,657
38122	Search & detection, navigation & guidance systems and equipment	27,057	29,504	30,911	31,145	30,840	32,420	31,763
38210	Laboratory apparatus and laboratory furniture [1] . . .	1,138	1,330	1,549	1,565	1,698	1,675	1,724
38220	Controls for monitoring residential and commercial environments and appliance regulating controls	1,926	1,966	2,093	2,207	2,224	1,982	1,981
38230	Process control instruments	3,963	3,895	4,084	4,348	4,743	5,224	4,816
38242	Integrating and totalizing meters for gas and liquids	549	526	589	610	647	725	708
38243	Counting devices.	175	177	198	193	206	210	201
38244	Motor vehicle instruments [2].	(NA)	197	232	682	637	1,457	1,325
38251	Integrating instruments, electrical	403	403	401	388	401	396	359
38252	Test equipment for testing electrical, radio and communication circuits, and motors	5,699	5,592	6,144	6,248	6,134	6,156	6,048
38253	Instruments to measure electricity	603	617	647	663	620	586	558
38260	Analytical, scientific instruments (except optical). . .	2,716	2,532	3,046	3,442	4,042	4,412	4,419
38271	Sighting, tracking, and fire-control equipment, optical type.	556	651	726	609	595	581	547
38272	Binoculars and astronomical instruments [3].	([3])	25	35	63	86	80	67
38273	Other optical instruments and lenses (except sighting, tracking, and fire control) [3]	1,346	1,221	1,180	1,207	1,188	1,172	1,137
38291	Aircraft engine instruments (except flight)	393	505	520	505	508	579	583
38292	Physical properties and kinematic testing equip. . . .	661	775	859	894	946	1,012	1,024
38294	Nuclear radiation detection and monitoring instruments.	542	587	637	654	606	567	583
38295	Commercial, geophysical, meteorological, and general purpose instruments	354	317	358	1,072	1,035	1,140	1,293
38296	Surveying and drafting instruments.	380	230	247	270	270	274	243

NA Not available. [1] Starting in 1987, product class 38210 (formerly 38112) includes laboratory furniture. Prior to 1987, laboratory furniture had been included in product class 38296 (formerly 38113). [2] The revision beginning 1990 is due to the classification of products in product code 38244 60. Previously, a large part of these data were collected in product class 37149. [3] Prior to 1987, "binoculars and astronomical instruments," and "other instruments and lenses" were combined under product class 38325. In 1987, these were separated into two distinct product classes, 38272 and 38273.

Source: U.S. Bureau of the Census, *Current Industrial Reports, MA38B,* annual.

No. 1297. Robots—Units Shipped and Value: 1985 to 1989

[Based on a survey of all known manufacturers of robots, robot accessories, and components. Shipment value represents the net sales price, f.o.b. plant, to the customer or branch to which the products are shipped, net of discounts, allowances, freight charges, and returns. A robot is a reprogrammable multifunctional manipulator designed to move materials, parts, tools, or specialized devices through variable programmed motions for the performance of a variety of tasks]

ROBOTS, ACCESSORIES, AND COMPONENTS	UNITS SHIPPED (number)			VALUE OF SHIPMENTS (mil. dol.)		
	1985	1988	1989	1985	1988	1989
Robots, robot accessories, and components	(X)	(X)	(X)	345.2	238.0	256.0
Robots, complete.	5,466	4,603	2,217	275.7	164.1	150.6
Servo-controlled robots	2,978	2,072	1,840	254.9	137.7	135.7
Point-to-point type:						
Welding, soldering, brazing, and/or cutting (welding type). .	839	304	273	74.6	32.3	29.3
Foundry, forging, and/or heat treating [1].	65	31	34	4.5	3.2	9.3
Assembly for nonelectronic and electronic products	547	296	238	17.8	8.0	8.1
Material handling and/or parts transfer	463	247	162	44.9	27.0	26.0
Continuous-path type:						
Welding, soldering, brazing, and/or cutting.	287	79	31	22.4	3.7	2.2
Spraying, painting, gluing, and/or sealing.	339	292	254	41.4	30.1	35.1
Fettling, grinding, polishing, and/or deburring [2].	438	823	848	49.4	33.4	25.6
Nonservo-controlled robots	460	336	377	18.0	17.1	14.9
Other robots.	2,028	2,195	([3])	2.8	9.3	([3])
Robot accessories, subassemblies, etc	(X)	(X)	(X)	69.5	73.9	105.4
Miscellaneous receipts	(X)	(X)	(X)	9.2	5.8	2.5

X Not applicable. [1] Includes all point-to-point robots, except assembly, material handling, and/or parts transfer. [2] Includes other continuous-path type, not elsewhere classified. [3] Beginning in 1989, other robots which included educational, hobby, experimental, and nonindustrial robots are no longer collected in this survey.

Source: U.S. Bureau of the Census, *Current Industrial Reports,* series MA35X(88-1).

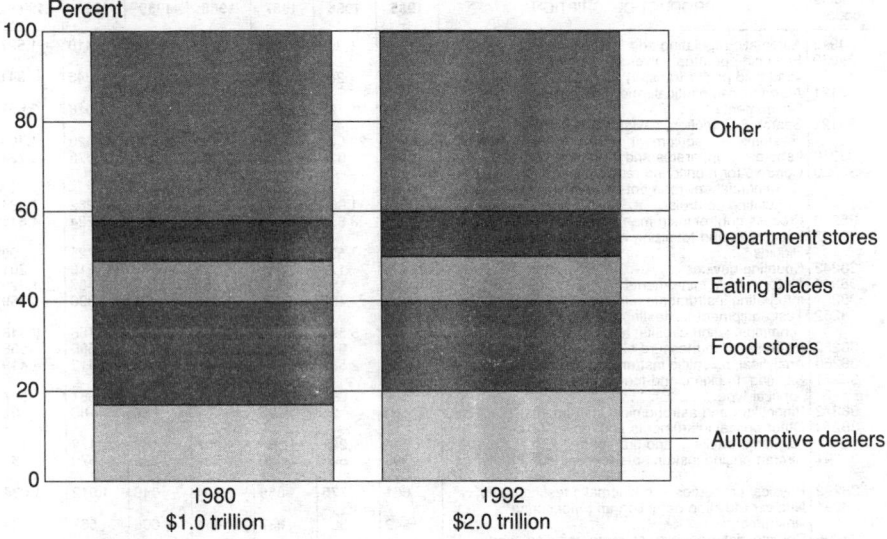

Figure 28.1
Distribution of Retail Sales, by Kind of Business: 1980 and 1992

Percent

- Other
- Department stores
- Eating places
- Food stores
- Automotive dealers

1980
$1.0 trillion

1992
$2.0 trillion

Source: Chart prepared by U.S. Bureau of the Census. For data, see table 1303.

Figure 28.2
Percent of Supermarkets Offering Selected Services and Products: 1990 and 1992

1990
1992

- Scanning checkouts
- Service delicatessen
- Reusable grocery bags
- Service meat
- Self-service delicatessen
- Accept credit cards
- Automated teller machines (ATM's)
- Salad bar
- Organic products

Percent

Source: Chart prepared by U.S. Bureau of the Census. For data, see table 1308.

Domestic Trade and Services

This section presents statistics relating to the distributive trades and service industries. Data shown for the trades, classified by kind of business, and for the various categories of services (e.g., personal, business, repair, hotel) cover sales or receipts, establishments, employees, payrolls, and other items. Also included are data for franchised businesses. The principal sources of these data are census reports and survey reports of the Bureau of the Census. Data on gross product in trade and service industries usually appear in the *Survey of Current Business*, issued by the U.S. Bureau of Economic Analysis. Financial data for firms engaged in retail, wholesale, or service activities appear in the annual *Statistics of Income*, published by the Internal Revenue Service.

Censuses.—Censuses of retail trade and wholesale trade have been taken at various intervals since 1929. Limited coverage of the service industries started in 1933. Beginning with the 1967 census, legislation provides for a census of each area to be conducted every 5 years (for years ending in "2" and "7"). The industries covered in the censuses and surveys of business are those classified in three divisions defined in the *Standard Industrial Classification Manual* (see text, section 13). *Retail trade* refers to places of business primarily engaged in selling merchandise for personal or household consumption; *wholesale trade,* to establishments primarily engaged in selling goods to dealers and distributors for resale or to purchasers who buy for business and farm uses; and *services,* to establishments primarily engaged in providing a wide range of services for individuals and for businesses.

Beginning with the 1954 Censuses of Retail Trade and Service Industries, data for nonemployer establishments are included and published separately. The census of wholesale trade excludes establishments with no paid employees. Beginning in 1977, sales taxes and finance charges are excluded from sales (or receipt) figures of the three censuses. In 1982 and prior censuses, the count of

In Brief

Retail sales, 1992:

Total	*$2.0 trillion*
Automotive dealers	*$.4 trillion*
Food stores	*$.4 trillion*

Annual receipts of taxable service firms ($ billions):

	1985	1991
Business services	*156*	*282*
Health services	*147*	*261*

establishments represented the number in business at the end of the year. For 1987, the count of establishments represents those in business at any time during 1987.

The 1987 Census of Service Industries includes hospitals whereas the 1982 census did not. For 1987, hospitals operated by governmental organizations are included. Government-operated facilities in other service kind-of-business classifications are excluded from the census. In 1982 and 1987, data were not collected for elementary and secondary schools, colleges and universities, labor unions and similar organizations, and political organizations.

The census of retail trade beginning in 1977, excludes nonemployer direct sellers. Beginning 1982, the census treated each leased department in a store as a separate establishment and classified it according to the kind of business it conducted. In prior years, data for leased departments were consolidated with the data for stores in which they were located.

Current surveys.—Current sample surveys conducted by the Bureau of the Census cover various aspects of the retail and wholesale trade and selected service industries. Its *Monthly Retail Trade Report* contains monthly estimates of sales, inventories, inventory/sales ratios, and sales of organizations operating 11 or more retail stores, for the United States, by kind of business. In addition, monthly retail sales data for census regions and divisions, large States, metropolitan areas, and cities are included. Annual figures on sales, year-end inventories, and sales/inventory ratios, by kind of business, appear in the *Combined Annual and Revised Monthly Retail Trade Report.*

Statistics from the Bureau's monthly wholesale trade survey include national estimates of merchant wholesalers' sales, inventories, and stock-sales ratios by major summary groups—durable and nondurable—and selected kinds of business. Merchant wholesalers are those wholesalers who take title to the goods they sell (e.g., jobbers, exporters, importers, major distributors). These data, based on reports submitted by a sample of firms, appear in the *Monthly Wholesale Trade Report.* Annual figures on sales, sales-inventory ratios, and year-end inventories appear in the *Combined Annual and Revised Monthly Wholesale Trade Report.* The *Service Annual Survey* provides annual estimates of receipts for selected service kinds of business for the United States as a whole.

For the current sample survey programs, retail trade coverage is the same as for the census; wholesale trade coverage is limited to merchant wholesalers; and selected services coverage is less inclusive than the census.

Estimates obtained from annual and monthly surveys are based on sample data and are not expected to agree exactly with results that would be obtained from a complete census of all establishments. Data include estimates for sampling units not reporting.

Statistical reliability.—For a discussion of statistical collection and estimation, sampling procedures, and measures of statistical reliability applicable to Census Bureau data, see Appendix III.

Historical statistics.—Tabular headnotes provide cross-references, where applicable, to *Historical Statistics of the United States, Colonial Times to 1970.* See Appendix IV.

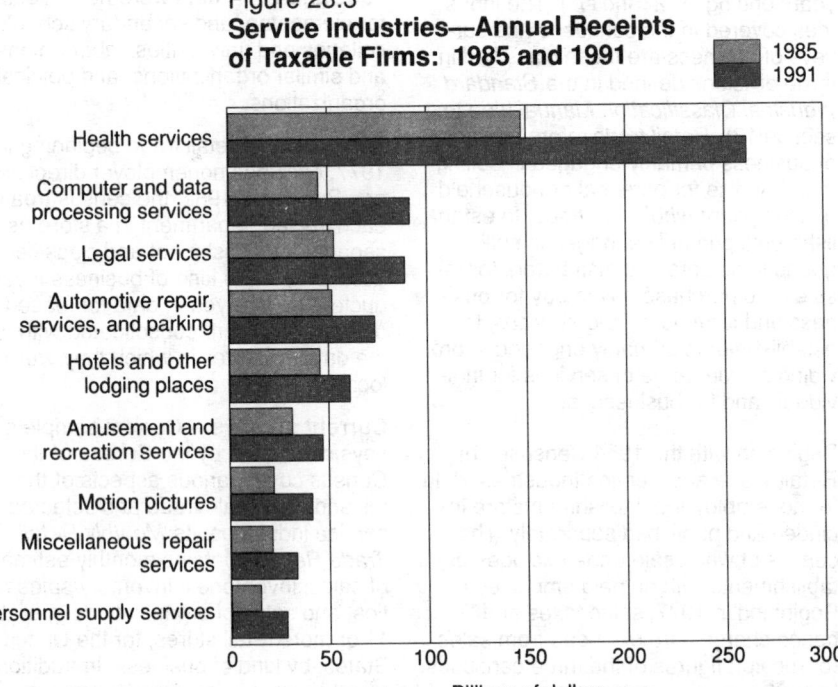

Figure 28.3
Service Industries—Annual Receipts of Taxable Firms: 1985 and 1991

Source: Chart prepared by U.S. Bureau of the Census. For data, see table 1327.

No. 1298. Gross National Product in Domestic Trade and Service Industries in Current and Constant (1982) Dollars: 1980 to 1989

[In billions of dollars, except percent. For definition of gross national product, see text, section 14. Based on 1972 Standard Industrial Classification]

INDUSTRY	CURRENT DOLLARS				CONSTANT (1982) DOLLARS			
	1980	1985	1988	1989	1980	1985	1988	1989
Wholesale and retail trade	438.8	658.2	777.3	825.4	481.8	621.5	689.8	716.6
Percent of gross national product	16.1	16.4	15.9	15.9	15.1	17.2	17.2	17.4
Wholesale trade.	193.9	280.8	317.4	339.5	200.1	267.1	290.6	304.7
Retail trade.	245.0	377.4	459.9	486.0	281.7	354.4	399.2	412.0
Services.	374.0	648.1	885.2	970.5	450.9	538.6	623.3	652.3
Percent of gross national product	13.7	16.1	18.2	18.7	14.1	14.9	15.5	15.8
Hotels and other lodging places	18.9	30.4	41.2	44.5	22.3	26.0	31.2	32.5
Personal services.	18.8	29.7	38.5	43.0	22.3	25.2	28.6	30.3
Business services.	68.8	145.8	202.1	222.9	83.9	120.8	147.7	158.7
Auto repair, services, and garages.	21.1	33.2	40.5	43.6	24.8	28.7	28.3	28.8
Miscellaneous repair services.	9.2	12.4	15.6	16.9	10.6	10.7	11.7	12.2
Motion pictures	5.0	9.0	13.5	14.7	5.7	7.5	9.5	9.8
Amusement and recreation services	12.4	19.9	27.4	29.8	13.4	17.5	21.8	22.8
Health services	108.1	184.6	250.3	273.3	133.8	148.6	161.1	164.4
Legal services	23.3	46.3	68.7	75.2	30.6	33.5	40.6	41.8
Educational services.	16.0	25.8	32.5	35.5	18.9	22.1	23.3	24.1
Social services, membership organizations	26.3	38.3	51.2	56.0	30.2	33.3	39.0	40.9
Miscellaneous professional services	39.6	63.6	93.9	104.9	47.0	56.0	71.3	76.4
Private households.	6.6	9.0	9.7	10.3	7.4	8.8	9.2	9.5

Source: U.S. Bureau of Economic Analysis, *Survey of Current Business*, January and April 1991.

No. 1299. Retail Trade—Summary: 1958 to 1987

[1972 through 1982 based on 1972 Standard Industrial Classification (SIC) code; 1987 based on 1987 SIC code. Prior years based on earlier editions of SIC. Comparability of data over time is affected by changes in the SIC code. See also *Historical Statistics, Colonial Times to 1970*, series T 43-47 and T 79-91]

ITEM	Unit	1958	1963	1967	1972	1977	1982	1987
Firms, total [1] . . . . [1] [2]	1,000	(NA)	1,532	1,577	1,665	1,567	1,573	1,992
Multiunit establishments [1] [2]	1,000	[3]183	220	220	301	343	415	498
Establishments, total [1].	1,000	1,795	1,708	1,763	1,780	1,855	1,923	2,420
With payroll	1,000	1,185	1,206	1,192	1,265	1,304	1,324	1,504
With sales of $1,000,000 or more.	1,000	(NA)	(NA)	(NA)	74	119	193	259
Consumer Price Index: [4]								
All items.	1982-84 = 100. .	28.9	30.6	33.4	41.8	60.6	96.5	113.6
All commodities.	1982-84 = 100. .	33.3	34.4	36.8	44.5	64.2	97.0	107.7
Sales	Bil. dol.	200	244	310	457	723	1,066	1,540
By establishments with payroll	Bil. dol.	188	233	295	440	700	1,039	1,493
By multiunit establishments [2]	Bil. dol.	[3]67	90	124	202	341	567	844
Percent of total sales	Percent	33.5	36.6	39.8	44.0	47.1	53.2	56.5
Percent of multiunit sales by 100-or-more establishment multiunits [2] [5]	Percent	42.4	43.1	46.7	55.8	55.8	54.5	54.6
In 1982 dollars [6]	Bil. dol.	(NA)	645	764	943	1,054	1,066	1,393
Percent of sales by corporations	Percent	53.0	61.9	67.4	76.4	79.8	84.6	88.9
Per capita sales: [7]								
Current dollars	Dollars	1,156	1,296	1,571	2,186	3,291	4,599	6,328
Constant (1982) dollars [6]	Dollars	(NA)	3,423	3,869	4,508	4,798	4,599	5,722
Sales as percent of personal income	Percent	[3]55.5	52.4	49.3	48.1	46.9	41.5	40.9
Sales, inside metropolitan areas [8]	Bil. dol.	[3]133	170	221	(NA)	552	845	[9]1,230
Percent of total sales	Percent	66.4	69.5	71.4	(NA)	76.3	79.3	[8]82.4
Payroll, entire year	Bil. dol.	21.7	27.6	36.2	55.4	85.9	123.6	177.5
Percent of sales	Percent	[3]11.5	11.3	11.7	12.1	11.9	11.6	11.5
Paid employees, March 12 pay period [10].	1,000	7,942	8,410	9,381	11,211	13,040	14,468	17,780

NA Not available. [1] Through 1982, represents the number of establishments and firms in business at the end of the year. For 1987, represents the number of establishments and firms in business at any time during year. [2] Establishments operated by firms which operate at two or more locations. Beginning 1982, includes single units operated by multiunit establishments. 1972 and 1977 data revised since originally published. [3] Excludes Alaska and Hawaii. [4] Source: U.S. Bureau of Labor Statistics, *Monthly Labor Review*. Beginning 1982, CPI-U annual averages, see text, section 14. [5] Prior to 1982, data provided for percent of multiunit sales by 101-or-more establishment units. [6] Based on implicit price deflators for retail sales supplied by U.S. Bureau of Economic Analysis. [7] Based on estimated resident population as of July 1. [8] Through 1982 based on Standard Metropolitan Statistical Area definitions. Data for 1987 based on Metropolitan Statistical Area definitions. See Appendix II. [9] Covers only establishments with payroll. [10] 1958 and 1963 data for week including November 15.

Source: Except as noted, U.S. Bureau of the Census, *U.S. Census of Business: 1958*, vol. I; *1963*, vol. I; *1967*, vol. I; and *Census of Retail Trade, 1972*, RC72-S-1; *1977*, RC77-52; *1982*, RC82-A-52 and RC82-I-1; and *1987*, RC87-A-52, RC87-N-1, and RC87-S-1.

No. 1300. Retail Trade—Establishments, Employees, and Payroll: 1988 to 1990

[Excludes government employees, railroad employees, self-employed persons, etc. For statement on methodology, see Appendix III]

1987 SIC code [1]	KIND OF BUSINESS	ESTABLISHMENTS (1,000)			EMPLOYEES (1,000)		PAYROLL (bil. dol.)	
		1988	1989	1990	1989	1990	1989	1990
(G)	**Retail trade, total**	**1,472.9**	**1,495.0**	**1,529.7**	**19,335**	**19,815**	**228.6**	**241.7**
52	Building materials and garden supplies [2] . . .	71.4	71.2	71.9	698	703	11.4	11.9
521	Lumber and other building materials.	27.1	27.0	27.5	402	403	7.3	7.5
523	Paint, glass, and wallpaper stores	10.2	10.0	10.2	54	54	0.9	0.9
525	Hardware stores.	19.1	19.3	19.0	142	143	1.8	1.9
526	Retail nurseries and garden stores.	10.4	9.9	10.1	72	76	1.0	1.0
53	General merchandise stores [2]	35.1	35.8	36.6	2,082	2,135	21.9	22.9
531	Department stores	10.0	10.1	10.1	1,675	1,710	17.7	18.3
533	Variety stores.	10.2	10.1	10.0	116	109	1.0	1.0
539	Misc. general merchandise stores	14.6	14.8	15.0	288	310	3.2	3.6
54	Food stores [2]	183.2	183.9	186.1	3,012	3,124	33.6	35.8
541	Grocery stores	132.3	132.8	132.5	2,661	2,757	30.5	32.4
542	Meat and fish markets.	10.3	9.7	9.3	55	54	0.6	0.6
546	Retail bakeries.	20.4	20.1	19.9	175	176	1.5	1.5
55	Automotive dealers and service stations [2] . .	208.3	208.2	207.3	2,129	2,104	39.4	40.0
551	New and used car dealers	27.4	26.7	26.1	960	917	24.1	23.9
552	Used car dealers	13.8	14.8	14.3	57	56	1.0	1.0
553	Auto and home supply stores	44.2	44.2	43.4	298	305	4.9	5.1
554	Gasoline service stations	108.1	105.8	104.8	699	701	7.3	7.5
56	Apparel and accessory stores [2]	148.3	147.5	150.2	1,168	1,193	11.5	12.2
561	Men's and boys' clothing stores	15.4	15.0	14.7	113	108	1.5	1.5
562	Women's clothing stores	52.8	50.1	50.2	434	439	3.8	4.0
563	Women's accessory and specialty stores .	7.1	7.2	7.7	40	46	0.4	0.5
565	Family clothing stores	17.8	17.3	17.8	269	283	2.7	3.0
566	Shoe stores.	38.5	38.4	37.4	213	206	2.1	2.2
569	Misc. apparel and accessory stores	8.1	8.2	9.1	44	47	0.5	0.5
57	Furniture and homefurnishings stores [2] . .	105.0	104.6	108.1	734	749	11.8	12.3
571	Furniture and homefurnishings stores [2]. . .	61.4	60.4	61.1	432	430	7.1	7.2
5712	Furniture stores.	31.3	31.0	30.8	248	245	4.3	4.3
5713	Floor covering stores	13.0	12.7	13.2	77	77	1.5	1.5
5719	Misc. homefurnishings stores.	13.4	13.0	13.3	90	92	1.1	1.1
572	Household appliance stores . . . . [2]. .	10.4	9.8	10.0	63	63	1.1	1.1
573	Radio, television, and computer stores [2] . .	32.3	32.5	34.2	233	245	3.5	3.9
5731	Radio, TV, and electronic stores.	17.8	16.4	16.5	120	120	2.0	2.1
5734	Computer and software stores	3.8	4.2	5.1	28	33	0.6	0.8
5735	Record and prerecorded tape stores. . .	6.3	6.4	7.1	55	60	0.5	0.6
58	Eating and drinking places [2]	378.5	391.5	402.6	6,288	6,461	46.1	49.6
5812	Eating places.	317.8	303.4	286.8	5,803	5,700	42.3	43.8
5813	Drinking places.	52.5	47.2	43.8	276	267	2.0	2.0
59	Miscellaneous retail [2]	326.6	334.7	349.0	2,386	2,487	30.7	33.2
591	Drug stores and proprietary stores.	50.8	50.6	50.0	588	593	7.6	8.3
592	Liquor stores	31.9	31.7	30.8	144	141	1.5	1.6
593	Used merchandise stores.	13.9	13.8	15.0	73	79	0.8	0.9
5941	Sporting goods and bicycle shops	20.6	20.8	21.4	133	139	1.5	1.6
5942	Book stores.	10.6	11.5	11.7	78	86	0.7	0.8
5944	Jewelry stores	27.0	27.4	26.6	159	161	2.3	2.3
5945	Hobby, toy, and game shops	9.2	9.0	9.4	83	83	0.8	0.8
5947	Gift, novelty, and souvenir shops.	30.2	28.8	29.5	159	164	1.3	1.4
5949	Sewing, needlework, and piece goods . . .	8.8	8.4	8.2	63	68	0.5	0.5
5961	Catalog and mail-order houses	6.9	6.9	7.2	137	141	2.4	2.6
5962	Merchandising machine operators	5.0	4.9	5.1	78	76	1.3	1.3
5963	Direct selling establishments.	9.3	8.9	8.8	107	107	1.6	1.7
598	Fuel dealers.	12.4	12.0	12.0	99	100	2.1	2.2
5992	Florists.	25.3	25.9	25.8	129	131	1.2	1.2
5995	Optical goods stores.	13.7	13.4	13.2	69	66	1.0	1.1
(X)	Administrative and auxiliary	16.4	17.6	18.0	838	860	22.2	23.7

X Not applicable.   [1] Based on 1987 Standard Industrial Classification; see text, section 13.   [2] Includes kinds of business not shown separately.

Source: U.S. Bureau of the Census, *County Business Patterns*, annual.

No. 1301. Retail Trade Establishments—Number, Sales, Payroll, and Employees, by Kind of Business: 1987

[Each kind-of-business classification includes leased departments classified in that kind of business as if they were separate establishments. See *Historical Statistics, Colonial Times to 1970*, series T 79-196 for similar but not comparable data]

1987 SIC code [1]	KIND OF BUSINESS	ALL ESTABLISHMENTS		ESTABLISHMENTS WITH PAYROLL				
		Num-ber [2] (1,000)	Sales (mil. dol.)	Num-ber [2] (1,000)	Sales Total (mil. dol.)	Sales Per estab-lish-ment ($1,000)	Annual payroll (mil. dol.)	Paid employ-ees [3] (1,000)
	Retail trade, total..........	[4]2,420	[4]1,540,263	1,504	1,493,309	993	177,548	17,780
52	Building materials & garden supplies. .	107	83,454	74	81,487	1,104	9,760	668
521, 3	Building materials, supply stores . . .	51	61,302	38	60,525	1,593	6,929	432
525	Hardware stores	27	11,036	20	10,535	525	1,564	138
526	Retail nurseries and garden stores .	21	5,809	11	5,411	506	822	71
527	Mobile home dealers	8	5,307	5	5,015	993	445	27
53	General merchandise stores	57	181,971	35	181,147	5,112	19,586	2,003
531	Department stores (incl. leased depts.) [5][6]	10	153,679	10	153,679	15,305	(NA)	(NA)
531	Department stores (excl. leased depts.) [5][6]	10	144,017	10	144,017	14,343	16,365	1,651
533	Variety stores	21	7,134	10	6,762	649	926	121
539	Misc. general merchandise stores . .	26	30,819	15	30,368	2,029	2,294	231
54	Food stores [7]	290	309,460	191	301,847	1,583	29,819	2,855
541	Grocery stores	197	290,979	138	285,481	2,075	27,084	2,502
542	Meat and fish markets.	(NA)	(NA)	11	5,616	494	606	59
546	Retail bakeries.	31	5,194	22	4,871	224	1,353	185
543	Fruit and vegetable markets.	(NA)	(NA)	3	1,802	551	186	20
544	Candy, nut, confectionery stores . . .	(NA)	(NA)	6	1,182	193	199	31
55 ex. 554	Automotive dealers [7]	194	342,896	103	333,420	3,246	28,688	1,373
551	New and used car dealers	28	280,529	28	280,529	9,906	22,205	940
552	Used car dealers	75	18,295	15	10,849	726	809	55
553	Auto and home supply stores.	67	26,622	46	25,460	551	4,152	286
555	Boat dealers	(NA)	(NA)	5	6,824	1,319	620	35
556	Recreational vehicle dealers	(NA)	(NA)	3	5,538	1,842	437	25
557	Motorcycle dealers	(NA)	(NA)	4	3,475	828	382	27
554	Gasoline service stations	137	104,769	115	101,997	889	6,414	702
56	Apparel and accessory stores [7]	197	79,322	149	77,391	518	9,725	1,121
561	Men's and boys' clothing stores . . .	19	9,017	17	8,869	537	1,361	115
562, 3	Women's clothing, specialty stores . .	77	29,208	60	28,531	477	3,519	455
562	Women's clothing stores	64	26,366	52	25,868	495	3,150	419
565	Family clothing stores	27	21,472	18	21,117	1,145	2,362	268
566	Shoe stores	43	14,594	39	14,411	365	1,880	205
564	Children's and infants' wear stores .	(NA)	(NA)	6	2,101	342	245	37
57	Furniture and homefurnishings stores .	180	78,072	110	74,783	682	9,904	703
5712	Furniture stores	46	26,740	33	25,997	793	3,828	247
5713, 4, 9	Homefurnishings stores.	63	17,737	32	16,374	512	2,389	176
572	Household appliance stores	17	8,642	11	8,332	744	953	65
573	Radio, television, computer stores. .	54	24,953	34	24,080	714	2,734	215
5734	Computer and software stores. . .	8	2,799	4	2,651	687	325	22
58	Eating and drinking places	490	153,462	391	148,776	380	38,582	6,100
5812	Eating places [7]	402	142,627	333	139,282	419	36,633	5,787
5812 pt.	Restaurants and lunchrooms. . . .	(NA)	(NA)	155	66,364	429	18,796	2,822
5812 pt.	Refreshment places.	(NA)	(NA)	138	56,870	412	13,269	2,352
5813	Drinking places	88	10,834	59	9,495	162	1,950	313
591	Drug stores and proprietary stores . . .	56	54,142	52	53,824	1,031	6,476	574
59 ex. 591	Miscellaneous retail stores [7]	[4]710	[4]152,716	284	138,636	489	18,594	1,682
592	Liquor stores.	45	19,826	35	18,597	528	1,454	157
593	Used merchandise stores	89	5,217	15	3,502	236	663	69
594	Misc. shopping goods stores [7]	263	53,777	123	49,460	403	6,481	706
5941	Sporting goods, bicycle shops . . .	50	11,256	22	10,077	467	1,218	121
5942	Book stores	19	5,338	11	5,116	462	581	72
5943	Stationery stores	7	1,942	5	1,814	376	287	27
5944	Jewelry stores	50	12,925	28	11,994	428	1,921	163
5945	Hobby, toy, and game shops. . . .	28	7,451	10	7,031	730	614	76
5946	Camera, photo supply stores. . . .	6	2,383	4	2,294	605	276	21
5947	Gift, novelty, souvenir shops	79	8,446	32	7,459	231	1,055	151
5949	Sewing, needlework, and piece goods	22	3,138	10	2,836	294	406	65
596	Nonstore retailers.	[4]66	[4]34,878	23	33,894	1,470	4,523	318
5961	Catalog and mail-order houses . .	31	20,765	7	20,347	2,815	1,932	123
5962	Merchandising machine operators	24	6,258	5	5,692	1,074	1,090	74
5963	Direct selling establishments	[4]11	[4]7,855	11	7,855	746	1,501	121
598	Fuel dealers	17	14,503	13	14,198	1,114	1,824	99
5992	Florists.	50	5,441	27	4,810	180	1,019	125
5995	Optical goods stores	15	3,480	14	3,415	251	811	54

NA Not available. [1] Based on 1987 Standard Industrial Classification; see text, section 13. [2] Represents the number of establishments in business at any time during year. [3] For pay period including March 12. [4] Excludes nonemployer direct sellers, SIC 5963. [5] Includes sales from catalog order desks. [6] Establishments defined as department stores with 50 employees or more. [7] Includes other kinds of businesses, not shown separately.
Source: U.S. Bureau of the Census, *1987 Census of Retail Trade*, RC87-A-52 and RC87-N-1.

No. 1302. Retail Trade Sales—Summary: 1970 to 1992

[Sales and inventories for leased departments and concessions are tabulated in the kind-of-business category of the leased department or concession. Based on Current Business Survey, see Appendix III. Minus sign (-) indicates decrease. See also *Historical Statistics, Colonial Times to 1970*, series T 245, 246, and 255]

| YEAR | CURRENT DOLLARS | | | | | | | CONSTANT (1987) DOLLARS [4] | | |
| | Total sales (bil. dol.) | Annual percent change [1] | Per capita [2] (dol.) | Index of sales (1982= 100) | Durable goods (bil. dol.) | Nondurable goods (bil. dol.) | | Total sales (bil. dol.) | Annual percent change [1] | Per capita [2] (dol.) |
						Total	Dept. stores [3]			
1970	375	6.4	1,839	35.1	115	260	36	908	(NA)	4,449
1971	414	10.4	2,002	38.7	135	279	41	964	6.3	4,663
1972	459	10.7	2,191	42.9	156	302	45	1,041	8.0	4,976
1973	512	11.6	2,422	47.9	177	335	49	1,095	5.1	5,181
1974	542	5.9	2,541	50.7	173	369	52	1,040	-5.0	4,876
1975	588	8.5	2,730	55.0	186	402	56	1,046	0.5	4,853
1976	656	11.6	3,017	61.4	220	436	62	1,112	6.3	5,111
1977	723	10.1	3,288	67.6	249	473	69	1,166	4.8	5,305
1978	804	11.3	3,621	75.2	281	523	76	1,221	4.7	5,497
1979	897	11.5	3,993	83.9	308	589	81	1,241	1.6	5,524
1980	957	6.7	4,213	89.5	299	658	86	1,193	-3.8	5,252
1981	1,039	8.5	4,527	97.1	325	714	96	1,201	0.6	5,232
1982	1,069	3.0	4,616	100.0	336	733	100	1,189	-1.0	5,130
1983	1,170	9.4	5,005	109.4	391	779	109	1,272	7.0	5,440
1984	1,287	10.0	5,457	120.3	454	832	121	1,360	6.9	5,767
1985	1,375	6.8	5,779	128.6	498	877	126	1,420	4.4	5,969
1986	1,450	5.4	6,037	135.6	541	909	135	1,498	5.5	6,240
1987	1,541	6.3	6,361	144.1	576	965	144	1,539	2.7	6,351
1988	1,658	7.5	6,780	155.0	630	1,028	152	1,599	3.9	6,543
1989	1,762	6.3	7,140	164.8	658	1,104	161	1,642	2.7	6,653
1990	1,850	5.0	7,417	173.0	671	1,179	166	1,654	0.7	6,632
1991	1,865	0.8	7,398	174.4	654	1,212	174	1,620	-2.0	6,426
1992	1,962	5.2	7,693	183.5	705	1,257	188	1,671	3.1	6,551

NA Not available. [1] Change from immediate prior year. [2] Based on Bureau of the Census estimates of resident population as of July 1. [3] Excludes leased departments. [4] Source: U.S. Bureau of Economic Analysis, *Survey of Current Business*, monthly; and unpublished data.

No. 1303. Retail Trade—Sales, by Kind of Business: 1980 to 1992

[In billions of dollars. See headnote, table 1302. Based on Current Business Survey, see Appendix III. See also *Historical Statistics, Colonial Times to 1970*, series T 245-271]

1987 SIC code [1]	KIND OF BUSINESS	1980	1985	1987	1988	1989	1990	1991	1992
	Retail trade, total	957.4	1,375.0	1,541.3	1,657.6	1,762.2	1,849.8	1,865.5	1,962.4
	Durable goods stores, total [2]	299.2	498.1	575.9	629.6	658.5	671.0	653.9	705.1
55 exc. 554	Automotive dealers	164.1	303.2	342.9	371.7	384.1	384.6	368.9	398.1
551,2,5,6,7,9	Motor vehicle, misc. automotive dealers [2]	146.2	278.0	316.3	341.4	352.5	350.4	334.6	363.8
551,2	Motor vehicle dealers	137.7	263.1	298.8	323.1	333.7	332.3	316.8	344.3
551	Motor vehicle dealers, franchised	130.5	251.6	280.5	302.1	309.2	312.1	296.5	320.0
553	Auto and home supply stores	18.0	25.2	26.6	30.3	31.7	34.2	34.3	34.3
52	Building materials, hardware, garden supply, mobile home dealers [2]	50.8	71.2	83.5	91.8	94.1	97.4	95.2	103.0
521,3	Building materials, supply stores	35.0	50.8	61.3	67.1	68.0	71.3	69.5	74.5
525	Hardware stores	8.3	10.5	11.0	11.8	12.5	12.4	11.9	12.8
57	Furniture, homefurnishings, equipment [2]	44.2	68.3	78.1	86.7	94.2	96.3	98.6	105.8
571	Furniture, homefurnishings stores	26.3	38.3	44.5	47.9	51.8	51.5	50.8	54.7
5722,31,34	Household appliance, radio, TV, and computer stores	14.0	25.1	27.1	31.5	34.7	36.3	38.5	41.0
	Nondurable goods stores, total [2]	658.1	876.9	965.4	1,028.0	1,103.7	1,178.8	1,211.6	1,257.3
56	Apparel and accessory stores [2]	49.3	70.2	79.3	85.3	92.4	95.8	97.5	105.0
561	Men's, boys' clothing, furnishings	7.7	8.5	9.0	9.5	9.8	9.4	9.0	9.1
562,3	Women's clothing specialty stores	17.6	26.1	29.2	31.1	33.4	34.7	35.4	38.2
562	Women's ready-to-wear stores	15.9	23.6	26.4	27.9	30.1	31.5	32.2	34.8
565	Family clothing stores	10.8	17.8	21.5	23.6	25.8	27.4	29.1	33.1
566	Shoe stores	10.5	13.1	14.6	15.5	17.3	18.1	17.6	17.7
591	Drug and proprietary stores	31.0	47.0	54.1	57.9	63.5	70.8	75.9	77.3
58	Eating and drinking places	90.1	127.9	153.5	168.2	178.3	191.0	196.9	201.9
5812	Eating places	80.4	117.6	142.6	157.2	167.5	179.2	184.6	190.6
54	Food stores	220.2	285.1	309.5	325.9	348.0	369.8	376.9	384.0
541	Grocery stores	205.6	269.5	291.0	307.3	328.4	348.8	355.3	360.8
554	Gasoline service stations	94.1	113.3	104.8	109.7	121.5	136.2	134.1	133.0
53	General merchandise group stores	109.0	158.6	182.0	192.7	206.9	216.5	228.5	247.4
531	Department stores [3]	85.5	126.4	144.0	151.6	160.8	166.2	173.5	187.7
533	Variety stores	7.8	8.5	7.1	7.1	7.2	7.2	7.1	6.7
539	Misc. gen. merchandise group stores	15.7	23.8	30.8	34.0	38.8	43.0	47.9	53.0
592	Liquor stores	16.9	19.5	19.8	20.0	20.9	22.9	24.0	25.6
596	Nonstore retailers	22.8	28.3	35.9	40.1	42.6	43.9	46.3	48.3
5961 pt.	Mail-order houses (department store merchandise)	4.3	4.7	4.1	4.1	4.0	3.7	3.7	4.1

[1] Based on 1987 Standard Industrial Classification code; see text, section 13. [2] Includes kinds of business, not shown separately. [3] Excludes leased departments.

Source of tables 1302 and 1303: Except as noted, U.S. Bureau of the Census, *Current Business Reports, Combined Annual and Revised Monthly Retail Trade, January 1983 Through December 1992*, (BR/92-RV) and prior issues.

No. 1304. Retail Trade—Sales of Multiunit Organizations, by Kind of Business: 1980 to 1992

[Data based on sales of companies which had 11 or more retail establishments according to the most recent update of multiestablishment files selected with certainty (i.e., their sales size exceeded specified dollar volume cutoffs which varied by kind of business). For details, see source. See also *Historical Statistics, Colonial Times to 1970*, series T 197-219]

1987 SIC code [1]	KIND OF BUSINESS	SALES (bil. dol.)						PERCENT OF TOTAL RETAIL SALES		
		1980	1985	1989	1990	1991	1992	1980	1990	1992
	Total	361.3	520.3	683.6	739.3	767.1	813.2	37.3	40.0	41.4
	Durable goods stores	35.2	55.1	87.9	98.9	103.0	112.4	11.4	14.7	15.9
553	Auto and home supply stores	4.7	5.9	9.2	10.7	11.2	11.9	26.2	31.3	34.7
	Nondurable goods stores [2]	326.0	465.2	595.7	640.4	664.1	700.9	49.1	54.3	55.7
56	Apparel and accessory stores [2]	21.1	35.9	53.4	58.0	61.1	66.3	42.7	60.5	63.1
562,3	Women's clothing specialty stores, furriers	8.3	13.6	19.1	20.6	21.9	23.6	47.1	59.4	61.8
566	Shoe stores	5.3	7.7	11.1	11.9	11.6	11.9	50.8	65.7	67.2
591	Drug and proprietary stores	16.8	27.9	37.8	42.8	46.0	47.8	54.3	60.5	61.8
54	Food stores	119.8	162.5	201.5	217.7	224.5	228.4	54.4	58.9	59.5
541	Grocery stores	118.1	160.2	198.6	214.4	220.9	224.6	57.4	61.5	62.3
53	General merchandise group	101.6	151.4	197.1	206.3	216.4	235.0	90.6	95.3	95.0
531	Department stores	83.2	124.0	157.4	163.2	170.7	184.9	96.1	98.2	98.5
533	Variety stores	6.3	7.0	5.2	4.8	4.5	4.6	80.9	66.7	68.7
539	Misc. general merchandise stores	12.1	20.4	34.5	38.2	41.2	45.5	58.1	88.8	85.8
5812	Eating places	22.6	33.8	44.1	45.9	45.6	48.1	28.1	25.6	25.2

[1] Based on 1987 Standard Industrial Classification code; see text, section 13.   [2] Includes kinds of business not shown separately.

Source: U.S. Bureau of the Census, *Current Business Reports, Combined Annual and Revised Monthly Retail Trade, January 1983 Through December 1992* (BR/92-RV); and unpublished data.

No. 1305. Retail Trade—Merchandise Inventories and Sales-Inventory Ratios, by Kind of Business: 1985 to 1992

[As of Dec. 31. Includes warehouses. See headnote, table 1302]

1987 SIC code [1]	KIND OF BUSINESS	INVENTORIES AT COST [2] (bil. dol.)				SALES-INVENTORY RATIOS [3]			
		1985	1990	1991	1992	1985	1990	1991	1992
	Total	176.9	238.0	242.2	253.6	7.8	7.8	7.7	7.7
	Excluding automotive group	130.5	173.1	179.8	187.1	8.2	8.5	8.3	8.4
	Durable goods stores [4]	87.6	122.5	121.0	130.5	5.7	5.5	5.4	5.4
55 exc. 554	Automotive dealers	46.4	64.8	62.3	66.5	6.5	5.9	5.9	6.0
52	Building materials, hardware, garden supply, mobile home dealers	13.1	16.9	16.9	18.4	5.5	5.8	5.6	5.6
57	Furniture, homefurnishings, equipment stores	13.7	18.1	18.7	20.5	5.0	5.3	5.3	5.2
	Nondurable goods stores [4]	89.3	115.4	121.2	123.1	9.8	10.2	10.0	10.2
56	Apparel and accessory stores	14.6	17.9	18.4	19.7	4.8	5.4	5.3	5.3
54	Food stores	19.5	25.8	26.6	26.7	14.6	14.3	14.2	14.4
53	General merchandise group stores	31.5	39.0	42.3	45.2	5.0	5.5	5.4	5.5
531	Department stores	23.0	30.8	33.4	35.6	5.4	5.4	5.2	5.3

[1] Based on 1987 Standard Industrial Classification code; see text, section 13.   [2] Excludes supplies and equipment used in store and warehouse operations that are not for resale. Not adjusted for seasonal variation.   [3] Relates annual sales to yearend inventories.   [4] Includes kinds of business not shown separately.

Source: U.S. Bureau of the Census, *Current Business Reports, Combined Annual and Revised Monthly Retail Trade, January 1983 Through December 1992* (BR/92-RV).

No. 1306. Retail Foodstores—Number and Sales, by Type: 1980 to 1991

TYPE OF FOODSTORE	NUMBER [1] (1,000)					SALES [2] (bil. dol.)					PERCENT DISTRIBUTION			
											Number		Sales	
	1980	1985	1989	1990	1991	1980	1985	1989	1990	1991	1980	1991	1980	1991
Total	253.4	255.9	254.4	253.0	251.7	220.2	285.1	348.0	369.8	376.9	100.0	100.0	100.0	100.0
Grocery stores [3]	178.3	177.2	172.3	170.1	168.0	205.6	269.5	328.4	348.7	355.3	70.4	66.7	93.4	94.3
Supermarkets [3]	26.3	26.2	24.1	23.8	23.7	157.0	201.8	247.3	260.1	268.9	10.4	9.4	71.3	71.3
Convenience stores [4]	35.8	45.4	52.0	51.7	50.7	18.9	33.7	43.9	46.5	47.3	14.1	20.1	8.6	12.5
Superette [5]	116.2	105.6	96.2	94.6	93.6	29.7	34.0	37.1	42.1	39.1	45.9	37.2	13.5	10.4
Specialized food stores [6]	75.0	78.7	82.1	83.0	83.7	14.6	15.5	19.6	21.1	21.6	29.6	33.3	6.6	5.7

[1] Estimated.   [2] Includes nonfood items.   [3] A grocery store, primarily self-service in operation, providing a full range of departments, and having at least $2.5 million in annual sales in 1985 dollars.   [4] A small grocery store selling a limited variety of food and nonfood products, typically open extended hours.   [5] A grocery store, primarily self-service in operation, selling a wide variety of food and nonfood products with annual sales below $2.5 million (1985 dollars).   [6] Primarily engaged in the retail sale of a single food category such as meat and seafood stores and retail bakeries.

Source: U.S. Dept. of Agriculture, Economic Research Service, *Food Marketing Review*, annual.

No. 1307. Supermarkets—Number and Sales, by Type of Format: 1980 to 1991

[For definition of supermarket, see footnote 3, table 1306]

SUPERMARKET FORMAT	NUMBER				SALES (bil. dol.)			PERCENT DISTRIBUTION			
								Number		Sales	
	1980	1985	1990	1991	1980	1990	1991	1980	1991	1980	1991
Supermarkets, total	26,321	26,229	23,813	23,722	157.0	260.1	268.9	100	100	100	100
Conventional.	21,009	16,568	12,550	11,647	114.7	90.7	81.8	80	49	73	30
Superstore [1]	3,150	4,854	5,810	5,900	27.8	87.6	91.1	12	25	18	34
Warehouse [2]	1,670	3,483	3,381	3,475	6.6	33.1	35.3	6	15	4	13
Combination food and drug [3] . . .	475	1,047	1,619	2,115	6.3	34.8	46.0	2	9	4	17
Superwarehouse [4]	7	207	333	465	1.6	12.6	13.8	(Z)	2	1	5
Hypermarket [5]	10	70	120	120	(NA)	1.3	0.9	(Z)	1	(NA)	(Z)

NA Not available.   Z Less than 0.5 percent.   [1] Contains greater variety of products than conventional supermarkets, including specialty and service departments, and considerable nonfood (general merchandise) products.   [2] Contains limited product variety and fewer services provided, incorporating case lot stocking and shelving practices.   [3] Contains a pharmacy, a nonprescription drug department, and a greater variety of health and beauty aids than that carried by conventional supermarkets.   [4] A larger warehouse store that offers expanded product variety and often service meat, deli, or seafood departments.   [5] A very large store offering a greater variety of general merchandise—like clothes, hardware, and seasonal goods—and personal care products than other grocery stores.

Source: U.S. Dept. of Agriculture, Economic Research Service, *Food Marketing Review*, annual.

No. 1308. Percent of Supermarkets Offering Selected Services and Product Lines: 1990 and 1992

[In percent. Based on a sample survey of chain and independent supermarkets and subject to sampling variability; for details, see source]

SERVICE OR PRODUCT LINE OFFERED	TOTAL		CHAINS		INDEPENDENTS	
	1990	1992	1990	1992	1990	1992
Service delicatessen	73	78	76	81	69	75
Service bakery	60	60	66	65	53	52
Hot takeout food	55	55	59	58	49	50
Chilled prepared food	50	48	55	53	42	41
Service meat	42	48	45	50	37	46
Self-service delicatessen	38	46	38	49	39	42
Service fish	33	41	43	53	20	24
Separate cheese department	33	33	43	44	19	18
Salad bar	18	22	22	29	13	12
Organic products	13	17	18	22	7	9
Plastic grocery bags	88	90	94	96	79	83
Reusable grocery bags	58	63	68	68	44	57
Carryout services	82	83	81	80	84	86
Scanning checkouts	71	81	79	90	61	70
Automated teller machines (ATM's)	20	28	28	38	10	15
Accept credit cards.	19	39	23	45	13	31
Pharmacy	15	18	22	26	6	7

Source: Maclean Hunter Media Inc., Stamford, CT, *Progressive Grocer, Annual Report of the Grocery Industry* (copyright).

No. 1309. Supermarket Shopping—Selected Characteristics: 1990 and 1992

[Based on a sample survey of 500 households and subject to sampling variability; for details, see source]

TYPE OF OUTLET	PERCENT OF HOUSEHOLDS SHOPPING AT OUTLET		AVERAGE NUMBER OF WEEKLY TRIPS		AVERAGE WEEKLY SPENDING (dollars)		NUMBER OF SUPER- MARKETS SHOPPED IN EACH WEEK	PERCENT DISTRIBUTION	
	1990	1992	1990	1992	1990	1992		1990	1992
Supermarket	100	100	2.3	2.1	72.65	68.04	Total	100	100
Convenience store	41	43	2.3	2.9	12.86	12.79	One.	31	27
Fast-food restaurant	67	63	1.9	2.0	16.17	13.49	Two.	45	46
Mass merchandiser	64	67	1.4	1.5	26.25	25.64	Three	20	22
Wholesale clubs.	(NA)	27	(NA)	2.0	(NA)	75.99	Four or more . . .	4	5

NA Not available.

Source: Maclean Hunter Media Inc., Stamford, CT, *Progressive Grocer, Annual Report of the Grocery Industry* (copyright).

No. 1310. Commercial and Institutional Groups—Food and Drink Sales: 1980 to 1993

[Excludes military. Data refer to sales to consumers of food and alcoholic beverages. Sales are estimated. For details, see source]

TYPE OF GROUP	Number, 1991	SALES (mil. dol.)							
		1980	1985	1988	1989	1990	1991	1992 [1]	1993 [1]
Total	729,364	119,004	172,787	212,859	225,644	237,700	245,418	253,769	266,009
Commercial foodservice [2][3]	553,739	101,529	151,762	189,289	200,583	211,083	217,983	225,454	236,495
Eating places [2]	344,061	72,276	111,657	138,542	146,716	154,227	159,272	165,341	173,590
Restaurants, lunchrooms	165,111	39,307	57,939	69,356	72,727	76,072	78,355	80,313	83,526
Limited menu restaurants [4]	152,936	28,699	47,477	61,397	65,775	69,458	71,889	75,627	80,241
Bars and taverns [5]	37,227	7,785	8,338	8,899	8,952	9,212	9,442	9,169	9,269
Food contractors [2]	15,739	6,818	9,460	12,071	13,198	14,149	14,829	15,494	16,376
Manufacturing and industrial plants. .	(NA)	2,121	2,721	3,356	3,669	3,856	3,918	4,021	4,241
Colleges and universities	(NA)	1,140	1,738	2,284	2,569	2,788	3,072	3,195	3,345
Lodging places [2]	27,364	6,768	10,557	12,933	13,606	14,272	14,601	15,170	15,974
Hotel restaurants.	17,028	4,964	8,986	11,533	12,215	12,907	13,281	13,856	14,645
Motel restaurants.	8,628	1,151	975	850	836	820	790	779	785
Retail hosts [2][6]	109,007	3,264	5,254	8,605	9,276	9,888	10,380	10,607	11,151
Department store restaurants	4,980	857	865	875	925	950	980	(NA)	(NA)
Grocery store restaurants [6]	44,966	830	2,074	4,979	5,379	5,733	6,013	(NA)	(NA)
Gasoline service stations	34,788	492	1,052	1,381	1,523	1,681	1,824	(NA)	(NA)
Recreation and sports.	14,447	1,452	1,972	2,546	2,787	2,916	2,949	3,045	3,189
Institutional foodservice [2]	175,625	17,475	21,025	23,570	25,061	26,617	27,436	28,314	29,514
Employee foodservice.	7,636	1,635	1,971	1,985	1,994	1,985	1,913	1,876	1,895
Industrial, commercial organizations .	3,012	1,377	1,682	1,658	1,641	1,603	1,535	(NA)	(NA)
Educational foodservice	96,356	4,610	5,978	6,883	7,237	7,671	8,223	8,353	8,664
Elementary and secondary schools .	93,535	2,312	2,919	3,347	3,478	3,700	3,878	3,984	4,129
Hospitals	6,606	6,668	7,104	7,826	8,396	8,968	9,018	9,643	10,067
Miscellaneous [2]	31,568	1,521	2,077	2,489	2,677	2,845	2,993	3,041	3,227
Clubs	10,310	1,056	1,537	1,809	1,914	1,993	2,039	(NA)	(NA)

NA Not available. [1] Projection. [2] Includes other types of groups, not shown separately. [3] Data for establishments with payroll. [4] Fast-food restaurants. [5] For establishments serving food. [6] Beginning 1988, a portion of delicatessen sales in grocery stores are considered foodservice.

Source: National Restaurant Association, Washington, DC, *Foodservice Numbers: A Statistical Digest for the Foodservice Industry*, 1992; *Foodservice Industry in Review*, annual; and *National Restaurant Association Foodservice Industry Forecast*, December 1992, (copyright).

No. 1311. Motor Vehicle Factory Sales and Retail Sales: 1980 to 1991

[**In thousands.** See also *Historical Statistics, Colonial Times to 1970*, series Q 148 and 150]

YEAR	1980	1982	1983	1984	1985	1986	1987	1988	1989	1990	1991
Factory sales, total.	8,067	6,955	9,153	10,696	11,359	10,909	10,907	11,225	10,869	9,769	8,783
Passenger cars	6,400	5,049	6,739	7,621	8,002	7,516	7,085	7,105	6,807	6,050	5,407
Trucks and buses	1,667	1,906	2,414	3,075	3,357	3,393	3,821	4,121	4,062	3,719	3,375
Retail sales, total.	11,466	10,542	12,311	14,483	15,724	16,323	15,189	15,679	14,713	14,146	12,540
Passenger cars (new), total	8,979	7,982	9,182	10,390	11,042	11,460	10,277	10,530	9,772	9,300	8,175
Domestic.	6,581	5,759	6,795	7,952	8,205	8,215	7,081	7,526	7,073	6,897	6,137
Imports	2,398	2,224	2,387	2,439	2,838	3,245	3,196	3,004	2,699	2,403	2,038
Trucks (new), total	2,487	2,560	3,129	4,093	4,682	4,863	4,912	5,149	4,941	4,846	4,365
Domestic.	2,001	2,146	2,658	3,475	3,902	3,921	4,055	4,508	4,403	4,215	3,813
Imports	486	414	471	618	780	942	857	641	538	631	551

Source: American Automobile Manufacturers Association, Detroit, MI, *AAMA Motor Vehicle Facts and Figures*, annual.

No. 1312. Franchised New Car Dealerships—Summary: 1980 to 1991

ITEM	Unit	1980	1983	1984	1985	1986	1987	1988	1989	1990	1991
Dealerships [1]	Number .	27,900	24,725	24,725	24,725	24,825	25,150	24,950	24,925	24,825	24,000
Sales	Bil. dol .	130.5	187.7	225.9	251.6	270.4	280.5	302.4	309.7	313.0	305.3
New cars.	1,000. .	8,979	9,182	10,390	11,038	11,455	10,277	10,639	9,771	9,296	8,176
Used vehicles.	1,000. .	9,717	10,630	12,410	13,360	13,540	13,260	14,600	14,610	14,180	14,190
Employment	1,000. .	745.2	722.4	794.8	856.9	896.7	926.0	960.1	959.2	926.4	886.4
Annual payroll	Bil. dol .	11.0	14.5	17.8	20.1	21.7	22.6	24.7	24.7	24.3	23.5
Advertising expenses	Bil. dol . .	1.2	1.7	2.1	2.8	3.2	3.7	4.1	3.9	3.6	3.5
Dealer pretax profits as a percentage of sales	Percent .	0.61	2.14	2.18	2.20	2.16	1.88	1.71	1.00	1.00	1.00
Inventory: [2]											
Domestic: [3]											
Total	1,000. . .	1,506	1,209	1,413	1,510	1,687	1,724	1,543	1,677	1,450	1,263
Days' supply	Days . . .	71	55	55	58	63	75	63	72	66	64
Imported: [3]											
Total	1,000. . .	458	260	216	271	392	551	626	648	597	584
Days' supply	Days . . .	55	34	26	30	37	53	62	70	74	86

[1] At beginning of year. [2] Annual average. [3] Classification based on where automobiles are produced (i.e., automobiles manufactured by foreign companies but produced in the U.S. are classified as domestic).

Source: National Automobile Dealers Association, McLean, VA, *NADA Data*, annual.

No. 1313. Domestic and International Franchising—Summary: 1980 to 1991

[Franchising is a form of marketing or distribution in which a parent company customarily grants an individual or a company the right, or privilege, to do business in a prescribed manner over a certain period of time in a specified place. The parent company is termed the franchisor; the receiver of the privilege the franchisee; and the right, or privilege, the franchise]

ITEM	Unit	1980	1983	1984	1985	1986	1987	1988	1989	1990	1991
DOMESTIC [1]											
Number of franchised establishments.	1,000 ..	442	442	444	455	462	479	481	493	521	542
Company-owned [2]	1,000 ..	85	86	87	86	88	89	94	95	97	100
Franchisee-owned	1,000 ..	357	355	357	369	374	390	387	398	424	442
Sales of products and services	Bil. dol .	336	423	492	543	569	599	648	678	714	758
Company-owned [2]	Bil. dol .	47	59	64	68	85	90	98	107	117	127
Franchisee-owned	Bil. dol .	289	364	428	475	484	509	550	570	597	631
Average sales per establishment	$1,000 .	760	958	1,108	1,193	1,231	1,251	1,348	1,376	1,370	1,399
Employment	1,000 ..	4,668	5,165	5,671	6,283	6,501	(NA)	(NA)	(NA)	(NA)	(NA)
INTERNATIONAL											
U.S. companies operating foreign outlets	Number.	279	305	328	342	354	(NA)	374	(NA)	(NA)	(NA)
Foreign outlets	1,000 ..	20.4	25.7	27.0	30.2	31.6	(NA)	35.0	(NA)	(NA)	(NA)

NA Not available. [1] Excludes foreign outlets of U.S. companies. [2] Represents establishments owned by the parent company.

Source: U.S. Dept. of Commerce, International Trade Administration, *Franchising in the Economy, 1986-88*, 1988. Beginning 1988, International Franchise Association Educational Foundation, Inc., Washington, DC, *Franchising in the Economy*, annual.

No. 1314. Domestic Franchising—Number of Establishments and Sales, by Kind of Franchised Business: 1980 to 1991

[See headnote, table 1313, for definition of franchising. Excludes foreign outlets of U.S. companies]

KIND OF FRANCHISED BUSINESS	NUMBER OF ESTABLISHMENTS (1,000)						SALES (bil. dol.)					
	1980	1985	1988	1989	1990	1991	1980	1985	1988	1989	1990	1991
All franchising, total	**442.4**	**455.2**	**480.8**	**492.5**	**521.2**	**542.5**	**336.2**	**543.0**	**648.1**	**677.9**	**713.8**	**757.8**
Auto and truck dealers [1]	29.4	27.5	27.8	26.9	26.8	26.5	143.9	282.6	345.1	351.0	345.9	354.5
Percent	6.6	6.0	5.8	5.5	5.1	4.9	42.8	52.0	53.2	51.8	48.5	46.8
Restaurants (all types)	60.0	73.9	90.3	92.0	99.3	103.3	27.9	47.7	64.3	70.1	77.9	85.5
Percent	13.6	16.2	18.8	18.7	19.1	19.0	8.3	8.8	9.9	10.3	10.9	11.3
Gasoline service stations [1]	158.5	124.6	113.2	111.5	107.5	107.0	94.5	100.8	101.9	109.4	126.6	143.2
Percent	35.8	27.4	23.5	22.6	20.6	19.7	28.1	18.6	15.7	16.1	18.0	18.9
Retailing (nonfood)	35.2	45.1	46.2	50.0	54.4	57.0	10.5	20.6	23.3	26.7	29.3	31.4
Percent	8.0	9.9	9.6	10.2	10.4	10.5	3.1	3.8	3.6	3.9	4.1	4.1
Auto, truck rental services	7.3	11.2	9.5	9.8	10.7	11.1	3.1	5.7	6.6	6.9	7.5	8.0
Automotive products and services [2]	40.2	36.5	34.7	36.2	39.2	42.2	7.1	10.7	11.4	12.5	13.9	15.5
Business aids and services	40.7	49.8	55.6	58.2	64.4	69.5	6.7	12.0	15.7	16.9	18.6	20.8
Employment services	4.4	4.8	6.5	6.6	7.5	8.3	1.6	2.7	4.7	5.0	5.7	6.4
Tax preparation services	9.2	8.1	8.3	8.2	8.3	8.5	0.3	0.4	0.6	0.7	0.7	0.7
Accounting, credit, collection, and general	2.4	2.1	1.7	1.7	1.8	1.9	0.1	0.2	0.2	0.2	0.2	0.2
Real estate [3]	17.3	13.9	15.3	15.8	16.4	18.2	3.6	4.6	5.9	6.2	6.8	7.7
Printing and copying	2.8	4.5	5.9	6.3	6.8	7.4	0.4	0.9	1.5	1.6	1.8	2.0
Other	4.8	16.4	17.9	19.5	23.6	25.3	0.8	3.1	3.0	3.4	3.5	3.8
Construction, home improvement, maintenance, and cleaning	14.3	17.5	22.0	24.1	27.4	30.6	1.5	4.1	5.3	5.8	6.5	7.1
Convenience stores	15.6	15.1	17.2	17.6	17.2	17.3	7.8	10.8	13.9	14.3	14.3	15.0
Educational products and services	3.2	8.2	11.6	11.1	12.5	13.9	0.3	0.8	1.7	1.7	2.0	2.3
Equipment rental services	2.2	2.5	3.0	2.6	2.7	2.9	0.4	0.7	0.7	0.7	0.7	0.8
Food retailing [4]	15.5	18.7	21.6	21.1	24.5	25.4	7.4	10.1	10.2	10.0	11.7	12.2
Hotels and motels [5]	6.4	7.5	9.3	10.1	11.0	11.4	9.5	14.8	19.7	21.6	23.8	26.0
Laundry, dry cleaning services	3.4	2.3	2.3	3.0	3.2	3.5	0.3	0.3	0.3	0.4	0.4	0.5
Recreation, entertainment, travel.	4.6	7.8	8.8	9.8	10.9	11.6	0.5	2.3	3.5	3.5	4.2	4.8
Soft drink bottlers [1] [6]	1.9	1.4	0.9	0.8	0.8	0.8	14.4	18.3	22.7	24.6	26.2	28.0
Miscellaneous	3.6	5.5	6.9	7.6	8.4	8.6	0.4	0.9	1.7	2.0	2.3	2.6

[1] Estimated by source on basis of Bureau of the Census and trade association data. [2] Includes some establishments with significant sales of nonautomotive products such as household appliances, garden supplies, etc. [3] Gross commissions. [4] Excludes convenience stores. [5] Includes campgrounds. [6] Includes soft drinks, fruit drinks and ades, syrups, flavoring agents and bases. Excludes independent private label and contract-filler bottling companies, which accounted for 22 percent of the value of shipments of the total industry in recent years.

Source: U.S. Dept. of Commerce, International Trade Administration, *Franchising in the Economy, 1986-88*, 1988. Beginning 1988, International Franchise Association Educational Foundation, Inc., Washington, DC, *Franchising in the Economy*, annual.

No. 1315. Shopping Centers—Number, Gross Leasable Area, and Retail Sales, by Gross Leasable Area: 1986 to 1992

[As of **December 31.** A shopping center is a group of architecturally unified commercial establishments built on a site that is planned, developed, owned, and managed as an operating unit related in its location, size, and type of shops to the trade area that the unit serves. The unit provides on-site parking in definite relationship to the types and total size of the stores. The data base attempts to include all centers with three or more stores. Estimates are based on a sample of data available on shopping center properties; for details, contact source]

YEAR	Total	GROSS LEASABLE AREA (sq. ft.)					
		Less than 100,001	100,001-200,000	200,001-400,000	400,001-800,000	800,001-1,000,000	More than 1 million
NUMBER							
1986.	28,496	18,230	6,692	2,083	918	261	312
1990.	36,515	23,231	8,756	2,781	1,102	288	357
1991.	37,975	23,997	9,226	2,953	1,141	294	364
1992.	38,966	24,578	9,467	3,086	1,170	294	371
Percent distribution	100.0	63.1	24.3	7.9	3.0	0.8	1.0
Percent change, 1991-92	2.6	2.4	2.6	4.5	2.5	-	1.9
GROSS LEASABLE AREA							
1986 (mil. sq. ft.)	3,523	901	917	555	522	234	393
1990 (mil. sq. ft.)	4,390	1,125	1,197	734	618	259	457
1991 (mil. sq. ft.)	4,564	1,162	1,258	775	639	264	466
1992 (mil. sq. ft.)	4,679	1,190	1,289	807	653	264	475
Percent distribution	100.0	25.4	27.5	17.2	14.0	5.7	10.2
Percent change, 1991-92	2.5	2.4	2.5	4.1	2.2	-	2.0
RETAIL SALES							
1986 (bil. dol.)	556.5	160.3	140.4	84.8	73.9	36.2	60.8
1990 (bil. dol.)	706.4	205.1	179.5	108.0	91.7	45.1	77.0
1991 (bil. dol.)	716.9	208.3	182.2	109.5	93.0	45.8	78.2
1992 (bil. dol.)	746.6	217.0	189.8	113.9	96.8	47.6	81.5
Percent distribution	100.0	29.1	25.4	15.3	13.0	6.4	10.9
Percent change, 1991-92	4.1	4.2	4.2	4.0	4.0	4.1	4.2

- Represents zero.

No. 1316. Shopping Centers—Number, Gross Leasable Area, and Retail Sales, by State: 1992

[Minus sign (-) indicates decrease. See headnote, table 1315]

DIVISION AND STATE	Number	Gross leasable area (mil. sq. ft.)	Retail sales (bil. dol.)	PERCENT CHANGE, 1991-92			DIVISION AND STATE	Number	Gross leasable area (mil. sq. ft.)	Retail sales (bil. dol.)	PERCENT CHANGE, 1991-92		
				Number	Gross leasable area	Retail sales per sq. ft.					Number	Gross leasable area	Retail sales per sq. ft.
U.S.	38,966	4,679	746.6	2.6	2.5	1.6	VA...	1,122	144	22.5	3.0	2.7	2.0
							WV..	154	21	2.9	0.7	0.6	1.7
N.E....	2,257	243	38.5	2.3	2.5	1.4	NC...	1,357	143	21.3	4.1	2.9	1.8
ME..	186	15	2.8	5.7	2.0	2.2	SC...	737	72	11.6	3.1	2.1	2.3
NH..	197	20	2.8	4.8	4.4	0.7	GA...	1,384	143	23.2	2.2	1.6	3.4
VT..	103	7	1.2	5.1	5.7	-1.3	FL...	2,999	378	65.7	2.1	2.4	3.0
MA..	894	100	16.4	1.4	2.6	1.1	**E.S.C**..	2,664	288	45.3	1.8	1.8	1.9
RI..	183	17	2.7	0.5	2.9	0.8	KY...	575	62	10.3	1.8	0.9	2.4
CT..	694	83	12.6	2.1	1.6	2.2	TN...	1,097	121	16.8	2.0	2.4	1.5
M.A..	3,944	553	81.1	3.4	3.0	0.3	AL...	587	67	11.7	0.7	1.1	2.6
NY..	1,512	208	32.4	3.7	2.3	0.9	MS..	405	38	6.4	2.5	2.4	1.1
NJ..	978	137	19.6	3.4	3.5	0.1	**W.S.C**..	4,321	488	93.7	0.9	1.1	3.0
PA..	1,454	208	29.0	3.0	3.3	-	AR...	332	32	5.7	0.3	0.8	2.9
							LA...	660	77	13.8	0.9	0.4	2.6
E.N.C..	5,739	740	105.2	2.5	2.3	0.8	OK...	549	57	10.2	0.5	1.1	2.2
OH..	1,515	213	30.6	3.4	2.9	0.3	TX...	2,780	322	64.0	1.0	1.3	3.2
IN...	818	108	15.9	1.9	1.3	1.8							
IL...	1,894	226	29.8	2.5	2.8	0.2	**Mt**....	2,589	309	53.0	2.4	2.5	2.3
MI...	940	123	18.4	1.5	1.5	1.6	MT...	90	9	1.5	1.1	7.9	-4.4
WI...	572	70	10.5	2.1	2.2	1.3	ID...	130	16	2.5	4.0	3.1	0.8
W.N.C..	2,305	291	47.6	1.9	2.2	1.1	WY..	53	6	1.0	3.9	3.6	-0.9
MN...	421	61	10.1	2.2	5.8	-2.0	CO..	665	86	16.1	0.8	0.9	3.4
IA...	270	35	5.5	1.5	1.8	0.8	NM...	276	26	4.8	4.5	3.9	1.0
MO...	808	100	16.7	1.8	1.4	2.1	AZ...	902	106	17.6	1.9	2.0	3.5
ND...	80	9	1.5	3.9	1.1	1.9	UT...	204	29	4.9	4.6	3.0	1.1
SD...	49	6	1.0	4.3	3.3	0.1	NV...	269	31	4.7	3.5	5.3	0.6
NE...	231	30	4.2	3.1	1.5	1.7							
KS...	446	49	8.6	0.9	0.6	2.8	**Pac**...	6,397	728	112.9	4.2	4.1	0.6
							WA..	638	84	12.6	3.1	2.0	2.4
S.A....	8,750	1,039	169.3	2.7	2.3	2.6	OR..	429	49	6.6	3.6	2.4	1.1
DE...	121	18	3.0	4.3	2.7	1.5	CA...	5,117	574	89.6	4.5	4.7	0.2
MD...	810	111	17.9	2.4	1.8	2.5	AK...	60	8	1.4	5.3	3.6	1.5
DC...	66	8	1.3	4.8	2.5	0.5	HI...	153	15	2.7	0.7	1.2	3.2

- Represents or rounds to zero.

Source of tables 1315 and 1316: National Research Bureau, 225 West Wacker Drive, Chicago, IL 60606-1229. Data for 1986 and 1991-92 published by Communication Channels Inc., Atlanta, GA, in *Shopping Center World*, February 1988 and March 1993, respectively, (copyright). Data for 1990 published by Monitor Publishing, Clearwater, FL, in *Monitor Magazine*, November/December 1991, (copyright).

No. 1317. Retail Sales—

[In millions of dollars, except as indicated. Kind-of-business classification based on

REGION, DIVISION, AND STATE	ALL STORES [1]				FOOD STORES				GENERAL MERCHANDISE STORES			
	1990, total	1991			Total		Supermarkets		Total		Department stores	
		Total	Sales per household [2]									
			Amount (dol.)	Percent change 1990-91	1990	1991	1990	1991	1990	1991	1990	1991
U.S. . . .	1,807,183	1,821,386	19,443	-0.2	362,667	370,255	340,455	347,716	211,806	217,494	167,761	173,960
Northeast .	383,482	377,542	19,852	-1.9	80,089	81,392	72,943	74,160	38,527	38,815	31,392	31,889
N.E	112,582	110,944	22,236	-1.8	23,176	22,367	21,216	20,471	10,656	10,918	8,387	8,689
ME . . .	10,399	10,092	21,309	-3.8	2,414	2,299	2,284	2,177	865	875	594	610
NH . . .	11,860	11,009	25,946	-8.6	2,532	2,314	2,413	2,206	1,250	1,213	887	875
VT . . .	4,512	4,450	20,716	-2.4	1,040	1,007	978	947	296	304	206	212
MA . . .	50,757	52,090	23,084	2.7	10,144	10,178	9,112	9,144	4,914	5,232	3,874	4,174
RI . . .	7,325	6,760	17,753	-7.9	1,512	1,361	1,319	1,188	785	752	616	597
CT . . .	27,729	26,544	21,415	-4.5	5,535	5,208	5,110	4,809	2,547	2,543	2,211	2,221
M.A . . .	270,900	266,598	19,004	-1.9	56,913	59,025	51,727	53,689	27,871	27,897	23,005	23,200
NY . . .	124,479	122,446	18,337	-1.8	26,457	27,261	23,612	24,345	12,572	12,504	10,073	10,099
NJ . . .	63,431	63,210	22,428	-0.7	13,222	13,970	12,182	12,876	6,039	6,161	5,120	5,262
PA . . .	82,990	80,942	17,856	-3.0	17,234	17,795	15,933	16,468	9,260	9,231	7,813	7,838
Midwest . .	422,324	432,340	19,195	1.7	77,593	78,561	72,926	73,872	55,423	58,063	45,614	48,105
E.N.C . . .	298,075	303,829	19,322	1.3	53,229	53,901	49,703	50,366	38,647	40,347	32,367	34,044
OH . . .	73,206	76,295	18,534	3.7	14,304	14,820	13,453	13,943	9,808	10,490	8,038	8,673
IN . . .	37,574	39,882	19,132	5.4	6,492	6,848	6,202	6,543	4,668	5,084	3,722	4,089
IL . . .	83,479	84,710	20,058	1.1	14,490	14,534	13,491	13,536	9,986	10,332	8,467	8,832
MI . . .	67,785	67,761	19,626	-0.7	11,420	11,360	10,443	10,397	9,739	9,988	8,607	8,879
WI . . .	36,031	35,181	19,041	-3.3	6,523	6,340	6,114	5,947	4,446	4,452	3,533	3,572
W.N.C	124,249	128,510	18,900	2.6	24,364	24,660	23,223	23,505	16,776	17,716	13,247	14,061
MN . . .	33,315	35,160	20,921	4.3	6,038	6,233	5,723	5,909	4,667	5,028	3,394	3,656
IA . . .	18,818	19,512	18,288	3.2	4,084	4,146	3,926	3,986	2,430	2,573	1,916	2,041
MO . . .	36,032	36,428	18,334	0.3	6,946	6,874	6,670	6,603	5,017	5,179	4,233	4,406
ND . . .	4,467	4,670	19,434	4.3	819	837	788	806	601	641	466	503
SD . . .	4,649	4,888	18,663	4.1	930	958	894	921	493	530	372	406
NE . . .	10,313	10,693	17,649	3.1	2,072	2,105	1,861	1,888	1,326	1,404	1,064	1,139
KS . . .	16,656	17,160	17,931	2.2	3,475	3,506	3,361	3,393	2,242	2,362	1,803	1,910
South	607,087	617,011	18,943	0.3	125,704	128,021	120,043	122,273	74,534	76,591	58,272	60,491
S.A	325,787	328,762	19,327	-0.7	64,629	65,621	61,489	62,438	37,645	37,894	29,679	30,189
DE . . .	6,041	6,060	23,907	-1.0	1,088	1,101	1,009	1,022	860	860	745	751
MD . . .	36,837	36,385	20,248	-2.6	7,045	7,004	6,616	6,579	4,388	4,324	3,493	3,470
DC . . .	3,815	3,606	14,732	-4.1	637	604	573	543	348	327	301	284
VA . . .	47,472	45,783	19,485	-4.8	9,856	9,571	9,517	9,244	5,373	5,170	4,168	4,047
WV . . .	10,060	10,147	14,777	0.4	2,404	2,439	2,262	2,295	1,481	1,490	1,003	1,021
NC . . .	45,756	46,078	17,862	-0.7	9,223	9,345	8,919	9,039	4,769	4,789	3,526	3,586
SC . . .	23,754	24,220	18,795	0.6	5,126	5,260	4,953	5,085	2,541	2,584	1,925	1,988
GA . . .	46,748	46,910	19,136	-1.4	9,419	9,115	8,700	8,795	5,809	5,820	4,708	4,751
FL . . .	105,304	109,571	20,446	1.9	20,231	21,181	18,940	19,836	12,077	12,530	9,809	10,291
E.S.C . . .	96,459	97,307	17,010	-	18,482	19,319	17,621	18,425	13,030	13,760	10,077	10,757
KY . . .	23,861	24,098	17,358	0.4	4,810	5,028	4,593	4,802	3,269	3,448	2,520	2,684
TN . . .	32,422	33,384	17,677	1.7	5,698	6,093	5,421	5,797	4,397	4,744	3,470	3,788
AL . . .	26,373	26,132	17,130	-1.7	4,963	5,108	4,727	4,867	3,349	3,479	2,696	2,825
MS . . .	13,803	13,692	14,916	-1.4	3,010	3,091	2,880	2,959	2,016	2,089	1,390	1,459
W.S.C . . .	184,842	190,942	19,404	2.1	42,593	43,081	40,933	41,411	23,859	24,937	18,516	19,545
AR . . .	15,386	15,584	17,281	0.4	3,406	3,381	3,293	3,268	2,196	2,252	1,825	1,885
LA . . .	28,778	28,997	19,271	0.1	7,508	7,423	7,173	7,094	3,950	4,033	2,949	3,040
OK . . .	20,218	20,200	16,678	-0.6	4,684	4,583	4,478	4,382	2,543	2,570	2,041	2,088
TX . . .	120,459	126,161	20,275	3.3	26,995	27,694	25,989	26,667	15,171	16,082	11,702	12,533
West	394,289	394,494	20,164	-1.5	79,282	82,280	74,543	77,411	43,323	44,025	32,482	33,475
Mt	94,172	96,491	18,546	0.4	20,409	21,898	19,689	21,130	10,827	11,441	8,166	8,764
MT . . .	5,333	5,473	17,810	1.9	1,240	1,331	1,198	1,287	518	548	398	426
ID . . .	6,004	6,192	16,853	1.6	1,375	1,488	1,335	1,444	589	628	448	482
WY . . .	2,726	2,794	16,543	1.4	575	617	562	604	284	301	209	226
CO . . .	24,383	25,216	19,207	1.8	4,987	5,401	4,817	5,217	2,967	3,169	2,314	2,521
NM . . .	9,378	9,645	17,217	1.0	1,944	2,096	1,854	2,000	1,103	1,170	784	845
AZ . . .	26,137	26,893	18,797	0.5	5,916	6,371	5,728	6,169	2,975	3,153	2,071	2,246
UT . . .	10,581	10,452	18,958	-2.8	2,367	2,452	2,270	2,353	1,288	1,313	1,006	1,031
NV . . .	9,630	9,826	19,496	-2.2	2,007	2,142	1,926	2,057	1,103	1,159	935	989
Pac	300,117	298,003	20,750	-2.1	58,872	60,383	54,854	56,281	32,496	32,585	24,316	24,711
WA . . .	36,762	37,717	19,575	1.1	8,010	8,476	7,669	8,116	3,945	4,077	2,938	3,082
OR . . .	22,417	23,262	20,575	2.1	4,468	4,582	4,015	4,312	2,953	3,102	2,088	2,226
CA . . .	225,066	220,871	20,563	-3.2	43,261	43,854	40,044	40,600	23,505	23,277	17,688	17,747
AK . . .	4,669	4,740	24,197	-1.4	1,197	1,246	1,161	1,209	592	601	412	432
HI . . .	11,204	11,412	31,095	-0.1	2,137	2,224	1,964	2,043	1,502	1,527	1,191	1,224

- Represents zero.   [1] Includes other types of stores, not shown separately.   [2] Based on number of households as of July 1 as estimated by source.   [3] Includes hardware dealers.   [4] Includes homefurnishings stores.

by Type of Store and State: 1990 and 1991

1987 Standard Industrial Classification code; see text, section 13. Data are estimates]

AUTOMOTIVE DEALERS		EATING AND DRINKING PLACES		GASOLINE SERVICE STATIONS		BUILDING MATERIALS DEALERS [3]		APPAREL AND ACCESSORIES STORES		FURNITURE AND APPLIANCE STORES [4]		REGION, DIVISION, AND STATE
1990	1991	1990	1991	1990	1991	1990	1991	1990	1991	1990	1991	
381,799	375,641	182,107	189,190	131,381	128,270	92,730	92,731	94,645	95,346	92,595	89,836	U.S.
76,991	73,946	38,489	38,276	22,359	22,129	17,209	16,810	23,396	22,841	21,577	19,428	Northeast
22,903	22,691	12,059	12,954	6,855	6,801	6,032	5,885	5,861	5,573	5,801	4,925	N.E
2,111	2,063	951	1,004	677	663	672	649	371	346	391	326	ME
2,658	2,494	1,038	1,052	599	563	806	744	482	430	686	533	NH
931	925	459	493	305	304	348	342	179	171	199	169	VT
10,175	10,476	6,093	6,774	2,900	2,993	2,333	2,376	2,900	2,859	2,605	2,339	MA
1,353	1,255	858	859	505	470	369	337	385	340	321	245	RI
5,676	5,480	2,660	2,773	1,869	1,809	1,505	1,437	1,544	1,427	1,599	1,312	CT
54,088	51,255	26,430	25,322	15,504	15,328	11,176	10,925	17,535	17,268	15,776	14,503	M.A
21,749	21,203	13,098	12,517	6,237	6,154	5,055	4,936	8,994	8,726	7,672	6,997	NY
14,185	13,354	5,656	5,505	3,839	3,852	2,499	2,481	4,288	4,338	4,037	3,793	NJ
18,154	16,698	7,675	7,300	5,428	5,322	3,623	3,508	4,253	4,204	4,066	3,714	PA
92,223	92,098	40,526	43,143	37,823	37,493	23,966	23,900	19,807	20,579	19,620	19,057	Midwest
64,296	62,483	28,767	30,930	25,908	25,680	16,720	16,615	14,490	15,226	15,131	14,779	E.N.C
15,950	15,863	7,184	7,910	6,596	6,690	3,889	3,958	3,018	3,250	3,499	3,507	OH
8,491	8,593	3,478	3,899	3,459	3,574	2,349	2,432	1,556	1,711	1,691	1,724	IN
17,140	16,501	8,189	8,736	6,563	6,446	4,307	4,244	4,991	5,206	4,466	4,335	IL
15,388	14,693	6,259	6,614	5,822	5,671	3,946	3,855	3,520	3,641	3,602	3,454	MI
7,328	6,833	3,656	3,770	3,468	3,299	2,229	2,127	1,404	1,418	1,873	1,759	WI
27,928	29,615	11,759	12,214	11,916	11,813	7,246	7,286	5,318	5,353	4,489	4,278	W.N.C
6,945	7,519	3,111	3,297	2,941	2,973	2,162	2,215	1,492	1,532	1,332	1,294	MN
4,305	4,582	1,691	1,762	1,918	1,907	1,056	1,063	790	797	615	587	IA
8,461	8,774	3,532	3,587	3,501	3,393	2,001	1,965	1,507	1,482	1,210	1,125	MO
1,063	1,139	403	423	478	479	282	286	199	202	128	123	ND
1,083	1,168	421	445	523	527	278	284	193	197	147	142	SD
2,229	2,373	1,034	1,078	1,027	1,023	536	541	447	452	437	418	NE
3,842	4,061	1,566	1,621	1,528	1,510	932	933	690	692	621	589	KS
136,393	138,702	58,025	59,296	43,879	42,786	30,498	30,786	29,546	30,464	28,801	29,309	South
70,886	71,254	32,715	33,303	23,197	22,419	18,114	18,240	15,350	15,973	16,856	17,074	S.A
1,242	1,240	540	547	360	346	360	360	258	267	314	317	DE
8,056	7,920	3,527	3,516	2,539	2,405	1,687	1,662	1,976	2,015	1,971	1,956	MD
170	159	910	865	147	132	71	67	343	334	205	194	DC
10,383	9,971	4,392	4,275	3,570	3,298	2,471	2,378	2,193	2,185	2,532	2,453	VA
2,020	2,027	827	841	814	787	630	633	358	372	376	380	WV
9,926	9,944	4,514	4,585	3,332	3,215	3,245	3,258	2,141	2,228	2,518	2,546	NC
4,839	4,908	2,313	2,379	1,943	1,899	1,603	1,631	1,232	1,297	1,175	1,203	SC
9,962	9,952	4,683	4,744	3,637	3,500	2,753	2,757	2,127	2,205	2,302	2,319	GA
24,288	25,134	11,008	11,553	6,855	6,837	5,294	5,494	4,722	5,070	5,462	5,707	FL
23,433	22,350	8,390	8,556	7,431	7,268	5,087	5,127	4,677	4,693	4,230	4,306	E.S.C
5,145	4,902	2,230	2,271	2,000	1,954	1,301	1,311	990	993	1,020	1,036	KY
8,256	8,046	2,912	3,031	2,563	2,562	1,683	1,733	1,586	1,627	1,565	1,625	TN
6,830	6,408	2,193	2,198	1,904	1,830	1,398	1,386	1,487	1,468	1,125	1,125	AL
3,202	2,995	1,056	1,056	964	922	705	697	614	605	520	519	MS
42,074	45,097	16,920	17,438	13,252	13,099	7,297	7,419	9,519	9,798	7,715	7,930	W.S.C
3,659	3,839	1,113	1,124	1,229	1,191	893	892	638	643	553	557	AR
5,566	5,615	2,552	2,567	2,015	1,943	1,169	1,161	1,373	1,379	1,159	1,161	LA
4,850	5,017	1,884	1,876	1,459	1,398	802	790	1,062	1,056	811	805	OK
27,999	30,426	11,370	11,870	8,549	8,567	4,432	4,576	6,447	6,721	5,192	5,407	TX
76,191	70,896	45,068	48,475	27,320	25,863	21,058	21,234	21,896	21,463	22,598	22,042	West
19,547	18,359	9,681	10,302	7,016	6,936	5,199	5,514	4,349	4,374	4,797	4,765	Mt
1,065	1,000	576	613	470	465	332	352	230	232	233	231	MT
1,331	1,260	549	588	511	509	382	409	261	265	282	282	ID
541	509	288	307	314	311	147	156	126	127	95	94	WY
4,915	4,664	2,732	2,930	1,707	1,704	1,237	1,323	1,159	1,178	1,313	1,317	CO
1,999	1,883	995	1,063	740	735	581	618	441	446	412	411	NM
5,556	5,239	2,611	2,787	1,782	1,769	1,360	1,447	1,103	1,114	1,403	1,399	AZ
2,185	1,978	940	965	847	808	570	588	562	546	617	594	UT
1,955	1,828	992	1,050	646	636	590	622	467	467	442	437	NV
56,644	52,537	35,387	38,173	20,304	18,927	15,859	15,720	17,547	17,089	17,801	17,277	Pac
6,503	6,229	4,155	4,627	2,650	2,552	2,190	2,240	1,977	1,989	1,957	1,964	WA
4,607	4,477	2,403	2,721	1,603	1,566	1,179	1,224	1,117	1,140	1,125	1,146	OR
43,475	39,890	26,290	28,044	15,110	13,916	11,908	11,670	13,289	12,808	14,153	13,607	CA
584	550	625	686	250	236	242	244	272	269	153	151	AK
1,476	1,390	1,913	2,095	692	655	339	343	892	883	413	409	HI

Source: Market Statistics, New York, NY, The Survey of Buying Power Data Service, annual (copyright).

No. 1318. Retail Trade—Summary of Establishments, by State: 1990

[Covers establishments with payroll. Excludes government employees, railroad employees, self-employed persons, etc. For statement on methodology, see Appendix III. Kind-of-business classification based on 1987 Standard Industrial Classification code; see text, section 13]

DIVISION AND STATE	Estab- lish- ments (1,000)	Paid employ- ees [1] (1,000)	Annual payroll (mil. dol.)	DIVISION AND STATE	Estab- lish- ments (1,000)	Paid employ- ees [1] (1,000)	Annual payroll (mil. dol.)	DIVISION AND STATE	Estab- lish- ments (1,000)	Paid employ- ees [1] (1,000)	Annual payroll (mil. dol.)
U.S ..	**1,529.7**	**19,815**	**241,710**	IA	19.9	236	2,346	MS	15.3	155	1,584
N.E . . .	**91.9**	**1,165**	**15,467**	MO	32.9	419	4,760	**W.S.C. . . .**	**155.0**	**1,957**	**22,566**
ME	9.4	101	1,220	ND	5.0	51	493	AR	14.9	160	1,814
NH	8.7	106	1,334	SD	5.2	55	540	LA. . . .	22.8	288	3,041
VT	5.2	51	589	NE	11.6	133	1,292	OK	19.4	215	2,246
MA	39.6	546	7,358	KS	16.8	201	2,178	TX	97.9	1,294	15,465
RI	6.8	80	950					**Mt . . . .**	**84.5**	**1,090**	**12,634**
CT	22.1	280	4,017	**S.A . . . .**	**280.9**	**3,719**	**43,855**	MT	6.1	60	620
M.A	**234.6**	**2,787**	**37,037**	DE	4.7	63	762	ID	6.7	74	814
NY	112.5	1,234	17,137	MD	28.1	412	5,563	WY	3.4	35	376
NJ	49.5	610	8,946	DC	3.9	56	806	CO	22.3	281	3,366
PA	72.6	943	10,954	VA	37.4	525	6,261	NM	9.0	111	1,198
				WV	10.7	115	1,190	AZ	21.2	298	3,477
E.N.C	**247.4**	**3,463**	**39,902**	NC	44.6	555	6,118	UT	8.7	128	1,391
OH	63.9	911	10,253	SC	22.4	276	2,949	NV	7.1	102	1,393
IN	33.6	466	4,936	GA	41.2	548	6,274	**Pac . . . . .**	**224.0**	**3,052**	**42,499**
IL	65.4	919	11,597	FL	88.0	1,169	13,932	WA	29.7	386	5,147
MI	52.5	752	8,779	**E.S.C . . . .**	**92.4**	**1,091**	**11,699**	OR	18.6	237	2,931
WI	32.0	416	4,337	KY	22.4	275	2,815	CA	164.5	2,277	32,212
W.N.C	**119.1**	**1,491**	**16,050**	TN	30.7	387	4,350	AK	3.5	38	648
MN . . .	27.7	396	4,440	AL	23.9	274	2,951	HI	7.7	114	1,560

[1] For pay period including March 12.
Source: U.S. Bureau of the Census, *County Business Patterns*, annual.

No. 1319. Wholesale Trade—Summary: 1958 to 1987

[Data prior to 1972 based on earlier editions of Standard Industrial Classification (SIC) code. Comparability of data over time is affected by changes in the SIC code; for details, see source. See also *Historical Statistics, Colonial Times to 1970*, series T 43-47, and T 274-279]

ITEM	Unit	1958	1963	1967	1972 [1]	1977 [1]	1982 [1]	1987 [1]	1987 [2]
Firms, total [3]	1,000. . .	(NA)	232	233	276	289	335	(NA)	364
Establishments, total [3]	1,000. . .	287	308	311	370	383	435	467	470
With sales of $1,000,000 or more.	1,000. . .	(NA)	62	75	103	152	(NA)	(NA)	222
Sales, all establishments.	Bil. dol . .	286	358	460	695	1,258	1,998	2,524	2,525
Merchant wholesalers	Bil. dol . .	122	157	206	354	678	1,159	1,477	1,478
Inventories, end of year.	Bil. dol . .	15.0	20.1	28.1	45.7	82.3	130.7	(NA)	165.1
Payroll, entire year	Bil. dol . .	13.2	18.1	23.9	36.9	56.8	95.2	133.2	133.4
Paid employees, Mar. 12 workweek [4] . . .	1,000. . .	2,808	3,089	3,519	4,026	4,397	4,985	5,581	5,596

NA Not available. [1] Based on 1972 SIC code. [2] Based on 1987 SIC code. [3] Through 1977 number of firms and establishments in business at end of year; beginning 1982 number of firms and establishments in business at any time during year. [4] 1958 and 1963 data for workweek including Nov. 15.

No. 1320. Wholesale Trade, by Type of Operation and Kind of Business: 1982 and 1987

[Based on 1972 Standard Industrial Classification code; see text, section 13. See *Historical Statistics, Colonial Times to 1970*, series T 274-287 and T 352-369 for similar but not comparable data]

TYPE OF OPERATION AND KIND OF BUSINESS	ESTABLISH- MENTS [1] (1,000)		SALES (mil. dol.)		ANNUAL PAYROLL (mil. dol.)		PAID EMPLOYEES [2] (1,000)	
	1982	1987	1982	1987	1982	1987	1982	1987
Wholesale trade	**435.1**	**466.7**	**1,997,895**	**2,523,688**	**95,209**	**133,153**	**4,985**	**5,581**
Durable goods	**267.4**	**292.8**	**881,212**	**1,258,483**	**57,368**	**82,248**	**2,913**	**3,303**
Motor vehicles, automotive equipment	41.1	43.0	187,607	(D)	7,524	(D)	433	(D)
Furniture, home furnishings	13.1	14.5	32,452	48,123	2,367	3,652	126	153
Lumber, construction materials . . . . [3]	17.9	19.1	50,694	79,946	3,429	5,476	184	231
Sporting, recreational, photographic goods [3] .	7.6	8.9	26,980	40,965	1,646	2,312	85	97
Metals and minerals, except petroleum	10.6	11.1	102,690	114,528	3,359	4,038	148	143
Electrical goods	30.4	35.3	120,062	(D)	7,462	(D)	357	(D)
Hardware, plumbing, heating equipment	21.6	23.1	43,529	57,126	4,051	5,610	217	235
Machinery, equipment, supplies	103.4	114.4	263,309	336,976	24,804	35,612	1,192	1,353
Miscellaneous.	21.7	23.4	53,889	75,506	2,726	3,777	171	184
Nondurable goods	**167.8**	**173.9**	**1,116,683**	**1,265,205**	**37,841**	**50,905**	**2,072**	**2,278**
Paper, paper products	14.5	16.8	53,493	83,173	3,586	5,202	187	228
Drugs, drug proprietaries [4]	4.0	4.9	33,987	64,280	1,975	2,968	106	120
Apparel, piece goods, notions	15.0	16.9	55,897	81,476	2,897	4,661	144	181
Groceries and related products	40.4	42.1	288,659	380,945	12,269	16,729	674	763
Farm-product raw materials.	14.4	12.6	153,419	117,606	1,839	1,847	136	117
Chemicals, allied products	11.2	12.7	76,103	94,620	2,902	3,847	124	131
Petroleum, petroleum products	20.3	16.7	296,995	234,874	3,433	3,658	188	175
Beer, wines, distilled alcoholic beverages . . .	6.7	5.8	54,222	49,433	3,091	3,849	141	146
Miscellaneous.	41.2	45.3	116,008	158,800	5,849	8,143	372	417

D Data withheld to avoid disclosure. [1] Number of establishments in business at any time during the year. [2] For pay period including March 12. [3] Includes toys, hobby goods, and supplies. [4] Includes druggists sundries.
Source of tables 1319 and 1320: U.S. Bureau of the Census, *U.S. Census of Business: 1958*, vol. III; *1963*, vol. IV; *1967*, vol. III; and *Census of Wholesale Trade: 1972*, vol. I; *1977*, WC77-A-52; *1982*, WC82-A-52; and *1987*, WC87-A-52.

No. 1321. Merchant Wholesalers—Summary: 1987 to 1992

[**Inventories and stock/sales ratios**, as of **December, seasonally adjusted**. Data reflect latest revision. Based on Current Business Survey; see Appendix III. See *Historical Statistics, Colonial Times to 1970*, series T 280-371, for related sales data]

1987 SIC code [1]	KIND OF BUSINESS	1987	1988	1989	1990	1991	1992
	SALES (bil. dol.)						
	Merchant wholesalers	**1,492.1**	**1,624.3**	**1,729.9**	**1,793.9**	**1,771.6**	**1,828.0**
50	**Durable goods**	**747.1**	**813.3**	**859.0**	**884.6**	**859.5**	**904.5**
501	Motor vehicles and automotive equipment....	156.2	166.4	166.2	172.1	164.5	167.7
502	Furniture and homefurnishings.	26.9	30.1	31.9	33.9	32.3	33.0
503	Lumber and other construction material	58.4	62.5	65.1	67.3	63.1	67.7
504	Professional and commercial equipment and supplies	84.7	93.5	108.3	112.1	121.0	130.7
505	Metals and minerals, except petroleum	67.6	78.0	78.2	74.9	70.9	73.8
506	Electrical goods	91.7	100.7	113.4	117.8	117.0	119.9
507	Hardware, plumbing and heating equipment...	41.4	44.4	47.3	50.2	46.7	47.8
508	Machinery, equipment and supplies	120.0	142.2	156.3	168.5	160.8	170.1
509	Miscellaneous durable goods	100.2	95.4	92.3	87.9	83.1	93.8
51	**Nondurable goods**	**745.0**	**810.9**	**870.9**	**909.2**	**912.1**	**923.5**
511	Paper and paper products.	40.8	46.6	50.0	50.7	50.7	51.0
512	Drugs, drug proprietaries and druggists' sundries.	34.0	40.1	44.9	51.1	58.9	64.3
513	Apparel, piece goods and notions	46.6	53.7	63.1	67.6	68.6	73.4
514	Groceries and related products	223.0	236.0	259.1	272.5	277.0	274.8
515	Farm-product raw materials.	102.2	124.2	119.9	108.2	105.8	109.1
516	Chemicals and allied products.	26.5	34.2	32.8	35.0	35.8	37.4
517	Petroleum and petroleum products.	124.9	118.9	130.0	139.4	126.9	125.8
518	Beer, wine, and distilled beverages.	41.6	44.0	46.9	51.7	55.0	56.5
519	Miscellaneous nondurable goods	105.5	113.4	124.0	132.9	133.5	131.1
	INVENTORIES (bil. dol.)						
	Merchant wholesalers	**165.8**	**180.5**	**188.5**	**196.9**	**201.3**	**209.2**
50	**Durable goods**	**110.0**	**118.9**	**124.0**	**128.0**	**129.0**	**134.2**
501	Motor vehicles and automotive equipment.	21.2	22.5	22.0	23.7	24.3	24.4
502	Furniture and homefurnishings.	4.2	4.6	4.7	4.7	4.6	4.7
503	Lumber and other construction material	5.5	5.9	6.3	6.3	6.3	6.8
504	Professional and commercial equipment and supplies	11.7	13.0	14.7	15.6	16.5	16.5
505	Metals and minerals, except petroleum	8.7	10.6	10.7	10.4	9.5	10.1
506	Electrical goods	13.0	14.1	15.5	16.0	16.6	17.8
507	Hardware, plumbing and heating equipment...	6.6	7.1	7.9	8.1	7.9	7.6
508	Machinery, equipment and supplies	27.7	30.4	31.7	34.0	32.9	35.4
509	Miscellaneous durable goods	11.4	10.6	10.5	9.3	10.3	11.0
51	**Nondurable goods**	**55.8**	**61.7**	**64.5**	**68.9**	**72.3**	**75.0**
511	Paper and paper products.	3.5	4.1	4.5	4.9	5.0	5.3
512	Drugs, drug proprietaries and druggists' sundries.	4.8	5.3	5.8	6.3	7.4	8.7
513	Apparel, piece goods and notions	7.7	8.2	9.9	10.4	10.3	11.6
514	Groceries and related products	12.5	12.8	14.0	14.6	15.5	15.9
515	Farm-product raw materials.	7.2	9.2	8.2	8.7	9.0	8.0
516	Chemicals and allied products.	2.5	2.9	2.6	2.9	2.9	3.1
517	Petroleum and petroleum products.	3.4	3.5	3.5	4.1	4.0	3.9
518	Beer, wine, and distilled beverages.	4.0	4.1	4.3	4.6	5.0	4.4
519	Miscellaneous nondurable goods	10.2	11.5	11.7	12.5	13.2	14.1
	STOCK/SALES RATIO						
	Merchant wholesalers	**1.29**	**1.28**	**1.28**	**1.32**	**1.36**	**1.35**
50	**Durable goods**	**1.74**	**1.66**	**1.72**	**1.76**	**1.79**	**1.72**
501	Motor vehicles and automotive equipment....	1.60	1.57	1.68	1.68	1.81	1.70
502	Furniture and homefurnishings.	1.78	1.66	1.74	1.70	1.79	1.55
503	Lumber and other construction material	1.09	1.06	1.19	1.26	1.17	1.08
504	Professional and commercial equipment and supplies	1.65	1.53	1.53	1.60	1.58	1.47
505	Metals and minerals, except petroleum	1.44	1.55	1.79	1.63	1.60	1.61
506	Electrical goods	1.75	1.55	1.55	1.69	1.71	1.72
507	Hardware, plumbing and heating equipment...	1.86	1.83	1.94	1.91	2.01	1.99
508	Machinery, equipment and supplies	2.72	2.39	2.38	2.46	2.41	2.39
509	Miscellaneous durable goods	1.35	1.35	1.34	1.30	1.49	1.35
51	**Nondurable goods**	**0.86**	**0.88**	**0.85**	**0.89**	**0.95**	**0.97**
511	Paper and paper products.	0.92	1.03	1.05	1.16	1.17	1.25
512	Drugs, drug proprietaries and druggists' sundries.	1.61	1.48	1.42	1.44	1.40	1.51
513	Apparel, piece goods, and notions	1.86	1.74	1.71	1.75	1.84	1.78
514	Groceries and related products	0.64	0.59	0.63	0.65	0.67	0.68
515	Farm-product raw materials.	0.81	0.90	0.88	1.00	1.04	0.85
516	Chemicals and allied products.	0.98	1.06	0.91	0.95	0.97	0.97
517	Petroleum and petroleum products.	0.34	0.37	0.29	0.33	0.39	0.40
518	Beer, wine, and distilled beverages.	1.13	1.09	1.06	0.97	1.04	0.96
519	Miscellaneous nondurable goods	1.11	1.17	1.07	1.13	1.19	1.41

[1] Based on 1987 Standard Industrial Classification code; see text, section 13.

Source: U.S. Bureau of the Census, *Current Business Reports, Combined Annual and Revised Monthly Wholesale Trade, January 1986 Through 1992*, (BW/92-RV).

No. 1322. Service Industries—Summary of Establishments, by Tax Status: 1987

[Data for firms subject to Federal income tax cover all establishments, except as noted. Data for firms exempt from Federal income tax cover only establishments with payroll. See *Historical Statistics, Colonial Times to 1970*, series T 391-443, for similar but not comparable data]

1987 SIC code [1]	KIND OF BUSINESS	Establishments [2] (1,000)	Receipts or revenues [3] (mil. dol.)	Annual payroll (mil. dol.)	Paid employees [4] (1,000)	Receipts or revenues per establishment [3] ($1,000)	Annual payroll per employee (dol.)
(X)	**Firms subject to Federal income tax [5]** . . .	**6,254.5**	**868,343**	**289,807**	**16,054.7**	**138.8**	**18,051**
70 ex. 704	Hotels, rooming houses, camps, and other lodging places [5][6] . . .	85.7	53,630	14,452	1,410.8	625.8	10,244
701	Hotels and motels . . .	63.4	51,633	14,135	1,380.2	814.4	10,241
72	Personal services [5] . . .	1,037.4	43,247	10,853	1,105.0	41.7	9,822
721	Laundry, cleaning, and garment services . . .	108.6	14,184	4,388	408.3	130.6	10,746
722	Photographic studios, portrait . . .	56.2	2,929	514	50.1	52.1	10,253
723, 4	Beauty and barber shops . . .	407.3	11,990	3,538	390.7	29.4	9,055
726	Funeral service and crematories . . .	22.3	5,668	1,362	82.6	254.2	16,479
73	Business services [5] . . .	1,433.2	188,856	66,456	4,414.4	131.8	15,054
731	Advertising . . .	79.2	16,802	5,537	181.6	212.1	30,493
732	Credit reporting and collection . . .	[7]7.1	[7]4,124	1,415	82.8	[7]582.8	17,078
733	Mailing, reproduction, stenographic . . .	[7]27.2	[7]12,407	3,945	210.6	[7]455.6	18,729
734	Services to dwellings and other buildings . . .	290.4	15,649	6,555	746.0	53.9	8,788
735	Miscellaneous equipment rental and leasing . .	49.1	15,472	3,579	185.3	315.1	19,319
736	Personnel supply services . . .	43.2	20,336	13,590	1,397.1	470.7	9,727
737	Computer and data processing services . . .	140.5	56,004	19,142	637.4	398.6	30,031
7381, 2	Detective agencies and protective services . .	45.2	9,303	5,040	475.8	205.8	10,594
75	Automotive repair, services, and parking . . .	388.2	58,278	11,690	785.3	150.1	14,886
751	Automotive rental and leasing, without drivers.	19.9	16,679	2,366	134.6	838.1	17,578
752	Automobile parking . . .	10.5	2,691	491	45.7	256.3	10,751
753	Automotive repair shops . . .	301.3	34,182	7,727	485.6	113.4	15,913
754	Automotive services, except repair . . .	56.4	4,726	1,106	119.4	83.8	9,258
76	Miscellaneous repair services [5] . . .	247.6	24,597	6,416	345.8	99.3	18,551
762	Electrical repair shops . . .	65.7	7,584	2,107	107.4	115.4	19,618
78, 79, 84	Amusement and recreation services [5][6] . . .	467.0	64,524	15,474	1,094.4	138.2	14,139
781, 2	Motion picture prod., distribution, services . . .	37.1	20,778	4,973	171.3	560.1	29,029
783	Motion picture theaters . . .	8.6	4,056	584	94.1	471.6	6,211
784	Video tape rental . . .	24.7	2,920	581	79.6	118.2	7,300
792	Producers, orchestras, entertainers [9] . . .	186.9	7,725	1,607	55.2	41.3	29,092
793	Bowling centers . . .	8.3	2,597	702	99.8	313.1	7,039
794	Commercial sports . . .	50.6	5,966	2,047	75.5	117.9	27,106
7991	Physical fitness facilities . . .	22.3	2,721	745	104.9	122.0	7,097
7996	Amusement parks . . .	0.7	[7]3,470	820	60.4	[7]4,663.8	13,566
7997	Membership sports and recreation clubs . . .	7.7	[7]3,000	1,173	112.7	[7]483.1	10,403
80	Health services [5] . . .	800.6	196,211	78,820	3,592.5	245.1	21,940
801	Offices and clinics of doctors of medicine . . .	297.7	96,698	43,856	1,131.6	324.8	38,756
802	Offices and clinics of dentists . . .	131.3	25,258	8,760	491.5	192.4	17,822
8041	Offices and clinics of chiropractors . . .	31.4	3,707	900	58.0	118.0	15,504
8042	Offices and clinics of optometrists . . .	23.1	3,755	893	57.9	162.8	15,429
805	Nursing and personal care facilities . . .	38.3	20,570	9,465	961.6	537.1	9,843
806	Hospitals . . .	[7]1.4	[7]19,720	6,582	366.5	[7]14,136.2	17,958
807	Medical and dental laboratories . . .	[7]14.8	[7]7,114	2,567	131.8	[7]479.4	19,474
808	Home health care services . . .	[7]5.1	[7]3,024	1,578	184.8	[7]595.3	8,542
81	Legal services . . .	273.2	72,115	26,078	807.6	264.0	32,291
823, 4, 9	Selected educational services [5] . . .	155.9	6,102	1,657	109.4	39.1	15,144
824	Vocational schools . . .	3.7	[7]3,058	1,086	65.3	[7]826.1	16,637
83	Social services [5] . . .	319.5	9,561	2,971	357.3	29.9	8,315
835	Child day care services . . .	248.7	4,284	1,307	199.7	17.2	6,547
871	Engineering and architectural services . . .	195.3	57,051	23,175	747.0	292.1	31,024
872	Accounting, auditing, and bookkeeping services.	250.1	26,612	10,204	448.1	106.4	22,768
873 ex. 8733	Research and testing services [10] . . .	[7]12.4	[7]14,184	5,615	222.2	[7]1,144.8	25,266
874	Management and public relations services . . .	418.8	43,381	14,515	551.8	103.6	26,303
(X)	**Firms exempt from Federal income tax [5]** . . .	**175.8**	**267,490**	**117,976**	**6,736.7**	**1,521.3**	**17,513**
7997	Membership sports and recreation clubs . . .	6.5	3,694	1,467	116.4	564.0	12,607
84	Museums, botanical, zoological gardens . . .	2.7	2,597	778	52.1	961.9	14,933
805	Nursing and personal care facilities . . .	4.1	8,201	4,264	371.5	1,995.5	11,479
806	Hospitals . . .	5.9	172,001	82,342	3,964.1	29,137.9	20,772
83	Social services [5] . . .	63.0	31,552	11,617	1,109.5	500.8	10,470
832	Individual and family social services . . .	21.9	8,585	3,629	312.7	392.7	11,606
833	Job training and related services . . .	5.0	3,664	1,741	238.2	732.0	7,307
836	Residential care . . .	10.5	6,125	2,768	240.5	584.8	11,507
861	Business associations . . .	12.3	6,756	1,996	87.5	549.3	22,819
862	Professional membership organizations . . .	5.6	4,110	1,133	49.3	732.6	22,981
864	Civic, social, and fraternal associations . . .	40.4	8,569	2,779	322.9	212.0	8,604
873	Research and testing services . . .	3.2	8,303	3,088	107.8	2,623.5	28,643

X Not applicable. [1] Based on 1987 Standard Industrial Classification; see text, section 13. [2] Represents the number of establishments in business at any time during year. [3] Receipts refer to establishments subject to Federal income tax. Revenues refer to establishments exempt from Federal income tax. [4] For pay period including March 12. [5] Includes other kinds of businesses, not shown separately. [6] Excludes membership lodging. [7] Covers only establishments with payroll. [8] Includes motion pictures and museums. [9] Excludes motion picture producers. [10] Excludes noncommercial research organizations.

Source: U.S. Bureau of the Census, *1987 Census of Service Industries*, SC87-A-52 and SC87-N-1.

No. 1323. Selected Service Industries—Summary: 1982 and 1987

[For establishments with payroll]

1972 SIC code [1]	KIND OF BUSINESS	ESTABLISH-MENTS [2] (1,000)		RECEIPTS OR EXPENSES [3] (mil. dol.)		PAID EMPLOYEES [4] (1,000)	
		1982	1987	1982	1987	1982	1987
(X)	**Firms subject to Federal income tax [5]**	**1,339.2**	**1,624.6**	**426,982**	**752,474**	**11,106**	**15,688**
70	Hotels, rooming houses, camps, and other lodging places	44.3	46.8	33,215	51,865	1,102	1,411
72	Personal services	179.6	196.1	22,980	35,133	970	1,209
73	Business services	230.1	339.3	106,866	216,807	3,152	5,250
75	Automotive repair, services, and parking	123.6	151.2	30,695	51,423	553	785
76	Miscellaneous repair services	58.2	65.5	14,133	20,838	300	346
78, 79	Amusement and recreation services [6]	73.0	74.3	33,115	52,808	804	929
80 ex. 806	Health services, except hospitals	360.4	405.4	95,610	162,569	2,433	3,226
81	Legal services	122.7	138.2	34,325	66,998	569	808
823, 4, 9	Selected educational services	7.8	10.6	2,400	4,882	68	109
83	Social services	29.7	43.1	3,636	7,330	222	357
891	Engineering, architectural, surveying services	47.6	62.3	34,315	53,563	581	747
893	Accounting, auditing, and bookkeeping services	55.3	69.8	14,596	24,483	330	448
(X)	**Firms exempt from Federal income tax [5]**	**151.6**	**169.9**	**54,522**	**87,448**	**2,280**	**2,773**
805, 8, 9	Selected health services	10.2	13.2	10,438	19,084	476	684
83	Social services	54.2	63.0	16,455	26,884	904	1,110
861,2,4,9	Selected membership organizations	63.2	68.0	15,093	22,028	493	539

X Not applicable. [1] Based on 1972 Standard Industrial Classification; see text, section 13. [2] Number of establishments in business at any time during the year. [3] Receipts refer to establishments subject to Federal income tax. Expenses refer to establishments exempt from Federal income tax. [4] For pay period including March 12. [5] Excludes hospitals. Includes other kinds of business, not shown separately. [6] Includes motion pictures.

Source: U.S. Bureau of the Census, *1987 Census of Service Industries*, Geographic Area Series, SC87-A-52.

No. 1324. Selected Service Industries—Revenue and Expenses for Tax-Exempt Firms: 1990 and 1991

[In billions of dollars. Estimated from a sample of employer firms only]

1987 SIC code [1]	KIND OF BUSINESS	REVENUE		EXPENSES	
		1990	1991	1990	1991
792,7991, 7997,7999	Selected amusement and recreation services [2]	8.2	8.5	8.1	8.5
805	Nursing and personal care facilities	9.3	10.5	9.2	10.3
806	Hospitals	247.2	274.4	217.4	238.6
808	Home health care services	3.2	3.9	3.1	3.6
809	Health and allied services, n.e.c.	4.5	5.0	4.6	5.2
83	Social services	44.6	48.3	39.8	43.5
8322	Individual and family social services	12.8	14.2	12.2	13.7
8331	Job training and related services	5.1	5.6	4.8	5.5
8351	Child day care services	2.9	3.2	3.0	3.2
8361	Residential care	8.6	9.3	8.4	9.2
84	Museums, botanical, zoological gardens	2.9	3.1	2.7	3.0
86 (pt)	Selected membership organizations [3]	34.0	36.1	29.3	31.8
873	Research and testing services	12.1	13.0	11.3	12.3

[1] Standard Industrial Classification; see text, section 13. [2] Covers theatrical producers, bands, orchestras, and entertainers (SIC 792); physical fitness facilities (SIC 7991); membership sports and recreation clubs (SIC 7997); and amusement and recreation services, not elsewhere classified (SIC 7999). [3] Includes business associations (SIC 861); professional membership organizations (SIC 862); civic, social, and fraternal organizations (SIC 864); and other membership organizations, except labor unions and political and religious organizations (SIC 869).

Source: U.S. Bureau of the Census, *Current Business Reports, Service Annual Survey: 1991* (BS/91-1).

No. 1325. National Nonprofit Associations—Number, by Type: 1980 to 1992

[Data compiled during last few months of year previous to year shown and the beginning months of year shown]

TYPE	1980	1985	1990	1992	TYPE	1980	1985	1990	1992
Total	**14,726**	**19,121**	**22,289**	**22,455**	Fraternal, foreign interest, nationality, ethnic	435	492	573	561
Trade, business, commercial	3,118	3,719	3,918	3,851	Religious	797	953	1,172	1,175
Agriculture	677	882	940	1,082	Veteran, hereditary, patriotic	208	281	462	586
Legal, governmental, public admin., military	529	658	792	790	Hobby, avocational	910	1,311	1,475	1,504
Scientific, engineering, tech.	1,039	1,270	1,417	1,365	Athletic sports	504	737	840	845
Educational	[1]2,376	[1]2,822	1,291	1,294	Labor unions	235	252	253	249
Cultural	[1]	[1]	1,886	1,887	Chambers of Commerce [2]	105	142	168	168
Social welfare	994	1,450	1,705	1,773	Greek and non-Greek letter societies	318	331	340	339
Health, medical	1,413	1,886	2,227	2,290	Fan clubs	(NA)	(NA)	581	506
Public affairs	1,068	1,935	2,249	2,190					

NA Not available. [1] Data for cultural associations included with educational associations. [2] National and binational.

Source: Gale Research Inc., Detroit, MI. Compiled from *Encyclopedia of Associations*, annual, (copyright).

No. 1326. Services—Establishments, Employees, and Payroll: 1988 to 1990

[Covers establishments with payroll. Excludes government employees, railroad employees, self-employed persons, etc. For statement on methodology, see Appendix III]

1987 SIC code [1]	KIND OF BUSINESS	ESTABLISHMENTS (1,000)			EMPLOYEES (1,000)		PAYROLL (bil. dol.)	
		1988	1989	1990	1989	1990	1989	1990
(I)	**Services, total [2]**	1,937.5	1,977.3	2,059.3	27,339	28,800	543.8	599.4
70	Hotels and other lodging places [2]	49.0	50.0	50.6	1,468	1,529	17.4	19.1
701	Hotels and motels	38.8	39.5	39.2	1,409	1,463	16.7	18.3
72	Personal services [2]	177.3	181.2	186.1	1,142	1,196	12.5	13.5
721	Laundry, cleaning, and garment services [2] . .	48.1	49.4	50.4	409	418	4.9	5.2
7215	Coin-operated laundries and cleaning . . .	11.7	11.6	11.1	45	45	0.4	0.4
7216	Drycleaning plants, except rug.	19.4	19.6	17.6	156	148	1.6	1.6
723	Beauty shops	75.3	74.9	76.1	357	371	3.6	3.9
726	Funeral service and crematories	15.1	15.1	14.9	85	85	1.6	1.7
73	Business services [2]	250.5	263.6	292.3	4,749	5,119	87.1	98.1
731	Advertising	17.9	17.7	19.1	199	204	6.8	7.3
7311	Advertising agencies	12.0	11.0	11.1	139	137	5.1	5.4
733	Mailing, reproduction, stenographic	25.2	24.5	26.2	221	233	4.7	5.1
734	Services to buildings.	44.0	45.3	48.5	765	802	7.7	8.3
735	Miscellaneous equipment rental and leasing	24.0	22.3	22.6	207	209	4.7	4.9
736	Personnel supply services [2]	24.4	25.2	27.0	1,390	1,518	18.1	20.6
7361	Employment agencies	11.8	12.0	12.8	202	247	3.4	4.3
7363	Help supply services	12.6	12.5	13.3	1,154	1,210	14.3	15.6
737	Computer and data processing services [2] . .	37.9	37.8	40.5	722	773	25.0	28.5
7371	Computer programming services	13.2	12.1	12.4	208	217	8.1	8.9
7374	Data processing and preparation	6.8	6.8	6.8	223	229	5.8	6.4
738	Miscellaneous business services.	60.5	55.4	62.7	1,019	1,093	15.6	17.2
7381	Detective and armored car services	9.4	8.9	9.4	438	467	4.7	5.2
75	Automotive repair, services, and parking [2] . .	145.5	151.1	156.6	843	877	14.0	15.2
751	Automotive rentals, no drivers	11.4	10.7	10.5	144	147	2.8	2.9
753	Automotive repair shops	108.2	111.2	112.7	495	507	9.0	9.6
7532	Top and body repair and paint shops	30.7	30.3	30.5	161	164	3.1	3.2
7538	General automotive repair shops	52.2	54.4	54.8	211	214	3.6	3.8
754	Automotive services, except repair	15.5	16.3	18.1	140	145	1.4	1.5
76	Miscellaneous repair services	61.8	62.9	67.4	373	403	7.8	8.7
762	Electrical repair shops.	17.1	16.5	17.2	111	115	2.5	2.6
78	Motion pictures [2]	33.5	35.2	35.4	348	430	6.9	8.6
781	Motion picture production and services . . .	9.0	8.8	9.2	129	189	4.6	5.9
784	Video tape rental	15.5	17.2	16.4	96	103	0.7	0.8
79	Amusement and recreation services [2]	70.5	70.3	75.2	956	1,032	14.1	16.1
7997	Membership sports and recreation clubs . .	13.5	13.1	13.1	232	242	3.2	3.4
80	Health services [2]	417.2	425.1	436.7	8,430	8,811	195.6	213.8
801	Offices and clinics of medical doctors	192.0	192.2	193.6	1,304	1,387	55.7	63.0
802	Offices and clinics of dentists.	102.2	103.3	104.7	513	533	10.6	11.6
8041	Offices and clinics of chiropractors	20.1	21.7	22.9	67	73	1.2	1.3
8042	Offices and clinics of optometrists.	15.3	15.0	15.3	59	63	1.0	1.1
805	Nursing and personal care facilities	18.0	18.2	19.1	1,420	1,461	16.6	18.6
806	Hospitals	5.2	6.2	6.3	4,197	4,325	94.5	99.2
807	Medical and dental laboratories	14.3	14.6	14.4	149	158	3.4	3.8
808	Home health care services	7.5	7.5	7.7	318	351	3.9	4.8
81	Legal services	135.7	137.3	142.4	892	932	32.9	36.0
82	Educational services [2]	33.2	34.1	36.0	1,704	1,755	27.2	29.5
821	Elementary and secondary schools	14.5	14.3	14.3	440	451	6.1	6.6
822	Colleges and universities	3.0	3.1	3.0	1,055	1,082	17.8	19.2
83	Social services [2]	104.8	108.5	115.6	1,630	1,750	18.4	20.9
832	Individual and family services	25.9	26.0	27.6	377	408	4.9	5.6
833	Job training and related services.	6.7	6.6	6.9	280	289	2.5	2.8
835	Child day care services	39.2	38.8	39.0	383	405	3.1	3.4
836	Residential care.	19.3	19.7	21.0	388	417	4.8	5.4
86	Membership organizations [2]	214.3	219.7	218.2	1,837	1,892	20.9	22.6
861	Business associations	12.0	12.2	12.7	95	99	2.5	2.7
863	Labor organizations	20.0	19.5	19.2	179	176	2.6	2.7
864	Civic and social associations	39.0	39.6	40.0	346	366	3.4	3.7
866	Religious organizations	126.8	131.8	128.8	1,072	1,096	9.4	10.1
87	Engineering and management services [2] . . .	199.0	189.6	201.1	2,384	2,473	72.7	79.8
8711	Engineering services.	35.6	32.7	33.1	624	652	22.5	24.9
8712	Architectural services	17.1	16.0	15.7	143	140	4.7	4.8
872	Accounting, auditing, and bookkeeping. . . .	66.2	64.9	67.9	509	524	12.7	13.8
873	Research and testing services	15.1	13.9	14.9	371	393	11.1	12.3
8731	Commercial physical research	3.9	3.4	3.7	159	165	6.0	6.5
8741	Management services.	17.1	15.1	15.3	285	286	7.3	7.7
8742	Management consulting services	26.0	22.7	24.5	217	226	7.7	8.6

[1] Based on 1987 Standard Industrial Classification; see text, section 13.   [2] Includes kinds of business not shown separately.

Source: U.S. Bureau of the Census, *County Business Patterns*, annual.

No. 1327. Service Industries—Annual Receipts of Taxable Firms: 1985 to 1991

[**In billions of dollars.** Covers employer and nonemployer firms except as noted. Estimated]

1987 SIC code [1]	KIND OF BUSINESS	1985	1986	1987	1988	1989	1990	1991
70, ex. 704	Hotels and other lodging places [2]	45.4	47.6	53.6	57.6	59.0	60.7	60.5
701	Hotels and motels	43.5	45.8	51.6	55.5	56.9	58.5	58.3
72	Personal services [3]	36.7	39.6	43.2	48.4	52.1	55.4	54.6
721	Laundry, cleaning, and garment services	12.8	13.3	14.2	15.5	16.3	17.0	17.2
7231	Beauty shops	9.0	9.7	10.6	11.3	12.1	12.1	12.1
7261	Funeral service and crematories	5.2	5.4	5.7	6.3	6.5	7.0	7.4
73	Business services [3]	155.9	170.4	188.9	222.4	249.0	276.2	282.0
731	Advertising	14.9	15.8	16.8	18.8	20.0	21.6	20.8
7311	Advertising agencies	11.1	11.7	12.0	13.8	15.0	16.3	15.5
732	Credit reporting and collection	4.4	4.7	5.5	5.8	6.3	6.9	7.1
733	Mailing, reproduction, stenographic [3]	13.6	14.8	16.6	18.2	19.4	21.0	20.8
7331	Direct mail advertising services	4.4	5.1	5.5	6.4	6.4	7.1	7.2
7336	Commercial art and graphic design	(NA)	(NA)	(NA)	(NA)	(NA)	6.5	6.5
734	Services to dwellings and other buildings	13.3	14.6	15.6	17.3	19.7	21.3	21.0
735	Miscellaneous equipment rental and leasing	(NA)	(NA)	(NA)	(NA)	(NA)	21.6	21.1
736	Personnel supply services	14.6	16.4	20.3	24.3	26.3	28.6	27.8
7361	Employment agencies	3.4	3.7	4.0	5.0	6.1	7.5	7.1
7363	Help supply services	(NA)	(NA)	(NA)	(NA)	(NA)	21.1	20.6
737	Computer and data processing services [3]	45.2	50.6	56.0	67.7	77.2	85.8	91.3
7371	Computer programming services	(NA)	(NA)	(NA)	(NA)	(NA)	19.0	20.9
7372	Prepackaged software	(NA)	(NA)	(NA)	(NA)	(NA)	11.4	12.6
7373	Computer integrated systems design	(NA)	(NA)	(NA)	(NA)	(NA)	18.7	19.9
7374	Data processing and preparation	(NA)	(NA)	(NA)	(NA)	(NA)	17.9	19.0
738	Miscellaneous business services [3]	(NA)	(NA)	(NA)	(NA)	(NA)	69.5	72.2
7381	Detective, guard, and armored car services	(NA)	(NA)	(NA)	(NA)	(NA)	9.3	9.9
7384	Photofinishing laboratories	4.9	5.1	5.4	6.0	6.5	6.4	6.8
75	Automotive repair, services, and parking [3]	51.7	53.9	58.3	66.4	71.7	75.0	73.3
751	Automotive rentals, no drivers [3]	14.6	15.5	16.7	19.5	21.1	23.2	22.8
7513	Truck rental and leasing, without drivers	5.5	5.8	6.5	7.6	8.2	8.9	8.4
7514	Passenger car rental	(NA)	(NA)	(NA)	(NA)	(NA)	9.7	10.3
753	Automotive repair shops [3]	30.5	31.6	34.2	38.6	41.9	43.4	41.9
7532	Top & body repair & paint shops	(NA)	(NA)	(NA)	(NA)	(NA)	13.4	12.7
7538	General automotive repair shops	(NA)	(NA)	(NA)	(NA)	(NA)	14.8	13.4
754	Automotive services, except repair	(NA)	(NA)	(NA)	(NA)	(NA)	6.2	6.4
76	Miscellaneous repair services	20.7	22.4	24.6	27.8	30.3	33.4	33.1
762	Electrical repair shops	(NA)	(NA)	(NA)	(NA)	(NA)	11.1	11.1
78	Motion pictures	21.6	23.8	27.8	31.2	35.0	38.1	41.1
781,2	Motion picture produc., distribution, allied services	15.1	17.0	20.8	22.6	24.7	26.1	28.5
783	Motion picture theaters	3.8	3.9	4.1	4.7	5.7	6.6	7.0
784	Video tape rental	(NA)	(NA)	(NA)	(NA)	(NA)	5.4	5.6
79	Amusement and recreation services [3]	31.2	34.0	36.6	40.2	42.2	46.5	46.7
792	Producers, orchestras, entertainers	6.4	7.6	7.7	8.1	7.5	9.2	9.5
794	Commercial sports	5.0	5.1	6.0	6.9	7.9	9.3	9.7
7941	Professional sports clubs and promoters	(NA)	(NA)	(NA)	(NA)	(NA)	4.6	5.2
80	Health services [3][4]	147.4	161.9	182.3	203.4	219.1	243.0	261.3
801	Offices and clinics of doctors of medicine	72.1	78.4	90.5	100.3	106.3	115.1	122.5
802	Offices and clinics of dentists	20.6	21.9	24.0	25.6	26.9	28.5	29.7
8041	Offices and clinics of chiropractors	2.7	3.0	3.3	4.0	4.4	4.8	5.0
805	Nursing and personal care facilities	17.5	19.0	20.1	21.4	23.3	26.4	28.8
8051	Skilled nursing care facilities	(NA)	(NA)	(NA)	(NA)	(NA)	21.8	23.6
806	Hospitals [3]	15.7	18.1	19.7	22.8	25.0	29.1	31.5
8062	General medical and surgical hospitals	(NA)	(NA)	(NA)	(NA)	(NA)	22.6	24.5
8063	Psychiatric hospitals	(NA)	(NA)	(NA)	(NA)	(NA)	5.1	5.4
8071	Medical laboratories	3.9	4.5	5.5	6.6	7.4	8.2	8.8
808	Home health care services	(NA)	(NA)	(NA)	(NA)	(NA)	6.2	7.4
811	Legal services [4]	52.8	58.9	67.0	75.0	80.9	87.5	88.7
83	Social services [4]	(NA)	(NA)	(NA)	(NA)	(NA)	12.3	13.1
8361	Residential care	(NA)	(NA)	(NA)	(NA)	(NA)	4.7	5.3
87	Engineering and management services	(NA)	(NA)	(NA)	(NA)	(NA)	190.3	194.9
871	Engineering & architectural services [3]	49.3	51.3	57.1	61.2	70.0	73.6	73.7
8711	Engineering services	(NA)	(NA)	(NA)	(NA)	(NA)	58.8	59.7
8712	Architectural services	(NA)	(NA)	(NA)	(NA)	(NA)	12.1	11.4
8721	Accounting, auditing, & bookkeeping	21.2	22.9	26.6	29.2	32.2	32.5	33.6
873, ex. 8733	Research and testing services [5]	(NA)	(NA)	(NA)	(NA)	(NA)	22.3	22.8
8731	Commercial physical research	6.0	6.9	7.2	8.9	10.3	11.7	11.8
874	Management and public relations	37.5	41.5	43.4	51.5	57.2	61.9	64.8
8741	Management services	(NA)	(NA)	(NA)	(NA)	(NA)	20.9	22.1
8742	Management consulting services	(NA)	(NA)	(NA)	(NA)	(NA)	25.3	26.1
8744	Facilities support services	(NA)	(NA)	(NA)	(NA)	(NA)	6.3	7.0
472	Arrangement of passenger transportation	6.3	6.6	7.3	8.0	8.7	9.0	8.5
653	Real estate agents and managers [4]	31.3	34.9	38.2	42.2	44.1	44.1	43.7

NA Not available. [1] Standard Industrial Classification; see text, section 13. [2] Excludes those on membership basis. [3] Includes other kinds of businesses, not shown separately. [4] Covers employer firms only. [5] Excludes noncommercial research organizations.

Source: U.S. Bureau of the Census, *Current Business Reports, Service Annual Survey: 1991* (BS/91-1).

Figure 29.1
U.S. International Transaction Balances: 1970 to 1992

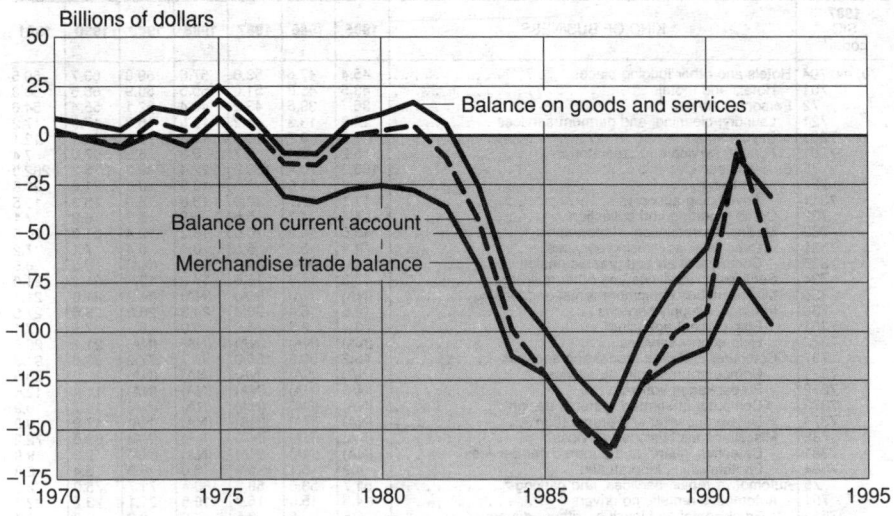

Source: Chart prepared by U.S. Bureau of the Census. For data, see table 1329.

Figure 29.2
Top Purchasers of U.S. Exports and Suppliers of U.S. General Imports: 1992

Total U.S. Exports $448.2 billion

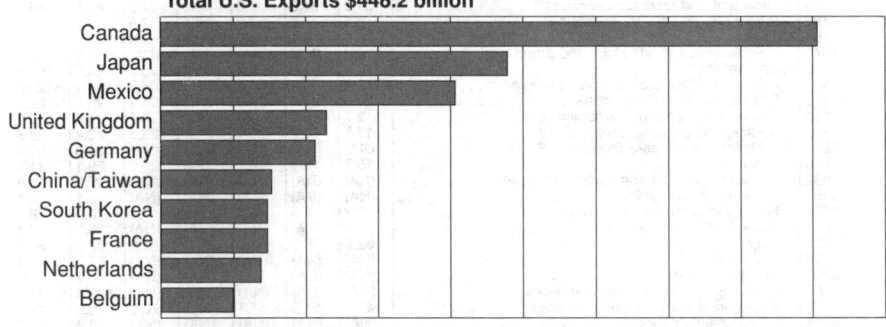

Total U.S. General Imports $532.5 billion

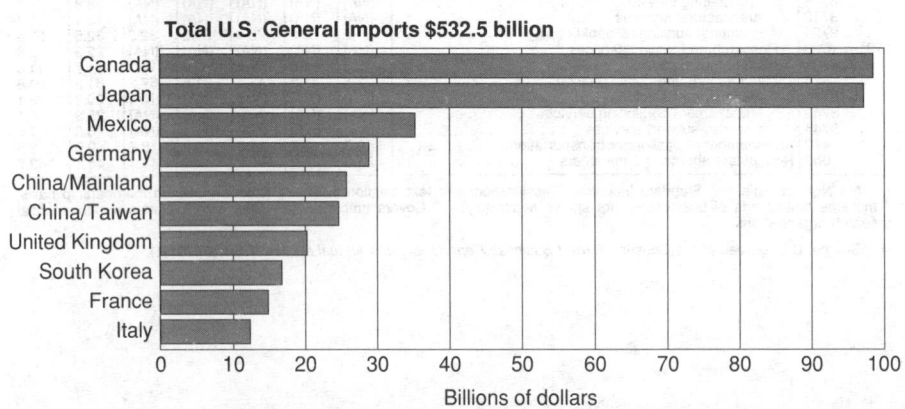

Billions of dollars

Source: Chart prepared by U.S. Bureau of the Census. For data, see table 1351.

Foreign Commerce and Aid

This section presents data on the flow of goods, services, and capital between the United States and other countries; changes in official reserve assets of the United States; international investments; foreign assistance programs; and import duties.

The Bureau of Economic Analysis publishes current figures on U.S. international transactions and the U.S. international investment position in its monthly *Survey of Current Business.* Statistics for the foreign aid programs are presented by the Agency for International Development (AID) in its annual *U.S. Overseas Loans and Grants and Assistance from International Organizations;* and by the Department of Agriculture in its *Foreign Agricultural Trade of the United States.*

The principal source of merchandise import and export data is the Bureau of the Census. Current data are presented monthly in *U.S. Merchandise Trade,* report series FT900, and *U.S. Merchandise Trade: Exports, General Imports, and Imports for Consumption,* report series FT925. The *Bureau of the Census Catalog* and the *Guide to Foreign Trade Statistics* lists the Bureau's monthly and annual reports in this field. In addition, the International Trade Administration and the Bureau of Economic Analysis present summary as well as selected commodity and country data for U.S. foreign trade in the *Overseas Business Reports* and the *Survey of Current Business,* respectively. The merchandise trade data in the latter source include balance of payments adjustments to the Census data. The Treasury Department's *Monthly Treasury Statement of Receipts and Outlays of the United States Government* contains information on import duties.

International accounts.—The international transactions tables (Nos. 1328 to 1330) show, for given time periods, the transfer of goods, services, grants, and financial assets and liabilities between the United States and the rest of the world. The international investment position table (No. 1331) presents, for specific dates, the value of U.S. investments

In Brief

U.S. current account deficit increased to –$62.4 billion in 1992.

U.S. merchandise trade deficit rose to –$84.3 billion in 1992

Trade surplus in "advance technology" products of $33 billion in 1992.

U.S. foreign assistance up 4.3% in 1991 to $16.4 billion.

abroad and of foreign investments in the United States. The movement of foreign and U.S. capital as presented in the balance of payments is not the only factor affecting the total value of foreign investments. Among the other factors are changes in the valuation of assets or liabilities, including changes in prices of securities, defaults, expropriations, and write-offs.

Direct investment abroad means the ownership or control, directly or indirectly, by one person of 10 percent or more of the voting securities of an incorporated business enterprise or an equivalent interest in an unincorporated business enterprise. Direct investment position is the value of U.S. parents' claims on the equity of, and receivables due from, foreign affiliates, less foreign affiliates' receivables due from their U.S. parents. Income consists of parents' shares in the earnings of their affiliates plus net interest received by parents on intercompany accounts, less withholding taxes on dividends and interest.

Foreign aid.—Foreign assistance is divided into three major categories—grants (military supplies and services and other grants), credits, and other assistance (through net accumulation of foreign currency claims from the sale of agricultural commodities). *Grants* are transfers for which no payment is expected (other than a limited percentage of the foreign currency "counterpart" funds generated by the grant), or which at most involve an obligation on the part of the receiver to extend aid to the United States or other countries to achieve a common objective. *Credits* are loan disbursements or transfers under other agreements which give rise to specific obligations to repay, over a period of years, usually with interest. All known returns to the U.S. Government stemming from grants and credits (reverse grants, returns of grants, and payments of principal) are taken into account in net grants and net credits, but no allowance is made for interest or commissions. *Other assistance* represents the transfer of U.S. farm products in exchange for foreign currencies (plus, since enactment of Public Law 87-128, currency claims from principal and interest collected on credits extended under the farm products program), *less* the Government's disbursements of the currencies as grants, credits, or for purchases. The net acquisition of currencies represents net transfers of resources to foreign countries under the agricultural programs, in addition to those classified as grants or credits.

The basic instrument for extending military aid to friendly nations has been the Mutual Defense Assistance Program authorized by the Congress in 1949. Prior to 1952, economic and technical aid was authorized in the Foreign Assistance Act of 1948, the 1950 Act for International Development, and other legislation which set up programs for specific countries. In 1952, these economic, technical, and military aid programs were combined under the Mutual Security Act, which in turn was followed by the Foreign Assistance Act passed in 1961. Appropriations to provide military assistance were also made in the Department of Defense Appropriation Act (rather than the Foreign Assistance Appropriation Act) beginning in 1966 for certain countries in Southeast Asia and in other legislation concerning program for specific countries (such as Israel). Figures on activity under the Foreign Assistance Act as reported in the *Foreign Grants and Credits* series differ from data published by AID or its immediate predecessors, due largely to differences in reporting, timing, and treatment of particular items.

Exports.—The Bureau of the Census compiles export data primarily from Shipper's Export Declarations required to be filed with customs officials for shipments leaving the United States. They include U.S. exports under mutual security programs and exclude shipments to U.S. Armed Forces for their own use.

The value reported in the export statistics is generally equivalent to a free alongside ship (f.a.s.) value at the U.S. port of export, based on the transaction price, including inland freight, insurance, and other charges incurred in placing the merchandise alongside the carrier at the U.S. port of exportation. This value, as defined, excludes the cost of loading merchandise aboard the exporting carrier and also excludes freight, insurance, and any other charges or transportation and other costs beyond the U.S. port of exportation. The country of destination is defined as the country of ultimate destination or country where the merchandise is to be consumed, further processed, or manufactured, as known to the shipper at the time of exportation. When ultimate destination is not known, the shipment is statistically credited to the last country to which the shipper knows the merchandise will be shipped in the same form as exported.

For certain "low-valued" shipments, the export statistics include estimates based upon selected samples of such shipments. The dollar value of the "low-valued" shipments has varied. For instance, effective January 1987 through September 1989, data are estimated for shipments valued under $1,501; from October 1989 through December 1989, data are estimated for shipments valued under $2,501 to all countries.

Effective January 1990, the United States began substituting Canadian import statistics for U.S. exports to Canada. As a result of the data exchange between the United States and Canada, the United States has adopted the Canadian import exemption level for its export statistics based on shipments to Canada.

Data are estimated for shipments valued under $2,501 to all countries, except Canada, using factors based on the ratios of low-valued shipments to individual country totals. These shipments represent slightly less than 2.5 percent of the monthly value of U.S. exports to those countries. Data are estimated for shipments reported on Canadian import documents which total less than $900 (Canadian). Such shipments represent 2 percent of the monthly value of U.S. exports to Canada.

Prior to 1989, exports were based on Schedule B, Statistical Classification of Domestic and Foreign Commodities Exported from the United States. These statistics were retabulated and published using Schedule E, Standard International Trade Classification, Revision 2. Beginning in 1989, Schedule B classifications were based on the Harmonized System and made to coincide with the Standard International Trade Classification, Revision 3. This revision will affect the comparability of most export series beginning with the 1989 data.

Imports.—The Bureau of the Census compiles import data from various customs forms required to be filed with customs officials. From 1974-1981, data on import values were presented on three bases: The transaction values f.a.s. (free alongside ship) at the foreign port of export, the c.i.f. (cost, insurance, and freight), and the previously reported customs import value (as appraised by the U.S. Customs Service in accordance with legal requirements of the Tariff Act of 1930, as amended). This latter valuation, primarily used for collection of import duties, frequently did not reflect the actual transaction value. Beginning 1982, import data are based on customs values, i.e., the price paid by the buyer to the seller in accordance with the 1979 Trade Agreement Act amendments to the 1930 Tariff Act. For the c.i.f. imports, the new customs value was substituted for the arms-length transaction value used for 1981 and earlier years. The f.a.s. transaction values were discontinued as of January 1982. Country of origin is defined as country where the merchandise was grown, mined, or manufactured. If country of origin is unknown, country of shipment is reported.

Imports are classified either as "General imports" or "Imports for consumption." General imports are a combination of entries for immediate consumption, entries into customs bonded warehouses, and entries into U.S. Foreign Trade Zones, thus generally reflecting total arrivals of merchandise. Imports for consumption are a combination of entries for immediate consumption, withdrawals from warehouses for consumption, and entries of merchandise into U.S. customs territory from U.S. Foreign Trade Zones, thus generally reflecting the total of the commodities entered into U.S. consumption channels.

Since July 1953, the import statistics include estimates, not classified by commodity, for certain low-valued shipments. For instance, from January 1985 through September 1989, import statistics include estimates for shipments valued under $1,001. Effective October 1989, import statistics are fully compiled on shipments valued over $1,250 or, under certain textile programs, for any article which must be reported on a formal entry. Value data for shipments valued under $1,251 and not required to be reported on formal entries are estimated for individual countries using factors based on the ratios of low-valued shipments to individual country totals for past periods. The estimated low-valued shipments generally amount to slightly less than 4 percent of the import total.

Prior to 1989, imports were based on the Tariff Schedule of the United States Annotated. The statistics were retabulated and published using Schedule A, Standard International Trade Classification, Revision 2. Beginning in 1989, the statistics are based on the Harmonized Tariff Schedule of the United States, which coincides with the Standard International Trade Classification, Revision 3. This revision will affect the comparability of most import series beginning with the 1989 data.

Area coverage.—Except as noted, the geographic area covered by the export and import trade statistics is the United States Customs area (includes the 50 States, the District of Columbia and Puerto Rico), the U.S. Virgin Islands (effective January 1981), and U.S. Foreign Trade Zones (effective July 1982). Data for selected tables and total values for 1980, have been revised to reflect the U.S. Virgin Islands' trade with foreign countries, where possible.

No. 1328. U.S. International Transactions, by Type of Transaction: 1980 to 1992

[In millions of dollars. Minus sign (-) indicates debits. See also Historical Statistics, Colonial Times to 1970, series U 1-25]

TYPE OF TRANSACTION	1980	1983	1984	1985	1986	1987	1988	1989	1990	1991	1992
Exports of goods and services [1]	**344,440**	**351,613**	**391,435**	**380,051**	**398,583**	**445,216**	**550,323**	**629,468**	**680,890**	**704,914**	**726,948**
Merchandise, excl. military [2][3]	224,250	201,799	219,926	215,915	223,344	250,208	320,230	361,697	388,705	415,962	439,272
Foods, feeds, and beverages	36,278	32,091	32,196	24,566	23,522	25,229	33,770	37,429	35,117	35,737	40,114
Industrial supplies and materials	72,088	58,936	64,120	61,159	64,720	70,052	90,019	99,907	105,682	109,977	109,570
Capital goods, except automotive	76,283	71,660	77,007	79,322	82,815	92,707	119,103	139,563	153,279	167,029	176,837
Automotive vehicles and parts [4]	17,443	18,461	22,422	24,945	25,097	27,583	33,397	34,940	36,504	40,045	46,686
Consumer goods (nonfood) [5]	17,751	14,925	15,085	14,593	16,730	20,307	26,981	36,565	42,779	45,944	50,386
Services	47,584	64,199	71,094	73,026	86,241	98,434	110,636	127,080	148,638	163,637	178,503
Transfers under U.S. military agency sales contracts	9,029	12,524	9,969	8,718	8,549	11,106	9,289	8,526	9,833	10,691	10,901
Travel	10,588	10,947	17,320	17,920	20,529	23,718	29,665	36,571	43,418	48,757	54,689
Passenger fares	2,591	3,610	4,058	4,382	5,545	6,966	8,925	10,526	15,140	15,627	16,868
Other transportation	11,618	12,590	13,809	14,674	15,784	17,334	19,456	21,095	22,942	23,625	24,672
Royalties and license fees	7,085	5,745	6,098	6,550	7,927	9,914	11,802	13,064	16,470	17,799	19,626
Other private services	6,276	[6]18,117	19,126	19,904	27,312	28,869	30,835	36,711	40,166	46,444	50,868
U.S. Government misc. services	398	666	714	878	595	526	664	587	668	693	879
Income on U.S. assets abroad	72,606	85,614	100,415	91,110	88,998	96,574	119,456	140,692	143,547	125,315	109,173
Direct investment	37,146	26,528	30,581	29,630	30,850	38,080	50,436	54,490	55,428	49,221	49,606
Other private receipts	32,898	54,255	64,607	55,981	51,735	53,183	62,318	80,567	77,612	67,990	53,139
U.S. Government receipts	2,562	4,832	5,227	5,499	6,413	5,311	6,703	5,635	10,508	8,104	6,428
Imports of goods, services and income	**-333,774**	**-377,495**	**-469,647**	**-478,821**	**-521,937**	**-585,637**	**-652,109**	**-705,005**	**-738,401**	**-716,624**	**-758,036**
Merchandise, excl. military [2][3]	-249,750	-268,901	-332,418	-338,088	-368,425	-409,765	-447,189	-477,365	-497,558	-489,398	-535,547
Foods, feeds, and beverages	-18,564	-18,824	-21,879	-21,850	-24,376	-24,809	-24,928	-25,077	-26,653	-26,467	-27,879
Industrial supplies and materials	-132,472	-108,794	-124,109	-114,008	-104,210	-113,746	-122,684	-135,112	-144,831	-132,032	-139,770
Capital goods, except automotive	-31,576	-43,735	-60,367	-61,287	-71,990	-85,128	-102,202	-112,453	-116,040	-120,735	-134,411
Automotive vehicles and parts [4]	-28,257	-43,044	-56,521	-65,905	-78,061	-85,174	-87,947	-87,380	-87,695	-84,941	-91,238
Consumer goods (nonfood) [5]	-34,268	-47,277	-61,094	-66,336	-79,355	-88,824	-96,425	-103,453	-105,294	-108,024	-123,003
Services	-41,491	-54,894	-67,657	-72,859	-79,892	-90,243	-97,930	-101,314	-116,583	-118,341	-123,378
Direct defense expenditures	-10,851	-13,087	-12,516	-13,108	-13,730	-14,918	-15,643	-15,364	-17,651	-16,215	-13,404
Travel	-10,397	-13,149	-22,913	-24,558	-25,913	-29,310	-32,114	-33,418	-37,349	-36,958	-43,534
Passenger Fares	-3,607	-6,003	-5,724	-6,484	-6,554	-7,318	-7,768	-8,258	-10,608	-10,636	-11,781
Other transportation	-11,790	-12,222	-14,843	-15,643	-16,715	-17,788	-19,534	-20,664	-23,401	-23,297	-23,401
Royalties and license fees	-724	-941	-1,164	-1,165	-1,392	-1,844	-2,585	-2,602	-3,133	-3,984	-4,290
Other private services	-2,909	[6]-7,924	-8,963	-10,166	-13,901	-17,172	-18,365	-19,137	-22,522	-25,154	-24,707
U.S. Government miscellaneous services	-1,214	-1,568	-1,534	-1,735	-1,686	-1,893	-1,921	-1,871	-1,919	-2,097	-2,262
Income on foreign assets in U.S.	-42,532	-53,700	-69,572	-67,875	-73,620	-85,629	-106,991	-126,326	-124,261	-108,886	-99,111
Direct investment	-8,635	-4,206	-8,723	-7,213	-7,058	-7,425	-11,693	-6,643	-1,083	3,675	-404
Other private payments	-21,214	-30,501	-39,694	-37,689	-42,491	-52,913	-65,133	-83,827	-85,308	-73,575	-59,846
U.S. Government payments	-12,684	-18,993	-21,155	-22,972	-24,071	-25,291	-30,164	-35,856	-37,870	-38,986	-38,861
Unilateral transfers (excl. military) grants, net [1]	**-8,349**	**-17,741**	**-20,612**	**-22,950**	**-24,176**	**-23,052**	**-24,869**	**-25,606**	**-32,916**	**8,028**	**-31,360**
U.S. Government grants	-5,486	-6,469	-8,696	-11,268	-11,867	-10,287	-10,506	-10,773	-17,597	24,487	-13,832
U.S. Government pensions	-1,818	-2,207	-2,159	-2,138	-2,197	-2,221	-2,501	-2,517	-2,945	-3,462	-3,736
Private remittances and other transfers	-1,044	[6]-9,066	-9,756	-9,545	-10,112	-10,544	-11,863	-12,316	-12,374	-12,996	-13,793

TYPE OF TRANSACTION	1980	1983	1984	1985	1986	1987	1988	1989	1990	1991	1992
U.S. assets abroad, net (increase/capital outflow (-))	-86,967	-58,856	-29,224	-34,069	-91,069	-62,402	-92,708	-114,944	-56,321	-62,220	-44,900
U.S. official reserve assets, net	-8,155	-1,196	-3,131	-3,858	312	9,149	-3,912	-25,293	-2,158	5,763	3,901
Special drawing rights	-16	-66	-979	-897	-246	-509	127	-535	-192	-177	2,316
Reserve position in the International Monetary Fund	-1,667	-4,434	-995	908	1,501	2,070	1,025	471	731	-367	-2,692
Foreign currencies	-6,472	3,304	-1,156	-3,869	-942	7,588	-5,064	-25,229	-2,697	6,307	4,277
U.S. Govt. assets, other than official reserve assets, net	-5,162	-5,006	-5,489	-2,821	-2,022	1,006	2,967	1,271	2,304	3,397	-959
U.S. credits and other long-term assets	-9,860	-9,967	-9,599	-7,657	-9,084	-6,506	-7,680	-5,580	-8,417	-12,123	-5,144
Repayments on U.S. credits and other long-term assets [7]	4,456	5,012	4,490	4,719	6,089	7,625	10,370	6,725	10,853	16,522	4,242
U.S. foreign currency holdings and U.S. short-term assets, net	242	-51	-379	117	973	-113	277	126	-131	-1,002	-57
U.S. private assets, net	-73,651	-52,654	-20,605	-27,391	-89,360	-72,556	-91,762	-90,922	-56,467	-71,379	-47,843
Direct investments abroad	-19,222	-4,889	-10,948	-13,401	-17,090	-27,181	-15,448	-28,995	-32,694	-27,135	-35,311
Foreign securities	-3,568	6,762	-4,756	-7,481	-4,271	-5,251	-7,846	-22,070	-28,765	-45,017	-48,646
U.S. claims on unaffiliated foreigners reported by U.S. nonbanking concerns	-4,023	-11,075	6,226	-5,186	-8,024	1,995	-12,146	11,398	-2,477	5,526	(NA)
U.S. claims reported by U.S. banks, n.i.e. [8]	-46,838	-29,928	-11,127	-1,323	-59,975	-42,119	-56,322	-51,255	7,469	-4,753	32,372
Foreign assets in the U.S., net (increase/capital inflow (+))	58,112	83,380	102,010	130,966	223,191	229,972	219,489	213,693	99,379	66,980	120,400
Foreign official assets in the U.S., net	15,497	5,845	3,140	-1,119	35,648	45,387	39,758	8,489	33,908	18,407	40,307
U.S. Government securities	11,895	6,496	4,703	-1,139	33,150	44,802	43,050	1,532	30,243	17,116	22,358
U.S. Treasury securities	9,708	6,972	4,690	-838	34,364	43,238	41,741	149	29,576	15,815	18,333
Other	2,187	-476	13	-301	-1,214	1,564	1,309	1,383	667	1,301	4,025
Other U.S. Government liabilities	615	602	739	844	2,195	-2,326	-467	146	1,866	1,600	2,469
U.S. liabilities reported by U.S. banks, n.i.e. [8]	-159	545	555	645	1,187	3,918	-319	4,976	3,385	-1,668	16,168
Other foreign official assets [8]	3,145	-1,798	-2,857	-1,469	-884	-1,007	-2,506	1,835	-1,586	1,359	-688
Other foreign assets in the U.S., net	42,615	77,534	98,870	132,084	187,542	184,585	179,731	205,204	65,471	48,573	80,093
Direct investments in U.S.	16,918	10,457	24,748	20,010	35,623	58,219	57,278	67,872	45,137	11,497	-3,948
U.S. Treasury securities	2,645	8,689	23,001	20,433	3,809	-7,643	20,239	29,618	-2,534	16,241	35,077
U.S. securities other than U.S. Treasury securities	5,457	8,164	12,568	50,962	70,969	42,120	26,353	38,767	1,592	34,918	29,884
U.S. liabilities to unaffiliated foreigners reported by U.S. nonbanking concerns	6,852	-118	4,704	-366	-2,641	2,863	5,626	5,565	4,906	-405	(NA)
U.S. liabilities reported by U.S. banks, n.i.e. [8]	10,743	50,342	33,849	41,045	79,783	89,026	70,235	63,382	16,370	-13,678	14,667
Allocations of special drawing rights	1,152										
Statistical discrepancy	25,386	19,099	26,038	24,825	15,407	-4,096	-126	2,394	47,370	-1,078	-13,052
Balance on merchandise trade	-25,500	-67,102	-112,492	-122,173	-145,081	-159,557	-126,959	-115,668	-108,853	-73,436	-96,275
Balance on services	6,093	9,306	3,437	167	6,350	8,191	12,707	25,766	32,055	45,296	55,125
Balance on investment income	30,073	31,915	30,843	23,235	15,378	10,945	12,466	14,366	19,287	16,429	10,062
Balance on goods, services, and income	10,666	-25,882	-78,212	-98,771	-129,354	-140,421	-101,787	-75,537	-57,511	-11,710	-31,088
Unilateral transfers, net	-8,349	-17,741	-20,612	-22,950	-24,176	-23,052	-24,869	-25,606	-32,916	8,028	-31,360
Balance on current account	2,317	-43,623	-98,824	-121,721	-147,529	-163,474	-126,656	-101,143	-90,428	-3,682	-62,448

- Represents zero. NA Not available. [1] Excludes transfers of goods and services under U.S. military grant programs. [2] Excludes exports of goods under U.S. military agency sales contracts identified in Bureau of the Census export documents, excludes imports of goods under direct defense expenditures identified in Census import documents, and reflects various other adjustments (for valuation, coverage, and timing) of Census statistics to a balance of payments basis. [3] Includes other end-use items, not shown separately. [4] Includes engines. [5] Excludes automotive. [6] Break in series due to inclusion of new data. See Technical Note in Survey of Current Business, June 1979. [7] Includes sales of foreign obligations to foreigners. [8] Not included elsewhere. [9] Includes foreign currency notes sold to private residents abroad.

Source: U.S. Bureau of Economic Analysis, *Survey of Current Business*, March 1993.

No. 1329. U.S. International Transactions—Summary: 1960 to 1992

[In billions of dollars. Reserve assets are for end of period. Minus sign (-) indicates debits, see headnote, table 1328]

YEAR	Merchandise trade balance [1]	Net investment income	Net military transactions	Net travel and transportation receipts	Other services, net	Balance on goods, services, and income.	Unilateral transfers [1]	Balance on current account	Net foreign assets in U.S.	Net U.S. assets abroad	Net U.S. official reserve assets
1960	4.9	3.4	-1.1	-1.0	0.6	6.9	-4.1	2.8	2.3	-4.1	19.4
1965	5.0	5.4	-0.5	-1.3	1.5	10.0	-4.6	5.4	0.7	-5.7	15.5
1966	3.8	5.0	-1.0	-1.3	1.5	8.0	-5.0	3.0	3.7	-7.3	14.9
1967	3.8	5.3	-1.2	-1.8	1.7	7.9	-5.3	2.6	7.4	-9.8	14.8
1968	0.6	6.0	-0.6	-1.5	1.8	6.2	-5.6	0.6	9.9	-11.0	15.7
1969	0.6	6.0	-0.7	-1.8	2.0	6.1	-5.7	0.4	12.7	-11.6	17.0
1970	2.6	6.2	-0.6	-2.0	2.3	8.5	-6.2	2.3	6.4	-9.3	14.5
1971	-2.3	7.3	0.7	-2.3	2.6	6.0	-7.4	-1.4	23.0	-12.5	12.2
1972	-6.4	8.2	1.1	-3.1	3.0	2.7	-8.5	-5.8	21.5	-14.5	13.2
1973	0.9	12.2	0.7	-3.2	3.4	14.1	-6.9	7.1	18.4	-22.9	14.4
1974	-5.5	15.5	0.2	-3.2	4.2	11.2	-9.2	2.0	34.2	-34.7	15.9
1975	8.9	12.8	1.5	-2.8	4.9	25.2	-7.1	18.1	15.7	-39.7	16.2
1976	-9.5	16.1	0.9	-2.6	5.0	10.0	-5.7	4.3	36.5	-51.3	18.7
1977	-31.1	18.1	1.7	-3.6	5.7	-9.1	-5.2	-14.3	51.3	-34.8	19.3
1978	-33.9	20.4	0.9	-3.6	6.9	-9.4	-5.8	-15.1	64.0	-61.1	18.7
1979	-27.6	30.9	-1.3	-2.9	7.3	6.3	-6.6	-0.3	38.8	-66.1	19.0
1980	-25.5	30.1	-1.8	-1.0	8.9	10.7	-8.3	2.3	58.1	-87.0	26.8
1981	-28.0	32.9	-0.8	0.1	12.6	16.7	-11.7	5.0	83.0	-114.1	30.1
1982	-36.5	29.8	0.1	-1.0	13.2	5.6	-17.1	-11.4	92.4	-122.3	34.0
1983	-67.1	31.9	-0.6	-4.2	14.1	-25.9	-17.7	-43.6	83.4	-58.9	33.7
1984	-112.5	30.8	-2.5	-8.3	14.3	-78.2	-20.6	-98.8	102.0	-29.2	34.9
1985	-122.2	23.2	-4.4	-9.7	14.3	-98.8	-23.0	-121.7	131.0	-34.1	43.2
1986	-145.1	15.4	-5.2	-7.3	18.9	-123.4	-24.2	-147.5	223.2	-91.1	48.5
1987	-159.6	10.9	-3.8	-6.4	18.4	-140.4	-23.1	-163.5	230.0	-62.4	45.8
1988	-127.0	12.5	-6.4	-1.4	20.4	-101.8	-24.9	-126.7	219.5	-92.7	47.8
1989	-115.7	14.4	-6.8	5.9	26.8	-75.5	-25.6	-101.1	213.7	-114.9	74.6
1990	-108.9	19.3	-7.8	10.1	29.7	-57.5	-32.9	-90.4	99.4	-56.3	83.3
1991	-73.4	16.4	-5.5	17.1	33.7	-11.7	8.0	-3.7	67.0	-62.2	77.7
1992, prel.	-96.3	10.1	-2.5	17.5	40.1	-31.1	-31.4	-62.4	120.4	-44.9	71.3

[1] Excludes military.

Source: U.S. Council of Economic Advisers, *Economic Indicators*, monthly; and *Economic Report of the President*, annual.

No. 1330. U.S. Balances on International Transactions, by Area and Selected Country: 1990 to 1992

[In millions of dollars. Minus sign (-) indicates debits]

AREA OR COUNTRY	1990, BALANCE ON—			1991, BALANCE ON—			1992, BALANCE ON—		
	Merchandise trade [1]	Goods, services, and income	Current account	Merchandise trade [1]	Goods, services, and income	Current account	Merchandise trade [1]	Goods, services, and income	Current account
All areas	-108,853	-57,511	-90,428	-73,436	-11,710	-3,682	-96,275	-31,088	-62,448
Western Europe	2,222	-558	33	14,918	13,910	18,754	2,962	608	410
European Economic Community [2]	4,931	1,823	3,202	15,578	13,662	20,040	6,552	3,561	4,471
United Kingdom	2,969	-7,792	-7,008	3,257	-8,456	-7,680	2,410	-9,932	-9,065
Belgium-Luxembourg	5,786	7,483	7,451	6,582	7,748	7,712	(NA)	(NA)	(NA)
France	640	4,367	4,285	2,157	5,766	5,669	(NA)	(NA)	(NA)
West Germany	-9,700	-14,696	-420	-5,266	-6,937	-420	(NA)	(NA)	(NA)
Italy	-4,812	-3,716	-3,985	-3,226	-1,810	-2,057	(NA)	(NA)	(NA)
Netherlands	7,840	12,073	12,046	8,408	12,610	12,582	(NA)	(NA)	(NA)
Eastern Europe	2,070	3,060	1,998	3,039	3,925	1,472	3,637	3,937	3,027
Canada	-10,233	5,910	5,616	-8,002	10,013	9,695	-10,301	6,155	5,816
Latin America, other Western Hemisphere	-10,068	-4,376	-12,636	262	8,453	-1,673	6,175	18,517	9,791
Mexico	-2,399	-134	-3,262	-1,645	4,988	1,866	(NA)	(NA)	(NA)
Venezuela	-6,441	-5,956	-6,007	-3,581	-2,867	-2,928	(NA)	(NA)	(NA)
Australia	3,894	7,710	7,651	4,285	6,461	6,392	5,065	8,560	8,477
Japan [3]	-44,289	-31,897	-23,097	-44,289	-31,897	-23,097	-50,002	-38,253	-38,446
Other Asia and Africa	-55,509	-44,585	-63,134	-44,039	-30,071	-16,794	-53,811	-38,536	-52,430
South Africa	37	519	465	387	1,033	964	(NA)	(NA)	(NA)
Int'l. and unallocated	558	7,579	2,066	390	7,496	1,569	(NA)	7,924	908

NA Not available. [1] Adjusted to balance of payments basis; excludes exports under U.S. military sales contracts and imports under direct defense expenditures. [2] Includes Denmark, Greece, Ireland, Spain, Portugal, European Atomic Energy Community, European Coal and Steel Community, and European Investment Bank, not shown separately. [3] Includes Ryukyu Islands.

Source: U.S. Bureau of Economic Analysis, *Survey of Current Business*, June 1992 and March 1993 issues.

No. 1331. International Investment Position: 1980 to 1991

[**In millions of dollars.** Estimates for end of year; subject to considerable error due to nature of basic data. See *Historical Statistics, Colonial Times to 1970*, series U 26-39, for similar data]

TYPE OF INVESTMENT	1980	1985	1986	1987	1988	1989	1990	1991
U.S. net international investment position:								
Current cost	392,547	138,950	18,735	−26,630	−183,715	−312,286	−294,836	−361,503
Market value	(NA)	142,205	109,146	54,240	−37,988	−158,782	−272,027	−381,835
U.S. assets abroad:								
Current cost	936,275	1,252,535	1,410,190	1,564,748	1,654,582	1,794,727	1,884,199	1,960,301
Market value	(NA)	1,244,460	1,507,734	1,648,367	1,817,494	2,049,801	1,977,053	2,107,041
U.S. official reserve assets	171,412	117,930	139,875	162,370	144,179	168,714	174,664	159,223
Gold	155,816	85,834	102,428	127,648	107,434	105,164	102,406	92,561
Special drawing rights	2,610	7,293	8,395	10,283	9,637	9,951	10,989	11,240
Reserve position in IMF	2,852	11,947	11,730	11,349	9,745	9,048	9,076	9,488
Foreign currencies	10,134	12,856	17,322	13,090	17,363	44,551	52,193	45,934
U.S. Government assets, other	63,865	87,752	89,637	88,880	85,860	84,553	82,230	78,729
U.S. loans and other long-term assets.	62,023	85,814	88,710	88,099	85,388	84,225	81,787	77,355
U.S. foreign currency holdings and short-term assets	1,842	1,938	927	781	472	328	443	1,374
U.S. private assets:								
Current cost	700,998	1,046,853	1,180,678	1,313,498	1,424,543	1,541,460	1,627,305	1,722,349
Market value	(NA)	1,038,778	1,278,222	1,397,117	1,587,455	1,796,534	1,720,159	1,869,089
Direct investments abroad:								
Current cost.	396,249	387,183	421,167	493,341	515,702	552,822	623,587	655,260
Market value	(NA)	379,108	518,711	576,960	678,614	807,896	716,441	802,000
Foreign securities.	62,454	114,670	145,878	164,717	183,061	220,865	241,748	305,886
U.S. claims on unaffiliated foreigners [1]	38,429	97,637	106,295	105,983	117,744	106,052	109,821	104,447
U.S. claims reported by U.S. banks [2]	203,866	447,363	507,338	549,457	608,036	661,721	652,149	656,756
Foreign assets in the U.S.								
Current cost	543,728	1,113,585	1,391,455	1,591,378	1,838,297	2,107,013	2,179,035	2,321,804
Market value	(NA)	1,102,255	1,398,589	1,594,127	1,855,482	2,208,583	2,249,080	2,488,876
Foreign official assets in the U.S.	176,062	202,482	241,226	283,058	322,036	337,277	371,101	396,607
U.S. Government securities . .	118,189	145,063	178,916	220,548	260,934	265,708	296,971	318,018
Other U.S. Government liabilities	13,367	15,803	17,993	15,667	15,200	15,346	17,212	18,812
U.S. liabilities reported by U.S. banks [2]	30,381	26,734	27,920	31,838	31,520	36,495	39,880	38,361
Other foreign official assets . .	14,125	14,882	16,397	15,005	14,382	19,728	17,038	21,416
Other foreign assets in the U.S:								
Current cost	367,666	911,103	1,150,229	1,308,320	1,516,261	1,769,736	1,807,934	1,925,197
Market value	(NA)	899,773	1,157,362	1,311,069	1,533,446	1,871,306	1,877,979	2,092,269
Direct investments:								
Current cost.	125,944	231,326	265,833	313,451	374,345	433,164	466,515	487,022
Market value	(NA)	219,996	272,966	316,200	391,530	534,734	536,560	645,094
U.S. securities other than U.S. Treasury securities	74,114	207,868	309,803	341,732	392,292	484,418	471,888	559,655
U.S. liabilities to unaffiliated foreigners [1]	30,426	29,458	26,902	29,818	35,003	40,549	45,379	43,761
U.S. liabilities reported by U.S. banks [2]	121,069	354,497	451,613	540,731	613,744	677,117	693,436	680,094
U.S. Treasury securities.	16,113	87,954	96,078	82,588	100,877	134,488	130,716	154,665

NA Not available.   [1] Reported by U.S. nonbanking concerns.   [2] Not included elsewhere.

Source: U.S. Bureau of Economic Analysis, *Survey of Current Business*, June 1992.

No. 1332. U.S. Reserve Assets: 1980 to 1992

[**In billions of dollars.** As of **end of year**, except as indicated]

TYPE	1980	1982	1983	1984	1985	1986	1987	1988	1989	1990	1991	1992
Total	26.8	34.0	33.7	34.9	43.2	48.5	45.8	47.8	74.6	83.3	77.7	71.3
Gold stock [1]	11.2	11.1	11.1	11.1	11.1	11.1	11.1	11.1	11.1	11.1	11.1	11.1
Special drawing rights	2.6	5.3	5.0	5.6	7.3	8.4	10.3	9.6	10.0	11.0	11.2	8.5
Foreign currencies	10.1	10.2	6.3	6.7	12.9	17.3	13.1	17.4	44.6	52.2	45.9	40.0
Reserve position in IMF [2]	2.9	7.3	11.3	11.5	11.9	11.7	11.3	9.7	9.0	9.1	9.5	11.8

[1] Includes gold in Exchange Stabilization Fund; excludes gold held under earmark at Federal Reserve banks for foreign and interternational accounts. Beginning 1975, gold assets were valued at $42.22 pursuant to the amending of Section 2 of the Par Value Modification Act, PL-93-110, approved September 21, 1973.   [2] International Monetary Fund.

Source: Board of Governors of the Federal Reserve System, *Federal Reserve Bulletin*, monthly; and Department of the Treasury, *Treasury Bulletin*, monthly.

No. 1333. Foreign Direct Investment Position in the United States on a Historical Cost Basis—Value, by Area and Industry: 1980 to 1991

[In millions of dollars. Book value at year end. Covers U.S. firms, including real estate investments in which foreign interest or ownership was 10 percent or more. Minus sign (-) indicates a negative position. See also *Historical Statistics, Colonial Times to 1970*, series U 47-74]

AREA AND INDUSTRY	1980	1983	1984	1985	1986	1987	1988	1989	1990	1991, prel.
All areas [1]	**83,046**	**137,061**	**164,583**	**184,615**	**220,414**	**263,394**	**314,754**	**368,924**	**396,702**	**407,577**
Petroleum	12,200	18,209	25,400	28,270	29,094	37,815	36,006	40,345	42,165	39,955
Manufacturing	32,993	47,665	51,802	59,584	71,963	93,865	122,582	150,949	157,431	162,853
Finance and insurance	12,027	10,934	24,881	27,429	34,978	39,455	44,010	59,597	53,782	63,157
Trade, wholesale and retail . .	15,210	26,513	31,219	35,873	42,920	45,399	53,590	54,005	59,627	59,692
Canada	**12,162**	**11,434**	**15,286**	**17,131**	**20,318**	**24,684**	**26,566**	**30,370**	**30,037**	**30,002**
Petroleum	1,817	1,391	1,544	1,589	1,432	1,088	1,181	1,141	1,394	913
Manufacturing	5,227	3,313	4,115	4,607	6,108	8,085	9,730	9,766	9,652	9,662
Finance and insurance	1,612	1,061	3,245	4,008	4,283	5,797	5,769	7,356	7,779	9,734
Europe	**54,688**	**92,936**	**108,211**	**121,413**	**144,181**	**181,006**	**208,942**	**239,190**	**250,973**	**258,127**
Petroleum	10,137	16,326	23,142	25,636	26,139	35,700	33,499	32,649	33,608	31,989
Manufacturing	21,953	36,866	39,083	45,841	56,016	74,300	95,641	118,129	121,292	126,809
Finance and insurance	8,673	8,450	15,945	17,022	21,787	26,336	27,121	33,157	29,400	32,414
United Kingdom	14,105	32,152	38,387	43,555	55,935	75,519	95,698	103,458	102,790	106,064
Petroleum	-257	5,955	10,991	12,155	11,758	17,950	19,522	16,666	15,841	14,238
Manufacturing	6,159	9,221	9,179	11,687	16,500	30,372	41,708	50,166	47,304	50,120
Finance and insurance . .	3,350	3,777	5,485	6,483	10,163	9,801	11,256	12,790	12,577	12,540
Netherlands	19,140	29,182	33,728	37,056	40,717	46,636	48,128	56,734	63,938	63,848
Petroleum	9,265	8,646	9,981	11,481	(D)	(D)	9,045	10,061	12,686	12,254
Manufacturing	4,777	11,222	12,497	13,351	13,293	15,615	17,843	23,090	24,717	24,137
Switzerland	5,070	7,464	8,146	10,568	12,058	13,772	14,372	18,746	17,745	17,594
Manufacturing	3,116	4,165	4,774	6,881	7,520	6,921	7,613	11,798	10,393	9,781
Finance and insurance . .	1,033	1,830	(D)	5,425	2,517	3,211	3,506	4,492	4,796	5,560
Germany [2]	7,596	10,845	12,330	14,816	17,250	21,905	25,250	28,386	28,309	28,171
Manufacturing	3,875	4,487	4,389	6,015	7,426	10,298	13,980	15,560	15,695	16,546
Finance and insurance . .	1,248	1,416	1,902	(D)	1,962	3,442	2,683	3,139	2,484	1,419
Other Europe [3]	8,777	13,293	15,620	15,417	18,221	23,174	25,494	31,866	38,191	42,450
Petroleum	991	1,679	2,080	(D)	(D)	(D)	4,580	4,786	4,806	4,800
Manufacturing	4,026	7,771	7,704	7,907	11,277	11,094	14,497	17,515	23,183	26,225
Finance and insurance . .	1,193	-908	(D)	(D)	(D)	2,189	406	2,519	1,408	2,605
Japan	**4,723**	**11,336**	**16,044**	**19,313**	**26,824**	**34,421**	**51,126**	**67,268**	**81,775**	**86,658**
Other areas	**11,472**	**21,356**	**25,043**	**26,758**	**29,091**	**23,283**	**28,120**	**32,096**	**33,917**	**32,790**

D Withheld to avoid disclosure of data of individual companies.   [1] Area totals include industries not shown separately.   [2] For 1989, includes only the Federal Republic of Germany. For 1990, also includes the former German Democratic Republic (GDR). This change has no effect on the data because, prior to 1990, there were no U.S. affiliates of the former GDR.   [3] Direct investments in 1991 (in millions of dollars): Belgium and Luxembourg, 4,627; France, 22,740; Italy, 2,859; and Sweden, 5,597.

Source: U.S. Bureau of Economic Analysis, *Survey of Current Business*, August 1992, and earlier issues.

No. 1334. U.S. Affiliates of Foreign Companies—Assets, Sales, Employment, Land, Exports, and Imports: 1990

[A U.S. affiliate is a U.S. business enterprise in which one foreign owner (individual, branch, partnership, association, trust, corporation, or government) has a direct or indirect voting interest of 10 percent or more. Universe estimates based on a sample survey of nonbank affiliates with assets, sales, or net income of $10 million or more]

INDUSTRY	Total assets (mil. dol.)	Sales [1] (mil. dol.)	Employ- ment [2] (1,000)	Employee compen- sation (mil. dol.)	GROSS BOOK VALUE (mil. dol.) Plant and equip- ment [3]	GROSS BOOK VALUE (mil. dol.) Land	Land owned (1,000 acres)	Merchan- dise exports [4] (mil. dol.)	Mer- chandise imports [4] (mil. dol.)
Total	**1,529,778**	**1,168,490**	**4,705.3**	**161,323**	**518,378**	**53,964**	**16,861**	**91,137**	**180,674**
Petroleum	101,323	116,785	151.0	6,483	99,749	3,517	1,375	2,916	18,842
Manufacturing	421,517	389,115	2,197.1	87,142	210,775	8,966	6,345	32,729	45,107
Chemicals and allied products	135,842	109,394	510.4	23,766	82,995	2,920	1,224	11,322	8,876
Wholesale trade [5]	162,663	381,462	436.8	16,298	36,012	2,271	460	52,072	113,439
Motor vehicles and auto parts and supplies	51,192	94,338	83.1	3,663	14,959	676	24	4,887	45,733
Farm-product raw materials . .	9,038	45,863	18.2	582	1,675	230	34	16,626	3,572
Retail trade	46,788	76,074	755.6	12,374	19,960	2,460	68	1,183	1,937
Finance, except banking	322,656	29,087	53.8	4,821	3,339	594	21	6	4
Insurance	205,313	63,377	126.6	5,080	8,489	783	47	-	-
Real estate	111,489	17,412	45.8	1,351	63,120	22,510	2,755	7	2
Services	81,681	37,930	553.5	13,197	30,793	5,084	144	523	389
Other	76,346	57,248	385.1	14,577	46,141	7,780	5,646	1,701	953

- Represents zero.   [1] Excludes returns, discounts, allowances, and sales and excise taxes.   [2] Average number of full-time and part-time employees.   [3] Includes other property, value of mineral rights owned and capitalized value of mineral rights leased.   [4] F.a.s. value at port of exportation.   [5] Includes industries not shown separately.

Source: U.S. Bureau of Economic Analysis, *Survey of Current Business*, May 1992, and *Foreign Direct Investment in the United States, Operations of U.S. Affiliates of Foreign Companies*, Preliminary 1990 Estimates.

No. 1335. Foreign Direct Investment in the United States—Gross Book Value and Employment of U.S. Affiliates of Foreign Companies, by State: 1981 and 1990

[A U.S. affiliate is a U.S. business enterprise in which one foreign owner (individual, branch, partnership, association, trust corporation, or government) has a direct or indirect voting interest of 10 percent or more. Universe estimates based on a sample survey of nonbank affiliates with assets, sales, or net income of $10 million or more]

DIVISION, STATE, AND OTHER AREA	GROSS BOOK VALUE OF PROPERTY, PLANT, AND EQUIPMENT (mil. dol.)		TOTAL EMPLOYMENT			MANUFACTURING EMPLOYMENT, 1990	
				1990			
	1981	1990	1981	Total (1,000)	Percent of all businesses	Total (1,000)	Percent of all manufacturing
Total	187,956	572,342	2,416.6	4,705.3	(X)	2,005.4	(X)
United States........	178,003	550,141	2,402.3	4,674.1	4.9	1,993.8	10.4
New England	5,686	19,402	143.9	284.1	5.0	116.5	9.5
Maine	1,637	2,077	17.7	27.1	5.9	7.7	7.5
New Hampshire	409	1,437	13.9	26.3	5.8	11.3	10.6
Vermont	315	625	6.0	8.0	3.6	3.8	8.1
Massachusetts	1,712	8,848	55.6	131.8	4.9	52.0	10.0
Rhode Island	359	1,081	9.9	12.7	3.1	6.8	6.8
Connecticut	1,254	5,334	40.8	78.3	5.3	34.9	10.2
Middle Atlantic.........	20,216	71,136	480.2	791.7	5.4	309.8	11.2
New York	7,892	36,203	210.3	349.2	5.0	101.5	8.9
New Jersey	6,552	18,447	134.9	225.5	7.2	95.3	15.8
Pennsylvania	5,772	16,486	135.0	217.0	4.7	113.0	11.0
East North Central	19,215	73,746	388.6	806.6	4.9	439.8	10.4
Ohio	5,178	20,308	99.9	217.9	5.1	120.0	10.8
Indiana	1,883	13,255	47.0	124.5	5.7	85.2	13.3
Illinois	5,646	23,229	113.6	242.8	5.2	113.0	11.5
Michigan	4,188	11,910	65.9	142.6	4.1	75.3	8.0
Wisconsin	2,320	5,044	62.2	78.8	3.9	46.3	8.2
West North Central.......	8,400	28,353	112.2	248.3	3.6	106.1	7.5
Minnesota	2,902	12,420	33.0	89.5	4.8	30.5	7.6
Iowa	1,032	2,615	21.6	36.7	3.5	21.6	9.1
Missouri............	1,894	5,775	32.6	71.8	3.5	32.5	7.4
North Dakota	1,155	1,200	3.5	3.0	1.4	1.1	6.3
South Dakota	299	552	1.3	4.5	1.9	2.4	7.0
Nebraska...........	241	760	5.6	14.6	2.4	7.3	7.3
Kansas	877	5,031	14.6	28.1	3.1	10.7	5.7
South Atlantic	33,271	93,221	476.0	926.8	5.5	400.3	12.7
Delaware...........	1,869	5,811	36.0	43.1	14.0	11.9	16.5
Maryland	2,103	5,784	45.1	80.9	4.4	30.7	14.8
District of Columbia	547	3,489	3.2	10.5	2.5	0.8	4.8
Virginia	3,046	10,618	49.8	112.2	4.7	49.3	11.5
West Virginia	3,992	8,023	35.4	35.2	6.9	17.9	20.3
North Carolina	5,543	15,160	89.0	180.8	6.7	107.3	12.4
South Carolina	5,318	10,153	65.1	104.2	8.0	63.4	16.5
Georgia............	4,558	16,506	78.5	159.8	6.3	71.6	12.7
Florida.............	6,295	17,677	73.9	200.1	4.2	47.4	9.1
East South Central	9,802	29,393	121.7	257.0	4.9	159.2	11.0
Kentucky	1,848	9,011	26.0	63.4	5.1	41.1	14.3
Tennessee..........	3,747	10,124	57.4	115.8	6.1	68.5	13.1
Alabama	2,776	7,346	27.0	55.0	4.1	34.8	9.0
Mississippi	1,431	2,912	11.3	22.8	3.0	14.8	6.0
West South Central.	34,651	82,951	268.5	434.9	4.8	162.6	10.3
Arkansas	636	2,478	17.5	29.7	3.7	18.7	8.0
Louisiana...........	7,872	17,221	47.0	61.2	4.7	20.9	11.4
Oklahoma	2,760	6,082	25.0	44.0	4.6	16.6	9.8
Texas	23,383	57,170	179.0	300.0	5.0	106.4	10.7
Mountain	12,353	33,077	97.9	194.8	3.9	42.5	6.5
Montana	1,235	2,151	3.0	5.1	2.1	1.4	6.2
Idaho	312	768	3.8	11.4	3.4	4.5	7.1
Wyoming	2,144	2,872	4.2	9.6	6.3	0.7	7.2
Colorado	2,369	6,268	24.7	53.1	4.1	11.0	5.7
New Mexico..........	997	4,334	7.9	17.4	3.9	3.3	7.4
Arizona	2,949	7,298	30.6	56.1	4.3	12.1	6.4
Utah	1,791	4,009	16.8	19.7	3.3	7.4	6.9
Nevada	556	5,377	6.9	22.4	3.9	2.1	8.1
Pacific..............	34,409	120,164	313.3	729.9	4.8	257.0	9.2
Washington	2,430	8,066	26.0	75.9	4.1	22.3	6.0
Oregon	845	3,205	13.1	38.1	3.6	13.8	6.2
California	20,404	77,497	248.4	552.5	4.8	214.2	10.0
Alaska.............	(D)	19,435	8.8	13.2	7.7	3.9	22.7
Hawaii.............	(D)	10,658	17.0	50.2	11.2	2.8	13.1
Puerto Rico.........	413	1,303	9.5	15.3	(X)	8.9	(X)
Other territories and offshore......	7,496	19,057	3.1	9.0	(X)	2.0	(X)
Foreign.............	2,044	1,841	1.6	6.9	(X)	0.7	(X)

D Withheld to avoid disclosure of data of individual companies.   X Not applicable.

Source: U.S. Bureau of Economic Analysis, *Survey of Current Business*, May 1992, and *Foreign Direct Investment in the United States, Operations of U.S. Affiliates of Foreign Companies*, Preliminary 1990 Estimates.

No. 1336. U.S. Businesses Acquired or Established by Foreign Direct Investors, by Industry of U.S. Business Enterprise: 1990 and 1991

[Foreign direct investment is the ownership or control, directly or indirectly, by one foreign individual branch, partnership, association, trust, corporation, or government of 10 percent or more of the voting securities of a U.S. business enterprise or an equivalent interest in an unincorporated business. Data represent number and full cost of acquisitions of existing U.S. business enterprises, including business segments or operating units of existing U.S. business enterprises and establishments of new enterprises. Investments may be made by the foreign direct investor itself, or indirectly by an existing U.S. affiliate of the foreign direct investor. Covers investments in U.S. business enterprises with assets of over $1 million, or ownership of 200 acres of U.S. land]

INDUSTRY	1990						1991					
	Investments			Investors			Investments			Investors		
	Total	Acqui-sition	Estab-lish-ments	Total	For-eign direct inves-tors	U.S. affili-ates	Total	Acqui-sition	Estab-lish-ments	Total	For-eign direct inves-tors	U.S. affili-ates
NUMBER OF INVESTMENTS [1]												
Total	1,617	839	778	1,768	670	1,098	971	501	470	1,092	428	664
Petroleum	23	17	6	24	3	21	(NA)	(NA)	(NA)	(NA)	(NA)	(NA)
Manufacturing	507	414	93	556	192	364	(NA)	(NA)	(NA)	(NA)	(NA)	(NA)
Wholesale trade. . . .	105	69	36	114	40	74	(NA)	(NA)	(NA)	(NA)	(NA)	(NA)
Retail trade	39	28	11	40	7	33	(NA)	(NA)	(NA)	(NA)	(NA)	(NA)
Banking	32	16	16	33	22	11	(NA)	(NA)	(NA)	(NA)	(NA)	(NA)
Finance, except banking	61	28	33	64	23	41	(NA)	(NA)	(NA)	(NA)	(NA)	(NA)
Insurance	26	21	5	26	7	19	(NA)	(NA)	(NA)	(NA)	(NA)	(NA)
Real estate	503	40	463	568	268	300	(NA)	(NA)	(NA)	(NA)	(NA)	(NA)
Services	203	139	64	217	68	149	(NA)	(NA)	(NA)	(NA)	(NA)	(NA)
Other [2]	118	67	51	126	40	86	(NA)	(NA)	(NA)	(NA)	(NA)	(NA)
INVESTMENT OUTLAYS (mil. dol.)												
Total	65,932	55,315	10,617	65,932	14,026	51,906	22,598	16,821	5,777	22,598	8,211	14,386
Petroleum	1,141	1,013	128	1,141	6	1,135	660	399	261	660	21	639
Manufacturing	23,898	22,789	1,109	23,898	5,708	18,190	10,553	9,141	1,413	10,553	4,509	6,044
Wholesale trade. . . .	1,676	1,484	192	1,676	509	1,167	443	370	73	443	101	341
Retail trade	1,250	1,197	53	1,250	28	1,222	1,365	1,205	160	1,365	459	906
Banking	897	816	81	897	115	781	433	393	40	433	290	143
Finance, except banking	2,121	875	1,246	2,121	252	1,869	1,899	1,472	427	1,899	381	1,518
Insurance	2,093	2,007	87	2,093	1,134	959	2,062	1,947	115	2,062	1,322	741
Real estate	7,771	1,873	5,898	7,771	4,330	3,441	2,919	210	2,709	2,919	839	2,080
Services	19,369	17,912	1,457	19,369	906	18,463	2,046	1,527	519	2,046	190	1,855
Other [2]	5,716	5,349	367	5,716	1,037	4,678	217	158	59	217	98	119

NA Not available. [1] Excludes investments that do not meet asset or acreage criteria in headnote. [2] Includes agriculture, forestry, and fishing; mining; construction; transportation; and communication and public utilities.
Source: U.S. Bureau of Economic Analysis, *Survey of Current Business,* May 1992, and unpublished data.

No. 1337. U.S. Businesses Acquired by Foreign Direct Investors—Assets, Sales, and Employment, by Industry of U.S. Business Enterprise: 1990 and 1991

[See headnote, table 1336. Minus sign (-) indicates loss]

INDUSTRY	1990					1991				
	Total assets (mil. dol.)	Sales (mil. dol.)	Net income (mil. dol.)	Employ-ment (1,000)	Acres of land owned (1,000)	Total assets (mil. dol.)	Sales (mil. dol.)	Net income (mil. dol.)	Employ-ment (1,000)	Acres of land owned (1,000)
Total	95,184	60,165	332	454.8	289.4	133,213	43,295	-32	213.0	266.1
Petroleum	(D)	864	22	2.9	1.5	538	395	10	1.7	(D)
Manufacturing	28,987	31,451	859	235.2	167.9	10,401	12,863	45	89.5	21.2
Wholesale trade.	2,156	4,320	26	9.2	4.8	484	996	-8	4.0	0.1
Retail trade	957	1,427	.11	36.2	0.5	(D)	(D)	(D)	66.2	(D)
Banking	10,057	438	˙51	2.7	(D)	(D)	(D)	-9	(D)	2.0
Finance, except banking . .	6,079	832	-56	3.6	(D)	13,245	1,254	33	3.8	0.0
Insurance	(D)	1,580	106	9.2	(D)	(D)	(D)	71	(D)	(D)
Real estate	4,322	1,123	110	3.0	4.1	(D)	100	(D)	0.2	5.1
Services	26,469	7,970	140	79.8	19.3	2,205	1,304	77	16.1	7.9
Other [1]	11,266	10,160	-937	73.1	87.0	242	315	-4	3.0	(D)

D Withheld to avoid disclosure of data of individual companies. [1] Includes agriculture, forestry, and fishing; mining; construction; transportation; and communication and public utilities.
Source: U.S. Bureau of Economic Analysis, *Survey of Current Business,* May 1992, and unpublished data.

No. 1338. U.S. Direct Investment Position Abroad, by Country: 1980 to 1991

[In millions of dollars. Direct investments represent private enterprises in one country owned or controlled by investors in another country or in the management of which foreign investors have an important role. Negative position occurs when U.S. parent company's liabilities to the foreign affiliate are greater than its equity in, and loans to the foreign affiliate. See also *Historical Statistics, Colonial Times to 1970*, series U 41-46]

COUNTRY	1980	1985	1988	1989	1990	1991 Total [1]	Manufacturing	Petroleum	Finance [2]
All countries	215,375	230,250	335,893	370,091	424,086	450,196	175,413	59,160	117,094
Developed countries	158,214	172,058	252,649	274,564	318,156	335,433	139,082	41,229	83,952
Canada . .	45,119	46,909	62,656	65,548	67,033	68,510	32,360	10,847	12,208
Europe [3]	96,287	105,171	157,077	175,213	211,194	224,554	89,090	22,829	67,423
Austria	524	493	669	588	889	1,238	223	(D)	1
Belgium	6,259	5,038	7,501	7,941	9,050	8,838	4,002	294	1,778
Denmark	1,266	1,281	1,161	1,234	1,597	1,835	313	(D)	306
France	9,347	7,643	13,041	14,069	18,874	20,495	11,952	(D)	2,170
Greece	347	210	195	264	288	291	101	26	(D)
Ireland	2,319	3,693	5,886	5,522	6,880	7,450	5,258	159	1,761
Italy	5,397	5,906	9,496	10,294	13,117	13,825	8,730	569	1,325
Luxembourg	652	690	841	1,127	1,390	1,455	784	15	425
Netherlands	8,039	7,129	16,145	18,133	22,658	24,711	7,715	1,822	11,028
Norway	1,679	3,215	4,371	3,547	3,815	4,248	104	3,638	(D)
Portugal	257	237	546	488	598	893	437	39	12
Spain	2,678	2,281	4,966	6,096	7,704	7,712	5,436	40	(D)
Sweden	1,474	933	1,119	1,129	1,600	1,693	1,213	(D)	(D)
Switzerland	11,280	15,766	18,734	19,209	25,199	26,443	1,249	836	15,432
Turkey	207	234	246	310	494	510	282	104	(Z)
United Kingdom	28,460	33,024	49,459	59,827	68,224	68,261	20,851	9,540	28,382
West Germany	15,415	16,764	21,832	24,550	27,269	32,942	20,086	3,621	4,289
Japan	6,225	9,235	18,009	18,488	20,997	22,918	10,437	4,195	2,555
Australia	7,654	8,772	12,823	13,331	14,846	15,627	6,141	2,828	1,508
New Zealand	579	576	833	1,140	3,131	2,809	558	(D)	(D)
South Africa	2,350	1,394	1,252	843	956	1,015	496	(D)	(D)
Developing countries	53,206	52,764	80,060	92,098	102,300	111,608	36,331	15,526	33,142
Latin America	38,761	28,261	53,506	62,727	71,593	77,342	25,687	4,339	29,888
South America [3]	16,342	17,623	21,815	23,612	23,760	25,996	15,441	2,262	2,398
Argentina	2,540	2,705	2,597	2,684	2,956	3,412	1,907	463	348
Brazil	7,704	8,893	12,609	14,522	14,918	15,222	11,002	859	1,379
Chile	536	88	672	1,069	1,368	1,555	188	(D)	531
Colombia	1,012	2,148	2,248	1,977	1,728	1,744	845	385	17
Ecuador	322	361	431	393	387	337	169	(D)	(D)
Peru	1,665	1,243	976	939	410	352	58	-37	(D)
Venezuela	1,908	1,588	1,903	1,503	1,490	2,785	1,164	262	97
Central America	10,193	9,658	13,380	16,050	17,719	23,408	9,302	1,176	9,465
Mexico	5,986	5,088	5,712	7,280	9,398	11,570	8,493	(D)	392
Panama	3,170	3,959	6,874	7,889	7,409	10,980	369	900	9,047
Other [3]	1,037	611	794	881	912	858	440	(D)	26
Costa Rica	303	113	169	163	(NA)	(NA)	(NA)	(NA)	(NA)
El Salvador	105	73	56	57	(NA)	(NA)	(NA)	(NA)	(NA)
Guatemala	229	213	201	215	(NA)	(NA)	(NA)	(NA)	(NA)
Honduras	288	171	240	317	(NA)	(NA)	(NA)	(NA)	(NA)
Other W. Hemisphere [3] . .	12,226	980	18,311	23,065	30,113	27,935	945	911	18,026
Bahamas, The	2,712	3,795	4,112	4,257	3,309	3,319	67	272	827
Bermuda	11,045	13,116	19,022	17,717	21,737	20,737	-	-165	19,535
Dominican Republic	316	212	138	361	(NA)	(NA)	(NA)	(NA)	(NA)
Jamaica	407	122	134	223	604	667	510	(D)	3
Netherlands Antilles	-4,336	-20,499	-9,983	-5,956	-2,229	-3,568	93	(D)	-3,919
Trinidad and Tobago . . .	951	484	447	503	503	526	(D)	(D)	7
Other Africa [3]	3,778	4,497	4,219	3,993	3,905	4,371	347	3,294	237
Egypt	1,038	1,926	1,637	1,744	1,465	1,515	44	1,110	-5
Libya	575	325	315	252	240	238	-	231	-
Nigeria	18	44	660	406	161	856	92	865	-
Middle East [3]	2,163	4,606	3,806	4,166	3,973	4,715	1,192	1,928	920
Israel	379	717	701	756	756	718	429	(D)	(D)
Saudi Arabia	1,037	2,442	1,782	1,955	1,981	2,317	746	(D)	(D)
United Arab Emirates . . .	384	792	672	652	519	544	14	472	(D)
Bahrain	-16	440	-311	-28	(NA)	(NA)	(NA)	(NA)	(NA)
Other Asia and Pacific	8,505	15,400	18,528	21,212	22,890	25,180	9,104	5,985	2,097
China: Taiwan	498	750	1,621	1,921	2,014	2,470	1,642	-4	131
Hong Kong	2,078	3,295	5,240	5,948	6,187	6,430	960	342	1,731
India	398	383	436	527	513	533	373	(D)	-2
Indonesia	1,314	4,475	2,921	3,770	3,226	3,458	206	2,889	42
Malaysia	632	1,140	1,135	1,174	1,384	1,440	687	516	50
Philippines	1,259	1,032	1,513	1,657	1,629	1,672	966	168	-63
Singapore	1,204	1,874	2,311	2,318	3,385	4,313	2,619	905	106
South Korea	575	743	1,501	1,855	2,178	2,392	960	(D)	86
Thailand	361	1,074	1,132	1,271	1,585	1,787	492	889	21
Other	186	635	719	772	788	684	224	240	-5
International	3,955	5,428	3,184	3,430	3,570	3,155	-	2,405	-
Addendum-OPEC [4]	6,090	10,383	8,827	9,046	8,470	11,028	2,392	5,383	1,069

- Represents zero.   D Suppressed to avoid disclosure of data of individual companies.   NA Not available.   Z Less than $500,000. [1] Includes industries not shown separately.   [2] Includes insurance.   [3] Includes countries not shown separately. [4] OPEC=Organization of Petroleum Exporting Countries. Includes Algeria, Ecuador, Gabon, Indonesia, Iran, Iraq, Kuwait, Libya, Nigeria, Qatar, Saudi Arabia, United Arab Emirates, and Venezuela.

Source: U.S. Bureau of Economic Analysis, *Survey of Current Business*, August 1992.

No. 1339. U.S. Government Foreign Grants and Credits: 1946 to 1991

[In millions of dollars. "P.L." means Public Law. For explanation of minus sign (-), see headnote, table 1340. See also text, section 29, and *Historical Statistics, Colonial Times to 1970*, series U 75-101]

PROGRAM	1946-1955, total	1956-1965, total	1966-1975, total	1976-1985, total	1987	1988	1989	1990	1991, prel.
Total, net.	**51,509**	**49,723**	**70,368**	**104,189**	**9,403**	**8,085**	**10,044**	**14,533**	**−29,047**
Investment in international financial institutions [1]	635	655	2,719	10,432	1,212	1,314	1,173	1,301	1,498
Under assistance programs, net	**50,875**	**49,067**	**67,649**	**93,757**	**8,191**	**6,771**	**8,871**	**13,233**	**−30,545**
Developed countries [2]	35,150	5,834	616	757	−801	−131	63	206	−14,894
Developing countries [2]	15,725	43,233	67,033	93,000	8,990	6,902	8,807	13,027	−15,651
Net new military grants	14,200	21,564	30,236	14,957	3,131	3,576	3,802	6,717	4,221
Developed countries [2]	8,910	7,931	691	1,369	261	305	321	551	448
Developing countries [2]	5,291	13,633	29,545	13,587	2,870	3,271	3,481	6,165	3,773
Gross new grants	14,434	21,805	30,281	14,993	3,136	3,578	3,805	6,721	4,223
Foreign Assistance Act [3]	13,427	21,769	30,281	14,993	3,136	3,578	3,805	6,721	4,223
Military supplies and services	12,282	20,662	9,802	2,438	57	92	119	151	468
Military assistance, service funded [4]	-	8	18,161	-	-	-	-	-	-
Financing of military purchases [5]	-	-	1,584	10,122	2,816	3,185	3,368	6,017	3,365
Relocation of facilities in Israel	-	-	-	800	-	-	-	-	-
Other special programs	1,145	1,100	734	1,633	263	301	319	553	390
Other	1,007	36	-	-	-	-	-	-	-
Less: Reverse grants and returns	234	241	45	36	5	2	3	5	1
Other grants, credits, and other assistance (through net accumulation of foreign currency claims)	36,675	27,503	37,413	78,800	5,060	3,195	5,069	6,516	−34,766
Developed countries [2]	26,240	−2,097	−75	−612	−1,062	−436	−258	−345	−15,342
Developing countries [2]	10,434	29,600	37,488	79,412	6,122	3,631	5,326	6,862	−19,424
Net new economic and technical aid grants [6]	27,529	17,675	21,748	43,302	7,419	7,231	7,395	10,254	−32,776
Developed countries [2]	19,424	780	−182	464	67	72	54	−593	−13,592
Developing countries [2]	8,104	16,896	21,929	42,839	7,352	7,160	7,341	10,847	−19,184
Gross new grants	28,769	17,993	22,003	43,311	7,419	7,231	7,395	15,771	14,117
Foreign Assistance Act [3]	17,711	12,189	12,191	31,525	5,886	5,559	5,784	6,767	6,887
Farm products disposals:									
Foreign currencies, P.L. 83-480 [7]	-	2,048	4,234	186	6	1	2	(Z)	(Z)
Famine and other urgent relief	530	2,704	2,862	5,026	687	740	615	842	853
Payment of transportation	-	494	946	1,890	222	177	113	156	240
Food for development loan forgiveness	-	-	-	353	37	133	7	166	27
Supplies to military or trusteeship administration areas	5,528	132	536	1,246	173	202	155	50	15
Peace Corps	-	232	912	979	126	151	151	179	178
Forgiveness of Foreign Debt	-	-	-	-	-	-	207	7,220	5,128
Other	5,000	194	321	2,106	284	269	360	391	788
Less: Reverse grants and returns	1,240	318	255	9	-	-	-	-	-
Less: Receipts from Persian Gulf partners	-	-	-	-	-	-	-	5,517	46,892
Net new credits [8]	8,605	7,025	16,955	35,785	2332	−4,002	−2,324	−3,705	−2,015
Developed countries [2]	6,627	−3,207	310	−1,019	−1,091	−481	−294	255	−1,747
Developing countries [2]	1,978	10,232	16,645	36,805	−1,241	−3,521	−2,029	−3,960	−267
New credits	11,958	15,429	37,424	72,195	4,845	5,910	3,951	6,654	12,917
Export-Import Bank Act	4,241	5,257	15,506	22,096	990	1,060	776	2,510	1,371
Foreign Assistance Act [3]	1,919	6,196	12,053	35,324	2,529	3,473	1,590	2,346	6,048
Country program loans	1,765	5,722	8,362	10,733	347	455	397	322	2,914
Financing or military purchases	9	247	3,089	24,288	2,169	2,989	1,159	1,993	3,057
Social Progress Trust Fund	-	226	487	142	−9	−4	−1	−14	2
Other	145	2	116	162	22	34	36	46	75
P.L. 83-480 [7]	48	3,839	7,161	8,142	826	959	793	870	3,100
Loans of foreign currency:									
To foreign governments	48	3,285	1,843	10	2	(Z)	(Z)	3	(Z)
To private enterprises	-	202	217	16	3	11	9	36	7
Long-term credit sales	-	352	5,101	8,116	821	948	784	830	3,094
P.L. 80-806 [9]	-	-	2,433	5,559	500	418	790	928	2,397
Other	5,750	137	271	1,074	-	-	-	-	-
Less: Principal collections	3,353	8,404	20,469	36,410	7,176	9,912	6,274	10,830	14,931
Export-Import Bank Act	1,787	4,458	9,282	15,222	4,293	1,501	1,395	1,834	1,863
Foreign Assistance Act [3]	38	1,263	3,557	11,234	2,336	7,715	3,860	7,355	5,540
Country program loans	1	944	2,481	4,212	470	489	744	691	4,727
Financing of military purchases	2	222	852	6,492	1,835	7,193	3,083	6,639	776
Social Progress Trust Fund	-	9	198	354	16	15	11	11	20
Other	35	88	25	177	14	18	21	14	17
P.L. 83-480 [7]	-	180	3,753	2,923	275	468	353	578	3,902
Loans of foreign currency:									
To foreign governments	-	111	2,354	551	29	24	27	31	47
To private enterprise	-	43	175	96	1	1	2	4	8
Long-term credit sales	-	27	1,223	2,276	245	444	325	542	3,848
Lend-lease, surplus property, and grant settlements	675	2,001	1,438	386	16	16	16	16	17
P.L. 80-806 [9]	-	-	1,763	4,748	152	106	548	469	3,504
Other	853	501	677	1,897	105	106	103	107	105

See footnotes at end of table.

No. 1339. U.S. Government Foreign Grants and Credits: 1946 to 1991—Continued

[In millions of dollars. See headnote, p. 802]

PROGRAM	1946-1955, total	1956-1965, total	1966-1975, total	1976-1985, total	1987	1988	1989	1990	1991, prel.
Other assistance (through net accumulation of foreign currency claims) [10]	541	2,802	-1,290	-287	-27	-34	-2	-33	24
Developed countries [3]	190	330	-203	-56	-38	-26	-17	-7	-3
Developing countries [2]	351	2,472	-1,086	-231	11	-8	15	-25	27
Currency claims acquired	813	11,498	6,888	1,227	84	81	64	76	100
Sales of farm products	813	11,170	3,013	114	41	35	25	13	25
Second-stage operations [11]	-	329	3,875	1,113	43	46	40	63	75
Less: Currencies disbursed	272	8,696	8,177	1,514	111	116	66	108	76
Economic grants and credits to purchasing country	182	6,863	6,238	180	15	16	10	36	10
Other uses	90	1,833	1,940	1,334	96	99	56	72	67

- Represents zero. Z Less than $500,000. [1] For details, see table 1340. [2] Developed countries include Australia, Canada, Japan, New Zealand, South Africa, all countries listed under "Western Europe" in table 1340, except Portugal, Spain (through 1981), Yugoslavia, and Malta, and all countries listed under "Eastern Europe" in table 1340. Developing countries include all other countries listed in table 1340 (including Spain through 1981). [3] Foreign Assistance Act of 1961 (P.L. 87-195), as amended. Also includes predecessor and related programs. [4] Includes military assistance under Dept. of Defense Appropriation Act, 1966 (P.L. 89-394) and later acts. [5] Includes funds made available under Public Law 93-199 and subsequent legislation to release Israel from its contractual liability to pay for defense articles and services purchased under other legislation. [6] Net new grants are not adjusted for settlements for postwar relief and other grants under agreements, and net new credits exclude prior grants converted into credits, which were as follows: 1946-55, $1,463 million; 1956-65, $491 million; 1972, $994 million. Repayments on these settlements are included in net new credits. [7] Agricultural Trade Development and Assistance Act. [8] Outstanding credits on Dec. 31, 1991, totaled $54,428 million representing net credits extended since organization of Export-Import Bank, Feb. 12, 1934, less chargeoffs and net adjustments due to exchange rates ($2,079 million), and excluding World War I debts. The amount repayable in dollars at U.S. Government option was $53,208 million; the remainder was repayable in foreign currencies, commodities, or services, at the option of the borrowers. [9] Commodity Credit Corporation Charter Act. [10] Equivalent value of currencies still available to be used, including some funds advanced from foreign governments and after loss by exchange rate fluctuation ($27,236 million), was $36 million on Dec. 31, 1991. [11] Includes foreign currencies acquired from triangular trade operations and principal and interest collections on credits, originally extended under P.L. 83-480, which—since enactment of P.L. 87-128—are available for the same purposes as P.L. 83-480 currencies.

Source: U.S. Bureau of Economic Analysis, press releases, and unpublished data.

No. 1340. U.S. Government Foreign Grants and Credits, by Type and Country: 1946 to 1991

[In millions of dollars. See text, section 29. Negative figures (-) occur when the total of grant returns, principal repayments, and/or foreign currencies disbursed by the U.S. Government exceeds new grants and new credits utilized and/or acquisitions of foreign currencies through new sales of farm products. See also Historical Statistics, Colonial Times to 1970, series U 75-186]

TYPE AND COUNTRY	1946-1955, total	1956-1965, total	1966-1975, total	1976-1985, total	1987	1988	1989	1990	1991, prel.
Total, net	51,509	49,723	70,368	104,189	9,403	8,085	10,044	14,533	-29,047
Investment in financial institutions	635	655	2,719	10,432	1,212	1,314	1,173	1,301	1,498
African Development Bank	-	-	-	54	20	9	7	19	(Z)
African Development Fund	-	-	-	125	45	40	34	75	78
Asian Development Bank	-	-	110	602	95	111	160	127	146
Inter-American Development Bank	-	300	1,321	2,770	189	124	97	90	74
Special Facility For Sub-Saharan Africa	-	-	-	-	65	48	-	-	-
International Bank for Reconstruction and Development	635	-	13	353	232	95	23	61	72
International Development Association	-	320	1,275	6,417	546	826	852	842	1,051
International Finance Corporation	-	35	-	111	7	25	-	75	40
Inter-American Investment Corporation	-	-	-	13	13	13	-	13	(Z)
Multinateral Investment Guarantee Agency	-	-	-	-	-	22	-	-	-
European Bank for Reconstruction and Development	-	-	-	-	-	-	-	-	36
Under assistance programs	50,875	49,067	67,649	93,757	8,191	6,771	8,871	13,233	-30,545
Developed Countries	35,150	5,834	616	757	-801	-131	63	206	-14,894
Developing Countries	15,725	43,233	67,033	92,999	8,992	6,902	8,807	13,027	-15,651
Western Europe	33,067	6,752	1,004	1,626	-167	121	-247	-58	-5,862
Austria	1,001	193	-19	34	-9	-9	-11	-10	-19
Belgium and Luxembourg	1,570	305	17	-46	-9	-9	-9	-9	-3
Denmark	596	276	64	-58	-6	-	-	-	-
Finland	86	-26	-19	21	8	6	7	-8	-5
France	8,661	-171	-93	-222	-13	-14	-14	-15	-8
Germany	-	-	-	-	-	-	-	-338	-6,117
Germany, Federal Republic of	3881	10	-117	-117	-3	-	-1	-	-
Iceland	34	33	-8	-12	-2	-4	(Z)	(Z)	-
Ireland	146	-16	-51	7	-2	-6	-7	2	-6
Italy	3,851	1,435	85	133	-21	-28	-28	-30	-14
Netherlands	1,716	322	116	-180	-1	-	-	-	-
Norway	697	362	379	-257	-4	-	-	-	-1
Portugal	248	241	34	1,003	8	69	71	56	44
Spain	258	1,203	607	965	-11	-113	-474	-122	-76
Sweden	107	-20	17	-1	-5	-3	-2	-	-
United Kingdom	7,458	105	-546	-964	-347	-105	-109	-111	-113
Yugoslavia	1,356	1,151	84	174	-41	-2	11	-39	-58
Other [1] and unspecified	1,399	1,351	454	1,146	290	338	320	566	514

See footnotes at end of table.

No. 1340. U.S. Government Foreign Grants and Credits, by Type and Country: 1946 to 1991—Continued

[In millions of dollars. See headnote, p. 803]

COUNTRY	1946-1955, total	1956-1965, total	1966-1975, total	1976-1985, total	1987	1988	1989	1990	1991, prel.
Eastern Europe	**823**	**501**	**226**	**1,029**	**-161**	**-121**	**419**	**954**	**274**
Czechoslovakia	136	-	-	-5	-	-	-	(Z)	1
Poland	350	555	-75	1,017	-44	-53	524	919	243
Romania	-	-	92	55	-50	-1	-59	64	22
Soviet Union	292	-59	214	-44	-66	-66	-46	-30	3
Other and unspecified	45	5	-5	6	-	-	-	1	3
Near East and South Asia	**4,944**	**16,828**	**17,195**	**50,793**	**6,276**	**2,128**	**4,442**	**6,675**	**-20,951**
Afghanistan	31	227	185	56	29	30	76	57	59
Bangladesh	-	-	701	1,670	150	170	138	175	139
Cyprus	-	19	20	138	17	14	19	16	18
Egypt	41	1,009	271	13,600	1,614	3,490	2,085	4,977	6,315
Greece	2,026	1,281	905	362	304	488	306	282	-181
India	370	4,890	3,810	1,021	66	139	71	-8	59
Iran	314	1,061	914	-847	-	-19	-	-	-23
Iraq	13	81	-5	5	21	29	-16	-7	336
Israel	390	483	3,760	25,417	3,115	-1,826	1,902	4,454	2,028
Jordan	26	495	618	1,320	109	-231	162	139	37
Kuwait	-	-	-	-	-	-	-	-2,506	-13,550
Lebanon	15	78	90	233	-4	-7	(Z)	8	2
Nepal	3	86	105	177	22	19	15	20	15
Oman	-	-	(Z)	79	-33	9	8	4	5
Pakistan	189	3,092	2,048	1,971	235	389	-387	524	333
Saudi Arabia	12	35	23	-20	-	-	-	-1,614	-13,913
Sri Lanka	(Z)	89	153	512	40	43	43	72	79
Syria	1	57	15	262	(Z)	(Z)	-	(Z)	-
Turkey	1,295	3,020	2,703	3,760	449	-720	-91	367	865
United Arab Emirates	-	-	-	-	-	(Z)	-	-361	-3,709
Yemen (Sanaa)	-	40	24	216	47	33	42	14	-
Yemen	-	-	-	-	-	-	-	28	19
UNRWA [2]	-	274	296	596	61	54	39	7	76
Other and unspecified	98	510	559	263	34	26	29	27	42
Africa	**147**	**2,272**	**3,610**	**11,074**	**1,110**	**1,260**	**982**	**18,396**	**1,282**
Algeria	1	135	263	345	-98	-58	-77	59	-42
Angola	-	-	-	6	115	24	2	-13	-15	-8
Benin	-	7	12	44	3	5	12	5	9
Botswana	-	(Z)	35	169	28	20	15	17	11
Burkina	-	5	40	287	24	18	14	15	29
Burundi	-	4	5	62	5	5	3	18	6
Cameroon	-	16	50	150	13	24	18	42	57
Cape Verde	-	-	1	68	7	6	4	6	5
Chad	(Z)	5	20	145	35	38	15	24	22
Ethiopia	13	200	297	310	13	71	37	54	89
Ghana	(Z)	64	203	152	10	17	46	14	26
Guinea	-	58	68	74	24	19	5	15	15
Ivory Coast	-	14	57	57	-3	27	2	25	57
Kenya	(Z)	34	76	549	46	47	56	110	81
Lesotho	-	(Z)	27	197	24	23	19	15	11
Liberia	24	139	86	459	23	27	-13	31	43
Madagascar	(Z)	7	13	86	17	21	7	33	20
Malawi	-	5	30	56	19	34	44	33	47
Mali	-	12	58	199	34	50	27	31	40
Mauritania	-	1	20	161	12	11	14	11	3
Morocco	7	464	413	948	85	185	-5	95	75
Mozambique	-	-	1	175	69	56	48	80	76
Niger	-	5	64	223	43	25	34	33	45
Nigeria	(Z)	87	284	267	1	169	44	156	34
Rwanda	-	2	13	91	16	16	9	13	27
Senegal	-	18	48	361	49	45	46	60	29
Sierra Leone	(Z)	22	36	85	12	8	12	2	9

See footnotes at end of table.

No. 1340. U.S. Government Foreign Grants and Credits, by Type and Country: 1946 to 1991—Continued

[In millions of dollars. See headnote, p. 803]

COUNTRY	1946-1955, total	1956-1965, total	1966-1975, total	1976-1985, total	1987	1988	1989	1990	1991, prel.
Africa—Continued									
Somalia	(Z)	42	47	582	69	62	38	77	9
Sudan	-	86	52	1,358	101	110	118	145	88
Swaziland	-	(Z)	8	58	16	12	11	14	13
Tanzania	2	34	123	259	40	16	16	40	42
Togo	-	9	18	60	13	9	15	10	18
Tunisia	2	407	376	563	-7	-175	56	38	5
Uganda	-	12	33	40	17	21	20	43	35
Zaire	(Z)	258	342	938	112	142	72	241	43
Zambia	-	1	35	331	36	18	21	58	44
Zimbabwe	-	(Z)	(Z)	271	33	6	12	10	28
Other and unspecified	96	118	350	781	154	133	157	176	139
Far East and Pacific	**9,678**	**16,199**	**34,780**	**9,635**	**-2,614**	**304**	**408**	**-124**	**-9,181**
Australia	-9	(Z)	276	-12	-30	-26	-18	-34	-26
Burma	25	134	43	31	10	9	1	1	-3
Cambodia	28	327	1,771	-	-	-	-	-	-
China: Mainland	-	-	-	49	9	48	35	71	55
Taiwan	1,267	2,681	1,523	648	-970	-8	-7	-7	-8
Hong Kong	3	35	41	11	-8	-8	-8	-8	-
Indonesia	246	501	1,390	1,661	-12	-3	36	46	20
Japan and Ryukyu Islands	3,267	1,318	-345	-210	-319	-4	-1	-635	-9,393
Laos	37	647	1,868	-	-	-	-	-	-
Malaysia	1	30	86	39	-12	-9	-36	-1	-2
New Zealand	3	2	95	-68	-4	-4	-4	-2	-2
Pacific Islands, Trust Territory of the [3]	28	89	488	1,260	166	138	156	52	16
Philippines	1,028	554	729	1,466	331	418	338	566	385
Singapore	-	(Z)	78	110	1	1	1	2	3
South Korea	1,420	4,744	5,426	3,518	-1,717	-383	-132	-192	-331
Thailand	192	727	996	733	-77	72	12	-19	49
Vietnam	244	3,566	19,721	-	-	-	-	-	-
Other and unspecified	1,898	844	595	400	18	65	36	39	42
Western Hemisphere	**1,248**	**5,181**	**6,816**	**9,861**	**2,100**	**1,448**	**1,133**	**2,033**	**1,797**
Argentina	86	342	34	21	27	16	-6	64	87
Bolivia	77	288	270	414	124	82	131	116	176
Brazil	509	1,400	1,518	399	34	(Z)	-202	260	-22
Canada	-1	4	272	317	-158	-50	-30	-41	-50
Chile	100	740	724	-565	26	11	-46	-32	-40
Colombia	43	446	846	298	22	-23	-29	-29	19
Costa Rica	15	83	103	687	159	107	143	108	63
Dominican Republic	2	184	360	550	78	52	52	28	22
Ecuador	32	131	144	153	60	47	24	61	22
El Salvador	3	56	93	1,681	418	405	406	303	291
Guatemala	23	146	160	270	159	142	161	96	75
Guyana	(Z)	7	71	36	8	5	8	42	11
Haiti	27	75	42	370	94	41	76	53	67
Honduras	6	53	113	801	212	194	133	223	182
Jamaica	16	3	120	643	92	95	148	108	101
Mexico	225	178	305	1,162	543	62	-100	141	8
Nicaragua	8	67	150	197	(Z)	(Z)	(Z)	100	382
Panama	10	103	210	205	10	13	8	102	148
Paraguay	4	67	86	22	(Z)	(Z)	1	(Z)	1
Peru	55	304	274	757	74	67	36	87	86
Trinidad and Tobago	-	35	21	151	-33	-11	16	5	5
Uruguay	8	90	116	-9	-3	9	-6	-4	-5
Venezuela	6	156	115	-35	-38	-28	-21	-18	-14
Central American Bank for Economic Integration	-	6	121	36	-4	-3	-1	-5	-5
Caribbean Development Bank	-	-	8	108	-1	-2	-2	-2	-6
Other [4] and unspecified	-6	218	543	1,193	197	219	233	268	192
Other international organizations and unspecified areas	**969**	**1,335**	**4,018**	**9,739**	**1,648**	**1,671**	**1,943**	**1,916**	**2,096**

- Represents zero.   Z Less than $500,000.   [1] Includes European Atomic Energy Community, European Coal and Steel Community, European Payments Union, European Productivity Agency, North Atlantic Treaty Organization, and Organization for European Economic Cooperation.   [2] United Nations Relief and Works Agency for Palestine refugees.   [3] Excludes transactions after October 1986, with Commonwealth of the Northern Mariana Islands; includes transactions with Federated States of Micronesia, Republic of the Marshall Islands, and Republic of Palau.   [4] Includes Andean Development Corporation, Eastern Caribbean Central Bank, Inter-American Institute of Agricultural Sciences, Organization of American States, and Pan American Health Organization.

Source: U.S. Bureau of Economic Analysis, press releases, and unpublished data.

No. 1341. U.S. Foreign Economic and Military Aid Programs: 1946 to 1991

[In millions of dollars. For years ending June 30 except, beginning 1977, ending Sept. 30. Economic aid shown here represents U.S. economic aid-not just aid under Foreign Assistance Act. Major components in recent years include AID, Food for Peace, Peace Corps, and paid-in subscriptions to international financial institutions, such as IBRD, and IDB. Cumulative totals for 1946-1991 are true totals net of deobligation; annual figures however, are gross unadjusted program figures. Military aid includes Military Assistance Program (MAP) grants, foreign military credit sales, service-funded programs, and excess defense articles]

PERIOD OR YEAR AND REGION	Total economic and military aid	ECONOMIC AID			MILITARY AID		
		Total	Loans	Grants	Total	Loans	Grants
1946 to 1991, total	**389,731**	**243,796**	**56,003**	**187,793**	**145,935**	**41,488**	**104,447**
1946 to 1952	41,661	31,116	8,518	22,598	10,545	-	10,545
1953 to 1961	43,358	24,053	5,850	18,203	19,305	161	19,144
1962 to 1969	50,254	33,392	15,421	17,972	16,862	1,620	15,242
1970 to 1979	65,714	26,902	9,995	16,907	38,812	14,179	24,633
1980 to 1989	140,130	92,082	13,740	78,342	48,048	21,884	26,164
1970	6,568	3,676	1,389	2,288	2,892	70	2,822
1975	6,916	4,908	1,679	3,229	2,009	750	1,259
1976	6,412	3,878	1,759	2,119	2,535	1,442	1,093
1976, TQ [1]	2,603	1,931	840	1,091	672	494	178
1977	7,784	5,594	2,083	3,511	2,190	1,411	779
1978	9,014	6,661	2,530	4,131	2,353	1,601	752
1979	13,845	7,120	1,900	5,220	6,725	5,173	1,552
1980	9,695	7,573	1,993	5,580	2,122	1,450	672
1981	10,550	7,305	1,460	5,845	3,245	2,546	699
1982	12,324	8,129	1,454	6,675	4,195	3,084	1,111
1983	14,202	8,603	1,619	6,984	5,599	3,932	1,667
1984	15,524	9,038	1,621	7,417	6,486	4,401	2,085
1985	18,128	12,327	1,579	10,748	5,801	2,365	3,436
1986	16,739	10,900	1,330	9,570	5,839	1,980	3,859
1987	14,488	9,386	1,138	8,248	5,102	953	4,149
1988	13,792	8,961	852	8,109	4,831	763	4,068
1989	14,688	9,860	694	9,166	4,828	410	4,418
1990	15,727	10,834	756	10,078	4,893	404	4,489
1991	**16,405**	**11,623**	**354**	**11,269**	**4,783**	**428**	**4,355**
Near East and South Asia	7,660	3,628	171	3,457	4,032	370	3,662
East Asia	806	574	14	560	232	25	207
Europe	519	415	-	415	104	-	104
Latin America	1,712	1,475	100	1,376	237	23	214
Africa	1,394	1,300	66	1,234	94	10	84
Oceania and other	29	28	-	28	-	-	-
Non-regional	4,285	4,201	3	4,198	85	-	85

- Represents zero. [1] Transition quarter, July-Sept.

No. 1342. U.S. Foreign Military Aid, by Region and Selected Countries: 1985 to 1991

[In millions of dollars. For years ending Sept. 30. Military aid data include Military Assistance Program (MAP) grants, foreign military credit sales, International Military Education and Training, and excess defense articles]

REGION AND COUNTRY	1985	1988	1989	1990	1991	REGION AND COUNTRY	1985	1988	1989	1990	1991
Total	**5,801**	**4,831**	**4,828**	**4,893**	**4,783**	Cameroon	5	(Z)	(Z)	-	1
Europe	**531**	**88**	**105**	**89**	**104**	Djibouti	3	1	1	2	2
Portugal	128	85	103	87	101	Gabon	(Z)	(Z)	(Z)	-	-
Spain	403	2	2	2	2	Kenya	22	6	16	11	1
Near East and						Liberia	13	1	1	-	-
South Asia	**4,248**	**4,231**	**4,202**	**4,241**	**4,032**	Morocco	50	53	53	44	44
Egypt	1,177	1,302	1,302	1,296	1,302	Niger	5	1	1	2	2
Greece	501	344	351	349	351	Somalia	34	7	1	1	-
Israel	1,400	1,800	1,800	1,792	1,800	Sudan	46	1	1	1	-
Jordan	92	28	12	70	21	Tunisia	67	28	31	31	12
Lebanon	1	(Z)	(Z)	-	-	Zaire	8	4	4	4	-
Oman	40	(Z)	(Z)	-	3	**Latin America [1]**	**269**	**144**	**164**	**234**	**237**
Pakistan	326	261	231	230	-	Colombia	1	4	8	73	50
Turkey	704	493	504	501	554	Costa Rica	11	(Z)	(Z)	-	-
Yemen	6	2	2	2	-	Dominican Rep	9	1	1	2	2
East Asia	**416**	**182**	**157**	**152**	**232**	Ecuador	7	1	5	1	3
Indonesia	34	6	3	2	27	El Salvador	136	82	81	81	67
Malaysia	5	1	1	1	-	Haiti	1	(Z)	(Z)	1	2
Philippines	42	128	128	143	203	Honduras	67	41	41	21	34
South Korea	232	2	2	1	1	Jamaica	8	(Z)	4	1	2
Thailand	102	46	24	5	1	Panama	11	-	-	-	-
Africa [1]	**279**	**116**	**118**	**114**	**94**	Peru	9	(Z)	3	2	25
Botswana	9	(Z)	1	1	1	**Non-regional**	**58**	**70**	**82**	**63**	**85**

- Represents zero. Z Less than $500,000. [1] Includes amounts not shown separately.
Source: U.S. Agency for International Development, U.S. Overseas Loans and Grants and Assistance from International Organizations, annual.

No. 1343. U.S. Foreign Aid—Commitments for Economic Assistance, by Region and Selected Countries: 1985 to 1991

[In millions of dollars. For years ending Sept. 30. Falls under economic portion of the Foreign Assistance Act. Data cover commitments for economic and technical assistance by AID. See text, section 29]

REGION AND COUNTRY	1985	1988	1989	1990	1991	REGION AND COUNTRY	1985	1988	1989	1990	1991
Total	8,132	5,705	6,136	6,964	7,668	Liberia	60	10	21	-	-
						Malawi	25	44	21	23	57
Europe	94	77	54	141	341	Mali	32	21	27	21	37
Italy	2	-	-	-	-	Mauritania	11	4	2	1	1
Portugal	80	32	50	39	43	Mauritius	7	15	2	-	3
Spain	12	3	-	-	-						
						Morocco	38	31	32	31	50
Near East and						Niger	28	35	24	20	28
South Asia [1]	3,867	2,523	2,562	2,565	3,192	Rwanda	19	5	9	12	40
Bangladesh	76	49	53	56	49	Senegal	44	24	49	37	25
Cyprus	15	10	20	5	15						
Egypt	1,065	718	817	901	783	Seychelles	2	3	3	3	3
						Sierra Leone	(Z)	1	1	1	1
Israel	1,950	1,200	1,200	1,195	1,850	Somalia	51	10	13	1	1
Jordan	100	24	16	4	31	Sudan	149	17	5	8	2
Lebanon	20	5	3	8	9	Swaziland	9	16	7	7	9
Nepal	18	12	15	17	24	Tanzania	(Z)	9	10	9	39
Oman	20	13	15	13	16	Togo	4	4	4	4	9
Pakistan	250	385	265	276	96	Tunisia	23	12	13	14	4
Sri Lanka	35	28	29	21	28	Uganda	9	25	14	43	45
Turkey	175	32	60	15	250						
Yemen (Sanaa)	28	22	24	23	3	Zaire	36	31	36	31	22
Regional	23	-	-	12	8	Zambia	42	13	7	17	35
						Zimbabwe	41	13	29	28	43
East Asia	313	225	541	482	522	Regional	96	65	110	73	12
Burma	15	6	-	-	-						
Indonesia	72	42	50	48	60	**Latin America** [1]	1,506	967	937	1,486	1,075
Philippines	183	78	347	314	328	Belize	23	8	8	6	7
						Bolivia	18	38	37	58	100
Thailand	36	25	23	14	3	Costa Rica	196	101	115	78	42
East Asia Regional	7	74	122	106	118						
						Dominican Rep.	126	33	20	18	14
Africa [1]	900	644	748	666	919	Ecuador	33	15	27	17	16
Botswana	10	13	9	9	8	El Salvador	376	266	253	200	180
Burkina	8	4	6	4	6						
Burundi	4	6	2	20	15	Grenada	11	-	-	-	-
						Guatemala	76	110	114	86	60
Cameroon	24	19	33	22	20	Guyana	-	-	-	2	1
Cape Verde	3	3	3	3	4	Haiti	31	31	40	42	51
Chad	16	17	16	11	16	Honduras	205	130	53	167	99
Congo	1	1	1	1	1	Jamaica	115	40	65	28	27
Djibouti	4	4	3	3	4						
Equatorial Guinea	1	1	1	1	1	Nicaragua	-	-	4	220	215
Gambia, The	6	4	4	5	15	Panama	74	1	-	396	40
Ghana	2	7	10	15	29	Paraguay	1	1	1	1	1
Guinea	4	18	16	15	31	Peru	38	28	22	22	69
						ROCAP [2]	107	59	48	30	21
Guinea-Bissau	4	1	2	3	4	Regional	30	74	100	88	96
Kenya	40	43	56	36	25						
Lesotho	11	26	10	7	11	**Non-regional**	1,453	1,269	1,296	1,607	1,598

- Represents zero. Z Less than $500,000. [1] Includes countries not shown separately. [2] Regional programs covering Costa Rica, El Salvador, Guatemala, Honduras, Nicaragua. and Panama.

Source: U.S. Agency for International Development, *U.S. Overseas Loans and Grants and Assistance from International Organizations*, annual; and unpublished data.

No. 1344. U.S. Exports and Imports of Merchandise: 1970 to 1992

[In billions of dollars, except percent. Includes silver ore and bullion; beginning 1974, includes shipments of nonmonetary gold. Data may differ from those shown in other tables due to revisions and inclusion of the Virgin Islands since 1974. For basis of dollar values, see text, section 29. See also *Historical Statistics, Colonial Times to 1970*, series U 190-195 and U 207-212]

YEAR	Merchandise trade balance	EXPORTS [1]					GENERAL IMPORTS [4]				AVERAGE ANNUAL PERCENT CHANGE [5]	
		Total [2]	Domestic				Total [3]	Petroleum	Machinery	Transport equipment	Domestic exports	General imports
			Total [3]	Agricultural	Machinery	Transport equipment						
1970	2.7	42.7	42.0	7.2	11.4	6.5	40.0	2.8	5.3	5.9	14.1	10.8
1971	-2.0	43.5	42.9	7.7	11.6	7.9	45.6	3.3	6.0	7.9	1.9	14.0
1972	-6.4	49.2	48.4	9.4	13.2	8.3	55.6	4.3	7.8	9.6	13.1	21.9
1973	1.3	70.8	69.7	17.7	17.1	10.7	69.5	7.6	10.0	11.1	43.9	25.0
1974	-4.5	98.1	96.5	22.0	23.7	14.5	102.6	24.3	11.6	12.5	38.6	47.6
1975	9.1	107.7	106.1	21.9	28.5	17.2	98.5	24.8	12.0	12.2	9.8	-4.0
1976	-8.3	115.2	113.5	23.0	31.3	18.2	123.5	31.8	15.2	14.6	7.0	25.4
1977	-29.2	121.2	118.9	23.7	32.5	18.5	150.4	41.5	17.7	17.8	5.2	21.8
1978	-31.1	143.7	141.0	29.4	37.0	22.3	174.8	39.1	24.4	23.2	18.6	16.2
1979	-27.6	181.9	178.6	34.8	44.7	25.8	209.5	56.0	28.0	25.6	26.6	19.9
1980	-24.2	220.6	216.5	41.3	55.8	28.8	244.9	77.6	31.9	28.6	21.3	16.9
1981	-27.3	233.7	228.9	43.3	62.9	32.8	261.0	75.6	38.2	31.4	5.9	6.6
1982	-31.8	212.3	207.1	36.6	60.3	23.6	244.0	59.4	39.7	33.6	-9.2	-6.5
1983	-57.5	200.5	196.0	36.1	54.3	28.3	258.0	52.3	47.0	39.2	-5.6	5.7
1984	-107.9	217.9	212.1	37.8	60.3	29.7	325.7	55.9	68.4	50.8	8.7	26.2
1985	-132.1	213.1	206.9	29.2	59.5	34.8	345.3	49.6	75.3	62.0	-2.2	6.0
1986	-152.7	217.3	206.4	26.1	60.4	34.9	370.0	34.1	87.5	74.0	2.0	7.2
1987	-152.1	254.1	243.9	28.6	69.6	39.0	406.2	41.5	99.4	78.4	16.9	9.8
1988	-118.6	322.4	310.0	37.0	88.4	46.7	441.0	38.8	117.3	79.8	26.9	8.6
1989	-109.6	363.8	349.4	40.0	98.3	50.5	473.4	49.1	126.8	79.0	12.8	7.3
1990	-101.7	393.6	375.1	38.7	122.4	32.1	495.3	60.5	134.8	72.4	8.2	4.6
1991	-65.4	421.7	401.1	38.5	139.7	34.9	487.1	50.1	131.8	70.6	7.1	1.7
1992	-84.3	448.2	425.7	42.1	126.3	36.6	532.5	50.4	148.4	75.3	6.3	9.3

[1] Includes "Special Category" items and beginning 1974, includes trade of Virgin Islands with foreign countries. F.a.s. value basis. [2] Domestic and foreign exports excluding M.A.P. Grant-Aid shipments, through 1985; 1986 through 1988 include Grant-Aid shipments. [3] Includes commodity groups not shown separately. [4] 1970-73, 1982-91, customs value basis; 1974-81, f.a.s. value basis. Beginning 1974, includes trade of Virgin Islands with foreign countries. [5] 1970, change from 1965; thereafter, from previous year. For explanation of average annual percent change, see Guide to Tabular Presentation.

Source: U.S. Bureau of the Census, 1970-88, *Highlights of U.S. Export and Import Trade*, FT 990, monthly; beginning 1989, *U.S. Merchandise Trade: Export, General Imports, and Imports for Consumption*, series FT 925, monthly.

No. 1345. U.S. Exports, by State of Origin: 1990 to 1992

[In millions of dollars. Exports are on a f.a.s. value basis]

STATE AND OTHER AREAS	1990	1991	1992		STATE AND OTHER AREAS	1990	1991	1992	
			Total	Rank				Total	Rank
Total	394,045	421,851	448,156	(X)	MT	229	279	268	48
					NE	693	960	1,233	40
U.S.	315,065	351,343	379,263	(X)	NV	394	427	507	44
AL	2,834	3,325	3,629	26	NH	973	988	917	39
AK	2,850	3,134	3,195	28	NJ	7,633	8,740	8,955	13
AZ	3,729	4,465	5,109	20	NM	249	309	356	47
AR	920	1,147	1,324	37	NY	22,072	23,261	22,628	4
CA	44,520	50,415	56,307	1	NC	8,010	8,540	10,374	14
CO	2,274	2,574	2,594	29	ND	360	335	336	45
CT	4,356	4,995	5,028	19	OH	13,378	14,855	16,306	7
DE	1,344	1,441	1,508	36	OK	1,646	1,770	1,987	33
DC	320	269	344	(X)	OR	4,065	4,264	4,890	22
FL	11,634	13,257	14,431	9	PA	8,491	9,411	10,329	12
GA	5,763	6,815	7,652	15	RI	595	679	859	43
HI	179	148	206	50	SC	3,116	3,741	4,222	23
ID	898	958	1,076	41	SD	205	218	232	49
IL	12,965	14,025	15,328	8	TN	3,746	4,344	5,156	21
IN	5,273	5,724	6,148	16	TX	32,931	40,079	43,553	2
IA	2,189	2,263	2,476	30	UT	1,596	1,906	2,706	32
KS	2,113	2,148	2,514	31	VT	1,154	1,091	1,314	38
KY	3,175	3,217	3,648	27	VA	9,333	10,004	9,784	11
LA	14,199	15,456	16,151	6	WA	24,432	27,053	28,041	3
ME	870	915	902	42	WV	1,550	1,656	1,746	35
MD	2,592	3,363	3,879	25	WI	5,158	5,319	6,173	18
MA	9,501	10,018	10,400	10	WY	264	328	368	46
MI	18,474	20,236	20,414	5					
MN	5,091	5,376	6,137	17	PR	3,600	3,657	3,872	(X)
MS	1,605	1,738	1,963	34	VI	51	171	121	(X)
MO	3,130	3,367	3,664	24	Other [1]	75,328	66,680	64,900	(X)

X Not applicable. [1] Includes unreported, not specified, special category, estimated shipments, foreign trade zone, re-exports, and any timing adjustments.

Source: U.S. Bureau of the Census, *U.S. Merchandise Trade*, series FT 900, December issues.

No. 1346. U.S. Exports and Imports for Consumption of Merchandise, by Coastal Area and Customs District: 1980 to 1992

[In billions of dollars. Exports are f.a.s. (free alongside ship) value all years; imports are on customs value basis. See also *Historical Statistics, Colonial Times to 1970*, series U 264-273]

U.S. COASTAL AREA AND CUSTOMS DISTRICT	EXPORTS							IMPORTS FOR CONSUMPTION						
	1980	1985	1988	1989	1990	1991	1992	1980	1985	1988	1989	1990	1991	1992
Total [1]	220.8	213.1	320.4	363.8	393.0	421.9	447.5	244.0	343.6	437.1	468.0	490.6	483.0	525.1
North Atlantic area	68.8	46.5	69.2	79.2	85.7	90.6	89.2	79.8	107.1	126.3	126.8	128.7	123.6	130.6
Portland, ME.	4.3	0.6	1.0	1.2	1.7	2.1	1.8	1.6	2.3	3.4	3.5	4.3	3.8	4.0
St. Albans, VT.	0.7	1.1	1.9	2.7	4.0	4.1	4.0	1.6	2.7	3.6	4.2	5.2	5.2	5.3
Boston, MA	0.8	3.0	5.7	6.2	5.6	4.3	4.4	5.0	8.2	12.6	12.0	12.2	11.8	12.0
Providence, RI	2.7	0.1	(Z)	(Z)	(Z)	(Z)	(Z)	1.5	2.3	1.5	1.4	1.3	1.1	1.1
New York, NY.	38.9	28.5	42.4	47.0	50.9	54.6	53.4	43.4	60.5	69.7	70.4	68.0	67.4	72.8
Philadelphia, PA	3.2	2.0	3.4	3.9	4.0	4.4	4.4	15.6	15.8	15.6	16.0	18.3	16.1	16.4
Baltimore, MD.	9.0	5.5	6.8	7.7	6.7	8.0	7.7	6.0	8.8	12.1	11.8	11.2	10.1	10.8
Norfolk, VA [2].	8.0	5.4	7.3	9.4	11.7	11.5	11.9	4.7	6.0	7.0	6.8	7.4	7.4	7.5
Washington, DC	0.3	0.5	0.7	1.1	1.1	1.6	1.6	0.4	0.5	0.8	0.7	0.8	0.7	0.8
South Atlantic area	14.7	15.0	24.2	27.7	31.0	34.5	38.7	15.5	20.4	28.4	31.5	34.5	33.6	37.8
Wilmington, NC [2]	1.3	1.3	1.4	2.1	3.0	2.8	3.9	1.1	1.9	2.9	3.0	3.3	3.4	4.6
Charleston, SC [2]	3.1	2.9	5.0	6.2	6.7	7.2	7.3	1.8	3.3	6.1	6.5	6.8	6.3	6.6
Savannah, GA.	2.4	3.4	6.0	6.8	7.4	8.4	8.9	2.2	5.1	8.3	4.5	9.8	10.1	11.3
San Juan, PR	0.9	1.2	1.7	2.1	2.5	2.4	2.5	3.7	4.0	4.1	4.7	5.4	4.8	5.0
Virgin Islands of the U.S..	0.1	0.1	0.1	0.1	0.2	0.3	0.1	4.1	1.7	1.0	1.6	2.1	1.7	1.8
Miami, FL.	6.9	6.1	9.9	10.4	11.2	13.4	16.0	2.6	4.4	6.0	6.2	7.1	7.3	8.4
Gulf area	51.1	38.4	49.7	56.9	58.2	66.0	70.9	62.3	50.5	56.3	64.1	72.3	67.6	70.4
Tampa, FL [2]	2.8	2.8	3.6	4.0	4.3	5.2	5.2	3.7	6.6	7.3	6.7	7.0	6.8	7.0
Mobile, AL [2]	2.6	1.1	1.4	1.9	1.9	2.2	2.2	3.0	2.8	2.8	3.4	3.4	3.3	3.2
New Orleans, LA	19.5	13.9	16.9	18.5	18.0	18.8	20.1	22.5	14.7	17.1	20.6	24.1	22.3	23.3
Port Arthur, TX	2.0	0.8	1.1	1.2	0.9	0.7	0.8	9.4	2.7	1.8	2.8	3.2	2.8	3.1
Laredo, TX	8.3	7.2	10.6	13.4	15.2	18.2	21.7	2.7	4.8	7.9	9.4	10.0	10.4	11.8
St. Louis, MO	0.2	0.1	0.2	0.5	0.3	0.4	0.7	0.9	1.6	2.7	3.0	3.0	2.8	3.4
Houston/Galveston, TX .	15.7	12.5	15.9	17.4	17.6	20.5	20.2	20.1	17.3	16.7	18.2	21.6	19.2	18.7
Pacific area	43.8	49.6	82.8	98.9	111.2	120.0	129.5	43.1	80.4	111.8	121.4	125.7	127.3	139.5
San Diego, CA	1.4	1.6	2.5	3.0	3.4	3.9	4.6	1.0	1.8	3.4	4.0	4.3	4.7	5.5
Los Angeles, CA	14.8	19.5	32.0	38.6	42.1	46.0	49.4	20.0	44.1	58.0	62.3	64.1	66.4	71.9
San Francisco, CA	10.6	11.3	19.1	21.4	23.1	23.9	27.1	8.3	15.5	25.1	27.1	28.0	29.2	33.2
Portland, OR.	3.8	3.5	5.6	6.2	5.8	6.0	7.2	2.6	3.8	5.8	5.7	5.6	5.3	5.1
Seattle, WA	12.0	12.1	20.9	26.6	32.6	35.0	35.5	9.2	13.4	17.8	20.2	20.9	18.9	20.5
Anchorage, AK	1.0	1.3	2.2	2.6	3.7	4.6	5.1	0.2	0.2	0.2	0.4	0.7	0.9	1.3
Honolulu, HI	0.2	0.4	0.6	0.5	0.5	0.6	0.6	1.8	1.6	1.6	1.7	2.1	1.9	2.1
Great Lakes area	35.0	46.5	62.6	63.9	78.7	80.6	85.7	37.0	72.3	95.9	103.7	107.5	108.1	121.3
Ogdensburg, NY	3.8	4.1	5.3	5.6	7.9	7.5	7.9	4.6	6.8	8.5	9.2	9.8	9.9	10.0
Buffalo, NY.	6.3	8.4	10.5	9.5	15.8	15.7	18.0	7.4	14.7	18.1	19.0	19.2	18.7	21.2
Pembina, ND	2.3	2.2	2.8	3.4	3.4	4.3	4.3	3.0	3.2	3.3	3.9	4.1	4.1	4.5
Minneapolis, MN	0.1	0.2	0.5	0.8	0.9	0.9	1.1	0.3	1.0	1.6	1.9	2.0	2.2	2.7
Duluth, MN	1.5	0.9	1.2	1.2	0.8	0.8	0.9	3.0	3.0	3.2	3.5	3.9	3.3	3.6
Milwaukee, WI.	0.4	0.2	0.1	0.1	0.1	0.1	0.1	0.4	1.0	1.1	0.9	1.1	1.1	1.2
Detroit, MI	14.6	22.8	30.1	28.9	35.6	36.0	37.4	12.7	27.4	35.7	38.7	37.8	37.6	42.0
Chicago, IL.	4.2	5.4	8.7	10.0	10.2	11.3	11.9	4.1	11.4	16.1	17.4	18.3	19.4	22.5
Cleveland, OH.	1.8	2.1	3.4	3.9	4.0	4.0	4.1	1.5	3.8	8.3	9.2	11.3	11.8	13.8
Other statistical areas [3]..	7.4	17.1	31.8	37.7	28.2	30.2	33.3	6.3	12.7	18.5	19.8	21.9	22.8	25.3
El Paso, TX	1.8	2.1	3.8	4.0	3.9	4.7	6.1	1.4	2.5	4.5	5.1	5.0	5.5	6.5
Nogales, AZ	0.8	0.8	1.3	1.5	2.1	2.2	2.8	1.2	2.0	3.2	3.7	4.2	4.4	4.6
Great Falls, MT.	1.8	1.5	1.6	1.8	2.4	3.3	3.1	3.2	4.0	4.0	4.1	4.7	4.6	4.9
Dallas/Fort Worth, TX .	0.5	1.0	2.1	2.7	3.4	2.6	3.9	1.2	2.4	4.1	4.1	4.8	4.9	5.3

Z Less than $50 million. [1] Totals shown for exports reflect the value of estimated parcel post and Special Category shipments, and beginning 1988, adjustments for undocumented exports to Canada which are not distributed by coastal area/customs district. Beginning 1985, the value of bituminous coal exported through Norfolk, VA; Charleston, SC; and Mobile, AL is reflected in the total but not distributed by district. [2] Beginning 1985, excludes exports of bituminous coal. [3] Includes estimated shipments and vessel-own power.

Source: U.S. Bureau of the Census, 1980-1988, *Highlights of U.S. Export and Import Trade*, FT 990; beginning 1989, *U.S. Merchandise Trade: Selected Highlights*, series FT 920, monthly.

No. 1347. Export and Import Unit Value Indexes—Selected Countries: 1988 to 1992

[Indexes in U.S. dollars, 1985 = 100. A unit value is an implicit price derived from value and quantity data. NA Not available]

COUNTRY	EXPORT UNIT VALUE					IMPORT UNIT VALUE				
	1988	1989	1990	1991	1992	1988	1989	1990	1991	1992
United States	109.9	112.8	113.9	114.9	115.0	108.6	111.9	115.6	115.6	116.5
Australia.	131.7	140.6	140.0	127.7	(NA)	126.6	126.8	130.2	131.3	129.3
Austria.	160.7	146.2	169.6	159.8	(NA)	147.1	141.0	160.0	156.1	(NA)
Belgium-Luxembourg	145.3	146.3	167.4	161.6	(NA)	134.8	134.9	156.0	151.6	(NA)
Canada	111.2	118.4	119.2	117.1	114.3	107.3	111.9	115.6	116.1	114.7
Denmark.	149.3	146.2	169.9	164.7	172.6	138.3	136.5	155.8	151.6	155.4
France.	145.9	144.1	166.1	159.0	(NA)	129.7	129.4	149.0	142.6	(NA)
Germany	159.2	155.5	178.9	173.1	182.7	133.4	133.9	151.9	150.4	154.9
Italy	148.5	149.8	175.2	174.1	(NA)	123.9	126.5	143.8	137.8	(NA)
Japan.	143.7	143.2	141.7	151.2	163.9	102.9	107.0	112.7	110.9	110.1
Norway.	95.9	101.4	116.8	108.2	104.1	139.5	139.5	155.0	147.2	149.9
Sweden	147.9	150.9	167.5	165.4	(NA)	138.3	136.5	151.6	147.4	(NA)
United Kingdom	130.4	129.5	148.1	147.5	148.7	134.5	132.6	149.3	149.0	148.4

Source: International Monetary Fund, Washington, DC, *International Financial Statistics*, monthly.

No. 1348. Characteristics of U.S. Exporters: 1987

SIC [1] code	INDUSTRY AND EMPLOYMENT-SIZE CLASS	Number of exporters	Number of employees (1,000)	Value of exports [2] (mil. dol.)	PERCENT DISTRIBUTION		
					Number of exporters	Number of employees (1,000)	Value of exports [2] (mil. dol.)
(X)	**All industries.**	129,883	10,276	241,273	100.0	100.0	100.0
	Less than 20 employees.	66,935	472	29,884	51.5	4.6	12.4
	20 to 99 employees.	28,071	1,068	18,244	21.6	10.4	7.6
	100 to 499 employees	13,722	1,582	21,171	10.6	15.4	8.8
	500 employees or more	21,155	7,155	171,973	16.3	69.6	71.3
(X)	Manufacturing.	54,045	8,654	155,607	41.6	84.2	64.5
20	Food and kindred products	2,751	446	15,298	2.1	4.3	6.3
21	Tobacco products	189	78	1,974	0.1	0.8	0.8
22	Textile mill products	1,177	239	1,188	0.9	2.3	0.5
23	Apparel and other textile products	1,477	130	509	1.1	1.3	0.2
24	Lumber and wood products	1,402	115	1,875	1.1	1.1	0.8
25	Furniture and fixtures	958	167	534	0.7	1.6	0.2
26	Paper and allied products	1,474	296	5,953	1.1	2.9	2.5
27	Printing, publishing & allied products	2,211	266	1,195	1.7	2.6	0.5
28	Chemicals and allied products	3,894	553	17,885	3.0	5.4	7.4
29	Petroleum and coal products	507	70	5,895	0.4	0.7	2.4
30	Rubber and misc. plastics products	3,193	349	2,645	2.5	3.4	1.1
31	Leather and leather products	395	40	274	0.3	0.4	0.1
32	Stone, clay, and glass products	1,353	185	1,352	1.0	1.8	0.6
33	Primary metal products	1,952	421	3,835	1.5	4.1	1.6
34	Fabricated metal products	5,317	497	3,634	4.1	4.8	1.5
35	Machinery, except electrical	9,729	1,064	21,076	7.5	10.4	8.7
36	Electronic & other electric equipment.	5,697	844	10,803	4.4	8.2	4.5
37	Transportation equipment	3,358	1,940	45,312	2.6	18.9	18.8
38	Instruments and related products	4,837	812	13,389	3.7	7.9	5.5
39	Misc. manufactured commodities	2,174	142	983	1.7	1.4	0.4
(X)	Wholesalers.	48,928	835	68,452	37.7	8.1	28.4
	Agricultural	2,096	30	12,614	1.6	0.3	5.2
	Manufactured	45,819	791	54,283	35.3	7.7	22.5
	Other	1,013	14	1,555	0.8	0.1	0.6
	Other intermediaries [3]	26,910	788	17,213	20.7	7.7	7.1

[1] Standard Industrial Classification.   [2] Based on f.o.b. (free on board) basis which excludes freight and wholesale margins.
[3] Includes retailers, brokers, freight forwarders, and others.

Source: U.S. Bureau of the Census, unpublished data.

No. 1349. U.S. Trade in Advanced Technology Products: 1989 to 1992

[In billions of dollars. Exports are f.a.s. value basis and imports are on customs value basis]

PRODUCT CATEGORY	EXPORTS				GENERAL IMPORTS				MERCHANDISE TRADE BALANCE			
	1989	1990	1991	1992	1989	1990	1991	1992	1989	1990	1991	1992
Total [1].	83.5	93.4	100.0	105.1	56.4	59.3	63.1	71.8	27.1	34.1	36.9	33.3
Advanced materials [2].	5.3	6.4	6.2	0.6	0.8	1.0	1.1	0.4	4.5	5.4	5.1	0.2
Aerospace.	30.6	37.0	41.9	42.5	9.2	10.7	12.1	12.8	21.4	26.3	29.8	29.7
Biotechnology [3]	0.5	0.6	0.7	0.7	(Z)	(Z)	(Z)	(Z)	0.5	0.6	0.7	0.7
Electronics.	7.3	7.5	8.9	16.5	10.7	11.0	12.4	15.4	-3.4	-3.5	-3.5	1.2
Flexible manufacturing [4].	3.1	3.1	3.3	3.4	2.0	1.7	1.8	1.7	1.1	1.4	1.5	1.7
Information and communications	28.1	31.4	30.7	32.5	29.4	30.2	29.2	33.9	-1.3	1.2	1.5	-1.4
Life science	4.2	4.9	5.5	5.8	3.0	3.4	4.3	4.8	1.2	1.5	1.2	1.1
Nuclear technology	1.4	1.3	1.3	1.5	(Z)	(Z)	(Z)	(Z)	1.4	1.3	1.3	1.5
Opto-electronics [5]	0.4	0.5	0.6	0.6	0.9	1.1	2.0	2.6	-0.5	-0.6	-1.4	-2.0
Weapons.	0.7	0.7	0.9	0.8	0.2	0.1	0.2	(Z)	0.5	0.6	0.7	0.6

Z Less than $50 million.   [1] 1989 includes end of year adjustments for carry-over and other corrections not carried to kind of product detail; therefore, detail will not add.   [2] Encompasses recent advances in the development of materials that allow for further development and application of other advanced technologies. Examples are semiconductor materials, optical fiber cable and video discs.   [3] Biotechnology is the medical and industrial application of advanced scientific discoveries in genetics to the creation of new drugs, hormones and other therapeutic items for both agricultural and human use.   [4] Encompasses advances in robotics, numerically—controlled machine tools, and similar products involving industrial automation that allow for greater flexibility to the manufacturing process and reduce the amount of human intervention. Includes robots, numerically controlled machine tools and semiconductor production and assembly machines.   [5] Encompasses electronic products and components that involve the emitting and/or detection of light. Examples of products included are optical scanners, optical disc players, solar cells, photo-sensitive semiconductors and laser printers.

Source: U. S. Bureau of the Census, *U. S. Merchandise Trade*, series FT 900, December issues.

No. 1350. U.S. Exports and General Imports of Selected Commodities—Value, by Area: 1991

[In millions of dollars. Includes nonmonetary gold. Exports are f.a.s. (free alongside ship) transaction value basis; imports are customs value basis. N.e.s. = Not elsewhere specified]

SELECTED MAJOR COMMODITIES	Total [1]	WESTERN HEMISPHERE		WESTERN EUROPE				ASIA		
		Canada	Mexico	United Kingdom	Germany[1]	France	Italy	Japan	China: Taiwan	South Korea
Exports, total	421,730	85,150	33,277	22,046	21,302	15,345	8,570	48,125	13,182	15,505
Meat and meat preparations	3,653	587	508	6	8	49	14	1,593	21	209
Fish (except marine mammal) crustaceans, etc., preparations	3,181	410	36	139	61	99	37	1,879	44	158
Cereals and cereal preparations	10,927	367	686	71	47	64	125	2,165	746	399
Vegetables and fruit	5,908	2,278	155	266	300	139	82	1,050	166	81
Feeding stuff for animals not including unmilled cereal	3,281	404	164	74	58	104	83	430	52	20
Miscellaneous edible products and preparations	1,364	318	74	12	13	17	2	99	99	39
Tobacco and tobacco manufactures	6,028	18	4	48	264	21	68	1,579	152	119
Hides, skins, and furskins, raw	1,389	60	140	3	13	10	38	282	130	603
Oil seeds and oleaginous fruits	4,320	100	390	111	202	30	59	891	467	244
Cork and wood	5,131	690	227	95	134	45	203	2,490	140	280
Pulp and waste paper	3,627	239	290	144	224	188	331	702	206	345
Textile fibers & their wastes (excluding wool tops, etc)	3,704	169	113	46	122	11	164	533	132	386
Crude fertilizers & crude minerals [2]	1,433	251	95	39	71	26	51	326	46	76
Metalliferous ores and metal scrap	4,163	1,002	178	103	68	34	55	709	228	600
Crude animal and vegetable materials, n.e.s.	1,128	210	133	40	70	27	33	155	16	31
Coal, coke and briquettes	4,781	489	22	286	69	389	516	536	190	171
Petroleum, petroleum products, and related materials	6,770	673	744	58	50	241	261	537	233	497
Organic chemicals	11,044	1,140	708	368	489	208	226	1,179	1,028	594
Inorganic chemicals	4,141	510	260	134	239	67	44	1,139	94	201
Dyeing, tanning and coloring materials	1,662	489	114	90	53	28	17	113	58	68
Medicinal and pharmaceutical products	4,679	564	121	235	325	288	361	812	61	65
Essential oils, etc; toilet, polishing, preparations	2,430	534	120	145	90	64	39	284	72	71
Fertilizers	2,994	202	52	7	27	56	13	166	3	75
Plastics in primary forms	7,560	1,279	608	235	222	74	63	519	360	312
Plastics in nonprimary forms	2,821	772	357	125	125	80	46	197	58	71
Chemical materials and products, n.e.s.	6,098	1,230	314	260	354	257	140	666	104	202
Rubber manufactures, n.e.s.	2,326	1,037	286	72	68	29	16	225	20	37
Cork and wood manufactures other than furniture	1,292	306	158	130	129	12	22	111	55	57
Paper, paperboard and articles	6,034	1,564	778	240	233	102	101	520	121	147
Textile yarn, fabrics, made-up articles, n.e.s.	5,610	1,410	547	307	196	99	134	266	67	124
Nonmetallic mineral manufactures, n.e.s.	4,720	1,215	246	167	120	84	55	447	94	103
Iron and steel	4,457	1,471	879	108	64	67	48	285	135	334
Nonferrous metals	5,822	1,285	426	294	136	120	58	1,778	425	210
Manufactures of metals, n.e.s.	6,700	2,360	1,109	326	295	129	116	395	90	182
Power generating machinery and equipment	17,368	4,175	1,082	1,200	851	2,354	226	881	351	869
Machinery specialized for particular industries	17,192	3,027	1,239	862	786	553	296	973	284	600
Metalworking machinery	2,805	448	244	169	217	98	64	243	91	181
General industrial machinery, equipment, parts	17,567	4,852	1,599	853	764	560	278	1,089	536	795
Office machines and automatic data processing machines	29,461	4,589	1,131	3,058	2,995	1,484	646	3,746	499	632
Telecommunications, sound recording, reproduction apparatus and equipment	10,896	1,763	1,643	581	433	230	288	1,086	432	420
Electrical machinery, apparatus, and appliances, n.e.s.	34,479	7,936	4,340	1,866	1,666	1,049	635	2,815	1,704	1,420
Road vehicles (incl. air-cushion vehicles)	33,133	17,648	3,650	394	1,596	345	106	1,344	838	361
Transport equipment, n.e.s.	37,188	1,870	754	3,167	2,966	2,196	1,025	3,278	1,150	1,457
Furniture, bedding, mattresses, etc.	2,172	941	536	72	58	36	7	95	11	14
Articles of apparel and clothing accessories	3,316	273	547	95	70	79	71	431	8	7
Professional scientific and control instruments and apparatus	14,062	1,990	1,028	982	1,154	834	489	1,821	335	519
Photo apparatus, equipment and optical goods n.e.s.; watch and clocks	4,247	647	220	527	232	390	101	656	67	37
Miscellaneous manufactured articles	21,212	4,459	1,335	1,710	1,644	854	323	2,499	439	542
Special transactions and commodities not classified by kind	3,737	1,264	187	138	105	43	13	213	94	145
Gold, nonmonetary (excluding ores and concentrates	3,337	411	80	608	61	328	5	81	55	8
Shipments under $10,000 and under $1,500 documented exports	9,854	1,493	1,423	690	556	415	204	621	181	140

See footnotes at end of table.

No. 1350. U.S. Exports and General Imports of Selected Commodities—Value, by Area: 1990—Continued

[In millions of dollars. See headnote, page 811]

SELECTED MAJOR COMMODITIES	Total [1]	WESTERN HEMISPHERE		WESTERN EUROPE				ASIA		
		Canada	Mexico	United Kingdom	Ger-many [1]	France	Italy	Japan	China: Taiwan	South Korea
Imports, total	487,129	91,064	31,130	18,413	26,137	13,333	11,764	91,511	23,023	17,018
Meat and meat preparations	2,908	603	2	(Z)	2	3	6	4	1	(Z)
Fish (except marine mammal) crustaceans, etc., preps	5,638	1,230	291	19	2	22	2	127	168	131
Vegetables and fruit.	5,391	273	1,382	12	92	20	36	41	60	14
Coffee, tea, cocoa, spices manufactures thereof	3,347	167	363	24	88	10	16	3	7	1
Beverages	3,609	569	234	602	158	812	340	31	4	5
Cork and wood	3,057	2,715	143	1	1	3	2	(Z)	4	(Z)
Pulp and waste paper	2,163	1,870	1	(Z)	6	(Z)	-	(Z)	1	-
Metalliferous ores and metal scrap. . . .	3,561	942	202	61	37	32	1	18	6	1
Petroleum, petroleum products, and related materials	49,762	6,636	4,564	1,391	54	303	447	19	(Z)	35
Gas, natural and manufactured	3,497	3,074	108	7	4	4	5	(Z)	(Z)	-
Organic chemicals.	8,133	757	248	917	1,139	449	385	979	52	74
Inorganic chemicals.	3,296	1,024	182	197	429	260	53	185	9	4
Medicinal and pharmaceutical products. .	3,047	118	18	587	403	128	216	268	4	2
Chemical materials and products, n.e.s.	2,122	302	55	201	331	139	42	280	11	3
Rubber manufactures, n.e.s	3,334	913	55	88	197	151	91	942	193	216
Cork and wood manufactures other than furniture	1,988	666	102	10	24	45	45	11	251	8
Paper, paperboard and articles	8,021	6,111	119	173	228	131	60	218	63	65
Textile yarn, fabrics, made-up articles, n.e.s.	6,981	500	324	269	327	184	499	615	500	554
Nonmetallic mineral manufactures, n.e.s. .	9,678	672	435	537	411	313	578	701	362	102
Iron and steel.	9,333	1,531	304	333	764	567	235	2,049	135	588
Nonferrous metals.	8,430	3,636	330	343	417	136	30	352	26	5
Manufactures of metals, n.e.s	8,834	1,270	569	260	548	257	223	1,724	1,585	503
Power generating machinery and equipment	14,195	2,324	1,131	1,698	1,507	2,200	227	3,123	89	100
Machinery specialized for particular industries	10,864	1,109	140	819	2,608	441	646	2,909	342	67
Metalworking machinery	3,605	232	7	173	718	61	134	1,562	144	26
General industrial machinery, equipment, parts	14,396	1,792	831	896	2,088	362	720	3,904	848	319
Office machines and automatic data processing machines	30,019	2,283	724	989	644	282	150	11,831	3,752	1,289
Telecommunications, sound recording, reproduction apparatus and equipment .	23,446	1,000	2,944	246	180	146	67	9,394	1,202	1,745
Electrical machinery, apparatus and appliances, n.e.s.	35,067	3,626	4,838	973	2,055	569	262	9,352	2,228	2,432
Road vehicles (incl air-cushion vehicles) .	70,576	25,577	4,273	867	5,425	712	528	28,344	804	1,223
Transport equipment, n.e.s.	8,197	2,428	33	1,075	169	1,441	502	633	43	84
Furniture, bedding, mattresses, etc.	4,936	1,066	651	100	175	56	444	208	1,106	50
Travel goods, handbags and similar containers.	2,346	16	52	5	12	78	190	9	370	379
Articles of apparel and clothing accessories	26,202	315	910	177	127	179	857	138	2,658	2,762
Footwear.	9,554	45	163	40	43	46	787	7	1,168	1,987
Professional scientific and control instruments and apparatus	6,733	577	643	624	1,012	274	75	1,796	194	83
Photo apparatus, equipment and optical goods,n.e.s.; watch and clocks.	7,469	221	150	270	353	214	303	2,996	355	152
Miscellaneous manufactured articles, n.e.s.	24,846	1,340	911	1,346	898	703	1,500	4,018	3,025	1,535
Special transactions and commodities not classified by kind	11,718	3,761	1,083	1,092	757	522	171	820	118	133
Estimate of low valued import transactions	3,424	879	302	201	323	115	108	543	160	38

- Represents zero.   Z Less than $500,000.   [1] Effective October 3, 1990 East Germany ceased to exist as a sovereign state and became a part of West Germany. However, trade statistics for Germany comprise of statistics for West Germany and East Germany combined for the period shown.   [2] Other than fertilizers covered in SITC division 56 (Fertilizers).   [3] Other than crude fertilizers covered in SITC division 272.

Source: U.S. Bureau of the Census, *U.S. Merchandise Trade: Exports, General Imports, and Imports for Consumption*, series FT 927.

No. 1351. U.S. Exports, Imports, and Merchandise Trade Balance, by Country: 1989 to 1992

[In millions of dollars. Includes silver ore and bullion. Country totals include exports of special category commodities, if any. Data include nonmonetary gold and includes trade of Virgin Islands with foreign countries, see footnote 2 for exception. Minus sign (-) denotes an excess of imports over exports. See Historical Statistics, Colonial Times to 1970, series U 317-352, for selected countries]

COUNTRY	EXPORTS, DOMESTIC AND FOREIGN				GENERAL IMPORTS [1]				MERCHANDISE TRADE BALANCE			
	1989	1990	1991	1992	1989	1990	1991	1992	1989	1990	1991	1992
Total [2]	363,812	393,592	421,730	448,156	473,211	495,311	487,129	532,498	-109,399	-101,718	-65,399	-84,341
Afghanistan	5	4	3	2	5	5	5	2	(Z)	-1	-2	(Z)
Albania	5	10	18	36	2	2	3	5	3	8	15	31
Algeria	756	951	727	677	1,829	2,626	2,103	1,589	-1,074	-1,674	-1,376	-912
Andorra	50	40	17	16	(Z)	(Z)	(Z)	(Z)	50	40	17	16
Angola	97	152	186	158	1,929	1,904	1,775	2,303	-1,832	-1,752	-1,589	-2,145
Anguilla	17	15	11	11	(Z)	(Z)	4	(Z)	17	15	10	11
Antigua	74	69	74	68	12	4	4	5	62	65	70	63
Argentina	1,039	1,179	2,045	3,222	1,391	1,511	1,287	1,254	-352	-333	758	1,967
Armenia	(X)	(X)	(X)	25	(X)	(X)	(X)	1	(X)	(X)	(X)	23
Aruba	127	202	235	288	1	1	100	212	126	201	135	76
Australia	8,331	8,538	8,404	8,913	3,873	4,447	3,988	3,692	4,458	4,091	4,416	5,221
Austria	873	875	1,056	1,257	1,136	1,318	1,264	1,306	-263	-444	-208	-49
Azerbaijan	(X)	(X)	(X)	(Z)	(X)	(X)	(X)	(Z)	(X)	(X)	(X)	(Z)
Bahamas, The	772	800	721	713	462	509	470	585	310	291	252	127
Bahrain	489	721	500	489	80	81	87	61	409	640	413	428
Bangladesh	282	181	179	188	428	539	524	832	-147	-357	-345	-644
Barbados	180	161	166	128	46	31	31	31	134	130	135	97
Belgium	8,381	10,318	10,572	9,779	4,351	4,375	3,929	4,479	4,029	5,942	6,643	5,300
Belize	101	105	114	117	43	47	45	59	58	58	69	58
Benin	18	24	26	27	11	17	23	10	6	6	4	17
Bermuda	354	255	233	242	11	12	8	24	343	242	225	219
Bolivia	145	138	192	222	118	203	209	161	27	-65	-17	61
Bosnia-Hercegovina	(X)	(X)	(X)	5	(X)	(X)	(X)	10	(X)	(X)	(X)	-4
Botswana	30	19	31	47	17	13	13	12	13	6	18	34
Brazil	4,804	5,048	6,148	5,740	8,410	7,898	6,717	7,611	-3,606	-2,850	-569	-1,871
British Virgin Islands	49	60	45	44	1	2	3	3	48	47	43	41
Brunei	63	143	162	453	75	96	27	30	-12	47	136	424
Bulgaria	181	84	142	85	59	47	56	79	122	37	86	7
Burkina	10	15	24	13	–	1	1	(Z)	10	14	23	13
Burma	5	20	23	4	17	23	27	38	-12	-3	-4	-34
Byelarus	(X)	(X)	(X)	25	(X)	(X)	(X)	25	(X)	(X)	(X)	(Z)
Cameroon	35	47	45	57	426	147	127	84	-391	-100	-82	-27
Canada	78,809	83,674	85,150	90,562	87,953	91,380	91,064	98,497	-9,144	-7,707	-5,914	-7,935
Cayman Islands	204	183	117	267	48	21	18	11	155	162	99	256
Chad	35	8	14	5	(X)	(Z)	(Z)	(Z)	35	8	14	5
Chile	1,414	1,664	1,839	2,455	1,292	1,313	1,302	1,387	122	351	537	1,068
China: Mainland	5,755	4,806	6,278	7,470	11,990	15,237	18,969	25,729	-6,235	-10,431	-12,691	-18,260
China: Taiwan	11,335	11,491	13,182	15,205	24,313	22,666	23,023	24,601	-12,978	-11,175	-9,841	-9,397
Colombia	1,924	2,029	1,952	3,282	2,555	3,168	2,736	2,849	-631	-1,139	-784	433
Congo (Brazzaville)	12	90	43	60	504	414	410	510	-492	-324	-367	-450
Costa Rica	882	986	1,034	1,351	962	1,005	1,154	1,411	-81	-19	-120	-60
Croatia	(X)	(X)	(X)	91	(X)	(X)	(X)	43	(X)	(X)	(X)	48
Cyprus	109	129	119	166	15	19	12	11	94	111	107	155
Czechoslovakia	53	85	123	413	85	87	145	242	-32	-2	-22	171
Denmark	1,051	1,311	1,574	1,477	1,535	1,678	1,661	1,668	-484	-367	-87	-192

See footnotes at end of table.

No. 1351. U.S. Exports, Imports, and Merchandise Trade Balance, by Country: 1989 to 1992—Continued

[See headnote, page 813]

COUNTRY	EXPORTS, DOMESTIC AND FOREIGN				GENERAL IMPORTS [1]				MERCHANDISE TRADE BALANCE			
	1989	1990	1991	1992	1989	1990	1991	1992	1989	1990	1991	1992
Djibouti	3	7	10	11	(Z)	(Z)	(Z)	(X)	3	7	10	11
Dominica	33	31	42	34	7	9	5	5	26	22	37	29
Dominican Republic	1,645	1,656	1,743	2,098	1,646	1,752	2,008	2,372	-1	-96	-265	-274
East Germany [3]	94	62	(X)	(X)	139	85	(X)	(X)	-45	-23	(X)	(X)
Ecuador	643	678	948	999	1,474	1,376	1,327	1,343	-832	-697	-379	-344
Egypt	2,612	2,249	2,720	3,087	227	398	206	435	2,385	1,851	2,514	2,653
El Salvador	520	554	534	741	245	238	303	384	275	316	231	357
Equatorial Guinea	(Z)	(Z)	13	11	(X)	(Z)	(Z)	(Z)	(Z)	(Z)	13	11
Estonia	(X)	(X)	(X)	59	(X)	(X)	(X)	13	(X)	(X)	(X)	46
Ethiopia	67	157	210	250	70	40	15	9	-3	117	196	241
Federated States of Micronesia	27	25	46	32	1	6	5	13	26	19	41	19
Fiji	22	25	18	59	16	34	43	73	6	-9	-25	-14
Finland	969	1,126	952	787	1,370	1,262	1,085	1,186	-402	-136	-133	-399
France	11,579	13,665	15,346	14,575	13,014	13,153	13,333	14,811	-1,435	511	2,013	-236
French Guiana	270	271	150	82	5	2	(X)	4	265	269	150	78
French Polynesia	70	70	80	82	8	10	12	11	62	60	68	71
Gabon	46	49	85	55	437	701	712	928	-390	-652	-627	-873
Gambia	10	9	11	10	1	2	2	(Z)	9	7	9	10
Georgia	(X)	(X)	(X)	16	(X)	(X)	(X)	7	(X)	(X)	(X)	9
Germany [3]	16,956	18,760	21,302	21,236	24,971	28,162	26,137	28,829	-8,015	-9,402	-4,835	-7,593
Ghana	121	140	142	124	127	169	152	96	-7	-29	-10	27
Gibraltar	2	32	10	11	(X)	1	1	7	2	31	9	4
Greece	697	763	1,039	897	473	509	429	370	224	255	610	527
Greenland	3	6	4	3	8	8	8	12	-5	-2	-4	-8
Grenada	28	35	31	24	24	8	8	8	4	27	23	16
Guadeloupe	34	53	83	60	2	2	2	1	32	52	81	59
Guatemala	662	764	945	1,204	609	794	899	1,075	53	-31	46	128
Guinea	40	43	88	61	132	141	138	102	-92	-98	-50	-41
Guyana	78	76	86	118	56	53	83	102	22	23	3	17
Haiti	472	477	395	217	374	343	284	107	97	134	111	110
Honduras	515	564	625	808	461	491	557	783	54	73	68	26
Hong Kong	6,291	6,817	8,137	9,069	9,722	9,622	9,279	9,799	-3,431	-2,805	-1,142	-731
Hungary	122	156	256	295	328	348	367	349	-207	-191	-111	-54
Iceland	179	232	156	119	208	163	209	166	-29	69	-53	-47
India	2,458	2,486	1,999	1,914	3,315	3,197	3,193	3,781	-857	-711	-1,194	-1,866
Indonesia	1,247	1,897	1,892	2,778	3,529	3,341	3,241	4,527	-2,282	-1,444	-1,349	-1,749
Iran	55	163	528	748	8	7	231	1	47	156	297	747
Iraq	1,169	732	(Z)	1	2,415	3,008	6	(X)	-1,246	-2,276	-6	1
Ireland	2,483	2,540	2,681	2,853	1,566	1,755	1,948	2,264	917	784	733	589
Israel	2,827	3,203	3,911	4,074	1,576	3,313	3,484	3,812	1,251	-110	427	262
Italy	7,215	7,992	8,570	8,698	11,933	12,751	11,764	12,300	-4,718	-4,760	-3,194	-3,602
Ivory Coast	79	81	81	87	234	200	223	188	-155	-121	-142	-100
Jamaica	1,006	943	961	939	509	569	576	599	497	374	385	340
Japan	44,494	48,580	48,125	47,764	93,553	89,684	91,511	97,181	-49,059	-41,105	-43,386	-49,418
Jordan	380	309	219	250	8	11	6	18	372	298	213	232
Kazakhstan	(X)	(X)	(X)	15	(X)	(X)	(X)	21	(X)	(X)	(X)	-6
Kenya	133	116	91	124	68	58	69	73	65	58	22	51
Kiribati	16	19	27	35	1	(Z)	1	1	14	19	26	35

COUNTRY	EXPORTS, DOMESTIC AND FOREIGN				GENERAL IMPORTS [1]				MERCHANDISE TRADE BALANCE			
	1989	1990	1991	1992	1989	1990	1991	1992	1989	1990	1991	1992
Kuwait	853	403	1,228	1,327	973	569	36	281	-120	-166	1,192	1,046
Kyrgyzstan	(X)	(X)	(X)	2	(X)	(X)	(X)	1	(X)	(X)	(X)	1
Laos	(Z)	1	1	1	1	2	2	6	-1	-1	-1	-5
Latvia	(X)	(X)	(X)	5	(X)	(X)	(X)	10	(X)	(X)	(X)	-5
Lebanon	94	98	165	311	31	24	27	28	63	74	138	283
Lesotho	4	3	4	3	19	25	27	53	-15	-22	-24	-50
Liberia	98	44	50	31	106	49	9	13	-8	-5	41	18
Libya	10	(Z)	(Z)	(X)	9	(Z)	(X)	(X)	1	(Z)	(Z)	(X)
Liechtenstein	(X)	12	10	12	(X)	15	21	36	(X)	-3	-11	-24
Lithuania	(X)	(X)	(X)	44	(X)	(X)	(X)	5	(X)	(X)	(X)	39
Luxembourg	142	134	217	272	218	210	188	227	-76	-76	29	45
Macao	11	8	10	19	654	736	581	721	-643	-728	-571	-702
Macedonia	(X)	(X)	(X)	4	(X)	(X)	(X)	46	(X)	(X)	(X)	-42
Madagascar	7	11	14	6	38	42	47	54	-30	-30	-33	-47
Malawi	14	14	55	14	39	49	73	59	-24	-36	-18	-45
Malaysia	2,870	3,425	3,900	4,396	4,744	5,272	6,102	8,294	-1,874	-1,847	-2,202	-3,898
Mali	11	9	18	11	9	3	2	1	3	6	16	10
Malta	48	45	57	58	60	40	65	91	-12	5	-8	-33
Marshall Islands	33	27	38	34	3	3	4	8	30	25	35	26
Martinique	25	34	36	33	10	1	1	2	15	33	35	31
Mauritania	13	15	22	59	10	24	11	9	2	-9	11	51
Mauritius	12	13	15	22	159	159	132	137	-147	-146	-117	-114
Mexico	24,982	28,279	33,277	40,598	27,162	30,157	31,130	35,189	-2,180	-1,878	2,147	5,408
Moldova	(X)	(X)	(X)	9	(X)	(X)	(X)	(Z)	(X)	(X)	(X)	9
Monaco	4	10	7	6	14	13	14	13	-9	-3	-7	-6
Montserrat	11	11	8	13	2	1	1	3	8	10	6	11
Morocco	394	495	403	493	98	109	154	178	296	386	249	315
Mozambique	41	50	101	150	20	29	23	19	21	21	78	130
Namibia	13	44	33	34	15	33	35	23	-2	11	-2	11
Nepal	9	10	6	5	47	51	55	73	-38	-41	-49	-68
Netherlands	11,364	13,022	13,511	13,740	4,810	4,952	4,811	5,287	6,554	8,071	8,700	8,453
Netherlands Antilles	412	543	627	476	383	429	647	646	29	114	-20	-170
New Caledonia	65	34	44	36	54	27	20	15	11	7	24	21
New Zealand	1,117	1,135	1,006	1,307	1,209	1,197	1,209	1,219	-91	-62	-203	88
Nicaragua	2	68	150	188	(Z)	15	60	69	2	52	91	119
Niger	9	12	10	10	2	46	5	3	7	-34	5	7
Nigeria	490	553	831	1,001	5,284	5,982	5,168	5,074	-4,794	-5,429	-4,337	-4,073
Norway	1,037	1,281	1,489	1,280	1,991	1,830	1,624	1,976	-955	-549	-135	-696
Oman	170	163	202	257	117	292	115	186	53	-129	87	71
Pakistan	1,134	1,143	950	877	523	610	663	865	612	533	288	12
Palau	10	14	14	10	(Z)	(Z)	(Z)	(Z)	10	14	14	10
Panama	724	869	978	1,100	268	234	269	254	455	635	709	847
Papua New Guinea	121	54	96	72	29	22	34	64	92	32	62	8
Paraguay	168	307	374	415	45	51	43	35	123	256	331	380
Peru	695	772	840	1,002	814	802	776	739	-119	-30	64	263
Philippines	2,202	2,471	2,265	2,753	3,068	3,384	3,471	4,358	-866	-913	-1,206	-1,605
Poland	414	406	459	637	387	408	357	374	26	-2	102	262
Portugal	925	922	792	1,024	800	832	695	664	125	91	97	360
Qatar	100	115	147	189	50	53	30	70	50	62	117	119

See footnotes at end of table.

No. 1351. U.S. Exports, Imports, and Merchandise Trade Balance, by Country: 1989 to 1992—Continued

[See headnote, page 813]

COUNTRY	EXPORTS, DOMESTIC AND FOREIGN 1989	1990	1991	1992	GENERAL IMPORTS[1] 1989	1990	1991	1992	MERCHANDISE TRADE BALANCE 1989	1990	1991	1992
Romania	155	369	209	248	354	231	69	87	-199	138	140	161
Russia	(X)	(X)	(X)	2,098	(X)	(X)	(X)	480	(X)	(X)	(X)	1,618
Saudi Arabia	3,574	4,049	6,557	7,163	7,157	10,021	10,900	10,367	-3,583	-5,971	-4,343	-3,204
Senegal	69	52	76	80	41	6	10	10	27	46	66	70
Sierra Leone	25	27	25	28	53	46	48	61	-28	-19	-23	-33
Singapore	7,345	8,023	8,804	9,624	9,003	9,800	9,957	11,318	-1,658	-1,778	-1,153	-1,694
Somalia	21	12	7	21	(Z)	(Z)	3	2	21	12	4	18
South Africa	1,659	1,732	2,113	2,425	1,531	1,698	1,728	1,723	128	34	385	702
South Korea	13,459	14,404	15,505	14,630	19,737	18,485	17,019	16,691	-6,278	-4,081	-1,514	-2,061
Spain	4,796	5,213	5,474	5,487	3,317	3,311	2,848	3,001	1,479	1,901	2,626	2,487
Sri Lanka	143	137	121	178	449	538	604	789	-306	-401	-483	-612
Sudan	81	42	92	53	20	16	16	11	61	26	76	42
Suriname	140	156	134	139	74	50	52	46	66	106	82	93
Sweden	3,139	3,405	3,287	2,844	4,892	4,937	4,525	4,716	-1,753	-1,533	-1,238	-1,872
Switzerland	4,911	4,943	5,557	4,536	4,714	5,587	5,576	5,643	197	-645	-19	-1,107
Syria	91	150	209	168	98	52	25	42	-7	98	184	126
Tajikistan	(X)	(X)	(X)	9	(X)	(X)	(X)	2	(X)	(X)	(X)	7
Tanzania	29	48	35	34	53	16	15	11	-24	33	20	23
Thailand	2,288	2,995	3,753	3,982	4,380	5,289	6,122	7,528	-2,091	-2,293	-2,369	-3,546
Togo	28	31	24	20	3	4	2	6	25	27	22	13
Trinidad and Tobago	563	428	468	447	768	1,020	866	862	-205	-592	-398	-414
Tunisia	160	177	172	233	55	40	25	48	105	137	147	184
Turkey	2,003	2,243	2,468	2,730	1,372	1,183	1,006	1,109	632	1,061	1,462	1,621
Turkmenistan	(X)	(X)	(X)	35	(X)	(X)	(X)	1	(X)	(X)	(X)	34
Turks and Caicos Islands	46	39	40	38	3	3	4	6	43	36	36	32
Uganda	23	26	13	15	41	15	18	12	-17	11	-5	3
Ukraine	(X)	(X)	(X)	305	(X)	(X)	(X)	89	(X)	(X)	(X)	216
United Arab Emirates	1,240	1,004	1,455	1,552	684	889	713	812	556	114	742	740
United Kingdom	20,837	23,490	22,046	22,808	18,319	20,188	18,413	20,152	2,518	3,302	3,633	2,657
Uruguay	134	144	216	231	219	206	237	266	-85	-62	-21	-35
U.S.S.R.	4,284	3,087	3,579	1,036	709	1,059	802	189	3,574	2,028	2,777	847
Uzbekistan	(X)	(X)	(X)	51	(X)	(X)	(X)	(Z)	(X)	(X)	(X)	51
Venezuela	3,025	3,108	4,656	5,438	6,771	9,480	8,179	8,168	-3,746	-6,371	-3,523	-2,730
Vietnam	11	7	4	7	(Z)	(Z)	(Z)	2	11	7	4	5
Western Samoa	4	5	7	73	3	1	1	1	1	4	6	72
Yemen (Sana & Aden)	80	110	192	321	260	391	152	41	-179	-281	40	281
Yugoslavia	499	565	371	6	799	776	674	225	-300	-211	-303	-219
Yugoslavia	(X)	(X)	(X)	169	(X)	(X)	(X)	41	(X)	(X)	(X)	128
Zaire	122	138	62	33	330	325	294	250	-208	-187	-232	-218
Zambia	50	80	24	68	24	29	42	70	26	52	-18	-2
Zimbabwe	121	135	53	143	127	119	90	107	-6	16	-37	37

- Represents zero.   Z Less than $500,000.   X Not applicable.   [1] Imports are on a customs value basis. Exports are f.a.s. value.   [2] Includes revisions not carried to area values; therefore, area values will not add to total.   [3] Effective October 3, 1990, East Germany ceased to exist as a sovereign state and became a part of West Germany. Accordingly, trade statistics for East Germany reflect trade for January through September 1990. Trade statistics for 1990 for former West Germany reflect this unification beginning with October 1990. Data for Germany reflect the consolidation of the two countries for 1991.

Source: U.S. Bureau of the Census, *U.S. Merchandise Trade*, series FT 900, monthly.

No. 1352. U.S. Exports and General Imports, by Selected Commodity Groups: 1989 to 1992

[In millions of dollars. N.e.s. = Not elsewhere specified]

COMMODITY GROUP	EXPORTS [1]				GENERAL IMPORTS [2]			
	1989	1990	1991	1992	1989	1990	1991	1992
Total	363,812	393,592	421,730	448,156	473,211	495,311	487,129	532,498
Agricultural commodities	41,319	38,723	38,510	42,078	22,036	22,343	22,140	23,433
Animal feeds	3,081	2,868	3,192	3,521	279	284	312	337
Bulbs	427	109	113	112	343	162	178	201
Cereal flour	695	686	813	925	558	569	641	726
Cocoa	22	38	23	31	732	783	823	774
Coffee	13	12	10	18	2,274	1,766	1,738	1,566
Corn	6,734	6,195	5,146	4,944	551	23	39	69
Cotton, raw and linters	2,268	2,799	2,514	2,010	10	20	16	11
Dairy products; eggs	447	372	455	709	405	501	452	507
Furskins, raw	173	144	107	95	116	78	57	61
Grains, unmilled	1,045	811	701	892	163	110	112	122
Hides and skins	1,577	1,612	1,276	1,260	98	94	110	124
Live animals	532	514	688	608	870	1,185	1,172	1,434
Meat and preparations	2,964	3,189	3,630	4,205	2,560	2,958	2,908	2,723
Oils/fats, animal	38	425	447	521	-	21	29	31
Oils/fats, vegetable	740	665	596	827	656	716	735	958
Plants	93	103	99	135	72	99	105	103
Rice	981	798	754	725	62	72	80	92
Seeds	224	246	274	298	126	119	132	153
Soybeans	4,011	3,597	3,995	4,416	24	15	27	16
Sugar	3	8	12	6	605	848	713	668
Tobacco, unmanufactured	1,340	1,445	1,430	1,651	668	680	989	949
Vegetables and fruit	4,530	5,015	5,342	5,719	4,909	5,795	5,391	5,698
Wheat	5,907	3,887	3,350	4,496	58	80	66	190
Other agricultural	3,475	3,184	3,546	3,954	5,877	5,365	5,313	5,922
Manufactured goods	272,166	298,236	325,978	347,512	379,425	388,820	392,433	434,256
ADP equipment, office machinery . . .	23,992	24,735	25,979	26,988	25,715	26,862	30,019	36,393
Airplanes	14,433	19,641	24,335	26,413	2,948	2,733	3,347	3,918
Airplane parts	8,792	9,815	10,284	9,329	2,929	3,556	4,046	3,397
Aluminum	2,988	2,857	3,128	2,666	3,144	2,843	2,409	2,538
Artwork/antiques	1,653	2,282	1,239	1,076	2,172	2,340	1,979	2,087
Basketware, etc	966	1,097	1,290	1,521	1,801	1,837	1,911	2,188
Chemicals, cosmetics	1,554	1,964	2,361	2,631	1,158	1,323	1,415	1,712
Chemicals, dyeing	1,249	1,591	1,649	1,867	1,131	1,287	1,416	1,626
Chemicals, fertilizers	2,708	2,578	2,977	2,372	1,003	921	918	952
Chemicals, inorganic	4,319	3,823	4,083	4,119	3,244	3,204	3,297	3,300
Chemicals, medicinal	3,693	4,103	4,609	5,357	2,088	2,491	3,047	3,812
Chemicals, organic	10,873	10,427	10,898	10,993	7,004	7,427	8,133	9,366
Chemicals, plastics	8,559	9,074	10,316	10,253	3,309	3,744	3,784	4,293
Chemicals, n.e.s	5,107	5,490	6,019	6,364	1,777	2,022	2,122	2,623
Clothing	2,291	2,472	3,215	4,093	24,537	25,622	26,202	31,242
Copper	946	1,213	1,328	1,177	2,140	1,774	1,573	1,635
Electrical machinery	25,409	28,406	30,050	32,039	32,373	33,564	35,067	39,729
Footwear	532	477	543	603	8,394	9,564	9,554	10,165
Furniture and parts	1,295	1,605	2,120	2,549	4,908	5,006	4,936	5,505
Gem diamonds	1,098	320	209	368	4,347	3,974	4,002	4,148
General industrial machinery	15,034	15,828	17,153	18,436	14,487	14,461	14,396	15,522
Glass	979	1,087	1,145	1,194	789	760	770	850
Glassware	343	401	449	496	889	939	937	1,016
Gold, nonmonetary	2,545	2,970	3,279	4,060	1,499	1,081	1,922	1,900
Iron and steel mill products	3,559	3,270	4,211	3,595	9,393	8,805	8,301	8,321
Lighting, plumbing	624	680	877	978	1,160	1,233	1,246	1,521
Metal manufactures, n.e.s.	4,494	4,783	5,189	5,491	6,372	6,441	6,372	6,730
Metalworking machinery	2,738	2,759	2,709	3,033	3,868	3,677	3,605	3,170
Motorcycles, bicycles	729	935	1,308	1,437	1,553	1,438	1,636	1,915
Nickel	244	228	219	196	1,522	1,102	1,061	797
Optical goods	544	639	713	766	1,371	1,470	1,484	1,645
Paper and paperboard	4,585	5,004	5,965	6,338	8,492	8,491	8,021	7,999
Photographic equipment	2,535	2,773	2,926	2,948	3,436	3,341	3,641	3,849
Plastic articles, n.e.s	1,700	1,945	2,240	2,773	2,999	3,138	3,114	3,571
Platinum	227	224	311	294	1,365	1,856	1,659	1,426
Pottery	70	71	87	103	1,244	1,222	1,242	1,403
Power generating machinery	15,349	15,796	16,960	17,950	14,257	14,552	14,195	15,910
Printed materials	3,002	3,164	3,589	3,801	1,618	1,669	1,702	1,876
Records/magnetic media	2,957	3,877	4,267	4,840	2,447	2,531	2,788	3,111
Rubber articles, n.e.s.	671	505	579	616	913	650	705	879
Rubber tires and tubes	819	1,148	1,274	1,408	2,384	2,591	2,309	2,512

See footnotes at end of table.

No. 1352. U.S. Exports and General Imports, by Selected SITC Commodity Groups: 1989 to 1992—Continued

[In millions of dollars]

COMMODITY GROUP	EXPORTS [1]				GENERAL IMPORTS [2]			
	1989	1990	1991	1992	1989	1990	1991	1992
Manufactured goods—Continued								
Scientific instruments	11,489	12,121	13,499	14,370	5,849	6,206	6,733	7,604
Ships, boats	1,050	1,277	1,155	1,422	579	329	249	320
Silver and bullion	68	163	237	209	577	451	363	449
Spacecraft	554	598	257	270	80	-	-	92
Specialized industrial machinery	14,352	15,277	16,686	16,680	12,839	12,990	10,864	11,826
Telecommunications equipment	8,132	9,139	9,999	11,205	23,234	22,230	23,446	25,819
Textile yarn, fabric	4,302	4,947	5,482	5,756	6,087	6,424	6,981	7,840
Toys/games/sporting goods	1,631	1,819	2,087	2,436	8,396	9,080	8,821	10,747
Travel goods	114	133	159	194	2,128	2,223	2,346	2,510
Vehicles/new cars, Canada	6,824	6,232	6,195	5,928	12,871	13,348	13,518	13,890
Vehicles/new cars, Japan	327	531	496	694	19,912	19,220	20,422	20,538
Vehicles/new cars, Other	2,274	2,465	3,070	5,091	11,371	12,542	10,813	11,564
Vehicles/trucks	2,843	3,084	3,879	3,678	8,807	8,580	8,293	9,784
Vehicles/chassis/bodies	207	207	241	311	1,095	518	352	353
Vehicles/parts	13,225	14,463	14,371	16,552	15,248	15,230	14,067	15,841
Watches/clocks/parts	177	209	225	207	908	2,247	2,285	2,321
Wood manufactures	1,065	1,222	1,251	1,387	2,029	2,034	1,907	2,409
Zinc	49	47	40	38	1,199	1,017	652	855
Other manufactured goods	17,281	22,246	24,570	27,559	28,043	30,605	30,042	32,948
Mineral fuel	10,124	12,233	12,081	11,122	52,779	64,661	54,056	55,028
Coal	4,087	4,636	4,776	4,325	84	288	310	419
Crude oil	205	137	33	27	35,529	43,785	36,902	38,544
Petroleum preparations	2,783	4,072	4,399	3,990	11,650	16,094	12,312	11,282
Liquified propane/butane	110	161	253	258	480	808	859	706
Natural gas	216	203	308	351	1,850	2,328	2,482	2,808
Electricity	189	493	44	64	521	463	487	590
Other mineral fuels	2,533	2,531	2,268	2,108	2,664	895	704	680
Selected commodities:								
Fish and preparations	2,396	2,801	3,063	3,377	5,389	5,192	5,638	5,657
Cork, wood, lumber	5,204	5,236	5,114	5,298	3,499	3,123	3,057	3,970
Pulp and waste paper	4,395	4,043	3,600	3,850	3,050	2,867	2,163	2,129
Metal ores; scrap	5,521	4,949	4,039	3,421	3,866	3,990	3,561	3,323
Crude fertilizers	1,359	1,266	1,385	1,385	1,146	1,129	982	914
Cigarettes	3,362	4,757	4,238	4,192	49	53	130	265
Alcoholic bev. distilled	222	254	279	343	1,588	1,725	1,595	1,837
All other	1,458	2,576	2,822	2,798	383	1,408	1,375	1,541
Re-exports	16,285	18,517	20,621	22,500	(X)	(X)	(X)	(X)
Agricultural commodities	885	848	857	892	(X)	(X)	(X)	(X)
Manufactured goods	14,851	17,119	19,153	21,052	(X)	(X)	(X)	(X)
Mineral fuels	127	151	206	78	(X)	(X)	(X)	(X)
Other, re-exports	549	399	405	479	(X)	(X)	(X)	(X)
Timing adjustment	(X)	(X)	(X)	279	(X)	(X)	(X)	146

- Represents zero.　X Not applicable.　[1] F.A.S. basis.　[2] Customs value basis.
Source: U.S. Bureau of the Census, *U.S. Merchandise Trade*, series FT 900, Final Reports, and December 1992 issue.

No. 1353. Imports for Consumption—Values and Duties: 1970 to 1992

[Imports are on customs value basis. Beginning 1970, includes silver ores and bullion, and beginning 1980, includes trade of Virgin Islands with foreign countries. For basis of dollar values and for area coverage, see text, section 29. See also *Historical Statistics, Colonial Times to 1970*, series U 207-212]

YEAR	VALUES				Duties calculated [1] (mil. dol.)	RATIO OF DUTIES TO VALUES		Duties per capita [2] (dollar)
	Total (mil. dol.)	Free (mil. dol.)	Dutiable (mil. dol.)	Percent free		Total imports (percent)	Dutiable imports (percent)	
1970	39,756	13,870	25,886	35	2,584	6.5	10.0	12.60
1975	96,516	31,030	65,486	32	3,780	3.9	5.8	17.50
1976	121,121	37,190	83,931	31	4,675	3.9	5.6	21.44
1977	[3]147,075	43,633	103,442	30	5,485	3.7	5.3	24.91
1978	[3]172,912	51,827	121,125	30	7,162	4.1	5.9	32.17
1979	[3]205,850	103,278	102,645	50	7,202	3.5	7.0	31.99
1980	[3]244,007	106,992	132,951	45	7,535	3.1	5.7	33.09
1981	259,012	76,338	182,674	29	8,893	3.4	4.9	38.67
1982	242,340	75,856	166,484	31	8,688	3.6	5.2	37.40
1983	256,679	83,397	173,283	32	9,430	3.7	5.4	40.21
1984	322,989	102,977	220,012	32	12,042	3.7	5.5	50.90
1985	343,553	106,035	237,518	31	13,067	3.8	5.5	54.73
1986	368,657	121,742	246,915	33	13,312	3.6	5.4	55.10
1987	402,066	132,152	269,914	33	13,923	3.5	5.2	57.08
1988	437,140	151,693	285,447	35	15,054	3.4	5.3	61.12
1989	468,012	156,365	311,647	33	16,096	3.4	5.2	64.70
1990	490,554	161,108	329,446	33	16,339	3.3	5.0	65.38
1991	483,028	167,641	315,386	35	16,197	3.4	5.1	64.10
1992	525,091	194,583	330,508	37	17,164	3.3	5.2	67.12

[1] Customs duties (including import excise taxes) calculated on the basis of reports of quantity and value of imports of merchandise entered directly for consumption or withdrawn from bonded customs warehouses.　[2] Based on estimated population including Armed Forces abroad as of July 1.　[3] Total includes revisions not carried to free and dutiable values.
Source: U.S. Bureau of the Census, 1970-1988, *Highlights of U.S. Export and Import Trade*, series FT 990, monthly; beginning 1989, *U.S. Merchandise Trade: Selected Highlights*, series FT 920, and unpublished data.

No. 1354. Domestic Exports and Imports for Consumption of Merchandise, by Selected SIC-Based Product Category: 1985 to 1992

[In millions of dollars. Includes nonmonetary gold]

SIC [1] code	SIC-BASED PRODUCT CATEGORY	1985	1987	1988	1989	1990	1991	1992
(X)	**Domestic exports, total** [2].....	212,961	243,859	310,346	349,433	374,537	400,842	425,377
	Agricultural, forestry and fishery							
(X)	products	20,074	17,718	24,464	27,198	26,225	25,052	26,785
01	Agricultural products	19,199	16,678	21,508	24,142	22,597	21,075	22,633
02	Livestock and livestock products	735	855	1,014	821	829	970	871
08	Forestry products	122	155	266	270	281	306	324
09	Fish, fresh or chilled; and other marine products [3]..........	18	30	1,676	1,965	2,518	2,701	2,959
(X)	Mineral commodities...........	6,394	5,058	6,559	7,030	7,335	7,442	7,210
10	Metallic ores and concentrates	686	597	883	1,247	1,137	1,014	1,084
11,12	Bituminous, lignite and anthracite coal	4,465	3,368	4,014	4,287	4,513	4,623	4,241
13	Crude petroleum and natural gas	476	271	485	490	638	675	737
14	Nonmetallic minerals, fuels	767	822	1,177	1,006	1,047	1,130	1,148
(X)	Manufactured commodities	175,752	208,438	261,755	290,536	330,403	359,635	383,082
20	Food and kindred products	10,055	12,320	14,788	15,205	16,160	17,492	19,761
21	Tobacco manufactures..........	1,268	2,310	2,901	3,632	5,040	4,574	4,509
22	Textile mill products...........	1,462	1,891	2,415	2,794	3,635	4,108	4,473
23	Apparel and related products	1,019	1,518	1,824	2,349	2,848	3,679	4,599
24	Lumber and related products.......	2,668	3,961	5,326	6,050	6,523	6,477	6,802
25	Furniture and fixtures..........	483	550	841	1,011	1,589	2,086	2,518
26	Paper and allied products........	3,886	5,676	7,197	8,126	8,631	9,214	9,969
27	Printing and publishing..........	1,250	1,525	1,996	2,598	3,150	3,590	3,808
28	Chemicals and allied products.....	21,797	26,090	31,722	35,825	37,806	41,483	41,953
29	Petroleum and coal products.......	5,433	4,479	3,926	5,019	6,794	7,026	6,403
30	Rubber and misc. plastics products ..	2,765	3,710	4,412	5,010	6,398	7,049	7,872
31	Leather and leather products.......	478	688	953	1,131	1,388	1,413	1,541
32	Stone, clay, and glass products.....	1,792	2,045	2,272	2,638	3,295	3,533	3,855
33	Primary metal products..........	4,747	5,806	12,362	12,110	13,116	15,243	15,105
34	Fabricated metal products	5,765	6,185	8,318	9,117	11,138	11,962	13,265
35	Machinery, except electrical	37,478	41,054	51,803	55,524	61,229	65,300	68,554
36	Electric and electronic machinery....	18,908	24,359	27,033	32,718	39,807	42,330	45,992
37	Transportation equipment.........	38,024	42,371	49,768	56,875	68,113	76,172	82,862
38	Instruments and related products....	8,623	10,191	17,160	17,327	19,524	21,699	22,815
39	Misc. manufactured commodities	1,773	2,719	4,443	4,553	4,296	4,621	5,446
(X)	**Imports for consumption, total** [2]...............	343,553	402,066	437,140	468,012	490,554	483,028	525,091
	Agricultural, forestry and fishery							
(X)	products	12,805	14,402	12,759	13,251	12,750	13,148	14,216
01	Agricultural products	7,483	7,444	5,786	6,109	5,925	6,107	6,716
02	Livestock and livestock products	933	999	1,235	1,290	1,453	1,501	1,873
08	Forestry products	830	933	1,326	1,235	1,015	978	1,088
09	Fish, fresh or chilled; and other marine products [3]..........	3,559	5,026	4,412	4,617	4,357	4,562	4,540
(X)	Mineral commodities...........	39,011	33,615	31,540	41,264	51,391	44,581	44,823
10	Metallic ores and concentrates	1,265	1,130	1,126	1,425	1,500	1,244	1,167
11,12	Bituminous, lignite and anthracite coal	70	56	65	97	93	112	127
13	Crude petroleum and natural gas	35,872	30,843	29,573	38,842	48,917	42,415	42,796
14	Nonmetallic minerals, exc. fuels.....	1,804	1,586	776	900	881	810	734
(X)	Manufactured commodities	280,089	341,141	379,172	396,903	407,043	406,550	445,127
20	Food and kindred products	12,521	13,180	15,043	15,122	16,564	16,298	17,445
21	Tobacco manufactures..........	78	90	86	88	94	199	285
22	Textile mill products...........	3,616	4,697	5,506	7,294	6,807	7,132	7,808
23	Apparel and related products	15,710	21,503	20,890	22,841	24,644	25,497	30,533
24	Lumber and related products.......	5,105	5,959	5,720	5,848	5,446	5,229	6,700
25	Furniture and fixtures..........	3,220	4,575	4,796	5,148	5,235	5,130	5,601
26	Paper and allied products........	7,493	9,461	11,001	11,880	11,669	10,431	10,382
27	Printing and publishing..........	1,200	1,583	1,776	1,807	1,849	1,878	2,046
28	Chemicals and allied products.....	12,790	14,400	18,602	20,118	21,611	22,999	25,849
29	Petroleum and coal products.......	18,282	13,123	11,027	11,979	14,472	11,097	10,410
30	Rubber and misc. plastics products ..	4,721	6,331	9,590	9,488	9,731	9,855	11,287
31	Leather and leather products.......	7,724	9,930	9,578	9,837	10,944	10,714	11,342
32	Stone, clay, and glass products.....	4,296	5,560	5,921	5,775	5,845	5,446	5,951
33	Primary metal products..........	20,439	19,254	25,075	25,563	23,232	22,262	22,891
34	Fabricated metal products	7,754	9,562	11,215	11,568	11,608	11,396	12,436
35	Machinery, except electrical	31,310	44,807	50,301	54,051	55,021	55,578	62,274
36	Electric and electronic machinery....	37,951	46,566	52,539	55,316	55,736	58,610	65,596
37	Transportation equipment.........	65,944	84,347	86,717	87,972	89,599	88,004	92,930
38	Instruments and related products....	8,805	11,547	15,430	15,430	16,846	18,668	20,338
39	Misc. manufactured commodities	11,130	14,666	18,359	19,844	20,090	20,015	23,025

X Not applicable. [1] Standard Industrial Classification. [2] Includes scrap and waste, used or secondhand merchandise, and manufactured commodities not identified by kind. [3] Includes frozen and packaged fish.

Source: U.S. Bureau of the Census, 1980-1988, *Highlights of U.S. Export and Import Trade*, series FT 990; beginning 1989, *U.S. Merchandise Trade*, series FT 900.

Figure 30.1
Selected Outlying Areas of the United States

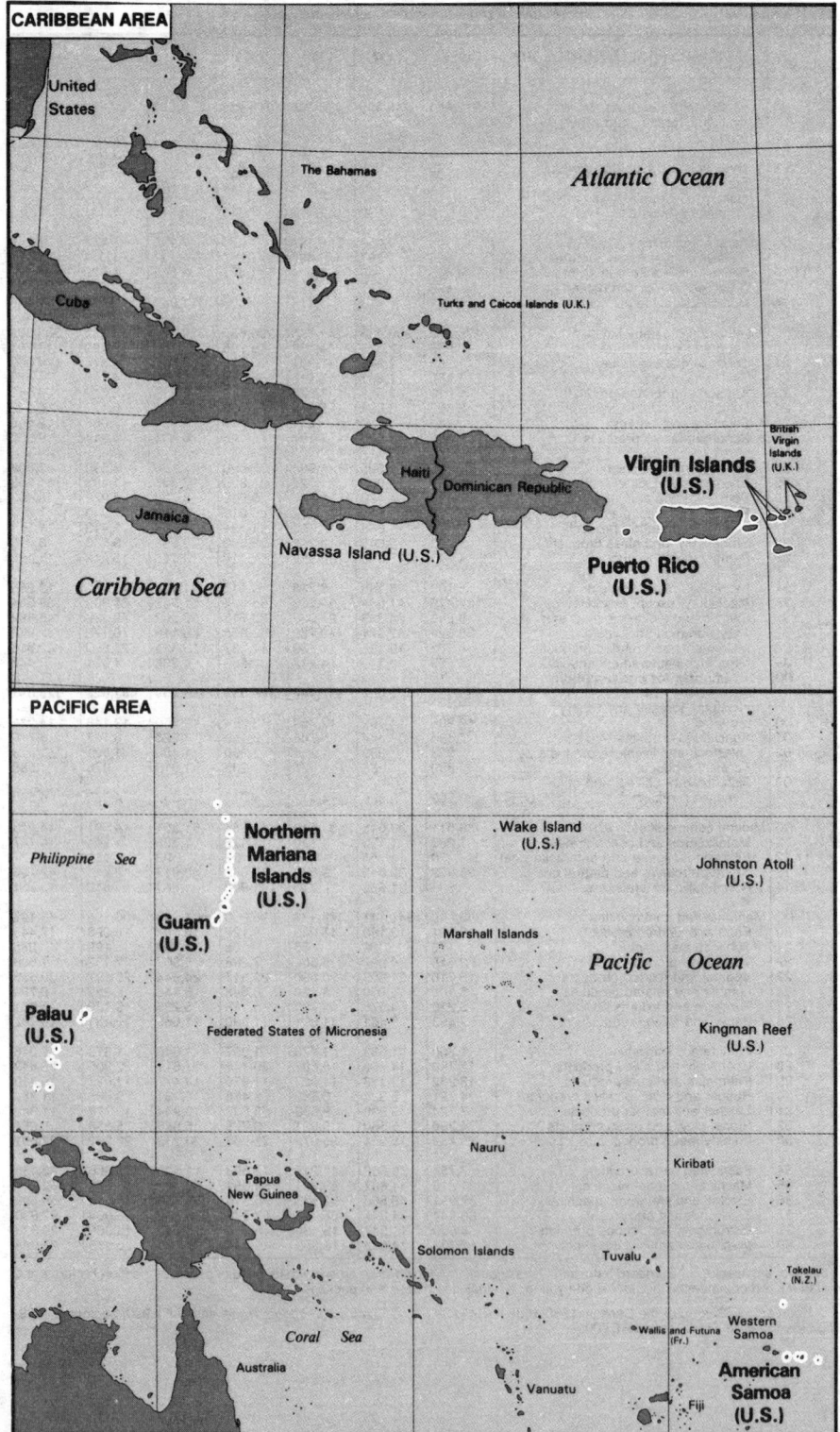

Outlying Areas

This section presents summary economic and social statistics for Puerto Rico, Virgin Islands, Guam, American Samoa, and the Northern Mariana Islands.

Primary sources are the decennial censuses of population and housing, and the censuses of agriculture, business, manufactures, and construction (taken every 5 years) conducted by the Bureau of the Census; the annual *Vital Statistics of the United States,* issued by the National Center for Health Statistics; and the annual *Income and Product* of the Puerto Rico Planning Board, San Juan.

Jurisdiction.—The United States gained jurisdiction over these areas as follows:

The islands of *Puerto Rico* and *Guam,* surrendered by Spain to the United States in October 1898, were ceded to the United States by the Treaty of Paris, ratified in 1899. Puerto Rico became a Commonwealth on July 25, 1952, thereby achieving a high degree of local autonomy under its own constitution. The *Virgin Islands,* comprising 50 islands and cays, was purchased by the United States from Denmark in 1917. *American Samoa,* a group of seven islands, was acquired by the United States in accordance with a convention among the United States, Great Britain, and Germany, ratified in 1900 (Swains Island was annexed in 1925).

By an agreement approved by the Security Council and the United States, the Northern Mariana Islands, previously under Japanese mandate, was administered by the United States between 1947 and 1986 under the United Nations trusteeship system. The Northern Mariana Islands became a Commonwealth in 1986.

For a brief summary of U.S. territorial development, see table 356.

Censuses.—Because characteristics of the outlying areas differ, the presentation of census data for them is not uniform. The 1960 Census of Population covered

In Brief	
Persons per household, 1990:	
Puerto Rico	*3.3*
Virgin Islands	*3.1*
Guam	*4.0*
American Samoa	*7.0*
Northern Mariana Islands	*4.6*

all of the places listed above except the Northern Mariana Islands (their census was conducted in April 1958 by the Office of the High Commissioner), while the 1960 Census of Housing also excluded American Samoa. The 1970, 1980 and 1990 Censuses of Population and Housing covered all five areas. The 1959, 1969, and 1978 Censuses of Agriculture covered Puerto Rico, American Samoa, Guam, and the Virgin Islands; the 1964, 1974, and 1982 censuses covered the same areas except American Samoa; and the 1969, 1978, and 1987 censuses included the Northern Mariana Islands. Beginning in 1967, Congress authorized the economic censuses, to be taken at 5-year intervals, for years ending in "2" and "7." Prior economic censuses were conducted in Puerto Rico for 1949, 1954, 1958, and 1963 and in Guam and the Virgin Islands for 1958 and 1963. In 1967, the census of construction industries was added for the first time in Puerto Rico; in 1972, Virgin Islands and Guam were covered. For 1982 and 1987, the economic censuses covered the Northern Mariana Islands.

Information in other sections.—In addition to the statistics presented in this section, other data are included as integral parts of many tables showing distribution by States in various sections of the *Abstract.* See "Outlying areas of the United States" in the index. For definition and explanation of terms used, see section 1, Population; section 4, Education; section 23, Agriculture; section 26, Construction and Housing; section 27, Manufactures; and section 28, Domestic Trade and Services.

No. 1355. Estimated Resident Population, by Area: 1950 to 1990

[In thousands. As of July 1, except 1990, as of April 1. Includes estimates of Armed Forces stationed in area]

AREA	1950	1960	1970	1975	1980	1985	1987	1988	1990
Puerto Rico.	2,218	2,362	2,716	2,933	3,206	3,282	3,292	3,291	3,522
American Samoa	19	20	27	30	32	36	38	40	47
Guam.	60	66	86	102	107	124	130	133	133
Virgin Islands.	27	32	63	94	98	111	106	103	102
Northern Mariana Islands [1]	(NA)	(NA)	12	15	17	19	20	21	43

NA Not available.　[1] Data consistent with apportionment census of September 1973 which showed a total population of 14,333 for the Marianas.

Source: U.S. Bureau of the Census, 1950-1988: *Current Population Reports*, P25-80, P25-336, P25-943, and P25-1049; 1990: press releases, CB91-142, 242, 276, 263, and 243.

No. 1356. Population and Median Age, by Area and Sex: 1960 to 1990

[As of April 1. For definition of median, see Guide to Tabular Presentation]

AREA AND SEX	POPULATION (1,000)				MEDIAN AGE (years)			
	1960	1970	1980	1990	1960	1970	1980	1990
Puerto Rico.	2,349.5	2,712.0	3,196.5	3,522.0	18.5	21.6	24.6	28.4
Male.	1,162.8	1,329.9	1,556.7	1,706.0	18.0	20.9	23.7	27.2
Female.	1,186.8	1,382.2	1,639.8	1,816.0	18.9	22.2	25.5	29.6
American Samoa.	20.1	27.2	32.3	46.8	15.2	16.1	18.8	20.9
Male.	10.2	13.7	16.4	24.0	14.6	16.1	18.4	20.6
Female.	9.9	13.6	15.9	22.8	15.8	16.1	19.2	21.2
Guam.	67.0	85.0	106.0	133.2	20.8	20.4	22.3	25.0
Male.	39.2	47.3	55.3	70.9	22.9	21.6	22.4	25.2
Female.	27.8	37.7	50.7	62.2	16.5	18.2	22.1	24.9
Virgin Islands.	32.1	62.5	96.6	101.8	20.7	23.0	22.5	28.2
Male.	15.9	31.3	46.2	49.2	20.3	23.1	21.1	27.1
Female.	16.2	31.3	50.4	52.6	21.2	23.0	23.6	29.2
Northern Mariana Islands.	(NA)	9.6	16.8	43.3	(NA)	15.2	19.7	27.4
Male.	(NA)	4.9	8.8	22.8	(NA)	15.4	20.9	29.9
Female.	(NA)	4.7	8.0	20.5	(NA)	15.0	18.5	24.9

NA Not available.

Source: U.S. Bureau of the Census, *Census pf Population: 1970*, vol. I, *Characteristics of the Population*, parts 53-58; *1980*, vol. 1, chapter B, *Characteristics of the Population*, parts 53-57a; and *1990*, CPH-1, parts 53A and 55; CPH-6, parts G (Guam), AS (American Samoa), and CNMI (Commonwealth of the Northern Mariana Islands); and Summary Tape File 1A, (Puerto Rico) and Summary Tape File 2 (Virgin Islands).

No. 1357. Population, by Place of Birth and Year of Immigration: 1990

[As of April 1]

ITEM	United States	Puerto Rico	Virgin Islands	Guam	American Samoa	Northern Mariana Islands
All persons	248,709,873	3,522,037	101,809	133,152	46,773	43,345
Born in this area	225,695,826	3,200,940	49,839	63,504	25,573	16,752
Percent of total	90.7	90.9	49.0	47.7	54.7	38.6
Born in the United States	225,695,826	229,304	14,246	28,010	3,519	1,271
Born elsewhere [1]	23,014,047	91,793	37,724	41,638	17,681	25,322
Born outside area.	23,014,047	321,097	51,970	69,648	21,200	26,593
Year of entry:						
1985 to 1990.	5,562,288	104,900	13,765	43,575	9,302	21,984
1980 to 1984.	4,222,420	52,487	7,951	8,768	5,025	2,491
1970 to 1979.	5,601,860	90,934	12,279	10,994	4,423	1,600
1960 to 1969.	3,410,665	58,278	13,072	4,143	1,758	274
Before 1960	4,216,814	14,498	4,903	2,168	692	244

[1] Includes persons born in other outlying areas under United States jurisdiction and persons born abroad with at least one parent who is a United States citizen, as well as foreign born persons.

Source: U.S. Bureau of the Census, *1990 Census of Population and Housing*, Summary Tape File, parts 3C, (United States), 3A and unpublished data, (Puerto Rico), and 3, (Virgin Islands); CPH-L-98, *The Foreign Born Population in the United States: 1990*; *1990 Census pf Population and Housing*, CPH-6, parts G (Guam), AS (American Samoa), and CNMI (Commonwealth of the Northern Mariana Islands).

No. 1358. Land Area and Population Characteristics, by Area: 1990

[As of **April 1**. See also table 356 for gross area (land and water). For definition of median, see Guide to Tabular Presentation]

ITEM	United States	Puerto Rico	Virgin Islands	Guam	American Samoa	Northern Mariana Islands
Land area (sq. miles)	3,536,338	3,427	134	209	77	184
Total resident population	**248,709,873**	**3,522,037**	**101,809**	**133,152**	**46,773**	**43,345**
Per square mile	70.3	1,027.9	760.9	637.1	607.4	235.6
Percent increase, 1980-90. . .	9.8	10.2	5.4	25.6	44.8	158.3
Urban	187,053,487	2,508,346	37,885	50,801	15,599	12,151
Rural.	61,656,386	1,013,691	63,924	82,351	31,174	31,194
Male	121,239,418	1,705,642	49,210	70,945	24,023	22,802
Female	127,470,455	1,816,395	52,599	62,207	22,750	20,543
Males per 100 females	95.1	93.9	93.6	114.0	105.6	111.0
Median age (years)	32.9	28.4	28.2	25.0	20.9	27.4
Male (years)	31.7	27.2	27.1	25.2	20.6	29.9
Female (years).	34.1	29.6	29.2	24.9	21.2	24.9
Marital status, persons						
15 years old and over	**195,142,002**	**2,563,818**	**72,365**	**93,200**	**28,952**	**33,030**
Never married.	52,559,853	711,470	27,539	30,759	11,412	13,810
Married [1]	111,498,578	1,499,449	35,199	54,717	15,958	17,869
Widowed or divorced.	31,083,571	352,899	9,627	7,724	1,582	1,351
Households and families:						
Households	91,947,410	1,054,924	32,020	31,373	6,607	6,873
Persons in households	242,012,129	3,487,667	100,488	124,596	46,267	31,856
Persons per household	2.63	3.31	3.14	3.97	7.00	4.63
Families.	64,517,947	886,339	23,012	27,313	6,301	5,312
Husband-wife families	50,708,322	634,872	13,197	21,342	5,153	3,947
Children ever born per						
1,000 females 15 to 44 years . .	1,223	1,512	1,662	1,523	1,757	1,226

[1] For Puerto Rico, includes consensually married couples and for all areas, includes separated couples.

Source: U.S. Bureau of the Census, *1990 Census of Population,* CP-1 parts 1, (United States), 53 (Puerto Rico), 55 (Virgin Islands); *1990 Census of Population and Housing,* CPH-1, parts 53A and 55; CPH-6, parts 53A (Guam), AS (American Samoa), and CNMI (Commonwealth of the Northern Mariana Islands); and Summary Tape File, parts 3C, (United States), 3A, (Puerto Rico), and 3, (Virgin Islands).

No. 1359. Selected Social and Economic Characteristics, by Area: 1990

[As of **April 1**]

CHARACTERISTIC	United States	Puerto Rico	Virgin Islands	Guam	American Samoa	Northern Mariana Islands
EDUCATIONAL ATTAINMENT						
Persons 25 years and over	158,868,436	1,952,297	55,639	66,700	19,570	24,633
Less than 9th grade	16,502,211	691,835	12,908	9,238	3,664	4,285
9th to 12th grade, no diploma.	22,841,507	290,173	11,278	8,602	5,239	4,016
High school graduate	47,642,763	410,559	14,021	22,220	6,253	8,659
Some college or associate degree	39,571,702	281,248	9,011	14,984	3,062	3,818
Bachelor's degree or higher	32,310,253	278,482	8,421	11,656	1,352	3,855
EMPLOYMENT STATUS						
Total persons, 16 years old						
and over	191,829,271	2,497,078	70,323	90,990	27,991	32,522
In labor force	125,182,378	1,180,162	47,553	66,138	14,198	26,589
Percent of total	65.3	47.3	67.6	72.7	50.7	81.8
Armed forces	1,708,928	5,486	110	11,952	11	8
Civilian labor force	123,473,450	1,174,676	47,443	54,186	14,187	26,581
Employed	115,681,202	934,736	44,267	52,144	13,461	25,965
Unemployed	7,792,248	239,940	3,176	2,042	726	616
Percent of civilian labor force. . . .	6.3	20.4	6.7	3.8	5.1	2.3
Not in labor force	66,646,893	1,316,916	22,770	24,852	13,793	5,933
FAMILY INCOME IN 1989						
Families, census year.	65,049,428	889,998	23,012	27,313	6,301	5,312
Percent distribution by income class	100.0	100.0	100.0	100.0	100.0	100.0
Less than $5,000	4.0	25.1	8.8	4.0	11.0	8.2
$5,000 to $9,999.	5.6	24.9	9.5	4.7	19.2	13.9
$10,000 to $14,999	7.2	16.5	12.8	8.3	17.0	13.1
$15,000 to $24,999	16.4	17.5	20.6	21.1	23.6	21.6
$25,000 or more	66.9	16.0	48.3	61.9	29.1	43.2
Median income (dollars)	35,225	9,988	24,036	31,178	15,979	21,275
RESIDENCE IN 1985						
Persons 5 years and over	230,445,777	3,219,765	92,579	118,055	39,821	39,206
Same house	122,796,970	2,190,479	56,098	54,665	30,759	11,479
Different house in this area	102,540,090	879,691	25,003	24,763	2,763	6,870
Outside area	5,108,710	149,595	11,478	38,627	6,299	20,857
LANGUAGE SPOKEN AT HOME						
Persons 5 years and over	230,445,777	3,219,765	92,579	118,055	39,821	39,206
Speak only English at home	198,600,798	(NA)	70,442	44,048	1,203	1,878

NA Not available.

Source: U.S. Bureau of the Census, *1990 Census of Population and Housing,* Summary Tape File, parts 3C, (United States), 3A and unpublished data, (Puerto Rico), and 3, (Virgin Islands); CPH-L-98, *The Foreign Born Population in the United States: 1990; 1990 Census of Population and Housing,* CPH-6, parts G (Guam), AS (American Samoa), and CNMI (Commonwealth of the Northern Mariana Islands).

No. 1360. Vital Statistics—Specified Areas: 1960 to 1990

[Births, deaths, and infant deaths by place of residence; marriages and divorces by place of occurrence. Rates for 1960, 1970, 1980, and 1990 based on population enumerated as of **April 1**; for other years, on population estimated as of **July 1**]

AREA AND YEAR	BIRTHS		DEATHS		INFANT DEATHS		MARRIAGES		DIVORCES [3]	
	Number	Rate [1]	Number	Rate [1]	Number	Rate [2]	Number	Rate [1]	Number	Rate [1]
Puerto Rico:										
1960	76,314	32.5	15,791	6.7	3,307	43.3	[4]20,212	[4]8.6	5,218	2.2
1970	67,628	24.8	18,080	6.7	1,930	28.6	29,905	11.0	9,688	3.6
1980	72,986	22.8	20,413	6.4	1,351	18.5	33,167	10.4	15,276	4.8
1985	63,547	19.4	23,071	7.0	944	14.9	30,355	9.2	14,686	4.5
1990	66,417	18.9	(NA)	(NA)	(NA)	(NA)	(NA)	(NA)	(NA)	(NA)
Guam:										
1965	2,523	32.8	336	4.4	82	32.5	471	6.2	53	0.7
1970	2,842	28.8	355	5.8	62	21.6	874	9.9	84	1.0
1980	2,945	27.8	393	3.7	43	14.6	(NA)	(NA)	(NA)	(NA)
1985	3,049	24.6	415	3.4	35	11.5	(NA)	(NA)	(NA)	(NA)
1990	3,839	28.8	(NA)	(NA)	(NA)	(NA)	(NA)	(NA)	(NA)	(NA)
Virgin Islands:										
1960	1,180	36.8	332	10.3	42	35.6	359	11.1	135	4.2
1970	2,898	46.8	469	7.9	72	24.6	1,149	18.4	270	4.3
1980	2,504	25.9	504	5.2	61	24.4	1,112	11.5	478	4.9
1985	2,375	21.4	506	4.6	42	17.7	1,448	13.1	363	3.3
1990	2,267	22.3	(NA)	(NA)	(NA)	(NA)	(NA)	(NA)	(NA)	(NA)

NA Not available. [1] Per 1,000 population. [2] Per 1,000 live births. [3] Includes reported annulments. [4] Data are incomplete.

Source: U.S. National Center for Health Statistics, *Vital Statistics of the United States*, annual.

No. 1361. Public Elementary and Secondary Schools, by Areas: 1990

[For school year ending in year shown, unless otherwise indicated]

ITEM	Puerto Rico	Guam	Virgin Islands	American Samoa	ITEM	Puerto Rico	Guam	Virgin Islands	American Samoa
Enrollment, fall	651,225	26,493	21,193	12,258	Staff, fall 1989	62,441	2,985	3,324	1,240
Elementary					School district staff	1,683	7	403	97
(kindergarten-					School staff	38,559	1,990	2,251	799
grade 8)	486,247	19,291	15,769	9,309	Teachers	33,427	1,622	1,595	659
Secondary (grades					Other support				
9-12 and post					services staff	22,199	988	670	344
graduates)	164,978	7,202	5,424	2,949	Current expenditures [1]				
Average daily					($1,000)	1,090,383	(NA)	128,066	21,837
attendance	597,436	(NA)	18,924	8,498	Per pupil [2] (dol.)	1,825	(NA)	6,767	2,570

NA Not available. [1] Public elementary and secondary day schools. [2] Annual expenditures per pupil in average daily attendance.

Source: U.S. National Center for Education Statistics, unpublished data.

No. 1362. Federal Direct Payments for Individuals, by Selected Program and Outlying Area: 1990 and 1992

[In thousands of dollars. For fiscal years ending **September 30**]

PROGRAM PAYMENTS	1990				1992			
	Puerto Rico	Guam	Virgin Islands	American Samoa	Puerto Rico	Guam	Virgin Islands	American Samoa
Total	3,487,697	83,199	95,396	14,615	4,086,581	127,067	105,364	16,998
Pell Grants	240,545	1,260	432	113	291,401	1,184	619	326
Medicare: Hospital Insurance	186,950	1,907	4,977	-	255,133	3,103	6,792	-
Supplemental medical insurance	209,525	2,273	3,722	-	260,308	2,767	4,624	-
Social Security:								
Disability insurance	560,910	1,907	5,692	2,410	660,884	4,558	7,574	3,019
Retirement insurance	1,077,133	11,372	31,601	4,330	1,246,085	23,589	37,497	5,114
Survivors insurance	461,999	6,430	11,056	3,873	539,050	14,425	13,259	5,093
Veterans:								
Pension and disability	280,799	3,578	1,794	1,354	311,838	4,124	1,734	1,554
Education assistance	3,086	178	28	37	2,687	73	28	18
Federal retirement and disability	161,315	34,150	8,326	1,605	149,771	39,562	6,809	1,767
Food Stamps	[1]931,131	14,362	18,403	-	[1]996,488	28,458	17,622	-
Other	305,435	5,782	9,365	893	369,424	5,224	8,806	107

- Represents or rounds to zero. [1] Food stamp program in Puerto Rico was replaced by the Nutritional Assistance Grant Program. Figures shown represent grants to State and local governments, not included in totals.

Source: U.S. Bureau of the Census, *Federal Expenditures by State for Fiscal Year*, annual.

No. 1363. Puerto Rico—Summary: 1970 to 1991

ITEM	Unit	1970	1980	1985	1986	1987	1988	1989	1990	1991
POPULATION										
Total [1]	1,000	2,722	3,184	3,378	3,406	3,433	3,461	3,497	3,522	3,550
Persons per family	Number	4.6	4.3	3.9	3.8	3.8	3.8	3.7	3.7	3.7
EDUCATION [2]										
Enrollment, total	1,000	922.6	1,090.9	1,107.9	1,127.8	1,112.0	1,114.0	(NA)	(NA)	(NA)
Public day school	1,000	672.3	716.1	692.9	686.9	679.5	672.8	660.6	651.2	644.7
Other public	1,000	103.9	149.5	152.0	153.7	152.1	156.3	(NA)	(NA)	(NA)
Private schools	1,000	89.1	95.2	107.3	130.4	121.8	129.2	137.2	145.8	134.2
College and university	1,000	57.3	130.1	155.7	156.8	158.6	155.7	156.9	156.1	157.5
Expenses	Mil. dol	288.8	825.0	1,171.8	1,212.9	1,282.3	1,434.0	1,564.2	1,686.4	1,760.3
As percent of GNP	Percent	6.2	7.5	7.8	7.6	7.5	7.7	7.8	7.8	7.7
Public	Mil. dol	254.6	612.2	810.2	814.4	847.9	932.7	990.8	1,054.2	1,095.4
Private	Mil. dol	34.2	212.8	361.6	398.5	434.4	501.3	573.4	632.2	664.9
LABOR FORCE [3]										
Total [4]	1,000	765	907	985	1,004	1,048	1,081	1,108	1,124	1,152
Employed [5]	1,000	686	753	774	798	863	909	948	963	977
Agriculture [6]	1,000	68	38	39	41	36	32	37	36	35
Manufacturing	1,000	132	143	141	144	157	163	165	168	164
Trade	1,000	128	138	150	153	165	180	186	185	195
Government	1,000	106	184	183	185	204	209	219	222	217
Unemployed	1,000	79	154	211	206	185	172	160	161	175
Unemployment rate [7]	Rate	10	17	21	21	18	16	14	14	15
Compensation of employees	Mil. dol	2,800	7,200	9,442	9,929	10,681	11,786	12,817	13,591	14,199
Avg. compensation	Dollar	4,082	9,563	12,456	12,779	12,806	13,447	14,131	14,854	15,351
Salary and wages	Mil. dol	2,555	6,290	8,137	8,496	9,182	10,118	10,965	11,632	12,136
INCOME [8]										
Personal income:										
Current dollars	Mil. dol	3,753	11,002	14,588	15,448	16,465	17,756	19,198	21,105	21,778
Constant (1954) dollars	Mil. dol	2,654	3,985	4,274	4,509	4,766	4,982	5,200	5,551	5,514
Disposable personal income:										
Current dollars	Mil. dol	3,565	10,403	13,760	14,391	15,420	16,529	18,170	19,914	20,577
Constant (1954) dollars	Mil. dol	2,521	3,768	4,032	4,200	4,463	4,638	4,921	5,238	5,197
Average family income:										
Current dollars	Dollar	6,366	14,858	16,914	17,305	18,297	19,572	20,416	22,231	22,772
Constant (1954) dollars	Dollar	4,503	5,381	4,957	5,050	5,297	5,491	5,530	5,847	5,765
BANKING [9]										
Assets	Mil. dol	3,322	10,223	21,209	22,534	26,101	24,660	27,179	27,902	27,946
TOURISM [8]										
Number of visitors	1,000	1,225.0	2,140.0	2,061.6	2,144.6	2,619.3	3,004.2	3,221.2	3,425.8	3,504.3
Visitor expenditures	Mil. dol	235.4	618.7	757.7	792.6	955.4	1,121.4	1,254.0	1,366.4	1,435.7
Average per visitor	Dollar	192	289	368	370	365	373	389	399	410
Net income from tourism	Mil. dol	89.8	202.2	223.1	239.3	285.8	333.1	372.8	383.3	423.0

NA Not available. [1] 1970, 1980, and 1990 enumerated as of April 1; all other years estimated as of July 1. [2] Enrollment for the first school month. Expenses for school year ending in year shown. [3] Annual average of monthly figures. For fiscal years. [4] Beginning 1980, for population 16 years old and over; 1970, for population 14 years and over. [5] Includes other employment not shown separately. [6] Includes forestry and fisheries. [7] Percent unemployed of the labor force. [8] For fiscal years. [9] As of June 30.

Source: Puerto Rico Planning Board, San Juan, PR, *Income and Product*, annual; and *Socioeconomics Statistics*, annual.

No. 1364. Puerto Rico—Employment Status, 1970 to 1992, and by Sex, 1992

[In thousands. For 1970, for persons 14 years old and over; beginning 1980, 16 years old and over. Annual averages for calendar years of the civilian noninstitutional population]

EMPLOYMENT STATUS	1970	1980	1985	1986	1987	1988	1989	1990	1991	1992 Total	1992 Male	1992 Female
Total	1,743	2,116	2,348	2,374	2,397	2,420	2,455	2,493	2,528	2,536	1,180	1,356
In the labor force	777	916	992	1,029	1,058	1,103	1,115	1,132	1,165	1,170	729	442
Employed	693	758	776	834	880	938	952	971	979	977	592	385
Working	657	712	710	768	804	848	858	(NA)	(NA)	(NA)	(NA)	(NA)
35 hours or more	569	535	508	579	570	614	651	(NA)	(NA)	(NA)	(NA)	(NA)
Less than 35 hours	88	177	203	189	235	234	207	(NA)	(NA)	(NA)	(NA)	(NA)
Unemployed	84	156	216	194	178	165	163	160	186	193	137	56
Percent	10.7	17.0	21.8	18.9	16.8	15.0	14.6	14.2	16.0	16.5	18.8	12.7
Not in labor force	966	1,200	1,356	1,345	1,340	1,317	1,340	1,362	1,363	1,366	451	915

NA Not available.

Source: Puerto Rico Dept. of Labor and Human Resources, Bureau of Labor Statistics, San Juan, PR.

No. 1365. Puerto Rico—Gross Product, by Major Industrial Sector: 1980 to 1992

[In millions of dollars. For fiscal years ending June 30. Data for 1992 are preliminary]

ITEM	1980	1984	1985	1986	1987	1988	1989	1990	1991	1992
Gross product	11,065	14,183	15,002	16,014	17,153	18,550	19,954	21,619	22,857	23,620
Agriculture	380	345	357	373	411	399	443	434	449	462
Manufacturing	5,306	7,371	7,909	8,549	9,483	10,513	11,133	12,126	12,762	13,155
Contract construction and mining [1] . . . . [2]	369	326	334	331	418	551	662	720	771	789
Transportation [2]	1,279	1,714	1,709	1,905	2,045	2,262	2,315	2,468	2,677	2,841
Trade	2,273	2,912	3,160	3,361	3,746	4,125	4,376	4,728	4,811	5,008
Finance, insurance, real estate	1,486	2,421	2,547	2,867	3,183	3,545	3,750	3,896	4,205	4,458
Services	1,279	1,715	1,837	1,993	2,184	2,505	2,699	3,015	3,284	3,547
Government	1,897	2,174	2,346	2,445	2,680	2,918	3,187	3,337	3,538	3,738
Commonwealth	1,574	1,850	1,996	2,078	2,293	2,506	2,745	2,884	3,052	3,213
Municipalities	323	324	350	367	387	413	442	453	486	525
Rest of the world	-3,372	-4,980	-5,287	-5,955	-6,725	-7,629	-8,313	-8,985	-9,734	-10,350
Statistical discrepancy . . .	166	186	91	147	-271	-640	-298	-121	94	-28

[1] Mining includes only quarries. [2] Includes other public utilities, and radio and television broadcasting.
Source: Puerto Rico Planning Board, San Juan, PR, *Economic Report of the Governor, 1991-92.*

No. 1366. Puerto Rico—Net Income, by Industrial Origin: 1980 to 1992

[See headnote, table 1365]

INDUSTRY	1980	1985	1986	1987	1988	1989	1990	1991	1992
All industries	9,007	12,182	13,166	14,414	15,699	16,662	17,941	18,854	19,535
Agriculture	435	410	420	465	447	494	486	503	518
Manufacturing	4,756	7,117	7,862	8,760	9,704	10,299	11,277	11,924	12,324
Mining	9	10	13	15	22	24	26	26	26
Contract construction . . . . [1]	337	309	299	380	516	624	679	728	745
Transp. and other public utilities [1] .	1,022	1,248	1,442	1,574	1,646	1,681	1,777	1,944	2,080
Trade	1,609	2,285	2,451	2,648	2,942	3,154	3,420	3,500	3,598
Finance, insurance, and real estate	1,200	2,141	2,442	2,707	2,978	3,136	3,280	3,544	3,739
Services	1,114	1,606	1,748	1,911	2,154	2,377	2,643	2,883	3,118
Commonwealth Government [2] . . .	1,897	2,346	2,445	2,680	2,918	3,187	3,337	3,538	3,738
Rest of the world	-3,372	-5,287	-5,955	-6,725	-7,629	-8,313	-8,985	-9,734	-10,350

[1] Includes radio and television. [2] Includes public enterprises not elsewhere classified.
Source: Puerto Rico Planning Board, San Juan, PR, *Economic Report of the Governor, 1991-92.*

No. 1367. Puerto Rico—Transfers Between Federal and State Governments and Other Nonresidents: 1983 to 1992

[See headnote, table 1365]

ITEM	1983	1985	1987	1988	1989	1990	1991	1992
Total receipts	3,310	3,531	3,992	4,073	4,289	4,871	4,973	5,225
Federal government	3,111	3,348	3,785	3,840	4,082	4,649	4,708	5,025
Transfers to individuals [1]	3,053	3,283	3,715	3,761	4,014	4,577	4,633	4,945
Veterans benefits	291	317	339	323	337	349	370	382
Medicare	184	220	273	292	320	368	415	481
Old age, disability, survivors	1,423	1,581	1,743	1,826	1,940	2,055	2,243	2,414
Nutritional assistance	775	780	804	822	853	880	916	957
Industry subsidies	59	65	70	80	68	72	75	80
U.S. State governments	15	17	15	15	17	18	18	26
Other nonresidents	183	166	192	217	191	205	246	174
Total payments	992	1,180	1,345	1,524	1,664	1,801	1,849	1,933
Federal government	979	1,145	1,332	1,512	1,651	1,756	1,832	1,864
Transfers from individuals	428	508	598	692	766	817	860	903
Contribution to Medicare	38	44	53	70	89	97	101	107
Employee contribution for Social Security . .	390	463	543	620	675	720	758	795
Transfers from industries	12	13	14	15	15	16	19	24
Unemployment insurance	171	189	213	223	237	247	243	193
Employer contribution for Social Security	368	435	508	582	633	675	710	744
Other nonresidents	13	35	13	11	13	45	17	69
Net balance	2,317	2,351	2,647	2,550	2,625	3,070	3,124	3,292
Federal government	2,132	2,203	2,452	2,328	2,431	2,893	2,877	3,161
U.S. State governments	13	14	13	14	14	16	15	21
Other nonresidents	173	134	181	208	180	162	232	109

[1] Includes other receipts and payments not shown separately.
Source: Puerto Rico Planning Board, San Juan, PR, *Economic Report of the Governor, 1991-92.*

No. 1368. Puerto Rico—Economic Summary, by Industry: 1990

[Excludes employees of establishments totally exempt from the Federal Insurance Contributions Act: government workers, railroad employment jointly covered by Social Security and railroad retirement programs, self-employed persons, domestic service, agriculture production employees, and employees on oceanborne vessels or in foreign countries]

1987 SIC code [1]	INDUSTRY	Total establishments	Employment-size class					Employees [2]	Annual payroll (mil. dol.)
			1 to 4	5 to 9	10 to 19	20 to 49	50 or more		
(X)	Total [3]	35,557	21,475	5,576	3,810	2,876	1,820	561,332	7,139.8
A	Agricultural services, forestry, and fishing	71	47	12	7	4	1	479	3.6
B	Mining	34	9	7	4	9	5	755	9.9
14	Nonmetallic minerals, except fuels	25	3	7	4	7	4	547	6.7
C	Construction [3]	890	329	141	129	128	163	34,798	361.7
15	General contractors and operative builders	364	102	52	46	57	107	22,399	216.9
17	Special trade contractors	452	208	78	66	56	44	8,946	99.4
D	Manufacturing [3]	1,701	359	209	250	329	554	151,269	2,314.7
20	Food and kindred products	243	73	39	37	44	50	18,093	285.1
22	Textile mill products	16	4	1	2	2	7	2,604	29.1
23	Apparel and other textile products	250	36	13	27	52	122	31,655	250.7
25	Furniture and fixtures	97	28	19	23	19	8	2,038	19.1
26	Paper and allied products	42	2	6	11	10	13	1,871	29.4
27	Printing and publishing	149	64	33	20	20	12	4,191	60.8
28	Chemicals and allied products	159	20	10	18	30	81	25,209	642.4
29	Petroleum and coal products	13	-	1	2	3	7	1,270	32.4
30	Rubber and misc. plastic products	85	9	5	15	24	32	6,197	90.0
31	Leather and leather products	25	1	-	3	5	16	6,047	58.1
32	Stone, clay, and glass products	115	25	19	28	31	12	3,519	64.6
34	Fabricated metal products	111	22	19	16	29	25	4,063	51.9
35	Industrial machinery and equip	74	18	16	7	14	19	6,960	129.6
36	ELectronic and other electronic equip	103	10	2	7	9	75	18,299	260.5
38	Instruments and related products	69	9	3	7	6	44	11,331	195.9
E	Transportation and public utilities [3]	819	419	151	106	86	57	24,837	459.1
42	Trucking and warehousing	310	173	58	37	35	7	2,772	32.3
44	Water transportation	55	21	8	5	9	12	4,547	71.6
45	Air transportation	58	16	14	12	6	10	3,769	71.6
47	Transportation services	235	160	36	18	15	6	2,034	30.4
48	Communication	88	6	20	27	18	17	10,723	240.4
49	Electric, gas, and sanitary services	15	3	4	1	2	5	716	10.8
F	Wholesale trade [3]	1,898	748	358	346	285	161	35,225	593.4
50	Durable goods	965	366	197	202	134	66	15,661	255.4
51	Nondurable goods	914	378	157	139	148	92	19,014	322.7
G	Retail trade [3]	9,210	4,994	1,831	1,188	833	364	107,637	976.5
52	Building materials, garden supplies	573	309	128	70	51	15	5,256	53.7
53	General merchandise stores	418	164	53	59	58	84	17,489	165.3
54	Food stores	1,206	675	203	123	90	115	20,973	156.4
55	Automotive dealers and service stations	1,478	945	314	135	67	17	9,255	98.3
56	Apparel and accessory stores	1,249	552	295	247	131	24	12,637	104.6
57	Furniture and home furnishings	650	359	169	85	33	4	4,234	44.3
58	Eating and drinking places [3]	1,647	800	261	267	269	50	19,768	148.6
H	Finance, insurance, and real estate [3]	1,864	978	332	242	205	107	36,085	607.7
60	Depository institutions	310	150	23	45	53	39	14,545	257.8
61	Nondepository institutions	423	105	126	103	69	20	7,796	112.4
63	Insurance carriers	80	19	14	8	24	15	3,915	79.0
64	Insurance agents, brokers, and service	240	127	43	28	25	17	4,025	73.2
65	Real estate	759	547	117	52	31	12	4,933	61.3
I	Services [3]	7,533	4,985	1,018	670	453	407	118,751	1,284.6
72	Personal services	508	355	74	57	16	6	3,201	26.0
73	Business services	631	268	115	74	66	108	27,429	253.3
75	Auto repair, services, and parking	482	340	86	35	15	6	2,688	27.6
78	Motion pictures	86	35	17	20	11	3	1,015	12.0
79	Amusement and recreation services	143	85	15	28	11	4	1,674	16.7
80	Health services	2,826	2,241	330	123	63	69	28,388	299.5
81	Legal services	726	603	43	52	19	9	3,143	53.0
82	Education services	441	112	52	75	103	99	20,705	226.5
83	Social services	223	94	46	43	17	23	5,151	46.3
86	Membership organizations	520	329	76	44	48	23	5,817	50.2
87	Engineering and management services	547	317	96	64	46	24	6,143	95.1

- Represents or rounds to zero. X Not applicable. [1] 1987 Standard Industrial Classification (SIC) code; see text, section 13. [2] For the pay period including March 12. [3] Includes other establishments not shown separately.
Source: U.S. Bureau of the Census, *County Business Patterns*, 1990.

No. 1369. Puerto Rico—Merchandise Imports and Exports: 1970 to 1991

[In millions of dollars. Imports are imports for consumption; see text, section 29]

ITEM	1970	1975	1980	1981	1982	1983	1984	1985	1986	1987	1988	1989	1990	1991
Imports	2,681	4,885	9,018	9,329	8,167	8,708	10,116	10,162	10,321	11,308	13,096	15,010	16,200	15,079
From U.S.	2,070	3,029	5,345	5,801	5,300	5,162	5,738	6,130	6,467	7,307	8,788	10,193	10,792	10,306
From other	611	1,856	3,673	3,528	2,867	3,546	4,378	4,032	3,854	4,001	4,308	4,817	5,408	4,773
Exports	1,680	3,000	6,576	7,047	8,888	8,242	9,426	11,087	11,854	12,508	14,436	17,455	20,402	21,128
To U.S.	1,563	2,633	5,643	6,024	7,624	6,936	8,074	9,873	10,524	11,153	12,756	15,334	17,915	18,729
To other	117	367	933	1,023	1,264	1,306	1,352	1,214	1,330	1,355	1,680	2,121	2,487	2,399

Source: U.S. Bureau of the Census, *Foreign Commerce and Navigation of the United States*, annual; *U.S. Trade with Puerto Rico and U.S. Possessions, FT 895*; and, through 1988, *Highlights of U.S. Export and Import Trade, FT990*; thereafter, FT990 supplement.

No. 1370. Puerto Rico, Guam, and Virgin Islands—Agriculture: 1982 and 1987

[1 cuerda = .97 acre. Tons specified are short tons]

ITEM	1982	1987	ITEM	1982	1987	ITEM	Unit	Harvested 1982	Harvested 1987	Sales 1982	Sales 1987
PUERTO RICO											
Farms.........	21,820	20,245	Tenure of operator: Percent—			Dairy products.	(X)	(X)	(X)	152,126	157,864
Percent—						Poultry [2].....	(X)	(X)	(X)	45,945	70,560
Less than 10 cuerdas	45.1	48.7	Full-owners .	79.3	77.5	Coffee......	1,000 cwt.[3]	243.9	246.2	39,302	41,786
10 to 19 cuerdas.	20.9	19.5	Part-owners .	11.5	13.1	Cattle and calves	(X)	(X)	(X)	28,579	30,206
20 to 49 cuerdas.	18.0	16.7	Managers ..	1.8	2.3	Sugarcane ...	1,000 tons	1,462	1,170	26,663	26,643
50 to 99 cuerdas.	7.1	6.7	Tenants....	7.4	7.1	Fruits/nuts ...	(X)	(X)	(X)	14,060	20,645
100 to 174 cuerdas	3.9	3.7	Avg. farm size—cuerdas—			Pineapples ...	1,000 tons	44	69	9,534	15,495
175 or more cuerdas	5.0	4.7	Full-owners .	31.1	30.6						
			Part-owners .	99.3	85.7	Hogs........	(X)	(X)	(X)	6,903	9,525
Cuerdas in farms	982,457	886,846	Managers .	122.8	128.0						
			Tenants....	90.9	84.0	Vegetables...	Cuerdas..	6,669	6,179	9,547	8,236
GUAM											
Farms.........	297	351	Tenure of operator: Percent—			Chicken eggs .	(X)	(X)	(X)	791.9	651.1
Percent—						Fish........	(X)	(X)	(X)	121.3	235.0
Less than 1 acre.	9.4	6.3	Full-owners .	62.0	64.1	Cucumbers...	1,000 lbs.	623.3	587.1	217.8	233.5
1 to 2 acres.	36.0	35.9	Permittees .	21.9	20.5	Green beans.	1,000 lbs.	116.5	303.8	81.7	230.2
3 to 7 acres....	28.6	29.1	Tenants....	9.1	4.3	Watermelons .	1,000 lbs.	400.3	632.6	115.6	178.6
8 or more acres .	26.0	28.8	Part-owners .	5.1	4.6	Tomatoes....	1,000 lbs.	88.0	142.7	64.3	108.6
			Non-permittees .	1.3	6.0	Hogs and pigs.	(X)	(X)	(X)	117.0	106.4
Acres in farms	17,787	13,134	Others....	0.7	0.6						
VIRGIN ISLANDS											
Farms.........	259	267	Tenure of operator: Percent—			Milk.........	(X)	(X)	(X)	922.8	1,042.7
Percent—						Cattle and calves	(X)	(X)	(X)	488.6	613.4
Less than 3 acres.	29.0	30.0									
3 to 9 acres....	34.7	30.3	Full-owners .	79.9	75.3	Hogs and pigs.	(X)	(X)	(X)	130.0	125.2
10 to 19 acres ..	9.3	12.0	Part-owners .	10.4	13.5						
			Tenants....	9.3	8.6	Tomatoes....	Acres ...	8	16	33.7	113.7
20 or more acres.	27.0	27.7				Lettuce	Acres ...	2	8	7.8	49.5
			Managers ..	0.4	2.6	Mangoes	1,000...	205.0	171.1	(D)	44.0
Acres in farms	17,778	17,785				Poultry [2]....	(X)	(X)	(X)	315.6	16.8

D Withheld to avoid disclosure of information pertaining to a specific organization or individual.　X Not applicable.
[1] Includes amounts not sold.　[2] Includes poultry products.　[3] Cwt = hundredweight (100 lbs.).
Source: U.S. Bureau of the Census, *1987 Census of Agriculture*, vol. 1, parts 52, 53, and 54.

No. 1371. Guam, Virgin Islands, and Northern Mariana Islands—Economic Summary: 1987

[Sales and payroll in millions of dollars]

ITEM	Guam	Virgin Islands	No. Mariana Islands	ITEM	Guam	Virgin Islands	No. Mariana Islands
Total: Establishments	1,490	2,604	768	**Wholesale trade:**			
Sales.................	1,510	(D)	374	Establishments	94	84	28
Annual payroll...........	221	255	57	Sales................	245	211	50
Paid employees [1]........	18,582	20,709	9,090	Annual payroll	19	20	2
Unpaid family workers [2]....	371	209	167	Paid employees [1].......	1,392	1,322	187
Construction: Establishments.	79	92	72	Unpaid family workers [2]....	6	2	-
Sales.................	127	124	43	**Retail trade:**			
Annual payroll...........	35	29	12	Establishments	804	1,311	383
Paid employees [1]........	2,705	2,170	2,061	Sales................	786	703	155
Unpaid family workers [2]....	1	3	6	Annual payroll	79	85	14
Manufacturing:				Paid employees [1].......	7,344	8,529	2,304
Establishments	38	66	39	Unpaid family workers [2]....	273	168	126
Sales.................	81	(D)	58	**Services: Establishments**	475	1,051	246
Annual payroll...........	17	44	14	Sales................	271	296	67
Paid employees [1]........	1,320	2,102	2,257	Annual payroll	71	76	16
Unpaid family workers [2]....	1	-	3	Paid employees [1].......	5,821	6,586	2,281
				Unpaid family workers [2]....	90	36	32

- Represents zero.　D Withheld to avoid disclosure of information pertaining to a specific organization or individual.　[1] For pay period including March 12.　[2] Includes those who worked 15 hours or more during the week including March 12.
Source: U.S. Bureau of the Census, *1987 Economic Census of Outlying Areas*, OAC 87-5 to OAC 87-7.

Comparative International Statistics

This section presents statistics for the world as a whole and for many countries on a comparative basis with the United States. Data are shown for population, births and deaths, social and industrial indicators, finances, agriculture, communication, and military affairs.

Statistics of the individual nations may be found primarily in official national publications, generally in the form of yearbooks, issued by most of the nations at various intervals in their own national languages and expressed in their own or customary units of measure. (For a listing of selected publications, see Guide to Sources.) For handier reference, especially for international comparisons, the Statistical Office of the United Nations compiles data as submitted by member countries and issues a number of international summary publications, generally in English and French. Among these are the *Statistical Yearbook*; the *Demographic Yearbook;* the *Yearbook of International Trade Statistics;* the *Yearbook of National Accounts Statistics: Vol. II, International Tables; Population and Vital Statistics Reports* (quarterly); the *Monthly Bulletin of Statistics;* and the *Energy Statistics Yearbook.* Specialized agencies of the United Nations also issue international summary publications on agricultural, labor, health, and education statistics. Among these are the *Production Yearbook* and *Trade Yearbook* issued by the Food and Agriculture Organization, the *Yearbook of Labour Statistics* issued by the International Labour Office, the *World Health Statistics* issued by the World Health Organization, and the *Statistical Yearbook* issued by the Educational, Scientific, and Cultural Organization.

The Bureau of the Census, in *Country Demographic Profiles,* series ISP-DP, presents data on individual countries for both a recent census year and the current period; and in the *World Population Profile* series, estimates of basic demographic measures for countries and regions of the world. The *International Population Statistics Reports,* series P-90 and P-91, issued by the Bureau of the Census, also present

In Brief

Ten largest countries in 1993:
(1,000 persons)

China, Mainland	1,177,585
India	903,159
United States	258,104
Indonesia	197,232
Brazil	156,664
Russia	149,300
Pakistan	125,214
Japan	124,712
Bangladesh	122,255
Nigeria	95,060

population figures for many foreign countries. Detailed population statistics are also available from the Bureau of the Census' computerized International Data Base.

The U.S. Arms Control and Disarmament Agency and the International Monetary Fund (IMF) also compile data on international statistics. In its *World Military Expenditures and Arms Transfers,* published annually, the ACDA presents data on various economic indicators, as well as basic military data. Among the topics presented have been military expenditures, gross national product, imports and exports, and armed forces, by region and/or country. The IMF publishes a series of reports relating to financial data. These include *International Financial Statistics, Direction of Trade,* and *Balance of Payments Yearbook,* published in English, French, and Spanish.

Statistical coverage, country names, and classifications.—Problems of space and availability of data limit the number of countries and the extent of statistical coverage shown. The list of countries included is based almost entirely on a list of sovereign nations, dependencies, and areas of special sovereignty published by the U.S. Department of State in *Status of the World's Nations.* Country names are shown here as specified in that publication. In the few cases where a lack of comparability exists between State Department and United Nations' terminology, the State Department's preferences are used.

In recent years, several important changes took place in the status of the world's nations. Two nations, Yemen and Germany, were formed in 1990, each by unification of two formerly separate nations. In the case of Germany, the former German Democratic Republic (East) was subsumed by the Federal Republic of Germany (West). In most cases, data presented in the *Statistical Abstract* are for former West Germany. The Republic of Yemen was formed by union of the former Yemen Arab Republic and the People's Democratic Republic of Yemen. Also in 1990, Namibia finally realized its independence; the United Nations terminated its status as a South African mandate in 1966.

The year 1990 also began a period of turmoil in the former Soviet Union. The independence of three Baltic States—Estonia, Latvia, and Lithuania—was recognized by the central Soviet government in August 1991. The United States established diplomatic relations with the democratically elected governments of the Baltic States in September 1991. In December 1991, the 12 former Soviet republics became separate sovereign nations—Armenia, Azerbaijan, Belarus, Georgia, Kazakhstan, Kyrgyzstan, Moldova, Russia, Tajikistan, Turkmenistan, Ukraine, and Uzbekistan. Eleven of the 12 have formed a Commonwealth of Independent States (Georgia has not joined). Most data presented in the *Statistical Abstract* are for former Soviet Union.

In 1992, the Socialist Federal Republic of Yugoslavia dissolved and none of the successor states represents its continuation. Bosnia and Herzegovina, Croatia, and Slovenia have been formally recognized as independent states by the United States. Macedonia has proclaimed independent statehood, but has not been formally recognized as a state by the U.S. Serbia and Montenegro have asserted the formation of a joint independent state, but this entity has not been formally recognized as a state by the U.S. In addition, on December 31, 1992, at midnight, Czechoslovakia ceased to exist and was succeeded by two separate and independent states, the Czech Republic and Slovakia. The United States formally recognized the Czech Republic and Slovakia as independent states on January 1, 1993. Finally, Eritrea announced its independence from Ethiopia on April 27, 1993. After this announcement, the U.S. recognized Eritrea as an independent state.

The population estimates and projections used in tables 1374-1376 were prepared by the Census Bureau. For each country, the data on population, by age and sex, fertility, mortality, and international migration were evaluated and, where necessary, adjusted for inconsistencies and errors in the data. In most instances, comprehensive projections were made by the component method, resulting in distributions of the population by age and sex, and requiring an assessment of probable future trends of fertility, mortality, and international migration.

Economic associations.—The Organization for European Economic Co-operation (OEEC), a regional grouping of Western European countries established in 1948 for the purpose of harmonizing national economic policies and conditions, was succeeded on September 30, 1961, by the Organization for Economic Cooperation and Development (OECD). The member nations of the OECD are Australia, Austria, Belgium, Canada, Denmark, Finland, France, Germany, Greece, Iceland, Ireland, Italy, Japan, Luxembourg, the Netherlands, New Zealand, Norway, Portugal, Spain, Sweden, Switzerland, Turkey, the United Kingdom, and the United States.

Quality and comparability of the data.— The quality and comparability of the data presented here are affected by a number of factors:

(1) The year for which data are presented may not be the same for all subjects for a particular country, or for a given subject for different countries, though the data shown are the most recent available. All such variations have been noted. The data shown are for calendar years except as otherwise specified.

(2) The bases, methods of estimating, methods of data collection, extent of coverage, precision of definition, scope of territory, and margins of error may vary for different items within a particular country, and for like items for different countries. Footnotes and headnotes to the tables give a few of the major time-period and coverage qualifications attached to the figures;

considerably more detail is presented in the source publications. Many of the measures shown are, at best, merely rough indicators of magnitude.

(3) Figures shown in this section for the United States may not always agree with figures shown in the preceding sections. Disagreements may be attributable to the use of differing original sources, a difference in the definition of geographic limits (the 50 States, conterminous United States only, or the United States including certain outlying areas and possessions), or to possible adjustments made in the U.S. figures by the United Nations or other sources in order to make them more comparable with figures from other countries.

International comparisons of national accounts data.—In order to compare national accounts data for different countries, it is necessary to convert each country's data into a common unit of currency, usually the U.S. dollar. The market exchange rates which are often used in converting national currencies do not necessarily reflect the relative purchasing power in the various countries. For example, using table 1387, it should not be concluded that the United Kingdom's individual standard of living in 1990 was only 78 percent of that of the United States, as the statistics may imply. It is obviously necessary that the goods and services produced in different countries should be valued consistently if the differences observed are meant to reflect real differences in the volumes of goods and services produced. The use of purchasing power parities (see table 1392) instead of exchange rates is intended to achieve this objective.

The method used to present the data shown in table 1392 is to construct volume measures directly by revaluing the goods and services sold in different countries at a common set of international prices. By dividing the ratio of the gross domestic products of two countries expressed in their own national currencies by the corresponding ratio calculated at constant international prices, it is possible to derive the implied purchasing power parity (PPP) between the two currencies concerned. PPP's show how many units of currency are needed in one country to buy the same amount of goods and services which one unit of currency will buy in the other country. For further information, see *National Accounts, Main Aggregates,* volume I, issued annually by the Organization for Economic Cooperation and Development, Paris, France.

International Standard Industrial Classification.—The original version of the International Standard Industrial Classification of All Economic Activities (ISIC) was adopted in 1948. Wide use has been made both nationally and internationally in classifying data according to kind of economic activity in the fields of production, employment, national income, and other economic statistics. A number of countries have utilized the ISIC as the basis for devising their industrial classification scheme. Substantial comparability has been attained between the industrial classifications of many other countries, including the United States, and the ISIC by ensuring, as far as practicable, that the categories at detailed levels of classification in national schemes fitted into only one category of the ISIC. For more detail, see Bureau of the Census, *The International Standard Industrial Classification and the U.S. Standard Industrial Classification,* Technical Paper No. 14 and text, section 27. The United Nations, the International Labour Organization, the Food and Agriculture Organization, and other international bodies have utilized the ISIC in publishing and analyzing statistical data. Revisions of the ISIC were issued in 1958, 1968, and 1989.

International maps. A series of regional world maps is provided on pages 832–838. References are included in table 1374 for easy location of individual countries on the maps. The Robinson map projection is used for this series of maps. A map projection is used to portray all or part of the round Earth on a flat surface, but this cannot be done without some distortion. For the Robinson projection, distortion is very low along the Equator and within 45 degrees of the center but is greatest near the poles. For additional information on map projections and maps, please contact the Earth Science Information Center, U.S. Geological Survey, 507 National Center, Reston, VA 22092.

Arctic Ocean

Faroe Islands

Russia

Finland

Sweden

Norway

Estonia

Russia

Latvia

Denmark

Lithuania

Russia

Netherlands

Germany

Poland

Belarus

Ireland

United Kingdom

Isle of Man

Guernsey

Jersey

Ukraine

France

Romania

Andorra

Monaco

San Marino

Italy

Serbia

Spain

Bulgaria

Albania

Macedonia

Portugal

Gibraltar

Greece

Atlantic Ocean

Netherlands

Belgium

Poland

Luxembourg

Germany

Czech Republic

Slovakia

Liechtenstein

Austria

Hungary

France

Switzerland

Slovenia

Croatia

Serbia

Italy

Bosnia & Herzegovina

Spain
Morocco
Western Sahara
Tunisia
Malta
Greece
Cyprus
Lebanon
West Bank
Gaza Strip
Syria
Iraq
Iran
Israel
Jordan
Kuwait
Bahrain
Qatar
United Arab Emirates
Algeria
Libya
Egypt
Saudi Arabia
Oman
Mauritania
Mali
Niger
Chad
Sudan
Djibouti
Yemen
Nigeria
Cameroon
Central African Republic
Ethiopia
Somalia
Sao Tome & Principe
Gabon
Congo
Zaire
Uganda
Rwanda
Burundi
Kenya
Tanzania
Indian Ocean
Equatorial Guinea
St. Helena
Angola
Zambia
Malawi
Mozambique
Seychelles
Comoros
Mayotte
Mauritius
Reunion
Atlantic Ocean
Namibia
Zimbabwe
Botswana
Madagascar
South Africa
Swaziland
Lesotho

Mauritania
Senegal
Niger
The Gambia
Mali
Burkina
Guinea-Bissau
Guinea
Benin
Sierra Leone
Cote d' Ivoire
Nigeria
Ghana
Liberia
Togo

China, Mainland

China, Taiwan

Macau

Burma · Laos

Hong Kong

Thailand

Pacific Ocean

Northern Mariana Islands

Guam

Marshall Islands

Trust Ter. of the Pac. Isl. (Palau)

Federated States of Micronesia

Kiribati

Papua New Guinea

Nauru

Indonesia

Solomon Islands

Tuvalu

Wallis & Futuna

Indian Ocean

Vanuatu

New Caledonia

Fiji

Australia

New Zealand

Pacific Ocean

Thailand

Vietnam

Philippines

Cambodia

Malaysia

Singapore

Indonesia

Indian Ocean

No. 1372. World Summary: 1970 to 1990

[See text, section 31, for general comments concerning quality of the data]

ITEM	Unit	1970	1980	1983	1984	1985	1986	1987	1988	1989	1990
Population	Millions	3,702	4,450	4,686	4,768	4,852	4,937	5,024	5,113	5,203	5,293
Agriculture, forestry, and fishing production: [1]											
Barley	Mil. metric tons	121.7	159.8	161.6	172.1	176.0	181.9	180.4	167.1	167.5	181.9
Coffee	Mil. metric tons	3.9	4.9	5.6	5.2	5.9	5.3	6.5	5.8	6.1	6.3
Corn	Mil. metric tons	266.4	397.5	348.5	452.0	487.0	478.0	450.9	400.2	474.1	479.3
Cotton (lint)	Mil. metric tons	12.0	13.8	14.3	18.2	17.4	15.2	16.6	18.3	17.1	18.4
Meats	Mil. metric tons	100.6	136.0	143.9	147.7	152.9	157.3	162.6	169.1	171.9	176.6
Peanuts (groundnuts)	Mil. metric tons	18.0	16.9	19.0	19.9	19.9	20.8	21.4	21.6	23.1	23.4
Rice	Mil. metric tons	316.7	399.4	451.6	468.6	471.6	471.4	464.4	491.0	517.3	521.7
Tobacco	Mil. metric tons	4.6	5.3	6.0	6.5	7.0	6.1	6.2	6.9	7.1	7.1
Wheat	Mil. metric tons	316.6	445.9	493.1	516.0	504.6	535.0	511.0	506.8	542.7	601.7
Wool, greasy	Mil. metric tons	2.9	2.8	2.9	2.9	3.0	3.0	3.1	3.2	3.2	3.3
Roundwood	Mil. cubic meters	2,614	2,942	3,048	3,163	3,200	3,305	3,372	3,426	3,456	3,450
Fish catches	Mil. metric tons	68.0	72.0	77.5	83.9	86.4	92.8	94.4	99.1	100.3	97.3
Industrial production:											
Wine [1]	Mil. metric tons	30.2	35.2	34.8	32.1	29.4	32.0	31.8	27.1	28.4	29.0
Sugar [1]	Mil. metric tons	72.5	84.3	97.5	99.7	98.6	100.9	101.9	103.9	105.5	110.8
Wheat flour	Mil. metric tons	121.2	187.2	197.3	202.8	206.7	211.3	200.7	205.4	203.2	203.4
Coal	Mil. metric tons	2,143	2,728	2,831	2,999	3,161	3,249	3,411	3,488	3,562	3,564
Lignite and brown coal	Mil. metric tons	793	1,042	1,130	1,153	1,202	1,219	1,250	1,261	1,274	1,219
Crude petroleum [2]	Bil. bbl.	16.74	21.66	19.33	19.78	19.58	20.39	20.55	21.35	21.74	22.03
Natural gas (dry) [2]	Trl. cu. ft	37.54	53.11	54.56	59.66	62.00	63.25	66.17	69.57	71.99	74.27
Electricity	Bil. kWh.	4,962	8,247	8,826	9,326	9,747	10,055	10,587	11,059	11,450	11,734
Iron ore	Mil. metric tons	421	841	740	829	862	868	890	916	920	921
Pig iron and ferroalloys	Mil. metric tons	440	542	466	500	507	496	503	504	506	505
Tin [3]	1,000 metric tons	184	231	195	196	196	191	194	210	210	211
Crude steel	Mil. metric tons	594	699	638	679	685	671	682	685	676	685
Cement	Mil. metric tons	570	872	906	933	949	997	1,045	1,109	1,137	1,140
Non-cellulosic fibers [3]	Mil. metric tons	4.9	10.0	10.4	11.0	11.5	11.7	12.4	13.0	13.2	11.8
Sawnwood	Mil. cubic meters	413	447	438	458	465	480	502	503	499	483
Woodpulp	Mil. metric tons	97.2	124.4	124.0	131.3	133.1	136.6	142.0	148.2	150.1	150.3
Newsprint	Mil. metric tons	21.6	25.4	2.6	27.8	28.3	29.3	30.6	3.2	32.3	33.1
Merchant vessels, launched	Mil. gross tons	21.7	13.9	14.9	17.7	17.3	14.9	9.6	11.8	12.7	14.7
Motor vehicles	Millions	29.3	38.9	39.0	41.9	44.8	45.3	45.9	48.1	48.9	48.1
External trade:											
Imports, c.i.f.	Bil. U.S. dollars	331	2,047	1,875	1,985	2,028	2,198	2,544	2,908	3,133	3,547
Exports, f.o.b.	Bil. U.S. dollars	314	1,998	1,807	1,903	1,927	2,121	2,465	2,814	3,013	3,482
Transport:											
Railway freight	Bil. metric ton-km	5,027	6,754	6,855	7,138	7,285	(NA)	(NA)	(NA)	(NA)	(NA)
Merchant shipping, freight [4]	Mil. metric tons	(NA)	3,676	3,290	3,410	3,362	3,459	3,506	3,692	3,891	(NA)
Civil aviation, kilometers flown [5]	Millions	4,353	9,362	9,320	9,950	10,565	11,455	12,208	13,026	13,564	14,339

NA Not available. [1] Source: U.S. Department of Agriculture, Economic Research Service, *World Agriculture-Trends and Indicators.* [2] Source: U.S. Energy Information Administration, *International Energy Annual* and *Annual Energy Review.* [3] Excludes China: Mainland. Tin and merchant vessels exclude Soviet Republics. For other exclusions, see source. [4] Freight loaded. [5] Scheduled services of members of International Civil Aviation Organization. Excludes Soviet Republics.

Source: Except as noted, Statistical Division of the United Nations, New York, NY, *Monthly Bulletin of Statistics,* (copyright).

No. 1373. U.S. Population Abroad, by Selected Area: 1993

[In thousands. As of October 15, 1992. Data taken from the annual noncombatant personnel evacuation requirements report, which is used solely to estimate the number of potential U.S. citizen evacuees from a given country in a crisis]

AREA	Resident U.S. citizens [1]	U.S. tourists	AREA	Resident U.S. citizens [1]	U.S. tourists
Argentina	13	11	Italy	104	105
Australia	62	56	Jerusalem	43	20
Canada	296	495	Mexico	539	1,088
Costa Rica	23	21	Netherlands	19	11
Dominican Republic	97	36	Panama	36	2
Egypt	17	11	Portugal	26	28
France	59	89	Saudi Arabia	40	6
Germany	354	1,060	South Korea	30	2
Greece	32	60	Spain	79	155
Hong Kong	24	23	Switzerland	27	29
Ireland	46	86	United Kingdom	255	377
Israel	112	61	Venezuela	24	2

[1] Totals represent broad estimates and may include some non-U.S. citizens, as well as dual nationals.

Source: U.S. Dept. of State, unpublished data.

No. 1374. Population, by Country, 1980, 1990, and 1993, and Projections, 2000

[Population data generally are de facto figures for the present territory. Population estimates were derived from information available as of early 1993. See text, section 31, for general comments concerning the data. For details of methodology, coverage, and reliability, see source. Minus sign (-) indicates decrease]

COUNTRY OR AREA	Map refer-ence	MIDYEAR POPULATION (1,000)				Popu-lation rank, 1993	ANNUAL RATE OF GROWTH [1] (percent)		Popula-tion per sq. mile, 1993
		1980	1990	1993	2000, proj.		1980-1990	1990-2000	
World total	S0	4,456,240	5,292,852	5,554,552	6,165,485	(X)	1.7	1.5	110
Afghanistan	S5	14,985	15,332	16,494	25,725	53	0.2	5.2	66
Albania	S3	2,673	3,249	3,334	3,610	125	2.0	1.1	315
Algeria	S4	18,862	25,352	27,256	31,743	37	3.0	2.2	30
Andorra	S3	34	53	62	73	203	4.5	3.3	356
Angola	S4	6,794	8,430	9,545	11,513	76	2.2	3.1	20
Antigua and Barbuda	S1	69	64	64	68	201	-0.7	0.7	379
Argentina	S2	28,237	32,386	33,533	36,202	31	1.4	1.1	32
Armenia	S5	3,115	3,363	3,481	3,685	123	0.8	0.9	303
Aruba	S1	60	64	65	68	200	0.6	0.6	874
Australia	S6	14,616	17,071	17,827	19,386	49	1.6	1.3	6
Austria	S3	7,549	7,718	7,915	8,108	85	0.2	0.5	248
Azerbaijan	S5	6,173	7,216	7,573	8,243	87	1.6	1.3	227
Bahamas, The	S1	210	255	269	298	174	2.0	1.5	69
Bahrain	S4	348	518	568	687	160	4.0	2.8	2,379
Bangladesh	S5	88,077	114,023	122,255	143,548	9	2.6	2.3	2,365
Barbados	S1	252	254	255	260	176	0.1	0.2	1,538
Belarus	S3	9,644	10,248	10,370	10,576	69	0.6	0.3	129
Belgium	S3	9,847	9,962	10,041	10,144	71	0.1	0.2	860
Belize	S1	144	190	204	242	180	2.7	2.4	23
Benin	S4	3,444	4,676	5,167	6,517	102	3.1	3.3	121
Bhutan	S5	1,281	1,585	1,699	1,996	141	2.1	2.3	94
Bolivia	S2	5,470	7,029	7,544	8,801	88	2.5	2.2	18
Bosnia and Herzegovina	S3	4,092	4,517	4,619	4,828	109	1.0	0.7	234
Botswana	S4	903	1,224	1,326	1,554	147	3.0	2.4	6
Brazil	S2	122,830	150,062	156,664	169,543	5	2.0	1.2	48
Brunei	S6	185	254	277	331	173	3.2	2.6	136
Bulgaria	S3	8,844	8,966	8,831	8,742	79	0.1	-0.3	207
Burkina	S4	6,939	9,042	9,853	11,871	74	2.6	2.7	93
Burma	S5	33,578	41,044	43,456	49,300	25	2.0	1.8	171
Burundi	S4	4,138	5,558	5,985	6,939	93	3.0	2.2	604
Cambodia	S5	6,499	8,731	9,899	12,098	73	3.0	3.3	145
Cameroon	S4	8,756	11,697	12,756	15,677	60	2.9	2.9	70
Canada	S1	24,070	26,620	27,770	29,867	34	1.0	1.2	8
Cape Verde	S1	296	375	411	503	166	2.4	2.9	264
Central African Republic	S4	2,269	2,866	3,074	3,511	128	2.3	2.0	13
Chad	S4	4,024	5,024	5,351	6,221	99	2.2	2.1	11
Chile	S2	11,094	13,108	13,740	15,207	58	1.7	1.5	48
China: Mainland	S5	984,736	1,136,626	1,177,585	1,260,154	1	1.4	1.0	327
Taiwan	S5	17,848	20,436	21,092	22,448	42	1.4	0.9	1,693
Colombia	S2	26,580	32,983	34,943	39,172	30	2.2	1.7	87
Comoros	S4	334	460	512	656	161	3.2	3.5	611
Congo	S4	1,620	2,215	2,389	2,784	135	3.1	2.3	18
Costa Rica	S2	2,307	3,031	3,265	3,797	126	2.7	2.3	167
Cote d'Ivoire	S4	8,418	12,399	13,808	17,371	57	3.9	3.4	112
Croatia	S3	4,593	4,686	4,694	4,717	107	0.2	0.1	215
Cuba	S1	9,653	10,622	10,957	11,617	61	1.0	0.9	256
Cyprus	S5	627	702	723	768	156	1.1	0.9	203
Czech Republic	S3	10,289	10,363	10,389	10,607	68	0.1	0.2	341
Denmark	S3	5,123	5,141	5,176	5,255	100	(Z)	0.2	316
Djibouti	S4	279	370	402	454	167	2.8	2.0	47
Dominica	S1	75	83	87	95	195	1.0	1.3	298
Dominican Republic	S1	5,847	7,249	7,684	8,644	86	2.2	1.8	411
Ecuador	S2	8,123	9,806	10,461	11,945	66	1.9	2.0	98
Egypt	S4	41,663	53,993	58,016	67,542	19	2.6	2.2	151
El Salvador	S1	4,655	5,303	5,637	6,459	95	1.3	2.0	705
Equatorial Guinea	S4	256	369	399	478	168	3.7	2.6	37
Eritrea [2]	S4	(NA)	(NA)	(NA)	(NA)	(NA)	(NA)	(NA)	(NA)
Estonia	S3	1,482	1,583	1,608	1,670	144	0.7	0.5	92
Ethiopia	S4	38,967	51,507	56,746	70,340	22	2.8	3.1	133
Fiji	S6	635	738	757	823	154	1.5	1.1	107
Finland	S3	4,780	4,986	5,051	5,153	104	0.4	0.3	43
France	S3	53,870	56,720	57,566	59,354	21	0.5	0.5	273
Gabon	S4	808	1,078	1,123	1,244	149	2.9	1.4	11
Gambia, The	S4	644	848	930	1,154	152	2.8	3.1	241
Georgia	S5	5,048	5,484	5,634	5,925	96	0.8	0.8	209
Germany	S3	78,298	79,357	80,768	82,239	12	0.1	0.4	597
Ghana	S4	10,777	15,195	16,699	20,608	52	3.4	3.0	188
Greece	S3	9,643	10,123	10,470	10,878	65	0.5	0.7	207
Grenada	S2	90	94	94	98	193	0.4	0.4	717
Guatemala	S1	7,232	9,633	10,446	12,408	67	2.9	2.5	250
Guinea	S4	4,320	5,930	6,237	7,372	92	3.2	2.2	66
Guinea-Bissau	S4	789	998	1,072	1,263	151	2.3	2.4	99
Guyana	S2	759	748	735	710	155	-0.2	-0.5	10
Haiti	S1	5,473	6,052	6,385	7,102	91	1.0	1.6	600
Honduras	S1	3,625	4,741	5,170	6,192	101	2.7	2.7	120
Hungary	S3	10,711	10,365	10,324	10,372	70	-0.3	(Z)	290
Iceland	S1	228	255	261	277	175	1.1	0.8	7
India	S5	692,394	852,656	903,159	1,018,105	2	2.1	1.8	787

See footnotes at end of table.

No. 1374. Population, by Country, 1980, 1990, and 1993, and Projections, 2000—Continued

[See headnote, page 840]

COUNTRY OR AREA	Map refer- ence	MIDYEAR POPULATION (1,000) 1980	1990	1993	2000, proj.	Popu- lation rank, 1993	ANNUAL RATE OF GROWTH[1] (percent) 1980- 1990	1990- 2000	Popula- tion per sq. mile, 1993
Indonesia	S6	154,936	187,728	197,232	219,496	4	1.9	1.6	280
Iran	S5	38,810	57,003	63,370	78,347	15	3.8	3.2	100
Iraq	S5	13,233	18,425	19,162	24,731	46	3.3	2.9	114
Ireland	S3	3,401	3,508	3,530	3,627	122	0.3	0.3	133
Israel	S4	3,737	4,303	4,919	5,507	105	1.4	2.5	627
Italy	S3	56,451	57,661	58,019	58,865	18	0.2	0.2	511
Jamaica	S1	2,229	2,466	2,530	2,746	134	1.0	1.1	605
Japan	S5	116,807	123,540	124,712	127,554	8	0.6	0.3	818
Jordan	S4	2,165	3,305	3,824	4,814	118	4.2	3.8	108
Kazakhstan	S5	14,994	16,749	17,156	17,886	51	1.1	0.7	16
Kenya	S4	16,681	24,229	27,372	32,479	35	3.7	2.9	125
Kiribati	S6	58	72	76	87	197	2.1	1.9	276
Kuwait	S5	1,370	2,117	1,698	2,494	142	4.4	1.6	247
Kyrgyzstan	S5	3,623	4,392	4,626	5,119	108	1.9	1.5	60
Laos	S5	3,293	4,191	4,569	5,557	110	2.4	2.8	51
Latvia	S3	2,525	2,693	2,736	2,833	131	0.6	0.5	110
Lebanon	S4	3,137	3,367	3,552	4,115	121	0.7	2.0	899
Lesotho	S4	1,347	1,755	1,896	2,242	140	2.6	2.4	162
Liberia	S4	1,900	2,311	2,875	3,620	129	2.0	4.5	77
Libya	S4	3,119	4,355	4,873	6,294	106	3.3	3.7	7
Liechtenstein	S3	25	29	30	32	214	1.3	1.2	481
Lithuania	S5	3,436	3,727	3,820	4,007	119	0.8	0.7	152
Luxembourg	S3	364	382	398	415	169	0.5	0.8	399
Madagascar	S4	8,700	11,811	13,006	16,232	59	3.1	3.2	58
Malawi	S4	6,128	9,289	9,832	11,045	75	4.2	1.7	271
Malaysia	S6	13,764	17,556	18,845	21,953	47	2.4	2.2	149
Maldives	S5	154	218	243	310	177	3.5	3.5	2,099
Mali	S4	6,693	8,234	8,869	10,911	78	2.1	2.8	19
Malta	S4	364	354	364	382	172	-0.3	0.8	2,935
Mauritania	S4	1,456	1,935	2,125	2,653	138	2.8	3.2	5
Mauritius	S4	964	1,074	1,107	1,194	150	1.1	1.1	1,550
Mexico	S1	68,686	85,121	90,420	102,912	11	2.1	1.9	122
Moldova	S5	3,996	4,389	4,456	4,565	112	0.9	0.4	342
Monaco	S3	27	30	31	32	212	1.2	0.7	40,155
Mongolia	S5	1,662	2,186	2,367	2,826	136	2.7	2.6	4
Morocco	S4	20,457	26,164	27,955	32,189	33	2.5	2.1	162
Mozambique	S4	12,103	14,438	16,342	20,868	54	1.8	3.7	54
Namibia	S4	967	1,387	1,541	1,957	145	3.6	3.4	5
Nauru	S6	8	9	10	11	222	2.0	1.3	1,219
Nepal	S5	15,001	19,104	20,535	24,364	43	2.4	2.4	389
Netherlands	S3	14,144	14,952	15,275	15,801	55	0.6	0.6	1,166
New Zealand	S6	3,113	3,300	3,369	3,476	124	0.6	0.5	32
Nicaragua	S2	2,776	3,617	3,987	4,759	116	2.6	2.7	86
Niger	S4	5,563	7,521	8,337	10,651	83	3.0	3.5	17
Nigeria	S4	65,699	86,551	95,060	118,620	10	2.8	3.2	270
North Korea	S5	17,999	21,412	22,646	25,491	40	1.7	1.7	487
Norway	S3	4,086	4,242	4,297	4,387	113	0.4	0.3	36
Oman	S5	984	1,481	1,644	2,098	143	4.1	3.5	20
Pakistan	S5	85,219	114,842	125,214	148,540	7	3.0	2.6	416
Panama	S2	1,956	2,427	2,579	2,934	133	2.2	1.9	88
Papua New Guinea	S6	2,991	3,823	4,101	4,812	115	2.5	2.3	24
Paraguay	S2	3,379	4,651	5,071	6,104	103	3.2	2.7	33
Peru	S2	17,295	21,879	23,210	26,258	38	2.4	1.8	47
Philippines	S6	50,864	64,405	68,464	77,747	14	2.4	1.9	595
Poland	S3	35,578	38,112	38,519	39,531	29	0.7	0.4	328
Portugal	S3	9,778	10,365	10,486	10,744	64	0.6	0.4	296
Qatar	S5	231	452	499	572	162	6.7	2.4	118
Romania	S5	22,201	23,191	23,172	23,383	39	0.4	0.1	261
Russia	S5	139,045	148,124	149,300	151,460	6	0.6	0.2	23
Rwanda	S4	5,170	7,415	8,139	9,715	84	3.6	2.7	845
Saint Kitts and Nevis	S1	44	40	40	43	210	-1.0	0.8	291
Saint Lucia	S1	122	142	144	151	186	1.5	0.6	612
Saint Vincent and the Grenadines	S1	98	112	115	122	190	1.4	0.8	875
San Marino	S3	21	23	24	25	215	0.8	0.9	1,030
Sao Tome and Principe	S4	94	123	133	159	188	2.7	2.6	359
Saudi Arabia	S4	10,139	16,271	17,615	22,070	50	4.7	3.0	21
Senegal	S4	5,731	7,715	8,463	10,533	82	3.0	3.1	114
Seychelles	S4	65	70	71	75	198	0.6	0.8	406
Sierra Leone	S4	3,315	4,230	4,511	5,421	111	2.4	2.5	163
Singapore	S6	2,414	2,720	2,826	3,025	130	1.2	1.1	11,731
Slovakia	S3	4,966	5,298	5,376	5,585	98	0.6	0.5	284
Slovenia	S3	1,885	1,954	1,968	1,998	139	0.4	0.2	252
Solomon Islands	S6	233	336	373	470	171	3.7	3.4	35
Somalia	S4	5,799	6,753	6,515	9,176	90	1.5	3.1	27
South Africa	S4	30,270	39,535	42,793	51,334	26	2.7	2.6	91
South Korea	S5	38,124	43,237	44,614	47,861	24	1.3	1.0	1,177
Spain	S3	37,488	38,964	39,207	39,972	28	0.4	0.3	203
Sri Lanka	S5	14,900	17,208	17,838	19,146	48	1.4	1.1	714
Sudan	S4	19,064	26,542	28,730	35,236	32	3.3	2.8	31
Suriname	S2	355	398	416	465	165	1.2	1.6	7

See footnotes at end of table.

No. 1374. Population, by Country, 1980, 1990, and 1993, and Projections, 2000—Continued

[See headnote, page 840]

COUNTRY OR AREA	Map refer-ence	MIDYEAR POPULATION (1,000)				Popu-lation rank, 1993	ANNUAL RATE OF GROWTH [1] (percent)		Popula-tion per sq. mile, 1993
		1980	1990	1993	2000, proj.		1980-1990	1990-2000	
Swaziland	S4	607	853	907	1,137	153	3.4	2.9	137
Sweden	S3	8,310	8,559	8,730	8,994	80	0.3	0.5	55
Switzerland	S3	6,385	6,779	6,987	7,268	89	0.6	0.7	455
Syria	S4	8,692	12,762	14,339	18,519	56	3.8	3.7	202
Tajikistan	S5	3,969	5,346	5,836	6,956	94	3.0	2.6	106
Tanzania	S4	18,695	25,155	27,286	32,254	36	3.0	2.5	80
Thailand	S5	47,026	56,220	58,722	63,620	17	1.8	1.2	297
Togo	S4	2,596	3,680	4,105	5,263	114	3.5	3.6	195
Tonga	S0	93	101	104	110	191	0.9	0.8	375
Trinidad and Tobago	S2	1,091	1,271	1,314	1,420	148	1.5	1.1	663
Tunisia	S4	6,452	8,084	8,571	9,599	81	2.3	1.7	143
Turkey	S5	45,121	57,130	60,898	69,624	16	2.4	2.0	205
Turkmenistan	S5	2,875	3,660	3,915	4,474	117	2.4	2.0	21
Tuvalu	S6	7	9	10	11	223	2.0	1.6	963
Uganda	S4	12,765	17,745	19,344	22,748	45	3.3	2.5	251
Ukraine	S5	50,047	51,674	51,821	51,931	23	0.3	-	222
United Arab Emirates	S5	1,000	2,252	2,657	3,582	132	8.1	4.6	82
United Kingdom	S3	56,314	57,418	57,970	58,951	20	0.2	0.3	621
United States	S1	227,726	249,924	258,104	275,327	3	0.9	1.0	73
Uruguay	S2	2,920	3,106	3,175	3,344	127	0.6	0.7	47
Uzbekistan	S5	16,000	20,615	22,128	25,467	41	2.5	2.1	128
Vanuatu	S6	117	154	166	193	184	2.8	2.2	29
Venezuela	S2	14,452	18,776	20,118	23,196	44	2.6	2.1	59
Vietnam	S5	54,234	67,718	71,788	80,533	13	2.2	1.7	571
Western Samoa	S0	155	186	200	235	181	1.8	2.3	182
Yemen	S5	7,324	9,746	10,742	13,603	63	2.9	3.3	53
Zaire	S4	27,954	37,903	41,346	51,413	27	3.0	3.0	47
Zambia	S4	5,638	8,233	8,926	10,625	77	3.8	2.6	31
Zimbabwe	S4	7,298	10,187	10,838	12,013	62	3.3	1.6	73
AREAS OF SPECIAL SOVEREIGNTY AND DEPENDENCIES									
American Samoa	S0	32	47	53	69	206	3.8	3.8	692
Anguilla	S1	7	7	7	7	224	0.5	0.7	199
Bermuda	S1	55	59	61	64	204	0.8	0.8	3,208
British Virgin Islands	S1	11	12	13	14	220	1.1	1.3	219
Cayman Islands	S1	17	27	30	41	213	4.4	4.3	303
Cook Islands	S0	18	18	19	20	216	0.1	1.1	203
Faroe Islands	S3	43	47	48	51	209	0.9	0.7	89
Federated States of Micronesia	S6	77	109	118	133	189	3.4	2.0	434
French Guiana	S2	68	116	133	173	187	5.4	4.0	4
French Polynesia	S0	151	196	210	245	178	2.6	2.2	149
Gaza Strip	S4	454	633	706	898	157	3.3	3.5	4,798
Gibraltar	S3	29	31	32	33	211	0.6	0.5	13,601
Greenland	S1	50	56	57	60	205	1.0	0.8	(Z)
Guadeloupe	S1	327	399	422	460	164	2.0	1.4	621
Guam	S6	107	134	146	171	185	2.3	2.4	699
Guernsey	S3	53	61	63	67	202	1.4	1.0	842
Hong Kong	S5	5,063	5,558	5,553	5,587	97	0.9	0.1	14,542
Isle of Man	S3	64	69	71	76	199	0.7	1.0	314
Jersey	S3	76	84	85	89	196	1.0	0.7	1,892
Macau [3]	S6	318	456	478	516	163	3.6	1.2	77,352
Macedonia [3]	S3	1,893	2,132	2,194	2,324	137	1.2	0.9	221
Marshall Islands	S6	31	46	52	68	207	4.1	3.9	744
Martinique	S1	339	374	388	419	170	1.0	1.2	948
Mayotte [3]	S4	52	80	90	117	194	4.3	3.8	620
Montenegro [3]	S5	579	645	661	696	158	1.1	0.8	124
Montserrat	S1	12	13	13	13	221	0.6	0.3	328
Netherlands Antilles	S2	170	183	185	193	182	0.8	0.5	499
New Caledonia	S6	139	168	178	200	183	1.9	1.7	25
Northern Mariana Islands	S6	17	44	49	57	208	9.7	2.6	264
Puerto Rico	S1	3,206	3,604	3,797	3,838	120	1.2	0.6	1,098
Reunion	S4	507	600	640	730	159	1.7	2.0	663
Saint Helena	S4	6	7	7	7	225	0.3	0.3	42
Saint Pierre and Miquelon	S1	6	6	7	7	226	0.8	0.8	71
Serbia [3]	S3	9,262	9,883	10,039	10,425	72	0.6	0.5	294
Trust Ter. of the Pac. Isl. (Palau)	S6	13	15	16	18	217	1.3	1.7	91
Turks and Caicos Islands	S1	7	12	13	15	219	4.5	2.7	79
Virgin Islands	S1	98	101	98	99	192	0.4	-0.2	726
Wallis and Futuna	S6	11	14	14	15	218	2.4	1.1	134
West Bank	S4	916	1,275	1,404	1,661	146	3.3	2.6	645
Western Sahara	S4	126	191	207	245	179	4.2	2.5	2

- Represents or rounds to zero.   NA Not available.   X Not applicable.   Z Less than .05 percent or one person per square mile.   [1] Computed by the exponential method. For explanation of average annual percent change, see Guide to Tabular Presentation.   [2] Eritrea included in Ethiopia totals.   [3] The U.S. view is that the Socialist Federal Republic of Yugoslavia has dissolved and no successor state represents its continuation. Macedonia has proclaimed independent statehood, but has not been recognized as a state by the United States. Serbia and Montenegro have asserted the formation of a joint independent state, but this entity has not been recognized by the United States.

Source: U.S. Bureau of the Census, International Data Base.

No. 1375. Population, by Age Group, 1993, and Projections, 2000

[In percent. Covers countries with 10 million or more population in 1993]

COUNTRY OR AREA	1993				2000			
	Under 5 years old	5 to 14 years old	15 to 64 years old	65 years old and over	Under 5 years old	5 to 14 years old	15 to 64 years old	65 years old and over
World total	11.4	20.5	61.8	6.3	10.6	20.0	62.7	6.8
Afghanistan	16.8	26.0	54.5	2.7	16.5	26.3	54.5	2.7
Algeria	14.1	27.7	54.5	3.6	12.5	23.9	59.6	3.9
Argentina	9.5	19.3	61.7	9.5	9.1	17.6	63.3	10.0
Australia	7.3	14.5	66.7	11.6	6.8	14.2	67.0	12.0
Bangladesh	14.8	26.5	55.7	3.0	14.1	23.8	59.1	3.1
Belarus	6.9	15.5	65.5	12.1	6.2	14.0	65.4	14.5
Belgium	6.0	12.0	66.4	15.6	5.4	11.8	65.6	17.2
Brazil	10.3	22.2	63.1	4.4	9.3	19.2	66.4	5.2
Burma	13.0	23.5	59.2	4.3	12.1	22.2	61.1	4.6
Cameroon	17.2	27.4	52.1	3.3	17.1	26.5	52.9	3.4
Canada	7.2	13.7	67.2	12.0	6.4	13.6	67.2	12.8
Chile	10.3	19.3	64.1	6.4	9.3	18.3	65.1	7.3
China: Mainland	9.3	17.6	67.2	5.9	7.7	17.3	68.2	6.8
Taiwan	8.0	17.4	67.6	7.0	7.2	14.6	69.8	8.4
Colombia	11.5	21.6	62.7	4.2	9.6	20.3	65.2	5.0
Cote d'Ivoire	19.3	28.0	50.6	2.0	18.7	29.2	49.9	2.3
Cuba	8.5	13.9	68.5	9.1	7.1	15.6	67.4	9.9
Czech Republic	6.3	13.7	67.2	12.8	6.7	12.4	67.4	13.4
Ecuador	12.7	24.4	58.7	4.1	10.9	22.0	62.5	4.5
Egypt	14.3	25.6	56.7	3.4	13.3	23.8	59.4	3.5
Ethiopia	18.5	27.1	51.5	2.8	17.9	27.9	51.4	2.8
France	6.6	12.6	65.5	15.2	6.2	12.8	64.5	16.4
Germany	5.5	10.8	68.5	15.2	5.2	11.1	67.2	16.5
Ghana	18.9	26.1	52.0	3.0	17.7	28.4	50.9	3.0
Greece	5.2	12.9	67.3	14.6	5.3	10.8	66.8	17.1
Guatemala	16.5	27.4	52.8	3.3	14.6	26.6	55.2	3.7
Hungary	6.0	12.7	67.4	13.9	6.4	11.9	66.8	14.9
India	13.0	22.6	60.5	3.9	11.5	21.8	62.3	4.4
Indonesia	11.3	22.4	63.0	3.3	10.5	19.7	65.6	4.3
Iran	18.7	28.1	49.7	3.6	17.5	28.3	50.3	3.9
Iraq	19.4	28.8	48.8	3.1	18.2	28.8	50.2	2.9
Italy	5.1	10.5	68.8	15.6	5.4	10.1	67.0	17.5
Japan	5.0	12.0	69.8	13.2	5.5	10.2	67.8	16.5
Kazakhstan	10.3	20.6	62.6	6.5	8.8	19.2	64.6	7.3
Kenya	18.8	29.8	49.2	2.2	16.9	29.3	51.4	2.4
Madagascar	19.1	27.7	50.0	3.2	18.3	28.3	50.4	3.0
Malaysia	13.6	23.1	59.5	3.8	12.4	23.0	60.6	4.0
Mexico	13.2	24.6	58.1	4.1	11.9	22.8	60.5	4.8
Morocco	13.6	25.6	56.6	4.2	12.1	23.3	60.1	4.6
Mozambique	18.1	26.8	52.6	2.5	17.4	27.4	52.6	2.6
Nepal	16.2	26.8	54.1	2.8	15.5	25.7	55.7	3.0
Netherlands	6.4	11.9	68.5	13.2	5.8	12.3	67.8	14.1
Nigeria	18.1	26.9	52.2	2.9	17.8	26.9	52.3	2.9
North Korea	11.1	18.4	66.6	3.9	10.2	19.2	65.9	4.7
Pakistan	17.5	26.4	52.1	4.0	16.8	26.9	52.5	3.9
Peru	12.3	24.0	59.8	3.9	10.8	21.3	63.4	4.5
Philippines	13.1	24.7	58.5	3.7	11.6	22.5	61.8	4.0
Poland	7.0	17.0	65.4	10.7	6.5	13.9	67.3	12.3
Portugal	5.7	13.5	67.1	13.8	5.8	11.5	67.7	15.1
Romania	6.9	15.2	66.5	11.3	6.6	13.8	65.9	13.6
Russia	6.8	15.8	66.3	11.2	6.1	14.0	67.2	12.6
Saudi Arabia	16.7	23.7	57.5	2.1	16.5	25.7	55.1	2.8
Serbia [1]	7.1	15.1	66.8	11.0	6.9	13.8	65.4	14.0
South Africa	15.2	24.6	56.2	4.0	14.7	24.7	56.5	4.1
South Korea	7.4	17.4	70.1	5.1	7.3	14.4	71.8	6.5
Spain	5.2	12.6	67.8	14.4	5.7	10.5	67.4	16.4
Sri Lanka	9.4	20.7	64.2	5.7	8.1	17.4	67.9	6.6
Sudan	18.2	28.0	51.5	2.2	16.9	27.7	53.1	2.3
Syria	19.4	29.0	48.8	2.8	18.4	29.1	49.7	2.8
Tanzania	18.5	28.3	50.3	2.8	18.1	28.6	50.5	2.8
Thailand	9.8	20.2	65.4	4.6	8.4	17.8	68.0	5.7
Turkey	12.5	23.0	59.5	5.0	11.0	21.5	61.8	5.8
Uganda	20.3	29.2	48.3	2.2	19.1	31.0	47.7	2.2
Ukraine	6.4	14.5	65.7	13.4	6.0	13.1	66.4	14.5
United Kingdom	6.8	12.7	64.7	15.8	6.2	13.2	64.7	15.9
United States	7.6	14.3	65.3	12.7	6.9	14.5	65.9	12.7
Uzbekistan	14.8	25.6	55.1	4.4	12.7	25.1	57.4	4.9
Venezuela	12.7	23.8	59.4	4.1	11.2	21.7	62.4	4.7
Vietnam	13.3	23.8	58.1	4.8	11.2	22.7	60.9	5.2
Yemen	20.2	28.9	48.2	2.6	20.0	29.5	47.9	2.6
Zaire	19.3	28.3	49.8	2.7	19.2	29.0	49.3	2.6
Zimbabwe	17.2	30.2	49.9	2.7	15.0	29.2	53.0	2.7

[1] The U.S. view is that the Socialist Federal Republic of Yugoslavia has dissolved and no successor state represents its continuation. Serbia and Montenegro have asserted the formation of a joint independent state, but this entity has not been recognized by the United States.

Source: U.S. Bureau of the Census, International Data Base.

No. 1376. Birth and Death Rates, and Other Vital Statistics, 1993, and Projections, 2000—Selected Countries

[Covers countries with 5 million or more population in 1993. AFR - Africa, EAS - East Asia, SAS - South Asia, CAR - Carribean, MAM - Middle America, SAM - South America, NAM - North America, EUR - Europe, SOV - Soviet republics, OCE - Oceania]

COUNTRY OR AREA	Region	CRUDE BIRTH RATE [1]		CRUDE DEATH RATE [2]		EXPECTATION OF LIFE AT BIRTH (years)		INFANT MORTALITY RATE [3]		TOTAL FERTILITY RATE [4]	
		1993	2000	1993	2000	1993	2000	1993	2000	1993	2000
United States	NAM	15.5	14.1	8.7	8.8	75.8	76.4	8.4	6.6	2.05	2.07
Afghanistan	SAS	43.8	41.6	19.3	16.6	44.4	47.8	158.9	137.5	6.34	5.87
Algeria	AFR	30.4	26.5	6.4	5.4	67.4	69.6	54.0	42.2	3.96	3.16
Angola	AFR	45.8	42.6	19.0	15.9	45.3	48.9	148.6	125.9	6.54	6.05
Argentina	SAM	19.8	19.1	8.6	8.6	71.2	72.3	30.0	26.1	2.72	2.50
Australia	OCE	14.4	13.2	7.4	7.4	77.4	78.7	7.4	6.4	1.83	1.80
Austria	EUR	11.5	10.1	10.4	10.0	76.4	78.0	7.3	6.2	1.47	1.50
Azerbaijan	SOV	24.1	18.5	6.6	6.5	70.6	72.5	35.7	28.7	2.76	2.39
Bangladesh	SAS	35.4	32.5	11.9	10.3	54.7	57.5	109.2	93.0	4.55	4.00
Belarus	SOV	13.3	12.6	11.1	11.3	70.7	72.2	19.2	16.4	1.89	1.83
Belgium	EUR	11.9	10.4	10.3	10.2	76.7	78.2	7.4	6.3	1.62	1.60
Benin	AFR	48.1	44.9	14.8	12.0	51.3	54.6	112.7	95.3	6.86	6.32
Bolivia	SAM	32.8	28.8	8.6	7.1	62.8	66.3	76.7	57.2	4.31	3.63
Bosnia and Herzegovina	EUR	13.5	12.2	6.4	6.7	74.8	76.9	13.2	10.1	1.62	1.60
Brazil	SAM	21.8	19.2	8.3	10.1	62.7	60.9	61.7	47.8	2.49	2.14
Bulgaria	EUR	11.7	11.7	11.5	10.9	72.8	75.5	12.6	9.4	1.71	1.70
Burkina	AFR	48.8	45.6	18.2	20.3	47.5	41.6	119.8	112.8	7.00	6.48
Burma	SAS	28.9	25.9	10.1	8.7	59.5	62.8	65.7	52.4	3.70	3.29
Burundi	AFR	44.7	40.9	21.3	21.3	40.8	39.1	115.6	102.2	6.76	6.25
Cambodia	SAS	45.5	41.0	16.6	14.3	49.1	51.5	111.5	100.5	5.81	5.81
Cameroon	AFR	40.7	40.1	11.6	10.2	56.7	59.4	78.8	67.5	5.88	5.61
Canada	NAM	14.5	12.3	7.4	7.7	78.0	79.1	7.0	6.2	1.84	1.80
Chad	AFR	42.2	39.7	20.9	18.4	40.4	43.3	134.0	118.6	5.33	5.05
Chile	SAM	20.9	19.0	5.6	5.3	74.2	76.4	15.9	11.4	2.51	2.43
China, Mainland	EAS	18.3	15.0	7.3	7.0	67.7	70.2	52.1	38.7	1.85	1.80
Taiwan	EAS	15.9	14.5	5.5	6.1	75.0	76.4	5.7	5.3	1.81	1.80
Colombia	SAM	23.4	19.0	4.8	4.6	71.7	74.2	29.7	21.3	2.54	2.17
Cote d'Ivoire	AFR	46.9	43.9	15.1	14.7	49.0	48.5	97.0	83.8	6.73	6.21
Cuba	CAR	17.1	13.6	6.5	6.7	76.7	77.8	10.5	9.2	1.83	1.80
Czech Republic	EUR	13.0	13.6	11.4	9.9	72.6	75.4	9.7	7.5	1.85	1.80
Denmark	EUR	12.5	11.7	11.4	10.7	75.5	77.4	7.1	6.1	1.68	1.70
Dominican Republic	CAR	25.7	21.1	6.4	5.6	68.0	70.4	53.6	40.8	2.89	2.42
Ecuador	SAM	26.5	22.5	5.8	5.2	69.6	72.0	40.8	31.1	3.19	2.59
Egypt	AFR	32.2	29.5	9.3	8.1	60.5	62.7	78.3	65.7	4.35	3.77
El Salvador	MAM	33.1	29.5	6.5	5.5	66.5	69.7	42.8	30.9	3.87	3.30
Ethiopia	AFR	45.4	42.3	14.2	11.9	52.2	55.4	108.8	92.1	6.88	6.36
Finland	EUR	12.6	11.4	9.9	9.7	75.7	77.5	5.4	4.9	1.79	1.80
France	EUR	13.2	12.3	9.3	9.3	78.0	79.2	6.8	5.9	1.80	1.80
Georgia	SOV	16.5	14.4	8.7	8.9	72.6	74.5	24.2	18.6	2.21	2.05
Germany	EUR	11.1	9.8	11.0	10.5	76.1	77.8	6.6	5.7	1.45	1.53
Ghana	AFR	44.7	40.5	12.5	10.8	55.2	57.5	84.5	74.8	6.21	5.76
Greece	EUR	10.4	10.6	9.4	9.5	77.5	78.8	8.9	7.3	1.44	1.50
Guatemala	MAM	36.2	31.2	7.7	6.5	64.0	66.9	55.6	44.6	4.90	4.00
Guinea	AFR	44.8	39.9	20.1	16.9	43.7	47.0	141.7	123.7	5.90	5.46
Haiti	CAR	40.8	35.0	18.9	18.3	45.5	43.9	109.5	102.2	6.05	5.16
Honduras	MAM	35.8	30.3	6.4	5.2	67.2	70.0	47.2	35.4	4.87	3.83
Hong Kong	EAS	12.3	11.2	5.7	6.8	80.0	80.6	5.9	5.5	1.34	1.50
Hungary	EUR	12.3	12.9	13.0	11.4	70.9	74.1	13.1	9.7	1.83	1.80
India	SAS	29.1	24.7	10.5	9.1	58.1	61.4	80.5	65.8	3.57	3.04
Indonesia	SAS	24.8	22.5	8.7	8.1	60.3	63.4	69.6	55.4	2.86	2.53
Iran	SAS	43.0	39.3	8.1	6.2	65.3	69.0	62.1	45.9	6.40	5.88
Iraq	SAS	44.6	40.8	7.7	5.6	65.0	68.7	71.8	50.1	6.86	5.81
Italy	EUR	10.7	10.9	9.7	10.0	77.4	78.7	7.8	6.6	1.37	1.50
Japan	EAS	10.3	11.4	7.2	8.3	79.2	80.0	4.3	4.1	1.54	1.60
Kazakhstan	SOV	19.6	18.3	8.0	7.9	67.8	69.6	41.8	34.6	2.45	2.32
Kenya	AFR	43.2	37.5	11.4	15.2	54.1	46.4	74.7	72.3	6.06	4.97
Madagascar	AFR	45.7	42.7	13.7	11.3	53.5	56.7	91.0	77.1	6.75	6.25
Malawi	AFR	51.1	46.9	22.9	25.7	40.5	35.2	141.9	134.2	7.50	6.94
Malaysia	SAS	28.9	25.6	5.8	5.2	68.8	71.0	26.5	20.9	3.54	3.31
Mali	AFR	51.7	49.3	20.8	17.5	45.5	48.7	108.0	95.6	7.33	6.91
Mexico	MAM	27.7	24.3	4.8	4.4	72.6	75.0	28.8	20.7	3.25	2.79
Morocco	AFR	29.2	25.0	6.6	5.1	67.5	71.8	53.4	32.9	3.96	3.13
Mozambique	AFR	45.4	42.1	16.7	14.1	48.0	51.3	131.4	112.8	6.31	5.84
Nepal	SAS	38.0	35.6	13.7	11.2	52.0	55.9	85.8	70.1	5.33	4.68
Netherlands	EUR	12.8	10.9	8.5	8.6	77.6	78.8	6.2	5.5	1.59	1.50
Niger	AFR	57.4	51.7	22.4	18.5	44.2	47.5	112.8	100.3	7.35	7.00
Nigeria	AFR	43.8	41.6	12.9	10.1	54.7	59.1	77.3	61.4	6.43	5.95
North Korea	EAS	24.1	19.9	5.5	5.4	69.5	71.5	28.6	22.2	2.40	2.21
Pakistan	SAS	42.6	39.7	12.6	10.8	57.1	59.7	103.6	90.3	6.50	5.94
Paraguay	SAM	32.6	29.1	4.6	4.1	73.0	74.9	26.4	19.6	4.37	3.86
Peru	SAM	26.2	22.7	7.2	6.3	64.2	68.1	56.4	42.9	3.22	2.63
Philippines	SAS	27.9	24.4	7.0	6.6	65.1	66.9	51.9	44.4	3.45	2.88
Poland	EUR	13.6	13.2	9.6	8.7	72.2	75.0	13.8	10.0	1.97	1.80
Portugal	EUR	11.6	11.7	9.8	9.5	74.9	76.9	9.8	7.8	1.45	1.50
Romania	EUR	13.7	13.5	10.2	9.5	71.3	74.4	21.2	14.3	1.83	1.80
Russia	SOV	12.7	12.7	11.3	11.2	68.7	70.5	27.6	22.6	1.83	1.80
Rwanda	AFR	49.9	45.9	20.9	23.8	41.2	35.7	119.4	110.2	8.27	7.64
Saudi Arabia	SAS	38.6	36.9	6.1	4.9	67.3	71.1	55.3	36.3	6.70	6.43
Senegal	AFR	43.4	41.3	12.4	10.0	56.0	59.9	77.8	63.5	6.15	5.71
Serbia [5]	EUR	14.4	13.9	9.1	8.7	73.0	75.6	22.4	16.6	2.07	2.01

See footnotes at end of table.

No. 1376. Birth and Death Rates, and Other Vital Statistics, 1993, and Projections, 2000—Selected Countries—Continued

[See headnote, page 844]

COUNTRY OR AREA	Region	CRUDE BIRTH RATE [1]		CRUDE DEATH RATE [2]		EXPECTATION OF LIFE AT BIRTH (years)		INFANT MORTALITY RATE [3]		TOTAL FERTILITY RATE [4]	
		1993	2000	1993	2000	1993	2000	1993	2000	1993	2000
Slovakia	EUR	14.6	14.1	9.5	8.5	72.4	75.1	10.8	8.4	1.99	1.80
Somalia	AFR	42.0	42.4	28.4	9.8	32.9	61.1	162.7	87.1	6.40	6.53
South Africa	AFR	33.8	32.3	7.7	6.9	64.8	67.0	48.3	39.8	4.40	4.23
South Korea	EAS	15.7	14.8	6.2	6.4	70.3	72.3	22.5	17.7	1.64	1.70
Spain	EUR	10.9	11.6	8.8	9.2	77.5	78.8	7.0	6.1	1.38	1.50
Sri Lanka	SAS	18.7	16.5	5.8	6.0	71.5	73.0	22.8	19.1	2.13	1.89
Sudan	AFR	42.7	38.8	12.5	10.3	53.9	56.8	81.3	69.2	6.19	5.47
Sweden	EUR	13.8	11.5	11.0	10.6	78.1	79.2	5.8	5.2	2.04	1.80
Switzerland	EUR	12.4	10.8	9.2	9.1	78.0	79.1	6.6	5.8	1.60	1.60
Syria	SAS	44.1	40.5	6.4	5.3	66.1	68.4	43.9	35.2	6.75	6.00
Tajikistan	SOV	35.5	30.4	6.9	6.0	68.5	70.5	63.6	52.1	4.70	4.10
Tanzania	AFR	45.7	43.6	19.0	22.4	44.0	38.4	110.4	104.3	6.25	5.85
Thailand	SAS	20.0	17.2	6.3	8.1	68.3	65.9	38.5	34.3	2.16	1.91
Tunisia	AFR	24.2	20.2	5.0	4.7	72.5	74.8	35.9	25.3	3.02	2.33
Turkey	SAS	26.6	22.8	6.0	5.1	70.4	73.8	52.0	33.3	3.30	2.78
Uganda	AFR	49.9	46.3	23.0	26.3	38.4	33.6	112.1	106.8	7.15	6.66
Ukraine	SOV	12.4	12.2	12.5	12.6	69.9	71.2	21.0	18.1	1.82	1.79
United Kingdom	EUR	13.6	11.9	10.9	10.3	76.5	78.1	7.4	6.3	1.83	1.80
Uzbekistan	SOV	30.6	26.8	6.6	6.0	68.4	70.1	54.4	45.1	3.78	3.37
Venezuela	SAM	26.4	22.9	4.7	4.5	72.7	74.4	28.9	22.6	3.14	2.68
Vietnam	SAS	28.0	22.9	7.9	7.0	65.1	67.1	46.4	39.9	3.45	2.80
Yemen	SAS	51.0	48.3	15.4	12.4	50.9	54.6	115.6	96.5	7.27	6.73
Zaire	AFR	48.4	46.1	16.9	15.5	47.3	48.4	113.2	97.9	6.70	6.39
Zambia	AFR	46.5	43.2	16.9	23.0	45.6	36.5	83.9	85.3	6.75	6.28
Zimbabwe	AFR	38.2	32.3	17.7	20.0	42.8	39.6	75.3	65.9	5.26	4.11

[1] Number of births during 1 year per 1,000 persons (based on midyear population). [2] Number of deaths during 1 year per 1,000 persons (based on midyear population). [3] Number of deaths of children under 1 year of age per 1,000 live births in a calendar year. [4] Average number of children that would be born if all women lived to the end of their childbearing years and, at each year of age, they experienced the birth rates occurring in the specified year. [5] The U.S. view is that the Socialist Federal Republic of Yugoslavia has dissolved and no successor state represents its continuation. Serbia and Montenegro have asserted the formation of a joint independent state, but this entity has not been recognized by the United States.

Source: U.S. Bureau of the Census, International Data Base.

No. 1377. Population and Average Annual Rates of Growth for World's Largest Cities: 1992 to 2000

[When these city projections were prepared in 1985, cities were defined as population clusters of continuous built-up area with a population density of at least 5,000 persons per square mile. Boundaries were determined by examining detailed maps of each city in conjunction with the most recent official population statistics. The ariel expansion of each city was not projected, hence, density figures for 1992 are based on areas as of 1985]

CITY AND COUNTRY	Rank	MIDYEAR POPULATION (1,000)			AVERAGE ANNUAL GROWTH RATE (percent)		Area (square miles)	Population per square mile, 1992
		1992	1995	2000	1992-1995	1995-2000		
Tokyo-Yokohama, Japan	1	27,540	28,447	29,971	1.1	1.0	1,089	25,290
Mexico City, Mexico	2	21,615	23,913	27,872	3.4	3.1	522	41,408
Sao Paulo, Brazil	3	19,373	21,539	25,354	3.5	3.3	451	42,956
Seoul, South Korea	4	17,334	19,065	21,976	3.2	2.8	342	50,684
New York, United States	5	14,628	14,638	14,648	(Z)	(Z)	1,274	11,482
Osaka-Kobe-Kyoto, Japan	6	13,919	14,060	14,287	0.3	0.3	495	28,119
Bombay, India	7	12,450	13,532	15,357	2.8	2.5	95	131,051
Calcutta, India	8	12,137	12,885	14,088	2.0	1.8	209	58,073
Rio de Janeiro, Brazil	9	12,009	12,786	14,169	2.1	2.1	260	46,190
Buenos Aires, Argentina	10	11,743	12,232	12,911	1.4	1.1	535	21,950
Manila, Philippines	11	10,554	11,342	12,846	2.4	2.5	188	56,141
Moscow, Russia	12	10,526	10,769	11,121	0.8	0.6	379	27,773
Cairo, Egypt	13	10,372	11,155	12,512	2.4	2.3	104	99,726
Jakarta, Indonesia	14	10,185	11,151	12,804	3.0	2.8	76	134,014
Tehran, Iran	15	10,102	11,681	14,251	4.8	4.0	112	90,198
Los Angeles, United States	16	10,072	10,414	10,714	1.1	0.6	1,110	9,074

See footnotes at end of table.

No. 1377. Population and Average Annual Rates of Growth for World's Largest Cities: 1992 to 2000—Continued

[See headnote, page 845]

CITY AND COUNTRY	Rank	MIDYEAR POPULATION (1,000)			AVERAGE ANNUAL GROWTH RATE (percent)		Area (square miles)	Popula-tion per square mile, 1992
		1992	1995	2000	1992-1995	1995-2000		
Delhi, India	17	9,243	10,105	11,849	3.0	3.2	138	66,976
London, United Kingdom	18	9,168	8,897	8,574	-1.0	-0.7	874	10,490
Paris, France	19	8,589	8,764	8,803	0.7	0.1	432	19,883
Lagos, Nigeria	20	8,487	9,799	12,528	4.8	4.9	56	151,548
Karachi, Pakistan	21	8,174	9,350	11,299	4.5	3.8	190	43,023
Essen, Germany	22	7,506	7,364	7,239	-0.6	-0.3	704	10,662
Lima, Peru	23	7,028	7,853	9,241	3.7	3.3	120	58,563
Shanghai, China	24	7,000	7,194	7,540	0.9	0.9	78	89,739
Istanbul, Turkey	25	6,937	7,624	8,875	3.2	3.0	165	42,040
Taipei, Taiwan	26	6,924	7,477	8,516	2.6	2.6	138	50,173
Chicago, United States.	27	6,493	6,541	6,568	0.2	0.1	762	8,521
Bogota, Colombia	28	6,176	6,801	7,935	3.2	3.1	79	78,173
Bangkok, Thailand	29	6,088	6,657	7,587	3.0	2.6	102	59,687
Madras, India	30	5,998	6,550	7,384	2.9	2.4	115	52,156
Beijing, China	31	5,791	5,865	5,993	0.4	0.4	151	38,354
Hong Kong, Hong Kong	32	5,762	5,841	5,956	0.5	0.4	23	250,524
Santiago, Chile	33	5,484	5,812	6,294	1.9	1.6	128	42,840
Pusan, South Korea	34	5,161	5,748	6,700	3.6	3.1	54	95,582
Bangalore, India	35	5,080	5,644	6,764	3.5	3.6	50	101,604
Nagoya, Japan	36	4,909	5,017	5,303	0.7	1.1	307	15,990
Tianjin, China	37	4,857	5,041	5,298	1.2	1.0	49	99,121
Milan, Italy	38	4,718	4,795	4,839	0.5	0.2	344	13,714
St. Petersburg, Russia	39	4,645	4,694	4,738	0.4	0.2	139	33,415
Dhaka, Bangladesh	40	4,640	5,296	6,492	4.4	4.1	32	144,991
Madrid, Spain	41	4,577	4,772	5,104	1.4	1.4	66	69,344
Lahore, Pakistan	42	4,475	4,986	5,864	3.6	3.2	57	78,500
Baghdad, Iraq	43	4,358	4,566	5,239	1.6	2.8	97	44,924
Shenyang, China	44	4,323	4,457	4,684	1.0	1.0	39	110,848
Barcelona, Spain	45	4,221	4,492	4,834	2.1	1.5	87	48,521
San Francisco, United States	46	4,005	4,104	4,214	0.8	0.5	428	9,358
Kinshasa, Zaire	47	3,997	4,520	5,646	4.1	4.5	57	70,130
Manchester, United Kingdom.	48	3,984	3,949	3,827	-0.3	-0.6	357	11,159
Philadelphia, United States.	49	3,970	3,988	3,979	0.2	-0.1	471	8,429
Belo Horizonte, Brazil.	50	3,920	4,373	5,125	3.6	3.2	79	49,625
Ahmadabad, India	51	3,826	4,200	4,837	3.1	2.8	32	119,555
Hyderabad, India.	52	3,787	4,149	4,765	3.0	2.8	88	43,031
Ho Chi Minh City, Vietnam	53	3,725	4,064	4,481	2.9	2.0	31	120,164
Athens, Greece	54	3,613	3,670	3,866	0.5	1.0	116	31,144
Sydney, Australia	55	3,528	3,619	3,708	0.9	0.5	338	10,437
Guadalajara, Mexico	56	3,525	3,839	4,451	2.8	3.0	78	45,192
Miami, United States	57	3,522	3,679	3,894	1.5	1.1	448	7,862
Surabaya, Indonesia	58	3,327	3,428	3,632	1.0	1.2	43	77,382
Guangzhou, China.	59	3,314	3,485	3,652	1.7	0.9	79	41,952
Caracas, Venezuela.	60	3,247	3,338	3,435	0.9	0.6	54	60,133
Wuhan, China.	61	3,231	3,325	3,495	1.0	1.0	65	49,700
Porto Alegre, Brazil	62	3,220	3,541	4,109	3.2	3.0	231	13,938
Toronto, Canada.	63	3,182	3,296	3,296	1.2	-	154	20,662
Casablanca, Morocco	64	3,136	3,327	3,795	2.0	2.6	35	89,604
Monterrey, Mexico.	65	3,084	3,385	3,974	3.1	3.2	77	40,057
Rome, Italy	66	3,028	3,079	3,129	0.6	0.3	69	43,889
Greater Berlin, Germany.	67	3,020	3,018	3,006	(Z)	-0.1	274	11,021
Ankara, Turkey	68	3,000	3,263	3,777	2.8	2.9	55	54,551
Naples, Italy	69	2,996	3,051	3,134	0.6	0.5	62	48,324
Alexandria, Egypt	70	2,981	3,114	3,304	1.5	1.2	35	85,180
Montreal, Canada	71	2,933	2,996	3,071	0.7	0.5	164	17,881
Detroit, United States [1]	72	2,890	2,865	2,735	-0.3	-0.9	468	6,175
Rangoon, Burma	73	2,876	3,075	3,332	2.2	1.6	47	61,198
Melbourne, Australia	74	2,865	2,946	2,968	0.9	0.2	327	8,763
Dallas, United States	75	2,856	2,972	3,257	1.3	1.8	419	6,817
Taegu, South Korea.	76	2,837	3,201	4,051	4.0	4.7	(NA)	(NA)
Kiev, Ukraine	77	2,837	2,983	3,237	1.7	1.6	62	45,751
Singapore, Singapore	78	2,743	2,816	2,913	0.9	0.7	78	35,164
Harbin, China	79	2,625	2,747	2,887	1.5	1.0	30	87,506
Poona, India.	80	2,617	2,987	3,647	4.4	4.0	(NA)	(NA)
Washington, United States	81	2,572	2,637	2,707	0.8	0.5	357	7,204
Lisbon, Portugal	82	2,505	2,551	2,717	0.6	1.3	(NA)	(NA)
Chongqing, China	83	2,468	2,632	2,961	2.1	2.4	(NA)	(NA)
Tashkent, Uzbekistan.	84	2,461	2,640	2,947	2.3	2.2	(NA)	(NA)
Boston, United States	85	2,460	2,480	2,485	0.3	(Z)	303	8,119
Vienna, Austria.	86	2,392	2,474	2,647	1.1	1.4	(NA)	(NA)
Houston, United States	87	2,369	2,456	2,651	1.2	1.5	310	7,642
Salvador, Brazil.	88	2,366	2,694	3,286	4.3	4.0	(NA)	(NA)
Chengdu, China	89	2,365	2,465	2,591	1.4	1.0	25	94,610
Budapest, Hungary	90	2,304	2,313	2,335	0.1	0.2	138	16,696
Kanpur, India	91	2,184	2,356	2,673	2.5	2.5	(NA)	(NA)
Birmingham, United Kingdom.	92	2,177	2,130	2,078	-0.7	-0.5	223	9,763
Bucharest, Romania	93	2,175	2,214	2,271	0.6	0.5	52	41,834
Havana, Cuba.	94	2,152	2,218	2,333	1.0	1.0	(NA)	(NA)

-Represents or rounds to zero. NA Not available. Z Less than .05 percent. [1] Includes Windsor, Canada.
Source: U.S. Bureau of the Census, International Data Base.

No. 1378. Percent Distribution of Households, by Type—Selected Countries

COUNTRY AND YEAR	Total	MARRIED-COUPLE [1]			Single parent [2]	One-person	Other [3]
		Total	With children [2]	Without children [2]			
United States:							
1960	100	74	44	30	4	13	8
1970	100	71	40	30	5	17	7
1980	100	61	31	30	8	23	9
1987	100	58	28	30	8	24	11
1988	100	57	27	30	8	24	11
1989	100	56	27	30	8	25	11
1990	100	56	26	30	8	25	11
1991	100	55	26	29	9	25	11
Canada:							
1961	100	[4]78	[4]51	[4]27	[4]4	9	[4]9
1971	100	74	47	28	5	13	8
1981	100	67	36	31	5	20	8
1986	100	65	32	32	6	22	8
Japan:							
1960	100	65	49	16	3	17	14
1970	100	64	45	20	2	20	13
1980	100	68	43	26	2	20	10
1985	100	67	39	28	3	21	9
1990	100	65	33	32	2	23	10
Denmark: [5]							
1976	100	45	24	21	5	(NA)	(NA)
1983	100	44	23	21	5	(NA)	(NA)
1988	100	41	20	21	5	(NA)	(NA)
1989	100	41	20	21	5	(NA)	(NA)
1990	100	40	19	21	5	(NA)	(NA)
France:							
1968	100	70	44	27	4	20	5
1975	100	69	42	27	4	22	5
1982	100	67	40	27	4	25	4
1988	100	63	36	27	5	27	4
1989	100	64	36	28	5	27	4
Netherlands:							
1961	100	78	55	22	6	12	5
1971	100	74	52	22	5	17	4
1981	100	67	44	23	6	21	6
1985	100	60	39	22	7	28	6
1989	100	57	35	22	7	29	7
Sweden:							
1960	100	66	36	31	4	20	10
1970	100	64	30	34	3	25	7
1980	100	58	25	33	3	33	6
1985	100	55	22	33	3	36	6
1990	100	52	20	32	3	40	5
United Kingdom: [6]							
1961	100	74	38	36	2	12	12
1971	100	70	34	35	3	18	9
1981	100	64	31	34	5	22	9
1987	100	64	28	36	4	25	7
1988	100	62	26	36	5	26	7
1989	100	62	26	36	5	25	8
1990	100	60	24	36	6	26	8
Germany: [7]							
1961	100	67	44	22	11	21	2
1970	100	65	42	23	6	27	3
1980	100	61	37	24	7	30	3
1988	100	54	31	23	7	35	4
1989	100	54	31	23	7	35	4
1990	100	54	31	23	6	35	4

NA Not available. [1] May include unmarried cohabitating couples. Such couples are explicitly included under married couples in Canada (beginning in 1981) and France. For Sweden, beginning in 1980, all cohabitants are included as married couples, and the figures for 1970 have been adjusted to include cohabitants. For Denmark, from 1983 onward, persons reported separately as living in consensual unions with joint children have been classified here as married couples. In other countries, some unmarried cohabitants are included as married couples, while some are classified under "other households," depending on responses to surveys and censuses. [2] Children are defined as unmarried children living at home according to the following age limits: Under 18 years old in the United States, Canada, Japan, Denmark, and the United Kingdom, except that the United Kingdom includes 16- and 17-year-olds only if they are in full-time education; under 25 years old in France; under 16 years old in Sweden; and children of all ages in the Netherlands and Germany. [3] Includes both family and nonfamily households not elsewhere classified. These households comprise, for example, siblings residing together, other households composed of relatives, and households made up of roommates. Some unmarried cohabitating couples may also be included in the "other" group. See footnote 1. [4] Estimated by the U.S. Bureau of Labor Statistics. [5] From family-based statistics. However, one person living alone constitutes a family in Denmark. In this respect, the Danish data are closer to household statistics. [6] Great Britain only (excludes Northern Ireland). [7] Former West Germany (prior to unification).

Source: U.S. Bureau of Labor Statistics, *Monthly Labor Review*, March 1990; and unpublished data.

No. 1379. Marriage and Divorce Rates, Selected Countries: 1960 to 1990

COUNTRY	MARRIAGE RATE PER 1,000 POPULATION, AGES 15 TO 64						DIVORCE RATE PER 1,000 MARRIED WOMEN					
	1960	1970	1980	1988	1989	1990	1960	1970	1980	1988	1989	1990
United States [1]	14	17	16	15	15	15	9	15	23	21	21	21
Canada	12	14	12	11	11	10	2	6	11	13	13	12
Denmark	12	12	8	9	9	9	6	8	11	13	14	13
France	11	12	10	7	8	8	3	3	6	8	8	(NA)
Germany [2]	14	12	9	9	9	9	4	5	6	9	9	8
Italy	12	11	9	8	8	8	(NA)	1	1	2	2	2
Japan	15	14	10	8	8	8	4	4	5	5	5	5
Netherlands	13	15	10	9	9	9	2	3	8	8	8	8
Sweden	10	8	7	8	[3]20	7	5	7	11	11	12	12
United Kingdom	12	14	12	11	11	(NA)	[4]2	[4]5	[4]12	12	(NA)	(NA)

NA Not available.   [1] Beginning 1980, includes unlicensed marriages registered in California.   [2] Former West Germany (prior to unification).   [3] Increase in Swedish marriage rate in 1989 is due to change in inheritance laws which caused many cohabiting couples to marry.   [4] England and Wales only.
Source: U.S. Bureau of Labor Statistics, *Monthly Labor Review*, March 1990; and unpublished data.

No. 1380. Births to Unmarried Women, Selected Countries: 1960 to 1990

[For U.S. figures, beginning 1980, marital status is inferred from a comparison of the childs' and parents' surnames on the birth certificate for those States that do not report on marital status. No estimates are included for misstatements on birth records or failures to register births]

COUNTRY	1960		1970		1980		1990	
	Total live births (1,000)	Percent born to unmarried women	Total live births (1,000)	Percent born to unmarried women	Total live births (1,000)	Percent born to unmarried women	Total live births (1,000)	Percent born to unmarried women
United States	4,258	5	3,731	11	3,612	18	4,179	28
Canada	479	4	372	10	360	13	3,979	24
Denmark	76	8	71	11	57	33	63	46
France	820	6	850	7	800	11	762	30
Germany [2]	969	6	811	6	621	8	727	11
Italy	910	2	902	2	640	4	581	6
Japan	1,624	1	1,932	1	1,616	1	1,240	1
Netherlands	239	1	239	2	181	4	198	11
Sweden	102	11	110	18	97	40	124	47
United Kingdom	918	5	904	8	754	12	799	28

[1] Beginning 1980, excludes Newfoundland.   [2] Former West Germany (prior to unification).
Source: U.S. Bureau of Labor Statistics, *Monthly Labor Review*, 1990; and unpublished data.

No. 1381. Death Rates, by Selected Causes—Selected Countries

[Age-standardized death rate per 100,000 population. For explanation of age-adjustment, see text, section 2. The standard population for this table is the European standard; see source for details. Deaths classified according to ninth revision of *International Classification of Diseases*; see text, section 2]

COUNTRY	Year	Ischemic heart disease	Cerebrovascular disease	MALIGNANT NEOPLASM OF—			Bronchitis,[1] emphysema, asthma	Chronic liver disease and cirrhosis	Motor vehicle traffic accidents	Suicide and self-inflicted injury
				Lung, trachea, bronchus	Stomach	Female breast				
United States	1988	188.1	53.6	55.4	5.4	32.0	9.1	11.7	18.7	12.2
Australia	1988	200.5	77.9	40.4	9.0	29.6	14.6	8.1	17.8	13.3
Austria	1990	151.0	96.9	34.3	17.8	32.1	18.2	25.8	16.8	21.7
Belgium	1986	110.4	83.0	55.5	13.8	38.1	26.3	12.6	19.6	21.0
Bulgaria	1990	230.1	226.2	30.7	22.7	21.1	13.0	16.0	15.5	14.1
Canada	1989	172.2	52.9	54.3	8.6	34.1	8.4	9.4	15.4	13.1
Czechoslovakia	1990	314.4	183.5	53.2	20.1	28.7	21.1	26.1	13.6	18.3
Denmark	1990	211.1	72.5	53.2	8.5	38.5	39.0	13.4	10.9	22.4
Finland	1989	243.2	98.5	33.8	15.5	28.1	17.2	10.0	14.0	27.5
France	1989	64.3	59.2	34.5	9.2	28.1	10.0	18.3	17.3	19.6
Germany [2]	1989	150.3	87.3	35.9	16.3	32.9	22.3	20.1	11.1	14.5
Hungary	1990	240.0	177.4	61.2	24.4	32.3	40.5	50.7	24.4	38.2
Italy	1988	97.4	102.3	44.1	20.5	29.5	23.9	24.9	14.2	7.0
Japan	1990	37.9	90.3	26.8	35.2	8.5	11.0	12.7	11.1	15.4
Netherlands	1989	134.9	67.8	54.6	13.4	39.0	18.2	5.5	8.9	10.0
New Zealand	1987	248.6	88.8	45.5	10.9	40.2	19.8	4.2	22.8	12.6
Norway	1989	186.9	84.2	27.5	12.3	27.3	13.6	5.7	8.5	15.3
Poland	1990	121.0	73.1	51.4	21.2	22.6	25.0	11.4	22.4	13.8
Portugal	1990	85.6	216.6	21.3	27.8	25.7	13.9	24.5	26.9	8.5
Spain	1987	75.3	100.2	30.6	17.1	23.2	10.1	20.6	16.6	7.1
Sweden	1988	209.3	69.0	23.9	10.3	26.8	13.1	6.1	8.8	17.8
Switzerland	1990	109.7	57.2	35.1	10.3	35.8	19.9	9.3	12.8	20.1
United Kingdom:										
England and Wales	1990	210.0	86.1	53.2	12.6	40.7	12.7	5.7	8.9	7.5
Scotland	1990	258.3	112.9	66.9	13.6	37.5	9.9	9.5	9.9	10.1

[1] Chronic and unspecified.   [2] Former West Germany (prior to unification).
Source: World Health Organization, Geneva, Switzerland, *1991 World Health Statistics Annual*.

No. 1382. Suicide Rates for Selected Countries, by Sex and Age Group

[Rate per 100,000 population. Includes deaths resulting indirectly from self-inflicted injuries. Deaths classified according to the ninth revision of the *International Classification of Diseases*; see text, section 2]

SEX AND AGE	United States, 1989	Aus- tralia, 1988	Aus- tria, 1990	Can- ada, 1990	Den- mark, 1990	France, 1989	Italy, 1988	Japan, 1990	Nether- lands, 1989	Poland, 1990	Swe- den, 1988	United King- dom,[1] 1990	West Ger- many, 1989
MALE													
Total [2]	20.0	21.0	34.8	20.4	32.2	30.5	11.1	20.4	13.0	22.0	26.4	12.1	23.5
15 to 24 years old. .	22.0	27.8	25.0	25.2	14.1	15.8	4.9	9.2	8.9	16.2	18.2	11.7	14.7
25 to 34 years old. .	24.4	28.2	32.7	29.3	26.7	32.2	9.1	18.4	15.4	30.4	29.8	16.0	22.7
35 to 44 years old. .	22.4	26.0	37.3	26.3	44.5	37.4	9.9	21.5	15.6	33.0	31.8	17.1	21.6
45 to 54 years old. .	22.7	24.4	47.7	22.7	53.0	39.2	12.1	32.0	17.3	38.4	38.2	16.4	30.8
55 to 64 years old. .	24.8	23.8	44.0	22.9	43.7	38.9	16.2	32.5	19.9	36.3	37.0	13.3	31.5
65 to 74 years old. .	33.6	27.7	66.8	20.8	47.3	52.9	28.3	36.6	21.1	28.0	36.4	13.6	39.4
75 yrs. old and over	54.5	39.8	107.6	32.7	76.7	107.2	47.4	62.9	29.0	27.3	47.2	19.4	75.6
FEMALE													
Total [2]	4.8	5.6	13.4	5.3	16.3	11.7	4.4	12.4	7.5	4.5	11.5	3.7	10.0
15 to 24 years old. .	4.2	4.5	5.5	5.1	4.0	4.6	1.4	4.7	4.4	2.8	5.9	2.0	4.2
25 to 34 years old. .	5.6	7.2	8.4	6.5	6.9	9.2	2.7	9.0	7.2	4.3	11.3	3.8	6.9
35 to 44 years old. .	6.6	7.5	13.9	8.9	18.4	13.0	3.6	9.2	7.5	6.0	17.1	4.5	7.9
45 to 54 years old. .	7.4	8.2	16.5	7.3	27.3	17.4	5.7	15.0	13.8	7.4	20.5	5.1	13.0
55 to 64 years old. .	7.3	8.7	20.8	5.5	31.5	19.4	7.3	17.6	12.6	8.7	14.5	5.3	13.7
65 to 74 years old. .	5.9	7.4	22.0	6.0	30.0	20.2	9.7	25.3	13.4	7.2	15.3	6.1	18.2
75 yrs. old and over	6.0	10.0	35.5	4.2	32.2	25.7	11.1	48.6	10.8	7.4	13.8	6.2	22.7

[1] England and Wales only.   [2] Includes under 15 years old not shown separately.

Source: World Health Organization, Geneva, Switzerland, *World Health Statistics Annual*, annual; and unpublished data.

No. 1383. Health Expenditures—Selected Countries: 1980 to 1991

[G.D.P.=gross domestic product; for explanation, see text, section 14. For explanation of purchasing power parities, see text, section 31]

COUNTRY	TOTAL HEALTH EXPENDITURES						PUBLIC HEALTH EXPENDITURES			
	Percent of gross domestic product					Per capita, 1991, on basis of G.D.P. pur- chasing power parities[1]	1980		1991	
	1980	1985	1989	1990	1991		Percent of gross domestic product	Percent of total health expendi- tures	Percent of gross domestic product	Percent of total health expendi- tures
United States	9.2	10.5	11.6	12.4	13.4	2,867	42.0	3.9	43.9	5.9
Australia	7.3	8.1	8.4	8.3	8.4	1,407	62.9	4.6	67.8	5.8
Austria	7.9	8.1	8.4	8.3	8.4	1,448	68.8	5.4	67.1	5.6
Belgium	6.6	7.4	7.6	7.6	7.9	1,377	83.4	5.5	88.9	7.0
Canada	7.4	8.5	9.0	9.5	10.0	1,915	74.7	5.5	72.2	7.2
Denmark	6.8	6.3	6.5	6.3	6.5	1,151	85.2	5.8	81.5	5.3
Finland	6.5	7.2	7.2	7.8	8.9	1,426	79.0	5.1	80.9	7.2
France	7.6	8.5	8.7	8.8	9.1	1,650	78.8	6.0	73.9	6.7
Germany [1]	8.4	8.7	8.3	8.3	8.5	1,659	75.0	6.3	71.8	6.1
Greece	4.3	4.9	5.4	5.4	5.2	404	82.2	3.6	[2]77.0	[2]4.1
Iceland	6.4	7.1	8.6	8.3	8.4	1,447	88.2	5.7	87.0	7.3
Ireland	9.2	8.2	6.9	7.0	7.3	845	82.2	7.5	75.8	5.6
Italy	6.9	7.0	7.6	8.1	8.3	1,408	81.1	5.6	77.5	6.5
Japan	6.6	6.5	6.6	6.7	6.8	1,307	70.8	4.6	70.1	[2]4.8
Luxembourg	6.8	6.8	6.9	7.2	7.2	1,494	92.8	6.3	[2]91.4	[2]6.6
Netherlands	8.0	8.0	8.1	8.2	8.3	1,360	74.7	6.0	73.1	6.1
New Zealand	7.2	6.5	7.2	7.3	7.6	1,047	83.6	6.0	78.9	6.0
Norway	6.6	6.4	7.4	7.4	7.6	1,305	98.4	6.5	96.6	7.3
Portugal	5.9	7.0	7.2	6.7	6.8	624	72.4	4.3	[2]61.7	[2]4.1
Spain	5.6	5.7	6.3	6.6	6.7	848	79.9	4.5	82.2	5.5
Sweden	9.4	8.8	8.6	8.6	8.6	1,443	92.5	8.7	78.0	6.7
Switzerland	7.3	7.6	7.5	7.8	7.9	1,713	67.5	4.9	68.3	5.4
Turkey	4.0	2.8	3.9	4.0	4.0	142	27.3	1.1	[2]35.6	[2]1.4
United Kingdom	5.8	6.0	6.1	6.2	6.6	1,043	89.6	5.2	83.3	5.5

[1] Former West Germany (prior to unification).   [2] 1990 data.

Source: Organization for Economic Cooperation and Development, Paris, France, *OECD Health Data*, 1993, and *OECD Health Systems: Facts and Trends*, 1993.

No. 1384. Education Expenditures: 1988

[For definitions of education levels, see table 1385. Includes both current and capital expenditures. Public expenditure refers to the spending of public authorities at all levels. Private expenditure refers to the spending of private sources- mainly households, private non- profit institutions, and firms and businesses. Expenditure per student based on full-time equivalent students enrolled in both public and private schools. Purchasing power parities (PPP's) are the rates of currency conversion that equalize the purchasing power of different countries. This means that a given sum of money, when converted into different currencies at the PPP rates, will buy the same basket of goods and services in all countries. Thus, PPP's are the rates of currency conversion that eliminate differences in price levels between countries]

COUNTRY	EXPENDITURES AS PERCENT OF GROSS DOMESTIC PRODUCT			PUBLIC EXPENDITURE FOR EDUCATION AS PERCENT OF TOTAL PUBLIC EXPENDITURES	EXPENDITURE PER STUDENT USING PURCHASING POWER PARITIES (U.S. dollars)					
	Total	Public sources	Private sources		Total	Primary and secondary levels				Higher education
						Total	Pre-primary	Primary	Secondary	
EDUCATION FUNDED BY PUBLIC AND PRIVATE SOURCES										
Canada [1]	7.2	6.4	0.8	14.4	5,337	4,268	(NA)	(NA)	(NA)	9,308
Denmark	6.9	6.8	0.1	11.6	4,656	3,753	2,632	3,227	4,283	10,847
France	5.7	5.1	0.7	10.2	3,161	2,550	1,649	1,976	3,387	4,362
Ireland	6.2	5.8	0.4	11.5	1,769	1,472	1,107	1,146	2,005	5,429
Japan	4.9	3.8	1.2	11.7	3,313	2,572	1,552	2,571	2,752	6,105
Netherlands	6.6	6.3	0.3	10.9	3,513	2,189	([2])	1,935	2,427	9,939
Portugal	4.9	4.7	0.2	10.7	1,600	1,359	858	1,368	1,438	4,637
Spain [3]	5.0	3.9	1.1	9.7	1,819	1,617	1,268	1,384	1,853	2,545
United States	5.7	5.0	0.7	13.7	[4]4,126	[3]3,654	1,762	[3]3,595	[4]4,346	[5]9,844
West Germany	6.2	4.3	1.9	9.1	[4]3,047	[4]2,263	941	[4]2,101	[4]2,659	[4]5,085
EDUCATION FUNDED BY PUBLIC SOURCES										
Australia	4.8	4.8	-	13.9	(NA)	(NA)	(NA)	1,930	2,959	(NA)
Austria	5.6	5.6	-	11.1	3,472	2,812	1,607	2,610	3,198	5,029
Belgium	6.1	6.1	-	10.5	3,111	2,838	1,524	2,115	4,050	4,987
Finland	6.8	6.8	-	17.1	4,536	3,557	4,361	3,145	3,786	5,293
Italy [6]	4.8	4.8	-	9.4	3,082	2,546	1,588	2,457	2,887	4,250
Luxembourg	6.0	6.0	-	(NA)	5,854	5,190	4,338	4,965	5,681	12,238
Norway	6.6	6.6	-	12.4	4,921	3,945	870	3,900	4,842	7,439
Sweden	5.7	5.7	-	9.6	4,818	4,606	2,240	4,423	5,146	6,334
Switzerland	5.1	5.1	-	14.7	4,621	4,089	(NA)	(NA)	(NA)	10,187
United Kingdom	4.7	4.7	-	11.4	3,008	2,430	1,659	2,105	2,763	7,960

- Represents or rounds to zero.   NA Not available.   [1] Expenditures per student estimated.   [2] Data included in another category.   [3] Public expenditure for education is underestimated because a large part of the pension costs are not included.   [4] Public expenditure only. Data not available for expenditure from private sources broken down by ISCED level.   [5] Data for private expenditures only.   [6] Low percentage of public expenditure for education relative to total public expenditure due to high level of public expenditure and not to low level of expenditure on education.

No. 1385. Educational Attainment: 1989

[Persons 25 to 64 years of age. Educational program levels classified according to the International Standard Classification for Education developed by United Nations Educational, Scientific, and Cultural Organization. Preprimary education covers young children participating in a program intended to foster learning, and emotional and social development. Upper secondary level includes general, technical, or vocational education for students who have completed the first cycle of secondary education. It may either be "terminal" (i.e., preparing students for entry directly into working life) and/or "preparatory" (i.e., preparing students for higher education]

COUNTRY	PERCENT OF POPULATION COMPLETING—						
	Total	Preprimary, Primary	Lower secondary	Upper secondary	Higher education (non-university)	Higher education (university)	Other
Australia	100	14	30	25	21	10	1
Austria	100	([1])	35	60	([1])	5	-
Belgium	100	33	30	20	10	7	-
Canada	100	14	14	41	15	15	-
Denmark [2]	100	([1])	43	40	7	10	-
Finland	100	([1])	42	40	8	10	-
France	100	24	26	33	7	7	3
Ireland	100	37	25	23	7	7	1
Italy	100	44	30	20	([1])	6	-
Japan [3]	100	([1])	30	48	8	13	1
Netherlands [4]	100	19	26	36	13	6	-
New Zealand [4]	100	33	10	25	22	9	1
Norway [4]	100	([1])	35	42	10	11	2
Portugal	100	89	4	2	2	4	-
Spain	100	67	13	10	([1])	9	-
Sweden	100	([1])	33	44	11	12	-
Switzerland	100	([1])	20	50	15	9	6
United Kingdom [5]	100	([1])	35	48	6	9	1
United States	100	8	10	46	12	23	-
West Germany	100	([1])	22	61	7	10	-

- Represents or rounds to zero.   [1] Data included in another category.   [2] 1988 data.   [3] 1987 data.   [4] 1990 data.   [5] Women 25 to 59 years.

Source of tables 1384 and 1385: Organization for Economic Cooperation and Development, Paris, France, *Education at a Glance*, (copyright).

No. 1386. Number of Women Per 100 Men, by Educational Attainment: 1989

[See headnote, table 1385]

COUNTRY	Total	Preprimary, Primary	Lower secondary	Upper secondary	Higher education (nonuniversity)	Higher education (university)
Australia	99	124	147	32	204	61
Austria	103	(1)	195	75	(1)	62
Belgium	100	128	91	88	137	43
Canada	102	95	99	113	115	78
Denmark [2]	98	(1)	125	77	189	61
Finland	99	(1)	101	109	103	62
France	102	120	122	81	149	63
Ireland	99	87	94	137	119	65
Italy	104	128	88	91	(1)	73
Japan [3]	102	(1)	111	118	252	25
Netherlands [4]	97	130	132	79	93	39
New Zealand [4]	103	127	170	50	163	67
Norway [4]	97	(1)	117	91	91	77
Portugal	110	111	79	86	340	78
Spain	104	114	98	71	(1)	84
Sweden	98	(1)	93	98	125	87
Switzerland	100	(1)	176	115	40	45
United Kingdom [5]	100	(1)	124	81	165	55
United States	105	91	113	122	99	81
West Germany	99	(1)	249	91	31	52

[1] Data included in another category.   [2] 1988 data.   [3] 1987 data.   [4] 1990 data.   [5] Women 25 to 59 years.

Source: Organization for Economic Cooperation and Development, Paris, France, *Education at a Glance,* (copyright).

No. 1387. Organization for Economic Cooperation and Development (OECD)—Gross National Product: 1980 to 1990

[For interpretation of the absolute levels of GNP and per capita GNP, the market exchange rates used in converting national currencies do not necessarily reflect the relative purchasing power in the various countries. As a consequence, it should not be concluded, for instance, that the United Kingdom's individual standard of living in 1990 was only 78 percent of that of the United States, as the statistics may imply. Minus sign (-) indicates decrease. For explanation of annual percent change, see Guide to Tabular Presentation]

COUNTRY	GROSS NATIONAL PRODUCT (GNP)					GNP PER CAPITA					Inflation rate, [2] 1989-1990 (percent)
	Total in constant (1990) dollars (bil.)			Annual percent change		In constant (1990) dollars [1]			Annual percent change		
	1980	1985	1990	1980-1990	1989-1990	1980	1985	1990	1980-1990	1989-1990	
United States	4,182.6	4,757.1	5,465.1	2.7	1.0	19,466	19,948	21,863	1.8	-0.1	4.1
OECD Europe [3]	5,526.7	5,974.4	6,974.1	2.4	2.8	14,505	14,798	16,639	1.7	1.8	5.9
Belgium	158.3	164.4	192.4	2.0	3.5	16,542	16,673	19,953	2.0	3.6	3.5
Denmark	103.0	117.4	123.5	1.8	1.0	22,016	22,975	24,027	1.8	0.8	2.7
France	954.0	1,028.6	1,187.7	2.2	2.5	18,369	18,644	21,044	1.7	2.0	2.7
Germany [4]	1,216.1	1,291.5	1,507.1	2.2	4.2	20,733	21,183	23,885	1.9	2.3	3.4
Greece	57.6	61.6	67.3	1.6	1.2	6,040	6,203	6,697	1.1	1.0	20.1
Ireland	31.2	32.4	37.4	1.8	4.4	9,065	9,153	10,685	1.5	4.8	3.6
Italy	855.1	925.5	1,078.0	2.4	2.6	15,825	16,197	18,696	2.1	2.3	7.5
Luxembourg	6.4	7.2	9.0	3.5	2.6	19,000	19,568	24,270	3.2	5.4	3.4
Netherlands	232.6	243.2	276.1	1.7	3.0	16,470	16,776	18,481	1.1	2.2	3.1
Portugal	44.7	46.7	58.0	2.6	3.9	4,490	4,596	5,505	1.8	3.3	14.2
Spain	364.6	390.4	486.9	2.9	3.5	9,953	10,148	12,497	2.5	3.3	7.5
United Kingdom	753.0	829.3	975.0	2.6	1.6	14,722	14,647	17,004	2.4	0.9	6.1
Austria	126.8	135.5	158.0	2.2	4.5	17,510	17,923	20,493	2.0	3.2	3.4
Finland	99.2	114.6	137.3	3.3	1.7	22,725	23,388	27,518	2.9	1.1	6.0
Iceland	4.4	4.8	5.4	2.1	-0.1	19,458	20,125	21,680	1.3	-0.2	12.5
Norway	75.8	83.4	105.0	3.3	3.0	20,507	21,672	24,764	2.9	2.7	4.0
Sweden	185.1	202.5	224.7	2.0	0.9	23,753	24,251	26,250	1.6	0.1	9.2
Switzerland	192.2	206.0	235.4	2.1	2.5	30,838	31,829	35,081	1.4	1.6	6.5
Turkey	66.6	83.4	109.9	5.1	7.6	1,619	1,660	1,873	2.2	4.1	53.1
Australia	213.5	250.0	294.2	3.3	2.2	15,259	15,833	17,215	1.7	0.6	3.8
Canada	415.1	477.8	558.0	3.0	1.1	18,267	18,990	21,094	2.0	-0.1	3.1
Japan	1,893.2	2,307.4	2,910.4	4.4	6.1	18,319	19,045	23,558	3.8	5.7	1.9
New Zealand	34.5	41.3	41.9	2.0	0.7	11,981	12,708	12,507	1.2	-0.5	2.9

[1] National currency values converted into dollars by the average 1989 Market Rate, as published by the International Monetary Fund, Washington, DC.   [2] GNP or GDP (gross domestic product) implicit price deflators; totals weighted by 1989 (base year) GNP.   [3] See text, section 31.   [4] Former West Germany (prior to unification).

Source: U.S. Department of State, Bureau of Intelligence and Research, *Economic Growth of OECD Countries, 1980-1990,* Report No. IRR 22.

No. 1388. Gross National Product in Current and Constant (1989) Dollars and Per Capita: 1980 to 1989

[In billions of dollars, except per capita. For explanation of conversion to U.S. dollars, see headnote, table 1432. For explanation of gross national product (GNP), see text, section 14]

COUNTRY	CURRENT DOLLARS				CONSTANT (1989) DOLLARS				Per capita (dol.)		
	1980	1985	1988	1989	1980	1985	1988	1989	1980	1985	1989
United States	2,732.0	4,015.0	4,874.0	5,201.0	4,025.0	4,571.0	5,073.0	5,201.0	17,670	[1]19,100	20,910
Afghanistan.	2.7	[1]2.9	(NA)	(NA)	4.0	[1]3.3	(NA)	(NA)	269	239	(NA)
Algeria.	23.9	40.0	42.4	45.3	35.3	45.6	44.1	45.3	1,870	2,054	1,831
Argentina	43.9	48.5	56.5	54.1	64.6	55.2	58.8	54.1	2,289	1,818	1,694
Austria	71.5	99.0	115.9	125.2	105.3	112.7	120.6	125.2	13,950	14,920	16,430
Bangladesh.	10.0	15.5	18.8	20.0	14.7	17.6	19.6	20.0	167	174	180
Belgium	89.4	119.4	141.8	154.6	131.8	135.9	147.6	154.6	13,380	13,780	15,620
Brazil	260.6	348.6	430.5	462.3	384.0	396.9	448.2	462.3	3,124	2,874	3,090
Bulgaria	30.6	41.2	48.0	49.6	45.0	46.9	49.9	49.6	5,093	5,246	5,530
Burma	9.8	15.8	14.6	16.3	14.4	17.9	15.2	16.3	429	482	404
Canada	270.2	401.3	496.5	531.0	398.0	456.9	516.8	531.0	16,540	18,140	20,240
Chile	12.6	15.2	20.2	23.3	18.5	17.4	21.1	23.3	1,670	1,438	1,809
China:											
Mainland [1]	186.4	386.3	559.1	603.5	274.6	439.8	582.0	603.5	279	422	547
Taiwan	49.7	90.6	134.6	150.2	73.3	103.2	140.1	150.2	4,104	5,317	7,390
Colombia	19.4	27.3	34.1	36.9	28.6	31.0	35.4	36.9	1,077	1,046	1,139
Czechoslovakia	71.2	97.8	117.1	123.2	104.9	111.3	121.9	123.2	6,874	7,182	7,876
East Germany	89.6	127.4	151.3	159.4	132.0	145.0	157.5	159.4	7,885	8,707	9,669
Egypt.	30.6	53.0	64.9	69.8	45.1	60.4	67.6	69.8	1,082	1,277	1,342
Ethiopia	3.3	4.3	5.6	6.0	4.9	4.8	5.8	6.0	128	111	120
France	536.2	740.9	884.2	954.1	790.0	843.5	920.5	954.1	14,660	15,290	17,000
Ghana	2.9	3.6	4.6	5.1	4.3	4.1	4.8	5.1	396	322	350
Greece	32.4	43.4	49.6	52.9	47.8	49.4	51.7	52.9	4,954	4,977	5,286
Hungary	39.3	52.6	63.3	64.7	57.9	59.9	65.9	64.7	5,408	5,621	6,119
India	112.4	188.2	246.2	267.4	165.5	214.2	256.3	267.4	240	279	321
Indonesia	35.1	61.1	79.8	89.4	51.7	69.5	83.1	89.4	334	403	479
Iran [1]	37.8	71.1	71.3	77.5	55.6	80.9	74.3	77.5	1,422	1,716	1,440
Iraq [1]	55.6	41.3	39.6	(NA)	81.9	47.0	41.3	(NA)	6,188	2,992	(NA)
Italy.	479.0	665.5	800.6	860.0	705.7	757.6	833.4	860.0	12,500	13,260	14,940
Japan.	1,328.0	2,090.0	2,586.0	2,820.0	1,956.0	2,379.0	2,692.0	2,820.0	16,750	19,700	22,900
Kenya	3.8	5.6	7.3	7.9	5.6	6.3	7.6	7.9	336	314	338
Madagascar	1.6	1.9	2.2	2.3	2.4	2.2	2.3	2.3	279	213	205
Malaysia.	15.1	24.1	31.2	36.0	22.3	27.4	32.5	36.0	1,619	1,765	2,099
Mexico.	114.1	159.2	174.1	186.7	168.1	181.2	181.3	186.7	2,415	2,310	2,170
Morocco.	10.7	15.8	20.3	21.7	15.7	18.0	21.1	21.7	764	780	866
Mozambique	0.9	0.9	1.0	1.1	1.4	1.0	1.0	1.1	114	76	78
Nepal.	1.3	2.1	2.7	2.8	1.8	2.3	2.8	2.8	123	138	150
Netherlands	129.9	176.4	205.0	222.5	191.4	200.8	213.4	222.5	13,530	13,860	14,980
Nigeria	18.9	22.4	25.2	27.5	27.8	25.5	26.2	27.5	309	248	239
North Korea [1]	21.9	26.3	29.2	30.0	32.3	29.9	30.4	30.0	1,793	1,527	1,427
Pakistan	14.3	25.6	33.7	36.8	21.1	29.1	35.1	36.8	247	293	330
Peru.	29.3	36.4	43.3	40.8	43.2	41.5	45.1	40.8	2,497	2,113	1,903
Philippines	25.9	31.8	40.0	44.0	38.2	36.2	41.7	44.0	750	629	697
Poland	108.1	144.4	170.9	174.7	159.3	164.3	177.9	174.7	4,477	4,417	4,625
Portugal	23.8	31.5	40.5	44.6	35.0	35.8	42.2	44.6	3,583	3,525	4,323
Romania.	75.0	99.3	112.3	113.4	110.5	113.1	117.0	113.4	4,977	4,977	4,896
South Africa	49.6	70.5	83.6	86.8	73.1	80.3	87.0	86.8	2,414	2,317	2,253
South Korea	62.3	120.6	188.4	210.1	91.9	137.2	196.1	210.1	2,409	3,343	4,920
Soviet Union	1,532.0	2,145.0	2,526.0	2,664.0	2,257.0	2,442.0	2,630.0	2,664.0	8,473	8,757	9,226
Spain.	196.2	271.0	340.2	370.7	289.1	308.5	354.2	370.7	7,711	8,014	9,471
Sri Lanka	3.3	5.5	6.5	6.9	4.9	6.3	6.8	6.9	330	392	409
Sudan	9.0	11.7	13.6	15.6	13.3	13.3	14.2	15.6	702	567	608
Sweden	106.0	147.6	174.8	185.8	156.1	168.0	182.0	185.8	18,790	20,110	21,900
Switzerland	103.7	146.4	172.3	184.3	152.8	166.7	179.4	184.3	23,930	25,510	27,510
Syria	11.2	16.7	19.5	19.3	16.6	19.0	20.3	19.3	1,904	1,832	1,608
Tanzania.	1.6	2.1	2.5	2.6	2.3	2.4	2.6	2.6	124	108	105
Thailand.	24.4	41.3	58.7	68.8	36.0	47.0	61.1	68.8	766	908	1,246
Turkey	34.1	55.6	73.1	77.3	50.3	63.2	76.1	77.3	1,115	1,241	1,380
Uganda	2.0	2.8	3.6	4.0	3.0	3.2	3.8	4.0	232	176	233
United Kingdom.	442.8	632.7	783.3	834.4	652.5	720.2	815.4	834.4	11,590	12,720	14,580
Venezuela.	29.3	34.7	44.7	41.5	43.1	39.6	46.6	41.5	2,869	2,285	2,158
West Germany.	685.6	942.9	1,112.0	1,207.0	1,010.0	1,073.0	1,158.0	1,207.0	16,410	17,590	19,520
Yugoslavia	39.0	51.2	55.9	58.6	57.4	58.2	58.2	58.6	2,574	2,518	2,474
Zaire	5.5	7.5	8.9	9.2	8.1	8.6	9.3	9.2	304	276	258

NA Not available.   [1] Estimated.

Source: U.S. Arms Control and Disarmament Agency, *World Military Expenditures and Arms Transfers,* annual. Data from International Bank for Reconstruction and Development and U.S. Central Intelligence Agency.

No. 1389. Annual Growth Rates of Real Gross Domestic Product: 1980 to 1990

[In percent. Minus sign (-) indicates decline. See also *Historical Statistics, Colonial Times to 1970,* series F 10-16]

COUNTRY	1980-81	1981-82	1982-83	1983-84	1984-85	1985-86	1986-87	1987-88	1988-89	1989-90
United States	2.3	-2.6	3.9	7.2	3.8	3.2	3.5	4.5	2.8	0.9
Per capita.................	1.2	-3.6	2.9	6.2	2.8	2.2	2.5	3.5	1.8	-0.1
Canada...................	3.7	-3.2	3.2	6.4	4.7	3.3	4.1	4.7	2.4	0.4
Per capita.................	2.4	-4.2	2.4	5.6	4.0	2.5	3.0	3.5	1.2	-1.0
France	1.2	2.3	0.8	1.5	1.8	2.4	2.2	3.8	3.6	2.6
Per capita.................	0.6	1.7	0.3	1.1	1.4	2.0	1.7	3.4	3.1	2.1
Germany [1]...............	0.2	-0.9	1.6	2.8	1.9	2.2	1.4	3.7	3.2	4.7
Per capita.................	-	0.9	1.9	3.2	2.1	2.2	1.4	3.1	2.2	2.8
Italy	0.6	0.2	1.0	2.7	2.6	2.9	3.1	4.1	3.0	2.0
Per capita.................	0.4	-	0.6	2.4	2.3	2.8	2.9	3.9	2.9	1.7
Japan....................	3.6	3.2	2.7	4.3	5.0	2.6	4.1	6.2	4.7	5.2
Per capita.................	2.8	2.5	2.0	3.6	4.3	2.0	3.6	5.8	4.3	4.9
United Kingdom	-1.3	1.7	3.7	2.2	3.6	3.9	4.8	4.2	2.3	0.8
Per capita.................	-1.4	1.8	3.6	2.0	3.3	3.7	4.5	4.0	2.0	0.5

- Represents or rounds to zero.   [1] Former West Germany (prior to unification).

Source: Organization for Economic Cooperation and Development, Paris, France, *National Accounts,* annual.

No. 1390. Gross Domestic Product of Selected Countries as Percent of United States: 1970 to 1989

[Comparisons are based on constant (1985) price data converted to U.S. dollars using 1985 exchange rates]

COUNTRY	GROSS DOMESTIC PRODUCT								PER CAPITA GROSS DOMESTIC PRODUCT							
	1970	1975	1980	1985	1986	1987	1988	1989	1970	1975	1980	1985	1986	1987	1988	1989
United States........	100	100	100	100	100	100	100	100	100	100	100	100	100	100	100	100
Canada...........	7	8	9	9	9	9	9	9	70	80	83	83	83	84	84	84
France	13	14	14	13	13	13	13	13	54	58	60	57	57	56	56	57
Italy	10	11	11	11	11	11	11	11	39	41	46	45	45	45	45	46
Japan............	26	29	32	33	33	33	34	35	52	57	62	66	66	67	68	70
United Kingdom......	13	13	12	11	11	12	12	12	48	49	48	48	49	50	50	51
West Germany.......	17	17	17	16	16	15	15	15	58	59	63	61	62	61	61	61

Source: Organization for Economic Cooperation and Development, Paris, France, *National Accounts, 1960-1989.*

No. 1391. Selected International Economic Indicators: 1970 to 1992

[Data cover gross domestic product (GDP) at market prices, except for Germany and Japan, which relate to gross national product. Gross fixed capital formation covers private and government sectors except military. Savings data are calculated by deducting outlays—such as personal consumption expenditures, interest paid, and transfer payments to foreigners—from disposable personal income. Minus sign (-) indicates decline]

YEAR	United States	France	Germany [1]	Italy	Netherlands	United Kingdom	Japan	Canada
GDP growth rates [2] (constant 1987 prices):								
1970	-	5.7	5.0	5.3	5.4	2.3	10.2	2.6
1980	-0.5	1.6	1.0	4.0	0.9	-1.9	3.5	1.5
1985	3.2	1.9	1.8	2.6	2.6	3.8	5.2	4.8
1990	0.8	2.2	4.9	2.1	3.9	0.5	4.8	-0.5
1991	-1.2	1.0	3.6	1.3	2.2	-2.2	4.1	-1.7
1992	2.1	1.8	0.8	0.9	(NA)	-0.6	1.5	0.9
Ratio of gross fixed capital formation to GDP (current prices):								
1970	18.0	24.3	25.5	24.6	27.2	18.8	35.6	21.3
1980	20.4	23.0	22.5	24.3	21.6	17.9	31.6	23.3
1985	19.4	19.3	19.4	20.7	19.7	16.9	27.4	19.7
1990	16.7	21.2	20.8	20.2	21.3	19.3	32.0	21.2
1991	15.2	20.7	21.5	19.8	20.8	16.6	31.4	19.6
1992	15.2	19.8	21.5	(NA)	(NA)	(NA)	30.3	18.9
Ratio of savings to disposable personal income:								
1970	8.0	18.7	14.7	29.4	13.2	9.0	18.2	5.5
1980	7.9	17.6	14.2	21.6	11.0	13.1	17.9	13.3
1985	6.4	14.0	12.7	18.0	13.1	9.7	15.6	13.1
1990	4.3	12.2	14.7	16.1	16.1	8.3	14.1	10.0
1991	4.7	12.5	14.5	15.6	13.1	9.7	14.6	10.3
1992	4.8	12.6	13.8	(NA)	(NA)	11.6	(NA)	10.2

- Represents or rounds to zero.   NA Not available.   [1] Former West Germany (prior to unification).   [2] Growth rates represent percentage change from preceding year.

Source: U.S. Dept. of Commerce, International Trade Administration, Office of Trade and Economic Analysis, based on official statistics of listed countries.

No. 1392. Gross Domestic Product, Total and Per Capita, Using Purchasing Power Parities—Selected Countries: 1970 to 1990

[The goods and services produced in different countries should be valued consistently if the differences observed are meant to reflect real differences in the volumes of goods and services produced. The use of purchasing power parities (PPP) instead of exchange rates is intended to achieve this objective. PPP's show how many units of currency are needed in one country to buy the same amount of goods and services which one unit of currency will buy in the other country. For further explanation of PPP, see text, section 31]

COUNTRY	GROSS DOMESTIC PRODUCT (bil. dol.)						GROSS DOMESTIC PRODUCT (dollars)					
	1970	1980	1985	1988	1989	1990	1970	1980	1985	1988	1989	1990
United States ...	1,009	2,686	3,962	4,809	5,132	5,392	4,919	11,794	16,559	19,525	20,630	21,449
OECD Europe [1] ..	1,128	3,088	4,275	5,111	5,478	5,871	3,060	7,847	10,586	12,460	13,262	14,070
Austria	24	69	94	109	117	128	3,158	9,081	12,408	14,356	15,402	16,620
Belgium	32	89	119	141	151	164	3,310	9,076	12,067	14,206	15,231	16,405
Denmark......	18	47	68	77	81	86	3,724	9,085	13,295	15,053	15,802	16,765
Finland	14	40	59	72	79	82	3,007	8,342	12,028	14,504	15,808	16,453
France	188	525	725	856	921	984	3,696	9,740	13,141	15,319	16,397	17,431
Germany	236	626	847	989	1,061	1,157	3,884	10,170	13,876	16,100	17,093	18,291
Greece	13	43	58	67	72	75	1,507	4,426	5,883	6,670	7,145	7,349
Iceland.......	1	2	3	4	4	4	2,674	9,448	12,532	15,211	15,400	15,851
Ireland	6	18	26	30	34	37	1,853	5,190	7,246	8,568	9,526	10,659
Italy	168	493	678	813	870	924	3,123	8,743	11,859	14,161	15,126	16,021
Luxembourg ..	1	4	5	6	7	7	3,919	9,610	13,825	14,802	18,345	19,340
Netherlands ...	48	131	176	202	218	236	3,699	9,233	12,137	13,664	14,671	15,766
Norway.......	11	35	53	61	64	68	2,812	8,622	12,818	14,532	15,079	15,921
Portugal	13	42	56	69	76	82	1,545	4,511	5,811	7,105	7,732	8,389
Spain........	80	229	314	392	426	459	2,366	6,126	8,159	10,089	10,952	11,792
Sweden	32	79	111	130	138	144	3,986	9,517	13,286	15,368	16,224	16,867
Switzerland	34	77	106	124	134	143	5,351	12,087	16,218	18,641	19,949	20,997
Turkey	22	75	121	159	167	190	628	1,673	2,390	2,948	3,018	3,316
United Kingdom.	189	465	656	810	860	903	3,399	8,259	11,590	14,188	15,023	15,720
Australia	47	132	198	238	258	273	3,644	9,003	12,548	14,412	15,324	15,951
Canada.......	80	253	374	458	487	509	3,733	10,509	14,852	17,648	18,544	19,120
Japan	304	961	1,479	1,824	1,981	2,179	2,932	8,225	12,246	14,875	16,090	17,634
New Zealand ..	10	25	37	41	43	45	3,474	7,836	11,159	12,164	12,745	13,258

[1] See text, section 31.
Source: Organization for Economic Cooperation and Development, Paris, France, *National Accounts of OECD Countries*, vol. I, annual.

No. 1393. Food and Beverage Expenditures as a Percent of Total Private Consumption Expenditures—Selected Countries: 1989

COUNTRY	Food	Nonalcoholic beverages	Alcoholic beverages	COUNTRY	Food	Nonalcoholic beverages	Alcoholic beverages
United States...	9.8	0.6	1.1	Italy.........	18.8	0.4	1.1
				Netherlands	14.2	0.6	1.7
Australia......	[1]14.8	(NA)	4.2	Norway	18.7	1.3	3.2
Austria.......	16.3	0.6	2.1	Philippines	52.8	2.4	(NA)
Belgium......	15.7	0.5	1.3	Portugal [3].....	34.1	0.3	2.0
Canada	[1]11.3	(NA)	2.7	South Africa	27.0	1.4	5.4
Denmark	14.7	0.6	3.4	Spain [4]	21.6	0.5	1.5
Finland	16.2	0.6	4.2	Sweden	16.2	0.6	3.2
France.......	15.9	0.5	2.0	Switzerland	19.1	[5]7.1	(NA)
Greece	31.3	1.2	3.0	Thailand......	27.1	3.6	4.1
India [2]......	51.3	0.1	1.1	United Kingdom. .	11.6	0.9	6.3
Ireland [2].....	21.3	1.6	11.9	Venezuela	35.5	3.7	(NA)
Israel........	24.0	2.4	0.6	West Germany ..	[6]20.2	(NA)	(NA)

NA Not available.   [1] Food expenditures include nonalcoholic beverages.   [2] Data for 1988.   [3] Data for 1986.   [4] Data for 1987.   [5] Nonalcoholic beverage expenditures include all beverages.   [6] Food expenditures include all beverages.
Source: U.S. Dept. of Agriculture, Economic Research Service. Based on data from the United Nations, New York, NY, *National Accounts Statistics*, annual.

No. 1394. Per Capita Consumption of Pork, Poultry, Beef, and Veal: 1992

[Preliminary. In pounds per capita. Beef, veal, and pork quantities are as of September and in carcass-weight equivalents; poultry quantities are as of July and are on ready-to-cook basis]

COUNTRY	PORK		COUNTRY	POULTRY		COUNTRY	BEEF AND VEAL	
	Quantity	Rank		Quantity	Rank		Quantity	Rank
Denmark.........	142.8	1	United States	94.8	1	Argentina........	155.2	1
Hungary	137.3	2	Israel	83.7	2	Uruguay.........	133.4	2
Sweden	120.6	3	Hong Kong	79.3	3	United States	96.6	3
Poland	113.9	4	Singapore	77.2	4	Australia	84.4	4
Czechoslovakia	112.7	5	Canada	61.7	5	Canada	80.7	5
Austria..........	112.5	6	Saudi Arabia.....	61.7	6	Baltic States.....	67.5	6
Spain...........	110.4	7	Australia	55.1	7	New Zealand	63.9	7
Germany	106.7	8	Spain	52.9	8	France	63.5	8
Belgium-Lux	104.1	9	Taiwan	52.9	9	Czechoslovakia....	60.2	9
Hong Kong.......	90.9	10	United Kingdom ...	50.7	10	Italy	58.6	10
United States.....	70.8	22						

Source: U.S. Department of Agriculture, Foreign Agricultural Service, *World Poultry Situation* and *World Livestock Situation*, annuals.

No. 1395. Percent of Households Owning Selected Appliances—Selected Countries: 1990

APPLIANCE	United States [1]	Bel-gium	Den-mark	France	Ger-many [2]	Italy	Nether-lands	Spain	Sweden	Swit-zerland	United King-dom
Cassette recorder...	(NA)	75	82	76	74	64	80	67	88	82	82
Clothes washer ...	76	88	76	88	88	96	91	87	72	78	78
Dishwasher......	45	26	26	33	34	18	12	11	31	32	11
Food processor ...	(NA)	91	83	83	92	48	84	50	77	91	80
Microwave oven....	79	21	14	25	36	6	19	9	37	15	48
Radio.........	(NA)	90	98	98	84	92	97	95	93	99	90
Television set, color/mono.....	96	97	98	94	97	98	98	98	97	93	98
Tumbledrier......	53	39	22	12	17	10	23	5	18	27	32
Vacuum cleaner....	(NA)	92	96	89	96	56	98	29	97	93	98
Video recorder....	(NA)	42	39	35	42	25	48	40	48	41	58

NA Not available.   [1] Represents appliances possessed and generally used by the household (as of November). Source: U.S. Energy Information Administration, *Annual Energy Review*, annual.   [2] Former West Germany (prior to unification).
Source: Except as noted, Euromonitor Publications Limited, London, England, *European Marketing Data and Statistics*, annual (copyright).

No. 1396. Motor Vehicle Deaths and Vehicle Registrations for Selected Nations

[Deaths are included if they occur within 30 days after the accident, except as noted. Death data must be compared cautiously because of differences in the volume and kinds of traffic, numbers of vehicles, population density, definitions of deaths, and other factors]

COUNTRY	MOTOR VEHICLE TRAFFIC DEATHS			1990 VEHICLE REGISTRATIONS			
				All vehicles		Passenger cars	
	Year	Number	Rate [1]	Number (mil.)	Persons per vehi-cle	Number (mil.)	Persons per car
Argentina	1987	3,054	9.8	5.8	5.6	4.3	7.5
Australia.......................	1989	4,210	16.1	9.8	1.7	7.7	2.2
Austria........................	1990	1,408	18.2	3.7	2.1	3.0	2.5
Belgium........................	1987	[2]1,937	[2]19.6	4.3	2.3	3.8	2.6
Bulgaria.......................	1990	1,409	15.7	1.5	6.0	1.3	6.9
Canada........................	1989	[3]4,210	[3]16.1	16.6	1.6	12.6	2.1
Chile	1989	941	7.3	1.0	13.0	0.7	18.0
Costa Rica	1989	389	13.2	0.3	12.0	0.2	20.0
Czechoslovakia	1990	2,127	13.6	3.5	4.5	3.2	4.8
Denmark.......................	1990	617	12.0	1.9	2.7	1.6	3.2
Dominican Republic	1985	557	8.9	0.3	27.0	0.2	45.0
East Germany (former)	1990	3,143	19.5	5.6	2.9	4.8	3.3
Ecuador	1990	2,049	19.4	0.2	44.0	0.1	136.0
Finland	1989	720	14.5	2.2	2.2	1.9	2.6
France........................	1989	[4]10,198	[4]18.2	28.5	2.0	23.6	2.4
Greece........................	1989	2,066	20.6	2.5	4.0	1.7	5.8
Hong Kong	1989	309	5.4	0.4	15.0	0.2	24.0
Hungary	1990	2,609	25.2	2.2	4.8	1.9	5.4
Ireland	1989	456	13.0	1.0	3.5	0.8	4.5
Israel	1988	439	9.9	0.9	4.6	0.8	5.6
Italy	1989	[4]8,717	[4]15.1	29.7	1.9	27.3	2.1
Japan.........................	1990	14,398	11.7	57.7	2.1	34.9	3.5
Kuwait	1987	343	18.3	0.6	3.3	0.5	4.2
Netherlands....................	1989	1,401	9.4	6.1	2.4	5.5	2.7
New Zealand....................	1989	766	22.9	1.9	1.8	1.6	2.2
Norway........................	1989	386	9.1	1.9	2.2	1.6	2.6
Panama	1989	320	13.5	0.2	11.0	0.2	16.0
Paraguay	1987	225	9.6	0.1	42.0	0.1	62.0
Poland	1990	8,266	21.7	6.3	6.1	5.3	7.3
Portugal	1990	2,784	28.2	2.2	4.8	1.6	6.6
Puerto Rico.....................	1989	577	15.8	1.5	2.2	1.3	2.5
Singapore	1989	226	8.4	0.4	6.6	0.3	9.4
Sweden	1988	809	9.6	3.9	2.1	3.6	2.3
Switzerland	1990	930	13.9	3.3	2.0	3.0	2.2
Syria	1985	176	1.7	0.2	51.0	0.1	111.0
Thailand.......................	1987	4,441	8.3	2.8	20.0	0.8	66.0
United States	**1989**	[3]**46,586**	[3]**18.8**	**188.7**	**1.3**	**143.5**	**1.7**
Uruguay	1989	477	15.4	0.3	12.0	0.2	17.0
West Germany (former)...........	1990	7,435	19.7	32.7	1.9	30.7	2.1
Yugoslavia	1989	3,692	15.6	4.4	5.4	3.5	6.8

[1] Deaths per 100,000 population.   [2] Deaths occurring at the accident scene only.   [3] Deaths occurring within 1 year after the accident.   [4] Deaths occurring within three days after the accident.
Source: World Health Organization, Geneva, Switzerland, *World Health Statistics*, annual, and unpublished data; and American Automobile Manufactures Association, Inc., Detroit, MI, *AAMA Motor Vehicle Facts & Figures*, annual (copyright).

No. 1397. Communications—Telephones, Newspapers, Television, and Radio, by Country: 1990

[See text, section 31, for general comments about the data. For additional data qualifications for countries, see source]

COUNTRY	Telephone main lines per 100 population [1]	Daily newspaper circulation, copies per 1,000 population [2]	Television receivers per 1,000 population [3]	Radio receivers per 1,000 population [4]	COUNTRY	Telephone main lines per 100 population [1]	Daily newspaper circulation, copies per 1,000 population [2]	Television receivers per 1,000 population [3]	Radio receivers per 1,000 population [4]
United States	51	250	815	2,123	Japan..........	[5]42	587	620	907
Algeria	3	51	74	233	Kenya..........	1	15	9	125
Argentina	11	124	222	681	Kuwait	[7]15	221	285	343
Australia	[5]45	249	486	1,280	Lebanon	(NA)	118	330	840
Austria	42	357	481	624	Luxembourg......	48	389	255	630
Bangladesh......	[6](Z)	6	5	42	Madagascar......	[8](Z)	4	20	200
Belgium	40	305	452	778	Malaysia	9	140	148	429
Bolivia	[5]3	55	163	599	Mexico	6	127	139	243
Brazil	6	54	213	379	Morocco	2	13	74	209
Bulgaria	[5]22	451	250	438	Netherlands......	46	[7]311	906	1,106
Burma	[7](Z)	5	2	82	New Zealand	43	324	442	929
Cambodia	(NA)	(NA)	9	113	Nicaragua	1	65	62	249
Canada	57	[5]228	641	1,026	Nigeria	[7](Z)	16	32	172
Chile	6	455	205	342	Norway	50	614	425	798
China, Mainland ...	1	[8]37	31	184	Pakistan	[7]1	15	17	87
Colombia........	7	61	115	170	Panama	9	70	165	223
Costa Rica	9	[9]102	149	259	Paraguay........	3	39	59	171
Cuba	3	124	207	345	Peru	3	79	97	253
Cyprus	36	111	150	292	Philippines.......	1	54	48	138
Czechoslovakia ...	15	507	412	587	Poland	9	127	293	429
Denmark........	57	352	535	1,030	Portugal	23	38	177	218
Dominican					Puerto Rico	(NA)	131	267	721
Republic	5	32	84	170	Romania........	10	[8]158	194	198
East Germany	11	[7]338	514	952	Saudi Arabia	10	42	283	318
Ecuador	5	87	83	315	Singapore	39	280	376	643
Egypt..........	3	57	109	324	South Africa.....	10	38	105	326
El Salvador	2	87	90	404	South Korea	32	280	210	1,006
Ethiopia	(Z)	[7]1	2	191	Soviet Union	[7]12	[5]482	329	686
Finland	53	559	497	998	Spain	32	[7]82	396	306
France	48	210	406	896	Sri Lanka	1	32	35	197
Ghana	(Z)	13	15	266	Sudan..........	[7](Z)	24	71	250
Greece	39	[7]140	196	423	Sweden	68	533	474	888
Guatemala.......	2	21	52	65	Switzerland	58	463	407	855
Honduras	2	39	72	385	Syria...........	4	22	59	251
Hong Kong	42	632	274	649	Thailand	2	72	112	185
Hungary	9	233	410	595	Trinidad and				
Iceland	50	[8]467	320	787	Tobago	14	(NA)	302	468
India...........	1	[8]26	32	79	Tunisia	4	37	80	196
Indonesia	[5](Z)	28	60	147	Turkey	12	72	175	161
Iran	4	27	70	247	United Kingdom ...	44	[7]395	435	1,146
Iraq	[8]5	34	69	205	Uruguay	14	233	233	603
Ireland	28	159	276	583	Venezuela.......	8	[1]142	167	436
Israel	34	261	266	471	West Germany....	48	[5]338	514	952
Italy	39	[5]107	424	797	Yugoslavia.......	16	96	198	246
Jamaica	4	63	130	411	Zimbabwe	1	21	31	85

NA Not available.   Z Less than 1 per 100 population.   [1] As of December 31.   [2] Publications containing general news and appearing at least 4 times a week; may range in size from a single sheet to 50 or more pages. Circulation data refer to average circulation per issue or number of printed copies per issue and include copies sold outside the country.   [3] Estimated number of sets in use.   [4] Data cover estimated number of receivers in use and apply to all types of receivers for radio broadcasts to the public, including receivers connected to a radio "redistribution system" but excluding television sets.   [5] For 1989.   [6] For 1979. [7] For 1988.   [8] For 1985.   [9] For 1991.

Source: International Telecommunications Union, Geneva, Switzerland, *Telecommunication Statistics*, (copyright); and United Nations Educational, Scientific, and Cultural Organization, Paris, France, *Statistical Yearbook* (copyright).

No. 1398. Tax Revenues—Selected Countries: 1980 to 1990

[Covers national and local taxes and Social Security contributions]

COUNTRY	TAX REVENUES, 1990		PERCENT CHANGE IN TOTAL TAX REVENUE AS EXPRESSED IN NATIONAL CURRENCY					TAX REVENUES AS PERCENT OF GROSS DOMESTIC PRODUCT				
	Total (bil. dol.)	Per capita (dol.)	1980-1990	1986-1987	1987-1988	1988-1989	1989-1990	1980	1985	1988	1989	1990
United States	1,598	6,358	106.5	10.2	6.7	8.2	5.0	29.5	29.2	29.4	29.6	29.9
Australia	91	5,300	190.9	13.8	12.0	8.6	2.9	28.5	30.0	30.5	30.4	30.8
Austria	65	8,473	81.6	2.8	4.9	4.3	8.4	41.2	43.1	42.1	41.2	41.6
Belgium	86	8,665	88.2	5.3	3.3	4.6	7.5	44.4	47.6	46.3	44.6	44.9
Canada	214	8,042	147.3	13.4	8.2	9.8	7.1	31.6	33.1	34.5	35.4	37.1
Denmark	63	12,235	129.0	6.6	4.8	2.6	0.3	45.5	49.0	51.7	50.4	48.6
Finland	52	10,469	214.1	2.3	18.6	11.3	7.5	33.0	37.0	37.8	37.4	38.0
France	521	9,229	142.1	6.4	6.0	7.0	5.4	41.7	44.5	43.8	43.7	43.7
Germany [1]	562	8,882	61.5	4.0	4.5	7.7	6.6	38.2	38.1	37.7	38.3	37.7
Greece	24	2,371	658.2	14.6	12.0	11.9	30.3	29.4	35.1	34.7	33.3	36.5
Ireland	16	4,519	200.3	7.5	12.3	1.7	6.3	34.0	38.0	40.6	37.0	37.2
Italy	428	7,432	338.8	9.7	12.9	12.8	13.6	30.2	34.4	37.0	37.9	39.1
Japan	939	7,601	117.7	9.3	8.6	8.4	9.9	25.4	27.6	30.3	30.7	31.3
Luxembourg	4	11,516	139.8	6.3	8.0	10.4	7.6	46.0	50.1	49.7	48.8	50.3
Netherlands	126	8,449	49.1	6.1	4.3	0.0	5.7	45.8	44.9	48.4	45.8	45.2
New Zealand	16	4,814	259.1	22.2	6.3	14.4	-1.1	33.1	34.1	37.2	39.3	38.2
Norway	49	11,533	128.1	4.8	3.6	2.5	7.1	47.1	47.6	47.8	46.0	46.3
Portugal	21	2,107	717.3	10.4	27.7	20.5	17.6	28.7	31.6	34.6	35.1	34.6
Spain	169	4,334	370.1	18.8	11.8	18.5	10.4	23.8	28.8	32.7	34.6	34.4
Sweden	130	15,154	196.2	14.0	7.8	11.4	11.8	49.1	50.4	55.5	56.0	56.9
Switzerland	71	10,490	88.9	3.0	7.1	5.4	7.5	30.8	32.0	32.6	31.7	31.7
Turkey	30	528	8,287.2	57.0	63.6	84.6	85.4	21.7	19.7	22.8	25.4	27.8
United Kingdom	358	6,232	146.6	8.4	11.7	8.5	6.7	35.3	37.9	37.3	37.0	36.7

[1] Former West Germany (prior to unification).

Source: Organization for Economic Cooperation and Development, Paris, France, *Revenue Statistics of OECD Member Countries,* annual.

No. 1399. Percent Distribution of Tax Receipts, by Type of Tax—Selected Countries: 1980 to 1990

COUNTRY	Total [1]	INCOME AND PROFITS TAXES [2]			SOCIAL SECURITY CONTRIBUTIONS			TAXES ON GOODS AND SERVICES [5]		
		Total [3]	Individual	Corporate	Total [4]	Employees	Employers	Total [3]	General consumption taxes [6]	Taxes on specific goods, services [7]
United States: 1980	100.0	47.0	36.9	10.2	26.2	10.0	15.5	16.6	6.6	7.8
1989	100.0	44.2	35.7	8.5	29.2	11.5	16.5	16.2	7.4	6.8
1990	100.0	43.2	35.8	7.3	29.5	11.6	16.6	16.5	7.6	6.8
Canada: 1980	100.0	46.6	34.1	11.6	10.5	3.7	6.6	32.5	11.5	13.0
1989	100.0	47.4	38.4	8.4	13.1	4.3	8.6	29.3	15.4	10.3
1990	100.0	48.3	40.8	6.8	14.2	4.3	9.7	27.4	13.9	9.9
France: 1980	100.0	18.1	12.9	5.1	42.7	11.1	28.4	30.4	21.1	8.4
1989	100.0	17.4	11.7	5.5	43.8	13.1	27.1	28.6	19.2	8.6
1990	100.0	17.3	11.8	5.4	44.2	13.3	27.3	28.2	18.8	8.5
Germany [8]: 1980	100.0	35.1	29.6	5.5	34.3	15.3	18.4	27.1	16.6	9.3
1989	100.0	35.0	29.5	5.5	36.3	15.7	18.5	25.6	15.5	9.0
1990	100.0	32.1	27.4	4.7	36.8	15.9	18.8	27.4	17.0	9.4
Italy: 1980	100.0	31.1	23.1	7.8	38.0	6.9	28.4	26.5	15.6	9.7
1989	100.0	37.0	26.7	10.0	33.1	6.4	23.8	27.0	14.1	10.3
1990	100.0	36.5	26.3	10.0	32.9	6.3	23.6	28.0	14.7	10.6
Japan: 1980	100.0	46.1	24.3	21.8	29.1	10.2	14.8	16.3	-	14.1
1989	100.0	48.9	24.7	24.3	28.1	10.2	14.7	12.5	3.3	7.6
1990	100.0	48.3	26.8	21.5	29.2	10.9	15.2	13.2	4.2	7.3
Netherlands: 1980	100.0	32.8	26.3	6.6	38.1	15.7	17.8	25.2	15.8	7.3
1989	100.0	28.5	21.3	7.2	41.2	18.4	16.7	26.2	16.3	7.5
1990	100.0	32.3	24.7	7.6	37.3	23.5	7.9	26.4	16.5	7.5
Sweden: 1980	100.0	43.5	41.0	2.5	28.8	-	27.6	24.0	13.4	9.2
1989	100.0	42.9	39.2	3.8	26.2	-	24.9	24.1	13.6	9.6
1990	100.0	41.0	37.9	3.1	27.6	-	25.4	24.6	14.6	9.0
United Kingdom: 1980	100.0	38.2	29.8	8.3	16.6	6.7	9.5	29.2	14.4	13.1
1989	100.0	38.7	26.5	12.2	17.7	7.3	9.5	30.6	16.7	12.4
1990	100.0	39.4	28.4	11.0	17.5	6.6	10.0	30.4	16.6	12.3

- Represents zero. [1] Includes property taxes, employer payroll taxes other than Social Security contributions, and miscellaneous taxes, not shown separately. [2] Includes taxes on capital gains. [3] Includes other taxes not shown separately. [4] Includes contributions of self-employed not shown separately. [5] Taxes on the production, sales, transfer, leasing, and delivery of goods and services and rendering of services. [6] Primary value-added and sales taxes. [7] For example, excise taxes on alcohol, tobacco, and gasoline. [8] Former West Germany (prior to unification).

Source: Organization for Economic Cooperation and Development, Paris, France, *Revenue Statistics of OECD Member Countries,* annual.

No. 1400. Employee-Employer Payroll Tax Rates for Social Security Programs—Selected Countries: 1981 to 1991

[In percent. Covers old-age, disability and survivors insurance, public health or sickness insurance, workers' compensation, unemployment insurance, and family allowance programs]

COUNTRY	ALL SOCIAL SECURITY PROGRAMS					OLD-AGE, DISABILITY, SURVIVORS INSUR.				
	1981, total	1985, total	1991			1981, total	1985, total	1991		
			Total	Employer	Employee			Total	Employer	Employee
United States ...	17.60	18.90	19.30	11.65	7.65	10.70	11.40	12.40	6.20	6.20
Austria	35.80	39.90	39.40	23.80	15.60	21.10	22.78	22.80	12.55	10.25
Belgium........	34.70	39.71	[1]61.75	49.68	12.07	15.11	16.36	16.36	8.86	7.50
Canada	[2]7.92	[2]9.24	10.00	5.45	4.55	3.60	3.60	4.60	2.30	2.30
France	47.55	51.23	54.41	35.90	[3]18.51	[4]13.00	[4]14.00	[4]17.00	8.20	8.80
Ireland.........	14.95	23.60	21.70	13.95	[5]7.75	12.00	20.7	18.70	12.20	[5]6.50
Italy	54.30	55.91	55.45	47.26	8.19	24.46	24.36	27.42	20.13	7.29
Japan	[6]21.41	[6]21.61	[6]24.44	12.44	12.00	[7]10.60	[7]10.60	[7]14.50	7.25	7.25
Luxembourg.....	34.25	34.30	38.10	20.90	17.20	16.00	16.00	16.00	8.00	8.00
Netherlands.....	54.85	51.18	43.08	12.14	[8]30.94	32.45	24.63	20.05	-	20.05
Sweden........	32.65	30.45	34.11	34.11	-	21.15	19.95	20.95	13.50	7.45
Switzerland	11.90	12.00	12.20	7.20	5.00	9.40	9.40	9.60	4.80	4.80
United Kingdom ..	21.45	19.45	21.45	[9]10.45	[10]11.00	(NA)	(NA)	(NA)	(NA)	(NA)
Germany [11] ...	34.80	34.30	36.16	18.76	17.40	18.50	18.70	17.70	8.85	8.85

- Represents zero.   NA Not available.   [1] Refers to blue collar workers in undertakings of 20 or more employees. [2] Excludes work-injury compensation program.   [3] Includes new 1.1 percent employee tax on all sources of income.   [4] Disability and survivors benefits financed through sickness insurance.   [5] Includes 1 percent tax to finance employment training for youth. [6] Total contribution rate for five social security programs, including contribution rates for pension and health insurance that are based on rates for male employees under Employee Pension Insurance and Employee Health Insurance programs.   [7] Rate refers to male employees and contributions for employee pension insurance only.   [8] In 1990 some employer contributions were shifted to the employee, however employer is required to make a special payment to the employee (11 percent in 1991) as compensation.   [9] Five to 10.45 percent.   [10] Two percent on first 46 pounds per week plus 9 percent of earnings between 46 and 350 pounds.   [11] Former West Germany (prior to unification).

Source: U.S. Social Security Administration, Office of International Policy, unpublished data.

No. 1401. Consumer Prices—Annual Percent Changes, by Country: 1987 to 1992

[See text, section 31, for general comments concerning the data. For additional qualifications of the data for individual countries, see source. Minus sign (-) indicates decrease]

COUNTRY	1987-1988	1988-1989	1989-1990	1990-1991	1991-1992	COUNTRY	1987-1988	1988-1989	1989-1990	1990-1991	1991-1992
United States ..	4.0	4.8	5.4	4.2	3.0	Italy	5.1	6.3	6.4	6.4	(NA)
Argentina	343.0	3,080	2,314	171.7	24.9	Japan........	0.7	2.3	3.1	3.3	1.7
Australia......	7.2	7.6	7.3	3.2	1.0	Malaysia......	2.6	2.8	2.6	4.4	(NA)
Austria	1.9	2.6	3.3	3.3	4.0	Mexico.......	114.2	20.0	26.7	22.7	15.5
Bangladesh....	9.3	10.0	8.1	7.2	(NA)	Netherlands ...	0.7	3.9	3.7	4.0	(NA)
Belgium	1.2	3.1	3.4	3.2	2.4	Norway.......	6.7	4.6	4.1	3.4	2.3
Bolivia	16.0	15.0	17.0	21.0	(NA)	Pakistan......	8.8	7.8	9.1	11.8	9.5
Brazil	682.3	1,287	2,938	440.8	(NA)	Peru.........	667.0	3,399	7,482	409.5	73.5
Canada	4.0	5.0	4.8	5.6	1.5	Philippines	8.8	12.2	14.1	18.7	8.9
Chile	14.7	17.0	26.0	21.8	15.4	Portugal......	9.6	12.6	13.4	11.4	8.9
Colombia	28.1	25.8	29.1	30.4	27.0	Romania......	2.8	0.7	4.2	(NA)	(NA)
Ecuador......	58.2	75.6	48.5	48.7	54.6	South Africa ...	12.8	14.7	14.4	15.3	13.9
Egypt........	17.7	21.3	16.8	19.8	13.6	South Korea ...	7.1	5.7	8.6	9.7	6.2
France	2.7	3.9	3.2	3.2	2.4	Spain........	4.8	6.8	6.7	5.9	5.8
Ghana	31.4	25.2	37.3	18.0	(NA)	Sweden	5.8	6.4	10.5	9.3	2.3
Greece	13.5	13.7	20.4	19.5	15.8	Switzerland	1.9	3.2	5.4	5.8	4.0
Guatemala	10.8	11.4	41.2	33.2	10.0	Thailand......	3.9	5.4	5.9	5.7	(NA)
India	9.4	6.2	9.0	13.9	11.8	Turkey.......	75.4	63.3	60.3	66.0	70.1
Indonesia	8.0	6.4	7.5	9.2	7.5	United Kingdom .	4.9	7.8	9.5	5.9	3.7
Iran	28.7	22.3	7.6	17.1	22.9	Venezuela.....	29.5	84.2	40.8	34.2	31.4
Israel........	16.3	20.2	17.2	19.0	11.9	Germany	1.3	2.8	2.7	3.5	4.0

NA Not available.
Source: International Monetary Fund, Washington, DC, *International Financial Statistics*, monthly.

No. 1402. Civilian Employment-Population Ratios, by Sex, and Females as Percent of Total Civilian Employment—Selected Countries: 1970 to 1991

[See headnote, table 1403]

COUNTRY	CIVILIAN EMPLOYMENT-POPULATION RATIOS [1]										CIVILIAN EMPLOYMENT, PERCENT FEMALE				
	Women					Men									
	1970	1980	1985	1990	1991	1970	1980	1985	1990	1991	1970	1980	1985	1990	1991
United States ..	40.8	47.7	50.4	54.4	53.7	76.2	72.0	70.9	71.9	70.2	37.7	42.4	44.1	45.4	45.6
Australia......	39.3	41.9	42.9	49.3	48.1	83.2	75.1	70.4	71.3	68.2	32.4	36.4	38.4	41.3	41.8
Canada	36.1	46.2	48.8	53.7	52.6	73.4	73.0	68.7	69.8	66.7	33.6	39.7	42.7	44.7	45.3
France	38.1	40.1	39.6	[2]40.3	[2]40.2	76.3	68.5	62.3	61.3	[2]60.9	36.0	39.5	41.4	42.3	[2]42.3
Germany [3] ...	(NA)	37.7	37.1	[2]40.3	(NA)	(NA)	70.9	66.4	[2]65.8	(NA)	(NA)	38.0	39.0	[2]40.7	41.2
Italy	25.0	27.9	27.8	[2]29.2	[2][4]29.6	71.9	66.0	62.5	[2]60.1	[2][4]60.4	27.7	31.7	32.8	[2][4]34.7	[2][4]34.9
Japan........	48.2	45.7	46.3	48.0	48.6	80.5	77.9	75.9	75.4	75.8	39.0	38.4	39.4	40.3	40.4
Netherlands ...	(NA)	31.0	33.4	(NA)	(NA)	(NA)	74.1	67.6	(NA)	(NA)	(NA)	30.2	34.0	(NA)	(NA)
Sweden	49.1	58.0	59.7	[2]62.7	[2]61.6	77.4	73.6	70.5	[2]71.7	[2]70.3	39.5	45.2	47.2	[2]47.8	[2]47.9
United Kingdom .	41.2	44.8	44.3	[2]49.8	[2]49.1	79.2	72.8	67.1	[2]70.1	[2]67.7	36.7	40.4	42.0	[2]43.6	[2]44.1

NA Not available.   [1] Civilian employment as a percent of the civilian working age population.   [2] Preliminary.   [3] Former West Germany (prior to unification).   [4] Break in series.

Source: U.S. Bureau of Labor Statistics, *Comparative Labor Force Statistics for Ten Countries, 1959-1991*, November 1992.

No. 1403. Civilian Labor Force, Employment, and Unemployment—Selected Countries: 1970 to 1991

[Data based on U.S. labor force definitions adopted in 1967 (see text, section 13) except that minimum age for population base varies as follows: United States, France, Sweden, and beginning 1980, United Kingdom, 16 years; Australia, Canada, Japan, Netherlands, Germany, and for 1970, United Kingdom, 15 years; Italy, 14 years]

YEAR	United States	Aus- tralia	Canada	France	Ger- many [1]	Italy	Japan	Nether- lands	Sweden	United King- dom
Civilian labor force (mil.):										
1970	82.8	5.5	8.4	20.8	26.2	19.7	50.7	(NA)	3.9	25.1
1980	106.9	6.7	11.6	22.8	27.3	21.1	55.7	5.9	4.3	26.5
1985	115.5	7.3	12.5	23.4	28.0	21.8	58.8	6.2	4.4	27.2
1990	124.8	8.5	13.7	23.9	[2]29.4	[2]22.7	63.0	6.8	4.6	[2]28.5
1991	125.3	8.5	13.8	24.1	[2]29.8	[2][3]22.9	64.3	[2]6.9	4.6	[2]28.4
Labor force participation rate: [4]										
1970	60.4	62.1	57.8	57.5	56.9	49.0	64.5	(NA)	64.0	61.1
1980	63.8	62.1	64.1	57.2	54.7	48.2	62.6	55.4	66.9	62.5
1985	64.8	61.6	65.3	56.3	54.7	47.2	62.3	55.5	66.9	62.2
1990	66.4	64.7	67.0	[2]55.2	[2]55.1	[2]47.3	62.6	56.8	[2]68.1	[2]63.9
1991	66.0	64.3	66.3	[2]55.3	[2]55.5	[2][3]47.7	63.2	[2]57.6	[2]67.6	[2]63.6
Civilian employment (mil.):										
1970	78.7	5.4	7.9	20.3	26.1	19.1	50.1	(NA)	3.8	24.3
1980	99.3	6.3	10.7	21.3	26.5	20.2	54.6	5.5	4.2	24.7
1985	107.2	6.7	11.2	20.9	26.0	20.5	57.3	5.6	4.3	24.2
1990	117.9	7.9	12.6	21.7	[2]28.0	[2]21.1	61.7	6.3	4.6	[2]26.6
1991	116.9	7.7	12.3	21.8	[2]28.5	[2][3]21.4	62.9	[2]6.4	4.5	[2]25.9
Employment-population ratio: [5]										
1970	57.4	61.1	54.5	56.0	56.6	47.4	63.8	(NA)	63.1	59.2
1980	59.2	58.3	59.3	53.5	53.1	46.1	61.3	52.1	65.6	58.1
1985	60.1	56.5	58.5	50.4	50.7	44.4	60.6	50.1	65.0	55.2
1990	62.7	60.2	61.5	[2]50.2	[2]52.3	[2]44.0	61.3	[2]52.6	67.0	[2]59.5
1991	61.6	58.1	59.5	[2]50.0	[2]53.0	[2][3]44.4	61.8	[2]53.5	65.8	[2]58.0
Unemployment rate:										
1970	4.9	1.6	5.7	2.5	0.5	3.2	1.2	(NA)	1.5	3.1
1980	7.1	6.1	7.5	6.4	2.8	4.4	2.0	6.0	2.0	7.0
1985	7.2	8.3	10.5	10.4	7.2	6.0	2.6	9.6	2.8	[1]11.2
1990	5.5	6.9	8.1	9.1	[2]5.0	[2]7.0	2.1	[2]7.5	1.5	[2]6.9
Under 25 years old	11.1	13.1	12.8	(NA)	4.7	[6]15.8	4.4	(NA)	3.5	[6]10.1
Teenagers [7]	15.5	16.9	14.2	(NA)	4.3	[6]27.3	6.7	(NA)	4.5	[6]11.5
20 to 24 years old	8.8	10.2	11.8	(NA)	4.9	[6]19.2	3.7	(NA)	3.0	[6]9.3
25 years old and over	4.4	5.1	7.0	(NA)	5.0	[6]4.3	1.8	(NA)	1.2	[6]5.9
1991	6.7	9.6	10.3	9.6	4.4	[2][3]6.9	2.1	[2]7.0	2.6	[2]8.8

NA Not available.   [1] Former West Germany (prior to unification).   [2] Preliminary.   [3] Break in series.   [4] Civilian labor force as a percent of the civilian working age population.   [5] Civilian employment as a percent of the civilian working age population.   [6] Italian data are for April; United Kingdom data are for April-June.   [7] 16 to 19 years old in the United States, France, Sweden, and the United Kingdom; 15 to 19 years old in Canada, Australia, and Japan; and 14 to 19 years old in Italy and Germany.

Source: U.S. Bureau of Labor Statistics, *Comparative Labor Force Statistics for Ten Countries, 1959-1991*, November 1992, and *Monthly Labor Review.*

No. 1404. Labor Force Participation Rates, by Sex and Age-Group—Selected Countries: 1980 and 1991

[Participation rates represent percent of population of each specified group in labor force]

COUNTRY AND SEX	15 TO 19 YEARS OLD		20 TO 24 YEARS OLD		25 TO 54 YEARS OLD		55 TO 64 YEARS OLD		65 YEARS AND OVER	
	1980	1991	1980	1991	1980	1991	1980	1991	1980	1991
United States: Male	[1]60.5	53.5	85.7	83.1	93.4	92.3	71.2	66.3	18.3	15.2
Female	[1]52.4	50.2	69.1	70.5	63.8	74.0	41.0	45.0	7.6	8.0
Canada: Male	57.9	55.8	86.3	81.5	94.8	92.5	76.2	62.5	14.8	11.3
Female	52.2	53.8	73.0	75.6	60.1	75.8	33.6	35.6	4.4	3.5
France: Male	25.7	12.3	80.2	62.3	96.4	95.3	68.5	44.5	7.5	3.5
Female	18.3	6.8	67.5	53.7	63.0	73.7	39.7	30.6	3.3	1.5
Italy: Male	33.3	23.2	72.5	69.5	[2]93.1	90.7	[3]39.6	34.9	9.0	5.2
Female	28.9	19.0	57.9	61.2	[2]39.9	49.9	[3]11.0	10.0	2.3	1.6
Japan: Male	17.4	19.1	69.6	72.8	97.0	97.2	85.4	84.5	41.0	38.0
Female	18.5	17.8	70.0	75.6	56.7	65.0	45.3	48.5	15.5	16.6
Sweden: Male	55.3	42.3	84.5	82.8	95.4	94.6	78.7	75.5	14.2	14.7
Female	55.8	47.1	81.6	77.5	82.9	90.5	55.3	66.9	3.7	5.1
United Kingdom: Male	73.6	73.6	86.0	85.7	95.4	93.4	81.6	67.5	10.3	8.4
Female	75.3	70.9	67.9	72.7	63.4	72.9	39.1	39.2	3.6	3.1

[1] Persons 16 to 19 years old.   [2] Persons 25 to 59 years old.   [3] Persons 60 to 64 years old.

Source: Organization for Economic Cooperation and Development, Paris, France, *Labour Force Statistics*, annual.

No. 1405. Poverty Rates in the Mid-1980's

[Percent of people with income below 40 percent of adjusted household median disposable income after taxes and transfers. (The U.S. official poverty line was approximately 41 percent of median adjusted income in both 1979 and 1986). Income: all forms of cash income (earnings, property income, and all cash transfers including the value of foodstamps in the United States and housing allowances in the United Kingdom and Sweden). Income is adjusted using the U.S. Poverty Line Equivalence Scale which weights a single person household at 1.0; two persons at 1.35; three persons at 1.70; four persons at 2.05; five persons at 2.40, etc. Adjusted income is then compared to the 40 percent poverty line. Data from Luxembourg Income Study, see text, section 31, and source for details]

ITEM	United States 1985	Canada 1987	Australia 1985	Sweden 1987	West Germany 1984	Nether-lands 1987	France 1984	United Kingdom 1986
All people.	13.3	7.0	6.7	4.3	2.8	3.4	4.5	5.2
Elderly, 65 years old and over	10.9	2.2	4.0	0.7	3.8	-	0.7	1.0
Adults, 18 to 64 years old	10.5	7.0	6.1	5.6	2.6	3.9	5.2	5.3
With children [1]	12.7	6.6	6.6	1.5	2.0	2.8	4.4	6.3
No children [1]	8.4	7.4	5.5	9.7	3.0	4.9	6.1	4.4
All children [1]	20.4	9.3	9.0	1.5	2.8	3.8	4.6	7.4

- Represents or rounds to zero.   [1] Children 17 years old and under.
Source: Timothy M. Smeeding, Syracuse, NY, "Why the U.S. Antipoverty System Doesn't Work Very Well," *Challenge*, January/February, 1992.

No. 1406. Child Poverty Rates

[Percent of children, 17 years old and under, in households with income below 40 percent of adjusted household median disposable income after taxes and transfers. See headnote, table 1405]

HOUSEHOLD TYPE	United States 1979	Canada 1981	Australia 1981	Sweden 1981	West Germany 1979	Nether-lands 1983	France 1979	United Kingdom 1986
All children [1]	14.7	10.2	8.6	2.1	1.3	4.0	4.7	3.3
One-parent households [2]	46.1	39.9	33.6	3.7	3.3	1.5	11.9	10.9
Two-parent households [3]	7.2	7.2	6.5	1.8	0.6	0.7	3.4	3.0
Extended households [4]	13.7	5.3	3.6	(NA)	3.5	18.6	8.0	0.5

HOUSEHOLD TYPE	United States 1985	Canada 1987	Australia 1985	Sweden 1987	West Germany [5] 1984	Nether-lands 1987	France 1984	United Kingdom 1986
All children [1]	20.4	9.3	9.0	1.5	2.8	3.8	4.6	7.4
One-parent households [2]	54.2	37.1	34.6	2.0	15.9	3.8	13.1	8.5
Two-parent households [3]	11.5	7.0	6.9	0.9	2.2	(NA)	(NA)	(NA)
Extended households [4]	22.4	4.9	4.4	(NA)	2.7	(NA)	(NA)	(NA)

NA Not available.   [1] All children regardless of living arrangements.   [2] Children living with one adult in the household. [3] Children living with two adults, a married couple, or two persons living as married and no other adults in the household. [4] Persons in all other living arrangements, including those with children over age 18.   [5] Not directly comparable with 1981 data.
Source: Timothy M. Smeeding, Syracuse, NY, "Cross National Perspectives on Trends in Child Poverty and the Effectiveness of Government Policies in Preventing Poverty Among Families with Children in the 1980's: The First Evidence from LIS."

No. 1407. Organization for Economic Cooperation and Development (OECD)—Index of Industrial Production: 1980 to 1991

[Industrial production index measures output in the manufacturing, mining, and electric and gas utilities industries. Minus sign (-) indicates decrease. For explanation of average annual percent change, see Guide to Tabular Presentation]

COUNTRY	INDEX (1985 = 100)							AVERAGE ANNUAL PERCENT CHANGE					
	1980	1986	1987	1988	1989	1990	1991	1980-1991	1986-1987	1987-1988	1988-1989	1989-1990	1990-1991
OECD, total	90.6	101.1	104.8	110.8	114.8	116.7	116.1	2.3	3.6	5.7	3.7	1.7	-0.5
United States	89.1	100.9	105.9	111.7	114.5	115.7	113.4	2.2	5.0	5.4	2.6	1.0	-2.0
Australia [1]	98.1	101.0	102.0	105.4	115.4	118.4	114.7	1.4	1.0	3.3	5.5	2.6	-3.1
Austria	92.2	101.1	102.1	106.6	112.9	121.2	123.4	2.6	1.0	4.4	6.0	7.4	1.8
Belgium [2]	96.0	100.8	103.0	109.7	113.4	117.7	115.3	1.7	2.1	6.5	3.4	3.8	-2.0
Canada [2]	86.2	99.3	104.1	109.8	109.1	104.6	100.3	1.4	4.9	5.5	-0.1	-4.6	-4.1
Finland	86.0	100.8	105.0	111.1	113.8	114.3	104.1	1.7	4.2	5.8	2.4	0.4	-8.9
France . . ., ...	101.9	100.9	102.8	107.6	112.0	114.1	114.3	1.0	1.9	4.6	4.1	1.9	0.2
Germany [3]	97.2	102.1	102.5	106.2	111.5	117.2	120.6	2.0	0.4	3.6	5.0	5.1	2.9
Greece	92.5	99.0	97.5	102.5	104.4	101.9	100.5	0.8	-1.5	5.2	1.8	-2.4	-1.4
Ireland	78.0	102.3	111.3	123.2	137.5	143.9	148.8	5.9	8.9	10.7	11.6	4.7	3.4
Italy	103.2	104.1	106.8	114.2	118.7	117.9	115.4	1.0	2.6	6.9	3.9	-0.7	-2.1
Japan	84.4	99.8	103.3	112.8	119.7	125.4	128.2	3.8	3.4	9.3	6.0	4.8	2.2
Luxembourg	82.3	101.9	101.2	110.0	118.6	118.0	118.6	3.3	-0.6	8.7	7.8	-0.5	0.5
Netherlands	94.6	100.2	101.3	101.3	106.5	109.0	113.2	1.6	1.1	-0.1	5.1	2.4	3.9
Norway	82.4	103.5	111.3	117.0	126.1	126.3	128.9	4.1	7.5	5.1	16.3	0.2	2.1
Portugal	84.9	107.3	112.0	116.2	124.1	135.2	135.3	4.2	4.4	3.8	6.7	8.9	0.1
Spain	96.7	103.1	107.8	111.1	116.1	116.2	115.1	1.6	4.6	3.1	4.5	0.1	-1.0
Sweden [4]	90.2	100.4	103.0	104.3	108.1	105.2	96.8	0.6	2.5	1.3	3.7	-2.7	-8.0
Switzerland [5]	96.8	103.8	105.0	111.6	114.9	118.0	119.0	1.9	1.2	6.2	3.0	2.6	0.9
United Kingdom	92.5	102.3	105.7	109.7	109.9	109.2	106.1	1.2	3.3	3.8	0.2	-0.6	-2.8

[1] Index of Real Gross Product in industry.   [2] Gross domestic product in industry at factor cost and 1986 prices.   [3] Former West Germany (prior to unification).   [4] Mining and manufacturing.   [5] Excludes mining and quarrying.
Source: Organization for Economic Cooperation and Development, Paris, France, *Main Economic Indicators, Historical Statistics, 1969-1988*, 1990; and *Main Economic Indicators*, monthly.

No. 1408. International Economic Composite Indexes—Average Annual Percent Change: 1980 to 1992

[The coincident index changes are for calendar years and the leading index changes are for years ending June 30 because they lead the coincident indexes by about 6 months, on average. The G-7 countries are United States, Canada, France, Germany, Italy, United Kingdom, and Japan. Average annual percent changes derived from indexes with base 1980=100. Minus sign (-) indicates decrease]

COUNTRIES	1980-1981	1981-1982	1982-1983	1983-1984	1984-1985	1985-1986	1986-1987	1987-1988	1988-1989	1989-1990	1990-1991	1991-1992
LEADING INDEX												
Total, 11 countries	-0.9	-0.8	1.6	9.2	2.9	2.1	4.7	7.8	5.0	2.2	-1.6	0.7
10 countries, excluding U.S.	-2.1	0.6	0.7	5.9	4.5	1.7	5.3	8.0	5.9	3.1	-1.1	-2.1
G-7 countries	-1.0	-0.9	1.6	9.2	2.8	1.9	4.5	7.6	4.9	2.2	-1.7	0.5
North America	1.0	-3.2	2.7	14.0	1.1	2.6	3.8	7.1	3.6	0.6	-2.7	4.6
United States	0.9	-2.9	2.9	14.2	0.9	2.5	3.9	7.3	3.8	0.9	-2.4	4.8
Canada	1.3	-6.3	0.5	11.3	4.3	3.0	2.7	6.1	1.0	-2.5	-5.1	1.5
4 European countries.	-1.4	0.7	1.2	4.0	2.3	2.4	3.7	3.1	4.2	1.3	0.6	1.0
France.	-0.7	0.9	0.7	4.0	2.5	2.1	6.1	5.1	6.2	0.3	1.4	2.7
Germany [1]	-2.9	-0.9	1.9	6.0	2.0	2.9	1.6	3.5	5.2	4.4	3.0	0.5
Italy.	5.1	-0.3	-0.6	1.3	2.8	4.6	4.9	-	1.6	-0.4	-1.8	-0.5
United Kingdom.	-4.3	3.6	2.1	3.4	2.0	0.5	3.4	2.1	2.5	-1.1	-2.0	0.2
5 Pacific region countries	-3.7	1.7	-0.2	8.2	7.8	0.8	7.8	15.9	8.6	6.3	-2.6	-6.4
Australia.	2.2	-4.1	-3.9	9.8	6.8	2.9	3.3	7.1	4.9	-1.9	-3.3	1.3
China: Taiwan	5.7	5.0	8.1	11.8	6.4	8.2	13.6	14.5	12.3	7.5	1.3	8.0
Japan	-5.2	2.0	-0.4	7.8	8.3	-0.4	7.6	17.6	8.9	7.3	-3.1	-8.7
South Korea	5.0	6.8	8.0	9.3	4.6	9.7	16.7	12.8	8.9	4.1	3.8	4.8
New Zealand	0.5	2.9	-1.7	6.4	5.3	-1.1	2.8	-1.5	0.9	1.5	-3.1	2.5
COINCIDENT INDEX												
Total, 11 countries	0.6	-2.0	1.6	6.0	3.7	3.2	4.1	6.0	4.8	3.3	-0.1	0.5
10 countries, excluding U.S.	0.6	0.5	1.2	3.6	3.9	3.5	4.4	6.9	6.4	5.6	2.5	0.7
G-7 countries	0.4	-2.1	1.7	5.8	3.6	3.0	3.9	5.9	4.7	3.4	-0.1	0.4
North America	0.8	-5.6	2.4	9.3	3.6	2.6	3.8	4.8	2.4	-0.4	-4.4	0.3
United States	0.5	-5.6	2.3	9.7	3.5	2.5	3.7	4.7	2.4	-0.4	-4.5	0.3
Canada	3.8	-4.8	2.0	6.3	5.2	3.5	4.9	5.9	2.6	0.1	-3.8	0.3
4 European countries.	-1.7	-0.3	0.6	2.0	3.0	3.5	3.8	5.9	5.9	5.7	1.7	0.1
France.	0.3	2.9	2.0	0.4	1.5	3.9	5.0	8.0	8.6	7.2	2.4	1.7
Germany [1]	-0.9	-2.4	-0.5	2.7	3.5	4.3	3.0	3.6	5.4	7.0	5.0	0.1
Italy.	-1.4	-0.3	-1.1	3.5	2.4	1.8	1.4	5.3	2.1	4.7	2.0	0.1
United Kingdom.	-5.4	-0.8	1.6	2.2	4.2	3.3	5.0	7.3	5.8	2.5	-4.1	-1.8
5 Pacific region countries	3.7	2.7	1.9	5.3	5.1	3.7	5.1	8.3	7.4	6.6	4.4	1.4
Australia.	6.0	-2.5	-6.8	9.4	7.5	5.1	3.7	8.3	10.2	0.6	-6.9	-0.4
China: Taiwan	5.1	2.9	7.3	12.1	4.9	10.8	11.6	6.0	6.1	1.7	4.3	5.5
Japan	3.3	3.2	2.3	4.6	4.7	2.7	4.6	8.4	7.3	7.4	5.6	1.3
South Korea	6.7	6.3	11.0	9.0	5.6	11.7	13.5	10.6	6.2	8.8	7.8	4.2
New Zealand	2.4	0.9	0.8	3.6	2.1	1.4	1.4	-1.0	-0.4	1.3	-0.7	1.5

- Represents or rounds to zero.   [1] Former West Germany (prior to unification).
Source: Center for International Business Cycle Research, Columbia Business School, New York, NY, *International Economic Outlook*, monthly.

No. 1409. Patents, Top Countries: 1991

[Includes only U.S. patents granted to residents of areas outside of the United States and its territories]

TOP COUNTRIES	Total [1]	Inventions	Designs	TOP COUNTRIES	Total [1]	Inventions	Designs
Total, foreign country residents	**49,042**	**45,338**	**3,496**	Netherlands	1,075	992	55
Japan	22,391	21,029	1,307	Sweden	831	716	112
Germany	7,984	7,680	257	Australia	571	463	98
France.	3,249	3,030	193	South Korea	446	402	44
United Kingdom.	3,050	2,801	238	Austria.	388	359	29
Canada	2,303	2,036	260	Belgium	366	324	40
Switzerland.	1,448	1,335	110	Finland	343	331	12
Italy.	1,388	1,209	176	Israel.	326	307	19
China: Taiwan.	1,094	904	190	Denmark	285	210	72
				Other countries	1,504	1,210	284

[1] Includes patents for botanical plants and reissues, not shown separately.
Source: U.S. Patent and Trademark Office, Technology Assessment and Forecast Data Base.

No. 1410. World's 500 Largest Industrial Corporations: 1991

[Sales as of December 31, 1991, assets as of company's fiscal year-end. Companies must have derived more than 50 percent of their sales from manufacturing and/or mining. Sales of consolidated subsidiaries are included and exclude excise taxes collected by manufacturers. Profits are shown after taxes and extraordinary credits or charges]

COUNTRY	Number of companies	Sales ($bil.)	Profits ($bil.)	Assets ($bil.)	Employees (1,000)	COUNTRY	Number of companies	Sales ($bil.)	Profits ($bil.)	Assets ($bil.)	Employees (1,000)
Australia. . . .	9	48	15	671	235	Japan	119	1,097	258	11,827	3,458
Canada	9	49	12	685	289	Netherlands .	7	58	12	576	405
Finland	5	28	-10	338	95	South Korea .	13	143	14	1,185	547
France.	32	337	75	4,376	1,866	Sweden	14	93	6	1,052	615
Germany . . .	33	473	91	3,998	3,017	Switzerland. .	10	117	53	1,306	754
India	6	27	7	328	966	U.K.	45	477	222	4,831	2,587
Italy.	7	186	7	1,235	851	U.S.	157	1,785	435	20,148	9,045

Source: Time Warner, New York, NY, *The Fortune Directories*, (copyright).

No. 1411. Indexes of Hourly Compensation Costs for Production Workers in Manufacturing—Selected Countries: 1980 to 1992

[United States=100. Compensation costs include pay for time worked, other direct pay, employer expenditures for legally required insurance programs and contractual and private benefit plans, and for some countries, other labor taxes. Data adjusted for exchange rates. Area averages are trade-weighted to account for differences in countries' relative importance to U.S. trade in manufactured goods. The trade weights used are the sum of U.S. imports of manufactured products for consumption (customs value) and U.S. domestic exports of manufactured products (f.a.s. value) in 1986; see source for detail

AREA OR COUNTRY	1980	1985	1989	1990	1991	1992	AREA OR COUNTRY	1980	1985	1989	1990	1991	1992
United States	100	100	100	100	100	100	Austria [6]	87	56	95	114	111	122
Total [1]	71	55	83	90	92	96	Belgium.	133	69	108	129	127	136
OECD [2]	84	65	97	105	107	111	Denmark.	110	62	101	120	117	124
Europe [3]	103	63	102	119	118	126	Finland [7]	83	63	116	139	132	116
Asian newly industrial-							France . [6] [8]	91	58	88	102	98	104
izing economies [4] . . .	12	12	23	25	27	30	Germany [6] [8].	125	74	124	147	145	160
Canada	88	84	104	107	110	105	Greece	38	28	38	45	44	(NA)
Mexico	22	12	10	11	13	15	Ireland	60	46	67	79	77	82
Australia	85	63	86	86	86	80	Italy	83	59	101	117	117	120
Hong Kong [5]	15	13	19	21	23	24	Luxembourg.	121	59	95	110	(NA)	(NA)
Israel	38	31	54	57	56	(NA)	Netherlands.	122	67	105	123	118	128
Japan	56	49	87	85	93	100	Norway	117	80	128	144	139	143
South Korea.	10	10	23	26	28	30	Portugal	21	12	20	25	27	31
New Zealand	54	34	54	56	54	49	Spain	60	36	62	76	78	83
Singapore	15	19	22	25	28	31	Sweden.	127	74	122	140	142	150
Sri Lanka.	2	2	2	2	(NA)	(NA)	Switzerland	112	74	117	140	139	144
China: Taiwan	10	12	25	26	28	32	United Kingdom	77	48	74	85	88	91

NA Not available. [1] The 25 foreign economies for which 1992 data are available. [2] Canada, Australia, Japan, New Zealand, and the 16 European countries for which 1992 data are available. [3] The 16 European countries for which 1992 data are available. [4] Hong Kong, South Korea, Singapore, and China: Taiwan. [5] Average of selected manufacturing industries. [6] Excludes workers in establishments considered handicraft manufactures (including all printing and publishing and miscellaneous manufacturing in Austria). [7] Includes workers in mining and electrical power plants. [8] Former West Germany (prior to unification).

Source: Bureau of Labor Statistics, *Report 844*, April 1993.

No. 1412. Structure of Manufacturing Industry for Selected Countries

[In percent. Contribution of each industry group to total manufacturing production. Based on International Standard Industrial Classification; see text, section 31, and source. Numbers in parentheses refer to ISIC codes]

COUNTRY	Food [1] (3100)	Textile [2] (3200)	Wood [3] (3300)	Paper [4] (3400)	Chemical [5] (3500)	Nonmetal [6] (3600)	Basic metal [7] (3700)	Machinery [8] (3800)	Other (3900)
United States: 1980	14.5	5.6	2.8	7.7	22.2	2.5	6.8	36.6	1.3
1985.	14.1	5.3	2.9	9.1	19.9	2.4	4.5	40.8	1.1
1988.	14.1	5.3	3.1	9.8	18.4	2.5	5.1	40.5	1.2
1989.	14.0	5.1	3.1	9.9	19.0	2.4	5.0	40.2	1.2
1990.	14.5	4.9	3.1	9.9	19.9	2.3	4.7	39.5	1.2
Japan: 1980	11.3	5.4	3.6	6.2	19.3	3.9	11.4	37.7	1.2
1985.	11.0	4.9	2.4	6.1	16.7	3.3	8.5	45.7	1.4
1988.	11.1	4.7	2.6	6.7	14.3	3.5	7.4	48.4	1.4
1989.	10.6	4.4	2.5	6.7	14.1	3.4	7.5	49.3	1.4
1990.	10.2	4.2	2.5	6.6	14.2	3.3	7.4	50.2	1.4
France: 1980.	17.0	6.9	3.1	5.6	21.4	3.5	8.4	32.6	1.3
1985.	17.6	6.9	2.5	6.5	21.6	3.0	7.3	33.3	1.3
1988.	16.8	6.4	2.8	7.3	18.4	3.4	7.0	36.6	1.3
1989.	16.5	6.1	2.8	7.4	18.4	3.3	7.2	37.2	1.3
1990.	16.5	5.9	2.8	7.4	18.4	3.4	6.5	37.9	1.3
Italy: 1980.	12.2	11.4	3.2	4.6	19.7	5.6	10.1	32.5	0.8
1985.	12.6	13.5	2.9	5.4	22.5	4.8	9.6	27.8	0.8
1986.	12.7	13.8	2.9	5.2	21.4	4.7	9.0	29.8	0.6
1987.	12.7	14.0	3.4	5.7	20.1	5.1	8.6	29.8	0.6
1988.	12.2	13.4	3.2	5.7	20.1	4.9	8.1	31.8	0.7
Portugal: 1980	18.2	18.9	6.0	6.3	24.5	6.1	2.2	17.6	0.2
1985.	19.5	18.5	3.6	6.8	28.5	4.8	3.3	15.0	0.2
1986.	20.7	20.4	3.9	7.3	24.1	5.2	2.9	15.3	0.2
1987.	20.4	20.8	4.2	8.0	22.0	5.5	2.9	15.9	0.2
Sweden: 1980	13.3	2.6	8.1	13.5	15.3	2.6	8.5	35.8	0.4
1985.	13.9	2.1	6.4	13.9	15.5	2.1	7.9	37.9	0.3
1987.	13.6	2.0	6.8	15.3	13.1	2.3	7.1	39.4	0.3
1988.	13.5	1.9	7.0	15.5	12.5	2.3	8.0	39.1	0.3
1989.	13.5	1.7	7.2	15.4	12.6	2.3	8.3	38.8	0.3
United Kingdom: 1980. . .	18.6	5.9	2.9	6.8	20.6	3.6	6.8	33.9	0.9
1985.	18.7	5.6	2.7	7.5	21.1	3.5	5.8	34.2	0.9
1988.	17.4	5.4	3.2	8.3	19.6	3.9	5.7	35.5	1.0
1989.	16.9	5.0	3.1	8.4	19.8	4.0	5.6	36.3	1.0
1990.	15.8	5.0	3.1	8.7	18.9	3.9	5.4	38.2	1.0
West Germany: 1980 . . .	12.4	5.4	3.4	4.1	22.9	3.4	7.6	40.3	0.5
1985.	12.2	4.8	2.4	4.2	23.7	2.7	6.6	43.1	0.4
1988.	11.7	4.6	2.7	4.4	20.4	2.9	6.1	46.7	0.5
1989.	11.5	4.4	2.7	4.4	20.6	2.8	6.3	46.9	0.5
1990.	11.7	4.4	2.8	(NA)	20.8	2.8	5.5	47.5	0.5

[1] Manufacture of food, beverages, and tobacco. [2] Textile, apparel, and leather. [3] Wood products and furniture. [4] Paper, paper products, and printing. [5] Chemical products, petroleum, coal, rubber, and plastic products. [6] Nonmetallic mineral products, except petroleum and coal products. [7] Basic metal industries, including iron, steel, and nonferrous metal. [8] Fabricated metal products, machinery and equipment.

Source: Organization for Economic Cooperation and Development, Paris, France, *OECD Industrial Structure Statistics*, 1988; and unpublished data.

No. 1413. Selected Indexes of Manufacturing Activity—Selected Countries: 1970 to 1991

[1982=100. Data relate to all employed persons in the United States and Canada; all employees in other countries. Minus sign (-) indicates decrease. For explanation of average annual percent change, see Guide to Tabular Presentation]

INDEX AND YEAR	United States	Bel- gium	Cana- da	Den- mark	France	Ger- many [1]	Italy	Japan	Neth- erlands	Swe- den	United King- dom
Output per hour:											
1970	(NA)	44.3	76.9	57.2	58.5	67.0	54.6	52.0	52.9	68.9	70.9
1980	94.4	87.5	99.9	98.0	90.6	98.4	95.5	92.1	93.9	96.2	89.9
1985	108.0	117.2	119.8	105.0	108.8	112.9	122.3	112.0	118.7	112.4	118.2
1989	122.5	131.2	119.0	105.6	127.9	119.0	135.1	135.2	126.3	120.0	143.5
1990	125.7	133.9	120.1	106.2	129.4	122.9	140.6	144.2	126.6	121.0	146.0
1991	128.1	137.0	121.7	109.3	129.1	125.4	145.2	146.5	128.6	122.4	149.8
Average annual percent change:											
1979-85	1.9	6.1	2.4	2.1	3.2	2.0	5.0	3.9	4.2	2.9	4.6
1985-91	2.9	2.6	0.3	0.7	2.9	1.8	2.9	4.6	1.3	1.4	4.0
1990-91	1.9	2.3	1.3	3.0	-0.2	2.0	3.2	1.6	1.6	1.2	2.6
Compensation per hour, national currency basis: [2]											
1970	(NA)	23.2	28.7	22.3	17.8	34.5	11.6	25.0	27.8	24.4	14.9
1980	83.1	86.3	48.6	83.4	72.8	89.2	70.2	89.0	88.5	84.4	79.8
1985	111.0	121.6	116.8	120.6	130.4	116.3	150.9	110.1	111.5	130.5	124.2
1989	127.3	138.1	137.4	148.3	153.2	138.2	191.1	128.2	118.1	177.4	162.8
1990	133.8	146.3	146.3	156.1	159.3	148.0	211.9	138.6	122.7	193.7	180.9
1991	140.6	154.6	156.0	163.0	166.2	158.3	232.4	147.1	127.6	206.9	197.1
Average annual percent change:											
1979-85	6.9	7.7	8.7	8.1	12.9	5.9	16.7	4.7	4.8	9.4	11.2
1985-91	4.0	4.1	4.9	5.1	4.1	5.3	7.5	4.9	2.3	8.0	8.0
1990-91	5.1	5.7	6.6	4.4	4.3	7.0	9.7	6.1	4.0	6.8	9.0
Real hourly compensation: [2][3]											
1970	(NA)	55.1	77.4	70.1	57.3	62.6	60.3	63.6	63.9	72.6	65.9
1980	97.4	101.0	97.9	102.6	92.3	99.9	96.9	96.0	100.0	103.0	97.1
1985	99.5	103.3	101.8	101.4	104.5	107.9	109.3	103.6	102.7	101.6	106.4
1989	99.1	107.2	100.8	105.5	109.1	123.3	111.4	116.3	107.1	113.5	114.6
1990	98.8	109.8	102.5	108.2	109.8	128.6	116.5	122.0	108.7	111.4	116.3
1991	99.6	112.2	103.4	110.4	111.1	132.9	119.9	125.3	108.8	109.3	119.7
Average annual percent change:											
1979-85	0.1	0.7	0.7	-0.5	2.4	1.8	1.5	1.1	0.3	-0.6	2.1
1985-91	-	1.7	0.3	1.4	1.0	3.5	1.6	3.2	1.0	1.2	2.0
1990-91	0.8	2.3	0.9	2.0	1.2	3.3	3.0	2.7	0.1	-1.8	2.9
Unit labor costs, national currency:											
1970	(NA)	52.2	37.3	39.0	30.4	51.4	21.3	48.0	52.7	35.4	21.0
1980	88.1	98.7	78.7	85.1	80.3	90.6	73.5	96.7	94.2	87.8	88.7
1985	102.8	103.8	97.6	114.9	119.9	103.0	123.4	98.4	93.9	116.1	105.1
1989	103.9	105.3	115.4	140.4	119.8	116.1	141.4	94.8	93.5	147.8	113.5
1990	106.4	109.2	121.8	146.9	123.1	120.3	150.7	96.1	96.9	160.1	123.9
1991	109.8	112.9	128.2	149.0	128.8	126.3	160.0	100.4	99.2	169.0	131.6
Average annual percent change:											
1979-85	4.9	1.5	6.1	5.9	9.4	3.8	11.1	0.7	0.6	6.3	6.3
1985-91	1.1	1.4	4.7	4.4	1.2	3.4	4.4	0.3	0.9	6.5	3.8
1990-91	3.2	3.3	5.2	1.4	4.6	4.9	6.2	4.4	2.4	5.5	6.2
Unit labor costs, U.S. dollar basis: [4]											
1970	(NA)	48.2	44.1	43.4	36.2	34.2	46.0	33.4	38.9	42.8	28.7
1980	88.1	154.7	83.1	126.2	125.2	121.2	116.3	106.7	126.8	130.5	118.1
1985	102.8	80.1	88.2	90.4	87.8	85.0	87.5	102.7	75.6	84.8	78.0
1989	103.9	122.3	120.3	160.1	123.6	149.9	139.5	171.1	117.7	143.9	106.3
1990	106.4	149.6	128.8	198.1	148.7	180.8	170.2	165.1	142.1	169.9	126.5
1991	109.8	151.2	138.1	194.2	150.0	184.6	174.6	185.8	141.6	175.5	133.0
Average annual percent change:											
1979-85	4.9	-9.7	3.4	-5.8	-3.4	-4.0	-3.3	-0.8	-7.5	-5.3	-2.0
1985-91	1.1	11.2	7.8	13.6	9.3	13.8	12.2	10.4	11.0	12.9	9.3
1990-91	3.2	1.0	7.1	-2.0	0.9	2.1	2.5	12.5	-0.3	3.3	5.2
Employment:											
1970	(NA)	137.7	96.3	119.6	107.3	115.2	97.6	99.9	135.4	114.8	141.8
1980	107.8	109.9	108.4	103.9	104.9	104.9	107.8	98.5	108.1	107.7	117.5
1985	102.3	95.1	103.6	112.4	92.0	97.4	89.8	106.9	96.5	101.3	91.7
1989	103.5	92.6	115.4	111.5	86.8	100.5	89.8	109.5	101.6	105.3	89.0
1990	102.0	92.9	109.9	112.1	87.4	103.4	89.9	112.0	103.7	102.3	87.9
1991	98.5	92.0	101.4	109.5	86.2	105.1	87.7	116.3	103.7	95.6	82.8
Average annual percent change:											
1979-85	-1.4	-2.7	-0.8	1.0	-2.4	-1.1	-2.9	1.7	-2.1	-1.0	-4.9
1985-91	-0.6	-0.5	-0.3	-0.4	-1.1	1.3	-0.4	1.4	1.2	-0.9	-1.7
1990-91	-3.4	-0.9	-7.7	-2.3	-1.3	1.7	-2.5	3.9	-	-6.5	-5.8
Aggregate hours:											
1970	(NA)	159.9	102.1	132.3	124.1	129.7	107.0	105.9	152.0	132.1	154.9
1980	109.9	110.1	110.8	103.7	111.0	106.3	108.0	99.3	108.1	106.4	118.1
1985	107.0	93.5	106.0	109.8	91.1	95.6	89.0	108.2	93.6	103.1	92.8
1989	109.8	93.0	118.6	107.6	86.4	95.9	96.0	110.4	97.8	104.3	90.8
1990	107.4	94.4	111.5	106.9	86.9	97.1	93.7	111.1	99.9	101.2	88.9
1991	103.0	91.9	102.8	104.7	85.5	97.7	90.4	112.9	99.7	94.7	82.1
Average annual percent change:											
1979-85	-1.2	-3.3	-0.9	0.8	-3.5	-1.8	-3.1	1.8	-2.5	-0.7	-5.3
1985-91	-0.6	-0.3	-0.5	-0.8	-1.0	0.4	0.3	0.7	1.1	-1.4	-2.0
1990-91	-4.1	-2.6	-7.8	-2.0	-1.5	0.7	-3.6	1.6	-0.2	-6.5	-7.6

- Represents or rounds to zero.   NA Not available.   [1] Former West Germany (prior to unification).   [2] Compensation includes, but real hourly compensation excludes, adjustments for payroll and employment taxes that are not compensation to employees, but are labor costs to employers.   [3] Index of hourly compensation divided by the index of consumer prices to adjust for changes in purchasing power.   [4] Indexes in national currency adjusted for changes in prevailing exchange rates.

Source: Bureau of Labor Statistics, Office of Productivity and Technology, unpublished data.

No. 1414. Crude Steel Production: 1980 to 1990

[In million metric tons. Data cover both ingots and steel for castings and excludes wrought (puddled) iron]

COUNTRY	1980	1982	1983	1984	1985	1986	1987	1988	1989	1990
World	718.2	645.3	662.6	715.9	715.6	708.8	729.3	770.6	777.3	762.0
United States [1]	101.5	67.7	76.8	83.9	80.1	74.0	80.9	91.8	[2]88.9	[2]88.6
Argentina	2.6	2.8	2.8	2.5	2.8	3.1	3.5	3.5	[2]3.9	[2]3.6
Australia [3]	7.9	7.3	5.4	4.6	6.3	6.8	6.2	6.1	6.7	6.7
Austria	4.6	4.3	4.4	4.9	4.7	4.3	4.3	4.4	4.9	[2]4.5
Belgium	12.3	10.1	10.3	11.4	10.8	9.8	9.8	11.3	11.0	11.5
Brazil	15.3	13.0	14.7	18.4	20.5	21.2	22.2	24.7	25.1	20.5
Bulgaria	2.6	2.6	2.8	2.9	2.9	3.0	3.0	2.9	2.9	2.2
Canada	15.9	11.9	12.8	14.7	13.5	14.1	14.7	14.8	[2]15.0	[2]12.2
China: Mainland	39.0	38.8	41.9	45.6	49.5	54.8	58.9	62.1	64.2	68.9
Czechoslovakia	15.2	15.0	15.0	14.8	15.0	15.1	15.4	15.4	15.5	14.9
East Germany (former)	7.3	7.2	7.2	7.6	7.9	8.0	8.2	8.1	7.8	(NA)
Finland	2.5	2.4	2.4	2.6	2.5	2.6	2.7	2.8	2.9	2.9
France	23.2	18.4	17.6	19.0	18.8	17.9	17.7	19.1	19.5	19.3
Greece	1.1	0.9	0.9	0.9	1.0	1.0	0.9	1.0	1.0	1.0
Hungary	3.8	3.6	3.5	3.6	3.5	3.6	3.5	3.5	3.3	2.9
India	9.4	10.9	10.1	10.3	11.2	11.4	12.3	13.0	12.9	13.0
Indonesia [4]	0.4	0.5	0.8	1.0	1.2	1.5	1.5	[2]2.0	[2]2.0	[2]2.1
Italy	26.5	24.0	21.8	24.1	23.9	22.9	22.9	23.9	25.6	[2]25.5
Japan	111.4	99.5	97.2	105.6	105.3	98.3	98.5	105.7	107.9	110.3
Luxembourg	4.6	3.5	3.3	4.0	3.9	3.7	3.3	3.7	3.7	3.6
Mexico	7.0	6.9	6.7	7.3	7.2	7.0	7.2	7.3	7.3	8.2
Netherlands [2,4]	5.3	4.3	4.5	5.7	5.5	5.3	5.1	5.5	5.7	5.4
North Korea [2,4]	5.8	5.8	6.1	6.5	6.5	6.5	6.5	8.0	8.0	8.0
Poland	18.6	14.1	16.2	15.2	15.4	16.3	16.3	15.9	13.1	12.2
Romania	10.7	10.1	9.3	10.1	9.7	9.7	9.9	9.8	14.4	9.8
South Africa	9.1	8.3	7.2	7.8	8.6	8.1	9.0	[4]9.0	[4]9.7	[4]8.9
South Korea	14.4	16.6	16.4	17.8	16.8	18.8	19.5	21.3	23.7	24.5
Soviet Union	147.9	147.2	152.5	154.2	154.7	160.6	161.9	163.0	160.1	154.4
Spain	12.6	13.4	13.3	13.4	14.7	[2]12.1	[2]11.6	[2]11.7	[2]12.6	[2]12.8
Sweden	4.2	3.9	4.2	4.7	4.9	4.7	4.7	4.8	4.7	[2]4.5
Turkey	1.7	2.0	3.6	4.1	4.7	6.0	7.0	8.0	7.9	9.4
United Kingdom	11.3	13.7	15.0	15.1	15.7	14.7	17.4	19.0	18.7	17.8
Venezuela	1.8	2.2	2.3	2.8	3.1	3.4	3.7	3.6	3.4	3.1
West Germany (former)	43.8	35.9	35.7	39.4	40.5	37.1	36.2	41.0	41.1	38.4
Yugoslavia	3.6	3.9	4.1	4.2	4.5	4.5	4.5	4.4	4.5	3.6

[2] NA Not available. [1] Excludes steel for castings made in foundries operated by companies not producing ingots. [2] Estimated. [3] For year ending June 30. [4] Source: U.S. Bureau of Mines.

Source: Except as noted, Statistical Office of the United Nations, New York, NY, *Statistical Yearbook*, and *Industrial Statistics Yearbook*, vol. II, annuals, (copyright).

No. 1415. World Production of Major Mineral Commodities, by Selected Commodity: 1985 to 1990

COUNTRY	Unit	1985	1988	1989, prel.	1990, est.	Leading producers, 1990
MINERAL FUELS [1]						
Coal	Mil. metric tons	4,353	4,652	4,785	4,750	China, U.S., Soviet Union
Dry natural gas	Tril. cu. ft.	62.0	69.6	72.0	73.2	Soviet Union, U.S., Canada
Natural gas plant liquids [2]	Mil. barrels [3]	1,437	1,663	1,676	1,728	U.S., Saudi Arabia, Soviet Union
Petroleum, crude	Mil. barrels [3]	19,703	21,412	21,817	22,072	Soviet Union, U.S., Saudi Arabia
Petroleum, refined	Mil. barrels [3]	21,114	22,626	22,812	23,791	U.S., Soviet Union, Japan
NONMETALLIC MINERALS						
Cement, hydraulic	Mil. metric tons	960	1,077	1,148	1,153	China, Soviet Union, Japan
Diamond, gem and industrial	1,000 carats	66,018	96,471	97,462	101,566	Australia, Zaire, Botswana
Nitrogen in ammonia	Mil. metric tons	91.0	99.3	99.1	97.6	Soviet Union, China, U.S.
Phosphate rock	Mil. metric tons	149	161	160	154	U.S., Soviet Union, Morocco
Potash, marketable	Mil. metric tons	29.2	31.8	29.6	27.7	Soviet Union, Canada
Salt	Mil. metric tons	173	183	190	182	U.S., China, Soviet Union
Sulfur, elemental basis	Mil. metric tons	53.8	59.1	59.5	58.2	U.S., Soviet Union, Canada
METALS						
Aluminum [4]	Mil. metric tons	15.4	17.5	18.2	18.0	U.S., Soviet Union, Canada
Bauxite, gross weight	Mil. metric tons	84.2	97.0	104.1	109.6	Australia, Guinea, Jamaica
Chromite, gross weight [2]	1,000 metric tons	10,945	12,890	14,190	12,848	South Africa, Soviet Union, India
Copper, metal content [5]	1,000 metric tons	7,988	8,323	8,667	8,693	Chile, U.S., Canada
Gold, metal content	Metric tons	1,532	1,848	2,023	2,127	South Africa, Soviet Union, U.S.
Iron ore, gross weight [6]	Mil. metric tons	861	926	953	929	Soviet Union, Brazil, China
Lead, metal content [5]	1,000 metric tons	3,431	3,359	3,285	3,390	Australia, U.S., Soviet Union
Manganese ore, gross weight	Mil. metric tons	25.4	25.0	26.6	25.4	Soviet Union, South Africa, China
Nickel, metal content [5]	1,000 metric tons	813	918	970	937	Soviet Union, Canada, New Caledonia
Steel, crude	Mil. metric tons	718	780	786	771	Soviet Union, Japan, U.S.
Tin, metal content [5]	1,000 metric tons	181	205	234	219	China, Brazil, Indonesia
Zinc, metal content [5]	1,000 metric tons	6,758	6,980	7,100	7,320	Canada, Australia, Soviet Union

[1] Source: Energy Information Administration, *International Energy Annual*. [2] Excludes China: Mainland. [3] 42-gallon barrels. [4] Unalloyed ingot metal. [5] Mine output. [6] Includes iron ore concentrates and iron ore agglomerates.

Source: Except as noted, U.S. Bureau of Mines, *Minerals Yearbook*.

No. 1416. Energy Consumption and Production, by Country: 1980 and 1990

[See text, section 31, for general comments about the data. For additional data qualifications for countries, see source]

| COUNTRY | ENERGY CONSUMED [1] (coal equiv.) | | | | ELECTRIC ENERGY PRODUCTION [2] (bil. kWh) | | CRUDE PETROLEUM PRODUCTION [3] (mil. metric tons) | | COAL PRODUCTION [4] (mil. metric tons) | |
| | Total (mil. metric tons) | | Per capita (kilograms) | | | | | | | |
	1980	1990	1980	1990	1980	1990	1980	1990	1980	1990
World, total	8,593	10,412	1,932	1,955	8,237	11,771	2,982	3,019	2,728	3,561
United States	2,364.4	2,572.3	10,381	10,321	[5]2,354.4	[5]3,040.9	424.2	371.0	710.4	853.6
Algeria	24.8	24.7	1,322	990	7.1	16.1	47.4	37.0	(Z)	[6](Z)
Argentina	49.1	59.0	1,739	1,825	39.7	50.9	25.3	24.8	0.4	0.3
Austria	31.2	31.8	4,138	4,196	41.6	50.4	1.5	1.1	-	-
Bahrain	4.4	8.0	12,615	15,595	1.7	3.5	2.4	2.1	(NA)	(NA)
Bangladesh [7]	4.0	8.5	45	73	2.7	8.1	(Z)	[6](Z)	(X)	(X)
Belgium	62.3	56.1	6,320	5,695	53.1	70.8	(X)	(X)	6.3	[8]1.0
Brazil	92.4	115.0	762	765	139.5	222.8	9.1	32.7	(NA)	4.6
Bulgaria	47.5	38.8	5,360	4,304	34.8	41.3	[6]0.3	0.1	0.3	[6]0.1
Burma [9]	2.0	2.5	60	59	1.5	2.6	1.6	[6]0.9	(Z)	[6](Z)
Canada	251.4	278.7	10,457	10,507	377.5	482.0	70.4	76.2	20.2	37.7
Chile	11.4	16.5	1,021	1,249	11.8	18.4	1.6	0.8	1.0	2.2
China: Mainland	545.5	893.4	557	787	300.6	621.2	105.9	138.3	595.8	[10]1,079.9
Taiwan [11]	37.8	67.1	2,126	3,285	(NA)	(NA)	0.2	0.2	2.6	0.5
Colombia	20.2	26.1	753	790	20.6	35.4	6.5	22.2	4.1	20.5
Cuba	13.7	15.3	1,412	1,447	10.0	16.2	0.3	[6]0.9	(X)	(X)
Czechoslovakia	95.2	89.8	6,215	5,729	72.7	89.3	0.1	0.1	[8]28.3	[6][8]22.8
Denmark	27.7	24.1	5,398	4,695	27.1	25.8	0.3	6.0	(X)	(X)
Ecuador	5.7	7.7	699	726	3.4	6.3	10.4	14.9	(NA)	(NA)
Egypt	20.9	36.5	512	696	18.9	39.4	29.4	44.0	(X)	(X)
Ethiopia	0.8	1.3	21	26	0.7	0.9	(X)	(X)	(NA)	(NA)
Finland [12]	25.7	29.5	5,384	5,926	[5]38.7	[5]54.4	(X)	(X)	(X)	(X)
France [12]	242.9	217.4	4,506	3,870	[5]245.7	[5]419.6	1.2	3.0	[8]20.2	[8]10.5
Germany	492.3	457.9	(NA)	(NA)	466.3	572.0	[13]5.3	[13]3.6	94.5	[6]76.4
Greece	20.2	30.6	2,098	3,048	22.7	35.0	-	[13]0.8	(X)	(X)
Hong Kong	7.3	10.4	1,447	1,782	12.6	28.9	(NA)	(NA)	(X)	(X)
Hungary	40.9	34.7	3,815	3,284	23.9	28.4	2.0	2.0	[8]3.1	[8]1.7
India [9]	139.3	264.9	202	311	119.3	286.0	9.4	33.3	109.2	201.8
Indonesia	36.1	57.3	239	311	14.2	44.3	77.6	70.4	0.3	7.3
Iran [14]	45.7	93.4	1,174	1,710	22.4	56.0	72.7	158.8	[6]0.9	[6]1.3
Iraq	10.7	16.0	802	848	11.4	29.2	130.1	100.6	(NA)	(NA)
Ireland	11.4	13.5	3,361	3,624	10.6	14.5	(X)	(X)	0.1	(Z)
Israel	8.8	14.7	2,277	3,190	12.5	20.7	(Z)	(Z)	(X)	(X)
Italy [15]	188.9	220.1	3,346	3,856	183.5	216.9	1.8	4.6	-	0.1
Japan	433.4	519.3	3,710	4,206	577.5	857.3	0.4	0.5	18.0	8.3
Kuwait [16]	12.0	14.8	8,735	7,247	9.4	20.6	84.1	59.6	(X)	(X)
Libya	7.3	19.7	2,399	4,344	4.8	19.0	88.3	67.2	(X)	(X)
Malaysia	11.3	26.7	821	1,490	10.1	23.0	13.4	30.0	(X)	0.1
Mexico	117.1	155.1	1,663	1,751	[5]67.0	[5]122.4	99.9	133.1	7.0	[6]10.0
Morocco	6.5	9.3	336	369	4.9	9.6	(Z)	(Z)	0.7	0.5
Netherlands	98.5	107.8	6,965	7,210	64.8	71.9	1.3	3.5	-	-
New Zealand [17]	10.0	16.4	3,208	4,822	22.0	30.2	0.3	1.8	2.0	2.2
Nigeria	12.0	22.9	153	211	7.2	9.9	104.2	86.0	0.2	[6]0.1
North Korea	48.5	91.5	2,658	4,203	35.0	53.5	(X)	(X)	[6]36.0	[6]40.7
Norway [18]	26.5	26.0	6,476	6,173	83.6	121.8	24.6	79.7	0.3	0.3
Pakistan [7]	16.6	34.4	195	280	15.0	43.9	0.5	2.6	1.6	2.8
Peru	11.0	10.6	637	491	10.0	13.8	9.7	6.9	(Z)	[6]0.1
Philippines	15.9	18.8	330	301	18.0	26.3	0.5	0.2	0.3	1.2
Poland	176.8	142.9	4,969	3,718	121.9	136.3	0.3	0.2	193.1	[6]147.0
Portugal	12.5	19.2	1,281	1,868	15.3	28.5	(X)	(X)	0.2	0.3
Romania	103.0	86.8	4,637	3,731	67.5	64.3	11.5	7.9	8.1	[6]4.5
Saudi Arabia [16]	25.3	99.1	2,703	7,010	18.9	46.7	495.9	320.4	(NA)	(NA)
South Africa [19]	84.3	106.2	2,604	2,594	89.6	166.7	(X)	(X)	116.6	175.7
South Korea	51.4	105.8	1,349	2,473	40.1	118.7	(X)	(X)	18.6	17.2
Soviet Union	1,507.5	1,931.3	5,677	6,692	1,293.9	1,726.0	603.2	565.5	492.9	543.0
Spain	87.1	100.5	2,321	2,565	109.2	151.8	1.6	0.8	[8]13.1	[8]14.7
Sudan	1.5	1.6	81	64	0.9	1.3	(X)	(X)	(NA)	(NA)
Sweden	44.2	40.4	5,318	4,785	96.3	146.4	(Z)	(Z)	(Z)	(Z)
Switzerland [20]	24.3	26.0	3,834	3,912	[5]47.1	55.8	(X)	(X)	(X)	(X)
Syria	8.6	13.6	981	1,084	3.8	11.5	9.2	22.9	(X)	(X)
Tanzania	0.9	1.0	46	36	0.8	0.9	(X)	(X)	(Z)	[6](Z)
Thailand	17.3	41.1	371	738	15.1	46.2	(Z)	1.3	-	-
Trinidad and Tobago . . .	7.5	9.1	6,901	7,066	2.1	3.5	11.0	7.9	(NA)	(NA)
Tunisia	4.1	6.6	643	807	2.8	5.5	5.6	4.5	(X)	(X)
Turkey	31.1	59.3	699	1,062	23.3	57.5	2.3	3.7	3.6	2.7
United Arab Emirates . . .	9.9	32.1	9,749	20,183	6.3	13.6	82.8	102.0	(NA)	(NA)

See footnotes at end of table.

No. 1416. Energy Consumption and Production, by Country: 1980 and 1990—Continued

[See text, section 31, for general comments about the data. For additional data qualifications for countries, see source]

COUNTRY	ENERGY CONSUMED [1] (coal equiv.)				ELECTRIC ENERGY PRODUCTION [2] (bil. kWh)		CRUDE PETROLEUM PRODUCTION [3] (mil. metric tons)		COAL PRODUCTION [4] (mil. metric tons)	
	Total (mil. metric tons)		Per capita (kilograms)							
	1980	1990	1980	1990	1980	1990	1980	1990	1980	1990
United Kingdom	271.8	290.0	4,809	5,049	283.7	319.0	78.9	88.0	[8]130.1	[8]94.4
Venezuela	49.2	64.7	3,278	3,277	35.9	55.8	114.8	112.0	(Z)	2.2
Vietnam	6.7	9.1	126	136	4.2	8.7	(X)	2.7	5.3	5.0
Yugoslavia	47.9	57.3	2,145	2,409	59.4	85.9	4.2	3.6	0.4	0.3
Zaire	2.0	2.3	75	66	4.4	6.2	1.0	[6]1.4	0.1	[6]0.1
Zambia	2.3	1.7	396	201	[5]9.2	7.8	(X)	(X)	0.6	0.4

- Represents or rounds to zero. NA Not available. X Not applicable. Z Less than 50,000 metric tons. [1] Based on apparent consumption of coal, lignite, petroleum products, natural gas, and hydro, nuclear, and geothermal electricity. [2] Comprises production by utilities generating primarily for public use, and production by industrial establishments generating primarily for own use. Relates to production at generating centers, including station use and transmission losses. [3] Includes shale oil, but excludes natural gasoline. [4] Excludes lignite and brown coal, except as noted. [5] Net production, i.e. excluding station use. [6] Provisional. [7] For year ending June of year shown. [8] Includes recovered slurries. [9] For year ending April of year shown. [10] Includes lignite. [11] Source: U.S. Bureau of the Census. Data from Republic of China publications. [12] Includes Monaco. [13] Includes inputs other than crude petroleum and natural gas liquids. [14] For year ending March 20 of year shown. [15] Includes San Marino. [16] Includes share of production and consumption in the Neutral Zone. [17] For year ending March 31 of year shown. [18] Includes Svalbard and Jan Mayen Islands. [19] Includes Botswana, Lesotho, Namibia, and Swaziland. [20] Includes Liechtenstein.

Source: Except as noted, Statistical Office of the United Nations, New York, NY, *Energy Statistics*, annual, (copyright).

No. 1417. Selected Petroleum Product Prices—Selected Countries: 1991

[As of January 1, 1991. Includes taxes]

COUNTRY	AUTOMOTIVE FUELS (U.S. dollars per gallon)		RESIDENTIAL (U.S. dollars per gallon)			INDUSTRIAL (U.S. dollars per barrel)	
	Premium gasoline	Diesel fuel	Light fuel oil	Kerosene	Liquified petroleum gases	Light fuel oil	Heavy fuel oil
United States [1]	[2]1.43	[2]0.91	[2]1.17	[2]1.05	[2]0.87	24.94	20.87
Argentina	3.07	1.53	1.53	1.28	1.19	64.26	29.01
Austria [1]	3.47	3.31	1.80	(NA)	2.01	28.32	21.70
Belgium [1]	3.61	(NA)	1.33	(NA)	(NA)	47.46	14.39
Bolivia	1.78	1.00	0.95	0.67	0.50	25.72	(NA)
Brazil	1.65	0.81	0.43	0.95	0.97	18.02	13.71
Canada [1]	2.06	1.98	1.55	1.24	1.21	65.10	27.08
Chile	1.71	1.48	1.44	1.32	(NA)	37.68	27.80
Denmark [1]	4.18	3.38	3.15	4.08	2.73	57.12	25.51
Ecuador	0.44	0.41	0.25	0.05	0.13	18.29	14.71
El Salvador	2.36	0.96	1.55	1.12	(NA)	65.10	(NA)
Ethiopia	2.93	1.44	(NA)	1.20	1.30	41.46	24.99
Finland [1]	4.45	3.53	1.69	(NA)	4.69	(NA)	36.58
France [1]	3.86	(NA)	2.03	(NA)	(NA)	(NA)	19.08
Germany [1]	2.87	2.69	1.34	(NA)	3.58	56.06	32.77
Ghana	1.49	1.24	(NA)	1.12	0.61	(NA)	35.39
Greece [1]	3.32	1.59	(NA)	2.12	0.96	27.74	27.74
India	3.09	1.05	(NA)	0.57	1.60	41.12	30.07
Ireland [1]	3.62	(NA)	1.43	(NA)	(NA)	42.84	21.80
Israel	2.70	2.01	0.80	2.05	0.54	24.52	22.96
Italy [1]	5.10	3.77	3.54	2.61	2.78	(NA)	54.64
Jamaica	1.94	2.04	2.05	(NA)	(NA)	85.68	35.91
Japan	3.90	2.40	1.69	(NA)	(NA)	(NA)	50.68
Luxembourg [1]	2.95	2.10	1.34	2.79	1.57	62.05	32.34
Mexico	0.87	0.66	(NA)	0.26	0.27	27.65	9.60
Morocco	2.92	1.67	0.83	1.50	0.70	31.64	29.78
Netherlands [1]	3.28	2.24	1.46	1.66	1.24	94.01	28.56
Norway [1]	4.80	2.33	2.07	2.35	(NA)	87.07	76.30
Pakistan	2.46	0.97	0.80	0.86	0.41	33.80	21.42
Panama	2.44	1.36	(NA)	1.10	0.81	21.28	21.15
Paraguay	2.34	1.40	(NA)	0.88	1.00	58.92	22.09
Peru	1.99	1.07	(NA)	0.98	1.16	45.05	38.17
Portugal [1]	4.25	3.02	(NA)	2.69	1.74	(NA)	30.73
Saudi Arabia	0.54	0.12	(NA)	0.20	0.49	3.60	5.30
South Africa	2.00	2.00	1.86	1.55	0.70	77.07	45.52
Spain [1]	3.53	(NA)	1.85	(NA)	(NA)	69.30	29.15
Sweden [1]	4.45	3.58	2.05	2.88	1.28	80.70	77.20
Switzerland [1]	3.21	3.42	1.19	(NA)	(NA)	(NA)	37.73
Thailand	1.67	1.27	(NA)	1.32	0.90	52.01	23.00
Turkey [1]	2.51	1.91	(NA)	2.10	0.68	(NA)	28.79
United Kingdom [1]	2.55	(NA)	0.81	(NA)	(NA)	30.24	19.59
Uruguay	3.05	1.79	1.22	1.34	1.46	46.14	37.11
Venezuela	0.27	0.19	(NA)	0.07	0.19	(NA)	6.55

NA Not available. [1] Average for January 1991. [2] Price excludes tax.
Source: Energy Information Administration, *International Energy Annual 1990*.

No. 1418. Indices of Food Production: 1980 to 1991

[1979-1981 = 100. For explanation of annual percent change, see Guide to Tabular Presentation. Minus sign (-) indicates decrease]

REGION AND COUNTRY	TOTAL FOOD PRODUCTION				Average annual percent change		PER CAPITA FOOD PRODUCTION				Average annual percent change	
	1980	1985	1990	1991	1980-1991	1990-1991	1980	1985	1990	1991	1980-1991	1990-1991
World.............	99	114	126	125	2.4	-0.6	99	105	106	103	0.4	-2.3
Developed countries.......	99	108	111	106	0.8	-3.9	99	105	104	99	0.1	-4.4
United States..........	96	108	106	103	0.3	-2.5	96	102	96	93	-0.6	-3.2
Canada.............	99	113	126	126	1.6	-0.2	99	108	115	114	0.5	-1.1
Europe (including Central)..	101	107	108	107	0.7	-0.9	101	106	105	104	0.4	-1.2
Japan	95	109	103	99	0.2	-3.2	95	105	97	94	-0.3	-3.5
Oceania	95	107	111	109	1.2	-1.6	95	101	96	94	-0.2	-2.8
South Africa	97	95	104	104	1.1	0.3	97	85	83	82	-1.0	-1.8
Soviet Union (former)	100	111	121	107	1.7	-11.8	100	106	111	97	0.8	-12.5
Developing countries.......	99	120	140	142	3.9	1.9	99	108	113	113	1.2	-0.2
Latin America	99	116	128	129	2.7	0.8	99	104	103	102	0.3	-1.2
Mexico	100	114	123	124	1.9	0.7	100	102	98	96	-0.6	-1.4
Brazil	102	155	166	167	6.3	0.2	102	139	134	132	3.0	-1.7
Argentina...........	96	107	111	110	0.8	-0.5	96	100	97	95	-0.5	-1.7
Africa..............	100	113	132	138	3.1	3.1	100	97	97	98	-0.2	0.1
Near East...........	100	115	130	130	2.7	-0.1	100	100	99	96	-0.4	-2.8
Far East............	99	123	147	150	4.6	2.2	99	113	122	123	2.0	0.3
India..............	98	123	149	151	4.8	1.1	98	111	120	119	1.9	-1.0
China: Mainland........	99	128	157	160	5.5	2.4	99	120	137	138	3.5	0.9

Source: Food and Agriculture Organization of the United Nations, Rome, Italy, FAO AGRISTAT Database.

No. 1419. Wheat, Rice, and Corn—Exports and Imports of 10 Leading Countries: 1980 to 1990

[In millions of dollars. Countries listed are the ten leading exporters or importers in 1990]

LEADING EXPORTERS	EXPORTS			LEADING IMPORTERS	IMPORTS		
	1980	1985	1990		1980	1985	1990
WHEAT				**WHEAT**			
United States........	6,376	3,602	3,887	Soviet Union........	2,891	2,975	2,490
France.............	2,110	2,351	3,296	China, Mainland	2,582	1,019	2,319
Canada.............	3,302	2,769	2,863	Italy	773	790	1,217
Australia............	2,425	2,222	1,971	Japan	1,236	991	1,019
Argentina...........	816	1,133	871	Egypt	839	814	965
United Kingdom.......	260	282	760	Iran...............	243	344	707
West Germany........	185	156	503	Netherlands	333	267	595
Netherlands	154	84	406	West Germany	309	488	429
Denmark............	23	65	229	Algeria	402	543	422
Saudi Arabia........	-	7	211	South Korea.........	367	442	419
RICE				**RICE**			
Thailand............	953	830	1,086	Saudi Arabia........	230	204	226
United States........	1,285	665	804	Iran...............	209	171	216
Vietnam............	10	15	375	France	154	146	216
Italy...............	289	304	357	United Kingdom	98	126	209
India	173	188	246	West Germany	96	92	165
Pakistan............	422	220	242	Hong Kong	158	115	150
Belgium-Luxembourg ...	91	114	168	Brazil	99	83	147
Spain	22	32	108	Philippines	-	123	128
Uruguay	64	81	104	Iraq...............	217	175	124
China, Mainland.......	510	233	98	United Arab Emirates...	123	65	120
CORN				**CORN**			
United States........	8,571	5,312	6,206	Japan	2,011	1,937	2,295
France	869	815	1,854	Soviet Union........	1,508	2,315	1,690
China, Mainland......	17	742	404	South Korea.........	376	422	837
Argentina	513	766	329	China, Mainland	716	437	750
South Africa	541	49	176	Netherlands	626	422	538
Thailand............	352	280	162	Mexico	589	255	473
Zimbabwe...........	17	22	87	United Kingdom	547	266	396
West Germany.......	39	25	71	West Germany	443	327	375
Hungary	27	39	51	Italy	450	212	363
Spain	1	1	41	Spain	668	495	307

- Represents or rounds to zero.

Source: U.S. Dept. of Agriculture, Economic Research Service, *World Agriculture-Trends and Indicators*.

No. 1420. Wheat, Rice, and Corn Production, by Country: 1980 to 1991

[In thousands of metric tons. Rice data cover paddy. Data for each country pertain to the calendar year in which all or most of the crop was harvested. See text, section 31, for general comments concerning quality of the data]

COUNTRY	WHEAT			RICE			CORN		
	1980	1990	1991	1980	1990	1991	1980	1990	1991
World, total	445,895	601,723	550,993	399,422	521,703	519,869	397,512	479,340	478,775
United States........	64,800	74,475	53,915	6,629	7,080	7,006	168,647	201,508	189,867
Argentina...........	7,780	11,014	9,000	266	467	347	6,400	5,049	7,768
Australia...........	10,856	15,402	9,633	613	924	726	173	200	159
Austria............	1,201	1,404	1,341	(X)	(X)	(X)	1,293	1,620	1,524
Belgium-Luxembourg ...	906	1,409	1,620	(X)	(X)	(X)	39	60	62
Brazil.............	2,702	3,094	3,077	9,776	7,419	9,503	20,372	21,339	22,604
Burma.............	91	124	123	13,317	13,969	13,201	166	187	190
Canada	19,292	32,709	32,822	(X)	(X)	(X)	5,753	7,157	7,319
China: Mainland.......	55,213	98,232	95,003	142,993	191,197	187,450	62,715	97,158	93,350
Egypt.............	1,736	4,268	4,483	2,382	3,167	3,152	3,231	4,799	5,270
France	23,781	33,312	34,483	24	121	109	9,365	9,291	12,787
Germany [1]	8,156	11,053	11,948	(X)	(X)	(X)	672	1,545	1,809
Greece............	2,970	1,965	2,750	80	110	127	1,279	1,992	1,700
Hungary...........	6,077	6,198	5,954	24	39	38	6,673	4,500	7,509
India	31,830	49,850	54,522	80,312	111,953	110,945	6,957	9,073	8,200
Indonesia	(X)	(X)	(X)	29,652	45,179	44,321	3,991	6,734	6,409
Iran..............	5,922	8,218	8,900	1,449	2,273	2,100	60	7	7
Iraq..............	976	1,196	525	167	229	125	60	185	74
Italy..............	9,156	8,109	9,289	968	1,291	1,236	6,377	5,864	6,208
Japan.............	583	952	860	12,189	13,124	12,005	4	1	1
Mexico............	2,785	3,931	4,115	445	394	354	12,374	14,635	13,527
Pakistan...........	10,857	14,316	14,505	4,685	4,897	4,903	970	1,185	1,190
South Korea	92	1	1	5,311	7,732	7,478	154	120	75
Soviet Union (former) ...	98,182	109,600	80,000	2,791	2,473	2,200	9,454	9,900	8,500
Sweden	1,193	2,243	1,524	(X)	(X)	(X)	(X)	(X)	(X)
Thailand...........	(X)	(X)	(X)	17,368	17,300	20,040	2,998	3,722	3,990
United Kingdom.......	8,470	14,000	14,300	(X)	(X)	(X)	1	(NA)	(NA)
Yugoslavia	5,091	6,359	6,530	42	28	32	9,317	6,724	8,800

NA Not available.　X Not applicable.　[1] Former West Germany (prior to unification).

Source: U.S. Department of Agriculture, Economic Research Service, *World Agriculture-Trends and Indicators.*

No. 1421. Fisheries—Commercial Catch, by Country: 1985 to 1990

[In thousand metric tons, live weight. Catch of fish, crustaceans, mollusks (including weight of shells). Does not include marine mammals and aquatic plants]

COUNTRY	1985	1987	1988	1989	1990	COUNTRY	1985	1987	1988	1989	1990
World, total [1] .	86,398	94,399	99,062	100,333	97,246	Japan..........	11,409	11,848	11,966	11,173	10,353
						Mexico........	1,226	1,419	1,372	1,469	1,401
United States	4,949	5,986	5,937	5,763	5,856	North Korea (est.)..	1,700	1,700	1,700	1,700	1,750
Canada........	1,453	1,565	1,609	1,572	1,624	Norway........	2,119	1,949	1,839	1,908	1,747
Chile	4,804	4,814	5,209	6,454	5,195	Peru..........	4,137	4,587	6,641	6,853	6,875
China: Mainland ...	6,779	9,346	10,358	11,219	12,095	Philippines......	1,865	1,988	2,010	2,098	2,208
Denmark.......	1,765	1,706	1,971	1,927	1,517	South Korea	2,650	2,876	2,727	2,832	2,750
Iceland........	1,680	1,632	1,759	1,504	1,507	Soviet Union	10,523	11,159	11,332	11,310	10,389
India..........	2,826	2,907	3,126	3,641	3,790	Spain	1,483	1,524	1,592	1,559	1,458
Indonesia	2,333	2,583	2,789	2,948	3,080	Thailand	2,225	2,779	2,642	2,781	2,650

[1] Includes other countries not shown separately.

Source: U.S. National Oceanic and Atmospheric Administration, National Marine Fisheries Service, *Fisheries of the United States,* annual. Data from Food and Agricultural Organization of the United Nations, Rome, Italy.

No. 1422. Meat—Production, by Country: 1980 to 1991

[In thousands of metric tons, carcass weight. Covers beef and veal (incl. buffalo meat), pork (incl. bacon and ham), mutton and lamb (incl. goat meat), horsemeat, and poultry. Refers to meat from animals slaughtered within the national boundaries irrespective of origin of animals, and relates to commercial and farm slaughter. Excludes lard, tallow, and edible offals. See text, section 31 for general comments concerning the data]

COUNTRY	1980	1990	1991	COUNTRY	1980	1990	1991
World............	134,407	176,629	178,830	France	5,300	5,506	5,764
United States.......	24,599	28,776	29,720	Italy	3,571	3,956	[2]3,956
Argentina.........	3,622	3,380	3,432	Japan............	3,046	3,529	3,489
Australia [1]	2,672	3,067	3,200	Mexico	2,537	3,478	3,403
Brazil	4,551	6,428	6,663	United Kingdom	3,070	3,356	3,508
Canada	2,556	2,838	2,769	West Germany.......	5,199	5,684	5,881
China: Mainland	13,744	29,725	31,907				

[1] Year ending June 30.　[2] Estimate.

Source: U.S. Department of Agriculture, Economic Research Service, *World Agriculture-Trends and Indicators,* and Food and Agriculture Organization of the United Nations, Rome, Italy, *FAO Production Yearbook, 1991.*

No. 1423. Foreign Trade of Selected Countries—Source of Imports and Destination of Exports: 1992

[In billions of dollars, except percent. All exports are f.o.b. (free on board) and all imports are c.i.f. (cost insurance freight) except for U.S. and Canadian imports, which are f.o.b.]

COUNTRY	Total [1]	O.E.C.D. [2]		C.E.E.C. [4]	China: Mainland, Vietnam, North Korea	O.P.E.C. [5]	Other developing countries [6]	Africa	America [7]	Middle East [8]	Far East [9]
		Total	E.E.C. [3]								
IMPORTS											
United States	531.3	310.1	94.1	2.0	25.7	33.0	160.6	14.3	68.7	15.7	119.7
Australia	40.8	29.1	8.2	0.1	1.8	1.9	7.7	0.1	0.4	1.1	8.7
Austria	54.2	45.8	36.8	3.5	0.6	1.1	3.3	1.0	0.5	0.5	2.4
Belgium-Lux	125.0	109.3	92.0	2.1	0.4	3.3	9.9	4.8	1.8	2.9	3.8
Canada	123.1	105.0	12.0	0.4	2.1	1.7	11.6	0.9	4.5	0.7	9.3
Denmark	33.6	29.1	18.0	1.1	0.6	0.2	2.7	0.2	1.0	0.1	1.9
France	238.8	191.9	142.3	5.5	3.6	9.4	23.8	11.2	5.0	5.7	13.7
Germany	408.5	326.3	212.5	22.5	7.8	9.8	41.8	10.6	9.4	4.2	30.9
Italy	164.4	127.1	96.7	6.7	2.4	10.1	17.6	11.4	4.0	4.3	8.2
Japan	232.7	112.3	31.4	3.1	18.1	38.9	60.4	3.5	8.3	29.1	75.5
Netherlands	130.4	110.6	85.5	2.2	1.0	6.3	10.3	2.8	2.4	4.6	7.4
Spain	99.8	78.9	60.6	1.5	1.7	5.9	11.6	6.5	4.4	2.0	6.1
Sweden	49.9	43.4	27.7	1.6	0.8	0.9	3.3	0.4	0.7	0.6	3.0
Switzerland	65.7	59.5	47.4	0.7	0.6	0.0	4.8	0.7	1.2	0.6	2.9
United Kingdom	220.3	183.3	115.0	2.7	1.7	4.9	26.5	4.7	4.2	4.1	19.1
Percent distribution:											
United States	100.0	58.4	17.7	0.4	4.8	6.2	30.2	2.7	12.9	3.0	22.5
Australia	100.0	71.5	20.1	0.2	4.5	4.7	18.9	0.4	1.1	2.8	21.4
Austria	100.0	84.4	67.9	6.5	1.1	1.9	6.1	1.9	0.9	0.9	4.5
Belgium-Lux	100.0	87.4	73.6	1.6	0.3	2.6	7.9	3.9	1.4	2.3	3.1
Canada	100.0	85.3	9.8	0.3	1.7	1.4	9.4	0.7	3.6	0.6	7.5
Denmark	100.0	86.7	53.5	3.2	1.7	0.5	7.9	0.5	3.0	0.2	5.7
France	100.0	80.4	59.6	2.3	1.5	3.9	10.0	4.7	2.1	2.4	5.8
Germany	100.0	79.9	52.0	5.5	1.9	2.4	10.2	2.6	2.3	1.0	7.6
Italy	100.0	77.3	58.8	4.1	1.5	6.2	10.7	6.9	2.4	2.6	5.0
Japan	100.0	48.3	13.5	1.3	7.8	16.7	25.9	1.5	3.6	12.5	32.5
Netherlands	100.0	84.8	65.6	1.7	0.7	4.8	7.9	2.1	1.9	3.5	5.7
Spain	100.0	79.0	60.8	1.5	1.7	5.9	11.6	6.5	4.4	2.0	6.1
Sweden	100.0	86.8	55.5	3.2	1.5	1.8	6.7	0.8	1.5	1.2	6.0
Switzerland	100.0	90.6	72.2	1.0	1.0	0.0	7.4	1.1	1.8	0.9	4.4
United Kingdom	100.0	83.2	52.2	1.2	0.8	2.2	12.0	2.1	1.9	1.9	8.7
EXPORTS											
United States	447.5	264.6	102.9	5.5	7.5	21.9	147.7	9.9	75.7	16.9	73.6
Australia	42.4	23.6	5.4	0.2	1.4	2.1	14.3	0.4	0.4	1.0	14.6
Austria	44.4	35.8	29.4	4.3	0.3	1.3	2.8	0.6	0.4	1.0	1.5
Belgium-Lux	123.0	106.7	92.1	1.7	0.5	2.6	10.7	2.8	1.2	4.3	5.1
Canada	134.9	122.8	9.5	1.2	1.9	1.7	7.2	0.8	2.7	0.8	6.4
Denmark	39.6	34.0	21.5	1.1	0.1	0.8	3.4	0.8	0.9	0.9	1.5
France	231.8	183.7	145.4	4.8	1.6	9.7	31.9	15.3	8.1	6.2	11.0
Germany	430.4	345.9	234.0	23.9	3.8	14.8	41.3	9.9	9.2	13.0	23.5
Italy	155.4	120.2	89.8	5.7	1.4	8.0	19.6	6.4	4.4	6.9	8.2
Japan	339.8	184.1	62.8	1.9	12.6	19.0	122.2	6.4	15.1	14.0	117.1
Netherlands	139.0	123.0	105.8	2.7	0.5	3.0	8.9	2.7	1.8	2.6	4.6
Spain	64.3	53.0	45.8	0.8	0.3	2.3	7.5	3.1	3.1	1.4	1.7
Sweden	56.1	48.5	31.3	1.4	0.4	1.4	4.3	0.7	1.1	1.3	2.8
Switzerland	65.5	52.4	38.6	1.3	0.5	2.4	9.0	1.2	1.9	2.7	5.6
United Kingdom	189.6	152.0	106.2	2.8	0.8	9.3	23.1	6.3	3.1	9.1	13.5
Percent distribution:											
United States	100.0	59.1	23.0	1.2	1.7	4.9	33.0	2.2	16.9	3.8	16.4
Australia	100.0	55.5	12.7	0.4	3.3	5.0	33.8	1.4	1.0	2.5	34.4
Austria	100.0	80.5	66.1	9.7	0.6	2.8	6.4	1.3	0.9	2.2	3.3
Belgium-Lux	100.0	86.7	74.9	1.4	0.4	2.1	8.7	2.3	0.9	3.5	4.2
Canada	100.0	91.0	7.1	0.9	1.4	1.3	5.3	0.6	2.0	0.6	4.8
Denmark	100.0	85.8	54.4	2.9	0.3	2.1	8.7	1.9	2.3	2.2	3.9
France	100.0	79.2	62.7	2.1	0.7	4.2	13.7	6.6	3.5	2.7	4.8
Germany	100.0	80.4	54.4	5.6	0.9	3.4	9.6	2.3	2.1	3.0	5.5
Italy	100.0	77.3	57.8	3.7	0.9	5.2	12.6	4.1	2.8	4.5	5.3
Japan	100.0	54.2	18.5	0.6	3.7	5.6	36.0	1.9	4.4	4.1	34.5
Netherlands	100.0	88.5	76.1	1.9	0.3	2.2	6.4	1.9	1.3	1.9	3.3
Spain	100.0	82.4	71.2	1.3	0.4	3.6	11.7	4.9	4.8	2.2	2.7
Sweden	100.0	86.5	55.8	2.5	0.8	2.5	7.7	1.3	2.0	2.3	5.0
Switzerland	100.0	79.9	58.9	2.0	0.7	3.6	13.8	1.9	2.9	4.2	8.6
United Kingdom	100.0	80.1	56.0	1.5	0.4	4.9	12.2	3.3	1.6	4.8	7.1

[1] Includes other areas not shown separately. [2] Organization for Economic Cooperation and Development. For member countries, see text, section 31. [3] European Economic Community comprises Belgium-Luxembourg, Denmark, France, Greece, Ireland, Italy, Netherlands, Portugal, Spain, United Kingdom, and Germany. [4] Central European Economic Community. [5] Organization of Petroleum Exporting Countries. For member countries, see footnote 4, table 1430. [6] Comprises trade with all countries other than China: Mainland, North Korea, Vietnam, South Africa, Eastern Europe, and members of O.P.E.C. and O.E.C.D. [7] All countries comprising the continent except Canada and the United States. [8] Comprises Syria, Lebanon, Israel, Gaza Strip, Jordan, Iraq, Saudi Arabia, Yemen, Kuwait, Bahrain, United Arab Emirates, Qatar, Oman, and Iran. [9] All countries comprising the continent of Asia except Japan, China: Mainland, North Korea, Vietnam, and those countries listed under Middle East.

Source: Organization for Economic Cooperation and Development, Paris, France. Data derived from Monthly Statistics of Foreign Trade.

No. 1424. Reserve Assets and International Transaction Balances: 1985 to 1992

[In millions of U.S. dollars. Assets include holdings of convertible foreign currencies, special drawing rights, and reserve position in International Monetary Fund and exclude gold holdings. Minus sign (-) indicates decrease]

COUNTRY	TOTAL RESERVE ASSETS				CURRENT ACCOUNT BALANCE			MERCHANDISE TRADE BALANCE		
	1985	1990	1992 Total	1992 Currency holdings[1]	1985	1990	1991	1985	1990	1991
United States	32,100	72,260	60,270	40,010	122,250	-90,460	-3,690	-122,160	-108,840	-73,440
Algeria	2,819	725	1,457	1,456	1,015	1,420	2,367	4,223	4,187	5,478
Argentina..................	3,273	4,592	(NA)	(NA)	-952	1,903	-2,803	4,878	8,628	4,578
Australia	5,768	16,264	11,199	10,526	9,015	-14,724	-9,853	-1,317	366	3,530
Austria	4,767	9,376	12,383	11,506	-273	1,174	116	-4,406	-8,328	-9,968
Bangladesh	337	629	1,825	1,783	-458	-397	65	-1,287	-1,587	-1,386
Belgium..................	4,849	12,151	10,135	9,159	669	4,950	4,731	-472	590	-66
Brazil	10,605	7,441	22,521	22,520	-273	-3,788	(NA)	12,466	10,747	(NA)
Burma..................	34	313	280	280	-206	(NA)	(NA)	-202	(NA)	(NA)
Cameroon	132	26	(NA)	(NA)	-562	(NA)	(NA)	490	621	(NA)
Canada	2,503	17,845	11,431	9,382	-2,279	-21,965	-25,529	12,574	9,181	5,929
Chile....................	2,450	6,069	9,168	9,167	-1,328	-598	142	850	1,273	1,575
China: Mainland	12,728	29,586	(NA)	(NA)	-11,417	11,997	13,272	-13,123	9,165	8,743
Colombia................	1,595	4,212	7,389	7,236	-1,809	542	2,349	-23	1,971	2,959
Cote d'Ivoire	5	4	7	7	64	-1,204	-1,451	1,351	1,419	1,162
Denmark	5,429	10,591	11,044	10,477	-2,767	1,380	2,167	-764	4,875	4,748
Ecuador	718	839	(NA)	(NA)	114	-166	-467	1,294	1,003	644
Egypt	792	2,684	10,810	10,677	-2,166	184	1,903	-5,215	-6,699	-5,975
Finland	3,750	9,644	5,213	4,774	-811	-6,682	-6,695	878	768	2,321
France	26,589	36,778	27,028	24,384	-35	-13,772	-6,148	-5,276	-13,667	-10,139
Germany[2]	44,380	67,902	90,967	85,887	16,960	46,280	-19,500	28,580	71,710	23,530
Ghana..................	479	280	(NA)	(NA)	-134	-229	(NA)	(NA)	-36	-308
Greece..................	868	3,412	4,794	4,633	-3,276	-3,537	-1,521	-5,053	-10,178	10,112
Hungary	2,153	1,070	(NA)	(NA)	-455	379	403	448	534	358
India....................	6,420	1,521	5,757	5,461	-4,177	(NA)	(NA)	-5,616	(NA)	(NA)
Indonesia...............	4,974	7,459	10,449	10,181	-1,923	-2,988	-4,080	5,822	5,352	4,804
Ireland	2,940	5,223	3,440	3,080	-690	921	(NA)	631	3,971	(NA)
Israel	3,680	6,275	5,127	5,127	1,120	575	-822	-2,364	-2,816	-4,765
Italy	15,595	62,927	27,643	24,966	3,408	-14,422	-21,454	-6,083	616	-898
Japan	26,719	78,496	71,623	61,888	49,170	35,870	72,910	55,990	63,580	103,090
Kenya..................	391	205	53	35	-113	-502	-231	-327	-998	-659
Kuwait..................	5,471	1,952	5,147	4,835	5,150	(NA)	(NA)	5,047	(NA)	(NA)
Libya	5,904	5,839	6,182	5,361	1,906	2,203	(NA)	4,599	3,780	(NA)
Malaysia	4,912	9,754	(NA)	(NA)	-613	-1,630	-4,530	3,577	1,910	-168
Mexico	4,906	9,863	(NA)	(NA)	1,130	-7,117	-13,282	8,451	-4,433	-11,063
Morocco	115	2,066	3,584	3,465	-891	-200	-396	-1,368	-2,071	-1,976
Nepal	56	295	470	462	-122	-289	-304	-283	-449	-482
Netherlands.............	10,782	17,484	21,937	20,237	4,190	8,856	7,772	5,393	10,330	10,740
Nigeria.................	1,667	3,864	966	966	2,566	4,988	1,203	5,616	8,653	4,441
Norway	13,917	15,332	11,940	11,101	3,052	3,886	4,939	4,728	7,770	8,717
Pakistan	807	296	850	850	-1,080	-1,654	-1,929	-3,230	-2,714	-2,247
Peru....................	1,842	1,040	2,849	2,849	135	-766	1,478	1,172	340	-165
Philippines	615	924	4,403	4,283	-35	-2,695	-1,034	-482	-4,020	-3,211
Poland	870	4,492	4,099	3,992	-982	3,067	-2,146	347	3,589	-711
Portugal	1,395	14,485	19,129	18,769	380	-181	-716	-1,504	-6,831	-7,848
Romania	199	373	223	212	1,381	-3,254	-1,184	1,772	-3,344	-1,220
Saudi Arabia	25,004	11,668	5,935	4,561	-12,932	-4,267	-25,738	7,029	22,806	22,096
Singapore	12,847	27,748	39,885	39,661	-4	2,170	4,208	-2,829	-5,119	-4,128
South Africa.............	315	1,008	(NA)	(NA)	2,622	2,253	2,664	5,842	6,338	6,267
South Korea.............	2,869	14,793	17,121	16,640	-887	-2,172	-8,726	-19	-2,004	-6,980
Spain	11,175	51,228	45,504	44,176	2,851	-16,819	-15,954	-4,171	-29,566	-30,027
Sri Lanka...............	451	423	927	899	-419	-298	-268	-523	-473	-474
Sudan..................	12	11	3	3	155	-369	-958	-139	-322	-836
Sweden.................	5,793	17,988	20,882	20,217	-1,231	-6,907	-3,115	2,385	3,402	6,059
Switzerland.............	18,016	29,223	33,255	32,440	6,040	6,942	9,847	-1,561	-6,391	-3,808
Syria...................	83	(NA)	(NA)	(NA)	-958	1,827	(NA)	-2,090	2,159	(NA)
Thailand	2,190	13,305	20,359	20,012	-1,537	-7,282	-7,564	-1,332	-6,751	-5,985
Trinidad and Tobago	1,129	492	172	172	-90	440	-17	756	988	541
Turkey	1,056	6,050	6,159	6,115	-1,013	-2,625	272	-2,975	-9,555	-7,326
United Kingdom	12,860	35,850	36,640	34,090	4,136	-29,390	-11,549	-3,850	-32,742	-18,286
Venezuela	10,251	8,321	9,562	9,288	3,327	8,279	1,663	6,782	10,637	4,791
Yugoslavia..............	1,095	5,474	(NA)	(NA)	833	-2,364	-1,161	-588	-2,676	512
Zaire...................	190	219	157	157	-289	-643	(NA)	606	600	(NA)

NA Not available.   [1] Holdings of convertible foreign currencies.   [2] Former West Germany (prior to unification).

Source: International Monetary Fund, Washington, DC, *International Financial Statistics*, monthly with annual supplements.

No. 1425. Foreign Exchange Rates: 1970 to 1992

[National currency units per dollar, except as noted. Except as indicated, data are annual averages of certified noon buying rates for cable transfers]

YEAR	Australia [1] (dollar)	Austria (schilling)	Belgium (franc)	Canada (dollar)	China: Taiwan (dollar)	Denmark (krone)	France (franc)	Greece (drachma)	Hong Kong (dollar)
1970	111.36	25.880	49.680	1.0103	40.050	7.4890	5.5200	30.00	6.0600
1980	114.00	12.945	29.237	1.1693	36.015	5.6345	4.2250	42.62	4.9760
1981	114.95	15.948	37.194	1.1990	36.849	7.1350	5.4396	55.41	5.5678
1982	101.65	17.060	45.780	1.2344	39.124	8.3443	6.5793	66.87	6.0697
1983	90.14	17.968	51.121	1.2325	40.065	9.1483	7.6203	87.90	7.2569
1984	87.94	20.005	57.749	1.2953	39.633	10.3540	8.7355	112.73	7.8188
1985	70.03	20.676	59.336	1.3658	39.889	10.5980	8.9799	138.40	7.7911
1986	67.09	15.260	44.662	1.3896	37.837	8.0954	6.9256	139.93	7.8037
1987	70.14	12.649	37.357	1.3259	31.756	6.8477	6.0121	135.47	7.7985
1988	78.41	12.357	36.783	1.2306	28.636	6.7411	5.9594	142.00	7.8071
1989	79.19	13.236	39.409	1.1842	26.407	7.3210	6.3802	162.60	7.8008
1990	78.07	11.331	33.424	1.1668	26.918	6.1899	5.4467	158.59	7.7899
1991	75.93	11.686	34.195	1.1460	26.759	6.4038	5.6468	182.63	7.7712
1992, Oct.	69.10	10.962	32.061	1.1968	25.109	6.0215	5.2760	187.54	7.7405

YEAR	India (rupee)	Ireland [1] (pound)	Italy (lira)	Japan (yen)	Malaysia (ringgit)	Netherlands (guilder)	New Zealand [1] (dollar)	Norway (krone)	Portugal (escudo)
1970	7.576	239.59	623.00	357.60	3.0900	3.5970	111.48	7.1400	28.75
1980	7.887	205.77	856.20	226.63	2.1767	1.9875	97.34	4.9381	50.08
1981	8.681	161.32	1,138.60	220.63	2.3048	2.4998	86.85	5.7430	61.74
1982	9.485	142.05	1,354.00	249.06	2.3395	2.6719	75.10	6.4567	80.10
1983	10.104	124.81	1,519.30	237.55	2.3204	2.8543	66.79	7.3012	111.61
1984	11.348	108.64	1,756.10	237.45	2.3448	3.2083	57.84	8.1596	147.70
1985	12.332	106.62	1,908.90	238.47	2.4806	3.3184	49.75	8.5933	172.07
1986	12.597	134.14	1,491.16	168.35	2.5830	2.4484	52.46	7.3984	149.80
1987	12.943	148.79	1,297.03	144.60	2.5185	2.0263	59.33	6.7408	141.20
1988	13.899	152.49	1,302.39	128.17	2.6189	1.9778	65.56	6.5242	144.26
1989	16.213	141.80	1,372.28	138.07	2.7079	2.1219	59.35	6.9131	157.53
1990	17.492	165.76	1,198.27	145.00	2.7057	1.8215	59.62	6.2541	142.70
1991	22.712	174.70	1,241.28	134.59	2.7503	1.8720	54.03	6.4912	144.77
1992, Oct.	28.043	167.90	1,202.28	127.31	2.5456	1.7541	52.18	6.1439	133.78

YEAR	Singapore (dollar)	South Africa (rand)	South Korea (won)	Spain (peseta)	Sweden (krona)	Switzerland (franc)	Thailand (baht)	United Kingdom [1] (pound)	Germany (deutsche mark)
1970	3.0800	0.7181	310.57	69.72	5.1700	4.3160	21.000	239.59	3.6464
1980	2.1412	0.7796	607.43	71.76	4.2309	1.6772	20.476	232.43	1.8175
1981	2.1053	0.8787	681.03	92.40	5.0659	1.9674	21.731	202.43	2.2632
1982	2.1406	1.0876	731.93	110.09	6.2838	2.0327	23.014	174.80	2.4281
1983	2.1136	1.1146	776.04	143.50	7.6717	2.1006	22.991	151.59	2.5539
1984	2.1325	1.4761	807.91	160.78	8.2706	2.3500	23.582	133.66	2.8455
1985	2.2008	2.2344	861.89	169.98	8.6031	2.4551	27.193	129.74	2.9420
1986	2.1782	2.2919	884.61	140.04	7.1272	1.7979	26.314	146.77	2.1705
1987	2.1059	2.0385	825.93	123.54	6.3468	1.4918	25.774	163.98	1.7981
1988	2.0132	2.2770	734.51	116.52	6.1369	1.4642	25.312	178.13	1.7570
1989	1.9511	2.6214	674.29	118.44	6.4559	1.6369	25.725	163.82	1.8808
1990	1.8134	2.5885	710.64	101.96	5.9231	1.3901	25.609	178.41	1.6166
1991	1.7283	2.7633	736.73	104.01	6.0521	1.4356	25.528	176.74	1.6610
1992, Oct.	1.6279	2.8233	783.58	100.31	5.6781	1.4027	25.398	180.88	1.5574

[1] Value is U.S. cents per unit of foreign currency.
Source: Board of Governors of the Federal Reserve System, *Federal Reserve Bulletin,* monthly.

No. 1426. Exchange Rates—Indexes of Value of Foreign Currency Relative to U.S. Dollar: 1970 to 1991

[1982=100]

YEAR	United States	Belgium	Canada	Denmark	France	Germany [1]	Italy	Japan	Netherlands	Norway	Sweden	United Kingdom
1970	100.0	92.2	118.3	111.3	119.0	66.6	215.9	69.5	73.9	90.3	121.2	137.1
1980	100.0	156.8	105.6	148.2	155.9	133.8	158.3	110.4	134.6	130.8	148.6	133.1
1981	100.0	123.6	103.0	116.9	121.0	107.7	118.9	112.9	107.4	112.4	124.0	115.8
1982	100.0	100.0	100.0	100.0	100.0	100.0	100.0	100.0	100.0	100.0	100.0	100.0
1983	100.0	89.5	100.2	91.2	86.3	95.1	89.1	104.8	93.6	88.4	81.9	86.7
1984	100.0	79.3	95.3	80.6	75.3	85.3	77.1	104.9	83.3	79.1	76.0	76.5
1985	100.0	77.2	90.4	78.7	73.3	82.5	70.9	104.4	80.5	75.1	73.0	74.2
1986	100.0	102.5	88.8	103.1	95.0	111.9	90.8	147.9	109.1	87.3	88.2	84.0
1987	100.0	122.5	93.1	121.9	109.4	135.0	104.4	172.2	131.9	95.8	99.0	93.8
1988	100.0	124.5	100.3	123.8	110.4	138.2	104.0	194.3	135.1	99.0	102.4	101.9
1989	100.0	116.2	104.2	114.0	103.1	129.1	98.7	180.4	125.9	93.4	97.3	93.7
1990	100.0	137.0	105.8	134.8	120.8	150.2	113.0	171.8	146.7	103.2	106.1	102.1
1991	100.0	133.9	107.7	130.3	116.5	146.2	109.1	185.1	142.7	99.5	103.8	101.1

[1] Former West Germany for years prior to 1991.

Source: U.S. Bureau of Labor Statistics, News Release USDL: 90-383, *"International Comparisons of Manufacturing Productivity and Labor Cost Trends";* July 27, 1990; and unpublished data.

No. 1427. Central Bank Discount Rates, Money Market Rates, and Government Bond Yields—Selected Countries: 1980 to 1993

[In percent per annum. **Central bank discount rates** refer to the rate at which the monetary authority lends or discounts eligible paper for deposit money banks. **Money market rates** refer to the rate at which short-term borrowings are effected between financial institutions. **Government bond yields** refer to one or more series representing average yields to maturity of government bonds or other bonds that would be indicative of longer term rates]

NATIONAL INTEREST RATE AND YEAR	United States	Canada	Japan	France	Germany [1]	Italy	Netherlands	Sweden	Switzerland	United Kingdom
Central bank discount rates: [2]										
1980	13.00	17.26	7.25	9.50	7.50	16.50	8.00	10.00	3.00	14.00
1985	7.50	9.49	5.00	9.50	4.00	15.00	5.00	10.50	4.00	(3)
1989	7.00	12.47	4.25	9.50	6.00	13.50	7.00	10.50	6.00	(3)
1990	6.50	11.78	6.00	9.50	6.00	12.50	7.25	11.50	6.00	(3)
1991	3.50	8.00	4.50	9.50	8.00	12.00	8.50	8.00	7.00	(3)
1992	3.00	7.00	3.25	9.50	8.25	12.00	7.75	10.00	6.00	(3)
1993, February	3.00	6.00	2.50	9.50	8.00	[4]12.00	7.50	9.00	5.50	(3)
Money market rates: [5]										
1980	13.36	13.28	10.93	11.85	9.10	17.17	10.13	12.17	2.29	15.62
1985	8.10	9.57	6.46	9.93	5.20	15.25	6.30	13.85	3.75	10.78
1989	9.22	12.06	4.87	9.07	6.59	12.69	6.99	11.52	6.50	13.88
1990	8.10	11.62	7.24	9.85	7.92	12.38	8.29	13.45	8.33	14.68
1991	5.70	7.40	7.46	9.49	8.84	12.18	9.01	11.81	7.73	11.75
1992	3.52	6.79	4.58	10.35	9.42	(NA)	9.27	18.42	7.47	9.55
1993, February	3.03	5.93	[4]3.83	11.46	8.65	(NA)	8.30	10.29	5.71	5.83
Government bond yields:										
1980	11.46	12.48	9.22	13.03	8.50	16.11	10.21	11.74	4.77	13.79
1985	10.62	11.04	6.34	10.94	6.87	13.00	7.34	13.09	4.78	10.62
1989	8.50	9.92	5.05	8.79	7.09	10.72	7.21	11.18	5.20	9.58
1990	8.55	10.85	7.36	9.96	8.88	11.51	8.93	13.08	6.68	11.08
1991	7.86	9.76	6.53	9.05	8.63	10.10	8.74	10.69	6.35	9.92
1992	7.01	8.77	4.94	8.60	7.96	(NA)	8.10	10.02	5.48	9.15
1993, February	6.26	8.19	3.76	7.79	6.77	(NA)	7.02	9.80	4.93	8.63

NA Not available. [1] Prior to 1990, data for former West Germany (prior to unification). [2] End of period. [3] Minimum lending rate suspended as of August 20, 1981. [4] January. [5] Period averages.

Source: International Monetary Fund, Washington, DC, *International Financial Statistics*, monthly.

No. 1428. External Debt of Eastern European Countries: 1980 to 1991

[In billions of dollars. **Gross debt:** total amount owed. **Commercial debt:** money owed to private institutions or indiviuals. **Official debt:** money owed to or guaranteed by a foreign government. Net debt represents gross debt minus assets held with Western commercial banks]

TYPE AND SOURCE	1980	1984	1985	1986	1987	1988	1989	1990	1991
Former Soviet Union: Gross debt	20.5	22.3	29.0	36.0	40.8	42.4	50.8	53.6	61.0
Commercial debt	11.0	13.2	19.5	25.9	30.1	33.7	40.5	35.6	31.8
Official debt	9.5	9.1	9.5	10.1	10.7	8.7	10.3	18.0	29.2
Net debt	10.5	10.8	15.7	21.1	25.9	26.9	36.3	45.4	(NA)
Bulgaria: Gross debt	3.5	2.2	3.7	4.9	6.1	7.5	10.0	11.4	11.9
Commercial debt	3.2	1.8	3.1	4.2	5.3	6.5	8.8	9.5	9.4
Official debt	0.3	0.5	0.6	0.7	0.9	1.0	1.2	1.9	2.5
Net debt	2.7	0.8	1.5	3.6	5.0	(NA)	(NA)	(NA)	(NA)
Czechoslovakia: Gross debt	4.9	3.6	3.8	4.5	5.8	6.1	7.8	8.1	9.3
Commercial debt	4.1	2.6	2.8	3.4	4.5	4.8	5.9	6.1	6.9
Official debt	0.9	1.0	1.0	1.1	1.3	1.3	1.9	2.0	2.4
Net debt	3.7	2.6	2.8	3.3	4.2	(NA)	(NA)	(NA)	(NA)
Hungary: Gross debt	9.1	8.8	11.8	15.1	17.8	18.0	21.9	21.3	22.7
Commercial debt	8.8	7.0	9.8	12.7	15.0	15.3	17.0	16.4	15.7
Official debt	0.3	0.8	0.8	0.9	1.0	1.0	3.2	2.3	3.1
BIS/IMF [1]	-	1.1	1.2	1.5	1.8	1.7	1.7	2.6	3.9
Net debt	7.0	6.7	8.6	12.0	15.5	(NA)	(NA)	(NA)	(NA)
Poland: Gross debt	25.0	26.8	29.3	33.5	39.2	38.5	39.7	48.5	46.3
Commercial debt	14.9	9.4	10.6	12.1	12.8	11.9	13.4	14.5	12.8
Official debt	10.1	17.4	18.7	21.4	26.4	26.6	26.3	33.5	30.6
IMF/World Bank [1]	-	-	-	-	-	-	-	0.5	2.9
Net debt	24.4	25.3	27.7	31.8	36.2	(NA)	(NA)	(NA)	(NA)
Romania: Gross debt	9.4	7.1	6.6	6.4	5.1	2.2	0.1	0.8	2.2
Commercial debt	6.5	3.4	2.9	2.7	1.7	0.4	0.1	0.7	0.3
Official debt	1.7	1.1	1.1	1.1	0.8	0.6	-	0.1	0.7
IMF/World Bank/CEMA bank [1]	1.2	2.6	2.6	2.6	2.6	1.2	-	-	1.2
Net debt	9.1	6.4	6.4	5.8	4.5	(NA)	(NA)	(NA)	(NA)
Yugoslavia: Gross debt	17.4	18.8	19.2	19.4	18.7	18.2	15.7	(NA)	(NA)
Commercial debt	12.8	9.0	7.8	7.4	7.6	7.8	6.7	(NA)	(NA)
Official debt	2.6	5.8	7.1	7.7	6.6	5.4	5.3	(NA)	(NA)
IMF/World Bank [1]	2.1	4.1	4.3	4.2	4.5	5.0	3.7	(NA)	(NA)
Net debt	16.2	17.7	18.1	17.9	18.0	(NA)	(NA)	(NA)	(NA)

- Represents zero. NA Not available. [1] IMF=International Monetary Fund. CEMA=Council for Mutual Economic Assistance.

Source: U.S. Central Intelligence Agency, *Handbook of International Economic Statistics, 1992;* and unpublished data.

No. 1429. Total External Public Debt, 1980 to 1991, and by Type of Creditor, 1991, and Debt Service Payments and Ratio, 1980 to 1991

[**External public debt** is defined as debt repayable to external creditors in foreign currency, goods, or services, with an original or extended maturity of more than 1 year, which is a direct obligation of, or has repayment guaranteed by, a public body in the borrowing country. Excludes undisbursed debt (amounts not yet drawn by recipient) and unguaranteed private debt, which for some countries is substantial. Debt contracted for the purchase of military equipment is not usually reported. **Debt service** payments represent the sum of interest payments and repayments of principal on external public debt]

COUNTRY	TOTAL EXTERNAL PUBLIC DEBT (mil. dol.)			1991				DEBT SERVICE PAYMENTS (mil. dol.)			DEBT SERVICE RATIO³ (percent)		
	1980	1985	1990	Total¹	Bilateral official	Banks²	International organizations	1980	1990	1991	1980	1990	1991
Argentina⁴	10,181	37,327	46,931	45,388	6,955	32,041	5,415	1,987	4,600	5,449	17.7	30.5	36.8
Bangladesh	3,417	5,966	11,440	12,103	4,931	-	6,998	110	523	412	9.4	15.0	11.1
Bolivia	2,182	3,511	3,682	3,524	1,501	245	1,718	290	289	221	(NA)	18.2	21.2
Brazil	40,895	74,739	83,760	87,477	14,779	53,191	11,068	8,065	5,575	7,604	27.7	28.9	23.4
Bulgaria	(NA)	3,964	9,564	11,023	2,063	5,534	549	(NA)	1,284	1,076	34.6	15.7	21.8
Cameroon	2,005	2,003	4,753	5,027	2,543	349	1,418	186	300	306	21.9	15.0	24.0
Chile	4,705	12,897	10,356	10,024	964	4,384	4,315	1,375	1,571	2,793	4.4	9.7	10.3
China: Mainland	4,504	9,963	45,284	50,502	9,514	20,322	7,527	930	5,896	7,269	23.9	14.6	13.5
Colombia	4,089	9,573	14,681	14,503	2,315	4,507	6,159	529	3,116	3,089	10.1	12.8	13.1
Congo	1,257	2,342	4,102	3,989	2,657	419	574	71	457	216	6.9	30.5	19.3
Costa Rica	1,700	3,534	3,076	3,316	1,460	616	1,189	206	433	341	8.9	30.8	27.6
Cote d'Ivoire	4,310	5,778	10,188	10,424	4,501	2,678	2,931	870	520	499	16.9	21.2	15.1
Dominican Republic	1,220	2,691	3,435	3,471	1,628	777	880	154	145	180	10.3	5.5	6.8
Ecuador	3,300	7,199	9,867	9,952	1,484	4,908	2,235	559	875	927	18.8	26.7	27.0
Egypt	16,212	34,978	34,318	36,028	27,828	774	3,339	747	2,734	1,828	8.1	16.5	10.0
Ethiopia	669	1,726	3,123	3,301	1,576	101	1,357	34	190	126	5.8	28.1	23.0
Gabon	1,271	945	2,925	2,935	1,891	182	350	398	144	78	16.4	5.5	3.0
Ghana	1,161	1,297	2,672	2,958	672	6	2,071	108	180	161	8.9	18.1	14.7
Guatemala	549	2,166	2,179	2,103	777	323	953	45	163	253	2.5	9.7	15.0
Honduras	974	2,137	3,217	2,866	967	156	1,618	98	313	261	10.1	29.0	25.0
Hungary	6,416	9,965	17,999	19,221	521	14,149	3,342	1,460	3,748	3,772	(NA)	30.4	30.1
India⁵	18,373	31,563	60,228	62,842	16,352	11,749	23,992	1,166	5,322	5,988	7.9	22.2	20.8
Indonesia	15,027	26,777	45,004	48,003	21,259	5,449	15,955	1,763	6,666	6,817	7.7	19.9	22.7
Jamaica	1,421	3,122	3,874	3,751	2,079	287	1,192	206	525	566	14.0	20.2	24.0
Jordan	1,486	3,404	7,143	7,670	3,822	1,358	936	182	517	583	7.3	14.4	16.7
Kenya	2,120	2,670	4,702	4,789	1,326	580	2,678	247	489	522	12.3	6.2	3.8
Madagascar	892	2,154	3,195	3,381	1,761	59	1,388	57	132	115	5.6	8.9	8.2
Malaysia	4,008	14,840	14,777	16,447	2,720	9,729	1,942	376	3,146	2,724	27.1	14.4	19.6
Mali	669	1,301	2,305	2,392	1,419	2	962	9	40	11	11.0	25.4	24.6
Mexico	33,915	72,703	76,752	78,456	9,694	48,141	15,475	7,890	7,977	9,378	35.6	17.5	19.9
Morocco	8,325	13,825	22,236	20,132	10,483	3,175	5,064	1,173	1,490	2,023	2.8	5.9	1.8
Nicaragua	1,661	4,892	8,067	8,703	5,554	2,088	957	87	10	386	2.5	9.0	6.9
Oman	436	1,908	2,205	2,270	237	1,619	132	223	757	541	16.9	2.5	110.9
Pakistan	8,507	10,565	16,486	17,632	9,014	317	8,048	592	1,365	1,472	5.7	12.8	10.6
Panama	2,271	3,320	3,988	3,939	601	2,307	956	466	140	181	12.4	13.3	14.9
Papua New Guinea	485	1,069	1,511	1,601	328	267	870	61	270	236	6.0	2.6	2.9
Peru	6,218	9,816	12,906	15,080	7,663	3,731	1,898	1,506	174	794	31.2	4.0	18.4
Philippines	6,363	13,697	23,695	24,530	10,161	6,776	6,672	596	2,866	2,787	7.3	21.1	18.4
Poland	(NA)	29,763	39,285	44,057	31,886	10,195	878	(NA)	840	834	5.6	18.1	13.3
Portugal	6,728	12,825	16,994	19,374	1,463	10,565	2,805	1,024	4,395	5,077	-	4.3	4.5
Senegal	1,105	2,058	2,946	2,838	1,283	77	1,412	219	212	222	12.0	21.9	22.9
South Korea	15,933	28,279	18,781	22,246	5,544	8,227	3,590	2,783	4,769	3,204	10.5	14.0	15.8
Sri Lanka	1,227	2,838	4,938	5,653	2,939	294	2,085	84	285	288	9.9	2.2	3.6
Sudan	3,822	6,602	9,156	9,221	5,782	1,579	1,856	102	23	23	24.2	12.7	13.5
Syria	2,918	9,502	14,959	14,932	13,069	-	1,048	302	1,374	627	9.0	23.5	12.7
Tanzania	1,915	2,957	5,598	5,786	3,569	16	1,968	63	106	98	5.1	10.5	4.9
Thailand	3,943	9,860	12,573	13,293	4,841	2,933	3,544	441	3,297	1,856	11.6	18.6	17.2
Tunisia	3,210	4,455	6,684	7,156	3,161	281	2,714	427	1,208	1,135	18.3	22.6	23.1
Turkey	15,040	19,564	38,617	39,207	8,618	17,426	10,142	1,053	6,433	6,605	8.2	19.3	18.3
Uganda	542	877	2,212	2,325	645	77	1,449	36	65	92	10.9	28.0	42.2
Uruguay	1,127	2,695	3,009	2,843	158	1,817	859	198	709	638	12.4	29.7	26.7
Venezuela	10,614	17,738	24,611	25,189	346	20,483	2,210	2,955	4,169	2,312	13.3	19.4	12.6
Yemen	1,453	2,968	5,126	5,207	3,991	80	1,059	35	107	111	(NA)	2.5	3.7
Yugoslavia⁶	4,581	11,149	12,986	11,641	4,001	4,735	2,784	617	2,719	2,339	3.4	6.8	11.3
Zaire	4,261	4,858	8,951	9,151	6,194	524	2,085	396	136	95	16.5	5.9	4.3
Zambia	2,141	3,141	4,858	4,954	2,944	73	1,518	287	166	483	17.7	11.5	40.7
Zimbabwe	696	1,778	2,465	2,604	907	413	728	50	370	465	2.9	18.5	22.6

- Represents or rounds to zero.   NA Not available.   ¹ Includes other types of creditors not shown separately.   ² Includes other private financial institutions.   ³ Debt service payments as percent of exports.   ⁴ The increase in debt outstanding from 1980 to 1985 includes the refinancing of short-term private debt by public debt, which matured in 1986-87.   ⁵ Fiscal year basis.   ⁶ The bulk of the debt of Yugoslovian enterprises is reported as nonguaranteed.

Source: The World Bank, Washington, DC, *World Debt Tables*, periodic.

No. 1430. Net Flow of Financial Resources to Developing Countries, by Origin and Type of Resource: 1970 to 1991

[In billions of U.S. dollars. Net flow covers loans, grants, and grant-like flows minus amortization on loans. Military flows are excluded. Developing countries cover countries designated by Development Assistance Committee as developing. Official development assistance covers all flows to developing countries and multilateral institutions provided by official agencies, including State and local governments, or by their executive agencies, which are administered with the promotion of economic development and welfare of developing countries as their main objective and whose financial terms are intended to be concessional in character with grant element of at least 25 percent. Other official flows cover export credits and portfolio investment from the official sector]

ORIGIN AND TYPE OF RESOURCE	1970	1980	1984	1985	1986	1987	1988	1989	1990	1991
Development Assistance Committee countries [1]	15.9	75.4	79.1	45.2	68.8	66.4	85.6	84.4	68.4	(NA)
Official development assistance .	6.9	27.3	28.7	29.4	36.7	41.6	48.1	45.7	53.0	56.7
Bilateral grants [2]	3.3	14.1	15.5	17.8	21.1	23.4	26.0	25.9	30.8	34.6
Bilateral loans	2.4	4.0	4.2	4.1	5.2	6.6	7.1	7.1	6.4	6.7
Multilateral contributions [3]	1.3	9.2	9.0	7.5	10.4	11.6	15.0	12.8	15.8	15.4
Other official flows	1.1	5.3	6.2	3.4	2.1	2.0	4.9	5.8	8.9	(NA)
Private flows at market terms	7.0	40.4	41.6	9.4	26.7	18.8	28.3	28.8	1.4	(NA)
Direct investment	3.7	10.1	10.9	6.5	11.0	21.0	25.1	30.1	26.8	(NA)
Private export credits	2.2	11.5	3.5	0.8	-1.7	-2.4	-1.3	5.7	-0.4	(NA)
Portfolio investment	1.2	18.7	27.2	2.1	17.4	0.3	4.4	-7.0	-25.2	(NA)
Private voluntary agencies	0.9	2.4	2.6	2.9	3.3	4.0	4.2	4.0	5.1	(NA)
Organization of Petroleum Exporting Countries [4]	0.6	10.8	3.7	4.1	(NA)	(NA)	(NA)	(NA)	(NA)	(NA)
Official development assistance .	0.4	9.7	4.6	3.6	4.7	3.3	2.4	2.4	6.4	2.7
Other official flows	0.2	1.1	-0.9	0.5	(NA)	(NA)	(NA)	(NA)	(NA)	(NA)
Centrally-planned economies: [5]										
Official development assistance .	1.0	2.6	3.4	3.6	4.6	5.0	5.0	4.7	-2.2	(NA)
Total net flow to developing countries, by DAC country [1]	15.9	75.4	79.1	45.2	68.8	66.4	85.6	84.4	68.4	(NA)
United States	6.4	13.9	28.6	1.8	18.2	13.8	17.5	16.4	11.1	20.8
Official development assistance	3.2	7.1	8.7	9.4	9.6	8.9	10.1	7.7	11.4	11.3
Bilateral grants [2]	1.4	3.0	5.6	7.3	7.0	6.7	6.5	6.8	8.5	12.1
Bilateral loans	1.3	1.4	0.8	0.9	0.6	0.3	0.3	(Z)	-0.2	-2.7
Multilateral contributions [3]	0.5	2.8	2.3	1.2	2.0	1.9	3.4	0.9	3.0	1.9
Other official flows	0.1	1.1	1.0	0.2	-0.6	-1.8	1.9	-0.5	-0.4	-0.8
Private flows at market terms	2.5	4.3	17.4	-9.3	7.5	4.4	3.2	7.3	-2.4	7.6
Direct investment	1.9	3.4	4.4	0.9	3.1	8.0	4.2	7.1	7.8	10.5
Private export credits and portfolio investment	0.6	0.9	13.0	-10.2	4.4	-3.6	-1.0	-0.3	-10.1	-2.9
Private voluntary agencies	0.6	1.3	1.5	1.5	1.7	1.6	2.3	1.9	2.5	2.7
Australia	0.4	0.9	1.5	1.2	1.1	0.9	3.6	1.5	1.5	-2.1
Austria	0.1	0.3	0.1	0.2	0.1	0.2	0.3	0.2	0.6	0.7
Belgium	0.3	2.9	3.5	1.3	-0.8	-0.3	1.8	1.5	0.1	1.5
Canada	0.6	3.2	2.8	1.7	1.6	2.5	2.7	2.7	3.2	4.0
Denmark	0.1	0.8	0.6	0.4	0.5	0.9	0.7	0.9	1.1	1.1
Finland	(Z)	0.2	0.3	0.3	0.4	0.6	0.8	0.9	1.0	1.0
France	1.8	11.6	8.9	8.9	9.2	8.7	7.2	5.6	6.1	(NA)
Germany [6]	1.5	10.6	6.5	5.8	7.9	8.8	11.8	12.1	13.6	13.1
Ireland	(NA)	(Z)	0.1	0.1	0.1	0.1	0.3	0.1	0.2	0.2
Italy	0.7	4.0	2.3	2.2	2.6	2.0	5.1	5.8	3.2	7.6
Japan	1.8	6.8	11.7	11.6	14.6	20.3	21.2	24.1	18.7	25.0
Netherlands	0.4	2.4	2.0	2.6	2.8	3.2	2.7	2.5	4.0	4.4
New Zealand	(Z)	0.1	0.1	0.1	0.1	0.1	0.1	0.1	0.1	0.1
Norway	0.1	0.9	0.6	0.6	0.7	0.9	0.9	0.9	1.2	1.4
Sweden	0.2	1.9	1.3	1.4	1.7	1.8	2.3	2.3	2.8	1.8
Switzerland	0.1	2.7	3.4	2.5	1.4	-1.6	2.0	2.7	4.6	0.8
United Kingdom	1.3	12.2	4.8	2.5	6.7	3.5	4.7	3.4	-4.4	(NA)

NA Not available.   Z Less than $50 million.   [1] Includes flows to OPEC countries (see footnote 4). Comprises as donors Australia, Austria, Belgium, Canada, Denmark, Finland, France, Ireland, Italy, Japan, Netherlands, New Zealand, Norway, Sweden, Switzerland, United Kingdom, United States, and Germany.   [2] Includes "grant-like" flows (i.e., loans repayable in recipients' currencies).   [3] Includes capital subscriptions to multilateral organizations in the form of demand instruments as of date of issue.   [4] Algeria, Ecuador, Gabon, Iran, Iraq, Kuwait, Libya, Nigeria, Qatar, Saudi Arabia, United Arab Emirates, and Venezuela.   [5] Bulgaria, Czechoslovakia, Hungary, Poland, Romania, and former Soviet Union.   [6] Former West Germany (prior to unification).
Source: Organization for Economic Cooperation and Development, Paris, France, unpublished data.

No. 1431. Per Capita Public and Private Aid to Developing Countries: 1980 to 1990

[In dollars. See headnote, table 1430. Private aid figures exclude government subsidies to voluntary agencies. Countries are ranked by per capita gross national product in 1990]

COUNTRY	OFFICIAL DEVELOPMENT ASSISTANCE			PRIVATE VOLUNTARY AID			COUNTRY	OFFICIAL DEVELOPMENT ASSISTANCE			PRIVATE VOLUNTARY AID		
	1980	1985	1990	1980	1985	1990		1980	1985	1990	1980	1985	1990
Switzerland	40	46	110	10	8	17	Austria	24	33	51	3	2	4
Finland	23	43	170	3	3	7	Belgium	60	45	89	5	2	6
Sweden	116	101	235	7	9	(NA)	Italy	12	19	59	(Z)	(Z)	(NA)
Norway	119	138	284	8	12	31	Netherlands	115	78	173	6	7	16
Denmark	92	86	228	3	3	6	Australia	45	47	56	3	3	3
Germany [1]	58	48	100	7	7	12	United Kingdom	33	27	46	3	3	6
Japan	29	31	73	(Z)	(Z)	1	New Zealand	23	16	28	2	3	4
United States	31	39	45	6	6	10	Spain	(NA)	(NA)	959	(NA)	(NA)	(NA)
Canada	45	64	93	4	7	10	Ireland	9	11	16	-	6	7
France	77	72	166	1	1	3	Portugal	(NA)	(NA)	148	(NA)	(NA)	(NA)

- Represents or rounds to zero.   NA Not available.   Z Less than 50 cents.   [1] Former West Germany (prior to unification).
Source: Organization for Economic Cooperation and Development, Paris, France, unpublished data.

No. 1432. Military Expenditures in Current and Constant (1989) Dollars: 1980 to 1989

[In millions of dollars, except as indicated. See also table 551. For most countries, data for expenditures and for GNP were based on local currencies which were deflated to constant 1989 local currency values before conversion to U.S. dollar equivalents. In general, the rates used for conversion are the 1989 average par/market exchange rates as supplied by the International Bank for Reconstruction and Development]

COUNTRY	CURRENT DOLLARS				CONSTANT (1989) DOLLARS				Per capita (dollars)		Percent of GNP [1]	
	1980	1985	1988	1989	1980	1985	1988	1989	1980	1989	1980	1989
United States	144,000	265,800	293,100	304,100	212,100	302,600	305,100	304,100	931	1,222	5.3	5.8
Algeria [2]	940	1,040	1,595	2,313	1,385	1,183	1,660	2,313	73	94	3.9	5.1
Argentina	1,559	[2]1,847	1,989	1,858	2,296	[2]2,103	2,070	1,858	81	58	3.6	3.4
Australia	3,226	5,856	6,093	6,153	4,753	6,666	6,342	6,153	325	368	2.3	2.3
Austria	820	[2]1,322	1,310	1,402	1,208	[2]1,505	1,364	1,402	160	184	1.1	1.1
Belgium	2,951	3,592	3,811	3,881	4,348	4,089	3,968	3,881	442	392	3.3	2.5
Brazil [2]	1,899	2,793	5,731	(NA)	2,799	3,180	5,966	(NA)	23	(NA)	0.7	(NA)
Bulgaria [2]	3,993	5,808	5,868	5,885	5,883	6,612	6,109	5,885	665	656	13.1	11.9
Canada	5,176	8,943	10,500	10,840	7,626	10,180	10,930	10,840	317	413	1.9	2.0
Chile [3]	449	619	[2]803	[2]790	662	704	[2]836	[2]790	60	[2]61	3.6	[2]3.4
China:												
Mainland [2]	16,370	19,850	21,830	22,330	24,120	22,600	22,720	22,330	25	20	8.8	3.7
Taiwan [2]	3,222	[2]6,377	[2]6,607	[2]8,060	4,748	[2]7,260	[2]6,877	[2]8,060	266	[2]397	6.5	[2]5.4
Cuba [3]	1,140	1,335	1,350	1,377	1,680	1,520	1,405	1,377	174	131	6.5	3.9
Czechoslovakia [2]	5,249	7,998	9,131	8,361	7,734	9,105	9,505	8,361	507	534	7.4	6.8
Denmark	1,454	1,909	2,135	2,184	2,143	2,173	2,222	2,184	418	426	2.5	2.2
East Germany [2]	7,040	10,810	12,770	13,970	10,370	12,310	13,290	13,970	620	848	7.9	8.8
Egypt [2]	2,923	6,785	5,559	3,499	4,306	7,724	5,786	3,499	103	67	9.5	5.0
El Salvador	120	[2]276	[2]237	[2]252	177	[2]314	[2]247	[2]252	38	[2]48	2.7	[2]4.0
Finland	909	1,435	1,687	1,788	1,339	1,633	1,756	1,788	280	360	1.6	1.6
France	21,230	29,600	33,490	35,260	31,270	33,690	34,860	35,260	581	628	4.0	3.7
Greece	1,779	3,052	3,170	3,097	2,621	3,474	3,300	3,097	272	309	5.5	5.9
Hungary [2]	2,832	3,782	4,396	4,064	4,173	4,305	4,576	4,064	390	384	7.2	6.3
India	3,608	6,662	8,377	8,174	5,316	7,584	8,721	8,174	8	10	3.2	3.1
Indonesia	1,093	1,446	1,402	1,510	1,611	1,646	1,460	1,510	10	8	3.1	1.7
Iran [2]	2,624	(NA)	(NA)	(NA)	3,867	(NA)	(NA)	(NA)	99	(NA)	7.0	(NA)
Israel	6,654	7,027	5,585	5,745	9,805	7,999	5,814	5,745	2,623	1,323	28.8	12.8
Italy	10,110	15,320	19,790	20,720	14,900	17,440	20,600	20,720	264	360	2.1	2.4
Japan	12,330	20,650	26,100	28,410	18,170	23,510	27,170	28,410	156	231	0.9	1.0
Kuwait	892	1,525	1,273	1,964	1,314	1,736	1,325	1,964	959	962	2.9	6.2
Malaysia	664	[2]920	832	1,039	978	[2]1,036	866	1,039	71	61	4.4	2.9
Mexico	456	1,049	962	875	671	1,194	1,002	875	10	10	0.4	0.5
Morocco [2]	763	(NA)	1,102	1,203	1,124	(NA)	1,147	1,203	55	48	7.2	5.5
Netherlands	4,048	5,433	6,070	6,399	5,965	6,185	6,319	6,399	422	431	3.1	2.9
Nicaragua [2]	53	192	(NA)	(NA)	78	218	(NA)	(NA)	28	(NA)	6.2	(NA)
Nigeria	447	294	201	130	658	335	210	130	7	1	2.4	0.2
North Korea [2]	4,380	5,260	5,840	6,000	6,454	5,988	6,079	6,000	359	285	20.0	20.0
Norway	1,320	2,152	2,680	2,925	1,945	2,450	2,790	2,925	476	691	3.0	3.3
Oman	1,059	1,937	1,350	1,552	1,560	2,205	1,405	1,552	1,585	1,085	22.1	20.3
Pakistan	777	[2]2,356	2,309	2,488	1,145	1,990	2,404	2,488	13	22	5.4	6.8
Peru	1,457	[2]2,356	(NA)	(NA)	2,147	[2]2,682	(NA)	(NA)	124	(NA)	5.0	(NA)
Philippines	501	405	675	960	738	461	702	960	15	15	1.9	2.2
Poland [2]	9,644	14,670	15,350	15,480	14,210	16,700	15,980	15,480	399	410	8.9	8.9
Portugal	858	1,051	1,338	1,457	1,265	1,196	1,393	1,457	129	141	3.6	3.3
Romania [2]	4,587	6,840	7,004	6,916	6,759	7,787	7,291	6,916	304	299	6.1	6.1
Saudi Arabia	14,990	21,340	13,600	14,690	22,090	24,290	14,160	14,690	2,176	897	14.3	16.0
Singapore	533	1,125	1,343	1,475	785	1,281	1,398	1,475	325	550	5.0	5.1
South Africa	2,563	2,612	3,555	3,786	3,777	2,974	3,701	3,786	125	98	5.2	4.4
South Korea	3,821	6,109	8,030	9,100	5,629	6,955	8,359	9,100	148	213	6.1	4.3
Soviet Union [2]	198,200	277,200	317,900	311,000	292,000	315,600	330,900	311,000	1,096	1,077	12.9	11.7
Spain	4,560	6,639	7,244	7,775	6,719	7,558	7,541	7,775	179	199	2.3	2.1
Sweden	3,257	4,390	4,875	4,872	4,799	4,998	5,075	4,872	577	574	3.1	2.6
Switzerland	2,461	[2]3,487	[2]3,468	[2]3,806	3,626	[2]3,970	[2]3,610	[2]3,806	568	[2]568	2.4	[2]2.1
Syria [3]	1,936	[2]3,627	[2]1,801	2,234	2,852	[2]4,129	[2]1,875	2,234	328	186	17.2	11.6
Thailand	1,011	1,814	1,741	1,843	1,489	2,065	1,813	1,843	32	33	4.1	2.7
Turkey	1,635	2,552	2,826	3,150	2,409	2,906	2,942	3,150	53	56	4.8	4.1
United Arab Emirates	1,724	[2]1,901	1,587	1,471	2,541	[2]2,165	1,652	1,471	2,540	695	5.5	5.3
United Kingdom	22,080	32,560	32,710	34,630	32,530	37,070	34,050	34,630	578	605	5.0	4.2
Venezuela	317	358	[2]647	[2]407	467	407	[2]674	[2]407	31	[2]21	1.1	[2]1.0
West Germany	22,400	29,980	32,300	33,600	33,000	34,130	33,630	33,600	536	544	3.3	2.8
Yugoslavia	1,669	1,884	2,528	2,126	2,459	2,144	2,631	2,126	110	90	4.3	3.6

NA Not available.   [1] Military expenditure as percent of gross national product.   [2] Estimated.   [3] Data probably omit a major share of total military expenditures, probably including most arms acquisitions.

Source: U.S. Arms Control and Disarmament Agency, *World Military Expenditures and Arms Transfers*, annual.

No. 1433. Armed Forces Personnel—Number and Rate, by Country: 1980 to 1989

[Personnel data as of July. Armed Forces refer to active-duty military personnel, including paramilitary forces where those forces resemble regular units in their organization, equipment, training, or mission. Reserve forces are not included]

COUNTRY	ARMED FORCES PERSONNEL (1,000)						ARMED FORCES PER 1,000 POPULATION					
	1980	1985	1986	1987	1988	1989	1980	1985	1986	1987	1988	1989
United States	2,050	2,244	2,269	2,279	2,246	2,241	9.0	9.4	9.4	9.3	9.1	9.0
Algeria	101	170	180	170	126	126	5.4	7.7	7.9	7.2	5.2	5.1
Argentina.	155	129	104	118	95	95	5.5	4.3	3.4	3.8	3.0	3.0
Australia	71	70	71	70	71	70	4.9	4.4	4.4	4.3	4.3	4.2
Austria	40	40	39	70	55	48	5.3	5.3	5.2	9.2	7.2	6.3
Belgium.	108	107	107	109	110	110	11.0	10.9	10.8	11.0	11.1	11.1
Brazil	450	496	527	541	319	319	3.7	3.6	3.7	3.8	2.2	2.1
Bulgaria.	188	189	190	191	160	150	21.2	21.2	21.2	21.3	17.8	16.7
Canada.	82	83	85	86	88	88	3.4	3.3	3.4	3.4	3.4	3.4
Chile.	116	124	127	127	96	95	10.5	10.3	10.3	10.1	7.6	7.4
China: Mainland	4,650	4,100	4,030	3,530	3,783	3,903	4.7	3.9	3.8	3.3	3.5	3.5
Taiwan.	465	440	390	365	390	379	26.1	22.7	19.9	18.4	19.4	18.6
Cuba	220	297	297	297	297	297	22.8	29.4	29.2	28.9	28.6	28.3
Czechoslovakia	190	210	214	215	211	175	12.5	13.5	13.8	13.8	13.5	11.2
Denmark	33	29	28	28	30	31	6.4	5.7	5.5	5.5	5.8	6.0
East Germany	228	242	242	241	242	262	13.6	14.5	14.6	14.5	14.6	15.9
Egypt	447	466	400	450	452	450	10.7	9.9	8.3	9.1	8.9	8.7
El Salvador	16	48	48	49	45	45	3.4	10.0	9.8	9.8	8.8	8.6
Finland	36	40	37	37	40	39	7.5	8.2	7.4	7.4	8.1	7.9
France	575	563	558	559	558	554	10.7	10.2	10.1	10.0	10.0	9.9
Greece	186	201	202	199	199	201	19.3	20.2	20.3	19.9	19.9	20.1
Honduras	14	21	22	22	19	19	3.9	5.0	5.1	4.9	4.2	4.1
Hungary	120	117	116	116	117	109	11.2	11.0	10.9	10.9	11.0	10.3
India	1,104	1,515	1,492	1,502	1,362	1,257	1.6	2.0	1.9	1.9	1.7	1.5
Indonesia	250	281	278	281	284	285	1.6	1.6	1.6	1.6	1.6	1.5
Iran	305	345	345	350	654	604	7.8	7.3	7.1	6.9	12.6	11.2
Iraq	430	788	800	900	1,000	1,000	32.5	50.2	49.2	53.5	57.4	55.3
Israel	196	195	180	180	191	191	52.4	47.8	43.5	42.8	44.7	44.0
Italy	500	531	529	531	533	533	8.9	9.3	9.2	9.3	9.3	9.3
Japan	242	241	245	244	245	247	2.1	2.0	2.0	2.0	2.0	2.0
Kuwait.	12	16	18	20	15	20	8.8	9.3	10.0	10.7	7.7	9.9
Malaysia	83	106	106	106	108	110	6.0	6.8	6.6	6.5	6.5	6.4
Mexico	120	140	141	141	154	154	1.7	1.8	1.8	1.7	1.8	1.8
Morocco	117	165	185	200	195	195	5.7	7.2	7.9	8.3	7.9	7.8
Netherlands	107	103	106	106	107	106	7.6	7.1	7.3	7.2	7.2	7.1
Nicaragua	24	74	75	80	74	74	8.6	22.5	22.2	23.2	21.0	20.4
Nigeria	150	134	138	138	107	107	1.7	1.3	1.3	1.3	1.0	0.9
North Korea.	700	784	838	838	842	1,040	38.9	40.0	42.0	41.3	40.8	49.5
Norway	40	36	38	38	40	43	9.7	8.7	9.1	9.1	9.5	10.2
Oman	15	25	26	27	27	29	15.2	20.2	20.3	22.3	19.3	20.3
Pakistan	467	644	573	572	484	520	5.5	6.5	5.6	5.4	4.5	4.7
Peru	151	128	127	127	111	110	8.7	6.5	6.3	6.2	5.3	5.1
Philippines	155	157	161	161	105	106	3.0	2.7	2.7	2.7	1.7	1.7
Poland	408	439	443	441	430	350	11.5	11.8	11.8	11.7	11.4	9.3
Portugal	88	102	101	105	104	104	9.0	10.0	9.9	10.2	10.1	10.1
Qatar	6	7	9	11	7	7	26.0	20.1	24.0	27.2	16.1	15.1
Romania	211	237	238	248	220	207	9.5	10.4	10.4	10.8	9.5	8.9
Saudi Arabia	79	80	80	80	84	82	7.8	5.9	5.6	5.4	5.3	5.0
Singapore	50	59	56	55	56	56	20.7	23.1	21.5	21.1	21.0	20.7
South Africa	70	95	90	102	100	100	2.3	2.7	2.5	2.8	2.7	2.6
South Korea.	600	600	604	604	626	647	15.7	14.6	14.5	14.4	14.8	15.1
Soviet Union	3,900	3,900	3,900	3,900	3,900	3,700	14.6	14.0	13.9	13.7	13.6	12.8
Spain	356	314	314	314	304	277	9.5	8.2	8.1	8.1	7.8	7.1
Sweden.	70	69	66	66	65	62	8.4	8.3	7.8	7.8	7.7	7.4
Switzerland	23	23	21	20	23	17	3.6	3.5	3.2	3.0	3.4	2.5
Syria.	250	402	400	400	400	400	28.8	38.8	37.2	35.9	34.5	33.3
Thailand	234	270	275	275	273	273	5.0	5.2	5.2	5.1	5.0	4.9
Turkey	717	814	860	879	847	780	15.9	16.0	16.5	16.4	15.5	13.9
United Arab Emirates.	44	44	44	44	43	43	44.0	28.0	25.7	23.8	21.7	20.3
United Kingdom	330	334	331	328	324	318	5.9	5.9	5.8	5.8	5.7	5.6
Venezuela	55	71	66	69	73	75	3.7	4.1	3.7	3.8	3.9	3.9
Vietnam	900	1,000	1,300	1,300	1,100	1,000	16.9	16.9	21.4	21.0	17.3	15.4
West Germany	490	495	495	495	495	503	8.0	8.1	8.1	8.1	8.1	8.1
Yugoslavia.	260	258	234	234	229	225	11.6	11.2	10.0	10.0	9.7	9.5

Source: U.S. Arms Control and Disarmament Agency, World Military Expenditures and Arms Transfers, annual.

Guide to—Sources of Statistics, State Statistical Abstracts, and Foreign Statistical Abstracts

Alphabetically arranged by subject, this guide contains references to the important primary sources of statistical information for the United States. Secondary sources have been included if the information contained in them is presented in a particularly convenient form or if primary sources are not readily available. Nonrecurrent publications presenting compilations or estimates for years later than 1982 or types of data not available in regular series are also included.

Much valuable information may also be found in State reports (see pp. 910-913) and foreign statistical abstracts (see pp. 914 and 915) and in reports for particular commodities, industries, or similar segments of our economic and social structures, many of which are not included here.

Publications listed under each subject are divided into two main groups: "U.S. Government" and "Other." The location of the publisher of each report is given except for Federal agencies located in Washington, DC. Most Federal publications may be purchased from the Superintendent of Documents, U.S. Government Printing Office, Washington, DC 20402, tel. 202-783-3238, or from Government Printing Office bookstores in certain major cities. In some cases, Federal publications may be obtained from the issuing agency.

Major reports, such as the Census of Population, which consist of many volumes, are listed by their general, all-inclusive titles.

Bureau of the Census Publications

In most cases, separate reports of the most recent censuses are available for each State, subject, industry, etc. Complete information on publications of all the censuses and current surveys conducted by the Bureau of the Census appears in the *Bureau of the Census Catalog,* published annually and available from the Superintendent of Documents.

Abortions—*see* Vital Statistics.

Accidents —*see also* Health; Insurance; and Vital Statistics

   U.S. Government

      Bureau of Labor Statistics

         Evaluating Your Firm's Injury and Illness Record, Construction Industries, Report 776 (1990).

         Handbook of Labor Statistics. 1989.

         Heatburn Injuries, Bulletin 2358 (1990).

         Injuries Involving Longshore Operation, Bulletin 2326 (1989).

         Occupational Injuries and Illnesses in the United States by Industry. Annual.

      Department of Transportation

         Transportation Safety Information Report. Quarterly.

      Federal Railroad Administration

Accidents —Con.

   U.S. Government —Con.

         Accident/Incident Bulletin. Summary, statistics, and analysis of accidents on railroads in the United States. Annual.

         Rail-Highway Crossing Accident/Incident and Inventory Bulletin. Annual.

      Mine Safety and Health Administration

         Informational Reports by Mining Industry: Coal; Metallic Minerals; Nonmetallic Minerals (except stone and coal); Stone, Sand, and Gravel. Annual.

         Mine Injuries and Worktime. (Some preliminary data.) Quarterly.

      National Center for Health Statistics

         Vital Statistics of the United States. Annual.

           Volume I, Natality

           Volume II, Mortality

           Volume III, Marriage and Divorce

      National Transportation Safety Board

Communications —Con.
Other —Con.

Statistics of the Independent Telephone Industry. Annual.

Warren Publishing, Inc., Washington, DC

Cable Action Update. Weekly.

Cable and Station Coverage Atlas. Annual.

Television Action Update. Weekly.

Television and Cable Factbook. Annual.

TV Station & Cable Ownership Directory. Semi-annual.

Construction, Housing, and Real Estate —*see also* Money *and* Roads

U.S. Government

Board of Governors of the Federal Reserve System

Federal Reserve Bulletin. Monthly.

Bureau of Census

Census of Construction Industries. Quinquennial. (1987, most recent.)

Census of Housing. Decennial. (1980, most recent.)

Current Construction Reports: Housing Starts, C20 (monthly); New Residential Construction in Selected Metropolitan Statistical Areas, C21 (quarterly); Housing Completions, C22 (monthly); New One-Family Houses Sold and for Sale, C25 (monthly with annual report, Characteristics of New Housing); Price Index of New One-Family Houses Sold, C27 (quarterly); Value of New Construction Put in Place, C30 (monthly with occasional historical supplement); Housing Units Authorized by Building Permits, C40 (monthly and annual); Residential Alterations and Repairs, C50 (quarterly and annual).

Current Housing Reports: Housing Vacancies, H-111 (quarterly and annual); Market Absorption of Apartments, H-130 (quarterly and annual); Characteristics of Apartments Completed, H-131 (annual); Annual Housing Survey, H-150 (series of six biennial reports); Annual Housing Survey—Housing Characteristics for Selected Metropolitan Areas, H-170.

Bureau of Economic Analysis

Business Statistics, 1963-91. 1992.

Fixed Reproducible Tangible Wealth in the United States, 1925-89. 1993.

The National Income and Product Accounts of the United States, 1929-88: Volume I, 1993 and Volume II, 1992.

Survey of Current Business. Monthly.

Bureau of Labor Statistics

Compensation and Working Conditions. Monthly.

Employment and Earnings. Monthly.

Employment, Hours, and Earnings, United States, 1909-90. 1991. Bulletin No. 2370.)

Construction, Housing, and Real Estate —Con.
U.S. Government —Con.

Supplement to Employment and Earnings

Evaluating Your Firm's Injury and Illness Record, Construction Industries Report 776, (1990).

Monthly Labor Review.

Occupational Employment in Mining, Construction, Finance, and Services. 1992. (Bulletin No. 2397.)

Occupational Injuries and Illnesses in the United States by Industry. Annual.

Department of Housing and Urban Development

Survey of Mortgage Lending Activity. Monthly and quarterly press releases.

Department of Veterans Affairs

Loan Guaranty Highlights. Quarterly. Trend Data 1964-1988.

Energy Information Administration

Residential Energy Consumption Survey: Housing Characteristics. Triennial.

International Trade Administration

Construction Review. Bimonthly.

Office of Thrift Supervision

Annual Report.

Savings and Home Financing Source Book. Annual. Discontinued after 1989.

Other

Dodge, F.W., National Information Services Division, McGraw-Hill Information Systems Co., New York, NY

Dodge Construction Potentials. Monthly.

NATIONAL ASSOCIATION OF REALTORS, Washington, DC

Home Sales. Monthly.

Consumer Income and Expenditures, and Personal Income —*see also* Agriculture; Economic Indexes; Investments; *and* National Income

U.S. Government

Board of Governors of the Federal Reserve System

Federal Reserve Bulletin. Monthly.

Bureau of the Census

Census of Population. Decennial. (1990, most recent.)

Current Population Reports. (Series on Consumer Income, P60.)

Current Population Reports. (Series on Household Economic Studies, P70.)

Special Studies Reports. (Series on Special Studies, P23.)

Bureau of Economic Analysis

Business Statistics, 1963-91. 1992.

Survey of Current Business. Monthly.

Bureau of Labor Statistics

Consumer Expenditure Survey, integrated Diary and Interview Survey data.

Annual press releases.

Consumer Expenditure Survey: 1988-89. 1991. (Bulletin No. 2383.)

Consumer Income and Expenditures, and Personal Income —Con.

U.S. Government —Con.

Consumer Expenditure Interview Survey. Quarterly.

Congressional Budget Office

The Changing Distribution of Federal Taxes: 1975-1990. October 1987.

Trends in Family Income: 1970-1986. February 1988.

Internal Revenue Service

Statistics of Income.

Individual Income Tax Returns. Annual.

Statistics of Income Bulletin. Quarterly.

National Science Foundation

Academic Science/Engineering: Graduate Enrollment and Support. Detailed Statistical Tables. Annual.

Characteristics of Doctoral Scientists and Engineers in the United States. Detailed Statistical Tables. Biennial.

Characteristics of Recent Science/Engineering Graduates. Detailed Statistical Tables. Biennial.

Federal Scientists and Engineers. Detailed Statistical Tables. Annual.

Profiles Aeronautical/Astronautical Engineering, Agricultural Science, Biological Science, Chemical Engineering, Chemistry, Civil Engineering, Computer Sciences, Economics, Electrical/Electronic Engineering, Mechanical Engineering, and Psychology: Human Resources and Funding. Special Reports. (NSF 89-314, 89-319, 89-318, 89-312, 87-307, 90-303, 88-324, 88-333, 88-326, 87-309, and 88-325, respectively.)

Science and Engineering Personnel: A National Overview. Report. Biennial.

Science Resources Studies. Data Brief. Frequent.

Steady Growth of Employed Ph.D. Scientists and Engineers Is Maintained. (NSF 91-303.)

U.S. Scientists and Engineers. Detailed Statistical Tables. Biennial.

Women and Minorities in Science and Engineering. Report. Biennial.

Social Security Administration

Trends since 1960 In the Economic Status of Aged Men and Women. (Research and Statistics Note No. 3. 1983.)

Other

American Financial Services Association, Washington, DC

AFSA Annual Research Report and Second Mortgage Lending Report on Finance Companies. Annual.

AFSA Annual Research Report and Second Mortgage Lending Report Supplements. Annual.

Finance Facts Yearbook. Annual. (Discontinued in 1988.)

Consumer Prices —*see* Commodity Prices.

Corporations —*see* Business; *and* Manufactures.

Correctional Institutions —*see* Law Enforcement.

Cost of Living —*see* Commodity Prices.

Courts —*see* Law Enforcement.

Crime —*see* Law Enforcement.

Crops —*see* Agriculture.

Deaths —*see* Vital Statistics.

Defense —*see* National Defense.

Divorce —*see* Vital Statistics.

Domestic Trade —*see* Retail and Wholesale Trade; *and* Service Establishments.

Economic Indexes —*see also* Agriculture; Business; Commodity Prices; Manufactures; *and* Science Resources

U.S. Government

Board of Governors of the Federal Reserve System

Federal Reserve Banks. Monthly review published by each Bank with special reference to its own Federal Reserve District.

Federal Reserve Bulletin. Monthly. (Also monthly releases on industrial production indexes.)

Bureau of Economic Analysis

Business Statistics, 1963-91. 1992.

The National Income and Product Accounts of the United States, 1929-88: Volume I, 1993 and Volume II, 1992.

Survey of Current Business. Monthly.

Bureau of Labor Statistics

CPE Detailed Report. Monthly.

Employment Cost Indexes and Levels. Annual.

Producer Price Indexes. Monthly, with annual supplement.

Handbook of Labor Statistics. 1989.

Monthly Labor Review.

Council of Economic Advisers

Economic Indicators. Monthly.

Economic Report of the President. Annual.

Other

The Conference Board, New York, NY

The Conference Board Statistical Bulletin. Monthly.

National Bureau of Economic Research, Cambridge, MA

The National Balance Sheet of the United States, 1953-80, by Raymond W. Goldsmith. 1982. (University of Chicago Press, Chicago, IL.)

The U.S. National Income and Product Accounts: Selected Topics, Murray F. Foss, editor. 1982. (Studies in Income and Wealth, No. 47.) (University of Chicago Press, Chicago, IL.)

Education —*see also* Science Resources; *and* Vocational Rehabilitation

U.S. Government

Bureau of the Census

Education —Con.

U.S. Government —Con.

Census of Population. Decennial. (1990, most recent.)

Current Population Reports. (Series on Population Characteristics, P20; and Special Studies, P23.)

Finances of Public School Systems. Annual. (GF No. 10.)

Bureau of Labor Statistics

Educational Attainment of Workers, March 1982-83. 1984. (Bulletin No. 2191.)

Handbook of Labor Statistics. 1989.

How Workers Get Their Training. 1985. (Bulletin No. 2226.)

Labor Force Statistics Derived From the Current Population Survey, 1948-87. 1988. (Bulletin No. 2307.)

Occupational Projections and Training Data. Biennial.

Students, Graduates, and Dropouts, October 1980-82. 1983. (Bulletin No. 2192.)

Department of Education

Annual Report.

Inflation Measures for Schools and Colleges. September 1983.

Employment and Training Administration

Employment and Training Report of the President. Annual.

National Center for Education Statistics

Associate Degrees and Other Formal Awards Below the Baccalaureate. Annual.

College and University Library Survey. (1985, most recent.)

The Condition of Education. Annual.

Digest of Education Statistics. Annual.

Earned Degrees Conferred. Annual.

Faculty Salaries, Tenure, and Benefits. Annual.

Fall Enrollment in Colleges and Universities. Annual.

High School and Beyond. Reports issued on 1980 high school sophomores and seniors and their transition to further education and labor force participation.

National Longitudinal Study. Reports issued on high school seniors from class of 1972 and their transition to higher education and the labor force.

Participation in Adult Education. (1984, most recent.)

Projections of Education Statistics. Annual.

Residence and Migration of College Students. (1986, most recent.)

Revenues and Expenditures for Public Elementary and Secondary Education. Annual.

National Science Foundation

Academic Research and Equipment Needs in the Physical Sciences. Report. Biennial.

Education —Con.

U.S. Government —Con.

Academic Research Equipment and Equipment Needs in Selected Science/Engineering Fields. Report. Biennial.

Academic Research Equipment in Computer Science, Central Computer Facilities and Engineering. Report. Biennial.

Academic Science and Engineering: Graduate Enrollment and Support. Detailed Statistical Tables. Annual.

Academic Science/Engineering: R&D Expenditures. Detailed Statistical Tables. Annual.

Blacks in Undergraduate Science and Engineering Education, April 1992. Special Report (NSF (92-305.))

Characteristics of Doctoral Scientists and Engineers in the United States. Detailed Statistical Tables. Biennial.

Characteristics of Recent Science/Engineering Graduates. Detailed Statistical Tables. Biennial.

Characteristics of Science/Engineering Equipment in Academic Settings: 1989-90. Report.

Federal Support to Universities, Colleges, and Nonprofit Institutions. A report to the President and Congress. Detailed Statistical Tables. Annual.

International Science and Technology Data Update. Report. Annual.

National Patterns of R&D Resources. Report. Annual.

Profiles—Aeronautical/Astronautical Engineering, Agricultural Science, Biological Science, Chemical Engineering, Chemistry, Civil Engineering, Computer Science, Economics, Electrical/ Electronic Engineering, Mechanical Engineering, and Psychology: Human Resources and Funding. Special Reports. (NSF 89-314, 89-319, 89-318, 89-312, 87-307, 90-303, 88-324, 88-333, 88-326, 87-309, and 88-325, respectively).

Research and Development Expenditures of State Government Agencies: Fiscal Years 1987 and 1988. Special Report. (NSF 90-309.)

Science and Engineering Degrees. A Source Book. Detailed Statistical Tables. Annual.

Science and Engineering Degrees, by Race/Ethnicity of Recipients: 1977-90. Detailed Statistical Tables. Biennial.

Science and Engineering Doctorates. Detailed Statistical Tables. Annual.

Science and Engineering Indicators. Report. Biennial.

Science and Engineering Personnel: A National Overview. Report. Biennial.

Science and Technology Data Book. Report. Annual.

Education —Con.

U.S. Government —Con.

Scientific and Engineering Research Facilities at Universities and Colleges. Report. Biennial.

Undergraduate Origins of Recent Science and Engineering Doctorate Recipients. Special Report (NSF 92-332.)

SRS (Division of Science Resources Studies) Data briefs. Frequent.

Foreign Citizens Continue to Increase U.S. Ranks of Science and Engineering Doctorate Recipients (NSF 92-311.)

Graduate Enrollment in S&E Fields Increased by 4 percent in 1990 (NSF 92-304.)

U.S. Universities and Colleges Report a 9-percent Net Increase in Research Space Since 1988, the Majority of it Within Doctorate-Granting Institutions (NSF 92-333.)

Women and Minorities in Science and Engineering. Report. Biennial.

Woman Continue to Earn Increasing Percentage of Science and Engineering Baccalaureates (NSF 92-313.)

Office for Civil Rights

Racial, Ethnic and Sex Enrollment Data, From Institutions of Higher Education. Fall 1982. Biennial.

State and National Summaries of Data from the fall 1982 Civil Rights Survey of Elementary and Secondary Schools. Biennial.

Other

American Council on Education, Washington, DC

A Fact Book on Higher Education. Quarterly.

National Norms for Entering College Freshmen. Annual.

Bowker (R.R.) Company, New Providence, NJ

American Library Directory. Annual.

Book Publishing Annual. (1985, most recent.)

Bowker Annual Library and Book Trade Almanac.

Chronicle of Higher Education, Inc., Washington, DC

Almanac. Annual.

College Entrance Examination Board, New York, NY

National Report on College-Bound Seniors. Annual.

National Catholic Educational Association, Washington, DC

Catholic Schools in America. Annual.

United States Catholic Elementary and Secondary Schools. Staffing and Enrollment. Annual.

U.S. Catholic Elementary Schools and their Finances. Biennial.

Education —Con.

Other —Con.

U.S. Catholic Secondary Schools and their Finances. Biennial.

National Education Association, Washington, DC

Estimates of School Statistics. Annual.

Rankings of the States. Annual.

Status of the American Public School Teacher, 1985-86. Quinquennial.

Research Associates of Washington, Washington, DC

Inflation Measures for Schools & Colleges. Annual.

State Profiles: Financing Public Higher Education. Annual.

Elections

U.S. Government

Bureau of the Census

Congressional District Data:

1990 Census of Population and Housing, 1990 CPH-4, Congressional Districts of the 103rd Congress.

Current Population Reports. (Series P20, Voting and Registration in the Election of November 19—. Biennial survey; and P25, Projections of the Population of Voting Age for States: November 19—, Biennial projection.)

Commission on Civil Rights

New Evidence on School Desegregation. 1987.

The Economic Status of Americans of Asian Descent. 1988.

The Economic Status of Americans of Southern and Eastern European Ancestry. 1986.

Congress. Clerk of the House

Statistics of the Presidential and Congressional Election Years. Biennial.

Congress. Joint Committee on Printing

Congressional Directory. Biennial.

Other

The Council of State Governments, Lexington, KY

The Book of the States. Biennial.

State Elective Officials and the Legislatures. Biennial.

State Legislative Leadership, Committees, and Staff. Biennial.

Elections Research Center, Chevy Chase MD

America Votes. A handbook of contemporary American election statistics, compiled and edited by Richard M. Scammon and Alice V. McGillivray. Biennial.

Joint Center for Political and Economic Studies, Washington, DC

Black Elected Officials: A National Roster. Annual.

Federal Government Finances and Employment —Con.

U.S. Government —Con.

Annual Report of the Commissioner and Chief Counsel.

Statistics of Income.

Corporation Income Tax Returns. Annual.

Statistics of Income Bulletin. Quarterly.

National Science Foundation

Federal Funds for Research and Development. (Includes geographic distribution and funding by function.) Detailed Statistical Tables. Annual.

Federal R&D Funding by Budget Function. Report. Annual.

Federal Scientists and Engineers. Detailed Statistical Tables. Annual.

Federal Support to Universities, Colleges, and Nonprofit Institutions. A report to the President and Congress. Detailed Statistical Tables. Annual.

Geographic Patterns: R&D in the United States. Special Report. (NSF 89-317.)

International Science and Technology Data Update. Report. Annual.

National Patterns of R&D Resources. Report. Annual.

Science and Engineering Indicators. Report. Biennial.

Science and Engineering Personnel: A National Overview. Report. Biennial.

Science and Technology Data Book. Report. Annual.

SRS (Science Resources Studies) Data Briefs.

Federal Academic R&D Support Increased by 6 Percent Between FY's 1989 and 1990. (NSF 92-328.)

Federal R&D Obligations to Reach About $70 Billion in FY 1992. (NSF 92-320.)

Slow Growth expected in U.S. R&D Spending for 1992. (NSF 92-308).

Office of Management and Budget

The Budget of the United States Government. Annual.

Office of Personnel Management

Affirmative Employment Statistics. Biennial. (Even Years.)

Compensation Report. Annual.

Employment by Geographic Area. Biennial. (Even Years.)

Employment and Trends. Bimonthly. (Odd Months.)

Occupations of Federal White-Collar and Blue-Collar Workers. Biennial. (Odd Years.)

Pay Structure of the Federal Civil Service. Annual.

Work Years and Personnel Costs. Annual.

Other

Advisory Commission on Intergovernmental Relations, Washington, DC

Federal Government Finances and Employment —Con.

Other —Con.

A Catalog of Federal Grant-in-Aid Programs to State and Local Governments, FY 89. 1989. Every 3 years.

Changing Public Attitudes on Governments and Taxes. Annual.

Significant Features of Fiscal Federalism. Annual.

Moody's Investors Service, New York, NY

Moody's Municipal and Government Manual. Annual with semiweekly supplements.

National Bureau of Economic Research, Cambridge, MA

The National Balance Sheet of the United States, 1953-80, by Raymond W. Goldsmith. 1982. (University of Chicago Press, Chicago, IL)

Tax Foundation, Washington, DC

Facts and Figures on Government Finance. Annual.

Finance —*see* Federal Government; Investments; Money; *and* State and Local Government.

Fisheries

U.S. Government

Department of Agriculture

Aquaculture. Biennially.

National Oceanic and Atmospheric Administration, National Marine Fisheries Service

Fisheries of the United States. Annual.

Fishery Statistics of the United States. (Statistical Digest.) Annual.

Marine Recreational Fishery Statistical Survey, Atlantic and Gulf Coasts. Annual.

Marine Recreational Fishery Statistical Survey, Pacific Coast. Annual.

Food —*see also* Agriculture

U.S. Government

Bureau of the Census

Bureau of Labor Statistics

Consumer Expenditure Survey, integrated Diary and Interview Survey data. Annual press releases.

Consumer Expenditure Survey, 1988-89. 1991. (Bulletin No. 2383.)

Consumer Expenditure Survey, 1987. (Bulletin 2354.) 1990.

Consumer Expenditure Survey: Quarterly Data from the Interview Survey.

Consumer Prices: Energy and Food. Monthly.

CPI Detailed Report. Monthly.

Handbook of Labor Statistics. 1989.

Monthly Labor Review.

Producer Price Indexes. Monthly, with annual supplement.

Department of Agriculture

Agricultural Outlook. 11 issues per year.

Food —Con.

  U.S. Government —Con.

      Food Consumption Prices, and Expenditures, 1968-89 (SB-804). Revised annually.

      Food Cost Review. 1989. (Agricultural Economic Report No. 651.) Revised annually.

      Food Review. Quarterly.

    Department of Agriculture, Food and Nutrition Service

      Annual Historical Review:

        Food and Nutrition Service Programs.

      Food Program Update. Monthly.

    Department of Agriculture, Science and Education Administration.

      Family Economics Review. Quarterly.

  Other

    American Frozen Food Institute, Burlingame, CA

      Frozen Food Pack Statistics. Annual.

    National Food Processors Association, Washington, DC

      Canned Fruit and Vegetable Pack and Stock Situation Reports. Quarterly.

Foreign Commerce —*see also* Economic Indexes; *and* International Accounts and Aid

  U.S. Government

    Army, Corps of Engineers

      Waterborne Commerce of the United States (in five parts). Annual.

    Bureau of the Census

      Highlights of U.S. Export and Import Trade. Monthly; includes cumulative data. (FT 990.)

      Summary of U.S. Export and Import Merchandise Trade. Monthly; includes cumulative data. (FT 900.)

      Survey of the Origin of Exports of Manufacturing Establishments. Triennial. (Current Industrial Reports M76(AS)-8.)

      U.S. Airborne Exports and General Imports. Monthly and annual. (FT 986.)

      U.S. Commodity Exports and Imports as Related to Output. Annual. (Series ES 2.)

      U.S. Exports of Domestic Merchandise, SIC-Based Products by World Areas. Annual. (FT 610.)

      U.S. Exports, Schedule B Commodity by Country. Annual. (FT 446.)

      U.S. Exports, Schedule E Commodity by Country. Monthly; includes cumulative data. (FT 410.)

      U.S. Exports, Schedule E Commodity Groupings by World Area and Country. Annual. (FT 450.)

      U.S. Exports, World Area and Country by Schedule E Commodity Groupings. Annual. (FT 455.)

      U.S. General Imports and Imports for Consumption, Schedule A Commodity by Country. Monthly; includes cumulative data. (FT 135.)

Foreign Commerce —Con.

  U.S. Government —Con.

      U.S. General Imports, Schedule A Commodity Groupings by World Area and Country. Annual. (FT 150.)

      U.S. General Imports, World Area by Schedule A Commodity Groupings. Annual. (FT 155.)

      U.S. Imports, SIC-Based Products. Annual. (FT 210.)

      U.S. Imports for Consumption and General Imports, TSUSA Commodity by Country of Origin. Annual. (FT 246.)

      U.S. Trade with Puerto Rico and U.S. Possessions. Monthly and Annual. (FT 800.)

      U.S. Waterborne Exports and General Imports. Monthly and Annual. (FT 985.)

    Bureau of Economic Analysis

      Business Statistics, 1963-91. 1992.

      Survey of Current Business. Monthly. (June issue contains detailed data on merchandise trade.)

      U.S. Merchandise Trade: Exports and Imports by End-Use Category. Annually.

    Department of Agriculture

      Foreign Agricultural Trade of the United States (FATUS). Bimonthly with annual supplements on calendar year and fiscal year trade statistics.

      World Agricultural Trends and Indicators, 1970-88 Statistical Bulletin No. 781. Annual.

    Department of Commerce

      Commerce America. Biweekly. (Issues in March, June, September, and December contain quarterly data on U.S. share of world exports of manufactures.)

      Export Administration Report, East-West Trade: Quarterly Report to the President, Senate, and House of Representatives.

    Department of the Treasury

      Statistical Appendix to Annual Report of the Secretary of the Treasury on the State of the Finances through 1980.

    Energy Information Administration

      Annual Energy Review.

      Monthly Energy Review.

    International Trade Administration

      Overseas Business Reports. Irregular.

      U.S. Trade Performance and Outlook. Annual.

    Maritime Administration

      Annual Report.

      United States Oceanborne Foreign Trade Routes. Annual.

    National Science Foundation

      International Science and Technology Data Update. Report. Annual.

      Science and Engineering Indicators. Report. Biennial.

      Science and Technology Data Book. Report. Annual.

Health and Medical Care —Con.
U.S. Government —Con.

Vital and Health Statistics. (A series of statistical reports covering health-related topics.)

Series 10: Health Interview Survey Statistics. Irregular.

Current Estimates from the Health Interview Survey. Annual.

Series 11: Health and Nutrition Examination Survey Statistics. Irregular.

Series 13: Health Resources Utilization Statistics. Irregular.

National Hospital Discharge Survey: Annual Summary. Annual.

Series 14: Health Resources: Manpower and Facilities Statistics. Irregular.

National Institute on Drug Abuse

High School Senior Survey. 1975-1991.

Substance Abuse and Mental Health Services Administration

Drug Abuse Warning Network. Annual Report, latest year available 1991.

National Drug and Alcoholism Treatment Utilization Survey, latest year available 1991.

National Household Survey on Drug Abuse. Starting in 1990 this survey will be annual: Main Findings, Highlights Population Estimates, latest year available 1991 Population Estimates, 1991 Highlights Main Findings.

Social Security Administration

Social Security Bulletin. Quarterly with annual statistical supplement.

Other

American Dental Association, Chicago, IL

Dental Statistics Handbook. Triennial.

Dental Students' Register. Annual.

Distribution of Dentists in the United States by Region and State. Triennial.

Survey of Dental Practice. Annual.

American Hospital Association, Chicago, IL

Hospital Statistics. Annual.

American Medical Association, Chicago, IL

Physician Characteristics and Distribution in the U.S. Annual.

Reference Data on the Profile of Medical Practice. Annual.

U.S. Medical Licensure Statistics, and License Requirements. Annual.

American Osteopathic Association, Chicago, IL

Yearbook and Directory of Osteopathic Physicians. Annual.

Medical Economics, Montvale, NJ

Physicians' Earnings and Expenses. Published annually in Medical Economics magazine.

Metropolitan Life Insurance Company, New York, NY

Health and Safety Education.

Health and Medical Care —Con.
Other —Con.

Statistical Bulletin. Quarterly.

Hospitals —see Health.

Hotels —see Service Establishments.

Household Appliances —see Construction, Housing, and Real Estate. Housing—see Construction.

Immigration and Naturalization
U.S. Government

Department of State, Bureau of Consular Affairs

Report of the Visa Office. Annual. (Dept. of State Pub. 8810.)

Department of Transportation

Report of Passenger Travel Between the United States and Foreign Countries. Annual, semiannual, quarterly, monthly.

Immigration and Naturalization Service

I&N Reporter. Quarterly.

Statistical Yearbook of the Immigration and Naturalization Service. Annual.

National Science Foundation

Foreign Citizens in U.S. Science and Engineering: History, Status, and Outlook. Special Report. (NSF 86-305, revised.)

Foreign Students Account for Most Growth in Graduate Science and Engineering Enrollment. Science Resources Studies Highlights. (NSF 88-316.)

Immigrant Scientists and Engineers. Detailed Statistical Tables. Annual.

Science and Engineering Doctoral Awards Reached Record Highs in 1990. SRS Data Brief. (NSF 91-308.)

Survey of Direct U.S. Private Capital Investment in Research and Development Facilities in Japan. (NSF 91-312)

Science and Engineering Doctorates. Detailed Statistical Tables. Annual.

Imports —see Foreign Commerce.

Income —see Consumer Income; and National Income.

Industry —see Business; Economic Indexes; and Manufactures.

Institutions —see Education; Health; and Law Enforcement.

Insurance—see also Social Insurance
U.S. Government

Department of Veterans Affairs

Annual Report of The Secretary of Veterans Affairs.

Government Life Insurance Programs for Veterans and Members of the Service. Annual.

Trend Data 1964-1988.

Other

American Council of Life Insurance, Washington, DC

Life Insurance Fact Book. Annual.(update odd years)

Health Insurance Association of America, Washington, DC

International Statistics —Con.

U.S. Government —Con.

National Patterns of R&D Resources. Report. Annual.

Science and Engineering Indicators. Report. Biennial.

Science and Technology Data Book. Report. Annual.

Survey of Direct U.S. Private Capital Investment in Research and Development Facilities in Japan. Report. (NSH 91-312.)

The Science and Technology Resources of Japan: A Comparison with the United States. Special Report. (NSF 88-318.)

The Science and Technology Resources of West Germany: A Comparison with the United States. Special Report. (NSF 86-310.)

Other

American Automobile Manufacturers Association, Detroit MI.

Motor Vehicle Facts and Figures. Annual

World Motor Vehicle Data. Annual.

The Economist Newspaper Ltd., London, England

The Economist Diary. 1987.

World Business Cycles. 1982.

The World in Figures. 1984.

Euromonitor, London, England

Consumer Asia 1993.

Consumer Eastern Europe 1992.

Consumer Europe.

Consumer Japan 1993.

Consumer Southern Europe 1993.

Consumer USA

European Marketing Data and Statistics. Annual.

International Marketing Data and Statistics. Annual.

Food and Agriculture Organization of the United Nations, Rome, Italy

Production Yearbook.

Trade Yearbook.

Yearbook of Fishery Statistics.

Yearbook of Forest Products.

Inter-American Development Bank, Washington, DC

Annual Report.

Economic and Social Progress in Latin America. Annual Survey.

The International Institute for Strategic Studies, London, England

The Military Balance. Annual.

International Labour Office, Geneva, Switzerland

Economically Active Population, Estimates and Projections: 1950-2025, Vols. 1-6. 3rd Edition. 1986.

Yearbook of Labour Statistics. 49th issue. 1989-1990.

International Statistics —Con.

Other —Con.

International Monetary Fund, Washington, DC

International Financial Statistics. Monthly with annual yearbook.

Jane's Information Group, Coulsdon, UK and Alexandria, VA

Jane's Air-Launched Weapons. (Binder-4 monthly update.)

Jane's All the World's Aircraft. Annual.

Jane's Armour and Artillery. Annual.

Jane's Avionics. Annual.

Jane's Fighting Ships. Annual.

Jane's Infantry Weapons. Annual.

Jane's Merchant Ships. Annual.

Jane's Military Communications. Annual.

Jane's Military Logistics. Annual.

Jane's Military Training Systems. Annual.

Jane's NATO Handbook. Annual.

Jane's Spaceflight Directory. Annual.

Organization for Economic Cooperation and Development, Paris, France

Annual Oil Market Report.

Coal Information. Annual.

Demographic Trends 1950-1990.

Energy Balances of OECD Countries. Annual.

Energy Prices and Taxes. Quarterly.

Energy Statistics. Annual.

Financial Market Trends. Triennial.

Financing and Delivering Health Care, 1987.

Food Consumption Statistics. Irregular.

Geographical Distribution of Financial Flows to Developing Countries.

Historical Statistics of Foreign Trade Series A. Annual.

Indicators of Industrial Activity. Quarterly.

Industrial Structure Statistics. Annual.

The Iron and Steel Industry. Annual.

Labour Force Statistics. Annual.

Latest Information on National Accounts of Developing Countries. Annual.

Living Conditions in OECD Countries. 1986.

Main Economic Indicators. Monthly.

Main Science and Technology Indicators. Biennial.

Maritime Transport. Annual.

Measuring Health Care, 1960-1983. 1985.

Meat Balances in OECD Countries. Annual.

Milk and Milk Products Balances in OECD Countries. Annual.

National Accounts of OECD Countries. Annual.

Vol. I: Main Aggregates.

Vol. II: Detailed Tables.

Labor —Con.

U.S. Government —Con.

Industry Wage Surveys. (Separate bulletins for selected industries; each industry on a 3- to 5-year cycle.)

Labor Force Statistics Derived from the Current Population Survey, 1948-87. 1988. (Bulletin No. 2307.)

Major Collective Bargaining Settlements. Quarterly.

Major Work Stoppages. Annual.

Mass Layoffs. Annual.

Monthly Labor Review.

Occupational Employment in Manufacturing Industries. 1991. (Bulletin No. 2376.)

Occupational Employment in Mining, Construction, Finance, and Services. 1992. (Bulletin No. 2397.)

Occupational Employment in Selected Nonmanufacturing Industries. 1990. (Bulletin No. 2348.)

Occupational Injuries and Illnesses in the United States, by Industry. Annual.

Occupational Projections and Training Data. Biennial.

Outlook 2000. 1990. (Bulletin No. 2352.)

Permanent Mass Layoffs and Plant Closings, 1987. 1988. (Bulletin 2310.)

Real Earnings. Monthly.

Revised Seasonally Adjusted Labor Force Statistics, 1978-87. 1988. (Bulletin 2506.)

State and Metropolitan Area Employment and Unemployment. Monthly.

Weekly Earnings of Wage and Salary Workers. Quarterly.

White-Collar Pay. Annual.

Work Experience of the Population. Annual.

Working Woman: A Chartbook. 1991 (Bulletin No. 2385.)

Department of Agriculture

Farm Labor. Monthly.

Department of Labor

Annual Report of the Secretary.

Employment and Training Administration

Employment and Training Report of the President. Annual.

Unemployment Insurance Claims. Weekly.

Interstate Commerce Commission

Monthly Report of Class I Railroad Employees, by Group. (Statement No. 350.)

Wage Statistics of Class I Railroads in the United States. Annual. (Statement No. 300.)

Maritime Administration

Labor —Con.

U.S. Government —Con.

Employment Report of United States Flag Merchant Fleet Ocean-going Vessels 1,000 Gross Tons and Over. Annual. (Monthly and quarterly data available from source.)

Seafaring Wage Rates. Biennial.

National Science Foundation

Characteristics of Doctoral Scientists and Engineers in the United States. Detailed Statistical Tables. Biennial.

Characteristics of Recent Science and Engineering Graduates. Detailed Statistical Tables. Biennial.

Immigrant Scientists and Engineers. Detailed Statistical Tables. Biennial.

U.S. Scientists and Engineers. Detailed Statistical Tables. Biennial.

U.S. Scientists and Engineers: 1984 Detailed Statistical Tables.

Woman and Minorities in Science and Engineering: An Update Report. Biennial.

Office of Personnel Management

Affirmative Employment Statistics. Biennial. (Even Years.)

Occupations of Federal White-Collar and Blue-Collar Workers. Biennial. (Odd Years.)

Women's Bureau

Handbook on Women Workers. Periodic.

Other

Aerospace Industries Association of America, Washington, DC

Employment in the Aerospace Industry. Monthly.

Survey of Aerospace Employment. Annual.

The Bureau of National Affairs, Inc., Washington, DC

Basic Patterns in Union Contracts. Annual.

BNA's Employment Outlook. Quarterly.

BNA's Job Absence and Turnover. Quarterly.

Briefing Sessions on Employee Relations Workbook. Annual.

Calendar of Negotiations. Annual.

Directory of U.S. Labor Organizations. Annual.

82 Key Statistics on Work and Family Issues. (The National Report on Work and Family. Special Report No. 9, September 1988.)

National Labor Relations Board Election Statistics. Annual.

NLRB Representation and Decertification Elections Statistics. Quarterly.

Manufactures —Con.
> *Other* —Con.
>> Annual Statistical Report.
>> Commodity Research Bureau, New York, NY
>>> Commodity Yearbook. Annual.
>> The Conference Board, New York, NY
>>> Quarterly Survey of Capital Appropriations.
>>> Quarterly Survey of Capital Investment and Supply Conditions in Manufacturing.
>> Dataquest Inc., San Jose, CA
>>> Consolidated Data Base.
>> Dealerscope Merchandising, Philadelphia, PA
>>> Merchandising. Annual.
>> Electronic Industries Association, Washington, DC
>>> Electronic Market Data Book. Annual.
>>> Electronic Market Trends. Monthly.
>>> Electronics Foreign Trade. Monthly.
>>> Electronics Foreign Trade 5-Year Summary. Annual.
>> National Association of Hosiery Manufacturers, Charlotte, NC
>>> Hosiery Statistics. Annual.
>> National Food Processors Association, Washington, DC
>>> Canned Fruit and Vegetable Pack and Stock Situation Reports. Quarterly.

Marine Corps —*see* National Defense.

Marriage —*see* Vital Statistics.

Medical Care; Mental Health —*see* Health.

Merchant Vessels —*see* Transportation

Military Services —see National Defense.

Minerals and Metals —*see also* Economic Indexes; Energy; Foreign Commerce; *and* Manufactures
> *U.S. Government*
>> Census of Mineral Industries. Quinquennial. (1987, Industry series MIC87-I; Geographic Area Series MIC87-A; Subject Series MIC87-S.)
>> Bureau of Mines Apparent Consumption of Industrial Explosives and Blasting Agents in the United States. Annual.
>>> Mineral Commodity Summaries. Annual.
>>> Mineral Industry Surveys. (Monthly, quarterly, or annual report.)
>>> Minerals Today. (Bimonthly survey.)
>>> Minerals Yearbook. Annual report.
>> Department of the Treasury
>>> Treasury Bulletin. Monthly through 1982; beginning 1983, quarterly.
>> Energy Information Administration
>>> Annual Energy Review.
>>> Coal Production. Annual.
>>> Domestic Uranium Mining and Milling Industry. Annual.
>>> International Energy Annual.
>>> Monthly Energy Review.

Minerals and Metals —Con.
> *U.S. Government* —Con.
>> Natural Gas Annual.
>> Petroleum Supply Annual.
>> Quarterly Coal Report.
>> U.S. Crude Oil, Natural Gas, and Natural Gas Liquids Reserves. Annual.
> *Other*
>> American Bureau of Metal Statistics, Inc., Secaucus, NJ
>>> Non-Ferrous Metal Data.
>> American Gas Association, Arlington, VA
>>> Gas Facts. Annual.
>>> Year Book.
>> American Metal Market, New York, NY
>>> Daily Newspapers.
>>> Metal Statistics. Annual.
>> American Petroleum Institute, Washington, DC
>>> Quarterly Review of Drilling Statistics for the United States.
>> American Petroleum Institute, Independent Petroleum Association of America, and MidContinent Oil and Gas Association
>>> Joint Association Survey on Drilling Costs. Annual.
>> Commodity Research Bureau, New York, NY
>>> Commodity Yearbook. Annual.
>> Independent Petroleum Association of America, Washington, DC
>>> IPAA Weekly Oil Trends.
>>> IPAA Wholesale Oil Prices. Monthly.
>>> The Oil & Natural Gas Producing Industry in Your State. Annual.
>>> U.S. Petroleum Statistics. Semiannual.
>> McGraw-Hill Publications Co., New York, NY
>>> Engineering and Mining Journal. Monthly.
>>> Keystone Coal Industry Manual. Annual.
>> National Coal Association, Washington, DC
>>> Coal Data. Annual.
>> PennWell Publishing Co., Tulsa, OK
>>> Offshore. Monthly.
>>> Oil and Gas Journal. Weekly.
>> Carl H. Pforzheimer & Co., New York, NY
>>> Comparative Oil Company Statistics, 19911990. Annual.

Money and Banking —*see also* Construction; Insurance; International Accounts; *and* Investments
> *U.S. Government*
>> Board of Governors of the Federal Reserve System
>>> Annual Statistical Digest.
>>> Domestic Offices, Commercial Bank Assets and Liabilities Consolidated Report of Condition. Quarterly.
>>> Federal Reserve Bulletin. Monthly.
>>> Flow of Funds Accounts: Seasonally Adjusted and Unadjusted. Z.1(780). Quarterly.

Recreation —Con.
Other —Con.

Americans' Attitudes Toward Golf in Their Community.

An Operational Profile of Canadian Golf Facilities.

Golf Consumer Spending and Facility Fees.

Golf Facilities in Canada.

Golf Facilities in the United States. 1992.

Golf Participation in Canada.

Golf Participation in the United States. 1992.

Golf Travel in the United States.

Stand-Alone Golf Ranges in the United States.

Trends in the Golf Industry 1987-1991.

Women in Golf.

National Marine Manufacturers Association, Chicago, IL

Boating. (A Statistical Report on America's Top Family Sport.) Annual.

State Boat Registration. Annual.

National Sporting Goods Association, Mt. Prospect, IL

The Sporting Goods Market in 1992. Annual.

Sports Participation in 1991. Annual.

Resources for the Future, Inc., Washington, DC

Statistics on Outdoor Recreation. 1984.

Part I: The Record Through 1956

Part II: The Record Since 1956

Religious Bodies

Other

American Jewish Committee and the Jewish Publication Society, New York, NY

American Jewish Year Book.

Glenmary Research Center, Atlanta, GA

Churches and Church Membership in the United States 1990 by M. Bradley; N.Green, Jr; D. Jones; M.Lynn; and L. McNeil. 1992.

National Council of the Churches of Christ in the U.S.A., New York, NY

Yearbook of American and Canadian Churches. Annual.

Research and Development —*see* Science Resources.

Retail and Wholesale Trade —*see also* Commodity Prices; Economic Indexes; *and* Service Establishments

U.S. Government

Board of Governors of the Federal Reserve System

Federal Reserve Bulletin. Monthly.

Bureau of the Census

Annual Retail Trade Report.

Annual Wholesale Trade Report.

Census of Retail Trade. Quinquennial. (1987, most recent.)

Retail and Wholesale Trade —Con.
U.S. Government —Con.

Census of Wholesale Trade. Quinquennial. (1987, most recent.)

County Business Patterns. Annual.

Merchant Wholesalers Measures of Value Produced, Capital Expenditures, Depreciable Assets, and Operating Expenses. (1982, most recent.)

Monthly Retail Trade Report. Sales and Inventories.

Monthly Wholesale Trade Report. Sales and Inventories.

Selected Characteristics of Retail Trade-Measures of Value Produced, Capital Expenditures, Depreciable Assets, and Operating Expenses. (1982, most recent.)

Bureau of Economic Analysis

Business Statistics, 1963-91. 1992.

Survey of Current Business. Monthly.

Bureau of Labor Statistics

Compensation and Working Conditions. Monthly

CPI Detailed Report. Monthly.

Employment and Earnings. Monthly, with annual supplement.

Employment, Hours, and Earnings, United States, 1909-90. 1991. (Bulletin No. 2370.)

Handbook of Labor Statistics. 1989.

Monthly Labor Review.

Occupational Employment in Selected Nonmanufacturing Industries. 1990. (Bulletin No. 2348.)

Occupational Injuries and Illnesses in the United States by Industry. Annual.

Producer Price Indexes. Monthly, with annual supplement.

Productivity Measures for Selected Industries and Government Services. Annual.

Technological Change and Its Labor Impact in Four Industries. 1988. (Bulletin 2316.)

Technology and Labor in Three Service Industries: Utilities, Retail Trade, and Lodging. 1990. (Bulletin 2367.)

International Trade Administration

Franchising in the Economy. Annual. (Last issued 1988.)

U.S. Industrial Outlook. Annual.

Other

Dealerscope Merchandising, Philadelphia, PA

Merchandising. Annual.

Lebhar-Friedman, Inc., New York, NY

Accounting Today. Biweekly.

Apparel Merchandising. Monthly.

Chain Store Age Executive. Census Issue, August 1989. Monthly.

Discount Store News. July 1989, Statistical Issue. Biweekly.

Science Resources —Con.

U.S. Government —Con.

Science and Engineering Degrees. A Source Book. Detailed Statistical Tables. Annual.

Science and Engineering Degrees, by Race/Ethnicity of Recipients: 1977-90. Detailed Statistical Tables. Biennial.

Science and Engineering Doctorates. Detailed Statistical Tables. Annual.

Science and Engineering Indicators. Report. Biennial.

Science and Engineering Personnel: A National Overview. Report. Biennial.

Science and Technology Data Book. Report. Annual.

Science and Technology Resources in U.S. Industry. Special Report. (NSF 88-321.)

The Science and Technology Resources of Japan: A Comparison with the United States. Special Report. (NSF 88-318.)

The Science and Technology Resources of West Germany: A Comparison with the United States. Special Report. (NSF 86-310.)

Scientific and Engineering Research Facilities at Universities and Colleges. Report. Biennial.

Scientists, Engineers, and Technicians in Manufacturing are Concentrated in High Technology Industries. (NSF 91-321.)

Scientists, Engineers, and Technicians in Manufacturing Industries. Detailed Statistical Tables. Triennial.

Scientists, Engineers, and Technicians in Nonmanufacturing Industries. Detailed Statistical Tables. Triennial.

Scientists, Engineers, and Technicians in Trade and Regulated Industries. Detailed Statistical Tables. Triennial.

Slow Growth Expected in U.S. R&D Spending for 1992. (NSF 92-308.)

Steady Growth of Employed Ph.D. Scientists and Engineers is Maintained (NSF 91-303.)

Superconductivity Research and Development Activities in U.S. Industry: 1987 and 1988. Special Report.

Survey of Direct U.S. Private Capital Investment in Research and Development Facilities in Japan. Special Report. (NSF 91-12.)

Undergraduate Origins of Recent Science and Engineering Doctorate Recipients. Special Report (NSF 92-332.)

U.S. Firms Report Real R&D Expenditures Declining in 1991 and 1992. (NSF 92-306.) U.S. Scientists and Engineers. Detailed Statistical Tables. Biennial.

Women and Minorities in Science and Engineering: An Update. Report. Biennial.

Science Resources —Con.

U.S. Government —Con.

Women Continue to Earn Increasing Percentage of Science and Engineering Baccalaureates. (NSF 92-313.)

Patent and Trademark Office

Commissioner of Patents and Trademarks Annual Report.

Technology Assessment and Forecast Reports "All Technologies" and State Country Report. Annual.

Other

National Academy of Sciences, Washington, DC

Science, Engineering, and Humanities Doctorates in the United States. Biennial. Summary Report. Doctorate Recipients from United States Universities. Annual.

Securities —*see* Investments; *and* Money.

Service Establishments—*see also* Retail and Wholesale Trade

U.S. Government

Bureau of the Census

Census of Service Industries. Quinquennial. (1987, most recent.)

Motor Freight Transportation and Warehousing Survey. Annual.

Selected Characteristics of Selected Service Industries—Capital Expenditures, Depreciable Assets, and Operating Expenses. (1987, most recent.)

Services Annual Survey Report.

Internal Revenue Service

Statistics of Income. (Annual report on Corporation Income Tax Returns. Periodic compendiums on Studies of International Income and Taxes.)

Statistics of Income Bulletin. Quarterly.

Other

Decker Communications, Inc., New York, NY

Marketing Communications. (Advertising.) Monthly.

Laventhol & Horwath, Philadelphia, PA

The Executive Conference Center: A Statistical and Financial Profile. Annual.

Gaming Industry Study. Annual.

Lifecare Industry. Annual. (Analysis of facilities by size and section of the country for selected financial data, resident census information, and medical costs.)

National Trends of Business in the Lodging Industry. Monthly. (Analysis of nationwide trends in sales, occupancy, and room rates of hotels, motor hotels, and economy lodging facilities.)

Separate reports on the segments of lodging industries. Annuals. (Reports covering economy, all-suite, and resort.)

Social Insurance and Human Services —Con.

Other —Con.

The Foundation Center, New York, NY

The Foundation Grants Index. Edition 21. 1992.

National Data Book of Foundations. Edition 16. 1992.

Girl Scouts of the U.S.A., New York, NY

Annual Report.

National Bureau of Economic Research, Cambridge, MA

Financial Aspects of the United States Pension System, Zvi Bodie and John B. Shoven, editors. 1983. (University of Chicago Press, Chicago, IL)

United Way of America, Alexandria, VA

Annual Directory.

Soil Conservation —*see* Agriculture.

Sports —*see* Recreation.

State and Local Government —*see also* Federal Government

U.S. Government

Bureau of the Census

Census of Governments. Quinquennial. (1987, most recent.)

City Employment. Annual. (GE No. 2.)

City Government Finances. Annual. (GF No. 4.)

County Government Employment. Annual. (GE No. 4.)

County Government Finances. Annual. (GF No. 8.)

Federal Expenditures by State. Annual.

Finances of Employee-Retirement Systems of State and Local Governments. Annual. (GF No. 2.)

Finances of Public School Systems. Annual. (GF No. 10.)

Finances of Selected Public Employee Retirement Systems. Quarterly. (GR Nos. 1-4.)

Government Finances. Annual. Covers Federal, State, and local governments. (GF No. 5.)

Local Government Employment in Major County Areas. Annual. (GE No. 3.)

Local Government Finances in Major County Areas. Annual. (GF No. 6.)

Public Employment. Annual. (GE No. 1.)

Quarterly Summary of Federal, State, and Local Tax Revenue. (GT Nos. 1-4.)

State Government Finances. Annual. (GF No. 3.)

State Government Tax Collections. Annual. (GF No. 1.)

Bureau of Labor Statistics

Employee Benefits in State and Local Governments. 1987.

Employment and Earnings. Monthly.

Employment, Hours, and Earnings, United States, 1909-90. 1991. (Bulletin No. 2370.)

State and Local Government —Con.

U.S. Government —Con.

Occupational Employment in Transportation, Communications, Utilities, and Trade. 1990. (Bulletin No. 2348.)

Federal Highway Administration

Highway Statistics. Annual.

Office of Management and Budget

The Budget of the United States Government. Annual.

Social Security Administration

Benefits and Beneficiaries Under Public Employee Retirement Systems, Fiscal Year 1989, Social Security Bulletin, Summer 1992.

Other

Advisory Commission on Intergovernmental Relations, Washington, DC

A Catalog of Federal Grant-in-Aid Programs to State and Local Governments, FY 89. 1989. Every 3 years.

1988 State Fiscal Capacity and Effort.

Significant Features of Fiscal Federalism. Annual.

The Council of State Governments, Lexington, KY

The Book of the States. Biennial.

State Administrative Officials Classified by Function. Biennial.

International City Management Association, Washington, DC

Baseline Data Reports. Bimonthly.

Compensation: An Annual Report on Local Government Executive Salaries and Fringe Benefits.

Municipal Year Book. Annual.

Special Data Issues. Periodical.

National Governors' Association, Washington, DC

Directory of Governors of the American States, Commonwealths & Territories. Annual.

Governors' Staff Directory. Biannual.

National Governors' Association and National Association of State Budget Officers, Washington, DC

The Fiscal Survey of States. Biannual.

The President's 1990 Budget-Impact on the States.

Tax Foundation, Washington, DC

Facts and Figures on Government Finance. Annual.

Stocks and Bonds —*see* Investments.

Stores —*see* Retail and Wholesale Trade *and* Service Establishments.

Tax Collections —*see* Federal Government; *and* State and Local Government.

Telephone and Telegraph Systems —*see* Communications.

Television —*see* Communications.

Trade —*see* Foreign Commerce; Retail and Wholesale Trade; *and* Service Establishments.

Transportation —*see also* Foreign Commerce; *and* Roads

U.S. Government

Army, Corps of Engineers

Waterborne Commerce of the United States (in five parts). Annual.

Bureau of the Census

Census of Transportation. Quinquennial. (1987, most recent.)

Motor Freight Transportation and Warehousing Survey. Annual.

Truck Inventory and Use Survey. (1987, most recent.)

Vessel Entrances and Clearances. Annual. (FT 975.)

Bureau of Economic Analysis

Business Statistics, 1963-91. 1992.

Survey of Current Business. Monthly.

Coast Guard

Marine Safety Statistical Review.

Merchant Vessels of the United States. Annual.

Polluting Incidents In And Around U.S. Waters. Annual.

Department of State, Bureau of Consular Affairs

Summary of Passport Statistics. Annual.

Department of Transportation

National Transportation Statistics. Annual.

Transportation Safety Information Report. Quarterly.

U.S. International Air Travel Statistics. Annual.

Federal Aviation Administration

Census of U.S. Civil Aircraft. Annual.

FAA Air Traffic Activity. Annual, for fiscal years.

FAA Aviation Forecasts, for fiscal years.

FAA Statistical Handbook of Aviation. Annual.

General Aviation Activity and Avionics Survey. Annual.

U.S. Civil Airman Statistics. Annual.

Federal Aviation Administration and Research and Special Programs Administration

Airport Activity Statistics of Certificated Route Air Carriers. Annual.

Federal Highway Administration

Drivers Licenses. Annual.

Highway Statistics. Annual.

Highway Statistics, Summary to 1985. (Published every 10 years.)

Selected Highway Statistics and Charts. Annual.

Interstate Commerce Commission

Class I Freight Railroads Selected Earnings Data. Quarterly.

Large Class I Household Goods Carriers Selected Earnings Data. Quarterly.

Transportation —Con.

U.S. Government —Con.

Large Class I Motor Carriers of Passengers Selected Earnings Data. Quarterly.

Large Class I Motor Carriers of Property Selected Earnings Data. Quarterly.

Quarterly Report.

Transport Statistics in the United States. Issued annually in two separate parts:

Part 1: Railroads

Part 2: Motor Carriers

Maritime Administration

Annual Report.

Bulk Carriers in the World Fleet. Annual.

Employment Report of United States Flag Merchant Fleet Ocean-Going Vessels 1,000 Gross Tons and Over. Annual. (Monthly and quarterly data available from source.)

Foreign Flag Merchant Ships Owned by U.S. Parent Companies. Annual.

Maritime Manpower Report. Monthly.

United States Oceanborne Foreign Trade Routes. Annual.

Research and Special Programs Administration

Air Carrier Financial Statistics. Quarterly.

Air Carrier Industry Scheduled Service Traffic Statistics. Quarterly.

Air Carrier Traffic Statistics. Monthly.

Other

Aerospace Industries Association of America, Washington, DC

Aerospace Facts and Figures. Annual.

Net New Orders, Shipments, and Backlog for Jet Transport Aircraft. Quarterly.

Commercial Helicopter Shipments. Quarterly.

Air Transport Association of America, Washington, DC

Air Transport Facts and Figures. Annual.

American Automobile Manufacturers Association, Detroit, MI.

Motor Vehicle Facts and Figures. Annual.

World Motor Vehicle Data. Annual.

American Bureau of Shipping, Paramus, NJ

The Record. Annual with one supplement.

American Public Transit Association, Washington, DC

Transit Fact Book. Annual.

Association of American Railroads, Washington, DC

Analysis of Class I Railroads. Annual.

Cars of Revenue Freight Loaded. Weekly with annual summary.

Freight Commodity Statistics, Class I Railroads in the United States. Annual.

Yearbook of Railroad Facts.

ENO Transportation Foundation, Leesburg, VA

Transportation —Con.

Other —Con.

Transportation in America. mid-year, annually with periodic supplements.

General Aviation Manufacturers Association, Washington, DC

Shipment Report. Quarterly and Annual.

Statistical Databook. Annual.

Lake Carriers' Association, Cleveland, OH

Annual Report.

Monthly Bulk Commodities Report.

Lloyd's Register of Shipping, London, England

Annual Summary of Merchant Ships Completed in the World.

Casualty Return. (Annual statistical summary of all merchant ships totally lost or reported broken up during year.)

Merchant Shipbuilding Returns. (Quarterly Statistical summary of world shipbuilding.)

Statistical Tables. (A mid-year analysis of world merchant fleet.)

National Air Carrier Association, Washington, DC

Annual Report.

Regional Airline Association, Washington, DC

Statistical Reports.

Shipbuilders Council of America, Arlington, VA

Annual Report.

Tanker Advisory Center, Inc., New York, NY

Worldwide Tanker Casualty Returns. Annual.

Travel —*see* Recreation *and* Transportation.

Unemployment Insurance —*see* Labor; *and* Social Insurance.

Utilities, Public—*see* Communications; Energy *and* Transportation.

Veterans —*see* National Defense; *and* Population.

Virgin Islands of the United States —*see* Outlying Areas.

Vital Statistics —*see also* Accidents; *and* Health

U.S. Government

Centers for Disease Control, Atlanta, GA

Morbidity and Mortality Weekly Report. Annual summary also.

National Center for Health Statistics

Monthly Vital Statistics Report. Provisional statistics. Annual summary also.

Vital and Health Statistics. (A series of statistical reports covering health-related topics.)

Series 20: Mortality Data. Irregular.

Series 21: Natality, Marriage, and Divorce Data. Irregular.

Series 23: National Survey of Family Growth Statistics. Irregular.

Vital Statistics of the United States. Annual.

Other

The Alan Guttmacher Institute, New York, NY

Vital Statistics —Con.

Other —Con.

Abortion Factbook, 1992 Edition: Readings, Trends, and State and Local Data to 1988. 1992.

Teenage Pregnancy in the United States: The Scope of the Problem and State Responses. 1989.

Family Planning Perspectives. Monthly.

United Nations Statistical Division, New York, NY

Demographic Yearbook.

Population and Vital Statistics Report. (Series A.) Quarterly.

World Health Organization, Geneva, Switzerland

Annual Epidemiological and Vital Statistics.

Epidemiological and Vital Statistics Report. Monthly.

World Health Statistics. Quarterly and annual.

Vocational Rehabilitation and Education

U.S. Government

Department of Education

Annual Report.

Dartment of Veterans Affairs

Annual Report of The Secretary of Veterans Affairs.

Disability Compensation Data. Semiannual.

Disability and Death Pension Data. Semiannual.

Historical Data on the Usage of Educational Benefits: 1944-1983. April 1984.

Office of Information Management and Statistics Monograph Selected Compensation and Pension Data, by State of Residence. Annual.

Office of Information Management and Statistics Monograph—Veterans Benefits under Current Educational Programs. Annual.

Trend Data 1964-1988.

Office of Management and Budget

The Budget of the United States Government. Annual.

Rehabilitation Services Administration

Caseload Statistics of State Vocational Rehabilitation Agencies in Fiscal Year. Annual.

Characteristics of Clients Rehabilitated in Fiscal Year. Annual.

Wages and Wage Rates —*see* Labor; *and* Social Insurance.

Wealth —*see* National Income.

Weather —*see* Climate.

Welfare Services —*see* Health; *and* Social Insurance.

Wholesale and Retail Trade —*see* Retail and Wholesale Trade.

Wholesale Prices —*see* Commodity Prices.

Work Relief —*see* Social Insurance.

Work Stoppages —*see* Labor.

Guide to State Statistical Abstracts

This bibliography includes the most recent statistical abstracts for States and Puerto Rico published since 1980 plus those that will be issued in late 1993 or early 1994. For some States, a near equivalent has been listed in substitution for, or in addition to, a statistical abstract. All sources contain statistical tables on a variety of subjects for the State as a whole, its component parts, or both. The page counts given for publications are approximate.

Alabama

University of Alabama, Center for Business and Economic Research, P.O. Box 870221, Tuscaloosa 35487 205-348-6191

*Economic Abstract of Alabama.*1992. 600 pp.

Alaska

Department of Commerce and Economic Development, Division of Economic Development, P.O. Box 110804, Juneau 99811 907-465-2017

The Alaska Economy Performance Report. 1990-1991

Arizona

University of Arizona, Economic and Business Research, College of Business and Public Administration, McClelland Hall 204 Tucson Arizona 85721-0001 602-621-2155 FAX 602-621-2150

Arizona Statistical Abstract: A 1993 Data Handbook. 616 pp.

Arizona Economic Indicators. 52 pp. (Biannual.)

Arizona's Economy. 20 pp. (Quarterly newsletter and data.)

Arkansas

University of Arkansas at Little Rock, Economic Research, Library 512, Little Rock 72204

Arkansas State and County Economic Data. 18 pp. (Revised annually.)

University of Arkansas at Little Rock, Census State Data Center, Library 508, Little Rock 72204 501-569-8530

Arkansas Statistical Abstract. 600 pp. (Revised biennially.)

California

Department of Finance, 915 L Street, 8th Floor, Sacramento 95814 916-322-2263

California Statistical Abstract, 1993. 210 pp.

Pacific Data Resources, P.O. Box 1922, Santa Barbara, CA 93116-1922 800-422-2546

California Almanac, 6th ed. Biennial. 275 pp.

Colorado

University of Colorado, Business Research Division, Campus Box 420, Boulder 80309 303-4928227

Statistical Abstract of Colorado, 1987. 600 pp.

Connecticut

Connecticut Department of Economic Development, 865 Brook St., Rocky Hill 06067-3405 1-800-392-2122

Connecticut Market Data. 1992-1993, Approx. 87 pp. No charge for single copy.

Delaware

Delaware Development Office, P.O. Box 1401, 99 Kings Highway, Dover 19903 302-739-4271

Delaware Data Book, 1993. 141 pp.

University of Delaware Bureau of Economic Research, College of Business and Economics, Newark 19716-2730 302-831-8401

Delaware Economic Report 1993-94. 200 pp. Annual

District of Columbia

Office of Planning, Data Management Division, Presidential Bldg., Suite 500, 415 12th St., N.W. Washington 20004 202-727-6533

Population Estimates and Housing Units, annual.

Office of Policy and Evaluation, Executive Office of the Mayor, 1 Judiciary Square, Suite 1000, 441 4th St., N.W., Washington 20001 202-727-4016

Indices—A Statistical Index to DC Services, Dec 1992. Annual. 366 pp.

Florida

University of Florida, Bureau of Economic and Business Research, Gainesville 32611-2017 904-392-0171

Florida Statistical Abstract, 1992. 26th ed. 760 pp.

National Data Consultants, P.O. Box 6381, Athens, Georgia 30604 706-548-8460

Florida County Perspectives: 1991. Annual. 110 pp.

Georgia

University of Georgia, Selig Center for Economic Growth, Terry College of Business, Athens 30602-6269 706-542-4085

Georgia Statistical Abstract, 1992-93. 1992. 535 pp.

University of Georgia, College of Agriculture and Environmental Sciences, Cooperative Extension Service, Athens 30602 706-542-8938

The Georgia County Guide. 1993. 12th ed. Annual. 197 pp.

Office of Planning and Budget, 254 Washington St., S.W., Atlanta 30334-8501 404-656-0911

Georgia Descriptions in Data. 1990-91. 249 pp.

Hawaii

Hawaii State Department of Business, and Economic Development & Tourism, Research and Economic Analysis Division, Statistics Branch P.O. Box 2359, Honolulu 96804. Inquiries 808-586-2481; Copies 808-586-2424

The State of Hawaii Data Book 1992: A Statistical Abstract. 26th ed. 1993. 618 pp.

Idaho

Department of Commerce, 700 West State St., Boise 83720 208-334-2470

County Profiles of Idaho, 1992

Idaho Community Profiles, 1992.

Idaho Facts, 1993.

Idaho Facts Data Book, 1993.

Profile of Rural Idaho 1993.

University of Idaho, Center for Business Development and Research, Moscow 83844-3227 208-885-6611

Idaho Statistical Abstract. 1980. 415 pp. (Out of print.)

Illinois

University of Illinois, Bureau of Economic and Business Research, 428 Commerce West, 1206 South 6th Street, Champaign 61820 217-333-2330

Illinois Statistical Abstract. 1992. 812 pages.

Indiana

Indiana University, Indiana Business Research Center, School of Business, 801 W. Michigan BS4015 Indianapolis 46202-5151 317-274-2204

Indiana Factbook, 1992. 413 pages.

Iowa

Iowa Department of Economic Development Research Bureau, 200 East Grand Ave., Des Moines 50309

1993 Statistical Profile of Iowa.

Kansas

University of Kansas, Institute for Public Policy and Business Research, 607 Blake Hall, Lawrence 66045-2960 913-864-3701

Kansas Statistical Abstract, 1991-92. 27th ed. 1993.

Kentucky

Department of Existing Business and Industry, Capital Plaza Office Tower, Frankfort 40601 502-564-4886

Kentucky Deskbook of Economic Statistics. 29th ed. 1993.

Louisiana

University of New Orleans, Division of Business and Economic Research, New Orleans 70148 504-286-6248

Statistical Abstract of Louisiana. 8th ed. 1990.

Maine

Maine Department of Economic and Community Development, State House Station 59, Augusta 04333 207-287-3153

Maine: A Statistical Summary. (Updated periodically.)

Maryland

Department of Economic and Employment Development, 217 E. Redwood St., Baltimore 21202 Inquiries 410-333-6953; Copies 410-333-6955

Maryland Statistical Abstract. 1990-91. 274 pp. (Biennial.) 1993-94 available in summer 1993.

Massachusetts

Massachusetts Institute for Social and Economic Research, 128 Thompson Hall, University of Massachusetts at Amherst 01003 413-5453460 FAX 413-545-3686

Projected Total Population and Age Distribution for 1995 and 2000: Massachusetts Cities and Towns. March 1992. 62 pages.

Michigan

Wayne State University, Bureau of Business Research, School of Business Administration, Detroit 48202

Michigan Statistical Abstract. 20th ed. 1986-87. 629 pp.

Minnesota

Department of Trade and Economic Development, Business Development and Analysis Division, 900 American Center Building, St. Paul 55101 612-296-8283

Compare Minnesota: An Economic and Statistical Factbook, 1992-93. 165 pp.

Economic Report to the Governor: State of Minnesota, 1992. 148 pp.

Office of State Demographer, Minnesota Planning, 300 Centennial Bldg., St. Paul 55155 612-296-2557

Minnesota Population and Household Estimates, 1988. 74 pp. Available on diskette in Lotus, dBase or ASCII files.

Mississippi

Mississippi State University, College of Business and Industry, Division of Research, Mississippi State 39762 601-325-3817

Mississippi Statistical Abstract. 1993. 750 pp.

Missouri

University of Missouri, Business and Public Administration Research Center, Columbia 65211 314-882-4805

Statistical Abstract for Missouri, 1991 Biennial. 350 pp.

Montana

Montana Department of Commerce, Census and Economic Information Center, 1424 9th Ave., Helena 59620 406-444-2896

Montana County Database. (Seperate county and state reports; will be available by subject section as well as complete reports by county and state, updated periodically, available in paper microfiche, and diskette.)

Nebraska

Department of Economic Development, Division of Research, Box 94666, Lincoln 68509 402-471-3779

Nebraska Statistical Handbook. 1990-1991. 300 pp.

Nevada

Department of Administration, Planning Division, Capitol Complex, Carson City 89710 702-687-4065

Nevada Statistical Abstract. 1992. Biennial. 405 pp.

New Hampshire

Office of State Planning, 2 1/2 Beacon St., Concord 03301 603-271-2155

Current Estimates and Trends in New Hampshire's Housing Supply. Update: 1991. 32 pp.

Selected Economic Characteristics of New Hampshire Municipalities. 1992. 12 pp. (Other series available on population estimates and projections, and taxation.)

New Jersey

New Jersey State Data Center, NJ Department of Labor, CN 388, Trenton 08625-0388 609-984-2593

New Jersey Statistical Factbook, 1992. 115 pp.

New Jersey Source Book, 1993. 156 pp.

New Mexico

University of New Mexico, Bureau of Business and Economic Research, 1920 Lomas N.E. Albuquerque 87131-6021 505-277-2216

New Mexico Statistical Abstract. 1989. 215 pp.

County Profiles. *(Occasionally.)*

New York

Energy Association of New York, 111 Washington Avenue, Suite 601, Albany 12210 518-449-3440

New York at a Glance, 1989-90. 230 pp.

Nelson Rockefeller Institute of Government, 411 State Street, Albany 12203-1003 518-443-5522

New York State Statistical Yearbook, 1993. 18th ed. 544 pp.

North Carolina

Office of Governor

Office of State Planning, 116 West Jones Street, Raleigh 27603-8003 919-733-4131

Statistical Abstract of North Carolina Counties, 1991. 6th edition.

North Dakota

University of North Dakota, Bureau of Business and Economic Research, Grand Forks 58202 701-777-3365

The Statistical Abstract of North Dakota. 1988. 700 pp.

North Dakota Department of Economic Development and Finance 1833 E. Bismarck Expressway, Bismarck 58504 701-221-5300

North Dakota Economic Data Book. 1988. 100 pp.

Ohio

Department of Development, Office of Statistical Research, P.O. Box 1001, Columbus 43266-0101 614-466-2115

Products and Services. (Updated continuously.)

The Ohio State University, School of Public Policy and Management, 1775 College Road, Columbus 43210-1399 614-292-8696

Benchmark Ohio, 1991. Biennial. 300 pp.

Oklahoma

University of Oklahoma, Center for Economic and Management Research, 307 West Brooks Street, Room 4, Norman 73019 405-325-2931

Statistical Abstract of Oklahoma, 1992. Annual. 626 pp.

Oregon

Secretary of State, Room 136, State Capitol, Salem 97310

Oregon Blue Book. 1993-1994. Biennial. 441 pp. $12.

Pennsylvania

Pennsylvania State Data Center, Institute of State and Regional Affairs, Penn State Harrisburg, 777 West Harrisburg Pike, Middleton Pennsylvania 17057-4898.

Pennsylvania Statistical Abstract, 1992. 30th ed. 1992. 249 pp.

Rhode Island

Department of Economic Development, 7 Jackson Walkway, Providence 02903 401-277-2601

Rhode Island Basic Economic Statistics. 1992. Population summary, Annual and Monthly Economic Trends.

South Carolina

Budget and Control Board, Division of Research and Statistical Services, R. C. Dennis Building, Room 425, Columbia 29201 803-734-3780

South Carolina Statistical Abstract: 1993. 422 pp.

South Dakota

University of South Dakota, State Data Center, Vermillion 57069 605-677-5287

Selected Social and Economic Characteristics. 550 pp.

1992 South Dakota Community Abstracts. 400 pp.

Tennessee

University of Tennessee, Center for Business and Economic Research, Knoxville 37996-4170 615-9745441

Tennessee Statistical Abstract, 1992-93. 14th ed. 800 pp. (Annual.)

Texas

Dallas Morning News, Communications Center,
P.O. Box 655237, Dallas 75265
214-977-8261

Texas Almanac, 1994-1995. 1993. 672 pp.

University of Texas, Bureau of Business
Research, Austin 78712 512-471-5180

Texas Fact Book, 1989. 6th ed. 250 pp.

Utah

University of Utah, Bureau of Economic and
Business Research, 401 Kendall D. Garff
Building, Salt Lake City 84112
801-581-6333

Statistical Abstract of Utah. 1993.
(Triennial.)

Utah Foundation, 10 West 100 South 323, Salt
Lake City 84101-1544 801-364-1837

Statistical Review of Government in Utah.
1993. 135 pp.

Vermont

Office of Policy and Information, Department of
Employment and Training, Montpelier 05601
802-828-4202 ext. 323

Demographic and Economic Profiles. Annual

Virginia

University of Virginia, Center for Public Service,
Dynamics Building, 4th Floor, 2015 Ivy Road,
Charlottesville 22903 804-924-3921

Virginia Statistical Abstract, 1992-93.
Biennial. 850 pp.

Washington

Washington State Office of Financial
Management, Forecasting Division
P.O. Box 43113 Olympia, WA 98504-3113
206-753-5617

Washington State Data Book, 1991.
Biennial. 306 pp. Current edition available:
1993 edition scheduled for release in
January/February 1994.

Population Trends for Washington State. Annual.
128 pages.

West Virginia

West Virginia Chamber of Commerce,
P.O. Box 2789, Charleston 25330
304-342-1115

*West Virginia: Economic-Statistical Profile,
1987-1988.* Biennial. 750 pp.

West Virginia Research League, Inc.,
405 Capitol Street, Suite 414,
Charleston 25301
304-346-9451

Economic Indicators. 1988. 110 pp.

The 1992 Statistical Handbook. 94 pp.

Wisconsin

Wisconsin Legislative Reference Bureau,
P.O. Box 2037, Madison 53701-2037
608-266-0341

1991-1992 Wisconsin Blue Book. 1,000 pp.
Biennial. 1993-94 edition will be published
September/October 1993.

Wyoming

Department of Administration and Information,
Division of Economic Analysis,
327 E. Emerson Building, Cheyenne 82002
307-777-7504

Wyoming Data Handbook, 1991. 310 pp.

Puerto Rico

Planning Board, Area of Economic and Social
Planning, Bureau of Economic Analysis and
Bureau of Statistics, Santurce 00940
809-722-2070

Economic Report to the Governor, 1992.
(In Spanish.)

*Historic Series of Employment, Unemploy-
ment and Labor Force, 1990.* (In Spanish.)

Social Statistics Abstract, 1988. (In Spanish.)

Socioeconomic Indicators by Municipios, 1991.
(In Spanish.)

*Economical Forecasts for Fiscal Years 1993
and 1994.* (In Spanish.)

Income Product, 1991. (In Spanish.)

National Accounts of Puerto Rico, 1992.
(In Spanish.)

Guide to Foreign Statistical Abstracts

This bibliography presents recent statistical abstracts for Mexico, the Soviet Union, and member nations of the Organization for Economic Cooperation and Development. All sources contain statistical tables on a variety of subjects for the individual countries. Many of the following publications provide text in English as well as in the national language(s). For further information on these publications, contact the named statistical agency which is responsible for editing the publication.

Austria

Osterreichisches Statistisches Zentralamt, P.O. Box 9000, A-1033 Vienna

Statistisches Handbuch for die Republik Osterreich. Annual. 1991 592 pp. (In German.)

Australia

Australian Bureau of Statistics, Canberra

Yearbook Australia. Annual. 1992 802 pp. (In English.)

Belgium

Institut National de Statistique, 44 rue de Louvain, 1000 Brussels

Annuaire statistique de la Belgique. Annual. 1990 791 pp. (In French and Dutch.)

Canada

Statistics Canada, Ottawa, Ontario, KIA OT6

Canada Yearbook: A review of economic, social and political developments in Canada. 1992 622 pp. Irregular. (In English and French.)

Croatia

Republika Hrvatska, Republicki Zavod Za Statistiku

Statisticki Godisnjak Republike Hrvatske 1991 472 pp.

Denmark

Danmarks Statistik, Postboks 2550 Sejrogade 11, DK 2100, Copenhagen 0

Statistical Yearbook. 1992. Annual. 566 pp. (In Danish with English translations of table headings.)

Finland

Central Statistical Office of Finland, Box 504 SF-00101 Helsinki

Statistical Yearbook of Finland. Annual. 1992 614 pp. (In English, Finnish, and Swedish.)

France

Institut National de la Statistique et des Etudes Economiques, Paris 18, Bld. Adolphe Pinard, 75675 Paris (Cedex 14)

Annuaire Statistique de la France. Annual. 1991/92 824 pp. (In French.)

Greece

National Statistical Office, 14-16 Lycourgou St., 101-66 Athens

Statistical Yearbook of Greece. Annual. 1989 535 pp. (plus 7 pages of diagrams). (In English and Greek.)

Iceland

Hagstofa Islands/Statistical Bureau, Hverfisgata 8-10, Reykjavik.

Statistical Abstract of Iceland. 1992. Irregular. 280 pp. (In English and Icelandic.)

Ireland

Central Statistics Office, Earlsfort Terrace, Dublin 2

Statistical Abstract. Annual. 1992 402 pp. (In English.)

Italy

ISTAT (Istituto Centrale di Statistica), Via Cesare Balbo 16, 00100 Rome

Annuario Statistico Italiano. Annual. 1992 211 pp. (In Italian.)

Japan

Statistics Bureau, Management & Coordination Agency, 19-1 Wakamatsucho, Shinjuku Tokyo 162

Japan Statistical Yearbook. Annual. 1992 840 pp. (In English and Japanese.)

Luxembourg

STATEC (Service Central de la Statistique et des Etudes), P.O. Box 304, L-2013, Luxembourg

Annuaire Statistique. Annual. 1991 529 pp. (In French.)

Mexico

Instituto Nacional de Estadistica Geografia e Informatica, Avda. Insurgentes Sur No. 795-PH Col. Napoles, Del. Benito Juarez 03810 Mexico, D.F.

Anuario estadistico de los Estados Unidos Mexicanos. Annual. 1986 706 pp. (In Spanish.)

Netherlands

Centraal Bureau voor de Statistiek. 428 Prinses Beatrixlaan P.O. Box 959, 2270 AZ Voorburg

Statistisch Yearbook 1993. 568 pp. (In Dutch.)

New Zealand

Department of Statistics, Wellington

New Zealand Official Yearbook. Annual. 1992 484 pp. (In English.)

Norway

Central Bureau of Statistics, Skippergate 15, P.B. 8131 Dep. N-Oslo 1

Statistical Yearbook. Annual. 1988 502 pp. (In English and Norwegian.)

Portugal

INE (Instituto Nacional de Estatistica), Avenida Antonio Jose de Almeida, P-1078 Lisbon Codex

Anuario Estatistico: de Portugal. 1991 378 pp. (In Portugese.)

Soviet Union

Central Statistical Board, Moscow

Narodnoe Khoziaistvo SSSR: Statisticheskii ezhegodnik. Annual. 767 pp. (In Russian.)

Spain

INE (Instituto Nacional de Estadistica), Paseo de la Castellana, 183, Madrid 16

Anuario Estadistico de Espana. Annual. 1991 867 pp. (In Spanish.)

Anuario Estadistico. 1988. (Edicion Manual.) 976 pp.

Sweden

Statistics Sweden, S-11581 Stockholm

Statistical Abstract of Sweden. Annual. 1993 565 pp. (In English and Swedish.)

Switzerland

Bundesamt fur Statistik, Hallwylstrasse 15, CH-3003, Bern

Statistisches Jahrbuch der Schweiz. Annual. 1991 420 pp. (In French and German.)

Turkey

State Institute of Statistics, Prime Ministry, 114 Necatibey Caddesi, Bakanliklar, Yenisehir, Ankara

Statistical Yearbook of Turkey. Published on odd numbered years. 1991 639 pp. (In English and Turkish.)

Statistical Pocketbook of Turkey. Published on even numbered years. 1986 294 pp. (In English and Turkish.)

United Kingdom

Central Statistical Office, Great George Street, London SW1P 3AQ

Annual Abstract of Statistics. Annual. 1991 349 pp. (In English.)

West Germany

Statistische Bundesamt, Postfach 5528, 6200 Wiesbaden

Statistisches Jahrbuch fur die Bundesrepublic Deutschland. Annual. 1990 740 pp. (In German.)

Yugoslavia

Savezni Zavod za Statistiku, P.O. Box 203, 11000 Belgrade

Statisticki Godisnjak Jugoslavije. Annual. 1991 779 pp. (In Serbo-Croation with English, French, and Russian translations of table headings.)

Statistical Pocketbook of Yugoslavia. 1991. 161 pp. (In English.)

Metropolitan Areas: Concepts, Components, and Population

Statistics for metropolitan areas (MA's) shown in the *Statistical Abstract* represent areas designated by the U.S. Office of Management and Budget (OMB) as metropolitan statistical areas (MSA's), consolidated metropolitan statistical areas (CMSA's), and primary metropolitan statistical areas (PMSA's). Currently defined MA's are based on application of 1990 standards (which appeared in the *Federal Register* on March 30, 1990) to 1990 decennial census data. These MA definitions were announced by OMB effective December 31, 1992.

The list of areas that follows (see p. 919) specifies geographic components and latest populations for each MA. As of the December 1992 OMB announcement there were 250 MSA's, as well as 18 CMSA's comprising 59 PMSA's in the United States. In addition, there were three MSA's, one CMSA, and three PMSA's in Puerto Rico. (The figures in tables A, B, and C below exclude the areas in Puerto Rico.)

Standard definitions of metropolitan areas were first issued in 1949 by the then Bureau of the Budget (predecessor of OMB), under the designation "standard metropolitan area" (SMA). The term was changed to "standard metropolitan statistical area" (SMSA) in 1959 and to "metropolitan statistical area" (MSA) in 1983. The current collective term "metropolitan area" for MSA's, CMSA's, and PMSA's became effective in 1990. OMB has been responsible for the official metropolitan areas since they were first defined, except for the period 1977 to 1981, when they were the responsibility of the Office of Federal Statistical Policy and Standards, Department of Commerce.

The standards for defining metropolitan areas were modified in 1958, 1971, 1975, 1980, and 1990.

Defining MA's. The general concept of a metropolitan area is that of a core area containing a large population nucleus, together with adjacent communities having a high degree of economic and social integration with that core.

The current standards provide that each MA must include at least: (a) one city with 50,000 or more inhabitants, or (b) a Census Bureau-defined urbanized area of at least 50,000 inhabitants and a total MA population of at least 100,000 (75,000 in New England).

Under the standards, the county (or counties) that contains the largest city becomes the central county (counties), along with any adjacent counties that have at least 50 percent of their population in the urbanized area surrounding the largest city. Additional "outlying counties" are included in the MA if they meet specified requirements of commuting to the central counties and selected requirements of metropolitan character (such as population density and percent urban). In New England the MA's are defined in terms of cities and towns rather than counties.

The standards provide that within MA's of a million or more population, separate component areas are defined if specified criteria are met and local opinion indicates need for the areas. Such areas are designated PMSA's, and any MA containing PMSA's is designated a CMSA. All MA's not designated as CMSA's and PMSA's are identified as MSA's, including 22 MSA's in the United States with a 1990 population greater than 1 million.

The largest city in each MA is designated a "central city," and additional cities may qualify as such if specified requirements are met concerning population size and commuting patterns. The title of each MSA consists of the names of up to three of its central cities and the name of each State into which the MSA extends. However, a central city generally is not included in an MSA title unless it has one-third the population of area's largest city or local opinion desires its inclusion. Titles of CMSA's and PMSA's also are limited to three names and typically use central city names (although PMSA's may use county names in their titles and these names may then also appear in CMSA titles). An MA may include other cities of 50,000 or more which are not central cities.

A 1990 census listing, CPH-L-118, showing 1990 and 1980 populations for current MA's and their component counties or New England subcounty areas is available through the Statistical Information Office, Population Division, 301-763-5002. A 1990 Census Supplementary Report showing population and housing characteristics for MA's as defined through June 1993 is being released in late 1993.

New England MA's and NECMA's. MA's in New England are defined in terms of cities and towns rather than counties, with the result that some statistical data available only for counties cannot be compiled for individual New England MA's. For that reason, OMB has established "New England county metropolitan areas" (NECMA's) as a county-based alternative for New England MA's (although NECMA's do not replace New England MA's as the standard areas). NECMA's are defined corresponding to the individual New England MSA's, for the Boston CMSA, and for the portion of the New York-Northern New Jersey-Long Island CMSA in Connecticut. There are no NECMA definitions corresponding to New England PMSA's.

Changes in MA definitions over time. Changes in the definitions of MA's since the 1950 census have consisted chiefly of (1) the recognition of new areas as they reached the minimum required city or area population; and (2) the addition of counties or New England cities and towns to existing areas as new census data showed them to qualify. Also, former separate MA's have been merged with other areas, and occasionally territory has been transferred from

one MA to another or from an MA to non-metropolitan territory. The large majority of changes have taken place on the basis of decennial census data, although the MA standards specify the bases for intercensal updates.

Because of these changes in definition, users must be cautious in comparing MA data from different dates. For some purposes, comparisons of data for MA's as defined at given dates may be appropriate. In this volume, however, data for earlier dates have been revised where possible to reflect the MA boundaries of the more recent date.

In tables A, B, and C that follow, data are given for MA's as defined for specific dates, thereby indicating the extent of change in population and land area resulting from revisions in definitions.

Table A. Number, Population, and Land Area of MA's as Defined at Specified Dates From 1950 to 1992

[The differences in population shown here for each year within each column of the table result entirely from net expansion of metropolitan territory through changes in the MA definitions. The differences in population over time shown for each MA definition (on the successive lines of the table) result entirely from population changes within that territory, unaffected by changes in MA definitions. The changes in 1990 land area result entirely from net change in MA territory. All data include Alaska and Hawaii and exclude Puerto Rico. Subtraction of any line of the table from the line below will show the net effect of change in population and land area undergone by the MA's as the result of changes in definitions between the specified dates. Such changes may have occurred throughout the period, not on any single date, and may have included reductions in, as well as additions to, MA territory. Census population data for 1970 include corrections made since publication. The area data for the 1950, 1960, 1970, and 1980 census definitions of MA's differ from the data published in those censuses because of subsequent remeasurement of land areas and changes in inland water area occurring for the 1990 census]

MA DEFINITION AS OF—	Number of MA's	POPULATION (as of April 1)					Land area, 1990 (sq. mi.)
		1950	1960	1970	1980	1990	
1950 census (Mar. 1952)	169	[1]84,853,700	106,344,548	122,184,836	128,839,422	139,837,352	206,802
1960 census (Nov. 1960)	212	89,316,903	[2]112,885,139	130,982,661	140,793,427	155,088,626	308,742
1964 (Aug. 31) [3]	217	91,644,188	115,876,343	134,700,911	145,503,863	160,500,956	348,400
1968 (Jan. 31) [4]	230	93,629,986	118,413,604	137,976,252	149,811,057	165,707,672	377,042
1970 census (Feb. 28, 1971). . .	243	94,579,008	[5]119,593,498	[6]139,479,806	151,662,221	167,896,646	386,241
1974 (Apr. 30) [7]	265	[8]100,219,707	[9]126,613,710	148,198,993	162,753,335	181,125,276	490,551
1977 (Dec. 31) [10]	277	101,109,145	127,674,818	149,482,664	164,383,496	182,989,860	509,841
1980 census (June 30, 1981) [11].	318	104,172,853	131,318,714	153,693,767	169,430,623	188,759,597	565,288
1983 (June 30).	[12]275	105,214,471	132,633,988	155,411,328	171,776,970	191,634,355	559,752
1984 (June 30).	[12]277	105,269,301	132,707,748	155,519,340	171,955,900	191,903,497	563,796
1985 (June 30).	[12]280	105,411,428	132,887,134	155,700,823	172,169,456	192,135,964	569,816
1986 (June 30).	[12]281	105,481,211	132,977,580	155,805,452	172,304,016	192,314,367	571,745
1987 (June 30) [13]	[12]281	105,502,909	133,003,445	155,832,688	172,334,547	192,345,395	572,284
1988 (June 30) [14]	[12]282	105,582,961	133,088,400	155,937,275	172,454,948	192,476,951	573,560
1989 (June 30) [14].	[12]283	105,718,150	133,233,777	156,084,580	172,601,873	192,618,846	574,622
1990 census (June 30, 1990) [14].	[12]284	105,742,856	133,275,412	156,137,337	172,679,870	192,725,741	580,136
1992 (Dec. 31) [14]	[12]268	(NA)	(NA)	(NA)	176,662,797	197,466,567	670,157

NA Not available. [1] Corresponds to total MA population for 1950 census (84,500,680) plus Honolulu MSA. [2] Corresponds to total MA population for 1960 census published in 1960 census (112,885,178), corrected by subtracting population (39) erroneously included in Franklin County, Ohio (Columbus MSA). [3] MA's as defined for the 1963 economic censuses. [4] MA's as defined for the 1967 economic censuses. [5] Corresponds to total 1960 population for 1970 MA's published in 1970 census (119,594,754), corrected by subtracting 1,256 population from Lawrence-Haverhill MSA; this represented an addition to the 1960 population of Andover town made subsequent to the original census tabulations, and therefore not reflected in State or national totals. [6] Corresponds to total MA population for 1970 published in 1970 census (139,418,811), plus net corrections made subsequent to publication. [7] MA's as defined for the 1972 economic censuses. [8] Includes estimated 1950 population (32,060) of Anchorage Census Division, as defined in 1970. [9] Includes 1960 population (82,833) of Anchorage Census Division, as defined in 1970. [10] MA's as defined for the 1977 economic censuses. [11] MA's as defined for the 1982 economic censuses. [12] MSA's and CMSA's. [13] MA's as defined for the 1987 economic censuses. [14] Data exclude the portion of Sullivan city in Crawford County, MO (1990 population 1,116) added to the St. Louis, MO-IL MSA by legislative action effective Dec. 22, 1987.

Source: U.S. Bureau of the Census, 1950-1970, *U.S. Census of Population,* vol. 1; *1980 Census of Population,* vol. 1, chapters A and B and *Supplementary Report, Metropolitan Statistical Areas* (PC80-S1-18); and *1990 Census of Population and Housing Data Paper Listing* (CPH-L-10 and CPH-L-118).

Table B. Nonmetropolitan Population and Land Area as Defined at Specified Dates From 1950 to 1992

[See headnote for table A. Nonmetropolitan population and land area are equivalent to that portion of the total national population and land area not included within MA's at the dates specified]

METROPOLITAN AREA DEFINITION AS OF—	POPULATION (as of April 1)					Land area, 1990 (sq. mi.)
	1950	1960	1970	1980	1990	
1950 census (Mar. 1952)	66,472,098	72,978,627	81,117,195	97,706,383	108,872,521	3,332,967
1960 census (Nov. 1960)	62,008,895	66,438,036	72,319,370	85,752,378	93,621,247	3,231,027
1964 (Aug. 31)	59,681,610	63,446,832	68,601,120	81,041,942	88,208,917	3,191,368
1968 (Jan. 31)	57,695,812	60,909,571	65,325,779	76,734,748	83,002,201	3,162,726
1970 census (Feb. 28, 1971)	56,746,790	59,729,677	63,822,225	74,883,584	80,813,227	3,153,527
1974 (Apr. 30)	51,106,091	52,709,465	55,103,038	63,792,470	67,584,597	3,049,218
1977 (Dec. 31)	50,216,653	51,648,357	53,819,367	62,162,309	65,720,013	3,029,928
1980 census (June 30, 1981)	47,152,945	48,004,461	49,608,264	57,115,182	59,950,276	2,974,481
1983 (June 30)	46,111,327	46,689,187	47,890,703	54,768,835	57,075,518	2,980,016
1984 (June 30)	46,056,497	46,615,427	47,782,691	54,589,905	56,806,376	2,975,972
1985 (June 30)	45,914,370	46,436,041	47,601,208	54,376,349	56,573,909	2,969,952
1986 (June 30)	45,844,587	46,345,595	47,496,579	54,241,789	56,395,506	2,968,023
1987 (June 30)	45,822,889	46,319,730	47,469,343	54,211,258	56,364,478	2,967,484
1988 (June 30)	45,742,837	46,234,775	47,364,756	54,090,857	56,232,922	2,966,208
1989 (June 30)	45,607,648	46,089,398	47,217,451	53,943,932	56,091,027	2,965,146
1990 census (June 30, 1990)	45,582,942	46,047,763	47,164,694	53,865,935	55,984,132	2,959,632
1992 (Dec. 31)	(NA)	(NA)	(NA)	49,883,008	51,243,306	2,869,611

NA Not available.

Table C. Percent of Total U.S. Population and Percent of Land Area Inside MA's as Defined at Specified Dates From 1950 to 1992

[See headnote for table A]

METROPOLITAN AREA DEFINITION AS OF—	PERCENT OF POPULATION (as of April 1)					Percent of land area, 1990
	1950	1960	1970	1980	1990	
1950 census (Mar. 1952)	56.1	59.3	60.1	56.9	56.2	5.8
1960 census (Nov. 1960)	59.0	63.0	64.4	62.1	62.4	8.7
1964 (Aug. 31)	60.6	64.6	66.3	64.2	64.5	9.8
1968 (Jan. 31)	61.9	66.0	67.9	66.1	66.6	10.7
1970 census (Feb. 28, 1971)	62.5	66.7	68.6	66.9	67.5	10.9
1974 (Apr. 30)	66.2	70.6	72.9	71.8	72.8	13.9
1977 (Dec. 31)	66.8	71.2	73.5	72.6	73.6	14.4
1980 census (June 30, 1981)	68.8	73.2	75.6	74.8	75.9	16.0
1983 (June 30)	69.5	74.0	76.4	75.8	77.1	15.8
1984 (June 30)	69.6	74.0	76.5	75.9	77.2	15.9
1985 (June 30)	69.7	74.1	76.6	76.0	77.3	16.1
1986 (June 30)	69.7	74.2	76.6	76.1	77.3	16.2
1987 (June 30)	69.7	74.2	76.7	76.1	77.3	16.2
1988 (June 30)	69.8	74.2	76.7	76.1	77.4	16.2
1989 (June 30)	69.9	74.3	76.8	76.2	77.4	16.2
1990 census (June 30, 1990)	69.9	74.3	76.8	76.2	77.5	16.4
1992 (Dec. 31)	(NA)	(NA)	(NA)	78.0	79.4	18.9

NA Not available.

Source of tables B and C: U.S. Bureau of the Census, 1950-1970, *U.S. Census of Population, vol. 1; 1980 Census of Population, vol. 1, chapters A and B* and *Supplementary Report, Metropolitan Statistical Areas* (PC80-S1-18); and *1990 Census of Population and Housing Data Paper Listing* (CPH-L-10 and CPH-L-118).

Table D. New England County Metropolitan Areas (NECMA's)

[In thousands. As of July 1]

NECMA	Popu-lation, 1991	NECMA	Popu-lation, 1991	NECMA	Popu-lation, 1991
Bangor, ME	147	**Burlington, VT**	178	**New London-Norwich, CT**	255
Penobscot County	147	Chittenden County	133	New London County	255
Barnstable-Yarmouth, MA	188	Franklin County	40		
Barnstable County	188	Grand Isle County	6	**Pittsfield, MA**	138
Boston-Brockton-Nashua,		**Hartford, CT**	1,125	Berkshire County	138
MA-NH	5,662	Hartford County	852	**Portland, ME**	244
Bristol County, MA	508	Middlesex County	144	Cumberland County	244
Essex County, MA	669	Tolland County	129	**Providence-Warwick, RI**	917
Middlesex County, MA	1,392	**Lewiston-Auburn, ME**	105	Bristol County	49
Norfolk County, MA	616	Androscoggin County	105	Kent County	162
Plymouth County, MA	437			Providence County	594
Suffolk County, MA	651	**New Haven-Bridgeport-**		Washington County	112
Worcester County, MA	707	**Stamford-Danbury-**		**Springfield, MA**	601
Hillsborough County, NH	336	**Waterbury, CT**	1,633	Hampden County	454
Rockingham County, NH	242	Fairfield County	829	Hampshire County	147
Strafford County, NH	103	New Haven County	804		

Source: U.S. Bureau of the Census, unpublished data.

Metropolitan Areas and Their Components as of December 31, 1992

[Population estimated as of **July 1, 1991**. All metropolitan areas are arranged alphabetically. For relationship of PMSA's to their CMSA's, see CMSA entry]

	1991 Population (1,000)
Abilene, TX MSA.	119
Taylor County.	119
Akron, OH PMSA	665
Portage County.	145
Summit County.	520
Albany, GA MSA.	114
Dougherty County	97
Lee County.	17
Albany-Schenectady-Troy, NY MSA.	869
Albany County	293
Montgomery County.	52
Rensselaer County	156
Saratoga County.	185
Schenectady County	151
Schoharie County	33
Albuquerque, NM MSA	602
Bernalillo County.	490
Sandoval County.	66
Valencia County	47
Alexandria, LA MSA	132
Rapides Parish	132
Allentown-Bethlehem-Easton, PA MSA	602
Carbon County, PA.	58
Lehigh County, PA.	294
Northampton County, PA . .	250
Altoona, PA MSA	131
Blair County	131
Amarillo, TX MSA	190
Potter County	99
Randall County.	90
Anchorage, AK MSA	236
Anchorage Borough.	236
Ann Arbor, MI PMSA.	499
Lenawee County.	92
Livingston County	119
Washtenaw County	287
Anniston, AL MSA	116
Calhoun County	116
Appleton-Oshkosh-Neenah, WI MSA	320
Calumet County	35
Outagamie County.	142
Winnebago County	143
Asheville, NC MSA	195
Buncombe County.	178
Madison County	17
Athens, GA MSA.	128
Clarke County.	88
Madison County	22
Oconee County.	18
Atlanta, GA MSA.	3,051
Barrow County	31
Bartow County	58
Carroll County.	73
Cherokee County	97
Clayton County	185
Cobb County	463

	1991 Population (1,000)
Coweta County.	57
De Kalb County	554
Douglas County	73
Fayette County.	66
Forsyth County.	47
Fulton County.	657
Gwinnett County.	371
Henry County	63
Newton County.	44
Paulding County	45
Pickens County.	15
Rockdale County.	57
Spalding County	56
Walton County	40
Atlantic-Cape May, NJ PMSA	323
Atlantic County	227
Cape May County	96
Augusta-Aiken, GA-SC MSA	407
Columbia County, GA. . . .	70
Richmond County, GA	192
Aiken County, SC	126
Edgefield County, SC.	19
Austin-San Marcos, TX MSA.	874
Bastrop County.	39
Caldwell County	27
Hays County.	67
Travis County.	595
Williamson County.	147
Bakersfield, CA MSA.	567
Kern County.	567
Baltimore, MD MSA.	2,414
Anne Arundel County.	434
Baltimore County.	701
Carroll County.	127
Harford County	190
Howard County.	193
Queen Anne's County	35
Baltimore city	734
Bangor, ME MSA	92
Penobscot County (pt.). . . .	89
Waldo County (pt.).	3
Barnstable-Yarmouth, MA MSA	136
Barnstable County (pt.). . . .	136
Baton Rouge, LA MSA	478
East Baton Rouge Parish . .	387
Livingston Parish.	72
West Baton Rouge Parish..	20
Beaumont-Port Arthur, TX MSA.	367
Hardin County.	42
Jefferson County.	243
Orange County.	82
Bellingham, WA MSA	133
Whatcom County.	133
Benton Harbor, MI MSA. . . .	161
Berrien County.	161
Billings, MT MSA.	115
Yellowstone County.	115
Biloxi-Gulfport-Pascagoula, MS MSA.	316
Hancock County	32
Harrison County	167
Jackson County	117

	1991 Population (1,000)
Binghamton, NY MSA	265
Broome County.	212
Tioga County.	53
Birmingham, AL MSA	849
Blount County.	40
Jefferson County.	655
St. Clair County.	52
Shelby County	103
Bismarck, ND MSA	85
Burleigh County	61
Morton County	23
Bloomington, IN MSA	110
Monroe County.	110
Bloomington-Normal, IL MSA.	132
McLean County.	132
Boise City, ID MSA	310
Ada County	216
Canyon County	94
Boston, MA-NH-ME-CT PMSA.	5,027
Bristol County, MA (pt.) . . .	253
Essex County, MA.	669
Hampden County, MA (pt.) .	2
Middlesex County, MA (pt.).	1,393
Norfolk County, MA (pt.). . .	612
Plymouth County, MA (pt.) .	235
Suffolk County, MA	651
Worcester County, MA (pt.).	682
Hillsborough County, NH (pt.)	142
Merrimack County, NH (pt.).	13
Rockingham County, NH (pt.)	233
Strafford County, NH (pt.). .	97
York County, ME (pt.).	36
Windham County, CT (pt.). .	9
Boston-Brockton-Nashua, MA-NH-ME-CT CMSA.	5,432
Boston, MA-NH-ME-CT PMSA	5,027
Brockton, MA PMSA	237
Nashua, NH PMSA	168
Boulder-Longmont, CO PMSA.	232
Boulder County.	232
Brazoria, TX PMSA	199
Brazoria County	199
Bremerton, WA PMSA.	201
Kitsap County	201
Bridgeport, CT PMSA	443
Fairfield County (pt.)	335
New Haven County (pt.). . .	108
Brockton, MA PMSA	237
Bristol County (pt.).	30
Norfolk County, (pt.).	5
Plymouth County, (pt.)	203
Brownsville-Harlingen, TX MSA.	269
Cameron County.	269
Bryan-College Station, TX MSA.	123
Brazos County	123

	1991 Population (1,000)

Buffalo-Niagara Falls, NY MSA. 1,193
Erie County 972
Niagara County 221

Burlington, VT MSA 153
Chittenden County (pt.) 126
Franklin County (pt.) 24
Grand Isle County (pt.) 3

Canton-Massillon, OH MSA 397
Carroll County 27
Stark County 370

Casper, WY MSA 62
Natrona County 62

Cedar Rapids, IA MSA 171
Linn County 171

Champaign-Urbana, IL MSA 174
Champaign County 174

Charleston, WV MSA 252
Kanawha County 207
Putnam County 44

Charleston-North Charleston, SC MSA 524
Berkeley County 133
Charleston County 304
Dorchester County 86

Charlotte-Gastonia-Rock Hill, NC-SC MSA 1,190
Cabarrus County, NC 101
Gaston County, NC 177
Lincoln County, NC 51
Mecklenburg County, NC 526
Rowan County, NC 112
Union County, NC 87
York County, SC 135

Charlottesville, VA MSA 134
Albemarle County 68
Fluvanna County 13
Greene County 11
Charlottesville city 41

Chattanooga, TN-GA MSA 403
Hamilton County, TN 288
Catoosa County, GA 43
Dade County, GA 13
Walker County, GA 59

Cheyenne, WY MSA 74
Laramie County 74

Chicago, IL PMSA 7,498
Cook County 5,130
DeKalb County 79
Du Page County 799
Grundy County 33
Kane County 326
Kendall County 41
Lake County 530
McHenry County 192
Will County 367

Chicago-Gary-Kenosha, IL-IN-WI CMSA 8,339
Chicago, IL PMSA 7,498
Gary, IN PMSA 611
Kankakee, IL PMSA 98
Kenosha, WI PMSA 132

Chico-Paradise, CA MSA 187
Butte County 187

Cincinnati, OH-KY-IN PMSA 1,539
Brown County, OH. 36
Clermont County, OH. 154
Hamilton County, OH. 870
Warren County, OH. 117
Boone County, KY 61

Campbell County, KY 84
Gallatin County, KY 5
Grant County, KY 16
Kenton County, KY 143
Pendleton County, KY 12
Dearborn County, IN 40
Ohio County, IN 5

Cincinnati-Hamilton, OH-KY-IN CMSA 1,843
Cincinnati, OH-KY-IN PMSA 1,544
Hamilton-Middletown, OH PMSA 299

Clarksville-Hopkinsville, TN-KY MSA 170
Montgomery County, TN. 103
Christian County, KY 67

Cleveland-Akron, OH CMSA 2,878
Akron, OH PMSA 665
Cleveland-Lorain-Elyria, OH PMSA 2,213

Cleveland-Lorain-Elyria, OH PMSA 2,213
Ashtabula County 100
Cuyahoga County 1,414
Geauga County 82
Lake County 218
Lorain County 273
Medina County 125

Colorado Springs, CO MSA 404
El Paso County 404

Columbia, MO MSA 115
Boone County 115

Columbia, SC MSA 464
Lexington County 173
Richland County 291

Columbus, GA-AL MSA 264
Chattahoochee County, GA. 17
Harris County, GA 18
Muscogee County, GA 181
Russell County, AL 48

Columbus, OH MSA 1,370
Delaware County 69
Fairfield County 106
Franklin County 978
Licking County 131
Madison County 38
Pickaway County 49

Corpus Christi, TX MSA 356
Nueces County 297
San Patricio County 60

Cumberland, MD-WV MSA 102
Allegany County, MD 75
Mineral County, WV 27

Dallas, TX PMSA 2,739
Collin County 277
Dallas County 1,887
Denton County 284
Ellis County 87
Henderson County 59
Hunt County 64
Kaufman County 54
Rockwall County 27

Dallas-Fort Worth, TX CMSA 4,135
Dallas, TX PMSA 2,739
Fort Worth-Arlington, TX PMSA 1,396

Danbury, CT PMSA 209
Fairfield County (pt.) 163
Litchfield County (pt.) 30
New Haven County (pt.) 16

Danville, VA MSA 109
Pittsylvania County 56
Danville city 54

Davenport-Moline-Rock Island, IA-IL MSA 354
Scott County, IA 153
Henry County, IL 51
Rock Island County, IL 150

Dayton-Springfield, OH MSA 956
Clark County 148
Greene County 138
Miami County 94
Montgomery County 576

Daytona Beach, FL MSA 414
Flagler County 31
Volusia County 382

Decatur, AL MSA 134
Lawrence County 32
Morgan County 102

Decatur, IL MSA 118
Macon County 118

Denver, CO PMSA 1,668
Adams County 273
Arapahoe County 407
Denver County 476
Douglas County 66
Jefferson County 447

Denver-Boulder-Greeley, CO CMSA 2,034
Boulder-Longmont, CO PMSA 232
Denver, CO PMSA 1,668
Greeley, CO PMSA 134

Des Moines, IA MSA 400
Dallas County 30
Polk County 333
Warren County 37

Detroit, MI PMSA 4,285
Lapeer County 77
Macomb County 722
Monroe County 134
Oakland County 1,100
St. Clair County 148
Wayne County 2,103

Detroit-Ann Arbor-Flint, MI CMSA 5,215
Ann Arbor, MI PMSA 499
Detroit, MI PMSA 4,285
Flint, MI PMSA 431

Dothan, AL MSA 132
Dale County 50
Houston County 82

Dover, DE MSA 114
Kent County 114

Dubuque, IA MSA 87
Dubuque County 87

Duluth, MN-WI MSA 241
St. Louis County, MN. 199
Douglas County, WI 42

Dutchess County, NY PMSA 261
Dutchess County 261

Eau Claire, WI MSA 139
Chippewa County 53
Eau Claire County 86

El Paso, TX MSA 612
El Paso County 612

Elkhart-Goshen, IN MSA 158
Elkhart County 158

	1991 Population (1,000)		1991 Population (1,000)		1991 Population (1,000)
Elmira, NY MSA	95	**Gadsden, AL MSA**	100	**Hickory-Morganton, NC MSA**	296
Chemung County	95	Etowah County	100	Alexander County	28
				Burke County	76
Enid, OK MSA	56	**Gainesville, FL MSA**	186	Caldwell County	71
Garfield County	56	Alachua County	186	Catawba County	120
Erie, PA MSA	278	**Galveston-Texas City, TX**		**Honolulu, HI MSA**	851
Erie County	278	**PMSA**	223	Honolulu County	851
		Galveston County	223		
Eugene-Springfield, OR				**Houma, LA MSA**	185
MSA	288	**Gary, IN PMSA**	611	Lafourche Parish	86
Lane County	288	Lake County	479	Terrebonne Parish	99
		Porter County	132		
Evansville-Henderson, IN-KY				**Houston, TX PMSA**	3,437
MSA	281	**Glens Falls, NY MSA**	120	Chambers County	20
Posey County, IN	26	Warren County	60	Fort Bend County	241
Vanderburgh County, IN . . .	166	Washington County	60	Harris County	2,905
Warrick County, IN	46			Liberty County	54
Henderson County, KY. . . .	43	**Goldsboro, NC MSA**	106	Montgomery County.	193
		Wayne County	106	Waller County.	24
Fargo-Moorhead, ND-MN					
MSA	155	**Grand Forks, ND-MN MSA** . .	103	**Houston-Galveston-**	
Cass County, ND	104	Grand Forks County, ND . .	70	**Brazoria, TX CMSA**	3,859
Clay County, MN	51	Polk County, MN.	33	Brazoria, TX PMSA	199
				Galveston-Texas City, TX	
Fayetteville, NC MSA	276	**Grand Rapids-Muskegon-Holland,**		PMSA	223
Cumberland County	276	**MI MSA**	953	Houston, TX PMSA	3,437
		Allegan County	92		
Fayetteville-Springdale-		Kent County.	508	**Huntington-Ashland,**	
Rogers, AR MSA	218	Muskegon County	160	**WV-KY-OH MSA**	289
Benton County	101	Ottawa County	193	Cabell County, WV	97
Washington County	117			Wayne County, WV	42
		Great Falls, MT MSA	79	Boyd County, KY.	51
Flint, MI PMSA	431	Cascade County	79	Greenup County, KY	37
Genesee County.	431			Lawrence County, OH	62
		Greeley, CO PMSA	134		
Florence, AL MSA	133	Weld County	134	**Huntsville, AL MSA**	300
Colbert County	52			Limestone County	56
Lauderdale County	81	**Green Bay, WI MSA**	199	Madison County	245
		Brown County.	199		
Florence, SC MSA	117			**Indianapolis, IN MSA**	1,406
Florence County	117	**Greensboro—Winston-**		Boone County.	38
		Salem—High Point, NC		Hamilton County	116
Fort Collins-Loveland, CO		**MSA**	1,066	Hancock County	46
MSA	193	Alamance County	110	Hendricks County	78
Larimer County	193	Davidson County.	128	Johnson County	92
		Davie County	28	Madison County	132
Fort Lauderdale, FL PMSA . .	1,287	Forsyth County.	268	Marion County.	807
Broward County	1,287	Guilford County	354	Morgan County	57
		Randolph County	109	Shelby County	41
Fort Myers-Cape Coral, FL		Stokes County	38		
MSA	347	Yadkin County	31	**Iowa City, IA MSA**	97
Lee County	347			Johnson County	97
		Greenville, NC MSA	111		
Fort Pierce-Port St. Lucie, FL		Pitt County	111	**Jackson, MI MSA**	151
MSA	260			Jackson County	151
Martin County.	104	**Greenville-Spartanburg-**			
St. Lucie County	156	**Anderson, SC MSA**	843	**Jackson, MS MSA**	400
		Anderson County	146	Hinds County	255
Fort Smith, AR-OK MSA . . .	179	Cherokee County	45	Madison County	56
Crawford County, AR	44	Greenville County	324	Rankin County	89
Sebastian County, AR	101	Pickens County	97		
Sequoyah County, OK . . .	34	Spartanburg County	231	**Jacksonville, FL MSA**	934
				Clay County	110
Fort Walton Beach, FL		**Hagerstown, MD PMSA**	123	Duval County	691
MSA	148	Washington County	123	Nassau County	45
Okaloosa County.	148			St. Johns County	87
		Hamilton-Middletown, OH			
Fort Wayne, IN MSA	460	**PMSA**	299	**Jacksonville, NC MSA**	144
Adams County	31	Butler County	299	Onslow County	144
Allen County.	303				
De Kalb County	36	**Harrisburg-Lebanon-**		**Jamestown, NY MSA**	142
Huntington County	36	**Carlisle, PA MSA**	595	Chautauqua County	142
Wells County	26	Cumberland County	198		
Whitley County	28	Dauphin County	240	**Janesville-Beloit, WI MSA** . .	141
		Lebanon County	115	Rock County	141
Fort Worth-Arlington, TX		Perry County	42		
PMSA	1,396			**Johnson City-Kingsport-**	
Hood County	30	**Hartford, CT MSA**	1,159	**Bristol, TN-VA MSA**	441
Johnson County	99	Hartford County (pt.)	850	Carter County, TN	52
Parker County.	66	Litchfield County (pt.)	38	Hawkins County, TN	45
Tarrant County	1,200	Middlesex County (pt.)	98	Sullivan County, TN	145
		New London County (pt.) . .	17	Unicoi County, TN	17
Fresno, CA MSA	781	Tolland County (pt.)	128	Washington County, TN . . .	94
Fresno County	688	Windham County (pt.)	28	Scott County, VA.	23
Madera County	93			Washington County, VA . . .	47
				Bristol city, VA	18

	1991 Population (1,000)
Johnstown, PA MSA	241
Cambria County	163
Somerset County	79
Joplin, MO MSA	136
Jasper County	91
Newton County	45
Kalamazoo-Battle Creek, MI MSA	433
Calhoun County	137
Kalamazoo County	224
Van Buren County	71
Kankakee, IL PMSA	98
Kankakee County	98
Kansas City, MO-KS MSA	1,602
Cass County, MO	66
Clay County, MO	156
Clinton County, MO	17
Jackson County, MO	634
Lafayette County, MO	31
Platte County, MO	60
Ray County, MO	22
Johnson County, KS	365
Leavenworth County, KS	67
Miami County, KS	24
Wyandotte County, KS	160
Kenosha, WI PMSA	132
Kenosha County	132
Killeen-Temple, TX MSA	248
Bell County	185
Coryell County	63
Knoxville, TN MSA	600
Anderson County	69
Blount County	89
Knox County	343
Loudon County	32
Sevier County	53
Union County	14
Kokomo, IN MSA	98
Howard County	82
Tipton County	16
La Crosse, WI-MN MSA	117
La Crosse County, WI	98
Houston County, MN	19
Lafayette, LA MSA	350
Acadia Parish	56
Lafayette Parish	169
St. Landry Parish	81
St. Martin Parish	44
Lafayette, IN MSA	164
Clinton County	31
Tippecanoe County	132
Lake Charles, LA MSA	170
Calcasieu Parish	170
Lakeland-Winter Haven, FL MSA	413
Polk County	413
Lancaster, PA MSA	430
Lancaster County	430
Lansing-East Lansing, MI MSA	436
Clinton County	59
Eaton County	94
Ingham County	283
Laredo, TX MSA	140
Webb County	140
Las Cruces, NM MSA	141
Dona Ana County	141
Las Vegas, NV-AZ MSA	925
Clark County, NV	806
Nye County, NV	19
Mohave County, AZ	100

	1991 Population (1,000)
Lawrence, KS MSA	84
Douglas County	84
Lawton, OK MSA	112
Comanche County	112
Lewiston-Auburn, ME MSA	93
Androscoggin County (pt.)	93
Lexington, KY MSA	412
Bourbon County	19
Clark County	30
Fayette County	228
Jessamine County	31
Madison County	58
Scott County	24
Woodford County	20
Lima, OH MSA	155
Allen County	109
Auglaize County	45
Lincoln, NE MSA	217
Lancaster County	217
Little Rock-North Little Rock, AR MSA	519
Faulkner County	62
Lonoke County	40
Pulaski County	352
Saline County	66
Longview-Marshall, TX MSA	197
Gregg County	107
Harrison County	57
Upshur County	32
Los Angeles-Long Beach, CA PMSA	8,978
Los Angeles County	8,978
Los Angeles-Riverside-Orange County, CA CMSA	14,818
Los Angeles-Long Beach, CA PMSA	8,978
Orange County, CA PMSA	2,442
Riverside-San Bernardino, CA PMSA	2,721
Ventura, CA PMSA	677
Louisville, KY-IN MSA	958
Bullitt County, KY	49
Jefferson County, KY	667
Oldham County, KY	35
Clark County, IN	89
Floyd County, IN	66
Harrison County, IN	31
Scott, IN	21
Lubbock, TX MSA	225
Lubbock County	225
Lynchburg, VA MSA	197
Amherst County	29
Bedford County	47
Campbell County	48
Bedford city	6
Lynchburg city	66
Macon, GA MSA	295
Bibb County	152
Houston County	91
Jones County	21
Peach County	21
Twiggs County	10
Madison, WI MSA	376
Dane County	376
Mansfield, OH MSA	174
Crawford County	48
Richland County	126
McAllen-Edinburg-Mission, TX MSA	399
Hidalgo County	399

	1991 Population (1,000)
Medford-Ashland, OR MSA	151
Jackson County	151
Melbourne-Titusville-Palm Bay, FL MSA	414
Brevard County	414
Memphis, TN-AR-MS MSA	1,020
Fayette County, TN	26
Shelby County, TN	835
Tipton County, TN	38
Crittenden County, AR	50
De Soto County, MS	71
Merced, CA MSA	185
Merced County	185
Miami, FL PMSA	1,977
Dade County	1,977
Miami-Fort Lauderdale, FL CMSA	3,264
Fort Lauderdale, FL PMSA	1,287
Miami, FL PMSA	1,977
Milwaukee-Racine, WI CMSA	1,622
Milwaukee-Waukesha, WI PMSA	1,444
Racine, WI PMSA	178
Milwaukee-Waukesha, WI PMSA	1,444
Milwaukee County	958
Ozaukee County	74
Washington County	99
Waukesha County	313
Minneapolis-St. Paul, MN-WI MSA	2,583
Anoka County, MN	252
Carver County, MN	50
Chisago County, MN	31
Dakota County, MN	286
Hennepin County, MN	1,039
Isanti County, MN	27
Ramsey County, MN	487
Scott County, MN	60
Sherburne County, MN	44
Washington County, MN	152
Wright County, MN	71
Pierce County, WI	33
St. Croix County, WI	51
Mobile, AL MSA	486
Baldwin County	102
Mobile County	384
Modesto, CA MSA	387
Stanislaus County	387
Monroe, LA MSA	143
Ouachita Parish	143
Montgomery, AL MSA	298
Autauga County	35
Elmore County	51
Montgomery County	212
Muncie, IN MSA	120
Delaware County	120
Myrtle Beach, SC MSA	149
Horry County	149
Naples, FL MSA	160
Collier County	160
Nashua, NH PMSA	168
Hillsborough County (pt.)	168
Nashville, TN MSA	1,003
Cheatham County	28
Davidson County	513
Dickson County	36
Robertson County	43
Rutherford County	124
Sumner County	105
Williamson County	85
Wilson County	70

	1991 Population (1,000)
New Haven-Meriden, CT PMSA	**530**
Middlesex County (pt.) . . .	18
New Haven County (pt.) . . .	512
New London-Norwich, CT-RI MSA	**290**
Middlesex County, CT (pt.) .	10
New London County, CT (pt.)	233
Windham County, CT (pt.) . .	19
Washington County, RI (pt.) .	29
New Orleans, LA MSA	**1,295**
Jefferson Parish	454
Orleans Parish	493
Plaquemines Parish	26
St. Bernard Parish	66
St. Charles Parish	43
St. James Parish	21
St. John the Baptist Parish .	41
St. Tammany Parish.	151
New York-Newark, NY-NJ-PA PMSA	**16,972**
Bergen County, NJ	827
Essex County, NJ	773
Hudson County, NJ	553
Hunterdon County, NJ	108
Middlesex County, NJ	674
Monmouth County, NJ	558
Morris County, NJ	423
Ocean County, NJ.	438
Passaic County, NJ	453
Somerset County, NJ	244
Sussex County, NJ	132
Union County, NJ	493
Warren County, NJ	93
Bronx County, NY	1,198
Kings County, NY	2,292
Nassau County, NY	1,293
New York County, NY	1,494
Putnam County, NY	86
Queens County, NY.	1,952
Richmond County, NY.	385
Rockland County, NY.	268
Suffolk County, NY	1,326
Westchester County, NY . . .	878
Pike County, PA	31
New York-Northern New Jersey-Long Island, NY-NJ-CT-PA CMSA	**19,384**
Bridgeport, CT PMSA.	443
Danbury, CT PMSA	209
Dutchess County, NY PMSA	261
New Haven-Meriden, CT PMSA	530
New York-Newark, NY-NJ-PA PMSA	16,972
Orange County, NY PMSA . .	312
Stamford-Norwalk, CT PMSA	331
Trenton, NJ PMSA	327
Norfolk-Virginia Beach-Newport News, VA-NC MSA	**1,465**
Currituck County, NC	14
Gloucester County, VA.	31
Isle of Wight County, VA. . . .	26
James City County, VA. . . .	36
Mathews County, VA	8
York County, VA	45
Chesapeake city, VA	159
Hampton city, VA	136
Newport News city, VA.	174
Norfolk city, VA.	255
Poquoson city, VA.	11
Portsmouth city, VA.	104
Suffolk city, VA.	53
Virginia Beach city, VA	402
Williamsburg city, VA	12
Oakland, CA PMSA	**2,112**
Alameda County	1,292
Contra Costa County	820
Ocala, FL MSA	**202**
Marion County	202

	1991 Population (1,000)
Odessa-Midland, TX MSA . .	**230**
Ector County	121
Midland County.	109
Oklahoma City, OK MSA . . .	**971**
Canadian County.	76
Cleveland County	178
Logan County	29
McClain County.	23
Oklahoma County	606
Pottawatomie County	59
Olympia, WA PMSA	**170**
Thurston County	170
Omaha, NE-IA MSA	**649**
Cass County, NE.	22
Douglas County, NE	422
Sarpy County, NE	106
Washington County, NE . . .	17
Pottawattamie County, IA . .	83
Orange County, CA PMSA . .	**2,442**
Orange County	2,442
Orange County, NY PMSA . .	**312**
Orange County	312
Orlando, FL MSA	**1,269**
Lake County.	158
Orange County.	696
Osceola County	115
Seminole County.	300
Owensboro, KY MSA.	**88**
Daviess County.	88
Panama City, FL MSA	**130**
Bay County	130
Parkersburg-Marietta, WV-OH MSA	**149**
Wood County, WV.	87
Washington County, OH . . .	62
Pensacola, FL MSA.	**354**
Escambia County	268
Santa Rosa County	86
Peoria-Pekin, IL MSA	**342**
Peoria County.	184
Tazewell County	125
Woodford County	33
Philadelphia, PA-NJ PMSA . .	**4,941**
Bucks County, PA	549
Chester County, PA.	383
Delaware County, PA.	549
Montgomery County, PA. . . .	686
Philadelphia County, PA. . . .	1,573
Burlington County, NJ	399
Camden County, NJ.	505
Gloucester County, NJ	233
Salem County, NJ	65
Philadelphia-Wilmington-Atlantic City, PA-NJ-DE-MD CMSA.	**5,925**
Atlantic-Cape May, NJ PMSA	323
Philadelphia, PA-NJ PMSA . .	4,941
Vineland-Millville-Bridgeton, NJ PMSA	139
Wilmington-Newark, DE-MD PMSA	522
Phoenix-Mesa, AZ MSA	**2,287**
Maricopa County.	2,169
Pinal County	118
Pine Bluff, AR MSA.	**85**
Jefferson County.	85
Pittsburgh, PA MSA	**2,404**
Allegheny County.	1,338
Beaver County	187
Butler County	155
Fayette County	146
Washington County	206
Westmoreland County	372

	1991 Population (1,000)
Pittsfield, MA MSA	**88**
Berkshire County (pt.)	88
Portland, ME MSA.	**222**
Cumberland County (pt.) . . .	201
York County (pt.).	21
Portland-Salem, OR-WA CMSA.	**1,857**
Portland-Vancouver, OR-WA PMSA	1,570
Salem, OR PMSA	287
Portland-Vancouver, OR-WA PMSA.	**1,570**
Clackamas County, OR . . .	289
Columbia County, OR.	39
Multnomah County, OR . . .	596
Washington County, OR . . .	327
Yamhill County, OR	68
Clark County, WA	252
Providence-Fall River-Warwick, RI-MA MSA.	**1,135**
Bristol County, RI	49
Kent County, RI	162
Newport County, RI (pt.) . . .	23
Providence County, RI	594
Washington County, RI (pt.).	82
Bristol County, MA (pt.) . . .	225
Provo-Orem, UT MSA	**270**
Utah County.	270
Pueblo, CO MSA.	**123**
Pueblo County	123
Punta Gorda, FL MSA	**117**
Charlotte County.	117
Racine, WI PMSA	**178**
Racine County.	178
Raleigh-Durham-Chapel Hill, NC MSA.	**883**
Chatham County.	40
Durham County.	186
Franklin County.	37
Johnston County.	84
Orange County	96
Wake County	441
Rapid City, SD MSA	**84**
Pennington County	84
Reading, PA MSA	**341**
Berks County	341
Redding, CA MSA.	**154**
Shasta County.	154
Reno, NV MSA	**263**
Washoe County	263
Richland-Kennewick-Pasco, WA MSA.	**155**
Benton County	116
Franklin County.	39
Richmond-Petersburg, VA MSA.	**881**
Charles City County	6
Chesterfield County	217
Dinwiddie County	20
Goochland County.	15
Hanover County	66
Henrico County.	220
New Kent County	11
Powhatan County	16
Prince George County	27
Colonial Heights city	16
Hopewell city	23
Petersburg city	40
Richmond city.	204

	1991 Population (1,000)
Riverside-San Bernardino, CA PMSA	**2,721**
Riverside County.	1,236
San Bernardino County . . .	1,485
Roanoke, VA MSA	**227**
Botetourt County	25
Roanoke County	80
Roanoke city	97
Salem city	24
Rochester, MN MSA	**109**
Olmsted County	109
Rochester, NY MSA	**1,073**
Genesee County	61
Livingston County	63
Monroe County	720
Ontario County	97
Orleans County	42
Wayne County	90
Rockford, IL MSA	**336**
Boone County	32
Ogle County.	47
Winnebago County	257
Rocky Mount, NC MSA . . .	**135**
Edgecombe County	56
Nash County	78
Sacramento, CA PMSA	**1,388**
El Dorado County	133
Placer County	180
Sacramento County	1,075
Sacramento-Yolo, CA CMSA. .	**1,532**
Sacramento, CA PMSA . . .	1,388
Yolo, CA PMSA	144
Saginaw-Bay City-Midland, MI MSA	**401**
Bay County	112
Midland County.	77
Saginaw County	212
St. Cloud, MN MSA	**151**
Benton County	31
Stearns County	120
St. Joseph, MO MSA	**98**
Andrew County	15
Buchanan County	83
St. Louis, MO-IL MSA	**2,507**
Franklin County, MO	82
Jefferson County, MO	175
Lincoln County, MO	30
St. Charles County, MO . . .	219
St. Louis County, MO. . . .	997
Warren County, MO.	20
St. Louis city, MO	392
Clinton County, IL	34
Jersey County, IL	21
Madison County, IL	252
Monroe County, IL.	23
St. Clair County, IL	263
Salem, OR PMSA	**287**
Marion County	236
Polk County	51
Salinas, CA MSA.	**363**
Monterey County	363
Salt Lake City-Ogden, UT MSA.	**1,103**
Davis County	194
Salt Lake County.	747
Weber County	162
San Angelo, TX MSA.	**99**
Tom Green County	99
San Antonio, TX MSA	**1,348**
Bexar County	1,206
Comal County.	53
Guadalupe County.	66
Wilson County	23

	1991 Population (1,000)
San Diego, CA MSA	**2,549**
San Diego County	2,549
San Francisco, CA PMSA. . .	**1,622**
Marin County	233
San Francisco County	733
San Mateo County.	656
San Francisco-Oakland-San Jose, CA CMSA.	**6,332**
Oakland, CA PMSA	2,112
San Francisco, CA PMSA . .	1,622
San Jose, CA PMSA	1,506
Santa Cruz-Watsonville, CA PMSA	229
Santa Rosa, CA PMSA. . . .	396
Vallejo-Fairfield-Napa, CA PMSA	466
San Jose, CA PMSA	**1,506**
Santa Clara County	1,506
San Luis Obispo-Atascadero-Paso Robles, CA MSA	**219**
San Luis Obispo County . . .	219
Santa Barbara-Santa Maria-Lompoc, CA MSA	**374**
Santa Barbara County	374
Santa Cruz-Watsonville, CA PMSA.	**229**
Santa Cruz County	229
Santa Fe, NM MSA	**120**
Los Alamos County	18
Santa Fe County.	102
Santa Rosa, CA PMSA.	**396**
Sonoma County	396
Sarasota-Bradenton, FL MSA	**501**
Manatee County	217
Sarasota County	285
Savannah, GA MSA.	**263**
Bryan County	16
Chatham County	220
Effingham County	26
Scranton—Wilkes-Barre—Hazleton, PA MSA.	**641**
Columbia County.	64
Lackawanna County	219
Luzerne County.	330
Wyoming County	28
Seattle-Bellevue-Everett, WA PMSA.	**2,078**
Island County	63
King County	1,532
Snohomish County	482
Seattle-Tacoma-Bremerton, WA CMSA	**3,054**
Bremerton, WA PMSA	201
Olympia, WA PMSA.	170
Seattle-Bellevue-Everett, WA PMSA	2,078
Tacoma, WA PMSA.	605
Sharon, PA MSA.	**122**
Mercer County	122
Sheboygan, WI MSA	**104**
Sheboygan County	104
Sherman-Denison, TX MSA.	**96**
Grayson County	96
Shreveport-Bossier City, LA MSA.	**374**
Bossier Parish	86
Caddo Parish	246
Webster Parish	42

	1991 Population (1,000)
Sioux City, IA-NE MSA	**116**
Woodbury County, IA	99
Dakota County, NE	17
Sioux Falls, SD MSA	**143**
Lincoln County	16
Minnehaha County	127
South Bend, IN MSA	**249**
St. Joseph County.	249
Spokane, WA MSA	**374**
Spokane County	374
Springfield, IL MSA	**191**
Menard County	11
Sangamon County.	180
Springfield, MA MSA.	**586**
Franklin County (pt.)	3
Hampden County (pt.)	443
Hampshire County (pt.). . . .	140
Springfield, MO MSA.	**270**
Christian County	35
Greene County	211
Webster County	24
Stamford-Norwalk, CT PMSA	**331**
Fairfield County (pt.)	331
State College, PA MSA	**125**
Centre County	125
Steubenville-Weirton, OH-WV MSA.	**142**
Jefferson County, OH.	80
Brooke County, WV	27
Hancock County, WV.	35
Stockton-Lodi, CA MSA.	**493**
San Joaquin County.	493
Sumter, SC MSA.	**105**
Sumter County	105
Syracuse, NY MSA	**749**
Cayuga County	83
Madison County	70
Onondaga County	473
Oswego County	123
Tacoma, WA PMSA.	**605**
Pierce County.	605
Tallahassee, FL MSA.	**240**
Gadsden County	42
Leon County.	199
Tampa-St. Petersburg-Clearwater, FL MSA.	**2,101**
Hernando County.	106
Hillsborough County.	846
Pasco County	286
Pinellas County.	863
Terre Haute, IN MSA.	**149**
Clay County	25
Vermillion County	17
Vigo County	107
Texarkana, TX-Texarkana, AR MSA.	**120**
Bowie County, TX	82
Miller County, AR	39
Toledo, OH MSA.	**614**
Fulton County	39
Lucas County	462
Wood County	114
Topeka, KS MSA.	**163**
Shawnee County.	163
Trenton, NJ PMSA	**327**
Mercer County	327

	1991 Population (1,000)		1991 Population (1,000)		1991 Population (1,000)
Tucson, AZ MSA.........	**677**	Charles County, MD.....	104	Wheeling, WV-OH MSA	**158**
Pima County...........	677	Frederick County, MD	155	Marshall County, WV	37
		Montgomery County, MD ..	768	Ohio County, WV	50
Tulsa, OK MSA..........	**723**	Prince George's County,		Belmont County, OH	71
Creek County..........	62	MD	743		
Osage County..........	42	Arlington County, VA	172	Wichita, KS MSA.........	**493**
Rogers County.........	57	Clarke County, VA......	12	Butler County	52
Tulsa County	514	Culpeper County, VA	29	Harvey County	31
Wagoner County........	49	Fairfax County, VA	834	Sedgwick County	410
		Fauquier County, VA	50		
Tuscaloosa, AL MSA......	**154**	King George County, VA...	14	Wichita Falls, TX MSA.....	**130**
Tuscaloosa County	154	Loudoun County, VA	89	Archer County	8
		Prince William County, VA..	221	Wichita County	122
Tyler, TX MSA	**154**	Spotsylvania County, VA...	59		
Smith County	154	Stafford County, VA	66	Williamsport, PA MSA.....	**120**
		Warren County, VA	27	Lycoming County	120
Utica-Rome, NY MSA	**318**	Alexandria city, VA	113		
Herkimer County........	66	Fairfax city, VA........	20	Wilmington, NC MSA......	**125**
Oneida County.........	252	Falls Church city, VA	10	New Hanover County.....	125
		Fredericksburg city, VA ...	20		
Vallejo-Fairfield-Napa, CA		Manassas city, VA......	29	Wilmington-Newark, DE-MD	
PMSA................	**466**	Manassas Park city, VA ...	7	PMSA................	**522**
Napa County	112	Berkeley County, WV	61	New Castle County, DE ...	449
Solano County	354	Jefferson County, WV	37	Cecil County, MD	73
Ventura, CA PMSA	**677**	**Washington-Baltimore, DC-MD-**		Yakima, WA MSA	**194**
Ventura County........	677	**VA-WV CMSA**...........	**6,830**	Yakima County	194
		Baltimore, MD PMSA ...	2,414		
Victoria, TX MSA	**76**	Hagerstown, MD PMSA ...	123	Yolo, CA PMSA..........	**144**
Victoria County........	76	Washington, DC-MD-VA-WV		Yolo County	144
		PMSA	4,293		
Vineland-Millville-Bridgeton,				York, PA MSA...........	**346**
NJ PMSA	**139**	**Waterbury, CT MSA**	**207**	York County...........	346
Cumberland County......	139	Litchfield County (pt.) ...	39		
		New Haven County (pt.) ...	168	Youngstown-Warren, OH	
Visalia-Tulare-Porterville,				MSA.................	**603**
CA MSA	**323**	**Waterloo-Cedar Falls, IA**		Columbiana County	109
Tulare County..........	323	**MSA**.................	**125**	Mahoning County	265
		Black Hawk County	125	Trumbull County	229
Waco, TX MSA..........	**191**				
McLennan County	191	**Wausau, WI MSA**	**117**	Yuba City, CA MSA	**127**
		Marathon County.......	117	Sutter County	67
Washington, DC-MD-VA-WV				Yuba County	59
PMSA.................	**4,293**	**West Palm Beach-Boca**			
District of Columbia	598	**Raton, FL MSA**	**887**	Yuma, AZ MSA..........	**111**
Calvert County, MD	55	Palm Beach County......	887	Yuma County	111

Statistical Methodology and Reliability

Introduction.—The data presented in this *Statistical Abstract* came from many sources. The sources include not only Federal statistical bureaus and other organizations that collect and issue statistics as their principal activity, but also governmental administrative and regulatory agencies, private research bodies, trade associations, insurance companies, health associations, and private organizations such as the National Education Association and philanthropic foundations. Consequently, the data vary considerably as to reference periods, definitions of terms and, for ongoing series, the number and frequency of time periods for which data are available.

The statistics presented were obtained and tabulated by various means. Some statistics are based on complete enumerations or censuses while others are based on samples. Some information is extracted from records kept for administrative or regulatory purposes (school enrollment, hospital records, securities registration, financial accounts, social security records, income tax returns, etc.), while other information is obtained explicitly for statistical purposes through interviews or by mail. The estimation procedures used vary from highly sophisticated scientific techniques, to crude "informed guesses."

Each set of data relates to a group of individuals or units of interest referred to as the *target universe* or *target population*, or simply as the *universe* or *population*. Prior to data collection the target universe should be clearly defined. For example, if data are to be collected for the universe of households in the United States, it is necessary to define a "household." The target universe may not be completely tractable. Cost and other considerations may restrict data collection to a *survey universe* of households on some available list, such list being inaccurate, out of date, defining "household" slightly differently, etc. This list is called a *survey frame* or *sampling frame.*

The data in many tables are based on data obtained for all population units, a *census,* or on data obtained for only a portion, or *sample,* of the population units. When the data presented are based on a sample, the sample is usually a scientifically selected *probability sample*. This is a sample selected from a list or sampling frame in such a way that every possible sample has a known chance of selection and usually each unit selected can be assigned a number, between zero and one, representing its likelihood or probability of selection.

For large-scale sample surveys, the probability sample of units is often selected as a multistage sample. The first stage of a multistage sample is the selection of a probability sample of large groups of population members, referred to as primary sampling units (PSU's). For example, in a national multistage household sample, PSU's are often counties or groups of counties. The second stage of a multistage sample is the selection, within each PSU selected at the first stage, of smaller groups of population units, referred to as secondary sampling units. In subsequent stages of selection, smaller and smaller nested groups are chosen until the ultimate sample of population units is obtained. To qualify a multistage sample as a probability sample, all stages of sampling must be carried out using probability sampling methods.

Prior to selection at each stage of a multistage (or a single stage) sample, a list of the sampling units or sampling frame for that stage must be obtained. For example, for the first stage of selection of a national household sample, a list of the counties and county groups that form the PSU's must be obtained. For the final stage of selection, lists of households, and sometimes persons within the households, have to be compiled in the field. For surveys of economic entities and for the economic census, the Census Bureau generally uses a frame constructed from the Bureau's Standard Statistical Establishment List (SSEL). The SSEL contains all establishments with payroll in the United States including small single establishment firms as well as large multi-establishment firms.

Wherever the quantities in a table refer to an entire universe, but are constructed from data collected in a sample survey, the table quantities are referred to as *sample estimates*. In constructing a sample estimate, an attempt is made to come as close as is feasible to the corresponding universe quantity that would be obtained from a complete census of the universe. Estimates based on a sample will, however, generally differ from the hypothetical census figures. Two classifications of errors are associated with estimates based on sample surveys: (1) *sampling error*—the error arising from the use of a sample, rather than a census, to estimate population quantities and (2) *nonsampling error*—those errors arising from nonsampling sources. As discussed below, the magnitude of the sampling error for an estimate can usually be estimated from the sample data. However, the magnitude of the nonsampling error for an estimate can rarely be estimated. Consequently, actual error in an estimate exceeds the estimated error in the estimate.

The particular sample used in a survey is only one of a large number of possible samples of the same size which could have been selected using the same sampling procedure. Estimates derived from the different samples would, in general, differ from each other. The *standard error* (SE) is a measure of the variation among the estimates derived from all possible samples. The standard error is the most commonly used measure of the sampling error of an estimate. Valid estimates of the standard errors of survey estimates can usually be calculated from the data collected in a probability sample. For convenience, the standard error is sometimes expressed as a percent of the estimate and is called the relative standard error or *coefficient of variation* (CV). For example, an estimate of 200 units with an estimated standard error of 10 units has an estimated CV of 5 percent.

A sample estimate and an estimate of its standard error or CV can be used to construct interval estimates that have a prescribed confidence that the interval includes the average of the estimates derived from all possible samples with a known probability. To illustrate, if all possible samples were selected under essentially the same general conditions, and using the same sample design, and if an estimate and its estimated standard error were calculated from each sample, then: 1) Approximately 68% of the intervals from one standard error below the estimate to one standard error above the estimate would include the average estimate derived from all possible samples; 2) approximately 90% of the intervals from 1.6 standard errors below the estimate to 1.6 standard errors above the estimate would include the average estimate derived from all possible samples; and 3) approximately 95% of the intervals from two standard errors below the estimate to two standard errors above the estimate would include the average estimate derived from all possible samples.

Thus, for a particular sample, one can say with the appropriate level of confidence (e.g., 90% or 95%) that the average of all possible samples is included in the constructed interval. Example of a confidence interval: An estimate is 200 units with a standard error of 10 units. An approximately 90% confidence interval (plus or minus 1.6 standard errors) is from 184 to 216.

All surveys and censuses are subject to nonsampling errors. Nonsampling errors are two kinds—*random* and *nonrandom*. Random nonsampling errors arise because of the varying interpretation of questions (by respondents or interviewers) and varying actions of coders, keyers, and other processors. Some randomness is also introduced when respondents must estimate values. These same errors usually have a nonrandom component. Nonrandom nonsampling errors result from total nonresponse (no usable data obtained for a sampled unit), partial or item nonresponse (only a portion of a response may be usable), inability or unwillingness on the part of respondents to provide correct information, difficulty interpreting questions, mistakes in recording or keying data, errors of collection or processing, and coverage problems (overcoverage and undercoverage of the target universe). Random nonresponse errors usually, but not always, result in an understatement of sampling errors and thus an overstatement of the precision of survey estimates. Estimating the magnitude of nonsampling errors would require special experiments or access to independent data and, consequently, the magnitudes are seldom available.

Nearly all types of nonsampling errors that affect surveys also occur in complete censuses. Since surveys can be conducted on a smaller scale than censuses, nonsampling errors can presumably be controlled more tightly. Relatively more funds and effort can perhaps be expended toward eliciting responses, detecting and correcting response error, and reducing processing errors. As a result, survey results can sometimes be more accurate than census results.

To compensate for suspected nonrandom errors, adjustments of the sample estimates are often made. For example, adjustments are frequently made for nonresponse, both total and partial. Adjustments made for either type of nonresponse are often referred to as *imputations*. Imputation for total nonresponse is usually made by substituting for the questionnaire responses of the nonrespondents the "average" questionnaire responses of the respondents. These imputations usually are made separately within various groups of sample members, formed by attempting to place respondents and nonrespondents together that have "similar" survey characteristics. Imputation for item nonresponse is usually made by substituting for a missing item the response to that item of a respondent having characteristics that are "similar" to those of the nonrespondent.

For an estimate calculated from a sample survey, the *total error* in the estimate is composed of the sampling error, which can usually be estimated from the sample, and the nonsampling error, which usually cannot be estimated from the sample. The total error present in a population quantity obtained from a complete census is composed of only nonsampling errors. Ideally, estimates of the total error associated with data given in the *Statistical Abstract* tables should be given. However, due to the unavailability of estimates of nonsampling errors, only estimates of the levels of sampling errors, in terms of estimated standard errors or coefficients of variation, are available. To obtain estimates of the estimated standard errors from the sample of interest, obtain a copy of the referenced report which appears at the end of each table.

Principal data bases.—Beginning below are brief descriptions of 35 of the sample surveys and censuses that provide a substantial portion of the data contained in this *Abstract*.

SECTION 1. POPULATION

Source and Title: Bureau of the Census, *Census of Population*

Tables: See tables citing *Census of Population* in section 1 and also in sections 2, 4, 6, 8, 13, 14, 26, 21, and 30.

Universe, Frequency, and Types of Data: Complete count of U.S. population conducted every 10 years since 1790. Data obtained on number and characteristics of inhabitants.

Type of Data Collection Operation: In 1970, 1980, and 1990 complete census for some items—age, sex, race, marital status, and relationship to household head. In 1970, other items collected from a 5% and a 15% probability (systematic) sample of the population. In 1980, approximately 19% of the housing units were included in the sample; in 1990, approximately 17%.

Data Collection and Imputation Procedures: In 1970, extensive use of mail questionnaires in urban areas; personal interviews in most rural areas. In 1980 and 1990, mail questionnaires were used in even more areas than in 1970, with personal interviews in the remainder. Extensive telephone and personal followup for nonrespondents was done in the censuses. Imputations were made for missing characteristics.

Estimates of Sampling Error: Sampling errors for data are estimated for all items collected by sample and vary by characteristic and geographic area. The CV's for national and State estimates are generally very small.

Other (nonsampling) Errors: Since 1950, evaluation programs have been conducted to provide information on the magnitude of some sources of nonsampling errors such as response bias and undercoverage in each census. Results from the evaluation program for the 1990 census indicate that the net under coverage amounted to about 1.5 to 2 percent of the total resident population.

Sources of Additional Material: U.S. Bureau of the Census, *The Coverage of Population in the 1980 Census,* PHC80-E4; *Content Reinterview Study: Accuracy of Data for Selected Population and Housing Characteristics as Measured by Reinterview,* PHC80-E2; *1980 Census of Population,* vol. 1., (PC80-1), appendixes B, C, and D.

Source and Title: U.S. Bureau of the Census, *Current Population Survey (CPS)*

Tables: See tables citing *Current Population Reports* primarily in section 1, but also in sections 2, 3, 4, 8, 12, 13, 14, 18, 23, and 30. Many Bureau of Labor Statistics' (BLS) tables in section 13 are CPS based.

Universe, Frequency, and Types of Data: Nationwide monthly sample survey of civilian noninstitutional population, 15 years old or over, to obtain data on employment, unemployment, and a number of other characteristics.

Type of Data Collection Operation: Multistage probability sample of about 60,000 households in 729 PSU's in 1989. Oversampling in some States and the largest MSA's to improve reliability for those areas of employment data on annual average basis. A continual sample rotation system is used. Households are in sample 4 months, out for 8 months, and in for 4 more. Month-to-month overlap is 75%; year-to-year overlap is 50%.

Data Collection and Imputation Procedures: For first and fifth months that a household is in sample, personal interviews; other months, approximately, 85% of the data collected by phone. Imputation is done for both item and total nonresponse. Adjustment for total nonresponse is done by a predefined cluster of units, by MSA size and residence; for item nonresponse imputation varies by subject matter.

Estimates of Sampling Error: Estimated CV's on national annual averages for labor force, total employment, and nonagricultural employment, 0.2%; for total unemployment and agricultural employment, 1.0% to 2.5%. The estimated CV's for family income and poverty rate for all persons in 1986 are 0.5% and 1.5%, respectively. CV's for subnational areas, such as States, would be larger and would vary by area.

Other (nonsampling) Errors: Estimates of response bias on unemployment are not available, but estimates of unemployment are usually 5% to 9% lower than estimates from reinterviews. Four to 5.0% of sample households unavailable for interviews.

Sources of Additional Material: U.S. Bureau of the Census and Bureau of Labor Statistics, *Concepts and Methods Used in Labor Force Statistics from Current Population Survey* (Census series P-23, No. 62; BLS Report No. 463) and Bureau of the Census, *Current Population Survey* (Tech. Paper 40) and Bureau of Labor Statistics, *Employment and Earnings,* monthly, Explanatory Notes, table 1-A through 1-H and *BLS Handbook of Methods,* Chapter 1 (Bulletin 2414.)

SECTION 2. VITAL STATISTICS

Source and Title: U.S. National Center for Health Statistics (NCHS), *Vital Registration System*

Tables: See tables citing *Vital Statistics of the United States;* 305 in section 5; and 1360 in section 30.

Universe, Frequency, and Types of Data: Annual data on births and deaths in the United States.

Type of Data Collection Operation: Mortality data based on complete file of death records, except 1972, based on 50% sample. Natality statistics 1951-71, based on 50% sample of birth certificates, except a 20% to 50% in 1967, received by NCHS. Beginning 1972, data from some States received through Vital Statistics Cooperative Program (VSCP) and complete file used; data from other States based on 50% sample. Beginning 1986, all reporting areas participated in the VSCP.

Data Collection and Imputation Procedures: Reports based on records from registration offices of all States, District of Columbia, New York City, Puerto Rico, Virgin Islands, and Guam.

Estimates of Sampling Error: For recent years, CV's for births are small due to large portion of total file in sample (except for very small estimated totals).

Other (nonsampling) Errors: Data on births and deaths believed to be at least 99% complete.

Sources of Additional Material: U.S. National Center for Health Statistics, *Vital Statistics of the United States,* vol. I and vol. II, annual, and *Monthly Vital Statistics Report.*

(See section 1 above for information pertaining to tables 103-108.)

SECTION 3. HEALTH AND NUTRITION

Source and Title: U.S. National Center for Health Statistics, *National Health Interview Survey (NHIS)*

Tables: 169, 174, 175, 196, 199, 200, 205, 206, 210, and 212-215.

Universe, Frequency, and Types of Data: Continuous data collection covering the civilian noninstitutional population to obtain information on personal and demographic characteristics, illnesses, injuries, impairments, and other health topics.

Type of Data Collection Operation: Multistage probability sample of 42,000 households (in 376 PSU's) selected in groups of about four adjacent households.

Data Collection and Imputation Procedures: Personal household interviews with extensive followup of nonrespondents. Data are adjusted for nonresponse by imputation procedure based on "average" characteristics of persons in interviewed households in the same geographic area.

Estimates of Sampling Error: Estimated CV's: For physician visits by males, 1.5%; for workdays lost by males, 3.5%; for persons injured at home, 4.7%.

Other (nonsampling) Errors: Response rate was 95.7% in 1985 for the NHIS.

Sources of Additional Material: U.S. National Center for Health Statistics, "Current Estimates from the National Health Interview Survey, U.S., 1983," Vital and Health Statistics, series 10.

(See section 13 for information pertaining to table 170 and section 15 for table 163.)

SECTION 4. EDUCATION

Source and Title: U.S. Department of Education, National Center for Education Statistics, *Higher Education General Information Survey (HEGIS), Fall Enrollment in Institutions of Higher Education;* beginning 1986, *Integrated Postsecondary Education Data Survey (IPEDS), Fall Enrollment*

Tables: 271, and 273-276.

Universe, Frequency, and Types of Data: Annual survey of all institutions and branches listed in the *Directory* to obtain data on total enrollment by sex, level of enrollment, type of program, racial/ethnic characteristics (in alternate years) and attendance status of student, and on first-time students.

Type of Data Collection Operation: Complete census.

Data Collection and Imputation Procedures: Survey package is usually mailed in the spring with surveys due at varying dates in the summer and fall; mail and phone followup procedures for nonrespondents. Missing data are imputed by using data of similar institutions.

Estimates of Sampling Error: Not applicable.

Other (nonsampling) Errors: Approximately 82% response rate.

Sources of Additional Material: U.S. Department of Education, National Center for Education Statistics, *Fall Enrollment in Higher Education,* annual.

Source and Title: U.S. Department of Education, National Center for Education Statistics, *Higher Education General Information Survey (HEGIS), Financial Statistics of Institutions of Higher Education;* beginning 1986, *Integrated Postsecondary Education Data Survey (IPEDS), Financial Statistics of Institutions of Higher Education*

Tables: 222, 225, 274, and 278.

Universe, Frequency, and Types of Data: Annual survey of all institutions and branches listed in the *Education Directory, Colleges and Universities* to obtain data on financial status and operations, including current funds revenues, current funds expenditures, and physical plant assets.

Type of Data Collection Operation: Complete census.

Data Collection and Imputation Procedures: Survey package is usually mailed in the spring with surveys due at varying dates in the summer and fall; mail and phone followup procedures for nonrespondents. Missing data are imputed by using data of similar institutions.

Estimates of Sampling Error: Not applicable.

Other (nonsampling) Errors: For 1990, a 87% response rate. Imputed expenditures amounted to about 2.8% of total expenditures.

Sources of Additional Material: U.S. Department of Education, National Center for Education Statistics, *Financial Statistics of Institutions of Higher Education,* annual.

Source and Title: U.S. Department of Education, National Center for Education Statistics, *Higher Education General Information Survey (HEGIS), Degrees and Other Formal Awards Conferred.* Beginning 1986, *Integrated Postsecondary Education Data Survey (IPEDS), Degrees and Other Formal Awards Conferred.*

Tables: 291-295.

Universe, Frequency, and Types of Data: Annual survey of all institutions and branches listed in the *Education Directory, Colleges and Universities* to obtain data on earned degrees and other formal awards, conferred by field of study, level of degree, sex, and by racial/ethnic characteristics (in alternate years).

Type of Data Collection Operation: Complete census.

Data Collection and Imputation Procedures: Survey package is usually mailed in the spring with surveys due at varying dates in the summer and fall; mail and phone followup procedures for nonrespondents. Missing data are imputed by using data of similar institutions.

Estimates of Sampling Error: Not applicable.

Other (nonsampling) Errors: For 1989-90, approximately 92.3% response rate.

Sources of Additional Material: U.S. Department of Education, National Center for Education Statistics, *Earned Degrees Conferred,* annual.

(See sections 1 and 9 for information pertaining to the Bureau of the Census and section 3 above for the National Center for Health Statistics.)

SECTION 5. LAW ENFORCEMENT, COURTS, AND PRISONS

Source and Title: U.S. Federal Bureau of Investigation, *Uniform Crime Reporting (UCR) Program*

Tables: 300-304, 306, 307, 313, 314, and 316.

Universe, Frequency, and Types of Data: Monthly reports on the number of criminal offenses that become known to law enforcement agencies. Data are collected on crimes cleared by arrest, by age, sex, and race of offender, and on assaults on law enforcement officers.

Type of Data Collection Operation: Crime statistics are based on reports of crime data submitted either directly to the FBI by contributing law enforcement agencies or through cooperating State UCR programs.

Data Collection and Imputation Procedures: States with UCR programs collect data directly from individual law enforcement agencies and forward reports, prepared in accordance with UCR standards, to FBI. Accuracy and consistency edits are performed by FBI.

Estimates of Sampling Error: Not applicable.

Other (nonsampling) Errors: Coverage of 96% of the population (98% in SMSA's, 93% in "other cities," and 89% in rural areas) by UCR program, though varying number of agencies report. Some error may be present through incorrect reporting.

Sources of Additional Material: U.S. Federal Bureau of Investigation, *Crime in the United States.*

Source and Title: U.S. Bureau of Justice Statistics (BJS), *National Crime Survey*

Tables: 308-312.

Universe, Frequency, and Types of Data: Monthly survey of individuals and households in the United States to obtain data on criminal victimization of those units for compilation of annual estimates.

Type of Data Collection Operation: National probability sample survey of about 50,000 interviewed households in 376 PSU's selected from a list of addresses

from the 1980 census, supplemented by new construction permits and an area sample where permits are not required.

Data Collection and Imputation Procedures: Interviews are conducted every 6 months for 3 years for each household in the sample; 8,000 households are interviewed monthly. Personal interviews are used in the first and fifth interviews; the intervening interviews are conducted by telephone whenever possible.

Estimates of Sampling Error: CV's in 1985: 2.2% for crimes of violence; 14.8% for estimate of rape counts; 5.5% for robbery counts; 2.5% for assault counts; 1.4% for personal larceny counts; 2.2% for burglary counts; 1.8% for household larceny; 1.3% for all household crimes; and 4.8% for motor vehicle theft counts.

Other (nonsampling) Errors: Respondent recall errors which may include reporting incidents for other than the reference period; interviewer coding and processing errors; and possible mistaken reporting or classifying of events. Adjustment is made for a household noninterview rate of about 4% and for a smaller within-household noninterview rate.

Sources of Additional Material: U.S. Bureau of Justice Statistics, *Criminal Victimization in the United States,* annual.

(See section 2 for details on table 305 and section 9 for details on table 325.)

SECTION 8. ELECTIONS

(See section 1 above for information pertaining to tables 434, 453, and 454.)

SECTION 9. STATE AND LOCAL GOVERNMENT FINANCES AND EMPLOYMENT

Source and Title: U.S. Bureau of the Census, *Census of Governments*

Tables: See tables in section 9 citing *Census of Governments.*

Universe, Frequency, and Types of Data: Survey of all governmental units in the United States conducted every 5 years to obtain data on government revenue, expenditures, debt, assets, employment and employee retirement systems, property values, public school systems, and number, size, and structure of governments.

Type of Data Collection Operation: Complete census. List of units derived through classification of government units recently authorized in each State and identification, counting, and classification of existing local governments and public school systems.

Data Collection and Imputation Procedures: Data collected through field and office compilation of financial data from official records and reports for States and large local governments; mail canvass of selected data items, like State tax revenue and employee retirement systems; and collection of local government statistics through central collection arrangements with State governments.

Estimates of Sampling Error: Not applicable.

Other (nonsampling) Errors: Some nonsampling errors may arise due to possible inaccuracies in classification, response, and processing.

Sources of Additional Material: U.S. Bureau of the Census, *Census of Governments, 1987,* various reports, and *State Government Finances in 1990,* GF 90, No. 3.

Source and Title: U.S. Bureau of the Census, *Annual Surveys of State and Local Government*

Tables: See tables citing *Public Employment* and *Governmental Finances* in section 9; table 250 in section 4; table 325 in section 5; and table 594 in section 12.

Universe, Frequency, and Types of Data: Sample survey conducted annually to obtain data on revenue, expenditure, debt, and employment of State and local governments. Universe is all governmental units in the United States (about 83,000).

Type of Data Collection Operation: Sample of about 22,000 units includes all State governments, county governments with 50,000+ population, municipalities and townships with 25,000+ population, all school districts with 10,000+ enrollment in October 1986, and other governments meeting certain criteria; probability sample for remaining units.

Data Collection and Imputation Procedures: Field and office compilation of data from official records and reports for States and large local governments; central collection of local governmental financial data through cooperative agreements with a number of State governments; mail canvass of other units with mail and telephone followups of nonrespondents. Data for nonresponses are imputed from previous year data or obtained from secondary sources, if available.

Estimates of Sampling Error: CV's for estimates of major employment and financial items are generally less than 2% for most States and less than 1.2% for the majority of States.

Other (nonsampling) Errors: Nonresponse rate is less than 15% for number of units. Other possible errors may result from undetected inaccuracies in classification, response, and processing.

Sources of Additional Material: U.S. Bureau of the Census, *Public Employment in 1990,* GE 90, No. 1, *Governmental Finances in 1989-90,* GF 90, No. 5, and *Census of Governments, 1987,* various reports.

SECTION 10. FEDERAL GOVERNMENT

Source and Title: U.S. Internal Revenue Service, *Statistics of Income, Individual Income Tax Returns*

Tables: 525-529.

Universe, Frequency, and Types of Data: Annual study of unaudited individual income tax returns, forms 1040, 1040A, and 1040EZ, filed by U.S. citizens and residents. Data provided on various financial characteristics by size of adjusted gross income, marital status, and by taxable and nontaxable returns. Data by State, based on 100% file, also include returns from 1040NR, filed by nonresident aliens plus certain self-employment tax returns.

Type of Data Collection Operation: Annual stratified probability sample of approximately 125,000 returns broken into sample strata based on the larger of total income or total loss amounts as well as the size of business plus farm receipts. Sampling rates for sample strata varied from .025% to 100%.

Data Collection and Imputation Procedures: Computer selection of sample of tax return records. Data adjusted during editing for incorrect, missing, or inconsistent entries to ensure consistency with other entries on return.

Estimates of Sampling Error: Estimated CV's for tax year 1987: Adjusted gross income less deficit .13%; salaries and wages .20%; and tax-exempt interest received 4.51%. (State data not subject to sampling error.)

Other (nonsampling) Errors: Processing errors and errors arising from the use of tolerance checks for the data.

Sources of Additional Material: U.S. Internal Revenue Service, *Statistics of Income, Individual Income Tax Returns,* annual.

SECTION 12. SOCIAL INSURANCE AND HUMAN SERVICES

Source and Title: U.S. Social Security Administration, *Benefit Data*

Tables: 589 and 590.

Universe, Frequency, and Types of Data: All persons receiving monthly benefits under Title 11 of Social Security Act. Data on number and amount of benefits paid by type and State.

Type of Data Collection Operation: Data based on administrative records. Data based on 100% files, as well as 10% and 1% sample files.

Data Collection and Imputation Procedures: Records used consist of actions pursuant to applications for benefits, updated by subsequent post-entitlement actions.

Estimates of Sampling Error: Varies by size of estimate and sample file size.

Other (nonsampling) Errors: Processing errors, which are believed to be small.

Sources of Additional Material: U.S. Social Security Administration, *Annual Statistical Supplement to the Social Security Bulletin.*

Source and Title: U.S. Social Security Administration, *Supplemental Security Income (SSI) Program*

Tables: 604-607.

Universe, Frequency, and Types of Data: All eligible aged, blind, or disabled persons receiving SSI benefit payments under SSI program. Data include number of persons receiving federally administered SSI, amounts paid, and State administered supplementation.

Type of Data Collection Operation: Data based on administrative records.

Data Collection and Imputation Procedures: Data adjusted to reflect returned checks and overpayment refunds. For federally administered payments, actual adjusted amounts are used.

Estimates of Sampling Error: Not applicable.

Other (nonsampling) Errors: Processing errors, which are believed to be small.

Sources of Additional Material: U.S. Social Security Administration, *Annual Statistical Supplement to the Social Security Bulletin.*

(See section 1 above for information pertaining to the Current Population Survey, section 3 for information pertaining to the National Center for Health Statistics, and section 9 for information pertaining to Annual Surveys of State and Local Government.)

SECTION 13. LABOR FORCE, EMPLOYMENT, AND EARNINGS

Source and Title: U.S. Bureau of Labor Statistics (BLS), *Current Employment Statistics (CES) Program*

Tables: 660-662, 667; in section 3, table 170; in section 21, table 1003; in section 22, table 1069; and in section 24, table 1152.

Universe, Frequency, and Types of Data: Monthly survey covering about 5 million nonagricultural establishments to obtain data on employment, hours, and earnings, by industry.

Type of Data Collection Operation: Sample survey of over 350,000 establishments in March 1990.

Data Collection and Imputation Procedures: Cooperating State agencies mail questionnaires to sample establishments to develop State and local estimates; information is forwarded to BLS where national estimates are prepared.

Estimates of Sampling Error: Estimated CV's for average weekly hours paid, 0.1% and for average hourly earnings, 0.2%.

Other (nonsampling) Errors: Estimates of employment adjusted annually to reflect complete universe. Average adjustment is 0.2%.

Sources of Additional Material: U.S. Bureau of Labor Statistics, *Employment and Earnings,* monthly, Explanatory Notes, tables 2-A through 2-F and *BLS Handbook of Methods,* Chapter 2, Bulletin 2414 (Sept. 1992).

(See section 1 above for information pertaining to the Current Population Survey.)

SECTION 14. INCOME, EXPENDITURES, AND WEALTH

Source and Title: Board of Governors of the Federal Reserve System, *Survey of Consumer Finances*

Tables: 751-753, and in secton 16, 788-791.

Universe, Frequency, and Types of Data: Periodic sample survey of families. In this survey a given household is divided into a primary economic unit and other economic units. The primary economic unity, which may be a single individual, is generally chosen as the unit that contains the person who either holds the title to the home or is the first person listed on the lease. The primary unit is used as the reference family. The survey collects detailed data on the composition of family balance sheets, the terms of loans, and relationships with financial institutions. It also gatherd information on the employment history and pension rights of the survey respondent and the spouse or partner of the respondent.

Type of Data Collection Operation: The survey employs a two-part strategy for sampling families. Some families were selected by standard multistage area-probability sampling methods from the forty-eight contiguous states. The remaining families in the survey were selected using tax data under the strict rules governing confidentiality and the rights of potential respondents to refuse participation.

Data Collection and Imputation Procedures: The Survey Research Center at the University of Michigan collected the 1989 survey data between August 1989 and March 1990. Adjustments for nonresponse errors are made through systematic imputation of unanswered questions and through weighting adjustments based on data used in the sample design for families that refused participation.

Estimates of Sampling Error: Because of the complex design of the survey, the estimation of potential sampling errors is not straightforward.

Other (nonsampling) Errors: The achieved sample of 3,143 families represents a response rate of about 69 percent in the area-probability sample and a rate of about 34 percent in the tax-data sample. Proper training of interviewers and careful design of questionnaires were used to control inaccurate survey responses.

Sources of Additional Material: Board of Governors of the Federal Reserve System, "Changes in Family Finances from 1983 to 1989: Evidence from the Survey of Consumer Finances", *Federal Reserve Bulletin,* January 1992.

(See section 1 above for information pertaining to the Bureau of the Census.)

SECTION 15. PRICES

Source and Title: U.S. Bureau of Labor Statistics (BLS), *Consumer Price Index (CPI)*

Tables: 755-761, 777, 778, and in section 3, table 163.

Universe, Frequency, and Types of Data: Monthly survey of price changes of all types of consumer goods and services purchased by urban wage earners and clerical workers prior to 1978, and urban consumers thereafter. Both indexes continue to be published.

Type of Data Collection Operation: Prior to 1978, sample of various consumer items in 56 urban areas; thereafter, in 85 PSU's, except from January 1987 through March 1988, when 91 areas were sampled.

Data Collection and Imputation Procedures: Prices of consumer items are obtained from about 57,000 housing units, and 19,000 other reporters in 85 areas. Prices of food, fuel, and a few other items are obtained monthly; prices of most other commodities and services are collected every month in the five largest geographic areas and every other month in others.

Estimates of Sampling Error: Estimates of standard errors are not available at present.

Other (nonsampling) Errors: Errors result from inaccurate reporting, difficulties in defining concepts and their operational implementation, and introduction of product quality changes and new products.

Sources of Additional Material: U.S. Bureau of Labor Statistics, *The Consumer Price Index:* 1987 Revision, Report 736, and *BLS Handbook of Methods,* Bulletin 2285.

Source and Title: U.S. Bureau of Labor Statistics, *Producer Price Index (PPI)*

Tables: 755, 764-767, and in section 21, table 1053; in section 24, table 1156; and in section 26, table 1212.

Universe, Frequency, and Types of Data: Monthly survey of producing companies to determine price changes of all commodities produced in the United States for sale in commercial transactions. Data on agriculture, forestry, fishing, manufacturing, mining, gas, electricity, public utilities, and a few services.

Type of Data Collection Operation: Probability sample of approximately 3,100 commodities and about 75,000 quotations per month.

Data Collection and Imputation Procedures: Data are collected by mail. If transaction prices are not supplied, list prices are used. Some prices are obtained from trade publications, organized exchanges, and government agencies. To calculate index, price changes are multiplied by their relative weights based on total net selling value of all commodities in 1982.

Estimates of Sampling Error: Not applicable.

Other (nonsampling) Errors: Not available at present.

Sources of Additional Material: U.S. Bureau of Labor Statistics, *BLS Handbook of Methods,* Bulletin 2285.

SECTION 16. BANKING, FINANCE, AND INSURANCE

(See section 14 for information pertaining to tables 788-791.)

SECTION 17. BUSINESS ENTERPRISE

Source and Title: U.S. Internal Revenue Service, *Statistics of Income, Sole Proprietorship Returns* and *Statistics of Income Bulletin*

Tables: 847-850.

Universe, Frequency, and Types of Data: Annual study of unaudited income tax returns of nonfarm sole proprietorships, form 1040 with business schedules. Data provided on various financial characteristics by industry.

Type of Data Collection Operation: Stratified probability sample of approximately 31,000 sole proprietorships for tax year 1990. The sample is classified based on presence or absence of certain business schedules; the larger of total income or loss; and size of business plus farm receipts. Sampling rates vary from .043% to 100%.

Data Collection and Imputation Procedures: Computer selection of sample of tax return records. Data adjusted during editing for incorrect, missing, or inconsistent entries to ensure consistency with other entries on return.

Estimates of Sampling Error: Estimated CV's for tax year 1990 are not available; for 1987 (the latest available): For sole proprietorships, business receipts, 1.66%; net income, (less loss), 1.33%; depreciation 2.17%; interest expense 2.80%; and employee benefit programs 7.55%.

Other (nonsampling) Errors: Processing errors and errors arising from the use of tolerance checks for the data.

Sources of Additional Material: U.S. Internal Revenue Service, *Statistics of Income, Sole Proprietorship Returns* (for years through 1980) and *Statistics of Income Bulletin,* vol. 10, No. 1 (summer 1990).

Source and Title: U.S. Internal Revenue Service, *Statistics of Income, Partnership Returns* and *Statistics of Income Bulletin*
Tables: 847-849, 851, and 852.

Universe, Frequency, and Types of Data: Annual study of unaudited income tax returns of partnerships, Form 1065. Data provided on various financial characteristics by industry.

Type of Data Collection Operation: Stratified probability sample of approximately 28,000 partnership returns from a population of 1,660,000 filed during calendar year 1990. The sample is classified based on combinations of gross receipts, net income or loss, and total assets, and on industry. Sampling rates vary from .04% to 100%.

Data Collection and Imputation Procedures: Computer selection of sample of tax return records. Data are adjusted during editing for incorrect, missing, or inconsistent entries to ensure consistency with other entries on return. Data not available due to regulations are not imputed.

Estimates of Sampling Error: Estimated CV's for tax year 1988 (latest available): For number of partnerships, .51%; business receipts, .78%; net income, 3.03%; net loss, 2.21% and total assets, 1.22%.

Other (nonsampling) Errors: Processing errors and errors arising from the use of tolerance checks for the data.

Sources of Additional Material: U.S. Internal Revenue Service, *Statistics of Income, Partnership Returns* and *Statistics of Income Bulletin,* vol. 10, No. 1 (summer 1990).

Source and Title: U.S. Internal Revenue Service, *Corporation Income Tax Returns*
Tables: 847-849 and 855-857.

Universe, Frequency, and Types of Data: Annual study of unaudited corporation income tax returns, Forms 1120 and 1120 (A, F, L, PC, REIT, RIC, and S), filed by corporations or businesses legally defined as corporations. Data provided on various financial characteristics by industry and size of total assets, and business receipts.

Type of Data Collection Operation: Stratified probability sample of approximately 85,000 returns for 1987, distributed by sample classes generally based on type of return, size of total assets, size of net income or deficit, and selected business activity. Sampling rates for sample strata varied from .25% to 100%.

Data Collection and Imputation Procedures: Computer selection of sample of tax return records. Data adjusted during editing for incorrect, missing, or inconsistent entries to ensure consistency with other entries on return and to achieve statistical definitions.

Estimates of Sampling Error: Estimated CV's for 1988: Number of returns in subgroups ranged from 1.4% with assets under $100,000, to 0% with assets over $100 mil.; for amount of net income and amount of income tax, .18%

Other (nonsampling) Errors: Processing errors and errors arising from the use of tolerance checks for the data.

Sources of Additional Material: U.S. Internal Revenue Service, *Statistics of Income, Corporation Income Tax Returns,* annual.

SECTION 18. COMMUNICATIONS

(See section 1 for information pertaining to table 905, and section 27 for table 914.)

SECTION 19. ENERGY

Source and Title: U.S. Energy Information Administration, *Residential Energy Consumption Survey*
Tables: 936-938, 968, and table 1244 in section 26.

Universe, Frequency, and Types of Data: Triennial survey of households and fuel suppliers. Data are obtained on energy-related household characteristics, housing unit characteristics, use of fuels, and energy consumption and expenditures by fuel type.

Type of Data Collection Operation: Probability sample of 7,183 eligible units in 129 PSU's. For responding units, fuel consumption and expenditure data obtained from fuel suppliers to those households.

Data Collection and Imputation Procedures: Personal interviews. Extensive followup of nonrespondents including mail questionnaires for some households. Adjustments for nonrespondents were made in weighting for respondents. Most item nonresponses were imputed.

Estimates of Sampling Error: Estimated CV's for household averages: For consumption, 1.3%; for expenditures, 1.0%; for various fuels, values ranged from 1.4% for electricity to 5.9% for LPG.

Other (nonsampling) Errors: Household response rate of 86.7%. Nonconsumption data were mostly imputed for mail respondents (5.2% of eligible units). Usable responses from fuel suppliers for various fuels ranged from 82.8% for electricity to 55.7% for fuel oil.

Sources of Additional Material: U.S. Energy Information Administration, *Household Energy Consumption and Expenditures, 1987* and *Housing Characteristics, 1987.*

SECTION 21. TRANSPORTATION—LAND

(See section 1 for information pertaining to table 1017, section 13 for table 1003, and section 15 for table 1053.)

SECTION 22. TRANSPORTATION—AIR AND WATER

Source and Title: U.S. Bureau of the Census, *Foreign Trade—Export Statistics*
Tables: See Bureau of the Census citations for export statistics in source notes in sections 22 and 29 and also tables 1179 and 1180 in section 24; 1194 in section 25; and 1369 in section 30.

Universe, Frequency, and Types of Data: The export declarations collected by Customs are processed each month to obtain data on the movement of U.S. merchandise exports to foreign countries. Data obtained include value, quantity, and shipping weight of exports by commodity, country of destination, Customs district of exportation, and mode of transportation.

Type of Data Collection Operation: Shipper's Export Declarations are required to be filed for the exportation of merchandise valued over $1,500. Customs officials collect and transmit the documents to the Bureau of the Census on a flow basis for data compilation. Value data for shipments valued under $1,501 are estimated, based on established percentages of individual country totals.

Data Collection and Imputation Procedures: Statistical copies of Shipper's Export Declarations are received on a daily basis from Customs ports throughout the country and subjected to a monthly processing cycle. They are fully processed to the extent

they reflect items valued over $1,500. Estimates for shipments valued at $1,500 or less are made, based on established percentages of individual country totals.

Estimates of Sampling Error: Not applicable.

Other (nonsampling) Errors: Clerical and complex computer checks intercept most processing errors and minimize otherwise significant reporting errors; other nonsampling errors are caused by undercounting of exports to Canada due to the nonreceipt of some Shipper's Export Declarations.

Sources of Additional Material: U.S. Bureau of the Census, *U.S. Merchandise Trade: Exports, General Imports, and Imports for Consumption, SITC, Commodity by Country,* FT 925.

Source and Title: U.S. Bureau of the Census, *Foreign Trade—Import Statistics*
Tables: See Bureau of the Census citations for import statistics in source notes in sections 22 and 29 and also tables 1179 and 1180 in section 24; 1194 in section 25; and 1369 in section 30.

Universe, Frequency, and Types of Data: The import entry documents collected by Customs are processed each month to obtain data on the movement of merchandise imported into the United States. Data obtained include value, quantity, and shipping weight by commodity, country of origin, Customs district of entry, and mode of transportation.

Type of Data Collection Operation: Import entry documents are required to be filed for the importation of goods into the United States valued over $1,000 or for articles which must be reported on formal entries. Customs officials collect and transmit statistical copies of the documents to the Bureau of the Census on a flow basis for data compilation. Estimates for shipments valued under $1,001 and not reported on formal entries are based on established percentages of individual country totals.

Data Collection and Imputation Procedures: Statistical copies of import entry documents, received on a daily basis from Customs ports of entry throughout the country, are subjected to a monthly processing cycle. They are fully processed to the extent they reflect items valued at $1,001 and over or items which must be reported on formal entries.

Estimates of Sampling Error: Not applicable.

Other (nonsampling) Errors: Verification of statistical data reporting by Customs officials prior to transmittal and a subsequent program of clerical and computer checks are utilized to hold nonsampling errors arising from reporting and/or processing errors to a minimum.

Sources of Additional Material: U.S. Bureau of the Census, *U.S. Merchandise Trade: Exports, General Imports and Imports for Consumption, SITC, Commodity by Country,* FT 925.

(See section 13 for information pertaining to table 1069.)

SECTION 23. AGRICULTURE

Source and Title: U.S. Department of Agriculture, National Agricultural Statistics Service (NASS), *Basic Area Frame Sample*

Tables: See tables citing NASS in source notes in section 23, which pertain to this or the following two surveys.

Universe, Frequency, and Types of Data: Two annual area sample surveys of U.S. farm operators: June agricultural survey collects data on planted acreage and livestock inventories; and a February Farm Costs and Returns survey that collects data on total farm production, expenses and specific commodity costs of production.

Type of Data Collection Operation: Stratified probability sample of about 16,000 land area units of about 1 sq. mile (range from 0.1 sq. mile in cities to several sq. miles in open grazing areas). Sample includes 60,000 parcels of agricultural land. About 20% of the sample replaced annually.

Data Collection and Imputation Procedures: Data collection is by personal enumeration. Imputation is based on enumerator observation or data reported by respondents having similar agricultural characteristics.

Estimates of Sampling Error: Estimated CV's range from 1% to 2% for regional estimates to 3% to 6% for State estimates of livestock inventories.

Other (nonsampling) Errors: Minimized through rigid quality controls on the collection process and careful review of all reported data.

Sources of Additional Material: U.S. Department of Agriculture, SRS, *Scope and Methods of the Statistical Reporting Service,* (name changed to National Agricultural Statistics Service), Miscellaneous Publication No. 1308, September 1983 (revised).

Source and Title: U.S. Department of Agriculture, National Agricultural Statistics Service (NASS), *Multiple Frame Surveys*

Tables: See tables citing NASS in source notes in section 23, which pertain to this or the following survey.

Universe, Frequency, and Types of Data: Surveys of U.S. farm operators to obtain data on major livestock inventories, selected crop acreages and production, grain stocks, and farm labor characteristics; and to obtain farm economic data for price indexing.

Type of Data Collection Operation: Primary frame is obtained from general or special purpose lists, supplemented by a probability sample of land areas used to estimate for list incompleteness.

Data Collection and Imputation Procedures: Mail, telephone, or personal interviews used for initial data collection. Mail nonrespondent followup by phone and personal interviews. Imputation based on average of respondents.

Estimates of Sampling Error: Estimated CV for number of hired farm workers is about 3%. Estimated CV's range from 1% to 2% for regional estimates to 3% to 6% for State estimates of livestock inventories.

Other (nonsampling) Errors: In addition to above, replicated sampling procedures used to monitor effects of changes in survey procedures.

Sources of Additional Material: U.S. Department of Agriculture, SRS, *Scope and Methods of the Statistical Reporting Service,* (name changed to National Agricultural Statistics Service), Miscellaneous Publication No. 1308, September 1983 (revised).

Source and Title: U.S. Department of Agriculture, National Agricultural Statistics Service (NASS), *Objective Yield Surveys*

Tables: See tables citing NASS in source notes in section 23, which pertain to this or the preceding survey.

Universe, Frequency, and Types of Data: Surveys for data on corn, cotton, potatoes, soybeans, wheat, and rice to forecast and estimate yields.

Type of Data Collection Operation: Random location of plots in probability sample of fields. Fields selected in June from Basic Area Frame Sample (see above).

Data Collection and Imputation Procedures: Enumerators count and measure plant characteristics in sample fields. Production measured from plots at harvest. Harvest loss measured from post harvest gleanings.

Estimates of Sampling Error: CV's for national estimates of production are about 2-3%.

Other (nonsampling) Errors: In addition to above, replicated sampling procedures used to monitor effects of changes in survey procedures.

Sources of Additional Material: U.S. Department of Agriculture, SRS, *Scope and Methods of the Statistical Reporting Service,* (name changed to National Agricultural Statistics Service), Miscellaneous Publication No. 1308, September 1983 (revised).

(See section 1 above for information pertaining to the Census of Population and Current Population Survey.)

SECTION 24. FORESTS AND FISHERIES

(See section 13 for information pertaining to table 1152, section 15 for table 1156, and section 22 for tables 1179 and 1180.)

SECTION 26. CONSTRUCTION AND HOUSING

Source and Title: U.S. Bureau of the Census, *Monthly Survey of Construction*
Tables: 1221, and 1223-1225.
Universe, Frequency, and Types of Data: Survey conducted monthly of newly constructed housing units (excluding mobile homes). Data are collected on the start, completion, and sale of housing. (Annual figures are aggregates of monthly estimates.)
Type of Data Collection Operation: Probability sample of housing units obtained from building permits selected from 17,000 places. For nonpermit places, multistage probability sample of new housing units selected in 169 PSU's. In those areas, all roads are canvassed in selected enumeration districts.
Data Collection and Imputation Procedures: Data are obtained by telephone inquiry and field visit.
Estimates of Sampling Error: Estimated CV of 3% to 4% for estimates of national totals, but are as high as 20% for estimated totals of more detailed characteristics, such as housing units in multiunit structures.
Other (nonsampling) Errors: Response rate is over 90% for most items. Nonsampling errors are attributed to definitional problems, differences in interpretation of questions, incorrect reporting, inability to obtain information about all cases in the sample, and processing errors.
Sources of Additional Material: U.S. Bureau of the Census, *Construction Reports,* series C20, *Housing Starts;* C22, *Housing Completions; and* C25, *New One-Family Houses Sold and For Sale.*

Source and Title: U.S. Bureau of the Census, *Value of New Construction Put in Place*
Tables: 1214-1216.
Universe, Frequency, and Types of Data: Survey conducted monthly on total value of all construction put in place in the current month, both public and private projects. Construction values include costs of materials and labor, contractors' profits, overhead costs, cost of architectural and engineering work, and miscellaneous project costs. (Annual figures are aggregates of monthly estimates.)
Type of Data Collection Operation: Varies by type of activity: Total cost of private one-family houses started each month is distributed into value put in place using fixed patterns of monthly construction progress; using a multistage probability sample, data for private multifamily housing are obtained by mail from owners of multiunit projects. Data for residential additions and alterations are obtained in a quarterly survey measuring expenditures; monthly estimates are interpolated from quarterly data. Estimates of value of private nonhousekeeping, nonresidential buildings, and State and local government construction are obtained by mail from owners (or agents) for a probability sample of projects. Estimates of farm nonresidential construction expenditures are based on U.S. Department of Agriculture annual estimates of construction; public utility estimates are obtained from reports submitted to Federal regulatory agencies and from private utility companies; estimates for all other private construction (nonbuilding) are obtained by phasing F. W. Dodge contract award data; estimates of Federal construction are based on monthly data supplied by Federal agencies.
Data Collection and Imputation Procedures: See "Type of Data Collection Operation." Imputation accounts for approximately 20% of estimated value of construction each month.
Estimates of Sampling Error: CV estimates for private nonresidential building construction range from 3% for estimated value of industrial buildings to 10% for miscellaneous buildings. CV is approximately 2% for total new private nonresidential buildings.
Other (nonsampling) Errors: For directly measured data series based on samples, some nonsampling errors may arise from processing errors, imputations, and misunderstanding of questions. Indirect data series are dependent on the validity of the underlying assumptions and procedures.
Sources of Additional Material: U.S. Bureau of the Census, *Construction Reports,* series C30, *Value of New Construction Put in Place.*

Source and Title: U.S. Bureau of the Census, *Census of Housing*
Tables: See tables citing *Census of Housing* in source notes in section 26.

Universe, Frequency, and Types of Data: Census of all occupied and vacant housing, excluding group quarters, conducted every 10 years as part of the decennial census (see section 1 above) to determine characteristics of U.S. housing.

Type of Data Collection Operation: For 1970, 1980, and 1990, a complete count of some housing items (e.g. Owned or rented, and value). In 1970, other items collected from 5% and 15% probability samples selected from two sets of detailed questions on housing (these two sets having some common items). In 1980, approximately 19% of the housing units were included in the sample; in 1990, approximately 17%.

Data Collection and Imputation Procedures: In 1970, a self-enumeration census using a mail-out/mail-back procedure was used in most areas. In 1980 and 1990, mail questionnaires were used in even more areas than in 1970, with personal interviews in the remainder. Followup for nonrespondents and identification of vacant units done by phone and personal visit.

Estimates of Sampling Error: Sampling errors for data are estimated for all items collected by sample and vary by characteristic and geographic area.

Other (nonsampling) Errors: Evaluation studies for 1980 estimated the underenumeration of occupied housing units at 1.5%. The missed rate in 1980 for all units was 2.6% or approximately 2.3 million units, 1 million of which were vacant housing units.

Sources of Additional Material: U.S. Bureau of the Census, *1980 Census of Population and Housing, The Coverage of Housing in the 1980 Census,* PHC80-E1, July 1985.

Source and Title: U.S. Bureau of the Census, *American Housing Survey*

Tables: See tables citing *American Housing Survey* in source notes.

Universe, Frequency, and Types of Data: Conducted nationally in the fall in odd numbered years to obtain data on the approximately 103 million occupied or vacant housing units in the United States (group quarters are excluded). Data include characteristics of occupied housing units, vacant units, new housing and mobile home units, financial characteristics, recent mover households, housing and neighborhood quality indicators, and energy characteristics.

Type of Data Collection Operation: The national sample was a multistage probability sample with about 51,300 units eligible for interview in 1987. Sample units, selected within 394 PSU's, were surveyed over a 5-month period.

Data Collection and Imputation Procedures: For 1987, the survey was conducted by personal interviews. The interviewers obtained the information from the occupants or, if the unit was vacant, from informed persons such as landlords, rental agents, or knowledgeable neighbors.

Estimates of Sampling Error: For the national sample, illustrations of the S.E. of the estimates are provided in the appendix B of the 1987 report. As an example, the estimated CV is about 0.5% for the estimated percentage of owner occupied units with two persons.

Other (nonsampling) Errors: Response rate was about 97%. Nonsampling errors may result from incorrect or incomplete responses, errors in coding and recording, and processing errors. For the 1985 national sample, approximately 6% of the total housing inventory was not adequately represented by the AHS sample.

Sources of Additional Material: U.S. Bureau of the Census, *Current Housing Reports,* series H-150 and H-170, *American Housing Survey.*

(See section 1 above for information pertaining to the Census of Population, section 15 pertaining to table 1212, and section 19 for table 1244.)

Section 27. MANUFACTURES

Source and Title: U.S. Bureau of the Census, *Census of Manufactures*

Tables: See tables citing *Census of Manufactures* in source notes in section 27 and also table 914 in section 18 and table 1371 in section 30.

Universe, Frequency, and Types of Data: Conducted every 5 years to obtain information on labor, materials, capital input and output characteristics, plant location, and legal form of organization for all plants in the United States with one or more paid employees. Universe was 350,000 manufacturing establishments in 1987.

Type of Data Collection Operation: Complete enumeration of data items obtained from 200,000 firms. Administrative records from Internal Revenue Service and Social Security Administration are used for 150,000 smaller single-location firms, which were determined by various cutoffs based on size and industry.

Data Collection and Imputation Procedures: Five mail and telephone followups for larger nonrespondents. Data for small single-location firms (generally those with fewer than 10 employees) not mailed census questionnaires were estimated from administrative records of IRS and SSA. Data for nonrespondents were imputed from related responses or administrative records from IRS and SSA. Approximately 8% of total value of shipments was represented by fully imputed records in 1987.

Estimates of Sampling Error: Not applicable.

Other (nonsampling) Errors: Based on evaluation studies, estimates of nonsampling errors for 1972 were about 1.3% for estimated total payroll; 2% for total employment; and 1% for value of shipments. Estimates for later years are not available.

Sources of Additional Material: U.S. Bureau of the Census, *1987 Census of Manufactures, Industry Series, Geographic Area Series, and Subject Series.*

Source and Title: U.S. Bureau of the Census, *Annual Survey of Manufactures*

Tables: See tables citing *Annual Survey of Manufactures* in source notes.

Universe, Frequency, and Types of Data: Conducted annually to provide basic measures of manufacturing activity for intercensal years for all manufacturing establishments having one or more paid employees.

Type of Data Collection Operation: Sampling frame is 350,000 establishments in the 1987 Census of Manufactures (see above), supplemented by Social Security Administration lists of new manufacturers and new manufacturing establishments of multi-establishment companies identified annually by the Census Bureau's Company Organization Survey. A probability sample of about 55,000 establishments is selected. All establishments of companies with more than $500 million of manufacturing shipments in 1987 are included with certainty. All establishments with 250+ employees are also included with certainty along with a probability sample of smaller establishments.

Data Collection and Imputation Procedures: Survey is conducted by mail with phone and mail followups of nonrespondents. Imputation (for all nonresponse items) is based on previous year reports, or for new establishments in survey, on industry averages.

Estimates of Sampling Error: Estimated standard errors for number of employees, new expenditure, and for value added totals are given in annual publications. For U.S. level industry statistics, most estimated standard errors are 2% or less, but vary considerably for detailed characteristics.

Other (nonsampling) Errors: Response rate is about 85%. Nonsampling errors include those due to collection, reporting, and transcription errors, many of which are corrected through computer and clerical checks.

Sources of Additional Material: U.S. Bureau of the Census, *Annual Survey of Manufactures,* and Technical Paper 24.

Section 28. DOMESTIC TRADE AND SERVICES

Source and Title: U.S. Bureau of the Census, *Census of Wholesale Trade, Census of Retail Trade, Census of Service Industries*

Tables: See tables citing the above censuses in source notes in section 28 and table 1371 in section 30.

Universe, Frequency, and Types of Data: Conducted every 5 years to obtain data on number of establishments, number of employees, total payroll size, total sales, and other industry-specific statistics. In 1987, the universe was all employer establishments primarily engaged in wholesale trade, and employer and nonemployer establishments in retail trade or service industries.

Type of Data Collection Operation: All wholesale firms with paid employees surveyed; all retail and service large employer firms surveyed (i.e. all employer firms above the payroll size cutoff established to separate large from small employers) plus a 10-percent sample of smaller employer firms. Firms with no employees were not required to file a census return.

Data Collection and Imputation Procedures: Mail questionnaire is utilized with both mail and telephone followups for nonrespondents. Data for nonrespondents and "nonselected" small employer firms in retail trade and service industries are obtained from administrative records of IRS and the Social Security Administration.

Estimates of Sampling Error: Not applicable.

Other (nonsampling) Errors: Response rate in 1987 of 80% for single establishment firms; 83% for multi-establishment firms. Item response ranged from 60% to 90% with higher rates for less detailed questions.

Sources of Additional Material: U.S. Bureau of the Census, Appendix A of *Census of Retail Trade; Census of Service Industries; Census of Wholesale Trade;* and *History of the 1987 Economic Censuses,* April 1992.

Source and Title: U.S. Bureau of the Census, *Current Business Surveys*

Tables: 1302-1305, 1321, 1324, 1327, and table 1005 in section 21.

Universe, Frequency, and Types of Data: Provides monthly estimates of retail sales by kind of business and geographic area, and end-of-month inventories of retail stores; wholesale sales and end-of-month inventories; and annual receipts of selected service industries.

Type of Data Collection Operation: Probability sample of all firms from a list frame and, additionally, for retail and service an area frame. The list frame is the Bureau's Standard Statistical Establishment List (SSEL) updated quarterly for recent birth Employer Identification (EI) Numbers issued by the Internal Revenue Service and assigned a kind-of-business code by the Social Security Administration. The largest firms are included monthly; a sample of others is included every three months on a rotating basis. The area frame covers businesses not subjected to sampling on the list frame.

Data Collection and Imputation Procedures: Data are collected by mail questionnaire with telephone followups for nonrespondents. Imputation made for each nonresponse item and each item failing edit checks.

Estimates of Sampling Error: For the 1989 monthly surveys, CV's are about 0.6% for estimated total retail sales, 1.7% for wholesale sales, 1.3% for wholesale inventories. For dollar volume of receipts, CV's from the *Service Annual Survey* vary by kind of business and range between 1.5% to 15.0%. Sampling errors are shown in monthly publications.

Other (nonsampling) Errors: Imputation rates are about 18% to 23% for monthly retail sales, 20% to 25% for wholesale sales, about 25% to 30% for monthly wholesale inventories and 14% for the *Service Annual Survey*.

Sources of Additional Material: U.S. Bureau of the Census, *Current Business Reports, Monthly Retail Trade, Monthly Wholesale Trade,* and *Service Annual Survey.*

Section 30. OUTLYING AREAS

(See section 1 for information pertaining to tables 1358 and 1359, section 2 for table 1360, section 22 for table 1369, section 27 for table 1371.)

Index to Tables Having Historical Statistics, Colonial Times to 1970 Series

[The most recent historical supplement to the *Statistical Abstract* is the bicentennial edition, *Historical Statistics of the United States, Colonial Times to 1970* (see inside back cover). Listed below are statistical time series (identified by number) appearing in this edition, for which tables in the *Statistical Abstract* present comparable figures. Historical series are listed only where related or comparable data are available for one or more years later than 1970. In a few instances, it may be necessary to combine figures shown in the *Abstract* to obtain totals comparable to the series shown in *Historical Statistics*]

Historical Statistics series	1993 Abstract table number	Historical Statistics series	1993 Abstract table number	Historical Statistics series	1993 Abstract table number	Historical Statistics series	1993 Abstract table number
N		**Q—Con.**		**T—Con.**		**X**	
N 1-29	1215	Q 414-416	1086	T 245-271	1303	X 114-147	787
N 66-69	1215	Q 438-448	1082	T 274-287	1320	X 192, 229	784
N 78-100	1217	Q 449-458	1084	T 280-371	1321	X 410-417	821
N 118-137	1213	Q 473-480	1088	T 391-443	1322	X 444-453	826
N 140-155	1212	Q 487-502	1083	T 444-471	922	X 454-455	825
N 156-163	1221	Q 507-517	1081	T 472-484	921	X 474-491	828
N 170	1221	Q 604-623	1067			X 492-498	827
N 186-191	1248					X 517-530	829
N 238-245	1235	**R**		**U**		X 536-539	837
N 249-258	1246	R 31-45	904	U 1-25	1328	X 551-560	815
N 273, 276	809	R 46-70	902	U 26-39	1331	X 716-724	793
		R 75-88	902	U 41-46	1338	X 741, 748	795
P		R 106-109	922	U 47-74	1333	X 756, 761	795
P 1-12	1255	R 123-126	922	U 75-186	1340	X 864-878	808
P 13	1260	R 140-148	907	U 190-195	1344	X 879-889	845
P 18-39	1260	R 163-171	896	U 207-212	1353	X 890-917	843
P 58-67	1256	R 172-186	897	U 264-273	1346	X 957-962	
P 74-92	1284	R 188-191	898	U 317-352	1351		
P 235, 236a	1270	R 191-216	402			**Y**	
P 239-241	1271	R 224-231	916	**V**		Y 79-83	427
P 265-269	1275	R 232-243	915	V 20-30	861	Y 84-134	430
				V 42-53	849	Y 135-186	431
Q		**S**		V 167-183	857	Y 189-198	439
Q 36-42	1003	S 1-14	927	V 197-212	964	Y 199-203	440
Q 50-51, 55	1009	S 32-52	955			Y 204-210	438
Q 69-75	1042	S 78-82	955	**W**		Y 211-214	436
Q 90-94	1013	S 86-107	955	W 14, 17, 19	663	Y 272-307	499
Q 136-147	1016	S 133-146	964	W 22-25	664	Y 318-331	537
Q 156-162	1037	S 160-175	965	W 30-54	663	Y 335-338	514
Q 199-207	1040	S 190-204	972	W 62-65	663	Y 339-342	509
Q 208	1027	S 205-218	970	W 82-95	919	Y 358-373	524
Q 224-232	1027			W 96-108	872	Y 393-411	525
Q 233-234	1015	**T**		W 109-125	975	Y 412-439	530
Q 238-250	1041	T 43-47	1299	W 126	978	Y 458-460	544
Q 284-312	1050	T 79-196	1301	W 142	977	Y 505-637	468
Q 319, 330	1050	T 197-219	1304	W 167	986	Y 638-651	472
Q 332	1052	T 245-246, 255	1302			Y 652-848	468
Q 356-378	1050					Y 710-782	480
Q 400-401	1050					Y 856-903	564
						Y 943-956	572
						Y 998-999	575

Tables Deleted From the 1992 Edition of the Statistical Abstract

Summary Social and Economic Characteristics—Congressional Districts
[As of **April** 1. For definition of median, see Guide to Tabular Presentation]

STATE AND DISTRICT	POPULATION					Percent high school graduate or higher[3]	Percent bachelor's degree or higher[3]	Median household income in 1989 (dol.)	Percent of persons below poverty level	OCCUPIED HOUSING UNITS		Median value of specified owner-occupied housing units[4] (dol.)
	Total population	Percent 65 years old and over	Percent Black	Percent Hispanic[1]	Voting-age[2] population					Total	Percent owner occupied	
AL.....	4,040,587	12.9	25.3	0.6	2,981,799	66.9	15.7	23,597	18.3	1,506,790	70.5	53,700
1st . . .	577,226	12.6	28.5	0.8	414,476	68.9	14.7	22,881	20.9	209,370	70.9	53,000
2d . . .	577,227	13.1	24.1	0.8	423,324	68.2	16.7	24,374	17.0	215,137	70.5	54,200
3d . . .	577,227	12.9	26.0	0.6	429,511	61.5	12.3	21,594	19.3	212,651	71.9	47,400
4th . . .	577,227	14.7	6.6	0.4	432,149	57.7	8.1	20,877	17.6	220,788	77.0	43,000
5th . . .	577,227	11.2	14.9	0.8	433,310	71.6	20.4	28,364	12.9	219,452	70.4	63,500
6th . . .	577,226	12.1	9.2	0.6	441,662	78.9	26.3	31,864	9.4	223,443	69.7	73,100
7th . . .	577,227	14.0	67.5	0.3	407,367	60.5	10.6	16,560	31.2	205,949	62.4	40,700
AK	550,043	4.1	4.1	3.2	377,699	86.5	23.0	41,408	9.0	188,915	56.1	94,400
AZ.....	3,665,228	13.1	3.0	18.8	2,684,109	78.7	20.3	27,540	15.7	1,368,843	64.2	80,100
1st . . .	610,872	9.2	3.2	13.2	457,975	86.1	27.6	31,288	11.5	241,398	55.1	88,700
2d . . .	610,871	9.8	6.8	50.5	414,281	59.1	9.2	20,258	27.9	196,480	57.9	54,900
3d . . .	610,871	19.8	1.9	11.8	457,293	79.0	16.2	27,627	12.1	234,162	74.4	80,100
4th . . .	610,871	11.3	1.9	7.8	464,379	86.7	26.3	33,681	8.6	246,345	62.8	91,100
5th . . .	610,871	14.8	3.0	16.5	465,370	84.4	25.0	27,047	13.2	242,990	63.1	81,200
6th . . .	610,872	13.6	1.3	13.0	424,811	73.8	15.9	25,710	21.3	207,468	72.2	76,400
AR	2,350,725	14.9	15.9	0.8	1,729,594	66.3	13.3	21,147	19.1	891,179	69.6	46,300
1st . . .	588,588	15.2	17.9	0.6	425,369	58.3	9.5	18,180	24.6	220,333	68.0	40,100
2d . . .	587,412	12.3	17.6	0.8	434,184	74.4	19.0	25,142	14.4	224,233	66.3	56,800
3d . . .	589,523	15.7	1.6	1.1	440,403	68.8	13.3	21,903	14.9	227,700	71.2	49,000
4th . . .	585,202	16.4	26.6	0.8	429,638	63.9	11.4	19,621	22.4	218,913	72.7	40,400
CA	29,760,021	10.5	7.4	25.8	22,009,296	76.2	23.4	35,798	12.5	10,381,206	55.6	195,500
1st . . .	573,082	12.8	3.9	11.2	423,418	79.6	18.2	30,943	11.4	208,711	63.2	136,400
2d . . .	573,322	15.4	1.5	6.0	424,975	78.3	16.4	24,807	15.1	219,020	61.4	94,300
3d . . .	571,374	11.0	3.2	14.2	417,336	79.0	19.9	30,296	12.9	209,586	59.1	118,400
4th . . .	571,033	12.0	1.8	7.4	426,723	85.1	21.1	35,772	7.5	210,045	59.3	152,400
5th . . .	573,684	11.4	12.8	14.7	421,787	79.5	24.0	29,974	15.7	223,134	53.0	122,500
6th . . .	571,227	13.0	2.4	8.9	443,956	87.8	33.0	40,564	6.7	226,960	62.0	257,400
7th . . .	572,773	10.3	16.6	13.3	421,122	82.0	23.2	38,608	9.6	208,202	62.0	168,100
8th . . .	573,247	13.6	12.8	15.7	481,160	76.3	33.8	31,659	14.1	245,820	29.0	274,700
9th . . .	573,458	11.8	31.8	12.0	446,911	80.2	35.4	30,067	16.5	227,756	43.0	223,900
10th . . .	572,008	10.4	2.3	8.7	431,405	90.1	35.8	52,374	4.4	213,366	71.5	275,100
11th . . .	571,772	10.8	5.8	21.1	404,673	71.5	14.7	31,605	14.7	192,038	58.1	124,000
12th . . .	571,535	13.8	4.1	14.3	455,454	84.4	31.6	44,720	6.0	215,787	59.4	324,100
13th . . .	572,441	9.4	7.4	18.4	426,316	80.6	22.4	43,877	6.4	198,910	62.0	223,700
14th . . .	571,131	11.4	4.9	13.5	456,226	88.0	44.2	50,078	6.1	223,976	54.7	404,400
15th . . .	572,485	9.5	2.3	10.8	444,446	88.3	34.8	50,823	5.0	214,252	63.2	291,500
16th . . .	571,551	7.1	5.2	36.8	409,054	69.7	19.4	42,223	11.6	168,563	60.9	234,500
17th . . .	570,981	10.5	4.4	31.6	419,952	74.5	23.0	33,911	11.7	189,099	52.8	220,800
18th . . .	571,393	10.3	2.8	26.0	391,176	66.4	12.5	28,324	16.0	186,489	58.7	114,800
19th . . .	573,043	11.2	3.3	23.6	404,642	74.4	20.2	29,153	16.4	202,858	58.9	90,800
20th . . .	573,282	8.8	6.4	55.4	373,560	47.9	6.4	21,140	27.9	158,379	51.3	64,000
21st . . .	571,300	10.8	4.0	20.3	398,248	72.7	15.0	29,943	15.1	199,642	61.3	85,000
22d . . .	572,891	13.1	2.8	21.3	442,869	81.4	25.3	33,680	13.0	205,198	56.7	230,100
23d . . .	571,483	9.6	2.5	30.0	412,637	77.1	20.5	42,989	7.9	183,312	63.3	235,600
24th . . .	572,563	11.0	2.1	13.5	450,849	86.2	33.4	46,433	6.2	219,354	62.5	305,700
25th . . .	573,105	7.5	4.5	16.4	414,953	82.8	22.9	46,480	7.2	190,996	71.5	214,100
26th . . .	571,523	8.0	6.2	52.7	410,112	60.6	15.4	32,134	15.8	177,447	44.5	186,600
27th . . .	572,594	13.0	8.3	20.6	445,260	80.2	31.4	37,929	11.5	219,623	49.3	296,000
28th . . .	572,927	11.1	5.7	24.1	423,910	82.5	25.6	43,508	7.1	192,695	67.4	233,700
29th . . .	571,566	16.0	3.5	13.2	496,536	86.3	43.5	37,540	11.7	278,690	35.3	500,000
30th . . .	572,538	8.1	3.5	61.5	415,463	52.8	16.1	23,435	24.1	177,284	24.4	189,000
31st . . .	572,643	9.0	1.7	58.5	403,689	56.4	13.3	30,667	18.1	158,775	48.2	180,100
32d . . .	572,595	11.5	40.3	30.2	435,038	69.9	23.3	28,332	19.2	212,744	36.4	234,800
33d . . .	570,943	6.5	4.5	83.7	384,158	33.6	5.3	20,708	28.0	145,328	24.7	156,200
34th . . .	573,047	9.0	1.9	62.3	402,266	61.7	12.0	36,224	11.6	162,272	62.8	174,400
35th . . .	570,882	7.4	42.7	43.1	389,470	57.1	10.1	25,481	24.6	174,747	36.4	150,500
36th . . .	573,663	10.4	3.2	14.9	462,022	86.7	36.8	48,522	6.8	233,720	52.8	371,100
37th . . .	572,049	6.9	33.6	45.1	375,216	54.8	9.2	27,127	23.3	153,884	50.4	142,800
38th . . .	572,657	11.8	7.7	25.7	435,049	76.5	21.0	34,364	12.5	215,601	45.7	224,700
39th . . .	573,574	9.4	2.6	22.8	430,089	81.6	25.4	46,196	7.0	190,832	64.6	239,000
40th . . .	573,625	11.8	5.4	16.1	407,236	78.3	16.0	30,408	12.5	201,282	64.1	110,300
41st . . .	572,663	6.0	6.8	31.5	400,070	76.8	21.4	44,607	9.9	172,941	67.8	204,600
42d . . .	571,844	7.3	11.1	34.3	381,173	72.2	17.2	33,737	14.2	181,408	62.1	127,000
43d . . .	571,231	8.5	5.9	25.0	401,020	76.4	15.7	37,806	10.2	182,767	66.5	153,700
44th . . .	571,583	18.2	5.1	28.1	417,411	71.3	13.2	29,049	13.1	209,956	68.3	121,800
45th . . .	570,874	10.2	1.2	14.8	450,058	84.5	27.7	45,074	7.4	213,006	56.4	266,300
46th . . .	571,380	7.0	2.5	50.0	405,602	59.8	12.5	35,416	15.5	155,659	48.2	188,500
47th . . .	571,518	10.8	1.8	13.1	441,680	89.7	37.1	51,554	5.6	212,084	65.6	280,800
48th . . .	572,928	10.4	4.0	17.2	426,279	86.3	27.7	42,389	7.7	200,215	63.9	237,300
49th . . .	573,362	12.5	5.3	12.8	480,143	87.7	33.9	32,562	10.9	233,952	42.2	226,000
50th . . .	573,463	8.5	14.4	40.6	398,704	67.9	13.9	27,655	18.5	175,606	47.9	137,300
51st . . .	572,982	11.4	1.8	13.6	431,928	87.6	34.5	45,186	7.0	207,876	65.0	231,000
52d . . .	573,203	10.9	3.1	22.6	415,866	77.9	17.1	33,046	11.9	199,359	59.5	155,400

See footnotes at end of table.

Summary Social and Economic Characteristics—Congressional Districts—Continued

[As of **April** 1. For definition of median, see Guide to Tabular Presentation]

STATE AND DIS-TRICT	POPULATION					Percent high school graduate or higher[3]	Percent bachelor's degree or higher[3]	Median household income in 1989 (dol.)	Percent of persons below poverty level	OCCUPIED HOUSING UNITS		Median value of specified owner-occupied housing units[2] (dol.)
	Total population	Percent 65 years old and over	Percent Black	Percent His-panic[1]	Voting-age population					Total	Percent owner occu-pied	
CO	3,294,394	10.0	4.0	12.9	2,433,128	84.4	27.0	30,140	11.7	1,282,489	62.2	82,700
1st . . .	549,068	13.3	12.9	21.9	424,133	78.9	26.8	24,870	17.1	242,791	49.7	75,500
2d . . .	549,072	7.8	0.8	9.5	407,402	87.7	29.5	35,117	8.7	210,000	65.4	89,900
3d . . .	549,062	12.6	0.7	17.4	403,933	79.8	20.5	24,521	15.9	210,794	66.0	62,300
4th . . .	549,070	11.0	0.7	14.7	396,906	79.7	21.5	26,577	13.8	202,437	65.4	70,200
5th . . .	549,066	7.3	5.6	7.4	394,039	89.5	30.1	33,348	8.9	199,048	64.0	90,600
6th . . .	549,056	7.9	3.5	6.4	406,715	91.1	33.4	37,333	5.7	217,419	65.0	92,400
CT.	3,287,116	13.6	8.3	6.5	2,537,535	79.2	27.2	41,721	6.8	1,230,479	65.6	177,800
1st . . .	548,016	14.3	14.2	10.1	423,317	77.9	26.6	39,961	9.3	208,723	61.0	172,000
2d . . .	548,041	11.8	3.7	3.0	421,044	79.7	23.2	38,524	6.2	200,769	65.8	151,300
3d . . .	547,765	14.6	11.9	4.9	426,557	79.7	26.8	39,815	7.7	207,515	64.7	173,800
4th . . .	547,765	13.9	13.1	11.1	426,140	79.3	34.0	47,636	7.5	204,373	63.5	277,400
5th . . .	547,764	12.8	4.8	6.2	416,643	79.2	26.9	44,056	5.6	201,115	68.7	183,900
6th . . .	547,765	13.9	2.3	3.5	423,834	79.5	25.3	42,817	4.6	207,984	70.1	166,400
DE. . . .	666,168	12.1	16.9	2.4	502,827	77.5	21.4	34,875	8.7	247,497	70.2	100,100
DC	606,900	12.8	65.8	5.4	489,808	73.1	33.3	30,727	16.9	249,634	38.9	123,900
FL.	12,937,926	18.3	13.6	12.2	10,071,689	74.4	18.3	27,483	12.7	5,134,869	67.2	77,100
1st . . .	562,518	11.3	12.8	2.1	419,490	77.5	18.4	25,866	14.9	211,725	67.0	62,400
2d . . .	562,519	11.6	23.2	2.0	419,703	71.6	19.5	23,388	19.0	207,785	68.0	58,200
3d . . .	562,519	12.1	55.0	2.8	400,759	63.2	9.9	19,780	25.1	201,260	57.5	47,400
4th . . .	562,518	14.1	5.8	3.1	436,058	82.5	23.4	31,707	7.8	225,237	66.8	81,200
5th . . .	562,518	25.6	5.6	2.8	460,123	71.4	15.4	21,374	15.1	239,193	74.6	62,400
6th . . .	562,518	17.8	7.4	2.9	427,389	72.8	12.4	26,025	10.5	214,839	77.1	66,800
7th . . .	562,518	15.8	4.0	5.5	435,985	81.3	20.5	30,921	7.7	222,116	71.3	80,600
8th . . .	562,518	11.2	5.2	11.4	436,210	81.4	22.7	31,251	8.7	216,066	60.0	85,100
9th . . .	562,518	21.8	3.4	4.1	447,843	79.9	19.8	29,293	8.0	233,442	74.4	85,300
10th . .	562,518	26.1	9.4	2.3	462,536	76.0	17.3	25,145	10.4	253,213	68.6	69,000
11th . .	562,519	12.0	17.2	13.9	430,766	74.5	19.4	26,166	15.2	225,942	56.7	66,600
12th . .	562,519	17.1	12.6	6.1	419,836	67.0	13.0	25,315	14.0	209,945	71.6	62,200
13th . .	562,518	30.9	5.4	4.3	465,139	77.8	18.5	27,616	8.8	247,257	74.9	81,800
14th . .	562,518	25.6	5.7	6.6	455,977	77.4	17.7	29,620	9.3	234,797	72.8	90,900
15th . .	562,519	18.6	7.6	3.4	440,627	79.8	18.9	29,755	9.1	226,294	71.1	75,500
16th . .	562,519	23.8	4.0	6.3	447,765	77.9	18.4	30,582	8.3	233,951	75.7	88,500
17th . .	562,519	9.9	58.4	23.0	391,015	57.7	11.0	21,899	26.6	182,462	50.4	64,100
18th . .	562,519	17.3	4.2	66.7	450,048	62.3	21.2	25,537	17.9	209,846	50.3	95,600
19th . .	562,519	28.2	2.7	6.2	461,448	82.7	22.8	34,396	5.5	244,747	76.4	107,600
20th . .	562,518	16.3	4.4	12.3	440,467	80.9	21.9	35,378	7.1	222,030	74.8	103,200
21st . .	562,519	10.0	4.1	69.6	424,355	67.7	19.4	32,043	12.2	188,480	59.3	91,300
22d. . .	562,519	31.0	3.0	12.8	490,832	79.5	24.1	29,595	9.8	284,067	62.9	118,200
23d. . .	562,519	13.1	51.6	9.4	407,318	61.4	11.0	23,039	21.5	200,175	54.9	67,600
GA	6,478,216	10.1	27.0	1.7	4,750,913	70.9	19.3	29,021	14.7	2,366,615	64.9	71,300
1st . . .	589,546	11.1	22.7	1.8	429,079	70.1	14.9	25,265	16.8	209,975	66.3	59,300
2d . . .	591,699	12.0	56.6	1.7	415,777	57.6	9.7	17,942	28.9	202,994	57.3	42,500
3d . . .	591,328	9.8	17.8	1.4	429,343	71.7	15.5	32,380	9.9	211,118	71.3	70,800
4th . . .	588,293	7.9	11.6	3.4	448,179	87.1	34.6	40,303	6.1	228,403	61.4	96,800
5th . . .	586,485	10.3	62.3	1.8	440,910	73.6	25.9	25,892	21.8	230,439	45.4	76,100
6th . . .	587,118	5.4	6.0	2.1	438,847	90.5	40.0	46,997	4.0	223,842	66.9	120,700
7th . . .	588,071	10.9	12.9	1.1	431,939	64.5	12.4	28,831	11.7	213,835	70.5	64,700
8th . . .	591,615	11.8	21.0	1.4	427,447	67.8	14.5	25,744	16.5	215,624	70.2	56,200
9th . . .	586,222	11.7	3.7	1.7	436,725	60.9	11.4	26,581	11.8	215,869	75.4	62,500
10th . .	591,644	10.5	18.1	1.2	439,254	67.7	17.9	27,553	14.8	213,372	68.5	68,000
11th . .	586,195	9.6	64.1	1.1	413,413	66.1	13.2	24,763	19.8	201,144	62.1	59,000
HI	1,108,229	11.3	2.5	7.3	828,103	80.1	22.9	38,829	8.3	356,267	53.9	245,300
1st . . .	554,119	12.5	2.5	5.5	431,485	81.4	26.6	40,257	7.0	188,969	50.4	311,200
2d . . .	554,110	10.0	2.4	9.2	396,618	78.6	18.8	37,247	9.5	167,298	57.8	190,900
ID	1,006,749	12.0	0.3	5.3	698,344	79.7	17.7	25,257	13.3	360,723	70.1	58,200
1st . . .	503,357	12.9	0.2	4.6	358,537	78.8	16.7	25,086	13.0	185,172	71.3	60,300
2d . . .	503,392	11.2	0.4	5.9	339,807	80.7	18.7	25,446	13.5	175,551	68.7	55,900
IL	11,430,602	12.6	14.8	7.9	8,484,236	76.2	21.0	32,252	11.9	4,202,240	64.2	80,900
1st . . .	571,530	13.9	69.7	3.6	418,800	70.7	18.4	24,140	23.8	210,872	44.7	73,100
2d . . .	571,530	9.6	68.5	6.8	402,216	70.1	13.1	30,217	18.0	183,227	62.9	65,000
3d . . .	571,531	16.2	1.9	7.4	442,224	74.5	15.7	36,250	5.4	214,647	73.8	92,800
4th . . .	571,530	7.7	6.3	65.0	383,497	46.5	8.4	23,083	23.8	170,646	36.0	64,900
5th . . .	571,530	15.2	1.5	13.3	467,584	73.6	26.1	33,262	8.0	243,577	48.8	109,900
6th . . .	571,530	12.0	1.5	5.3	437,195	85.1	28.6	44,216	3.3	210,552	73.7	130,400
7th . . .	571,530	10.0	65.6	4.3	406,971	66.6	20.9	25,220	29.5	204,386	36.9	89,500
8th . . .	571,530	7.4	1.7	5.5	420,358	87.1	30.2	47,374	3.3	205,605	74.2	132,300
9th . . .	571,530	16.4	12.1	9.7	467,139	81.1	36.6	32,183	11.9	245,104	45.8	145,800
10th . .	571,530	10.4	6.2	7.1	425,243	87.6	40.4	50,355	4.4	199,839	74.4	181,400
11th . .	571,528	13.1	8.6	6.5	417,917	75.8	13.4	33,632	8.2	204,630	73.7	67,400
12th . .	571,530	13.6	17.0	1.3	421,442	71.9	13.9	25,032	17.4	213,212	66.6	48,000
13th . .	571,531	7.8	3.2	3.0	412,733	89.0	35.0	50,087	2.5	197,921	77.4	140,300
14th . .	571,530	9.2	4.2	9.8	407,741	80.4	22.7	39,815	6.9	192,838	71.1	100,600
15th . .	571,532	12.8	7.4	1.6	433,424	79.7	21.1	26,760	13.6	213,068	64.0	52,500
16th . .	571,530	12.0	4.7	3.1	415,480	78.9	17.1	34,668	7.6	210,646	72.5	73,700
17th . .	571,530	16.5	3.3	3.0	427,877	76.3	13.3	25,195	12.8	221,563	70.0	41,600
18th . .	571,580	14.2	5.1	0.9	422,030	79.0	17.5	30,189	10.6	217,008	70.3	52,000

See footnotes at end of table.

Summary Social and Economic Characteristics—Congressional Districts—Continued

[As of April 1. For definition of median, see Guide to Tabular Presentation]

STATE AND DISTRICT	POPULATION					Percent high school graduate or higher[3]	Percent bachelor's degree or higher[3]	Median household income in 1989 (dol.)	Percent of persons below poverty level	OCCUPIED HOUSING UNITS		Median value of specified owner-occupied housing units[4] (dol.)
	Total population	Percent 65 years old and over	Percent Black	Percent Hispanic[1]	Voting-age[2] population					Total	Percent owner occupied	
19th ..	571,530	17.4	3.9	0.5	429,589	70.7	11.1	22,979	15.3	223,161	74.6	38,800
20th ..	571,480	15.8	4.2	0.7	424,776	73.9	13.2	26,173	12.2	219,738	73.1	47,200
IN	5,544,159	12.6	7.8	1.8	4,088,195	75.6	15.6	28,797	10.7	2,065,355	70.2	53,900
1st ...	554,416	11.9	21.1	8.5	400,197	75.0	14.2	31,300	12.8	198,750	68.6	57,000
2d ...	554,416	13.7	4.1	0.6	416,400	73.1	12.3	26,185	12.7	209,961	71.2	43,400
3d ...	554,416	12.9	7.4	1.9	407,768	74.8	16.1	29,470	8.8	203,314	72.5	55,500
4th ...	554,416	12.0	5.5	1.6	396,224	78.2	15.0	30,859	7.8	202,849	74.3	56,500
5th ...	554,415	13.4	2.2	1.3	403,843	75.1	10.9	27,893	9.8	205,013	75.1	46,700
6th ...	554,416	11.1	1.1	0.8	408,057	85.3	26.7	38,644	4.5	209,027	72.8	81,400
7th ...	554,416	12.4	2.0	0.8	418,523	78.8	17.4	28,080	10.7	200,596	71.4	54,700
8th ...	554,416	13.9	3.1	0.6	421,765	74.5	15.7	25,242	13.4	211,519	70.1	49,200
9th ...	554,416	12.8	1.7	0.4	404,813	69.9	10.2	26,900	10.7	202,651	76.0	49,300
10th ...	554,416	11.5	29.8	1.2	410,605	71.6	16.9	25,304	15.8	221,675	52.0	46,200
IA	2,776,755	15.3	1.7	1.2	2,057,875	80.1	16.9	26,229	11.5	1,064,325	70.0	45,900
1st ...	555,229	11.9	2.6	2.0	413,721	82.8	22.7	29,544	11.5	211,466	66.7	55,800
2d ...	555,494	16.4	1.7	0.7	408,469	77.9	13.8	25,010	12.3	209,760	72.2	42,600
3d ...	555,299	16.5	0.9	0.8	417,743	79.3	15.7	24,767	12.7	212,356	71.2	41,400
4th ...	555,276	13.7	2.8	1.5	412,171	82.5	18.9	28,591	9.8	216,874	68.3	52,900
5th ...	555,457	18.2	0.6	0.9	405,771	80.3	14.3	24,150	11.3	213,869	71.7	37,200
KS.	2,477,574	13.8	5.8	3.8	1,815,960	81.3	21.1	27,291	11.5	944,726	67.9	52,200
1st ...	619,370	17.2	1.3	5.2	452,729	77.9	15.2	23,433	12.3	239,568	71.2	38,200
2d ...	619,391	14.3	6.3	3.0	458,157	80.7	18.4	24,903	13.4	230,344	67.7	44,500
3d ...	619,439	10.3	8.9	3.3	455,833	85.9	31.5	34,275	9.4	235,450	65.7	75,800
4th ...	619,374	13.5	6.6	3.7	449,241	80.6	19.6	28,308	10.9	239,364	67.0	52,500
KY.	3,685,296	12.7	7.1	0.6	2,731,202	64.6	13.6	22,534	19.0	1,379,782	69.6	50,500
1st ...	614,226	15.3	7.8	0.7	460,899	62.0	9.5	20,331	19.0	232,748	73.4	40,500
2d ...	614,833	11.4	5.5	0.8	448,234	65.1	11.2	23,212	16.8	222,251	72.8	48,200
3d ...	613,603	13.9	18.3	0.7	465,371	74.1	19.7	26,614	14.3	246,351	63.3	57,000
4th ...	614,245	12.1	2.1	0.4	449,764	67.6	13.4	26,362	15.0	224,334	71.9	57,100
5th ...	614,119	11.9	1.0	0.3	441,744	48.1	7.6	15,052	32.7	221,146	74.5	35,400
6th ...	614,270	11.5	8.1	0.7	465,190	70.0	19.9	25,377	16.2	232,952	62.7	61,900
LA.	4,219,973	11.1	30.8	2.2	2,992,704	68.3	16.1	21,949	23.6	1,499,269	65.9	58,500
1st ...	602,859	11.9	10.1	4.1	444,144	76.3	22.0	27,877	14.2	227,357	68.9	75,000
2d ...	602,689	11.0	61.0	3.7	426,275	65.8	17.5	18,367	31.3	218,508	45.8	62,600
3d ...	602,950	9.1	21.8	2.4	414,995	62.8	9.8	23,813	21.5	200,571	75.0	58,100
4th ...	602,884	11.4	66.4	0.9	413,500	58.0	11.1	14,515	38.5	200,250	61.9	40,600
5th ...	602,816	13.0	22.1	1.1	437,021	72.9	17.5	22,903	20.0	222,839	70.5	55,500
6th ...	602,854	10.7	14.6	2.0	434,678	75.2	19.9	25,251	17.3	215,242	69.1	63,400
7th ...	602,921	10.7	19.5	1.3	422,091	65.7	14.1	21,442	22.6	214,502	70.4	50,100
ME	1,227,928	13.3	0.4	0.6	918,926	78.8	18.8	27,854	10.8	465,312	70.5	87,400
1st ...	636,486	13.3	0.4	0.6	478,547	81.7	22.4	30,952	8.5	243,870	69.6	106,700
2d ...	591,442	13.3	0.4	0.5	440,379	75.6	14.7	24,672	13.3	221,442	71.5	66,400
MD	4,781,468	10.8	24.9	2.6	3,619,227	78.4	26.5	39,386	8.3	1,748,991	65.0	116,500
1st ...	597,684	12.4	15.0	1.1	454,906	74.7	19.9	35,115	8.4	221,366	70.3	101,300
2d ...	597,683	12.0	5.9	1.2	457,201	78.1	22.3	40,120	5.2	222,476	70.5	110,900
3d ...	597,680	13.3	17.5	1.7	459,113	75.1	27.2	35,970	9.0	232,681	63.3	91,000
4th ...	597,690	7.4	58.5	6.4	447,123	83.0	27.7	41,081	6.5	216,758	52.8	124,000
5th ...	597,681	7.6	18.6	2.4	450,198	83.2	25.4	46,936	4.9	204,414	71.9	132,100
6th ...	597,688	11.4	4.5	0.9	447,788	77.6	20.9	36,883	7.0	214,745	71.9	113,700
7th ...	597,680	12.1	71.0	0.9	448,177	64.0	16.1	25,684	21.4	216,574	46.9	60,100
8th ...	597,682	10.4	8.2	6.3	454,721	91.3	51.1	56,789	3.7	219,977	72.8	207,200
MA	6,016,425	13.6	5.0	4.8	4,663,350	80.0	27.2	36,952	8.9	2,247,110	59.3	162,800
1st ...	601,643	14.0	1.7	4.8	457,863	78.0	21.4	31,903	10.2	222,811	62.8	123,700
2d ...	601,642	14.1	5.6	6.0	454,404	74.7	18.8	33,401	9.9	222,230	63.9	129,100
3d ...	601,642	13.7	1.8	3.7	458,187	76.6	24.2	36,873	7.9	220,174	61.7	150,800
4th ...	601,642	13.7	2.2	2.5	461,073	77.5	30.9	39,005	7.7	218,092	63.8	170,600
5th ...	601,643	10.5	2.3	8.1	446,756	79.9	28.8	42,701	8.9	209,525	64.4	174,200
6th ...	601,643	13.8	1.9	2.9	465,983	83.3	27.4	40,836	6.8	225,496	65.5	181,100
7th ...	601,642	15.2	2.3	3.0	485,704	84.0	30.6	41,318	5.9	232,429	57.4	193,600
8th ...	601,643	10.8	23.3	10.6	494,335	76.7	36.0	30,417	17.4	238,103	29.1	189,700
9th ...	601,643	14.6	6.7	4.6	472,887	81.6	27.8	38,646	8.9	226,665	57.4	172,800
10th ..	601,642	15.9	2.1	1.4	466,158	86.7	26.4	37,489	6.3	231,585	68.7	163,700
MI	9,295,297	11.9	13.9	2.2	6,836,532	76.8	17.4	31,020	13.1	3,419,331	71.0	60,600
1st ...	580,956	15.7	0.8	0.6	431,643	77.0	14.5	22,788	13.3	219,934	75.8	44,900
2d ...	580,956	12.3	4.4	3.0	414,968	75.9	13.6	28,905	11.4	206,301	78.7	58,400
3d ...	580,956	10.8	7.5	2.8	416,628	79.9	19.1	31,917	9.4	208,512	70.8	66,000
4th ...	580,956	12.3	1.1	1.8	425,655	76.2	13.5	25,898	15.2	207,299	78.1	49,300
5th ...	580,956	13.0	8.4	3.4	418,962	73.8	10.7	26,312	15.0	214,348	75.7	47,400
6th ...	580,956	12.2	9.5	1.8	426,902	77.2	18.6	28,453	13.8	216,367	70.0	54,600
7th ...	580,957	12.2	5.6	2.4	424,301	78.2	13.9	29,976	11.4	210,201	74.0	50,700
8th ...	580,956	9.0	5.8	2.9	431,535	84.0	24.1	35,911	10.6	208,151	70.1	72,100
9th ...	580,956	9.1	17.8	2.8	420,886	78.0	17.7	34,737	14.2	213,603	67.9	65,200
10th ..	580,956	12.1	2.0	1.3	434,093	77.3	12.8	36,536	6.6	214,512	76.8	71,500
11th ..	580,956	12.3	4.1	1.3	444,245	87.7	34.4	49,021	3.4	220,558	77.9	111,100
12th ..	580,956	12.8	3.7	1.2	442,863	78.6	19.9	38,760	6.0	220,490	73.9	76,200
13th ..	580,956	8.6	11.0	1.7	442,445	81.6	27.3	36,596	10.1	215,487	61.6	77,500

See footnotes at end of table.

Summary Social and Economic Characteristics—Congressional Districts—Continued

[As of **April** 1. For definition of median, see Guide to Tabular Presentation]

STATE AND DISTRICT	POPULATION					Percent high school graduate or higher [3]	Percent bachelor's degree or higher [3]	Median household income in 1989 (dol.)	Percent of persons below poverty level	OCCUPIED HOUSING UNITS		Median value of specified owner-occupied housing units [3] (dol.)
	Total population	Percent 65 years old and over	Percent Black	Percent Hispanic [1]	Voting-age population [2]					Total	Percent owner occupied	
14th ..	580,956	11.5	69.1	1.1	408,963	69.2	12.5	25,079	24.6	206,555	64.9	29,800
15th ..	580,956	14.0	70.0	4.3	418,224	58.6	11.1	15,264	36.6	220,864	45.2	23,200
16th ..	580,956	13.0	1.4	2.4	434,219	74.0	12.9	35,315	8.4	216,149	75.4	62,400
MN	4,375,099	12.5	2.2	1.2	3,208,316	82.4	21.8	30,909	10.2	1,647,853	71.8	74,000
1st ...	546,887	14.2	0.3	1.0	399,063	79.7	18.3	28,371	9.8	201,192	75.3	58,700
2d ...	546,887	15.5	0.2	1.0	390,480	75.8	13.5	27,024	10.0	200,982	77.2	55,100
3d ...	546,888	8.1	1.3	1.1	398,813	92.3	33.2	43,963	3.8	203,897	74.5	100,600
4th ...	546,887	12.1	4.2	2.9	410,455	85.3	28.3	32,670	10.6	213,928	63.3	84,300
5th ...	546,887	13.7	9.6	1.8	434,263	84.5	29.3	28,634	14.2	235,257	54.8	78,600
6th ...	546,888	5.6	1.2	0.9	382,305	89.3	22.7	42,346	4.8	187,782	79.9	91,100
7th ...	546,888	15.4	0.2	0.8	394,926	74.3	14.4	22,893	15.4	198,870	74.8	50,300
8th ...	546,887	15.4	0.4	0.5	398,011	77.4	13.9	24,667	13.4	205,945	78.8	49,300
MS	2,573,216	12.5	35.6	0.6	1,826,455	64.3	14.7	20,136	25.2	911,374	71.5	45,600
1st ...	514,548	13.2	22.8	0.5	373,928	59.6	10.8	20,867	20.1	186,772	77.2	43,900
2d ...	514,845	12.9	63.0	0.5	345,943	55.3	13.5	15,530	37.7	170,188	64.4	40,200
3d ...	515,314	12.2	31.3	0.6	370,290	66.6	16.1	21,625	22.0	184,721	74.0	47,100
4th ...	513,853	13.2	40.7	0.4	367,753	67.7	18.1	20,234	25.3	185,716	71.3	47,900
5th ...	514,656	10.9	20.0	1.1	368,541	71.6	15.1	21,702	20.8	183,977	70.0	49,700
MO	5,117,073	14.0	10.7	1.2	3,802,247	73.9	17.8	26,362	13.3	1,961,206	68.8	59,800
1st ...	568,285	13.9	52.3	0.9	418,731	70.6	19.5	24,963	19.1	220,470	56.6	55,800
2d ...	568,306	10.3	3.7	1.0	420,651	86.4	33.6	43,957	3.7	210,097	75.5	95,300
3d ...	568,326	14.8	2.3	1.1	428,779	73.1	17.2	30,863	7.9	225,237	70.0	72,100
4th ...	569,146	14.8	3.2	1.1	420,347	72.0	12.7	23,064	13.7	211,458	72.8	49,600
5th ...	569,130	13.7	23.7	3.2	428,226	78.8	20.0	26,968	13.9	230,604	60.0	56,700
6th ...	569,131	14.3	2.1	1.5	421,046	78.4	16.0	27,165	11.4	216,556	70.8	55,300
7th ...	568,017	15.6	0.9	0.8	428,827	72.9	14.6	21,712	15.2	222,201	70.7	48,400
8th ...	568,385	16.2	4.4	0.5	418,339	69.0	9.5	18,207	22.4	216,430	71.3	37,900
9th ...	568,347	12.8	3.7	0.7	417,301	73.6	16.6	26,055	12.9	208,153	72.3	55,400
MT	799,065	13.3	0.3	1.5	576,961	81.0	19.8	22,988	16.1	306,163	67.3	56,600
NE.	1,578,385	14.1	3.6	2.3	1,149,373	81.8	18.9	26,016	11.1	602,363	66.5	50,400
1st ...	526,297	14.7	1.1	1.4	389,852	81.4	18.5	25,763	10.9	200,847	66.9	50,100
2d ...	526,567	10.1	9.7	2.8	379,331	85.6	24.8	30,889	9.5	197,804	62.8	61,300
3d ...	525,521	17.6	0.2	2.9	380,190	78.5	13.8	22,344	13.0	203,712	69.6	38,300
NV.	1,201,833	10.6	6.6	10.4	904,885	78.8	15.3	31,011	10.2	466,297	54.8	95,700
1st ...	600,957	11.0	10.5	12.2	456,137	75.9	13.3	29,611	11.4	236,070	50.1	89,300
2d ...	600,876	10.3	2.7	8.5	448,748	81.7	17.3	32,413	8.9	230,227	59.6	104,100
NH	1,109,252	11.3	0.6	1.0	830,497	82.2	24.4	36,329	6.4	411,186	68.2	129,400
1st ...	554,360	11.0	0.7	1.0	415,884	82.4	23.8	36,511	6.3	206,495	66.3	132,500
2d ...	554,892	11.5	0.6	1.0	414,613	81.9	24.9	36,145	6.5	204,691	70.1	125,800
NJ.	7,730,188	13.4	13.4	9.6	5,930,726	76.7	24.9	40,927	7.6	2,794,711	64.9	162,300
1st ...	594,630	11.7	15.8	6.3	435,857	74.2	16.9	35,250	9.9	211,962	69.1	94,100
2d ...	594,630	14.8	14.1	6.6	450,384	71.3	14.9	32,410	9.9	218,043	69.0	93,900
3d ...	594,630	15.1	8.0	2.6	451,821	80.5	24.1	41,257	4.3	212,334	82.3	129,200
4th ...	594,630	16.7	12.5	5.2	451,927	75.5	18.7	36,888	6.9	220,574	73.6	130,500
5th ...	594,630	12.5	1.3	2.8	452,587	85.4	32.6	53,433	3.2	206,078	80.8	214,400
6th ...	594,630	12.1	11.2	6.1	465,699	79.5	24.9	42,309	6.4	215,093	63.1	160,600
7th ...	594,629	13.8	10.2	5.0	467,393	82.7	32.4	50,996	3.4	215,596	74.6	186,900
8th ...	594,629	14.7	13.0	17.8	461,457	72.4	24.5	39,944	8.7	212,344	57.2	193,600
9th ...	594,630	16.1	6.5	11.4	480,677	74.9	24.7	40,816	6.0	234,586	54.6	195,700
10th ..	594,630	11.7	60.2	12.3	444,087	65.7	14.6	28,849	17.1	212,001	35.7	137,600
11th ..	594,630	10.8	2.7	4.1	458,657	87.3	37.4	57,219	2.6	209,150	76.4	215,600
12th ..	594,630	11.4	5.2	2.7	455,824	87.5	39.7	54,630	2.9	209,601	78.3	205,700
13th ..	594,630	12.1	13.7	41.5	454,356	58.0	15.9	28,721	17.1	217,349	31.0	143,900
NM	1,515,069	10.8	2.0	38.2	1,068,328	75.1	20.4	24,087	20.6	542,709	67.4	70,100
1st ...	505,491	10.5	2.7	38.1	371,875	81.6	26.0	27,074	14.8	194,425	61.9	84,600
2d ...	504,659	11.8	2.1	42.1	350,557	69.5	15.0	21,456	23.5	175,354	69.4	52,700
3d ...	504,919	9.9	1.2	34.6	345,896	73.7	19.7	23,610	23.6	172,930	71.7	68,600
NY.	17,990,455	13.1	15.9	12.3	13,730,906	74.8	23.1	32,965	13.0	6,639,322	52.2	131,600
1st ...	580,338	11.8	4.1	4.7	433,173	82.3	22.8	45,464	5.2	192,807	79.1	159,000
2d ...	580,337	9.6	9.8	9.7	437,435	80.2	18.9	50,076	4.9	178,664	79.6	159,600
3d ...	580,337	13.5	2.0	4.4	455,840	86.4	29.9	56,060	3.0	195,063	83.8	205,300
4th ...	580,338	14.7	16.2	7.5	450,745	81.3	26.2	50,887	4.5	191,210	78.1	197,800
5th ...	580,337	15.5	3.5	7.3	462,505	83.9	34.8	50,103	4.8	212,262	66.6	256,900
6th ...	580,337	11.2	56.2	16.9	432,187	69.0	14.6	36,223	11.4	180,632	54.5	159,600
7th ...	580,337	17.1	10.1	21.3	472,528	67.9	18.0	30,324	12.2	235,147	32.5	206,100
8th ...	580,337	15.2	8.6	12.7	486,296	78.6	42.1	32,784	16.8	282,170	22.9	223,000
9th ...	580,338	19.7	3.3	8.5	469,579	75.2	24.2	34,758	9.4	238,905	42.9	212,300
10th ..	580,335	9.7	60.7	19.7	414,607	61.9	16.8	23,164	28.3	202,579	23.6	167,900
11th ..	580,337	8.4	74.0	11.5	414,564	67.0	17.5	26,148	21.7	199,404	18.5	183,900
12th ..	580,340	8.4	13.7	57.9	417,933	47.4	10.5	20,444	30.4	184,010	15.3	176,300
13th ..	580,337	14.0	5.6	7.5	449,571	74.2	19.3	38,437	9.0	215,118	52.4	190,700
14th ..	580,337	15.6	4.6	10.9	515,981	84.9	51.4	42,184	9.4	316,747	25.8	235,700
15th ..	580,337	11.7	46.9	46.4	437,484	56.9	17.6	19,238	33.0	214,632	6.4	186,600
16th ..	580,338	7.0	42.2	60.2	385,188	47.0	6.1	15,060	41.8	188,194	8.2	144,300
17th ..	580,337	14.3	41.9	29.1	438,290	66.6	17.1	27,227	18.3	217,580	21.8	176,400
18th ..	580,337	17.0	7.5	10.4	467,381	80.3	33.4	43,754	6.1	222,962	53.7	288,500

See footnotes at end of table.

Summary Social and Economic Characteristics—Congressional Districts—Continued

[As of **April 1**. For definition of median, see Guide to Tabular Presentation]

STATE AND DIS-TRICT	POPULATION					Percent high school graduate or higher [3]	Percent bachelor's degree or higher [3]	Median household income in 1989 (dol.)	Percent of persons below poverty level	OCCUPIED HOUSING UNITS		Median value of specified owner-occupied housing units [3] (dol.)
	Total population	Percent 65 years old and over	Percent Black	Percent Hispanic [1]	Voting-age [2] population					Total	Percent owner occupied	
19th ..	580,337	11.1	7.3	5.2	444,315	83.4	32.4	50,239	4.8	199,080	71.0	199,200
20th ..	580,338	11.1	8.2	6.1	429,329	81.7	29.6	47,107	7.1	192,825	71.8	193,600
21st ..	580,337	15.4	6.3	2.1	451,775	79.3	24.2	31,489	9.8	228,409	59.1	99,200
22d ..	580,337	12.8	2.2	1.5	434,538	79.0	20.4	33,306	7.4	210,874	73.6	99,600
23d ..	580,337	14.9	2.9	1.5	436,162	75.4	15.9	26,155	11.9	211,591	70.0	67,900
24th ..	580,338	11.8	2.6	1.6	426,525	73.8	13.7	25,687	13.6	202,380	68.3	56,700
25th ..	580,337	12.9	6.6	1.4	435,923	79.9	22.7	31,080	10.3	217,749	64.9	78,100
26th ..	580,338	13.2	5.7	4.3	446,405	77.4	22.5	30,335	12.2	213,391	63.9	94,500
27th ..	580,337	12.9	2.5	1.3	433,948	80.3	22.0	34,573	6.9	206,855	75.8	81,300
28th ..	580,337	13.1	14.0	4.3	439,156	79.5	27.4	33,899	11.7	225,411	62.3	90,700
29th ..	580,337	14.7	4.5	2.8	441,716	77.2	17.8	28,951	10.9	225,954	64.5	71,600
30th ..	580,337	14.9	16.7	1.5	441,308	72.7	14.6	26,263	13.7	223,708	63.5	68,300
31st ..	580,337	14.5	2.3	1.5	428,519	75.5	15.0	25,124	13.1	213,009	70.9	48,500
NC	6,628,637	12.1	22.0	1.2	5,022,488	70.0	17.4	26,647	13.0	2,517,026	68.0	65,800
1st ..	552,394	13.9	57.3	0.7	399,878	57.8	9.3	18,226	26.1	202,736	62.2	50,800
2d ..	552,378	13.0	21.9	1.2	420,178	70.5	18.1	27,271	12.7	212,833	68.4	67,600
3d ..	552,387	11.6	21.5	1.6	413,263	71.6	14.4	24,553	14.5	205,941	69.4	63,100
4th ..	552,387	8.4	20.1	1.3	428,984	84.0	35.9	34,569	9.3	215,806	61.0	96,000
5th ..	552,386	13.8	15.2	0.8	428,782	65.3	14.8	25,543	12.3	217,545	70.3	59,500
6th ..	552,385	12.4	7.5	0.7	428,096	72.1	19.0	30,628	7.5	216,882	73.7	73,300
7th ..	552,386	8.8	18.7	2.9	414,413	74.9	15.8	24,708	14.4	184,729	65.2	64,000
8th ..	552,387	11.8	23.2	1.4	403,678	65.8	11.4	26,180	12.2	200,750	73.0	57,100
9th ..	552,387	10.2	8.9	1.1	421,616	78.5	26.2	35,346	6.6	215,438	69.0	83,600
10th ..	552,386	12.2	5.5	0.7	421,456	65.4	13.6	28,511	8.8	212,320	78.9	64,000
11th ..	552,387	17.7	7.2	0.7	430,457	68.2	15.3	23,564	13.7	221,168	74.3	59,700
12th ..	552,387	11.6	56.6	0.9	411,687	65.6	14.3	23,068	17.7	210,878	50.0	58,400
ND	638,800	14.3	0.6	0.7	463,415	76.7	18.1	23,213	14.4	240,878	65.5	50,800
OH	10,847,115	13.0	10.6	1.3	8,047,371	75.7	17.0	28,706	12.5	4,087,546	67.5	63,500
1st ..	570,900	13.4	30.1	0.6	420,468	72.2	18.7	25,405	17.4	223,619	52.2	65,100
2d ..	570,902	11.5	2.3	0.5	417,784	76.9	23.7	34,688	8.0	211,251	71.6	79,400
3d ..	570,901	12.6	17.8	0.8	429,073	77.8	20.1	30,083	12.7	225,198	62.8	65,000
4th ..	570,901	13.2	4.6	0.9	417,141	75.3	11.3	27,312	11.1	210,326	73.0	50,600
5th ..	570,901	12.9	2.1	3.1	411,006	77.0	12.4	30,117	8.6	206,472	76.0	58,000
6th ..	570,901	13.1	2.1	0.4	421,059	68.3	11.4	21,761	20.1	209,760	71.3	46,600
7th ..	570,902	11.9	5.3	0.7	421,456	76.2	15.3	30,364	11.0	205,376	70.8	62,900
8th ..	570,901	11.5	2.8	0.5	415,676	75.4	14.8	31,171	9.4	204,772	72.3	66,300
9th ..	570,901	12.6	12.2	3.4	421,341	76.9	16.3	28,856	14.1	214,332	66.3	58,700
10th ..	570,903	15.2	2.1	4.0	435,467	75.5	19.5	30,323	10.4	228,377	65.6	63,700
11th ..	570,901	14.9	58.6	1.1	424,718	68.5	13.2	22,459	22.1	227,958	51.7	58,800
12th ..	570,902	9.4	23.2	0.8	416,053	80.2	23.5	30,859	13.4	215,958	57.6	75,800
13th ..	570,894	10.8	4.5	2.9	413,086	78.6	16.5	34,725	8.5	198,819	76.9	77,000
14th ..	570,900	13.4	10.9	0.6	433,423	78.2	19.7	28,184	12.9	219,388	67.1	60,600
15th ..	570,902	10.0	4.9	1.0	443,164	81.0	27.0	31,020	10.8	223,084	58.0	73,200
16th ..	570,902	13.7	4.8	0.6	419,742	74.0	13.7	27,524	11.7	209,545	70.8	58,200
17th ..	570,900	15.9	9.8	1.3	428,405	74.4	12.3	25,220	14.4	217,693	72.5	44,400
18th ..	570,900	15.1	2.4	0.3	421,743	71.4	8.5	22,808	15.5	216,909	74.1	44,400
19th ..	570,901	15.3	1.8	0.9	436,566	79.8	19.4	34,385	6.1	219,378	75.4	77,900
OK	3,145,585	13.5	7.4	2.7	2,308,578	74.6	17.8	23,577	16.7	1,206,135	68.1	48,100
1st ..	524,264	11.4	9.6	2.3	386,158	81.7	23.4	27,472	13.0	209,563	61.3	61,100
2d ..	524,264	15.1	5.1	1.1	382,426	67.9	11.6	20,633	19.7	196,048	75.3	41,300
3rd ..	524,264	16.0	4.0	1.4	388,310	66.7	13.3	18,394	22.4	199,724	71.7	36,100
4th ..	524,265	10.9	7.2	4.0	381,702	77.5	18.7	25,391	14.6	192,106	66.6	51,200
5th ..	524,264	12.8	5.6	3.2	388,030	81.8	26.4	28,348	11.9	209,157	65.7	58,700
6th ..	524,264	14.7	13.2	4.4	381,952	71.8	13.3	21,797	18.8	199,537	68.4	40,000
OR	2,842,321	13.8	1.6	4.0	2,118,191	81.5	20.6	27,250	12.4	1,103,313	63.1	67,100
1st ..	568,461	11.7	0.8	4.0	425,695	87.3	30.8	33,227	8.6	225,335	59.7	84,800
2d ..	568,464	15.7	0.3	5.4	418,063	77.6	15.2	23,949	14.7	219,958	64.8	62,600
3d ..	568,465	13.5	5.9	3.2	428,542	81.5	19.0	27,150	12.5	226,909	58.7	59,800
4th ..	568,465	14.6	0.5	2.4	424,702	79.4	17.1	24,593	14.4	221,212	64.4	60,600
5th ..	568,466	13.5	0.6	5.0	421,189	81.6	20.7	28,608	11.8	209,899	66.2	69,200
PA	11,881,643	15.4	9.2	2.0	9,086,833	74.7	17.9	29,069	11.1	4,495,966	70.6	69,700
1st ..	565,842	12.7	52.4	9.9	412,588	58.1	14.0	20,372	28.0	202,744	59.4	37,600
2d ..	565,650	14.9	62.2	1.6	439,005	69.2	21.9	24,880	20.9	222,487	55.6	42,800
3d ..	565,866	17.8	4.9	4.7	437,241	66.6	12.7	29,157	10.9	218,642	71.1	65,800
4th ..	565,792	16.4	3.2	0.5	431,903	77.5	15.3	26,792	10.6	215,984	76.0	55,700
5th ..	565,813	13.9	1.0	0.6	431,688	75.7	15.3	23,934	14.6	205,789	72.2	47,900
6th ..	565,760	16.9	2.5	3.3	435,116	69.8	12.6	28,766	8.9	218,537	74.1	66,500
7th ..	565,746	15.1	3.8	0.9	440,851	84.6	31.0	41,710	4.6	211,077	74.3	134,500
8th ..	565,787	10.8	2.8	1.6	421,078	83.2	25.1	43,483	3.9	199,677	75.4	140,700
9th ..	565,803	15.3	1.2	0.4	425,600	70.2	10.0	24,309	12.1	212,351	75.2	49,700
10th ..	565,681	16.8	1.1	0.8	428,771	75.0	13.9	25,648	11.0	212,813	71.8	70,600
11th ..	565,913	18.7	0.9	0.7	441,306	71.7	12.7	24,310	10.7	218,969	72.0	58,000
12th ..	565,794	17.0	1.3	0.4	431,900	71.6	10.8	22,024	14.9	213,386	75.0	44,400
13th ..	565,793	15.5	6.1	1.2	439,132	84.5	33.5	44,764	3.5	211,735	73.0	147,500
14th ..	565,787	17.5	17.8	0.8	449,638	76.0	22.6	24,751	16.3	231,642	58.6	52,000
15th ..	565,810	15.0	2.2	4.7	434,888	74.1	18.2	33,049	7.1	213,418	71.6	102,100

See footnotes at end of table.

Summary Social and Economic Characteristics—Congressional Districts—Continued
[As of April 1. For definition of median, see Guide to Tabular Presentation]

STATE AND DISTRICT	POPULATION					Percent high school graduate or higher[3]	Percent bachelor's degree or higher[3]	Median household income in 1989 (dol.)	Percent of persons below poverty level	OCCUPIED HOUSING UNITS		Median value of specified owner-occupied housing units[4] (dol.)
	Total population	Percent 65 years old and over	Percent Black	Percent Hispanic[1]	Voting-age[2] population					Total	Percent owner occupied	
16th ..	565,835	12.0	5.2	3.8	416,976	76.4	24.3	37,553	7.2	197,885	70.9	115,800
17th ..	565,742	13.5	6.7	1.9	427,245	75.4	16.3	31,841	7.7	216,856	68.9	76,700
18th ..	565,781	18.5	7.8	0.6	447,927	80.0	21.0	29,003	9.0	232,220	69.9	55,800
19th ..	565,831	13.3	2.6	1.3	432,100	74.2	16.0	32,424	6.4	212,004	73.3	80,600
20th ..	565,815	16.8	3.2	0.5	436,822	75.7	17.2	26,294	12.8	217,875	74.8	56,900
21st ..	565,802	14.8	3.9	0.8	425,058	76.5	14.6	25,845	12.9	209,875	71.8	50,600
RI	1,003,464	15.0	3.9	4.6	777,774	72.0	21.3	32,181	9.6	377,977	59.5	133,500
1st ...	501,677	15.6	3.3	3.8	392,873	70.7	21.9	31,675	9.2	191,853	55.6	137,300
2d ...	501,787	14.4	4.5	5.3	384,901	73.3	20.7	32,729	10.0	186,124	63.4	130,200
SC.....	3,486,703	11.4	29.8	0.9	2,566,496	68.3	16.6	26,256	15.4	1,258,044	69.8	61,100
1st ...	581,125	9.3	20.1	1.4	427,603	77.9	19.8	28,705	12.5	211,114	65.4	75,700
2d ...	581,111	10.2	25.4	1.4	431,032	78.1	24.0	30,500	12.3	210,510	69.4	73,700
3d ...	581,104	12.9	20.7	0.5	435,406	64.3	14.4	25,897	13.3	215,780	74.5	54,400
4th ...	581,113	12.3	19.7	0.8	437,837	67.3	17.6	27,703	11.3	220,099	68.2	59,500
5th ...	581,131	11.8	30.8	0.6	422,575	62.9	12.5	25,215	16.0	205,042	73.5	53,300
6th ...	581,119	11.8	62.2	0.6	412,043	59.2	11.4	19,254	26.9	195,499	67.8	48,500
SD.....	696,004	14.7	0.5	0.8	497,542	77.1	17.2	22,503	15.9	259,034	66.1	45,200
TN.....	4,877,185	12.7	16.0	0.7	3,660,581	67.1	16.0	24,807	15.7	1,853,725	68.0	58,400
1st ...	541,875	14.0	1.9	0.4	418,894	61.9	12.7	21,952	16.6	210,363	74.6	51,200
2d ...	541,864	13.0	6.6	0.6	416,775	70.0	19.3	25,267	14.1	212,752	68.5	59,700
3d ...	541,866	13.7	11.6	0.6	410,195	67.5	16.0	24,687	15.1	209,558	68.7	55,200
4th ...	541,868	14.4	3.6	0.4	405,759	56.4	9.0	20,685	18.3	204,747	75.7	44,600
5th ...	541,910	11.6	22.8	0.9	416,547	75.0	23.3	28,208	12.9	218,369	54.8	74,500
6th ...	541,977	10.9	5.7	0.6	399,124	68.2	17.2	29,234	11.3	197,185	74.2	71,400
7th ...	541,937	10.1	12.4	1.1	396,773	72.5	18.6	29,242	12.0	197,446	70.9	69,600
8th ...	541,907	14.1	19.7	0.7	402,139	62.8	10.4	22,622	16.8	200,919	70.3	47,400
9th ...	541,981	12.4	59.2	0.7	394,375	69.5	17.3	22,117	24.2	202,386	55.5	55,700
TX.....	16,986,510	10.1	11.9	25.5	12,150,671	72.1	20.3	27,016	18.1	6,070,937	60.9	59,600
1st ...	566,217	16.0	18.1	3.2	416,554	68.1	13.1	21,697	20.1	212,663	72.5	44,100
2d ...	566,217	14.2	16.7	5.6	414,273	64.9	10.4	21,216	20.5	202,546	74.2	42,200
3d ...	566,217	8.5	4.4	6.0	419,575	91.3	41.3	45,232	4.0	218,161	66.9	101,000
4th ...	566,217	13.7	8.4	4.3	413,296	73.7	16.3	26,974	13.7	211,624	70.6	57,500
5th ...	566,217	11.8	16.3	17.9	414,181	66.2	14.3	24,045	19.6	207,288	59.0	53,600
6th ...	566,217	6.0	4.4	5.4	411,725	90.0	32.8	41,697	4.5	213,897	65.0	92,500
7th ...	566,217	5.7	5.9	11.9	412,822	90.1	40.7	42,157	5.8	222,256	56.0	88,500
8th ...	566,217	7.0	5.2	7.2	408,226	83.0	29.2	35,454	10.7	200,327	64.0	78,800
9th . , .	566,217	11.2	21.7	9.4	410,971	76.4	18.9	29,420	15.8	212,633	63.4	53,300
10th ...	566,217	7.1	11.2	21.4	430,148	83.2	34.5	27,280	16.2	228,606	45.2	77,400
11th ...	566,217	12.6	15.9	12.3	413,528	72.6	14.8	22,283	18.4	200,738	59.4	50,400
12th ...	566,217	11.6	8.0	16.3	412,814	70.9	15.3	27,366	14.1	207,789	61.5	57,800
13th ...	566,217	14.3	8.0	19.4	409,490	66.9	13.7	20,907	21.3	209,996	64.8	38,600
14th ...	566,217	13.5	10.6	23.6	407,375	66.1	13.8	23,812	20.0	201,932	68.9	52,800
15th ...	566,217	11.0	1.1	74.5	369,299	50.8	11.5	17,866	37.5	164,944	69.9	37,200
16th ...	566,217	8.3	3.6	70.4	382,985	63.3	15.4	22,632	27.0	170,915	58.1	57,600
17th ...	566,217	15.9	3.6	17.2	412,570	66.2	13.4	21,532	19.1	210,111	70.6	38,900
18th ...	566,217	8.8	50.9	15.3	414,418	66.6	17.5	22,531	25.2	208,958	46.8	47,000
19th ...	566,217	10.2	2.5	19.6	403,001	76.0	20.8	27,267	14.7	208,449	65.1	55,400
20th ...	566,217	9.6	5.8	60.7	398,984	68.4	15.6	22,372	24.4	192,134	50.1	48,900
21st ...	566,217	13.5	2.5	14.1	420,498	83.7	28.0	32,103	9.7	217,836	66.8	79,400
22d ...	566,217	6.6	7.8	16.1	406,687	84.3	32.6	40,654	7.9	201,164	64.1	76,100
23d ...	566,217	9.0	2.9	62.5	374,947	59.7	16.6	21,555	29.5	174,390	68.1	48,200
24th ...	566,217	8.7	19.1	21.8	396,176	68.7	15.4	27,535	15.9	194,359	59.5	59,400
25th ...	566,217	7.0	26.9	16.7	405,030	78.3	22.5	30,614	13.7	209,966	51.5	57,600
26th ...	566,217	5.0	4.2	9.2	422,747	88.3	37.0	40,533	5.8	224,668	53.7	99,500
27th ...	566,217	10.3	2.4	66.2	380,622	60.5	14.8	21,552	29.7	177,612	61.0	47,700
28th ...	566,217	10.6	8.5	60.4	382,636	58.4	8.3	20,276	28.2	178,888	68.6	40,400
29th ...	566,217	7.6	10.2	60.6	377,455	46.0	6.5	20,612	27.9	175,663	46.2	38,500
30th ...	566,217	7.9	50.0	17.1	407,638	68.6	16.4	23,144	22.6	210,424	37.4	60,100
UT.....	1,722,850	8.7	0.7	4.9	1,095,406	85.1	22.3	29,470	11.4	537,273	68.1	68,900
1st ...	574,286	9.4	0.9	4.7	360,394	85.6	20.5	30,563	10.1	176,881	71.5	69,000
2d ...	574,241	9.0	0.6	4.9	379,147	87.4	27.1	30,960	8.9	193,316	64.9	76,900
3d ...	574,323	7.7	0.5	5.1	355,865	82.1	18.6	26,570	15.2	167,076	68.3	60,100
VT.....	562,758	11.8	0.3	0.7	419,675	80.8	24.3	29,792	9.9	210,650	69.0	95,500
VA.....	6,187,358	10.7	18.8	2.6	4,682,620	75.2	24.5	33,328	10.2	2,291,830	66.3	91,000
1st ...	562,677	11.3	17.9	1.6	418,734	77.3	21.1	33,285	8.3	205,478	70.3	93,200
2d ...	562,276	7.2	16.6	3.3	419,231	85.3	23.6	32,576	8.1	192,765	57.0	93,100
3d ...	562,431	11.8	64.1	1.4	414,401	64.0	12.7	22,556	21.6	209,391	50.7	62,400
4th ...	562,466	11.5	32.1	1.1	415,002	69.3	14.1	30,425	11.4	199,069	71.2	73,200
5th ...	562,268	14.4	24.8	0.6	433,192	60.7	13.3	24,807	14.1	212,145	72.0	56,000
6th ...	562,572	14.6	11.5	0.7	437,920	69.8	16.7	27,155	11.1	215,001	68.1	65,100
7th ...	562,643	11.0	10.0	1.0	424,882	81.9	30.5	38,865	5.3	217,794	70.4	91,800
8th ...	562,484	9.4	13.4	8.7	453,533	88.6	48.0	48,839	5.4	232,754	54.8	209,900
9th ...	562,380	13.4	2.5	0.5	433,970	57.6	11.7	20,857	19.1	210,961	73.9	49,100
10th ...	562,664	7.5	5.8	2.2	411,822	81.2	30.3	46,205	4.9	197,675	74.2	155,400
11th ...	562,497	6.0	8.2	7.4	419,933	90.4	44.3	54,369	3.9	198,797	67.6	191,000

See footnotes at end of table.

Summary Social and Economic Characteristics—Congressional Districts—Continued
[As of April 1. For definition of median, see Guide to Tabular Presentation]

STATE AND DISTRICT	POPULATION					Percent high school graduate or higher[3]	Percent bachelor's degree or higher[3]	Median household income in 1989 (dol.)	Percent of persons below poverty level	OCCUPIED HOUSING UNITS		Median value of specified owner-occupied housing units[4] (dol.)
	Total population	Percent 65 years old and over	Percent Black	Percent Hispanic[1]	Voting-age[2] population					Total	Percent owner occupied	
WA	4,866,692	11.8	3.1	4.4	3,605,305	83.8	22.9	31,183	10.9	1,872,431	62.6	93,400
1st ...	540,745	9.5	1.3	2.3	401,047	90.7	31.2	40,390	5.1	205,181	66.8	148,200
2d ...	540,739	12.3	0.9	3.0	396,004	83.4	17.7	31,305	9.4	202,215	65.7	100,500
3d ...	540,745	12.7	0.9	2.5	392,267	81.5	16.9	29,154	11.3	206,863	64.9	70,400
4th ...	540,744	12.5	1.0	15.9	380,303	73.0	16.1	25,055	17.6	196,812	63.2	60,300
5th ...	540,744	13.4	1.2	3.4	398,869	83.0	20.3	25,107	15.3	207,264	63.8	57,700
6th ...	540,742	14.3	5.4	3.1	403,037	82.3	17.8	27,882	12.7	211,878	61.5	74,700
7th ...	540,747	14.7	10.0	3.5	447,790	86.4	37.0	29,707	12.2	244,606	49.7	133,300
8th ...	540,742	7.9	1.6	2.3	388,671	88.7	29.0	42,379	5.3	195,943	72.1	142,200
9th ...	540,744	9.2	5.4	3.7	397,317	84.6	18.2	32,194	9.6	201,669	58.3	93,300
WV	1,793,477	15.0	3.1	0.5	1,349,900	66.0	12.3	20,795	19.7	688,557	74.1	47,900
1st ...	598,056	15.6	1.6	0.5	456,552	70.9	13.7	21,903	17.3	230,990	73.9	46,700
2d ...	597,921	14.4	3.3	0.5	448,825	67.3	13.1	22,253	17.6	230,330	73.9	55,600
3d ...	597,500	15.0	4.5	0.4	444,523	59.7	10.2	18,166	24.1	227,237	74.4	41,900
WI	4,891,769	13.3	5.0	1.9	3,602,787	78.6	17.7	29,442	10.7	1,822,118	66.7	62,500
1st ...	543,530	12.5	5.4	3.4	397,289	77.1	14.8	31,431	9.8	198,940	68.5	61,700
2d ...	543,532	11.3	2.1	1.2	412,393	84.8	26.7	30,625	10.1	208,577	60.6	70,000
3d ...	543,533	14.0	0.2	0.5	398,432	78.1	16.3	25,758	13.0	197,728	69.7	52,600
4th ...	543,527	13.3	0.9	6.3	410,090	78.7	16.6	32,260	8.0	210,102	60.5	71,800
5th ...	543,530	12.8	35.2	2.6	395,942	76.3	23.6	26,267	21.0	207,859	47.9	63,200
6th ...	543,652	14.8	0.4	0.9	400,512	76.4	13.1	28,038	8.7	201,139	73.2	55,000
7th ...	543,529	15.1	0.2	0.5	395,676	75.6	13.2	25,277	11.6	202,076	74.3	48,600
8th ...	543,404	13.8	0.3	0.6	396,279	78.4	14.8	28,169	9.9	202,772	72.4	58,100
9th ...	543,532	12.2	0.4	1.0	396,174	82.1	20.8	37,579	4.3	192,925	74.7	82,800
WY	453,588	10.4	0.8	5.7	318,063	83.0	18.8	27,096	11.9	168,839	67.8	61,600

[1] Persons of Hispanic origin may be of any race.   [2] Persons 18 years old and over.   [3] Persons 25 years old and over.
[4] Specified owner-occupied housing units are limited to one-unit structures on less than 10 acres and no business on property.

Source: U.S. Bureau of the Census, *1990 Census of Population and Housing, Population and Housing Characteristics for Congressional Districts of the 103rd Congress* (1990 CPH-4).

Index

NOTE: Index citations refer to table numbers, not page numbers.

NOTE: Index citations refer to table numbers, not page numbers.

NOTE: Index citations refer to table numbers, not page numbers.

NOTE: Index citations refer to table numbers, not page numbers.

NOTE: Index citations refer to table numbers, not page numbers.

NOTE: Index citations refer to table numbers, not page numbers.

NOTE: Index citations refer to table numbers, not page numbers.

NOTE: Index citations refer to table numbers, not page numbers.

NOTE: Index citations refer to table numbers, not page numbers.

NOTE: Index citations refer to table numbers, not page numbers.

NOTE: Index citations refer to table numbers, not page numbers.

NOTE: Index citations refer to table numbers, not page numbers.

Index

Table | Table

Education: —Con.
Non-resident aliens 295
Dormitory population 85
Enrollment ... 221, 223, 226, 228, 229, 270,
271, 272, 273, 274, 275, 276, 286, 287
College freshmen 285, 286
Foreign languages 288
Foreign students 273, 287
Projections 221, 223, 226, 271
States 276, 280
U.S. service schools 276
Expenditures . 222, 225, 274, 275, 278, 282
Price indexes 277
Scientific purposes, by type 980
Faculty 274, 283, 284
Finances . 222, 223, 225, 274, 275, 278, 280
Financial aid 278, 279
Libraries 296, 298
Number 221, 274, 276
Price indexes 277
Scientists and engineers, employed 987
Tuition and fees 281
Voluntary financial support 282
High school dropouts 262, 263, 264
Loans and grants, Federal government 279
Medical schools, students, graduates 171
National Assessment of Educational Progress
Tests (NAEP) 267
Nursing programs, students, graduates 172
Outlying areas of U.S. 1361, 1363
Philanthropy 616, 617, 619, 620
Price indexes 758
Private schools:
Computer use 252
Elementary and secondary .. 221, 222, 225,
226, 228, 239, 257, 259, 260
Expenditures 222, 225
Number 221
Teachers 258
Public elementary and secondary schools:
Computer use 252
Enrollment ... 221, 223, 226, 228, 238, 241,
242, 243
Projections 221, 226, 239
Size 240
States 241, 242
Finances 222, 223, 225, 250, 251
High school graduates 268
Number 221
Personnel 248
Salaries 247
Price indexes 249
Special education programs 255
Teachers 223, 238, 244, 245, 248
Projections 223, 645
Scholastic Aptitude Test 265
School districts 489
School-loss days 199
School years completed. See Education
attainment.
Special education programs 255, 256
State data:
Elementary and secondary .. 241, 242, 245,
251, 268
Higher education 276, 280
Teachers:
Catholic schools 257

Education: —Con.
Elementary and secondary ... 238, 239, 245
Employment projections 223, 239, 645
Higher education 274, 283
Occupational tenure 650
Test scores:
American College Testing (ACT)
Program 266
National Assessment of Educational
Progress
(NAEP) Tests 267
Scholastic Aptitude Tests (SAT) 265
Volunteers 614
Educational expense indexes 758
Educational services 1325
Advertising expenditures 926
Earnings 662, 1322, 1326, 1368
Employees 662, 1322, 1323, 1326, 1368
Establishments .. 1314, 1322, 1323, 1326, 1368
Finances 1322
Gross national product 1298
Occupational safety 685
Receipts 1314, 1322, 1323
Eggplant 1136
Eggs (see also Poultry):
Consumption 218, 1146
Farm marketings, sales 1111
Foreign trade 1146
Prices 758, 777, 1146
Production 1121, 1146
Supply and use 1146
Egypt. See Foreign countries.
Elderly (see also Population):
Adult education 299
Age and/or sex 14, 15, 16, 17, 22, 23, 24,
25, 26, 48
AIDS 203
Alcohol use 213
Arrests 309
Arthritis and rheumatism 206
Black population 16, 23, 24, 25, 26, 48, 49
Book purchasing 401
Cancer 127, 128, 129, 133, 186, 212
Cerebrovascular disease 128, 129, 186
Charitable contributions 615
Children under 18 years old living with elderly
parents 79
Chronic conditions 206
Cigarette smoking 210, 213
Deaths and death rates 128, 129, 132
Disability days 199
Education, attainment 48, 232, 234
Eldercare 502, 679
Elections, voter registration and turnout 454
Farm workers 1120
Health care expenditures 164, 165
Health insurance coverage 161, 165, 166
Hearing impaired 206
Heart disease 127, 129, 132, 186, 206
Height distribution 216
Hispanic origin population 22, 23, 24, 26, 53
Homes for the aged 85, 178, 191, 192
Hospital use 185, 186, 190
Housing, tenure 1237
Illness/injuries 196, 205
Income 234
Labor force 622, 623, 631, 639, 652

NOTE: Index citations refer to table numbers, not page numbers.

NOTE: Index citations refer to table numbers, not page numbers.

NOTE: Index citations refer to table numbers, not page numbers.

NOTE: Index citations refer to table numbers, not page numbers.

NOTE: Index citations refer to table numbers, not page numbers.

NOTE: Index citations refer to table numbers, not page numbers.

NOTE: Index citations refer to table numbers, not page numbers.

NOTE: Index citations refer to table numbers, not page numbers.

NOTE: Index citations refer to table numbers, not page numbers.

NOTE: Index citations refer to table numbers, not page numbers.

NOTE: Index citations refer to table numbers, not page numbers.

NOTE: Index citations refer to table numbers, not page numbers.

NOTE: Index citations refer to table numbers, not page numbers.

Table

NOTE: Index citations refer to table numbers, not page numbers.

NOTE: Index citations refer to table numbers, not page numbers.

NOTE: Index citations refer to table numbers, not page numbers.

NOTE: Index citations refer to table numbers, not page numbers.

Table

Table

NOTE: Index citations refer to table numbers, not page numbers.

NOTE: Index citations refer to table numbers, not page numbers.

NOTE: Index citations refer to table numbers, not page numbers.

NOTE: Index citations refer to table numbers, not page numbers.

NOTE: Index citations refer to table numbers, not page numbers.

NOTE: Index citations refer to table numbers, not page numbers.

NOTE: Index citations refer to table numbers, not page numbers.

NOTE: Index citations refer to table numbers, not page numbers.

NOTE: Index citations refer to table numbers, not page numbers.

NOTE: Index citations refer to table numbers, not page numbers.

NOTE: Index citations refer to table numbers, not page numbers.

NOTE: Index citations refer to table numbers, not page numbers.

NOTE: Index citations refer to table numbers, not page numbers.

NOTE: Index citations refer to table numbers, not page numbers.

NOTE: Index citations refer to table numbers, not page numbers.

NOTE: Index citations refer to table numbers, not page numbers.

NOTE: Index citations refer to table numbers, not page numbers.

NOTE: Index citations refer to table numbers, not page numbers.

NOTE: Index citations refer to table numbers, not page numbers.

NOTE: Index citations refer to table numbers, not page numbers.

U.S. Census Bureau Announces
Census Catalog and Guide: 1993

Helps you select from all the products

Every Census Bureau product issued mid-1988–1992:

- Reports
- Microfiche
- Computer tapes
- CD-ROM
- Floppy disks
- Online access
- Maps

Statistical publications from other Federal agencies

Features facts about each product

Topics   Dates
Areas   Prices

Makes finding the right product easy

Title index   Detailed subject index

Guides to statistics from all censuses and surveys, covering population, housing, business, construction, and more.

Identifies sources of assistance

1,700 data center organizations
200 Census Bureau data specialists
1,500 depository libraries
Other Federal statistical agencies
5 other directory lists

Superintendent of Documents **Publications** Order Form
*7136

☐ **YES,** please send me the following indicated publications:

_____ copies of **Census Catalog and Guide: 1993**
at $21, S/N 003-024-08690-5.

The total cost of my order is $ _____ . Prices include regular domestic
postage and handling and are subject to change. International customers
please add 25%.

_____
(Company or personal name)   (Please type or print)

_____
(Additional address/attention line)

_____
(Street address)

_____
(City, State, ZIP Code)

_____
(Daytime phone including area code)

_____
(Purchase Order No.)

*Charge
your
order.
It's
easy!*

VISA

MasterCard

P3S

Please Choose Method of Payment:

☐ Check payable to the Superintendent of Documents
☐ GPO Deposit Account ☐☐☐☐☐☐☐☐–☐
☐ VISA or MasterCard Account

☐☐☐☐☐☐☐☐☐☐☐☐☐☐☐☐☐☐☐☐☐☐

☐☐☐☐☐ (Credit card expiration date)

**To fax
your orders
(202) 512-2250**

_____
(Authorizing Signature)

Mail To: Superintendent of Documents
P.O. Box 371954, Pittsburgh, PA 15250-7954

*Thank you for
your order!*